Sporting News
BOOKS

HOCKEY GUIDE

2006-2007 EDITION

Editors: Zach Bodendieck, Chris Bergeron Linton, Lauren Parajon, Ray Slover. **Cover design and page layout by:** Chad Painter.

ON THE COVER: Carolina Hurricane Rod Brind'Amour by Robert Seale / SN.

NHL statistics compiled by STATS, Inc., a News Corporation company; 8130 Lehigh Avenue, Morton Grove, IL 60053. STATS is a trademark of Sports Team Analysis and Tracking Systems, Inc.

ISBN: 0-89204-853-0

10 9 8 7 6 5 4 3 2 1

CONTENTS

ANAHEIM DUCKS

WESTERN CONFERENCE, PACIFIC DIVISION

Ducks Schedule

Home games shaded.

October

SUN	MON	TUE	WED	THU	FRI	SAT
1	2	3	4	5	6 LA	7 PHO
8	9 STL	10	11 NYI	12	13	14
15 DAL	16	17	18 DET	19	20 MIN	21
22 LA	23	24	25 EDM	26	27 MIN	28 CHI
29	30 STL	31				

November

SUN	MON	TUE	WED	THU	FRI	SAT
			1 NYR	2	3 PHO	4
5	6 PIT	7	8	9 VAN	10 CAL	11
12 MIN	13	14	15 PHI	16	17 CHI	18
19 PHO	20	21 SJ	22 COL	23	24 NJ	25
26 CAL	27	28 EDM	29	30 VAN		

December

SUN	MON	TUE	WED	THU	FRI	SAT
					1	2 LA
3 LA	4	5	6 NAS	7	8 WAS	9 TB
10	11	12 FLA	13 ATL	14	15	16 SJ
17	18 CAL	19	20 DAL	21	22	23 PHO
24	25	26 SJ	27	28	29 CAR	30
31 MIN						

January

SUN	MON	TUE	WED	THU	FRI	SAT
	1	2 DET	3	4	5 CLB	6
7 DET	8	9 NAS	10	11 DAL	12	13 COL
14	15	16 STL	17	18 EDM	19 CAL	20
21	22	23	24	25	26	27
28 DAL	29	30	31 PHO			

February

SUN	MON	TUE	WED	THU	FRI	SAT
				1	2	3 NAS
4	5	6 SJ	7 SJ	8	9	10 DAL
11	12	13 COL	14	15 PHO	16	17 LA
18 LA	19	20 VAN	21	22	23 DAL	24
25 COL	26 SJ	27	28			

March

SUN	MON	TUE	WED	THU	FRI	SAT
				1 LA	2 SJ	3
4 NAS	5	6	7 PHO	8	9 EDM	10
11 VAN	12	13	14 CLB	15	16 CHI	17
18 LA	19	20	21	22 PHO	23 DAL	24
25	26 DET	27	28 CHI	29 CLB	30	31 STL

April

SUN	MON	TUE	WED	THU	FRI	SAT
1	2	3	4 SJ	5	6 DAL	7 CLB

2006-07 SEASON

CLUB DIRECTORY

Executive vice president, general manager
Brian Burke
Senior v.p. of hockey operation
Bob Murray
Assistant general manager
David McNab
Head coach
Randy Carlyle
Director of communications/team services
Alex Gilchrist
Manager of communications/team services
Merit Tully
Communications and team services coordinator
Ryan Lichtenfels
Strength and conditioning coordinator
Sean Skahan
Equipment manager
Mark O'Neill
Assistant equipment manager
John Allaway

2006 DRAFT CHOICES

Rd.-Overall		Ht., Wt.	Amateur league, team	Position
1-19	MARK MITERA	6-3, 202	CCHA, U. of Michigan	D
2-38	BRYCE SWAN	6-2, 191	QMJHL, Halifax	RW
3-83	JOHN DEGRAY	6-4, 204	OHL, Brampton	D
4-112	MATT BELESKEY	5-11, 202	OHL, Belleville	LW
6-172	PETTERI WIRTANEN	6-1, 202	FIN, HPK	C

MISCELLANEOUS DATA

Home ice (capacity)
Honda Center
(17,174)
Address
2695 E. Katella Avenue
P.O. Box 61077
Anaheim, CA 92803-6177
Business phone
714-940-2900
Ticket information
714-704-2445
Website
www.anaheimducks.com
Training site
Anaheim
Club colors
Black, orange, gold
Radio affiliation
Mighty 1090 AM
TV affiliation
KCAL (Channel 9), FOX Sports West 2 (Cable)

ATLANTA THRASHERS

EASTERN CONFERENCE, SOUTHEAST DIVISION

Thrashers Schedule

Home games shaded.

October

SUN	MON	TUE	WED	THU	FRI	SAT
1	2	3	4	5 TB	6	7 FLA
8	9 TB	10	11 BOS	12	13 CAR	14 WAS
15	16	17	18	19 WAS	20	21 FLA
22	23 FLA	24	25 CAR	26 PHI	27	28 BUF
29	30 TOR	31				

November

SUN	MON	TUE	WED	THU	FRI	SAT
			1 CAR	2	3 WAS	4 NYI
5	6 BOS	7	8 OTT	9	10 NYR	11 TB
12	13	14	15	16	17 DAL	18 MON
19	20	21	22 WAS	23	24 TB	25 FLA
26	27	28 NYR	29	30 TOR		

December

SUN	MON	TUE	WED	THU	FRI	SAT
					1	2 FLA
3	4	5 TOR	6	7 TB	8	9 PIT
10	11	12	13 ANA	14	15 WAS	16 NYI
17	18	19 NJ	20	21 PIT	22	23 NJ
24	25	26 TB	27 PIT	28	29	30 BUF
31						

January

SUN	MON	TUE	WED	THU	FRI	SAT
	1 OTT	2 MIN	3	4	5 PHO	6 WAS
7	8	9 MON	10	11	12 NJ	13 CAR
14	15	16 LA	17	18 MON	19	20 NYR
21	22	23	24	25	26 NYI	27
28 PHI	29	30 NJ	31			

February

SUN	MON	TUE	WED	THU	FRI	SAT
				1 NYI	2	3 PHI
4	5	6 BUF	7	8 COL	9	10 VAN
11 EDM	12	13 CAL	14	15	16	17 OTT
18	19	20 CAR	21	22 TB	23	24 CAR
25	26 BOS	27	28			

March

SUN	MON	TUE	WED	THU	FRI	SAT
				1	2 OTT	3
4 CAR	5	6 FLA	7	8 MON	9	10 FLA
11	12 WAS	13	14	15 PHI	16 NYR	17
18 BUF	19	20	21	22 SJ	23	24 PIT
25	26	27	28 FLA	29 TOR	30	31 BOS

April

SUN	MON	TUE	WED	THU	FRI	SAT
1	2	3	4 WAS	5	6 CAR	7 TB

2006-07 SEASON

CLUB DIRECTORY

President and CEO
Bernard J. Mullin
Executive v.p./g.m., Thrashers
Don Waddell
President, Philips Arena
Bob Williams
Exec. v.p. and chief marketing officer
Lou DePaoli
Exec. v.p. and chief financial officer
Bill Duffy
Senior v.p., broadcast and corporate partnerships
Tracy White
Senior v.p., communications
Tom Hughes
V.p., ticket sales and services
Brendan Donohue
V.p., community development
LaVerne Henderson
V.p., business development
David Lee
V.p., strategic planning
Ailey Penningroth
V.p., marketing, advertising, branding
Jim Pfeifer
V.p., human resources
Ginni Siler
V.p. and team counsel
Scott Wilkinson
V.p. and asst. general manager
Larry Simmons
Head coach
Bob Hartley
Assistant coaches
Brad McCrimmon, Steve Weeks
Director of player personnel
Jack Ferriera
Dir. of amateur scouting and player dev.
Dan Marr
Head scout
Marcel Comeau
Senior director of team services
Michele Zarzaca
Full-time scouts
Evgeny Bogdanovich, Mark Dobson, Bernd Freimuller, Mark Hillier, Peter Mahovlich, Bob Owen, John Perpich, Normand Poisson
Part-time scouts
Terry Brennan, Pat Carmichael
Head trainer
Craig Brewer
Assistant athletic trainer
Step Roberts
Equipment manager
Bobby Stewart
Assistant equipment managers
Joe Guilmet, Jim Guilmet
Strength and conditioning coach
Ray Bear
Massage therapist
Inar Treiguts
Video/hockey operations coordinator
Tony Borgford

2006 DRAFT CHOICES

Rd.-Overall	Ht., Wt.	Amateur league, team	Position
1-12 BRYAN LITTLE	5-10, 190	OHL, Barrie	C
2-43 RILEY HOLZAPFEL	5-11, 170	WHL,Moose Jaw	C
3-80 MICHAEL FORNEY	6-2, 185	USHSW, Thief River Falls	LW
5-135 ALEX KANGAS	6-1, 175	USHL, Sioux Falls	G
6-165 JONAS ENLUND	6-0, 185	Finland Jr., IFK JR.	C
7-195 JESSE MARTIN	5-11, 170	AJHL, Spruce Grove	C
7-200 ARTURS KULDA	6-2, 194	RPL, CSKA 2	D
7-210 WILL O'NEILL	6-0, 193	USHSE, Tabor Academy	D

MISCELLANEOUS DATA

Home ice (capacity)
Philips Arena (18,545)
Address
One Philips Drive
Atlanta, GA 30303
Business phone
404-878-3000
Ticket information
866-715-1500
Website
www.atlantathrashers.com
Training site
IceForum, Duluth, GA
Club colors
Navy, blue, copper, red, gold
Radio affiliation
WCNN (680 The Fan AM)
TV affiliation
TBD

BOSTON BRUINS

EASTERN CONFERENCE, NORTHEAST DIVISION

Bruins Schedule

Home games shaded.

October

SUN	MON	TUE	WED	THU	FRI	SAT
1	2	3	4	5	6 FLA	7 TB
8	9	10	11 ATL	12 STL	13	14 NYI
15	16	17	18	19 CAL	20	21 BUF
22	23	24	25	26 MON	27	28 OTT
29	30	31				

November

SUN	MON	TUE	WED	THU	FRI	SAT
			1	2 BUF	3	4 TB
5	6 ATL	7	8	9 TOR	10	11 OTT
12	13	14	15 WAS	16 TOR	17	18 WAS
19	20 FLA	21	22 PIT	23	24 CAR	25 TOR
26	27	28 TOR	29	30 TB		

December

SUN	MON	TUE	WED	THU	FRI	SAT
					1	2 CAR
3	4 MON	5	6	7 TOR	8	9 NJ
10	11	12 MON	13	14 NJ	15	16 FLA
17	18	19 OTT	20	21 VAN	22	23 MON
24	25	26 CLB	27	28	29 CHI	30 NAS
31						

January

SUN	MON	TUE	WED	THU	FRI	SAT
	1 TOR	2	3	4 TOR	5	6 PHI
7	8	9 OTT	10	11 NYI	12	13 NYR
14	15 BUF	16	17 BUF	18 PIT	19	20 OTT
21	22	23	24	25	26	27 OTT
28	29 NYR	30 BUF	31			

February

SUN	MON	TUE	WED	THU	FRI	SAT
				1 BUF	2	3 CAR
4	5	6 WAS	7	8 CAR	9	10 NYI
11	12	13 EDM	14	15 NYI	16	17 BUF
18	19 PHI	20 TOR	21	22	23 TB	24 FLA
25	26 ATL	27	28			

March

SUN	MON	TUE	WED	THU	FRI	SAT
				1 PHI	2	3 MON
4 NJ	5	6 COL	7	8 MIN	9	10 PHI
11 DET	12	13	14	15 WAS	16	17 NYR
18	19	20 MON	21	22 MON	23	24 NYR
25 PIT	26	27 OTT	28	29 PIT	30	31 ATL

April

SUN	MON	TUE	WED	THU	FRI	SAT
1 NJ	2	3 MON	4	5 BUF	6	7 OTT

2006-07 SEASON

CLUB DIRECTORY

Owner and governor
Jeremy M. Jacobs
Alternative governors
Charles Jacobs, Jeremy Jacobs Jr., Louis Jacobs, Harry Sinden
President
Harry Sinden
Executive vice president
Charles Jacobs
Senior assistant to the president
Nate Greenberg
Chief legal officer
Michael Wall
Chief financial officer
Jessica Rahuba
General manager
Peter Chiarelli
Director of administration
Dale Hamilton-Powers
Assistant general manager
Jeff Gorton
Head coach
Dave Lewis
Associate coach
Marc Habscheid
Assistant coach
Doug Houda
Goaltending coach
Bob Essensa
Director of player development
Don Sweeney
Director of player personnel
Jim Benning
Director of amateur scouting
Scott Bradley
Director of European scouting
Nikolai Bobrov
Scouting staff
Adam Creighton, Daniel Dore, Oto Huscak, Bill Lesuk, Don Matheson, Mike McGraw, Tom McVie, Tom Songin, Svenake Svensson
Video coordinator
Brant Berglund
Director of media relations
Heidi Holland
Media relations manager
Ryan Nadeau
Strength & conditioning coach
John Whitesides
Athletic trainer
Don Del Negro
Physical therapist
Scott Waugh
Equipment manager
Peter Henderson
Assistant equipment managers
Chris "Muggsy" Aldrich
Keith Robinson

2006 DRAFT CHOICES

Rd.-Overall		Ht., Wt.	Amateur league, team	Position
1-5	PHIL KESSEL	6-0, 189	WCHA, U. of Minnesota	C
2-37	YURI ALEXANDROV	6-0, 185	RUSSIA, Cherepovec	D
2-50	MILAN LUCIC	6-2, 204	WHL, Vancouver	LW
3-71	BRAD MARCHAND	5-9, 183	QMJHL, Moncton	C
5-128	ANDREW BODNARCHUK	5-10, 172	QMJHL, Halifax	D
6-158	LEVI NELSON	5-11, 167	WHL, Swift Current	C

MISCELLANEOUS DATA

Home ice (capacity)
TD Banknorth Garden (17,565)
Address
100 Legends Way
Boston, MA 02114-1303
Business phone
617-624-1900
Ticket information
(617) 624-BEAR (2327)
Website
www.bostonbruins.com
Training site
Ristuccia Exposition Center (Wilmington, MA)
Club colors
Gold, black and white
Radio affiliation
WBZ (1030 AM)
TV affiliation
NESN

BUFFALO SABRES

EASTERN CONFERENCE, NORTHEAST DIVISION

Sabres Schedule

Home games shaded.

October

SUN	MON	TUE	WED	THU	FRI	SAT
1	2	3	4 CAR	5	6 MON	7 OTT
8	9	10	11	12	13 DET	14 NYR
15	16	17 PHI	18	19	20 CAR	21 BOS
22	23 MON	24	25	26 NYI	27	28 ATL
29	30	31				

November

SUN	MON	TUE	WED	THU	FRI	SAT
			1	2 BOS	3	4 TOR
5 NYR	6	7	8	9	10 FLA	11 PHI
12	13 CAR	14	15 OTT	16	17 PIT	18 OTT
19	20 TB	21	22 TOR	23	24 MON	25
26 NYR	27	28	29	30		

December

SUN	MON	TUE	WED	THU	FRI	SAT
					1 NYR	2 WAS
3	4	5 TB	6	7 FLA	8	9 MON
10	11	12 NJ	13	14 FLA	15	16 OTT
17	18	19 MON	20	21 NAS	22	23 STL
24	25	26 WAS	27	28 CAR	29	30 ATL
31						

January

SUN	MON	TUE	WED	THU	FRI	SAT
	1 NYI	2	3 OTT	4	5 PIT	6 TOR
7	8	9	10 CHI	11 TOR	12	13 TB
14	15 BOS	16	17 BOS	18	19 VAN	20 MON
21	22	23	24	25	26 CLB	27 NYI
28	29	30 BOS	31			

February

SUN	MON	TUE	WED	THU	FRI	SAT
				1 BOS	2	3 NJ
4	5	6 ATL	7 OTT	8	9	10 CAL
11	12	13	14	15 EDM	16	17 BOS
18	19	20 PHI	21	22 OTT	23	24 OTT
25	26	27 TOR	28			

March

SUN	MON	TUE	WED	THU	FRI	SAT
				1	2 MON	3 TOR
4	5	6	7 COL	8	9 MIN	10 NJ
11	12	13 PIT	14	15 FLA	16 TB	17
18 ATL	19	20	21 WAS	22	23 TOR	24 TOR
25	26	27	28 NJ	29	30 NYI	31 MON

April

SUN	MON	TUE	WED	THU	FRI	SAT
1	2	3 PIT	4	5 BOS	6	7 WAS
8 PHI	9	10	11	12	13	14

2006-07 SEASON

CLUB DIRECTORY

Owner
Tom Golisano
Managing partner
Lawrence Quinn
Chief operating officer
Daniel DiPofi
Director of public relations
Michael Gilbert
Director of marketing
Rob Kopacz
General manager
Darcy Regier
Head coach
Lindy Ruff
Assistant coaches
Brian McCutcheon
Manager of media relations
Chris Bandura
Manager, publications/hockey info.
Kevin Snow
Professional scout
Kevin Devine
Scouting staff
Bo Berglund, Jon Christiano, Iouri Khmylev, Paul Merritt, Rudy Migay, Darryl Plandowski, Mike Racicot, David Volek
Strength & conditioning coach
Doug McKenney
Goaltender coach
Jim Corsi
Administrative assistant coach
Corey Smith
Head equipment manager
Rip Simonick
Assistant equipment managers
George Babcock , Dave Williams
Team doctor
William Hartich

2006 DRAFT CHOICES

Rd.-Overall	Ht., Wt.	Amateur league, team	Position
1-24 DENNIS PERSSON	6-1, 181	SWE, Vasteras	D
2-46 JHONAS ENROTH	5-10, 174	SWE, Sodertalje	G
2-57 MIKE WEBER	6-2, 199	OHL, Windsor	D
4-117 FELIX SCHUTZ	5-11, 187	QMJHL, Saint John	C
5-147 ALEX BIEGA	5-10, 191	USHSE, Salisbury	D
7-207 BENJAMIN BREAULT	5-10, 177	QMJHL, Baie Comeau	C

MISCELLANEOUS DATA

Home ice (capacity)
HSBC Arena (18,690)
Address
One Seymour H. Knox III Plaza
Buffalo, NY 14203
Business phone
716-855-4100
Ticket information
888-223-6000
Website
www.sabres.com
Training site
Buffalo, NY
Club colors
Black, white, red, gray and silver
Radio affiliation
WGR (550 AM)
TV affiliation
MSG Network

CALGARY FLAMES

WESTERN CONFERENCE, NORTHWEST DIVISION

Flames Schedule

Home games shaded.

October

SUN	MON	TUE	WED	THU	FRI	SAT
1	2	3	4	5 EDM	6	7 EDM
8	9 SJ	10	11	12 OTT	13	14 TOR
15	16	17 MON	18	19 BOS	20	21
22	23	24 PHO	25	26	27	28 NAS
29	30 WAS	31				

November

SUN	MON	TUE	WED	THU	FRI	SAT
			1 DET	2	3 CLB	4 STL
5	6	7 DAL	8	9	10 ANA	11 VAN
12	13	14 STL	15	16	17 DET	18
19	20	21 EDM	22 CHI	23	24	25 LA
26 ANA	27	28 COL	29	30		

December

SUN	MON	TUE	WED	THU	FRI	SAT
					1 CLB	2
3	4	5 CAR	6	7 MIN	8	9 VAN
10	11	12 MIN	13	14 VAN	15	16 PHO
17	18 ANA	19 LA	20	21 COL	22	23 SJ
24	25	26 VAN	27 VAN	28	29 LA	30
31 EDM						

January

SUN	MON	TUE	WED	THU	FRI	SAT
	1	2 VAN	3	4 FLA	5	6 DAL
7	8	9 MIN	10	11 COL	12	13 EDM
14	15 NAS	16	17 DAL	18	19 ANA	20 EDM
21	22	23	24	25	26 MIN	27
28 CHI	29	30 LA	31			

February

SUN	MON	TUE	WED	THU	FRI	SAT
				1	2 CLB	3 VAN
4	5	6 CHI	7	8 CLB	9	10 BUF
11 DET	12	13 ATL	14	15 COL	16	17 COL
18	19	20 COL	21	22 PHO	23	24 SJ
25	26 PHO	27	28 MIN			

March

SUN	MON	TUE	WED	THU	FRI	SAT
				1	2	3 EDM
4	5	6 STL	7	8 NAS	9	10 TB
11	12 STL	13	14 COL	15 DAL	16	17 MIN
18	19	20 DET	21	22	23 NAS	24
25 CHI	26	27 MIN	28	29 MIN	30	31 VAN

April

SUN	MON	TUE	WED	THU	FRI	SAT
1	2	3 COL	4	5 SJ	6	7 EDM

2006-07 SEASON

CLUB DIRECTORY

Co-owners
N. Murray Edwards, Harley N. Hotchkiss, Alvin G. Libin, Allan P. Markin, J.R. (Bud) McCaig, Byron J. Seaman, Daryl K. Seaman, Clayton H. Riddell

President & chief executive officer
Ken King

General manager/head coach
Darryl Sutter

Vice president, hockey administration
Michael Holditch

Vice president, building operations
Libby Raines

Vice president, business development
Jim Peplinski

Vice president, advertising/marketing
Jim Bagshaw

Vice president, sales
Rollie Cyr

Director, hockey administration
Mike Burke

Special assistant to the G.M.
Al MacNeil

Assistant coaches
Jim Playfair, Rich Preston, Rob Cookson

Development coach
Jamie Hislop

Goaltending coach
David Marcoux

Team services manager
Kelly Chesla

Director of scouting
Tod Button

Director of amateur scouting
Mike Sands

Pro scouts
Ron Sutter, Tom Webster

Scouts
Tomas Jelinek, Randy Hansch, Sergei Samoilov, Al Tuer, Craig Demetrick, Fred Devereaux, Ralph Schmidt, Anders Steen, Rich Thibeau

Athletic therapist
Morris Boyer

Assistant athletic therapist
Gerry Kurylowich

Strength & conditioning coach
Rich Hesketh

Equipment manager
Gus Thorson

Assistant equipment manager
Les Jarvis

Team physicians
Dr. Kelly Brett, Dr. Jim Thorne

Team dentist
Dr. Bill Blair

V.p., communications
Peter Hanlon

Manager, media relations
Sean O'Brien

Admin. assistant, communications
Bernie Hargrave

2006 DRAFT CHOICES

Rd.-Overall		Ht., Wt.	Amateur league, team	Position
1-26	LELAND IRVING	6-0, 177	WHL, Everett	G
3-87	JOHN ARMSTRONG	6-2, 188	OHL, Plymouth	C/RW
3-89	AARON MARVIN	6-2, 191	USHSW, Warroad	C/W
4-118	HUGO CARPENTIER	6-1, 200	QMJHL, Rouyn Noranda	C
5-149	JUUSO PUUSTINEN	6-1, 185	FIN JR., Kalpa Jr.	RW
6-179	JORDAN FULTON	6-1, 191	USHSW, Breck	C
7-187	DEVIN DIDIOMETE	5-11, 200	OHL, Sudbury	LW
7-209	PER JONSSON	6-0, 172	SWE JR., Farjestad Jr.	F

MISCELLANEOUS DATA

Home ice (capacity)
Pengrowth Saddledome (17,439)

Address
P.O. Box 1540, Station M, Calgary, Alta. T2P 3B9

Business phone
403-777-2177

Ticket information
403-777-0000

Website
www.calgaryflames.com

Training site
Pengrowth Saddledome

Club colors
Red, white, gold and black

Radio affiliation
The Fan 960 (960 AM)

TV affiliations
Rogers Sportsnet, CBC, TSN, PPV

CAROLINA HURRICANES
EASTERN CONFERENCE, SOUTHEAST DIVISION

Hurricanes Schedule
Home games shaded.

October

SUN	MON	TUE	WED	THU	FRI	SAT
1	2	3	4 BUF	5	6 NJ	7 WAS
8	9	10	11 FLA	12	13 ATL	14 PIT
15	16 TB	17	18	19	20 BUF	21 NYI
22	23	24	25 ATL	26 TB	27	28 TB
29	30	31				

November

SUN	MON	TUE	WED	THU	FRI	SAT
			1 ATL	2 MON	3	4 OTT
5	6	7 NJ	8	9 WAS	10	11 PIT
12	13 BUF	14	15 NYR	16	17 WAS	18 DAL
19	20	21 NYR	22 NYI	23	24 BOS	25
26	27	28 OTT	29	30 MON		

December

SUN	MON	TUE	WED	THU	FRI	SAT
					1	2 BOS
3	4	5 CAL	6 EDM	7	8 VAN	9
10	11 COL	12	13	14	15 TOR	16 TB
17	18	19 PHI	20	21	22 NYI	23 FLA
24	25	26 FLA	27	28 BUF	29 ANA	30
31 PHI						

January

SUN	MON	TUE	WED	THU	FRI	SAT
	1	2 PIT	3	4 PHO	5	6 NYI
7	8	9 TOR	10	11 FLA	12	13 ATL
14	15	16 FLA	17	18 WAS	19	20 TB
21	22	23	24	25	26 WAS	27 WAS
28	29	30 TOR	31			

February

SUN	MON	TUE	WED	THU	FRI	SAT
				1 TB	2	3 BOS
4	5	6 MON	7	8 BOS	9	10 MIN
11	12	13 LA	14	15 NYR	16	17 MON
18	19	20 ATL	21	22 PHI	23	24 ATL
25	26	27 OTT	28 OTT			

March

SUN	MON	TUE	WED	THU	FRI	SAT
				1	2 PIT	3
4 ATL	5	6	7	8	9 WAS	10
11 NYR	12	13 FLA	14	15 NJ	16	17 NJ
18	19	20	21	22 WAS	23	24 SJ
25	26	27 TOR	28 PHI	29	30 TB	31

April

SUN	MON	TUE	WED	THU	FRI	SAT
1 FLA	2	3 TB	4	5	6 ATL	7 FLA

2006-07 SEASON
CLUB DIRECTORY

CEO/Owner/governor
Peter Karmanos Jr.
General partner
Thomas Thewes
President/general manager
Jim Rutherford
Vice president/asst. general manager
Jason Karmanos
Chief financial officer
Mike Amendola
V.p., business operations
Matt West
V.p., general manager of RBC Center
Davin Olsen
Head coach
Peter Laviolette
Assistant coaches
Jeff Daniels
Kevin McCarthy
Goaltending coach/pro scout
Greg Stefan
Director of amateur scouting
Sheldon Ferguson
Director of professional scouting
Marshall Johnston
Amateur scouts
Martin Madden
Tony MacDonald
Bert Marshall
Pro scout
Claude Larose, Ron Smith
Video coordinator
Chris Huffine
Head athletic therapist/strength and conditioning coach
Peter Friesen
Associate athletic therapist
Chris Stewart
Equipment managers
Skip Cunningham
Bob Gorman
Wally Tatomir
Director of media relations
Mike Sundheim
Manager of media relations
Kyle Hanlin
Hockey event coordinator
Kelly Kirwin

2006 DRAFT CHOICES

Rd.-Overall	Ht., Wt.	Amateur league, team	Position
2-63 JAMIE MCBAIN	6-2, 190	USA, U.S. National	D
3-93 HARRISON REED	6-1, 178	OHL, Sarnia	RW
4-123 BOBBY HUGHES	5-11, 170	OHL, Kingston	C
5-153 STEFAN CHAPUT	6-2, 190	QMJHL, Lewiston	C
6-183 NICK DODGE	5-10, 175	ECAC, Clarkson University	RW
7-213 JUSTIN KRUEGER	6-2, 205	BCHL, Penticton	D

MISCELLANEOUS DATA

Home ice (capacity)
RBC Center (18,730)
Address
1400 Edwards Mill Road
Raleigh, NC 27607
Business phone
919-467-7825
Ticket information
866-NHL-CANES (645-2263)
Website
www.carolinahurricanes.com
Training site
RecZone
Club colors
Red, white, black and silver
Radio affiliation
102.9 FM
TV affiliation
FOX Sports Net South

CHICAGO BLACKHAWKS
WESTERN CONFERENCE, CENTRAL DIVISION

Blackhawks Schedule
Home games shaded.

October

SUN	MON	TUE	WED	THU	FRI	SAT
1	2	3	4	5 NAS	6	7 CLB
8	9	10	11	12 NAS	13	14 STL
15	16 COL	17	18 MON	19	20 DAL	21 STL
22	23	24	25 VAN	26	27	28 ANA
29	30 PHI	31 NYI				

November

SUN	MON	TUE	WED	THU	FRI	SAT
			1	2 DET	3	4
5	6	7	8	9 NJ	10 STL	11
12 CLB	13	14	15	16 PHO	17 ANA	18
19 VAN	20	21	22 CAL	23	24 EDM	25
26	27	28	29 DAL	30		

December

SUN	MON	TUE	WED	THU	FRI	SAT
					1 STL	2 NAS
3	4	5 MIN	6	7 PHO	8	9 MIN
10 EDM	11	12 STL	13	14 DET	15	16 CLB
17 COL	18	19	20 NAS	21	22 TOR	23 COL
24	25	26 DAL	27	28	29 BOS	30
31 CLB						

January

SUN	MON	TUE	WED	THU	FRI	SAT
	1	2 STL	3	4 STL	5 NAS	6
7 PHO	8	9	10 BUF	11	12	13 DET
14 MIN	15	16 CLB	17	18	19 MIN	20 NAS
21	22	23	24	25	26 NAS	27
28 CAL	29	30	31			

February

SUN	MON	TUE	WED	THU	FRI	SAT
				1 LA	2	3 SJ
4	5	6 CAL	7 VAN	8	9 EDM	10
11 CLB	12	13	14 PIT	15	16 VAN	17
18 NYR	19	20	21 DET	22 SJ	23	24
25 STL	26	27 DET	28			

March

SUN	MON	TUE	WED	THU	FRI	SAT
				1 COL	2 DET	3
4 OTT	5	6 LA	7	8	9	10 PHO
11	12	13 SJ	14	15 LA	16 ANA	17
18	19	20 CLB	21 SJ	22	23 LA	24
25 CAL	26	27	28 ANA	29	30 CLB	31

April

SUN	MON	TUE	WED	THU	FRI	SAT
1 EDM	2	3 NAS	4	5 DET	6	7 DET
8 DAL	9	10	11	12	13	14

2006-07 SEASON
CLUB DIRECTORY

President
William W. Wirtz
Senior vice president
Robert J. Pulford
Vice presidents
Peter R. Wirtz, Jack Davison
General manager
Dale Tallon
Assistant general manager
Rick Dudley
Head coach
Trent Yawney
Assistant coaches
Denis Savard
Mark Hardy
Strength and conditioning coach
Phil Walker
Goaltending consultant
Vladislav Tretiak
Goaltending coach
Stephane Waite
Pro scout
Marc Bergevin
Scouts
Ron Anderson, Bruce Franklin, Rob Pulford, Chris Valentine, Tim Keown
Chief amateur scout
Michel Dumas
European scouting coordinator
Sakari Pietela
European scouts
Karl Pavlik, Rushan Shabanov
Director of hockey operations
Stan Bowman
Skating coach
Dan Jansen
Head trainer
Michael Gapski
Equipment manager
Troy Parchman
Massage therapist
Pawel Prylinski
Executive director of communications
Jim De Maria
Director of community outreach
Jim Blaney
Manager of p.r. and team services
Tony Ommen
Exec. dir. of marketing and sales
Jim Sofranko
Manager, game operations
Ben Broder
Manager, community outreach
Angela Armbruster
Director of ticket operations
James K. Bare
Sales manager
Doug Ryan
Website producer
Adam Kempenaar
Executive assistant
Alison Finley

2006 DRAFT CHOICES

Rd.-Overall		Ht., Wt.	Amateur league, team	Position
1-3	JONATHAN TOEWS	6-1, 195	WCHA, U. of North Dakota	C/W
2-33	IGOR MAKAROV	6-1,183	Russia, KRYLJA	RW
2-61	SIMON DANIS-PEPIN	6-7, 208	H-EAST, U. of Maine	D
3-76	TONY LAGERSTROM	6-1, 189	SWE. Jr., Sodertalje Jr.	C
4-95	BEN SHUTRON	5-11, 186	OHL, Kingston	D
4-96	JOSEPH PALMER	6-1, 205	USA, U.S. National U-18	G
6-156	JAN-MIKAEL JUUTILAINEN	5-11, 183	FIN JR., Jokerit Jr.	C
6-169	CHRIS AUGER	5-10, 160	OPJRA, Wellington	C
7-186	PETER LEBLANC	5-10, 175	OPJRA, Hamilton	C/LW

MISCELLANEOUS DATA

Home ice (capacity)
United Center (20,500)
Address
1901 W. Madison Street
Chicago, IL 60612
Business phone
312-455-7000
Ticket information
312-943-4295
Website
www.chicagoblackhawks.com
Training site
Bensenville, Ill.
Club colors
Red, black and white
Radio affiliation
WSCR (670 AM)
TV affiliation
Comcast SportsNet Chicago

COLORADO AVALANCHE

WESTERN CONFERENCE, NORTHWEST DIVISION

Avalanche Schedule

Home games shaded.

October

SUN	MON	TUE	WED	THU	FRI	SAT
1	2	3	4 DAL	5 MIN	6	7
8 VAN	9	10	11	12	13	14 EDM
15	16 CHI	17	18 TOR	19 OTT	20	21 MON
22	23 LA	24	25 WAS	26	27	28
29 MIN	30	31				

November

SUN	MON	TUE	WED	THU	FRI	SAT
			1 CLB	2 STL	3	4 VAN
5	6	7 LA	8	9	10	11 NAS
12	13 EDM	14	15 SJ	16	17 CLB	18 MIN
19	20 DAL	21	22 ANA	23	24	25 VAN
26	27	28 CAL	29	30 EDM		

December

SUN	MON	TUE	WED	THU	FRI	SAT
					1	2 VAN
3	4	5 CLB	6	7 SJ	8	9 LA
10	11 CAR	12	13 STL	14	15 EDM	16
17 CHI	18	19 EDM	20	21 CAL	22	23 CHI
24	25	26	27 DAL	28	29 STL	30 STL
31						

January

SUN	MON	TUE	WED	THU	FRI	SAT
	1 NAS	2	3	4	5 TB	6 MIN
7	8	9 DET	10	11 CAL	12	13 ANA
14	15 SJ	16	17 PHO	18	19	20 DET
21	22	23	24	25	26 PHO	27
28 DET	29	30 NAS	31			

February

SUN	MON	TUE	WED	THU	FRI	SAT
				1 MIN	2	3 EDM
4	5	6 FLA	7	8 ATL	9	10
11 DAL	12	13 ANA	14	15 CAL	16	17 CAL
18 VAN	19	20 CAL	21	22 MIN	23	24 LA
25 ANA	26	27 CLB	28			

March

SUN	MON	TUE	WED	THU	FRI	SAT
				1 CHI	2	3
4 DET	5	6 BOS	7 BUF	8	9	10
11 MIN	12	13	14 CAL	15	16	17 PHO
18 SJ	19	20	21 EDM	22	23 EDM	24
25 VAN	26	27 VAN	28	29 PHO	30	31 MIN

April

SUN	MON	TUE	WED	THU	FRI	SAT
1	2	3 CAL	4	5 VAN	6	7 NAS

2006-07 SEASON

CLUB DIRECTORY

Owner & governor
E. Stanley Kroenke
President
Pierre Lacroix
Exec. vice president/general manager
Francois Giguere
Head coach
Joel Quenneville
Assistant coaches
Jacques Cloutier, Tony Granato
Director of player personnel
Brad Smith
Assistant to the general manager
Greg Sherman
Special assistant to the president
Michel Goulet
Director of player development
Craig Billington
Goaltending coach
Jeff Hackett
Senior director of hockey administration
Charlotte Grahame
Video coordinator
Bryan Vines
Team services assistant
Ronnie Jameson
Chief scout
Jim Hammett
Pro scout
Terry Martin
Scouts
Glen Cochrane, Paul Fixter, Luc Gauthier, Alan Hepple, Kiril Ladygin, Chris O'Sullivan, Don Paarup, Richard Pracey, Joni Lehto
Strength and conditioning coach
Paul Goldberg
Head athletic trainer
Matt Sokolowski
Assistant athletic trainer
Scott Woodward
Massage therapist
Gregorio Pradera
Inventory manager
Wayne Flemming
Head equipment manager
Mark Miller
Assistant equipment managers
Terry Geer, Cliff Halstead
Senior v.p., communications & team services
Jean Martineau
Director of communications
Damen Zier
Director of media services/Internet
Brendan McNicholas

2006 DRAFT CHOICES

Rd.-Overall		Ht., Wt.	Amateur league, team	Position
1-18	CHRIS STEWART	6-1, 228	OHL, Kingston	RW
2-51	NIGEL WILLIAMS	6-4, 226	USA, U.S. National U-18	D
2-59	CODEY BURKI	6-0, 190	WHL, Brandon	C
3-81	MICHAEL CARMAN	6-0, 180	USA, U.S. National U-18	C
4-110	KEVIN MONTGOMERY	6-1, 185	USA, U.S. National U-18	D
7-201	BILLY SAUER	6-2, 170	CCHA, U. of Michigan	G

MISCELLANEOUS DATA

Home ice (capacity)
Pepsi Center (18,007)
Address
1000 Chopper Cr.
Denver, CO 80204
Business phone
303-405-1100
Ticket information
303-405-1100
Website
www.coloradoavalanche.com
Training site
South Suburban Family Sports Center - Englewood, CO
Club colors
Burgundy, silver, blue and black
Radio affiliation
KKFN (950 AM)
TV affiliation
FoxSports Net Rocky Mountain

COLUMBUS BLUE JACKETS
WESTERN CONFERENCE, CENTRAL DIVISION

Blue Jackets Schedule
Home games shaded.

October

SUN	MON	TUE	WED	THU	FRI	SAT
1	2	3	4	5	6 VAN	7 CHI
8	9 PHO	10	11	12	13	14 MIN
15	16	17	18	19	20 TOR	21 PIT
22	23 SJ	24	25	26	27 LA	28 NJ
29	30	31				

November

SUN	MON	TUE	WED	THU	FRI	SAT
			1 COL	2	3 CAL	4 DET
5	6	7	8	9 STL	10 EDM	11
12 CHI	13	14	15 NAS	16	17 COL	18 NAS
19	20 NAS	21	22 STL	23	24 PHI	25 MIN
26	27	28 VAN	29	30		

December

SUN	MON	TUE	WED	THU	FRI	SAT
					1 CAL	2 EDM
3	4	5 COL	6	7	8	9 STL
10 OTT	11	12 DAL	13	14 PHO	15	16 CHI
17	18 DET	19	20 DET	21	22 VAN	23 NYI
24	25	26 BOS	27	28 DET	29 MIN	30
31 CHI						

January

SUN	MON	TUE	WED	THU	FRI	SAT
	1	2	3 LA	4	5 ANA	6 SJ
7	8	9 STL	10	11	12 NAS	13 NAS
14	15	16 CHI	17	18 NAS	19 DET	20
21	22	23	24	25	26 BUF	27 MIN
28	29	30 VAN	31 EDM			

February

SUN	MON	TUE	WED	THU	FRI	SAT
				1	2 CAL	3
4	5	6 PHO	7	8 CAL	9	10
11 CHI	12	13	14 STL	15	16 SJ	17
18 MON	19	20 STL	21	22 EDM	23	24 NYR
25 NAS	26	27 COL	28			

March

SUN	MON	TUE	WED	THU	FRI	SAT
				1	2 DAL	3 PHO
4	5	6	7 LA	8	9 DAL	10 NAS
11	12	13	14 ANA	15	16 SJ	17 LA
18	19	20 CHI	21	22 DET	23	24
25 STL	26	27 STL	28	29 ANA	30 CHI	31

April

SUN	MON	TUE	WED	THU	FRI	SAT
1 DET	2	3 DET	4	5 DAL	6	7 ANA

2006-07 SEASON

CLUB DIRECTORY

Majority owner/governor
John H. McConnell
Alternate governor
John P. McConnell
President/g.m./alternate governor
Doug MacLean
Exec. v.p./assistant general manager
Jim Clark
Senior v.p., business operations
Larry Hoepfner
V.p., ticketing
David Paitson
V.p., corporate development
Paul D'Aiuto
V.p., marketing
Marc Gregory
V.p., public relations
Todd Sharrock
General counsel
Greg Kirstein
Chief financial officer
T.J. LaMendola
Head coach
Gerard Gallant
Associate coach
Gary Agnew
Assistant coach
Gord Murphy
Director of player personnel
Don Boyd
Director of pro scouting
Bob Strumm
Director of amateur scouting
Paul Castron
Player development
Dean Blais
Manager of hockey operations
Chris MacFarland
Manager of team services
Jim Rankin
Pro scout
Peter Dineen
Amateur scouts
Sam McMaster, John Williams
European scout
Kjell Larsson
Regional scouts
Brian Bates, Denis LeBlanc, John McNamara, Artem Telepin, Bryan Raymond, Andrew Shaw, Milan Tichy
Video coordinator
Dan Singleton
Athletic trainer
Chris Mizer
Strength and conditioning coach
Barry Brennan
Equipment manager
Tim LeRoy

2006 DRAFT CHOICES

Rd.-Overall		Ht., Wt.	Amateur league, team	Position
1-6	DERICK BRASSARD	6-0, 172	QMJHL, Drummondville	C
3-69	STEVE MASON	6-3, 186	OHL, London	G
3-85	TOMMY SESTITO	6-4, 209	OHL, Plymouth	LW
4-113	BEN WRIGHT	6-2, 189	WHL, Lethbridge	D
5-129	ROBERT NYHOLM	6-1, 194	Finland Jr., IFK JR.	RW
5-136	NICK SUCHARSKI	6-1, 165	CCHA, Michigan State	LW
5-142	MAXIME FRECHETTE	6-4, 200	QMJHL, Drummondville	D
6-159	JESSE DUDAS	6-1, 214	WHL, Prince George	D
7-189	DEREK DORSETT	5-11, 176	WHL, Medicine Hat	RW
7-194	MATT MARQUARDT	6-2, 222	QMJHL, Moncton	LW

MISCELLANEOUS DATA

Home ice (capacity)
Nationwide Arena (18,136)
Office address
Nationwide Arena
200 W. Nationwide Blvd.
Columbus, OH 43215
Business phone
614-246-4625
Ticket information
1-800-645-2657
Website
www.bluejackets.com
Training site
Dispatch Ice Haus
Club colors
Blue, Red, White, Silver
Radio affiliation
WBNS (1460 AM), WWCD (101.1 FM)
TV affiliation
Fox Sports Net Ohio

DALLAS STARS
WESTERN CONFERENCE, PACIFIC DIVISION

Stars Schedule
Home games shaded.

October

SUN	MON	TUE	WED	THU	FRI	SAT
1	2	3	4 COL	5	6	7 NJ
8	9	10	11	12 LA	13	14 LA
15 ANA	16	17 SJ	18	19	20 CHI	21 PHO
22	23 VAN	24	25	26	27 DET	28 LA
29	30	31				

November

SUN	MON	TUE	WED	THU	FRI	SAT
			1 STL	2	3 EDM	4
5	6 VAN	7 CAL	8	9 PHO	10	11
12	13	14	15 NYI	16	17 ATL	18 CAR
19	20 COL	21	22 NAS	23	24 LA	25
26	27 DET	28	29 CHI	30 WAS		

December

SUN	MON	TUE	WED	THU	FRI	SAT
					1	2 MIN
3	4 SJ	5	6 PHO	7	8 EDM	9 PHO
10	11	12 CLB	13	14 NYR	15	16 LA
17	18	19	20 ANA	21 SJ	22	23 EDM
24	25	26 CHI	27 COL	28	29 NAS	30
31 SJ						

January

SUN	MON	TUE	WED	THU	FRI	SAT
	1	2	3 VAN	4 EDM	5	6 CAL
7	8	9 PHO	10	11 ANA	12	13
14	15 LA	16	17 CAL	18	19	20 MIN
21	22	23	24	25	26 PIT	27
28 ANA	29	30 SJ	31			

February

SUN	MON	TUE	WED	THU	FRI	SAT
				1 SJ	2	3 STL
4	5	6 MIN	7	8	9	10 ANA
11 COL	12	13	14 DET	15	16	17
18 SJ	19	20 MIN	21	22	23 ANA	24
25 VAN	26	27 TB	28			

March

SUN	MON	TUE	WED	THU	FRI	SAT
				1 FLA	2 CLB	3
4 SJ	5	6	7	8 STL	9 CLB	10
11 LA	12	13 PHI	14	15 CAL	16	17 NAS
18 PHO	19	20	21 LA	22	23 ANA	24 PHO
25	26	27 PHO	28	29	30 DET	31 NAS

April

SUN	MON	TUE	WED	THU	FRI	SAT
1	2 STL	3	4	5 CLB	6 ANA	7
8 CHI	9	10	11	12	13	14

2006-07 SEASON
CLUB DIRECTORY

Chairman of the board and owner
Thomas O. Hicks
President
James R. Lites
General manager
Doug Armstrong
Assistant general managers
Les Jackson, Frank Provenzao
Head coach
Dave Tippett
Associate coach
Rick Wilson
Assistant coaches
Mark Lamb, Ulf Dahlen
Player development/goaltending coach
Andy Moog
Video coach
Derek MacKinnon
Director, hockey administration
Lesa Moake
Director of pro scouting
Doug Overton
Director of amateur scouting
Tim Bernhardt
Professional scouts
Paul McIntosh, John Weisbrod, Kevin Maxwell
Senior dir., communications
Rob Scichili
Director, public relations
Mark Janko
Manager of media and team services
Jason Rademan
Head athletic trainer
Dave Surprenant
Head equipment manager
Steve Sumner
Strength and conditioning coach
J.J. McQueen

2006 DRAFT CHOICES

Rd.-Overall	Ht., Wt.	Amateur league, team	Position
1-27 IVAN VISHNEVSKIY	5-11, 176	QMJHL, Rouyn Noranda	D
3-90 AARON SNOW	6-0, 199	OHL, Brampton	LW
4-120 RICHARD BACHMAN	5-11, 160	USHSE, Cushing Academy	G
5-138 DAVID MCINTYRE	5-11, 171	OPJRA, Newmarket	C
5-150 MAX WARN	6-2, 194	Finland Jr., IFK JR.	LW

MISCELLANEOUS DATA

Home ice (capacity)
American Airlines Center (18,532)
Address
2500 Victory Avenue,
Dallas, Texas 75219
Business phone
214-387-5500
Ticket information
214-467-8277
Website
www.dallasstars.com
Training site
Frisco, TX
Club colors
Green, black, gold
Radio affiliation
WBAP (820 AM)
TV affiliation
FOX Sports Southwest (Cable), KDFI

DETROIT RED WINGS

WESTERN CONFERENCE, CENTRAL DIVISION

Red Wings Schedule

Home games shaded.

October

SUN	MON	TUE	WED	THU	FRI	SAT
1	2	3	4	5 VAN	6	7 PIT
8	9	10	11 PHO	12	13 BUF	14
15	16 LA	17	18 ANA	19 SJ	20	21 EDM
22	23	24	25 SJ	26	27 DAL	28 STL
29	30	31				

November

SUN	MON	TUE	WED	THU	FRI	SAT
			1 CAL	2 CHI	3	4 CLB
5	6	7	8 EDM	9	10 NAS	11
12	13	14 VAN	15	16	17 CAL	18 EDM
19	20	21 VAN	22	23	24 STL	25 NAS
26	27 DAL	28	29	30		

December

SUN	MON	TUE	WED	THU	FRI	SAT
					1 MIN	2 SJ
3	4	5 STL	6	7 STL	8	9 TOR
10	11	12 OTT	13	14 CHI	15	16 NJ
17	18 CLB	19	20 CLB	21	22 MIN	23 MIN
24	25	26	27 MIN	28 CLB	29	30
31 LA						

January

SUN	MON	TUE	WED	THU	FRI	SAT
	1	2 ANA	3	4 SJ	5	6 LA
7 ANA	8	9 COL	10	11 PHO	12	13 CHI
14	15 MON	16	17 NAS	18	19 CLB	20 COL
21	22	23	24	25	26 STL	27
28 COL	29	30 NYI	31			

February

SUN	MON	TUE	WED	THU	FRI	SAT
				1	2 STL	3
4	5 NYR	6	7 PHO	8 STL	9	10
11 CAL	12 PHI	13	14 DAL	15	16	17 PHO
18	19	20	21 CHI	22	23 EDM	24 NAS
25	26	27 CHI	28			

March

SUN	MON	TUE	WED	THU	FRI	SAT
				1	2 CHI	3
4 COL	5	6 NAS	7	8	9 LA	10
11 BOS	12	13 NAS	14 NAS	15	16	17 VAN
18	19	20 CAL	21	22 CLB	23	24 STL
25	26 ANA	27	28	29 NAS	30 DAL	31

April

SUN	MON	TUE	WED	THU	FRI	SAT
1 CLB	2	3 CLB	4	5 CHI	6	7 CHI

2006-07 SEASON

CLUB DIRECTORY

Owner/governor
Mike Ilitch
Owner/secretary-treasurer
Marian Ilitch
President, Ilitch Holdings
Christopher Ilitch
Sr. vice president/alternate governor
Jim Devellano
General manager
Ken Holland
Assistant general manager
Jim Nill
Head coach
Mike Babcock
Assistant coaches
Paul MacLean
Todd McLellan
Goaltending consultant
Jim Bedard
NHL scouts
Mark Howe, Bob McCammon
Scouts
Hakan Andersson, Evgeni Erfilov, Bruce Haralson, Vladimir Havluj, David Kolb, Mark Leach, Joe McDonnell, Glenn Merkosky, Marty Stein
Athletic trainer
Piet VanZant
Equipment manager
Paul Boyer
Assistant athletic trainer
Russ Baumann
Masseur
Sergei Tchekmarev
Team doctors
David Collon, M.D.
Anthony Colucci, M.D.
Team dentist
C.J. Regula, D.M.D.
Senior director of communications
John Hahn
Community relations manager
AnneMarie Krappmann

2006 DRAFT CHOICES

Rd.-Overall		Ht., Wt.	Amateur league, team	Position
2-41	CORY EMMERTON	5-11, 177	OHL, Kingston	C/LW
2-47	SHAWN MATTHIAS	6-3, 211	OHL, Belleville	C
2-62	DICK AXELSSON	6-2, 198	SWE, Huddinge	W
3-92	DANIEL LARSSON	6-0, 170	SWE, Hammarby	G
6-182	JAN MURSAK	5-11, 167	CZECH JR., Budejovice Jr.	LW
7-191	NICK OSLUND	6-3, 195	USHSW, Burnsville	RW
7-212	LOGAN PYETT	5-10, 199	WHL, Regina	D

MISCELLANEOUS DATA

Home ice (capacity)
Joe Louis Arena (20,066)
Address
600 Civic Center Drive
Detroit, MI 48226
Business phone
313-396-7544
Ticket information
313-396-7575
Website
www.detroitredwings.com
Training site
Center I.C.E., Traverse City, Mich.
Club colors
Red and white
Radio affiliation
Team 1270 WXYT (AM)
TV affiliation
FOX Sports Net Detroit (Cable)

EDMONTON OILERS

WESTERN CONFERENCE, NORTHWEST DIVISION

Oilers Schedule

Home games shaded.

October

SUN	MON	TUE	WED	THU	FRI	SAT
1	2	3	4	5 CAL	6	7 CAL
8	9	10	11	12 SJ	13	14 COL
15	16 VAN	17 VAN	18	19	20	21 DET
22	23 PHO	24	25 ANA	26 PHO	27	28 WAS
29	30	31				

November

SUN	MON	TUE	WED	THU	FRI	SAT
			1 NAS	2	3 DAL	4
5	6	7 MON	8 DET	9	10 CLB	11
12 STL	13 COL	14	15	16 STL	17	18 DET
19	20	21 CAL	22	23	24 CHI	25
26	27	28 ANA	29	30 COL		

December

SUN	MON	TUE	WED	THU	FRI	SAT
					1	2 CLB
3	4 VAN	5	6 CAR	7	8 DAL	9
10 CHI	11	12 NAS	13	14 MIN	15 COL	16
17	18	19 COL	20	21 PHO	22	23 DAL
24	25	26	27	28 LA	29	30 VAN
31 CAL						

January

SUN	MON	TUE	WED	THU	FRI	SAT
	1	2 FLA	3	4 DAL	5 VAN	6
7	8 LA	9	10 SJ	11	12 MIN	13 CAL
14	15	16 MIN	17	18 ANA	19	20 CAL
21	22	23	24	25	26 SJ	27 LA
28	29	30	31 CLB			

February

SUN	MON	TUE	WED	THU	FRI	SAT
				1 VAN	2	3 COL
4	5	6 VAN	7	8	9 CHI	10
11 ATL	12	13 BOS	14	15 BUF	16	17 TOR
18	19	20 OTT	21	22 CLB	23 DET	24
25 MIN	26	27 PHO	28			

March

SUN	MON	TUE	WED	THU	FRI	SAT
				1 MIN	2	3 CAL
4	5	6	7 TB	8	9 ANA	10
11 SJ	12 LA	13	14	15 MIN	16	17 STL
18	19 VAN	20	21 COL	22	23 COL	24 NAS
25	26	27 NAS	28	29 STL	30	31

April

SUN	MON	TUE	WED	THU	FRI	SAT
1 CHI	2	3 MIN	4	5 MIN	6	7 CAL

2006-07 SEASON

CLUB DIRECTORY

Owner
Edmonton Investors Group, Ltd.
Chairman of the board, governor
Cal Nichols
Alternate governors
Patrick LaForge, Bill Butler, Kevin Lowe
President & chief executive officer
Patrick LaForge
General manager, exec. v.p.
Kevin Lowe
Assistant general manager
Scott Howson
V.p. of hockey operations
Kevin Prendergast
Head coach
Craig MacTavish
Assistant coaches
Charlie Huddy, Bill Moores, Craig Simpson
Video coach
Brian Ross
Goaltending coach
Pete Peeters
Development coach
Kelly Buchberger
Director, research, analysis & software
Sean Draper
Scouting staff
Mike Abbamont, Bob Brown, Bill Dandy, Brad Davis, Lorne Davis, Morey Gare, Kent Hawley, Stu MacGregor, Chris McCarthy, Frank Musil, Kent Nilsson, Dave Semenko
Head medical trainer
Ken Lowe
Head equipment manager
Barrie Stafford
Equipment managers
Lyle Kulchisky, Jeff Lang
Massage therapist
Stewart Poirier
V.p. of communications/broadcasting
Allan Watt
Information coordinator
Steve Knowles
Coordinator of communications/media
J.J. Hebert
Team services coordinator
Patrick Garland
Vice president, finance & CFO
Darryl Boessenkool
Exec. v.p., commercial operations
Stew MacDonald
V.p., sales & customer relationships
Eric Upton
V.p., corporate sales
Brad MacGregor
Manager, corporate communications
Darren Krill
New media production
Andreas Schwabe, Marc Ciampa

2006 DRAFT CHOICES

Rd.-Overall	Ht., Wt.	Amateur league, team	Position
2-45 JEFF PETRY	6-2, 176	USHL, Des Moines	D
3-75 THEO PECKHAM	6-2, 216	OHL, Owen Sound	D
5-133 BRYAN PITTON	6-1, 168	OHL, Brampton	G
5-140 CODY WILD	6-1, 183	H-EAST, Providence	D
6-170 ALEXANDER BUMAGIN	6-0, 180	RUSSIA, Togliatti	W

MISCELLANEOUS DATA

Home ice (capacity)
Rexall Place (16,839)
Address
11230 110 Street
Edmonton, AB T5G 3H7
Business phone
780-414-4000
Ticket information
780-414-4625
Website
www.edmontonoilers.com
Training site
Rexall Place; Coca-Cola Arena & Crystal Centre
Club colors
White, midnight blue, metallic copper and red
Radio affiliation
CHED (630 AM)
TV affiliation
SportsNet & CBXT-TV

FLORIDA PANTHERS

EASTERN CONFERENCE, SOUTHEAST DIVISION

Panthers Schedule

Home games shaded.

October

SUN	MON	TUE	WED	THU	FRI	SAT
1	2	3	4	5	6 BOS	7 ATL
8	9 TOR	10	11 CAR	12	13 TB	14 TB
15	16	17	18 WAS	19	20 PHI	21 ATL
22	23 ATL	24	25 NYR	26 NJ	27	28 NYI
29	30	31 SJ				

November

SUN	MON	TUE	WED	THU	FRI	SAT
			1	2 TOR	3	4
5	6	7	8 NYR	9	10 BUF	11 NJ
12	13 WAS	14	15	16 MON	17	18 NYI
19	20 BOS	21	22 TB	23	24 OTT	25 ATL
26	27	28 MON	29	30 OTT		

December

SUN	MON	TUE	WED	THU	FRI	SAT
					1	2 ATL
3	4	5 PIT	6	7 BUF	8	9 NYI
10 NYR	11	12 ANA	13	14 BUF	15	16 BOS
17	18	19 TOR	20	21 NYR	22	23 CAR
24	25	26 CAR	27 PHI	28	29 MON	30
31						

January

SUN	MON	TUE	WED	THU	FRI	SAT
	1	2 EDM	3	4 CAL	5	6
7 VAN	8	9	10 PIT	11 CAR	12	13 WAS
14	15	16 CAR	17	18 TOR	19	20 WAS
21	22	23	24	25	26	27 NJ
28	29	30 PIT	31			

February

SUN	MON	TUE	WED	THU	FRI	SAT
				1 WAS	2	3 LA
4	5	6 COL	7	8 MIN	9	10 PHO
11	12	13 MON	14 OTT	15	16	17 TB
18	19	20 TB	21	22 PIT	23	24 BOS
25	26	27 WAS	28			

March

SUN	MON	TUE	WED	THU	FRI	SAT
				1 DAL	2	3 TB
4	5	6 ATL	7	8 PHI	9	10 ATL
11	12	13 CAR	14	15 BUF	16	17 NYI
18	19	20 PHI	21	22 OTT	23	24 NJ
25	26	27 TB	28 ATL	29	30 WAS	31

April

SUN	MON	TUE	WED	THU	FRI	SAT
1 CAR	2	3 WAS	4	5	6 TB	7 CAR

2006-07 SEASON

CLUB DIRECTORY

General partner and chairman of the board/CEO
Alan Cohen
General manager, alternate governor
Mike Keenan
Chief operating officer
Michael Yormark
Head coach
Jacques Martin
Assistant coaches
Guy Charron, George Kingston
Goaltending coach
Phil Myre
Video coach
Pierre Grouix
Director of hockey operations
Jack Birch
Director of player development
Duane Sutter
Strength & conditioning coach
Andy O'Brien
Director of scouting
Scott Luce
Head amateur scout
Darwin Bennett
Physical therapist
Steve Dischiavi
Medical trainer
Curtis Bell
Medical trainer/massage therapist
Jim Pizzutelli
Head equipment manager
Robert McLean
Assistant equipment managers
Chris Moody, Rob Kennedy

2006 DRAFT CHOICES

Rd.-Overall	Ht., Wt.	Amateur league, team	Position
1-10 MICHAEL FROLIK	6-1, 185	CZECH, Kladno	C/W
3-73 BRADY CALLA	6-0, 190	WHL, Everett	RW
4-103 MICHAEL CARUSO	6-2, 191	OHL, Guelph	D
4-116 DERRICK LAPOINT	6-2, 175	USHSW, Eau Claire North	D
6-155 PETER ASTON	6-1, 205	OHL, Windsor	D
7-193 MARC CHEVERIE	6-3, 183	BCHL, Nanaimo	G

MISCELLANEOUS DATA

Home ice (capacity)
BankAtlantic Center (19,250)
Address
One Panther Parkway
Sunrise, FL 33323
Business phone
954-835-7000
Ticket information
954-835-7825
Website
www.floridapanthers.com; sselive.com
Training site
Incredible Ice in Coral Springs, Fla.
Club colors
Red, navy, yellow and gold
Radio affiliation
WQAM (560 AM)
TV affiliation
FOX SportsNet Florida

LOS ANGELES KINGS
WESTERN CONFERENCE, PACIFIC DIVISION

Kings Schedule
Home games shaded.

October

SUN	MON	TUE	WED	THU	FRI	SAT
1	2	3	4	5	6 ANA	7 STL
8	9	10 NYI	11	12 DAL	13	14 DAL
15	16 DET	17	18 MIN	19 PHO	20	21
22 ANA	23 COL	24	25 MIN	26	27 CLB	28 DAL
29	30 NYR	31				

November

SUN	MON	TUE	WED	THU	FRI	SAT
			1 PIT	2	3	4 PHO
5	6	7 COL	8	9 SJ	10	11 MIN
12	13 SJ	14	15	16 PHI	17	18 PHO
19	20	21	22 SJ	23	24 DAL	25 CAL
26	27 NJ	28	29	30 PHO		

December

SUN	MON	TUE	WED	THU	FRI	SAT
					1	2 ANA
3 ANA	4	5	6	7 NAS	8	9 COL
10	11	12 SJ	13	14 SJ	15	16 DAL
17	18	19 CAL	20	21 STL	22	23 NAS
24	25	26 PHO	27	28 EDM	29 CAL	30
31 DET						

January

SUN	MON	TUE	WED	THU	FRI	SAT
	1	2	3 CLB	4	5	6 DET
7	8 EDM	9	10	11 SJ	12	13 STL
14	15 DAL	16 ATL	17	18 STL	19	20 PHO
21	22	23	24	25	26 VAN	27 EDM
28	29	30 CAL	31			

February

SUN	MON	TUE	WED	THU	FRI	SAT
				1 CHI	2	3 FLA
4	5	6 TB	7	8 WAS	9	10 NAS
11	12	13 CAR	14	15	16	17 ANA
18 ANA	19	20	21	22 VAN	23	24 COL
25	26	27	28			

March

SUN	MON	TUE	WED	THU	FRI	SAT
				1 ANA	2	3 NAS
4	5	6 CHI	7 CLB	8	9 DET	10
11 DAL	12 EDM	13	14	15 CHI	16	17 CLB
18 ANA	19	20	21 DAL	22	23 CHI	24 MIN
25	26	27 SJ	28	29 VAN	30	31

April

SUN	MON	TUE	WED	THU	FRI	SAT
1 SJ	2	3 VAN	4	5 PHO	6	7 PHO

2006-07 SEASON
CLUB DIRECTORY

Owners
Philip F. Anschutz
Edward P. Roski, Jr.
Governor
Tim Leiweke
President, general manager
Dean Lombardi
Coach
Marc Crawford
Assistant coaches
Mike Johnston, Jamie Kompon, Nelson Emerson, Bill Ranford
Assistant g.m.
Ron Hextall
Director of amateur scouting
Al Murray
Asst. director of amateur scouting
Grant Sonier
Director of operations
Marshall Dickerson
Scouting coordinator
Lee Callans
Exec. asst., president/general manager
Kely Lyon
Scouting staff
Jan Vopat, Ari Vuori, Mike Donnelly, Viacheslav Golovin, Victor Tjumenev, Mike O'Connell, Rob Laird, Bob Crocker, Brent McEwen, Terry McDonnell, Tony Gasparini, Bob Berry
Vice president of sales and marketing
Chris McGowan
V.p., communications and broadcasting
Michael Altieri
Director, communications
Jeff Moeller
Manager, communications
Mike Kalinowski
Comm./broadcasting supervisor
Stephanie Krauss
Trainers
Mike Kadar, Darren Granger, Corey Osmak, Dana Bryson

2006 DRAFT CHOICES

Rd.-Overall		Ht., Wt.	Amateur league, team	Position
1-11	JONATHAN BERNIER	5-11, 177	QMJHL, Lewiston	G
1-17	TREVOR LEWIS	6-1, 192	USHL, Des Moines	C
2-48	JOE RYAN	6-1, 189	QMJHL, Quebec	D
3-74	JEFF ZATKOFF	6-1, 150	CCHA, Miami University	G
3-86	BUD HOLLOWAY	6-0, 190	WHL, Seattle	C/RW
4-114	NICLAS ANDERSEN	6-1, 207	SWE, Leksand	D
5-134	DAVID MECKLER	6-0, 184	ECAC, Yale	C
5-144	MARTIN NOLET	6-3, 209	QAAAJHL, Champlain	D
6-164	CONSTANTIN BRAUN	6-3, 198	GERMANY, Eisbaren	LW

MISCELLANEOUS DATA

Home ice (capacity)
Staples Center (18,118)
Address
Staples Center
1111 South Figueroa St.
Los Angeles, CA 90015
Business phone
213-742-7100
Ticket information
888-546-4752
Website
www.lakings.com
Training site
Toyota Sports Center
Club colors
Purple, silver, black and white
Radio affiliation
TBA
TV affiliation
FOX Sports West

MINNESOTA WILD
WESTERN CONFERENCE, NORTHWEST DIVISION

MINNESOTA WILD

Wild Schedule
Home games shaded.

October

SUN	MON	TUE	WED	THU	FRI	SAT
1	2	3	4	5 COL	6	7 NAS
8	9	10 VAN	11	12 WAS	13	14 CLB
15	16	17	18 LA	19	20 ANA	21 SJ
22	23	24	25 LA	26	27 ANA	28
29 COL	30	31				

November

SUN	MON	TUE	WED	THU	FRI	SAT
			1	2 VAN	3	4 NAS
5	6	7 SJ	8	9	10	11 LA
12 ANA	13	14 PHO	15	16 NAS	17	18 COL
19	20 OTT	21	22 MON	23	24 PHO	25 CLB
26	27	28	29 SJ	30		

December

SUN	MON	TUE	WED	THU	FRI	SAT
					1 DET	2 DAL
3	4	5 CHI	6	7 CAL	8	9 CHI
10	11	12 CAL	13	14 EDM	15	16 VAN
17	18	19 VAN	20	21	22 DET	23 DET
24	25	26 TOR	27 DET	28	29 CLB	30
31 ANA						

January

SUN	MON	TUE	WED	THU	FRI	SAT
	1	2 ATL	3	4 TB	5	6 COL
7	8	9 CAL	10	11 VAN	12 EDM	13
14 CHI	15	16 EDM	17	18	19 CHI	20 DAL
21	22	23	24	25	26 CAL	27 CLB
28	29	30 STL	31			

February

SUN	MON	TUE	WED	THU	FRI	SAT
				1 COL	2	3 PHO
4	5	6 DAL	7	8 FLA	9	10 CAR
11	12	13	14 VAN	15	16	17 NAS
18 STL	19	20 DAL	21	22 COL	23	24
25 EDM	26	27	28 CAL			

March

SUN	MON	TUE	WED	THU	FRI	SAT
				1 EDM	2	3
4 VAN	5	6 SJ	7	8 BOS	9 BUF	10
11 COL	12	13 VAN	14	15 EDM	16	17 CAL
18	19	20 PHO	21	22 STL	23	24 LA
25	26	27 CAL	28	29 CAL	30	31 COL

April

SUN	MON	TUE	WED	THU	FRI	SAT
1	2	3 EDM	4	5 EDM	6	7 STL

2006-07 SEASON
CLUB DIRECTORY

Chairman
Robert O. Naegele Jr.
Vice chairman
Jac Sperling
President and general manager
Doug Risebrough
Executive vice president
Matt Majka
V.p., communications & broadcasting
Bill Robertson
Assistant general manager/hockey operations
Tom Lynn
Assistant general manager/player personnel
Tom Thompson
Head coach
Jacques Lemaire
Assistant coaches
Mike Ramsey, Mario Tremblay
Goaltending coach
Bob Mason
Director of strength & conditioning
Kirk Olson
Director of pro scouting
Blair Mackasey
Coordinator, amateur scouting
Guy Lapointe
Coordinator, player development
Barry MacKenzie
Scouts
Paul Charles, Marc Chamard, Christopher Hamel, Glen Sonmor, Ernie Vargas, Doug Mosher, Darryl Porter, Frank Effinger, Thomas Steen, Matti Vaisanen, Branislav Gaborik, Ken Hoodikoff, Jiri Koluch
Head athletic therapist
Don Fuller
Head equipment manager
Tony DaCosta
Medical director
Dr. Sheldon Burns
Orthopedic surgeon
Dr. Joel Boyd
Team dentist
Dr. Michael Nanne

2006 DRAFT CHOICES

Rd.-Overall		Ht., Wt.	Amateur league, team	Position
1-9	JAMES SHEPPARD	6-1, 204	QMJHL, Cape Breton	C
2-40	ONDREJ FIALA	6-1, 183	WHL, Everett	C
3-72	CAL CLUTTERBUCK	5-10, 196	OHL, Oshawa	RW
4-102	KYLE MEDVEC	6-5, 191	USHSW, Apple Valley	D
5-132	NIKO HOVINEN	6-7, 200	FINLAND, Jokerit	G
6-162	JULIAN WALKER	6-2, 209	SUI, Basel	W
7-192	CHRIS HICKEY	6-1, 190	USHSW, Cretin Derham Hall	C

MISCELLANEOUS DATA

Home ice (capacity)
Xcel Energy Center (18,064)
Office address
317 Washington Street
St. Paul, MN 55102
Business phone
651-602-6000
Ticket information
651-222-9453
Website
www.wild.com
Training site
Parade Ice Garden, Minneapolis
Club colors
Red, green, gold and wheat
Radio affiliation
WCCO (830 AM)
TV affiliation
FOX Sports Net (Cable), KSTC TV (Channel 45)

MONTREAL CANADIENS
EASTERN CONFERENCE, NORTHEAST DIVISION

Canadiens Schedule
Home games shaded.

October

SUN	MON	TUE	WED	THU	FRI	SAT
1	2	3	4	5	6 BUF	7 TOR
8	9	10	11 PHI	12	13	14 OTT
15	16	17 CAL	18 CHI	19	20	21 COL
22	23 BUF	24	25	26 BOS	27	28 TOR
29	30	31 OTT				

November

SUN	MON	TUE	WED	THU	FRI	SAT
			1	2 CAR	3	4 NJ
5	6	7 EDM	8	9	10	11 TOR
12	13 OTT	14	15 TB	16 FLA	17	18 ATL
19	20	21	22 MIN	23	24 BUF	25 PHI
26	27	28 FLA	29	30 CAR		

December

SUN	MON	TUE	WED	THU	FRI	SAT
					1	2 TOR
3	4 BOS	5	6 NJ	7 NYI	8	9 BUF
10	11	12 BOS	13	14 TB	15	16 PIT
17	18	19 BUF	20	21 PHI	22	23 BOS
24	25	26	27 WAS	28	29 FLA	30 TB
31						

January

SUN	MON	TUE	WED	THU	FRI	SAT
	1	2 TB	3	4 WAS	5	6 NYR
7 NJ	8	9 ATL	10	11 PHI	12	13 OTT
14	15 DET	16 VAN	17	18 ATL	19	20 BUF
21	22	23	24	25	26	27 TOR
28	29 OTT	30	31			

February

SUN	MON	TUE	WED	THU	FRI	SAT
				1 PIT	2	3 NYI
4 PIT	5	6 CAR	7	8 OTT	9	10 OTT
11	12	13 FLA	14 NJ	15	16	17 CAR
18 CLB	19	20 WAS	21	22 NAS	23	24 NYI
25	26 TOR	27 NYR	28			

March

SUN	MON	TUE	WED	THU	FRI	SAT
				1	2 BUF	3 BOS
4	5	6	7	8 ATL	9	10 STL
11	12	13 NYI	14	15	16 PIT	17 TOR
18	19	20 BOS	21	22 BOS	23	24 WAS
25	26	27 NYR	28	29	30 OTT	31 BUF

April

SUN	MON	TUE	WED	THU	FRI	SAT
1	2	3 BOS	4	5 NYR	6	7 TOR

2006-07 SEASON
CLUB DIRECTORY

Owner and governor
George N. Gillett Jr.
Vice chairman
Jeff Joyce
President of club de hockey Canadien and the Bell Centre
Pierre Boivin
Assistant to the president
Foster Gillett
Executive v.p. and general manager
Bob Gainey
Chief financial officer
Fred Steer
Vice president, marketing and sales
Ray Lalonde
V.p., comm. and community relations
Donald Beauchamp
V.p., operations, Bell Centre
Alain Gauthier
Vice president of hockey operations and legal affairs
Julien BriseBois
Director of player personnel
Trevor Timmins
Asst. g.m./head of pro scouting
Pierre Gauthier
Head coach
Guy Carbonneau
Assistant coaches
Roland Melanson, Kirk Muller, Doug Jarvis
Pro scouts
Gordie Roberts, Richard Green
Amateur scouting coordinator
Pierre Dorion
Scouting staff
Elmer Benning, William A. Berglund, Hannu Laine, Dave Mayville, Vaughn Karpan Antonin Routa, Nikolai Vakourov, Patrik Allvin, Denis Morel, Michael Boucher
Equipment manager
Pierre Gervais
Assistant to the equipment manager
Pierre Ouellette
Video supervisor
Mario Leblanc
Club physician and chief surgeon
Dr. David Mulder
Head athletic therapist
Graham Rynbend
Strength & conditioning coordinator
Scott Livingston
Director of media relations
Dominick Saillant

2006 DRAFT CHOICES

Rd.-Overall		Ht., Wt.	Amateur league, team	Position
1-20	DAVID FISCHER	6-3, 185	USHSW, Apple Valley	D
2-49	BEN MAXWELL	6-0, 177	WHL, Kootenay	C
2-53	MATHIEU CARLE	6-0, 206	QMJHL, Acadie-Bathurst	D
3-66	RYAN WHITE	5-11, 200	WHL, Calgary	C
5-139	PAVEL VALENTENKO	6-2, 202	RPL, Neftekamsk	D
7-199	CAMERON CEPEK	6-1, 170	WHL, Portland	D

MISCELLANEOUS DATA

Home ice (capacity)
Bell Centre (21,273)
Address
1260 rue de la Gauchetiere Ouest
Montreal, Que. H3B 5E8
Business phone
514-932-2582
Ticket information
1-800-361-4595
Website
www.canadiens.com
Training site
Centre Bell, Montreal
Club colors
Red, white and blue
Radio affiliation
CJAD (800 AM), CKAC (730 AM)
TV affiliation
RDS (33)

NASHVILLE PREDATORS

WESTERN CONFERENCE, CENTRAL DIVISION

Predators Schedule

Home games shaded.

October

SUN	MON	TUE	WED	THU	FRI	SAT
1	2	3	4	5 CHI	6	7 MIN
8	9	10	11	12 CHI	13	14 PHO
15	16 NYI	17	18 NYR	19 NJ	20	21 VAN
22	23	24	25	26 SJ	27	28 CAL
29	30	31 VAN				

November

SUN	MON	TUE	WED	THU	FRI	SAT
			1 EDM	2	3	4 MIN
5	6	7	8	9	10 DET	11 COL
12	13	14	15 CLB	16 MIN	17	18 CLB
19	20 CLB	21	22 DAL	23 VAN	24	25 DET
26	27	28	29 PHI	30 STL		

December

SUN	MON	TUE	WED	THU	FRI	SAT
					1	2 CHI
3	4 PHO	5	6 ANA	7 LA	8	9 SJ
10	11	12 EDM	13	14 OTT	15	16 STL
17 STL	18	19	20 CHI	21 BUF	22	23 LA
24	25	26 STL	27	28	29 DAL	30 BOS
31						

January

SUN	MON	TUE	WED	THU	FRI	SAT
	1 COL	2	3	4	5 CHI	6 STL
7	8	9 ANA	10	11	12 CLB	13 CLB
14	15 CAL	16	17 DET	18 CLB	19	20 CHI
21	22	23	24	25	26 CHI	27 STL
28	29	30 COL	31			

February

SUN	MON	TUE	WED	THU	FRI	SAT
				1 PHO	2	3 ANA
4	5	6 PIT	7	8 TOR	9	10 LA
11	12	13	14 SJ	15	16 STL	17 MIN
18	19 PHO	20	21	22 MON	23	24 DET
25 CLB	26	27	28 SJ			

March

SUN	MON	TUE	WED	THU	FRI	SAT
				1	2	3 LA
4 ANA	5	6 DET	7	8 CAL	9	10 CLB
11	12	13 DET	14 DET	15	16	17 DAL
18	19	20	21 VAN	22	23 CAL	24 EDM
25	26	27 EDM	28	29 DET	30	31 DAL

April

SUN	MON	TUE	WED	THU	FRI	SAT
1	2	3 CHI	4	5 STL	6	7 COL

2006-07 SEASON

CLUB DIRECTORY

Owner, chairman and governor
Craig Leipold
Exec. v.p. hockey operations/g.m.
David Poile
V.p. finance and admin./CFO
Ed Lang
Exec. v. p. business affairs
Steve Violetta
Asst. g.m./Director of player personnel
Paul Fenton
Director of hockey operations
Michael Santos
Senior v.p., comm./development
Gerry Helper
Head coach
Barry Trotz
Associate coach
Brent Peterson
Assistant coach
Peter Horachek
Goaltending coach
Mitch Korn
Head athletic trainer
Dan Redmond
Equipment manager
Pete Rogers
Video coach
Robert Bouchard
Pro scouts
Nick Beverley, Dan MacKinnon
North American amateur scouts
Gord Donnelly, Jeff Kealty, Rick Knickle, Glen Sanders, David Westby
European scouts
Lucas Bergman, Janne Kekalainen, Martin Bakula

2006 DRAFT CHOICES

Rd.-Overall	Ht., Wt.	Amateur league, team	Position
2-56 BLAKE GEOFFRION	6-1, 190	USA, U.S. National U-18	LW
4-105 NIKO SNELLMAN	6-1, 191	FINLAND JR., Ilves Jr.	W
5-146 MARK DEKANICH	6-2, 192	ECAC, Colgate	G
6-176 RYAN FLYNN	6-2, 212	USA, U.S. National U-18	RW
7-206 VIKTOR SJODIN	6-0, 207	SJL, Vasteras Jr.	W

MISCELLANEOUS DATA

Home ice (capacity)
Gaylord Entertainment Center (17,113)
Address
501 Broadway
Nashville, TN 37203
Business phone
615-770-2000
Ticket information
615-770-7825
Website
www.nashvillepredators.com
Training site
Centennial Sportsplex, Nashville
Club colors
Blue, gold, silver, steel and orange
Radio affiliation
WGFX 104.5 (The Zone) and WNSR Sports56
TV affiliation
FOX Sports Net South

NEW JERSEY DEVILS
EASTERN CONFERENCE, ATLANTIC DIVISION

Devils Schedule
Home games shaded.

October

SUN	MON	TUE	WED	THU	FRI	SAT
1	2	3	4	5	6 CAR	7 DAL
8	9	10	11	12 TOR	13	14 PHI
15	16 NYR	17	18 PIT	19 NAS	20	21 OTT
22	23	24 PIT	25	26 FLA	27	28 CLB
29	30	31				

November

SUN	MON	TUE	WED	THU	FRI	SAT
			1	2 NYI	3	4 MON
5	6	7 CAR	8	9 CHI	10	11 FLA
12	13	14 NYR	15	16	17 OTT	18 TOR
19	20	21	22 PHO	23	24 ANA	25 SJ
26	27 LA	28	29	30		

December

SUN	MON	TUE	WED	THU	FRI	SAT
					1 PIT	2 PHI
3	4	5	6 MON	7	8 PHI	9 BOS
10	11	12 BUF	13	14 BOS	15	16 DET
17 NYR	18	19 ATL	20	21	22 WAS	23 ATL
24	25	26 PIT	27	28	29 WAS	30 NYI
31						

January

SUN	MON	TUE	WED	THU	FRI	SAT
	1	2 NYR	3	4 NYI	5	6 OTT
7 MON	8	9	10 STL	11	12 ATL	13 NYI
14	15	16 NYR	17	18 TB	19	20 PHI
21	22	23	24	25	26 TB	27 FLA
28	29	30 ATL	31			

February

SUN	MON	TUE	WED	THU	FRI	SAT
				1 PHI	2	3 BUF
4	5	6 NYR	7	8 NYI	9	10
11 TB	12	13	14 MON	15	16 PIT	17 NYI
18	19	20 NYR	21	22 NYR	23	24 WAS
25 WAS	26	27 PIT	28			

March

SUN	MON	TUE	WED	THU	FRI	SAT
				1	2 TOR	3
4 BOS	5	6 PHI	7	8 PIT	9	10 BUF
11	12	13	14 PIT	15 CAR	16	17 CAR
18	19	20 TOR	21	22 TB	23	24 FLA
25	26	27 NYI	28 BUF	29	30 PHI	31

April

SUN	MON	TUE	WED	THU	FRI	SAT
1 BOS	2	3 OTT	4	5 PHI	6	7
8 NYI	9	10	11	12	13	14

2006-07 SEASON
CLUB DIRECTORY

CEO/president and general manager
Lou Lamoriello
Chairman and managing partner
Jeff Vanderbeek
Exec. v.p./chief operating officer
Chris Modrzynski
Executive vice president
Peter S. McMullen
CFO/vice president
Scott Strubie
V.p., general counsel
Joseph C. Benedetti
V.p., ticket operations
Terry Farmer
V.p.,corporate partnerships
Kenneth F. Ferriter
V.p., facilities
Mark A. Gheduzzi
V.p., administration
Gordon Lavalette
V.p., information/publications
Mike Levine
V.p., marketing/community development
Jason Siegel
Head coach
Claude Julien
Assistant coaches
Jacques Laperriere
John MacLean
Goaltending coach
Jacques Caron
Special assignment coach
Larry Robinson
Director of scouting
David Conte
Assistant director, scouting
Claude Carrier
Scouts
Marcel Pronovost, Glen Dirk, Milt Fisher, Ferny Flaman, Dan Labraaten, Chris Lamoriello, Vladimir Lokotko, Pierra Mondou, Larry Perris, Lou Reycroft, Vaclav Slansky Jr.
Massage therapist
Tommy Plasko
Strength & conditioning coordinator
Michael Vasalani
Equipment manager
Rich Matthews
Assistant equipment manager
Alex Abasto, Paul Emmick
Exercise physiologist
Dr. Garret Caffrey
Fitness consultant
Vladimir Bure

2006 DRAFT CHOICES

Rd.-Overall		Ht., Wt.	Amateur league, team	Position
1-30	MATTHEW CORRENTE	5-11, 189	OHL, Saginaw	D
2-58	ALEXANDER VASYUNOV	6-0, 189	RPL, Yaroslavl 2	LW
3-67	KIRILL TULUPOV	6-3, 220	RUSSIA, Alemetjevsk	D
3-77	VLADIMIR ZHARKOV	6-0, 187	Russia, CSKA 2	RW
4-107	T.J. MILLER	6-4, 200	BCHL, Penticton	D
5-148	OLIVIER MAGNAN	6-2, 190	QMJHL, Rouyn Noranda	D
6-178	TONY ROMANO	5-10, 170	AJHL, N.Y. Bobcats	C
7-208	KYLE HENEGAN	6-4, 204	QMJHL, Shawinigan	D

MISCELLANEOUS DATA

Home ice (capacity)
Continental Airlines Arena (19,040)
Address
P.O. Box 504
50 Route 120 North
East Rutherford, N.J. 07073
Business phone
201-935-6050
Ticket information
201-935-3900
Website
www.newjerseydevils.com
Training site
Richard J. Codey Arena
Club colors
Red, black and white
Radio affiliation
WFAN (660 AM)
TV affiliation
FOX Sports Net New York

NEW YORK ISLANDERS

EASTERN CONFERENCE, ATLANTIC DIVISION

Islanders Schedule

Home games shaded.

October

SUN	MON	TUE	WED	THU	FRI	SAT
1	2	3	4	5 PHO	6	7 SJ
8	9	10 LA	11 ANA	12	13	14 BOS
15	16 NAS	17	18	19 PIT	20	21 CAR
22	23	24	25	26 BUF	27	28 FLA
29	30	31 CHI				

November

SUN	MON	TUE	WED	THU	FRI	SAT
			1	2 NJ	3	4 ATL
5	6 TB	7	8	9 PHI	10	11
12	13	14	15 DAL	16	17 TB	18 FLA
19	20 TOR	21	22 CAR	23	24 PIT	25 WAS
26	27	28 PIT	29	30 PHI		

December

SUN	MON	TUE	WED	THU	FRI	SAT
					1	2 PIT
3 NYR	4	5 OTT	6	7 MON	8	9 FLA
10	11	12	13	14	15 PIT	16 ATL
17	18	19 NYR	20	21	22 CAR	23 CLB
24	25	26 NYR	27 OTT	28	29	30 NJ
31						

January

SUN	MON	TUE	WED	THU	FRI	SAT
	1 BUF	2 PHI	3	4 NJ	5	6 CAR
7	8	9 NYR	10	11 BOS	12	13 NJ
14	15 TB	16 PIT	17	18 PHI	19	20
21	22	23	24	25	26 ATL	27 BUF
28	29	30 DET	31			

February

SUN	MON	TUE	WED	THU	FRI	SAT
				1 ATL	2	3 MON
4 WAS	5	6	7 PHI	8 NJ	9	10 BOS
11	12	13 TOR	14	15 BOS	16	17 NJ
18	19 PIT	20	21	22 TOR	23	24 MON
25	26	27 PHI	28			

March

SUN	MON	TUE	WED	THU	FRI	SAT
				1 STL	2	3 WAS
4	5 NYR	6	7	8 NYR	9	10 WAS
11	12	13 MON	14	15 OTT	16	17 FLA
18	19	20 TB	21	22 PIT	23	24 PHI
25 NYR	26	27 NJ	28	29	30 BUF	31 OTT

April

SUN	MON	TUE	WED	THU	FRI	SAT
1	2	3 NYR	4	5 TOR	6	7 PHI
8 NJ	9	10	11	12	13	14

2006-07 SEASON

CLUB DIRECTORY

Owner and governor
Charles B. Wang

General manager and alt. governor
Garth Snow

Head coach
Ted Nolan

Assistant coaches
Dan Flynn, Daniel Lacroix

Director of pro scouting
Ken Morrow

Head amateur scout
Tony Feltrin

2006 DRAFT CHOICES

Rd.-Overall	Ht., Wt.	Amateur league, team	Position
1-7 KYLE OKPOSO	6-0, 195	USHL, Des Moines	RW
2-60 JESSE JOENSUU	6-4, 207	FINLAND, Assat	W
3-70 ROBIN FIGREN	5-11, 176	SJL, Frolunda Jr.	W
4-100 RHETT RAKHSHANI	5-10, 170	USA, U.S. National U-18	RW
4-108 JASE WESLOSKY	6-2, 170	AJHL, Sherwood Park	G
4-115 TOMAS MARCINKO	6-4, 187	SVK, Kosice	C
4-119 DOUG ROGERS	6-0, 175	USHSE, St. Sebastian's	C
5-126 SHANE SIMS	5-11, 192	USHL, Des Moines	D
5-141 KIM JOHANSSON	6-1, 172	SJL, Malmo Jr.	W
6-160 ANDREW MACDONALD	6-0, 188	QMJHL, Moncton	D
6-171 BRIAN DAY	6-0, 186	USHSE, Governor Dummer	RW
6-173 STEFAN RIDDERWALL	6-1, 189	SJL, Djurgarden Jr.	G
7-190 TROY MATTILA	6-2, 176	NAHL, Springfield	LW

MISCELLANEOUS DATA

Home ice (capacity)
Nassau Veterans Memorial Coliseum (16,234)

Address
1535 Old Country Road
Plainview, NY 11803

Business phone
516-501-6700

Ticket information
1-800-882-4753

Website
www.newyorkislanders.com

Training site
Iceworks, Syosset, NY

Club colors
Blue and orange

Radio affiliation
Bloomberg Radio (1130 AM)

TV affiliation
FOX Sports Net New York

NEW YORK RANGERS

EASTERN CONFERENCE, ATLANTIC DIVISION

Rangers Schedule

Home games shaded.

October

SUN	MON	TUE	WED	THU	FRI	SAT
1	2	3	4	5 WAS	6	7 PHI
8	9	10 PHI	11	12 PIT	13	14 BUF
15	16 NJ	17	18 NAS	19	20	21 TOR
22	23	24	25 FLA	26	27	28 PHO
29	30 LA	31				

November

SUN	MON	TUE	WED	THU	FRI	SAT
			1 ANA	2 SJ	3	4
5 BUF	6	7	8 FLA	9	10 ATL	11 WAS
12	13	14 NJ	15 CAR	16	17	18 PIT
19 TB	20	21 CAR	22	23	24	25 PIT
26 BUF	27	28 ATL	29	30		

December

SUN	MON	TUE	WED	THU	FRI	SAT
					1 BUF	2
3 NYI	4	5	6	7 PIT	8	9 OTT
10 FLA	11	12 PHI	13	14 DAL	15	16 TOR
17 NJ	18	19 NYI	20	21 FLA	22	23 TB
24	25	26 NYI	27	28	29 OTT	30 WAS
31						

January

SUN	MON	TUE	WED	THU	FRI	SAT
	1	2 NJ	3	4 PHI	5	6 MON
7	8	9 NYI	10	11 OTT	12	13 BOS
14	15	16 NJ	17	18	19	20 ATL
21	22	23	24	25	26	27 PHI
28	29 BOS	30	31 TOR			

February

SUN	MON	TUE	WED	THU	FRI	SAT
				1	2	3 TB
4	5 DET	6 NJ	7	8	9 TB	10 WAS
11	12	13	14	15 CAR	16	17 PHI
18 CHI	19	20 NJ	21	22 NJ	23	24 CLB
25	26	27 MON	28			

March

SUN	MON	TUE	WED	THU	FRI	SAT
				1 PIT	2	3 STL
4	5 NYI	6	7	8 NYI	9	10 PIT
11 CAR	12	13 OTT	14	15	16 ATL	17 BOS
18	19 PIT	20	21 PHI	22	23	24 BOS
25 NYI	26	27 MON	28	29	30	31 PHI

April

SUN	MON	TUE	WED	THU	FRI	SAT
1 TOR	2	3 NYI	4	5 MON	6	7 PIT

2006-07 SEASON

CLUB DIRECTORY

Chairman, MSG
James L. Dolan
Vice chairman, MSG
Hank J. Ratner
President and G.M., alternate governor
Glen Sather
President & CEO, MSG sports; alt. gov
Steve Mills
Vice president, player personnel and assistant G.M.
Don Maloney
Head coach
Tom Renney
Vice president of hockey administration, research and development
Cameron Hope
Assistant coaches
Perry Pearn, Mike Pelino, Benoit Allaire
Director, player personnel—Europe
Christer Rockstrom
Head amateur scout
Gordie Clark
Amateur scouting staff
Andre Beaulieu, Rich Brown, Ray Clearwater, Pierre Dorion, Jan Gajdosik, Ernie Gare, Vladimir Lutchenko, Tim Murray, Shanon Sather
Professional scouting staff
Gilles Leger, Nick Fotiu, Peter Stephen
Manager of scouting
Victor Saljanin
Video analyst
Jerry Dineen
V.p., public relations
John Rosasco
Director, public relations
Sammy Steinlight
Manager, public relations
Jody Sowa
Coordinator, public relations
Dave Martella
Senior v.p., sports team operations
Mark Piazza
V.p., sports team operations
Jason Vogel
V.p., marketing
Jeanie Baumgartner
V.p., marketing services
Janet Duch
V.p. of sponsorship for NY Rangers & NY Knicks
Rob Scolaro
V.p., community/fan development
Kerryann Tomlinson
Dir., special projects/community relations
Rod Gilbert
Medical trainer
Jim Ramsay
Equipment manager
Acacio Marques
Assistant equipment manager
James Johnson
Massage therapist
Bruce Lifrieri
Strength & conditioning coordinator
Reg Grant
Manager, training center operations
Pat Boller

2006 DRAFT CHOICES

Rd.-Overall		Ht., Wt.	Amateur league, team	Position
1-21	BOBBY SANGUINETTI	6-1, 174	OHL, Owen Sound	D
2-54	ARTEM ANISIMOV	6-3, 187	RUSSIA, Yaroslavl	C
3-84	RYAN HILLIER	6-0, 179	QMJHL, Halifax	LW
4-104	DAVID KVETON	5-11, 180	CZECH, Vsetin	RW
5-137	TOMAS ZABORSKY	5-11, 180	SVK, Trencin	W
6-174	ERIC HUNTER	6-1, 194	WHL, Prince George	C
7-204	LUKAS ZELISKA	5-11, 176	CZECH JR., Trinec Jr.	C

MISCELLANEOUS DATA

Home ice (capacity)
Madison Square Garden (18,200)
Address
2 Pennsylvania Plaza
New York, NY 10121
Business phone
212-465-6486
Ticket information
212-307-7171
Website
www.newyorkrangers.com
Training site
MSG Training Center—Tarrytown, NY
Club colors
Blue, red and white
Radio affiliation
MSG Radio
TV affiliation
MSG Network

OTTAWA SENATORS

EASTERN CONFERENCE, NORTHEAST DIVISION

Senators Schedule

Home games shaded.

October

SUN	MON	TUE	WED	THU	FRI	SAT
1	2	3	4 TOR	5 TOR	6	7 BUF
8	9	10	11	12 CAL	13	14 MON
15	16	17	18	19 COL	20	21 NJ
22	23	24 TOR	25	26 TOR	27	28 BOS
29	30	31 MON				

November

SUN	MON	TUE	WED	THU	FRI	SAT
			1	2	3	4 CAR
5	6 WAS	7	8 ATL	9	10 PIT	11 BOS
12	13 MON	14	15 BUF	16	17 NJ	18 BUF
19	20 MIN	21	22 PHI	23	24 FLA	25
26 TB	27	28 CAR	29	30 FLA		

December

SUN	MON	TUE	WED	THU	FRI	SAT
					1	2 TB
3	4	5 NYI	6 WAS	7	8	9 NYR
10 CLB	11	12 DET	13	14 NAS	15	16 BUF
17	18	19 BOS	20	21 TB	22	23 PHI
24	25	26	27 NYI	28	29 NYR	30 TOR
31						

January

SUN	MON	TUE	WED	THU	FRI	SAT
	1 ATL	2	3 BUF	4	5	6 NJ
7 PHI	8	9 BOS	10	11 NYR	12	13 MON
14	15	16 WAS	17	18 VAN	19	20 BOS
21	22	23	24	25	26	27 BOS
28	29 MON	30 WAS	31			

February

SUN	MON	TUE	WED	THU	FRI	SAT
				1	2	3 TOR
4	5	6	7 BUF	8 MON	9	10 MON
11	12	13	14 FLA	15	16	17 ATL
18	19	20 EDM	21	22 BUF	23	24 BUF
25	26	27 CAR	28 CAR			

March

SUN	MON	TUE	WED	THU	FRI	SAT
				1	2 ATL	3
4 CHI	5	6 PIT	7	8 TOR	9	10 TOR
11	12	13 NYR	14	15 NYI	16	17 PHI
18 PIT	19	20 STL	21	22 FLA	23	24 TB
25	26	27 BOS	28	29	30 MON	31 NYI

April

SUN	MON	TUE	WED	THU	FRI	SAT
1	2	3 NJ	4	5 PIT	6	7 BOS

2006-07 SEASON

CLUB DIRECTORY

Owner, governor, and chairman
Eugene Melnyk
President and CEO & alt. governor
Roy Mlakar
General manager
John Muckler
Chief operating officer
Cyril Leeder
V.p. and exec. director, Scotiabank Place
Tom Conroy
Director, hockey administration
Kevin Billet
Head coach
Bryan Murray
Assistant coaches
Greg Carvel
John Paddock
Director of player personnel, pro scout
Anders Hedberg
Conditioning coach
Randy Lee
Goaltending coach, pro scout
Ron Low
Assistant to general manager
Allison Vaughan
Team services and scouting coordinator
Alex Lepore
Video coordinator
Tim Pattyson
Head equipment manager
Scott Allegrino
Assistant equipment manager
Chris Cook
Head athletic trainer, therapist
Gerry Townend
Assistant athletic therapist
Andy Playter
Scouts
Frank Jay, Arne Andersen, Vaclav Burda, George Fargher, Bob Janecyk, Bill McCarthy, Lewis Mongelluzzo, Gord Pell, Nick Polano, Mikko Ruutu, Patrick Savard, Boris Shagas
Vice president, broadcast
Jim Steel
Vice president, communications
Phil Legault
Director, communications
Steve Keogh
Communications coordinator
Brian Morris

2006 DRAFT CHOICES

Rd.-Overall		Ht., Wt.	Amateur league, team	Position
1-28	NICK FOLIGNO	6-0, 188	OHL, Sudbury	LW
3-68	ERIC GRYBA	6-3, 215	USHL, Green Bay	D
3-91	KASPARS DAUGAVINS	5-11, 181	LATVIA, Riga	LW
4-121	PIERRE-LUC LESSARD	6-0, 180	QMJHL, Gatineau	L
5-151	RYAN DANIELS	6-1, 205	OHL, Saginaw	G
6-181	KEVIN KOOPMAN	6-3, 200	KIJHL, Beaver Valley Jr.	D
7-211	ERIK CONDRA	5-11, 180	CCHA, U. of Notre Dame	RW

MISCELLANEOUS DATA

Home ice (capacity)
Scotiabank Place (19,153)
Address
1000 Palladium Drive
Ottawa, Ont. K2V 1A5
Business phone
613-599-0250
Ticket information
613-599-3267
Website
www.ottawasenators.com
Training site
Bell Sensplex
Club colors
Red, black and gold
Radio affiliation
Team 1200 (1200 AM), English
Radio 1150 CJRC (1150 AM), French
TV affiliation
Rogers Sportsnet, A-Channel and RDS

PHILADELPHIA FLYERS
EASTERN CONFERENCE, ATLANTIC DIVISION

Flyers Schedule
Home games shaded.

October

SUN	MON	TUE	WED	THU	FRI	SAT
1	2	3	4	5 PIT	6	7 NYR
8	9	10 NYR	11 MON	12	13	14 NJ
15	16	17 BUF	18	19 TB	20 FLA	21
22	23	24	25	26 ATL	27	28 PIT
29	30 CHI	31				

November

SUN	MON	TUE	WED	THU	FRI	SAT
			1	2 TB	3	4 WAS
5	6 TOR	7	8	9 NYI	10	11 BUF
12	13 PIT	14	15 ANA	16 LA	17	18 SJ
19	20 PIT	21	22 OTT	23	24 CLB	25 MON
26	27	28	29 NAS	30 NYI		

December

SUN	MON	TUE	WED	THU	FRI	SAT
					1	2 NJ
3	4	5	6	7	8 NJ	9 WAS
10	11	12 NYR	13 PIT	14	15	16 WAS
17	18	19 CAR	20	21 MON	22	23 OTT
24	25	26	27 FLA	28 TB	29	30
31 CAR						

January

SUN	MON	TUE	WED	THU	FRI	SAT
	1	2 NYI	3	4 NYR	5	6 BOS
7 OTT	8	9 WAS	10	11 MON	12	13 PIT
14	15	16	17	18 NYI	19	20 NJ
21	22	23	24	25	26	27 NYR
28 ATL	29	30 TB	31			

February

SUN	MON	TUE	WED	THU	FRI	SAT
				1 NJ	2	3 ATL
4	5	6	7 NYI	8 PIT	9	10 STL
11	12 DET	13	14	15 TOR	16	17 NYR
18	19 BOS	20 BUF	21	22 CAR	23	24 TOR
25	26	27 NYI	28			

March

SUN	MON	TUE	WED	THU	FRI	SAT
				1 BOS	2	3
4 PIT	5	6 NJ	7	8 FLA	9	10 BOS
11	12 PHO	13 DAL	14	15 ATL	16	17 OTT
18	19	20 FLA	21 NYR	22	23	24 NYI
25	26	27	28 CAR	29	30 NJ	31 NYR

April

SUN	MON	TUE	WED	THU	FRI	SAT
1	2	3 TOR	4	5 NJ	6	7 NYI
8 BUF	9	10	11	12	13	14

2006-07 SEASON
CLUB DIRECTORY

Chairman and governor
Ed Snider
President & COO, Comcast-Spectacor
Peter Luukko
Alternate governors
Bob Clarke, Peter Luukko, Ron Ryan, Phil Weinberg
General manager
Bob Clarke
Executive vice president
Keith Allen
Senior vice president, sales
Joe Croce
V.p., marketing/communications
Shawn Tilger
Assistant general manager
Paul Holmgren
Head coach
Ken Hitchcock
Assistant coaches
Terry Murray
John Stevens
Goaltending coach
Reggie Lemelin
Director of player personnel
Dave Brown
Pro scout
Al Hill
Scouts
John Chapman, Inge Hammarstrom, Vaclav Slansky, Simon Nolet, Dennis Patterson, Chris Pryor, Evgeny Zimin, Ilkka Sinisalo, Steve Leach, Patrick Burke, Ross Fitzpatrick
Assistant to general manager
Barry Hanrahan
Video coordinator
Adam Patterson
Scouting information coordinator
Bryan Hardenbergh
Executive assistant
Dianna Taylor

2006 DRAFT CHOICES

Rd.-Overall	Ht., Wt.	Amateur league, team	Position
1-22 CLAUDE GIROUX	5-10, 169	QMJHL, Gatineau	RW
2-39 ANDREAS NODL	6-1, 196	USHL, Sioux Falls	RW
2-42 MICHAEL RATCHUK	5-10, 175	USA, U.S. National U-18	D
2-55 DENIS BODROV	6-0, 185	RUSSIA, Togliatti	D
3-79 JONATHAN MATSUMOTO	6-0, 184	CCHA, Bowling Green	C
4-101 JOONAS LEHTIVUORI	5-11, 167	FINLAND JR., Ilves Jr.	D
4-109 JAKUB KOVAR	6-0, 176	CZECH JR., Budejovice Jr.	G
5-145 JONATHAN RHEAULT	5-10, 202	H-EAST, Providence	RW
6-175 MICHAEL DUPONT	6-0, 175	QMJHL, Baie Comeau	G
7-205 ANDREI POPOV	6-0, 187	RUSSIA, Chelyabinsk	RW

MISCELLANEOUS DATA

Home ice (capacity)
Wachovia Center (19,519)
Address
3601 South Broad Street
Philadelphia, PA 19148
Business phone
215-465-4500
Ticket information
215-218-7825
Website
www.philadelphiaflyers.com
Training site
Sovereign Bank Flyers Skate Zone, Voorhees, NJ
Club colors
Orange, white and black
Radio affiliation
WIP (610 AM)
TV affiliation
Comcast SportsNet

PHOENIX COYOTES

WESTERN CONFERENCE, PACIFIC DIVISION

Coyotes Schedule

Home games shaded.

October

SUN	MON	TUE	WED	THU	FRI	SAT
1	2	3	4	5 NYI	6	7 ANA
8	9 CLB	10	11 DET	12	13	14 NAS
15	16	17 STL	18	19 LA	20	21 DAL
22	23 EDM	24 CAL	25	26 EDM	27	28 NYR
29	30	31				

November

SUN	MON	TUE	WED	THU	FRI	SAT
			1	2	3 ANA	4 LA
5	6	7	8	9 DAL	10	11 SJ
12	13	14 MIN	15	16 CHI	17	18 LA
19 ANA	20	21	22 NJ	23	24 MIN	25 STL
26	27	28	29	30 LA		

December

SUN	MON	TUE	WED	THU	FRI	SAT
					1	2
3	4 NAS	5	6 DAL	7 CHI	8	9 DAL
10	11 SJ	12 VAN	13	14 CLB	15	16 CAL
17	18	19	20	21 EDM	22	23 ANA
24	25	26 LA	27	28 SJ	29	30 SJ
31						

January

SUN	MON	TUE	WED	THU	FRI	SAT
	1 WAS	2	3	4 CAR	5 ATL	6
7 CHI	8	9 DAL	10	11 DET	12	13 SJ
14	15 STL	16	17 COL	18 SJ	19	20 LA
21	22	23	24	25	26 COL	27 PIT
28	29	30	31 ANA			

February

SUN	MON	TUE	WED	THU	FRI	SAT
				1 NAS	2	3 MIN
4	5	6 CLB	7 DET	8	9	10 FLA
11	12	13 TB	14	15 ANA	16	17 DET
18	19 NAS	20	21	22 CAL	23	24
25	26 CAL	27 EDM	28			

March

SUN	MON	TUE	WED	THU	FRI	SAT
				1 VAN	2	3 CLB
4	5	6	7 ANA	8 VAN	9	10 CHI
11	12 PHI	13	14	15 SJ	16	17 COL
18 DAL	19	20 MIN	21	22 ANA	23	24 DAL
25	26	27 DAL	28	29 COL	30 SJ	31

April

SUN	MON	TUE	WED	THU	FRI	SAT
1	2	3 STL	4	5 LA	6	7 LA
8 VAN	9	10	11	12	13	14

2006-07 SEASON

CLUB DIRECTORY

Majority investor
Jerry Moyes
CEO
Jeff A. Shumway
Managing partner/alt. gov./head coach
Wayne Gretzky
President/chief operating officer/alt. gov.
Douglas Moss
Sr. executive v.p. of hockey operations
Cliff Fletcher
G.M./exec. v.p./ general manager
Michael Barnett
Exec. v.p., business development
John Browne
Senior v.p. and assistant g.m.
Laurence Gilman
Senior v.p. and chief marketing officer
Michael Bucek
Senior v.p., corporate communications
Jeff Holbrook
Senior v.p., ticket sales
Jim Van Stone
Senior v.p. and CFO
Mike Nealy
Senior v.p., media and player relations
Richard Nairn
Associate coach
Barry Smith
Assistant coaches
Ulf Samuelsson
Goaltending coach
Grant Fuhr
Director of player personnel
Tom Kurvers
Director of player development
Eddie Mio
Director of hockey administration
Stuart Judge
Video coordinator
Steve Peters
Manager of team services
Lesa Guth
Pro scout
Rich Sutter
Amateur scouts
Gus Baldali, Keith Gretzky, Charles Henry, Willy Lindstrom, Steve Lyones, Blair Reid, Greg Royce, Evzen Slansky, Boris, Yemeljano
Strength and conditioning
Mike Bahn
Massage therapist
Jukka Nieminen
Athletic therapist
Chris Broadhurs
Head equipment manager
Stan Wilson

2006 DRAFT CHOICES

Rd.-Overall		Ht., Wt.	Amateur league, team	Position
1-8	PETER MUELLER	6-2, 205	WHL, Everett	C
1-29	CHRIS SUMMERS	6-1, 180	USA, U.S. National U-18	D
3-88	JONAS AHNELOV	6-3, 205	SWEDEN, Frolunda	D
5-130	BRETT BENNETT	6-1, 185	USA, U.S. National U-18	G
5-131	MARTIN LATAL	5-11, 174	CZECH, Kladno	RW
5-152	JORDAN BENDFELD	6-2, 216	WHL, Medicine Hat	D
7-188	CHRIS FRANK	6-0, 213	CCHA, Western Michigan	D
7-196	BENN FERRIERO	5-10, 185	H-EAST, Boston College	C/RW

MISCELLANEOUS DATA

Home ice (capacity)
Glendale Center (17,799)
Address
5800 W. Glenn Avenue
Glendale, AZ 85301
Business phone
623-463-8800
Ticket information
480-563-7825
Website
www.phoenixcoyotes.com
Training site
Glendale, AZ
Club colors
Brick red, desert sand and black
Radio affiliation
KDUS (1060 AM) and KDKB (93.3 FM)
TV affiliation
FOX Sports Arizona, WB 6/61, KTVK (Channel 3)

PITTSBURGH PENGUINS

EASTERN CONFERENCE, ATLANTIC DIVISION

Penguins Schedule

Home games shaded.

October

SUN	MON	TUE	WED	THU	FRI	SAT
1	2	3	4	5 PHI	6	7 DET
8	9	10	11	12 NYR	13	14 CAR
15	16	17	18 NJ	19 NYI	20	21 CLB
22	23	24 NJ	25	26	27	28 PHI
29	30	31				

November

SUN	MON	TUE	WED	THU	FRI	SAT
			1 LA	2	3	4 SJ
5	6 ANA	7	8 TB	9	10 OTT	11 CAR
12	13 PHI	14	15	16	17 BUF	18 NYR
19	20 PHI	21	22 BOS	23	24 NYI	25 NYR
26	27	28 NYI	29	30		

December

SUN	MON	TUE	WED	THU	FRI	SAT
					1 NJ	2 NYI
3	4	5 FLA	6	7 NYR	8	9 ATL
10	11 WAS	12	13 PHI	14	15 NYI	16 MON
17	18	19 STL	20	21 ATL	22	23
24	25	26 NJ	27 ATL	28	29 TOR	30
31						

January

SUN	MON	TUE	WED	THU	FRI	SAT
	1	2 CAR	3	4	5 BUF	6
7 TB	8	9 TB	10 FLA	11	12	13 PHI
14	15	16 NYI	17	18 BOS	19	20 TOR
21	22	23	24	25	26 DAL	27 PHO
28	29	30 FLA	31			

February

SUN	MON	TUE	WED	THU	FRI	SAT
				1 MON	2	3 WAS
4 MON	5	6 NAS	7	8 PHI	9	10 TOR
11	12	13	14 CHI	15	16 NJ	17
18 WAS	19 NYI	20	21	22 FLA	23	24
25 TB	26	27 NJ	28			

March

SUN	MON	TUE	WED	THU	FRI	SAT
				1 NYR	2 CAR	3
4 PHI	5	6 OTT	7	8 NJ	9	10 NYR
11	12	13 BUF	14 NJ	15	16 MON	17
18 OTT	19 NYR	20	21	22 NYI	23	24 ATL
25 BOS	26	27 WAS	28	29 BOS	30	31 TOR

April

SUN	MON	TUE	WED	THU	FRI	SAT
1	2	3 BUF	4	5 OTT	6	7 NYR

2006-07 SEASON

CLUB DIRECTORY

Chairman
Mario Lemieux
President and CEO
Ken Sawyer
Executive v.p./general manager
Ray Shero
Assistant general manager
Chuck Fletcher
Senior adviser, hockey operations
Ed Johnston
Head coach
Michel Therrien
Assistant coaches
Mike Yeo, Andre Savard
Scouts
Gilles Meloche, Rick Kehoe, Chuck Grillo, Mark Kelley, Kevin Stevens, Neil Shea
Equipment manager
Steve Latin
Assistant equipment manager
Paul Flati
Equipment staff
Paul DeFazio
Team physician
Dr. Charles Burke
Strength and conditioning coach
Stephane Dube
Video coordinator
Paul Fink
Athletic trainers
Scott Johnson, Mark Mortland
Massage therapist
David Sampson

2006 DRAFT CHOICES

Rd.-Overall		Ht., Wt.	Amateur league, team	Position
1-2	JORDAN STAAL	6-4, 215	OHL, Peterborough	C
2-32	CARL SNEEP	6-4, 210	USHSW, Brainerd	D
3-65	BRIAN STRAIT	6-0, 200	USA, U.S. National U-18	D
5-125	CHAD JOHNSON	6-2, 175	CCHA, Alaska-Fairbanks	G
7-185	TIMO SEPPANEN	6-1, 209	Finland, IFK	D

MISCELLANEOUS DATA

Home ice (capacity)
Mellon Arena (16,958)
Address
Mellon Arena
66 Mario Lemieux Place
Pittsburgh, PA 15219
Business phone
412-642-1300
Ticket information
412-642-7367 and 1-800-642-7367
Website
www.pittsburghpenguins.com
Training site
Canonsburg, PA
Club colors
Black, gold and white
Radio affiliation
3WS (94.5FM), Fox Sports Radio 970AM
TV affiliation
Fox Sports Net Pittsburgh

ST. LOUIS BLUES
WESTERN CONFERENCE, CENTRAL DIVISION

Blues Schedule
Home games shaded.

October

SUN	MON	TUE	WED	THU	FRI	SAT
1	2	3	4	5 SJ	6	7 LA
8	9 ANA	10	11	12 BOS	13	14 CHI
15	16	17 PHO	18	19	20 VAN	21 CHI
22	23	24	25	26	27	28 DET
29	30 ANA	31				

November

SUN	MON	TUE	WED	THU	FRI	SAT
			1 DAL	2 COL	3	4 CAL
5	6	7	8	9 CLB	10 CHI	11
12 EDM	13	14 CAL	15	16 EDM	17 VAN	18
19	20	21	22 CLB	23	24 DET	25 PHO
26	27	28 SJ	29	30 NAS		

December

SUN	MON	TUE	WED	THU	FRI	SAT
					1 CHI	2
3	4	5 DET	6	7 DET	8	9 CLB
10	11	12 CHI	13 COL	14	15	16 NAS
17 NAS	18	19 PIT	20	21 LA	22	23 BUF
24	25	26 NAS	27	28	29 COL	30 COL
31						

January

SUN	MON	TUE	WED	THU	FRI	SAT
	1	2 CHI	3	4 CHI	5	6 NAS
7	8	9 CLB	10 NJ	11	12	13 LA
14	15 PHO	16 ANA	17	18 LA	19	20 SJ
21	22	23	24	25	26 DET	27 NAS
28	29	30 MIN	31			

February

SUN	MON	TUE	WED	THU	FRI	SAT
				1	2 DET	3 DAL
4	5	6 TOR	7	8 DET	9	10 PHI
11	12	13 SJ	14 CLB	15	16 NAS	17
18 MIN	19	20 CLB	21	22	23	24
25 CHI	26	27 VAN	28			

March

SUN	MON	TUE	WED	THU	FRI	SAT
				1 NYI	2	3 NYR
4	5	6 CAL	7	8 DAL	9	10 MON
11	12 CAL	13	14	15 VAN	16	17 EDM
18	19	20 OTT	21	22 MIN	23	24 DET
25 CLB	26	27 CLB	28	29 EDM	30	31 ANA

April

SUN	MON	TUE	WED	THU	FRI	SAT
1	2 DAL	3 PHO	4	5 NAS	6	7 MIN

2006-07 SEASON
CLUB DIRECTORY

Chairman
David W. Checketts
Partners
Kenneth W. Munoz, Michael McCarthy
President of hockey operations
John Davidson
CEO, St. Louis Blues enterprises
Peter McLoughlin
Sr. v.p. and G.M.
Larry Pleau
Sr. v.p., finance and hockey admin.
Jerry Jasiek
Senior v.p. and g.m., Savvis Center
Dennis Petrullo
V.p. of sales
Bruce Affleck
V.p. of marketing
Jo Ann Miles
V.p. of human resources
Dave Coverstone
V.p. of building operations
Fred Corsi
Asst. g.m./director, amateur scouting
Jo Ann Miles
Head coach
Mike Kitchen
Assistant coach/goaltending coach
Rick Wamsley
Assistant coach
Brad Shaw
Strength and conditioning coach
Nelson Ayotte
Director, pro scouting/Peoria g.m.
Kevin McDonald
Director of player evaluation
Ted Hampson
Special assignments
Al MacInnis
Pro scout
Wayne Mundey
Amateur scouts
Mike Antonovich, Craig Channell, Rick Meagher, Ville Siren
Part-time amateur scouts
Bill Armstrong, Thomas Carlsson, Paul Gallagher, Dan Ginnell, Vladimir Havluj Jr., Barclay Parneta, Georgi Zhuravlev

2006 DRAFT CHOICES

Rd.-Overall		Ht., Wt.	Amateur league, team	Position
1-1	ERIK JOHNSON	6-4, 222	USA, U.S. National U-18	D
1-25	PATRIK BERGLUND	6-4, 187	SWEDEN, Vasteras	C
2-31	TOMAS KANA	6-0, 202	CZECH, Vitkovice	C
3-64	JONAS JUNLAND	6-2, 198	SWEDEN, Linkoping	D
4-94	RYAN TUREK	5-11, 170	USHL, Omaha	C
4-106	RETO BERRA	6-4, 189	SUI, Zurich/Kusnacht	G
5-124	ANDY SACKRISON	6-1, 178	USHSW, St. Louis Park	C/LW
6-154	MATTHEW MCCOLLEM	6-0, 185	USHSE, Belmont Hill	LW
7-184	ALEXANDER HELLSTROM	6-2, 207	SWEDEN, Bjorkloven	D

MISCELLANEOUS DATA

Home ice (capacity)
Savvis Center (19,022)
Address
1401 Clark
St. Louis, MO 63103
Business phone
314-622-2500; fax, 314-622-2582
Ticket information
314-241-1888
Website
www.stlouisblues.com
Training site
Ice Zone at St. Louis Mills, Hazelwood, MO
Club colors
Blue, gold, navy and white
Radio affiliation
KTRS (550 AM)
TV affiliation
KPLR (Channel 11) & FOX Sports Midwest

SAN JOSE SHARKS

WESTERN CONFERENCE, PACIFIC DIVISION

SAN JOSE SHARKS

Sharks Schedule

Home games shaded.

October

SUN	MON	TUE	WED	THU	FRI	SAT
1	2	3	4	5 STL	6	7 NYI
8	9 CAL	10	11	12 EDM	13 VAN	14
15	16	17 DAL	18	19 DET	20	21 MIN
22	23 CLB	24	25 DET	26 NAS	27	28
29 TB	30	31 FLA				

November

SUN	MON	TUE	WED	THU	FRI	SAT
			1	2 NYR	3	4 PIT
5	6	7 MIN	8	9 LA	10	11 PHO
12	13 LA	14	15 COL	16	17	18 PHI
19	20	21 ANA	22 LA	23	24	25 NJ
26	27	28 STL	29 MIN	30		

December

SUN	MON	TUE	WED	THU	FRI	SAT
					1	2 DET
3	4 DAL	5	6	7 COL	8	9 NAS
10	11 PHO	12 LA	13	14 LA	15	16 ANA
17	18	19	20	21 DAL	22	23 CAL
24	25	26 ANA	27	28 PHO	29	30 PHO
31 DAL						

January

SUN	MON	TUE	WED	THU	FRI	SAT
	1	2	3	4 DET	5	6 CLB
7	8	9	10 EDM	11 LA	12	13 PHO
14	15 COL	16	17	18 PHO	19	20 STL
21	22	23	24	25	26 EDM	27
28 VAN	29	30 DAL	31			

February

SUN	MON	TUE	WED	THU	FRI	SAT
				1 DAL	2	3 CHI
4	5	6 ANA	7 ANA	8	9	10
11	12	13 STL	14 NAS	15	16 CLB	17
18 DAL	19	20	21 WAS	22 CHI	23	24 CAL
25	26 ANA	27	28 NAS			

March

SUN	MON	TUE	WED	THU	FRI	SAT
				1	2 ANA	3
4 DAL	5	6 MIN	7	8	9 VAN	10
11 EDM	12	13 CHI	14	15 PHO	16 CLB	17
18 COL	19	20	21 CHI	22 ATL	23	24 CAR
25	26	27 LA	28	29	30 PHO	31

April

SUN	MON	TUE	WED	THU	FRI	SAT
1 LA	2	3	4 ANA	5 CAL	6	7 VAN

2006-07 SEASON

CLUB DIRECTORY

President, CEO and manager of the SJSEE Ownership Group
Greg Jamison
Exec. v.p., business operations
Malcolm Bordelon
Exec. v.p., g.m. HP Pavilion arena
Jim Goddard
Exec. v.p., general counsel
Don Gralnek
Exec. v.p., g.m. Sharks
Doug Wilson
Exec. v.p., CFO
Charlie Faas
Vice president, finance
Ken Caveney
Vice president, sales and marketing
Kent Russell
Vice president, building operations
Rich Sotelo
Vice president, assistant g.m.
Wayne Thomas
Head coach
Ron Wilson
Assistant coaches
Tim Hunter, Rob Zettler
Goaltender coach
Warren Strelow
Special consultant to g.m.
John Ferguson
Director of scouting
Tim Burke
Director, hockey operations
Joe Will
Scouts
Gilles Cote, Pelle Eklund, Pat Funk, Jack Gardiner, Rob Grillo, Brian Gross, Barry Long, Karel Masopust, Cap Raeder, Graeme Townshend
Director, hockey administration
Rosemary Tebaldi
Video scouting coordinator
Bob Friedlander
Head athletic trainer
Ray Tufts, A.T.C.
Strength & conditioning
Mac Read
Equipment manager
Mike Aldrich
Director, media relations
Scott Emmert
Media relations coordinator
Tom Holy
Team physician
Arthur J. Ting, M.D.
Team internist
John Chiu, M.D.
Team Dentist
Robert Bonahoom, D.D.S.
Team vision specialist
Vincent S. Zuccaro, O.D., F.A.A.O.
Medical staff
Warren King, M.D., Mark Sontag, M.D.

2006 DRAFT CHOICES

Rd.-Overall	Ht., Wt.	Amateur league, team	Position
1-16 TY WISHART	6-4, 205	WHL, Prince George	D
2-36 JAMIE MCGINN	5-11, 179	OHL, Ottawa	LW
4-98 JAMES DELORY	6-4, 212	OHL, Oshawa	D
5-143 ASHTON ROME	6-1, 202	WHL, Kamloops	RW
7-202 JOHN MCCARTHY	6-0, 200	H-EAST, Boston U.	LW
7-203 JAY BARRIBALL	5-9, 155	USHL, Sioux Falls	F

MISCELLANEOUS DATA

Home ice (capacity)
HP Pavilion at San Jose (17,496)
Address
525 West Santa Clara Street
San Jose, CA 95113
Business phone
408-287-7070
Ticket information
408-999-5757
Website
sjsharks.com
Training site
Logitech Ice at San Jose
Club colors
Deep pacific teal, gray, burnt orange and black
Radio affiliation
KUFX (98.5 FM)
TV affiliation
FOX Sports Net Bay Area

TAMPA BAY LIGHTNING

EASTERN CONFERENCE, SOUTHEAST DIVISION

Lightning Schedule

Home games shaded.

October

SUN	MON	TUE	WED	THU	FRI	SAT
1	2	3	4	5 ATL	6	7 BOS
8	9 ATL	10	11	12	13 FLA	14 FLA
15	16 CAR	17	18	19 PHI	20	21 WAS
22	23	24	25	26 CAR	27	28 CAR
29 SJ	30	31				

November

SUN	MON	TUE	WED	THU	FRI	SAT
			1 TOR	2 PHI	3	4 BOS
5	6 NYI	7	8 PIT	9	10	11 ATL
12	13	14	15 MON	16	17 NYI	18
19 NYR	20 BUF	21	22 FLA	23	24 ATL	25
26 OTT	27	28 WAS	29	30 BOS		

December

SUN	MON	TUE	WED	THU	FRI	SAT
					1	2 OTT
3	4	5 BUF	6	7 ATL	8	9 ANA
10	11	12 TOR	13	14 MON	15	16 CAR
17	18	19 WAS	20	21 OTT	22	23 NYR
24	25	26 ATL	27	28 PHI	29	30 MON
31						

January

SUN	MON	TUE	WED	THU	FRI	SAT
	1	2 MON	3	4 MIN	5 COL	6
7 PIT	8	9 PIT	10	11 WAS	12	13 BUF
14	15 NYI	16 TOR	17	18 NJ	19	20 CAR
21	22	23	24	25	26 NJ	27
28	29	30 PHI	31			

February

SUN	MON	TUE	WED	THU	FRI	SAT
				1 CAR	2	3 NYR
4	5	6 LA	7	8	9 NYR	10
11 NJ	12	13 PHO	14	15 WAS	16	17 FLA
18	19	20 FLA	21	22 ATL	23 BOS	24
25 PIT	26	27 DAL	28			

March

SUN	MON	TUE	WED	THU	FRI	SAT
				1 WAS	2	3 FLA
4	5	6 VAN	7 EDM	8	9	10 CAL
11	12	13 TOR	14	15	16 BUF	17
18 WAS	19	20 NYI	21	22 NJ	23	24 OTT
25	26	27 FLA	28	29	30 CAR	31 WAS

April

SUN	MON	TUE	WED	THU	FRI	SAT
1	2	3 CAR	4	5	6 FLA	7 ATL

2006-07 SEASON

CLUB DIRECTORY

Owner
Bill Davidson, Palace Sports & Entertainment
President, Palace Sports/governor
Tom Wilson
President, TB Lightning/alt. governor
Ron Campbell
Executive v.p./C.O.O
Sean Henry
Executive v.p./G.M./alt. governor
Jay H. Feaster
Director, player personnel
Bill Barber
Assistant general manager
Claude Loiselle
Head coach
John Tortorella
Associate coach
Craig Ramsay
Assistant coach
Jeff Reese
Video coach
Nigel Kirwan
Associate goaltending coach
Corey Schwab
Strength & conditioning
Eric Lawson
Chief scout
Jake Goertzen
Scouting staff
Mikael Andersson, Stephen Baker, Larry Bernard, Angelo Bumbacco, Dave Heitz, Charlie Hodge, Kari Kettunen, Gerry O'Flaherty, Miroslav Prihoda, Darrell Young, Glen Zacharias
Senior v.p., communications
Bill Wickett
Head medical trainer
Thomas Mulligan
Director, team services
Phil Thibodeau
Massage therapist
Mike Griebel
Equipment manager
Ray Thill
Medical director
Dr. Ira Guttentag
Associate medical director
Dr. David Shapiro
Team internist
Dr. Stan Watkins

2006 DRAFT CHOICES

Rd.-Overall	Ht., Wt.	Amateur league, team	Position
1-15 RIKU HELENIUS	6-3, 202	FINLAND, Ilves	G
3-78 KEVIN QUICK	6-0, 175	USHSE, Salisbury	D
6-168 DANE CROWLEY	6-2, 210	WHL, Swift Current	D
7-198 DENIS KAZIONOV	6-3, 187	Russia, TVER	LW

MISCELLANEOUS DATA

Home ice (capacity)
St. Pete Times Forum (19,758)
Address
401 Channelside Drive
Tampa, Fla. 33602
Business phone
813-301-6500
Ticket information
813-301-6600
Website
www.tampabaylightning.com
Training site
Brandon Ice Sports Forum, Brandon, FL
Club colors
Black, blue, silver and white
Radio affiliation
WDAE (620 AM)
TV affiliation
Sun Sports (Cable)

TORONTO MAPLE LEAFS

EASTERN CONFERENCE, NORTHEAST DIVISION

Maple Leafs Schedule

Home games shaded.

October

SUN	MON	TUE	WED	THU	FRI	SAT
1	2	3	4 OTT	5 OTT	6	7 MON
8	9 FLA	10	11	12 NJ	13	14 CAL
15	16	17	18 COL	19	20 CLB	21 NYR
22	23	24 OTT	25	26 OTT	27	28 MON
29	30 ATL	31				

November

SUN	MON	TUE	WED	THU	FRI	SAT
			1 TB	2 FLA	3	4 BUF
5	6 PHI	7	8	9 BOS	10	11 MON
12	13	14	15	16 BOS	17	18 NJ
19	20 NYI	21	22 BUF	23	24 WAS	25 BOS
26	27	28 BOS	29	30 ATL		

December

SUN	MON	TUE	WED	THU	FRI	SAT
					1	2 MON
3	4	5 ATL	6	7 BOS	8	9 DET
10	11	12 TB	13	14	15 CAR	16 NYR
17	18	19 FLA	20	21	22 CHI	23 WAS
24	25	26 MIN	27	28	29 PIT	30 OTT
31						

January

SUN	MON	TUE	WED	THU	FRI	SAT
	1 BOS	2	3	4 BOS	5	6 BUF
7	8	9 CAR	10	11 BUF	12	13 VAN
14	15	16 TB	17	18 FLA	19	20 PIT
21	22	23	24	25	26	27 MON
28	29	30 CAR	31 NYR			

February

SUN	MON	TUE	WED	THU	FRI	SAT
				1	2	3 OTT
4	5	6 STL	7	8 NAS	9	10 PIT
11	12	13 NYI	14	15 PHI	16	17 EDM
18	19	20 BOS	21	22 NYI	23	24 PHI
25	26 MON	27 BUF	28			

March

SUN	MON	TUE	WED	THU	FRI	SAT
				1	2 NJ	3 BUF
4	5	6 WAS	7	8 OTT	9	10 OTT
11	12	13 TB	14	15	16 WAS	17 MON
18	19	20 NJ	21	22	23 BUF	24 BUF
25	26	27 CAR	28	29 ATL	30	31 PIT

April

SUN	MON	TUE	WED	THU	FRI	SAT
1 NYR	2	3 PHI	4	5 NYI	6	7 MON

2006-07 SEASON

CLUB DIRECTORY

Chairman of the board and NHL governor
Larry Tanenbaum
Alternate governors
John Ferguson, Dale Lastman, Dean Metcalf, Richard Peddie
President, CEO and alt. governor
Richard Peddie
Exec. v.p., chief operating officer
Tom Anselmi
Exec. v.p./ g.m., venues and entertainment
Bob Hunter
Exec. v.p., chief financial officer & business development
Ian Clarke
Senior v.p., communications & community development
John Lashway
Vice president, people
Mardi Walker
Sr. v.p. and general counsel & corporate secretary
Robin Brudner
General manager & vice president
John Ferguson
Head Coach
Paul Maurice
Assistant general manager
Mike Penny
Assistant coaches
Keith Acton, Dallas Eakins, Randy Ladouceur
Player development coach
Paul Dennis
Director, hockey administration
Jeff Jackson
Community representatives
Wendel Clark, Darryl Sittler
Chief European scout
Thommie Bergman
Director, amateur scouting
Dave Morrison
Scouts
George Armstrong, Fred Bandel, Garth Malarchuk, Mike Palmateer, Mark Yannetti
European scouts
Jan Kovac, Nikolai Ladygin
Director, media relations
Pat Park
Coordinators, media relations
Craig Downey, James Lamont
Manager, hockey administration
Reid Mitchell
Manager, team services
Dave Griffiths
Director, community development
Bev Deeth
Equipment manager
Brian Papineau

2006 DRAFT CHOICES

Rd.-Overall	Ht., Wt.	Amateur league, team	Position
1-13 JIRI TLUSTY	6-0, 196	CZECH, Kladno	C/W
2-44 NIKOLAI KULEMIN	6-1, 183	RUSSIA, Magnitogorsk	W
4-99 JAMES REIMER	6-2, 208	WHL, Red Deer	G
4-111 KORBINIAN HOLZER	6-3, 190	GERMANY, Bad Tolz	D
6-161 VIKTOR STAHLBERG	6-3, 191	SWEDEN, Frolunda	LW
6-166 TYLER RUEGSEGGER	5-11, 170	USHSW, Shattuck-St. Mary's	C/RW
6-180 LEO KOMAROV	5-10, 187	FINLAND, Assat	C

MISCELLANEOUS DATA

Home ice (capacity)
Air Canada Centre (18,819)
Address
Air Canada Centre
40 Bay Street
Toronto, Ont. M5J 2X2
Business phone
416-815-5700
Ticket information
416-815-5700
Website
www.mapleleafs.com
Training site
Toronto
Club colors
Blue and white
Radio affiliation
Toronto Radio (640 AM)
TV affiliation
Leafs TV, CBC, TSN, Rogers Sportsnet

VANCOUVER CANUCKS

WESTERN CONFERENCE, NORTHWEST DIVISION

Canucks Schedule

Home games shaded.

October

SUN	MON	TUE	WED	THU	FRI	SAT
1	2	3	4	5 DET	6 CLB	7
8 COL	9	10 MIN	11	12	13 SJ	14
15	16 EDM	17 EDM	18	19	20 STL	21 NAS
22	23 DAL	24	25 CHI	26	27 WAS	28
29	30	31 NAS				

November

SUN	MON	TUE	WED	THU	FRI	SAT
			1	2 MIN	3	4 COL
5	6 DAL	7	8	9 ANA	10	11 CAL
12	13	14 DET	15	16	17 STL	18
19 CHI	20	21 DET	22	23 NAS	24	25 COL
26	27	28 CLB	29	30 ANA		

December

SUN	MON	TUE	WED	THU	FRI	SAT
					1	2 COL
3	4 EDM	5	6	7	8 CAR	9 CAL
10	11	12 PHO	13	14 CAL	15	16 MIN
17	18	19 MIN	20	21 BOS	22 CLB	23
24	25	26 CAL	27 CAL	28	29	30 EDM
31						

January

SUN	MON	TUE	WED	THU	FRI	SAT
	1	2 CAL	3 DAL	4	5 EDM	6
7 FLA	8	9	10	11 MIN	12	13 TOR
14	15	16 MON	17	18 OTT	19 BUF	20
21	22	23	24	25	26 LA	27
28 SJ	29	30 CLB	31			

February

SUN	MON	TUE	WED	THU	FRI	SAT
				1 EDM	2	3 CAL
4	5	6 EDM	7 CHI	8	9	10 ATL
11	12	13	14 MIN	15	16 CHI	17
18 COL	19	20 ANA	21	22 LA	23	24
25 DAL	26	27 STL	28			

March

SUN	MON	TUE	WED	THU	FRI	SAT
				1 PHO	2	3
4 MIN	5	6 TB	7	8 PHO	9 SJ	10
11 ANA	12	13 MIN	14	15 STL	16	17 DET
18	19 EDM	20	21 NAS	22	23	24
25 COL	26	27 COL	28	29 LA	30	31 CAL

April

SUN	MON	TUE	WED	THU	FRI	SAT
1	2	3 LA	4	5 COL	6	7 SJ
8 PHO	9	10	11	12	13	14

2006-07 SEASON

CLUB DIRECTORY

Chairman/OBSE & Governor
John E McCaw, Jr.
Deputy chairman/OBSE & alt. governor
Francesco Aquilini
Sr. v.p./g.m./alternate governor
David M. Nonis
General counsel
James Conrad
Exec. v.p., business
Jon Festinger
V.p., finance and CFO
Victor de Bonis
V.p./g.m./arena operations
Harvey Jones
V.p., people development
Susanne Haine
V.p., broadcast and new media
Chris Hebb
Executive assistants
Chris Stephens, Lori Meehan
Vice president/assistant g.m.
Steve Tambellini
Head coach
Alain Vigneault
Assistant coaches
Rick Bowness, Mike Kelly, Barry Smith
Goaltending consultant
Ian Clark
Strength & conditioning coach
Roger Takahashi
Director, player development
Stan Smyl
Chief scout
Ron Delorme
Professional scouts
Lucien DeBlois, Eric Crawford, Lorne Henning
European scout
Thomas Gradin
Russian scout
Sergei Chibisov
Amateur scouts
Jack McCartan, Barry Dean, Jim Eagle, Mario Marois, John McMorrow, Gary Lupul, Tim Lenardon, Branislav Pulis, Harold Snepsts
Manager, scouting & player info.
Jonathan Wall
Medical trainer
Mike Burnstein
Assistant medical trainers
Jon Sanderson, Marty Dudgeon
Equipment manager
Pat O'Neill
Assistant equipment manager
Jamie Hendricks
Assistant equipment trainer
Brian Hamilton

2006 DRAFT CHOICES

Rd.-Overall		Ht., Wt.	Amateur league, team	Position
1-14	MICHAEL GRABNER	6-0, 170	WHL, Spokane	RW
3-82	DANIEL RAHIMI	6-3, 213	SJL, Bjorkloven Jr.	D
6-163	SERGEI SHIROKOV	5-10, 176	Russia, CSKA	W
6-167	JURAJ SIMEK	6-1, 189	SUI, Kloten	W
7-197	EVAN FULLER	6-1, 196	WHL, Prince George	RW

MISCELLANEOUS DATA

Home ice (capacity)
General Motors Place (18,630)
Address
800 Griffiths Way
Vancouver, B.C. V6B 6G1
Business phone
604-899-4600
Ticket information
604-899-4625
Website
www.canucks.com
Training site
Ice Sports Burnaby 8-Rinks; Burnaby, B.C.
Club colors
Deep blue, sky blue, deep red, white and silver
Radio affiliation
The Team Sports Radio (1040 AM)

WASHINGTON CAPITALS

EASTERN CONFERENCE, SOUTHEAST DIVISION

Capitals Schedule

Home games shaded.

October

SUN	MON	TUE	WED	THU	FRI	SAT
1	2	3	4	5 NYR	6	7 CAR
8	9	10	11	12 MIN	13	14 ATL
15	16	17	18 FLA	19 ATL	20	21 TB
22	23	24	25 COL	26	27 VAN	28 EDM
29	30 CAL	31				

November

SUN	MON	TUE	WED	THU	FRI	SAT
			1	2	3 ATL	4 PHI
5	6 OTT	7	8	9 CAR	10	11 NYR
12	13 FLA	14	15 BOS	16	17 CAR	18 BOS
19	20	21	22 ATL	23	24 TOR	25 NYI
26	27	28 TB	29	30 DAL		

December

SUN	MON	TUE	WED	THU	FRI	SAT
					1	2 BUF
3	4	5	6 OTT	7	8 ANA	9 PHI
10	11 PIT	12	13	14	15 ATL	16 PHI
17	18	19 TB	20	21	22 NJ	23 TOR
24	25	26 BUF	27 MON	28	29 NJ	30 NYR
31						

January

SUN	MON	TUE	WED	THU	FRI	SAT
	1 PHO	2	3	4 MON	5	6 ATL
7	8	9 PHI	10	11 TB	12	13 FLA
14	15	16 OTT	17	18 CAR	19	20 FLA
21	22	23	24	25	26 CAR	27 CAR
28	29	30 OTT	31			

February

SUN	MON	TUE	WED	THU	FRI	SAT
				1 FLA	2	3 PIT
4 NYI	5	6 BOS	7	8 LA	9	10 NYR
11	12	13	14	15 TB	16	17
18 PIT	19	20 MON	21 SJ	22	23	24 NJ
25 NJ	26	27 FLA	28			

March

SUN	MON	TUE	WED	THU	FRI	SAT
				1 TB	2	3 NYI
4	5	6 TOR	7	8	9 CAR	10 NYI
11	12 ATL	13	14	15 BOS	16 TOR	17
18 TB	19	20	21 BUF	22 CAR	23	24 MON
25	26	27 PIT	28	29	30 FLA	31 TB

April

SUN	MON	TUE	WED	THU	FRI	SAT
1	2	3 FLA	4 ATL	5	6	7 BUF

2006-07 SEASON

CLUB DIRECTORY

Chairman and majority owner
Ted Leonsis

President and owner
Dick Patrick

Owners
Jack Davies, Richard Fairbank, Raul Fernandez, Joshua Freeman, Sheila Johnson, Richard Kay, Jeong Kim, Mark Lerner, George Stamas

Vice president/general manager
George McPhee

Director of player personnel
Brian MacLellan

Head coach
Glen Hanlon

Assistant coaches
Jay Leach, Dean Evason

Goaltending coach
Dave Prior

Director of amateur scouting
Ross Mahoney

Pro scouts
Larry Carriere, Dave Draper

Amateur scouts
Steve Bowman, Ed McColgan, Ray Payne, Martin Pouliot, Steve Richmond

European scouts
Gleb Chistyakov, Vojtech Kucera

2006 DRAFT CHOICES

Rd.-Overall		Ht., Wt.	Amateur league, team	Position
1-4	NICKLAS BACKSTROM	6-0, 183	SWEDEN, Brynas	C
1-23	SEMEN VARLAMOV	6-1, 183	RPL, Yaroslavl 2	G
2-34	MICHAL NEUVIRTH	6-0, 174	CZECH JR., Sparta Jr.	G
2-35	FRANCOIS BOUCHARD	6-0, 180	QMJHL, Baie Comeau	RW
2-52	KEITH SEABROOK	6-0, 198	BCHL, Burnaby	D
4-97	OSKAR OSALA	6-4, 217	OHL, Mississauga	LW
4-122	LUKE LYNES	6-1, 195	OHL, Brampton	C/LW
5-127	MAXIME LACROIX	6-0, 180	QMJHL, Quebec	LW
6-157	BRENT GWIDT	6-2, 198	USHSW, Lakeland H.S.	C
6-177	MATHIEU PERREAULT	5-8, 151	QMJHL, Acadie-Bathurst	C

MISCELLANEOUS DATA

Home ice (capacity)
Verizon Center (18,277)

Address
601 F Street, NW
Washington, DC 20004

Business phone
202-628-3200

Ticket information
202-397-SEAT (7328)
Season tickets: 202-266-2277

Website
www.washingtoncaps.com

Training site (temporary)
Capitals Ice Center
4238 Wilson Boulevard
Suite 2152
Arlington, VA 22203

Club colors
Bronze, blue and black

Radio affiliation
WTNT-AM 570, Sportstalk 980

TV affiliation
Comcast SportsNet

SCHEDULE

DAY BY DAY

All times Eastern

Wednesday, Oct. 4
Buffalo at Carolina, 7 p.m.
Ottawa at Toronto, 7:30 p.m.
Dallas at Colorado, 10 p.m.

Thursday, Oct. 5
Toronto at Ottawa, 7 p.m.
Washington at N.Y. Rangers, 7 p.m.
Tampa Bay at Atlanta, 7 p.m.
Philadelphia at Pittsburgh, 7:30 p.m.
Vancouver at Detroit, 7:30 p.m.
Chicago at Nashville, 8 p.m.
Colorado at Minnesota, 8:30 p.m.
Calgary at Edmonton, 10 p.m.
N.Y. Islanders at Phoenix, 10 p.m.
St. Louis at San Jose, 10:30 p.m.

Friday, Oct. 6
New Jersey at Carolina, 7 p.m.
Vancouver at Columbus, 7 p.m.
Boston at Florida, 7:30 p.m.
Montreal at Buffalo, 8 p.m.
Los Angeles at Anaheim, 10 p.m.

Saturday, Oct. 7
Montreal at Toronto, 7 p.m.
Buffalo at Ottawa, 7 p.m.
N.Y. Rangers at Philadelphia, 7 p.m.
Carolina at Washington, 7 p.m.
Florida at Atlanta, 7 p.m.
Detroit at Pittsburgh, 7:30 p.m.
Boston at Tampa Bay, 7:30 p.m.
Nashville at Minnesota, 8 p.m.
New Jersey at Dallas, 8 p.m.
Columbus at Chicago, 8:30 p.m.
Edmonton at Calgary, 10 p.m.
Anaheim at Phoenix, 10 p.m.
St. Louis at Los Angeles, 10:30 p.m.
N.Y. Islanders at San Jose, 10:30 p.m.

Sunday, Oct. 8
Vancouver at Colorado, 8 p.m.

Monday, Oct. 9
St. Louis at Anaheim, 4 p.m.
Phoenix at Columbus, 7 p.m.
Florida at Toronto, 7:30 p.m.
Atlanta at Tampa Bay, 7:30 p.m.
San Jose at Calgary, 8 p.m.

Tuesday, Oct. 10
Philadelphia at N.Y. Rangers, 7 p.m.
Vancouver at Minnesota, 9 p.m.
N.Y. Islanders at Los Angeles, 10:30 p.m.

Wednesday, Oct. 11
Montreal at Philadelphia, 7 p.m.
Boston at Atlanta, 7 p.m.
Carolina at Florida, 7:30 p.m.
Phoenix at Detroit, 7:30 p.m.
N.Y. Islanders at Anaheim, 10 p.m.

Thursday, Oct. 12
Pittsburgh at N.Y. Rangers, 7 p.m.
Calgary at Ottawa, 7:30 p.m.
Toronto at New Jersey, 7:30 p.m.
Boston at St. Louis, 8 p.m.
Washington at Minnesota, 8 p.m.
Nashville at Chicago, 8:30 p.m.
San Jose at Edmonton, 9 p.m.
Dallas at Los Angeles, 10:30 p.m.

Friday, Oct. 13
Carolina at Atlanta, 7:30 p.m.
Tampa Bay at Florida, 7:30 p.m.
Buffalo at Detroit, 7:30 p.m.
San Jose at Vancouver, 10 p.m.

Saturday, Oct. 14
N.Y. Rangers at Buffalo, 7 p.m.
Calgary at Toronto, 7 p.m.
Ottawa at Montreal, 7 p.m.
Boston at N.Y. Islanders, 7 p.m.
Atlanta at Washington, 7 p.m.
Philadelphia at New Jersey, 7:30 p.m.
Carolina at Pittsburgh, 7:30 p.m.
Florida at Tampa Bay, 7:30 p.m.
Chicago at St. Louis, 8 p.m.
Phoenix at Nashville, 8 p.m.
Columbus at Minnesota, 8 p.m.
Edmonton at Colorado, 10 p.m.
Dallas at Los Angeles, 10:30 p.m.

Sunday, Oct. 15
Dallas at Anaheim, 8 p.m.

Monday, Oct. 16
New Jersey at N.Y. Rangers, 7 p.m.
Carolina at Tampa Bay, 7 p.m.
Nashville at N.Y. Islanders, 7:30 p.m.
Chicago at Colorado, 9 p.m.
Edmonton at Vancouver, 10 p.m.
Detroit at Los Angeles, 10:30 p.m.

Tuesday, Oct. 17
Philadelphia at Buffalo, 7 p.m.
Calgary at Montreal, 7:30 p.m.
Phoenix at St. Louis, 8 p.m.
Vancouver at Edmonton, 9 p.m.
Dallas at San Jose, 10:30 p.m.

Wednesday, Oct. 18
Nashville at N.Y. Rangers, 7 p.m.
Florida at Washington, 7 p.m.
Colorado at Toronto, 7:30 p.m.
New Jersey at Pittsburgh, 7:30 p.m.
Montreal at Chicago, 8:30 p.m.
Detroit at Anaheim, 10 p.m.
Minnesota at Los Angeles, 10:30 p.m.

Thursday, Oct. 19
Calgary at Boston, 7 p.m.
Washington at Atlanta, 7 p.m.
Colorado at Ottawa, 7:30 p.m.
Nashville at New Jersey, 7:30 p.m.
Pittsburgh at N.Y. Islanders, 7:30 p.m.
Philadelphia at Tampa Bay, 7:30 p.m.
Los Angeles at Phoenix, 10 p.m.
Detroit at San Jose, 10:30 p.m.

Friday, Oct. 20
Toronto at Columbus, 7 p.m.
Philadelphia at Florida, 7:30 p.m.
Carolina at Buffalo, 8 p.m.
Vancouver at St. Louis, 8 p.m.
Chicago at Dallas, 8:30 p.m.
Minnesota at Anaheim, 10 p.m.

Saturday, Oct. 21
Buffalo at Boston, 7 p.m.
N.Y. Rangers at Toronto, 7 p.m.
Colorado at Montreal, 7 p.m.
New Jersey at Ottawa, 7 p.m.
Carolina at N.Y. Islanders, 7 p.m.
Tampa Bay at Washington, 7 p.m.
Florida at Atlanta, 7 p.m.
Columbus at Pittsburgh, 7:30 p.m.
Vancouver at Nashville, 8 p.m.
St. Louis at Chicago, 8:30 p.m.
Detroit at Edmonton, 10 p.m.
Dallas at Phoenix, 10 p.m.
Minnesota at San Jose, 10:30 p.m.

Sunday, Oct. 22
Anaheim at Los Angeles, 6 p.m.

Monday, Oct. 23
San Jose at Columbus, 7 p.m.
Buffalo at Montreal, 7:30 p.m.
Atlanta at Florida, 7:30 p.m.
Los Angeles at Colorado, 8 p.m.
Vancouver at Dallas, 8:30 p.m.
Phoenix at Edmonton, 9 p.m.

Tuesday, Oct. 24
New Jersey at Pittsburgh, 7 p.m.
Ottawa at Toronto, 7:30 p.m.
Phoenix at Calgary, 9 p.m.

Wednesday, Oct. 25
Florida at N.Y. Rangers, 7 p.m.
Atlanta at Carolina, 7 p.m.
San Jose at Detroit, 7:30 p.m.
Los Angeles at Minnesota, 8 p.m.
Vancouver at Chicago, 8:30 p.m.
Washington at Colorado, 9 p.m.
Edmonton at Anaheim, 10 p.m.

Thursday, Oct. 26
Montreal at Boston, 7 p.m.
Atlanta at Philadelphia, 7 p.m.
Toronto at Ottawa, 7:30 p.m.
Florida at New Jersey, 7:30 p.m.
Buffalo at N.Y. Islanders, 7:30 p.m.
Carolina at Tampa Bay, 7:30 p.m.
San Jose at Nashville, 8 p.m.
Edmonton at Phoenix, 10 p.m.

Friday, Oct. 27
Los Angeles at Columbus, 7 p.m.
Anaheim at Minnesota, 8 p.m.
Detroit at Dallas, 8:30 p.m.
Washington at Vancouver, 10 p.m.

Saturday, Oct. 28
Ottawa at Boston, 7 p.m.
Atlanta at Buffalo, 7 p.m.
Toronto at Montreal, 7 p.m.
Florida at N.Y. Islanders, 7 p.m.

Pittsburgh at Philadelphia, 7 p.m.
Tampa Bay at Carolina, 7 p.m.
Columbus at New Jersey, 7:30 p.m.
Detroit at St. Louis, 8 p.m.
Washington at Edmonton, 8 p.m.
Los Angeles at Dallas, 8 p.m.
Anaheim at Chicago, 8:30 p.m.
Nashville at Calgary, 10 p.m.
N.Y. Rangers at Phoenix, 10 p.m.

Sunday, Oct. 29
San Jose at Tampa Bay, 5 p.m.
Minnesota at Colorado, 8 p.m.

Monday, Oct. 30
Chicago at Philadelphia, 7 p.m.
Atlanta at Toronto, 7:30 p.m.
Anaheim at St. Louis, 8 p.m.
Washington at Calgary, 9 p.m.
N.Y. Rangers at Los Angeles, 10:30 p.m.

Tuesday, Oct. 31
Chicago at N.Y. Islanders, 7 p.m.
Ottawa at Montreal, 7:30 p.m.
San Jose at Florida, 7:30 p.m.
Nashville at Vancouver, 10 p.m.

Wednesday, Nov. 1
Carolina at Atlanta, 7 p.m.
Colorado at Columbus, 7 p.m.
Toronto at Tampa Bay, 7:30 p.m.
Calgary at Detroit, 7:30 p.m.
St. Louis at Dallas, 8:30 p.m.
Nashville at Edmonton, 9 p.m.
N.Y. Rangers at Anaheim, 10 p.m.
Pittsburgh at Los Angeles, 10:30 p.m.

Thursday, Nov. 2
Buffalo at Boston, 7 p.m.
Tampa Bay at Philadelphia, 7 p.m.
Montreal at Carolina, 7 p.m.
N.Y. Islanders at New Jersey, 7:30 p.m.
Toronto at Florida, 7:30 p.m.
Colorado at St. Louis, 8 p.m.
Vancouver at Minnesota, 8 p.m.
Detroit at Chicago, 8:30 p.m.
N.Y. Rangers at San Jose, 10:30 p.m.

Friday, Nov. 3
Atlanta at Washington, 7 p.m.
Calgary at Columbus, 7 p.m.
Dallas at Edmonton, 9p.m.
Phoenix at Anaheim, 10 p.m.

Saturday, Nov. 4
Tampa Bay at Boston, 7 p.m.
Toronto at Buffalo, 7 p.m.
New Jersey at Montreal, 7 p.m.
Carolina at Ottawa, 7 p.m.
Atlanta at N.Y. Islanders, 7 p.m.
Washington at Philadelphia, 7 p.m.
Columbus at Detroit, 7 p.m.
Calgary at St. Louis, 8 p.m.
Nashville at Minnesota, 8 p.m.
Los Angeles at Phoenix, 9 p.m.
Vancouver at Colorado, 10 p.m.
Pittsburgh at San Jose, 10:30 p.m.

Sunday, Nov. 5
Buffalo at N.Y. Rangers, 5 p.m.

Monday, Nov. 6
Ottawa at Washington, 7 p.m.
Boston at Atlanta, 7 p.m.
Philadelphia at Toronto, 7:30 p.m.
Tampa Bay at N.Y. Islanders, 7:30 p.m.
Dallas at Vancouver, 10 p.m.
Pittsburgh at Anaheim, 10 p.m.

Tuesday, Nov. 7
Carolina at New Jersey, 7 p.m.
Edmonton at Montreal, 7:30 p.m.
Los Angeles at Colorado, 9 p.m.
Dallas at Calgary, 9 p.m.
Minnesota at San Jose, 10:30 p.m.

Wednesday, Nov. 8
Ottawa at Atlanta, 7 p.m.
Tampa Bay at Pittsburgh, 7:30 p.m.
N.Y. Rangers at Florida, 7:30 p.m.
Edmonton at Detroit, 7:30 p.m.

Thursday, Nov. 9
Toronto at Boston, 7 p.m.
N.Y. Islanders at Philadelphia, 7 p.m.
Washington at Carolina, 7 p.m.
Chicago at New Jersey, 7:30 p.m.
Columbus at St. Louis, 8 p.m.
Dallas at Phoenix, 9 p.m.
Anaheim at Vancouver, 10 p.m.
San Jose at Los Angeles, 10:30 p.m.

Friday, Nov. 10
Edmonton at Columbus, 7 p.m.
Ottawa at Pittsburgh, 7:30 p.m.
N.Y. Rangers at Atlanta, 7:30 p.m.
Nashville at Detroit, 7:30 p.m.
Florida at Buffalo, 8 p.m.
St. Louis at Chicago, 8:30 p.m.
Anaheim at Calgary, 9 p.m.

Saturday, Nov. 11
Ottawa at Boston, 7 p.m.
Montreal at Toronto, 7 p.m.
Buffalo at Philadelphia, 7 p.m.
N.Y. Rangers at Washington, 7 p.m.
Pittsburgh at Carolina, 7 p.m.
Florida at New Jersey, 7:30 p.m.
Atlanta at Tampa Bay, 7:30 p.m.
Colorado at Nashville, 8 p.m.
San Jose at Phoenix, 9 p.m.
Calgary at Vancouver, 10 p.m.
Minnesota at Los Angeles, 10:30 p.m.

Sunday, Nov. 12
Edmonton at St. Louis, 2 p.m.
Columbus at Chicago, 7 p.m.
Minnesota at Anaheim, 8 p.m.

Monday, Nov. 13
Buffalo at Carolina, 7 p.m.
Montreal at Ottawa, 7:30 p.m.
Philadelphia at Pittsburgh, 7:30 p.m.
Washington at Florida, 7:30 p.m.
Edmonton at Colorado, 9 p.m.
San Jose at Los Angeles, 10:30 p.m.

Tuesday, Nov. 14
New Jersey at N.Y. Rangers, 7 p.m.
St. Louis at Calgary, 9 p.m.
Minnesota at Phoenix, 9 p.m.
Detroit at Vancouver, 10 p.m.

Wednesday, Nov. 15
Ottawa at Buffalo, 7 p.m.
Boston at Washington, 7 p.m.
N.Y. Rangers at Carolina, 7 p.m.
Nashville at Columbus, 7 p.m.
Montreal at Tampa Bay, 7:30 p.m.
N.Y. Islanders at Dallas, 8:30 p.m.
San Jose at Colorado, 9 p.m.
Philadelphia at Anaheim, 10 p.m.

Thursday, Nov. 16
Toronto at Boston, 7 p.m.
Montreal at Florida, 7:30 p.m.
Minnesota at Nashville, 8 p.m.
St. Louis at Edmonton, 9 p.m.
Chicago at Phoenix, 9 p.m.
Philadelphia at Los Angeles, 10:30 p.m.

Friday, Nov. 17
Carolina at Washington, 7 p.m.
Colorado at Columbus, 7 p.m.
Ottawa at New Jersey, 7:30 p.m.
Dallas at Atlanta, 7:30 p.m.
Pittsburgh at Buffalo, 8 p.m.
N.Y. Islanders at Tampa Bay, 8 p.m.
Detroit at Calgary, 9 p.m.
St. Louis at Vancouver, 10 p.m.
Chicago at Anaheim, 10 p.m.

Saturday, Nov. 18
Phoenix at Los Angeles, 4p.m.
Washington at Boston, 7 p.m.
New Jersey at Toronto, 7 p.m.
Atlanta at Montreal, 7 p.m.
Buffalo at Ottawa, 7 p.m.
Dallas at Carolina, 7 p.m.
N.Y. Rangers at Pittsburgh, 7:30 p.m.
N.Y. Islanders at Florida, 7:30 p.m.
Columbus at Nashville, 8 p.m.
Colorado at Minnesota, 8 p.m.
Detroit at Edmonton, 10 p.m.
Philadelphia at San Jose, 10:30 p.m.

Sunday, Nov. 19
Tampa Bay at N.Y. Rangers, 7 p.m.
Phoenix at Anaheim, 8 p.m.
Chicago at Vancouver, 10 p.m.

Monday, Nov. 20
Florida at Boston, 7 p.m.
Tampa Bay at Buffalo, 7 p.m.
Pittsburgh at Philadelphia, 7 p.m.
Nashville at Columbus, 7 p.m.
N.Y. Islanders at Toronto, 7:30 p.m.
Minnesota at Ottawa, 7:30 p.m.
Colorado at Dallas, 8 p.m.

Tuesday, Nov. 21
Carolina at N.Y. Rangers, 7 p.m.
Vancouver at Detroit, 7:30 p.m.
Calgary at Edmonton, 9 p.m.
San Jose at Anaheim, 10 p.m.

Wednesday, Nov. 22
Toronto at Buffalo, 7 p.m.
Ottawa at Philadelphia, 7 p.m.
Atlanta at Washington, 7 p.m.
St. Louis at Columbus, 7 p.m.
Minnesota at Montreal, 7:30 p.m.
Carolina at N.Y. Islanders, 7:30 p.m.
Boston at Pittsburgh, 7:30 p.m.
Tampa Bay at Florida, 7:30 p.m.
Nashville at Dallas, 8:30 p.m.
Anaheim at Colorado, 9 p.m.
Chicago at Calgary, 9 p.m.
New Jersey at Phoenix, 9 p.m.

Los Angeles at San Jose, 10:30 p.m.

Thursday, Nov. 23
Vancouver at Nashville, 8 p.m.

Friday, Nov. 24
Carolina at Boston, 12 p.m.
Columbus at Philadelphia, 1 p.m.
Pittsburgh at N.Y. Islanders, 2 p.m.
Phoenix at Minnesota, 2 p.m.
New Jersey at Anaheim, 4 p.m.
Toronto at Washington, 7 p.m.
Ottawa at Florida, 7:30 p.m.
St. Louis at Detroit, 7:30 p.m.
Montreal at Buffalo, 8 p.m.
Atlanta at Tampa Bay, 8 p.m.
Los Angeles at Dallas, 8:30 p.m.
Chicago at Edmonton, 9 p.m.

Saturday, Nov. 25
Boston at Toronto, 7 p.m.
Philadelphia at Montreal, 7 p.m.
Washington at N.Y. Islanders, 7 p.m.
Florida at Atlanta, 7 p.m.
Minnesota at Columbus, 7 p.m.
N.Y. Rangers at Pittsburgh, 7:30 p.m.
Phoenix at St. Louis, 8 p.m.
Detroit at Nashville, 8 p.m.
Vancouver at Colorado, 10 p.m.
Calgary at Los Angeles, 10:30 p.m.
New Jersey at San Jose, 10:30 p.m.

Sunday, Nov. 26
Ottawa at Tampa Bay, 5 p.m.
Buffalo at N.Y. Rangers, 7 p.m.
Calgary at Anaheim, 8 p.m.

Monday, Nov. 27
Dallas at Detroit, 7 p.m.
New Jersey at Los Angeles, 10 p.m.

Tuesday, Nov. 28
Atlanta at N.Y. Rangers, 7 p.m.
N.Y. Islanders at Pittsburgh, 7 p.m.
Ottawa at Carolina, 7 p.m.
Boston at Toronto, 7:30 p.m.
Florida at Montreal, 7:30 p.m.
Washington at Tampa Bay, 7:30 p.m.
San Jose at St. Louis, 8 p.m.
Colorado at Calgary, 9 p.m.
Anaheim at Edmonton, 9 p.m.
Columbus at Vancouver, 10 p.m.

Wednesday, Nov. 29
Nashville at Philadelphia, 7 p.m.
San Jose at Minnesota, 8 p.m.
Dallas at Chicago, 8:30 p.m.

Thursday, Nov. 30
Tampa Bay at Boston, 7 p.m.
Dallas at Washington, 7 p.m.
Montreal at Carolina, 7 p.m.
Toronto at Atlanta, 7 p.m.
Florida at Ottawa, 7:30 p.m.
Philadelphia at N.Y. Islanders, 7:30 p.m.
Nashville at St. Louis, 8 p.m.
Colorado at Edmonton, 9 p.m.
Los Angeles at Phoenix, 9 p.m.
Anaheim at Vancouver, 10 p.m.

Friday, Dec. 1
Pittsburgh at New Jersey, 7:30 p.m.
N.Y. Rangers at Buffalo, 8 p.m.
Detroit at Minnesota, 8 p.m.
St. Louis at Chicago, 8:30 p.m.
Columbus at Calgary, 9 p.m.

Saturday, Dec. 2
Anaheim at Los Angeles, 4 p.m.
Toronto at Montreal, 7 p.m.
Tampa Bay at Ottawa, 7 p.m.
Boston at Carolina, 7 p.m.
San Jose at Detroit, 7 p.m.
New Jersey at Philadelphia, 7:30 p.m.
N.Y. Islanders at Pittsburgh, 7:30 p.m.
Atlanta at Florida, 7:30 p.m.
Buffalo at Washington, 8 p.m.
Chicago at Nashville, 8 p.m.
Columbus at Edmonton, 8 p.m.
Minnesota at Dallas, 8 p.m.
Colorado at Vancouver, 10 p.m.

Sunday, Dec. 3
N.Y. Islanders at N.Y. Rangers, 5 p.m.
Los Angeles at Anaheim, 8 p.m.

Monday, Dec. 4
Boston at Montreal, 7 p.m.
San Jose at Dallas, 9 p.m.
Nashville at Phoenix, 9 p.m.
Edmonton at Vancouver, 10 p.m.

Tuesday, Dec. 5
Atlanta at Toronto, 7:30 p.m.
Ottawa at N.Y. Islanders, 7:30 p.m.
Florida at Pittsburgh, 7:30 p.m.
Buffalo at Tampa Bay, 7:30 p.m.
Detroit at St. Louis, 8 p.m.
Chicago at Minnesota, 8 p.m.
Columbus at Colorado, 9 p.m.
Carolina at Calgary, 9 p.m.

Wednesday, Dec. 6
Ottawa at Washington, 7 p.m.
Montreal at New Jersey, 7:30 p.m.
Phoenix at Dallas, 8:30 p.m.
Carolina at Edmonton, 9 p.m.
Nashville at Anaheim, 10 p.m.

Thursday, Dec. 7
Toronto at Boston, 7 p.m.
Pittsburgh at N.Y. Rangers, 7 p.m.
Montreal at N.Y. Islanders, 7:30 p.m.
Atlanta at Tampa Bay, 7:30 p.m.
Buffalo at Florida, 7:30 p.m.
St. Louis at Detroit, 7:30 p.m.
Calgary at Minnesota, 8 p.m.
Phoenix at Chicago, 8:30 p.m.
Nashville at Los Angeles, 10:30 p.m.
Colorado at San Jose, 10:30 p.m.

Friday, Dec. 8
Anaheim at Washington, 7 p.m.
Philadelphia at New Jersey, 7:30 p.m.
Edmonton at Dallas, 8:30 p.m.
Carolina at Vancouver, 10 p.m.

Saturday, Dec. 9
New Jersey at Boston, 7 p.m.
Buffalo at Montreal, 7 p.m.
N.Y. Rangers at Ottawa, 7 p.m.
Florida at N.Y. Islanders, 7 p.m.
Washington at Philadelphia, 7 p.m.
Pittsburgh at Atlanta, 7 p.m.
Toronto at Detroit, 7 p.m.
Anaheim at Tampa Bay, 7:30 p.m.
Columbus at St. Louis, 8 p.m.
Chicago at Minnesota, 8 p.m.
Dallas at Phoenix, 9 p.m.
Vancouver at Calgary, 10 p.m.
Colorado at Los Angeles, 10:30 p.m.
Nashville at San Jose, 10:30 p.m.

Sunday, Dec. 10
Ottawa at Columbus, 6 p.m.
Florida at N.Y. Rangers, 7 p.m.
Edmonton at Chicago, 7 p.m.

Monday, Dec. 11
Pittsburgh at Washington, 7 p.m.
Carolina at Colorado, 9 p.m.
Phoenix at San Jose, 10 p.m.

Tuesday, Dec. 12
Buffalo at New Jersey, 7 p.m.
N.Y. Rangers at Philadelphia, 7 p.m.
Tampa Bay at Toronto, 7:30 p.m.
Boston at Montreal, 7:30 p.m.
Anaheim at Florida, 7:30 p.m.
Ottawa at Detroit, 7:30 p.m.
Chicago at St. Louis, 8 p.m.
Edmonton at Nashville, 8 p.m.
Columbus at Dallas, 8:30 p.m.
Minnesota at Calgary, 9 p.m.
Phoenix at Vancouver, 10 p.m.
San Jose at Los Angeles, 10:30 p.m.

Wednesday, Dec. 13
Anaheim at Atlanta, 7 p.m.
Philadelphia at Pittsburgh, 7:30 p.m.
St. Louis at Colorado, 9 p.m.

Thursday, Dec. 14
New Jersey at Boston, 7 p.m.
Florida at Buffalo, 7 p.m.
Tampa Bay at Montreal, 7:30 p.m.
Ottawa at Nashville, 8 p.m.
Detroit at Chicago, 8:30 p.m.
N.Y. Rangers at Dallas, 8:30 p.m.
Minnesota at Edmonton, 9 p.m.
Columbus at Phoenix, 9 p.m.
Calgary at Vancouver, 10 p.m.
Los Angeles at San Jose, 10:30 p.m.

Friday, Dec. 15
Toronto at Carolina, 7 p.m.
N.Y. Islanders at Pittsburgh, 7:30 p.m.
Washington at Atlanta, 7:30 p.m.
Edmonton at Colorado, 9 p.m.

Saturday, Dec. 16
Detroit at New Jersey, 1 p.m.
Dallas at Los Angeles, 4 p.m.
Florida at Boston, 7 p.m.
Ottawa at Buffalo, 7 p.m.
N.Y. Rangers at Toronto, 7 p.m.
Pittsburgh at Montreal, 7 p.m.
Atlanta at N.Y. Islanders, 7 p.m.
Philadelphia at Washington, 7 p.m.
Chicago at Columbus, 7 p.m.
Carolina at Tampa Bay, 7:30 p.m.
St. Louis at Nashville, 8 p.m.
Calgary at Phoenix, 9 p.m.
Minnesota at Vancouver, 10 p.m.
Anaheim at San Jose, 10:30 p.m.

Sunday, Dec. 17
Nashville at St. Louis, 6 p.m.
New Jersey at N.Y. Rangers, 7 p.m.

Colorado at Chicago, 7 p.m.

Monday, Dec. 18
Detroit at Columbus, 7 p.m.
Calgary at Anaheim, 10 p.m.

Tuesday, Dec. 19
Montreal at Buffalo, 7 p.m.
N.Y. Islanders at N.Y. Rangers, 7 p.m.
Carolina at Philadelphia, 7 p.m.
St. Louis at Pittsburgh, 7 p.m.
Tampa Bay at Washington, 7 p.m.
Florida at Toronto, 7:30 p.m.
Boston at Ottawa, 7:30 p.m.
Atlanta at New Jersey, 7:30 p.m.
Vancouver at Minnesota, 8 p.m.
Colorado at Edmonton, 9 p.m.
Calgary at Los Angeles, 10:30 p.m.

Wednesday, Dec. 20
Columbus at Detroit, 7:30 p.m.
Nashville at Chicago, 8:30 p.m.
Dallas at Anaheim, 10 p.m.

Thursday, Dec. 21
Vancouver at Boston, 7 p.m.
Pittsburgh at Atlanta, 7 p.m.
Philadelphia at Montreal, 7:30 p.m.
Tampa Bay at Ottawa, 7:30 p.m.
N.Y. Rangers at Florida, 7:30 p.m.
Los Angeles at St. Louis, 8 p.m.
Buffalo at Nashville, 8 p.m.
Calgary at Colorado, 9 p.m.
Edmonton at Phoenix, 9 p.m.
Dallas at San Jose, 10:30 p.m.

Friday, Dec. 22
New Jersey at Washington, 7 p.m.
N.Y. Islanders at Carolina, 7 p.m.
Vancouver at Columbus, 7 p.m.
Minnesota at Detroit, 7:30 p.m.
Toronto at Chicago, 8:30 p.m.

Saturday, Dec. 23
Ottawa at Philadelphia, 1 p.m.
Montreal at Boston, 7 p.m.
Washington at Toronto, 7 p.m.
Columbus at N.Y. Islanders, 7 p.m.
New Jersey at Atlanta, 7 p.m.
N.Y. Rangers at Tampa Bay, 7:30 p.m.
Carolina at Florida, 7:30 p.m.
Buffalo at St. Louis, 8 p.m.
Los Angeles at Nashville, 8 p.m.
Detroit at Minnesota, 8 p.m.
Edmonton at Dallas, 8 p.m.
Chicago at Colorado, 9 p.m.
Anaheim at Phoenix, 9 p.m.
Calgary at San Jose, 10 p.m.

Tuesday, Dec. 26
Washington at Buffalo, 7 p.m.
Florida at Carolina, 7 p.m.
Tampa Bay at Atlanta, 7 p.m.
Boston at Columbus, 7 p.m.
Dallas at Chicago, 7 p.m.
Minnesota at Toronto, 7:30 p.m.
Pittsburgh at New Jersey, 7:30 p.m.
N.Y. Rangers at N.Y. Islanders, 7:30 p.m.
St. Louis at Nashville, 8 p.m.
Vancouver at Calgary, 9 p.m.
Phoenix at Los Angeles, 10:30 p.m.
Anaheim at San Jose, 10:30 p.m.

Wednesday, Dec. 27
Montreal at Washington, 7 p.m.
N.Y. Islanders at Ottawa, 7:30 p.m.
Atlanta at Pittsburgh, 7:30 p.m.
Philadelphia at Florida, 7:30 p.m.
Minnesota at Detroit, 7:30 p.m.
Dallas at Colorado, 9 p.m.
Calgary at Vancouver, 10 p.m.

Thursday, Dec. 28
Carolina at Buffalo, 7 p.m.
Detroit at Columbus, 7 p.m.
Philadelphia at Tampa Bay, 7:30 p.m.
Los Angeles at Edmonton, 9 p.m.
Phoenix at San Jose, 10:30 p.m.

Friday, Dec. 29
Anaheim at Carolina, 7 p.m.
N.Y. Rangers at Ottawa, 7:30 p.m.
Washington at New Jersey, 7:30 p.m.
Toronto at Pittsburgh, 7:30 p.m.
Montreal at Florida, 7:30 p.m.
Columbus at Minnesota, 8 p.m.
Boston at Chicago, 8:30 p.m.
Nashville at Dallas, 8:30 p.m.
St. Louis at Colorado, 9 p.m.
Los Angeles at Calgary, 9 p.m.

Saturday, Dec. 30
Atlanta at Buffalo, 7 p.m.
Ottawa at Toronto, 7 p.m.
New Jersey at N.Y. Islanders, 7 p.m.
Washington at N.Y. Rangers, 7 p.m.
Montreal at Tampa Bay, 7:30 p.m.
Colorado at St. Louis, 8 p.m.
Boston at Nashville, 8 p.m.
San Jose at Phoenix, 9 p.m.
Vancouver at Edmonton, 10 p.m.

Sunday, Dec. 31
Anaheim at Minnesota, 6 p.m.
Los Angeles at Detroit, 7 p.m.
Chicago at Columbus, 7 p.m.
Philadelphia at Carolina, 8 p.m.
Edmonton at Calgary, 8 p.m.
San Jose at Dallas, 8 p.m.

Monday, Jan. 1
Atlanta at Ottawa, 2 p.m.
Phoenix at Washington, 2 p.m.
Colorado at Nashville, 3 p.m.
N.Y. Islanders at Buffalo, 5 p.m.
Boston at Toronto, 7 p.m.

Tuesday, Jan. 2
Chicago at St. Louis, 7 p.m.
Tampa Bay at Montreal, 7:30 p.m.
N.Y. Rangers at New Jersey, 7:30 p.m.
Philadelphia at N.Y. Islanders, 7:30 p.m.
Carolina at Pittsburgh, 7:30 p.m.
Anaheim at Detroit, 7:30 p.m.
Atlanta at Minnesota, 8 p.m.
Vancouver at Calgary, 9 p.m.
Florida at Edmonton, 9 p.m.

Wednesday, Jan. 3
Buffalo at Ottawa, 7:30 p.m.
Dallas at Vancouver, 10 p.m.
Columbus at Los Angeles, 10:30 p.m.

Thursday, Jan. 4
Toronto at Boston, 7 p.m.
Philadelphia at N.Y. Rangers, 7 p.m.
Montreal at Washington, 7 p.m.
Phoenix at Carolina, 7 p.m.
N.Y. Islanders at New Jersey, 7:30 p.m.
Chicago at St. Louis, 8 p.m.
Tampa Bay at Minnesota, 8 p.m.
Florida at Calgary, 9 p.m.
Dallas at Edmonton, 9 p.m.
Detroit at San Jose, 10:30 p.m.

Friday, Jan. 5
Phoenix at Atlanta, 7:30 p.m.
Pittsburgh at Buffalo, 8 p.m.
Nashville at Chicago, 8:30 p.m.
Tampa Bay at Colorado, 9 p.m.
Edmonton at Vancouver, 10 p.m.
Columbus at Anaheim, 10 p.m.

Saturday, Jan. 6
Philadelphia at Boston, 1 p.m.
New Jersey at Ottawa, 2 p.m.
N.Y. Rangers at Montreal, 3 p.m.
Buffalo at Toronto, 7 p.m.
Atlanta at Washington, 7 p.m.
N.Y. Islanders at Carolina, 7 p.m.
St. Louis at Nashville, 8 p.m.
Colorado at Minnesota, 8 p.m.
Dallas at Calgary, 10 p.m.
Detroit at Los Angeles, 10:30 p.m.
Columbus at San Jose, 10:30 p.m.

Sunday, Jan. 7
Philadelphia at Ottawa, 2 p.m.
New Jersey at Montreal, 3 p.m.
Phoenix at Chicago, 3 p.m.
Tampa Bay at Pittsburgh, 7:30 p.m.
Detroit at Anaheim, 8 p.m.
Florida at Vancouver, 10 p.m.

Monday, Jan. 8
Edmonton at Los Angeles, 10:30 p.m.

Tuesday, Jan. 9
N.Y. Islanders at N.Y. Rangers, 7 p.m.
Philadelphia at Washington, 7 p.m.
St. Louis at Columbus, 7 p.m.
Carolina at Toronto, 7:30 p.m.
Atlanta at Montreal, 7:30 p.m.
Boston at Ottawa, 7:30 p.m.
Pittsburgh at Tampa Bay, 7:30 p.m.
Anaheim at Nashville, 8 p.m.
Phoenix at Dallas, 8:30 p.m.
Detroit at Colorado, 9 p.m.
Minnesota at Calgary, 9 p.m.

Wednesday, Jan. 10
St. Louis at New Jersey, 7:30 p.m.
Pittsburgh at Florida, 7:30 p.m.
Buffalo at Chicago, 8:30 p.m.
Edmonton at San Jose, 10 p.m.

Thursday, Jan. 11
N.Y. Islanders at Boston, 7 p.m.
Toronto at Buffalo, 7 p.m.
Ottawa at N.Y. Rangers, 7 p.m.
Montreal at Philadelphia, 7 p.m.
Florida at Carolina, 7 p.m.
Washington at Tampa Bay, 7:30 p.m.
Anaheim at Dallas, 8:30 p.m.
Calgary at Colorado, 9 p.m.
Detroit at Phoenix, 9 p.m.
Minnesota at Vancouver, 10 p.m.
San Jose at Los Angeles, 10:30 p.m.

Friday, Jan. 12
Atlanta at New Jersey, 7:30 p.m.
Columbus at Nashville, 8 p.m.
Minnesota at Edmonton, 9 p.m.

Saturday, Jan. 13
Montreal at Ottawa, 2 p.m.
Boston at N.Y. Rangers, 2 p.m.
Pittsburgh at Philadelphia, 2 p.m.
Los Angeles at St. Louis, 2 p.m.
Tampa Bay at Buffalo, 7 p.m.
Vancouver at Toronto, 7 p.m.
New Jersey at N.Y. Islanders, 7 p.m.
Atlanta at Carolina, 7 p.m.
Chicago at Detroit, 7 p.m.
Nashville at Columbus, 7 p.m.
Washington at Florida, 7:30 p.m.
San Jose at Phoenix, 9 p.m.
Edmonton at Calgary, 10 p.m.
Colorado at Anaheim, 10 p.m.

Sunday, Jan. 14
Minnesota at Chicago, 7 p.m.

Monday, Jan. 15
Tampa Bay at N.Y. Islanders, 12 p.m.
Buffalo at Boston, 1 p.m.
Los Angeles at Dallas, 4 p.m.
St. Louis at Phoenix, 4 p.m.
Calgary at Nashville, 6 p.m.
Montreal at Detroit, 7 p.m.
Colorado at San Jose, 10 p.m.

Tuesday, Jan. 16
N.Y. Islanders at Pittsburgh, 7 p.m.
Los Angeles at Atlanta, 7 p.m.
Vancouver at Montreal, 7:30 p.m.
Washington at Ottawa, 7:30 p.m.
N.Y. Rangers at New Jersey, 7:30 p.m.
Toronto at Tampa Bay, 7:30 p.m.
Carolina at Florida, 7:30 p.m.
Edmonton at Minnesota, 8 p.m.
Columbus at Chicago, 8:30 p.m.
St. Louis at Anaheim, 10 p.m.

Wednesday, Jan. 17
Boston at Buffalo, 7 p.m.
Nashville at Detroit, 7:30 p.m.
Calgary at Dallas, 8:30 p.m.
Phoenix at Colorado, 9 p.m.

Thursday, Jan. 18
Pittsburgh at Boston, 7 p.m.
N.Y. Islanders at Philadelphia, 7 p.m.
Washington at Carolina, 7 p.m.
Montreal at Atlanta, 7 p.m.
Vancouver at Ottawa, 7:30 p.m.
Tampa Bay at New Jersey, 7:30 p.m.
Toronto at Florida, 7:30 p.m.
Columbus at Nashville, 8 p.m.
Anaheim at Edmonton, 9 p.m.
St. Louis at Los Angeles, 10:30 p.m.
Phoenix at San Jose, 10:30 p.m.

Friday, Jan. 19
Detroit at Columbus, 7 p.m.
Vancouver at Buffalo, 8 p.m.
Minnesota at Chicago, 8:30 p.m.
Anaheim at Calgary, 9 p.m.

Saturday, Jan. 20
Philadelphia at New Jersey, 1 p.m.
Atlanta at N.Y. Rangers, 1 p.m.
Florida at Washington, 1 p.m.
Ottawa at Boston, 7 p.m.
Buffalo at Montreal, 7 p.m.
Toronto at Pittsburgh, 7 p.m.
Chicago at Nashville, 8 p.m.
Dallas at Minnesota, 8 p.m.
Tampa Bay at Carolina, 8:30 p.m.
Detroit at Colorado, 9 p.m.
Calgary at Edmonton, 10 p.m.
Phoenix at Los Angeles, 10:30 p.m.
St. Louis at San Jose, 10:30 p.m.

Friday, Jan. 26
Washington at Carolina, 7 p.m.
Buffalo at Columbus, 7 p.m.
N.Y. Islanders at Atlanta, 7:30 p.m.
New Jersey at Tampa Bay, 8 p.m.
Detroit at St. Louis, 8 p.m.
Calgary at Minnesota, 8 p.m.
Nashville at Chicago, 8:30 p.m.
Pittsburgh at Dallas, 8:30 p.m.
Phoenix at Colorado, 9 p.m.
San Jose at Edmonton, 9 p.m.
Los Angeles at Vancouver, 10 p.m.

Saturday, Jan. 27
N.Y. Rangers at Philadelphia, 1 p.m.
Montreal at Toronto, 7 p.m.
Boston at Ottawa, 7 p.m.
Buffalo at N.Y. Islanders, 7 p.m.
Carolina at Washington, 7 p.m.
Minnesota at Columbus, 7 p.m.
New Jersey at Florida, 7:30 p.m.
Nashville at St. Louis, 8 p.m.
Pittsburgh at Phoenix, 9 p.m.
Los Angeles at Edmonton, 10 p.m.

Sunday, Jan. 28
Calgary at Chicago, 3 p.m.
Philadelphia at Atlanta, 3:30 p.m.
Colorado at Detroit, 3:30 p.m.
Dallas at Anaheim, 3:30 p.m.
San Jose at Vancouver, 10 p.m.

Monday, Jan. 29
N.Y. Rangers at Boston, 7 p.m.
Ottawa at Montreal, 7:30 p.m.

Tuesday, Jan. 30
Boston at Buffalo, 7 p.m.
Tampa Bay at Philadelphia, 7 p.m.
Toronto at Carolina, 7 p.m.
New Jersey at Atlanta, 7 p.m.
Washington at Ottawa, 7:30 p.m.
Detroit at N.Y. Islanders, 7:30 p.m.
Florida at Pittsburgh, 7:30 p.m.
Minnesota at St. Louis, 8 p.m.
Nashville at Colorado, 8 p.m.
Los Angeles at Calgary, 9 p.m.
Columbus at Vancouver, 10 p.m.
Dallas at San Jose, 10:30 p.m.

Wednesday, Jan. 31
Toronto at N.Y. Rangers, 7 p.m.
Columbus at Edmonton, 9 p.m.
Phoenix at Anaheim, 10 p.m.

Thursday, Feb. 1
Buffalo at Boston, 7 p.m.
New Jersey at Philadelphia, 7 p.m.
Tampa Bay at Carolina, 7 p.m.
N.Y. Islanders at Atlanta, 7 p.m.
Montreal at Pittsburgh, 7:30 p.m.
Washington at Florida, 7:30 p.m.
Minnesota at Colorado, 9 p.m.
Nashville at Phoenix, 9 p.m.
Edmonton at Vancouver, 10 p.m.
Chicago at Los Angeles, 10:30 p.m.
Dallas at San Jose, 10:30 p.m.

Friday, Feb. 2
St. Louis at Detroit, 7:30 p.m.
Columbus at Calgary, 9 p.m.

Saturday, Feb. 3
Washington at Pittsburgh, 1 p.m.
N.Y. Islanders at Montreal, 2 p.m.
Edmonton at Colorado, 3 p.m.
Chicago at San Jose, 4 p.m.
Toronto at Ottawa, 7 p.m.
Philadelphia at Atlanta, 7 p.m.
Buffalo at New Jersey, 7:30 p.m.
N.Y. Rangers at Tampa Bay, 7:30 p.m.
Los Angeles at Florida, 7:30 p.m.
Dallas at St. Louis, 8 p.m.
Anaheim at Nashville, 8 p.m.
Boston at Carolina, 8:30 p.m.
Minnesota at Phoenix, 9 p.m.
Vancouver at Calgary, 10 p.m.

Sunday, Feb. 4
N.Y. Islanders at Washington, 1 p.m.
Pittsburgh at Montreal, 2 p.m.

Monday, Feb. 5
Detroit at N.Y. Rangers, 7 p.m.

Tuesday, Feb. 6
Boston at Washington, 7 p.m.
Buffalo at Atlanta, 7 p.m.
Phoenix at Columbus, 7 p.m.
Carolina at Montreal, 7:30 p.m.
N.Y. Rangers at New Jersey, 7:30 p.m.
Nashville at Pittsburgh, 7:30 p.m.
Los Angeles at Tampa Bay, 7:30 p.m.
Toronto at St. Louis, 8 p.m.
Minnesota at Dallas, 8 p.m.
Florida at Colorado, 9 p.m.
Chicago at Calgary, 9 p.m.
Vancouver at Edmonton, 9 p.m.
Anaheim at San Jose, 10:30 p.m.

Wednesday, Feb. 7
Ottawa at Buffalo, 7 p.m.
Philadelphia at N.Y. Islanders, 7:30 p.m.
Phoenix at Detroit, 7:30 p.m.
Chicago at Vancouver, 10 p.m.
San Jose at Anaheim, 10 p.m.

Thursday, Feb. 8
Carolina at Boston, 7 p.m.
Pittsburgh at Philadelphia, 7 p.m.
Los Angeles at Washington, 7 p.m.
Calgary at Columbus, 7 p.m.
Montreal at Ottawa, 7:30 p.m.
N.Y. Islanders at New Jersey, 7:30 p.m.
Detroit at St. Louis, 8 p.m.
Toronto at Nashville, 8 p.m.
Florida at Minnesota, 8 p.m.
Atlanta at Colorado, 9 p.m.

Friday, Feb. 9
Tampa Bay at N.Y. Rangers, 7 p.m.
Chicago at Edmonton, 9 p.m.

Saturday, Feb. 10
Anaheim at Dallas, 3:30 p.m.
N.Y. Islanders at Boston, 7 p.m.

Calgary at Buffalo, 7 p.m.
Pittsburgh at Toronto, 7 p.m.
Ottawa at Montreal, 7 p.m.
St. Louis at Philadelphia, 7 p.m.
N.Y. Rangers at Washington, 7 p.m.
Phoenix at Florida, 7:30 p.m.
Los Angeles at Nashville, 8 p.m.
Carolina at Minnesota, 8 p.m.
Atlanta at Vancouver, 10 p.m.

Sunday, Feb. 11
Tampa Bay at New Jersey, 3:30 p.m.
Chicago at Columbus, 3:30 p.m.
Colorado at Dallas, 3:30 p.m.
Calgary at Detroit, 6 p.m.
Atlanta at Edmonton, 8 p.m.

Monday, Feb. 12
Detroit at Philadelphia, 7 p.m.

Tuesday, Feb. 13
Edmonton at Boston, 7 p.m.
Los Angeles at Carolina, 7 p.m.
N.Y. Islanders at Toronto, 7:30 p.m.
Florida at Montreal, 7:30 p.m.
Phoenix at Tampa Bay, 7:30 p.m.
San Jose at St. Louis, 8 p.m.
Anaheim at Colorado, 9 p.m.
Atlanta at Calgary, 9 p.m.

Wednesday, Feb. 14
St. Louis at Columbus, 7 p.m.
Florida at Ottawa, 7:30 p.m.
Montreal at New Jersey, 7:30 p.m.
Chicago at Pittsburgh, 7:30 p.m.
San Jose at Nashville, 8 p.m.
Vancouver at Minnesota, 8 p.m.
Detroit at Dallas, 8:30 p.m.

Thursday, Feb. 15
Edmonton at Buffalo, 7 p.m.
Toronto at Philadelphia, 7 p.m.
N.Y. Rangers at Carolina, 7 p.m.
Boston at N.Y. Islanders, 7:30 p.m.
Washington at Tampa Bay, 7:30 p.m.
Colorado at Calgary, 9 p.m.
Anaheim at Phoenix, 9 p.m.

Friday, Feb. 16
San Jose at Columbus, 7 p.m.
Pittsburgh at New Jersey, 7:30 p.m.
Nashville at St. Louis, 8 p.m.
Vancouver at Chicago, 8:30 p.m.

Saturday, Feb. 17
Philadelphia at N.Y. Rangers, 1 p.m.
Boston at Buffalo, 7 p.m.
Edmonton at Toronto, 7 p.m.
Carolina at Montreal, 7 p.m.
Atlanta at Ottawa, 7 p.m.
New Jersey at N.Y. Islanders, 7 p.m.
Tampa Bay at Florida, 7:30 p.m.
Minnesota at Nashville, 8 p.m.
Detroit at Phoenix, 9 p.m.
Colorado at Calgary, 10 p.m.
Anaheim at Los Angeles, 10:30 p.m.

Sunday, Feb. 18
Chicago at N.Y. Rangers, 3:30 p.m.
Washington at Pittsburgh, 3:30 p.m.
San Jose at Dallas, 3:30 p.m.
Montreal at Columbus, 6 p.m.
Minnesota at St. Louis, 6 p.m.
Los Angeles at Anaheim, 8 p.m.
Colorado at Vancouver, 10 p.m.

Monday, Feb. 19
Pittsburgh at N.Y. Islanders, 1 p.m.
Phoenix at Nashville, 6 p.m.
Boston at Philadelphia, 7 p.m.

Tuesday, Feb. 20
Philadelphia at Buffalo, 7 p.m.
Boston at Toronto, 7 p.m.
Atlanta at Carolina, 7 p.m.
Washington at Montreal, 7:30 p.m.
Edmonton at Ottawa, 7:30 p.m.
N.Y. Rangers at New Jersey, 7:30 p.m.
Florida at Tampa Bay, 7:30 p.m.
Columbus at St. Louis, 8 p.m.
Dallas at Minnesota, 8 p.m.
Calgary at Colorado, 9 p.m.
Vancouver at Anaheim, 10 p.m.

Wednesday, Feb. 21
San Jose at Washington, 7 p.m.
Chicago at Detroit, 7:30 p.m.

Thursday, Feb. 22
Ottawa at Buffalo, 7 p.m.
New Jersey at N.Y. Rangers, 7 p.m.
Philadelphia at Carolina, 7 p.m.
Tampa Bay at Atlanta, 7 p.m.
Edmonton at Columbus, 7 p.m.
Toronto at N.Y. Islanders, 7:30 p.m.
Pittsburgh at Florida, 7:30 p.m.
Montreal at Nashville, 8 p.m.
San Jose at Chicago, 8:30 p.m.
Minnesota at Colorado, 9 p.m.
Calgary at Phoenix, 9 p.m.
Vancouver at Los Angeles, 10:30 p.m.

Friday, Feb. 23
Edmonton at Detroit, 7:30 p.m.
Boston at Tampa Bay, 8 p.m.
Anaheim at Dallas, 8:30 p.m.

Saturday, Feb. 24
Washington at New Jersey, 1 p.m.
Montreal at N.Y. Islanders, 1 p.m.
Buffalo at Ottawa, 7 p.m.
Columbus at N.Y. Rangers, 7 p.m.
Toronto at Philadelphia, 7 p.m.
Carolina at Atlanta, 7 p.m.
Boston at Florida, 7:30 p.m.
Detroit at Nashville, 8 p.m.
San Jose at Calgary, 10 p.m.
Colorado at Los Angeles, 10:30 p.m.

Sunday, Feb. 25
New Jersey at Washington, 1 p.m.
Edmonton at Minnesota, 2 p.m.
St. Louis at Chicago, 3 p.m.
Vancouver at Dallas, 3:30 p.m.
Pittsburgh at Tampa Bay, 5 p.m.
Nashville at Columbus, 6 p.m.
Colorado at Anaheim, 8 p.m.

Monday, Feb. 26
Atlanta at Boston, 7 p.m.
Toronto at Montreal, 7:30 p.m.
Phoenix at Calgary, 9 p.m.
Anaheim at San Jose, 10 p.m.

Tuesday, Feb. 27
Montreal at N.Y. Rangers, 7 p.m.
Florida at Washington, 7 p.m.
Ottawa at Carolina, 7 p.m.
Buffalo at Toronto, 7:30 p.m.
Philadelphia at N.Y. Islanders, 7:30 p.m.
New Jersey at Pittsburgh, 7:30 p.m.
Dallas at Tampa Bay, 7:30 p.m.
Vancouver at St. Louis, 8 p.m.
Detroit at Chicago, 8:30 p.m.
Columbus at Colorado, 9 p.m.
Phoenix at Edmonton, 9 p.m.

Wednesday, Feb. 28
Carolina at Ottawa, 7:30 p.m.
Minnesota at Calgary, 9 p.m.
Nashville at San Jose, 10:30 p.m.

Thursday, Mar. 1
Philadelphia at Boston, 7 p.m.
Pittsburgh at N.Y. Rangers, 7 p.m.
Tampa Bay at Washington, 7 p.m.
St. Louis at N.Y. Islanders, 7:30 p.m.
Dallas at Florida, 7:30 p.m.
Colorado at Chicago, 8:30 p.m.
Minnesota at Edmonton, 9 p.m.
Phoenix at Vancouver, 10 p.m.
Anaheim at Los Angeles, 10:30 p.m.

Friday, Mar. 2
Pittsburgh at Carolina, 7 p.m.
Toronto at New Jersey, 7:30 p.m.
Ottawa at Atlanta, 7:30 p.m.
Chicago at Detroit, 7:30 p.m.
Montreal at Buffalo, 8 p.m.
Columbus at Dallas, 8:30 p.m.
San Jose at Anaheim, 10 p.m.

Saturday, Mar. 3
St. Louis at N.Y. Rangers, 1 p.m.
Nashville at Los Angeles, 4 p.m.
Montreal at Boston, 7 p.m.
Buffalo at Toronto, 7 p.m.
N.Y. Islanders at Washington, 7 p.m.
Tampa Bay at Florida, 7:30 p.m.
Columbus at Phoenix, 9 p.m.
Calgary at Edmonton, 10 p.m.

Sunday, Mar. 4
Philadelphia at Pittsburgh, 12:30 p.m.
Carolina at Atlanta, 12:30 p.m.
Colorado at Detroit, 12:30 p.m.
Ottawa at Chicago, 3 p.m.
San Jose at Dallas, 3:30 p.m.
Boston at New Jersey, 7 p.m.
Nashville at Anaheim, 8 p.m.
Minnesota at Vancouver, 10 p.m.

Monday, Mar. 5
N.Y. Islanders at N.Y. Rangers, 7 p.m.

Tuesday, Mar. 6
Colorado at Boston, 7 p.m.
New Jersey at Philadelphia, 7 p.m.
Florida at Atlanta, 7 p.m.
Washington at Toronto, 7:30 p.m.
Pittsburgh at Ottawa, 7:30 p.m.
Nashville at Detroit, 7:30 p.m.
Calgary at St. Louis, 8 p.m.
San Jose at Minnesota, 8 p.m.
Los Angeles at Chicago, 8:30 p.m.
Tampa Bay at Vancouver, 10 p.m.

Wednesday, Mar. 7
Colorado at Buffalo, 7 p.m.
Los Angeles at Columbus, 7 p.m.

Tampa Bay at Edmonton, 9 p.m.
Phoenix at Anaheim, 10 p.m.

Thursday, Mar. 8
Minnesota at Boston, 7 p.m.
Florida at Philadelphia, 7 p.m.
Montreal at Atlanta, 7 p.m.
Toronto at Ottawa, 7:30 p.m.
N.Y. Rangers at N.Y. Islanders, 7:30 p.m.
New Jersey at Pittsburgh, 7:30 p.m.
Dallas at St. Louis, 8 p.m.
Calgary at Nashville, 8 p.m.
Vancouver at Phoenix, 9 p.m.

Friday, Mar. 9
Carolina at Washington, 7 p.m.
Dallas at Columbus, 7 p.m.
Los Angeles at Detroit, 7:30 p.m.
Minnesota at Buffalo, 8 p.m.
Edmonton at Anaheim, 10 p.m.
Vancouver at San Jose, 10:30 p.m.

Saturday, Mar. 10
Boston at Philadelphia, 1 p.m.
N.Y. Rangers at Pittsburgh, 1 p.m.
New Jersey at Buffalo, 7 p.m.
Ottawa at Toronto, 7 p.m.
Washington at N.Y. Islanders, 7 p.m.
Atlanta at Florida, 7:30 p.m.
Montreal at St. Louis, 8 p.m.
Columbus at Nashville, 8 p.m.
Chicago at Phoenix, 9 p.m.
Tampa Bay at Calgary, 10 p.m.

Sunday, Mar. 11
Carolina at N.Y. Rangers, 12:30 p.m.
Boston at Detroit, 12:30 p.m.
Colorado at Minnesota, 3 p.m.
Los Angeles at Dallas, 3:30 p.m.
Vancouver at Anaheim, 8 p.m.
Edmonton at San Jose, 8 p.m.

Monday, Mar. 12
Washington at Atlanta, 7 p.m.
St. Louis at Calgary, 9 p.m.
Philadelphia at Phoenix, 10 p.m.
Edmonton at Los Angeles, 10:30 p.m.

Tuesday, Mar. 13
Ottawa at N.Y. Rangers, 7 p.m.
Florida at Carolina, 7 p.m.
Tampa Bay at Toronto, 7:30 p.m.
N.Y. Islanders at Montreal, 7:30 p.m.
Buffalo at Pittsburgh, 7:30 p.m.
Detroit at Nashville, 8 p.m.
Philadelphia at Dallas, 8 p.m.
Minnesota at Vancouver, 10 p.m.
Chicago at San Jose, 10:30 p.m.

Wednesday, Mar. 14
Pittsburgh at New Jersey, 7:30 p.m.
Nashville at Detroit, 7:30 p.m.
Calgary at Colorado, 9 p.m.
Columbus at Anaheim, 10 p.m.

Thursday, Mar. 15
Washington at Boston, 7 p.m.
Atlanta at Philadelphia, 7 p.m.
New Jersey at Carolina, 7 p.m.
N.Y. Islanders at Ottawa, 7:30 p.m.
Buffalo at Florida, 7:30 p.m.
Calgary at Dallas, 8:30 p.m.
Minnesota at Edmonton, 9 p.m.
San Jose at Phoenix, 10 p.m.
St. Louis at Vancouver, 10 p.m.
Chicago at Los Angeles, 10:30 p.m.

Friday, Mar. 16
Toronto at Washington, 7 p.m.
Montreal at Pittsburgh, 7:30 p.m.
N.Y. Rangers at Atlanta, 7:30 p.m.
Buffalo at Tampa Bay, 8 p.m.
Chicago at Anaheim, 10 p.m.
Columbus at San Jose, 10:30 p.m.

Saturday, Mar. 17
Carolina at New Jersey, 1 p.m.
Toronto at Montreal, 7 p.m.
Philadelphia at Ottawa, 7 p.m.
Boston at N.Y. Rangers, 7 p.m.
N.Y. Islanders at Florida, 7:30 p.m.
Dallas at Nashville, 8 p.m.
St. Louis at Edmonton, 8 p.m.
Minnesota at Calgary, 9 p.m.
Colorado at Phoenix, 10 p.m.
Detroit at Vancouver, 10 p.m.
Columbus at Los Angeles, 10:30 p.m.

Sunday, Mar. 18
Tampa Bay at Washington, 1 p.m.
Buffalo at Atlanta, 2 p.m.
Ottawa at Pittsburgh, 7:30 p.m.
San Jose at Colorado, 8 p.m.
Phoenix at Dallas, 8 p.m.
Los Angeles at Anaheim, 8 p.m.

Monday, Mar. 19
Pittsburgh at N.Y. Rangers, 7 p.m.
Vancouver at Edmonton, 9 p.m.

Tuesday, Mar. 20
Boston at Montreal, 7 p.m.
Florida at Philadelphia, 7 p.m.
Chicago at Columbus, 7 p.m.
New Jersey at Toronto, 7:30 p.m.
N.Y. Islanders at Tampa Bay, 7:30 p.m.
Ottawa at St. Louis, 8 p.m.
Phoenix at Minnesota, 8 p.m.
Detroit at Calgary, 9 p.m.

Wednesday, Mar. 21
Washington at Buffalo, 7 p.m.
Philadelphia at N.Y. Rangers, 7 p.m.
San Jose at Chicago, 8:30 p.m.
Colorado at Edmonton, 9 p.m.
Nashville at Vancouver, 10 p.m.
Dallas at Los Angeles, 10:30 p.m.

Thursday, Mar. 22
Montreal at Boston, 7 p.m.
Washington at Carolina, 7 p.m.
San Jose at Atlanta, 7 p.m.
Pittsburgh at N.Y. Islanders, 7:30 p.m.
New Jersey at Tampa Bay, 7:30 p.m.
Ottawa at Florida, 7:30 p.m.
Columbus at Detroit, 7:30 p.m.
St. Louis at Minnesota, 8 p.m.
Anaheim at Phoenix, 10 p.m.

Friday, Mar. 23
Toronto at Buffalo, 8 p.m.
Los Angeles at Chicago, 8:30 p.m.
Nashville at Calgary, 9 p.m.
Colorado at Edmonton, 9 p.m.
Dallas at Anaheim, 10 p.m.

Saturday, Mar. 24
N.Y. Rangers at Boston, 1 p.m.
N.Y. Islanders at Philadelphia, 1 p.m.
Atlanta at Pittsburgh, 1 p.m.
St. Louis at Detroit, 2 p.m.
Buffalo at Toronto, 7 p.m.
Washington at Montreal, 7 p.m.
San Jose at Carolina, 7 p.m.
Ottawa at Tampa Bay, 7:30 p.m.
New Jersey at Florida, 7:30 p.m.
Los Angeles at Minnesota, 8 p.m.
Dallas at Phoenix, 10 p.m.
Nashville at Edmonton, 10 p.m.

Sunday, Mar. 25
N.Y. Rangers at N.Y. Islanders, 12:30 p.m
Boston at Pittsburgh, 12:30 p.m.
St. Louis at Columbus, 12:30 p.m.
Calgary at Chicago, 3 p.m.
Colorado at Vancouver, 10 p.m.

Monday, Mar. 26
Anaheim at Detroit, 7 p.m.

Tuesday, Mar. 27
Pittsburgh at Washington, 7 p.m.
Florida at Tampa Bay, 7 p.m.
Carolina at Toronto, 7:30 p.m.
N.Y. Rangers at Montreal, 7:30 p.m.
Boston at Ottawa, 7:30 p.m.
New Jersey at N.Y. Islanders, 7:30 p.m.
Columbus at St. Louis, 8 p.m.
Edmonton at Nashville, 8 p.m.
Calgary at Minnesota, 8 p.m.
Phoenix at Dallas, 8:30 p.m.
Vancouver at Colorado, 9 p.m.
Los Angeles at San Jose, 10:30 p.m.

Wednesday, Mar. 28
New Jersey at Buffalo, 7 p.m.
Carolina at Philadelphia, 7 p.m.
Atlanta at Florida, 7:30 p.m.
Anaheim at Chicago, 8:30 p.m.

Thursday, Mar. 29
Pittsburgh at Boston, 7 p.m.
Toronto at Atlanta, 7 p.m.
Anaheim at Columbus, 7 p.m.
Edmonton at St. Louis, 8 p.m.
Detroit at Nashville, 8 p.m.
Calgary at Minnesota, 8 p.m.
Colorado at Phoenix, 10 p.m.
Vancouver at Los Angeles, 10:30 p.m.

Friday, Mar. 30
Tampa Bay at Carolina, 7 p.m.
Montreal at Ottawa, 7:30 p.m.
Philadelphia at New Jersey, 7:30 p.m.
Washington at Florida, 7:30 p.m.
Dallas at Detroit, 7:30 p.m.
N.Y. Islanders at Buffalo, 8 p.m.
Columbus at Chicago, 8:30 p.m.
Phoenix at San Jose, 10:30 p.m.

Saturday, Mar. 31
Atlanta at Boston, 1 p.m.
Minnesota at Colorado, 3 p.m.
Pittsburgh at Toronto, 7 p.m.
Buffalo at Montreal, 7 p.m.
Ottawa at N.Y. Islanders, 7 p.m.
N.Y. Rangers at Philadelphia, 7 p.m.
Washington at Tampa Bay, 7:30 p.m.
Anaheim at St. Louis, 8 p.m.

Dallas at Nashville, 8 p.m.
Calgary at Vancouver, 10 p.m.

Sunday, Apr. 1
Boston at New Jersey, 12:30 p.m.
Detroit at Columbus, 12:30 p.m.
Edmonton at Chicago, 3 p.m.
Carolina at Florida, 5 p.m.
Los Angeles at San Jose, 6 p.m.
Toronto at N.Y. Rangers, 7 p.m.

Monday, Apr. 2
St. Louis at Dallas, 8 p.m.

Tuesday, Apr. 3
Buffalo at Pittsburgh, 7 p.m.
Florida at Washington, 7 p.m.
Philadelphia at Toronto, 7:30 p.m.
Boston at Montreal, 7:30 p.m.
Ottawa at New Jersey, 7:30 p.m.
N.Y. Rangers at N.Y. Islanders, 7:30 p.m.
Carolina at Tampa Bay, 7:30 p.m.
Columbus at Detroit, 7:30 p.m.
Chicago at Nashville, 8 p.m.
Edmonton at Minnesota, 8 p.m.
Colorado at Calgary, 9 p.m.
Los Angeles at Vancouver, 10 p.m.
St. Louis at Phoenix, 10 p.m.

Wednesday, Apr. 4
Washington at Atlanta, 7 p.m.
San Jose at Anaheim, 10 p.m.

Thursday, Apr. 5
Boston at Buffalo, 7 p.m.
Montreal at N.Y. Rangers, 7 p.m.
New Jersey at Philadelphia, 7 p.m.
Dallas at Columbus, 7 p.m.
Pittsburgh at Ottawa, 7:30 p.m.
Toronto at N.Y. Islanders, 7:30 p.m.
St. Louis at Nashville, 8 p.m.
Edmonton at Minnesota, 8 p.m.
Detroit at Chicago, 8:30 p.m.
Colorado at Vancouver, 10 p.m.
Los Angeles at Phoenix, 10 p.m.
Calgary at San Jose, 10:30 p.m.

Friday, Apr. 6
Atlanta at Carolina, 7 p.m.
Florida at Tampa Bay, 8 p.m.
Anaheim at Dallas, 8:30 p.m.

Saturday, Apr. 7
N.Y. Islanders at Philadelphia, 1 p.m.
Buffalo at Washington, 1 p.m.
Chicago at Detroit, 1 p.m.
Phoenix at Los Angeles, 4 p.m.
Vancouver at San Jose, 4 p.m.
Ottawa at Boston, 7 p.m.
Montreal at Toronto, 7 p.m.
Florida at Carolina, 7 p.m.
Tampa Bay at Atlanta, 7 p.m.
Anaheim at Columbus, 7 p.m.
N.Y. Rangers at Pittsburgh, 7:30 p.m.
St. Louis at Minnesota, 8 p.m.
Nashville at Colorado, 9 p.m.
Edmonton at Calgary, 10 p.m.

Sunday, Apr. 8
N.Y. Islanders at New Jersey, 1 p.m.
Buffalo at Philadelphia, 1 p.m.
Chicago at Dallas, 1 p.m.
Vancouver at Phoenix, 5 p.m.

2005-06 REVIEW

Regular season

Stanley Cup playoffs

2006 entry draft

REGULAR SEASON

2005-06 FINAL STANDINGS

EASTERN CONFERENCE

ATLANTIC DIVISION

	G	W	L	OTL	Pts.	GF	GA	Home	Away	Div. Rec.
New Jersey Devils	82	46	27	9	101	242	229	27-11—3	19-16—6	16-12—4
Philadelphia Flyers	82	45	26	11	101	267	259	22-13—6	23-13—5	19-9—4
New York Rangers	82	44	26	12	100	257	215	25-10—6	19-16—6	18-9—5
New York Islanders	82	36	40	6	78	230	278	20-18—3	16-22—3	15-15—2
Pittsburgh Penguins	82	22	46	14	58	244	316	12-21—8	10-25—6	12-14—6

NORTHEAST DIVISION

	G	W	L	OTL	Pts.	GF	GA	Home	Away	Div. Rec.
Ottawa Senators	82	52	21	9	113	314	211	29-9—3	23-12—6	20-8—4
Buffalo Sabres	82	52	24	6	110	281	239	27-11—3	25-13—3	21-9—2
Montreal Canadiens	82	42	31	9	93	243	247	24-13—4	18-18—5	18-9—5
Toronto Maple Leafs	82	41	33	8	90	257	270	26-12—3	15-21—5	11-16—5
Boston Bruins	82	29	37	16	74	230	266	16-15—10	13-22—6	10-19—3

SOUTHEAST DIVISION

	G	W	L	OTL	Pts.	GF	GA	Home	Away	Div. Rec.
Carolina Hurricanes	82	52	22	8	112	294	260	31-8—2	21-14—6	18-11—3
Tampa Bay Lightning	82	43	33	6	92	252	260	25-14—2	18-19—4	16-11—5
Atlanta Thrashers	82	41	33	8	90	281	275	24-13—4	17-20—4	17-10—5
Florida Panthers	82	37	34	11	85	240	257	25-11—5	12-23—6	18-11—3
Washington Capitals	82	29	41	12	70	237	306	16-18—7	13-23—5	11-14—7

WESTERN CONFERENCE

CENTRAL DIVISION

	G	W	L	OTL	Pts.	GF	GA	Home	Away	Div. Rec.
Detroit Red Wings	82	58	16	8	124	305	209	27-9—5	31-7—3	25-3—4
Nashville Predators	82	49	25	8	106	259	227	32-8—1	17-17—7	23-8—1
Columbus Blue Jackets	82	35	43	4	74	223	279	23-18—0	12-25—4	14-15—3
Chicago Blackhawks	82	26	43	13	65	211	285	16-19—6	10-24—7	11-17—4
St. Louis Blues	82	21	46	15	57	197	292	12-23—6	9-23—9	7-20—5

NORTHWEST DIVISION

	G	W	L	OTL	Pts.	GF	GA	Home	Away	Div. Rec.
Calgary Flames	82	46	25	11	103	218	200	30-7—4	16-18—7	20-8—4
Colorado Avalanche	82	43	30	9	95	283	257	25-10—6	18-20—3	16-12—4
Edmonton Oilers	82	41	28	13	95	256	251	20-15—6	21-13—7	15-15—2
Vancouver Canucks	82	42	32	8	92	256	255	25-10—6	17-22—2	15-12—5
Minnesota Wild	82	38	36	8	84	231	215	23-16—2	15-20—6	14-17—1

PACIFIC DIVISION

	G	W	L	OTL	Pts.	GF	GA	Home	Away	Div. Rec.
Dallas Stars	82	53	23	6	112	265	218	28-11—2	25-12—4	17-11—4
San Jose Sharks	82	44	27	11	99	266	242	25-9—7	19-18—4	16-10—6
Mighty Ducks of Anaheim	82	43	27	12	98	254	229	26-10—5	17-17—7	18-9—5
Los Angeles Kings	82	42	35	5	89	249	270	26-14—1	16-21—4	14-14—4
Phoenix Coyotes	82	38	39	5	81	244	271	19-18—4	19-21—1	15-15—2

Note: OTL denotes overtime loss; teams receive two points for each victory and one for each overtime loss, including shootouts.

INDIVIDUAL LEADERS

SCORING

TOP SCORERS

Player, Team	GP	G	A	Pts.	+/-	PIM	SHG	PPG	ESG	GWG	OTG	Shots	ATOI
Joe Thornton, Boston-San Jose	81	29	96	125	31	61	0	11	18	6	1	195	21:20
Jaromir Jagr, N.Y. Rangers	82	54	69	123	34	72	0	24	30	9	2	368	22:04
Alexander Ovechkin, Washington	81	52	54	106	2	52	3	21	28	5	2	425	21:37
Dany Heatley, Ottawa	82	50	53	103	29	86	2	23	25	7	0	300	21:09
Daniel Alfredsson, Ottawa	77	43	60	103	29	50	5	16	22	8	0	249	21:41
Sidney Crosby, Pittsburgh	81	39	63	102	-1	110	0	16	23	5	3	278	20:07
Eric Staal, Carolina	82	45	55	100	-8	81	4	19	22	4	0	279	19:38
Ilya Kovalchuk, Atlanta	78	52	46	98	-6	68	0	27	25	7	0	323	22:22
Marc Savard, Atlanta	82	28	69	97	7	100	1	14	13	4	2	212	20:30
Jonathan Cheechoo, San Jose	82	56	37	93	23	58	2	24	30	11	0	317	19:57
Marian Hossa, Atlanta	80	39	53	92	17	67	7	14	18	7	1	341	21:41
Brad Richards, Tampa Bay	82	23	68	91	0	32	4	7	12	0	0	282	22:45
Teemu Selanne, Anaheim	80	40	50	90	28	44	0	18	22	5	0	267	17:47
Jason Spezza, Ottawa	68	19	71	90	23	33	0	7	12	5	1	156	19:00
Brian Gionta, New Jersey	82	48	41	89	18	46	1	24	23	10	3	291	19:49
Olli Jokinen, Florida	82	38	51	89	14	88	1	14	23	9	4	351	20:29
Joe Sakic, Colorado	82	32	55	87	10	60	0	10	22	6	1	263	19:54
Pavel Datsyuk, Detroit	75	28	59	87	26	22	0	11	17	4	1	146	17:53
Patrick Marleau, San Jose	82	34	52	86	-12	26	1	20	13	4	2	260	19:55
Henrik Zetterberg, Detroit	77	39	46	85	29	30	1	17	21	9	0	270	18:57
Andy McDonald, Anaheim	82	34	51	85	24	32	0	13	21	7	0	229	16:48
Paul Kariya, Nashville	82	31	54	85	-6	40	0	14	17	3	1	245	19:04

GOALTENDING

TOP GOALTENDERS

(Based on save percentage, minimum 25 games played)

Goalie, Team	GP	Mins.	W	L	OTL	SA	GA	GAA	SV	SV%	SO
Cristobal Huet, Montreal	36	2103	18	11	4	1085	77	2.2	1008	92.9	7
Dominik Hasek, Ottawa	43	2584	28	10	4	1202	90	2.09	1112	92.5	5
Miikka Kiprusoff, Calgary	74	4380	42	20	11	1951	151	2.07	1800	92.3	10
Henrik Lundqvist, N.Y. Rangers	53	3112	30	12	9	1485	116	2.24	1369	92.2	2
Tomas Vokoun, Nashville	61	3601	36	18	7	1984	160	2.67	1824	91.9	4
Manny Fernandez, Minnesota	58	3411	30	18	7	1612	130	2.29	1482	91.9	1
Tim Thomas, Boston	38	2187	12	13	10	1213	101	2.77	1112	91.7	1
Manny Legace, Detroit	51	2905	37	8	3	1244	106	2.19	1138	91.5	7
Roberto Luongo, Florida	75	4305	35	30	9	2488	213	2.97	2275	91.4	4
Ryan Miller, Buffalo	48	2862	30	14	3	1440	124	2.6	1316	91.4	1
Jean-Sebastien Giguere, Anaheim	60	3381	30	15	11	1692	150	2.66	1542	91.1	2
Martin Brodeur, New Jersey	73	4365	43	23	7	2105	187	2.57	1918	91.1	5
Pascal Leclaire, Columbus	33	1804	11	15	3	1084	97	3.23	987	91.1	0
Ilya Bryzgalov, Anaheim	31	1575	13	12	1	733	66	2.51	667	91	1
Curtis Sanford, St. Louis	34	1830	13	13	5	885	81	2.66	804	90.8	3
Dwayne Roloson, Minn.-Edm.	43	2524	14	24	5	1256	115	2.73	1141	90.8	2
Martin Gerber, Carolina	60	3493	38	14	6	1719	162	2.78	1557	90.6	3
Kari Lehtonen, Atlanta	38	2166	20	15	0	1123	106	2.94	1017	90.6	2
Brent Johnson, Washington	26	1413	9	12	1	854	81	3.44	773	90.5	1
Martin Biron, Buffalo	35	1934	21	8	3	980	93	2.89	887	90.5	1
Alexander Auld, Vancouver	67	3859	33	26	6	1938	189	2.94	1749	90.2	0
Ray Emery, Ottawa	39	2168	23	11	4	1045	102	2.82	943	90.2	3
Curtis Joseph, Phoenix	60	3424	32	21	3	1690	166	2.91	1524	90.2	4
Vesa Toskala, San Jose	37	2039	23	7	4	878	87	2.56	791	90.1	2
Peter Budaj, Colorado	34	1803	14	10	6	864	86	2.86	778	90	2
Rick DiPietro, N.Y. Islanders	63	3572	30	24	5	1797	180	3.02	1617	90	1
Jason LaBarbera, Los Angeles	29	1433	11	9	2	688	69	2.89	619	90	1
Marc Denis, Columbus	49	2786	21	25	1	1505	151	3.25	1354	90	1
David Aebischer, Colo.-Mont.	50	2895	29	17	2	1473	149	3.09	1324	89.9	3
Marty Turco, Dallas	68	3910	41	19	5	1624	166	2.55	1458	89.8	3
Marc-Andre Fleury, Pittsburgh	50	2809	13	27	6	1485	152	3.25	1333	89.8	1
Chris Osgood, Detroit	32	1846	20	6	5	828	85	2.76	743	89.7	2

STANLEY CUP PLAYOFFS

2005-06 RESULTS

CONFERENCE QUARTERFINALS

EASTERN CONFERENCE

Score	Win. goalie	GWG	Period	Time
Ottawa 4, Tampa Bay 1	Emery	Spezza	3	6:13
Tampa Bay 4, Ottawa 3	Grahame	St. Louis	3	6:19
Ottawa 8, Tampa Bay 4	Emery	Vermette	2	9:11
Ottawa 5, Tampa Bay 2	Emery	Heatley	2	17:10
Ottawa 3, Tampa Bay 2	Emery	Havlat	2	15:02

(Ottawa wins Eastern Conference quarterfinals, 4-1)

Score	Win. goalie	GWG	Period	Time
Montreal 6, Carolina 1	Huet	Bonk	1	16:17
Montreal 6, Carolina 5 (2OT)	Huet	Ryder	2OT	2:32
Carolina 2, Montreal 1 (OT)	Ward	Staal	OT	3:38
Carolina 3, Montreal 2	Ward	Brind'Amour	3	5:54
Carolina 2, Montreal 1	Ward	Cullen	2	13:57
Carolina 2, Montreal 1 (OT)	Ward	Stillman	OT	1:19

(Carolina wins Eastern Conference quarterfinals, 4-2)

Score	Win. goalie	GWG	Period	Time
New Jersey 6, NY Rang. 1	Brodeur	Gomez	2	7:48
New Jersey 4, NY Rang. 1	Brodeur	Gionta	1	14:13
New Jersey 3, NY Rang. 0	Brodeur	Langenbrunner	1	1:08
New Jersey 4, NY Rang. 2	Brodeur	Gionta	3	4:30

(New Jersey wins Eastern Conference quarterfinals, 4-0)

Score	Win. goalie	GWG	Period	Time
Buffalo 3, Phila. 2 (2OT)	Miller	Briere	2OT	7:31
Buffalo 8, Phila. 2	Miller	Kotalik	1	12:26
Phila. 4, Buffalo 2	Esche	Forsberg	2	12:37
Phila. 5, Buffalo 4	Esche	Forsberg	3	19:11
Buffalo 3, Phila. 0	Miller	Connolly	1	6:05
Buffalo 7, Phila. 1	Miller	Kotalik	1	17:34

(Buffalo wins Eastern Conference quarterfinals, 4-2)

WESTERN CONFERENCE

Score	Win. goalie	GWG	Period	Time
Detroit 3, Edm. 2 (2OT)	Legace	Maltby	2OT	2:39
Edm. 4, Detroit 2	Roloson	Winchester	2	18:46
Edm. 4, Detroit 3 (2OT)	Roloson	Stoll	2OT	8:44
Detroit 4, Edm. 2	Legace	Lidstrom	3	6:44
Edm. 3, Detroit 2	Roloson	Horcoff	2	12:36
Edm. 4, Detroit 3	Roloson	Hemsky	3	18:54

(Edmonton wins Western Conference quarterfinals, 4-2)

Score	Win. goalie	GWG	Period	Time
Colorado 5, Dallas 2	Theodore	Blake	2	9:08
Colorado 5, Dallas 4 (OT)	Theodore	Sakic	OT	4:36
Colorado 4, Dallas 3 (OT)	Theodore	Tanguay	OT	1:09
Dallas 4, Colorado 1	Turco	Hagman	2	3:50
Colorado 3, Dallas 2 (OT)	Theodore	Brunette	OT	13:55

(Colorado wins Western Conference quarterfinals, 4-1)

Score	Win. goalie	GWG	Period	Time
Calgary 2, Anaheim 1 (OT)	Kiprusoff	McCarty	OT	9:45
Anaheim 4, Calgary 3	Giguere	Pahlsson	3	7:55
Calgary 5, Anaheim 2	Kiprusoff	Kobasew	2	15:34
Anaheim 3, Calgary 2 (OT)	Giguere	O'Donnell	OT	1:36
Calgary 3, Anaheim 2	Kiprusoff	Iginla	2	1:03
Anaheim 2, Calgary 1	Bryzgalov	Niedermayer	3	14:23
Anaheim 3, Calgary 0	Bryzgalov	Selanne	2	5:12

(Anaheim wins Western Conference quarterfinals, 4-3)

Score	Win. goalie	GWG	Period	Time
Nashville 4, San Jose 3	Mason	Hall	3	12:06
San Jose 3, Nashville 0	Toskala	Cheechoo	1	5:37
San Jose 4, Nashville 1	Toskala	Bernier	2	18:48
San Jose 5, Nashville 4	Toskala	Marleau	3	4:13
San Jose 2, Nashville 1	Toskala	Marleau	2	13:24

(San Jose wins Western Conference quarterfinals, 4-1)

CONFERENCE SEMIFINALS

EASTERN CONFERENCE

Score	Win. goalie	GWG	Period	Time
Buffalo 7, Ottawa 6 (OT)	Miller	Drury	OT	0:18
Buffalo 2, Ottawa 1	Miller	Hecht	2	6:00
Buffalo 3, Ottawa 2 (OT)	Miller	Dumont	OT	5:05
Ottawa 2, Buffalo 1	Emery	Redden	3	2:52
Buffalo 3, Ottawa 2 (OT)	Miller	Pominville	OT	2:26

(Buffalo wins Eastern Conference semifinals, 4-1)

Score	Win. goalie	GWG	Period	Time
Carolina 6, New Jersey 0	Ward	Whitney	1	11:37
Carolina 3, New Jersey 2 (OT)	Ward	Wallin	OT	3:09
Carolina 3, New Jersey 2	Ward	Brind'Amour	2	18:59
New Jersey 5, Carolina 1	Brodeur	Pandolfo	1	11:02
Carolina 4, New Jersey 1	Ward	Stillman	2	14:20

(Carolina wins Eastern Conference semifinals, 4-1)

WESTERN CONFERENCE

Score	Win. goalie	GWG	Period	Time
San Jose 2, Edm. 1	Toskala	Ehrhoff	2	3:14
San Jose 2, Edm. 1	Toskala	Thornton	2	17:29
Edm. 3, San Jose 2 (3OT)	Roloson	Horcoff	3OT	2:24
Edm. 6, San Jose 3	Roloson	J. Smith	3	2:57
Edm. 6, San Jose 3	Roloson	Pisani	3	4:03
Edm. 2, San Jose 0	Roloson	Peca	1	8:21

(Edmonton wins Western Conference semifinals, 4-2)

Score	Win. goalie	GWG	Period	Time
Anaheim 5, Colorado 0	Bryzgalov	Pahlsson	2	2:38
Anaheim 3, Colorado 0	Bryzgalov	Getzlaf	1	18:17
Anaheim 4, Colorado 3 (OT)	Bryzgalov	Lupul	OT	16:30
Anaheim 4, Colorado 1	Bryzgalov	Selanne	2	2:22

(Anaheim wins Western Conference semifinals, 4-0)

CONFERENCE FINALS

EASTERN CONFERENCE

Score	Win. goalie	GWG	Period	Time
Buffalo 3, Carolina 2	Miller	McKee	3	13:40
Carolina 4, Buffalo 3	Ward	J. Williams	3	6:58
Buffalo 4, Carolina 3	Miller	Kotalik	2	12:55
Carolina 4, Buffalo 0	Gerber	Recchi	1	6:54
Carolina 4, Buffalo 3 (OT)	Ward	Stillman	OT	8:46
Buffalo 2, Carolina 1 (OT)	Miller	Briere	OT	4:22
Carolina 4, Buffalo 2	Ward	Brind'Amour	3	11:22

(Carolina wins Eastern Conference finals, 4-3)

WESTERN CONFERENCE

Score	Win. goalie	GWG	Period	Time
Edm. 3, Anaheim 1	Roloson	Hemsky	2	11:35
Edm. 3, Anaheim 1	Roloson	Pisani	2	17:09
Edm. 5, Anaheim 4	Roloson	Pisani	3	14:14
Anaheim 6, Edm. 3	Giguere	Salei	2	5:42
Edm. 2, Anaheim 1	Roloson	Torres	2	8:31

(Edmonton wins Western Conference finals, 4-1)

STANLEY CUP FINALS

Score	Winning goalie	Game winning goal scorer	Period	Time
Carolina 5, Edmonton 4	Cam Ward	Rod Brind'Amour	3	19:28
Carolina 5, Edmonton 0	Cam Ward	Andrew Ladd	1	6:21
Edmonton 2, Carolina 1	Jussi Markkanen	Ryan Smyth	3	17:45
Carolina 2, Edmonton 1	Cam Ward	Mark Recchi	2	15:56
Edmonton 4, Carolina 3 (OT)	Jussi Markkanen	Fernando Pisani	OT	0:00
Edmonton 4, Carolina 0	Jussi Markkanen	Fernando Pisani	2	1:45
Carolina 3, Edmonton 1	Cam Ward	Frantisek Kaberle	2	4:18

(Carolina wins Stanley Cup finals, 4-3)

INDIVIDUAL LEADERS

SCORING

TOP SCORERS

	GP	G	A	Pts.	PIM
Eric Staal, Carolina	25	9	19	28	8
Cory Stillman, Carolina	25	9	17	26	14
Chris Pronger, Edmonton	24	5	16	21	26
Daniel Briere, Buffalo	18	8	11	19	12
Shawn Horcoff, Edmonton	24	7	12	19	12
Fernando Pisani, Edmonton	24	14	4	18	10
Rod Brind'Amour, Carolina	25	12	6	18	16
Chris Drury, Buffalo	18	9	9	18	10
Justin Williams, Carolina	25	7	11	18	34
Matt Cullen, Carolina	25	4	14	18	12
Ales Hemsky, Edmonton	24	6	11	17	14
Ryan Smyth, Edmonton	24	7	9	16	22
Mark Recchi, Carolina	25	7	9	16	18
Patrik Elias, New Jersey	9	6	10	16	4
Doug Weight, Carolina	23	3	13	16	20
Ray Whitney, Carolina	24	9	6	15	14
Derek Roy, Buffalo	18	5	10	15	16
Sergei Samsonov, Edmonton	24	4	11	15	14
Patrick Marleau, San Jose	11	9	5	14	8
J.P. Dumont, Buffalo	18	7	7	14	14
Teemu Selanne, Anaheim	16	6	8	14	6
Jason Spezza, Ottawa	10	5	9	14	2
Jaroslav Spacek, Edmonton	24	3	11	14	24

GOALTENDING

TOP GOALTENDERS

(Based on save percentage, minimum seven games)

	GP	S%	W	L	GAA	SO	GA
Ilya Bryzgalov, Anaheim	11	94.4	6	4	1.46	3	16
Dwayne Roloson, Edmonton	18	92.7	12	5	2.33	1	45
Martin Brodeur. New Jersey	9	92.3	5	4	2.25	1	20
Miikka Kiprusoff, Calgary	7	92.1	3	4	2.24	0	16
Cam Ward, Carolina	23	92	15	8	2.14	2	47
Vesa Toskala, San Jose	11	91	6	5	2.45	1	28
Ryan Miller, Buffalo	18	90.8	11	7	2.56	1	48
Jose Theodore, Colorado	9	90.2	4	5	3.04	0	29
Ray Emery, Ottawa	10	90	5	5	2.88	0	29

TEAM-BY-TEAM STATISTICS

ANAHEIM DUCKS

(Lost Western Conference finals to Edmonton, 4-1)

SCORING

Pos., No., Name	GP	ATOI	G	A	Pts	+/-	PIM	PPG	SHG	GWG	OTG	Shots	S%
RW, 13, Teemu Selanne	16	17:55	6	8	14	0	6	1	0	2	0	53	11.3
C, 22, Todd Marchant	16	17:33	3	10	13	14	14	0	0	0	0	26	11.5
RW, 15, Joffrey Lupul	16	16:43	9	2	11	9	31	1	0	1	1	62	14.5
D, 27, Scott Niedermayer	16	28:53	2	9	11	1	14	1	1	1	0	48	4.2
C, 76, Dustin Penner*	13	13:15	3	6	9	10	12	0	0	0	0	41	7.3
D, 23, Francois Beauchemin*	16	27:26	3	6	9	0	11	3	0	0	0	35	8.6
C, 19, Andy McDonald	16	16:33	2	7	9	0	10	2	0	0	0	48	4.2
LW, 38, Chris Kunitz*	16	12:30	3	5	8	-1	8	0	0	0	0	34	8.8
C, 51, Ryan Getzlaf*	16	15:49	3	4	7	-3	13	2	0	1	0	38	7.9
D, 24, Ruslan Salei	16	22:08	3	2	5	10	18	0	0	1	0	27	11.1
D, 21, Sean O'Donnell	16	16:43	2	3	5	8	23	0	0	1	1	10	20
C, 26, Samuel Pahlsson	16	17:06	2	3	5	2	18	0	0	2	0	22	9.1
LW, 12, Jeff Friesen	16	11:14	3	1	4	-1	6	0	0	0	0	15	20
C, 44, Rob Niedermayer	16	19:35	1	3	4	-1	10	1	0	0	0	24	4.2
D, 5, Vitaly Vishnevski	16	13:40	0	4	4	2	10	0	0	0	0	8	0
RW, 61, Corey Perry*	11	9:32	0	3	3	-4	16	0	0	0	0	14	0
LW, 32, Travis Moen	9	8:25	1	0	1	1	10	0	0	0	0	5	20
RW, 17, Jonathan Hedstrom	3	16:57	0	1	1	0	2	0	0	0	0	1	0
G, 35, Jean-Sebastien Giguere (goalie)	6	_	0	0	0	0	0	0	0	0	0	0	_
G, 30, Ilya Bryzgalov (goalie)	11	_	0	0	0	0	2	0	0	0	0	0	_
LW, 29, Todd Fedoruk	12	8:19	0	0	0	-1	16	0	0	0	0	12	0
D, 33, Joe DiPenta	16	11:34	0	0	0	1	13	0	0	0	0	5	0

GOALTENDING

	GP	Mins.	GAA	W	L	EN	SO	GA	SA	SV%	PIM
Ilya Bryzgalov*	11	659	1.46	6	4	2	3	16	285	0.944	2
Jean-Sebastien Giguere	6	318	3.4	3	3	0	0	18	132	0.864	0

BUFFALO SABRES

(Lost Eastern Conference finals to Carolina, 4-3)

SCORING

Pos., No., Name	GP	ATOI	G	A	Pts	+/-	PIM	PPG	SHG	GWG	OTG	Shots	S%
C, 48, Daniel Briere	18	18:47	8	11	19	0	12	3	0	2	2	47	17
C, 23, Chris Drury	18	19:20	9	9	18	5	10	5	1	1	1	42	21.4
C, 9, Derek Roy	18	17:03	5	10	15	7	16	1	1	0	0	33	15.2
RW, 17, J.P. Dumont	18	16:39	7	7	14	1	14	3	0	1	1	25	28
C, 19, Tim Connolly	8	17:29	5	6	11	3	0	1	1	1	0	11	45.5
RW, 12, Ales Kotalik	18	15:15	4	7	11	4	8	0	0	3	0	51	7.8
RW, 29, Jason Pominville*	18	12:11	5	5	10	0	8	0	1	1	1	22	22.7
RW, 61, Maxim Afinogenov	18	16:53	3	5	8	3	10	0	0	0	0	43	7
RW, 25, Mike Grier	18	16:16	3	5	8	3	2	0	1	0	0	32	9.4
D, 10, Henrik Tallinder	14	22:15	2	6	8	14	16	0	0	0	0	12	16.7
C, 55, Jochen Hecht	15	17:28	2	6	8	4	8	0	0	1	0	36	5.6
D, 51, Brian Campbell	18	20:28	0	6	6	-5	12	0	0	0	0	29	0
D, 74, Jay McKee	17	20:17	2	3	5	3	30	0	0	1	0	21	9.5
D, 5, Toni Lydman	18	23:03	1	4	5	14	18	0	0	0	0	14	7.1
LW, 24, Taylor Pyatt	14	11:07	0	5	5	-2	10	0	0	0	0	17	0
D, 8, Rory Fitzpatrick	11	17:11	0	4	4	-1	16	0	0	0	0	3	0
C, 28, Paul Gaustad*	18	12:21	0	4	4	1	14	0	0	0	0	13	0
LW, 26, Thomas Vanek*	10	10:44	2	0	2	-1	6	2	0	0	0	16	12.5
D, 27, Teppo Numminen	12	18:45	1	1	2	3	4	1	0	0	0	7	14.3
D, 45, Dmitri Kalinin	8	16:53	0	2	2	4	2	0	0	0	0	11	0
D, 33, Doug Janik*	5	10:29	1	0	1	-2	2	0	0	0	0	4	25
D, 38, Nathan Paetsch*	1	12:06	0	0	0	0	0	0	0	0	0	3	0
C, 22, Adam Mair	3	9:16	0	0	0	-2	0	0	0	0	0	5	0
D, 34, Jeff Jillson	4	11:40	0	0	0	-4	0	0	0	0	0	5	0
C, 13, Jiri Novotny*	4	10:27	0	0	0	-1	0	0	0	0	0	3	0
G, 30, Ryan Miller (goalie)	18	_	0	0	0	0	2	0	0	0	0	0	_

GOALTENDING

	GP	Mins.	GAA	W	L	EN	SO	GA	SA	SV%	PIM
Ryan Miller*	18	1123	2.56	11	7	1	1	48	522	0.908	2

*rookie

CALGARY FLAMES

(Lost Western Conference quarterfinals to Anaheim, 4-3)

SCORING

Pos., No., Name	GP	ATOI	G	A	Pts	+/-	PIM	PPG	SHG	GWG	OTG	Shots	S%
RW, 12, Jarome Iginla	7	24:14	5	3	8	3	11	1	1	1	0	24	20.8
RW, 20, Kristian Huselius	7	15:35	2	4	6	1	4	2	0	0	0	14	14.3
C, 22, Daymond Langkow	7	19:41	1	5	6	4	6	1	0	0	0	18	5.6
D, 28, Robyn Regehr	7	22:22	1	3	4	3	6	1	0	0	0	9	11.1
D, 21, Andrew Ference	7	23:08	0	4	4	3	12	0	0	0	0	7	0
RW, 10, Tony Amonte	7	17:27	2	1	3	2	10	0	1	0	0	13	15.4
RW, 25, Darren McCarty	7	9:50	2	0	2	1	15	0	0	1	1	7	28.6
D, 4, Roman Hamrlik	7	19:43	0	2	2	-7	2	0	0	0	0	10	0
C, 8, Matthew Lombardi	7	15:50	0	2	2	-4	2	0	0	0	0	9	0
RW, 19, Chuck Kobasew	7	12:28	1	0	1	-3	0	0	0	1	0	13	7.7
D, 3, Dion Phaneuf*	7	18:37	1	0	1	-8	7	1	0	0	0	13	7.7
C, 11, Stephane Yelle	7	15:27	1	0	1	-1	8	0	0	0	0	7	14.3
C, 24, Jamie Lundmark	4	9:44	0	1	1	0	7	0	0	0	0	2	0
LW, 17, Chris Simon	6	10:12	0	1	1	-3	7	0	0	0	0	6	0
D, 6, Jordan Leopold	7	19:13	0	1	1	2	4	0	0	0	0	5	0
C, 29, Craig MacDonald	1	7:50	0	0	0	-1	0	0	0	0	0	2	0
LW, 27, Mike Leclerc	3	10:29	0	0	0	0	2	0	0	0	0	2	0
RW, 16, Shean Donovan	7	11:23	0	0	0	-2	6	0	0	0	0	4	0
G, 34, Miikka Kiprusoff (goalie)	7	_	0	0	0	0	2	0	0	0	0	0	_
C, 15, Byron Ritchie	7	9:14	0	0	0	-2	0	0	0	0	0	7	0
D, 44, Rhett Warrener	7	19:56	0	0	0	4	14	0	0	0	0	5	0

GOALTENDING

	GP	Mins.	GAA	W	L	EN	SO	GA	SA	SV%	PIM
Miikka Kiprusoff	7	428	2.24	3	4	1	0	16	202	0.921	2

CAROLINA HURRICANES

(Won Stanley Cup finals against Edmonton, 4-3)

SCORING

Pos., No., Name	GP	ATOI	G	A	Pts	+/-	PIM	PPG	SHG	GWG	OTG	Shots	S%
C, 12, Eric Staal	25	19:47	9	19	28	0	8	7	0	1	1	87	10.3
LW, 61, Cory Stillman	25	18:41	9	17	26	12	14	4	0	3	2	75	12
C, 17, Rod Brind'Amour	25	23:51	12	6	18	9	16	6	0	4	0	75	16
RW, 11, Justin Williams	25	21:36	7	11	18	12	34	0	1	1	0	71	9.9
C, 8, Matt Cullen	25	15:37	4	14	18	2	12	2	0	1	0	56	7.1
RW, 18, Mark Recchi	25	16:33	7	9	16	-5	18	2	0	2	0	45	15.6
C, 39, Doug Weight	23	15:26	3	13	16	-3	20	2	0	0	0	35	8.6
LW, 13, Ray Whitney	24	14:07	9	6	15	-1	14	5	0	1	0	40	22.5
D, 5, Frantisek Kaberle	25	18:24	4	9	13	-7	8	3	0	1	0	35	11.4
D, 6, Bret Hedican	25	22:40	2	9	11	6	42	0	0	0	0	23	8.7
LW, 16, Andrew Ladd*	17	9:27	2	3	5	0	4	0	0	1	0	13	15.4
D, 4, Aaron Ward	25	21:41	2	3	5	0	18	0	0	0	0	18	11.1
D, 7, Niclas Wallin	25	16:39	1	4	5	3	14	0	0	1	1	19	5.3
D, 22, Mike Commodore	25	19:27	2	2	4	1	33	0	1	0	0	27	7.4
D, 2, Glen Wesley	25	16:10	0	2	2	1	16	0	0	0	0	15	0
C, 59, Chad LaRose*	21	8:57	0	1	1	-2	10	0	0	0	0	15	0
G, 30, Cam Ward (goalie)	23	_	0	1	1	0	0	0	0	0	0	0	_
LW, 26, Erik Cole	2	15:29	0	0	0	-1	0	0	0	0	0	3	0
D, 70, Oleg Tverdovsky	5	5:16	0	0	0	-1	0	0	0	0	0	2	0
G, 29, Martin Gerber (goalie)	6	_	0	0	0	0	4	0	0	0	0	0	_
C, 63, Josef Vasicek	8	10:04	0	0	0	-2	2	0	0	0	0	13	0
C, 14, Kevyn Adams	25	11:43	0	0	0	-4	14	0	0	0	0	36	0
RW, 27, Craig Adams	25	8:15	0	0	0	-4	10	0	0	0	0	18	0

GOALTENDING

	GP	Mins.	GAA	W	L	EN	SO	GA	SA	SV%	PIM
Cam Ward*	23	1320	2.14	15	8	0	2	47	584	0.92	0
Martin Gerber	6	221	3.53	1	1	0	1	13	90	0.856	4

*rookie

COLORADO AVALANCHE

(Lost Western Conference semifinals to Anaheim, 4-0)

SCORING

Pos., No., Name	GP	ATOI	G	A	Pts	+/-	PIM	PPG	SHG	GWG	OTG	Shots	S%
C, 19, Joe Sakic	9	21:38	4	5	9	-1	6	1	0	1	1	21	19
LW, 15, Andrew Brunette	9	17:46	3	6	9	-2	8	1	0	1	1	15	20
RW, 23, Milan Hejduk	9	20:55	2	6	8	3	2	0	0	0	0	24	8.3

Pos., No., Name	GP	ATOI	G	A	Pts	+/-	PIM	PPG	SHG	GWG	OTG	Shots	S%
LW, 18, Alex Tanguay	9	18:20	2	4	6	1	12	0	0	1	1	20	10
C, 38, Jim Dowd	9	14:10	2	3	5	3	20	0	1	0	0	6	33.3
D, 4, Rob Blake	9	28:19	3	1	4	1	8	2	0	1	0	42	7.1
D, 5, Brett Clark	9	24:16	2	2	4	-2	2	0	1	0	0	19	10.5
LW, 8, Wojtek Wolski*	8	12:05	1	3	4	-3	2	0	0	0	0	9	11.1
D, 26, John-Michael Liles	9	17:35	1	2	3	-1	6	1	0	0	0	15	6.7
RW, 13, Dan Hinote	9	13:27	1	1	2	-2	31	0	0	0	0	10	10
C, 87, Pierre Turgeon	5	11:40	0	2	2	-3	6	0	0	0	0	9	0
LW, 24, Antti Laaksonen	9	15:22	0	2	2	-3	2	0	0	0	0	16	0
C, 12, Brad Richardson*	9	11:41	1	0	1	-3	6	0	0	0	0	7	14.3
C, 53, Brett McLean	8	10:39	0	1	1	-5	4	0	0	0	0	8	0
D, 71, Patrice Brisebois	9	22:18	0	1	1	-7	4	0	0	0	0	10	0
RW, 14, Ian Laperriere	9	13:39	0	1	1	-6	27	0	0	0	0	9	0
D, 3, Karlis Skrastins	9	23:24	0	1	1	-3	10	0	0	0	0	9	0
D, 27, Ossi Vaananen	1	13:58	0	0	0	0	0	0	0	0	0	1	0
LW, 22, Steve Konowalchuk	2	14:09	0	0	0	-1	4	0	0	0	0	1	0
LW, 10, Brad May	3	9:21	0	0	0	-3	0	0	0	0	0	5	0
D, 34, Kurt Sauer	9	8:39	0	0	0	-3	4	0	0	0	0	1	0
G, 60, Jose Theodore (goalie)	9	_	0	0	0	0	0	0	0	0	0	0	_

GOALTENDING

	GP	Mins.	GAA	W	L	EN	SO	GA	SA	SV%	PIM
Jose Theodore	9	573	3.04	4	5	2	0	29	296	0.902	0

DALLAS STARS

(Lost Western Conference quarterfinals to Colorado, 4-1)

SCORING

Pos., No., Name	GP	ATOI	G	A	Pts	+/-	PIM	PPG	SHG	GWG	OTG	Shots	S%
LW, 10, Brenden Morrow	5	21:57	1	5	6	-1	6	0	0	0	0	10	10
D, 56, Sergei Zubov	5	29:41	1	5	6	-1	6	1	0	0	0	11	9.1
RW, 13, Bill Guerin	5	16:13	3	1	4	-2	0	1	0	0	0	18	16.7
RW, 26, Jere Lehtinen	5	22:09	3	1	4	-1	0	1	0	0	0	17	17.6
C, 9, Mike Modano	5	22:14	1	3	4	0	4	1	0	0	0	12	8.3
LW, 15, Niklas Hagman	5	10:50	2	1	3	-1	4	0	0	1	0	9	22.2
LW, 36, Jussi Jokinen*	5	13:39	2	1	3	1	0	1	0	0	0	12	16.7
C, 44, Jason Arnott	5	20:03	0	3	3	-1	4	0	0	0	0	17	0
C, 14, Stu Barnes	5	17:33	1	1	2	0	0	0	1	0	0	4	25
D, 3, Stephane Robidas	5	16:42	0	2	2	-1	4	0	0	0	0	3	0
D, 42, Jon Klemm	5	15:44	1	0	1	-1	0	0	0	0	0	5	20
D, 4, Janne Niinimaa	4	14:06	0	1	1	0	8	0	0	0	0	5	0
D, 43, Philippe Boucher	5	21:34	0	1	1	0	2	0	0	0	0	9	0
C, 38, Niko Kapanen	5	14:51	0	1	1	-2	10	0	0	0	0	5	0
RW, 20, Antti Miettinen*	5	12:10	0	1	1	-1	8	0	0	0	0	8	0
C, 29, Steve Ott	5	7:40	0	1	1	0	2	0	0	0	0	2	0
LW, 25, Jeremy Stevenson	1	3:46	0	0	0	0	0	0	0	0	0	1	0
LW, 11, Jaroslav Svoboda	2	6:35	0	0	0	-1	2	0	0	0	0	1	0
D, 6, Trevor Daley	3	11:30	0	0	0	-3	0	0	0	0	0	1	0
D, 2, Willie Mitchell	5	23:21	0	0	0	0	2	0	0	0	0	6	0
G, 35, Marty Turco (goalie)	5	_	0	0	0	0	2	0	0	0	0	0	_

GOALTENDING

	GP	Mins.	GAA	W	L	EN	SO	GA	SA	SV%	PIM
Marty Turco	5	319	3.39	1	4	0	0	18	136	0.868	2

*rookie

DETROIT RED WINGS

(Lost Western Conference quarterfinals to Edmonton, 4-2)

SCORING

Pos., No., Name	GP	ATOI	G	A	Pts	+/-	PIM	PPG	SHG	GWG	OTG	Shots	S%
D, 23, Mathieu Schneider	6	26:43	1	7	8	-1	6	0	0	0	0	17	5.9
LW, 40, Henrik Zetterberg	6	21:42	6	0	6	-2	2	4	0	0	0	23	26.1
C, 20, Robert Lang	6	19:11	3	3	6	-2	2	2	0	0	0	18	16.7
C, 19, Steve Yzerman	4	16:38	0	4	4	-2	4	0	0	0	0	10	0
LW, 18, Kirk Maltby	6	13:01	2	1	3	2	4	0	0	1	1	12	16.7
C, 39, Johan Franzen*	6	11:59	1	2	3	0	4	0	0	0	0	11	9.1
LW, 96, Tomas Holmstrom	6	17:04	1	2	3	-1	12	1	0	0	0	10	10
C, 13, Pavel Datsyuk	5	20:05	0	3	3	0	0	0	0	0	0	11	0
D, 55, Niklas Kronwall*	6	22:43	0	3	3	0	2	0	0	0	0	7	0
D, 5, Nicklas Lidstrom	6	31:54	1	1	2	-4	2	1	0	1	0	21	4.8

Pos., No., Name	GP	ATOI	G	A	Pts	+/-	PIM	PPG	SHG	GWG	OTG	Shots	S%
LW, 14, Brendan Shanahan	6	18:53	1	1	2	0	6	0	0	0	0	21	4.8
C, 29, Jason Williams	6	18:09	1	1	2	-3	6	0	0	0	0	16	6.3
RW, 11, Daniel Cleary	6	10:44	0	1	1	2	6	0	0	0	0	14	0
D, 3, Andreas Lilja	6	19:21	0	1	1	-4	6	0	0	0	0	3	0
RW, 37, Mikael Samuelsson	6	15:32	0	1	1	-1	6	0	0	0	0	16	0
RW, 44, Mark Mowers	3	9:27	0	0	0	0	0	0	0	0	0	4	0
D, 24, Chris Chelios	6	19:25	0	0	0	2	6	0	0	0	0	3	0
C, 33, Kris Draper	6	19:57	0	0	0	3	6	0	0	0	0	14	0
D, 22, Brett Lebda*	6	13:08	0	0	0	3	4	0	0	0	0	7	0
G, 34, Manny Legace (goalie)	6	_	0	0	0	0	0	0	0	0	0	0	_

GOALTENDING

	GP	Mins.	GAA	W	L	EN	SO	GA	SA	SV%	PIM
Manny Legace	6	408	2.65	2	4	1	0	18	155	0.884	0

EDMONTON OILERS

(Lost Stanley Cup finals to Carolina, 4-3)

SCORING

Pos., No., Name	GP	ATOI	G	A	Pts	+/-	PIM	PPG	SHG	GWG	OTG	Shots	S%
D, 44, Chris Pronger	24	30:57	5	16	21	10	26	3	0	0	0	61	8.2
C, 10, Shawn Horcoff	24	21:37	7	12	19	4	12	1	1	2	1	41	17.1
RW, 34, Fernando Pisani	24	17:11	14	4	18	4	10	3	1	5	1	49	28.6
RW, 83, Ales Hemsky	24	16:05	6	11	17	-3	14	4	0	2	0	47	12.8
LW, 94, Ryan Smyth	24	21:27	7	9	16	-2	22	4	0	1	0	60	11.7
LW, 12, Sergei Samsonov	24	14:30	4	11	15	2	14	1	0	0	0	40	10
D, 6, Jaroslav Spacek	24	25:52	3	11	14	-3	24	2	0	0	0	43	7
C, 37, Michael Peca	24	19:05	6	5	11	5	20	0	1	1	0	43	14
LW, 14, Raffi Torres	22	13:14	4	7	11	2	16	1	0	1	0	42	9.5
C, 16, Jarret Stoll	24	17:05	4	6	10	-4	24	2	0	1	1	49	8.2
D, 24, Steve Staios	24	21:31	1	5	6	0	28	1	0	0	0	28	3.6
D, 21, Jason Smith	24	22:28	1	4	5	5	16	0	0	1	0	14	7.1
C, 22, Rem Murray	24	8:37	0	4	4	0	2	0	0	0	0	14	0
D, 47, Marc-Andre Bergeron	18	14:55	2	1	3	0	14	2	0	0	0	17	11.8
LW, 18, Ethan Moreau	21	14:35	2	1	3	0	19	0	0	0	0	40	5
C, 26, Brad Winchester*	10	9:13	1	2	3	-2	4	0	0	1	0	9	11.1
LW, 13, Todd Harvey	10	7:56	1	1	2	0	4	0	0	0	0	6	16.7
RW, 27, Georges Laraque	15	5:31	1	1	2	2	44	0	0	0	0	6	16.7
D, 23, Dick Tarnstrom	12	13:59	0	2	2	1	10	0	0	0	0	7	0
RW, 20, Radek Dvorak	16	13:28	0	2	2	-1	4	0	0	0	0	32	0
G, 35, Dwayne Roloson (goalie)	18	_	0	2	2	0	14	0	0	0	0	0	_
C, 45, Toby Petersen	2	6:22	1	0	1	1	0	0	0	0	0	3	33.3
D, 2, Matt Greene*	18	10:03	0	1	1	1	34	0	0	0	0	4	0
G, 29, Ty Conklin (goalie)	1	_	0	0	0	0	0	0	0	0	0	0	_
G, 30, Jussi Markkanen (goalie)	6	_	0	0	0	0	0	0	0	0	0	0	_

GOALTENDING

	GP	Mins.	GAA	W	L	EN	SO	GA	SA	SV%	PIM
Jussi Markkanen	6	360	2.17	3	3	1	1	13	137	0.905	0
Dwayne Roloson	18	1160	2.33	12	5	1	1	45	618	0.927	14
Ty Conklin	1	6	10	0	1	0	0	1	3	0.667	0

*rookie

MONTREAL CANADIENS

(Lost Eastern Conference quarterfinals to Carolina, 4-2)

SCORING

Pos., No., Name	GP	ATOI	G	A	Pts	+/-	PIM	PPG	SHG	GWG	OTG	Shots	S%
RW, 27, Alexei Kovalev	6	19:20	4	3	7	3	4	1	0	0	0	15	26.7
D, 44, Sheldon Souray	6	18:46	3	2	5	-1	8	2	0	0	0	16	18.8
RW, 73, Michael Ryder	6	16:09	2	3	5	-4	0	1	0	1	1	13	15.4
C, 21, Christopher Higgins*	6	17:03	1	3	4	-3	0	0	0	0	0	7	14.3
C, 35, Tomas Plekanec*	6	18:00	0	4	4	2	6	0	0	0	0	11	0
D, 51, Francis Bouillon	6	22:24	1	2	3	0	10	1	0	0	0	15	6.7
RW, 37, Niklas Sundstrom	5	9:28	0	3	3	3	4	0	0	0	0	4	0
D, 25, Mathieu Dandenault	6	19:47	0	3	3	1	4	0	0	0	0	8	0
C, 14, Radek Bonk	6	15:36	2	0	2	-1	2	0	0	1	0	7	28.6
LW, 20, Richard Zednik	6	15:12	2	0	2	0	4	1	0	0	0	10	20
C, 38, Jan Bulis	6	16:41	1	1	2	1	2	0	0	0	0	7	14.3
RW, 42, Alexander Perezhogin*	6	13:41	1	1	2	2	4	0	0	0	0	8	12.5
C, 11, Saku Koivu	3	14:24	0	2	2	1	2	0	0	0	0	1	0

Pos., No., Name	GP	ATOI	G	A	Pts	+/-	PIM	PPG	SHG	GWG	OTG	Shots	S%
C, 71, Mike Ribeiro	6	18:21	0	2	2	1	0	0	0	0	0	12	0
D, 52, Craig Rivet	6	24:09	0	2	2	0	2	0	0	0	0	9	0
D, 79, Andrei Markov	6	25:29	0	1	1	2	4	0	0	0	0	6	0
RW, 47, Aaron Downey	1	6:17	0	0	0	0	0	0	0	0	0	0	–
D, 32, Mark Streit	1	3:29	0	0	0	0	0	0	0	0	0	0	–
C, 22, Steve Begin	2	13:41	0	0	0	-1	2	0	0	0	0	6	0
G, 39, Cristobal Huet (goalie)	6	–	0	0	0	0	0	0	0	0	0	0	–
D, 8, Mike Komisarek	6	18:34	0	0	0	2	10	0	0	0	0	8	0
LW, 57, Garth Murray	6	12:38	0	0	0	2	0	0	0	0	0	4	0

GOALTENDING

	GP	Mins.	GAA	W	L	EN	SO	GA	SA	SV%	PIM
Cristobal Huet	6	386	2.33	2	4	0	0	15	212	0.929	0

NASHVILLE PREDATORS

(Lost Western Conference quarterfinals to San Jose, 4-1)

SCORING

Pos., No., Name	GP	ATOI	G	A	Pts	+/-	PIM	PPG	SHG	GWG	OTG	Shots	S%
LW, 9, Paul Kariya	5	20:46	2	5	7	0	0	2	0	0	0	12	16.7
D, 44, Kimmo Timonen	5	24:42	1	3	4	0	4	0	1	0	0	17	5.9
RW, 81, Mike Sillinger	5	17:09	2	1	3	-1	12	1	0	0	0	7	28.6
D, 6, Shea Weber*	4	14:12	2	0	2	-3	8	1	0	0	0	4	50
LW, 10, Martin Erat	5	19:30	1	1	2	-1	6	1	0	0	0	8	12.5
D, 2, Dan Hamhuis	5	19:41	0	2	2	-2	2	0	0	0	0	9	0
RW, 26, Steve Sullivan	5	17:02	0	2	2	-2	0	0	0	0	0	12	0
RW, 18, Adam Hall	5	12:09	1	0	1	-3	0	1	0	1	0	7	14.3
LW, 17, Scott Hartnell	5	12:12	1	0	1	0	4	0	0	0	0	9	11.1
C, 38, Vernon Fiddler	2	8:48	0	1	1	-1	0	0	0	0	0	1	0
D, 3, Marek Zidlicky	2	15:18	0	1	1	0	2	0	0	0	0	7	0
C, 22, Greg Johnson	5	14:42	0	1	1	0	2	0	0	0	0	3	0
C, 11, David Legwand	5	17:21	0	1	1	-1	8	0	0	0	0	11	0
C, 94, Yanic Perreault	1	10:09	0	0	0	0	2	0	0	0	0	2	0
RW, 7, Scottie Upshall	2	11:56	0	0	0	0	0	0	0	0	0	4	0
C, 12, Scott Nichol	3	7:44	0	0	0	-2	2	0	0	0	0	2	0
C, 25, Jerred Smithson	3	9:26	0	0	0	0	4	0	0	0	0	0	–
RW, 14, Jordin Tootoo	3	4:04	0	0	0	-1	0	0	0	0	0	3	0
D, 4, Mark Eaton	5	17:48	0	0	0	0	8	0	0	0	0	3	0
D, 55, Danny Markov	5	19:21	0	0	0	-1	6	0	0	0	0	6	0
G, 30, Chris Mason (goalie)	5	–	0	0	0	0	0	0	0	0	0	0	–
RW, 24, Scott Walker	5	16:00	0	0	0	0	6	0	0	0	0	5	0
D, 19, Brendan Witt	5	17:07	0	0	0	-3	12	0	0	0	0	5	0

GOALTENDING

	GP	Mins.	GAA	W	L	EN	SO	GA	SA	SV%	PIM
Chris Mason	5	296	3.45	1	4	0	0	17	171	0.901	0

*rookie

NEW JERSEY DEVILS

(Lost Eastern Conference semifinals to Carolina, 4-1)

SCORING

Pos., No., Name	GP	ATOI	G	A	Pts	+/-	PIM	PPG	SHG	GWG	OTG	Shots	S%
C, 26, Patrik Elias	9	18:42	6	10	16	5	4	4	0	0	0	32	18.8
RW, 15, Jamie Langenbrunner	9	19:46	3	10	13	5	16	1	0	1	0	17	17.6
C, 23, Scott Gomez	9	18:14	5	4	9	-1	6	4	0	1	0	39	12.8
D, 28, Brian Rafalski	9	27:26	1	8	9	3	2	1	0	0	0	9	11.1
RW, 14, Brian Gionta	9	20:05	3	4	7	-1	2	1	1	2	0	29	10.3
C, 11, John Madden	9	18:56	4	1	5	2	8	0	2	0	0	27	14.8
LW, 20, Jay Pandolfo	9	18:36	1	4	5	1	0	0	1	1	0	4	25
C, 9, Zach Parise*	9	15:03	1	2	3	0	2	0	0	0	0	21	4.8
D, 7, Paul Martin	9	24:16	0	3	3	6	4	0	0	0	0	6	0
LW, 18, Sergei Brylin	9	16:33	2	0	2	5	2	0	0	0	0	14	14.3
D, 2, David Hale	8	12:06	0	2	2	-1	12	0	0	0	0	3	0
D, 8, Ken Klee	6	12:04	1	0	1	-1	6	0	0	0	0	2	50
RW, 29, Grant Marshall	7	14:06	0	1	1	0	8	0	0	0	0	4	0
G, 40, Scott Clemmensen (goalie)	1	–	0	0	0	0	0	0	0	0	0	0	–
D, 6, Tommy Albelin	2	10:37	0	0	0	0	2	0	0	0	0	0	–
RW, 22, Viktor Kozlov	3	14:04	0	0	0	-1	0	0	0	0	0	4	0
D, 5, Colin White	4	17:39	0	0	0	0	4	0	0	0	0	1	0
D, 24, Richard Matvichuk	7	16:41	0	0	0	5	4	0	0	0	0	1	0

Pos., No., Name	GP	ATOI	G	A	Pts	+/-	PIM	PPG	SHG	GWG	OTG	Shots	S%
C, 16, Jason Wiemer	8	5:32	0	0	0	0	16	0	0	0	0	2	0
G, 30, Martin Brodeur (goalie)	9	_	0	0	0	0	2	0	0	0	0	1	0
RW, 25, Cam Janssen*	9	3:43	0	0	0	0	26	0	0	0	0	3	0
D, 21, Brad Lukowich	9	21:27	0	0	0	0	4	0	0	0	0	6	0
C, 10, Erik Rasmussen	9	6:44	0	0	0	-1	8	0	0	0	0	4	0

GOALTENDING

	GP	Mins.	GAA	W	L	EN	SO	GA	SA	SV%	PIM
Scott Clemmensen	1	7	0	0	0	0	0	0	3	1	0
Martin Brodeur	9	533	2.25	5	4	1	1	20	261	0.923	2

NEW YORK RANGERS

(Lost Eastern Conference quarterfinals to New Jersey, 4-0)

SCORING

Pos., No., Name	GP	ATOI	G	A	Pts	+/-	PIM	PPG	SHG	GWG	OTG	Shots	S%
C, 19, Blair Betts	4	16:12	1	1	2	-1	2	0	0	0	0	4	25
RW, 41, Jed Ortmeyer	4	11:40	1	0	1	1	4	0	0	0	0	4	25
RW, 25, Petr Prucha*	4	14:12	1	0	1	-3	0	1	0	0	0	6	16.7
C, 20, Steve Rucchin	4	13:50	1	0	1	-2	0	1	0	0	0	9	11.1
LW, 26, Martin Rucinsky	2	13:29	0	1	1	-1	2	0	0	0	0	5	0
RW, 68, Jaromir Jagr	3	13:46	0	1	1	0	2	0	0	0	0	10	0
C, 44, Ryan Hollweg*	4	10:25	0	1	1	-1	19	0	0	0	0	2	0
D, 8, Marek Malik	4	20:43	0	1	1	-2	6	0	0	0	0	3	0
C, 92, Michael Nylander	4	20:32	0	1	1	-3	0	0	0	0	0	10	0
D, 3, Michal Rozsival	4	24:30	0	1	1	-2	8	0	0	0	0	5	0
D, 51, Fedor Tyutin*	4	17:49	0	1	1	-1	0	0	0	0	0	7	0
RW, 28, Colton Orr*	1	4:17	0	0	0	0	2	0	0	0	0	0	_
RW, 14, Jason Ward	1	2:39	0	0	0	0	2	0	0	0	0	1	0
G, 80, Kevin Weekes (goalie)	1	_	0	0	0	0	2	0	0	0	0	0	_
LW, 21, Chad Wiseman*	1	6:00	0	0	0	0	2	0	0	0	0	0	_
D, 6, Darius Kasparaitis	2	16:22	0	0	0	-1	0	0	0	0	0	1	0
G, 30, Henrik Lundqvist (goalie)	3	_	0	0	0	0	0	0	0	0	0	0	_
D, 24, Sandis Ozolinsh	3	21:27	0	0	0	-3	6	0	0	0	0	9	0
D, 34, Jason Strudwick	3	13:35	0	0	0	-1	0	0	0	0	0	2	0
LW, 81, Marcel Hossa	4	13:17	0	0	0	-1	6	0	0	0	0	6	0
C, 18, Dominic Moore*	4	11:21	0	0	0	-1	2	0	0	0	0	8	0
D, 16, Tom Poti	4	19:38	0	0	0	-4	2	0	0	0	0	7	0
LW, 82, Martin Straka	4	20:29	0	0	0	-4	2	0	0	0	0	6	0
RW, 17, Petr Sykora	4	17:44	0	0	0	-5	0	0	0	0	0	9	0

GOALTENDING

	GP	Mins.	GAA	W	L	EN	SO	GA	SA	SV%	PIM
Kevin Weekes	1	60	4	0	1	0	0	4	25	0.84	2
Henrik Lundqvist*	3	177	4.41	0	3	0	0	13	79	0.835	0

*rookie

OTTAWA SENATORS

(Lost Eastern Conference semifinals to Buffalo, 4-1)

SCORING

Pos., No., Name	GP	ATOI	G	A	Pts	+/-	PIM	PPG	SHG	GWG	OTG	Shots	S%
C, 19, Jason Spezza	10	17:59	5	9	14	-1	2	3	0	1	0	23	21.7
LW, 9, Martin Havlat	10	17:13	7	6	13	0	4	3	0	1	0	27	25.9
LW, 15, Dany Heatley	10	18:56	3	9	12	1	11	3	0	1	0	32	9.4
D, 6, Wade Redden	9	25:06	2	8	10	-2	10	2	0	1	0	19	10.5
RW, 11, Daniel Alfredsson	10	21:09	2	8	10	2	4	1	0	0	0	24	8.3
LW, 27, Peter Schaefer	10	16:38	2	5	7	2	14	0	0	0	0	18	11.1
C, 21, Bryan Smolinski	10	12:34	3	3	6	3	2	1	0	0	0	23	13
C, 12, Mike Fisher	10	18:50	2	2	4	1	12	0	1	0	0	20	10
D, 3, Zdeno Chara	10	27:32	1	3	4	0	23	1	0	0	0	17	5.9
D, 24, Anton Volchenkov	9	13:53	0	4	4	1	8	0	0	0	0	10	0
D, 2, Brian Pothier	8	15:02	2	1	3	1	2	0	0	0	0	10	20
D, 4, Chris Phillips	9	21:40	2	0	2	-2	6	0	0	0	0	8	25
C, 20, Antoine Vermette	10	15:00	2	0	2	-1	4	0	0	1	0	17	11.8
RW, 26, Vaclav Varada	8	6:04	0	2	2	-2	12	0	0	0	0	7	0
RW, 44, Patrick Eaves*	10	11:40	1	0	1	-3	10	0	0	0	0	20	5
D, 14, Andrej Meszaros*	10	17:49	1	0	1	0	18	0	0	0	0	17	5.9
RW, 25, Chris Neil	10	6:57	1	0	1	-1	14	0	0	0	0	10	10
D, 5, Christoph Schubert*	7	7:52	0	1	1	3	4	0	0	0	0	9	0
G, 1, Ray Emery (goalie)	10	_	0	1	1	0	0	0	0	0	0	0	_
C, 22, Chris Kelly*	10	11:49	0	0	0	-4	2	0	0	0	0	14	0

		GOALTENDING									
	GP	Mins.	GAA	W	L	EN	SO	GA	SA	SV%	PIM
Ray Emery*	10	604	2.88	5	5	0	0	29	289	0.9	0

PHILADELPHIA FLYERS

(Lost Eastern Conference quarterfinals to Buffalo, 4-2)

SCORING

Pos., No., Name	GP	ATOI	G	A	Pts	+/-	PIM	PPG	SHG	GWG	OTG	Shots	S%
C, 21, Peter Forsberg	6	18:54	4	4	8	2	6	1	0	2	0	12	33.3
LW, 12, Simon Gagne	6	21:44	3	1	4	2	2	1	0	0	0	26	11.5
D, 37, Eric Desjardins	6	24:59	1	3	4	-3	6	0	0	0	0	10	10
RW, 22, Mike Knuble	6	19:17	1	3	4	1	8	0	0	0	0	17	5.9
C, 93, Petr Nedved	6	17:28	2	0	2	-4	8	1	0	0	0	7	28.6
C, 26, Michal Handzus	6	15:56	0	2	2	-2	2	0	0	0	0	4	0
D, 2, Derian Hatcher	6	21:35	0	2	2	-4	10	0	0	0	0	5	0
D, 44, Joni Pitkanen	6	24:12	0	2	2	0	2	0	0	0	0	10	0
RW, 19, Branko Radivojevic	5	10:34	1	0	1	-1	0	0	0	0	0	6	16.7
C, 20, R.J. Umberger*	5	11:15	1	0	1	-3	2	0	0	0	0	6	16.7
LW, 49, Brian Savage	6	14:13	1	0	1	-4	4	0	1	0	0	7	14.3
D, 23, Denis Gauthier	6	18:20	0	1	1	-5	19	0	0	0	0	3	0
D, 34, Freddy Meyer*	6	18:23	0	1	1	-5	8	0	0	0	0	5	0
C, 18, Mike Richards*	6	15:40	0	1	1	-5	0	0	0	0	0	9	0
LW, 87, Donald Brashear	1	4:20	0	0	0	0	0	0	0	0	0	1	0
LW, 55, Ben Eager*	2	7:05	0	0	0	-4	26	0	0	0	0	3	0
G, 30, Antero Niittymaki (goalie)	2	_	0	0	0	0	0	0	0	0	0	0	_
RW, 15, Niko Dimitrakos	5	10:07	0	0	0	-2	2	0	0	0	0	4	0
C, 17, Jeff Carter*	6	13:03	0	0	0	-4	10	0	0	0	0	10	0
G, 42, Robert Esche (goalie)	6	_	0	0	0	0	2	0	0	0	0	0	_
RW, 24, Sami Kapanen	6	20:18	0	0	0	-4	2	0	0	0	0	12	0
D, 3, Mike Rathje	6	16:26	0	0	0	-1	6	0	0	0	0	3	0

GOALTENDING

	GP	Mins.	GAA	W	L	EN	SO	GA	SA	SV%	PIM
Antero Niittymaki*	2	73	4.11	0	0	0	0	5	29	0.828	0
Robert Esche	6	314	4.2	2	4	0	0	22	176	0.875	2

*rookie

SAN JOSE SHARKS

(Lost Western Conference semifinals to Edmonton, 4-2)

SCORING

Pos., No., Name	GP	ATOI	G	A	Pts	+/-	PIM	PPG	SHG	GWG	OTG	Shots	S%
C, 12, Patrick Marleau	11	21:06	9	5	14	2	8	4	0	2	0	38	23.7
RW, 14, Jonathan Cheechoo	11	24:00	4	5	9	-1	8	1	0	1	0	46	8.7
C, 19, Joe Thornton	11	25:08	2	7	9	-4	12	1	0	1	0	23	8.7
D, 44, Christian Ehrhoff	11	19:47	2	6	8	2	18	1	0	1	0	27	7.4
D, 42, Tom Preissing	11	23:49	1	6	7	0	4	0	0	0	0	18	5.6
RW, 26, Steve Bernier*	11	15:16	1	5	6	4	8	1	0	1	0	14	7.1
RW, 9, Milan Michalek*	9	15:11	1	4	5	4	8	1	0	0	0	23	4.3
LW, 28, Nils Ekman	11	15:13	2	2	4	-2	8	1	0	0	0	24	8.3
C, 16, Mark Smith	11	13:20	3	0	3	2	6	1	0	0	0	23	13
C, 34, Pat Rissmiller	11	8:06	2	1	3	1	6	0	0	0	0	11	18.2
D, 25, Matt Carle*	11	15:17	0	3	3	1	4	0	0	0	0	13	0
C, 11, Marcel Goc*	11	12:37	0	3	3	0	0	0	0	0	0	9	0
D, 4, Kyle McLaren	11	20:41	0	3	3	2	4	0	0	0	0	7	0
LW, 17, Scott Thornton	11	11:18	2	0	2	-1	6	0	0	0	0	23	8.7
LW, 15, Ville Nieminen	11	15:39	0	2	2	-1	24	0	0	0	0	18	0
C, 10, Alyn McCauley	6	11:17	0	1	1	0	4	0	0	0	0	4	0
D, 6, Josh Gorges*	11	18:55	0	1	1	-1	4	0	0	0	0	6	0
D, 22, Scott Hannan	11	25:15	0	1	1	0	6	0	0	0	0	12	0
RW, 29, Ryane Clowe*	1	5:06	0	0	0	-1	0	0	0	0	0	0	_
D, 5, Rob Davison	1	8:00	0	0	0	0	0	0	0	0	0	1	0
G, 20, Evgeni Nabokov (goalie)	1	_	0	0	0	0	0	0	0	0	0	0	_
C, 37, Grant Stevenson*	5	6:58	0	0	0	-1	4	0	0	0	0	6	0
G, 35, Vesa Toskala (goalie)	11	_	0	0	0	0	0	0	0	0	0	0	_

GOALTENDING

	GP	Mins.	GAA	W	L	EN	SO	GA	SA	SV%	PIM
Vesa Toskala	11	686	2.45	6	5	0	1	28	311	0.91	0
Evgeni Nabokov	1	12	5	0	0	0	0	1	4	0.75	0

TAMPA BAY LIGHTNING

(Lost Eastern Conference quarterfinals to Ottawa, 4-1)

SCORING

Pos., No., Name	GP	ATOI	G	A	Pts	+/-	PIM	PPG	SHG	GWG	OTG	Shots	S%
C, 19, Brad Richards	5	24:11	3	5	8	-5	6	0	0	0	0	24	12.5
D, 54, Paul Ranger*	5	21:43	2	4	6	0	0	1	0	0	0	13	15.4
RW, 26, Martin St. Louis	5	22:53	4	0	4	-2	2	1	0	1	0	15	26.7
D, 22, Dan Boyle	5	25:53	1	3	4	-1	6	0	0	0	0	6	16.7
C, 4, Vincent Lecavalier	5	22:17	1	3	4	0	7	1	0	0	0	17	5.9
D, 13, Pavel Kubina	5	20:09	1	1	2	-6	26	1	0	0	0	9	11.1
C, 20, Vaclav Prospal	5	15:56	0	2	2	1	0	0	0	0	0	10	0
RW, 76, Evgeny Artyukhin*	5	8:14	1	0	1	1	6	0	0	0	0	10	10
LW, 29, Dmitry Afanasenkov	5	15:46	0	1	1	-1	2	0	0	0	0	12	0
D, 21, Cory Sarich	5	15:45	0	1	1	-1	4	0	0	0	0	5	0
D, 5, Darryl Sydor	5	17:54	0	1	1	-3	0	0	0	0	0	5	0
RW, 18, Rob DiMaio	2	2:12	0	0	0	-1	0	0	0	0	0	1	0
G, 1, Sean Burke (goalie)	3	_	0	0	0	0	0	0	0	0	0	0	_
LW, 11, Chris Dingman	3	2:23	0	0	0	0	19	0	0	0	0	1	0
G, 47, John Grahame (goalie)	4	_	0	0	0	0	0	0	0	0	0	0	_
C, 8, Martin Cibak	5	3:56	0	0	0	-1	0	0	0	0	0	2	0
C, 34, Ryan Craig*	5	12:58	0	0	0	-3	10	0	0	0	0	6	0
LW, 17, Ruslan Fedotenko	5	14:38	0	0	0	-1	20	0	0	0	0	11	0
LW, 33, Fredrik Modin	5	18:45	0	0	0	-6	6	0	0	0	0	11	0
D, 44, Nolan Pratt	5	15:29	0	0	0	0	7	0	0	0	0	6	0
C, 27, Tim Taylor	5	11:05	0	0	0	-2	2	0	0	0	0	7	0

GOALTENDING

	GP	Mins.	GAA	W	L	EN	SO	GA	SA	SV%	PIM
Sean Burke	3	109	3.85	0	1	0	0	7	57	0.877	0
John Grahame	4	188	4.79	1	3	1	0	15	98	0.847	0

*rookie

ENTRY DRAFT

JUNE 24, 2006, Vancouver

FIRST ROUND

No.—Selecting club	Player	Pos.	Previous team (league/country)
1—St. Louis	ERIK JOHNSON	D	U.S. National U-18
2—Pittsburgh	JORDAN STAAL	C	Peterborough (OHL)
3—Chicago	JONATHAN TOEWS	C/W	U. of North Dakota (WCHA)
4—Washington	NICKLAS BACKSTROM	C	Brynas (Sweden)
5—Boston	PHIL KESSEL	C	U. of Minnesota (WCHA)
6—Columbus	DERICK BRASSARD	C	Drummondville (QMJHL)
7—New York Islanders	KYLE OKPOSO	RW	Des Moines (USHL)
8—Phoenix	PETER MUELLER	C	Everett (WHL)
9—Minnesota	JAMES SHEPPARD	C	Cape Breton (QMJHL)
10—Florida	MICHAEL FROLIK	C/W	Kladno (Czech Rep.)
11—Los Angeles	JONATHAN BERNIER	G	Lewiston (QMJHL)
12—Atlanta	BRYAN LITTLE	C	Barrie (OHL)
13—Toronto	JIRI TLUSTY	C/W	Kladno (Czech Rep.)
14—Vancouver	MICHAEL GRABNER	RW	Spokane (WHL)
15—Tampa Bay	RIKU HELENIUS	G	Ilves (Finland)
16—San Jose (from Montreal)	TY WISHART	D	Prince George (WHL)
17—Los Angeles (from Edmonton)	TREVOR LEWIS	C	Des Moines (USHL)
18—Colorado	CHRIS STEWART	RW	Kingston (OHL)
19—Anaheim	MARK MITERA	D	U. of Michigan (CCHA)
20—Montreal (from San Jose.)	DAVID FISCHER	D	Apple Valley (USHSW)
21—New York Rangers	BOBBY SANGUINETTI	D	Owen Sound (OHL)
22—Philadelphia	CLAUDE GIROUX	RW	Gatineau (QMJHL)
23—Washington (from Nashville)	SEMEN VARLAMOV	G	Yaroslavl 2 (Russia)
24—Buffalo	DENNIS PERSSON	D	Vasteras (Sweden)
25—St. Louis (from New Jersey)	PATRIK BERGLUND	C	Vasteras (Sweden)
26—Calgary	LELAND IRVING	G	Everett (WHL)
27—Dallas	IVAN VISHNEVSKIY	D	Rouyn Noranda (QMJHL)
28—Ottawa	NICK FOLIGNO	LW	Sudbury (OHL)
29—Phoenix (from Detroit)	CHRIS SUMMERS	D	U.S. National U-18
30—New Jersey (from Carolina)	MATTHEW CORRENTE	D	Saginaw (OHL)

SECOND ROUND

No.—Selecting club	Player	Pos.	Previous team (league/country)
31—St. Louis	TOMAS KANA	C	Vitkovice (Czech Rep.)
32—Pittsburgh	CARL SNEEP	D	Brainerd (USHSW)
33—Chicago	IGOR MAKAROV	RW	Krylja (Russia)
34—Washington	MICHAL NEUVIRTH	G	Sparta Jr. (Czech Rep. Jr.)
35—Washington (from Boston)	FRANCOIS BOUCHARD	RW	Baie Comeau (QMJHL)
36—San Jose (from Columbus)	JAMIE MCGINN	LW	Ottawa (OHL)
37—Boston	YURI ALEXANDROV	D	Cherepovec (Russia)
38—Anaheim (from New York Islanders)	BRYCE SWAN	RW	Halifax (QMJHL)
39—Philadelphia (from Phoenix)	ANDREAS NODL	RW	Sioux Falls (USHL)
40—Minnesota	ONDREJ FIALA	C	Everett (WHL)
41—Detroit (from Florida)	CORY EMMERTON	C/LW	Kingston (OHL)
42—Philadelphia (from LA)	MICHAEL RATCHUK	D	U.S. National U-18
43—Atlanta	RILEY HOLZAPFEL	C	Moose Jaw (WHL)
44—Toronto	NIKOLAI KULEMIN	W	Magnitogorsk (Russia)
45—Edmonton	JEFF PETRY	D	Des Moines (USHL)
46—Buffalo (from Vancouver)	JHONAS ENROTH	G	Sodertalje (Sweden)
47—Detroit from Tampa Bay	SHAWN MATTHIAS	C	Belleville (OHL)
48—Los Angeles	JOE RYAN	D	Quebec (QMJHL)
49—Montreal	BEN MAXWELL	C	Kootenay (WHL)
50—Boston (from Edmonton)	MILAN LUCIC	LW	Vancouver (WHL)
51—Colorado	NIGEL WILLIAMS	D	U.S. National U-18
52—Washington (from Anaheim)	KEITH SEABROOK	D	Burnaby (BCHL)
53—Montreal (from San Jose)	MATHIEU CARLE	D	Acadie-Bathurst (QMJHL)
54—New York Rangers	ARTEM ANISIMOV	C	Yaroslavl (Russia)
55—Philadelphia	DENIS BODROV	D	Togliatti (Russia)
56—Nashville	BLAKE GEOFFRION	LW	U.S. National U-18
57—Buffalo	MIKE WEBER	D	Windsor (OHL)
58—New Jersey	ALEXANDER VASYUNOV	LW	Yaroslavl 2 (Russia)
59—Colorado (from Calgary)	CODEY BURKI	C	Brandon (WHL)
60—New York Islanders (from Dallas)	JESSE JOENSUU	W	Assat (Finland)

No.—Selecting club	Player	Pos.	Previous team (league/country)
61—Chicago (from Ottawa)	SIMON DANIS-PEPIN	D	U. of Maine (H-EAST)
62—Detroit	DICK AXELSSON	W	Huddinge (Sweden)
63—Carolina	JAMIE MCBAIN	D	U.S. National U-18

THIRD ROUND

No.—Selecting club	Player	Pos.	Previous team (league/country)
64—St. Louis	JONAS JUNLAND	D	Linkoping (Sweden)
65—Pittsburgh	BRIAN STRAIT	D	U.S. National U-18
66—Montreal (from Chicago)	RYAN WHITE	C	Calgary (WHL)
67—New Jersey (from Washington)	KIRILL TULUPOV	D	Alemetjevsk (Russia)
68—Ottawa (from Boston)	ERIC GRYBA	D	Green Bay (USHL)
69—Columbus	STEVE MASON	G	London (OHL)
70—New York Islanders	ROBIN FIGREN	W	Frolunda Jr. (Sweden Jr.)
71—Boston (from Phoenix)	BRAD MARCHAND	C	Moncton (QMJHL)
72—Minnesota	CAL CLUTTERBUCK	RW	Oshawa (OHL)
73—Florida	BRADY CALLA	RW	Everett (WHL)
74—Los Angeles	JEFF ZATKOFF	G	Miami University (CCHA)
75—Edmonton (from Atlanta)	THEO PECKHAM	D	Owen Sound (OHL)
76—Chicago (from Toronto)	TONY LAGERSTROM	C	Sodertalje Jr. (Sweden Jr.)
77—New Jersey (from Vancouver)	VLADIMIR ZHARKOV	RW	CSKA 2 (Russia)
78—Tampa Bay	KEVIN QUICK	D	Salisbury (USHSE)
79—Philadelphia (from Montreal)	JONATHAN MATSUMOTO	C	Bowling Green (CCHA)
80—Atlanta (from Edmonton)	MICHAEL FORNEY	LW	Thief River Falls (USHSW)
81—Colorado	MICHAEL CARMAN	C	U.S. National U-18
82—Vancouver (from Anaheim)	DANIEL RAHIMI	D	Bjorkloven Jr. (Sweden Jr.)
83—Anaheim (from San Jose)	JOHN DEGRAY	D	Brampton (OHL)
84—New York Rangers	RYAN HILLIER	LW	Halifax (QMJHL)
85—Columbus (from Phoenix)	TOMMY SESTITO	LW	Plymouth (OHL)
86—Los Angeles (from Nashville)	BUD HOLLOWAY	C/RW	Seattle (WHL)
87—Calgary (from Buffalo)	JOHN ARMSTRONG	C/RW	Plymouth (OHL)
88—Phoenix (from New Jersey)	JONAS AHNELOV	D	Frolunda (Sweden)
89—Calgary	AARON MARVIN	C/W	Warroad (USHSW)
90—Dallas	AARON SNOW	LW	Brampton (OHL)
91—Ottawa	KASPARS DAUGAVINS	LW	Riga (Latvia)
92—Detroit	DANIEL LARSSON	G	Hammarby (Sweden)
93—Carolina	HARRISON REED	RW	Sarnia (OHL)

FOURTH ROUND

No.—Selecting club	Player	Pos.	Previous team (league/country)
94—St. Louis	RYAN TUREK	C	Omaha (USHL)
95—Chicago (from Pittsburgh)	BEN SHUTRON	D	Kingston (OHL)
96—Chicago	JOSEPH PALMER	G	U.S. National U-18
97—Washington	OSKAR OSALA	LW	Mississauga (OHL)
98—San Jose (from Boston)	JAMES DELORY	D	Oshawa (OHL)
99—Toronto (from Columbus)	JAMES REIMER	G	Red Deer (WHL)
100—New York Islanders	RHETT RAKHSHANI	RW	U.S. National U-18
101—Philadelphia	JOONAS LEHTIVUORI	D	Ilves Jr. (Finland Jr.).
102—Minnesota	KYLE MEDVEC	D	Apple Valley (USHSW)
103—Florida	MICHAEL CARUSO	D	Guelph (OHL)
104—New York Rangers (from L.A.)	DAVID KVETON	RW	Vsetin (Czech Rep.)
105—Nashville (from Atlanta)	NIKO SNELLMAN	W	Ilves Jr. (Finland Jr.).
106—St. Louis (from Toronto)	RETO BERRA	G	Zurich/Kusnacht (SUI)
107—New Jersey (from Vancouver)	T.J. MILLER	D	Penticton (BCHL)
108—New York Islanders (from T.B.)	JASE WESLOSKY	G	Sherwood Park (AJHL)
109—Philadelphia (from Montreal)	JAKUB KOVAR	G	Budejovice Jr. (Czech Rep. Jr.)
110—Colorado (from Edmonton)	KEVIN MONTGOMERY	D	U.S. National U-18
111—Toronto (from Colorado)	KORBINIAN HOLZER	D	Bad Tolz (Germany)
112—Anaheim	MATT BELESKEY	LW	Belleville (OHL)
113—Columbus (from San Jose)	BEN WRIGHT	D	Lethbridge (WHL)
114—Los Angeles (from N.Y. Rangers)	NICLAS ANDERSEN	D	Leksand (Sweden)
115—New York Islanders (from Phoenix)	TOMAS MARCINKO	C	Kosice (SVK)
116—Florida (from Nashville)	DERRICK LAPOINT	D	Eau Claire North (USHSW)
117—Buffalo	FELIX SCHUTZ	C	Saint John (QMJHL)
118—Calgary (from NJ)	HUGO CARPENTIER	C	Rouyn Noranda (QMJHL)
119—New York Islanders (from Calgary)	DOUG ROGERS	C	St. Sebastian's (USHSE)
120—Dallas	RICHARD BACHMAN	G	Cushing Academy (USHSE)
121—Ottawa	PIERRE-LUC LESSARD	L	Gatineau (QMJHL)
122—Washington (from Detroit)	LUKE LYNES	C/LW	Brampton (OHL)
123—Carolina	BOBBY HUGHES	C	Kingston (OHL)

FIFTH ROUND

No.—Selecting club	Player	Pos.	Previous team (league/country)
124—St. Louis	ANDY SACKRISON	C/LW	St. Louis Park (USHSW)
125—Pittsburgh	CHAD JOHNSON	G	Alaska-Fairbanks (CCHA)
126—New York Islanders (from Chicago)	SHANE SIMS	D	Des Moines (USHL)
127—Washington	MAXIME LACROIX	LW	Quebec (QMJHL)
128—Boston	ANDREW BODNARCHUK	D	Halifax (QMJHL)
129—Columbus	ROBERT NYHOLM	RW	IFK Jr. (Finland Jr.).
130—Phoenix (from New York Islanders)	BRETT BENNETT	G	U.S. National U-18
131—Phoenix	MARTIN LATAL	RW	Kladno (Czech Rep.)
132—Minnesota	NIKO HOVINEN	G	Jokerit (Finland)
133—Edmonton (from Florida)	BRYAN PITTON	G	Brampton (OHL)
134—Los Angeles	DAVID MECKLER	C	Yale (ECAC)
135—Atlanta	ALEX KANGAS	G	Sioux Falls (USHL)
136—Columbus (from Toronto)	NICK SUCHARSKI	LW	Michigan State (CCHA)
137—N.Y. Rangers (from Vancouver)	TOMAS ZABORSKY	W	Trencin (SVK)
138—Dallas (from Tampa Bay)	DAVID MCINTYRE	C	Newmarket (OPJRA)
139—Montreal	PAVEL VALENTENKO	D	Neftekamsk (Russia)
140—Edmonton	CODY WILD	D	Providence (H-EAST)
141—New York Islanders (from Colorado)	KIM JOHANSSON	W	Malmo Jr. (Sweden Jr.)
142—Columbus (from Anaheim)	MAXIME FRECHETTE	D	Drummondville (QMJHL)
143—San Jose	ASHTON ROME	RW	Kamloops (WHL)
144—Los Angeles (from N.Y. Rangers)	MARTIN NOLET	D	Champlain (QAAAJHL)
145—Philadelphia	JONATHAN RHEAULT	RW	Providence (H-EAST)
146—Nashville	MARK DEKANICH	G	Colgate (ECAC)
147—Buffalo	ALEX BIEGA	D	Salisbury (USHSE)
148—New Jersey	OLIVIER MAGNAN	D	Rouyn Noranda (QMJHL)
149—Calgary	JUUSO PUUSTINEN	RW	Kalpa Jr. (Finland Jr.).
150—Dallas	MAX WARN	LW	IFK Jr. (Finland Jr.).
151—Ottawa	RYAN DANIELS	G	Saginaw (OHL)
152—Phoenix (from Detroit)	JORDAN BENDFELD	D	Medicine Hat (WHL)
153—Carolina	STEFAN CHAPUT	C	Lewiston (QMJHL)

SIXTH ROUND

No.—Selecting club	Player	Pos.	Previous team (league/country)
154—St. Louis	MATTHEW MCCOLLEM	LW	Belmont Hill (USHSE)
155—Florida (from Pittsburgh)	PETER ASTON	D	Windsor (OHL)
156—Chicago	JAN-MIKAEL JUUTILAINEN	C	Jokerit Jr. (Finland Jr.).
157—Washington	BRENT GWIDT	C	Lakeland H.S. (USHSW)
158—Boston	LEVI NELSON	C	Swift Current (WHL)
159—Columbus	JESSE DUDAS	D	Prince George (WHL)
160—New York Islanders	ANDREW MACDONALD	D	Moncton (QMJHL)
161—Toronto (from Phoenix)	VIKTOR STAHLBERG	LW	Frolunda (Sweden)
162—Minnesota	JULIAN WALKER	W	Basel (SUI)
163—Vancouver (from Florida)	SERGEI SHIROKOV	W	CSKA (Russia)
164—Los Angeles	CONSTANTIN BRAUN	LW	Eisbaren (Germany)
165—Atlanta	JONAS ENLUND	C	IFK Jr. (Finland Jr.).
166—Toronto	TYLER RUEGSEGGER	C/RW	Shattuck-St. Mary's (USHSW)
167—Vancouver	JURAJ SIMEK	W	Kloten (SUI)
168—Tampa Bay	DANE CROWLEY	D	Swift Current (WHL)
169—Chicago (from Montreal)	CHRIS AUGER	C	Wellington (OPJRA)
170—Edmonton	ALEXANDER BUMAGIN	W	Togliatti (Russia)
171—New York Islanders (from Colorado)	BRIAN DAY	RW	Governor Dummer (USHSE)
172—Anaheim	PETTERI WIRTANEN	C	HPK (Finland)
173—New York Islanders (from S.J.)	STEFAN RIDDERWALL	G	Djurgarden Jr. (Sweden Jr.)
174—New York Rangers	ERIC HUNTER	C	Prince George (WHL)
175—Philadelphia	MICHAEL DUPONT	G	Baie Comeau (QMJHL)
176—Nashville	RYAN FLYNN	RW	U.S. National U-18
177—Washington (from Buffalo)	MATHIEU PERREAULT	C	Acadie-Bathurst (QMJHL)
178—New Jersey	TONY ROMANO	C	N.Y. Bobcats (AJHL)
179—Calgary	JORDAN FULTON	C	Breck (USHSW)
180—Toronto (from Dallas)	LEO KOMAROV	C	Assat (Finland)
181—Ottawa	KEVIN KOOPMAN	D	Beaver Valley Jr. B (KIJHL)
182—Detroit	JAN MURSAK	LW	Budejovice (Czech Rep. Jr.)
183—Carolina	NICK DODGE	RW	Clarkson University (ECAC)

SEVENTH ROUND

No.—Selecting club	Player	Pos.	Previous team (league/country)
184—St. Louis	ALEXANDER HELLSTROM	D	Bjorkloven (Sweden)
185—Pittsburgh	TIMO SEPPANEN	D	IFK (Finland)

No.—Selecting club	Player	Pos.	Previous team (league/country)
186—Chicago	PETER LEBLANC	C/LW	Hamilton (OPJRA)
187—Calgary (from Washington)	DEVIN DIDIOMETE	LW	Sudbury (OHL)
188—Phoenix (from Boston)	CHRIS FRANK	D	Western Michigan (CCHA)
189—Columbus	DEREK DORSETT	RW	Medicine Hat (WHL)
190—New York Islanders	TROY MATTILA	LW	Springfield (NAHL)
191—Detroit (from Phoenix)	NICK OSLUND	RW	Burnsville (USHSW)
192—Minnesota	CHRIS HICKEY	C	Cretin Derham Hall (USHSW)
193—Florida	MARC CHEVERIE	G	Nanaimo (BCHL)
194—Columbus (from Los Angeles)	MATT MARQUARDT	LW	Moncton (QMJHL)
195—Atlanta	JESSE MARTIN	C	Spruce Grove (AJHL)
196—Phoenix (from Toronto)	BENN FERRIERO	C/RW	Boston College (H-EAST)
197—Vancouver	EVAN FULLER	RW	Prince George (WHL)
198—Tampa Bay	DENIS KAZIONOV	LW	TVER (Russia)
199—Montreal	CAMERON CEPEK	D	Portland (WHL)
200—Atlanta (from Edmonton)	ARTURS KULDA	D	CSKA 2 (Russia)
201—Colorado	BILLY SAUER	G	U. of Michigan (CCHA)
202—San Jose (from Anaheim)	JOHN MCCARTHY	LW	Boston U. (H-EAST)
203—San Jose	JAY BARRIBALL	F	Sioux Falls (USHL)
204—New York Rangers	LUKAS ZELISKA	C	Trinec Jr. (Czech Rep. Jr.)
205—Philadelphia	ANDREI POPOV	RW	Chelyabinsk (Russia)
206—Nashville	VIKTOR SJODIN	W	Vasteras Jr. (Sweden Jr.)
207—Buffalo	BENJAMIN BREAULT	C	Baie Comeau (QMJHL)
208—New Jersey	KYLE HENEGAN	D	Shawinigan (QMJHL)
209—Calgary	PER JONSSON	F	Farjestad Jr. (Sweden Jr.)
210—Atlanta (from Dallas)	WILL O'NEILL	D	Tabor Academy (USHSE)
211—Ottawa	ERIK CONDRA	RW	U. of Notre Dame (CCHA)
212—Detroit	LOGAN PYETT	D	Regina (WHL)
213—Carolina	JUSTIN KRUEGER	D	Penticton (BCHL)

Compensatory pick notes:

Pick 37—assigned to Boston for club not signing 2000 first-round pick Lars Jonsson.
Pick 42—assigned to Philadelphia for loss of G.M. Dean Lombardi.
Pick 45—assigned to Edmonton for club not signing 2002 first-round pick Jesse Niinimaki.
Pick 48—assigned to Los Angeles for club not signing 2001 first-round pick Jens Karlsson.
Pick 68—assigned to Ottawa for loss of G.M. Peter Chiarelli.
Pick 82—assigned to Vancouver for loss of coach Randy Carlyle.

NHL HISTORY

Stanley Cup champions

All-Star games

Year-by-year standings

Award winners

Sporting News awards

Hall of Fame

Team by team

STANLEY CUP CHAMPIONS

LIST OF WINNERS

The Stanley Cup was donated in 1893 to be awarded to signify supremacy in Canadian amateur hockey. Eventually, other teams, including professional clubs and clubs outside of Canada, began vying for the trophy. Since 1926 only NHL clubs have competed for the Stanley Cup.

Season	Club	Coach
1892-93	Montreal Amateur Athletic Association*	
1893-94	Montreal Amateur Athletic Association*	
1894-95	Montreal Victorias*	Mike Grant†
1895-96	(Feb. '96) Winnipeg Victorias*	J. Armitage†
1895-96	(Dec. '96) Montreal Victorias*	Mike Grant†
1896-97	Montreal Victorias*	Mike Grant†
1897-98	Montreal Victorias*	F. Richardson†
1898-99	Montreal Shamrocks*	H.J. Trihey†
1899-1900	Montreal Shamrocks*	H.J. Trihey†
1900-01	Winnipeg Victorias*	D.H. Bain†
1901-02	Montreal Am. Ath. Assn.*	C. McKerrow
1902-03	Ottawa Silver Seven*	A.T. Smith
1903-04	Ottawa Silver Seven*	A.T. Smith
1904-05	Ottawa Silver Seven*	A.T. Smith
1905-06	Montreal Wanderers*	Cecil Blachford†
1906-07	(Jan. '07) Kenora Thistles*	Tommy Phillips†
1906-07	(Mar. '07) Montreal Wanderers*	Cecil Blachford†
1907-08	Montreal Wanderers*	Cecil Blachford†
1908-09	Ottawa Senators*	Bruce Stuart†
1909-10	Montreal Wanderers*	Pud Glass†
1910-11	Ottawa Senators*	Bruce Stuart†
1911-12	Quebec Bulldogs*	C. Nolan
1912-13	Quebec Bulldogs*	Joe Malone†
1913-14	Toronto Blueshirts*	Scotty Davidson†
1914-15	Vancouver Millionaires*	Frank Patrick
1915-16	Montreal Canadiens*	George Kennedy
1916-17	Seattle Metropolitans*	Pete Muldoon
1917-18	Toronto Arenas	Dick Carroll
1919-20	Ottawa Senators	Pete Green
1920-21	Ottawa Senators	Pete Green
1921-22	Toronto St. Pats	George O'Donoghue
1922-23	Ottawa Senators	Pete Green
1923-24	Montreal Canadiens	Leo Dandurand
1924-25	Victoria Cougars*	Lester Patrick
1925-26	Montreal Maroons	Eddie Gerard
1926-27	Ottawa Senators	Dave Gill
1927-28	New York Rangers	Lester Patrick
1928-29	Boston Bruins	Cy Denneny
1929-30	Montreal Canadiens	Cecil Hart
1930-31	Montreal Canadiens	Cecil Hart
1931-32	Toronto Maple Leafs	Dick Irvin
1932-33	New York Rangers	Lester Patrick
1933-34	Chicago Black Hawks	Tommy Gorman
1934-35	Montreal Maroons	Tommy Gorman
1935-36	Detroit Red Wings	Jack Adams
1936-37	Detroit Red Wings	Jack Adams
1937-38	Chicago Black Hawks	Bill Stewart
1938-39	Boston Bruins	Art Ross
1939-40	New York Rangers	Frank Boucher
1940-41	Boston Bruins	Cooney Weiland
1941-42	Toronto Maple Leafs	Hap Day
1942-43	Detroit Red Wings	Jack Adams
1943-44	Montreal Canadiens	Dick Irvin
1944-45	Toronto Maple Leafs	Hap Day
1945-46	Montreal Canadiens	Dick Irvin
1946-47	Toronto Maple Leafs	Hap Day
1947-48	Toronto Maple Leafs	Hap Day
1948-49	Toronto Maple Leafs	Hap Day
1949-50	Detroit Red Wings	Tommy Ivan
1950-51	Toronto Maple Leafs	Joe Primeau
1951-52	Detroit Red Wings	Tommy Ivan
1952-53	Montreal Canadiens	Dick Irvin
1953-54	Detroit Red Wings	Tommy Ivan
1954-55	Detroit Red Wings	Jimmy Skinner
1955-56	Montreal Canadiens	Toe Blake
1956-57	Montreal Canadiens	Toe Blake
1957-58	Montreal Canadiens	Toe Blake
1958-59	Montreal Canadiens	Toe Blake
1959-60	Montreal Canadiens	Toe Blake
1960-61	Chicago Black Hawks	Rudy Pilous
1961-62	Toronto Maple Leafs	Punch Imlach
1962-63	Toronto Maple Leafs	Punch Imlach
1963-64	Toronto Maple Leafs	Punch Imlach
1964-65	Montreal Canadiens	Toe Blake
1965-66	Montreal Canadiens	Toe Blake
1966-67	Toronto Maple Leafs	Punch Imlach
1967-68	Montreal Canadiens	Toe Blake
1968-69	Montreal Canadiens	Claude Ruel
1969-70	Boston Bruins	Harry Sinden
1970-71	Montreal Canadiens	Al MacNeil
1971-72	Boston Bruins	Tom Johnson
1972-73	Montreal Canadiens	Scotty Bowman
1973-74	Philadelphia Flyers	Fred Shero
1974-75	Philadelphia Flyers	Fred Shero
1975-76	Montreal Canadiens	Scotty Bowman
1976-77	Montreal Canadiens	Scotty Bowman
1977-78	Montreal Canadiens	Scotty Bowman
1978-79	Montreal Canadiens	Scotty Bowman
1979-80	New York Islanders	Al Arbour
1980-81	New York Islanders	Al Arbour
1981-82	New York Islanders	Al Arbour
1982-83	New York Islanders	Al Arbour
1983-84	Edmonton Oilers	Glen Sather
1984-85	Edmonton Oilers	Glen Sather
1985-86	Montreal Canadiens	Jean Perron
1986-87	Edmonton Oilers	Glen Sather
1987-88	Edmonton Oilers	Glen Sather
1988-89	Calgary Flames	Terry Crisp
1989-90	Edmonton Oilers	John Muckler
1990-91	Pittsburgh Penguins	Bob Johnson
1991-92	Pittsburgh Penguins	Scotty Bowman
1992-93	Montreal Canadiens	Jacques Demers
1993-94	New York Rangers	Mike Keenan
1994-95	New Jersey Devils	Jacques Lemaire
1995-96	Colorado Avalanche	Marc Crawford
1996-97	Detroit Red Wings	Scotty Bowman
1997-98	Detroit Red Wings	Scotty Bowman
1998-99	Dallas Stars	Ken Hitchcock
1999-00	New Jersey Devils	Larry Robinson
2000-01	Colorado Avalanche	Bob Hartley
2001-02	Detroit Red Wings	Scotty Bowman
2002-03	New Jersey Devils	Pat Burns
2003-04	Tampa Bay Lightning	John Tortorella
2004-05	No Cup awarded	
2005-06	Carolina Hurricanes	Peter Laviolette

NOTE: 1918-19 series between Montreal and Seattle canceled after five games because of influenza epidemic. 2004-05 series not contested because of lockout.

*Stanley Cups won by non-NHL clubs.

†Team captain.

ALL-STAR GAMES

RESULTS

Date	Site	Winning team, score	Losing team, score	Att.
2-14-34†	Maple Leaf Gardens, Toronto	Toronto Maple Leafs, 7	NHL All-Stars, 3	*14,000
11-3-37‡	Montreal Forum	NHL All-Stars, 6	Montreal All-Stars§, 5	8,683
10-29-39∞	Montreal Forum	NHL All-Stars, 5	Montreal Canadiens, 2	*6,000
10-13-47	Maple Leaf Gardens, Toronto	NHL All-Stars, 4	Toronto Maple Leafs, 3	14,169
11-3-48	Chicago Stadium	NHL All-Stars, 3	Toronto Maple Leafs, 1	12,794
10-10-49	Maple Leaf Gardens, Toronto	NHL All-Stars, 3	Toronto Maple Leafs, 1	13,541
10-8-50	Olympia Stadium, Detroit	Detroit Red Wings, 7	NHL All-Stars, 1	9,166
10-9-51	Maple Leaf Gardens, Toronto	First Team, 2	Second Team, 2	11,469
10-5-52	Olympia Stadium, Detroit	First Team, 1	Second Team, 1	10,680
10-3-53	Montreal Forum	NHL All-Stars, 3	Montreal Canadiens, 1	14,153
10-2-54	Olympia Stadium, Detroit	NHL All-Stars, 2	Detroit Red Wings, 2	10,689
10-2-55	Olympia Stadium, Detroit	Detroit Red Wings, 3	NHL All-Stars, 1	10,111
10-9-56	Montreal Forum	NHL All-Stars, 1	Montreal Canadiens, 1	13,095
10-5-57	Montreal Forum	NHL All-Stars, 5	Montreal Canadiens, 3	13,095
10-4-58	Montreal Forum	Montreal Canadiens, 6	NHL All-Stars, 3	13,989
10-3-59	Montreal Forum	Montreal Canadiens, 6	NHL All-Stars, 1	13,818
10-1-60	Montreal Forum	NHL All-Stars, 2	Montreal Canadiens, 1	13,949
10-7-61	Chicago Stadium	NHL All-Stars, 3	Chicago Blackhawks, 1	14,534
10-6-62	Maple Leaf Gardens, Toronto	Toronto Maple Leafs, 4	NHL All-Stars, 1	14,236
10-5-63	Maple Leaf Gardens, Toronto	NHL All-Stars, 3	Toronto Maple Leafs, 3	14,034
10-10-64	Maple Leaf Gardens, Toronto	NHL All-Stars, 3	Toronto Maple Leafs, 2	14,232
10-20-65	Montreal Forum	NHL All-Stars, 5	Montreal Canadiens, 2	14,284
1-18-67	Montreal Forum	Montreal Canadiens, 3	NHL All-Stars, 0	14,284
1-16-68	Maple Leaf Gardens, Toronto	Toronto Maple Leafs, 4	NHL All-Stars, 3	15,753
1-21-69	Montreal Forum	West Division, 3	East Division, 3	16,260
1-20-70	St. Louis Arena	East Division, 4	West Division, 1	16,587
1-19-71	Boston Garden	West Division, 2	East Division, 1	14,790
1-25-72	Met Sports Center, Bloomington, Minn.	East Division, 3	West Division, 2	15,423
1-30-73	Madison Square Garden, New York	East Division, 5	West Division, 4	16,986
1-29-74	Chicago Stadium	West Division, 6	East Division, 4	16,426
1-21-75	Montreal Forum	Wales Conference, 7	Campbell Conference, 1	16,080
1-20-76	The Spectrum, Philadelphia	Wales Conference, 7	Campbell Conference, 5	16,436
1-25-77	Pacific Coliseum, Vancouver	Wales Conference, 4	Campbell Conference, 3	15,607
1-24-78	Buffalo Memorial Auditorium	Wales Conference, 3	Campbell Conference, 2 (OT)	16,433
1979 All-Star Game replaced by Challenge Cup series between Team NHL and Soviet Union				
2-5-80	Joe Louis Arena, Detroit	Wales Conference, 6	Campbell Conference, 3	21,002
2-10-81	The Forum, Los Angeles	Campbell Conference, 4	Wales Conference, 1	15,761
2-9-82	Capital Centre, Landover, Md.	Wales Conference, 4	Campbell Conference, 2	18,130
2-8-83	Nassau Coliseum, Long Island, N.Y.	Campbell Conference, 9	Wales Conference, 3	15,230
1-31-84	Meadowlands Arena, East Rutherford, N.J.	Wales Conference, 7	Campbell Conference, 6	18,939
2-12-85	Olympic Saddledome, Calgary	Wales Conference, 6	Campbell Conference, 4	16,683
2-4-86	Hartford Civic Center	Wales Conference, 4	Campbell Conference, 3 (OT)	15,126
1987 All-Star Game replaced by Rendez-Vous '87 between Team NHL and Soviet Union				
2-9-88	St. Louis Arena	Wales Conference, 6	Campbell Conference, 5 (OT)	17,878
2-7-89	Northlands Coliseum, Edmonton	Campbell Conference, 9	Wales Conference, 5	17,503
1-21-90	Pittsburgh Civic Arena	Wales Conference, 12	Campbell Conference, 7	17,503
1-19-91	Chicago Stadium	Campbell Conference, 11	Wales Conference, 5	18,472
1-18-92	The Spectrum, Philadelphia	Campbell Conference, 10	Wales Conference, 6	17,380
2-6-93	Montreal Forum	Wales Conference, 16	Campbell Conference, 6	17,137
1-22-94	Madison Square Garden, New York	Eastern Conference, 9	Western Conference, 8	18,200
1995 All-Star Game canceled because of NHL lockout				
1-20-96	FleetCenter, Boston	Eastern Conference, 5	Western Conference, 4	17,565
1-18-97	San Jose Arena	Eastern Conference, 11	Western Conference, 7	17,442
1-18-98	General Motors Place, Vancouver	North America, 8	World, 7	18,422
1-24-99	Ice Palace, Tampa	North America, 8	World, 6	19,758
2-6-00	Air Canada Centre, Toronto	World, 9	North America, 4	19,300
2-4-01	Pepsi Center, Denver	North America, 14	World, 12	18,646
2-2-02	Staples Center, Los Angeles	World, 8	North America, 5	18,118
2-2-03	Office Depot Center, Sunrise, Florida	Western Conference, 6	Eastern Conference, 5 (2OT; SO)	19,250
2-8-04	Xcel Energy Center, St. Paul, Minnesota	Eastern Conference 6	Western Conference 4	19,434
2005 All-Star Game canceled because of NHL lockout				
2006 All-Star Game canceled because of players' participation in Winter Olympics				

*Estimated figure.
†Benefit game for Toronto Maple Leafs left winger Ace Bailey, who suffered a career-ending skull injury earlier in the season.
‡Benefit game for the family of Montreal Canadiens center Howie Morenz, who died of a heart attack earlier in the year.
§Montreal All-Star roster made up of players from Montreal Canadiens and Maroons.
∞Benefit game for the family of Montreal Canadiens defenseman Babe Siebert, who drowned earlier in the year.

MOST VALUABLE PLAYERS

Date	Player, All-Star Game team (regular-season team)
10-6-62	Eddie Shack, Toronto Maple Leafs
10-5-63	Frank Mahovlich, Toronto Maple Leafs
10-10-64	Jean Beliveau, All-Stars (Montreal Canadiens)
10-20-65	Gordie Howe, All-Stars (Detroit Red Wings)
1-18-67	Henri Richard, Montreal Canadiens
1-16-68	Bruce Gamble, Toronto Maple Leafs
1-21-69	Frank Mahovlich, East Div. (Detroit Red Wings)
1-20-70	Bobby Hull, East Div. (Chicago Blackhawks)
1-19-71	Bobby Hull, West Div. (Chicago Blackhawks)
1-25-72	Bobby Orr, East Division (Boston Bruins)
1-30-73	Greg Polis, West Division (Pittsburgh Penguins)
1-29-74	Garry Unger, West Division (St. Louis Blues)
1-21-75	Syl Apps Jr., Wales Conf. (Pittsburgh Penguins)
1-20-76	Peter Mahovlich, Wales Conf. (Montreal Canadiens)
1-25-77	Rick Martin, Wales Conference (Buffalo Sabres)
1-24-78	Billy Smith, Campbell Conf. (New York Islanders)
2-5-80	Reggie Leach, Campbell Conf. (Philadelphia Flyers)
2-10-81	Mike Liut, Campbell Conf. (St. Louis Blues)
2-9-82	Mike Bossy, Wales Conf. (New York Islanders)
2-8-83	Wayne Gretzky, Campbell Conf. (Edmonton Oilers)
1-31-84	Don Maloney, Wales Conf. (New York Rangers)
2-12-85	Mario Lemieux, Wales Conf. (Pittsburgh Penguins)
2-4-86	Grant Fuhr, Campbell Conf. (Edmonton Oilers)
2-9-88	Mario Lemieux, Wales Conf. (Pittsburgh Penguins)
2-7-89	Wayne Gretzky, Campbell Conf. (Los Angeles Kings)
1-21-90	Mario Lemieux, Wales Conf. (Pittsburgh Penguins)
1-19-91	Vincent Damphousse, Camp. Conf. (Tor. Maple Leafs)
1-18-92	Brett Hull, Campbell Conf. (St. Louis Blues)
2-6-93	Mike Gartner, Wales Conf. (New York Rangers)
1-22-94	Mike Richter, Eastern Conf. (New York Rangers)
1-20-96	Ray Bourque, Eastern Conf. (Boston Bruins)
1-18-97	Mark Recchi, Eastern Conf. (Montreal Canadiens)
1-18-98	Teemu Selanne, North America (Ana. Mighty Ducks)
1-24-99	Wayne Gretzky, North America (New York Rangers)
2-6-00	Pavel Bure, World (Florida Panthers)
2-4-01	Bill Guerin, North America (Boston Bruins)
2-2-02	Eric Daze, North America (Chicago Blackhawks)
2-2-03	Dany Heatley, Eastern Conference (Atlanta Thrashers)
2-8-04	Joe Sakic, Western Conference (Colorado Avalanche)

YEAR-BY-YEAR STANDINGS

Note: Prior to 1926-27 season, clubs outside the NHL also competed for the Stanley Cup. Non-NHL clubs are denoted in parentheses. Sometimes playoff rounds were decided by total goals scored, rather than by games won.

1917-18

Team	W	L	T	Pts.	GF	GA
Montreal Canadiens	13	9	0	26	115	84
Toronto Arenas	13	9	0	26	108	109
Ottawa Senators	9	13	0	18	102	114
Montreal Wanderers	1	5	0	2	17	35

PLAYOFFS

Semifinals: Toronto 10 goals, Montreal Canadiens 7 goals (2-game series); Vancouver (PCHL) 3 goals, Seattle (PCHL) 2 goals (2-game series).

Stanley Cup finals: Toronto 3, Vancouver (PCHL) 2.

1918-19

Team	W	L	T	Pts.	GF	GA
Ottawa Senators	12	6	0	24	71	53
Montreal Canadiens	10	8	0	20	88	78
Toronto Arenas	5	13	0	10	64	92

PLAYOFFS

Semifinals: Seattle (PCHL) 7 goals, Vancouver 5 goals (2-game series); Montreal Canadiens 3, Ottawa 1.

Stanley Cup finals: Series between Montreal Canadiens and Seattle (PCHL) abandoned (with each team winning two games and one game tied) due to influenza epidemic.

1919-20

Team	W	L	T	Pts.	GF	GA
Ottawa Senators	19	5	0	38	121	64
Montreal Canadiens	13	11	0	26	129	113
Toronto St. Patricks	12	12	0	24	119	106
Quebec Bulldogs	4	20	0	8	91	177

PLAYOFFS

Semifinals: Seattle (PCHL) 7 goals, Vancouver (PCHL) 3 goals (2-game series).

Stanley Cup finals: Ottawa 3, Seattle (PCHL) 2.

1920-21

Team	W	L	T	Pts.	GF	GA
Toronto St. Patricks	15	9	0	30	105	100
Ottawa Senators	14	10	0	28	97	75
Montreal Canadiens	13	11	0	26	112	99
Hamilton Tigers	6	18	0	12	92	132

PLAYOFFS

Semifinals: Vancouver (PCHL) 2, Seattle (PCHL) 0; Ottawa 2, Toronto 0.

Stanley Cup finals: Ottawa 3, Vancouver (PCHL) 2.

1921-22

Team	W	L	T	Pts.	GF	GA
Ottawa Senators	14	8	2	30	106	84
Toronto St. Patricks	13	10	1	27	98	97
Montreal Canadiens	12	11	1	25	88	94
Hamilton Tigers	7	17	0	14	88	105

PLAYOFFS

Preliminaries: Regina (WCHL) 2 goals, Calgary (WCHL) 1 goal (2-game series); Regina (WCHL) 3, Edmonton (WCHL) 2; Vancouver (PCHL) 2, Seattle (PCHL) 0; Vancouver (PCHL) 5 goals, Regina (WCHL) 2 goals (2-game series); Toronto 5 goals, Ottawa 4 goals (2-game series).

Stanley Cup finals: Toronto 3, Vancouver (PCHL) 2.

1922-23

Team	W	L	T	Pts.	GF	GA
Ottawa Senators	14	9	1	29	77	54
Montreal Canadiens	13	9	2	28	73	61
Toronto St. Patricks	13	10	1	27	82	88
Hamilton Tigers	6	18	0	12	81	110

PLAYOFFS

Quarterfinals: Ottawa 3 goals, Montreal Canadiens 2 goals (2-game series); Vancouver (PCHL) 5 goals, Victoria (PCHL) 3 goals (2-game series). **Semifinals:** Ottawa 3, Vancouver (PCHL) 1; Edmonton (WCHL) 4 goals, Regina (WCHL) 3 goals (2-game series).

Stanley Cup finals: Ottawa 2, Edmonton (WCHL) 0.

1923-24

Team	W	L	T	Pts.	GF	GA
Ottawa Senators	16	8	0	32	74	54
Montreal Canadiens	13	11	0	26	59	48
Toronto St. Patricks	10	14	0	20	59	85
Hamilton Tigers	9	15	0	18	63	68

PLAYOFFS

First round: Vancouver (PCHL) 4 goals, Seattle (PCHL) 3 goals (2-game series); Calgary (WCHL) 4 goals, Regina (WCHL) 2 goals (2-game series). **Second round:** Montreal Canadiens 2, Ottawa 0; Calgary (WCHL) 2, Vancouver (PCHL) 1. **Third round:** Montreal Canadiens 2, Vancouver (PCHL) 0.

Stanley Cup finals: Montreal Canadiens 2, Calgary (WCHL) 0.

1924-25

Team	W	L	T	Pts.	GF	GA
Hamilton Tigers	19	10	1	39	90	60
Toronto St. Patricks	19	11	0	38	90	84
Montreal Canadiens	17	11	2	36	93	56
Ottawa Senators	17	12	1	35	83	66
Montreal Maroons	9	19	2	20	45	65
Boston Bruins	6	24	0	12	49	119

PLAYOFFS

Quarterfinals: Victoria (WCHL) 6 goals, Saskatoon (WCHL) 4 goals (2-game series). **Semifinals:** Montreal Canadiens 2, Toronto 0; Victoria (WCHL) 3 goals, Calgary (WCHL) 1 goal (2-game series).

Stanley Cup finals: Victoria (WCHL) 3, Montreal Canadiens 1.

1925-26

Team	W	L	T	Pts.	GF	GA
Ottawa Senators	24	8	4	52	77	42
Montreal Maroons	20	11	5	45	91	73
Pittsburgh Pirates	19	16	1	39	82	70
Boston Bruins	17	15	4	38	92	85
New York Americans	12	20	4	28	68	89
Toronto St. Patricks	12	21	3	27	92	114
Montreal Canadiens	11	24	1	23	79	108

PLAYOFFS

Quarterfinals: Victoria (WHL) 4 goals, Saskatoon (WHL) 3 goals (2-game series); Montreal Maroons 6 goals, Pittsburgh 4 goals (2-game series). **Semifinals:** Victoria (WHL) 5 goals, Edmonton (WHL) 3 goals (2-game series); Montreal Maroons 2 goals, Ottawa 1 goal (2-game series).

Stanley Cup finals: Montreal Maroons 3, Victoria (WHL) 1.

1926-27

AMERICAN DIVISION

Team	W	L	T	Pts.	GF	GA
New York Rangers	25	13	6	56	95	72
Boston Bruins	21	20	3	45	97	89
Chicago Blackhawks	19	22	3	41	115	116
Pittsburgh Pirates	15	26	3	33	79	108
Detroit Cougars	12	28	4	28	76	105

CANADIAN DIVISION

Team	W	L	T	Pts.	GF	GA
Ottawa Senators	30	10	4	64	89	69
Montreal Canadiens	28	14	2	58	99	67
Montreal Maroons	20	20	4	44	71	68
New York Americans	17	25	2	36	82	91
Toronto St. Patricks	15	24	5	35	79	94

PLAYOFFS

League quarterfinals: Montreal Canadiens 2 goals, Montreal Maroons 1 goal (2-game series); Boston 10 goals, Chicago 5 goals (2-game series). **Semifinals:** Ottawa 5 goals, Montreal Canadiens 1 goal (2-game series); Boston 3 goals, N.Y. Rangers 1 goal (2-game series).

Stanley Cup finals: Ottawa 2, Boston 0 (two ties).

1927-28

AMERICAN DIVISION

Team	W	L	T	Pts.	GF	GA
Boston Bruins	20	13	11	51	77	70
New York Rangers	19	16	9	47	94	79
Pittsburgh Pirates	19	17	8	46	67	76
Detroit Cougars	19	19	6	44	88	79
Chicago Blackhawks	7	34	3	17	68	134

CANADIAN DIVISION

Team	W	L	T	Pts.	GF	GA
Montreal Canadiens	26	11	7	59	116	48
Montreal Maroons	24	14	6	54	96	77
Ottawa Senators	20	14	10	50	78	57
Toronto Maple Leafs	18	18	8	44	89	88
New York Americans	11	27	6	28	63	128

PLAYOFFS

League quarterfinals: Montreal Maroons 3 goals, Ottawa 1 goal (2-game series); N.Y. Rangers 6 goals, Pittsburgh 4 goals (2-game series). **Semifinals:** Montreal Maroons 3 goals, Montreal Canadiens 2 goals (2-game series); N.Y. Rangers 5 goals, Boston 2 goals (2-game series).

Stanley Cup finals: N.Y. Rangers 3, Montreal Maroons 2.

1928-29

AMERICAN DIVISION

Team	W	L	T	Pts.	GF	GA
Boston Bruins	26	13	5	57	89	52
New York Rangers	21	13	10	52	72	65
Detroit Cougars	19	16	9	47	72	63
Pittsburgh Pirates	9	27	8	26	46	80
Chicago Blackhawks	7	29	8	22	33	85

CANADIAN DIVISION

Team	W	L	T	Pts.	GF	GA
Montreal Canadiens	22	7	15	59	71	43
New York Americans	19	13	12	50	53	53
Toronto Maple Leafs	21	18	5	47	85	69
Ottawa Senators	14	17	13	41	54	67
Montreal Maroons	15	20	9	39	67	65

PLAYOFFS

League quarterfinals: N.Y. Rangers 1 goal, N.Y. Americans 0 goals (2-game series); Toronto 7 goals, Detroit 2 goals (2-game series). **Semifinals:** Boston 3, Montreal Canadiens 0; N.Y. Rangers 2, Toronto 0.

Stanley Cup finals: Boston 2, N.Y. Rangers 0.

1929-30

AMERICAN DIVISION

Team	W	L	T	Pts.	GF	GA
Boston Bruins	38	5	1	77	179	98
Chicago Blackhawks	21	18	5	47	117	111
New York Rangers	17	17	10	44	136	143
Detroit Cougars	14	24	6	34	117	133
Pittsburgh Pirates	5	36	3	13	102	185

CANADIAN DIVISION

Team	W	L	T	Pts.	GF	GA
Montreal Maroons	23	16	5	51	141	114
Montreal Canadiens	21	14	9	51	142	114
Ottawa Senators	21	15	8	50	138	118
Toronto Maple Leafs	17	21	6	40	116	124
New York Americans	14	25	5	33	113	161

PLAYOFFS

League quarterfinals: Montreal Canadiens 3 goals, Chicago 2 goals (2-game series); N.Y. Rangers 6 goals, Ottawa 3 goals (2-game series). **Semifinals:** Boston 3, Montreal Maroons 1; Montreal Canadiens 2, N.Y. Rangers 0.

Stanley Cup finals: Montreal Canadiens 2, Boston 0.

1930-31

AMERICAN DIVISION

Team	W	L	T	Pts.	GF	GA
Boston Bruins	28	10	6	62	143	90
Chicago Blackhawks	24	17	3	51	108	78
New York Rangers	19	16	9	47	106	87
Detroit Falcons	16	21	7	39	102	105
Philadelphia Quakers	4	36	4	12	76	184

CANADIAN DIVISION

Team	W	L	T	Pts.	GF	GA
Montreal Canadiens	26	10	8	60	129	89
Toronto Maple Leafs	22	13	9	53	118	99
Montreal Maroons	20	18	6	46	105	106
New York Americans	18	16	10	46	76	74
Ottawa Senators	10	30	4	24	91	142

PLAYOFFS

League quarterfinals: Chicago 4 goals, Toronto 3 goals (2-game series); N.Y. Rangers 8 goals, Montreal Maroons 1 goal (2-game series). **Semifinals:** Montreal Canadiens 3, Boston 2; Chicago 3 goals, N.Y. Rangers 0 goals (2-game series).

Stanley Cup finals: Montreal Canadiens 3, Chicago 2.

1931-32

AMERICAN DIVISION

Team	W	L	T	Pts.	GF	GA
New York Rangers	23	17	8	54	134	112
Chicago Blackhawks	18	19	11	47	86	101
Detroit Falcons	18	20	10	46	95	108
Boston Bruins	15	21	12	42	122	117

CANADIAN DIVISION

Team	W	L	T	Pts.	GF	GA
Montreal Canadiens	25	16	7	57	128	111
Toronto Maple Leafs	23	18	7	53	155	127
Montreal Maroons	19	22	7	45	142	139
New York Americans	16	24	8	40	95	142

PLAYOFFS

League quarterfinals: Toronto 6 goals, Chicago 2 goals (2-game series); Montreal Maroons 3 goals, Detroit 1 goal (2-game series). **Semifinals:** N.Y. Rangers 3, Montreal Canadiens 1; Toronto 4 goals, Montreal Maroons 3 (2-game series).

Stanley Cup finals: Toronto 3, N.Y. Rangers 0.

1932-33

AMERICAN DIVISION

Team	W	L	T	Pts.	GF	GA
Boston Bruins	25	15	8	58	124	88
Detroit Red Wings	25	15	8	58	111	93
New York Rangers	23	17	8	54	135	107
Chicago Blackhawks	16	20	12	44	88	101

CANADIAN DIVISION

Team	W	L	T	Pts.	GF	GA
Toronto Maple Leafs	24	18	6	54	119	111
Montreal Maroons	22	20	6	50	135	119
Montreal Canadiens	18	25	5	41	92	115
New York Americans	15	22	11	41	91	118
Ottawa Senators	11	27	10	32	88	131

PLAYOFFS

League quarterfinals: Detroit 5 goals, Montreal Maroons 2 goals (2-game series); N.Y. Rangers 8 goals, Montreal Canadiens 5 goals (2-game series). **Semifinals:** Toronto 3, Boston 2; N.Y. Rangers 6 goals, Detroit 3 goals (2-game series).

Stanley Cup finals: N.Y. Rangers 3, Toronto 1.

1933-34

AMERICAN DIVISION

Team	W	L	T	Pts.	GF	GA
Detroit Red Wings	24	14	10	58	113	98
Chicago Blackhawks	20	17	11	51	88	83
New York Rangers	21	19	8	50	120	113
Boston Bruins	18	25	5	41	111	130

CANADIAN DIVISION

Team	W	L	T	Pts.	GF	GA
Toronto Maple Leafs	26	13	9	61	174	119
Montreal Canadiens	22	20	6	50	99	101
Montreal Maroons	19	18	11	49	117	122
New York Americans	15	23	10	40	104	132
Ottawa Senators	13	29	6	32	115	143

PLAYOFFS

League quarterfinals: Chicago 4 goals, Montreal Canadiens 3 goals (2-game series); Montreal Maroons 2 goals, N.Y. Rangers 1 goal (2-game series). **Semifinals:** Detroit 3, Toronto 2; Chicago 6 goals, Montreal Maroons 2 goals (2-game series).

Stanley Cup finals: Chicago 3, Detroit 1.

1934-35

AMERICAN DIVISION

Team	W	L	T	Pts.	GF	GA
Boston Bruins	26	16	6	58	129	112
Chicago Blackhawks	26	17	5	57	118	88
New York Rangers	22	20	6	50	137	139
Detroit Red Wings	19	22	7	45	127	114

CANADIAN DIVISION

Team	W	L	T	Pts.	GF	GA
Toronto Maple Leafs	30	14	4	64	157	111
Montreal Maroons	24	19	5	53	123	92
Montreal Canadiens	19	23	6	44	110	145
New York Americans	12	27	9	33	100	142
St. Louis Eagles	11	31	6	28	86	144

PLAYOFFS

League quarterfinals: Montreal Maroons 1 goal, Chicago 0 goals (2-game series); N.Y. Rangers 6 goals, Montreal Canadiens 5 goals (2-game series). **Semifinals:** Toronto 3, Boston 1; Montreal Maroons 5 goals, N.Y. Rangers 4 (2-game series).

Stanley Cup finals: Montreal Maroons 3, Toronto 0.

1935-36

AMERICAN DIVISION

Team	W	L	T	Pts.	GF	GA
Detroit Red Wings	24	16	8	56	124	103
Boston Bruins	22	20	6	50	92	83
Chicago Blackhawks	21	19	8	50	93	92
New York Rangers	19	17	12	50	91	96

CANADIAN DIVISION

Team	W	L	T	Pts.	GF	GA
Montreal Maroons	22	16	10	54	114	106
Toronto Maple Leafs	23	19	6	52	126	106
New York Americans	16	25	7	39	109	122
Montreal Canadiens	11	26	11	33	82	123

PLAYOFFS

League quarterfinals: Toronto 8 goals, Boston 6 goals (2-game series); N.Y. Americans 7 goals, Chicago 5 goals (2-game series). **Semifinals:** Detroit 3, Montreal Maroons 0; Toronto 2, N.Y. Americans 1.

Stanley Cup finals: Detroit 3, Toronto 1.

1936-37

AMERICAN DIVISION

Team	W	L	T	Pts.	GF	GA
Detroit Red Wings	25	14	9	59	128	102
Boston Bruins	23	18	7	53	120	110
New York Rangers	19	20	9	47	117	106
Chicago Blackhawks	14	27	7	35	99	131

CANADIAN DIVISION

Team	W	L	T	Pts.	GF	GA
Montreal Canadiens	24	18	6	54	115	111
Montreal Maroons	22	17	9	53	126	110
Toronto Maple Leafs	22	21	5	49	119	115
New York Americans	15	29	4	34	122	161

PLAYOFFS

League quarterfinals: Montreal Maroons 2, Boston 1; N.Y. Rangers 2, Toronto 0. **Semifinals:** Detroit 3, Montreal Canadiens 2; N.Y. Rangers 2, Montreal Maroons 0.

Stanley Cup finals: Detroit 3, N.Y. Rangers 2.

1937-38

AMERICAN DIVISION

Team	W	L	T	Pts.	GF	GA
Boston Bruins	30	11	7	67	142	89
New York Rangers	27	15	6	60	149	96
Chicago Blackhawks	14	25	9	37	97	139
Detroit Red Wings	12	25	11	35	99	133

CANADIAN DIVISION

Team	W	L	T	Pts.	GF	GA
Toronto Maple Leafs	24	15	9	57	151	127
New York Americans	19	18	11	49	110	111
Montreal Canadiens	18	17	13	49	123	128
Montreal Maroons	12	30	6	30	101	149

PLAYOFFS

League quarterfinals: N.Y. Americans 2, N.Y. Rangers 1; Chicago 2, Montreal Canadiens 1. **Semifinals:** Toronto 3, Boston 0; Chicago 2, N.Y. Americans 1.

Stanley Cup finals: Chicago 3, Toronto 1.

1938-39

Team	W	L	T	Pts.	GF	GA
Boston Bruins	36	10	2	74	156	76
New York Rangers	26	16	6	58	149	105
Toronto Maple Leafs	19	20	9	47	114	107
New York Americans	17	21	10	44	119	157
Detroit Red Wings	18	24	6	42	107	128
Montreal Canadiens	15	24	9	39	115	146
Chicago Blackhawks	12	28	8	32	91	132

PLAYOFFS

League quarterfinals: Toronto 2, N.Y. Americans 0; Detroit 2, Montreal 1. **Semifinals:** Boston 4, N.Y. Rangers 3; Toronto 2, Detroit 1.
Stanley Cup finals: Boston 4, Toronto 1.

1939-40

Team	W	L	T	Pts.	GF	GA
Boston Bruins	31	12	5	67	170	98
New York Rangers	27	11	10	64	136	77
Toronto Maple Leafs	25	17	6	56	134	110
Chicago Blackhawks	23	19	6	52	112	120
Detroit Red Wings	16	26	6	38	90	126
New York Americans	15	29	4	34	106	140
Montreal Canadiens	10	33	5	25	90	168

PLAYOFFS

League quarterfinals: Toronto 2, Chicago 0; Detroit 2, N.Y. Americans 1. **Semifinals:** N.Y. Rangers 4, Boston 2; Toronto 2, Detroit 0.
Stanley Cup finals: N.Y. Rangers 4, Toronto 2.

1940-41

Team	W	L	T	Pts.	GF	GA
Boston Bruins	27	8	13	67	168	102
Toronto Maple Leafs	28	14	6	62	145	99
Detroit Red Wings	21	16	11	53	112	102
New York Rangers	21	19	8	50	143	125
Chicago Blackhawks	16	25	7	39	112	139
Montreal Canadiens	16	26	6	38	121	147
New York Americans	8	29	11	27	99	186

PLAYOFFS

League quarterfinals: Detroit 2, N.Y. Rangers 1; Chicago 2, Montreal 1. **Semifinals:** Boston 4, Toronto 3; Detroit 2, Chicago 0.
Stanley Cup finals: Boston 4, Detroit 0.

1941-42

Team	W	L	T	Pts.	GF	GA
New York Rangers	29	17	2	60	177	143
Toronto Maple Leafs	27	18	3	57	158	136
Boston Bruins	25	17	6	56	160	118
Chicago Blackhawks	22	23	3	47	145	155
Detroit Red Wings	19	25	4	42	140	147
Montreal Canadiens	18	27	3	39	134	173
Brooklyn Americans	16	29	3	35	133	175

PLAYOFFS

League quarterfinals: Boston 2, Chicago 1; Detroit 2, Montreal 1. **Semifinals:** Toronto 4, New York 2; Detroit 2, Boston 0.
Stanley Cup finals: Toronto 4, Detroit 3.

1942-43

Team	W	L	T	Pts.	GF	GA
Detroit Red Wings	25	14	11	61	169	124
Boston Bruins	24	17	9	57	195	176
Toronto Maple Leafs	22	19	9	53	198	159
Montreal Canadiens	19	19	12	50	181	191
Chicago Blackhawks	17	18	15	49	179	180
New York Rangers	11	31	8	30	161	253

PLAYOFFS

League semifinals: Detroit 4, Toronto 2; Boston 4, Montreal 1.
Stanley Cup finals: Detroit 4, Boston 0.

1943-44

Team	W	L	T	Pts.	GF	GA
Montreal Canadiens	38	5	7	83	234	109
Detroit Red Wings	26	18	6	58	214	177
Toronto Maple Leafs	23	23	4	50	214	174
Chicago Blackhawks	22	23	5	49	178	187
Boston Bruins	19	26	5	43	223	268
New York Rangers	6	39	5	17	162	310

PLAYOFFS

League semifinals: Montreal 4, Toronto 1; Chicago 4, Detroit 1.
Stanley Cup finals: Montreal 4, Chicago 0.

1944-45

Team	W	L	T	Pts.	GF	GA
Montreal Canadiens	38	8	4	80	228	121
Detroit Red Wings	31	14	5	67	218	161
Toronto Maple Leafs	24	22	4	52	183	161
Boston Bruins	16	30	4	36	179	219
Chicago Blackhawks	13	30	7	33	141	194
New York Rangers	11	29	10	32	154	247

PLAYOFFS

League semifinals: Toronto 4, Montreal 2; Detroit 4, Boston 3.
Stanley Cup finals: Toronto 4, Detroit 3.

1945-46

Team	W	L	T	Pts.	GF	GA
Montreal Canadiens	28	17	5	61	172	134
Boston Bruins	24	18	8	56	167	156
Chicago Blackhawks	23	20	7	53	200	178
Detroit Red Wings	20	20	10	50	146	159
Toronto Maple Leafs	19	24	7	45	174	185
New York Rangers	13	28	9	35	144	191

PLAYOFFS

League semifinals: Montreal 4, Chicago 0; Boston 4, Detroit 1.
Stanley Cup finals: Montreal 4, Boston 1.

1946-47

Team	W	L	T	Pts.	GF	GA
Montreal Canadiens	34	16	10	78	189	138
Toronto Maple Leafs	31	19	10	72	209	172
Boston Bruins	26	23	11	63	190	175
Detroit Red Wings	22	27	11	55	190	193
New York Rangers	22	32	6	50	167	186
Chicago Blackhawks	19	37	4	42	193	274

PLAYOFFS

League semifinals: Montreal 4, Boston 1; Toronto 4, Detroit 1.
Stanley Cup finals: Toronto 4, Montreal 2.

1947-48

Team	W	L	T	Pts.	GF	GA
Toronto Maple Leafs	32	15	13	77	182	143
Detroit Red Wings	30	18	12	72	187	148
Boston Bruins	23	24	13	59	167	168
New York Rangers	21	26	13	55	176	201
Montreal Canadiens	20	29	11	51	147	169
Chicago Blackhawks	20	34	6	46	195	225

PLAYOFFS

League semifinals: Toronto 4, Boston 1; Detroit 4, New York 2.
Stanley Cup finals: Toronto 4, Detroit 0.

1948-49

Team	W	L	T	Pts.	GF	GA
Detroit Red Wings	34	19	7	75	195	145
Boston Bruins	29	23	8	66	178	163
Montreal Canadiens	28	23	9	65	152	126
Toronto Maple Leafs	22	25	13	57	147	161
Chicago Blackhawks	21	31	8	50	173	211
New York Rangers	18	31	11	47	133	172

PLAYOFFS

League semifinals: Detroit 4, Montreal 3; Toronto 4, Boston 1.
Stanley Cup finals: Toronto 4, Detroit 0.

1949-50

Team	W	L	T	Pts.	GF	GA
Detroit Red Wings	37	19	14	88	229	164
Montreal Canadiens	29	22	19	77	172	150
Toronto Maple Leafs	31	27	12	74	176	173
New York Rangers	28	31	11	67	170	189
Boston Bruins	22	32	16	60	198	228
Chicago Blackhawks	22	38	10	54	203	244

PLAYOFFS

League semifinals: Detroit 4, Toronto 3; New York 4, Montreal 1.
Stanley Cup finals: Detroit 4, New York 3.

1950-51

Team	W	L	T	Pts.	GF	GA
Detroit Red Wings	44	13	13	101	236	139
Toronto Maple Leafs	41	16	13	95	212	138
Montreal Canadiens	25	30	15	65	173	184
Boston Bruins	22	30	18	62	178	197
New York Rangers	20	29	21	61	169	201
Chicago Blackhawks	13	47	10	36	171	280

PLAYOFFS

League semifinals: Montreal 4, Detroit 2; Toronto 4, Boston 1.
Stanley Cup finals: Toronto 4, Montreal 1.

1951-52

Team	W	L	T	Pts.	GF	GA
Detroit Red Wings	44	14	12	100	215	133
Montreal Canadiens	34	26	10	78	195	164
Toronto Maple Leafs	29	25	16	74	168	157
Boston Bruins	25	29	16	66	162	176
New York Rangers	23	34	13	59	192	219
Chicago Blackhawks	17	44	9	43	158	241

PLAYOFFS

League semifinals: Detroit 4, Toronto 0; Montreal 4, Boston 3.
Stanley Cup finals: Detroit 4, Montreal 0.

1952-53

Team	W	L	T	Pts.	GF	GA
Detroit Red Wings	36	16	18	90	222	133
Montreal Canadiens	28	23	19	75	155	148
Boston Bruins	28	29	13	69	152	172
Chicago Blackhawks	27	28	15	69	169	175
Toronto Maple Leafs	27	30	13	67	156	167
New York Rangers	17	37	16	50	152	211

PLAYOFFS

League semifinals: Boston 4, Detroit 2; Montreal 4, Chicago 3.
Stanley Cup finals: Montreal 4, Boston 1.

1953-54

Team	W	L	T	Pts.	GF	GA
Detroit Red Wings	37	19	14	88	191	132
Montreal Canadiens	35	24	11	81	195	141
Toronto Maple Leafs	32	24	14	78	152	131
Boston Bruins	32	28	10	74	177	181
New York Rangers	29	31	10	68	161	182
Chicago Blackhawks	12	51	7	31	133	242

PLAYOFFS

League semifinals: Detroit 4, Toronto 1; Montreal 4, Boston 0.
Stanley Cup finals: Detroit 4, Montreal 3.

1954-55

Team	W	L	T	Pts.	GF	GA
Detroit Red Wings	42	17	11	95	204	134
Montreal Canadiens	41	18	11	93	228	157
Toronto Maple Leafs	24	24	22	70	147	135
Boston Bruins	23	26	21	67	169	188
New York Rangers	17	35	18	52	150	210
Chicago Blackhawks	13	40	17	43	161	235

PLAYOFFS

League semifinals: Detroit 4, Toronto 0; Montreal 4, Boston 1.
Stanley Cup finals: Detroit 4, Montreal 3.

1955-56

Team	W	L	T	Pts.	GF	GA
Montreal Canadiens	45	15	10	100	222	131
Detroit Red Wings	30	24	16	76	183	148
New York Rangers	32	28	10	74	204	203
Toronto Maple Leafs	24	33	13	61	153	181
Boston Bruins	23	34	13	59	147	185
Chicago Blackhawks	19	39	12	50	155	216

PLAYOFFS

League semifinals: Montreal 4, New York 1; Detroit 4, Toronto 1.
Stanley Cup finals: Montreal 4, Detroit 1.

1956-57

Team	W	L	T	Pts.	GF	GA
Detroit Red Wings	38	20	12	88	198	157
Montreal Canadiens	35	23	12	82	210	155
Boston Bruins	34	24	12	80	195	174
New York Rangers	26	30	14	66	184	227
Toronto Maple Leafs	21	34	15	57	174	192
Chicago Blackhawks	16	39	15	47	169	225

PLAYOFFS

League semifinals: Boston 4, Detroit 1; Montreal 4, New York 1.
Stanley Cup finals: Montreal 4, Boston 1.

1957-58

Team	W	L	T	Pts.	GF	GA
Montreal Canadiens	43	17	10	96	250	158
New York Rangers	32	25	13	77	195	188
Detroit Red Wings	29	29	12	70	176	207
Boston Bruins	27	28	15	69	199	194
Chicago Blackhawks	24	39	7	55	163	202
Toronto Maple Leafs	21	38	11	53	192	226

PLAYOFFS

League semifinals: Montreal 4, Detroit 0; Boston 4, New York 2.
Stanley Cup finals: Montreal 4, Boston 2.

1958-59

Team	W	L	T	Pts.	GF	GA
Montreal Canadiens	39	18	13	91	258	158
Boston Bruins	32	29	9	73	205	215
Chicago Blackhawks	28	29	13	69	197	208
Toronto Maple Leafs	27	32	11	65	189	201
New York Rangers	26	32	12	64	201	217
Detroit Red Wings	25	37	8	58	167	218

PLAYOFFS

League semifinals: Montreal 4, Chicago 2; Toronto 4, Boston 3.
Stanley Cup finals: Montreal 4, Toronto 1.

1959-60

Team	W	L	T	Pts.	GF	GA
Montreal Canadiens	40	18	12	92	255	178
Toronto Maple Leafs	35	26	9	79	199	195
Chicago Blackhawks	28	29	13	69	191	180
Detroit Red Wings	26	29	15	67	186	197
Boston Bruins	28	34	8	64	220	241
New York Rangers	17	38	15	49	187	247

PLAYOFFS

League semifinals: Montreal 4, Chicago 0; Toronto 4, Detroit 2.
Stanley Cup finals: Montreal 4, Toronto 0.

1960-61

Team	W	L	T	Pts.	GF	GA
Montreal Canadiens	41	19	10	92	254	188
Toronto Maple Leafs	39	19	12	90	234	176
Chicago Blackhawks	29	24	17	75	198	180
Detroit Red Wings	25	29	16	66	195	215
New York Rangers	22	38	10	54	204	248
Boston Bruins	15	42	13	43	176	254

PLAYOFFS

League semifinals: Chicago 4, Montreal 2; Detroit 4, Toronto 1.
Stanley Cup finals: Chicago 4, Detroit 2.

1961-62

Team	W	L	T	Pts.	GF	GA
Montreal Canadiens	42	14	14	98	259	166
Toronto Maple Leafs	37	22	11	85	232	180
Chicago Blackhawks	31	26	13	75	217	186
New York Rangers	26	32	12	64	195	207
Detroit Red Wings	23	33	14	60	184	219
Boston Bruins	15	47	8	38	177	306

PLAYOFFS

League semifinals: Chicago 4, Montreal 2; Toronto 4, New York 2.
Stanley Cup finals: Toronto 4, Chicago 2.

1962-63

Team	W	L	T	Pts.	GF	GA
Toronto Maple Leafs	35	23	12	82	221	180
Chicago Blackhawks	32	21	17	81	194	178
Montreal Canadiens	28	19	23	79	225	183
Detroit Red Wings	32	25	13	77	200	194
New York Rangers	22	36	12	56	211	233
Boston Bruins	14	39	17	45	198	281

PLAYOFFS

League semifinals: Toronto 4, Montreal 1; Detroit 4, Chicago 2.
Stanley Cup finals: Toronto 4, Detroit 1.

1963-64

Team	W	L	T	Pts.	GF	GA
Montreal Canadiens	36	21	13	85	209	167
Chicago Blackhawks	36	22	12	84	218	169
Toronto Maple Leafs	33	25	12	78	192	172
Detroit Red Wings	30	29	11	71	191	204
New York Rangers	22	38	10	54	186	242
Boston Bruins	18	40	12	48	170	212

PLAYOFFS

League semifinals: Toronto 4, Montreal 3; Detroit 4, Chicago 3.
Stanley Cup finals: Toronto 4, Detroit 3.

1964-65

Team	W	L	T	Pts.	GF	GA
Detroit Red Wings	40	23	7	87	224	175
Montreal Canadiens	36	23	11	83	211	185
Chicago Blackhawks	34	28	8	76	224	176
Toronto Maple Leafs	30	26	14	74	204	173
New York Rangers	20	38	12	52	179	246
Boston Bruins	21	43	6	48	166	253

PLAYOFFS

League semifinals: Chicago 4, Detroit 3; Montreal 4, Toronto 2.
Stanley Cup finals: Montreal 4, Chicago 3.

1965-66

Team	W	L	T	Pts.	GF	GA
Montreal Canadiens	41	21	8	90	239	173
Chicago Blackhawks	37	25	8	82	240	187
Toronto Maple Leafs	34	25	11	79	208	187
Detroit Red Wings	31	27	12	74	221	194
Boston Bruins	21	43	6	48	174	275
New York Rangers	18	41	11	47	195	261

PLAYOFFS

League semifinals: Montreal 4, Toronto 0; Detroit 4, Chicago 2.
Stanley Cup finals: Montreal 4, Detroit 2.

1966-67

Team	W	L	T	Pts.	GF	GA
Chicago Blackhawks	41	17	12	94	264	170
Montreal Canadiens	32	25	13	77	202	188
Toronto Maple Leafs	32	27	11	75	204	211
New York Rangers	30	28	12	72	188	189
Detroit Red Wings	27	39	4	58	212	241
Boston Bruins	17	43	10	44	182	253

PLAYOFFS

League semifinals: Toronto 4, Chicago 2; Montreal 4, New York 0.
Stanley Cup finals: Toronto 4, Montreal 2.

1967-68

EAST DIVISION

Team	W	L	T	Pts.	GF	GA
Montreal Canadiens	42	22	10	94	236	167
New York Rangers	39	23	12	90	226	183
Boston Bruins	37	27	10	84	259	216
Chicago Blackhawks	32	26	16	80	212	222
Toronto Maple Leafs	33	31	10	76	209	176
Detroit Red Wings	27	35	12	66	245	257

WEST DIVISION

Team	W	L	T	Pts.	GF	GA
Philadelphia Flyers	31	32	11	73	173	179
Los Angeles Kings	31	33	10	72	200	224

Team	W	L	T	Pts.	GF	GA
St. Louis Blues	27	31	16	70	177	191
Minnesota North Stars	27	32	15	69	191	226
Pittsburgh Penguins	27	34	13	67	195	216
Oakland Seals	15	42	17	47	153	219

PLAYOFFS

Division semifinals: Montreal 4, Boston 0; Chicago 4, New York 2; St. Louis 4, Philadelphia 3; Minnesota 4, Los Angeles 3. **Division finals:** Montreal 4, Chicago 1; St. Louis 4, Minnesota 3.

Stanley Cup finals: Montreal 4, St. Louis 0.

1968-69

EAST DIVISION

Team	W	L	T	Pts.	GF	GA
Montreal Canadiens	46	19	11	103	271	202
Boston Bruins	42	18	16	100	303	221
New York Rangers	41	26	9	91	231	196
Toronto Maple Leafs	35	26	15	85	234	217
Detroit Red Wings	33	31	12	78	239	221
Chicago Blackhawks	34	33	9	77	280	246

WEST DIVISION

Team	W	L	T	Pts.	GF	GA
St. Louis Blues	37	25	14	88	204	157
Oakland Seals	29	36	11	69	219	251
Philadelphia Flyers	20	35	21	61	174	225
Los Angeles Kings	24	42	10	58	185	260
Pittsburgh Penguins	20	45	11	51	189	252
Minnesota North Stars	18	43	15	51	189	270

PLAYOFFS

Division semifinals: Montreal 4, New York 0; Boston 4, Toronto 0; St. Louis 4, Philadelphia 0; Los Angeles 4, Oakland 3. **Division finals:** Montreal 4, Boston 2; St. Louis 4, Los Angeles 0.

Stanley Cup finals: Montreal 4, St. Louis 0.

1969-70

EAST DIVISION

Team	W	L	T	Pts.	GF	GA
Chicago Blackhawks	45	22	9	99	250	170
Boston Bruins	40	17	19	99	277	216
Detroit Red Wings	40	21	15	95	246	199
New York Rangers	38	22	16	92	246	189
Montreal Canadiens	38	22	16	92	244	201
Toronto Maple Leafs	29	34	13	71	222	242

WEST DIVISION

Team	W	L	T	Pts.	GF	GA
St. Louis Blues	37	27	12	86	224	179
Pittsburgh Penguins	26	38	12	64	182	238
Minnesota North Stars	19	35	22	60	224	257
Oakland Seals	22	40	14	58	169	243
Philadelphia Flyers	17	35	24	58	197	225
Los Angeles Kings	14	52	10	38	168	290

PLAYOFFS

Division semifinals: Chicago 4, Detroit 0; Boston 4, N.Y. Rangers 2; St. Louis 4, Minnesota 2; Pittsburgh 4, Oakland 0. **Division finals:** Boston 4, Chicago 0; St. Louis 4, Pittsburgh 2.

Stanley Cup finals: Boston 4, St. Louis 0.

1970-71

EAST DIVISION

Team	W	L	T	Pts.	GF	GA
Boston Bruins	57	14	7	121	399	207
New York Rangers	49	18	11	109	259	177
Montreal Canadiens	42	23	13	97	291	216
Toronto Maple Leafs	37	33	8	82	248	211
Buffalo Sabres	24	39	15	63	217	291
Vancouver Canucks	24	46	8	56	229	296
Detroit Red Wings	22	45	11	55	209	308

WEST DIVISION

Team	W	L	T	Pts.	GF	GA
Chicago Blackhawks	49	20	9	107	277	184
St. Louis Blues	34	25	19	87	223	208
Philadelphia Flyers	28	33	17	73	207	225
Minnesota North Stars	28	34	16	72	191	223
Los Angeles Kings	25	40	13	63	239	303
Pittsburgh Penguins	21	37	20	62	221	240
California Golden Seals	20	53	5	45	199	320

PLAYOFFS

Division semifinals: Montreal 4, Boston 3; N.Y Rangers 4, Toronto 2; Chicago 4, Philadelphia 0; Minnesota 4, St. Louis 2. **Division finals:** Montreal 4, Minnesota 2; Chicago 4, N.Y. Rangers 3.

Stanley Cup finals: Montreal 4, Chicago 3.

1971-72

EAST DIVISION

Team	W	L	T	Pts.	GF	GA
Boston Bruins	54	13	11	119	330	204
New York Rangers	48	17	13	109	317	192
Montreal Canadiens	46	16	16	108	307	205
Toronto Maple Leafs	33	31	14	80	209	208
Detroit Red Wings	33	35	10	76	261	262
Buffalo Sabres	16	43	19	51	203	289
Vancouver Canucks	20	50	8	48	203	297

WEST DIVISION

Team	W	L	T	Pts.	GF	GA
Chicago Blackhawks	46	17	15	107	256	166
Minnesota North Stars	37	29	12	86	212	191
St. Louis Blues	28	39	11	67	208	247
Pittsburgh Penguins	26	38	14	66	220	258
Philadelphia Flyers	26	38	14	66	200	236
California Golden Seals	21	39	18	60	216	288
Los Angeles Kings	20	49	9	49	206	305

PLAYOFFS

Division semifinals: Boston 4, Toronto 1; N.Y. Rangers 4, Montreal 2; Chicago 4, Pittsburgh 0; St. Louis 4, Minnesota 3. **Division finals:** N.Y. Rangers 4, Chicago 0; Boston 4, St. Louis 0.

Stanley Cup finals: Boston 4, N.Y. Rangers 2.

1972-73

EAST DIVISION

Team	W	L	T	Pts.	GF	GA
Montreal Canadiens	52	10	16	120	329	184
Boston Bruins	51	22	5	107	330	235
New York Rangers	47	23	8	102	297	208
Buffalo Sabres	37	27	14	88	257	219
Detroit Red Wings	37	29	12	86	265	243
Toronto Maple Leafs	27	41	10	64	247	279
Vancouver Canucks	22	47	9	53	233	339
New York Islanders	12	60	6	30	170	347

WEST DIVISION

Team	W	L	T	Pts.	GF	GA
Chicago Blackhawks	42	27	9	93	284	225
Philadelphia Flyers	37	30	11	85	296	256
Minnesota North Stars	37	30	11	85	254	230
St. Louis Blues	32	34	12	76	233	251
Pittsburgh Penguins	32	37	9	73	257	265

Team	W	L	T	Pts.	GF	GA
Los Angeles Kings	31	36	11	73	232	245
Atlanta Flames	25	38	15	65	191	239
California Golden Seals	16	46	16	48	213	323

PLAYOFFS

Division semifinals: Montreal 4, Buffalo 2; N.Y. Rangers 4, Boston 1; Chicago 4, St. Louis 1; Philadelphia 4, Minnesota 2. **Division finals:** Montreal 4, Philadelphia 1; Chicago 4, N.Y. Rangers 1.

Stanley Cup finals: Montreal 4, Chicago 2.

1973-74

EAST DIVISION

Team	W	L	T	Pts.	GF	GA
Boston Bruins	52	17	9	113	349	221
Montreal Canadiens	45	24	9	99	293	240
New York Rangers	40	24	14	94	300	251
Toronto Maple Leafs	35	27	16	86	274	230
Buffalo Sabres	32	34	12	76	242	250
Detroit Red Wings	29	39	10	68	255	319
Vancouver Canucks	24	43	11	59	224	296
New York Islanders	19	41	18	56	182	247

WEST DIVISION

Team	W	L	T	Pts.	GF	GA
Philadelphia Flyers	50	16	12	112	273	164
Chicago Blackhawks	41	14	23	105	272	164
Los Angeles Kings	33	33	12	78	233	231
Atlanta Flames	30	34	14	74	214	238
Pittsburgh Penguins	28	41	9	65	242	273
St. Louis Blues	26	40	12	64	206	248
Minnesota North Stars	23	38	17	63	235	275
California Golden Seals	13	55	10	36	195	342

PLAYOFFS

Division semifinals: Boston 4, Toronto 0; N.Y. Rangers 4, Montreal 2; Philadelphia 4, Atlanta 0; Chicago 4, Los Angeles 1. **Division finals:** Boston 4, Chicago 2; Philadelphia 4, N.Y. Rangers 3.

Stanley Cup finals: Philadelphia 4, Boston 2.

1974-75

PRINCE OF WALES CONFERENCE

ADAMS DIVISION

Team	W	L	T	Pts.	GF	GA
Buffalo Sabres	49	16	15	113	354	240
Boston Bruins	40	26	14	94	345	245
Toronto Maple Leafs	31	33	16	78	280	309
California Golden Seals	19	48	13	51	212	316

NORRIS DIVISION

Team	W	L	T	Pts.	GF	GA
Montreal Canadiens	47	14	19	113	374	225
Los Angeles Kings	42	17	21	105	269	185
Pittsburgh Penguins	37	28	15	89	326	289
Detroit Red Wings	23	45	12	58	259	335
Washington Capitals	8	67	5	21	181	446

CLARENCE CAMPBELL CONFERENCE

PATRICK DIVISION

Team	W	L	T	Pts.	GF	GA
Philadelphia Flyers	51	18	11	113	293	181
New York Rangers	37	29	14	88	319	276
New York Islanders	33	25	22	88	264	221
Atlanta Flames	34	31	15	83	243	233

SMYTHE DIVISION

Team	W	L	T	Pts.	GF	GA
Vancouver Canucks	38	32	10	86	271	254
St. Louis Blues	35	31	14	84	269	267
Chicago Blackhawks	37	35	8	82	268	241
Minnesota North Stars	23	50	7	53	221	341
Kansas City Scouts	15	54	11	41	184	328

PLAYOFFS

Preliminaries: Toronto 2, Los Angeles 1; Chicago 2, Boston 1; Pittsburgh 2, St. Louis 0; N.Y. Islanders 2, N.Y. Rangers 1. **Quarterfinals:** Philadelphia 4, Toronto 0; Buffalo 4, Chicago 1; Montreal 4, Vancouver 1; N.Y. Islanders 4, Pittsburgh 3. **Semifinals:** Philadelphia 4, N.Y. Islanders 3; Buffalo 4, Montreal 2.

Stanley Cup finals: Philadelphia 4, Buffalo 2.

1975-76

PRINCE OF WALES CONFERENCE

ADAMS DIVISION

Team	W	L	T	Pts.	GF	GA
Boston Bruins	48	15	17	113	313	237
Buffalo Sabres	46	21	13	105	339	240
Toronto Maple Leafs	34	31	15	83	294	276
California Golden Seals	27	42	11	65	250	278

NORRIS DIVISION

Team	W	L	T	Pts.	GF	GA
Montreal Canadiens	58	11	11	127	337	174
Los Angeles Kings	38	33	9	85	263	265
Pittsburgh Penguins	35	33	12	82	339	303
Detroit Red Wings	26	44	10	62	226	300
Washington Capitals	11	59	10	32	224	394

CLARENCE CAMPBELL CONFERENCE

PATRICK DIVISION

Team	W	L	T	Pts.	GF	GA
Philadelphia Flyers	51	13	16	118	348	209
New York Islanders	42	21	17	101	297	190
Atlanta Flames	35	33	12	82	262	237
New York Rangers	29	42	9	67	262	333

SMYTHE DIVISION

Team	W	L	T	Pts.	GF	GA
Chicago Blackhawks	32	30	18	82	254	261
Vancouver Canucks	33	32	15	81	271	272
St. Louis Blues	29	37	14	72	249	290
Minnesota North Stars	20	53	7	47	195	303
Kansas City Scouts	12	56	12	36	190	351

PLAYOFFS

Preliminaries: Buffalo 2, St. Louis 1; N.Y. Islanders 2, Vancouver 0; Los Angeles 2, Atlanta 0; Toronto 2, Pittsburgh 1. **Quarterfinals:** Montreal 4, Chicago 0; Philadelphia 4, Toronto 3; Boston 4, Los Angeles 3; N.Y. Islanders 4, Buffalo 2. **Semifinals:** Montreal 4, N.Y. Islanders 1; Philadelphia 4, Boston 1.

Stanley Cup finals: Montreal 4, Philadelphia 0.

1976-77

PRINCE OF WALES CONFERENCE

ADAMS DIVISION

Team	W	L	T	Pts.	GF	GA
Boston Bruins	49	23	8	106	312	240
Buffalo Sabres	48	24	8	104	301	220
Toronto Maple Leafs	33	32	15	81	301	285
Cleveland Barons	25	42	13	63	240	292

NORRIS DIVISION

Team	W	L	T	Pts.	GF	GA
Montreal Canadiens	60	8	12	132	387	171
Los Angeles Kings	34	31	15	83	271	241
Pittsburgh Penguins	34	33	13	81	240	252
Washington Capitals	24	42	14	62	221	307
Detroit Red Wings	16	55	9	41	183	309

CLARENCE CAMPBELL CONFERENCE

PATRICK DIVISION

Team	W	L	T	Pts.	GF	GA
Philadelphia Flyers	48	16	16	112	323	213
New York Islanders	47	21	12	106	288	193
Atlanta Flames	34	34	12	80	264	265
New York Rangers	29	37	14	72	272	310

SMYTHE DIVISION

Team	W	L	T	Pts.	GF	GA
St. Louis Blues	32	39	9	73	239	276
Minnesota North Stars	23	39	18	64	240	310
Chicago Blackhawks	26	43	11	63	240	298
Vancouver Canucks	25	42	13	63	235	294
Colorado Rockies	20	46	14	54	226	307

PLAYOFFS

Preliminaries: N.Y. Islanders 2, Chicago 0; Buffalo 2, Minnesota 0; Los Angeles 2, Atlanta 1; Toronto 2, Pittsburgh 1. **Quarterfinals:** Montreal 4, St. Louis 0; Philadelphia 4, Toronto 2; Boston 4, Los Angeles 2; N.Y. Islanders 4, Buffalo 0. **Semifinals:** Montreal 4, N.Y. Islanders 2; Boston 4, Philadelphia 0.

Stanley Cup finals: Montreal 4, Boston 0.

1977-78

PRINCE OF WALES CONFERENCE

ADAMS DIVISION

Team	W	L	T	Pts.	GF	GA
Boston Bruins	51	18	11	113	333	218
Buffalo Sabres	44	19	17	105	288	215
Toronto Maple Leafs	41	29	10	92	271	237
Cleveland Barons	22	45	13	57	230	325

NORRIS DIVISION

Team	W	L	T	Pts.	GF	GA
Montreal Canadiens	59	10	11	129	359	183
Detroit Red Wings	32	34	14	78	252	266
Los Angeles Kings	31	34	15	77	243	245
Pittsburgh Penguins	25	37	18	68	254	321
Washington Capitals	17	49	14	48	195	321

CLARENCE CAMPBELL CONFERENCE

PATRICK DIVISION

Team	W	L	T	Pts.	GF	GA
New York Islanders	48	17	15	111	334	210
Philadelphia Flyers	45	20	15	105	296	200
Atlanta Flames	34	27	19	87	274	252
New York Rangers	30	37	13	73	279	280

SMYTHE DIVISION

Team	W	L	T	Pts.	GF	GA
Chicago Blackhawks	32	29	19	83	230	220
Colorado Rockies	19	40	21	59	257	305
Vancouver Canucks	20	43	17	57	239	320
St. Louis Blues	20	47	13	53	195	304
Minnesota North Stars	18	53	9	45	218	325

PLAYOFFS

Preliminaries: Philadelphia 2, Colorado 0; Buffalo 2, N.Y. Rangers 1; Toronto 2, Los Angeles 0; Detroit 2, Atlanta 0. **Quarterfinals:** Montreal 4, Detroit 1; Boston 4, Chicago 0; Toronto 4, N.Y. Islanders 3; Philadelphia 4, Buffalo 1. **Semifinals:** Montreal 4, Toronto 0; Boston 4, Philadelphia 1.

Stanley Cup finals: Montreal 4, Boston 2.

1978-79

PRINCE OF WALES CONFERENCE

ADAMS DIVISION

Team	W	L	T	Pts.	GF	GA
Boston Bruins	43	23	14	100	316	270
Buffalo Sabres	36	28	16	88	280	263
Toronto Maple Leafs	34	33	13	81	267	252
Minnesota North Stars	28	40	12	68	257	289

NORRIS DIVISION

Team	W	L	T	Pts.	GF	GA
Montreal Canadiens	52	17	11	115	337	204
Pittsburgh Penguins	36	31	13	85	281	279
Los Angeles Kings	34	34	12	80	292	286
Washington Capitals	24	41	15	63	273	338
Detroit Red Wings	23	41	16	62	252	295

CLARENCE CAMPBELL CONFERENCE

PATRICK DIVISION

Team	W	L	T	Pts.	GF	GA
New York Islanders	51	15	14	116	358	214
Philadelphia Flyers	40	25	15	95	281	248
New York Rangers	40	29	11	91	316	292
Atlanta Flames	41	31	8	90	327	280

SMYTHE DIVISION

Team	W	L	T	Pts.	GF	GA
Chicago Blackhawks	29	36	15	73	244	277
Vancouver Canucks	25	42	13	63	217	291
St. Louis Blues	18	50	12	48	249	348
Colorado Rockies	15	53	12	42	210	331

PLAYOFFS

Preliminaries: Philadelphia 2, Vancouver 1; N.Y. Rangers 2, Los Angeles 0; Toronto 2, Atlanta 0; Pittsburgh 2, Buffalo 1. **Quarterfinals:** N.Y. Islanders 4, Chicago 0; Montreal 4, Toronto 0; Boston 4, Pittsburgh 0; N.Y. Rangers 4, Philadelphia 1. **Semifinals:** N.Y. Rangers 4, N.Y. Islanders 2; Montreal 4, Boston 3.

Stanley Cup finals: Montreal 4, N.Y. Rangers 1.

1979-80

PRINCE OF WALES CONFERENCE

ADAMS DIVISION

Team	W	L	T	Pts.	GF	GA
Buffalo Sabres	47	17	16	110	318	201
Boston Bruins	46	21	13	105	310	234
Minnesota North Stars	36	28	16	88	311	253
Toronto Maple Leafs	35	40	5	75	304	327
Quebec Nordiques	25	44	11	61	248	313

NORRIS DIVISION

Team	W	L	T	Pts.	GF	GA
Montreal Canadiens	47	20	13	107	328	240
Los Angeles Kings	30	36	14	74	290	313
Pittsburgh Penguins	30	37	13	73	251	303
Hartford Whalers	27	34	19	73	303	312
Detroit Red Wings	26	43	11	63	268	306

CLARENCE CAMPBELL CONFERENCE

PATRICK DIVISION

Team	W	L	T	Pts.	GF	GA
Philadelphia Flyers	48	12	20	116	327	254
New York Islanders	39	28	13	91	281	247

Team	W	L	T	Pts.	GF	GA
New York Rangers	38	32	10	86	308	284
Atlanta Flames	35	32	13	83	282	269
Washington Capitals	27	40	13	67	261	293

SMYTHE DIVISION

Team	W	L	T	Pts.	GF	GA
Chicago Blackhawks	34	27	19	87	241	250
St. Louis Blues	34	34	12	80	266	278
Vancouver Canucks	27	37	16	70	256	281
Edmonton Oilers	28	39	13	69	301	322
Winnipeg Jets	20	49	11	51	214	314
Colorado Rockies	19	48	13	51	234	308

PLAYOFFS

Preliminaries: Philadelphia 3, Edmonton 0; Buffalo 3, Vancouver 1; Montreal 3, Hartford 0; Boston 3, Pittsburgh 2; N.Y. Islanders 3, Los Angeles 1; Minnesota 3, Toronto 0; Chicago 3, St. Louis 0; N.Y. Rangers 3, Atlanta 1. **Quarterfinals:** Philadelphia 4, N.Y. Rangers 1; Buffalo 4, Chicago 0; Minnesota 4, Montreal 3; N.Y. Islanders 4, Boston 1. **Semifinals:** Philadelphia 4, Minnesota 1; N.Y. Islanders 4, Buffalo 2.

Stanley Cup finals: N.Y. Islanders 4, Philadelphia 2.

1980-81

PRINCE OF WALES CONFERENCE

ADAMS DIVISION

Team	W	L	T	Pts.	GF	GA
Buffalo Sabres	39	20	21	99	327	250
Boston Bruins	37	30	13	87	316	272
Minnesota North Stars	35	28	17	87	291	263
Quebec Nordiques	30	32	18	78	314	318
Toronto Maple Leafs	28	37	15	71	322	367

NORRIS DIVISION

Team	W	L	T	Pts.	GF	GA
Montreal Canadiens	45	22	13	103	332	232
Los Angeles Kings	43	24	13	99	337	290
Pittsburgh Penguins	30	37	13	73	302	345
Hartford Whalers	21	41	18	60	292	372
Detroit Red Wings	19	43	18	56	252	339

CLARENCE CAMPBELL CONFERENCE

PATRICK DIVISION

Team	W	L	T	Pts.	GF	GA
New York Islanders	48	18	14	110	355	260
Philadelphia Flyers	41	24	15	97	313	249
Calgary Flames	39	27	14	92	329	298
New York Rangers	30	36	14	74	312	317
Washington Capitals	26	36	18	70	286	317

SMYTHE DIVISION

Team	W	L	T	Pts.	GF	GA
St. Louis Blues	45	18	17	107	352	281
Chicago Blackhawks	31	33	16	78	304	315
Vancouver Canucks	28	32	20	76	289	301
Edmonton Oilers	29	35	16	74	328	327
Colorado Rockies	22	45	13	57	258	344
Winnipeg Jets	9	57	14	32	246	400

PLAYOFFS

Preliminaries: N.Y. Islanders 3, Toronto 0; St. Louis 3, Pittsburgh 2; Edmonton 3, Montreal 0; N.Y. Rangers 3, Los Angeles 1; Buffalo 3, Vancouver 0; Philadelphia 3, Quebec 2; Calgary 3, Chicago 0; Minnesota 3, Boston 0. **Quarterfinals:** N.Y. Islanders 4, Edmonton 2; N.Y. Rangers 4, St. Louis 2; Minnesota 4, Buffalo 1; Calgary 4, Philadelphia 3. **Semifinals:** N.Y. Islanders 4, N.Y. Rangers 0; Minnesota 4, Calgary 2.

Stanley Cup finals: N.Y. Islanders 4, Minnesota 1.

1981-82

PRINCE OF WALES CONFERENCE

ADAMS DIVISION

Team	W	L	T	Pts.	GF	GA
Montreal Canadiens	46	17	17	109	360	223
Boston Bruins	43	27	10	96	323	285
Buffalo Sabres	39	26	15	93	307	273
Quebec Nordiques	33	31	16	82	356	345
Hartford Whalers	21	41	18	60	264	351

PATRICK DIVISION

Team	W	L	T	Pts.	GF	GA
New York Islanders	54	16	10	118	385	250
New York Rangers	39	27	14	92	316	306
Philadelphia Flyers	38	31	11	87	325	313
Pittsburgh Penguins	31	36	13	75	310	337
Washington Capitals	26	41	13	65	319	338

CLARENCE CAMPBELL CONFERENCE

NORRIS DIVISION

Team	W	L	T	Pts.	GF	GA
Minnesota North Stars	37	23	20	94	346	288
Winnipeg Jets	33	33	14	80	319	332
St. Louis Blues	32	40	8	72	315	349
Chicago Blackhawks	30	38	12	72	332	363
Toronto Maple Leafs	20	44	16	56	298	380
Detroit Red Wings	21	47	12	54	270	351

SMYTHE DIVISION

Team	W	L	T	Pts.	GF	GA
Edmonton Oilers	48	17	15	111	417	295
Vancouver Canucks	30	33	17	77	290	286
Calgary Flames	29	34	17	75	334	345
Los Angeles Kings	24	41	15	63	314	369
Colorado Rockies	18	49	13	49	241	362

PLAYOFFS

Wales Conference division semifinals: Quebec 3, Montreal 2; Boston 3, Buffalo 1; N.Y. Islanders 3, Pittsburgh 2; N.Y. Rangers 3, Philadelphia 1. **Division finals:** Quebec 4, Boston 3; N.Y. Islanders 4, N.Y. Rangers 2. **Conference finals:** N.Y. Islanders 4, Quebec 0.

Campbell Conference division semifinals: Chicago 3, Minnesota 1; St. Louis 3, Winnipeg 1; Los Angeles 3, Edmonton 2; Vancouver 3, Calgary 0. **Division finals:** Chicago 4, St. Louis 2; Vancouver 4, Los Angeles 1. **Conference finals:** Vancouver 4, Chicago 1.

Stanley Cup finals: N.Y. Islanders 4, Vancouver 0.

1982-83

PRINCE OF WALES CONFERENCE

ADAMS DIVISION

Team	W	L	T	Pts.	GF	GA
Boston Bruins	50	20	10	110	327	228
Montreal Canadiens	42	24	14	98	350	286
Buffalo Sabres	38	29	13	89	318	285
Quebec Nordiques	34	34	12	80	343	336
Hartford Whalers	19	54	7	45	261	403

PATRICK DIVISION

Team	W	L	T	Pts.	GF	GA
Philadelphia Flyers	49	23	8	106	326	240
New York Islanders	42	26	12	96	302	226
Washington Capitals	39	25	16	94	306	283
New York Rangers	35	35	10	80	306	287
New Jersey Devils	17	49	14	48	230	338
Pittsburgh Penguins	18	53	9	45	257	394

CLARENCE CAMPBELL CONFERENCE

NORRIS DIVISION

Team	W	L	T	Pts.	GF	GA
Chicago Blackhawks	47	23	10	104	338	268
Minnesota North Stars	40	24	16	96	321	290
Toronto Maple Leafs	28	40	12	68	293	330
St. Louis Blues	25	40	15	65	285	316
Detroit Red Wings	21	44	15	57	263	344

SMYTHE DIVISION

Team	W	L	T	Pts.	GF	GA
Edmonton Oilers	47	21	12	106	424	315
Calgary Flames	32	34	14	78	321	317
Vancouver Canucks	30	35	15	75	303	309
Winnipeg Jets	33	39	8	74	311	333
Los Angeles Kings	27	41	12	66	308	365

PLAYOFFS

Wales Conference division semifinals: Boston 3, Quebec 1; Buffalo 3, Montreal 0; N.Y. Rangers 3, Philadelphia 0; N.Y. Islanders 3, Washington 1. **Division finals:** Boston 4, Buffalo 3; N.Y. Islanders 4, N.Y. Rangers 2. **Conference finals:** N.Y. Islanders 4, Boston 2.

Campbell Conference division semifinals: Chicago 3, St. Louis 1; Minnesota 3, Toronto 1; Edmonton 3, Winnipeg 0; Calgary 3, Vancouver 1. **Division finals:** Chicago 4, Minnesota 1; Edmonton 4, Calgary 1. **Conference finals:** Edmonton 4, Chicago 0.

Stanley Cup finals: N.Y. Islanders 4, Edmonton 0.

1983-84

PRINCE OF WALES CONFERENCE

ADAMS DIVISION

Team	W	L	T	Pts.	GF	GA
Boston Bruins	49	25	6	104	336	261
Buffalo Sabres	48	25	7	103	315	257
Quebec Nordiques	42	28	10	94	360	278
Montreal Canadiens	35	40	5	75	286	295
Hartford Whalers	28	42	10	66	288	320

PATRICK DIVISION

Team	W	L	T	Pts.	GF	GA
New York Islanders	50	26	4	104	357	269
Washington Capitals	48	27	5	101	308	226
Philadelphia Flyers	44	26	10	98	350	290
New York Rangers	42	29	9	93	314	304
New Jersey Devils	17	56	7	41	231	350
Pittsburgh Penguins	16	58	6	38	254	390

CLARENCE CAMPBELL CONFERENCE

NORRIS DIVISION

Team	W	L	T	Pts.	GF	GA
Minnesota North Stars	39	31	10	88	345	344
St. Louis Blues	32	41	7	71	293	316
Detroit Red Wings	31	42	7	69	298	323
Chicago Blackhawks	30	42	8	68	277	311
Toronto Maple Leafs	26	45	9	61	303	387

SMYTHE DIVISION

Team	W	L	T	Pts.	GF	GA
Edmonton Oilers	57	18	5	119	446	314
Calgary Flames	34	32	14	82	311	314
Vancouver Canucks	32	39	9	73	306	328
Winnipeg Jets	31	38	11	73	340	374
Los Angeles Kings	23	44	13	59	309	376

PLAYOFFS

Wales Conference division semifinals: Montreal 3, Boston 0; Quebec 3, Buffalo 0; N.Y. Islanders 3, N.Y. Rangers 2; Washington 3, Philadelphia 0. **Division finals:** Montreal 4, Quebec 2; N.Y. Islanders 4, Washington 1. **Conference finals:** N.Y. Islanders 4, Montreal 2.

Campbell Conference division semifinals: Minnesota 3, Chicago 2; St. Louis 3, Detroit 1; Edmonton 3, Winnipeg 0; Calgary 3, Vancouver 1. **Division finals:** Minnesota 4, St. Louis 3; Edmonton 4, Calgary 3. **Conference finals:** Edmonton 4, Minnesota 0.

Stanley Cup finals: Edmonton 4, N.Y. Islanders 1.

1984-85

PRINCE OF WALES CONFERENCE

ADAMS DIVISION

Team	W	L	T	Pts.	GF	GA
Montreal Canadiens	41	27	12	94	309	262
Quebec Nordiques	41	30	9	91	323	275
Buffalo Sabres	38	28	14	90	290	237
Boston Bruins	36	34	10	82	303	287
Hartford Whalers	30	41	9	69	268	318

PATRICK DIVISION

Team	W	L	T	Pts.	GF	GA
Philadelphia Flyers	53	20	7	113	348	241
Washington Capitals	46	25	9	101	322	240
New York Islanders	40	34	6	86	345	312
New York Rangers	26	44	10	62	295	345
New Jersey Devils	22	48	10	54	264	346
Pittsburgh Penguins	24	51	5	53	276	385

CLARENCE CAMPBELL CONFERENCE

NORRIS DIVISION

Team	W	L	T	Pts.	GF	GA
St. Louis Blues	37	31	12	86	299	288
Chicago Blackhawks	38	35	7	83	309	299
Detroit Red Wings	27	41	12	66	313	357
Minnesota North Stars	25	43	12	62	268	321
Toronto Maple Leafs	20	52	8	48	253	358

SMYTHE DIVISION

Team	W	L	T	Pts.	GF	GA
Edmonton Oilers	49	20	11	109	401	298
Winnipeg Jets	43	27	10	96	358	332
Calgary Flames	41	27	12	94	363	302
Los Angeles Kings	34	32	14	82	339	326
Vancouver Canucks	25	46	9	59	284	401

PLAYOFFS

Wales Conference division semifinals: Montreal 3, Boston 2; Quebec 3, Buffalo 2; Philadelphia 3, N.Y. Rangers 0; N.Y. Islanders 3, Washington 2. **Division finals:** Quebec 4, Montreal 3; Philadelphia 4, N.Y. Islanders 1. **Conference finals:** Philadelphia 4, Quebec 2.

Campbell Conference division semifinals: Minnesota 3, St. Louis 0; Chicago 3, Detroit 0; Edmonton 3, Los Angelse 0; Winnipeg 3, Calgary 1. **Division finals:** Chicago 4, Minnesota 2; Edmonton 4, Winnipeg 0. **Conference finals:** Edmonton 4, Chicago 2.

Stanley Cup finals: Edmonton 4, Philadelphia 1.

1985-86

PRINCE OF WALES CONFERENCE

ADAMS DIVISION

Team	W	L	T	Pts.	GF	GA
Quebec Nordiques	43	31	6	92	330	289
Montreal Canadiens	40	33	7	87	330	280
Boston Bruins	37	31	12	86	311	288
Hartford Whalers	40	36	4	84	332	302
Buffalo Sabres	37	37	6	80	296	291

PATRICK DIVISION

Team	W	L	T	Pts.	GF	GA
Philadelphia Flyers	53	23	4	110	335	241
Washington Capitals	50	23	7	107	315	272
New York Islanders	39	29	12	90	327	284
New York Rangers	36	38	6	78	280	276
Pittsburgh Penguins	34	38	8	76	313	305
New Jersey Devils	28	49	3	59	300	374

CLARENCE CAMPBELL CONFERENCE

NORRIS DIVISION

Team	W	L	T	Pts.	GF	GA
Chicago Blackhawks	39	33	8	86	351	349
Minnesota North Stars	38	33	9	85	327	305
St. Louis Blues	37	34	9	83	302	291
Toronto Maple Leafs	25	48	7	57	311	386
Detroit Red Wings	17	57	6	40	266	415

SMYTHE DIVISION

Team	W	L	T	Pts.	GF	GA
Edmonton Oilers	56	17	7	119	426	310
Calgary Flames	40	31	9	89	354	315
Winnipeg Jets	26	47	7	59	295	372
Vancouver Canucks	23	44	13	59	282	333
Los Angeles Kings	23	49	8	54	284	389

PLAYOFFS

Wales Conference division semifinals: Hartford 3, Quebec 0; Montreal 3, Boston 0; N.Y. Rangers 3, Philadelphia 2; Washington 3, N.Y. Islanders 0. **Division finals:** Montreal 4, Hartford 3; N.Y. Rangers 4, Washington 2. **Conference finals:** Montreal 4, N.Y. Rangers 1.

Campbell Conference division semifinals: Toronto 3, Chicago 0; St. Louis 3, Minnesota 2; Edmonton 3, Vancouver 0; Calgary 3, Winnipeg 0. **Division finals:** St. Louis 4, Toronto 3; Calgary 4, Edmonton 3. **Conference finals:** Calgary 4, St. Louis 3.

Stanley Cup finals: Montreal 4, Calgary 1.

1986-87

PRINCE OF WALES CONFERENCE

ADAMS DIVISION

Team	W	L	T	Pts.	GF	GA
Hartford Whalers	43	30	7	93	287	270
Montreal Canadiens	41	29	10	92	277	241
Boston Bruins	39	34	7	85	301	276
Quebec Nordiques	31	39	10	72	267	276
Buffalo Sabres	28	44	8	64	280	308

PATRICK DIVISION

Team	W	L	T	Pts.	GF	GA
Philadelphia Flyers	46	26	8	100	310	245
Washington Capitals	38	32	10	86	285	278
New York Islanders	35	33	12	82	279	281
New York Rangers	34	38	8	76	307	323
Pittsburgh Penguins	30	38	12	72	297	290
New Jersey Devils	29	45	6	64	293	368

CLARENCE CAMPBELL CONFERENCE

NORRIS DIVISION

Team	W	L	T	Pts.	GF	GA
St. Louis Blues	32	33	15	79	281	293
Detroit Red Wings	34	36	10	78	260	274
Chicago Blackhawks	29	37	14	72	290	310
Toronto Maple Leafs	32	42	6	70	286	319
Minnesota North Stars	30	40	10	70	296	314

SMYTHE DIVISION

Team	W	L	T	Pts.	GF	GA
Edmonton Oilers	50	24	6	106	372	284
Calgary Flames	46	31	3	95	318	289
Winnipeg Jets	40	32	8	88	279	271
Los Angeles Kings	31	41	8	70	318	341
Vancouver Canucks	29	43	8	66	282	314

PLAYOFFS

Wales Conference division semifinals: Quebec 4, Hartford 2; Montreal 4, Boston 0; Philadelphia 4, N.Y. Rangers 2; N.Y. Islanders 4, Washington 3. **Division finals:** Montreal 4, Quebec 3; Philadelphia 4, N.Y. Islanders 3. **Conference finals:** Philadelphia 4, Montreal 2.

Campbell Conference division semifinals: Toronto 4, St. Louis 2; Detroit 4, Chicago 0; Edmonton 4, Los Angeles 1; Winnipeg 4, Calgary 2. **Division finals:** Detroit 4, Toronto 3; Edmonton 4, Winnipeg 0. **Conference finals:** Edmonton 4, Detroit 1.

Stanley Cup finals: Edmonton 4, Philadelphia 3.

1987-88

PRINCE OF WALES CONFERENCE

ADAMS DIVISION

Team	W	L	T	Pts.	GF	GA
Montreal Canadiens	45	22	13	103	298	238
Boston Bruins	44	30	6	94	300	251
Buffalo Sabres	37	32	11	85	283	305
Hartford Whalers	35	38	7	77	249	267
Quebec Nordiques	32	43	5	69	271	306

PATRICK DIVISION

Team	W	L	T	Pts.	GF	GA
New York Islanders	39	31	10	88	308	267
Philadelphia Flyers	38	33	9	85	292	292
Washington Capitals	38	33	9	85	281	249
New Jersey Devils	38	36	6	82	295	296
New York Rangers	36	34	10	82	300	283
Pittsburgh Penguins	36	35	9	81	319	316

CLARENCE CAMPBELL CONFERENCE

NORRIS DIVISION

Team	W	L	T	Pts.	GF	GA
Detroit Red Wings	41	28	11	93	322	269
St. Louis Blues	34	38	8	76	278	294
Chicago Blackhawks	30	41	9	69	284	328
Toronto Maple Leafs	21	49	10	52	273	345
Minnesota North Stars	19	48	13	51	242	349

SMYTHE DIVISION

Team	W	L	T	Pts.	GF	GA
Calgary Flames	48	23	9	105	397	305
Edmonton Oilers	44	25	11	99	363	288
Winnipeg Jets	33	36	11	77	292	310
Los Angeles Kings	30	42	8	68	318	359
Vancouver Canucks	25	46	9	59	272	320

PLAYOFFS

Wales Conference division semifinals: Montreal 4, Hartford 2; Boston 4, Buffalo 2; New Jersey 4, N.Y. Islanders 2; Washington 4, Philadelphia 3. **Division finals:** Boston 4, Montreal 1; New Jersey 4, Washington 3. **Conference finals:** Boston 4, New Jersey 3.

Campbell Conference division semifinals: Detroit 4, Toronto 2; St. Louis 4, Chicago 1; Calgary 4, Los Angeles 1; Edmonton 4, Winnipeg 1. **Division finals:** Detroit 4, St. Louis 1; Edmonton 4, Calgary 0. **Conference finals:** Edmonton 4, Detroit 1.

Stanley Cup finals: Edmonton 4, Boston 0.

1988-89

PRINCE OF WALES CONFERENCE

ADAMS DIVISION

Team	W	L	T	Pts.	GF	GA
Montreal Canadiens	53	18	9	115	315	218
Boston Bruins	37	29	14	88	289	256
Buffalo Sabres	38	35	7	83	291	299
Hartford Whalers	37	38	5	79	299	290
Quebec Nordiques	27	46	7	61	269	342

PATRICK DIVISION

Team	W	L	T	Pts.	GF	GA
Washington Capitals	41	29	10	92	305	259
Pittsburgh Penguins	40	33	7	87	347	349
New York Rangers	37	35	8	82	310	307
Philadelphia Flyers	36	36	8	80	307	285
New Jersey Devils	27	41	12	66	281	325
New York Islanders	28	47	5	61	265	325

CLARENCE CAMPBELL CONFERENCE

NORRIS DIVISION

Team	W	L	T	Pts.	GF	GA
Detroit Red Wings	34	34	12	80	313	316
St. Louis Blues	33	35	12	78	275	285
Minnesota North Stars	27	37	16	70	258	278
Chicago Blackhawks	27	41	12	66	297	335
Toronto Maple Leafs	28	46	6	62	259	342

SMYTHE DIVISION

Team	W	L	T	Pts.	GF	GA
Calgary Flames	54	17	9	117	354	226
Los Angeles Kings	42	31	7	91	376	335
Edmonton Oilers	38	34	8	84	325	306
Vancouver Canucks	33	39	8	74	251	253
Winnipeg Jets	26	42	12	64	300	355

PLAYOFFS

Wales Conference division semifinals: Montreal 4, Hartford 0; Boston 4, Buffalo 1; Philadelphia 4, Washington 2; Pittsburgh 4, N.Y. Rangers 0. **Division finals:** Montreal 4, Boston 1; Philadelphia 4, Pittsburgh 3. **Conference finals:** Montreal 4, Philadelphia 2.

Campbell Conference division semifinals: Chicago 4, Detroit 2; St. Louis 4, Minnesota 1; Calgary 4, Vancouver 3; Los Angeles 4, Edmonton 3. **Division finals:** Chicago 4, St. Louis 1; Calgary 4, Los Angeles 0. **Conference finals:** Calgary 4, Chicago 1.

Stanley Cup finals: Calgary 4, Montreal 2.

1989-90

PRINCE OF WALES CONFERENCE

ADAMS DIVISION

Team	W	L	T	Pts.	GF	GA
Boston Bruins	46	25	9	101	289	232
Buffalo Sabres	45	27	8	98	286	248
Montreal Canadiens	41	28	11	93	288	234
Hartford Whalers	38	33	9	85	275	268
Quebec Nordiques	12	61	7	31	240	407

PATRICK DIVISION

Team	W	L	T	Pts.	GF	GA
New York Rangers	36	31	13	85	279	267
New Jersey Devils	37	34	9	83	295	288
Washington Capitals	36	38	6	78	284	275
New York Islanders	31	38	11	73	281	288
Pittsburgh Penguins	32	40	8	72	318	359
Philadelphia Flyers	30	39	11	71	290	297

CLARENCE CAMPBELL CONFERENCE

NORRIS DIVISION

Team	W	L	T	Pts.	GF	GA
Chicago Blackhawks	41	33	6	88	316	294
St. Louis Blues	37	34	9	83	295	279
Toronto Maple Leafs	38	38	4	80	337	358
Minnesota North Stars	36	40	4	76	284	291
Detroit Red Wings	28	38	14	70	288	323

SMYTHE DIVISION

Team	W	L	T	Pts.	GF	GA
Calgary Flames	42	23	15	99	348	265
Edmonton Oilers	38	28	14	90	315	283
Winnipeg Jets	37	32	11	85	298	290
Los Angeles Kings	34	39	7	75	338	337
Vancouver Canucks	25	41	14	64	245	306

PLAYOFFS

Wales Conference division semifinals: Boston 4, Hartford 3; Montreal 4, Buffalo 2; N.Y. Rangers 4, N.Y. Islanders 1; Washington 4, New Jersey 2. **Division finals:** Boston 4, Montreal 1; Washington 4, N.Y. Rangers 1. **Conference finals:** Boston 4, Washington 0.

Campbell Conference division semifinals: Chicago 4, Minnesota 3; St. Louis 4, Toronto 1; Los Angeles 4, Calgary 2; Edmonton 4, Winnipeg 3. **Division finals:** Chicago 4, St. Louis 3; Edmonton 4, Los Angeles 0. **Conference finals:** Edmonton 4, Chicago 2.

Stanley Cup finals: Edmonton 4, Boston 1.

1990-91

PRINCE OF WALES CONFERENCE

ADAMS DIVISION

Team	W	L	T	Pts.	GF	GA
Boston Bruins	44	24	12	100	299	264
Montreal Canadiens	39	30	11	89	273	249
Buffalo Sabres	31	30	19	81	292	278
Hartford Whalers	31	38	11	73	238	276
Quebec Nordiques	16	50	14	46	236	354

PATRICK DIVISION

Team	W	L	T	Pts.	GF	GA
Pittsburgh Penguins	41	33	6	88	342	305
New York Rangers	36	31	13	85	297	265
Washington Capitals	37	36	7	81	258	258
New Jersey Devils	32	33	15	79	272	264
Philadelphia Flyers	33	37	10	76	252	267
New York Islanders	25	45	10	60	223	290

CLARENCE CAMPBELL CONFERENCE

NORRIS DIVISION

Team	W	L	T	Pts.	GF	GA
Chicago Blackhawks	49	23	8	106	284	211
St. Louis Blues	47	22	11	105	310	250
Detroit Red Wings	34	38	8	76	273	298
Minnesota North Stars	27	39	14	68	256	266
Toronto Maple Leafs	23	46	11	57	241	318

SMYTHE DIVISION

Team	W	L	T	Pts.	GF	GA
Los Angeles Kings	46	24	10	102	340	254
Calgary Flames	46	26	8	100	344	263
Edmonton Oilers	37	37	6	80	272	272
Vancouver Canucks	28	43	9	65	243	315
Winnipeg Jets	26	43	11	63	260	288

PLAYOFFS

Wales Conference division semifinals: Boston 4, Hartford 2; Montreal 4, Buffalo 2; Pittsburgh 4, New Jersey 3; Washington

4, N.Y. Rangers 2. **Division finals:** Boston 4, Montreal 3; Pittsburgh 4, Washington 1. **Conference finals:** Pittsburgh 4, Boston 2.

Campbell Conference division semifinals: Minnesota 4, Chicago 2; St. Louis 4, Detroit 3; Los Angeles 4, Vancouver 2; Edmonton 4, Calgary 3. **Division finals:** Minnesota 4, St. Louis 2; Edmonton 4, Los Angeles 2. **Conference finals:** Minnesota 4, Edmonton 1.

Stanley Cup finals: Pittsburgh 4, Minnesota 2.

1991-92

PRINCE OF WALES CONFERENCE

ADAMS DIVISION

Team	W	L	T	Pts.	GF	GA
Montreal Canadiens	41	28	11	93	267	207
Boston Bruins	36	32	12	84	270	275
Buffalo Sabres	31	37	12	74	289	299
Hartford Whalers	26	41	13	65	247	283
Quebec Nordiques	20	48	12	52	255	318

PATRICK DIVISION

Team	W	L	T	Pts.	GF	GA
New York Rangers	50	25	5	105	321	246
Washington Capitals	45	27	8	98	330	275
Pittsburgh Penguins	39	32	9	87	343	308
New Jersey Devils	38	31	11	87	289	259
New York Islanders	34	35	11	79	291	299
Philadelphia Flyers	32	37	11	75	252	273

CLARENCE CAMPBELL CONFERENCE

NORRIS DIVISION

Team	W	L	T	Pts.	GF	GA
Detroit Red Wings	43	25	12	98	320	256
Chicago Blackhawks	36	29	15	87	257	236
St. Louis Blues	36	33	11	83	279	266
Minnesota North Stars	32	42	6	70	246	278
Toronto Maple Leafs	30	43	7	67	234	294

SMYTHE DIVISION

Team	W	L	T	Pts.	GF	GA
Vancouver Canucks	42	26	12	96	285	250
Los Angeles Kings	35	31	14	84	287	296
Edmonton Oilers	36	34	10	82	295	297
Winnipeg Jets	33	32	15	81	251	244
Calgary Flames	31	37	12	74	296	305
San Jose Sharks	17	58	5	39	219	359

PLAYOFFS

Wales Conference division semifinals: Montreal 4, Hartford 3; Boston 4, Buffalo 3; N.Y. Rangers 4, New Jersey 3; Pittsburgh 4, Washington 3. **Division finals:** Boston 4, Montreal 0; Pittsburgh 4, N.Y. Rangers 2. **Conference finals:** Pittsburgh 4, Boston 0.

Campbell Conference division semifinals: Detroit 4, Minnesota 3; Chicago 4, St. Louis 2; Vancouver 4, Winnipeg 3; Edmonton 4, Los Angeles 2. **Division finals:** Chicago 4, Detroit 0; Edmonton 4, Vancouver 2. **Conference finals:** Chicago 4, Edmonton 0.

Stanley Cup finals: Pittsburgh 4, Chicago 0.

1992-93

PRINCE OF WALES CONFERENCE

ADAMS DIVISION

Team	W	L	T	Pts.	GF	GA
Boston Bruins	51	26	7	109	332	268
Quebec Nordiques	47	27	10	104	351	300
Montreal Canadiens	48	30	6	102	326	280
Buffalo Sabres	38	36	10	86	335	297
Hartford Whalers	26	52	6	58	284	369
Ottawa Senators	10	70	4	24	202	395

PATRICK DIVISION

Team	W	L	T	Pts.	GF	GA
Pittsburgh Penguins	56	21	7	119	367	268
Washington Capitals	43	34	7	93	325	286
New York Islanders	40	37	7	87	335	297
New Jersey Devils	40	37	7	87	308	299
Philadelphia Flyers	36	37	11	83	319	319
New York Rangers	34	39	11	79	304	308

CLARENCE CAMPBELL CONFERENCE

NORRIS DIVISION

Team	W	L	T	Pts.	GF	GA
Chicago Blackhawks	47	25	12	106	279	230
Detroit Red Wings	47	28	9	103	369	280
Toronto Maple Leafs	44	29	11	99	288	241
St. Louis Blues	37	36	11	85	282	278
Minnesota North Stars	36	38	10	82	272	293
Tampa Bay Lightning	23	54	7	53	245	332

SMYTHE DIVISION

Team	W	L	T	Pts.	GF	GA
Vancouver Canucks	46	29	9	101	346	278
Calgary Flames	43	30	11	97	322	282
Los Angeles Kings	39	35	10	88	338	340
Winnipeg Jets	40	37	7	87	322	320
Edmonton Oilers	26	50	8	60	242	337
San Jose Sharks	11	71	2	24	218	414

PLAYOFFS

Wales Conference division semifinals: Buffalo 4, Boston 0; Montreal 4, Quebec 2; Pittsburgh 4, New Jersey 1; N.Y. Islanders 4, Washington 2. **Division finals:** Montreal 4, Buffalo 0; N.Y. Islanders 4, Pittsburgh 3. **Conference finals:** Montreal 4, N.Y. Islanders 1.

Campbell Conference division semifinals: St. Louis 4, Chicago 0; Toronto 4, Detroit 3; Vancouver 4, Winnipeg 2; Los Angeles 4, Calgary 2. **Division finals:** Toronto 4, St. Louis 3; Los Angeles 4, Vancouver 2. **Conference finals:** Los Angeles 4, Toronto 3.

Stanley Cup finals: Montreal 4, Los Angeles 1.

1993-94

EASTERN CONFERENCE

ATLANTIC DIVISION

Team	W	L	T	Pts.	GF	GA
New York Rangers	52	24	8	112	299	231
New Jersey Devils	47	25	12	106	306	220
Washington Capitals	39	35	10	88	277	263
New York Islanders	36	36	12	84	282	264
Florida Panthers	33	34	17	83	233	233
Philadelphia Flyers	35	39	10	80	294	314
Tampa Bay Lightning	30	43	11	71	224	251

NORTHEAST DIVISION

Team	W	L	T	Pts.	GF	GA
Pittsburgh Penguins	44	27	13	101	299	285
Boston Bruins	42	29	13	97	289	252
Montreal Canadiens	41	29	14	96	283	248
Buffalo Sabres	43	32	9	95	282	218
Quebec Nordiques	34	42	8	76	277	292
Hartford Whalers	27	48	9	63	227	288
Ottawa Senators	14	61	9	37	201	397

WESTERN CONFERENCE

CENTRAL DIVISION

Team	W	L	T	Pts.	GF	GA
Detroit Red Wings	46	30	8	100	356	275
Toronto Maple Leafs	43	29	12	98	280	243
Dallas Stars	42	29	13	97	286	265
St. Louis Blues	40	33	11	91	270	283
Chicago Blackhawks	39	36	9	87	254	240
Winnipeg Jets	24	51	9	57	245	344

PACIFIC DIVISION

Team	W	L	T	Pts.	GF	GA
Calgary Flames	42	29	13	97	302	256
Vancouver Canucks	41	40	3	85	279	276
San Jose Sharks	33	35	16	82	252	265
Mighty Ducks of Anaheim	33	46	5	71	229	251
Los Angeles Kings	27	45	12	66	294	322
Edmonton Oilers	25	45	14	64	261	305

PLAYOFFS

Eastern Conference quarterfinals: N.Y. Rangers 4, N.Y. Islanders 0; Washington 4, Pittsburgh 2; New Jersey 4, Buffalo 3; Boston 4, Montreal 3. **Semifinals:** N.Y. Rangers 4, Washington 1; New Jersey 4, Boston 2. **Finals:** N.Y. Rangers 4, New Jersey 3.

Western Conference quarterfinals: San Jose 4, Detroit 3; Vancouver 4, Calgary 3; Toronto 4, Chicago 2; Dallas 4, St. Louis 0. **Semifinals:** Toronto 4, San Jose 3; Vancouver 4, Dallas 1. **Finals:** Vancouver 4, Toronto 1.

Stanley Cup finals: N.Y. Rangers 4, Vancouver 3.

1994-95

EASTERN CONFERENCE

ATLANTIC DIVISION

Team	W	L	T	Pts.	GF	GA
Philadelphia Flyers	28	16	4	60	150	132
New Jersey Devils	22	18	8	52	136	121
Washington Capitals	22	18	8	52	136	120
New York Rangers	22	23	3	47	139	134
Florida Panthers	20	22	6	46	115	127
Tampa Bay Lightning	17	28	3	37	120	144
New York Islanders	15	28	5	35	126	158

NORTHEAST DIVISION

Team	W	L	T	Pts.	GF	GA
Quebec Nordiques	30	13	5	65	185	134
Pittsburgh Penguins	29	16	3	61	181	158
Boston Bruins	27	18	3	57	150	127
Buffalo Sabres	22	19	7	51	130	119
Hartford Whalers	19	24	5	43	127	141
Montreal Canadiens	18	23	7	43	125	148
Ottawa Senators	9	34	5	23	117	174

WESTERN CONFERENCE

CENTRAL DIVISION

Team	W	L	T	Pts.	GF	GA
Detroit Red Wings	33	11	4	70	180	117
St. Louis Blues	28	15	5	61	178	135
Chicago Blackhawks	24	19	5	53	156	115
Toronto Maple Leafs	21	19	8	50	135	146
Dallas Stars	17	23	8	42	136	135
Winnipeg Jets	16	25	7	39	157	177

PACIFIC DIVISION

Team	W	L	T	Pts.	GF	GA
Calgary Flames	24	17	7	55	163	135
Vancouver Canucks	18	18	12	48	153	148
San Jose Sharks	19	25	4	42	129	161
Los Angeles Kings	16	23	9	41	142	174
Edmonton Oilers	17	27	4	38	136	183
Mighty Ducks of Anaheim	16	27	5	37	125	164

PLAYOFFS

Eastern Conference quarterfinals: N.Y. Rangers 4, Quebec 2; Pittsburgh 4, Washington 3; Philadelphia 4, Buffalo 1; New Jersey 4, Boston 1. **Semifinals:** New Jersey 4, Pittsburgh 1; Philadelphia 4, N.Y. Rangers 0. **Finals:** New Jersey 4, Philadelphia 2.

Western Conference quarterfinals: Detroit 4, Dallas 1; Vancouver 4, St. Louis 3; Chicago 4, Toronto 3; San Jose 4, Calgary 3. **Semifinals:** Detroit 4, San Jose 0; Chicago 4, Vancouver 0. **Finals:** Detroit 4, Chicago 1.

Stanley Cup finals: New Jersey 4, Detroit 0.

1995-96

EASTERN CONFERENCE

ATLANTIC DIVISION

Team	W	L	T	Pts.	GF	GA
Philadelphia Flyers	45	24	13	103	282	208
New York Rangers	41	27	14	96	272	237
Florida Panthers	41	31	10	92	254	234
Washington Capitals	39	32	11	89	234	204
Tampa Bay Lightning	38	32	12	88	238	248
New Jersey Devils	37	33	12	86	215	202
New York Islanders	22	50	10	54	229	315

NORTHEAST DIVISION

Team	W	L	T	Pts.	GF	GA
Pittsburgh Penguins	49	29	4	102	362	284
Boston Bruins	40	31	11	91	282	269
Montreal Canadiens	40	32	10	90	265	248
Hartford Whalers	34	39	9	77	237	259
Buffalo Sabres	33	42	7	73	247	262
Ottawa Senators	18	59	5	41	191	291

WESTERN CONFERENCE

CENTRAL DIVISION

Team	W	L	T	Pts.	GF	GA
Detroit Red Wings	62	13	7	131	325	181
Chicago Blackhawks	40	28	14	94	273	220
Toronto Maple Leafs	34	36	12	80	247	252
St. Louis Blues	32	34	16	80	219	248
Winnipeg Jets	36	40	6	78	275	291
Dallas Stars	26	42	14	66	227	280

PACIFIC DIVISION

Team	W	L	T	Pts.	GF	GA
Colorado Avalanche	47	25	10	104	326	240
Calgary Flames	34	37	11	79	241	240
Vancouver Canucks	32	35	15	79	278	278
Mighty Ducks of Anaheim	35	39	8	78	234	247
Edmonton Oilers	30	44	8	68	240	304
Los Angeles Kings	24	40	18	66	256	302
San Jose Sharks	20	55	7	47	252	357

PLAYOFFS

Eastern Conference quarterfinals: Philadelphia 4, Tampa Bay 2; Pittsburgh 4, Washington 2; N.Y. Rangers 4, Montreal 2; Florida 4, Boston 1. **Semifinals:** Florida 4, Philadelphia 2; Pittsburgh 4, N.Y. Rangers 1. **Finals:** Florida 4, Pittsburgh 3.

Western Conference quarterfinals: Detroit 4, Winnipeg 2; Colorado 4, Vancouver 2; Chicago 4, Calgary 0; St. Louis 4, Toronto 2. **Semifinals:** Detroit 4, St. Louis 3; Colorado 4, Chicago 2. **Finals:** Colorado 4, Detroit 2.

Stanley Cup finals: Colorado 4, Florida 0.

1996-97

EASTERN CONFERENCE

ATLANTIC DIVISION

Team	W	L	T	Pts.	GF	GA
New Jersey Devils	45	23	14	104	231	182
Philadelphia Flyers	45	24	13	103	274	217
Florida Panthers	35	28	19	89	221	201
New York Rangers	38	34	10	86	258	231
Washington Capitals	33	40	9	75	214	231
Tampa Bay Lightning	32	40	10	74	217	247
New York Islanders	29	41	12	70	240	250

NORTHEAST DIVISION

Team	W	L	T	Pts.	GF	GA
Buffalo Sabres	40	30	12	92	237	208
Pittsburgh Penguins	38	36	8	84	285	280
Ottawa Senators	31	36	15	77	226	234
Montreal Canadiens	31	36	15	77	249	276
Hartford Whalers	32	39	11	75	226	256
Boston Bruins	26	47	9	61	234	300

WESTERN CONFERENCE

CENTRAL DIVISION

Team	W	L	T	Pts.	GF	GA
Dallas Stars	48	26	8	104	252	198
Detroit Red Wings	38	26	18	94	253	197
Phoenix Coyotes	38	37	7	83	240	243
St. Louis Blues	36	35	11	83	236	239
Chicago Blackhawks	34	35	13	81	223	210
Toronto Maple Leafs	30	44	8	68	230	273

PACIFIC DIVISION

Team	W	L	T	Pts.	GF	GA
Colorado Avalanche	49	24	9	107	277	205
Mighty Ducks of Anaheim	36	33	13	85	245	233
Edmonton Oilers	36	37	9	81	252	247
Vancouver Canucks	35	40	7	77	257	273
Calgary Flames	32	41	9	73	214	239
Los Angeles Kings	28	43	11	67	214	268
San Jose Sharks	27	47	8	62	211	278

PLAYOFFS

Eastern Conference quarterfinals: New Jersey 4, Montreal 1; Buffalo 4, Ottawa 3; Philadelphia 4, Pittsburgh 1; N.Y. Rangers 4, Florida 1. **Semifinals:** N.Y. Rangers 4, New Jersey 1; Philadelphia 4, Buffalo 1. **Finals:** Philadelphia 4, N.Y. Rangers 1.

Western Conference quarterfinals: Colorado 4, Chicago 2; Edmonton 4, Dallas 3; Detroit 4, St. Louis 2; Anaheim 4, Phoenix 3. **Semifinals:** Colorado 4, Edmonton 1; Detroit 4, Anaheim 0. **Finals:** Detroit 4, Colorado 2.

Stanley Cup finals: Detroit 4, Philadelphia 0.

1997-98

EASTERN CONFERENCE

ATLANTIC DIVISION

Team	W	L	T	Pts.	GF	GA
New Jersey Devils	48	23	11	107	225	166
Philadelphia Flyers	42	29	11	95	242	193
Washington Capitals	40	30	12	92	219	202
New York Islanders	30	41	11	71	212	225
New York Rangers	25	39	18	68	197	231
Florida Panthers	24	43	15	63	203	256
Tampa Bay Lightning	17	55	10	44	151	269

NORTHEAST DIVISION

Team	W	L	T	Pts.	GF	GA
Pittsburgh Penguins	40	24	18	98	228	188
Boston Bruins	39	30	13	91	221	194
Buffalo Sabres	36	29	17	89	211	187
Montreal Canadiens	37	32	13	87	235	208
Ottawa Senators	34	33	15	83	193	200
Carolina Hurricanes	33	41	8	74	200	219

WESTERN CONFERENCE

CENTRAL DIVISION

Team	W	L	T	Pts.	GF	GA
Dallas Stars	49	22	11	109	242	167
Detroit Red Wings	44	23	15	103	250	196
St. Louis Blues	45	29	8	98	256	204
Phoenix Coyotes	35	35	12	82	224	227
Chicago Blackhawks	30	39	13	73	192	199
Toronto Maple Leafs	30	43	9	69	194	237

PACIFIC DIVISION

Team	W	L	T	Pts.	GF	GA
Colorado Avalanche	39	26	17	95	231	205
Los Angeles Kings	38	33	11	87	227	225
Edmonton Oilers	35	37	10	80	215	224
San Jose Sharks	34	38	10	78	210	216
Calgary Flames	26	41	15	67	217	252
Mighty Ducks of Anaheim	26	43	13	65	205	261
Vancouver Canucks	25	43	14	64	224	273

PLAYOFFS

Eastern Conference quarterfinals: Ottawa 4, New Jersey 2; Washington 4, Boston 2; Buffalo 4, Philadelphia 1; Montreal 4, Pittsburgh 2. **Semifinals:** Washington 4, Ottawa 1; Buffalo 4, Montreal 0. **Finals:** Washington 4, Buffalo 2.

Western Conference quarterfinals: Edmonton 4, Colorado 3; Dallas 4, San Jose 2; Detroit 4, Phoenix 2; St. Louis 4, Los Angeles 0. **Semifinals:** Dallas 4, Edmonton 1; Detroit 4, St. Louis 2. **Finals:** Detroit 4, Dallas 2.

Stanley Cup finals: Detroit 4, Washington 0.

1998-99

EASTERN CONFERENCE

ATLANTIC DIVISION

Team	W	L	T	Pts.	GF	GA
New Jersey Devils	47	24	11	105	248	196
Philadelphia Flyers	37	26	19	93	231	196
Pittsburgh Penguins	38	30	14	90	242	225
New York Rangers	33	38	11	77	217	227
New York Islanders	24	48	10	58	194	244

NORTHEAST DIVISION

Team	W	L	T	Pts.	GF	GA
Ottawa Senators	44	23	15	103	239	179
Toronto Maple Leafs	45	30	7	97	268	231
Boston Bruins	39	30	13	91	214	181
Buffalo Sabres	37	28	17	91	207	175
Montreal Canadiens	32	39	11	75	184	209

SOUTHEAST DIVISION

Team	W	L	T	Pts.	GF	GA
Carolina Hurricanes	34	30	18	86	210	202
Florida Panthers	30	34	18	78	210	228
Washington Capitals	31	45	6	68	200	218
Tampa Bay Lightning	19	54	9	47	179	292

WESTERN CONFERENCE

CENTRAL DIVISION

Team	W	L	T	Pts.	GF	GA
Detroit Red Wings	43	32	7	93	245	202
St. Louis Blues	37	32	13	87	237	209
Chicago Blackhawks	29	41	12	70	202	248
Nashville Predators	28	47	7	63	190	261

PACIFIC DIVISION

Team	W	L	T	Pts.	GF	GA
Dallas Stars	51	19	12	114	236	168
Phoenix Coyotes	39	31	12	90	205	197
Anaheim Mighty Ducks	35	34	13	83	215	206
San Jose Sharks	31	33	18	80	196	191
Los Angeles Kings	32	45	5	69	189	222

NORTHWEST DIVISION

Team	W	L	T	Pts.	GF	GA
Colorado Avalanche	44	28	10	98	239	205
Edmonton Oilers	33	37	12	78	230	226
Calgary Flames	30	40	12	72	211	234
Vancouver Canucks	23	47	12	58	192	258

PLAYOFFS

Eastern Conference quarterfinals: Pittsburgh 4, New Jersey 3; Buffalo 4, Ottawa 0; Boston 4, Carolina 2; Toronto 4, Philadelphia 2. **Semifinals:** Toronto 4, Pittsburgh 2; Buffalo 4, Boston 2. **Finals:** Buffalo 4, Toronto 1.

Western Conference quarterfinals: Dallas 4, Edmonton 0; Colorado 4, San Jose 2; Detroit 4, Anaheim 0; St. Louis 4, Phoenix 3. **Semifinals:** Dallas 4, St. Louis 2; Colorado 4, Detroit 2. **Finals:** Dallas 4, Colorado 3.

Stanley Cup finals: Dallas 4, Buffalo 2.

1999-2000

EASTERN CONFERENCE

ATLANTIC DIVISION

Team	W	L	T	OTL	Pts.	GF	GA
Philadelphia Flyers	45	22	12	3	105	237	179
New Jersey Devils	45	24	8	5	103	251	203
Pittsburgh Penguins	37	31	8	6	88	241	236
New York Rangers	29	38	12	3	73	218	246
New York Islanders	24	48	9	1	58	194	275

NORTHEAST DIVISION

Team	W	L	T	OTL	Pts.	GF	GA
Toronto Maple Leafs	45	27	7	3	100	246	222
Ottawa Senators	41	28	11	2	95	244	210
Buffalo Sabres	35	32	11	4	85	213	204
Montreal Canadiens	35	34	9	4	83	196	194
Boston Bruins	24	33	19	6	73	210	248

SOUTHEAST DIVISION

Team	W	L	T	OTL	Pts.	GF	GA
Washington Capitals	44	24	12	2	102	227	194
Florida Panthers	43	27	6	6	98	244	209
Carolina Hurricanes	37	35	10	0	84	217	216
Tampa Bay Lightning	19	47	9	7	54	204	310
Atlanta Thrashers	14	57	7	4	39	170	313

WESTERN CONFERENCE

CENTRAL DIVISION

Team	W	L	T	OTL	Pts.	GF	GA
St. Louis Blues	51	19	11	1	114	248	165
Detroit Red Wings	48	22	10	2	108	278	210
Chicago Blackhawks	33	37	10	2	78	242	245
Nashville Predators	28	40	7	7	70	199	240

PACIFIC DIVISION

Team	W	L	T	OTL	Pts.	GF	GA
Dallas Stars	43	23	10	6	102	211	184
Los Angeles Kings	39	27	12	4	94	245	228
Phoenix Coyotes	39	31	8	4	90	232	228
San Jose Sharks	35	30	10	7	87	225	214
Mighty Ducks of Anaheim	34	33	12	3	83	217	227

NORTHWEST DIVISION

Team	W	L	T	OTL	Pts.	GF	GA
Colorado Avalanche	42	28	11	1	96	233	201
Edmonton Oilers	32	26	16	8	88	226	212
Vancouver Canucks	30	29	15	8	83	227	237
Calgary Flames	31	36	10	5	77	211	256

PLAYOFFS

Eastern Conference quarterfinals: Philadelphia 4, Buffalo 1; Pittsburgh 4, Washington 1; Toronto 4, Ottawa 2; New Jersey 4, Florida 0. **Semifinals:** Philadelphia 4, Pittsburgh 2; New Jersey 4, Toronto 2. **Finals:** New Jersey 4, Philadelphia 3.

Western Conference quarterfinals: San Jose 4, St. Louis 3; Dallas 4, Edmonton 1; Colorado 4, Phoenix 1; Detroit 4, Los Angeles 0. **Semifinals:** Dallas 4, San Jose 1; Colorado 4, Detroit 1. **Finals:** Dallas 4, Colorado 3.

Stanley Cup finals: New Jersey 4, Dallas 2.

2000-01

EASTERN CONFERENCE

ATLANTIC DIVISION

Team	W	L	T	OTL	Pts.	GF	GA
New Jersey Devils	48	19	12	3	111	295	195
Philadelphia Flyers	43	25	11	3	100	240	207
Pittsburgh Penguins	42	28	9	3	96	281	256
New York Rangers	33	43	5	1	72	250	290
New York Islanders	21	51	7	3	52	185	268

NORTHEAST DIVISION

Team	W	L	T	OTL	Pts.	GF	GA
Ottawa Senators	48	21	9	4	109	274	205
Buffalo Sabres	46	30	5	1	98	218	184
Toronto Maple Leafs	37	29	11	5	90	232	207
Boston Bruins	36	30	8	8	88	227	249
Montreal Canadiens	28	40	8	6	70	206	232

SOUTHEAST DIVISION

Team	W	L	T	OTL	Pts.	GF	GA
Washington Capitals	41	27	10	4	96	233	211
Carolina Hurricanes	38	32	9	3	88	212	225
Florida Panthers	22	38	13	9	66	200	246
Atlanta Thrashers	23	45	12	2	60	211	289
Tampa Bay Lightning	24	47	6	5	59	201	280

WESTERN CONFERENCE

CENTRAL DIVISION

Team	W	L	T	OTL	Pts.	GF	GA
Detroit Red Wings	49	20	9	4	111	253	202
St. Louis Blues	43	22	12	5	103	249	195
Nashville Predators	34	36	9	3	80	186	200
Chicago Blackhawks	29	40	8	5	71	210	246
Columbus Blue Jackets	28	39	9	6	71	190	233

PACIFIC DIVISION

Team	W	L	T	OTL	Pts.	GF	GA
Dallas Stars	48	24	8	2	106	241	187
San Jose Sharks	40	27	12	3	95	217	192
Los Angeles Kings	38	28	13	3	92	252	228
Phoenix Coyotes	35	27	17	3	90	214	212
Mighty Ducks of Anaheim	25	41	11	5	66	188	245

NORTHWEST DIVISION

Team	W	L	T	OTL	Pts.	GF	GA
Colorado Rockies	52	16	10	4	118	270	192
Edmonton Oilers	39	28	12	3	93	243	222
Vancouver Canucks	36	28	11	7	90	239	238
Calgary Flames	27	36	15	4	73	197	236
Minnesota Wild	25	39	13	5	68	168	210

PLAYOFFS

Eastern Conference quarterfinals: New Jersey 4, Carolina 2; Toronto 4, Ottawa 0; Pittsburgh 4, Washington 2; Buffalo 4, Philadelphia 2. **Semifinals:** New Jersey 4, Toronto 3; Pittsburgh 4, Buffalo 3. **Finals:** New Jersey 4, Pittsburgh 1.

Western Conference quarterfinals: Colorado 4, Vancouver 0; Los Angeles 4, Detroit 2; Dallas 4, Edmonton 2; St. Louis 4, San Jose 2. **Semifinals:** Colorado 4, Los Angeles 3; St. Louis 4, Dallas 0. **Finals:** Colorado 4, St. Louis 1.

Stanley Cup finals: Colorado 4, New Jersey 3.

2001-02

EASTERN CONFERENCE

NORTHEAST DIVISION

Team	W	L	T	OTL	Pts.	GF	GA
Boston Bruins	43	24	6	9	101	236	201
Toronto Maple Leafs	43	25	10	4	100	249	207
Ottawa Senators	39	27	9	7	94	243	208
Montreal Canadiens	36	31	12	3	87	207	209
Buffalo Sabres	35	35	11	1	82	213	200

ATLANTIC DIVISION

Team	W	L	T	OTL	Pts.	GF	GA
Philadelphia Flyers	42	27	10	3	97	234	192
New York Islanders	42	28	8	4	96	239	220
New Jersey Devils	41	28	9	4	95	205	187
New York Rangers	36	38	4	4	80	227	258
Pittsburgh Penguins	28	41	8	5	69	198	249

SOUTHEAST DIVISION

Team	W	L	T	OTL	Pts.	GF	GA
Carolina Hurricanes	35	26	16	5	91	217	217
Washington Capitals	36	33	11	2	85	228	240
Tampa Bay Lightning	27	40	11	4	69	178	219
Florida Panthers	22	44	10	6	60	180	250
Atlanta Thrashers	19	47	11	5	54	187	288

WESTERN CONFERENCE

CENTRAL DIVISION

Team	W	L	T	OTL	Pts.	GF	GA
Detroit Red Wings	51	17	10	4	116	251	187
St. Louis Blues	43	27	8	4	98	227	188
Chicago Blackhawks	41	27	13	1	96	216	207
Nashville Predators	28	41	13	0	69	196	230
Columbus Blue Jackets	22	47	8	5	57	164	255

PACIFIC DIVISION

Team	W	L	T	OTL	Pts.	GF	GA
San Jose Sharks	44	27	8	3	99	248	199
Phoenix Coyotes	40	27	9	6	95	228	210
Los Angeles Kings	40	27	11	4	95	214	190
Dallas Stars	36	28	13	5	90	215	213
Mighty Ducks of Anaheim	29	42	8	3	69	175	198

NORTHWEST DIVISION

Team	W	L	T	OTL	Pts.	GF	GA
Colorado Avalanche	45	28	8	1	99	212	169
Vancouver Canucks	42	30	7	3	94	254	211
Edmonton Oilers	38	28	12	4	92	205	182
Calgary Flames	32	35	12	3	79	201	220
Minnesota Wild	26	35	12	9	73	195	238

PLAYOFFS

Eastern Conference quarterfinals: Ottawa 4, Philadelphia 1; Montreal 4, Boston 2; Carolina 4, New Jersey 2; Toronto 4, N.Y. Islanders 3. **Semifinals:** Toronto 4, Ottawa 3; Carolina 4, Montreal 2. **Finals:** Carolina 4, Toronto 2.

Western Conference quarterfinals: San Jose 4, Phoenix 1; St. Louis 4, Chicago 1; Colorado 4, Los Angeles 3; Detroit 4, Vancouver 2. **Semifinals:** Colorado 4, San Jose 3; Detroit 4, St. Louis 1. **Finals:** Detroit 4, Colorado 3.

Stanley Cup finals: Detroit 4, Carolina 1.

2002-03

EASTERN CONFERENCE

NORTHEAST DIVISION

Team	W	L	T	OTL	Pts.	GF	GA
Ottawa Senators	52	21	8	1	113	263	182
Toronto Maple Leafs	44	28	7	3	98	236	208
Boston Bruins	36	31	11	4	87	245	237
Montreal Canadiens	30	35	8	9	77	206	234
Buffalo Sabres	27	37	10	8	72	190	219

ATLANTIC DIVISION

Team	W	L	T	OTL	Pts.	GF	GA
New Jersey Devils	46	20	10	6	108	216	166
Philadelphia Flyers	45	20	13	4	107	211	166
New York Islanders	35	34	11	2	83	224	231
New York Rangers	32	36	10	4	78	210	231
Pittsburgh Penguins	27	44	6	5	65	189	255

SOUTHEAST DIVISION

Team	W	L	T	OTL	Pts.	GF	GA
Tampa Bay Lightning	36	25	16	5	93	219	210
Washington Capitals	39	29	8	6	92	224	220
Atlanta Thrashers	31	39	7	5	74	226	284
Florida Panthers	24	36	13	9	70	176	237
Carolina Hurricanes	22	43	11	6	61	171	240

WESTERN CONFERENCE

CENTRAL DIVISION

Team	W	L	T	OTL	Pts.	GF	GA
Detroit Red Wings	48	20	10	4	110	269	203
St. Louis Blues	41	24	11	6	99	253	222
Chicago Blackhawks	30	33	13	6	79	207	226
Nashville Predators	27	35	13	7	74	183	206
Columbus Blue Jackets	29	42	8	3	69	213	263

PACIFIC DIVISION

Team	W	L	T	OTL	Pts.	GF	GA
Dallas Stars	46	17	15	4	111	245	169
Mighty Ducks of Anaheim	40	27	9	6	95	203	193
Los Angeles Kings	33	37	6	7	78	203	221
Phoenix Coyotes	31	35	11	5	78	204	230
San Jose Sharks	28	37	9	8	73	214	239

NORTHWEST DIVISION

Team	W	L	T	OTL	Pts.	GF	GA
Colorado Avalanche	42	19	13	8	105	251	194
Vancouver Canucks	45	23	13	1	104	264	208
Minnesota Wild	42	29	10	1	95	198	178
Edmonton Oilers	36	26	11	9	92	231	230
Calgary Flames	29	36	13	4	75	186	228

PLAYOFFS

Eastern Conference quarterfinals: Ottawa 4, N.Y. Islanders 1; New Jersey 4, Boston 1; Tampa Bay 4, Washington 2; Philadelphia 4, Toronto 2. **Semifinals:** Ottawa 4, Philadelphia 2; New Jersey 4, Tampa Bay 2. **Finals:** New Jersey 4, Ottawa 3.

Western Conference quarterfinals: Dallas 4, Edmonton 2; Anaheim 4, Detroit 0; Minnesota 4, Colorado 3; Vancouver 4, St. Louis 3. **Semifinals:** Anaheim 4, Dallas 2; Minnesota 4, Vancouver 3. **Finals:** Anaheim 4, Minnesota 0.

Stanley Cup finals: New Jersey 4, Anaheim 3.

2003-04

EASTERN CONFERENCE

NORTHEAST DIVISION

Team	W	L	T	OTL	Pts.	GF	GA
Boston Bruins	41	19	15	7	104	209	188
Toronto Maple Leafs	45	24	10	3	103	242	204
Ottawa Senators	43	23	10	6	102	262	189
Montreal Canadiens	41	30	7	4	93	208	192
Buffalo Sabres	37	34	7	4	85	220	221

ATLANTIC DIVISION

Team	W	L	T	OTL	Pts.	GF	GA
Philadelphia Flyers	40	21	15	6	101	229	186
New Jersey Devils	43	25	12	2	100	213	164
New York Islanders	38	29	11	4	91	237	210
New York Rangers	27	40	7	8	69	206	250
Pittsbugh Penguins	23	47	8	4	58	190	303

SOUTHEAST DIVISION

Team	W	L	T	OTL	Pts.	GF	GA
Tampa Bay Lightning	46	22	8	6	106	245	192
Atlanta Thrashers	33	37	8	4	78	214	243
Carolina Hurricanes	28	34	14	6	76	172	209
Florida Panthers	28	35	15	4	75	188	221
Washington Capitals	23	46	10	3	59	186	253

WESTERN CONFERENCE

CENTRAL DIVISION

Team	W	L	T	OTL	Pts.	GF	GA
Detroit Red Wings	48	21	11	2	109	255	189
St. Louis Blues	39	30	11	2	91	191	198
Nashville Predators	38	29	11	4	91	216	217
Columbus Blue Jackets	25	45	8	4	62	177	238
Chicago Blackhawks	20	43	11	8	59	188	259

PACIFIC DIVISION

Team	W	L	T	OTL	Pts.	GF	GA
San Jose Sharks	43	21	12	6	104	219	183
Dallas Stars	41	26	13	2	97	194	175
Los Angeles Kings	28	29	16	9	81	205	217
Anaheim Mighty Ducks	29	35	10	8	76	184	213
Phoenix Coyotes	22	36	18	6	68	188	245

NORTHWEST DIVISION

Team	W	L	T	OTL	Pts.	GF	GA
Vancouver Canucks	43	24	10	5	101	235	194
Colorado Avalanche	40	22	13	7	100	236	198
Calgary Flames	42	30	7	3	94	200	176
Edmonton Oilers	36	29	12	5	89	221	208
Minnesota Wild	30	29	20	3	83	188	183

PLAYOFFS

Eastern Conference quarterfinals: Tampa Bay 4, NY Islanders 1; Montreal 4, Boston 3; Philadelphia 4, New Jersey 1; Toronto 4, Ottawa 3. **Semifinals:** Tampa Bay 4, Montreal 0; Philadelphia 4, Toronto 2. **Finals:** Tampa Bay 4, Philadelphia 3.

Western Conference quarterfinals: Detroit 4, Nashville 2; San Jose 4, St. Louis 1; Calgary 4, Vancouver 3; Colorado 4, Dallas 1. **Semifinals:** Calgary 4, Detroit 2; San Jose 4, Colorado 2. **Finals:** Calgary 4, San Jose 2.

Stanley Cup finals: Tampa Bay 4, Calgary 3.

AWARD WINNERS

LEAGUE AWARDS

ART ROSS TROPHY

(Leading scorer)

Season	Player, Team	Pts.
1917-18	Joe Malone, Montreal	48
1918-19	Newsy Lalonde, Montreal	32
1919-20	Joe Malone, Quebec Bulldogs	49
1920-21	Newsy Lalonde, Montreal	43
1921-22	Punch Broadbent, Ottawa	46
1922-23	Babe Dye, Toronto	37
1923-24	Cy Denneny, Ottawa	24
1924-25	Babe Dye, Toronto	46
1925-26	Nels Stewart, Montreal Maroons	42
1926-27	Bill Cook, N.Y. Rangers	37
1927-28	Howie Morenz, Montreal	51
1928-29	Ace Bailey, Toronto	32
1929-30	Cooney Weiland, Boston	73
1930-31	Howie Morenz, Montreal	51
1931-32	Harvey Jackson, Toronto	53
1932-33	Bill Cook, N.Y. Rangers	50
1933-34	Charlie Conacher, Toronto	52
1934-35	Charlie Conacher, Toronto	57
1935-36	Dave Schriner, N.Y. Americans	45
1936-37	Dave Schriner, N.Y. Americans	46
1937-38	Gordie Drillion, Toronto	52
1938-39	Toe Blake, Montreal	47
1939-40	Milt Schmidt, Boston	52
1940-41	Bill Cowley, Boston	62
1941-42	Bryan Hextall, N.Y. Rangers	56
1942-43	Doug Bentley, Chicago	73
1943-44	Herbie Cain, Boston	82
1944-45	Elmer Lach, Montreal	80
1945-46	Max Bentley, Chicago	61
1946-47	Max Bentley, Chicago	72
1947-48	Elmer Lach, Montreal	61
1948-49	Roy Conacher, Chicago	68
1949-50	Ted Lindsay, Detroit	78
1950-51	Gordie Howe, Detroit	86
1951-52	Gordie Howe, Detroit	86
1952-53	Gordie Howe, Detroit	95
1953-54	Gordie Howe, Detroit	81
1954-55	Bernie Geoffrion, Montreal	75
1955-56	Jean Beliveau, Montreal	88
1956-57	Gordie Howe, Detroit	89
1957-58	Dickie Moore, Montreal	84
1958-59	Dickie Moore, Montreal	96
1959-60	Bobby Hull, Chicago	81
1960-61	Bernie Geoffrion, Montreal	95
1961-62	Bobby Hull, Chicago	84
1962-63	Gordie Howe, Detroit	86
1963-64	Stan Mikita, Chicago	89
1964-65	Stan Mikita, Chicago	87
1965-66	Bobby Hull, Chicago	97
1966-67	Stan Mikita, Chicago	97
1967-68	Stan Mikita, Chicago	87
1968-69	Phil Esposito, Boston	126
1969-70	Bobby Orr, Boston	120
1970-71	Phil Esposito, Boston	152
1971-72	Phil Esposito, Boston	133
1972-73	Phil Esposito, Boston	130

Season	Player, Team	Pts.
1973-74	Phil Esposito, Boston	145
1974-75	Bobby Orr, Boston	135
1975-76	Guy Lafleur, Montreal	125
1976-77	Guy Lafleur, Montreal	136
1977-78	Guy Lafleur, Montreal	132
1978-79	Bryan Trottier, N.Y. Islanders	134
1979-80	Marcel Dionne, Los Angeles	137
1980-81	Wayne Gretzky, Edmonton	164
1981-82	Wayne Gretzky, Edmonton	212
1982-83	Wayne Gretzky, Edmonton	196
1983-84	Wayne Gretzky, Edmonton	205
1984-85	Wayne Gretzky, Edmonton	208
1985-86	Wayne Gretzky, Edmonton	215
1986-87	Wayne Gretzky, Edmonton	183
1987-88	Mario Lemieux, Pittsburgh	168
1988-89	Mario Lemieux, Pittsburgh	199
1989-90	Wayne Gretzky, Los Angeles	142
1990-91	Wayne Gretzky, Los Angeles	163
1991-92	Mario Lemieux, Pittsburgh	131
1992-93	Mario Lemieux, Pittsburgh	160
1993-94	Wayne Gretzky, Los Angeles	130
1994-95	Jaromir Jagr, Pittsburgh	70
1995-96	Mario Lemieux, Pittsburgh	161
1996-97	Mario Lemieux, Pittsburgh	122
1997-98	Jaromir Jagr, Pittsburgh	102
1998-99	Jaromir Jagr, Pittsburgh	127
1999-00	Jaromir Jagr, Pittsburgh	96
2000-01	Jaromir Jagr, Pittsburgh	121
2001-02	Jarome Iginla, Calgary	96
2002-03	Peter Forsberg, Colorado	106
2003-04	Martin St. Louis, Tampa Bay	94
2005-06	Joe Thornton, San Jose	125

The award was originally known as the Leading Scorer Trophy. The present trophy, first given in 1947, was presented to the NHL by Art Ross, former manager-coach of the Boston Bruins. In event of a tie, the player with the most goals receives the award.

MAURICE RICHARD TROPHY

(Leading goal scorer)

Season	Player, Team	Goals
1998-99	Teemu Selanne, Anaheim	47
1999-00	Pavel Bure, Florida	58
2000-01	Pavel Bure, Florida	59
2001-02	Jarome Iginla, Calgary	52
2002-03	Milan Hejduk, Colorado	50
2003-04	I. Kovalchuk, Atl., J. Iginla, Cal., R. Nash, Clb.	41
2005-06	Jonathan Cheechoo, San Jose	56

HART MEMORIAL TROPHY

(Most Valuable Player)

Season	Player, Team
1923-24	Frank Nighbor, Ottawa
1924-25	Billy Burch, Hamilton
1925-26	Nels Stewart, Montreal Maroons
1926-27	Herb Gardiner, Montreal
1927-28	Howie Morenz, Montreal
1928-29	Roy Worters, N.Y. Americans
1929-30	Nels Stewart, Montreal Maroons
1930-31	Howie Morenz, Montreal
1931-32	Howie Morenz, Montreal
1932-33	Eddie Shore, Boston
1933-34	Aurel Joliat, Montreal
1934-35	Eddie Shore, Boston
1935-36	Eddie Shore, Boston
1936-37	Babe Siebert, Montreal
1937-38	Eddie Shore, Boston
1938-39	Toe Blake, Montreal
1939-40	Ebbie Goodfellow, Detroit
1940-41	Bill Cowley, Boston
1941-42	Tom Anderson, Brooklyn
1942-43	Bill Cowley, Boston
1943-44	Babe Pratt, Toronto
1944-45	Elmer Lach, Montreal
1945-46	Max Bentley, Chicago
1946-47	Maurice Richard, Montreal
1947-48	Buddy O'Connor, N.Y. Rangers
1948-49	Sid Abel, Detroit
1949-50	Chuck Rayner, N.Y. Rangers
1950-51	Milt Schmidt, Boston
1951-52	Gordie Howe, Detroit
1952-53	Gordie Howe, Detroit
1953-54	Al Rollins, Chicago
1954-55	Ted Kennedy, Toronto
1955-56	Jean Beliveau, Montreal
1956-57	Gordie Howe, Detroit
1957-58	Gordie Howe, Detroit
1958-59	Andy Bathgate, N.Y. Rangers
1959-60	Gordie Howe, Detroit
1960-61	Bernie Geoffrion, Montreal
1961-62	Jacques Plante, Montreal
1962-63	Gordie Howe, Detroit
1963-64	Jean Beliveau, Montreal
1964-65	Bobby Hull, Chicago
1965-66	Bobby Hull, Chicago
1966-67	Stan Mikita, Chicago
1967-68	Stan Mikita, Chicago
1968-69	Phil Esposito, Boston
1969-70	Bobby Orr, Boston
1970-71	Bobby Orr, Boston
1971-72	Bobby Orr, Boston
1972-73	Bobby Clarke, Philadelphia
1973-74	Phil Esposito, Boston
1974-75	Bobby Clarke, Philadelphia
1975-76	Bobby Clarke, Philadelphia
1976-77	Guy Lafleur, Montreal
1977-78	Guy Lafleur, Montreal
1978-79	Bryan Trottier, N.Y. Islanders
1979-80	Wayne Gretzky, Edmonton
1980-81	Wayne Gretzky, Edmonton
1981-82	Wayne Gretzky, Edmonton
1982-83	Wayne Gretzky, Edmonton
1983-84	Wayne Gretzky, Edmonton
1984-85	Wayne Gretzky, Edmonton
1985-86	Wayne Gretzky, Edmonton
1986-87	Wayne Gretzky, Edmonton
1987-88	Mario Lemieux, Pittsburgh
1988-89	Wayne Gretzky, Los Angeles
1989-90	Mark Messier, Edmonton
1990-91	Brett Hull, St. Louis
1991-92	Mark Messier, N.Y. Rangers
1992-93	Mario Lemieux, Pittsburgh
1993-94	Sergei Fedorov, Detroit
1994-95	Eric Lindros, Philadelphia
1995-96	Mario Lemieux, Pittsburgh
1996-97	Dominik Hasek, Buffalo
1997-98	Dominik Hasek, Buffalo
1998-99	Jaromir Jagr, Pittsburgh
1999-00	Chris Pronger, St. Louis
2000-01	Joe Sakic, Colorado
2001-02	Jose Theodore, Montreal
2002-03	Peter Forsberg, Colorado
2003-04	Martin St. Louis, Tampa Bay
2005-06	Joe Thornton, San Jose

JAMES NORRIS MEMORIAL TROPHY

(Outstanding defenseman)

Season	Player, Team
1953-54	Red Kelly, Detroit
1954-55	Doug Harvey, Montreal
1955-56	Doug Harvey, Montreal
1956-57	Doug Harvey, Montreal
1957-58	Doug Harvey, Montreal

Season	Player, Team
1958-59	Tom Johnson, Montreal
1959-60	Doug Harvey, Montreal
1960-61	Doug Harvey, Montreal
1961-62	Doug Harvey, N.Y. Rangers
1962-63	Pierre Pilote, Chicago
1963-64	Pierre Pilote, Chicago
1964-65	Pierre Pilote, Chicago
1965-66	Jacques Laperriere, Montreal
1966-67	Harry Howell, N.Y. Rangers
1967-68	Bobby Orr, Boston
1968-69	Bobby Orr, Boston
1969-70	Bobby Orr, Boston
1970-71	Bobby Orr, Boston
1971-72	Bobby Orr, Boston
1972-73	Bobby Orr, Boston
1973-74	Bobby Orr, Boston
1974-75	Bobby Orr, Boston
1975-76	Denis Potvin, N.Y. Islanders
1976-77	Larry Robinson, Montreal
1977-78	Denis Potvin, N.Y. Islanders
1978-79	Denis Potvin, N.Y. Islanders
1979-80	Larry Robinson, Montreal
1980-81	Randy Carlyle, Pittsburgh
1981-82	Doug Wilson, Chicago
1982-83	Rod Langway, Washington
1983-84	Rod Langway, Washington
1984-85	Paul Coffey, Edmonton
1985-86	Paul Coffey, Edmonton
1986-87	Ray Bourque, Boston
1987-88	Ray Bourque, Boston
1988-89	Chris Chelios, Montreal
1989-90	Ray Bourque, Boston
1990-91	Ray Bourque, Boston
1991-92	Brian Leetch, N.Y. Rangers
1992-93	Chris Chelios, Chicago
1993-94	Ray Bourque, Boston
1994-95	Paul Coffey, Detroit
1995-96	Chris Chelios, Chicago
1996-97	Brian Leetch, N.Y. Rangers
1997-98	Rob Blake, Los Angeles
1998-99	Al MacInnis, St. Louis
1999-00	Chris Pronger, St. Louis
2000-01	Nicklas Lidstrom, Detroit
2001-02	Nicklas Lidstrom, Detroit
2002-03	Nicklas Lidstrom, Detroit
2003-04	Scott Niedermayer, New Jersey
2005-06	Nicklas Lidstrom, Detroit

VEZINA TROPHY

(Outstanding goaltender)

Season	Player, Team	GAA
1926-27	George Hainsworth, Montreal	1.52
1927-28	George Hainsworth, Montreal	1.09
1928-29	George Hainsworth, Montreal	0.98
1929-30	Tiny Thompson, Boston	2.23
1930-31	Roy Worters, N.Y. Americans	1.68
1931-32	Charlie Gardiner, Chicago	2.10
1932-33	Tiny Thompson, Boston	1.83
1933-34	Charlie Gardiner, Chicago	1.73
1934-35	Lorne Chabot, Chicago	1.83
1935-36	Tiny Thompson, Boston	1.71
1936-37	Normie Smith, Detroit	2.13
1937-38	Tiny Thompson, Boston	1.85
1938-39	Frank Brimsek, Boston	1.60
1939-40	Dave Kerr, N.Y. Rangers	1.60
1940-41	Turk Broda, Toronto	2.60
1941-42	Frank Brimsek, Boston	2.38
1942-43	Johnny Mowers, Detroit	2.48
1943-44	Bill Durnan, Montreal	2.18
1944-45	Bill Durnan, Montreal	2.42
1945-46	Bill Durnan, Montreal	2.60
1946-47	Bill Durnan, Montreal	2.30
1947-48	Turk Broda, Toronto	2.38
1948-49	Bill Durnan, Montreal	2.10
1949-50	Bill Durnan, Montreal	2.20
1950-51	Al Rollins, Toronto	1.75
1951-52	Terry Sawchuk, Detroit	1.98
1952-53	Terry Sawchuk, Detroit	1.94
1953-54	Harry Lumley, Toronto	1.85
1954-55	Terry Sawchuk, Detroit	1.94
1955-56	Jacques Plante, Montreal	1.86
1956-57	Jacques Plante, Montreal	2.02
1957-58	Jacques Plante, Montreal	2.09
1958-59	Jacques Plante, Montreal	2.15
1959-60	Jacques Plante, Montreal	2.54
1960-61	Johnny Bower, Toronto	2.50
1961-62	Jacques Plante, Montreal	2.37
1962-63	Glenn Hall, Chicago	2.51
1963-64	Charlie Hodge, Montreal	2.26
1964-65	Terry Sawchuk, Toronto	2.56
	Johnny Bower, Toronto	2.38
1965-66	Lorne Worsley, Montreal	2.36
	Charlie Hodge, Montreal	2.58
1966-67	Glenn Hall, Chicago	2.38
	Denis DeJordy, Chicago	2.46
1967-68	Lorne Worsley, Montreal	1.98
	Rogatien Vachon, Montreal	2.48
1968-69	Glenn Hall, St. Louis	2.17
	Jacques Plante, St. Louis	1.96
1969-70	Tony Esposito, Chicago	2.17
1970-71	Ed Giacomin, N.Y. Rangers	2.16
	Gilles Villemure, N.Y. Rangers	2.30
1971-72	Tony Esposito, Chicago	1.77
	Gary Smith, Chicago	2.42
1972-73	Ken Dryden, Montreal	2.26
1973-74	Bernie Parent, Philadelphia	1.89
	Tony Esposito, Chicago	2.04
1974-75	Bernie Parent, Philadelphia	2.03
1975-76	Ken Dryden, Montreal	2.03
1976-77	Ken Dryden, Montreal	2.14
	Michel Larocque, Montreal	2.09
1977-78	Ken Dryden, Montreal	2.05
	Michel Larocque, Montreal	2.67
1978-79	Ken Dryden, Montreal	2.30
	Michel Larocque, Montreal	2.84
1979-80	Bob Sauve, Buffalo	2.36
	Don Edwards, Buffalo	2.57
1980-81	Richard Sevigny, Montreal	2.40
	Michel Larocque, Montreal	3.03
	Denis Herron, Montreal	3.50
1981-82	Billy Smith, N.Y. Islanders	2.97
1982-83	Pete Peeters, Boston	2.36
1983-84	Tom Barrasso, Buffalo	2.84
1984-85	Pelle Lindbergh, Philadelphia	3.02
1985-86	John Vanbiesbrouck, N.Y. Rangers	3.32
1986-87	Ron Hextall, Philadelphia	3.00
1987-88	Grant Fuhr, Edmonton	3.43
1988-89	Patrick Roy, Montreal	2.47
1989-90	Patrick Roy, Montreal	2.53
1990-91	Ed Belfour, Chicago	2.47
1991-92	Patrick Roy, Montreal	2.36
1992-93	Ed Belfour, Chicago	2.59
1993-94	Dominik Hasek, Buffalo	1.95
1994-95	Dominik Hasek, Buffalo	2.11
1995-96	Jim Carey, Washington	2.26
1996-97	Dominik Hasek, Buffalo	2.27
1997-98	Dominik Hasek, Buffalo	2.09
1998-99	Dominik Hasek, Buffalo	1.87
1999-00	Olaf Kolzig, Washington	2.24
2000-01	Dominik Hasek, Buffalo	2.11

Season	Player, Team	GAA
2001-02	Jose Theodore, Montreal	2.11
2002-03	Martin Brodeur, New Jersey	2.02
2003-04	Martin Brodeur, New Jersey	2.02
2005-06	Miikka Kiprusoff, Calgary	2.07

The award was formerly presented to the goaltender(s) having played a minimum of 25 games for the team with the fewest goals scored against. Beginning with the 1981-82 season, it was awarded to the outstanding goaltender.

LESTER B. PEARSON AWARD

(Most outstanding player as selected by NHL Players' Association members)

Season Player, Team

1970-71—Phil Esposito, Boston
1971-72—Jean Ratelle, N.Y. Rangers
1972-73—Bobby Clarke, Philadelphia
1973-74—Phil Esposito, Boston
1974-75—Bobby Orr, Boston
1975-76—Guy Lafleur, Montreal
1976-77—Guy Lafleur, Montreal
1977-78—Guy Lafleur, Montreal
1978-79—Marcel Dionne, Los Angeles
1979-80—Marcel Dionne, Los Angeles
1980-81—Mike Liut, St. Louis
1981-82—Wayne Gretzky, Edmonton
1982-83—Wayne Gretzky, Edmonton
1983-84—Wayne Gretzky, Edmonton
1984-85—Wayne Gretzky, Edmonton
1985-86—Mario Lemieux, Pittsburgh
1986-87—Wayne Gretzky, Edmonton
1987-88—Mario Lemieux, Pittsburgh
1988-89—Steve Yzerman, Detroit
1989-90—Mark Messier, Edmonton
1990-91—Brett Hull, St. Louis
1991-92—Mark Messier, N.Y. Rangers
1992-93—Mario Lemieux, Pittsburgh
1993-94—Sergei Fedorov, Detroit
1994-95—Eric Lindros, Philadelphia
1995-96—Mario Lemieux, Pittsburgh
1996-97—Dominik Hasek, Buffalo
1997-98—Dominik Hasek, Buffalo
1998-99—Jaromir Jagr, Pittsburgh
1999-00—Jaromir Jagr, Pittsburgh
2000-01—Joe Sakic, Colorado
2001-02—Jarome Iginla, Calgary
2002-03—Markus Naslund, Vancouver
2003-04—Martin St. Louis, Tampa Bay
2005-06—Jaromir Jagr, N.Y. Rangers

WILLIAM M. JENNINGS TROPHY

(Leading goaltender)

Season	Player, Team	GAA
1981-82	Denis Herron, Montreal	2.64
	Rick Wamsley, Montreal	2.75
1982-83	Roland Melanson, N.Y. Islanders	2.66
	Billy Smith, N.Y. Islanders	2.87
1983-84	Pat Riggin, Washington	2.66
	Al Jensen, Washington	2.91
1984-85	Tom Barrasso, Buffalo	2.66
	Bob Sauve, Buffalo	3.22
1985-86	Bob Froese, Philadelphia	2.55
	Darren Jensen, Philadelphia	3.68
1986-87	Brian Hayward, Montreal	2.81
	Patrick Roy, Montreal	2.93
1987-88	Brian Hayward, Montreal	2.86
	Patrick Roy, Montreal	2.90
1988-89	Patrick Roy, Montreal	2.47
	Brian Hayward, Montreal	2.90
1989-90	Rejean Lemelin, Boston	2.81
	Andy Moog, Boston	2.89
1990-91	Ed Belfour, Chicago	2.47
1991-92	Patrick Roy, Montreal	2.36
1992-93	Ed Belfour, Chicago	2.59
1993-94	Dominik Hasek, Buffalo	1.95
	Grant Fuhr, Buffalo	3.68
1994-95	Ed Belfour, Chicago	2.28
1995-96	Chris Osgood, Detroit	2.17
	Mike Vernon, Detroit	2.26
1996-97	Martin Brodeur, New Jersey	1.88
	Mike Dunham, New Jersey	2.55
1997-98	Martin Brodeur, New Jersey	1.89
1998-99	Ed Belfour, Dallas	1.99
	Roman Turek, Dallas	2.08
1999-00	Roman Turek, St. Louis	1.95
2000-01	Dominik Hasek, Buffalo	2.11
2001-02	Patrick Roy, Colorado	1.94
2002-03	Roman Cechmanek, Philadelphia	1.83
	Robert Esche, Philadelphia	2.20
	Martin Brodeur, New Jersey	2.02
2003-04	Martin Brodeur, New Jersey	2.03
2005-06	Miikka Kiprusoff, Calgary	2.07

The award is presented to the goaltender(s) who played a minimum of 25 games for his team with the fewest goals against average.

CALDER MEMORIAL TROPHY

(Rookie of the year)

Season Player, Team

1932-33—Carl Voss, Detroit
1933-34—Russ Blinco, Montreal Maroons
1934-35—Dave Schriner, N.Y. Americans
1935-36—Mike Karakas, Chicago
1936-37—Syl Apps, Toronto
1937-38—Cully Dahlstrom, Chicago
1938-39—Frank Brimsek, Boston
1939-40—Kilby Macdonald, N.Y. Rangers
1940-41—John Quilty, Montreal
1941-42—Grant Warwick, N.Y. Rangers
1942-43—Gaye Stewart, Toronto
1943-44—Gus Bodnar, Toronto
1944-45—Frank McCool, Toronto
1945-46—Edgar Laprade, N.Y. Rangers
1946-47—Howie Meeker, Toronto
1947-48—Jim McFadden, Detroit
1948-49—Pentti Lund, N.Y. Rangers
1949-50—Jack Gelineau, Boston
1950-51—Terry Sawchuk, Detroit
1951-52—Bernie Geoffrion, Montreal
1952-53—Lorne Worsley, N.Y. Rangers
1953-54—Camille Henry, N.Y. Rangers
1954-55—Ed Litzenberger, Chicago
1955-56—Glenn Hall, Detroit
1956-57—Larry Regan, Boston
1957-58—Frank Mahovlich, Toronto
1958-59—Ralph Backstrom, Montreal
1959-60—Bill Hay, Chicago
1960-61—Dave Keon, Toronto
1961-62—Bobby Rousseau, Montreal
1962-63—Kent Douglas, Toronto
1963-64—Jacques Laperriere, Montreal
1964-65—Roger Crozier, Detroit
1965-66—Brit Selby, Toronto
1966-67—Bobby Orr, Boston
1967-68—Derek Sanderson, Boston
1968-69—Danny Grant, Minnesota
1969-70—Tony Esposito, Chicago
1970-71—Gilbert Perreault, Buffalo
1971-72—Ken Dryden, Montreal
1972-73—Steve Vickers, N.Y. Rangers

Season Player, Team
1973-74—Denis Potvin, N.Y. Islanders
1974-75—Eric Vail, Atlanta
1975-76—Bryan Trottier, N.Y. Islanders
1976-77—Willi Plett, Atlanta
1977-78—Mike Bossy, N.Y. Islanders
1978-79—Bobby Smith, Minnesota
1979-80—Ray Bourque, Boston
1980-81—Peter Stastny, Quebec
1981-82—Dale Hawerchuk, Winnipeg
1982-83—Steve Larmer, Chicago
1983-84—Tom Barrasso, Buffalo
1984-85—Mario Lemieux, Pittsburgh
1985-86—Gary Suter, Calgary
1986-87—Luc Robitaille, Los Angeles
1987-88—Joe Nieuwendyk, Calgary
1988-89—Brian Leetch, N.Y. Rangers
1989-90—Sergei Makarov, Calgary
1990-91—Ed Belfour, Chicago
1991-92—Pavel Bure, Vancouver
1992-93—Teemu Selanne, Winnipeg
1993-94—Martin Brodeur, New Jersey
1994-95—Peter Forsberg, Quebec
1995-96—Daniel Alfredsson, Ottawa
1996-97—Bryan Berard, N.Y. Islanders
1997-98—Sergei Samsonov, Boston
1998-99—Chris Drury, Colorado
1999-00—Scott Gomez, New Jersey
2000-01—Evgeni Nabokov, San Jose
2001-02—Dany Heatley, Atlanta
2002-03—Barret Jackman, St. Louis
2003-04—Andrew Raycroft, Boston
2005-06—Alexander Ovechkin, Washington

The award was originally known as the Leading Rookie Award. It was renamed the Calder Trophy in 1936-37 and became the Calder Memorial Trophy in 1942-43, following the death of NHL President Frank Calder.

LADY BYNG MEMORIAL TROPHY

(Most gentlemanly player)

Season Player, Team
1924-25—Frank Nighbor, Ottawa
1925-26—Frank Nighbor, Ottawa
1926-27—Billy Burch, N.Y. Americans
1927-28—Frank Boucher, N.Y. Rangers
1928-29—Frank Boucher, N.Y. Rangers
1929-30—Frank Boucher, N.Y. Rangers
1930-31—Frank Boucher, N.Y. Rangers
1931-32—Joe Primeau, Toronto
1932-33—Frank Boucher, N.Y. Rangers
1933-34—Frank Boucher, N.Y. Rangers
1934-35—Frank Boucher, N.Y. Rangers
1935-36—Doc Romnes, Chicago
1936-37—Marty Barry, Detroit
1937-38—Gordie Drillon, Toronto
1938-39—Clint Smith, N.Y. Rangers
1939-40—Bobby Bauer, Boston
1940-41—Bobby Bauer, Boston
1941-42—Syl Apps, Toronto
1942-43—Max Bentley, Chicago
1943-44—Clint Smith, Chicago
1944-45—Bill Mosienko, Chicago
1945-46—Toe Blake, Montreal
1946-47—Bobby Bauer, Boston
1947-48—Buddy O'Connor, N.Y. Rangers
1948-49—Bill Quackenbush, Detroit
1949-50—Edgar Laprade, N.Y. Rangers
1950-51—Red Kelly, Detroit
1951-52—Sid Smith, Toronto
1952-53—Red Kelly, Detroit
1953-54—Red Kelly, Detroit

Season Player, Team
1954-55—Sid Smith, Toronto
1955-56—Earl Reibel, Detroit
1956-57—Andy Hebenton, N.Y. Rangers
1957-58—Camille Henry, N.Y. Rangers
1958-59—Alex Delvecchio, Detroit
1959-60—Don McKenney, Boston
1960-61—Red Kelly, Toronto
1961-62—Dave Keon, Toronto
1962-63—Dave Keon, Toronto
1963-64—Ken Wharram, Chicago
1964-65—Bobby Hull, Chicago
1965-66—Alex Delvecchio, Detroit
1966-67—Stan Mikita, Chicago
1967-68—Stan Mikita, Chicago
1968-69—Alex Delvecchio, Detroit
1969-70—Phil Goyette, St. Louis
1970-71—John Bucyk, Boston
1971-72—Jean Ratelle, N.Y. Rangers
1972-73—Gilbert Perreault, Buffalo
1973-74—John Bucyk, Boston
1974-75—Marcel Dionne, Detroit
1975-76—Jean Ratelle, N.Y. R.-Boston
1976-77—Marcel Dionne, Los Angeles
1977-78—Butch Goring, Los Angeles
1978-79—Bob MacMillan, Atlanta
1979-80—Wayne Gretzky, Edmonton
1980-81—Rick Kehoe, Pittsburgh
1981-82—Rick Middleton, Boston
1982-83—Mike Bossy, N.Y. Islanders
1983-84—Mike Bossy, N.Y. Islanders
1984-85—Jari Kurri, Edmonton
1985-86—Mike Bossy, N.Y. Islanders
1986-87—Joe Mullen, Calgary
1987-88—Mats Naslund, Montreal
1988-89—Joe Mullen, Calgary
1989-90—Brett Hull, St. Louis
1990-91—Wayne Gretzky, Los Angeles
1991-92—Wayne Gretzky, Los Angeles
1992-93—Pierre Turgeon, N.Y. Islanders
1993-94—Wayne Gretzky, Los Angeles
1994-95—Ron Francis, Pittsburgh
1995-96—Paul Kariya, Anaheim
1996-97—Paul Kariya, Anaheim
1997-98—Ron Francis, Pittsburgh
1998-99—Wayne Gretzky, N.Y. Rangers
1999-00—Pavol Demitra, St. Louis
2000-01—Joe Sakic, Colorado
2001-02—Ron Francis, Carolina
2002-03—Alexander Mogilny, Toronto
2003-04—Brad Richards, Tampa Bay
2005-06—Pavel Datsyuk, Detroit

The award was originally known as the Lady Byng Trophy. After winning the award seven times, Frank Boucher received permanent possession and a new trophy was donated to the NHL in 1936. After Lady Byng's death in 1949, the NHL changed the name to Lady Byng Memorial Trophy.

CONN SMYTHE TROPHY

(Playoff MVP)

Season Player, Team
1964-65—Jean Beliveau, Montreal
1965-66—Roger Crozier, Detroit
1966-67—Dave Keon, Toronto
1967-68—Glenn Hall, St. Louis
1968-69—Serge Savard, Montreal
1969-70—Bobby Orr, Boston
1970-71—Ken Dryden, Montreal
1971-72—Bobby Orr, Boston
1972-73—Yvan Cournoyer, Montreal
1973-74—Bernie Parent, Philadelphia

Season Player, Team
1974-75—Bernie Parent, Philadelphia
1975-76—Reggie Leach, Philadelphia
1976-77—Guy Lafleur, Montreal
1977-78—Larry Robinson, Montreal
1978-79—Bob Gainey, Montreal
1979-80—Bryan Trottier, N.Y. Islanders
1980-81—Butch Goring, N.Y. Islanders
1981-82—Mike Bossy, N.Y. Islanders
1982-83—Billy Smith, N.Y. Islanders
1983-84—Mark Messier, Edmonton
1984-85—Wayne Gretzky, Edmonton
1985-86—Patrick Roy, Montreal
1986-87—Ron Hextall, Philadelphia
1987-88—Wayne Gretzky, Edmonton
1988-89—Al MacInnis, Calgary
1989-90—Bill Ranford, Edmonton
1990-91—Mario Lemieux, Pittsburgh
1991-92—Mario Lemieux, Pittsburgh
1992-93—Patrick Roy, Montreal
1993-94—Brian Leetch, N.Y. Rangers
1994-95—Claude Lemieux, New Jersey
1995-96—Joe Sakic, Colorado
1996-97—Mike Vernon, Detroit
1997-98—Steve Yzerman, Detroit
1998-99—Joe Nieuwendyk, Dallas
1999-00—Scott Stevens, New Jersey
2000-01—Patrick Roy, Colorado
2001-02—Niklas Lidstrom, Detroit
2002-03—Jean-Sebastien Giguere, Anaheim
2003-04—Brad Richards, Tampa Bay
2005-06—Cam Ward, Carolina

FRANK J. SELKE TROPHY

(Best defensive forward)

Season Player, Team
1977-78—Bob Gainey, Montreal
1978-79—Bob Gainey, Montreal
1979-80—Bob Gainey, Montreal
1980-81—Bob Gainey, Montreal
1981-82—Steve Kasper, Boston
1982-83—Bobby Clarke, Philadelphia
1983-84—Doug Jarvis, Washington
1984-85—Craig Ramsay, Buffalo
1985-86—Troy Murray, Chicago
1986-87—Dave Poulin, Philadelphia
1987-88—Guy Carbonneau, Montreal
1988-89—Guy Carbonneau, Montreal
1989-90—Rick Meagher, St. Louis
1990-91—Dirk Graham, Chicago
1991-92—Guy Carbonneau, Montreal
1992-93—Doug Gilmour, Toronto
1993-94—Sergei Fedorov, Detroit
1994-95—Ron Francis, Pittsburgh
1995-96—Sergei Fedorov, Detroit
1996-97—Michael Peca, Buffalo
1997-98—Jere Lehtinen, Dallas
1998-99—Jere Lehtinen, Dallas
1999-00—Steve Yzerman, Detroit
2000-01—John Madden, New Jersey
2001-02—Michael Peca, N.Y. Islanders
2002-03—Jere Lehtinen, Dallas
2003-04—Kris Draper, Detroit
2005-06—Rod Brind'Amour, Carolina

BILL MASTERTON MEMORIAL TROPHY

(Sportsmanship, dedication to hockey)

Season Player, Team
1967-68—Claude Provost, Montreal
1968-69—Ted Hampson, Oakland
1969-70—Pit Martin, Chicago
1970-71—Jean Ratelle, N.Y. Rangers
1971-72—Bobby Clarke, Philadelphia
1972-73—Lowell MacDonald, Pittsburgh
1973-74—Henri Richard, Montreal
1974-75—Don Luce, Buffalo
1975-76—Rod Gilbert, N.Y. Rangers
1976-77—Ed Westfall, N.Y. Islanders
1977-78—Butch Goring, Los Angeles
1978-79—Serge Savard, Montreal
1979-80—Al MacAdam, Minnesota
1980-81—Blake Dunlop, St. Louis
1981-82—Glenn Resch, Colorado
1982-83—Lanny McDonald, Calgary
1983-84—Brad Park, Detroit
1984-85—Anders Hedberg, N.Y. Rangers
1985-86—Charlie Simmer, Boston
1986-87—Doug Jarvis, Hartford
1987-88—Bob Bourne, Los Angeles
1988-89—Tim Kerr, Philadelphia
1989-90—Gord Kluzak, Boston
1990-91—Dave Taylor, Los Angeles
1991-92—Mark Fitzpatrick, N.Y. Islanders
1992-93—Mario Lemieux, Pittsburgh
1993-94—Cam Neely, Boston
1994-95—Pat LaFontaine, Buffalo
1995-96—Gary Roberts, Calgary
1996-97—Tony Granato, San Jose
1997-98—Jamie McLennan, St. Louis
1998-99—John Cullen, Tampa Bay
1999-00—Ken Daneyko, New Jersey
2000-01—Adam Graves, N.Y. Rangers
2001-02—Saku Koivu, Montreal
2002-03—Steve Yzerman, Detroit
2003-04—Bryan Berard, Chicago
2005-06—Teemu Selanne, Anaheim

Presented by the Professional Hockey Writers' Association to the player who best exemplifies the qualities of perseverance, sportsmanship and dedication to hockey.

JACK ADAMS AWARD

(Coach of the year)

Season Coach, Team
1973-74—Fred Shero, Philadelphia
1974-75—Bob Pulford, Los Angeles
1975-76—Don Cherry, Boston
1976-77—Scotty Bowman, Montreal
1977-78—Bobby Kromm, Detroit
1978-79—Al Arbour, N.Y. Islanders
1979-80—Pat Quinn, Philadelphia
1980-81—Red Berenson, St. Louis
1981-82—Tom Watt, Winnipeg
1982-83—Orval Tessier, Chicago
1983-84—Bryan Murray, Washington
1984-85—Mike Keenan, Philadelphia
1985-86—Glen Sather, Edmonton
1986-87—Jacques Demers, Detroit
1987-88—Jacques Demers, Detroit
1988-89—Pat Burns, Montreal
1989-90—Bob Murdoch, Winnipeg
1990-91—Brian Sutter, St. Louis
1991-92—Pat Quinn, Vancouver
1992-93—Pat Burns, Toronto
1993-94—Jacques Lemaire, New Jersey
1994-95—Marc Crawford, Quebec
1995-96—Scotty Bowman, Detroit
1996-97—Ted Nolan, Buffalo
1997-98—Pat Burns, Boston
1998-99—Jacques Martin, Ottawa

Season Coach, Team
1999-00—Joel Quenneville, St. Louis
2000-01—Bill Barber, Philadelphia
2001-02—Bob Francis, Phoenix
2002-03—Jacques Lemaire, Minnesota
2003-04—John Tortorella, Tampa Bay
2005-06—Lindy Ruff, Buffalo

KING CLANCY TROPHY

(Humanitarian contributions)

Season Player, Team
1987-88—Lanny McDonald, Calgary
1988-89—Bryan Trottier, N.Y. Islanders
1989-90—Kevin Lowe, Edmonton
1990-91—Dave Taylor, Los Angeles
1991-92—Ray Bourque, Boston
1992-93—Dave Poulin, Boston
1993-94—Adam Graves, N.Y. Rangers
1994-95—Joe Nieuwendyk, Calgary
1995-96—Kris King, Winnipeg
1996-97—Trevor Linden, Vancouver
1997-98—Kelly Chase, St. Louis
1998-99—Rob Ray, Buffalo
1999-00—Curtis Joseph, Toronto
2000-01—Shjon Podein, Colorado
2001-02—Ron Francis, Carolina
2002-03—Brendan Shanahan, Detroit
2003-04—Jarome Iginla, Calgary
2005-06—Olaf Kolzig, Washington

SPORTING NEWS AWARDS

PLAYER OF THE YEAR

Season Player, Team
1967-68—E. Div.: Stan Mikita, Chicago
W. Div.: Red Berenson, St. Louis
1968-69—E. Div.: Phil Esposito, Boston
W. Div.: Red Berenson, St. Louis
1969-70—E. Div.: Bobby Orr, Boston
W. Div.: Red Berenson, St. Louis
1970-71—E. Div.: Phil Esposito, Boston
W. Div.: Bobby Hull, Chicago
1971-72—E. Div.: Jean Ratelle, N.Y. Rangers
W. Div.: Bobby Hull, Chicago
1972-73—E. Div.: Phil Esposito, Boston
W. Div.: Bobby Clarke, Philadelphia
1973-74—E. Div.: Phil Esposito, Boston
W. Div.: Bernie Parent, Philadelphia
1974-75—Camp. Conf.: Bobby Clarke, Philadelphia
Wales Conf.: Guy Lafleur, Montreal
1975-76—Bobby Clarke, Philadelphia
1976-77—Guy Lafleur, Montreal
1977-78—Guy Lafleur, Montreal
1978-79—Bryan Trottier, N.Y. Islanders
1979-80—Marcel Dionne, Los Angeles
1980-81—Wayne Gretzky, Edmonton
1981-82—Wayne Gretzky, Edmonton
1982-83—Wayne Gretzky, Edmonton
1983-84—Wayne Gretzky, Edmonton
1984-85—Wayne Gretzky, Edmonton
1985-86—Wayne Gretzky, Edmonton
1986-87—Wayne Gretzky, Edmonton
1987-88—Mario Lemieux, Pittsburgh
1988-89—Mario Lemieux, Pittsburgh
1989-90—Mark Messier, Edmonton
1990-91—Brett Hull, St. Louis
1991-92—Mark Messier, N.Y. Rangers
1992-93—Mario Lemieux, Pittsburgh
1993-94—Sergei Fedorov, Detroit
1994-95—Eric Lindros, Philadelphia

Season Player, Team
1995-96—Mario Lemieux, Pittsburgh
1996-97—Dominik Hasek, Buffalo
1997-98—Dominik Hasek, Buffalo
1998-99—Jaromir Jagr, Pittsburgh
1999-00—Jaromir Jagr, Pittsburgh
2000-01—Joe Sakic, Colorado
2001-02—Jarome Iginla, Calgary
2002-03—Peter Forsberg, Colorado
2003-04—Martin St. Louis, Tampa Bay
2005-06—Jaromir Jagr, N.Y. Rangers

ROOKIE OF THE YEAR

Season Player, Team
1967-68—E. Div.: Derek Sanderson, Boston
W. Div.: Bill Flett, Los Angeles
1968-69—E. Div.: Brad Park, N.Y. Rangers
W. Div.: Norm Ferguson, Oakland
1969-70—E. Div.: Tony Esposito, Chicago
W. Div.: Bobby Clarke, Philadelphia
1970-71—E. Div.: Gil Perreault, Buffalo
W. Div.: Jude Drouin, Minnesota
1971-72—E. Div.: Richard Martin, Buffalo
W. Div.: Gilles Meloche, California
1972-73—E. Div.: Steve Vickers, N.Y. Rangers
W. Div.: Bill Barber, Philadelphia
1973-74—E. Div.: Denis Potvin, N.Y. Islanders
W. Div.: Tom Lysiak, Atlanta
1974-75—Camp. Conf.: Eric Vail, Atlanta
Wales Conf.: Pierre Larouche, Pittsburgh
1975-76—Bryan Trottier, N.Y. Islanders
1976-77—Willi Plett, Atlanta
1977-78—Mike Bossy, N.Y. Islanders
1978-79—Bobby Smith, Minnesota
1979-80—Ray Bourque, Boston
1980-81—Peter Stastny, Quebec
1981-82—Dale Hawerchuk, Winnipeg
1982-83—Steve Larmer, Chicago
1983-84—Steve Yzerman, Detroit
1984-85—Mario Lemieux, Pittsburgh
1985-86—Wendel Clark, Toronto
1986-87—Ron Hextall, Philadelphia
1987-88—Joe Nieuwendyk, Calgary
1988-89—Brian Leetch, N.Y. Rangers
1989-90—Jeremy Roenick, Chicago
1990-91—Ed Belfour, Chicago
1991-92—Tony Amonte, N.Y. Rangers
1992-93—Teemu Selanne, Winnipeg
1993-94—Jason Arnott, Edmonton
1994-95—Peter Forsberg, Quebec
1995-96—Eric Daze, Chicago
1996-97—Bryan Berard, N.Y. Islanders
1997-98—Sergei Samsonov, Boston
1998-99—Chris Drury, Colorado
1999-00—Scott Gomez, New Jersey
2000-01—Evgeni Nabokov, San Jose
2001-02—Dany Heatley, Atlanta
2002-03—Henrik Zetterberg, Detroit
2003-04—Michael Ryder, Montreal
2005-06—Alexander Ovechkin, Washington

NHL COACH OF THE YEAR

Season Player, Team
1944-45—Dick Irvin, Montreal
1945-46—Johnny Gottselig, Chicago
1979-80—Pat Quinn, Philadelphia
1980-81—Red Berenson, St. Louis
1981-82—Herb Brooks, N.Y. Rangers
1982-83—Gerry Cheevers, Boston
1983-84—Bryan Murray, Washington
1984-85—Mike Keenan, Philadelphia

Season	Player, Team

1985-86—Jacques Demers, St. Louis
1986-87—Jacques Demers, Detroit
1987-88—Terry Crisp, Calgary
1988-89—Pat Burns, Montreal
1989-90—Mike Milbury, Boston
1990-91—Tom Webster, Los Angeles
1991-92—Pat Quinn, Vancouver
1992-93—Pat Burns, Toronto
1993-94—Jacques Lemaire, New Jersey
1994-95—Marc Crawford, Quebec
1995-96—Scotty Bowman, Detroit
1996-97—Ken Hitchcock, Dallas
1997-98—Pat Burns, Boston
1998-99—Jacques Martin, Ottawa
1999-00—Joel Quenneville, St. Louis
2000-01—Scotty Bowman, Detroit
2001-02—Brian Sutter, Chicago
2002-03—Jacques Lemaire, Minnesota
2003-04—John Tortorella, Tampa Bay
2005-06—Lindy Ruff, Buffalo

NOTE: The Coach of the Year Award was not given from 1946-47 through 1978-79 seasons.

NHL EXECUTIVE OF THE YEAR

Season Player, Team

1972-73—Sam Pollock, Montreal
1973-74—Keith Allen, Philadelphia
1974-75—Bill Torrey, N.Y. Islanders
1975-76—Sam Pollock, Montreal
1976-77—Harry Sinden, Boston
1977-78—Ted Lindsay, Detroit
1978-79—Bill Torrey, N.Y. Islanders
1979-80—Scotty Bowman, Buffalo
1980-81—Emile Francis, St. Louis
1981-82—John Ferguson, Winnipeg
1982-83—David Poile, Washington
1983-84—David Poile, Washington
1984-85—John Ferguson, Winnipeg
1985-86—Emile Francis, Hartford
1986-87—John Ferguson, Winnipeg
1987-88—Cliff Fletcher, Calgary
1988-89—Bruce McNall, Los Angeles
1989-90—Harry Sinden, Boston
1990-91—Craig Patrick, Pittsburgh
1991-92—Neil Smith, N.Y. Rangers
1992-93—Cliff Fletcher, Toronto
1993-94—Bobby Clarke, Florida
1994-95—Bobby Clarke, Philadelphia
1995-96—Bryan Murray, Florida
1996-97—John Muckler, Buffalo
1997-98—Craig Patrick, Pittsburgh
1998-99—Craig Patrick, Pittsburgh
1999-00—Larry Pleau, St. Louis
2000-01—Brian Burke, Vancouver
2001-02—Mike Smith, Chicago
2002-03—Doug Risebrough, Minnesota
2003-04—Jay Feaster, Tampa Bay
2005-06—Jim Rutherford, Carolina

SPORTING NEWS ALL-STAR TEAMS

(As selected by six hockey writers in 1944-45 and 1945-46 and by a vote of league players since 1967-68; no teams selected from 1946-47 through 1966-67)

1944-45

First team		Second team
Maurice Richard, Mon.	W	Bill Mosienko, Chi.
Toe Blake, Mon.	W	Sweeney Schriner, Tor.
Elmer Lach, Mon.	C	Bill Cowley, Bos.
Emile Bouchard, Mon.	D	Earl Seibert, Det.
Bill Hollett, Det.	D	Babe Pratt, Tor.
Bill Durnan, Mon.	G	Frank McCool, Tor.

1945-46

First team		Second team
Gaye Stewart, Tor.	LW	Doug Bentley, Chi.
Max Bentley, Chi.	C	Elmer Lach, Mon.
Bill Mosienko, Chi.	RW	Maurice Richard, Mon.
Emile Bouchard, Mon.	D	Jack Crawford, Bos.
Jack Stewart, Det.	D	Babe Pratt, Tor.
Bill Durnan, Mon.	G	Harry Lumley, Det.

1967-68

EAST DIVISION		WEST DIVISION
First team		**First team**
Bobby Hull, Chi.	LW	Ab McDonald, Pit.
Stan Mikita, Chi.	C	Red Berenson, St.L.
Gordie Howe, Det.	RW	Wayne Connelly, Min.
Bobby Orr, Bos.	D	Bill White, L.A.
Tim Horton, Tor.	D	Mike McMahon, Min.
Ed Giacomin, N.Y.R.	G	Glenn Hall, St.L.
Second team		**Second team**
Johnny Bucyk, Bos.	LW	Bill Sutherland, Phi.
Phil Esposito, Bos.	C	Ray Cullen, Min.
Rod Gilbert, N.Y.R.	RW	Bill Flett, L.A.
J.C. Tremblay, Mon.	D	Al Arbour, St.L.
Gary Bergman, Det.	D	Ed Van Impe, Phi.
Gump Worsley, Mon.	G	Doug Favell, Phi.

1968-69

EAST DIVISION		WEST DIVISION
First team		**First team**
Bobby Hull, Chi.	LW	Danny Grant, Min.
Phil Esposito, Bos.	C	Red Berenson, St.L.
Gordie Howe, Det.	RW	Norm Ferguson, Oak.
Bobby Orr, Bos.	D	Bill White, L.A.
Tim Horton, Tor.	D	Al Arbour, St.L.
Ed Giacomin, N.Y.R.	G	Glenn Hall, St.L.
Second team		**Second team**
Frank Mahovlich, Det.	LW	Ab McDonald, St.L.
Stan Mikita, Chi.	C	Ted Hampson, Oak.
Yvan Cournoyer, Mon.	RW	Claude LaRose, Min.
J.C. Tremblay, Mon.	D	Carol Vadnais, Oak.
Jim Neilson, N.Y.R.	D	Ed Van Impe, Phi.
Bruce Gamble, Tor.	G	Bernie Parent, Phi.

1969-70

EAST DIVISION		WEST DIVISION
Bobby Hull, Chi.	LW	Dean Prentice, Pit.
Stan Mikita, Chi.	C	Red Berenson, St.L.
Ron Ellis, Tor.	RW	Bill Goldsworthy, Min.
Bobby Orr, Bos.	D	Al Arbour, St.L.
Brad Park, N.Y.R.	D	Bob Woytowich, Pit.
Tony Esposito, Chi.	G	Bernie Parent, Phi.

1970-71

EAST DIVISION		WEST DIVISION
Johnny Bucyk, Bos.	LW	Bobby Hull, Chi.
Phil Esposito, Bos.	C	Stan Mikita, Chi.
Ken Hodge, Bos.	RW	Bill Goldsworthy, Min.
Bobby Orr, Bos.	D	Pat Stapleton, Chi.
J.C. Tremblay, Mon.	D	Bill White, Chi.
Ed Giacomin, N.Y.R.	G	Tony Esposito, Chi.

1971-72

EAST DIVISION		WEST DIVISION
Vic Hadfield, N.Y.R.	LW	Bobby Hull, Chi.

EAST DIVISION		WEST DIVISION
Phil Esposito, Bos.	C	Bobby Clarke, Phi.
Rod Gilbert, N.Y.R.	RW	Bill Goldsworthy, Min.
Bobby Orr, Bos.	D	Pat Stapleton, Chi.
Brad Park, N.Y.R.	D	Bill White, Chi.
Ken Dryden, Mon.	G	Tony Esposito, Chi.

1972-73

EAST DIVISION		WEST DIVISION
Frank Mahovlich, Mon.	LW	Dennis Hull, Chi.
Phil Esposito, Bos.	C	Bobby Clarke, Phi.
Mickey Redmond, Det.	RW	Bill Flett, Phi.
Bobby Orr, Bos.	D	Bill White, Chi.
Guy Lapointe, Mon.	D	Barry Gibbs, Min.
Ken Dryden, Mon.	G	Tony Esposito, Chi.

1973-74

EAST DIVISION		WEST DIVISION
First team		**First team**
Richard Martin, Buf.	LW	Lowell MacDonald, Pit.
Phil Esposito, Bos.	C	Bobby Clarke, Phi.
Ken Hodge, Bos.	RW	Bill Goldsworthy, Min.
Bobby Orr, Bos.	D	Bill White, Chi.
Brad Park, N.Y.R.	D	Barry Ashbee, Phi.
Gilles Gilbert, Bos.	G	Bernie Parent, Phi.
Second team		**Second team**
Frank Mahovlich, Mon.	LW	Dennis Hull, Chi.
Darryl Sittler, Tor.	C	Stan Mikita, Chi.
Mickey Redmond, Det.	RW	Jean Pronovost, Pit.
Guy Lapointe, Mon.	D	Don Awrey, St.L.
Borje Salming, Tor.	D	Dave Burrows, Pit.
Ed Giacomin, N.Y.R.	D	Tony Esposito, Chi.

1974-75

CAMPBELL CONFERENCE		WALES CONFERENCE
First team		**First team**
Steve Vickers, N.Y.R.	LW	Richard Martin, Buf.
Bobby Clarke, Phi.	C	Phil Esposito, Bos.
Rod Gilbert, N.Y.R.	RW	Guy Lafleur, Mon.
Denis Potvin, N.Y.I.	D	Bobby Orr, Bos.
Brad Park, N.Y.R.	D	Guy Lapointe, Mon.
Bernie Parent, Phi.	G	Rogie Vachon, L.A.
Second team		**Second team**
Eric Vail, Atl.	LW	Danny Grant, Det.
Stan Mikita, Chi.	C	Gilbert Perreault, Buf.
Reggie Leach, Phi.	RW	Rene Robert, Buf.
Jim Watson, Phi.	D	Borje Salming, Tor.
Phil Russell, Chi.	D	Terry Harper, L.A.
Gary Smith, Van.	G	Ken Dryden, Mon.

1975-76

First team		Second team
Bill Barber, Phi.	LW	Richard Martin, Buf.
Bobby Clarke, Phi.	C	Pete Mahovlich, Mon.
Guy Lafleur, Mon.	RW	Reggie Leach, Phi.
Denis Potvin, N.Y.I.	D	Guy Lapointe, Mon.
Brad Park, Bos.	D	Borje Salming, Tor.
Ken Dryden, Mon.	G	Glenn Resch, N.Y.I.

1976-77

First team		Second team
Steve Shutt, Mon.	LW	Clark Gillies, N.Y.I.
Marcel Dionne, L.A.	C	Gilbert Perreault, Buf.
Guy Lafleur, Mon.	RW	Lanny McDonald, Tor.
Larry Robinson, Mon.	D	Guy Lapointe, Mon.
Borje Salming, Tor.	D	Serge Savard, Mon.
	(tied)	Denis Potvin, N.Y.I.
Rogie Vachon, L.A.	G	Ken Dryden, Mon.

1977-78

First team		Second team
Clark Gillies, N.Y.I.	LW	Steve Shutt, Mon.
Bryan Trottier, N.Y.I.	C	Darryl Sittler, Tor.
Guy Lafleur, Mon.	RW	Terry O'Reilly, Bos.
Borje Salming, Tor.	D	Denis Potvin, N.Y.I.
Larry Robinson, Mon.	D	Serge Savard, Mon.
Ken Dryden, Mon.	G	Don Edwards, Buf.

1978-79

First team		Second team
Clark Gillies, N.Y.I.	LW	Bob Gainey, Mon.
Bryan Trottier, N.Y.I.	C	Marcel Dionne, L.A.
Guy Lafleur, Mon.	RW	Mike Bossy, N.Y.I.
Denis Potvin, N.Y.I.	D	Borje Salming, Tor.
Larry Robinson, Mon.	D	Serge Savard, Mon.
Ken Dryden, Mon.	G	Glenn Resch, N.Y.I.

1979-80

First team		Second team
Charlie Simmer, L.A.	LW	Steve Shutt, Mon.
Marcel Dionne, L.A.	C	Wayne Gretzky, Edm.
Guy Lafleur, Mon.	RW	Danny Gare, Buf.
Larry Robinson, Mon.	D	Barry Beck, Col., N.Y.R.
Borje Salming, Tor.	D	Mark Howe, Har.
Tony Esposito, Chi.	G	Don Edwards, Buf.

1980-81

First team		Second team
Charlie Simmer, L.A.	LW	Bill Barber, Phi.
Wayne Gretzky, Edm.	C	Marcel Dionne, L.A.
Mike Bossy, N.Y.I.	RW	Dave Taylor, L.A.
Randy Carlyle, Pit.	D	Larry Robinson, Mon.
Denis Potvin, N.Y.I.	D	Ray Bourque, Bos.
Mike Liut, St.L.	G	Don Beaupre, Min.

1981-82

First team		Second team
Mark Messier, Edm.	LW	John Tonelli, N.Y.I.
Wayne Gretzky, Edm.	C	Bryan Trottier, N.Y.I.
Mike Bossy, N.Y.I.	RW	Rick Middleton, Bos.
Doug Wilson, Chi.	D	Paul Coffey, Edm.
Ray Bourque, Bos.	D	Larry Robinson, Mon.
Bill Smith, N.Y.I.	G	Grant Fuhr, Edm.

1982-83

First team		Second team
Mark Messier, Edm.	LW	Michel Goulet, Que.
Wayne Gretzky, Edm.	C	Denis Savard, Chi.
Lanny McDonald, Cal.	RW	Mike Bossy, N.Y.I.
Mark Howe, Phi.	D	Ray Bourque, Bos.
Rod Langway, Was.	D	Paul Coffey, Edm.
Pete Peeters, Bos.	G	Andy Moog, Edm.

1983-84

First team		Second team
Michel Goulet, Que.	LW	John Ogrodnick, Det.
Wayne Gretzky, Edm.	C	Bryan Trottier, N.Y.I.
Rick Middleton, Bos.	RW	Mike Bossy, N.Y.I.
Ray Bourque, Bos.	D	Paul Coffey, Edm.
Rod Langway, Was.	D	Denis Potvin, N.Y.I.
Pat Riggin, Was.	G	Tom Barrasso, Buf.

1984-85

First team		Second team
Michel Goulet, Que.	LW	John Ogrodnick, Det.
Wayne Gretzky, Edm.	C	Dale Hawerchuk, Win.
Jari Kurri, Edm.	RW	Mike Bossy, N.Y.I.
Ray Bourque, Bos.	D	Rod Langway, Was.
Paul Coffey, Edm.	D	Doug Wilson, Chi.
Pelle Lindbergh, Phi.	G	Tom Barrasso, Buf.

1985-86

First team		Second team
Michel Goulet, Que.	LW	Mats Naslund, Mon.
Wayne Gretzky, Edm.	C	Mario Lemieux, Pit.
Mike Bossy, N.Y.I.	RW	Jari Kurri, Edm.
Paul Coffey, Edm.	D	Ray Bourque, Bos.
Mark Howe, Phi.	D	Larry Robinson, Mon.
John Vanbiesbrouck, N.Y.R.	G	Grant Fuhr, Edm.

1986-87

First team		Second team
Michel Goulet, Que.	LW	Luc Robitaille, L.A.
Wayne Gretzky, Edm.	C	Mark Messier, Edm.
Tim Kerr, Phi.	RW	Kevin Dineen, Har.
Ray Bourque, Bos.	D	Larry Murphy, Was.
Mark Howe, Phi.	D	Paul Coffey, Edm.
Mike Liut, Har.	G	Ron Hextall, Phi.

1987-88

First team		Second team
Luc Robitaille, L.A.	LW	Michel Goulet, Que.
Mario Lemieux, Pit.	C	Wayne Gretzky, Edm.
Cam Neely, Bos.	RW	Hakan Loob, Cal.
Ray Bourque, Bos.	D	Scott Stevens, Was.
Gary Suter, Cal.	D	Brad McCrimmon, Cal.
Grant Fuhr, Edm.	G	Tom Barrasso, Buf.

1988-89

First team		Second team
Luc Robitaille, L.A.	LW	Mats Naslund, Mon.
Mario Lemieux, Pit.	C	Wayne Gretzky, L.A.
Joe Mullen, Cal.	RW	Jari Kurri, Edm.
Paul Coffey, Pit.	D	Ray Bourque, Bos.
Chris Chelios, Mon.	D	Gary Suter, Cal.
Patrick Roy, Mon.	G	Mike Vernon, Cal.

1989-90

First team		Second team
Luc Robitaille, L.A.	LW	Brian Bellows, Min.
Mark Messier, Edm.	C	Pat LaFontaine, N.Y.I.
Brett Hull, St.L.	RW	Cam Neely, Bos.
Ray Bourque, Bos.	D	Doug Wilson, Chi.
Al MacInnis, Cal.	D	Paul Coffey, Pit.
Patrick Roy, Mon.	G	Daren Puppa, Buf.

1990-91

First team		Second team
Luc Robitaille, L.A.	LW	Kevin Stevens, Pit.
Wayne Gretzky, L.A.	C	Adam Oates, St.L.
Brett Hull, St.L.	RW	Cam Neely, Bos.
Ray Bourque, Bos.	D	Brian Leetch, N.Y.R.
Al MacInnis, Cal.	D	Chris Chelios, Chi.
Ed Belfour, Chi.	G	Patrick Roy, Mon.

1991-92

First team		Second team
Kevin Stevens, Pit.	LW	Luc Robitaille, L.A.
Mark Messier, N.Y.R.	C	Wayne Gretzky, L.A.
Brett Hull, St.L.	RW	Joe Mullen, Pit.
Brian Leetch, N.Y.R.	D	Phil Housley, Win.
Ray Bourque, Bos.	D	Chris Chelios, Chi.
Patrick Roy, Mon.	G	Kirk McLean, Van.

1992-93

First team		Second team
Luc Robitaille, L.A.	LW	Kevin Stevens, Pit.
Mario Lemieux, Pit.	C	Doug Gilmour, Tor.
Teemu Selanne, Win.	RW	Alexander Mogilny, Buf.
Chris Chelios, Chi.	D	Larry Murphy, Pit.
Ray Bourque, Bos.	D	Al Iafrate, Was.
Tom Barrasso, Pit.	G	Ed Belfour, Chi.

1993-94

First team		Second team
Adam Graves, N.Y.R.	LW	Dave Andreychuk, Tor.
Sergei Fedorov, Det.	C	Wayne Gretzky, L.A.
Cam Neely, Bos.	RW	Pavel Bure, Van.
Ray Bourque, Bos.	D	Brian Leetch, N.Y.R.
Scott Stevens, N.J.	D	Al MacInnis, Cal.
John Vanbiesbrouck, Fla.	G	Dominik Hasek, Buf.

1994-95

John LeClair, Mon.-Phi.	LW
Eric Lindros, Phi.	C
Jaromir Jagr, Pit.	RW
Paul Coffey, Det.	D
Ray Bourque, Bos.	D
Dominik Hasek, Buf.	G

1995-96

Keith Tkachuk, Win.	LW
Mario Lemieux, Pit.	C
Jaromir Jagr, Pit.	RW
Chris Chelios, Chi.	D
Ray Bourque, Bost.	D
Chris Osgood, Det.	G

1996-97

John LeClair, Phil.	LW
Mario Lemieux, Pit.	C
Teemu Selanne, Ana.	RW
Chris Chelios, Chi.	D
Brian Leetch, N.Y. Rangers	D
Dominik Hasek, Buf.	G

1997-98

John LeClair, Phi.	LW
Peter Forsberg, Colo.	C
Teemu Selanne, Ana.	RW
Rob Blake, L.A.	D
Nicklas Lidstrom, Det.	D
Dominik Hasek, Buf.	G

1998-99

Paul Kariya, Ana.	LW
Alexei Yashin, Ott.	C
Jaromir Jagr, Pit.	RW
Al MacInnis, St.L.	D
Nicklas Lidstrom, Det.	D
Dominik Hasek, Buf.	G

1999-2000

Paul Kariya, Ana.	LW
Steve Yzerman, Det.	C
Jaromir Jagr, Pit.	RW
Nicklas Lidstrom, Det.	D
Chris Pronger, St.L.	D
Roman Turek, St.L.	G

2000-01

First team		Second team
Alexei Kovalev, Pit.	LW	Patrik Elias, N.J.
Joe Sakic, Colo.	C	Mario Lemieux, Pit.
Jaromir Jagr, Pit.	RW	Pavel Bure, Fla.
Rob Blake, L.A.-Col.	D	Brian Leetch, N.Y.R.
Nicklas Lidstrom, Det.	D	Chris Pronger, St.L.
Martin Brodeur, N.J.	G	Sean Burke, Pho.

2001-02

Markus Naslund, Van.	LW
Joe Sakic, Col.	C
Jarome Iginla, Cal.	RW
Rob Blake, Col.	D
Nicklas Lidstrom, Det.	D
Patrick Roy, Col.	G

2002-03

First team		Second team
Markus Naslund, Van.	LW	Marian Hossa, Ott.
Peter Forsberg, Colo.	C	Joe Thornton, Bost.
Todd Bertuzzi, Van.	RW	Milan Hejduk, Colo.
Nicklas Lidstrom, Det.	D	Rob Blake, Colo.
Al MacInnis, St.L.	D	Sergei Gonchar, Was.
Martin Brodeur, N.J.	G	Marty Turco, Dal.

2003-04

First team		Second team
Markus Naslund, Van.	LW	Alex Tanguay, Colo.
Joe Sakic, Colo.	C	Joe Thornton, Bost.
Martin St. Louis, T.B.	RW	Jarome Iginla, Cal.
Nicklas Lidstrom, Det.	D	Scott Niedermayer, N.J.
Zdeno Chara, Ott.	D	Rob Blake, Colo.
Roberto Luongo, Fla.	G	Martin Brodeur, N.J.

2005-06

First team	
Alexander Ovechkin, Was.	LW
Joe Thornton, S.J.	C
Jaromir Jagr, N.Y. Rangers	RW
Nicklas Lidstrom, Det.	D
Scott Niedermayer, Ana.	D
Miikka Kiprusoff, Cal.	G

HOCKEY HALL OF FAME

ROSTER OF MEMBERS

NOTE: Leagues other than the NHL with which Hall of Fame members are associated are denoted in parentheses. Abbreviations: **AAHA:** Alberta Amateur Hockey Association. **AHA:** Amateur Hockey Association of Canada. **CAHL:** Canadian Amateur Hockey League. **EAA:** Eaton Athletic Association. **ECAHA:** Eastern Canada Amateur Hockey Association. **ECHA:** Eastern Canada Hockey Association. **FAHL:** Federal Amateur Hockey League. **IHL:** International Professional Hockey League. **MHL:** Manitoba Hockey League. **MNSHL:** Manitoba and Northwestern Senior Hockey League. **MPHL:** Maritime Pro Hockey League. **MSHL:** Manitoba Senior Hockey League. **NHA:** National Hockey Association. **NOHA:** Northern Ontario Hockey Association. **OHA:** Ontario Hockey Association. **OPHL:** Ontario Professional Hockey League. **PCHA:** Pacific Coast Hockey Association. **WCHL:** Western Canada Hockey League. **WHA:** World Hockey Association. **WHL:** Western Hockey League. **WinHL:** Winnipeg Hockey League. **WOHA:** Western Ontario Hockey Association.

PLAYERS

Player	Elec. year/ how elected*	Pos.†	First season	Last season	Stanley Cup wins‡	Teams as player
Abel, Sid	1969/P	C	1938-39	1953-54	3	Detroit Red Wings, Chicago Blackhawks
Adams, Jack	1959/P	C	1917-18	1926-27	2	Toronto Arenas, Vancouver Millionaires (PCHA), Toronto St. Pats, Ottawa Senators
Apps, Syl	1961/P	C	1936-37	1947-48	3	Toronto Maple Leafs
Armstrong, George	1975/P	RW	1949-50	1970-71	4	Toronto Maple Leafs
Bailey, Ace	1975/P	RW	1926-27	1933-34	1	Toronto Maple Leafs
Bain, Dan	1945/P	C	1895-96	1901-02	3	Winnipeg Victorias (MHL)
Baker, Hobey	1945/P	Ro.	1910	1915	0	Princeton University, St. Nicholas
Barber, Bill	1990/P	LW	1972-73	1983-84	2	Philadelphia Flyers
Barry, Marty	1965/P	C	1927-28	1939-40	2	New York Americans, Boston Bruins, Detroit Red Wings, Montreal Canadiens
Bathgate, Andy	1978/P	RW	1952-53	1974-75	1	New York Rangers, Toronto Maple Leafs, Detroit Red Wings, Pittsburgh Penguins, Vancouver Blazers (WHA)
Bauer, Bobby	1996/V	LW	1936-37	1951-52	2	Boston Bruins
Beliveau, Jean	1972/P	C	1950-51	1970-71	10	Montreal Canadiens
Benedict, Clint	1965/P	G	1917-18	1929-30	4	Ottawa Senators, Montreal Maroons
Bentley, Doug	1964/P	LW	1939-40	1953-54	0	Chicago Blackhawks, New York Rangers
Bentley, Max	1966/P	C	1940-41	1953-54	3	Chicago Blackhawks, Toronto Maple Leafs, New York Rangers
Blake, Toe	1966/P	LW	1934-35	1947-48	3	Montreal Maroons, Montreal Canadiens
Boivin, Leo	1986/P	D	1951-52	1969-70	0	Toronto Maple Leafs, Boston Bruins, Detroit Red Wings, Pittsburgh Penguins, Minnesota North Stars
Boon, Dickie	1952/P	D	1897	1905	2	Montreal Monarchs, Montreal AAA (CAHL), Montreal Wanderers (FAHL)
Bossy, Mike	1991/P	RW	1977-78	1986-87	4	New York Islanders
Bouchard, Butch	1966/P	D	1941-42	1955-56	4	Montreal Canadiens
Boucher, Frank	1958/P	C	1921-22	1943-44	2	Ottawa Senators, Vancouver Maroons, New York Rangers
Boucher, Georges	1960/P	F/D	1917-18	1931-32	4	Ottawa Senators, Montreal Maroons, Chicago Blackhawks
Bourque, Raymond	2004/P	D	1979-80	2000-01	1	Boston Bruins, Colorado Avalanche
Bower, Johnny	1976/P	G	1953-54	1969-70	0	New York Rangers, Toronto Maple Leafs
Bowie, Russell	1945/P	C	1898-99	1907-08	1	Montreal Victorias
Brimsek, Frank	1966/P	G	1938-39	1949-50	2	Boston Bruins, Chicago Blackhawks
Broadbent, Punch	1962/P	RW	1912-13	1928-29	4	Ottawa Senators, Montreal Maroons, New York Americans
Broda, Turk	1967/P	G	1936-37	1951-52	0	Toronto Maple Leafs
Bucyk, John	1981/P	LW	1955-56	1977-78	2	Detroit Red Wings, Boston Bruins
Burch, Billy	1974/P	C	1922-23	1932-33	0	Hamilton Tigers, New York Americans, Boston Bruins, Chicago Blackhawks
Cameron, Harry	1962/P	D	1912-13	1925-26	3	Toronto Blueshirts, Toronto Arenas, Montreal Wanderers, Ottawa Senators, Toronto St. Pats, Montreal Canadiens, Saskatoon (WCHL)
Cheevers, Gerry	1985/P	G	1961-62	1979-80	2	Toronto Maple Leafs, Boston Bruins, Cleveland Crusaders (WHA)

Player	Elec. year/ how elected*	Pos.†	First season	Last season	Stanley Cup wins‡	Teams as player
Abel, Sid	1969/P	C	1938-39	1953-54	3	Detroit Red Wings, Chicago Blackhawks
Clancy, King	1958/P	D	1921-22	1936-37	3	Ottawa Senators, Toronto Maple Leafs
Clapper, Dit	1947/P	RW	1927-28	1946-47	3	Boston Bruins
Clarke, Bobby	1987/P	C	1969-70	1983-84	2	Philadelphia Flyers
Cleghorn, Sprague	1958/P	D	1909-10	1927-28	3	New York Crescents, Renfrew Creamery Kings (NHA), Montreal Wanderers, Ottawa Senators, Toronto St. Pats, Montreal Canadiens, Boston Bruins
Coffey, Paul	2004/P	D	1980-81	2000-01	4	Edmonton Oilers, Pittsburgh Penguins, Los Angeles Kings, Detroit Red Wings, Hartford Whalers, Philadelphia Flyers, Chicago Blackhawks, Carolina Hurricanes, Boston Bruins
Colville, Neil	1967/P	C/D	1935-36	1948-49	1	New York Rangers
Conacher, Charlie	1961/P	RW	1929-30	1940-41	1	Toronto Maple Leafs, Detroit Red Wings, New York Americans
Conacher, Lionel	1994/V	D	1925-26	1936-37	2	Pittsburgh Pirates, New York Americans, Montreal Maroons, Chicago Blackhawks
Conacher, Roy	1998/V	LW	1938-39	1951-52	2	Boston Bruins, Detroit Red Wings, Chicago Blackhawks
Connell, Alex	1958/P	G	1924-25	1936-37	2	Ottawa Senators, Detroit Falcons, New York Americans, Montreal Maroons
Cook, Bill	1952/P	RW	1921-22	1936-37	2	Saskatoon (WCHL/WHL), New York Rangers
Cook, Bun	1995/V	LW	1926-27	1936-37	2	New York Rangers, Boston Bruins
Coulter, Art	1974/P	D	1931-32	1941-42	2	Chicago Blackhawks, New York Rangers
Cournoyer, Yvan	1982/P	RW	1963-64	1978-79	10	Montreal Canadiens
Cowley, Bill	1968/P	C	1934-35	1946-47	2	St. Louis Eagles, Boston Bruins
Crawford, Rusty	1962/P	LW	1912-13	1925-26	1	Quebec Bulldogs, Ottawa Senators, Toronto Arenas, Saskatoon (WCHL), Calgary (WCHL), Vancouver (WHL)
Darragh, Jack	1962/P	RW	1910-11	1923-24	4	Ottawa Senators
Davidson, Scotty	1950/P	RW	1912-13	1913-14	0	Toronto (NHA)
Day, Hap	1961/P	D	1924-25	1937-38	1	Toronto St. Pats, Toronto Maple Leafs, New York Americans
Delvecchio, Alex	1977/P	C	1950-51	1973-74	3	Detroit Red Wings
Denneny, Cy	1959/P	LW	1914-15	1928-29	5	Toronto Shamrocks (NHA), Toronto Blueshirts (NHA), Ottawa Senators, Boston Bruins
Dionne, Marcel	1992/P	C	1971-72	1988-89	0	Detroit Red Wings, Los Angeles Kings, New York Rangers
Drillon, Gord	1975/P	RW	1936-37	1942-43	1	Toronto Maple Leafs, Montreal Canadiens
Drinkwater, Graham	1950/P	F/D	1892-93	1898-99	5	Montreal Victorias
Dryden, Ken	1983/P	G	1970-71	1978-79	6	Montreal Canadiens
Duff, Dick	2006/P	F	1954-55	1971-72	6	Toronto Maple Leafs, New York Rangers, Montreal Canadiens, Los Angeles Kings, Buffalo Sabres
Dumart, Woody	1992/V	LW	1935-36	1953-54	2	Boston Bruins
Dunderdale, Tommy	1974/P	C	1906-07	1923-24	0	Winnipeg Maple Leafs (MHL), Montreal Shamrocks (NHA), Quebec Bulldogs (NHA), Victoria (PCHA), Portland (PCHA), Saskatoon (WCHL), Edmonton (WCHL)
Durnan, Bill	1964/P	G	1943-44	1949-50	2	Montreal Canadiens
Dutton, Red	1958/P	D	1921-22	1935-36	0	Calgary Tigers (WCHL), Montreal Maroons, New York Americans
Dye, Babe	1970/P	RW	1919-20	1930-31	1	Toronto St. Pats, Hamilton Tigers, Chicago Blackhawks, New York Americans, Toronto Maple Leafs
Esposito, Phil	1984/P	C	1963-64	1980-81	2	Chicago Blackhawks, Boston Bruins, New York Rangers
Esposito, Tony	1988/P	G	1968-69	1983-84	1	Montreal Canadiens, Chicago Blackhawks
Farrell, Arthur	1965/P	F	1896-97	1900-01	2	Montreal Shamrocks (AHA/CAHL)
Federko, Bernie	2002/P	C	1976-77	1989-90	0	St. Louis Blues, Detroit Red Wings
Fetisov, Viacheslav	2001/P	D	1974-75	1997-98	2	CSKA Moscow, New Jersey Devils, Detroit Red Wings
Flaman, Fern	1990/V	D	1944-45	1960-61	1	Boston Bruins, Toronto Maple Leafs
Foyston, Frank	1958/P	C	1912-13	1927-28	3	Toronto Blueshirts (NHA), Seattle Metropolitans (PCHA), Victoria Cougars (WCHL/WHL), Detroit Cougars
Fredrickson, Frank	1958/P	C	1920-21	1930-31	1	Victoria Aristocrats (PCHA), Victoria Cougars (PCHA/WCHL/WHL), Detroit Cougars, Boston Bruins, Pittsburgh Pirates, Detroit Falcons
Fuhr, Grant	2003/P	G	1979-80	1999-00	5	Victoria Cougars (WHL), Edmonton Oilers, Toronto Maple Leafs, Buffalo Sabres, St. Louis Blues, Calgary Flames
Gadsby, Bill	1970/P	D	1946-47	1965-66	0	Chicago Blackhawks, New York Rangers, Detroit Red Wings
Gainey, Bob	1992/P	LW	1973-74	1988-89	5	Montreal Canadiens
Gardiner, Chuck	1945/P	G	1927-28	1933-34	1	Chicago Blackhawks
Gardiner, Herb	1958/P	D	1921-22	1928-29	0	Calgary Tigers (WCHL), Montreal Canadiens, Chicago Blackhawks
Gardner, Jimmy	1962/P	LW	1900-01	1914-15	3	Montreal Hockey Club (CAHL), Montreal Wanderers (FAHL/ECHA/NHA), Calumet (IHL), Pittsburgh (IHL), Montreal Shamrocks (ECAHA),New Westminster Royals (PCHA), Montreal Canadiens (NHA)
Gartner, Mike	2001/P	RW	1978-79	1997-98	0	Cincinnati Stingers (WHA), Washington Capitals, Minnesota North Stars, New York Rangers, Toronto Maple Leafs, Phoenix Coyotes
Geoffrion, Boom Boom	1972/P	RW	1950-51	1967-68	6	Montreal Canadiens, New York Rangers
Gerard, Eddie	1945/P	F/D	1913-14	1922-23	4	Ottawa Senators (NHA/NHL), Toronto St. Pats
Giacomin, Eddie	1987/P	G	1965-66	1977-78	0	New York Rangers, Detroit Red Wings

Player	Elec. year/ how elected*	Pos.†	First season	Last season	Stanley Cup wins‡	Teams as player
Abel, Sid	1969/P	C	1938-39	1953-54	3	Detroit Red Wings, Chicago Blackhawks
Gilbert, Rod	1982/P	RW	1960-61	1977-78	0	New York Rangers
Gillies, Clark	2002/P	LW	1974-75	1987-88	4	New York Islanders, Buffalo Sabres
Gilmour, Billy	1962/P	RW	1902-03	1915-16	5	Ottawa Silver Seven (CAHL/FAHL/ECAHA), Montreal Victorias (ECAHA), Ottawa Senators (ECHA/NHA)
Goheen, Moose	1952/P	D	1914	1918	0	St. Paul Athletic Club, 1920 U.S. Olympic Team
Goodfellow, Ebbie	1963/P	C	1929-30	1942-43	3	Detroit Cougars, Detroit Falcons, Detroit Red Wings
Goulet, Michel	1998/P	LW	1978-79	1993-94	0	Birmingham Bulls (WHA), Quebec Nordiques, Chicago Blackhawks
Grant, Mike	1950/P	D	1893-94	1901-02	5	Montreal Victorias (AHA/CAHL), Montreal Shamrocks (CAHL)
Green, Shorty	1962/P	RW	1923-24	1926-27	0	Hamilton Tigers, New York Americans
Gretzky, Wayne	1999/P	C	1978-79	1998-99	4	Indianapolis Racers (WHA), Edmonton (WHA/NHL), Los Angeles Kings, St. Louis Blues, New York Rangers
Griffis, Si	1950/P	Ro./D	1902-03	1918-19	2	Rat Portage Thistles (MNSHL), Kenora Thistles (MSHL), Vancouver Millionaires (PCHA)
Hainsworth, George	1961/P	G	1923-24	1936-37	2	Saskatoon Crescents (WCHL/WHL), Montreal Canadiens, Toronto Maple Leafs
Hall, Glenn	1975/P	G	1952-53	1970-71	1	Detroit Red Wings, Chicago Blackhawks, St. Louis Blues
Hall, Joe	1961/P	F/D	1903-04	1918-19	2	Winnipeg (MSHL), Quebec Bulldogs (ECAHA/NHA), Brandon (MHL), Montreal (ECAHA), Montreal Shamrocks (ECAHA/NHA), Montreal Wanderers (ECHA), Montreal Canadiens
Harvey, Doug	1973/P	D	1947-48	1968-69	6	Montreal Canadiens, New York Rangers, Detroit Red Wings, St. Louis Blues
Hawerchuk, Dale	2001/P	C	1981-82	1996-97	0	Winnipeg Jets, Buffalo Sabres, St. Louis Blues, Philadelphia Flyers
Hay, George	1958/P	LW	1921-22	1933-34	0	Regina Capitals (WCHL), Portland Rosebuds (WHL), Chicago Blackhawks, Detroit Cougars, Detroit Falcons, Detroit Red Wings
Hern, Riley	1962/P	G	1906-07	1910-11	3	Montreal Wanderers (ECAHA/ECHA/NHA)
Hextall, Bryan	1969/P	RW	1936-37	1947-48	1	New York Rangers
Holmes, Hap	1972/P	G	1912-13	1927-28	0	Toronto Blueshirts (NHA), Seattle Metropolitans (PCHA), Toronto Arenas, Victoria Cougars (WCHL/WHL), Detroit Cougars
Hooper, Tom	1962/P	F	1904-05	1907-08	2	Rat Portage Thistles (MNSHL), Kenora Thistles (SHL), Montreal Wanderers (ECAHA), Montreal (ECAHA)
Horner, Red	1965/P	D	1928-29	1939-40	1	Toronto Maple Leafs
Horton, Tim	1977/P	D	1949-50	1973-74	4	Toronto Maple Leafs, New York Rangers, Pittsburgh Penguins, Buffalo Sabres
Howe, Gordie	1972/P	RW	1946-47	1979-80	4	Detroit Red Wings, Houston Aeros (WHA), New England Whalers (WHA), Hartford Whalers
Howe, Syd	1965/P	F/D	1929-30	1945-46	3	Ottawa Senators, Philadelphia Quakers, Toronto Maple Leafs, St. Louis Eagles, Detroit Red Wings
Howell, Harry	1979/P	D	1952-53	1975-76	0	New York Rangers, Oakland Seals, California Golden Seals, Los Angeles Kings, New York Golden Blades/Jersey Knights (WHA), San Diego Mariners (WHA), Calgary Cowboys (WHA)
Hull, Bobby	1983/P	LW	1957-58	1979-80	1	Chicago Blackhawks, Winnipeg Jets (WHA/NHL), Hartford Whalers
Hutton, Bouse	1962/P	G	1898-99	1903-04	1	Ottawa Silver Seven (CAHL)
Hyland, Harry	1962/P	RW	1908-09	1917-18	1	Montreal Shamrocks (ECHA), Montreal Wanderers (NHA), New Westminster Royals (PCHA), Ottawa Senators
Irvin, Dick	1958/P	C	1916-17	1928-29	0	Portland Rosebuds (PCHA), Regina Capitals (WCHL), Chicago Blackhawks
Jackson, Busher	1971/P	LW	1929-30	1943-44	1	Toronto Maple Leafs, New York Americans, Boston Bruins
Johnson, Ching	1958/P	D	1926-27	1937-38	2	New York Rangers, New York Americans
Johnson, Moose	1952/P	LW/D	1903-04	1921-22	4	Montreal AAA (CAHL), Montreal Wanderers (ECAHA/ECHA/NHA), New Westminster Royals (PCHA), Portland Rosebuds (PCHA), Victoria Aristocrats (PCHA)
Johnson, Tom	1970/P	D	1947-48	1964-65	6	Montreal Canadiens, Boston Bruins
Joliat, Aurel	1947/P	LW	1922-23	1937-38	3	Montreal Canadiens
Keats, Duke	1958/P	C	1915-16	1928-29	0	Toronto Blueshirts (NHA), Edmonton Eskimos (WCHL/WHL), Boston Bruins, Detroit Cougars, Chicago Blackhawks
Kelly, Red	1969/P	C	1947-48	1966-67	8	Detroit Red Wings, Toronto Maple Leafs
Kennedy, Ted	1966/P	C	1942-43	1956-57	5	Toronto Maple Leafs
Keon, Dave	1986/P	C	1960-61	1981-82	4	Toronto Maple Leafs, Minnesota Fighting Saints (WHA) Indianapolis Racers (WHA), New England Whalers (WHA), Hartford Whalers
Kharlamov, Valeri	2005/P	W	1967-68	1980-81	0	CSKA Moscow
Kurri, Jari	2001/P	C/RW	1980-81	1997-98	5	Edmonton Oilers, Los Angeles Kings, New York Rangers, Mighty Ducks of Anaheim, Colorado Avalanche
Lach, Elmer	1966/P	C	1940-41	1953-54	3	Montreal Canadiens
Lafleur, Guy	1988/P	RW	1971-72	1990-91	5	Montreal Canadiens, New York Rangers, Quebec Nordiques

Player	Elec. year/ how elected*	Pos.†	First season	Last season	Stanley Cup wins‡	Teams as player
Abel, Sid	1969/P	C	1938-39	1953-54	3	Detroit Red Wings, Chicago Blackhawks
LaFontaine, Pat	2003/P	C	1983-84	1997-98	0	New York Islanders, Buffalo Sabres, New York Rangers
Lalonde, Newsy	1950/P	C/Ro.	1904-05	1926-27	1	Cornwall (FAHL), Portage La Prairie (MHL), Toronto (OPHL), Montreal Canadiens (NHA/NHL), Renfrew Creamery Kings (NHA), Vancouver Millionaires (PCHA), Saskatoon Sheiks (WCHL), Saskatoon Crescents (WCHL/WHL), New York Americans
Langway, Rod	2002/P	D	1978-79	1992-93	1	Montreal Canadiens, Washington Capitals
Laperriere, Jacques	1987/P	D	1962-63	1973-74	6	Montreal Canadiens
Lapointe, Guy	1993/P	D	1968-69	1983-84	6	Montreal Canadiens, St. Louis Blues, Boston Bruins
Laprade, Edgar	1993/V	C	1945-46	1954-55	0	New York Rangers
Laviolette, Jack	1962/P	D/LW	1903-04	1917-18	1	Montreal Nationals (FAHL), Montreal Shamrocks (ECAHA/ECHA), Montreal Canadiens (NHA/NHL)
Lehman, Hugh	1958/P	G	1908-09	1927-28	1	Berlin Dutchmen (OPHL), Galt (OPHL), New Westminster Royals (PCHA), Vancouver Millionaires (PCHA), Vancouver Maroons (PCHA), Chicago Blackhawks
Lemaire, Jacques	1984/P	C	1967-68	1978-79	8	Montreal Canadiens
Lemieux, Mario	1997/P	C	1984-85	2002-03	2	Pittsburgh Penguins
LeSueur, Percy	1961/P	G	1905-06	1915-16	3	Smith Falls (FAHL), Ottawa Senators (ECAHA/ECHA/NHA), Toronto Shamrocks (NHA), Toronto Blueshirts (NHA)
Lewis, Herbie	1989/V	LW	1928-29	1938-39	2	Detroit Cougars, Detroit Falcons, Detroit Red Wings
Lindsay, Ted	1966/P	LW	1944-45	1964-65	4	Detroit Red Wings, Chicago Blackhawks
Lumley, Harry	1980/P	G	1943-44	1959-60	1	Detroit Red Wings, New York Rangers, Chicago Blackhawks, Toronto Maple Leafs, Boston Bruins
MacKay, Mickey	1952/P	C/Ro.	1914-15	1929-30	1	Vancouver Millionaires (PCHA), Vancouver Maroons (PCHA/WCHL/WHL), Chicago Blackhawks, Pittsburgh Pirates, Boston Bruins
Mahovlich, Frank	1981/P	LW	1956-57	1977-78	6	Toronto Maple Leafs, Detroit Red Wings, Montreal Canadiens, Toronto Toros (WHA), Birmingham Bulls (WHA)
Malone, Joe	1950/P	C/LW	1908-09	1923-24	3	Quebec (ECHA), Waterloo (OPHL), Quebec Bulldogs (NHA/NHL), Montreal Canadiens, Hamilton Tigers
Mantha, Sylvio	1960/P	D	1923-24	1936-37	3	Montreal Canadiens, Boston Bruins
Marshall, Jack	1965/P	C/D	1900-01	1916-17	6	Winnipeg Victorias, Montreal AAA (CAHL), Montreal Wanderers (FAHL/ECAHA/NHA), Ottawa Montagnards (FAHL), Montreal Shamrocks (ECAHA/ECHA), Toronto Blueshirts (NHA)
Maxwell, Fred	1962/P	Ro.	1914	1925	0	Winnipeg Monarchs (MSHL), Winnipeg Falcons (MSHL)
McDonald, Lanny	1992/P	RW	1973-74	1988-89	1	Toronto Maple Leafs, Colorado Rockies, Calgary Flames
McGee, Frank	1945/P	C/Ro.	1902-03	1905-06	4	Ottawa Silver Seven
McGimsie, Billy	1962/P	F	1902-03	1906-07	1	Rat Portage Thistles (MNSHL/MSHL), Kenora Thistles (MSHL)
McNamara, George	1958/P	D	1907-08	1916-17	1	Montreal Shamrocks (ECAHA/ECHA), Waterloo (OPHL), Toronto Tecumsehs (NHA), Toronto Ontarios (NHA), Toronto Blueshirts (NHA), Toronto Shamrocks (NHA), 228th Battalion (NHA)
Mikita, Stan	1983/P	C	1958-59	1979-80	1	Chicago Blackhawks
Moore, Dickie	1974/P	LW	1951-52	1967-68	6	Montreal Canadiens, Toronto Maple Leafs, St. Louis Blues
Moran, Paddy	1958/P	G	1901-02	1916-17	2	Quebec Bulldogs (CAHL/ECAHA/ECHA/NHA), Haileybury (NHA)
Morenz, Howie	1945/P	C	1923-24	1936-37	3	Montreal Canadiens, Chicago Blackhawks, New York Rangers
Mosienko, Bill	1965/P	RW	1941-42	1954-55	0	Chicago Blackhawks
Mullen, Joe	2000/P	RW	1979-80	1996-97	3	St. Louis Blues, Calgary Flames, Pittsburgh Penguins, Boston Bruins
Murphy, Larry	2004/P	D	1980-81	2000-01	4	Los Angeles Kings, Washington Capitals, Minnesota North Stars, Pittsburgh Penguins, Toronto Maple Leafs, Detroit Red Wings
Neely, Cam	2005/P	RW	1983-84	1995-96	0	Vancouver Canucks, Boston Bruins
Nighbor, Frank	1947/P	LW/C	1912-13	1929-30	5	Toronto Blueshirts (NHA), Vancouver Millionaires, (PCHA), Ottawa Senators, Toronto Maple Leafs
Noble, Reg	1962/P	LW/C/D	1916-17	1932-33	3	Toronto Blueshirts (NHA), Montreal Canadiens (NHA), Toronto Arenas, Toronto St. Pats, Montreal Maroons, Detroit Cougars, Detroit Falcons, Detroit Red Wings
O'Connor, Buddy	1988/V	C	1941-42	1950-51	2	Montreal Canadiens, New York Rangers
Oliver, Harry	1967/P	RW	1921-22	1936-37	1	Calgary Tigers (WCHL/WHL), Boston Bruins, New York Americans
Olmstead, Bert	1985/P	LW	1948-49	1961-62	5	Chicago Blackhawks, Montreal Canadiens, Toronto Maple Leafs
Orr, Bobby	1979/P	D	1966-67	1978-79	2	Boston Bruins, Chicago Blackhawks
Parent, Bernie	1984/P	G	1965-66	1978-79	2	Boston Bruins, Philadelphia Flyers, Toronto Maple Leafs, Philadelphia Blazers (WHA)

Player	Elec. year/ how elected*	Pos.†	First season	Last season	Stanley Cup wins‡	Teams as player
Park, Brad	1988/P	D	1968-69	1984-85	0	New York Rangers, Boston Bruins, Detroit Red Wings
Patrick, Lester	1947/P	D	1903-04	1926-27	3	Brandon, Westmount (CAHL), Montreal Wanderers (ECAHA), Edmonton Eskimos (AAHA), Renfrew Creamery Kings (NHA), Victoria Aristocrats (PCHA), Spokane Canaries (PCHA), Seattle Metropolitans (PCHA), Seattle Metropolitans(PCHA), Victoria Cougars (WHL), New York Rangers
Patrick, Lynn	1980/P	LW	1934-35	1945-46	1	New York Rangers
Perreault, Gilbert	1990/P	C	1970-71	1986-87	0	Buffalo Sabres
Phillips, Tommy	1945/P	LW	1902-03	1911-12	1	Montreal AAA (CAHL), Toronto Marlboros (OHA), Rat Portage Thistles, Kenora Thistles (MHL), Ottawa Ottawa Senators (ECAHA), Edmonton Eskimos (AAHA), Vancouver Millionaires (PCHA)
Pilote, Pierre	1975/P	D	1955-56	1968-69	1	Chicago Blackhawks, Toronto Maple Leafs
Pitre, Didier	1962/P	D/RW	1903-04	1922-23	0	Montreal Nationals (FAHL/CAHL), Montreal Shamrocks (ECAHA), Edmonton Eskimos (AAHA), Montreal Canadiens (NHA/NHL), Vancouver Millionaires (PCHA)
Plante, Jacques	1978/P	G	1952-53	1974-75	6	Montreal Canadiens, New York Rangers, St. Louis Blues, Toronto Maple Leafs, Boston Bruins, Edmonton Oilers (WHA)
Potvin, Denis	1991/P	D	1973-74	1987-88	4	New York Islanders
Pratt, Babe	1966/P	D	1935-36	1946-47	2	New York Rangers, Toronto Maple Leafs, Boston Bruins
Primeau, Joe	1963/P	C	1927-28	1935-36	1	Toronto Maple Leafs
Pronovost, Marcel	1978/P	D	1949-50	1969-70	5	Detroit Red Wings, Toronto Maple Leafs
Pulford, Bob	1991/P	LW	1956-57	1971-72	4	Toronto Maple Leafs, Los Angeles Kings
Pulford, Harvey	1945/P	D	1893-94	1907-08	4	Ottawa Silver Seven/Senators (AHA/CAHL/FAHL/ECAHA)
Quackenbush, Bill	1976/P	D	1942-43	1955-56	0	Detroit Red Wings, Boston Bruins
Rankin, Frank	1961/P	Ro.	1906	1914	0	Stratford (OHA), Eatons (EAA), Toronto St. Michaels (OHA)
Ratelle, Jean	1985/P	C	1960-61	1980-81	0	New York Rangers, Boston Bruins
Rayner, Chuck	1973/P	G	1940-41	1952-53	0	New York Americans, New York Rangers
Reardon, Ken	1966/P	D	1940-41	1949-50	1	Montreal Canadiens
Richard, Henri	1979/P	C	1955-56	1974-75	11	Montreal Canadiens
Richard, Rocket	1961/P	RW	1942-43	1959-60	8	Montreal Canadiens
Richardson, George	1950/P		1906	1912	0	14th Regiment, Queen's University
Roberts, Gordon	1971/P	LW	1909-10	1919-20	0	Ottawa Senators (NHA), Montreal Wanderers (NHA), Vancouver Millionaires (PCHA), Seattle Metropolitans (PCHA)
Robinson, Larry	1995/P	D	1972-73	1991-92	6	Montreal Canadiens, Los Angeles Kings
Ross, Art	1945/P	D	1904-05	1917-18	2	Westmount (CAHL), Brandon (MHL), Kenora Thistles (MHL), Montreal Wanderers (ECAHA/ECHA/NHA/NHL), Haileybury (NHA), Ottawa Senators (NHA)
Roy, Patrick	2006/P	G	1984-85	2002-03	4	Montreal Canadiens, Colorado Avalanche
Russell, Blair	1965/P	RW/C	1899-00	1907-08	0	Montreal Victorias (CAHL/ECAHA)
Russell, Ernie	1965/P	Ro./C	1904-05	1913-14	4	Montreal Winged Wheelers (CAHL), Montreal Wanderers (ECAHA/NHA)
Ruttan, Jack	1962/P		1905	1913	0	Armstrong's Point, Rustler, St. John's College, Manitoba Varsity (WSHL), Winnipeg (WinHL)
Salming, Borje	1996/P	D	1973-74	1989-90	0	Toronto Maple Leafs, Detroit Red Wings
Savard, Dennis	2000/P	C	1980-81	1996-97	1	Chicago Blackhawks, Montreal Canadiens, Tampa Bay Lightning
Savard, Serge	1986/P	D	1966-67	1982-83	7	Montreal Canadiens, Winnipeg Jets
Sawchuk, Terry	1971/P	G	1949-50	1969-70	4	Detroit Red Wings, Boston Bruins, Toronto Maple Leafs, Los Angeles Kings, New York Rangers
Scanlan, Fred	1965/P	F	1897-98	1902-03	3	Montreal Shamrocks (AHA/CAHL), Winnipeg Victorias (MSHL)
Schmidt, Milt	1961/P	C	1936-37	1954-55	2	Boston Bruins
Schriner, Sweeney	1962/P	LW	1934-35	1945-46	2	New York Americans, Toronto Maple Leafs
Seibert, Earl	1963/P	D	1931-32	1945-46	2	New York Rangers, Chicago Blackhawks, Detroit Red Wings
Seibert, Oliver	1961/P	D	1900	1906	0	Berlin Rangers (WOHA), Houghton (IHL), Guelph (OPHL), London (OPHL)
Shore, Eddie	1947/P	D	1924-25	1939-40	2	Regina Capitals (WCHL), Edmonton Eskimos (WHL), Boston Bruins, New York Americans
Shutt, Steve	1993/P	LW	1972-73	1984-85	5	Montreal Canadiens, Los Angeles Kings
Siebert, Babe	1964/P	LW/D	1925-26	1938-39	2	Montreal Maroons, New York Rangers, Boston Bruins, Montreal Canadiens
Simpson, Joe	1962/P	D	1921-22	1930-31	0	Edmonton Eskimos (WCHL), New York Americans
Sittler, Darryl	1989/P	C	1970-71	1984-85	0	Toronto Maple Leafs, Philadelphia Flyers, Detroit Red Wings
Smith, Alf	1962/P	RW	1894-95	1907-08	4	Ottawa Silver Seven/Senators (AHA/CAHL/FAHL/ECAHA), Kenora Thistles (MHL)
Smith, Billy	1993/P	G	1971-72	1988-89	4	Los Angeles Kings, New York Islanders

Player	Elec. year/ how elected*	Pos.†	First season	Last season	Stanley Cup wins‡	Teams as player
Smith, Clint	1991/V	C	1936-37	1946-47	1	New York Rangers, Chicago Blackhawks
Smith, Hooley	1972/P	RW	1924-25	1940-41	2	1924 Canadian Olympic Team, Ottawa Senators, Montreal Maroons, Boston Bruins, New York Americans
Smith, Tommy	1973/P	LW/C	1905-06	1919-20	1	Ottawa Vics (FAHL), Ottawa Senators (ECAHA), Brantford (OPHL), Moncton (MPHL), Quebec Bulldogs (NHA/NHL), Toronto Shamrocks (NHA), Montreal Canadiens (NHA)
Stanley, Allan	1981/P	D	1948-49	1968-69	4	New York Rangers, Chicago Blackhawks, Boston Bruins, Toronto Maple Leafs, Philadelphia Flyers
Stanley, Barney	1962/P	RW/D	1914-15	1927-28	1	Vancouver Millionaires (PCHA), Calgary Tigers (WCHL), Regina Capitals (WCHL), Edmonton Eskimos (WCHL/WHL), Chicago Blackhawks
Stastny, Peter	1998/P	C	1980-81	1994-95	0	Quebec Nordiques, New Jersey Devils, St. Louis Blues
Stewart, Black Jack	1964/P	D	1938-39	1951-52	2	Detroit Red Wings, Chicago Blackhawks
Stewart, Nels	1962/P	C	1925-26	1939-40	1	Montreal Maroons, Boston Bruins, New York Americans
Stuart, Bruce	1961/P	F	1989-99	1910-11	3	Ottawa Senators (CAHL/ECHA/NHA), Quebec Bulldogs (CAHL), Pittsburgh (IHL), Houghton (IHL), Portage Lake (IHL), Montreal Wanderers (ECAHA)
Stuart, Hod	1945/P	D	1898-99	1906-07	1	Ottawa Senators, Quebec Bulldogs, Calumet (IHL), Pittsburgh (IHL), Montreal Wanderers
Taylor, Cyclone	1947/P	D/Ro./C	1907-08	1922-23	2	Ottawa Senators (ECAHA/ECHA), Renfrew Creamery Kings (NHA), Vancouver Maroons (PCHA)
Thompson, Tiny	1959/P	G	1928-29	1939-40	1	Boston Bruins, Detroit Red Wings
Tretiak, Vladislav	1989/P	G	1969	1984	0	CSKA Moscow
Trihey, Harry	1950/P	C	1896-97	1900-01	2	Montreal Shamrocks (AHA/CAHL)
Trottier, Bryan	1997/P	C	1975-76	1993-94	6	New York Islanders, Pittsburgh Penguins
Ullman, Norm	1982/P	C	1955-56	1976-77	0	Detroit Red Wings, Toronto Maple Leafs, Edmonton Oilers (WHA)
Vezina, Georges	1945/P	G	1910-11	1925-26	2	Montreal Canadiens (NHA/NHL)
Walker, Jack	1960/P	LW/Ro.	1912-13	1927-28	3	Port Arthur, Toronto Blueshirts (NHA), Seattle Metropolitans (PCHA), Victoria Cougars (WCHL/WHL), Detroit Cougars
Walsh, Marty	1962/P	C	1905-06	1911-12	2	Queens University (OHA), Ottawa Senators (ECAHA/ECHA/NHA)
Watson, Harry E.	1962/P	C	1915	1931	0	St. Andrews (OHA), Aura Lee Juniors (OHA), Toronto Dentals (OHA), Toronto Granites (OHA), 1924 Canadian Olympic Team, Toronto National Sea Fleas (OHA)
Watson, Harry P.	1994/V	LW	1941-42	1956-57	5	Brooklyn Americans, Detroit Red Wings, Toronto Maple Leafs, Chicago Blackhawks
Weiland, Cooney	1971/P	C	1928-29	1938-39	2	Boston Bruins, Ottawa Senators, Detroit Red Wings
Westwick, Harry	1962/P	Ro.	1894-95	1907-08	4	Ottawa Senators/Silver Seven (AHA/CAHL/FAHL/ECAHA), Kenora Thistles
Whitcroft, Frederick	1962/P	Ro.	1906-07	1909-10	0	Kenora Thistles (MSHL), Edmonton Eskimos (AAHA), Renfrew Creamery Kings (NHA)
Wilson, Gord	1962/P	D	1918	1933	0	Port Arthur War Veterans (OHA), Iroquois Falls (NOHA), Port Arthur Bearcats (OHA)
Worsley, Gump	1980/P	G	1952-53	1973-74	4	New York Rangers, Montreal Canadiens, Minnesota North Stars
Worters, Roy	1969/P	G	1925-26	1936-37	0	Pittsburgh Pirates, New York Americans, Montreal Canadiens

*Denotes whether enshrinee was elected by regular election (P) or veterans committee (V).
†Primary positions played during career: C—center; D—defense; G—goaltender; LW—left wing; Ro.—rover; RW—right wing.
‡Stanley Cup wins column refers to wins as a player in the players section and as a coach in the coaches section.

BUILDERS

Builder	Election year	Stanley Cup wins‡	Designation for induction
Adams, Charles F.	1960		Founder, Boston Bruins (1924)
Adams, Weston W.	1972		President and chairman, Boston Bruins(1936-69)
Aheam, Frank	1962		Owner, Ottawa Senators (1924-34)
Ahearne, Bunny	1977		President, International Hockey Federation (1957-75)
Allan, Sir Montagu	1945		Donator of Allan Cup, awarded anually to senior amateur champion of Canada (1908)
Allen, Keith	1992	0	Coach, Philadelphia Flyers (1967-68 and 1968-69); general manager and executive, Philadelphia Flyers (1966-present)
Arbour, Al	1996	4	Coach, St. Louis Blues, New York Islanders, 1970-71, 1971-72 to 1972-73, 1973-74 through 1985-86 and 1988-89 to 1993-94; vice president of hockey operations and consultant, New York Islanders (1994 to 1998)

Builder	Election year	Stanley Cup wins‡	Designation for induction
Ballard, Harold	1977		Owner and chief executive, Toronto Maple Leafs (1961-90)
Bauer, Father David	1989		Developer and coach of first Canadian National Hockey Team
Bickell, J.P.	1978		First president and chairman of the board, Toronto Maple Leafs (1927-51)
Bowman, Scotty	1991	9	Coach, St. Louis Blues, Montreal Canadiens, Buffalo Sabres, Pittsburgh Penguins, Detroit Red Wings (1967-68 through 1979-80, 1981-82 through 1986-87 and 1991-92 through 2001-02); general manager, St. Louis Blues, Buffalo Sabres (1969-70, 1970-71 and 1979-80 through 1986-87)
Brooks, Herb	2006		Coach, U.S. Olympic team (1980), U. of Minnesota (1971-79), Davos (1980), New York Rangers (1981-85), St. Cloud State (1986), Minnesota North Stars (1987), Utica (1991), New Jersey Devils (1992) and Pittsburgh Penguins (1999).
Brown, George V.	1961		U.S. hockey pioneer; organizer, Boston Athletic Association hockey team (1910); general manager, Boston Arena and Boston Garden (1934-37)
Brown, Walter A.	1962		Co-owner and president, Boston Bruins (1951-64); general manager, Boston Gardens
Buckland, Frank	1975		Amateur hockey coach and manager; president and treasurer, Ontario Hockey Association
Bush, Walter L.	2000		President, Minnesota North Stars (1967-1978); president, USA Hockey; vice president, International Ice Hockey Federation
Butterfield, Jack	1980		President, American Hockey League
Calder, Frank	1947		First president, National Hockey League (1917-43)
Campbell, Angus	1964		First president, Northern Ontario Hockey Association (1919); executive, Ontario Hockey Association
Campbell, Clarence	1966		Referee (1929-40); president, National Hockey League (1946-77)
Cattarinich, Joseph	1977		General manager, Montreal Canadiens (1909-10); co-owner, Montreal Canadiens (1921-35)
Costello, Murray	2005	0	President, Canadian Hockey Association (1979-1998); Hockey Hall of Fame selection committee and board member; member of IIHF
Dandurand, Leo	1963	1	Co-owner, Montreal Canadiens (1921-35); coach, Montreal Canadiens (1920-21 through 1925-26 and 1934-35); general manager, Montreal Canadiens (1920-21 through 1934-35)
Dilio, Frank	1964		Secretary and president, Junior Amateur Hockey Association; registrar and secretary, Quebec Amateur Hockey League (1943-62)
Dudley, George	1958		President, Canadian Amateur Hockey Association (1940-42); treasurer, Ontario Hockey Association; president, International Ice Hockey Federation
Dunn, Jimmy	1968		President, Manitoba Amateur Hockey Association (1945-51); president, Canadian Amateur Hockey Association
Fletcher, Cliff	2004		General manager, Altanta and Calgary Flames, Toronto Maple Leafs (1972-1997), Phoenix Coyotes (2001); first G.M. to sign a Soviet player with official consent
Francis, Emile	1982	0	General manager, New York Rangers,St. Louis Blues, Hartford Whalers (1964-65 through 1988-89); coach, New York Rangers, St. Louis Blues (1965-66 through 1974-75, 1976-77, 1981-82 and 1982-83); president, Hartford Whalers (1983-1993)
Gibson, Jack	1976		Organizer, International League (1903-07), world's first professional hockey league
Gorman, Tommy	1963	2	Co-founder, National Hockey League (1917); coach, Ottawa Senators, New York Americans, Chicago Blackhawks, Montreal Maroons (1917-1938); general manager, Montreal Canadiens (1941-42 through 1945-46)
Griffiths, Frank	1993		Chairman, Vancouver Canucks (1974 through 1994)
Hanley, Bill	1986		Secretary-manager, Ontario Hockey Association
Hay, Charles	1974		Coordinator, 1972 series between Canada and Soviet Union; president, Hockey Canada
Hendy, Jim	1968		President, United States Hockey League; general manager, Cleveland Barons (AHL); publisher, Hockey Guide (1933-51)
Hewitt, Foster	1965		Hockey broadcaster
Hewitt, William	1947		Sports editor, Toronto Star; secretary, Ontario Hockey Association (1903-61); registrar and treasurer, Canadian Amateur Hockey Association
Hotchkiss, Harley	2006		Governor, Calgary Flames; director, Hockey Hall of Fame; and Chairman of NHL Board of Governors (1995-2006).
Hume, Fred	1962		Co-developer, Western Hockey League, New Westminster Royals
Ilitch, Mike	2003	3	Owner, Detroit Red Wings (1982-83 through 2002-03)
Imlach, Punch	1984	4	Coach, Toronto Maple Leafs, Buffalo Sabres (1958-59 through 1968-69, 1970-71, 1971-72 and 1979-80); general manager, Toronto Maple Leafs, Buffalo Sabres (1958-59 through 1968-69, 1970-71 through 1977-78 and 1979-80 through 1981-82)
Ivan, Tommy	1974	3	Coach, Detroit Red Wings, Chicago Blackhawks (1947-48 through 1953-54, 1956-57 and 1957-58); general manager, Chicago Blackhawks (1954-55 through 1976-77)
Jennings, Bill	1975		President, New York Rangers
Johnson, Bob	1992	1	Coach, Calgary Flames, Pittsburgh Penguins (1982-83 through 1986-87, 1990-91 and 1991-92)
Juckes, Gordon	1979		President, Saskatchewan Amateur Hockey Association; director, Canadian Amateur Hockey Association (1960-78)
Kilpatrick,General J.R.	1960		President, New York Rangers, Madison Square Garden; director, NHL Players' Pension Society; NHL Governor
Kilrea, Brian	2003		Player, Detroit Red Wings (1957-58) and Los Angeles Kings (1967-68); general manager and head coach, Ottawa 67's of the Ontario Hockey League (1974-75 through 1983-84, 1986-87 through 1993-94 and 1995-96 through 2002-03); assistant coach, New York Islanders (1984-85 through 1985-86)
Knox III, Seymour	1993		Chairman and president, Buffalo Sabres (1970-71 through 1995-96)
Leader, Al	1969		President, Western Hockey League (1944-69)
LeBel, Bob	1970		Founder and president, Interprovincial Senior League (1944-47); president, Quebec Amateur Hockey League, Canadian Amateur Hockey Association, International Ice Hockey Federation (1955-63)

Builder	Election year	Stanley Cup wins‡	Designation for induction
Lockhart, Tommy	1965		Organizer and president, Eastern Amateur Hockey League, Amateur Hockey Association of the United States; business manager, New York Rangers
Loicq, Paul	1961		President and referee, International Ice Hockey Federation (1922-47)
Mariucci, John	1985		Minnesota hockey pioneer; coach, 1956 U.S. Olympic Team
Mathers, Frank	1992		Coach, president and general manager, Hershey Bears (AHL)
McLaughlin, Major Frederic	1963		Owner and first president, Chicago Blackhawks; general manager, Chicago Blackhawks (1926-27 through 1941-42)
Milford, Jake	1984		Coach, New York Rangers organization; general manager, Los Angeles Kings, Vancouver Canucks (1973-74 through 1981-82)
Molson, Senator Hartland De Montarville	1973		President and chairman, Montreal Canadiens (1957-68)
Morrison, Scotty	1999		Referee-in-chief; chairman, Hall of Fame
Murray, Monsignor Athol	1998		Founded hockey programs in Saskatchewan; founded Notre Dame College in Wilcox
Neilson, Roger	2002		Coach, Toronto Maple Leafs, Buffalo Sabres, Vancouver Canucks, Los Angeles Kings, New York Rangers, Florida Panthers, Philadelphia Flyers, Ottawa Senators (1977-78 through 1983-84, 1989-90 through 1994-95, 1997-98 through 1999-2000 and 2001-02)
Nelson, Francis	1947		Sports editor, Toronto Globe; vice president, Ontario Hockey Association (1903-05); Governor, Amateur Athletic Union of Canada
Norris, Bruce	1969		Owner, Detroit Red Wings, Olympic Stadium (1955-82)
Norris, James Sr.	1958		Co-owner, Detroit Red Wings (1933-43)
Norris, James Dougan	1962		Co-owner, Detroit Red Wings (1933-43), Chicago Blackhawks (1946-66)
Northey, William	1947		President, Montreal Amateur Athletic Association; managing director, Montreal Forum; first trustee, Allan Cup (1908)
O'Brien, J. Ambrose	1962		Organizer, National Hockey Association (1909); co-founder, Montreal Canadiens
O'Neil, Brian	1994		Director of administration, NHL (1966); executive director, NHL (1971); executive vice-president, NHL (1977)
Page, Fred	1993		President, Canadian Amateur Hockey Association (1966-68); chairman of the board, British Columbia Junior Hockey League (1983 through 1997)
Patrick, Craig	2001		Builder of U.S. National & Olympic programs; general manager, New York Rangers (1981 through 1986), general manager, Pittsburgh Penguins (1989 to present), coach, Pittsburgh Penguins (1989-90 and1996-97)
Patrick, Frank	1958		Co-organizer and president, Pacific Coast Hockey Association (1911); owner, manager, player/coach, Vancouver Millionaires (PCHA), managing director, National Hockey League (1933-34); coach, Boston Bruins (1934-35 and 1935-36); business manager, Montreal Canadiens (1941-42)
Pickard, Allan	1958		President, Saskatchewan Amateur Hockey Association, Saskatchewan Senior League (1933-34), Western Canada Senior League;governor, Saskatchewan Junior League, Western Canada Junior League; president, Canadian Amateur Hockey Association (1947-50)
Pilous, Rudy	1985	1	Coach, Chicago Blackhawks, Winnipeg Jets (1957-58 through 1962-63 and 1974-75); manager, Winnipeg Jets (WHA); scout, Detroit Red Wings, Los Angeles Kings
Poile, Bud	1990		General manager, Philadelphia Flyers, Vancouver Canucks (1967-68 through 1972-73); vice president, World Hockey Association; commissioner, Central Hockey League, International Hockey League
Pollock, Sam	1978		Director of personnel, Montreal Canadiens (1950-64); general manager, Montreal Canadiens (1964-65 through 1977-78)
Raymond, Sen. Donat	1958		President, Canadian Arena Company (Montreal Maroons, Montreal Canadiens) (1924-25 through 1955); chairman, Canadian Arena Company (1955-63)
Robertson, John Ross	1947		President, Ontario Hockey Association (1901-05)
Robinson, Claude	1947		First secretary, Canadian Amateur Hockey Association (1914); manager, 1932 Canadian Olympic Team
Ross, Philip	1976		Trustee, Stanley Cup (1893-1949)
Sabetzki, Gunther	1995		President, International Ice Hockey Federation (1975-1994)
Sather, Glen	1997	4	Coach, Edmonton Oilers (1976-89 and 1993-94); general manager, Edmonton Oilers (1979 to 2000); general manager, New York Rangers (2000 to present)
Selke, Frank	1960		Assistant general manager, Toronto Maple Leafs; general manager, Montreal Canadiens (1946-47 through 1963-64)
Sinden, Harry	1983	1	Coach, Boston Bruins (1966-67 through 1969-70, 1979-80 and 1984-85); coach, 1972 Team Canada; general manager, Boston Bruins (1972-73 through 1988-89); President, Boston bruins (1989-90 through present)
Smith, Frank	1962		Co-founder and secretary, Beaches Hockey League (later Metropolitan Toronto Hockey League (1911-62)
Smythe, Conn	1958	0	President, Toronto Maple Leafs, Maple Leaf Gardens, general manager, Toronto Maple Leafs (1927-28 through 1956-57); coach, Toronto Maple Leafs (1927-28 through 1930-31)
Snider, Ed	1988		Owner, Philadelphia Flyers (1967-68 through present)

Builder	Election year	Stanley Cup wins‡	Designation for induction
Stanley of Preston, Lord	1945		Donator, Stanley Cup (1893)
Sutherland, Capt. James	1947		President, Ontario Hockey Association (1915-17); president, Canadian Amateur Hockey Association (1919-21)
Tarasov, Anatoli	1974		Coach, Soviet National Team
Torrey, Bill	1995		Executive vice president, California Seals; general manager, New York Islanders; president, Florida Panthers (1967-present)
Turner, Lloyd	1958		Co-organizer, Western Canadian Hockey League (1918); organizer, Calgary Tigers
Tutt, Thayer	1978		President, International Ice Hockey Federation (1966-69), Amateur Hockey Association of the United States
Voss, Carl	1974		President, U.S. Hockey League; first NHL referee-in-chief
Waghorne, Fred	1961		Pioneer and hockey official, Toronto Hockey League
Wirtz, Arthur	1971		Co-owner, Detroit Red Wings, Olympia Stadium, Chicago Stadium, St. Louis Arena, Madison Square Garden, Chicago Blackhawks
Wirtz, Bill	1976		President, Chicago Blackhawks (1966 through present); chairman, NHL Board of Governors
Ziegler, John	1987		President, National Hockey League (1977-92)

‡Stanley Cup wins column refers to wins as a player in the players section and as a coach in the builders section.

REFEREES/LINESMEN

Referee/linesman	Election year	First season	Last season	Position
Armstrong, Neil	1991	1957	1977	Linesman and referee
Ashley, John	1981	1959	1972	Referee
Chadwick, Bill	1964	1940	1955	Linesman and referee
D'Amico, John	1993	1964-65	1987-88	Linesman
Elliott, Chaucer	1961	1903	1913	Referee (OHA)
Hayes, George	1988	1946-47	1964-65	Linesman
Hewitson, Bobby	1963	1924	1934	Referee
Ion, Mickey	1961	1913	1943	Referee (PCHL/NHL)
Pavelich, Matt	1987	1956-57	1978-79	Linesman
Rodden, Mike	1962			Referee
Smeaton, Cooper	1961			Referee (NHA/NHL); referee-in-chief (NHL) (1931-37); trustee, Stanley Cup (1946-78)
Storey, Red	1967	1951	1959	Referee
Udvari, Frank	1973	1951-52	1965-66	Referee; supervisor of NHL officials
Van Hellemond, Andy	1999	1972-73	1995-96	Referee

TEAM BY TEAM

ANAHEIM DUCKS

YEAR-BY-YEAR RECORDS

	REGULAR SEASON						PLAYOFFS			
Season	W	L	T	OTL	Pts.	Finish	W	L	Highest round	Coach
1993-94	33	46	5	—	71	4th/Pacific	—	—		Ron Wilson
1994-95	16	27	5	—	37	6th/Pacific	—	—		Ron Wilson
1995-96	35	39	8	—	78	4th/Pacific	—	—		Ron Wilson
1996-97	36	33	13	—	85	2nd/Pacific	4	7	Conference semifinals	Ron Wilson
1997-98	26	43	13	—	65	6th/Pacific	—	—		Pierre Page
1998-99	35	34	13	—	83	3rd/Pacific	0	4	Conference quarterfinals	Craig Hartsburg
1999-00	34	33	12	3	83	5th/Pacific	—	—		Craig Hartsburg
2000-01	25	41	11	5	66	5th/Pacific	—	—		Craig Hartsburg, Guy Charron
2001-02	29	42	8	3	69	5th/Pacific	—	—		Bryan Murray
2002-03	40	27	9	6	95	2nd/Pacific	15	6	Stanley Cup finals	Mike Babcock
2003-04	29	35	10	8	76	4th/Pacific	—	—		Mike Babcock
2004-05	No season—Lockout									
2005-06	43	27	—	12	98	3rd/Pacific	9	7	Conference finals	Randy Carlyle

FIRST-ROUND ENTRY DRAFT CHOICES

Year Player, Overall, Last amateur team (league)
1993—Paul Kariya, 4, University of Maine
1994—Oleg Tverdovsky, 2, Krylja Sovetov, CIS
1995—Chad Kilger, 4, Kingston (OHL)
1996—Ruslan Salei, 9, Las Vegas (IHL)
1997—Mikael Holmqvist, 18, Djurgarden Stockholm, Sweden
1998—Vitali Vishnevsky, 5, Torpedo Yaroslavl, Russia
1999—No first-round selection
2000—Alexei Smirnov, 12, Dynamo, Russia

Year Player, Overall, Last amateur team (league)
2001—Stanislav Chistov, 5, OMDK, Russia
2002—Joffrey Lupul, 7, Medicine Hat (WHL)
2003—Ryan Getzlaf, 19, Calgary (WHL)
Corey Perry, 28, London (OHL)
2004—Ladislav Smid, 9, Liberec, Czech. Rep.
2005—Bobby Ryan, 2, Owen Sound (OHL)
2006—Mark Mitera, 19, U. of Michigan (CCHA)

SINGLE-SEASON INDIVIDUAL RECORDS

FORWARDS/DEFENSEMEN

Most goals
52—Teemu Selanne, 1997-98

Most assists
62—Paul Kariya, 1998-99

Most points
109—Teemu Selanne, 1996-97

Most penalty minutes
285—Todd Ewen, 1995-96

Most power play goals
25—Teemu Selanne, 1998-99

Most shorthanded goals
3—Bob Corkum, 1993-94
Paul Kariya, 1995-96
Paul Kariya, 1996-97
Paul Kariya, 1999-2000
Paul Kariya, 2000-01
Samuel Pahlsson, 2005-06

Most games with three or more goals
3—Teemu Selanne, 1997-98

Most shots
429—Paul Kariya, 1998-99

GOALTENDERS

Most games
69—Guy Hebert, 1998-99

Most minutes
4,083—Guy Hebert, 1998-99

Most shots against
2,133—Guy Hebert, 1996-97

Most goals allowed
172—Guy Hebert, 1996-97

Lowest goals-against average
2.13—Jean-Sebastien Giguere, 2001-02

Most shutouts
8—Jean-Sebastien Giguere, 2002-03

Most wins
34—Jean-Sebastien Giguere, 2002-03

Most losses
31—Guy Hebert, 1999-2000
Jean-Sebastien Giguere, 2003-04

Most ties
12—Guy Hebert, 1996-97

ATLANTA THRASHERS

YEAR-BY-YEAR RECORDS

	REGULAR SEASON						PLAYOFFS			
Season	W	L	T	OTL	Pts.	Finish	W	L	Highest round	Coach
1999-00	14	57	7	4	39	5th/Southeast	—	—		Curt Fraser
2000-01	23	45	12	2	60	4th/Southeast	—	—		Curt Fraser
2001-02	19	47	11	5	54	5th/Southeast	—	—		Curt Fraser
2002-03	31	39	7	5	74	3rd/Southeast	—	—		C. Fraser, Don Waddell, Bob Hartley
2003-04	33	37	8	4	78	2nd/Southeast	—	—		Bob Hartley
2004-05	No season—Lockout									
2005-06	41	33	—	8	90	3rd/Southeast	—	—		Bob Hartley

FIRST-ROUND ENTRY DRAFT CHOICES

Year Player, Overall, Last amateur team (league)
1999—Patrik Stefan, 1, Long Beach (IHL)
2000—Dany Heatley, 2, Wisconsin (WCHA)
2001—Ilja Kovalchuk, 1, Spartak Jr., Russia
2002—Kari Lehtonen, 2, Jokerit, Finland
Jim Slater, 30, Michigan State (CCHA)

Year Player, Overall, Last amateur team (league)
2003—Braydon Coburn, 8, Portland (WHL)
2004—Boris Valabik, 10, Kitchener (OHL)
2005—Alex Bourret, 16, Lewiston (QMJHL)
2006—Bryan Little, 12, Barrie (OHL)

SINGLE-SEASON INDIVIDUAL RECORDS

FORWARDS/DEFENSEMEN

Most goals
52—Ilya Kovalchuk, 2005-06

Most assists
69—Marc Savard, 2005-06

Most points
98—Ilya Kovalchuk, 2005-06

Most penalty minutes
226—Jeff Odgers, 2000-01

Most power play goals
27—Ilya Kovalchuk, 2005-06

Most shorthanded goals
7—Marian Hossa, 2005-06

Most games with three or more goals
2—Donald Audette, 2000-01
Ray Ferraro, 2000-01
Ilya Kovalchuk, 2003-04
Ilya Kovalchuk, 2005-06

Most shots
341—Ilya Kovalchuk, 2003-04
Marian Hossa, 2005-06

GOALTENDERS

Most games
64—Pasi Nurminen, 2003-04

Most minutes
3,738—Pasi Nurminen, 2003-04

Most shots against
1,956—Milan Hnilicka, 2001-02

Most goals allowed
179—Milan Hnilicka, 2001-02

Lowest goals-against average
2.78—Pasi Nurminen, 2003-04

Most shutouts
3—Milan Hnilicka, 2001-02
Pasi Nurminen, 2003-04

Most wins
25—Pasi Nurminen, 2003-04

Most losses
33—Milan Hnilicka, 2001-02

Most ties
10—Milan Hnilicka, 2001-02

BOSTON BRUINS

YEAR-BY-YEAR RECORDS

	REGULAR SEASON						PLAYOFFS			
Season	W	L	T	OTL	Pts.	Finish	W	L	Highest round	Coach
1924-25	6	24	0	—	12	6th	—	—		Art Ross
1925-26	17	15	4	—	38	4th	—	—		Art Ross
1926-27	21	20	3	—	45	2nd/American	*2	2	Stanley Cup finals	Art Ross
1927-28	20	13	11	—	51	1st/American	*0	1	Semifinals	Art Ross
1928-29	26	13	5	—	57	1st/American	5	0	Stanley Cup champ	Cy Denneny
1929-30	38	5	1	—	77	1st/American	3	3	Stanley Cup finals	Art Ross
1930-31	28	10	6	—	62	1st/American	2	3	Semifinals	Art Ross
1931-32	15	21	12	—	42	4th/American	—	—		Art Ross
1932-33	25	15	8	—	58	1st/American	2	3	Semifinals	Art Ross
1933-34	18	25	5	—	41	4th/American	—	—		Art Ross
1934-35	26	16	6	—	58	1st/American	1	3	Semifinals	Frank Patrick
1935-36	22	20	6	—	50	2nd/American	1	1	Quarterfinals	Frank Patrick
1936-37	23	18	7	—	53	2nd/American	1	2	Quarterfinals	Art Ross
1937-38	30	11	7	—	67	1st/American	0	3	Semifinals	Art Ross
1938-39	36	10	2	—	74	1st	8	4	Stanley Cup champ	Art Ross
1939-40	31	12	5	—	67	1st	2	4	Semifinals	Ralph (Cooney) Weiland
1940-41	27	8	13	—	67	1st	8	3	Stanley Cup champ	Ralph (Cooney) Weiland
1941-42	25	17	6	—	56	3rd	2	3	Semifinals	Art Ross
1942-43	24	17	9	—	57	2nd	4	5	Stanley Cup finals	Art Ross
1943-44	19	26	5	—	43	5th	—	—		Art Ross
1944-45	16	30	4	—	36	4th	3	4	League semifinals	Art Ross
1945-46	24	18	8	—	56	2nd	5	5	Stanley Cup finals	Dit Clapper
1946-47	26	23	11	—	63	3rd	1	4	League semifinals	Dit Clapper
1947-48	23	24	13	—	59	3rd	1	4	League semifinals	Dit Clapper
1948-49	29	23	8	—	66	2nd	1	4	League semifinals	Dit Clapper
1949-50	22	32	16	—	60	5th	—	—		George Boucher
1950-51	22	30	18	—	62	4th	†1	4	League semifinals	Lynn Patrick
1951-52	25	29	16	—	66	4th	3	4	League semifinals	Lynn Patrick
1952-53	28	29	13	—	69	3rd	5	6	Stanley Cup finals	Lynn Patrick
1953-54	32	28	10	—	74	4th	0	4	League semifinals	Lynn Patrick
1954-55	23	26	21	—	67	4th	1	4	League semifinals	Lynn Patrick, Milt Schmidt
1955-56	23	34	13	—	59	5th	—	—		Milt Schmidt
1956-57	34	24	12	—	80	3rd	5	5	Stanley Cup finals	Milt Schmidt
1957-58	27	28	15	—	69	4th	6	6	Stanley Cup finals	Milt Schmidt
1958-59	32	29	9	—	73	2nd	3	4	League semifinals	Milt Schmidt
1959-60	28	34	8	—	64	5th	—	—		Milt Schmidt
1960-61	15	42	13	—	43	6th	—	—		Milt Schmidt
1961-62	15	47	8	—	38	6th	—	—		Phil Watson
1962-63	14	39	17	—	45	6th	—	—		Phil Watson, Milt Schmidt
1963-64	18	40	12	—	48	6th	—	—		Milt Schmidt

	REGULAR SEASON						PLAYOFFS			
Season	W	L	T	OTL	Pts.	Finish	W	L	Highest round	Coach
1964-65	21	43	6	—	48	6th	—	—		Milt Schmidt
1965-66	21	43	6	—	48	5th	—	—		Milt Schmidt
1966-67	17	43	10	—	44	6th	—	—		Harry Sinden
1967-68	37	27	10	—	84	3rd/East	0	4	Division semifinals	Harry Sinden
1968-69	42	18	16	—	100	2nd/East	6	4	Division finals	Harry Sinden
1969-70	40	17	19	—	99	2nd/East	12	2	Stanley Cup champ	Harry Sinden
1970-71	57	14	7	—	121	1st/East	3	4	Division semifinals	Tom Johnson
1971-72	54	13	11	—	119	1st/East	12	3	Stanley Cup champ	Tom Johnson
1972-73	51	22	5	—	107	2nd/East	1	4	Division semifinals	Tom Johnson, Bep Guidolin
1973-74	52	17	9	—	113	1st/East	10	6	Stanley Cup finals	Bep Guidolin
1974-75	40	26	14	—	94	2nd/Adams	1	2	Preliminaries	Don Cherry
1975-76	48	15	17	—	113	1st/Adams	5	7	Semifinals	Don Cherry
1976-77	49	23	8	—	106	1st/Adams	8	6	Stanley Cup finals	Don Cherry
1977-78	51	18	11	—	113	1st/Adams	10	5	Stanley Cup finals	Don Cherry
1978-79	43	23	14	—	100	1st/Adams	7	4	Semifinals	Don Cherry
1979-80	46	21	13	—	105	2nd/Adams	4	6	Quarterfinals	Fred Creighton, Harry Sinden
1980-81	37	30	13	—	87	2nd/Adams	0	3	Preliminaries	Gerry Cheevers
1981-82	43	27	10	—	96	2nd/Adams	6	5	Division finals	Gerry Cheevers
1982-83	50	20	10	—	110	1st/Adams	9	8	Conference finals	Gerry Cheevers
1983-84	49	25	6	—	104	1st/Adams	0	3	Division semifinals	Gerry Cheevers
1984-85	36	34	10	—	82	4th/Adams	2	3	Division semifinals	Gerry Cheevers, Harry Sinden
1985-86	37	31	12	—	86	3rd/Adams	0	3	Division semifinals	Butch Goring
1986-87	39	34	7	—	85	3rd/Adams	0	4	Division semifinals	Butch Goring, Terry O'Reilly
1987-88	44	30	6	—	94	2nd/Adams	12	10	Stanley Cup finals	Terry O'Reilly
1988-89	37	29	14	—	88	2nd/Adams	5	5	Division finals	Terry O'Reilly
1989-90	46	25	9	—	101	1st/Adams	13	8	Stanley Cup finals	Mike Milbury
1990-91	44	24	12	—	100	1st/Adams	10	9	Conference finals	Mike Milbury
1991-92	36	32	12	—	84	2nd/Adams	8	7	Conference finals	Rick Bowness
1992-93	51	26	7	—	109	1st/Adams	0	4	Division semifinals	Brian Sutter
1993-94	42	29	13	—	97	2nd/Northeast	6	7	Conference semifinals	Brian Sutter
1994-95	27	18	3	—	57	3rd/Northeast	1	4	Conference quarterfinals	Brian Sutter
1995-96	40	31	11	—	91	2nd/Northeast	1	4	Conference quarterfinals	Steve Kasper
1996-97	26	47	9	—	61	6th/Northeast	—	—		Steve Kasper
1997-98	39	30	13	—	91	2nd/Northeast	2	4	Conference quarterfinals	Pat Burns
1998-99	39	30	13	—	91	3th/Northeast	6	6	Conference semifinals	Pat Burns
1999-00	24	33	19	6	73	5th/Northeast	—	—		Pat Burns
2000-01	36	30	8	8	88	4th/Northeast	—	—		Pat Burns, Mike Keenan
2001-02	43	24	6	9	101	1st/Northeast	2	4	Conference quarterfinals	Robbie Ftorek
2002-03	36	31	11	4	87	3rd/Northeast	1	4	Conference quarterfinals	Robbie Ftorek, Mike O'Connell
2003-04	41	19	15	7	104	1st/Northeast	3	4	Conference quarterfinals	Mike Sullivan
2004-05	No season—Lockout									
2005-06	29	37	—	16	74	5th/Northeast	—	—		Mike Sullivan

*Won-lost record does not indicate tie(s) resulting from two-game, total-goals series that year (two-game, total-goals series were played from 1917-18 through 1935-36).

†Tied after one overtime (curfew law).

FIRST-ROUND ENTRY DRAFT CHOICES

Year Player, Overall, Last amateur team (league)

1969—Don Tannahill, 3, Niagara Falls (OHL)
Frank Spring, 4, Edmonton (WCHL)
Ivan Boldirev, 11, Oshawa (OHL)
1970—Reggie Leach, 3, Flin Flon (WCHL)
Rick MacLeish, 4, Peterborough (OHL)
Ron Plumb, 9, Peterborough (OHL)
Bob Stewart, 13, Oshawa (OHL)
1971—Ron Jones, 6, Edmonton (WCHL)
Terry O'Reilly, 14, Oshawa (OHL)
1972—Mike Bloom, 16, St. Catharines (OHL)
1973—Andre Savard, 6, Quebec (QMJHL)
1974—Don Laraway, 18, Swift Current (WCHL)
1975—Doug Halward, 14, Peterborough (OHL)
1976—Clayton Pachal, 16, New Westminster (WCHL)
1977—Dwight Foster, 16, Kitchener (OHL)
1978—Al Secord, 16, Hamilton (OHL)
1979—Ray Bourque, 8, Verdun (QMJHL)
Brad McCrimmon, 15, Brandon (WHL)
1980—Barry Pederson, 18, Victoria (WHL)
1981—Norm Leveille, 14, Chicoutimi (QMJHL)
1982—Gord Kluzak, 1, Billings (WHL)
1983—Nevin Markwart, 21, Regina (WHL)
1984—Dave Pasin, 19, Prince Albert (WHL)
1985—No first-round selection
1986—Craig Janney, 13, Boston College

Year Player, Overall, Last amateur team (league)

1987—Glen Wesley, 3, Portland (WHL)
Stephane Quintal, 14, Granby (QMJHL)
1988—Robert Cimetta, 18, Toronto (OHL)
1989—Shayne Stevenson, 17, Kitchener (OHL)
1990—Bryan Smolinski, 21, Michigan State University
1991—Glen Murray, 18, Sudbury (OHL)
1992—Dmitri Kvartalnov, 16, San Diego (IHL)
1993—Kevyn Adams, 25, Miami of Ohio
1994—Evgeni Riabchikov, 21, Molot-Perm (Russia)
1995—Kyle McLaren, 9, Tacoma (WHL)
Sean Brown, 21, Belleville (OHL)
1996—Johnathan Aitken, 8, Medicine Hat (WHL)
1997—Joe Thornton, 1, Sault Ste. Marie (OHL)
Sergei Samsonov, 8, Detroit (IHL)
1998—No first-round selection
1999—Nicholas Boynton, 21, Ottawa (OHL)
2000—Lars Jonsson, 7, Leksand, Sweden
Martin Samuelsson, 27, MoDo, Sweden
2001—Shaone Morrisonn, 19, Kamloops (WHL)
2002—Hannu Toivonen, 29, HPK, Finland
2003—Mark Stuart, 21, Colorado College (WCHA)
2004—No first-round selection
2005—Matt Lashoff, 22, Kitchener (OHL)
2006—Phil Kessel, 5, U. of Minnesota (WCHA)

SINGLE-SEASON INDIVIDUAL RECORDS

FORWARDS/DEFENSEMEN

Most goals
76—Phil Esposito, 1970-71

Most assists
102—Bobby Orr, 1970-71

Most points
152—Phil Esposito, 1970-71

Most penalty minutes
302—Jay Miller, 1987-88

Most power play goals
28—Phil Esposito, 1971-72

Most shorthanded goals
9—Brian Rolston, 2001-02

Most games with three or more goals
7—Phil Esposito, 1970-71

Most shots
550—Phil Esposito, 1970-71

GOALTENDERS

Most games
70—Jack Gelineau, 1950-51
Jim Henry, 1951-52
Jim Henry, 1952-53
Jim Henry, 1953-54
Eddie Johnston, 1963-64

Most minutes
4,200—Jack Gelineau, 1950-51
Jim Henry, 1951-52
Jim Henry, 1952-53
Jim Henry, 1953-54
Eddie Johnston, 1963-64

Most goals allowed
220—Jack Gelineau, 1949-50

Lowest goals-against average
1.18—Tiny Thompson, 1928-29

Most shutouts
15—Hal Winkler, 1927-28

Most wins
40—Pete Peeters, 1982-83

Most losses
40—Eddie Johnston, 1963-64

Most ties
18—Jack Gelineau, 1950-51

BUFFALO SABRES

YEAR-BY-YEAR RECORDS

	REGULAR SEASON						PLAYOFFS			
Season	W	L	T	OTL	Pts.	Finish	W	L	Highest round	Coach
1970-71	24	39	15	—	63	5th/East	—	—		Punch Imlach
1971-72	16	43	19	—	51	6th/East	—	—		Punch Imlach, Joe Crozier
1972-73	37	27	14	—	88	4th/East	2	4	Division semifinals	Joe Crozier
1973-74	32	34	12	—	76	5th/East	—	—		Joe Crozier
1974-75	49	16	15	—	113	1st/Adams	10	7	Stanley Cup finals	Floyd Smith
1975-76	46	21	13	—	105	2nd/Adams	4	5	Quarterfinals	Floyd Smith
1976-77	48	24	8	—	104	2nd/Adams	2	4	Quarterfinals	Floyd Smith
1977-78	44	19	17	—	105	2nd/Adams	3	5	Quarterfinals	Marcel Pronovost
1978-79	36	28	16	—	88	2nd/Adams	1	2	Preliminaries	Marcel Pronovost, Bill Inglis
1979-80	47	17	16	—	110	1st/Adams	9	5	Semifinals	Scotty Bowman
1980-81	39	20	21	—	99	1st/Adams	4	4	Quarterfinals	Roger Neilson
1981-82	39	26	15	—	93	3rd/Adams	1	3	Division semifinals	Jim Roberts, Scotty Bowman
1982-83	38	29	13	—	89	3rd/Adams	6	4	Division finals	Scotty Bowman
1983-84	48	25	7	—	103	2nd/Adams	0	3	Division semifinals	Scotty Bowman
1984-85	38	28	14	—	90	3rd/Adams	2	3	Divison semifinals	Scotty Bowman
1985-86	37	37	6	—	80	5th/Adams	—	—		Jim Schoenfeld, Scotty Bowman
1986-87	28	44	8	—	64	5th/Adams	—	—		Scotty Bowman, Craig Ramsay
1987-88	37	32	11	—	85	3rd/Adams	2	4	Division semifinals	Ted Sator
1988-89	38	35	7	—	83	3rd/Adams	1	4	Division semifinals	Ted Sator
1989-90	45	27	8	—	98	2nd/Adams	2	4	Division semifinals	Rick Dudley
1990-91	31	30	19	—	81	3rd/Adams	2	4	Division semifinals	Rick Dudley
										Ted Sator
1991-92	31	37	12	—	74	3rd/Adams	3	4	Division semifinals	Rick Dudley, John Muckler
1992-93	38	36	10	—	86	4th/Adams	4	4	Division finals	John Muckler
1993-94	43	32	9	—	95	4th/Northeast	3	4	Conference quarterfinals	John Muckler
1994-95	22	19	7	—	51	4th/Northeast	1	4	Conference quarterfinals	John Muckler
1995-96	33	42	7	—	73	5th/Northeast	—	—		Ted Nolan
1996-97	40	30	12	—	92	1st/Northeast	5	7	Conference semifinals	Ted Nolan
1997-98	36	29	17	—	89	3rd/Northeast	10	5	Conference finals	Lindy Ruff
1998-99	37	28	17	—	91	4rd/Northeast	14	7	Stanley Cup finals	Lindy Ruff
1999-00	35	32	11	4	85	3rd/Northeast	1	4	Conference quarterfinals	Lindy Ruff
2000-01	46	30	5	1	98	2nd/Northeast	7	6	Conference semifinals	Lindy Ruff
2001-02	35	35	11	1	82	5th/Northeast	—	—		Lindy Ruff
2002-03	27	37	10	8	72	5th/Northeast	—	—		Lindy Ruff
2003-04	37	34	7	4	85	5th/Northeast	—	—		Lindy Ruff
2004-05			No season—Lockout							
2005-06	52	24	—	6	110	2nd/Northeast	11	7	Conference finals	Lindy Ruff

FIRST-ROUND ENTRY DRAFT CHOICES

Year Player, Overall, Last amateur team (league)
1970—Gilbert Perreault, 1, Montreal (OHL)
1971—Rick Martin, 5, Montreal (OHL)
1972—Jim Schoenfeld, 5, Niagara Falls (OHL)
1973—Morris Titanic, 12, Sudbury (OHL)
1974—Lee Fogolin, 11, Oshawa (OHL)
1975—Robert Sauve, 17, Laval (QMJHL)
1976—No first-round selection

Year Player, Overall, Last amateur team (league)
1977—Ric Seiling, 14, St. Catharines (OHL)
1978—Larry Playfair, 13, Portland (WHL)
1979—Mike Ramsey, 11, University of Minnesota
1980—Steve Patrick, 20, Brandon (WHL)
1981—Jiri Dudacek, 17, Kladno (Czechoslovakia)
1982—Phil Housley, 6, South St. Paul H.S. (Minn.)
Paul Cyr, 9, Victoria (WHL)

Year	Player, Overall, Last amateur team (league)
	Dave Andreychuk, 16, Oshawa (OHL)
1983—	Tom Barrasso, 5, Acton Boxboro H.S. (Mass.)
	Norm Lacombe, 10, Univ. of New Hampshire
	Adam Creighton, 11, Ottawa (OHL)
1984—	Bo Andersson, 18, Vastra Frolunda, Sweden
1985—	Carl Johansson, 14, Vastra Frolunda, Sweden
1986—	Shawn Anderson, 5, Team Canada
1987—	Pierre Turgeon, 1, Granby (QMJHL)
1988—	Joel Savage, 13, Victoria (WHL)
1989—	Kevin Haller, 14, Regina (WHL)
1990—	Brad May, 14, Niagara Falls (OHL)
1991—	Philippe Boucher, 13, Granby (QMJHL)
1992—	David Cooper, 11, Medicine Hat (WHL)
1993—	No first-round selection

Year	Player, Overall, Last amateur team (league)
1994—	Wayne Primeau, 17, Owen Sound (OHL)
1995—	Jay McKee, 14, Niagara Falls (OHL)
	Martin Biron, 16, Beauport (QMJHL)
1996—	Erik Rasmussen, 7, University of Minnesota
1997—	Mika Noronen, 21, Tappara Tampere, Finland
1998—	Dimitri Kalinin, 18, Traktor Chelyabinsk, Russia
1999—	Barrett Heisten, 20, Maine (H. East)
2000—	Artem Kriukov, 15, Yaroslavl, Russia
2001—	Jiri Novotny, 22, Budejovice, Czech Republic
2002—	Keith Ballard, 11, University of Minnesota (WCHA)
	Daniel Paille, 20, Guelph (OHL)
2003—	Thomas Vanek, 5, Minnesota (WCHA)
2004—	Drew Stafford, 13, North Dakota (WCHA)
2005—	Marek Zagrapan, 13, Chicoutimi (QMJHL)
2006—	Dennis Persson, 24, Vasteras (Sweden)

SINGLE-SEASON INDIVIDUAL RECORDS

FORWARDS/DEFENSEMEN

Most goals
76—Alexander Mogilny, 1992-93

Most assists
95—Pat LaFontaine, 1992-93

Most points
148—Pat LaFontaine, 1992-93

Most penalty minutes
354—Rob Ray, 1991-92

Most power play goals
28—Dave Andreychuk, 1991-92

Most shorthanded goals
8—Don Luce, 1974-75

Most games with three or more goals
7—Rick Martin, 1975-76
Alexander Mogilny, 1992-93

Most shots
360—Alexander Mogilny, 1992-93

GOALTENDERS

Most games
72—Don Edwards, 1977-78
Dominik Hasek, 1997-98
Martin Biron, 2001-02

Most minutes
4,220—Dominik Hasek, 1997-98

Most shots against
2,190—Roger Crozier, 1971-72

Most goals allowed
214—Roger Crozier, 1971-72
Tom Barrasso, 1985-86

Lowest goals-against average
1.87—Dominik Hasek, 1998-99

Most shutouts
13—Dominik Hasek, 1997-98

Most wins
38—Don Edwards, 1977-78

Most losses
34—Roger Crozier, 1971-72

Most ties
17—Don Edwards, 1977-78

CALGARY FLAMES

YEAR-BY-YEAR RECORDS

	REGULAR SEASON						PLAYOFFS			
Season	W	L	T	OTL	Pts.	Finish	W	L	Highest round	Coach
1972-73*	25	38	15	—	65	7th/West	—	—		Bernie Geoffrion
1973-74*	30	34	14	—	74	4th/West	0	4	Division semifinals	Bernie Geoffrion
1974-75*	34	31	15	—	83	4th/Patrick	—	—		Bernie Geoffrion, Fred Creighton
1975-76*	35	33	12	—	82	3rd/Patrick	0	2	Preliminaries	Fred Creighton
1976-77*	34	34	12	—	80	3rd/Patrick	1	2	Preliminaries	Fred Creighton
1977-78*	34	27	19	—	87	3rd/Patrick	0	2	Preliminaries	Fred Creighton
1978-79*	41	31	8	—	90	4th/Patrick	0	2	Preliminaries	Fred Creighton
1979-80*	35	32	13	—	83	4th/Patrick	1	3	Preliminaries	Al MacNeil
1980-81	39	27	14	—	92	3rd/Patrick	9	7	Semifinals	Al MacNeil
1981-82	29	34	17	—	75	3rd/Smythe	0	3	Division semifinals	Al MacNeil
1982-83	32	34	14	—	78	2nd/Smythe	4	5	Division finals	Bob Johnson
1983-84	34	32	14	—	82	2nd/Smythe	6	5	Division finals	Bob Johnson
1984-85	41	27	12	—	94	3rd/Smythe	1	3	Division semifinals	Bob Johnson
1985-86	40	31	9	—	89	2nd/Smythe	12	10	Stanley Cup finals	Bob Johnson
1986-87	46	31	3	—	95	2nd/Smythe	2	4	Division semifinals	Bob Johnson
1987-88	48	23	9	—	105	1st/Smythe	4	5	Division finals	Terry Crisp
1988-89	54	17	9	—	117	1st/Smythe	16	6	Stanley Cup champ	Terry Crisp
1989-90	42	23	15	—	99	1st/Smythe	2	4	Division semifinals	Terry Crisp
1990-91	46	26	8	—	100	2nd/Smythe	3	4	Division semifinals	Doug Risebrough
1991-92	31	37	12	—	74	5th/Smythe	—	—		Doug Risebrough, Guy Charron
1992-93	43	30	11	—	97	2nd/Smythe	2	4	Division semifinals	Dave King
1993-94	42	29	13	—	97	1st/Pacific	3	4	Conference quarterfinals	Dave King
1994-95	24	17	7	—	55	1st/Pacific	3	4	Conference quarterfinals	Dave King
1995-96	34	37	11	—	79	2nd/Pacific	0	4	Conference quarterfinals	Pierre Page
1996-97	32	41	9	—	73	5th/Pacific	—	—		Pierre Page
1997-98	26	41	15	—	67	5th/Pacific	—	—		Brian Sutter
1998-99	30	40	12	—	72	3rd/Northwest	—	—		Brian Sutter
1999-00	31	36	10	5	77	4th/Northwest	—	—		Brian Sutter
2000-01	27	36	15	4	73	4th/Northwest	—	—		Don Hay, Greg Gilbert
2001-02	32	35	12	3	79	4th/Northwest	—	—		Greg Gilbert
2002-03	29	36	13	4	75	5th/Northwest	—	—		G. Gilbert, A. MacNeil, D. Sutter
2003-04	42	30	7	3	94	3rd/Northwest	15	11	Stanley Cup finals	Darryl Sutter
2004-05	No season—Lockout									
2005-06	46	25	—	11	103	1st/Northwest	3	4	Conference quarterfinals	Darryl Sutter

*Atlanta Flames.

FIRST-ROUND ENTRY DRAFT CHOICES

Year Player, Overall, Last amateur team (league)
1972—Jacques Richard, 2, Quebec (QMJHL)
1973—Tom Lysiak, 2, Medicine Hat (WCHL)
Vic Mercredi, 16, New Westminster (WCHL)
1974—No first-round selection
1975—Richcard Mulhern, 8, Sherbrooke (QMJHL)
1976—Dave Shand, 8, Peterborough (OHL)
Harold Phillipoff, 10, New Westminster (WCHL)
1977—No first-round selection
1978—Brad Marsh, 11, London (OHL)
1979—Paul Reinhart, 12, Kitchener (OHL)
1980—Denis Cyr, 13, Montreal (OHL)
1981—Al MacInnis, 15, Kitchener (OHL)
1982—No first-round selection
1983—Dan Quinn, 13, Belleville (OHL)
1984—Gary Roberts, 12, Ottawa (OHL)
1985—Chris Biotti, 17, Belmont Hill H.S. (Mass.)
1986—George Pelawa, 16, Bemidji H.S. (Minn.)
1987—Bryan Deasley, 19, University of Michigan
1988—Jason Muzzatti, 21, Michigan State University

Year Player, Overall, Last amateur team (league)
1989—No first-round selection
1990—Trevor Kidd, 11, Brandon (WHL)
1991—Niklas Sundblad, 19, AIK, Sweden
1992—Cory Stillman, 6, Windsor (OHL)
1993—Jesper Mattsson, 18, Malmo, Sweden
1994—Chris Dingman, 19, Brandon (WHL)
1995—Denis Gauthier, 20, Drummondville (QMJHL)
1996—Derek Morris, 13, Regina (WHL)
1997—Daniel Tkaczuk, 6, Barrie (OHL)
1998—Rico Fata, 6, London (OHL)
1999—Oleg Saprykin, 11, Seattle (WHL)
2000—Brent Krahn, 9, Calgary (WHL)
2001—Chuck Kobasew, 14, Boston College
2002—Eric Nystrom, 10, University of Michigan (CCHA)
2003—Dion Phaneuf, 9, Red Deer (WHL)
2004—Kris Chucko, 24, Salmon Arm (BCHL)
2005—Matt Pelech, 26, Sarnia (OHL)
2006—Leland Irving, 26, Calgary, Everett (WHL)

SINGLE-SEASON INDIVIDUAL RECORDS

FORWARDS/DEFENSEMEN

Most goals
66—Lanny McDonald, 1982-83

Most assists
82—Kent Nilsson, 1980-81

Most points
131—Kent Nilsson, 1980-81

Most penalty minutes
375—Tim Hunter, 1988-89

Most power play goals
31—Joe Nieuwendyk, 1987-88

Most shorthanded goals
9—Kent Nilsson, 1984-85

Most games with three or more goals
5—Hakan Loob, 1987-88
Theo Fleury, 1990-91

Most shots
353—Theo Fleury, 1995-96

GOALTENDERS

Most games
74—Miikka Kiprusoff, 2005-06

Most minutes
4,380—Miikka Kiprusoff, 2005-06

Most shots against
1,951—Miikka Kiprusoff, 2005-06

Most goals allowed
229—Rejean Lemelin, 1985-86

Lowest goals-against average
2.07—Miikka Kiprusoff, 2005-06

Most shutouts
10—Miikka Kiprusoff, 2005-06

Most wins
42—Miikka Kiprusoff, 2005-06

Most losses
30—Mike Vernon, 1991-92

Most ties
19—Dan Bouchard, 1977-78

CAROLINA HURRICANES

YEAR-BY-YEAR RECORDS

	REGULAR SEASON						PLAYOFFS			
Season	W	L	T	OTL	Pts.	Finish	W	L	Highest round	Coach
1972-73*	46	30	2	—	94	1st	12	3	Avco World Cup champ	Jack Kelley
1973-74*	43	31	4	—	90	1st	3	4	League quarterfinals	Ron Ryan
1974-75*	43	30	5	—	91	1st	2	4	League quarterfinals	Ron Ryan, Jack Kelley
1975-76*	33	40	7	—	73	3rd	10	7	League semifinals	Jack Kelley, Don Blackburn, Harry Neale
1976-77*	35	40	6	—	76	4th	1	4	League quarterfinals	Harry Neale
1977-78*	44	31	5	—	93	2nd	8	6	Avco World Cup finals	Harry Neale
1978-79*	37	34	9	—	83	4th	5	5	League semifinals	Bill Dineen, Don Blackburn
1979-80†	27	34	19	—	73	4th/Norris	0	3	Preliminaries	Don Blackburn
1980-81†	21	41	18	—	60	4th/Norris	—	—		Don Blackburn, Larry Pleau
1981-82†	21	41	18	—	60	5th/Adams	—	—		Larry Pleau
1982-83†	19	54	7	—	45	5th/Adams	—	—		Larry Kish, Larry Pleau, John Cunniff
1983-84†	28	42	10	—	66	5th/Adams	—	—		Jack Evans
1984-85†	30	41	9	—	69	5th/Adams	—	—		Jack Evans
1985-86†	40	36	4	—	84	4th/Adams	6	4	Division finals	Jack Evans
1986-87†	43	30	7	—	93	1st/Adams	2	4	Division semifinals	Jack Evans
1987-88†	35	38	7	—	77	4th/Adams	2	4	Division semifinals	Jack Evans, Larry Pleau
1988-89†	37	38	5	—	79	4th/Adams	0	4	Division semifinals	Larry Pleau
1989-90†	38	33	9	—	85	4th/Adams	3	4	Division semifinals	Rick Ley
1990-91†	31	38	11	—	73	4th/Adams	2	4	Division semifinals	Rick Ley
1991-92†	26	41	13	—	65	4th/Adams	3	4	Division semifinals	Jim Roberts
1992-93†	26	52	6	—	58	5th/Adams	—	—		Paul Holmgren

Season	W	L	T	OTL	Pts.	Finish	W	L	Highest round	Coach
		REGULAR SEASON					PLAYOFFS			
1993-94†	27	48	9	—	63	6th/Northeast	—	—		Paul Holmgren, Pierre McGuire
1994-95†	19	24	5	—	43	5th/Northeast	—	—		Paul Holmgren
1995-96†	34	39	9	—	77	4th/Northeast	—	—		Paul Holmgren, Paul Maurice
1996-97†	32	39	11	—	75	5th/Northeast	—	—		Paul Maurice
1997-98	33	41	8	—	74	6th/Northeast	—	—		Paul Maurice
1998-99	34	30	18	—	86	1st/Southeast	2	4	Conference quarterfinals	Paul Maurice
1999-00	37	35	10	0	84	3rd/Southeast	—	—		Paul Maurice
2000-01	38	32	9	3	88	2nd/Southeast	2	4	Conference quarterfinals	Paul Maurice
2001-02	35	26	16	5	91	1st/Southeast	13	10	Stanley Cup finals	Paul Maurice
2002-03	22	43	11	6	61	5th/Southeast	—	—		Paul Maurice
2003-04	28	34	14	6	76	3rd/Southeast	—	—		Paul Maurice, Peter Laviolette
2004-05			No season—Lockout							
2005-06	52	22	—	8	112	1st/Southeast	16	9	Stanley Cup champs	Peter Laviolette

*New England Whalers, members of World Hockey Association.
†Hartford Whalers.

FIRST-ROUND ENTRY DRAFT CHOICES

Year Player, Overall, Last amateur team (league)

1979—Ray Allison, 18, Brandon (WHL)
1980—Fred Arthur, 8, Cornwall (QMJHL)
1981—Ron Francis, 4, Sault Ste. Marie (OHL)
1982—Paul Lawless, 14, Windsor (OHL)
1983—Sylvain Turgeon, 2, Hull (QMJHL)
David A. Jensen, 20, Lawrence Academy (Mass.)
1984—Sylvain Cote, 11, Quebec (QMJHL)
1985—Dana Murzyn, 5, Calgary (WHL)
1986—Scott Young, 11, Boston University
1987—Jody Hull, 18, Peterborough (OHL)
1988—Chris Govedaris, 11, Toronto (OHL)
1989—Robert Holik, 10, Jihlava, Czechoslovakia
1990—Mark Greig, 15, Lethbridge (WHL)
1991—Patrick Poulin, 9, St. Hyacinthe (QMJHL)
1992—Robert Petrovicky, 9, Dukla Trencin, Czech Republic
1993—Chris Pronger, 2, Peterborough (OHL)

Year Player, Overall, Last amateur team (league)

1994—Jeff O'Neill, 5, Guelph (OHL)
1995—Jean-Sebastien Giguere, 13, Halifax (QMJHL)
1996—No first-round selection
1997—Nikos Tselios, 22, Belleville (OHL)
1998—Jeff Heerema, 11, Sarnia (OHL)
1999—David Tanabe, 16, Wisconsin (WCHA)
2000—No first-round selection
2001—Igor Knyazev, 15, Spartak Jr., Russia
2002—Cam Ward, 25, Red Deer (WHL)
2003—Eric Staal, 2, Peterborough (OHL)
2004—Andrew Ladd, 4, Calgary (WHL)
2005—Jack Johnson, 3, U.S. National team
2006—No first-round selection
NOTE: Hartford chose Jordy Douglas, John Garrett and Mark Howe as priority selections before the 1979 expansion draft.

SINGLE-SEASON INDIVIDUAL RECORDS

FORWARDS/DEFENSEMEN

Most goals
56—Blaine Stoughton, 1979-80

Most assists
69—Ron Francis, 1989-90

Most points
105—Mike Rogers, 1979-80
Mike Rogers, 1980-81

Most penalty minutes
358—Torrie Robertson, 1985-86

Most power play goals
21—Geoff Sanderson, 1992-93

Most shorthanded goals
5—Kevyn Adams, 2003-04

Most games with three or more goals
3—Mike Rogers, 1980-81
Blaine Stoughton, 1981-82

Most shots
316—Jeff O'Neill, 2002-03

GOALTENDERS

Most games
77—Arturs Irbe, 2000-01

Most minutes
4,406—Arturs Irbe, 2000-01

Most shots against
1,947—Arturs Irbe, 2000-01

Most goals allowed
282—Greg Millen, 1982-83

Lowest goals-against average
2.17—Trevor Kidd, 1997-98

Most shutouts
6—Arturs Irbe, 1998-99
Arturs Irbe, 2000-01
Kevin Weekes, 2003-04

Most wins
38—Martin Gerber, 2005-06

Most losses
38—Greg Millen, 1982-83

Most ties
12—John Garrett, 1980-81
Greg Millen, 1982-83
Arturs Irbe, 1998-99

CHICAGO BLACKHAWKS

YEAR-BY-YEAR RECORDS

Season	W	L	T	OTL	Pts.	Finish	W	L	Highest round	Coach
		REGULAR SEASON					PLAYOFFS			
1926-27	19	22	3	—	41	3rd/American	*0	1	Quarterfinals	Pete Muldoon
1927-28	7	34	3	—	17	5th/American	—	—		Barney Stanley, Hugh Lehman
1928-29	7	29	8	—	22	5th/American	—	—		Herb Gardiner
1929-30	21	18	5	—	47	2nd/American	*0	1	Quarterfinals	Tom Schaughnessy, Bill Tobin
1930-31	24	17	3	—	51	2nd/American	*5	3	Stanley Cup finals	Dick Irvin
1931-32	18	19	11	—	47	2nd/American	1	1	Quarterfinals	Dick Irvin, Bill Tobin
1932-33	16	20	12	—	44	4th/American	—	—		Godfrey Matheson, Emil Iverson

	REGULAR SEASON						PLAYOFFS			
Season	W	L	T	OTL	Pts.	Finish	W	L	Highest round	Coach
1933-34	20	17	11	—	51	2nd/American	*6	1	Stanley Cup champ	Tom Gorman
1934-35	26	17	5	—	57	2nd/American	*0	1	Quarterfinals	Clem Loughlin
1935-36	21	19	8	—	50	3rd/American	1	1	Quarterfinals	Clem Loughlin
1936-37	14	27	7	—	35	4th/American	—	—		Clem Loughlin
1937-38	14	25	9	—	37	3rd/American	7	3	Stanley Cup champ	Bill Stewart
1938-39	12	28	8	—	32	7th	—	—		Bill Stewart, Paul Thompson
1939-40	23	19	6	—	52	4th	0	2	Quarterfinals	Paul Thompson
1940-41	16	25	7	—	39	5th	2	3	Semifinals	Paul Thompson
1941-42	22	23	3	—	47	4th	1	2	Quarterfinals	Paul Thompson
1942-43	17	18	15	—	49	5th	—	—		Paul Thompson
1943-44	22	23	5	—	49	4th	4	5	Stanley Cup finals	Paul Thompson
1944-45	13	30	7	—	33	5th	—	—		Paul Thompson, John Gottselig
1945-46	23	20	7	—	53	3rd	0	4	League semifinals	John Gottselig
1946-47	19	37	4	—	42	6th	—	—		John Gottselig
1947-48	20	34	6	—	46	6th	—	—		John Gottselig, Charlie Conacher
1948-49	21	31	8	—	50	5th	—	—		Charlie Conacher
1949-50	22	38	10	—	54	6th	—	—		Charlie Conacher
1950-51	13	47	10	—	36	6th	—	—		Ebbie Goodfellow
1951-52	17	44	9	—	43	6th	—	—		Ebbie Goodfellow
1952-53	27	28	15	—	69	4th	3	4	League semifinals	Sid Abel
1953-54	12	51	7	—	31	6th	—	—		Sid Abel
1954-55	13	40	17	—	43	6th	—	—		Frank Eddolls
1955-56	19	39	12	—	50	6th	—	—		Dick Irvin
1956-57	16	39	15	—	47	6th	—	—		Tommy Ivan
1957-58	24	39	7	—	55	5th	—	—		Tommy Ivan, Rudy Pilous
1958-59	28	29	13	—	69	3rd	2	4	League semifinals	Rudy Pilous
1959-60	28	29	13	—	69	3rd	0	4	League semifinals	Rudy Pilous
1960-61	29	24	17	—	75	3rd	8	4	Stanley Cup champ	Rudy Pilous
1961-62	31	26	13	—	75	3rd	6	6	Stanley Cup finals	Rudy Pilous
1962-63	32	21	17	—	81	2nd	2	4	League semifinals	Rudy Pilous
1963-64	36	22	12	—	84	2nd	3	4	League semifinals	Billy Reay
1964-65	34	28	8	—	76	3rd	7	7	Stanley Cup finals	Billy Reay
1965-66	37	25	8	—	82	2nd	2	4	League semifinals	Billy Reay
1966-67	41	17	12	—	94	1st	2	4	League semifinals	Billy Reay
1967-68	32	26	16	—	80	4th/East	5	6	Division finals	Billy Reay
1968-69	34	33	9	—	77	6th/East	—	—		Billy Reay
1969-70	45	22	9	—	99	1st/East	4	4	Division finals	Billy Reay
1970-71	49	20	9	—	107	1st/West	11	7	Stanley Cup finals	Billy Reay
1971-72	46	17	15	—	107	1st/West	4	4	Division finals	Billy Reay
1972-73	42	27	9	—	93	1st/West	10	6	Stanley Cup finals	Billy Reay
1973-74	41	14	23	—	105	2nd/West	6	5	Division finals	Billy Reay
1974-75	37	35	8	—	82	3rd/Smythe	3	5	Quarterfinals	Billy Reay
1975-76	32	30	18	—	82	1st/Smythe	0	4	Quarterfinals	Billy Reay
1976-77	26	43	11	—	63	3rd/Smythe	0	2	Preliminaries	Billy Reay, Bill White
1977-78	32	29	19	—	83	1st/Smythe	0	4	Quarterfinals	Bob Pulford
1978-79	29	36	15	—	73	1st/Smythe	0	4	Quarterfinals	Bob Pulford
1979-80	34	27	19	—	87	1st/Smythe	3	4	Quarterfinals	Eddie Johnston
1980-81	31	33	16	—	78	2nd/Smythe	0	3	Preliminaries	Keith Magnuson
1981-82	30	38	12	—	72	4th/Norris	8	7	Conference finals	Keith Magnuson, Bob Pulford
1982-83	47	23	10	—	104	1st/Norris	7	6	Conference finals	Orval Tessier
1983-84	30	42	8	—	68	4th/Norris	2	3	Division semifinals	Orval Tessier
1984-85	38	35	7	—	83	2nd/Norris	9	6	Conference finals	Orval Tessier, Bob Pulford
1985-86	39	33	8	—	86	1st/Norris	0	3	Division semifinals	Bob Pulford
1986-87	29	37	14	—	72	3rd/Norris	0	4	Division semifinals	Bob Pulford
1987-88	30	41	9	—	69	3rd/Norris	1	4	Division semifinals	Bob Murdoch
1988-89	27	41	12	—	66	4th/Norris	9	7	Conference finals	Mike Keenan
1989-90	41	33	6	—	88	1st/Norris	10	10	Conference finals	Mike Keenan
1990-91	49	23	8	—	106	1st/Norris	2	4	Division semifinals	Mike Keenan
1991-92	36	29	15	—	87	2nd/Norris	12	6	Stanley Cup finals	Mike Keenan
1992-93	47	25	12	—	106	1st/Norris	0	4	Division semifinals	Darryl Sutter
1993-94	39	36	9	—	87	5th/Central	2	4	Conference quarterfinals	Darryl Sutter
1994-95	24	19	5	—	53	3rd/Central	9	7	Conference finals	Darryl Sutter
1995-96	40	28	14	—	94	2nd/Central	6	4	Conference semifinals	Craig Hartsburg
1996-97	34	35	13	—	81	5th/Central	2	4	Conference quarterfinals	Craig Hartsburg
1997-98	30	39	13	—	73	5th/Central	—	—		Craig Hartsburg
1998-99	29	41	12	—	70	3rd/Central	—	—		Dirk Graham, Lorne Molleken
1999-00	33	37	10	2	78	3rd/Central	—	—		Lorne Molleken, Bob Pulford
2000-01	29	40	8	5	71	4th/Central	—	—		Alpo Suhonen, Denis Savard, Al MacAdam
2001-02	41	27	13	1	96	3rd/Central	1	4	Conference quarterfinals	Brian Sutter
2002-03	30	33	13	6	79	3rd/Central	—	—		Brian Sutter
2003-04	20	43	11	8	59	5th/Central	—	—		Brian Sutter
2004-05			No season—Lockout							
2005-06	26	43	—	13	65	4th/Central	—	—		Trent Yawney

*Won-lost record does not indicate tie(s) resulting from two-game, total-goals series that year (two-game, total-goals series were played from 1917-18 through 1935-36).

FIRST-ROUND ENTRY DRAFT CHOICES

Year Player, Overall, Last amateur team (league)

1969—J.P. Bordeleau, 13, Montreal (OHL)
1970—Dan Maloney, 14, London (OHL)
1971—Dan Spring, 12, Edmonton (WCHL)
1972—Phil Russell, 13, Edmonton (WCHL)
1973—Darcy Rota, 13, Edmonton (WCHL)
1974—Grant Mulvey, 16, Calgary (WCHL)
1975—Greg Vaydik, 7, Medicine Hat (WCHL)
1976—Real Cloutier, 9, Quebec (WHA)
1977—Doug Wilson, 6, Ottawa (OHL)
1978—Tim Higgins, 10, Ottawa (OHL)
1979—Keith Brown, 7, Portland (WHL)
1980—Denis Savard, 3, Montreal (QMJHL)
Jerome Dupont, 15, Toronto (OHL)
1981—Tony Tanti, 12, Oshawa (OHL)
1982—Ken Yaremchuk, 7, Portland (WHL)
1983—Bruce Cassidy, 18, Ottawa (OHL)
1984—Ed Olczyk, 3, U.S. Olympic Team
1985—Dave Manson, 11, Prince Albert (WHL)
1986—Everett Sanipass, 14, Verdun (QMJHL)
1987—Jimmy Waite, 8, Chicoutimi (QMJHL)
1988—Jeremy Roenick, 8, Thayer Academy (Mass.)

Year Player, Overall, Last amateur team (league)

1989—Adam Bennett, 6, Sudbury (OHL)
1990—Karl Dykhuis, 16, Hull (QMJHL)
1991—Dean McAmmond, 22, Prince Albert (WHL)
1992—Sergei Krivokrasov, 12, Central Red Army, CIS
1993—Eric Lecompte, 24, Hull (QMJHL)
1994—Ethan Moreau, 14, Niagara Falls (OHL)
1995—Dimitri Nabokov, 19, Krylja Sovetov, CIS
1996—No first-round selection
1997—Daniel Cleary, 13, Belleville (OHL)
Ty Jones, 16, Spokane (WHL)
1998—Mark Bell, 8, Ottawa (OHL)
1999—Steve McCarthy, 23, Kootenay (WHL)
2000—Mikhail Yakubov, 10, Togliatta, Russia
Pavel Vorobiev, 11, Yaroslavl, Russia
2001—Tuomo Ruutu, 9, Jokerit, Finland
Adam Munro, 29, Erie (OHL)
2002—Anton Babchuk, 21, Elektrostal Jr., Russia
2003—Brent Seabrook, 14, Lethbridge (WHL)
2004—Cameron Barker, 3, Medicine Hat (WHL)
2005—Jack Skille, 7, U.S. National team
2006—Jonathan Toews, 3, U. of North Dakota (WCHA)

SINGLE-SEASON INDIVIDUAL RECORDS

FORWARDS/DEFENSEMEN

Most goals
58—Bobby Hull, 1968-69

Most assists
87—Denis Savard, 1981-82
Denis Savard, 1987-88

Most points
131—Denis Savard, 1987-88

Most penalty minutes
408—Mike Peluso, 1991-92

Most power play goals
24—Jeremy Roenick, 1993-94

Most shorthanded goals
10—Dirk Graham, 1988-89

Most games with three or more goals
4—Bobby Hull, 1959-60
Bobby Hull, 1965-66

Most shots
414—Bobby Hull, 1968-69

GOALTENDERS

Most games
74—Ed Belfour, 1990-91

Most minutes
4,219—Tony Esposito, 1974-75

Most goals allowed
246—Harry Lumley, 1950-51
Tony Esposito, 1980-81

Lowest goals-against average
1.73—Charles Gardiner, 1933-34

Most shutouts
15—Tony Esposito, 1969-70

Most wins
43—Ed Belfour, 1990-91

Most losses
47—Al Rollins, 1953-54

Most ties
21—Tony Esposito, 1973-74

CLEVELAND BARONS (DEFUNCT)

YEAR-BY-YEAR RECORDS

	REGULAR SEASON					PLAYOFFS			
Season	W	L	T	Pts.	Finish	W	L	Highest round	Coach
1967-68*	15	42	17	47	6th/West	—	—		Bert Olmstead, Gordie Fashoway
1968-69*	29	36	11	69	2nd/West	3	4	Division semifinals	Fred Glover
1969-70*	22	40	14	58	4th/West	0	4	Division semifinals	Fred Glover
1970-71†	20	53	5	45	7th/West	—	—		Fred Glover
1971-72†	21	39	18	60	6th/West	—	—		Fred Glover, Vic Stasiuk
1972-73†	16	46	16	48	8th/West	—	—		Garry Young, Fred Glover
1973-74†	13	55	10	36	8th/West	—	—		Fred Glover, Marsh Johnston
1974-75†	19	48	13	51	4th/Adams	—	—		Marsh Johnston
1975-76†	27	42	11	65	4th/Adams	—	—		Jack Evans
1976-77	25	42	13	63	4th/Adams	—	—		Jack Evans
1977-78	22	45	13	57	4th/Adams	—	—		Jack Evans

*Oakland Seals.
†California Golden Seals.
Barons disbanded after 1977-78 season. Owners merged with Minnesota franchise and a number of Cleveland players were awarded to North Stars; remaining players were dispersed to other clubs in draft.

COLORADO AVALANCHE

YEAR-BY-YEAR RECORDS

	REGULAR SEASON						PLAYOFFS			
Season	W	L	T	OTL	Pts.	Finish	W	L	Highest round	Coach
1972-73*	33	40	5	—	71	5th	—	—		Maurice Richard, Maurice Filion

	REGULAR SEASON						PLAYOFFS			
Season	W	L	T	OTL	Pts.	Finish	W	L	Highest round	Coach
1973-74*	38	36	4	—	80	5th	—	—		Jacques Plante
1974-75*	46	32	0	—	92	1st	8	7	Avco World Cup finals	Jean-Guy Gendron
1975-76*	50	27	4	—	104	2nd	1	4	League quarterfinals	Jean-Guy Gendron
1976-77*	47	31	3	—	97	1st	12	5	Avco World Cup champ	Marc Boileau
1977-78*	40	37	3	—	83	4th	5	6	League semifinals	Marc Boileau
1978-79*	41	34	5	—	87	2nd	0	4	League semifinals	Jacques Demers
1979-80†	25	44	11	—	61	5th/Adams	—	—		Jacques Demers
1980-81†	30	32	18	—	78	4th/Adams	2	3	Preliminaries	Maurice Filion, Michel Bergeron
1981-82†	33	31	16	—	82	4th/Adams	7	9	Conference finals	Michel Bergeron
1982-83†	34	34	12	—	80	4th/Adams	1	3	Division semifinals	Michel Bergeron
1983-84†	42	28	10	—	94	3rd/Adams	5	4	Division finals	Michel Bergeron
1984-85†	41	30	9	—	91	2nd/Adams	9	9	Conference finals	Michel Bergeron
1985-86†	43	31	6	—	92	1st/Adams	0	3	Division semifinals	Michel Bergeron
1986-87†	31	39	10	—	72	4th/Adams	7	6	Division finals	Michel Bergeron
1987-88†	32	43	5	—	69	5th/Adams	—	—		Andre Savard, Ron Lapointe
1988-89†	27	46	7	—	61	5th/Adams	—	—		Ron Lapointe, Jean Perron
1989-90†	12	61	7	—	31	5th/Adams	—	—		Michel Bergeron
1990-91†	16	50	14	—	46	5th/Adams	—	—		Dave Chambers
1991-92†	20	48	12	—	52	5th/Adams	—	—		Dave Chambers, Pierre Page
1992-93†	47	27	10	—	104	2nd/Adams	2	4	Division semifinals	Pierre Page
1993-94†	34	42	8	—	76	5th/Northeast	—	—		Pierre Page
1994-95†	30	13	5	—	65	1st/Northeast	2	4	Conference quarterfinals	Marc Crawford
1995-96	47	25	10	—	104	1st/Pacific	16	6	Stanley Cup champ	Marc Crawford
1996-97	49	24	9	—	107	1st/Pacific	10	7	Conference finals	Marc Crawford
1997-98	39	26	17	—	95	1st/Pacific	3	4	Conference quarterfinals	Marc Crawford
1998-99	44	28	10	—	98	1st/Northwest	11	8	Conference finals	Bob Hartley
1999-00	42	28	11	1	96	1st/Northwest	11	6	Conference finals	Bob Hartley
2000-01	52	16	10	4	118	1st/Northwest	16	7	Stanley Cup champ	Bob Hartley
2001-02	45	28	8	1	99	1st/Northwest	11	10	Conference finals	Bob Hartley
2002-03	42	19	13	8	105	1st/Northwest	3	4	Conference quarterfinals	Bob Hartley, Tony Granato
2003-04	40	22	13	7	100	2nd/Northwest	6	5	Conference semifinals	Tony Granato
2004-05	No season—Lockout									
2005-06	43	30	—	9	95	2nd/Northwest	4	5	Conference semifinals	Joel Quenneville

*Quebec Nordiques, members of World Hockey Association.
†Quebec Nordiques.

FIRST-ROUND ENTRY DRAFT CHOICES

Year Player, Overall, Last amateur team (league)
1979—Michel Goulet, 20, Birmingham (WHA)
1980—No first-round selection
1981—Randy Moller, 11, Lethbridge (WHL)
1982—David Shaw, 13, Kitchener (OHL)
1983—No first-round selection
1984—Trevor Steinburg, 15, Guelph (OHL)
1985—Dave Latta, 15, Kitchener (OHL)
1986—Ken McRae, 18, Sudbury (OHL)
1987—Bryan Fogarty, 9, Kingston (OHL)
Joe Sakic, 15, Swift Current (WHL)
1988—Curtis Leschyshyn, 3, Saskatoon (WHL)
Daniel Dore, 5, Drummondville (QMJHL)
1989—Mats Sundin, 1, Nacka (Sweden)
1990—Owen Nolan, 1, Cornwall (OHL)
1991—Eric Lindros, 1, Oshawa (OHL)
1992—Todd Warriner, 4, Windsor (OHL)
1993—Jocelyn Thibault, 10, Sherbrooke (QMJHL)
Adam Deadmarsh, 14, Portland (WHL)

Year Player, Overall, Last amateur team (league)
1994—Wade Belak, 12, Saskatoon (WHL)
Jeffrey Kealty, 22, Catholic Memorial H.S.
1995—Marc Denis, 25, Chicoutimi (QMJHL)
1996—Peter Ratchuk, 25, Shattuck-St. Mary's H.S. (Min.)
1997—Kevin Grimes, 26, Kingston (OHL)
1998—Alex Tanguay, 12, Halifax (QMJHL)
Martin Skoula, 17, Barrie (OHL)
Robyn Regehr, 19, Kamloops (WHL)
Scott Parker, 20, Kelowna (WHL)
1999—Mihail Kuleshov, 25, Cherepovec, Russia
2000—Vaclav Nedorost, 14, Budejovice, Czech Republic
2001—No first-round selection
2002—Jonas Johansson, 28, HV 71, Sweden
2003—No first-round selection.
2004—Wojtek Wolski, 21, Brampton (OHL)
2005—No first-round selection.
2006—Chris Stewart, 18, Kingston (OHL)
NOTE: Quebec chose Paul Baxter, Richard Brodeur and Garry Larivierre as priority selections before the 1979 expansion draft.

SINGLE-SEASON INDIVIDUAL RECORDS

FORWARDS/DEFENSEMEN

Most goals
57—Michel Goulet, 1982-83

Most assists
93—Peter Stastny, 1981-82

Most points
139—Peter Stastny, 1981-82

Most penalty minutes
301—Gord Donnelly, 1987-88

Most power play goals
29—Michel Goulet, 1987-88

Most shorthanded goals
6—Michel Goulet, 1981-82
Scott Young, 1992-93
Joe Sakic, 1995-96

Most games with three or more goals
4—Miroslav Frycer, 1981-82
Peter Stastny, 1982-83

Most shots
332—Joe Sakic, 2000-01

GOALTENDERS

Most games
65—Patrick Roy, 1997-98

Most minutes
3,835—Patrick Roy, 1997-98

Most shots against
1,861—Patrick Roy, 1996-97

Most goals allowed
230—Dan Bouchard, 1981-82

Lowest goals-against average
1.94—Patrick Roy, 2001-02

Most shutouts
9—Patrick Roy, 2001-02

Most wins
40—Patrick Roy, 2000-01

Most losses
29—Ron Tugnutt, 1990-91

Most ties
13—Patrick Roy, 1997-98

COLUMBUS BLUE JACKETS

YEAR-BY-YEAR RECORDS

	REGULAR SEASON						PLAYOFFS			
Season	W	L	T	OTL	Pts.	Finish	W	L	Highest round	Coach
2000-01	28	39	9	6	71	5th/Central	—	—		Dave King
2001-02	22	47	8	5	57	5th/Central	—	—		Dave King
2002-03	29	42	8	3	69	5th/Central	—	—		Dave King, Doug MacLean
2003-04	25	45	8	4	62	4th/Central	—	—		Doug MacLean, Gerard Gallant
2004-05	No season—Lockout									
2005-06	35	43	—	4	74	3rd/Central	—	—		Gerard Gallant

FIRST-ROUND ENTRY DRAFT CHOICES

Year Player, Overall, Last amateur team (league)
2000—Rostislav Klesla, 4, Brampton (OHL)
2001—Pascal LeClaire, 8, Halifax (QMJHL)
2002—Rick Nash, 1, London (OHL)
2003—Nikolai Zherdev, 4, Russia

Year Player, Overall, Last amateur team (league)
2004—Alexandre Picard, 8, Lewiston (QMJHL)
2005—Gilbert Brule, 6, Vancouver (WHL)
2006—Derick Brassard, 6, Drummondville (QMJHL)

SINGLE-SEASON INDIVIDUAL RECORDS

FORWARDS/DEFENSEMEN

Most goals
41—Rick Nash, 2003-04

Most assists
52—Ray Whitney, 2002-03

Most points
76—Ray Whitney, 2002-03

Most penalty minutes
249—Jody Shelley, 2001-02

Most power play goals
19—Rick Nash, 2003-04

Most shorthanded goals
4—David Vyborny, 2003-04

Most games with three or more goals
1—Deron Quint, 2000-01
Geoff Sanderson, 2000-01
Tyler Wright, 2000-01
Espen Knutsen, 2001-02
David Vyborny, 2003-04
Bryan Berard, 2005-06
Rick Nash, 2005-06

Most shots
286—Geoff Sanderson, 2002-03

GOALTENDERS

Most games
77—Marc Denis, 2002-03

Most minutes
3,129—Ron Tugnutt, 2000-01

Most shots against
2,404—Marc Denis, 2002-03

Most goals allowed
232—Marc Denis, 2002-03

Lowest goals-against average
2.44—Ron Tugnutt, 2000-01

Most shutouts
5—Marc Denis, 2002-03
Marc Denis, 2003-04

Most wins
27—Marc Denis, 2002-03

Most losses
41—Marc Denis, 2002-03

Most ties
8—Marc Denis, 2002-03

DALLAS STARS

YEAR-BY-YEAR RECORDS

	REGULAR SEASON						PLAYOFFS			
Season	W	L	T	OTL	Pts.	Finish	W	L	Highest round	Coach
1967-68*	27	32	15	—	69	4th/West	7	7	Division finals	Wren Blair
1968-69*	18	43	15	—	51	6th/West	—	—		Wren Blair, John Muckler
1969-70*	19	35	22	—	60	3rd/West	2	4	Division semifinals	Wren Blair, Charlie Burns
1970-71*	28	34	16	—	72	4th/West	6	6	Division finals	Jack Gordon
1971-72*	37	29	12	—	86	2nd/West	3	4	Division semifinals	Jack Gordon
1972-73*	37	30	11	—	85	3rd/West	2	4	Division semifinals	Jack Gordon
1973-74*	23	38	17	—	63	7th/West	—	—		Jack Gordon, Parker MacDonald
1974-75*	23	50	7	—	53	4th/Smythe	—	—		Jack Gordon, Charlie Burns
1975-76*	20	53	7	—	47	4th/Smythe	—	—		Ted Harris
1976-77*	23	39	18	—	64	2nd/Smythe	0	2	Preliminaries	Ted Harris
1977-78*	18	53	9	—	45	5th/Smythe	—	—		Ted Harris, Andre Beaulieu, Lou Nanne

Season	W	L	T	OTL	Pts.	Finish	W	L	Highest round	Coach
			REGULAR SEASON						PLAYOFFS	
1978-79*	28	40	12	—	68	4th/Adams	—	—		Harry Howell, Glen Sonmor
1979-80*	36	28	16	—	88	3rd/Adams	8	7	Semifinals	Glen Sonmor
1980-81*	35	28	17	—	87	3rd/Adams	12	7	Stanley Cup finals	Glen Sonmor
1981-82*	37	23	20	—	94	1st/Norris	1	3	Division semifinals	Glen Sonmor, Murray Oliver
1982-83*	40	24	16	—	96	2nd/Norris	4	5	Division finals	Glen Sonmor, Murray Oliver
1983-84*	39	31	10	—	88	1st/Norris	7	9	Conference finals	Bill Maloney
1984-85*	25	43	12	—	62	4th/Norris	5	4	Division finals	Bill Maloney, Glen Sonmor
1985-86*	38	33	9	—	85	2nd/Norris	2	3	Division semifinals	Lorne Henning
1986-87*	30	40	10	—	70	5th/Norris	—	—		Lorne Henning, Glen Sonmor
1987-88*	19	48	13	—	51	5th/Norris	—	—		Herb Brooks
1988-89*	27	37	16	—	70	3rd/Norris	1	4	Division semifinals	Pierre Page
1989-90*	36	40	4	—	76	4th/Norris	3	4	Division semifinals	Pierre Page
1990-91*	27	39	14	—	68	4th/Norris	14	9	Stanley Cup finals	Bob Gainey
1991-92*	32	42	6	—	70	4th/Norris	3	4	Division semifinals	Bob Gainey
1992-93*	36	38	10	—	82	5th/Norris	—	—		Bob Gainey
1993-94	42	29	13	—	97	3rd/Central	5	4	Conference semifinals	Bob Gainey
1994-95	17	23	8	—	42	5th/Central	1	4	Conference quarterfinals	Bob Gainey
1995-96	26	42	14	—	66	6th/Central	—	—		Bob Gainey, Ken Hitchcock
1996-97	48	26	8	—	104	1st/Central	3	4	Conference quarterfinals	Ken Hitchcock
1997-98	49	22	11	—	109	1st/Central	10	7	Conference finals	Ken Hitchcock
1998-99	51	19	12	—	114	1st/Pacific	16	7	Stanley Cup champ	Ken Hitchcock
1999-00	43	23	10	6	102	1st/Pacific	14	9	Stanley Cup finals	Ken Hitchcock
2000-01	48	24	8	2	106	1st/Pacific	4	6	Conference semifinals	Ken Hitchcock
2001-02	36	28	13	5	90	4th/Pacific	—	—		Ken Hitchcock, Rick Wilson
2002-03	46	17	15	4	111	1st/Pacific	6	6	Conference semifinals	Dave Tippett
2003-04	41	26	13	2	97	2nd/Pacific	1	4	Conference quarterfinals	Dave Tippett
2004-05			No season—Lockout							
2005-06	53	23	—	6	112	1st/Pacific	1	4	Conference quarterfinals	Dave Tippett

*Minnesota North Stars.

FIRST-ROUND ENTRY DRAFT CHOICES

Year Player, Overall, Last amateur team (league)

1969—Dick Redmond, 5, St. Catharines (OHL)
Dennis O'Brien, 14, St. Catharines (OHL)
1970—No first-round selection
1971—No first-round selection
1972—Jerry Byers, 12, Kitchener (OHL)
1973—No first-round selection
1974—Doug Hicks, 6, Flin Flon (WCHL)
1975—Brian Maxwell, 4, Medicine Hat (WCHL)
1976—Glen Sharpley, 3, Hull (QMJHL)
1977—Brad Maxwell, 7, New Westminster (WCHL)
1978—Bobby Smith, 1, Ottawa (OHL)
1979—Craig Hartsburg, 6, Birmingham (WHA)
Tom McCarthy, 10, Oshawa (OHL)
1980—Brad Palmer, 16, Victoria (WHL)
1981—Ron Meighan, 13, Niagara Falls (OHL)
1982—Brian Bellows, 2, Kitchener (OHL)
1983—Brian Lawton, 1, Mount St. Charles H.S. (R.I.)
1984—David Quinn, 13, Kent H.S. (Ct.)
1985—No first-round selection
1986—Warren Babe, 12, Lethbridge (WHL)

Year Player, Overall, Last amateur team (league)

1987—Dave Archibald, 6, Portland (WHL)
1988—Mike Modano, 1, Prince Albert (WHL)
1989—Doug Zmolek, 7, John Marshall H.S. (Minn.)
1990—Derian Hatcher, 8, North Bay (OHL)
1991—Richard Matvichuk, 8, Saskatoon (WHL)
1992—No first-round selection
1993—Todd Harvey, 9, Detroit (OHL)
1994—Jason Botterill, 20, Michigan (CCHA)
1995—Jarome Iginla, 11, Kamloops (WHL)
1996—Richard Jackman, 5, Sault Ste. Marie (OHL)
1997—Brenden Morrow, 25, Portland (WHL)
1998—No first-round selection
1999—No first-round selection
2000—Steve Ott, 25, Windsor (OHL)
2001—Jason Bacashihua, 26, Chicago (NAHL)
2002—Martin Vagner, 26, Hull (QMJHL)
2003—No first-round selection
2004—Mark Fistric, 28, Vancouver (WHL)
2005—Matt Niskanen, 28, Virginia (USHSW)
2006—Ivan Vishnevskiy, 27, Rouyn Noranda (QMJHL)

SINGLE-SEASON INDIVIDUAL RECORDS

FORWARDS/DEFENSEMEN

Most goals
55—Dino Ciccarelli, 1981-82
Brian Bellows, 1989-90

Most assists
76—Neal Broten, 1985-86

Most points
114—Bobby Smith, 1981-82

Most penalty minutes
382—Basil McRae, 1987-88

Most power play goals
22—Dino Ciccarelli, 1986-87

Most shorthanded goals
6—Bill Collins, 1969-70

Most games with three or more goals
3—Bill Goldsworthy, 1973-74
Dino Ciccarelli, 1981-82
Dino Ciccarelli, 1983-84
Tom McCarthy, 1984-85
Scott Bjugstad, 1985-86
Dino Ciccarelli, 1985-86
Mike Modano, 1998-99

Most shots
321—Bill Goldsworthy, 1973-74

GOALTENDERS

Most games
73—Marty Turco, 2003-04

Most minutes
4,359—Marty Turco, 2003-04

Most shots against
1,648—Marty Turco, 2003-04

Most goals allowed
216—Pete LoPresti, 1977-78

Lowest goals-against average
1.88—Ed Belfour, 1997-98

Most shutouts

9—Ed Belfour, 1997-98
Marty Turco, 2003-04

Most wins

41—Marty Turco, 2005-06

Most losses

35—Pete LoPresti, 1977-78

Most ties

16—Cesare Maniago, 1969-70

DETROIT RED WINGS

YEAR-BY-YEAR RECORDS

	REGULAR SEASON						PLAYOFFS			
Season	W	L	T	OTL	Pts.	Finish	W	L	Highest round	Coach
1926-27†	12	28	4	—	28	5th/American	—	—		Art Duncan, Duke Keats
1927-28†	19	19	6	—	44	4th/American	—	—		Jack Adams
1928-29†	19	16	9	—	47	3rd/American	0	2	Quarterfinals	Jack Adams
1929-30†	14	24	6	—	34	4th/American	—	—		Jack Adams
1930-31‡	16	21	7	—	39	4th/American	—	—		Jack Adams
1931-32‡	18	20	10	—	46	3rd/American	*0	1	Quarterfinals	Jack Adams
1932-33	25	15	8	—	58	2nd/American	2	2	Semifinals	Jack Adams
1933-34	24	14	10	—	58	1st/American	4	5	Stanley Cup finals	Jack Adams
1934-35	19	22	7	—	45	4th/American	—	—		Jack Adams
1935-36	24	16	8	—	56	1st/American	6	1	Stanley Cup champ	Jack Adams
1936-37	25	14	9	—	59	1st/American	6	4	Stanley Cup champ	Jack Adams
1937-38	12	25	11	—	35	4th/American	—	—		Jack Adams
1938-39	18	24	6	—	42	5th	3	3	Semifinals	Jack Adams
1939-40	16	26	6	—	38	5th	2	3	Semifinals	Jack Adams
1940-41	21	16	11	—	53	3rd	4	5	Stanley Cup finals	Jack Adams
1941-42	19	25	4	—	42	5th	7	5	Stanley Cup finals	Jack Adams
1942-43	25	14	11	—	61	1st	8	2	Stanley Cup champ	Jack Adams
1943-44	26	18	6	—	58	2nd	1	4	League semifinals	Jack Adams
1944-45	31	14	5	—	67	2nd	7	7	Stanley Cup finals	Jack Adams
1945-46	20	20	10	—	50	4th	1	4	League semifinals	Jack Adams
1946-47	22	27	11	—	55	4th	1	4	League semifinals	Jack Adams
1947-48	30	18	12	—	72	2nd	4	6	Stanley Cup finals	Tommy Ivan
1948-49	34	19	7	—	75	1st	4	7	Stanley Cup finals	Tommy Ivan
1949-50	37	19	14	—	88	1st	8	6	Stanley Cup champ	Tommy Ivan
1950-51	44	13	13	—	101	1st	2	4	League semifinals	Tommy Ivan
1951-52	44	14	12	—	100	1st	8	0	Stanley Cup champ	Tommy Ivan
1952-53	36	16	18	—	90	1st	2	4	League semifinals	Tommy Ivan
1953-54	37	19	14	—	88	1st	8	4	Stanley Cup champ	Tommy Ivan
1954-55	42	17	11	—	95	1st	8	3	Stanley Cup champ	Jimmy Skinner
1955-56	30	24	16	—	76	2nd	5	5	Stanley Cup finals	Jimmy Skinner
1956-57	38	20	12	—	88	1st	1	4	League semifinals	Jimmy Skinner
1957-58	29	29	12	—	70	3rd	0	4	League semifinals	Jimmy Skinner, Sid Abel
1958-59	25	37	8	—	58	6th	—	—		Sid Abel
1959-60	26	29	15	—	67	4th	2	4	League semifinals	Sid Abel
1960-61	25	29	16	—	66	4th	6	5	Stanley Cup finals	Sid Abel
1961-62	23	33	14	—	60	5th	—	—		Sid Abel
1962-63	32	25	13	—	77	4th	5	6	Stanley Cup finals	Sid Abel
1963-64	30	29	11	—	71	4th	7	7	Stanley Cup finals	Sid Abel
1964-65	40	23	7	—	87	1st	3	4	League semifinals	Sid Abel
1965-66	31	27	12	—	74	4th	6	6	Stanley Cup finals	Sid Abel
1966-67	27	39	4	—	58	5th	—	—		Sid Abel
1967-68	27	35	12	—	66	6th/East	—	—		Sid Abel
1968-69	33	31	12	—	78	5th/East	—	—		Bill Gadsby
1969-70	40	21	15	—	95	3rd/East	0	4	Division semifinals	Bill Gadsby, Sid Abel
1970-71	22	45	11	—	55	7th/East	—	—		Ned Harkness, Doug Barkley
1971-72	33	35	10	—	76	5th/East	—	—		Doug Barkley, Johnny Wilson
1972-73	37	29	12	—	86	5th/East	—	—		Johnny Wilson
1973-74	29	39	10	—	68	6th/East	—	—		Ted Garvin, Alex Delvecchio
1974-75	23	45	12	—	58	4th/Norris	—	—		Alex Delvecchio
1975-76	26	44	10	—	62	4th/Norris	—	—		Ted Garvin, Alex Delvecchio
1976-77	16	55	9	—	41	5th/Norris	—	—		Alex Delvecchio, Larry Wilson
1977-78	32	34	14	—	78	2nd/Norris	3	4	Quarterfinals	Bobby Kromm
1978-79	23	41	16	—	62	5th/Norris	—	—		Bobby Kromm
1979-80	26	43	11	—	63	5th/Norris	—	—		Bobby Kromm, Ted Lindsay
1980-81	19	43	18	—	56	5th/Norris	—	—		Ted Lindsay, Wayne Maxner
1981-82	21	47	12	—	54	6th/Norris	—	—		Wayne Maxner, Billy Dea
1982-83	21	44	15	—	57	5th/Norris	—	—		Nick Polano
1983-84	31	42	7	—	69	3rd/Norris	1	3	Division semifinals	Nick Polano
1984-85	27	41	12	—	66	3rd/Norris	0	3	Division semifinals	Nick Polano
1985-86	17	57	6	—	40	5th/Norris	—	—		Harry Neale, Brad Park, Dan Belisle
1986-87	34	36	10	—	78	2nd/Norris	9	7	Conference finals	Jacques Demers
1987-88	41	28	11	—	93	1st/Norris	9	7	Conference finals	Jacques Demers
1988-89	34	34	12	—	80	1st/Norris	2	4	Division semifinals	Jacques Demers

Season	W	L	T	OTL	Pts.	Finish	W	L	Highest round	Coach
			REGULAR SEASON				PLAYOFFS			
1989-90	28	38	14	—	70	5th/Norris	—	—		Jacques Demers
1990-91	34	38	8	—	76	3rd/Norris	3	4	Division semifinals	Bryan Murray
1991-92	43	25	12	—	98	1st/Norris	4	7	Division finals	Bryan Murray
1992-93	47	28	9	—	103	2nd/Norris	3	4	Division semifinals	Bryan Murray
1993-94	46	30	8	—	100	1st/Central	3	4	Division semifinals	Scotty Bowman
1994-95	33	11	4	—	70	1st/Central	12	6	Stanley Cup finals	Scotty Bowman
1995-96	62	13	7	—	131	1st/Central	10	9	Conference finals	Scotty Bowman
1996-97	38	26	18	—	94	2nd/Central	16	4	Stanley Cup champ	Scotty Bowman
1997-98	44	23	15	—	103	2nd/Central	16	6	Stanley Cup champ	Scotty Bowman
1998-99	43	32	7	—	93	1st/Central	6	4	Conference semifinals	Dave Lewis, Barry Smith, Scotty Bowman
1999-00	48	22	10	2	108	2nd/Central	5	4	Conference semifinals	Scotty Bowman
2000-01	49	20	9	4	111	1st/Central	2	4	Conference quarterfinals	Scotty Bowman
2001-02	51	17	10	4	116	1st/Central	16	7	Stanley Cup champ	Scotty Bowman
2002-03	48	20	10	4	110	1st/Central	0	4	Conference quarterfinals	Dave Lewis
2003-04	48	21	11	2	109	2nd/Central	6	6	Conference semifinals	Dave Lewis
2004-05	No season—Lockout									
2005-06	58	16	—	8	124	1st/Central	2	4	Conference quarterfinals	Mike Babcock

*Won-lost record does not indicate tie(s) resulting from two-game, total goals series that year (two-game, total-goals series were played from 1917-18 through 1935-36).

†Detroit Cougars.

‡Detroit Falcons.

FIRST-ROUND ENTRY DRAFT CHOICES

Year Player, Overall, Last amateur team (league)

1969—Jim Rutherford, 10, Hamilton (OHL)
1970—Serge Lajeunesse, 12, Montreal (OHL)
1971—Marcel Dionne, 2, St. Catharines (OHL)
1972—No first-round selection
1973—Terry Richardson, 11, New Westminster (WCHL)
1974—Bill Lochead, 9, Oshawa (OHL)
1975—Rick Lapointe, 5, Victoria (WCHL)
1976—Fred Williams, 4, Saskatoon (WCHL)
1977—Dale McCourt, 1, St. Catharines (OHL)*
1978—Willie Huber, 9, Hamilton (OHL)
Brent Peterson, 12, Portland (WCHL)
1979—Mike Foligno, 3, Sudbury (OHL)
1980—Mike Blaisdell, 11, Regina (WHL)
1981—No first-round selection
1982—Murray Craven, 17, Medicine Hat (WHL)
1983—Steve Yzerman, 4, Peterborough (OHL)
1984—Shawn Burr, 7, Kitchener (OHL)
1985—Brent Fedyk, 8, Regina (WHL)
1986—Joe Murphy, 1, Michigan State University

Year Player, Overall, Last amateur team (league)

1987—Yves Racine, 11, Longueuil (QMJHL)
1988—Kory Kocur, 17, Saskatoon (WHL)
1989—Mike Sillinger, 11, Regina (WHL)
1990—Keith Primeau, 3, Niagara Falls (OHL)
1991—Martin Lapointe, 10, Laval (QMJHL)
1992—Curtis Bowen, 22, Ottawa (OHL)
1993—Anders Eriksson, 22, MoDo, Sweden
1994—Yan Golvbovsky, 23, Dynamo Moscow, CIS
1995—Maxim Kuznetsov, 26, Dynamo Moscow, CIS
1996—Jesse Wallin, 26, Red Deer (WHL)
1997—No first-round selection
1998—Jiri Fischer, 25, Hull (QMJHL)
1999—No first-round selection
2000—Niklas Kronvall, 29, Djurgarden, Sweden
2001—No first-round selection
2002—No first-round selection
2003—No first-round selection
2004—No first-round selection
2005—Jakub Kindl, 19, Kitchener (OHL)
2006—No first-round selection

SINGLE-SEASON INDIVIDUAL RECORDS

FORWARDS/DEFENSEMEN

Most goals
65—Steve Yzerman, 1988-89

Most assists
90—Steve Yzerman, 1988-89

Most points
155—Steve Yzerman, 1988-89

Most penalty minutes
398—Bob Probert, 1987-88

Most power play goals
21—Mickey Redmond, 1973-74
Dino Ciccarelli, 1992-93

Most shorthanded goals
10—Marcel Dionne, 1974-75

Most games with three or more goals
4—Frank Mahovlich, 1968-69

Most shots
388—Steve Yzerman, 1988-89

GOALTENDERS

Most games
72—Tim Cheveldae, 1991-92

Most minutes
4,236—Tim Cheveldae, 1991-92

Most goals allowed
226—Tim Cheveldae, 1991-92

Lowest goals-against average
1.43—Dolly Dodson, 1928-29

Most shutouts
12—Terry Sawchuk, 1951-52
Terry Sawchuk, 1953-54
Terry Sawchuk, 1954-55
Glenn Hall, 1955-56

Most wins
44—Terry Sawchuk, 1950-51
Terry Sawchuk, 1951-52

Most losses
36—Terry Sawchuk, 1959-60

Most ties
16—Terry Sawchuk, 1952-53
GlennHall, 1955-56

EDMONTON OILERS

YEAR-BY-YEAR RECORDS

Season	W	L	T	OTL	Pts.	Finish	W	L	Highest round	Coach
			REGULAR SEASON				PLAYOFFS			
1972-73*	38	37	3	—	79	5th	—	—		Ray Kinasewich
1973-74†	38	37	3	—	79	3rd	1	4	League quarterfinals	Brian Shaw

	REGULAR SEASON						PLAYOFFS			
Season	W	L	T	OTL	Pts.	Finish	W	L	Highest round	Coach
1974-75†	36	38	4	—	76	5th	—	—		Brian Shaw, Bill Hunter
1975-76†	27	49	5	—	59	4th	0	4	League quarterfinals	Clare Drake, Bill Hunter
1976-77†	34	43	4	—	72	4th	1	4	League quarterfinals	Bep Guidolin, Glen Sather
1977-78†	38	39	3	—	79	5th	1	4	League quarterfinals	Glen Sather
1978-79†	48	30	2	—	98	1st	6	7	Avco World Cup finals	Glen Sather
1979-80	28	39	13	—	69	4th/Smythe	0	3	Preliminaries	Glen Sather
1980-81	29	35	16	—	74	4th/Smythe	5	4	Quarterfinals	Glen Sather
1981-82	48	17	15	—	111	1st/Smythe	2	3	Division semifinals	Glen Sather
1982-83	47	21	12	—	106	1st/Smythe	11	5	Stanley Cup finals	Glen Sather
1983-84	57	18	5	—	119	1st/Smythe	15	4	Stanley Cup champ	Glen Sather
1984-85	49	20	11	—	109	1st/Smythe	15	3	Stanley Cup champ	Glen Sather
1985-86	56	17	7	—	119	1st/Smythe	6	4	Division finals	Glen Sather
1986-87	50	24	6	—	106	1st/Smythe	16	5	Stanley Cup champ	Glen Sather
1987-88	44	25	11	—	99	2nd/Smythe	16	2	Stanley Cup champ	Glen Sather
1988-89	38	34	8	—	84	3rd/Smythe	3	4	Division semifinals	Glen Sather
1989-90	38	28	14	—	90	2nd/Smythe	16	6	Stanley Cup champ	John Muckler
1990-91	37	37	6	—	80	3rd/Smythe	9	9	Conference finals	John Muckler
1991-92	36	34	10	—	82	3rd/Smythe	8	8	Conference finals	Ted Green
1992-93	26	50	8	—	60	5th/Smythe	—	—		Ted Green
1993-94	25	45	14	—	64	6th/Pacific	—	—		Ted Green, Glen Sather
1994-95	17	27	4	—	38	5th/Pacific	—	—		George Burnett, Ron Low
1995-96	30	44	8	—	68	5th/Pacific	—	—		Ron Low
1996-97	36	37	9	—	81	3rd/Pacific	5	7	Conference semifinals	Ron Low
1997-98	35	37	10	—	80	3rd/Pacific	5	7	Conference semifinals	Ron Low
1998-99	33	37	12	—	78	2nd/Northwest	0	4	Conference quarterfinals	Ron Low
1999-00	32	26	16	8	88	2nd/Northwest	1	4	Conference quarterfinals	Kevin Lowe
2000-01	39	28	12	3	93	2nd/Northwest	2	4	Conference quarterfinals	Craig MacTavish
2001-02	38	28	12	4	92	3rd/Northwest	—	—		Craig MacTavish
2002-03	36	26	11	9	92	4th/Northwest	2	4	Conference quarterfinals	Craig MacTavish
2003-04	36	29	12	5	89	4th/Pacific	—	—		Craig MacTavish
2004-05	No season—Lockout									
2005-06	41	28	—	13	95	3rd/Northwest	15	9	Stanley Cup finals	Craig MacTavish

*Alberta Oilers, members of World Hockey Association.
†Members of World Hockey Association.

FIRST-ROUND ENTRY DRAFT CHOICES

Year Player, Overall, Last amateur team (league)

1979—Kevin Lowe, 21, Quebec (QMJHL)
1980—Paul Coffey, 6, Kitchener (OHL)
1981—Grant Fuhr, 8, Victoria (WHL)
1982—Jim Playfair, 20, Portland (WHL)
1983—Jeff Beukeboom, 19, Sault Ste. Marie (OHL)
1984—Selmar Odelein, 21, Regina (WHL)
1985—Scott Metcalfe, 20, Kingston (OHL)
1986—Kim Issel, 21, Prince Albert (WHL)
1987—Peter Soberlak, 21, Swift Current (WHL)
1988—Francois Leroux, 19, St. Jean (QMJHL)
1989—Jason Soules, 15, Niagara Falls (OHL)
1990—Scott Allison, 17, Prince Albert (WHL)
1991—Tyler Wright, 12, Swift Current (WHL)
Martin Rucinsky, 20, Litvinov, Czechoslovakia
1992—Joe Hulbig, 13, St. Sebastian H.S. (Mass.)
1993—Jason Arnott, 7, Oshawa (OHL)
Nick Stajduhar, 16, London (OHL)

Year Player, Overall, Last amateur team (league)

1994—Jason Bonsignore, 4, Niagara Falls (OHL)
Ryan Smyth, 6, Moose Jaw (WHL)
1995—Steve Kelly, 6, Prince Albert (WHL)
1996—Boyd Devereaux, 6, Kitchener (OHL)
Matthieu Descoteaux, 19, Shawinigan (QMJHL)
1997—Michel Riessen, 14, HC Biel, Switzerland
1998—Michael Henrich, 13, Barrie (OHL)
1999—Jani Rita, 13, Jokerit Helsinki, Finland
2000—Alexei Mikhnov, 17, Yaroslavl, Russia
2001—Ales Hemsky, 13, Hull (QMJHL)
2002—Jesse Niinimaki, 15, Ilves, Finland
2003—Marc-Antoine Pouliot, 22, Rimouski (QMJHL)
2004—Devan Dubnyk, 14, Kamloops (WHL)
Rob Schremp, 25, London (OHL)
2005—Andrew Cogliano, 25, St. Michael's Jr. A
2006—No first-round selection

NOTE: Edmonton chose Dave Dryden, Bengt Gustafsson and Ed Mio as priority selections before the 1979 expansion draft.

SINGLE-SEASON INDIVIDUAL RECORDS

FORWARDS/DEFENSEMEN

Most goals
92—Wayne Gretzky, 1981-82

Most assists
163—Wayne Gretzky, 1985-86

Most points
215—Wayne Gretzky, 1985-86

Most penalty minutes
286—Steve Smith, 1987-88

Most power play goals
20—Wayne Gretzky, 1983-84
Ryan Smyth, 1996-97

Most shorthanded goals
12—Wayne Gretzky, 1983-84

Most games with three or more goals
10—Wayne Gretzky, 1981-82
Wayne Gretzky, 1983-84

Most shots
369—Wayne Gretzky, 1981-82

GOALTENDERS

Most games
75—Grant Fuhr, 1987-88

Most minutes
4,364—Tommy Salo, 2000-01

Most goals allowed
246—Grant Fuhr, 1987-88

Lowest goals-against average
2.22—Tommy Salo, 2001-02

Most shutouts
8—Curtis Joseph, 1997-98
Tommy Salo, 2000-01

Most wins
40—Grant Fuhr, 1987-88

Most losses
38—Bill Ranford, 1992-93

Most ties
14—Grant Fuhr, 1981-82

FLORIDA PANTHERS

YEAR-BY-YEAR RECORDS

	REGULAR SEASON						PLAYOFFS			
Season	W	L	T	OTL	Pts.	Finish	W	L	Highest round	Coach
1993-94	33	34	17	—	83	5th/Atlantic	—	—		Roger Neilson
1994-95	20	22	6	—	46	5th/Atlantic	—	—		Roger Neilson
1995-96	41	31	10	—	92	3rd/Atlantic	12	10	Stanley Cup finals	Doug MacLean
1996-97	35	28	19	—	89	3rd/Atlantic	1	4	Conference quarterfinals	Doug MacLean
1997-98	24	43	15	—	63	6th/Atlantic	—	—		Doug MacLean, Bryan Murray
1998-99	30	34	18	—	78	2nd/Southeast	—	—		Terry Murray
1999-00	43	27	6	6	98	2nd/Southeast	0	4	Conference quarterfinals	Terry Murray
2000-01	22	38	13	9	66	3rd/Southeast	—	—		Terry Murray, Duane Sutter
2001-02	22	44	10	6	60	4th/Southeast	—	—		Duane Sutter, Mike Keenan
2002-03	24	36	13	9	70	4th/Southeast	—	—		Mike Keenan
2003-04	28	35	15	4	75	4th/Southeast	—	—		M.Keenan, R.Dudley, J.Torchetti
2004-05			No season—Lockout							
2005-06	37	34	—	11	85	4th/Southeast	—	—		Jacques Martin

FIRST-ROUND ENTRY DRAFT CHOICES

Year Player, Overall, Last amateur team (league)
1993—Rob Niedermayer, 5, Medicine Hat (WHL)
1994—Ed Jovanovski, 1, Windsor (OHL)
1995—Radek Dvorak, 10, Budejovice, Czech Republic
1996—Marcus Nilson, 20, Djurgarden-Stockholm, Sweden
1997—Mike Brown, 20, Red Deer (WHL)
1998—No first-round selection
1999—Denis Shvidki, 12, Barrie (OHL)
2000—No first-round selection
2001—Stephen Weiss, 4, Plymouth (OHL)

Year Player, Overall, Last amateur team (league)
Lukas Krajicek, 24, Peterborough (OHL)
2002—Jay Bouwmeester, 3, Medicine Hat (WHL)
Petr Taticek, 9, Sault Ste. Marie (OHL)
2003—Nathan Horton, 3, Oshawa (OHL)
Anthony Stewart, 25, Kingston (OHL)
2004—Rostislav Olesz, 7, Vitkovic, Czech. Rep.
2005—Kenndal McArdle, 20, Moose Jaw (WHL)
2006—Michael Frolik, 10, Kladno, Czech Republic

SINGLE-SEASON INDIVIDUAL RECORDS

FORWARDS/DEFENSEMEN

Most goals
59—Pavel Bure, 2000-01

Most assists
53—Viktor Kozlov, 1999-2000

Most points
94—Pavel Bure, 1999-2000

Most penalty minutes
354—Peter Worrell, 2001-02

Most power play goals
19—Scott Mellanby, 1995-96
Pavel Bure, 2000-01

Most shorthanded goals
6—Tom Fitzgerald, 1995-96

Most games with three or more goals
4—Pavel Bure, 1999-2000
Pavel Bure, 2000-01

Most shots
384—Pavel Bure, 2000-01

GOALTENDERS

Most games
75—Roberto Luongo, 2005-06

Most minutes
4,304—Roberto Luongo, 2005-06

Most shots against
2,488—Roberto Luongo, 2005-06

Most goals allowed
213—Roberto Luongo, 2005-06

Lowest goals-against average
2.29—John Vanbiesbrouck, 1996-97

Most shutouts
5—Roberto Luongo, 2000-01

Most wins
35—Roberto Luongo, 2005-06

Most losses
33—Roberto Luongo, 2001-02

Most ties
14—Sean Burke, 1998-99

LOS ANGELES KINGS

YEAR-BY-YEAR RECORDS

	REGULAR SEASON						PLAYOFFS			
Season	W	L	T	OTL	Pts.	Finish	W	L	Highest round	Coach
1967-68	31	33	10	—	72	2nd/West	3	4	Division semifinals	Red Kelly
1968-69	24	42	10	—	58	4th/West	4	7	Division finals	Red Kelly
1969-70	14	52	10	—	38	6th/West	—	—		Hal Laycoe, Johnny Wilson
1970-71	25	40	13	—	63	5th/West	—	—		Larry Regan
1971-72	20	49	9	—	49	7th/West	—	—		Larry Regan, Fred Glover
1972-73	31	36	11	—	73	6th/West	—	—		Bob Pulford
1973-74	33	33	12	—	78	3rd/West	1	4	Division semifinals	Bob Pulford
1974-75	42	17	21	—	105	2nd/Norris	1	2	Preliminaries	Bob Pulford

	REGULAR SEASON						PLAYOFFS			
Season	W	L	T	OTL	Pts.	Finish	W	L	Highest round	Coach
1975-76	38	33	9	—	85	2nd/Norris	5	4	Quarterfinals	Bob Pulford
1976-77	34	31	15	—	83	2nd/Norris	4	5	Quarterfinals	Bob Pulford
1977-78	31	34	15	—	77	3rd/Norris	0	2	Preliminaries	Ron Stewart
1978-79	34	34	12	—	80	3rd/Norris	0	2	Preliminaries	Bob Berry
1979-80	30	36	14	—	74	2nd/Norris	1	3	Preliminaries	Bob Berry
1980-81	43	24	13	—	99	2nd/Norris	1	3	Preliminaries	Bob Berry
1981-82	24	41	15	—	63	4th/Smythe	4	6	Division finals	Parker MacDonald, Don Perry,
1982-83	27	41	12	—	66	5th/Smythe	—	—		Don Perry
1983-84	23	44	13	—	59	5th/Smythe	—	—		Don Perry, Rogie Vachon, Roger Neilson
1984-85	34	32	14	—	82	4th/Smythe	0	3	Division semifinals	Pat Quinn
1985-86	23	49	8	—	54	5th/Smythe	—	—		Pat Quinn
1986-87	31	41	8	—	70	4th/Smythe	1	4	Division semifinals	Pat Quinn, Mike Murphy
1987-88	30	42	8	—	68	4th/Smythe	1	4	Division semifinals	Mike Murphy, Rogie Vachon, Robbie Ftorek
1988-89	42	31	7	—	91	2nd/Smythe	4	7	Division finals	Robbie Ftorek
1989-90	34	39	7	—	75	4th/Smythe	4	6	Division finals	Tom Webster
1990-91	46	24	10	—	102	1st/Smythe	6	6	Division finals	Tom Webster
1991-92	35	31	14	—	84	2nd/Smythe	2	4	Division semifinals	Tom Webster
1992-93	39	35	10	—	88	3rd/Smythe	13	11	Stanley Cup finals	Barry Melrose
1993-94	27	45	12	—	66	5th/Pacific	—	—		Barry Melrose
1994-95	16	23	9	—	41	4th/Pacific	—	—		Barry Melrose, Rogie Vachon
1995-96	24	40	18	—	66	6th/Pacific	—	—		Larry Robinson
1996-97	28	43	11	—	67	6th/Pacific	—	—		Larry Robinson
1997-98	38	33	11	—	87	2nd/Pacific	0	4	Conference quarterfinals	Larry Robinson
1998-99	32	45	5	—	69	5th/Pacific	—	—		Larry Robinson
1999-00	39	27	12	4	94	2nd/Pacific	0	4	Conference quarterfinals	Andy Murray
2000-01	38	28	13	3	92	3rd/Pacific	7	6	Conference semifinals	Andy Murray
2001-02	40	27	11	4	95	3rd/Pacific	3	4	Conference quarterfinals	Andy Murray
2002-03	33	37	6	6	78	3rd/Pacific	—	—		Andy Murray, Dave Tippett
2003-04	28	29	16	9	81	3rd/Pacific	—	—		Andy Murray
2004-05	No season—Lockout									
2005-06	42	35	—	5	89	4th/Pacific	—	—		Andy Murray, John Torchetti

FIRST-ROUND ENTRY DRAFT CHOICES

Year Player, Overall, Last amateur team (league)

1969—No first-round selection
1970—No first-round selection
1971—No first-round selection
1972—No first-round selection
1973—No first-round selection
1974—No first-round selection
1975—Tim Young, 16, Ottawa (OHL)
1976—No first-round selection
1977—No first-round selection
1978—No first-round selection
1979—Jay Wells, 16, Kingston (OHL)
1980—Larry Murphy, 4, Peterborough (OHL)
Jim Fox, 10, Ottawa (OHL)
1981—Doug Smith, 2, Ottawa (OHL)
1982—No first-round selection
1983—No first-round selection
1984—Craig Redmond, 6, Canadian Olympic Team
1985—Craig Duncanson, 9, Sudbury (OHL)
Dan Gratton, 10, Oshawa (OHL)
1986—Jimmy Carson, 2, Verdun (QMJHL)
1987—Wayne McBean, 4, Medicine Hat (WHL)
1988—Martin Gelinas, 7, Hull (QMJHL)
1989—No first-round selection

Year Player, Overall, Last amateur team (league)

1990—Darryl Sydor, 7, Kamloops (WHL)
1991—No first-round selection
1992—No first-round selection
1993—No first-round selection
1994—Jamie Storr, 7, Owen Sound (OHL)
1995—Aki-Petteri Berg, 3, TPS Jrs., Finland
1996—No first-round selection
1997—Olli Jokinen, 3, IFK Helsinki, Finland
Matt Zultek, 15, Ottawa (OHL)
1998—Mathieu Biron, 21, Shawinigan (QMJHL)
1999—No first-round selection
2000—Alexander Frolov, 20, Yaroslavl, Russia
2001—Jens Karlsson, 18, Frolunda, Sweden
David Steckel, 30, Ohio State
2002—Denis Grebeshkov, 18, Yaroslavl, Russia
2003—Dustin Brown, 13, Guelph (OHL)
Brian Boyle, 26, St. Sebastian's (U.S. high school)
Jeff Tambellini, 27, Michigan (CCHA)
2004—Lauri Tukonen, 11, Espoo, Finland
2005—Anze Kopitar, 11, Sodertalje, Sweden
2006—Jonathan Bernier, 11, Lewiston (QMJHL)
Trevor Lewis, 17, Des Moines (USHL)

SINGLE-SEASON INDIVIDUAL RECORDS

FORWARDS/DEFENSEMEN

Most goals
70—Bernie Nicholls, 1988-89

Most assists
122—Wayne Gretzky, 1990-91

Most points
168—Wayne Gretzky, 1988-89

Most penalty minutes
399—Marty McSorley, 1992-93

Most power play goals
26—Luc Robitaille, 1991-92

Most shorthanded goals
8—Bernie Nicholls, 1988-89

Most games with three or more goals
5—Jimmy Carson, 1987-88

Most shots
385—Bernie Nicholls, 1988-89

GOALTENDERS

Most games
71—Felix Potvin, 2001-02

Most minutes
4,107—Rogie Vachon, 1977-78

Most shots against
2,219—Kelly Hrudey, 1993-94

Most goals allowed
228—Kelly Hrudey, 1993-94

Lowest goals-against average
2.24—Rogie Vachon, 1974-75

Most shutouts
8—Rogie Vachon, 1976-77

Most wins
35—Mario Lessard, 1980-81

Most losses
31—Kelly Hrudey, 1993-94

Most ties
13—Rogie Vachon, 1974-75
Rogie Vachon, 1977-78
Kelly Hrudey, 1991-92

MINNESOTA WILD

YEAR-BY-YEAR RECORDS

	REGULAR SEASON						PLAYOFFS			
Season	W	L	T	OTL	Pts.	Finish	W	L	Highest round	Coach
2000-01	25	39	13	5	68	5th/Northwest	—	—		Jacques Lemaire
2001-02	26	35	12	9	73	5th/Northwest	—	—		Jacques Lemaire
2002-03	42	29	10	1	95	3rd/Northwest	8	10	Conference finals	Jacques Lemaire
2003-04	30	29	20	3	83	5th/Northwest	—	—		Jacques Lemaire
2004-05			No season—Lockout							
2005-06	38	36	—	8	84	5th/Northwest	—	—		Jacques Lemaire

FIRST-ROUND ENTRY DRAFT CHOICES

Year Player, Overall, Last amateur team (league)
2000—Marian Gaborik, 3, Trencin, Slovakia
2001—Mikko Koivu, 6, TPS, Finland
2002—Pierre-Marc Bouchard, 8, Chicoutimi
2003—Brent Burns, 20, Brampton (OHL)

Year Player, Overall, Last amateur team (league)
2004—A.J. Thelen, 12, Michigan State (CCHA)
2005—Benoit Pouliot, 4, Sudbury (OHL)
2006—James Sheppard, 9, Cape Breton (QMJHL)

SINGLE-SEASON INDIVIDUAL RECORDS

FORWARDS/DEFENSEMEN

Most goals
38—Marian Gaborik, 2005-06

Most assists
48—Andrew Brunette, 2001-02

Most points
79—Brian Rolston, 2005-06

Most penalty minutes
201—Matt Johnson, 2002-03

Most power play goals
15—Brian Rolston, 2005-06

Most shorthanded goals
7—Wes Walz, 2000-01

Most games with three or more goals
2—Marian Gaborik, 2001-02

Most shots
293—Brian Rolston, 2005-06

GOALTENDERS

Most games
58—Manny Fernandez, 2005-06

Most minutes
3,411—Manny Fernandez, 2005-06

Most shots against
1,612—Manny Fernandez, 2005-06

Most goals allowed
130—Manny Fernandez, 2005-06

Lowest goals-against average
1.88—Dwayne Roloson, 2003-04

Most shutouts
5—Dwayne Roloson, 2001-02
Dwayne Roloson, 2003-04

Most wins
30—Manny Fernandez, 2005-06

Most losses
24—Manny Fernandez, 2001-02

Most ties
11—Dwayne Roloson, 2003-04

MONTREAL CANADIENS

YEAR-BY-YEAR RECORDS

	REGULAR SEASON						PLAYOFFS			
Season	W	L	T	OTL	Pts.	Finish	W	L	Highest round	Coach
1917-18	13	9	0	—	26	1st/3rd	1	1	Semifinals	George Kennedy
1918-19	10	8	0	—	20	1st/2nd	†*6	3	Stanley Cup finals	George Kennedy
1919-20	13	11	0	—	26	2nd/3rd	—	—		George Kennedy
1920-21	13	11	0	—	26	3rd/2nd	—	—		George Kennedy
1921-22	12	11	1	—	25	3rd	—	—		Leo Dandurand
1922-23	13	9	2	—	28	2nd	1	1	Quarterfinals	Leo Dandurand
1923-24	13	11	0	—	26	2nd	6	0	Stanley Cup champ	Leo Dandurand
1924-25	17	11	2	—	36	3rd	3	3	Stanley Cup finals	Leo Dandurand
1925-26	11	24	1	—	23	7th	—	—		Cecil Hart
1926-27	28	14	2	—	58	2nd/Canadian	*1	1	Semifinals	Cecil Hart
1927-28	26	11	7	—	59	1st/Canadian	*0	1	Semifinals	Cecil Hart
1928-29	22	7	15	—	59	1st/Canadian	0	3	Semifinals	Cecil Hart
1929-30	21	14	9	—	51	2nd/Canadian	*5	0	Stanley Cup champ	Cecil Hart
1930-31	26	10	8	—	60	1st/Canadian	6	4	Stanley Cup champ	Cecil Hart
1931-32	25	16	7	—	57	1st/Canadian	1	3	Semifinals	Cecil Hart
1932-33	18	25	5	—	41	3rd/Canadian	*0	1	Quarterfinals	Newsy Lalonde
1933-34	22	20	6	—	50	2nd/Canadian	*0	1	Quarterfinals	Newsy Lalonde
1934-35	19	23	6	—	44	3rd/Canadian	*0	1	Quarterfinals	Newsy Lalonde, Leo Dandurand
1935-36	11	26	11	—	33	4th/Canadian	—	—		Sylvio Mantha
1936-37	24	18	6	—	54	1st/Canadian	2	3	Semifinals	Cecil Hart

	REGULAR SEASON						PLAYOFFS			
Season	W	L	T	OTL	Pts.	Finish	W	L	Highest round	Coach
1937-38	18	17	13	—	49	3rd/Canadian	1	2	Quarterfinals	Cecil Hart
1938-39	15	24	9	—	39	6th	1	2	Quarterfinals	Cecil Hart, Jules Dugal
1939-40	10	33	5	—	25	7th	—	—		Pit Lepine
1940-41	16	26	6	—	38	6th	1	2	Quarterfinals	Dick Irvin
1941-42	18	27	3	—	39	6th	1	2	Quarterfinals	Dick Irvin
1942-43	19	19	12	—	50	4th	1	4	League semifinals	Dick Irvin
1943-44	38	5	7	—	83	1st	8	1	Stanley Cup champ	Dick Irvin
1944-45	38	8	4	—	80	1st	2	4	League semifinals	Dick Irvin
1945-46	28	17	5	—	61	1st	8	1	Stanley Cup champ	Dick Irvin
1946-47	34	16	10	—	78	1st	6	5	Stanley Cup finals	Dick Irvin
1947-48	20	29	11	—	51	5th	—	—		Dick Irvin
1948-49	28	23	9	—	65	3rd	3	4	League semifinals	Dick Irvin
1949-50	29	22	19	—	77	2nd	1	4	League semifinals	Dick Irvin
1950-51	25	30	15	—	65	3rd	5	6	Stanley Cup finals	Dick Irvin
1951-52	34	26	10	—	78	2nd	4	7	Stanley Cup finals	Dick Irvin
1952-53	28	23	19	—	75	2nd	8	4	Stanley Cup champ	Dick Irvin
1953-54	35	24	11	—	81	2nd	7	4	Stanley Cup finals	Dick Irvin
1954-55	41	18	11	—	93	2nd	7	5	Stanley Cup finals	Dick Irvin
1955-56	45	15	10	—	100	1st	8	2	Stanley Cup champ	Toe Blake
1956-57	35	23	12	—	82	2nd	8	2	Stanley Cup champ	Toe Blake
1957-58	43	17	10	—	96	1st	8	2	Stanley Cup champ	Toe Blake
1958-59	39	18	13	—	91	1st	8	3	Stanley Cup champ	Toe Blake
1959-60	40	18	12	—	92	1st	8	0	Stanley Cup champ	Toe Blake
1960-61	41	19	10	—	92	1st	2	4	League semifinals	Toe Blake
1961-62	42	14	14	—	98	1st	2	4	League semifinals	Toe Blake
1962-63	28	19	23	—	79	3rd	1	4	League semifinals	Toe Blake
1963-64	36	21	13	—	85	1st	3	4	League semifinals	Toe Blake
1964-65	36	23	11	—	83	2nd	8	5	Stanley Cup champ	Toe Blake
1965-66	41	21	8	—	90	1st	8	2	Stanley Cup champ	Toe Blake
1966-67	32	25	13	—	77	2nd	6	4	Stanley Cup finals	Toe Blake
1967-68	42	22	10	—	94	1st/East	12	1	Stanley Cup champ	Toe Blake
1968-69	46	19	11	—	103	1st/East	12	2	Stanley Cup champ	Claude Ruel
1969-70	38	22	16	—	92	5th/East	—	—		Claude Ruel
1970-71	42	23	13	—	97	3rd/East	12	8	Stanley Cup champ	Claude Ruel, Al MacNeil
1971-72	46	16	16	—	108	3rd/East	2	4	Division semifinals	Scotty Bowman
1972-73	52	10	16	—	120	1st/East	12	5	Stanley Cup champ	Scotty Bowman
1973-74	45	24	9	—	99	2nd/East	2	4	Division semifinals	Scotty Bowman
1974-75	47	14	19	—	113	1st/Norris	6	5	Semifinals	Scotty Bowman
1975-76	58	11	11	—	127	1st/Norris	12	1	Stanley Cup champ	Scotty Bowman
1976-77	60	8	12	—	132	1st/Norris	12	2	Stanley Cup champ	Scotty Bowman
1977-78	59	10	11	—	129	1st/Norris	12	3	Stanley Cup champ	Scotty Bowman
1978-79	52	17	11	—	115	1st/Norris	12	4	Stanley Cup champ	Scotty Bowman
1979-80	47	20	13	—	107	1st/Norris	6	4	Quarterfinals	Bernie Geoffrion, Claude Ruel
1980-81	45	22	13	—	103	1st/Norris	0	3	Preliminaries	Claude Ruel
1981-82	46	17	17	—	109	1st/Adams	2	3	Division semifinals	Bob Berry
1982-83	42	24	14	—	98	2nd/Adams	0	3	Division semifinals	Bob Berry
1983-84	35	40	5	—	75	4th/Adams	9	6	Conference finals	Bob Berry, Jacques Lemaire
1984-85	41	27	12	—	94	1st/Adams	6	6	Division finals	Jacques Lemaire
1985-86	40	33	7	—	87	2nd/Adams	15	5	Stanley Cup champ	Jean Perron
1986-87	41	29	10	—	92	2nd/Adams	10	7	Conference finals	Jean Perron
1987-88	45	22	13	—	103	1st/Adams	5	6	Division finals	Jean Perron
1988-89	53	18	9	—	115	1st/Adams	14	7	Stanley Cup finals	Pat Burns
1989-90	41	28	11	—	93	3rd/Adams	5	6	Division finals	Pat Burns
1990-91	39	30	11	—	89	2nd/Adams	7	6	Division finals	Pat Burns
1991-92	41	28	11	—	93	1st/Adams	4	7	Division finals	Pat Burns
1992-93	48	30	6	—	102	3rd/Adams	16	4	Stanley Cup champ	Jacques Demers
1993-94	41	29	14	—	96	3rd/Northeast	3	4	Conference quarterfinals	Jacques Demers
1994-95	18	23	7	—	43	6th/Northeast	—	—		Jacques Demers
1995-96	40	32	10	—	90	3rd/Northeast	2	4	Conference quarterfinals	Jacques Demers, Mario Tremblay
1996-97	31	36	15	—	77	4th/Northeast	1	4	Conference quarterfinals	Mario Tremblay
1997-98	37	32	13	—	87	4th/Northeast	4	6	Conference semifinals	Alain Vigneault
1998-99	32	39	11	—	75	5th/Northeast	—	—		Alain Vigneault
1999-00	35	34	9	4	83	4th/Northeast	—	—		Alain Vigneault
2000-01	28	40	8	6	70	5th/Northeast	—	—		Alain Vigneault, Michel Therrien
2001-02	36	31	12	3	87	4th/Northeast	6	6	Conference semifinals	Michel Therrien
2002-03	30	35	8	9	77	4th/Northeast	—	—		Michel Therrien, Claude Julien
2003-04	41	30	7	4	93	4th/Northeast	4	7	Conference semifinals	Claude Julien
2004-05		No season—Lockout								
2005-06	42	31	—	9	93	3rd/Northeast	2	4	Conference quarterfinals	Claude Julien, Bob Gainey

*Won-lost record does not indicate tie(s) resulting from two-game, total-goals series that year (two-game, total-goals series were played from 1917-18 through 1935-36).

†1918-19 series abandoned with no Cup holder due to influenza epidemic.

FIRST-ROUND ENTRY DRAFT CHOICES

Year Player, Overall, Last amateur team (league)

1969—Rejean Houle, 1, Montreal (OHL)
Marc Tardif, 2, Montreal (OHL)
1970—Ray Martiniuk, 5, Flin Flon (WCHL)
Chuck Lefley, 6, Canadian Nationals
1971—Guy Lafleur, 1, Quebec (QMJHL)
Chuck Arnason, 7, Flin Flon (WCHL)
Murray Wilson, 11, Ottawa (OHL)
1972—Steve Shutt, 4, Toronto (OHL)
Michel Larocque, 6, Ottawa (OHL)
Dave Gardner, 8, Toronto (OHL)
John Van Boxmeer, 14, Guelph (SOJHL)
1973—Bob Gainey, 8, Peterborough (OHL)
1974—Cam Connor, 5, Flin Flon (WCHL)
Doug Risebrough, 7, Kitchener (OHL)
Rick Chartraw, 10, Kitchener (OHL)
Mario Tremblay, 12, Montreal (OHL)
Gord McTavish, 15, Sudbury (OHL)
1975—Robin Sadler, 9, Edmonton (WCHL)
Pierre Mondou, 15, Montreal (QMJHL)
1976—Peter Lee, 12, Ottawa (OHL)
Rod Schutt, 13, Sudbury (OHL)
Bruce Baker, 18, Ottawa (OHL)
1977—Mark Napier, 10, Birmingham (WHA)
Normand Dupont, 18, Montreal (QMJHL)
1978—Danny Geoffrion, 8, Cornwall (QMJHL)
Dave Hunter, 17, Sudbury (OHL)
1979—No first-round selection
1980—Doug Wickenheiser, 1, Regina (WHL)
1981—Mark Hunter, 7, Brantford (OHL)
Gilbert Delorme, 18, Chicoutimi (QMJHL)

Year Player, Overall, Last amateur team (league)

Jan Ingman, 19, Farjestads (Sweden)
1982—Alain Heroux, 19, Chicoutimi (QMJHL)
1983—Alfie Turcotte, 17, Portland (WHL)
1984—Petr Svoboda, 5, Czechoslovakia
Shayne Corson, 8, Brantford (OHL)
1985—Jose Charbonneau, 12, Drummondville (QMJHL)
Tom Chorske, 16, Minneapolis SW H.S. (Minn.)
1986—Mark Pederson, 15, Medicine Hat (WHL)
1987—Andrew Cassels, 17, Ottawa (OHL)
1988—Eric Charron, 20, Trois-Rivieres (QMJHL)
1989—Lindsay Vallis, 13, Seattle (WHL)
1990—Turner Stevenson, 12, Seattle (WHL)
1991—Brent Bilodeau, 17, Seattle (WHL)
1992—David Wilkie, 20, Kamloops (WHL)
1993—Saku Koivu, 21, TPS Turku (Finland)
1994—Brad Brown, 18, North Bay (OHL)
1995—Terry Ryan, 8, Tri-City (WHL)
1996—Matt Higgins, 18, Moose Jaw (WHL)
1997—Jason Ward, 11, Erie (OHL)
1998—Eric Chouinard, 16, Quebec (QMJHL)
1999—No first-round selection
2000—Ron Hainsey, 13, Univ. of Mass.-Lowell
Marcel Hossa, 16, Portland (WHL)
2001—Michael Komisarek, 7, Univ. of Michigan
Alexander Perezhogin, 25, OMSK, Russia
2002—Christopher Higgins, 14, Yale (ECAC)
2003—Andrei Kastsitsyn, 10, Belarus
2004—Kyle Chipchura, 18, Prince Albert (WHL)
2005—Carey Price, 5, Tri-City (WHL)
2006—David Fischer, 20, Apple Valley (USHSW)

SINGLE-SEASON INDIVIDUAL RECORDS

FORWARDS/DEFENSEMEN

Most goals
60—Steve Shutt, 1976-77
Guy Lafleur, 1977-78

Most assists
82—Pete Mahovlich, 1974-75

Most points
136—Guy Lafleur, 1976-77

Most penalty minutes
358—Chris Nilan, 1984-85

Most power play goals
20—Yvan Cournoyer, 1966-67

Most shorthanded goals
8—Guy Carbonneau, 1983-84

Most games with three or more goals
7—Joe Malone, 1917-18

GOALTENDERS

Most games
70—Gerry McNeil, 1950-51
Gerry McNeil, 1951-52
Jacques Plante, 1961-62

Most minutes
4,200—Gerry McNeil, 1950-51
Gerry McNeil, 1951-52
Jacques Plante, 1961-62

Most goals allowed
192—Patrick Roy, 1992-93

Lowest goals-against average
0.92—George Hainsworth, 1928-29

Most shutouts
22—George Hainsworth, 1928-29

Most wins
42—Jacques Plante, 1955-56
Jacques Plante, 1961-62
Ken Dryden, 1975-76

Most losses
31—Jose Theodore, 2002-03

Most ties
19—Jacques Plante, 1962-63

MONTREAL MAROONS (DEFUNCT)

YEAR-BY-YEAR RECORDS

	REGULAR SEASON					PLAYOFFS			
Season	W	L	T	Pts.	Finish	W	L	Highest round	Coach
1924-25	9	19	2	20	5th	—	—		Eddie Gerard
1925-26	20	11	5	45	2nd	3	1	Stanley Cup champ	Eddie Gerard
1926-27	20	20	4	44	3rd/Canadian	*0	1	Quarterfinals	Eddie Gerard
1927-28	24	14	6	54	2nd/Canadian	*5	3	Stanley Cup finals	Eddie Gerard
1928-29	15	20	9	39	5th/Canadian	—	—		Eddie Gerard
1929-30	23	16	5	51	1st/Canadian	1	3	Semifinals	Dunc Munro
1930-31	20	18	6	46	3rd/Canadian	*0	2	Quarterfinals	Dunc Munro, George Boucher
1931-32	19	22	7	45	3rd/Canadian	*1	1	Semifinals	Sprague Cleghorn
1932-33	22	20	6	50	2nd/Canadian	0	2	Quarterfinals	Eddie Gerard
1933-34	19	18	11	49	3rd/Canadian	*1	2	Semifinals	Eddie Gerard
1934-35	24	19	5	53	2nd/Canadian	*5	0	Stanley Cup champ	Tommy Gorman
1935-36	22	16	10	54	1st/Canadian	0	3	Semifinals	Tommy Gorman
1936-37	22	17	9	53	2nd/Canadian	2	3	Semifinals	Tommy Gorman
1937-38	12	30	6	30	4th/Canadian	—	—		King Clancy, Tommy Gorman

*Won-lost record does not indicate tie(s) resulting from two-game, total goals series that year (two-game, total-goals series were played from 1917-18 through 1935-36).

MONTREAL WANDERERS (DEFUNCT)

YEAR-BY-YEAR RECORDS

	REGULAR SEASON					PLAYOFFS			
Season	W	L	T	Pts.	Finish	W	L	Highest round	Coach
1917-18*	1	5	0	2	4th	—	—		Art Ross

*Franchise disbanded after Montreal Arena burned down. Montreal Canadiens and Toronto each counted one win for defaulted games with Wanderers.

NASHVILLE PREDATORS

YEAR-BY-YEAR RECORDS

	REGULAR SEASON						PLAYOFFS			
Season	W	L	T	OTL	Pts.	Finish	W	L	Highest round	Coach
1998-99	28	47	7	—	63	4th/Central	—	—		Barry Trotz
1999-00	28	40	7	7	70	4th/Central	—	—		Barry Trotz
2000-01	34	36	9	3	80	3rd/Central	—	—		Barry Trotz
2001-02	28	41	13	0	69	4th/Central	—	—		Barry Trotz
2002-03	27	35	13	7	74	4th/Central	—	—		Barry Trotz
2003-04	38	29	11	4	91	3rd/Central	2	4	Conference quarterfinals	Barry Trotz
2004-05	No season—Lockout									
2005-06	49	25	—	8	106	2nd/Central	1	4	Conference quarterfinals	Barry Trotz

FIRST-ROUND ENTRY DRAFT CHOICES

Year Player, Overall, Last amateur team (league)
1998—David Legwand, 2, Plymouth (OHL)
1999—Brian Finley, 6, Barrie (OHL)
2000—Scott Hartnell, 6, Prince Albert (WHL)
2001—Dan Hamhuis, 12, Prince George (WHL)
2002—Scottie Upshall, 6, Kamloops (WHL)

Year Player, Overall, Last amateur team (league)
2003—Ryan Suter, 7, U.S. National under-18 (NTDP)
2004—Alexander Radulov, 15, Dynamo 2, Russia
2005—Ryan Parent, 18, Guelph (OHL)
2006—No first-round selection

SINGLE-SEASON INDIVIDUAL RECORDS

FORWARDS/DEFENSEMEN

Most goals
31—Steve Sullivan, 2005-06
Paul Kariya, 2005-06

Most assists
54—Paul Kariya, 2005-06

Most points
85—Paul Kariya, 2005-06

Most penalty minutes
242—Patrick Cote, 1998-99

Most power play goals
14—Andy Delmore, 2002-03
Paul Kariya, 2005-06

Most shorthanded goals
4—Greg Johnson, 2003-04
Steve Sullivan, 2005-06

Most games with three or more goals
1—Robert Valicevic, 1999-2000
Scott Walker, 2000-01
Petr Tenkrat, 2001-02
Vladimir Orszagh, 2003-04
Steve Sullivan, 2003-04
Scott Walker, 2003-04
Scott Hartnell, 2005-06
Paul Kariya, 2005-06
Steve Sullivan, 2005-06

Most shots
248—Cliff Ronning, 1999-2000

GOALTENDERS

Most games
73—Tomas Vokoun, 2003-04

Most minutes
4,221—Tomas Vokoun, 2003-04

Most shots against
1,984—Tomas Vokoun, 2005-06

Most goals allowed
178—Tomas Vokoun, 2003-04

Lowest goals-against average
2.20—Tomas Vokoun, 2002-03

Most shutouts
4—Mike Dunham, 2000-01
Tomas Vokoun, 2005-06

Most wins
36—Tomas Vokoun, 2005-06

Most losses
31—Tomas Vokoun, 2002-03

Most ties
11—Tomas Vokoun, 2002-03

NEW JERSEY DEVILS

YEAR-BY-YEAR RECORDS

	REGULAR SEASON						PLAYOFFS			
Season	W	L	T	OTL	Pts.	Finish	W	L	Highest round	Coach
1974-75*	15	54	11	—	41	5th/Smythe	—	—		Bep Guidolin
1975-76*	12	56	12	—	36	5th/Smythe	—	—		Bep Guidolin, Sid Abel, Eddie Bush
1976-77†	20	46	14	—	54	5th/Smythe	—	—		John Wilson
1977-78†	19	40	21	—	59	2nd/Smythe	0	2	Preliminaries	Pat Kelly
1978-79†	15	53	12	—	42	4th/Smythe	—	—		Pat Kelly, Bep Guidolin
1979-80†	19	48	13	—	51	6th/Smythe	—	—		Don Cherry
1980-81†	22	45	13	—	57	5th/Smythe	—	—		Billy MacMillan
1981-82†	18	49	13	—	49	5th/Smythe	—	—		Bert Marshall, Marshall Johnston
1982-83	17	49	14	—	48	5th/Patrick	—	—		Billy MacMillan
1983-84	17	56	7	—	41	5th/Patrick	—	—		Billy MacMillan, Tom McVie

Season	W	L	T	OTL	Pts.	Finish	W	L	Highest round	Coach
			REGULAR SEASON						PLAYOFFS	
1984-85	22	48	10	—	54	5th/Patrick	—	—		Doug Carpenter
1985-86	28	49	3	—	59	6th/Patrick	—	—		Doug Carpenter
1986-87	29	45	6	—	64	6th/Patrick	—	—		Doug Carpenter
1987-88	38	36	6	—	82	4th/Patrick	11	9	Conference finals	Doug Carpenter, Jim Schoenfeld
1988-89	27	41	12	—	66	5th/Patrick	—	—		Jim Schoenfeld
1989-90	37	34	9	—	83	2nd/Patrick	2	4	Division semifinals	Jim Schoenfeld, John Cunniff
1990-91	32	33	15	—	79	4th/Patrick	3	4	Division semifinals	John Cunniff, Tom McVie
1991-92	38	31	11	—	87	4th/Patrick	3	4	Division semifinals	Tom McVie
1992-93	40	37	7	—	87	4th/Patrick	1	4	Division semifinals	Herb Brooks
1993-94	47	25	12	—	106	2nd/Atlantic	11	9	Conference finals	Jacques Lemaire
1994-95	22	18	8	—	52	2nd/Atlantic	16	4	Stanley Cup champ	Jacques Lemaire
1995-96	37	33	12	—	86	6th/Atlantic	—	—		Jacques Lemaire
1996-97	45	23	14	—	104	1st/Atlantic	5	5	Conference semifinals	Jacques Lemaire
1997-98	48	23	11	—	107	1st/Atlantic	2	4	Conference quarterfinals	Jacques Lemaire
1998-99	47	24	11	—	105	1st/Atlantic	3	4	Conference quarterfinals	Robbie Ftorek
1999-00	45	24	8	5	103	2nd/Atlantic	16	7	Stanley Cup champ	Robbie Ftorek, Larry Robinson
2000-01	48	19	12	3	111	1st/Atlantic	15	10	Stanley Cup finals	Larry Robinson
2001-02	41	28	9	4	95	3rd/Atlantic	2	4	Conference quarterfinals	Larry Robinson, Kevin Constantine
2002-03	46	20	10	6	108	1st/Atlantic	16	8	Stanley Cup finals	Pat Burns
2003-04	43	25	12	2	100	2nd/Atlantic	1	4	Conference quarterfinals	Pat Burns
2004-05			No season—Lockout							
2005-06	46	27	—	9	101	3rd/Atlantic	5	4	Conference semifinals	Larry Robinson, Lou Lamoriello

*Kansas City Scouts.
†Colorado Rockies.

FIRST-ROUND ENTRY DRAFT CHOICES

Year Player, Overall, Last amateur team (league)
1974—Wilf Paiement, 2, St. Catharines (OHL)
1975—Barry Dean, 2, Medicine Hat (WCHL)
1976—Paul Gardner, 11, Oshawa (OHL)
1977—Barry Beck, 2, New Westminster (WCHL)
1978—Mike Gillis, 5, Kingston (OHL)
1979—Rob Ramage, 1, Birmingham (WHA)
1980—Paul Gagne, 19, Windsor (OHL)
1981—Joe Cirella, 5, Oshawa (OHL)
1982—Rocky Trottier, 8, Billings (WHL)
Ken Daneyko, 18, Seattle (WHL)
1983—John MacLean, 6, Oshawa (OHL)
1984—Kirk Muller, 2, Guelph (OHL)
1985—Craig Wolanin, 3, Kitchener (OHL)
1986—Neil Brady, 3, Medicine Hat (WHL)
1987—Brendan Shanahan, 2, London (OHL)
1988—Corey Foster, 12, Peterborough (OHL)
1989—Bill Guerin, 5, Springfield (Mass.) Jr.
Jason Miller, 18, Medicine Hat (WHL)
1990—Martin Brodeur, 20, St. Hyacinthe (QMJHL)

Year Player, Overall, Last amateur team (league)
1991—Scott Niedermayer, 3, Kamloops (WHL)
Brian Rolston, 11, Detroit Compuware Jr.
1992—Jason Smith, 18, Regina (WHL)
1993—Denis Pederson, 13, Prince Albert (WHL)
1994—Vadim Sharifjanov, 25, Salavat (Russia)
1995—Petr Sykora, 18, Detroit (IHL)
1996—Lance Ward, 10, Red Deer (WHL)
1997—Jean-Francois Damphousse, 24, Moncton (QMJHL)
1998—Mike Van Ryn, 26, Michigan
Scott Gomez, 27, Tri-City (WHL)
1999—Ari Ahonen, 27, Jyvaskyla, Finland
2000—David Hale, 22, Sioux City (USHL)
2001—Adrian Foster, 28, Saskatoon (WHL)
2002—No first-round selection
2003—Zach Parise, 17, North Dakota (WCHA)
2004—Travis Zajac, 20, Salmon Arm (BCHL)
2005—Nicklas Bergfors, 23, Sodertalje (Sweden Jr.)
2006—Matthew Corrente, 30, Saginaw (OHL)

SINGLE-SEASON INDIVIDUAL RECORDS

FORWARDS/DEFENSEMEN

Most goals
48—Brian Gionta, 2005-06

Most assists
60—Scott Stevens, 1993-94

Most points
96—Patrik Elias, 2000-01

Most penalty minutes
295—Krzysztof Oliwa, 1997-98

Most power play goals
24—Brian Gionta, 2005-06

Most shorthanded goals
6—John Madden, 1999-2000

Most games with three or more goals
3—Kirk Muller, 1987-88
John MacLean, 1988-89
Patrik Elias, 2000-01

Most shots
322—John MacLean, 1989-90

GOALTENDERS

Most games
77—Martin Brodeur, 1995-96

Most minutes
4,555—Martin Brodeur, 2003-04

Most shots against
2,105—Martin Brodeur, 2005-06

Most goals allowed
243—Denis Herron, 1975-76

Lowest goals-against average
1.88—Martin Brodeur, 1996-97

Most shutouts
11—Martin Brodeur, 2003-04

Most wins
43—Martin Brodeur, 1997-98
Martin Brodeur, 1999-2000
Martin Brodeur, 2005-06

Most losses
39—Denis Herron, 1975-76

Most ties
13—Martin Brodeur, 1996-97

NEW YORK AMERICANS (DEFUNCT)

YEAR-BY-YEAR RECORDS

	REGULAR SEASON					PLAYOFFS			
Season	W	L	T	Pts.	Finish	W	L	Highest round	Coach
1919-20	4	20	0	8	4th/4th	—	—		Mike Quinn
1920-21†	6	18	0	12	4th/4th	—	—		Percy Thompson
1921-22†	7	17	0	14	4th	—	—		Percy Thompson
1922-23†	6	18	0	12	4th	—	—		Art Ross
1923-24†	9	15	0	18	4th	—	—		Percy Lesueur
1924-25†	19	10	1	39	1st	‡—	—		Jimmy Gardner
1925-26	12	20	4	28	5th	—	—		Tommy Gorman
1926-27	17	25	2	36	4th/Canadian	—	—		Newsy Lalonde
1927-28	11	27	6	28	5th/Canadian	—	—		Wilf Green
1928-29	19	13	12	50	2nd/Canadian	§0	1	Semifinals	Tommy Gorman
1929-30	14	25	5	33	5th/Canadian	—	—		Lionel Conacher
1930-31	18	16	10	46	4th/Canadian	—	—		Eddie Gerard
1931-32	16	24	8	40	4th/Canadian	—	—		Eddie Gerard
1932-33	15	22	11	41	4th/Canadian	—	—		Joe Simpson
1933-34	15	23	10	40	4th/Canadian	—	—		Joe Simpson
1934-35	12	27	9	33	4th/Canadian	—	—		Joe Simpson
1935-36	16	25	7	39	3rd/Canadian	2	3	Semifinals	Red Dutton
1936-37	15	29	4	34	4th/Canadian	—	—		Red Dutton
1937-38	19	18	11	49	2nd/Canadian	3	3	Semifinals	Red Dutton
1938-39	17	21	10	44	4th	0	2	Quarterfinals	Red Dutton
1939-40	15	29	4	34	6th	1	2	Quarterfinals	Red Dutton
1940-41	8	29	11	27	7th	—	—		Red Dutton
1941-42∞	16	29	3	35	7th	—	—		Red Dutton

*Quebec Bulldogs.

†Hamilton Tigers.

∞Brooklyn Americans.

‡Refused to participate in playoffs—held out for more compensation.

§Won-lost record does not indicate tie(s) resulting from two-game, total goals series that year (two-game, total-goals series were played from 1917-18 through 1935-36).

NEW YORK ISLANDERS

YEAR-BY-YEAR RECORDS

	REGULAR SEASON						PLAYOFFS			
Season	W	L	T	OTL	Pts.	Finish	W	L	Highest round	Coach
1972-73	12	60	6	—	30	8th/East	—	—		Phil Goyette, Earl Ingarfield
1973-74	19	41	18	—	56	8th/East	—	—		Al Arbour
1974-75	33	25	22	—	88	3rd/Patrick	9	8	Semifinals	Al Arbour
1975-76	42	21	17	—	101	2nd/Patrick	7	6	Semifinals	Al Arbour
1976-77	47	21	12	—	106	2nd/Patrick	8	4	Semifinals	Al Arbour
1977-78	48	17	15	—	111	1st/Patrick	3	4	Quarterfinals	Al Arbour
1978-79	51	15	14	—	116	1st/Patrick	6	4	Semifinals	Al Arbour
1979-80	39	28	13	—	91	2nd/Patrick	15	6	Stanley Cup champ	Al Arbour
1980-81	48	18	14	—	110	1st/Patrick	15	3	Stanley Cup champ	Al Arbour
1981-82	54	16	10	—	118	1st/Patrick	15	4	Stanley Cup champ	Al Arbour
1982-83	42	26	12	—	96	2nd/Patrick	15	5	Stanley Cup champ	Al Arbour
1983-84	50	26	4	—	104	1st/Patrick	12	9	Stanley Cup finals	Al Arbour
1984-85	40	34	6	—	86	3rd/Patrick	4	6	Division finals	Al Arbour
1985-86	39	29	12	—	90	3rd/Patrick	0	3	Division semifinals	Al Arbour
1986-87	35	33	12	—	82	3rd/Patrick	7	7	Division finals	Terry Simpson
1987-88	39	31	10	—	88	1st/Patrick	2	4	Division semifinals	Terry Simpson
1988-89	28	47	5	—	61	6th/Patrick	—	—		Terry Simpson, Al Arbour
1989-90	31	38	11	—	73	4th/Patrick	1	4	Division semifinals	Al Arbour
1990-91	25	45	10	—	60	6th/Patrick	—	—		Al Arbour
1991-92	34	35	11	—	79	5th/Patrick	—	—		Al Arbour
1992-93	40	37	7	—	87	3rd/Patrick	9	9	Conference finals	Al Arbour
1993-94	36	36	12	—	84	4th/Atlantic	0	4	Conference quarterfinals	Al Arbour, Lorne Henning
1994-95	15	28	5	—	35	7th/Atlantic	—	—		Lorne Henning
1995-96	22	50	10	—	54	7th/Atlantic	—	—		Mike Milbury
1996-97	29	41	12	—	70	7th/Atlantic	—	—		Mike Milbury, Rick Bowness
1997-98	30	41	11	—	71	4th/Atlantic	—	—		Rick Bowness, Mike Milbury
1998-99	24	48	10	—	58	5th/Atlantic	—	—		Mike Milbury, Bill Stewart

Season	W	L	T	OTL	Pts.	Finish	W	L	Highest round	Coach
	REGULAR SEASON						PLAYOFFS			
1999-00	24	48	9	1	58	5th/Atlantic	—	—		Butch Goring
2000-01	21	51	7	3	52	5th/Atlantic	—	—		Butch Goring, Lorne Henning
2001-02	42	28	8	4	96	2nd/Atlantic	3	4	Conference quarterfinals	Peter Laviolette
2002-03	35	34	11	2	83	3rd/Atlantic	1	4	Conference quarterfinals	Peter Laviolette
2003-04	38	29	11	4	91	3rd/Atlantic	1	5	Conference quarterfinals	Steve Stirling
2004-05	No season—Lockout									
2005-06	36	40	—	6	78	4th/Atlantic	—	—	—	Steve Stirling, Brad Shaw

FIRST-ROUND ENTRY DRAFT CHOICES

Year Player, Overall, Last amateur team (league)
1972—Billy Harris, 1, Toronto (OHL)
1973—Denis Potvin, 1, Ottawa (OHL)
1974—Clark Gillies, 4, Regina (WCHL)
1975—Pat Price, 11, Vancouver (WHA)
1976—Alex McKendry, 14, Sudbury (OHL)
1977—Mike Bossy, 15, Laval (QMJHL)
1978—Steve Tambellini, 15, Lethbridge (WCHL)
1979—Duane Sutter, 17, Lethbridge (WHL)
1980—Brent Sutter, 17, Red Deer (AJHL)
1981—Paul Boutilier, 21, Sherbrooke (QMJHL)
1982—Pat Flatley, 21, University of Wisconsin
1983—Pat LaFontaine, 3, Verdun (QMJHL)
Gerald Diduck, 16, Lethbridge (WHL)
1984—Duncan MacPherson, 20, Saskatoon (WHL)
1985—Brad Dalgarno, 6, Hamilton (OHL)
Derek King, 13, Sault Ste. Marie (OHL)
1986—Tom Fitzgerald, 17, Austin Prep (Mass.)
1987—Dean Chynoweth, 13, Medicine Hat (WHL)
1988—Kevin Cheveldayoff, 16, Brandon (WHL)
1989—Dave Chyzowski, 2, Kamloops (WHL)
1990—Scott Scissons, 6, Saskatoon (WHL)

Year Player, Overall, Last amateur team (league)
1991—Scott Lachance, 4, Boston University
1992—Darius Kasparaitis, 5, Dynamo Moscow (CIS)
1993—Todd Bertuzzi, 23, Guelph (OHL)
1994—Brett Lindros, 9, Kingston (OHL)
1995—Wade Redden, 2, Brandon (WHL)
1996—Jean-Pierre Dumont, 3, Val-d'Or (QMJHL)
1997—Roberto Luongo, 4, Val d'Or (QMJHL)
Eric Brewer, 5, Prince George (WHL)
1998—Michael Rupp, 9, Erie (OHL)
1999—Tim Connolly, 5, Erie (OHL)
Taylor Pyatt, 8, Sudbury (OHL)
Branislav Mezei, 10, Belleville (OHL)
Kristian Kudroc, 28, Michalovce, Slovakia
2000—Rick DiPietro, 1, Boston University
Raffi Torres, 5, Brampton (OHL)
2001—No first-round selection
2002—Sean Bergenheim, 22, Jokerit, Finland
2003—Robert Nilsson, 15, Sweden
2004—Petteri Nokelainen, 16, Saipa, Finland
2005—Ryan O'Marra, 15, Erie (OHL)
2006—Kyle Okposo, 7, Des Moines (USHL)

SINGLE-SEASON INDIVIDUAL RECORDS

FORWARDS/DEFENSEMEN

Most goals
69—Mike Bossy, 1978-79

Most assists
87—Bryan Trottier, 1978-79

Most points
147—Mike Bossy, 1981-82

Most penalty minutes
356—Brian Curran, 1986-87

Most power play goals
28—Mike Bossy, 1980-81

Most shorthanded goals
7—Bob Bourne, 1980-81

Most games with three or more goals
9—Mike Bossy, 1980-81

Most shots
315—Mike Bossy, 1980-81

GOALTENDERS

Most games
66—Chris Osgood, 2001-02

Most minutes
3,743—Chris Osgood, 2001-02

Most shots against
1,801—Ron Hextall, 1993-94

Most goals allowed
195—Gerry Desjardins, 1972-73

Lowest goals-against average
2.07—Chico Resch, 1975-76

Most shutouts
7—Chico Resch, 1975-76

Most wins
32—Billy Smith, 1981-82
Chris Osgood, 2001-02

Most losses
35—Gerry Desjardins, 1972-73

Most ties
17—Billy Smith, 1974-75

NEW YORK RANGERS

YEAR-BY-YEAR RECORDS

Season	W	L	T	OTL	Pts.	Finish	W	L	Highest round	Coach
	REGULAR SEASON						PLAYOFFS			
1926-27	25	13	6	—	56	1st/American	*0	1	Semifinals	Lester Patrick
1927-28	19	16	9	—	47	2nd/American	*5	3	Stanley Cup champ	Lester Patrick
1928-29	21	13	10	—	52	2nd/American	*3	2	Stanley Cup finals	Lester Patrick
1929-30	17	17	10	—	44	3rd/American	*1	2	Semifinals	Lester Patrick
1930-31	19	16	9	—	47	3rd/American	2	2	Semifinals	Lester Patrick
1931-32	23	17	8	—	54	1st/American	3	4	Stanley Cup finals	Lester Patrick
1932-33	23	17	8	—	54	3rd/American	*6	1	Stanley Cup champ	Lester Patrick
1933-34	21	19	8	—	50	3rd/American	*0	1	Quarterfinals	Lester Patrick
1934-35	22	20	6	—	50	3rd/American	*1	1	Semifinals	Lester Patrick
1935-36	19	17	12	—	50	4th/American	—	—		Lester Patrick
1936-37	19	20	9	—	47	3rd/American	6	3	Stanley Cup finals	Lester Patrick

Season	REGULAR SEASON W	L	T	OTL	Pts.	Finish	PLAYOFFS W	L	Highest round	Coach
1937-38	27	15	6	—	60	2nd/American	1	2	Quarterfinals	Lester Patrick
1938-39	26	16	6	—	58	2nd	3	4	Semifinals	Lester Patrick
1939-40	27	11	10	—	64	2nd	8	4	Stanley Cup champ	Frank Boucher
1940-41	21	19	8	—	50	4th	1	2	Quarterfinals	Frank Boucher
1941-42	29	17	2	—	60	1st	2	4	Semifinals	Frank Boucher
1942-43	11	31	8	—	30	6th	—	—		Frank Boucher
1943-44	6	39	5	—	17	6th	—	—		Frank Boucher
1944-45	11	29	10	—	32	6th	—	—		Frank Boucher
1945-46	13	28	9	—	35	6th	—	—		Frank Boucher
1946-47	22	32	6	—	50	5th	—	—		Frank Boucher
1947-48	21	26	13	—	55	4th	2	4	League semifinals	Frank Boucher
1948-49	18	31	11	—	47	6th	—	—		Frank Boucher, Lynn Patrick
1949-50	28	31	11	—	67	4th	7	5	Stanley Cup finals	Lynn Patrick
1950-51	20	29	21	—	61	5th	—	—		Neil Colville
1951-52	23	34	13	—	59	5th	—	—		Neil Colville, Bill Cook
1952-53	17	37	16	—	50	6th	—	—		Bill Cook
1953-54	29	31	10	—	68	5th	—	—		Frank Boucher, Muzz Patrick
1954-55	17	35	18	—	52	5th	—	—		Muzz Patrick
1955-56	32	28	10	—	74	3rd	1	4	League semifinals	Phil Watson
1956-57	26	30	14	—	66	4th	1	4	League semifinals	Phil Watson
1957-58	32	25	13	—	77	2nd	2	4	League semifinals	Phil Watson
1958-59	26	32	12	—	64	5th	—	—		Phil Watson
1959-60	17	38	15	—	49	6th	—	—		Phil Watson, Alf Pike
1960-61	22	38	10	—	54	5th	—	—		Alf Pike
1961-62	26	32	12	—	64	4th	2	4	League semifinals	Doug Harvey
1962-63	22	36	12	—	56	5th	—	—		Muzz Patrick, Red Sullivan
1963-64	22	38	10	—	54	5th	—	—		Red Sullivan
1964-65	20	38	12	—	52	5th	—	—		Red Sullivan
1965-66	18	41	11	—	47	6th	—	—		Red Sullivan, Emile Francis
1966-67	30	28	12	—	72	4th	0	4	League semifinals	Emile Francis
1967-68	39	23	12	—	90	2nd/East	2	4	Division semifinals	Emile Francis
1968-69	41	26	9	—	91	3rd/East	0	4	Division semifinals	Bernie Geoffrion, Emile Francis
1969-70	38	22	16	—	92	4th/East	2	4	Division semifinals	Emile Francis
1970-71	49	18	11	—	109	2nd/East	7	6	Division finals	Emile Francis
1971-72	48	17	13	—	109	2nd/East	10	6	Stanley Cup finals	Emile Francis
1972-73	47	23	8	—	102	3rd/East	5	5	Division finals	Emile Francis
1973-74	40	24	14	—	94	3rd/East	7	6	Division finals	Larry Popein, Emile Francis
1974-75	37	29	14	—	88	2nd/Patrick	1	2	Preliminaries	Emile Francis
1975-76	29	42	9	—	67	4th/Patrick	—	—		Ron Stewart, John Ferguson
1976-77	29	37	14	—	72	4th/Patrick	—	—		John Ferguson
1977-78	30	37	13	—	73	4th/Patrick	1	2	Preliminaries	Jean-Guy Talbot
1978-79	40	29	11	—	91	3rd/Patrick	11	7	Stanley Cup finals	Fred Shero
1979-80	38	32	10	—	86	3rd/Patrick	4	5	Quarterfinals	Fred Shero
1980-81	30	36	14	—	74	4th/Patrick	7	7	Semifinals	Fred Shero, Craig Patrick
1981-82	39	27	14	—	92	2nd/Patrick	5	5	Division finals	Herb Brooks
1982-83	35	35	10	—	80	4th/Patrick	5	4	Division finals	Herb Brooks
1983-84	42	29	9	—	93	4th/Patrick	2	3	Division semifinals	Herb Brooks
1984-85	26	44	10	—	62	4th/Patrick	0	3	Division semifinals	Herb Brooks, Craig Patrick
1985-86	36	38	6	—	78	4th/Patrick	8	8	Conference finals	Ted Sator
1986-87	34	38	8	—	76	4th/Patrick	2	4	Division semifinals	T. Sator, T. Webster, P. Esposito
1987-88	36	34	10	—	82	5th/Patrick	—	—		Michel Bergeron
1988-89	37	35	8	—	82	3rd/Patrick	0	4	Division semifinals	Michel Bergeron, Phil Esposito
1989-90	36	31	13	—	85	1st/Patrick	5	5	Division finals	Roger Neilson
1990-91	36	31	13	—	85	2nd/Patrick	2	4	Division semifinals	Roger Neilson
1991-92	50	25	5	—	105	1st/Patrick	6	7	Division finals	Roger Neilson
1992-93	34	39	11	—	79	6th/Patrick	—	—		Roger Neilson, Ron Smith
1993-94	52	24	8	—	112	1st/Atlantic	16	7	Stanley Cup champ	Mike Keenan
1994-95	22	23	3	—	47	4th/Atlantic	4	6	Conference semifinals	Colin Campbell
1995-96	41	27	14	—	96	2nd/Atlantic	5	6	Conference semifinals	Colin Campbell
1996-97	38	34	10	—	86	4th/Atlantic	9	6	Conference finals	Colin Campbell
1997-98	25	39	18	—	68	5th/Atlantic	—	—		Colin Campbell, John Muckler
1998-99	33	38	11	—	77	4th/Atlantic	—	—		John Muckler
1999-00	29	38	12	3	73	4th/Atlantic	—	—		John Muckler, John Tortorella
2000-01	33	43	5	1	72	4th/Atlantic	—	—		Ron Low
2001-02	36	38	4	4	80	4th/Atlantic	—	—		Ron Low
2002-03	32	36	10	4	78	4th/Atlantic	—	—		Bryan Trottier, Glen Sather
2003-04	27	40	7	8	69	4th/Atlantic	—	—		Glen Sather, Tom Renney
2004-05		No season—Lockout								
2005-06	44	26	—	12	100	3rd/Atlantic	0	4	Conference quarterfinals	Tom Renney

*Won-lost record does not indicate tie(s) resulting from two-game, total goals series that year (two-game, total-goals series were played from 1917-18 through 1935-36).

FIRST-ROUND ENTRY DRAFT CHOICES

Year Player, Overall, Last amateur team (league)
1969—Andre Dupont, 8, Montreal (OHL)
Pierre Jarry, 12, Ottawa (OHL)
1970—Normand Gratton, 11, Montreal (OHL)
1971—Steve Vickers, 10, Toronto (OHL)
Steve Durbano, 13, Toronto (OHL)
1972—Albert Blanchard, 10, Kitchener (OHL)
Bobby MacMillan, 15, St. Catharines (OHL)
1973—Rick Middleton, 14, Oshawa (OHL)
1974—Dave Maloney, 14, Kitchener (OHL)
1975—Wayne Dillon, 12, Toronto (WHA)
1976—Don Murdoch, 6, Medicine Hat (WCHL)
1977—Lucien DeBlois, 8, Sorel (QMJHL)
Ron Duguay, 13, Sudbury (OHL)
1978—No first-round selection
1979—Doug Sulliman, 13, Kitchener (OHL)
1980—Jim Malone, 14, Toronto (OHL)
1981—James Patrick, 9, Prince Albert (AJHL)
1982—Chris Kontos, 15, Toronto (OHL)
1983—Dave Gagner, 12, Brantford (OHL)
1984—Terry Carkner, 14, Peterborough (OHL)
1985—Ulf Dahlen, 7, Ostersund (Sweden)
1986—Brian Leetch, 9, Avon Old Farms Prep (Ct.)

Year Player, Overall, Last amateur team (league)
1987—Jayson More, 10, New Westminster (WCHL)
1988—No first-round selection
1989—Steven Rice, 20, Kitchener (OHL)
1990—Michael Stewart, 13, Michigan State University
1991—Alexei Kovalev, 15, Dynamo Moscow, USSR
1992—Peter Ferraro, 24, Waterloo (USHL)
1993—Niklas Sundstrom, 8, Ornskoldsvik, Sweden
1994—Dan Cloutier, 26, Sault Ste. Marie (OHL)
1995—No first-round selection
1996—Jeff Brown, 22, Sarnia (OHL)
1997—Stefan Cherneski, 19, Brandon (WHL)
1998—Manny Malhotra, 7, Guelph (OHL)
1999—Pavel Brendl, 4, Calgary (WHL)
Jamie Lundmark, 9, Moose Jaw (WHL)
2000—No first-round selection
2001—Daniel Blackburn, 10, Kootenay (WHL)
2002—No first-round selection
2003—Hugh Jessiman, 12, Dartmouth (ECAC)
2004—Al Montoya, 6, Michigan (CCHA)
Lauri Korpikoski, 19, TPS Jr., Finland
2005—Marc Staal, 12, Sudbury (OHL)
2006—Bobby Sanguinetti, 21, Owen Sound (OHL)

SINGLE-SEASON INDIVIDUAL RECORDS

FORWARDS/DEFENSEMEN

Most goals
54—Jaromir Jagr, 2005-06

Most assists
80—Brian Leetch, 1991-92

Most points
123—Jaromir Jagr, 2005-06

Most penalty minutes
305—Troy Mallette, 1989-90

Most power play goals
24—Jaromir Jagr, 2005-06

Most shorthanded goals
7—Theo Fleury, 2000-01

Most games with three or more goals
4—Tomas Sandstrom, 1986-87

Most shots
368—Jaromir Jagr, 2005-06

GOALTENDERS

Most games
72—Mike Richter, 1997-98

Most minutes
4,200—Johnny Bower, 1953-54
Gump Worsley, 1955-56

Most goals allowed
310—Ken McAuley, 1943-44

Lowest goals-against average
1.48—John Ross Roach, 1928-29

Most shutouts
13—John Ross Roach, 1928-29

Most wins
42—Mike Richter, 1993-94

Most losses
39—Ken McAuley, 1943-44

Most ties
20—Chuck Rayner, 1950-51

OTTAWA SENATORS (MODERN ERA)

YEAR-BY-YEAR RECORDS

	REGULAR SEASON						PLAYOFFS			
Season	W	L	T	OTL	Pts.	Finish	W	L	Highest round	Coach
1992-93	10	70	4	—	24	6th/Adams	—	—		Rick Bowness
1993-94	14	61	9	—	37	7th/Northeast	—	—		Rick Bowness
1994-95	9	34	5	—	23	7th/Northeast	—	—		Rick Bowness
1995-96	18	59	5	—	41	6th/Northeast	—	—		Rick Bowness, Dave Allison, Jacques Martin
1996-97	31	36	15	—	77	3rd/Northeast	3	4	Conference quarterfinals	Jacques Martin
1997-98	34	33	15	—	83	5th/Northeast	5	6	Conference semifinals	Jacques Martin
1998-99	44	23	15	—	103	1st/Northeast	0	4	Conference quarterfinals	Jacques Martin
1999-00	41	28	11	2	95	2nd/Northeast	2	4	Conference quarterfinals	Jacques Martin
2000-01	48	21	9	4	109	1st/Northeast	0	4	Conference quarterfinals	Jacques Martin
2001-02	39	27	9	7	94	3rd/Northeast	7	5	Conference semifinals	Jacques Martin, Roger Neilson
2002-03	52	21	8	1	113	1st/Northeast	11	7	Conference finals	Jacques Martin
2003-04	43	23	10	6	102	3rd/Northeast	3	4	Conference quarterfinals	Jacques Martin
2004-05	No season—Lockout									
2005-06	52	21	—	9	113	1st/Northeast	5	5	Conference semifinals	Bryan Murray

FIRST-ROUND ENTRY DRAFT CHOICES

Year Player, Overall, Last amateur team (league)
1992—Alexei Yashin, 2, Dynamo Moscow (CIS)
1993—Alexandre Daigle, 1, Victoriaville (QMJHL)
1994—Radek Bonk, 3, Las Vegas (IHL)
1995—Bryan Berard, 1, Detroit (OHL)
1996—Chris Phillips, 1, Prince Albert (WHL)
1997—Marian Hossa, 12, Dukla Trencin, Czechoslovakia

Year Player, Overall, Last amateur team (league)
1998—Mathieu Chouinard, 15, Shawinigan (QMJHL)
1999—Martin Havlat, 26, Trinec, Czech Republic
2000—Anton Volchenkov, 21, CSKA, Russia
2001—Jason Spezza, 2, Windsor (OHL)
Tim Gleason, 23, Windsor (OHL)
2002—Jakub Klepis, 16, Portland (WHL)

Year	Player, Overall, Last amateur team (league)
2003	Patrick Eaves, 29, Boston College (HE)
2004	Andrej Meszaros, 23, Trencin (Slovakia)
2005	Brian Lee, 9, Moorhead (USHSW)
2006	Nick Foligno, 28, Sudbury (OHL)

SINGLE-SEASON INDIVIDUAL RECORDS

FORWARDS/DEFENSEMEN

Most goals
50—Dany Heatley, 2005-06

Most assists
71—Jason Spezza, 2005-06

Most points
103—Daniel Alfredsson, 2005-06
Dany Heatley, 2005-06

Most penalty minutes
318—Mike Peluso, 1992-93

Most power play goals
23—Dany Heatley, 2005-06

Most shorthanded goals
6—Antoine Vermette, 2005-06

Most games with three or more goals
2—Daniel Alfredsson, 2001-02

Most shots
337—Alexei Yashin, 1998-99

GOALTENDERS

Most games
67—Patrick Lalime, 2002-03

Most minutes
3,943—Patrick Lalime, 2002-03

Most shots against
1,801—Craig Billington, 1993-94

Most goals allowed
254—Craig Billington, 1993-94

Lowest goals-against average
1.79—Ron Tugnutt, 1998-99

Most shutouts
8—Patrick Lalime, 2002-03

Most wins
39—Patrick Lalime, 2002-03

Most losses
46—Peter Sidorkiewicz, 1992-93

Most ties
14—Damian Rhodes, 1996-97

PHILADELPHIA FLYERS

YEAR-BY-YEAR RECORDS

	REGULAR SEASON						PLAYOFFS			
Season	W	L	T	OTL	Pts.	Finish	W	L	Highest round	Coach
1967-68	31	32	11	—	73	1st/West	3	4	Division semifinals	Keith Allen
1968-69	20	35	21	—	61	3rd/West	0	4	Division semifinals	Keith Allen
1969-70	17	35	24	—	58	5th/West	—	—		Vic Stasiuk
1970-71	28	33	17	—	73	3rd/West	0	4	Division semifinals	Vic Stasiuk
1971-72	26	38	14	—	66	5th/West	—	—		Fred Shero
1972-73	37	30	11	—	85	2nd/West	5	6	Division finals	Fred Shero
1973-74	50	16	12	—	112	1st/West	12	5	Stanley Cup champ	Fred Shero
1974-75	51	18	11	—	113	1st/Patrick	12	5	Stanley Cup champ	Fred Shero
1975-76	51	13	16	—	118	1st/Patrick	8	8	Stanley Cup finals	Fred Shero
1976-77	48	16	16	—	112	1st/Patrick	4	6	Semifinals	Fred Shero
1977-78	45	20	15	—	105	2nd/Patrick	7	5	Semifinals	Fred Shero
1978-79	40	25	15	—	95	2nd/Patrick	3	5	Quarterfinals	Bob McCammon, Pat Quinn
1979-80	48	12	20	—	116	1st/Patrick	13	6	Stanley Cup finals	Pat Quinn
1980-81	41	24	15	—	97	2nd/Patrick	6	6	Quarterfinals	Pat Quinn
1981-82	38	31	11	—	87	3rd/Patrick	1	3	Division semifinals	Pat Quinn, Bob McCammon
1982-83	49	23	8	—	106	1st/Patrick	0	3	Division semifinals	Bob McCammon
1983-84	44	26	10	—	98	3rd/Patrick	0	3	Division semifinals	Bob McCammon
1984-85	53	20	7	—	113	1st/Patrick	12	7	Stanley Cup finals	Mike Keenan
1985-86	53	23	4	—	110	1st/Patrick	2	3	Division semifinals	Mike Keenan
1986-87	46	26	8	—	100	1st/Patrick	15	11	Stanley Cup finals	Mike Keenan
1987-88	38	33	9	—	85	3rd/Patrick	3	4	Division semifinals	Mike Keenan
1988-89	36	36	8	—	80	4th/Patrick	10	9	Conference finals	Paul Holmgren
1989-90	30	39	11	—	71	6th/Patrick	—	—		Paul Holmgren
1990-91	33	37	10	—	76	5th/Patrick	—	—		Paul Holmgren
1991-92	32	37	11	—	75	6th/Patrick	—	—		Paul Holmgren, Bill Dineen
1992-93	36	37	11	—	83	5th/Patrick	—	—		Bill Dineen
1993-94	35	39	10	—	80	6th/Atlantic	—	—		Terry Simpson
1994-95	28	16	4	—	60	1st/Atlantic	10	5	Conference finals	Terry Murray
1995-96	45	24	13	—	103	1st/Atlantic	6	6	Conference semifinals	Terry Murray
1996-97	45	24	13	—	103	2nd/Atlantic	12	7	Stanley Cup finals	Terry Murray
1997-98	42	29	11	—	95	2nd/Atlantic	1	4	Conference quarterfinals	Wayne Cashman, Roger Neilson
1998-99	37	26	19	—	93	2nd/Atlantic	2	4	Conference quarterfinals	Roger Neilson
1999-00	45	22	12	3	105	1st/Atlantic	11	7	Conference finals	Roger Neilson, Craig Ramsay
2000-01	43	25	11	3	100	2nd/Atlantic	2	4	Conference quarterfinals	Craig Ramsay, Bill Barber
2001-02	42	27	10	3	97	1st/Atlantic	1	4	Conference quarterfinals	Bill Barber
2002-03	45	20	13	4	107	2nd/Atlantic	6	7	Conference semifinals	Ken Hitchcock
2003-04	40	21	15	6	101	1st/Atlantic	11	7	Conference finals	Ken Hitchcock
2004-05		No season—Lockout								
2005-06	45	26	—	11	101	2nd/Atlantic	2	4	Conference quarterfinals	Ken Hitchcock

FIRST-ROUND ENTRY DRAFT CHOICES

Year Player, Overall, Last amateur team (league)

1969—Bob Currier, 6, Cornwall (QMJHL)
1970—No first-round selection
1971—Larry Wright, 8, Regina (WCHL)
Pierre Plante, 9, Drummondville (QMJHL)
1972—Bill Barber, 7, Kitchener (OHL)
1973—No first-round selection
1974—No first-round selection
1975—Mel Bridgman, 1, Victoria (WCHL)
1976—Mark Suzor, 17, Kingston (OHL)
1977—Kevin McCarthy, 17, Winnipeg (WCHL)
1978—Behn Wilson, 6, Kingston (OHL)
Ken Linseman, 7, Birmingham (WHA)
Dan Lucas, 14, Sault Ste. Marie (OHL)
1979—Brian Propp, 14, Brandon (WHL)
1980—Mike Stothers, 21, Kingston (OHL)
1981—Steve Smith, 16, Sault Ste. Marie (OHL)
1982—Ron Sutter, 4, Lethbridge (WHL)
1983—No first-round selection
1984—No first-round selection
1985—Glen Seabrooke, 21, Peterborough (OHL)
1986—Kerry Huffman, 20, Guelph (OHL)

Year Player, Overall, Last amateur team (league)

1987—Darren Rumble, 20, Kitchener (OHL)
1988—Claude Boivin, 14, Drummondville (QMJHL)
1989—No first-round selection
1990—Mike Ricci, 4, Peterborough (OHL)
1991—Peter Forsberg, 6, Modo, Sweden
1992—Ryan Sittler, 7, Nichols H.S. (N.Y.)
Jason Bowen, 15, Tri-City (WHL)
1993—No first-round selection
1994—No first-round selection
1995—Brian Boucher, 22, Tri-City (WHL)
1996—Dainius Zubrus, 15, Pembroke, Tier II
1997—No first-round selection
1998—Simon Gagne, 22, Quebec (QMJHL)
1999—Maxime Ouellet, 22, Quebec (QMJHL)
2000—Justin Williams, 28, Plymouth (OHL)
2001—Jeff Woywitka, 27, Red Deer (WHL)
2002—Joni Pitkanen, 4, Karpat, Finland
2003—Jeff Carter, 11, Sault Ste. Marie (OHL)
Mike Richards, 24, Kitchener (OHL)
2004—No first-round selection
2005—Steve Downie, 29, Windsor (OHL)
2006—Claude Giroux, 22, Gatineau (QMJHL)

SINGLE-SEASON INDIVIDUAL RECORDS

FORWARDS/DEFENSEMEN

Most goals
61—Reggie Leach, 1975-76

Most assists
89—Bobby Clarke, 1974-75
Bobby Clarke, 1975-76

Most points
123—Mark Recchi, 1992-93

Most penalty minutes
472—Dave Schultz, 1974-75

Most power play goals
34—Tim Kerr, 1985-86

Most shorthanded goals
7—Brian Propp, 1984-85
Mark Howe, 1985-86

Most games with three or more goals
5—Tim Kerr, 1984-85

Most shots
380—Bill Barber, 1975-76

GOALTENDERS

Most games
73—Bernie Parent, 1973-74

Most minutes
4,314—Bernie Parent, 1973-74

Most goals allowed
208—Ron Hextall, 1987-88

Lowest goals-against average
1.83—Roman Cechmanek, 2002-03

Most shutouts
12—Bernie Parent, 1973-74
Bernie Parent, 1974-75

Most wins
47—Bernie Parent, 1973-74

Most losses
29—Bernie Parent, 1969-70

Most ties
20—Bernie Parent, 1969-70

PHOENIX COYOTES

YEAR-BY-YEAR RECORDS

	REGULAR SEASON						PLAYOFFS			
Season	W	L	T	OTL	Pts.	Finish	W	L	Highest round	Coach
1972-73*	43	31	4	—	90	1st	9	5	Avco World Cup finals	Nick Mickoski, Bobby Hull
1973-74*	34	39	5	—	73	4th	0	4	League quarterfinals	Nick Mickoski, Bobby Hull
1974-75*	38	35	5	—	81	3rd	—	—		Rudy Pilous
1975-76*	52	27	2	—	106	1st	12	1	Avco World Cup champ	Bobby Kromm
1976-77*	46	32	2	—	94	2nd	11	9	Avco World Cup finals	Bobby Kromm
1977-78*	50	28	2	—	102	1st	8	1	Avco World Cup champ	Larry Hillman
1978-79*	39	35	6	—	84	3rd	8	2	Avco World Cup champ	Larry Hillman, Tom McVie
1979-80†	20	49	11	—	51	5th/Smythe	—	—		Tom McVie
1980-81†	9	57	14	—	32	6th/Smythe	—	—		T. McVie, Bill Sutherland, M. Smith
1981-82†	33	33	14	—	80	2nd/Norris	1	3	Division semifinals	Tom Watt
1982-83†	33	39	8	—	74	4th/Smythe	0	3	Division semifinals	Tom Watt
1983-84†	31	38	11	—	73	4th/Smythe	0	3	Division semifinals	Tom Watt, Barry Long
1984-85†	43	27	10	—	96	2nd/Smythe	3	5	Division finals	Barry Long
1985-86†	26	47	7	—	59	3rd/Smythe	0	3	Division semifinals	Barry Long, John Ferguson
1986-87†	40	32	8	—	88	3rd/Smythe	4	6	Division finals	Dan Maloney
1987-88†	33	36	11	—	77	3rd/Smythe	1	4	Division semifinals	Dan Maloney
1988-89†	26	42	12	—	64	5th/Smythe	—	—		Dan Maloney, Rick Bowness
1989-90†	37	32	11	—	85	3rd/Smythe	3	4	Division semifinals	Bob Murdoch
1990-91†	26	43	11	—	63	5th/Smythe	—	—		Bob Murdoch
1991-92†	33	32	15	—	81	4th/Smythe	3	4	Division semifinals	John Paddock
1992-93†	40	37	7	—	87	4th/Smythe	2	4	Division semifinals	John Paddock
1993-94†	24	51	9	—	57	6th/Central	—	—		John Paddock

Season	W	L	T	OTL	Pts.	Finish	W	L	Highest round	Coach
			REGULAR SEASON				PLAYOFFS			
1994-95†	16	25	7	—	39	6th/Central	—	—		John Paddock, Terry Simpson
1995-96†	36	40	6	—	78	5th/Central	—	—		Terry Simpson
1996-97	38	37	7	—	83	3rd/Central	3	4	Conference quarterfinals	Don Hay
1997-98	35	35	12	—	82	4th/Central	2	4	Conference quarterfinals	Jim Schoenfeld
1998-99	39	31	12	—	90	2nd/Pacific	3	4	Conference quarterfinals	Jim Schoenfeld
1999-00	39	31	8	4	90	3rd/Pacific	1	4	Conference quarterfinals	Bob Francis
2000-01	35	27	17	3	90	4th/Pacific	—	—		Bob Francis
2001-02	40	27	9	6	95	2nd/Pacific	1	4	Conference quarterfinals	Bob Francis
2002-03	31	35	11	5	78	4th/Pacific	—	—		Bob Francis
2003-04	22	36	18	6	68	5th/Pacific	—	—		Bob Francis, Rick Bowness
2004-05			No season—Lockout							
2005-06	38	39	—	5	81	5th/Pacific	—	—		Wayne Gretzky

*Winnipeg Jets, members of World Hockey Association. †Winnipeg Jets.

FIRST-ROUND ENTRY DRAFT CHOICES

Year Player, Overall, Last amateur team (league)

1979—Jimmy Mann, 19, Sherbrooke (QMJHL)
1980—David Babych, 2, Portland (WHL)
1981—Dale Hawerchuk, 1, Cornwall (QMJHL)*
1982—Jim Kyte, 12, Cornwall (OHL)
1983—Andrew McBain, 8, North Bay (OHL)
Bobby Dollas, 14, Laval (QMJHL)
1984—No first-round selection
1985—Ryan Stewart, 18, Kamloops (WHL)
1986—Pat Elynuik, 8, Prince Albert (WHL)
1987—Bryan Marchment, 16, Belleville (OHL)
1988—Teemu Selanne, 10, Jokerit, Finland
1989—Stu Barnes, 4, Tri-City (WHL)
1990—Keith Tkachuk, 19, Malden Cath. H.S. (Mass.)
1991—Aaron Ward, 5, University of Michigan
1992—Sergei Bautin, 17, Dynamo Moscow (CIS)
1993—Mats Lindgren, 15, Skelleftea, Sweden
1994—No first-round selection

Year Player, Overall, Last amateur team (league)

1995—Shane Doan, 7, Kamloops (WHL)
1996—Dan Focht, 11, Tri-City (WHL)
Daniel Briere, 24, Drummondville (QMJHL)
1997—No first-round selection
1998—Patrick DesRochers, 14, Sarnia (OHL)
1999—Scott Kelman, 15, Seattle (WHL)
Kirill Safronov, 19, SKA St. Petersburg, Russia
2000—Krystofer Kolanos, 19, Boston College
2001—Fredrik Sjostrom, 11, Frolunda, Sweden
2002—Jakub Koreis, 19, Plzen, Czechoslovakia
Ben Eager, 23, Oshawa (OHL)
2003—No first-round selection
2004—Blake Wheeler, 5, Breck (USHSW)
2005—Martin Hanzal, 17, Budejovice (Czech Rep. Jr.)
2006—Peter Mueller, 8, Everett (WHL)
Chris Summers, 29, U.S. National U-18

NOTE: Winnipeg chose Scott Campbell, Morris Lukowich and Markus Mattsson as priority selections before the 1979 expansion draft.

SINGLE-SEASON INDIVIDUAL RECORDS

FORWARDS/DEFENSEMEN

Most goals
76—Teemu Selanne, 1992-93

Most assists
79—Phil Housley, 1992-93

Most points
132—Teemu Selanne, 1992-93

Most penalty minutes
347—Tie Domi, 1993-94

Most power play goals
24—Teemu Selanne, 1992-93

Most shorthanded goals
7—Dave McLlwain, 1989-90

Most games with three or more goals
5—Teemu Selanne, 1992-93

Most shots
387—Teemu Selanne, 1992-93

GOALTENDERS

Most games
72—Nikolai Khabibulin, 1996-97

Most minutes
4,091—Nikolai Khabibulin, 1996-97

Most shots against
2,119—Bob Essensa, 1992-93

Most goals allowed
227—Bob Essensa, 1992-93

Lowest goals-against average
2.13—Nikolai Khabibulin, 1998-99

Most shutouts
8—Nikolai Khabibulin, 1998-99

Most wins
33—Brian Hayward, 1984-85
Bob Essensa, 1992-93
Sean Burke, 2001-02

Most losses
33—Nikolai Khabibulin, 1996-97

Most ties
13—Sean Burke, 2000-01

PITTSBURGH PENGUINS

YEAR-BY-YEAR RECORDS

Season	W	L	T	OTL	Pts.	Finish	W	L	Highest round	Coach
			REGULAR SEASON				PLAYOFFS			
1967-68	27	34	13	—	67	5th/West	—	—		Red Sullivan
1968-69	20	45	11	—	51	5th/West	—	—		Red Sullivan
1969-70	26	38	12	—	64	2nd/West	6	4	Division finals	Red Kelly
1970-71	21	37	20	—	62	6th/West	—	—		Red Kelly
1971-72	26	38	14	—	66	4th/West	0	4	Division semifinals	Red Kelly
1972-73	32	37	9	—	73	5th/West	—	—		Red Kelly, Ken Schinkel
1973-74	28	41	9	—	65	5th/West	—	—		Ken Schinkel, Marc Boileau
1974-75	37	28	15	—	89	3rd/Norris	5	4	Quarterfinals	Marc Boileau
1975-76	35	33	12	—	82	3rd/Norris	1	2	Preliminaries	Marc Boileau, Ken Schinkel

Season	W	L	T	OTL	Pts.	Finish	W	L	Highest round	Coach
	REGULAR SEASON						PLAYOFFS			
1976-77	34	33	13	—	81	3rd/Norris	1	2	Preliminaries	Ken Schinkel
1977-78	25	37	18	—	68	4th/Norris	—	—		Johnny Wilson
1978-79	36	31	13	—	85	2nd/Norris	2	5	Quarterfinals	Johnny Wilson
1979-80	30	37	13	—	73	3rd/Norris	2	3	Preliminaries	Johnny Wilson
1980-81	30	37	13	—	73	3rd/Norris	2	3	Preliminaries	Eddie Johnston
1981-82	31	36	13	—	75	4th/Patrick	2	3	Division semifinals	Eddie Johnston
1982-83	18	53	9	—	45	6th/Patrick	—	—		Eddie Johnston
1983-84	16	58	6	—	38	6th/Patrick	—	—		Lou Angotti
1984-85	24	51	5	—	53	6th/Patrick	—	—		Bob Berry
1985-86	34	38	8	—	76	5th/Patrick	—	—		Bob Berry
1986-87	30	38	12	—	72	5th/Patrick	—	—		Bob Berry
1987-88	36	35	9	—	81	6th/Patrick	—	—		Pierre Creamer
1988-89	40	33	7	—	87	2nd/Patrick	7	4	Division finals	Gene Ubriaco
1989-90	32	40	8	—	72	5th/Patrick	—	—		Gene Ubriaco, Craig Patrick
1990-91	41	33	6	—	88	1st/Patrick	16	8	Stanley Cup champ	Bob Johnson
1991-92	39	32	9	—	87	3rd/Patrick	16	5	Stanley Cup champ	Scotty Bowman
1992-93	56	21	7	—	119	1st/Patrick	7	5	Division finals	Scotty Bowman
1993-94	44	27	13	—	101	1st/Northeast	2	4	Conference quarterfinals	Eddie Johnston
1994-95	29	16	3	—	61	2nd/Northeast	5	7	Conference semifinals	Eddie Johnston
1995-96	49	29	4	—	102	1st/Northeast	11	7	Conference finals	Eddie Johnston
1996-97	38	36	8	—	84	2nd/Northeast	1	4	Conference quarterfinals	Eddie Johnston, Craig Patrick
1997-98	40	24	18	—	98	1st/Northeast	2	4	Conference quarterfinals	Kevin Constantine
1998-99	38	30	14	—	90	3rd/Atlantic	6	7	Conference semifinals	Kevin Constantine
1999-00	37	31	8	6	88	3rd/Atlantic	6	5	Conference semifinals	Kevin Constantine, Herb Brooks
2000-01	42	28	9	3	96	3rd/Atlantic	9	9	Conference finals	Ivan Hlinka
2001-02	28	41	8	5	69	5th/Atlantic	—	—		Ivan Hlinka, Rick Kehoe
2002-03	27	44	6	5	65	5th/Atlantic	—	—		Rick Kehoe
2003-04	23	47	8	4	58	5th/Atlantic	—	—		Ed Olczyk
2004-05			No season—Lockout							
2005-06	22	46	—	14	58	5th/Atlantic	—	—		Ed Olczyk, Michel Therrien

FIRST-ROUND ENTRY DRAFT CHOICES

Year Player, Overall, Last amateur team (league)

1969—No first-round selection
1970—Greg Polis, 7, Estevan (WCHL)
1971—No first-round selection
1972—No first-round selection
1973—Blaine Stoughton, 7, Flin Flon (WCHL)
1974—Pierre Larouche, 8, Sorel (QMJHL)
1975—Gord Laxton, 13, New Westminster (WCHL)
1976—Blair Chapman, 2, Saskatoon (WCHL)
1977—No first-round selection
1978—No first-round selection
1979—No first-round selection
1980—Mike Bullard, 9, Brantford (OHL)
1981—No first-round selection
1982—Rich Sutter, 10, Lethbridge (WHL)
1983—Bob Errey, 15, Peterborough (OHL)
1984—Mario Lemieux, 1, Laval (QMJHL)
Doug Bodger, 9, Kamloops (WHL)
Roger Belanger, 16, Kingston (OHL)
1985—Craig Simpson, 2, Michigan State University
1986—Zarley Zalapski, 4, Team Canada

Year Player, Overall, Last amateur team (league)

1987—Chris Joseph, 5, Seattle (WHL)
1988—Darrin Shannon, 4, Windsor (OHL)
1989—Jamie Heward, 16, Regina (WHL)
1990—Jaromir Jagr, 5, Poldi Kladno, Czech. Republic
1991—Markus Naslund, 16, MoDo, Sweden
1992—Martin Straka, 19, Skoda Plzen, Czech. Republic
1993—Stefan Bergqvist, 26, Leksand, Sweden
1994—Chris Wells, 24, Seattle (WHL)
1995—Alexei Morozov, 24, Krylja Sovetov, CIS
1996—Craig Hillier, 23, Ottawa (OHL)
1997—Robert Dome, 17, Las Vegas (IHL)
1998—Milan Kraft, 23, Plzen (Czech.)
1999—Konstantin Koltsov, 18, Cherepovec, Russia
2000—Brooks Orpik, 18, Boston College
2001—Colby Armstrong, 21, Red Deer (WHL)
2002—Ryan Whitney, 5, Boston University (H. East)
2003—Marc-Andre Fleury, 1, Cape Breton (QMJHL)
2004—Evgeni Malkin, 2, Magnitogorsk, Russia
2005—Sidney Crosby, 1, Rimouski (QMJHL)
2006—Jordan Staal, 2, Peterborough (OHL)

SINGLE-SEASON INDIVIDUAL RECORDS

FORWARDS/DEFENSEMEN

Most goals
85—Mario Lemieux, 1988-89

Most assists
114—Mario Lemieux, 1988-89

Most points
199—Mario Lemieux, 1988-89

Most penalty minutes
409—Paul Baxter, 1981-82

Most power play goals
31—Mario Lemieux, 1988-89
Mario Lemieux, 1995-96

Most shorthanded goals
13—Mario Lemieux, 1988-89

Most games with three or more goals
9—Mario Lemieux, 1988-89

Most shots
403—Jaromir Jagr, 1995-96

GOALTENDERS

Most games
66—Johan Hedberg, 2001-02

Most minutes
3,877—Johan Hedberg, 2001-02

Most shots against
1,885—Tom Barrasso, 1992-93

Most goals allowed
258—Greg Millen, 1980-81

Lowest goals-against average
2.07—Tom Barrasso, 1997-98

Most shutouts
7—Tom Barrasso, 1997-98

Most wins
43—Tom Barrasso, 1992-93

Most losses
34—Johan Hedberg, 2001-02

Most ties
15—Denis Herron, 1977-78

PITTSBURGH PIRATES (DEFUNCT)

YEAR-BY-YEAR RECORDS

	REGULAR SEASON					PLAYOFFS			
Season	W	L	T	Pts.	Finish	W	L	Highest round	Coach
1925-26	19	16	1	39	3rd	—	—		Odie Cleghorn
1926-27	15	26	3	33	4th/American	—	—		Odie Cleghorn
1927-28	19	17	8	46	3rd/American	1	1	Quarterfinals	Odie Cleghorn
1928-29	9	27	8	26	4th/American	—	—		Odie Cleghorn
1929-30	5	36	3	13	5th/American	—	—		Frank Frederickson
1930-31*	4	36	4	12	5th/American	—	—		Cooper Smeaton

*Philadelphia Quakers.

ST. LOUIS BLUES

YEAR-BY-YEAR RECORDS

	REGULAR SEASON						PLAYOFFS			
Season	W	L	T	OTL	Pts.	Finish	W	L	Highest round	Coach
1967-68	27	31	16	—	70	3rd/West	8	10	Stanley Cup finals	Lynn Patrick, Scotty Bowman
1968-69	37	25	14	—	88	1st/West	8	4	Stanley Cup finals	Scotty Bowman
1969-70	37	27	12	—	86	1st/West	8	8	Stanley Cup finals	Scotty Bowman
1970-71	34	25	19	—	87	2nd/West	2	4	Division semifinals	Al Arbour, Scotty Bowman
1971-72	28	39	11	—	67	3rd/West	4	7	Division finals	Sid Abel, Bill McCreary, Al Arbour
1972-73	32	34	12	—	76	4th/West	1	4	Division semifinals	Al Arbour, Jean-Guy Talbot
1973-74	26	40	12	—	64	6th/West	—	—		Jean-Guy Talbot, Lou Angotti
1974-75	35	31	14	—	84	2nd/Smythe	0	2	Preliminaries	Lou Angotti, Lynn Patrick, Garry Young
1975-76	29	37	14	—	72	3rd/Smythe	1	2	Preliminaries	Garry Young, Lynn Patrick, Leo Boivin
1976-77	32	39	9	—	73	1st/Smythe	0	4	Quarterfinals	Emile Francis
1977-78	20	47	13	—	53	4th/Smythe	—	—		Leo Boivin, Barclay Plager
1978-79	18	50	12	—	48	3rd/Smythe	—	—		Barclay Plager
1979-80	34	34	12	—	80	2nd/Smythe	0	3	Preliminaries	Barclay Plager, Red Berenson
1980-81	45	18	17	—	107	1st/Smythe	5	6	Quarterfinals	Red Berenson
1981-82	32	40	8	—	72	3rd/Norris	5	5	Division finals	Red Berenson, Emile Francis
1982-83	25	40	15	—	65	4th/Norris	1	3	Division semifinals	Emile Francis, Barclay Plager
1983-84	32	41	7	—	71	2nd/Norris	6	5	Division finals	Jacques Demers
1984-85	37	31	12	—	86	1st/Norris	0	3	Division semifinals	Jacques Demers
1985-86	37	34	9	—	83	3rd/Norris	10	9	Conference finals	Jacques Demers
1986-87	32	33	15	—	79	1st/Norris	2	4	Division semifinals	Jacques Martin
1987-88	34	38	8	—	76	2nd/Norris	5	5	Division finals	Jacques Martin
1988-89	33	35	12	—	78	2nd/Norris	5	5	Division finals	Brian Sutter
1989-90	37	34	9	—	83	2nd/Norris	7	5	Division finals	Brian Sutter
1990-91	47	22	11	—	105	2nd/Norris	6	7	Division finals	Brian Sutter
1991-92	36	33	11	—	83	3rd/Norris	2	4	Division semifinals	Brian Sutter
1992-93	37	36	11	—	85	4th/Norris	7	4	Division finals	Bob Plager, Bob Berry
1993-94	40	33	11	—	91	4th/Central	0	4	Conference quarterfinals	Bob Berry
1994-95	28	15	5	—	61	2nd/Central	3	4	Conference quarterfinals	Mike Keenan
1995-96	32	34	16	—	80	4th/Central	7	6	Conference semifinals	Mike Keenan
1996-97	36	35	11	—	83	4th/Central	2	4	Conference quarterfinals	Mike Keenan, Jimmy Roberts, Joel Quenneville
1997-98	45	29	8	—	98	3rd/Central	6	4	Conference semifinals	Joel Quenneville
1998-99	37	32	13	—	87	2nd/Central	6	7	Conference semifinals	Joel Quenneville
1999-00	51	19	11	1	114	1st/Central	3	4	Conference quarterfinals	Joel Quenneville
2000-01	43	22	12	5	103	2nd/Central	9	6	Conference finals	Joel Quenneville
2001-02	43	27	8	4	98	2nd/Central	5	5	Conference semifinals	Joel Quenneville
2002-03	41	24	11	6	99	2nd/Central	3	4	Conference quarterfinals	Joel Quenneville
2003-04	39	30	11	2	91	2nd/Central	1	4	Conference quarterfinals	Joel Quenneville, Mike Kitchen
2004-05	No season—Lockout									
2005-06	21	46	—	15	57	5th/Central	—	—	—	Mike Kitchen

FIRST-ROUND ENTRY DRAFT CHOICES

Year Player, Overall, Last amateur team (league)
1969—No first-round selection
1970—No first-round selection
1971—Gene Carr, 4, Flin Flon (WCHL)
1972—Wayne Merrick, 9, Ottawa (OHL)
1973—John Davidson, 5, Calgary (WCHL)
1974—No first-round selection

Year Player, Overall, Last amateur team (league)
1975—No first-round selection
1976—Bernie Federko, 7, Saskatoon (WCHL)
1977—Scott Campbell, 9, London (OHL)
1978—Wayne Babych, 3, Portland (WCHL)
1979—Perry Turnbull, 2, Portland (WHL)
1980—Rik Wilson, 12, Kingston (OHL)

Year Player, Overall, Last amateur team (league)
1981—Marty Ruff, 20, Lethbridge (WHL)
1982—No first-round selection
1983—No first-round selection
1984—No first-round selection
1985—No first-round selection
1986—Jocelyn Lemieux, 10, Laval (QMJHL)
1987—Keith Osborne, 12, North Bay (OHL)
1988—Rod Brind'Amour, 9, Notre Dame Academy (Sask.)
1989—Jason Marshall, 9, Vernon (B.C.) Tier II
1990—No first-round selection
1991—No first-round selection
1992—No first-round selection
1993—No first-round selection
1994—No first-round selection

Year Player, Overall, Last amateur team (league)
1995—No first-round selection
1996—Marty Reasoner, 14, Boston College
1997—No first-round selection
1998—Christian Backman, 24, Frolunda Goteborg, Sweden
1999—Barret Jackman, 17, Regina (WHL)
2000—Jeff Taffe, 30, University of Minnesota
2001—No first-round selection
2002—No first-round selection
2003—Shawn Belle, 30, Tri-City (WHL)
2004—Marek Schwarz, 17, Sparta Prague, Czech Republic
2005—T.J. Oshie, 24, Warroad (USHSW)
2006—Erik Johnson, 1, U.S. National U-18
Patrik Berglund, 25, Vasteras, Sweden

SINGLE-SEASON INDIVIDUAL RECORDS

FORWARDS/DEFENSEMEN

Most goals
86—Brett Hull, 1990-91

Most assists
90—Adam Oates, 1990-91

Most points
131—Brett Hull, 1990-91

Most penalty minutes
306—Bob Gassoff, 1975-76

Most power play goals
29—Brett Hull, 1990-91
Brett Hull, 1992-93

Most shorthanded goals
8—Chuck Lefley, 1975-76
Larry Patey, 1980-81

Most games with three or more goals
8—Brett Hull, 1991-92

Most shots
408—Brett Hull, 1991-92

GOALTENDERS

Most games
79—Grant Fuhr, 1995-96

Most minutes
4,365—Grant Fuhr, 1995-96

Most shots against
2,382—Curtis Joseph, 1993-94

Most goals allowed
250—Mike Liut, 1991-92

Lowest goals-against average
1.95—Roman Turek, 1999-2000

Most shutouts
8—Glenn Hall, 1968-69

Most wins
42—Roman Turek, 1999-2000

Most losses
29—Mike Liut, 1983-84

Most ties
16—Grant Fuhr, 1995-96

ST. LOUIS EAGLES (DEFUNCT)

YEAR-BY-YEAR RECORDS

	REGULAR SEASON					PLAYOFFS			
Season	W	L	T	Pts.	Finish	W	L	Highest round	Coach
1917-18*	9	13	0	18	3rd/2nd	—	—		Eddie Gerard
1918-19*	12	6	0	24	2nd/1st	1	4	Semifinals	Alf Smith
1919-20*	19	5	0	38	1st/1st	3	2	Stanley Cup champ	Pete Green
1920-21*	14	10	0	28	1st/3rd	†4	2	Stanley Cup champ	Pete Green
1921-22*	14	8	2	30	1st	†0	1	Semifinals	Pete Green
1922-23*	14	9	1	29	1st	6	2	Stanley Cup champ	Pete Green
1923-24*	16	8	0	32	1st	0	2	Semifinals	Pete Green
1924-25*	17	12	1	35	4th	—	—		Pete Green
1925-26*	24	8	4	52	1st	†0	1	Semifinals	Pete Green
1926-27*	30	10	4	64	1st/Canadian	†3	0	Stanley Cup champ	Dave Gill
1927-28*	20	14	10	50	3rd/Canadian	0	2	Quarterfinals	Dave Gill
1928-29*	14	17	13	41	4th/Canadian	—	—		Dave Gill
1929-30*	21	15	8	50	3rd/Canadian	†0	1	Semifinals	Newsy Lalonde
1930-31*	10	30	4	24	5th/Canadian	—	—		Newsy Lalonde
1931-32*					Club suspended operations for one season.				
1932-33*	11	27	10	32	5th/Canadian	—	—		Cy Denneny
1933-34*	13	29	6	32	5th/Canadian	—	—		George Boucher
1934-35	11	31	6	28	5th/Canadian	—	—		Eddie Gerard, George Boucher

*Ottawa Senators (first club).
†Won-lost record does not indicate tie(s) resulting from two-game, total goals series that year (two-game, total-goals series were played from 1917-18 through 1935-36).

SAN JOSE SHARKS

YEAR-BY-YEAR RECORDS

	REGULAR SEASON						PLAYOFFS			
Season	W	L	T	OTL	Pts.	Finish	W	L	Highest round	Coach
1991-92	17	58	5	—	39	6th/Smythe	—	—		George Kingston
1992-93	11	71	2	—	24	6th/Smythe	—	—		George Kingston
1993-94	33	35	16	—	82	3rd/Pacific	7	7	Conference semifinals	Kevin Constantine
1994-95	19	25	4	—	42	3rd/Pacific	4	7	Conference semifinals	Kevin Constantine
1995-96	20	55	7	—	47	7th/Pacific	—	—		Kevin Constantine, Jim Wiley

Season	W	L	T	OTL	Pts.	Finish	W	L	Highest round	Coach
	REGULAR SEASON						PLAYOFFS			
1996-97	27	47	8	—	62	7th/Pacific	—	—		Al Sims
1997-98	34	38	10	—	78	4th/Pacific	2	4	Conference quarterfinals	Darryl Sutter
1998-99	31	33	18	—	80	4th/Pacific	2	4	Conference quarterfinals	Darryl Sutter
1999-00	35	30	10	7	87	4th/Pacific	5	7	Conference semifinals	Darryl Sutter
2000-01	40	27	12	3	95	2nd/Pacific	2	4	Conference quarterfinals	Darryl Sutter
2001-02	44	27	8	3	99	1st/Pacific	7	5	Conference semifinals	Darryl Sutter
2002-03	28	37	9	8	73	5th/Pacific	—	—		Darryl Sutter, Doug Wilson, Cap Raeder, Ron Wilson
2003-04	43	21	12	6	104	1st/Pacific	10	7	Conference finals	Ron Wilson
2004-05	No season—Lockout									
2005-06	44	27	—	11	99	2nd/Pacific	6	5	Conference semifinals	Ron Wilson

FIRST-ROUND ENTRY DRAFT CHOICES

Year Player, Overall, Last amateur team (league)
1991—Pat Falloon, 2, Spokane (WHL)
1992—Mike Rathje, 3, Medicine Hat (WHL)
Andrei Nazarov, 10, Dynamo Moscow, CIS
1993—Viktor Kozlov, 6, Moscow, CIS
1994—Jeff Friesen, 11, Regina (WHL)
1995—Teemu Riihijarvi, 12, Espoo Jrs., Finland
1996—Andrei Zyuzin, 2, Salavat Yulayev UFA, CIS
Marco Sturm, 21, Landshut, Germany
1997—Patrick Marleau, 2, Seattle (WHL)
Scott Hannan, 23, Kelowna (WHL)

Year Player, Overall, Last amateur team (league)
1998—Brad Stuart, 3, Regina (WHL)
1999—Jeff Jillson, 14, University of Michigan
2000—No first-round selection
2001—Marcel Goc, 20, Schwennigen, Germany
2002—Mike Morris, 27, St. Sebastian's (USHSE)
2003—Milan Michalek, 6, Czech Republic
Steve Bernier, 16, Moncton (QMJHL)
2004—Lukas Kaspar, 22, Litvinov, Czech Republic
2005—Devin Setoguchi, 8, Saskatoon (WHL)
2006—Ty Wishart, 16, Prince George (WHL)

SINGLE-SEASON INDIVIDUAL RECORDS

FORWARDS/DEFENSEMEN

Most goals
56—Jonathan Cheechoo, 2005-06

Most assists
72—Joe Thornton, 2005-06

Most points
93—Jonathan Cheechoo, 2005-06

Most penalty minutes
326—Link Gaetz, 1991-92

Most power play goals
24—Jonathan Cheechoo, 2005-06

Most shorthanded goals
6—Jamie Baker, 1995-96
Jeff Friesen, 1997-98

Most games with three or more goals
5—Jonathan Cheechoo, 2005-06

Most shots
317—Jonathan Cheechoo, 2005-06

GOALTENDERS

Most games
74—Arturs Irbe, 1993-94

Most minutes
4,412—Arturs Irbe, 1993-94

Most shots against
2,064—Arturs Irbe, 1993-94

Most goals allowed
209—Arturs Irbe, 1993-94

Lowest goals-against average
2.06—Vesa Toskala, 2003-04

Most shutouts
7—Evgeni Nabokov, 2001-02

Most wins
37—Evgeni Nabokov, 2001-02

Most losses
30—Jeff Hackett, 1992-93
Steve Shields, 1999-2000

Most ties
16—Arturs Irbe, 1993-94

TAMPA BAY LIGHTNING

YEAR-BY-YEAR RECORDS

Season	W	L	T	OTL	Pts.	Finish	W	L	Highest round	Coach
	REGULAR SEASON						PLAYOFFS			
1992-93	23	54	7	—	53	6th/Norris	—	—		Terry Crisp
1993-94	30	43	11	—	71	7th/Atlantic	—	—		Terry Crisp
1994-95	17	28	3	—	37	6th/Atlantic	—	—		Terry Crisp
1995-96	38	32	12	—	88	5th/Atlantic	2	4	Conference quarterfinals	Terry Crisp
1996-97	32	40	10	—	74	6th/Atlantic	—	—		Terry Crisp
1997-98	17	55	10	—	44	7th/Atlantic	—	—		Terry Crisp, Rick Paterson, Jacques Demers
1998-99	19	54	9	—	47	4th/Southeast	—	—		Jacques Demers
1999-00	19	47	9	7	54	4th/Southeast	—	—		Steve Ludzik
2000-01	24	47	6	5	59	5th/Southeast	—	—		Steve Ludzik, John Tortorella
2001-02	27	40	11	4	69	3rd/Southeast	—	—		John Tortorella
2002-03	36	25	16	5	93	1st/Southeast	5	6	Conference semifinals	John Tortorella
2003-04	46	22	8	6	106	1st/Southeast	16	7	Stanley Cup champ	John Tortorella
2004-05	No season—Lockout									
2005-06	43	33	—	6	92	2nd/Southeast	1	4	Conference quarterfinals	John Tortorella

FIRST-ROUND ENTRY DRAFT CHOICES

Year Player, Overall, Last amateur team (league)
1992—Roman Hamrlik, 1, Zlin, Czechoslovakia
1993—Chris Gratton, 3, Kingston (OHL)

Year Player, Overall, Last amateur team (league)
1994—Jason Weimer, 8, Portland (WHL)
1995—Daymond Langkow, 5, Tri-City (WHL)

Year	Player, Overall, Last amateur team (league)
1996	Mario Larocque, 16, Hull (QMJHL)
1997	Paul Mara, 7, Sudbury (OHL)
1998	Vincent Lecavalier, 1, Rimouski (QMJHL)
1999	No first-round selection
2000	Nikita Alexeev, 8, Erie (OHL)
2001	Alexander Svitov, 3, OMSK, Russia
2002	No first-round selection
2003	No first-round selection
2004	Andy Rogers, 30, Calgary (WHL)
2005	Vladimir Mihalik, 30, Presov (Slovakia 2)
2006	Riku Helenius, 15, Ilves, Finland

SINGLE-SEASON INDIVIDUAL RECORDS

FORWARDS/DEFENSEMEN

Most goals
42—Brian Bradley, 1992-93

Most assists
68—Brad Richards, 2005-06

Most points
94—Martin St. Louis, 2003-04

Most penalty minutes
258—Enrico Ciccone, 1995-96

Most power play goals
16—Brian Bradley, 1992-93

Most shorthanded goals
8—Martin St. Louis, 2003-04

Most games with three or more goals
3—Wendel Clark, 1998-99

Most shots
309—Vincent Lecavalier, 2005-06

GOALTENDERS

Most games
70—Nikolai Khabibulin, 2001-02

Most minutes
3,896—Nikolai Khabibulin, 2001-02

Most shots against
1,914—Nikolai Khabibulin, 2001-02

Most goals allowed
177—Kevin Weekes, 2000-01

Lowest goals-against average
2.33—Nikolai Khabibulin, 2003-04

Most shutouts
7—Nikolai Khabibulin, 2001-02

Most wins
30—Nikolai Khabibulin, 2002-03

Most losses
33—Daren Puppa, 1993-94
Kevin Weekes, 2000-01

Most ties
11—Nikolai Khabibulin, 2002-03

TORONTO MAPLE LEAFS

YEAR-BY-YEAR RECORDS

	REGULAR SEASON						PLAYOFFS			
Season	W	L	T	OTL	Pts.	Finish	W	L	Highest round	Coach
1917-18‡	13	9	0	—	26	2nd/1st	4	3	Stanley Cup champ	Dick Carroll
1918-19‡	5	13	0	—	10	3rd/3rd	—	—		Dick Carroll
1919-20§	12	12	0	—	24	3rd/2nd	—	—		Frank Heffernan, Harry Sproule
1920-21§	15	9	0	—	30	2nd/1st	0	2	Semifinals	Dick Carroll
1921-22§	13	10	1	—	27	2nd	*4	2	Stanley Cup champ	Eddie Powers
1922-23§	13	10	1	—	27	3rd	—	—		Charlie Querrie, Jack Adams
1923-24§	10	14	0	—	20	3rd	—	—		Eddie Powers
1924-25§	19	11	0	—	38	2nd	0	2	Semifinals	Eddie Powers
1925-26§	12	21	3	—	27	6th	—	—		Eddie Powers
1926-27§	15	24	5	—	35	5th/Canadian	—	—		Conn Smythe
1927-28	18	18	8	—	44	4th/Canadian	—	—		Alex Roveril, Conn Smythe
1928-29	21	18	5	—	47	3rd/Canadian	2	2	Semifinals	Alex Roveril, Conn Smythe
1929-30	17	21	6	—	40	4th/Canadian	—	—		Alex Roveril, Conn Smythe
1930-31	22	13	9	—	53	2nd/Canadian	*0	1	Quarterfinals	Conn Smythe, Art Duncan
1931-32	23	18	7	—	53	2nd/Canadian	*5	1	Stanley Cup champ	Art Duncan, Dick Irvin
1932-33	24	18	6	—	54	1st/Canadian	4	5	Stanley Cup finals	Dick Irvin
1933-34	26	13	9	—	61	1st/Canadian	2	3	Semifinals	Dick Irvin
1934-35	30	14	4	—	64	1st/Canadian	3	4	Stanley Cup finals	Dick Irvin
1935-36	23	19	6	—	52	2nd/Canadian	4	5	Stanley Cup finals	Dick Irvin
1936-37	22	21	5	—	49	3rd/Canadian	0	2	Quarterfinals	Dick Irvin
1937-38	24	15	9	—	57	1st/Canadian			Stanley Cup finals	Dick Irvin
1938-39	19	20	9	—	47	3rd	5	5	Stanley Cup finals	Dick Irvin
1939-40	25	17	6	—	56	3rd	6	4	Stanley Cup finals	Dick Irvin
1940-41	28	14	6	—	62	2nd	3	4	Semifinals	Hap Day
1941-42	27	18	3	—	57	2nd	8	5	Stanley Cup champ	Hap Day
1942-43	22	19	9	—	53	3rd	2	4	League semifinals	Hap Day
1943-44	23	23	4	—	50	3rd	1	4	League semifinals	Hap Day
1944-45	24	22	4	—	52	3rd	8	5	Stanley Cup champ	Hap Day
1945-46	19	24	7	—	45	5th	—	—		Hap Day
1946-47	31	19	10	—	72	2nd	8	3	Stanley Cup champ	Hap Day
1947-48	32	15	13	—	77	1st	8	1	Stanley Cup champ	Hap Day
1948-49	22	25	13	—	57	4th	8	1	Stanley Cup champ	Hap Day
1949-50	31	27	12	—	74	3rd	3	4	League semifinals	Hap Day
1950-51	41	16	13	—	95	2nd	†8	2	Stanley Cup champ	Joe Primeau
1951-52	29	25	16	—	74	3rd	0	4	League semifinals	Joe Primeau
1952-53	27	30	13	—	67	5th	—	—		Joe Primeau
1953-54	32	24	14	—	78	3rd	1	4	League semifinals	King Clancy
1954-55	24	24	22	—	70	3rd	0	4	League semifinals	King Clancy
1955-56	24	33	13	—	61	4th	1	4	League semifinals	King Clancy
1956-57	21	34	15	—	57	5th	—	—		Howie Meeker

Season	W	L	T	OTL	Pts.	Finish	W	L	Highest round	Coach
	REGULAR SEASON						PLAYOFFS			
1957-58	21	38	11	—	53	6th	—	—		Billy Reay
1958-59	27	32	11	—	65	4th	5	7	Stanley Cup finals	Billy Reay, Punch Imlach
1959-60	35	26	9	—	79	2nd	4	6	Stanley Cup finals	Punch Imlach
1960-61	39	19	12	—	90	2nd	1	4	League semifinals	Punch Imlach
1961-62	37	22	11	—	85	2nd	8	4	Stanley Cup champ	Punch Imlach
1962-63	35	23	12	—	82	1st	8	2	Stanley Cup champ	Punch Imlach
1963-64	33	25	12	—	78	3rd	8	6	Stanley Cup champ	Punch Imlach
1964-65	30	26	14	—	74	4th	2	4	League semifinals	Punch Imlach
1965-66	34	25	11	—	79	3rd	0	4	League semifinals	Punch Imlach
1966-67	32	27	11	—	75	3rd	8	4	Stanley Cup champ	Punch Imlach
1967-68	33	31	10	—	76	5th/East	—	—		Punch Imlach
1968-69	35	26	15	—	85	4th/East	0	4	Division semifinals	Punch Imlach
1969-70	29	34	13	—	71	6th/East	—	—		John McLellan
1970-71	37	33	8	—	82	4th/East	2	4	Division semifinals	John McLellan
1971-72	33	31	14	—	80	4th/East	1	4	Division semifinals	John McLellan
1972-73	27	41	10	—	64	6th/East	—	—		John McLellan
1973-74	35	27	16	—	86	4th/East	0	4	Division semifinals	Red Kelly
1974-75	31	33	16	—	78	3rd/Adams	2	5	Quarterfinals	Red Kelly
1975-76	34	31	15	—	83	3rd/Adams	5	5	Quarterfinals	Red Kelly
1976-77	33	32	15	—	81	3rd/Adams	4	5	Quarterfinals	Red Kelly
1977-78	41	29	10	—	92	3rd/Adams	6	7	Semifinals	Roger Neilson
1978-79	34	33	13	—	81	3rd/Adams	2	4	Quarterfinals	Roger Neilson
1979-80	35	40	5	—	75	4th/Adams	0	3	Preliminaries	Floyd Smith
1980-81	28	37	15	—	71	5th/Adams	0	3	Preliminaries	Punch Imlach, Joe Crozier
1981-82	20	44	16	—	56	5th/Norris	—	—		Mike Nykoluk
1982-83	28	40	12	—	68	3rd/Norris	1	3	Division semifinals	Mike Nykoluk
1983-84	26	45	9	—	61	5th/Norris	—	—		Mike Nykoluk
1984-85	20	52	8	—	48	5th/Norris	—	—		Dan Maloney
1985-86	25	48	7	—	57	4th/Norris	6	4	Division finals	Dan Maloney
1986-87	32	42	6	—	70	4th/Norris	7	6	Division finals	John Brophy
1987-88	21	49	10	—	52	4th/Norris	2	4	Division semifinals	John Brophy
1988-89	28	46	6	—	62	5th/Norris	—	—		John Brophy, George Armstrong
1989-90	38	38	4	—	80	3rd/Norris	1	4	Division semifinals	Doug Carpenter
1990-91	23	46	11	—	57	5th/Norris	—	—		Doug Carpenter, Tom Watt
1991-92	30	43	7	—	67	5th/Norris	—	—		Tom Watt
1992-93	44	29	11	—	99	3rd/Norris	11	10	Conference finals	Pat Burns
1993-94	43	29	12	—	98	2nd/Central	9	9	Conference finals	Pat Burns
1994-95	21	19	8	—	50	4th/Central	3	4	Conference quarterfinals	Pat Burns
1995-96	34	36	12	—	80	3rd/Central	2	4	Conference quarterfinals	Pat Burns, Nick Beverley
1996-97	30	44	8	—	68	6th/Central	—	—		Mike Murphy
1997-98	30	43	9	—	69	6th/Central	—	—		Mike Murphy
1998-99	45	30	7	—	97	2nd/Northeast	9	8	Conference finals	Pat Quinn
1999-00	45	27	7	3	100	1st/Northeast	6	6	Conference semifinals	Pat Quinn
2000-01	37	29	11	5	90	3rd/Northeast	7	4	Conference semifinals	Pat Quinn
2001-02	43	25	10	4	100	2nd/Northeast	10	10	Conference finals	Pat Quinn
2002-03	44	28	7	3	98	2nd/Northeast	3	4	Conference quarterfinals	Pat Quinn
2003-04	45	24	10	3	104	2nd/Northeast	6	7	Conference semifinals	Pat Quinn
2004-05		No season—Lockout								
2005-06	41	33	—	8	90	4th/Northeast	—	—	—	Pat Quinn

*Won-lost record does not indicate tie(s) resulting from two-game, total-goals series that year (two-game, total-goals series were played from 1917-18 through 1935-36).

†Game 2 semifinals vs. Boston tied 1-1 after one overtime (curfew law).

‡Toronto Arenas.

§Toronto St. Patricks (until April 14, 1927).

FIRST-ROUND ENTRY DRAFT CHOICES

Year Player, Overall, Last amateur team (league)

1969—Ernie Moser, 9, Esteven (WCHL)
1970—Darryl Sittler, 8, London (OHL)
1971—No first-round selection
1972—George Ferguson, 11, Toronto (OHL)
1973—Lanny McDonald, 4, Medicine Hat (WCHL)
Bob Neely, 10, Peterborough (OHL)
Ian Turnbull, 15, Ottawa (OHL)
1974—Jack Valiquette, 13, Sault Ste. Marie (OHL)
1975—Don Ashby, 6, Calgary (WCHL)
1976—No first-round selection
1977—John Anderson, 11, Toronto (OHA)
Trevor Johansen, 12, Toronto (OHA)
1978—No first-round selection

Year Player, Overall, Last amateur team (league)

1979—Laurie Boschman, 9, Brandon (WHL)
1980—No first-round selection
1981—Jim Benning, 6, Portland (WHL)
1982—Gary Nylund, 3, Portland (WHL)
1983—Russ Courtnall, 7, Victoria (WHL)
1984—Al Iafrate, 4, U.S. Olympics/Belleville (OHL)
1985—Wendel Clark, 1, Saskatoon (WHL)
1986—Vincent Damphousse, 6, Laval (QMJHL)
1987—Luke Richardson, 7, Peterborough (OHL)
1988—Scott Pearson, 6, Kingston (OHL)
1989—Scott Thornton, 3, Belleville (OHL)
Rob Pearson, 12, Belleville (OHL)
Steve Bancroft, 21, Belleville (OHL)

Year	Player, Overall, Last amateur team (league)
1990	Drake Berehowsky, 10, Kingston (OHL)
1991	No first-round selection
1992	Brandon Convery, 8, Sudbury (OHL) Grant Marshall, 23, Ottawa (OHL)
1993	Kenny Jonsson, 12, Rogle (Sweden) Landon Wilson, 19, Dubuque (USHL)
1994	Eric Fichaud, 16, Chicoutimi (QMJHL)
1995	Jeff Ware, 15, Oshawa (OHL)
1996	No first-round selection
1997	No first-round selection

Year	Player, Overall, Last amateur team (league)
1998	Nikolai Antropov, 10, Torpedo (Russia)
1999	Luca Cereda, 24, Ambri (Switzerland)
2000	Brad Boyes, 24, Erie (OHL)
2001	Carlo Colaiacovo, 17, Erie (OHL)
2002	Alexander Steen, 24, Frolunda (Sweden)
2003	No first-round selection
2004	No first-round selection
2005	Tuuka Rask, 21, Ilves (Finland Jr.)
2006	Jiri Tlusty, 13, Kladno, Czech Republic

SINGLE-SEASON INDIVIDUAL RECORDS

FORWARDS/DEFENSEMEN

Most goals
54—Rick Vaive, 1981-82

Most assists
95—Doug Gilmour, 1992-93

Most points
127—Doug Gilmour, 1992-93

Most penalty minutes
365—Tie Domi, 1997-98

Most power play goals
21—Dave Andreychuk, 1993-94
Wendell Clark, 1993-94

Most shorthanded goals
8—Dave Keon, 1970-71
Dave Reid, 1990-91

Most games with three or more goals
5—Darryl Sittler, 1980-81

Most shots
346—Darryl Sittler, 1975-76

GOALTENDERS

Most games
74—Felix Potvin, 1996-97

Most minutes
4,271—Felix Potvin, 1996-97

Most goals allowed
230—Grant Fuhr, 1991-92

Lowest goals-against average
1.61—Lorne Chabot, 1928-29

Most shutouts
13—Harry Lumley, 1953-54

Most wins
37—Ed Belfour, 2002-03

Most losses
38—Ed Chadwick, 1957-58

Most ties
22—Harry Lumley, 1954-55

VANCOUVER CANUCKS

YEAR-BY-YEAR RECORDS

	REGULAR SEASON						PLAYOFFS			
Season	W	L	T	OTL	Pts.	Finish	W	L	Highest round	Coach
1970-71	24	46	8	—	56	6th/East	—	—		Hal Laycoe
1971-72	20	50	8	—	48	7th/East	—	—		Hal Laycoe
1972-73	22	47	9	—	53	7th/East	—	—		Vic Stasiuk
1973-74	24	43	11	—	59	7th/East	—	—		Bill McCreary, Phil Maloney
1974-75	38	32	10	—	86	1st/Smythe	1	4	Quarterfinals	Phil Maloney
1975-76	33	32	15	—	81	2nd/Smythe	0	2	Preliminaries	Phil Maloney
1976-77	25	42	13	—	63	4th/Smythe	—	—		Phil Maloney, Orland Kurtenbach
1977-78	20	43	17	—	57	3rd/Smythe	—	—		Orland Kurtenbach
1978-79	25	42	13	—	63	2nd/Smythe	1	2	Preliminaries	Harry Neale
1979-80	27	37	16	—	70	3rd/Smythe	1	3	Preliminaries	Harry Neale
1980-81	28	32	20	—	76	3rd/Smythe	0	3	Preliminaries	Harry Neale
1981-82	30	33	17	—	77	2nd/Smythe	11	6	Stanley Cup finals	Harry Neale, Roger Neilson
1982-83	30	35	15	—	75	3rd/Smythe	1	3	Division semifinals	Roger Neilson
1983-84	32	39	9	—	73	3rd/Smythe	1	3	Division semifinals	Roger Neilson, Harry Neale
1984-85	25	46	9	—	59	5th/Smythe	—	—		Bill Laforge, Harry Neale
1985-86	23	44	13	—	59	4th/Smythe	0	3	Division semifinals	Tom Watt
1986-87	29	43	8	—	66	5th/Smythe	—	—		Tom Watt
1987-88	25	46	9	—	59	5th/Smythe	—	—		Bob McCammon
1988-89	33	39	8	—	74	4th/Smythe	3	4	Division semifinals	Bob McCammon
1989-90	25	41	14	—	64	5th/Smythe	—	—		Bob McCammon
1990-91	28	43	9	—	65	4th/Smythe	2	4	Division semifinals	Bob McCammon, Pat Quinn
1991-92	42	26	12	—	96	1st/Smythe	6	7	Division finals	Pat Quinn
1992-93	46	29	9	—	101	1st/Smythe	6	6	Division finals	Pat Quinn
1993-94	41	40	3	—	85	2nd/Pacific	15	9	Stanley Cup finals	Pat Quinn
1994-95	18	18	12	—	48	2nd/Pacific	4	7	Conference semifinals	Rick Ley
1995-96	32	35	15	—	79	3rd/Pacific	2	4	Conference quarterfinals	Rick Ley, Pat Quinn
1996-97	35	40	7	—	77	4th/Pacific	—	—		Tom Renney
1997-98	25	43	14	—	64	7th/Pacific	—	—		Tom Renney, Mike Keenan
1998-99	23	47	12	—	58	4th/Northwest	—	—		Mike Keenan, Marc Crawford
1999-00	30	29	15	8	83	3rd/Northwest	—	—		Marc Crawford
2000-01	36	28	11	7	90	3rd/Northwest	0	4	Conference quarterfinals	Marc Crawford
2001-02	42	30	7	3	94	2nd/Northwest	2	4	Conference quarterfinals	Marc Crawford
2002-03	45	23	13	1	104	2nd/Northwest	7	7	Conference semifinals	Marc Crawford
2003-04	43	24	10	5	101	1st/Northwest	3	4	Conference quarterfinals	Marc Crawford
2004-05			No season—Lockout							
2005-06	42	32	—	8	92	4th/Northwest	—	—	—	Marc Crawford

FIRST-ROUND ENTRY DRAFT CHOICES

Year Player, Overall, Last amateur team (league)
1970—Dale Tallon, 2, Toronto (OHL)
1971—Jocelyn Guevremont, 3, Montreal (OHL)
1972—Don Lever, 3, Niagara Falls (OHL)
1973—Dennis Ververgaert, 3, London (OHL)
Bob Dailey, 9, Toronto (OHL)
1974—No first-round selection
1975—Rick Blight, 10, Brandon (WCHL)
1976—No first-round selection
1977—Jere Gillis, 4, Sherbrooke (QMJHL)
1978—Bill Derlago, 4, Brandon (WCHL)
1979—Rick Vaive, 5, Birmingham (WHA)
1980—Rick Lanz, 7, Oshawa (OHL)
1981—Garth Butcher, 10, Regina (WHL)
1982—Michel Petit, 11, Sherbrooke (QMJHL)
1983—Cam Neely, 9, Portland (WHL)
1984—J.J. Daigneault, 10, Can. Ol./Longueuil (QMJHL)
1985—Jim Sandlak, 4, London (OHL)
1986—Dan Woodley, 7, Portland (WHL)
1987—No first-round selection
1988—Trevor Linden, 2, Medicine Hat (WHL)
1989—Jason Herter, 8, University of North Dakota

Year Player, Overall, Last amateur team (league)
1990—Petr Nedved, 2, Seattle (WHL)
Shawn Antoski, 18, North Bay (OHL)
1991—Alex Stojanov, 7, Hamilton (OHL)
1992—Libor Polasek, 21, TJ Vikovice (Czech.)
1993—Mike Wilson, 20, Sudbury (OHL)
1994—Mattias Ohlund, 13, Pitea Div. I (Sweden)
1995—No first-round selection
1996—Josh Holden, 12, Regina (WHL)
1997—Brad Ference, 10, Spokane (WHL)
1998—Bryan Allen, 4, Oshawa (OHL)
1999—Daniel Sedin, 2, Modo Ornskoldsvik, Sweden
Henrik Sedin, 3, Modo Ornskoldsvik, Sweden
2000—Nathan Smith, 23, Swift Current (WHL)
2001—R.J. Umberger, 16, Ohio State
2002—No first-round selection
2003—Ryan Kesler, 23, Ohio State (CCHA)
2004—Cory Schneider, 26, Phillips-Andover (USHSE)
2005—Luc Bourdon, 10, Val d'Or (QMJHL)
2006—Michael Grabner, 14, Spokane (WHL)

SINGLE-SEASON INDIVIDUAL RECORDS

FORWARDS/DEFENSEMEN

Most goals
60—Pavel Bure, 1992-93
Pavel Bure, 1993-94

Most assists
62—Andre Boudrias, 1974-75

Most points
110—Pavel Bure, 1992-93

Most penalty minutes
372—Donald Brashear, 1997-98

Most power play goals
25—Pavel Bure, 1993-94
Todd Bertuzzi, 2002-03

Most shorthanded goals
7—Pavel Bure, 1992-93

Most games with three or more goals
4—Petri Skriko, 1986-87

Most shots
407—Pavel Bure, 1992-93

GOALTENDERS

Most games
72—Gary Smith, 1974-75

Most minutes
3,859—Alexander Auld, 2005-06

Most shots against
1,938—Alexander Auld, 2005-06

Most goals allowed
240—Richard Brodeur, 1985-86

Lowest goals-against average
2.27—Dan Cloutier, 2003-04

Most shutouts
7—Dan Cloutier, 2002-03

Most wins
38—Kirk McLean, 1991-92

Most losses
33—Gary Smith, 1973-74

Most ties
16—Richard Brodeur, 1980-81

WASHINGTON CAPITALS

YEAR-BY-YEAR RECORDS

	REGULAR SEASON						PLAYOFFS			
Season	W	L	T	OTL	Pts.	Finish	W	L	Highest round	Coach
1974-75	8	67	5	—	21	5th/Norris	—	—		Jim Anderson, Red Sullivan, Milt Schmidt
1975-76	11	59	10	—	32	5th/Norris	—	—		Milt Schmidt, Tom McVie
1976-77	24	42	14	—	62	4th/Norris	—	—		Tom McVie
1977-78	17	49	14	—	48	5th/Norris	—	—		Tom McVie
1978-79	24	41	15	—	63	4th/Norris	—	—		Dan Belisle
1979-80	27	40	13	—	67	5th/Patrick	—	—		Dan Belisle, Gary Green
1980-81	26	36	18	—	70	5th/Patrick	—	—		Gary Green
1981-82	26	41	13	—	65	5th/Patrick	—	—		Gary Green, Roger Crozier, Bryan Murray
1982-83	39	25	16	—	94	3rd/Patrick	1	3	Division semifinals	Bryan Murray
1983-84	48	27	5	—	101	2nd/Patrick	4	4	Division finals	Bryan Murray
1984-85	46	25	9	—	101	2nd/Patrick	2	3	Division semifinals	Bryan Murray
1985-86	50	23	7	—	107	2nd/Patrick	5	4	Division finals	Bryan Murray
1986-87	38	32	10	—	86	2nd/Patrick	3	4	Division semifinals	Bryan Murray
1987-88	38	33	9	—	85	2nd/Patrick	7	7	Division finals	Bryan Murray
1988-89	41	29	10	—	92	1st/Patrick	2	4	Division semifinals	Bryan Murray
1989-90	36	38	6	—	78	3rd/Patrick	8	7	Conference finals	Bryan Murray, Terry Murray
1990-91	37	36	7	—	81	3rd/Patrick	5	6	Division finals	Terry Murray
1991-92	45	27	8	—	98	2nd/Patrick	3	4	Division semifinals	Terry Murray
1992-93	43	34	7	—	93	2nd/Patrick	2	4	Division semifinals	Terry Murray

	REGULAR SEASON						PLAYOFFS			
Season	W	L	T	OTL	Pts.	Finish	W	L	Highest round	Coach
1993-94	39	35	10	—	88	3rd/Atlantic	5	6	Conference semifinals	Terry Murray, Jim Schoenfeld
1994-95	22	18	8	—	52	3rd/Atlantic	3	4	Conference quarterfinals	Jim Schoenfeld
1995-96	39	32	11	—	89	4th/Atlantic	2	4	Conference quarterfinals	Jim Schoenfeld
1996-97	33	40	9	—	75	5th/Atlantic	—	—		Jim Schoenfeld
1997-98	40	30	12	—	92	3rd/Atlantic	12	9	Stanley Cup finals	Ron Wilson
1998-99	31	45	6	—	68	3rd/Southeast	—	—		Ron Wilson
1999-00	44	24	12	2	102	1st/Southeast	1	4	Conference quarterfinals	Ron Wilson
2000-01	41	27	10	4	96	1st/Southeast	2	4	Conference quarterfinals	Ron Wilson
2001-02	36	33	11	2	85	2nd/Southeast	—	—		Ron Wilson
2002-03	39	29	8	6	92	2nd/Southeast	2	4	Conference quarterfinals	Bruce Cassidy
2003-04	23	46	10	3	59	5th/Southeast	—	—		Bruce Cassidy, Glen Hanlon
2004-05	No season—Lockout									
2005-06	29	41	—	12	70	5th/Southeast	—	—		Glen Hanlon

FIRST-ROUND ENTRY DRAFT CHOICES

Year Player, Overall, Last amateur team (league)

1974—Greg Joly, 1, Regina (WCHL)
1975—Alex Forsyth, 18, Kingston (OHA)
1976—Rick Green, 1, London (OHL)
Greg Carroll, 15, Medicine Hat (WCHL)
1977—Robert Picard, 3, Montreal (QMJHL)
1978—Ryan Walter, 2, Seattle (WCHL)
Tim Coulis, 18, Hamilton (OHL)
1979—Mike Gartner, 4, Cincinnati (WHA)
1980—Darren Veitch, 5, Regina (WHL)
1981—Bobby Carpenter, 3, St. John's H.S. (Mass.)
1982—Scott Stevens, 5, Kitchener (OHL)
1983—No first-round selection
1984—Kevin Hatcher, 17, North Bay (OHL)
1985—Yvon Corriveau, 19, Toronto (OHL)
1986—Jeff Greenlaw, 19, Team Canada
1987—No first-round selection
1988—Reggie Savage, 15, Victoriaville (QMJHL)
1989—Olaf Kolzig, 19, Tri-City (WHL)
1990—John Slaney, 9, Cornwall (OHL)
1991—Pat Peake, 14, Detroit (OHL)
Trevor Halverson, 21, North Bay (OHL)
1992—Sergei Gonchar, 14, Dynamo Moscow, CIS
1993—Brendan Witt, 11, Seattle (WHL)
Jason Allison, 17, London (OHL)

Year Player, Overall, Last amateur team (league)

1994—Nolan Baumgartner, 10, Kamloops (WHL)
Alexander Kharlamov, 15, CSKA Moscow, CIS
1995—Brad Church, 17, Prince Albert (WHL)
Miikka Elomo, 23, Kiekko-67, Finland
1996—Alexander Volchkov, 4, Barrie (OHL)
Jaroslav Svejkovsky, 17, Tri-City (WHL)
1997—Nick Boynton, 9, Ottawa (OHL)
1998—No first-round selection
1999—Kris Breech, 7, Calgary (WHL)
2000—Brian Sutherby, 26, Moose Jaw (WHL)
2001—No first-round selection
2002—Steve Eminger, 12, Kitchener (OHL)
Alexander Syemin, 13, Chelyabinsk, Russia
Boyd Gordon, 17, Red Deer (WHL)
2003—Eric Fehr, 18, Brandon (WHL)
2004—Alexander Ovechkin, 1, Dynamo Moscow, Russia
Jeff Schultz, 27, Calgary (WHL)
Mike Green, 29, Saskatoon (WHL)
2005—Sasha Pokulok, 14, Cornell (ECAC)
Joe Finley, 27, Sioux Falls (USHL)
2006—Nicklas Backstrom, 4, Brynas, Sweden
Semen Varlamov, 23, Yaroslavl 2, Russia

SINGLE-SEASON INDIVIDUAL RECORDS

FORWARDS/DEFENSEMEN

Most goals
60—Dennis Maruk, 1981-82

Most assists
76—Dennis Maruk, 1981-82

Most points
136—Dennis Maruk, 1981-82

Most penalty minutes
339—Alan May, 1989-90

Most power play goals
22—Peter Bondra, 2000-01

Most shorthanded goals
6—Mike Gartner, 1986-87
Peter Bondra, 1994-95

Most games with three or more goals
4—Dennis Maruk, 1980-81
Dennis Maruk, 1981-82
Peter Bondra, 1995-96

Most shots
425—Alexander Ovechkin, 2005-06

GOALTENDERS

Most games
73—Olaf Kolzig, 1999-2000

Most minutes
4,371—Olaf Kolzig, 1999-2000

Most shots against
1,987—Olaf Kolzig, 2005-06

Most goals allowed
235—Ron Low, 1974-75

Lowest goals-against average
2.13—Jim Carey, 1994-95

Most shutouts
9—Jim Carey, 1995-96

Most wins
41—Olaf Kolzig, 1999-2000

Most losses
36—Ron Low, 1974-75

Most ties
11—Olaf Kolzig, 1999-2000

Sporting News
BOOKS

PLAYER REGISTER

2006-2007 EDITION

:S AND ABBREVIATIONS

* National Hockey Leagu

† Indicates tied for NHL l

. . . Statistic unavailable, ucalculate.

— Statistic inapplicable.

POSITIONS: C: center. **D:** de **RW:** right winger.

STATISTICS: A: assists. **GAA**als against. **GP:** games played. **L:** losses. **Min.:** minutes. **PIM.:** penalties in minutes. **+/-:** plus. **SH:** shorthanded goals. **SO:** shutouts. **SV%:** save percentage. **T:** ties. **W:** wins.

TEAMS: Bloom. Jefferson: Chemopetrol Litvinov. **Chem. Litvinov Jrs.:** Chemopetrol Litvinov Juniors. **Culver Mil. Acad.: : team:** Czechoslovakian Olympic team. **Czech Rep. Oly. team:** Czech Republic Olympic teakian Junior national team. **Det. Little Caesars:** Detroit Little Caesars. **Djur. Stockholm: Yek.:** Dynamo-Energiya Yekaterinburg. **Dyn.-Energiya 2 Yek.:** Dynamo-Energiya 2 YekateriUst-Kamenogorsk. **Fin. Olympic team:** Finnish Olympic team. **German Oly. team:** German ce Budejovice. **HK 32 Lip. Mikulas:** HK 32 Liptovsky Mikulas. **IS Banska Byst.:** IS Banska Byarhut Jodusuu. **Krylja Sov. Moscow:** Krylja Sovetov Moscow. **Mass.-Lowell:** Massachusetg Cherepovets. **Metal. Magnitogorsk:** Metallurg Magnitogorsk. **Metallurg-2 Novok.:** Metall: Modo Ornskoldsvik Jrs. **Motor Ceske Bude.:** Motor Ceske Budejovice. **N. Yarmouth Azona Univ.:** Northern Arizona University. **N. Michigan Univ.:** Northern Michigan Universiericans Junior B. **Poji. Pardubice Jrs.:** Pojistovna Pardubice Juniors. **Prin. Edward Islandm:** Russian Olympic team. **Sault Ste. Marie:** Sault Sainte Marie. **Sever. Cherepovets:** Severstvakian Olympic team. **Sov. Olympic team:** Soviet Olympic team. **Spisska N.V.:** Spisska Nova dec Kralove. **Swed. Olympic team:** Swedish Olympic team. **Tor. Nizhny Nov.:** Torpedo NizhnyUst-Kamenogorsk. **Ukrainian Oly. team:** Ukrainian Olympic team. **Unif. Olympic team:** Unified versity of New Hampshire. **Univ. of West. Ontario:** University of Western Ontario. **V. Frolund**

LEAGUES: AAHL: All Americ Hockey League. **AHL:** American Hockey League. **AJHL:** Alberta Junior Hockey League. **AMHI**tlantic Universities Athletic Association. **BCJHL:** British Columbia Junior Hockey League. **CAHL:** Central Alberta Junior Hockey League. **Can. College:** Canadian College. **Can.HL:** Canadian iate Hockey Association. **CHL:** Central Hockey League. **CIS:** Commonwealth of Independy League. **COJHL:** Central Ontario Junior Hockey League. **CPHL:** Central Professional Hockeyity Athletic Association. **Conn. H.S.:** Connecticut High School. **Czech.:** Czechoslovakia. **Czeep.:** Czech Republic. **ECAC:** Eastern College Athletic Conference. **ECAC-II:** Eastern College Ath Coast Hockey League. **EEHL:** Eastern European Hockey League. **EHL:** Eastern Hockey Leagueermany. **GWHC:** Great Western Hockey Conference. **Hoc. East:** Hockey East. **IHL:** Internation School. **Indiana H.S.:** Indiana High School. **Int'l:** International. **KIJHL:** Kootenay Internationassachusetts High School. **Md. H.S.:** Maryland High School. **Met. Bos.:** Metro Boston. **Mich. S.:** Minnesota High School. **MJHL:** Manitoba Junior Hockey League. **MTHL:** Metro TorAmerican Hockey League. **NAJHL:** North American Junior Hockey League. **N.B. H.S.II:** National Collegiate Athletic Association, Division II. **N.D. H.S.:** North Dakota High Hockey League. **NHL:** National Hockey League. **N.H. H.S.:** New Hampshire High School. **Nia. D. Jr. C:** Niagara District Junior C. **NSJHL:** Nova Scotia Junior Hockey LeaA. **N.Y. H.S.:** New York High School. **NYMJHL:** New York Major Junior Hockey Leagkey League. **ODHA:** Ottawa & District Hockey Association. **OHA:** Ontario Hockey Assy Association Junior A. **OHA Mjr. Jr. A:** Ontario Hockey Association Major Junior ciation Senior. **OHL:** Ontario Hockey League. **O.H.S.:** Ohio High School. **OJHA:** OntaL: Ontario Junior Hockey League. **OMJHL:** Ontario Major Junior Hockey League. **OP**y League. **OUAA:** Ontario Universities Athletic Association. **PCJHL:** Peace Caribou JuEdward Island Hockey Association. **PEIJHL:** Prince Edward Island Junior Hockey LeagSchool. **QMJHL:** Quebec Major Junior Hockey League. **R.I. H.S.:** Rhode Island High ision II, III. **SAJHL:** Southern Alberta Junior Hockey League. **SJHL:** Saskatchewan Junior lan High School. **SOJHL:** Southern Ontario Junior Hockey League. **Swed. Jr.:** Sweden Junior. **S**Amateur Hockey Association. **TBJHL:** Thunder Bay Junior Hockey League. **UHL:** United Hockeyeague. **USHS:** United States High School. **USSR:** Union of Soviet Socialist Republics. **Vt. H.S, W. Ger.:** West Germany. **WCHA:** Western Collegiate Hockey Association. **WCHL:** WesterHockey Association. **WHL:** Western Hockey League. **Wisc. H.S.:** Wisconsin High School. **Yuk**

VETERANS AND TOP F

ABID, RAMZI LW

PERSONAL: Born March 24, 1980, in Montreal. ... 6-2/210. ... Shoots left.... Name pron

TRANSACTIONS/CAREER NOTES: Selected by Colorado Avalanche in second round (fifaft (June 27, 1998). ... Returned to draft pool by Avalanche and selected by Phoenix Coyotes in tl of entry draft (June 24, 2000). ... Traded by Coyotes with D Dan Focht and LW Guillaume Lefebna and D Francois Leroux (March 11, 2003). ... Injured knee (March 18, 2003); missed nine gamesed final 57 games of season. ... Signed as free agent by Atlanta Thrashers (August 8, 2005). ... S(July 21, 2006).

Season Team	League	GP	G	A	Pts.	PIM	+/-	PP	PIM
		REGULAR SEASON							
96-97—Chicoutimi	QMJHL	65	13	24	37	151	...	...	—
97-98—Chicoutimi	QMJHL	68	50	85	135	266	...	...	10
98-99—Chicoutimi	QMJHL	21	11	15	26	97	-4	2	—
—Acadie-Bathurst	QMJHL	24	14	22	36	102	11	3	84
99-00—Acadie-Bathurst	QMJHL	13	10	11	21	61	10	0	—
—Halifax	QMJHL	59	57	80	137	148	29	18	18
00-01—Springfield	AHL	17	6	4	10	38	...	...	—
01-02—Springfield	AHL	66	18	25	43	214	-4	7	—
02-03—Springfield	AHL	27	15	10	25	50	-1	9	—
—Phoenix	NHL	30	10	8	18	30	1	4	—
—Pittsburgh	NHL	3	0	0	0	2	-5	0	—
03-04—Pittsburgh	NHL	16	3	2	5	27	-5	2	—
04-05—Wilkes-Barre/Scranton	AHL	78	26	29	55	119	1	10	18
05-06—Chicago	AHL	75	34	42	76	165	-3	18	—
—Atlanta	NHL	6	0	2	2	6	1	0	—
NHL Totals (3 years)		55	13	12	25	65	-8	6	

ADAMS, CRAIG RW

PERSONAL: Born April 26, 1977, in Seria, Brunei. ... 6-0/200. ... Shoots right.

TRANSACTIONS/CAREER NOTES: Selected by Hartford Whalers in the ninth round (ninthraft (June 22, 1996). ... Whalers franchise moved to North Carolina and renamed Carolina Hurricane on June 25, 1997. ... Bruised chest (November 30, 2000); missed four games. ... Suspended 10 g3, 2002). ... Signed as free agent by Anaheim Mighty Ducks (August 25, 2005). ... Traded by the Mig Jacques (October 3, 2005).

Season Team	League	GP	G	A	Pts.	PIM	+/-	PP	PIM
		REGULAR SEASON							
95-96—Harvard	ECAC	34	8	9	17	56	...	...	—
96-97—Harvard	ECAC	32	6	4	10	36	...	0	—
97-98—Harvard	ECAC	23	6	6	12	12	...	...	—
98-99—Harvard	ECAC	31	9	14	23	53	...	...	—
99-00—Cincinnati	IHL	73	12	12	24	124	...	...	14
00-01—Carolina	NHL	44	1	0	1	20	-7	0	0
—Cincinnati	IHL	4	0	1	1	9	...	...	2
01-02—Carolina	NHL	33	0	1	1	38	2	0	0
—Lowell	AHL	22	5	4	9	51	2	0	—
02-03—Carolina	NHL	81	6	12	18	71	-11	1	—
03-04—Carolina	NHL	80	7	10	17	69	-5	0	—
04-05—Milano	Italy	30	15	14	29	82	...	...	26
05-06—Lowell	AHL	13	4	3	7	20	-1	1	—
—Carolina	NHL	67	10	11	21	51	1	1	10
NHL Totals (5 years)		305	24	34	58	249	-20	2	10

ADAMS, KEVYN C

PERSONAL: Born October 8, 1974, in Washington, D.C. ... 6-2/195. ... Shoots right.

TRANSACTIONS/CAREER NOTES: Selected by Boston Bruins in first round (first Bruins 1993). ... Signed as free agent by Toronto Maple Leafs (August 1, 1997). ... Selected by Columbus 2000). ... Strained gluteal muscle (December 13, 2000); missed two games. ... Traded by Blue JacWoodford) in 2001 draft to Florida Panthers for LW Ray Whitney and future considerations (March 13 Hedican, D Tomas Malec and future considerations to Carolina Hurricanes for D Sandis Ozolinsh . Infected knee (january 21, 2004); missed one game. ... Injured left knee (january 30, 2004); misse

Season Team	League	GP	G	A	Pts.	PIM	+/-	PP	PIM
		REGULAR SEASON							
90-91—Niagara	NAJHL	55	17	20	37	24	...	...	—
91-92—Niagara	NAJHL	40	25	33	58	51	...	...	—
92-93—Miami (Ohio)	CCHA	41	17	16	33	18	...	2	—
93-94—Miami (Ohio)	CCHA	36	15	28	43	24	9	3	—
94-95—Miami (Ohio)	CCHA	38	20	29	49	30	5	5	—
95-96—Miami (Ohio)	CCHA	36	17	30	47	30	...	...	—
96-97—Grand Rapids	IHL	82	22	25	47	47	...	...	4
97-98—Toronto	NHL	5	0	0	0	7	0	0	—
—St. John's	AHL	58	17	21	38	99	-5	3	4

Season Team	League	GP	G	A	Pts.	PIM	+/-	PP	SH	GP	G	A	Pts.	PIM
		REGULAR SEASON								PLAYOFFS				
98-99—St. John's	AHL	80	15	35	50	85	-2	1	1	5	2	0	2	4
—Toronto	NHL	1	0	0	0	0	0	0	0	7	0	2	2	14
99-00—St. John's	AHL	23	6	11	17	24	...	...	...	—	—	—	—	—
—Toronto	NHL	52	5	8	13	39	-7	0	0	12	1	0	1	7
00-01—Columbus	NHL	66	8	12	20	52	-4	0	0	—	—	—	—	—
—Florida	NHL	12	3	6	9	2	7	0	0	—	—	—	—	—
01-02—Florida	NHL	44	4	8	12	28	-3	0	0	—	—	—	—	—
—Carolina	NHL	33	2	3	5	15	-2	0	0	23	1	0	1	4
02-03—Carolina	NHL	77	9	9	18	57	-8	0	0	—	—	—	—	—
03-04—Carolina	NHL	73	10	12	22	43	6	0	5	—	—	—	—	—
04-05—DEG Metro Stars	Germany	9	1	2	3	4	0	0	0	—	—	—	—	—
05-06—Carolina	NHL	82	15	8	23	36	0	0	2	25	0	0	0	14
NHL Totals (8 years)		445	56	66	122	279	-11	0	7	67	2	2	4	39

AEBISCHER, DAVID G

PERSONAL: Born February 7, 1978, in Fribourg, Switzerland. ... 6-1/190. ... Catches left. ... Name pronounced EH-bih-shuhr.
TRANSACTIONS/CAREER NOTES: Selected by Colorado Avalanche in sixth round (seventh Avalanche pick, 161st overall) of NHL draft (June 21, 1997). ... Pharyngitis (November 25, 2000); missed one game. ... Traded by Avalanche to Montreal Canadiens for G Jose Theodore (March 8, 2006).

Season Team	League	GP	Min.	W	L	OTL	T	GA	SO	GAA	SV%	GP	Min.	W	L	GA	SO	GAA	SV%
		REGULAR SEASON										PLAYOFFS							
96-97—Fribourg-Gotteron	Switzerland	10	577	...	...	...	...	34	...	3.54	...	3	184	1	2	13	0	4.24	...
97-98—Fribourg-Gotteron	Switzerland	1	60	...	...	...	...	1	0	1.00	...	4	240	...	...	17	...	4.25	...
—Hershey	AHL	2	80	0	0	...	1	5	0	3.75	.853	—	—	—	—	—	—	—	—
—Chesapeake	ECHL	17	930	5	7	...	2	52	0	3.35	...	—	—	—	—	—	—	—	—
—Wheeling	ECHL	10	564	5	3	...	1	30	1	3.19	...	—	—	—	—	—	—	—	—
98-99—Hershey	AHL	38	1932	17	10	...	5	79	2	2.45	.920	3	152	1	2	6	0	2.37	.925
99-00—Hershey	AHL	58	3259	29	23	...	2	180	1	3.31	...	14	788	7	6	40	2	3.05	...
00-01—Colorado	NHL	26	1393	12	7	...	3	52	3	2.24	.903	1	1	0	0	0	0	0.00	...
01-02—Colorado	NHL	21	1184	13	6	...	0	37	2	1.88	.931	1	34	0	0	1	0	1.76	.929
—Swiss Olympic team	Int'l	2	81	0	1	...	1	6	0	4.44	.806	—	—	—	—	—	—	—	—
02-03—Colorado	NHL	22	1235	7	12	...	0	50	1	2.43	.916	—	—	—	—	—	—	—	—
03-04—Colorado	NHL	62	3703	32	19	...	9	129	4	2.09	.924	11	662	6	5	23	1	2.08	.922
04-05—Lugano	Switzerland	18	1019	12	2	...	3	41	0	2.41	...	4	...	1	3	8	0	2.02	...
05-06—Colorado	NHL	43	2477	25	14	2	...	123	3	2.98	.900	—	—	—	—	—	—	—	—
—Montreal	NHL	7	418	4	3	...	...	26	0	3.73	.892	—	—	—	—	—	—	—	—
—Swiss Olympic team	Int'l	4	...	...	...	...	...	...	0	2.10	.940	—	—	—	—	—	—	—	—
NHL Totals (5 years)		181	10410	93	61	2	12	417	13	2.40	.914	13	697	6	5	24	1	2.07	.922

AFANASENKOV, DIMITRY LW/RW

PERSONAL: Born May 12, 1980, in Arkhangelsk, U.S.S.R. ... 6-1/195. ... Shoots right. ... Name pronounced ah-fahn-ah-SEHN-kov.
TRANSACTIONS/CAREER NOTES: Selected by Tampa Bay Lightning in third round (third Lightning pick, 72nd overall) of draft (June 27, 1998).

Season Team	League	GP	G	A	Pts.	PIM	+/-	PP	SH	GP	G	A	Pts.	PIM
		REGULAR SEASON								PLAYOFFS				
95-96—Torpedo Yaroslavl	CIS Div. II	25	10	5	15	10	...	...	...	—	—	—	—	—
—Torpedo Yaroslavl	CIS Jr.	35	28	16	44	8	...	...	...	—	—	—	—	—
96-97—Torpedo Yaroslavl	Rus. Div.	45	20	15	35	14	...	...	...	—	—	—	—	—
97-98—Torpedo-Yaroslavl	Russian	45	19	11	30	28	...	...	...	—	—	—	—	—
98-99—Moncton	QMJHL	15	5	5	10	12	...	...	...	—	—	—	—	—
—Sherbrooke	QMJHL	51	23	30	53	22	...	...	...	13	10	6	16	6
99-00—Sherbrooke	QMJHL	60	56	43	99	70	6	18	3	5	3	2	5	4
00-01—Detroit	IHL	65	15	22	37	26	...	...	...	—	—	—	—	—
—Tampa Bay	NHL	9	1	1	2	4	1	0	0	—	—	—	—	—
01-02—Springfield	AHL	28	4	5	9	4	-2	0	0	—	—	—	—	—
—Grand Rapids	AHL	18	1	2	3	2	2	0	0	—	—	—	—	—
—Tampa Bay	NHL	5	0	0	0	0	-1	0	0	—	—	—	—	—
02-03—Springfield	AHL	41	4	9	13	25	...	...	...	—	—	—	—	—
03-04—Tampa Bay	NHL	71	6	10	16	12	-4	0	0	23	1	2	3	6
04-05—Lada Togliatti	Russian	30	2	9	11	12	11	...	...	9	0	0	0	4
05-06—Tampa Bay	NHL	68	9	6	15	16	-7	1	0	5	0	1	1	2
NHL Totals (4 years)		153	16	17	33	32	-11	1	0	28	1	3	4	8

AFINOGENOV, MAXIM RW

PERSONAL: Born September 4, 1979, in Moscow, U.S.S.R. ... 6-0/195. ... Shoots left. ... Name pronounced ah-FEEN-o-gin-ov.
TRANSACTIONS/CAREER NOTES: Selected by Buffalo Sabres in third round (third Sabres pick, 69th overall) of entry draft (June 21, 1997). ... Flu (january 10, 2002); missed one game. ... Concussion (September 5, 2002); missed first 46 games of season. ... Injured ribs (November 11, 2005); missed five games.
STATISTICAL PLATEAUS: Three-goal games: 2003-04 (1).

Season Team	League	GP	G	A	Pts.	PIM	+/-	PP	SH	GP	G	A	Pts.	PIM
		REGULAR SEASON								PLAYOFFS				
95-96—Dynamo Moscow	CIS	1	0	0	0	0	...	...	...	—	—	—	—	—
96-97—Dynamo Moscow	Russian	29	6	5	11	10	...	...	...	4	0	2	2	0

Season Team	League	GP	G	A	Pts.	PIM	+/-	PP	SH	GP	G	A	Pts.	PIM
		REGULAR SEASON								PLAYOFFS				
—Dynamo Moscow........	Rus. Div.	14	9	2	11	10	...	...	...	—	—	—	—	—
97-98—Dynamo Moscow........	Russian	35	10	5	15	53	...	...	...	—	—	—	—	—
98-99—Dynamo Moscow........	Russian	38	8	13	21	24	15	...	...	16	10	6	16	14
99-00—Rochester..................	AHL	15	6	12	18	8	...	...	...	8	3	1	4	4
—Buffalo........................	NHL	65	16	18	34	41	-4	2	0	5	0	1	1	2
00-01—Buffalo........................	NHL	78	14	22	36	40	1	3	0	11	2	3	5	4
01-02—Buffalo........................	NHL	81	21	19	40	69	-9	3	1	—	—	—	—	—
—Russian Oly. team.......	Int'l	6	2	2	4	4	...	...	...	—	—	—	—	—
02-03—Buffalo........................	NHL	35	5	6	11	21	-12	2	0	—	—	—	—	—
03-04—Buffalo........................	NHL	73	17	14	31	57	-4	3	0	—	—	—	—	—
04-05—Dynamo Moscow........	Russian	36	13	14	27	91	7	...	...	10	4	4	8	8
05-06—Buffalo........................	NHL	77	22	51	73	84	6	11	0	18	3	5	8	10
—Russian Oly. team.......	Int'l	8	1	0	1	10	-1	0	0	—	—	—	—	—
NHL Totals (6 years)...........		409	95	130	225	312	-22	24	1	34	5	9	14	16

ALBELIN, TOMMY D

PERSONAL: Born May 21, 1964, in Stockholm, Sweden. ... 6-2/195. ... Shoots left. ... Name pronounced AL-buh-leen.
TRANSACTIONS/CAREER NOTES: Selected by Quebec Nordiques in eighth round (seventh Nordiques pick, 152nd overall) of entry draft (June 8, 1983). ... Traded by Nordiques to New Jersey Devils for fourth-round pick (LW Niclas Andersson) in 1989 draft (December 12, 1988). ... Injured right knee (March 2, 1990); missed four games. ... Injured groin (November 21, 1992); missed two games. ... Urinary infection (1993-94 season); missed nine games. ... Bruised thigh (December 16, 1995); missed six games. ... Traded by Devils with D Cale Hulse and RW Jocelyn Lemieux to Calgary Flames for D Phil Housley and D Dan Keczmer (February 26, 1996). ... Strained groin (November 9, 1996); missed four games. ... Reinjured groin (November 25, 1996); missed two games. ... Strained abdominal muscle (December 7, 1996); missed five games. ... Concussion (November 11, 1997); missed three games. ... Pulled groin (November 27, 1997); missed three games. ... Reinjured groin (December 9, 1997); missed four games. ... Injured ribs (February 2, 1998); missed three games. ... Strained groin (November 20, 1998); missed six games. ... Injured shoulder (January 6, 2000); missed final 41 games of season. ... Concussion (October 27, 2000); missed five games. ... Signed as free agent by Devils (July 5, 2001). ... Flu (March 1, 2003); missed five games.

Season Team	League	GP	G	A	Pts.	PIM	+/-	PP	SH	GP	G	A	Pts.	PIM
		REGULAR SEASON								PLAYOFFS				
82-83—Djurgarden Stockholm	Sweden	17	2	5	7	4	...	...	...	6	1	0	1	2
83-84—Djurgarden Stockholm	Sweden	37	9	8	17	36	...	...	...	4	0	1	1	2
84-85—Djurgarden Stockholm	Sweden	32	9	8	17	22	...	...	...	8	2	1	3	4
85-86—Djurgarden Stockholm	Sweden	35	4	8	12	26	...	...	...	—	—	—	—	—
86-87—Djurgarden Stockholm	Sweden	33	7	5	12	49	...	...	...	2	0	0	0	0
87-88—Quebec.......................	NHL	60	3	23	26	47	-7	0	0	—	—	—	—	—
88-89—Halifax........................	AHL	8	2	5	7	4	...	...	...	—	—	—	—	—
—Quebec.......................	NHL	14	2	4	6	27	-6	1	0	—	—	—	—	—
—New Jersey.................	NHL	46	7	24	31	40	18	1	1	—	—	—	—	—
89-90—New Jersey.................	NHL	68	6	23	29	63	-1	4	0	—	—	—	—	—
90-91—Utica...........................	AHL	14	4	2	6	10	...	...	...	—	—	—	—	—
—New Jersey.................	NHL	47	2	12	14	44	1	1	0	3	0	1	1	2
91-92—New Jersey.................	NHL	19	0	4	4	4	7	0	0	1	1	1	2	0
—Utica...........................	AHL	11	4	6	10	4	...	...	...	—	—	—	—	—
92-93—New Jersey.................	NHL	36	1	5	6	14	0	1	0	5	2	0	2	0
93-94—Albany.........................	AHL	4	0	2	2	17	-2	0	0	—	—	—	—	—
—New Jersey.................	NHL	62	2	17	19	36	20	1	0	20	2	5	7	14
94-95—New Jersey.................	NHL	48	5	10	15	20	9	2	0	20	1	7	8	2
95-96—New Jersey.................	NHL	53	1	12	13	14	0	0	0	—	—	—	—	—
—Calgary.......................	NHL	20	0	1	1	4	1	0	0	4	0	0	0	0
96-97—Calgary.......................	NHL	72	4	11	15	14	-8	2	0	—	—	—	—	—
97-98—Calgary.......................	NHL	69	2	17	19	32	9	1	0	—	—	—	—	—
—Swedish Oly. team......	Int'l	3	0	0	0	4	0	0	0	—	—	—	—	—
98-99—Calgary.......................	NHL	60	1	5	6	8	-11	0	0	—	—	—	—	—
99-00—Calgary.......................	NHL	41	4	6	10	12	-3	1	1	—	—	—	—	—
00-01—Calgary.......................	NHL	77	1	19	20	22	2	1	0	—	—	—	—	—
01-02—New Jersey.................	NHL	42	1	3	4	4	0	0	0	6	0	0	0	0
02-03—Albany.........................	AHL	5	0	2	2	2	-2	0	0	—	—	—	—	—
—New Jersey.................	NHL	37	1	6	7	6	10	0	1	16	1	0	1	2
03-04—New Jersey.................	NHL	45	1	3	4	4	7	0	0	4	0	1	1	0
05-06—New Jersey.................	NHL	36	0	6	6	2	4	0	0	2	0	0	0	2
NHL Totals (18 years)..........		952	44	211	255	417	52	16	3	81	7	15	22	22

ALBERTS, ANDREW D

PERSONAL: Born June 30, 1981, in Minneapolis. ... 6-4/218. ... Shoots left.
COLLEGE: Boston College.
TRANSACTIONS/CAREER NOTES: Selected by Boston Bruins in the sixth round (179th overall) in NHL entry draft (June 23, 2001).

Season Team	League	GP	G	A	Pts.	PIM	+/-	PP	SH	GP	G	A	Pts.	PIM
		REGULAR SEASON								PLAYOFFS				
99-00—Waterloo.....................	USHL	49	2	2	4	55	...	...	...	—	—	—	—	—
00-01—Waterloo.....................	USHL	54	4	10	14	54	...	...	...	—	—	—	—	—
01-02—Boston College...........	Hockey East	38	2	10	12	52	...	...	...	—	—	—	—	—
02-03—Boston College...........	Hockey East	39	6	16	22	60	...	...	...	—	—	—	—	—
03-04—Boston College...........	Hockey East	41	4	12	16	32	...	...	...	—	—	—	—	—
04-05—Boston College...........	Hockey East	30	4	12	16	67	...	...	...	—	—	—	—	—
—Providence..................	AHL	8	0	0	0	16	-3	0	0	16	1	4	5	40
05-06—Boston.........................	NHL	73	1	6	7	68	3	0	1	—	—	—	—	—
—Providence..................	AHL	6	0	1	1	7	4	0	0	—	—	—	—	—
NHL Totals (1 year).............		73	1	6	7	68	3	0	1					

ALEXANDROV, YURI — D

PERSONAL: Born June 24, 1988, in Cherepovets, Rus. ... 6-0/185. ... Shoots left.
TRANSACTIONS/CAREER NOTES: Selected by Boston Bruins in second round (second Bruins pick; 37th overall) of entry draft (June 24, 2006).

		REGULAR SEASON								PLAYOFFS				
Season Team	League	GP	G	A	Pts.	PIM	+/-	PP	SH	GP	G	A	Pts.	PIM
05-06—Severstal Cherepovets	Russian	37	1	0	1	18	...	...	...	2	0	0	0	2

ALFREDSSON, DANIEL — RW

PERSONAL: Born December 11, 1972, in Gothenburg, Sweden. ... 5-11/199. ... Shoots right.
TRANSACTIONS/CAREER NOTES: Selected by Ottawa Senators in sixth round (fifth Senators pick, 133rd overall) of entry draft (June 29, 1994). ... Strained abdominal muscle (january 29, 1997); missed six games. ... Injured right ankle (November 3, 1997); missed eight games. ... Fractured right leg (December 11, 1997); missed 13 games. ... Torn left knee ligament (September 16, 1998); missed first nine games of season. ... Injured right eye (November 12, 1998); missed four games. ... Flu (December 30, 1998); missed one game. ... Sprained left knee (january 26, 1999); missed five games. ... Strained abdominal muscle (March 17, 1999); missed five games. ... Torn right knee ligament (October 21, 1999); missed 20 games. ... Sprained left knee (February 15, 2000); missed three games. ... Bruised left foot (March 31, 2000); missed one game. ... Strained hip flexor (October 19, 2001); missed 13 games. ... Injured right wrist (April 6, 2001); missed final game of regular season. ... Injured hip (December 8, 2001); missed four games. ... Strained lower back (December 4, 2002); missed three games. ... Injured hip flexor (March 21, 2003); missed one game. ... Sprained right knee (November 21, 2003); missed one game. ... Flu (january 15, 2004); missed one game. ... Bruised thigh (March 15, 2004); missed three games. ... Broken rib (December 30, 2005); missed four games. ... Flu (April 3, 2006); missed one game.
STATISTICAL PLATEAUS: Three-goal games: 1995-96 (1), 2000-01 (1), 2001-02 (2). Total: 4.

		REGULAR SEASON								PLAYOFFS				
Season Team	League	GP	G	A	Pts.	PIM	+/-	PP	SH	GP	G	A	Pts.	PIM
91-92—Molndal	Sweden Dv. 2	32	12	8	20	43	...	...	...	—	—	—	—	—
92-93—Vastra Frolunda	Sweden	20	1	5	6	8	...	...	...	—	—	—	—	—
93-94—Vastra Frolunda	Sweden	39	20	10	30	18	...	...	...	4	1	1	2	...
94-95—Vastra Frolunda	Sweden	22	7	11	18	22	...	...	...	—	—	—	—	—
95-96—Ottawa	NHL	82	26	35	61	28	-18	8	2	—	—	—	—	—
96-97—Ottawa	NHL	76	24	47	71	30	5	11	1	7	5	2	7	6
97-98—Ottawa	NHL	55	17	28	45	18	7	7	0	11	7	2	9	20
—Swedish Oly. team	Int'l	4	2	3	5	2	3	1	0	—	—	—	—	—
98-99—Ottawa	NHL	58	11	22	33	14	8	3	0	4	1	2	3	4
99-00—Ottawa	NHL	57	21	38	59	28	11	4	2	6	1	3	4	2
00-01—Ottawa	NHL	68	24	46	70	30	11	10	0	4	1	0	1	2
01-02—Ottawa	NHL	78	37	34	71	45	3	9	1	12	7	6	13	4
—Swedish Oly. team	Int'l	4	1	4	5	2	...	...	...	—	—	—	—	—
02-03—Ottawa	NHL	78	27	51	78	42	15	9	0	18	4	4	8	12
03-04—Ottawa	NHL	77	32	48	80	24	12	9	0	7	1	2	3	2
04-05—Vastra Frolunda	Sweden	15	8	9	17	10	9	1	0	14	12	6	18	8
05-06—Ottawa	NHL	77	43	60	103	50	29	16	5	10	2	8	10	4
—Swedish Oly. team	Int'l	8	5	5	10	4	2	2	0	—	—	—	—	—
NHL Totals (10 years)		706	262	409	671	309	83	86	11	79	29	29	58	56

ALLEN, BRYAN — D

PERSONAL: Born August 21, 1980, in Kingston, Ont. ... 6-4/220. ... Shoots left.
TRANSACTIONS/CAREER NOTES: Selected by Vancouver Canucks in first round (first Canucks pick, fourth overall) of entry draft (June 27, 1998). ... Injured knee (September 15, 1999); missed first 57 games of season. ... Suspended two games for slashing incident (November 5, 2003). ... Injured shoulder (March 27, 2004); missed final four games of regular season and three playoff games. ... Bruised knee (October 25, 2005); missed five games. ... Traded by Canucks with G Alex Auld and F Todd Bertuzzi to Florida Panthers for G Roberto Luongo, D Lukas Krajicek and a sixth-round pick (W Sergei Shirokov) in 2006 draft (June 23, 2006).

		REGULAR SEASON								PLAYOFFS				
Season Team	League	GP	G	A	Pts.	PIM	+/-	PP	SH	GP	G	A	Pts.	PIM
95-96—Ernestown	Jr. C	36	1	16	17	71	...	...	...	—	—	—	—	—
96-97—Oshawa	OHL	60	2	4	6	76	...	...	...	18	1	3	4	26
97-98—Oshawa	OHL	48	6	13	19	126	11	...	...	5	0	5	5	18
98-99—Oshawa	OHL	37	7	15	22	77	14	...	...	17	0	3	3	30
99-00—Oshawa	OHL	3	0	2	2	12	1	0	0	3	0	0	0	13
—Syracuse	AHL	9	1	1	2	11	...	...	...	2	0	0	0	2
00-01—Kansas City	IHL	75	5	20	25	99	...	...	...	—	—	—	—	—
—Vancouver	NHL	6	0	0	0	0	0	0	0	2	0	0	0	2
01-02—Vancouver	NHL	11	0	0	0	6	1	0	0	—	—	—	—	—
—Manitoba	AHL	68	7	18	25	121	1	2	0	5	0	1	1	8
02-03—Manitoba	AHL	7	0	1	1	4	3	0	0	—	—	—	—	—
—Vancouver	NHL	48	5	3	8	73	8	0	0	1	0	0	0	2
03-04—Vancouver	NHL	74	2	5	7	94	-10	0	0	4	0	0	0	2
04-05—Khimik Voskresensk	Russian	19	0	3	3	34	0	...	...	—	—	—	—	—
05-06—Vancouver	NHL	77	7	10	17	115	4	1	0	—	—	—	—	—
NHL Totals (5 years)		216	14	18	32	288	3	1	0	7	0	0	0	6

ALLISON, JAMIE — D/LW

PERSONAL: Born May 13, 1975, in Lindsay, Ont. ... 6-1/200. ... Shoots left.
TRANSACTIONS/CAREER NOTES: Selected by Calgary Flames in second round (second Flames pick, 44th overall) of entry draft (June 26,

1993). ... Concussion (December 20, 1996); missed three games. ... Fractured thumb (january 9, 1998); missed 11 games. ... Concussion (March 28, 1998); missed 10 games. ... Traded by Flames with C/LW Marty McInnis and RW Erik Andersson to Chicago Blackhawks for C Jeff Shantz and C/LW Steve Dubinsky (October 27, 1998). ... Sprained wrist (November 17, 1998); missed 23 games. ... Strained groin (March 31, 1999); missed three games. ... Strained groin (December 26, 1999); missed four games. ... Injured rib cage muscle (February 23, 2000); missed eight games. ... Stiff neck (March 26, 2000); missed one game. ... Bruised foot (December 21, 2000); missed one game. ... Sprained knee (February 10, 2001); missed 13 games. ... Claimed by Flames from Blackhawks in waiver draft (September 28, 2001). ... Injured groin (November 3, 2001); missed three games. ... Traded by Flames to Columbus Blue Jackets for RW Blake Sloan (March 19, 2002). ... Strained back (March 25, 2002); missed one game. ... Injured neck (November 20, 2002); missed four games. ... Sprained hand (November 30, 2002); missed 14 games. ... Injured groin (March 13, 2003); missed two games. ... Signed as free agent by the Nashville Predators (September 10, 2003). ... Injured rib (October 9, 2003); missed seven games. ... Sprained thumb (November 8, 2003); missed one game. ... Injured groin (December 13, 2003); missed eight games. ... Concussion (january 7, 2004); missed five games. ... Suspended one game for unsportsmanlike conduct (january 30, 2004). ... Strained groin (September 2005); missed first four games of season. ... Claimed off waivers by Panthers (February 13, 2006).

		REGULAR SEASON								PLAYOFFS				
Season Team	**League**	**GP**	**G**	**A**	**Pts.**	**PIM**	**+/-**	**PP**	**SH**	**GP**	**G**	**A**	**Pts.**	**PIM**
90-91—Waterloo Jr. B	OHA	45	3	8	11	91	...	...	...	—	—	—	—	—
91-92—Windsor	OHL	59	4	8	12	52	...	...	...	4	1	1	2	2
92-93—Det. Jr. Red Wings	OHL	61	0	13	13	64	...	...	...	15	2	5	7	23
93-94—Det. Jr. Red Wings	OHL	40	2	22	24	69	...	0	0	17	2	9	11	35
94-95—Det. Jr. Red Wings	OHL	50	1	14	15	119	...	0	0	18	2	7	9	35
—Calgary	NHL	1	0	0	0	0	0	0	0	—	—	—	—	—
95-96—Saint John	AHL	71	3	16	19	223	...	...	...	14	0	2	2	16
96-97—Saint John	AHL	46	3	6	9	139	-10	1	0	5	0	1	1	4
—Calgary	NHL	20	0	0	0	35	-4	0	0	—	—	—	—	—
97-98—Saint John	AHL	16	0	5	5	49	3	0	0	—	—	—	—	—
—Calgary	NHL	43	3	8	11	104	3	0	0	—	—	—	—	—
98-99—Saint John	AHL	5	0	0	0	23	-1	0	0	—	—	—	—	—
—Chicago	NHL	39	2	2	4	62	0	0	0	—	—	—	—	—
—Indianapolis	IHL	3	1	0	1	10	1	0	0	—	—	—	—	—
99-00—Chicago	NHL	59	1	3	4	102	-5	0	0	—	—	—	—	—
00-01—Chicago	NHL	44	1	3	4	53	7	0	0	—	—	—	—	—
01-02—Calgary	NHL	37	0	2	2	24	-3	0	0	—	—	—	—	—
—Columbus	NHL	7	0	0	0	28	-4	0	0	—	—	—	—	—
02-03—Columbus	NHL	48	0	1	1	99	-15	0	0	—	—	—	—	—
03-04—Nashville	NHL	47	0	3	3	76	-7	0	0	—	—	—	—	—
05-06—Nashville	NHL	20	0	1	1	45	-6	0	0	—	—	—	—	—
—Florida	NHL	7	0	0	0	11	0	0	0	—	—	—	—	—
NHL Totals (10 years)		372	7	23	30	639	-34	0	0					

ALLISON, JASON C

PERSONAL: Born May 29, 1975, in North York, Ont. ... 6-3/222. ... Shoots right.

TRANSACTIONS/CAREER NOTES: Selected by Washington Capitals in first round (second Capitals pick, 17th overall) of entry draft (June 26, 1993). ... Injured ankle (February 15, 1997); missed one game. ... Traded by Capitals with G Jim Carey, C Anson Carter and third-round pick (RW Lee Goren) in 1997 draft to Boston Bruins for C Adam Oates, RW Rick Tocchet and G Bill Ranford (March 1, 1997). ... Injured hip (March 1, 1998); missed one game. ... Injured wrist (October 30, 1999); missed two games. ... Injured wrist (December 23, 1999); missed three games. ... Injured ligaments in left thumb (january 8, 2000) and had surgery; missed 15 games. ... Injured wrist (February 12, 2000) and had surgery; missed final 25 games of season. ... Missed first nine games of 2001-02 season in contract dispute. ... Traded by Bruins with C/LW Mikko Eloranta to Los Angeles Kings for C Jozef Stumpel and RW Glen Murray (October 24, 2001). ... Sprained knee (October 29, 2002); missed 15 games. ... Reinjured knee (December 22, 2002); missed eight games. ... Hip, concussion (january 25, 2003); missed 33 games. ... Missed 2003-04 season with postconcussion syndrome. ... Signed as free agent by Toronto Maple Leafs (August 5, 2005). ... Injured finger (December 27, 2005); missed four games. ... Broken left hand (March 27, 2006); missed final 12 games of regular season.

STATISTICAL PLATEAUS: Three-goal games: 1997-98 (2), 1998-99 (1), 2000-01 (1). Total: 4.

		REGULAR SEASON								PLAYOFFS				
Season Team	**League**	**GP**	**G**	**A**	**Pts.**	**PIM**	**+/-**	**PP**	**SH**	**GP**	**G**	**A**	**Pts.**	**PIM**
91-92—London	OHL	65	11	18	29	15	...	...	...	7	0	0	0	0
92-93—London	OHL	66	42	76	118	50	...	...	...	12	7	13	20	8
93-94—London	OHL	56	55	87	142	68	...	21	6	5	2	13	15	13
—Washington	NHL	2	0	1	1	0	1	0	0	—	—	—	—	—
—Portland	AHL	6	2	1	3	0	...	...	...	—	—	—	—	—
94-95—London	OHL	15	15	21	36	43	...	3	1	—	—	—	—	—
—Washington	NHL	12	2	1	3	6	-3	2	0	—	—	—	—	—
—Portland	AHL	8	5	4	9	2	-1	1	1	7	3	8	11	2
95-96—Washington	NHL	19	0	3	3	2	-3	0	0	—	—	—	—	—
—Portland	AHL	57	28	41	69	42	...	...	...	6	1	6	7	9
96-97—Washington	NHL	53	5	17	22	25	-3	1	0	—	—	—	—	—
—Boston	NHL	19	3	9	12	9	-3	1	0	—	—	—	—	—
97-98—Boston	NHL	81	33	50	83	60	33	5	0	6	2	6	8	4
98-99—Boston	NHL	82	23	53	76	68	5	5	1	12	2	9	11	6
99-00—Boston	NHL	37	10	18	28	20	5	3	0	—	—	—	—	—
00-01—Boston	NHL	82	36	59	95	85	-8	11	3	—	—	—	—	—
01-02—Los Angeles	NHL	73	19	55	74	68	2	5	0	7	3	3	6	4
02-03—Los Angeles	NHL	26	6	22	28	22	9	2	0	—	—	—	—	—
03-04—Los Angeles	NHL	Did not play — injured												
05-06—Toronto	NHL	66	17	43	60	76	-18	9	0	—	—	—	—	—
NHL Totals (12 years)		552	154	331	485	441	17	44	4	25	7	18	25	14

AMONTE, TONY RW

PERSONAL: Born August 2, 1970, in Hingham, Mass. ... 6-0/200. ... Shoots left. ... Name pronounced ah-MAHN-tee.

TRANSACTIONS/CAREER NOTES: Selected by New York Rangers in fourth round (third Rangers pick, 68th overall) of NHL draft (June 11,

1988). ... Traded by Rangers with rights to LW Matt Oates to Chicago Blackhawks for LW Stephane Matteau and RW Brian Noonan (March 21, 1994). ... Injured groin (1993-94 season); missed three games. ... Signed as free agent by Phoenix Coyotes (July 12, 2002). ... Bruised ribs (january 11, 2003); missed eight games. ... Contract bought out by Flyers (July 23, 2005). ... Signed as free agent by Calgary Flames (August 2, 2005). ... Rib injury (December 29, 2005); missed two games.

STATISTICAL PLATEAUS: Three-goal games: 1991-92 (1), 1995-96 (1), 1996-97 (2), 1998-99 (2), 1999-00 (1). Total: 7.

		REGULAR SEASON								PLAYOFFS				
Season Team	**League**	**GP**	**G**	**A**	**Pts.**	**PIM**	**+/-**	**PP**	**SH**	**GP**	**G**	**A**	**Pts.**	**PIM**
86-87—Thayer Academy	Mass. H.S.	25	25	32	57	...	...	...	...	—	—	—	—	—
87-88—Thayer Academy	Mass. H.S.	28	30	38	68	...	...	...	...	—	—	—	—	—
88-89—Thayer Academy	Mass. H.S.	25	35	38	73	...	...	...	...	—	—	—	—	—
—Team USA Juniors	Int'l	7	1	3	4	...	...	...	...	—	—	—	—	—
89-90—Boston University	Hockey East	41	25	33	58	52	...	...	...	—	—	—	—	—
90-91—Boston University	Hockey East	38	31	37	68	82	...	...	...	—	—	—	—	—
—New York Rangers	NHL	...	...	...	...	...	...	...	...	2	0	2	2	2
91-92—New York Rangers	NHL	79	35	34	69	55	12	9	0	13	3	6	9	2
92-93—New York Rangers	NHL	83	33	43	76	49	0	13	0	—	—	—	—	—
93-94—New York Rangers	NHL	72	16	22	38	31	5	3	0	—	—	—	—	—
—Chicago	NHL	7	1	3	4	6	-5	1	0	6	4	2	6	4
94-95—Fassa	Italy	14	22	16	38	10	...	...	...	—	—	—	—	—
—Chicago	NHL	48	15	20	35	41	7	6	1	16	3	3	6	10
95-96—Chicago	NHL	81	31	32	63	62	10	5	4	7	2	4	6	6
96-97—Chicago	NHL	81	41	36	77	64	35	9	2	6	4	2	6	8
97-98—Chicago	NHL	82	31	42	73	66	21	7	3	—	—	—	—	—
—U.S. Olympic team	Int'l	4	0	1	1	4	-4	0	0	—	—	—	—	—
98-99—Chicago	NHL	82	44	31	75	60	0	14	3	—	—	—	—	—
99-00—Chicago	NHL	82	43	41	84	48	10	11	5	—	—	—	—	—
00-01—Chicago	NHL	82	35	29	64	54	-22	9	1	—	—	—	—	—
01-02—Chicago	NHL	82	27	39	66	67	11	6	1	5	0	1	1	4
—U.S. Olympic team	Int'l	6	2	2	4	0	...	...	...	—	—	—	—	—
02-03—Phoenix	NHL	59	13	23	36	26	-12	6	0	—	—	—	—	—
—Philadelphia	NHL	13	7	8	15	2	12	1	1	13	1	6	7	4
03-04—Philadelphia	NHL	80	20	33	53	38	13	4	0	18	3	5	8	6
05-06—Calgary	NHL	80	14	28	42	43	3	3	1	7	2	1	3	10
NHL Totals (15 years)		1093	406	464	870	712	100	107	22	93	22	32	54	56

ANDERSON, CRAIG — G

PERSONAL: Born May 21, 1981, in Park Ridge, Ill. ... 6-2/174. ... Catches left. ... Also known as Craig Andersson.

TRANSACTIONS/CAREER NOTES: Selected by Calgary Flames in third round (third Flames pick, 77th overall) of NHL entry draft (June 26, 1999). ... Returned to draft pool by Flames and selected by Chicago Blackhawks in third round (fourth Blackhawks pick, 73th overall) of NHL entry draft (June 23, 2001). ... Acquired off waivers by Bruins (january 19, 2006). ... Acquired off waivers by St. Louis Blues (january 31, 2006). ... Acquired off waivers by Blackhawks (February 3, 2006). ... Traded by Blackhawks to Panthers for sixth-round selection in 2008 draft (June 24, 2006).

		REGULAR SEASON										PLAYOFFS							
Season Team	**League**	**GP**	**Min.**	**W**	**L**	**OTL**	**T**	**GA**	**SO**	**GAA**	**SV%**	**GP**	**Min.**	**W**	**L**	**GA**	**SO**	**GAA**	**SV%**
98-99—Chicago	NAHL	14	821	11	3	...	0	35	0	2.56	...	—	—	—	—	—	—	—	—
—Guelph	OHL	21	1006	12	5	...	1	52	1	3.10	...	3	114	0	2	9	0	4.74	...
99-00—Guelph	OHL	38	1955	12	17	...	2	117	0	3.59	.903	3	110	0	1	5	0	2.73	.900
00-01—Guelph	OHL	59	3555	30	19	...	9	156	3	2.63	.918	4	240	0	4	17	0	4.25	...
01-02—Norfolk	AHL	28	1567	9	13	...	4	77	2	2.95	.871	1	21	0	1	1	0	2.86	.938
02-03—Norfolk	AHL	32	1794	15	11	...	5	58	4	1.94	.923	5	344	2	3	15	0	2.61	...
—Chicago	NHL	6	270	0	3	...	2	18	0	4.00	.856	—	—	—	—	—	—	—	—
03-04—Chicago	NHL	21	1205	6	14	...	0	57	1	2.84	.905	—	—	—	—	—	—	—	—
—Norfolk	AHL	37	2108	17	20	...	0	74	3	2.11	.905	5	326	2	3	10	0	1.84	.929
04-05—Norfolk	AHL	15	885	9	4	...	...	27	2	1.83	.929	6	355	2	4	14	0	2.37	.925
05-06—Chicago	NHL	29	1553	6	12	4	...	86	1	3.32	.886	—	—	—	—	—	—	—	—
NHL Totals (3 years)		56	3028	12	29	4	2	161	2	3.19	.892								

ANDREYCHUK, DAVE — LW

PERSONAL: Born September 29, 1963, in Hamilton, Ont. ... 6-4/220. ... Shoots right. ... Name pronounced AN-druh-chuhk.

TRANSACTIONS/CAREER NOTES: Selected by Buffalo Sabres in first round (third Sabres pick, 16th overall) of entry draft (June 9, 1982). ... Sprained knee (March 1983). ... Fractured collarbone (March 1985). ... Twisted knee (September 1985). ... Injured right knee (September 1986). ... Strained left knee ligaments (November 27, 1988). ... Fractured left thumb (February 18, 1990). ... Suspended two off-days and fined $500 for cross-checking incident (November 16, 1992). ... Traded by Sabres with G Daren Puppa and first-round pick (D Kenny Jonsson) in 1993 draft to Toronto Maple Leafs for G Grant Fuhr and fifth-round pick (D Kevin Popp) in 1995 draft (February 2, 1993). ... Injured knee (December 27, 1993); missed one game. ... Separated shoulder (December 2, 1995); missed five games. ... Flu (December 27, 1995); missed one game. ... Thumb surgery (january 15, 1996); missed two games. ... Traded by Maple Leafs to New Jersey Devils for second-round pick (D Marek Posmyk) in 1996 draft and third-round pick (traded back to New Jersey) in 1999 draft (March 13, 1996). ... Bruised left foot (October 23, 1997); missed six games. ... Bruised sternum (November 7, 1998); missed six games. ... Fractured right ankle (january 5, 1999); missed 21 games. ... Signed as free agent by Boston Bruins (July 28, 1999). ... Injured knee (january 11, 2000); missed two games. ... Traded by Bruins with D Ray Bourque to Colorado Avalanche for LW Brian Rolston, D Martin Grenier, C Samuel Pahlsson and first-round pick (LW Martin Samuelsson) in 2000 draft (March 6, 2000). ... Signed as free agent by Sabres (July 13, 2000). ... Injured knee (February 13, 2001); missed two games. ... Signed as free agent by Tampa Bay Lightning (July 13, 2001). ... Fractured foot (December 5, 2002); missed nine games. ... Signed as free agent by Lightning (August 25, 2005). ... Placed on waivers by Lightning (january 10, 2006). ... Retired (2006).

STATISTICAL PLATEAUS: Three-goal games: 1987-88 (3), 1988-89 (1), 1989-90 (1), 1991-92 (1), 1993-94 (1). Total: 7. ... Four-goal games: 1991-92 (1), 1992-93 (1), 1999-00 (1). Total: 3. ... Five-goal games: 1985-86 (1). ... Total hat tricks: 11.

Season Team	League	REGULAR SEASON GP	G	A	Pts.	PIM	+/-	PP	SH	PLAYOFFS GP	G	A	Pts.	PIM
80-81—Oshawa	OMJHL	67	22	22	44	80	...	...	...	10	3	2	5	20
81-82—Oshawa	OHL	67	58	43	101	71	...	...	...	3	1	4	5	16
82-83—Oshawa	OHL	14	8	24	32	6	...	...	...	—	—	—	—	—
—Buffalo	NHL	43	14	23	37	16	6	3	0	4	1	0	1	4
83-84—Buffalo	NHL	78	38	42	80	42	20	10	0	2	0	1	1	2
84-85—Buffalo	NHL	64	31	30	61	54	-4	14	0	5	4	2	6	4
85-86—Buffalo	NHL	80	36	51	87	61	3	12	0	—	—	—	—	—
86-87—Buffalo	NHL	77	25	48	73	46	2	13	0	—	—	—	—	—
87-88—Buffalo	NHL	80	30	48	78	112	1	15	0	6	2	4	6	0
88-89—Buffalo	NHL	56	28	24	52	40	0	7	0	5	0	3	3	0
89-90—Buffalo	NHL	73	40	42	82	42	6	18	0	6	2	5	7	2
90-91—Buffalo	NHL	80	36	33	69	32	11	13	0	6	2	2	4	8
91-92—Buffalo	NHL	80	41	50	91	71	-9	*28	0	7	1	3	4	12
92-93—Buffalo	NHL	52	29	32	61	48	-8	20	0	—	—	—	—	—
—Toronto	NHL	31	25	13	38	8	12	12	0	21	12	7	19	35
93-94—Toronto	NHL	83	53	46	99	98	22	21	5	18	5	5	10	16
94-95—Toronto	NHL	48	22	16	38	34	-7	8	0	7	3	2	5	25
95-96—Toronto	NHL	61	20	24	44	54	-11	12	2	—	—	—	—	—
—New Jersey	NHL	15	8	5	13	10	2	2	0	—	—	—	—	—
96-97—New Jersey	NHL	82	27	34	61	48	38	4	1	1	0	0	0	0
97-98—New Jersey	NHL	75	14	34	48	26	19	4	0	6	1	0	1	4
98-99—New Jersey	NHL	52	15	13	28	20	1	4	0	4	2	0	2	4
99-00—Boston	NHL	63	19	14	33	28	-11	7	0	—	—	—	—	—
—Colorado	NHL	14	1	2	3	2	-9	1	0	17	3	2	5	18
00-01—Buffalo	NHL	74	20	13	33	32	0	8	0	13	1	2	3	4
01-02—Tampa Bay	NHL	82	21	17	38	109	-12	9	1	—	—	—	—	—
02-03—Tampa Bay	NHL	72	20	14	34	34	-12	15	0	11	3	3	6	10
03-04—Tampa Bay	NHL	82	21	18	39	42	-9	10	0	23	1	13	14	14
05-06—Tampa Bay	NHL	42	6	12	18	16	-13	4	1	—	—	—	—	—
NHL Totals (23 years)		1639	640	698	1338	1125	38	274	10	162	43	54	97	162

ANISIMOV, ARTEM — C

PERSONAL: Born May 24, 1988, in Yaroslavl, Rus. ... 6-3/187. ... Shoots left.
TRANSACTIONS/CAREER NOTES: Selected by New York Rangers in second round (second Rangers pick; 54th overall) of NHL draft (June 24, 2006).

Season Team	League	REGULAR SEASON GP	G	A	Pts.	PIM	+/-	PP	SH	PLAYOFFS GP	G	A	Pts.	PIM
05-06—Lokomotive Yaroslavl .	Russian Jr.	32	15	12	27	28	...	...	...	—	—	—	—	—
—Lokomotiv Yaroslavl	Russian	10	0	1	1	4	...	...	...	—	—	—	—	—

ANTROPOV, NIK — C/RW

PERSONAL: Born February 18, 1980, in Vost, U.S.S.R. ... 6-6/230. ... Shoots left.
TRANSACTIONS/CAREER NOTES: Selected by Toronto Maple Leafs in first round (first Maple Leafs pick, 10th overall) of entry draft (June 27, 1998). ... Injured (November 27, 1999); missed seven games. ... Injured (january 5, 2000); missed two games. ... Injured (March 29, 2000); missed one game. ... Sprained knee (November 5, 2002); missed five games. ... Injured shoulder (january 3, 2003); missed three games. ... Injured groin (March 22, 2003); missed two games. ... Fractured foot (April 9, 2003); missed four playoff games. ... Injured shoulder (October 27, 2003); missed 20 games. ... Left team for personal reasons and upper-body injury (October 20, 2005); missed nine games. ... Injured knee (December 17, 2005); missed 12 games. ... Arm injury (March 4, 2006); missed two games. ... Right knee surgery (April 18, 2006); missed final game of regular season.
STATISTICAL PLATEAUS: Three-goal games: 1999-00 (1).

Season Team	League	REGULAR SEASON GP	G	A	Pts.	PIM	+/-	PP	SH	PLAYOFFS GP	G	A	Pts.	PIM
95-96—Torpedo Ust-Kam	CIS Jr.	20	18	20	38	30	...	...	...	—	—	—	—	—
96-97—Torpedo Ust-Kam	Rus. Div.	8	2	1	3	6	...	...	...	—	—	—	—	—
97-98—Torpedo Ust-Kam	Rus. Div.	42	15	24	39	62	...	...	...	—	—	—	—	—
98-99—Dynamo Moscow	Russian	30	5	9	14	30	...	...	...	11	0	1	1	4
99-00—St. John's	AHL	2	0	0	0	4	...	...	...	—	—	—	—	—
—Toronto	NHL	66	12	18	30	41	14	0	0	3	0	0	0	4
00-01—Toronto	NHL	52	6	11	17	30	5	0	0	9	2	1	3	12
01-02—Toronto	NHL	11	1	1	2	4	-1	0	0	—	—	—	—	—
—St. John's	AHL	34	11	24	35	47	9	2	0	—	—	—	—	—
02-03—Toronto	NHL	72	16	29	45	124	11	2	1	3	0	0	0	0
03-04—Toronto	NHL	62	13	18	31	62	7	1	1	13	0	2	2	18
04-05—Ak Bars Kazan	Russian	10	2	3	5	6	3	...	...	—	—	—	—	—
—Lokomotiv Yaroslavl	Russian	26	4	15	19	44	6	...	...	9	3	4	7	18
05-06—Toronto	NHL	57	12	19	31	56	13	2	1	—	—	—	—	—
—Kazak. Oly. team	Int'l	5	1	0	1	4	2	0	0	—	—	—	—	—
NHL Totals (6 years)		320	60	96	156	317	49	5	3	28	2	3	5	34

ARMSTRONG, COLBY — RW

PERSONAL: Born November 23, 1982, in Lloydminster, Sask. ... 6-2/195. ... Shoots right.
TRANSACTIONS/CAREER NOTES: Selected by Pittsburgh Penguins in first round (first Penguins pick, 21st overall) of NHL draft (June 23, 2001). ... Re-signed by Penguins as free agent (August 12, 2005).

Season Team	League	REGULAR SEASON								PLAYOFFS				
		GP	G	A	Pts.	PIM	+/-	PP	SH	GP	G	A	Pts.	PIM
98-99—Red Deer	WHL	1	0	1	1	0	...	...	...	—	—	—	—	—
99-00—Red Deer	WHL	68	13	25	38	122	...	...	...	2	0	1	1	11
00-01—Red Deer	WHL	72	36	42	78	156	...	...	...	21	6	6	12	39
01-02—Red Deer	WHL	64	27	41	68	115	...	...	...	23	6	10	16	32
02-03—Wilkes-Barre/Scranton	AHL	73	7	11	18	76	...	...	...	3	0	0	0	4
03-04—Wilkes-Barre/Scranton	AHL	67	10	17	27	71	6	3	0	24	3	2	5	45
04-05—Wilkes-Barre/Scranton	AHL	80	18	37	55	89	9	6	3	10	4	2	6	14
05-06—Wilkes-Barre/Scranton	AHL	31	11	18	29	44	14	4	0	—	—	—	—	—
—Pittsburgh	NHL	47	16	24	40	58	15	7	2	—	—	—	—	—
NHL Totals (1 year)		47	16	24	40	58	15	7	2					

ARMSTRONG, DEREK C

PERSONAL: Born April 23, 1973, in Ottawa. ... 6-0/190. ... Shoots right.
TRANSACTIONS/CAREER NOTES: Selected by New York Islanders in sixth round (fifth Islanders pick, 128th overall) of entry draft (June 20, 1992). ... Food poisoning (january 28, 1997); missed one game. ... Signed as free agent by Ottawa Senators (July 10, 1997). ... Signed as free agent by New York Rangers (July 20, 1998). ... Traded by Rangers to Los Angeles Kings for sixth-round pick (G Chris Holt) in 2003 (July 16, 2002). ... Groin (December 11, 2002); missed six games. ... Knee (january 2, 2003); missed two games. ... Fractured finger (November 15, 2003); missed 22 games. ... Groin (October 25, 2005); missed five games. ... Groin (November 9, 2005); missed five games. ... Back (March 25, 2006); missed six games. ... Back (April 6, 2006); missed season's final four games.

Season Team	League	REGULAR SEASON								PLAYOFFS				
		GP	G	A	Pts.	PIM	+/-	PP	SH	GP	G	A	Pts.	PIM
89-90—Hawkesbury	COJHL	48	8	10	18	30	...	...	...	—	—	—	—	—
90-91—Hawkesbury	COJHL	54	27	45	72	49	...	...	...	—	—	—	—	—
—Sudbury	OHL	2	0	2	2	0	...	...	...	—	—	—	—	—
91-92—Sudbury	OHL	66	31	54	85	22	...	...	...	9	2	2	4	2
92-93—Sudbury	OHL	66	44	62	106	56	...	...	...	14	9	10	19	26
93-94—Salt Lake City	IHL	76	23	35	58	61	-17	8	0	—	—	—	—	—
—New York Islanders	NHL	1	0	0	0	0	0	0	0	—	—	—	—	—
94-95—Denver	IHL	59	13	18	31	65	6	3	0	6	0	2	2	0
95-96—Worcester	AHL	51	11	15	26	33	...	...	...	4	2	1	3	0
—New York Islanders	NHL	19	1	3	4	14	-6	0	0	—	—	—	—	—
96-97—New York Islanders	NHL	50	6	7	13	33	-8	0	0	—	—	—	—	—
—Utah	IHL	17	4	8	12	10	...	...	...	6	0	4	4	4
97-98—Detroit	IHL	10	0	1	1	2	-1	0	0	—	—	—	—	—
—Hartford	AHL	54	16	30	46	40	15	1	0	15	2	6	8	22
—Ottawa	NHL	9	2	0	2	9	1	0	0	—	—	—	—	—
98-99—Hartford	AHL	59	29	51	80	73	16	6	2	7	5	4	9	10
—New York Rangers	NHL	3	0	0	0	0	0	0	0	—	—	—	—	—
99-00—Hartford	AHL	77	28	54	82	101	...	...	...	23	7	16	23	24
—New York Rangers	NHL	1	0	0	0	0	0	0	0	—	—	—	—	—
00-01—Hartford	AHL	75	32	69	101	73	...	...	...	5	0	6	6	6
—New York Rangers	NHL	3	0	0	0	0	0	0	0	—	—	—	—	—
01-02—Bern	Switzerland	44	17	36	53	62	...	...	...	6	3	5	8	8
02-03—Manchester	AHL	2	3	0	3	4	...	...	...	—	—	—	—	—
—Los Angeles	NHL	66	12	26	38	30	5	2	0	—	—	—	—	—
03-04—Los Angeles	NHL	57	14	21	35	33	4	5	0	—	—	—	—	—
04-05—Rapperswil	Switzerland	3	1	3	4	4	...	0	1	—	—	—	—	—
—Geneva	Switzerland	9	6	7	13	18	...	3	0	—	—	—	—	—
05-06—Los Angeles	NHL	62	13	28	41	46	-2	7	0	—	—	—	—	—
NHL Totals (10 years)		271	48	85	133	165	-6	14	0					

ARNASON, TYLER C

PERSONAL: Born March 16, 1979, in Oklahoma City, Okla. ... 5-11/192. ... Shoots left. ... Son of Chuck Arnason, RW with eight NHL teams (1971-79).
COLLEGE: St. Cloud State.
TRANSACTIONS/CAREER NOTES: Selected by Chicago Blackhawks in sixth round (sixth Blackhawks pick, 183rd overall) of NHL draft (June 28, 1998). ... Traded by Blackhawks to Ottawa Senators for RW Brandon Bochenski and second-round pick (D Simon Danis-Pepin) in 2006 draft (March 9, 2006). ... Signed as free agent by Colorado Avalanche (July 1, 2006).
STATISTICAL PLATEAUS: Three-goal games: 2002-03 (1), 2003-04 (1). Total: 2.

Season Team	League	REGULAR SEASON								PLAYOFFS				
		GP	G	A	Pts.	PIM	+/-	PP	SH	GP	G	A	Pts.	PIM
96-97—Winnipeg	MJHL	56	35	30	65	18	...	...	...	—	—	—	—	—
97-98—Fargo	USHL	52	37	45	82	16	...	...	...	—	—	—	—	—
98-99—St. Cloud State	WCHA	38	14	17	31	16	...	...	...	—	—	—	—	—
99-00—St. Cloud State	WCHA	39	19	30	49	18	...	...	...	—	—	—	—	—
00-01—St. Cloud State	WCHA	41	28	28	56	14	...	...	...	—	—	—	—	—
01-02—Norfolk	AHL	60	26	30	56	42	-2	11	0	—	—	—	—	—
—Chicago	NHL	21	3	1	4	4	-3	0	0	3	0	0	0	0
02-03—Chicago	NHL	82	19	20	39	20	7	3	0	—	—	—	—	—
03-04—Chicago	NHL	82	22	33	55	16	-13	6	0	—	—	—	—	—
04-05—Brynas IF	Sweden	4	0	0	0	0	-1	0	0	—	—	—	—	—
05-06—Chicago	NHL	60	13	28	41	40	5	5	0	—	—	—	—	—
—Ottawa	NHL	19	0	4	4	4	-4	0	0	—	—	—	—	—
NHL Totals (4 years)		264	57	86	143	84	-8	14	0	3	0	0	0	0

ARNOTT, JASON C

PERSONAL: Born October 11, 1974, in Collingwood, Ont. ... 6-4/220. ... Shoots right. ... Name pronounced AHR-niht.

TRANSACTIONS/CAREER NOTES: Selected by Edmonton Oilers in first round (first Oilers pick, seventh overall) of entry draft (June 26, 1993). ... Tonsillitis (November 3, 1993); missed one game. ... Bruised sternum (November 27, 1993); missed one game. ... Sprained back (December 7, 1993); missed one game. ... Appendectomy (December 28, 1993); missed three games. ... Flu (February 22, 1995); missed one game. ... Concussion (March 23, 1995); missed two games. ... Strained knee (April 19, 1995); missed two games. ... Suspended one game for game misconduct penalties (April 22, 1995). ... Concussion, facial cut (October 8, 1995); missed seven games. ... Sprained knee (February 11, 1996); missed nine games. ... Strained knee (March 19, 1996); missed one game. ... Inner ear infection (April 8, 1996); missed one game. ... Fractured ankle (December 27, 1996); missed seven games. ... Ankle (january 22, 1997); missed two games. ... Flu (February 12, 1997); missed two games. ... Strained lower back (March 23, 1997); missed four games. ... Separated right shoulder (December 10, 1997); missed five games. ... Shoulder (january 2, 1998); missed two games. ... Traded by Oilers with D Bryan Muir to New Jersey Devils for RW Bill Guerin and RW Valeri Zelepukin (January 4, 1998). ... Back spasms (March 21, 1998); missed one game. ... Bruised hip (April 8, 1998); missed three games. ... Hip (April 16, 1998); missed two games. ... Had offseason finger surgery; missed first game of 1998-99 season. ... Bruised thigh (December 28, 1998); missed one game. ... Flu (January 15, 1999); missed two games ... Bruised foot (January 20, 1999); missed one game ... Bruised hip (March 28, 1999); missed one game. ... Hip (April 4, 1999); missed two games. ... Mouth (October 23, 1999); missed three games. ... Flu (February 21, 2000); missed two games. ... Bruised ribs (March 17, 2000); missed one game. ... Missed 2000-01 season's first 18 games in contract dispute. ... Back (February 16, 2001); missed six games. ... Flu (December 20, 2001); missed two games. ... Back (March 10, 2002); missed five games. ... Traded by Devils with RW Randy McKay and first-round pick (traded to Columbus; traded to Buffalo; Sabres selected LW Dan Paille) in 2002 to Dallas Stars for C Joe Nieuwendyk and RW Jamie Langenbrunner (March 19, 2002). ... Strained groin (April 10, 2002); missed remainder of season. ... Sprained right ankle (October 10, 2002); missed nine games. ... Knee (March 16, 2003); missed one game. ... Groin (December 3, 2003); missed four games. ... Ankle (December 27, 2003); missed one game. ... Groin (March 24, 2004); missed one game. ... Groin (March 31, 2004); missed regular season's final three games. ... Signed as free agent by Nashville Predators (July 2, 2006).

STATISTICAL PLATEAUS: Three-goal games: 1994-95 (1), 1995-96 (1), 2001-02 (1), 2002-03 (1), 2003-04 (1). Total: 5.

		REGULAR SEASON								PLAYOFFS				
Season Team	League	GP	G	A	Pts.	PIM	+/-	PP	SH	GP	G	A	Pts.	PIM
89-90—Stayner	Jr. C	34	21	31	52	12	...	...	...	—	—	—	—	—
90-91—Lindsay Jr. B	OHA	42	17	44	61	10	...	...	...	—	—	—	—	—
91-92—Oshawa	OHL	57	9	15	24	12	...	...	...	—	—	—	—	—
92-93—Oshawa	OHL	56	41	57	98	74	...	...	...	13	9	9	18	20
93-94—Edmonton	NHL	78	33	35	68	104	1	10	0	—	—	—	—	—
94-95—Edmonton	NHL	42	15	22	37	128	-14	7	0	—	—	—	—	—
95-96—Edmonton	NHL	64	28	31	59	87	-6	8	0	—	—	—	—	—
96-97—Edmonton	NHL	67	19	38	57	92	-21	10	1	12	3	6	9	18
97-98—Edmonton	NHL	35	5	13	18	78	-16	1	0	—	—	—	—	—
—New Jersey	NHL	35	5	10	15	21	-8	3	0	5	0	2	2	0
98-99—New Jersey	NHL	74	27	27	54	79	10	8	0	7	2	2	4	4
99-00—New Jersey	NHL	76	22	34	56	51	22	7	0	23	8	12	20	18
00-01—New Jersey	NHL	54	21	34	55	75	23	8	0	23	8	7	15	16
01-02—New Jersey	NHL	63	22	19	41	59	3	8	0	—	—	—	—	—
—Dallas	NHL	10	3	1	4	6	-1	2	0	—	—	—	—	—
02-03—Dallas	NHL	72	23	24	47	51	9	7	0	11	3	2	5	6
03-04—Dallas	NHL	73	21	36	57	66	23	5	0	5	1	1	2	2
05-06—Dallas	NHL	81	32	44	76	102	13	11	1	5	0	3	3	4
NHL Totals (12 years)		824	276	368	644	999	38	95	2	91	25	35	60	68

ARTYUKHIN, EVGENY RW/LW

PERSONAL: Born April 4, 1983, in Moscow, U.S.S.R. ... 6-5/254. ... Shoots left.... Name pronounced: yahv-GEH-nee ahr-TOO-kihn

TRANSACTIONS/CAREER NOTES: Selected by Tampa Bay Lightning in third round (fourth Lightning pick, 94th overall) of NHL entry draft (June 23, 2001). ... Suspended two games by NHL for hitting opponent with his helmet (March 7, 2006).

		REGULAR SEASON								PLAYOFFS				
Season Team	League	GP	G	A	Pts.	PIM	+/-	PP	SH	GP	G	A	Pts.	PIM
99-00—Podolsk	Russian	3	0	0	0	2	...	...	...	—	—	—	—	—
00-01—Podolsk	Russian	24	0	1	1	14	...	...	...	—	—	—	—	—
01-02—Podolsk	Russian	49	15	7	22	94	...	...	...	12	0	1	1	18
02-03—Moncton	QMJHL	53	13	27	40	204	...	...	...	6	1	2	3	29
03-04—Hershey	AHL	36	3	3	6	11	...	...	...	—	—	—	—	—
—Pensacola	ECHL	6	1	0	1	14	...	...	...	—	—	—	—	—
04-05—Springfield	AHL	62	9	19	28	142	1	3	0	—	—	—	—	—
05-06—Tampa Bay	NHL	72	4	13	17	90	-4	1	0	5	1	0	1	6
—Springfield	AHL	4	2	1	3	4	-2	0	0	—	—	—	—	—
NHL Totals (1 year)		72	4	13	17	90	-4	1	0	5	1	0	1	6

ASHAM, ARRON RW/LW

PERSONAL: Born April 13, 1978, in Portage-La-Prairie, Man. ... 5-11/209. ... Shoots right.

TRANSACTIONS/CAREER NOTES: Selected by Montreal Canadiens in third round (third Canadiens pick, 71st overall) of entry draft (June 22, 1996). ... Injured back (October 23, 1999); missed one game. ... Flu (December 27, 1999); missed one game. ... Strained groin (January 22, 2000); missed 23 games. ... Strained hip flexor (February 17, 2001); missed eight games. ... Flu (March 19, 2001); missed one game. ... Traded by Canadiens with fifth-round pick (W Markus Pahlsson) in 2002 draft to New York Islanders for RW Mariusz Czerkawski (June 22, 2002). ... Injured neck (November 3, 2003); missed three games. ... Re-signed by Islanders as restricted free agent (August 15, 2005). ... Bruised ribs (October 1, 2005); missed season's first game. ... Ankle sprain (March 15, 2006); missed final 18 games of regular season.

		REGULAR SEASON								PLAYOFFS				
Season Team	League	GP	G	A	Pts.	PIM	+/-	PP	SH	GP	G	A	Pts.	PIM
94-95—Red Deer	WHL	62	11	16	27	126	...	...	...	—	—	—	—	—
95-96—Red Deer	WHL	70	32	45	77	174	...	...	...	10	6	3	9	20

Season Team	League	REGULAR SEASON GP	G	A	Pts.	PIM	+/-	PP	SH	PLAYOFFS GP	G	A	Pts.	PIM
96-97—Red Deer	WHL	67	45	51	96	149	12	14	7	16	12	14	26	36
97-98—Red Deer	WHL	67	43	49	92	153	-3	16	2	5	0	2	2	8
—Fredericton	AHL	2	1	1	2	0	0	0	0	2	0	1	1	0
98-99—Fredericton	AHL	60	16	18	34	118	-3	5	0	13	8	6	14	11
—Montreal	NHL	7	0	0	0	0	-4	0	0	—	—	—	—	—
99-00—Montreal	NHL	33	4	2	6	24	-7	0	1	—	—	—	—	—
—Quebec	AHL	13	4	5	9	32	...	...	...	2	0	0	0	2
00-01—Quebec	AHL	15	7	9	16	51	...	...	...	7	1	2	3	2
—Montreal	NHL	46	2	3	5	59	-9	0	0	—	—	—	—	—
01-02—Quebec	AHL	24	9	14	23	35	1	2	0	—	—	—	—	—
—Montreal	NHL	35	5	4	9	55	7	0	0	3	0	1	1	0
02-03—New York Islanders	NHL	78	15	19	34	57	1	4	0	5	0	0	0	16
03-04—New York Islanders	NHL	79	12	12	24	92	-12	1	0	5	0	1	1	4
04-05—Visp	Switzerland	5	2	4	6	6	...	0	0	4	1	2	3	8
05-06—New York Islanders	NHL	63	9	15	24	103	-5	2	1	—	—	—	—	—
NHL Totals (7 years)		341	47	55	102	390	-29	7	2	13	0	2	2	20

AUBIN, JEAN-SEBASTIEN G

PERSONAL: Born July 17, 1977, in Montreal. ... 5-11/180. ... Catches right. ... Name pronounced OH-ban.

TRANSACTIONS/CAREER NOTES: Selected by Pittsburgh Penguins in third round (second Penguins pick, 76th overall) of entry draft (July 8, 1995). ... Strained hamstring (April 3, 1999); missed six games. ... Injured shoulder (November 23, 1999); missed two games. ... Sprained ankle (April 3, 2000); missed final three games of season. ... Injured knee (December 3, 2000); missed 14 games. ... Bruised hand (February 8, 2003); missed nine games. ... Signed as free agent by Toronto Maple Leafs (August 18, 2005).

Season Team	League	REGULAR SEASON GP	Min.	W	L	OTL	T	GA	SO	GAA	SV%	PLAYOFFS GP	Min.	W	L	GA	SO	GAA	SV%
94-95—Sherbrooke	QMJHL	27	1287	13	10	...	1	73	1	3.40	...	3	185	1	2	11	0	3.57	.891
95-96—Sherbrooke	QMJHL	40	2084	18	14	...	2	127	0	3.66	...	4	174	1	3	16	0	5.52	...
96-97—Sherbrooke	QMJHL	4	249	3	1	...	0	8	0	1.93	...	—	—	—	—	—	—	—	—
—Moncton	QMJHL	23	1311	9	13	...	0	72	1	3.30	...	—	—	—	—	—	—	—	—
—Laval	QMJHL	11	532	2	6	...	1	41	0	4.62	...	2	128	0	2	10	0	4.69	.872
97-98—Syracuse	AHL	8	380	2	4	...	1	26	0	4.11	.855	—	—	—	—	—	—	—	—
—Dayton	ECHL	21	1177	15	2	...	2	59	1	3.01	...	3	142	1	1	4	0	1.69	...
98-99—Kansas City	IHL	13	751	5	7	...	1	41	0	3.28	.900	—	—	—	—	—	—	—	—
—Pittsburgh	NHL	17	756	4	3	...	6	28	2	2.22	.908	—	—	—	—	—	—	—	—
99-00—Wilkes-Barre/Scranton	AHL	11	538	2	8	...	0	39	0	4.35	...	—	—	—	—	—	—	—	—
—Pittsburgh	NHL	51	2789	23	21	...	3	120	2	2.58	.914	—	—	—	—	—	—	—	—
00-01—Pittsburgh	NHL	36	2050	20	14	...	1	107	0	3.13	.890	1	1	0	0	0	0	0.00	...
01-02—Pittsburgh	NHL	21	1094	3	12	...	1	65	0	3.56	.879	—	—	—	—	—	—	—	—
02-03—Pittsburgh	NHL	21	1132	6	13	...	0	59	1	3.13	.900	—	—	—	—	—	—	—	—
—Wilkes-Barre/Scranton	AHL	16	919	8	6	...	1	29	3	1.89	.937	6	355	3	3	12	0	2.03	.930
03-04—Pittsburgh	NHL	22	1067	7	9	...	0	53	1	2.98	.908	—	—	—	—	—	—	—	—
—Wilkes-Barre/Scranton	AHL	13	670	4	5	...	2	31	0	2.78	.890	—	—	—	—	—	—	—	—
04-05—St. John's	AHL	23	1335	12	9	...	...	64	3	2.88	.921	1	47	0	0	1	0	1.28	.957
05-06—Toronto	AHL	46	2491	19	18	2	...	126	2	3.03	.899	5	359	1	4	17	0	2.84	.917
—Toronto	NHL	11	677	9	0	2	...	25	1	2.22	.924	—	—	—	—	—	—	—	—
NHL Totals (7 years)		179	9565	72	72	2	11	457	7	2.87	.903	1	1	0	0	0	0	0.00	...

AUBIN, SERGE LW/C

PERSONAL: Born February 15, 1975, in Val d'Or, Que. ... 6-1/200. ... Shoots left. ... Name pronounced AH-ban.

TRANSACTIONS/CAREER NOTES: Selected by Pittsburgh Penguins in seventh round (ninth Penguins pick, 161st overall) of entry draft (June 29, 1994). ... Signed as free agent by Colorado Avalanche (December 18, 1998). ... Signed as free agent by Columbus Blue Jackets (July 11, 2000). ... Flu (January 15, 2001); missed one game. ... Cut knee (November 25, 2001); missed two games. ... Bruised thigh (December 8, 2001); missed two games. ... Concussion (January 26, 2002); missed two games. ... Flu (March 14, 2002); missed one game. ... Injured mouth (March 26, 2002); missed two games. ... Signed as free agent by Avalanche (August 27, 2002). ... Injured ankle (December 26, 2002); missed three games. ... Injured ankle (January 4, 2003); missed two games. ... Bruised foot (January 23, 2003); missed one game. ... Claimed by Atlanta Thrashers in waiver draft (October3, 2003). ... Concussion, neck strain; (December 21, 2003); missed 16 games. ... Flu (December 22, 2005); missed one game. ... Sprained right knee (March 20, 2006); missed five games.

Season Team	League	REGULAR SEASON GP	G	A	Pts.	PIM	+/-	PP	SH	PLAYOFFS GP	G	A	Pts.	PIM
92-93—Drummondville	QMJHL	65	16	34	50	30	...	...	...	8	0	1	1	16
93-94—Granby	QMJHL	63	42	32	74	80	...	...	...	7	2	3	5	8
94-95—Granby	QMJHL	60	37	73	110	55	...	...	...	11	8	15	23	4
95-96—Cleveland	IHL	2	0	0	0	0	...	...	...	2	0	0	0	0
—Hampton Roads	ECHL	62	24	62	86	74	...	...	...	3	1	4	5	10
96-97—Cleveland	IHL	57	9	16	25	38	...	...	...	2	0	0	0	0
97-98—Syracuse	AHL	55	6	14	20	57	-11	2	0	—	—	—	—	—
—Hershey	AHL	5	2	1	3	0	0	1	0	7	1	3	4	6
98-99—Hershey	AHL	64	30	39	69	58	-2	13	1	3	0	1	1	2
—Colorado	NHL	1	0	0	0	0	0	0	0	—	—	—	—	—
99-00—Hershey	AHL	58	42	38	80	56	...	...	...	—	—	—	—	—
—Colorado	NHL	15	2	1	3	6	1	0	0	17	0	1	1	6
00-01—Columbus	NHL	81	13	17	30	107	-20	0	0	—	—	—	—	—
01-02—Columbus	NHL	71	8	8	16	32	-20	1	0	—	—	—	—	—
02-03—Colorado	NHL	66	4	6	10	64	-2	0	0	5	0	0	0	4

Season Team	League	REGULAR SEASON GP	G	A	Pts.	PIM	+/-	PP	SH	PLAYOFFS GP	G	A	Pts.	PIM
03-04—Atlanta	NHL	66	10	15	25	73	0	1	0	—	—	—	—	—
04-05—Geneva	Switzerland	6	2	1	3	8	...	0	0	3	1	2	3	2
05-06—Atlanta	NHL	74	7	17	24	79	-4	1	0	—	—	—	—	—
NHL Totals (7 years)		374	44	64	108	361	-45	3	0	22	0	1	1	10

AUCOIN, ADRIAN D

PERSONAL: Born July 3, 1973, in Ottawa. ... 6-2/215. ... Shoots right. ... Name pronounced oh-COYN.

TRANSACTIONS/CAREER NOTES: Selected by Vancouver Canucks in fifth round (seventh Canucks pick, 117th overall) of entry draft (June 20, 1992). ... Sprained shoulder (January 10, 1997); missed six games. ... Strained groin (October 30, 1997); missed five games. ... Reinjured groin (November 12, 1997); missed 10 games. ... Sprained ankle (December 13, 1997); missed seven games. ... Injured groin (December 4, 1999); missed four games. ... Fractured finger (February 9, 2000); missed 20 games. ... Strained groin (November 4, 2000); missed two games. ... Reinjured groin (November 9, 2000); missed three games. ... Traded by Canucks with second-round pick (C/LW Alexander Polushin) in 2001 draft to Tampa Bay Lightning for G Dan Cloutier (February 7, 2001). ... Traded by Lightning with RW Alexander Kharitonov to New York Islanders for D Mathieu Biron and second-round pick (traded to Washington; traded to Vancouver; Canucks selected Denis Grot) in 2002 draft (June 22, 2001). ... Injured heel (March 28, 2002); missed one game. ... Injured groin (January 15, 2003); missed eight games. ... Injured groin (April 1, 2003); missed one game. ... Signed as free agent by Chicago Blackhawks (August 2, 2005). ... Strained groin (October 9, 2005); missed four games. ... Strained groin (October 23, 2005); missed two games. ... Strained groin (December 3, 2005); missed two games. ... Reinjured groin (December 13, 2005); missed four games. ... Re-injured groin (January 13, 2006); missed six games. ... Injured shoulder (January 31, 2006); missed remainder of season.

Season Team	League	REGULAR SEASON GP	G	A	Pts.	PIM	+/-	PP	SH	PLAYOFFS GP	G	A	Pts.	PIM
91-92—Boston University	Hockey East	33	2	10	12	62	...	...	...	—	—	—	—	—
92-93—Canadian nat'l team	Int'l	42	8	10	18	71	...	...	...	—	—	—	—	—
93-94—Canadian nat'l team	Int'l	59	5	12	17	80	...	...	...	—	—	—	—	—
—Can. Olympic team	Int'l	4	0	0	0	2	4	0	0	—	—	—	—	—
—Hamilton	AHL	13	1	2	3	19	-6	1	0	4	0	2	2	6
94-95—Syracuse	AHL	71	13	18	31	52	-14	5	0	—	—	—	—	—
—Vancouver	NHL	1	1	0	1	0	1	0	0	4	1	0	1	0
95-96—Syracuse	AHL	29	5	13	18	47	...	...	...	—	—	—	—	—
—Vancouver	NHL	49	4	14	18	34	8	2	0	6	0	0	0	2
96-97—Vancouver	NHL	70	5	16	21	63	0	1	0	—	—	—	—	—
97-98—Vancouver	NHL	35	3	3	6	21	-4	1	0	—	—	—	—	—
98-99—Vancouver	NHL	82	23	11	34	77	-14	18	2	—	—	—	—	—
99-00—Vancouver	NHL	57	10	14	24	30	7	4	0	—	—	—	—	—
00-01—Vancouver	NHL	47	3	13	16	20	13	1	0	—	—	—	—	—
—Tampa Bay	NHL	26	1	11	12	25	-8	1	0	—	—	—	—	—
01-02—New York Islanders	NHL	81	12	22	34	62	23	7	0	7	2	5	7	4
02-03—New York Islanders	NHL	73	8	27	35	70	-5	5	0	5	1	2	3	4
03-04—New York Islanders	NHL	81	13	31	44	54	29	4	0	5	0	0	0	6
04-05—MoDo Ornskoldsvik	Sweden	14	2	4	6	32	3	1	0	6	1	0	1	16
05-06—Chicago	NHL	33	1	5	6	38	-13	1	0	—	—	—	—	—
NHL Totals (11 years)		635	84	167	251	494	37	45	2	27	4	7	11	16

AUCOIN, KEITH C

PERSONAL: Born November 6, 1978, in Waltham, Mass. ... 5-9/185. ... Shoots right.

COLLEGE: Norwich.

TRANSACTIONS/CAREER NOTES: Signed as free agent by Providence of the AHL (August 7, 2002). ... Signed as free agent by Anaheim Mighty Ducks (August 30, 2003). ... Signed as free agent by Carolina Hurricanes (August 8, 2005).

Season Team	League	REGULAR SEASON GP	G	A	Pts.	PIM	+/-	PP	SH	PLAYOFFS GP	G	A	Pts.	PIM
97-98—Norwich	ECAC	26	19	14	33	...	...	...	...	—	—	—	—	—
98-99—Norwich	ECAC	31	33	39	72	...	...	...	...	—	—	—	—	—
99-00—Norwich	ECAC	31	36	41	77	14	...	...	...	—	—	—	—	—
00-01—Norwich	ECAC	28	26	30	56	26	...	...	...	—	—	—	—	—
01-02—Florida	ECHL	1	0	2	2	0	...	...	...	—	—	—	—	—
—B.C.	UHL	44	23	35	58	42	...	...	...	10	3	5	8	4
—Lowell	AHL	30	6	10	16	8	...	...	...	—	—	—	—	—
02-03—Providence	AHL	78	25	51	76	71	...	...	...	4	0	1	1	6
03-04—Cincinnati	AHL	80	18	30	48	64	-28	6	0	9	0	3	3	4
04-05—Providence	AHL	72	21	45	66	49	3	10	0	17	4	14	18	18
—Memphis	CHL	5	4	5	9	10	...	...	...	—	—	—	—	—
05-06—Lowell	AHL	72	29	56	85	68	-8	12	1	—	—	—	—	—
—Carolina	NHL	7	0	1	1	4	-4	0	0	—	—	—	—	—
NHL Totals (1 year)		7	0	1	1	4	-4	0	0					

AULD, ALEX G

PERSONAL: Born January 7, 1981, in Cold Lake, Alta. ... 6-4/200. ... Catches left.

TRANSACTIONS/CAREER NOTES: Selected by Florida Panthers in second round (second Panthers pick, 40th overall) of NHL draft (June 26, 1999). ... Traded by Panthers to Vancouver Canucks for second-round pick (traded to New Jersey; Devils selected Tuomas Pihlman) in 2001 draft and (traded to Atlanta; traded Buffalo; Sabres selected John Adams) in 2002 draft (May 31, 2001). ... Traded by Canucks with F Todd Bertuzzi and D Bryan Allen to Florida Panthers for G Roberto Luongo, D Lukas Krajicek and a sixth-round pick (W Sergei Shirokov) in 2006 draft (June 23, 2006).

Season Team	League	GP	Min.	W	L	OTL	T	GA	SO	GAA	SV%	GP	Min.	W	L	GA	SO	GAA	SV%
		REGULAR SEASON										PLAYOFFS							
97-98—North Bay	OHL	6	206	0	4	...	0	17	0	4.95	...	—	—	—	—	—	—	—	—
98-99—North Bay	OHL	37	1894	9	20	...	1	106	1	3.36	.899	3	170	0	3	10	0	3.53	.905
99-00—North Bay	OHL	55	3047	21	26	...	6	167	2	3.29	.891	6	374	2	4	12	0	1.93	.950
00-01—North Bay	OHL	40	2319	22	11	...	5	98	1	2.54	.917	4	240	0	4	15	0	3.75	...
01-02—Manitoba	AHL	21	1103	11	9	...	0	65	1	3.54	.865	1	20	0	0	0	0	0.00	1.000
—Columbia	ECHL	6	375	3	1	...	2	12	0	1.92	.921	—	—	—	—	—	—	—	—
—Vancouver	NHL	1	60	1	0	...	0	2	0	2.00	.909	—	—	—	—	—	—	—	—
02-03—Manitoba	AHL	37	2208	15	19	...	3	97	3	2.64	.908	—	—	—	—	—	—	—	—
—Vancouver	NHL	7	382	3	3	...	0	10	1	1.57	.939	1	20	0	0	1	0	3.00	.800
03-04—Manitoba	AHL	40	2329	18	16	...	4	99	4	2.55	.908	—	—	—	—	—	—	—	—
—Vancouver	NHL	6	349	2	2	...	2	12	0	2.06	.929	3	222	1	2	9	0	2.43	.898
04-05—Manitoba	AHL	50	2763	25	18	...	...	118	2	2.56	.909	3	127	0	2	7	0	3.31	.860
05-06—Vancouver	NHL	67	3859	33	26	6	...	189	0	2.94	.902	—	—	—	—	—	—	—	—
NHL Totals (4 years)		81	4650	39	31	6	2	213	1	2.75	.907	4	242	1	2	10	0	2.48	.892

AVERY, SEAN C/LW

PERSONAL: Born April 10, 1980, in Pickering, Ont. ... 5-9/185. ... Shoots left.

TRANSACTIONS/CAREER NOTES: Signed as free agent by Detroit Red Wings (September 21, 1999). ... Traded by Red Wings with D Maxim Kuznetsov, first-round pick (Jeff Tambellini) in 2003 and second-round pick (later traded to Boston; Bruins selected RW Martins Karsum) in 2004 to Los Angeles Kings for D Mathieu Schneider (March 11, 2003). ... Back (March 27, 2003); missed one game. ... Sprained ankle (October 19, 2005); missed one game. ... Fined $1,000 by NHL in diving incident (November 15, 2005).

Season Team	League	GP	G	A	Pts.	PIM	+/-	PP	SH	GP	G	A	Pts.	PIM
		REGULAR SEASON								PLAYOFFS				
95-96—Markham Waxers	OJHL	1	0	0	0	4	...	...	...	—	—	—	—	—
96-97—Owen Sound	OHL	58	10	21	31	86	...	...	...	4	1	0	1	4
97-98—Owen Sound	OHL	47	13	41	54	105	...	...	...	—	—	—	—	—
98-99—Owen Sound	OHL	28	22	23	45	70	...	...	...	—	—	—	—	—
—Kingston	OHL	33	14	25	39	88	...	...	...	5	1	3	4	13
99-00—Kingston	OHL	55	28	56	84	215	...	...	...	5	2	2	4	26
00-01—Cincinnati	AHL	58	8	15	23	304	...	...	...	4	1	0	1	19
01-02—Cincinnati	AHL	36	14	7	21	106	-4	6	0	—	—	—	—	—
—Detroit	NHL	36	2	2	4	68	1	0	0	—	—	—	—	—
02-03—Grand Rapids	AHL	15	6	6	12	82	2	2	0	—	—	—	—	—
—Detroit	NHL	39	5	6	11	120	7	0	0	—	—	—	—	—
—Los Angeles	NHL	12	1	3	4	33	0	0	0	—	—	—	—	—
—Manchester	AHL	...	...	...	...	...	...	...	...	3	2	1	3	8
03-04—Los Angeles	NHL	76	9	19	28	*261	2	0	0	—	—	—	—	—
04-05—Reipas Lahti	Finland	2	3	0	3	26	-3	...	...	—	—	—	—	—
—Motor City	UHL	16	15	11	26	149	19	4	2	—	—	—	—	—
05-06—Los Angeles	NHL	75	15	24	39	*257	-5	1	3	—	—	—	—	—
NHL Totals (4 years)		238	32	54	86	739	5	1	3					

AXELSSON, DICK LW

PERSONAL: Born April 25, 1987, in Stockholm, Swe. ... 6-2/198. ... Shoots left.

TRANSACTIONS/CAREER NOTES: Selected by Detroit Red Wings in second round (third Red Wings pick; 6second overall) of NHL draft (June 24, 2006).

Season Team	League	GP	G	A	Pts.	PIM	+/-	PP	SH	GP	G	A	Pts.	PIM
		REGULAR SEASON								PLAYOFFS				
04-05—Huddinge	Sweden Jr.	31	12	4	16	34	...	...	...	—	—	—	—	—
05-06—Huddinge	Sweden Jr.	28	19	15	34	157	...	...	...	—	—	—	—	—

AXELSSON, P.J. LW/RW

PERSONAL: Born February 26, 1975, in Kungalv, Sweden. ... 6-1/184. ... Shoots left.

TRANSACTIONS/CAREER NOTES: Selected by Boston Bruins in seventh round (seventh Bruins pick, 177th overall) of entry draft (June 8, 1995). ... Concussion (October 28, 1998); missed one game. ... Concussion (November 3, 1998); missed three games. ... Flu (April 17, 1999); missed one game. ... Charley horse (October 23, 1999); missed one game. ... Strained shoulder (December 15, 2001); missed three games. ... Knee (November 19, 2002); missed four games. ... Back (December 7, 2002); missed six games. ... Flu (January 3, 2003); missed two games. ... Back (January 23, 2003); missed four games. ... Collarbone (November 22, 2003); missed two games. ... Shoulder (November 30, 2003); missed 10 games. ... Sprained right knee (January 8, 2004); missed two games. ... Left knee injury (March 1, 2006); missed final 23 games of regular season.

Season Team	League	GP	G	A	Pts.	PIM	+/-	PP	SH	GP	G	A	Pts.	PIM
		REGULAR SEASON								PLAYOFFS				
93-94—Frolunda	Sweden	11	0	0	0	4	...	...	...	4	0	0	0	0
94-95—Frolunda	Sweden	8	2	1	3	6	...	...	...	—	—	—	—	—
95-96—Frolunda	Sweden	36	15	5	20	10	...	...	...	13	3	0	3	10
96-97—Vastra Frolunda	Sweden	50	19	15	34	34	...	...	...	3	0	2	2	0
97-98—Boston	NHL	82	8	19	27	38	-14	2	0	6	1	0	1	0
98-99—Boston	NHL	77	7	10	17	18	-14	0	0	12	1	1	2	4
99-00—Boston	NHL	81	10	16	26	24	1	0	0	—	—	—	—	—
00-01—Boston	NHL	81	8	15	23	27	-12	0	0	—	—	—	—	—
01-02—Boston	NHL	78	7	17	24	16	6	0	2	6	2	1	3	6

Season Team	League	REGULAR SEASON GP	G	A	Pts.	PIM	+/-	PP	SH	PLAYOFFS GP	G	A	Pts.	PIM
—Swedish Oly. team	Int'l	4	0	0	0	2	...	...	...	—	—	—	—	—
02-03—Boston	NHL	66	17	19	36	24	8	2	2	5	0	0	0	6
03-04—Boston	NHL	68	6	14	20	42	2	0	0	7	0	0	0	4
04-05—Vastra Frolunda	Sweden	45	8	9	17	95	6	3	0	14	1	10	11	18
05-06—Boston	NHL	59	10	18	28	4	-3	1	2	—	—	—	—	—
—Swedish Oly. team	Int'l	8	3	3	6	0	0	1	0	—	—	—	—	—
NHL Totals (8 years)		592	73	128	201	193	-26	5	6	36	4	2	6	20

BABCHUK, ANTON D

PERSONAL: Born May 6, 1984, in Kiev, U.S.S.R. ... 6-5/202. ... Shoots right.

TRANSACTIONS/CAREER NOTES: Selected by Chicago Blackhawks in first round (first Blackhawks pick, 21st overall) of entry draft (June 22, 2002). ... Traded by Blackhawks to Carolina Hurricanes for D Danny Richmond and fourth-round pick (traded to Toronto; Maple Leafs selected G James Reimer) in 2006 draft (January 20, 2006).

Season Team	League	REGULAR SEASON GP	G	A	Pts.	PIM	+/-	PP	SH	PLAYOFFS GP	G	A	Pts.	PIM
01-02—Elektrostal	Russian Div. 1	40	7	8	15	90	...	...	...	—	—	—	—	—
02-03—Ak Bars Kazan	Russian	10	0	0	0	4	...	...	...	—	—	—	—	—
—St. Petersburg	Rus. Div.	20	3	0	3	10	...	...	...	—	—	—	—	—
03-04—Norfolk	AHL	73	8	14	22	89	9	3	0	8	0	2	2	6
—Chicago	NHL	5	0	2	2	2	-1	0	0	—	—	—	—	—
04-05—Norfolk	AHL	66	8	16	24	88	-15	3	0	2	0	0	0	2
05-06—Norfolk	AHL	24	5	7	12	22	0	2	0	—	—	—	—	—
—Lowell	AHL	5	1	3	4	0	-1	1	0	—	—	—	—	—
—Chicago	NHL	17	2	3	5	16	-5	1	0	—	—	—	—	—
—Carolina	NHL	22	3	2	5	6	-2	2	0	—	—	—	—	—
NHL Totals (2 years)		44	5	7	12	24	-8	3	0					

BACASHIHUA, JASON G

PERSONAL: Born September 20, 1982, in Garden City, Mich. ... 5-11/175. ... Catches left. ... Name pronounced bah-kah-SHIH-wah.

TRANSACTIONS/CAREER NOTES: Selected by Dallas Stars in first round (first Stars pick, 26th overall) of entry draft (June 23, 2001). ... Traded by Stars to St. Louis Blues for D Shawn Belle (June 25, 2004). ... Injured left shoulder (January 21, 2006); missed 29 games.

Season Team	League	REGULAR SEASON GP	Min.	W	L	OTL	T	GA	SO	GAA	SV%	PLAYOFFS GP	Min.	W	L	GA	SO	GAA	SV%
99-00—Chicago	NAHL	41	2432	20	19	...	2	118	2	2.91	...	2	103	0	2	12	0	6.99	...
00-01—Chicago	NAHL	39	2246	24	14	...	0	121	1	3.23	...	3	190	1	2	12	0	3.79	...
01-02—Plymouth	OHL	46	2688	26	12	...	7	105	5	2.34	...	6	360	2	4	15	0	2.50	...
—Utah	AHL	1	60	0	1	...	0	3	0	3.00	.925	—	—	—	—	—	—	—	—
02-03—Utah	AHL	39	2244	18	18	...	2	118	3	3.16	.907	1	58	0	1	2	0	2.07	.941
03-04—Utah	AHL	39	2234	13	19	...	5	99	3	2.66	.908	—	—	—	—	—	—	—	—
04-05—Worcester	AHL	35	1908	18	13	...	...	80	2	2.52	.902	—	—	—	—	—	—	—	—
05-06—Peoria	AHL	15	820	9	4	0	...	36	2	2.63	.903	—	—	—	—	—	—	—	—
—St. Louis	NHL	19	966	4	10	1	...	52	0	3.23	.899	—	—	—	—	—	—	—	—
NHL Totals (1 year)		19	966	4	10	1	0	52	0	3.23	.899								

BACKMAN, CHRISTIAN D

PERSONAL: Born April 28, 1980, in Alingsas, Sweden. ... 6-3/208. ... Shoots left. ... Name pronounced BEK-man.

TRANSACTIONS/CAREER NOTES: Selected by St. Louis Blues in first round (first Blues pick, 24th overall) of entry draft (June 27, 1998). ... Bruised shoulder (December 31, 2003); missed 10 games. ... Lleft shoulder (October 28, 2005); missed one game. ... Fractured left foot (December 1, 2005); missed 21 games. ... Hip (February 2, 2006); missed one game. ... Wrist (April 11, 2006); missed one game.

Season Team	League	REGULAR SEASON GP	G	A	Pts.	PIM	+/-	PP	SH	PLAYOFFS GP	G	A	Pts.	PIM
96-97—Vastra Frolunda	Sweden Jr.	26	2	5	7	16	...	...	...	—	—	—	—	—
97-98—Vastra Frolunda	Sweden Jr.	28	5	14	19	12	...	...	...	2	0	1	1	4
98-99—Vastra Frolunda	Sweden	49	0	4	4	4	...	...	...	4	0	0	0	0
99-00—Vastra Frolunda	Sweden	27	1	0	1	14	...	...	...	5	0	0	0	0
00-01—Vastra Frolunda	Sweden	50	1	10	11	32	...	...	...	3	0	2	2	2
01-02—Vastra Frolunda	Sweden	44	7	4	11	38	...	...	...	10	0	0	0	8
02-03—St. Louis	NHL	4	0	0	0	0	-3	0	0	—	—	—	—	—
—Worcester	AHL	72	8	19	27	66	-2	4	0	3	0	1	1	5
03-04—Worcester	AHL	4	1	2	3	2	3	1	0	—	—	—	—	—
—St. Louis	NHL	66	5	13	18	16	3	1	0	5	0	2	2	4
04-05—Vastra Frolunda	Sweden	—	—	—	—	—	—	—	—	14	2	7	9	10
—Vastra Frolunda	Sweden	50	4	15	19	40	29	2	0	—	—	—	—	—
05-06—St. Louis	NHL	52	6	12	18	48	-15	3	0	—	—	—	—	—
—Swedish Oly. team	Int'l	8	1	2	3	6	-1	0	0	—	—	—	—	—
NHL Totals (3 years)		122	11	25	36	64	-15	4	0	5	0	2	2	4

BACKSTROM, NICKLAS C

PERSONAL: Born November 23, 1987, in Gavle, Swe. ... 6-0/183. ... Shoots left.

TRANSACTIONS/CAREER NOTES: Selected by Washington Capitals in first round (first Capitals pick, fourth overall) of NHL draft (June 24, 2006).

Season Team	League	REGULAR SEASON								PLAYOFFS				
		GP	G	A	Pts.	PIM	+/-	PP	SH	GP	G	A	Pts.	PIM
04-05—Brynas IF	Sweden	19	0	0	0	2	-5	...	...	—	—	—	—	—
05-06—Brynas IF	Sweden	46	10	16	26	30	...	...	...	4	1	0	1	2

BALASTIK, JAROSLAV RW/LW

PERSONAL: Born November 28, 1979, in Gottwaldow, Czechoslovakia. ... 6-0/198. ... Shoots left. ... Name pronounced ba-LASH-tihk.
TRANSACTIONS/CAREER NOTES: Selected by Columbus Blue Jackets in sixth round (ninth Blue Jackets pick, 184th overall) of entry draft (June 23, 2002).

Season Team	League	REGULAR SEASON								PLAYOFFS				
		GP	G	A	Pts.	PIM	+/-	PP	SH	GP	G	A	Pts.	PIM
97-98—Zlin	Czech Rep.	6	0	2	2	0	...	...	...	—	—	—	—	—
98-99—Zlin	Czech Rep.	41	4	8	12	10	...	...	...	9	1	0	1	27
99-00—Zlin	Czech Rep.	48	7	10	17	14	7	...	...	4	0	1	1	2
00-01—Zlin	Czech Rep.	52	8	17	25	32	14	...	...	6	1	1	2	6
01-02—Zlin	Czech Rep.	50	25	19	44	32	13	...	...	11	3	5	8	14
02-03—Zlin	Czech Rep.	31	14	8	22	26	7	...	...	—	—	—	—	—
—Hameenlinna	Finland	13	5	7	12	2	8	...	...	—	—	—	—	—
03-04—Zlin	Czech Rep.	51	29	18	47	54	13	...	...	17	9	9	18	32
04-05—Zlin	Czech Rep.	52	30	16	46	74	10	...	...	17	4	9	13	52
05-06—Columbus	NHL	66	12	10	22	26	-1	7	0	—	—	—	—	—
—Syracuse	AHL	14	3	3	6	6	5	0	0	—	—	—	—	—
NHL Totals (1 year)		66	12	10	22	26	-1	7	0					

BALEJ, JOZEF RW

PERSONAL: Born February 22, 1982, in Myjava, Czech. ... 6-1/191. ... Shoots right. ... Name pronounced BAH-lee.
TRANSACTIONS/CAREER NOTES: Selected by Montreal Canadiens in third round (third Canadiens pick, 78th overall) of entry draft (June 24, 2000). ... Traded by Canadiens with second-round pick (C Bruce Graham) in 2004 draft to New York Rangers for RW Alexei Kovalev (March 2, 2004). ... Traded by Rangers with conditional draft pick to Vancouver Canucks for C Fedor Fedorov (October 7, 2005).

Season Team	League	REGULAR SEASON								PLAYOFFS				
		GP	G	A	Pts.	PIM	+/-	PP	SH	GP	G	A	Pts.	PIM
97-98—Dukla Trencin	Slovakia Jrs.	52	57	40	97	60	...	...	...	—	—	—	—	—
98-99—Thunder Bay Flyers	USHL	38	8	7	15	9	...	...	...	—	—	—	—	—
99-00—Portland	WHL	65	22	23	45	33	...	...	...	—	—	—	—	—
00-01—Portland	WHL	46	32	21	53	18	...	...	...	16	6	9	15	6
01-02—Portland	WHL	65	51	41	92	52	...	...	...	7	0	2	2	6
02-03—Hamilton	AHL	56	5	15	20	29	0	2	0	3	1	0	1	2
03-04—Hamilton	AHL	55	26	32	58	32	19	3	2	—	—	—	—	—
—Montreal	NHL	4	0	0	0	0	-1	0	0	—	—	—	—	—
—New York Rangers	NHL	13	1	4	5	4	0	0	0	—	—	—	—	—
—Hartford	AHL	5	1	3	4	21	0	0	0	16	9	7	16	10
04-05—Hartford	AHL	69	20	22	42	46	2	5	2	6	0	0	0	4
05-06—Manitoba	AHL	39	14	15	29	20	3	4	0	4	1	0	1	4
—Vancouver	NHL	1	0	1	1	0	1	0	0	—	—	—	—	—
NHL Totals (2 years)		18	1	5	6	4	0	0	0					

BALLARD, KEITH D

PERSONAL: Born November 26, 1982, in Baudette, Minn. ... 5-11/202. ... Shoots left.
TRANSACTIONS/CAREER NOTES: Selected by Buffalo Sabres in first round (first Sabres pick, 11th overall) of entry draft (June 22, 2002). ... Traded by Sabres to Colorado Avalanche for C/W Steve Reinprecht (July 2, 2003). ... Traded by Avalanche with D Derek Morris to Phoenix Coyotes for F Chris Gratton, D Ossi Vaananen and second-round pick (C Paul Stastny) in 2005 (March 9, 2004).

Season Team	League	REGULAR SEASON								PLAYOFFS				
		GP	G	A	Pts.	PIM	+/-	PP	SH	GP	G	A	Pts.	PIM
99-00—U.S. National	USHL	58	12	21	33	...	...	...	...	—	—	—	—	—
00-01—Omaha	USHL	56	22	29	51	168	...	...	...	10	1	6	7	8
01-02—Minnesota	WCHA	34	6	12	18	28	...	...	...	—	—	—	—	—
02-03—Minnesota	WCHA	45	12	29	41	78	...	...	...	—	—	—	—	—
03-04—Minnesota	WCHA	37	11	25	36	83	...	6	1	—	—	—	—	—
04-05—Utah	AHL	60	2	18	20	88	-29	2	0	—	—	—	—	—
05-06—Phoenix	NHL	82	8	31	39	99	-18	1	3	—	—	—	—	—
NHL Totals (1 year)		82	8	31	39	99	-18	1	3					

BARINKA, MICHAL D

PERSONAL: Born June 12, 1984, in Vyskov, Czechoslovakia. ... 6-3/217. ... Shoots left.
TRANSACTIONS/CAREER NOTES: Drafted by Chicago Blackhawks in second round (59th overall) of NHL entry draft (June 20, 2003). ... Concussion (December 16, 2005); missed six games. ... Traded by Blackhawks with D Tom Preissing, D Josh Hennessy and a second-round pick in 2008 draft to Ottawa Senators for Fs Martin Havlat and Bryan Smolinski in three-team trade in which Blackhawks traded F Mark Bell to San Jose Sharks for Preissing and Hennessy (July 10, 2006).

Season Team	League	REGULAR SEASON								PLAYOFFS				
		GP	G	A	Pts.	PIM	+/-	PP	SH	GP	G	A	Pts.	PIM
01-02—HC Ceske Budejovice	Czech Rep.	3	0	0	0	0	0	...	...	—	—	—	—	—
02-03—HC Ceske Budejovice	Czech Rep.	31	0	1	1	14	...	...	...	4	0	0	0	2

Season Team	League	GP	G	A	Pts.	PIM	+/-	PP	SH	GP	G	A	Pts.	PIM
		REGULAR SEASON								PLAYOFFS				
03-04—Norfolk	AHL	40	4	2	6	80	-2	1	0	—	—	—	—	—
—Chicago	NHL	9	0	1	1	6	-5	0	0	—	—	—	—	—
04-05—Norfolk	AHL	59	1	10	11	77	-3	0	0	0	0	0	0	0
05-06—Norfolk	AHL	54	1	11	12	86	5	0	0	4	0	0	0	11
—Chicago	NHL	25	0	1	1	20	-7	0	0	—	—	—	—	—
NHL Totals (2 years)		34	0	2	2	26	-12	0	0					

BARKER, CAM D

PERSONAL: Born April 4, 1986, in Winnipeg. ... 6-3/214. ... Shoots left.

TRANSACTIONS/CAREER NOTES: Selected by Chicago Blackhawks in first round (first Blackhawks pick, third overall) of NHL entry draft (June 26, 2004). ... Signed by Blackhawks (July 26, 2005).

Season Team	League	GP	G	A	Pts.	PIM	+/-	PP	SH	GP	G	A	Pts.	PIM
		REGULAR SEASON								PLAYOFFS				
01-02—Medicine Hat	WHL	3	0	1	1	0	...	...	...	—	—	—	—	—
02-03—Medicine Hat	WHL	64	10	37	47	79	...	...	...	11	3	4	7	17
03-04—Medicine Hat	WHL	69	21	44	65	105	...	...	...	20	3	9	12	18
04-05—Medicine Hat	WHL	52	15	33	48	99	19	6	0	12	3	3	6	16
05-06—Chicago	NHL	1	0	0	0	0	0	0	0	—	—	—	—	—
NHL Totals (1 year)		1	0	0	0	0	0	0	0					

BARNABY, MATTHEW RW/LW

PERSONAL: Born May 4, 1973, in Ottawa. ... 6-1/190. ... Shoots left.

TRANSACTIONS/CAREER NOTES: Selected by Buffalo Sabres in fourth round (fifth Sabres pick, 83rd overall) of NHL draft (June 20, 1992). ... Had back spasms (March 28, 1995); missed one game. ... Suspended one game for accumulating three game misconduct penalties (March 31, 1996). ... Injured groin (April 3, 1996); missed five games. ... Sprained knee ligament (April 2, 1997); missed final six games of regular season and four playoff games. ... Injured sternum (October 10, 1997); missed five games. ... Strained shoulder (February 2, 1998); missed one game. ... Suspended four games and fined $1,000 for striking another player in the head (November 5, 1998). ... Back spasms (December 12, 1998); missed one game. ... Injured ankle (December 18, 1998); missed one game. ... Flu (January 11, 1999); missed one game. ... Traded by Sabres to Pittsburgh Penguins for C Stu Barnes (March 11, 1999). ... Strained knee (November 2, 1999); missed five games. ... Suffered concussion (December 15, 1999); missed seven games. ... Suffered concussion (January 13, 2000); missed one game. ... Suspended five games for fighting incident (February 13, 2000). ... Traded by Penguins to Tampa Bay Lightning for C Wayne Primeau (February 1, 2001). ... Injured elbow (October 14, 2001); missed one game. ... Traded by Lightning to New York Rangers for LW Zdeno Ciger (December 12, 2001). ... Injured knee (December 5, 2002); missed three games. ... Traded by Rangers with third-round pick (LW Denis Pershin) in 2004 entry draft to Colorado Avalanche for D Chris McAllister, D David Liffiton and future considerations (March 8, 2004). ... Signed as free agent by Chicago Blackhawks (July 2, 2004). ... Signed as free agent by Dallas Stars (July 5, 2006).

Season Team	League	GP	G	A	Pts.	PIM	+/-	PP	SH	GP	G	A	Pts.	PIM
		REGULAR SEASON								PLAYOFFS				
90-91—Beauport	QMJHL	52	9	5	14	262	...	...	...	—	—	—	—	—
91-92—Beauport	QMJHL	63	29	37	66	476	...	...	...	—	—	—	—	—
92-93—Victoriaville	QMJHL	65	44	67	111	448	...	...	...	6	2	4	6	44
—Buffalo	NHL	2	1	0	1	10	0	1	0	1	0	1	1	4
93-94—Buffalo	NHL	35	2	4	6	106	-7	1	0	3	0	0	0	17
—Rochester	AHL	42	10	32	42	153	-8	6	0	—	—	—	—	—
94-95—Rochester	AHL	56	21	29	50	274	7	6	0	—	—	—	—	—
—Buffalo	NHL	23	1	1	2	116	-2	0	0	—	—	—	—	—
95-96—Buffalo	NHL	73	15	16	31	*335	-2	0	0	—	—	—	—	—
96-97—Buffalo	NHL	68	19	24	43	249	16	2	0	8	0	4	4	36
97-98—Buffalo	NHL	72	5	20	25	289	8	0	0	15	7	6	13	22
98-99—Buffalo	NHL	44	4	14	18	143	-2	0	0	—	—	—	—	—
—Pittsburgh	NHL	18	2	2	4	34	-10	1	0	13	0	0	0	35
99-00—Pittsburgh	NHL	64	12	12	24	197	3	0	0	11	0	2	2	29
00-01—Pittsburgh	NHL	47	1	4	5	168	-7	0	0	—	—	—	—	—
—Tampa Bay	NHL	29	4	4	8	97	-3	1	0	—	—	—	—	—
01-02—Tampa Bay	NHL	29	0	0	0	70	-7	0	0	—	—	—	—	—
—New York Rangers	NHL	48	8	13	21	144	-3	0	0	—	—	—	—	—
02-03—New York Rangers	NHL	79	14	22	36	142	9	1	0	—	—	—	—	—
03-04—New York Rangers	NHL	69	12	20	32	120	15	0	0	—	—	—	—	—
—Colorado	NHL	13	4	5	9	37	3	1	0	11	0	2	2	27
05-06—Chicago	NHL	82	8	20	28	178	-11	0	0	—	—	—	—	—
NHL Totals (13 years)		795	112	181	293	2435	0	8	0	62	7	15	22	170

BARNES, STU C/RW

PERSONAL: Born December 25, 1970, in Spruce Grove, Alta. ... 5-11/180. ... Shoots right.

TRANSACTIONS/CAREER NOTES: Selected by Winnipeg Jets in first round (first Jets pick, fourth overall) of NHL draft (June 17, 1989). ... Traded by Jets to Florida Panthers for C Randy Gilhen (November 26, 1993). ... Strained left calf (January 1, 1994); missed one game. ... Cut, bruised left eye (February 15, 1995); missed seven games. ... Sprained left knee (March 10, 1996); missed 10 games. ... Traded by Panthers with D Jason Woolley to Pittsburgh Penguins for C Chris Wells (November 19, 1996). ... Hip (April 11, 1997); missed one game. ... Back spasms (October 9, 1997); missed one game. ... Hip flexor (April 16, 1998); missed one game. ... Traded by Penguins to Buffalo Sabres for RW Matthew Barnaby (March 11, 1999). ... Groin (November 3, 2000); missed seven games. ... Concussion (March 17, 2002); missed remainder of season. ... Traded by Sabres to Dallas Stars for C Mike Ryan and second-round pick (RW Branislav Fabry) in 2003 (March 10, 2003). ... Upper-body injury (March 24, 2004); missed five games. ... Hip flexor (December 27, 2005); missed three games.

STATISTICAL PLATEAUS: Three-goal games: 1991-92 (1), 1997-98 (1), 1998-99 (1). Total: 3.

Season Team	League	GP	G	A	Pts.	PIM	+/-	PP	SH	GP	G	A	Pts.	PIM
		REGULAR SEASON								PLAYOFFS				
86-87—St. Albert	AJHL	57	43	32	75	80	...	...	...	—	—	—	—	—
87-88—New Westminster	WHL	71	37	64	101	88	...	...	...	5	2	3	5	6
88-89—Tri-City	WHL	70	59	82	141	117	...	...	...	7	6	5	11	10
89-90—Tri-City	WHL	63	52	92	144	165	...	...	...	7	1	5	6	26
90-91—Canadian nat'l team	Int'l	53	22	27	49	68	...	...	...	—	—	—	—	—
91-92—Winnipeg	NHL	46	8	9	17	26	-2	4	0	—	—	—	—	—
—Moncton	AHL	30	13	19	32	10	...	...	...	11	3	9	12	6
92-93—Moncton	AHL	42	23	31	54	58	3	4	0	—	—	—	—	—
—Winnipeg	NHL	38	12	10	22	10	-3	3	0	6	1	3	4	2
93-94—Winnipeg	NHL	18	5	4	9	8	-1	2	0	—	—	—	—	—
—Florida	NHL	59	18	20	38	30	5	6	1	—	—	—	—	—
94-95—Florida	NHL	41	10	19	29	8	7	1	0	—	—	—	—	—
95-96—Florida	NHL	72	19	25	44	46	-12	8	0	22	6	10	16	4
96-97—Florida	NHL	19	2	8	10	10	-3	1	0	—	—	—	—	—
—Pittsburgh	NHL	62	17	22	39	16	-20	4	0	5	0	1	1	0
97-98—Pittsburgh	NHL	78	30	35	65	30	15	15	1	6	3	3	6	2
98-99—Pittsburgh	NHL	64	20	12	32	20	-12	13	0	—	—	—	—	—
—Buffalo	NHL	17	0	4	4	10	1	0	0	21	7	3	10	6
99-00—Buffalo	NHL	82	20	25	45	16	-3	8	2	5	3	0	3	2
00-01—Buffalo	NHL	75	19	24	43	26	-2	3	2	13	4	4	8	2
01-02—Buffalo	NHL	68	17	31	48	26	6	5	0	—	—	—	—	—
02-03—Buffalo	NHL	68	11	21	32	20	-13	2	1	—	—	—	—	—
—Dallas	NHL	13	2	5	7	8	2	2	0	12	2	3	5	0
03-04—Dallas	NHL	77	11	18	29	18	7	0	1	5	0	0	0	0
05-06—Dallas	NHL	78	15	21	36	44	9	0	1	5	1	1	2	0
NHL Totals (14 years)		975	236	313	549	372	-19	77	9	100	27	28	55	18

B

BARNEY, SCOTT RW

PERSONAL: Born March 27, 1979, in Oshawa, Ont. ... 6-4/208. ... Shoots right.

TRANSACTIONS/CAREER NOTES: Selected by Los Angeles Kings in second round (third Kings pick, 29th overall) of entry draft (June 21, 1997). ... Injured back (September 28, 1999); missed 1999-2000, 2000-01 and 2001-02. ... Shoulder (February 14, 2004); missed 12 games. ... Abdominal surgery; missed 2004-05 season. ... Signed as free agent by Atlanta Thrashers (August 8, 2005).

Season Team	League	GP	G	A	Pts.	PIM	+/-	PP	SH	GP	G	A	Pts.	PIM
		REGULAR SEASON								PLAYOFFS				
94-95—North York	MTHL	41	16	19	35	88	...	...	...	—	—	—	—	—
95-96—Peterborough	OHL	60	22	24	46	52	...	...	...	24	6	8	14	38
96-97—Peterborough	OHL	64	21	33	54	110	...	...	...	9	0	3	3	16
97-98—Peterborough	OHL	62	44	32	76	60	...	...	...	4	1	0	1	6
98-99—Peterborough	OHL	44	41	26	67	80	15	...	...	5	4	1	5	4
—Springfield	AHL	5	0	0	0	2	0	0	0	1	0	0	0	2
02-03—Manchester	AHL	57	13	5	18	74	-11	5	0	—	—	—	—	—
—Los Angeles	NHL	5	0	0	0	0	-1	0	0	—	—	—	—	—
03-04—Los Angeles	NHL	19	5	6	11	4	3	2	0	—	—	—	—	—
—Manchester	AHL	44	20	14	34	28	12	8	0	6	2	3	5	8
04-05—Manchester	AHL	Did not play — injured												
05-06—Chicago	AHL	53	32	19	51	54	-8	15	0	—	—	—	—	—
—Atlanta	NHL	3	0	0	0	0	-1	0	0	—	—	—	—	—
NHL Totals (3 years)		27	5	6	11	4	1	2	0					

BARTOVIC, MILAN LW/RW

PERSONAL: Born April 9, 1981, in Trencin, Czechoslovakia. ... 5-11/192. ... Shoots left.

TRANSACTIONS/CAREER NOTES: Selected by Buffalo Sabres in second round (second Sabres pick, 35th overall) of entry draft (June 26, 1999). ... Traded by Sabres to Chicago Blackhawks for G Michael Leighton (October 4, 2005).

Season Team	League	GP	G	A	Pts.	PIM	+/-	PP	SH	GP	G	A	Pts.	PIM
		REGULAR SEASON								PLAYOFFS				
97-98—Dukla Trencin	Slovakia Jrs.	26	2	6	8	15	...	...	...	—	—	—	—	—
98-99—Dukla Trencin	Slovakia Jrs.	46	36	35	71	62	...	...	...	6	9	3	12	10
99-00—Tri-City	WHL	18	8	9	17	12	...	...	...	—	—	—	—	—
—Brandon	WHL	38	18	22	40	28	-7	9	3	—	—	—	—	—
00-01—Brandon	WHL	34	15	25	40	40	...	...	...	6	1	2	3	8
—Rochester	AHL	2	1	1	2	0	...	...	...	4	0	1	1	2
01-02—Rochester	AHL	73	15	11	26	56	10	0	3	2	0	0	0	0
02-03—Buffalo	NHL	3	1	0	1	0	0	0	0	—	—	—	—	—
—Rochester	AHL	74	18	10	28	84	-6	2	0	3	0	0	0	0
03-04—Buffalo	NHL	23	1	8	9	18	1	0	0	—	—	—	—	—
—Rochester	AHL	52	18	11	29	52	1	4	1	2	0	0	0	2
04-05—Rochester	AHL	69	10	18	28	83	8	1	1	9	0	3	3	22
05-06—Norfolk	AHL	49	10	14	24	34	1	2	0	3	0	0	0	8
—Chicago	NHL	24	1	6	7	8	0	0	0	—	—	—	—	—
NHL Totals (3 years)		50	3	14	17	26	1	0	0					

BATES, SHAWN C/LW

PERSONAL: Born April 3, 1975, in Melrose, Mass. ... 6-0/205. ... Shoots right.

TRANSACTIONS/CAREER NOTES: Selected by Boston Bruins in fourth round (fourth Bruins pick, 10third overall) of entry draft (June 26,

1993). ... Involved in car accident (November 8, 1997); missed one game. ... Flu (December 1, 1998); missed one game. ... Injured hamstring (April 15, 1999); missed two games. ... Injured shoulder (October 30, 1999); missed four games. ... Sprained wrist (December 9, 1999); missed 25 games. ... Sprained wrist (March 25, 2000); missed seven games. ... Strained groin (December 16, 2000); missed three games. ... Reinjured groin (January 10, 2001); missed 16 games. ... Signed as free agent by New York Islanders (July 8, 2001). ... Injured groin (November 23, 2001); missed 10 games. ... Strained groin (March 28, 2002); missed one game. ... Injured groin (December 19, 2002); missed eight games. ... Injured groin (March 11, 2004); missed final 13 games of regular season. ... Re-signed by Islanders as restricted free agent (August 22, 2005). ... Injured hip (October 13, 2005); missed four games. ... Strained hamstring (November 19, 2005); missed 12 games. ... Signed by Islanders to three-year contract extension (March 6, 2006).

		REGULAR SEASON								PLAYOFFS				
Season Team	League	GP	G	A	Pts.	PIM	+/-	PP	SH	GP	G	A	Pts.	PIM
90-91—Medford H.S.	Mass. H.S.	22	18	43	61	6	...	...	...	—	—	—	—	—
91-92—Medford H.S.	Mass. H.S.	22	38	41	79	10	...	...	...	—	—	—	—	—
92-93—Medford H.S.	Mass. H.S.	25	49	46	95	20	...	...	...	—	—	—	—	—
93-94—Boston University	Hockey East	41	10	19	29	24	25	1	1	—	—	—	—	—
94-95—Boston University	Hockey East	38	18	12	30	48	13	1	3	—	—	—	—	—
95-96—Boston University	Hockey East	40	28	22	50	54	...	...	...	—	—	—	—	—
96-97—Boston University	Hockey East	41	17	18	35	64	16	4	3	—	—	—	—	—
97-98—Boston	NHL	13	2	0	2	2	-3	0	0	—	—	—	—	—
—Providence	AHL	50	15	19	34	22	-24	5	4	—	—	—	—	—
98-99—Providence	AHL	37	25	21	46	39	8	10	5	—	—	—	—	—
—Boston	NHL	33	5	4	9	2	3	0	0	12	0	0	0	4
99-00—Boston	NHL	44	5	7	12	14	-17	0	0	—	—	—	—	—
00-01—Boston	NHL	45	2	3	5	26	-12	0	0	—	—	—	—	—
—Providence	AHL	11	5	8	13	12	...	...	...	8	2	6	8	8
01-02—New York Islanders	NHL	71	17	35	52	30	18	1	4	7	2	4	6	11
02-03—New York Islanders	NHL	74	13	29	42	52	-9	1	*6	5	1	0	1	0
03-04—New York Islanders	NHL	69	9	23	32	46	-8	0	1	5	0	0	0	4
05-06—New York Islanders	NHL	66	15	19	34	60	-11	1	1	—	—	—	—	—
NHL Totals (8 years)		415	68	120	188	232	-39	3	12	29	3	4	7	19

BAUMGARTNER, NOLAN D

PERSONAL: Born March 23, 1976, in Calgary. ... 6-2/205. ... Shoots right.

TRANSACTIONS/CAREER NOTES: Selected by Washington Capitals in first round (first Capitals pick, 10th overall) of NHL draft (June 28, 1994). ... Traded by Capitals to Chicago Blackhawks for D Remi Royer (July 21, 2000). ... Signed as free agent by Vancouver Canucks (July 11, 2002). ... Claimed by Pittsburgh Penguins from Canucks in waiver draft (October 3, 2003). ... Claimed by Canucks off waivers from Penguins (November 1, 2003). ... Injured finger (December 22, 2005); missed three games. ... Injured foot (February 4, 2006); missed six games. ... Signed as free agent by Philadelphia Flyers (July 1, 2006).

		REGULAR SEASON								PLAYOFFS				
Season Team	League	GP	G	A	Pts.	PIM	+/-	PP	SH	GP	G	A	Pts.	PIM
92-93—Kamloops	WHL	43	0	5	5	30	...	...	...	11	1	1	2	0
93-94—Kamloops	WHL	69	13	42	55	109	62	5	1	19	3	14	17	33
94-95—Kamloops	WHL	62	8	36	44	71	50	3	0	21	4	13	17	16
95-96—Washington	NHL	1	0	0	0	0	-1	0	0	1	0	0	0	10
—Kamloops	WHL	28	13	15	28	45	...	...	...	16	1	9	10	26
96-97—Portland	AHL	8	2	2	4	4	-6	1	0	—	—	—	—	—
97-98—Portland	AHL	70	2	24	26	70	-12	1	0	10	1	4	5	10
—Washington	NHL	4	0	1	1	0	0	0	0	—	—	—	—	—
98-99—Portland	AHL	38	5	14	19	62	-16	2	0	—	—	—	—	—
—Washington	NHL	5	0	0	0	0	-3	0	0	—	—	—	—	—
99-00—Portland	AHL	71	5	18	23	56	...	...	...	4	1	2	3	10
—Washington	NHL	8	0	1	1	2	1	0	0	—	—	—	—	—
00-01—Norfolk	AHL	63	5	28	33	75	...	...	...	9	2	3	5	11
—Chicago	NHL	8	0	0	0	6	-4	0	0	—	—	—	—	—
01-02—Norfolk	AHL	76	10	24	34	72	1	4	0	4	0	1	1	2
02-03—Vancouver	NHL	8	1	2	3	4	4	1	0	2	0	0	0	0
—Manitoba	AHL	59	8	31	39	82	15	5	0	1	0	0	0	4
03-04—Pittsburgh	NHL	5	0	0	0	2	-7	0	0	—	—	—	—	—
—Manitoba	AHL	55	6	21	27	101	-2	1	0	—	—	—	—	—
—Vancouver	NHL	9	0	3	3	2	3	0	0	—	—	—	—	—
04-05—Manitoba	AHL	78	9	30	39	51	-5	7	0	14	0	4	4	10
05-06—Vancouver	NHL	70	5	29	34	30	11	4	1	—	—	—	—	—
NHL Totals (8 years)		118	6	36	42	46	4	5	1	3	0	0	0	10

BEAUCHEMIN, FRANCOIS D

PERSONAL: Born June 4, 1980, in Sorel, Que. ... 6-0/215. ... Shoots left. ... Name pronounced frahn-SWUH boh-sheh-MEH.

TRANSACTIONS/CAREER NOTES: Selected by Montreal Canadiens in third round (third Canadiens pick, 75th overall) of entry draft (June 27, 1998). ... Claimed by Columbus Blue Jackets off waivers (September 14, 2004). ... Traded by Blue Jackets with C Tyler Wright to Anaheim Mighty Ducks for C Sergei Fedorov and fifth-round pick (D Maxime Frechette) in 2006 draft (November 15, 2005).

		REGULAR SEASON								PLAYOFFS				
Season Team	League	GP	G	A	Pts.	PIM	+/-	PP	SH	GP	G	A	Pts.	PIM
96-97—Laval	QMJHL	66	7	20	27	112	...	...	...	3	0	0	0	2
97-98—Laval	QMJHL	70	12	35	47	132	...	...	...	16	1	3	4	23
98-99—Acadie-Bathurst	QMJHL	31	4	17	21	53	27	1	1	23	2	16	18	55
99-00—Acadie-Bathurst	QMJHL	38	11	36	47	64	7	1	0	—	—	—	—	—
—Moncton	QMJHL	33	8	31	39	35	43	1	0	16	2	11	13	14
00-01—Quebec	AHL	56	3	6	9	44	...	...	...	—	—	—	—	—
01-02—Quebec	AHL	56	8	11	19	88	-11	3	0	3	0	1	1	0

Season Team	League	REGULAR SEASON								PLAYOFFS				
		GP	G	A	Pts.	PIM	+/-	PP	SH	GP	G	A	Pts.	PIM
—Mississippi	ECHL	7	1	3	4	2	-1	0	0	—	—	—	—	—
02-03—Montreal	NHL	1	0	0	0	0	-1	0	0	—	—	—	—	—
—Hamilton	AHL	75	7	21	28	92	25	3	0	23	1	9	10	16
03-04—Hamilton	AHL	77	9	27	36	57	7	...	...	10	2	4	6	18
04-05—Syracuse	AHL	72	3	27	30	55	17	1	0	—	—	—	—	—
05-06—Columbus	NHL	11	0	2	2	11	-6	0	0	—	—	—	—	—
—Anaheim	NHL	61	8	26	34	41	8	4	0	16	3	6	9	11
NHL Totals (2 years)		73	8	28	36	52	1	4	0	16	3	6	9	11

BEECH, KRIS C

PERSONAL: Born February 5, 1981, in Salmon Arm, B.C. ... 6-2/209. ... Shoots left.

TRANSACTIONS/CAREER NOTES: Selected by Washington Capitals in first round (first Capitals pick, seventh overall) of entry draft (June 26, 1999). ... Traded by Capitals with C Michal Sivek, D Ross Lupaschuk and future considerations to Pittsburgh Penguins for RW Jaromir Jagr and D Frantisek Kucera (July 11, 2001). ... Appendectomy (December 15, 2002); missed 15 games. ... Signed as free agent by Wilkes-Barre/Scranton of the AHL (September 26, 2004). ... Traded by Penguins to Nashville Predators for fourth-round pick (traded to Florida; Panthers selected D Derrick LaPoint) in 2006 draft (September 9, 2005). ... Trade by Predators with first-round pick (G Semen Varlomov) in 2006 draft to Capitals for D Brendan Witt (March 9, 2006).

Season Team	League	REGULAR SEASON								PLAYOFFS				
		GP	G	A	Pts.	PIM	+/-	PP	SH	GP	G	A	Pts.	PIM
96-97—Sicamous	Jr. A	49	34	36	70	80	...	...	...	—	—	—	—	—
—Calgary	WHL	8	1	1	2	0	...	...	...	—	—	—	—	—
97-98—Calgary	WHL	68	26	41	67	103	...	...	...	—	—	—	—	—
98-99—Calgary	WHL	58	10	25	35	24	...	...	...	—	—	—	—	—
99-00—Calgary	WHL	66	32	54	86	99	25	15	2	5	3	5	8	16
00-01—Washington	NHL	4	0	0	0	2	-2	0	0	—	—	—	—	—
—Calgary	WHL	40	22	44	66	103	...	...	...	10	2	8	10	26
01-02—Pittsburgh	NHL	79	10	15	25	45	-25	2	0	—	—	—	—	—
02-03—Pittsburgh	NHL	12	0	1	1	6	-3	0	0	—	—	—	—	—
—Wilkes-Barre/Scranton	AHL	50	19	24	43	76	-4	10	1	5	1	1	2	0
03-04—Wilkes-Barre/Scranton	AHL	53	20	26	46	97	15	9	0	22	9	5	14	22
—Pittsburgh	NHL	4	0	1	1	6	0	0	0	—	—	—	—	—
04-05—Wilkes-Barre/Scranton	AHL	68	14	48	62	146	17	3	0	11	4	6	10	14
05-06—Milwaukee	AHL	48	18	32	50	48	4	9	3	—	—	—	—	—
—Hershey	AHL	10	8	6	14	6	1	2	2	14	8	10	18	20
—Nashville	NHL	5	1	2	3	0	1	0	0	—	—	—	—	—
—Washington	NHL	5	0	0	0	4	0	0	0	—	—	—	—	—
NHL Totals (5 years)		109	11	19	30	63	-29	2	0					

BEGIN, STEVE C/LW

PERSONAL: Born June 14, 1978, in Trois-Rivieres, Que. ... 5-11/185. ... Shoots left. ... Name pronounced BAY-zhin.

TRANSACTIONS/CAREER NOTES: Selected by Calgary Flames in second round (third Flames pick, 40th overall) of entry draft (June 22, 1996). ... Shoulder (October 10, 1997); missed six games. ... Dislocated fibula (March 18, 2000); missed season's final 10 games. ... Shoulder (January 17, 2002); missed nine games. ... Head (April 2, 2002); missed remainder of season. ... Traded by Flames to Buffalo Sabres with C Chris Drury for D Rhett Warrener and C Steve Reinprecht (July 2, 2003). ... Claimed by Montreal Canadiens in waiver draft (October 3, 2003). ... Shoulder (October 16, 2003); missed three games. ... Left shoulder (December 10, 2003); surgery (December 18, 2003); missed 23 games. ... Flu (March 16, 2004); missed one game. ... Strained neck (December 31, 2005); missed one game. ... Injured knee (April 10, 2006); missed final five games of regular season and four playoff games.

Season Team	League	REGULAR SEASON								PLAYOFFS				
		GP	G	A	Pts.	PIM	+/-	PP	SH	GP	G	A	Pts.	PIM
95-96—Val-d'Or	QMJHL	64	13	23	36	218	...	...	...	13	1	3	4	33
96-97—Val-d'Or	QMJHL	58	13	33	46	207	...	...	...	10	0	3	3	8
—Saint John	AHL	...	...	...	...	...	...	...	...	4	0	2	2	6
97-98—Calgary	NHL	5	0	0	0	23	0	0	0	—	—	—	—	—
—Val-d'Or	QMJHL	35	18	17	35	73	...	...	...	15	2	12	14	34
98-99—Saint John	AHL	73	11	9	20	156	-16	3	0	7	2	0	2	18
99-00—Calgary	NHL	13	1	1	2	18	-3	0	0	—	—	—	—	—
—Saint John	AHL	47	13	12	25	99	...	...	...	—	—	—	—	—
00-01—Saint John	AHL	58	14	14	28	109	...	...	...	19	10	7	17	18
—Calgary	NHL	4	0	0	0	21	0	0	0	—	—	—	—	—
01-02—Calgary	NHL	51	7	5	12	79	-3	1	0	—	—	—	—	—
02-03—Calgary	NHL	50	3	1	4	51	-7	0	0	—	—	—	—	—
03-04—Montreal	NHL	52	10	5	15	41	6	0	1	9	0	1	1	10
04-05—Hamilton	AHL	21	10	3	13	20	6	0	2	4	0	2	2	8
05-06—Montreal	NHL	76	11	12	23	113	9	1	2	2	0	0	0	2
NHL Totals (7 years)		251	32	24	56	346	2	2	3	11	0	1	1	12

BELAK, WADE D/RW

PERSONAL: Born July 3, 1976, in Saskatoon, Sask. ... 6-5/221. ... Shoots right. ... Brother of Graham Belak, defenseman, Colorado Avalanche organization (1997-98 and 1998-99). ... Name pronounced BEE-lak.

TRANSACTIONS/CAREER NOTES: Selected by Quebec Nordiques in first round (first Nordiques pick, 12th overall) of NHL draft (June 28, 1994). ... Nordiques franchise moved to Colorado and renamed Avalanche for 1995-96 season (June 21, 1995). ... Injured abdominal muscle (March 5, 1998); missed six games. ... Strained groin (October 9, 1998); missed first two games of season. ... Strained groin (October 26, 1998); missed one game. ... Reinjured groin (November 2, 1998); missed 10 games. ... Traded by Avalanche with LW Rene Corbet and future considerations to Calgary Flames for RW Theo Fleury and LW Chris Dingman (February 28, 1999); Flames acquired D Robyn Regehr to complete deal (March 27, 1999). ... Had concussion (November 10, 1999); missed one game. ... Injured shoulder (February 10, 2000); missed 18 games. ... Injured groin (March 22, 2000); missed three games. ... Claimed off waivers by Toronto Maple Leafs (February 16, 2001). ... Injured (March 29, 2001); missed final four games of regular season. ... Flu (March 2, 2002); missed three games. ... Had concussion (October 15, 2002); missed seven games. ... Suspended two games for elbowing incident (November 27, 2002). ... Injured abdomen (November 21, 2003); missed 10 games. ... Injured left knee (January 7, 2004); missed 28 games. ... Suspended final six regular-season games and two playoff games for high-sticking incident (March 22, 2004). ... Injured foot (October 5, 2005); missed one game.

		REGULAR SEASON								PLAYOFFS				
Season Team	**League**	**GP**	**G**	**A**	**Pts.**	**PIM**	**+/-**	**PP**	**SH**	**GP**	**G**	**A**	**Pts.**	**PIM**
91-92—North Battleford	SJHL	57	6	20	26	186	...	...	...	—	—	—	—	—
92-93—North Battleford	SJHL	32	3	13	16	142	...	...	...	—	—	—	—	—
93-94—Saskatoon	WHL	69	4	13	17	226	20	0	0	16	2	2	4	43
94-95—Saskatoon	WHL	72	4	14	18	290	12	0	0	9	0	0	0	36
—Cornwall	AHL	...	...	...	...	...	...	...	...	11	1	2	3	40
95-96—Saskatoon	WHL	63	3	15	18	207	...	...	...	4	0	0	0	9
—Cornwall	AHL	5	0	0	0	18	...	...	...	2	0	0	0	2
96-97—Colorado	NHL	5	0	0	0	11	-1	0	0	—	—	—	—	—
—Hershey	AHL	65	1	7	8	320	-1	0	0	16	0	1	1	61
97-98—Colorado	NHL	8	1	1	2	27	-3	0	0	—	—	—	—	—
—Hershey	AHL	11	0	0	0	30	-5	0	0	—	—	—	—	—
98-99—Colorado	NHL	22	0	0	0	71	-2	0	0	—	—	—	—	—
—Hershey	AHL	17	0	1	1	49	8	0	0	—	—	—	—	—
—Saint John	AHL	12	0	2	2	43	-3	0	0	6	0	1	1	23
—Calgary	NHL	9	0	1	1	23	3	0	0	—	—	—	—	—
99-00—Calgary	NHL	40	0	2	2	122	-4	0	0	—	—	—	—	—
00-01—Calgary	NHL	23	0	0	0	79	-2	0	0	—	—	—	—	—
—Toronto	NHL	16	1	1	2	31	-4	0	0	—	—	—	—	—
01-02—Toronto	NHL	63	1	3	4	142	2	0	0	16	1	0	1	18
02-03—Toronto	NHL	55	3	6	9	196	-2	0	0	2	0	0	0	4
03-04—Toronto	NHL	34	1	1	2	109	0	0	0	4	0	0	0	14
04-05—Coventry	England	34	6	9	15	170	...	...	...	8	1	1	2	16
05-06—Toronto	NHL	55	0	3	3	109	-13	0	0	—	—	—	—	—
NHL Totals (9 years)		330	7	18	25	920	-26	0	0	22	1	0	1	36

BELANGER, ERIC — C

PERSONAL: Born December 16, 1977, in Sherbrooke, Que. ... 6-0/185. ... Shoots left. ... Name pronounced buh-LAH-zhay.

TRANSACTIONS/CAREER NOTES: Selected by Los Angeles Kings in fourth round (fifth Kings pick, 96th overall) of entry draft (June 22, 1996). ... Back spasms (February 25, 2001); missed two games. ... Left wrist surgery (January 15, 2002); missed 29 games. ... Back (December 29, 2002); missed six games. ... Back (January 13, 2003); missed 14 games. ... Groin (December 21, 2005); missed two games. ... Groin (December 29, 2005); missed 13 games. ... Elbow (March 14, 2006); missed one game. ... Concussion (March 1, 2006); missed one game.

STATISTICAL PLATEAUS: Three-goal games: 2002-03 (1).

		REGULAR SEASON								PLAYOFFS				
Season Team	**League**	**GP**	**G**	**A**	**Pts.**	**PIM**	**+/-**	**PP**	**SH**	**GP**	**G**	**A**	**Pts.**	**PIM**
94-95—Beauport	QMJHL	71	12	28	40	24	...	...	...	—	—	—	—	—
95-96—Beauport	QMJHL	59	35	48	83	18	...	...	...	20	13	14	27	6
96-97—Beauport	QMJHL	31	13	37	50	30	...	...	...	—	—	—	—	—
—Rimouski	QMJHL	31	26	41	67	36	...	...	...	4	2	3	5	10
97-98—Fredericton	AHL	56	17	34	51	28	-1	6	0	4	2	1	3	2
98-99—Springfield	AHL	33	8	18	26	10	8	1	0	3	0	1	1	2
—Long Beach	IHL	1	0	0	0	0	0	0	0	—	—	—	—	—
99-00—Lowell	AHL	65	15	25	40	20	...	...	...	7	3	3	6	2
00-01—Los Angeles	NHL	62	9	12	21	16	14	1	2	13	1	4	5	2
—Lowell	AHL	13	8	10	18	4	...	...	...	—	—	—	—	—
01-02—Los Angeles	NHL	53	8	16	24	21	2	2	1	7	0	0	0	4
02-03—Los Angeles	NHL	62	16	19	35	26	-5	0	3	—	—	—	—	—
03-04—Los Angeles	NHL	81	13	20	33	44	-16	0	1	—	—	—	—	—
04-05—Bolzano	Italy	12	13	10	23	20	...	...	...	—	—	—	—	—
05-06—Los Angeles	NHL	65	17	20	37	62	-5	5	0	—	—	—	—	—
NHL Totals (5 years)		323	63	87	150	169	-10	8	7	20	1	4	5	6

BELANGER, KEN — LW

PERSONAL: Born May 14, 1974, in Sault Ste. Marie, Ont. ... 6-4/225. ... Shoots left. ... Name pronounced buh-LAHN-zhay.

TRANSACTIONS/CAREER NOTES: Selected by Hartford Whalers in seventh round (seventh Whalers pick, 153rd overall) of entry draft (June 20, 1992). ... Traded by Whalers to Toronto Maple Leafs for ninth-round pick (RW Matt Ball) in 1994 entry draft (March 18, 1994). ... Traded by Maple Leafs with G Damian Rhodes to New York Islanders for C Kirk Muller (January 23, 1996). ... Concussion (February 6, 1996); missed two games. ... Concussion (February 12, 1996); missed remainder of season. ... Concussion (October 13, 1997); missed four games. ... Injured hand (November 15, 1997); missed three games. ... Flu (November 26, 1997); missed three games. ... Reinjured hand (January 8, 1998); missed two games. ... Thumb surgery (January 14, 1998); missed 22 games. ... Traded by Islanders to Boston Bruins for LW Ted Donato (November 7, 1998). ... Cut face (November 8, 1998); missed two games. ... Strained neck (December 28, 1998); missed two games. ... Injured hand (April 3, 1999); missed one game. ... Concussion (November 10, 1999); missed 34 games. ... Injured groin (March 29, 2000); missed final six games of season. ... Strained hip (December 8, 2000); missed three games. ... Reinjured hip (January 10, 2001) and had surgery; missed 18 games. ... Signed as free agent by Los Angeles Kings (July 2, 2001). ... Fractured thumb (January 2, 2002); missed 20 games. ... Concussion (November 5, 2002); missed remainder of season and all of 2003-04. ... Retired (November 14, 2005).

		REGULAR SEASON								PLAYOFFS				
Season Team	**League**	**GP**	**G**	**A**	**Pts.**	**PIM**	**+/-**	**PP**	**SH**	**GP**	**G**	**A**	**Pts.**	**PIM**
91-92—Ottawa	OHL	51	4	4	8	174	...	...	...	11	0	0	0	24
92-93—Ottawa	OHL	34	6	12	18	139	...	...	...	—	—	—	—	—

Season Team	League	REGULAR SEASON								PLAYOFFS				
		GP	G	A	Pts.	PIM	+/-	PP	SH	GP	G	A	Pts.	PIM
—Guelph	OHL	29	10	14	24	86	...	...	...	5	2	1	3	14
93-94—Guelph	OHL	55	11	22	33	185	...	...	...	9	2	3	5	30
94-95—St. John's	AHL	47	5	5	10	246	-15	0	0	4	0	0	0	30
—Toronto	NHL	3	0	0	0	9	0	0	0	—	—	—	—	—
95-96—St. John's	AHL	40	16	14	30	222	...	...	...	—	—	—	—	—
—New York Islanders	NHL	7	0	0	0	27	-2	0	0	—	—	—	—	—
96-97—Kentucky	AHL	38	10	12	22	164	-1	4	0	4	0	1	1	27
—New York Islanders	NHL	18	0	2	2	102	-1	0	0	—	—	—	—	—
97-98—New York Islanders	NHL	37	3	1	4	101	1	0	0	—	—	—	—	—
98-99—New York Islanders	NHL	9	1	1	2	30	1	0	0	—	—	—	—	—
—Boston	NHL	45	1	4	5	152	-2	0	0	12	1	0	1	16
99-00—Boston	NHL	37	2	2	4	44	-4	0	0	—	—	—	—	—
00-01—Boston	NHL	40	2	2	4	121	-6	0	0	—	—	—	—	—
—Providence	AHL	10	1	4	5	47	...	...	...	2	0	0	0	4
01-02—Los Angeles	NHL	43	2	0	2	85	-5	0	0	—	—	—	—	—
02-03—Los Angeles	NHL	4	0	0	0	17	0	0	0	—	—	—	—	—
03-04—	injured													
04-05—Adirondack	UHL	1	0	0	0	5	...	...	...	—	—	—	—	—
05-06—Los Angeles	NHL	5	0	0	0	7	-1	0	0	—	—	—	—	—
NHL Totals (10 years)		248	11	12	23	695	-19	0	0	12	1	0	1	16

BELFOUR, ED — G

PERSONAL: Born April 21, 1965, in Carman, Man. ... 5-11/202. ... Catches left.

TRANSACTIONS/CAREER NOTES: Signed as free agent by Chicago Blackhawks (June 18, 1987). ... Strained hip muscle (1993-94 season); missed four games. ... Sprained knee (January 31, 1996); missed one game. ... Injured back (February 19, 1996); missed three games. ... Traded by Blackhawks to San Jose Sharks for G Chris Terreri, D Michal Sykora and RW Ulf Dahlen (January 25, 1997). ... Injured knee ligament (February 1, 1997); missed 13 games. ... Bulging disk in back (March 1, 1997); missed seven games. ... Signed as free agent by Dallas Stars (July 2, 1997). ... Strained lower back (February 2, 1998); missed three games. ... Strained groin (November 10, 1999); missed one game. ... Injured back (March 23, 2001); missed one game. ... Injured back (March 29, 2002); missed two games. ... Traded by Stars with RW Cameron Mann to Nashville Predators for C David Gosselin and fifth-round pick (G Eero Kilpelainen) in 2003 entry draft (June 29, 2002). ... Signed as free agent by Toronto Maple Leafs (July 2, 2002). ... Infected thumb (October 13, 2002); missed four games. ... Back spasms (January 17, 2003); missed four games. ... Injured groin (January 4, 2004); missed three games. ... Injured back (February 3, 2004); missed three games. ... Reinjured back (February 14, 2004); missed eight games. ... Injured groin (December 10, 2005); missed one game. ... Injured back (March 14, 2006); missed final 19 games of regular season. ... Signed as a free agent by Florida Panthers (July 25, 2006).

Season Team	League	REGULAR SEASON										PLAYOFFS							
		GP	Min.	W	L	OTL	T	GA	SO	GAA	SV%	GP	Min.	W	L	GA	SO	GAA	SV%
85-86—Winkler	MJHL	48	2880	...	...	...	...	124	1	2.58	...	—	—	—	—	—	—	—	—
86-87—North Dakota	WCHA	34	2049	29	4	...	0	81	3	2.37	...	—	—	—	—	—	—	—	—
87-88—Saginaw	IHL	61	3446	32	25	...	0	183	3	3.19	...	9	561	4	5	33	0	3.53	...
88-89—Chicago	NHL	23	1148	4	12	...	3	74	0	3.87	.878	—	—	—	—	—	—	—	—
—Saginaw	IHL	29	1760	12	10	...	0	92	0	3.14	...	5	298	2	3	14	0	2.82	...
89-90—Canadian nat'l team	Int'l	33	1808	...	...	...	...	93	...	3.09	...	—	—	—	—	—	—	—	—
—Chicago	NHL	...	...	...	...	...	...	...	...	...	...	9	409	4	2	17	0	2.49	.915
90-91—Chicago	NHL	*74	*4127	*43	19	...	7	170	4	*2.47	*.910	6	295	2	4	20	0	4.07	.891
91-92—Chicago	NHL	52	2928	21	18	...	10	132	†5	2.70	.894	18	949	12	4	39	1	*2.47	.902
92-93—Chicago	NHL	*71	*4106	41	18	...	11	177	*7	2.59	.906	4	249	0	4	13	0	3.13	.866
93-94—Chicago	NHL	70	3998	37	24	...	6	178	†7	2.67	.906	6	360	2	4	15	0	2.50	.921
94-95—Chicago	NHL	42	2450	22	15	...	3	93	†5	2.28	.906	16	1014	9	†7	37	1	2.19	.923
95-96—Chicago	NHL	50	2956	22	17	...	10	135	1	2.74	.902	9	666	6	3	23	1	*2.07	.929
96-97—Chicago	NHL	33	1966	11	15	...	6	88	1	2.69	.907	—	—	—	—	—	—	—	—
—San Jose	NHL	13	757	3	9	...	0	43	1	3.41	.884	—	—	—	—	—	—	—	—
97-98—Dallas	NHL	61	3581	37	12	...	10	112	9	*1.88	.916	17	1039	10	7	31	1	1.79	.922
98-99—Dallas	NHL	61	3536	35	15	...	9	117	5	1.99	.915	*23	*1544	*16	7	43	*3	*1.67	.930
99-00—Dallas	NHL	62	3620	32	21	...	7	127	4	2.10	†.919	†23	1443	14	*9	*45	*4	1.87	.931
00-01—Dallas	NHL	63	3687	35	20	...	7	144	8	2.34	.905	10	671	4	6	25	0	2.24	.910
01-02—Dallas	NHL	60	3467	21	27	...	†11	153	1	2.65	.895	—	—	—	—	—	—	—	—
—Can. Olympic team	Int'l	Did not play																	
02-03—Toronto	NHL	62	3738	37	20	...	5	141	7	2.26	.922	7	532	3	4	24	0	2.71	.915
03-04—Toronto	NHL	59	3444	34	19	...	6	122	10	2.13	.918	13	774	6	7	27	3	2.09	.929
05-06—Toronto	NHL	49	2897	22	22	4	...	159	0	3.29	.892	—	—	—	—	—	—	—	—
NHL Totals (17 years)		905	52406	457	303	4	111	2165	75	2.48	.907	161	9945	88	68	359	14	2.17	.920

BELL, BRENDAN — D

PERSONAL: Born March 31, 1983, in Ottawa. ... 6-1/198. ... Shoots left.

TRANSACTIONS/CAREER NOTES: Selected by Toronto Maple Leafs in third round (third Maple Leafs pick, 65th overall) of NHL draft (June 23, 2001).

Season Team	League	REGULAR SEASON								PLAYOFFS				
		GP	G	A	Pts.	PIM	+/-	PP	SH	GP	G	A	Pts.	PIM
99-00—Ottawa	OHL	48	1	32	33	34	...	...	...	5	0	1	1	4
00-01—Ottawa	OHL	68	7	32	39	59	...	...	...	20	1	11	12	22
01-02—Ottawa	OHL	67	10	36	46	56	...	...	...	13	2	5	7	25
02-03—Ottawa	OHL	55	14	39	53	46	...	...	...	23	8	19	27	25
03-04—St. John's	AHL	74	7	19	26	62	-19	1	0	—	—	—	—	—
04-05—St. John's	AHL	75	6	25	31	57	-15	4	0	5	0	1	1	2

Season Team	League	REGULAR SEASON GP	G	A	Pts.	PIM	+/-	PP	SH	PLAYOFFS GP	G	A	Pts.	PIM
05-06—Toronto	AHL	70	6	37	43	99	-1	3	0	5	0	4	4	10
—Toronto	NHL	1	0	0	0	0	0	0	0	—	—	—	—	—
NHL Totals (1 year)		1	0	0	0	0	0	0	0					

BELL, MARK C/LW

PERSONAL: Born August 5, 1980, in St. Paul's, Ont. ... 6-4/205. ... Shoots left.

TRANSACTIONS/CAREER NOTES: Selected by Chicago Blackhawks in first round (first Blackhawks pick, eighth overall) of NHL draft (June 27, 1998). ... Bruised hip (March 18, 2002); missed two games. ... Traded by Blackhawks to San Jose Sharks for D Tom Preissing and D Josh Hennessy in three-team trade in which Blackhawks then traded Preissing, Hennessy, D Michal Barinka and second-round pick in 2008 draft to Ottawa Senators for Fs Martin Havlat and Bryan Smolinski (July 10, 2006).

Season Team	League	REGULAR SEASON GP	G	A	Pts.	PIM	+/-	PP	SH	PLAYOFFS GP	G	A	Pts.	PIM
95-96—Stratford Jr. B	OHA	47	8	15	23	32	...	...	...	—	—	—	—	—
96-97—Ottawa	OHL	65	8	12	20	40	...	...	...	24	4	7	11	13
97-98—Ottawa	OHL	55	34	26	60	87	...	...	...	13	6	5	11	14
98-99—Ottawa	OHL	44	29	26	55	69	28	...	...	9	6	5	11	8
99-00—Ottawa	OHL	48	34	38	72	95	11	12	7	2	0	1	1	0
00-01—Norfolk	AHL	61	15	27	42	126	...	...	...	9	4	3	7	10
—Chicago	NHL	13	0	1	1	4	0	0	0	—	—	—	—	—
01-02—Chicago	NHL	80	12	16	28	124	-6	1	0	5	0	0	0	8
02-03—Chicago	NHL	82	14	15	29	113	0	0	2	—	—	—	—	—
03-04—Chicago	NHL	82	21	24	45	106	-14	2	0	—	—	—	—	—
04-05—Trondheim	Norway	25	10	17	27	87	5	...	...	11	6	6	12	44
05-06—Chicago	NHL	82	25	23	48	107	-14	11	1	—	—	—	—	—
NHL Totals (5 years)		339	72	79	151	454	-34	14	3	5	0	0	0	8

BERARD, BRYAN D

PERSONAL: Born March 5, 1977, in Woonsocket, R.I. ... 6-2/220. ... Shoots left. ... Name pronounced buh-RAHRD.

TRANSACTIONS/CAREER NOTES: Selected by Ottawa Senators in first round (first Senators pick, first overall) of NHL draft (July 8, 1995). ... Traded by Senators with C Martin Straka to New York Islanders for D Wade Redden and G Damian Rhodes (January 23, 1996). ... Groin (October 16, 1997); missed one game. ... Groin (November 10, 1997); missed two games. ... Groin (November 15, 1997); missed three games. ... Bruised elbow (March 24, 1998); missed one game. ... Groin (December 18, 1998); missed nine games. ... Traded by Islanders with sixth-round pick (RW Jan Sochor) in draft to Toronto Maple Leafs for G Felix Potvin and sixth-round pick (C Fedor Fedorov) in 1999 (January 9, 1999). ... Groin (January 7, 1999); missed three games. ... Flu (March 28, 1999); missed two games. ... Suspended two games for illegal check (October 19, 1999). ... Injured (November 23, 1999); missed three games. ... Eye (March 11, 2000); missed remainder of season. ... Missed 2000-01 season recovering from eye injury. ... Signed as free agent by New York Rangers (October 4, 2001). ... Signed as free agent by Boston Bruins (August 13, 2002). ... Signed as free agent by Chicago Blackhawks (October 31, 2003). ... Groin (November 22, 2003); missed one game. ... Groin (December 12, 2003); missed 10 games. ... Signed as free agent by Columbus Blue Jackets (August 3, 2005). ... Strained lower back (December 17, 2005); missed seven games. ... Back (February 28, 2006); missed final 31 games of regular season.

Season Team	League	REGULAR SEASON GP	G	A	Pts.	PIM	+/-	PP	SH	PLAYOFFS GP	G	A	Pts.	PIM
91-92—Mt. St. Charles H.S.	R.I.H.S.	32	3	15	18	10	...	...	...	—	—	—	—	—
92-93—Mt. St. Charles H.S.	R.I.H.S.	32	8	12	20	18	...	...	...	—	—	—	—	—
93-94—Mt. St. Charles H.S.	R.I.H.S.	32	11	36	47	5	...	...	...	—	—	—	—	—
94-95—Det. Jr. Red Wings	OHL	58	20	55	75	97	...	13	1	21	4	20	24	38
95-96—Det. Jr. Red Wings	OHL	56	31	58	89	116	...	...	...	17	7	18	25	41
96-97—New York Islanders	NHL	82	8	40	48	86	1	3	0	—	—	—	—	—
97-98—New York Islanders	NHL	75	14	32	46	59	-32	8	1	—	—	—	—	—
—U.S. Olympic team	Int'l	2	0	0	0	0	-1	0	0	—	—	—	—	—
98-99—New York Islanders	NHL	31	4	11	15	26	-6	2	0	—	—	—	—	—
—Toronto	NHL	38	5	14	19	22	7	2	0	17	1	8	9	8
99-00—Toronto	NHL	64	3	27	30	42	11	1	0	—	—	—	—	—
00-01—Toronto	NHL	Did not play — injured												
01-02—New York Rangers	NHL	82	2	21	23	60	-1	0	0	—	—	—	—	—
02-03—Boston	NHL	80	10	28	38	64	-4	4	0	3	1	0	1	2
03-04—Chicago	NHL	58	13	34	47	53	-24	6	0	—	—	—	—	—
05-06—Columbus	NHL	44	12	20	32	32	-29	11	0	—	—	—	—	—
NHL Totals (9 years)		554	71	227	298	444	-77	37	1	20	2	8	10	10

BERG, AKI D

PERSONAL: Born July 28, 1977, in Turku, Finland. ... 6-3/213. ... Shoots left. ... Name pronounced AH-kee BUHRG.

TRANSACTIONS/CAREER NOTES: Selected by Los Angeles Kings in first round (first Kings pick, third overall) of NHL draft (July 8, 1995). ... Charley horse (January 25, 1997); missed one game. ... Concussion (February 3, 1997); missed two games. ... Sprained left ankle (April 9, 1997); missed final two games of regular season. ... Bruised right foot (December 4, 1997); missed one game. ... Sprained right wrist (March 10, 1998); missed two games. ... Injured ribs (December 23, 1999); missed two games. ... Concussion (March 13, 2000); missed two games. ... Injured (January 4, 2001); missed three games. ... Traded by Kings to Toronto Maple Leafs for C Adam Mair and second-round pick (C Mike Cammalleri) in 2001 draft (March 13, 2001). ... Injured (March 16, 2002); missed one game. ... Injured finger (February 8, 2003); missed two games. ... Reinjured finger (February 15, 2003); missed two games. ... Flu (December 19, 2003); missed three games. ... Rib injury (October 27, 2005); missed one game. ... Knee injury (November 6, 2005); missed one game. ... Rib injury (January 26, 2006); missed five games.

Season Team	League	REGULAR SEASON GP	G	A	Pts.	PIM	+/-	PP	SH	PLAYOFFS GP	G	A	Pts.	PIM
92-93—TPS Turku	Finland Jr.	39	18	24	42	59	...	...	...	—	—	—	—	—
93-94—TPS Turku	Finland Jr.	21	3	11	14	24	...	...	...	7	0	0	0	10

Season Team	League	REGULAR SEASON GP	G	A	Pts.	PIM	+/-	PP	SH	PLAYOFFS GP	G	A	Pts.	PIM
—TPS Turku	Finland	6	0	3	3	4	...	...	...	—	—	—	—	—
94-95—Kiekko-67	Finland Div. 2	20	3	9	12	34	...	...	...	—	—	—	—	—
—TPS Turku	Finland Jr.	8	1	0	1	30	...	...	...	—	—	—	—	—
—TPS Turku	Finland	5	0	0	0	4	3	...	...	—	—	—	—	—
95-96—Los Angeles	NHL	51	0	7	7	29	-13	0	0	—	—	—	—	—
—Phoenix	IHL	20	0	3	3	18	...	...	...	2	0	0	0	4
96-97—Los Angeles	NHL	41	2	6	8	24	-9	2	0	—	—	—	—	—
—Phoenix	IHL	23	1	3	4	21	...	...	...	—	—	—	—	—
97-98—Los Angeles	NHL	72	0	8	8	61	3	0	0	4	0	3	3	0
—Fin. Olympic team	Int'l	6	0	0	0	6	2	0	0	—	—	—	—	—
98-99—TPS Turku	Finland	48	8	7	15	137	...	...	...	9	1	1	2	45
99-00—Los Angeles	NHL	70	3	13	16	45	-1	0	0	2	0	0	0	2
00-01—Los Angeles	NHL	47	0	4	4	43	3	0	0	—	—	—	—	—
—Toronto	NHL	12	3	0	3	2	-6	3	0	11	0	2	2	4
01-02—Toronto	NHL	81	1	10	11	46	14	0	0	20	0	1	1	37
—Fin. Olympic team	Int'l	4	1	0	1	2	...	...	...	—	—	—	—	—
02-03—Toronto	NHL	78	4	7	11	28	3	0	0	7	1	1	2	2
03-04—Toronto	NHL	79	2	7	9	40	-1	0	0	10	0	0	0	2
04-05—Timra	Sweden	47	6	14	20	46	11	2	1	7	0	0	0	6
05-06—Toronto	NHL	75	0	8	8	56	-5	0	0	—	—	—	—	—
—Fin. Olympic team	Int'l	8	0	0	0	4	4	0	0	—	—	—	—	—
NHL Totals (9 years)		606	15	70	85	374	-12	5	0	54	1	7	8	47

BERGENHEIM, SEAN — LW

PERSONAL: Born February 8, 1984, in Helsinki, Finland. ... 5-11/194. ... Shoots left.
TRANSACTIONS/CAREER NOTES: Selected by New York Islanders in first round (first Islanders pick, 22nd overall) of NHL draft (June 22, 2002).

Season Team	League	REGULAR SEASON GP	G	A	Pts.	PIM	+/-	PP	SH	PLAYOFFS GP	G	A	Pts.	PIM
01-02—Jokerit Helsinki	Finland	28	2	2	4	4	...	...	...	—	—	—	—	—
02-03—Jokerit Helsinki	Finland	38	3	3	6	4	...	...	...	—	—	—	—	—
03-04—Bridgeport	AHL	—	—	—	—	—	—	—	—	7	2	3	5	10
—New York Islanders	NHL	18	1	1	2	4	-4	0	1	—	—	—	—	—
04-05—Bridgeport	AHL	61	15	14	29	69	1	5	1	—	—	—	—	—
05-06—Bridgeport	AHL	55	25	22	47	112	4	7	4	7	0	2	2	24
—New York Islanders	NHL	28	4	5	9	20	-11	0	0	—	—	—	—	—
NHL Totals (2 years)		46	5	6	11	24	-15	0	1					

BERGERON, MARC-ANDRE — D

PERSONAL: Born October 13, 1980, in St-Louis-de-France, Que. ... 5-10/190. ... Shoots left.
TRANSACTIONS/CAREER NOTES: Signed as free agent by Edmonton Oilers (July 20, 2001). ... Broken finger (November 4, 2005); missed three games. ... Injured knee (March 25, 2006); missed three games.

Season Team	League	REGULAR SEASON GP	G	A	Pts.	PIM	+/-	PP	SH	PLAYOFFS GP	G	A	Pts.	PIM
97-98—Baie-Comeau	QMJHL	40	6	14	20	48	...	...	...	—	—	—	—	—
98-99—Baie-Comeau	QMJHL	46	8	14	22	57	...	...	...	—	—	—	—	—
—Shawinigan	QMJHL	24	6	7	13	66	...	...	...	5	2	2	4	24
99-00—Shawinigan	QMJHL	70	24	50	74	173	...	...	...	13	4	7	11	45
00-01—Shawinigan	QMJHL	69	42	59	101	185	...	...	...	10	4	11	15	24
01-02—Hamilton	AHL	50	2	13	15	61	5	0	0	9	1	4	5	8
02-03—Edmonton	NHL	5	1	1	2	9	2	0	0	1	0	1	1	0
—Hamilton	AHL	66	8	31	39	73	34	3	0	20	0	7	7	25
03-04—Edmonton	NHL	54	9	17	26	26	13	3	0	—	—	—	—	—
—Toronto	AHL	17	4	3	7	23	4	2	0	—	—	—	—	—
04-05—Brynas IF	Sweden	10	3	2	5	72	-1	0	0	9	1	2	3	8
05-06—Edmonton	NHL	75	15	20	35	38	3	8	0	18	2	1	3	14
NHL Totals (3 years)		134	25	38	63	73	18	11	0	19	2	2	4	14

BERGERON, PATRICE — C/RW

PERSONAL: Born July 24, 1985, in Ancienne-Lorette, Que. ... 6-1/190. ... Shoots right. ... Name pronounced BUHR-zhur-uhn.
TRANSACTIONS/CAREER NOTES: Selected by Boston Bruins in second round (second Bruins pick, 45th overall) of entry draft (June 21, 2003). ... Injured shoulder (February 24, 2004); missed 11 games. ... Flu (November 17, 2006); missed one game.

Season Team	League	REGULAR SEASON GP	G	A	Pts.	PIM	+/-	PP	SH	PLAYOFFS GP	G	A	Pts.	PIM
01-02—Acadie-Bathurst	QMJHL	4	0	1	1	0	...	...	...	—	—	—	—	—
02-03—Acadie-Bathurst	QMJHL	70	23	50	73	62	...	...	...	11	6	9	15	6
03-04—Boston	NHL	71	16	23	39	22	5	7	0	7	1	3	4	0
04-05—Providence	AHL	68	21	40	61	59	2	6	1	16	5	7	12	4
05-06—Boston	NHL	81	31	42	73	22	3	12	1	—	—	—	—	—
NHL Totals (2 years)		152	47	65	112	44	8	19	1	7	1	3	4	0

BERGLUND, PATRIK — C

PERSONAL: Born June 2, 1988, in Vesteras, Swe. ... 6-4/187. ... Shoots left.
TRANSACTIONS/CAREER NOTES: Selected by St. Louis Blues in first round (second Blues pick; 25th overall) of NHL draft (June 24, 2006).

		REGULAR SEASON								PLAYOFFS				
Season Team	League	GP	G	A	Pts.	PIM	+/-	PP	SH	GP	G	A	Pts.	PIM
04-05—Vasteras	Sweden Jr.	25	5	5	10	14	...	...	...	—	—	—	—	—
05-06—Vasteras	Sweden Jr.	27	17	12	29	38	...	...	...	—	—	—	—	—
—Vasteras	Sweden Dv. 2	21	3	1	4	4	-4	...	...	—	—	—	—	—

BERKHOEL, ADAM — G

PERSONAL: Born May 16, 1981, in St. Paul, Minn. ... 5-11/190. ... Catches left.
TRANSACTIONS/CAREER NOTES: Selected by Chicago Blackhawks in eighth round (12th Blackhawks pick, 240th overall) of entry draft (June 25, 2000). ... Traded by Blackhawks to Atlanta Thrashers for seventh-round pick (C Adam Hobson) in 2005 draft (June 27, 2004).

		REGULAR SEASON										PLAYOFFS							
Season Team	League	GP	Min.	W	L	OTL	T	GA	SO	GAA	SV%	GP	Min.	W	L	GA	SO	GAA	SV%
99-00—Twin Cities	USHL	49	2848	25	15	...	7	129	5	2.72	...	—	—	—	—	—	—	—	—
00-01—Denver	WCHA	15	745	7	6	...	1	38	1	3.06	...	—	—	—	—	—	—	—	—
01-02—Denver	WCHA	18	1026	12	4	...	1	40	1	2.34	...	—	—	—	—	—	—	—	—
02-03—Denver	WCHA	26	1436	12	6	...	4	55	3	2.30	...	—	—	—	—	—	—	—	—
03-04—Denver	WCHA	39	2225	24	11	...	4	91	7	2.45	...	—	—	—	—	—	—	—	—
04-05—Chicago	AHL	1	59	0	1	...	...	4	0	4.07	.875	0	0	0	0	0	0	...	...
—Gwinnett	ECHL	24	1458	9	10	...	5	59	2	2.43	...	7	353	4	1	9	0	1.53	...
05-06—Atlanta	NHL	9	473	2	4	1	...	30	0	3.81	.882	—	—	—	—	—	—	—	—
—Chicago	AHL	11	526	3	6	0	...	32	0	3.65	.882	—	—	—	—	—	—	—	—
NHL Totals (1 year)		9	473	2	4	1	0	30	0	3.81	.882								

BERNIER, JONATHAN — G

PERSONAL: Born August 7, 1988, in Laval, Quebec. ... 5-11/177. ... Catches left.
TRANSACTIONS/CAREER NOTES: Selected by Los Angeles Kings in first round (first Kings pick; 11th overall) of NHL draft (June 24, 2006).

		REGULAR SEASON										PLAYOFFS							
Season Team	League	GP	Min.	W	L	OTL	T	GA	SO	GAA	SV%	GP	Min.	W	L	GA	SO	GAA	SV%
04-05—Lewiston	QMJHL	23	1353	7	12	...	3	67	0	2.97	.909	1	20	0	0	0	...	0.00	1.000
05-06—Lewiston	QMJHL	54	3240	27	26	...	...	146	2	2.70	.908	6	358	2	4	17	1	2.84	.914

BERNIER, STEVE — RW

PERSONAL: Born March 31, 1985, in Quebec City. ... 6-2/233. ... Shoots right.
TRANSACTIONS/CAREER NOTES: Selected by San Jose Sharks (second Sharks pick, 16th overall) in 2003 entry draft (June 23, 2003).

		REGULAR SEASON								PLAYOFFS				
Season Team	League	GP	G	A	Pts.	PIM	+/-	PP	SH	GP	G	A	Pts.	PIM
01-02—Moncton	QMJHL	66	31	28	59	51	...	...	...	—	—	—	—	—
02-03—Moncton	QMJHL	71	49	52	101	90	...	...	...	—	—	—	—	—
03-04—Moncton	QMJHL	66	36	46	82	80	...	...	...	20	7	10	17	17
04-05—Moncton	QMJHL	68	35	36	71	114	18	12	1	12	6	13	19	22
05-06—Cleveland	AHL	49	20	23	43	33	-2	11	0	—	—	—	—	—
—San Jose	NHL	39	14	13	27	35	4	2	1	11	1	5	6	8
NHL Totals (1 year)		39	14	13	27	35	4	2	1	11	1	5	6	8

BERTUZZI, TODD — RW

PERSONAL: Born February 2, 1975, in Sudbury, Ont. ... 6-3/245. ... Shoots left. ... Name pronounced buhr-TOO-zee.
TRANSACTIONS/CAREER NOTES: Selected by New York Islanders in first round (first Islanders pick, 23rd overall) of NHL draft (June 26, 1993). ... Injured eye (February 22, 1996); missed two games. ... Suspended three games for attempting to break free of a linesman (April 2, 1996). ... Bone chips in elbow (November 23, 1996); missed one game. ... Traded by Islanders with D Bryan McCabe and third-round pick (LW Jarkko Ruutu) in 1998 entry draft to Vancouver Canucks for C Trevor Linden (February 6, 1998). ... Bruised thigh (March 17, 1998); missed four games. ... Fractured leg (November 1, 1998); missed 31 games. ... Tore knee ligament (March 5, 1999); missed remainder of season. ... Concussion (October 20, 1999); missed one game. ... Injured thumb (February 23, 2000); missed one game. ... Bruised shoulder (January 28, 2001); missed three games. ... Suspended 10 games for elbowing incident (October 15, 2001). ... Suspended indefinitely for match penalty for deliberate attempt to injure Colorado Avalanche C Steve Moore (March 8, 2004); missed remainder of season and playoffs. Reinstated (August 8, 2005); missed total of 13 regular season games and 7 playoff games. ... Traded by Canucks with G Alex Auld and D Bryan Allen to Florida Panthers for G Roberto Luongo, D Lukas Krajicek and a sixth-round pick (W Sergei Shirokov) in 2006 draft (June 23, 2006).
STATISTICAL PLATEAUS: Three-goal games: 2000-01 (1), 2001-02 (1), 2002-03 (1). Total: 3.

		REGULAR SEASON								PLAYOFFS				
Season Team	League	GP	G	A	Pts.	PIM	+/-	PP	SH	GP	G	A	Pts.	PIM
91-92—Guelph	OHL	47	7	14	21	145	...	...	...	—	—	—	—	—
92-93—Guelph	OHL	59	27	32	59	164	...	...	...	5	2	2	4	6
93-94—Guelph	OHL	61	28	54	82	165	...	8	0	9	2	6	8	30
94-95—Guelph	OHL	62	54	65	119	58	...	15	0	14	15	18	33	41
95-96—New York Islanders	NHL	76	18	21	39	83	-14	4	0	—	—	—	—	—

Season Team	League	GP	G	A	Pts.	PIM	+/-	PP	SH	GP	G	A	Pts.	PIM
		REGULAR SEASON								PLAYOFFS				
96-97—New York Islanders.....	NHL	64	10	13	23	68	-3	3	0	—	—	—	—	—
—Utah..........................	IHL	13	5	5	10	16	...	...	...	—	—	—	—	—
97-98—New York Islanders.....	NHL	52	7	11	18	58	-19	1	0	—	—	—	—	—
—Vancouver..................	NHL	22	6	9	15	63	2	1	1	—	—	—	—	—
98-99—Vancouver..................	NHL	32	8	8	16	44	-6	1	0	—	—	—	—	—
99-00—Vancouver..................	NHL	80	25	25	50	126	-2	4	0	—	—	—	—	—
00-01—Vancouver..................	NHL	79	25	30	55	93	-18	14	0	4	2	2	4	8
01-02—Vancouver..................	NHL	72	36	49	85	110	21	14	0	6	2	2	4	14
02-03—Vancouver..................	NHL	82	46	51	97	144	2	*25	0	14	2	4	6	*60
03-04—Vancouver..................	NHL	69	17	43	60	122	21	8	0	—	—	—	—	—
05-06—Vancouver..................	NHL	82	25	46	71	120	-17	12	0	—	—	—	—	—
—Canadian Oly. team.....	Int'l	6	0	3	3	6	1	0	0	—	—	—	—	—
NHL Totals (10 years).........		710	223	306	529	1031	-33	87	1	24	6	8	14	82

BETTS, BLAIR C

PERSONAL: Born February 16, 1980, in Edmonton. ... 6-3/200. ... Shoots left.

TRANSACTIONS/CAREER NOTES: Selected by Calgary Flames in second round (second Flames pick, 33rd overall) of NHL draft (June 27, 1998). ... Injured shoulder (November 25, 2003); missed 15 games. ... Reinjured shoulder (December 31, 2003); missed final 46 games of season. ... Traded by Flames with G Jamie McLennan and RW Greg Moore to New York Rangers for LW Chris Simon and seventh-round pick (C Matt Schneider) in 2004 draft (March 6, 2004). ... Signed as free agent by New York Rangers (August 11, 2005). ... Left knee sprain (January 7, 2006); missed 16 games.

Season Team	League	GP	G	A	Pts.	PIM	+/-	PP	SH	GP	G	A	Pts.	PIM
		REGULAR SEASON								PLAYOFFS				
96-97—Prince George............	WHL	58	12	18	30	19	...	...	...	15	2	2	4	6
97-98—Prince George............	WHL	71	35	41	76	38	14	15	1	11	4	6	10	8
98-99—Prince George............	WHL	42	20	22	42	39	2	8	1	7	3	2	5	8
99-00—Prince George............	WHL	44	24	35	59	38	19	6	2	13	11	11	22	6
00-01—Saint John	AHL	75	13	15	28	28	...	...	...	19	2	3	5	4
01-02—Saint John	AHL	67	20	29	49	10	-3	10	0	—	—	—	—	—
—Calgary	NHL	6	1	0	1	2	-1	0	0	—	—	—	—	—
02-03—Saint John	AHL	19	6	7	13	6	2	0	0	—	—	—	—	—
—Calgary	NHL	9	1	3	4	0	3	0	0	—	—	—	—	—
03-04—Calgary	NHL	20	1	2	3	10	-1	1	0	—	—	—	—	—
04-05—Hartford	AHL	16	5	4	9	4	3	1	1	0	0	0	0	0
05-06—New York Rangers......	NHL	66	8	2	10	24	-10	0	1	4	1	1	2	2
NHL Totals (4 years)...........		101	11	7	18	36	-9	1	1	4	1	1	2	2

BIEKSA, KEVIN D

PERSONAL: Born June 16, 1981, in Grimsby, Ont. ... 6-1/180. ... Shoots right. ... Name pronounced BEEKS-ah.

TRANSACTIONS/CAREER NOTES: Selected by Vancouver Canucks in fifth round (fourth Canucks pick, 151th overall) of entry draft (June 24, 2001).

Season Team	League	GP	G	A	Pts.	PIM	+/-	PP	SH	GP	G	A	Pts.	PIM
		REGULAR SEASON								PLAYOFFS				
00-01—Bowling Green...........	CCHA	35	4	9	13	90	...	...	...	—	—	—	—	—
01-02—Bowling Green...........	CCHA	40	5	10	15	68	...	...	...	—	—	—	—	—
02-03—Bowling Green...........	CCHA	34	8	17	25	92	...	...	...	—	—	—	—	—
03-04—Bowling Green...........	CCHA	38	7	15	22	66	...	...	...	—	—	—	—	—
—Manitoba.....................	AHL	4	0	2	2	2	...	...	...	—	—	—	—	—
04-05—Manitoba.....................	AHL	80	12	27	39	192	21	4	0	14	1	1	2	52
05-06—Manitoba.....................	AHL	23	3	17	20	71	3	2	0	13	0	10	10	38
—Vancouver..................	NHL	39	0	6	6	77	-1	0	0	—	—	—	—	—
NHL Totals (1 year).............		39	0	6	6	77	-1	0	0					

BIRON, MARTIN G

PERSONAL: Born August 15, 1977, in Lac St. Charles, Que. ... 6-3/163. ... Catches left. ... Brother of Mathieu Biron, D, Washington Capitals.

TRANSACTIONS/CAREER NOTES: Selected by Buffalo Sabres in first round (second Sabres pick, 16th overall) of entry draft (July 8, 1995). ... Missed first 12 games of 2000-01 season in contract dispute.

Season Team	League	GP	Min.	W	L	OTL	T	GA	SO	GAA	SV%	GP	Min.	W	L	GA	SO	GAA	SV%
		REGULAR SEASON										PLAYOFFS							
94-95—Beauport....................	QMJHL	56	3193	29	16	...	9	132	3	2.48	.898	16	902	8	7	37	4	2.46	.909
95-96—Beauport....................	QMJHL	55	3207	29	17	...	7	152	1	2.84	...	19	1132	12	8	64	0	3.39	...
—Buffalo	NHL	3	119	0	2	...	0	10	0	5.04	.844	—	—	—	—	—	—	—	—
96-97—Beauport....................	QMJHL	18	935	6	10	...	1	62	1	3.98	...	—	—	—	—	—	—	—	—
—Hull............................	QMJHL	16	972	11	4	...	1	43	2	2.65	...	6	326	3	1	19	0	3.50	.871
97-98—Rochester...................	AHL	41	2312	14	18	...	6	113	5	2.93	.907	4	239	1	3	16	0	4.02	.885
—South Carolina	ECHL	2	86	0	1	...	1	3	0	2.09	...	—	—	—	—	—	—	—	—
98-99—Rochester...................	AHL	52	3129	36	13	...	3	108	6	2.07	.930	20	1167	12	8	42	/d1	2.16	.934
—Buffalo	NHL	6	281	1	2	...	1	10	0	2.14	.917	—	—	—	—	—	—	—	—
99-00—Rochester...................	AHL	6	344	6	0	...	0	12	1	2.09	...	—	—	—	—	—	—	—	—
—Buffalo	NHL	41	2229	19	18	...	2	90	5	2.42	.909	—	—	—	—	—	—	—	—
00-01—Rochester...................	AHL	4	239	3	1	...	0	4	1	1.00	.955	—	—	—	—	—	—	—	—
—Buffalo	NHL	18	918	7	7	...	1	39	2	2.55	.909	—	—	—	—	—	—	—	—

Season Team	League	GP	Min.	W	L	OTL	T	GA	SO	GAA	SV%	GP	Min.	W	L	GA	SO	GAA	SV%
		REGULAR SEASON										PLAYOFFS							
01-02—Buffalo	NHL	72	4085	31	28	...	10	151	4	2.22	.915	—	—	—	—	—	—	—	—
02-03—Buffalo	NHL	54	3170	17	28	...	6	135	4	2.56	.908	—	—	—	—	—	—	—	—
03-04—Buffalo	NHL	52	2972	26	18	...	5	125	2	2.52	.913	—	—	—	—	—	—	—	—
05-06—Buffalo	NHL	35	1934	21	8	3	...	93	1	2.89	.905	—	—	—	—	—	—	—	—
NHL Totals (8 years)		281	15708	122	111	3	25	653	18	2.49	.910								

BIRON, MATHIEU — D

PERSONAL: Born April 29, 1980, in Lac St. Charles, Que. ... 6-6/230. ... Shoots right. ... Brother of Martin Biron, G, Buffalo Sabres.

TRANSACTIONS/CAREER NOTES: Selected by Los Angeles Kings in first round (first Kings pick, 21st overall) of entry draft (June 27, 1998). ... Traded by Kings with C Olli Jokinen, LW Josh Green and first-round pick (LW Taylor Pyatt) in 1999 draft to New York Islanders for RW Zigmund Palffy, C Bryan Smolinski, G Marcel Cousineau and fourth-round pick (C Daniel Johansson) in 1999 draft (June 20, 1999). ... Traded by Islanders with second-round pick (traded to Washington; traded to Vancouver; Canucks selected Denis Grot) in 2002 draft to Tampa Bay Lightning for RW Alexander Kharitonov and D Adrian Aucoin (June 22, 2001). ... Claimed by Columbus Blue Jackets in waiver draft (October 4, 2002). ... Traded by Blue Jackets to Florida Panthers for RW Petr Tenkrat (October 4, 2002). ... Fractured thumb (October 3, 2003); missed 17 games. ... Contract bought out by Panthers (July 28, 2005). ... Signed as free agent by Washington Capitals (August 10, 2005).

Season Team	League	GP	G	A	Pts.	PIM	+/-	PP	SH	GP	G	A	Pts.	PIM
		REGULAR SEASON								PLAYOFFS				
97-98—Shawinigan	QMJHL	59	8	28	36	60	...	...	...	6	0	1	1	10
98-99—Shawinigan	QMJHL	69	13	32	45	116	7	7	2	6	0	2	2	6
99-00—New York Islanders	NHL	60	4	4	8	38	-13	2	0	—	—	—	—	—
00-01—Lowell	AHL	22	1	3	4	17	...	...	...	—	—	—	—	—
—New York Islanders	NHL	14	0	1	1	12	2	0	0	—	—	—	—	—
—Springfield	AHL	34	0	6	6	18	...	...	...	—	—	—	—	—
01-02—Springfield	AHL	35	4	9	13	16	5	1	0	—	—	—	—	—
—Tampa Bay	NHL	36	0	0	0	12	-16	0	0	—	—	—	—	—
02-03—Florida	NHL	34	1	8	9	14	-18	0	1	—	—	—	—	—
—San Antonio	AHL	43	3	8	11	58	...	...	...	—	—	—	—	—
03-04—Florida	NHL	57	3	10	13	51	-13	0	0	—	—	—	—	—
04-05—Thetford Mines	LNAH	19	7	15	22	8	...	...	...	—	—	—	—	—
05-06—Washington	NHL	52	4	9	13	50	-11	3	0	—	—	—	—	—
NHL Totals (6 years)		253	12	32	44	177	-69	5	1					

BLAKE, JASON — LW/RW

PERSONAL: Born September 2, 1973, in Moorhead, Minn. ... 5-10/180. ... Shoots left.

TRANSACTIONS/CAREER NOTES: Signed as free agent by Los Angeles Kings (April 17, 1999). ... Concussion (December 19, 1999); missed four games. ... Traded by Kings to New York Islanders for fifth-round pick (D Joel Andersen) in 2002 draft (January 3, 2001). ... Concussion (February 9, 2001); missed one game. ... Granted personal leave for final 13 games of 2000-01 season. ... Sprained knee (November 4, 2003); missed two games. ... High ankle sprain (March 25, 2004); missed remainder of regular season. ... Concussion (December 14, 2005); missed one game. ... Bruised ribs (January 4, 2006); missed three games. ... Groin (April 2, 2006); missed one game.

STATISTICAL PLATEAUS: Three-goal games: 2002-03 (1), 2003-04 (1). Total: 2.

Season Team	League	GP	G	A	Pts.	PIM	+/-	PP	SH	GP	G	A	Pts.	PIM
		REGULAR SEASON								PLAYOFFS				
94-95—Ferris State	CCHA	36	16	16	32	46	...	...	...	—	—	—	—	—
96-97—Univ. of North Dakota	WCHA	43	19	32	51	44	17	4	2	—	—	—	—	—
97-98—Univ. of North Dakota	WCHA	38	24	27	51	62	...	...	...	—	—	—	—	—
98-99—North Dakota	WCHA	38	28	/d41	69	49	...	...	...	—	—	—	—	—
—Orlando	IHL	5	3	5	8	6	5	0	0	13	3	4	7	20
—Los Angeles	NHL	1	1	0	1	0	1	0	0	—	—	—	—	—
99-00—Los Angeles	NHL	64	5	18	23	26	4	0	0	3	0	0	0	0
—Long Beach	IHL	7	3	6	9	2	...	...	...	—	—	—	—	—
00-01—Los Angeles	NHL	17	1	3	4	10	-8	0	0	—	—	—	—	—
—Lowell	AHL	2	0	1	1	2	...	...	...	—	—	—	—	—
—New York Islanders	NHL	30	4	8	12	24	-12	1	1	—	—	—	—	—
01-02—New York Islanders	NHL	82	8	10	18	36	-11	0	0	7	0	1	1	13
02-03—New York Islanders	NHL	81	25	30	55	58	16	3	1	5	0	1	1	2
03-04—New York Islanders	NHL	75	22	25	47	56	11	1	4	4	2	0	2	2
04-05—Lugano	Switzerland	7	2	2	4	4	...	0	0	—	—	—	—	—
05-06—New York Islanders	NHL	76	28	29	57	60	0	12	2	—	—	—	—	—
—U.S. Olympic team	Int'l	6	0	0	0	2	2	0	0	—	—	—	—	—
NHL Totals (7 years)		426	94	123	217	270	1	17	8	19	2	2	4	17

BLAKE, ROB — D

PERSONAL: Born December 10, 1969, in Simcoe, Ont. ... 6-4/225. ... Shoots right.

TRANSACTIONS/CAREER NOTES: Selected by Los Angeles Kings in fourth round (fourth Kings pick, 70th overall) of NHL draft (June 11, 1988). ... Sprained knee (April 1990). ... Injured knee (February 12, 1991); missed two games. ... Injured shoulder (October 8, 1991); missed 11 games. ... Sprained knee ligaments (November 28, 1991); missed six games. ... Flu (January 23, 1992); missed one game. ... Flu (February 13, 1992); missed one game. ... Strained shoulder (March 14, 1992); missed four games. ... Fractured rib (December 19, 1992); missed three games. ... Bruised lower back (April 3, 1993); missed final five games of regular season and one playoff game. ... Strained groin (January 23, 1995); missed 11 games. ... Strained groin (March 11, 1995); missed 12 games. ... Strained groin (April 7, 1995); missed one game. ... Tore left knee ligaments (October 20, 1995); missed 76 games. ... Fractured hand (December 26, 1996); missed 11 games. ... Suspended two games and fined $1,000 by NHL for high-sticking incident (February 5, 1997). ... Tendinitis in left knee (February 22, 1997); missed seven games. ... Fractured right foot (November 6, 1998); missed 15 games. ... Suspended three games and fined $1,000 for slashing incident

(December 14, 1998). ... Suspended two games for cross-checking incident (April 9, 1999). ... Strained groin (December 8, 1999); missed two games. ... Bruised knee (April 1, 2000); missed three games. ... Fractured lumbar vertebrae (October 13, 2000); missed three games. ... Bruised shoulder (February 21, 2001); missed two games. ... Traded by Kings with C Steve Reinprecht to Colorado Avalanche for RW Adam Deadmarsh, D Aaron Miller, first-round pick (C David Steckel) in 2001 draft, C Jared Aulin and first-round pick (Brian Boyle) in 2003 draft (February 21, 2001). ... Sprained knee (March 20, 2001); missed eight games. ... Injured groin (November 27, 2001); missed three games. ... Flu (February 13, 2002); missed one game. ... Bruised knee (February 11, 2002); missed one game. ... Reinjured knee (February 26, 2002); missed two games. ... Injured groin (November 8, 2002); missed one game. ... Back spasms (January 2, 2003); missed two games. ... Fractured left leg (February 10, 2004); missed seven games. ... Hand injury (January 3, 2006); missed one game. ... Signed as free agent by Kings (July 1, 2006).

STATISTICAL PLATEAUS: Three-goal games: 2000-01 (1).

		REGULAR SEASON								PLAYOFFS				
Season Team	**League**	**GP**	**G**	**A**	**Pts.**	**PIM**	**+/-**	**PP**	**SH**	**GP**	**G**	**A**	**Pts.**	**PIM**
86-87—Stratford Jr. B	OHA	31	11	20	31	115	...	...	...	—	—	—	—	—
87-88—Bowling Green	CCHA	36	5	8	13	72	...	...	...	—	—	—	—	—
88-89—Bowling Green	CCHA	46	11	21	32	140	...	...	...	—	—	—	—	—
89-90—Bowling Green	CCHA	42	23	36	59	140	...	...	...	—	—	—	—	—
—Los Angeles	NHL	4	0	0	0	4	0	0	0	8	1	3	4	4
90-91—Los Angeles	NHL	75	12	34	46	125	3	9	0	12	1	4	5	26
91-92—Los Angeles	NHL	57	7	13	20	102	-5	5	0	6	2	1	3	12
92-93—Los Angeles	NHL	76	16	43	59	152	18	10	0	23	4	6	10	46
93-94—Los Angeles	NHL	84	20	48	68	137	-7	7	0	—	—	—	—	—
94-95—Los Angeles	NHL	24	4	7	11	38	-16	4	0	—	—	—	—	—
95-96—Los Angeles	NHL	6	1	2	3	8	0	0	0	—	—	—	—	—
96-97—Los Angeles	NHL	62	8	23	31	82	-28	4	0	—	—	—	—	—
97-98—Los Angeles	NHL	81	23	27	50	94	-3	11	0	4	0	0	0	6
—Can. Olympic team	Int'l	6	1	1	2	2	8	0	0	—	—	—	—	—
98-99—Los Angeles	NHL	62	12	23	35	128	-7	5	1	—	—	—	—	—
99-00—Los Angeles	NHL	77	18	39	57	112	10	12	0	4	0	2	2	4
00-01—Los Angeles	NHL	54	17	32	49	69	-8	9	0	—	—	—	—	—
—Colorado	NHL	13	2	8	10	8	11	1	0	23	6	13	19	16
01-02—Colorado	NHL	75	16	40	56	58	16	10	0	20	6	6	12	16
—Can. Olympic team	Int'l	6	1	2	3	2	...	...	...	—	—	—	—	—
02-03—Colorado	NHL	79	17	28	45	57	20	8	2	7	1	2	3	8
03-04—Colorado	NHL	74	13	33	46	61	6	8	0	9	0	5	5	6
05-06—Colorado	NHL	81	14	37	51	94	2	7	1	9	3	1	4	8
—Canadian Oly. team	Int'l	6	0	1	1	2	0	0	0	—	—	—	—	—
NHL Totals (16 years)		984	200	437	637	1329	12	110	4	125	24	43	67	152

BLATNY, ZDENEK C/LW

PERSONAL: Born January 14, 1981, in Brno, Czech. ... 6-1/190. ... Shoots left.

TRANSACTIONS/CAREER NOTES: Selected by Atlanta Thrashers in third round (third Thrashers pick, 68th overall) of entry draft (June 26, 1999). ... Signed as free agent by Boston Bruins (September 29, 2005). ... Traded by Bruins to Tampa Bay Lightning for G Brian Eklund (February 8, 2005).

		REGULAR SEASON								PLAYOFFS				
Season Team	**League**	**GP**	**G**	**A**	**Pts.**	**PIM**	**+/-**	**PP**	**SH**	**GP**	**G**	**A**	**Pts.**	**PIM**
97-98—Kometa Brno	Czech. Jrs.	42	22	21	43	40	...	...	...	—	—	—	—	—
98-99—Seattle	WHL	44	18	15	33	25	7	6	0	11	4	0	4	24
99-00—Seattle	WHL	7	4	5	9	12	...	...	...	—	—	—	—	—
—Kootenay	WHL	61	43	39	82	119	42	20	5	21	10	17	27	46
00-01—Kootenay	WHL	58	37	48	85	120	...	...	...	11	8	10	18	24
01-02—Chicago	AHL	41	4	3	7	30	-8	0	1	3	2	0	2	0
—Greenville	ECHL	12	5	5	10	17	1	2	0	9	2	8	10	14
02-03—Chicago	AHL	72	12	9	21	62	7	3	0	9	0	2	2	20
—Atlanta	NHL	4	0	0	0	0	-1	0	0	—	—	—	—	—
03-04—Chicago	AHL	61	11	23	34	115	5	2	0	10	0	4	4	24
—Atlanta	NHL	16	3	0	3	6	0	0	0	—	—	—	—	—
04-05—Reipas Lahti	Finland	9	1	1	2	22	-8	...	...	—	—	—	—	—
—HC Znojemsti Orli	Czech Rep.	15	3	4	7	28	-4	...	...	—	—	—	—	—
05-06—Providence	AHL	35	8	22	30	21	6	1	2	—	—	—	—	—
—Springfield	AHL	31	14	15	29	20	-2	5	0	—	—	—	—	—
—Boston	NHL	5	0	0	0	2	-2	0	0	—	—	—	—	—
NHL Totals (3 years)		25	3	0	3	8	-3	0	0					

BOCHENSKI, BRANDON LW/RW

PERSONAL: Born April 4, 1982, in Blaine, Minn. ... 6-0/180. ... Shoots right.

COLLEGE: North Dakota.

TRANSACTIONS/CAREER NOTES: Selected by Ottawa Senators in seventh round (ninth Senators pick, 223rd overall) of entry draft (June 24, 2001). ... Separated right shoulder (December 17, 2005); missed 11 games. ... Shoulder injury (January 13, 2006); missed four games. ... Traded by Senators with a second-round pick (D Simon Danis-Pepin) in 2006 draft to Chicago for C Tyler Arnason (March 9, 2006).

		REGULAR SEASON								PLAYOFFS				
Season Team	**League**	**GP**	**G**	**A**	**Pts.**	**PIM**	**+/-**	**PP**	**SH**	**GP**	**G**	**A**	**Pts.**	**PIM**
00-01—Lincoln	USHL	55	47	33	80	22	...	...	...	11	5	7	12	4
01-02—North Dakota	WCHA	36	17	15	32	36	...	...	...	—	—	—	—	—
02-03—Univ. of North Dakota	WCHA	43	35	27	62	42	...	...	...	—	—	—	—	—
03-04—Univ. of North Dakota	WCHA	41	27	33	60	40	...	...	...	—	—	—	—	—

Season Team	League	REGULAR SEASON								PLAYOFFS				
		GP	G	A	Pts.	PIM	+/-	PP	SH	GP	G	A	Pts.	PIM
04-05—Binghamton	AHL	75	34	36	70	16	16	12	0	6	1	0	1	2
05-06—Norfolk	AHL	—	—	—	—	—	—	—	—	3	1	1	2	0
—Binghamton	AHL	33	22	24	46	36	-3	15	0	—	—	—	—	—
—Ottawa	NHL	20	6	7	13	14	7	2	0	—	—	—	—	—
—Chicago	NHL	20	2	2	4	8	-9	0	0	—	—	—	—	—
NHL Totals (1 year)		40	8	9	17	22	-2	2	0					

BODROV, DENIS D

PERSONAL: Born August 22, 1986, in Moscow, Rus. ... 6-0/185. ... Shoots left.

TRANSACTIONS/CAREER NOTES: Selected by Philadelphia Flyers in second round (fourth Flyers pick; 55th overall) of NHL draft (June 24, 2006).

Season Team	League	REGULAR SEASON								PLAYOFFS				
		GP	G	A	Pts.	PIM	+/-	PP	SH	GP	G	A	Pts.	PIM
05-06—Lada Togliatti	Russian	35	2	2	4	42	...	...	...	—	—	—	—	—

BOGUNIECKI, ERIC RW

PERSONAL: Born May 6, 1975, in New Haven, Conn. ... 5-8/192. ... Shoots right. ... Name pronounced BOH-guh-nih-kee.

TRANSACTIONS/CAREER NOTES: Selected by St. Louis Blues in eighth round (sixth Blues pick, 193rd overall) of entry draft (June 29, 1993). ... Signed as free agent by Florida Panthers (July 20, 1999). ... Traded by Panthers to Blues for C Andrei Podkonicky (December 18, 2000). ... Injured shoulder (October 10, 2003); missed season's first 18 games. ... Reinjured shoulder (December 20, 2003); missed 14 games. ... Concussion (February 29, 2004); missed 18 games. ... Signed as free agent by Worcester of the AHL (December 17, 2004). ... Re-signed by Blues as restricted free agent (August 9, 2005). ... Injured shoulder (September 2005); missed first 12 games of season. ... Traded by Blues to Pittsburgh Penguins for D Steve Poapst (December 9, 2005). ... Injured knee (December 31, 2006); missed seven games.

Season Team	League	REGULAR SEASON								PLAYOFFS				
		GP	G	A	Pts.	PIM	+/-	PP	SH	GP	G	A	Pts.	PIM
92-93—Westminster School	Conn. H.S.	24	30	24	54	55	...	...	...	—	—	—	—	—
93-94—New Hampshire	Hockey East	40	17	16	33	66	...	3	0	—	—	—	—	—
94-95—New Hampshire	Hockey East	34	12	19	31	62	...	5	1	—	—	—	—	—
95-96—New Hampshire	Hockey East	32	23	28	51	46	...	...	...	—	—	—	—	—
96-97—New Hampshire	Hockey East	36	26	31	57	58	...	14	0	—	—	—	—	—
97-98—Dayton	ECHL	26	19	18	37	36	...	...	...	—	—	—	—	—
—Fort Wayne	IHL	35	4	8	12	29	-4	0	0	4	1	2	3	10
98-99—Fort Wayne	IHL	72	32	34	66	100	2	11	0	2	0	1	1	2
99-00—Louisville	AHL	57	33	42	75	148	...	...	...	4	3	2	5	20
—Florida	NHL	4	0	0	0	2	-1	0	0	—	—	—	—	—
00-01—Louisville	AHL	28	13	12	25	56	...	...	...	—	—	—	—	—
—Worcester	AHL	45	17	28	45	100	...	...	...	9	3	2	5	10
—St. Louis	NHL	1	0	0	0	0	-1	0	0	—	—	—	—	—
01-02—Worcester	AHL	63	/d38	46	84	181	22	9	3	3	2	0	2	4
—St. Louis	NHL	8	0	1	1	4	-2	0	0	1	0	1	1	0
02-03—St. Louis	NHL	80	22	27	49	38	22	3	1	7	1	2	3	2
03-04—Worcester	AHL	3	0	1	1	0	-2	0	0	—	—	—	—	—
—St. Louis	NHL	27	6	4	10	20	-1	2	0	1	0	0	0	0
04-05—Langenthal	Switzerland	10	5	3	8	47	...	3	1	—	—	—	—	—
—Worcester	AHL	30	14	11	25	46	-3	6	1	—	—	—	—	—
05-06—Peoria	AHL	2	0	0	0	4	0	0	0	—	—	—	—	—
—St. Louis	NHL	9	1	4	5	4	-1	1	0	—	—	—	—	—
—Pittsburgh	NHL	38	5	6	11	29	-2	1	0	—	—	—	—	—
NHL Totals (6 years)		167	34	42	76	97	14	7	1	9	1	3	4	2

BONDRA, PETER RW

PERSONAL: Born February 7, 1968, in Luck, U.S.S.R. ... 6-1/202. ... Shoots left. ... Name pronounced BAHN-druh.

TRANSACTIONS/CAREER NOTES: Selected by Washington Capitals in eighth round (ninth Capitals pick, 156th overall) of entry draft (June 16, 1990). ... Dislocated left shoulder (January 17, 1991). ... Recurring shoulder problems (February 13, 1991); missed 13 games. ... Injured throat (April 4, 1993); missed one game. ... Fractured left hand (November 26, 1993); missed 12 games. ... Flu (April 8, 1995); missed one game. ... Signed by IHL Detroit during contract dispute (September 28, 1995); re-signed by Capitals (October 20, 1995). ... Separated shoulder (November 11, 1995); missed six games. ... Injured groin (February 24, 1996); missed four games. ... Strained groin (December 4, 1996); missed three games. ... Suspended one game and fined $1,000 for kneeing (February 4, 1997). ... Back spasms (April 1, 1997); missed one game. ... Injured foot (November 29, 1997); missed three games. ... Injured knee (April 8, 1998); missed two games. ... Injured hip (November 28, 1998); missed one game. ... Fractured hand (March 15, 1999); missed remainder of season. ... Knee surgery (December 5, 1999); missed eight games. ... Injured knee (January 4, 2000); missed seven games. ... Injured shoulder (March 30, 1999); missed five games. ... Flu (January 9, 2002); missed three games. ... Flu (February 26, 2002); missed one game. ... Flu (March 2, 2002); missed one game. ... Injured back (November 23, 2002); missed three games. ... Flu (January 1, 2003); missed three games. ... Injured groin (December 31, 2003); missed four games. ... Flu (January 17, 2004); missed one game. ... Traded by Capitals for LW/C Brooks Laich and second-round pick (later traded to Colorado; Avalanche selected C Chris Durand) in 2005 (February 18, 2004). ... Signed as free agent by Atlanta Thrashers (September 18, 2005). ... Strained groin (December 3, 2005); missed 22 games.

STATISTICAL PLATEAUS: Three-goal games: 1990-91 (1), 1994-95 (1), 1995-96 (2), 1996-97 (1), 1997-98 (1), 1998-99 (2), 1999-00 (1), 2000-01 (2), 2001-02 (1), 2003-04 (1). Total: 13. ... Four-goal games: 1995-96 (2), 1996-97 (1), 1998-99 (1), 2000-01 (1). Total: 5. ... Five-goal games: 1993-94 (1). ... Total hat tricks: 19.

Season Team	League	REGULAR SEASON								PLAYOFFS				
		GP	G	A	Pts.	PIM	+/-	PP	SH	GP	G	A	Pts.	PIM
86-87—Kosice	Czech.	32	4	5	9	24	...	...	...	—	—	—	—	—
87-88—Kosice	Czech.	45	27	11	38	20	...	...	...	—	—	—	—	—

Season Team	League	GP	G	A	Pts.	PIM	+/-	PP	SH	GP	G	A	Pts.	PIM
		REGULAR SEASON								PLAYOFFS				
88-89—Kosice	Czech.	40	30	10	40	20	...	...	...	—	—	—	—	—
89-90—Kosice	Czech.	42	29	17	46	...	...	...	...	—	—	—	—	—
90-91—Washington	NHL	54	12	16	28	47	-10	4	0	4	0	1	1	2
91-92—Washington	NHL	71	28	28	56	42	16	4	0	7	6	2	8	4
92-93—Washington	NHL	83	37	48	85	70	8	10	0	6	0	6	6	0
93-94—Washington	NHL	69	24	19	43	40	22	4	0	9	2	4	6	4
94-95—HC Kosice	Slovakia	2	1	0	1	0	1	...	...	—	—	—	—	—
—Washington	NHL	47	*34	9	43	24	9	12	*6	7	5	3	8	10
95-96—Detroit	IHL	7	8	1	9	0	...	...	...	—	—	—	—	—
—Washington	NHL	67	52	28	80	40	18	11	4	6	3	2	5	8
96-97—Washington	NHL	77	46	31	77	72	7	10	4	—	—	—	—	—
97-98—Washington	NHL	76	†52	26	78	44	14	11	5	17	7	5	12	12
—Slovakian Oly. team	Int'l	2	1	0	1	25	-1	1	0	—	—	—	—	—
98-99—Washington	NHL	66	31	24	55	56	-1	6	3	—	—	—	—	—
99-00—Washington	NHL	62	21	17	38	30	5	5	3	5	1	1	2	4
00-01—Washington	NHL	82	45	36	81	60	8	*22	4	6	2	0	2	2
01-02—Washington	NHL	77	39	31	70	80	-2	*17	1	—	—	—	—	—
02-03—Washington	NHL	76	30	26	56	52	-3	9	2	6	4	2	6	8
03-04—Washington	NHL	54	21	14	35	22	-17	12	0	—	—	—	—	—
—Ottawa	NHL	23	5	9	14	16	1	2	0	7	0	0	0	6
04-05—HC SKP Poprad	Slovakia	6	4	2	6	4	2	...	...	—	—	—	—	—
05-06—Atlanta	NHL	60	21	18	39	40	-3	8	0	—	—	—	—	—
—Slovakian Oly. team	Int'l	6	4	0	4	2	0	2	0	—	—	—	—	—
NHL Totals (15 years)		1044	498	380	878	735	72	147	32	80	30	26	56	60

B

BONK, RADEK C

PERSONAL: Born January 9, 1976, in Krnov, Czech. ... 6-3/220. ... Shoots left. ... Name pronounced BAHNK.

TRANSACTIONS/CAREER NOTES: Selected by Ottawa Senators in first round (first Senators pick, third overall) of entry draft (June 28, 1994). ... Injured ankle (April 26, 1995); missed final five games of season. ... Injured hand (1995-96 season); missed one game. ... Strained abdomen (November 8, 1996); missed six games. ... Fractured left wrist (November 23, 1996); missed 23 games. ... Bruised knee (March 5, 1998); missed one game. ... Injured hip flexor (November 7, 1998); missed one game. ... Flu (January 4, 2000); missed two games. ... Flu (February 19, 2001); missed one game. ... Fractured left thumb (March 24, 2001); missed final seven games of regular season and two playoff games. ... Chest (October 23, 2002); missed five games. ... Shoulder, reinjured chest (November 9, 2002); missed three games. ... Back (February 12, 2003); missed two games. ... Bruised left leg (March 15, 2003); missed two games. ... Flu (December 30, 2003); missed two games. ... Fractured right foot (February 10, 2004); missed 14 games. ... Traded by Senators to Los Angeles Kings for third-round pick (LW Shawn Weller) in 2004 draft (June 26, 2004). ... Traded by Kings with G Cristobal Huet to Montreal Canadiens for G Mathieu Garon and third-round pick (D Paul Baier) in 2004 draft (June 26, 2004). ... Strained groin (October 31, 2005); missed five games. ... Thigh (November 15, 2005); missed two games. ... Strained groin (December 3, 2005); missed 11 games. ... Leg (April 10, 2006); missed one game.

STATISTICAL PLATEAUS: Three-goal games: 2000-01 (1).

Season Team	League	GP	G	A	Pts.	PIM	+/-	PP	SH	GP	G	A	Pts.	PIM
		REGULAR SEASON								PLAYOFFS				
90-91—Opava	Czech.	35	47	42	89	25	...	...	...	—	—	—	—	—
91-92—ZPS Zlin	Czech Dv.I	45	47	36	83	30	...	...	...	—	—	—	—	—
92-93—ZPS Zlin	Czech.	30	5	5	10	10	...	...	...	—	—	—	—	—
93-94—Las Vegas	IHL	76	42	45	87	208	42	11	0	5	1	2	3	10
94-95—Las Vegas	IHL	33	7	13	20	62	-8	5	0	—	—	—	—	—
—Ottawa	NHL	42	3	8	11	28	-5	1	0	—	—	—	—	—
—Prince Edward	AHL	...	...	...	...	...	...	...	...	1	0	0	0	0
95-96—Ottawa	NHL	76	16	19	35	36	-5	5	0	—	—	—	—	—
96-97—Ottawa	NHL	53	5	13	18	14	-4	0	1	7	0	1	1	4
97-98—Ottawa	NHL	65	7	9	16	16	-13	1	0	5	0	0	0	2
98-99—Ottawa	NHL	81	16	16	32	48	15	0	1	4	0	0	0	6
99-00—HC Pardubice	Czech Rep.	3	1	0	1	4	...	...	...	—	—	—	—	—
—Ottawa	NHL	80	23	37	60	53	-2	10	0	6	0	0	0	8
00-01—Ottawa	NHL	74	23	36	59	52	27	5	2	2	0	0	0	2
01-02—Ottawa	NHL	82	25	45	70	52	3	6	2	12	3	7	10	6
02-03—Ottawa	NHL	70	22	32	54	36	6	11	0	18	6	5	11	10
03-04—Ottawa	NHL	66	12	32	44	66	2	6	0	7	0	2	2	0
04-05—Trinec	Czech Rep.	27	6	10	16	44	5	...	...	—	—	—	—	—
—Zlin	Czech Rep.	6	3	2	5	4	3	...	...	6	0	2	2	8
05-06—Montreal	NHL	61	6	15	21	52	-3	0	2	6	2	0	2	2
NHL Totals (11 years)		750	158	262	420	453	21	45	8	67	11	15	26	40

BOOGAARD, DEREK LW

PERSONAL: Born June 23, 1982, in Saskatoon, Sask. ... 6-7/250. ... Shoots left. ... Brother of Aaron Boogaard, Minnesota Wild organization.

TRANSACTIONS/CAREER NOTES: Selected by Minnesota Wild in seventh round (fifth Wild selection, 20second overall) of entry draft (June 24, 2001). ... Lower-body injury (October 28, 2005); missed one game. ... Back (January 18, 2006); missed one game.

Season Team	League	GP	G	A	Pts.	PIM	+/-	PP	SH	GP	G	A	Pts.	PIM
		REGULAR SEASON								PLAYOFFS				
99-00—Regina	WHL	5	0	0	0	17	...	...	...	—	—	—	—	—
—Prince George	WHL	33	0	0	0	149	...	...	...	—	—	—	—	—
00-01—Prince George	WHL	61	1	8	9	245	...	...	...	6	1	0	1	31
01-02—Prince George	WHL	2	0	0	0	16	...	...	...	—	—	—	—	—
—Medicine Hat	WHL	46	1	8	9	178	...	...	...	—	—	—	—	—
02-03—Medicine Hat	WHL	27	1	2	3	65	...	...	...	—	—	—	—	—

Season Team	League	REGULAR SEASON GP	G	A	Pts.	PIM	+/-	PP	SH	PLAYOFFS GP	G	A	Pts.	PIM
—Louisiana	ECHL	33	1	2	3	240	-3	0	0	2	0	0	0	0
03-04—Houston	AHL	53	0	4	4	207	...	...	...	2	0	1	1	16
04-05—Houston	AHL	56	1	4	5	259	0	0	0	5	0	0	0	38
05-06—Minnesota	NHL	65	2	4	6	158	2	0	0	—	—	—	—	—
NHL Totals (1 year)		65	2	4	6	158	2	0	0					

BOUCHARD, FRANCOIS RW

PERSONAL: Born April 26, 1988, in Sherbrooke, Quebec. ... 6-0/180. ... Shoots left.
TRANSACTIONS/CAREER NOTES: Selected by Washington Capitals in second round (fourth Capitals pick; 35th overall) of NHL draft (June 24, 2006).

Season Team	League	REGULAR SEASON GP	G	A	Pts.	PIM	+/-	PP	SH	PLAYOFFS GP	G	A	Pts.	PIM
04-05—Baie-Comeau	QMJHL	54	11	13	24	13	-4	...	...	6	1	1	2	2
05-06—Baie-Comeau	QMJHL	69	33	69	102	66	-6	...	...	4	1	0	1	6

BOUCHARD, JOEL D

PERSONAL: Born January 23, 1974, in Montreal. ... 6-1/209. ... Shoots left.
TRANSACTIONS/CAREER NOTES: Selected by Calgary Flames in sixth round (sixth Flames pick, 129th overall) of entry draft (June 20, 1992). ... Strained abdominal muscle (September 30, 1997); missed one game. ... Concussion (January 24, 1998); missed six games. ... Selected by Nashville Predators in expansion draft (June 26, 1998). ... Sprained ankle (October 27, 1998); missed 11 games. ... Sprained ankle (December 19, 1998); missed seven games. ... Concussion (December 15, 1999); missed nine games. ... Claimed off waivers by Dallas Stars (March 14, 2000). ... Signed as free agent by Phoenix Coyotes (August 31, 2000). ... Back spasms (December 30, 2000); missed two games. ... Signed as free agent by New Jersey Devils (October 25, 2001). ... Signed as free agent by New York Rangers (August 7, 2002). ... Traded by Rangers with RW Rico Fata, RW Mikael Samuelsson, D Richard Lintner and cash to Pittsburgh Penguins for RW Alexei Kovalev, LW Dan LaCouture, D Janne Laukkanen and D Mike Wilson (February 10, 2003). ... Fractured jaw (February 22, 2003); missed 20 games. ... Signed as free agent by Buffalo Sabres (July 14, 2003). ... Claimed by Rangers in waiver draft (October 3, 2003). ... Injured hamstring (January 3, 2004); missed six games. ... Concussion (February 14, 2004); missed four games. ... Signed as free agent by New York Islanders (August 19, 2005). ... Knee (March 16, 2006); missed one game. ... Knee (April 5, 2006); missed final eight games of regular season.

Season Team	League	REGULAR SEASON GP	G	A	Pts.	PIM	+/-	PP	SH	PLAYOFFS GP	G	A	Pts.	PIM
90-91—Longueuil	QMJHL	53	3	19	22	34	...	...	...	8	0	1	1	11
91-92—Verdun	QMJHL	70	9	37	46	55	...	...	...	19	1	7	8	20
92-93—Verdun	QMJHL	60	10	49	59	126	...	...	...	4	0	2	2	4
93-94—Verdun	QMJHL	60	15	55	70	62	37	6	2	4	1	0	1	6
—Saint John	AHL	1	0	0	0	0	0	0	0	2	0	0	0	0
94-95—Saint John	AHL	77	6	25	31	63	2	0	0	5	1	0	1	4
—Calgary	NHL	2	0	0	0	0	0	0	0	—	—	—	—	—
95-96—Saint John	AHL	74	8	25	33	104	...	...	...	16	1	4	5	10
—Calgary	NHL	4	0	0	0	4	0	0	0	—	—	—	—	—
96-97—Calgary	NHL	76	4	5	9	49	-23	0	1	—	—	—	—	—
97-98—Calgary	NHL	44	5	7	12	57	0	0	1	—	—	—	—	—
—Saint John	AHL	3	2	1	3	6	4	1	0	—	—	—	—	—
98-99—Nashville	NHL	64	4	11	15	60	-10	0	0	—	—	—	—	—
99-00—Nashville	NHL	52	1	4	5	23	-11	0	0	—	—	—	—	—
—Dallas	NHL	2	0	0	0	2	1	0	0	—	—	—	—	—
00-01—Grand Rapids	IHL	19	3	9	12	8	...	...	...	—	—	—	—	—
—Phoenix	NHL	32	1	2	3	22	-8	0	0	—	—	—	—	—
01-02—Albany	AHL	70	9	22	31	28	-30	4	1	—	—	—	—	—
—New Jersey	NHL	1	0	1	1	0	1	0	0	—	—	—	—	—
02-03—New York Rangers	NHL	27	5	7	12	14	6	1	0	—	—	—	—	—
—Hartford	AHL	22	6	14	20	22	5	4	0	—	—	—	—	—
—Pittsburgh	NHL	7	0	1	1	0	-6	0	0	—	—	—	—	—
03-04—New York Rangers	NHL	28	1	7	8	10	2	0	0	—	—	—	—	—
04-05—Hartford	AHL	7	1	2	3	6	2	0	0	6	0	2	2	20
05-06—Bridgeport	AHL	15	4	9	13	10	-4	2	0	—	—	—	—	—
—New York Islanders	NHL	25	1	8	9	23	5	0	0	—	—	—	—	—
NHL Totals (11 years)		364	22	53	75	264	-43	1	2					

BOUCHARD, PIERRE-MARC RW

PERSONAL: Born April 27, 1984, in Sherbrooke, Que. ... 5-10/162. ... Shoots left.
TRANSACTIONS/CAREER NOTES: Selected by Minnesota Wild in first round (first Wild pick, eighth overall) of entry draft (June 22, 2002). ... Neck (January 5, 2006); missed two games.

Season Team	League	REGULAR SEASON GP	G	A	Pts.	PIM	+/-	PP	SH	PLAYOFFS GP	G	A	Pts.	PIM
00-01—Chicoutimi	QMJHL	67	38	57	95	20	...	...	...	6	5	8	13	0
01-02—Chicoutimi	QMJHL	69	46	94	140	54	...	...	...	4	2	3	5	4
02-03—Minnesota	NHL	50	7	13	20	18	1	5	0	5	0	1	1	2
03-04—Minnesota	NHL	61	4	18	22	22	-7	2	0	—	—	—	—	—
04-05—Houston	AHL	67	12	42	54	46	-2	7	0	5	0	1	1	0
05-06—Minnesota	NHL	80	17	42	59	28	3	7	0	—	—	—	—	—
NHL Totals (3 years)		191	28	73	101	68	-3	14	0	5	0	1	1	2

BOUCHER, BRIAN G

PERSONAL: Born January 2, 1977, in Woonsocket, R.I. ... 6-2/198. ... Catches left. ... Name pronounced boo-SHAY.

TRANSACTIONS/CAREER NOTES: Selected by Philadelphia Flyers in first round (first Flyers pick, 22nd overall) of NHL draft (July 8, 1995). ... Throat infection (January 16, 2001); missed one game. ... Strained left hamstring (November 15, 2001); missed nine games. ... Traded by Flyers with third-round pick (D Joe Callahan) in 2002 draft to Phoenix Coyotes for G Robert Esche and C Michal Handzus (June 12, 2002). ... Bruised knee (January 3, 2003); missed five games. ... Groin (September 16, 2005); missed season's first 13 games. ... Traded by Coyotes with LW Mike Leclerc to Calgary Flames for C Steve Reinprecht and G Philippe Sauve (February 1, 2006).

		REGULAR SEASON										PLAYOFFS							
Season Team	**League**	**GP**	**Min.**	**W**	**L**	**OTL**	**T**	**GA**	**SO**	**GAA**	**SV%**	**GP**	**Min.**	**W**	**L**	**GA**	**SO**	**GAA**	**SV%**
93-94—Mt. St. Charles H.S.	R.I.H.S.	23	1170	...	...	...	...	23	12	1.18	...	—	—	—	—	—	—	—	—
94-95—Wexford	Tier II Jr. A	8	425	...	...	...	...	23	0	3.25	...	—	—	—	—	—	—	—	—
—Tri-City	WHL	35	1969	17	11	...	2	108	1	3.29	.908	13	795	6	5	50	0	3.77	.904
95-96—Tri-City	WHL	55	3183	33	19	...	2	181	1	3.41	...	11	653	6	5	37	2	3.40	...
96-97—Tri-City	WHL	41	2458	10	24	...	6	149	1	3.64	.901	—	—	—	—	—	—	—	—
97-98—Philadelphia	AHL	34	1901	16	12	...	3	101	0	3.19	.888	2	31	0	0	1	0	1.94	.944
98-99—Philadelphia	AHL	36	2061	20	8	...	5	89	2	2.59	.911	16	947	9	7	45	0	2.85	.906
99-00—Philadelphia	NHL	35	2038	20	10	...	3	65	4	*1.91	.918	18	1183	11	7	40	1	2.03	.917
—Philadelphia	AHL	1	65	0	0	...	1	3	0	2.77	...	—	—	—	—	—	—	—	—
00-01—Philadelphia	NHL	27	1470	8	12	...	5	80	1	3.27	.876	1	37	0	0	3	0	4.86	.824
01-02—Philadelphia	NHL	41	2295	18	16	...	4	92	2	2.41	.905	2	88	0	1	2	0	1.36	.939
02-03—Phoenix	NHL	45	2544	15	20	...	8	128	0	3.02	.894	—	—	—	—	—	—	—	—
03-04—Phoenix	NHL	40	2364	10	19	...	10	108	5	2.74	.906	—	—	—	—	—	—	—	—
04-05—HV 71 Jonkoping	Sweden	4	235	...	...	...	...	13	0	3.32	.884	—	—	—	—	—	—	—	—
05-06—San Antonio	AHL	6	345	2	3	0	...	8	1	1.39	.950	—	—	—	—	—	—	—	—
—Phoenix	NHL	11	512	3	6	0	...	33	0	3.87	.877	—	—	—	—	—	—	—	—
—Calgary	NHL	3	182	1	2	0	...	15	0	4.95	.854	—	—	—	—	—	—	—	—
NHL Totals (6 years)		202	11405	75	85	0	30	521	12	2.74	.899	21	1308	11	8	45	1	2.06	.916

BOUCHER, PHILIPPE D

PERSONAL: Born March 24, 1973, in St. Apollinaire, Que. ... 6-3/221. ... Shoots right. ... Name pronounced fih-LEEP boo-SHAY.

TRANSACTIONS/CAREER NOTES: Selected by Buffalo Sabres in first round (first Sabres pick, 13th overall) of entry draft (June 22, 1991). ... Traded by Sabres with G Grant Fuhr and D Denis Tsygurov to Los Angeles Kings for D Alexei Zhitnik, D Charlie Huddy, G Robb Stauber and fifth-round pick (D Marian Menhart) in 1995 (February 14, 1995). ... Sprained wrist (February 25, 1995); missed season's final 31 games. ... Tendinitis in right wrist (October 6, 1995); missed first 25 games of season. ... Left hand (February 19, 1996); missed four games. ... Sprained right shoulder (October 4, 1996); missed 10 games. ... Flu (December 18, 1997); missed two games. ... Injured (January 10, 1998); missed 12 games. ... Flu (March 3, 1999); missed two games. ... Foot surgery (April 27, 1999); missed 1999-2000 season's first 71 games. ... Flu (December 16, 2001); missed one game. ... Concussion (January 17, 2002); missed one game. ... Signed as free agent by Dallas Stars (July 2, 2002). ... Groin (October 24, 2003); missed one game. ... Eye (November 29, 2003); missed nine games. ... Flu (January 5, 2004); missed two games. ... Broken finger (December 2, 2005), surgery (December 3, 2005); missed six games. ... Hand (December 26, 2005); missed six games. ... Knee (February 4, 2006); missed three games. ... Knee (April 18, 2006); missed one game.

		REGULAR SEASON								PLAYOFFS				
Season Team	**League**	**GP**	**G**	**A**	**Pts.**	**PIM**	**+/-**	**PP**	**SH**	**GP**	**G**	**A**	**Pts.**	**PIM**
90-91—Granby	QMJHL	69	21	46	67	92	...	...	...	—	—	—	—	—
91-92—Granby	QMJHL	49	22	37	59	47	...	...	...	—	—	—	—	—
—Laval	QMJHL	16	7	11	18	36	...	...	...	10	5	6	11	8
92-93—Laval	QMJHL	16	12	15	27	37	...	...	...	13	6	15	21	12
—Rochester	AHL	5	4	3	7	8	-1	1	0	3	0	1	1	2
—Buffalo	NHL	18	0	4	4	14	1	0	0	—	—	—	—	—
93-94—Buffalo	NHL	38	6	8	14	29	-1	4	0	7	1	1	2	2
—Rochester	AHL	31	10	22	32	51	-1	6	0	—	—	—	—	—
94-95—Rochester	AHL	43	14	27	41	26	-1	5	0	—	—	—	—	—
—Buffalo	NHL	9	1	4	5	0	6	0	0	—	—	—	—	—
—Los Angeles	NHL	6	1	0	1	4	-3	0	0	—	—	—	—	—
95-96—Los Angeles	NHL	53	7	16	23	31	-26	5	0	—	—	—	—	—
—Phoenix	IHL	10	4	3	7	4	...	...	...	—	—	—	—	—
96-97—Los Angeles	NHL	60	7	18	25	25	0	2	0	—	—	—	—	—
97-98—Los Angeles	NHL	45	6	10	16	49	6	1	0	—	—	—	—	—
—Long Beach	IHL	2	0	1	1	4	1	0	0	—	—	—	—	—
98-99—Los Angeles	NHL	45	2	6	8	32	-12	1	0	—	—	—	—	—
99-00—Long Beach	IHL	14	4	11	15	8	...	...	...	6	0	9	9	8
—Los Angeles	NHL	1	0	0	0	0	0	0	0	—	—	—	—	—
00-01—Manitoba	IHL	45	10	22	32	99	...	...	...	—	—	—	—	—
—Los Angeles	NHL	22	2	4	6	20	4	2	0	13	0	1	1	2
01-02—Los Angeles	NHL	80	7	23	30	94	0	4	0	5	0	1	1	2
02-03—Dallas	NHL	80	7	20	27	94	28	1	1	11	1	2	3	11
03-04—Dallas	NHL	70	8	16	24	64	15	2	0	5	1	0	1	6
05-06—Dallas	NHL	66	16	27	43	77	28	8	0	5	0	1	1	2
NHL Totals (13 years)		593	70	156	226	533	46	30	1	46	3	6	9	25

BOUCK, TYLER RW/LW

PERSONAL: Born January 13, 1980, in Camrose, Alta. ... 6-0/196. ... Shoots left.

TRANSACTIONS/CAREER NOTES: Selected by Dallas Stars in second round (second Stars pick, 57th overall) of entry draft (June 27, 1998). ... Traded by Stars to Phoenix Coyotes for D Jyrki Lumme (June 23, 2001). ... Traded by Coyotes with LW Todd Warriner, C Trevor Letowski and third-round pick (traded back to Phoenix; Coyotes selected Dimitri Pestrunov) in 2003 draft to Vancouver Canucks for C Denis Pederson and D Drake Berehowsky (December 28, 2001). ... Strained groin (October 5, 2005); missed 37 games.

Season Team	League	GP	G	A	Pts.	PIM	+/-	PP	SH	GP	G	A	Pts.	PIM
		REGULAR SEASON								PLAYOFFS				
96-97—Prince George	WHL	12	0	2	2	11	...	...	...	—	—	—	—	—
97-98—Prince George	WHL	65	11	26	37	90	...	...	...	11	1	0	1	21
98-99—Prince George	WHL	56	22	25	47	178	8	4	1	2	0	2	2	10
99-00—Prince George	WHL	57	30	33	63	183	17	9	5	13	6	13	19	36
00-01—Dallas	NHL	48	2	5	7	29	-3	0	0	1	0	0	0	0
—Utah	IHL	24	2	6	8	39	...	...	...	—	—	—	—	—
01-02—Phoenix	NHL	7	0	0	0	4	-1	0	0	—	—	—	—	—
—Springfield	AHL	21	1	2	3	33	-2	0	0	—	—	—	—	—
—Manitoba	AHL	41	5	6	11	58	-5	0	2	—	—	—	—	—
02-03—Manitoba	AHL	76	10	28	38	103	8	2	2	14	2	2	4	10
03-04—Manitoba	AHL	49	11	14	25	100	-3	2	0	—	—	—	—	—
—Vancouver	NHL	18	1	2	3	23	-4	0	1	1	0	0	0	0
04-05—TPS Turku	Finland	—	—	—	—	—	—	—	—	6	1	0	1	12
—TPS Turku	Finland	40	3	7	10	100	-2	...	...	—	—	—	—	—
05-06—Manitoba	AHL	8	0	1	1	8	0	0	0	—	—	—	—	—
—Vancouver	NHL	12	1	1	2	21	0	0	0	—	—	—	—	—
NHL Totals (4 years)		85	4	8	12	77	-8	0	1	2	0	0	0	0

BOUGHNER, BOB D

PERSONAL: Born March 8, 1971, in Windsor, Ont. ... 6-0/203. ... Shoots right. ... Name pronounced BOOG-nuhr.

TRANSACTIONS/CAREER NOTES: Selected by Detroit Red Wings in second round (second Red Wings pick, 3second overall) of draft (June 17, 1989). ... Signed as free agent by Florida Panthers (August 10, 1994). ... Traded by Panthers to Buffalo Sabres for third-round pick (D Chris Allen) in 1996 (February 1, 1996). ... Bruised left thigh (February 28, 1996); missed one game. ... Bruised shoulder (February 7, 1998); missed two games. ... Injured wrist (March 12, 1998); missed three games. ... Bruised foot (April 29, 1998); missed one game. ... Selected by Nashville Predators in expansion draft (June 26, 1998). ... Flu (October 27, 1998); missed one game. ... Flu (January14, 1999); missed two games. ... Flu (November, 1999); missed two games. ... Sprained ankle (December 1999); missed two games. ... Fractured finger (February 2, 2000); missed three games. ... Traded by Predators to Pittsburgh Penguins for D Pavel Skrbek (March 13, 2000). ... Fractured wrist (November 11, 2000); missed 23 games. ... Bruised chest (March 2, 2001); missed one game. ... Signed as free agent by Calgary Flames (July 2, 2001). ... Injured (November 10, 2001); missed one game. ... Injured (March 9, 2002); missed one game. ... Injured (March 16, 2002); missed one game. ... Traded by Flames to Carolina Hurricanes for fourth-round pick (LW Kris Hogg) in 2004 and fifth-round pick (G Kevin Lalande) in 2005 (July 16, 2003). ... Fractured left hand (October 4, 2003); missed seven games. ... Injured left knee (November 18, 2003); missed four games. ... Injured knee (February 3, 2004); missed five games. ... Traded by Hurricanes to Avalanche for D Chris Bahen and third-round pick (D Casey Borer) in 2004 (February 20, 2004). ... Reinjured knee (February 24, 2004) and had surgery (February 26, 2004); missed 11 games. ... Hip pointer (February 2, 2006); missed one game. ... Sprained right wrist (February 9, 2006); missed one game. ... Announced retirement (June 2006).

Season Team	League	GP	G	A	Pts.	PIM	+/-	PP	SH	GP	G	A	Pts.	PIM
		REGULAR SEASON								PLAYOFFS				
87-88—St. Mary's Jr. B	OHA	36	4	18	22	177	...	...	...	—	—	—	—	—
88-89—Sault Ste. Marie	OHL	64	6	15	21	182	...	...	...	—	—	—	—	—
89-90—Sault Ste. Marie	OHL	49	7	23	30	122	...	...	...	—	—	—	—	—
90-91—Sault Ste. Marie	OHL	64	13	33	46	156	...	...	...	14	2	9	11	35
91-92—Adirondack	AHL	1	0	0	0	7	...	...	...	—	—	—	—	—
—Toledo	ECHL	28	3	10	13	79	...	...	...	5	2	0	2	15
92-93—Adirondack	AHL	69	1	16	17	190	5	0	0	—	—	—	—	—
93-94—Adirondack	AHL	72	8	14	22	292	3	1	1	10	1	1	2	18
94-95—Cincinnati	IHL	81	2	14	16	192	10	0	0	10	0	0	0	18
95-96—Carolina	AHL	46	2	15	17	127	...	...	...	—	—	—	—	—
—Buffalo	NHL	31	0	1	1	104	3	0	0	—	—	—	—	—
96-97—Buffalo	NHL	77	1	7	8	225	12	0	0	11	0	1	1	9
97-98—Buffalo	NHL	69	1	3	4	165	5	0	0	14	0	4	4	15
98-99—Nashville	NHL	79	3	10	13	137	-6	0	0	—	—	—	—	—
99-00—Nashville	NHL	62	2	4	6	97	-13	0	0	—	—	—	—	—
—Pittsburgh	NHL	11	1	0	1	69	2	1	0	11	0	2	2	15
00-01—Pittsburgh	NHL	58	1	3	4	147	18	0	0	18	0	1	1	22
01-02—Calgary	NHL	79	2	4	6	170	9	0	0	—	—	—	—	—
02-03—Calgary	NHL	69	3	14	17	126	5	0	0	—	—	—	—	—
03-04—Carolina	NHL	43	0	5	5	80	-9	0	0	—	—	—	—	—
—Colorado	NHL	11	0	0	0	8	-1	0	0	11	0	4	4	6
05-06—Colorado	NHL	41	1	6	7	54	2	0	0	—	—	—	—	—
NHL Totals (10 years)		630	15	57	72	1382	27	1	0	65	0	12	12	67

BOUILLON, FRANCIS D

PERSONAL: Born October 17, 1975, in New York City. ... 5-8/196. ... Shoots left.

TRANSACTIONS/CAREER NOTES: Signed as free agent by Montreal Canadiens (August 18, 1998). ... Fractured hand (November 14, 2000); missed 13 games. ... Sprained ankle (December 30, 2000); missed 23 games. ... Claimed by Nashville Predators in waiver draft (October 4, 2002). ... Claimed off waivers by Canadiens (October 25, 2002). ... Took personal leave (February 2, 2004); missed one game. ... Re-signed by Canadiens as restricted free agent (August 2, 2005). ... Sprained ankle (March 18, 2006); missed three weeks.

Season Team	League	GP	G	A	Pts.	PIM	+/-	PP	SH	GP	G	A	Pts.	PIM
		REGULAR SEASON								PLAYOFFS				
92-93—Laval	QMJHL	46	0	7	7	45	...	...	...	—	—	—	—	—
93-94—Laval	QMJHL	68	3	15	18	129	...	...	...	19	2	9	11	48
94-95—Laval	QMJHL	72	8	25	33	115	...	...	...	20	3	11	14	21
95-96—Granby	QMJHL	68	11	35	46	156	...	...	...	21	2	12	14	30
96-97—Wheeling	ECHL	69	10	32	42	77	...	...	...	3	0	2	2	10
97-98—Quebec	IHL	71	8	27	35	76	...	...	...	—	—	—	—	—

Season Team	League	REGULAR SEASON GP	G	A	Pts.	PIM	+/-	PP	SH	PLAYOFFS GP	G	A	Pts.	PIM
98-99—Fredericton	AHL	79	19	36	55	174	7	7	1	5	2	1	3	0
99-00—Montreal	NHL	74	3	13	16	38	-7	2	0	—	—	—	—	—
00-01—Montreal	NHL	29	0	6	6	26	3	0	0	—	—	—	—	—
—Quebec	AHL	4	0	0	0	0	...	...	...	—	—	—	—	—
01-02—Quebec	AHL	38	8	14	22	30	2	4	0	—	—	—	—	—
—Montreal	NHL	28	0	5	5	33	-5	0	0	—	—	—	—	—
02-03—Nashville	NHL	4	0	0	0	2	-1	0	0	—	—	—	—	—
—Montreal	NHL	20	3	1	4	2	-1	0	1	—	—	—	—	—
—Hamilton	AHL	29	1	12	13	31	9	0	0	—	—	—	—	—
03-04—Montreal	NHL	73	2	16	18	70	1	0	0	11	0	0	0	7
04-05—Leksand	Sweden Dv. 2	8	3	4	7	10	11	0	0	10	4	9	13	12
05-06—Montreal	NHL	67	3	19	22	34	-6	3	0	6	1	2	3	10
NHL Totals (6 years)		295	11	60	71	205	-16	5	1	17	1	2	3	17

BOULERICE, JESSE — RW/LW

PERSONAL: Born August 10, 1978, in Plattsburgh, N.Y. ... 6-2/203. ... Shoots right. ... Name pronounced: BOH-luh-rihz

TRANSACTIONS/CAREER NOTES: Selected by Philadelphia in fifth round (fourth Flyers pick, 133rd overall) of draft (June 22, 1996). ... Traded by Flyers to Carolina Hurricanes for C Greg Koehler (February 13, 2002). ... Concussion (February 11, 2003); missed 24 games. ... Traded by Hurricanes with LW Magnus Kahnberg, C Mike Zigomanis, first-round (traded to New Jersey; Devils selected D Matthew Correntes) and fourth-round (G Reto Berra) picks in 2006 draft and fourth-round pick in 2007 draft to St. Louis Blues for C Doug Weight and LW Erkki Rajamaki (January 30, 2006). ... Released by Blues (April 3, 2006).

Season Team	League	REGULAR SEASON GP	G	A	Pts.	PIM	+/-	PP	SH	PLAYOFFS GP	G	A	Pts.	PIM
95-96—Det. Jr. Red Wings	OHL	64	2	5	7	150	...	...	...	16	0	0	0	12
96-97—Detroit	OHL	33	10	14	24	209	-13	3	0	—	—	—	—	—
97-98—Plymouth	OHL	53	20	23	43	170	...	...	...	13	2	4	6	35
98-99—Philadelphia	AHL	24	1	2	3	82	-5	0	0	—	—	—	—	—
—New Orleans	ECHL	12	0	1	1	38	-2	0	0	—	—	—	—	—
99-00—Philadelphia	AHL	40	3	4	7	85	...	...	...	4	0	2	2	4
—Trenton	ECHL	25	8	8	16	90	...	...	...	—	—	—	—	—
00-01—Philadelphia	AHL	60	3	4	7	256	...	...	...	10	1	1	2	28
01-02—Philadelphia	NHL	3	0	0	0	5	-1	0	0	—	—	—	—	—
—Philadelphia	AHL	41	2	5	7	204	1	0	0	—	—	—	—	—
—Lowell	AHL	56	4	9	13	284	2	0	0	5	0	2	2	6
02-03—Carolina	NHL	48	2	1	3	108	-2	0	0	—	—	—	—	—
03-04—Carolina	NHL	76	6	1	7	127	-5	0	0	—	—	—	—	—
05-06—Lowell	AHL	1	0	2	2	0	1	0	0	—	—	—	—	—
—Carolina	NHL	26	0	0	0	51	-3	0	0	—	—	—	—	—
—St. Louis	NHL	12	0	0	0	13	-4	0	0	—	—	—	—	—
NHL Totals (4 years)		165	8	2	10	304	-15	0	0					

BOULTON, ERIC — LW

PERSONAL: Born August 17, 1976, in Halifax, N.S. ... 6-1/215. ... Shoots left.

TRANSACTIONS/CAREER NOTES: Selected by New York Rangers in ninth round (12th Rangers pick, 234th overall) of entry draft (June 29, 1994). ... Signed as free agent by Buffalo Sabres (August 20, 1999). ... Injured thumb (September 16, 2003); missed first 10 games of season. ... Signed as free agent by Atlanta Thrashers (August 5, 2005). ... Suspended six games in elbowing incident (October 24, 2005).

Season Team	League	REGULAR SEASON GP	G	A	Pts.	PIM	+/-	PP	SH	PLAYOFFS GP	G	A	Pts.	PIM
93-94—Oshawa	OHL	45	4	3	7	149	...	...	...	5	0	0	0	16
94-95—Oshawa	OHL	27	7	5	12	125	...	2	0	—	—	—	—	—
—Sarnia	OHL	24	3	7	10	134	...	2	0	4	0	1	1	10
95-96—Sarnia	OHL	66	14	29	43	243	...	...	...	9	0	3	3	29
96-97—Binghamton	AHL	23	2	3	5	67	-5	0	0	3	0	0	0	4
—Charlotte	ECHL	44	14	11	25	325	...	...	...	3	0	1	1	6
97-98—Charlotte	ECHL	53	11	16	27	202	...	...	...	4	1	0	1	0
—Fort Wayne	IHL	8	0	2	2	42	...	...	...	—	—	—	—	—
98-99—Houston	IHL	7	1	0	1	41	1	0	0	—	—	—	—	—
—Florida	ECHL	26	9	13	22	143	5	1	0	—	—	—	—	—
—Kentucky	AHL	34	3	3	6	154	1	1	0	10	0	1	1	36
99-00—Rochester	AHL	76	2	2	4	276	...	...	...	18	2	1	3	53
00-01—Buffalo	NHL	35	1	2	3	94	-1	0	0	—	—	—	—	—
01-02—Buffalo	NHL	35	2	3	5	129	-1	0	0	—	—	—	—	—
02-03—Buffalo	NHL	58	1	5	6	178	1	0	0	—	—	—	—	—
03-04—Buffalo	NHL	44	1	2	3	110	-2	0	0	—	—	—	—	—
04-05—Columbia	ECHL	48	23	16	39	124	10	8	...	4	2	3	5	8
05-06—Atlanta	NHL	51	4	5	9	87	-4	0	0	—	—	—	—	—
NHL Totals (5 years)		223	9	17	26	598	-7	0	0					

BOURQUE, RENE — LW

PERSONAL: Born December 10, 1981, in Lac La Biche, Alta. ... 6-2/205. ... Shoots left.

COLLEGE: Wisconsin.

TRANSACTIONS/CAREER NOTES: Signed as free agent by Chicago Blackhawks (July 29, 2004). ... Hip flexor (December 9, 2005); missed one game.

Season Team	League	REGULAR SEASON GP	G	A	Pts.	PIM	+/-	PP	SH	PLAYOFFS GP	G	A	Pts.	PIM
00-01—Wisconsin	WCHA	32	10	5	15	18	...	...	...	—	—	—	—	—
01-02—Wisconsin	WCHA	38	12	7	19	26	...	...	...	—	—	—	—	—
02-03—Wisconsin	WCHA	40	19	8	27	54	...	...	...	—	—	—	—	—
03-04—Wisconsin	WCHA	42	16	20	36	74	...	...	...	—	—	—	—	—
04-05—Norfolk	AHL	78	33	27	60	105	-3	10	1	6	1	0	1	8
05-06—Chicago	NHL	77	16	18	34	56	3	4	0	—	—	—	—	—
NHL Totals (1 year)		77	16	18	34	56	3	4	0					

BOUWMEESTER, JAY — D

PERSONAL: Born September 27, 1983, in Edmonton. ... 6-4/218. ... Shoots left. ... Name pronounced boh-MEES-tuhr.

TRANSACTIONS/CAREER NOTES: Selected by Florida Panthers in first round (first Panthers pick, third overall) of NHL draft (June 22, 2002). ... Fractured left foot (January 19, 2004); missed 18 games.

Season Team	League	REGULAR SEASON GP	G	A	Pts.	PIM	+/-	PP	SH	PLAYOFFS GP	G	A	Pts.	PIM
98-99—Medicine Hat	WHL	8	2	1	3	2	...	...	...	—	—	—	—	—
99-00—Medicine Hat	WHL	34	13	21	34	26	...	...	...	—	—	—	—	—
00-01—Medicine Hat	WHL	61	14	39	53	44	...	...	...	—	—	—	—	—
01-02—Medicine Hat	WHL	61	12	49	61	42	...	...	...	—	—	—	—	—
02-03—Florida	NHL	82	4	12	16	14	-29	2	0	—	—	—	—	—
03-04—Florida	NHL	61	2	18	20	30	-15	0	0	—	—	—	—	—
—San Antonio	AHL	2	0	1	1	2	0	0	0	—	—	—	—	—
04-05—Chicago	AHL	18	6	3	9	12	4	3	0	18	0	0	0	14
—San Antonio	AHL	64	4	13	17	50	-22	1	1	—	—	—	—	—
05-06—Florida	NHL	82	5	41	46	79	1	0	0	—	—	—	—	—
—Canadian Oly. team	Int'l	6	0	0	0	0	4	0	0	—	—	—	—	—
NHL Totals (3 years)		225	11	71	82	123	-43	2	0					

BOYES, BRAD — C/RW

PERSONAL: Born April 17, 1982, in Mississauga, Ont. ... 6-1/195. ... Shoots right.

TRANSACTIONS/CAREER NOTES: Selected by Toronto Maple Leafs in first round (first Maple Leafs pick, 24th overall) of entry draft (June 24, 2000). ... Traded by Maple Leafs with C Alyn McCauley and 2003 first-round pick (traded to Boston; Bruins selected D Mark Stuart) to San Jose Sharks for RW Owen Nolan (March 5, 2003). ... Traded by Sharks to Bruins for D Jeff Jillson (March 9, 2004).

Season Team	League	REGULAR SEASON GP	G	A	Pts.	PIM	+/-	PP	SH	PLAYOFFS GP	G	A	Pts.	PIM
98-99—Erie	OHL	59	24	36	60	30	...	...	...	5	1	2	3	10
99-00—Erie	OHL	68	36	46	82	38	...	...	...	13	6	8	14	10
00-01—Erie	OHL	59	45	45	90	42	27	13	5	15	10	13	23	8
01-02—Erie	OHL	47	36	41	77	42	...	...	...	21	22	19	41	27
02-03—St. John's	AHL	65	23	28	51	45	1	6	2	—	—	—	—	—
—Cleveland	AHL	15	7	6	13	21	-6	3	1	—	—	—	—	—
03-04—San Jose	NHL	1	0	0	0	2	-2	0	0	—	—	—	—	—
—Cleveland	AHL	61	25	35	60	38	9	7	0	—	—	—	—	—
—Providence	AHL	17	6	6	12	13	4	1	0	2	1	0	1	0
04-05—Providence	AHL	80	33	42	75	58	-6	20	2	16	8	7	15	23
05-06—Boston	NHL	82	26	43	69	30	11	8	0	—	—	—	—	—
NHL Totals (2 years)		83	26	43	69	32	9	8	0					

BOYLE, DAN — D

PERSONAL: Born July 12, 1976, in Ottawa. ... 5-11/190. ... Shoots right.

TRANSACTIONS/CAREER NOTES: Signed as free agent by Florida Panthers (March 30, 1998). ... Traded by Panthers to Tampa Bay Lightning for fifth-round pick (D Martin Tuma) in 2003 draft (January 7, 2002). ... Fractured finger (January 7, 2003); missed four games. ... Had concussion (December 6, 2003); missed four games. ... Injured right ankle (March 26, 2006); missed three games.

Season Team	League	REGULAR SEASON GP	G	A	Pts.	PIM	+/-	PP	SH	PLAYOFFS GP	G	A	Pts.	PIM
94-95—Miami (Ohio)	CCHA	35	8	18	26	24	...	...	...	—	—	—	—	—
95-96—Miami (Ohio)	CCHA	36	7	20	27	70	...	...	...	—	—	—	—	—
96-97—Miami (Ohio)	CCHA	40	11	43	54	52	...	...	...	—	—	—	—	—
97-98—Miami (Ohio)	CCHA	37	14	26	40	58	...	...	...	—	—	—	—	—
—Cincinnati	IHL	8	0	3	3	20	1	0	0	5	0	1	1	4
98-99—Kentucky	AHL	53	8	34	42	87	21	4	0	12	3	5	8	16
—Florida	NHL	22	3	5	8	6	0	1	0	—	—	—	—	—
99-00—Louisville	AHL	58	14	38	52	75	...	...	...	4	0	2	2	8
—Florida	NHL	13	0	3	3	4	-2	0	0	—	—	—	—	—
00-01—Florida	NHL	69	4	18	22	28	-14	1	0	—	—	—	—	—
—Louisville	AHL	6	0	5	5	12	...	...	...	—	—	—	—	—
01-02—Florida	NHL	25	3	3	6	12	-1	1	0	—	—	—	—	—
—Tampa Bay	NHL	41	5	15	20	27	-15	2	0	—	—	—	—	—
02-03—Tampa Bay	NHL	77	13	40	53	44	9	8	0	11	0	7	7	6
03-04—Tampa Bay	NHL	78	9	30	39	60	23	3	0	23	2	8	10	16
04-05—Djurgarden Stockholm	Sweden	32	9	9	18	47	4	3	1	12	2	3	5	26
05-06—Tampa Bay	NHL	79	15	38	53	38	-8	6	0	5	1	3	4	6
NHL Totals (7 years)		404	52	152	204	219	-8	22	0	39	3	18	21	28

BOYNTON, NICK — D

PERSONAL: Born January 14, 1979, in Nobleton, Ont. ... 6-2/212. ... Shoots right.

TRANSACTIONS/CAREER NOTES: Selected by Washington Capitals in first round (first Capitals pick, ninth overall) of entry draft (June 21, 1997). ... Returned to draft pool by Capitals; selected by Boston Bruins in first round (first Bruins pick, 21st overall) of entry draft (June 26, 1999). ... Food poisoning (December 12, 2001); missed two games. ... Injured hand (November 21, 2002); missed one game. ... Flu (December 21, 2002); missed two games. ... Injured shoulder (February 24, 2004); missed one game. ... Missed first four games of 2005-06 in contract dispute; re-signed by Bruins to one-year contract (October 13, 2006). ... Fractured kneecap (December 4, 2005); missed 12 games. ... Suspended one game by NHL for threatening gesture (March 10, 2006). ... Shoulder (March 31, 2006); missed final eight games of regular season. ... Traded by Bruins with a fourth-round pick in 2007 entry draft to Phoenix Coyotes for D Paul Mara and an unconditional draft choice (June 26, 2006).

		REGULAR SEASON								PLAYOFFS				
Season Team	**League**	**GP**	**G**	**A**	**Pts.**	**PIM**	**+/-**	**PP**	**SH**	**GP**	**G**	**A**	**Pts.**	**PIM**
94-95—Caledon	Jr. A	44	10	35	45	139	...	...	...	—	—	—	—	—
95-96—Ottawa	OHL	64	10	14	24	90	...	...	...	4	0	3	3	10
96-97—Ottawa	OHL	63	13	51	64	143	81	6	0	24	4	24	28	38
97-98—Ottawa	OHL	40	7	31	38	94	...	...	...	13	0	4	4	24
98-99—Ottawa	OHL	51	11	48	59	83	53	...	...	9	1	9	10	18
99-00—Providence	AHL	53	5	14	19	66	...	...	...	12	1	0	1	6
—Boston	NHL	5	0	0	0	0	-5	0	0	—	—	—	—	—
00-01—Providence	AHL	78	6	27	33	105	...	...	...	17	0	2	2	35
—Boston	NHL	1	0	0	0	0	-1	0	0	—	—	—	—	—
01-02—Boston	NHL	80	4	14	18	107	18	0	0	6	1	2	3	8
02-03—Boston	NHL	78	7	17	24	99	8	0	1	5	0	1	1	4
03-04—Boston	NHL	81	6	24	30	98	17	1	1	7	0	2	2	2
04-05—Nottingham	England	13	2	3	5	10	...	...	...	6	1	2	3	22
05-06—Boston	NHL	54	5	7	12	93	-7	1	1	—	—	—	—	—
NHL Totals (6 years)		299	22	62	84	397	30	2	3	18	1	5	6	14

BRADLEY, MATT — RW/LW

PERSONAL: Born June 13, 1978, in Stittsville, Ont. ... 6-3/199. ... Shoots right.

TRANSACTIONS/CAREER NOTES: Selected by San Jose Sharks in fourth round (fourth Sharks pick, 10second overall) of entry draft (June 22, 1996). ... Injured shoulder (February 14, 2001); missed seven games. ... Injured back (March 3, 2002); missed one game. ... Injured wrist (April 10, 2002); missed final two games of season. ... Injured wrist (March 8, 2003); missed three games. ... Traded by Sharks to Pittsburgh Penguins for C Wayne Primeau (March 11, 2003); missed final 12 games of season because of wrist injury. ... Signed as unrestricted free agent by Washington Capitals (August 18, 2005). ... Lower-body injury (October 29, 2005); missed two games. ... Bruised foot (January 31, 2006); missed six games.

		REGULAR SEASON								PLAYOFFS				
Season Team	**League**	**GP**	**G**	**A**	**Pts.**	**PIM**	**+/-**	**PP**	**SH**	**GP**	**G**	**A**	**Pts.**	**PIM**
94-95—Cumberland	CJHL	49	13	20	33	18	...	...	...	—	—	—	—	—
95-96—Kingston	OHL	55	10	14	24	17	...	...	...	6	0	1	1	6
96-97—Kingston	OHL	65	24	24	48	41	17	5	0	5	0	4	4	2
—Kentucky	AHL	1	0	1	1	0	0	0	0	—	—	—	—	—
97-98—Kingston	OHL	55	33	50	83	24	13	...	...	8	3	4	7	7
—Kentucky	AHL	1	0	1	1	0	...	...	...	—	—	—	—	—
98-99—Kentucky	AHL	79	23	20	43	57	9	5	1	10	1	4	5	4
99-00—Kentucky	AHL	80	22	19	41	81	...	...	...	9	6	3	9	9
00-01—Kentucky	AHL	22	5	8	13	16	...	...	...	1	1	0	1	5
—San Jose	NHL	21	1	1	2	19	0	0	0	—	—	—	—	—
01-02—San Jose	NHL	54	9	13	22	43	22	0	0	10	0	0	0	0
02-03—San Jose	NHL	46	2	3	5	37	-1	0	0	—	—	—	—	—
03-04—Pittsburgh	NHL	82	7	9	16	65	-27	0	0	—	—	—	—	—
04-05—Dornbirner	Austria	6	5	2	7	18	...	...	...	—	—	—	—	—
05-06—Washington	NHL	74	7	12	19	72	-8	0	0	—	—	—	—	—
NHL Totals (5 years)		277	26	38	64	236	-14	0	0	10	0	0	0	0

BRASHEAR, DONALD — LW

PERSONAL: Born January 7, 1972, in Bedford, Ind. ... 6-2/230. ... Shoots left. ... Name pronounced brah-SHEER.

TRANSACTIONS/CAREER NOTES: Signed as free agent by Montreal Canadiens (July 28, 1992). ... Bruised knee (November 23, 1993); missed one game. ... Injured shoulder (February 27, 1995); missed one game. ... Bruised hand (March 20, 1995); missed one game. ... Cut right thigh (December 30, 1995); missed seven games. ... Traded by Canadiens to Vancouver Canucks for D Jassen Cullimore (November 13, 1996). ... Strained back (February 8, 1997); missed three games. ... Suspended four games and fined $1,000 for fighting (February 25, 1997). ... Injured shoulder (March 11, 1998); missed two games. ... Suspended two games for illegal check (October 24, 1999). ... Suffered concussion (February 21, 2000); missed 20 games. ... Strained knee (October 18, 2000); missed one game. ... Strained back (November 21, 2000); missed two games. ... Injured leg (November 11, 2001); missed five games. ... Traded by Canucks with sixth-round pick (traded to Columbus; Blue Jackets selected Jaroslav Balastik) in 2002 draft to Philadelphia Flyers for LW Jan Hlavac and third-round pick (Brett Skinner) in 2002 (December 17, 2001). ... Bruised right hand (March 29, 2003); missed two games. ... Injured left knee (October 14, 2003); missed nine games. ... Sprained left knee (February 5, 2004); missed three games. ... Sprained left knee (February 17, 2004); missed six games. ... Strained left shoulder (December 13, 2005); missed three games. ... Strained muscle (January 11, 2006); missed two games. ... Suspended one game by NHL in fighting incident (March 3, 2006). ... Signed as free agent by Washington Capitals (July 14, 2006).

		REGULAR SEASON								PLAYOFFS				
Season Team	**League**	**GP**	**G**	**A**	**Pts.**	**PIM**	**+/-**	**PP**	**SH**	**GP**	**G**	**A**	**Pts.**	**PIM**
89-90—Longueuil	QMJHL	64	12	14	26	169	...	...	...	7	0	0	0	11
90-91—Longueuil	QMJHL	68	12	26	38	195	...	...	...	8	0	3	3	33
91-92—Verdun	QMJHL	65	18	24	42	283	...	...	...	18	4	2	6	98
92-93—Fredericton	AHL	76	11	3	14	261	...	...	...	5	0	0	0	8

Season Team	League	GP	G	A	Pts.	PIM	+/-	PP	SH	GP	G	A	Pts.	PIM
		REGULAR SEASON								PLAYOFFS				
93-94—Fredericton	AHL	62	38	28	66	250	6	9	3	—	—	—	—	—
—Montreal	NHL	14	2	2	4	34	0	0	0	2	0	0	0	0
94-95—Montreal	NHL	20	1	1	2	63	-5	0	0	—	—	—	—	—
—Fredericton	AHL	29	10	9	19	182	1	3	0	17	7	5	12	77
95-96—Montreal	NHL	67	0	4	4	223	-10	0	0	6	0	0	0	2
96-97—Montreal	NHL	10	0	0	0	38	-2	0	0	—	—	—	—	—
—Vancouver	NHL	59	8	5	13	207	-6	0	0	—	—	—	—	—
97-98—Vancouver	NHL	77	9	9	18	*372	-9	0	0	—	—	—	—	—
98-99—Vancouver	NHL	82	8	10	18	209	-25	2	0	—	—	—	—	—
99-00—Vancouver	NHL	60	11	2	13	136	-9	1	0	—	—	—	—	—
00-01—Vancouver	NHL	79	9	19	28	145	0	0	0	4	0	0	0	0
01-02—Vancouver	NHL	31	5	8	13	90	-8	1	0	—	—	—	—	—
—Philadelphia	NHL	50	4	15	19	109	0	0	0	5	0	0	0	19
02-03—Philadelphia	NHL	80	8	17	25	161	5	0	0	13	1	2	3	21
03-04—Philadelphia	NHL	64	6	7	13	212	-1	0	0	18	1	3	4	61
04-05—Quebec	LNAH	47	18	32	50	260	...	...	...	14	7	9	16	46
05-06—Philadelphia	NHL	76	4	5	9	166	-2	0	0	1	0	0	0	0
NHL Totals (12 years)		769	75	104	179	2165	-72	4	0	49	2	5	7	103

BRASSARD, DERICK C

PERSONAL: Born September 22, 1987, in Hull, QC. ... 6-0/172. ... Shoots left.

TRANSACTIONS/CAREER NOTES: Selected by Columbus Blue Jackets in first round (first Blue Jackets pick, sixth overall) of NHL draft (June 24, 2006).

Season Team	League	GP	G	A	Pts.	PIM	+/-	PP	SH	GP	G	A	Pts.	PIM
		REGULAR SEASON								PLAYOFFS				
03-04—Drummondville	QMJHL	10	0	1	1	0	-1	...	...	7	0	0	0	0
04-05—Drummondville	QMJHL	69	25	51	76	25	-6	...	...	6	1	5	6	6
05-06—Drummondville	QMJHL	58	44	72	116	92	19	...	...	7	5	4	9	10

BRATHWAITE, FRED G

PERSONAL: Born November 24, 1972, in Ottawa. ... 5-8/178. ... Catches left. ... Name pronounced BRATH-wayt.

TRANSACTIONS/CAREER NOTES: Signed as free agent by Edmonton Oilers (October 6, 1993). ... Signed as free agent by Calgary Flames (January 7, 1999). ... Injured groin (November 7, 2000); missed two games. ... Traded by Flames with C Daniel Tkaczuk, RW Sergei Varlamov and ninth-round pick (C Grant Jacobsen) in 2001 draft to St. Louis Blues for G Roman Turek and fourth-round pick (LW Egor Shastin) in 2001 draft (June 23, 2001). ... Injured mouth (March 7, 2002); missed one game. ... Released by Blues (March 18, 2003). ... Signed as free agent by Columbus Blue Jackets (June 3, 2003). ... Injured groin (December 29, 2003); missed two games. ... Signed as free agent by Atlanta Thrashers (July 4, 2006).

Season Team	League	GP	Min.	W	L	OTL	T	GA	SO	GAA	SV%	GP	Min.	W	L	GA	SO	GAA	SV%
		REGULAR SEASON										PLAYOFFS							
89-90—Oshawa	OHL	20	901	11	2	...	1	45	1	3.00	...	10	451	4	2	22	0	2.93	...
90-91—Oshawa	OHL	39	1986	25	6	...	3	112	1	3.38	...	13	677	9	2	43	0	3.81	...
91-92—Oshawa	OHL	24	1248	12	7	...	2	81	0	3.89	...	—	—	—	—	—	—	—	—
—London	OHL	23	1325	23	10	...	4	61	4	2.76	...	10	615	5	5	36	0	3.51	...
92-93—Det. Jr. Red Wings	OHL	37	2192	23	10	...	4	134	0	3.67	...	15	858	9	6	48	1	3.36	...
93-94—Cape Breton	AHL	2	119	1	1	...	0	6	0	3.03	.880	—	—	—	—	—	—	—	—
—Edmonton	NHL	19	982	3	10	...	3	58	0	3.54	.889	—	—	—	—	—	—	—	—
94-95—Edmonton	NHL	14	601	2	5	...	1	40	0	3.99	.863	—	—	—	—	—	—	—	—
95-96—Cape Breton	AHL	31	1699	12	16	...	0	110	1	3.88	...	—	—	—	—	—	—	—	—
—Edmonton	NHL	7	293	0	2	...	0	12	0	2.46	.914	—	—	—	—	—	—	—	—
96-97—Manitoba	IHL	58	2945	22	22	...	5	167	1	3.40	.901	—	—	—	—	—	—	—	—
97-98—Manitoba	IHL	51	2737	23	18	...	4	138	1	3.03	.908	2	73	0	1	4	0	3.29	.905
98-99—Canadian nat'l team	Int'l	24	989	6	8	...	3	47	...	2.85	...	—	—	—	—	—	—	—	—
—Calgary	NHL	28	1663	11	9	...	7	68	1	2.45	.915	—	—	—	—	—	—	—	—
99-00—Calgary	NHL	61	3448	25	25	...	7	158	5	2.75	.905	—	—	—	—	—	—	—	—
—Saint John	AHL	2	120	2	0	...	0	4	0	2.00	...	—	—	—	—	—	—	—	—
00-01—Calgary	NHL	49	2742	15	17	...	10	106	5	2.32	.910	—	—	—	—	—	—	—	—
01-02—St. Louis	NHL	25	1446	9	11	...	4	54	2	2.24	.901	1	1	0	0	0	0	0.00	...
02-03—St. Louis	NHL	30	1615	12	9	...	4	74	2	2.75	.883	—	—	—	—	—	—	—	—
03-04—Columbus	NHL	21	1050	4	11	...	1	59	0	3.37	.897	—	—	—	—	—	—	—	—
—Syracuse	AHL	3	188	0	2	...	1	7	1	2.23	.918	—	—	—	—	—	—	—	—
04-05—Ak Bars Kazan	Russian	35	1958	20	9	...	2	61	9	1.87	...	2	128	1	1	2	1	0.93	...
05-06—Ak Bars Kazan	Russian	32	1866	...	...	...	...	66	6	2.12	.900	11	623	...	...	16	1	1.54	...
NHL Totals (9 years)		254	13840	81	99	...	37	629	15	2.73	.901	1	1	0	0	0	0	0.00	...

BRENDL, PAVEL RW

PERSONAL: Born March 23, 1981, in Opocno, Czech. ... 6-1/204. ... Shoots right.

TRANSACTIONS/CAREER NOTES: Selected by New York Rangers in first round (first Rangers pick, fourth overall) of entry draft (June 26, 1999). ... Traded by Rangers with LW Jan Hlavac, D Kim Johnsson and third-round pick (LW Stefan Ruzicka) in 2003 to Philadelphia Flyers for rights to C Eric Lindros (August 20, 2001). ... Right ankle (October 4, 2001); missed first seven games of season. ... Traded by Flyers with D Bruno St. Jacques to Carolina Hurricanes for RW Sami Kapanen and D Ryan Bast (February 7, 2003). ... Knee (February 25, 2003) and had surgery; missed 19 games. ... Fractured collarbone (February 25, 2004); missed final 21 games of season. ... Traded by Hurricanes to Phoenix Coyotes for C Krys Kolanos (December 28, 2005).

Season Team	League	REGULAR SEASON								PLAYOFFS				
		GP	G	A	Pts.	PIM	+/-	PP	SH	GP	G	A	Pts.	PIM
96-97—Olomouc	Czech. Jrs.	40	35	17	52	...	...	...	...	—	—	—	—	—
97-98—Olomouc	Czech. Jrs.	38	29	23	52	...	...	...	...	—	—	—	—	—
—Olomouc	Czech Dv.I	12	1	1	2	...	...	...	...	—	—	—	—	—
98-99—Calgary	WHL	68	73	61	134	40	68	20	10	20	21	25	46	18
99-00—Calgary	WHL	61	59	52	111	94	41	16	8	10	7	12	19	8
—Hartford	AHL	...	...	...	...	...	...	...	...	2	0	0	0	0
00-01—Calgary	WHL	49	40	35	75	66	...	...	...	10	7	6	13	6
01-02—Philadelphia	NHL	8	1	0	1	2	-1	0	0	2	0	0	0	0
—Philadelphia	AHL	64	15	22	37	22	-15	7	0	5	4	1	5	0
02-03—Philadelphia	NHL	42	5	7	12	4	8	1	0	—	—	—	—	—
—Carolina	NHL	8	0	1	1	2	-3	0	0	—	—	—	—	—
03-04—Lowell	AHL	33	17	16	33	34	-6	3	0	—	—	—	—	—
—Carolina	NHL	18	5	3	8	8	0	1	0	—	—	—	—	—
04-05—Trinec	Czech Rep.	2	0	0	0	0	-1	0	0	—	—	—	—	—
—HC Olomouc	Czech Rep.	3	0	0	0	12	-4	...	...	—	—	—	—	—
—Thurgau	Switz. Div. 2	4	3	0	3	4	...	1	0	—	—	—	—	—
—Kiek.-Karhut Joensuu .	Finland Div. 2	21	9	10	19	48	...	...	...	—	—	—	—	—
05-06—Lowell	AHL	25	6	7	13	10	-6	3	0	—	—	—	—	—
—Phoenix	NHL	2	0	0	0	0	-3	0	0	—	—	—	—	—
—San Antonio	AHL	38	13	11	24	8	-5	6	0	—	—	—	—	—
NHL Totals (4 years)		78	11	11	22	16	1	2	0	2	0	0	0	0

BRENNAN, KIP — LW

PERSONAL: Born August 27, 1980, in Kingston, Ont. ... 6-4/228. ... Shoots left.

TRANSACTIONS/CAREER NOTES: Selected by Los Angeles Kings in fourth round (fourth Kings pick, 10third overall) of entry draft (June 27, 1998). ... Bruised foot, hip (January 4, 2003); missed three games. ... Strained left knee (January 16, 2003); missed eight games. ... Charley horse (December 2, 2003); missed 10 games. ... Suspended 10 games for returning to ice after being ejected (December 26, 2003). ... Traded by Kings to Atlanta Thrashers for LW Jeff Cowan (March 9, 2004). ... Injured hand (March 19, 2004); missed six games. ... Signed as free agent by Chicago of the AHL (September 27, 2004). ... Traded by Thrashers to Anaheim Mighty Ducks for D Mark Popvic (August 25, 2005). ... Shoulder (November 3, 2005); missed seven games.

Season Team	League	REGULAR SEASON								PLAYOFFS				
		GP	G	A	Pts.	PIM	+/-	PP	SH	GP	G	A	Pts.	PIM
96-97—Windsor	OHL	42	0	10	10	156	...	...	...	5	0	1	1	16
97-98—Windsor	OHL	24	0	7	7	103	...	...	...	—	—	—	—	—
—Sudbury	OHL	24	0	3	3	85	...	...	...	—	—	—	—	—
98-99—Sudbury	OHL	38	9	12	21	160	-4	...	...	—	—	—	—	—
99-00—Sudbury	OHL	55	16	16	32	228	-2	4	1	12	3	3	6	67
00-01—Lowell	AHL	23	2	3	5	117	...	...	...	—	—	—	—	—
—Sudbury	OHL	27	7	14	21	94	12	3	0	12	5	6	11	92
01-02—Manchester	AHL	44	4	1	5	269	-2	0	0	4	0	1	1	26
—Los Angeles	NHL	4	0	0	0	22	1	0	0	—	—	—	—	—
02-03—Los Angeles	NHL	19	0	0	0	57	0	0	0	—	—	—	—	—
—Manchester	AHL	35	3	2	5	195	-2	0	0	3	0	0	0	0
03-04—Los Angeles	NHL	18	1	0	1	79	-1	0	0	—	—	—	—	—
—Manchester	AHL	2	0	0	0	6	0	0	0	2	0	1	1	2
—Atlanta	NHL	5	0	0	0	17	0	0	0	—	—	—	—	—
04-05—Chicago	AHL	48	7	6	13	267	-4	3	0	18	1	1	2	105
05-06—Portland	AHL	9	2	1	3	22	1	0	0	—	—	—	—	—
—Anaheim	NHL	12	0	1	1	35	-2	0	0	—	—	—	—	—
NHL Totals (4 years)		58	1	1	2	210	-2	0	0					

BREWER, ERIC — D

PERSONAL: Born April 17, 1979, in Vernon, B.C. ... 6-3/220. ... Shoots left.

TRANSACTIONS/CAREER NOTES: Selected by New York Islanders in first round (second Islanders pick, fifth overall) of entry draft (June 21, 1997). ... Strained ankle tendon (April 8, 1999); missed four games. ... Toe (November 19, 1999); missed six games. ... Traded by Islanders with LW Josh Green and second-round pick (LW Brad Winchester) in 2000 draft to Edmonton Oilers for D Roman Hamrlik (June 24, 2000). ... Strained buttocks (October 6, 2000); missed four games. ... Sprained left shoulder (January 21, 2002); missed one game. ... Sprained left shoulder (November 1, 2002); missed two games. ... Groin (November 26, 2003); missed five games. ... Traded by Oilers with D Jeff Woywitka and D Doug Lynch to St. Louis Blues for D Chris Pronger (August 2, 2005). ... Separated right shoulder (November 16, 2005); missed 10 games. ... Dislocated left shoulder (January 14, 2006) and had surgery; missed remainder of season (40 games).

Season Team	League	REGULAR SEASON								PLAYOFFS				
		GP	G	A	Pts.	PIM	+/-	PP	SH	GP	G	A	Pts.	PIM
95-96—Prince George	WHL	63	4	10	14	25	...	...	...	—	—	—	—	—
96-97—Prince George	WHL	71	5	24	29	81	...	...	...	15	2	4	6	16
97-98—Prince George	WHL	34	5	28	33	45	11	3	0	11	4	2	6	19
98-99—New York Islanders	NHL	63	5	6	11	32	-14	2	0	—	—	—	—	—
99-00—New York Islanders	NHL	26	0	2	2	20	-11	0	0	—	—	—	—	—
—Lowell	AHL	25	2	2	4	26	...	...	...	7	0	0	0	0
00-01—Edmonton	NHL	77	7	14	21	53	15	2	0	6	1	5	6	2
01-02—Edmonton	NHL	81	7	18	25	45	-5	6	0	—	—	—	—	—
—Can. Olympic team	Int'l	6	2	0	2	0	...	...	...	—	—	—	—	—
02-03—Edmonton	NHL	80	8	21	29	45	-11	1	0	6	1	3	4	6
03-04—Edmonton	NHL	77	7	18	25	67	-6	3	0	—	—	—	—	—
05-06—St. Louis	NHL	32	6	3	9	45	-17	1	0	—	—	—	—	—
NHL Totals (7 years)		436	40	82	122	307	-49	15	0	12	2	8	10	8

BRIERE, DANIEL C

PERSONAL: Born October 6, 1977, in Gatineau, Que. ... 5-10/179. ... Shoots right.

TRANSACTIONS/CAREER NOTES: Selected by Phoenix Coyotes in first round (second Coyotes pick, 24th overall) of entry draft (June 22, 1996). ... Separated shoulder (March 21, 1998); missed five games. ... Concussion (October 6, 1998); missed first two games of season. ... Strained groin (September 25, 2000); missed first game of season. ... Strained groin (October 6, 2001); missed one game. ... Traded by Coyotes with third-round pick (D Andrej Sekera) in 2004 draft to Buffalo Sabres for C Chris Gratton and fourth-round pick (later traded to Edmonton Oilers; LW Liam Reddox) in 2004 draft (March 10, 2003). ... Re-signed by Sabres as restricted free agent (August 15, 2005). ... Abdominal muscle strain (November 22, 2005); missed eight games. ... Aggravated abdominal injury (December 16, 2005) and had surgery (January 6, 2006); missed 24 games. ... Suspended two games in high-sticking incident (March 30, 2006).

		REGULAR SEASON								PLAYOFFS				
Season Team	League	GP	G	A	Pts.	PIM	+/-	PP	SH	GP	G	A	Pts.	PIM
94-95—Drummondville	QMJHL	72	51	72	123	54	...	...	...	—	—	—	—	—
95-96—Drummondville	QMJHL	67	67	96	163	84	...	...	...	6	6	12	18	8
96-97—Drummondville	QMJHL	59	52	78	130	86	...	...	...	8	7	7	14	14
97-98—Springfield	AHL	68	36	56	92	42	23	12	0	4	1	2	3	4
—Phoenix	NHL	5	1	0	1	2	1	0	0	—	—	—	—	—
98-99—Las Vegas	IHL	1	1	1	2	0	2	0	0	—	—	—	—	—
—Phoenix	NHL	64	8	14	22	30	-3	2	0	—	—	—	—	—
—Springfield	AHL	13	2	6	8	20	-2	0	0	3	0	1	1	2
99-00—Springfield	AHL	58	29	42	71	56	...	...	...	—	—	—	—	—
—Phoenix	NHL	13	1	1	2	0	0	0	0	1	0	0	0	0
00-01—Phoenix	NHL	30	11	4	15	12	-2	9	0	—	—	—	—	—
—Springfield	AHL	30	21	25	46	30	...	...	...	—	—	—	—	—
01-02—Phoenix	NHL	78	32	28	60	52	6	12	0	5	2	1	3	2
02-03—Phoenix	NHL	68	17	29	46	50	-21	4	0	—	—	—	—	—
—Buffalo	NHL	14	7	5	12	12	1	5	0	—	—	—	—	—
03-04—Buffalo	NHL	82	28	37	65	70	-7	11	0	—	—	—	—	—
04-05—Bern	Switzerland	36	17	29	46	26	...	5	0	11	1	6	7	2
05-06—Buffalo	NHL	48	25	33	58	48	3	11	0	18	8	11	19	12
NHL Totals (8 years)		402	130	151	281	276	-22	54	0	24	10	12	22	14

BRIND'AMOUR, ROD C

PERSONAL: Born August 9, 1970, in Ottawa. ... 6-1/200. ... Shoots left. ... Name pronounced BRIHN-duh-MOHR.

TRANSACTIONS/CAREER NOTES: Selected by St. Louis Blues in first round (first Blues pick, ninth overall) of NHL draft (June 11, 1988). ... Traded by Blues with C Dan Quinn to Philadelphia Flyers for C Ron Sutter and D Murray Baron (September 22, 1991). ... Cut elbow (November 19, 1992); missed two games. ... Bruised right hand (February 20, 1993); missed one game. ... Fractured foot (September 25, 1999) and had surgery; missed first 34 games of season. ... Traded by Flyers with G Jean-Marc Pelletier and second-round pick (traded to Colorado; Avalanche selected Agris Saviels) in 2000 draft to Carolina Hurricanes for rights to C Keith Primeau and fifth-round pick (traded to New York Islanders; Islanders selected Kristofer Ottosson) in 2000 draft (January 23, 2000). ... Suffered concussion (April 3, 2000); missed one game. ... Injured groin (December 27, 2000); missed three games. ... Injured eye (February 8, 2002); missed one game. ... Injured hand (January 22, 2003) and had surgery; missed 34 games. ... Strained groin (January 23, 2004); missed three games. ... Injured elbow (February 14, 2004); missed one game. ... Injured groin (November 15, 2005); missed four games.

STATISTICAL PLATEAUS: Three-goal games: 1992-93 (1), 2000-01 (1). Total: 2.

		REGULAR SEASON								PLAYOFFS				
Season Team	League	GP	G	A	Pts.	PIM	+/-	PP	SH	GP	G	A	Pts.	PIM
87-88—Notre Dame	SJHL	56	46	61	107	136	...	...	...	—	—	—	—	—
88-89—Michigan State	CCHA	42	27	32	59	63	...	...	...	—	—	—	—	—
—St. Louis	NHL	...	...	...	...	...	...	...	...	5	2	0	2	4
89-90—St. Louis	NHL	79	26	35	61	46	23	10	0	12	5	8	13	6
90-91—St. Louis	NHL	78	17	32	49	93	2	4	0	13	2	5	7	10
91-92—Philadelphia	NHL	80	33	44	77	100	-3	8	4	—	—	—	—	—
92-93—Philadelphia	NHL	81	37	49	86	89	-8	13	4	—	—	—	—	—
93-94—Philadelphia	NHL	84	35	62	97	85	-9	14	1	—	—	—	—	—
94-95—Philadelphia	NHL	48	12	27	39	33	-4	4	1	15	6	9	15	8
95-96—Philadelphia	NHL	82	26	61	87	110	20	4	4	12	2	5	7	6
96-97—Philadelphia	NHL	82	27	32	59	41	2	8	2	19	†13	8	21	10
97-98—Philadelphia	NHL	82	36	38	74	54	-2	10	2	5	2	2	4	7
—Can. Olympic team	Int'l	6	1	2	3	0	3	0	0	—	—	—	—	—
98-99—Philadelphia	NHL	82	24	50	74	47	3	10	0	6	1	3	4	0
99-00—Philadelphia	NHL	12	5	3	8	4	-1	4	0	—	—	—	—	—
—Carolina	NHL	33	4	10	14	22	-12	0	1	—	—	—	—	—
00-01—Carolina	NHL	79	20	36	56	47	-7	5	1	6	1	3	4	6
01-02—Carolina	NHL	81	23	32	55	40	3	5	2	23	4	8	12	16
02-03—Carolina	NHL	48	14	23	37	37	-9	7	1	—	—	—	—	—
03-04—Carolina	NHL	78	12	26	38	28	0	1	0	—	—	—	—	—
04-05—Kloten	Switzerland	2	2	1	3	0	...	1	0	5	2	4	6	6
05-06—Carolina	NHL	78	31	39	70	68	8	19	2	25	12	6	18	16
NHL Totals (17 years)		1187	382	599	981	944	6	126	25	141	50	57	107	89

BRISEBOIS, PATRICE D

PERSONAL: Born January 27, 1971, in Montreal. ... 6-2/202. ... Shoots right. ... Name pronounced pa-TREEZ BREES-bwah.

TRANSACTIONS/CAREER NOTES: Selected by Montreal Canadiens in second round (second Canadiens pick, 30th overall) of entry draft (June 17, 1989). ... Sprained right ankle (October 10, 1992); missed two games. ... Charley horse (December 16, 1992); missed two games. ... Injured knee (October 30, 1993); missed 10 games. ... Fractured ankle (December 1, 1993); missed 14 games. ... Sprained ankle (February 21, 1994); missed seven games. ... Acute herniated disc (April 3, 1995); missed 12 games. ... Injured rib cage (November 1, 1995). ... Sprained back (February 17, 1996); missed four games. ... Mild disc irritation (March 25, 1996); missed final nine games of regular season. ... Separated shoulder (January 4, 1997); missed 27 games. ... Strained shoulder (March 22, 1997); missed four games. ... Injured rib (April 10, 1997); missed remainder of regular season and two playoff games. ... Sprained knee (April 15, 1998); missed three games. ... Injured back (October 2, 1998); missed first six games of season. ... Separated shoulder (December 23, 1998); missed nine games. ... Sprained knee (February 20, 1999); missed one game. ... Injured shoulder (March 11, 1999); missed 12 games. ... Injured back before start of 1999-2000 season; missed first 27 games. ... Injured back (January 28, 2001); missed five games. ... Fractured ankle (January 17, 2002); missed 10 games. ... Irregular heartbeat (February 8, 2003); missed nine games. ... Injured groin (March 18, 2003); missed one game. ... Injured groin (December 11, 2003); missed seven games. ... Injured groin (March 19, 2004); missed four games. ... Contract bought out by Canadiens (July 25, 2005). ... Signed as free agent by Colorado Avalanche (August 3, 2005). ... Injured back (December 30, 2005); missed two games.

		REGULAR SEASON								PLAYOFFS				
Season Team	League	GP	G	A	Pts.	PIM	+/-	PP	SH	GP	G	A	Pts.	PIM
87-88—Laval	QMJHL	48	10	34	44	95	...	...	...	6	0	2	2	2
88-89—Laval	QMJHL	50	20	45	65	95	...	...	...	17	8	14	22	45
89-90—Laval	QMJHL	56	18	70	88	108	...	...	...	13	7	9	16	26
90-91—Montreal	NHL	10	0	2	2	4	1	0	0	—	—	—	—	—
—Drummondville	QMJHL	54	17	44	61	72	...	...	...	14	6	18	24	49
91-92—Fredericton	AHL	53	12	27	39	51	...	...	...	—	—	—	—	—
—Montreal	NHL	26	2	8	10	20	9	0	0	11	2	4	6	6
92-93—Montreal	NHL	70	10	21	31	79	6	4	0	20	0	4	4	18
93-94—Montreal	NHL	53	2	21	23	63	5	1	0	7	0	4	4	6
94-95—Montreal	NHL	35	4	8	12	26	-2	0	0	—	—	—	—	—
95-96—Montreal	NHL	69	9	27	36	65	10	3	0	6	1	2	3	6
96-97—Montreal	NHL	49	2	13	15	24	-7	0	0	3	1	1	2	24
97-98—Montreal	NHL	79	10	27	37	67	16	5	0	10	1	0	1	0
98-99—Montreal	NHL	54	3	9	12	28	-8	1	0	—	—	—	—	—
99-00—Montreal	NHL	54	10	25	35	18	-1	5	0	—	—	—	—	—
00-01—Montreal	NHL	77	15	21	36	28	-31	11	0	—	—	—	—	—
01-02—Montreal	NHL	71	4	29	33	25	9	2	1	10	1	1	2	2
02-03—Montreal	NHL	73	4	25	29	32	-14	1	0	—	—	—	—	—
03-04—Montreal	NHL	71	4	27	31	22	17	2	0	11	2	1	3	4
04-05—Kloten	Switzerland	10	3	1	4	2	...	0	0	—	—	—	—	—
05-06—Colorado	NHL	80	10	28	38	55	1	4	0	9	0	1	1	4
NHL Totals (15 years)		871	89	291	380	556	11	39	1	87	8	18	26	70

BRODEUR, MARTIN G

PERSONAL: Born May 6, 1972, in Montreal. ... 6-2/210. ... Catches left. ... Son of Denis Brodeur, goaltender with bronze medal-winning Canadian Olympic team (1956). ... Name pronounced MAHR-tan broh-DOOR.

TRANSACTIONS/CAREER NOTES: Selected by New Jersey Devils in first round (first Devils pick, 20th overall) of entry draft (June 16, 1990). ... Flu (December 30, 1997); missed two games. ... Right knee injury (October 26, 2005); missed six games. ... Re-signed by Devils to six-year contract extension (January 27, 2006).

		REGULAR SEASON										PLAYOFFS							
Season Team	League	GP	Min.	W	L	OTL	T	GA	SO	GAA	SV%	GP	Min.	W	L	GA	SO	GAA	SV%
89-90—St. Hyacinthe	QMJHL	42	2333	23	13	...	2	156	0	4.01	...	12	678	5	7	46	0	4.07	...
90-91—St. Hyacinthe	QMJHL	52	2946	22	24	...	4	162	2	3.30	...	4	232	0	4	16	0	4.14	...
91-92—St. Hyacinthe	QMJHL	48	2846	27	16	...	4	161	2	3.39	...	5	317	2	3	14	0	2.65	...
—New Jersey	NHL	4	179	2	1	...	0	10	0	3.35	.882	1	32	0	1	3	0	5.63	.800
92-93—Utica	AHL	32	1952	14	13	...	5	131	0	4.03	.884	4	258	1	3	18	0	4.19	.871
93-94—New Jersey	NHL	47	2625	27	11	...	8	105	3	2.40	.915	17	1171	8	†9	38	1	1.95	.928
94-95—New Jersey	NHL	40	2184	19	11	...	6	89	3	2.45	.902	*20	*1222	*16	4	34	*3	*1.67	*.927
95-96—New Jersey	NHL	77	*4433	34	†30	...	12	173	6	2.34	.911	—	—	—	—	—	—	—	—
96-97—New Jersey	NHL	67	3838	37	14	...	13	120	*10	*1.88	.927	10	659	5	5	19	2	1.73	.929
97-98—New Jersey	NHL	70	4128	*43	17	...	8	130	10	1.89	.917	6	366	2	4	12	0	1.97	.927
98-99—New Jersey	NHL	*70	*4239	*39	21	...	10	162	4	2.29	.906	7	425	3	4	20	0	2.82	.856
99-00—New Jersey	NHL	72	4312	*43	20	...	8	161	6	2.24	.910	†23	*1450	*16	7	39	2	*1.61	.927
00-01—New Jersey	NHL	72	4297	*42	17	...	11	166	*9	2.32	.906	25	1505	15	10	52	4	2.07	.897
01-02—New Jersey	NHL	*73	*4347	38	26	...	9	156	4	2.15	.906	6	381	2	4	9	1	1.42	.938
—Can. Olympic team	Int'l	5	300	4	0	...	1	9	0	1.80	.917	—	—	—	—	—	—	—	—
02-03—New Jersey	NHL	73	4374	*41	23	...	9	147	*9	2.02	.914	*24	*1491	*16	8	41	*7	1.65	.934
03-04—New Jersey	NHL	*75	*4555	*38	26	...	11	154	*11	2.03	.917	5	298	1	4	13	0	2.62	.902
05-06—New Jersey	NHL	73	4365	*43	23	7	...	187	5	2.57	.911	9	533	5	4	20	1	2.25	.923
—Canadian Oly. team	Int'l	4	...	...	...	...	...	...	0	2.01	.923	—	—	—	—	—	—	—	—
NHL Totals (13 years)		813	47876	446	240	7	105	1760	80	2.21	.912	153	9533	89	64	300	21	1.89	.921

BRODZIAK, KYLE C

PERSONAL: Born May 25, 1984, in St. Paul, Alta. ... 6-1/191. ... Shoots right.

TRANSACTIONS/CAREER NOTES: Selected by Edmonton Oilers in seventh round (ninth Oilers pick, 214th overall) of NHL entry draft (June 21, 2003).

		REGULAR SEASON								PLAYOFFS				
Season Team	League	GP	G	A	Pts.	PIM	+/-	PP	SH	GP	G	A	Pts.	PIM
99-00—Moose Jaw	WHL	2	0	0	0	0	...	...	...	—	—	—	—	—
00-01—Moose Jaw	WHL	57	2	8	10	49	...	...	...	3	0	0	0	0
01-02—Moose Jaw	WHL	72	8	12	20	56	...	...	...	12	0	3	3	11
02-03—Moose Jaw	WHL	72	32	30	62	84	...	...	...	13	5	3	8	16
03-04—Moose Jaw	WHL	70	39	54	93	58	30	9	9	10	5	4	9	10
04-05—Edmonton	AHL	56	6	26	32	49	1	1	0	—	—	—	—	—
05-06—Iowa	AHL	55	12	19	31	41	7	3	0	7	1	3	4	2
—Edmonton	NHL	10	0	0	0	4	-4	0	0	—	—	—	—	—
NHL Totals (1 year)		10	0	0	0	4	-4	0	0					

BROOKBANK, WADE D/LW

PERSONAL: Born September 29, 1977, in Lanigan, Sask. ... 6-4/221. ... Shoots left. ... Brother of Sheldon Brookbank, D, Nashville Predators organization.

TRANSACTIONS/CAREER NOTES: Signed as free agent by Ottawa Senators (July 27, 2001). ... Claimed by Nashville Predators in waiver draft (October 3, 2003). ... Traded by Senators to Vancouver Canucks for future considerations (December 17, 2003). ... Claimed by Senators off waivers from Canucks (December19, 2003). ... Traded by Senators to Florida Panthers for future considerations (December29, 2003). ... Claimed by Canucks off waivers from Panthers (January 3, 2004). ... Concussion (December 15, 2005); missed seven games. ... Concussion (January 28, 2006); missed seven games. ... Signed as free agent by Boston Bruins (July 21, 2006).

		REGULAR SEASON								PLAYOFFS				
Season Team	League	GP	G	A	Pts.	PIM	+/-	PP	SH	GP	G	A	Pts.	PIM
97-98—Anchorage	WCHL	7	0	0	0	46	...	...	...	4	0	0	0	20
98-99—Anchorage	WCHL	56	0	4	4	337	...	...	...	5	0	0	0	47
99-00—Oklahoma City	CHL	68	3	9	12	354	...	...	...	7	1	1	2	29
00-01—Oklahoma City	CHL	46	1	13	14	267	...	...	...	5	0	0	0	24
—Orlando	IHL	29	0	1	1	122	...	...	...	4	0	0	0	6
01-02—Grand Rapids	AHL	73	1	6	7	337	...	...	...	3	0	1	1	14
02-03—Binghamton	AHL	8	0	0	0	28	-4	0	0	—	—	—	—	—
03-04—Nashville	NHL	9	0	0	0	38	-4	0	0	—	—	—	—	—
—Milwaukee	AHL	6	0	0	0	6	-2	0	0	—	—	—	—	—
—Vancouver	NHL	20	2	0	2	95	3	0	0	—	—	—	—	—
—Binghamton	AHL	4	0	0	0	31	0	0	0	—	—	—	—	—
—Manitoba	AHL	4	0	0	0	12	0	0	0	—	—	—	—	—
04-05—Manitoba	AHL	68	0	10	10	285	2	0	0	9	0	0	0	10
05-06—Vancouver	NHL	32	1	2	3	81	3	0	0	—	—	—	—	—
NHL Totals (2 years)		61	3	2	5	214	2	0	0					

BROWN, CURTIS C/LW

PERSONAL: Born February 12, 1976, in Unity, Sask. ... 6-0/196. ... Shoots left.

TRANSACTIONS/CAREER NOTES: Selected by Buffalo Sabres in second round (second Sabres pick, 43rd overall) of entry draft (June 28, 1994). ... Injured ankle before 1995-96 season; missed two games. ... Bruised knee (February 11, 1999); missed two games. ... Bruised knee (March 27, 1999); missed one game. ... Missed first game of 1999-2000 season in contract dispute. ... Concussion (October 22, 1999); missed one game. ... Flu (February 10, 2000); missed five games. ... Knee (December 23, 2000); missed eight games. ... Back spasms (January 30, 2001); missed four games. ... Sprained right knee (March 12, 2003); missed two games. ... Ankle (March 29, 2003); missed five games. ... Traded by Sabres with D Andy Delmore to San Jose Sharks for D Jeff Jillson and seventh-round pick (D Andrew Orpik) in entry draft (March 9, 2004). ... Signed as free agent by Chicago Blackhawks (July 2, 2004). ... Sprained knee (January 10, 2006); missed five games. ... Concussion (April 8, 2006); missed final six games of regular season. ... Signed as free agent by San Jose Sharks (July 1, 2006).

STATISTICAL PLATEAUS: Three-goal games: 2002-03 (1).

		REGULAR SEASON								PLAYOFFS				
Season Team	League	GP	G	A	Pts.	PIM	+/-	PP	SH	GP	G	A	Pts.	PIM
92-93—Moose Jaw	WHL	71	13	16	29	30	...	...	...	—	—	—	—	—
93-94—Moose Jaw	WHL	72	27	38	65	82	15	14	2	—	—	—	—	—
94-95—Moose Jaw	WHL	70	51	53	104	63	11	19	7	10	8	7	15	20
—Buffalo	NHL	1	1	1	2	2	2	0	0	—	—	—	—	—
95-96—Buffalo	NHL	4	0	0	0	0	0	0	0	—	—	—	—	—
—Moose Jaw	WHL	25	20	18	38	30	...	...	...	—	—	—	—	—
—Prince Albert	WHL	19	12	21	33	8	...	...	...	18	10	15	25	18
—Rochester	AHL	...	...	...	...	...	...	...	...	12	0	1	1	2
96-97—Buffalo	NHL	28	4	3	7	18	4	0	0	—	—	—	—	—
—Rochester	AHL	51	22	21	43	30	17	7	0	10	4	6	10	4
97-98—Buffalo	NHL	63	12	12	24	34	11	1	1	13	1	2	3	10
98-99—Buffalo	NHL	78	16	31	47	56	23	5	1	21	7	6	13	10
99-00—Buffalo	NHL	74	22	29	51	42	19	5	0	5	1	3	4	6
00-01—Buffalo	NHL	70	10	22	32	34	15	2	1	13	5	0	5	8
01-02—Buffalo	NHL	82	20	17	37	32	-4	4	1	—	—	—	—	—
02-03—Buffalo	NHL	74	15	16	31	40	4	3	4	—	—	—	—	—
03-04—Buffalo	NHL	68	9	12	21	30	2	2	1	—	—	—	—	—
—San Jose	NHL	12	2	2	4	6	1	0	0	17	0	2	2	18
04-05—San Diego	ECHL	47	9	29	38	24	5	3	2	—	—	—	—	—
05-06—Chicago	NHL	71	5	10	15	38	-9	0	1	—	—	—	—	—
NHL Totals (11 years)		625	116	155	271	332	68	22	10	69	14	13	27	52

BROWN, DUSTIN RW/LW

PERSONAL: Born November 4, 1984, in Ithaca, N.Y. ... 6-0/200. ... Shoots right.

TRANSACTIONS/CAREER NOTES: Selected by Los Angeles Kings in first round (first Kings pick, 13th overall) of entry draft (June 23, 2003). ... Left ankle (November 30, 2003); missed 26 games. ... Right ankle (January 31, 2004); missed 14 games. ... Bruised chest (January 2, 2006); missed three games.

		REGULAR SEASON								PLAYOFFS				
Season Team	League	GP	G	A	Pts.	PIM	+/-	PP	SH	GP	G	A	Pts.	PIM
00-01—Guelph	OHL	53	23	22	45	45	...	...	...	4	0	0	0	10
01-02—Guelph	OHL	63	41	32	73	56	...	...	...	9	8	5	13	14
02-03—Guelph	OHL	58	34	42	76	89	...	...	...	11	7	8	15	6
03-04—Los Angeles	NHL	31	1	4	5	16	0	0	0	—	—	—	—	—
04-05—Manchester	AHL	79	29	45	74	96	7	12	0	6	5	2	7	10
05-06—Los Angeles	NHL	79	14	14	28	80	-10	6	0	—	—	—	—	—
NHL Totals (2 years)		110	15	18	33	96	-10	6	0					

BROWN, MIKE — LW

PERSONAL: Born April 29, 1979, in Surrey, B.C. ... 6-5/227. ... Shoots left.
TRANSACTIONS/CAREER NOTES: Selected by Florida Panthers in first round (first Panthers pick, 20th overall) of entry draft (June 21, 1997). ... Traded by Panthers with D Ed Jovanovski, G Kevin Weekes, C Dave Gagner and first-round pick (C Nathan Smith) in 2000 draft to Vancouver Canucks for RW Pavel Bure, D Bret Hedican, D Brad Ference and third-round pick (RW Robert Fried) in 2000 draft (January 17, 1999). ... Claimed on waivers by Anaheim Mighty Ducks (October 11, 2002). ... Strained back (December 29, 2002); missed nine games. ... Signed as free agent by Chicago Blackhawks (August 9, 2005).

		REGULAR SEASON								PLAYOFFS				
Season Team	League	GP	G	A	Pts.	PIM	+/-	PP	SH	GP	G	A	Pts.	PIM
94-95—Merritt	BCJHL	45	3	4	7	128	...	...	...	—	—	—	—	—
95-96—Red Deer	WHL	62	4	5	9	125	...	...	...	10	0	0	0	18
96-97—Red Deer	WHL	70	19	13	32	243	...	...	...	16	1	2	3	47
97-98—Kamloops	WHL	72	23	33	56	305	-13	10	0	7	2	1	3	22
98-99—Kamloops	WHL	69	28	16	44	285	20	8	1	15	3	7	10	68
99-00—Syracuse	AHL	71	13	18	31	284	...	...	...	4	0	0	0	0
00-01—Kansas City	IHL	78	14	13	27	214	...	...	...	—	—	—	—	—
—Vancouver	NHL	1	0	0	0	5	0	0	0	—	—	—	—	—
01-02—Manitoba	AHL	31	7	9	16	155	1	0	0	6	0	1	1	16
—Vancouver	NHL	15	0	0	0	72	1	0	0	—	—	—	—	—
02-03—Anaheim	NHL	16	1	1	2	44	0	0	0	—	—	—	—	—
—Cincinnati	AHL	27	3	3	6	85	...	...	...	—	—	—	—	—
03-04—St. John's	AHL	21	3	3	6	74	...	...	...	—	—	—	—	—
—Binghamton	AHL	38	4	7	11	131	...	...	...	—	—	—	—	—
04-05—Norfolk	AHL	68	7	8	15	284	-3	0	0	0	0	0	0	0
05-06—Chicago	NHL	2	0	1	1	9	0	0	0	—	—	—	—	—
—Norfolk	AHL	53	2	13	15	146	12	0	0	1	0	0	0	17
NHL Totals (4 years)		34	1	2	3	130	1	0	0					

BROWN, SEAN — D

PERSONAL: Born November 5, 1976, in Oshawa, Ont. ... 6-3/215. ... Shoots left.
TRANSACTIONS/CAREER NOTES: Selected by Boston Bruins in first round (second Bruins pick, 21st overall) of NHL draft (July 8, 1995). ... Traded by Bruins with RW Mariusz Czerkawski and first-round pick (D Mattieu Descoteaux) in 1996 draft to Edmonton Oilers for G Bill Ranford (January 11, 1996). ... Suspended three games for high-sticking incident (November 13, 1998). ... Traded by Oilers to Bruins for D Bobby Allen (March 19, 2002). ... Suspended one game for cross-checking incident (November 11, 2002). ... Signed as free agent by New Jersey Devils (July 24, 2003). ... Traded by Devils to Vancouver Canucks for fourth-round pick (D T.J. Miller) in 2006 draft (March 9, 2006).

		REGULAR SEASON								PLAYOFFS				
Season Team	League	GP	G	A	Pts.	PIM	+/-	PP	SH	GP	G	A	Pts.	PIM
92-93—Oshawa	Tier II Jr. A	15	0	1	1	9	...	...	...	—	—	—	—	—
93-94—Wellington	OJHL	32	5	14	19	165	...	...	...	—	—	—	—	—
—Belleville	OHL	28	1	2	3	53	...	...	...	8	0	0	0	17
94-95—Belleville	OHL	58	2	16	18	200	...	0	0	16	4	2	6	67
95-96—Belleville	OHL	37	10	23	33	150	...	...	...	—	—	—	—	—
—Sarnia	OHL	26	8	17	25	112	...	...	...	10	1	0	1	38
96-97—Hamilton	AHL	61	1	7	8	238	-8	1	0	19	1	0	1	47
—Edmonton	NHL	5	0	0	0	4	-1	0	0	—	—	—	—	—
97-98—Edmonton	NHL	18	0	1	1	43	-1	0	0	—	—	—	—	—
—Hamilton	AHL	43	4	6	10	166	-4	2	0	6	0	2	2	38
98-99—Edmonton	NHL	51	0	7	7	188	1	0	0	1	0	0	0	10
99-00—Edmonton	NHL	72	4	8	12	192	1	0	0	3	0	0	0	23
00-01—Edmonton	NHL	62	2	3	5	110	2	0	0	—	—	—	—	—
01-02—Edmonton	NHL	61	6	4	10	127	8	3	0	—	—	—	—	—
—Boston	NHL	12	0	1	1	47	-1	0	0	4	0	0	0	2
02-03—Boston	NHL	69	1	5	6	117	-6	0	0	—	—	—	—	—
03-04—New Jersey	NHL	39	0	3	3	44	5	0	0	1	0	0	0	2
—Albany	AHL	21	1	6	7	56	-5	1	0	—	—	—	—	—
05-06—Albany	AHL	1	0	1	1	2	0	0	0	—	—	—	—	—
—New Jersey	NHL	35	1	11	12	27	-14	0	0	—	—	—	—	—
—Vancouver	NHL	12	0	0	0	8	-3	0	0	—	—	—	—	—
NHL Totals (9 years)		436	14	43	57	907	-9	3	0	9	0	0	0	37

BRULE, GILBERT — C

PERSONAL: Born January 1, 1987, in Edmonton. ... 5-10/175. ... Shoots right. ... Name pronounced jihl-BAIR BROO-lay.
TRANSACTIONS/CAREER NOTES: Selected by Columbus Blue Jackets in first round (first Blue Jackets pick, sixth overall) of entry draft (July 30, 2005). ... Sternal clavicular sprain (October 7, 2005); missed 17 games. ... Broken right leg (November 30, 2005); missed 18 games.

		REGULAR SEASON								PLAYOFFS				
Season Team	League	GP	G	A	Pts.	PIM	+/-	PP	SH	GP	G	A	Pts.	PIM
02-03—Vancouver	WHL	1	0	0	0	0	-1	...	...	4	1	0	1	0
03-04—Vancouver	WHL	67	25	35	60	100	-2	...	...	11	4	5	9	10
04-05—Vancouver	WHL	70	39	48	87	169	4	13	4	6	1	3	4	8
05-06—Columbus	NHL	7	2	2	4	0	-2	0	0	—	—	—	—	—
—Vancouver	WHL	27	23	15	38	40	...	...	...	18	16	14	30	44
NHL Totals (1 year)		7	2	2	4	0	-2	0	0					

BRUNETTE, ANDREW — LW/RW

PERSONAL: Born August 24, 1973, in Sudbury, Ont. ... 6-1/210. ... Shoots left. ... Name pronounced broo-NEHT.
TRANSACTIONS/CAREER NOTES: Selected by Washington Capitals in sixth round (sixth Capitals pick, 174th overall) of NHL draft (June 26,

1993). ... Selected by Nashville Predators in expansion draft (June 26, 1998). ... Traded by Predators to Atlanta Thrashers for fifth-round pick (C Matt Hendricks) in 2000 draft (June 21, 1999). ... Concussion (January 13, 2001); missed four games. ... Bruised thigh (February 15, 2001); missed one game. ... Signed as free agent by Minnesota Wild (July 6, 2001). ... Bruised shoulder (December 29, 2001); missed one game. ... Signed as free agent by Colorado Avalanche (August 6, 2005).

		REGULAR SEASON								PLAYOFFS				
Season Team	**League**	**GP**	**G**	**A**	**Pts.**	**PIM**	**+/-**	**PP**	**SH**	**GP**	**G**	**A**	**Pts.**	**PIM**
90-91—Owen Sound	OHL	63	15	20	35	15	...	...	...	—	—	—	—	—
91-92—Owen Sound	OHL	66	51	47	98	42	...	...	...	5	5	0	5	8
92-93—Owen Sound	OHL	66	62	100	162	91	...	...	...	8	8	6	14	16
93-94—Portland	AHL	23	9	11	20	10	...	...	...	2	0	1	1	0
—Hampton	ECHL	20	12	18	30	32	...	...	...	7	7	6	13	18
—Providence	AHL	3	0	0	0	0	...	...	...	—	—	—	—	—
94-95—Portland	AHL	79	30	50	80	53	...	...	...	7	3	3	6	10
95-96—Portland	AHL	69	28	66	94	125	...	...	...	20	11	18	29	15
—Washington	NHL	11	3	3	6	0	5	0	0	6	1	3	4	0
96-97—Portland	AHL	50	22	51	73	48	7	10	0	5	1	2	3	0
—Washington	NHL	23	4	7	11	12	-3	2	0	—	—	—	—	—
97-98—Portland	AHL	43	21	46	67	64	-17	12	1	10	1	11	12	12
—Washington	NHL	28	11	12	23	12	2	4	0	—	—	—	—	—
98-99—Nashville	NHL	77	11	20	31	26	-10	7	0	—	—	—	—	—
99-00—Atlanta	NHL	81	23	27	50	30	-32	9	0	—	—	—	—	—
00-01—Atlanta	NHL	77	15	44	59	26	-5	6	0	—	—	—	—	—
01-02—Minnesota	NHL	81	21	48	69	18	-4	10	0	—	—	—	—	—
02-03—Minnesota	NHL	82	18	28	46	30	-10	9	0	18	7	6	13	4
03-04—Minnesota	NHL	82	15	34	49	12	3	7	0	—	—	—	—	—
05-06—Colorado	NHL	82	24	39	63	48	9	11	0	9	3	6	9	8
NHL Totals (10 years)		624	145	262	407	214	-45	65	0	33	11	15	26	12

BRYLIN, SERGEI C/RW

PERSONAL: Born January 13, 1974, in Moscow, U.S.S.R. ... 5-10/190. ... Shoots left. ... Name pronounced BREE-lihn.

TRANSACTIONS/CAREER NOTES: Selected by New Jersey Devils in second round (second Devils pick, 42nd overall) of NHL draft (June 20, 1992). ... Tonsillitis (May 3, 1995); missed last game of season. ... Fractured hand (November 16, 1995); missed 13 games. ... Injured knee (September 19, 1997); missed 19 games. ... Injured knee (November 28, 2000); missed one game. ... Injured knee (February 22, 2001); missed five games. ... Bruised knee (November 13, 2001); missed five games. ... Fractured wrist (February 7, 2003); missed final 30 games of season and five playoff games.

		REGULAR SEASON								PLAYOFFS				
Season Team	**League**	**GP**	**G**	**A**	**Pts.**	**PIM**	**+/-**	**PP**	**SH**	**GP**	**G**	**A**	**Pts.**	**PIM**
91-92—CSKA Moscow	CIS	44	1	6	7	4	...	...	...	—	—	—	—	—
92-93—CSKA Moscow	CIS	42	5	4	9	36	...	...	...	—	—	—	—	—
93-94—CSKA Moscow	CIS	39	4	6	10	36	...	...	...	3	0	1	1	0
—Russian Penguins	IHL	13	4	5	9	18	-5	0	0	—	—	—	—	—
94-95—Albany	AHL	63	19	35	54	78	8	7	0	—	—	—	—	—
—New Jersey	NHL	26	6	8	14	8	12	0	0	12	1	2	3	4
95-96—New Jersey	NHL	50	4	5	9	26	-2	0	0	—	—	—	—	—
96-97—New Jersey	NHL	29	2	2	4	20	-13	0	0	—	—	—	—	—
—Albany	AHL	43	17	24	41	38	12	6	0	16	4	8	12	12
97-98—New Jersey	NHL	18	2	3	5	0	4	0	0	—	—	—	—	—
—Albany	AHL	44	21	22	43	60	25	4	1	—	—	—	—	—
98-99—New Jersey	NHL	47	5	10	15	28	8	3	0	5	3	1	4	4
99-00—New Jersey	NHL	64	9	11	20	20	0	1	0	17	3	5	8	0
00-01—New Jersey	NHL	75	23	29	52	24	25	3	1	20	3	4	7	6
01-02—New Jersey	NHL	76	16	28	44	10	21	5	0	6	0	2	2	2
02-03—New Jersey	NHL	52	11	8	19	16	-2	3	1	19	1	3	4	8
03-04—New Jersey	NHL	82	14	19	33	20	10	7	0	5	0	0	0	0
04-05—Khimik Voskresensk	Russian	35	8	19	27	40	-3	...	...	—	—	—	—	—
05-06—New Jersey	NHL	82	15	22	37	46	-4	4	0	9	2	0	2	2
NHL Totals (11 years)		601	107	145	252	218	59	26	2	93	13	17	30	26

BRYZGALOV, ILYA G

PERSONAL: Born June 22, 1980, in Togliatti, U.S.S.R. ... 6-3/194. ... Catches left. ... Name pronounced breez-GAH-lahf.

TRANSACTIONS/CAREER NOTES: Selected by Anaheim Mighty Ducks in second round (second Mighty Ducks pick, 44th overall) of entry draft (June 24, 2000).

		REGULAR SEASON										PLAYOFFS							
Season Team	**League**	**GP**	**Min.**	**W**	**L**	**OTL**	**T**	**GA**	**SO**	**GAA**	**SV%**	**GP**	**Min.**	**W**	**L**	**GA**	**SO**	**GAA**	**SV%**
97-98—Lada-2 Togliatti	Rus. Div.	8	480	...	...	...	...	28	...	3.50	...	—	—	—	—	—	—	—	—
98-99—Lada-2 Togliatti	Rus.-4	20	1200	...	...	...	...	43	...	2.15	...	—	—	—	—	—	—	—	—
99-00—Spartak Moscow	Russian	9	500	...	...	...	...	21	...	2.52	...	—	—	—	—	—	—	—	—
—Lada Togliatti	Russian	14	796	...	...	...	...	18	3	1.36	...	7	407	...	...	10	1	1.47	...
00-01—Lada Togliatti	Russian	34	1992	...	...	...	...	61	8	1.84	...	5	249	...	...	8	0	1.93	...
01-02—Anaheim	NHL	1	32	0	0	...	0	1	0	1.88	.917	—	—	—	—	—	—	—	—
—Cincinnati	AHL	45	2398	20	16	...	4	99	4	2.48	.909	—	—	—	—	—	—	—	—
02-03—Cincinnati	AHL	54	3019	12	26	...	9	142	1	2.82	.910	—	—	—	—	—	—	—	—
03-04—Anaheim	NHL	1	60	1	0	...	0	2	0	2.00	.929	—	—	—	—	—	—	—	—
—Cincinnati	AHL	64	3747	27	25	...	10	145	6	2.32	.912	9	535	5	4	27	1	3.03	.900
04-05—Cincinnati	AHL	36	2006	17	13	...	...	87	4	2.60	.902	7	314	3	3	13	0	2.48	.904
05-06—Anaheim	NHL	31	1575	13	12	1	...	66	1	2.51	.910	11	659	6	4	16	*3	*1.46	*.944
—Russian Oly. Team	Int'l	1	...	...	...	...	...	...	...	5.00	.861	—	—	—	—	—	—	—	—
NHL Totals (3 years)		33	1667	14	12	1	0	69	1	2.48	.911	11	659	6	4	16	3	1.46	.944

BUDAJ, PETER G

PERSONAL: Born September 18, 1982, in Banska Bystrica, Czech. ... 6-1/200. ... Catches left.
TRANSACTIONS/CAREER NOTES: Selected by Colorado Avalanche in second round (first Avalanche pick, 63rd overall) of entry draft (June 23, 2001).

		REGULAR SEASON										PLAYOFFS							
Season Team	League	GP	Min.	W	L	OTL	T	GA	SO	GAA	SV%	GP	Min.	W	L	GA	SO	GAA	SV%
99-00 —Toronto St. Michael's..	OHL	34	1676	6	18	...	1	...	1	4.01	...	—	—	—	—	—	—	—	—
00-01 —Toronto St. Michael's..	OHL	37	1996	17	12	...	3	95	3	2.86	...	11	621	6	4	26	1	2.51	...
01-02 —Toronto St. Michael's..	OHL	42	2329	26	9	...	5	89	2	2.29	...	12	620	5	6	34	1	3.29	...
02-03 —Hershey	AHL	28	1467	10	10	...	2	65	2	2.66	...	1	6	0	0	2	0	20.81	...
03-04 —Hershey	AHL	46	2574	17	20	...	6	120	3	2.80	.916	—	—	—	—	—	—	—	—
04-05 —Hershey	AHL	59	3356	29	25	...	...	148	5	2.65	.919	—	—	—	—	—	—	—	—
05-06 —Colorado	NHL	34	1803	14	10	6	...	86	2	2.86	.900	—	—	—	—	—	—	—	—
—Slovak. Oly. team	Int'l	3	...	...	...	...	...	...	0	2.01	.924	—	—	—	—	—	—	—	—
NHL Totals (1 year)		34	1803	14	10	6	0	86	2	2.86	.900								

BULIS, JAN C

PERSONAL: Born March 18, 1978, in Pardubice, Czechoslovakia. ... 6-1/208. ... Shoots left. ... Name pronounced YAHN BOO-lihsh.
TRANSACTIONS/CAREER NOTES: Selected by Washington Capitals in second round (third Capitals pick, 43rd overall) of NHL draft (June 22, 1996). ... Suffered concussion (November 11, 1997); missed one game. ... Sprained ankle before 1998-99 season; missed first 13 games of season. ... Sprained ankle (November 21, 1998); missed 15 games. ... Back spasms (November 11, 1999); missed one game. ... Bruised ribs (November 20, 1999); missed two games. ... Injured groin (December 15, 1999); missed three games. ... Separated shoulder (February 26, 2000); missed remainder of season. ... Fractured right thumb (November 22, 2000); missed 18 games. ... Traded by Capitals with RW Richard Zednik and first-round pick (C Alexander Perezhogin) in 2001 draft to Montreal Canadiens for C Trevor Linden, RW Dainius Zubrus and second-round pick (traded to Tampa Bay; Lightning selected D Andreas Holmqvist) in 2001 draft (March 13, 2001). ... Sprained knee (December 1, 2001); missed 20 games. ... Injured knee (February 24, 2004); missed 10 games. ... Injured left shoulder (November 8, 2005); missed four games. ... Signed as free agent by Vancouver Canucks (July 24, 2006).

		REGULAR SEASON								PLAYOFFS				
Season Team	League	GP	G	A	Pts.	PIM	+/-	PP	SH	GP	G	A	Pts.	PIM
94-95—Kelowna	BCJHL	51	23	25	48	36	...	...	...	17	7	9	16	...
95-96—Barrie	OHL	59	29	30	59	22	...	...	...	7	2	3	5	2
96-97—Barrie	OHL	64	42	61	103	42	17	13	1	9	3	7	10	10
97-98—Washington	NHL	48	5	11	16	18	-5	0	0	—	—	—	—	—
—Portland	AHL	3	1	4	5	12	1	1	0	—	—	—	—	—
—Kingston	OHL	2	0	1	1	0	-1	...	...	12	8	10	18	12
98-99—Washington	NHL	38	7	16	23	6	3	3	0	—	—	—	—	—
—Cincinnati	IHL	10	2	2	4	14	-5	0	0	—	—	—	—	—
99-00—Washington	NHL	56	9	22	31	30	7	0	0	—	—	—	—	—
00-01—Washington	NHL	39	5	13	18	26	0	1	0	—	—	—	—	—
—Portland	AHL	4	0	2	2	0	...	...	...	—	—	—	—	—
—Montreal	NHL	12	0	5	5	0	-1	0	0	—	—	—	—	—
01-02—Montreal	NHL	53	9	10	19	8	-2	1	0	6	0	0	0	6
02-03—Montreal	NHL	82	16	24	40	30	9	0	0	—	—	—	—	—
03-04—Montreal	NHL	72	13	17	30	30	-8	1	1	11	1	1	2	4
04-05—Pardubice	Czech Rep.	45	24	25	49	113	22	...	...	16	7	4	11	43
05-06—Montreal	NHL	73	20	20	40	50	2	6	1	6	1	1	2	2
—Czech Rep. Oly. team	Int'l	8	0	0	0	10	-1	0	0	—	—	—	—	—
NHL Totals (8 years)		473	84	138	222	198	5	12	2	23	2	2	4	12

BURKE, SEAN G

PERSONAL: Born January 29, 1967, in Windsor, Ont. ... 6-4/209. ... Catches left. ... Name pronounced BUHRK.
TRANSACTIONS/CAREER NOTES: Selected by New Jersey Devils in second round (second Devils pick, 24th overall) of NHL draft (June 15, 1985). ... Injured groin (December 1988). ... Arthroscopic right knee surgery (September 5, 1989). ... Traded by Devils with D Eric Weinrich to Hartford Whalers for RW Bobby Holik and second-round pick (LW Jay Pandolfo) in 1993 draft (August 28, 1992). ... Sprained ankle (December 27, 1992); missed seven games. ... Back spasms (March 13, 1993); missed remainder of season. ... Injured hamstring (September 29, 1993); missed seven games. ... Reinjured hamstring (October 27, 1993); missed 14 games. ... Back spasms (December 23, 1993); missed one game. ... Strained groin (February 28, 1995); missed two games. ... Back spasms (November 19, 1995); missed two games. ... Back spasms (February 7, 1996); missed three games. ... Dislocated thumb (November 30, 1996); missed 19 games. ... Strained hip flexor (February 26, 1997); missed one game. ... Whalers franchise moved to North Carolina and renamed Carolina Hurricanes for 1997-98 season; NHL approved move on June 25, 1997. ... Traded by Hurricanes with LW Geoff Sanderson and D Enrico Ciccone to Vancouver Canucks for LW Martin Gelinas and G Kirk McLean (January 3, 1998). ... Traded by Canucks to Philadelphia Flyers for G Garth Snow (March 4, 1998). ... Lower back spasms (March 8, 1998); missed six games. ... Signed as free agent by Florida Panthers (September 11, 1998). ... Strained hip flexor (April 10, 1999); missed final three games of season. ... Traded by Panthers with fifth-round pick (D Nate Kiser) in 2000 draft to Phoenix Coyotes for G Mikhail Shtalenkov and fourth-round pick (D Chris Eade) in 2000 draft (November 19, 1999). ... Tore thumb ligament (November 26, 1999); missed 16 games. ... Strained hip flexor (January 12, 2000); missed one game. ... Injured groin (February 1, 2000); missed one game. ... Strained groin (March 1, 2000); missed one game. ... Injured elbow (November 30, 2000); missed one game. ... Bruised knee (February 11, 2001); missed two games. ... Strained groin (March 2, 2001); missed four games. ... Strained groin (November 17, 2001); missed three games. ... Strained groin (January 9, 2002); missed seven games. ... Flu (March 17, 2002); missed one game. ... High ankle sprain (October 22, 2002); missed 29 games. ... Sprained knee (January 3, 2003); missed 20 games. ... Strained groin (March 30, 2003); missed seven games. ... Traded by Coyotes with RW Branko Radivojevic and rights to LW Ben Eager to Philadelphia Flyers for C Mike Comrie (February 9, 2004). ... Signed as free agent by Tampa Bay Lightning (August 9, 2005). ... Sore groin (October 29, 2005); missed eight games. ... Fractured finger (March 16, 2006); missed seven games.

		REGULAR SEASON										PLAYOFFS							
Season Team	League	GP	Min.	W	L	OTL	T	GA	SO	GAA	SV%	GP	Min.	W	L	GA	SO	GAA	SV%
83-84—St. Michael's H.S.	MTHL	25	1482	...	...	...	...	120	0	4.86	...	—	—	—	—	—	—	—	—
84-85—Toronto	OHL	49	2987	25	21	...	3	211	0	4.24	...	5	266	1	3	25	0	5.64	...

Season	Team	League	GP	Min.	W	L	OTL	T	GA	SO	GAA	SV%	GP	Min.	W	L	GA	SO	GAA	SV%
			REGULAR SEASON										PLAYOFFS							
85-86	—Toronto	OHL	47	2840	16	27	...	3	233	0	4.92	...	4	238	0	4	24	0	6.05	...
	—Canadian nat'l team	Int'l	5	284	...	...	...	...	22	0	4.65	...	—	—	—	—	—	—	—	—
86-87	—Canadian nat'l team	Int'l	42	2550	27	13	...	2	130	0	3.06	...	—	—	—	—	—	—	—	—
87-88	—Canadian nat'l team	Int'l	37	1962	19	9	...	2	92	1	2.81	...	—	—	—	—	—	—	—	—
	—Can. Olympic team	Int'l	4	238	1	2	...	1	12	0	3.03	.893	—	—	—	—	—	—	—	—
	—New Jersey	NHL	13	689	10	1	...	0	35	1	3.05	.883	17	1001	9	8	*57	†1	3.42	.889
88-89	—New Jersey	NHL	62	3590	22	31	...	9	†230	3	3.84	.874	—	—	—	—	—	—	—	—
89-90	—New Jersey	NHL	52	2914	22	22	...	6	175	0	3.60	.880	2	125	0	2	8	0	3.84	.860
90-91	—New Jersey	NHL	35	1870	8	12	...	8	112	0	3.59	.872	—	—	—	—	—	—	—	—
91-92	—Canadian nat'l team	Int'l	31	1721	18	6	...	4	75	1	2.61	...	—	—	—	—	—	—	—	—
	—Can. Olympic team	Int'l	7	429	5	2	...	0	17	0	2.38	.928	—	—	—	—	—	—	—	—
	—San Diego	IHL	7	424	4	2	...	1	17	0	2.41	...	3	160	0	3	13	0	4.88	...
92-93	—Hartford	NHL	50	2656	16	27	...	3	184	0	4.16	.876	—	—	—	—	—	—	—	—
93-94	—Hartford	NHL	47	2750	17	24	...	5	137	2	2.99	.906	—	—	—	—	—	—	—	—
94-95	—Hartford	NHL	42	2418	17	19	...	4	108	0	2.68	.912	—	—	—	—	—	—	—	—
95-96	—Hartford	NHL	66	3669	28	28	...	6	190	4	3.11	.907	—	—	—	—	—	—	—	—
96-97	—Hartford	NHL	51	2985	22	22	...	6	134	4	2.69	.914	—	—	—	—	—	—	—	—
97-98	—Carolina	NHL	25	1415	7	11	...	5	66	1	2.80	.899	—	—	—	—	—	—	—	—
	—Vancouver	NHL	16	838	2	9	...	4	49	0	3.51	.876	—	—	—	—	—	—	—	—
	—Philadelphia	NHL	11	632	7	3	...	0	27	1	2.56	.913	5	283	1	4	17	0	3.60	.860
98-99	—Florida	NHL	59	3402	21	24	...	14	151	3	2.66	.907	—	—	—	—	—	—	—	—
99-00	—Florida	NHL	7	418	2	5	...	0	18	0	2.58	.913	—	—	—	—	—	—	—	—
	—Phoenix	NHL	35	2074	17	14	...	3	88	3	2.55	.914	5	296	1	4	16	0	3.24	.904
00-01	—Phoenix	NHL	62	3644	25	22	...	*13	138	4	2.27	.922	—	—	—	—	—	—	—	—
01-02	—Phoenix	NHL	60	3587	33	21	...	6	137	5	2.29	.920	5	297	1	4	13	0	2.63	.902
02-03	—Phoenix	NHL	22	1248	12	6	...	2	44	2	2.12	.930	—	—	—	—	—	—	—	—
03-04	—Phoenix	NHL	32	1795	10	15	...	5	84	1	2.81	.908	—	—	—	—	—	—	—	—
	—Philadelphia	NHL	15	825	6	5	...	2	35	1	2.55	.910	1	40	0	0	1	0	1.50	.889
05-06	—Tampa Bay	NHL	35	1713	14	10	4	...	80	2	2.80	.895	3	109	0	1	7	0	3.85	.877
NHL Totals (17 years)			797	45132	318	331	4	101	2222	37	2.95	.902	38	2151	12	23	119	1	3.32	.888

BURKI, CODEY C

PERSONAL: Born November 17, 1987, in Winnipeg. ... 6-0/190. ... Shoots left.

TRANSACTIONS/CAREER NOTES: Selected by Colorado Avalanche in second round (third Avalanche pick; 59th overall) of NHL draft (June 24, 2006).

Season	Team	League	GP	G	A	Pts.	PIM	+/-	PP	SH	GP	G	A	Pts.	PIM
			REGULAR SEASON								PLAYOFFS				
03-04	—Brandon	WHL	53	1	11	12	14	-3	...	...	8	0	0	0	0
04-05	—Brandon	WHL	68	10	13	23	48	-7	...	...	24	6	5	11	13
05-06	—Brandon	WHL	70	27	34	61	69	5	...	...	6	0	3	3	2

BURNS, BRENT RW/D

PERSONAL: Born March 9, 1985, in Ajax, Ont. ... 6-4/210. ... Shoots right.

TRANSACTIONS/CAREER NOTES: Selected by Minnesota Wild in first round (first Wild pick, 20th overall) of entry draft (June 23, 2003). ... Separated shoulder (October 26, 2003); missed eight games. ... Neck (February 2, 2004); missed eight games.

Season	Team	League	GP	G	A	Pts.	PIM	+/-	PP	SH	GP	G	A	Pts.	PIM
			REGULAR SEASON								PLAYOFFS				
02-03	—Brampton	OHL	68	15	25	40	14	...	...	...	—	—	—	—	—
03-04	—Minnesota	NHL	36	1	5	6	12	-10	0	0	—	—	—	—	—
	—Houston	AHL	1	0	1	1	2	-1	0	0	—	—	—	—	—
04-05	—Houston	AHL	73	11	16	27	57	-11	6	2	5	0	0	0	4
05-06	—Minnesota	NHL	72	4	12	16	32	-7	1	0	—	—	—	—	—
NHL Totals (2 years)			108	5	17	22	44	-17	1	0					

BURROWS, ALEX RW

PERSONAL: Born April 11, 1981, in Pointe-Claire, Quebec. ... 6-1/190. ... Shoots left.

TRANSACTIONS/CAREER NOTES: Signed as free agent by Vancouver Canucks (October 21, 2003).

Season	Team	League	GP	G	A	Pts.	PIM	+/-	PP	SH	GP	G	A	Pts.	PIM
			REGULAR SEASON								PLAYOFFS				
00-01	—Shawinigan	QMJHL	63	16	14	30	105	...	...	...	10	2	1	3	8
01-02	—Shawinigan	QMJHL	64	35	35	70	184	...	...	...	10	9	10	19	20
02-03	—Baton Rouge	ECHL	13	4	2	6	64	...	...	...	—	—	—	—	—
	—Greenville	ECHL	53	9	17	26	201	...	...	...	—	—	—	—	—
03-04	—Manitoba	AHL	2	0	0	0	0	...	...	...	—	—	—	—	—
	—Columbia	ECHL	64	29	44	73	194	...	...	...	4	2	0	2	28
04-05	—Columbia	ECHL	4	5	1	6	4	...	...	...	—	—	—	—	—
	—Manitoba	AHL	72	9	17	26	107	...	...	...	14	0	3	3	37
05-06	—Manitoba	AHL	33	12	18	30	57	...	...	...	13	6	7	13	27
	—Vancouver	NHL	43	7	5	12	61	5	0	1	—	—	—	—	—
NHL Totals (1 year)			43	7	5	12	61	5	0	1					

BUTENSCHON, SVEN — D/LW

PERSONAL: Born March 22, 1976, in Itzehoe, West Germany. ... 6-4/215. ... Shoots left. ... Name pronounced BOO-tihn-shohn.

TRANSACTIONS/CAREER NOTES: Selected by Pittsburgh Penguins in 3ird round (third Penguins pick, 57th overall) of entry draft (June 29, 1994). ... Flu (November 7, 1997); missed two games. ... Injured shoulder (March 3, 2001); missed four games. ... Traded by Penguins to Edmonton Oilers for LW Dan LaCouture (March 13, 2001). ... Signed as free agent by Florida Panthers (July 9, 2002). ... Traded by Panthers to New York Islanders for RW Juraj Kolnik and ninth-round pick (traded to San Jose; Sharks selected RW Carter Lee) in 2003 draft (October 11, 2002). ... Virus (December 21, 2003); missed four games. ... Signed as free agent by Vancouver Canucks (August 22, 2005).

		REGULAR SEASON								PLAYOFFS				
Season Team	League	GP	G	A	Pts.	PIM	+/-	PP	SH	GP	G	A	Pts.	PIM
93-94—Brandon	WHL	70	3	19	22	51	15	1	0	4	0	0	0	6
94-95—Brandon	WHL	21	1	5	6	44	15	0	0	18	1	2	3	11
95-96—Brandon	WHL	70	4	37	41	99	...	...	...	19	1	12	13	18
96-97—Cleveland	IHL	75	3	12	15	68	...	...	...	10	0	1	1	4
97-98—Syracuse	AHL	65	14	23	37	66	-7	7	0	5	1	2	3	0
—Pittsburgh	NHL	8	0	0	0	6	-1	0	0	—	—	—	—	—
98-99—Houston	IHL	57	1	4	5	81	15	0	0	—	—	—	—	—
—Pittsburgh	NHL	17	0	0	0	6	-7	0	0	—	—	—	—	—
99-00—Wilkes-Barre/Scranton	AHL	75	19	21	40	101	...	...	...	—	—	—	—	—
—Pittsburgh	NHL	3	0	0	0	0	3	0	0	—	—	—	—	—
00-01—Wilkes-Barre/Scranton	AHL	55	7	28	35	85	...	...	...	—	—	—	—	—
—Pittsburgh	NHL	5	0	1	1	2	1	0	0	—	—	—	—	—
—Edmonton	NHL	7	1	1	2	2	2	0	0	—	—	—	—	—
01-02—Hamilton	AHL	61	9	35	44	88	16	2	0	—	—	—	—	—
—Edmonton	NHL	14	0	0	0	4	0	0	0	—	—	—	—	—
02-03—New York Islanders	NHL	37	0	4	4	26	-6	0	0	—	—	—	—	—
—Bridgeport	AHL	36	3	13	16	58	-15	2	0	9	3	6	9	6
03-04—Bridgeport	AHL	5	0	1	1	4	-1	0	0	—	—	—	—	—
—New York Islanders	NHL	41	1	6	7	30	-3	0	0	4	0	0	0	0
04-05—Mannheim	Germany	50	1	5	6	54	1	0	0	14	0	1	1	16
05-06—Manitoba	AHL	60	15	22	37	30	5	10	1	13	0	6	6	12
—Vancouver	NHL	8	0	0	0	10	1	0	0	—	—	—	—	—
NHL Totals (8 years)		140	2	12	14	86	-10	0	0	4	0	0	0	0

BYFUGLIEN, DUSTIN — D

PERSONAL: Born March 27, 1985, in Roseau, Minn. ... 6-3/246. ... Shoots right. ... Name pronounced BUHF-lihn.

TRANSACTIONS/CAREER NOTES: Selected by Chicago Blackhawks in eighth round (eighth Blackhawks pick, 245th overall) of NHL entry draft (June 22, 2003).

		REGULAR SEASON								PLAYOFFS				
Season Team	League	GP	G	A	Pts.	PIM	+/-	PP	SH	GP	G	A	Pts.	PIM
02-03—Brandon	WHL	8	1	1	2	4	...	...	...	—	—	—	—	—
—Prince George	WHL	56	10	29	39	78	...	...	...	5	1	3	4	12
03-04—Prince George	WHL	66	16	29	45	137	-1	...	...	—	—	—	—	—
04-05—Prince George	WHL	64	22	36	58	184	-5	8	0	—	—	—	—	—
05-06—Norfolk	AHL	53	8	15	23	75	-1	2	0	4	1	2	3	4
—Chicago	NHL	25	3	2	5	24	-6	0	0	—	—	—	—	—
NHL Totals (1 year)		25	3	2	5	24	-6	0	0					

CAIRNS, ERIC — D

PERSONAL: Born June 27, 1974, in Oakville, Ont. ... 6-6/230. ... Shoots left. ... Name pronounced KAIR-ihns.

TRANSACTIONS/CAREER NOTES: Selected by New York Rangers in third round (third Rangers pick, 72nd overall) of entry draft (June 20, 1992). ... Claimed on waivers by New York Islanders (December 22, 1998). ... Strained back (January 6, 2000); missed one game. ... Suspended four games for fighting incident (February 13, 2000). ... Fractured thumb (October 1, 2000); missed first 18 games of season. ... Hand surgery (December 8, 2000); missed 17 games. ... Sprained left wrist (February 18, 2001); missed two games. ... Strained oblique muscle (December 2, 2001); missed five games. ... Bruised ribs (January 24, 2002); missed one game. ... Suspended two games for unsportsmanlike conduct (March 28, 2002). ... Injured knee (December 21, 2002); missed one game. ... Injured shoulder (January 24, 2003); missed 20 games. ... Injured toe (December 9, 2003); missed two games. ... Back spasms (January 6, 2004); missed three games. ... Signed as free agent by Florida Panthers (July 5, 2004). ... Injured ankle (October 5, 2005); missed first three games of season. ... Traded by Panthers to Pittsburgh Penguins for sixth-round pick (D Peter Aston) in 2006 draft (January 18, 2006). ... Suspended three games by NHL for misconduct (March 23, 2006).

		REGULAR SEASON								PLAYOFFS				
Season Team	League	GP	G	A	Pts.	PIM	+/-	PP	SH	GP	G	A	Pts.	PIM
90-91—Burlington Jr. B	OHA	37	5	16	21	120	...	...	...	—	—	—	—	—
91-92—Det. Jr. Red Wings	OHL	64	1	11	12	237	...	...	...	7	0	0	0	31
92-93—Det. Jr. Red Wings	OHL	64	3	13	16	194	...	...	...	15	0	3	3	24
93-94—Det. Jr. Red Wings	OHL	59	7	35	42	204	...	3	0	17	0	4	4	46
94-95—Birmingham	ECHL	11	1	3	4	49	2	0	0	—	—	—	—	—
—Binghamton	AHL	27	0	3	3	134	5	0	0	9	1	1	2	28
95-96—Binghamton	AHL	46	1	13	14	192	...	...	...	4	0	0	0	37
—Charlotte	ECHL	6	0	1	1	34	...	...	...	—	—	—	—	—
96-97—New York Rangers	NHL	40	0	1	1	147	-7	0	0	3	0	0	0	0
—Binghamton	AHL	10	1	1	2	96	-1	1	0	—	—	—	—	—
97-98—New York Rangers	NHL	39	0	3	3	92	-3	0	0	—	—	—	—	—
—Hartford	AHL	7	1	2	3	43	10	0	0	—	—	—	—	—
98-99—Hartford	AHL	11	0	2	2	49	-2	0	0	—	—	—	—	—
—Lowell	AHL	24	0	0	0	91	7	0	0	3	1	0	1	32
—New York Islanders	NHL	9	0	3	3	23	1	0	0	—	—	—	—	—

Season Team	League	REGULAR SEASON								PLAYOFFS				
		GP	G	A	Pts.	PIM	+/-	PP	SH	GP	G	A	Pts.	PIM
99-00—Providence	AHL	4	1	1	2	14	...	...	...	—	—	—	—	—
—New York Islanders	NHL	67	2	7	9	196	-5	0	0	—	—	—	—	—
00-01—New York Islanders	NHL	45	2	2	4	106	-18	0	0	—	—	—	—	—
01-02—New York Islanders	NHL	74	2	5	7	176	-2	0	0	7	0	0	0	15
02-03—New York Islanders	NHL	60	1	4	5	124	-7	0	0	5	0	0	0	13
03-04—New York Islanders	NHL	72	2	6	8	189	-5	0	0	1	0	0	0	0
04-05—London	England	33	3	7	10	119	...	1	0	—	—	—	—	—
05-06—Florida	NHL	23	0	1	1	37	1	0	0	—	—	—	—	—
—Pittsburgh	NHL	27	1	0	1	87	0	0	0	—	—	—	—	—
NHL Totals (9 years)		456	10	32	42	1177	-45	0	0	16	0	0	0	28

CAJANEK, PETR — C

PERSONAL: Born August 18, 1975, in Zlin, Czech. ... 5-11/191. ... Shoots left. ... Name pronounced chuh-YA-nihk.
TRANSACTIONS/CAREER NOTES: Selected by St. Louis Blues in eighth round (sixth Blues pick, 253rd overall) of entry draft (June 23, 2001). ... Fractured leg (January 2, 2003); missed 24 games. ... Facial cuts (March 23, 2003); missed four games. ... Ribs (October 28, 2003); missed five games. ... Neck (December 20, 2003); missed seven games. ... Strained groin (December 2, 2005); missed six games. ... Wrist (March 1, 2006); missed three games. ... Hip flexor (April 8, 2006); missed two games.

Season Team	League	REGULAR SEASON								PLAYOFFS				
		GP	G	A	Pts.	PIM	+/-	PP	SH	GP	G	A	Pts.	PIM
97-98—HC Continental Zlin	Czech Rep.	46	19	27	46	125	...	...	...	—	—	—	—	—
98-99—HC Continental Zlin	Czech Rep.	49	15	33	48	131	...	...	...	11	5	7	12	...
99-00—HC Continental Zlin	Czech Rep.	50	23	34	57	64	...	...	...	4	1	0	1	0
00-01—HC Continental Zlin	Czech Rep.	52	18	31	49	105	...	...	...	6	0	4	4	22
01-02—HC Continental Zlin	Czech Rep.	49	20	44	64	64	...	...	...	11	5	7	12	10
—Czech Rep. Oly. team	Int'l	4	0	0	0	0	...	...	...	—	—	—	—	—
02-03—St. Louis	NHL	51	9	29	38	20	16	2	2	2	0	0	0	2
03-04—St. Louis	NHL	70	12	14	26	16	12	3	0	5	0	2	2	2
04-05—Zlin	Czech Rep.	49	10	15	25	91	12	...	...	19	5	6	11	28
05-06—St. Louis	NHL	71	10	31	41	54	-22	3	0	—	—	—	—	—
—Czech Rep. Oly. team	Int'l	7	1	0	1	4	-1	0	0	—	—	—	—	—
NHL Totals (3 years)		192	31	74	105	90	6	8	2	7	0	2	2	4

CALDER, KYLE — LW/RW

PERSONAL: Born January 5, 1979, in Mannville, Alta. ... 5-11/176. ... Shoots left.
TRANSACTIONS/CAREER NOTES: Selected by Chicago Blackhawks in fifth round (seventh Blackhawks pick, 130th overall) of NHL draft (June 21, 1997). ... Concussion (January 9, 2002); missed one game. ... Broken leg (March 4, 2004); missed remainder of season. ... Injured elbow (October 23, 2005); missed three games.

Season Team	League	REGULAR SEASON								PLAYOFFS				
		GP	G	A	Pts.	PIM	+/-	PP	SH	GP	G	A	Pts.	PIM
95-96—Regina	WHL	27	1	8	9	10	...	...	...	11	0	0	0	0
96-97—Regina	WHL	62	25	34	59	17	...	...	...	5	3	0	3	6
97-98—Regina	WHL	62	27	50	77	58	...	...	...	2	0	1	1	0
98-99—Regina	WHL	34	23	28	51	29	...	...	...	—	—	—	—	—
—Kamloops	WHL	27	19	18	37	30	...	...	...	15	6	10	16	6
99-00—Cleveland	IHL	74	14	22	36	43	...	...	...	9	2	2	4	14
—Chicago	NHL	8	1	1	2	2	-3	0	0	—	—	—	—	—
00-01—Norfolk	AHL	37	12	15	27	21	...	...	...	9	2	6	8	2
—Chicago	NHL	43	5	10	15	14	-4	0	0	—	—	—	—	—
01-02—Chicago	NHL	81	17	36	53	47	8	6	0	5	2	0	2	2
02-03—Chicago	NHL	82	15	27	42	40	-6	7	0	—	—	—	—	—
03-04—Chicago	NHL	66	21	18	39	29	-18	10	0	—	—	—	—	—
04-05—Sodertalje	Sweden	12	5	1	6	6	-6	2	0	10	5	1	6	2
05-06—Chicago	NHL	79	26	33	59	52	-4	6	2	—	—	—	—	—
NHL Totals (6 years)		359	85	125	210	184	-27	29	2	5	2	0	2	2

CALDWELL, RYAN — D

PERSONAL: Born June 15, 1981, in Deloraine, Man. ... 6-2/174. ... Shoots left.
COLLEGE: Denver.
TRANSACTIONS/CAREER NOTES: Selected by New York Islanders in seventh round (seventh Islanders pick, 202nd overall) of entry draft (June 25, 2000).

Season Team	League	REGULAR SEASON								PLAYOFFS				
		GP	G	A	Pts.	PIM	+/-	PP	SH	GP	G	A	Pts.	PIM
99-00—Thunder Bay Flyers	USHL	46	3	20	23	152	...	...	...	—	—	—	—	—
00-01—Denver	WCHA	36	3	20	23	76	...	...	...	—	—	—	—	—
01-02—Denver	WCHA	40	3	16	19	76	...	...	...	—	—	—	—	—
02-03—Denver	WCHA	38	5	14	19	58	...	...	...	—	—	—	—	—
03-04—Denver	WCHA	42	15	12	27	96	...	...	...	—	—	—	—	—
04-05—Bridgeport	AHL	73	2	19	21	65	...	...	...	—	—	—	—	—
05-06—Bridgeport	AHL	61	3	12	15	38	-9	1	0	7	1	1	2	2
—New York Islanders	NHL	2	0	0	0	2	-2	0	0	—	—	—	—	—
NHL Totals (1 year)		2	0	0	0	2	-2	0	0					

CAMMALLERI, MICHAEL C

PERSONAL: Born June 8, 1982, in Richmond Hill, Ont. ... 5-9/180. ... Shoots left.
TRANSACTIONS/CAREER NOTES: Selected by Los Angeles Kings in second round (third Kings pick, 49th overall) of entry draft (June 23, 2001). ... Concussion (January 28, 2003); missed 31 games. ... Knee (September 22, 2003); missed season's first eight games.

		REGULAR SEASON								PLAYOFFS				
Season Team	**League**	**GP**	**G**	**A**	**Pts.**	**PIM**	**+/-**	**PP**	**SH**	**GP**	**G**	**A**	**Pts.**	**PIM**
99-00—Univ. of Michigan........	CCHA	39	13	13	26	32	...	...	...	—	—	—	—	—
00-01—Univ. of Michigan........	CCHA	42	29	32	61	24	...	...	...	—	—	—	—	—
01-02—Univ. of Michigan........	CCHA	28	23	20	43	24	...	...	...	—	—	—	—	—
02-03—Manchester................	AHL	13	5	15	20	12	-4	1	1	—	—	—	—	—
—Los Angeles...............	NHL	28	5	3	8	22	-4	2	0	—	—	—	—	—
03-04—Los Angeles...............	NHL	31	9	6	15	20	1	2	0	—	—	—	—	—
—Manchester................	AHL	41	20	18	38	28	13	4	0	1	0	1	1	0
04-05—Manchester................	AHL	79	46	63	109	60	25	17	2	6	1	5	6	0
05-06—Los Angeles...............	NHL	80	26	29	55	50	-14	15	0	—	—	—	—	—
NHL Totals (3 years)...........		139	40	38	78	92	-17	19	0					

CAMPBELL, BRIAN D

PERSONAL: Born May 23, 1979, in Strathroy, Ont. ... 6-0/190. ... Shoots left.
TRANSACTIONS/CAREER NOTES: Selected by Buffalo Sabres in sixth round (seventh Sabres pick, 156th overall) of entry draft (June 21, 1997). ... Separated shoulder (April 1, 2002); missed remainder of season.

		REGULAR SEASON								PLAYOFFS				
Season Team	**League**	**GP**	**G**	**A**	**Pts.**	**PIM**	**+/-**	**PP**	**SH**	**GP**	**G**	**A**	**Pts.**	**PIM**
94-95—Petrolia.......................	Jr. B	50	1	2	3	...	...	...	...	—	—	—	—	—
95-96—Ottawa.......................	OHL	66	5	22	27	23	...	...	...	4	0	1	1	2
96-97—Ottawa.......................	OHL	66	7	36	43	12	...	...	...	24	2	11	13	8
97-98—Ottawa.......................	OHL	66	14	39	53	31	...	...	...	13	1	14	15	0
98-99—Ottawa.......................	OHL	62	12	75	87	27	45	...	...	9	2	10	12	6
—Rochester..................	AHL	...	...	...	...	...	...	...	...	2	0	0	0	0
99-00—Buffalo.......................	NHL	12	1	4	5	4	-2	0	0	—	—	—	—	—
—Rochester..................	AHL	67	2	24	26	22	...	...	...	21	0	3	3	0
00-01—Rochester..................	AHL	65	7	25	32	24	...	...	...	4	0	1	1	0
—Buffalo.......................	NHL	8	0	0	0	2	-2	0	0	—	—	—	—	—
01-02—Rochester..................	AHL	45	2	35	37	13	9	1	0	—	—	—	—	—
—Buffalo.......................	NHL	29	3	3	6	12	0	0	0	—	—	—	—	—
02-03—Buffalo.......................	NHL	65	2	17	19	20	-8	0	0	—	—	—	—	—
03-04—Buffalo.......................	NHL	53	3	8	11	12	-8	0	0	—	—	—	—	—
04-05—Jokerit Helsinki...........	Finland	44	12	13	25	12	14	...	...	12	3	4	7	6
05-06—Buffalo.......................	NHL	79	12	32	44	16	-14	5	0	18	0	6	6	12
NHL Totals (6 years)...........		246	21	64	85	66	-34	5	0	18	0	6	6	12

CAMPBELL, GREGORY C

PERSONAL: Born December 17, 1983, in London, Ont. ... 6-0/197. ... Shoots left. ... Son of Colin Campbell, NHL director of hockey operations, who played for five NHL teams from 1970-85.
TRANSACTIONS/CAREER NOTES: Selected by Florida Panthers in third round (fourth Panthers pick, 67th overall) of NHL draft (June 22, 2002). ... Concussion (January 24, 2006); missed four games.

		REGULAR SEASON								PLAYOFFS				
Season Team	**League**	**GP**	**G**	**A**	**Pts.**	**PIM**	**+/-**	**PP**	**SH**	**GP**	**G**	**A**	**Pts.**	**PIM**
00-01—Plymouth....................	OHL	65	2	12	14	40	...	...	...	21	15	4	19	34
01-02—Plymouth....................	OHL	65	17	36	53	105	...	...	...	6	0	2	2	13
02-03—Kitchener....................	OHL	55	23	33	56	116	...	...	...	21	15	4	19	34
03-04—Florida........................	NHL	2	0	0	0	5	-1	0	0	—	—	—	—	—
—San Antonio................	AHL	76	13	16	29	73	-13	1	0	—	—	—	—	—
04-05—San Antonio................	AHL	70	12	16	28	113	-17	3	1	—	—	—	—	—
05-06—Rochester....................	AHL	11	3	3	6	30	1	0	1	—	—	—	—	—
—Florida........................	NHL	64	3	6	9	40	-11	0	0	—	—	—	—	—
NHL Totals (2 years)...........		66	3	6	9	45	-12	0	0					

CAMPBELL, JIM RW

PERSONAL: Born April 3, 1973, in Worcester, Mass. ... 6-2/205. ... Shoots right.
TRANSACTIONS/CAREER NOTES: Selected by Montreal Canadiens in second round (second Canadiens pick, 28th overall) of NHL entry draft (June 22, 1991). ... Traded by Canadiens to Anaheim Mighty Ducks for D Robert Dirk (January 21, 1996). ... Signed as free agent by St. Louis Blues (July 3, 1996). ... Strained thumb (February 25, 1997); missed 10 games. ... Reinjured thumb (April 6, 1997); missed remainder of regular season. ... Strained groin (December 6, 1997); missed one game. ... Injured left heel (January 20, 1998); missed five games. ... Bruised right shoulder (October 23, 1998); missed two games. ... Injured groin (February 9, 1999); missed three games. ... Injured abdominal muscle (March 18, 1999) and had surgery; missed remainder of season. ... Signed as free agent by Canadiens (August 22, 2000). ... Suffered concussion (October 17, 2000); missed one game. ... Strained groin (November 14, 2000); missed nine games. ... Signed as free agent by Chicago Blackhawks (November 19, 2001). ... Signed as free agent by Florida Panthers (July 19, 2002). ... Signed as free agent by Chicago of the AHL (December 10, 2003). ... Signed as free agent by New York Islanders (August 11, 2004).

		REGULAR SEASON								PLAYOFFS				
Season Team	**League**	**GP**	**G**	**A**	**Pts.**	**PIM**	**+/-**	**PP**	**SH**	**GP**	**G**	**A**	**Pts.**	**PIM**
88-89—Northwood School......	N.Y. H.S.	12	12	8	20	6	...	...	...	—	—	—	—	—
89-90—Northwood School......	N.Y. H.S.	8	14	7	21	8	...	...	...	—	—	—	—	—

Season Team	League	GP	G	A	Pts.	PIM	+/-	PP	SH	GP	G	A	Pts.	PIM
		REGULAR SEASON								PLAYOFFS				
90-91—Northwood School	N.Y. H.S.	26	36	47	83	36	...	...	...	—	—	—	—	—
91-92—Hull	QMJHL	64	41	44	85	51	...	...	...	6	7	3	10	8
92-93—Hull	QMJHL	50	42	29	71	66	...	...	...	8	11	4	15	43
93-94—U.S. national team	Int'l	56	24	33	57	59	...	0	0	—	—	—	—	—
—U.S. Olympic team	Int'l	8	0	0	0	6	-5	0	0	—	—	—	—	—
—Fredericton	AHL	19	6	17	23	6	-9	2	0	—	—	—	—	—
94-95—Fredericton	AHL	77	27	24	51	103	-9	7	2	12	0	7	7	8
95-96—Fredericton	AHL	44	28	23	51	24	...	...	...	—	—	—	—	—
—Baltimore	AHL	16	13	7	20	8	...	...	...	12	7	5	12	10
—Anaheim	NHL	16	2	3	5	36	0	1	0	—	—	—	—	—
96-97—St. Louis	NHL	68	23	20	43	68	3	5	0	4	1	0	1	6
97-98—St. Louis	NHL	76	22	19	41	55	0	7	0	10	7	3	10	12
98-99—St. Louis	NHL	55	4	21	25	41	-8	1	0	—	—	—	—	—
99-00—Manitoba	IHL	10	1	3	4	10	...	...	...	—	—	—	—	—
—Worcester	AHL	66	31	34	65	88	...	...	...	9	1	2	3	6
—St. Louis	NHL	2	0	0	0	9	0	0	0	—	—	—	—	—
00-01—Montreal	NHL	57	9	11	20	53	-3	6	0	—	—	—	—	—
—Quebec	AHL	3	5	0	5	6	...	...	...	—	—	—	—	—
01-02—Norfolk	AHL	44	11	14	25	26	6	5	0	4	3	1	4	2
—Chicago	NHL	9	1	1	2	4	-3	0	0	—	—	—	—	—
02-03—Florida	NHL	1	0	0	0	0	0	0	0	—	—	—	—	—
—San Antonio	AHL	64	16	37	53	55	-10	11	0	1	0	0	0	0
03-04—Chicago	AHL	41	10	13	23	41	1	...	...	—	—	—	—	—
04-05—Bridgeport	AHL	46	8	12	20	64	-13	5	0	—	—	—	—	—
—Springfield	AHL	13	2	5	7	8	-7	2	0	—	—	—	—	—
05-06—Springfield	AHL	32	12	12	24	24	-8	5	0	—	—	—	—	—
—Philadelphia	AHL	35	12	17	29	46	7	4	0	—	—	—	—	—
—Tampa Bay	NHL	1	0	0	0	2	0	0	0	—	—	—	—	—
NHL Totals (9 years)		285	61	75	136	268	-11	20	0	14	8	3	11	18

CAMPOLI, CHRIS D

PERSONAL: Born July 9, 1984, in North York, Ont. ... 6-0/190. ... Shoots left.

TRANSACTIONS/CAREER NOTES: Selected by New York Islanders in seventh round (eighth Islanders pick, 227th overall) of NHL entry draft (June 28, 2004).

Season Team	League	GP	G	A	Pts.	PIM	+/-	PP	SH	GP	G	A	Pts.	PIM
		REGULAR SEASON								PLAYOFFS				
00-01—Erie	OHL	52	1	9	10	47	...	...	...	15	0	0	0	4
01-02—Erie	OHL	68	2	24	26	117	...	...	...	20	0	5	5	18
02-03—Erie	OHL	60	8	40	48	82	...	...	...	—	—	—	—	—
03-04—Erie	OHL	67	20	46	66	66	...	...	...	8	0	6	6	16
04-05—Bridgeport	AHL	79	15	34	49	78	13	7	2	—	—	—	—	—
05-06—New York Islanders	NHL	80	9	25	34	46	-16	2	0	—	—	—	—	—
NHL Totals (1 year)		80	9	25	34	46	-16	2	0					

CARKNER, MATT D

PERSONAL: Born November 3, 1980, in Winchester, Ont. ... 6-4/222. ... Shoots right.

TRANSACTIONS/CAREER NOTES: Selected by Montreal Canadiens in second round (second Canadiens pick, 58th overall) of entry draft (June 26, 1999). ... Signed as free agent by San Jose Sharks (June 12, 2001). ... Signed as free agent by Pittsburgh Penguins (July 21, 2006).

Season Team	League	GP	G	A	Pts.	PIM	+/-	PP	SH	GP	G	A	Pts.	PIM
		REGULAR SEASON								PLAYOFFS				
96-97—Winchester	Jr. B	29	1	18	19	...	...	...	...	—	—	—	—	—
97-98—Peterborough	OHL	57	0	6	6	121	...	...	...	4	0	0	0	2
98-99—Peterborough	OHL	60	2	16	18	173	15	...	...	5	0	0	0	20
99-00—Peterborough	OHL	62	3	13	16	177	5	0	0	5	0	1	1	6
00-01—Peterborough	OHL	53	8	8	16	128	7	1	0	7	0	3	3	25
01-02—Cleveland	AHL	74	0	3	3	335	-3	0	0	—	—	—	—	—
02-03—Cleveland	AHL	39	1	4	5	104	-12	0	0	—	—	—	—	—
03-04—Cleveland	AHL	60	2	11	13	115	...	...	...	9	0	3	3	39
04-05—Cleveland	AHL	73	0	10	10	192	-5	0	0	—	—	—	—	—
05-06—San Jose	NHL	1	0	1	1	2	0	0	0	—	—	—	—	—
—Cleveland	AHL	69	10	20	30	202	-17	3	0	—	—	—	—	—
NHL Totals (1 year)		1	0	1	1	2	0	0	0					

CARLE, MATHIEU D

PERSONAL: Born September 30, 1987, in Gatineau, Quebec. ... 6-0/206. ... Shoots right.

TRANSACTIONS/CAREER NOTES: Selected by Montreal Canadiens in second round (third Canadiens pick; 53rd overall) of NHL draft (June 24, 2006).

Season Team	League	GP	G	A	Pts.	PIM	+/-	PP	SH	GP	G	A	Pts.	PIM
		REGULAR SEASON								PLAYOFFS				
03-04—Acadie-Bathurst	QMJHL	59	11	12	23	57	-9	...	...	—	—	—	—	—
04-05—Acadie-Bathurst	QMJHL	69	4	29	33	53	-27	...	...	—	—	—	—	—
05-06—Acadie-Bathurst	QMJHL	67	18	51	69	122	20	8	3	17	1	14	15	29

CARLE, MATT — D

PERSONAL: Born September 25, 1984, in Anchorage, Alaska. ... 6-0/182. ... Shoots left.

TRANSACTIONS/CAREER NOTES: Selected by San Jose Sharks in second round (fourth Sharks pick, 47th overall) of entry draft (June 20, 2003).

		REGULAR SEASON								PLAYOFFS				
Season Team	League	GP	G	A	Pts.	PIM	+/-	PP	SH	GP	G	A	Pts.	PIM
01-02—U.S. Jr. national team	Int'l	12	0	0	0	21	...	...	...	—	—	—	—	—
—River City	USHL	72	4	18	22	...	...	...	...	—	—	—	—	—
02-03—River City	USHL	59	12	30	42	98	...	...	...	11	2	2	4	20
03-04—Denver	WCHA	30	5	20	25	33	15	2	0	4	0	2	2	...
04-05—Denver	WCHA	39	12	27	39	58	...	...	...	4	1	4	5	10
05-06—Denver	WCHA	39	11	42	53	58	...	...	...	—	—	—	—	—
—San Jose	NHL	12	3	3	6	14	-2	2	0	11	0	3	3	4
NHL Totals (1 year)		12	3	3	6	14	-2	2	0	11	0	3	3	4

CARNEY, KEITH — D

PERSONAL: Born February 3, 1970, in Providence, R.I. ... 6-1/217. ... Shoots left.

TRANSACTIONS/CAREER NOTES: Selected by Buffalo Sabres in fourth round (third Sabres pick, 76th overall) of NHL draft (June 11, 1988). ... Traded by Sabres to Chicago Blackhawks for D Craig Muni (October 27, 1993). ... Traded by Blackhawks with RW Jim Cummins to Phoenix Coyotes for C Chad Kilger and D Jayson More (March 4, 1998). ... Traded by Coyotes to Anaheim Mighty Ducks for second-round pick (traded to New Jersey) in 2001 draft (June 19, 2001). ... Fractured right hand (November 7, 2001); missed 17 games. ... Had hip pointer and cut right elbow (March 30, 2002); missed one game. ... Reinjured elbow (April 3, 2002); missed four games. ... Stomach virus (December 19, 2002); missed one game. ... Fractured right foot (October 3, 2003); missed 11 games. ... Back spasms (December 13, 2003); missed 2 games. ... Traded by Mighty Ducks with D Juha Alen to Vancouver Canucks for second-round pick (RW Bryce Swan) in 2006 draft and D Brett Skinner (March 9, 2006). ... Signed as free agent by Minnesota Wild (July 1, 2006).

		REGULAR SEASON								PLAYOFFS				
Season Team	League	GP	G	A	Pts.	PIM	+/-	PP	SH	GP	G	A	Pts.	PIM
88-89—Maine	Hockey East	40	4	22	26	24	...	...	...	—	—	—	—	—
89-90—Maine	Hockey East	41	3	41	44	43	...	...	...	—	—	—	—	—
90-91—Maine	Hockey East	40	7	49	56	38	...	...	...	—	—	—	—	—
91-92—U.S. national team	Int'l	49	2	17	19	16	...	...	...	—	—	—	—	—
—Rochester	AHL	24	1	10	11	2	...	...	...	2	0	2	2	0
—Buffalo	NHL	14	1	2	3	18	-3	1	0	7	0	3	3	0
92-93—Buffalo	NHL	30	2	4	6	55	3	0	0	8	0	3	3	6
—Rochester	AHL	41	5	21	26	32	8	0	1	—	—	—	—	—
93-94—Louisville	ECHL	15	1	4	5	14	-6	0	0	—	—	—	—	—
—Buffalo	NHL	7	1	3	4	4	-1	0	0	—	—	—	—	—
—Indianapolis	IHL	28	0	14	14	20	-13	0	0	—	—	—	—	—
—Chicago	NHL	30	3	5	8	35	15	0	0	6	0	1	1	4
94-95—Chicago	NHL	18	1	0	1	11	-1	0	0	4	0	1	1	0
95-96—Chicago	NHL	82	5	14	19	94	31	1	0	10	0	3	3	4
96-97—Chicago	NHL	81	3	15	18	62	26	0	0	6	1	1	2	2
97-98—Chicago	NHL	60	2	13	15	73	-7	0	1	—	—	—	—	—
—U.S. Olympic team	Int'l	4	0	0	0	2	0	0	0	—	—	—	—	—
—Phoenix	NHL	20	1	6	7	18	5	1	0	6	0	0	0	4
98-99—Phoenix	NHL	82	2	14	16	62	15	0	2	7	1	2	3	10
99-00—Phoenix	NHL	82	4	20	24	87	11	0	0	5	0	0	0	17
00-01—Phoenix	NHL	82	2	14	16	86	15	0	0	—	—	—	—	—
01-02—Anaheim	NHL	60	5	9	14	30	14	0	0	—	—	—	—	—
02-03—Anaheim	NHL	81	4	18	22	65	8	0	0	21	0	4	4	16
03-04—Anaheim	NHL	69	2	5	7	42	-5	1	0	—	—	—	—	—
05-06—Anaheim	NHL	61	2	16	18	48	13	1	0	—	—	—	—	—
—Vancouver	NHL	18	0	2	2	14	-5	0	0	—	—	—	—	—
NHL Totals (14 years)		877	40	160	200	804	134	5	3	80	2	18	20	63

CARON, SEBASTIEN — G

PERSONAL: Born June 25, 1980, in Amqui, Que. ... 6-1/170. ... Catches left.

TRANSACTIONS/CAREER NOTES: Selected by Pittsburgh Penguins in third round (fourth Penguins pick, 86th overall) of NHL draft (June 26, 1999). ... Strained quadriceps (November 9, 2005); missed five games.

		REGULAR SEASON										PLAYOFFS							
Season Team	League	GP	Min.	W	L	OTL	T	GA	SO	GAA	SV%	GP	Min.	W	L	GA	SO	GAA	SV%
98-99—Rimouski	QMJHL	30	1570	13	10	...	3	85	0	3.25	...	2	68	1	0	0	0	0.00	...
99-00—Rimouski	QMJHL	54	3040	38	11	...	3	179	1	3.53	.896	14	828	12	2	50	0	3.62	.900
00-01—Wilkes-Barre/Scranton	AHL	30	1746	12	14	...	3	103	4	3.54	.882	—	—	—	—	—	—	—	—
01-02—Wilkes-Barre/Scranton	AHL	46	2670	14	22	...	8	139	1	3.12	.892	—	—	—	—	—	—	—	—
02-03—Wilkes-Barre/Scranton	AHL	27	1560	12	14	...	1	81	1	3.12	.904	—	—	—	—	—	—	—	—
—Pittsburgh	NHL	24	1408	7	14	...	2	62	2	2.64	.916	—	—	—	—	—	—	—	—
03-04—Pittsburgh	NHL	40	2213	9	24	...	5	138	1	3.74	.883	—	—	—	—	—	—	—	—
—Wilkes-Barre/Scranton	AHL	14	811	7	3	...	4	26	2	1.92	.924	7	394	3	4	23	0	3.50	.823
04-05—Saguenay	LNAH	18	...	...	...	...	...	...	...	...	...	—	—	—	—	—	—	—	—
—Sorel-Tracy	LNAH	24	...	...	...	...	...	...	...	...	...	4	164	1	2	14	0	5.12	.829
05-06—Wilkes-Barre/Scranton	AHL	6	357	3	3	0	...	7	2	1.18	.954	—	—	—	—	—	—	—	—
—Pittsburgh	NHL	26	1312	8	9	5	...	87	1	3.98	.881	—	—	—	—	—	—	—	—
NHL Totals (3 years)		90	4933	24	47	5	7	287	4	3.49	.892								

CARTER, ANSON — RW

PERSONAL: Born June 6, 1974, in Toronto. ... 6-1/209. ... Shoots right.

TRANSACTIONS/CAREER NOTES: Selected by Quebec Nordiques in 10th round (10th Nordiques pick, 220th overall) of entry draft (June 20, 1992). ... Nordiques franchise moved to Colorado and renamed Avalanche for 1995-96 season (June 21, 1995). ... Traded by Avalanche to Washington Capitals for fourth-round pick (D Ben Storey) in 1996 draft (April 3, 1996). ... Sprained thumb (February 7, 1997); missed five games. ... Traded by Capitals with G Jim Carey, C Jason Allison and third-round pick (RW Lee Goren) in 1997 draft to Boston Bruins for C Adam Oates, RW Rick Tocchet and G Bill Ranford (March 1, 1997). ... Strained hip flexor (October 7, 1997); missed two games. ... Upper respiratory infection (November 22, 1997); missed two games. ... Missed first 12 games of 1998-99 season in contract dispute. ... Sprained ankle (January 2, 1999); missed 15 games. ... Bruised shoulder (February 21, 2000); missed eight games. ... Wrist surgery (March 10, 2000); missed final 15 games of season. ... Traded by Bruins with second-round pick (D Doug Lynch) in 2001 draft and swap of first-round picks in 2001 to Edmonton Oilers for RW Bill Guerin (November 15, 2000); with first-round picks, Bruins selected D Shaonne Morrisonn and Oilers selected RW Ales Hemsky. ... Traded by Oilers with D Ales Pisa to New York Rangers for RW Radek Dvorak and D Cory Cross (March 11, 2003). ... Injured wrist (November 27, 2003); missed two games. ... Injured ribs (December 26, 2003); missed three games. ... Traded by Rangers to Capitals for RW Jaromir Jagr (January 23, 2004). ... Traded by Capitals to Los Angeles Kings for C Jared Aulin (March 8, 2004). ... Signed as free agent by Vancouver Canucks (August 17, 2005). ... Bruised foot (February 6, 2006); missed one game.

STATISTICAL PLATEAUS: Three-goal games: 1998-99 (1).

		REGULAR SEASON								PLAYOFFS				
Season Team	**League**	**GP**	**G**	**A**	**Pts.**	**PIM**	**+/-**	**PP**	**SH**	**GP**	**G**	**A**	**Pts.**	**PIM**
91-92—Wexford	OHA Jr. A	42	18	22	40	24	...	...	...	—	—	—	—	—
92-93—Michigan State	CCHA	36	19	11	30	20	...	...	...	—	—	—	—	—
93-94—Michigan State	CCHA	39	30	24	54	36	...	...	...	—	—	—	—	—
94-95—Michigan State	CCHA	39	34	17	51	40	11	13	7	—	—	—	—	—
95-96—Michigan State	CCHA	42	23	20	43	36	...	...	...	—	—	—	—	—
96-97—Washington	NHL	19	3	2	5	7	0	1	0	—	—	—	—	—
—Portland	AHL	27	19	19	38	11	15	5	4	—	—	—	—	—
—Boston	NHL	19	8	5	13	2	-7	1	1	—	—	—	—	—
97-98—Boston	NHL	78	16	27	43	31	7	6	0	6	1	1	2	0
98-99—Utah	IHL	6	1	1	2	0	-2	0	0	—	—	—	—	—
—Boston	NHL	55	24	16	40	22	7	6	0	12	4	3	7	0
99-00—Boston	NHL	59	22	25	47	14	8	4	0	—	—	—	—	—
00-01—Edmonton	NHL	61	16	26	42	23	1	7	1	6	3	1	4	4
01-02—Edmonton	NHL	82	28	32	60	25	3	12	0	—	—	—	—	—
02-03—Edmonton	NHL	68	25	30	55	20	-11	10	0	—	—	—	—	—
—New York Rangers	NHL	11	1	4	5	6	0	0	0	—	—	—	—	—
03-04—New York Rangers	NHL	43	10	7	17	14	-12	4	1	—	—	—	—	—
—Washington	NHL	19	5	5	10	6	2	2	0	—	—	—	—	—
—Los Angeles	NHL	15	0	1	1	0	-5	0	0	—	—	—	—	—
05-06—Vancouver	NHL	81	33	22	55	41	-1	15	0	—	—	—	—	—
NHL Totals (9 years)		610	191	202	393	211	-8	68	3	24	8	5	13	4

CARTER, JEFF — C/RW

PERSONAL: Born January 1, 1985, in London, Ont. ... 6-3/200. ... Shoots right.

TRANSACTIONS/CAREER NOTES: Selected by Philadelphia Flyers in first round (first Flyers pick, 11th overall) of entry draft (June 23, 2003). ... Lacerated left ear (December 15, 2005); missed one game.

		REGULAR SEASON								PLAYOFFS				
Season Team	**League**	**GP**	**G**	**A**	**Pts.**	**PIM**	**+/-**	**PP**	**SH**	**GP**	**G**	**A**	**Pts.**	**PIM**
01-02—Sault Ste. Marie	OHL	63	18	17	35	12	...	...	...	—	—	—	—	—
02-03—Sault Ste. Marie	OHL	61	35	36	71	55	...	...	...	—	—	—	—	—
03-04—Sault Ste. Marie	OHL	57	36	30	66	26	...	...	...	—	—	—	—	—
—Philadelphia	AHL	...	...	...	...	...	...	...	...	12	4	1	5	0
04-05—Sault Ste. Marie	OHL	55	34	40	74	40	20	14	1	7	5	5	10	6
—Philadelphia	AHL	3	0	1	1	4	-1	0	0	21	12	11	23	12
05-06—Philadelphia	NHL	81	23	19	42	40	10	6	2	6	0	0	0	10
NHL Totals (1 year)		81	23	19	42	40	10	6	2	6	0	0	0	10

CASSELS, ANDREW — C

PERSONAL: Born July 23, 1969, in Bramalea, Ont. ... 6-1/178. ... Shoots left. ... Name pronounced KAS-uhls.

TRANSACTIONS/CAREER NOTES: Selected by Montreal Canadiens in first round (first Canadiens pick, 17th overall) of entry draft (June 13, 1987). ... Separated right shoulder (November 22, 1989); missed 10 games. ... Traded by Canadiens to Hartford Whalers for second-round pick (RW Valeri Bure) in 1992 draft (September 17, 1991). ... Bruised kneecap (December 4, 1993); missed one game. ... Facial injury (March 13, 1994); missed four games. ... Bruised forearm (December 2, 1995); missed one game. ... Charley horse (March 6, 1997); missed one game. ... Whalers franchise moved to North Carolina and renamed Carolina Hurricanes for 1997-98 season; NHL approved move on June 25, 1997. ... Traded by Hurricanes with G Jean-Sebastien Giguere to Calgary Flames for LW Gary Roberts and G Trevor Kidd (August 25, 1997). ... Strained rib cage (October 9, 1997); missed one game. ... Injured groin (February 1, 1999); missed 12 games. ... Signed as free agent by Vancouver Canucks (July 13, 1999). ... Sprained thumb (October 19, 1999); missed three games. ... Fractured toe (January 20, 2001); missed 10 games. ... Sprained ankle (March 25, 2001); missed remainder of season. ... Sprained knee (October 23, 2001); missed 20 games. ... Concussion (March 9, 2002); missed eight games. ... Signed as free agent by Columbus Blue Jackets (August 15, 2002). ... Injured elbow (December 26, 2002); missed three games. ... Back spasms (October 18, 2003); missed three games. ... Fractured foot (January 8, 2004); missed 22 games. ... Contract bought out by Blue Jackets (July 29, 2005). ... Signed as free agent by Washington Capitals (August 9, 2005).

STATISTICAL PLATEAUS: Three-goal games: 2000-01 (1).

		REGULAR SEASON								PLAYOFFS				
Season Team	**League**	**GP**	**G**	**A**	**Pts.**	**PIM**	**+/-**	**PP**	**SH**	**GP**	**G**	**A**	**Pts.**	**PIM**
85-86—Bramalea Jr. B	OHA	33	18	25	43	26	...	...	...	—	—	—	—	—
86-87—Ottawa	OHL	66	26	66	92	28	...	...	...	11	5	9	14	7

Season Team	League	GP	G	A	Pts.	PIM	+/-	PP	SH	GP	G	A	Pts.	PIM
		REGULAR SEASON								PLAYOFFS				
87-88—Ottawa	OHL	61	48	103	151	39	...	...	...	16	8	24	32	13
88-89—Ottawa	OHL	56	37	97	134	66	...	...	...	12	5	10	15	10
89-90—Sherbrooke	AHL	55	22	45	67	25	...	...	...	12	2	11	13	6
—Montreal	NHL	6	2	0	2	2	1	0	0	—	—	—	—	—
90-91—Montreal	NHL	54	6	19	25	20	2	1	0	8	0	2	2	2
91-92—Hartford	NHL	67	11	30	41	18	3	2	2	7	2	4	6	6
92-93—Hartford	NHL	84	21	64	85	62	-11	8	3	—	—	—	—	—
93-94—Hartford	NHL	79	16	42	58	37	-21	8	1	—	—	—	—	—
94-95—Hartford	NHL	46	7	30	37	18	-3	1	0	—	—	—	—	—
95-96—Hartford	NHL	81	20	43	63	39	8	6	0	—	—	—	—	—
96-97—Hartford	NHL	81	22	44	66	46	-16	8	0	—	—	—	—	—
97-98—Calgary	NHL	81	17	27	44	32	-7	6	1	—	—	—	—	—
98-99—Calgary	NHL	70	12	25	37	18	-12	4	1	—	—	—	—	—
99-00—Vancouver	NHL	79	17	45	62	16	8	6	0	—	—	—	—	—
00-01—Vancouver	NHL	66	12	44	56	10	1	2	0	—	—	—	—	—
01-02—Vancouver	NHL	53	11	39	50	22	5	7	0	6	2	1	3	0
02-03—Columbus	NHL	79	20	48	68	30	-4	9	1	—	—	—	—	—
03-04—Columbus	NHL	58	6	20	26	26	-24	2	0	—	—	—	—	—
05-06—Washington	NHL	31	4	8	12	14	-3	2	0	—	—	—	—	—
NHL Totals (16 years)		1015	204	528	732	410	-73	72	9	21	4	7	11	8

C

CASSIVI, FREDERIC G

PERSONAL: Born June 12, 1975, in Sorel, Que. ... 6-4/215. ... Catches left. ... Name pronounced kuh-SIH-vee.

TRANSACTIONS/CAREER NOTES: Selected by Ottawa Senators in ninth round (seventh Senators pick, 210th overall) of entry draft (June 29, 1994). ... Signed as free agent by Colorado Avalanche (August 3, 1999). ... Traded by Avalanche to Atlanta Thrashers for D Brett Clark (January 24, 2002). ... Signed as free agent by Washington Capitals (August 12, 2005).

Season Team	League	GP	Min.	W	L	OTL	T	GA	SO	GAA	SV%	GP	Min.	W	L	GA	SO	GAA	SV%
		REGULAR SEASON										PLAYOFFS							
93-94—St. Hyacinthe	QMJHL	35	1751	15	13	...	3	127	1	4.35	.879	0	0	0	0	0	0	...	...
94-95—Halifax	QMJHL	24	1362	9	12	...	1	105	0	4.63	...	—	—	—	—	—	—	—	—
—St. Jean	QMJHL	19	1021	12	6	...	0	55	1	3.23	.959	5	258	2	3	18	0	4.19	.888
95-96—Prince Edward	AHL	41	2346	20	14	...	3	128	1	3.27	...	5	317	2	3	24	0	4.54	...
—Thunder Bay	Col.HL	12	714	6	4	...	2	51	0	4.29	...	—	—	—	—	—	—	—	—
96-97—Syracuse	AHL	55	3069	23	22	...	8	164	2	3.21	.889	1	60	0	1	3	0	3.00	.893
97-98—Worcester	AHL	45	2594	20	22	...	2	140	1	3.24	.891	6	326	3	3	18	0	3.31	.901
98-99—Cincinnati	IHL	44	2418	21	17	...	2	123	1	3.05	.903	3	139	1	2	6	0	2.59	.917
99-00—Hershey	AHL	31	1554	14	9	...	3	78	1	3.01	...	2	63	0	1	5	0	4.76	...
00-01—Hershey	AHL	49	2620	17	24	...	3	124	2	2.84	.906	9	564	7	2	14	1	1.49	...
01-02—Hershey	AHL	21	1201	6	10	...	4	50	0	2.50	.912	—	—	—	—	—	—	—	—
—Chicago	AHL	12	624	6	2	...	1	26	0	2.50	.913	5	264	2	2	11	0	2.50	.923
—Atlanta	NHL	6	307	2	3	...	0	17	0	3.32	.918	—	—	—	—	—	—	—	—
02-03—Atlanta	NHL	2	123	1	1	...	0	11	0	5.37	.810	—	—	—	—	—	—	—	—
—Chicago	AHL	21	1170	10	8	...	1	62	0	3.18	.892	2	90	0	2	3	0	2.00	.925
03-04—Chicago	AHL	34	1911	15	12	...	5	82	1	2.57	...	—	—	—	—	—	—	—	—
04-05—Cincinnati	AHL	46	2549	25	18	...	...	88	10	2.07	.924	8	444	2	4	21	0	2.84	.903
05-06—Hershey	AHL	61	3538	34	19	6	...	153	3	2.59	.908	14	889	11	3	28	4	1.89	.936
—Washington	NHL	1	59	0	1	0	...	4	0	4.07	.867	—	—	—	—	—	—	—	—
NHL Totals (3 years)		9	489	3	5	0	0	32	0	3.93	.892								

CHARA, ZDENO D

PERSONAL: Born March 18, 1977, in Trencin, Czech. ... 6-9/260. ... Shoots left. ... Name pronounced zuh-DAY-noh CHAH-ruh.

TRANSACTIONS/CAREER NOTES: Selected by New York Islanders in third round (third Islanders pick, 56th overall) of entry draft (June 22, 1996). ... Left shoulder (January 10, 2000); missed 16 games. ... Flu (April 9, 2000); missed one game. ... Traded by Islanders with RW Bill Muckalt and first-round pick (C Jason Spezza) in 2001 draft to Ottawa Senators for C Alexei Yashin (June 23, 2001). ... Left shoulder (January 12, 2002); missed three games. ... Flu (March 23, 2002); missed four games. ... Bruised chest (February 15, 2003); missed eight games. ... Upper body (February 3, 2004); missed two games. ... Bruised right foot (March 5, 2004); missed one game. ... Suspended one game for instigating an altercation with Kings D Tim Gleason in the last five minutes of play (December 3, 2005). ... Hand (March 23, 2006); missed 10 games. ... Signed as a free agent by Boston Bruins (July 1, 2006).

Season Team	League	GP	G	A	Pts.	PIM	+/-	PP	SH	GP	G	A	Pts.	PIM
		REGULAR SEASON								PLAYOFFS				
94-95—Dukla Trencin	Slovakia Jrs.	2	0	0	0	2	...	...	...	—	—	—	—	—
95-96—Dukla Trencin	Slovakia Jrs.	22	1	13	14	80	...	...	...	—	—	—	—	—
—HC Piestany	Slov. Div.	10	1	3	4	10	...	...	...	—	—	—	—	—
—Sparta Praha Jrs.	Czech Rep.	15	1	2	3	42	...	...	...	—	—	—	—	—
—Sparta Praha	Czech Rep.	1	0	0	0	0	...	...	...	—	—	—	—	—
96-97—Prince George	WHL	49	3	19	22	120	-5	0	1	15	1	7	8	45
97-98—Kentucky	AHL	48	4	9	13	125	0	0	0	1	0	0	0	4
—New York Islanders	NHL	25	0	1	1	50	1	0	0	—	—	—	—	—
98-99—Lowell	AHL	23	2	2	4	47	5	0	0	—	—	—	—	—
—New York Islanders	NHL	59	2	6	8	83	-8	0	1	—	—	—	—	—
99-00—New York Islanders	NHL	65	2	9	11	57	-27	0	0	—	—	—	—	—
00-01—New York Islanders	NHL	82	2	7	9	157	-27	0	1	—	—	—	—	—
01-02—Dukla Trencin	Slovakia	8	2	2	4	32	...	...	...	—	—	—	—	—
—Ottawa	NHL	75	10	13	23	156	30	4	1	10	0	1	1	12

Season Team	League	REGULAR SEASON GP	G	A	Pts.	PIM	+/-	PP	SH	PLAYOFFS GP	G	A	Pts.	PIM
02-03—Ottawa	NHL	74	9	30	39	116	29	3	0	18	1	6	7	14
03-04—Ottawa	NHL	79	16	25	41	147	33	7	0	7	1	1	2	8
04-05—Farjestad Karlstad	Sweden	33	10	15	25	132	24	5	0	13	3	5	8	82
05-06—Ottawa	NHL	71	16	27	43	135	17	10	1	10	1	3	4	23
—Slovakian Oly. team	Int'l	6	1	1	2	2	6	0	0	—	—	—	—	—
NHL Totals (8 years)		530	57	118	175	901	48	24	4	45	3	11	14	57

CHEECHOO, JONATHAN RW

PERSONAL: Born July 15, 1980, in Moose Factory, Ont. ... 6-1/190. ... Shoots right.
TRANSACTIONS/CAREER NOTES: Selected by San Jose Sharks in second round (second Sharks pick, 29th overall) of entry draft (June 27, 1998). ... Injured torso (January 10, 2004); missed two games.

Season Team	League	REGULAR SEASON GP	G	A	Pts.	PIM	+/-	PP	SH	PLAYOFFS GP	G	A	Pts.	PIM
96-97—Kitchener Jr. B	OHA	43	35	41	76	33	...	...	...	—	—	—	—	—
97-98—Belleville	OHL	64	31	45	76	62	...	...	...	10	4	2	6	10
98-99—Belleville	OHL	63	35	47	82	74	23	...	...	21	15	15	30	27
99-00—Belleville	OHL	66	45	46	91	102	25	13	3	16	5	12	17	16
00-01—Kentucky	AHL	75	32	34	66	63	...	...	...	3	0	0	0	0
01-02—Cleveland	AHL	53	21	25	46	54	-6	7	2	—	—	—	—	—
02-03—Cleveland	AHL	9	3	4	7	16	0	1	0	—	—	—	—	—
—San Jose	NHL	66	9	7	16	39	-5	0	0	—	—	—	—	—
03-04—San Jose	NHL	81	28	19	47	33	5	8	0	17	4	6	10	10
04-05—HV 71 Jonkoping	Sweden	20	5	0	5	10	-11	1	0	—	—	—	—	—
05-06—San Jose	NHL	82	*56	37	93	58	23	24	2	11	4	5	9	8
NHL Totals (3 years)		229	93	63	156	130	23	32	2	28	8	11	19	18

CHELIOS, CHRIS D

PERSONAL: Born January 25, 1962, in Chicago. ... 6-1/190. ... Shoots right. ... Name pronounced CHEH-lee-ohz.
TRANSACTIONS/CAREER NOTES: Selected by Montreal Canadiens in second round (fifth Canadiens pick, 40th overall) of entry draft (June 10, 1981). ... Right ankle (January 1985). ... Left knee (April 1985). ... Knee (December 19, 1985). ... Knee (January 20, 1986). ... Back spasms (October 1986). ... Fractured finger on left hand (December 1987). ... Bruised tailbone (February 7, 1988). ... Knee (February 1990). ... Abdominal surgery (April 30, 1990). ... Traded by Canadiens with second-round pick (C Michael Pomichter) in 1991 to Chicago Blackhawks for C Denis Savard (June 29, 1990). ... Cut left temple (February 9, 1991). ... Suspended four games (October 15, 1993). ... Suspended four games in eye-scratching incident (February 5, 1994). ... Knee (March 1, 1997); missed eight games. ... Back (April 6, 1997); missed one game. ... Groin (November 12, 1998); missed five games. ... Traded by Blackhawks to Detroit Red Wings for D Anders Eriksson, first-round pick (D Steve McCarthy) in 1999 and first-round pick (G Adam Munro) in 2001 (March 23, 1999). ... Groin (April 7, 1999); missed two games. ... Injured (April 7, 2000); missed one game. ... Knee surgery (October 18, 2000); missed five games. ... Knee surgery (November 20, 2000); missed 44 games. ... Fractured thumb (March 17, 2001); missed final seven games of regular season. ... Knee (December 9, 2003); missed 10 games. ... Right shoulder (February 25, 2004); missed three games. ... Upper-body injury (April 27, 2004); missed final four games of playoffs.

Season Team	League	REGULAR SEASON GP	G	A	Pts.	PIM	+/-	PP	SH	PLAYOFFS GP	G	A	Pts.	PIM
79-80—Moose Jaw	SJHL	53	12	31	43	118	...	...	...	—	—	—	—	—
80-81—Moose Jaw	SJHL	54	23	64	87	175	...	...	...	—	—	—	—	—
81-82—Wisconsin	WCHA	43	6	43	49	50	...	...	...	—	—	—	—	—
82-83—Wisconsin	WCHA	45	16	32	48	62	...	...	...	—	—	—	—	—
83-84—U.S. national team	Int'l	60	14	35	49	58	...	...	...	—	—	—	—	—
—U.S. Olympic team	Int'l	6	0	3	3	8	...	...	...	—	—	—	—	—
—Montreal	NHL	12	0	2	2	12	-5	0	0	15	1	9	10	17
84-85—Montreal	NHL	74	9	55	64	87	11	2	1	9	2	8	10	17
85-86—Montreal	NHL	41	8	26	34	67	4	2	0	20	2	9	11	49
86-87—Montreal	NHL	71	11	33	44	124	-5	6	0	17	4	9	13	38
87-88—Montreal	NHL	71	20	41	61	172	14	10	1	11	3	1	4	29
88-89—Montreal	NHL	80	15	58	73	185	35	8	0	21	4	15	19	28
89-90—Montreal	NHL	53	9	22	31	136	20	1	2	5	0	1	1	8
90-91—Chicago	NHL	77	12	52	64	192	23	5	2	6	1	7	8	46
91-92—Chicago	NHL	80	9	47	56	245	24	2	2	18	6	15	21	37
92-93—Chicago	NHL	84	15	58	73	282	14	8	0	4	0	2	2	14
93-94—Chicago	NHL	76	16	44	60	212	12	7	1	6	1	1	2	8
94-95—Biel-Bienne	Switzerland	3	0	3	3	4	...	...	...	—	—	—	—	—
—Chicago	NHL	48	5	33	38	72	17	3	1	16	4	7	11	12
95-96—Chicago	NHL	81	14	58	72	140	25	7	0	9	0	3	3	8
96-97—Chicago	NHL	72	10	38	48	112	16	2	0	6	0	1	1	8
97-98—Chicago	NHL	81	3	39	42	151	-7	1	0	—	—	—	—	—
—U.S. Olympic team	Int'l	4	2	0	2	2	-2	1	0	—	—	—	—	—
98-99—Chicago	NHL	65	8	26	34	89	-4	2	1	—	—	—	—	—
—Detroit	NHL	10	1	1	2	4	5	1	0	10	0	4	4	14
99-00—Detroit	NHL	81	3	31	34	103	48	0	0	9	0	1	1	8
00-01—Detroit	NHL	24	0	3	3	45	4	0	0	5	1	0	1	2
01-02—Detroit	NHL	79	6	33	39	126	*40	1	0	23	1	13	14	44
—U.S. Olympic team	Int'l	6	1	0	1	4	...	...	...	—	—	—	—	—
02-03—Detroit	NHL	66	2	17	19	78	4	0	1	4	0	0	0	2
03-04—Detroit	NHL	69	2	19	21	61	12	0	0	8	0	1	1	4
04-05—Motor City	UHL	23	5	19	24	25	13	3	1	—	—	—	—	—
05-06—Detroit	NHL	81	4	7	11	108	22	1	1	6	0	0	0	6
—U.S. Olympic team	Int'l	6	0	1	1	2	-1	0	0	—	—	—	—	—
NHL Totals (22 years)		1476	182	743	925	2803	329	69	13	228	30	107	137	399

CHIMERA, JASON — LW

PERSONAL: Born May 2, 1979, in Edmonton. ... 6-2/206. ... Shoots left. ... Name pronounced chihm-AIR-uh.

TRANSACTIONS/CAREER NOTES: Selected by Edmonton Oilers in fifth round (fifth Oilers pick, 121st overall) of entry draft (June 21, 1997). ... Traded by Oilers with third-round pick (traded to New York Rangers; Rangers selected C Billy Ryan) in 2004 to Phoenix Coyotes for second- (LW Geoff Pankovich) and fourth-round (LW Liam Reddox) picks in 2004 (June 26, 2004). ... Ribs (October 2, 2005); missed two games. ... Traded by Coyotes with D Cale Hulse and C Mike Rupp to Columbus Blue Jackets for LW Geoff Sanderson and RW Tim Jackman (October 8, 2005).

		REGULAR SEASON								PLAYOFFS				
Season Team	**League**	**GP**	**G**	**A**	**Pts.**	**PIM**	**+/-**	**PP**	**SH**	**GP**	**G**	**A**	**Pts.**	**PIM**
96-97—Medicine Hat	WHL	71	16	23	39	64	...	...	...	4	0	1	1	4
97-98—Medicine Hat	WHL	72	34	32	66	93	-34	13	0	—	—	—	—	—
—Hamilton	AHL	4	0	0	0	8	-2	0	0	—	—	—	—	—
98-99—Medicine Hat	WHL	37	18	22	40	84	...	...	...	—	—	—	—	—
—Brandon	WHL	21	14	12	26	32	...	...	...	5	4	1	5	8
99-00—Hamilton	AHL	78	15	13	28	77	...	...	...	10	0	2	2	12
00-01—Hamilton	AHL	78	29	25	54	93	...	...	...	—	—	—	—	—
—Edmonton	NHL	1	0	0	0	0	0	0	0	—	—	—	—	—
01-02—Hamilton	AHL	77	26	51	77	158	28	7	3	15	4	6	10	10
—Edmonton	NHL	3	1	0	1	0	-3	0	0	—	—	—	—	—
02-03—Edmonton	NHL	66	14	9	23	36	-2	0	1	2	0	2	2	0
03-04—Edmonton	NHL	60	4	8	12	57	-1	0	0	—	—	—	—	—
04-05—Varese	Italy	15	6	3	9	34	...	...	...	5	2	1	3	31
05-06—Columbus	NHL	80	17	13	30	95	-10	1	1	—	—	—	—	—
NHL Totals (5 years)		210	36	30	66	188	-16	1	2	2	0	2	2	0

CHOUINARD, ERIC — RW

PERSONAL: Born July 8, 1980, in Atlanta. ... 6-3/215. ... Shoots left. ... Son of Guy Chouinard, C with Atlanta/Calgary Flames (1974-83) and St. Louis Blues (1983-84); and cousin of Marc Chouinard, C, Vancouver Canucks. ... Name pronounced Shwee-NAHRD.

TRANSACTIONS/CAREER NOTES: Selected by Montreal Canadiens in first round (first Canadiens pick, 16th overall) of entry draft (June 27, 1998). ... Traded by Canadiens to Philadelphia Flyers for second-round pick (C Maxime Lapierre) in 2003 (January 29, 2003). ... Traded by Flyers to Minnesota Wild for fifth-round pick (D Chris Zarb) in 2004 (December 17, 2003). ... Signed as free agent by Flyers (August 22, 2005). ... Traded by Flyers to Phoenix Coyotes for C Kiel McLeod (December 28, 2005).

		REGULAR SEASON								PLAYOFFS				
Season Team	**League**	**GP**	**G**	**A**	**Pts.**	**PIM**	**+/-**	**PP**	**SH**	**GP**	**G**	**A**	**Pts.**	**PIM**
97-98—Quebec	QMJHL	68	41	42	83	18	...	...	...	14	7	10	17	6
98-99—Quebec	QMJHL	62	50	59	109	56	35	15	7	13	8	10	18	8
99-00—Quebec	QMJHL	50	57	47	104	105	23	16	6	11	14	4	18	8
—Fredericton	AHL	...	...	...	...	...	...	...	...	6	3	2	5	0
00-01—Quebec	AHL	48	12	21	33	6	...	...	...	9	2	0	2	2
—Montreal	NHL	13	1	3	4	0	0	1	0	—	—	—	—	—
01-02—Quebec	AHL	65	19	23	42	18	-7	1	0	2	0	0	0	0
02-03—Utah	AHL	32	12	12	24	16	2	4	0	—	—	—	—	—
—Philadelphia	NHL	28	4	4	8	8	2	1	0	—	—	—	—	—
03-04—Philadelphia	NHL	17	3	0	3	0	-3	0	0	—	—	—	—	—
—Philadelphia	AHL	1	0	0	0	0	...	0	0	—	—	—	—	—
—Minnesota	NHL	31	3	4	7	6	-7	0	0	—	—	—	—	—
04-05—Salzburg	Austria	16	5	5	10	42	-7	...	...	—	—	—	—	—
05-06—Philadelphia	AHL	24	7	7	14	4	-8	1	0	—	—	—	—	—
—Philadelphia	NHL	1	0	0	0	2	0	0	0	—	—	—	—	—
—San Antonio	AHL	47	8	12	20	22	-19	3	0	—	—	—	—	—
NHL Totals (4 years)		90	11	11	22	16	-8	2	0					

CHOUINARD, MARC — C

PERSONAL: Born May 6, 1977, in Charlesbourg, Que. ... 6-5/218. ... Shoots right. ... Cousin of Eric Chouinard, RW, Phoenix Coyotes; and nephew of Guy Chouinard, C with Atlanta/Calgary Flames (1974-83) and St. Louis Blues (1983-84). ... Name pronounced shwee-NAHRD.

TRANSACTIONS/CAREER NOTES: Selected by Winnipeg Jets in second round (second Jets pick, 3second overall) of entry draft (July 8, 1995). ... Traded by Jets with RW Teemu Selanne and fourth-round pick (traded to Toronto; traded to Montreal; Canadiens picked C Kim Staal) in 1996 to Anaheim Mighty Ducks for C Chad Kilger, D Oleg Tverdovsky and third-round pick (D Per-Anton Lundstrom) in 1996 (February 7, 1996). ... Tore Achilles' tendon (October 31, 1997); missed remainder of season. ... Injured (October 8, 2001); missed one game. ... Knee (October 14, 2001); missed one game. ... Shoulder (February 27, 2002); missed remainder of season. ... Strained neck, concussion (January 5, 2003); missed three games. ... Signed as free agent by Minnesota Wild (July 28, 2003). ... Fractured jaw (November 14, 2003); missed 32 games. ... Bruised left thumb (February 27, 2004); missed four games. ... Shoulder (November 3, 2005); missed seven games. ... Neck strain (January 31. 2006); missed one game. ... Signed as free agent by Vancouver Canucks (July 10, 2006).

		REGULAR SEASON								PLAYOFFS				
Season Team	**League**	**GP**	**G**	**A**	**Pts.**	**PIM**	**+/-**	**PP**	**SH**	**GP**	**G**	**A**	**Pts.**	**PIM**
93-94—Beauport	QMJHL	62	11	19	30	23	...	...	...	13	2	5	7	2
94-95—Beauport	QMJHL	68	24	40	64	32	40	5	0	18	1	6	7	4
95-96—Beauport	QMJHL	30	14	21	35	19	...	...	...	—	—	—	—	—
—Halifax	QMJHL	24	6	12	18	17	...	...	...	6	2	1	3	2
96-97—Halifax	QMJHL	63	24	49	73	52	...	...	...	18	10	16	26	12
97-98—Cincinnati	AHL	8	1	2	3	4	0	0	0	—	—	—	—	—
98-99—Cincinnati	AHL	69	7	8	15	20	-11	2	0	3	0	0	0	4
99-00—Cincinnati	AHL	70	17	16	33	29	...	...	...	—	—	—	—	—
00-01—Cincinnati	AHL	32	10	9	19	4	...	...	...	—	—	—	—	—
—Anaheim	NHL	44	3	4	7	12	-5	0	0	—	—	—	—	—

		REGULAR SEASON								PLAYOFFS				
Season Team	**League**	**GP**	**G**	**A**	**Pts.**	**PIM**	**+/-**	**PP**	**SH**	**GP**	**G**	**A**	**Pts.**	**PIM**
01-02—Anaheim	NHL	45	4	5	9	10	2	0	0	—	—	—	—	—
02-03—Anaheim	NHL	70	3	4	7	40	-9	0	1	15	1	0	1	0
03-04—Minnesota	NHL	45	11	10	21	17	4	3	1	—	—	—	—	—
04-05—Frisk	Norway	16	9	8	17	26	5	...	...	3	5	2	7	24
05-06—Minnesota	NHL	74	14	16	30	34	1	6	2	—	—	—	—	—
NHL Totals (5 years)		278	35	39	74	113	-7	9	4	15	1	0	1	0

CHRISTENSEN, ERIK C

PERSONAL: Born December 17, 1983, in Edmonton. ... 6-1/185. ... Shoots left.
TRANSACTIONS/CAREER NOTES: Selected by Pittsburgh Penguins in third round (third Penguins pick, 69th overall) of NHL entry draft (June 22, 2002).

		REGULAR SEASON								PLAYOFFS				
Season Team	**League**	**GP**	**G**	**A**	**Pts.**	**PIM**	**+/-**	**PP**	**SH**	**GP**	**G**	**A**	**Pts.**	**PIM**
99-00—Kamloops	WHL	66	9	5	14	41	...	...	...	—	—	—	—	—
00-01—Kamloops	WHL	72	21	23	44	36	...	...	...	—	—	—	—	—
01-02—Kamloops	WHL	70	22	36	58	68	...	...	...	—	—	—	—	—
02-03—Kamloops	WHL	67	54	54	108	60	...	...	...	6	1	7	8	14
03-04—Kamloops	WHL	29	10	14	24	40	...	...	...	—	—	—	—	—
—Brandon	WHL	34	17	21	38	20	...	...	...	11	8	4	12	8
04-05—Wilkes-Barre/Scranton	AHL	77	14	13	27	33	-1	4	0	11	1	6	7	4
05-06—Pittsburgh	NHL	33	6	7	13	34	-3	2	0	—	—	—	—	—
—Wilkes-Barre/Scranton	AHL	48	24	22	46	50	10	11	1	11	2	2	4	2
NHL Totals (1 year)		33	6	7	13	34	-3	2	0					

CIBAK, MARTIN C

PERSONAL: Born May 17, 1980, in Liptovmikulas, Czechoslovakia. ... 6-1/196. ... Shoots left. ... Name pronounced SEE-back.
TRANSACTIONS/CAREER NOTES: Selected by Tampa Bay Lightning in eighth round (11th Lightning pick, 252nd overall) of NHL draft (June 28, 1998).

		REGULAR SEASON								PLAYOFFS				
Season Team	**League**	**GP**	**G**	**A**	**Pts.**	**PIM**	**+/-**	**PP**	**SH**	**GP**	**G**	**A**	**Pts.**	**PIM**
95-96—Liptovsky Mikulas	Slovakia Jrs.	48	38	35	73	...	...	...	...	—	—	—	—	—
96-97—Liptovsky Mikulas	Slovakia Jrs.	45	22	18	40	...	...	...	...	—	—	—	—	—
97-98—Liptovsky Mikulas	Slovakia Jrs.	42	31	21	52	...	...	...	...	—	—	—	—	—
—HK 32 Lip. Mikulas	Slovakia	28	1	3	4	10	...	...	...	—	—	—	—	—
98-99—Medicine Hat	WHL	66	21	26	47	72	-21	6	1	—	—	—	—	—
99-00—Medicine Hat	WHL	58	16	29	45	77	5	4	0	—	—	—	—	—
00-01—Detroit	IHL	79	10	28	38	88	...	...	...	—	—	—	—	—
01-02—Springfield	AHL	52	5	9	14	44	-10	0	0	—	—	—	—	—
—Tampa Bay	NHL	26	1	5	6	8	-6	0	0	—	—	—	—	—
02-03—Springfield	AHL	62	5	15	20	78	-6	0	0	—	—	—	—	—
03-04—Tampa Bay	NHL	63	2	7	9	30	-1	0	0	6	0	1	1	0
—Hershey	AHL	1	0	0	0	2	-1	0	0	—	—	—	—	—
04-05—HK 32 Lip. Mikulas	Slovakia	4	0	0	0	6	-3	...	...	—	—	—	—	—
—Plzen	Czech Rep.	30	4	11	15	52	5	...	...	—	—	—	—	—
—HC Kosice	Slovakia	6	1	3	4	8	2	...	...	10	2	5	7	36
05-06—Tampa Bay	NHL	65	2	6	8	22	-9	0	0	5	0	0	0	0
NHL Totals (3 years)		154	5	18	23	60	-16	0	0	11	0	1	1	0

CLARK, BRETT D

PERSONAL: Born December 23, 1976, in Wapella, Sask. ... 6-0/195. ... Shoots left.
TRANSACTIONS/CAREER NOTES: Selected by Montreal Canadiens in sixth round (seventh Canadiens pick, 154th overall) of NHL draft (June 22, 1996). ... Suffered concussion (November 19, 1998); missed four games. ... Selected by Atlanta Thrashers in expansion draft (June 25, 1999). ... Traded by Thrashers to Colorado Avalanche for G Frederic Cassivi (January 24, 2002). ... Flu (November 21, 2005); missed one game.

		REGULAR SEASON								PLAYOFFS				
Season Team	**League**	**GP**	**G**	**A**	**Pts.**	**PIM**	**+/-**	**PP**	**SH**	**GP**	**G**	**A**	**Pts.**	**PIM**
94-95—Melville	SJHL	62	19	32	51	77	...	...	...	—	—	—	—	—
95-96—Maine	Hockey East	39	7	31	38	22	...	...	...	—	—	—	—	—
96-97—Canadian nat'l team	Int'l	60	12	20	32	87	...	...	...	—	—	—	—	—
97-98—Montreal	NHL	41	1	0	1	20	-3	0	0	—	—	—	—	—
—Fredericton	AHL	20	0	6	6	6	1	0	0	4	0	1	1	17
98-99—Montreal	NHL	61	2	2	4	16	-3	0	0	—	—	—	—	—
—Fredericton	AHL	3	1	0	1	0	2	0	0	—	—	—	—	—
99-00—Orlando	IHL	63	9	17	26	31	...	...	...	6	0	1	1	0
—Atlanta	NHL	14	0	1	1	4	-12	0	0	—	—	—	—	—
00-01—Atlanta	NHL	28	1	2	3	14	-12	0	0	—	—	—	—	—
—Orlando	IHL	43	2	9	11	32	...	...	...	15	1	6	7	2
01-02—Chicago	AHL	42	3	17	20	18	15	1	1	—	—	—	—	—
—Atlanta	NHL	2	0	0	0	0	-3	0	0	—	—	—	—	—
—Hershey	AHL	32	7	9	16	12	...	...	...	8	0	2	2	6
02-03—Hershey	AHL	80	8	27	35	26	-1	5	0	5	0	4	4	4

Season Team	League	GP	G	A	Pts.	PIM	+/-	PP	SH		GP	G	A	Pts.	PIM
		REGULAR SEASON									PLAYOFFS				
03-04—Hershey	AHL	64	11	21	32	35	-7	6	0		—	—	—	—	—
—Colorado	NHL	12	1	1	2	6	3	0	0		—	—	—	—	—
04-05—Hershey	AHL	67	7	37	44	54	1	3	0		—	—	—	—	—
05-06—Colorado	NHL	80	9	27	36	56	3	4	0		9	2	2	4	2
NHL Totals (7 years)		238	14	33	47	116	-27	4	0		9	2	2	4	2

CLARK, CHRIS — RW

PERSONAL: Born March 8, 1976, in South Windsor, Conn. ... 6-0/200. ... Shoots right.

TRANSACTIONS/CAREER NOTES: Selected by Calgary Flames in third round (third Flames pick, 77th overall) of NHL draft (June 29, 1994). ... Injured shoulder (January 15, 2000); missed one game. ... Injured (March 31, 2000); missed remainder of season. ... Injured hip (November 7, 2001); missed two games. ... Injured (December 6, 2001); missed one game. ... Bruised thigh (December 19, 2001); missed two games. ... Injured knee (January 19, 2002); missed 10 games. ... Traded by Flames with seventh-round pick in 2007 draft to Washington Capitals for sixth-round pick (LW Devin Didiomete) in 2006 draft and seventh-round pick in 2007 draft (August 4, 2005). ... Injured rib (September 2005); missed first game of season. ... Fined $2,000 for unpenalized elbow to the head of Flyers D Eric Desjardins (November 4, 2005). ... Groin strain (February 4, 2006); missed three games.

Season Team	League	GP	G	A	Pts.	PIM	+/-	PP	SH		GP	G	A	Pts.	PIM
		REGULAR SEASON									PLAYOFFS				
93-94—Springfield Jr. B	NEJHL	35	31	26	57	185	...	...	...		—	—	—	—	—
94-95—Clarkson	ECAC	32	12	11	23	92	...	5	0		—	—	—	—	—
95-96—Clarkson	ECAC	38	10	8	18	108	...	...	...		—	—	—	—	—
96-97—Clarkson	ECAC	37	23	25	48	86	...	8	0		—	—	—	—	—
97-98—Clarkson	ECAC	35	18	21	39	106	...	...	...		—	—	—	—	—
98-99—Saint John	AHL	73	13	27	40	123	-10	2	0		7	2	4	6	15
99-00—Saint John	AHL	48	16	17	33	134	...	...	...		—	—	—	—	—
—Calgary	NHL	22	0	1	1	14	-3	0	0		—	—	—	—	—
00-01—Saint John	AHL	48	18	17	35	131	...	...	...		18	4	10	14	49
—Calgary	NHL	29	5	1	6	38	0	1	0		—	—	—	—	—
01-02—Calgary	NHL	64	10	7	17	79	-12	2	1		—	—	—	—	—
02-03—Calgary	NHL	81	10	12	22	126	-11	2	0		—	—	—	—	—
03-04—Calgary	NHL	82	10	15	25	106	-3	4	0		26	3	3	6	30
04-05—Bern	Switzerland	3	0	0	0	6	...	0	0		—	—	—	—	—
—Storhamar	Norway	15	10	4	14	86	6	...	...		7	4	4	8	14
05-06—Washington	NHL	78	20	19	39	110	9	1	3		—	—	—	—	—
NHL Totals (6 years)		356	55	55	110	473	-20	10	4		26	3	3	6	30

CLARKE, NOAH — LW

PERSONAL: Born June 11, 1979, in LaVerne, Calif. ... 5-10/193. ... Shoots left.

TRANSACTIONS/CAREER NOTES: Selected by Los Angeles Kings in 10th round (10th Kings pick, 250th overall) in entry draft (June 26, 1999).

Season Team	League	GP	G	A	Pts.	PIM	+/-	PP	SH		GP	G	A	Pts.	PIM
		REGULAR SEASON									PLAYOFFS				
99-00—Colorado College	WCHA	39	17	20	37	30	...	...	...		—	—	—	—	—
00-01—Colorado College	WCHA	41	12	20	32	22	...	...	...		—	—	—	—	—
01-02—Colorado College	WCHA	42	13	24	37	32	...	...	...		—	—	—	—	—
02-03—Colorado College	WCHA	42	21	49	70	15	...	...	...		—	—	—	—	—
—Manchester	AHL	3	1	1	2	0	...	...	...		—	—	—	—	—
03-04—Manchester	AHL	71	25	26	51	24	20	6	0		6	3	1	4	4
—Los Angeles	NHL	2	0	1	1	0	1	0	0		—	—	—	—	—
04-05—Manchester	AHL	61	21	24	45	24	24	6	4		6	1	0	1	4
05-06—Manchester	AHL	69	14	30	44	33	6	6	1		7	4	4	8	2
—Los Angeles	NHL	5	0	0	0	0	0	0	0		—	—	—	—	—
NHL Totals (2 years)		7	0	1	1	0	1	0	0						

CLEARY, DANIEL — RW/LW

PERSONAL: Born December 18, 1978, in Carbonear, Nfld. ... 6-0/203. ... Shoots left.

TRANSACTIONS/CAREER NOTES: Selected by Chicago Blackhawks in first round (first Blackhawks pick, 13th overall) of entry draft (June 21, 1997). ... Traded by Blackhawks with C Chad Kilger, LW Ethan Moreau and D Christian Laflamme to Edmonton Oilers for D Boris Mironov, LW Dean McAmmond and D Jonas Elofsson (March 20, 1999). ... Left knee surgery (December 8, 2001); missed 14 games. ... Signed as free agent by Phoenix Coyotes (July 15, 2003). ... Elbow (November 19, 2003); missed one game. ... Separated shoulder (December 12, 2003); missed six games. ... Signed as free agent by Detroit Red Wings (October 4, 2005). ... Flu (March 23, 2005); missed two games. ... Right shoulder (April 2, 2006); missed three games.

Season Team	League	GP	G	A	Pts.	PIM	+/-	PP	SH		GP	G	A	Pts.	PIM
		REGULAR SEASON									PLAYOFFS				
93-94—Kingston	Tier II Jr. A	41	18	28	46	33	...	...	...		—	—	—	—	—
94-95—Belleville	OHL	62	26	55	81	62	...	...	...		16	7	10	17	23
95-96—Belleville	OHL	64	53	62	115	74	...	...	...		14	10	17	27	40
96-97—Belleville	OHL	64	32	48	80	88	-11	12	1		6	3	4	7	6
97-98—Chicago	NHL	6	0	0	0	0	-2	0	0		—	—	—	—	—
—Indianapolis	IHL	4	2	1	3	6	1	0	0		—	—	—	—	—
—Belleville	OHL	30	16	31	47	14	9	...	...		10	6	17	23	10
98-99—Chicago	NHL	35	4	5	9	24	-1	0	0		—	—	—	—	—
—Portland	AHL	30	9	17	26	74	-3	4	0		—	—	—	—	—
—Hamilton	AHL	9	0	1	1	7	-5	0	0		3	0	0	0	0

Season Team	League	REGULAR SEASON GP	G	A	Pts.	PIM	+/-	PP	SH	PLAYOFFS GP	G	A	Pts.	PIM
99-00—Hamilton	AHL	58	22	52	74	108	...	...	...	5	2	3	5	18
—Edmonton	NHL	17	3	2	5	8	-1	0	0	4	0	1	1	2
00-01—Edmonton	NHL	81	14	21	35	37	5	2	0	6	1	1	2	8
01-02—Edmonton	NHL	65	10	19	29	51	-1	2	1	—	—	—	—	—
02-03—Edmonton	NHL	57	4	13	17	31	5	0	0	—	—	—	—	—
03-04—Phoenix	NHL	68	6	11	17	42	-8	0	3	—	—	—	—	—
04-05—Mora	Sweden Dv. 2	47	11	26	37	138	-18	2	1	—	—	—	—	—
05-06—Detroit	NHL	77	3	12	15	40	5	0	0	6	0	1	1	6
NHL Totals (8 years)		406	44	83	127	233	2	4	4	16	1	3	4	16

CLEMMENSEN, SCOTT G

PERSONAL: Born July 23, 1977, in Des Moines, Iowa. ... 6-3/205. ... Catches left.
TRANSACTIONS/CAREER NOTES: Selected by New Jersey Devils in eighth round (seventh Devils pick, 215th overall) of NHL draft (June 21, 1997). ... Flu (April 5, 2006); missed one game.

Season Team	League	REGULAR SEASON GP	Min.	W	L	OTL	T	GA	SO	GAA	SV%	PLAYOFFS GP	Min.	W	L	GA	SO	GAA	SV%
96-97—Des Moines	USHL	36	2042	...	...	...	...	111	1	3.26	...	—	—	—	—	—	—	—	—
97-98—Boston College	Hockey East	37	2205	24	9	...	4	102	4	2.78	...	—	—	—	—	—	—	—	—
98-99—Boston College	Hockey East	42	2507	26	12	...	4	120	1	2.87	...	—	—	—	—	—	—	—	—
99-00—Boston College	Hockey East	29	1610	19	7	...	0	59	3	2.20	...	—	—	—	—	—	—	—	—
00-01—Boston College	Hockey East	39	2312	30	7	...	2	82	3	2.13	...	—	—	—	—	—	—	—	—
01-02—New Jersey	NHL	2	20	0	0	...	0	1	0	3.00	.800	—	—	—	—	—	—	—	—
—Albany	AHL	29	1676	5	19	...	4	92	0	3.29	.899	—	—	—	—	—	—	—	—
02-03—Albany	AHL	47	2694	12	24	...	8	119	1	2.65	.910	—	—	—	—	—	—	—	—
03-04—New Jersey	NHL	4	238	3	1	...	0	4	2	1.01	.952	—	—	—	—	—	—	—	—
—Albany	AHL	22	1309	5	12	...	4	67	0	3.07	.891	—	—	—	—	—	—	—	—
04-05—Albany	AHL	46	2644	13	25	...	...	124	2	2.81	.916	—	—	—	—	—	—	—	—
05-06—Albany	AHL	1	59	0	1	0	...	5	0	5.08	.848	—	—	—	—	—	—	—	—
—New Jersey	NHL	13	627	3	4	2	...	35	0	3.35	.881	1	7	0	0	0	0	0.00	1.000
NHL Totals (3 years)		19	885	6	5	2	0	40	2	2.71	.896	1	7	0	0	0	0	0.00	1.000

CLOUTIER, DAN G

PERSONAL: Born April 22, 1976, in Mont-Laurier, Que. ... 6-1/195. ... Catches left. ... Brother of Sylvain Cloutier, C, New Jersey Devils organization (1999-2004). ... Name pronounced KLOO-tee-yay.
TRANSACTIONS/CAREER NOTES: Selected by New York Rangers in first round (first Rangers pick, 26th overall) of entry draft (June 28, 1994). ... Traded by Rangers with LW Niklas Sundstrom and first- (RW Nikita Alexeev) and third-round (traded to San Jose) picks in 2000 draft to Tampa Bay Lightning for first-round pick (RW Pavel Brendl) in 1999 draft (June 26, 1999). ... Strained groin (November 18, 1999); missed two games. ... Suspended four games for kicking incident (January 14, 2000). ... Strained groin (February 21, 2000); missed three games. ... Injured neck (March 14, 2000); missed four games. ... Strained knee (March 28, 2000); missed five games. ... Strained biceps (October 22, 2000); missed nine games. ... Flu (December 8, 2000); missed one game. ... Traded by Lightning to Vancouver Canucks for D Adrian Aucoin and second-round pick (C/LW Alexander Polushin) in 2001 draft (February 7, 2001). ... Injured ankle (January 23, 2002); missed nine games. ... Injured knee (December 28, 2002); missed three games. ... Sprained knee (March 18, 2003); missed 10 games. ... Injured knee (March 27, 2003); missed two games. ... Injured knee (March 30, 2003); missed one game. ... Injured groin (December 9, 2003); missed three games. ... Injured hip flexor (March 18, 2004); missed two games. ... Concussion and whiplash (October 29, 2005); missed five games. ... Partially torn ACL in left knee (November 20, 2005) and surgery (December 15, 2005); missed final 60 games of regular season. ... Traded by Canucks to Kings for second-round selection in 2007 draft and conditional pick in 2009 draft (July 5, 2006).

Season Team	League	REGULAR SEASON GP	Min.	W	L	OTL	T	GA	SO	GAA	SV%	PLAYOFFS GP	Min.	W	L	GA	SO	GAA	SV%
91-92—St. Thomas	Jr. B	14	823	...	...	...	...	80	...	5.83	...	—	—	—	—	—	—	—	—
92-93—Sault Ste. Marie	OHL	12	572	4	6	...	0	44	0	4.62	...	4	231	1	2	12	0	3.12	...
93-94—Sault Ste. Marie	OHL	55	2934	28	14	...	6	174	2	3.56	.890	14	833	10	4	52	0	3.75	.887
94-95—Sault Ste. Marie	OHL	45	2517	15	25	...	2	184	1	4.39	.881	—	—	—	—	—	—	—	—
95-96—Sault Ste. Marie	OHL	13	641	9	3	...	0	43	0	4.02	...	—	—	—	—	—	—	—	—
—Guelph	OHL	17	1004	12	2	...	2	35	2	2.09	...	16	993	11	5	52	2	3.14	...
96-97—Binghamton	AHL	60	3367	23	28	...	8	199	3	3.55	.892	4	236	1	3	13	0	3.31	.893
97-98—Hartford	AHL	24	1417	12	8	...	3	62	0	2.63	.917	8	479	5	3	24	0	3.01	.921
—New York Rangers	NHL	12	551	4	5	...	1	23	0	2.50	.907	—	—	—	—	—	—	—	—
98-99—New York Rangers	NHL	22	1097	6	8	...	3	49	0	2.68	.914	—	—	—	—	—	—	—	—
99-00—Tampa Bay	NHL	52	2492	9	30	...	3	145	0	3.49	.885	—	—	—	—	—	—	—	—
00-01—Detroit	IHL	1	59	0	1	...	0	3	0	3.05	...	—	—	—	—	—	—	—	—
—Tampa Bay	NHL	24	1005	3	13	...	3	59	1	3.52	.891	—	—	—	—	—	—	—	—
—Vancouver	NHL	16	914	4	6	...	5	37	0	2.43	.894	2	117	0	2	9	0	4.62	.842
01-02—Vancouver	NHL	62	3502	31	22	...	5	142	7	2.43	.901	6	273	2	3	16	0	3.52	.870
02-03—Vancouver	NHL	57	3376	33	16	...	7	136	2	2.42	.908	14	833	7	7	45	0	3.24	.868
03-04—Vancouver	NHL	60	3539	33	21	...	6	134	5	2.27	.914	3	138	1	1	5	0	2.17	.922
04-05—KAC	Austria	23	1362	13	5	...	4	52	2	2.29	.924	—	—	—	—	—	—	—	—
05-06—Vancouver	NHL	13	681	8	3	1	...	36	0	3.17	.892	—	—	—	—	—	—	—	—
NHL Totals (8 years)		318	17157	131	124	1	33	761	15	2.66	.902	25	1361	10	13	75	0	3.31	.872

CLOWE, RYANE LW/RW

PERSONAL: Born September 30, 1982, in St. John's, Nfld. ... 6-2/205. ... Shoots right.
TRANSACTIONS/CAREER NOTES: Selected by San Jose Sharks in sixth round (fifth Sharks pick, 175th overall) of entry draft (June 24, 2001). ... Ankle (December 30, 2005); missed six games.

Season Team	League	GP	G	A	Pts.	PIM	+/-	PP	SH	GP	G	A	Pts.	PIM
		REGULAR SEASON								PLAYOFFS				
00-01—Rimouski	QMJHL	32	15	10	25	43	...	...	...	11	8	1	9	12
01-02—Rimouski	QMJHL	53	28	45	73	120	...	...	...	7	1	6	7	2
02-03—Rimouski	QMJHL	17	8	19	27	44	...	...	...	—	—	—	—	—
—Montreal	QMJHL	43	18	30	48	60	...	...	...	7	3	7	10	6
03-04—Cleveland	AHL	72	11	29	40	97	...	...	...	8	3	1	4	9
04-05—Cleveland	AHL	74	27	35	62	101	19	14	0	—	—	—	—	—
05-06—Cleveland	AHL	35	13	21	34	35	-22	7	1	—	—	—	—	—
—San Jose	NHL	18	0	2	2	9	-2	0	0	1	0	0	0	0
NHL Totals (1 year)		18	0	2	2	9	-2	0	0	1	0	0	0	0

CLYMER, BEN RW/LW

PERSONAL: Born April 11, 1978, in Edina, Minn. ... 6-1/199. ... Shoots right.

TRANSACTIONS/CAREER NOTES: Selected by Boston Bruins in second round (third Bruins pick, 27th overall) of NHL draft (June 21, 1997). ... Signed as free agent by Tampa Bay Lightning (October 2, 1999). ... Bruised foot (November 2, 2002); missed one game. ... Strained groin (January 2, 2003); missed four games. ... Reinjured groin (January 17, 2003); missed five games. ... Reinjured groin (January 28, 2003); missed two games. ... Reinjured groin (March 20, 2003); missed four games. ... Concussion (December 7, 2003); missed four games. ... Signed as free agent by Washington Capitals (August 8, 2005). ... Groin (October 22, 2005); missed one game. ... Flu (January 25, 2006); missed one game.

C

Season Team	League	GP	G	A	Pts.	PIM	+/-	PP	SH	GP	G	A	Pts.	PIM
		REGULAR SEASON								PLAYOFFS				
93-94—Thomas Jefferson	Minn. H.S.	23	3	7	10	6	...	...	...	—	—	—	—	—
94-95—Thomas Jefferson	Minn. H.S.	28	6	20	26	26	...	...	...	—	—	—	—	—
95-96—Thomas Jefferson	Minn. H.S.	19	12	28	40	38	...	...	...	—	—	—	—	—
96-97—Minnesota	WCHA	29	7	13	20	64	...	...	...	—	—	—	—	—
97-98—Minnesota	WCHA	1	0	0	0	2	...	...	...	—	—	—	—	—
98-99—Seattle	WHL	70	12	44	56	93	21	3	0	11	1	5	6	12
99-00—Detroit	IHL	19	1	9	10	30	...	...	...	—	—	—	—	—
—Tampa Bay	NHL	60	2	6	8	87	-26	2	0	—	—	—	—	—
00-01—Detroit	IHL	53	5	8	13	88	...	...	...	—	—	—	—	—
—Tampa Bay	NHL	23	5	1	6	21	-7	3	0	—	—	—	—	—
01-02—Tampa Bay	NHL	81	14	20	34	36	-10	4	0	—	—	—	—	—
02-03—Tampa Bay	NHL	65	6	12	18	57	-2	1	0	11	0	2	2	6
03-04—Tampa Bay	NHL	66	2	8	10	50	5	0	0	5	0	0	0	0
04-05—Biel-Bienne	Switz. Div. 2	19	12	13	25	30	...	4	1	11	6	11	17	24
05-06—Washington	NHL	77	16	17	33	72	-7	3	0	—	—	—	—	—
NHL Totals (6 years)		372	45	64	109	323	-47	13	0	16	0	2	2	6

COBURN, BRAYDON D

PERSONAL: Born February 27, 1985, in Calgary. ... 6-5/205. ... Shoots left.

TRANSACTIONS/CAREER NOTES: Selected by Atlanta Thrashers in first round (first Thrashers pick, eighth overall) in 2003 NHL entry draft (June 23, 2003).

Season Team	League	GP	G	A	Pts.	PIM	+/-	PP	SH	GP	G	A	Pts.	PIM
		REGULAR SEASON								PLAYOFFS				
00-01—Portland	WHL	2	0	1	1	0	...	...	...	14	0	4	4	2
01-02—Portland	WHL	68	4	33	37	100	...	...	...	—	—	—	—	—
02-03—Portland	WHL	53	3	16	19	147	...	...	...	—	—	—	—	—
03-04—Portland	WHL	55	10	20	30	92	-19	7	0	5	0	1	1	10
04-05—Chicago	AHL	3	0	1	1	5	-1	0	0	18	0	1	1	36
—Portland	WHL	60	12	32	44	144	9	7	0	7	1	5	6	6
05-06—Chicago	AHL	73	6	20	26	136	12	1	0	—	—	—	—	—
—Atlanta	NHL	9	0	1	1	4	-2	0	0	—	—	—	—	—
NHL Totals (1 year)		9	0	1	1	4	-2	0	0					

COLAIACOVO, CARLO D

PERSONAL: Born January 27, 1983, in Toronto. ... 6-1/188. ... Shoots left. ... Name pronounced KOH-lee-ah-kovo.

TRANSACTIONS/CAREER NOTES: Selected by Toronto Maple Leafs in first round (first Maple Leafs pick, 17th overall) of entry draft (June 23, 2001). ... Injured wrist (December 27, 2005); missed five games. ... Concussion (January 23, 2006); missed final 34 games of regular season.

Season Team	League	GP	G	A	Pts.	PIM	+/-	PP	SH	GP	G	A	Pts.	PIM
		REGULAR SEASON								PLAYOFFS				
99-00—Erie	OHL	52	4	18	22	12	...	...	...	13	2	4	6	9
00-01—Erie	OHL	62	12	27	39	59	...	...	...	14	4	7	11	16
01-02—Erie	OHL	60	13	27	40	49	...	...	...	21	7	10	17	20
02-03—Toronto	NHL	2	0	1	1	0	0	0	0	—	—	—	—	—
—Erie	OHL	35	14	21	35	12	...	...	...	—	—	—	—	—
03-04—St. John's	AHL	62	6	25	31	50	-15	1	0	—	—	—	—	—
—Toronto	NHL	2	0	1	1	2	1	0	0	—	—	—	—	—
04-05—St. John's	AHL	49	4	20	24	59	9	2	0	5	0	1	1	2
05-06—Toronto	AHL	14	5	6	11	14	-3	2	0	—	—	—	—	—
—Toronto	NHL	21	2	5	7	17	0	1	0	—	—	—	—	—
NHL Totals (3 years)		25	2	7	9	19	1	1	0					

COLE, ERIK — LW

PERSONAL: Born November 6, 1978, in Oswego, N.Y. ... 6-2/200. ... Shoots left.

TRANSACTIONS/CAREER NOTES: Selected by Carolina Hurricanes in third round (third Hurricanes pick, 71st overall) of NHL draft (June 27, 1998). ... Flu (November 8, 2001); missed one game. ... Fractured leg (February 5, 2003); missed 28 games. ... Injured elbow (November 8, 2003); missed one game. ... Injured hamstring (March 23, 2004); missed one game. ... Injured neck (March 4, 2006); missed remainder of regular season.

STATISTICAL PLATEAUS: Three-goal games: 2001-02 (1), 2002-03 (1). Total: 2.

		REGULAR SEASON								PLAYOFFS				
Season Team	League	GP	G	A	Pts.	PIM	+/-	PP	SH	GP	G	A	Pts.	PIM
96-97—Des Moines	USHL	48	30	34	64	185	...	...	...	—	—	—	—	—
97-98—Clarkson	ECAC	34	11	20	31	55	...	...	...	—	—	—	—	—
98-99—Clarkson	ECAC	36	22	20	42	50	...	...	...	—	—	—	—	—
99-00—Clarkson	ECAC	33	19	11	30	46	...	...	...	—	—	—	—	—
—Cincinnati	IHL	9	4	3	7	2	...	...	...	7	1	1	2	2
00-01—Cincinnati	IHL	69	23	20	43	28	...	...	...	5	1	0	1	2
01-02—Carolina	NHL	81	16	24	40	35	-10	3	0	23	6	3	9	30
02-03—Carolina	NHL	53	14	13	27	72	1	6	2	—	—	—	—	—
03-04—Carolina	NHL	80	18	24	42	93	-4	2	2	—	—	—	—	—
04-05—Eisbaren Berlin	Germany	39	6	21	27	76	7	2	0	8	5	1	6	37
05-06—Carolina	NHL	60	30	29	59	54	19	3	3	2	0	0	0	0
—U.S. Olympic team	Int'l	6	1	2	3	0	0	0	0	—	—	—	—	—
NHL Totals (4 years)		274	78	90	168	254	6	14	7	25	6	3	9	30

COLEMAN, GERALD — G

PERSONAL: Born April 3, 1985, in Chicago. ... 6-4/189. ... Catches right.

TRANSACTIONS/CAREER NOTES: Selected by Tampa Bay Lightning in seventh round (fifth Lightning pick, 224th overall) in NHL entry draft (June 21, 2003).

		REGULAR SEASON										PLAYOFFS							
Season Team	League	GP	Min.	W	L	OTL	T	GA	SO	GAA	SV%	GP	Min.	W	L	GA	SO	GAA	SV%
02-03—London	OHL	26	1074	6	9	...	3	59	1	3.30	...	—	—	—	—	—	—	—	—
03-04—London	OHL	—	—	—	—	...	—	—	—	—	—	8	442	5	2	...	1	2.58	...
04-05—London	OHL	38	2224	32	2	...	2	63	8	1.70	.940	8	455	7	1	13	0	1.71	.940
05-06—Tampa Bay	NHL	2	43	0	0	1	...	2	0	2.79	.882	—	—	—	—	—	—	—	—
—Springfield	AHL	43	2413	14	21	3	...	156	2	3.88	.880	—	—	—	—	—	—	—	—
NHL Totals (1 year)		2	43	0	0	1	0	2	0	2.79	.882								

COLLEY, KEVIN — RW

PERSONAL: Born January 4, 1979, in New Haven, Conn. ... 5-11/175. ... Shoots right.

TRANSACTIONS/CAREER NOTES: Signed as free agent by New York Islanders (June 2004). ... Announced retirement (February 6, 2006).

		REGULAR SEASON								PLAYOFFS				
Season Team	League	GP	G	A	Pts.	PIM	+/-	PP	SH	GP	G	A	Pts.	PIM
96-97—Oshawa	OHL	64	19	17	36	46	...	...	...	16	2	4	6	25
97-98—Oshawa	OHL	57	27	41	68	107	...	...	...	7	1	5	6	14
98-99—Oshawa	OHL	63	39	62	101	68	...	...	...	14	7	13	20	32
99-00—Dayton	ECHL	24	8	6	14	111	...	...	...	2	1	0	1	4
—Charlotte	ECHL	5	2	1	3	10	...	...	...	—	—	—	—	—
—Hartford	AHL	5	0	0	0	0	...	...	...	—	—	—	—	—
00-01—Pensacola	ECHL	23	6	11	17	44	...	...	...	—	—	—	—	—
—New Orleans	ECHL	23	11	8	19	27	...	...	...	8	1	1	2	12
01-02—Altantic City	ECHL	—	—	—	—	—	—	—	—	41	23	30	53	90
—Providence	AHL	4	0	1	1	27	...	...	...	—	—	—	—	—
—Rochester	AHL	25	3	4	7	70	...	...	...	2	0	1	1	0
02-03—Worcester	AHL	6	1	1	2	27	...	...	...	—	—	—	—	—
—Syracuse	AHL	16	2	3	5	6	...	...	...	—	—	—	—	—
—Altantic City	ECHL	50	33	38	71	190	...	...	...	17	13	7	20	27
03-04—Bridgeport	AHL	78	12	19	31	122	...	...	...	3	1	0	1	12
04-05—Bridgeport	AHL	59	11	13	24	212	...	...	...	—	—	—	—	—
05-06—New York Islanders	NHL	16	0	0	0	52	-2	0	0	—	—	—	—	—
—Bridgeport	AHL	21	5	5	10	60	3	2	0	—	—	—	—	—
NHL Totals (1 year)		16	0	0	0	52	-2	0	0					

COLLINS, ROB — RW/C

PERSONAL: Born March 15, 1978, in Whitby, Ont. ... 5-10/185. ... Shoots right. ... Nephew of Bob Gainey, former NHL player, Montreal Canadiens GM and member of Hockey Hall of Fame.

COLLEGE: Ferris State.

TRANSACTIONS/CAREER NOTES: Signed as free agent by Grand Rapids of the AHL (March 21, 2002). ... Signed as free agent by New York Islanders (September 11, 2003).

		REGULAR SEASON								PLAYOFFS				
Season Team	League	GP	G	A	Pts.	PIM	+/-	PP	SH	GP	G	A	Pts.	PIM
98-99—Ferris State	CCHA	36	3	9	12	14	...	...	...	—	—	—	—	—
99-00—Ferris State	CCHA	38	11	20	31	39	...	...	...	—	—	—	—	—

Season Team	League	REGULAR SEASON								PLAYOFFS				
		GP	G	A	Pts.	PIM	+/-	PP	SH	GP	G	A	Pts.	PIM
00-01—Ferris State	CCHA	35	15	17	32	23	...	...	...	—	—	—	—	—
01-02—Grand Rapids	AHL	5	0	2	2	0	...	...	...	—	—	—	—	—
—Ferris State	CCHA	36	15	33	48	30	...	...	...	—	—	—	—	—
02-03—Grand Rapids	AHL	73	11	20	31	16	...	...	...	15	3	8	11	10
03-04—Bridgeport	AHL	75	9	23	32	42	...	...	...	7	3	5	8	10
04-05—Bridgeport	AHL	78	23	39	62	67	-2	5	1	—	—	—	—	—
05-06—New York Islanders	NHL	8	1	1	2	0	1	1	0	—	—	—	—	—
—Bridgeport	AHL	67	21	48	69	54	-6	8	2	7	4	2	6	10
NHL Totals (1 year)		8	1	1	2	0	1	1	0					

COLLITON, JEREMY C

PERSONAL: Born January 13, 1985, in Blackie, Alta. ... 6-2/195. ... Shoots right.
TRANSACTIONS/CAREER NOTES: Selected by New York Islanders in second round (fourth Islanders pick, 58th overall) of entry draft (June 20, 2003).

Season Team	League	REGULAR SEASON								PLAYOFFS				
		GP	G	A	Pts.	PIM	+/-	PP	SH	GP	G	A	Pts.	PIM
01-02—Prince Albert	WHL	68	11	21	32	53	...	...	...	—	—	—	—	—
02-03—Prince Albert	WHL	58	20	28	48	76	...	...	...	—	—	—	—	—
03-04—Prince Albert	WHL	62	24	26	50	73	12	8	1	6	5	5	10	8
04-05—Prince Albert	WHL	41	16	30	46	25	9	5	0	17	3	4	7	21
05-06—Bridgeport	AHL	66	21	32	53	44	-4	8	2	6	0	1	1	2
—New York Islanders	NHL	19	1	1	2	6	2	0	0	—	—	—	—	—
NHL Totals (1 year)		19	1	1	2	6	2	0	0					

COMMODORE, MIKE D

PERSONAL: Born November 7, 1979, in Fort Saskatchewan, Alta. ... 6-4/230. ... Shoots right.
TRANSACTIONS/CAREER NOTES: Selected by New Jersey Devils in second round (second Devils pick, 42nd overall) of NHL draft (June 26, 1999). ... Flu (March 20, 2002); missed two games. ... Traded by Devils with RW Petr Sykora, C Igor Pohanka and G J.F. Damphousse to Anaheim Mighty Ducks for D Oleg Tverdovsky, LW Jeff Friesen and RW Maxin Balmochnykh (July 7, 2002). ... Traded by Mighty Ducks with G J.F. Damphousse to Calgary Flames for C Rob Niedermayer (March 11, 2003). ... Injured shoulder (February 11, 2004); missed 19 games. ... Traded by Flames to Carolina Hurricanes for third-round pick (Carolina obtained pick from Atlanta; Calgary selected D Gord Baldwin) in 2005 draft (July 29, 2005). ... Leg bruise (January 15, 2006); missed two games. ... Injured thigh (January 23, 2006); missed four games. ... Upper body injury (March 10, 2006); missed two games.

Season Team	League	REGULAR SEASON								PLAYOFFS				
		GP	G	A	Pts.	PIM	+/-	PP	SH	GP	G	A	Pts.	PIM
96-97—Fort Saskatchewan	Tier II Jr. A	51	3	8	11	244	...	...	...	—	—	—	—	—
97-98—Univ. of North Dakota	WCHA	29	0	5	5	74	...	...	...	—	—	—	—	—
98-99—Univ. of North Dakota	WCHA	39	5	8	13	154	...	...	...	—	—	—	—	—
99-00—Univ. of North Dakota	WCHA	38	5	7	12	154	...	...	...	—	—	—	—	—
00-01—Albany	AHL	41	2	5	7	59	...	...	...	—	—	—	—	—
—New Jersey	NHL	20	1	4	5	14	5	0	0	—	—	—	—	—
01-02—Albany	AHL	14	0	3	3	31	0	0	0	—	—	—	—	—
—New Jersey	NHL	37	0	1	1	30	-12	0	0	—	—	—	—	—
02-03—Cincinnati	AHL	61	2	9	11	210	-12	0	0	—	—	—	—	—
—Calgary	NHL	6	0	1	1	19	2	0	0	—	—	—	—	—
—Saint John	AHL	7	0	3	3	18	1	0	0	—	—	—	—	—
03-04—Lowell	AHL	37	5	11	16	75	-1	1	1	—	—	—	—	—
—Calgary	NHL	12	0	0	0	25	-4	0	0	20	0	2	2	19
04-05—Lowell	AHL	73	6	29	35	175	23	3	2	11	1	2	3	18
05-06—Carolina	NHL	72	3	10	13	138	12	0	0	25	2	2	4	33
NHL Totals (5 years)		147	4	16	20	226	3	0	0	45	2	4	6	52

COMRIE, MIKE C

PERSONAL: Born September 11, 1980, in Edmonton. ... 5-9/185. ... Shoots left. ... Brother of Paul Comrie, C, Edmonton Oilers organization, 1998-2000.
TRANSACTIONS/CAREER NOTES: Selected by Edmonton Oilers in third round (fifth Oilers pick, 91st overall) on entry draft (June 25, 1999). ... Fractured thumb (January 6, 2003); missed 13 games. ... Missed first 30 games of 2003-04 season in contract dispute. ... Traded by Oilers to Philadelphia Flyers for D Jeff Woywitka, first-round pick (C Robbie Schremp) in 2004 and third-round pick in (D Danny Syvret) 2005 (December 16, 2003). ... Traded by Flyers to Phoenix Coyotes for G Sean Burke, RW Branko Radivojevic and rights to LW Ben Eager (February 9, 2004). ... Knee (January 24, 2006); missed one game.

Season Team	League	REGULAR SEASON								PLAYOFFS				
		GP	G	A	Pts.	PIM	+/-	PP	SH	GP	G	A	Pts.	PIM
98-99—Univ. of Michigan	CCHA	42	19	25	44	38	...	...	...	—	—	—	—	—
99-00—Univ. of Michigan	CCHA	40	24	35	59	95	...	...	...	—	—	—	—	—
00-01—Kootenay	WHL	37	39	40	79	79	...	...	...	—	—	—	—	—
—Edmonton	NHL	41	8	14	22	14	6	3	0	6	1	2	3	0
01-02—Edmonton	NHL	82	33	27	60	45	16	8	0	—	—	—	—	—
02-03—Edmonton	NHL	69	20	31	51	90	-18	8	0	6	1	0	1	10
03-04—Philadelphia	NHL	21	4	5	9	12	2	0	0	—	—	—	—	—
—Phoenix	NHL	28	8	7	15	16	-8	1	1	—	—	—	—	—
04-05—Farjestad Karlstad	Sweden	10	1	6	7	10	-5	0	0	—	—	—	—	—
05-06—Phoenix	NHL	80	30	30	60	55	2	10	0	—	—	—	—	—
NHL Totals (5 years)		321	103	114	217	232	0	30	1	12	2	2	4	10

CONKLIN, TY — G

PERSONAL: Born March 30, 1976, in Anchorage, Alaska. ... 6-0/180. ... Catches left.
TRANSACTIONS/CAREER NOTES: Signed as free agent by Edmonton Oilers (April 18, 2000). ... Groin (October 23, 2003); missed two games. ... Fractured right hand (February 14, 2004); missed 11 games. ... Groin (November 6, 2005); missed 12 games. ... Signed as free agent by Columbus Blue Jackets (July 6, 2006).

		REGULAR SEASON										PLAYOFFS							
Season Team	**League**	**GP**	**Min.**	**W**	**L**	**OTL**	**T**	**GA**	**SO**	**GAA**	**SV%**	**GP**	**Min.**	**W**	**L**	**GA**	**SO**	**GAA**	**SV%**
98-99—New Hampshire	Hockey East	22	1338	18	3	...	1	41	0	1.84	...	—	—	—	—	—	—	—	—
99-00—New Hampshire	Hockey East	37	2194	22	8	...	6	91	1	2.49	...	—	—	—	—	—	—	—	—
00-01—New Hampshire	Hockey East	34	2048	17	12	...	5	70	4	2.05	...	—	—	—	—	—	—	—	—
01-02—Hamilton	AHL	37	2043	13	12	...	8	89	1	2.61	.908	7	416	4	2	18	0	2.60	.917
—Edmonton	NHL	4	148	2	0	...	0	4	0	1.62	.939	—	—	—	—	—	—	—	—
02-03—Hamilton	AHL	38	2140	19	13	...	3	91	4	2.55	.914	17	1023	9	6	38	1	2.23	.933
03-04—Edmonton	NHL	38	2086	17	14	...	4	84	1	2.42	.912	—	—	—	—	—	—	—	—
04-05—Wolfsburg	Ger. Div. II	11	623	...	...	...	...	31	0	2.99	.920	7	414	...	...	11	2	1.59	.946
05-06—Hamilton	AHL	3	152	1	2	0	...	8	0	3.16	.907	—	—	—	—	—	—	—	—
—Hartford	AHL	2	130	1	0	1	...	5	0	2.31	.932	—	—	—	—	—	—	—	—
—Edmonton	NHL	18	922	8	5	1	...	43	1	2.80	.880	1	6	0	1	1	0	10.00	.667
NHL Totals (3 years)		60	3156	27	19	1	4	131	2	2.49	.905	1	6	0	1	1	0	10.00	.667

CONNOLLY, TIM — C

PERSONAL: Born May 7, 1981, in Syracuse, N.Y. ... 6-1/182. ... Shoots right.
TRANSACTIONS/CAREER NOTES: Selected by New York Islanders in first round (first Islanders pick, fifth overall) of entry draft (June 26, 1999). ... Traded by Islanders with LW Taylor Pyatt to Buffalo Sabres for C Michael Peca (June 24, 2001). ... Suspended four games for high-sticking incident (April 3, 2003). ... Concussion (October 9, 2003); missed entire season. ... Injured left knee (January 24, 2006); missed 12 games. ... Sore left knee (March 14, 2006); missed seven games. ... Upper-body injury (May 8, 2006); missed 10 playoff games.

		REGULAR SEASON								PLAYOFFS				
Season Team	**League**	**GP**	**G**	**A**	**Pts.**	**PIM**	**+/-**	**PP**	**SH**	**GP**	**G**	**A**	**Pts.**	**PIM**
96-97—Syracuse	Jr. A	50	42	62	104	34	...	...	...	—	—	—	—	—
97-98—Erie	OHL	59	30	32	62	32	...	...	...	7	1	6	7	6
98-99—Erie	OHL	46	34	34	68	50	5	...	...	—	—	—	—	—
99-00—New York Islanders	NHL	81	14	20	34	44	-25	2	1	—	—	—	—	—
00-01—New York Islanders	NHL	82	10	31	41	42	-14	5	0	—	—	—	—	—
01-02—Buffalo	NHL	82	10	35	45	34	4	3	0	—	—	—	—	—
02-03—Buffalo	NHL	80	12	13	25	32	-28	6	0	—	—	—	—	—
03-04—Buffalo	NHL	Did not play; injured												
04-05—SC Langnau	Switzerland	16	8	3	11	14	...	2	2	—	—	—	—	—
05-06—Buffalo	NHL	63	16	39	55	28	5	7	0	8	5	6	11	0
NHL Totals (6 years)		388	62	138	200	180	-58	23	1	8	5	6	11	0

CONROY, CRAIG — C

PERSONAL: Born September 4, 1971, in Potsdam, N.Y. ... 6-2/197. ... Shoots right. ... Nickname: Connie.
COLLEGE: Clarkson.
TRANSACTIONS/CAREER NOTES: Selected by Montreal Canadiens in sixth round (seventh Canadiens pick, 123rd overall) of entry draft (June 16, 1990). ... Traded by Canadiens with C Pierre Turgeon and D Rory Fitzpatrick to St. Louis Blues for LW Shayne Corson, D Murray Baron and fifth-round pick (D Gennady Razin) in 1997 (October 29, 1996). ... Ankle (March 12, 1999); missed 11 games. ... Ankle (April 7, 1999); missed two games. ... Flu (October 2, 1999); missed one game. ... Traded by Blues with seventh-round pick (LW David Moss) in 2001 to Calgary Flames for LW Cory Stillman (March 13, 2001). ... Injured (November 20, 2001); missed one game. ... Foot (November 4, 2002); missed two games. ... Right shoulder (December 21, 2002); missed one game. ... Knee (December 7, 2003); missed 19 games. ... Signed as free agent by Los Angeles Kings (July 6, 2004). ... Flu (December 21, 2005); missed one game. ... Left eye (March 14, 2006); missed two games. ... Knee (April 15, 2006); missed season's final game.
STATISTICAL PLATEAUS: Three-goal games: 1998-99 (1).

		REGULAR SEASON								PLAYOFFS				
Season Team	**League**	**GP**	**G**	**A**	**Pts.**	**PIM**	**+/-**	**PP**	**SH**	**GP**	**G**	**A**	**Pts.**	**PIM**
89-90—Northwood School	N.Y. H.S.	31	33	43	76	...	...	...	...	—	—	—	—	—
90-91—Clarkson	ECAC	40	8	21	29	24	...	...	...	—	—	—	—	—
91-92—Clarkson	ECAC	31	19	17	36	36	...	...	...	—	—	—	—	—
92-93—Clarkson	ECAC	35	10	23	33	26	...	...	...	—	—	—	—	—
93-94—Clarkson	ECAC	34	26	40	66	66	...	...	...	—	—	—	—	—
94-95—Fredericton	AHL	55	26	18	44	29	-5	11	0	11	7	3	10	6
—Montreal	NHL	6	1	0	1	0	-1	0	0	—	—	—	—	—
95-96—Fredericton	AHL	67	31	38	69	65	...	...	...	10	5	7	12	6
—Montreal	NHL	7	0	0	0	2	-4	0	0	—	—	—	—	—
96-97—Fredericton	AHL	9	10	6	16	10	2	3	0	—	—	—	—	—
—St. Louis	NHL	61	6	11	17	43	0	0	0	6	0	0	0	8
—Worcester	AHL	5	5	6	11	2	3	1	0	—	—	—	—	—
97-98—St. Louis	NHL	81	14	29	43	46	20	0	3	10	1	2	3	8
98-99—St. Louis	NHL	69	14	25	39	38	14	0	1	13	2	1	3	6
99-00—St. Louis	NHL	79	12	15	27	36	5	1	2	7	0	2	2	2
00-01—St. Louis	NHL	69	11	14	25	46	2	0	3	—	—	—	—	—
—Calgary	NHL	14	3	4	7	14	0	0	1	—	—	—	—	—
01-02—Calgary	NHL	81	27	48	75	32	24	7	2	—	—	—	—	—
02-03—Calgary	NHL	79	22	37	59	36	-4	5	0	—	—	—	—	—

Season Team	League	GP	G	A	Pts.	PIM	+/-	PP	SH	GP	G	A	Pts.	PIM
		REGULAR SEASON								PLAYOFFS				
03-04—Calgary	NHL	63	8	39	47	44	13	2	0	26	6	11	17	12
05-06—Los Angeles	NHL	78	22	44	66	78	13	5	3	—	—	—	—	—
—U.S. Olympic team	Int'l	6	1	4	5	2	0	0	0	—	—	—	—	—
NHL Totals (11 years)		687	140	266	406	415	82	20	15	62	9	16	25	36

COOKE, MATT LW/RW

PERSONAL: Born September 7, 1978, in Belleville, Ont. ... 5-11/205. ... Shoots left.
TRANSACTIONS/CAREER NOTES: Selected by Vancouver Canucks in sixth round (eighth Canucks pick, 144th overall) of entry draft (June 21, 1997). ... Injured knee (March 2, 2001); missed one game. ... Injured shoulder (November 25, 2003); missed 13 games. ... Injured knee (January 10, 2004); missed 14 games. ... Suspended two games for spearing incident (February 21, 2004). ... Missed part of training camp in contract dispute (October 2005). ... Broken jaw (November 1, 2005); missed 17 games. ... Injured ankle (January 19, 2006); missed 11 games. ... Concussion (March 27, 2006); missed final nine games of regular season

Season Team	League	GP	G	A	Pts.	PIM	+/-	PP	SH	GP	G	A	Pts.	PIM
		REGULAR SEASON								PLAYOFFS				
95-96—Windsor	OHL	61	8	11	19	102	...	...	...	7	1	3	4	6
96-97—Windsor	OHL	65	45	50	95	146	...	...	...	5	5	5	10	4
97-98—Windsor	OHL	23	14	19	33	50	1	...	...	—	—	—	—	—
—Kingston	OHL	25	8	13	21	49	-6	...	...	12	8	8	16	20
98-99—Vancouver	NHL	30	0	2	2	27	-12	0	0	—	—	—	—	—
—Syracuse	AHL	37	15	18	33	119	-28	8	0	—	—	—	—	—
99-00—Syracuse	AHL	18	5	8	13	27	...	...	...	—	—	—	—	—
—Vancouver	NHL	51	5	7	12	39	3	0	1	—	—	—	—	—
00-01—Vancouver	NHL	81	14	13	27	94	5	0	2	4	0	0	0	4
01-02—Vancouver	NHL	82	13	20	33	111	4	1	0	6	3	2	5	0
02-03—Vancouver	NHL	82	15	27	42	82	21	1	4	14	2	1	3	12
03-04—Vancouver	NHL	53	11	12	23	73	5	1	1	7	3	1	4	12
05-06—Vancouver	NHL	45	8	10	18	71	-8	0	0	—	—	—	—	—
NHL Totals (7 years)		424	66	91	157	497	18	3	8	31	8	4	12	28

C

CORRENTE, MATTHEW D

PERSONAL: Born March 17, 1988, in Mississauga, Ont. ... 5-11/189. ... Shoots right.
TRANSACTIONS/CAREER NOTES: Selected by New Jersey Devils in first round (first Devils pick; 30th overall) of NHL draft (June 24, 2006).

Season Team	League	GP	G	A	Pts.	PIM	+/-	PP	SH	GP	G	A	Pts.	PIM
		REGULAR SEASON								PLAYOFFS				
04-05—Saginaw	OHL	62	6	9	15	89	-38	...	...	—	—	—	—	—
05-06—Saginaw	OHL	61	6	24	30	172	2	...	...	4	1	1	2	8

CORVO, JOE D

PERSONAL: Born June 20, 1977, in Oak Park, Ill. ... 6-1/205. ... Shoots right.
TRANSACTIONS/CAREER NOTES: Selected by Los Angeles Kings in fourth round (fourth Kings pick, 83rd overall) of entry draft (June 21, 1997). ... Missed 1999-2000 season in contract dispute. ... Suspended three games by Kings for off-ice issues (October 30, 2003). ... Signed as free agent by Ottawa Senators (July 1, 2006).

Season Team	League	GP	G	A	Pts.	PIM	+/-	PP	SH	GP	G	A	Pts.	PIM
		REGULAR SEASON								PLAYOFFS				
95-96—Western Michigan	CCHA	41	5	25	30	38	...	...	...	—	—	—	—	—
96-97—Western Michigan	CCHA	32	12	21	33	85	...	...	...	—	—	—	—	—
97-98—Western Michigan	CCHA	32	5	12	17	93	...	...	...	—	—	—	—	—
98-99—Springfield	AHL	50	5	15	20	32	9	4	0	—	—	—	—	—
—Hampton Roads	ECHL	5	0	0	0	15	-1	0	0	4	0	1	1	0
99-00—Springfield	AHL	Did not play.												
00-01—Lowell	AHL	77	10	23	33	31	...	...	...	4	3	1	4	0
01-02—Manchester	AHL	80	13	37	50	30	6	7	0	5	0	5	5	0
02-03—Manchester	AHL	26	8	18	26	8	7	4	0	3	0	0	0	0
—Los Angeles	NHL	50	5	7	12	14	2	2	0	—	—	—	—	—
03-04—Los Angeles	NHL	72	8	17	25	36	7	0	0	—	—	—	—	—
04-05—Chicago	AHL	23	7	7	14	14	7	3	1	18	4	5	9	12
05-06—Los Angeles	NHL	81	14	26	40	38	16	7	0	—	—	—	—	—
NHL Totals (3 years)		203	27	50	77	88	25	9	0					

COTE, JEAN-PHILIPPE D

PERSONAL: Born April 22, 1982, in Quebec City. ... 6-1/193. ... Shoots left. ... Son of Alain Cote, defenseman, Quebec Nordiques (1979-80 through 1988-89).
TRANSACTIONS/CAREER NOTES: Selected by Toronto Maple Leafs in ninth round (10th Maple Leafs pick, 265th overall) of NHL entry draft (June 25, 2000). ... Signed as free agent by Hamilton of the AHL (September 16, 2003). ... Signed as free agent by Montreal Canadiens (August 19, 2004).

Season Team	League	GP	G	A	Pts.	PIM	+/-	PP	SH	GP	G	A	Pts.	PIM
		REGULAR SEASON								PLAYOFFS				
98-99—Quebec	QMJHL	8	0	0	0	2	...	...	...	—	—	—	—	—
99-00—Quebec	QMJHL	34	0	10	10	15	...	...	...	—	—	—	—	—

Season Team	League	REGULAR SEASON GP	G	A	Pts.	PIM	+/-	PP	SH	PLAYOFFS GP	G	A	Pts.	PIM
—Cape Breton	QMJHL	28	0	4	4	21	...	...	...	4	0	1	1	4
00-01—Cape Breton	QMJHL	71	6	29	35	90	...	...	...	12	0	0	0	18
01-02—Cape Breton	QMJHL	61	4	20	24	72	...	...	...	16	1	6	7	38
02-03—Cape Breton	QMJHL	16	1	3	4	12	...	...	...	—	—	—	—	—
—Acadie-Bathurst	QMJHL	48	8	18	26	87	...	...	...	11	2	3	5	20
03-04—Hamilton	AHL	75	2	7	9	79	...	...	...	10	0	4	4	24
04-05—Hamilton	AHL	51	1	8	9	58	14	0	0	4	0	1	1	0
—Drummondville	QMJHL	24	0	0	0	14	-3	0	0	5	0	0	0	2
—Rouyn-Noranda	QMJHL	31	5	4	9	29	3	1	0	—	—	—	—	—
05-06—Hamilton	AHL	61	3	8	11	113	8	0	1	—	—	—	—	—
—Montreal	NHL	8	0	0	0	4	2	0	0	—	—	—	—	—
NHL Totals (1 year)		8	0	0	0	4	2	0	0					

COWAN, JEFF LW/RW

PERSONAL: Born September 27, 1976, in Scarborough, Ont. ... 6-2/205. ... Shoots left. ... Name pronounced KOW-ihn.

TRANSACTIONS/CAREER NOTES: Signed as free agent by Calgary Flames (October 2, 1995). ... Injured (March 3, 2000); missed one game. ... Flu (March 25, 2000); missed season's final six games. ... Knee (February 10, 2001); missed 19 games. ... Knee (March 28, 2001); missed three games. ... Traded by Flames with D Kurtis Foster to Atlanta Thrashers for D Petr Buzek (December 18, 2001). ... Fractured hand (January 19, 2002); missed 10 games. ... Knee (November 2, 2002); missed seven games. ... Groin (December 27, 2002); missed two games. ... Concussion (January 21, 2003); missed one game. ... Ribs (February 15, 2003); missed two games. ... Concussion (December 16, 2003); missed four games. ... Postconcussion syndrome (December 31, 2003); missed six games. ... Traded by Thrashers to Los Angeles Kings for LW Kip Brennan (March 9, 2004). ... Groin (October 6, 2005); missed nine games. ... Hamstring (December 10, 2005); missed 13 games. ... Back spasms (March 14, 2006); missed five games.

Season Team	League	REGULAR SEASON GP	G	A	Pts.	PIM	+/-	PP	SH	PLAYOFFS GP	G	A	Pts.	PIM
92-93—Guelph	Jr. B	45	8	8	16	22	...	...	...	—	—	—	—	—
93-94—Guelph	Jr. B	43	30	26	56	96	...	...	...	—	—	—	—	—
—Guelph	OHL	17	1	0	1	5	...	...	...	0	0	0	0	0
94-95—Guelph	OHL	51	10	7	17	14	...	0	1	14	1	1	2	0
95-96—Barrie	OHL	66	38	14	52	29	...	...	...	5	1	2	3	6
96-97—Saint John	AHL	22	5	5	10	8	-8	1	1	—	—	—	—	—
—Roanoke	ECHL	47	21	13	34	42	...	...	...	—	—	—	—	—
97-98—Saint John	AHL	69	15	13	28	23	9	5	0	13	4	1	5	14
98-99—Saint John	AHL	71	7	12	19	117	-18	0	0	4	0	1	1	10
99-00—Saint John	AHL	47	15	10	25	77	...	...	...	—	—	—	—	—
—Calgary	NHL	13	4	1	5	16	2	0	0	—	—	—	—	—
00-01—Calgary	NHL	51	9	4	13	74	-8	2	0	—	—	—	—	—
01-02—Calgary	NHL	19	1	0	1	40	-3	0	0	—	—	—	—	—
—Atlanta	NHL	38	4	1	5	50	-11	0	0	—	—	—	—	—
02-03—Atlanta	NHL	66	3	5	8	115	-15	0	0	—	—	—	—	—
03-04—Atlanta	NHL	58	9	15	24	68	2	1	0	—	—	—	—	—
—Los Angeles	NHL	13	2	1	3	24	-1	1	0	—	—	—	—	—
05-06—Los Angeles	NHL	46	8	1	9	73	-8	0	0	—	—	—	—	—
NHL Totals (6 years)		304	40	28	68	460	-42	4	0					

CRAIG, RYAN C

PERSONAL: Born January 6, 1982, in Abbotsford, B.C. ... 6-1/208. ... Shoots left.

TRANSACTIONS/CAREER NOTES: Selected by Tampa Bay Lightning in eighth round (10th Lightning pick, 255th overall) of NHL entry draft (June 23, 2002).

Season Team	League	REGULAR SEASON GP	G	A	Pts.	PIM	+/-	PP	SH	PLAYOFFS GP	G	A	Pts.	PIM
97-98—Brandon	WHL	1	0	0	0	0	...	...	...	—	—	—	—	—
98-99—Brandon	WHL	54	11	12	23	46	...	...	...	5	0	0	0	4
99-00—Brandon	WHL	65	17	19	36	40	...	...	...	—	—	—	—	—
00-01—Brandon	WHL	70	38	33	71	49	...	...	...	6	3	0	3	7
01-02—Brandon	WHL	52	29	35	64	52	...	...	...	19	11	10	21	13
02-03—Brandon	WHL	60	42	32	74	69	...	...	...	17	5	8	13	29
03-04—Pensacola	ECHL	5	3	5	8	0	...	...	...	—	—	—	—	—
—Hershey	AHL	61	4	8	12	12	...	...	...	—	—	—	—	—
04-05—Springfield	AHL	80	27	14	41	50	-21	12	0	—	—	—	—	—
05-06—Springfield	AHL	28	12	10	22	14	-3	5	0	—	—	—	—	—
—Tampa Bay	NHL	48	15	13	28	6	-4	6	0	5	0	0	0	10
NHL Totals (1 year)		48	15	13	28	6	-4	6	0	5	0	0	0	10

CRAWFORD, COREY G

PERSONAL: Born December 31, 1984, in Montreal. ... 6-2/183. ... Catches right.

TRANSACTIONS/CAREER NOTES: Selected by Chicago Blackhawks in second round (Blackhawks' second choice, 52nd overall) of NHL entry draft (June 20, 2003).

Season Team	League	REGULAR SEASON GP	Min.	W	L	OTL	T	GA	SO	GAA	SV%	PLAYOFFS GP	Min.	W	L	GA	SO	GAA	SV%
01-02—Moncton	QMJHL	38	1863	9	20	...	3	116	1	3.74	.900	—	—	—	—	—	—	—	—
02-03—Moncton	QMJHL	50	2855	24	17	...	6	130	2	2.73	.922	6	360	2	3	20	0	3.33	.900

Season Team	League	GP	Min.	W	L	OTL	T	GA	SO	GAA	SV%	Playoffs GP	Min.	W	L	GA	SO	GAA	SV%
		REGULAR SEASON										PLAYOFFS							
03-04—Moncton	QMJHL	54	...	35	15	...	3	132	2	...	.919	20	1170	13	6	42	0	2.15	.940
04-05—Moncton	QMJHL	51	2942	28	16	...	6	121	6	2.47	.920	12	725	6	6	33	1	2.73	.918
05-06—Norfolk	AHL	48	2734	22	23	1	...	134	1	2.94	.898	1	17	0	0	1	0	3.53	.750
—Chicago	NHL	2	86	0	0	1	...	5	0	3.49	.878	—	—	—	—	—	—	—	—
NHL Totals (1 year)		2	86	0	0	1	0	5	0	3.49	.878								

CROSBY, SIDNEY — C

PERSONAL: Born August 7, 1987, in Dartmouth, Nova Scotia. ... 5-11/193. ... Shoots left.
TRANSACTIONS/CAREER NOTES: Selected by Pittsburgh Penguins in first round (first Penguins pick, first overall) of entry draft (July 30, 2005). ... Signed by Penguins to entry-level contract (September 9, 2005). ... Flu (February 2, 2006); missed one game.

Season Team	League	GP	G	A	Pts.	PIM	+/-	PP	SH	Playoffs GP	G	A	Pts.	PIM
		REGULAR SEASON								PLAYOFFS				
03-04—Rimouski	QMJHL	59	54	81	135	74	...	...	...	—	—	—	—	—
04-05—Rimouski	QMJHL	62	66	102	168	84	78	15	7	13	14	17	31	16
05-06—Pittsburgh	NHL	81	39	63	102	110	-1	16	0	—	—	—	—	—
NHL Totals (1 year)		81	39	63	102	110	-1	16	0					

CROSS, CORY — D

PERSONAL: Born January 3, 1971, in Lloydminster, Alta. ... 6-5/220. ... Shoots left.
TRANSACTIONS/CAREER NOTES: Selected by Tampa Bay Lightning in NHL supplemental draft (June 19, 1992). ... Foot (November 3, 1995); missed one game. ... Bruised right foot (November 10, 1996); missed five games. ... Flu (March 28, 1998); missed one game. ... Ankle (January 4, 1999); missed two games. ... Hip pointer (January 30, 1999); missed 12 games. ... Traded by Lightning with seventh-round pick (F Ivan Kolozvary) in 2001 to Toronto Maple Leafs for RW Fredrik Modin (October 1, 1999). ... Injured (November 15, 1999); missed two games. ... Injured (March 29, 2000); missed two games. ... Injured (November 10, 2000); missed five games. ... Hip (November 29, 2000); missed 14 games. ... Foot (February 10, 2001); missed 12 games. ... Injured (March 20, 2001); missed five games. ... Groin (December 29, 2001); missed 19 games. ... Injured (March 12, 2002); missed one game. ... Signed as free agent by New York Rangers (December 17, 2002). ... Flu (January 13, 2003); missed one game. ... Back spasms (January 18, 2003); missed one game. ... Strained abdomen (February 5, 2003); missed six games. ... Traded by Rangers with RW Radek Dvorak to Edmonton Oilers for RW Anson Carter and D Ales Pisa (March 11, 2003). ... Shoulder (October 18, 2003); missed two games. ... Back spasms (December 28, 2003); missed five games. ... Fractured nose (January 17, 2004); missed one game. ... Back (March 26, 2004); missed two games. ... Back spasms (March 31, 2004); missed final two games of season. ... Knee sprain (November 4, 2005); missed nine games. ... Traded by Oilers with RW Jani Rita to Pittsburgh Penguins for D Dick Tarnstrom (January 26, 2006). ... Traded by Penguins to Detroit Red Wings for fourth-round pick in 2007 (March 9, 2006).

Season Team	League	GP	G	A	Pts.	PIM	+/-	PP	SH	Playoffs GP	G	A	Pts.	PIM
		REGULAR SEASON								PLAYOFFS				
90-91—Alberta	CIS	20	2	5	7	16	...	...	...	—	—	—	—	—
91-92—Alberta	CIS	39	3	10	13	76	...	...	...	—	—	—	—	—
92-93—Alberta	CIS	43	11	28	39	105	...	...	...	—	—	—	—	—
—Atlanta	IHL	7	0	1	1	2	4	0	0	4	0	0	0	6
93-94—Atlanta	IHL	70	4	14	18	72	13	0	0	9	1	2	3	14
—Tampa Bay	NHL	5	0	0	0	6	-3	0	0	—	—	—	—	—
94-95—Atlanta	IHL	41	5	10	15	67	10	1	0	—	—	—	—	—
—Tampa Bay	NHL	43	1	5	6	41	-6	0	0	—	—	—	—	—
95-96—Tampa Bay	NHL	75	2	14	16	66	4	0	0	6	0	0	0	22
96-97—Tampa Bay	NHL	72	4	5	9	95	6	0	0	—	—	—	—	—
97-98—Tampa Bay	NHL	74	3	6	9	77	-24	0	1	—	—	—	—	—
98-99—Tampa Bay	NHL	67	2	16	18	92	-25	0	0	—	—	—	—	—
99-00—Toronto	NHL	71	4	11	15	64	13	0	0	12	0	2	2	2
00-01—Toronto	NHL	41	3	5	8	50	7	1	0	11	2	1	3	10
01-02—Toronto	NHL	50	3	9	12	54	11	0	0	12	0	0	0	8
02-03—Hartford	AHL	2	0	0	0	2	0	0	0	—	—	—	—	—
—New York Rangers	NHL	26	0	4	4	16	13	0	0	—	—	—	—	—
—Edmonton	NHL	11	2	3	5	8	3	1	0	6	0	1	1	20
03-04—Edmonton	NHL	68	7	14	21	56	9	1	0	—	—	—	—	—
05-06—Edmonton	NHL	34	2	3	5	38	-5	0	1	—	—	—	—	—
—Pittsburgh	NHL	6	0	1	1	6	-1	0	0	—	—	—	—	—
—Detroit	NHL	16	1	1	2	15	3	0	0	—	—	—	—	—
NHL Totals (12 years)		659	34	97	131	684	5	3	2	47	2	4	6	62

CULLEN, MARK — C/LW

PERSONAL: Born October 28, 1978, in Moorhead, Minn. ... 5-11/175. ... Shoots right. ... Brother of Matt Cullen, C, New York Rangers; and Joe Cullen, C, Ottawa Senators organization.
COLLEGE: Colorado College.
TRANSACTIONS/CAREER NOTES: Signed as free agent by Minnesota Wild (April 8, 2002). ... Signed as free agent by Chicago Blackhawks (August 4, 2005). ... Signed as free agent by Philadelphia Flyers (July 5, 2006).

Season Team	League	GP	G	A	Pts.	PIM	+/-	PP	SH	Playoffs GP	G	A	Pts.	PIM
		REGULAR SEASON								PLAYOFFS				
98-99—Colorado College	WCHA	42	8	25	33	22	...	...	...	—	—	—	—	—
99-00—Colorado College	WCHA	37	11	20	31	22	...	...	...	—	—	—	—	—
00-01—Colorado College	WCHA	43	14	36	50	14	...	...	...	—	—	—	—	—
01-02—Colorado College	WCHA	43	14	36	50	14	...	...	...	—	—	—	—	—
02-03—Houston	AHL	72	22	25	47	20	14	9	0	15	3	7	10	4
03-04—Houston	AHL	53	10	28	38	28	...	...	...	2	0	0	0	0

Season Team	League	GP	G	A	Pts.	PIM	+/-	PP	SH	GP	G	A	Pts.	PIM
		REGULAR SEASON								PLAYOFFS				
—Houston	AHL	64	10	24	34	26	-5	3	1	5	1	1	2	0
05-06—Chicago	NHL	29	7	9	16	2	7	0	0	—	—	—	—	—
—Norfolk	AHL	54	29	39	68	48	6	13	1	4	2	2	4	0
NHL Totals (1 year)		29	7	9	16	2	7	0	0					

CULLEN, MATT C

PERSONAL: Born November 2, 1976, in Virginia, Minn. ... 6-2/199. ... Shoots left. ... Brother of Mark Cullen, C, Philaelphia Flyers; and Joe Cullen, C, Ottawa Senators organization.

TRANSACTIONS/CAREER NOTES: Selected by Anaheim Mighty Ducks in second round (second Mighty Ducks pick, 35th overall) of entry draft (June 22, 1996). ... Sprained ankle (December 16, 1998); missed one game. ... Traded by Mighty Ducks with D Pavel Trnka and fourth-round pick (D James Pemberton) in 2003 draft to Florida Panthers for D Sandis Ozolinsh and D Lance Ward (January 30, 2003). ... Injured groin (October 14, 2003); missed 14 games. ... Signed as free agent by Carolina Hurricanes (August 5, 2004). ... Broken jaw (January 26, 2006); missed four games. ... Signed as free agent by New York Rangers (July 1, 2006).

Season Team	League	GP	G	A	Pts.	PIM	+/-	PP	SH	GP	G	A	Pts.	PIM
		REGULAR SEASON								PLAYOFFS				
94-95—Moorhead Senior	Minn. H.S.	28	47	42	89	78	...	...	...	—	—	—	—	—
95-96—St. Cloud State	WCHA	39	12	29	41	28	...	...	...	—	—	—	—	—
96-97—St. Cloud State	WCHA	36	15	30	45	70	...	4	3	—	—	—	—	—
—Baltimore	AHL	6	3	3	6	7	-4	1	0	3	0	2	2	0
97-98—Anaheim	NHL	61	6	21	27	23	-4	2	0	—	—	—	—	—
—Cincinnati	AHL	18	15	12	27	2	12	3	1	—	—	—	—	—
98-99—Anaheim	NHL	75	11	14	25	47	-12	5	1	4	0	0	0	0
—Cincinnati	AHL	3	1	2	3	8	1	0	0	—	—	—	—	—
99-00—Anaheim	NHL	80	13	26	39	24	5	1	0	—	—	—	—	—
00-01—Anaheim	NHL	82	10	30	40	38	-23	4	0	—	—	—	—	—
01-02—Anaheim	NHL	79	18	30	48	24	-1	3	1	—	—	—	—	—
02-03—Anaheim	NHL	50	7	14	21	12	-4	1	0	—	—	—	—	—
—Florida	NHL	30	6	6	12	22	-4	2	1	—	—	—	—	—
03-04—Florida	NHL	56	6	13	19	24	-2	1	0	—	—	—	—	—
04-05—Cortina	Italy	36	27	34	61	58	...	...	...	—	—	—	—	—
05-06—Carolina	NHL	78	25	24	49	40	4	8	0	25	4	14	18	12
NHL Totals (8 years)		591	102	178	280	254	-41	27	3	29	4	14	18	12

CULLIMORE, JASSEN D

PERSONAL: Born December 4, 1972, in Simcoe, Ont. ... 6-5/247. ... Shoots left. ... Name pronounced KUHL-ih-MOHR.

TRANSACTIONS/CAREER NOTES: Selected by Vancouver Canucks in second round (second Canucks pick, 29th overall) of entry draft (June 22, 1991). ... Injured knee (March 31, 1995); missed three games. ... Traded by Canucks to Montreal Canadiens for LW Donald Brashear (November 13, 1996). ... Bruised eye (March 1, 1997); missed one game. ... Claimed off waivers by Tampa Bay Lightning (January 22, 1998). ... Sprained knee (April 4, 1998); missed final seven games of season. ... Injured neck (October 14, 1998); missed two games. ... Injured wrist (December 11, 1998); missed one game. ... Injured knee (April 2, 2000); missed final four games of season. ... Bruised hand (November 27, 2000); missed one game. ... Injured knee (January 10, 2001); missed one game. ... Injured shin (February 10, 2001); missed one game. ... Strained abdomen muscle (March 8, 2001); missed two games. ... Sprained left ankle (October 30, 2001); missed two games. ... Bruised right thigh (February 9, 2002); missed one game. ... Injured shoulder (November 27, 2002) and had surgery (December 9, 2002); missed 54 games. ... Injured shoulder (February 26, 2004); missed three games. ... Injured wrist (April 14, 2004); missed 12 playoff games. ... Signed as free agent by Chicago Blackhawks (July 21, 2004). ... Flu (November 6, 2005); missed three games. ... Strained groin (December 7, 2005); missed nine games.

Season Team	League	GP	G	A	Pts.	PIM	+/-	PP	SH	GP	G	A	Pts.	PIM
		REGULAR SEASON								PLAYOFFS				
88-89—Peterborough	OHL	20	2	1	3	6	...	...	...	—	—	—	—	—
—Peterborough	Jr. B	29	11	17	28	88	...	...	...	—	—	—	—	—
89-90—Peterborough	OHL	59	2	6	8	61	...	...	...	11	0	2	2	8
90-91—Peterborough	OHL	62	8	16	24	74	...	...	...	4	1	0	1	7
91-92—Peterborough	OHL	54	9	37	46	65	...	...	...	10	3	6	9	8
92-93—Hamilton	AHL	56	5	7	12	60	-16	2	0	—	—	—	—	—
93-94—Hamilton	AHL	71	8	20	28	86	-1	0	1	3	0	1	1	2
94-95—Syracuse	AHL	33	2	7	9	66	4	0	0	—	—	—	—	—
—Vancouver	NHL	34	1	2	3	39	-2	0	0	11	0	0	0	12
95-96—Vancouver	NHL	27	1	1	2	21	4	0	0	—	—	—	—	—
96-97—Vancouver	NHL	3	0	0	0	2	-2	0	0	—	—	—	—	—
—Montreal	NHL	49	2	6	8	42	4	0	1	2	0	0	0	2
97-98—Montreal	NHL	3	0	0	0	4	0	0	0	—	—	—	—	—
—Fredericton	AHL	5	1	0	1	8	5	0	0	—	—	—	—	—
—Tampa Bay	NHL	25	1	2	3	22	-4	1	0	—	—	—	—	—
98-99—Tampa Bay	NHL	78	5	12	17	81	-22	1	1	—	—	—	—	—
99-00—Providence	AHL	16	5	10	15	31	...	...	...	—	—	—	—	—
—Tampa Bay	NHL	46	1	1	2	66	-12	0	0	—	—	—	—	—
00-01—Tampa Bay	NHL	74	1	6	7	80	-6	0	0	—	—	—	—	—
01-02—Tampa Bay	NHL	78	4	9	13	58	-1	0	0	—	—	—	—	—
02-03—Tampa Bay	NHL	28	1	3	4	31	3	0	0	11	1	1	2	4
03-04—Tampa Bay	NHL	79	2	5	7	58	8	0	0	11	0	2	2	6
05-06—Chicago	NHL	54	1	6	7	53	-24	1	0	—	—	—	—	—
NHL Totals (11 years)		578	20	53	73	557	-54	3	2	35	1	3	4	24

CZERKAWSKI, MARIUSZ RW/LW

PERSONAL: Born April 13, 1972, in Radomsko, Poland. ... 6-1/195. ... Shoots right. ... Name pronounced MAIR-ee-uhz chuhr-KAHV-skee.

TRANSACTIONS/CAREER NOTES: Selected by Boston Bruins (fifth Bruins pick, 106th overall) of NHL draft (June 22, 1991). ... Traded by Bruins with D Sean Brown and first-round pick (D Mathieu Descoteaux) in 1996 draft to Edmonton Oilers for G Bill Ranford (January 11, 1996). ... Injured finger (March 23, 1996); missed two games. ... Hip pointer (January 11, 1997); missed two games. ... Traded by Oilers to New York Islanders for LW Dan LaCouture (August 25, 1997). ... Strained rib cage muscle (December 15, 1999); missed three games. ... Traded by Islanders to Montreal Canadiens for RW/C Aaron Asham and fifth-round pick (W Markus Pahlsson) in 2002 draft (June 22, 2002). ... Signed as free agent by New York Islanders (July 17, 2003). ... Irregular heartbeat (December 2, 2003); missed one game. ... Signed as free agent by Toronto Maple Leafs (September 9, 2005). ... Shoulder (October 29, 2005); missed 12 games. ... Flu (January 13, 2006); missed two games. ... Claimed on waivers by Bruins (March 8, 2006).

STATISTICAL PLATEAUS: Three-goal games: 1996-97 (2), 1999-00 (1), 2001-02 (1). Total: 4.

		REGULAR SEASON								PLAYOFFS				
Season Team	**League**	**GP**	**G**	**A**	**Pts.**	**PIM**	**+/-**	**PP**	**SH**	**GP**	**G**	**A**	**Pts.**	**PIM**
90-91—GKS Tychy	Poland	24	25	15	40	...	...	...	...	—	—	—	—	—
91-92—Djurgarden Stockholm	Sweden	39	8	5	13	4	...	...	...	3	0	0	0	2
—Polish Olympic Team	Int'l	5	0	1	1	4	-6	0	0	—	—	—	—	—
92-93—Hammarby	Sweden Dv. 2	32	39	30	69	74	...	...	...	—	—	—	—	—
93-94—Djurgarden Stockholm	Sweden	39	13	21	34	20	...	...	...	—	—	—	—	—
—Boston	NHL	4	2	1	3	0	-2	1	0	13	3	3	6	4
94-95—Kiekko-Espoo	Finland	7	9	3	12	10	-1	...	...	—	—	—	—	—
—Boston	NHL	47	12	14	26	31	4	1	0	5	1	0	1	0
95-96—Boston	NHL	33	5	6	11	10	-11	1	0	—	—	—	—	—
—Edmonton	NHL	37	12	17	29	8	7	2	0	—	—	—	—	—
96-97—Edmonton	NHL	76	26	21	47	16	0	4	0	12	2	1	3	10
97-98—New York Islanders	NHL	68	12	13	25	23	11	2	0	—	—	—	—	—
98-99—New York Islanders	NHL	78	21	17	38	14	-10	4	0	—	—	—	—	—
99-00—New York Islanders	NHL	79	35	35	70	34	-16	16	0	—	—	—	—	—
00-01—New York Islanders	NHL	82	30	32	62	48	-24	10	1	—	—	—	—	—
01-02—New York Islanders	NHL	82	22	29	51	48	-8	6	0	7	2	2	4	4
02-03—Montreal	NHL	43	5	9	14	16	-7	1	0	—	—	—	—	—
—Hamilton	AHL	20	8	12	20	12	0	3	0	6	1	3	4	6
03-04—New York Islanders	NHL	81	25	24	49	16	8	9	0	5	0	1	1	0
04-05—Djurgarden Stockholm	Sweden	46	15	9	24	20	-10	4	0	5	1	0	1	2
05-06—Toronto	NHL	19	4	1	5	6	-2	1	0	—	—	—	—	—
—Boston	NHL	16	4	1	5	4	-4	0	0	—	—	—	—	—
NHL Totals (12 years)		745	215	220	435	274	-54	58	1	42	8	7	15	18

DAGENAIS, PIERRE RW/LW

PERSONAL: Born March 4, 1978, in Blainville, Que. ... 6-5/215. ... Shoots left. ... Name pronounced da-zhih-NAY.

TRANSACTIONS/CAREER NOTES: Selected by New Jersey Devils in second round (fourth Devils pick, 47th overall) of NHL draft (June 22, 1996). ... Returned to draft pool by Devils; selected by Devils in fourth round (sixth Devils pick, 105th overall) of draft (June 27, 1998). ... Claimed on waivers by Florida Panthers (January 12, 2002). ... Injured ankle (April 10, 2002); missed remainder of season. ... Signed as free agent by Montreal Canadiens (July 3, 2003). ... Suspended two games for high-sticking (January 24, 2004).

		REGULAR SEASON								PLAYOFFS				
Season Team	**League**	**GP**	**G**	**A**	**Pts.**	**PIM**	**+/-**	**PP**	**SH**	**GP**	**G**	**A**	**Pts.**	**PIM**
95-96—Moncton	QMJHL	67	43	25	68	59	...	...	...	—	—	—	—	—
96-97—Moncton	QMJHL	6	4	2	6	0	...	...	...	—	—	—	—	—
—Laval	QMJHL	37	16	14	30	40	...	...	...	—	—	—	—	—
—Rouyn-Noranda	QMJHL	27	21	8	29	22	...	...	...	—	—	—	—	—
97-98—Rouyn-Noranda	QMJHL	60	66	67	133	50	...	...	...	6	6	2	8	2
98-99—Albany	AHL	69	17	13	30	37	-2	3	0	4	0	0	0	0
99-00—Albany	AHL	80	35	30	65	47	...	...	...	5	1	0	1	14
00-01—Albany	AHL	69	34	28	62	52	...	...	...	—	—	—	—	—
—New Jersey	NHL	9	3	2	5	6	1	1	0	—	—	—	—	—
01-02—New Jersey	NHL	16	3	3	6	4	-5	1	0	—	—	—	—	—
—Albany	AHL	6	0	2	2	2	0	0	0	—	—	—	—	—
—Florida	NHL	26	7	1	8	4	-5	2	0	—	—	—	—	—
—Utah	AHL	4	1	1	2	2	...	...	...	—	—	—	—	—
02-03—San Antonio	AHL	49	21	14	35	28	4	7	3	3	2	0	2	2
—Florida	NHL	9	0	0	0	4	-1	0	0	—	—	—	—	—
03-04—Montreal	NHL	50	17	10	27	24	15	4	0	8	0	1	1	6
—Hamilton	AHL	20	12	9	21	19	4	4	0	—	—	—	—	—
04-05—Ajoie	Switz. Div. 2	7	5	5	10	12	...	4	0	6	7	7	14	6
05-06—Hamilton	AHL	38	12	13	25	23	2	5	0	—	—	—	—	—
—Montreal	NHL	32	5	7	12	16	-5	2	0	—	—	—	—	—
NHL Totals (5 years)		142	35	23	58	58	0	10	0	8	0	1	1	6

DAIGLE, ALEXANDRE RW/LW

PERSONAL: Born February 7, 1975, in Montreal. ... 6-0/202. ... Shoots left. ... Name pronounced DAYG.

TRANSACTIONS/CAREER NOTES: Selected by Ottawa Senators in first round (first Senators pick, first overall) of NHL draft (June 26, 1993). ... Fractured left forearm (February 3, 1996); missed remainder of season. ... Traded by Senators to Flyers for C Vaclav Prospal, RW Pat Falloon and second round pick (LW Chris Bala) in 1998 draft (January 17, 1998). ... Had concussion (October 29, 1998); missed two games. ... Strained left groin (November 14, 1998); missed one game. ... Traded by Flyers to Edmonton Oilers for RW Andrei Kovalenko (January 29, 1999). ... Traded by Oilers to Tampa Bay Lightning for RW Alexander Selivanov (January 29, 1999). ... Injured wrist (March 19, 1999); missed one game. ... Reinjured wrist (March 31, 1999); missed one game. ... Traded by Lightning to New York Rangers for cash (October 3, 1999).

... Did not play in 2000-01 and 2001-02 seasons. ... Signed as free agent by Pittsburgh Penguins (October 4, 2002). ... Signed as free agent by Minnesota Wild (September 30, 2003). ... Flu (December 9, 2003); missed one game. ... Waived by Wild (March 5, 2006).
STATISTICAL PLATEAUS: Three-goal games: 1994-95 (1), 1997-98 (1). Total: 2.

		REGULAR SEASON								PLAYOFFS				
Season Team	**League**	**GP**	**G**	**A**	**Pts.**	**PIM**	**+/-**	**PP**	**SH**	**GP**	**G**	**A**	**Pts.**	**PIM**
91-92—Victoriaville	QMJHL	66	35	75	110	63	...	...	...	—	—	—	—	—
92-93—Victoriaville	QMJHL	53	45	92	137	85	...	...	...	6	5	6	11	4
93-94—Ottawa	NHL	84	20	31	51	40	-45	4	0	—	—	—	—	—
94-95—Victoriaville	QMJHL	18	14	20	34	16	...	...	...	—	—	—	—	—
—Ottawa	NHL	47	16	21	37	14	-22	4	1	—	—	—	—	—
95-96—Ottawa	NHL	50	5	12	17	24	-30	1	0	—	—	—	—	—
96-97—Ottawa	NHL	82	26	25	51	33	-33	4	0	7	0	0	0	2
97-98—Ottawa	NHL	38	7	9	16	8	-7	4	0	—	—	—	—	—
—Philadelphia	NHL	37	9	17	26	6	-1	4	0	5	0	2	2	0
98-99—Philadelphia	NHL	31	3	2	5	2	-1	1	0	—	—	—	—	—
—Tampa Bay	NHL	32	6	6	12	2	-12	3	0	—	—	—	—	—
99-00—Hartford	AHL	16	6	13	19	4	...	...	...	—	—	—	—	—
—New York Rangers	NHL	58	8	18	26	23	-5	1	0	—	—	—	—	—
02-03—Pittsburgh	NHL	33	4	3	7	8	-10	1	0	—	—	—	—	—
—Wilkes-Barre/Scranton	AHL	40	9	29	38	18	-10	3	2	4	0	1	1	0
03-04—Minnesota	NHL	78	20	31	51	14	-4	6	0	—	—	—	—	—
04-05—Morges	Switzerland	—	—	—	—	—	—	—	—	2	1	1	2	0
05-06—Manchester	AHL	16	6	8	14	4	-7	2	0	7	4	7	11	6
—Minnesota	NHL	46	5	23	28	12	-6	2	0	—	—	—	—	—
NHL Totals (10 years)		616	129	198	327	186	-176	35	1	12	0	2	2	2

DALEY, TREVOR D

PERSONAL: Born October 9, 1983, in Toronto. ... 5-9/197. ... Shoots left.
TRANSACTIONS/CAREER NOTES: Selected by Dallas Stars in second round (fifth Stars pick, 43rd overall) of NHL entry draft (June 22, 2002). ... Flu (Jan 25, 2006); missed one game.

		REGULAR SEASON								PLAYOFFS				
Season Team	**League**	**GP**	**G**	**A**	**Pts.**	**PIM**	**+/-**	**PP**	**SH**	**GP**	**G**	**A**	**Pts.**	**PIM**
99-00—Sault Ste. Marie	OHL	54	16	30	46	77	...	...	...	15	3	7	10	12
00-01—Sault Ste. Marie	OHL	58	14	27	41	105	...	...	...	—	—	—	—	—
01-02—Sault Ste. Marie	OHL	47	9	39	48	38	...	...	...	6	2	2	4	4
02-03—Sault Ste. Marie	OHL	57	20	33	53	128	...	...	...	1	0	0	0	2
03-04—Dallas	NHL	27	1	5	6	14	-6	1	0	1	0	0	0	0
—Utah	AHL	40	8	6	14	76	-22	3	0	—	—	—	—	—
04-05—Hamilton	AHL	78	7	27	34	109	-4	4	0	4	0	1	1	2
05-06—Dallas	NHL	81	3	11	14	87	-2	0	0	3	0	0	0	0
NHL Totals (2 years)		108	4	16	20	101	-8	1	0	4	0	0	0	0

DALLMAN, KEVIN D

PERSONAL: Born February 26, 1981, in Niagara Falls, Ont. ... 5-11/195. ... Shoots right.
TRANSACTIONS/CAREER NOTES: Signed as undrafted free agent by Boston Bruins (July 18, 2002). ... Foot (November 5, 2005); missed one game. ... Claimed off waivers by St. Louis Blues (December 5, 2005). ... Left hand (January 30, 2006); missed one game. ... Signed as free agent by Los Angeles Kings (July 10, 2006).

		REGULAR SEASON								PLAYOFFS				
Season Team	**League**	**GP**	**G**	**A**	**Pts.**	**PIM**	**+/-**	**PP**	**SH**	**GP**	**G**	**A**	**Pts.**	**PIM**
98-99—Guelph	OHL	68	8	30	38	52	...	...	...	11	1	4	5	2
99-00—Guelph	OHL	67	13	46	59	38	...	...	...	6	0	2	2	11
00-01—Guelph	OHL	66	25	52	77	88	...	...	...	1	0	0	0	0
01-02—Guelph	OHL	67	23	63	86	68	...	...	...	9	8	8	16	22
02-03—Providence	AHL	72	2	19	21	53	...	...	...	—	—	—	—	—
03-04—Providence	AHL	65	6	23	29	44	...	...	...	2	0	0	0	0
04-05—Providence	AHL	71	8	26	34	48	-8	3	0	17	4	6	10	20
05-06—Boston	NHL	21	0	1	1	8	1	0	0	—	—	—	—	—
—St. Louis	NHL	46	4	9	13	21	-15	3	0	—	—	—	—	—
NHL Totals (1 year)		67	4	10	14	29	-14	3	0					

DANDENAULT, MATHIEU D

PERSONAL: Born February 3, 1976, in Sherbrooke, Que. ... 6-2/200. ... Shoots right. ... Cousin of Eric Dandenault, D with Philadelphia Flyers organization (1991-94). ... Name pronounced DAN-dih-noh.
TRANSACTIONS/CAREER NOTES: Selected by Detroit Red Wings in second round (second Red Wings pick, 49th overall) of entry draft (June 28, 1994). ... Flu (November 11, 1995); missed one game. ... Bruised ribs (March 10, 1997); missed four games. ... Injured eye (December 14, 2002); missed eight games. ... Injured groin (November 5, 2003); missed one game. ... Flu (December 15, 2003); missed one game. ... Fractured right foot (March 3, 2004); missed 15 games. ... Signed as free agent by Montreal Canadiens (August 3, 2005).

		REGULAR SEASON								PLAYOFFS				
Season Team	**League**	**GP**	**G**	**A**	**Pts.**	**PIM**	**+/-**	**PP**	**SH**	**GP**	**G**	**A**	**Pts.**	**PIM**
91-92—Gloucester	OPJHL	6	3	4	7	0	...	...	...	—	—	—	—	—
92-93—Gloucester	OPJHL	55	11	26	37	64	...	...	...	—	—	—	—	—
93-94—Sherbrooke	QMJHL	67	17	36	53	67	...	...	...	12	4	10	14	12
94-95—Sherbrooke	QMJHL	67	37	70	107	76	41	12	1	7	1	7	8	10
95-96—Detroit	NHL	34	5	7	12	6	6	1	0	—	—	—	—	—
—Adirondack	AHL	4	0	0	0	0	...	...	...	—	—	—	—	—

Season Team	League	GP	G	A	Pts.	PIM	+/-	PP	SH	Playoffs GP	G	A	Pts.	PIM
		REGULAR SEASON								PLAYOFFS				
96-97—Detroit	NHL	65	3	9	12	28	-10	0	0	—	—	—	—	—
97-98—Detroit	NHL	68	5	12	17	43	5	0	0	3	1	0	1	0
98-99—Detroit	NHL	75	4	10	14	59	17	0	0	10	0	1	1	0
99-00—Detroit	NHL	81	6	12	18	20	-12	0	0	6	0	0	0	2
00-01—Detroit	NHL	73	10	15	25	38	11	2	0	6	0	1	1	0
01-02—Detroit	NHL	81	8	12	20	44	-5	2	0	23	1	2	3	8
02-03—Detroit	NHL	74	4	15	19	64	25	1	0	4	0	0	0	2
03-04—Detroit	NHL	65	3	9	12	40	9	0	1	12	1	1	2	6
04-05—Asiago	Italy	10	0	2	2	2	...	...	...	9	1	5	6	4
05-06—Montreal	NHL	82	5	15	20	83	8	0	0	6	0	3	3	4
NHL Totals (10 years)		698	53	116	169	425	54	6	1	70	3	8	11	22

DANIS, YANN G

PERSONAL: Born June 21, 1981, in Lafontaine, Que. ... 6-0/175. ... Catches left.
COLLEGE: Brown.
TRANSACTIONS/CAREER NOTES: Signed as undrafted free agent by Montreal Canadiens (March 19, 2004).

Season Team	League	GP	Min.	W	L	OTL	T	GA	SO	GAA	SV%	Playoffs GP	Min.	W	L	GA	SO	GAA	SV%
		REGULAR SEASON										PLAYOFFS							
00-01—Brown	ECAC	12	667	2	8	...	1	40	0	3.60	...	—	—	—	—	—	—	—	—
01-02—Brown	ECAC	24	1451	11	10	...	2	45	3	1.86	...	—	—	—	—	—	—	—	—
02-03—Brown	ECAC	34	2074	15	14	...	5	80	5	2.31	...	—	—	—	—	—	—	—	—
03-04—Brown	ECAC	30	1821	15	11	...	4	55	5	1.81	...	—	—	—	—	—	—	—	—
—Hamilton	AHL	2	120	2	0	...	0	3	1	1.50	...	—	—	—	—	—	—	—	—
04-05—Hamilton	AHL	53	3075	28	17	...	...	120	5	2.34	.924	4	237	0	4	13	0	3.29	.893
05-06—Hamilton	AHL	39	2242	17	17	3	...	111	0	2.97	.902	—	—	—	—	—	—	—	—
—Montreal	NHL	6	312	3	2	0	...	14	1	2.69	.908	—	—	—	—	—	—	—	—
NHL Totals (1 year)		6	312	3	2	0	0	14	1	2.69	.908								

DANIS-PEPIN, SIMON D

PERSONAL: Born April 11, 1988, in Montreal. ... 6-7/208. ... Shoots right.
TRANSACTIONS/CAREER NOTES: Selected by Chicago Blackhawks in second round (third Blackhawks pick; 61st overall) of NHL draft (June 24, 2006).

Season Team	League	GP	G	A	Pts.	PIM	+/-	PP	SH	Playoffs GP	G	A	Pts.	PIM
		REGULAR SEASON								PLAYOFFS				
05-06—Maine	Hockey East	23	0	5	5	14	...	...	...	—	—	—	—	—

DATSYUK, PAVEL C

PERSONAL: Born July 20, 1978, in Sverdolvsk, U.S.S.R. ... 5-11/185. ... Shoots left.
TRANSACTIONS/CAREER NOTES: Selected by Detroit Red Wings in sixth round (eighth Red Wings pick, 171st overall) of entry draft (June 27, 1998). ... Flu (February 26, 2002); missed one game. ... Knee (December 1, 2002); missed 28 games. ... Left thigh (April 3, 2006); missed regular season's final seven games and one playoff game.

Season Team	League	GP	G	A	Pts.	PIM	+/-	PP	SH	Playoffs GP	G	A	Pts.	PIM
		REGULAR SEASON								PLAYOFFS				
96-97—HC Yekaterinburg	Russian	18	2	2	4	4	...	...	...	—	—	—	—	—
—HC Yekaterinburg	Rus. Div. 2	36	12	10	22	12	...	...	...	—	—	—	—	—
97-98—HC Yekaterinburg	Russian	24	3	5	8	4	...	...	...	—	—	—	—	—
—HC Yekaterinburg	Rus. Div. 2	22	7	8	15	4	...	...	...	—	—	—	—	—
98-99—Yekaterinburg 2.	Russian Div.2	22	12	15	27	12	...	...	...	—	—	—	—	—
—HC Yekaterinburg	Rus. Div. 2	13	9	8	17	2	...	...	...	9	3	7	10	10
99-00—HC Yekaterinburg	Russian	15	1	3	4	4	...	...	...	—	—	—	—	—
00-01—Ak Bars Kazan	Russian	42	9	18	27	10	...	...	...	4	0	1	1	2
01-02—Detroit	NHL	70	11	24	35	4	4	2	0	21	3	3	6	2
—Russian Oly. team	Int'l	6	1	2	3	0	...	...	...	—	—	—	—	—
02-03—Detroit	NHL	64	12	39	51	16	20	1	0	4	0	0	0	0
03-04—Detroit	NHL	75	30	38	68	35	-2	8	1	12	0	6	6	2
04-05—Dynamo Moscow	Russian	47	15	17	32	16	22	...	...	10	6	3	9	4
05-06—Detroit	NHL	75	28	59	87	22	26	11	0	5	0	3	3	0
—Russian Oly. team	Int'l	8	1	7	8	10	5	0	0	—	—	—	—	—
NHL Totals (4 years)		284	81	160	241	77	48	22	1	42	3	12	15	4

DAVISON, ROB D

PERSONAL: Born May 1, 1980, in St. Catharines, Ont. ... 6-3/220. ... Shoots left.
TRANSACTIONS/CAREER NOTES: Selected by San Jose Sharks in fourth round (fourth Sharks pick, 98th overall) of entry draft (June 27, 1998). ... Injured neck (February 2, 2006); missed two games.

Season Team	League	GP	G	A	Pts.	PIM	+/-	PP	SH	Playoffs GP	G	A	Pts.	PIM
		REGULAR SEASON								PLAYOFFS				
96-97—St. Michael's	Tier II Jr. A	45	2	6	8	93	...	...	...	—	—	—	—	—
97-98—North Bay	OHL	59	0	11	11	200	-28	...	...	—	—	—	—	—
98-99—North Bay	OHL	59	2	17	19	150	-1	...	...	4	0	1	1	12

Season Team	League	REGULAR SEASON GP	G	A	Pts.	PIM	+/-	PP	SH	PLAYOFFS GP	G	A	Pts.	PIM
99-00—North Bay	OHL	67	4	6	10	194	-15	1	0	6	0	1	1	8
00-01—Kentucky	AHL	72	0	4	4	230	...	...	...	3	0	0	0	0
01-02—Cleveland	AHL	70	1	3	4	206	-12	0	1	—	—	—	—	—
02-03—Cleveland	AHL	42	1	3	4	82	-8	0	0	—	—	—	—	—
—San Jose	NHL	15	1	2	3	22	4	0	0	—	—	—	—	—
03-04—San Jose	NHL	55	0	3	3	92	-3	0	0	5	0	2	2	4
04-05—Cardiff	England	42	7	7	14	148	...	...	...	8	0	1	1	12
05-06—San Jose	NHL	69	1	5	6	76	6	0	0	1	0	0	0	0
NHL Totals (3 years)		139	2	10	12	190	7	0	0	6	0	2	2	4

DAZE, ERIC LW/RW

PERSONAL: Born July 2, 1975, in Montreal. ... 6-6/235. ... Shoots left. ... Name pronounced dah-ZAY.

TRANSACTIONS/CAREER NOTES: Selected by Chicago Blackhawks in fourth round (fifth Blackhawks pick, 90th overall) of entry draft (June 26, 1993). ... Sprained left ankle (September 1996); missed first eight games of season. ... Flu (January 20, 1997); missed one game. ... Injured back (March 27, 1998); missed two games. ... Bruised ankle (October 22, 1998); missed three games. ... Back spasms (October 27, 1999); missed three games. ... Flu (January 2, 2000); missed one game. ... Migraine headache (February 16, 2000); missed one game. ... Back spasms (March 3, 2000) and surgery; missed final 18 games of season. ... Disk surgery (September 25, 2002); missed 15 games. ... Injured back (January 5, 2003); missed three games ... Injured groin (January 30, 2003); missed five games. ... Infected ankle (February 27, 2003); missed five games. ... Injured back (October 16, 2003) and had surgery; missed 63 games. ... Injured back (October 7, 2005); out indefinitely.

STATISTICAL PLATEAUS: Three-goal games: 1996-97 (1), 2001-02 (2), 2002-03 (2). Total: 5. ... Four-goal games: 1997-98 (1). ... Total hat tricks: 6.

Season Team	League	REGULAR SEASON GP	G	A	Pts.	PIM	+/-	PP	SH	PLAYOFFS GP	G	A	Pts.	PIM
92-93—Beauport	QMJHL	68	19	36	55	24	...	...	...	—	—	—	—	—
93-94—Beauport	QMJHL	66	59	48	107	31	22	17	3	15	16	8	24	2
94-95—Beauport	QMJHL	57	54	45	99	20	42	14	3	16	9	12	21	23
—Chicago	NHL	4	1	1	2	2	2	0	0	16	0	1	1	4
95-96—Chicago	NHL	80	30	23	53	18	16	2	0	10	3	5	8	0
96-97—Chicago	NHL	71	22	19	41	16	-4	11	0	6	2	1	3	2
97-98—Chicago	NHL	80	31	11	42	22	4	10	0	—	—	—	—	—
98-99—Chicago	NHL	72	22	20	42	22	-13	8	0	—	—	—	—	—
99-00—Chicago	NHL	59	23	13	36	28	-16	6	0	—	—	—	—	—
00-01—Chicago	NHL	79	33	24	57	16	1	9	1	—	—	—	—	—
01-02—Chicago	NHL	82	38	32	70	36	17	12	0	5	0	0	0	2
02-03—Chicago	NHL	54	22	22	44	14	10	3	0	—	—	—	—	—
03-04—Chicago	NHL	19	4	7	11	0	-7	1	0	—	—	—	—	—
05-06—Chicago	NHL	1	0	0	0	2	-2	0	0	—	—	—	—	—
NHL Totals (11 years)		601	226	172	398	176	8	62	1	37	5	7	12	8

DE VRIES, GREG D

PERSONAL: Born January 4, 1973, in Sundridge, Ont. ... 6-3/215. ... Shoots left. ... Name pronounced duh-VREES.

TRANSACTIONS/CAREER NOTES: Signed as free agent by Edmonton Oilers (March 28, 1994). ... Sprained ankle (January 26, 1997); missed four games. ... Traded by Oilers with G Eric Fichaud and D Drake Berehowsky to Nashville Predators for C Jim Dowd and G Mikhail Shtalenkov (October 1, 1998). ... Traded by Predators to Colorado Avalanche for third-round pick (RW Branko Radivojevic) in 1999 entry draft (October 25, 1998). ... Flu (December 27, 1999); missed two games. ... Separated shoulder (February 19, 2001); missed three games. ... Signed as free agent by New York Rangers (July 14, 2003). ... Sprained right knee (January 8, 2004); missed 15 games. ... Flu (February 16, 2004); missed one game. ... Traded by Rangers to Ottawa Senators for D Karel Rachunek and C/LW Alexandre Giroux (March 9, 2004). ... Traded by Senators with RW Marian Hossa to Atlanta Thrashers for RW Dany Heatley (August 23, 2005).

Season Team	League	REGULAR SEASON GP	G	A	Pts.	PIM	+/-	PP	SH	PLAYOFFS GP	G	A	Pts.	PIM
91-92—Bowling Green	CCHA	24	0	3	3	20	...	...	...	—	—	—	—	—
92-93—Niagara Falls	OHL	62	3	23	26	86	...	...	...	4	0	1	1	6
93-94—Niagara Falls	OHL	64	5	40	45	135	...	...	...	—	—	—	—	—
—Cape Breton	AHL	9	0	0	0	11	...	...	...	1	0	0	0	0
94-95—Cape Breton	AHL	77	5	19	24	68	-13	1	1	—	—	—	—	—
95-96—Edmonton	NHL	13	1	1	2	12	-2	0	0	—	—	—	—	—
—Cape Breton	AHL	58	9	30	39	174	...	...	...	—	—	—	—	—
96-97—Hamilton	AHL	34	4	14	18	26	-1	2	0	—	—	—	—	—
—Edmonton	NHL	37	0	4	4	52	-2	0	0	12	0	1	1	8
97-98—Edmonton	NHL	65	7	4	11	80	-17	1	0	7	0	0	0	21
98-99—Nashville	NHL	6	0	0	0	4	-4	0	0	—	—	—	—	—
—Colorado	NHL	67	1	3	4	60	-3	0	0	19	0	2	2	22
99-00—Colorado	NHL	69	2	7	9	73	-7	0	0	5	0	0	0	4
00-01—Colorado	NHL	79	5	12	17	51	23	0	0	23	0	1	1	20
01-02—Colorado	NHL	82	8	12	20	57	18	1	1	21	4	9	13	2
02-03—Colorado	NHL	82	6	26	32	70	15	0	0	7	2	0	2	0
03-04—New York Rangers	NHL	53	3	12	15	37	12	0	0	—	—	—	—	—
—Ottawa	NHL	13	0	1	1	6	0	0	0	7	0	1	1	8
05-06—Atlanta	NHL	82	7	28	35	76	1	3	0	—	—	—	—	—
NHL Totals (10 years)		648	40	110	150	578	34	5	1	101	6	14	20	85

DELMORE, ANDY D

PERSONAL: Born December 26, 1976, in LaSalle, Ont. ... 6-0/201. ... Shoots right.

TRANSACTIONS/CAREER NOTES: Signed as free agent by Philadelphia Flyers (July 9, 1997). ... Sprained right knee (March 5, 2000); missed nine games. ... Traded by Flyers to Nashville Predators for third-round pick (traded to Phoenix; Coyotes selected D Clayton Stoner) in 2002 (July 31, 2001). ... Strained hamstring (December 17, 2001); missed one game. ... Reinjured hamstring (December 23, 2001); missed eight games. ... Shoulder (November 7, 2002); missed five games. ... Wrist (March 12, 2003); missed two games. ... Wrist (March 20, 2003); missed one game. ... Traded by Predators to the Buffalo Sabres for a third-round pick (later traded to Minnesota; Wild picked D Andrew Orpik) in 2004 (June 27, 2003). ... Groin (December 9, 2003); missed 11 games. ... Traded by Sabres with C Curtis Brown to San Jose Sharks for D Jeff Jillson and ninth-round pick in 2005; then traded by Sharks to Boston Bruins for future considerations (March 9, 2004). ... Signed as free agent by Detroit Red Wings (August 16, 2005). ... Claimed off waivers by Columbus Blue Jackets (October 4, 2005). ... Signed as free agent by Tampa Bay Lightning (July 1, 2006).

		REGULAR SEASON								PLAYOFFS				
Season Team	League	GP	G	A	Pts.	PIM	+/-	PP	SH	GP	G	A	Pts.	PIM
92-93—Chatham Jr. B	OHA	47	4	21	25	38	...	...	...	—	—	—	—	—
93-94—North Bay	OHL	45	2	7	9	33	...	...	...	17	0	0	0	2
94-95—North Bay	OHL	40	2	14	16	21	...	0	0	—	—	—	—	—
—Sarnia	OHL	27	5	13	18	27	...	3	0	3	0	0	0	2
95-96—Sarnia	OHL	64	21	38	59	45	...	...	...	10	3	7	10	2
96-97—Sarnia	OHL	63	18	60	78	39	21	11	1	12	2	10	12	10
—Fredericton	AHL	4	0	1	1	0	2	0	0	—	—	—	—	—
97-98—Philadelphia	AHL	73	9	30	39	46	-4	5	0	18	4	4	8	21
98-99—Philadelphia	AHL	70	5	18	23	51	1	1	1	15	1	4	5	6
—Philadelphia	NHL	2	0	1	1	0	-1	0	0	—	—	—	—	—
99-00—Philadelphia	AHL	39	12	14	26	31	...	...	...	—	—	—	—	—
—Philadelphia	NHL	27	2	5	7	8	-1	0	0	18	5	2	7	14
00-01—Philadelphia	NHL	66	5	9	14	16	2	2	0	2	1	0	1	2
01-02—Nashville	NHL	73	16	22	38	22	-13	11	0	—	—	—	—	—
02-03—Nashville	NHL	71	18	16	34	28	-17	14	0	—	—	—	—	—
03-04—Buffalo	NHL	37	2	5	7	29	-5	2	0	—	—	—	—	—
—Rochester	AHL	8	0	2	2	2	-3	0	0	—	—	—	—	—
04-05—Mannheim	Germany	50	7	16	23	59	-2	4	0	14	1	6	7	12
05-06—Syracuse	AHL	66	17	55	72	46	4	11	0	6	0	1	1	19
—Columbus	NHL	7	0	0	0	2	-1	0	0	—	—	—	—	—
NHL Totals (7 years)		283	43	58	101	105	-36	29	0	20	6	2	8	16

DEMITRA, PAVOL RW/C

PERSONAL: Born November 29, 1974, in Dubnica, Czech. ... 6-0/206. ... Shoots left. ... Name pronounced PA-vuhl dih-MEE-truh.

TRANSACTIONS/CAREER NOTES: Selected by Ottawa Senators in ninth round (ninth Senators pick, 227th overall) of entry draft (June 26, 1993). ... Fractured ankle (October 14, 1993); missed 23 games. ... Traded by Senators to St. Louis Blues for D Christer Olsson (November 27, 1996). ... Back spasms, bruised tailbone (December 8, 1997); missed 10 games. ... Fractured jaw (March 7, 1998); missed 11 games. ... Triceps (December 26, 1999); missed three games. ... Concussion (March 24, 2000); missed remainder of season. ... Eye (December 30, 2000); missed 17 games. ... Hamstring (February 10, 2001); missed 14 games. ... Hamstring (March 14, 2001); missed seven games. ... Chicken pox (December 8, 2002); missed four games. ... Flu (November 1, 2003); missed one game. ... Neck (December 29, 2003); missed four games. ... Hip (January 28, 2004); missed nine games. ... Signed as free agent by Los Angeles Kings (August 2, 2005). ... Bruised right leg (January 5, 2006); missed 10 games. ... Fractured nose, bleeding behind right eye (February 24, 2006); missed six games. ... Concussion (March 16, 2006); had facial surgery (March 25, 2006); missed eight games. ... Traded by Kings to Minnesota Wild for C Patrick O'Sullivan and first-round pick (D Trevor Lewis) in 2006 (June 24, 2006).

STATISTICAL PLATEAUS: Three-goal games: 1999-00 (1), 2000-01 (1), 2002-03 (1). Total: 3.

		REGULAR SEASON								PLAYOFFS				
Season Team	League	GP	G	A	Pts.	PIM	+/-	PP	SH	GP	G	A	Pts.	PIM
91-92—Sparta Dubnica	Czech Dv.I	28	13	10	23	12	...	...	...	—	—	—	—	—
92-93—Dukla Trencin	Czech.	46	11	17	28	0	...	...	...	—	—	—	—	—
—CAPEH Dubnica	Czech Dv.I	4	3	0	3	...	...	...	...	—	—	—	—	—
93-94—Ottawa	NHL	12	1	1	2	4	-7	1	0	—	—	—	—	—
—Prince Edward	AHL	41	18	23	41	8	-13	4	0	—	—	—	—	—
94-95—Prince Edward	AHL	61	26	48	74	23	20	4	0	5	0	7	7	0
—Ottawa	NHL	16	4	3	7	0	-4	1	0	—	—	—	—	—
95-96—Prince Edward	AHL	48	28	53	81	44	...	...	...	—	—	—	—	—
—Ottawa	NHL	31	7	10	17	6	-3	2	0	—	—	—	—	—
96-97—Las Vegas	IHL	22	8	13	21	10	...	...	...	—	—	—	—	—
—Grand Rapids	IHL	42	20	30	50	24	...	...	...	—	—	—	—	—
—Dukla Trencin	Slovakia	1	1	1	2	...	...	...	...	—	—	—	—	—
—St. Louis	NHL	8	3	0	3	2	0	2	0	6	1	3	4	6
97-98—St. Louis	NHL	61	22	30	52	22	11	4	4	10	3	3	6	2
98-99—St. Louis	NHL	82	37	52	89	16	13	14	0	13	5	4	9	4
99-00—St. Louis	NHL	71	28	47	75	8	34	8	0	—	—	—	—	—
00-01—St. Louis	NHL	44	20	25	45	16	27	5	0	15	2	4	6	2
01-02—St. Louis	NHL	82	35	43	78	46	13	11	0	10	4	7	11	6
—Slovakian Oly. team	Int'l	2	1	2	3	2	...	...	...	—	—	—	—	—
02-03—St. Louis	NHL	78	36	57	93	32	0	11	0	7	2	4	6	2
03-04—St. Louis	NHL	68	23	35	58	18	1	8	0	5	1	0	1	4
04-05—Dukla Trencin	Slovakia	54	28	54	82	39	49	...	...	12	4	13	17	14
05-06—Los Angeles	NHL	58	25	37	62	42	21	7	5	—	—	—	—	—
—Slovakian Oly. team	Int'l	6	2	5	7	2	10	0	1	—	—	—	—	—
NHL Totals (12 years)		611	241	340	581	212	106	74	9	66	18	25	43	26

DEMPSEY, NATHAN D

PERSONAL: Born July 14, 1974, in Spruce Grove, Alta. ... 6-0/190. ... Shoots left.

TRANSACTIONS/CAREER NOTES: Selected by Toronto Maple Leafs in 11th round (11th Leafs pick, 245th overall) of entry draft (June 20, 1992). ... Signed as free agent by Chicago Blackhawks (July 12, 2002). ... Elbow (January 8, 2004); missed four games. ... Concussion

(February 24, 2004); missed three games. ... Traded by Blackhawks to Los Angeles Kings for fourth-round pick (C/LW Nathan Davis) in 2005 (March 2, 2004). ... Flu (January 2, 2006); missed one game. ... Concussion (March 29, 2006); missed six games.

Season Team	League	REGULAR SEASON								PLAYOFFS				
		GP	G	A	Pts.	PIM	+/-	PP	SH	GP	G	A	Pts.	PIM
91-92—Regina	WHL	70	4	22	26	72	...	...	...	—	—	—	—	—
92-93—Regina	WHL	72	12	29	41	95	...	...	...	13	3	8	11	14
—St. John's	AHL	0	0	0	0	0	...	...	...	2	0	0	0	0
93-94—Regina	WHL	56	14	36	50	100	...	...	...	4	0	0	0	4
94-95—St. John's	AHL	74	7	30	37	91	19	1	1	5	1	0	1	11
95-96—St. John's	AHL	73	5	15	20	103	...	...	...	4	1	0	1	9
96-97—St. John's	AHL	52	8	18	26	108	-5	2	0	6	1	0	1	4
—Toronto	NHL	14	1	1	2	2	-2	0	0	—	—	—	—	—
97-98—St. John's	AHL	68	12	16	28	85	-12	5	0	4	0	0	0	0
98-99—St. John's	AHL	67	2	29	31	70	-12	0	0	5	0	1	1	2
99-00—St. John's	AHL	44	15	12	27	40	...	...	...	—	—	—	—	—
—Toronto	NHL	6	0	2	2	2	2	0	0	—	—	—	—	—
00-01—St. John's	AHL	55	11	28	39	60	...	...	...	4	0	4	4	8
—Toronto	NHL	25	1	9	10	4	13	1	0	—	—	—	—	—
01-02—St. John's	AHL	75	13	48	61	66	4	6	1	11	1	5	6	8
—Toronto	NHL	3	0	0	0	0	1	0	0	6	0	2	2	0
02-03—Chicago	NHL	67	5	23	28	26	-7	1	0	—	—	—	—	—
03-04—Chicago	NHL	58	8	17	25	30	-5	2	0	—	—	—	—	—
—Los Angeles	NHL	17	4	3	7	2	-7	1	0	—	—	—	—	—
04-05—Eisbaren Berlin	Germany	10	2	3	5	26	2	1	0	12	0	3	3	14
05-06—Los Angeles	NHL	53	2	11	13	48	0	0	0	—	—	—	—	—
NHL Totals (7 years)		243	21	66	87	114	-5	5	0	6	0	2	2	0

DENIS, MARC G

PERSONAL: Born August 1, 1977, in Montreal. ... 6-1/193. ... Catches left. ... Name pronounced deh-NEE.

TRANSACTIONS/CAREER NOTES: Selected by Colorado Avalanche in first round (first Avalanche pick, 25th overall) of entry draft (July 8, 1995). ... Traded by Avalanche to Columbus Blue Jackets for second-round pick (traded to Carolina; Hurricanes selected LW Tomas Kurka) in 2000 (June 7, 2000). ... Groin (March 6, 2002); missed four games. ... Flu (November 22, 2003); missed one game. ... Bruised collarbone (October 24, 2005); missed three games. ... Groin (November 20, 2005); missed six games. ... Traded by Blue Jackets to Tampa Bay Lightning for LW Fredrik Modin and G Fredrik Norrena (June 30, 2006).

Season Team	League	REGULAR SEASON										PLAYOFFS							
		GP	Min.	W	L	OTL	T	GA	SO	GAA	SV%	GP	Min.	W	L	GA	SO	GAA	SV%
94-95—Chicoutimi	QMJHL	32	1688	17	9	...	1	98	0	3.48	.891	6	374	4	2	19	1	3.05	.915
95-96—Chicoutimi	QMJHL	51	2895	23	21	...	4	157	2	3.25	...	16	917	8	8	66	0	4.32	...
96-97—Chicoutimi	QMJHL	41	2317	22	15	...	2	104	4	2.69	...	21	1226	11	10	70	1	3.43	.883
—Colorado	NHL	1	60	0	1	...	0	3	0	3.00	.885	—	—	—	—	—	—	—	—
—Hershey	AHL	...	...	...	...	...	...	...	...	...	...	4	56	1	0	1	0	1.07	.960
97-98—Hershey	AHL	47	2589	17	23	...	4	125	1	2.90	.899	6	347	3	3	15	0	2.59	.894
98-99—Hershey	AHL	52	2908	20	23	...	5	137	4	2.83	.914	3	143	1	1	7	0	2.94	.909
—Colorado	NHL	4	217	1	1	...	1	9	0	2.49	.918	—	—	—	—	—	—	—	—
99-00—Colorado	NHL	23	1203	9	8	...	3	51	3	2.54	.917	—	—	—	—	—	—	—	—
00-01—Columbus	NHL	32	1830	6	20	...	4	99	0	3.25	.895	—	—	—	—	—	—	—	—
01-02—Columbus	NHL	42	2335	9	24	...	5	121	1	3.11	.899	—	—	—	—	—	—	—	—
02-03—Columbus	NHL	*77	*4511	27	41	...	8	232	5	3.09	.903	—	—	—	—	—	—	—	—
03-04—Columbus	NHL	66	3796	21	*36	...	7	162	5	2.56	.918	—	—	—	—	—	—	—	—
05-06—Columbus	NHL	49	2786	21	25	1	...	151	1	3.25	.900	—	—	—	—	—	—	—	—
NHL Totals (8 years)		294	16738	94	156	1	28	828	15	2.97	.906								

DESJARDINS, ERIC D

PERSONAL: Born June 14, 1969, in Rouyn, Que. ... 6-1/205. ... Shoots right. ... Name pronounced day-zhar-DAN.

TRANSACTIONS/CAREER NOTES: Selected by Montreal Canadiens in second round (third Canadiens pick, 38th overall) of NHL draft (June 13, 1987). ... Flu (January 1989). ... Injured groin (November 2, 1989); missed seven games. ... Sprained left ankle (January 26, 1991); missed 16 games. ... Fractured right thumb (December 8, 1991); missed two games. ... Traded by Canadiens with LW Gilbert Dionne and C John LeClair to Philadelphia Flyers for RW Mark Recchi and third-round pick (C Martin Hohenberger) in 1995 draft (February 9, 1995). ... Strained groin (March 28, 1995); missed one game. ... Reinjured groin (April 1, 1995); missed three games. ... Flu (December 26, 1995); missed one game. ... Inflamed pelvic bone (October 1, 1997); missed five games. ... Strained groin (October 27, 1998); missed four games. ... Stomach virus (March 6, 1999); missed three games. ... Sprained left knee (March 21, 1999); missed seven games. ... Injured head (September 1999); missed first game of season. ... Stromach virus (December 21, 2000); missed one game. ... Concussion (March 8, 2001); missed two games. ... Strained lower back and injured left elbow (October 27, 2001); missed three games. ... Fractured finger (December 10, 2001); missed 12 games. ... Strained lower back (April 4, 2002); missed two games. ... Injured back (December 4, 2002); missed two games. ... Bruised left knee (March 31, 2003); missed one game. ... Fractured foot (April 19, 2003); missed final eight playoff games. ... Back spasms (November 5, 2003); missed two games. ... Fractured right forearm (January 17, 2004); missed 32 games. ... Reinjured right forearm (April 6, 2004); missed remainder of season and all of playoffs. ... Concussion (November 3, 2005); missed eight games. ... Dislocated right shoulder (December 6, 2005); missed 28 games.

Season Team	League	REGULAR SEASON								PLAYOFFS				
		GP	G	A	Pts.	PIM	+/-	PP	SH	GP	G	A	Pts.	PIM
86-87—Granby	QMJHL	66	14	24	38	75	...	...	...	8	3	2	5	10
87-88—Granby	QMJHL	62	18	49	67	138	...	...	...	5	0	3	3	10
—Sherbrooke	AHL	3	0	0	0	6	...	...	...	4	0	2	2	2
88-89—Montreal	NHL	36	2	12	14	26	9	1	0	14	1	1	2	6
89-90—Montreal	NHL	55	3	13	16	51	1	1	0	6	0	0	0	10
90-91—Montreal	NHL	62	7	18	25	27	7	0	0	13	1	4	5	8

Season Team	League	REGULAR SEASON GP	G	A	Pts.	PIM	+/-	PP	SH	PLAYOFFS GP	G	A	Pts.	PIM
91-92—Montreal	NHL	77	6	32	38	50	17	4	0	11	3	3	6	4
92-93—Montreal	NHL	82	13	32	45	98	20	7	0	20	4	10	14	23
93-94—Montreal	NHL	84	12	23	35	97	-1	6	1	7	0	2	2	4
94-95—Montreal	NHL	9	0	6	6	2	2	0	0	—	—	—	—	—
—Philadelphia	NHL	34	5	18	23	12	10	1	0	15	4	4	8	10
95-96—Philadelphia	NHL	80	7	40	47	45	19	5	0	12	0	6	6	2
96-97—Philadelphia	NHL	82	12	34	46	50	25	5	1	19	2	8	10	12
97-98—Philadelphia	NHL	77	6	27	33	36	11	2	1	5	0	1	1	0
—Can. Olympic team	Int'l	6	0	0	0	2	1	0	0	—	—	—	—	—
98-99—Philadelphia	NHL	68	15	36	51	38	18	6	0	6	2	2	4	4
99-00—Philadelphia	NHL	81	14	41	55	32	20	8	0	18	2	10	12	2
00-01—Philadelphia	NHL	79	15	33	48	50	-3	6	1	6	1	1	2	0
01-02—Philadelphia	NHL	65	6	19	25	24	-1	2	1	5	0	1	1	2
02-03—Philadelphia	NHL	79	8	24	32	35	30	1	0	5	2	1	3	0
03-04—Philadelphia	NHL	48	1	11	12	28	11	0	0	—	—	—	—	—
05-06—Philadelphia	NHL	45	4	20	24	56	3	3	0	6	1	3	4	6
NHL Totals (16 years)		1143	136	439	575	757	198	58	5	168	23	57	80	93

DEVEREAUX, BOYD — C

PERSONAL: Born April 16, 1978, in Seaforth, Ont,. ... 6-2/195. ... Shoots left. ... Name pronounced DEH-vuh-roh.
TRANSACTIONS/CAREER NOTES: Selected by Edmonton Oilers in first round (first Oilers pick, sixth overall) of entry draft (June 22, 1996). ... Concussion (April 1, 2000); missed remainder of season. ... Signed as free agent by Detroit Red Wings (August 23, 2000). ... Fractured thumb (October 10, 2002); missed three games. ... Face (February 23, 2004); missed five games. ... Signed as free agent by Phoenix Coyotes (July 5, 2004). ... Ankle (February 2, 2006); missed two games.
STATISTICAL PLATEAUS: Three-goal games: 1999-00 (1).

Season Team	League	REGULAR SEASON GP	G	A	Pts.	PIM	+/-	PP	SH	PLAYOFFS GP	G	A	Pts.	PIM
93-94—Stratford	OPJHL	46	12	27	39	8	...	...	...	—	—	—	—	—
94-95—Stratford	OPJHL	45	31	74	105	21	...	...	...	—	—	—	—	—
95-96—Kitchener	OHL	66	20	38	58	35	...	...	...	12	3	7	10	4
96-97—Kitchener	OHL	54	28	41	69	37	15	8	3	13	4	11	15	8
—Hamilton	AHL	...	...	...	...	...	...	...	...	1	0	1	1	0
97-98—Edmonton	NHL	38	1	4	5	6	-5	0	0	—	—	—	—	—
—Hamilton	AHL	14	5	6	11	6	0	1	0	9	1	1	2	8
98-99—Edmonton	NHL	61	6	8	14	23	2	0	1	1	0	0	0	0
—Hamilton	AHL	7	4	6	10	2	3	2	0	8	0	3	3	4
99-00—Edmonton	NHL	76	8	19	27	20	7	0	1	—	—	—	—	—
00-01—Detroit	NHL	55	5	6	11	14	1	0	0	2	0	0	0	0
01-02—Detroit	NHL	79	9	16	25	24	9	0	0	21	2	4	6	4
02-03—Detroit	NHL	61	3	9	12	16	4	0	0	—	—	—	—	—
03-04—Detroit	NHL	61	6	9	15	20	-1	0	0	3	1	0	1	0
05-06—Phoenix	NHL	78	8	14	22	44	-13	1	0	—	—	—	—	—
NHL Totals (8 years)		509	46	85	131	167	4	1	2	27	3	4	7	4

DIMAIO, ROB — RW

PERSONAL: Born February 19, 1968, in Calgary. ... 5-10/190. ... Shoots right. ... Name pronounced duh-MIGH-oh.
TRANSACTIONS/CAREER NOTES: Selected by New York Islanders in sixth round (sixth Islanders pick, 118th overall) of NHL draft (June 13, 1987). ... Bruised left hand (February 1989). ... Sprained clavicle (November 1989). ... Sprained wrist (February 20, 1992); missed four games. ... Reinjured wrist (February 29, 1992); missed remainder of season. ... Selected by Tampa Bay Lightning in expansion draft (June 18, 1992). ... Bruised wrist (November 28, 1992); missed four games. ... Sprained ankle (February 14, 1993); missed nine games. ... Reinjured right ankle (March 20, 1993); missed three games. ... Reinjured right ankle (April 1, 1993); missed remainder of season. ... Fractured left leg (October 16, 1993); missed 27 games. ... Traded by Lightning to Philadelphia Flyers for RW Jim Cummins and fourth-round pick (traded back to Flyers) in 1995 draft (March 18, 1994). ... Bruised foot (February 28, 1995); missed two games. ... Flu (April 16, 1995); missed one game. ... Bruised bone in left leg (December 16, 1995); missed 14 games. ... Sprained right knee (March 29, 1996); missed final eight games of regular season. ... Selected by San Jose Sharks from Flyers in waiver draft (September 30, 1996). ... Traded by Sharks to Boston Bruins for fifth-round pick (RW Adam Nittel) in 1997 draft (September 30, 1996). ... Strained knee (November 6, 1996); missed five games. ... Flu (December 17, 1996); missed one game. ... Sprained knee (March 8, 1997); missed two games. ... Injured hip (April 5, 1997); missed two games. ... Strained groin (January 12, 1998); missed one game. ... Suffered concussion (February 26, 1998); missed one game. ... Injured ankle (November 3, 1998); missed one game. ... Had viral meningitis (December 26, 1998); missed five games. ... Strained elbow (April 1, 1999); missed one game. ... Reinjured elbow (April 7, 1999); missed two games. ... Injured hip (October 20, 1999); missed one game. ... Bruised foot (November 10, 1999); missed two games. ... Fractured foot (November 17, 1999); missed eight games. ... Injured wrist (February 25, 2000); missed seven games. ... Traded by Bruins to New York Rangers for RW Mike Knuble (March 10, 2000). ... Suffered concussion (March 19, 2000); missed one game. ... Traded by Rangers with LW Darren Langdon to Carolina Hurricanes for RW Sandy McCarthy and fourth-round (D Bryce Lampman) in 2001 draft (August 4, 2000). ... Back spasms (November 4, 2000); missed three games. ... Strained shoulder (March 21, 2001); missed two games. ... Bruised sternum (March 30, 2001); missed three games. ... Signed as free agent by Dallas Stars (July 1, 2001). ... Strained back (December 13, 2002); missed one game. ... Injured neck (January 29, 2003); missed one game. ... Bruised chest (February 27, 2003); missed nine games. ... Injured hip flexor (November 8, 2003); missed one game. ... Injured ankle (January 13, 2004); missed 11 games. ... Signed as free agent by Tampa Bay Lightning (August 9, 2005). ... Injured back (January 2, 2006); missed three games. ... Injured back (March 4, 2006); missed 11 games.

Season Team	League	REGULAR SEASON GP	G	A	Pts.	PIM	+/-	PP	SH	PLAYOFFS GP	G	A	Pts.	PIM
84-85—Kamloops	WHL	55	9	18	27	29	...	...	...	—	—	—	—	—
85-86—Kamloops	WHL	6	1	0	1	0	...	...	...	—	—	—	—	—
—Medicine Hat	WHL	55	20	30	50	82	...	...	...	—	—	—	—	—
86-87—Medicine Hat	WHL	70	27	43	70	130	...	...	...	20	7	11	18	46

Season Team	League	REGULAR SEASON GP	G	A	Pts.	PIM	+/-	PP	SH	PLAYOFFS GP	G	A	Pts.	PIM
87-88—Medicine Hat	WHL	54	47	43	90	120	...	...	...	14	12	19	31	59
88-89—New York Islanders	NHL	16	1	0	1	30	-6	0	0	—	—	—	—	—
—Springfield	AHL	40	13	18	31	67	...	...	...	—	—	—	—	—
89-90—New York Islanders	NHL	7	0	0	0	2	0	0	0	1	1	0	1	4
—Springfield	AHL	54	25	27	52	69	...	...	...	16	4	7	11	45
90-91—New York Islanders	NHL	1	0	0	0	0	0	0	0	—	—	—	—	—
—Capital District	AHL	12	3	4	7	22	...	...	...	—	—	—	—	—
91-92—New York Islanders	NHL	50	5	2	7	43	-23	0	2	—	—	—	—	—
92-93—Tampa Bay	NHL	54	9	15	24	62	0	2	0	—	—	—	—	—
93-94—Tampa Bay	NHL	39	8	7	15	40	-5	2	0	—	—	—	—	—
—Philadelphia	NHL	14	3	5	8	6	1	0	0	—	—	—	—	—
94-95—Philadelphia	NHL	36	3	1	4	53	8	0	0	15	2	4	6	4
95-96—Philadelphia	NHL	59	6	15	21	58	0	1	1	3	0	0	0	0
96-97—Boston	NHL	72	13	15	28	82	-21	0	3	—	—	—	—	—
97-98—Boston	NHL	79	10	17	27	82	-13	0	0	6	1	0	1	8
98-99—Boston	NHL	71	7	14	21	95	-14	1	0	12	2	0	2	8
99-00—Boston	NHL	50	5	16	21	42	-1	0	0	—	—	—	—	—
—New York Rangers	NHL	12	1	3	4	8	-8	0	0	—	—	—	—	—
00-01—Carolina	NHL	74	6	18	24	54	-14	0	2	6	0	0	0	4
01-02—Dallas	NHL	61	6	6	12	25	-2	0	2	—	—	—	—	—
—Utah	AHL	3	1	1	2	0	0	1	0	—	—	—	—	—
02-03—Dallas	NHL	69	10	9	19	76	18	0	0	12	1	4	5	10
03-04—Dallas	NHL	69	9	15	24	52	2	0	1	5	0	1	1	2
04-05—SC Langnau	Switzerland	9	2	3	5	8	...	0	0	—	—	—	—	—
—Milano	Italy	9	4	8	12	4	...	...	...	15	9	10	19	16
05-06—Tampa Bay	NHL	61	4	13	17	30	-7	2	0	2	0	0	0	0
NHL Totals (17 years)		894	106	171	277	840	-85	8	11	62	7	9	16	40

DIMITRAKOS, NIKO RW

PERSONAL: Born May 21, 1979, in Somersville, Mass. ... 5-10/205. ... Shoots right. ... Name pronounced NIK-oh DIH-mih-tra-kohs.
COLLEGE: Maine.
TRANSACTIONS/CAREER NOTES: Selected by San Jose Sharks in fifth round (fourth Sharks pick, 155th overall) of NHL draft (June 26, 1999). ... Flu (December 30, 2005); missed two games. ... Traded by Sharks to Philadelphia Flyers for third-round pick (traded to Columbus; Blue Jackets selected LW Tommy Sestito) in 2006 entry draft (March 9, 2006).

Season Team	League	REGULAR SEASON GP	G	A	Pts.	PIM	+/-	PP	SH	PLAYOFFS GP	G	A	Pts.	PIM
98-99—Maine	Hockey East	35	8	19	27	33	...	1	0	—	—	—	—	—
99-00—Maine	Hockey East	32	11	16	27	16	...	...	...	—	—	—	—	—
00-01—Maine	Hockey East	29	11	14	25	43	...	...	...	—	—	—	—	—
01-02—Maine	Hockey East	43	20	31	51	44	...	...	...	—	—	—	—	—
02-03—Cleveland	AHL	55	15	29	44	30	-18	10	0	—	—	—	—	—
—San Jose	NHL	21	6	7	13	8	-7	3	0	—	—	—	—	—
03-04—San Jose	NHL	68	9	15	24	49	6	2	0	15	1	8	9	8
—Cleveland	AHL	7	4	4	8	4	7	1	0	—	—	—	—	—
04-05—SC Langnau	Switzerland	3	0	1	1	2	...	0	0	6	3	3	6	16
05-06—San Jose	NHL	45	4	12	16	26	0	0	0	—	—	—	—	—
—Philadelphia	NHL	19	5	4	9	6	4	1	0	5	0	0	0	2
NHL Totals (3 years)		153	24	38	62	89	3	6	0	20	1	8	9	10

DINGMAN, CHRIS LW/RW

PERSONAL: Born July 6, 1976, in Edmonton. ... 6-4/235. ... Shoots left.
TRANSACTIONS/CAREER NOTES: Selected by Calgary Flames in first round (first Flames pick, 19th overall) of NHL draft (June 28, 1994). ... Traded by Flames with RW Theo Fleury to Colorado Avalanche for LW Rene Corbet, D Wade Belak and future considerations (February 28, 1999); Flames acquired D Robyn Regehr to complete deal (March 27, 1999). ... Partially dislocated right shoulder (November 15, 1999); missed six games. ... Sprained knee (November 13, 2000); missed 13 games. ... Traded by Avalanche to Carolina Hurricanes for fifth-round pick (D Mikko Viitanen) in 2001 draft (June 24, 2001). ... Strained groin (September 26, 2001); missed season's first eight games. ... Injured groin (November 9, 2001); missed two games. ... Injured knee (December 12, 2001); missed 16 games. ... Traded by Hurricanes with RW Shane Willis to Tampa Bay Lightning for G Kevin Weekes (March 5, 2002). ... Back spasms (March 30, 2002); missed five games. ... Suspended two games for high-sticking incident (October 16, 2002). ... Injured shoulder (December 27, 2003); missed four games.

Season Team	League	REGULAR SEASON GP	G	A	Pts.	PIM	+/-	PP	SH	PLAYOFFS GP	G	A	Pts.	PIM
92-93—Brandon	WHL	50	10	17	27	64	...	...	...	4	0	0	0	0
93-94—Brandon	WHL	45	21	20	41	77	10	5	0	13	1	7	8	39
94-95—Brandon	WHL	66	40	43	83	201	40	11	1	3	1	0	1	9
95-96—Brandon	WHL	40	16	29	45	109	...	...	...	19	12	11	23	60
—Saint John	AHL	...	...	...	...	...	...	...	...	1	0	0	0	0
96-97—Saint John	AHL	71	5	6	11	195	-9	0	0	—	—	—	—	—
97-98—Calgary	NHL	70	3	3	6	149	-11	1	0	—	—	—	—	—
98-99—Saint John	AHL	50	5	7	12	140	-12	0	0	—	—	—	—	—
—Calgary	NHL	2	0	0	0	17	-2	0	0	—	—	—	—	—
—Hershey	AHL	17	1	3	4	102	-8	0	0	5	0	2	2	6
—Colorado	NHL	1	0	0	0	7	0	0	0	—	—	—	—	—
99-00—Colorado	NHL	68	8	3	11	132	-2	2	0	—	—	—	—	—
00-01—Colorado	NHL	41	1	1	2	108	-3	0	0	16	0	4	4	14
01-02—Carolina	NHL	30	0	1	1	77	-2	0	0	—	—	—	—	—

		REGULAR SEASON								PLAYOFFS				
Season Team	**League**	**GP**	**G**	**A**	**Pts.**	**PIM**	**+/-**	**PP**	**SH**	**GP**	**G**	**A**	**Pts.**	**PIM**
—Tampa Bay	NHL	14	0	4	4	26	-8	0	0	—	—	—	—	—
02-03—Tampa Bay	NHL	51	2	1	3	91	-11	0	0	10	1	0	1	4
03-04—Tampa Bay	NHL	74	1	5	6	140	-9	0	0	23	1	1	2	63
05-06—Springfield	AHL	27	8	8	16	30	-11	3	0	—	—	—	—	—
—Tampa Bay	NHL	34	0	1	1	22	-10	0	0	3	0	0	0	19
NHL Totals (8 years)		385	15	19	34	769	-58	3	0	52	2	5	7	100

DIPENTA, JOE — D

PERSONAL: Born February 25, 1979, in Barrie, Ont. ... 6-2/235. ... Shoots right.

TRANSACTIONS/CAREER NOTES: Selected by Florida Panthers in third round (second Panthers pick, 61st overall) of entry draft (June 27, 1998). ... Signed as free agent by Philadelphia Flyers (August 1, 2000). ... Traded by Flyers to Atlanta Thrashers for C Jarrod Skalde (March 4, 2002). ... Signed as free agent by Vancouver Canucks (August 19, 2004). ... Signed as free agent by Anaheim Mighty Ducks (August 11, 2005).

		REGULAR SEASON								PLAYOFFS				
Season Team	**League**	**GP**	**G**	**A**	**Pts.**	**PIM**	**+/-**	**PP**	**SH**	**GP**	**G**	**A**	**Pts.**	**PIM**
96-97—Smith Falls	OJHL	54	13	22	35	92	...	...	...	—	—	—	—	—
97-98—Boston University	Hockey East	38	2	16	18	50	...	...	...	—	—	—	—	—
98-99—Boston University	Hockey East	36	2	15	17	72	...	...	...	—	—	—	—	—
99-00—Halifax	QMJHL	63	13	43	56	83	32	6	0	10	3	4	7	26
00-01—Philadelphia	AHL	71	3	5	8	65	...	...	...	10	1	2	3	15
01-02—Philadelphia	AHL	61	2	4	6	71	7	0	0	—	—	—	—	—
—Chicago	AHL	15	0	2	2	15	...	...	...	25	1	3	4	22
02-03—Chicago	AHL	76	2	17	19	107	22	1	0	9	0	1	1	7
—Atlanta	NHL	3	1	1	2	0	3	0	0	—	—	—	—	—
03-04—Chicago	AHL	73	0	6	6	105	1	0	0	10	1	0	1	13
—Cincinnati	AHL	7	0	0	0	9	...	...	...	—	—	—	—	—
04-05—Manitoba	AHL	73	2	10	12	48	18	0	0	14	0	5	5	2
05-06—Anaheim	NHL	72	2	6	8	46	8	0	0	16	0	0	0	13
NHL Totals (2 years)		75	3	7	10	46	11	0	0	16	0	0	0	13

DIPIETRO, RICK — G

PERSONAL: Born September 19, 1981, in Winthrop, Mass. ... 6-0/190. ... Catches right.

TRANSACTIONS/CAREER NOTES: Selected by New York Islanders in first round (first Islanders pick, first overall) of entry draft (June 24, 2000). ... Re-signed by Islanders as restricted free agent (September 7, 2005). ... Mild concussion (October 13, 2005); missed one game. ... Bruised knee (November 1, 2005); missed one game. ... Sprained left knee (December 30, 2005); missed five games.

		REGULAR SEASON										PLAYOFFS							
Season Team	**League**	**GP**	**Min.**	**W**	**L**	**OTL**	**T**	**GA**	**SO**	**GAA**	**SV%**	**GP**	**Min.**	**W**	**L**	**GA**	**SO**	**GAA**	**SV%**
97-98 —U.S. Jr. national team	Int'l	46	2526	21	19	...	0	131	2	3.11	.893	—	—	—	—	—	—	—	—
98-99 —U.S. Jr. national team	Int'l	30	1733	22	6	...	2	67	3	2.32	.907	—	—	—	—	—	—	—	—
99-00 —Boston University	Hockey East	30	1791	18	5	...	5	73	2	2.45	.913	—	—	—	—	—	—	—	—
00-01 —Chicago	IHL	14	778	4	5	...	2	44	0	3.39	...	—	—	—	—	—	—	—	—
—New York Islanders	NHL	20	1083	3	15	...	1	63	0	3.49	.878	—	—	—	—	—	—	—	—
01-02 —Bridgeport	AHL	59	3471	30	22	...	7	134	4	2.32	.905	20	1270	12	8	45	3	2.13	.906
02-03 —New York Islanders	NHL	10	585	2	5	...	2	29	0	2.97	.894	1	15	0	0	0	0	0.00	1.00
—Bridgeport	AHL	34	2044	16	10	...	8	73	3	2.14	.924	5	298	2	3	10	1	2.01	.925
03-04 —Bridgeport	AHL	2	119	0	2	...	0	3	0	1.51	.942	—	—	—	—	—	—	—	—
—New York Islanders	NHL	50	2844	23	18	...	5	112	5	2.36	.911	5	303	1	4	11	1	2.18	.908
05-06 —New York Islanders	NHL	63	3572	30	24	5	...	180	1	3.02	.900	—	—	—	—	—	—	—	—
—U.S. Oly. team	Int'l	4	...	...	...	...	...	...	0	2.28	.893	—	—	—	—	—	—	—	—
NHL Totals (4 years)		143	8084	58	62	5	8	384	6	2.85	.900	6	318	1	4	11	1	2.08	.911

DISALVATORE, JON — RW

PERSONAL: Born March 30, 1981, in Bangor, Maine. ... 6-1/180. ... Shoots right.

TRANSACTIONS/CAREER NOTES: Selected by San Jose Sharks in fourth round (second Sharks pick, 104th overall) of entry draft (June 24, 2000). ... Signed as free agent by St. Louis Blues (June 30, 2004).

		REGULAR SEASON								PLAYOFFS				
Season Team	**League**	**GP**	**G**	**A**	**Pts.**	**PIM**	**+/-**	**PP**	**SH**	**GP**	**G**	**A**	**Pts.**	**PIM**
98-99—New England	EJHL	...	45	75	120	...	...	...	...	—	—	—	—	—
99-00—Providence College	Hockey East	38	15	12	27	12	...	...	...	—	—	—	—	—
00-01—Providence College	Hockey East	36	9	16	25	29	...	...	...	—	—	—	—	—
01-02—Providence College	Hockey East	38	16	26	42	6	...	...	...	—	—	—	—	—
02-03—Providence College	Hockey East	36	19	29	48	12	...	...	...	—	—	—	—	—
03-04—Cleveland	AHL	74	22	24	46	30	...	...	...	8	1	1	2	2
04-05—Worcester	AHL	79	22	23	45	42	-17	8	1	—	—	—	—	—
05-06—St. Louis	NHL	5	0	0	0	2	-1	0	0	—	—	—	—	—
—Peoria	AHL	72	22	45	67	42	2	8	2	4	0	0	0	0
NHL Totals (1 year)		5	0	0	0	2	-1	0	0					

DIVIS, REINHARD — G

PERSONAL: Born July 4, 1975, in Vienna, Austria. ... 6-0/192. ... Catches left.

TRANSACTIONS/CAREER NOTES: Selected by St. Louis Blues in 8th round (8th Blues pick, 261st overall) of entry draft (June 25, 2000).

		REGULAR SEASON										PLAYOFFS							
Season Team	**League**	**GP**	**Min.**	**W**	**L**	**OTL**	**T**	**GA**	**SO**	**GAA**	**SV%**	**GP**	**Min.**	**W**	**L**	**GA**	**SO**	**GAA**	**SV%**
95-96 —VEU Feldkirch	Austria	37	2200	...	...	...	...	85	0	2.32	...	—	—	—	—	—	—	—	—
96-97 —VEU Feldkirch	Alpenliga	45	2792	...	...	...	...	105	0	2.26	...	—	—	—	—	—	—	—	—
—VEU Feldkirch	Austria	...	...	...	...	...	...	27	0	...	...	11	620	...	...	...	...	...	...
97-98 —VEU Feldkirch	Austria	13	779	...	...	...	...	22	0	1.69	...	—	—	—	—	—	—	—	—
—VEU Feldkirch	Alpenliga	27	1620	...	...	...	...	55	0	2.04	...	—	—	—	—	—	—	—	—
98-99 —VEU Feldkirch	Austria	15	900	...	...	...	...	58	0	3.87	...	—	—	—	—	—	—	—	—
99-00 —Leksand	Sweden Dv. 2	48	2839	...	...	...	...	160	3	3.38	...	—	—	—	—	—	—	—	—
00-01 —Leksand	Sweden Dv. 2	41	2451	...	...	...	...	141	3	3.45	...	—	—	—	—	—	—	—	—
01-02 —Worcester	AHL	55	3173	28	20	...	5	137	3	2.59	.892	3	204	1	2	8	0	2.35	.930
—Austrian Olympic team	Int'l	4	238	1	3	...	0	12	0	3.03	.875	—	—	—	—	—	—	—	—
—St. Louis	NHL	1	25	0	0	...	0	0	0	0.00	1.000	—	—	—	—	—	—	—	—
02-03 —Worcester	AHL	9	452	6	1	...	0	17	0	2.26	.923	—	—	—	—	—	—	—	—
—St. Louis	NHL	2	83	2	0	...	0	1	0	0.72	.971	—	—	—	—	—	—	—	—
03-04 —Worcester	AHL	31	1710	12	10	...	8	63	3	2.21	.911	—	—	—	—	—	—	—	—
—St. Louis	NHL	13	629	4	4	...	2	29	0	2.77	.900	1	18	0	0	0	0	0.00	1.000
04-05 —VSV	Austria	29	1651	10	13	...	4	73	2	2.65	.920	—	—	—	—	—	—	—	—
05-06 —Peoria	AHL	31	1646	16	10	2	...	76	2	2.77	.899	—	—	—	—	—	—	—	—
—St. Louis	NHL	12	475	0	5	1	...	37	0	4.67	.840	—	—	—	—	—	—	—	—
NHL Totals (4 years)		28	1212	6	9	1	2	67	0	3.32	.880	1	18	0	0	0	0	0.00	1.000

DOAN, SHANE — RW

PERSONAL: Born October 10, 1976, in Halkirk, Alta. ... 6-2/216. ... Shoots right. ... Name pronounced DOHN.

TRANSACTIONS/CAREER NOTES: Selected by Winnipeg Jets in first round (first Jets pick, seventh overall) of entry draft (July 8, 1995). ... Flu (January 8, 1996); missed one game. ... Ribs (January 14, 1996); missed two games. ... Back (February 23, 1996); missed two games. ... Jets franchise moved to Phoenix and renamed Coyotes for 1996-97 season; NHL approved move on January 18, 1996. ... Ankle (October 14, 1996); missed two games. ... Foot (November 8, 1996); missed eight games. ... Hand (February 22, 1997); missed four games. ... Eye (February 20, 1999); missed one game. ... Forearm (March 15, 1999); missed one game. ... Knee (December 10, 2000); missed one game. ... Abdominal strain (January 24, 2001); missed five games. ... Ankle (March 17, 2002); missed one game. ... Charley horse (March 12, 2004); missed two games. ... Knee (April 2, 2004); missed final game of season.

		REGULAR SEASON								PLAYOFFS				
Season Team	**League**	**GP**	**G**	**A**	**Pts.**	**PIM**	**+/-**	**PP**	**SH**	**GP**	**G**	**A**	**Pts.**	**PIM**
92-93—Kamloops	WHL	51	7	12	19	55	...	...	...	13	0	1	1	8
93-94—Kamloops	WHL	52	24	24	48	88	...	...	...	—	—	—	—	—
94-95—Kamloops	WHL	71	37	57	94	106	47	12	1	21	6	10	16	16
95-96—Winnipeg	NHL	74	7	10	17	101	-9	1	0	6	0	0	0	6
96-97—Phoenix	NHL	63	4	8	12	49	-3	0	0	4	0	0	0	2
97-98—Phoenix	NHL	33	5	6	11	35	-3	0	0	6	1	0	1	6
—Springfield	AHL	39	21	21	42	64	20	6	0	—	—	—	—	—
98-99—Phoenix	NHL	79	6	16	22	54	-5	0	0	7	2	2	4	6
99-00—Phoenix	NHL	81	26	25	51	66	6	1	1	4	1	2	3	8
00-01—Phoenix	NHL	76	26	37	63	89	0	6	1	—	—	—	—	—
01-02—Phoenix	NHL	81	20	29	49	61	11	6	0	5	2	2	4	6
02-03—Phoenix	NHL	82	21	37	58	86	3	7	0	—	—	—	—	—
03-04—Phoenix	NHL	79	27	41	68	47	-11	9	2	—	—	—	—	—
05-06—Phoenix	NHL	82	30	36	66	123	-9	17	0	—	—	—	—	—
—Canadian Oly. team	Int'l	6	2	1	3	2	3	0	0	—	—	—	—	—
NHL Totals (10 years)		730	172	245	417	711	-20	47	4	32	6	6	12	34

DOMI, TIE — RW

PERSONAL: Born November 1, 1969, in Windsor, Ont. ... 5-10/213. ... Shoots right. ... Name pronounced TIGH DOH-mee.

TRANSACTIONS/CAREER NOTES: Selected by Toronto Maple Leafs in second round (second Maple Leafs pick, 27th overall) of NHL draft (June 11, 1988). ... Traded by Maple Leafs with G Mark Laforest to New York Rangers for RW Greg Johnston (June 28, 1990). ... Sprained right knee (March 11, 1992); missed eight games. ... Traded by Rangers with LW Kris King to Winnipeg Jets for C Ed Olczyk (December 28, 1992). ... Fined $500 for premeditated fight (January 4, 1993). ... Sprained knee (January 25, 1994); missed three games. ... Traded by Jets to Maple Leafs for C Mike Eastwood and third-round pick (RW Brad Isbister) in 1995 draft (April 7, 1995). ... Strained groin (April 8, 1995); missed two games. ... Flu (April 19, 1995); missed one game. ... Suspended eight games for fighting (October 17, 1995). ... Sprained knee (December 2, 1995); missed two games. ... Fined $1,000 for fighting (November 13, 1996). ... Sprained ankle (April 2, 1997); missed two games. ... Strained abdominal muscle (October 25, 1997); missed two games. ... Sprained knee (January 7, 1999); missed 10 games. ... Injured (October 30, 1999); missed five games. ... Injured (January 14, 2000); missed seven games. ... Suspended remainder of playoffs and first eight games of 2001-02 season game for elbowing incident (May 4, 2001). ... Traded by Maple Leafs to Nashville Predators for eighth-round pick (C Shaun Landolt) in 2003 draft (June 30, 2002). ... Signed as free agent by Maple Leafs (July 12, 2002). ... Suspended two games for unsportsmanlike conduct (March 5, 2003). ... Shoulder injury (December 17, 2005); missed two games.

		REGULAR SEASON								PLAYOFFS				
Season Team	**League**	**GP**	**G**	**A**	**Pts.**	**PIM**	**+/-**	**PP**	**SH**	**GP**	**G**	**A**	**Pts.**	**PIM**
85-86—Windsor Jr. B	OHA	32	8	17	25	346	...	...	...	—	—	—	—	—
86-87—Peterborough	OHL	18	1	1	2	79	...	...	...	—	—	—	—	—
87-88—Peterborough	OHL	60	22	21	43	292	...	...	...	12	3	9	12	24
88-89—Peterborough	OHL	43	14	16	30	175	...	...	...	17	10	9	19	70
89-90—Newmarket	AHL	57	14	11	25	285	...	...	...	—	—	—	—	—
—Toronto	NHL	2	0	0	0	42	0	0	0	—	—	—	—	—

Season Team	League	GP	G	A	Pts.	PIM	+/-	PP	SH	GP	G	A	Pts.	PIM
		REGULAR SEASON								PLAYOFFS				
90-91—New York Rangers......	NHL	28	1	0	1	185	-5	0	0	—	—	—	—	—
—Binghamton	AHL	25	11	6	17	219	...	...	...	7	3	2	5	16
91-92—New York Rangers......	NHL	42	2	4	6	246	-4	0	0	6	1	1	2	32
92-93—New York Rangers......	NHL	12	2	0	2	95	-1	0	0	—	—	—	—	—
—Winnipeg	NHL	49	3	10	13	249	2	0	0	6	1	0	1	23
93-94—Winnipeg	NHL	81	8	11	19	*347	-8	0	0	—	—	—	—	—
94-95—Winnipeg	NHL	31	4	4	8	128	-6	0	0	—	—	—	—	—
—Toronto	NHL	9	0	1	1	31	1	0	0	7	1	0	1	0
95-96—Toronto	NHL	72	7	6	13	297	-3	0	0	6	0	2	2	4
96-97—Toronto	NHL	80	11	17	28	275	-17	2	0	—	—	—	—	—
97-98—Toronto	NHL	80	4	10	14	365	-5	0	0	—	—	—	—	—
98-99—Toronto	NHL	72	8	14	22	198	5	0	0	14	0	2	2	24
99-00—Toronto	NHL	70	5	9	14	198	-5	0	0	12	0	1	1	20
00-01—Toronto	NHL	82	13	7	20	214	2	1	0	8	0	1	1	20
01-02—Toronto	NHL	74	9	10	19	157	3	0	0	19	1	3	4	61
02-03—Toronto	NHL	79	15	14	29	171	-1	4	0	7	1	0	1	13
03-04—Toronto	NHL	80	7	13	20	208	-2	1	0	13	2	2	4	41
05-06—Toronto	NHL	77	5	11	16	109	-10	1	0	—	—	—	—	—
NHL Totals (16 years)..........		1020	104	141	245	3515	-54	9	0	98	7	12	19	238

DONOVAN, SHEAN RW

PERSONAL: Born January 22, 1975, in Timmins, Ont. ... 6-2/200. ... Shoots right. ... Name pronounced SHAWN DAHN-ih-vihn.

TRANSACTIONS/CAREER NOTES: Selected by San Jose Sharks in second round (second Sharks pick, 28th overall) of NHL entry draft (June 26, 1993). ... Suffered concussion (October 5, 1996); missed two games. ... Injured knee (December 21, 1996); missed two games. ... Traded by Sharks with first-round pick (C Alex Tanguay) in 1998 entry draft to Colorado Avalanche for C Mike Ricci and second-round pick (RW Jonathan Cheechoo) in 1998 entry draft (November 20, 1997). ... Bruised knee (January 3, 1998); missed one game. ... Bruised knee (January 21, 1998); missed three games. ... Suffered concussion (October 24, 1998); missed one game. ... Injured shoulder and jaw (February 5, 1999); missed one game. ... Injured hip (March 20, 1999); missed two games. ... Traded by Avalanche to Atlanta Thrashers for G Rick Tabaracci (December 8, 1999). ... Strained abdominal muscle (January 1, 2000); missed three games. ... Fractured right foot (January 27, 2000); missed 20 games. ... Sprained knee (December 9, 2000); missed 13 games. ... Bruised heel (January 22, 2002); missed one game. ... Claimed on waivers by Pittsburgh Penguins (March 15, 2002). ... Cut elbow (April 8, 2002); missed two games. ... Injured knee (November 2, 2002); missed seven games. ... Fractured foot (November 30, 2002); missed 11 games. ... Traded by Penguins to Calgary Flames for D Micki Dupont and C Mathias Johansson (March 11, 2003). ... Signed as free agent by Boston Bruins (July 2, 2006).

STATISTICAL PLATEAUS: Three-goal games: 2000-01 (1), 2003-04 (1). Total: 2.

Season Team	League	GP	G	A	Pts.	PIM	+/-	PP	SH	GP	G	A	Pts.	PIM
		REGULAR SEASON								PLAYOFFS				
91-92—Ottawa	OHL	58	11	8	19	14	...	...	...	11	1	0	1	5
92-93—Ottawa	OHL	66	29	23	52	33	...	...	...	—	—	—	—	—
93-94—Ottawa	OHL	62	35	49	84	63	...	8	4	17	10	11	21	14
94-95—Ottawa	OHL	29	22	19	41	41	...	4	1	—	—	—	—	—
—San Jose....................	NHL	14	0	0	0	6	-6	0	0	7	0	1	1	6
—Kansas City................	IHL	5	0	2	2	7	-2	0	0	14	5	3	8	23
95-96—Kansas City................	IHL	4	0	0	0	8	...	...	...	5	0	0	0	8
—San Jose....................	NHL	74	13	8	21	39	-17	0	1	—	—	—	—	—
96-97—San Jose....................	NHL	73	9	6	15	42	-18	0	1	—	—	—	—	—
—Kentucky.....................	AHL	3	1	3	4	18	2	0	0	—	—	—	—	—
—Canadian nat'l team....	Int'l	10	0	1	1	31	...	...	...	—	—	—	—	—
97-98—San Jose....................	NHL	20	3	3	6	22	3	0	0	—	—	—	—	—
—Colorado....................	NHL	47	5	7	12	48	3	0	0	—	—	—	—	—
98-99—Colorado....................	NHL	68	7	12	19	37	4	1	0	5	0	0	0	2
99-00—Colorado....................	NHL	18	1	0	1	8	-4	0	0	—	—	—	—	—
—Atlanta	NHL	33	4	7	11	18	-13	1	0	—	—	—	—	—
00-01—Atlanta	NHL	63	12	11	23	47	-14	1	3	—	—	—	—	—
01-02—Atlanta	NHL	48	6	6	12	40	-16	1	0	—	—	—	—	—
—Pittsburgh.................	NHL	13	2	1	3	4	-5	0	0	—	—	—	—	—
02-03—Pittsburgh.................	NHL	52	4	5	9	30	-6	0	1	—	—	—	—	—
—Calgary	NHL	13	1	2	3	7	-2	0	0	—	—	—	—	—
03-04—Calgary	NHL	82	18	24	42	72	14	3	3	24	5	5	10	23
04-05—Geneva........................	Switzerland	12	5	3	8	30	...	1	1	—	—	—	—	—
05-06—Calgary	NHL	80	9	11	20	82	9	0	1	7	0	0	0	6
NHL Totals (11 years)..........		698	94	103	197	502	-68	7	10	43	5	6	11	37

DOULL, DOUG LW

PERSONAL: Born May 31, 1974, in Glace Bay, N.S. ... 6-2/216. ... Shoots left.

TRANSACTIONS/CAREER NOTES: Signed as free agent by Toronto Maple Leafs (July 25, 2001). ... Signed as free agent by Boston Bruins (July 28, 2003). ... Flu (January 7, 2004); missed one game. ... Suspended one game for charging incident (January 20, 2004). ... Signed as free agent by Phoenix Coyotes (September 2, 2004). ... Traded by Coyotes to Washington Capitals for D Dwayne Zinger (February 3, 2006).

Season Team	League	GP	G	A	Pts.	PIM	+/-	PP	SH	GP	G	A	Pts.	PIM
		REGULAR SEASON								PLAYOFFS				
91-92—Belleville	OHL	62	6	11	17	123	...	...	...	—	—	—	—	—
92-93—Belleville	OHL	65	19	37	56	143	...	...	...	—	—	—	—	—
93-94—Belleville	OHL	62	13	24	37	143	...	...	...	—	—	—	—	—
94-95—Belleville	OHL	29	7	12	19	71	...	...	...	16	2	13	15	39
95-96—St. Mary's University ..	AUAA	11	4	4	8	54	...	...	...	—	—	—	—	—
96-97—St. Mary's University ..	AUAA	18	3	10	13	138	...	...	...	—	—	—	—	—

Season Team	League	GP	G	A	Pts.	PIM	+/-	PP	SH	GP	G	A	Pts.	PIM
		REGULAR SEASON								PLAYOFFS				
97-98—St. Mary's University ..	AUAA	25	4	11	15	227	...	...	...	—	—	—	—	—
98-99—Michigan	IHL	55	4	11	15	227	...	...	...	3	1	1	2	4
99-00—Manitoba	AHL	45	4	4	8	184	...	...	...	2	0	0	0	2
—Detroit	IHL	17	0	2	2	69	...	...	...	—	—	—	—	—
00-01—Manchester	England	15	1	6	7	51	...	...	...	—	—	—	—	—
—Saint John	AHL	49	3	10	13	167	...	...	...	16	0	1	1	32
01-02—St. John's	AHL	36	5	8	13	166	...	...	...	9	0	1	1	17
02-03—St. John's	AHL	70	15	10	25	257	...	...	...	—	—	—	—	—
03-04—Providence	AHL	22	1	0	1	98	-7	0	0	—	—	—	—	—
—Boston	NHL	35	0	1	1	132	2	0	0	—	—	—	—	—
04-05—Utah	AHL	40	1	1	2	232	-11	0	0	—	—	—	—	—
05-06—San Antonio	AHL	26	1	2	3	84	1	0	0	—	—	—	—	—
—Hershey	AHL	21	1	2	3	117	-2	0	0	1	0	0	0	4
—Washington	NHL	2	0	0	0	19	-1	0	0	—	—	—	—	—
NHL Totals (2 years)		37	0	1	1	151	1	0	0					

DOWD, JIM C

PERSONAL: Born December 25, 1968, in Brick, N.J. ... 6-1/190. ... Shoots right.

TRANSACTIONS/CAREER NOTES: Selected by New Jersey Devils in eighth round (seventh Devils pick, 149th overall) of NHL draft (June 13, 1987). ... Injured shoulder (February 2, 1995) and had shoulder surgery; missed 35 games. ... Traded by Devils with second-round pick (traded to Calgary; Flames selected Dmitri Kokorev) in 1997 draft to Hartford Whalers for RW Jocelyn Lemieux and second-round pick (traded to Dallas; Stars picked D John Erskine) in 1998 draft (December 19, 1995). ... Traded by Whalers with D Frantisek Kucera and second-round pick (D Ryan Bonni) in 1997 draft to Vancouver Canucks for D Jeff Brown and third-round pick (traded to Dallas; Stars picked D Paul Manning) in 1998 draft (December 19, 1995). ... Selected by New York Islanders from Canucks in waiver draft (September 30, 1996). ... Signed as free agent by Calgary Flames (July 10, 1997). ... Traded by Flames to Nashville Predators for future considerations (June 27, 1998). ... Traded by Predators with G Mikhail Shtalenkov to Edmonton Oilers for G Eric Fichaud, D Drake Berehowsky and D Greg de Vries (October 1, 1998). ... Selected by Minnesota Wild in expansion draft (June 23, 2000). ... Injured ribs (January 6, 2001); missed 10 games. ... Strained neck (March 31, 2001); missed four games. ... Flu (December 14, 2002); missed one game. ... Injured groin (February 10, 2004); missed 10 games. ... Traded by Wild to Montreal Canadiens for fourth-round pick (W Julien Sprunger) in 2004 draft (March 4, 2004). ... Signed as free agent by Chicago Blackhawks (August 5, 2005). ... Traded by Blackhawks to Colorado Avalanche for fourth-round pick (traded to Toronto; Maple Leafs selected D Korbinian Holzer) in 2006 draft (March 9, 2006).

Season Team	League	GP	G	A	Pts.	PIM	+/-	PP	SH	GP	G	A	Pts.	PIM
		REGULAR SEASON								PLAYOFFS				
83-84—Brick Township	N.J. H.S.	...	19	30	49	...	...	...	...	—	—	—	—	—
84-85—Brick Township	N.J. H.S.	...	58	55	113	...	...	...	...	—	—	—	—	—
85-86—Brick Township	N.J. H.S.	...	47	51	98	...	...	...	...	—	—	—	—	—
86-87—Brick Township	N.J. H.S.	24	22	33	55	...	...	...	...	—	—	—	—	—
87-88—Lake Superior St.	CCHA	45	18	27	45	16	...	...	...	—	—	—	—	—
88-89—Lake Superior St.	CCHA	46	24	35	59	40	...	...	...	—	—	—	—	—
89-90—Lake Superior St.	CCHA	46	25	67	92	30	...	...	...	—	—	—	—	—
90-91—Lake Superior St.	CCHA	44	24	54	78	53	...	...	...	—	—	—	—	—
91-92—Utica	AHL	78	17	42	59	47	...	...	...	4	2	2	4	4
—New Jersey	NHL	1	0	0	0	0	0	0	0	—	—	—	—	—
92-93—Utica	AHL	78	27	45	72	62	-6	3	2	5	1	7	8	10
—New Jersey	NHL	1	0	0	0	0	-1	0	0	—	—	—	—	—
93-94—Albany	AHL	58	26	37	63	76	15	3	3	—	—	—	—	—
—New Jersey	NHL	15	5	10	15	0	8	2	0	19	2	6	8	8
94-95—New Jersey	NHL	10	1	4	5	0	-5	1	0	11	2	1	3	8
95-96—New Jersey	NHL	28	4	9	13	17	-1	0	0	—	—	—	—	—
—Vancouver	NHL	38	1	6	7	6	-8	0	0	1	0	0	0	0
96-97—New York Islanders	NHL	3	0	0	0	0	-1	0	0	—	—	—	—	—
—Utah	IHL	48	10	21	31	27	...	...	...	—	—	—	—	—
—Saint John	AHL	24	5	11	16	18	-5	2	0	5	1	2	3	0
97-98—Saint John	AHL	35	8	30	38	20	5	1	1	19	3	13	16	10
—Calgary	NHL	48	6	8	14	12	10	0	1	—	—	—	—	—
98-99—Hamilton	AHL	51	15	29	44	82	3	5	2	11	3	6	9	8
—Edmonton	NHL	1	0	0	0	0	0	0	0	—	—	—	—	—
99-00—Edmonton	NHL	69	5	18	23	45	10	2	0	5	2	1	3	4
00-01—Minnesota	NHL	68	7	22	29	80	-6	0	0	—	—	—	—	—
01-02—Minnesota	NHL	82	13	30	43	54	-14	5	0	—	—	—	—	—
02-03—Minnesota	NHL	78	8	17	25	31	-1	3	1	15	0	2	2	0
03-04—Minnesota	NHL	55	4	20	24	38	6	2	0	—	—	—	—	—
—Montreal	NHL	14	3	2	5	6	6	0	1	11	0	2	2	2
04-05—Hamburg	Germany	20	4	9	13	12	1	1	1	...	...	...	...	...
05-06—Chicago	NHL	60	3	12	15	38	-5	0	0	—	—	—	—	—
—Colorado	NHL	18	2	1	3	2	-6	0	1	9	2	3	5	20
NHL Totals (14 years)		589	62	159	221	329	-8	15	4	71	8	15	23	42

DOWNEY, AARON RW

PERSONAL: Born August 27, 1974, in Shelburne, Ont. ... 6-1/216. ... Shoots right.

TRANSACTIONS/CAREER NOTES: Signed as free agent by Boston Bruins (January 20, 1998). ... Signed as free agent by Chicago Blackhawks (August 8, 2000). ... Signed as free agent by Dallas Stars (July 3, 2002). ... Injured hip flexor (November 11, 2003); missed 17 games. ... Signed as free agent by St. Louis Blues (August 1, 2005). ... Strained left oblique muscle (December 22, 2005); missed nine games. ... Claimed on waivers by Montreal Canadiens (January 23, 2006).

Season Team	League	REGULAR SEASON GP	G	A	Pts.	PIM	+/-	PP	SH	PLAYOFFS GP	G	A	Pts.	PIM
92-93—Guelph	OHL	53	3	3	6	88	...	...	...	5	1	0	1	0
93-94—Cole Harbor	MWJHL	35	8	20	28	210	...	...	...	—	—	—	—	—
94-95—Cole Harbor	MWJHL	40	10	31	41	320	...	...	...	—	—	—	—	—
95-96—Hampton	ECHL	65	12	11	23	354	...	...	...	—	—	—	—	—
96-97—Hampton	ECHL	64	8	8	16	338	...	...	...	9	0	3	3	26
—Portland	AHL	3	0	0	0	19	...	...	...	—	—	—	—	—
—Manitoba	IHL	2	0	0	0	17	...	...	...	—	—	—	—	—
97-98—Providence	AHL	78	5	10	15	407	-8	0	0	—	—	—	—	—
98-99—Providence	AHL	75	10	12	22	401	3	1	0	19	1	1	2	46
99-00—Providence	AHL	47	6	4	10	221	...	...	...	14	1	0	1	24
—Boston	NHL	1	0	0	0	0	0	0	0	—	—	—	—	—
00-01—Norfolk	AHL	67	6	15	21	234	...	...	...	9	0	0	0	4
—Chicago	NHL	3	0	0	0	6	-1	0	0	—	—	—	—	—
01-02—Chicago	NHL	36	1	0	1	76	-2	0	0	4	0	0	0	8
—Norfolk	AHL	12	0	2	2	21	1	0	0	—	—	—	—	—
02-03—Dallas	NHL	43	1	1	2	69	1	0	0	—	—	—	—	—
03-04—Dallas	NHL	37	1	1	2	77	2	0	0	—	—	—	—	—
05-06—St. Louis	NHL	17	2	0	2	45	0	0	0	—	—	—	—	—
—Montreal	NHL	25	1	4	5	50	2	0	0	1	0	0	0	0
NHL Totals (6 years)		162	6	6	12	323	2	0	0	5	0	0	0	8

DRAKE, DALLAS RW/LW

PERSONAL: Born February 4, 1969, in Trail, B.C. ... 6-0/195. ... Shoots left.

TRANSACTIONS/CAREER NOTES: Selected by Detroit Red Wings in sixth round (sixth Red Wings pick, 116th overall) of entry draft (June 17, 1989). ... Bruised left leg (November 27, 1992); missed three games. ... Back spasms (December 28, 1992); missed one game. ... Bruised kneecap (January 23, 1993); missed three games. ... Concussion (February 13, 1993); missed one game. ... Right wrist (October 16, 1993); missed three games. ... Tendon in right hand (December 14, 1993); missed 16 games. ... Traded by Red Wings with G Tim Cheveldae to Winnipeg Jets for G Bob Essensa and D Sergei Bautin (March 8, 1994). ... Back spasms (March 17, 1995); missed four games. ... Bruised right shoulder (October 22, 1995); missed seven games. ... Ear infection (November 21, 1995); missed two games. ... Strained Achilles' tendon (December 28, 1995); missed two games. ... Jets franchise moved to Phoenix and renamed Coyotes for 1996-97 season; NHL approved move on January 18, 1996. ... Sprained ankle (November 16, 1996); missed eight games. ... Sprained knee (January 29, 1997); missed 10 games. ... Flu (October 19, 1997); missed one game. ... Knee (December 3, 1997); missed 12 games. ... Bruised knee (March 2, 1998); missed one game. ... Wrist (March 18, 1998); missed five games. ... Bruised ankle (October 21, 1998); missed one game. ... Concussion (November 6, 1998); missed two games. ... Bruised elbow (December 28, 1998); missed one game. ... Suspended four games for illegal hit (December 29, 1998). ... Separated shoulder (January 29, 1999); missed 13 games. ... Strained shoulder (March 15, 1999); missed two games. ... Bruised shoulder (March 23, 1999); missed five games. ... Sprained shoulder (October 30, 1999); missed three games. ... Selected by Columbus Blue Jackets in expansion draft (June 23, 2000). ... Signed as free agent by St. Louis Blues (July 1, 2000). ... Knee (November 6, 2001); missed one game. ... Ankle (November 20, 2002); missed one game. ... Flu (December 20, 2002); missed one game. ... Fractured cheekbone (October 9, 2003); missed two games. ... Suspended two games (forfeiting $12,408.16) for illegal hit on Anaheim's Corey Perry (October 29, 2005) ... Back (December 8, 2005); missed seven games. ... Broken ribs (March 27, 2006); missed final 11 games of regular season.

Season Team	League	REGULAR SEASON GP	G	A	Pts.	PIM	+/-	PP	SH	PLAYOFFS GP	G	A	Pts.	PIM
84-85—Rossland	KIJHL	30	13	37	50	...	...	...	...	—	—	—	—	—
85-86—Rossland	KIJHL	41	53	73	126	...	...	...	...	—	—	—	—	—
86-87—Rossland	KIJHL	40	55	80	135	...	...	...	...	—	—	—	—	—
87-88—Vernon	BCHL	47	39	85	124	50	...	...	...	11	9	17	26	30
88-89—N. Michigan Univ.	WCHA	45	18	24	42	26	...	...	...	—	—	—	—	—
89-90—N. Michigan Univ.	WCHA	36	13	24	37	42	...	...	...	—	—	—	—	—
90-91—N. Michigan Univ.	WCHA	44	22	36	58	89	...	...	...	—	—	—	—	—
91-92—N. Michigan Univ.	WCHA	40	39	44	83	58	...	...	...	—	—	—	—	—
92-93—Detroit	NHL	72	18	26	44	93	15	3	2	7	3	3	6	6
93-94—Detroit	NHL	47	10	22	32	37	5	0	1	—	—	—	—	—
—Adirondack	AHL	1	2	0	2	0	2	0	0	—	—	—	—	—
—Winnipeg	NHL	15	3	5	8	12	-6	1	1	—	—	—	—	—
94-95—Winnipeg	NHL	43	8	18	26	30	-6	0	0	—	—	—	—	—
95-96—Winnipeg	NHL	69	19	20	39	36	-7	4	4	3	0	0	0	0
96-97—Phoenix	NHL	63	17	19	36	52	-11	5	1	7	0	1	1	2
97-98—Phoenix	NHL	60	11	29	40	71	17	3	0	4	0	1	1	2
98-99—Phoenix	NHL	53	9	22	31	65	17	0	0	7	4	3	7	4
99-00—Phoenix	NHL	79	15	30	45	62	11	0	2	5	0	1	1	4
00-01—St. Louis	NHL	82	12	29	41	71	18	2	0	15	4	2	6	16
01-02—St. Louis	NHL	80	11	15	26	87	8	1	3	8	0	0	0	8
02-03—St. Louis	NHL	80	20	10	30	66	-7	4	1	7	1	4	5	23
03-04—St. Louis	NHL	79	13	22	35	65	10	3	2	5	1	1	2	2
05-06—St. Louis	NHL	62	2	24	26	59	-13	1	0	—	—	—	—	—
NHL Totals (13 years)		884	168	291	459	806	51	27	17	68	13	16	29	67

DRAPER, KRIS C

PERSONAL: Born May 24, 1971, in Toronto. ... 5-10/190. ... Shoots left.

TRANSACTIONS/CAREER NOTES: Selected by Winnipeg Jets in third round (fourth Jets pick, 6second overall) of entry draft (June 17, 1989). ... Traded by Jets to Detroit Red Wings for future considerations (June 30, 1993). ... Right knee (February 4, 1995); missed eight games. ... Flu (January 5, 1996); missed one game. ... Right knee (February 15, 1996); missed 12 games. ... Right knee (March 25, 1996); missed three games. ... Dislocated thumb (December 17, 1997) and had surgery; missed 18 games. ... Suspended two games for slashing incident (January 29, 1999). ... Cut face (November 15, 1999); missed three games. ... Fractured wrist (November 24, 1999); missed 25 games. ... Rotator cuff (March 3, 2004); missed 14 games. ... Eye (October 20, 2005); missed one game.

Season Team	League	REGULAR SEASON GP	G	A	Pts.	PIM	+/-	PP	SH	PLAYOFFS GP	G	A	Pts.	PIM
88-89—Canadian nat'l team	Int'l	60	11	15	26	16	...	...	...	—	—	—	—	—
89-90—Canadian nat'l team	Int'l	61	12	22	34	44	...	...	...	—	—	—	—	—
90-91—Winnipeg	NHL	3	1	0	1	5	0	0	0	—	—	—	—	—
—Moncton	AHL	7	2	1	3	2	...	...	...	—	—	—	—	—
—Ottawa	OHL	39	19	42	61	35	...	...	...	17	8	11	19	20
91-92—Moncton	AHL	61	11	18	29	113	...	...	...	4	0	1	1	6
—Winnipeg	NHL	10	2	0	2	2	0	0	0	2	0	0	0	0
92-93—Winnipeg	NHL	7	0	0	0	2	-6	0	0	—	—	—	—	—
—Moncton	AHL	67	12	23	35	40	-13	0	4	5	2	2	4	18
93-94—Adirondack	AHL	46	20	23	43	49	10	1	2	—	—	—	—	—
—Detroit..........................	NHL	39	5	8	13	31	11	0	1	7	2	2	4	4
94-95—Detroit..........................	NHL	36	2	6	8	22	1	0	0	18	4	1	5	12
95-96—Detroit..........................	NHL	52	7	9	16	32	2	0	1	18	4	2	6	18
96-97—Detroit..........................	NHL	76	8	5	13	73	-11	1	0	20	2	4	6	12
97-98—Detroit..........................	NHL	64	13	10	23	45	5	1	0	19	1	3	4	12
98-99—Detroit..........................	NHL	80	4	14	18	79	2	0	1	10	0	1	1	6
99-00—Detroit..........................	NHL	51	5	7	12	28	3	0	0	9	2	0	2	6
00-01—Detroit..........................	NHL	75	8	17	25	38	17	0	1	6	0	1	1	2
01-02—Detroit..........................	NHL	82	15	15	30	56	26	0	2	23	2	3	5	20
02-03—Detroit..........................	NHL	82	14	21	35	82	6	0	1	4	0	0	0	4
03-04—Detroit..........................	NHL	67	24	16	40	31	22	2	5	12	1	3	4	6
05-06—Detroit..........................	NHL	80	10	22	32	58	3	0	1	6	0	0	0	6
—Canadian Oly. team.....	Int'l	6	0	0	0	0	2	0	0	—	—	—	—	—
NHL Totals (15 years).........		804	118	150	268	584	81	4	13	154	18	20	38	108

DRURY, CHRIS — C/LW

PERSONAL: Born August 20, 1976, in Trumbull, Conn. ... 5-10/180. ... Shoots right. ... Brother of Ted Drury, C, played for six NHL teams (1993-2001).

TRANSACTIONS/CAREER NOTES: Selected by Quebec Nordiques in third round (fifth Nordiques pick, 72nd overall) of entry draft (June 29, 1994). ... Nordiques franchise moved to Colorado and renamed Avalanche for 1995-96 season (June 21, 1995). ... Hip pointer (October 29, 1998); missed two games. ... Sprained knee (November 1, 2000); missed 11 games. ... Traded by Avalanche with C Stephane Yelle to Calgary Flames for D Derek Morris, LW Deam McAmmond and C Jeff Shantz (October 1, 2002). ... Traded by Flames with C Steve Begin to Buffalo Sabres for D Rhett Warrener and C Steve Reinprecht (July 2, 2003). ... Separated shoulder (December 16, 2003); missed four games. ... Concussion (March 15, 2004); missed two games. ... Strained groin (January 7, 2006); missed one game.

Season Team	League	REGULAR SEASON GP	G	A	Pts.	PIM	+/-	PP	SH	PLAYOFFS GP	G	A	Pts.	PIM
92-93—Fairfield College Prep..	Conn. H.S.	24	25	32	57	15	...	...	...	—	—	—	—	—
93-94—Fairfield College Prep..	Conn. H.S.	24	37	18	55	...	...	...	...	—	—	—	—	—
94-95—Boston University	Hockey East	39	12	15	27	38	15	1	0	—	—	—	—	—
95-96—Boston University	Hockey East	37	35	33	68	46	...	...	...	—	—	—	—	—
96-97—Boston University	Hockey East	41	38	24	62	64	29	10	4	—	—	—	—	—
97-98—Boston University	Hockey East	38	28	29	57	88	...	...	...	—	—	—	—	—
98-99—Colorado	NHL	79	20	24	44	62	9	6	0	19	6	2	8	4
99-00—Colorado	NHL	82	20	47	67	42	8	7	0	17	4	10	14	4
00-01—Colorado	NHL	71	24	41	65	47	6	11	0	23	11	5	16	4
01-02—Colorado	NHL	82	21	25	46	38	1	5	0	21	5	7	12	10
02-03—Calgary	NHL	80	23	30	53	33	-9	5	1	—	—	—	—	—
03-04—Buffalo	NHL	76	18	35	53	68	8	5	1	—	—	—	—	—
05-06—Buffalo	NHL	81	30	37	67	32	-11	16	2	18	9	9	18	10
—U.S. Olympic team......	Int'l	6	0	3	3	2	2	0	0	—	—	—	—	—
NHL Totals (7 years)...........		551	156	239	395	322	12	55	4	98	35	33	68	32

DUBIELEWICZ, WADE — G

PERSONAL: Born January 30, 1979, in Invermere, B.C. ... 5-10/180. ... Catches left.

TRANSACTIONS/CAREER NOTES: Signed as free agent by New York Islanders (July 2, 2003).

Season Team	League	REGULAR SEASON GP	Min.	W	L	OTL	T	GA	SO	GAA	SV%	PLAYOFFS GP	Min.	W	L	GA	SO	GAA	SV%
99-00—Denver	WCHA	13	596	3	5	...	1	27	1	2.72	.902	—	—	—	—	—	—	—	—
00-01—Denver	WCHA	29	1542	12	9	...	3	59	2	2.30	.921	—	—	—	—	—	—	—	—
01-02—Denver	WCHA	24	1431	20	4	...	0	41	2	1.72	.943	—	—	—	—	—	—	—	—
02-03—Denver	WCHA	19	1060	9	8	...	2	43	3	2.43	.912	—	—	—	—	—	—	—	—
03-04—New York Islanders	NHL	2	105	1	0	...	1	3	0	1.71	.940	—	—	—	—	—	—	—	—
—Bridgeport	AHL	33	1959	20	8	...	5	45	9	1.38	.943	3	181	2	1	11	0	3.65	.864
04-05—Bridgeport	AHL	43	2538	18	23	...	...	113	1	2.67	.911	—	—	—	—	—	—	—	—
05-06—Bridgeport	AHL	46	2575	20	21	2	...	134	3	3.12	.910	7	435	3	4	16	0	2.21	.933
—New York Islanders	NHL	7	310	2	3		...	15	0	2.90	.897	—	—	—	—	—	—	—	—
NHL Totals (2 years)...........		9	415	3	3		1	18	0	2.60	.908								

DUMONT, J.P. — LW/RW

PERSONAL: Born April 1, 1978, in Montreal. ... 6-1/203. ... Shoots left.

TRANSACTIONS/CAREER NOTES: Selected by New York Islanders in first round (first Islanders pick, third overall) of entry draft (June 22, 1996). ... Traded by Islanders with fifth-round pick (traded to Philadelphia; Flyers selected Francis Belanger) in 1998 draft to Chicago

Blackhawks for C/LW Dmitri Nabokov (May 30, 1998). ... Injured back (April 8, 1999); missed two games. ... Traded by Blackhawks with C Doug Gilmour to Buffalo Sabres for LW Michal Grosek (March 10, 2000). ... Injured rib (February 13, 2001); missed two games. ... Injured shoulder (April 1, 2002); missed remainder of season. ... Flu (December 13, 2002); missed two games. ... Injured hip (December 26, 2003); missed five games. ... Sports hernia (November 17, 2005) and had surgery (December 7, 2005); missed 28 games.

STATISTICAL PLATEAUS: Three-goal games: 1998-99 (1), 2000-01 (1), 2001-02 (1). Total: 3.

		REGULAR SEASON								PLAYOFFS				
Season Team	**League**	**GP**	**G**	**A**	**Pts.**	**PIM**	**+/-**	**PP**	**SH**	**GP**	**G**	**A**	**Pts.**	**PIM**
93-94—Val-d'Or	QMJHL	25	9	11	20	10	...	...	...	—	—	—	—	—
94-95—Val-d'Or	QMJHL	48	5	14	19	24	...	...	...	—	—	—	—	—
95-96—Val-d'Or	QMJHL	66	48	57	105	109	...	...	...	13	12	8	20	22
96-97—Val-d'Or	QMJHL	62	44	64	108	88	...	...	...	13	9	7	16	12
97-98—Val-d'Or	QMJHL	55	57	42	99	63	...	...	...	19	31	15	46	18
98-99—Portland	AHL	50	32	14	46	39	-2	12	0	—	—	—	—	—
—Chicago	NHL	25	9	6	15	10	7	0	0	—	—	—	—	—
99-00—Chicago	NHL	47	10	8	18	18	-6	0	0	—	—	—	—	—
—Cleveland	IHL	7	5	2	7	8	...	...	...	—	—	—	—	—
—Rochester	AHL	13	7	10	17	18	...	...	...	21	14	7	21	32
00-01—Buffalo	NHL	79	23	28	51	54	1	9	0	13	4	3	7	8
01-02—Buffalo	NHL	76	23	21	44	42	-10	7	0	—	—	—	—	—
02-03—Buffalo	NHL	76	14	21	35	44	-14	2	0	—	—	—	—	—
03-04—Buffalo	NHL	77	22	31	53	40	-9	10	0	—	—	—	—	—
04-05—Bern	Switzerland	3	2	2	4	6	...	0	0	10	4	1	5	14
05-06—Buffalo	NHL	54	20	20	40	38	-1	9	0	18	7	7	14	14
NHL Totals (7 years)		434	121	135	256	246	-32	37	0	31	11	10	21	22

DUNHAM, MIKE G

PERSONAL: Born June 1, 1972, in Johnson City, N.Y. ... 6-2/190. ... Catches left.

TRANSACTIONS/CAREER NOTES: Selected by New Jersey Devils in third round (fourth Devils pick, 53rd overall) of entry draft (June 16, 1990). ... Hand (January 1, 1998); missed three games. ... Knee surgery (March 5, 1998); missed 18 games. ... Selected by Nashville Predators in expansion draft (June 26, 1998). ... Strained right groin (November 29, 1998); missed seven games. ... Reinjured groin (December 19, 1998); missed 13 games. ... Strained groin (March 27, 1999); missed six games. ... Flu (December 26, 1999); missed one game. ... Sprained right thumb (February 3, 2000); missed four games. ... Sprained left knee (October 27, 2000); missed 15 games. ... Knee (December 4, 2000); missed two games. ... Strained neck (February 20, 2001); missed one game. ... Concussion (April 6, 2002); missed remainder of season. ... Strained groin (December 5, 2002); missed three games. ... Traded by Predators to New York Rangers for LW Rem Murray, D Tomas Kloucek and D Marek Zidlicky (December 12, 2002). ... Groin (February 5, 2003); missed two games. ... Hamstring (March 22, 2003); missed one game. ... Injured hip (November 18, 2003); missed three games. ... Concussion (January 22, 2004); missed two games. ... Flu (February 16, 2004); missed one game. ... Bruised shoulder (March 27, 2004); missed two games. ... Signed as free agent by Atlanta Thrashers (September 2, 2005). ... Groin (October 12, 2005); missed eight games. ... Reinjured groin (November 15, 2005); missed 28 games.

		REGULAR SEASON										PLAYOFFS							
Season Team	**League**	**GP**	**Min.**	**W**	**L**	**OTL**	**T**	**GA**	**SO**	**GAA**	**SV%**	**GP**	**Min.**	**W**	**L**	**GA**	**SO**	**GAA**	**SV%**
87-88—Canterbury School	Conn. H.S.	29	1740	...	...	...	...	69	4	2.38	...	—	—	—	—	—	—	—	—
88-89—Canterbury School	Conn. H.S.	25	1500	...	...	...	...	63	2	2.52	...	—	—	—	—	—	—	—	—
89-90—Canterbury School	Conn. H.S.	32	1558	...	...	...	...	55	3	2.12	...	—	—	—	—	—	—	—	—
90-91—Maine	Hockey East	23	1275	14	5	...	2	63	2	2.96	...	—	—	—	—	—	—	—	—
91-92—Maine	Hockey East	7	382	6	0	...	0	14	1	2.20	...	—	—	—	—	—	—	—	—
—U.S. national team	Int'l	3	157	0	1	...	1	10	0	3.82	...	—	—	—	—	—	—	—	—
92-93—Maine	Hockey East	25	1429	21	1	...	1	63	0	2.65	...	—	—	—	—	—	—	—	—
—U.S. national team	Int'l	1	60	0	0	...	1	1	0	1.00	...	—	—	—	—	—	—	—	—
93-94—U.S. national team	Int'l	33	1983	22	9	...	2	125	2	3.78	...	—	—	—	—	—	—	—	—
—U.S. Olympic team	Int'l	3	180	0	1	...	2	15	0	5.00	.826	—	—	—	—	—	—	—	—
—Albany	AHL	5	305	2	2	...	1	26	0	5.11	.858	—	—	—	—	—	—	—	—
94-95—Albany	AHL	35	2120	20	7	...	8	99	1	2.80	.898	7	420	6	1	20	1	2.86	.895
95-96—Albany	AHL	44	2591	30	10	...	2	109	1	2.52	...	3	181	1	2	5	1	1.66	...
96-97—Albany	AHL	3	184	1	1	...	1	12	0	3.91	.871	—	—	—	—	—	—	—	—
—New Jersey	NHL	26	1013	8	7	...	1	43	2	2.55	.906	—	—	—	—	—	—	—	—
97-98—New Jersey	NHL	15	773	5	5	...	3	29	1	2.25	.913	—	—	—	—	—	—	—	—
98-99—Nashville	NHL	44	2472	16	23	...	3	127	1	3.08	.908	—	—	—	—	—	—	—	—
99-00—Milwaukee	IHL	1	60	2	0	...	0	1	0	1.00	...	—	—	—	—	—	—	—	—
—Nashville	NHL	52	3077	19	27	...	6	146	0	2.85	.908	—	—	—	—	—	—	—	—
00-01—Nashville	NHL	48	2810	21	21	...	4	107	4	2.28	.923	—	—	—	—	—	—	—	—
01-02—Nashville	NHL	58	3316	23	24	...	9	144	3	2.61	.906	—	—	—	—	—	—	—	—
—U.S. Olympic team	Int'l	1	60	1	0	...	0	0	1	0.00	1.000	—	—	—	—	—	—	—	—
02-03—Nashville	NHL	15	819	2	9	...	2	43	0	3.15	.892	—	—	—	—	—	—	—	—
—New York Rangers	NHL	43	2467	19	17	...	5	94	5	2.29	.924	—	—	—	—	—	—	—	—
03-04—New York Rangers	NHL	57	3148	16	30	...	6	159	2	3.03	.896	—	—	—	—	—	—	—	—
04-05—Skelleftea	Sweden Dv. 2	3	176	...	...	...	...	4	1	1.36	.945	10	550	...	...	32	3	3.49	.879
05-06—Atlanta	NHL	17	779	8	5	2	...	36	1	2.77	.893	—	—	—	—	—	—	—	—
NHL Totals (9 years)		375	20674	137	168	2	39	928	19	2.69	.909								

DUPUIS, PASCAL LW/RW

PERSONAL: Born April 7, 1979, in Laval, Que. ... 6-0/196. ... Shoots left. ... Name pronounced DU-pwee.

TRANSACTIONS/CAREER NOTES: Signed as free agent by Minnesota Wild (September 18, 2000). ... Leg (October 18, 2002); missed one game. ... Missed 2003-04 first nine games of season in holdout. ... Left team for personal reasons (December 20, 2003); missed two games. ... Ankle (January 9, 2004); missed one game. ... Ankle (March 7, 2004); missed nine games. ... Groin (October 16, 2005); missed four games. ... Flu (December 10, 2005); missed three games. ... Shoulder (January 16, 2006); missed three games. ... Shoulder (January 26, 2006); missed one game. ... Personal absence (February 9, 2006); missed one game. ... Ankle (April 11, 2006); missed one game.

Season Team	League	REGULAR SEASON GP	G	A	Pts.	PIM	+/-	PP	SH	PLAYOFFS GP	G	A	Pts.	PIM
96-97—Rouyn-Noranda	QMJHL	44	9	15	24	20	...	...	...	—	—	—	—	—
97-98—Rouyn-Noranda	QMJHL	39	9	17	26	36	...	...	...	—	—	—	—	—
—Shawinigan	QMJHL	28	7	13	20	10	...	...	...	6	2	0	2	4
98-99—Shawinigan	QMJHL	57	30	42	72	118	...	...	...	6	1	8	9	18
99-00—Shawinigan	QMJHL	61	50	55	105	164	31	17	7	13	15	7	22	4
00-01—Cleveland	IHL	70	19	24	43	37	...	...	...	4	0	0	0	0
—Minnesota	NHL	4	1	0	1	4	0	1	0	—	—	—	—	—
01-02—Minnesota	NHL	76	15	12	27	16	-10	3	2	—	—	—	—	—
02-03—Minnesota	NHL	80	20	28	48	44	17	6	0	16	4	4	8	8
03-04—Minnesota	NHL	59	11	15	26	20	5	2	0	—	—	—	—	—
04-05—Ajoie	Switz. Div. 2	8	5	5	10	26	...	1	3	6	6	8	14	8
05-06—Minnesota	NHL	67	10	16	26	40	-10	4	0	—	—	—	—	—
NHL Totals (5 years)		286	57	71	128	124	2	16	2	16	4	4	8	8

DVORAK, RADEK RW

PERSONAL: Born March 9, 1977, in Tabor, Czech. ... 6-2/200. ... Shoots right. ... Name pronounced RA-dihk duh-VOHR-ak.

TRANSACTIONS/CAREER NOTES: Selected by Florida Panthers in first round (first Panthers pick, 10th overall) of entry draft (July 8, 1995). ... Fractured left wrist (October 30, 1997); missed 15 games. ... Traded by Panthers to San Jose Sharks for G Mike Vernon and third-round pick (RW Sean O'Connor) in 2000 entry draft (December 30, 1999). ... Traded by Sharks to New York Rangers for RW Todd Harvey and fourth-round pick (G Dimitri Patzold) in 2001 entry draft (December 30, 1999). ... Sprained left knee (November 23, 2001); missed three games. ... Torn right knee ligament (March 13, 2002); missed remainder of season. ... Injured knee (October 15, 2002); missed four games. ... Back spasms (November 28, 2002); missed one game. ... Concussion (January 21, 2003); missed three games. ... Traded by Rangers with D Cory Cross to Edmonton Oilers for RW Anson Carter and D Ales Pisa (March 11, 2003). ... Injured groin (February 16, 2004); missed four games. ... Strained groin (December 5, 2005); missed two games. ... Reaggravated groin injury (December 13, 2005); missed 13 games. ... Sore hip flexor (March 22, 2006); missed three games.

STATISTICAL PLATEAUS: Three-goal games: 1999-00 (1). ... Four-goal games: 2000-01 (1). ... Total hat tricks: 2.

Season Team	League	REGULAR SEASON GP	G	A	Pts.	PIM	+/-	PP	SH	PLAYOFFS GP	G	A	Pts.	PIM
92-93—Motor-Ceske Bude.	Czech.	35	44	46	90	...	...	...	...	—	—	—	—	—
93-94—HC Ceske Budejovice..	Czech Rep.	8	0	0	0	...	...	...	...	—	—	—	—	—
—Motor-Ceske Bude.	Czech Rep.	20	17	18	35	...	...	...	...	—	—	—	—	—
94-95—HC Ceske Budejovice..	Czech Rep.	10	3	5	8	...	...	...	...	9	5	1	6	...
95-96—Florida	NHL	77	13	14	27	20	5	0	0	16	1	3	4	0
96-97—Florida	NHL	78	18	21	39	30	-2	2	0	3	0	0	0	0
97-98—Florida	NHL	64	12	24	36	33	-1	2	3	—	—	—	—	—
98-99—Florida	NHL	82	19	24	43	29	7	0	4	—	—	—	—	—
99-00—Florida	NHL	35	7	10	17	6	5	0	0	—	—	—	—	—
—New York Rangers	NHL	46	11	22	33	10	0	2	1	—	—	—	—	—
00-01—New York Rangers	NHL	82	31	36	67	20	9	5	2	—	—	—	—	—
01-02—New York Rangers	NHL	65	17	20	37	14	-20	3	3	—	—	—	—	—
—Czech Rep. Oly. team..	Int'l	4	0	0	0	0	...	...	...	—	—	—	—	—
02-03—New York Rangers	NHL	63	6	21	27	16	-3	2	0	—	—	—	—	—
—Edmonton	NHL	12	4	4	8	14	-3	1	0	4	1	0	1	0
03-04—Edmonton	NHL	78	15	35	50	26	18	6	0	—	—	—	—	—
04-05—Budejovice	Czech Dv.I	32	23	35	58	18	50	...	...	16	5	13	18	20
05-06—Edmonton	NHL	64	8	20	28	26	-2	2	0	16	0	2	2	4
NHL Totals (10 years)		746	161	251	412	244	13	25	13	39	2	5	7	4

E

EAGER, BEN LW

PERSONAL: Born January 22, 1984, in Ottawa. ... 6-2/225. ... Shoots left.

TRANSACTIONS/CAREER NOTES: Selected by Phoenix Coyotes in first round (second Coyotes pick, 23rd overall) of NHL entry draft (June 22, 2002). ... Traded by Coyotes with G Sean Burke and RW Branko Radivojevic to Philadelphia Flyers for C Mike Comrie (February 9, 2004).

Season Team	League	REGULAR SEASON GP	G	A	Pts.	PIM	+/-	PP	SH	PLAYOFFS GP	G	A	Pts.	PIM
00-01—Oshawa	OHL	61	4	6	10	120	...	...	...	—	—	—	—	—
01-02—Oshawa	OHL	63	14	23	37	255	...	...	...	5	0	1	1	13
02-03—Oshawa	OHL	58	16	24	40	216	...	...	...	8	0	4	4	8
03-04—Oshawa	OHL	61	25	27	52	204	...	...	...	7	2	3	5	31
—Philadelphia	AHL	5	0	0	0	0	0	0	0	3	0	1	1	8
04-05—Philadelphia	AHL	66	7	10	17	232	12	2	0	16	1	1	2	71
05-06—Philadelphia	AHL	49	6	12	18	256	-6	1	0	—	—	—	—	—
—Philadelphia	NHL	25	3	5	8	18	0	0	0	2	0	0	0	26
NHL Totals (1 year)		25	3	5	8	18	0	0	0	2	0	0	0	26

EATON, MARK D

PERSONAL: Born May 6, 1977, in Wilmington, Del. ... 6-2/208. ... Shoots left.

TRANSACTIONS/CAREER NOTES: Signed as free agent by Philadelphia Flyers (July 28, 1998). ... Stomach virus (March 26, 2000); missed one game. ... Traded by Flyers to Nashville Predators for third-round pick (C Patrick Sharp) in 2001 (September 29, 2000). ... Back (October 18, 2001); missed seven games. ... Shoulder (December 20, 2001); missed two games. ... Knee, shoulder (December 3, 2002); missed five games. ... Groin (October 18, 2003); missed two games. ... Back spasms (March 13, 2004); missed four games. ... Back (December 21, 2005); missed one game. ... Left knee (March 1, 2006); missed 12 games. ... Signed as free agent by Pittsbugh Penguins (July 3, 2006).

Season Team	League	GP	G	A	Pts.	PIM	+/-	PP	SH	GP	G	A	Pts.	PIM
		REGULAR SEASON								PLAYOFFS				
97-98—Notre Dame	CCHA	41	12	17	29	32	...	...	...	—	—	—	—	—
98-99—Philadelphia	AHL	74	9	27	36	38	13	7	0	16	4	8	12	0
99-00—Philadelphia	NHL	27	1	1	2	8	1	0	0	7	0	0	0	0
—Philadelphia	AHL	47	9	17	26	6	...	...	...	—	—	—	—	—
00-01—Milwaukee	IHL	34	3	12	15	27	...	...	...	—	—	—	—	—
—Nashville	NHL	34	3	8	11	14	7	1	0	—	—	—	—	—
01-02—Nashville	NHL	58	3	5	8	24	-12	0	0	—	—	—	—	—
02-03—Milwaukee	AHL	3	1	0	1	2	3	1	0	—	—	—	—	—
—Nashville	NHL	50	2	7	9	22	1	0	0	—	—	—	—	—
03-04—Nashville	NHL	75	4	9	13	26	16	0	0	6	0	0	0	2
04-05—Grand Rapids	AHL	29	3	3	6	21	2	1	1	—	—	—	—	—
05-06—Nashville	NHL	69	3	1	4	44	-2	0	0	5	0	0	0	8
NHL Totals (6 years)		313	16	31	47	138	11	1	0	18	0	0	0	10

EAVES, PATRICK RW

PERSONAL: Born May 1, 1984, in Calgary. ... 5-11/174. ... Shoots right. ... Son of Mike Eaves, RW with two NHL teams (1976-86).
TRANSACTIONS/CAREER NOTES: Selected by Ottawa Senators in first round (Senators' first pick, ninth overall) in NHL entry draft (June 21, 2003). ... Flu (December 30, 2005); missed one game. ... Lower-body injury (April 11, 2006); missed one game.

Season Team	League	GP	G	A	Pts.	PIM	+/-	PP	SH	GP	G	A	Pts.	PIM
		REGULAR SEASON								PLAYOFFS				
02-03—Boston College	Hockey East	14	10	8	18	61	...	...	...	—	—	—	—	—
03-04—Boston College	Hockey East	34	18	23	41	66	...	...	...	—	—	—	—	—
04-05—Boston College	ECAC	36	19	29	48	36	...	...	...	—	—	—	—	—
05-06—Binghamton	AHL	18	5	8	13	10	-8	3	1	—	—	—	—	—
—Ottawa	NHL	58	20	9	29	22	7	5	1	10	1	0	1	10
NHL Totals (1 year)		58	20	9	29	22	7	5	1	10	1	0	1	10

EHRHOFF, CHRISTIAN D

PERSONAL: Born July 6, 1982, in Moers, West Germany. ... 6-2/195. ... Shoots left.
TRANSACTIONS/CAREER NOTES: Selected by San Jose Sharks in fourth round (second Sharks pick, 106th overall) of entry draft (June 23, 2001).

Season Team	League	GP	G	A	Pts.	PIM	+/-	PP	SH	GP	G	A	Pts.	PIM
		REGULAR SEASON								PLAYOFFS				
00-01—Krefeld Pinguine	Germany	58	3	11	14	73	...	...	...	—	—	—	—	—
01-02—Krefeld Pinguine	Germany	46	7	17	24	81	...	...	...	3	0	0	0	2
—German Oly. team	Int'l	7	0	0	0	8	...	...	...	—	—	—	—	—
02-03—Krefeld Pinguine	Germany	48	10	17	27	54	...	...	...	14	3	6	9	24
03-04—San Jose	NHL	41	1	11	12	14	4	0	0	—	—	—	—	—
—Cleveland	AHL	27	4	10	14	43	14	2	0	9	2	6	8	11
04-05—Cleveland	AHL	79	12	23	35	103	-12	7	0	—	—	—	—	—
05-06—San Jose	NHL	64	5	18	23	32	10	2	0	11	2	6	8	18
—German Oly. team	Int'l	5	1	1	2	4	0	0	0	—	—	—	—	—
NHL Totals (2 years)		105	6	29	35	46	14	2	0	11	2	6	8	18

EKLUND, BRIAN G

PERSONAL: Born May 24, 1980, in Braintree, Mass. ... 6-5/200. ... Catches left.
HIGH SCHOOL: Archbishop Prep.
COLLEGE: Brown.
TRANSACTIONS/CAREER NOTES: Selected by Tampa Bay Lightning in seventh round (Lightning's eighth choice, 226th overall) of NHL entry draft (June 24, 2000). ... Traded by Lightning to Boston Bruins for LW Zdenek Blatny (February 8, 2005).

Season Team	League	GP	Min.	W	L	OTL	T	GA	SO	GAA	SV%	GP	Min.	W	L	GA	SO	GAA	SV%
		REGULAR SEASON										PLAYOFFS							
98-99—Brown	ECAC	8	...	1	3	...	0	...	0	3.41	...	—	—	—	—	—	—	—	—
99-00—Brown	ECAC	12	...	1	6	...	2	...	1	2.95	...	—	—	—	—	—	—	—	—
00-01—Brown	ECAC	18	1019	2	13	...	2	...	0	3.48	...	—	—	—	—	—	—	—	—
01-02—Brown	ECAC	9	454	3	5	...	0	30	0	3.96	...	—	—	—	—	—	—	—	—
02-03—Pensacola	ECHL	19	998	10	6	...	0	61	0	3.67	.896	—	—	—	—	—	—	—	—
—Springfield	AHL	1	60	1	0	...	0	1	0	1.00	.974	—	—	—	—	—	—	—	—
03-04—Pensacola	ECHL	62	3725	38	17	...	7	187	1	3.01	.921	5	333	2	3	16	0	2.88	...
04-05—Springfield	AHL	43	2415	14	23	...	...	121	0	3.01	.911	—	—	—	—	—	—	—	—
05-06—Springfield	AHL	17	960	5	11	1	...	67	0	4.19	.876	—	—	—	—	—	—	—	—
—Tampa Bay	NHL	1	58	0	1	0	...	3	0	3.10	.842	—	—	—	—	—	—	—	—
—Providence	AHL	12	597	3	6	1	...	35	0	3.52	.870	—	—	—	—	—	—	—	—
NHL Totals (1 year)		1	58	0	1	0	0	3	0	3.10	.842								

EKMAN, NILS LW/RW

PERSONAL: Born March 11, 1976, in Stockholm, Sweden. ... 6-0/185. ... Shoots left.
TRANSACTIONS/CAREER NOTES: Selected by Calgary Flames in fifth round (sixth Flames pick, 107th overall) of entry draft (June 29, 1994). ... Rights traded by Flames with fourth-round pick (traded to New York Islanders; Islanders selected RW Vladimir Gorbunov) in 2000 to Tampa

Bay Lightning for C/LW Andreas Johansson (November 20, 1999). ... Injured hip (January 20, 2000); missed one game. ... Traded by Lightning with LW Kyle Freadrich to New York Rangers for C Tim Taylor (July 1, 2001). ... Traded by Rangers to San Jose Sharks for LW Chad Wiseman (August 12, 2003). ... Personal leave (March 16, 2006); missed one game. ... Traded by Sharks with G Patrick Ehelechner to Pittsburgh Penguins for a second-round pick in 2007 draft (July 20, 2006).

		REGULAR SEASON								PLAYOFFS				
Season Team	**League**	**GP**	**G**	**A**	**Pts.**	**PIM**	**+/-**	**PP**	**SH**	**GP**	**G**	**A**	**Pts.**	**PIM**
93-94—Hammarby	Sweden Dv. 2	18	7	2	9	4	...	...	...	—	—	—	—	—
94-95—Hammarby	Sweden Dv. 2	29	10	7	17	18	...	...	...	—	—	—	—	—
95-96—Hammarby	Sweden Dv. 2	22	9	7	16	20	...	...	...	—	—	—	—	—
96-97—Kiekko-Espoo	Finland	50	24	19	43	60	...	...	...	4	2	0	2	4
97-98—Kiekko-Espoo	Finland	43	14	14	28	86	...	...	...	7	2	2	4	27
—Saint John	AHL	...	...	...	...	...	...	...	...	1	0	0	0	2
98-99—Blues Espoo	Finland	52	20	14	34	96	...	...	...	3	1	1	2	6
99-00—Tampa Bay	NHL	28	2	2	4	36	-8	1	0	—	—	—	—	—
—Detroit	IHL	10	7	2	9	8	...	...	...	—	—	—	—	—
—Long Beach	IHL	27	11	12	23	26	...	...	...	5	3	3	6	4
00-01—Detroit	IHL	33	22	14	36	63	...	...	...	—	—	—	—	—
—Tampa Bay	NHL	43	9	11	20	40	-15	2	1	—	—	—	—	—
01-02—Djurgarden Stockholm	Sweden	38	16	15	31	57	...	...	...	4	1	0	1	32
02-03—Hartford	AHL	57	30	36	66	73	6	9	3	2	0	2	2	4
03-04—San Jose	NHL	82	22	33	55	34	30	1	4	16	0	3	3	8
04-05—Djurgarden Stockholm	Sweden	44	18	27	45	106	2	7	1	12	4	5	9	20
05-06—San Jose	NHL	77	21	36	57	54	20	5	0	11	2	2	4	8
NHL Totals (4 years)		230	54	82	136	164	27	9	5	27	2	5	7	16

ELIAS, PATRIK — LW

PERSONAL: Born April 13, 1976, in Trebic, Czechoslovakia. ... 6-1/195. ... Shoots left. ... Name pronounced EH-lee-ahsh.
TRANSACTIONS/CAREER NOTES: Selected by New Jersey Devils in second round (second Devils pick, 51st overall) of entry draft (June 28, 1994). ... Flu (January 14, 1999); missed five games. ... Missed first nine games of 1999-2000 season in contract dispute. ... Infected finger (January 3, 2002); missed five games. ... Flu (March 20, 2002); missed two games. ... Back spasms (January 17, 2003); missed one game. ... Re-signed by Devils as restricted free agent (August 23, 2005). ... Contracted hepatitis-A while playing in Russia (spring 2005); missed first 39 games of 2005-06 season. ... Injured ribs during Olympics (February 17, 2006); missed four NHL games.
STATISTICAL PLATEAUS: Three-goal games: 2000-01 (3), 2001-02 (2). Total: 5. ... Four-goal games: 2002-03 (1). ... Total hat tricks: 6.

		REGULAR SEASON								PLAYOFFS				
Season Team	**League**	**GP**	**G**	**A**	**Pts.**	**PIM**	**+/-**	**PP**	**SH**	**GP**	**G**	**A**	**Pts.**	**PIM**
92-93—HC Kladno	Czech.	2	0	0	0	0	...	...	...	—	—	—	—	—
93-94—HC Kladno	Czech Rep.	15	1	2	3	...	...	...	...	11	2	2	4	...
—Czech Rep. Oly. team	Int'l	5	2	5	7	...	...	...	...	—	—	—	—	—
94-95—HC Kladno	Czech Rep.	28	4	3	7	...	...	...	...	7	1	2	3	...
95-96—Albany	AHL	74	27	36	63	83	...	...	...	4	1	1	2	2
—New Jersey	NHL	1	0	0	0	0	-1	0	0	—	—	—	—	—
96-97—Albany	AHL	57	24	43	67	76	22	6	0	6	1	2	3	8
—New Jersey	NHL	17	2	3	5	2	-4	0	0	8	2	3	5	4
97-98—New Jersey	NHL	74	18	19	37	28	18	5	0	4	0	1	1	0
—Albany	AHL	3	3	0	3	2	-2	1	1	—	—	—	—	—
98-99—New Jersey	NHL	74	17	33	50	34	19	3	0	7	0	5	5	6
99-00—SK Trebic	Czech Dv.I	2	2	1	3	2	...	...	...	—	—	—	—	—
—HC Pardubice	Czech Rep.	5	1	4	5	6	...	...	...	—	—	—	—	—
—New Jersey	NHL	72	35	37	72	58	16	9	0	23	7	†13	20	9
00-01—New Jersey	NHL	82	40	56	96	51	†45	8	3	25	9	14	23	10
01-02—New Jersey	NHL	75	29	32	61	36	4	8	1	6	2	4	6	6
—Czech Rep. Oly. team	Int'l	4	1	1	2	0	...	...	...	—	—	—	—	—
02-03—New Jersey	NHL	81	28	29	57	22	17	6	0	24	5	8	13	26
03-04—New Jersey	NHL	82	38	43	81	44	26	9	3	5	3	2	5	2
04-05—HC Znojemsti Orli	Czech Rep.	28	8	20	28	65	7	...	...	—	—	—	—	—
—Metal. Magnitogorsk	Russian	17	5	9	14	28	10	...	...	—	—	—	—	—
05-06—New Jersey	NHL	38	16	29	45	20	11	6	0	9	6	10	16	4
—Czech Rep. Oly. team	Int'l	1	0	0	0	2	0	0	0	—	—	—	—	—
NHL Totals (10 years)		596	223	281	504	295	151	54	7	111	34	60	94	67

ELLISON, MATT — RW/C

PERSONAL: Born December 8, 1983, in Duncan, B.C. ... 5-11/189. ... Shoots right.
TRANSACTIONS/CAREER NOTES: Selected by Chicago Blackhawks in fourth round (fourth Blackhawks pick, 128th overall) of entry draft (June 23, 2002). ... Traded by Blackhawks with third-round pick (traded to Montreal; Canadiens selected C Ryan White) in 2006 to Philadelphia Flyers for C Patrick Sharp and RW Eric Meloche (December 5, 2005).

		REGULAR SEASON								PLAYOFFS				
Season Team	**League**	**GP**	**G**	**A**	**Pts.**	**PIM**	**+/-**	**PP**	**SH**	**GP**	**G**	**A**	**Pts.**	**PIM**
99-00—Cowichan	BCJHL	60	11	23	34	95	...	...	...	—	—	—	—	—
00-01—Cowichan	BCJHL	60	22	44	66	102	...	...	...	—	—	—	—	—
02-03—Red Deer	WHL	72	40	56	96	80	...	...	...	22	7	13	20	28
03-04—Norfolk	AHL	71	14	21	35	115	-10	6	0	7	0	1	1	4
—Chicago	NHL	10	0	1	1	0	-3	0	0	—	—	—	—	—
04-05—Norfolk	AHL	71	14	37	51	44	8	5	1	5	0	1	1	2
05-06—Philadelphia	AHL	48	12	13	25	35	-8	6	1	—	—	—	—	—
—Chicago	NHL	26	3	9	12	17	-4	1	0	—	—	—	—	—
—Philadelphia	NHL	5	0	1	1	2	2	0	0	—	—	—	—	—
NHL Totals (2 years)		41	3	11	14	19	-5	1	0					

EMERY, RAY G

PERSONAL: Born September 28, 1982, in Cayuga, Ont. ... 6-2/203. ... Catches left.
TRANSACTIONS/CAREER NOTES: Selected by Ottawa Senators in fourth round (fourth Senators pick, 99th overall) of NHL entry draft (June 23, 2001).

		REGULAR SEASON										PLAYOFFS							
Season Team	League	GP	Min.	W	L	OTL	T	GA	SO	GAA	SV%	GP	Min.	W	L	GA	SO	GAA	SV%
99-00—Sault Ste. Marie	OHL	16	716	9	3	...	0	36	1	3.02	...	15	883	8	7	33	3	2.24	...
00-01—Sault Ste. Marie	OHL	52	2938	18	29	...	2	174	1	3.55	.904	—	—	—	—	—	—	—	—
01-02—Sault Ste. Marie	OHL	59	3477	33	17	...	9	158	4	2.73	...	6	360	2	4	19	1	3.17	...
02-03—Ottawa	NHL	3	85	1	0	...	0	2	0	1.41	.923	—	—	—	—	—	—	—	—
—Binghamton	AHL	50	2923	27	17	...	6	118	7	2.42	.924	14	848	8	6	40	2	2.83	.912
03-04—Ottawa	NHL	3	126	2	0	...	0	5	0	2.38	.904	—	—	—	—	—	—	—	—
—Binghamton	AHL	53	3108	21	23	...	7	128	3	2.47	.916	2	119	0	2	6	0	3.03	.903
04-05—Binghamton	AHL	51	2992	28	18	...	...	132	0	2.65	.910	6	409	2	4	14	0	2.05	.925
05-06—Ottawa	NHL	39	2168	23	11	4	...	102	3	2.82	.902	10	604	5	5	29	0	2.88	.900
NHL Totals (3 years)		45	2379	26	11	4	0	109	3	2.75	.903	10	604	5	5	29	0	2.88	.900

EMINGER, STEVE D

PERSONAL: Born October 31, 1983, in Woodbridge, Ont. ... 6-2/203. ... Shoots right.
TRANSACTIONS/CAREER NOTES: Selected by Washington Capitals in first round (first Capitals pick, 12th overall) of NHL entry draft (June 22, 2002). ... Suffered concussion (November 8, 2003); missed two games. ... Bruised thigh (December 29, 2003); missed four games. ... Ankle sprain (January 13, 2006); missed 16 games.

		REGULAR SEASON								PLAYOFFS				
Season Team	League	GP	G	A	Pts.	PIM	+/-	PP	SH	GP	G	A	Pts.	PIM
99-00—Kitchener	OHL	50	2	14	16	74	...	...	...	5	0	0	0	0
00-01—Kitchener	OHL	54	6	26	32	66	...	...	...	—	—	—	—	—
01-02—Kitchener	OHL	64	19	39	58	93	...	...	...	4	0	2	2	10
02-03—Washington	NHL	17	0	2	2	24	-3	0	0	—	—	—	—	—
—Kitchener	OHL	23	2	27	29	40	...	...	...	21	3	8	11	44
03-04—Washington	NHL	41	0	4	4	45	-11	0	0	—	—	—	—	—
—Portland	AHL	41	0	4	4	40	-5	0	0	7	0	1	1	2
04-05—Portland	AHL	62	3	17	20	40	-8	1	0	—	—	—	—	—
05-06—Washington	NHL	66	5	13	18	81	-12	1	0	—	—	—	—	—
NHL Totals (3 years)		124	5	19	24	150	-26	1	0					

EMMERTON, CORY C/LW

PERSONAL: Born June 1, 1988, in St. Thomas, Ont. ... 5-11/177. ... Shoots left.
TRANSACTIONS/CAREER NOTES: Selected by Detroit Red Wings in second round (first Red Wings pick; 41st overall) of NHL draft (June 24, 2006).

		REGULAR SEASON								PLAYOFFS				
Season Team	League	GP	G	A	Pts.	PIM	+/-	PP	SH	GP	G	A	Pts.	PIM
04-05—Kingston	OHL	58	17	21	38	8	-7	...	...	—	—	—	—	—
05-06—Kingston	OHL	66	26	64	90	32	37	...	...	6	2	0	2	6

E

ENDICOTT, SHANE C/LW

PERSONAL: Born December 21, 1981, in Saskatoon, Sask. ... 6-4/214. ... Shoots left.
TRANSACTIONS/CAREER NOTES: Selected by Pittsburgh Penguins in second round (second Penguins pick, 52nd overall) of NHL entry draft (June 24, 2000). ... Signed as free agent by AHL Wilkes-Barre/Scranton (September 26, 2004). ... Ankle (October 30, 2005); missed 20 games. ... Re-injured ankle (November 22, 2005); missed five games. ... Re-signed by Penguins as restricted free agent (August 11, 2005).

		REGULAR SEASON								PLAYOFFS				
Season Team	League	GP	G	A	Pts.	PIM	+/-	PP	SH	GP	G	A	Pts.	PIM
97-98—Seattle	WHL	5	0	0	0	0	...	...	...	5	0	0	0	0
98-99—Seattle	WHL	72	13	26	39	27	...	...	...	11	0	1	1	0
99-00—Seattle	WHL	70	23	32	55	62	...	...	...	7	1	6	7	6
00-01—Seattle	WHL	72	36	43	79	86	...	...	...	9	4	5	9	12
01-02—Wilkes-Barre/Scranton	AHL	63	19	20	39	46	-12	8	1	—	—	—	—	—
—Pittsburgh	NHL	4	0	1	1	4	-1	0	0	—	—	—	—	—
02-03—Wilkes-Barre/Scranton	AHL	74	13	26	39	68	-7	3	0	6	0	2	2	4
03-04—Wilkes-Barre/Scranton	AHL	79	17	22	39	68	-2	6	2	24	8	4	12	26
04-05—Wilkes-Barre/Scranton	AHL	68	24	23	47	89	3	7	2	11	2	2	4	31
05-06—Wilkes-Barre/Scranton	AHL	8	0	2	2	4	-1	0	0	10	1	3	4	2
—Pittsburgh	NHL	41	1	1	2	43	-9	0	1	—	—	—	—	—
NHL Totals (2 years)		45	1	2	3	47	-10	0	1					

ENROTH, JHONAS G

PERSONAL: Born June 25, 1988, in Stockholm, Swe. ... 5-10/174. ... Catches left.
TRANSACTIONS/CAREER NOTES: Selected by Buffalo Sabres in second round (second Sabres pick; 46th overall) of NHL draft (June 24, 2006).

Season Team	League	GP	Min.	W	L	OTL	T	GA	SO	GAA	SV%	GP	Min.	W	L	GA	SO	GAA	SV%
		REGULAR SEASON										PLAYOFFS							
04-05—Huddinge	Sweden Jr.	19	1144	...	...	...	...	49	3	2.57	.904	—	—	—	—	—	—	—	—
05-06—Sodertalje	Sweden Jr.	26	1594	...	...	...	...	62	0	2.33	.918	—	—	—	—	—	—	—	—

ERAT, MARTIN LW/RW

PERSONAL: Born August 28, 1981, in Trebic, Czech. ... 6-0/195. ... Shoots left.

TRANSACTIONS/CAREER NOTES: Selected by Nashville Predators in seventh round (12th Predators pick, 191st overall) of entry draft (June 26, 1999). ... Shoulder (March 6, 2004); missed one game. ... Hip flexor (January 23, 2006); missed two games.

Season Team	League	GP	G	A	Pts.	PIM	+/-	PP	SH	GP	G	A	Pts.	PIM
		REGULAR SEASON								PLAYOFFS				
97-98—ZPS Zlin	Czech. Jrs.	46	35	30	65	...	...	...	...	—	—	—	—	—
98-99—ZPS Zlin	Czech. Jrs.	35	21	23	44	...	...	...	...	—	—	—	—	—
—ZPS Zlin	Czech.	5	0	0	0	2	...	...	...	—	—	—	—	—
99-00—Saskatoon	WHL	66	27	26	53	82	...	...	...	11	4	8	12	16
00-01—Saskatoon	WHL	31	19	35	54	48	...	...	...	—	—	—	—	—
—Red Deer	WHL	17	4	24	28	24	...	...	...	22	15	21	36	32
01-02—Nashville	NHL	80	9	24	33	32	-11	2	0	—	—	—	—	—
02-03—Milwaukee	AHL	45	10	22	32	41	-3	0	2	—	—	—	—	—
—Nashville	NHL	27	1	7	8	14	-9	1	0	—	—	—	—	—
03-04—Nashville	NHL	76	16	33	49	38	10	4	0	6	0	1	1	6
04-05—Zlin	Czech Rep.	48	20	23	43	129	7	...	...	18	8	6	14	12
05-06—Nashville	NHL	80	20	29	49	76	0	5	0	5	1	1	2	6
—Czech Rep. Oly. team	Int'l	8	1	1	2	4	1	0	0	—	—	—	—	—
NHL Totals (4 years)		263	46	93	139	160	-10	12	0	11	1	2	3	12

ERIKSSON, ANDERS D

PERSONAL: Born January 9, 1975, in Bollnas, Sweden. ... 6-3/215. ... Shoots left.

TRANSACTIONS/CAREER NOTES: Selected by Detroit Red Wings in first round (first Red Wings pick, 22nd overall) of NHL draft (June 26, 1993). ... Traded by Red Wings with first-round pick (D Steve McCarthy) in 1999 draft and first-round pick (G Adam Munro) in 2001 draft to Chicago Blackhawks for D Chris Chelios (March 23, 1999). ... Traded by Blackhawks to Florida Panthers for D Jaroslav Spacek (November 6, 2000). ... Injured knee (November 10, 2000); missed one game. ... Sprained knee (February 22, 2001); missed nine games. ... Signed as free agent by Toronto Maple Leafs (July 4, 2001). ... Signed as free agent by Columbus Blue Jackets (October 10, 2003). ... Signed as free agent by Calgary Flames (September 15, 2004). ... Signed as free agent by Columbus Blue Jackets (July 1, 2006).

Season Team	League	GP	G	A	Pts.	PIM	+/-	PP	SH	GP	G	A	Pts.	PIM
		REGULAR SEASON								PLAYOFFS				
92-93—MoDo Ornskoldsvik	Sweden	20	0	2	2	2	...	...	...	—	—	—	—	—
93-94—MoDo Ornskoldsvik	Sweden	38	2	8	10	42	...	...	...	11	0	0	0	8
94-95—MoDo Ornskoldsvik	Sweden	39	3	6	9	54	...	...	...	—	—	—	—	—
95-96—Adirondack	AHL	75	6	36	42	64	...	...	...	3	0	0	0	0
—Detroit	NHL	1	0	0	0	2	1	0	0	3	0	0	0	0
96-97—Detroit	NHL	23	0	6	6	10	5	0	0	—	—	—	—	—
—Adirondack	AHL	44	3	25	28	36	10	0	0	4	0	1	1	4
97-98—Detroit	NHL	66	7	14	21	32	21	1	0	18	0	5	5	16
98-99—Detroit	NHL	61	2	10	12	34	5	0	0	—	—	—	—	—
—Chicago	NHL	11	0	8	8	0	6	0	0	—	—	—	—	—
99-00—Chicago	NHL	73	3	25	28	20	4	0	0	—	—	—	—	—
00-01—Chicago	NHL	13	2	3	5	2	-4	1	0	—	—	—	—	—
—Florida	NHL	60	0	21	21	28	2	0	0	—	—	—	—	—
01-02—Toronto	NHL	34	0	2	2	12	-1	0	0	10	0	0	0	0
—St. John's	AHL	25	4	6	10	14	3	3	0	11	0	5	5	6
02-03—St. John's	AHL	72	5	34	39	133	-9	2	0	—	—	—	—	—
—Toronto	NHL	4	0	0	0	0	1	0	0	—	—	—	—	—
03-04—Columbus	NHL	66	7	20	27	18	-6	2	0	—	—	—	—	—
—Syracuse	AHL	9	1	3	4	12	-5	1	0	—	—	—	—	—
04-05—HV 71 Jonkoping	Sweden	32	1	9	10	54	-13	1	0	—	—	—	—	—
05-06—Springfield	AHL	12	1	8	9	10	0	0	0	—	—	—	—	—
—Mag. Metallurg	Russia	17	2	8	10	10	...	...	...	—	—	—	—	—
NHL Totals (9 years)		412	21	109	130	158	34	4	0	31	0	5	5	16

ERSKINE, JOHN D

PERSONAL: Born June 26, 1980, in Kingston, Ont. ... 6-4/215. ... Shoots left.

TRANSACTIONS/CAREER NOTES: Selected by Dallas Stars in second round (first Stars pick, 39th overall) of entry draft (June 27, 1998). ... Fractured foot (March 8, 2002); missed 13 games. ... Injured ankle (December 29, 2003); missed 7 games. ... Injured calf (January 16, 2004); missed four games. ... Hernia (March 3, 2004); missed final 15 games of season and playoffs. ... Signed as a free agent by Houston of the AHL (September 27, 2004). ... Re-signed by Stars as restricted free agent (August 19, 2005). ... Traded by Stars with second-round pick (W Jesse Joensuu) in 2006 draft to Islanders for D Janne Niinimaa and fifth-round pick in 2007 (January 10, 2006).

Season Team	League	GP	G	A	Pts.	PIM	+/-	PP	SH	GP	G	A	Pts.	PIM
		REGULAR SEASON								PLAYOFFS				
96-97—Quinte	Tier II Jr. A	48	4	16	20	241	...	...	...	—	—	—	—	—
97-98—London	OHL	55	0	9	9	205	...	...	...	16	0	5	5	25
98-99—London	OHL	57	8	12	20	208	21	...	...	25	5	10	15	38
99-00—London	OHL	58	12	31	43	177	-17	6	1	—	—	—	—	—
00-01—Utah	IHL	77	1	8	9	284	...	...	...	—	—	—	—	—
01-02—Utah	AHL	39	2	6	8	118	1	1	0	3	0	0	0	10
—Dallas	NHL	33	0	1	1	62	-8	0	0	—	—	—	—	—

Season Team	League	GP	G	A	Pts.	PIM	+/-	PP	SH	GP	G	A	Pts.	PIM
		REGULAR SEASON								PLAYOFFS				
02-03—Dallas	NHL	16	2	0	2	29	1	0	0	—	—	—	—	—
—Utah	AHL	52	2	8	10	274	2	0	0	1	0	1	1	15
03-04—Utah	AHL	5	0	0	0	18	0	0	0	—	—	—	—	—
—Dallas	NHL	32	0	1	1	84	-9	0	0	—	—	—	—	—
04-05—Houston	AHL	61	3	7	10	238	-5	0	0	5	0	1	1	20
05-06—Iowa	AHL	3	0	0	0	6	2	0	0	—	—	—	—	—
—Dallas	NHL	26	0	0	0	62	-3	0	0	—	—	—	—	—
—New York Islanders	NHL	34	1	0	1	99	-12	0	0	—	—	—	—	—
NHL Totals (4 years)		141	3	2	5	336	-31	0	0					

ESCHE, ROBERT G

PERSONAL: Born January 22, 1978, in Whitesboro, N.Y. ... 6-1/210. ... Catches left. ... Name pronounced EHSH.

TRANSACTIONS/CAREER NOTES: Selected by Phoenix Coyotes in sixth round (fifth Coyotes pick, 139th overall) of entry draft (June 22, 1996). ... Strained hamstring (April 12, 2002); missed final game of season. ... Traded by Coyotes with C Michal Handzus to Philadelphia Flyers for G Brian Boucher and third-round pick (D Joe Callahan) in 2002 draft (June 12, 2002). ... Groin (December 8, 2003); missed six games. ... Reinjured groin (December 23, 2003): missed one game. ... Sprained left knee (February 4, 2004); missed 10 games. ... Tore abductor tendon (December 5, 2005); missed four games. ... Groin (December 17, 2005); missed 17 games. ... Flu (April 15, 2006); missed one game.

Season Team	League	GP	Min.	W	L	OTL	T	GA	SO	GAA	SV%	GP	Min.	W	L	GA	SO	GAA	SV%
		REGULAR SEASON										PLAYOFFS							
95-96—Det. Jr. Red Wings	OHL	23	1219	13	6	...	0	76	1	3.74	...	3	105	0	2	4	0	2.29	...
96-97—Det. Jr. Red Wings	OHL	58	3241	24	28	...	2	206	2	3.81	.878	5	317	1	4	19	0	3.60	.907
97-98—Plymouth	OHL	48	2810	29	13	...	4	135	3	2.88	.896	15	869	8	7	45	0	3.11	.914
98-99—Springfield	AHL	55	2957	24	20	...	6	138	1	2.80	.905	1	60	0	1	4	0	4.00	.867
—Phoenix	NHL	3	130	0	1	...	0	7	0	3.23	.860	—	—	—	—	—	—	—	—
99-00—Houston	IHL	7	419	4	2	...	1	16	2	2.29	...	—	—	—	—	—	—	—	—
—Phoenix	NHL	8	408	2	5	...	0	23	0	3.38	.893	—	—	—	—	—	—	—	—
—Springfield	AHL	21	1207	9	9	...	2	61	2	3.03	...	3	180	1	2	12	0	4.00	...
00-01—Phoenix	NHL	25	1350	10	8	...	4	68	2	3.02	.896	—	—	—	—	—	—	—	—
01-02—Phoenix	NHL	22	1145	6	10	...	2	52	1	2.72	.902	—	—	—	—	—	—	—	—
—Springfield	AHL	1	60	1	0	...	0	0	1	0.00	1.000	—	—	—	—	—	—	—	—
02-03—Philadelphia	NHL	30	1638	12	9	...	3	60	2	2.20	.907	1	30	0	0	1	0	2.00	.929
03-04—Philadelphia	NHL	40	2322	21	11	...	7	79	3	2.04	.915	18	1061	11	7	41	1	2.32	.918
05-06—Philadelphia	NHL	40	2286	22	11	5	...	113	1	2.97	.897	6	314	2	4	22	0	4.20	.875
—U.S. Olympic team	Int'l	1	...	...	...	...	...	...	...	5.10	.762	—	—	—	—	—	—	—	—
NHL Totals (7 years)		168	9279	73	55	5	16	402	9	2.60	.903	25	1405	13	11	64	1	2.73	.907

EXELBY, GARNET D

PERSONAL: Born August 16, 1981, in Craik, Sask. ... 6-1/215. ... Shoots left.

TRANSACTIONS/CAREER NOTES: Selected by Atlanta Thrashers in eighth round (ninth Thrashers pick, 217th overall) of entry draft (June 27, 1999). ... Injured hip (January 22, 2004); missed six games. ... Injured ankle (February 5, 2004); missed two games. ... Flu (March 29, 2004); missed final three games of season. ... Leg injury (September 2005); missed first game of season. ... Illness (March 10, 2006); missed two games.

Season Team	League	GP	G	A	Pts.	PIM	+/-	PP	SH	GP	G	A	Pts.	PIM
		REGULAR SEASON								PLAYOFFS				
01-02—Chicago	AHL	75	3	4	7	257	-8	0	0	25	0	4	4	49
02-03—Chicago	AHL	53	3	6	9	140	11	0	0	—	—	—	—	—
—Atlanta	NHL	15	0	2	2	41	0	0	0	—	—	—	—	—
03-04—Atlanta	NHL	71	1	9	10	134	-10	0	0	—	—	—	—	—
05-06—Atlanta	NHL	75	1	9	10	75	11	0	0	—	—	—	—	—
NHL Totals (3 years)		161	2	20	22	250	1	0	0					

FAHEY, JIM D

PERSONAL: Born May 11, 1979, in Boston. ... 6-0/205. ... Shoots right.

TRANSACTIONS/CAREER NOTES: Selected by San Jose Sharks in eighth round (ninth Sharks pick, 212th overall) of NHL draft (June 27, 1998). ... Suffered concussion (March 1, 2003); missed three games.

Season Team	League	GP	G	A	Pts.	PIM	+/-	PP	SH	GP	G	A	Pts.	PIM
		REGULAR SEASON								PLAYOFFS				
97-98—Catholic Memorial	Mass. H.S.	24	12	12	24	28	...	...	...	—	—	—	—	—
98-99—Northeastern Univ.	Hockey East	32	5	13	18	34	...	...	...	—	—	—	—	—
99-00—Northeastern Univ.	Hockey East	36	3	17	20	62	...	...	...	—	—	—	—	—
00-01—Northeastern Univ.	Hockey East	36	4	23	27	48	...	...	...	—	—	—	—	—
01-02—Northeastern Univ.	Hockey East	39	14	32	46	50	...	...	...	—	—	—	—	—
02-03—Cleveland	AHL	25	3	14	17	42	-2	2	0	—	—	—	—	—
—San Jose	NHL	43	1	19	20	33	-3	0	0	—	—	—	—	—
03-04—Cleveland	AHL	32	1	18	19	64	-2	0	0	—	—	—	—	—
—San Jose	NHL	15	0	2	2	18	-2	0	0	2	0	0	0	0
04-05—Cleveland	AHL	69	4	22	26	146	-6	1	1	—	—	—	—	—
05-06—San Jose	NHL	21	0	2	2	14	-11	0	0	—	—	—	—	—
NHL Totals (3 years)		79	1	23	24	65	-16	0	0	2	0	0	0	0

FATA, RICO C/LW

PERSONAL: Born February 12, 1980, in Sault Ste. Marie, Ont. ... 6-0/205. ... Shoots left. ... Brother of Drew Fata, D, Pittsburgh Penguins organization.

TRANSACTIONS/CAREER NOTES: Selected by Calgary Flames in first round (first Flames pick, sixth overall) of NHL draft (June 27, 1998). ... Claimed off waivers by New York Rangers (October 3, 2001). ... Concussion (January 4, 2003); missed one game. ... Traded by Rangers with RW Mikael Samuelsson, D Joel Bouchard, D Richard Lintner and cash to Pittsburgh Penguins for RW Alexei Kovalev, LW Dan LaCouture, D Janne Laukkanen and D Mike Wilson (February 10, 2003). ... Injured hamstring (November 12, 2003); missed three games. ... Injured knee (November 29, 2003); missed five games. ... Claimed on waivers by Atlanta Thrasher (January 31, 2006). ... Claimed on waivers by Washington Capitals (March 9, 2006).

		REGULAR SEASON								PLAYOFFS				
Season Team	**League**	**GP**	**G**	**A**	**Pts.**	**PIM**	**+/-**	**PP**	**SH**	**GP**	**G**	**A**	**Pts.**	**PIM**
95-96—Sault Ste. Marie	OMJHL	62	11	15	26	52	...	...	...	—	—	—	—	—
96-97—London	OHL	59	19	34	53	76	...	...	...	—	—	—	—	—
97-98—London	OHL	64	43	33	76	110	...	...	...	16	9	5	14	49
98-99—Calgary	NHL	20	0	1	1	4	0	0	0	—	—	—	—	—
—London	OHL	23	15	18	33	41	3	...	...	25	10	12	22	42
99-00—Calgary	NHL	2	0	0	0	0	-1	0	0	—	—	—	—	—
—Saint John	AHL	76	29	29	58	65	...	...	...	3	0	0	0	4
00-01—Saint John	AHL	70	23	29	52	129	...	...	...	19	2	3	5	22
—Calgary	NHL	5	0	0	0	6	-3	0	0	—	—	—	—	—
01-02—New York Rangers	NHL	10	0	0	0	0	-2	0	0	—	—	—	—	—
—Hartford	AHL	61	35	36	71	36	27	8	2	10	2	5	7	4
02-03—New York Rangers	NHL	36	2	4	6	6	-1	0	0	—	—	—	—	—
—Hartford	AHL	9	8	6	14	6	4	1	1	—	—	—	—	—
—Pittsburgh	NHL	27	5	8	13	10	-6	0	0	—	—	—	—	—
03-04—Pittsburgh	NHL	73	16	18	34	54	-46	6	2	—	—	—	—	—
04-05—Asiago	Italy	35	18	20	38	36	...	...	...	—	—	—	—	—
05-06—Wilkes-Barre/Scranton	AHL	25	8	10	18	39	7	2	0	—	—	—	—	—
—Pittsburgh	NHL	20	0	0	0	10	-5	0	0	—	—	—	—	—
—Atlanta	NHL	6	0	1	1	4	-2	0	0	—	—	—	—	—
—Washington	NHL	21	3	3	6	8	3	1	0	—	—	—	—	—
NHL Totals (7 years)		220	26	35	61	102	-63	7	2					

FEDOROV, FEDOR C

PERSONAL: Born June 11, 1981, in Moscow, U.S.S.R. ... 6-3/230. ... Shoots left. ... Brother of Sergei Fedorov, C, Columbus Blue Jackets. ... Name pronounced feh-DUHR FEH-duhr-rahf.

TRANSACTIONS/CAREER NOTES: Selected by Tampa Bay Lightning in sixth round (seventh Lightning pick, 182nd overall) of entry draft (June 26, 1999). ... Returned to draft pool by Lightning; selected by Vancouver Canucks in third round (second Canucks pick, 66th overall) of entry draft (June 23, 2001). ... Traded by Canucks to New York Rangers for RW Josef Balej and conditional pick (October 7, 2005). ... Eye (March 15, 2005); missed two games.

		REGULAR SEASON								PLAYOFFS				
Season Team	**League**	**GP**	**G**	**A**	**Pts.**	**PIM**	**+/-**	**PP**	**SH**	**GP**	**G**	**A**	**Pts.**	**PIM**
97-98—Detroit Little Caesars	MNHL	13	3	7	10	18	...	...	...	—	—	—	—	—
98-99—Port Huron	UHL	42	2	5	7	20	...	...	...	—	—	—	—	—
99-00—Windsor	OHL	60	7	10	17	115	-5	0	0	12	1	0	1	4
00-01—Sudbury	OHL	37	33	45	78	88	25	11	1	12	4	6	10	36
01-02—Manitoba	AHL	8	2	1	3	6	3	1	0	—	—	—	—	—
—Columbia	ECHL	2	0	2	2	0	2	0	0	—	—	—	—	—
02-03—Vancouver	NHL	7	0	1	1	4	0	0	0	—	—	—	—	—
—Manitoba	AHL	50	10	13	23	61	-4	3	1	3	1	2	3	0
03-04—Manitoba	AHL	58	23	16	39	52	-8	10	0	—	—	—	—	—
—Vancouver	NHL	8	0	1	1	4	0	0	0	—	—	—	—	—
04-05—Spartak Moscow	Russian	19	4	7	11	52	0	...	...	—	—	—	—	—
—Metal. Magnitogorsk	Russian	10	3	0	3	22	-1	...	...	5	2	0	2	30
05-06—Hartford	AHL	38	2	15	17	80	-1	1	0	—	—	—	—	—
—Syracuse	AHL	12	2	3	5	22	-7	1	0	3	0	0	0	2
—New York Rangers	NHL	3	0	0	0	6	0	0	0	—	—	—	—	—
NHL Totals (3 years)		18	0	2	2	14	0	0	0					

FEDOROV, SERGEI C

PERSONAL: Born December 13, 1969, in Pskov, USSR. ... 6-2/205. ... Shoots left. ... Brother of Fedor Fedorov, C, New York Rangers. ... Name pronounced SAIR-gay FEH-duh-rahf.

TRANSACTIONS/CAREER NOTES: Selected by Detroit Red Wings in fourth round (fourth Red Wings pick, 74th overall) of entry draft (June 17, 1989). ... Bruised left shoulder (October 1990). ... Reinjured left shoulder (January 16, 1991). ... Sprained left shoulder (November 27, 1992); missed seven games. ... Flu (January 30, 1993); missed two games. ... Charley horse (February 11, 1993); missed one game. ... Concussion (April 5, 1994); missed two games. ... Suspended four games without pay and fined $500 for high-sticking incident in playoff game (May 17, 1994); suspension reduced to three games due to abbreviated 1994-95 season. ... Flu (February 7, 1995); missed one game. ... Bruised right hamstring (April 9, 1995); missed one game. ... Tonsillitis (October 6, 1995); missed three games. ... Sprained left wrist (December 15, 1995); missed one game. ... Groin (January 9, 1997); missed two games. ... Groin (January 20, 1997); missed six games. ... Missed 1997-98 season's first 59 games in contract dispute. ... Tendered offer sheet by Carolina Hurricanes (February 19, 1998). ... Offer matched by Red Wings (February 26, 1998). ... Suspended two games and fined $1,000 for illegal check (March 31, 1998). ... Suspended five games for slashing incident (March 3, 1999). ... Head (November 20, 1999); missed six games. ... Neck (January 16, 2000); missed three games. ... Wrist (February 18, 2000); missed five games. ... Fractured nose (February 23, 2001); missed six games. ... Signed as free agent by Anaheim Mighty Ducks (July 20, 2003). ... Stomach virus (January 21, 2004); missed one game. ... Flu (March 8, 2004); missed one game. ... Groin (October 14, 2005); missed 13 games. ... Traded by Mighty Ducks with a fifth-round pick (D Maxime Frechette) in 2006 draft to

Columbus Blue Jackets for C Tyler Wright and D Francois Beauchemin (November 15, 2005). ... Back (March 17, 2005); missed two games.
STATISTICAL PLATEAUS: Three-goal games: 1993-94 (1), 2000-01 (1), 2002-03 (2). Total: 4. ... Four-goal games: 1994-95 (1). ... Five-goal games: 1996-97 (1). ... Total hat tricks: 6.

		REGULAR SEASON								PLAYOFFS				
Season Team	League	GP	G	A	Pts.	PIM	+/-	PP	SH	GP	G	A	Pts.	PIM
85-86—Dynamo Minsk	USSR	15	6	1	7	10	...	...	...	—	—	—	—	—
86-87—CSKA Moscow	USSR	29	6	6	12	12	...	...	...	—	—	—	—	—
87-88—CSKA Moscow	USSR	48	7	9	16	20	...	...	...	—	—	—	—	—
88-89—CSKA Moscow	USSR	44	9	8	17	35	...	...	...	—	—	—	—	—
89-90—CSKA Moscow	USSR	48	19	10	29	20	...	...	...	—	—	—	—	—
90-91—Detroit	NHL	77	31	48	79	66	11	11	3	7	1	5	6	4
91-92—Detroit	NHL	80	32	54	86	72	26	7	2	11	5	5	10	8
92-93—Detroit	NHL	73	34	53	87	72	33	13	4	7	3	6	9	23
93-94—Detroit	NHL	82	56	64	120	34	48	13	4	7	1	7	8	6
94-95—Detroit	NHL	42	20	30	50	24	6	7	3	17	7	*17	*24	6
95-96—Detroit	NHL	78	39	68	107	48	49	11	3	19	2	*18	20	10
96-97—Detroit	NHL	74	30	33	63	30	29	9	2	20	8	12	20	12
97-98—Russian Oly. team	Int'l	6	1	5	6	8	6	0	0	—	—	—	—	—
—Detroit	NHL	21	6	11	17	25	10	2	0	22	*10	10	20	12
98-99—Detroit	NHL	77	26	37	63	66	9	6	2	10	1	8	9	8
99-00—Detroit	NHL	68	27	35	62	22	8	4	4	9	4	4	8	4
00-01—Detroit	NHL	75	32	37	69	40	12	14	2	6	2	5	7	0
01-02—Detroit	NHL	81	31	37	68	36	20	10	0	23	5	14	19	20
—Russian Oly. team	Int'l	6	2	2	4	4	...	...	...	—	—	—	—	—
02-03—Detroit	NHL	80	36	47	83	52	15	10	2	4	1	2	3	0
03-04—Anaheim	NHL	80	31	34	65	42	-5	9	2	—	—	—	—	—
05-06—Anaheim	NHL	5	0	1	1	2	-1	0	0	—	—	—	—	—
—Columbus	NHL	62	12	31	43	64	-1	3	1	—	—	—	—	—
NHL Totals (15 years)		1055	443	620	1063	695	269	129	34	162	50	113	163	113

FEDORUK, TODD LW

PERSONAL: Born February 13, 1979, in Redwater, Alta. ... 6-2/235. ... Shoots left.
TRANSACTIONS/CAREER NOTES: Selected by Philadelphia Flyers in seventh round (sixth Flyers pick, 16th overall) of entry draft (June 21, 1997). ... Strained elbow (January 13, 2001); missed two games. ... Cut eyelid (January 31, 2001); missed one game. ... Strained right thumb (October 24, 2002); missed three games. ... Facial cuts and headaches (December 21, 2002); missed two games. ... Sprained right thumb (February 25, 2003); missed three games. ... Bruised left tight (March 18, 2003); missed four games. ... Cheekbone (November 12, 2003); missed six games. ... Fractured cheekbone (December 1, 2003); missed eight games. ... Knee (February 18, 2004); missed four games. ... Traded by Flyers to Anaheim Mighty Ducks for second-round pick (later traded to Phoenix; Coyotes selected G Pier-Olivier Pelletier) in 2005 draft (July 29, 2005). ... Back (November 5, 2005); missed one game. ... Suspended three games for match penalty issued after hit on Coyotes C Petr Nedved (November 23, 2005).

		REGULAR SEASON								PLAYOFFS				
Season Team	League	GP	G	A	Pts.	PIM	+/-	PP	SH	GP	G	A	Pts.	PIM
96-97—Kelowna	WHL	31	1	5	6	87	...	...	...	6	0	0	0	13
97-98—Kelowna	WHL	31	3	5	8	120	...	...	...	—	—	—	—	—
—Regina	WHL	21	4	3	7	80	...	...	...	9	1	2	3	23
98-99—Regina	WHL	39	12	12	24	107	...	...	...	—	—	—	—	—
—Prince Albert	WHL	28	6	4	10	75	...	...	...	—	—	—	—	—
99-00—Philadelphia	AHL	19	1	2	3	40	...	...	...	5	0	1	1	2
—Trenton	ECHL	18	2	5	7	118	...	...	...	—	—	—	—	—
00-01—Philadelphia	AHL	14	0	1	1	49	...	...	...	—	—	—	—	—
—Philadelphia	NHL	53	5	5	10	109	0	0	0	2	0	0	0	20
01-02—Philadelphia	NHL	55	3	4	7	141	-2	0	0	3	0	0	0	0
—Philadelphia	AHL	7	0	1	1	54	-3	0	0	—	—	—	—	—
02-03—Philadelphia	NHL	63	1	5	6	105	1	0	0	1	0	0	0	0
03-04—Philadelphia	NHL	49	1	4	5	136	-4	0	0	1	0	0	0	2
—Philadelphia	AHL	2	0	2	2	2	2	0	0	—	—	—	—	—
04-05—Philadelphia	AHL	42	4	12	16	142	8	0	0	16	2	2	4	33
05-06—Anaheim	NHL	76	4	19	23	174	6	0	0	12	0	0	0	16
NHL Totals (5 years)		296	14	37	51	665	1	0	0	19	0	0	0	38

FEDOTENKO, RUSLAN LW/RW

PERSONAL: Born January 18, 1979, in Kiev, U.S.S.R. ... 6-2/195. ... Shoots left.
TRANSACTIONS/CAREER NOTES: Signed as free agent by Philadelphia Flyers (August 3, 1999). ... Sprained right knee (February 27, 2002); missed four games. ... Traded by Flyers with two second-round picks (traded to Ottawa [Tobias Stephan] and traded to Phoenix [Dan Spang]) in 2002 draft to Tampa Bay Lightning for first-round pick (D Joni Pitkanen) in 2002 draft (June 21, 2002). ... Injured shoulder (November 21, 2002); missed one game. ... Fractured finger (February 25, 2003); missed five games. ... Facial injury (May 29, 2004); missed one playoff game. ... Injured hip (December 15, 2005); missed two games.

		REGULAR SEASON								PLAYOFFS				
Season Team	League	GP	G	A	Pts.	PIM	+/-	PP	SH	GP	G	A	Pts.	PIM
97-98—Melfort	SJHL	68	35	31	66	...	...	...	...	—	—	—	—	—
98-99—Sioux City	USHL	55	43	34	77	139	...	...	...	5	5	1	6	9
99-00—Philadelphia	AHL	67	16	34	50	42	...	...	...	2	0	0	0	0
—Trenton	ECHL	8	5	3	8	9	...	...	...	—	—	—	—	—
00-01—Philadelphia	AHL	8	1	0	1	8	...	...	...	—	—	—	—	—
—Philadelphia	NHL	74	16	20	36	72	8	3	0	6	0	1	1	4
01-02—Philadelphia	NHL	78	17	9	26	43	15	0	1	5	1	0	1	2

Season Team	League	REGULAR SEASON GP	G	A	Pts.	PIM	+/-	PP	SH	PLAYOFFS GP	G	A	Pts.	PIM
—Ukranian Oly. team	Int'l	1	1	0	1	4	...	...	...	—	—	—	—	—
02-03—Tampa Bay	NHL	76	19	13	32	44	-7	6	0	11	0	1	1	2
03-04—Tampa Bay	NHL	77	17	22	39	30	14	0	0	22	12	2	14	14
05-06—Tampa Bay	NHL	80	26	15	41	44	-4	4	0	5	0	0	0	20
NHL Totals (5 years)		385	95	79	174	233	26	13	1	49	13	4	17	42

FEHR, ERIC — RW

PERSONAL: Born September 7, 1985, in Winkler, Man. ... 6-3/187. ... Shoots right.
TRANSACTIONS/CAREER NOTES: Selected by Washington Capitals in first round (first Capitals pick, 18th overall) in 2003 NHL entry draft (June 23, 2003).

Season Team	League	REGULAR SEASON GP	G	A	Pts.	PIM	+/-	PP	SH	PLAYOFFS GP	G	A	Pts.	PIM
01-02—Brandon	WHL	63	11	16	27	29	...	...	...	—	—	—	—	—
02-03—Brandon	WHL	70	26	29	55	76	...	...	...	—	—	—	—	—
03-04—Brandon	WHL	71	50	34	84	129	...	...	...	7	5	0	5	16
04-05—Brandon	WHL	71	59	52	111	91	26	31	2	24	16	16	32	47
05-06—Hershey	AHL	70	25	28	53	70	-12	14	0	12	4	3	7	8
—Washington	NHL	11	0	0	0	2	0	0	0	—	—	—	—	—
NHL Totals (1 year)		11	0	0	0	2	0	0	0					

FERENCE, ANDREW — D

PERSONAL: Born March 17, 1979, in Edmonton. ... 5-10/196. ... Shoots left.
TRANSACTIONS/CAREER NOTES: Selected by Pittsburgh Penguins in eighth round (eighth Penguins pick, 20eighth overall) of 1997 entry draft (June 21, 2004). ... Flu (December 9, 1999); missed four games. ... Flu (December 26, 2001); missed one game. ... Hernia (October 10, 2002); missed 21 games. ... Traded by Penguins to Calgary Flames for third-round pick (C Brian Gifford) in 2004 draft (February 10, 2003). ... Ankle (March 18, 2003); missed season's final nine games. ... Groin (December 2, 2003); missed two games. ... Right shoulder (January 8, 2004); missed two games.

Season Team	League	REGULAR SEASON GP	G	A	Pts.	PIM	+/-	PP	SH	PLAYOFFS GP	G	A	Pts.	PIM
95-96—Portland	WHL	72	9	31	40	159	...	...	...	7	1	3	4	12
96-97—Portland	WHL	72	12	32	44	163	...	...	...	—	—	—	—	—
97-98—Portland	WHL	72	11	57	68	142	75	5	1	16	2	18	20	28
98-99—Portland	WHL	40	11	21	32	104	-13	6	1	4	1	4	5	10
—Kansas City	IHL	5	1	2	3	4	-5	0	0	3	0	0	0	9
99-00—Pittsburgh	NHL	30	2	4	6	20	3	0	0	—	—	—	—	—
—Wilkes-Barre/Scranton	AHL	44	8	20	28	58	...	...	...	—	—	—	—	—
00-01—Wilkes-Barre/Scranton	AHL	43	6	18	24	95	...	...	...	3	1	0	1	12
—Pittsburgh	NHL	36	4	11	15	28	6	1	0	18	3	7	10	16
01-02—Pittsburgh	NHL	75	4	7	11	73	-12	1	0	—	—	—	—	—
02-03—Pittsburgh	NHL	22	1	3	4	36	-16	1	0	—	—	—	—	—
—Wilkes-Barre/Scranton	AHL	1	0	0	0	2	1	0	0	—	—	—	—	—
—Calgary	NHL	16	0	4	4	6	1	0	0	—	—	—	—	—
03-04—Calgary	NHL	72	4	12	16	53	5	1	0	26	0	3	3	25
04-05—Budejovice	Czech Dv.I	19	5	6	11	45	16	...	...	12	2	7	9	10
05-06—Calgary	NHL	82	4	27	31	85	-12	2	0	7	0	4	4	12
NHL Totals (6 years)		333	19	68	87	301	-25	6	0	51	3	14	17	53

FERGUSON, SCOTT — D

PERSONAL: Born January 6, 1973, in Camrose, Alta. ... 6-1/195. ... Shoots left.
TRANSACTIONS/CAREER NOTES: Signed as free agent by Edmonton Oilers (June 2, 1994). ... Traded by Oilers to Ottawa Senators for D Frank Musil (March 9, 1998). ... Signed as free agent by Anaheim Mighty Ducks (July 22, 1998). ... Signed as free agent by Oilers (July 5, 2000). ... Stomach virus (February 27, 2003); missed one game. ... Signed as free agent by Minnesota Wild (August 4, 2005).

Season Team	League	REGULAR SEASON GP	G	A	Pts.	PIM	+/-	PP	SH	PLAYOFFS GP	G	A	Pts.	PIM
90-91—Kamloops	WHL	4	0	0	0	0	...	...	...	—	—	—	—	—
91-92—Kamloops	WHL	62	4	10	14	148	...	...	...	12	0	2	2	21
92-93—Kamloops	WHL	71	4	19	23	206	...	...	...	13	0	2	2	24
93-94—Kamloops	WHL	68	5	49	54	180	...	3	1	19	5	11	16	48
94-95—Wheeling	ECHL	5	1	5	6	16	5	0	0	—	—	—	—	—
—Cape Breton	AHL	58	4	6	10	103	-7	2	0	—	—	—	—	—
95-96—Cape Breton	AHL	80	5	16	21	196	...	...	...	—	—	—	—	—
96-97—Hamilton	AHL	74	6	14	20	115	4	2	1	21	5	7	12	59
97-98—Hamilton	AHL	77	7	17	24	150	6	2	1	9	0	3	3	16
—Edmonton	NHL	1	0	0	0	0	1	0	0	—	—	—	—	—
98-99—Cincinnati	AHL	78	4	31	35	144	4	3	0	3	0	0	0	4
—Anaheim	NHL	2	0	1	1	0	0	0	0	—	—	—	—	—
99-00—Cincinnati	AHL	77	7	25	32	166	...	...	...	—	—	—	—	—
00-01—Hamilton	AHL	42	3	18	21	79	...	...	...	—	—	—	—	—
—Edmonton	NHL	20	0	1	1	13	2	0	0	6	0	0	0	0
01-02—Edmonton	NHL	50	3	2	5	75	11	0	0	—	—	—	—	—
02-03—Edmonton	NHL	78	3	5	8	120	11	0	0	5	0	0	0	8
03-04—Edmonton	NHL	52	1	5	6	80	-5	0	0	—	—	—	—	—

		REGULAR SEASON								PLAYOFFS				
Season Team	**League**	**GP**	**G**	**A**	**Pts.**	**PIM**	**+/-**	**PP**	**SH**	**GP**	**G**	**A**	**Pts.**	**PIM**
04-05—Skovde	Sweden	10	0	2	2	57	3	0	0	—	—	—	—	—
05-06—Houston	AHL	46	5	8	13	105	6	1	0	8	0	2	2	21
—Minnesota	NHL	15	0	0	0	22	-3	0	0	—	—	—	—	—
NHL Totals (7 years)		218	7	14	21	310	17	0	0	11	0	0	0	8

FERLAND, JONATHAN RW

PERSONAL: Born February 9, 1983, in Quebec City. ... 6-2/208. ... Shoots right.
TRANSACTIONS/CAREER NOTES: Selected by Montreal Canadiens in seventh round (fifth Canadiens pick, 212th overall) of NHL entry draft (June 23, 2002).

		REGULAR SEASON								PLAYOFFS				
Season Team	**League**	**GP**	**G**	**A**	**Pts.**	**PIM**	**+/-**	**PP**	**SH**	**GP**	**G**	**A**	**Pts.**	**PIM**
99-00—Moncton	QMJHL	52	3	6	9	21	...	...	...	11	0	1	1	0
00-01—Acadie-Bathurst	QMJHL	70	17	11	28	135	...	...	...	13	0	4	4	47
01-02—Acadie-Bathurst	QMJHL	55	28	46	74	104	...	...	...	16	5	12	17	16
02-03—Acadie-Bathurst	QMJHL	68	45	44	89	94	...	...	...	11	4	5	9	16
03-04—Hamilton	AHL	70	5	10	15	43	...	...	...	10	0	0	0	6
04-05—Hamilton	AHL	62	6	8	14	24	-7	0	0	4	0	0	0	4
05-06—Montreal	NHL	7	1	0	1	2	-2	0	0	—	—	—	—	—
—Hamilton	AHL	39	7	8	15	65	-4	3	0	—	—	—	—	—
NHL Totals (1 year)		7	1	0	1	2	-2	0	0					

FERNANDEZ, MANNY G

PERSONAL: Born August 27, 1974, in Etobicoke, Ont. ... 6-0/180. ... Catches left. ... Nephew of Jacques Lemaire, coach, Minnesota Wild, and Hall of Fame center with Montreal Canadiens (1967-68 through 1978-79).
TRANSACTIONS/CAREER NOTES: Selected by Quebec Nordiques in third round (fourth Nordiques pick, 52nd overall) of entry draft (June 20, 1992). ... Traded by Nordiques to Dallas Stars for D Tommy Sjodin and third-round pick (C Chris Drury) in 1994 (February 13, 1994). ... Traded by Stars with D Brad Lukowich to Minnesota Wild for third-round pick (C Joel Lundqvist) in 2000 and fourth-round pick (traded back to Minnesota; traded to Los Angeles; Kings selected D Aaron Rome) in 2002 (June 12, 2000). ... Ankle (October 14, 2000); missed five games. ... Knee (March 6, 2001); missed two games. ... Ankle (March 15, 2001); missed remainder of season. ... Ankle (April 10, 2002); missed remainder of season. ... Knee (January 6, 2003); missed 10 games. ... Neck, back spasms (October 4, 2005); missed season's first two games.

		REGULAR SEASON										PLAYOFFS							
Season Team	**League**	**GP**	**Min.**	**W**	**L**	**OTL**	**T**	**GA**	**SO**	**GAA**	**SV%**	**GP**	**Min.**	**W**	**L**	**GA**	**SO**	**GAA**	**SV%**
91-92—Laval	QMJHL	31	1593	14	13	...	2	99	1	3.73	...	9	468	3	5	39	0	5.00	...
92-93—Laval	QMJHL	43	2348	26	14	...	2	141	1	3.60	.887	13	818	12	1	42	0	3.08	...
93-94—Laval	QMJHL	51	2776	29	14	...	1	143	5	3.09	.906	19	1116	14	5	49	1	2.63	.914
94-95—Kalamazoo	IHL	46	2470	21	10	...	9	115	2	2.79	.905	12	655	9	1	30	1	2.75	.901
—Dallas	NHL	1	59	0	1	...	0	3	0	3.05	.889	—	—	—	—	—	—	—	—
95-96—Michigan	IHL	47	2663	22	15	...	9	133	4	3.00	...	6	372	5	1	14	0	2.26	...
—Dallas	NHL	5	249	0	1	...	1	19	0	4.58	.843	—	—	—	—	—	—	—	—
96-97—Michigan	IHL	48	2721	20	24	...	2	142	2	3.13	...	4	277	1	3	15	0	3.25	...
97-98—Michigan	IHL	55	3023	27	17	...	5	139	5	2.76	.916	2	89	0	2	7	0	4.72	.860
—Dallas	NHL	2	69	1	0	...	0	2	0	1.74	.943	1	2	0	0	0	0	0.00	...
98-99—Houston	IHL	50	2949	34	6	...	9	116	2	2.36	.916	19	1126	11	8	49	1	2.61	.904
—Dallas	NHL	1	60	0	1	...	0	2	0	2.00	.931	—	—	—	—	—	—	—	—
99-00—Dallas	NHL	24	1353	11	8	...	3	48	1	2.13	.920	1	17	0	0	1	0	3.53	.875
00-01—Minnesota	NHL	42	2461	19	17	...	4	92	4	2.24	.920	—	—	—	—	—	—	—	—
01-02—Minnesota	NHL	44	2463	12	24	...	5	125	1	3.05	.892	—	—	—	—	—	—	—	—
02-03—Minnesota	NHL	35	1979	19	13	...	2	74	2	2.24	.924	9	552	3	4	18	0	1.96	.929
03-04—Minnesota	NHL	37	2166	11	14	...	9	90	2	2.49	.915	—	—	—	—	—	—	—	—
04-05—Lulea	Sweden	19	1083	...	...	...	...	50	2	2.77	.895	3	159	...	...	13	0	4.90	.849
05-06—Minnesota	NHL	58	3411	30	18	7	...	130	1	2.29	.919	—	—	—	—	—	—	—	—
NHL Totals (10 years)		249	14270	103	97	7	24	585	11	2.46	.913	11	571	3	4	19	0	2.00	.927

F

FIALA, ONDREJ C

PERSONAL: Born November 4, 1987, in Stenberk, Czech. ... 6-1/183. ... Shoots left.
TRANSACTIONS/CAREER NOTES: Selected by Minnesota Wild in second round (second Wild pick; 40th overall) of NHL draft (June 24, 2006).

		REGULAR SEASON								PLAYOFFS				
Season Team	**League**	**GP**	**G**	**A**	**Pts.**	**PIM**	**+/-**	**PP**	**SH**	**GP**	**G**	**A**	**Pts.**	**PIM**
04-05—Kladno	Czech. Jrs.	40	9	11	20	89	...	...	...	—	—	—	—	—
—HC Ocelari Trinec	Czech.	3	0	0	0	0	...	...	...	—	—	—	—	—
05-06—Everett	WHL	51	21	14	35	26	4	...	...	8	4	4	8	4

FIDDLER, VERNON C

PERSONAL: Born May 9, 1980, in Edmonton. ... 5-11/204. ... Shoots left.
TRANSACTIONS/CAREER NOTES: Signed as free agent by Nashville Predators (May 6, 2002). ... Concussion (February 9, 2006); missed two games. ... Concussion (March 1, 2006); missed 16 games.

Season Team	League	GP	G	A	Pts.	PIM	+/-	PP	SH	GP	G	A	Pts.	PIM
		REGULAR SEASON								PLAYOFFS				
97-98—Kelowna	WHL	65	10	11	21	31	...	...	...	7	0	1	1	4
98-99—Kelowna	WHL	68	22	21	43	82	...	...	...	6	2	0	2	8
99-00—Kelowna	WHL	64	20	28	48	60	...	...	...	5	1	3	4	4
00-01—Medicine Hat	WHL	67	33	38	71	100	...	...	...	—	—	—	—	—
—Kelowna	WHL	3	0	2	2	0	...	...	...	—	—	—	—	—
—Arkansas	ECHL	3	0	1	1	2	...	...	...	5	3	0	3	5
01-02—Norfolk	AHL	38	8	5	13	28	...	...	...	4	1	3	4	2
—Roanoke	ECHL	44	27	28	55	71	...	...	...	—	—	—	—	—
02-03—Milwaukee	AHL	54	8	16	24	70	9	0	0	6	1	2	3	14
—Nashville	NHL	19	4	2	6	14	2	0	0	—	—	—	—	—
03-04—Milwaukee	AHL	47	9	15	24	72	13	0	0	22	5	3	8	36
—Nashville	NHL	17	0	0	0	23	-6	0	0	—	—	—	—	—
04-05—Milwaukee	AHL	73	20	22	42	70	19	1	2	7	0	0	0	18
05-06—Milwaukee	AHL	11	1	6	7	20	1	1	0	—	—	—	—	—
—Nashville	NHL	40	8	4	12	42	-2	3	0	2	0	1	1	0
NHL Totals (3 years)		76	12	6	18	79	-6	3	0	2	0	1	1	0

FILPPULA, VALTTERI C

PERSONAL: Born March 20, 1984, in Vantaa, Finland. ... 5-11/180. ... Shoots left. ... Name pronounced: val-TAIR-ee fihl-POO-luh
TRANSACTIONS/CAREER NOTES: Selected by Detroit Red Wings in third round (third Red Wings pick, 95th overall) of entry draft (June 22, 2002).

Season Team	League	GP	G	A	Pts.	PIM	+/-	PP	SH	GP	G	A	Pts.	PIM
		REGULAR SEASON								PLAYOFFS				
00-01—Jokerit Helsinki	Finland Jr. B	31	18	29	47	4	...	...	...	—	—	—	—	—
—Jokerit Helsinki	Finland Jr.	1	0	1	1	0	...	...	...	—	—	—	—	—
01-02—Jokerit Helsinki	Finland Jr. B	1	0	1	1	0	...	...	...	—	—	—	—	—
—Jokerit Helsinki	Finland Jr.	40	8	15	23	14	...	...	...	9	4	9	13	2
02-03—Jokerit Helsinki	Finland Jr.	35	16	37	53	39	...	...	...	11	4	10	14	4
03-04—Jokerit Helsinki	Finland	49	5	13	18	6	...	...	...	—	—	—	—	—
04-05—Jokerit Helsinki	Finland	55	10	20	30	20	...	...	...	12	5	6	11	2
05-06—Grand Rapids	AHL	74	20	50	70	30	23	5	1	16	7	9	16	4
—Detroit	NHL	4	0	1	1	2	1	0	0	—	—	—	—	—
NHL Totals (1 year)		4	0	1	1	2	1	0	0					

FINLEY, BRIAN G

PERSONAL: Born July 3, 1981, in Sault Ste. Marie, Ont. ... 6-3/205. ... Catches right.
TRANSACTIONS/CAREER NOTES: Selected by Nashville Predators in first round (first Predators pick, sixth overall) of draft (June 26, 1999). ... Injured groin; missed 2001-02 season. ... Signed as free agent by Boston Bruins (July 17, 2006).

Season Team	League	GP	Min.	W	L	OTL	T	GA	SO	GAA	SV%	GP	Min.	W	L	GA	SO	GAA	SV%
		REGULAR SEASON										PLAYOFFS							
97-98—Barrie	OHL	41	2154	23	14	...	1	105	3	2.92	.909	5	260	1	3	13	0	3.00	.911
98-99—Barrie	OHL	52	3063	36	10	...	4	136	3	2.66	.913	5	323	4	1	15	0	2.79	.910
99-00—Barrie	OHL	47	2540	24	12	...	6	130	2	3.07	.908	23	1353	14	8	58	1	1.00	.917
00-01—Barrie	OHL	16	818	5	8	...	0	42	0	3.08	.904	—	—	—	—	—	—	—	—
—Brampton	OHL	11	631	7	3	...	1	31	0	2.95	.889	9	503	5	4	26	1	3.10	...
02-03—Milwaukee	AHL	22	1207	7	11	...	2	59	2	2.93	.898	—	—	—	—	—	—	—	—
—Toledo	ECHL	7	305	4	2	...	0	12	0	2.36	.918	1	60	0	1	4	0	4.00	.889
—Nashville	NHL	1	47	0	0	...	0	3	0	3.83	.769	—	—	—	—	—	—	—	—
03-04—Milwaukee	AHL	43	2562	23	15	...	4	100	2	2.34	.911	1	58	0	1	2	0	2.07	.909
04-05—Milwaukee	AHL	64	3642	36	22	...	...	139	7	2.29	.921	7	457	3	4	20	1	2.63	.913
05-06—Milwaukee	AHL	32	1712	18	7	2	...	77	4	2.70	.908	6	310	3	2	14	0	2.71	.896
—Nashville	NHL	1	60	0	1	0	...	7	0	7.00	.829	—	—	—	—	—	—	—	—
NHL Totals (2 years)		2	107	0	1	0	0	10	0	5.61	.815								

FISCHER, DAVID D

PERSONAL: Born February 19, 1988, in Minneapolis, Minn. ... 6-3/185. ... Shoots right.
TRANSACTIONS/CAREER NOTES: Selected by Montreal Canadiens in first round (first Canadiens pick; 20th overall) of NHL draft (June 24, 2006).

Season Team	League	GP	G	A	Pts.	PIM	+/-	PP	SH	GP	G	A	Pts.	PIM
		REGULAR SEASON								PLAYOFFS				
04-05—Apple Valley	USHS (West)	28	8	23	31	32	...	...	...	—	—	—	—	—
05-06—Apple Valley	USHS (West)	25	8	30	38	34	...	...	...	—	—	—	—	—

FISCHER, JIRI D

PERSONAL: Born July 31, 1980, in Horovice, Czech. ... 6-5/235. ... Shoots left.
TRANSACTIONS/CAREER NOTES: Selected by Detroit Red Wings in first round (first Red Wings pick, 25th overall) of entry draft (June 27, 1998). ... Ankle (December 2, 2000); missed eight games. ... Suspended one playoff game for cross-checking incident (June 11, 2002). ... Heart abnormality (September 2002). ... Knee (November 15, 2002); missed remainer of season (67 games). ... Suspended for one game for head-butting incident (January 24, 2004). ... Heart abnormality (November 21, 2005); missed remainder of season (60 games).

Season Team	League	REGULAR SEASON GP	G	A	Pts.	PIM	+/-	PP	SH	PLAYOFFS GP	G	A	Pts.	PIM
95-96—Poldi Kladno	Czech Rep.	39	6	10	16	...	...	...	...	—	—	—	—	—
96-97—Poldi Kladno	Czech Rep.	38	11	16	27	...	...	...	...	—	—	—	—	—
97-98—Hull	QMJHL	70	3	19	22	112	-18	2	0	11	1	4	5	16
98-99—Hull	QMJHL	65	22	56	78	141	11	15	2	23	6	17	23	44
99-00—Detroit	NHL	52	0	8	8	45	1	0	0	—	—	—	—	—
—Cincinnati	AHL	7	0	2	2	10	...	...	...	—	—	—	—	—
00-01—Detroit	NHL	55	1	8	9	59	3	0	0	5	0	0	0	9
—Cincinnati	AHL	18	2	6	8	22	...	...	...	—	—	—	—	—
01-02—Detroit	NHL	80	2	8	10	67	17	0	0	22	3	3	6	30
02-03—Detroit	NHL	15	1	5	6	16	0	0	0	—	—	—	—	—
03-04—Detroit	NHL	81	4	15	19	75	0	1	0	—	—	—	—	—
04-05—Liberec	Czech Rep.	27	6	12	18	52	15	...	...	11	1	4	5	22
05-06—Detroit	NHL	22	3	5	8	33	8	0	1	—	—	—	—	—
NHL Totals (6 years)		305	11	49	60	295	29	1	1	27	3	3	6	39

FISHER, MIKE C/LW

PERSONAL: Born June 5, 1980, in Peterborough, Ont. ... 6-1/203. ... Shoots right.

TRANSACTIONS/CAREER NOTES: Selected by Ottawa Senators in second round (second Senators pick, 44th overall) of entry draft (June 27, 1998). ... Hip pointer (October 5, 1999); missed three games. ... Torn right knee ligament (December 30, 1999); missed remainder of season. ... Injured left shoulder (November 2, 2000); missed 22 games. ... Injured left shoulder (February 8, 2002); missed five games. ... Injured right shoulder (March 7, 2002); missed final 19 games of season. ... Flu (December 17, 2002); missed one game. ... Bruised right knee (January 2, 2003); missed two games. ... Separated left shoulder (March 25, 2003); missed four games. ... Injured left elbow (October 4, 2003); missed 33 games. ... Injured left elbow (December 30, 2003); missed 25 games. ... Sprained left shoulder (October 11, 2005); missed four games. ... Flu (February 6, 2006); missed one game. ... Sprained right ankle (March 18, 2006); missed nine games.

Season Team	League	REGULAR SEASON GP	G	A	Pts.	PIM	+/-	PP	SH	PLAYOFFS GP	G	A	Pts.	PIM
96-97—Peterborough	Tier II Jr. A	51	26	30	56	33	...	...	...	—	—	—	—	—
97-98—Sudbury	OHL	66	24	25	49	65	...	...	...	9	2	2	4	13
98-99—Sudbury	OHL	68	41	65	106	55	10	...	...	4	2	1	3	4
99-00—Ottawa	NHL	32	4	5	9	15	-6	0	0	—	—	—	—	—
00-01—Ottawa	NHL	60	7	12	19	46	-1	0	0	4	0	1	1	4
01-02—Ottawa	NHL	58	15	9	24	55	8	0	3	10	2	1	3	0
02-03—Ottawa	NHL	74	18	20	38	54	13	5	1	18	2	2	4	16
03-04—Ottawa	NHL	24	4	6	10	39	-3	1	0	7	1	0	1	4
04-05—Zug	Switzerland	21	9	17	26	32	11	4	2	9	2	3	5	10
05-06—Ottawa	NHL	68	22	22	44	64	23	2	4	10	2	2	4	12
NHL Totals (6 years)		316	70	74	144	273	34	8	8	49	7	6	13	36

FITZGERALD, TOM C/RW

PERSONAL: Born August 28, 1968, in Billerica, Mass. ... 6-0/190. ... Shoots right. ... Cousin of Keith Tkachuk, LW, St. Louis Blues.

TRANSACTIONS/CAREER NOTES: Selected by New York Islanders in first round (first Islanders pick, 17th overall) of entry draft (June 21, 1986). ... Bruised left knee (November 7, 1990). ... Strained abdominal muscle (October 22, 1991); missed 16 games. ... Torn rib cage muscle (October 24, 1992); missed four games. ... Selected by Florida Panthers in expansion draft (June 24, 1993). ... Sore hip (March 18, 1994); missed one game. ... Bruised eye (November 13, 1996); missed one game. ... Flu (December 29, 1996); missed one game. ... Strained abdominal muscle (January 25, 1997); missed three games. ... Reinjured abdominal muscle (February 22, 1997); missed five games. ... Traded by Panthers to Colorado Avalanche for rights to LW Mark Parrish and third-round pick (D Lance Ward) in 1998 entry draft (March 24, 1998). ... Signed as free agent by Nashville Predators (July 6, 1998). ... Strained neck (December 8, 1998); missed one game. ... Injured ribs (December 15, 2001); missed three games. ... Traded by Predators to Chicago Blackhawks for fourth-round pick (traded to Anaheim; Mighty Ducks selected Nathan Saunders) in 2003 draft (March 13, 2002). ... Signed as free agent by Toronto Maple Leafs (July 17, 2002). ... Injured upper body (January 13, 2003); missed four games. ... Injured left leg (March 3, 2003); missed six games. ... Injured shoulder (October 8, 2003); missed two games. ... Injured foot (January 21, 2004); missed nine games. ... Signed as free agent by Boston Bruins (July 28, 2004).

Season Team	League	REGULAR SEASON GP	G	A	Pts.	PIM	+/-	PP	SH	PLAYOFFS GP	G	A	Pts.	PIM
84-85—Austin Prep.	Mass. H.S.	18	20	21	41	...	...	...	...	—	—	—	—	—
85-86—Austin Prep.	Mass. H.S.	24	35	38	73	...	...	...	...	—	—	—	—	—
86-87—Providence College	Hockey East	27	8	14	22	22	...	...	...	—	—	—	—	—
87-88—Providence College	Hockey East	36	19	15	34	50	...	...	...	—	—	—	—	—
88-89—Springfield	AHL	61	24	18	42	43	...	...	...	—	—	—	—	—
—New York Islanders	NHL	23	3	5	8	10	1	0	0	—	—	—	—	—
89-90—Springfield	AHL	53	30	23	53	32	...	...	...	14	2	9	11	13
—New York Islanders	NHL	19	2	5	7	4	-3	0	0	4	1	0	1	4
90-91—New York Islanders	NHL	41	5	5	10	24	-9	0	0	—	—	—	—	—
—Capital District	AHL	27	7	7	14	50	...	...	...	—	—	—	—	—
91-92—New York Islanders	NHL	45	6	11	17	28	-3	0	2	—	—	—	—	—
—Capital District	AHL	4	1	1	2	4	...	...	...	—	—	—	—	—
92-93—New York Islanders	NHL	77	9	18	27	34	-2	0	3	18	2	5	7	18
93-94—Florida	NHL	83	18	14	32	54	-3	0	3	—	—	—	—	—
94-95—Florida	NHL	48	3	13	16	31	-3	0	0	—	—	—	—	—
95-96—Florida	NHL	82	13	21	34	75	-3	1	6	22	4	4	8	34
96-97—Florida	NHL	71	10	14	24	64	7	0	2	5	0	1	1	0
97-98—Florida	NHL	69	10	5	15	57	-4	0	1	—	—	—	—	—
—Colorado	NHL	11	2	1	3	22	0	0	1	7	0	1	1	20
98-99—Nashville	NHL	80	13	19	32	48	-18	0	0	—	—	—	—	—
99-00—Nashville	NHL	82	13	9	22	66	-18	0	3	—	—	—	—	—
00-01—Nashville	NHL	82	9	9	18	71	-5	0	2	—	—	—	—	—

Season Team	League	REGULAR SEASON GP	G	A	Pts.	PIM	+/-	PP	SH	PLAYOFFS GP	G	A	Pts.	PIM
01-02—Nashville	NHL	63	7	9	16	33	-4	0	1	—	—	—	—	—
—Chicago	NHL	15	1	3	4	6	-3	0	1	5	0	0	0	4
02-03—Toronto	NHL	66	4	13	17	57	10	0	0	7	0	1	1	4
03-04—Toronto	NHL	69	7	10	17	52	-2	1	0	10	0	0	0	6
05-06—Boston	NHL	71	4	6	10	40	-10	0	0	—	—	—	—	—
NHL Totals (17 years)		1097	139	190	329	776	-72	2	25	78	7	12	19	90

FITZPATRICK, RORY D

PERSONAL: Born January 11, 1975, in Rochester, N.Y. ... 6-2/208. ... Shoots right.

TRANSACTIONS/CAREER NOTES: Selected by Montreal Canadiens in second round (second Canadiens pick, 47th overall) of entry draft (June 26, 1993). ... Traded by Canadiens with C Pierre Turgeon and C Craig Conroy to St. Louis Blues for LW Shayne Corson, D Murray Baron and fifth-round pick (D Gennady Razin) in 1997 entry draft (October 29, 1996). ... Selected by Boston Bruins in waiver draft (October 5, 1998). ... Claimed off waivers by Blues (October 7, 1998). ... Traded by Blues to Nashville Predators for D Dan Keczmer (February 9, 2000). ... Traded by Predators to Edmonton Oilers for future considerations (January 12, 2001). ... Signed as free agent by Buffalo Sabres (August 14, 2001). ... Concussion (December 14, 2002); missed five games. ... Injured thigh (March 31, 2003); missed one game. ... Bruised knee (November 19, 2003); missed one game. ... Fractured nose (February 16, 2004); missed two games. ... Injured knee (February 28, 2004); missed final 17 games of season. ... Infection (January 5, 2006); missed eight games.

Season Team	League	REGULAR SEASON GP	G	A	Pts.	PIM	+/-	PP	SH	PLAYOFFS GP	G	A	Pts.	PIM
90-91—Rochester Jr. B	OHA	40	0	5	5	...	...	...	...	—	—	—	—	—
91-92—Rochester Jr. B	OHA	28	8	28	36	141	...	...	...	—	—	—	—	—
92-93—Sudbury	OHL	58	4	20	24	68	...	...	...	14	0	0	0	17
93-94—Sudbury	OHL	65	12	34	46	112	...	8	0	10	2	5	7	10
94-95—Sudbury	OHL	56	12	36	48	72	...	9	0	18	3	15	18	21
—Fredericton	AHL	...	...	...	...	...	...	...	...	10	1	2	3	5
95-96—Fredericton	AHL	18	4	6	10	36	...	...	...	—	—	—	—	—
—Montreal	NHL	42	0	2	2	18	-7	0	0	6	1	1	2	0
96-97—Montreal	NHL	6	0	1	1	6	-2	0	0	—	—	—	—	—
—Worcester	AHL	49	4	13	17	78	8	2	0	5	1	2	3	0
—St. Louis	NHL	2	0	0	0	2	-2	0	0	—	—	—	—	—
97-98—Worcester	AHL	62	8	22	30	111	-3	6	0	11	0	3	3	26
98-99—Worcester	AHL	53	5	16	21	82	-11	4	0	4	0	1	1	17
—St. Louis	NHL	1	0	0	0	2	-3	0	0	—	—	—	—	—
99-00—Worcester	AHL	28	0	5	5	48	...	...	...	—	—	—	—	—
—Milwaukee	IHL	27	2	1	3	27	...	...	...	3	0	2	2	2
00-01—Hamilton	AHL	34	3	17	20	29	...	...	...	—	—	—	—	—
—Nashville	NHL	2	0	0	0	2	-2	0	0	—	—	—	—	—
—Milwaukee	IHL	22	0	2	2	32	...	...	...	—	—	—	—	—
01-02—Rochester	AHL	60	4	8	12	83	12	1	0	2	0	1	1	0
—Buffalo	NHL	5	0	0	0	4	-2	0	0	—	—	—	—	—
02-03—Rochester	AHL	41	5	11	16	65	-2	2	0	—	—	—	—	—
—Buffalo	NHL	36	1	3	4	16	-7	0	0	—	—	—	—	—
03-04—Buffalo	NHL	60	4	7	11	44	-5	2	0	—	—	—	—	—
04-05—Rochester	AHL	20	1	1	2	18	-8	0	1	9	0	1	1	12
05-06—Buffalo	NHL	56	4	5	9	50	-18	2	0	11	0	4	4	16
NHL Totals (8 years)		210	9	18	27	144	-48	4	0	17	1	5	6	16

FLEISCHMANN, TOMAS C

PERSONAL: Born May 16, 1984, in Koprivnice, Czechoslovakia. ... 6-1/172. ... Shoots left.

TRANSACTIONS/CAREER NOTES: Selected by Detroit Red Wings in second round (second Red Wings pick, 63rd overall) of NHL entry draft (June 22, 2002). ... Traded by Red Wings with a first-round pick (D Mike Green) in 2004 draft and a fourth-round pick (C/LW Luke Lynes) in 2006 draft to Washington Capitals for C Robert Lang (February 27, 2004).

Season Team	League	REGULAR SEASON GP	G	A	Pts.	PIM	+/-	PP	SH	PLAYOFFS GP	G	A	Pts.	PIM
99-00—Vitkovice	Czech. Jrs.	46	9	13	22	6	...	...	...	—	—	—	—	—
00-01—Vitkovice	Czech. Jrs.	21	4	9	13	8	...	...	...	—	—	—	—	—
01-02—Vitkovice	Czech. Jrs.	46	26	35	51	16	...	...	...	—	—	—	—	—
—Novy Jicin	Czech. Div. 3	8	3	2	5	8	...	...	...	7	3	4	7	35
02-03—Moose Jaw	WHL	65	21	50	71	36	...	...	...	12	4	11	15	6
03-04—Moose Jaw	WHL	60	33	42	75	32	...	...	...	10	3	4	7	10
04-05—Portland	AHL	53	7	12	19	14	-5	2	0	—	—	—	—	—
05-06—Hershey	AHL	57	30	33	63	32	14	13	3	13	8	12	20	4
—Washington	NHL	14	0	2	2	0	-7	0	0	—	—	—	—	—
NHL Totals (1 year)		14	0	2	2	0	-7	0	0					

FLEURY, MARC-ANDRE G

PERSONAL: Born November 28, 1984, in Sorel, Que. ... 6-2/176. ... Catches left.

TRANSACTIONS/CAREER NOTES: Selected by Pittsburgh Penguins in first round (first Penguins pick, first overall) in 2003 draft June 23, 2003). ... Flu (December 7, 2005); missed one game.

Season Team	League	REGULAR SEASON GP	Min.	W	L	OTL	T	GA	SO	GAA	SV%	PLAYOFFS GP	Min.	W	L	GA	SO	GAA	SV%
00-01—Cape Breton	QMJHL	35	1705	12	13	...	2	115	0	4.05	...	2	32	0	1	4	0	7.50	...
01-02—Cape Breton	QMJHL	55	3043	26	14	...	8	141	2	2.78	...	16	1003	9	7	55	0	3.29	...
02-03—Cape Breton	QMJHL	51	2889	17	24	...	6	162	2	3.36	...	—	—	—	—	—	—	—	—

Season Team	League	GP	Min.	W	L	OTL	T	GA	SO	GAA	SV%	GP	Min.	W	L	GA	SO	GAA	SV%
		REGULAR SEASON										PLAYOFFS							
03-04—Pittsburgh	NHL	21	1154	4	14	...	2	70	1	3.64	.896	—	—	—	—	—	—	—	—
—Cape Breton	QMJHL	10	606	8	1	...	1	20	0	1.98	.933	—	—	—	—	—	—	—	—
—Wilkes-Barre/Scranton	AHL	...	...	...	...	...	...	...	...	...	...	2	92	0	1	6	0	3.91	.750
04-05—Wilkes-Barre/Scranton	AHL	54	3029	26	19	...	...	127	5	2.52	.901	4	151	0	2	11	0	4.37	.843
05-06—Wilkes-Barre/Scranton	AHL	12	727	10	2	0	...	19	0	1.57	.939	5	311	2	3	18	0	3.47	.883
—Pittsburgh	NHL	50	2809	13	27	6	...	152	1	3.25	.898	—	—	—	—	—	—	—	—
NHL Totals (2 years)		71	3963	17	41	6	2	222	2	3.36	.897								

FLINN, RYAN — LW

PERSONAL: Born April 20, 1980, in Halifax, N.S. ... 6-5/248. ... Shoots left.
TRANSACTIONS/CAREER NOTES: Selected by New Jersey Devils in fifth round (eighth Devils pick, 143rd overall) of entry draft (June 27, 1998). ... Signed as free agent by Los Angeles Kings (January 9, 2002). ... Concussion (November 26, 2005); missed season's final 58 games.

Season Team	League	GP	G	A	Pts.	PIM	+/-	PP	SH	GP	G	A	Pts.	PIM
		REGULAR SEASON								PLAYOFFS				
96-97—Laval	QMJHL	23	3	2	5	66	...	...	...	2	0	0	0	0
97-98—Laval	QMJHL	59	4	12	16	217	...	...	...	15	1	0	1	63
98-99—Acadie-Bathurst	QMJHL	44	3	4	7	195	-9	1	0	23	2	0	2	37
99-00—Halifax	QMJHL	67	14	19	33	365	4	5	0	—	—	—	—	—
00-01—Cape Breton	QMJHL	57	16	17	33	280	5	4	0	9	1	1	2	43
01-02—Reading	ECHL	20	1	3	4	130	-10	0	0	—	—	—	—	—
—Manchester	AHL	37	0	1	1	113	-6	0	0	1	0	0	0	0
—Los Angeles	NHL	10	0	0	0	51	0	0	0	—	—	—	—	—
02-03—Manchester	AHL	27	2	2	4	95	0	0	0	—	—	—	—	—
—Los Angeles	NHL	19	1	0	1	28	0	0	0	—	—	—	—	—
03-04—Manchester	AHL	59	3	5	8	164	-7	0	0	6	0	0	0	4
04-05—Manchester	AHL	14	1	1	2	112	-1	1	0	0	0	0	0	0
05-06—Manchester	AHL	6	0	1	1	38	0	0	0	—	—	—	—	—
—Los Angeles	NHL	2	0	0	0	5	0	0	0	—	—	—	—	—
NHL Totals (3 years)		31	1	0	1	84	0	0	0					

FOLIGNO, NICK — LW

PERSONAL: Born October 31, 1987, in Buffalo, N.Y. ... 6-0/188. ... Shoots left. ... Son of Mike Foligno, forward with four NHL teams (1979-94).
TRANSACTIONS/CAREER NOTES: Selected by Ottawa Senators in first round (first Senators pick; 28th overall) of NHL draft (June 24, 2006).

Season Team	League	GP	G	A	Pts.	PIM	+/-	PP	SH	GP	G	A	Pts.	PIM
		REGULAR SEASON								PLAYOFFS				
04-05—Sudbury	OHL	65	10	28	38	111	5	...	...	12	5	5	10	16
05-06—Sudbury	OHL	65	24	46	70	146	19	...	...	10	1	3	4	28

FOOTE, ADAM — D

PERSONAL: Born July 10, 1971, in Toronto. ... 6-2/215. ... Shoots right.
TRANSACTIONS/CAREER NOTES: Selected by Quebec Nordiques in second round (second Nordiques pick, 22nd overall) of NHL draft (June 17, 1989). ... Fractured right thumb (February 1992); missed remainder of season. ... Knee (October 21, 1992); missed one game. ... Flu (January 28, 1993); missed two games. ... Groin (January 18, 1994); missed eight games. ... Herniated disc (February 11, 1994) and had surgery; missed remainder of season. ... Back (February 9, 1995); missed two games. ... Groin (February 28, 1995); missed two games. ... Groin (March 26, 1995); missed four games. ... Groin (April 6, 1995); missed five games. ... Nordiques franchise moved to Colorado and renamed Avalanche for 1995-96 season (June 21, 1995). ... Fractured wrist; missed 1995-96 season's first two games. ... Separated left shoulder (January 6, 1996); missed five games. ... Bruised left knee (February 8, 1997); missed two games. ... Bruised knee (January 2, 1998); missed one game. ... Bruised knee (January 10, 1998); missed three games. ... Elbow (October 24, 1998); missed 15 games. ... Concussion (December 4, 1998); missed three games. ... Shoulder (October 10, 1999); missed one game. ... Shoulder (October 21, 1999); missed six games. ... Shoulder (November 17, 1999); missed eight games. ... Groin (January 9, 2000); missed one game. ... Groin (February 10, 2000); missed six games. ... Stress fracture in heel (November 9, 2000); missed 12 games. ... Separated right shoulder (January 4, 2001); missed 35 games. ... Shoulder surgery (summer 2000); missed season's first 16 games. ... Knee (December 27, 2001); missed six games. ... Finger (March 14, 2002); missed two games. ... Suspended two games in cross-checking incident (April 1, 2002). ... Groin (April 12, 2002); missed final game of season. ... Groin (December 2, 2002); missed two games. ... Hamstring (March 5, 2003); missed two games. ... Hamstring (November 5, 2003); missed four games. ... Flu (December 4, 2003); missed one game. ... Headache (January 30, 2004); missed two games. ... Groin (February 20, 2004); missed two games. ... Signed as free agent by Columbus Blue Jackets (August 1, 2005). ... Strained groin (November 23, 2005); missed four games. ... Pulled groin muscle (December 15, 2005); missed four games. ... Hip (December 28, 2005); missed nine games.

Season Team	League	GP	G	A	Pts.	PIM	+/-	PP	SH	GP	G	A	Pts.	PIM
		REGULAR SEASON								PLAYOFFS				
88-89—Sault Ste. Marie	OHL	66	7	32	39	120	...	...	...	—	—	—	—	—
89-90—Sault Ste. Marie	OHL	61	12	43	55	199	...	...	...	—	—	—	—	—
90-91—Sault Ste. Marie	OHL	59	18	51	69	93	...	...	...	14	5	12	17	28
91-92—Quebec	NHL	46	2	5	7	44	-4	0	0	—	—	—	—	—
—Halifax	AHL	6	0	1	1	2	...	...	...	—	—	—	—	—
92-93—Quebec	NHL	81	4	12	16	168	6	0	1	6	0	1	1	2
93-94—Quebec	NHL	45	2	6	8	67	3	0	0	—	—	—	—	—
94-95—Quebec	NHL	35	0	7	7	52	17	0	0	6	0	1	1	14
95-96—Colorado	NHL	73	5	11	16	88	27	1	0	22	1	3	4	36
96-97—Colorado	NHL	78	2	19	21	135	16	0	0	17	0	4	4	62
97-98—Colorado	NHL	77	3	14	17	124	-3	0	0	7	0	0	0	23

Season Team	League	GP	G	A	Pts.	PIM	+/-	PP	SH	GP	G	A	Pts.	PIM
		REGULAR SEASON								PLAYOFFS				
—Can. Olympic team	Int'l	6	0	1	1	4	-2	0	0	—	—	—	—	—
98-99—Colorado	NHL	64	5	16	21	92	20	3	0	19	2	3	5	24
99-00—Colorado	NHL	59	5	13	18	98	5	1	0	16	0	7	7	28
00-01—Colorado	NHL	35	3	12	15	42	6	1	1	23	3	4	7	*47
01-02—Colorado	NHL	55	5	22	27	55	7	1	1	21	1	6	7	28
—Can. Olympic team	Int'l	6	1	0	1	2	...	...	...	—	—	—	—	—
02-03—Colorado	NHL	78	11	20	31	88	30	3	0	6	0	1	1	8
03-04—Colorado	NHL	73	8	22	30	87	13	5	0	11	0	4	4	10
05-06—Columbus	NHL	65	6	16	22	89	-16	2	2	—	—	—	—	—
—Canadian Oly. team	Int'l	6	0	1	1	6	1	0	0	—	—	—	—	—
NHL Totals (14 years)		864	61	195	256	1229	127	17	5	154	7	34	41	282

FORBES, COLIN C/RW

PERSONAL: Born February 16, 1976, in New Westminster, B.C. ... 6-3/220. ... Shoots left.

TRANSACTIONS/CAREER NOTES: Selected by Philadelphia Flyers in seventh round (fifth Flyers pick, 166th overall) of entry draft (June 29, 1994). ... Bruised thumb (November 7, 1998); missed one game. ... Stomach virus (January 7, 1999); missed one game. ... Traded by Flyers with fifth-round pick (G Michal Lanicek) in 1999 draft to Tampa Bay Lightning for RW Mikael Andersson and RW Sandy McCarthy (March 20, 1999). ... Traded by Lightning to Ottawa Senators for C Bruce Gardiner (November 11, 1999). ... Traded by Senators to New York Rangers for LW Eric Lacroix (March 1, 2001). ... Signed as free agent by Washington Capitals (January 8, 2002). ... Signed as free agent by Colorado Avalanche (September 11, 2003). ... Signed as free agent by Capitals (December 20, 2003). ... Signed as free agent by Carolina Hurricanes (August 11, 2004). ... Traded by Hurricanes to Washington Capitals for RW Stephen Peat (December 28, 2005).

Season Team	League	GP	G	A	Pts.	PIM	+/-	PP	SH	GP	G	A	Pts.	PIM
		REGULAR SEASON								PLAYOFFS				
93-94—Sherwood Park	AJHL	47	18	22	40	76	...	...	...	—	—	—	—	—
94-95—Portland	WHL	72	24	31	55	108	-17	7	0	9	1	3	4	10
95-96—Portland	WHL	72	33	44	77	137	...	...	...	7	2	5	7	14
—Hershey	AHL	2	1	0	1	2	...	...	...	4	0	2	2	2
96-97—Philadelphia	AHL	74	21	28	49	108	4	1	1	10	5	5	10	33
—Philadelphia	NHL	3	1	0	1	0	0	0	0	3	0	0	0	0
97-98—Philadelphia	AHL	13	7	4	11	22	-4	2	0	—	—	—	—	—
—Philadelphia	NHL	63	12	7	19	59	2	2	0	5	0	0	0	2
98-99—Philadelphia	NHL	66	9	7	16	51	0	0	0	—	—	—	—	—
—Tampa Bay	NHL	14	3	1	4	10	-5	0	1	—	—	—	—	—
99-00—Tampa Bay	NHL	8	0	0	0	18	-4	0	0	—	—	—	—	—
—Ottawa	NHL	45	2	5	7	12	-1	0	0	5	1	0	1	14
00-01—Ottawa	NHL	39	0	1	1	31	-3	0	0	—	—	—	—	—
—New York Rangers	NHL	19	1	4	5	15	-3	0	0	—	—	—	—	—
01-02—Utah	AHL	4	0	0	0	21	-1	0	0	—	—	—	—	—
—Portland	AHL	14	4	5	9	18	...	1	0	—	—	—	—	—
—Washington	NHL	38	5	3	8	15	-2	0	1	—	—	—	—	—
02-03—Washington	NHL	5	0	0	0	0	-2	0	0	—	—	—	—	—
—Portland	AHL	69	22	38	60	73	10	7	2	3	2	2	4	4
03-04—Portland	AHL	69	16	32	48	59	-10	5	0	7	0	6	6	16
—Washington	NHL	2	0	0	0	0	0	0	0	—	—	—	—	—
04-05—Lowell	AHL	76	27	37	64	80	32	7	0	11	3	1	4	20
05-06—Lowell	AHL	34	10	18	28	24	-1	4	0	—	—	—	—	—
—Hershey	AHL	36	11	12	23	16	-6	7	0	14	3	2	5	10
—Washington	NHL	9	0	0	0	2	-2	0	0	—	—	—	—	—
NHL Totals (9 years)		311	33	28	61	213	-20	2	2	13	1	0	1	16

FORSBERG, PETER C/LW

PERSONAL: Born July 20, 1973, in Ornskoldsvik, Sweden. ... 6-1/205. ... Shoots left. ... Son of Kent Forsberg, head coach, Swedish Olympic team and Swedish National team (1995-98).

TRANSACTIONS/CAREER NOTES: Selected by Philadelphia Flyers in first round (first Flyers pick, sixth overall) of NHL draft (June 22, 1991). ... Traded by Flyers with G Ron Hextall, C Mike Ricci, D Steve Duchesne, D Kerry Huffman, first-round pick (G Jocelyn Thibault) in 1993 draft, cash and future considerations to Quebec Nordiques for C Eric Lindros (June 20, 1992); Nordiques acquired LW Chris Simon and first-round pick (traded to Toronto; traded to Washington; Capitals selected D Nolan Baumgartner) in 1994 draft to complete deal (July 21, 1992). ... Flu (March 1, 1995); missed one game. ... Nordiques franchise moved to Colorado and renamed Avalanche for 1995-96 season (June 21, 1995). ... Bruised thigh (December 14, 1996); missed 17 games. ... Bruised shoulder (November 8, 1997); missed three games. ... Groin (March 26, 1998); missed seven games. ... Concussion (May 7, 1998); missed two playoff games. ... Charley horse (May 22, 1998); missed one playoff game. ... Groin (December 14, 1998); missed one game. ... Elbow (March 4, 1999); missed three games. ... Shoulder surgery (summer 1999); missed first 23 games of season. ... Hip pointer (November 30, 1999); missed two games. ... Concussion (February 1, 2000); missed five games. ... Bruised shoulder (March 26, 2000); missed two games. ... Separated shoulder (April 7, 2000); missed final game of season. ... Ribs (November 11, 2000); missed eight games. ... Spleen removed (May 10, 2001); missed remainder of playoffs. ... Missed 2001-02 regular season because of spleen, shoulder and ankle surgery. ... Wrist, groin (November 30, 2002); missed two games. ... Stiff neck (December 13, 2002); missed three games. ... Flu (December 26, 2002); missed one game. ... Charley horse (March 15, 2003); missed two games. ... Groin (November 1, 2003); missed three games. ... Groin (November 11, 2003); missed 19 games. ... Groin (January 17, 2004); missed four games. ... Strained groin (February 18, 2004); missed 17 games. ... Signed as free agent by Flyers (August 3, 2005). ... Strained grain (November 25, 2005); missed six games. ... Groin (January 18, 2006); missed two games. ... Groin (January 25, 2006); missed eight games. ... Knee (March 18, 2006); missed one game. ... Groin (April 7, 2006); missed four games. ... Groin (April 16, 2006); missed one game. ... Offseason ankle surgery (May 16, 2006).

STATISTICAL PLATEAUS: Three-goal games: 1995-96 (2), 1996-97 (1), 1998-99 (1), 2002-03 (2), 2003-04 (1). Total: 7.

Season Team	League	GP	G	A	Pts.	PIM	+/-	PP	SH	GP	G	A	Pts.	PIM
		REGULAR SEASON								PLAYOFFS				
89-90—MoDo Hockey	Sweden Jr.	30	15	12	27	42	...	...	...	—	—	—	—	—
90-91—MoDo Ornskoldsvik	Sweden	23	7	10	17	22	...	...	...	—	—	—	—	—

Season Team	League	REGULAR SEASON GP	G	A	Pts.	PIM	+/-	PP	SH	PLAYOFFS GP	G	A	Pts.	PIM
91-92—MoDo Ornskoldsvik	Sweden	39	9	19	28	78	...	...	...	—	—	—	—	—
92-93—MoDo Ornskoldsvik	Sweden	39	23	24	47	92	...	...	...	3	4	1	5	...
93-94—MoDo Ornskoldsvik	Sweden	39	18	26	44	82	...	...	...	11	9	7	16	14
—Swedish Oly. team	Int'l	8	2	6	8	6	4	0	0	—	—	—	—	—
94-95—MoDo Ornskoldsvik	Sweden	11	5	9	14	20	...	...	...	—	—	—	—	—
—Quebec	NHL	47	15	35	50	16	17	3	0	6	2	4	6	4
95-96—Colorado	NHL	82	30	86	116	47	26	7	3	22	10	11	21	18
96-97—Colorado	NHL	65	28	58	86	73	31	5	4	14	5	12	17	10
97-98—Colorado	NHL	72	25	66	91	94	6	7	3	7	6	5	11	12
—Swedish Oly. team	Int'l	4	1	4	5	6	5	0	0	—	—	—	—	—
98-99—Colorado	NHL	78	30	67	97	108	27	9	2	19	8	16	*24	31
99-00—Colorado	NHL	49	14	37	51	52	9	3	0	16	7	8	15	12
00-01—Colorado	NHL	73	27	62	89	54	23	12	2	11	4	10	14	6
01-02—Colorado	NHL	...	...	...	...	...	...	...	...	20	9	*18	*27	20
02-03—Colorado	NHL	75	29	*77	*106	70	52	8	0	7	2	6	8	6
03-04—Colorado	NHL	39	18	37	55	30	16	3	1	11	4	7	11	12
04-05—MoDo Ornskoldsvik	Sweden	33	13	26	39	88	14	1	0	1	0	0	0	2
05-06—Philadelphia	NHL	60	19	56	75	46	21	8	1	6	4	4	8	6
—Swedish Oly. team	Int'l	6	0	6	6	0	1	0	0	—	—	—	—	—
NHL Totals (11 years)		640	235	581	816	590	228	65	16	139	61	101	162	137

FOSTER, KURTIS D

PERSONAL: Born November 24, 1981, in Carp, Ontario. ... 6-5/235. ... Shoots right.
TRANSACTIONS/CAREER NOTES: Selected by Calgary Flames in second round (second Flames pick, 40th overall) of entry draft (June 24, 2000). ... Traded by Flames with LW Jeff Cowan to Atlanta Thrashers for D Petr Buzek and sixth-round pick (D Adam Pardy) in 2004 (December 18, 2001). ... Traded by Thrashers to Anaheim Mighty Ducks for D Niclas Havelid (June 26, 2004). ... Signed as free agent by Minnesota Wild (August 4, 2005). ... Head (January 5, 2006); missed one game. ... Food poisoning (March 31, 2006); missed two games.

Season Team	League	REGULAR SEASON GP	G	A	Pts.	PIM	+/-	PP	SH	PLAYOFFS GP	G	A	Pts.	PIM
97-98—Peterborough	OHL	39	1	1	2	45	...	...	...	4	0	0	0	2
98-99—Peterborough	OHL	54	2	13	15	59	...	...	...	5	0	0	0	6
99-00—Peterborough	OHL	68	6	18	24	116	...	...	...	5	1	2	3	4
00-01—Peterborough	OHL	62	17	24	41	78	19	8	0	7	1	1	2	10
01-02—Peterborough	OHL	33	10	4	14	58	...	...	...	—	—	—	—	—
—Chicago	AHL	39	6	9	15	59	6	1	0	14	1	1	2	21
02-03—Chicago	AHL	75	15	27	42	159	-15	9	0	9	1	3	4	14
—Atlanta	NHL	2	0	0	0	0	-2	0	0	—	—	—	—	—
03-04—Chicago	AHL	67	11	19	30	95	-2	7	0	10	0	3	3	12
—Atlanta	NHL	3	0	1	1	0	0	0	0	—	—	—	—	—
04-05—Cincinnati	AHL	78	17	25	42	71	16	8	0	9	2	3	5	28
05-06—Houston	AHL	19	4	11	15	32	2	1	0	—	—	—	—	—
—Minnesota	NHL	58	10	18	28	60	-3	6	0	—	—	—	—	—
NHL Totals (3 years)		63	10	19	29	60	-5	6	0					

FOY, MATT RW

PERSONAL: Born May 18, 1983, in Oakville, Ont. ... 6-2/219. ... Shoots right.
TRANSACTIONS/CAREER NOTES: Selected by Minnesota Wild in sixth round (sixth Wild pick, 175th overall) of entry draft (June 23, 2002).

Season Team	League	REGULAR SEASON GP	G	A	Pts.	PIM	+/-	PP	SH	PLAYOFFS GP	G	A	Pts.	PIM
01-02—Merrimack	Hockey East	29	6	17	23	44	...	...	...	—	—	—	—	—
02-03—Ottawa	OHL	68	61	71	132	112	...	...	...	21	11	20	31	47
03-04—Houston	AHL	51	11	13	24	74	...	...	...	1	0	0	0	0
04-05—Houston	AHL	69	12	13	25	78	-1	1	0	5	1	2	3	6
05-06—Houston	AHL	51	15	25	40	122	-3	8	0	8	5	3	8	29
—Minnesota	NHL	19	2	3	5	16	-4	1	0	—	—	—	—	—
NHL Totals (1 year)		19	2	3	5	16	-4	1	0					

FRANZEN, JOHAN C/LW

PERSONAL: Born December 23, 1979, in Vetlanda, Sweden. ... 6-0/210. ... Shoots left.
TRANSACTIONS/CAREER NOTES: Selected by Detroit Red Wings in third round (first Red Wings pick, 97th overall) of entry draft (June 27, 2004). ... Chest (January 6, 2006); missed two games.

Season Team	League	REGULAR SEASON GP	G	A	Pts.	PIM	+/-	PP	SH	PLAYOFFS GP	G	A	Pts.	PIM
01-02—Linkopings	Sweden	36	2	6	8	64	-13	...	...	—	—	—	—	—
02-03—Linkopings	Sweden	37	2	4	6	14	-3	...	...	—	—	—	—	—
03-04—Linkopings	Sweden	49	12	18	30	26	24	...	...	5	0	1	1	8
04-05—Linkopings	Sweden	43	7	7	14	45	...	...	...	6	2	0	2	16
05-06—Detroit	NHL	80	12	4	16	36	4	0	2	6	1	2	3	4
NHL Totals (1 year)		80	12	4	16	36	4	0	2	6	1	2	3	4

FRIESEN, JEFF — LW

PERSONAL: Born August 5, 1976, in Meadow Lake, Sask. ... 6-1/205. ... Shoots left. ... Name pronounced FREE-sihn.
TRANSACTIONS/CAREER NOTES: Selected by San Jose Sharks in first round (first Sharks pick, 11th overall) of entry draft (June 28, 1994). ... Injured hand (October 18, 1996); missed two games. ... Missed first two games of 1997-98 season due to contract dispute. ... Injured shoulder (December 26, 1998); missed two games. ... Traded by Sharks with G Steve Shields and second-round pick (traded to Dallas Stars) in 2004 draft to Anaheim Mighty Ducks for RW Teemu Selanne (March 5, 2001). ... Sprained left ankle (January 12, 2002); missed one game. ... Traded by Mighty Ducks with D Oleg Tverdovsky and RW Maxim Balmochnykh to New Jersey Devils for RW Petr Sykora, C Igor Pohanka, D Mike Commodore and G J.F. Damphousse (July 7, 2002). ... Flu (January 25, 2003); missed one game. ... Pinched nerve (March 30, 2004); missed one game. ... Traded by Devils to Washington Capitals for third-round pick (D Kirill Tulupov) in 2006 draft (September 26, 2005). ... Strained groin (November 6, 2005) and abdominal surgery; missed 28 games. ... Traded by Capitals to Mighty Ducks for second-round pick (D Keith Seabrook) in 2006 draft (March 9, 2006). ... Signed as free agent by Calgary Flames (July 5, 2006).
STATISTICAL PLATEAUS: Three-goal games: 1995-96 (1), 1999-00 (1). Total: 2.

		REGULAR SEASON								PLAYOFFS				
Season Team	League	GP	G	A	Pts.	PIM	+/-	PP	SH	GP	G	A	Pts.	PIM
91-92—Regina	WHL	4	3	1	4	2	...	...	...	—	—	—	—	—
92-93—Regina	WHL	70	45	38	83	23	...	...	...	13	7	10	17	8
93-94—Regina	WHL	66	51	67	118	48	3	20	5	4	3	2	5	2
94-95—Regina	WHL	25	21	23	44	22	6	5	1	—	—	—	—	—
—San Jose	NHL	48	15	10	25	14	-8	5	1	11	1	5	6	4
95-96—San Jose	NHL	79	15	31	46	42	-19	2	0	—	—	—	—	—
96-97—San Jose	NHL	82	28	34	62	75	-8	6	2	—	—	—	—	—
97-98—San Jose	NHL	79	31	32	63	40	8	7	6	6	0	1	1	2
98-99—San Jose	NHL	78	22	35	57	42	3	10	1	6	2	2	4	14
99-00—San Jose	NHL	82	26	35	61	47	-2	11	3	11	2	2	4	10
00-01—San Jose	NHL	64	12	24	36	56	7	2	0	—	—	—	—	—
—Anaheim	NHL	15	2	10	12	10	-2	2	0	—	—	—	—	—
01-02—Anaheim	NHL	81	17	26	43	44	-1	1	1	—	—	—	—	—
02-03—New Jersey	NHL	81	23	28	51	26	23	3	0	24	10	4	14	6
03-04—New Jersey	NHL	81	17	20	37	26	8	5	0	5	0	0	0	4
05-06—Washington	NHL	33	3	4	7	24	-11	0	0	—	—	—	—	—
—Anaheim	NHL	18	1	3	4	8	-4	0	0	16	3	1	4	6
NHL Totals (11 years)		821	212	292	504	454	-6	54	14	79	18	15	33	46

FRITSCHE, DAN — C

PERSONAL: Born July 13, 1985, in Parma, Ohio. ... 6-1/198. ... Shoots right.
TRANSACTIONS/CAREER NOTES: Selected by Columbus Blue Jackets in the second round (second Blue Jackets selection, 46th overall) of entry draft (June 21, 2003). ... Ankle (October 16, 2005); missed four games. ... Concussion (January 7, 2006); missed two games.

		REGULAR SEASON								PLAYOFFS				
Season Team	League	GP	G	A	Pts.	PIM	+/-	PP	SH	GP	G	A	Pts.	PIM
01-02—Sarnia	OHL	17	5	13	18	20	...	...	...	—	—	—	—	—
02-03—Sarnia	OHL	61	32	39	71	79	...	...	...	5	2	2	4	4
03-04—Columbus	NHL	19	1	0	1	12	-5	0	0	—	—	—	—	—
—Sarnia	OHL	27	16	13	29	26	...	...	...	5	1	5	6	0
—Syracuse	AHL	4	2	0	2	0	2	0	0	4	0	1	1	4
04-05—Sarnia	OHL	2	1	1	2	0	-1	0	0	—	—	—	—	—
—London	OHL	28	17	18	35	18	27	5	0	17	9	13	22	12
05-06—Syracuse	AHL	19	5	4	9	12	3	0	1	6	2	2	4	8
—Columbus	NHL	59	6	7	13	22	-14	0	0	—	—	—	—	—
NHL Totals (2 years)		78	7	7	14	34	-19	0	0					

FROLIK, MICHAEL — C

PERSONAL: Born February 17, 1988, in Kladno, Czech. ... 6-1/185. ... Shoots left.
TRANSACTIONS/CAREER NOTES: Selected by Florida Panthers in first round (first Panthers pick; 10th overall) of NHL draft (June 24, 2006).

		REGULAR SEASON								PLAYOFFS				
Season Team	League	GP	G	A	Pts.	PIM	+/-	PP	SH	GP	G	A	Pts.	PIM
04-05—HC Kladno	Czech.	27	3	1	4	6	-4	...	...	1	0	0	0	0
05-06—HC Kladno	Czech.	48	2	7	9	32	-8	...	...	—	—	—	—	—

FROLOV, ALEXANDER — LW

PERSONAL: Born June 19, 1982, in Moscow, U.S.S.R. ... 6-2/210. ... Shoots right.
TRANSACTIONS/CAREER NOTES: Selected by Los Angeles Kings in first round (first Kings pick, 20th overall) of entry draft (June 24, 2000). ... Cut face (December 29, 2002); missed two games. ... Leg (March 27, 2004); missed final five games of regular season. ... Flu (January 17, 2006); missed three games. ... Shoulder (February 25, 2006); missed 10 games.

		REGULAR SEASON								PLAYOFFS				
Season Team	League	GP	G	A	Pts.	PIM	+/-	PP	SH	GP	G	A	Pts.	PIM
99-00—Torpedo Yaroslavl	Rus. Div.	36	27	13	40	30	...	...	...	—	—	—	—	—
00-01—Krylja Sovetov	Rus. Div.	44	20	19	39	8	...	...	...	—	—	—	—	—
01-02—Kryla Sov. Moscow	Russian	43	18	12	30	16	...	...	...	3	1	0	1	0
02-03—Los Angeles	NHL	79	14	17	31	34	12	1	0	—	—	—	—	—
03-04—Los Angeles	NHL	77	24	24	48	24	8	5	2	—	—	—	—	—
04-05—CSKA Moscow	Russian	42	20	17	37	10	16	...	...	—	—	—	—	—
—Dynamo Moscow	Russian	6	2	1	3	2	2	...	...	6	2	1	3	0
05-06—Los Angeles	NHL	69	21	33	54	40	17	4	3	—	—	—	—	—
—Russian Oly. team	Int'l	3	0	1	1	0	1	0	0	—	—	—	—	—
NHL Totals (3 years)		225	59	74	133	98	37	10	5					

GABORIK, MARIAN — RW/LW

PERSONAL: Born February 14, 1982, in Trencin, Czech. ... 6-1/190. ... Shoots left.
TRANSACTIONS/CAREER NOTES: Selected by Minnesota Wild in first round (first Wild pick, third overall) of entry draft (June 24, 2000). ... Leg (November 15, 2000); missed six games. ... Strained abdominal muscle (March 31, 2001); missed four games. ... Hernia surgery (summer 2001); missed one game. ... Strained right quadriceps (December 20, 2001); missed three games. ... Flu (December 15, 2002); missed one game. ... Missed 2003-04 season's first 12 games in contract dispute. ... Hip flexor (January 22, 2004); missed five games. ... Groin (September 13, 2005); missed rest of preseason and first six games of season. ... Hip flexor (October 23, 2005); missed 11 games.
STATISTICAL PLATEAUS: Three-goal games: 2001-02 (2), 2002-03 (3), 2003-04 (2). Total: 7.

		REGULAR SEASON								PLAYOFFS				
Season Team	**League**	**GP**	**G**	**A**	**Pts.**	**PIM**	**+/-**	**PP**	**SH**	**GP**	**G**	**A**	**Pts.**	**PIM**
98-99—Dukla Trencin	Slovakia	33	11	9	20	6	...	...	...	3	1	0	1	2
99-00—Dukla Trencin	Slovakia	50	25	21	46	34	...	...	...	5	1	2	3	2
00-01—Minnesota	NHL	71	18	18	36	32	-6	6	0	—	—	—	—	—
01-02—Minnesota	NHL	78	30	37	67	34	0	10	0	—	—	—	—	—
02-03—Minnesota	NHL	81	30	35	65	46	12	5	1	18	9	8	17	6
03-04—Minnesota	NHL	65	18	22	40	20	10	3	0	—	—	—	—	—
04-05—Dukla Trencin	Slovakia	29	25	27	52	46	43	...	...	12	8	9	17	26
—Farjestad Karlstad	Sweden	12	6	4	10	45	8	0	0	—	—	—	—	—
05-06—Minnesota	NHL	65	38	28	66	64	6	10	2	—	—	—	—	—
—Slovakian. Oly. team	Int'l	6	3	4	7	4	6	0	0	—	—	—	—	—
NHL Totals (5 years)		360	134	140	274	196	22	34	3	18	9	8	17	6

GAGNE, SIMON — LW

PERSONAL: Born February 29, 1980, in Ste-Foy, Que. ... 6-0/195. ... Shoots left. ... Name pronounced see-MONE gahn-YAY.
TRANSACTIONS/CAREER NOTES: Selected by Philadelphia Flyers in first round (first Flyers pick, 22nd overall) of entry draft (June 27, 1998). ... Flu (January 2, 2000); missed one game. ... Flu (March 23, 2000); missed one game. ... Strained lower back (February 19, 2001); missed one game. ... Separated shoulder (February 24, 2001); missed 12 games. ... Bruised left shoulder (December 31, 2001); missed two games. ... Injured (April 13, 2002); missed final game of season. ... Concussion (December 28, 2002); missed five games. ... Strained groin (January 25, 2003); missed three games. ... Reinjured groin (February 4, 2003); missed 13 games. ... Reinjured groin (March 8, 2003); missed 13 games. ... Bruised right shoulder (October 21, 2003); missed two games. ... Strained groin (December 9, 2005); missed five games. ... Flu (December 31, 2005); missed one game. ... Flu (February 8, 2006); missed one game. ... Bruised knee (February 22, 2006) during Olympics; missed three games.
STATISTICAL PLATEAUS: Three-goal games: 2001-02 (1).

		REGULAR SEASON								PLAYOFFS				
Season Team	**League**	**GP**	**G**	**A**	**Pts.**	**PIM**	**+/-**	**PP**	**SH**	**GP**	**G**	**A**	**Pts.**	**PIM**
96-97—Beauport	QMJHL	51	9	22	31	39	...	...	...	—	—	—	—	—
97-98—Quebec	QMJHL	53	30	39	69	26	...	...	...	12	11	5	16	23
98-99—Quebec	QMJHL	61	50	70	120	42	51	15	5	13	9	8	17	4
99-00—Philadelphia	NHL	80	20	28	48	22	11	8	1	17	5	5	10	2
00-01—Philadelphia	NHL	69	27	32	59	18	24	6	0	6	3	0	3	0
01-02—Philadelphia	NHL	79	33	33	66	32	31	4	1	5	0	0	0	2
—Can. Olympic team	Int'l	6	1	3	4	0	...	...	...	—	—	—	—	—
02-03—Philadelphia	NHL	46	9	18	27	16	20	1	1	13	4	1	5	6
03-04—Philadelphia	NHL	80	24	21	45	29	12	6	0	18	5	4	9	12
05-06—Philadelphia	NHL	72	47	32	79	38	31	12	2	6	3	1	4	2
—Canadian Oly. team	Int'l	6	1	2	3	6	1	0	0	—	—	—	—	—
NHL Totals (6 years)		426	160	164	324	155	129	37	5	65	20	11	31	24

GAINEY, STEVE — LW/C

PERSONAL: Born January 26, 1979, in Montreal. ... 6-1/192. ... Shoots left. ... Son of Bob Gainey, coach of Minnesota/Dallas Stars (1990-91 through January 8, 1996), G.M. of Stars (1992-93 through January 25, 2002), G.M. of Montreal Canadiens (June 2, 2003 to present) and Hall of Fame C with Montreal Canadiens (1973-74 through 1988-89).
TRANSACTIONS/CAREER NOTES: Selected by Dallas Stars in third round (third Stars pick, 77th overall) of NHL draft (June 21, 1997). ... Traded by Stars to Philadelphia Flyers for F/D Mike Siklenka (February 16, 2004). ... Signed as free agent by Phoenix Coyotes (November4, 2005).

		REGULAR SEASON								PLAYOFFS				
Season Team	**League**	**GP**	**G**	**A**	**Pts.**	**PIM**	**+/-**	**PP**	**SH**	**GP**	**G**	**A**	**Pts.**	**PIM**
95-96—Kamloops	WHL	49	1	4	5	40	...	...	...	3	0	0	0	0
96-97—Kamloops	WHL	60	9	18	27	60	...	...	...	2	0	0	0	9
97-98—Kamloops	WHL	68	21	34	55	93	1	6	3	7	1	7	8	15
98-99—Kamloops	WHL	68	30	34	64	155	37	11	4	15	5	4	9	38
99-00—Michigan	IHL	58	8	10	18	41	...	...	...	—	—	—	—	—
—Fort Wayne	UHL	1	0	0	0	0	...	...	...	—	—	—	—	—
00-01—Utah	IHL	61	7	7	14	167	...	...	...	—	—	—	—	—
—Dallas	NHL	1	0	0	0	0	0	0	0	—	—	—	—	—
01-02—Utah	AHL	58	16	18	34	87	4	4	1	—	—	—	—	—
—Dallas	NHL	5	0	1	1	7	-1	0	0	—	—	—	—	—
02-03—Utah	AHL	68	9	17	26	106	-4	4	1	2	0	0	0	11
03-04—Dallas	NHL	7	0	0	0	7	1	0	0	—	—	—	—	—
—Utah	AHL	45	7	8	15	74	-15	1	2	—	—	—	—	—
—Philadelphia	AHL	27	2	7	9	27	-3	1	0	11	0	1	1	14
04-05—Epinal	France	30	10	13	23	97	-7	1	1	4	1	3	4	6
05-06—San Antonio	AHL	56	10	20	30	85	-13	5	0	—	—	—	—	—
—Phoenix	NHL	20	0	1	1	20	-3	0	0	—	—	—	—	—
NHL Totals (4 years)		33	0	2	2	34	-3	0	0					

GAMACHE, SIMON RW

PERSONAL: Born January 3, 1981, in Thetford Mines, Que. ... 5-10/186. ... Shoots left. ... Name pronounced: see-MOHN guh-MAHSH

TRANSACTIONS/CAREER NOTES: Selected by Atlanta Thrashers in ninth round (14th Thrashers pick, 290th overall) of entry draft (June 25, 2000). ... Traded by Thrashers with D Kirill Safronov to Nashville Predators for D Tomas Kloucek and C Ben Simon (December 2, 2003). ... Claimed on waivers by St. Louis Blues (November 29, 2005). ... Claimed on waivers by Predators (January 28, 2006).

		REGULAR SEASON								PLAYOFFS				
Season Team	League	GP	G	A	Pts.	PIM	+/-	PP	SH	GP	G	A	Pts.	PIM
98-99—Val-d'Or	QMJHL	70	19	43	62	54	...	...	...	—	—	—	—	—
99-00—Val-d'Or	QMJHL	72	64	79	143	74	...	...	...	—	—	—	—	—
00-01—Val-d'Or	QMJHL	72	74	110	184	70	64	16	8	21	22	35	57	18
01-02—Chicago	AHL	26	2	4	6	11	-7	1	0	—	—	—	—	—
—Greenville	ECHL	31	19	19	38	35	4	7	2	17	15	9	24	22
02-03—Atlanta	NHL	2	0	0	0	2	-1	0	0	—	—	—	—	—
—Chicago	AHL	76	35	42	77	37	15	16	0	9	7	2	9	4
03-04—Chicago	AHL	16	5	6	11	4	5	2	0	—	—	—	—	—
—Atlanta	NHL	2	0	1	1	0	0	0	0	—	—	—	—	—
—Nashville	NHL	7	1	0	1	0	-3	1	0	—	—	—	—	—
—Milwaukee	AHL	52	19	27	46	26	-2	4	0	22	6	18	24	14
04-05—Milwaukee	AHL	80	29	57	86	93	11	16	0	7	6	4	10	18
05-06—Milwaukee	AHL	39	18	18	36	46	-2	8	1	15	10	12	22	12
—Nashville	NHL	11	0	0	0	0	-6	0	0	—	—	—	—	—
—St. Louis	NHL	15	3	4	7	10	1	0	0	—	—	—	—	—
NHL Totals (3 years)		37	4	5	9	12	-9	1	0					

GARNETT, MICHAEL G

PERSONAL: Born November 25, 1982, in Saskatoon, Sask. ... 6-1/200. ... Catches left.

TRANSACTIONS/CAREER NOTES: Selected by Atlanta Thrashers in third round (second Thrashers pick, 80th overall) of entry draft (June 23, 2001).

		REGULAR SEASON										PLAYOFFS							
Season Team	League	GP	Min.	W	L	OTL	T	GA	SO	GAA	SV%	GP	Min.	W	L	GA	SO	GAA	SV%
00-01—Saskatoon	WHL	28	1501	7	17	...	2	83	1	3.32	...	—	—	—	—	—	—	—	—
01-02—Saskatoon	WHL	67	3738	27	34	...	4	205	2	3.29	...	7	450	3	4	15	0	2.00	...
—Chicago	AHL	0	...	...	...	...	...	...	...	...	...	—	—	—	—	—	—	—	—
02-03—Chicago	AHL	2	33	0	1	...	0	2	0	3.64	.875	—	—	—	—	—	—	—	—
—Greenville	ECHL	38	2092	16	15	...	3	119	0	3.41	.895	3	178	1	2	13	0	4.38	.885
03-04—Chicago	AHL	13	730	7	3	...	2	32	0	2.63	...	—	—	—	—	—	—	—	—
—Gwinnett	ECHL	33	1936	21	10	...	2	69	4	2.14	...	12	770	7	5	34	0	2.65	...
04-05—Chicago	AHL	24	1321	11	9	...	...	63	1	2.86	.911	2	119	2	0	3	0	1.51	.957
05-06—Chicago	AHL	35	1892	15	12	4	...	106	1	3.36	.881	—	—	—	—	—	—	—	—
—Atlanta	NHL	24	1271	10	7	4	...	73	2	3.45	.885	—	—	—	—	—	—	—	—
NHL Totals (1 year)		24	1271	10	7	4	0	73	2	3.45	.885								

GARON, MATHIEU G

PERSONAL: Born January 9, 1978, in Chandler, Que. ... 6-2/192. ... Catches right.

TRANSACTIONS/CAREER NOTES: Selected by Montreal Canadiens in second round (second Canadiens pick, 44th overall) of entry draft (June 22, 1996). ... Traded by Canadiens with C Radek Bonk to Los Angeles Kings for G Cristobal Huet and third-round pick (D Paul Baier) in 2004 (June 27, 2004). ... Injured shoulder (Jan 19, 2006); missed one game.

		REGULAR SEASON										PLAYOFFS							
Season Team	League	GP	Min.	W	L	OTL	T	GA	SO	GAA	SV%	GP	Min.	W	L	GA	SO	GAA	SV%
95-96—Victoriaville	QMJHL	51	2709	18	27	...	0	189	1	4.00	...	12	676	7	4	38	1	3.37	...
96-97—Victoriaville	QMJHL	53	3026	29	18	...	3	148	6	2.93	...	6	330	2	4	23	0	4.18	.903
97-98—Victoriaville	QMJHL	47	2802	27	18	...	2	125	5	2.68	.909	6	345	2	4	22	0	3.83	.851
98-99—Fredericton	AHL	40	2222	14	22	...	2	114	3	3.08	.904	6	208	1	1	12	0	3.46	.911
99-00—Quebec	AHL	53	2884	17	28	...	3	149	2	3.10	...	1	20	0	0	3	0	9.00	...
00-01—Montreal	NHL	11	589	4	5	...	1	24	2	2.44	.897	—	—	—	—	—	—	—	—
—Quebec	AHL	31	1768	16	13	...	1	86	1	2.92	.920	8	459	4	4	22	1	2.88	...
01-02—Quebec	AHL	50	2987	21	15	...	12	136	2	2.73	.911	3	198	0	3	12	0	3.64	.874
—Montreal	NHL	5	261	1	4	...	0	19	0	4.37	.871	—	—	—	—	—	—	—	—
02-03—Hamilton	AHL	20	1150	15	2	...	2	34	4	1.77	.937	—	—	—	—	—	—	—	—
—Montreal	NHL	8	482	3	5	...	0	16	2	1.99	.940	—	—	—	—	—	—	—	—
03-04—Montreal	NHL	19	1003	8	6	...	2	38	0	2.27	.921	1	12	0	0	0	0	0.00	1.000
04-05—Manchester	AHL	52	2969	32	14	...	...	105	8	2.12	.927	6	284	2	4	17	0	3.59	.893
05-06—Los Angeles	NHL	63	3446	31	26	3	...	185	4	3.22	.894	—	—	—	—	—	—	—	—
NHL Totals (5 years)		106	5781	47	46	3	3	282	8	2.93	.902	1	12	0	0	0	0	0.00	1.000

GAUSTAD, PAUL C/LW

PERSONAL: Born February 3, 1982, in Fargo, N.D. ... 6-4/217. ... Shoots left.

TRANSACTIONS/CAREER NOTES: Selected by Buffalo Sabres in seventh round (sixth Sabres pick, 220th overall) of entry draft (June 24, 2000). ... Concussion (January 11, 2006); missed three games. ... Flu (February 7, 2006); missed one game.

Season Team	League	GP	G	A	Pts.	PIM	+/-	PP	SH	GP	G	A	Pts.	PIM
		REGULAR SEASON								PLAYOFFS				
99-00—Portland	WHL	56	6	8	14	110	...	...	...	—	—	—	—	—
00-01—Portland	WHL	70	11	30	41	168	...	...	...	—	—	—	—	—
01-02—Portland	WHL	72	36	44	80	202	...	...	...	—	—	—	—	—
02-03—Buffalo	NHL	1	0	0	0	0	0	0	0	—	—	—	—	—
—Rochester	AHL	80	14	39	53	137	2	4	3	3	0	0	0	4
03-04—Rochester	AHL	78	9	22	31	169	...	...	...	16	3	10	13	30
04-05—Rochester	AHL	76	18	25	43	192	2	7	0	9	6	5	11	16
05-06—Buffalo	NHL	78	9	15	24	65	4	0	0	18	0	4	4	14
NHL Totals (2 years)		79	9	15	24	65	4	0	0	18	0	4	4	14

GAUTHIER, DENIS — D

PERSONAL: Born October 1, 1976, in Montreal. ... 6-2/224. ... Shoots left. ... Name pronounced GO-tee-ay.

TRANSACTIONS/CAREER NOTES: Selected by Calgary Flames in first round (first Flames pick, 20th overall) of entry draft (July 8, 1995). ... Concussion (September 27, 1997); missed two games. ... Concussion (January 10, 1999); missed two games. ... Groin (March 25, 1999); missed two games. ... Shoulder (October 26, 1999); missed 11 games. ... Suspended two games by NHL in elbowing incident (December 7, 1999). ... Hip pointer (February 1, 2000); missed remainder of season. ... Wrist (October 15, 2000); missed 17 games. ... Shoulder (March 16, 2001); missed two games. ... Strained oblique muscle (October 22, 2001); missed five games. ... Facial injury (December 31, 2001); missed five games. ... Shoulder (April 2, 2002); missed remainder of season. ... Suspended one game for illegal checking incident (November 16, 2002). ... Strained left shoulder (February 4, 2003); missed four games. ... Concussion (March 29, 2003); missed season's final four games. ... Suspended two games for kneeing incident (December 26, 2003). ... Leg (April 17, 2004); missed remainder of playoffs. ... Traded by Flames with LW Oleg Saprykin to Phoenix Coyotes for C Daymond Langkow (August 26, 2004). ... Broken finger (October 17, 2005); missed 14 games. ... Left shoulder (February 1, 2006); missed three games. ... Traded by Coyotes to Philadelphia Flyers for LW Josh Gratton and two second-rounds picks (pick 41 traded to Detroit; Red Wings selected C/LW Cory Emmerton; pick 47 traded to Detroit; Red Wings selected C Shawn Matthias) in 2006 draft (March 9, 2006). ... Suspended two games for checking from behind (April 10, 2006).

Season Team	League	GP	G	A	Pts.	PIM	+/-	PP	SH	GP	G	A	Pts.	PIM
		REGULAR SEASON								PLAYOFFS				
92-93—Drummondville	QMJHL	61	1	7	8	136	...	...	...	10	0	5	5	40
93-94—Drummondville	QMJHL	60	0	7	7	176	...	...	...	9	2	0	2	41
94-95—Drummondville	QMJHL	64	9	31	40	190	...	...	...	4	0	5	5	12
95-96—Drummondville	QMJHL	53	25	49	74	140	...	...	...	6	4	4	8	32
—Saint John	AHL	5	2	0	2	8	...	...	...	16	1	6	7	20
96-97—Saint John	AHL	73	3	28	31	74	2	2	0	5	0	0	0	6
97-98—Calgary	NHL	10	0	0	0	16	-5	0	0	—	—	—	—	—
—Saint John	AHL	68	4	20	24	154	-5	2	0	21	0	4	4	83
98-99—Saint John	AHL	16	0	3	3	31	-3	0	0	—	—	—	—	—
—Calgary	NHL	55	3	4	7	68	3	0	0	—	—	—	—	—
99-00—Calgary	NHL	39	1	1	2	50	-4	0	0	—	—	—	—	—
00-01—Calgary	NHL	62	2	6	8	78	3	0	0	—	—	—	—	—
01-02—Calgary	NHL	66	5	8	13	91	9	0	1	—	—	—	—	—
02-03—Calgary	NHL	72	1	11	12	99	5	0	0	—	—	—	—	—
03-04—Calgary	NHL	80	1	15	16	113	4	0	0	6	0	1	1	4
05-06—Phoenix	NHL	45	2	9	11	61	-4	0	0	—	—	—	—	—
—Philadelphia	NHL	17	0	0	0	37	6	0	0	6	0	1	1	19
NHL Totals (8 years)		446	15	54	69	613	17	0	1	12	0	2	2	23

GAVEY, AARON — LW/RW

PERSONAL: Born February 22, 1974, in Sudbury, Ont. ... 6-2/189. ... Shoots left. ... Name pronounced GAY-vee.

TRANSACTIONS/CAREER NOTES: Selected by Tampa Bay Lightning in fourth round (fourth Lightning pick, 74th overall) of entry draft (June 20, 1992). ... Cut face (February 4, 1996); missed eight games. ... Traded by Lightning to Calgary Flames for G Rick Tabaracci (November 19, 1996). ... Strained neck (February 28, 1997); missed 14 games. ... Strained abdominal muscle (January 11, 1997); missed 37 games. ... Sprained thumb (April 15, 1998); missed two games. ... Traded by Flames to Dallas Stars for C Bob Bassen (July 14, 1998). ... Fractured hand (September 22, 1998); missed first three games of 1998-99 season. ... Sprained knee (February 2, 2000); missed one game. ... Traded by Stars with C Pavel Patera, eighth-round pick (C Eric Johansson) in 2000 entry draft and fourth-round pick (traded to Los Angeles) in 2002 draft to Minnesota Wild for D Brad Lukowich, third-(C Yared Hagos) and ninth-round (RW Dale Sullivan) picks in 2001 draft (June 25, 2000). ... Bruised foot (November 14, 2000); missed three games. ... Cut face (October 27, 2001); missed three games. ... Flu (March 18, 2002); missed two games. ... Fractured left foot (April 10, 2002); missed remainder of season. ... Signed as free agent by Toronto Maple Leafs (July 24, 2002). ... Signed as free agent by Anaheim Mighty Ducks (September 12, 2005).

Season Team	League	GP	G	A	Pts.	PIM	+/-	PP	SH	GP	G	A	Pts.	PIM
		REGULAR SEASON								PLAYOFFS				
90-91—Peterborough Jr. B	OHA	42	26	30	56	68	...	...	...	—	—	—	—	—
91-92—Sault Ste. Marie	OHL	48	7	11	18	27	...	...	...	19	5	1	6	10
92-93—Sault Ste. Marie	OHL	62	45	39	84	114	...	...	...	18	5	9	14	36
93-94—Sault Ste. Marie	OHL	60	42	60	102	116	...	16	0	14	11	10	21	22
94-95—Atlanta	IHL	66	18	17	35	85	-16	2	0	5	0	1	1	9
95-96—Tampa Bay	NHL	73	8	4	12	56	-6	1	1	6	0	0	0	4
96-97—Tampa Bay	NHL	16	1	2	3	12	-1	0	0	—	—	—	—	—
—Calgary	NHL	41	7	9	16	34	-11	3	0	—	—	—	—	—
97-98—Calgary	NHL	26	2	3	5	24	-5	0	0	—	—	—	—	—
—Saint John	AHL	8	4	3	7	28	2	1	0	—	—	—	—	—
98-99—Dallas	NHL	7	0	0	0	10	-1	0	0	—	—	—	—	—
—Michigan	IHL	67	24	33	57	128	-9	9	2	5	2	3	5	4
99-00—Michigan	IHL	28	14	15	29	73	...	...	...	—	—	—	—	—
—Dallas	NHL	41	7	6	13	44	0	1	0	13	1	2	3	10
00-01—Minnesota	NHL	75	10	14	24	52	-8	1	0	—	—	—	—	—
01-02—Minnesota	NHL	71	6	11	17	38	-21	1	0	—	—	—	—	—

Season Team	League	REGULAR SEASON GP	G	A	Pts.	PIM	+/-	PP	SH	PLAYOFFS GP	G	A	Pts.	PIM
02-03—St. John's	AHL	70	14	29	43	83	-13	3	1	—	—	—	—	—
—Toronto	NHL	5	0	1	1	0	1	0	0	—	—	—	—	—
03-04—St. John's	AHL	75	22	45	67	100	0	7	2	—	—	—	—	—
04-05—Utah	AHL	60	5	14	19	58	-24	2	0	—	—	—	—	—
05-06—Portland	AHL	72	16	31	47	106	18	5	0	18	1	3	4	43
—Anaheim	NHL	5	0	0	0	2	0	0	0	—	—	—	—	—
NHL Totals (9 years)		360	41	50	91	272	-52	7	1	19	1	2	3	14

GELINAS, MARTIN — LW

PERSONAL: Born June 5, 1970, in Shawinigan, Que. ... 5-11/196. ... Shoots left. ... Name pronounced MAHR-tahn ZHEHL-ih-nuh.

TRANSACTIONS/CAREER NOTES: Selected by Los Angeles Kings in first round (first Kings pick, seventh overall) of NHL draft (June 11, 1988). ... Traded by Kings with C Jimmy Carson, first-round picks in 1989 (traded to New Jersey), 1991 (LW Martin Rucinsky) and 1993 (D Nick Stajduhar) drafts and cash to Edmonton Oilers for C Wayne Gretzky, RW/D Marty McSorley and LW/C Mike Krushelnyski (August 9, 1988). ... Suspended five games (March 9, 1990). ... Shoulder surgery (June 1990). ... Traded by Oilers with sixth-round pick (C Nicholas Checco) in 1993 draft to Quebec Nordiques for LW Scott Pearson (June 20, 1993). ... Injured thigh (October 20, 1993); missed one game. ... Separated left shoulder (November 25, 1993); missed 10 games. ... Claimed off waivers by Vancouver Canucks (January 15, 1994). ... Charley horse (March 27, 1994); missed six games. ... Injured knee (April 30, 1995); missed last game of season and eight playoff games. ... Fractured rib (November 2, 1996); missed eight games. ... Sprained knee (October 13, 1997); missed 16 games. ... Traded by Canucks with G Kirk McLean to Carolina Hurricanes for LW Geoff Sanderson, D Enrico Ciccone and G Sean Burke (January 3, 1998). ... Strained quadriceps (October 27, 1998); missed two games. ... Bruised thigh (April 3, 1999); missed four games. ... Injured knee (February 8, 2001); missed three games. ... Injured ankle (October 11, 2001); missed three games. ... Concussion (January 25, 2002); missed seven games. ... Signed as free agent by Calgary Flames (July 2, 2002). ... Injured thumb (January 23, 2003); missed one game. ... Injured ankle (November 15, 2003); missed two games. ... Injured neck (March 4, 2004); missed four games. ... Signed as free agent by Florida Panthers (August 2, 2005).

STATISTICAL PLATEAUS: Three-goal games: 1989-90 (1), 1996-97 (1). Total: 2. ... Four-goal games: 1996-97 (1). ... Total hat tricks: 3.

Season Team	League	REGULAR SEASON GP	G	A	Pts.	PIM	+/-	PP	SH	PLAYOFFS GP	G	A	Pts.	PIM
87-88—Hull	QMJHL	65	63	68	131	74	...	...	...	17	15	18	33	32
88-89—Edmonton	NHL	6	1	2	3	0	-1	0	0	—	—	—	—	—
—Hull	QMJHL	41	38	39	77	31	...	...	...	9	5	4	9	14
89-90—Edmonton	NHL	46	17	8	25	30	0	5	0	20	2	3	5	6
90-91—Edmonton	NHL	73	20	20	40	34	-7	4	0	18	3	6	9	25
91-92—Edmonton	NHL	68	11	18	29	62	14	1	0	15	1	3	4	10
92-93—Edmonton	NHL	65	11	12	23	30	3	0	0	—	—	—	—	—
93-94—Quebec	NHL	31	6	6	12	8	-2	0	0	—	—	—	—	—
—Vancouver	NHL	33	8	8	16	26	-6	3	0	24	5	4	9	14
94-95—Vancouver	NHL	46	13	10	23	36	8	1	0	3	0	1	1	0
95-96—Vancouver	NHL	81	30	26	56	59	8	3	4	6	1	1	2	12
96-97—Vancouver	NHL	74	35	33	68	42	6	6	1	—	—	—	—	—
97-98—Vancouver	NHL	24	4	4	8	10	-6	1	1	—	—	—	—	—
—Carolina	NHL	40	12	14	26	30	1	2	1	—	—	—	—	—
98-99—Carolina	NHL	76	13	15	28	67	3	0	0	6	0	3	3	2
99-00—Carolina	NHL	81	14	16	30	40	-10	3	0	—	—	—	—	—
00-01—Carolina	NHL	79	23	29	52	59	-4	6	1	6	0	1	1	6
01-02—Carolina	NHL	72	13	16	29	30	-1	3	0	23	3	4	7	10
02-03—Calgary	NHL	81	21	31	52	51	-3	6	0	—	—	—	—	—
03-04—Calgary	NHL	76	17	18	35	70	10	5	0	26	8	7	15	35
04-05—Morges	Switzerland	41	38	23	61	81	...	9	2	4	2	2	4	24
—Lugano	Switzerland	1	0	0	0	0	...	0	0	5	0	1	1	2
05-06—Florida	NHL	82	17	24	41	80	27	4	0	—	—	—	—	—
NHL Totals (17 years)		1134	286	310	596	764	40	53	8	147	23	33	56	120

GEOFFRION, BLAKE — LW

PERSONAL: Born February 3, 1988, in Plantation, Fla. ... 6-1/190. ... Shoots left. ... Son of Danny Geoffrion, RW with Montreal Canadiens and Winnipeg Jets (1979-82); grandson of Bernie "Boom Boom" Geoffrion, RW with Montreal Canadiens (1950-64) and New York Rangers (1966-68) and coach of Rangers and Atlanta Flames; great grandson of Howie Morenz, member of Montreal Canadiens, Chicago Blackhawks and New York Rangers.

TRANSACTIONS/CAREER NOTES: Selected by Nashville Predators in second round (first Predators pick; 56th overall) of NHL draft (June 24, 2006).

Season Team	League	REGULAR SEASON GP	G	A	Pts.	PIM	+/-	PP	SH	PLAYOFFS GP	G	A	Pts.	PIM
04-05—U.S. National	USHL	34	7	11	18	62	...	...	...	—	—	—	—	—
05-06—U.S. National	USHL	46	17	17	34	56	...	...	...	—	—	—	—	—

GERBER, MARTIN — G

PERSONAL: Born September 3, 1974, in Burgdorf, Switzerland. ... 6-0/185. ... Catches left.

TRANSACTIONS/CAREER NOTES: Selected by Anaheim Mighty Ducks in eighth round (10th Mighty Ducks pick, 232nd overall) of NHL draft (June 24, 2001). ... Traded by Mighty Ducks to Carolina Hurricanes for D Tomas Malec and third-round pick (D Kyle Klubertanz) in 2004 draft (June 18, 2004). ... Pulled hip muscle (October 5, 2005); missed five games. ... Signed as free agent by Ottawa Senators (July 1, 2006).

Season Team	League	REGULAR SEASON GP	Min.	W	L	OTL	T	GA	SO	GAA	SV%	PLAYOFFS GP	Min.	W	L	GA	SO	GAA	SV%
01-02—Farjestad Karlstad	Sweden	44	2664	...	...	...	...	87	4	1.96	...	10	657	...	...	18	2	1.64	...
02-03—Cincinnati	AHL	1	60	1	0	...	0	2	0	2.00	.951	—	—	—	—	—	—	—	—
—Anaheim	NHL	22	1203	6	11	...	3	39	1	1.95	.929	2	20	0	0	1	0	3.00	.833

Season Team	League	REGULAR SEASON GP	Min.	W	L	OTL	T	GA	SO	GAA	SV%	PLAYOFFS GP	Min.	W	L	GA	SO	GAA	SV%
03-04—Anaheim	NHL	32	1698	11	12	...	4	64	2	2.26	.918	—	—	—	—	—	—	—	—
04-05—SC Langnau	Switzerland	20	1217	6	10	...	4	57	0	2.87	...	—	—	—	—	—	—	—	—
—Farjestad Karlstad	Sweden	30	1828	...	...	...	...	58	4	1.90	.929	15	901	...	...	36	1	2.41	.925
05-06—Carolina	NHL	60	3493	38	14	6	...	162	3	2.78	.906	6	221	1	1	13	1	3.53	.856
—Swiss Olympic team	Int'l	3	...	...	...	...	...	...	...	4.13	.890	—	—	—	—	—	—	—	—
NHL Totals (3 years)		114	6394	55	37	6	7	265	6	2.49	.913	8	241	1	1	14	1	3.49	.854

GERMYN, CARSEN — RW

PERSONAL: Born February 22, 1982, in Campbell River, B.C. ... 5-10/185. ... Shoots right. ... Name pronounced: GUHR mihn
TRANSACTIONS/CAREER NOTES: Signed as free agent by Calgary Flames (July 6, 2004).

Season Team	League	REGULAR SEASON GP	G	A	Pts.	PIM	+/-	PP	SH	PLAYOFFS GP	G	A	Pts.	PIM
98-99—Kelowna	WHL	59	6	10	16	61	...	...	...	5	0	0	0	2
99-00—Kelowna	WHL	71	16	29	45	111	...	...	...	5	3	3	6	4
00-01—Kelowna	WHL	71	35	52	87	102	...	...	...	6	2	6	8	10
01-02—Kelowna	WHL	23	10	18	28	43	...	...	...	—	—	—	—	—
—Red Deer	WHL	37	23	25	48	83	...	...	...	23	4	12	16	24
02-03—Red Deer	WHL	63	26	33	59	108	...	...	...	23	4	9	13	25
03-04—Norfolk	AHL	77	11	16	27	104	...	...	...	6	1	0	1	2
04-05—Lowell	AHL	60	9	11	20	115	10	2	0	10	0	0	0	25
05-06—Omaha Ak-Sar-Ben	AHL	77	24	31	55	127	-13	11	0	—	—	—	—	—
—Calgary	NHL	2	0	0	0	0	-1	0	0	—	—	—	—	—
NHL Totals (1 year)		2	0	0	0	0	-1	0	0					

GERVAIS, BRUNO — D

PERSONAL: Born October 3, 1984, in Longueuil, Que. ... 6-1/195. ... Shoots right. ... Name pronounced: zhuhr VAY
TRANSACTIONS/CAREER NOTES: Selected by New York Islanders in sixth round (sixth Islanders pick, 182nd overall) of NHL entry draft (June 21, 2003). ... Injured knee in Canadian juniors evaluation camp (December 12, 2003); missed remainder of season.

Season Team	League	REGULAR SEASON GP	G	A	Pts.	PIM	+/-	PP	SH	PLAYOFFS GP	G	A	Pts.	PIM
01-02—Acadie-Bathurst	QMJHL	65	4	12	16	42	...	...	...	10	3	1	4	6
02-03—Acadie-Bathurst	QMJHL	72	22	28	50	73	47	17	0	11	3	5	8	14
03-04—Acadie-Bathurst	QMJHL	23	4	6	10	28	-6	3	0	—	—	—	—	—
04-05—Bridgeport	AHL	76	8	22	30	58	0	4	2	—	—	—	—	—
05-06—Bridgeport	AHL	55	16	25	41	70	5	8	1	7	1	2	3	0
—New York Islanders	NHL	27	3	4	7	8	-1	1	0	—	—	—	—	—
NHL Totals (1 year)		27	3	4	7	8	-1	1	0					

GETZLAF, RYAN — C

PERSONAL: Born May 10, 1985, in Regina, Sask. ... 6-3/213. ... Shoots right.
TRANSACTIONS/CAREER NOTES: Selected by Anaheim Mighty Ducks in first round (first Mighty Ducks pick, 19th overall) in entry draft (June 23, 2003). ... Strained left shoulder (October 23, 2005); missed five games.

Season Team	League	REGULAR SEASON GP	G	A	Pts.	PIM	+/-	PP	SH	PLAYOFFS GP	G	A	Pts.	PIM
01-02—Calgary	WHL	63	9	9	18	34	...	...	...	7	2	1	3	4
02-03—Calgary	WHL	70	29	39	68	121	...	...	...	5	1	1	2	6
03-04—Calgary	WHL	49	28	47	75	97	...	...	...	7	5	1	6	12
04-05—Calgary	WHL	51	29	25	54	102	22	7	2	12	4	13	17	18
05-06—Portland	AHL	17	8	25	33	36	5	5	0	—	—	—	—	—
—Anaheim	NHL	57	14	25	39	22	6	10	0	16	3	4	7	13
NHL Totals (1 year)		57	14	25	39	22	6	10	0	16	3	4	7	13

GIGUERE, JEAN-SEBASTIEN — G

PERSONAL: Born May 16, 1977, in Montreal. ... 6-1/200. ... Catches left. ... Name pronounced zhee-GAIR.
TRANSACTIONS/CAREER NOTES: Selected by Hartford Whalers in first round (first Whalers pick, 13th overall) of entry draft (July 8, 1995). ... Whalers franchise moved to North Carolina and renamed Carolina Hurricanes for 1997-98 season; NHL approved move on June 25, 1997. ... Traded by Hurricanes with C Andrew Cassels to Calgary Flames for LW Gary Roberts and G Trevor Kidd (August 25, 1997). ... Strained hamstring (December 27, 1998); missed seven games. ... Traded by Flames to Anaheim Mighty Ducks for second-round pick (later traded to Washington; Capitals selected LW Matt Pettinger) in 2000 draft (June 10, 2000). ... Strained groin (September 2001); missed first five games of season. ... Injured neck (January 3, 2003); missed three games. ... Strained groin (October 19, 2005); missed three games. ... Dehydration (November 15, 2005); missed two games. ... Strained hamstring (November 22, 2005); missed six games.

Season Team	League	REGULAR SEASON GP	Min.	W	L	OTL	T	GA	SO	GAA	SV%	PLAYOFFS GP	Min.	W	L	GA	SO	GAA	SV%
93-94—Verdun	QMJHL	25	1234	13	5	...	2	66	0	3.21	...	—	—	—	—	—	—	—	—
94-95—Halifax	QMJHL	47	2755	14	27	...	5	181	2	3.94	.889	7	417	3	4	17	1	2.45	.934
95-96—Verdun	QMJHL	55	3228	26	23	...	2	185	1	3.44	...	6	356	1	5	24	0	4.04	...
96-97—Halifax	QMJHL	50	3009	28	19	...	3	169	2	3.37	...	16	954	9	7	58	0	3.65	.899
—Hartford	NHL	8	394	1	4	...	0	24	0	3.65	.881	—	—	—	—	—	—	—	—

Season Team	League	GP	Min.	W	L	OTL	T	GA	SO	GAA	SV%	GP	Min.	W	L	GA	SO	GAA	SV%
		REGULAR SEASON										PLAYOFFS							
97-98—Saint John	AHL	31	1758	16	10	...	3	72	2	2.46	.926	10	537	5	3	27	0	3.02	.897
98-99—Saint John	AHL	39	2145	18	16	...	3	123	3	3.44	.905	7	304	3	2	21	0	4.14	.859
—Calgary	NHL	15	860	6	7	...	1	46	0	3.21	.897	—	—	—	—	—	—	—	—
99-00—Saint John	AHL	41	2243	17	17	...	3	114	0	3.05	...	3	178	0	3	9	0	3.03	...
—Calgary	NHL	7	330	1	3	...	1	15	0	2.73	.914	—	—	—	—	—	—	—	—
00-01—Cincinnati	AHL	23	1306	12	7	...	2	53	0	2.43	.917	—	—	—	—	—	—	—	—
—Anaheim	NHL	34	2031	11	17	...	5	87	4	2.57	.911	—	—	—	—	—	—	—	—
01-02—Anaheim	NHL	53	3127	20	25	...	6	111	4	2.13	.920	—	—	—	—	—	—	—	—
02-03—Anaheim	NHL	65	3775	34	22	...	6	145	8	2.30	.920	21	1407	15	6	38	5	*1.62	.945
03-04—Anaheim	NHL	55	3210	17	31	...	6	140	3	2.62	.914	—	—	—	—	—	—	—	—
04-05—Hamburg	Germany	6	301	...	...	...	...	12	0	2.39	.925	2	100	...	...	7	0	4.20	.881
05-06—Anaheim	NHL	60	3381	30	15	*11	...	150	2	2.66	.911	6	318	3	3	18	0	3.40	.864
NHL Totals (8 years)		297	17108	120	124	11	25	718	21	2.52	.914	27	1725	18	9	56	5	1.95	.932

GILL, HAL — D

PERSONAL: Born April 6, 1975, in Concord, Mass. ... 6-7/250. ... Shoots left.

TRANSACTIONS/CAREER NOTES: Selected by Boston Bruins in eighth round (eighth Bruins pick, 207th overall) of entry draft (June 26, 1993). ... Flu (January 21, 1998); missed one game. ... Strained hip flexor (April 7, 1999); missed two games. ... Flu (January 11, 2000); missed one game. ... Tendinitis in shoulder (December 4, 2001); missed two games. ... Bruised foot (April 6, 2002); missed one game. ... Injured finger (February 15, 2003); missed six games. ... Pinched nerve (January 11, 2006); missed two games. ... Signed as free agent by Toronto Maple Leafs (July 1, 2006).

Season Team	League	GP	G	A	Pts.	PIM	+/-	PP	SH	GP	G	A	Pts.	PIM
		REGULAR SEASON								PLAYOFFS				
93-94—Providence College	Hockey East	31	1	2	3	26	...	...	...	—	—	—	—	—
94-95—Providence College	Hockey East	26	1	3	4	22	7	0	1	—	—	—	—	—
95-96—Providence College	Hockey East	39	5	12	17	54	...	...	...	—	—	—	—	—
96-97—Providence College	Hockey East	35	5	16	21	52	-3	1	1	—	—	—	—	—
97-98—Boston	NHL	68	2	4	6	47	4	0	0	6	0	0	0	4
—Providence	AHL	4	1	0	1	23	-2	0	0	—	—	—	—	—
98-99—Boston	NHL	80	3	7	10	63	-10	0	0	12	0	0	0	14
99-00—Boston	NHL	81	3	9	12	51	0	0	0	—	—	—	—	—
00-01—Boston	NHL	80	1	10	11	71	-2	0	0	—	—	—	—	—
01-02—Boston	NHL	79	4	18	22	77	16	0	0	6	0	1	1	2
02-03—Boston	NHL	76	4	13	17	56	21	0	0	5	0	0	0	4
03-04—Boston	NHL	82	2	7	9	99	16	0	0	7	0	1	1	4
04-05—Lukko Rauma	Finland	31	2	8	10	110	-2	...	...	8	0	0	0	57
05-06—Boston	NHL	80	1	9	10	124	-4	0	0	—	—	—	—	—
NHL Totals (8 years)		626	20	77	97	588	41	0	0	36	0	2	2	28

GILLIES, TREVOR — D

PERSONAL: Born January 30, 1979, in Cambridge, Ont. ... 6-3/210. ... Shoots left.

TRANSACTIONS/CAREER NOTES: Signed as free agent by New York Rangers (July 20, 2004). ... Traded by Rangers with conditional 2007 pick to Anaheim Ducks for C Steve Rucchin (August 23, 2005).

Season Team	League	GP	G	A	Pts.	PIM	+/-	PP	SH	GP	G	A	Pts.	PIM
		REGULAR SEASON								PLAYOFFS				
96-97—North Bay	OHL	26	0	3	3	72	...	...	...	—	—	—	—	—
97-98—Sarnia	OHL	17	0	1	1	33	...	...	...	—	—	—	—	—
—Oshawa	OHL	45	1	2	3	184	...	...	...	7	0	1	1	12
—North Bay	OHL	2	0	0	0	4	...	...	...	—	—	—	—	—
98-99—Oshawa	OHL	66	6	9	15	270	...	...	...	11	0	2	2	28
99-00—Lowell	AHL	8	0	0	0	38	...	...	...	—	—	—	—	—
—Mississippi	ECHL	53	0	6	6	202	...	...	...	—	—	—	—	—
00-01—Worcester	AHL	0	...	...	...	...	...	...	...	6	0	0	0	24
—Greensboro	ECHL	63	1	6	7	303	...	...	...	—	—	—	—	—
01-02—Providence	AHL	5	0	0	0	21	...	...	...	—	—	—	—	—
—Richmond	ECHL	18	0	1	1	51	...	...	...	—	—	—	—	—
—Augusta	ECHL	46	0	1	1	269	...	...	...	—	—	—	—	—
02-03—Lowell	AHL	25	0	1	1	132	...	...	...	—	—	—	—	—
—Richmond	ECHL	6	0	0	0	20	...	...	...	—	—	—	—	—
—Peoria	ECHL	24	0	1	1	180	...	...	...	—	—	—	—	—
03-04—Springfield	AHL	61	2	1	3	277	...	...	...	—	—	—	—	—
04-05—Hartford	AHL	49	0	2	2	277	-4	0	0	0	0	0	0	0
05-06—Anaheim	NHL	1	0	0	0	21	0	0	0	—	—	—	—	—
—Portland	AHL	50	2	3	5	169	2	0	0	4	0	0	0	0
NHL Totals (1 year)		1	0	0	0	21	0	0	0					

GIONTA, BRIAN — RW

PERSONAL: Born January 18, 1979, in Rochester, N.Y. ... 5-7/175. ... Shoots right. ... Name pronounced: jee AHN tuh

TRANSACTIONS/CAREER NOTES: Selected by New Jersey Devils in third round (fourth Devils pick, 82nd overall) of NHL draft (June 27, 1998). ... Injured ankle (December 14, 2002); missed two games. ... Fractured leg (January 4, 2003); missed 19 games. ... Injured ankle (February 18, 2003); missed three games. ... Cut face (March 5, 2004); missed seven games.

Season Team	League	REGULAR SEASON GP	G	A	Pts.	PIM	+/-	PP	SH	PLAYOFFS GP	G	A	Pts.	PIM
97-98—Boston College	Hockey East	40	30	32	62	44	...	...	...	—	—	—	—	—
98-99—Boston College	Hockey East	39	27	33	60	46	...	...	...	—	—	—	—	—
99-00—Boston College	Hockey East	42	33	23	56	66	...	...	...	—	—	—	—	—
00-01—Boston College	Hockey East	43	33	21	54	47	...	...	...	—	—	—	—	—
01-02—Albany	AHL	37	9	16	25	18	0	1	0	—	—	—	—	—
—New Jersey	NHL	33	4	7	11	8	10	0	0	6	2	2	4	0
02-03—New Jersey	NHL	58	12	13	25	23	5	2	0	24	1	8	9	6
03-04—New Jersey	NHL	75	21	8	29	36	19	0	0	5	2	3	5	0
04-05—Albany	AHL	15	5	7	12	10	0	2	0	—	—	—	—	—
05-06—New Jersey	NHL	82	48	41	89	46	18	24	1	9	3	4	7	2
—U.S. Olympic team	Int'l	6	4	0	4	2	-1	3	0	—	—	—	—	—
NHL Totals (4 years)		248	85	69	154	113	52	26	1	44	8	17	25	8

GIORDANO, MARK — D

PERSONAL: Born October 3, 1983, in Toronto. ... 6-0/203. ... Shoots left.
TRANSACTIONS/CAREER NOTES: Signed as free agent by Calgary Flames (July 6, 2004).

Season Team	League	REGULAR SEASON GP	G	A	Pts.	PIM	+/-	PP	SH	PLAYOFFS GP	G	A	Pts.	PIM
02-03—Owen Sound	OHL	68	18	30	48	109	...	...	...	4	1	3	4	2
03-04—Owen Sound	OHL	65	14	35	49	72	...	...	...	7	1	3	4	5
04-05—Lowell	AHL	66	6	10	16	85	13	3	0	11	0	1	1	41
05-06—Omaha Ak-Sar-Ben	AHL	73	16	42	58	141	-1	12	0	—	—	—	—	—
—Calgary	NHL	7	0	1	1	8	2	0	0	—	—	—	—	—
NHL Totals (1 year)		7	0	1	1	8	2	0	0					

GIROUX, ALEXANDRE — C/LW

PERSONAL: Born August 16, 1981, in Quebec City. ... 6-2/165. ... Shoots left. ... Name pronounced zhih-ROO.
TRANSACTIONS/CAREER NOTES: Selected by Ottawa Senators in seventh round (ninth Senators pick, 213th overall) of NHL entry draft (June 26, 1999). ... Traded by Senators with D Karel Rachunek to New York Rangers for D Greg de Vries (March 9, 2004).

Season Team	League	REGULAR SEASON GP	G	A	Pts.	PIM	+/-	PP	SH	PLAYOFFS GP	G	A	Pts.	PIM
98-99—Hull	QMJHL	67	15	22	37	124	...	...	...	22	2	2	4	8
99-00—Hull	QMJHL	72	52	47	99	117	...	...	...	15	12	6	18	30
00-01—Hull	QMJHL	38	31	32	63	62	...	...	...	—	—	—	—	—
—Rouyn-Noranda	QMJHL	25	13	14	27	56	...	...	...	9	2	6	8	22
01-02—Grand Rapids	AHL	70	11	16	27	74	5	2	0	—	—	—	—	—
02-03—Binghamton	AHL	67	19	16	35	101	-4	9	0	10	1	0	1	10
03-04—Binghamton	AHL	60	19	23	42	79	15	6	1	—	—	—	—	—
—Hartford	AHL	16	6	3	9	13	-2	2	0	16	3	4	7	28
04-05—Hartford	AHL	78	32	22	54	128	15	13	0	6	3	3	6	23
05-06—Hartford	AHL	73	36	31	67	102	14	10	6	13	7	9	16	17
—New York Rangers	NHL	1	0	0	0	0	-1	0	0	—	—	—	—	—
NHL Totals (1 year)		1	0	0	0	0	-1	0	0					

GIROUX, CLAUDE — RW

PERSONAL: Born January 12, 1988, in Hearst, Ont. ... 5-10/169. ... Shoots right.
TRANSACTIONS/CAREER NOTES: Selected by Philadelphia Flyers in first round (first Flyers pick; 22nd overall) of NHL draft (June 24, 2006).

Season Team	League	REGULAR SEASON GP	G	A	Pts.	PIM	+/-	PP	SH	PLAYOFFS GP	G	A	Pts.	PIM
04-05—Cumberland	CJHL	48	13	27	40	35	...	...	...	—	—	—	—	—
05-06—Gatineau	QMJHL	69	39	64	103	64	30	...	...	17	5	15	20	24

GIULIANO, JEFF — C/LW

PERSONAL: Born June 20, 1979, in Nashua, N.H. ... 5-9/205. ... Shoots left.
COLLEGE: Boston College.
TRANSACTIONS/CAREER NOTES: Signed as free agent by AHL Manchester (August 20, 2003). ... Signed as free agent by Los Angeles Kings (August 12, 2005).

Season Team	League	REGULAR SEASON GP	G	A	Pts.	PIM	+/-	PP	SH	PLAYOFFS GP	G	A	Pts.	PIM
98-99—Boston College	Hockey East	43	10	...	...	...	...	...	...	—	—	—	—	—
99-00—Boston College	Hockey East	42	10	13	23	16	...	...	...	—	—	—	—	—
00-01—Boston College	Hockey East	43	14	21	35	28	...	...	...	—	—	—	—	—
01-02—Boston College	Hockey East	38	11	24	35	14	...	...	...	—	—	—	—	—
02-03—Reading	ECHL	38	7	23	30	6	...	...	...	—	—	—	—	—
—Manchester	AHL	47	4	11	15	8	...	...	...	—	—	—	—	—
03-04—Manchester	AHL	80	6	14	20	16	...	...	...	—	—	—	—	—
04-05—Manchester	AHL	69	8	16	24	21	16	0	1	2	0	0	0	0
05-06—Los Angeles	NHL	48	3	4	7	26	0	0	0	—	—	—	—	—
—Manchester	AHL	19	5	6	11	17	10	0	1	7	3	1	4	2
NHL Totals (1 year)		48	3	4	7	26	0	0	0					

GLEASON, TIM D

PERSONAL: Born January 29, 1983, in Southfield, Mich. ... 6-1/202. ... Shoots left.

TRANSACTIONS/CAREER NOTES: Selected by Ottawa Senators in first round (second Senators pick, 23rd overall) of entry draft (June 23, 2001). ... Traded by Senators to Los Angeles Kings for C Bryan Smolinski (March 11, 2003). ... Bruised knee (January 26, 2006); missed two games.

		REGULAR SEASON								PLAYOFFS				
Season Team	**League**	**GP**	**G**	**A**	**Pts.**	**PIM**	**+/-**	**PP**	**SH**	**GP**	**G**	**A**	**Pts.**	**PIM**
99-00—Windsor	OHL	55	5	13	18	101	...	...	...	12	2	4	6	14
00-01—Windsor	OHL	47	8	26	34	124	...	...	...	9	1	2	3	23
01-02—Windsor	OHL	67	17	42	59	109	...	...	...	16	7	13	20	40
02-03—Windsor	OHL	45	7	31	38	75	...	...	...	7	5	2	7	17
03-04—Los Angeles	NHL	47	0	7	7	21	1	0	0	—	—	—	—	—
—Manchester	AHL	22	0	8	8	19	10	0	0	6	0	1	1	4
04-05—Manchester	AHL	67	10	14	24	112	17	2	1	5	0	0	0	4
05-06—Los Angeles	NHL	78	2	19	21	77	0	0	0	—	—	—	—	—
NHL Totals (2 years)		125	2	26	28	98	1	0	0					

GLOBKE, ROB RW/C

PERSONAL: Born October 24, 1982, in Farmington, Mich. ... 6-2/200. ... Shoots right.

COLLEGE: Notre Dame.

TRANSACTIONS/CAREER NOTES: Selected by Florida Panthers in second round (third Panthers pick, 40th overall) of NHL entry draft (June 22, 2002).

		REGULAR SEASON								PLAYOFFS				
Season Team	**League**	**GP**	**G**	**A**	**Pts.**	**PIM**	**+/-**	**PP**	**SH**	**GP**	**G**	**A**	**Pts.**	**PIM**
00-01— Notre Dame	CCHA	33	17	9	26	74	...	...	...	—	—	—	—	—
01-02— Notre Dame	CCHA	29	11	11	22	73	...	...	...	—	—	—	—	—
02-03— Notre Dame	CCHA	40	21	15	36	44	...	...	...	—	—	—	—	—
03-04— Notre Dame	CCHA	39	19	21	40	42	2	5	1	—	—	—	—	—
04-05—San Antonio	AHL	63	6	6	12	21	-3	0	0	—	—	—	—	—
—Texas	ECHL	10	8	4	12	13	...	...	...	—	—	—	—	—
05-06—Rochester	AHL	52	6	9	15	52	-13	1	0	—	—	—	—	—
—Florida	NHL	18	1	0	1	6	0	0	0	—	—	—	—	—
NHL Totals (1 year)		18	1	0	1	6	0	0	0					

GLUMAC, MIKE RW

PERSONAL: Born April 5, 1980, in Niagara Falls, Ont. ... 6-2/203. ... Shoots right.

COLLEGE: Miami (Ohio).

TRANSACTIONS/CAREER NOTES: Signed as free agent by St. Louis Blues (October 6, 2003).

		REGULAR SEASON								PLAYOFFS				
Season Team	**League**	**GP**	**G**	**A**	**Pts.**	**PIM**	**+/-**	**PP**	**SH**	**GP**	**G**	**A**	**Pts.**	**PIM**
98-99—Miami (Ohio)	CCHA	35	2	0	2	44	...	...	...	—	—	—	—	—
99-00—Miami (Ohio)	CCHA	36	8	5	13	52	...	...	...	—	—	—	—	—
00-01—Miami (Ohio)	CCHA	37	9	10	19	46	...	...	...	—	—	—	—	—
01-02—Miami (Ohio)	CCHA	36	15	8	23	28	...	...	...	—	—	—	—	—
02-03—Cleveland	AHL	2	0	0	0	0	...	...	...	—	—	—	—	—
—Pee Dee	ECHL	69	37	32	69	49	...	...	...	—	—	—	—	—
03-04—Worcester	AHL	80	28	24	52	74	...	...	...	10	3	3	6	11
04-05—Worcester	AHL	45	12	17	29	27	-7	7	0	—	—	—	—	—
05-06—St. Louis	NHL	33	7	5	12	33	-8	5	0	—	—	—	—	—
—Peoria	AHL	49	25	32	57	64	18	10	0	4	1	1	2	5
NHL Totals (1 year)		33	7	5	12	33	-8	5	0					

GOC, MARCEL C/LW

PERSONAL: Born August 24, 1983, in Calw, West Germany. ... 6-1/187. ... Shoots left. ... Brother of Sascha Goc, D, New Jersey Devils (1998-2001) and Tampa Bay Lightning (2001-02). ... Name pronounced: GAHCH

TRANSACTIONS/CAREER NOTES: Selected by San Jose Sharks in first round (first Sharks pick, 20th overall) of NHL entry draft (June 23, 2001).

		REGULAR SEASON								PLAYOFFS				
Season Team	**League**	**GP**	**G**	**A**	**Pts.**	**PIM**	**+/-**	**PP**	**SH**	**GP**	**G**	**A**	**Pts.**	**PIM**
99-00—Schwenningen	Germany	62	1	4	5	6	...	...	...	—	—	—	—	—
00-01—Schwenningen	Germany	58	13	28	41	12	...	...	...	—	—	—	—	—
01-02—Schwenningen	Germany	45	8	9	17	24	...	...	...	—	—	—	—	—
—Mannheim	Germany	8	0	2	2	0	...	...	...	—	—	—	—	—
02-03—Mannheim	Germany	36	6	14	20	16	...	...	...	8	1	2	3	0
03-04—Cleveland	AHL	78	16	21	37	24	3	0	1	—	—	—	—	—
—San Jose	NHL	...	...	...	...	...	...	...	...	5	1	1	2	0
04-05—Cleveland	AHL	76	16	34	50	28	6	5	3	—	—	—	—	—
05-06—San Jose	NHL	81	8	14	22	22	-7	2	0	11	0	3	3	0
—German Oly. team	Int'l	5	1	0	1	6	-4	1	0	—	—	—	—	—
NHL Totals (2 years)		81	8	14	22	22	-7	2	0	16	1	4	5	0

GODARD, ERIC — RW

PERSONAL: Born March 7, 1980, in Vernon, B.C. ... 6-4/235. ... Shoots right.

TRANSACTIONS/CAREER NOTES: Signed as free agent by Florida Panthers (September 24, 1999). ... Traded by Panthers to New York Islanders for third-round pick (C/LW Gregory Campbell) in 2002 draft (June 22, 2002). ... Suspended one playoff game for high-sticking incident (April 10, 2003). ... Injured shoulder (November 28, 2003); missed three games. ... Signed by Islanders as restricted free agent (September 29, 2005). ... Suspended two games by NHL for punching incident (January 7, 2006). ... Viral infection (February 8, 2006); missed seven games.

		REGULAR SEASON								PLAYOFFS				
Season Team	**League**	**GP**	**G**	**A**	**Pts.**	**PIM**	**+/-**	**PP**	**SH**	**GP**	**G**	**A**	**Pts.**	**PIM**
97-98—Lethbridge	WHL	7	0	0	0	26	...	0	0	2	0	0	0	0
98-99—Lethbridge	WHL	66	2	5	7	213	...	...	...	4	0	0	0	14
99-00—Lethbridge	WHL	60	3	5	8	310	...	...	...	—	—	—	—	—
—Louisville	AHL	4	0	1	1	16	...	...	...	—	—	—	—	—
00-01—Louisville	AHL	45	0	0	0	132	...	...	...	—	—	—	—	—
01-02—Bridgeport	AHL	67	1	4	5	198	1	0	0	20	0	4	4	30
02-03—Bridgeport	AHL	46	2	2	4	199	-10	2	0	6	0	0	0	16
—New York Islanders	NHL	19	0	0	0	48	-3	0	0	2	0	1	1	4
03-04—New York Islanders	NHL	31	0	1	1	97	-2	0	0	—	—	—	—	—
—Bridgeport	AHL	7	0	0	0	13	-2	0	0	—	—	—	—	—
04-05—Bridgeport	AHL	75	7	11	18	295	-10	2	0	—	—	—	—	—
05-06—New York Islanders	NHL	57	2	2	4	115	-2	0	0	—	—	—	—	—
NHL Totals (3 years)		107	2	3	5	260	-7	0	0	2	0	1	1	4

GOERTZEN, STEVEN — RW

PERSONAL: Born May 26, 1984, in Stony Plane, Alta. ... 6-1/190. ... Shoots right. ... Name pronounced: GUHRT zehn

TRANSACTIONS/CAREER NOTES: Selected by Columbus Blue Jackets in seventh round (11th Blue Jackets pick, 225th overall) of NHL entry draft (June 23, 2002).

		REGULAR SEASON								PLAYOFFS				
Season Team	**League**	**GP**	**G**	**A**	**Pts.**	**PIM**	**+/-**	**PP**	**SH**	**GP**	**G**	**A**	**Pts.**	**PIM**
01-02—Seattle	WHL	66	6	9	15	44	-14	...	...	11	2	0	2	4
02-03—Seattle	WHL	71	12	19	31	95	21	...	...	14	4	3	7	9
03-04—Syracuse	AHL	8	0	3	3	4	-3	...	...	1	0	0	0	0
—Seattle	WHL	69	15	18	33	115	16	...	...	—	—	—	—	—
04-05—Syracuse	AHL	57	2	7	9	100	4	0	0	—	—	—	—	—
—Dayton	ECHL	11	0	3	3	2	2	...	...	—	—	—	—	—
05-06—Columbus	NHL	39	0	0	0	44	-17	0	0	—	—	—	—	—
—Syracuse	AHL	40	7	8	15	55	3	2	1	6	0	1	1	34
NHL Totals (1 year)		39	0	0	0	44	-17	0	0					

GOMEZ, SCOTT — C/LW

PERSONAL: Born December 23, 1979, in Anchorage, Alaska. ... 5-11/200. ... Shoots left.

TRANSACTIONS/CAREER NOTES: Selected by New Jersey Devils in first round (second Devils pick, 27th overall) of NHL draft (June 27, 1998). ... Injured back (February 17, 2001); missed six games. ... Fractured left hand (April 1, 2002); missed remainder of season. ... Bruised ribs (December 2, 2003); missed two games.

STATISTICAL PLATEAUS: Three-goal games: 1999-00 (1).

		REGULAR SEASON								PLAYOFFS				
Season Team	**League**	**GP**	**G**	**A**	**Pts.**	**PIM**	**+/-**	**PP**	**SH**	**GP**	**G**	**A**	**Pts.**	**PIM**
96-97—Surrey Jr. A	BCJHL	56	48	76	124	94	...	...	...	—	—	—	—	—
97-98—Tri-City	WHL	45	12	37	49	57	-11	6	0	—	—	—	—	—
98-99—Tri-City	WHL	58	30	78	108	55	43	9	1	10	6	13	19	31
99-00—New Jersey	NHL	82	19	51	70	78	14	7	0	23	4	6	10	4
00-01—New Jersey	NHL	76	14	49	63	46	-1	2	0	25	5	9	14	24
01-02—New Jersey	NHL	76	10	38	48	36	-4	1	0	—	—	—	—	—
02-03—New Jersey	NHL	80	13	42	55	48	17	2	0	24	3	9	12	2
03-04—New Jersey	NHL	80	14	†56	70	70	18	3	0	5	0	6	6	0
04-05—Alaska	ECHL	61	13	73	86	69	26	1	1	4	1	3	4	4
05-06—New Jersey	NHL	82	33	51	84	42	8	9	0	9	5	4	9	6
—U.S. Olympic team	Int'l	6	1	4	5	10	-3	1	0	—	—	—	—	—
NHL Totals (6 years)		476	103	287	390	320	52	24	0	86	17	34	51	36

GONCHAR, SERGEI — D

PERSONAL: Born April 13, 1974, in Chelyabinsk, U.S.S.R. ... 6-2/215. ... Shoots left. ... Name pronounced GAHN-shahr.

TRANSACTIONS/CAREER NOTES: Selected by Washington Capitals in first round (first Capitals pick, 14th overall) of NHL draft (June 20, 1992). ... Injured groin (November 30, 1995); missed two games. ... Flu (December 13, 1995); missed one game. ... Flu (November 7, 1996); missed one game. ... Hyperextended elbow (November 18, 1996); missed one game. ... Back spasms (December 28, 1996); missed eight games. ... Bruised knee (January 29, 1997); missed two games. ... Sprained knee (February 26, 1997); missed 12 games. ... Sprained knee (October 23, 1998); missed 10 games. ... Strained groin (January 1, 1999); missed one game. ... Sprained wrist (January 30, 1999); missed eight games. ... Sprained ankle (March 13, 1999); missed two games. ... Reinjured ankle (April 7, 1999); missed remainder of season. ... Injured (November 11, 1999); missed five games. ... Injured neck (February 28, 2000); missed two games. ... Reinjured neck (March 5, 2000); missed two games. ... Missed first two games of 2000-01 season in contract dispute. ... Injured neck (December 21, 2000); missed one game. ... Bruised shoulder (January 18, 2001); missed three games. ... Injured (November 27, 2001); missed one game. ... Concussion (March 21, 2002); missed five games. ... Injured shoulder (January 14, 2004); missed seven games. ... Flu (February 27, 2004); missed three games. ...

Traded by Capitals to Boston Bruins for D Shaone Morrisonn and first- (D Jeff Schultz) and second-round (C/W Mihail Yunkov) picks in 2004 draft (March 3, 2004). ... Signed as free agent by Pittsburgh Penguins (August 3, 2005). ... Groin (November 12, 2005); missed three games. ... Dizzyness (February 6, 2006); missed two games.
STATISTICAL PLATEAUS: Three-goal games: 1999-00 (1).

		REGULAR SEASON								PLAYOFFS				
Season Team	**League**	**GP**	**G**	**A**	**Pts.**	**PIM**	**+/-**	**PP**	**SH**	**GP**	**G**	**A**	**Pts.**	**PIM**
90-91—Mechel Chelyabinsk....	USSR	2	0	0	0	0	...	...	...	—	—	—	—	—
91-92—Traktor Chelyabinsk....	CIS	31	1	0	1	6	...	...	...	—	—	—	—	—
92-93—Dynamo Moscow........	CIS	31	1	3	4	70	...	...	...	10	0	0	0	12
93-94—Dynamo Moscow........	CIS	44	4	5	9	36	...	...	...	10	0	3	3	14
—Portland....................	AHL	...	...	...	...	...	...	...	...	2	0	0	0	0
94-95—Portland....................	AHL	61	10	32	42	67	39	1	0	—	—	—	—	—
—Washington	NHL	31	2	5	7	22	4	0	0	7	2	2	4	2
95-96—Washington	NHL	78	15	26	41	60	25	4	0	6	2	4	6	4
96-97—Washington	NHL	57	13	17	30	36	-11	3	0	—	—	—	—	—
97-98—Washington	NHL	72	5	16	21	66	2	2	0	21	7	4	11	30
—Russian Oly. team.......	Int'l	6	0	2	2	0	0	0	0	—	—	—	—	—
98-99—Washington	NHL	53	21	10	31	57	1	13	1	—	—	—	—	—
99-00—Washington	NHL	73	18	36	54	52	26	5	0	5	1	0	1	6
00-01—Washington	NHL	76	19	38	57	70	12	8	0	6	1	3	4	2
01-02—Washington	NHL	76	26	33	59	58	-1	7	0	—	—	—	—	—
—Russian Oly. team.......	Int'l	6	0	0	0	2	...	...	...	—	—	—	—	—
02-03—Washington	NHL	82	18	49	67	52	13	7	0	6	0	5	5	4
03-04—Washington	NHL	56	7	42	49	44	-20	4	0	—	—	—	—	—
—Boston........................	NHL	15	4	5	9	12	6	2	0	7	1	4	5	4
04-05—Metal. Magnitogorsk...	Russian	40	2	17	19	54	11	...	...	4	1	1	2	6
05-06—Pittsburgh..................	NHL	75	12	46	58	100	-13	8	0	—	—	—	—	—
—Russian Oly. team.......	Int'l	8	0	2	2	8	-2	0	0	—	—	—	—	—
NHL Totals (11 years).........		744	160	323	483	629	44	63	1	58	14	22	36	52

GORDON, BOYD RW/C

PERSONAL: Born October 19, 1983, in Unity, Sask. ... 6-1/201. ... Shoots right.
TRANSACTIONS/CAREER NOTES: Selected by Washington Capitals in first round (third Capitals pick, 17th overall) of NHL entry draft (June 22, 2002).

		REGULAR SEASON								PLAYOFFS				
Season Team	**League**	**GP**	**G**	**A**	**Pts.**	**PIM**	**+/-**	**PP**	**SH**	**GP**	**G**	**A**	**Pts.**	**PIM**
99-00—Red Deer.....................	WHL	66	10	26	36	24	...	...	...	4	0	1	1	2
00-01—Red Deer.....................	WHL	72	12	27	39	39	...	...	...	22	3	6	9	2
01-02—Red Deer.....................	WHL	66	22	29	51	19	...	...	...	23	10	12	22	8
02-03—Red Deer.....................	WHL	56	33	48	81	28	...	...	...	23	8	12	20	14
03-04—Washington	NHL	41	1	5	6	8	-9	0	0	—	—	—	—	—
—Portland.....................	AHL	43	5	17	22	16	-1	0	0	7	2	1	3	0
04-05—Portland.....................	AHL	80	17	22	39	35	-20	7	1	—	—	—	—	—
05-06—Hershey......................	AHL	58	16	22	38	23	9	7	2	14	3	5	8	6
—Washington	NHL	25	0	1	1	4	-4	0	0	—	—	—	—	—
NHL Totals (2 years)...........		66	1	6	7	12	-13	0	0					

GOREN, LEE RW

PERSONAL: Born December 26, 1977, in Winnipeg. ... 6-3/205. ... Shoots right.
TRANSACTIONS/CAREER NOTES: Selected by Boston Bruins in third round (fifth Bruins pick, 63rd overall) of NHL draft (June 21, 1997). ... Signed as free agent by Florida Panthers (July 24, 2003). ... Signed as free agent by Vancouver Canucks (July 7, 2004).

		REGULAR SEASON								PLAYOFFS				
Season Team	**League**	**GP**	**G**	**A**	**Pts.**	**PIM**	**+/-**	**PP**	**SH**	**GP**	**G**	**A**	**Pts.**	**PIM**
95-96—Minote........................	Jr. A	64	31	55	86	...	...	...	...	—	—	—	—	—
96-97—Univ. of North Dakota.	WCHA		Did not play											
97-98—Univ. of North Dakota.	WCHA	29	3	13	16	26	...	...	...	—	—	—	—	—
98-99—Univ. of North Dakota.	WCHA	38	26	19	45	20	...	...	...	—	—	—	—	—
99-00—Univ. of North Dakota.	WCHA	44	34	29	63	42	...	...	...	—	—	—	—	—
00-01—Providence.................	AHL	54	15	18	33	72	...	...	...	17	5	2	7	11
—Boston........................	NHL	21	2	0	2	7	-3	1	0	—	—	—	—	—
01-02—Providence.................	AHL	71	11	26	37	121	-19	6	0	—	—	—	—	—
02-03—Providence.................	AHL	65	32	37	69	106	9	17	0	—	—	—	—	—
—Boston........................	NHL	14	2	1	3	7	-2	2	0	5	0	0	0	5
03-04—Florida.........................	NHL	2	0	1	1	0	-4	0	0	—	—	—	—	—
—San Antonio...............	AHL	65	27	22	49	72	-4	9	3	—	—	—	—	—
04-05—Manitoba....................	AHL	79	32	30	62	117	24	16	1	14	10	3	13	23
05-06—Manitoba....................	AHL	42	22	19	41	84	2	11	0	13	3	7	10	27
—Vancouver.................	NHL	28	1	2	3	30	-6	0	0	—	—	—	—	—
NHL Totals (4 years)...........		65	5	4	9	44	-15	3	0	5	0	0	0	5

GORGES, JOSH D

PERSONAL: Born August 14, 1984, in Kelowna, B.C. ... 6-1/185. ... Shoots left.
TRANSACTIONS/CAREER NOTES: Signed as free agent by San Jose Sharks (September 20, 2002). ... Flu (March 24, 2006); missed one game.

		REGULAR SEASON								PLAYOFFS				
Season Team	**League**	**GP**	**G**	**A**	**Pts.**	**PIM**	**+/-**	**PP**	**SH**	**GP**	**G**	**A**	**Pts.**	**PIM**
00-01—Kelowna	WHL	57	4	6	10	24	...	...	...	6	1	1	2	4
01-02—Kelowna	WHL	72	7	34	41	74	...	...	...	15	1	7	8	8
02-03—Kelowna	WHL	54	11	48	59	76	...	...	...	19	3	17	20	16
03-04—Kelowna	WHL	62	11	31	42	38	...	...	...	17	2	13	15	6
04-05—Cleveland	AHL	74	4	8	12	37	...	...	...	—	—	—	—	—
05-06—San Jose	NHL	49	0	6	6	31	5	0	0	11	0	1	1	4
—Cleveland	AHL	18	2	3	5	12	1	0	0	—	—	—	—	—
NHL Totals (1 year)		49	0	6	6	31	5	0	0	11	0	1	1	4

GOVE, DAVID LW

PERSONAL: Born May 4, 1978, in Centerville, Mass. ... 5-9/190. ... Shoots left.
COLLEGE: Western Michigan.
TRANSACTIONS/CAREER NOTES: Signed as free agent by Providence of the AHL (September 21, 2004). ... Signed as free agent by the Carolina Hurricanes (August 4, 2005).

		REGULAR SEASON								PLAYOFFS				
Season Team	**League**	**GP**	**G**	**A**	**Pts.**	**PIM**	**+/-**	**PP**	**SH**	**GP**	**G**	**A**	**Pts.**	**PIM**
97-98—Western Michigan	CCHA	36	8	7	15	8	...	...	...	—	—	—	—	—
98-99—Western Michigan	CCHA	33	9	14	23	12	...	...	...	—	—	—	—	—
99-00—Western Michigan	CCHA	36	18	28	46	22	...	...	...	—	—	—	—	—
00-01—Western Michigan	CCHA	39	22	37	59	16	...	...	...	—	—	—	—	—
—Orlando	IHL	9	1	1	2	2	...	...	...	1	0	0	0	0
01-02—Johnstown	ECHL	54	17	32	49	32	-19	6	1	8	1	3	4	4
—Grand Rapids	AHL	17	2	4	6	8	2	2	0	—	—	—	—	—
02-03—Laredo	CHL	8	4	12	16	15	-1	3	0	—	—	—	—	—
—San Antonio	AHL	72	15	20	35	30	...	...	...	3	0	1	1	0
03-04—Utah	AHL	75	14	22	36	28	...	...	...	—	—	—	—	—
04-05—Providence	AHL	70	13	18	31	30	14	3	0	17	3	3	6	14
05-06—Lowell	AHL	65	20	26	46	50	-17	3	2	—	—	—	—	—
—Carolina	NHL	1	0	1	1	0	2	0	0	—	—	—	—	—
NHL Totals (1 year)		1	0	1	1	0	2	0	0					

GRABNER, MICHAEL RW

PERSONAL: Born October 5, 1987, in Villach, Austria. ... 6-0/170. ... Shoots left.
TRANSACTIONS/CAREER NOTES: Selected by Vancouver Canucks in first round (first Canucks pick; 14th overall) of NHL draft (June 24, 2006).

		REGULAR SEASON								PLAYOFFS				
Season Team	**League**	**GP**	**G**	**A**	**Pts.**	**PIM**	**+/-**	**PP**	**SH**	**GP**	**G**	**A**	**Pts.**	**PIM**
04-05—Spokane	WHL	58	13	11	24	18	-2	...	...	—	—	—	—	—
05-06—Spokane	WHL	67	36	14	50	28	-2	...	...	—	—	—	—	—

GRAHAME, JOHN G

PERSONAL: Born August 31, 1975, in Denver. ... 6-2/220. ... Catches left. ... Son of Ron Grahame, goaltender with three NHL teams (1977-78 through 1980-81). ... Name pronounced GRAY-ihm.
TRANSACTIONS/CAREER NOTES: Selected by Boston Bruins in ninth round (seventh Bruins pick, 229th overall) of NHL draft (June 29, 1994). ... Injured ankle (December 19, 2000) and had surgery; missed seven games. ... Injured shoulder (October 17, 2002); missed seven games. ... Traded by Bruins to Tampa Bay Lightning for fourth-round pick (later traded to San Jose Sharks) in 2004 draft (January 13, 2003). ... Signed as free agent by Carolina Hurricanes (July 1, 2006).

		REGULAR SEASON										PLAYOFFS							
Season Team	**League**	**GP**	**Min.**	**W**	**L**	**OTL**	**T**	**GA**	**SO**	**GAA**	**SV%**	**GP**	**Min.**	**W**	**L**	**GA**	**SO**	**GAA**	**SV%**
93-94—Sioux City	USHL	20	1136	...	...	...	...	72	0	3.80	...	—	—	—	—	—	—	—	—
94-95—Lake Superior St.	CCHA	28	1616	16	7	...	3	75	1	2.78	.887	—	—	—	—	—	—	—	—
95-96—Lake Superior St.	CCHA	29	1658	21	4	...	2	67	2	2.42	...	—	—	—	—	—	—	—	—
96-97—Lake Superior St.	CCHA	37	2197	19	13	...	4	134	3	3.66	.876	—	—	—	—	—	—	—	—
97-98—Providence	AHL	55	3054	15	31	...	4	164	3	3.22	.898	—	—	—	—	—	—	—	—
98-99—Providence	AHL	48	2771	37	9	...	1	134	3	2.90	.896	19	1209	15	4	48	1	2.38	.912
99-00—Boston	NHL	24	1344	7	10	...	5	55	2	2.46	.910	—	—	—	—	—	—	—	—
—Providence	AHL	27	1528	11	13	...	2	86	1	3.38	...	13	839	10	3	35	0	2.50	...
00-01—Boston	NHL	10	471	3	4	...	0	28	0	3.57	.867	—	—	—	—	—	—	—	—
—Providence	AHL	16	893	4	7	...	3	47	0	3.16	.899	17	1043	8	9	46	2	2.65	...
01-02—Boston	NHL	19	1079	8	7	...	2	52	1	2.89	.897	—	—	—	—	—	—	—	—
02-03—Boston	NHL	23	1352	11	9	...	2	61	1	2.71	.902	1	111	0	1	2	0	1.08	.958
—Tampa Bay	NHL	17	914	6	5	...	4	34	2	2.23	.920	...	...	...	...	...	...	...	...
03-04—Tampa Bay	NHL	29	1688	18	9	...	1	58	1	2.06	.913	1	34	0	0	2	0	3.53	.882
05-06—Tampa Bay	NHL	57	3152	29	22	1	...	161	5	3.06	.889	4	188	1	3	15	0	4.79	.847
—U.S. Olympic team	Int'l	1	...	...	...	...	...	...	...	3.00	.880	—	—	—	—	—	—	—	—
NHL Totals (6 years)		179	10000	82	66	1	14	449	12	2.69	.900	6	333	1	4	19	0	3.42	.883

GRATTON, CHRIS C/LW

PERSONAL: Born July 5, 1975, in Brantford, Ont. ... 6-4/220. ... Shoots left. ... Name pronounced GRA-tuhn. ... Cousin of Josh Gratton, LW with Phoenix Coyotes.

G

TRANSACTIONS/CAREER NOTES: Selected by Tampa Bay Lightning in first round (first Lightning pick, third overall) of NHL draft (June 26, 1993). ... Bruised shoulder (April 2, 1995); missed two games. ... Traded by Lightning to Philadelphia Flyers for RW Mikael Renberg and D Karl Dykhuis (August 20, 1997). ... Traded by Flyers with C/RW Mike Sillinger to Lightning for RW Mikael Renberg and C Daymond Langkow (December 12, 1998). ... Suspended three games for spitting at referee (December 25, 1998). ... Bruised right foot (February 17, 2000); missed seven games. ... Traded by Lightning with second-round pick (C Derek Roy) in 2001 draft to Buffalo Sabres for C/RW Brian Holzinger, C Wayne Primeau, D Cory Sarich and third-round pick (RW Alexandre Kharitonov) in 2000 draft (March 9, 2000). ... Concussion (January 30, 2003); missed two games. ... Traded by Sabres with fourth-round pick (later traded to Edmonton Oilers; LW Liam Reddox) in 2004 draft to Phoenix Coyotes for C Daniel Briere and third-round pick (D Andrej Sekera) in 2004 entry draft (March 10, 2003). ... Traded by Coyotes with D Ossi Vaananen and second-round pick (C Paul Stastny) in 2005 draft to Colorado Avalanche for D Derek Morris and D Keith Ballard (March 9, 2004). ... Contract bought out by Avalanche (July 28, 2005). ... Signed as free agent by Florida Panthers (August 12, 2005). ... Groin (October 13, 2005); missed three games. ... Hip injury (November 3, 2005); missed two games. ... Broken foot (April 15, 2005); missed final game of regular season.

STATISTICAL PLATEAUS: Three-goal games: 1996-97 (1).

		REGULAR SEASON								PLAYOFFS				
Season Team	**League**	**GP**	**G**	**A**	**Pts.**	**PIM**	**+/-**	**PP**	**SH**	**GP**	**G**	**A**	**Pts.**	**PIM**
90-91—Brantford Jr. B	OHA	31	30	30	60	28	...	...	...	—	—	—	—	—
91-92—Kingston	OHL	62	27	39	66	35	...	...	...	—	—	—	—	—
92-93—Kingston	OHL	58	55	54	109	125	...	...	...	16	11	18	29	42
93-94—Tampa Bay	NHL	84	13	29	42	123	-25	5	1	—	—	—	—	—
94-95—Tampa Bay	NHL	46	7	20	27	89	-2	2	0	—	—	—	—	—
95-96—Tampa Bay	NHL	82	17	21	38	105	-13	7	0	6	0	2	2	27
96-97—Tampa Bay	NHL	82	30	32	62	201	-28	9	0	—	—	—	—	—
97-98—Philadelphia	NHL	82	22	40	62	159	11	5	0	5	2	0	2	10
98-99—Philadelphia	NHL	26	1	7	8	41	-8	0	0	—	—	—	—	—
—Tampa Bay	NHL	52	7	19	26	102	-20	1	0	—	—	—	—	—
99-00—Tampa Bay	NHL	58	14	27	41	121	-24	4	0	—	—	—	—	—
—Buffalo	NHL	14	1	7	8	15	1	0	0	5	0	1	1	4
00-01—Buffalo	NHL	82	19	21	40	102	0	5	0	13	6	4	10	14
01-02—Buffalo	NHL	82	15	24	39	75	0	1	0	—	—	—	—	—
02-03—Buffalo	NHL	66	15	29	44	86	-5	4	0	—	—	—	—	—
—Phoenix	NHL	14	0	1	1	21	-11	0	0	—	—	—	—	—
03-04—Phoenix	NHL	68	11	18	29	93	-19	3	0	—	—	—	—	—
—Colorado	NHL	13	2	1	3	18	1	0	0	11	0	0	0	27
05-06—Florida	NHL	76	17	22	39	104	6	4	1	—	—	—	—	—
NHL Totals (12 years)		927	191	318	509	1455	-136	50	2	40	8	7	15	82

GRATTON, JOSH LW

PERSONAL: Born September 9, 1982, in Scarborough, Ont. ... 6-2/210. ... Shoots left. ... Cousin of Chris Gratton, C with Florida Panthers.

TRANSACTIONS/CAREER NOTES: Signed as free agent by Philadelphia Flyers (July 27, 2004). ... Traded by Flyers with two second-round picks (pick 41 traded to Detroit; Red Wings selected C/LW Cory Emmerton; pick 47 traded to Detroit; Red Wings selected C Shawn Matthias) in 2006 draft to Phoenix Coyotes for D Denis Gauthier (March 9, 2006). ... Knee infection (March 10, 2006); missed three games.

		REGULAR SEASON								PLAYOFFS				
Season Team	**League**	**GP**	**G**	**A**	**Pts.**	**PIM**	**+/-**	**PP**	**SH**	**GP**	**G**	**A**	**Pts.**	**PIM**
00-01—Sudbury	OHL	44	5	13	18	110	...	...	...	9	1	1	2	25
01-02—Kingston	OHL	46	14	14	28	140	...	...	...	1	1	0	1	7
—Sudbury	OHL	14	5	4	9	47	...	...	...	—	—	—	—	—
02-03—Windsor	OHL	62	26	30	56	192	...	...	...	6	2	1	3	8
03-04—Cincinnati	AHL	21	2	2	4	69	...	...	...	8	0	0	0	35
—San Diego	ECHL	30	4	6	10	239	...	...	...	—	—	—	—	—
04-05—Trenton	ECHL	1	0	0	0	0	...	...	...	—	—	—	—	—
—Philadelphia	AHL	57	9	5	14	246	8	4	0	21	3	3	6	78
05-06—Philadelphia	NHL	3	0	0	0	14	0	0	0	—	—	—	—	—
—Philadelphia	AHL	53	9	10	19	265	-1	4	0	—	—	—	—	—
—Phoenix	NHL	11	1	0	1	30	-3	0	0	—	—	—	—	—
NHL Totals (1 year)		14	1	0	1	44	-3	0	0					

GREBESHKOV, DENIS D

PERSONAL: Born October 11, 1983, in Yaroslavl, U.S.S.R. ... 6-1/195. ... Shoots left. ... Name pronounced: gruh BEHSH kahv

TRANSACTIONS/CAREER NOTES: Selected by Los Angeles Kings in first round (first Kings pick, 18th overall) of NHL entry draft (June 22, 2002). ... Traded by Kings with LW Jeff Tambellini to New York Islanders for LW Mark Parrish and D Brent Sopel (March 8, 2006).

		REGULAR SEASON								PLAYOFFS				
Season Team	**League**	**GP**	**G**	**A**	**Pts.**	**PIM**	**+/-**	**PP**	**SH**	**GP**	**G**	**A**	**Pts.**	**PIM**
01-02—Lokomotiv Yaroslavl	Russian	27	1	2	3	10	...	...	...	—	—	—	—	—
02-03—Lokomotiv Yaroslavl	Russian	48	0	7	7	26	...	...	...	—	—	—	—	—
03-04—Los Angeles	NHL	4	0	1	1	0	-4	0	0	—	—	—	—	—
—Manchester	AHL	43	2	7	9	34	6	0	0	6	0	1	1	6
04-05—Manchester	AHL	75	5	44	49	87	21	3	0	6	0	4	4	2
05-06—Bridgeport	AHL	—	—	—	—	—	—	—	—	7	1	1	2	8
—Manchester	AHL	48	2	25	27	59	7	1	0	—	—	—	—	—
—Los Angeles	NHL	8	0	2	2	12	-4	0	0	—	—	—	—	—
—New York Islanders	NHL	21	0	3	3	8	-8	0	0	—	—	—	—	—
NHL Totals (2 years)		33	0	6	6	20	-16	0	0					

GREEN, JOSH LW

PERSONAL: Born November 16, 1977, in Camrose, Alta. ... 6-3/215. ... Shoots left.

TRANSACTIONS/CAREER NOTES: Selected by Los Angeles Kings in second round (first Kings pick, 30th overall) of entry draft (June 22,

1996). ... Strained shoulder (October 18, 1998); missed three games. ... Traded by Kings with C Olli Jokinen, D Mathieu Biron and first-round pick (LW Taylor Pyatt) in 1999 draft to New York Islanders for RW Zigmund Palffy, C Bryan Smolinski, G Marcel Cousineau and fourth-round pick (C Daniel Johansson) in 1999 draft (June 20, 1999). ... Injured shoulder (March 21, 2000); missed remainder of season. ... Traded by Islanders with D Eric Brewer and second-round pick (LW Brad Winchester) in 2000 draft to Edmonton Oilers for D Roman Hamrlik (June 24, 2000). ... Dislocated shoulder (September 11, 2000); missed 39 games. ... Reinjured shoulder (December 30, 2000); missed final 42 games of season. ... Bruised right hand (January 21, 2002); missed one game. ... Injured back (October 8, 2002); missed seven games. ... Traded by Oilers to New York Rangers for future considerations (December 12, 2002). ... Sprained wrist (December 19, 2002); missed seven games. ... Claimed off waivers by Washington Capitals (January 15, 2003). ... Signed as free agent by Calgary Flames (July 17, 2003). ... Claimed off waivers by Rangers (March 6, 2004). ... Signed as free agent by Vancouver Canucks (August 23, 2005). ... Surgery to repair tendon in finger on right hand (December 5, 2005); missed six weeks.

		REGULAR SEASON								PLAYOFFS				
Season Team	**League**	**GP**	**G**	**A**	**Pts.**	**PIM**	**+/-**	**PP**	**SH**	**GP**	**G**	**A**	**Pts.**	**PIM**
93-94—Medicine Hat	WHL	63	22	22	44	43	...	...	...	3	0	0	0	4
94-95—Medicine Hat	WHL	68	32	23	55	64	...	...	...	5	5	1	6	2
95-96—Medicine Hat	WHL	46	18	25	43	55	...	...	...	5	2	2	4	4
96-97—Medicine Hat	WHL	51	25	32	57	61	17	5	1	—	—	—	—	—
—Swift Current	WHL	23	10	15	25	33	9	1	1	10	9	7	16	19
97-98—Swift Current	WHL	5	9	1	10	9	...	...	...	—	—	—	—	—
—Portland	WHL	31	35	19	54	36	22	14	1	—	—	—	—	—
—Fredericton	AHL	43	16	15	31	14	7	8	0	4	1	3	4	6
98-99—Los Angeles	NHL	27	1	3	4	8	-5	1	0	—	—	—	—	—
—Springfield	AHL	41	15	15	30	29	1	7	0	—	—	—	—	—
99-00—Lowell	AHL	17	6	2	8	19	...	...	...	—	—	—	—	—
—New York Islanders	NHL	49	12	14	26	41	-7	2	0	—	—	—	—	—
00-01—Hamilton	AHL	2	2	0	2	2	...	...	...	—	—	—	—	—
—Edmonton	NHL	...	...	...	...	...	...	...	...	3	0	0	0	0
01-02—Edmonton	NHL	61	10	5	15	52	9	1	0	—	—	—	—	—
02-03—Edmonton	NHL	20	0	2	2	12	-3	0	0	—	—	—	—	—
—New York Rangers	NHL	4	0	0	0	2	-1	0	0	—	—	—	—	—
—Washington	NHL	21	1	2	3	7	1	0	0	—	—	—	—	—
03-04—Lowell	AHL	22	6	9	15	46	1	3	0	—	—	—	—	—
—Calgary	NHL	36	2	4	6	24	-3	0	0	—	—	—	—	—
—New York Rangers	NHL	14	3	2	5	8	0	0	0	—	—	—	—	—
04-05—Manitoba	AHL	67	21	19	40	72	6	5	0	14	9	5	14	26
05-06—Manitoba	AHL	35	7	24	31	33	0	3	0	10	5	5	10	23
—Vancouver	NHL	33	4	2	6	14	2	0	0	—	—	—	—	—
NHL Totals (7 years)		265	33	34	67	168	-7	4	0	3	0	0	0	0

GREEN, MIKE — D

PERSONAL: Born October 12, 1985, in Calgary. ... 6-1/198. ... Shoots right.
TRANSACTIONS/CAREER NOTES: Selected by Washington Capitals in first round (third Capitals pick, 29th overall) of NHL entry draft (June 26, 2004).

		REGULAR SEASON								PLAYOFFS				
Season Team	**League**	**GP**	**G**	**A**	**Pts.**	**PIM**	**+/-**	**PP**	**SH**	**GP**	**G**	**A**	**Pts.**	**PIM**
00-01—Saskatoon	WHL	7	0	2	2	0	...	...	...	—	—	—	—	—
01-02—Saskatoon	WHL	62	3	20	23	57	...	...	...	7	0	1	1	2
02-03—Saskatoon	WHL	72	6	36	42	70	...	...	...	6	0	2	2	6
03-04—Saskatoon	WHL	59	14	25	39	92	...	...	...	—	—	—	—	—
04-05—Saskatoon	WHL	67	14	52	66	105	36	6	2	4	0	0	0	6
05-06—Hershey	AHL	56	9	34	43	79	1	3	0	14	1	9	10	16
—Washington	NHL	22	1	2	3	18	-8	0	0	—	—	—	—	—
NHL Totals (1 year)		22	1	2	3	18	-8	0	0					

GREEN, TRAVIS — C/RW

PERSONAL: Born December 20, 1970, in Castlegar, B.C. ... 6-2/200. ... Shoots right.
TRANSACTIONS/CAREER NOTES: Selected by New York Islanders in second round (second Islanders pick, 23rd overall) of entry draft (June 17, 1989). ... Sore groin (November 30, 1995); missed four games. ... Sprained knee (February 8, 1996); missed nine games. ... Traded by Islanders with D Doug Houda and RW Tony Tuzzolino to Anaheim Mighty Ducks for D J.J. Daigneault, C Mark Janssens and RW Joe Sacco (February 6, 1998). ... Strained groin (February 7, 1998); missed five games. ... Sprained right knee (November 20, 1998); missed three games. ... Traded by Mighty Ducks with first-round pick (C Scott Kelman) in 1999 draft to Phoenix Coyotes for D Oleg Tverdovsky (June 26, 1999). ... Infected knee (November 25, 1999); missed three games. ... Concussion (March 21, 2000); missed one game. ... Strained knee (January 6, 2001); missed nine games. ... Bruised knee (March 4, 2001); missed three games. ... Traded by Coyotes with C Robert Reichel and RW Craig Mills to Toronto Maple Leafs for D Danny Markov (June 12, 2001). ... Bruised ribs (March 25, 2003); missed six games. ... Claimed by Columbus Blue Jackets in waiver draft (October 3, 2003). ... Traded by Blue Jackets to Boston Bruins for sixth-round pick (C/W Lennart Petrell) in 2004 draft (October 3, 2003). ... Injured ribs (January 13, 2004); missed eight games. ... Reinjured ribs (February 3, 2004); missed 10 games.
STATISTICAL PLATEAUS: Three-goal games: 1993-94 (1).

		REGULAR SEASON								PLAYOFFS				
Season Team	**League**	**GP**	**G**	**A**	**Pts.**	**PIM**	**+/-**	**PP**	**SH**	**GP**	**G**	**A**	**Pts.**	**PIM**
85-86—Castlegar	KIJHL	35	30	40	70	41	...	...	...	—	—	—	—	—
86-87—Spokane	WHL	64	8	17	25	27	...	...	...	3	0	0	0	0
87-88—Spokane	WHL	72	33	53	86	42	...	...	...	15	10	10	20	13
88-89—Spokane	WHL	72	51	51	102	79	...	...	...	—	—	—	—	—
89-90—Spokane	WHL	50	45	44	89	80	...	...	...	—	—	—	—	—
—Medicine Hat	WHL	25	15	24	39	19	...	...	...	3	0	0	0	2
90-91—Capital District	AHL	73	21	34	55	26	...	...	...	—	—	—	—	—
91-92—Capital District	AHL	71	23	27	50	10	...	...	...	7	0	4	4	21

G

Season Team	League	REGULAR SEASON GP	G	A	Pts.	PIM	+/-	PP	SH	PLAYOFFS GP	G	A	Pts.	PIM
92-93—Capital District	AHL	20	12	11	23	39	4	2	0	—	—	—	—	—
—New York Islanders	NHL	61	7	18	25	43	4	1	0	12	3	1	4	6
93-94—New York Islanders	NHL	83	18	22	40	44	16	1	0	4	0	0	0	2
94-95—New York Islanders	NHL	42	5	7	12	25	-10	0	0	—	—	—	—	—
95-96—New York Islanders	NHL	69	25	45	70	42	-20	14	1	—	—	—	—	—
96-97—New York Islanders	NHL	79	23	41	64	38	-5	10	0	—	—	—	—	—
97-98—New York Islanders	NHL	54	14	12	26	66	-19	8	0	—	—	—	—	—
—Anaheim	NHL	22	5	11	16	16	-10	1	0	—	—	—	—	—
98-99—Anaheim	NHL	79	13	17	30	81	-7	3	1	4	0	1	1	4
99-00—Phoenix	NHL	78	25	21	46	45	-4	6	0	5	2	1	3	2
00-01—Phoenix	NHL	69	13	15	28	63	-11	3	0	—	—	—	—	—
01-02—Toronto	NHL	82	11	23	34	61	13	3	0	20	3	6	9	34
02-03—Toronto	NHL	75	12	12	24	67	2	2	1	4	2	1	3	4
03-04—Boston	NHL	64	11	5	16	67	-6	2	0	7	0	1	1	8
05-06—Boston	NHL	82	10	12	22	79	-2	0	2	—	—	—	—	—
NHL Totals (13 years)		939	192	261	453	737	-59	54	5	56	10	11	21	60

GREENE, MATT — D

PERSONAL: Born May 13, 1983, in Grand Ledge. Mich. ... 6-2/210. ... Shoots right.
COLLEGE: North Dakota.
TRANSACTIONS/CAREER NOTES: Selected by Edmonton Oilers in second round (fourth Oilers pick, 44th overall) of entry draft (June 22, 2002). ... Bruised leg (February 25, 2006); missed six games.

Season Team	League	REGULAR SEASON GP	G	A	Pts.	PIM	+/-	PP	SH	PLAYOFFS GP	G	A	Pts.	PIM
00-01—U.S. National	USHL	54	0	10	10	109	...	...	...	—	—	—	—	—
01-02—Green Bay	USHL	47	3	16	19	134	...	...	...	—	—	—	—	—
02-03—Univ. of North Dakota	WCHA	39	0	4	4	135	...	...	...	—	—	—	—	—
03-04—Univ. of North Dakota	WCHA	40	1	16	17	86	33	0	0	—	—	—	—	—
04-05—Univ. of North Dakota	WCHA	43	2	8	10	126	...	...	...	—	—	—	—	—
05-06—Iowa	AHL	26	2	5	7	47	5	1	1	—	—	—	—	—
—Edmonton	NHL	27	0	2	2	43	-6	0	0	18	0	1	1	34
NHL Totals (1 year)		27	0	2	2	43	-6	0	0	18	0	1	1	34

GRIER, MIKE — RW

PERSONAL: Born January 5, 1975, in Detroit. ... 6-1/227. ... Shoots right.
TRANSACTIONS/CAREER NOTES: Selected by St. Louis Blues in ninth round (seventh Blues pick, 219th overall) of entry draft (June 26, 1993). ... Rights traded by Blues with rights to G Curtis Joseph to Edmonton Oilers for first-round picks in 1996 (C Marty Reasoner) and 1997 (traded to Los Angeles; Kings selected Matt Zultek) drafts (August 4, 1995). ... Strained left knee (November 19, 1997); missed 14 games. ... Fractured clavicle (November 24, 1999); missed four games. ... Torn triceps (March 13, 2000) and had surgery; missed remainder of season. ... Dislocated right shoulder (December 3, 2000); missed eight games. ... Traded by Oilers to Washington Capitals for second- (traded to New York Islanders; Islanders selected Evgeni Tunik) and third-round (RW Zachary Stortini) picks in 2003 draft (October 7, 2002). ... Suspended one game for elbowing incident (October 14, 2003). ... Traded by Capitals to Buffalo Sabres for C Jakub Klepis (March 9, 2004). ... Injured hip flexor (November 3, 2005); missed one game. ... Signed as free agent by San Jose Sharks (July 3, 2006).
STATISTICAL PLATEAUS: Three-goal games: 1998-99 (1).

Season Team	League	REGULAR SEASON GP	G	A	Pts.	PIM	+/-	PP	SH	PLAYOFFS GP	G	A	Pts.	PIM
92-93—St. Sebastian's	USHS (East)	22	16	27	43	32	...	...	...	—	—	—	—	—
93-94—Boston University	Hockey East	39	9	9	18	56	...	...	...	—	—	—	—	—
94-95—Boston University	Hockey East	37	29	26	55	85	24	13	3	—	—	—	—	—
95-96—Boston University	Hockey East	38	21	25	46	82	...	...	...	—	—	—	—	—
96-97—Edmonton	NHL	79	15	17	32	45	7	4	0	12	3	1	4	4
97-98—Edmonton	NHL	66	9	6	15	73	-3	1	0	12	2	2	4	13
98-99—Edmonton	NHL	82	20	24	44	54	5	3	2	4	1	1	2	6
99-00—Edmonton	NHL	65	9	22	31	68	9	0	3	—	—	—	—	—
00-01—Edmonton	NHL	74	20	16	36	20	11	2	3	6	0	0	0	8
01-02—Edmonton	NHL	82	8	17	25	32	1	0	2	—	—	—	—	—
02-03—Washington	NHL	82	15	17	32	36	-14	2	2	6	1	1	2	2
03-04—Washington	NHL	68	8	12	20	32	-19	1	1	—	—	—	—	—
—Buffalo	NHL	14	1	8	9	4	10	0	0	—	—	—	—	—
05-06—Buffalo	NHL	81	7	16	23	28	-7	0	0	18	3	5	8	2
NHL Totals (9 years)		693	112	155	267	392	0	13	13	58	10	10	20	35

GUERIN, BILL — RW

PERSONAL: Born November 9, 1970, in Worcester, Mass. ... 6-2/210. ... Shoots right. ... Name pronounced GAIR-ihn.
TRANSACTIONS/CAREER NOTES: Selected by New Jersey Devils in first round (first Devils pick, fifth overall) of entry draft (June 17, 1989). ... Flu (February 1992); missed three games. ... Leg (March 19, 1994); missed two games. ... Flu (December 6, 1995); missed two games. ... Missed 1997-98 season's first 21 games in contract dispute. ... Traded by Devils with RW Valeri Zelepukin to Edmonton Oilers for C Jason Arnott and D Bryan Muir (January 4, 1998). ... Sprained left knee (April 12, 1999); missed regular seasonÔøΩs final two games and one playoff game. ... Flu (December 9, 1999); missed one game. ... Traded by Oilers to Boston Bruins for C Anson Carter, second-round pick (D Doug Lynch) in 2001 and swap of first-round picks in 2001 (Oilers selected RW Ales Hemsky; Bruins selected D Shaone Morrisonn) (November 15, 2000). ... Suspended three games for high-sticking incident (October 8, 2001). ... Charley horse (December 13, 2001); missed one game. ... Signed as free agent by Dallas Stars (July 3, 2002). ... Bruised thigh (February 28, 2003); missed 16 games. ... Back spasms (October 29,

2005); missed one game. ... Face/eye (March 14, 2006); missed 11 games. ... Waived by Stars (June 29, 2006). ... Signed by St. Louis Blues (July 5, 2006).

STATISTICAL PLATEAUS: Three-goal games: 1996-97 (1), 2003-04 (3). Total: 4.

		REGULAR SEASON								PLAYOFFS				
Season Team	**League**	**GP**	**G**	**A**	**Pts.**	**PIM**	**+/-**	**PP**	**SH**	**GP**	**G**	**A**	**Pts.**	**PIM**
85-86—Springfield Jr. B	NEJHL	48	26	19	45	71	...	...	...	—	—	—	—	—
86-87—Springfield Jr. B	NEJHL	32	34	20	54	40	...	...	...	—	—	—	—	—
87-88—Springfield Jr. B	NEJHL	38	31	44	75	146	...	...	...	—	—	—	—	—
88-89—Springfield Jr. B	NEJHL	31	32	37	69	90	...	...	...	—	—	—	—	—
89-90—Boston College	Hockey East	39	14	11	25	64	...	...	...	—	—	—	—	—
90-91—Boston College	Hockey East	38	26	19	45	102	...	...	...	—	—	—	—	—
91-92—U.S. national team	Int'l	46	12	15	27	67	...	...	...	—	—	—	—	—
—Utica	AHL	22	13	10	23	6	...	...	...	4	1	3	4	14
—New Jersey	NHL	5	0	1	1	9	1	0	0	6	3	0	3	4
92-93—New Jersey	NHL	65	14	20	34	63	14	0	0	5	1	1	2	4
—Utica	AHL	18	10	7	17	47	-4	0	0	—	—	—	—	—
93-94—New Jersey	NHL	81	25	19	44	101	14	2	0	17	2	1	3	35
94-95—New Jersey	NHL	48	12	13	25	72	6	4	0	20	3	8	11	30
95-96—New Jersey	NHL	80	23	30	53	116	7	8	0	—	—	—	—	—
96-97—New Jersey	NHL	82	29	18	47	95	-2	7	0	8	2	1	3	18
97-98—New Jersey	NHL	19	5	5	10	13	0	1	0	—	—	—	—	—
—Edmonton	NHL	40	13	16	29	80	1	8	0	12	7	1	8	17
—U.S. Olympic team	Int'l	4	0	3	3	2	2	0	0	—	—	—	—	—
98-99—Edmonton	NHL	80	30	34	64	133	7	13	0	3	0	2	2	2
99-00—Edmonton	NHL	70	24	22	46	123	4	11	0	5	3	2	5	9
00-01—Edmonton	NHL	21	12	10	22	18	11	4	0	—	—	—	—	—
—Boston	NHL	64	28	35	63	122	-4	7	1	—	—	—	—	—
01-02—Boston	NHL	78	41	25	66	91	-1	10	1	6	4	2	6	6
—U.S. Olympic team	Int'l	6	4	0	4	4	...	...	...	—	—	—	—	—
02-03—Dallas	NHL	64	25	25	50	113	5	11	0	4	0	0	0	4
03-04—Dallas	NHL	82	34	35	69	109	14	9	0	5	0	1	1	4
05-06—Dallas	NHL	70	13	27	40	115	0	3	0	5	3	1	4	0
—U.S. Olympic team	Int'l	6	1	0	1	0	0	0	0	—	—	—	—	—
NHL Totals (14 years)		949	328	335	663	1373	77	98	2	96	28	20	48	133

GUITE, BEN RW

PERSONAL: Born July 17, 1978, in Montreal. ... 6-1/205. ... Shoots right. ... Name pronounced: GEE tay

COLLEGE: Maine.

TRANSACTIONS/CAREER NOTES: Selected by Montreal Canadiens in seventh round (eighth Canadiens pick, 172nd overall) of NHL entry draft (June 21, 1997). ... Signed as free agent by New York Islanders (August 1, 2001). ... Traded by Islanders with D Bjorn Melin to Anaheim Mighty Ducks for LW Dave Roche (March 19, 2002). ... Signed as free agent by Bridgeport of the AHL (December 11, 2003). ... Signed as free agent by Boston Bruins (August 15, 2005). ... Signed as free agent by Colorado Avalanche (July 12, 2006).

		REGULAR SEASON								PLAYOFFS				
Season Team	**League**	**GP**	**G**	**A**	**Pts.**	**PIM**	**+/-**	**PP**	**SH**	**GP**	**G**	**A**	**Pts.**	**PIM**
96-97—Maine	Hockey East	34	7	7	14	21	...	...	...	—	—	—	—	—
97-98—Maine	Hockey East	32	6	12	18	20	...	...	...	—	—	—	—	—
98-99—Maine	Hockey East	40	12	16	28	30	...	...	...	—	—	—	—	—
99-00—Maine	Hockey East	40	22	14	36	36	...	...	...	—	—	—	—	—
00-01—Tallahassee	ECHL	68	11	18	29	34	...	...	...	—	—	—	—	—
01-02—Bridgeport	AHL	68	12	18	30	39	15	0	1	—	—	—	—	—
—Cincinnati	AHL	10	2	5	7	4	2	1	0	3	0	0	0	2
02-03—Cincinnati	AHL	80	13	16	29	44	-9	2	2	—	—	—	—	—
03-04—Bridgeport	AHL	79	6	18	24	73	...	...	...	7	0	0	0	6
04-05—Providence	AHL	77	9	15	24	69	-4	0	0	17	3	4	7	34
05-06—Providence	AHL	73	22	31	53	87	2	10	2	6	1	3	4	14
—Boston	NHL	1	0	0	0	0	0	0	0	—	—	—	—	—
NHL Totals (1 year)		1	0	0	0	0	0	0	0					

HAGMAN, NIKLAS LW/RW

PERSONAL: Born December 5, 1979, in Espoo, Finland. ... 6-0/205. ... Shoots left.

TRANSACTIONS/CAREER NOTES: Selected by Florida Panthers in third round (third Panthers pick, 70th overall) of entry draft (June 26, 1999). ... Traded by Panthers to Dallas Stars for seventh-round pick (December 13, 2005).

		REGULAR SEASON								PLAYOFFS				
Season Team	**League**	**GP**	**G**	**A**	**Pts.**	**PIM**	**+/-**	**PP**	**SH**	**GP**	**G**	**A**	**Pts.**	**PIM**
96-97—HIFK Helsinki	Finland Jr.	30	13	12	25	30	...	...	...	4	1	1	2	0
97-98—HIFK Helsinki	Finland	8	1	0	1	0	...	...	...	—	—	—	—	—
—HIFK Helsinki	Finland Jr.	26	9	5	14	16	...	...	...	—	—	—	—	—
98-99—HIFK Helsinki	Finland	17	1	1	2	14	...	...	...	—	—	—	—	—
—HIFK Helsinki	Finland Jr.	14	4	9	13	43	...	...	...	—	—	—	—	—
99-00—Espoo	Finland	14	1	1	2	2	...	...	...	—	—	—	—	—
—Karpat Oulu	Finland	41	17	18	35	12	...	...	...	7	4	2	6	...
00-01—Karpat Oulu	Finland	56	28	18	46	32	...	...	...	8	3	1	4	0
01-02—Florida	NHL	78	10	18	28	8	-6	0	1	—	—	—	—	—
—Fin. Olympic team	Int'l	4	1	2	3	0	...	...	...	—	—	—	—	—
02-03—Florida	NHL	80	8	15	23	20	-8	2	0	—	—	—	—	—
03-04—Florida	NHL	75	10	13	23	22	-5	0	1	—	—	—	—	—

H

Season Team	League	REGULAR SEASON GP	G	A	Pts.	PIM	+/-	PP	SH	PLAYOFFS GP	G	A	Pts.	PIM
04-05—Davos	Switzerland	44	17	22	39	20	...	2	3	15	10	7	17	6
05-06—Florida	NHL	30	2	4	6	2	-8	0	0	—	—	—	—	—
—Dallas	NHL	54	6	9	15	16	-2	0	1	5	2	1	3	4
—Fin. Olympic team	Int'l	7	0	1	1	2	1	0	0	—	—	—	—	—
NHL Totals (4 years)		317	36	59	95	68	-29	2	3	5	2	1	3	4

HAINSEY, RON — D

PERSONAL: Born March 24, 1981, in Bolton, Conn. ... 6-3/211. ... Shoots left.

TRANSACTIONS/CAREER NOTES: Selected by Montreal Canadiens in first round (first Canadiens pick, 13th overall) of entry draft (June 24, 2000). ... Claimed off waivers by Columbus Blue Jackets (November 29, 2005). ... Knee (March 2, 2006); missed three games.

Season Team	League	REGULAR SEASON GP	G	A	Pts.	PIM	+/-	PP	SH	PLAYOFFS GP	G	A	Pts.	PIM
98-99—U.S. National	USHL	48	5	12	17	45	...	...	...	—	—	—	—	—
99-00—Mass.-Lowell	Hockey East	30	3	8	11	20	...	...	...	—	—	—	—	—
00-01—Mass.-Lowell	Hockey East	33	10	26	36	51	...	...	...	—	—	—	—	—
—Quebec	AHL	4	1	0	1	0	...	...	...	1	0	0	0	0
01-02—Quebec	AHL	63	7	24	31	26	16	4	0	3	0	0	0	0
02-03—Montreal	NHL	21	0	0	0	2	-1	0	0	—	—	—	—	—
—Hamilton	AHL	33	2	11	13	26	-2	1	0	23	1	10	11	20
03-04—Hamilton	AHL	54	7	24	31	35	14	3	0	10	0	5	5	6
—Montreal	NHL	11	1	1	2	4	3	0	0	—	—	—	—	—
04-05—Hamilton	AHL	68	9	14	23	45	-3	8	0	4	1	1	2	0
05-06—Hamilton	AHL	22	3	14	17	19	-10	2	1	—	—	—	—	—
—Columbus	NHL	55	2	15	17	43	13	1	0	—	—	—	—	—
NHL Totals (3 years)		87	3	16	19	49	15	1	0					

HALE, DAVID — D

PERSONAL: Born June 18, 1981, in Colorado Springs, Colo. ... 6-1/215. ... Shoots left.

COLLEGE: North Dakota.

TRANSACTIONS/CAREER NOTES: Selected by New Jersey Devils in first round (first Devils pick, 22nd overall) of NHL entry draft (June 24, 2000). ... Injured groin (October 24, 2003); missed four games. ... Flu (December 18, 2003); missed three games. ... Sprained knee (February 5, 2004); missed five games. ... Re-signed by Devils as restricted free agent (September 29, 2005).

Season Team	League	REGULAR SEASON GP	G	A	Pts.	PIM	+/-	PP	SH	PLAYOFFS GP	G	A	Pts.	PIM
98-99—Sioux City	USHL	56	3	15	18	127	...	...	...	—	—	—	—	—
99-00—Sioux City	USHL	54	6	18	24	187	...	...	...	—	—	—	—	—
00-01—Univ. of North Dakota	WCHA	44	4	5	9	79	...	...	...	—	—	—	—	—
01-02—Univ. of North Dakota	WCHA	34	4	5	9	63	...	...	...	—	—	—	—	—
02-03—Univ. of North Dakota	WCHA	26	2	6	8	49	...	...	...	—	—	—	—	—
03-04—New Jersey	NHL	65	0	4	4	72	12	0	0	1	0	0	0	0
04-05—Albany	AHL	30	2	3	5	39	-3	0	0	—	—	—	—	—
05-06—Albany	AHL	30	2	5	7	64	-1	0	0	—	—	—	—	—
—New Jersey	NHL	38	0	4	4	21	5	0	0	8	0	2	2	12
NHL Totals (2 years)		103	0	8	8	93	17	0	0	9	0	2	2	12

HALL, ADAM — RW

PERSONAL: Born August 14, 1980, in Kalamazoo, Mich. ... 6-3/205. ... Shoots right.

TRANSACTIONS/CAREER NOTES: Selected by Nashville Predators in second round (third Predators pick, 52nd overall) of entry draft (June 26, 1999). ... Had the flu (February 13, 2004); missed three games. ... Injured ankle (October 29, 2005); missed one game. ... Injured ankle (November 2, 2005); missed four games. ... Traded by Predators to New York Rangers for C Dominic Moore (July 19, 2006).

Season Team	League	REGULAR SEASON GP	G	A	Pts.	PIM	+/-	PP	SH	PLAYOFFS GP	G	A	Pts.	PIM
97-98—U.S. National	NAHL	72	43	23	66	63	...	12	0	—	—	—	—	—
98-99—Michigan State	CCHA	36	16	7	23	74	...	...	...	—	—	—	—	—
99-00—Michigan State	CCHA	39	25	13	38	36	...	...	...	—	—	—	—	—
00-01—Michigan State	CCHA	42	18	12	30	42	...	...	...	—	—	—	—	—
01-02—Michigan State	CCHA	41	19	15	34	36	...	...	...	—	—	—	—	—
—Milwaukee	AHL	6	2	2	4	4	4	0	0	—	—	—	—	—
—Nashville	NHL	1	0	1	1	0	0	0	0	—	—	—	—	—
02-03—Milwaukee	AHL	1	0	0	0	2	0	0	0	—	—	—	—	—
—Nashville	NHL	79	16	12	28	31	-8	8	0	—	—	—	—	—
03-04—Nashville	NHL	79	13	14	27	37	-8	6	0	6	2	1	3	2
04-05—KalPa Kuopio	Finland	36	23	17	40	28	22	...	...	9	2	3	5	4
05-06—Nashville	NHL	75	14	15	29	40	0	10	0	5	1	0	1	0
NHL Totals (4 years)		234	43	42	85	108	-16	24	0	11	3	1	4	2

HALPERN, JEFF — C/RW

PERSONAL: Born May 3, 1976, in Potomac, Md. ... 6-0/198. ... Shoots right.

TRANSACTIONS/CAREER NOTES: Signed as free agent by Washington Capitals (March 29, 1999). ... Had back spasms (February 19, 2000); missed three games. ... Strained groin (January 8, 2001); missed two games. ... Torn left knee ligament (January 18, 2002); missed remainder of season. ... Personal absence (October 12, 2005); missed one game. ... Knee (January 1, 2006); missed four games. ... Knee (January 16, 2006); missed three games. ... Back (February 3, 2006); missed four games. ... Signed as free agent by Dallas Stars (July 5, 2006).

		REGULAR SEASON								PLAYOFFS				
Season Team	League	GP	G	A	Pts.	PIM	+/-	PP	SH	GP	G	A	Pts.	PIM
95-96—Princeton	ECAC	29	3	11	14	30	...	...	...	—	—	—	—	—
96-97—Princeton	ECAC	33	7	24	31	35	...	...	...	—	—	—	—	—
97-98—Princeton	ECAC	36	28	25	53	46	...	...	...	—	—	—	—	—
98-99—Princeton	ECAC	33	22	22	44	32	...	...	...	—	—	—	—	—
—Portland	AHL	6	2	1	3	4	-1	1	0	—	—	—	—	—
99-00—Washington	NHL	79	18	11	29	39	21	4	4	5	2	1	3	0
00-01—Washington	NHL	80	21	21	42	60	13	2	1	6	2	3	5	17
01-02—Washington	NHL	48	5	14	19	29	-9	0	0	—	—	—	—	—
02-03—Washington	NHL	82	13	21	34	88	6	1	2	6	0	1	1	2
03-04—Washington	NHL	79	19	27	46	56	-21	7	0	—	—	—	—	—
04-05—Kloten	Switzerland	9	7	4	11	6	...	4	0	—	—	—	—	—
—Ajoie	Switz. Div. 2	15	5	12	17	54	...	0	1	—	—	—	—	—
05-06—Washington	NHL	70	11	33	44	79	-8	6	0	—	—	—	—	—
NHL Totals (6 years)		438	87	127	214	351	2	20	7	17	4	5	9	19

HAMEL, DENIS — LW/C

PERSONAL: Born May 10, 1977, in Lachute, Que. ... 6-2/203. ... Shoots left. ... Name pronounced uh-MEHL.
TRANSACTIONS/CAREER NOTES: Selected by St. Louis Blues in sixth round (fifth Blues pick, 153rd overall) of NHL entry draft (July 8, 1995). ... Traded by Blues to Buffalo Sabres for D Charlie Huddy and seventh-round pick (C Daniel Corso) in 1996 draft (March 19, 1996). ... Tore knee ligament (January 27, 2001); missed remainder of season. ... Claimed by Washington Capitals in waiver draft (October 3, 2003). ... Traded by Capitals to Senators for future considerations (October 5, 2003).

		REGULAR SEASON								PLAYOFFS				
Season Team	League	GP	G	A	Pts.	PIM	+/-	PP	SH	GP	G	A	Pts.	PIM
94-95—Chicoutimi	QMJHL	66	15	12	27	155	-3	4	0	13	2	0	2	29
95-96—Chicoutimi	QMJHL	65	40	49	89	199	...	...	...	17	10	14	24	64
96-97—Chicoutimi	QMJHL	70	50	50	100	339	...	...	...	20	15	10	25	65
97-98—Rochester	AHL	74	10	15	25	98	-1	4	1	4	1	2	3	0
98-99—Rochester	AHL	74	16	17	33	121	20	2	1	20	3	4	7	10
99-00—Rochester	AHL	76	34	24	58	122	...	...	...	21	6	7	13	49
—Buffalo	NHL	3	1	0	1	0	-1	0	0	—	—	—	—	—
00-01—Buffalo	NHL	41	8	3	11	22	-2	1	1	—	—	—	—	—
01-02—Buffalo	NHL	61	2	6	8	28	-1	0	0	—	—	—	—	—
02-03—Buffalo	NHL	25	2	0	2	17	-4	0	0	—	—	—	—	—
—Rochester	AHL	48	27	20	47	64	15	7	4	3	3	2	5	4
03-04—Binghamton	AHL	78	29	38	67	116	2	5	4	2	0	0	0	2
—Ottawa	NHL	5	0	0	0	0	-3	0	0	—	—	—	—	—
04-05—Binghamton	AHL	80	39	39	78	75	10	17	2	5	1	0	1	4
05-06—Binghamton	AHL	77	56	35	91	65	-5	27	2	—	—	—	—	—
—Ottawa	NHL	4	1	0	1	0	1	0	0	—	—	—	—	—
NHL Totals (6 years)		139	14	9	23	67	-10	1	1					

HAMHUIS, DAN — D

PERSONAL: Born December 13, 1982, in Smithers, B.C. ... 6-0/205. ... Shoots left. ... Name pronounced HAM-hoos.
TRANSACTIONS/CAREER NOTES: Selected by Nashville Predators in first round (first Predators pick, 12th overall) of entry draft (June 23, 2001).

		REGULAR SEASON								PLAYOFFS				
Season Team	League	GP	G	A	Pts.	PIM	+/-	PP	SH	GP	G	A	Pts.	PIM
98-99—Prince George	WHL	56	1	3	4	45	...	...	...	7	1	2	3	8
99-00—Prince George	WHL	70	10	23	33	140	...	...	...	13	2	3	5	35
00-01—Prince George	WHL	62	13	46	59	125	...	...	...	6	2	3	5	15
01-02—Prince George	WHL	72	10	50	60	135	...	...	...	7	0	5	5	16
02-03—Milwaukee	AHL	68	6	21	27	81	-3	2	0	6	0	3	3	2
03-04—Nashville	NHL	80	7	19	26	57	-12	2	0	6	0	2	2	6
04-05—Milwaukee	AHL	76	13	38	51	85	10	8	0	7	0	2	2	10
05-06—Nashville	NHL	82	7	31	38	70	11	4	1	5	0	2	2	2
NHL Totals (2 years)		162	14	50	64	127	-1	6	1	11	0	4	4	8

HAMILTON, JEFF — C

PERSONAL: Born September 4, 1977, in Englewood, Ohio. ... 5-10/185. ... Shoots right.
TRANSACTIONS/CAREER NOTES: Signed as free agent by New York Islanders (August 6, 2002).

		REGULAR SEASON								PLAYOFFS				
Season Team	League	GP	G	A	Pts.	PIM	+/-	PP	SH	GP	G	A	Pts.	PIM
96-97—Yale	ECAC	31	10	13	23	26	...	...	...	—	—	—	—	—
97-98—Yale	ECAC	33	27	20	47	28	...	...	...	—	—	—	—	—
98-99—Yale	ECAC	30	20	28	48	51	...	...	...	—	—	—	—	—
99-00—Yale	ECAC	2	0	1	1	0	...	...	...	—	—	—	—	—
00-01—Yale	ECAC	31	23	32	55	39	...	...	...	—	—	—	—	—
01-02—Karpat Oulu	Finland	39	18	15	33	16	...	...	...	3	0	0	0	0
02-03—Bridgeport	AHL	67	22	16	38	35	8	7	0	9	3	3	6	0
03-04—Bridgeport	AHL	67	43	25	68	26	16	20	0	7	4	0	4	4
—New York Islanders	NHL	1	0	0	0	0	0	0	0	—	—	—	—	—

Season Team	League	REGULAR SEASON GP	G	A	Pts.	PIM	+/-	PP	SH	PLAYOFFS GP	G	A	Pts.	PIM
04-05—Hartford	AHL	60	23	30	53	32	15	6	0	6	4	3	7	0
05-06—Bridgeport	AHL	39	24	25	49	28	-8	15	0	—	—	—	—	—
—New York Islanders	NHL	13	2	6	8	8	0	1	0	—	—	—	—	—
NHL Totals (2 years)		14	2	6	8	8	0	1	0					

HAMRLIK, ROMAN D

PERSONAL: Born April 12, 1974, in Ziln, Czech. ... 6-2/210. ... Shoots left. ... Brother of Martin Hamrlik, defenseman with Hartford Whalers (1991-92 through 1993-94) and St. Louis Blues (1993-94 and 1994-95) organizations. ... Name pronounced ROH-muhn HAM-uhr-lihk.

TRANSACTIONS/CAREER NOTES: Selected by Tampa Bay Lightning in first round (first Lightning pick, first overall) of entry draft (June 20, 1992). ... Bruised shoulder (November 3, 1993); missed six games. ... Bruised shoulder (March 1, 1994); missed seven games. ... Back spasms (January 9, 1997); missed two games. ... Traded by Lightning with C Paul Comrie to Edmonton Oilers for C Steve Kelly, D Bryan Marchment and C Jason Bonsignore (December 30, 1997). ... Fractured toe (January 5, 1999); missed six games. ... Bruised finger (December 1, 1999); missed two games. ... Traded by Oilers to New York Islanders for D Eric Brewer, LW Josh Green and second-round pick (LW Brad Winchester) in 2000 draft (June 24, 2000). ... Strained groin (December 21, 2000); missed five games. ... Strained hip flexor (January 31, 2001); missed one game. ... Sprained knee (November 27, 2001); missed one game. ... Right knee (December 29, 2001); missed 11 games. ... Shoulder (December 13, 2002); missed six games. ... Hip (March 6, 2003); missed two games. ... Sinuses (April 6, 2003); missed one game. ... Flu (December 23, 2003); missed one game. ... Signed as free agent by Calgary Flames (August 14, 2005). ... Sprained right knee (December 7, 2005); missed 12 games. ... Right knee (January 12, 2006); missed six games. ... Broken left hand (January 29, 2006); missed 13 games.

Season Team	League	REGULAR SEASON GP	G	A	Pts.	PIM	+/-	PP	SH	PLAYOFFS GP	G	A	Pts.	PIM
90-91—TJ Zlin	Czech.	14	2	2	4	18	...	...	...	—	—	—	—	—
91-92—ZPS Zlin	Czech.	34	5	5	10	34	...	...	...	—	—	—	—	—
92-93—Tampa Bay	NHL	67	6	15	21	71	-21	1	0	—	—	—	—	—
—Atlanta	IHL	2	1	1	2	2	2	0	0	—	—	—	—	—
93-94—Tampa Bay	NHL	64	3	18	21	135	-14	0	0	—	—	—	—	—
94-95—ZPS Zlin	Czech Rep.	2	1	0	1	10	...	...	...	—	—	—	—	—
—Tampa Bay	NHL	48	12	11	23	86	-18	7	1	—	—	—	—	—
95-96—Tampa Bay	NHL	82	16	49	65	103	-24	12	0	5	0	1	1	4
96-97—Tampa Bay	NHL	79	12	28	40	57	-29	6	0	—	—	—	—	—
97-98—Tampa Bay	NHL	37	3	12	15	22	-18	1	0	—	—	—	—	—
—Edmonton	NHL	41	6	20	26	48	3	4	1	12	0	6	6	12
—Czech Rep. Oly. team	Int'l	6	1	0	1	2	4	0	0	—	—	—	—	—
98-99—Edmonton	NHL	75	8	24	32	70	9	3	0	3	0	0	0	2
99-00—Edmonton	NHL	80	8	37	45	68	1	5	0	5	0	1	1	4
00-01—New York Islanders	NHL	76	16	30	46	92	-20	5	1	—	—	—	—	—
01-02—New York Islanders	NHL	70	11	26	37	78	7	4	1	7	1	6	7	6
—Czech Rep. Oly. team	Int'l	4	0	1	1	2	...	...	...	—	—	—	—	—
02-03—New York Islanders	NHL	73	9	32	41	87	21	3	0	5	0	2	2	2
03-04—New York Islanders	NHL	81	7	22	29	68	2	2	0	5	0	1	1	2
04-05—Zlin	Czech Rep.	45	2	14	16	70	16	...	...	17	1	3	4	24
05-06—Calgary	NHL	51	7	19	26	56	8	1	1	7	0	2	2	2
NHL Totals (12 years)		924	124	343	467	1041	-93	54	5	49	1	19	20	34

HANDZUS, MICHAL C/LW

PERSONAL: Born March 11, 1977, in Banska Bystrica, Czechoslovakia. ... 6-5/215. ... Shoots left. ... Name pronounced han-ZOOZ.

TRANSACTIONS/CAREER NOTES: Selected by St. Louis Blues in fourth round (third Blues pick, 101st overall) of NHL draft (July 8, 1995). ... Bruised shoulder (February 26, 1999); missed five games. ... Bruised shoulder (March 25, 1999); missed final 11 games of regular season and two playoffs games. ... Injured groin (October 1, 2000); missed first five games of season. ... Strained abdominal muscle (January 11, 2001) and had surgery; missed 33 games. ... Traded by Blues with RW Ladislav Nagy, C Jeff Taffe and first-round pick (LW Ben Eager) in 2002 draft to Phoenix Coyotes for LW Keith Tkachuk (March 13, 2001). ... Strained groin (January 17, 2002); missed three games. ... Traded by Coyotes with G Robert Esche to Philadelphia Flyers for G Brian Boucher and third-round pick (D Joe Callahan) in 2002 draft (June 12, 2002). ... Torn left labrum (February 11, 2006); missed eight games. ... Fatigue (March 18, 2006); missed one game.

STATISTICAL PLATEAUS: Three-goal games: 2000-01 (1).

Season Team	League	REGULAR SEASON GP	G	A	Pts.	PIM	+/-	PP	SH	PLAYOFFS GP	G	A	Pts.	PIM
93-94—IS Banska Byst.	Slovakia Jrs.	40	23	36	59	...	...	...	...	—	—	—	—	—
94-95—IS Banska Bystrica	Slov. Div.	22	15	14	29	10	...	...	...	—	—	—	—	—
95-96—IS Banska Bystrica	Slov. Div.	19	3	1	4	8	...	...	...	—	—	—	—	—
96-97—Poprad	Slovakia	44	15	18	33	...	...	...	...	—	—	—	—	—
97-98—Worcester	AHL	69	27	36	63	54	-8	6	1	11	2	6	8	10
98-99—St. Louis	NHL	66	4	12	16	30	-9	0	0	11	0	2	2	8
99-00—St. Louis	NHL	81	25	28	53	44	19	3	4	7	0	3	3	6
00-01—St. Louis	NHL	36	10	14	24	12	11	3	2	—	—	—	—	—
—Phoenix	NHL	10	4	4	8	21	5	0	1	—	—	—	—	—
01-02—Phoenix	NHL	79	15	30	45	34	-8	3	1	5	0	0	0	2
—Slovakian Oly. team	Int'l	2	1	0	1	6	...	...	...	—	—	—	—	—
02-03—Philadelphia	NHL	82	23	21	44	46	13	1	1	13	2	6	8	6
03-04—Philadelphia	NHL	82	20	38	58	82	18	7	1	18	5	5	10	10
04-05—Zvolen	Slovakia	34	14	25	39	34	33	...	...	17	5	10	15	6
05-06—Philadelphia	NHL	73	11	33	44	38	-2	2	1	6	0	2	2	2
NHL Totals (7 years)		509	112	180	292	307	47	19	11	60	7	18	25	34

HANNAN, SCOTT D

PERSONAL: Born January 23, 1979, in Richmond, B.C. ... 6-1/220. ... Shoots left.
TRANSACTIONS/CAREER NOTES: Selected by San Jose Sharks in first round (second Sharks pick, 23rd overall) of NHL entry draft (June 21, 1997). ... Injured ankle (October 24, 2000); missed three games. ... Injured knee (March 3, 2002); missed six games. ... Had the flu (February 14, 2003); missed two games.

		REGULAR SEASON								PLAYOFFS				
Season Team	**League**	**GP**	**G**	**A**	**Pts.**	**PIM**	**+/-**	**PP**	**SH**	**GP**	**G**	**A**	**Pts.**	**PIM**
94-95—Tacoma	WHL	2	0	0	0	0	...	...	...	—	—	—	—	—
95-96—Kelowna	WHL	69	4	5	9	76	...	...	...	6	0	1	1	4
96-97—Kelowna	WHL	70	17	26	43	101	...	...	...	6	0	0	0	8
97-98—Kelowna	WHL	47	10	30	40	70	...	...	...	—	—	—	—	—
98-99—San Jose	NHL	5	0	2	2	6	0	0	0	—	—	—	—	—
—Kelowna	WHL	47	15	30	45	92	-7	9	0	6	1	2	3	14
—Kentucky	AHL	2	0	0	0	2	0	0	0	12	0	2	2	10
99-00—Kentucky	AHL	41	5	12	17	40	...	...	...	—	—	—	—	—
—San Jose	NHL	30	1	2	3	10	7	0	0	1	0	1	1	0
00-01—San Jose	NHL	75	3	14	17	51	10	0	0	6	0	1	1	6
01-02—San Jose	NHL	75	2	12	14	57	10	0	0	12	0	2	2	12
02-03—San Jose	NHL	81	3	19	22	61	0	1	0	—	—	—	—	—
03-04—San Jose	NHL	82	6	15	21	48	10	0	0	17	1	5	6	22
05-06—San Jose	NHL	81	6	18	24	58	7	2	0	11	0	1	1	6
NHL Totals (7 years)		429	21	82	103	291	44	3	0	47	1	10	11	46

HARDING, JOSH G

PERSONAL: Born June 18, 1984, in Regina, Sask. ... 6-1/180. ... Catches right.
TRANSACTIONS/CAREER NOTES: Selected by Minnesota Wild in second round (second Wild pick, 38th overall) of NHL entry draft (June 22, 2002).

		REGULAR SEASON										PLAYOFFS							
Season Team	**League**	**GP**	**Min.**	**W**	**L**	**OTL**	**T**	**GA**	**SO**	**GAA**	**SV%**	**GP**	**Min.**	**W**	**L**	**GA**	**SO**	**GAA**	**SV%**
01-02—Regina	WHL	42	2389	27	13	...	1	95	4	2.39	...	6	325	2	4	16	0	2.95	...
02-03—Regina	WHL	57	3385	18	24	...	13	155	3	2.75	.914	5	...	1	4	...	...	2.43	...
03-04—Regina	WHL	28	1665	12	14	...	2	67	2	2.41	.927	—	—	—	—	—	—	—	—
—Brandon	WHL	27	1612	13	11	...	3	65	5	2.42	.920	11	660	5	6	36	0	3.27	.897
04-05—Houston	AHL	42	2387	21	16	...	...	80	4	2.01	.930	2	119	0	2	8	0	4.03	.893
05-06—Houston	AHL	38	2215	29	8	0	...	99	2	2.68	.922	8	476	4	4	30	0	3.78	.886
—Minnesota	NHL	3	185	2	1	0	...	8	1	2.59	.904	—	—	—	—	—	—	—	—
NHL Totals (1 year)		3	185	2	1	0	0	8	1	2.59	.904								

HARRISON, JAY D

PERSONAL: Born November 3, 1982, in Oshawa, Ont. ... 6-3/200. ... Shoots left.
TRANSACTIONS/CAREER NOTES: Selected by Toronto Maple Leafs in third round (fourth Maple Leafs pick, 82nd overall) of NHL entry draft (June 23, 2001).

		REGULAR SEASON								PLAYOFFS				
Season Team	**League**	**GP**	**G**	**A**	**Pts.**	**PIM**	**+/-**	**PP**	**SH**	**GP**	**G**	**A**	**Pts.**	**PIM**
98-99—Brampton	OHL	63	1	14	15	108	...	...	...	—	—	—	—	—
99-00—Brampton	OHL	68	2	18	20	139	...	...	...	6	0	2	2	15
00-01—Brampton	OHL	53	4	15	19	112	...	...	...	9	1	1	2	17
01-02—Brampton	OHL	61	12	31	43	116	...	...	...	—	—	—	—	—
—St. John's	AHL	7	0	1	1	2	2	0	0	10	0	0	0	4
02-03—St. John's	AHL	72	2	8	10	72	2	0	0	—	—	—	—	—
03-04—St. John's	AHL	70	4	5	9	141	...	...	...	—	—	—	—	—
04-05—St. John's	AHL	60	0	4	4	108	-9	0	0	4	0	1	1	14
05-06—Toronto	AHL	57	9	20	29	100	10	6	0	5	1	3	4	8
—Toronto	NHL	8	0	1	1	2	5	0	0	—	—	—	—	—
NHL Totals (1 year)		8	0	1	1	2	5	0	0					

HARTIGAN, MARK C/LW

PERSONAL: Born October 15, 1977, in Fort St. John, B.C. ... 6-0/205. ... Shoots left.
TRANSACTIONS/CAREER NOTES: Signed as free agent by Atlanta Thrashers (March 27, 2002). ... Tore hamstring (April 3, 2002); missed remainder of season. ... Signed as free agent by Columbus Blue Jackets (July 15, 2003).

		REGULAR SEASON								PLAYOFFS				
Season Team	**League**	**GP**	**G**	**A**	**Pts.**	**PIM**	**+/-**	**PP**	**SH**	**GP**	**G**	**A**	**Pts.**	**PIM**
99-00—St. Cloud State	WCHA	37	22	20	42	24	...	...	...	—	—	—	—	—
00-01—St. Cloud State	WCHA	40	27	21	48	20	...	...	...	—	—	—	—	—
01-02—St. Cloud State	WCHA	42	37	38	75	42	...	...	...	—	—	—	—	—
—Atlanta	NHL	2	0	0	0	2	-2	0	0	—	—	—	—	—
02-03—Atlanta	NHL	23	5	2	7	6	-8	1	0	—	—	—	—	—
—Chicago	AHL	55	15	31	46	43	6	5	0	9	1	2	3	10
03-04—Columbus	NHL	9	1	3	4	6	-2	1	0	—	—	—	—	—
—Syracuse	AHL	69	23	23	46	81	-5	4	0	7	1	4	5	8
04-05—Syracuse	AHL	69	31	28	59	105	2	15	0	—	—	—	—	—
05-06—Syracuse	AHL	49	34	41	75	48	18	17	1	6	1	2	3	33
—Columbus	NHL	33	9	3	12	22	-1	3	0	—	—	—	—	—
NHL Totals (4 years)		67	15	8	23	36	-13	5	0					

HARTNELL, SCOTT LW/RW

PERSONAL: Born April 18, 1982, in Regina, Sask. ... 6-2/210. ... Shoots left. ... Cousin of Mark Deyell, C, Toronto Maple Leafs organization (1996-99).

TRANSACTIONS/CAREER NOTES: Selected by Nashville Predators in first round (first Predators pick, sixth overall) of entry draft (June 24, 2000). ... Concussion (November 26, 2000); missed six games. ... Bruised left eye (October 27, 2001); missed five games. ... Concussion (April 9, 2002); missed remainder of season. ... Right ankle (December 17, 2003); missed 13 games. ... Concussion (February 21, 2004); missed 10 games.

		REGULAR SEASON								PLAYOFFS				
Season Team	**League**	**GP**	**G**	**A**	**Pts.**	**PIM**	**+/-**	**PP**	**SH**	**GP**	**G**	**A**	**Pts.**	**PIM**
97-98—Lloydminster	Jr. A	56	9	16	25	82	...	...	...	4	2	1	3	8
—Prince Albert	WHL	1	0	1	1	2	...	...	...	—	—	—	—	—
98-99—Prince Albert	WHL	65	10	34	44	104	...	...	...	14	0	5	5	22
99-00—Prince Albert	WHL	62	27	55	82	124	...	...	...	6	3	2	5	6
00-01—Nashville	NHL	75	2	14	16	48	-8	0	0	—	—	—	—	—
01-02—Nashville	NHL	75	14	27	41	111	5	3	0	—	—	—	—	—
02-03—Nashville	NHL	82	12	22	34	101	-3	2	0	—	—	—	—	—
03-04—Nashville	NHL	59	18	15	33	87	-5	5	0	6	1	2	3	2
04-05—Valerengen	Norway	28	17	12	29	103	26	...	...	11	12	7	19	24
05-06—Nashville	NHL	81	25	23	48	101	8	10	2	5	1	0	1	4
NHL Totals (5 years)		372	71	101	172	448	-3	20	2	11	2	2	4	6

HARVEY, TODD RW/C

PERSONAL: Born February 17, 1975, in Hamilton, Ont. ... 6-0/210. ... Shoots right.

TRANSACTIONS/CAREER NOTES: Selected by Dallas Stars in first round (first Stars pick, ninth overall) of entry draft (June 26, 1993). ... Strained back (March 13, 1995); missed one game. ... Sprained knee (October 30, 1995); missed two games. ... Strained groin (November 3, 1996); missed one game. ... Sprained knee (November 19, 1996); missed five games. ... Flu (December 29, 1996); missed one game. ... Suspended two games and fined $1,000 for elbowing incident (February 2, 1997). ... Bruised hand (April 4, 1997); missed one game. ... Concussion (November 16, 1997); missed one game. ... Strained hip flexor (December 20, 1997); missed one game. ... Sprained knee (January 7, 1998); missed five games. ... Injured hand (February 4, 1998); missed one game. ... Strained lower back (March 13, 1998); missed one game. ... Right knee surgery (March 22, 1998); missed 12 games. ... Traded by Stars with LW Bob Errey and fourth-round pick (LW Boyd Kane) in 1998 draft to New York Rangers for RW Mike Keane, C Brian Skrudland and sixth-round pick (RW Pavel Patera) in 1998 draft (March 24, 1998). ... Strained hip flexor (October 9, 1998); missed first two games of season. ... Suspended one game and fined $1,000 for roughing incident (December 13, 1998). ... Bruised right thumb (December 11, 1998); missed two games. ... Sprained knee (January 13, 1999); missed 10 games. ... Fractured thumb (February 17, 1999); missed final 27 games of season. ... Sprained knee (November 18, 1999); missed three games. ... Traded by Rangers with fourth-round pick (G Dimitri Patzold) in 2001 draft to San Jose Sharks for RW Radek Dvorak (December 30, 1999). ... Concussion and whiplash (January 1, 2001); missed 10 games. ... Injured knee (November 27, 2001); missed three games. ... Injured shoulder (March 10, 2002); missed 10 games. ... Injured shoulder (November 23, 2002); missed four games. ... Signed as free agent by Edmonton Oilers (September 16, 2004). ... Bruised right foot (October 10, 2005); missed eight games. ... Undisclosed upper-body injury (April 27, 2006); missed eight playoff games.

STATISTICAL PLATEAUS: Three-goal games: 1994-95 (1), 2000-01 (1). Total: 2.

		REGULAR SEASON								PLAYOFFS				
Season Team	**League**	**GP**	**G**	**A**	**Pts.**	**PIM**	**+/-**	**PP**	**SH**	**GP**	**G**	**A**	**Pts.**	**PIM**
89-90—Cambridge Jr. B	OHA	41	35	27	62	213	...	...	...	—	—	—	—	—
90-91—Cambridge Jr. B	OHA	35	32	39	71	174	...	...	...	—	—	—	—	—
91-92—Det. Jr. Red Wings	OHL	58	21	43	64	141	...	...	...	7	3	5	8	32
92-93—Det. Jr. Red Wings	OHL	55	50	50	100	83	...	...	...	15	9	12	21	39
93-94—Det. Jr. Red Wings	OHL	49	34	51	85	75	...	13	2	17	10	12	22	26
94-95—Det. Jr. Red Wings	OHL	11	8	14	22	12	...	3	0	—	—	—	—	—
—Dallas	NHL	40	11	9	20	67	-3	2	0	5	0	0	0	8
95-96—Dallas	NHL	69	9	20	29	136	-13	3	0	—	—	—	—	—
—Michigan	IHL	5	1	3	4	8	...	...	...	—	—	—	—	—
96-97—Dallas	NHL	71	9	22	31	142	19	1	0	7	0	1	1	10
97-98—Dallas	NHL	59	9	10	19	104	5	0	0	—	—	—	—	—
98-99—New York Rangers	NHL	37	11	17	28	72	-1	6	0	—	—	—	—	—
99-00—New York Rangers	NHL	31	3	3	6	62	-9	0	0	—	—	—	—	—
—San Jose	NHL	40	8	4	12	78	-2	2	0	12	1	0	1	8
00-01—San Jose	NHL	69	10	11	21	72	6	1	0	6	0	0	0	8
01-02—San Jose	NHL	69	9	13	22	73	16	0	0	12	0	2	2	12
02-03—San Jose	NHL	76	3	16	19	74	5	0	0	—	—	—	—	—
03-04—San Jose	NHL	47	4	5	9	38	3	0	0	16	1	2	3	2
—Cleveland	AHL	13	6	1	7	29	2	1	0	—	—	—	—	—
04-05—Cambridge	OHA Sr.	16	9	15	24	31	...	...	...	—	—	—	—	—
05-06—Edmonton	NHL	63	5	2	7	32	-7	0	0	10	1	1	2	4
NHL Totals (11 years)		671	91	132	223	950	19	15	0	68	3	6	9	52

HASEK, DOMINIK G

PERSONAL: Born January 29, 1965, in Pardubice, Czech. ... 5-11/180. ... Catches left. ... Name pronounced HA-shehk.

TRANSACTIONS/CAREER NOTES: Selected by Chicago Blackhawks in 10th round (11th Blackhawks pick, 199th overall) of NHL draft (June 8, 1983). ... Traded by Blackhawks to Buffalo Sabres for G Stephane Beauregard and fourth-round pick (LW Eric Daze) in 1993 entry draft (August 7, 1992). ... Injured groin (November 25, 1992); missed three games. ... Strained abdominal muscle (January 6, 1993); missed six games. ... Strained rotator cuff (March 16, 1995); missed three games. ... Injured abdominal muscle (December 15, 1995); missed 10 games. ... Sprained left knee (April 6, 1996); missed last two games of season. ... Fractured rib (March 19, 1997); missed five games. ... Sprained knee (April 21, 1997); missed six playoff games. ... Suspended three playoff games and fined $10,000 for assaulting a journalist (May 1, 1997). ... Ear infection (April 15, 1998); missed one game. ... Strained groin (February 17, 1999); missed 12 games. ... Strained back (March 23, 1999); missed one game. ... Tore groin muscle (October 29, 1999); missed 40 games. ... Injured knee (October 5, 2000); missed one game. ... Traded by Sabres to Detroit Red Wings for LW Slava Kozlov, first-round pick (traded to Columbus; traded to Atlanta; Thrashers selected Jim Slater) in 2002 draft and future considerations (July 1, 2001). ... Announced retirement (June 25, 2002). ... Announced return from retirement (July 8, 2003). ... Injured groin (October 30, 2003); missed five games. ... Reinjured groin (November 19, 2003); missed seven games. ... Reinjured groin (December 10, 2003); missed remainer of season and playoffs. ... Signed as free agent by Ottawa Senators (July 6, 2004). ... Strained adductor muscle during Olympics (February 15, 2006); missed final 25 games of regular season and all of playoffs.

		REGULAR SEASON										PLAYOFFS							
Season Team	**League**	**GP**	**Min.**	**W**	**L**	**OTL**	**T**	**GA**	**SO**	**GAA**	**SV%**	**GP**	**Min.**	**W**	**L**	**GA**	**SO**	**GAA**	**SV%**
81-82—Pardubice	Czech Rep.	12	661	...	...	...	...	34	...	3.09	...	—	—	—	—	—	—	—	—
82-83—Pardubice	Czech Rep.	42	2358	...	...	...	...	105	...	2.67	...	—	—	—	—	—	—	—	—
83-84—Pardubice	Czech Rep.	40	2304	...	...	...	...	108	...	2.81	...	—	—	—	—	—	—	—	—
84-85—Pardubice	Czech Rep.	42	2419	...	...	...	...	131	...	3.25	...	—	—	—	—	—	—	—	—
85-86—Pardubice	Czech Rep.	45	2689	...	...	...	...	138	...	3.08	...	—	—	—	—	—	—	—	—
86-87—Pardubice	Czech Rep.	23	2515	...	...	...	...	103	...	2.46	...	—	—	—	—	—	—	—	—
87-88—Pardubice	Czech Rep.	31	1863	...	...	...	...	93	...	3.00	...	—	—	—	—	—	—	—	—
—Czech. Olympic Team	Int'l	5	217	3	2	...	0	18	1	4.98	.833	—	—	—	—	—	—	—	—
88-89—Pardubice	Czech Rep.	42	2507	...	...	...	...	114	...	2.73	...	—	—	—	—	—	—	—	—
89-90—Dukla Jihlava	Czech.	40	2251	...	...	...	...	80	...	2.13	...	—	—	—	—	—	—	—	—
90-91—Chicago	NHL	5	195	3	0	...	1	8	0	2.46	.914	3	69	0	0	3	0	2.61	.923
—Indianapolis	IHL	33	1903	20	11	...	4	80	5	2.52	...	1	60	1	0	3	0	3.00	...
91-92—Indianapolis	IHL	20	1162	7	10	...	3	69	1	3.56	...	—	—	—	—	—	—	—	—
—Chicago	NHL	20	1014	10	4	...	1	44	1	2.60	.893	3	158	0	2	8	0	3.04	.886
92-93—Buffalo	NHL	28	1429	11	10	...	4	75	0	3.15	.896	1	45	1	0	1	0	1.33	.958
93-94—Buffalo	NHL	58	3358	30	20	...	6	109	†7	*1.95	*.930	7	484	3	4	13	2	*1.61	*.950
94-95—HC Pardubice	Czech Rep.	2	125	...	...	...	...	6	...	2.88	...	—	—	—	—	—	—	—	—
—Buffalo	NHL	41	2416	19	14	...	7	85	†5	*2.11	*.930	5	309	1	4	18	0	3.50	.863
95-96—Buffalo	NHL	59	3417	22	†30	...	6	161	2	2.83	*.920	—	—	—	—	—	—	—	—
96-97—Buffalo	NHL	67	4037	37	20	...	10	153	5	2.27	*.930	3	153	1	1	5	0	1.96	.926
97-98—Buffalo	NHL	*72	*4220	33	23	...	13	147	*13	2.09	.932	15	948	10	5	32	1	2.03	.938
—Czech Rep. Oly. team	Int'l	6	369	5	1	...	0	6	2	0.98	.961	—	—	—	—	—	—	—	—
98-99—Buffalo	NHL	64	3817	30	18	...	14	119	9	1.87	*.937	19	1217	13	6	36	2	1.77	.939
99-00—Buffalo	NHL	35	2066	15	11	...	6	76	3	2.21	†.919	5	301	1	4	12	0	2.39	.918
00-01—Buffalo	NHL	67	3904	37	24	...	4	137	*11	2.11	.921	13	833	7	6	29	1	2.09	.916
01-02—Detroit	NHL	65	3872	*41	15	...	8	140	5	2.17	.915	*23	*1455	*16	7	45	*6	1.86	.920
—Czech Rep. Oly. team	Int'l	4	239	1	2	...	1	8	0	2.01	.924	—	—	—	—	—	—	—	—
02-03—Detroit	NHL	Did not play																	
03-04—Detroit	NHL	14	817	8	3	...	2	30	2	2.20	.907	—	—	—	—	—	—	—	—
05-06—Ottawa	NHL	43	2584	28	10	4	...	90	5	2.09	.925	—	—	—	—	—	—	—	—
—Czech Oly. team	Int'l	1	...	...	...	...	...	...	0	0.00	1.00	—	—	—	—	—	—	—	—
NHL Totals (15 years)		638	37146	324	202		82	1374	68	2.22	.924	97	5972	53	39	202	12	2.03	.927

HATCHER, DERIAN — D

PERSONAL: Born June 4, 1972, in Sterling Heights, Mich. ... 6-4/244. ... Shoots left. ... Brother of Kevin Hatcher, D with five NHL teams (1984-01).

TRANSACTIONS/CAREER NOTES: Selected by Minnesota North Stars in first round (first North Stars pick, eighth overall) of entry draft (June 16, 1990). ... Suspended 10 games (December 1991). ... Fractured ankle in off-ice incident (January 19, 1992); missed 21 games. ... Sprained knee (January 6, 1993); missed 14 games. ... Suspended one game for game misconduct penalties (March 9, 1993). ... North Stars franchise moved from Minnesota to Dallas and renamed Stars for 1993-94 season. ... Sprained ankle (February 2, 1995); missed one game. ... Staph infection on finger (February 14, 1995); missed four games. ... Injured right knee (May 1, 1995); missed playoffs. ... Injured shoulder (November 14, 1995); missed three games. ... Strained knee (December 8, 1996); missed 14 games. ... Knee surgery (March 19, 1997); missed five games. ... Injured knee (March 8, 1998); missed seven games. ... Suspended four preseason games and fined $1,000 for injuring another player (September 23, 1998). ... Suspended seven games for illegal check (April 17, 1999); missed final two games of season and first five playoff games. ... Lacerated calf (December 17, 1999); missed 24 games. ... Strained Achilles' tendon (March 8, 2000); missed one game. ... Suspended two games for elbowing incident (March 27, 2001). ... Strained hamstring (November 21, 2001); missed two games. ... Suspended one playoff game for receiving second game misconduct during the playoffs (April 12, 2003). ... Signed as free agent by Detroit Red Wings (July 2, 2003). ... Torn knee ligament (October 16, 2003); missed 64 games. ... Bruised shoulder (March 16, 2004); missed three games. ... Suspended three games (served in first three games of 2005-06 season) for elbowing incident (May 11, 2004). ... Placed on waivers by Red Wings (July 25, 2005). ... Signed as free agent by the Philadelphia Flyers (August 2, 2005). ... Bruised right knee (March 11, 2006); missed two games.

		REGULAR SEASON								PLAYOFFS				
Season Team	**League**	**GP**	**G**	**A**	**Pts.**	**PIM**	**+/-**	**PP**	**SH**	**GP**	**G**	**A**	**Pts.**	**PIM**
88-89—Detroit G.P.D.	MNHL	51	19	35	54	100	...	...	...	—	—	—	—	—
89-90—North Bay	OHL	64	14	38	52	81	...	...	...	5	2	3	5	8
90-91—North Bay	OHL	64	13	50	63	163	...	...	...	10	2	10	12	28
91-92—Minnesota	NHL	43	8	4	12	88	7	0	0	5	0	2	2	8
92-93—Minnesota	NHL	67	4	15	19	178	-27	0	0	—	—	—	—	—
—Kalamazoo	IHL	2	1	2	3	21	-3	0	0	—	—	—	—	—
93-94—Dallas	NHL	83	12	19	31	211	19	2	1	9	0	2	2	14
94-95—Dallas	NHL	43	5	11	16	105	3	2	0	—	—	—	—	—
95-96—Dallas	NHL	79	8	23	31	129	-12	2	0	—	—	—	—	—
96-97—Dallas	NHL	63	3	19	22	97	8	0	0	7	0	2	2	20
97-98—Dallas	NHL	70	6	25	31	132	9	3	0	17	3	3	6	39
—U.S. Olympic team	Int'l	4	0	0	0	0	-1	0	0	—	—	—	—	—
98-99—Dallas	NHL	80	9	21	30	102	21	3	0	18	1	6	7	24
99-00—Dallas	NHL	57	2	22	24	68	6	0	0	23	1	3	4	29
00-01—Dallas	NHL	80	2	21	23	77	5	1	0	10	0	1	1	16
01-02—Dallas	NHL	80	4	21	25	87	12	1	0	—	—	—	—	—
02-03—Dallas	NHL	82	8	22	30	106	37	1	1	11	1	2	3	33

Season Team	League	GP	G	A	Pts.	PIM	+/-	PP	SH	GP	G	A	Pts.	PIM
		REGULAR SEASON								PLAYOFFS				
03-04—Detroit	NHL	15	0	4	4	8	4	0	0	12	0	1	1	15
04-05—Motor City	UHL	24	5	12	17	27	9	4	0	—	—	—	—	—
05-06—Philadelphia	NHL	77	4	13	17	93	2	1	1	6	0	2	2	10
—U.S. Olympic team	Int'l	6	0	0	0	12	-1	0	0	—	—	—	—	—
NHL Totals (14 years)		919	75	240	315	1481	94	16	3	118	6	24	30	208

HAUSER, ADAM G

PERSONAL: Born May 27, 1980, in Bovey, Minn. ... 6-2/192. ... Catches left.
COLLEGE: Minnesota.
TRANSACTIONS/CAREER NOTES: Selected by Edmonton Oilers in third round (fourth Oilers pick, 81st overall) of entry draft (June 26, 1999). ... Signed as free agent by Los Angeles Kings (July 8, 2004).

Season Team	League	GP	Min.	W	L	OTL	T	GA	SO	GAA	SV%	GP	Min.	W	L	GA	SO	GAA	SV%
		REGULAR SEASON										PLAYOFFS							
97-98—U.S. National	NAHL	38	2110	19	10	...	3	94	4	2.67	...	—	—	—	—	—	—	—	—
98-99—Minnesota	WCHA	40	2350	14	18	...	8	136	3	3.47	.876	—	—	—	—	—	—	—	—
99-00—Minnesota	WCHA	36	2114	20	14	...	2	104	1	2.95	...	—	—	—	—	—	—	—	—
00-01—Minnesota	WCHA	40	2366	26	12	...	2	101	3	2.56	...	—	—	—	—	—	—	—	—
01-02—Minnesota	WCHA	35	2002	23	6	...	4	80	1	2.40	...	—	—	—	—	—	—	—	—
02-03—Providence	AHL	1	64	0	0	...	1	3	0	2.81	.917	—	—	—	—	—	—	—	—
—Jackson	ECHL	34	2021	20	9	...	4	83	5	2.46	.916	—	—	—	—	—	—	—	—
03-04—Manchester	AHL	43	2536	20	15	...	7	82	7	1.94	...	—	—	—	—	—	—	—	—
04-05—Manchester	AHL	32	1867	19	11	...	...	60	5	1.93	.933	2	70	0	0	2	0	1.71	.905
05-06—Los Angeles	NHL	1	51	0	0	0	...	6	0	7.06	.750	—	—	—	—	—	—	—	—
—Manchester	AHL	45	2600	22	17	2	...	111	3	2.56	.919	3	177	1	2	9	0	3.05	.913
NHL Totals (1 year)		1	51	0	0	0	0	6	0	7.06	.750								

HAVELID, NICLAS D

PERSONAL: Born April 12, 1973, in Stockholm, Sweden. ... 6-0/200. ... Shoots left. ... Name pronounced: NIHK-luhz HAV-lihd
TRANSACTIONS/CAREER NOTES: Selected by Anaheim Mighty Ducks in third round (second Mighty Ducks pick, 83rd overall) of NHL draft (June 26, 1999). ... Fractured finger (January 15, 2000); missed 23 games. ... Tore knee ligament (January 15, 2001); missed remainder of season. ... Traded by Mighty Ducks to Atlanta Thrashers for D Kurtis Foster (June 26, 2004).

Season Team	League	GP	G	A	Pts.	PIM	+/-	PP	SH	GP	G	A	Pts.	PIM
		REGULAR SEASON								PLAYOFFS				
91-92—AIK Solna	Sweden	10	0	0	0	2	...	...	...	—	—	—	—	—
92-93—AIK Solna	Sweden	22	1	0	1	16	...	...	...	3	0	0	0	2
93-94—AIK Solna	Sweden Dv. 2	22	3	9	12	14								
94-95—AIK Solna	Sweden Dv. 2	40	3	7	10	38	...	...	...	—	—	—	—	—
95-96—AIK Solna	Sweden	40	5	6	11	30	...	...	...	—	—	—	—	—
96-97—AIK Solna	Sweden	49	3	6	9	42	...	...	...	7	1	2	3	8
97-98—AIK Solna	Sweden	43	8	4	12	42	...	...	...	—	—	—	—	—
98-99—Malmo	Sweden	50	10	12	22	42	...	...	...	8	0	4	4	10
99-00—Anaheim	NHL	50	2	7	9	20	0	0	0	—	—	—	—	—
—Cincinnati	AHL	2	0	0	0	0	...	...	...	—	—	—	—	—
00-01—Anaheim	NHL	47	4	10	14	34	-6	2	0	—	—	—	—	—
01-02—Anaheim	NHL	52	1	2	3	40	-13	0	0	—	—	—	—	—
02-03—Anaheim	NHL	82	11	22	33	30	5	4	0	21	0	4	4	2
03-04—Anaheim	NHL	79	6	20	26	28	-28	5	0	—	—	—	—	—
04-05—Sodertalje	Sweden Dv. 2	46	2	2	4	60	-5	1	0	10	1	1	2	18
05-06—Atlanta	NHL	82	4	28	32	48	9	2	0	—	—	—	—	—
—Swedish Oly. team	Int'l	5	0	0	0	4	2	0	0	—	—	—	—	—
NHL Totals (6 years)		392	28	89	117	200	-33	13	0	21	0	4	4	2

HAVLAT, MARTIN RW/LW

PERSONAL: Born April 19, 1981, in Mlada Boleslav, Czechoslovakia. ... 6-1/194. ... Shoots left.
TRANSACTIONS/CAREER NOTES: Selected by Ottawa Senators in first round (first Senators pick, 26th overall) of entry draft (June 26, 1999). ... Injured shoulder (November 23, 2000); missed eight games. ... Strained groin (April 6, 2001); missed final game of regular season. ... Injured groin (January 30, 2002); missed one game. ... Strained groin (March 17, 2002); missed two games. ... Reinjured groin (March 28, 2002); missed final seven games of regular season. ... Injured groin (October 29, 2002); missed six games. ... Bruised right elbow (January 20, 2003); missed two games. ... Injured groin (February 19, 2003); missed four games. ... Injured groin (March 4, 2003); missed two games. ... Missed first two games of 2003-04 season in contract dispute. ... Injured hamstring (November 22, 2003); missed 3 games. ... Suspended for two games for kicking incident (January 1, 2004). ... Injured groin (January 29, 2004); missed two games. ... Suspended two games for high-sticking incident (February 27, 2004). ... Suspended five games (forfeiting $66,326.55) for kicking incident (October 17, 2005). ... Injured hamstring (November 22, 2005); missed one game. ... Dislocated right shoulder (November 29, 2005) and had surgery (December 7, 2005); missed final 58 games of regular season. ... Traded by Senators with F Bryan Smolinski to Chicago Blackhawks in three-team deal in which San Jose Sharks traded D Tom Preissing and D Josh Hennessy to Blackhawks for F Mark Bell. Blackhawks then traded Preissing, Hennessy, D Michal Barinka and a second-round pick in 2008 draft (July 10, 2006).
STATISTICAL PLATEAUS: Three-goal games: 2000-01 (1), 2001-02 (1), 2002-03 (1), 2003-04 (1). Total: 4.

Season Team	League	GP	G	A	Pts.	PIM	+/-	PP	SH	GP	G	A	Pts.	PIM
		REGULAR SEASON								PLAYOFFS				
96-97—Ytong Brno	Czech. Jrs.	34	43	27	70	...	...	...	...	—	—	—	—	—
97-98—Ytong Brno	Czech. Jrs.	32	38	29	67	...	...	...	...	—	—	—	—	—

H

		Regular Season								Playoffs				
Season Team	**League**	**GP**	**G**	**A**	**Pts.**	**PIM**	**+/-**	**PP**	**SH**	**GP**	**G**	**A**	**Pts.**	**PIM**
98-99—Zelezarny Trinec..........	Czech. Jrs.	31	28	23	51	...	...	...	...	—	—	—	—	—
—Zelezarny Trinec..........	Czech Rep.	24	2	3	5	4	...	...	...	8	0	0	0	...
99-00—Zelezarny Trinec..........	Czech Rep.	46	13	29	42	42	...	...	...	4	0	2	2	8
00-01—Ottawa	NHL	73	19	23	42	20	8	7	0	4	0	0	0	2
01-02—Ottawa	NHL	72	22	28	50	66	-7	9	0	12	2	5	7	14
—Czech Rep. Oly. team..	Int'l	4	3	1	4	27	...	...	...	—	—	—	—	—
02-03—Ottawa	NHL	67	24	35	59	30	20	9	0	18	5	6	11	14
03-04—Ottawa	NHL	68	31	37	68	46	12	13	0	7	0	3	3	2
04-05—HC Znojemsti Orli	Czech Rep.	12	10	4	14	16	5	...	...	—	—	—	—	—
—Dynamo Moscow........	Russian	10	2	0	2	14	1	...	...	—	—	—	—	—
—Sparta Praha..............	Czech Rep.	9	5	4	9	37	4	...	...	5	0	0	0	20
05-06—Ottawa	NHL	18	9	7	16	4	6	2	1	10	7	6	13	4
NHL Totals (5 years)...........		298	105	130	235	166	39	40	1	51	14	20	34	36

HEALEY, ERIC LW

PERSONAL: Born January 20, 1975, in Hull, Mass. ... 5-11/300. ... Shoots left.

TRANSACTIONS/CAREER NOTES: Signed as undrafted free agent by Calgary Flames (September 22, 1998). ... Signed as free agent by Phoenix Coyotes (July 26, 1999). ... Signed as free agent by Los Angeles Kings (September 4, 2002). ... Signed as free agent by Atlanta Thrashers (August 12, 2003). ... Signed as free agent by Adler Mannheim of German league (July 9, 2004). ... Signed as free agent by Tampa Bay Lightning (July 14, 2006).

		Regular Season								Playoffs				
Season Team	**League**	**GP**	**G**	**A**	**Pts.**	**PIM**	**+/-**	**PP**	**SH**	**GP**	**G**	**A**	**Pts.**	**PIM**
94-95—R.P.I.	ECAC	37	13	11	24	33	...	...	...	—	—	—	—	—
95-96—R.P.I.	ECAC	35	18	22	40	55	...	...	...	—	—	—	—	—
96-97—R.P.I.	ECAC	36	30	26	56	62	...	...	...	—	—	—	—	—
97-98—R.P.I.	ECAC	35	21	27	48	42	...	...	...	—	—	—	—	—
98-99—Saint John	AHL	64	14	24	38	77	-16	1	1	—	—	—	—	—
—Orlando....................	IHL	13	5	4	9	13	0	1	0	8	1	0	1	12
99-00—Springfield	AHL	32	14	15	29	51	...	...	...	1	0	0	0	2
00-01—Springfield	AHL	66	16	17	33	53	...	...	...	—	—	—	—	—
01-02—Manchester................	AHL	65	24	34	58	45	-2	6	0	5	2	2	4	8
—Jackson	ECHL	2	1	1	2	0	-1	1	0	—	—	—	—	—
02-03—Manchester................	AHL	75	42	31	73	47	4	14	1	3	1	0	1	2
03-04—Chicago.......................	AHL	71	31	20	51	52	-7	12	0	10	3	6	9	10
04-05—Mannheim....................	Germany	50	16	13	29	54	...	...	...	13	2	4	6	12
05-06—Providence..................	AHL	66	29	42	71	49	15	11	0	5	2	3	5	0
—Boston	NHL	2	0	0	0	2	0	0	0	—	—	—	—	—
NHL Totals (1 year).............		2	0	0	0	2	0	0	0					

HEALEY, PAUL RW

PERSONAL: Born March 20, 1975, in Edmonton. ... 6-2/198. ... Shoots right.

TRANSACTIONS/CAREER NOTES: Selected by Philadelphia Flyers in eighth round (seventh Flyers pick, 192nd overall) of entry draft (June 26, 1993). ... Traded by Flyers to Nashville Predators for RW Matt Henderson (September 27, 1999). ... Signed as free agent by Edmonton Oilers (August 31, 2000). ... Signed as free agent by Toronto Maple Leafs (July 24, 2001). ... Signed as free agent by New York Rangers (July 28, 2003). ... Injured ribs (November 6, 2003); missed four games. ... Traded by Rangers to Atlanta Thrashers for D Jeff Paul (March 9, 2004). ... Signed as free agent by Colorado Avalanche (August 16, 2005).

		Regular Season								Playoffs				
Season Team	**League**	**GP**	**G**	**A**	**Pts.**	**PIM**	**+/-**	**PP**	**SH**	**GP**	**G**	**A**	**Pts.**	**PIM**
92-93—Prince Albert..............	WHL	72	12	20	32	66	...	...	...	—	—	—	—	—
93-94—Prince Albert..............	WHL	63	23	26	49	70	...	...	...	—	—	—	—	—
94-95—Prince Albert..............	WHL	71	43	50	93	67	25	6	8	12	3	4	7	2
95-96—Hershey	AHL	61	7	15	22	35	...	...	...	—	—	—	—	—
96-97—Philadelphia	AHL	64	21	19	40	56	9	5	1	10	4	1	5	10
—Philadelphia	NHL	2	0	0	0	0	0	0	0	—	—	—	—	—
97-98—Philadelphia	AHL	71	34	18	52	48	8	8	2	20	6	2	8	4
—Philadelphia	NHL	4	0	0	0	12	0	0	0	—	—	—	—	—
98-99—Philadelphia	AHL	72	26	20	46	39	-2	10	3	15	4	6	10	11
99-00—Milwaukee...................	IHL	76	21	18	39	28	...	...	...	3	1	2	3	0
00-01—Hamilton......................	AHL	79	39	32	71	34	...	...	...	—	—	—	—	—
01-02—St. John's....................	AHL	58	27	29	56	30	20	6	2	2	1	1	2	8
—Toronto	NHL	21	3	7	10	2	7	0	0	18	0	1	1	2
02-03—St. John's....................	AHL	17	6	10	16	12	-6	3	0	—	—	—	—	—
—Toronto	NHL	44	3	7	10	16	8	1	0	4	0	1	1	2
03-04—New York Rangers......	NHL	4	0	0	0	0	0	0	0	—	—	—	—	—
—Hartford	AHL	50	11	10	21	37	2	2	2	—	—	—	—	—
—San Antonio	AHL	18	5	5	10	20	-1	2	1	—	—	—	—	—
04-05—Edmonton	AHL	17	3	6	9	29	-3	1	0	—	—	—	—	—
—San Antonio	AHL	62	6	17	23	50	-9	0	0	—	—	—	—	—
05-06—Lowell	AHL	59	19	21	40	51	-21	12	1	—	—	—	—	—
—Colorado	NHL	2	0	0	0	14	0	0	0	—	—	—	—	—
NHL Totals (6 years)...........		77	6	14	20	44	15	1	0	22	0	2	2	4

H

HEATLEY, DANY LW/RW

PERSONAL: Born January 21, 1981, in Freiburg, W. Germany. ... 6-3/215. ... Shoots left.
TRANSACTIONS/CAREER NOTES: Selected by Atlanta Thrashers in first round (first Thrashers pick, second overall) of entry draft (June 24, 2000). ... Injured knee (December 14, 2002); missed five games. ... Injured knees and fractured jaw in offseason auto accident (September 29, 2003); missed 51 games. ... Traded by Thrashers to Ottawa Senators for D Greg de Vries and RW Marian Hossa (August 23, 2005).
STATISTICAL PLATEAUS: Three-goal games: 2002-03 (2).

		REGULAR SEASON								PLAYOFFS				
Season Team	League	GP	G	A	Pts.	PIM	+/-	PP	SH	GP	G	A	Pts.	PIM
98-99—Calgary Royals	AJHL	60	70	56	126	91	...	...	...	13	22	13	35	6
99-00—Wisconsin	WCHA	38	28	28	56	32	...	...	...	—	—	—	—	—
00-01—Wisconsin	WCHA	39	24	33	57	74	...	...	...	—	—	—	—	—
01-02—Atlanta	NHL	82	26	41	67	56	-19	7	0	—	—	—	—	—
02-03—Atlanta	NHL	77	41	48	89	58	-8	19	1	—	—	—	—	—
03-04—Atlanta	NHL	31	13	12	25	18	-8	5	0	—	—	—	—	—
04-05—Bern	Switzerland	16	14	10	24	58	...	7	0	—	—	—	—	—
—Ak Bars Kazan	Russian	11	3	1	4	22	1	...	...	4	2	1	3	4
05-06—Ottawa	NHL	82	50	53	103	86	29	23	2	10	3	9	12	11
—Canadian Oly. team	Int'l	6	2	1	3	8	1	0	0	—	—	—	—	—
NHL Totals (4 years)		272	130	154	284	218	-6	54	3	10	3	9	12	11

HECHT, JOCHEN C/LW

PERSONAL: Born June 21, 1977, in Mannheim, W. Germany. ... 6-1/200. ... Shoots left.
TRANSACTIONS/CAREER NOTES: Selected by St. Louis Blues in second round (first Blues pick, 49th overall) of entry draft (July 8, 1995). ... Sprained ankle (January 13, 2000); missed 13 games. ... Reinjured ankle (February 23, 2000); missed six games. ... Strained oblique muscle (January 27, 2001); missed one game. ... Strained oblique muscle (February 1, 2001); missed two games. ... Strained oblique muscle (March 24, 2001); missed seven games. ... Traded by Blues with C Marty Reasoner and D Jan Horacek to Edmonton Oilers for C Doug Weight and LW Michel Riesen (July 1, 2001). ... Traded by Oilers to Buffalo Sabres for two second-round (G Jeff Deslauriers and C Jarrett Stoll) picks in 2002 draft (June 22, 2002). ... Bruised right knee (October 22, 2002); missed two games. ... Concussion, injured ear (December 7, 2002); missed 20 games. ... Injured wrist (February 11, 2003); missed two games. ... Bruised right wrist (February 19, 2003); missed nine games. ... Concussion (March 14, 2003); missed two games. ... Fractured left arm (October 4, 2003); missed 17 games. ... Bruised left shoulder (January 30, 2004); missed one game. ... Sprained knee (February 9, 2006); missed two games. ... Aggravated right knee injury (March 17, 2006); missed nine games. ... Knee (April 3, 2006); missed final seven games of regular season.

		REGULAR SEASON								PLAYOFFS				
Season Team	League	GP	G	A	Pts.	PIM	+/-	PP	SH	GP	G	A	Pts.	PIM
94-95—Mannheim	Germany	43	11	12	23	68	...	...	...	10	5	4	9	12
95-96—Mannheim	Germany	44	12	16	28	68	...	...	...	8	3	2	5	6
96-97—Mannheim	Germany	46	21	21	42	36	...	...	...	—	—	—	—	—
97-98—Mannheim	Germany	44	7	19	26	42	...	...	...	10	1	1	2	14
—German Oly. team	Int'l	4	1	0	1	6	-1	0	0	—	—	—	—	—
98-99—Worcester	AHL	74	21	35	56	48	-2	9	3	4	1	1	2	2
—St. Louis	NHL	3	0	0	0	0	-2	0	0	5	2	0	2	0
99-00—St. Louis	NHL	63	13	21	34	28	20	5	0	7	4	6	10	2
00-01—St. Louis	NHL	72	19	25	44	48	11	8	3	15	2	4	6	4
01-02—Edmonton	NHL	82	16	24	40	60	4	5	0	—	—	—	—	—
—German Oly. team	Int'l	4	1	1	2	2	...	...	...	—	—	—	—	—
02-03—Buffalo	NHL	49	10	16	26	30	4	2	0	—	—	—	—	—
03-04—Buffalo	NHL	64	15	37	52	49	17	2	1	—	—	—	—	—
04-05—Mannheim	Germany	48	16	34	50	151	11	6	1	14	10	10	20	14
05-06—Buffalo	NHL	64	18	24	42	34	10	4	2	15	2	6	8	8
NHL Totals (7 years)		397	91	147	238	249	64	26	6	42	10	16	26	14

HEDBERG, JOHAN G

PERSONAL: Born May 3, 1973, in Leksand, Sweden. ... 6-0/190. ... Catches left.
TRANSACTIONS/CAREER NOTES: Selected by Philadelphia Flyers in ninth round (eighth Flyers pick, 218th overall) of NHL draft (June 29, 1994). ... Traded by Flyers to San Jose Sharks for seventh-round pick (C Pavel Kasparik) in 1999 (July 6, 1998). ... Traded by Sharks with D Bobby Dollas to Pittsburgh Penguins for D Jeff Norton (March 12, 2001). ... Fractured collarbone (February 8, 2003); missed 14 games. ... Traded by Penguins to Vancouver Canucks for a second-round pick (D Alex Goligoski) in 2004 (August 25, 2003). ... Foot (November 11, 2003); missed one game. ... Fractured wrist (December 16, 2003); missed 16 games. ... Signed as free agent by Dallas Stars (August 5, 2005). ... Signed as free agent by Atlanta Thrashers (July 1, 2006).

		REGULAR SEASON										PLAYOFFS							
Season Team	League	GP	Min.	W	L	OTL	T	GA	SO	GAA	SV%	GP	Min.	W	L	GA	SO	GAA	SV%
92-93—Leksand	Sweden Dv. 2	10	600	...	...	...	...	24	...	2.40	...	—	—	—	—	—	—	—	—
93-94—Leksand	Sweden Dv. 2	17	1020	...	...	...	...	48	0	2.82	...	—	—	—	—	—	—	—	—
94-95—Leksand	Sweden Dv. 2	17	986	...	...	...	...	58	1	3.53	...	—	—	—	—	—	—	—	—
95-96—Leksand	Sweden Dv. 2	34	2013	...	...	...	...	95	...	2.83	...	4	240	...	...	13	...	3.25	...
96-97—Leksand	Sweden Dv. 2	38	2260	...	...	...	...	95	3	2.52	...	4	581	...	...	18	1	1.86	...
97-98—Baton Rouge	ECHL	2	100	1	1	...	0	7	0	4.20	...	—	—	—	—	—	—	—	—
—Detroit	IHL	16	726	7	2	...	2	32	1	2.64	.899	—	—	—	—	—	—	—	—
—Manitoba	IHL	14	745	8	4	...	1	32	1	2.58	.922	2	106	0	2	6	0	3.40	.905
98-99—Leksand	Sweden Dv. 2	48	2940	...	...	...	...	140	0	2.86	...	4	255	...	...	15	0	3.53	...
99-00—Kentucky	AHL	33	1973	18	9	...	5	88	3	2.68	...	5	311	3	2	10	1	1.93	...
00-01—Manitoba	IHL	46	2697	23	13	...	7	115	1	2.56	...	—	—	—	—	—	—	—	—
—Pittsburgh	NHL	9	545	7	1	...	1	24	0	2.64	.905	18	1123	9	9	43	2	2.30	.911
01-02—Pittsburgh	NHL	66	3877	25	*34	...	7	178	6	2.75	.904	—	—	—	—	—	—	—	—

Season Team	League	GP	Min.	W	L	OTL	T	GA	SO	GAA	SV%	GP	Min.	W	L	GA	SO	GAA	SV%
		REGULAR SEASON										PLAYOFFS							
—Swedish Oly. team	Int'l	1	60	1	0	...	0	1	0	1.00	.950	—	—	—	—	—	—	—	—
02-03—Pittsburgh	NHL	41	2410	14	22	...	4	126	1	3.14	.895	—	—	—	—	—	—	—	—
03-04—Vancouver	NHL	21	1098	8	6	...	2	46	3	2.51	.900	2	98	1	1	4	0	2.45	.922
—Manitoba	AHL	2	124	0	2	...	0	9	0	4.35	.868	—	—	—	—	—	—	—	—
04-05—Leksand	Sweden Dv. 2	12	724	...	...	...	...	26	0	2.15	.909	9	550	...	...	19	1	2.07	.918
05-06—Dallas	NHL	19	1079	12	4	1	...	48	0	2.67	.898	—	—	—	—	—	—	—	—
NHL Totals (5 years)		156	9009	66	67	1	14	422	10	2.81	.900	20	1221	10	10	47	2	2.31	.912

HEDICAN, BRET D

PERSONAL: Born August 10, 1970, in St. Paul, Minn. ... 6-2/205. ... Shoots left. ... Name pronounced HEHD-ih-kihn.

TRANSACTIONS/CAREER NOTES: Selected by St. Louis Blues in 10th round (10th Blues pick, 198th overall) of NHL draft (June 11, 1988). ... Strained knee ligaments (September 27, 1992); missed first 15 games of season. ... Injured shoulder (October 24, 1993); missed three games. ... Injured groin (January 18, 1994); missed six games. ... Traded by Blues with D Jeff Brown and C Nathan LaFayette to Vancouver Canucks for C Craig Janney (March 21, 1994). ... Strained groin (March 27, 1994); missed three games. ... Injured back (February 1, 1996); missed three games. ... Strained back (October 5, 1996); missed six games. ... Strained groin (December 4, 1996); missed five games. ... Strained groin (December 26, 1996); missed four games. ... Personal absence (December 13, 1997); missed one game. ... Strained back (January 21, 1998); missed one game. ... Strained abdominal muscle (February 17, 1998); missed six games. ... Sprained ankle (September 23, 1998); missed first game of season. ... Traded by Canucks with RW Pavel Bure, D Brad Ference and third-round pick (RW Robert Fried) in 2000 draft to Florida Panthers for D Ed Jovanovski, G Kevin Weekes, C Dave Gagner, C Mike Brown and first-round pick (C Nathan Smith) in 2000 draft (January 17, 1999). ... Eye (February 11, 1999); missed eight games. ... Strained groin (March 31, 1999); missed eight games. ... Suspended three games in slashing incident (November 3, 1999). ... Strained groin (October 22, 1999); missed two games. ... Strained groin (February 26, 2000); missed one game. ... Concussion (December 4, 2000); missed three games. ... Sprained left ankle (December 29, 2000); missed nine games. ... Fractured jaw (September 29, 2001); missed first 14 games of season. ... Traded by Panthers with C Kevyn Adams, D Tomas Malec and future considerations to Carolina Hurricanes for D Sandis Ozolinsh and C Byron Ritchie (January 16, 2002). ... Strained back (January 25, 2002); missed seven games. ... Concussion (December 15, 2002); missed five games. ... Concussion (January 3, 2003); missed five games. ... Injured knee (February 4, 2004); missed one game. ... Sore groin (December 18, 2005); missed one game. ... Sore shoulder (January 19, 2006); missed one game. ... Ill (March 14, 2006); missed one game. ... Injured lower body (March 23, 2006); missed four games.

Season Team	League	GP	G	A	Pts.	PIM	+/-	PP	SH	GP	G	A	Pts.	PIM
		REGULAR SEASON								PLAYOFFS				
88-89—St. Cloud State	WCHA	28	5	3	8	28	...	...	...	—	—	—	—	—
89-90—St. Cloud State	WCHA	36	4	17	21	37	...	...	...	—	—	—	—	—
90-91—St. Cloud State	WCHA	41	18	30	48	52	...	...	...	—	—	—	—	—
91-92—U.S. national team	Int'l	54	1	8	9	59	...	...	...	—	—	—	—	—
—U.S. Olympic team	Int'l	8	0	0	0	4	...	...	...	—	—	—	—	—
—St. Louis	NHL	4	1	0	1	0	1	0	0	5	0	0	0	0
92-93—Peoria	IHL	19	0	8	8	10	-2	0	0	—	—	—	—	—
—St. Louis	NHL	42	0	8	8	30	-2	0	0	10	0	0	0	14
93-94—St. Louis	NHL	61	0	11	11	64	-8	0	0	—	—	—	—	—
—Vancouver	NHL	8	0	1	1	0	1	0	0	24	1	6	7	16
94-95—Vancouver	NHL	45	2	11	13	34	-3	0	0	11	0	2	2	6
95-96—Vancouver	NHL	77	6	23	29	83	8	1	0	6	0	1	1	10
96-97—Vancouver	NHL	67	4	15	19	51	-3	2	0	—	—	—	—	—
97-98—Vancouver	NHL	71	3	24	27	79	3	1	0	—	—	—	—	—
98-99—Vancouver	NHL	42	2	11	13	34	7	0	2	—	—	—	—	—
—Florida	NHL	25	3	7	10	17	-2	0	0	—	—	—	—	—
99-00—Florida	NHL	76	6	19	25	68	4	2	0	4	0	0	0	0
00-01—Florida	NHL	70	5	15	20	72	-7	4	0	—	—	—	—	—
01-02—Florida	NHL	31	3	7	10	12	-4	0	0	—	—	—	—	—
—Carolina	NHL	26	2	4	6	10	3	0	0	23	1	4	5	20
02-03—Carolina	NHL	72	3	14	17	75	-24	1	0	—	—	—	—	—
03-04—Carolina	NHL	81	7	17	24	64	-10	2	0	—	—	—	—	—
05-06—Carolina	NHL	74	5	22	27	58	11	2	1	25	2	9	11	42
—U.S. Olympic team	Int'l	6	0	1	1	6	1	0	0	—	—	—	—	—
NHL Totals (14 years)		872	52	209	261	751	-25	15	3	108	4	22	26	108

HEDSTROM, JONATHAN RW/LW

PERSONAL: Born December 27, 1977, in Skelleftea, Sweden. ... 5-11/201. ... Shoots left.

TRANSACTIONS/CAREER NOTES: Selected by Toronto Maple Leafs in 9nth round (eighth Maple Leafs pick, 239th overall) of entry draft (June 21, 1997). ... Rights traded by Maple Leafs to Anaheim Mighty Ducks for sixth-(C Vadim Sozinov) and seventh-round (D Markus Seikola) picks in 2000 entry draft (June 25, 2000). ... Signed as free agent by Djurgardens IF of Swedish league (September 1, 2003). ... Strained groin (October 5, 2005); missed two games.

Season Team	League	GP	G	A	Pts.	PIM	+/-	PP	SH	GP	G	A	Pts.	PIM
		REGULAR SEASON								PLAYOFFS				
95-96—Skelleftea	Sweden Dv. 2	7	0	0	0	0	...	...	...	—	—	—	—	—
96-97—Skelleftea	Sweden Dv. 2	12	1	1	2	10	...	...	...	6	0	0	0	2
—Skelleftea	Sweden Jr.	9	4	4	8	...	...	...	...	—	—	—	—	—
97-98—Skelleftea	Sweden Dv. 2	16	2	3	5	...	...	...	...	—	—	—	—	—
—Skelleftea	Sweden Jr.	1	0	0	0	2	...	...	...	—	—	—	—	—
98-99—Skelleftea	Sweden Dv. 2	36	15	28	43	74	...	...	...	—	—	—	—	—
99-00—Lulea	Sweden	48	9	17	26	46	...	...	...	9	2	1	3	12
00-01—Lulea	Sweden	46	9	19	28	68	...	...	...	12	1	6	7	16
01-02—Lulea	Sweden	47	11	7	18	38	...	...	...	4	2	1	3	6
02-03—Cincinnati	AHL	50	14	21	35	62	-3	1	1	—	—	—	—	—
—Anaheim	NHL	4	0	0	0	0	-1	0	0	—	—	—	—	—

Season Team	League	REGULAR SEASON GP	G	A	Pts.	PIM	+/-	PP	SH	PLAYOFFS GP	G	A	Pts.	PIM
03-04—Djurgarden Stockholm	Sweden	48	12	22	34	94	...	...	...	3	0	2	2	12
04-05—Timra	Sweden	46	14	21	35	92	...	...	...	7	3	5	8	16
05-06—Anaheim	NHL	79	13	14	27	48	2	2	2	3	0	1	1	2
NHL Totals (2 years)		83	13	14	27	48	1	2	2	3	0	1	1	2

HEJDUK, MILAN RW

PERSONAL: Born February 14, 1976, in Usti-nad-Labem, Czech. ... 6-0/190. ... Shoots right. ... Name pronounced MEE-lan HAY-dook.
TRANSACTIONS/CAREER NOTES: Selected by Quebec Nordiques in fourth round (sixth Nordiques pick, 72nd overall) of NHL draft (June 29, 1994). ... Nordiques franchise moved to Colorado and renamed Avalanche for 1995-96 season (June 21, 1995). ... Strained back (January 7, 2000); missed one game. ... Strained abdominal muscle (February 28, 2002); missed final 20 games of season. ... Arthoscopic knee surgery (September 19, 2005); missed first six games of season. ... Neck injury (February 2, 2006); missed one game. ... Flu (March 25, 2006); missed one game.
STATISTICAL PLATEAUS: Three-goal games: 2002-03 (1), 2003-04 (1). Total: 2.

Season Team	League	REGULAR SEASON GP	G	A	Pts.	PIM	+/-	PP	SH	PLAYOFFS GP	G	A	Pts.	PIM
93-94—HC Pardubice	Czech Rep.	22	6	3	9	...	...	...	...	10	5	1	6	...
94-95—HC Pardubice	Czech Rep.			Did not play										
95-96—HC Pardubice	Czech Rep.	37	13	7	20	...	...	...	...	—	—	—	—	—
96-97—HC Pardubice	Czech Rep.	51	27	11	38	10	...	...	...	10	6	0	6	27
97-98—Pojistovna Pardubice	Czech Rep.	48	26	19	45	20	...	...	...	3	0	0	0	2
—Czech Rep. Oly. team	Int'l	4	0	0	0	2	2	0	0	—	—	—	—	—
98-99—Colorado	NHL	82	14	34	48	26	8	4	0	16	6	6	12	4
99-00—Colorado	NHL	82	36	36	72	16	14	13	0	17	5	4	9	6
00-01—Colorado	NHL	80	41	38	79	36	32	12	1	23	7	*16	23	6
01-02—Colorado	NHL	62	21	23	44	24	0	7	1	16	3	3	6	4
—Czech Rep. Oly. team	Int'l	4	1	0	1	0	...	...	...	—	—	—	—	—
02-03—Colorado	NHL	82	*50	48	98	32	52	18	0	7	2	2	4	2
03-04—Colorado	NHL	82	35	40	75	20	19	16	0	11	5	2	7	0
04-05—Pardubice	Czech Rep.	48	25	26	51	14	12	...	...	16	6	2	8	6
05-06—Colorado	NHL	74	24	34	58	24	13	14	1	9	2	6	8	2
—Czech Rep. Oly. team	Int'l	8	2	1	3	2	-5	0	0	—	—	—	—	—
NHL Totals (7 years)		544	221	253	474	178	138	84	3	99	30	39	69	24

HELBLING, TIMO D

PERSONAL: Born July 21, 1981, in Basel, Switz. ... 6-3/209. ... Shoots right.
TRANSACTIONS/CAREER NOTES: Selected by Nashville Predators in sixth round (12th Predators pick, 16second overall) of entry draft (June 26, 1999). ... Traded by Predators to Tampa Bay Lightning for eighth-round pick (G Pekka Rinne) in 2004 entry draft (February 25, 2004).

Season Team	League	REGULAR SEASON GP	G	A	Pts.	PIM	+/-	PP	SH	PLAYOFFS GP	G	A	Pts.	PIM
97-98—Davos	Switz. Jr.	40	6	7	13	48	...	...	...	—	—	—	—	—
98-99—Davos	Switz. Jr.	22	8	10	18	108	...	...	...	—	—	—	—	—
—Davos	Switzerland	25	0	1	1	12	...	...	...	4	0	0	0	0
99-00—Davos HC	Switzerland	44	0	0	0	49	...	0	0	5	0	0	0	0
00-01—Windsor	OHL	54	7	14	21	90	16	2	0	7	0	2	2	11
—Milwaukee	IHL	...	...	...	...	...	...	...	...	1	0	0	0	0
01-02—Milwaukee	AHL	67	2	6	8	59	-10	0	0	—	—	—	—	—
02-03—Milwaukee	AHL	23	0	1	1	37	1	0	0	—	—	—	—	—
—Toledo	ECHL	35	3	8	11	75	6	0	0	7	0	1	1	2
03-04—Milwaukee	AHL	37	0	2	2	46	...	...	...	—	—	—	—	—
—Utah	AHL	23	3	2	5	47	...	...	...	—	—	—	—	—
04-05—Kloten	Switzerland	44	2	9	11	118	...	...	...	5	1	3	4	8
05-06—Springfield	AHL	60	7	14	21	56	-22	2	0	—	—	—	—	—
—Tampa Bay	NHL	9	0	1	1	6	-3	0	0	—	—	—	—	—
NHL Totals (1 year)		9	0	1	1	6	-3	0	0					

HELENIUS, RIKU G

PERSONAL: Born March 1, 1988, in Palkane, Finland. ... 6-3/202. ... Catches left.
TRANSACTIONS/CAREER NOTES: Selected by Tampa Bay Lightning in first round (first Lightning pick; 15th overall) of NHL draft (June 24, 2006).

Season Team	League	REGULAR SEASON GP	Min.	W	L	OTL	T	GA	SO	GAA	SV%	PLAYOFFS GP	Min.	W	L	GA	SO	GAA	SV%
04-05—Ilves Tampere	Finland Jr.	2	86	...	...	...	...	4	...	2.79	.913	—	—	—	—	—	—	—	—
05-06—Ilves Tampere	Finland Jr.	26	1565	...	...	...	...	70	...	2.68	.919	—	—	—	—	—	—	—	—

HELMER, BRYAN D

PERSONAL: Born July 15, 1972, in Sault Ste. Marie, Ont. ... 6-2/208. ... Shoots right.
TRANSACTIONS/CAREER NOTES: Signed as free agent by New Jersey Devils (October 1, 1993). ... Signed as free agent by Phoenix Coyotes (July 22, 1998). ... Claimed off waivers by St. Louis Blues (December 19, 1998). ... Signed as free agent by Vancouver Canucks (August 21, 2000). ... Traded by Canucks to Phoenix Coyotes for D Martin Grenier (July 27, 2003). ... Injured left shoulder (October 7, 2003); missed 53 games. ... Signed as free agent by Detroit Red Wings (July 20, 2004). ... Signed as free agent by Coyotes (July 19, 2006).

Season Team	League	GP	G	A	Pts.	PIM	+/-	PP	SH	GP	G	A	Pts.	PIM
		REGULAR SEASON								PLAYOFFS				
89-90—Wellington	OJHL	51	6	22	28	204	...	...	...	—	—	—	—	—
—Belleville	OHL	6	0	1	1	0	...	...	...	—	—	—	—	—
90-91—Wellington	OJHL	50	11	14	25	109	...	...	...	—	—	—	—	—
91-92—Wellington	OJHL	45	19	32	51	66	...	...	...	—	—	—	—	—
92-93—Wellington	OJHL	57	25	62	87	62	...	...	...	—	—	—	—	—
93-94—Albany	AHL	65	4	19	23	79	...	...	...	5	0	0	0	9
94-95—Albany	AHL	77	7	36	43	101	17	4	0	7	1	0	1	0
95-96—Albany	AHL	80	14	30	44	107	...	...	...	4	2	0	2	6
96-97—Albany	AHL	77	12	27	39	113	22	5	0	16	1	7	8	10
97-98—Albany	AHL	80	14	49	63	101	15	8	0	13	4	9	13	18
98-99—Phoenix	NHL	11	0	0	0	23	2	0	0	—	—	—	—	—
—Las Vegas	IHL	8	1	3	4	28	-4	1	0	—	—	—	—	—
—St. Louis	NHL	29	0	4	4	19	3	0	0	—	—	—	—	—
—Worcester	AHL	16	7	8	15	18	0	4	0	4	0	0	0	12
99-00—Worcester	AHL	54	10	25	35	124	...	...	...	9	1	4	5	10
—St. Louis	NHL	15	1	1	2	10	-3	1	0	—	—	—	—	—
00-01—Kansas City	IHL	42	4	15	19	76	...	...	...	—	—	—	—	—
—Vancouver	NHL	20	2	4	6	18	0	0	0	—	—	—	—	—
01-02—Manitoba	AHL	34	6	18	24	69	18	1	1	—	—	—	—	—
—Vancouver	NHL	40	5	5	10	53	10	2	0	6	0	0	0	0
02-03—Vancouver	NHL	2	0	0	0	0	1	0	0	—	—	—	—	—
—Manitoba	AHL	60	7	24	31	82	-10	5	0	14	0	4	4	20
03-04—Springfield	AHL	9	1	6	7	6	5	1	0	—	—	—	—	—
—Phoenix	NHL	17	0	1	1	10	-5	0	0	—	—	—	—	—
04-05—Grand Rapids	AHL	80	7	18	25	64	11	5	1	—	—	—	—	—
05-06—Grand Rapids	AHL	80	12	44	56	138	25	9	0	16	1	8	9	24
NHL Totals (6 years)		134	8	15	23	133	8	3	0	6	0	0	0	0

HEMINGWAY, COLIN RW

PERSONAL: Born August 12, 1980, in Surrey, B.C. ... 6-0/170. ... Shoots right.
TRANSACTIONS/CAREER NOTES: Selected by St. Louis Blues in eighth round (seventh Blues pick, 221st overall) of entry draft (June 26, 1999).

Season Team	League	GP	G	A	Pts.	PIM	+/-	PP	SH	GP	G	A	Pts.	PIM
		REGULAR SEASON								PLAYOFFS				
99-00—New Hampshire	Hockey East	22	3	5	8	6	...	...	...	—	—	—	—	—
00-01—New Hampshire	Hockey East	37	9	18	27	16	...	...	...	—	—	—	—	—
01-02—New Hampshire	Hockey East	40	33	33	66	30	...	...	...	—	—	—	—	—
02-03—New Hampshire	Hockey East	40	22	25	47	51	...	...	...	—	—	—	—	—
03-04—Worcester	AHL	13	2	0	2	11	...	...	...	—	—	—	—	—
—Peoria	ECHL	36	20	24	44	34	...	...	...	2	0	0	0	0
04-05—Worcester	AHL	24	5	2	7	6	-4	3	0	—	—	—	—	—
—Peoria	ECHL	20	8	10	18	6	...	...	...	—	—	—	—	—
05-06—Peoria	AHL	29	7	9	16	19	-1	3	0	—	—	—	—	—
—St. Louis	NHL	3	0	0	0	0	-2	0	0	—	—	—	—	—
—Alaska	ECHL	5	1	2	3	2	...	...	...	—	—	—	—	—
NHL Totals (1 year)		3	0	0	0	0	-2	0	0					

HEMSKY, ALES RW

PERSONAL: Born August 13, 1983, in Pardubice, Czech. ... 6-0/192. ... Shoots right. ... Name pronounced: AL-ihsh HEHM-skee
TRANSACTIONS/CAREER NOTES: Selected by Edmonton Oilers in first round (first Oilers pick, 13th overall) of NHL draft (June 23, 2001). ... Flu and abdominal soreness (January 22, 2003); missed one game. ... Strained abdomen (January 29, 2003); missed two games. ... Flu and abdominal soreness (February 18, 2003); missed four games.

Season Team	League	GP	G	A	Pts.	PIM	+/-	PP	SH	GP	G	A	Pts.	PIM
		REGULAR SEASON								PLAYOFFS				
99-00—Pardubice	Czech. Jrs.	52	24	50	74	90	...	...	...	—	—	—	—	—
—HC Pardubice	Czech Rep.	4	0	1	1	0	...	...	...	—	—	—	—	—
00-01—Hull	QMJHL	68	36	64	100	67	...	...	...	5	2	3	5	2
01-02—Hull	QMJHL	53	27	70	97	86	...	...	...	10	6	10	16	6
02-03—Edmonton	NHL	59	6	24	30	14	5	0	0	6	0	0	0	0
03-04—Edmonton	NHL	71	12	22	34	14	-7	4	0	—	—	—	—	—
04-05—Pardubice	Czech Rep.	47	13	18	31	28	5	...	...	16	4	10	14	26
05-06—Edmonton	NHL	81	19	58	77	64	-5	7	1	24	6	11	17	14
—Czech Rep. Oly. team	Int'l	8	1	2	3	2	0	1	0	—	—	—	—	—
NHL Totals (3 years)		211	37	104	141	92	-7	11	1	30	6	11	17	14

HENRY, ALEX D/LW

PERSONAL: Born October 18, 1979, in Elliot Lake, Ont. ... 6-5/220. ... Shoots left.
TRANSACTIONS/CAREER NOTES: Selected by Edmonton Oilers in third round (second Oilers pick, 67th overall) of draft (June 27, 1998). ... Claimed off waivers by Washington Capitals (October 24, 2002). ... Flu (January 25, 2003); missed four games. ... Concussion (October 3, 2003); missed five games. ... Claimed off waivers by Minnesota Wild (October 9, 2003). ... Groin (November 19, 2003); missed three games. ... Groin (October 16, 2005); missed two games. ... Leg (October 25, 2005); missed five games. ... Chest (January 24, 2006); missed one game.

Season Team	League	GP	G	A	Pts.	PIM	+/-	PP	SH	GP	G	A	Pts.	PIM
		REGULAR SEASON								PLAYOFFS				
96-97—London	OHL	61	1	10	11	65	...	...	...	—	—	—	—	—
97-98—London	OHL	62	5	9	14	97	...	...	...	16	0	3	3	14
98-99—London	OHL	68	5	23	28	105	33	...	...	25	3	10	13	22
99-00—Hamilton	AHL	60	1	0	1	69	...	...	...	—	—	—	—	—
00-01—Hamilton	AHL	56	2	3	5	87	...	...	...	—	—	—	—	—
01-02—Hamilton	AHL	69	4	8	12	143	12	0	0	15	1	2	3	16
02-03—Edmonton	NHL	3	0	0	0	0	-1	0	0	—	—	—	—	—
—Washington	NHL	38	0	0	0	80	-4	0	0	—	—	—	—	—
—Portland	AHL	3	0	1	1	0	1	0	0	—	—	—	—	—
03-04—Minnesota	NHL	71	2	4	6	106	4	0	0	—	—	—	—	—
04-05—Kaufbeuren	Germany	16	4	4	8	20	...	...	...	—	—	—	—	—
05-06—Minnesota	NHL	63	0	5	5	73	-4	0	0	—	—	—	—	—
NHL Totals (3 years)		175	2	9	11	259	-5	0	0					

HEWARD, JAMIE D

PERSONAL: Born March 30, 1971, in Regina, Sask. ... 6-2/207. ... Shoots right. ... Name pronounced HYOO-uhrd.
TRANSACTIONS/CAREER NOTES: Selected by Pittsburgh in first round (first Penguins pick, 16th overall) of entry draft (June 17, 1989). ... Signed as free agent by Toronto (May 4, 1995). ... Signed as free agent by Philadelphia (July 10, 1997). ... Signed as free agent by Nashville (August 6, 1998). ... Sprained ankle (December 8, 1998); missed five games. ... Injured heel (March 14, 1999); missed five games. ... Signed as free agent by New York Islanders (July 7, 1999). ... Concussion (October 23, 1999); missed two games. ... Strained lower back (December 9, 1999); missed two games. ... Fractured right ankle (February 17, 2000); missed remainder of season. ... Claimed off waivers by Columbus (May 26, 2000). ... Sprained wrist (January 7, 2001); missed two games. ... Injured wrist (February 6, 2002); missed one game. ... Signed as free agent by Washington Capitals (August 12, 2005). ... Arm muscle strain (November 6, 2005); missed one game. ... Undisclosed lower body injury (January 18, 2006); missed five games. ... Head injury (March 4, 2006); missed two games. ... Upper-body injury (April 15, 2006); missed final three games of regular season.

Season Team	League	GP	G	A	Pts.	PIM	+/-	PP	SH	GP	G	A	Pts.	PIM
		REGULAR SEASON								PLAYOFFS				
87-88—Regina	WHL	68	10	17	27	17	...	...	...	4	1	1	2	2
88-89—Regina	WHL	52	31	28	59	29	...	...	...	—	—	—	—	—
89-90—Regina	WHL	72	14	44	58	42	...	...	...	11	2	2	4	10
90-91—Regina	WHL	71	23	61	84	41	...	...	...	8	2	9	11	6
91-92—Muskegon	IHL	54	6	21	27	37	...	...	...	14	1	4	5	4
92-93—Cleveland	IHL	58	9	18	27	64	-11	4	0	—	—	—	—	—
93-94—Cleveland	IHL	73	8	16	24	72	-7	2	0	—	—	—	—	—
94-95—Canadian nat'l team	Int'l	51	11	35	46	32	...	...	...	—	—	—	—	—
95-96—St. John's	AHL	73	22	34	56	33	...	...	...	3	1	1	2	6
—Toronto	NHL	5	0	0	0	0	-1	0	0	—	—	—	—	—
96-97—Toronto	NHL	20	1	4	5	6	-6	0	0	—	—	—	—	—
—St. John's	AHL	27	8	19	27	26	-9	2	1	9	1	3	4	6
97-98—Philadelphia	AHL	72	17	48	65	54	21	5	0	20	3	16	19	10
98-99—Nashville	NHL	63	6	12	18	44	-24	4	0	—	—	—	—	—
99-00—New York Islanders	NHL	54	6	11	17	26	-9	2	0	—	—	—	—	—
00-01—Columbus	NHL	69	11	16	27	33	3	9	0	—	—	—	—	—
01-02—Columbus	NHL	28	1	2	3	7	-9	0	0	—	—	—	—	—
—Syracuse	AHL	14	3	10	13	6	2	2	0	10	0	4	4	6
02-03—Geneva	Switzerland	39	8	23	31	60	...	...	...	6	1	1	2	22
03-04—ZSC Lions Zurich	Switzerland	25	5	9	14	57	...	...	...	6	0	1	1	24
04-05—SC Langnau	Switzerland	44	3	14	17	83	...	...	...	5	0	0	0	40
05-06—Washington	NHL	71	7	21	28	54	-5	4	0	—	—	—	—	—
NHL Totals (7 years)		310	32	66	98	170	-51	19	0					

HIGGINS, CHRIS LW

PERSONAL: Born June 2, 1983, in Smithtown, N.Y. ... 6-0/192. ... Shoots left.
TRANSACTIONS/CAREER NOTES: Selected by Montreal Canadiens in first round (first Canadiens pick, 14th overall) of NHL draft (June 22, 2002). ... Injured groin (January 21, 2006); missed two games.

Season Team	League	GP	G	A	Pts.	PIM	+/-	PP	SH	GP	G	A	Pts.	PIM
		REGULAR SEASON								PLAYOFFS				
00-01—Avon Old Farms	USHS (East)	24	22	14	36	29	...	...	...	—	—	—	—	—
01-02—Yale	ECAC	25	13	16	29	32	...	...	...	—	—	—	—	—
02-03—Yale	ECAC	28	20	21	41	41	...	...	...	—	—	—	—	—
03-04—Montreal	NHL	2	0	0	0	0	0	0	0	—	—	—	—	—
—Hamilton	AHL	67	21	27	48	18	16	4	1	10	3	2	5	0
04-05—Hamilton	AHL	76	28	23	51	33	9	8	4	4	3	3	6	4
05-06—Montreal	NHL	80	23	15	38	26	-1	7	3	6	1	3	4	0
NHL Totals (2 years)		82	23	15	38	26	-1	7	3	6	1	3	4	0

HILBERT, ANDY C/LW

PERSONAL: Born February 6, 1981, in Lansing, Mich. ... 5-11/194. ... Shoots left.
TRANSACTIONS/CAREER NOTES: Selected by Boston Bruins in second round (third Bruins pick, 37th overall) of entry draft (June 24, 2000). ... Signed as free agent by AHL Providence (September 27, 2004). ... Traded by Bruins to Chicago Blackhawks for fifth-round pick (traded to New York Islanders; Islanders selected D Shane Sims) in 2006 draft (November 6, 2005). ... Claimed on waivers by Pittsburgh Penguins (March 9, 2006). ... Signed as free agent by New York Islanders (July 4, 2006).

Season Team	League	GP	G	A	Pts.	PIM	+/-	PP	SH	GP	G	A	Pts.	PIM
		REGULAR SEASON								PLAYOFFS				
98-99—U.S. National	USHL	46	23	35	58	140	...	...	...	—	—	—	—	—
99-00—Univ. of Michigan	CCHA	35	17	15	32	39	...	...	...	—	—	—	—	—
00-01—Univ. of Michigan	CCHA	42	26	38	64	72	...	...	...	—	—	—	—	—
01-02—Providence	AHL	72	26	27	53	74	-2	10	2	—	—	—	—	—
—Boston	NHL	6	1	0	1	2	-2	0	0	—	—	—	—	—
02-03—Providence	AHL	64	35	35	70	119	0	11	2	—	—	—	—	—
—Boston	NHL	14	0	3	3	7	-1	0	0	—	—	—	—	—
03-04—Boston	NHL	18	2	0	2	9	1	0	0	5	1	0	1	0
—Providence	AHL	19	3	5	8	20	2	1	1	—	—	—	—	—
04-05—Providence	AHL	79	37	42	79	83	11	16	3	17	7	14	21	27
05-06—Norfolk	AHL	5	3	4	7	2	2	1	0	—	—	—	—	—
—Chicago	NHL	28	5	4	9	22	-4	0	0	—	—	—	—	—
—Pittsburgh	NHL	19	7	11	18	16	8	3	0	—	—	—	—	—
NHL Totals (4 years)		85	15	18	33	56	2	3	0	5	1	0	1	0

HILL, SEAN — D

PERSONAL: Born February 14, 1970, in Duluth, Minn. ... 6-0/205. ... Shoots right.

TRANSACTIONS/CAREER NOTES: Selected by Montreal Canadiens in eighth round (ninth Canadiens pick, 167th overall) of entry draft (June 11, 1988). ... Strained abdominal muscle (October 13, 1992); missed 14 games. ... Selected by Anaheim Mighty Ducks in expansion draft (June 24, 1993). ... Sprained shoulder (January 6, 1994); missed nine games. ... Traded by Mighty Ducks with ninth-round pick (G Frederic Cassivi) in 1994 entry draft to Ottawa Senators for third-round pick (traded to Tampa Bay; Lightning selected Vadim Epanchintsev) in 1994 entry draft (June 29, 1994). ... Strained abdominal muscle during 1995-96 season; missed two games. ... Torn left knee ligament (October 18, 1996); missed remainder of season. ... Traded by Senators to Carolina Hurricanes for RW Chris Murray (November 18, 1997). ... Strained hip flexor (December 1, 1997); missed three games. ... Fractured leg (March 26, 1998); missed final 11 games of season. ... Fractured ankle and strained abdominal muscle (December 21, 1998); missed 20 games. ... Strained abdominal muscle (February 13, 1999); missed one game. ... Sprained ankle (March 21, 1999); missed four games. ... Fractured cheekbone (April 14, 1999); missed final two games of season. ... Strained groin (December 22, 1999); missed 18 games. ... Reinjured groin (April 3, 2000); missed final two games of season. ... Signed as free agent by St. Louis Blues (July 1, 2000). ... Strained muscle in abdomen (November 29, 2000); missed 32 games. ... Strained groin (October 31, 2001); missed two games. ... Traded by Blues to Hurricanes for D Steve Halko and fourth-round pick (later traded to Atlanta; Thrashers selected Lane Manson) in 2002 draft (December 5, 2001). ... Strained groin (October 28, 2003); missed two games. ... Signed as free agent by Florida Panthers (July 15, 2004). ... Groin (December 1, 2005); missed four games.

Season Team	League	GP	G	A	Pts.	PIM	+/-	PP	SH	GP	G	A	Pts.	PIM
		REGULAR SEASON								PLAYOFFS				
88-89—Wisconsin	WCHA	45	2	23	25	69	...	...	...	—	—	—	—	—
89-90—Wisconsin	WCHA	42	14	39	53	78	...	...	...	—	—	—	—	—
90-91—Wisconsin	WCHA	37	19	32	51	122	...	...	...	—	—	—	—	—
—Fredericton	AHL	...	...	...	...	...	...	...	...	3	0	2	2	2
—Montreal	NHL	...	...	...	...	...	...	...	...	1	0	0	0	0
91-92—Fredericton	AHL	42	7	20	27	65	...	...	...	7	1	3	4	6
—U.S. national team	Int'l	12	4	3	7	16	...	...	...	—	—	—	—	—
—U.S. Olympic team	Int'l	8	2	0	2	6	...	...	...	—	—	—	—	—
—Montreal	NHL	...	...	...	...	...	...	...	...	4	1	0	1	2
92-93—Montreal	NHL	31	2	6	8	54	-5	1	0	3	0	0	0	4
—Fredericton	AHL	6	1	3	4	10	3	1	0	—	—	—	—	—
93-94—Anaheim	NHL	68	7	20	27	78	-12	2	1	—	—	—	—	—
94-95—Ottawa	NHL	45	1	14	15	30	-11	0	0	—	—	—	—	—
95-96—Ottawa	NHL	80	7	14	21	94	-26	2	0	—	—	—	—	—
96-97—Ottawa	NHL	5	0	0	0	4	1	0	0	—	—	—	—	—
97-98—Ottawa	NHL	13	1	1	2	6	-3	0	0	—	—	—	—	—
—Carolina	NHL	42	0	5	5	48	-2	0	0	—	—	—	—	—
98-99—Carolina	NHL	54	0	10	10	48	9	0	0	—	—	—	—	—
99-00—Carolina	NHL	62	13	31	44	59	3	8	0	—	—	—	—	—
00-01—St. Louis	NHL	48	1	10	11	51	5	0	0	15	0	1	1	12
01-02—St. Louis	NHL	23	0	3	3	28	1	0	0	—	—	—	—	—
—Carolina	NHL	49	7	23	30	61	-1	4	0	23	4	4	8	20
02-03—Carolina	NHL	82	5	24	29	141	4	1	0	—	—	—	—	—
03-04—Carolina	NHL	80	13	26	39	84	-2	6	0	—	—	—	—	—
05-06—Florida	NHL	78	2	18	20	80	3	1	0	—	—	—	—	—
NHL Totals (15 years)		760	59	205	264	866	-36	25	1	46	5	5	10	38

HINOTE, DAN — RW/C

PERSONAL: Born January 30, 1977, in Leesburg, Fla. ... 6-0/195. ... Shoots right.

TRANSACTIONS/CAREER NOTES: Selected by Colorado Avalanche in seventh round (ninth Avalanche pick, 167th overall) of NHL draft (June 22, 1996). ... Sprained knee (February 19, 2001); missed one game. ... Injured finger (November 10, 2001); missed one game. ... Injured knee (December 12, 2001); missed one game. ... Injured heel (January 5, 2002); missed 11 games. ... Injured shoulder (March 6, 2002); missed 11 games. ... Fractured leg (October 8, 2002); missed nine games. ... Injured head, leg (February 2, 2003); missed 12 games. ... Concussion (January 30, 2003); missed 14 games. ... Dislocated shoulder (March 14, 2004); missed nine games. ... Back spasms (October 19, 2005); missed six games. ... Knee injury (November 10, 2005); missed three games. ... Signed as free agent by St. Louis Blues (July 3, 2006).

Season Team	League	GP	G	A	Pts.	PIM	+/-	PP	SH	GP	G	A	Pts.	PIM
		REGULAR SEASON								PLAYOFFS				
95-96—Army	AH	33	20	24	44	20	...	...	...	—	—	—	—	—
96-97—Oshawa	OHL	60	15	13	28	58	...	...	...	18	4	5	9	8
97-98—Hershey	AHL	24	1	4	5	25	-6	0	0	—	—	—	—	—
—Oshawa	OHL	35	12	15	27	39	7	...	...	5	2	2	4	7
98-99—Hershey	AHL	65	4	16	20	95	3	0	0	5	3	1	4	6

Season Team	League	GP	G	A	Pts.	PIM	+/-	PP	SH	GP	G	A	Pts.	PIM
		REGULAR SEASON								PLAYOFFS				
99-00—Colorado	NHL	27	1	3	4	10	0	0	0	—	—	—	—	—
—Hershey	AHL	55	28	31	59	96	...	...	...	14	4	5	9	19
00-01—Colorado	NHL	76	5	10	15	51	1	1	0	23	2	4	6	21
01-02—Colorado	NHL	58	6	6	12	39	8	0	1	19	1	2	3	9
02-03—Colorado	NHL	60	6	4	10	49	4	0	0	7	1	2	3	2
03-04—Colorado	NHL	59	4	7	11	57	-6	0	2	11	1	0	1	0
04-05—MoDo Ornskoldsvik	Sweden	18	2	1	3	106	-1	1	0	5	0	0	0	56
05-06—Colorado	NHL	73	5	8	13	48	-5	0	1	9	1	1	2	31
NHL Totals (6 years)		353	27	38	65	254	2	1	4	69	6	9	15	63

HNIDY, SHANE — D

PERSONAL: Born November 8, 1975, in Neepawa, Man. ... 6-1/210. ... Shoots right. ... Name pronounced NIGH-dee.

TRANSACTIONS/CAREER NOTES: Selected by Buffalo Sabres in seventh round (Sabres seventh pick, 173rd overall) of NHL draft (June 28, 1994). ... Signed as free agent by Detroit Red Wings (August 6, 1998). ... Traded by Red Wings to Ottawa Senators for eighth-round pick (RW Todd Jackson) in 2000 draft (June 25, 2000). ... Bruised left foot (December 14, 2000); missed four games. ... Strained groin (March 26, 2001); missed final six games of regular season. ... Injured left ankle (December 23, 2001); missed 11 games. ... Injured left eye (November 21, 2002); missed eight games. ... Fractured finger (January 9, 2003); missed three games. ... Bruised neck (April 1, 2003); missed 1 game. ... Bruised right foot (November 8, 2003); missed 11 games. ... Bruised leg (January 17, 2004); missed two games. ... Flu (February 10, 2004); missed one game. ... Traded by Senators to Nashville Predators for third-round pick (C/W Peter Regin) in 2004 draft (March 9, 2004). ... Left team for personal reasons (March 23, 2004); missed one game. ... Traded by the Predators to Atlanta Thrashers for fourth-round pick (W Niko Snellman) in 2006 (July 30, 2005) ... Separated shoulder (September 2005); missed first seven games of season.

Season Team	League	GP	G	A	Pts.	PIM	+/-	PP	SH	GP	G	A	Pts.	PIM
		REGULAR SEASON								PLAYOFFS				
91-92—Swift Current	WHL	56	1	3	4	11	...	...	...	—	—	—	—	—
92-93—Swift Current	WHL	72	7	22	29	105	...	...	...	—	—	—	—	—
93-94—Prince Albert	WHL	69	7	26	33	113	18	2	1	—	—	—	—	—
94-95—Prince Albert	WHL	72	5	29	34	169	18	0	0	15	4	7	11	29
95-96—Prince Albert	WHL	58	11	42	53	100	...	...	...	18	4	11	15	34
96-97—Baton Rouge	ECHL	21	3	10	13	50	...	...	...	—	—	—	—	—
—Saint John	AHL	44	2	12	14	112	-16	0	0	—	—	—	—	—
97-98—Grand Rapids	IHL	77	6	12	18	210	2	0	0	3	0	2	2	23
98-99—Adirondack	AHL	68	9	20	29	121	-29	4	0	3	0	1	1	0
99-00—Cincinnati	AHL	68	9	19	28	153	...	...	...	—	—	—	—	—
00-01—Ottawa	NHL	52	3	2	5	84	8	0	0	1	0	0	0	0
—Grand Rapids	IHL	2	0	0	0	2	...	...	...	—	—	—	—	—
01-02—Ottawa	NHL	33	1	1	2	57	-10	0	0	12	1	1	2	12
02-03—Ottawa	NHL	67	0	8	8	130	-1	0	0	1	0	0	0	0
03-04—Ottawa	NHL	37	0	5	5	72	2	0	0	—	—	—	—	—
—Nashville	NHL	9	0	2	2	10	3	0	0	5	0	0	0	6
04-05—Florida	ECHL	19	1	4	5	56	7	0	...	17	0	4	4	6
05-06—Atlanta	NHL	66	0	3	3	33	1	0	0	—	—	—	—	—
NHL Totals (5 years)		264	4	21	25	386	3	0	0	19	1	1	2	18

HOGGAN, JEFF — LW/RW

PERSONAL: Born February 1, 1978, in Hope. B.C. ... 6-0/200. ... Shoots right.

COLLEGE: Nebraska-Omaha.

TRANSACTIONS/CAREER NOTES: Signed as free agent by Minnesota Wild (August 20, 2002). ... Signed as free agent by St. Louis Blues (August 2, 2005). ... Fractured collarbone (January 26, 2006); missed 26 games. ... Signed as free agent by Boston Bruins (July 21, 2006).

Season Team	League	GP	G	A	Pts.	PIM	+/-	PP	SH	GP	G	A	Pts.	PIM
		REGULAR SEASON								PLAYOFFS				
99-00—U. of Neb.-Omaha	CCHA	34	16	9	25	82	...	...	...	—	—	—	—	—
00-01—U. of Neb.-Omaha	CCHA	42	12	17	29	78	...	...	...	—	—	—	—	—
01-02—Houston	AHL	0	...	...	...	...	...	...	...	4	0	0	0	2
—U. of Neb.-Omaha	CCHA	41	24	21	45	92	...	...	...	—	—	—	—	—
02-03—Houston	AHL	65	6	5	11	45	...	...	...	14	1	2	3	23
03-04—Houston	AHL	77	21	15	36	88	...	...	...	2	0	1	1	4
04-05—Worcester	AHL	47	16	9	25	55	-7	5	0	—	—	—	—	—
05-06—St. Louis	NHL	52	2	6	8	34	-16	0	0	—	—	—	—	—
NHL Totals (1 year)		52	2	6	8	34	-16	0	0					

HOLIK, BOBBY — C

PERSONAL: Born January 1, 1971, in Jihlava, Czech. ... 6-4/235. ... Shoots right. ... Name pronounced hoh-LEEK.

TRANSACTIONS/CAREER NOTES: Selected by Hartford Whalers in first round (first Whalers pick, 10th overall) of entry draft (June 17, 1989). ... Traded by Whalers with second-round pick (LW Jay Pandolfo) in 1993 draft to New Jersey Devils for G Sean Burke and D Eric Weinrich (August 28, 1992). ... Bruised left shoulder (December 8, 1993); missed 11 games. ... Fractured left index finger (October 7, 1995); missed 13 games. ... Sprained left ankle (February 28, 1996); missed six games. ... Suspended two games and fined $1,000 for tripping incident (November 8, 1998). ... Suspended two games for slashing incident (March 23, 1999). ... Suspended three games for slashing incident (November 25, 1999). ... Injured knee (February 15, 2001); missed two games. ... Suspended one game for high-sticking incident (March 24, 2002). ... Signed as free agent by New York Rangers (July 1, 2002). ... Injured hip flexor (October 16, 2002); missed 18 games. ... Contract bought out by Rangers (July 29, 2005). ... Signed as a free agent by the Atlanta Thrashers (August 2, 2005). ... Broken left foot (January 1, 2006); missed 18 games.

STATISTICAL PLATEAUS: Three-goal games: 1992-93 (2), 1998-99 (1). Total: 3.

Season Team	League	GP	G	A	Pts.	PIM	+/-	PP	SH	GP	G	A	Pts.	PIM
		REGULAR SEASON								PLAYOFFS				
87-88—Dukla Jihlava	Czech.	31	5	9	14	...	...	...	...	—	—	—	—	—
88-89—Dukla Jihlava	Czech.	24	7	10	17	...	...	...	...	—	—	—	—	—
89-90—Dukla Jihlava	Czech.	42	15	26	41	...	...	...	...	—	—	—	—	—
—Czech. national team	Int'l	10	1	5	6	0	...	...	...	—	—	—	—	—
90-91—Hartford	NHL	78	21	22	43	113	-3	8	0	6	0	0	0	7
91-92—Hartford	NHL	76	21	24	45	44	4	1	0	7	0	1	1	6
92-93—Utica	AHL	1	0	0	0	2	-1	0	0	—	—	—	—	—
—New Jersey	NHL	61	20	19	39	76	-6	7	0	5	1	1	2	6
93-94—New Jersey	NHL	70	13	20	33	72	28	2	0	20	0	3	3	6
94-95—New Jersey	NHL	48	10	10	20	18	9	0	0	20	4	4	8	22
95-96—New Jersey	NHL	63	13	17	30	58	9	1	0	—	—	—	—	—
96-97—New Jersey	NHL	82	23	39	62	54	24	5	0	10	2	3	5	4
97-98—New Jersey	NHL	82	29	36	65	100	23	8	0	5	0	0	0	8
98-99—New Jersey	NHL	78	27	37	64	119	16	5	0	7	0	7	7	6
99-00—New Jersey	NHL	79	23	23	46	106	7	7	0	23	3	7	10	14
00-01—New Jersey	NHL	80	15	35	50	97	19	3	0	25	6	10	16	37
01-02—New Jersey	NHL	81	25	29	54	97	7	6	0	6	4	1	5	2
02-03—New York Rangers	NHL	64	16	19	35	50	-1	3	0	—	—	—	—	—
03-04—New York Rangers	NHL	82	25	31	56	96	4	8	0	—	—	—	—	—
05-06—Atlanta	NHL	64	15	18	33	79	-6	5	0	—	—	—	—	—
NHL Totals (15 years)		1088	296	379	675	1179	134	69	0	134	20	37	57	118

HOLLWEG, RYAN — LW

PERSONAL: Born April 23, 1983, in Langley, B.C. ... 5-10/210. ... Shoots left.

TRANSACTIONS/CAREER NOTES: Selected by New York Rangers in eighth round (10th Rangers pick, 238th overall) of NHL entry draft (June 24, 2001). ... Eye (December 3, 2005); missed two games. ... Suspended three games by NHL for checking from behind (March 23, 2006).

Season Team	League	GP	G	A	Pts.	PIM	+/-	PP	SH	GP	G	A	Pts.	PIM
		REGULAR SEASON								PLAYOFFS				
99-00—Medicine Hat	WHL	54	19	27	46	107	...	...	...	—	—	—	—	—
00-01—Medicine Hat	WHL	65	19	39	58	125	...	...	...	—	—	—	—	—
01-02—Medicine Hat	WHL	58	30	40	70	121	...	...	...	—	—	—	—	—
—Hartford	AHL	8	1	1	2	2	...	...	...	9	0	2	2	19
02-03—Medicine Hat	WHL	4	1	1	2	8	...	...	...	—	—	—	—	—
03-04—Medicine Hat	WHL	52	25	32	57	117	...	...	...	20	6	9	15	22
04-05—Hartford	AHL	73	8	6	14	239	-4	0	0	6	1	0	1	9
05-06—Hartford	AHL	7	2	1	3	11	1	0	0	—	—	—	—	—
—New York Rangers	NHL	52	2	3	5	84	-3	0	0	4	0	1	1	19
NHL Totals (1 year)		52	2	3	5	84	-3	0	0	4	0	1	1	19

HOLMQVIST, MIKAEL — LW/RW

PERSONAL: Born June 8, 1979, in Stockholm, Sweden. ... 6-3/205. ... Shoots left.

TRANSACTIONS/CAREER NOTES: Selected by Anaheim Mighty Ducks in first round (first Mighty Ducks pick, 18th overall) of entry draft (June 21, 1997). ... Injured stomach muscle (January 18, 2004); missed 22 games. ... Traded by Mighty Ducks to Chicago Blackhawks for LW Travis Moen (July 30, 2005).

Season Team	League	GP	G	A	Pts.	PIM	+/-	PP	SH	GP	G	A	Pts.	PIM
		REGULAR SEASON								PLAYOFFS				
95-96—Djurgarden Stockholm	Sweden Jr.	24	7	2	9	4	...	...	...	—	—	—	—	—
96-97—Sweden	Int'l	6	1	3	4	4	...	...	...	—	—	—	—	—
—Djurgarden Stockholm	Sweden Jr.	39	29	35	64	110	...	...	...	—	—	—	—	—
—Djurgarden Stockholm	Sweden	9	0	0	0	0	...	...	...	—	—	—	—	—
97-98—Farjestad Karlstad	Sweden	41	2	3	5	6	...	...	...	7	0	0	0	0
—Swedish nat. Jr.	Sweden	7	0	1	1	28	...	...	...	—	—	—	—	—
98-99—Farjestad Karlstad	Sweden	15	0	0	0	6	-1	...	...	—	—	—	—	—
99-00—TPS Turku	Finland	54	12	3	15	14	...	...	...	11	2	3	5	4
00-01—TPS Turku	Finland	46	4	5	9	8	...	...	...	10	1	3	4	2
01-02—TPS Turku	Finland	56	9	13	22	16	...	...	...	8	1	0	1	12
02-03—TPS Turku	Finland	56	15	25	40	36	...	...	...	7	0	0	0	4
03-04—Anaheim	NHL	21	2	0	2	25	-6	0	0	—	—	—	—	—
—Cincinnati	AHL	24	7	7	14	20	0	1	2	—	—	—	—	—
04-05—Cincinnati	AHL	79	14	32	46	111	-2	6	0	11	2	2	4	10
05-06—Chicago	NHL	72	10	10	20	16	-14	2	0	—	—	—	—	—
NHL Totals (2 years)		93	12	10	22	41	-20	2	0					

HOLMSTROM, TOMAS — LW

PERSONAL: Born January 23, 1973, in Pieta, Sweden. ... 6-0/200. ... Shoots left.

TRANSACTIONS/CAREER NOTES: Selected by Detroit Red Wings in 10th round (ninth Red Wings pick, 257th overall) of entry draft (June 29, 1994). ... Knee (October 30, 1996); missed seven games. ... Shoulder (March 28, 1997); missed one game. ... Knee (November 17, 1999); missed five games. ... Injured (March 3, 2000); missed one game. ... Cut face (March 29, 2000); missed two games. ... Charley horse (November 12, 2000); missed one game. ... Back spasms (December 31, 2000); missed three games. ... Injured (October 16, 2001); missed two games. ... Wrist (November 2, 2001); missed five games. ... Flu (January 4, 2002); missed three games. ... Sternum (October 29, 2002); missed three games. ... Flu (December 8, 2002); missed one game. ... Sternum (January 28, 2003); missed two games. ... Flu (March 22, 2003); missed two games. ... Separated right shoulder (November 27, 2003); missed 15 games.

STATISTICAL PLATEAUS: Three-goal games: 2000-01 (1).

Season Team	League	GP	G	A	Pts.	PIM	+/-	PP	SH	GP	G	A	Pts.	PIM
		REGULAR SEASON								PLAYOFFS				
94-95—Lulea	Sweden	40	14	14	28	56	...	...	...	8	1	2	3	20
95-96—Lulea	Sweden	34	12	11	23	78	...	...	...	11	6	2	8	22
96-97—Detroit	NHL	47	6	3	9	33	-10	3	0	1	0	0	0	0
—Adirondack	AHL	6	3	1	4	7	-1	1	0	—	—	—	—	—
97-98—Detroit	NHL	57	5	17	22	44	6	1	0	22	7	12	19	16
98-99—Detroit	NHL	82	13	21	34	69	-11	5	0	10	4	3	7	4
99-00—Detroit	NHL	72	13	22	35	43	4	4	0	9	3	1	4	16
00-01—Detroit	NHL	73	16	24	40	40	-12	9	0	6	1	3	4	8
01-02—Detroit	NHL	69	8	18	26	58	-12	6	0	23	8	3	11	8
—Swedish Oly. team	Int'l	4	1	0	1	2	...	...	...	—	—	—	—	—
02-03—Detroit	NHL	74	20	20	40	62	11	12	0	4	1	1	2	4
03-04—Detroit	NHL	67	15	15	30	38	8	6	0	12	2	2	4	10
04-05—Lulea	Sweden	47	14	16	30	50	-10	6	0	4	0	0	0	18
05-06—Detroit	NHL	81	29	30	59	66	14	11	0	6	1	2	3	12
—Swedish Oly. team	Int'l	8	1	3	4	10	0	0	0	—	—	—	—	—
NHL Totals (9 years)		622	125	170	295	453	-2	57	0	93	27	27	54	78

HOLT, CHRIS — G

PERSONAL: Born June 5, 1985, in Vancouver. ... 6-2/218. ... Catches left.
COLLEGE: Nebraska-Omaha.
TRANSACTIONS/CAREER NOTES: Selected by New York Rangers in sixth round (eighth Rangers pick, 180th overall) of entry draft (June 21, 2002).

Season Team	League	GP	Min.	W	L	OTL	T	GA	SO	GAA	SV%	GP	Min.	W	L	GA	SO	GAA	SV%
		REGULAR SEASON										PLAYOFFS							
02-03—U.S. Jr. national team	Int'l	29	1631	11	15	...	2	...	1	...	...	—	—	—	—	—	—	—	—
03-04—U. of Neb.-Omaha	CCHA	27	1498	5	17	...	2	81	0	3.24	.900	—	—	—	—	—	—	—	—
04-05—U. of Neb.-Omaha	CCHA	37	...	19	14	...	4	...	...	2.94	...	—	—	—	—	—	—	—	—
05-06—New York Rangers	NHL	1	10	0	0	0	...	0	0	0.00	1.000	—	—	—	—	—	—	—	—
—Hartford	AHL	9	459	3	2	1	...	31	0	4.05	.879	8	487	4	4	24	0	2.96	.912
—Charlotte	ECHL	23	1229	7	11	...	1	84	0	4.10	.887	—	—	—	—	—	—	—	—
NHL Totals (1 year)		1	10	0	0	0	0	0	0	0.00	1.000								

HOLZAPFEL, RILEY — C

PERSONAL: Born August 18, 1988, in Regina, Sask. ... 5-11/170. ... Shoots left.
TRANSACTIONS/CAREER NOTES: Selected by Atlanta Thrashers in second round (second Thrashers pick; 43rd overall) of NHL draft (June 24, 2006).

Season Team	League	GP	G	A	Pts.	PIM	+/-	PP	SH	GP	G	A	Pts.	PIM
		REGULAR SEASON								PLAYOFFS				
04-05—Moose Jaw	WHL	63	15	13	28	32	2	...	...	5	1	2	3	8
05-06—Moose Jaw	WHL	64	19	38	57	46	35	...	...	22	7	9	16	20

HORCOFF, SHAWN — C/LW

PERSONAL: Born September 17, 1978, in Trail, B.C. ... 6-1/204. ... Shoots left.
TRANSACTIONS/CAREER NOTES: Selected by Edmonton Oilers in fourth round (third Oilers pick, 99th overall) of NHL draft (June 27, 1998). ... Back spasms (November 20, 2003); missed one game. ... Injured right shoulder (October 15, 2005); missed two games.

Season Team	League	GP	G	A	Pts.	PIM	+/-	PP	SH	GP	G	A	Pts.	PIM
		REGULAR SEASON								PLAYOFFS				
95-96—Chilliwack	BCJHL	58	49	96	145	44	...	...	...	—	—	—	—	—
96-97—Michigan State	CCHA	40	10	13	23	20	...	...	...	—	—	—	—	—
97-98—Michigan State	CCHA	34	14	13	27	50	...	...	...	—	—	—	—	—
98-99—Michigan State	CCHA	39	12	25	37	70	...	...	...	—	—	—	—	—
99-00—Michigan State	CCHA	41	14	48	62	46	...	...	...	—	—	—	—	—
00-01—Hamilton	AHL	24	10	18	28	19	...	...	...	—	—	—	—	—
—Edmonton	NHL	49	9	7	16	10	8	0	0	5	0	0	0	0
01-02—Edmonton	NHL	61	8	14	22	18	3	0	0	—	—	—	—	—
—Hamilton	AHL	2	1	2	3	6	2	0	0	—	—	—	—	—
02-03—Edmonton	NHL	78	12	21	33	55	10	2	0	6	3	1	4	6
03-04—Edmonton	NHL	80	15	25	40	73	0	0	2	—	—	—	—	—
04-05—Mora	Sweden Dv. 1	50	19	27	46	117	-11	6	1	—	—	—	—	—
05-06—Edmonton	NHL	79	22	51	73	85	0	3	3	24	7	12	19	12
NHL Totals (5 years)		347	66	118	184	241	21	5	5	35	10	13	23	18

HORDICHUK, DARCY — LW/RW

PERSONAL: Born August 10, 1980, in Kamsack, Sask. ... 6-1/215. ... Shoots left.
TRANSACTIONS/CAREER NOTES: Selected by Atlanta Thrashers in sixth round (eighth Thrashers pick, 180th overall) of entry draft (June 24, 2000). ... Traded by Thrashers with fourth- (RW Lance Monych) and fifth-round (RW John Zeiler) picks in 2002 to Phoenix Coyotes for D Kirill Safronov, RW Ruslan Zainullin and fourth-round pick (RW Patrick Dwyer) in 2002 (March 19, 2002). ... Suspended 10 games for abuse of an official (November 1, 2002). ... Ankle (March 15, 2003); missed 10 games. ... Traded by Coyotes with second-round pick (Matt Smaby) in 2003 to Florida Panthers for D Brad Ference (March 9, 2003). ... Fractured foot (November 13, 2003); missed 21 games. ... Fractured left hand (March 27, 2004) and had surgery; missed remainder of season. ... Traded by Panthers to Nashville Predators for fourth-round pick (D Matt Duffy) in 2005 (July 27, 2005). ... Suspended three games by NHL in on-ice altercation (March 27, 2006).

Season Team	League	REGULAR SEASON GP	G	A	Pts.	PIM	+/-	PP	SH	PLAYOFFS GP	G	A	Pts.	PIM
96-97—Calgary	WHL	3	0	0	0	2	...	...	...	—	—	—	—	—
—Yorkton	SMHL	57	6	15	21	230	...	...	...	—	—	—	—	—
97-98—Dauphin	MJHL	58	12	21	33	279	...	...	...	—	—	—	—	—
98-99—Saskatoon	WHL	66	3	2	5	246	...	...	...	—	—	—	—	—
99-00—Saskatoon	WHL	63	6	8	14	269	...	...	...	—	—	—	—	—
00-01—Orlando	IHL	69	7	3	10	369	...	...	...	16	3	3	6	41
—Atlanta	NHL	11	0	0	0	38	-3	0	0	—	—	—	—	—
01-02—Chicago	AHL	34	5	4	9	127	2	0	0	—	—	—	—	—
—Atlanta	NHL	33	1	1	2	127	-5	0	0	—	—	—	—	—
—Phoenix	NHL	1	0	0	0	14	0	0	0	—	—	—	—	—
02-03—Phoenix	NHL	25	0	0	0	82	-1	0	0	—	—	—	—	—
—Springfield	AHL	22	1	3	4	38	-3	0	0	—	—	—	—	—
—Florida	NHL	3	0	0	0	15	-1	0	0	—	—	—	—	—
03-04—Florida	NHL	57	3	1	4	158	-10	0	0	—	—	—	—	—
05-06—Nashville	NHL	74	7	6	13	163	9	0	0	—	—	—	—	—
NHL Totals (5 years)		204	11	8	19	597	-11	0	0					

HORTON, NATHAN — RW

PERSONAL: Born May 29, 1985, in Welland, Ont. ... 6-2/201. ... Shoots right.

TRANSACTIONS/CAREER NOTES: Selected by Florida Panthers in first round (first Panthers pick, third overall) in entry draft (June 23, 2003). ... Injured left shoulder (January 13, 2004) and had surgery (January 16, 2004); missed 21 games. ... Sore shoulder (March 9, 2004); missed one game. ... Injured shoulder (March 29, 2004) and had surgery; missed remainder of season. ... Sprained left knee (November 9, 2005); missed 10 games. ... Flu (March 18, 2006); missed one game.

Season Team	League	REGULAR SEASON GP	G	A	Pts.	PIM	+/-	PP	SH	PLAYOFFS GP	G	A	Pts.	PIM
01-02—Oshawa	OHL	64	31	36	67	84	...	...	...	—	—	—	—	—
02-03—Oshawa	OHL	54	33	35	68	111	...	...	...	—	—	—	—	—
03-04—Florida	NHL	55	14	8	22	57	-5	6	1	—	—	—	—	—
04-05—San Antonio	AHL	21	5	4	9	21	1	1	0	—	—	—	—	—
05-06—Florida	NHL	71	28	19	47	89	8	3	0	—	—	—	—	—
NHL Totals (2 years)		126	42	27	69	146	3	9	1					

HOSSA, MARCEL — LW/RW

PERSONAL: Born October 12, 1981, in Ilava, Czech. ... 6-2/215. ... Shoots left. ... Brother of Marian Hossa, RW, Atlanta Thrashers. ... Name pronounced HOH-suh.

TRANSACTIONS/CAREER NOTES: Selected by Montreal Canadiens in first round (second Canadiens pick, 16th overall) of entry draft (June 24, 2000). ... Injured wrist (January 14, 2002); missed two games. ... Reinjured wrist (January 19, 2002); missed five games. ... Re-signed by Canadiens as restricted free agent (August 15, 2005). ... Traded by Canadiens to New York Rangers for C/LW Garth Murray (September 30, 2005). ... Chest injury (October 22, 2005); missed one game. ... Dental surgery (January 21, 2006); missed two games.

Season Team	League	REGULAR SEASON GP	G	A	Pts.	PIM	+/-	PP	SH	PLAYOFFS GP	G	A	Pts.	PIM
96-97—Dukla Trencin	Slovakia Jrs.	45	30	21	51	30	...	...	...	—	—	—	—	—
97-98—Dukla Trencin	Slovakia Jrs.	39	11	38	49	44	...	...	...	—	—	—	—	—
98-99—Portland	WHL	70	7	14	21	66	...	...	...	2	0	0	0	0
99-00—Portland	WHL	60	24	29	53	58	...	...	...	—	—	—	—	—
00-01—Portland	WHL	58	34	56	90	58	...	...	...	16	5	7	12	14
01-02—Quebec	AHL	50	17	15	32	24	-5	4	0	3	0	0	0	4
—Montreal	NHL	10	3	1	4	2	2	0	0	—	—	—	—	—
02-03—Hamilton	AHL	37	19	13	32	18	22	7	0	21	4	7	11	12
—Montreal	NHL	34	6	7	13	14	3	2	0	—	—	—	—	—
03-04—Montreal	NHL	15	1	1	2	8	-3	0	0	—	—	—	—	—
—Hamilton	AHL	57	18	22	40	45	7	6	0	10	2	3	5	8
04-05—Mora	Sweden Dv. 1	48	18	6	24	69	-6	8	1	—	—	—	—	—
05-06—New York Rangers	NHL	64	10	6	16	28	-6	3	0	4	0	0	0	6
—Slovakian Oly. team	Int'l	6	0	0	0	0	1	0	0	—	—	—	—	—
NHL Totals (4 years)		123	20	15	35	52	-4	5	0	4	0	0	0	6

HOSSA, MARIAN — RW

PERSONAL: Born January 12, 1979, in Stara Lubovna, Czech. ... 6-1/208. ... Shoots left. ... Brother of Marcel Hossa, LW/RW, New York Rangers. ... Name pronounced HOH-suh.

TRANSACTIONS/CAREER NOTES: Selected by Ottawa Senators in first round (first Senators pick, 12th overall) of entry draft (June 21, 1997). ... Torn knee ligaments (May 21, 1998); missed first 22 games of season. ... Concussion (November 18, 1999); missed one game. ... Bruised left wrist (January 6, 2000); missed two games. ... Flu (February 1, 2000); missed one game. ... Bruised calf (February 18, 2001); missed one game. ... Injured left knee (February 4, 2002); missed one game. ... Flu (April 13, 2002); missed one game. ... Flu (February 4, 2003); missed two games. ... Injured foot (November 11, 2003); missed one game. ... Traded by Senators with D Greg deVries to Atlanta Thrashers for RW Dany Heatley (August 23, 2005). ... Flu (March 20, 2006); missed two games.

STATISTICAL PLATEAUS: Three-goal games: 2000-01 (1), 2002-03 (2). Total: 3. ... Four-goal games: 2002-03 (1). ... Total hat tricks: 4.

Season Team	League	REGULAR SEASON GP	G	A	Pts.	PIM	+/-	PP	SH	PLAYOFFS GP	G	A	Pts.	PIM
95-96—Dukla Trencin	Slovakia Jrs.	53	42	49	91	26	...	...	...	—	—	—	—	—
96-97—Dukla Trencin	Slovakia	46	25	19	44	33	...	...	...	7	5	5	10	...
97-98—Ottawa	NHL	7	0	1	1	0	-1	0	0	—	—	—	—	—
—Portland	WHL	53	45	40	85	50	41	11	1	16	13	6	19	6

Season Team	League	GP	G	A	Pts.	PIM	+/-	PP	SH	GP	G	A	Pts.	PIM
		REGULAR SEASON								PLAYOFFS				
98-99—Ottawa	NHL	60	15	15	30	37	18	1	0	4	0	2	2	4
99-00—Ottawa	NHL	78	29	27	56	32	5	5	0	6	0	0	0	2
00-01—Ottawa	NHL	81	32	43	75	44	19	11	2	4	1	1	2	4
01-02—Dukla Trencin	Slovakia	8	3	4	7	16	...	...	...	—	—	—	—	—
—Ottawa	NHL	80	31	35	66	50	11	9	1	12	4	6	10	2
—Slovakian Oly. team	Int'l	2	4	2	6	0	...	...	...	—	—	—	—	—
02-03—Ottawa	NHL	80	45	35	80	34	8	14	0	18	5	11	16	6
03-04—Ottawa	NHL	81	36	46	82	46	4	14	1	7	3	1	4	0
04-05—Mora	Sweden Dv. 1	24	18	14	32	22	8	3	1	—	—	—	—	—
—Dukla Trencin	Slovakia	25	22	20	42	38	34	...	...	5	4	5	9	14
05-06—Atlanta	NHL	80	39	53	92	67	17	14	*7	—	—	—	—	—
—Slovakian Oly. team	Int'l	6	5	5	10	4	9	1	0	—	—	—	—	—
NHL Totals (8 years)		547	227	255	482	310	81	68	11	51	13	21	34	18

HOWARD, JIMMY G

PERSONAL: Born March 26, 1984, in Ogensburgh, N.Y. ... 6-1/204. ... Catches left.
COLLEGE: Maine.
TRANSACTIONS/CAREER NOTES: Selected by Detroit Red Wings in second round (first Red Wings pick, 64th overall) of entry draft (June 20, 2003).

Season Team	League	GP	Min.	W	L	OTL	T	GA	SO	GAA	SV%	GP	Min.	W	L	GA	SO	GAA	SV%
		REGULAR SEASON										PLAYOFFS							
01-02—U.S. Jr. national team	Int'l	8	425	4	3	...	0	14	0	1.98	.927	—	—	—	—	—	—	—	—
02-03—University of Maine	ECAC	21	1151	14	6	...	0	47	3	2.45	.916	—	—	—	—	—	—	—	—
03-04—University of Maine	ECAC	23	...	14	4	...	3	...	6	1.19	...	—	—	—	—	—	—	—	—
04-05—Maine	Hockey East	39	...	19	13	...	7	...	6	1.92	...	—	—	—	—	—	—	—	—
05-06—Grand Rapids	AHL	38	2141	27	6	2	...	92	2	2.58	.910	13	763	5	7	44	0	3.46	.885
—Detroit	NHL	4	201	1	2	0	...	10	0	2.99	.904	—	—	—	—	—	—	—	—
NHL Totals (1 year)		4	201	1	2	0	0	10	0	2.99	.904								

HRDINA, JAN C/LW

PERSONAL: Born February 5, 1976, in Hradec Kralove, Czech. ... 6-0/206. ... Shoots right. ... Name pronounced YAHN huhr-DEE-nuh.
TRANSACTIONS/CAREER NOTES: Selected by Pittsburgh Penguins in fifth round (fourth Penguins pick, 128th overall) of entry draft (July 8, 1995). ... Sprained ankle (October 14, 1999); missed 12 games. ... Strained groin (December 5, 2000); missed three games. ... Bruised hip (January 12, 2001); missed one game. ... Strained back (January 23, 2002); missed two games. ... Flu (April 3, 2002); missed one game. ... Back spasms (January 7, 2003); missed two games. ... Hip (February 14, 2003); missed four games. ... Hip (February 27, 2003); missed seven games. ... Traded by Penguins with D Francois Leroux to Phoenix Coyotes for LW Ramzi Abid, D Dan Focht and LW Guillaume Lefebvre (March 11, 2003). ... Hip flexor (March 14, 2003); missed 10 games. ... Fractured toe (November 17, 2003); missed 11 games. ... Traded by Coyotes to New Jersey Devils for C Mike Rupp and second-round pick (traded to Edmonton; Oilers picked LW Geoff Paukovich) in 2004 draft (March 5, 2004). ... Signed as free agent by Columbus Blue Jackets (August 10, 2005). ... Chest (December 28, 2005); missed two games. ... Dizzyness (January 11, 2006); missed one game. ... Broken toe (March 13, 2006); missed one game.

Season Team	League	GP	G	A	Pts.	PIM	+/-	PP	SH	GP	G	A	Pts.	PIM
		REGULAR SEASON								PLAYOFFS				
93-94—Std.Hradec Kralove	Czech Rep.	21	1	5	6	...	...	...	...	—	—	—	—	—
94-95—Seattle	WHL	69	41	59	100	79	24	12	4	4	0	1	1	8
95-96—Seattle	WHL	30	19	28	47	37	...	...	...	—	—	—	—	—
—Spokane	WHL	18	10	16	26	25	...	...	...	18	5	14	19	49
96-97—Cleveland	IHL	68	23	31	54	82	...	...	...	13	1	2	3	8
97-98—Syracuse	AHL	72	20	24	44	82	-3	3	0	5	1	3	4	10
98-99—Pittsburgh	NHL	82	13	29	42	40	-2	3	0	13	4	1	5	12
99-00—Pittsburgh	NHL	70	13	33	46	43	13	3	0	9	4	8	12	2
00-01—Pittsburgh	NHL	78	15	28	43	48	19	3	0	18	2	5	7	8
01-02—Pittsburgh	NHL	79	24	33	57	50	-7	6	0	—	—	—	—	—
—Czech Rep. Oly. team	Int'l	4	0	0	0	0	...	...	...	—	—	—	—	—
02-03—Pittsburgh	NHL	57	14	25	39	34	1	11	0	—	—	—	—	—
—Phoenix	NHL	4	0	4	4	8	3	0	0	—	—	—	—	—
03-04—Phoenix	NHL	55	11	15	26	30	-10	5	0	—	—	—	—	—
—New Jersey	NHL	13	1	6	7	10	4	0	0	5	2	0	2	2
04-05—HC Kladno	Czech Rep.	23	4	3	7	38	-7	...	...	7	3	3	6	4
05-06—Columbus	NHL	75	10	23	33	78	-8	4	1	—	—	—	—	—
NHL Totals (7 years)		513	101	196	297	341	13	35	1	45	12	14	26	24

HUDLER, JIRI C

PERSONAL: Born January 4, 1984, in Olomouc, Czechoslovakia. ... 5-9/154. ... Shoots left.
TRANSACTIONS/CAREER NOTES: Selected by Detroit Red Wings in second round (first Red Wings pick, 58th overall) of entry draft (June 22, 2002).

Season Team	League	GP	G	A	Pts.	PIM	+/-	PP	SH	GP	G	A	Pts.	PIM
		REGULAR SEASON								PLAYOFFS				
01-02—HC Vsetin	Czech Rep.	46	15	31	46	54	...	...	...	—	—	—	—	—
02-03—HC Vsetin	Czech Rep.	11	1	5	6	12	...	...	...	—	—	—	—	—
—Kazan	Rus. Div.	11	1	5	6	12	...	...	...	1	0	0	0	0
03-04—Grand Rapids	AHL	57	17	32	49	46	15	4	0	4	1	5	6	2
—Detroit	NHL	12	1	2	3	10	-1	1	0	—	—	—	—	—

H

Season Team	League	GP	G	A	Pts.	PIM	+/-	PP	SH	GP	G	A	Pts.	PIM
		REGULAR SEASON								PLAYOFFS				
04-05—HC Vsetin	Czech Rep.	7	5	2	7	10	-1	...	...	—	—	—	—	—
—Grand Rapids	AHL	52	12	22	34	10	1	4	0	—	—	—	—	—
05-06—Grand Rapids	AHL	76	36	60	96	56	5	11	1	16	6	16	22	20
—Detroit	NHL	4	0	0	0	2	0	0	0	—	—	—	—	—
NHL Totals (2 years)		16	1	2	3	12	-1	1	0					

HUET, CRISTOBAL G

PERSONAL: Born July 3, 1975, in St. Martin D'Heres, France. ... 6-0/194. ... Name pronounced oo-AY.

TRANSACTIONS/CAREER NOTES: Selected by Los Angeles Kings in seventh round (ninth Kings pick, 214th overall) of entry draft (June 24, 2001). ... Traded by Kings with C Radek Bonk to Montreal Canadiens for G Mathieu Garon and third-round pick (D Paul Baier) in 2004 draft (June 26, 2004). ... Torn ACL (June 2005); missed first 18 games of season.

Season Team	League	GP	Min.	W	L	OTL	T	GA	SO	GAA	SV%	GP	Min.	W	L	GA	SO	GAA	SV%
		REGULAR SEASON										PLAYOFFS							
97-98—French Olympic Team	Int'l	2	120	1	1	...	0	5	0	2.50	...	—	—	—	—	—	—	—	—
98-99—Lugano	Switzerland	21	1275	...	...	...	...	58	1	2.73	...	...	...	...	...	18	1	...	...
99-00—Lugano	Switzerland	31	1886	...	...	...	...	50	8	1.59	...	...	...	...	...	29	0	...	...
00-01—Lugano	Switzerland	39	2365	...	...	...	...	77	6	1.95	...	...	...	...	...	39	2	...	...
01-02—Lugano	Switzerland	39	2313	...	...	...	...	107	4	2.78	...	...	...	...	...	3	0	...	...
—French Olympic Team	Int'l	3	179	0	2	...	1	10	0	3.35	...	—	—	—	—	—	—	—	—
02-03—Los Angeles	NHL	12	541	4	4	...	1	21	1	2.33	.913	—	—	—	—	—	—	—	—
—Manchester	AHL	30	1784	16	8	...	5	68	1	2.29	...	1	29	0	1	4	0	8.28	...
03-04—Los Angeles	NHL	41	2199	10	16	...	10	89	3	2.43	.907	—	—	—	—	—	—	—	—
04-05—Mannheim	Germany	36	2001	...	...	...	...	93	1	2.79	.915	14	850	...	...	40	2	2.82	.919
05-06—Hamilton	AHL	4	...	...	...	0	...	...	...	...	...	—	—	—	—	—	—	—	—
—Montreal	NHL	36	2103	18	11	4	...	77	7	2.20	*.929	6	386	2	4	15	0	2.33	.929
NHL Totals (3 years)		89	4843	32	31	4	11	187	11	2.32	.918	6	386	2	4	15	0	2.33	.929

HULL, BRETT RW

PERSONAL: Born August 9, 1964, in Belleville, Ont. ... 5-11/203. ... Shoots right. ... Son of Bobby Hull, Hall of Fame LW with three NHL teams (1957-72 and 1979-80) and Winnipeg Jets of WHA (1972-79); and nephew of Dennis Hull, LW with two NHL teams (1964-78).

TRANSACTIONS/CAREER NOTES: Selected by Calgary Flames in sixth round (sixth Flames pick, 117th overall) of NHL draft (June 9, 1984). ... Traded by Flames with LW Steve Bozek to St. Louis Blues for D Rob Ramage and G Rick Wamsley (March 7, 1988). ... Sprained left ankle (January 15, 1991); missed two regular-season games and All-Star Game. ... Back spasms (March 12, 1992); missed seven games. ... Sore wrist (March 20, 1993); missed four games. ... Injured abdominal muscle (October 7, 1993); missed three games. ... Strained groin (November 1, 1995); missed two games. ... Reinjured groin (November 10, 1995); missed five games. ... Injured hamstring (March 28, 1996); missed four games. ... Strained groin (March 30, 1997); missed four games. ... Strained buttocks (December 8, 1997); missed two games. ... Fractured left hand (December 27, 1997); missed 13 games. ... Signed as free agent by Dallas Stars (July 3, 1998). ... Bruised kidney (November 20, 1998); missed two games. ... Strained groin (November 25, 1998); missed one game. ... Reinjured groin (December 2, 1998); missed six games. ... Strained back (January 10, 1999); missed one game. ... Strained hamstring (February 24, 1999); missed 11 games. ... Injured groin (January 12, 2000); missed one game. ... Fractured nose (February 9, 2000); missed one game. ... Strained hip flexor (March 8, 2000); missed one game. ... Strained lower back (December 23, 2000); missed three games. ... Signed as free agent by Detroit Red Wings (August 22, 2001). ... Sore back (October 16, 2003); missed one game. ... Signed as a free agent by Phoenix Coyotes (August 6, 2004). ... Announced retirement (October 15, 2005).

STATISTICAL PLATEAUS: Three-goal games: 1987-88 (1), 1989-90 (5), 1990-91 (4), 1991-92 (8), 1993-94 (3), 1994-95 (1), 1995-96 (1), 1996-97 (2), 1997-98 (1), 2000-01 (1), 2001-02 (1), 2002-03 (2). Total: 30. ... Four-goal games: 1994-95 (1), 1995-96 (1), 2000-01 (1). Total: 3. ... Total hat tricks: 33.

Season Team	League	GP	G	A	Pts.	PIM	+/-	PP	SH	GP	G	A	Pts.	PIM
		REGULAR SEASON								PLAYOFFS				
82-83—Penticton	BCJHL	50	48	56	104	27	...	...	...	—	—	—	—	—
83-84—Penticton	BCJHL	56	105	83	188	20	...	...	...	—	—	—	—	—
84-85—Minnesota-Duluth	WCHA	48	32	28	60	24	...	...	...	—	—	—	—	—
85-86—Minnesota-Duluth	WCHA	42	52	32	84	46	...	...	...	—	—	—	—	—
—Calgary	NHL	...	...	...	...	...	...	...	...	2	0	0	0	0
86-87—Moncton	AHL	67	50	42	92	16	...	...	...	3	2	2	4	2
—Calgary	NHL	5	1	0	1	0	-1	0	0	4	2	1	3	0
87-88—Calgary	NHL	52	26	24	50	12	10	4	0	—	—	—	—	—
—St. Louis	NHL	13	6	8	14	4	4	2	0	10	7	2	9	4
88-89—St. Louis	NHL	78	41	43	84	33	-17	16	0	10	5	5	10	6
89-90—St. Louis	NHL	80	*72	41	113	24	-1	*27	0	12	13	8	21	17
90-91—St. Louis	NHL	78	*86	45	131	22	23	*29	0	13	11	8	19	4
91-92—St. Louis	NHL	73	*70	39	109	48	-2	20	5	6	4	4	8	4
92-93—St. Louis	NHL	80	54	47	101	41	-27	29	0	11	8	5	13	2
93-94—St. Louis	NHL	81	57	40	97	38	-3	†25	3	4	2	1	3	0
94-95—St. Louis	NHL	48	29	21	50	10	13	9	3	7	6	2	8	0
95-96—St. Louis	NHL	70	43	40	83	30	4	16	5	13	6	5	11	10
96-97—St. Louis	NHL	77	42	40	82	10	-9	12	2	6	2	7	9	2
97-98—St. Louis	NHL	66	27	45	72	26	-1	10	0	10	3	3	6	2
—U.S. Olympic team	Int'l	4	2	1	3	0	-1	1	0	—	—	—	—	—
98-99—Dallas	NHL	60	32	26	58	30	19	15	0	22	8	7	15	4
99-00—Dallas	NHL	79	24	35	59	43	-21	11	0	23	*11	†13	*24	4
00-01—Dallas	NHL	79	39	40	79	18	10	11	0	10	2	5	7	6
01-02—Detroit	NHL	82	30	33	63	35	18	7	1	23	*10	8	18	4
—U.S. Olympic team	Int'l	6	3	5	8	6	...	...	...	—	—	—	—	—
02-03—Detroit	NHL	82	37	39	76	22	11	12	1	4	0	1	1	0

H

Season Team	League	GP	G	A	Pts.	PIM	+/-	PP	SH	GP	G	A	Pts.	PIM
		REGULAR SEASON								PLAYOFFS				
03-04—Detroit	NHL	81	25	43	68	12	-4	10	0	12	3	2	5	4
05-06—Phoenix	NHL	5	0	1	1	0	-3	0	0	—	—	—	—	—
NHL Totals (20 years)		1269	741	650	1391	458	23	265	20	202	103	87	190	73

HULSE, CALE D

PERSONAL: Born November 10, 1973, in Edmonton. ... 6-3/220. ... Shoots right. ... Name pronounced HUHLZ.

TRANSACTIONS/CAREER NOTES: Selected by New Jersey Devils in third round (third Devils pick, 66th overall) of entry draft (June 20, 1992). ... Traded by Devils with D Tommy Albelin and RW Jocelyn Lemieux to Calgary Flames for D Phil Housley and D Dan Keczmer (February 26, 1996). ... Bruised ankle (February 28, 1997); missed four games. ... Reinjured ankle (March 7, 1997); missed one game. ... Reinjured ankle (March 21, 1997); missed one game. ... Bruised ribs (April 1, 1999); missed six games. ... Fractured hand (September 18, 1999); missed first four games of season. ... Sprained ankle (February 23, 2000); missed nine games. ... Traded by Flames with third-round pick (C/LW Denis Platonov) in 2001 entry draft to Nashville Predators for RW Sergei Krivokrasov (March 14, 2000); missed Predators final 12 games with sprained ankle. ... Fractured right hand (September 29, 2001); missed first 18 games of season. ... Strained right knee (March 10, 2002); missed one game. ... Suspended one game for cross-checking incident (February 23, 2003). ... Signed by Phoenix Coyotes as free agent (July 9, 2003). ... Traded by Coyotes with LW Jason Chimera and C Mike Rupp to Columbus Blue Jackets for LW Geoff Sanderson and RW Tim Jackman (October 8, 2005). ... Traded by Blue Jackets to Flames for LW Cam Severson (February 28, 2006). ... Shoulder (April 7, 2006); missed final six games of regular season and seven playoff games.

Season Team	League	GP	G	A	Pts.	PIM	+/-	PP	SH	GP	G	A	Pts.	PIM
		REGULAR SEASON								PLAYOFFS				
90-91—Calgary Royals	AJHL	49	3	23	26	220	...	...	...	—	—	—	—	—
91-92—Portland	WHL	70	4	18	22	250	...	...	...	6	0	2	2	27
92-93—Portland	WHL	72	10	26	36	284	38	0	0	16	4	4	8	65
93-94—Albany	AHL	79	7	14	21	186	-3	0	1	5	0	3	3	11
94-95—Albany	AHL	77	5	13	18	215	5	1	0	12	1	1	2	17
95-96—Albany	AHL	42	4	23	27	107	...	...	...	—	—	—	—	—
—New Jersey	NHL	8	0	0	0	15	-2	0	0	—	—	—	—	—
—Saint John	AHL	13	2	7	9	39	...	...	...	—	—	—	—	—
—Calgary	NHL	3	0	0	0	5	3	0	0	1	0	0	0	0
96-97—Calgary	NHL	63	1	6	7	91	-2	0	1	—	—	—	—	—
97-98—Calgary	NHL	79	5	22	27	169	1	1	1	—	—	—	—	—
98-99—Calgary	NHL	73	3	9	12	117	-8	0	0	—	—	—	—	—
99-00—Calgary	NHL	47	1	6	7	47	-11	0	0	—	—	—	—	—
00-01—Nashville	NHL	82	1	7	8	128	-5	0	0	—	—	—	—	—
01-02—Nashville	NHL	63	0	2	2	121	-18	0	0	—	—	—	—	—
02-03—Nashville	NHL	80	2	6	8	121	-11	0	0	—	—	—	—	—
03-04—Phoenix	NHL	82	3	17	20	123	-4	1	0	—	—	—	—	—
05-06—Columbus	NHL	27	0	3	3	43	-9	0	0	—	—	—	—	—
—Calgary	NHL	12	0	1	1	20	1	0	0	—	—	—	—	—
NHL Totals (10 years)		619	16	79	95	1000	-65	2	2	1	0	0	0	0

HUNTER, TRENT RW/LW

PERSONAL: Born July 5, 1980, in Red Deer, Alta. ... 6-3/210. ... Shoots right.

TRANSACTIONS/CAREER NOTES: Selected by Anaheim Mighty Ducks in sixth round (fourth Mighty Ducks pick, 150th overall) of NHL draft (June 27, 1998). ... Traded by Mighty Ducks to New York Islanders for fourth-round pick (RW/LW Jonas Ronnqvist) in 2000 draft (May 23, 2000). ... Re-signed by Islanders as restricted free agent (August 13, 2005).

Season Team	League	GP	G	A	Pts.	PIM	+/-	PP	SH	GP	G	A	Pts.	PIM
		REGULAR SEASON								PLAYOFFS				
96-97—Red Deer	AMHL	42	30	25	55	50	...	...	...	—	—	—	—	—
97-98—Prince George	WHL	60	13	14	27	34	...	...	...	8	1	0	1	4
98-99—Prince George	WHL	50	18	20	38	34	13	2	0	7	2	5	7	2
99-00—Prince George	WHL	67	46	49	95	47	21	16	4	13	7	15	22	6
00-01—Springfield	AHL	57	18	17	35	14	...	...	...	—	—	—	—	—
01-02—Bridgeport	AHL	80	30	35	65	30	27	8	0	17	8	11	19	6
—New York Islanders	NHL	...	...	...	...	...	...	...	...	4	1	1	2	2
02-03—New York Islanders	NHL	8	0	4	4	4	5	0	0	—	—	—	—	—
—Bridgeport	AHL	70	30	41	71	39	0	13	1	9	7	4	11	10
03-04—New York Islanders	NHL	77	25	26	51	16	23	4	0	5	0	0	0	4
04-05—Nykoping	Sweden	24	9	6	15	53	0	5	0	14	5	3	8	24
05-06—New York Islanders	NHL	82	16	19	35	34	-9	5	0	—	—	—	—	—
NHL Totals (4 years)		167	41	49	90	54	19	9	0	9	1	1	2	6

HUSELIUS, KRISTIAN LW

PERSONAL: Born November 10, 1978, in Osterhaninge, Sweden. ... 6-1/190. ... Shoots left. ... Name pronounced hoo-say-LE-US.

TRANSACTIONS/CAREER NOTES: Selected by Florida Panthers in second round (second Panthers pick, 47th overall) of entry draft (June 21, 1997). ... Intestinal infection (December 15, 2001); missed three games. ... Knee (September 12, 2002); missed three games. ... Traded by Panthers to Calgary Flames for D Steve Montador and C Dustin Johner (December 2, 2005).

Season Team	League	GP	G	A	Pts.	PIM	+/-	PP	SH	GP	G	A	Pts.	PIM
		REGULAR SEASON								PLAYOFFS				
94-95—Hammarby	Sweden Jr.	17	6	2	8	2	...	...	...	—	—	—	—	—
95-96—Hammarby	Sweden Jr.	25	13	8	21	14	...	...	...	—	—	—	—	—
—Hammarby	Sweden Dv. 2	6	1	0	1	0	...	...	...	—	—	—	—	—
96-97—Farjestad Karlstad	Sweden	13	2	0	2	4	...	...	...	5	1	0	1	0

H

Season Team	League	REGULAR SEASON GP	G	A	Pts.	PIM	+/-	PP	SH	PLAYOFFS GP	G	A	Pts.	PIM
97-98—Farjestad Karlstad	Sweden	34	2	1	3	2	...	...	...	11	0	0	0	0
98-99—Farjestad Karlstad	Sweden	28	4	4	8	4	...	...	...	—	—	—	—	—
—Vastra Frolunda	Sweden	20	2	2	4	2	...	...	...	4	1	0	1	0
99-00—Vastra Frolunda	Sweden	50	21	23	44	20	...	...	...	5	2	2	4	8
00-01—Vastra Frolunda	Sweden	49	32	35	67	26	...	...	...	5	4	5	9	14
01-02—Florida	NHL	79	23	22	45	14	-4	6	1	—	—	—	—	—
02-03—Florida	NHL	78	20	23	43	20	-6	3	0	—	—	—	—	—
03-04—Florida	NHL	76	10	21	31	24	-6	2	0	—	—	—	—	—
04-05—Rapperswil	Switzerland	—	—	—	—	—	—	—	—	4	1	3	4	2
—Linkopings	Sweden	34	14	35	49	10	20	5	2	—	—	—	—	—
05-06—Florida	NHL	24	5	3	8	4	-11	2	0	—	—	—	—	—
—Calgary	NHL	54	15	24	39	36	2	6	0	7	2	4	6	4
NHL Totals (4 years)		311	73	93	166	98	-25	19	1	7	2	4	6	4

HUSSEY, MATT C

PERSONAL: Born May 28, 1979, in New Haven, Conn. ... 6-2/212. ... Shoots left.

TRANSACTIONS/CAREER NOTES: Selected by Pittsburgh Penguins in ninth round (Penguins' 10th pick, 254th overall) of entry draft (June 27, 1998). ... Signed as free agent by Detroit Red Wings (July 13, 2006).

Season Team	League	REGULAR SEASON GP	G	A	Pts.	PIM	+/-	PP	SH	PLAYOFFS GP	G	A	Pts.	PIM
98-99—Wisconsin	WCHA	37	10	5	15	18	...	...	...	—	—	—	—	—
99-00—Wisconsin	WCHA	35	5	11	16	8	...	...	...	—	—	—	—	—
00-01—Wisconsin	WCHA	40	9	11	20	24	...	...	...	—	—	—	—	—
01-02—Wisconsin	WCHA	39	18	15	33	16	...	...	...	—	—	—	—	—
02-03—Wilkes-Barre/Scranton	AHL	69	12	11	23	28	...	...	...	2	0	0	0	0
03-04—Pittsburgh	NHL	3	2	1	3	0	-1	2	0	—	—	—	—	—
—Wilkes-Barre/Scranton	AHL	55	2	1	3	6	-3	1	0	6	2	2	4	0
04-05—Wilkes-Barre/Scranton	AHL	80	16	14	30	19	3	3	2	10	1	2	3	2
05-06—Wilkes-Barre/Scranton	AHL	65	21	30	51	34	11	6	1	9	1	0	1	0
—Pittsburgh	NHL	13	0	1	1	0	-5	0	0	—	—	—	—	—
NHL Totals (2 years)		16	2	2	4	0	-6	2	0					

HUTCHINSON, ANDREW D

PERSONAL: Born March 24, 1980, in Evanston, Ill. ... 6-2/204. ... Shoots right.

TRANSACTIONS/CAREER NOTES: Selected by Nashville Predators in second round (fourth Predators pick, 54th overall) of entry draft (June 26, 1999). ... Traded by Predators to Carolina Hurricanes for third-round pick (acquired from Phoenix; Predators selected Teemu Laakso) in 2005 draft (July 29, 2005). ... Injured hip (November 11, 2005); missed seven games. ... Injured wrist (February 2, 2006) and had surgery; missed 21 games.

Season Team	League	REGULAR SEASON GP	G	A	Pts.	PIM	+/-	PP	SH	PLAYOFFS GP	G	A	Pts.	PIM
97-98—U.S. National	NAHL	60	7	22	29	63	...	2	0	—	—	—	—	—
98-99—Michigan State	CCHA	37	3	12	15	26	...	...	...	—	—	—	—	—
99-00—Michigan State	CCHA	41	4	11	15	62	...	...	...	—	—	—	—	—
00-01—Michigan State	CCHA	42	5	19	24	46	...	...	...	—	—	—	—	—
01-02—Michigan State	CCHA	39	6	16	22	24	...	...	...	—	—	—	—	—
—Milwaukee	AHL	5	0	1	1	0	-2	0	0	—	—	—	—	—
02-03—Toledo	ECHL	10	2	5	7	4	8	1	0	—	—	—	—	—
—Milwaukee	AHL	63	9	17	26	40	-10	4	0	3	1	0	1	0
03-04—Milwaukee	AHL	46	12	12	24	39	7	4	0	22	5	11	16	33
—Nashville	NHL	18	4	4	8	4	1	2	0	—	—	—	—	—
04-05—Milwaukee	AHL	76	10	35	45	79	1	4	1	7	1	3	4	8
05-06—Carolina	NHL	36	3	8	11	18	-2	2	0	—	—	—	—	—
NHL Totals (2 years)		54	7	12	19	22	-1	4	0					

IGINLA, JAROME RW

PERSONAL: Born July 1, 1977, in Edmonton. ... 6-1/207. ... Shoots right. ... Name pronounced ih-GIHN-luh.

TRANSACTIONS/CAREER NOTES: Selected by Dallas Stars in first round (first Stars pick, 11th overall) of entry draft (July 8, 1995). ... Traded by Stars with C Corey Millen to Calgary Flames for C Joe Nieuwendyk (December 19, 1995). ... Fractured right hand (January 21, 1998); missed 10 games. ... Missed first three games of 1999-2000 season in contract dispute. ... Bruised knee (March 22, 2000); missed two games. ... Knee (December 13, 2000); missed one game. ... Fractured wrist (March 31, 2001); missed remainder of season. ... Hip, groin (December 21, 2002); missed five games. ... Shoulder (March 21, 2003); missed two games. ... Sprained knee (January 18, 2004); missed one game.

STATISTICAL PLATEAUS: Three-goal games: 2001-02 (1), 2002-03 (1), 2003-04 (1). Total: 3. ... Four-goal games: 2002-03 (1). ... Total hat tricks: 4.

Season Team	League	REGULAR SEASON GP	G	A	Pts.	PIM	+/-	PP	SH	PLAYOFFS GP	G	A	Pts.	PIM
93-94—Kamloops	WHL	48	6	23	29	33	...	...	...	19	3	6	9	10
94-95—Kamloops	WHL	72	33	38	71	111	29	8	0	21	7	11	18	34
95-96—Kamloops	WHL	63	63	73	136	120	...	...	...	16	16	13	29	44
—Calgary	NHL	...	...	...	...	...	...	...	...	2	1	1	2	0
96-97—Calgary	NHL	82	21	29	50	37	-4	8	1	—	—	—	—	—
97-98—Calgary	NHL	70	13	19	32	29	-10	0	2	—	—	—	—	—
98-99—Calgary	NHL	82	28	23	51	58	1	7	0	—	—	—	—	—

Season Team	League	GP	G	A	Pts.	PIM	+/-	PP	SH	GP	G	A	Pts.	PIM
		REGULAR SEASON								PLAYOFFS				
99-00—Calgary	NHL	77	29	34	63	26	0	12	0	—	—	—	—	—
00-01—Calgary	NHL	77	31	40	71	62	-2	10	0	—	—	—	—	—
01-02—Calgary	NHL	82	*52	44	*96	77	27	16	1	—	—	—	—	—
—Can. Olympic team	Int'l	6	3	1	4	0	...	...	...	—	—	—	—	—
02-03—Calgary	NHL	75	35	32	67	49	-10	11	3	—	—	—	—	—
03-04—Calgary	NHL	81	†41	32	73	84	21	8	4	26	*13	9	22	45
05-06—Calgary	NHL	82	35	32	67	86	5	17	1	7	5	3	8	11
—Canadian Oly. team	Int'l	6	2	1	3	4	1	2	0	—	—	—	—	—
NHL Totals (10 years)		708	285	285	570	508	28	89	12	35	19	13	32	56

IMMONEN, JARKKO — C

PERSONAL: Born April 19, 1982, in Rantasalmi, Finland. ... 6-0/209. ... Shoots right.

TRANSACTIONS/CAREER NOTES: Selected by Toronto Maple Leafs in eighth round (eighth Leafs pick, 254th overall) of NHL entry draft (June 23, 2002). ... Traded by Maple Leafs with D Maxim Kondratiev, first-round pick (later traded to Calgary; Flames picked LW Kris Chucko) in 2004 entry draft and second-round pick of 2005 entry draft to New York Rangers for D Brian Leetch and conditional draft pick (March 3, 2004). ... Signed by Rangers to entry-level contract (August 22, 2005).

Season Team	League	GP	G	A	Pts.	PIM	+/-	PP	SH	GP	G	A	Pts.	PIM
		REGULAR SEASON								PLAYOFFS				
99-00—Sapko	Finland Jr.	42	18	16	34	34	...	...	...	—	—	—	—	—
00-01—TPS Turku	Finland Jr.	41	20	20	40	22	...	...	...	—	—	—	—	—
01-02—Assat Pori	Finland	44	0	2	2	6	...	...	...	8	5	1	6	10
02-03—JyP Jyvaskyla	Finland	56	10	23	33	34	...	...	...	7	1	1	2	8
03-04—JyP Jyvaskyla	Finland	52	23	26	49	28	...	...	...	2	0	0	0	0
04-05—JyP Jyvaskyla	Finland	54	19	28	47	24	...	...	...	3	0	2	2	2
05-06—Hartford	AHL	74	30	40	70	34	16	16	1	6	2	3	5	2
—New York Rangers	NHL	6	2	0	2	0	-1	1	0	—	—	—	—	—
NHL Totals (1 year)		6	2	0	2	0	-1	1	0					

IRVING, LELAND — G

PERSONAL: Born April 11, 1988, in Barrhead, Alb. ... 6-0/177. ... Catches left.

TRANSACTIONS/CAREER NOTES: Selected by Calgary Flames in first round (first Flames pick; 26th overall) of NHL draft (June 24, 2006).

Season Team	League	GP	Min.	W	L	OTL	T	GA	SO	GAA	SV%	GP	Min.	W	L	GA	SO	GAA	SV%
		REGULAR SEASON										PLAYOFFS							
03-04—Everett	WHL	1	8	...	...	...	...	0	...	0.00	1.000	3	104	1	0	2	...	1.15	.967
04-05—Everett	WHL	23	1132	9	8	...	1	34	2	1.80	.930	—	—	—	—	—	—	—	—
05-06—Everett	WHL	67	3791	37	22	...	4	121	4	1.92	.925	12	747	8	3	21	3	1.68	.938

ISBISTER, BRAD — LW/RW

PERSONAL: Born May 7, 1977, in Edmonton. ... 6-4/231. ... Shoots right. ... Name pronounced ihs-BIH-stuhr.

TRANSACTIONS/CAREER NOTES: Selected by Winnipeg Jets in third round (fourth Jets pick, 67th overall) of entry draft (July 8, 1995). ... Jets franchise moved to Phoenix and renamed Coyotes for 1996-97 season; NHL approved move on January 18, 1996. ... Strained abdominal muscle (November 22, 1997); missed six games. ... Strained groin (January 8, 1999); missed six games. ... Hernia (January 27, 1999); missed 19 games. ... Strained groin (March 11, 1999); missed remainder of season. ... Traded by Coyotes with third-round pick (C Brian Collins) in 1999 entry draft to New York Islanders for C Robert Reichel and third- (C/LW Jason Jaspers) and fourth-round (C Preston Mizzi) picks in 1999 entry draft (March 20, 1999). ... Sprained ankle (January 26, 2000); missed 18 games. ... Fractured jaw (December 12, 2000); missed 15 games. ... Flu (February 1, 2001); missed one game. ... Sprained right knee (March 3, 2001); missed remainder of season. ... Injured back (February 26, 2002); missed three games. ... Injured ankle (December 23, 2002); missed one game. ... Reinjured ankle (January 7, 2003); missed seven games. ... Reinjured ankle (January 28, 2003); missed six games. ... Traded by Islanders with LW Raffi Torres to Edmonton Oilers for D Janne Niinimaa and second-round pick (C Evgeni Tunik) in 2003 draft (March 11, 2003). ... Injured neck (November 8, 2003); missed five games. ... Back spasms (November 30, 2003); missed four games. ... Back spasms (January 11, 2004); missed one game. ... Injured right leg (January 31, 2004); missed four games. ... Injured ankle (February 16, 2004); missed 12 games. ... Traded by Oilers to Boston Bruins for fourth-round pick in 2006 draft (August 1, 2005). ... Strained groin (October 24, 2005); missed three games. ... Injured groin (November 1, 2005); missed four games. ... Sprained left ankle (January 28, 2006); missed 17 games.

Season Team	League	GP	G	A	Pts.	PIM	+/-	PP	SH	GP	G	A	Pts.	PIM
		REGULAR SEASON								PLAYOFFS				
93-94—Portland	WHL	64	7	10	17	45	...	...	...	10	0	2	2	0
94-95—Portland	WHL	67	16	20	36	123	-13	3	1	—	—	—	—	—
95-96—Portland	WHL	71	45	44	89	184	...	...	...	7	2	4	6	20
96-97—Springfield	AHL	7	3	1	4	14	-1	1	0	9	1	2	3	10
—Portland	WHL	24	15	18	33	45	18	3	3	6	2	1	3	16
97-98—Phoenix	NHL	66	9	8	17	102	4	1	0	5	0	0	0	2
—Springfield	AHL	9	8	2	10	36	8	0	0	—	—	—	—	—
98-99—Las Vegas	IHL	2	0	0	0	9	1	0	0	—	—	—	—	—
—Springfield	AHL	4	1	1	2	12	1	0	0	—	—	—	—	—
—Phoenix	NHL	32	4	4	8	46	1	0	0	—	—	—	—	—
99-00—New York Islanders	NHL	64	22	20	42	100	-18	9	0	—	—	—	—	—
00-01—New York Islanders	NHL	51	18	14	32	59	-19	7	1	—	—	—	—	—
01-02—New York Islanders	NHL	79	17	21	38	113	1	4	0	3	1	1	2	17
02-03—New York Islanders	NHL	53	10	13	23	34	-9	2	0	—	—	—	—	—
—Edmonton	NHL	13	3	2	5	9	0	0	0	6	0	1	1	12
03-04—Edmonton	NHL	51	10	8	18	54	-2	1	0	—	—	—	—	—
04-05—Innsbruck	Austria	11	7	4	11	41	-1	...	...	5	3	1	4	6
05-06—Boston	NHL	58	6	17	23	46	-2	1	0	—	—	—	—	—
NHL Totals (8 years)		467	99	107	206	563	-44	25	1	14	1	2	3	31

IVANANS, RAITAS — D

PERSONAL: Born January 1, 1979, in Riga, U.S.S.R. ... 6-3/200. ... Shoots left.
TRANSACTIONS/CAREER NOTES: Signed as free agent by Montreal Canadiens (July 16, 2004). ... Injured hand (October 12, 2005), missed 13 games. ... Signed as free agent by the Los Angeles Kings (July 13, 2006).

		REGULAR SEASON								PLAYOFFS				
Season Team	League	GP	G	A	Pts.	PIM	+/-	PP	SH	GP	G	A	Pts.	PIM
97-98—Flint	UHL	18	0	1	1	20	...	...	...	—	—	—	—	—
98-99—Macon	CHL	16	1	1	2	20	...	...	...	—	—	—	—	—
—Tulsa	CHL	32	2	7	9	39	...	...	...	—	—	—	—	—
99-00—Pensacola	ECHL	59	3	7	10	146	...	...	...	2	0	0	0	0
00-01—Hew Haven	UHL	66	4	10	14	270	...	...	...	8	1	0	1	4
—Hershey	AHL	2	0	0	0	0	...	...	...	—	—	—	—	—
01-02—Toledo	ECHL	16	2	2	4	59	...	...	...	—	—	—	—	—
—Baton Rouge	ECHL	40	4	5	9	59	...	...	...	—	—	—	—	—
02-03—Milwaukee	AHL	17	0	0	0	38	...	...	...	1	0	0	0	15
—Rockford	UHL	50	4	2	6	208	...	...	...	—	—	—	—	—
03-04—Milwaukee	AHL	54	1	7	8	166	...	...	...	7	0	1	1	2
—Rockford	UHL	1	0	0	0	0	...	...	...	—	—	—	—	—
04-05—Hamilton	AHL	75	2	5	7	259	...	...	...	2	0	1	1	0
05-06—Hamilton	AHL	43	2	0	2	120	-7	0	0	—	—	—	—	—
—Montreal	NHL	4	0	0	0	9	-1	0	0	—	—	—	—	—
NHL Totals (1 year)		4	0	0	0	9	-1	0	0					

JACINA, GREG — C

PERSONAL: Born May 22, 1982, in Guelph, Ontario. ... 6-0/203. ... Shoots right.
TRANSACTIONS/CAREER NOTES: Signed as free agent by Florida Panthers to an entry-level contract (August 12, 2003).

		REGULAR SEASON								PLAYOFFS				
Season Team	League	GP	G	A	Pts.	PIM	+/-	PP	SH	GP	G	A	Pts.	PIM
98-99—Guelph	OHL	6	0	1	1	0	...	...	...	—	—	—	—	—
99-00—Owen Sound	OHL	66	12	29	41	62	...	...	...	—	—	—	—	—
00-01—Owen Sound	OHL	57	25	26	51	101	...	...	...	4	0	1	1	15
01-02—Owen Sound	OHL	33	15	20	35	64	...	...	...	—	—	—	—	—
—Mississauga	OHL	28	14	26	40	43	...	...	...	—	—	—	—	—
02-03—Mississauga	OHL	—	—	—	—	—	—	—	—	5	6	5	11	17
03-04—Augusta	ECHL	58	15	23	38	170	...	...	...	—	—	—	—	—
—San Antonio	AHL	13	0	4	4	22	...	...	...	—	—	—	—	—
04-05—San Antonio	AHL	78	11	20	31	150	...	...	...	—	—	—	—	—
05-06—Rochester	AHL	35	7	4	11	152	1	0	1	—	—	—	—	—
—Florida	NHL	11	0	1	1	4	-1	0	0	—	—	—	—	—
NHL Totals (1 year)		11	0	1	1	4	-1	0	0					

JACKMAN, BARRET — D

PERSONAL: Born March 5, 1981, in Trail, B.C. ... 6-0/209. ... Shoots left.
TRANSACTIONS/CAREER NOTES: Selected by St. Louis Blues in first round (first Blues pick, 17th overall) of entry draft (June 26, 1999). ... Dislocated shoulder (October 22, 2003); missed six games. ... Shoulder (November 26, 2003); missed 17 games. ... Reinjured shoulder (January 5, 2004) and had surgery; missed remainder of season. ... Separated left shoulder (September 27, 2005); missed three games. ... Fractured jaw (March 21, 2006); missed final 16 games of regular season.

		REGULAR SEASON								PLAYOFFS				
Season Team	League	GP	G	A	Pts.	PIM	+/-	PP	SH	GP	G	A	Pts.	PIM
97-98—Regina	WHL	68	2	11	13	224	...	...	...	9	0	3	3	32
98-99—Regina	WHL	70	8	36	44	259	-9	4	0	—	—	—	—	—
99-00—Regina	WHL	53	9	37	46	175	-10	3	0	6	1	1	2	19
—Worcester	AHL	...	...	...	...	...	...	...	...	2	0	0	0	13
00-01—Regina	WHL	43	9	27	36	138	...	...	...	6	0	3	3	8
01-02—Worcester	AHL	75	2	12	14	266	16	1	0	3	0	1	1	4
—St. Louis	NHL	1	0	0	0	0	0	0	0	1	0	0	0	2
02-03—St. Louis	NHL	82	3	16	19	190	23	0	0	7	0	0	0	14
03-04—St. Louis	NHL	15	1	2	3	41	-1	0	0	—	—	—	—	—
04-05—Missouri	UHL	28	3	17	20	61	10	2	0	—	—	—	—	—
05-06—St. Louis	NHL	63	4	6	10	156	-6	0	0	—	—	—	—	—
NHL Totals (4 years)		161	8	24	32	387	16	0	0	8	0	0	0	16

JACKMAN, RIC — D

PERSONAL: Born June 28, 1978, in Toronto. ... 6-2/197. ... Shoots right.
TRANSACTIONS/CAREER NOTES: Selected by Dallas Stars in first round (first Stars pick, fifth overall) of NHL draft (June 22, 1996). ... Traded by Stars to Boston Bruins for RW Cameron Mann (June 24, 2001). ... Separated shoulder (September 20, 2001); missed first four games of season. ... Traded by Bruins to Toronto Maple Leafs for C Kris Vernarsky (May 13, 2002). ... Traded by Maple Leafs to Pittsburgh Penguins for D Drake Berehowsky (February 11, 2004). ... Flu (March 2, 2004); missed one game. ... Traded by Penguins to Florida Panthers for C Petr Taticeck (March 9, 2006).

		REGULAR SEASON								PLAYOFFS				
Season Team	League	GP	G	A	Pts.	PIM	+/-	PP	SH	GP	G	A	Pts.	PIM
95-96—Sault Ste. Marie	OHL	66	13	29	42	97	...	...	...	4	1	0	1	15
96-97—Sault Ste. Marie	OHL	53	13	34	47	116	12	9	0	10	2	6	8	24

Season Team	League	REGULAR SEASON GP	G	A	Pts.	PIM	+/-	PP	SH	PLAYOFFS GP	G	A	Pts.	PIM
97-98—Sault Ste. Marie	OHL	60	33	40	73	111	...	...	...	—	—	—	—	—
—Michigan	IHL	14	1	5	6	10	-1	0	0	4	0	0	0	10
98-99—Michigan	IHL	71	13	17	30	106	-12	8	0	5	0	4	4	6
99-00—Michigan	IHL	50	3	16	19	51	...	...	...	—	—	—	—	—
—Dallas	NHL	22	1	2	3	6	-1	1	0	—	—	—	—	—
00-01—Dallas	NHL	16	0	0	0	18	-6	0	0	—	—	—	—	—
—Utah	IHL	57	9	19	28	24	...	...	...	—	—	—	—	—
01-02—Boston	NHL	2	0	0	0	2	-1	0	0	—	—	—	—	—
—Providence	AHL	9	0	1	1	8	-1	0	0	—	—	—	—	—
02-03—St. John's	AHL	8	2	6	8	24	-4	1	0	—	—	—	—	—
—Toronto	NHL	42	0	2	2	41	-10	0	0	—	—	—	—	—
03-04—St. John's	AHL	3	2	1	3	0	3	1	0	—	—	—	—	—
—Toronto	NHL	29	2	4	6	13	-11	1	0	—	—	—	—	—
—Pittsburgh	NHL	25	7	17	24	14	-5	6	0	—	—	—	—	—
04-05—Bjorkloven	Sweden	32	13	19	32	148	6	5	0	—	—	—	—	—
05-06—Pittsburgh	NHL	49	6	22	28	46	-20	3	0	—	—	—	—	—
—Florida	NHL	15	1	1	2	6	0	0	0	—	—	—	—	—
NHL Totals (6 years)		200	17	48	65	146	-54	11	0					

JACKMAN, TIM RW

PERSONAL: Born November 14, 1981, in Minot, N.D. ... 6-4/210. ... Shoots right.

TRANSACTIONS/CAREER NOTES: Selected by Columbus Blue Jackets in second round (second Blue Jackets pick, 38th overall) of entry draft (June 23, 2001). ... Traded by Blue Jackets with LW Geoff Sanderson to Phoenix Coyotes for D Cale Hulse, LW Jason Chimera and C Mike Rupp (October 8, 2005). ... Traded by Coyotes to Los Angeles Kings for C Yanick Lehoux (March 9, 2006).

Season Team	League	REGULAR SEASON GP	G	A	Pts.	PIM	+/-	PP	SH	PLAYOFFS GP	G	A	Pts.	PIM
99-00—Park Center	USHS (West)	19	34	22	56	...	...	...	...	—	—	—	—	—
00-01—Minnesota-Mankato	WCHA	35	11	14	25	82	...	...	...	—	—	—	—	—
01-02—Minnesota-Mankato	WCHA	36	14	14	28	86	...	...	...	—	—	—	—	—
02-03—Syracuse	AHL	77	9	7	16	48	-13	3	0	—	—	—	—	—
03-04—Columbus	NHL	19	1	2	3	16	-7	0	0	—	—	—	—	—
—Syracuse	AHL	65	23	13	36	61	12	5	0	7	2	3	5	12
04-05—Syracuse	AHL	73	14	21	35	98	0	4	1	—	—	—	—	—
05-06—San Antonio	AHL	50	7	13	20	127	-8	3	0	—	—	—	—	—
—Phoenix	NHL	8	0	0	0	21	1	0	0	—	—	—	—	—
—Manchester	AHL	18	2	3	5	33	-3	0	0	7	0	3	3	20
NHL Totals (2 years)		27	1	2	3	37	-6	0	0					

JACQUES, JEAN-FRANCOIS LW

PERSONAL: Born April 29, 1985, in Terrebonne, Que. ... 6-4/217. ... Shoots left. ... Nickname: J.F..

TRANSACTIONS/CAREER NOTES: Selected by Edmonton Oilers in second round (third Oilers pick, 68th overall) of entry draft (June 20, 2003).

Season Team	League	REGULAR SEASON GP	G	A	Pts.	PIM	+/-	PP	SH	PLAYOFFS GP	G	A	Pts.	PIM
01-02—Baie-Comeau	QMJHL	66	10	14	24	136	...	...	...	5	1	0	1	2
02-03—Baie-Comeau	QMJHL	67	12	21	33	123	...	...	...	12	4	2	6	13
03-04—Baie-Comeau	QMJHL	59	20	24	44	70	-14	5	3	4	1	0	1	4
04-05—Edmonton	AHL	6	0	0	0	5	...	...	...	—	—	—	—	—
—Baie-Comeau	QMJHL	69	36	42	78	56	...	...	...	6	3	5	8	6
05-06—Hamilton	AHL	65	24	20	44	131	-10	13	0	—	—	—	—	—
—Edmonton	NHL	7	0	0	0	0	-3	0	0	—	—	—	—	—
NHL Totals (1 year)		7	0	0	0	0	-3	0	0					

JAGR, JAROMIR RW

PERSONAL: Born February 15, 1972, in Kladno, Czechoslovakia. ... 6-2/233. ... Shoots left. ... Name pronounced YAHR-oh-meer YAH-gihr.

TRANSACTIONS/CAREER NOTES: Selected by Pittsburgh Penguins in first round (Penguins' first pick, fifth overall) of NHL draft (June 16, 1990). ... Separated shoulder (February 23, 1993); missed three games. ... Strained groin (January 21, 1994); missed four games. ... Flu (January 11, 1997); missed one game. ... Strained groin (February 16, 1997); missed three games. ... Injured groin (February 27, 1997); missed 13 games. ... Strained groin (April 10, 1997); missed two games. ... Strained hip flexor and groin (November 14, 1997); missed four games. ... Injured groin (April 16, 1998); missed one game. ... Injured groin (April 5, 1999); missed one game. ... Bruised thigh (November 18, 1999); missed one game. ... Strained abdominal muscle (January 15, 2000); missed four games. ... Injured hamstring (February 21, 2000); missed 12 games. ... Bruised upper back (March 26, 2000); missed two games. ... Bruised finger (April 7, 2001); missed one game. ... Traded by Penguins with D Frantisek Kucera to Washington Capitals for C Kris Beech, C Michal Sivek, D Ross Lupaschuk and future considerations (July 11, 2001). ... Injured knee (October 10, 2001); missed three games. ... Strained knee (November 2, 2001); missed four games. ... Strained groin (January 11, 2002); missed six games. ... Injured groin (November 27, 2002); missed one game. ... Fractured wrist (March 10, 2003); missed six games. ... Injured thumb (December 16, 2003); missed two games. ... Traded by Capitals to New York Rangers for RW Anson Carter (January 23, 2004). ... Strained groin (February 14, 2004); missed two games. ... Injured hip flexor (April 3, 2004); missed final game of season.

STATISTICAL PLATEAUS: Three-goal games: 1990-91 (1), 1994-95 (1), 1996-97 (2), 1999-00 (2), 2000-01 (2), 2002-03 (2). Total: 10. ... Four-goal games: 2000-01 (1). ... Total hat tricks: 11.

Season Team	League	REGULAR SEASON GP	G	A	Pts.	PIM	+/-	PP	SH	PLAYOFFS GP	G	A	Pts.	PIM
88-89—Poldi Kladno	Czech.	39	8	10	18	...	...	...	...	—	—	—	—	—
89-90—Poldi Kladno	Czech.	51	30	30	60	...	...	...	...	—	—	—	—	—

Season Team	League	REGULAR SEASON								PLAYOFFS				
		GP	G	A	Pts.	PIM	+/-	PP	SH	GP	G	A	Pts.	PIM
90-91—Pittsburgh	NHL	80	27	30	57	42	-4	7	0	24	3	10	13	6
91-92—Pittsburgh	NHL	70	32	37	69	34	12	4	0	†21	11	13	24	6
92-93—Pittsburgh	NHL	81	34	60	94	61	30	10	1	12	5	4	9	23
93-94—Pittsburgh	NHL	80	32	67	99	61	15	9	0	6	2	4	6	16
94-95—HC Kladno	Czech Rep.	11	8	14	22	10	...	...	...	—	—	—	—	—
—HC Bolzano	Euro	5	8	8	16	4	...	...	...	—	—	—	—	—
—HC Bolzano	Italy	1	0	0	0	0	...	...	...	—	—	—	—	—
—Schalker Haie	Ger. Div. II	1	1	10	11	0	...	...	...	—	—	—	—	—
—Pittsburgh	NHL	48	32	38	†70	37	23	8	3	12	10	5	15	6
95-96—Pittsburgh	NHL	82	62	87	149	96	31	20	1	18	11	12	23	18
96-97—Pittsburgh	NHL	63	47	48	95	40	22	11	2	5	4	4	8	4
97-98—Pittsburgh	NHL	77	35	†67	*102	64	17	7	0	6	4	5	9	2
—Czech Rep. Oly. team	Int'l	6	1	4	5	2	3	0	0	—	—	—	—	—
98-99—Pittsburgh	NHL	81	44	*83	*127	66	17	10	1	9	5	7	12	16
99-00—Pittsburgh	NHL	63	42	54	*96	50	25	10	0	11	8	8	16	6
00-01—Pittsburgh	NHL	81	52	†69	*121	42	19	14	1	16	2	10	12	18
01-02—Washington	NHL	69	31	48	79	30	0	10	0	—	—	—	—	—
—Czech Rep. Oly. team	Int'l	4	2	3	5	4	...	...	...	—	—	—	—	—
02-03—Washington	NHL	75	36	41	77	38	5	13	2	6	2	5	7	2
03-04—Washington	NHL	46	16	29	45	26	-4	6	0	—	—	—	—	—
—New York Rangers	NHL	31	15	14	29	12	-1	4	0	—	—	—	—	—
04-05—HC Kladno	Czech Rep.	17	11	17	28	16	7	...	...	—	—	—	—	—
—Avangard Omsk	Russian	32	16	22	38	63	1	...	...	14	6	11	17	32
05-06—New York Rangers	NHL	82	54	69	123	72	34	24	0	3	0	1	1	2
—Czech Rep. Oly. team	Int'l	8	2	5	7	6	1	0	0	—	—	—	—	—
NHL Totals (15 years)		1109	591	841	1432	771	241	167	11	149	67	88	155	125

JAMES, CONNOR — RW

PERSONAL: Born August 25, 1982, in Calgary. ... 5-10/168. ... Shoots right.
COLLEGE: Denver.
TRANSACTIONS/CAREER NOTES: Selected by Los Angeles Kings in ninth round (11th Kings pick, 279th overall) of entry draft (June 23, 2002).

Season Team	League	REGULAR SEASON								PLAYOFFS				
		GP	G	A	Pts.	PIM	+/-	PP	SH	GP	G	A	Pts.	PIM
02-03—Denver	WCHA	41	20	23	43	12	...	...	...	—	—	—	—	—
03-04—Denver	WCHA	40	13	25	38	16	...	...	...	—	—	—	—	—
04-05—Manchester	AHL	14	2	1	3	10	3	0	0	3	0	0	0	0
—Bakersfield	ECHL	51	21	25	46	34	...	...	...	—	—	—	—	—
05-06—Manchester	AHL	77	17	25	42	43	9	1	2	7	0	0	0	2
—Los Angeles	NHL	2	0	0	0	0	-1	0	0	—	—	—	—	—
NHL Totals (1 year)		2	0	0	0	0	-1	0	0					

JANCEVSKI, DAN — D

PERSONAL: Born June 15, 1981, in Windsor, Ont. ... 6-3/212. ... Shoots left. ... Name pronounced: jan SEHV skee
TRANSACTIONS/CAREER NOTES: Selected by Dallas Stars in second round (second Stars pick, 66th overall) of entry draft (June 22, 1999). ... Signed as free agent by Montreal Canadiens (July 13, 2006).

Season Team	League	REGULAR SEASON								PLAYOFFS				
		GP	G	A	Pts.	PIM	+/-	PP	SH	GP	G	A	Pts.	PIM
97-98—Tecumseh	Jr. B	49	3	11	14	145	...	...	...	—	—	—	—	—
98-99—London	OHL	68	2	12	14	115	21	...	...	25	1	7	8	24
99-00—London	OHL	59	8	15	23	138	-7	4	0	—	—	—	—	—
00-01—London	OHL	39	4	23	27	95	...	...	...	—	—	—	—	—
—Sudbury	OHL	31	3	14	17	42	...	...	...	12	0	9	9	17
01-02—Utah	AHL	77	0	13	13	147	3	0	0	5	0	0	0	4
02-03—Utah	AHL	76	1	10	11	172	-12	0	0	2	0	1	1	12
03-04—Utah	AHL	80	5	17	22	171	...	...	...	—	—	—	—	—
04-05—Hamilton	AHL	80	6	20	26	163	8	4	0	4	0	0	0	2
05-06—Iowa	AHL	77	9	29	38	91	7	6	0	7	1	1	2	6
—Dallas	NHL	2	0	0	0	0	1	0	0	—	—	—	—	—
NHL Totals (1 year)		2	0	0	0	0	1	0	0					

JANSSEN, CAM — RW

PERSONAL: Born April 15, 1984, in St. Louis. ... 5-11/205. ... Shoots right.
TRANSACTIONS/CAREER NOTES: Selected by New Jersey Devils in fourth round (sixth Devils pick, 117th overall) of NHL entry draft (June 23, 2002). ... Illness (January 7, 2006); missed one game.

Season Team	League	REGULAR SEASON								PLAYOFFS				
		GP	G	A	Pts.	PIM	+/-	PP	SH	GP	G	A	Pts.	PIM
00-01—St. Louis	NAJHL	45	1	2	3	244	...	...	...	—	—	—	—	—
01-02—Windsor	OHL	64	5	17	22	268	...	...	...	10	0	0	0	13
02-03—Windsor	OHL	50	1	12	13	211	...	...	...	7	0	1	1	22
03-04—Guelph	OHL	29	7	4	11	125	...	...	...	22	3	3	6	49
—Windsor	OHL	35	4	9	13	144	...	...	...	—	—	—	—	—

Season Team	League	REGULAR SEASON GP	G	A	Pts.	PIM	+/-	PP	SH	PLAYOFFS GP	G	A	Pts.	PIM
04-05—Albany	AHL	70	1	3	4	337	-16	0	0	—	—	—	—	—
05-06—Albany	AHL	26	1	3	4	117	-2	0	0	—	—	—	—	—
—New Jersey	NHL	47	0	0	0	91	-3	0	0	9	0	0	0	26
NHL Totals (1 year)		47	0	0	0	91	-3	0	0	9	0	0	0	26

JARRETT, COLE — D

PERSONAL: Born January 4, 1983, in Sault Ste. Marie, Ont. ... 5-10/200. ... Shoots left. ... Cousin of former NHL goaltender Mike Liut.
TRANSACTIONS/CAREER NOTES: Selected by Columbus Blue Jackets in fifth round (sixth Blue Jackets pick, 141st overall) of entry draft (June 23, 2001). ... Signed as free agent by New York Islanders (September 9, 2003).

Season Team	League	REGULAR SEASON GP	G	A	Pts.	PIM	+/-	PP	SH	PLAYOFFS GP	G	A	Pts.	PIM
99-00—Plymouth	OHL	57	3	7	10	47	...	...	...	23	3	7	10	19
00-01—Plymouth	OHL	60	12	36	48	98	...	...	...	19	6	12	18	29
01-02—Plymouth	OHL	51	14	24	38	92	...	...	...	6	1	1	2	18
02-03—Plymouth	OHL	58	14	41	55	138	...	...	...	14	5	6	11	29
03-04—Bridgeport	AHL	59	2	14	16	38	...	...	...	—	—	—	—	—
04-05—Bridgeport	AHL	61	7	13	20	65	-12	1	2	—	—	—	—	—
05-06—Bridgeport	AHL	78	3	20	23	88	-13	0	1	7	0	0	0	13
—New York Islanders	NHL	1	0	0	0	0	1	0	0	—	—	—	—	—
NHL Totals (1 year)		1	0	0	0	0	1	0	0					

JILLSON, JEFF — D

PERSONAL: Born July 24, 1980, in North Smithfield, R.I. ... 6-3/220. ... Shoots right.
TRANSACTIONS/CAREER NOTES: Selected by San Jose Sharks in first round (first Sharks pick, 14th overall) of NHL entry draft (June 26, 1999). ... Traded by Sharks with G Jeff Hackett to Boston Bruins for D Kyle McLaren and fourth-round pick (G Jason Churchill) in 2004 entry draft (January 23, 2003). ... Traded by Bruins to Sharks for C Brad Boyes; then traded by Sharks with ninth-round pick in 2005 entry draft to Buffalo Sabres for C Curtis Brown and D Andy Delmore (March 9, 2004).

Season Team	League	REGULAR SEASON GP	G	A	Pts.	PIM	+/-	PP	SH	PLAYOFFS GP	G	A	Pts.	PIM
96-97—Mount St. Charles	USHS (East)	15	16	14	30	20	...	...	...	—	—	—	—	—
97-98—Mount St. Charles	USHS (East)	15	10	13	23	32	...	...	...	—	—	—	—	—
98-99—Univ. of Michigan	CCHA	38	5	19	24	71	...	...	...	—	—	—	—	—
99-00—Univ. of Michigan	CCHA	36	8	26	34	111	...	...	...	—	—	—	—	—
00-01—Univ. of Michigan	CCHA	43	10	20	30	74	...	...	...	—	—	—	—	—
01-02—San Jose	NHL	48	5	13	18	29	2	3	0	4	0	0	0	0
—Cleveland	AHL	27	2	13	15	45	-10	1	0	—	—	—	—	—
02-03—Cleveland	AHL	19	3	5	8	12	-13	1	0	—	—	—	—	—
—San Jose	NHL	26	0	6	6	9	-7	0	0	—	—	—	—	—
—Providence	AHL	30	4	11	15	26	4	2	0	—	—	—	—	—
03-04—Boston	NHL	50	4	10	14	35	-1	1	0	—	—	—	—	—
—Buffalo	NHL	14	0	3	3	19	-3	0	0	—	—	—	—	—
04-05—Rochester	AHL	78	12	17	29	46	6	8	0	9	1	1	2	12
05-06—Rochester	AHL	73	10	20	30	94	-2	7	0	—	—	—	—	—
—Buffalo	NHL	2	0	0	0	4	0	0	0	4	0	0	0	0
NHL Totals (4 years)		140	9	32	41	96	-9	4	0	8	0	0	0	0

JOENSUU, JESSE — LW

PERSONAL: Born October 5, 1987, in Pori, Finland. ... 6-4/207. ... Shoots left.
TRANSACTIONS/CAREER NOTES: Selected by New York Islanders in second round (second Islanders pick; 60th overall) of NHL draft (June 24, 2006).

Season Team	League	REGULAR SEASON GP	G	A	Pts.	PIM	+/-	PP	SH	PLAYOFFS GP	G	A	Pts.	PIM
04-05—Assat Pori	Finland	39	1	1	2	4	...	...	...	—	—	—	—	—
05-06—Assat Pori	Finland	51	4	8	12	57	...	...	...	14	0	2	2	12

JOHANSSON, JONAS — RW/LW

PERSONAL: Born March 18, 1984, in Jonkoping, Sweden. ... 6-1/180. ... Shoots right.
TRANSACTIONS/CAREER NOTES: Selected by Colorado Avalanche in first round (first Avalanche pick, 28th overall) of entry draft (June 22, 2002). ... Traded by Avalanche to Washington Capitals with LW Bates Battaglia for LW Steve Konowalchuk and third-round pick (later traded to Carolina; Hurricanes selected D Casy Borer) in the 2004 entry draft (October 22, 2003).

Season Team	League	REGULAR SEASON GP	G	A	Pts.	PIM	+/-	PP	SH	PLAYOFFS GP	G	A	Pts.	PIM
01-02—HV 71 Jonkoping	Sweden Jr.	26	15	19	34	20	...	...	...	—	—	—	—	—
—HV 71 Jonkoping	Sweden	5	0	0	0	0	...	...	...	2	0	0	0	0
02-03—Kamloops	WHL	26	10	25	35	8	...	...	...	6	1	2	3	4
03-04—Kamloops	WHL	72	18	19	37	70	...	...	...	5	2	2	4	4
04-05—Portland	AHL	50	3	6	9	8	-10	1	0	—	—	—	—	—
—South Carolina	ECHL	5	4	2	6	10	4	1	0	—	—	—	—	—
05-06—Hershey	AHL	37	5	5	10	24	-2	1	0	2	1	0	1	4
—Washington	NHL	1	0	0	0	2	0	0	0	—	—	—	—	—
NHL Totals (1 year)		1	0	0	0	2	0	0	0					

JOHNSON, AARON D

PERSONAL: Born April 30, 1983, in Point Hawkesbury, N.S. ... 6-0/197. ... Shoots left.
TRANSACTIONS/CAREER NOTES: Selected by Columbus Blue Jackets in third round (fourth Blue Jackets pick, 85th overall) of entry draft (June 23, 2001). ... Sprained knee (December 23, 2005); missed eight games.

		REGULAR SEASON								PLAYOFFS				
Season Team	League	GP	G	A	Pts.	PIM	+/-	PP	SH	GP	G	A	Pts.	PIM
00-01—Rimouski	QMJHL	64	12	41	53	128	...	...	...	11	2	4	6	35
01-02—Rimouski	QMJHL	68	17	49	66	172	...	...	...	7	1	2	3	12
02-03—Rimouski	QMJHL	25	6	31	37	41	...	...	...	—	—	—	—	—
—Quebec	QMJHL	32	6	31	37	41	...	...	...	11	4	4	8	25
03-04—Syracuse	AHL	49	6	15	21	83	0	4	0	7	2	3	5	27
—Columbus	NHL	29	2	6	8	32	-2	0	0	—	—	—	—	—
04-05—Syracuse	AHL	77	6	17	23	140	-13	2	0	—	—	—	—	—
05-06—Syracuse	AHL	49	5	24	29	122	-4	4	0	6	1	3	4	19
—Columbus	NHL	26	2	6	8	23	9	1	0	—	—	—	—	—
NHL Totals (2 years)		55	4	12	16	55	7	1	0					

JOHNSON, BRENT G

PERSONAL: Born March 12, 1977, in Farmington, Mich. ... 6-3/205. ... Catches left. ... Son of Bob Johnson, G with two NHL teams (1972-75). Grandson of Hall of Fame member Sid Abel, F with two NHL teams (1938-54) and coach and general manager.
TRANSACTIONS/CAREER NOTES: Selected by Colorado Avalanche in fifth round (fifth Avalanche pick, 129th overall) of entry draft (July 8, 1995). ... Traded by Avalanche to St. Louis Blues for third-round pick (D Rick Berry) in 1997 draft (May 30, 1997). ... Injured knee (January 23, 2001); missed three games. ... Flu (November 23, 2001); missed one game. ... Strained hip flexor (April 7, 2002); missed one game. ... Ankle sprain (September 15, 2002); missed season's first 27 games. ... Groin (February 27, 2003); missed five games. ... Traded by Blues to Phoenix Coyotes for C Mike Sillinger (March 4, 2004). ... Signed as free agent by Vancouver Canucks (September 1, 2005). ... Claimed off waivers by Washington Capitals (October 4, 2005). ... Groin (December 31, 2005); missed two games.

		REGULAR SEASON										PLAYOFFS							
Season Team	League	GP	Min.	W	L	OTL	T	GA	SO	GAA	SV%	GP	Min.	W	L	GA	SO	GAA	SV%
94-95 —Owen Sound	OHL	18	904	3	9	...	1	75	0	4.98	...	4	253	0	4	24	0	5.69	.865
95-96 —Owen Sound	OHL	58	3211	24	28	...	1	243	1	4.54	...	6	371	2	4	29	0	4.69	...
96-97 —Owen Sound	OHL	50	2798	20	28	...	1	201	1	4.31	.891	4	253	0	4	24	0	5.69	.865
97-98 —Worcester	AHL	42	2241	14	15	...	7	119	0	3.19	.899	6	332	3	2	19	0	3.43	.885
98-99 —Worcester	AHL	49	2925	22	22	...	4	146	2	2.99	.896	4	238	1	3	12	0	3.03	.916
—St. Louis	NHL	6	286	3	2	...	0	10	0	2.10	.921	—	—	—	—	—	—	—	—
99-00 —Worcester	AHL	58	3319	24	27	...	5	161	3	2.91	...	9	561	4	5	23	1	2.46	...
00-01 —St. Louis	NHL	31	1744	19	9	...	2	63	4	2.17	.907	2	62	0	1	2	0	1.94	.944
01-02 —St. Louis	NHL	58	3491	34	20	...	4	127	5	2.18	.902	10	590	5	5	18	3	1.83	.929
02-03 —Worcester	AHL	2	125	0	1	...	1	8	0	3.84	.881	—	—	—	—	—	—	—	—
—St. Louis	NHL	38	2042	16	13	...	5	84	2	2.47	.900	—	—	—	—	—	—	—	—
03-04 —St. Louis	NHL	10	493	4	3	...	1	20	1	2.43	.901	—	—	—	—	—	—	—	—
—Phoenix	NHL	8	486	1	6	...	1	21	0	2.59	.914	—	—	—	—	—	—	—	—
—Worcester	AHL	8	365	2	2	...	2	14	0	2.30	.901	—	—	—	—	—	—	—	—
05-06 —Washington	NHL	26	1413	9	12	1	...	81	1	3.44	.905	—	—	—	—	—	—	—	—
NHL Totals (6 years)		177	9955	86	65	1	13	406	13	2.45	.904	12	652	5	6	20	3	1.84	.931

JOHNSON, ERIK D

PERSONAL: Born March 21, 1988, in Bloomington, Minn. ... 6-4/222. ... Shoots right.
TRANSACTIONS/CAREER NOTES: Selected by St. Louis Blues in first round (first Blues pick, first overall) of NHL draft (June 24, 2006).

		REGULAR SEASON								PLAYOFFS				
Season Team	League	GP	G	A	Pts.	PIM	+/-	PP	SH	GP	G	A	Pts.	PIM
04-05—U.S. National	USHL	57	11	15	26	26	...	...	...	—	—	—	—	—
05-06—U.S. National	USHL	47	16	33	49	88	...	...	...	—	—	—	—	—

JOHNSON, GREG C

PERSONAL: Born March 16, 1971, in Thunder Bay, Ont. ... 5-11/200. ... Shoots left. ... Brother of Ryan Johnson, C, St. Louis Blues.
TRANSACTIONS/CAREER NOTES: Selected by Philadelphia Flyers in second round (first Flyers pick, 33rd overall) of entry draft (June 17, 1989). ... Shoulder (November 24, 1990). ... Rights traded by Flyers with fifth-round pick (G Frederic Deschenes) in 1994 to Detroit Red Wings for RW Jim Cummins and fourth-round pick (traded to Boston; Bruins selected D Charles Paquette) in 1993 (June 20, 1993). ... Loaned to Canadian Olympic Team (January 19, 1994). ... Returned to Red Wings (March 1, 1994). ... Ankle (April 14, 1995); missed season's final nine games. ... Hand (October 8, 1995); missed two games. ... Knee (March 19, 1996); missed 12 games. ... Traded by Red Wings to Pittsburgh Penguins for RW Tomas Sandstrom (January 27, 1997). ... Shoulder (April 3, 1997); missed one game. ... Strained groin (October 3, 1997); missed five games. ... Traded by Penguins to Chicago Blackhawks for D Tuomas Gronman (October 27, 1997). ... Groin (October 31, 1997); missed three games. ... Selected by Nashville Predators in expansion draft (June 26, 1998). ... Concussion (December 10, 1998); missed four games. ... Groin (February 20, 1999); missed five games. ... Stress fracture in ankle (April 7, 1999); missed season's final five games. ... Concussion (October 22, 2002); missed 44 games. ... Foot (October 25, 2005); missed one game. ... Groin (November 19, 2005); missed 13 games.

		REGULAR SEASON								PLAYOFFS				
Season Team	League	GP	G	A	Pts.	PIM	+/-	PP	SH	GP	G	A	Pts.	PIM
88-89—Thunder Bay Jrs.	USHL	47	32	64	96	4	...	...	...	12	5	13	18	...
89-90—North Dakota	WCHA	44	17	38	55	11	...	...	...	—	—	—	—	—
90-91—North Dakota	WCHA	38	18	61	79	6	...	...	...	—	—	—	—	—

Season Team	League	REGULAR SEASON GP	G	A	Pts.	PIM	+/-	PP	SH	PLAYOFFS GP	G	A	Pts.	PIM
91-92—North Dakota	WCHA	39	20	54	74	8	...	...	...	—	—	—	—	—
92-93—Canadian nat'l team	Int'l	23	6	14	20	2	...	...	...	—	—	—	—	—
—North Dakota	WCHA	34	19	45	64	18	...	...	...	—	—	—	—	—
93-94—Detroit	NHL	52	6	11	17	22	-7	1	1	7	2	2	4	2
—Canadian nat'l team	Int'l	6	2	6	8	4	...	...	...	—	—	—	—	—
—Can. Olympic team	Int'l	8	0	3	3	0	0	0	0	—	—	—	—	—
—Adirondack	AHL	3	2	4	6	0	3	1	0	4	0	4	4	2
94-95—Detroit	NHL	22	3	5	8	14	1	2	0	1	0	0	0	0
95-96—Detroit	NHL	60	18	22	40	30	6	5	0	13	3	1	4	8
96-97—Detroit	NHL	43	6	10	16	12	-5	0	0	—	—	—	—	—
—Pittsburgh	NHL	32	7	9	16	14	-13	1	0	5	1	0	1	2
97-98—Pittsburgh	NHL	5	1	0	1	2	0	0	0	—	—	—	—	—
—Chicago	NHL	69	11	22	33	38	-2	4	0	—	—	—	—	—
98-99—Nashville	NHL	68	16	34	50	24	-8	2	3	—	—	—	—	—
99-00—Nashville	NHL	82	11	33	44	40	-15	2	0	—	—	—	—	—
00-01—Nashville	NHL	82	15	17	32	46	-6	1	0	—	—	—	—	—
01-02—Nashville	NHL	82	18	26	44	38	-14	3	0	—	—	—	—	—
02-03—Nashville	NHL	38	8	9	17	22	7	0	0	—	—	—	—	—
03-04—Nashville	NHL	82	14	18	32	33	-21	1	4	6	1	2	3	0
04-05—Pee Dee	ECHL	70	27	36	63	46	1	5	2	—	—	—	—	—
05-06—Nashville	NHL	68	11	8	19	10	5	0	4	5	0	1	1	2
NHL Totals (12 years)		785	145	224	369	345	-72	22	12	37	7	6	13	14

JOHNSON, MIKE C/RW

PERSONAL: Born October 3, 1974, in Scarborough, Ont. ... 6-2/201. ... Shoots right.

TRANSACTIONS/CAREER NOTES: Signed as free agent by Toronto Maple Leafs (March 16, 1997). ... Suspended two games for elbowing (April 8, 1999). ... Traded by Maple Leafs with D Marek Posmyk and fifth- (F Pavel Sedov) and sixth-round (D Aaron Gionet) picks in 2000 to Tampa Bay Lightning for C Darcy Tucker and fourth-round pick (RW Miguel Delisle) in 2000 (February 9, 2000). ... Injured (November 27, 1999); missed two games. ... Fractured facial bone (March 17, 2000); missed one game. ... Ribs (December 2, 2000); missed two games. ... Traded by Lightning with D Paul Mara, RW Ruslan Zainullin and second-round pick (D Matthew Spiller) in 2001 to Phoenix Coyotes for G Nikolai Khabibulin and D Stan Neckar (March 5, 2001). ... Shoulder (March 8, 2001); missed four games. ... Neck (November 23, 2001); missed one game. ... Knee (November 29, 2001); missed 11 games. ... Knee (December 28, 2001); missed 11 games. ... Shoulder (November 6, 2003), had surgery; missed remainder of season. ... Flu (October 18, 2005); missed one game. ... Neck (January 14, 2006); missed one game. ... Traded by Coyotes to Montreal Canadiens for fourth-round pick in 2007 draft (July 12, 2006).

Season Team	League	REGULAR SEASON GP	G	A	Pts.	PIM	+/-	PP	SH	PLAYOFFS GP	G	A	Pts.	PIM
92-93—Aurora	OPJHL	48	25	40	65	18	...	...	...	—	—	—	—	—
93-94—Bowling Green	CCHA	38	6	14	20	18	...	...	...	—	—	—	—	—
94-95—Bowling Green	CCHA	37	16	33	49	35	...	...	...	—	—	—	—	—
95-96—Bowling Green	CCHA	30	12	19	31	22	...	...	...	—	—	—	—	—
96-97—Bowling Green	CCHA	38	30	32	62	46	8	...	...	—	—	—	—	—
—Toronto	NHL	13	2	2	4	4	-2	0	1	—	—	—	—	—
97-98—Toronto	NHL	82	15	32	47	24	-4	5	0	—	—	—	—	—
98-99—Toronto	NHL	79	20	24	44	35	13	5	3	17	3	2	5	4
99-00—Toronto	NHL	52	11	14	25	23	8	2	1	—	—	—	—	—
—Tampa Bay	NHL	28	10	12	22	4	-2	4	0	—	—	—	—	—
00-01—Tampa Bay	NHL	64	11	27	38	38	-10	3	1	—	—	—	—	—
—Phoenix	NHL	12	2	3	5	4	0	1	0	—	—	—	—	—
01-02—Phoenix	NHL	57	5	22	27	28	14	1	2	5	1	1	2	6
02-03—Phoenix	NHL	82	23	40	63	47	9	8	0	—	—	—	—	—
03-04—Phoenix	NHL	11	1	9	10	10	-1	1	0	—	—	—	—	—
04-05—Farjestad Karlstad	Sweden	8	1	2	3	4	2	0	0	6	0	2	2	4
05-06—Phoenix	NHL	80	16	38	54	50	7	6	1	—	—	—	—	—
NHL Totals (9 years)		560	116	223	339	267	32	36	9	22	4	3	7	10

JOHNSON, RYAN C/LW

PERSONAL: Born June 14, 1976, in Thunder Bay, Ont. ... 6-1/205. ... Shoots left. ... Brother of Greg Johnson, C, Nashville Predators.

TRANSACTIONS/CAREER NOTES: Selected by Florida Panthers in second round (fourth Panthers pick, 36th overall) of entry draft (June 28, 1994). ... Loaned to Canadian national team before 1995-96 season. ... Bruised left ankle (October 16, 1999); missed two games. ... Flu (January 6, 2000); missed one game. ... Traded by Panthers with LW Dwayne Hay to Tampa Bay Lightning for C Mike Sillinger (March 14, 2000). ... Virus (December 2, 2000); missed two games. ... Traded by Lightning with sixth-round pick (later traded back to Lightning, who selected D Doug O'Brien) in 2003 draft to Florida Panthers for C Vaclav Prospal (July 10, 2001). ... Fractured left foot (November 24, 2001); missed five games. ... Concussion (December 22, 2001); missed remainder of season. ... Claimed off waivers by St. Louis Blues (February 19, 2003). ... Groin (April 15, 2004); missed final two games of playoffs. ... Left team for personal reasons (December 6, 2005); missed one game. ... Broken foot (March 5, 2006); missed 13 games.

Season Team	League	REGULAR SEASON GP	G	A	Pts.	PIM	+/-	PP	SH	PLAYOFFS GP	G	A	Pts.	PIM
93-94—Thunder Bay Jrs.	USHL	48	14	36	50	28	...	...	...	—	—	—	—	—
94-95—North Dakota	WCHA	38	6	22	28	39	...	2	1	—	—	—	—	—
95-96—Canadian nat'l team	Int'l	28	5	12	17	14	...	...	...	—	—	—	—	—
—North Dakota	WCHA	21	2	17	19	14	...	...	...	—	—	—	—	—
96-97—Carolina	AHL	79	18	24	42	28	-25	0	1	—	—	—	—	—
97-98—New Haven	AHL	64	19	48	67	12	10	5	5	3	0	1	1	0
—Florida	NHL	10	0	2	2	0	-4	0	0	—	—	—	—	—
98-99—New Haven	AHL	37	8	19	27	18	-15	4	0	—	—	—	—	—
—Florida	NHL	1	1	0	1	0	0	0	0	—	—	—	—	—

Season Team	League	GP	G	A	Pts.	PIM	+/-	PP	SH	GP	G	A	Pts.	PIM
		REGULAR SEASON								PLAYOFFS				
99-00—Florida	NHL	66	4	12	16	14	1	0	0	—	—	—	—	—
—Tampa Bay	NHL	14	0	2	2	2	-9	0	0	—	—	—	—	—
00-01—Tampa Bay	NHL	80	7	14	21	44	-20	1	0	—	—	—	—	—
01-02—Florida	NHL	29	1	3	4	10	-5	0	0	—	—	—	—	—
02-03—Florida	NHL	58	2	5	7	26	-13	0	0	—	—	—	—	—
—St. Louis	NHL	17	0	0	0	12	0	0	0	6	0	2	2	6
03-04—St. Louis	NHL	69	4	7	11	8	-2	0	1	3	0	0	0	0
04-05—Missouri	UHL	29	7	14	21	12	8	1	0	—	—	—	—	—
05-06—St. Louis	NHL	65	3	6	9	33	-21	1	1	—	—	—	—	—
NHL Totals (8 years)		409	22	51	73	149	-73	2	2	9	0	2	2	6

J

JOHNSSON, KIM — D

PERSONAL: Born March 16, 1976, in Malmo, Sweden. ... 6-1/193. ... Shoots left.

TRANSACTIONS/CAREER NOTES: Selected by New York Rangers in 11th round (15th Rangers pick, 286th overall) of NHL draft (June 29, 1994). ... Injured eye (February 8, 2000); missed one game. ... Fractured hand (November 2, 2000); missed five games. ... Traded by Rangers with LW Jan Hlavac, RW Pavel Brendl and third-round pick (LW Stefan Ruzicka) in 2003 draft to Philadelphia Flyers for rights to C Eric Lindros (August 20, 2001). ... Flu (December 3, 2003); missed two games. ... Fractured hand (April 30, 2004); missed three playoff games. ... Signed as restricted free agent by Flyers (August 9, 2005). ... Injured groin (November 3, 2005); missed one game. ... Concussion (January 21, 2006); missed three games. ... Post-concussion symptoms (January 28, 2006); missed one month. ... Signed as free agent by Minnesota Wild (July 1, 2006).

Season Team	League	GP	G	A	Pts.	PIM	+/-	PP	SH	GP	G	A	Pts.	PIM
		REGULAR SEASON								PLAYOFFS				
94-95—Malmo	Sweden	13	0	0	0	4	...	...	...	1	0	0	0	0
95-96—Malmo	Sweden	38	2	0	2	30	...	...	...	4	0	1	1	8
96-97—Malmo	Sweden	49	4	9	13	42	...	...	...	4	0	0	0	2
97-98—Malmo	Sweden	45	5	9	14	29	...	...	...	—	—	—	—	—
98-99—Malmo	Sweden	49	9	8	17	76	...	...	...	8	2	3	5	12
99-00—New York Rangers	NHL	76	6	15	21	46	-13	1	0	—	—	—	—	—
00-01—New York Rangers	NHL	75	5	21	26	40	-3	4	0	—	—	—	—	—
01-02—Philadelphia	NHL	82	11	30	41	42	12	5	0	5	0	0	0	2
—Swedish Oly. team	Int'l	4	1	1	2	0	...	...	...	—	—	—	—	—
02-03—Philadelphia	NHL	82	10	29	39	38	11	5	0	13	0	3	3	8
03-04—Philadelphia	NHL	80	13	29	42	26	16	4	0	15	2	6	8	8
04-05—Ambri-Piotta	Switzerland	24	4	10	14	61	...	3	0	—	—	—	—	—
05-06—Philadelphia	NHL	47	6	19	25	34	5	3	0	—	—	—	—	—
NHL Totals (6 years)		442	51	143	194	226	28	22	0	33	2	9	11	18

JOKINEN, JUSSI — LW

PERSONAL: Born April 1, 1983, in Kalajoki, Finland. ... 5-11/183. ... Shoots left. ... Name pronounced: YOO-see YOH-kih-nehn

TRANSACTIONS/CAREER NOTES: Selected by Dallas Stars in sixth round (seventh Stars pick, 192nd overall) of entry draft (June 24, 2001). ... Lower-body injury (December 7, 2005); missed one game.

Season Team	League	GP	G	A	Pts.	PIM	+/-	PP	SH	GP	G	A	Pts.	PIM
		REGULAR SEASON								PLAYOFFS				
01-02—Karpat Oulu	Finland	54	10	6	16	34	...	...	...	4	1	0	1	0
02-03—Karpat Oulu	Finland	51	14	23	37	10	...	...	...	15	2	1	3	33
03-04—Karpat Oulu	Finland	55	15	23	38	20	...	...	...	15	3	4	7	6
04-05—Karpat Oulu	Finland	56	23	24	47	24	...	...	...	12	3	4	7	2
05-06—Dallas	NHL	81	17	38	55	30	2	8	0	5	2	1	3	0
—Fin. Olympic team	Int'l	8	1	3	4	2	2	1	0	—	—	—	—	—
NHL Totals (1 year)		81	17	38	55	30	2	8	0	5	2	1	3	0

JOKINEN, OLLI — C

PERSONAL: Born December 5, 1978, in Kuopio, Finland. ... 6-3/215. ... Shoots left. ... Name pronounced OH-lee YOH-kih-nehn.

TRANSACTIONS/CAREER NOTES: Selected by Los Angeles Kings in first round (first Kings pick, third overall) of NHL draft (June 21, 1997). ... Traded by Kings with LW Josh Green, D Mathieu Biron and first-round pick (LW Taylor Pyatt) in 1999 draft to New York Islanders for RW Zigmund Palffy, C Bryan Smolinski, G Marcel Cousineau and fourth-round pick (C Daniel Johansson) in 1999 draft (June 20, 1999). ... Traded by Islanders with G Roberto Luongo to Florida Panthers for RW Mark Parrish and LW Oleg Kvasha (June 24, 2000). ... Flu (December 23, 2002); missed one game.

Season Team	League	GP	G	A	Pts.	PIM	+/-	PP	SH	GP	G	A	Pts.	PIM
		REGULAR SEASON								PLAYOFFS				
94-95—KalPa Kuopio	Finland Jr.	6	0	1	1	6	...	...	...	—	—	—	—	—
95-96—KalPa Kuopio	Finland Jr.	15	1	1	2	2	...	...	...	—	—	—	—	—
—KalPa Kuopio	Finland	15	1	1	2	2	...	...	...	—	—	—	—	—
96-97—HIFK Helsinki	Finland	50	14	27	41	88	...	...	...	—	—	—	—	—
97-98—Los Angeles	NHL	8	0	0	0	6	-5	0	0	—	—	—	—	—
—HIFK Helsinki	Finland	30	11	28	39	8	...	...	...	9	7	2	9	2
98-99—Springfield	AHL	9	3	6	9	6	-1	1	0	—	—	—	—	—
—Los Angeles	NHL	66	9	12	21	44	-10	3	1	—	—	—	—	—
99-00—New York Islanders	NHL	82	11	10	21	80	0	1	2	—	—	—	—	—
00-01—Florida	NHL	78	6	10	16	106	-22	0	0	—	—	—	—	—
01-02—Florida	NHL	80	9	20	29	98	-16	3	1	—	—	—	—	—
—Fin. Olympic team	Int'l	4	2	1	3	0	...	...	...	—	—	—	—	—

Season Team	League	GP	G	A	Pts.	PIM	+/-	PP	SH	GP	G	A	Pts.	PIM
		REGULAR SEASON								PLAYOFFS				
02-03—Florida	NHL	81	36	29	65	79	-17	13	3	—	—	—	—	—
03-04—Florida	NHL	82	26	32	58	81	-16	8	2	—	—	—	—	—
04-05—Kloten	Switzerland	8	6	1	7	14	1	1	1	—	—	—	—	—
—Sodertalje SK	Sweden	23	13	9	22	52	-5	4	0	—	—	—	—	—
—HIFK Helsinki	Finland	14	9	8	17	10	8	...	...	5	2	0	2	24
05-06—Florida	NHL	82	38	51	89	88	14	14	1	—	—	—	—	—
—Fin. Olympic team	Int'l	8	6	2	8	2	5	4	0	—	—	—	—	—
NHL Totals (8 years)		559	135	164	299	582	-72	42	10					

JONES, MATT — D

PERSONAL: Born August 8, 1983, in Downers Grove, Ill. ... 6-0/214. ... Shoots left.
COLLEGE: North Dakota.
TRANSACTIONS/CAREER NOTES: Selected by Phoenix Coyotes in third round (fifth Coyotes pick, 80th overall) of entry draft (June 22, 2002).

Season Team	League	GP	G	A	Pts.	PIM	+/-	PP	SH	GP	G	A	Pts.	PIM
		REGULAR SEASON								PLAYOFFS				
99-00—Green Bay	USHL	54	1	4	5	59	...	...	...	13	0	0	0	2
00-01—Green Bay	USHL	52	3	10	13	58	...	...	...	4	0	0	0	2
01-02—Univ. of North Dakota	WCHA	37	2	5	7	20	...	...	...	—	—	—	—	—
02-03—Univ. of North Dakota	WCHA	39	1	6	7	26	...	...	...	—	—	—	—	—
03-04—Univ. of North Dakota	WCHA	31	7	14	21	40	...	...	...	—	—	—	—	—
04-05—Univ. of North Dakota	WCHA	45	6	11	17	66	...	...	...	—	—	—	—	—
05-06—San Antonio	AHL	59	2	11	13	46	-17	0	0	—	—	—	—	—
—Phoenix	NHL	16	0	2	2	14	-2	0	0	—	—	—	—	—
NHL Totals (1 year)		16	0	2	2	14	-2	0	0					

JONES, RANDY — D

PERSONAL: Born July 23, 1981, in Quispamsis, New Brunswick. ... 6-2/195. ... Shoots left.
TRANSACTIONS/CAREER NOTES: Signed as free agent by Philadelphia Flyers (July 24, 2003).

Season Team	League	GP	G	A	Pts.	PIM	+/-	PP	SH	GP	G	A	Pts.	PIM
		REGULAR SEASON								PLAYOFFS				
01-02—Clarkson	ECAC	34	9	11	20	32	...	...	...	—	—	—	—	—
02-03—Clarkson	ECAC	33	13	20	33	65	...	...	...	—	—	—	—	—
03-04—Philadelphia	NHL	5	0	0	0	0	1	0	0	—	—	—	—	—
—Philadelphia	AHL	55	8	24	32	63	0	2	0	12	0	1	1	17
04-05—Philadelphia	AHL	69	5	19	24	32	1	2	0	18	0	5	5	10
05-06—Philadelphia	AHL	21	2	3	5	53	-7	0	0	—	—	—	—	—
—Philadelphia	NHL	28	0	8	8	16	-6	0	0	—	—	—	—	—
NHL Totals (2 years)		33	0	8	8	16	-5	0	0					

JOSEPH, CURTIS — G

PERSONAL: Born April 29, 1967, in Keswick, Ont. ... 5-11/190. ... Catches left.
TRANSACTIONS/CAREER NOTES: Signed as free agent by St. Louis Blues (June 16, 1989). ... Dislocated left shoulder (April 11, 1990); surgery (May 10, 1990). ... Right knee (February 26, 1991); missed remainder of season. ... Ankle (March 12, 1992); missed seven games. ... Knee (January 2, 1993); missed three games. ... Flu (February 9, 1993); missed one game. ... Groin (January 26, 1995); missed three games. ... Hamstring (April 16, 1995); missed four games. ... Traded by Blues with rights to RW Michael Grier to Edmonton Oilers for first-round picks in 1996 (C Marty Reasoner) and 1997 (traded to Los Angeles; Kings selected LW Matt Zultek) (August 4, 1995); picks had been awarded to Oilers as compensation for Blues signing free agent LW Shayne Corson (July 28, 1995). ... Right knee (March 30, 1996); missed three games. ... Groin (December 18, 1996); missed seven games. ... Signed as free agent by Toronto Maple Leafs (July 15, 1998). ... Groin (January 21, 1999); missed one game. ... Fractured hand (February 26, 2002); missed 20 games. ... Traded by Maple Leafs to Calgary Flames for third-round pick (traded to Minnesota; Wild selected Danny Irmen) in 2003 and future considerations (June 30, 2002). ... Signed as free agent by Detroit Red Wings (July 2, 2002). ... Ankle (September 10, 2003); missed season's first four games. ... Ankle (February 11, 2004); missed 10 games. ... Ankle (March 23, 2004); missed regular season's final 11 games. ... Signed as free agent by Phoenix Coyotes (August 17, 2005). ... Groin (October 8, 2005); missed two games.

Season Team	League	GP	Min.	W	L	OTL	T	GA	SO	GAA	SV%	GP	Min.	W	L	GA	SO	GAA	SV%
		REGULAR SEASON										PLAYOFFS							
87-88—Notre Dame	SCMHL	36	2174	25	4	...	7	94	1	2.59	...	—	—	—	—	—	—	—	—
88-89—Wisconsin	WCHA	38	2267	21	11	...	5	94	1	2.49	...	—	—	—	—	—	—	—	—
89-90—Peoria	IHL	23	1241	10	8	...	2	80	0	3.87	...	—	—	—	—	—	—	—	—
—St. Louis	NHL	15	852	9	5	...	1	48	0	3.38	.890	6	327	4	1	18	0	3.30	.892
90-91—St. Louis	NHL	30	1710	16	10	...	2	89	0	3.12	.898	—	—	—	—	—	—	—	—
91-92—St. Louis	NHL	60	3494	27	20	...	10	175	2	3.01	.910	6	379	2	4	23	0	3.64	.894
92-93—St. Louis	NHL	68	3890	29	28	...	9	196	1	3.02	*.911	11	715	7	4	27	2	2.27	.938
93-94—St. Louis	NHL	71	4127	36	23	...	11	213	1	3.10	.911	4	246	0	4	15	0	3.66	.905
94-95—St. Louis	NHL	36	1914	20	10	...	1	89	1	2.79	.902	7	392	3	3	24	0	3.67	.865
95-96—Las Vegas	IHL	15	873	12	2	...	1	29	1	1.99	...	—	—	—	—	—	—	—	—
—Edmonton	NHL	34	1936	15	16	...	2	111	0	3.44	.886	—	—	—	—	—	—	—	—
96-97—Edmonton	NHL	72	4100	32	29	...	9	200	6	2.93	.907	12	767	5	7	36	2	2.82	.911
97-98—Edmonton	NHL	71	4132	29	31	...	9	181	8	2.63	.905	12	716	5	7	23	3	1.93	.928
98-99—Toronto	NHL	67	4001	35	24	...	7	†171	3	2.56	.910	17	1011	9	†8	41	1	2.43	.907
99-00—Toronto	NHL	63	3801	36	20	...	7	158	4	2.49	.915	12	729	6	6	25	1	2.06	.932
00-01—Toronto	NHL	68	4100	33	27	...	8	163	6	2.39	.915	11	685	7	4	24	3	2.10	.927

Season Team	League	REGULAR SEASON GP	Min.	W	L	OTL	T	GA	SO	GAA	SV%	PLAYOFFS GP	Min.	W	L	GA	SO	GAA	SV%
01-02—Toronto	NHL	51	3065	29	17	...	5	114	4	2.23	.906	20	1253	10†	10	48	3	2.30	.914
—Can. Olympic team	Int'l	1	60	0	1	...	0	5	0	5.00	.800	—	—	—	—	—	—	—	—
02-03—Detroit	NHL	61	3566	34	19	...	6	148	5	2.49	.912	4	289	0	4	10	0	2.08	.917
03-04—Detroit	NHL	31	1708	16	10	...	3	68	2	2.39	.909	9	518	4	4	12	1	*1.39	†.939
—Grand Rapids	AHL	1	60	1	0	...	0	1	0	1.00	.950	—	—	—	—	—	—	—	—
05-06—Phoenix	NHL	60	3424	32	21	3	...	166	4	2.91	.902	—	—	—	—	—	—	—	—
NHL Totals (16 years)		858	49820	428	310	3	90	2290	47	2.76	.907	131	8027	62	66	326	16	2.44	.916

JOVANOVSKI, ED D

PERSONAL: Born June 26, 1976, in Windsor, Ont. ... 6-2/210. ... Shoots left. ... Name pronounced joh-vuh-NAHV-skee.

TRANSACTIONS/CAREER NOTES: Selected by Florida Panthers in first round (first Panthers pick, first overall) of entry draft (June 28, 1994). ... Fractured right index finger (September 29, 1995); missed first 11 games of season. ... Sprained knee (January 15, 1997); missed 16 games. ... Traded by Panthers with G Kevin Weekes, C Dave Gagner, C Mike Brown and first-round pick (C Nathan Smith) in 2000 draft to Vancouver Canucks for RW Pavel Bure, D Bret Hedican, D Brad Ference and third-round pick (RW Robert Fried) in 2000 draft (January 17, 1999). ... Fractured foot (February 9, 1999); missed eight games. ... Injured groin (January 12, 2000); missed six games. ... Injured hip (March 13, 2000); missed one game. ... Strained oblique muscle (October 27, 2000); missed one game. ... Fractured heel (December 28, 2002); missed 14 games. ... Injured quadriceps muscle (November 11, 2003); missed one game. ... Sprained right shoulder (January 26, 2004); missed 25 games. ... Strained groin (December 28, 2005); missed 11 games. ... Strained groin (January 25, 2006), had surgery (February 2, 2006); missed 27 games. ... Signed as free agent by Phoenix Coyotes (July 1, 2006).

Season Team	League	REGULAR SEASON GP	G	A	Pts.	PIM	+/-	PP	SH	PLAYOFFS GP	G	A	Pts.	PIM
92-93—Windsor	OHL Jr. B	48	7	46	53	88	...	...	...	—	—	—	—	—
93-94—Windsor	OHL	62	15	35	50	221	...	7	...	4	0	0	0	15
94-95—Windsor	OHL	50	23	42	65	198	...	9	1	9	2	7	9	39
95-96—Florida	NHL	70	10	11	21	137	-3	2	0	22	1	8	9	52
96-97—Florida	NHL	61	7	16	23	172	-1	3	0	5	0	0	0	4
97-98—Florida	NHL	81	9	14	23	158	-12	2	1	—	—	—	—	—
98-99—Florida	NHL	41	3	13	16	82	-4	1	0	—	—	—	—	—
—Vancouver	NHL	31	2	9	11	44	-5	0	0	—	—	—	—	—
99-00—Vancouver	NHL	75	5	21	26	54	-3	1	0	—	—	—	—	—
00-01—Vancouver	NHL	79	12	35	47	102	-1	4	0	4	1	1	2	0
01-02—Vancouver	NHL	82	17	31	48	101	-7	7	1	6	1	4	5	8
—Can. Olympic team	Int'l	6	0	3	3	4	...	...	...	—	—	—	—	—
02-03—Vancouver	NHL	67	6	40	46	113	19	2	0	14	7	1	8	22
03-04—Vancouver	NHL	56	7	16	23	64	2	2	0	7	0	4	4	6
05-06—Vancouver	NHL	44	8	25	33	58	-8	6	0	—	—	—	—	—
NHL Totals (10 years)		687	86	231	317	1085	-23	30	2	58	10	18	28	92

JURCINA, MILAN D

PERSONAL: Born June 7, 1983, in Liptovsky Mikulas, Czech. ... 6-4/235. ... Shoots right.

TRANSACTIONS/CAREER NOTES: Selected by Boston Bruins in eighth round (seventh Bruins pick, 241st overall) of entry draft (June 24, 2001). ... Shoulder (March 11, 2006); missed 10 games.

Season Team	League	REGULAR SEASON GP	G	A	Pts.	PIM	+/-	PP	SH	PLAYOFFS GP	G	A	Pts.	PIM
00-01—Halifax	QMJHL	68	0	5	5	56	...	...	...	6	0	2	2	12
01-02—Halifax	QMJHL	61	4	16	20	58	...	...	...	13	5	3	8	10
02-03—Halifax	QMJHL	51	15	13	28	102	...	...	...	25	6	6	12	40
03-04—Providence	AHL	73	5	12	17	52	-1	1	0	2	0	1	1	2
04-05—Providence	AHL	79	6	17	23	92	6	4	0	17	1	3	4	30
05-06—Providence	AHL	7	0	3	3	8	2	0	0	—	—	—	—	—
—Boston	NHL	51	6	5	11	54	3	2	0	—	—	—	—	—
—Slovakian Oly. team	Int'l	6	0	1	1	8	-2	0	0	—	—	—	—	—
NHL Totals (1 year)		51	6	5	11	54	3	2	0					

KABERLE, FRANTISEK D

PERSONAL: Born November 8, 1973, in Kladno, Czechoslovakia. ... 6-0/190. ... Shoots left. ... Brother of Tomas Kaberle, D, Toronto Maple Leafs. ... Name pronounced KA-buhr-lay.

TRANSACTIONS/CAREER NOTES: Selected by Los Angeles Kings in third round (third Kings pick, 76th overall) of entry draft (June 26, 1999). ... Traded by Kings with RW Donald Audette to Atlanta Thrashers for RW Kelly Buchberger and RW Nelson Emerson (March 13, 2000). ... Bruised foot (October 15, 2000); missed one game. ... Flu (January 25, 2001); missed one game. ... Fractured foot (February 1, 2001); missed 25 games. ... Strained groin (April 1, 2001); missed season's final three games. ... Strained right shoulder (November 23, 2001); missed four games. ... Strained groin and hamstring (March 1, 2002); missed 17 games. ... Foot (December 11, 2002); missed three games. ... Sprained right knee (February 19, 2004); missed 12 games. ... Signed as free agent by Carolina Hurricanes (July 15, 2004). ... Ill (April 1, 2006); missed one game. ... Facial cut (April 8, 2006); missed one game.

Season Team	League	REGULAR SEASON GP	G	A	Pts.	PIM	+/-	PP	SH	PLAYOFFS GP	G	A	Pts.	PIM
91-92—Poldi Kladno	Czech.	37	1	4	5	8	...	...	...	8	0	1	1	0
92-93—Poldi Kladno	Czech.	49	6	9	15	...	...	...	...	—	—	—	—	—
93-94—HC Kladno	Czech Rep.	40	4	15	19	...	...	...	...	9	1	2	3	...
94-95—HC Kladno	Czech Rep.	40	7	17	24	...	...	...	...	8	0	3	3	...
95-96—MoDo Ornskoldsvik	Sweden	40	5	7	12	34	...	...	...	8	0	1	1	0
96-97—MoDo Ornskoldsvik	Sweden	50	3	11	14	28	...	...	...	—	—	—	—	—

Season Team	League	REGULAR SEASON GP	G	A	Pts.	PIM	+/-	PP	SH	PLAYOFFS GP	G	A	Pts.	PIM
97-98—MoDo Ornskoldsvik ..	Sweden	46	5	4	9	22	...	...	...	9	1	1	2	4
98-99—MoDo Ornskoldsvik ..	Sweden	45	15	18	33	4	...	...	...	13	2	5	7	8
99-00—Los Angeles.............	NHL	37	0	9	9	4	3	0	0	—	—	—	—	—
—Long Beach	IHL	18	2	8	10	8	...	...	...	—	—	—	—	—
—Lowell......................	AHL	4	0	2	2	0	...	...	...	—	—	—	—	—
—Atlanta......................	NHL	14	1	6	7	6	-13	0	1	—	—	—	—	—
00-01—Atlanta......................	NHL	51	4	11	15	18	11	1	0	—	—	—	—	—
01-02—Atlanta......................	NHL	61	5	20	25	24	-11	1	0	—	—	—	—	—
02-03—Atlanta......................	NHL	79	7	19	26	32	-19	3	1	—	—	—	—	—
03-04—Atlanta......................	NHL	67	3	26	29	30	2	2	0	—	—	—	—	—
04-05—HC Kladno	Czech Rep.	22	5	11	16	34	6	...	...	—	—	—	—	—
—MoDo Ornskoldsvik ..	Sweden	8	2	2	4	0	-6	2	0	6	1	0	1	27
05-06—Carolina....................	NHL	77	6	38	44	46	8	1	0	25	4	9	13	8
—Czech Rep. Oly. team	Int'l	8	0	1	1	6	4	0	0	—	—	—	—	—
NHL Totals (6 years)		386	26	129	155	160	-19	8	2	25	4	9	13	8

KABERLE, TOMAS D

PERSONAL: Born March 2, 1978, in Rakovnik, Czech. ... 6-1/198. ... Shoots left. ... Brother of Frantisek Kaberle, D, Carolina Hurricanes. ... Name pronounced KA-buhr-lay.

TRANSACTIONS/CAREER NOTES: Selected by Toronto Maple Leafs in eighth round (13th Maple Leafs pick, 20fourth overall) of NHL draft (June 22, 1996). ... Missed first 12 games of 2001-02 season in contract dispute. ... Injured shoulder (December 19, 2003); missed five games. ... Injured shoulder (January 7, 2004); missed five games.

Season Team	League	REGULAR SEASON GP	G	A	Pts.	PIM	+/-	PP	SH	PLAYOFFS GP	G	A	Pts.	PIM
94-95—Kladno	Czech. Jrs.	38	7	10	17	...	...	...	...	—	—	—	—	—
—Poldi Kladno	Czech Rep.	1	0	1	1	0	...	0	0	3	0	0	0	2
95-96—Poldi Kladno	Czech. Jrs.	23	6	13	19	19	...	...	...	—	—	—	—	—
—Poldi Kladno	Czech Rep.	23	0	1	1	2	...	...	...	2	0	0	0	0
96-97—Poldi Kladno	Czech Rep.	49	0	5	5	26	...	...	...	3	0	0	0	0
97-98—Poldi Kladno	Czech Rep.	47	4	19	23	12	...	...	...	—	—	—	—	—
—St. John's....................	AHL	2	0	0	0	0	0	0	0	—	—	—	—	—
98-99—Toronto	NHL	57	4	18	22	12	3	0	0	14	0	3	3	2
99-00—Toronto	NHL	82	7	33	40	24	3	2	0	12	1	4	5	0
00-01—Toronto	NHL	82	6	39	45	24	10	0	0	11	1	3	4	0
01-02—HC Kladno..................	Czech Rep.	9	1	7	8	4	...	...	...	—	—	—	—	—
—Toronto	NHL	69	10	29	39	2	5	5	0	20	2	8	10	16
—Czech Rep. Oly. team..	Int'l	4	0	1	1	2	...	...	...	—	—	—	—	—
02-03—Toronto	NHL	82	11	36	47	30	20	4	1	7	2	1	3	0
03-04—Toronto	NHL	71	3	28	31	18	16	0	0	13	0	3	3	6
04-05—HC Kladno..................	Czech Rep.	49	8	31	39	38	11	...	...	7	1	0	1	0
05-06—Toronto	NHL	82	9	58	67	46	-1	6	0	—	—	—	—	—
—Czech Rep. Oly. team	Int'l	8	2	2	4	2	2	2	0	—	—	—	—	—
NHL Totals (7 years)............		525	50	241	291	156	56	17	1	77	6	22	28	24

KALININ, DMITRI D

PERSONAL: Born July 22, 1980, in Cheljabinsk, U.S.S.R. ... 6-2/206. ... Shoots left.

TRANSACTIONS/CAREER NOTES: Selected by Buffalo Sabres in first round (first Sabres pick, 18th overall) of entry draft (June 27, 1998). ... Fractured thumb (October 26, 2001); missed 18 games. ... Flu (April 5, 2002); missed one game. ... Separated left shoulder (March 12, 2003); missed seven games. ... Flu (March 28, 2003); missed one game. ... Strained groin (October 5, 2005); missed first three games of season. ... Hairline fracture in finger (December 11, 2005); missed 10 games. ... Separated shoulder (February 1, 2006); missed 10 games. ... Broken left ankle (May 9, 2006); missed 10 playoff games.

Season Team	League	REGULAR SEASON GP	G	A	Pts.	PIM	+/-	PP	SH	PLAYOFFS GP	G	A	Pts.	PIM
95-96—Traktor Chelyabinsk	CIS Jr.	30	10	10	20	60	...	...	...	—	—	—	—	—
—Nadezhda Chelyabinsk	CIS Div. II	20	0	3	3	10	...	...	...	—	—	—	—	—
96-97—Traktor Chelyabinsk	Russian	2	0	0	0	0	...	...	...	0	...	...	...	...
—Traktor-2 Chelyabinsk.	Rus. Div.	20	0	0	0	10	...	...	...	—	—	—	—	—
97-98—Traktor Chelyabinsk	Russian	26	0	2	2	24	...	...	...	—	—	—	—	—
98-99—Moncton	QMJHL	39	7	18	25	44	-8	4	0	4	1	1	2	0
—Rochester	AHL	3	0	1	1	14	2	0	0	7	0	0	0	6
99-00—Rochester	AHL	75	2	19	21	52	...	...	...	21	2	9	11	8
—Buffalo	NHL	4	0	0	0	4	0	0	0	—	—	—	—	—
00-01—Buffalo	NHL	79	4	18	22	38	-2	2	0	13	0	2	2	4
01-02—Buffalo	NHL	58	2	11	13	26	-6	0	0	—	—	—	—	—
02-03—Rochester	AHL	1	0	0	0	0	0	0	0	—	—	—	—	—
—Buffalo	NHL	65	8	13	21	57	-7	3	1	—	—	—	—	—
03-04—Buffalo	NHL	77	10	24	34	42	0	2	1	—	—	—	—	—
04-05—Metal. Magnitogorsk...	Russian	—	—	—	—	—	—	—	—	5	0	0	0	2
—Metal. Magnitogorsk...	Russian	48	2	8	10	14	3	...	...	48	2	8	10	14
05-06—Buffalo	NHL	55	2	16	18	54	14	0	0	8	0	2	2	2
NHL Totals (6 years)............		338	26	82	108	221	-1	7	2	21	0	4	4	6

KANA, TOMAS C

PERSONAL: Born November 29, 1987, in Opava, Cze. ... 6-0/202. ... Shoots right.

TRANSACTIONS/CAREER NOTES: Selected by St. Louis Blues in second round (third Blues pick; 31st overall) of NHL draft (June 24, 2006).

Season Team	League	GP	G	A	Pts.	PIM	+/-	PP	SH	GP	G	A	Pts.	PIM
		REGULAR SEASON								PLAYOFFS				
04-05—HC Vitkovice	Czech. Jrs.	46	12	22	34	155	...	...	...	—	—	—	—	—
05-06—HC Vitkovice	Czech.	42	5	9	14	50	4	...	...	6	0	1	1	2

KANE, BOYD — LW

PERSONAL: Born April 18, 1978, in Swift Current, Sask. ... 6-2/222. ... Shoots left.

TRANSACTIONS/CAREER NOTES: Selected by Pittsburgh Penguins in third round (third Penguins pick, 72nd overall) of NHL entry draft (June 22, 1996). ... Returned to draft pool by Penguins and selected by New York Rangers in fourth round (fourth Rangers pick, 114th overall) of NHL entry draft (June 27, 1998). ... Traded by Rangers to Tampa Bay Lightning for LW Gordie Dwyer (October 10, 2002). ... Signed as free agent by Philadelphia Flyers (July 14, 2003). ... Signed as free agent by Washington Capitals (August 12, 2005). ... Signed as free agent by Flyers (July 13, 2006).

Season Team	League	GP	G	A	Pts.	PIM	+/-	PP	SH	GP	G	A	Pts.	PIM
		REGULAR SEASON								PLAYOFFS				
94-95—Regina	WHL	25	6	5	11	6	...	...	...	4	0	0	0	0
95-96—Regina	WHL	72	21	42	63	155	...	...	...	11	5	7	12	12
96-97—Regina	WHL	66	25	50	75	154	25	11	1	5	1	1	2	15
97-98—Regina	WHL	68	48	45	93	133	38	20	2	9	5	7	12	29
98-99—Hartford	AHL	56	3	5	8	23	-8	0	0	—	—	—	—	—
—Charlotte	ECHL	12	5	6	11	14	-6	2	0	—	—	—	—	—
99-00—B.C.	UHL	3	0	2	2	4	...	...	...	—	—	—	—	—
—Hartford	AHL	8	0	0	0	9	...	...	...	—	—	—	—	—
—Charlotte	ECHL	47	10	19	29	110	...	...	...	—	—	—	—	—
00-01—Hartford	AHL	56	11	17	28	81	...	...	...	5	2	0	2	2
—Charlotte	ECHL	12	9	8	17	6	...	...	...	—	—	—	—	—
01-02—Hartford	AHL	78	17	22	39	193	2	7	1	10	1	2	3	50
02-03—Springfield	AHL	72	15	22	37	121	-2	4	0	—	—	—	—	—
03-04—Philadelphia	NHL	7	0	0	0	7	-4	0	0	—	—	—	—	—
—Philadelphia	AHL	73	13	22	35	177	12	6	2	12	0	1	1	39
04-05—Philadelphia	AHL	58	9	15	24	112	-5	0	1	21	0	7	7	28
05-06—Hershey	AHL	74	20	29	49	185	-6	10	2	14	2	8	10	8
—Washington	NHL	5	0	1	1	2	1	0	0	—	—	—	—	—
NHL Totals (2 years)		12	0	1	1	9	-3	0	0					

KANKO, PETR — RW

PERSONAL: Born February 7, 1984, in Pribram, Czech. ... 5-9/195. ... Shoots left.

TRANSACTIONS/CAREER NOTES: Selected by Los Angeles Kings in third round (third Kings pick, 66th overall) of NHL entry draft (June 22, 2002).

Season Team	League	GP	G	A	Pts.	PIM	+/-	PP	SH	GP	G	A	Pts.	PIM
		REGULAR SEASON								PLAYOFFS				
00-01—Sparta Prague	Czech. Jrs.	32	23	10	33	20	...	...	...	—	—	—	—	—
01-02—Kitchener	OHL	61	28	32	60	54	...	...	...	—	—	—	—	—
02-03—Kitchener	OHL	60	33	34	67	123	...	...	...	—	—	—	—	—
03-04—Manchester	AHL	6	1	3	4	0	...	...	...	—	—	—	—	—
—Kitchener	OHL	55	26	42	68	97	...	...	...	—	—	—	—	—
04-05—Manchester	AHL	60	4	14	18	118	-5	1	0	6	0	0	0	18
05-06—Manchester	AHL	60	15	12	27	52	-8	4	4	7	1	1	2	5
—Los Angeles	NHL	10	1	0	1	0	1	0	0	—	—	—	—	—
NHL Totals (1 year)		10	1	0	1	0	1	0	0					

KAPANEN, NIKO — C

PERSONAL: Born April 29, 1978, in Hattula, Finland. ... 5-9/180. ... Shoots left. ... Name pronounced KAP-ih-nehn.

TRANSACTIONS/CAREER NOTES: Selected by Dallas Stars in sixth round (fifth Stars pick, 173rd overall) of entry draft (June 27, 1998). ... Flu (January 26, 2005); missed one game. ... Traded by Stars with a seventh-round pick (D Will O'Neill) in 2006 entry draft to Atlanta Thrashers for F Patrik Stefan and D Jaroslav Modry (June 24, 2006).

Season Team	League	GP	G	A	Pts.	PIM	+/-	PP	SH	GP	G	A	Pts.	PIM
		REGULAR SEASON								PLAYOFFS				
93-94—HPK Hameenlinna	Finland Jr.	31	17	33	50	34	...	...	...	—	—	—	—	—
94-95—HPK Hameenlinna	Finland Jr.	37	19	44	63	40	...	...	...	—	—	—	—	—
95-96—HPK Hameenlinna	Finland Jr.	26	15	22	37	34	...	...	...	—	—	—	—	—
—HPK Hameenlinna	Finland	7	1	0	1	0	...	...	...	—	—	—	—	—
96-97—HPK Hameenlinna	Finland	41	6	9	15	12	...	...	...	10	4	5	9	2
—HPK Hameenlinna	Finland Jr.	5	1	7	8	2	...	...	...	2	0	1	1	2
97-98—HPK Hameenlinna	Finland	48	8	18	26	44	...	...	...	—	—	—	—	—
—HPK Hameenlinna	Finland Jr.	2	1	1	2	0	...	...	...	—	—	—	—	—
98-99—HPK Hameenlinna	Finland	53	14	29	43	49	13	...	...	8	3	4	7	4
99-00—HPK Hameenlinna	Finland	53	20	28	48	40	...	...	...	8	1	9	10	4
00-01—TPS Turku	Finland	56	11	21	32	20	...	...	...	10	2	1	3	4
01-02—Dallas	NHL	9	0	1	1	2	-1	0	0	—	—	—	—	—
—Utah	AHL	59	13	28	41	40	-3	2	3	5	2	1	3	0
02-03—Dallas	NHL	82	5	29	34	44	25	0	1	12	4	3	7	12
03-04—Dallas	NHL	67	1	5	6	16	-15	0	0	1	1	0	1	0
04-05—Zug	Switzerland	44	10	34	44	24	8	4	0	9	2	5	7	35
05-06—Dallas	NHL	81	14	21	35	36	-10	5	2	5	0	1	1	10
—Fin. Olympic team	Int'l	8	2	1	3	2	1	1	0	—	—	—	—	—
NHL Totals (4 years)		239	20	56	76	98	-1	5	3	18	5	4	9	22

KAPANEN, SAMI RW/LW/D

PERSONAL: Born June 14, 1973, in Vantaa, Finland. ... 5-9/181. ... Shoots left. ... Name pronounced KAP-ih-nehn.

TRANSACTIONS/CAREER NOTES: Selected by Hartford Whalers in fourth round (fourth Whalers pick, 87th overall) of entry draft (July 8, 1995). ... Flu (October 20, 1996); missed two games. ... Sprained knee (November 30, 1996); missed 16 games. ... Sprained knee (January 10, 1997); missed nine games. ... Sprained knee (February 26, 1997); missed three games. ... Sprained knee (March 15, 1997); missed six games. ... Flu (April 5, 1997); missed one game. ... Whalers franchise moved to North Carolina and renamed Carolina Hurricanes for 1997-98 season; NHL approved move on June 25, 1997. ... Flu (March 12, 1998); missed one game. ... Bruised knee (October 24, 1998); missed one game. ... Bruised shoulder (February 19, 2000); missed two games. ... Concussion (March 29, 2000); missed four games. ... Injured back (October 18, 2001); missed two games. ... Cut hand (February 8, 2002); missed one game. ... Strained groin (November 15, 2002); missed 11 games. ... Traded by Hurricanes with D Ryan Bast to Philadelphia Flyers for RW Pavel Brendl and D Bruno St. Jacques (February 7, 2003). ... Bruised kidney (December 27, 2003); missed four games. ... Bruised ribs (January 25, 2004); missed two games. ... Flu (January 28, 2004); missed one game. ... Torn cartilage in right shoulder (September 2005) and had surgery; missed first 20 games of season. ... Flu (December 28, 2005); missed one game. ... Sore right shoulder (January 9, 2006); missed one game. ... Injured shoulder (March 17, 2006); missed one game.

STATISTICAL PLATEAUS: Three-goal games: 1997-98 (2), 2001-02 (1). Total: 3.

		REGULAR SEASON								PLAYOFFS				
Season Team	**League**	**GP**	**G**	**A**	**Pts.**	**PIM**	**+/-**	**PP**	**SH**	**GP**	**G**	**A**	**Pts.**	**PIM**
90-91—KalPa Kuopio	Finland	14	1	2	3	2	...	...	...	8	2	1	3	2
91-92—KalPa Kuopio	Finland	42	15	10	25	8	...	...	...	—	—	—	—	—
92-93—KalPa Kuopio	Finland	37	4	17	21	12	...	...	...	—	—	—	—	—
93-94—KalPa Kuopio	Finland	48	23	32	55	16	...	...	...	—	—	—	—	—
94-95—HIFK Helsinki	Finland	49	14	28	42	42	...	...	...	3	0	0	0	0
95-96—Springfield	AHL	28	14	17	31	4	...	...	...	3	1	2	3	0
—Hartford	NHL	35	5	4	9	6	0	0	0	—	—	—	—	—
96-97—Hartford	NHL	45	13	12	25	2	6	3	0	—	—	—	—	—
97-98—Carolina	NHL	81	26	37	63	16	9	4	0	—	—	—	—	—
—Fin. Olympic team	Int'l	6	0	1	1	0	-4	0	0	—	—	—	—	—
98-99—Carolina	NHL	81	24	35	59	10	-1	5	0	5	1	1	2	0
99-00—Carolina	NHL	76	24	24	48	12	10	7	0	—	—	—	—	—
00-01—Carolina	NHL	82	20	37	57	24	-12	7	0	6	2	3	5	0
01-02—Carolina	NHL	77	27	42	69	23	9	11	0	23	1	8	9	6
—Fin. Olympic team	Int'l	4	1	2	3	4	...	...	...	—	—	—	—	—
02-03—Carolina	NHL	43	6	12	18	12	-17	3	0	—	—	—	—	—
—Philadelphia	NHL	28	4	9	13	6	-1	2	0	13	4	3	7	6
03-04—Philadelphia	NHL	74	12	18	30	14	9	0	1	18	3	7	10	6
04-05—KalPa Kuopio	Finland	10	6	3	9	2	4	...	...	9	5	3	8	4
05-06—Philadelphia	NHL	58	12	22	34	12	-9	3	4	6	0	0	0	2
NHL Totals (10 years)		680	173	252	425	137	3	45	5	71	11	22	33	20

KARIYA, PAUL LW

PERSONAL: Born October 16, 1974, in Vancouver. ... 5-10/176. ... Shoots left. ... Brother of Steve Kariya, LW, Vancouver Canucks (1999 through 2001). ... Name pronounced kuh-REE-uh.

TRANSACTIONS/CAREER NOTES: Selected by Anaheim Mighty Ducks in first round (first Mighty Ducks pick, fourth overall) of NHL draft (June 26, 1993). ... Lower back spasms (February 12, 1995); missed one game. ... Strained abdominal muscle; missed first 11 games of 1996-97 season. ... Mild concussion (November 13, 1996); missed two games. ... Missed first 32 games of 1997-98 season in contract dispute. ... Concussion (February 1, 1998); missed remainder of season. ... Injured hip (September 1999); missed one game. ... Fractured right foot (February 18, 2000); missed seven games. ... Fractured right foot (December 20, 2000); missed 16 games. ... Signed as free agent by Colorado Avalanche (July 2, 2003). ... Sprained right wrist (October 22, 2003); missed 10 games. ... Reinjured wrist (November 15, 2003); missed 21 games. ... Sprained left ankle (April 4, 2004); missed 10 playoff games. ... Signed as free agent by Nashville Predators (August 5, 2005).

STATISTICAL PLATEAUS: Three-goal games: 1996-97 (2), 1997-98 (1), 2000-01 (2), 2001-02 (2), 2002-03 (1). Total: 8.

		REGULAR SEASON								PLAYOFFS				
Season Team	**League**	**GP**	**G**	**A**	**Pts.**	**PIM**	**+/-**	**PP**	**SH**	**GP**	**G**	**A**	**Pts.**	**PIM**
90-91—Penticton	BCJHL	54	45	67	112	8	...	...	...	—	—	—	—	—
91-92—Penticton	BCJHL	40	46	86	132	16	...	...	...	—	—	—	—	—
92-93—Maine	Hockey East	39	25	75	100	12	...	...	...	—	—	—	—	—
93-94—Canadian nat'l team	Int'l	23	7	34	41	2	...	...	...	—	—	—	—	—
—Can. Olympic team	Int'l	8	3	4	7	2	6	1	0	—	—	—	—	—
—Maine	Hockey East	12	8	16	24	4	8	1	0	—	—	—	—	—
94-95—Anaheim	NHL	47	18	21	39	4	-17	7	1	—	—	—	—	—
95-96—Anaheim	NHL	82	50	58	108	20	9	20	3	—	—	—	—	—
96-97—Anaheim	NHL	69	44	55	99	6	36	15	3	11	7	6	13	4
97-98—Anaheim	NHL	22	17	14	31	23	12	3	0	—	—	—	—	—
98-99—Anaheim	NHL	82	39	62	101	40	17	11	2	3	1	3	4	0
99-00—Anaheim	NHL	74	42	44	86	24	22	11	3	—	—	—	—	—
00-01—Anaheim	NHL	66	33	34	67	20	-9	18	3	—	—	—	—	—
01-02—Anaheim	NHL	82	32	25	57	28	-15	11	0	—	—	—	—	—
—Can. Olympic team	Int'l	6	3	1	4	0	...	...	...	—	—	—	—	—
02-03—Anaheim	NHL	82	25	56	81	48	-3	11	1	21	6	6	12	6
03-04—Colorado	NHL	51	11	25	36	22	-5	5	1	1	0	1	1	0
05-06—Nashville	NHL	82	31	54	85	40	-6	14	0	5	2	5	7	0
NHL Totals (11 years)		739	342	448	790	275	41	126	17	41	16	21	37	10

KARPOVTSEV, ALEXANDER D

PERSONAL: Born April 7, 1970, in Moscow, U.S.S.R. ... 6-3/221. ... Shoots right. ... Name pronounced KAHR-puht-sehf.

TRANSACTIONS/CAREER NOTES: Selected by Quebec Nordiques in seventh round (seventh Nordiques pick, 158th overall) of NHL draft (June

16, 1990). ... Traded by Nordiques to New York Rangers for D Mike Hurlbut (September 9, 1993). ... Bruised buttocks (October 9, 1993); missed one game. ... Bruised hip (November 3, 1993); missed six games. ... Reinjured hip (November 23, 1993); missed one game. ... Injured face (February 28, 1994); missed two games. ... Injured (March 14, 1994); missed two games. ... Played in Europe during 1994-95 lockout. ... Sore ankle (April 14, 1995); missed one game. ... Hyperextended elbow (October 29, 1995); missed one game. ... Back spasms (February 10, 1996); missed one game. ... Back spasms (February 18, 1996); missed two games. ... Bruised thumb (March 13, 1996); missed two games. ... Back spasms (March 27, 1996); missed six games. ... Bruised toe (April 3, 1997); missed one game. ... Hyperextended elbow (April 10, 1997); missed one game. ... Throat infection (October 10, 1997); missed one game. ... Sprained wrist (January 19, 1998); missed one game. ... Had wrist surgery (February 2, 1998); missed 28 games. ... Bruised knee (October 13, 1998); missed two games. ... Traded by Rangers with fourth-round pick (LW Mirko Murovic) in 1999 draft to Toronto Maple Leafs for D Mathieu Schneider (October 14, 1998). ... Fractured thumb (November 14, 1998); missed 12 games. ... Sprained wrist (January 2, 1999); missed three games ... Strained wrist (February 2, 1999); missed three games. ... Fractured finger (March 17, 1999); missed three games. ... Strained shoulder (April 26, 1999); missed three playoff games. ... Injured (November 5, 1999); missed one game. ... Sprained shoulder (November 26, 1999); missed five games. ... Fractured hand (January 11, 2000); missed four games. ... Injured (March 16, 2000); missed one game. ... Injured (March 23, 2000); missed one game. ... Traded by Maple Leafs with fourth-round pick (D Vladimir Gusev) in 2001 draft to Chicago Blackhawks for D Bryan McCabe (October 2, 2000). ... Bruised ankle (November 2, 2000); missed one game. ... Reinjured ankle (November 5, 2000); missed two games. ... Injured knee (December 3, 2000); missed one game. ... Had knee surgery (December 10, 2000); missed 11 games. ... Cut arm (January 7, 2001); missed one game. ... Suspended two games by NHL for elbowing (February 10, 2001). ... Bruised knee (February 27, 2001); missed three games. ... Injured elbow (March 24, 2001); missed remainder of season. ... Sprained ankle (October 23, 2001); missed one game. ... Sprained knee (November 9, 2001); missed two games. ... Strained groin (November 19, 2001); missed three games. ... Bruised ribs (Janaury 10, 2002); missed three games. ... Had knee surgery (March 3, 2002); missed final seven games of season. ... Fractured ankle (November 5, 2002); missed 18 games. ... Bruised foot (January 15, 2003); missed seven games. ... Bruised ankle (February 5, 2003); missed three games. ... Fractured facial bones (February 20, 2003); missed 13 games. ... Injured back (November 9, 2003); missed four games. ... Injured ankle (November 28, 2003); missed 36 games. ... Injured shoulder (February 29, 2004); missed three games. ... Traded by Blackhawks to New York Islanders for fourth-round pick in 2005 draft (March 9, 2004). ... Bruised lower left leg (March 17, 2004); missed final 10 games of season and playoffs. ... Signed as free agent by Florida Panthers (July 14, 2004).

		REGULAR SEASON								PLAYOFFS				
Season Team	**League**	**GP**	**G**	**A**	**Pts.**	**PIM**	**+/-**	**PP**	**SH**	**GP**	**G**	**A**	**Pts.**	**PIM**
89-90—Dynamo Moscow	USSR	35	1	1	2	27	...	...	...	—	—	—	—	—
90-91—Dynamo Moscow	USSR	40	0	5	5	15	...	...	...	—	—	—	—	—
91-92—Dynamo Moscow	CIS	28	3	2	5	22	...	...	...	—	—	—	—	—
92-93—Dynamo Moscow	CIS	40	3	11	14	100	...	...	...	—	—	—	—	—
93-94—New York Rangers	NHL	67	3	15	18	58	12	1	0	17	0	4	4	12
94-95—Dynamo Moscow	CIS	13	0	2	2	10	...	...	...	—	—	—	—	—
—New York Rangers	NHL	47	4	8	12	30	-4	1	0	8	1	0	1	0
95-96—New York Rangers	NHL	40	2	16	18	26	12	1	0	6	0	1	1	4
96-97—New York Rangers	NHL	77	9	29	38	59	1	6	1	13	1	3	4	20
97-98—New York Rangers	NHL	47	3	7	10	38	-1	1	0	—	—	—	—	—
98-99—New York Rangers	NHL	2	1	0	1	0	1	0	0	—	—	—	—	—
—Toronto	NHL	56	2	25	27	52	38	1	0	14	1	3	4	12
99-00—Toronto	NHL	69	3	14	17	54	9	3	0	11	0	3	3	4
00-01—Dynamo Moscow	Russian	5	0	1	1	0	...	...	...	—	—	—	—	—
—Chicago	NHL	53	2	13	15	39	-4	1	0	—	—	—	—	—
01-02—Chicago	NHL	65	1	9	10	40	10	0	1	5	1	0	1	0
02-03—Chicago	NHL	40	4	10	14	12	-8	3	0	—	—	—	—	—
03-04—Chicago	NHL	24	0	7	7	14	-17	0	0	—	—	—	—	—
—New York Islanders	NHL	3	0	1	1	4	1	0	0	—	—	—	—	—
04-05—Sibir Novosibirsk	Russian	5	0	1	1	16	-3	...	...	—	—	—	—	—
—Lokomotiv Yaroslavl	Russian	33	2	5	7	45	-2	...	...	9	0	0	0	0
05-06—Sibir Novosibirsk	Russian	18	1	2	3	39	...	...	...	—	—	—	—	—
—Florida	NHL	6	0	0	0	4	-3	0	0	—	—	—	—	—
NHL Totals (12 years)		596	34	154	188	430	47	18	2	74	4	14	18	52

KASPARAITIS, DARIUS D

PERSONAL: Born October 16, 1972, in Elektrenai, U.S.S.R. ... 5-11/212. ... Shoots left. ... Name pronounced kas-puhr-IGH-tihz.

TRANSACTIONS/CAREER NOTES: Selected by New York Islanders in first round (first Islanders pick, fifth overall) of entry draft (June 20, 1992). ... Back spasms (February 12, 1993); missed two games. ... Strained back (April 15, 1993); missed one game. ... Strained lower back (November 10, 1993); missed two games. ... Jammed wrist (March 5, 1994); missed four games. ... Tore knee ligament (February 20, 1995); missed remainder of season and first 15 games of 1995-96 season. ... Flu (December 2, 1995); missed two games. ... Severed two tendons in right hand (December 9, 1995); missed 16 games. ... Groin (February 8, 1996); missed two games. ... Traded by Islanders with C Andreas Johansson to Pittsburgh Penguins for C Bryan Smolinski (November 17, 1996). ... Concussion (December 23, 1996); missed two games. ... Cut face (January 2, 1997); missed one game. ... Twisted ankle (January 23, 1997); missed one game. ... Concussion (March 18, 1997); missed three games. ... Flu (March 29, 1998); missed one game. ... Knee (September 20, 1998); missed season's first eight games. ... Strained knee (December 21, 1998); missed one game. ... Strained groin (February 24, 1999); missed two games. ... Strained knee (March 5, 1999) and had surgery; missed remainder of season. ... Injured knee; missed first four games of 1999-2000 season. ... Suspended two games in elbowing incident (October 20, 1999). ... Headaches (December 30, 1999); missed two games. ... Suspended one game for second major penalty and game misconduct in season (January 19, 2000). ... Bruised foot (December 16, 2000); missed three games. ... Injured (April 4, 2001); missed season's final two games. ... Traded by Penguins to Colorado Avalanche for LW Ville Nieminen and D Rick Berry (March 19, 2002). ... Signed as free agent by New York Rangers (July 2, 2002). ... Rib muscle (December 1, 2002); missed one game. ... Flu (January 27, 2003); missed one game. ... Strained ribs (December 30, 2003); missed two games. ... Injured left knee (January 19, 2004) and had right shoulder surgery (March 24, 2004); missed season's final 36 games. ... Knee (January 14, 2006); missed three games. ... Groin (March 22, 2006); missed four games. ... Groin (March 30, 2006); missed eight games.

		REGULAR SEASON								PLAYOFFS				
Season Team	**League**	**GP**	**G**	**A**	**Pts.**	**PIM**	**+/-**	**PP**	**SH**	**GP**	**G**	**A**	**Pts.**	**PIM**
88-89—Dynamo Moscow	USSR	3	0	0	0	0	...	...	...	—	—	—	—	—
89-90—Dynamo Moscow	USSR	1	0	0	0	0	...	...	...	—	—	—	—	—
90-91—Dynamo Moscow	USSR	17	0	1	1	10	...	...	...	—	—	—	—	—
91-92—Dynamo Moscow	CIS	31	2	10	12	14	...	...	...	—	—	—	—	—
—Unif. Olympic team	Int'l	8	0	2	2	2	4	0	0	—	—	—	—	—
92-93—Dynamo Moscow	CIS	7	1	3	4	8	...	...	...	—	—	—	—	—
—New York Islanders	NHL	79	4	17	21	166	15	0	0	18	0	5	5	31
93-94—New York Islanders	NHL	76	1	10	11	142	-6	0	0	4	0	0	0	8

Season Team	League	REGULAR SEASON								PLAYOFFS				
		GP	G	A	Pts.	PIM	+/-	PP	SH	GP	G	A	Pts.	PIM
94-95—New York Islanders.....	NHL	13	0	1	1	22	-11	0	0	—	—	—	—	—
95-96—New York Islanders.....	NHL	46	1	7	8	93	-12	0	0	—	—	—	—	—
96-97—New York Islanders.....	NHL	18	0	5	5	16	-7	0	0	—	—	—	—	—
—Pittsburgh..................	NHL	57	2	16	18	84	24	0	0	5	0	0	0	6
97-98—Pittsburgh..................	NHL	81	4	8	12	127	3	0	2	5	0	0	0	8
—Russian Oly. team.......	Int'l	6	0	2	2	6	8	0	0	—	—	—	—	—
98-99—Pittsburgh..................	NHL	48	1	4	5	70	12	0	0	—	—	—	—	—
99-00—Pittsburgh..................	NHL	73	3	12	15	146	-12	1	0	11	1	1	2	10
00-01—Pittsburgh..................	NHL	77	3	16	19	111	11	1	0	17	1	1	2	26
01-02—Pittsburgh..................	NHL	69	2	12	14	123	-1	0	0	—	—	—	—	—
—Russian Oly. team.......	Int'l	6	1	0	1	4	...	...	...	—	—	—	—	—
—Colorado.....................	NHL	11	0	0	0	19	1	0	0	21	0	3	3	18
02-03—New York Rangers......	NHL	80	3	11	14	85	5	0	0	—	—	—	—	—
03-04—New York Rangers......	NHL	44	1	9	10	48	11	0	0	—	—	—	—	—
04-05—Ak Bars Kazan............	Russian	29	1	3	4	118	8	...	...	3	0	0	0	6
05-06—New York Rangers......	NHL	67	0	6	6	97	7	0	0	2	0	0	0	0
—Russian Oly. team.......	Int'l	8	0	1	1	8	1	0	0	—	—	—	—	—
NHL Totals (13 years)..........		839	25	134	159	1349	40	2	2	83	2	10	12	107

K

KAVANAGH, PAT RW

PERSONAL: Born March 14, 1979, in Ottawa. ... 6-3/205. ... Shoots right.
TRANSACTIONS/CAREER NOTES: Selected by Philadelphia Flyers in second round (second Flyers pick, 50th overall) of NHL entry draft (June 21, 1997). ... Traded by Flyers to Vancouver Canucks for sixth-round pick (F Konstantin Rudenko) in 1999 entry draft (June 1, 1999). ... Signed as free agent by Ottawa Senators (July 27, 2004).

Season Team	League	REGULAR SEASON								PLAYOFFS				
		GP	G	A	Pts.	PIM	+/-	PP	SH	GP	G	A	Pts.	PIM
96-97—Peterborough.............	OHL	43	6	8	14	53	...	...	...	11	1	1	2	12
97-98—Peterborough.............	OHL	66	10	16	26	85	...	...	...	4	1	0	1	6
98-99—Peterborough.............	OHL	68	26	43	69	118	14	...	...	5	0	5	5	10
99-00—Syracuse..................	AHL	68	12	8	20	56	...	...	...	4	0	0	0	0
00-01—Kansas City................	IHL	78	26	15	41	86	...	...	...	—	—	—	—	—
—Vancouver..................	NHL	...	...	...	...	...	...	...	...	3	0	0	0	2
01-02—Manitoba....................	AHL	70	13	19	32	100	4	1	1	7	1	0	1	6
02-03—Vancouver..................	NHL	3	1	0	1	2	2	0	0	—	—	—	—	—
—Manitoba....................	AHL	63	15	15	30	96	7	3	3	14	7	4	11	20
03-04—Manitoba....................	AHL	73	23	22	45	69	3	6	4	—	—	—	—	—
—Vancouver..................	NHL	3	1	0	1	0	0	0	0	—	—	—	—	—
04-05—Binghamton................	AHL	80	14	17	31	87	7	0	3	6	0	1	1	10
05-06—Philadelphia...............	AHL	73	20	23	43	81	6	4	4	—	—	—	—	—
—Philadelphia...............	NHL	8	0	0	0	2	-2	0	0	—	—	—	—	—
NHL Totals (4 years)...........		14	2	0	2	4	0	0	0	3	0	0	0	2

KEITH, DUNCAN D

PERSONAL: Born July 16, 1983, in Winnipeg. ... 6-0/182. ... Shoots left.
COLLEGE: Michigan State.
TRANSACTIONS/CAREER NOTES: Selected by Chicago Blackhawks in second round (second Blackhawks pick, 54th overall) of NHL entry draft (June 22, 2002).

Season Team	League	REGULAR SEASON								PLAYOFFS				
		GP	G	A	Pts.	PIM	+/-	PP	SH	GP	G	A	Pts.	PIM
01-02—Michigan State............	CCHA	41	3	12	15	18	...	...	...	—	—	—	—	—
02-03—Kelowna......................	WHL	37	11	35	46	60	...	...	...	19	3	11	14	12
—Michigan State............	CCHA	13	3	5	8	8	...	...	...	—	—	—	—	—
03-04—Norfolk........................	AHL	75	7	18	25	44	...	...	...	8	1	1	2	6
04-05—Norfolk........................	AHL	79	9	17	26	78	0	3	0	6	0	0	0	14
05-06—Chicago.......................	NHL	81	9	12	21	79	-11	1	1	—	—	—	—	—
NHL Totals (1 year).............		81	9	12	21	79	-11	1	1					

KEITH, MATT RW

PERSONAL: Born April 11, 1983, in Edmonton. ... 6-2/200. ... Shoots right.
TRANSACTIONS/CAREER NOTES: Selected by Chicago Blackhawks in second round (third Blackhawks pick, 59th overall) of entry draft (June 23, 2001).

Season Team	League	REGULAR SEASON								PLAYOFFS				
		GP	G	A	Pts.	PIM	+/-	PP	SH	GP	G	A	Pts.	PIM
98-99—Spokane......................	WHL	7	1	0	1	4	...	...	...	—	—	—	—	—
99-00—Spokane......................	WHL	39	1	3	4	37	...	...	...	15	1	2	3	11
00-01—Spokane......................	WHL	33	13	14	27	63	...	...	...	12	1	3	4	14
01-02—Spokane......................	WHL	68	34	33	67	71	...	...	...	11	5	5	10	16
02-03—Spokane......................	WHL	7	2	2	4	11	...	...	...	—	—	—	—	—
—Red Deer....................	WHL	49	25	26	51	32	...	...	...	23	6	7	13	30
03-04—Chicago.......................	NHL	20	2	3	5	10	-5	1	0	—	—	—	—	—
—Norfolk.......................	AHL	66	13	13	26	57	-4	5	0	8	1	2	3	10
04-05—Norfolk........................	AHL	80	18	31	49	74	10	9	0	6	0	1	1	0
05-06—Norfolk........................	AHL	72	26	19	45	61	-6	7	0	3	0	1	1	0
—Chicago.......................	NHL	2	0	0	0	0	0	0	0	—	—	—	—	—
NHL Totals (2 years)...........		22	2	3	5	10	-5	1	0					

KELLY, CHRIS — C

PERSONAL: Born November 11, 1980, in Toronto. ... 6-0/194. ... Shoots left.
TRANSACTIONS/CAREER NOTES: Selected by Ottawa Senators in third round (fourth Senators pick, 94th overall) of NHL entry draft (June 26, 1999). ... Injured knee (February 14, 2004); missed 12 games.

		REGULAR SEASON								PLAYOFFS				
Season Team	**League**	**GP**	**G**	**A**	**Pts.**	**PIM**	**+/-**	**PP**	**SH**	**GP**	**G**	**A**	**Pts.**	**PIM**
96-97—Aurora	OPJHL	49	14	20	34	11	...	...	...	—	—	—	—	—
97-98—London	OHL	54	15	14	29	4	...	...	...	16	4	5	9	12
98-99—London	OHL	68	36	41	77	60	17	...	...	25	9	17	26	22
99-00—London	OHL	63	29	43	72	57	-6	7	1	—	—	—	—	—
00-01—London	OHL	31	21	34	55	46	...	...	...	—	—	—	—	—
—Sudbury	OHL	19	5	16	21	17	...	...	...	12	11	5	16	14
01-02—Grand Rapids	AHL	31	3	3	6	20	0	0	1	5	1	1	2	5
02-03—Binghamton	AHL	77	17	14	31	73	7	5	3	14	2	3	5	8
03-04—Binghamton	AHL	54	15	19	34	40	5	3	1	2	0	0	0	4
—Ottawa	NHL	4	0	0	0	0	-2	0	0	—	—	—	—	—
04-05—Binghamton	AHL	77	24	36	60	57	30	4	4	6	1	2	3	11
05-06—Ottawa	NHL	82	10	20	30	76	21	1	0	10	0	0	0	2
NHL Totals (2 years)		86	10	20	30	76	19	1	0	10	0	0	0	2

K

KESLER, RYAN — C

PERSONAL: Born August 31, 1984, in Detroit. ... 6-2/205. ... Shoots right.
TRANSACTIONS/CAREER NOTES: Selected by Vancouver Canucks in first round (23rd overall) of NHL entry draft (June 21, 2003).

		REGULAR SEASON								PLAYOFFS				
Season Team	**League**	**GP**	**G**	**A**	**Pts.**	**PIM**	**+/-**	**PP**	**SH**	**GP**	**G**	**A**	**Pts.**	**PIM**
02-03—Ohio State	CCHA	40	11	20	31	44	...	...	...	—	—	—	—	—
03-04—Manitoba	AHL	33	3	8	11	29	-4	0	1	—	—	—	—	—
—Vancouver	NHL	28	2	3	5	16	-2	0	0	—	—	—	—	—
04-05—Manitoba	AHL	78	30	27	57	105	22	8	1	14	4	5	9	8
05-06—Vancouver	NHL	82	10	13	23	79	1	1	0	—	—	—	—	—
NHL Totals (2 years)		110	12	16	28	95	-1	1	0					

KESSEL, PHIL — C

PERSONAL: Born October 2, 1987, in Madison, Wis. ... 6-0/189. ... Shoots right.
TRANSACTIONS/CAREER NOTES: Selected by Boston Bruins in first round (first Bruins pick, fifth overall) of NHL draft (June 24, 2006).

		REGULAR SEASON								PLAYOFFS				
Season Team	**League**	**GP**	**G**	**A**	**Pts.**	**PIM**	**+/-**	**PP**	**SH**	**GP**	**G**	**A**	**Pts.**	**PIM**
05-06—Minnesota	WCHA	39	18	33	51	28	...	10	...	—	—	—	—	—

KHABIBULIN, NIKOLAI — G

PERSONAL: Born January 13, 1973, in Sverdlovsk, U.S.S.R. ... 6-1/203. ... Catches left. ... Name pronounced hah-bee-BOO-lihn.
TRANSACTIONS/CAREER NOTES: Selected by Winnipeg Jets in ninth round (eighth Jets pick, 20fourth overall) of entry draft (June 20, 1992). ... Sprained knee (November 30, 1995); missed 20 games. ... Jets franchise moved to Phoenix and renamed Coyotes for 1996-97 season; NHL approved move on January 18, 1996. ... Bruised hand (November 6, 1998); missed two games. ... Strained groin (March 2, 1999); missed one game. ... Traded by Coyotes with D Stan Neckar to Tampa Bay Lightning for D Paul Mara, RW Mike Johnson, RW Ruslan Zainullin and second-round pick (D Matthew Spiller) in 2001 draft (March 5, 2001). ... Signed as free agent by Chicago Blackhawks (August 5, 2005). ... Strained groin (December 28, 2005); missed 10 games. ... Injured knee (January 20, 2006); missed 13 games.

		REGULAR SEASON										PLAYOFFS							
Season Team	**League**	**GP**	**Min.**	**W**	**L**	**OTL**	**T**	**GA**	**SO**	**GAA**	**SV%**	**GP**	**Min.**	**W**	**L**	**GA**	**SO**	**GAA**	**SV%**
91-92—CSKA Moscow	CIS	2	34	...	...	...	...	2	...	3.53	...	—	—	—	—	—	—	—	—
92-93—CSKA Moscow	CIS	13	491	...	...	...	...	27	...	3.30	...	—	—	—	—	—	—	—	—
93-94—Russian Penguins	IHL	12	639	2	7	...	2	47	0	4.41	.873	—	—	—	—	—	—	—	—
—CSKA Moscow	CIS	46	2625	...	...	...	...	116	5	2.65	...	3	193	1	2	11	0	3.42	...
94-95—Springfield	AHL	23	1240	9	9	...	3	80	0	3.87	.874	—	—	—	—	—	—	—	—
—Winnipeg	NHL	26	1339	8	9	...	4	76	0	3.41	.895	—	—	—	—	—	—	—	—
95-96—Winnipeg	NHL	53	2914	26	20	...	3	152	2	3.13	.908	6	359	2	4	19	0	3.18	.911
96-97—Phoenix	NHL	72	4091	30	33	...	6	193	7	2.83	.908	7	426	3	4	15	1	2.11	.932
97-98—Phoenix	NHL	70	4026	30	28	...	10	†184	4	2.74	.900	4	185	2	1	13	0	4.22	.877
98-99—Phoenix	NHL	63	3657	32	23	...	7	130	8	2.13	.923	7	449	3	4	18	0	2.41	.924
99-00—Long Beach	IHL	33	1936	26	11	...	1	59	5	1.83	...	5	321	2	3	15	0	2.80	...
00-01—Tampa Bay	NHL	2	123	1	1	...	0	6	0	2.93	.913	—	—	—	—	—	—	—	—
01-02—Tampa Bay	NHL	70	3896	24	32	...	10	153	7	2.36	.920	—	—	—	—	—	—	—	—
—Russian Oly. team	Int'l	6	359	3	2	...	1	14	1	2.34	.930	—	—	—	—	—	—	—	—
02-03—Tampa Bay	NHL	65	3787	30	22	...	11	156	4	2.47	.911	10	644	5	5	26	0	2.42	.913
03-04—Tampa Bay	NHL	55	3274	28	19	...	7	127	3	2.33	.910	23	1401	*16	7	40	5	1.71	.933
04-05—Ak Bars Kazan	Russian	24	1457	...	...	...	...	40	5	1.65	...	2	118	...	...	6	0	3.04	...
05-06—Chicago	NHL	50	2815	17	26	6	...	157	0	3.35	.886	—	—	—	—	—	—	—	—
NHL Totals (10 years)		526	29922	226	213	6	58	1334	35	2.67	.908	57	3464	31	25	131	6	2.27	.922

KHAVANOV, ALEXANDER — D

PERSONAL: Born January 30, 1972, in Moscow, U.S.S.R. ... 6-2/205. ... Shoots left.

TRANSACTIONS/CAREER NOTES: Selected by St. Louis Blues in eighth round (eighth Blues pick, 232nd overall) of NHL draft (June 24, 2000). ... Fractured toe (October 12, 2003); missed five games. ... Bruised foot (January 31, 2003); missed 15 games. ... Fractured foot (March 20, 2004); missed final eight games of regular season and five playoff games. ... Signed as free agent by Toronto Maple Leafs (August 9, 2005). ... Injured left foot (January 31, 2006); missed six games. ... Broken foot (March 26, 2006); missed final 12 games of regular season.

		REGULAR SEASON								PLAYOFFS				
Season Team	League	GP	G	A	Pts.	PIM	+/-	PP	SH	GP	G	A	Pts.	PIM
92-93—Birmingham	ECHL	19	0	3	3	14	...	...	...	—	—	—	—	—
—Raleigh	ECHL	17	0	6	6	8	...	...	...	—	—	—	—	—
93-94—St. Petersburg	CIS	41	1	2	3	24	...	...	...	—	—	—	—	—
94-95—St. Petersburg	CIS	49	7	0	7	32	...	...	...	3	0	0	0	0
95-96—St. Petersburg	CIS	32	1	5	6	41	...	...	...	—	—	—	—	—
—HPK Hameenlinna	Finland	16	0	2	2	4	...	...	...	9	0	0	0	0
96-97—Cherepovets	Russian	39	3	8	11	56	...	...	...	3	1	0	1	4
97-98—Cherepovets	Russian	44	3	5	8	46	...	...	...	—	—	—	—	—
98-99—Dynamo	Russian	40	2	7	9	14	...	...	...	16	1	5	6	35
99-00—Dynamo	Russian	38	5	12	17	49	...	...	...	17	0	3	3	4
00-01—St. Louis	NHL	74	7	16	23	52	16	2	0	15	3	2	5	14
01-02—St. Louis	NHL	81	3	21	24	55	9	0	0	4	0	0	0	2
02-03—St. Louis	NHL	81	8	25	33	48	-1	2	1	7	2	3	5	2
03-04—St. Louis	NHL	48	3	7	10	18	2	2	0	—	—	—	—	—
04-05—SKA St. Petersburg	Russian	3	0	0	0	27	...	...	...	—	—	—	—	—
05-06—Toronto	NHL	64	6	6	12	60	-11	2	1	—	—	—	—	—
NHL Totals (5 years)		348	27	75	102	233	15	8	2	26	5	5	10	18

KILGER, CHAD — LW/C

PERSONAL: Born November 27, 1976, in Cornwall, Ont. ... 6-4/224. ... Shoots left. ... Son of Bob Kilger, NHL referee (1970-80).

TRANSACTIONS/CAREER NOTES: Selected by Mighty Ducks of Anaheim in first round (first Mighty Ducks pick, fourth overall) of NHL entry draft (July 8, 1995). ... Traded by Mighty Ducks with D Oleg Tverdovsky and third-round pick (D Per-Anton Lundstrom) in 1996 entry draft to Winnipeg Jets for C Marc Chouinard, RW Teemu Selanne and fourth-round pick (traded to Toronto) in 1996 entry draft (February 7, 1996). ... Flu (February 21, 1996); missed one game. ... Jets franchise moved to Phoenix and renamed Coyotes for 1996-97 season; NHL approved move on January 18, 1996. ... Bruised thigh (October 7, 1996); missed one game. ... Traded by Coyotes with D Jayson More to Chicago Blackhawks for D Keith Carney and RW Jim Cummins (March 4, 1998). ... Suffered concussion (February 19, 1999); missed three games. ... Traded by Blackhawks with LW Daniel Cleary, LW Ethan Moreau and D Christian Laflamme to Edmonton Oilers for D Boris Mironov, LW Dean McAmmond and D Jonas Elofsson (March 20, 1999). ... Had hip pointer (December 30, 1999); missed five games. ... Had hip pointer (February 23, 2000); missed two games. ... Traded by Oilers to Montreal Canadiens for C Sergei Zholtok (December 18, 2000). ... Suffered concussion (March 3, 2001); missed five games. ... Strained groin (April 2, 2001); missed one game. ... Strained neck (January 8, 2002); missed seven games. ... Injured knee (January 17, 2003); missed five games. ... Injured finger (March 31, 2003); missed two games. ... Injured eye (September 16, 2003); missed 10 games. ... Claimed off waivers by Toronto Maple Leafs (March 9, 2004). ... Injured ankle (October 15, 2005); missed one game.

		REGULAR SEASON								PLAYOFFS				
Season Team	League	GP	G	A	Pts.	PIM	+/-	PP	SH	GP	G	A	Pts.	PIM
92-93—Cornwall	CJHL	55	30	36	66	26	...	...	...	6	0	0	0	0
93-94—Kingston	OHL	66	17	35	52	23	...	...	...	6	7	2	9	8
94-95—Kingston	OHL	65	42	53	95	95	...	12	1	6	5	2	7	10
95-96—Anaheim	NHL	45	5	7	12	22	-2	0	0	—	—	—	—	—
—Winnipeg	NHL	29	2	3	5	12	-2	0	0	4	1	0	1	0
96-97—Phoenix	NHL	24	4	3	7	13	-5	1	0	—	—	—	—	—
—Springfield	AHL	52	17	28	45	36	7	5	0	16	5	7	12	56
97-98—Springfield	AHL	35	14	14	28	33	-8	3	0	—	—	—	—	—
—Phoenix	NHL	10	0	1	1	4	-2	0	0	—	—	—	—	—
—Chicago	NHL	22	3	8	11	6	2	2	0	—	—	—	—	—
98-99—Chicago	NHL	64	14	11	25	30	-1	2	1	—	—	—	—	—
—Edmonton	NHL	13	1	1	2	4	-3	0	0	4	0	0	0	4
99-00—Edmonton	NHL	40	3	2	5	18	-6	0	0	3	0	0	0	0
—Hamilton	AHL	3	3	3	6	0	...	...	...	—	—	—	—	—
00-01—Edmonton	NHL	34	5	2	7	17	-7	1	0	—	—	—	—	—
—Montreal	NHL	43	9	16	25	34	-1	1	1	—	—	—	—	—
01-02—Montreal	NHL	75	8	15	23	27	-7	0	1	12	0	1	1	9
02-03—Montreal	NHL	60	9	7	16	21	-4	0	0	—	—	—	—	—
03-04—Montreal	NHL	36	2	2	4	14	2	0	0	—	—	—	—	—
—Hamilton	AHL	2	1	0	1	0	-1	1	0	—	—	—	—	—
—Toronto	NHL	5	1	1	2	2	2	0	0	13	2	1	3	0
05-06—Toronto	NHL	79	17	11	28	63	-6	1	1	—	—	—	—	—
NHL Totals (10 years)		579	83	90	173	287	-40	8	4	36	3	2	5	13

KIPRUSOFF, MIIKKA — G

PERSONAL: Born October 26, 1976, in Turku, Finland. ... 6-2/190. ... Catches left. ... Brother of Marko Kiprusoff, defenseman, Montreal Canadiens (1995-96) and New York Islanders (2001-02).

TRANSACTIONS/CAREER NOTES: Selected by San Jose Sharks in fifth round (fifth Sharks pick, 115th overall) of entry draft (July 8, 1995). ... Knee (March 22, 2003); missed nine games. ... Traded by Sharks to Calgary Flames for second-round pick (D Marc-Edouard Vlasic) in 2005 draft (November 16, 2003). ... Left knee (December 31, 2003); missed 19 games.

Season	Team	League	GP	Min.	W	L	OTL	T	GA	SO	GAA	SV%	Playoffs GP	Min.	W	L	GA	SO	GAA	SV%
			REGULAR SEASON										PLAYOFFS							
93-94	—TPS Turku	Finland Jr.	35	...	...	...	...	...	...	...	3.00	...	6	...	...	...	...	...	4.00	...
94-95	—TPS Turku	Finland Jr.	31	1880	...	...	...	...	93	...	2.97	...	—	—	—	—	—	—	—	—
	—TPS Turku	Finland	4	240	...	...	...	...	12	0	3.00	...	2	120	...	...	7	...	3.50	...
95-96	—TPS Turku	Finland	12	550	...	...	...	...	38	...	4.15	...	—	—	—	—	—	—	—	—
	—Kiekko	Finland	5	300	...	...	...	...	7	...	1.40	...	—	—	—	—	—	—	—	—
96-97	—AIK	Sweden	42	2466	...	...	...	...	104	3	2.53	...	7	420	...	...	23	0	3.29	...
97-98	—AIK Solna	Sweden	42	2457	...	...	...	...	110	...	2.69	...	—	—	—	—	—	—	—	—
98-99	—TPS Turku	Finland	39	2259	26	6	...	6	70	4	1.86	...	10	580	9	1	15	3	1.55	...
99-00	—Kentucky	AHL	47	2759	23	19	...	4	114	3	2.48	...	5	239	1	3	13	0	3.26	...
00-01	—Kentucky	AHL	36	2038	19	9	...	6	76	2	2.24	.926	—	—	—	—	—	—	—	—
	—San Jose	NHL	5	154	2	1	...	0	5	0	1.95	.902	3	149	1	1	5	0	2.01	.937
01-02	—San Jose	NHL	20	1037	7	6	...	3	43	2	2.49	.915	1	8	0	0	0	0	0.00	1.000
	—Cleveland	AHL	4	242	4	0	...	0	7	0	1.74	.946	—	—	—	—	—	—	—	—
02-03	—San Jose	NHL	22	1199	5	14	...	0	65	1	3.25	.879	—	—	—	—	—	—	—	—
03-04	—Calgary	NHL	38	2301	24	10	...	4	65	4	*1.69	*.933	26	1655	15	11	51	5	1.85	.928
04-05	—Timra	Sweden Dv. 2	46	2719	...	...	...	...	97	5	2.14	.916	6	356	...	...	13	0	2.19	.890
05-06	—Calgary	NHL	74	*4380	42	20	*11	...	151	*10	*2.07	.923	7	428	3	4	16	0	2.24	.921
	NHL Totals (5 years)		159	9071	80	51	11	7	329	17	2.18	.918	37	2240	19	16	72	5	1.93	.927

KLEE, KEN D

PERSONAL: Born April 24, 1971, in Indianapolis, Ind. ... 6-0/214. ... Shoots right.

TRANSACTIONS/CAREER NOTES: Selected by Washington Capitals in ninth round (11th Capitals pick, 177th overall) of entry draft (June 16, 1990). ... Injured foot (January 27, 1995); missed six games. ... Injured groin (March 12, 1996); missed 13 games. ... Sprained knee (April 10, 1996); missed two games. ... Fractured facial bone (March 28, 1998); missed eight games. ... Bruised foot (February 12, 2000); missed one game. ... Injured wrist (October 19, 2000); missed six games. ... Strained left knee (December 12, 2000); missed one game. ... Strained back (February 13, 2001); missed six games. ... Concussion (March 7, 2001); missed two games. ... Injured ribs (November 8, 2001); missed three games. ... Injured groin (January 18, 2002); missed four games. ... Injured foot (March 29, 2002); missed five games. ... Signed as free agent by Toronto Maple Leafs (September 27, 2003). ... Strained abdominal muscle (January 13, 2004); missed five games. ... Reinjured abdominal muscle (March 13, 2004); missed four games. ... Injured shoulder (March 20, 2004); missed final seven games of season and one playoff game. ... Knee surgery (May 4, 2004); missed final playoff game. ... Injured ankle (October 4, 2005); missed one game. ... Injured ankle (February 4, 2006); missed four games. ... Traded by Maple Leafs to Devils for F Aleksander Suglobov (March 8, 2006). ... Signed as free agent by Colorado Avalanche (July 24, 2006).

Season	Team	League	GP	G	A	Pts.	PIM	+/-	PP	SH	Playoffs GP	G	A	Pts.	PIM
			REGULAR SEASON								PLAYOFFS				
89-90	—Bowling Green	CCHA	39	0	5	5	52	...	...	...	—	—	—	—	—
90-91	—Bowling Green	CCHA	37	7	28	35	50	...	...	...	—	—	—	—	—
91-92	—Bowling Green	CCHA	10	0	1	1	14	...	...	...	—	—	—	—	—
92-93	—Baltimore	AHL	77	4	14	18	68	...	...	...	7	0	1	1	15
93-94	—Portland	AHL	65	2	9	11	87	0	0	0	17	1	2	3	14
94-95	—Portland	AHL	49	5	7	12	89	12	0	0	—	—	—	—	—
	—Washington	NHL	23	3	1	4	41	2	0	0	7	0	0	0	4
95-96	—Washington	NHL	66	8	3	11	60	-1	0	1	1	0	0	0	0
96-97	—Washington	NHL	80	3	8	11	115	-5	0	0	—	—	—	—	—
97-98	—Washington	NHL	51	4	2	6	46	-3	0	0	9	1	0	1	10
98-99	—Washington	NHL	78	7	13	20	80	-9	0	0	—	—	—	—	—
99-00	—Washington	NHL	80	7	13	20	79	8	0	0	5	0	1	1	10
00-01	—Washington	NHL	54	2	4	6	60	-5	0	0	6	0	1	1	8
01-02	—Washington	NHL	68	8	8	16	38	4	2	0	—	—	—	—	—
02-03	—Washington	NHL	70	1	16	17	89	22	0	0	6	0	0	0	6
03-04	—Toronto	NHL	66	4	25	29	36	-1	3	0	11	0	0	0	6
05-06	—Toronto	NHL	56	3	12	15	66	-1	1	0	—	—	—	—	—
	—New Jersey	NHL	18	0	0	0	14	-3	0	0	6	1	0	1	6
	NHL Totals (11 years)		710	50	105	155	724	8	6	1	51	2	2	4	50

KLEIN, KEVIN D

PERSONAL: Born December 13, 1984, in Kitchener, Ont. ... 6-1/187. ... Shoots right.

TRANSACTIONS/CAREER NOTES: Selected by Nashville Predators in second round (third Predators pick, 37th overall) of entry draft (June 20, 2003).

Season	Team	League	GP	G	A	Pts.	PIM	+/-	PP	SH	Playoffs GP	G	A	Pts.	PIM
			REGULAR SEASON								PLAYOFFS				
00-01	—Toronto St. Michael's	OHL	58	3	16	19	21	...	...	...	18	0	5	5	17
01-02	—Toronto St. Michael's	OHL	68	5	22	27	35	...	...	...	15	2	7	9	12
02-03	—Toronto St. Michael's	OHL	67	11	33	44	88	...	...	...	17	1	9	10	8
03-04	—Toronto St. Michael's	OHL	5	0	1	1	2	-3	0	0	—	—	—	—	—
	—Guelph	OHL	46	6	23	29	40	33	4	0	22	10	11	21	12
04-05	—Rockford	UHL	3	2	1	3	0	...	...	...	—	—	—	—	—
	—Milwaukee	AHL	65	4	12	16	22	9	1	0	7	0	0	0	11
05-06	—Milwaukee	AHL	76	10	32	42	31	4	3	2	15	3	5	8	0
	—Nashville	NHL	2	0	0	0	0	-1	0	0	—	—	—	—	—
	NHL Totals (1 year)		2	0	0	0	0	-1	0	0					

KLEMM, JON D

PERSONAL: Born January 8, 1970, in Cranbrook, B.C. ... 6-2/200. ... Shoots right.

TRANSACTIONS/CAREER NOTES: Signed as free agent by Quebec Nordiques (May 14, 1991). ... Abdomen (March 28, 1995); missed five games. ... Abdomen (April 8, 1995); missed remainder of season. ... Nordiques franchise moved to Colorado and renamed Avalanche for 1995-96 season (June 21, 1995). ... Groin (January 27, 1996); missed one game. ... Thumb (October 30, 1997), had surgery; missed 11 games. ... Groin (December 27, 1997); missed one game. ... Knee (November 15, 1998); missed 29 games. ... Appendicitis (March 25, 1999); missed six games. ... Groin (October 20, 1999); missed seven games. ... Back spasms (February 25, 2000); missed one game. ... Hamstring (December 5, 2000); missed three games. ... Signed as free agent by Chicago Blackhawks (July 1, 2001). ... Fractured finger (December 20, 2002); missed 12 games. ... Traded by Blackhawks to Dallas Stars with fourth-round pick (RW Fredrik Naslund) in 2004 for D Stephane Robidas and second-round pick (C Jakub Sindel) in 2004 (November 17, 2003). ... Groin (January 10, 2004); missed one game. ... Groin (March 24, 2004); missed five games. ... Groin (April 7, 2004); missed playoffs. ... Back spasms (October 5, 2005); missed first two games of season. ... Groin (November 16, 2005); missed two games. ... Shoulder (Jan 16, 2006); missed one game.

		REGULAR SEASON								PLAYOFFS				
Season Team	**League**	**GP**	**G**	**A**	**Pts.**	**PIM**	**+/-**	**PP**	**SH**	**GP**	**G**	**A**	**Pts.**	**PIM**
87-88—Seattle	WHL	68	6	7	13	24	...	...	...	—	—	—	—	—
88-89—Seattle	WHL	2	1	1	2	0	...	...	...	—	—	—	—	—
—Spokane	WHL	66	6	34	40	42	...	...	...	—	—	—	—	—
89-90—Spokane	WHL	66	3	28	31	100	...	...	...	6	1	1	2	5
90-91—Spokane	WHL	72	7	58	65	65	...	...	...	15	3	6	9	8
91-92—Halifax	AHL	70	6	13	19	40	...	...	...	—	—	—	—	—
—Quebec	NHL	4	0	1	1	0	2	0	0	—	—	—	—	—
92-93—Halifax	AHL	80	3	20	23	32	-2	0	0	—	—	—	—	—
93-94—Cornwall	AHL	66	4	26	30	78	15	1	0	13	1	2	3	6
—Quebec	NHL	7	0	0	0	4	-1	0	0	—	—	—	—	—
94-95—Cornwall	AHL	65	6	13	19	84	-12	1	0	—	—	—	—	—
—Quebec	NHL	4	1	0	1	2	3	0	0	—	—	—	—	—
95-96—Colorado	NHL	56	3	12	15	20	12	0	1	15	2	1	3	0
96-97—Colorado	NHL	80	9	15	24	37	12	1	2	17	1	1	2	6
97-98—Colorado	NHL	67	6	8	14	30	-3	0	0	4	0	0	0	0
98-99—Colorado	NHL	39	1	2	3	31	4	0	0	19	0	1	1	10
99-00—Colorado	NHL	73	5	7	12	34	26	0	0	17	2	1	3	9
00-01—Colorado	NHL	78	4	11	15	54	22	2	0	22	1	2	3	16
01-02—Chicago	NHL	82	4	16	20	42	-3	2	0	5	0	1	1	4
02-03—Chicago	NHL	70	2	14	16	44	-9	1	0	—	—	—	—	—
03-04—Chicago	NHL	19	0	1	1	20	6	0	0	—	—	—	—	—
—Dallas	NHL	58	2	4	6	24	10	0	0	—	—	—	—	—
05-06—Dallas	NHL	76	4	7	11	60	-3	1	0	5	1	0	1	0
NHL Totals (13 years)		713	41	98	139	402	78	7	3	104	7	7	14	45

KLEPIS, JAKUB C/RW

PERSONAL: Born June 5, 1984, in Prague, Czechoslovakia. ... 6-0/200. ... Shoots right. ... Name pronounced KLEH-pihsh.

TRANSACTIONS/CAREER NOTES: Selected by Ottawa Senators in first round (first Senators pick, 16th pick overall) of NHL entry draft (June 22, 2002). ... Traded by Senators to Buffalo Sabres for RW Vaclav Varada and fifth-round pick (Tim Cook) in 2003 entry draft (February 25, 2003). ... Traded by Sabres to Washington Capitals for RW Mike Grier (March 9, 2004).

		REGULAR SEASON								PLAYOFFS				
Season Team	**League**	**GP**	**G**	**A**	**Pts.**	**PIM**	**+/-**	**PP**	**SH**	**GP**	**G**	**A**	**Pts.**	**PIM**
01-02—Portland	WHL	70	14	50	64	111	...	...	...	7	0	3	3	22
02-03—Slavia Praha	Czech. Jrs.	38	2	6	8	22	...	...	...	—	—	—	—	—
03-04—Slavia Praha	Czech Rep.	44	4	9	13	43	...	...	...	17	5	3	8	10
04-05—Portland	AHL	78	13	14	27	76	-26	5	0	—	—	—	—	—
05-06—Hershey	AHL	54	11	20	31	49	-13	2	0	8	1	2	3	2
—Washington	NHL	25	1	3	4	8	-11	0	0	—	—	—	—	—
NHL Totals (1 year)		25	1	3	4	8	-11	0	0					

KLESLA, ROSTISLAV D

PERSONAL: Born March 21, 1982, in Novy Jicin, Czech. ... 6-3/208. ... Shoots left. ... Nickname: Rusty. ... Name pronounced: RAHZ-tih-slav KLEHZ-luh

TRANSACTIONS/CAREER NOTES: Selected by Columbus Blue Jackets in first round (first Blue Jackets pick, fourth overall) of entry draft (June 24, 2000). ... Strained shoulder (January 24, 2002); missed seven games. ... Sore shoulder (January 10, 2003); missed eight games. ... Flu (February 15, 2003); missed one game. ... Hip pointer (October 25, 2003); missed five games. ... Sprained knee (November 29, 2003); missed 13 games. ... Sprained wrist (February 25, 2004); missed 15 games. ... Charley horse (March 31, 2004); missed season's final two games. ... Broken right leg (September 26, 2005); missed season's first 12 games. ... Broken hand (November 9, 2005); missed 16 games. ... Groin (April 13, 2006); missed season's final three games.

		REGULAR SEASON								PLAYOFFS				
Season Team	**League**	**GP**	**G**	**A**	**Pts.**	**PIM**	**+/-**	**PP**	**SH**	**GP**	**G**	**A**	**Pts.**	**PIM**
97-98—Opava	Czech. Jrs.	40	11	16	27	...	...	...	...	—	—	—	—	—
98-99—Sioux City	USHL	54	4	12	16	100	...	...	...	—	—	—	—	—
99-00—Brampton	OHL	67	16	29	45	174	...	...	...	6	1	1	2	21
00-01—Columbus	NHL	8	2	0	2	6	-1	0	0	—	—	—	—	—
—Brampton	OHL	45	18	36	54	59	22	7	1	9	2	9	11	26
01-02—Columbus	NHL	75	8	8	16	74	-6	1	0	—	—	—	—	—
02-03—Columbus	NHL	72	2	14	16	71	-22	0	0	—	—	—	—	—
03-04—Columbus	NHL	47	2	11	13	27	-16	0	0	—	—	—	—	—
04-05—HPK Hameenlinna	Finland	9	1	2	3	12	0	...	...	10	0	2	2	12
—HC Vsetin	Czech Rep.	34	6	15	21	134	3	...	...	—	—	—	—	—
—HC Ceske Budejovice	Czech Rep.	7	1	2	3	2	0	...	...	—	—	—	—	—
05-06—Columbus	NHL	51	6	13	19	75	-4	2	0	—	—	—	—	—
NHL Totals (5 years)		253	20	46	66	253	-49	3	0					

KLOUCEK, TOMAS D

PERSONAL: Born March 7, 1980, in Prague, Czechoslovakia. ... 6-3/225. ... Shoots left.

TRANSACTIONS/CAREER NOTES: Selected by New York Rangers in fifth round (sixth Rangers pick, 131st overall) of NHL draft (June 27, 1998). ... Bruised ankle (February 19, 2001); missed one game. ... Bruised shoulder (March 10, 2001): mised two games. ... Bruised heel (March 25, 2001); missed two games. ... Injured knee (April 1, 2001); missed final three games of season. ... Had knee surgery; missed first five games of 2001-02 season. ... Reinjured knee (October 19, 2001); missed one game. ... Had back spasms (November 18, 2001); missed two games. ... Traded with LW Rem Murray and D Marek Zidlicky to Nashville Predators for G Mike Dunham (December 12, 2002). ... Injured knee (October 9, 2003); missed five games. ... Traded with C Ben Simon to Atlanta Thrashers for C Simon Gamache and D Kirill Safronov (December 2, 2003). ... Bruised shoulder (December 5, 2003); missed nine games. ... Bruised shoulder (December 21, 2003); missed nine games. ... Suffered concussion (February 22, 2004); missed six games. ... Signed as free agent by Columbus Blue Jackets (July 6, 2006).

		REGULAR SEASON								PLAYOFFS				
Season Team	League	GP	G	A	Pts.	PIM	+/-	PP	SH	GP	G	A	Pts.	PIM
95-96—Slavia Praha	Czech. Jrs.	40	2	8	10	...	...	...	...	—	—	—	—	—
96-97—Slavia Praha	Czech. Jrs.	43	4	14	18	44	...	...	...	—	—	—	—	—
97-98—Slavia Praha	Czech. Jrs.	43	1	9	10	...	...	...	...	—	—	—	—	—
98-99—Cape Breton	QMJHL	59	4	17	21	162	10	1	0	2	0	0	0	4
99-00—Hartford	AHL	73	2	8	10	113	...	...	...	23	0	4	4	18
00-01—Hartford	AHL	21	0	2	2	44	...	...	...	—	—	—	—	—
—New York Rangers	NHL	43	1	4	5	74	-3	0	0	—	—	—	—	—
01-02—New York Rangers	NHL	52	1	3	4	137	-2	0	0	—	—	—	—	—
—Hartford	AHL	9	0	2	2	27	1	0	0	10	1	1	2	8
02-03—Nashville	NHL	3	0	0	0	2	1	0	0	—	—	—	—	—
—Hartford	AHL	20	3	4	7	102	5	2	0	—	—	—	—	—
—Milwaukee	AHL	34	0	6	6	80	1	0	0	—	—	—	—	—
03-04—Nashville	NHL	5	0	1	1	10	3	0	0	—	—	—	—	—
—Atlanta	NHL	37	0	0	0	25	-8	0	0	—	—	—	—	—
04-05—Slavia Praha	Czech Rep.	29	1	1	2	28	4	...	...	—	—	—	—	—
—Trinec	Czech Rep.	11	1	2	3	24	-2	...	...	—	—	—	—	—
—Liberec	Czech Rep.	8	0	1	1	12	8	...	...	9	0	1	1	35
05-06—Chicago	AHL	33	0	1	1	94	-3	0	0	—	—	—	—	—
—Atlanta	NHL	1	0	0	0	2	0	0	0	—	—	—	—	—
NHL Totals (5 years)		141	2	8	10	250	-9	0	0					

KNUBLE, MIKE LW/RW

PERSONAL: Born July 4, 1972, in Toronto. ... 6-2/232. ... Shoots right. ... Name pronounced kuh-NOO-buhl.

COLLEGE: Michigan

TRANSACTIONS/CAREER NOTES: Selected by Detroit Red Wings in fourth round (fourth Red Wings pick, 76th overall) of NHL draft (June 22, 1991). ... Traded by Red Wings to New York Rangers for third-round pick (traded back to Rangers; Rangers selected Tomas Kopecky) in 2000 draft (October 1, 1998). ... Traded by Rangers to Boston Bruins for LW Rob DiMaio (March 10, 2000). ... Fractured vetebra (November 20, 2001); missed nine games. ... Injured back (March 1, 2002); missed four games. ... Injured back (November 27, 2002); missed nine games. ... Had concussion (November 14, 2002); missed three games. ... Flu (December 27, 2002); missed two games. ... Signed as free agent by Philadelphia Flyers (July 3, 2004).

		REGULAR SEASON								PLAYOFFS				
Season Team	League	GP	G	A	Pts.	PIM	+/-	PP	SH	GP	G	A	Pts.	PIM
88-89—East Kentwood H.S.	Mich. H.S.	28	52	37	89	60	...	...	...	—	—	—	—	—
89-90—East Kentwood H.S.	Mich. H.S.	29	63	40	103	40	...	...	...	—	—	—	—	—
90-91—Kalamazoo	NAJHL	36	18	24	42	30	...	...	...	—	—	—	—	—
91-92—Univ. of Michigan	CCHA	43	7	8	15	48	...	...	...	—	—	—	—	—
92-93—Univ. of Michigan	CCHA	39	26	16	42	57	...	...	...	—	—	—	—	—
93-94—Univ. of Michigan	CCHA	41	32	26	58	71	6	21	0	—	—	—	—	—
94-95—Univ. of Michigan	CCHA	34	38	22	60	62	26	15	0	—	—	—	—	—
95-96—Adirondack	AHL	80	22	23	45	59	...	...	...	3	1	0	1	0
96-97—Adirondack	AHL	68	28	35	63	54	...	...	...	—	—	—	—	—
—Detroit	NHL	9	1	0	1	0	-1	0	0	—	—	—	—	—
97-98—Detroit	NHL	53	7	6	13	16	2	0	0	3	0	1	1	0
98-99—New York Rangers	NHL	82	15	20	35	26	-7	3	0	—	—	—	—	—
99-00—New York Rangers	NHL	59	9	5	14	18	-5	1	0	—	—	—	—	—
—Boston	NHL	14	3	3	6	8	-2	1	0	—	—	—	—	—
00-01—Boston	NHL	82	7	13	20	37	0	0	1	—	—	—	—	—
01-02—Boston	NHL	54	8	6	14	42	9	0	0	2	0	0	0	0
02-03—Boston	NHL	75	30	29	59	45	18	9	0	5	0	2	2	2
03-04—Boston	NHL	82	21	25	46	32	19	4	0	7	2	0	2	0
04-05—Linkopings	Sweden	49	26	13	39	40	24	5	0	6	0	1	1	2
05-06—Philadelphia	NHL	82	34	31	65	80	25	13	2	6	1	3	4	8
—U.S. Olympic team	Int'l	6	1	1	2	4	1	0	0	—	—	—	—	—
NHL Totals (9 years)		592	135	138	273	304	58	31	3	23	3	6	9	10

KOALSKA, MATT C/LW

PERSONAL: Born May 16, 1980, in St. Paul, Minn. ... 5-11/188. ... Shoots left. ... Name pronounced: koh WAHL skuh

COLLEGE: Minnesota.

TRANSACTIONS/CAREER NOTES: Selected by Nashville Predators in fifth round (seventh Predators pick, 154th overall) of entry draft (June 24, 2000). ... Signed as free agent by New York Islanders (August 10, 2004).

Season Team	League	REGULAR SEASON GP	G	A	Pts.	PIM	+/-	PP	SH	PLAYOFFS GP	G	A	Pts.	PIM
99-00—Twin Cities	USHL	57	24	34	58	19	...	...	...	13	5	5	10	4
00-01—Minnesota	WCHA	42	10	14	24	36	...	...	...	—	—	—	—	—
01-02—Minnesota	WCHA	44	10	23	33	34	...	...	...	—	—	—	—	—
02-03—Minnesota	WCHA	41	9	31	40	26	...	...	...	—	—	—	—	—
03-04—Minnesota	WCHA	44	13	26	39	44	...	...	...	—	—	—	—	—
04-05—Bridgeport	AHL	60	7	8	15	22	-1	1	0	—	—	—	—	—
05-06—Bridgeport	AHL	75	19	30	49	82	0	7	0	7	2	1	3	0
—New York Islanders	NHL	3	0	0	0	2	-1	0	0	—	—	—	—	—
NHL Totals (1 year)		3	0	0	0	2	-1	0	0					

KOBASEW, CHUCK RW/LW

PERSONAL: Born April 17, 1982, in Osoyoos, B.C. ... 6-1/190. ... Shoots right.
TRANSACTIONS/CAREER NOTES: Selected by Calgary Flames in first round (first Flames pick, 14th overall) of entry draft (June 23, 2001). ... Right shoulder (January 3, 2004); missed eight games. ... Groin (April 7, 2006); missed five games.

Season Team	League	REGULAR SEASON GP	G	A	Pts.	PIM	+/-	PP	SH	PLAYOFFS GP	G	A	Pts.	PIM
98-99—Penticton	BCHL	30	11	17	28	18	...	...	...	—	—	—	—	—
99-00—Penticton	BCHL	58	54	52	106	83	...	...	...	—	—	—	—	—
00-01—Boston College	Hockey East	43	27	22	49	38	...	...	...	—	—	—	—	—
01-02—Kelowna	WHL	55	41	21	62	114	...	...	...	15	10	5	15	22
02-03—Calgary	NHL	23	4	2	6	8	-3	1	0	—	—	—	—	—
—Saint John	AHL	48	21	12	33	61	-5	9	1	—	—	—	—	—
03-04—Calgary	NHL	70	6	11	17	51	-12	3	0	26	0	1	1	24
04-05—Lowell	AHL	79	38	37	75	110	37	9	1	11	6	3	9	27
05-06—Calgary	NHL	77	20	11	31	64	-10	10	0	7	1	0	1	0
NHL Totals (3 years)		170	30	24	54	123	-25	14	0	33	1	1	2	24

KOIVU, MIKKO C

PERSONAL: Born March 12, 1983, in Turku, Finland. ... 6-2/205. ... Shoots left. ... Brother of Saku Koivu, C, Montreal Canadiens. ... Name pronounced: MEE-koh KOY-voo
TRANSACTIONS/CAREER NOTES: Selected by Minnesota Wild in first round (first Wild pick, sixth overall) of entry draft (June 23, 2001). ... Knee (September 30, 2005); missed season's first 14 games. ... Knee (January 22, 2006); missed one game. ... Foot (January 30, 2006); missed one game. ... Flu (March 7, 2006); missed one game.

Season Team	League	REGULAR SEASON GP	G	A	Pts.	PIM	+/-	PP	SH	PLAYOFFS GP	G	A	Pts.	PIM
99-00—TPS Turku	Finland Jr.	30	4	8	12	22	...	...	...	—	—	—	—	—
00-01—TPS Turku	Finland Jr.	30	11	38	49	34	...	...	...	—	—	—	—	—
—TPS Turku	Finland	21	0	1	1	2	...	...	...	—	—	—	—	—
01-02—TPS Turku	Finland	48	4	3	7	34	...	...	...	8	0	3	3	4
02-03—TPS Turku	Finland	37	7	13	20	20	...	...	...	—	—	—	—	—
03-04—TPS Turku	Finland	45	6	24	30	36	...	...	...	13	1	7	8	8
04-05—Houston	AHL	67	20	28	48	47	-1	4	1	5	1	0	1	2
05-06—Minnesota	NHL	64	6	15	21	40	-9	3	0	—	—	—	—	—
—Fin. Olympic team	Int'l	8	0	0	0	6	-1	0	0	—	—	—	—	—
NHL Totals (1 year)		64	6	15	21	40	-9	3	0					

KOIVU, SAKU C

PERSONAL: Born November 23, 1974, in Turku, Finland. ... 5-10/181. ... Shoots left. ... Brother of Mikko Koivu, C, Minnesota Wild. ... Name pronounced SAK-oo KOY-voo.
TRANSACTIONS/CAREER NOTES: Selected by Montreal Canadiens in first round (first Canadiens pick, 21st overall) of entry draft (June 26, 1993). ... Torn knee ligament (December 7, 1996); missed 26 games. ... Sprained shoulder (March 10, 1997); missed five games. ... Tonsillitis (March 29, 1997); missed one game. ... Strained ribcage (January 8, 1998); missed seven games. ... Fractured hand (April 7, 1998); missed six games. ... Strained abdominal muscle (October 24, 1998); missed 12 games. ... Infected elbow (January 18, 1999); missed three games. ... Injured knee (March 24, 1999); missed two games. ... Injured (October 30, 1999); missed five games. ... Separated shoulder (November 2, 1999); missed 40 games. ... Torn knee ligament (March 11, 2000); missed remainder of season. ... Torn knee ligament (October 11, 2000) and had surgery; missed 28 games. ... Diagnosed with non-Hodgkin's lymphoma; missed first 79 games of 2001-02 season. ... Injured right knee (September 22, 2003); missed first 13 games of season. ... Concussion (December 30, 2003); missed one game. ... Strained groin (November 30, 2005); missed five games. ... Aggravated groin injury (December 20, 2005); missed five games.
STATISTICAL PLATEAUS: Three-goal games: 2002-03 (1).

Season Team	League	REGULAR SEASON GP	G	A	Pts.	PIM	+/-	PP	SH	PLAYOFFS GP	G	A	Pts.	PIM
90-91—TPS Turku	Finland Jr.	24	20	28	48	26	...	...	...	—	—	—	—	—
91-92—TPS Turku	Finland Jr.	42	30	37	67	63	...	...	...	—	—	—	—	—
92-93—TPS Turku	Finland	46	3	7	10	28	...	...	...	—	—	—	—	—
93-94—TPS Turku	Finland	47	23	30	53	42	...	...	...	11	4	8	12	16
—Fin. Olympic team	Int'l	8	4	3	7	12	3	2	0	—	—	—	—	—
94-95—TPS Turku	Finland	45	27	47	74	73	...	...	...	13	7	10	17	16
95-96—Montreal	NHL	82	20	25	45	40	-7	8	3	6	3	1	4	8
96-97—Montreal	NHL	50	17	39	56	38	7	5	0	5	1	3	4	10
97-98—Montreal	NHL	69	14	43	57	48	8	2	2	6	2	3	5	2
—Fin. Olympic team	Int'l	6	2	8	10	4	1	1	0	—	—	—	—	—
98-99—Montreal	NHL	65	14	30	44	38	-7	4	2	—	—	—	—	—

Season Team	League	GP	G	A	Pts.	PIM	+/-	PP	SH	GP	G	A	Pts.	PIM
		REGULAR SEASON								PLAYOFFS				
99-00—Montreal	NHL	24	3	18	21	14	7	1	0	—	—	—	—	—
00-01—Montreal	NHL	54	17	30	47	40	2	7	0	—	—	—	—	—
01-02—Montreal	NHL	3	0	2	2	0	0	0	0	12	4	6	10	4
02-03—Montreal	NHL	82	21	50	71	72	5	5	1	—	—	—	—	—
03-04—Montreal	NHL	68	14	41	55	52	-5	5	0	11	3	8	11	10
04-05—TPS Turku	Finland	20	8	8	16	28	11	...	...	6	3	2	5	30
05-06—Montreal	NHL	72	17	45	62	70	1	5	0	3	0	2	2	2
—Fin. Olympic team	Int'l	8	3	8	11	12	5	3	0	—	—	—	—	—
NHL Totals (10 years)		569	137	323	460	412	11	42	8	43	13	23	36	36

KOLANOS, KRYSTOFER — C

PERSONAL: Born July 27, 1981, in Calgary. ... 6-3/206. ... Shoots right.
TRANSACTIONS/CAREER NOTES: Selected by Phoenix Coyotes in first round (first Coyotes pick, 19th overall) of entry draft (June 24, 2000). ... Concussion (January 19, 2002); missed 22 games. ... Postconcussion syndrome (fall 2002); missed first 80 games of season. ... Claimed off waivers by Edmonton Oilers (November 11, 2005). ... Claimed off waivers by Coyotes (December 19, 2005). ... Traded by Coyotes to Carolina Hurricanes for RW Pavel Brendl (December 28, 2005). ... Traded by Hurricanes with D Niklas Nordgren and second-round pick in 2007 draft to Penguins for LW Mark Recchi (March 9, 2006).

Season Team	League	GP	G	A	Pts.	PIM	+/-	PP	SH	GP	G	A	Pts.	PIM
		REGULAR SEASON								PLAYOFFS				
98-99—Calgary Royals	AJHL	58	43	67	110	98	...	...	...	—	—	—	—	—
99-00—Boston College	Hockey East	34	14	13	27	44	...	...	...	—	—	—	—	—
00-01—Boston College	Hockey East	41	25	25	50	54	...	...	...	—	—	—	—	—
01-02—Phoenix	NHL	57	11	11	22	48	6	0	0	2	0	0	0	6
02-03—Phoenix	NHL	2	0	0	0	0	0	0	0	—	—	—	—	—
03-04—Phoenix	NHL	41	4	6	10	24	-9	1	0	—	—	—	—	—
—Springfield	AHL	32	10	11	21	38	-2	1	0	—	—	—	—	—
04-05—Krefeld Pinguine	Germany	7	3	2	5	16	2	1	0	—	—	—	—	—
—Blues Espoo	Finland	15	7	9	16	40	4	...	...	—	—	—	—	—
05-06—Lowell	AHL	19	10	11	21	40	-2	6	0	—	—	—	—	—
—San Antonio	AHL	3	0	1	1	0	-3	0	0	—	—	—	—	—
—Phoenix	NHL	9	2	1	3	2	2	1	0	—	—	—	—	—
—Wilkes-Barre/Scranton	AHL	18	10	8	18	19	3	2	0	11	2	0	2	16
—Edmonton	NHL	6	0	0	0	2	-1	0	0	—	—	—	—	—
NHL Totals (4 years)		115	17	18	35	76	-2	2	0	2	0	0	0	6

KOLESNIK, VITALY — G

PERSONAL: Born August 20, 1979, in Ust-Kamenogorsk, USSR. ... 6-2/198. ... Catches left.
TRANSACTIONS/CAREER NOTES: Signed as nondrafted free agent by Colorado Avalanche (August 16, 2005).

Season Team	League	GP	Min.	W	L	T	GA	SO	GAA	SV%	GP	Min.	W	L	GA	SO	GAA	SV%
		REGULAR SEASON									PLAYOFFS							
05-06—Lowell	AHL	29	1717	15	13	...	80	3	2.80	.918	—	—	—	—	—	—	—	—
—Colorado	NHL	8	370	3	3	...	20	0	3.24	.888	—	—	—	—	—	—	—	—
NHL Totals (1 year)		8	370	3	3	0	20	0	3.24	.888								

KOLNIK, JURAJ — RW

PERSONAL: Born November 13, 1980, in Nitra, Czechoslovakia. ... 5-10/190. ... Shoots right.
TRANSACTIONS/CAREER NOTES: Selected by New York Islanders in fourth round (seventh Islanders pick, 10first overall) of entry draft (June 26, 1999). ... Traded by Islanders with ninth-round pick (later traded to San Jose; Sharks selected Carter Lee) in 2003 entry draft to Florida Panthers for D Sven Butenschon (October 11, 2002). ... Injured ankle (December 31, 2003); missed seven games. ... Flu (March 17, 2004); missed one game. ... Sprained knee (December 22, 2005); missed five games.

Season Team	League	GP	G	A	Pts.	PIM	+/-	PP	SH	GP	G	A	Pts.	PIM
		REGULAR SEASON								PLAYOFFS				
97-98—Plastika Nitra	Slovakia	28	1	3	4	6	...	...	...	—	—	—	—	—
98-99—Quebec	QMJHL	12	6	5	11	6	...	...	...	—	—	—	—	—
—Rimouski	QMJHL	50	36	37	73	34	...	...	...	11	9	6	15	6
99-00—Rimouski	QMJHL	47	53	53	106	53	48	11	2	14	10	17	27	16
00-01—Lowell	AHL	25	2	6	8	18	...	...	...	—	—	—	—	—
—Springfield	AHL	29	15	20	35	20	...	...	...	—	—	—	—	—
—New York Islanders	NHL	29	4	3	7	12	-8	0	0	—	—	—	—	—
01-02—Bridgeport	AHL	67	18	30	48	40	4	1	1	20	7	14	21	17
—New York Islanders	NHL	7	2	0	2	0	-2	1	0	—	—	—	—	—
02-03—Florida	NHL	10	0	1	1	0	1	0	0	—	—	—	—	—
—San Antonio	AHL	65	25	15	40	36	5	4	2	3	0	1	1	4
03-04—Florida	NHL	53	14	11	25	14	-7	2	0	—	—	—	—	—
—San Antonio	AHL	15	2	14	16	21	1	0	0	—	—	—	—	—
04-05—San Antonio	AHL	74	13	16	29	24	-1	6	0	—	—	—	—	—
05-06—Florida	NHL	77	15	20	35	40	1	4	1	—	—	—	—	—
NHL Totals (5 years)		176	35	35	70	66	-15	7	1					

K

KOLTSOV, KONSTANTIN RW/LW

PERSONAL: Born April 17, 1981, in Minsk, U.S.S.R. ... 6-0/206. ... Shoots left.
TRANSACTIONS/CAREER NOTES: Selected by Pittsburgh Penguins in first round (first Penguins pick, 18th overall) of entry draft (June 26, 1999). ... Re-signed by Penguins as free agent (August 16, 2005).

		REGULAR SEASON								PLAYOFFS				
Season Team	League	GP	G	A	Pts.	PIM	+/-	PP	SH	GP	G	A	Pts.	PIM
97-98—Minsk	Belarus	52	15	18	33	60	...	...	...	—	—	—	—	—
—Severstal Cherepovets	Russian	2	0	0	0	2	...	...	...	—	—	—	—	—
—Severstal-2 Cherepovets	Rus. Div.	44	11	12	23	16	...	...	...	—	—	—	—	—
98-99—Severstal Cherepovets	Russian	33	3	0	3	8	...	...	...	1	0	0	0	2
99-00—Metallurg Novokuznetsk	Russian	30	3	4	7	28	...	...	...	14	1	1	2	8
00-01—Ak Bars Kazan	Russian	24	7	8	15	10	...	...	...	2	0	0	0	4
01-02—Ak Bars Kazan	Russian	10	1	2	3	2	...	...	...	—	—	—	—	—
—Spartak Moscow	Russian	23	1	0	1	12	...	...	...	—	—	—	—	—
—Belarus Oly. team	Int'l	2	0	0	0	0	...	...	...	—	—	—	—	—
02-03—Wilkes-Barre/Scranton	AHL	65	9	21	30	41	-8	1	0	6	2	4	6	4
—Pittsburgh	NHL	2	0	0	0	0	-2	0	0	—	—	—	—	—
03-04—Wilkes-Barre/Scranton	AHL	3	0	4	4	4	3	0	0	24	6	11	17	18
—Pittsburgh	NHL	82	9	20	29	30	-30	2	0	—	—	—	—	—
04-05—Dynamo Minsk	Belarus	11	6	2	8	38	...	...	...	—	—	—	—	—
—Spartak Moscow	Russian	31	6	10	16	48	3	...	...	—	—	—	—	—
05-06—Wilkes-Barre/Scranton	AHL	18	7	5	12	13	9	3	1	—	—	—	—	—
—Pittsburgh	NHL	60	3	6	9	20	-10	0	1	—	—	—	—	—
NHL Totals (3 years)		144	12	26	38	50	-42	2	1					

KOLZIG, OLAF G

PERSONAL: Born April 6, 1970, in Johannesburg, South Africa. ... 6-3/225. ... Catches left. ... Name pronounced OH-lahf KOHL-zihg.
TRANSACTIONS/CAREER NOTES: Selected by Washington Capitals in first round (first Capitals pick, 19th overall) of entry draft (June 17, 1989). ... Dislocated kneecap (October 13, 1993); missed 14 games. ... Mononucleosis (October 8, 1996); missed three games. ... Knee injury (September 26, 2000); missed first two games of regular season. ... Sprained ankle (December 14, 2001); missed one game. ... Injured knee (February 8, 2002); missed two games. ... Injured hand (October 30, 2002); missed four games. ... Injured groin (December 7, 2002); missed four games. ... Injured groin (November 8, 2005); missed four games.

		REGULAR SEASON										PLAYOFFS							
Season Team	League	GP	Min.	W	L	OTL	T	GA	SO	GAA	SV%	GP	Min.	W	L	GA	SO	GAA	SV%
87-88—New Westminster	WHL	15	650	6	5	...	0	48	1	4.43	...	3	149	0	0	11	0	4.43	...
88-89—Tri-City	WHL	30	1671	16	10	...	2	97	1	3.48	...	—	—	—	—	—	—	—	—
89-90—Washington	NHL	2	120	0	2	...	0	12	0	6.00	.810	—	—	—	—	—	—	—	—
—Tri-City	WHL	48	2504	27	27	...	3	187	1	4.48	...	6	318	4	0	27	0	5.09	...
90-91—Baltimore	AHL	26	1367	10	12	...	1	72	0	3.16	...	—	—	—	—	—	—	—	—
—Hampton Roads	ECHL	21	1248	11	9	...	1	71	2	3.41	...	3	180	1	2	14	0	4.67	...
91-92—Baltimore	AHL	28	1503	5	17	...	2	105	1	4.19	...	—	—	—	—	—	—	—	—
—Hampton Roads	ECHL	14	847	11	3	...	0	41	0	2.90	...	—	—	—	—	—	—	—	—
92-93—Rochester	AHL	49	2737	25	16	...	4	168	0	3.68	.882	17	1040	9	8	61	0	3.52	.911
—Washington	NHL	1	20	0	0	...	0	2	0	6.00	.714	—	—	—	—	—	—	—	—
93-94—Portland	AHL	29	1726	16	8	...	5	88	3	3.06	.906	17	1035	12	5	44	0	2.55	.918
—Washington	NHL	7	224	0	3	...	0	20	0	5.36	.844	—	—	—	—	—	—	—	—
94-95—Washington	NHL	14	724	2	8	...	2	30	0	2.49	.902	2	44	1	0	1	0	1.36	.952
—Portland	AHL	2	125	1	0	...	1	3	0	1.44	.952	—	—	—	—	—	—	—	—
95-96—Washington	NHL	18	897	4	8	...	2	46	0	3.08	.887	5	341	2	3	11	0	*1.94	.934
—Portland	AHL	5	300	5	0	...	0	7	1	1.40	...	—	—	—	—	—	—	—	—
96-97—Washington	NHL	29	1645	8	15	...	4	71	2	2.59	.906	—	—	—	—	—	—	—	—
97-98—Washington	NHL	64	3788	33	18	...	10	139	5	2.20	.920	21	1351	12	9	44	*4	1.95	.941
—German Oly. team	Int'l	2	120	2	0	...	0	2	1	1.00	.966	—	—	—	—	—	—	—	—
98-99—Washington	NHL	64	3586	26	†31	...	3	154	4	2.58	.900	—	—	—	—	—	—	—	—
99-00—Washington	NHL	73	*4371	41	20	...	11	163	5	2.24	.917	5	284	1	4	16	0	3.38	.845
00-01—Washington	NHL	72	4279	37	26	...	8	177	5	2.48	.909	6	375	2	4	14	1	2.24	.908
01-02—Washington	NHL	71	4131	31	29	...	8	*192	6	2.79	.903	—	—	—	—	—	—	—	—
02-03—Washington	NHL	66	3894	33	25	...	6	156	4	2.40	.919	6	404	2	4	14	1	2.08	.927
03-04—Washington	NHL	63	3738	19	35	...	9	180	2	2.89	.908	—	—	—	—	—	—	—	—
04-05—Eisbaren Berlin	Germany	8	452	...	...	...	...	19	2	2.52	.905	3	178	...	...	7	1	2.36	.879
05-06—Washington	NHL	59	3506	20	28	*11	...	206	0	3.53	.896	—	—	—	—	—	—	—	—
—German Oly. team	Int'l	3	...	...	...	...	...	...	...	2.68	.899	—	—	—	—	—	—	—	—
NHL Totals (14 years)		603	34923	254	248	11	63	1548	33	2.66	.907	45	2799	20	24	100	6	2.14	.927

KOMISAREK, MIKE D

PERSONAL: Born January 19, 1982, in West Islip, N.Y. ... 6-4/237. ... Shoots right. ... Name pronounced: kah mih SAIR ihk
TRANSACTIONS/CAREER NOTES: Selected by Montreal Canadiens in first round (first Canadiens pick, seventh overall) of NHL entry draft (June 23, 2001). ... Personal leave (December 10, 2005); missed 10 games.

		REGULAR SEASON								PLAYOFFS				
Season Team	League	GP	G	A	Pts.	PIM	+/-	PP	SH	GP	G	A	Pts.	PIM
99-00—U.S. National	USHL	51	5	8	13	124	...	...	...	—	—	—	—	—
00-01—Univ. of Michigan	CCHA	41	4	12	16	77	...	...	...	—	—	—	—	—
01-02—Univ. of Michigan	CCHA	39	11	19	30	68	...	...	...	—	—	—	—	—

Season Team	League	GP	G	A	Pts.	PIM	+/-	PP	SH	Playoffs GP	G	A	Pts.	PIM
		REGULAR SEASON								PLAYOFFS				
02-03—Montreal	NHL	21	0	1	1	28	-6	0	0	—	—	—	—	—
—Hamilton	AHL	56	5	25	30	79	27	3	0	23	1	5	6	60
03-04—Hamilton	AHL	18	2	7	9	47	0	0	0	—	—	—	—	—
—Montreal	NHL	46	0	4	4	34	4	0	0	7	0	0	0	8
04-05—Hamilton	AHL	20	1	4	5	49	6	1	0	4	0	1	1	8
05-06—Montreal	NHL	71	2	4	6	116	-1	0	0	6	0	0	0	10
NHL Totals (3 years)		138	2	9	11	178	-3	0	0	13	0	0	0	18

KONDRATIEV, MAXIM D

PERSONAL: Born January 20, 1983, in Togliatti, U.S.S.R. ... 6-1/176. ... Shoots left. ... Name pronounced: MAK-seem kahn-DRAHT-yehf
TRANSACTIONS/CAREER NOTES: Selected by Toronto Maple Leafs in sixth round (seventh Leafs pick, 168th overall) of entry draft (June 24, 2001). ... Traded by Maple Leafs with C Jarkko Immonen, first-round pick in 2004 draft (traded to Calgary; Flames selected RW Kris Chucko) and second-round pick in 2005 draft (D Michael Sauer) to New York Rangers for D Brian Leetch and fourth-round pick (C Roman Kukumberg) in 2004 draft (March 3, 2004). ... Traded by Rangers with fourth-round pick in 2007 to Anaheim Mighty Ducks for RW Petr Sykora (January 8, 2006).

Season Team	League	GP	G	A	Pts.	PIM	+/-	PP	SH	Playoffs GP	G	A	Pts.	PIM
		REGULAR SEASON								PLAYOFFS				
01-02—Lada Togliatti	Russian	43	3	3	6	32	...	...	...	4	0	0	0	0
02-03—Lada Togliatti	Russian	47	2	3	5	56	...	...	...	10	0	0	0	6
03-04—Toronto	NHL	7	0	0	0	2	0	0	0	—	—	—	—	—
—St. John's	AHL	18	3	5	8	10	4	1	0	—	—	—	—	—
04-05—Lada Togliatti	Russian	32	2	4	6	65	12	...	...	5	0	2	2	0
—Hartford	AHL	13	1	4	5	8	-1	1	0	—	—	—	—	—
05-06—Hartford	AHL	4	0	0	0	0	4	0	0	—	—	—	—	—
—Portland	AHL	37	4	13	17	19	4	0	1	12	5	7	12	10
—New York Rangers	NHL	29	1	2	3	22	-2	1	0	—	—	—	—	—
NHL Totals (2 years)		36	1	2	3	24	-2	1	0					

KONOPKA, ZENON C

PERSONAL: Born January 2, 1981, in Niagara Falls, Ont. ... 6-0/206. ... Shoots left. ... Name pronounced KOHNO-ah-PKA.
TRANSACTIONS/CAREER NOTES: Signed as free agent by Anaheim Mighty Ducks (September 2, 2004). ... Sprained ankle (January 19, 2006); missed 15 games.

Season Team	League	GP	G	A	Pts.	PIM	+/-	PP	SH	Playoffs GP	G	A	Pts.	PIM
		REGULAR SEASON								PLAYOFFS				
98-99—Ottawa	OHL	56	7	8	15	62	...	...	...	7	0	0	0	2
99-00—Ottawa	OHL	59	8	11	19	107	...	...	...	11	1	2	3	8
00-01—Ottawa	OHL	66	20	45	65	120	...	...	...	20	7	13	20	47
01-02—Ottawa	OHL	61	18	68	86	100	...	...	...	13	8	6	14	49
02-03—Wilkes-Barre/Scranton	AHL	4	0	1	1	9	...	...	...	—	—	—	—	—
—Wheeling	ECHL	68	22	48	70	231	...	...	...	—	—	—	—	—
03-04—Utah	AHL	43	7	4	11	198	...	...	...	—	—	—	—	—
—Idaho	ECHL	23	6	22	28	82	...	...	...	17	9	8	17	30
04-05—Cincinnati	AHL	75	17	29	46	212	7	7	2	12	3	3	6	26
05-06—Portland	AHL	34	18	26	44	57	27	8	0	18	11	18	29	46
—Anaheim	NHL	23	4	3	7	48	-4	2	0	—	—	—	—	—
NHL Totals (1 year)		23	4	3	7	48	-4	2	0					

KONOWALCHUK, STEVE LW

PERSONAL: Born November 11, 1972, in Salt Lake City, Utah. ... 6-2/204. ... Shoots left. ... Name pronounced kah-nah-WAHL-chuhk.
TRANSACTIONS/CAREER NOTES: Selected by Washington Capitals in third round (fifth Capitals pick, 58th overall) of entry draft (June 22, 1991). ... Separated shoulder (October 13, 1995); missed four games. ... Left hand (March 26, 1996); missed eight games. ... Separated rib cartilage; missed four games of 1996-97 season. ... Strained groin (January 28, 1998); missed two games. ... Sprained ankle (October 10, 1998); missed 15 games. ... Concussion (March 2, 1999); missed remainder of season. ... Shoulder (October 13, 2001), had surgery; missed 54 games. ... Groin (January 25, 2003); missed three games. ... Foot (March 22, 2003); missed one game. ... Foot (April 5, 2003); missed one game. ... Traded by Capitals with a third-round pick (later traded to Carolina Hurricanes; Hurricanes selected D Casey Borer) in 2004 draft to Colorado Avalanche for LW Bates Battaglia and RW Jonas Johansson (October 22, 2003). ... Torn ligaments in right wrist (November 21, 2005); had surgery (November 30, 2005); missed 61 regular-season games and five playoff games.
STATISTICAL PLATEAUS: Three-goal games: 1995-96 (2), 2000-01 (1). Total: 3.

Season Team	League	GP	G	A	Pts.	PIM	+/-	PP	SH	Playoffs GP	G	A	Pts.	PIM
		REGULAR SEASON								PLAYOFFS				
90-91—Portland	WHL	72	43	49	92	78	...	...	...	—	—	—	—	—
91-92—Portland	WHL	64	51	53	104	95	...	...	...	6	3	6	9	12
—Baltimore	AHL	3	1	1	2	0	...	...	...	—	—	—	—	—
—Washington	NHL	1	0	0	0	0	0	0	0	—	—	—	—	—
92-93—Baltimore	AHL	37	18	28	46	74	2	4	1	—	—	—	—	—
—Washington	NHL	36	4	7	11	16	4	1	0	2	0	1	1	0
93-94—Portland	AHL	8	11	4	15	4	6	3	1	—	—	—	—	—
—Washington	NHL	62	12	14	26	33	9	0	0	11	0	1	1	10
94-95—Washington	NHL	46	11	14	25	44	7	3	3	7	2	5	7	12
95-96—Washington	NHL	70	23	22	45	92	13	7	1	2	0	2	2	0
96-97—Washington	NHL	78	17	25	42	67	-3	2	1	—	—	—	—	—
97-98—Washington	NHL	80	10	24	34	80	9	2	0	—	—	—	—	—

Season Team	League	GP	G	A	Pts.	PIM	+/-	PP	SH	GP	G	A	Pts.	PIM
		REGULAR SEASON								PLAYOFFS				
98-99—Washington	NHL	45	12	12	24	26	0	4	1	—	—	—	—	—
99-00—Washington	NHL	82	16	27	43	80	19	3	0	5	1	0	1	2
00-01—Washington	NHL	82	24	23	47	87	8	6	0	6	2	3	5	14
01-02—Washington	NHL	28	2	12	14	23	-2	0	0	—	—	—	—	—
02-03—Washington	NHL	77	15	15	30	71	3	2	0	6	0	0	0	6
03-04—Washington	NHL	6	0	1	1	0	-5	0	0	—	—	—	—	—
—Colorado	NHL	76	19	20	39	70	2	3	0	11	4	0	4	12
05-06—Colorado	NHL	21	6	9	15	14	5	1	2	2	0	0	0	4
NHL Totals (14 years)		790	171	225	396	703	69	34	8	52	9	12	21	60

KOPECKY, TOMAS C

PERSONAL: Born February 5, 1982, in Ilava, Czech. ... 6-3/187. ... Shoots left.
TRANSACTIONS/CAREER NOTES: Selected by Detroit Red Wings in second round (second Red Wings pick, 38th overall) of NHL draft (June 24, 2000).

Season Team	League	GP	G	A	Pts.	PIM	+/-	PP	SH	GP	G	A	Pts.	PIM
		REGULAR SEASON								PLAYOFFS				
98-99—Dukla Trencin	Slovakia Jrs.	44	13	16	29	...	...	...	...	—	—	—	—	—
99-00—Dukla Trencin	Slovakia	52	3	4	7	24	...	...	...	5	0	0	0	0
—Dukla Trencin	Slovakia Jrs.	12	11	13	24	10	...	...	...	—	—	—	—	—
00-01—Lethbridge	WHL	49	22	28	50	52	...	...	...	5	1	1	2	6
—Cincinnati	AHL	1	0	0	0	0	...	...	...	—	—	—	—	—
01-02—Lethbridge	WHL	60	34	42	76	94	...	...	...	4	2	1	3	15
—Cincinnati	AHL	2	1	1	2	6	1	0	0	2	0	0	0	0
02-03—Grand Rapids	AHL	70	17	21	38	32	18	3	0	14	0	0	0	6
03-04—Grand Rapids	AHL	48	6	6	12	28	-3	2	0	1	0	0	0	2
04-05—Grand Rapids	AHL	48	8	8	16	35	1	2	0	—	—	—	—	—
05-06—Grand Rapids	AHL	77	32	40	72	123	24	8	0	16	3	4	7	25
—Detroit	NHL	1	0	0	0	2	1	0	0	—	—	—	—	—
NHL Totals (1 year)		1	0	0	0	2	1	0	0					

KOSTITSYN, ANDREI RW/LW

PERSONAL: Born February 3, 1985, in Novopolosk, U.S.S.R. ... 6-0/189. ... Shoots left.
TRANSACTIONS/CAREER NOTES: Selected by Montreal Canadiens in first round (first Canadiens pick, 10th overall) of 2003 NHL entry draft (June 23, 2003).

Season Team	League	GP	G	A	Pts.	PIM	+/-	PP	SH	GP	G	A	Pts.	PIM
		REGULAR SEASON								PLAYOFFS				
00-01—Yunost	Belarus	3	1	4	5	8	...	...	...	—	—	—	—	—
—Novopolotsk	Russian Jr.	5	1	0	1	0	...	...	...	—	—	—	—	—
—Vitebsk	Belarus	17	17	6	23	42	...	...	...	—	—	—	—	—
—Novopolotsk	Belarus	1	2	1	3	2	...	...	...	—	—	—	—	—
01-02—Novopolotsk	Belarus	17	9	6	15	28	...	...	...	—	—	—	—	—
—Novopolotsk	Russian Jr.	29	9	8	17	16	...	...	...	—	—	—	—	—
—Yunost	Belarus	6	2	0	2	8	...	...	...	—	—	—	—	—
02-03—CSKA	Rus. Div.	3	2	2	4	25	...	...	...	—	—	—	—	—
—Khimik Voskresensk	Russian	2	1	1	2	2	...	...	...	—	—	—	—	—
—HC CSKA Moscow	Russian	6	0	0	0	2	...	...	...	—	—	—	—	—
03-04—Minsk	Belarus	2	0	2	2	14	...	...	...	6	4	4	8	16
—CSKA Moscow	Russian	11	0	1	1	2	...	...	...	—	—	—	—	—
04-05—Hamilton	AHL	66	12	11	23	24	6	1	1	3	0	0	0	0
05-06—Hamilton	AHL	64	18	29	47	76	-14	6	2	—	—	—	—	—
—Montreal	NHL	12	2	1	3	2	1	0	0	—	—	—	—	—
NHL Totals (1 year)		12	2	1	3	2	1	0	0					

KOSTOPOULOS, TOM RW

PERSONAL: Born January 24, 1979, in Mississauga, Ont. ... 6-0/205. ... Shoots right. ... Name pronounced: kuh STAH puh luhz
TRANSACTIONS/CAREER NOTES: Selected by Pittsburgh Penguins in ninth round (ninth Penguins pick, 20fourth overall) of entry draft (June 26, 1999). ... Signed as free agent by Los Angeles Kings (July 12, 2004).

Season Team	League	GP	G	A	Pts.	PIM	+/-	PP	SH	GP	G	A	Pts.	PIM
		REGULAR SEASON								PLAYOFFS				
96-97—London	OHL	64	13	12	25	67	...	...	...	—	—	—	—	—
97-98—London	OHL	66	24	26	50	108	...	...	...	16	6	4	10	26
98-99—London	OHL	66	27	60	87	114	...	...	...	25	19	16	35	32
99-00—Wilkes-Barre/Scranton	AHL	76	26	32	58	121	...	...	...	—	—	—	—	—
00-01—Wilkes-Barre/Scranton	AHL	80	16	36	52	120	...	...	...	21	3	9	12	6
01-02—Wilkes-Barre/Scranton	AHL	70	27	26	53	112	-1	10	2	—	—	—	—	—
—Pittsburgh	NHL	11	1	2	3	9	-1	0	0	—	—	—	—	—
02-03—Wilkes-Barre/Scranton	AHL	71	21	42	63	131	-4	9	0	6	1	2	3	7
—Pittsburgh	NHL	8	0	1	1	0	-4	0	0	—	—	—	—	—
03-04—Pittsburgh	NHL	60	9	13	22	67	-14	2	1	—	—	—	—	—
—Wilkes-Barre/Scranton	AHL	21	7	13	20	43	13	1	0	24	7	16	23	32
04-05—Manchester	AHL	64	25	46	71	99	30	9	2	6	0	7	7	10
05-06—Los Angeles	NHL	76	8	14	22	100	-8	0	0	—	—	—	—	—
NHL Totals (4 years)		155	18	30	48	176	-27	2	1					

KOTALIK, ALES — RW/LW

PERSONAL: Born December 23, 1978, in Jindrichuv Hradec, Czech. ... 6-1/217. ... Shoots right.
TRANSACTIONS/CAREER NOTES: Selected by Buffalo Sabres in sixth round (seventh Sabres pick, 164th overall) of entry draft (June 27, 1998). ... Flu (March 28, 2003); missed three games. ... Injured shoulder (February 27, 2004); missed final 19 games of season.

		REGULAR SEASON								PLAYOFFS				
Season Team	League	GP	G	A	Pts.	PIM	+/-	PP	SH	GP	G	A	Pts.	PIM
93-94—HC Ceske Budejovice..	Czech. Jrs.	28	12	12	24	...	...	...	...	—	—	—	—	—
94-95—HC Ceske Budejovice..	Czech. Jrs.	36	26	17	43	...	...	...	...	—	—	—	—	—
95-96—HC Ceske Budejovice..	Czech. Jrs.	28	6	7	13	...	...	...	...	—	—	—	—	—
96-97—HC Ceske Budejovice..	Czech. Jrs.	36	15	16	31	24	...	...	...	—	—	—	—	—
97-98—ZPS Zlin	Czech.	47	9	7	16	14	...	...	...	—	—	—	—	—
98-99—HC Ceske Budejovice..	Czech Rep.	41	8	13	21	16	4	...	...	3	0	0	0	0
99-00—HC Ceske Budejovice..	Czech Rep.	43	7	12	19	34	...	...	...	3	0	1	1	6
00-01—HC Ceske Budejovice..	Czech Rep.	52	19	29	48	54	...	...	...	—	—	—	—	—
01-02—Rochester	AHL	68	18	25	43	55	-2	5	0	1	0	0	0	0
—Buffalo	NHL	13	1	3	4	2	-1	0	0	—	—	—	—	—
02-03—Rochester	AHL	8	0	2	2	4	-5	0	0	—	—	—	—	—
—Buffalo	NHL	68	21	14	35	30	-2	4	0	—	—	—	—	—
03-04—Buffalo	NHL	62	15	11	26	41	-1	2	0	—	—	—	—	—
04-05—Liberec	Czech Rep.	25	8	8	16	46	10	...	...	12	2	5	7	12
05-06—Buffalo	NHL	82	25	37	62	62	-3	10	0	18	4	7	11	8
—Czech Rep. Oly. team	Int'l	4	0	0	0	0	0	0	0	—	—	—	—	—
NHL Totals (4 years)		225	62	65	127	135	-7	16	0	18	4	7	11	8

KOVALCHUK, ILYA — LW

PERSONAL: Born April 15, 1983, in Tver, U.S.S.R. ... 6-2/220. ... Shoots right. ... Name pronounced: IHL-yuh KOH-vuhl-chuhk
TRANSACTIONS/CAREER NOTES: Selected by Atlanta Thrashers in first round (first Thrashers pick, first overall) of entry draft (June 23, 2001). ... Injured shoulder (March 10, 2002); missed remainder of season. ... Signed with Khimik Voskresensk of the Russian League (September 1, 2005); missed first three games of NHL season in contract holdout. ... Suspended one game for throwing stick into the stands (December 22, 2005).
STATISTICAL PLATEAUS: Three-goal games: 2002-03 (1), 2003-04 (2). Total: 3.

		REGULAR SEASON								PLAYOFFS				
Season Team	League	GP	G	A	Pts.	PIM	+/-	PP	SH	GP	G	A	Pts.	PIM
00-01—Spartak	Russian Div. 1	40	28	18	46	78	...	...	...	—	—	—	—	—
01-02—Atlanta	NHL	65	29	22	51	28	-19	7	0	—	—	—	—	—
—Russian Oly. team	Int'l	6	1	2	3	14	...	...	...	—	—	—	—	—
02-03—Atlanta	NHL	81	38	29	67	57	-24	9	0	—	—	—	—	—
03-04—Atlanta	NHL	81	†41	46	87	63	-10	16	1	—	—	—	—	—
04-05—Ak Bars Kazan	Russian	53	19	23	42	72	16	...	...	4	0	1	1	0
05-06—Atlanta	NHL	78	52	46	98	68	-6	*27	0	—	—	—	—	—
—Russian Oly. team	Int'l	8	4	1	5	31	3	0	0	—	—	—	—	—
NHL Totals (4 years)		305	160	143	303	216	-59	59	1					

KOVALEV, ALEXEI — RW

PERSONAL: Born February 24, 1973, in Togliatti, U.S.S.R. ... 6-2/220. ... Shoots left. ... Name pronounced KOH-vuh-lahf.
TRANSACTIONS/CAREER NOTES: Selected by New York Rangers in first round (first Rangers pick, 15th overall) of entry draft (June 22, 1991). ... Back spasms (January 16, 1993); missed one game. ... Suspended one game (November 10, 1993). ... Suspended five games for tripping incident (November 30, 1993). ... Suspended two games (February 12, 1994). ... Flu (December 2, 1995); missed one game. ... Torn knee ligament (January 8, 1997); missed remainder of season. ... Sprained knee and had arthroscopic surgery (January 22, 1998); missed eight games. ... Separated shoulder (October 27, 1998); missed five games. ... Bruised shoulder (November 21, 1998); missed one game. ... Traded by Rangers with C Harry York to Pittsburgh Penguins for C Petr Nedved, C Sean Pronger and D Chris Tamer (November 25, 1998). ... Bruised shoulder (November 21, 1998); missed one game. ... Suspended three games for unsportsmanlike conduct (March 24, 2001). ... Knee surgery (October 16, 2001); missed 13 games. ... Injured hip (April 6, 2002); missed one game. ... Reinjured hip (April 12, 2002); missed remainder of season. ... Bruised arm (December 7, 2003); missed one game. ... Traded by Penguins with LW Dan LaCouture, D Janne Laukkanen and D Mike Wilson to Rangers for RW Rico Fata, RW Mikael Samuelsson, D Joel Bouchard, D Richard Lintner and cash (February 10, 2003). ... Traded by Rangers to Montreal Canadiens for RW Jozef Balej and second-round pick (C Bruce Graham) in 2004 draft (March 2, 2004). ... Injured knee (November 12, 2005) and had surgery (November 14, 2005); missed 13 games.
STATISTICAL PLATEAUS: Three-goal games: 1992-93 (1), 1996-97 (1), 2000-01 (4), 2001-02 (3), 2002-03 (1). Total: 10.

		REGULAR SEASON								PLAYOFFS				
Season Team	League	GP	G	A	Pts.	PIM	+/-	PP	SH	GP	G	A	Pts.	PIM
89-90—Dynamo Moscow	USSR	1	0	0	0	0	...	...	...	—	—	—	—	—
90-91—Dynamo Moscow	USSR	18	1	2	3	4	...	...	...	—	—	—	—	—
91-92—Dynamo Moscow	CIS	33	16	9	25	20	...	...	...	—	—	—	—	—
—Unif. Olympic team	Int'l	8	1	2	3	14	4	0	0	—	—	—	—	—
92-93—New York Rangers	NHL	65	20	18	38	79	-10	3	0	—	—	—	—	—
—Binghamton	AHL	13	13	11	24	35	12	8	0	9	3	5	8	14
93-94—New York Rangers	NHL	76	23	33	56	154	18	7	0	23	9	12	21	18
94-95—Lada Togliatti	CIS	12	8	8	16	49	...	...	...	—	—	—	—	—
—New York Rangers	NHL	48	13	15	28	30	-6	1	1	10	4	7	11	10
95-96—New York Rangers	NHL	81	24	34	58	98	5	8	1	11	3	4	7	14
96-97—New York Rangers	NHL	45	13	22	35	42	11	1	0	—	—	—	—	—
97-98—New York Rangers	NHL	73	23	30	53	44	-22	8	0	—	—	—	—	—
98-99—New York Rangers	NHL	14	3	4	7	12	-6	1	0	—	—	—	—	—
—Pittsburgh	NHL	63	20	26	46	37	8	5	1	10	5	7	12	14
99-00—Pittsburgh	NHL	82	26	40	66	94	-3	9	2	11	1	5	6	10

Season Team	League	GP	G	A	Pts.	PIM	+/-	PP	SH	GP	G	A	Pts.	PIM
		REGULAR SEASON								PLAYOFFS				
00-01—Pittsburgh	NHL	79	44	51	95	96	12	12	2	18	5	5	10	16
01-02—Pittsburgh	NHL	67	32	44	76	80	2	8	1	—	—	—	—	—
—Russian Oly. team	Int'l	6	3	1	4	4	...	...	...	—	—	—	—	—
02-03—Pittsburgh	NHL	54	27	37	64	50	-11	8	0	...	...	...	...	...
—New York Rangers	NHL	24	10	3	13	20	2	3	0	—	—	—	—	—
03-04—New York Rangers	NHL	66	13	29	42	54	-5	3	0	—	—	—	—	—
—Montreal	NHL	12	1	2	3	12	-4	0	0	11	6	4	10	8
04-05—Ak Bars Kazan	Russian	35	10	11	21	80	-1	...	...	4	0	0	0	8
05-06—Montreal	NHL	69	23	42	65	76	-1	9	0	6	4	3	7	4
—Russian Oly. team	Int'l	8	4	2	6	4	4	2	0	—	—	—	—	—
NHL Totals (13 years)		918	315	430	745	978	-10	86	8	100	37	47	84	94

KOZLOV, VIKTOR C/RW

PERSONAL: Born February 14, 1975, in Togliatti, U.S.S.R. ... 6-5/235. ... Shoots right. ... Name pronounced KAHZ-lahf.
TRANSACTIONS/CAREER NOTES: Selected by San Jose Sharks in first round (first Sharks pick, sixth overall) of NHL draft (June 26, 1993). ... Fractured ankle (November 27, 1994); missed 13 games. ... Played in Europe during 1994-95 NHL lockout. ... Bruised ankle (March 26, 1997); missed four games. ... Traded by Sharks with fifth-round pick (D Jaroslav Spacek) in 1998 draft to Florida Panthers for LW Dave Lowry and first-round pick (traded to Tampa Bay; Lightning selected C Vincent Lecavalier) in 1998 draft (November 13, 1997). ... Separated right shoulder (November 18, 1997); missed 16 games. ... Had concussion (April 1, 1998); missed three games. ... Separated shoulder (October 30, 1998); missed six games. ... Reinjured shoulder (January 8, 1999); missed one game. ... Strained shoulder (January 20, 1999); missed three games. ... Fractured finger (April 3, 1999); missed final seven games of season. ... Sprained shoulder (March 8, 2000); missed two games. ... Injured shoulder (October 25, 2000); missed six games. ... Injured left shoulder (December 13, 2000); missed nine games. ... Injured groin (March 14, 2001); missed five games. ... Reinjured groin (March 28, 2001); missed final five games of season. ... Injured groin and hip (December 6, 2001); missed seven games. ... Strained muscle in abdomen (February 9, 2002); missed remainder of season. ... Injured groin (October 15, 2002); missed eight games. ... Injured face (November 11, 2003); missed four games. ... Injured toe (January 17, 2004); missed two games. ... Injured thumb (January 28, 2004); missed four games. ... Had concussion (February 18, 2004); missed 15 games. ... Traded by Panthers to New Jersey Devils for F Christian Berglund and D Victor Uchevatov (March 1, 2004). ... Injured (April 10, 2004); missed one playoff game. ... Re-signed by Devils as restricted free agent (September 21, 2005). ... Illness (November 15, 2005); missed one game.
STATISTICAL PLATEAUS: Three-goal games: 1999-00 (1).

Season Team	League	GP	G	A	Pts.	PIM	+/-	PP	SH	GP	G	A	Pts.	PIM
		REGULAR SEASON								PLAYOFFS				
90-91—Lada Togliatti	USSR Div.	2	2	0	2	0	...	...	...	—	—	—	—	—
91-92—Lada Togliatti	CIS	3	0	0	0	0	...	...	...	—	—	—	—	—
92-93—Dynamo Moscow	CIS	30	6	5	11	4	...	...	...	10	3	0	3	0
93-94—Dynamo Moscow	CIS	42	16	9	25	14	...	...	...	7	3	2	5	0
94-95—Dynamo Moscow	CIS	3	1	1	2	2	...	...	...	—	—	—	—	—
—San Jose	NHL	16	2	0	2	2	-5	0	0	—	—	—	—	—
—Kansas City	IHL	...	...	...	...	...	...	...	...	13	4	5	9	12
95-96—Kansas City	IHL	15	4	7	11	12	...	...	...	—	—	—	—	—
—San Jose	NHL	62	6	13	19	6	-15	1	0	—	—	—	—	—
96-97—San Jose	NHL	78	16	25	41	40	-16	4	0	—	—	—	—	—
97-98—San Jose	NHL	18	5	2	7	2	-2	2	0	—	—	—	—	—
—Florida	NHL	46	12	11	23	14	-1	3	2	—	—	—	—	—
98-99—Florida	NHL	65	16	35	51	24	13	5	1	—	—	—	—	—
99-00—Florida	NHL	80	17	53	70	16	24	6	0	4	0	1	1	0
00-01—Florida	NHL	51	14	23	37	10	-4	6	0	—	—	—	—	—
01-02—Florida	NHL	50	9	18	27	20	-16	6	0	—	—	—	—	—
02-03—Florida	NHL	74	22	34	56	18	-8	7	1	—	—	—	—	—
03-04—Florida	NHL	48	11	16	27	16	-4	3	1	—	—	—	—	—
—New Jersey	NHL	11	2	4	6	2	0	0	0	2	0	0	0	0
04-05—Lada Togliatti	Russian	52	15	22	37	22	19	...	...	10	3	3	6	6
05-06—New Jersey	NHL	69	12	13	25	16	0	2	0	3	0	0	0	0
—Russian Oly. team	Int'l	8	2	3	5	2	2	0	0	—	—	—	—	—
NHL Totals (11 years)		668	144	247	391	186	-34	45	5	9	0	1	1	0

KOZLOV, VYACHESLAV LW/C

PERSONAL: Born May 3, 1972, in Voskresensk, U.S.S.R. ... 5-10/185. ... Shoots left. ... Name pronounced VYACH-ih-slav KAHS-lahf.
TRANSACTIONS/CAREER NOTES: Selected by Detroit Red Wings in third round (second Red Wings pick, 45th overall) of NHL draft (June 16, 1990). ... Played in Europe during 1994-95 NHL lockout. ... Bruised left foot (April 16, 1995); missed one game. ... Sprained knee (April 15, 1998); missed two games. ... Suspended three games by NHL for elbowing incident (December 18, 1998). ... Injured ankle (December 22, 1999); missed three games. ... Reinjured ankle (January 4, 2000); missed four games. ... Had concussion (March 29, 2000); missed two games. ... Traded by Red Wings with first-round pick (traded to Columbus; traded to Atlanta; Thrashers selected C Jim Slater) in 2002 draft and future considerations to Buffalo Sabres for G Dominik Hasek (July 1, 2001). ... Injured Achilles' tendon (December 29, 2001); missed remainder of season. ... Traded by Sabres with second-round pick (traded to Nashville; Predators selected LW Konstantin Glazachev) in 2002 draft to Atlanta Thrashers for second-(traded to Florida; Panthers selected C Kamil Kreps) and third-round (traded to Phoenix; Coyotes selected C Tyler Redenbach) picks in 2002 draft (June 22, 2002). ... Suspended three games by NHL for abuse of official (January 3, 2003). ... Injured shoulder (February 16, 2004); missed six games.
STATISTICAL PLATEAUS: Three-goal games: 1993-94 (1), 1998-99 (1). Total: 2. ... Four-goal games: 1995-96 (1). ... Total hat tricks: 3.

Season Team	League	GP	G	A	Pts.	PIM	+/-	PP	SH	GP	G	A	Pts.	PIM
		REGULAR SEASON								PLAYOFFS				
87-88—Khimik	USSR	2	0	1	1	0	...	...	...	—	—	—	—	—
88-89—Khimik	USSR	13	0	1	1	2	...	...	...	—	—	—	—	—
89-90—Khimik	USSR	45	14	12	26	38	...	...	...	—	—	—	—	—
90-91—Khimik	USSR	45	11	13	24	46	...	...	...	—	—	—	—	—
91-92—Khimik	USSR	11	6	5	11	12	...	...	...	—	—	—	—	—
—Detroit	NHL	7	0	2	2	2	-2	0	0	—	—	—	—	—

		REGULAR SEASON								PLAYOFFS				
Season Team	**League**	**GP**	**G**	**A**	**Pts.**	**PIM**	**+/-**	**PP**	**SH**	**GP**	**G**	**A**	**Pts.**	**PIM**
92-93—Detroit	NHL	17	4	1	5	14	-1	0	0	4	0	2	2	2
—Adirondack	AHL	45	23	36	59	54	10	1	2	4	1	1	2	4
93-94—Detroit	NHL	77	34	39	73	50	27	8	2	7	2	5	7	12
—Adirondack	AHL	3	0	1	1	15	-1	0	0	—	—	—	—	—
94-95—CSKA Moscow	CIS	10	3	4	7	14	...	...	...	—	—	—	—	—
—Detroit	NHL	46	13	20	33	45	12	5	0	18	9	7	16	10
95-96—Detroit	NHL	82	36	37	73	70	33	9	0	19	5	7	12	10
96-97—Detroit	NHL	75	23	22	45	46	21	3	0	20	8	5	13	14
97-98—Detroit	NHL	80	25	27	52	46	14	6	0	22	6	8	14	10
98-99—Detroit	NHL	79	29	29	58	45	10	6	1	10	6	1	7	4
99-00—Detroit	NHL	72	18	18	36	28	11	4	0	8	2	1	3	12
00-01—Detroit	NHL	72	20	18	38	30	9	4	0	6	4	1	5	2
01-02—Buffalo	NHL	38	9	13	22	16	0	3	0	—	—	—	—	—
02-03—Atlanta	NHL	79	21	49	70	66	-10	9	1	—	—	—	—	—
03-04—Atlanta	NHL	76	20	32	52	74	-12	6	0	—	—	—	—	—
04-05—Khimik Voskresensk	Russian	38	12	18	30	69	1	...	...	—	—	—	—	—
—Ak Bars Kazan	Russian	8	2	4	6	0	0	...	...	4	1	0	1	8
05-06—Atlanta	NHL	82	25	46	71	33	14	8	0	—	—	—	—	—
NHL Totals (14 years)		882	277	353	630	565	126	71	4	114	42	37	79	76

KRAJICEK, LUKAS D

PERSONAL: Born March 11, 1983, in Prostejov, Czechoslovakia. ... 6-2/182. ... Shoots left. ... Name pronounced LOO-kahsh KRIGH-ee-chehk.
TRANSACTIONS/CAREER NOTES: Selected by Florida Panthers in first round (second Panthers pick, 24th overall) of NHL entry draft (June 23, 2001). ... Knee (January 12, 2006); missed one game. ... Illness (March 10, 2006); missed 11 games. ... Traded by Panthers with G Roberto Luongo and a sixth-round pick (W Sergei Shirokov) in the 2006 draft to Vancouver Canucks for F Todd Bertuzzi, G Alex Auld and D Bryan Allen (June 23, 2006).

		REGULAR SEASON								PLAYOFFS				
Season Team	**League**	**GP**	**G**	**A**	**Pts.**	**PIM**	**+/-**	**PP**	**SH**	**GP**	**G**	**A**	**Pts.**	**PIM**
99-00—Detroit	NAHL	53	5	22	27	61	...	...	...	—	—	—	—	—
00-01—Peterborough	OHL	61	8	27	35	53	...	...	...	7	0	5	5	0
01-02—Peterborough	OHL	55	10	32	42	56	...	...	...	6	0	5	5	6
—Florida	NHL	5	0	0	0	0	0	0	0	—	—	—	—	—
02-03—Peterborough	OHL	52	11	42	53	42	...	...	...	7	0	3	3	0
—San Antonio	AHL	3	0	1	1	0	-1	0	0	3	0	0	0	0
03-04—San Antonio	AHL	54	5	12	17	24	-7	3	0	—	—	—	—	—
—Florida	NHL	18	1	6	7	12	-2	1	0	—	—	—	—	—
04-05—San Antonio	AHL	78	2	22	24	57	-20	0	0	—	—	—	—	—
05-06—Florida	NHL	67	2	14	16	50	1	2	0	—	—	—	—	—
NHL Totals (3 years)		90	3	20	23	62	-1	3	0					

KRONWALL, NIKLAS D

PERSONAL: Born January 12, 1981, in Stockholm, Sweden. ... 6-0/158. ... Shoots left. ... Brother of Staffan Kronwall, D, Toronto Maple Leafs.
TRANSACTIONS/CAREER NOTES: Selected by Detroit Red Wings in first round (first Red Wings pick, 29th overall) of entry draft (June 24, 2000). ... Fractured right leg (January 22, 2004); missed regular season's final 33 games and all of playoffs. ... Torn left knee ligaments (September 27, 2005); missed 52 games.

		REGULAR SEASON								PLAYOFFS				
Season Team	**League**	**GP**	**G**	**A**	**Pts.**	**PIM**	**+/-**	**PP**	**SH**	**GP**	**G**	**A**	**Pts.**	**PIM**
98-99—Huddinge	Sweden	14	0	1	1	10	...	...	...	—	—	—	—	—
99-00—Djurgarden Stockholm	Sweden	37	1	4	5	16	...	...	...	8	0	0	0	8
00-01—Djurgarden Stockholm	Sweden	31	1	9	10	32	...	...	...	15	0	1	1	8
01-02—Djurgarden Stockholm	Sweden	48	5	7	12	34	...	...	...	5	0	0	0	0
02-03—Djurgarden Stockholm	Sweden	50	5	13	18	46	...	...	...	12	3	2	5	18
03-04—Detroit	NHL	20	1	4	5	16	5	0	0	—	—	—	—	—
—Grand Rapids	AHL	25	2	11	13	20	6	1	0	—	—	—	—	—
04-05—Grand Rapids	AHL	76	13	40	53	53	6	3	0	—	—	—	—	—
05-06—Grand Rapids	AHL	1	0	0	0	0	-1	0	0	—	—	—	—	—
—Detroit	NHL	27	1	8	9	28	11	1	0	6	0	3	3	2
—Swedish Oly. team	Int'l	2	1	1	2	8	2	1	0	—	—	—	—	—
NHL Totals (2 years)		47	2	12	14	44	16	1	0	6	0	3	3	2

KRONWALL, STAFFAN D

PERSONAL: Born September 10, 1983, in Jarfalla, Sweden. ... 6-3/209. ... Shoots left. ... Brother of Niklas Kronwall, D, Detroit Red Wings.
TRANSACTIONS/CAREER NOTES: Selected by Toronto Maple Leafs in ninth round (ninth Maple Leafs pick, 285th overall) of NHL entry draft (June 23, 2002).

		REGULAR SEASON								PLAYOFFS				
Season Team	**League**	**GP**	**G**	**A**	**Pts.**	**PIM**	**+/-**	**PP**	**SH**	**GP**	**G**	**A**	**Pts.**	**PIM**
99-00—Huddinge	Sweden Jr.	34	2	0	2	38	...	...	...	—	—	—	—	—
00-01—Huddinge	Sweden Jr.	23	6	1	7	16	...	...	...	—	—	—	—	—
01-02—Huddinge	Sweden Dv. 2	42	4	7	11	30	...	...	...	—	—	—	—	—
—Huddinge	Sweden Jr.	1	0	0	0	0	...	...	...	4	2	1	3	27
02-03—Djurgarden Stockholm	Sweden	48	4	6	10	65	...	...	...	12	1	1	2	8
03-04—Djurgarden Stockholm	Sweden	44	1	5	6	54	...	...	...	4	0	1	1	2

Season Team	League	REGULAR SEASON GP	G	A	Pts.	PIM	+/-	PP	SH	PLAYOFFS GP	G	A	Pts.	PIM
04-05—Brynas Gavle	Sweden	3	0	1	1	4	...	...	...	—	—	—	—	—
—Djurgarden Stockholm	Sweden	35	1	4	5	43	...	...	...	12	2	0	2	10
05-06—Toronto	AHL	16	1	10	11	12	-2	1	0	4	0	2	2	2
—Toronto	NHL	34	0	1	1	14	-3	0	0	—	—	—	—	—
NHL Totals (1 year)		34	0	1	1	14	-3	0	0					

KUBA, FILIP D

PERSONAL: Born December 29, 1976, in Ostrava, Czech. ... 6-3/205. ... Shoots left. ... Name pronounced KOO-buh.

TRANSACTIONS/CAREER NOTES: Selected by Florida Panthers in eighth round (eighth Panthers pick, 192nd overall) of entry draft (July 8, 1995). ... Traded by Panthers to Calgary Flames for RW Rocky Thompson (March 16, 2000). ... Selected by Minnesota Wild in expansion draft (June 23, 2000). ... Ribs (November 15, 2000); missed five games. ... Knee (January 19, 2001); missed one game. ... Fractured right hand (Fe. 10, 2002); missed 20 games. ... Fractured finger (March 27, 2004); missed remainder of season. ... Back spasms (October 25, 2005); missed one game. ... Back spasms (December 6, 2005); missed four games. ... Abdominal strain (March 5, 2006); missed five games. ... Groin (April 6, 2006); missed final six games of regular season. ... Signed as free agent by Tampa Bay Lightning (July 1, 2006).

Season Team	League	REGULAR SEASON GP	G	A	Pts.	PIM	+/-	PP	SH	PLAYOFFS GP	G	A	Pts.	PIM
94-95—Vitkovice	Czech. Jrs.	35	10	15	25	...	...	...	...	—	—	—	—	—
—Vitkovice	Czech Rep.	...	...	...	...	...	...	...	...	4	0	0	0	2
95-96—Vitkovice	Czech Rep.	19	0	1	1	...	...	...	...	—	—	—	—	—
96-97—Carolina	AHL	51	0	12	12	38	...	...	...	—	—	—	—	—
97-98—New Haven	AHL	77	4	13	17	58	11	2	0	3	1	1	2	0
98-99—Kentucky	AHL	45	2	8	10	33	13	1	0	10	0	1	1	4
—Florida	NHL	5	0	1	1	0	2	0	0	—	—	—	—	—
99-00—Florida	NHL	13	1	5	6	2	-3	1	0	—	—	—	—	—
—Houston	IHL	27	3	6	9	13	...	...	...	11	1	2	3	4
00-01—Minnesota	NHL	75	9	21	30	28	-6	4	0	—	—	—	—	—
01-02—Minnesota	NHL	62	5	19	24	32	-6	3	0	—	—	—	—	—
02-03—Minnesota	NHL	78	8	21	29	29	0	4	2	18	3	5	8	24
03-04—Minnesota	NHL	77	5	19	24	28	-7	2	1	—	—	—	—	—
05-06—Minnesota	NHL	65	6	19	25	44	0	1	1	—	—	—	—	—
—Czech Rep. Oly. team	Int'l	8	1	0	1	0	1	0	0	—	—	—	—	—
NHL Totals (7 years)		375	34	105	139	163	-20	15	4	18	3	5	8	24

KUBINA, PAVEL D

PERSONAL: Born April 15, 1977, in Caledna, Czechoslovakia. ... 6-4/230. ... Shoots right. ... Name pronounced koo-BEE-nuh.

TRANSACTIONS/CAREER NOTES: Selected by Tampa Bay Lightning in seventh round (sixth Lightning pick, 179th overall) of NHL draft (June 22, 1996). ... Injured knee (November 8, 1998); missed two games. ... Injured shoulder (November 29, 1998); missed three games. ... Bruised rib (January 5, 2000); missed two games. ... Bruised hand (March 1, 2000); missed one game. ... Injured ankle (March 21, 2000); missed final nine games of season. ... Had concussion (November 3, 2000); missed two games. ... Cut finger (December 30, 2000); missed two games. ... Injured leg (February 24, 2001); missed eight games. ... Bruised foot (December 12, 2002); missed one game. ... Injured neck (February 19, 2003); missed three games. ... Strained groin (December 10, 2005); missed two games. ... Lower-body injury (March 27, 2006); missed three games. ... Signed as free agent by Toronto Maple Leafs (July 1, 2006).

Season Team	League	REGULAR SEASON GP	G	A	Pts.	PIM	+/-	PP	SH	PLAYOFFS GP	G	A	Pts.	PIM
93-94—HC Vitkovice	Czech Rep.	1	0	0	0	0	...	...	...	—	—	—	—	—
94-95—HC Vitkovice	Czech Rep.	8	2	0	2	0	...	...	...	4	0	0	0	0
95-96—HC Vitkovice	Czech Rep.	32	3	4	7	0	...	...	...	4	0	0	0	0
96-97—Moose Jaw	WHL	61	12	32	44	116	...	...	...	11	2	5	7	27
—HC Vitkovice	Czech Rep.	1	0	0	0	0	...	...	...	—	—	—	—	—
97-98—Adirondack	AHL	55	4	8	12	86	20	0	0	1	1	0	1	14
—Tampa Bay	NHL	10	1	2	3	22	-1	0	0	—	—	—	—	—
98-99—Tampa Bay	NHL	68	9	12	21	80	-33	3	1	—	—	—	—	—
—Cleveland	IHL	6	2	2	4	16	-1	1	0	—	—	—	—	—
99-00—Tampa Bay	NHL	69	8	18	26	93	-19	6	0	—	—	—	—	—
00-01—Tampa Bay	NHL	70	11	19	30	103	-14	6	1	—	—	—	—	—
01-02—Tampa Bay	NHL	82	11	23	34	106	-22	5	2	—	—	—	—	—
—Czech Rep. Oly. team	Int'l	4	0	1	1	0	...	...	...	—	—	—	—	—
02-03—Tampa Bay	NHL	75	3	19	22	78	-7	0	0	11	0	0	0	12
03-04—Tampa Bay	NHL	81	17	18	35	85	9	8	1	22	0	4	4	50
04-05—Vitkovice	Czech Rep.	28	6	5	11	46	2	...	...	12	4	6	10	34
05-06—Tampa Bay	NHL	76	5	33	38	96	-12	4	0	5	1	1	2	26
—Czech Rep. Oly. team	Int'l	8	1	1	2	12	2	1	0	—	—	—	—	—
NHL Totals (8 years)		531	65	144	209	663	-99	32	5	38	1	5	6	88

KULEMIN, NIKOLAI LW

PERSONAL: Born July 14, 1986, in Magnitogorsk, Rus. ... 6-1/183. ... Shoots left.

TRANSACTIONS/CAREER NOTES: Selected by Toronto Maple Leafs in second round (second Maple Leafs pick; 44th overall) of NHL draft (June 24, 2006).

Season Team	League	REGULAR SEASON GP	G	A	Pts.	PIM	+/-	PP	SH	PLAYOFFS GP	G	A	Pts.	PIM
04-05—Magnitogorsk	Russian	43	9	13	22	44	...	...	...	—	—	—	—	—
05-06—Magnitogorsk	Russian	31	5	7	12	8	...	...	...	11	2	4	6	6

KUNITZ, CHRIS — LW

PERSONAL: Born September 26, 1979, in Regina, Sask. ... 6-0/200. ... Shoots left.

TRANSACTIONS/CAREER NOTES: Signed as free agent by Anaheim Mighty Ducks (April 1, 2003). ... Claimed on waivers by Atlanta Thrashers (October 4, 2005). ... Claimed on waivers by Mighty Ducks (October 18, 2005).

		REGULAR SEASON								PLAYOFFS				
Season Team	League	GP	G	A	Pts.	PIM	+/-	PP	SH	GP	G	A	Pts.	PIM
99-00—Ferris State	CCHA	38	20	9	29	70	...	...	...	—	—	—	—	—
00-01—Ferris State	CCHA	37	16	13	29	81	...	...	...	—	—	—	—	—
01-02—Ferris State	CCHA	35	28	10	38	68	...	...	...	—	—	—	—	—
02-03—Ferris State	CCHA	42	35	44	79	56	...	...	...	—	—	—	—	—
03-04—Anaheim	NHL	21	0	6	6	12	1	0	0	—	—	—	—	—
—Cincinnati	AHL	59	19	25	44	101	4	5	1	9	4	2	6	24
04-05—Cincinnati	AHL	54	22	17	39	71	13	10	2	12	1	7	8	20
05-06—Portland	AHL	5	0	4	4	12	1	0	0	—	—	—	—	—
—Atlanta	NHL	2	0	0	0	2	-3	0	0	—	—	—	—	—
—Anaheim	NHL	67	19	22	41	69	19	5	1	16	3	5	8	8
NHL Totals (2 years)		90	19	28	47	83	17	5	1	16	3	5	8	8

KVASHA, OLEG — C/LW

PERSONAL: Born July 26, 1978, in Moscow, U.S.S.R. ... 6-5/230. ... Shoots right. ... Name pronounced kuh-VA-shuh.

TRANSACTIONS/CAREER NOTES: Selected by Florida Panthers in third round (third Panthers pick, 65th overall) of entry draft (June 22, 1996). ... Ankle (December 16, 1998); missed one game. ... Shoulder (February 27, 1999); missed one game. ... Separated left shoulder (March 31, 1999); missed final nine games of season. ... Knee (March 7, 2000); missed two games. ... Traded by Panthers with RW Mark Parrish to New York Islanders for C Olli Jokinen and G Roberto Luongo (June 24, 2000). ... Back (December 6, 2000); missed two games. ... Knee (January 12, 2001); missed 10 games. ... Left knee (February 10, 2001); missed eight games. ... Shoulder (November 21, 2001); missed two games. ... Flu (December 18, 2001); missed one game. ... Knee, had surgery (February 28, 2002); missed five games. ... Fractured ankle (October 24, 2002); missed seven games. ... Ankle (November 20, 2002); missed three games. ... Fractured nose (December 10, 2003); missed one game. ... Ankle (November 26, 2005); missed 12 games. ... Traded by Islanders with conditional fifth-round pick (G Brett Bennett) in 2006 to Phoenix Coyotes for third-round pick (traded to Boston; Bruins selected C Brad Marchand) in 2006 draft (March 9, 2006). ... Knee (April 5, 2006), surgery; missed four games.

		REGULAR SEASON								PLAYOFFS				
Season Team	League	GP	G	A	Pts.	PIM	+/-	PP	SH	GP	G	A	Pts.	PIM
94-95—CSKA	CIS Jr.	Statistics unavailable												
95-96—CSKA Moscow	CIS	38	2	3	5	14	...	...	...	2	0	0	0	0
96-97—CSKA Moscow	USSR	44	20	22	42	115	...	...	...	—	—	—	—	—
97-98—New Haven	AHL	57	13	16	29	46	11	4	0	3	2	1	3	0
98-99—Florida	NHL	68	12	13	25	45	5	4	0	—	—	—	—	—
99-00—Florida	NHL	78	5	20	25	34	3	2	0	4	0	0	0	0
00-01—New York Islanders	NHL	62	11	9	20	46	-15	0	0	—	—	—	—	—
01-02—New York Islanders	NHL	71	13	25	38	80	-4	2	0	7	0	1	1	6
—Russian Oly. team	Int'l	5	0	0	0	0	...	...	...	—	—	—	—	—
02-03—New York Islanders	NHL	69	12	14	26	44	4	0	1	5	0	1	1	2
03-04—New York Islanders	NHL	81	15	36	51	48	4	5	3	5	1	0	1	0
04-05—Severstal Cherepovets	Russian	22	6	5	11	24	3	...	...	—	—	—	—	—
—CSKA Moscow	Russian	26	3	6	9	20	-7	...	...	—	—	—	—	—
05-06—New York Islanders	NHL	49	9	12	21	32	-2	1	0	—	—	—	—	—
—Phoenix	NHL	15	4	7	11	6	5	0	0	—	—	—	—	—
NHL Totals (7 years)		493	81	136	217	335	0	14	4	21	1	2	3	8

KWIATKOWSKI, JOEL — D

PERSONAL: Born March 22, 1977, in Kindersley, Sask. ... 6-2/210. ... Shoots left. ... Name pronounced kwee-iht-KOW-skee.

TRANSACTIONS/CAREER NOTES: Signed as free agent by Mighty Ducks (June 18, 1998). ... Traded by Mighty Ducks to Senators for D Patrick Traverse (June 12, 2000). ... Injured ankle (December 31, 2002); missed three games. ... Traded by Senators to Capitals for ninth-round pick (F Mark Olafson) in 2003 draft (January 15, 2003). ... Signed as free agent by Panthers (July 16, 2004). ... Signed as free agent by San Antonio of the AHL (September 26, 2004). ... Head injury (December 8, 2005); missed one game.

		REGULAR SEASON								PLAYOFFS				
Season Team	League	GP	G	A	Pts.	PIM	+/-	PP	SH	GP	G	A	Pts.	PIM
94-95—Tacoma	WHL	70	4	13	17	66	...	...	...	4	0	0	0	2
95-96—Prince George	WHL	72	12	28	40	133	...	...	...	—	—	—	—	—
96-97—Prince George	WHL	72	16	36	52	94	...	...	...	4	4	2	6	24
97-98—Prince George	WHL	62	21	43	64	65	16	8	0	11	3	6	9	6
98-99—Cincinnati	AHL	80	12	21	33	48	7	2	0	3	2	0	2	0
99-00—Cincinnati	AHL	70	4	22	26	28	...	...	...	—	—	—	—	—
00-01—Grand Rapids	IHL	77	4	17	21	58	...	...	...	10	1	0	1	4
—Ottawa	NHL	4	1	0	1	0	1	0	0	—	—	—	—	—
01-02—Grand Rapids	AHL	65	8	21	29	94	21	1	0	5	1	2	3	12
—Ottawa	NHL	11	0	0	0	12	5	0	0	—	—	—	—	—
02-03—Ottawa	NHL	20	0	2	2	6	2	0	0	—	—	—	—	—
—Binghamton	AHL	1	0	0	0	2	...	...	...	—	—	—	—	—
—Washington	NHL	34	0	3	3	12	1	0	0	6	0	0	0	2
03-04—Washington	NHL	80	6	6	12	89	-28	2	0	—	—	—	—	—
04-05—San Antonio	AHL	64	13	19	32	76	-1	5	0	—	—	—	—	—
—St. John's	AHL	17	7	6	13	16	8	4	0	5	0	4	4	23
05-06—Florida	NHL	73	4	8	12	86	3	1	0	—	—	—	—	—
NHL Totals (5 years)		222	11	19	30	205	-16	3	0	6	0	0	0	2

LAAKSONEN, ANTTI LW/RW

PERSONAL: Born October 3, 1973, in Tammela, Finland. ... 6-0/180. ... Shoots left. ... Name pronounced AHN-tee lah-AHK-soh-nehn.
TRANSACTIONS/CAREER NOTES: Selected by Boston Bruins in eighth round (10th Bruins pick, 191st overall) of NHL draft (July 21, 1997). ... Signed as free agent by Minnesota Wild (July 20, 2000). ... Signed as free agent by Colorado Avalanche (July 2, 2004).
STATISTICAL PLATEAUS: Three-goal games: 2000-01 (1).

		REGULAR SEASON								PLAYOFFS				
Season Team	League	GP	G	A	Pts.	PIM	+/-	PP	SH	GP	G	A	Pts.	PIM
92-93—HPK Hameenlinna	Finland	2	0	0	0	0	...	0	0	—	—	—	—	—
93-94—Denver	WCHA	36	12	9	21	38	...	...	...	—	—	—	—	—
94-95—Denver	WCHA	40	17	18	35	42	...	...	...	—	—	—	—	—
95-96—Denver	WCHA	39	25	28	53	71	...	...	...	—	—	—	—	—
96-97—Denver	WCHA	39	21	17	38	63	...	...	...	—	—	—	—	—
97-98—Providence	AHL	38	3	2	5	14	-13	0	0	—	—	—	—	—
—Charlotte	ECHL	15	4	3	7	12	...	...	...	6	0	3	3	0
98-99—Boston	NHL	11	1	2	3	2	-1	0	0	—	—	—	—	—
—Providence	AHL	66	25	33	58	52	40	5	1	19	7	2	9	28
99-00—Providence	AHL	40	10	12	22	57	...	...	...	14	5	4	9	4
—Boston	NHL	27	6	3	9	2	3	0	0	—	—	—	—	—
00-01—Minnesota	NHL	82	12	16	28	24	-7	0	2	—	—	—	—	—
01-02—Minnesota	NHL	82	16	17	33	22	-5	0	0	—	—	—	—	—
02-03—Minnesota	NHL	82	15	16	31	26	4	1	2	16	1	3	4	4
03-04—Minnesota	NHL	77	12	14	26	20	0	0	1	—	—	—	—	—
05-06—Colorado	NHL	81	16	18	34	40	-2	0	2	9	0	2	2	2
—Fin. Olympic team	Int'l	8	0	0	0	6	0	0	0	—	—	—	—	—
NHL Totals (7 years)		442	78	86	164	136	-8	1	7	25	1	5	6	6

LABARBERA, JASON G

PERSONAL: Born January 18, 1980, in Prince George, B.C. ... 6-3/224. ... Catches left.
TRANSACTIONS/CAREER NOTES: Selected by New York Rangers in third round (third Rangers pick, 66th overall) of entry draft (June 27, 1998). ... Signed as free agent by Los Angeles Kings (August 2, 2005). ... Personal leave (November 14, 2005); missed two games.

		REGULAR SEASON										PLAYOFFS							
Season Team	League	GP	Min.	W	L	OTL	T	GA	SO	GAA	SV%	GP	Min.	W	L	GA	SO	GAA	SV%
96-97—Tri-City	WHL	2	...	1	0	...	0	...	...	3.81	...	—	—	—	—	—	—	—	—
—Portland	WHL	9	443	5	1	...	1	18	0	2.44	...	—	—	—	—	—	—	—	—
97-98—Portland	WHL	23	1305	18	4	...	0	72	1	3.31	...	—	—	—	—	—	—	—	—
98-99—Portland	WHL	51	2991	18	23	...	9	170	4	3.41	.904	4	252	0	4	19	0	4.52	.899
99-00—Portland	WHL	34	2005	8	24	...	2	123	1	3.68	.903	—	—	—	—	—	—	—	—
—Spokane	WHL	21	1146	12	6	...	2	50	0	2.62	.900	9	435	6	1	18	1	2.48	.890
00-01—Hartford	AHL	4	156	1	1	...	0	12	0	4.62	.871	—	—	—	—	—	—	—	—
—New York Rangers	NHL	1	10	0	0	...	0	0	0	0.00	1.000	—	—	—	—	—	—	—	—
—Charlotte	ECHL	35	2100	18	10	...	7	112	1	3.20	...	2	143	1	1	5	0	2.10	...
01-02—Hartford	AHL	20	1057	7	11	...	1	55	0	3.12	.904	—	—	—	—	—	—	—	—
—Charlotte	ECHL	13	743	9	3	...	1	29	0	2.34	.918	4	212	2	2	12	0	3.40	.910
02-03—Hartford	AHL	46	2451	18	17	...	6	105	2	2.57	.915	2	117	0	2	6	0	3.08	.867
03-04—New York Rangers	NHL	4	198	1	2	...	0	16	0	4.85	.824	—	—	—	—	—	—	—	—
—Hartford	AHL	59	3393	34	9	...	9	90	13	1.59	.932	16	1042	11	5	30	3	1.73	.930
04-05—Hartford	AHL	53	2937	31	16	...	...	90	6	1.84	.934	4	237	1	3	9	0	2.28	.940
05-06—Manchester	AHL	3	185	1	1	1	...	10	0	3.24	.907	—	—	—	—	—	—	—	—
—Los Angeles	NHL	29	1433	11	9	2	...	69	1	2.89	.900	—	—	—	—	—	—	—	—
NHL Totals (3 years)		34	1641	12	11	2	0	85	1	3.11	.891								

LACOUTURE, DAN LW

PERSONAL: Born April 18, 1977, in Hyannis, Mass. ... 6-2/208. ... Shoots left. ... Name pronounced LA-kuh-toor.
TRANSACTIONS/CAREER NOTES: Selected by New York Islanders in second round (second Islanders pick, 29th overall) of entry draft (June 22, 1996). ... Traded by Islanders to Edmonton Oilers for RW Mariusz Czerkawski (August 25, 1997). ... Traded by Oilers to Pittsburgh Penguins for D Sven Butenschon (March 13, 2001). ... Concussion (December 7, 2002); missed four games. ... Traded by Penguins with RW Alexei Kovalev, D Janne Laukkanen and D Mike Wilson to New York Rangers for RW Rico Fata, RW Mikael Samuelsson, D Joel Bouchard, D Richard Lintner and cash (February 10, 2003). ... Separated shoulder (November 24, 2003); missed six games. ... Concussion (January 6, 2004); missed seven games. ... Postconcussion syndrome (January 24, 2004); missed eight games. ... Signed to training camp tryout by Detroit Red Wings (September 2005). ... Released by Red Wings (October 3, 2005). ... Signed as free agent by Boston Bruins (November 29, 2005).

		REGULAR SEASON								PLAYOFFS				
Season Team	League	GP	G	A	Pts.	PIM	+/-	PP	SH	GP	G	A	Pts.	PIM
94-95—Springfield Jr. B	EJHL	49	37	39	76	100	...	...	...	—	—	—	—	—
95-96—Jr. Whalers	EJHL	42	36	48	84	102	...	9	8	—	—	—	—	—
96-97—Boston University	Hockey East	31	13	12	25	18	13	6	0	—	—	—	—	—
97-98—Hamilton	AHL	77	15	10	25	31	-2	4	0	5	1	0	1	0
98-99—Hamilton	AHL	72	17	14	31	73	-5	1	4	9	2	1	3	2
—Edmonton	NHL	3	0	0	0	0	1	0	0	—	—	—	—	—
99-00—Hamilton	AHL	70	23	17	40	85	...	...	...	6	2	1	3	0
—Edmonton	NHL	5	0	0	0	10	0	0	0	1	0	0	0	0
00-01—Edmonton	NHL	37	2	4	6	29	-2	0	0	—	—	—	—	—
—Pittsburgh	NHL	11	0	0	0	14	0	0	0	5	0	0	0	2
01-02—Pittsburgh	NHL	82	6	11	17	71	-19	0	1	—	—	—	—	—

Season Team	League	REGULAR SEASON GP	G	A	Pts.	PIM	+/-	PP	SH	PLAYOFFS GP	G	A	Pts.	PIM
02-03—Pittsburgh	NHL	44	2	2	4	72	-8	0	0	—	—	—	—	—
—New York Rangers	NHL	24	1	4	5	0	4	0	0	—	—	—	—	—
03-04—New York Rangers	NHL	59	5	2	7	82	-13	1	0	—	—	—	—	—
04-05—Providence	AHL	64	12	15	27	52	9	3	2	6	1	1	2	4
05-06—Boston	NHL	55	2	2	4	53	-6	0	1	—	—	—	—	—
NHL Totals (7 years)		320	18	25	43	331	-43	1	2	6	0	0	0	2

LADD, ANDREW — LW

PERSONAL: Born December 12, 1985, in Maple Ridge,B.C. ... 6-2/200. ... Shoots left.
TRANSACTIONS/CAREER NOTES: Selected by Carolina Hurricanes in first round (first Hurricanes pick, fourth overall) of entry draft (June 26, 2004). ... Injured right knee (December 3, 2005); missed 18 games. ... Lower-body injury (March 29, 2006); missed six games.

Season Team	League	REGULAR SEASON GP	G	A	Pts.	PIM	+/-	PP	SH	PLAYOFFS GP	G	A	Pts.	PIM
02-03—Vancouver	WHL	1	0	0	0	0	...	...	...	—	—	—	—	—
03-04—Calgary	WHL	71	30	45	75	119	...	...	...	7	1	6	7	10
04-05—Calgary	WHL	65	19	26	45	167	16	6	2	12	7	4	11	18
05-06—Lowell	AHL	25	11	8	19	28	-9	4	1	—	—	—	—	—
—Carolina	NHL	29	6	5	11	4	0	3	0	17	2	3	5	4
NHL Totals (1 year)		29	6	5	11	4	0	3	0	17	2	3	5	4

LAICH, BROOKS — C/LW

PERSONAL: Born June 23, 1983, in Wawota, Alta. ... 6-2/199. ... Shoots left.
TRANSACTIONS/CAREER NOTES: Selected by Ottawa Senators in sixth round (193rd overall) in NHL draft (June 24, 2001). ... Traded by Senators with second-round pick in 2005 draft to Washington for RW Peter Bondra (February 18, 2004).

Season Team	League	REGULAR SEASON GP	G	A	Pts.	PIM	+/-	PP	SH	PLAYOFFS GP	G	A	Pts.	PIM
00-01—Moose Jaw	WHL	71	9	21	30	28	...	...	...	4	0	0	0	5
01-02—Moose Jaw	WHL	28	6	14	20	12	...	...	...	—	—	—	—	—
—Seattle	WHL	47	22	36	58	42	...	...	...	11	5	3	8	11
02-03—Seattle	WHL	60	41	53	94	65	...	...	...	15	5	14	19	24
03-04—Binghamton	AHL	44	15	18	33	16	3	7	1	—	—	—	—	—
—Ottawa	NHL	1	0	0	0	2	0	0	0	—	—	—	—	—
—Portland	AHL	22	1	3	4	12	-9	0	0	6	0	0	0	0
—Washington	NHL	4	0	1	1	0	-1	0	0	—	—	—	—	—
04-05—Portland	AHL	68	16	10	26	33	-20	8	1	—	—	—	—	—
05-06—Hershey	AHL	10	7	6	13	8	1	5	0	14	5	4	9	17
—Washington	NHL	73	7	14	21	26	-9	1	0	—	—	—	—	—
NHL Totals (2 years)		78	7	15	22	28	-10	1	0					

LALIME, PATRICK — G

PERSONAL: Born July 7, 1974, in St. Bonaventure, Que. ... 6-3/192. ... Catches left. ... Name pronounced luh-LEEM.
TRANSACTIONS/CAREER NOTES: Selected by Pittsburgh Penguins in sixth round (sixth Penguins pick, 156th overall) of entry draft (June 26, 1993). ... Rights traded by Penguins to Anaheim Mighty Ducks for C Sean Pronger (March 24, 1998). ... Traded by Mighty Ducks to Ottawa Senators for LW Ted Donato and D Antti-Jussi Niemi (June 18, 1999). ... Flu (February 1, 2000); missed one game. ... Sprained left knee (October 14, 2000); missed 10 games. ... Flu (February 6, 2003); missed two games. ... Flu (December 2, 2003); missed two games. ... Sprained left knee (March 27, 2004); missed remainder of regular season. ... Traded by Senators to St. Louis Blues for fourth-round pick (C Ilja Zubov) in 2005 draft (June 27, 2004). ... Bruised left knee (October 28, 2005); missed one game. ... Torn ACL (April 1, 2006); missed final nine games of regular season. ... Signed as free agent by Chicago Blackhawks (July 1, 2006).

Season Team	League	REGULAR SEASON GP	Min.	W	L	OTL	T	GA	SO	GAA	SV%	PLAYOFFS GP	Min.	W	L	GA	SO	GAA	SV%
92-93—Shawinigan	QMJHL	44	2467	10	24	...	4	192	0	4.67	.863	—	—	—	—	—	—	—	—
93-94—Shawinigan	QMJHL	48	2733	22	20	...	2	192	1	4.22	.874	5	223	1	3	25	0	6.73	.793
94-95—Hampton Roads	ECHL	26	1471	15	7	...	3	82	2	3.34	.894	—	—	—	—	—	—	—	—
—Cleveland	IHL	23	1230	7	10	...	4	91	0	4.44	.882	—	—	—	—	—	—	—	—
95-96—Cleveland	IHL	41	2314	20	12	...	7	149	0	3.86	...	—	—	—	—	—	—	—	—
96-97—Cleveland	IHL	14	834	6	6	...	2	45	1	3.24	...	—	—	—	—	—	—	—	—
—Pittsburgh	NHL	39	2058	21	12	...	2	101	3	2.94	.913	—	—	—	—	—	—	—	—
97-98—Grand Rapids	IHL	31	1749	10	10	...	9	76	2	2.61	.918	1	77	0	1	4	0	3.12	.892
98-99—Kansas City	IHL	66	3789	39	20	...	4	190	2	3.01	.900	3	179	1	2	6	1	2.01	.942
99-00—Ottawa	NHL	38	2038	19	14	...	3	79	3	2.33	.905	—	—	—	—	—	—	—	—
00-01—Ottawa	NHL	60	3607	36	19	...	5	141	7	2.35	.914	4	251	0	4	10	0	2.39	.899
01-02—Ottawa	NHL	61	3583	27	24	...	8	148	7	2.48	.903	12	778	7	5	18	4	*1.39	.946
02-03—Ottawa	NHL	67	3943	39	20	...	7	142	8	2.16	.911	18	1122	11	7	34	1	1.82	.924
03-04—Ottawa	NHL	57	3324	25	23	...	7	127	5	2.29	.905	7	398	3	4	13	0	1.96	.906
05-06—Peoria	AHL	14	798	6	6	1	...	38	1	2.86	.903	—	—	—	—	—	—	—	—
—St. Louis	NHL	31	1699	4	18	8	...	103	0	3.64	.881	—	—	—	—	—	—	—	—
NHL Totals (7 years)		353	20252	171	130	8	32	841	33	2.49	.906	41	2549	21	20	75	5	1.77	.926

LAMPMAN, BRYCE — D

PERSONAL: Born August 31, 1982, in Rochester, Minn. ... 6-2/201. ... Shoots left.
TRANSACTIONS/CAREER NOTES: Selected by New York Rangers in fourth round (fourth Rangers pick, 113th overall) of NHL entry draft (June 23, 2001).

Season Team	League	GP	G	A	Pts.	PIM	+/-	PP	SH	GP	G	A	Pts.	PIM
		REGULAR SEASON								PLAYOFFS				
00-01—Omaha	USHL	55	10	11	21	77	...	...	...	—	—	—	—	—
01-02—U. of Neb.-Omaha	CCHA	26	0	4	4	28	...	...	...	—	—	—	—	—
02-03—Hartford	AHL	45	0	6	6	32	11	0	0	2	0	1	1	0
—Kamloops	WHL	29	1	17	18	32	...	...	...	—	—	—	—	—
03-04—Hartford	AHL	68	4	11	15	52	12	2	0	16	1	3	4	14
—New York Rangers	NHL	8	0	0	0	0	-4	0	0	—	—	—	—	—
04-05—Hartford	AHL	74	7	18	25	74	19	2	0	4	0	0	0	4
05-06—Hartford	AHL	11	2	3	5	16	6	0	1	—	—	—	—	—
—New York Rangers	NHL	1	0	0	0	2	-1	0	0	—	—	—	—	—
NHL Totals (2 years)		9	0	0	0	2	-5	0	0					

LANG, ROBERT C

PERSONAL: Born December 19, 1970, in Teplice, Czech. ... 6-2/217. ... Shoots right.

TRANSACTIONS/CAREER NOTES: Selected by Los Angeles Kings in seventh round (sixth Kings pick, 133rd overall) of entry draft (June 16, 1990). ... Dislocated shoulder (April 3, 1994); missed remainder of season. ... Strained left shoulder (March 26, 1995); missed one game. ... Strained back (November 20, 1995); missed seven games. ... Signed as free agent by Edmonton Oilers (October 19, 1996). ... Loaned by Oilers to Sparta Praha of Czech league (October 19, 1996). ... Signed as free agent by Pittsburgh Penguins (September 2, 1997). ... Claimed by Boston Bruins in waiver draft (September 28, 1997). ... Claimed off waivers by Penguins (October 25, 1997). ... Fractured thumb (March 21, 1998); missed nine games. ... Bruised ankle (March 23, 1999); missed 10 games. ... Back spasms (October 16, 1999); missed one game. ... Thumb (December 14, 1999); missed one game. ... Face (March 9, 2000); missed two games. ... Oral surgery (January 26, 2002); missed two games. ... Fractured hand (March 5, 2002); missed seven games. ... Reinjured hand (March 23, 2002); missed remainder of season. ... Signed as free agent by Washington Capitals (July 1, 2002). ... Traded by Capitals to Detroit Red Wings for C Tomas Fleischmann, first-round pick (D Mike Green) in 2004 and a fourth-round pick (C/LW Luke Lynes) in 2006 (February 27, 2004). ... Cracked ribs (March 9, 2004); missed 11 games. ... Reinjured ribs (April 1, 2004); missed 1 game. ... Strained groin (December 1, 2005); missed eight games. ... Upper body (April 11, 2006); missed two games.

STATISTICAL PLATEAUS: Three-goal games: 2003-04 (1).

Season Team	League	GP	G	A	Pts.	PIM	+/-	PP	SH	GP	G	A	Pts.	PIM
		REGULAR SEASON								PLAYOFFS				
88-89—Litvinov	Czech.	7	3	2	5	0	...	...	...	—	—	—	—	—
89-90—Litvinov	Czech.	39	11	10	21	20	...	...	...	—	—	—	—	—
90-91—Litvinov	Czech.	56	26	26	52	38	...	...	...	—	—	—	—	—
91-92—Litvinov	Czech.	43	12	31	43	34	...	...	...	—	—	—	—	—
—Czech. national team	Int'l	8	5	8	13	8	...	...	...	—	—	—	—	—
—Czech. Olympic Team	Int'l	8	5	8	13	8	8	2	0	—	—	—	—	—
92-93—Los Angeles	NHL	11	0	5	5	2	-3	0	0	—	—	—	—	—
—Phoenix	IHL	38	9	21	30	20	-2	4	0	—	—	—	—	—
93-94—Phoenix	IHL	44	11	24	35	34	-14	4	0	—	—	—	—	—
—Los Angeles	NHL	32	9	10	19	10	7	0	0	—	—	—	—	—
94-95—Chem. Litvinov	Czech Rep.	16	4	19	23	28	...	...	...	—	—	—	—	—
—Los Angeles	NHL	36	4	8	12	4	-7	0	0	—	—	—	—	—
95-96—Los Angeles	NHL	68	6	16	22	10	-15	0	2	—	—	—	—	—
96-97—Sparta Praha	Czech Rep.	38	14	27	41	30	...	...	...	5	1	2	3	4
97-98—Boston	NHL	3	0	0	0	2	1	0	0	—	—	—	—	—
—Houston	IHL	9	1	7	8	4	1	0	0	—	—	—	—	—
—Pittsburgh	NHL	51	9	13	22	14	6	1	1	6	0	3	3	2
—Czech Rep. Oly. team	Int'l	6	0	3	3	0	4	0	0	—	—	—	—	—
98-99—Pittsburgh	NHL	72	21	23	44	24	-10	7	0	12	0	2	2	0
99-00—Pittsburgh	NHL	78	23	42	65	14	-9	13	0	11	3	3	6	0
00-01—Pittsburgh	NHL	82	32	48	80	28	20	10	0	16	4	4	8	4
01-02—Pittsburgh	NHL	62	18	32	50	16	9	5	1	—	—	—	—	—
—Czech Rep. Oly. team	Int'l	4	1	2	3	2	...	...	...	—	—	—	—	—
02-03—Washington	NHL	82	22	47	69	22	12	10	0	6	2	1	3	2
03-04—Washington	NHL	63	29	45	74	24	2	10	0	—	—	—	—	—
—Detroit	NHL	6	1	4	5	0	2	0	0	12	4	5	9	6
05-06—Detroit	NHL	72	20	42	62	72	17	8	0	6	3	3	6	2
—Czech Rep. Oly. team	Int'l	8	0	4	4	4	0	0	0	—	—	—	—	—
NHL Totals (12 years)		718	194	335	529	242	32	64	4	69	16	21	37	16

LANGDON, DARREN LW

PERSONAL: Born January 8, 1971, in Deer Lake, Nfld. ... 6-1/205. ... Shoots left.

TRANSACTIONS/CAREER NOTES: Signed as free agent by New York Rangers (August 16, 1993). ... Suspended three games for abuse of an official in preseason game (September 23, 1995). ... Sprained right knee (December 13, 1996); missed 13 games. ... Suspended two games for initiating altercation (March 7, 1997). ... Sprained knee (November 21, 1997); missed six games. ... Bruised sternum (March 4, 1998); missed three games. ... Strained groin (January 2, 2000); missed remainder of season. ... Traded by Rangers with RW Rob DiMaio to Carolina Hurricanes for RW Sandy McCarthy and fourth-round pick (D Bryce Lampman) in 2001 entry draft (August 4, 2000). ... Injured groin (February 7, 2001); missed nine games. ... Injured shoulder (March 26, 2002); missed four games. ... Injured knee (October 16, 2002); missed two games. ... Traded by Hurricanes with D Marek Malik to Vancouver Canucks for LW Jan Hlavac and C Harold Druken (November 1, 2002). ... Injured hand (March 3, 2003); missed 17 games. ... Claimed by Montreal Canadiens in waiver draft (October 3, 2003). ... Injured groin (October 14, 2003); missed nine games. ... Signed as free agent by New Jersey Devils (July 3, 2004). ... Groin injury (March 11, 2006); missed final 18 games of regular season and all nine playoff games.

Season Team	League	GP	G	A	Pts.	PIM	+/-	PP	SH	GP	G	A	Pts.	PIM
		REGULAR SEASON								PLAYOFFS				
91-92—Summerside	MJHL	44	34	49	83	441	...	...	...	—	—	—	—	—
92-93—Binghamton	AHL	18	3	4	7	115	...	...	...	8	0	1	1	14
—Dayton	ECHL	54	23	22	45	429	...	...	...	3	0	1	1	40

Season Team	League	GP	G	A	Pts.	PIM	+/-	PP	SH	GP	G	A	Pts.	PIM
		REGULAR SEASON								PLAYOFFS				
93-94—Binghamton	AHL	54	2	7	9	327	...	...	...	...	...	...	...	...
94-95—Binghamton	AHL	55	6	14	20	296	5	1	0	11	1	3	4	84
—New York Rangers	NHL	18	1	1	2	62	0	0	0	—	—	—	—	—
95-96—New York Rangers	NHL	64	7	4	11	175	2	0	0	2	0	0	0	0
—Binghamton	AHL	1	0	0	0	12	...	...	...	—	—	—	—	—
96-97—New York Rangers	NHL	60	3	6	9	195	-1	0	0	10	0	0	0	2
97-98—New York Rangers	NHL	70	3	3	6	197	0	0	0	—	—	—	—	—
98-99—New York Rangers	NHL	44	0	0	0	80	-3	0	0	—	—	—	—	—
99-00—New York Rangers	NHL	21	0	1	1	26	-2	0	0	—	—	—	—	—
00-01—Carolina	NHL	54	0	2	2	94	-4	0	0	4	0	0	0	12
01-02—Carolina	NHL	58	2	1	3	106	2	0	0	—	—	—	—	—
02-03—Carolina	NHL	9	0	0	0	16	0	0	0	—	—	—	—	—
—Vancouver	NHL	45	0	1	1	143	-2	0	0	—	—	—	—	—
03-04—Montreal	NHL	64	0	3	3	135	-2	0	0	9	1	0	1	6
05-06—New Jersey	NHL	14	0	1	1	22	-3	0	0	—	—	—	—	—
NHL Totals (11 years)		521	16	23	39	1251	-13	0	0	25	1	0	1	20

LANGENBRUNNER, JAMIE RW

PERSONAL: Born July 24, 1975, in Duluth, Minn. ... 6-1/200. ... Shoots right. ... Name pronounced LANG-ihn-BRUH-nuhr.

TRANSACTIONS/CAREER NOTES: Selected by Dallas Stars in second round (second Stars pick, 35th overall) of NHL draft (June 26, 1993). ... Had back spasms (February 21, 1997); missed one game. ... Had whiplash (January 12, 1998); missed one game. ... Injured shoulder (January 6, 1999); missed five games. ... Strained abdominal muscle (March 26, 1999); missed one game. ... Had concussion (November 30, 1999); missed one game. ... Sprained shoulder (December 17, 1999); missed one game. ... Pinched nerve in neck (January 7, 2000); missed 11 games. ... Strained neck (February 16, 2000); missed three games. ... Strained abdominal muscle (December 20, 2000); missed 22 games. ... Reinjured abdominal muscle (March 4, 2001); missed five games. ... Strained back (March 31, 2001); missed one game. ... Traded by Stars with C Joe Nieuwendyk to New Jersey Devils for C Jason Arnott, RW Randy McKay and first-round pick (later traded to Columbus; Blue Jackets selected LW Dan Paille) in 2002 draft (March 19, 2002). ... Viral infection (November 19, 2002); missed four games. ... Injured knee (November 29, 2003) and had surgery (January 19, 2004); missed 28 games. ... Re-signed with Devils as restricted free agent (September 21, 2005). ... Virus (November 18, 2005); missed two games.

Season Team	League	GP	G	A	Pts.	PIM	+/-	PP	SH	GP	G	A	Pts.	PIM
		REGULAR SEASON								PLAYOFFS				
90-91—Cloquet H.S.	Minn. H.S.	20	6	16	22	8	...	...	...	—	—	—	—	—
91-92—Cloquet H.S.	Minn. H.S.	23	16	23	39	24	...	...	...	—	—	—	—	—
92-93—Cloquet H.S.	Minn. H.S.	27	27	62	89	18	...	...	...	—	—	—	—	—
93-94—Peterborough	OHL	62	33	58	91	53	...	10	0	7	4	6	10	2
94-95—Peterborough	OHL	62	42	57	99	84	...	19	1	11	8	14	22	12
—Dallas	NHL	2	0	0	0	2	0	0	0	—	—	—	—	—
—Kalamazoo	IHL	...	...	...	...	...	...	...	...	11	1	3	4	2
95-96—Michigan	IHL	59	25	40	65	129	...	...	...	10	3	10	13	8
—Dallas	NHL	12	2	2	4	6	-2	1	0	—	—	—	—	—
96-97—Dallas	NHL	76	13	26	39	51	-2	3	0	5	1	1	2	14
97-98—Dallas	NHL	81	23	29	52	61	9	8	0	16	1	4	5	14
—U.S. Olympic team	Int'l	3	0	0	0	4	-2	0	0	—	—	—	—	—
98-99—Dallas	NHL	75	12	33	45	62	10	4	0	23	10	7	17	16
99-00—Dallas	NHL	65	18	21	39	68	16	4	2	15	1	7	8	18
00-01—Dallas	NHL	53	12	18	30	57	4	3	2	10	2	2	4	6
01-02—Dallas	NHL	68	10	16	26	54	-11	0	1	—	—	—	—	—
—New Jersey	NHL	14	3	3	6	23	2	0	0	5	0	1	1	8
02-03—New Jersey	NHL	78	22	33	55	65	17	5	1	24	11	7	18	16
03-04—New Jersey	NHL	53	10	16	26	43	9	1	2	5	0	2	2	2
04-05—Ingolstadt ERC	Germany	11	2	2	4	22	-3	1	0	11	2	6	8	6
05-06—New Jersey	NHL	80	19	34	53	74	-1	8	1	9	3	10	13	16
NHL Totals (11 years)		657	144	231	375	566	51	37	9	112	29	41	70	110

LANGFELD, JOSH RW/LW

PERSONAL: Born July 17, 1977, in Fridley, Minn. ... 6-3/215. ... Shoots right.

TRANSACTIONS/CAREER NOTES: Selected by Ottawa Senators in third round (third Senators pick, 66th overall) of entry draft (June 21, 1997). ... Concussion (March 30, 2002); missed two games. ... Signed to one-year contract by San Jose as unrestricted free agent (September 12, 2005). ... Claimed off waivers by Bruins (January 31, 2006).

Season Team	League	GP	G	A	Pts.	PIM	+/-	PP	SH	GP	G	A	Pts.	PIM
		REGULAR SEASON								PLAYOFFS				
96-97—Lincoln	Jr. A	38	35	23	58	100	...	...	...	—	—	—	—	—
97-98—Univ. of Michigan	CCHA	46	19	17	36	66	...	...	...	—	—	—	—	—
98-99—Univ. of Michigan	CCHA	41	21	14	35	84	...	...	...	—	—	—	—	—
99-00—Univ. of Michigan	CCHA	37	9	20	29	56	...	...	...	—	—	—	—	—
00-01—Univ. of Michigan	CCHA	42	16	12	28	44	...	...	...	—	—	—	—	—
01-02—Grand Rapids	AHL	68	21	16	37	29	1	8	1	5	2	0	2	0
—Ottawa	NHL	1	0	0	0	2	0	0	0	—	—	—	—	—
02-03—Ottawa	NHL	12	0	1	1	4	2	0	0	—	—	—	—	—
—Binghamton	AHL	59	14	21	35	38	-4	4	0	13	5	3	8	8
03-04—Binghamton	AHL	30	13	14	27	25	12	4	0	2	0	0	0	0
—Ottawa	NHL	38	7	10	17	16	6	2	0	—	—	—	—	—
04-05—Binghamton	AHL	74	32	25	57	75	17	9	6	6	2	2	4	2
05-06—San Jose	NHL	39	2	9	11	16	4	0	1	—	—	—	—	—
—Boston	NHL	18	0	1	1	10	-6	0	0	—	—	—	—	—
NHL Totals (4 years)		108	9	21	30	48	6	2	1					

LANGKOW, DAYMOND — C

PERSONAL: Born September 27, 1976, in Edmonton. ... 5-11/192. ... Shoots left. ... Brother of Scott Langkow, G with three NHL teams (1995-2000).

TRANSACTIONS/CAREER NOTES: Selected by Tampa Bay Lightning in first round (first Lightning pick, fifth overall) of NHL entry draft (July 8, 1995). ... Had the flu (October 1, 1997); missed one game. ... Suffered concussion (January 7, 1998); missed two games. ... Had the flu (January 31, 1998); missed three games ... Traded by Lightning with RW Mikael Renberg to Philadelphia Flyers for C Chris Gratton and C/RW Mike Sillinger (December 12, 1998). ... Fractured right foot (February 25, 2001); missed 11 games. ... Traded by Flyers to Phoenix Coyotes for second-round pick (later traded to Tampa Bay Lightning) in 2002 entry draft and first-round pick (C Jeff Carter) in 2003 entry draft (July 2, 2001). ... Fractured toe (January 3, 2002); missed two games. ... Traded by Coyotes to Calgary Flames for D Denis Gauthier and LW Oleg Saprykin (August 26, 2004).

STATISTICAL PLATEAUS: Three-goal games: 2001-02 (1), 2002-03 (1). Total: 2.

		REGULAR SEASON								PLAYOFFS				
Season Team	League	GP	G	A	Pts.	PIM	+/-	PP	SH	GP	G	A	Pts.	PIM
91-92—Tri-City	WHL	1	0	0	0	0	...	...	...	4	2	2	4	15
92-93—Tri-City	WHL	65	22	42	64	96	...	...	...	4	1	0	1	4
93-94—Tri-City	WHL	61	40	43	83	174	...	...	...	4	2	2	4	15
94-95—Tri-City	WHL	72	67	73	140	142	32	26	5	17	12	15	27	52
95-96—Tampa Bay	NHL	4	0	1	1	0	-1	0	0	—	—	—	—	—
—Tri-City	WHL	48	30	61	91	103	...	...	...	11	14	13	27	20
96-97—Adirondack	AHL	2	1	1	2	0	-1	0	0	—	—	—	—	—
—Tampa Bay	NHL	79	15	13	28	35	1	3	1	—	—	—	—	—
97-98—Tampa Bay	NHL	68	8	14	22	62	-9	2	0	—	—	—	—	—
98-99—Cleveland	IHL	4	1	1	2	18	-4	1	0	—	—	—	—	—
—Tampa Bay	NHL	22	4	6	10	15	0	1	0	—	—	—	—	—
—Philadelphia	NHL	56	10	13	23	24	-8	3	1	6	0	2	2	2
99-00—Philadelphia	NHL	82	18	32	50	56	1	5	0	16	5	5	10	23
00-01—Philadelphia	NHL	71	13	41	54	50	12	3	0	6	2	4	6	2
01-02—Phoenix	NHL	80	27	35	62	36	18	6	3	5	1	0	1	0
02-03—Phoenix	NHL	82	20	32	52	56	20	4	2	—	—	—	—	—
03-04—Phoenix	NHL	81	21	31	52	40	4	4	1	—	—	—	—	—
05-06—Calgary	NHL	82	25	34	59	46	2	11	0	7	1	5	6	6
NHL Totals (10 years)		707	161	252	413	420	40	42	8	40	9	16	25	33

L

LAPERRIERE, IAN — C/RW

PERSONAL: Born January 19, 1974, in Montreal. ... 6-1/201. ... Shoots right. ... Name pronounced EE-ihn luh-PAIR-ee-AIR.

TRANSACTIONS/CAREER NOTES: Selected by St. Louis Blues in seventh round (sixth Blues pick, 158th overall) of NHL draft (June 20, 1992). ... Concussion (March 26, 1995); missed three games. ... Traded by Blues to New York Rangers for LW Stephane Matteau (December 28, 1995). ... Traded by Rangers with C Ray Ferraro, C Nathan LaFayette, D Mattias Norstrom and fourth-round pick (D Sean Blanchard) in 1997 entry draft to Los Angeles Kings for RW Shane Churla, LW Jari Kurri and D/RW Marty McSorley (March 14, 1996). ... Sprained left shoulder (March 16, 1996); missed two games. ... Strained shoulder (October 29, 1996); missed three games. ... Strained hip flexor (February 1, 1997); missed three games. ... Concussion (February 25, 1997); missed two games. ... Shoulder surgery (March 17, 1997); missed final 11 games of regular season. ... Blurred vision (December 31, 1997); missed three games. ... Tore knee ligament (October 12, 1998); missed nine games. ... Inflamed left knee (January 2, 1999); missed one game. ... Sprained knee (December 30, 1999); missed three games. ... Strained hip flexor (October 15, 2000); missed one game. ... Concussion (April 3, 2001); missed two games. ... Cervical strain (November 27, 2002); missed four games. ... Injured back (January 18, 2003); missed one game. ... Injured right knee and had surgery (February 3, 2003); missed three games. ... Concussion (November 27, 2003); missed 19 games. ... Signed as free agent by Colorado Avalanche (July 2, 2004).

STATISTICAL PLATEAUS: Three-goal games: 2000-01 (1).

		REGULAR SEASON								PLAYOFFS				
Season Team	League	GP	G	A	Pts.	PIM	+/-	PP	SH	GP	G	A	Pts.	PIM
90-91—Drummondville	QMJHL	65	19	29	48	117	...	...	...	—	—	—	—	—
91-92—Drummondville	QMJHL	70	28	49	77	160	...	...	...	—	—	—	—	—
92-93—Drummondville	QMJHL	60	44	96	140	188	...	...	...	10	6	13	19	20
93-94—Drummondville	QMJHL	62	41	72	113	150	17	13	1	9	4	6	10	35
—St. Louis	NHL	1	0	0	0	0	0	0	0	—	—	—	—	—
—Peoria	IHL	...	...	...	...	...	...	...	...	5	1	3	4	2
94-95—Peoria	IHL	51	16	32	48	111	11	5	1	—	—	—	—	—
—St. Louis	NHL	37	13	14	27	85	12	1	0	7	0	4	4	21
95-96—St. Louis	NHL	33	3	6	9	87	-4	1	0	—	—	—	—	—
—Worcester	AHL	3	2	1	3	22	...	...	...	—	—	—	—	—
—New York Rangers	NHL	28	1	2	3	53	-5	0	0	—	—	—	—	—
—Los Angeles	NHL	10	2	3	5	15	-2	0	0	—	—	—	—	—
96-97—Los Angeles	NHL	62	8	15	23	102	-25	0	1	—	—	—	—	—
97-98—Los Angeles	NHL	77	6	15	21	131	0	0	1	4	1	0	1	6
98-99—Los Angeles	NHL	72	3	10	13	138	-5	0	0	—	—	—	—	—
99-00—Los Angeles	NHL	79	9	13	22	185	-14	0	0	4	0	0	0	2
00-01—Los Angeles	NHL	79	8	10	18	141	5	0	0	13	1	2	3	12
01-02—Los Angeles	NHL	81	8	14	22	125	5	0	0	7	0	1	1	9
02-03—Los Angeles	NHL	73	7	12	19	122	-9	1	1	—	—	—	—	—
03-04—Los Angeles	NHL	62	10	12	22	58	-4	1	0	—	—	—	—	—
05-06—Colorado	NHL	82	21	24	45	116	3	1	1	9	0	1	1	27
NHL Totals (12 years)		776	99	150	249	1358	-43	5	4	44	2	8	10	77

LAPIERRE, MAXIM — C

PERSONAL: Born March 29, 1985, in St. Leonard, Que. ... 6-2/174. ... Shoots right.

TRANSACTIONS/CAREER NOTES: Selected by Montreal Canadiens in second round (third Canadiens pick, 61st overall) of NHL entry draft (June 20, 2003).

Season Team	League	GP	G	A	Pts.	PIM	+/-	PP	SH	GP	G	A	Pts.	PIM
		REGULAR SEASON								PLAYOFFS				
01-02—Montreal	QMJHL	9	2	0	2	2	...	...	...	—	—	—	—	—
02-03—Montreal	QMJHL	72	22	21	43	55	...	...	...	7	1	3	4	6
03-04—PEI	QMJHL	67	25	36	61	138	10	3	2	11	7	2	9	14
04-05—PEI	QMJHL	69	25	27	52	139	...	...	...	—	—	—	—	—
05-06—Hamilton	AHL	73	13	23	36	214	0	0	2	—	—	—	—	—
—Montreal	NHL	1	0	0	0	0	-1	0	0	—	—	—	—	—
NHL Totals (1 year)		1	0	0	0	0	-1	0	0					

LAPOINTE, MARTIN RW

PERSONAL: Born September 12, 1973, in Ville Ste-Pierre, Que. ... 5-11/215. ... Shoots right. ... Name pronounced MAHR-tahn luh-POYNT.
TRANSACTIONS/CAREER NOTES: Selected by Detroit Red Wings in first round (first Red Wings pick, 10th overall) of entry draft (June 22, 1991). ... Fractured wrist (October 9, 1991); missed 22 games. ... Injured left knee (February 29, 1996); missed eight games. ... Injured leg (April 10, 1996); missed two games. ... Fractured finger (December 1, 1996); missed four games. ... Strained hamstring (February 25, 1998); missed one game. ... Suspended two games and fined $1,000 for cross-checking incident (March 18, 1998). ... Back spasms (December 22, 1998); missed one game. ... Bruised knee (February 12, 1999); missed three games. ... Signed as free agent by Boston Bruins (July 2, 2001). ... Strained hamstring (January 30, 2002); missed seven games. ... Reinjured hamstring (March 6, 2002); missed five games. ... Injured hamstring (February 5, 2003); missed seven games. ... Injured hamstring (March 8, 2003); missed five games. ... Had offseason knee surgery; missed first three games of 2003-04 season. ... Suspended one game for high-sticking incident (December 29, 2003). ... Signed as free agent by Chicago Blackhawks (August 4, 2005).
STATISTICAL PLATEAUS: Three-goal games: 1999-00 (1), 2002-03 (1). Total: 2.

Season Team	League	GP	G	A	Pts.	PIM	+/-	PP	SH	GP	G	A	Pts.	PIM
		REGULAR SEASON								PLAYOFFS				
89-90—Laval	QMJHL	65	42	54	96	77	...	...	...	14	8	17	25	54
90-91—Laval	QMJHL	64	44	54	98	66	...	...	...	13	7	14	21	26
91-92—Detroit	NHL	4	0	1	1	5	2	0	0	3	0	1	1	4
—Laval	QMJHL	31	25	30	55	84	...	...	...	10	4	10	14	32
—Adirondack	AHL	...	...	...	...	...	...	...	...	8	2	2	4	4
92-93—Adirondack	AHL	8	1	2	3	9	1	0	0	—	—	—	—	—
—Detroit	NHL	3	0	0	0	0	-2	0	0	—	—	—	—	—
—Laval	QMJHL	35	38	51	89	41	...	...	...	13	13	17	30	22
93-94—Adirondack	AHL	28	25	21	46	47	13	14	0	4	1	1	2	8
—Detroit	NHL	50	8	8	16	55	7	2	0	4	0	0	0	6
94-95—Adirondack	AHL	39	29	16	45	80	12	10	5	—	—	—	—	—
—Detroit	NHL	39	4	6	10	73	1	0	0	2	0	1	1	8
95-96—Detroit	NHL	58	6	3	9	93	0	1	0	11	1	2	3	12
96-97—Detroit	NHL	78	16	17	33	167	-14	5	1	20	4	8	12	60
97-98—Detroit	NHL	79	15	19	34	106	0	4	0	21	9	6	15	20
98-99—Detroit	NHL	77	16	13	29	141	7	7	1	10	0	2	2	20
99-00—Detroit	NHL	82	16	25	41	121	17	1	1	9	3	1	4	20
00-01—Detroit	NHL	82	27	30	57	127	3	13	0	6	0	1	1	8
01-02—Boston	NHL	68	17	23	40	101	12	4	0	6	1	2	3	12
02-03—Boston	NHL	59	8	10	18	87	-19	1	0	5	1	0	1	14
03-04—Boston	NHL	78	15	10	25	67	-5	9	0	7	0	0	0	14
05-06—Chicago	NHL	82	14	17	31	106	-30	6	0	—	—	—	—	—
NHL Totals (14 years)		839	162	182	344	1249	-21	53	3	104	19	24	43	198

LARAQUE, GEORGES RW

PERSONAL: Born December 7, 1976, in Montreal. ... 6-3/245. ... Shoots right. ... Name pronounced zhawrzh la-RAHK.
TRANSACTIONS/CAREER NOTES: Selected by Edmonton Oilers in second round (second Oilers pick, 31st overall) of entry draft (July 8, 1995). ... Fractured left foot (November 17, 1997); missed five games. ... Right knee (December 5, 1997); missed seven games. ... Suspended two games by AHL for checking from behind (October 21, 1998). ... Bruised sternum (January 17, 1999); missed two games. ... Sprained ankle (March 24, 1999); missed three games. ... Concussion (April 1, 1999); missed three games. ... Eye (December 19, 1999); missed two games. ... Sprained knee (March 27, 2000); missed one game. ... Tendinitis in right forearm (January 18, 2002); missed two games. ... Sprained left wrist (November 8, 2002); missed five games. ... Elbow (November 30, 2002); missed five games. ... Knee (January 18, 2003); missed six games. ... Shoulder (February 22, 2003); missed one game. ... Thumb (October 30, 2003); missed 1 game. ... Reinjured thumb (November 4, 2003); missed two games. ... Thumb (November 11, 2005); missed one game. ... Hip flexor (March 28, 2006); missed two games. ... Hip flexor (April 3, 2006); missed five games. ... Signed as free agent by Phoenix Coyotes (July 5, 2006).
STATISTICAL PLATEAUS: Three-goal games: 1999-00 (1).

Season Team	League	GP	G	A	Pts.	PIM	+/-	PP	SH	GP	G	A	Pts.	PIM
		REGULAR SEASON								PLAYOFFS				
93-94—St. Jean	QMJHL	70	11	11	22	142	...	...	...	4	0	0	0	7
94-95—St. Jean	QMJHL	62	19	22	41	259	-1	8	0	7	1	1	2	42
95-96—Laval	QMJHL	11	8	13	21	76	...	...	...	—	—	—	—	—
—St. Hyacinthe	QMJHL	8	3	4	7	59	...	...	...	—	—	—	—	—
—Granby	QMJHL	22	9	7	16	125	...	...	...	18	7	6	13	104
96-97—Hamilton	AHL	73	14	20	34	179	-11	6	0	15	1	3	4	12
97-98—Hamilton	AHL	46	10	20	30	154	6	2	0	3	0	0	0	11
—Edmonton	NHL	11	0	0	0	59	-4	0	0	—	—	—	—	—
98-99—Hamilton	AHL	25	6	8	14	93	-2	0	0	—	—	—	—	—
—Edmonton	NHL	39	3	2	5	57	-1	0	0	4	0	0	0	2
99-00—Edmonton	NHL	76	8	8	16	123	5	0	0	5	0	1	1	6
00-01—Edmonton	NHL	82	13	16	29	148	5	1	0	6	1	1	2	8
01-02—Edmonton	NHL	80	5	14	19	157	6	1	0	—	—	—	—	—
02-03—Edmonton	NHL	64	6	7	13	110	-4	0	0	6	1	3	4	4

Season Team	League	REGULAR SEASON GP	G	A	Pts.	PIM	+/-	PP	SH	PLAYOFFS GP	G	A	Pts.	PIM
03-04—Edmonton	NHL	66	6	11	17	99	7	1	0	—	—	—	—	—
04-05—AIK Solna	Sweden Dv. 2	16	11	5	16	24	...	...	...	—	—	—	—	—
05-06—Edmonton	NHL	72	2	10	12	73	-5	0	0	15	1	1	2	*44
NHL Totals (8 years)		490	43	68	111	826	9	3	0	36	3	6	9	64

LAROSE, CHAD RW

PERSONAL: Born March 27, 1982, in Fraser, Mich. ... 5-10/173. ... Shoots right.
TRANSACTIONS/CAREER NOTES: Signed as undrafted free agent by Carolina Hurricanes (August 6, 2003).

Season Team	League	REGULAR SEASON GP	G	A	Pts.	PIM	+/-	PP	SH	PLAYOFFS GP	G	A	Pts.	PIM
99-00—Sioux Falls	USHL	54	29	26	55	28	...	...	...	3	0	1	1	0
00-01—Plymouth	OHL	32	18	7	25	24	...	...	...	19	10	10	20	22
—Sioux Falls	USHL	24	11	22	33	50	...	...	...	—	—	—	—	—
01-02—Plymouth	OHL	53	32	27	59	40	...	...	...	6	3	4	7	16
02-03—Plymouth	OHL	67	61	56	117	52	...	...	...	...	...	...	...	...
03-04—Lowell	AHL	36	7	9	16	29	...	...	...	—	—	—	—	—
—Florida	ECHL	41	16	19	35	16	...	...	...	14	3	4	7	20
04-05—Lowell	AHL	66	20	22	42	32	10	10	2	11	3	5	8	10
05-06—Lowell	AHL	23	14	11	25	10	11	4	3	—	—	—	—	—
—Carolina	NHL	49	1	12	13	35	7	0	0	21	0	1	1	10
NHL Totals (1 year)		49	1	12	13	35	7	0	0	21	0	1	1	10

LARSEN, BRAD LW

PERSONAL: Born January 28, 1977, in Nakusp, B.C. ... 6-0/200. ... Shoots left.
TRANSACTIONS/CAREER NOTES: Selected by Ottawa Senators in third round (third Senators pick, 53rd overall) of entry draft (July 8, 1995). ... Rights traded by Senators to Colorado Avalanche for D Janne Laukkanen (January 25, 1996). ... Returned to draft pool by Avalanche; selected by Avalanche in fourth round (fifth Avalanche pick, 87th overall) of entry draft (June 21, 1997). ... Injured ribs (December 27, 2001); missed 11 games. ... Strained back (April 1, 2002); missed four games. ... Injured groin (October 27, 2002); missed 18 games. ... Injured back (December 10, 2002); missed 28 games. ... Injured groin (October 26, 2003); missed four games. ... Reinjured groin (November 11, 2003); missed six games. ... Reinjured groin (February 14, 2004); missed seven games. ... Claimed on waivers by Atlanta Thrashers (February 25, 2004). ... Bruised ribs (March 5, 2004); missed 12 games. ... Strained groin (December 17, 2005); missed 11 games.

Season Team	League	REGULAR SEASON GP	G	A	Pts.	PIM	+/-	PP	SH	PLAYOFFS GP	G	A	Pts.	PIM
92-93—Nelson	Tier II Jr. A	42	31	37	68	164	...	...	...	—	—	—	—	—
93-94—Swift Current	WHL	64	15	18	33	37	...	...	...	7	1	2	3	4
94-95—Swift Current	WHL	62	24	33	57	73	-18	7	0	6	0	1	1	2
95-96—Swift Current	WHL	51	30	47	77	67	...	...	...	6	3	2	5	13
96-97—Swift Current	WHL	61	36	46	82	61	27	11	2	—	—	—	—	—
97-98—Hershey	AHL	65	12	10	22	80	-6	3	0	7	3	2	5	2
—Colorado	NHL	1	0	0	0	0	0	0	0	—	—	—	—	—
98-99—Hershey	AHL	18	3	4	7	11	-4	1	0	5	1	0	1	6
99-00—Hershey	AHL	52	13	26	39	66	...	...	...	14	5	2	7	29
00-01—Hershey	AHL	67	21	25	46	93	...	...	...	10	1	3	4	6
—Colorado	NHL	9	0	0	0	0	1	0	0	—	—	—	—	—
01-02—Colorado	NHL	50	2	7	9	47	4	1	0	21	1	1	2	13
02-03—Colorado	NHL	6	0	3	3	2	3	0	0	—	—	—	—	—
—Hershey	AHL	25	3	6	9	25	-5	1	0	4	1	1	2	8
03-04—Colorado	NHL	26	2	2	4	11	2	0	0	—	—	—	—	—
—Hershey	AHL	21	4	13	17	40	9	2	0	—	—	—	—	—
—Atlanta	NHL	6	0	0	0	2	-2	0	0	—	—	—	—	—
04-05—Chicago	AHL	75	26	23	49	112	9	10	1	18	4	7	11	22
05-06—Atlanta	NHL	62	7	8	15	21	-3	0	3	—	—	—	—	—
NHL Totals (6 years)		160	11	20	31	83	5	1	3	21	1	1	2	13

LEACH, JAY D

PERSONAL: Born September 2, 1979, in Syracuse, N.Y. ... 6-3/202. ... Shoots left. ... Nephew of Steve Leach, RW with seven NHL teams (1985 through 2000).
COLLEGE: Providence College.
TRANSACTIONS/CAREER NOTES: Selected by Phoenix Coyotes in fifth round (fifth Coyotes pick, 115th overall) of entry draft (June 27, 1998). ... Signed as free agent by Boston Bruins (September 26, 2003).

Season Team	League	REGULAR SEASON GP	G	A	Pts.	PIM	+/-	PP	SH	PLAYOFFS GP	G	A	Pts.	PIM
96-97—Capital District (N.Y.)	Jr. A	57	8	50	58	140	...	...	...	—	—	—	—	—
97-98—Providence College	Hockey East	32	0	8	8	33	...	...	...	—	—	—	—	—
98-99—Providence College	Hockey East	33	1	8	9	42	...	...	...	—	—	—	—	—
99-00—Providence College	Hockey East	37	1	9	10	101	...	...	...	—	—	—	—	—
00-01—Providence College	Hockey East	40	4	21	25	104	...	...	...	—	—	—	—	—
01-02—Mississippi	ECHL	70	3	13	16	116	9	0	1	10	1	1	2	8
02-03—Springfield	AHL	9	0	0	0	0	-4	0	0	—	—	—	—	—
—Augusta	ECHL	65	8	11	19	162	4	2	0	—	—	—	—	—
03-04—Providence	AHL	3	0	0	0	4	...	...	...	—	—	—	—	—
—Bridgeport	AHL	23	0	1	1	33	...	...	...	7	0	1	1	10

		REGULAR SEASON								PLAYOFFS				
Season Team	League	GP	G	A	Pts.	PIM	+/-	PP	SH	GP	G	A	Pts.	PIM
—Trenton	ECHL	31	2	11	13	45	...	...	...	—	—	—	—	—
—Long Beach	ECHL	3	0	1	1	4	...	...	...	—	—	—	—	—
04-05—Trenton	ECHL	11	0	2	2	17	...	...	...	—	—	—	—	—
—Providence	AHL	62	4	5	9	92	5	0	0	17	0	0	0	28
05-06—Providence	AHL	71	5	11	16	100	12	0	1	6	0	1	1	15
—Boston	NHL	2	0	0	0	7	1	0	0	—	—	—	—	—
NHL Totals (1 year)		2	0	0	0	7	1	0	0					

LEAHY, PAT — RW

PERSONAL: Born June 9, 1979, in Brighton, Mass. ... 6-3/200. ... Shoots right.
TRANSACTIONS/CAREER NOTES: Selected by New York Rangers in fifth round (fifth Rangers pick, 122nd overall) of entry draft (June 27, 1998). ... Signed as free agent by Boston Bruins (July 28, 2003). ... Signed as free agent by Providence of the AHL (October 1, 2004). ... Broken finger (November 1, 2005); missed 22 games. ... Signed as free agent by Nashville Predators (July 17, 2006).

		REGULAR SEASON								PLAYOFFS				
Season Team	League	GP	G	A	Pts.	PIM	+/-	PP	SH	GP	G	A	Pts.	PIM
97-98—Miami (Ohio)	CCHA	28	0	1	1	24	...	...	...	—	—	—	—	—
98-99—Miami (Ohio)	CCHA	34	10	20	30	40	...	...	...	—	—	—	—	—
99-00—Miami (Ohio)	CCHA	36	16	22	38	89	...	...	...	—	—	—	—	—
00-01—Miami (Ohio)	CCHA	37	13	19	32	52	...	...	...	—	—	—	—	—
01-02—Trenton	ECHL	41	20	21	41	64	9	7	2	—	—	—	—	—
—Hershey	AHL	9	1	2	3	8	-1	0	0	—	—	—	—	—
—Portland	AHL	9	1	1	2	8	2	0	0	—	—	—	—	—
—Bridgeport	AHL	14	2	2	4	2	4	0	0	20	3	4	7	4
02-03—Providence	AHL	66	20	23	43	63	14	5	1	—	—	—	—	—
03-04—Boston	NHL	6	0	0	0	0	1	0	0	—	—	—	—	—
—Providence	AHL	55	14	16	30	37	3	6	2	2	0	0	0	0
04-05—Providence	AHL	38	1	14	15	18	2	0	0	17	4	6	10	20
05-06—Providence	AHL	4	1	2	3	4	1	1	0	—	—	—	—	—
—Boston	NHL	43	4	4	8	19	-2	0	0	—	—	—	—	—
NHL Totals (2 years)		49	4	4	8	19	-1	0	0					

LEBDA, BRETT — D

PERSONAL: Born January 15, 1982, in Buffalo Grove, Ill. ... 5-10/195. ... Shoots left.
TRANSACTIONS/CAREER NOTES: Signed as free agent by Detroit Red Wings (April 2, 2004).

		REGULAR SEASON								PLAYOFFS				
Season Team	League	GP	G	A	Pts.	PIM	+/-	PP	SH	GP	G	A	Pts.	PIM
98-99—U.S. National	USHL	3	0	0	0	0	...	...	...	—	—	—	—	—
99-00—U.S. National	USHL	22	6	7	13	28	...	...	...	—	—	—	—	—
00-01—Notre Dame	CCHA	39	7	19	26	109	...	...	...	—	—	—	—	—
—Chicago	USHL	1	0	0	0	0	...	...	...	—	—	—	—	—
01-02—Notre Dame	CCHA	34	6	8	14	54	...	...	...	—	—	—	—	—
02-03—Notre Dame	CCHA	40	7	14	21	48	...	...	...	—	—	—	—	—
03-04—Notre Dame	CCHA	39	6	18	24	42	...	...	...	—	—	—	—	—
—Grand Rapids	AHL	6	0	1	1	0	...	...	...	4	0	0	0	2
04-05—Grand Rapids	AHL	80	2	10	12	34	-1	0	0	—	—	—	—	—
05-06—Grand Rapids	AHL	25	4	14	18	42	13	2	0	11	1	4	5	8
—Detroit	NHL	46	3	9	12	20	9	1	0	6	0	0	0	4
NHL Totals (1 year)		46	3	9	12	20	9	1	0	6	0	0	0	4

LECAVALIER, VINCENT — C

PERSONAL: Born April 21, 1980, in Ile-Bizard, Que. ... 6-4/207. ... Shoots left.
TRANSACTIONS/CAREER NOTES: Selected by Tampa Bay Lightning in first round (first Lightning pick, first overall) of entry draft (June 27, 1998). ... Injured ankle (April 6, 2000); missed final two games of season. ... Fractured left foot (January 12, 2001); missed 14 games. ... Fractured left ankle (February 9, 2002); missed four games. ... Sprained knee (October 21, 2002); missed two games. ... Suspended one game for kicking incident (January 11, 2004). ... Suspended one game (forfeiting $35,076.53) for high-sticking incident with Rangers C Dominic Moore (December 22, 2005). ... Upper-body injury (January 31, 2006); missed one game.
STATISTICAL PLATEAUS: Three-goal games: 2002-03 (2), 2003-04 (1). Total: 3.

		REGULAR SEASON								PLAYOFFS				
Season Team	League	GP	G	A	Pts.	PIM	+/-	PP	SH	GP	G	A	Pts.	PIM
95-96—Notre Dame	SJHL	22	52	52	104	...	...	...	...	—	—	—	—	—
96-97—Rimouski	QMJHL	64	42	60	102	36	...	...	...	4	4	3	7	2
97-98—Rimouski	QMJHL	58	44	71	115	117	...	...	...	18	15	26	41	46
98-99—Tampa Bay	NHL	82	13	15	28	23	-19	2	0	—	—	—	—	—
99-00—Tampa Bay	NHL	80	25	42	67	43	-25	6	0	—	—	—	—	—
00-01—Tampa Bay	NHL	68	23	28	51	66	-26	7	0	—	—	—	—	—
01-02—Tampa Bay	NHL	76	20	17	37	61	-18	5	0	—	—	—	—	—
02-03—Tampa Bay	NHL	80	33	45	78	39	0	11	2	11	3	3	6	22
03-04—Tampa Bay	NHL	81	32	34	66	52	23	5	2	23	9	7	16	25
04-05—Ak Bars Kazan	Russian	30	7	9	16	78	4	...	...	4	1	0	1	6
05-06—Tampa Bay	NHL	80	35	40	75	90	0	13	2	5	1	3	4	7
—Canadian Oly. team	Int'l	6	0	3	3	16	2	0	0	—	—	—	—	—
NHL Totals (7 years)		547	181	221	402	374	-65	49	6	39	13	13	26	54

LECLAIR, JOHN LW

PERSONAL: Born July 5, 1969, in St. Albans, Vt. ... 6-3/225. ... Shoots left.

TRANSACTIONS/CAREER NOTES: Selected by Montreal Canadiens in second round (second Canadiens pick, 33rd overall) of entry draft (June 13, 1987). ... Injured shoulder (January 15, 1992); missed four games. ... Charley horse (January 20, 1993); missed four games. ... Sprained knee (October 2, 1993); missed eight games. ... Bruised sternum (March 28, 1994); missed two games. ... Traded by Canadiens with LW Gilbert Dionne and D Eric Desjardins to Philadelphia Flyers for RW Mark Recchi and third-round pick (C Martin Hohenberger) in 1995 entry draft (February 9, 1995). ... Strained right hip (April 18, 1995); missed one playoff game. ... Strained hip flexor (March 9, 1999); missed four games. ... Back spasms (April 1, 1999); missed two games. ... Injured back (October 9, 2000); missed 20 games. ... Strained lower back (December 9, 2000); missed 46 games. ... Dislocated right shoulder (November 29, 2002), required surgery; missed 47 games. ... Fractured left foot (October 8, 2003); missed seven games. ... Contract bought out by Flyers (July 23, 2005). ... Signed as free agent by Pittsburgh Penguins (August 15, 2005). ... Facial cuts (November 5, 2005); missed three games. ... Groin (December 8, 2005); missed five games.

STATISTICAL PLATEAUS: Three-goal games: 1994-95 (2), 1995-96 (2), 1996-97 (1), 1997-98 (1), 1998-99 (1), 2000-01 (1). Total: 8. ... Four-goal games: 1996-97 (1), 1998-99 (1), 2002-03 (1). Total: 3. ... Total hat tricks: 11.

		REGULAR SEASON								PLAYOFFS				
Season Team	League	GP	G	A	Pts.	PIM	+/-	PP	SH	GP	G	A	Pts.	PIM
85-86—Bellows Free Acad.	VT. H.S.	22	41	28	69	14	...	...	...	—	—	—	—	—
86-87—Bellows Free Acad.	VT. H.S.	23	44	40	84	25	...	...	...	—	—	—	—	—
87-88—Vermont	ECAC	31	12	22	34	62	...	...	...	—	—	—	—	—
88-89—Vermont	ECAC	19	9	12	21	40	...	...	...	—	—	—	—	—
89-90—Vermont	ECAC	10	10	6	16	38	...	...	...	—	—	—	—	—
90-91—Vermont	ECAC	33	25	20	45	58	...	...	...	—	—	—	—	—
—Montreal	NHL	10	2	5	7	2	1	0	0	3	0	0	0	0
91-92—Montreal	NHL	59	8	11	19	14	5	3	0	8	1	1	2	4
—Fredericton	AHL	8	7	7	14	10	...	...	...	2	0	0	0	4
92-93—Montreal	NHL	72	19	25	44	33	11	2	0	20	4	6	10	14
93-94—Montreal	NHL	74	19	24	43	32	17	1	0	7	2	1	3	8
94-95—Montreal	NHL	9	1	4	5	10	-1	1	0	—	—	—	—	—
—Philadelphia	NHL	37	25	24	49	20	21	5	0	15	5	7	12	4
95-96—Philadelphia	NHL	82	51	46	97	64	21	19	0	11	6	5	11	6
96-97—Philadelphia	NHL	82	50	47	97	58	*44	10	0	19	9	12	21	10
97-98—Philadelphia	NHL	82	51	36	87	32	30	16	0	5	1	1	2	8
—U.S. Olympic team	Int'l	4	0	1	1	0	-2	0	0	—	—	—	—	—
98-99—Philadelphia	NHL	76	43	47	90	30	36	16	0	6	3	0	3	12
99-00—Philadelphia	NHL	82	40	37	77	36	8	13	0	18	6	7	13	6
00-01—Philadelphia	NHL	16	7	5	12	0	2	3	0	6	1	2	3	2
01-02—Philadelphia	NHL	82	25	26	51	30	5	4	0	5	0	0	0	2
—U.S. Olympic team	Int'l	6	6	1	7	2	...	...	...	—	—	—	—	—
02-03—Philadelphia	NHL	35	18	10	28	16	10	8	0	13	2	3	5	10
03-04—Philadelphia	NHL	75	23	32	55	51	20	8	0	18	2	2	4	8
05-06—Pittsburgh	NHL	73	22	29	51	61	-24	8	1	—	—	—	—	—
NHL Totals (15 years)		946	404	408	812	489	206	117	1	154	42	47	89	94

LECLAIRE, PASCAL G

PERSONAL: Born November 7, 1982, in Repentigny, Que. ... 6-2/190. ... Catches left.

TRANSACTIONS/CAREER NOTES: Selected by Columbus Blue Jackets in first round (first Blue Jackets pick, eighth overall) of entry draft (June 23, 2001). ... Back (February 6, 2006); missed three games.

		REGULAR SEASON										PLAYOFFS							
Season Team	League	GP	Min.	W	L	OTL	T	GA	SO	GAA	SV%	GP	Min.	W	L	GA	SO	GAA	SV%
98-99—Halifax	QMJHL	33	1828	19	11	...	1	96	2	3.15	...	1	17	0	0	2	0	7.06	...
99-00—Halifax	QMJHL	31	1729	16	8	...	4	103	1	3.57	...	5	198	1	2	12	0	3.64	...
00-01—Halifax	QMJHL	33	2111	14	16	...	5	126	1	3.58	...	2	109	0	2	10	0	5.50	...
01-02—Montreal	QMJHL	45	2513	15	23	...	4	138	1	3.29	...	—	—	—	—	—	—	—	—
02-03—Syracuse	AHL	36	1886	8	21	...	3	112	0	3.56	.890	—	—	—	—	—	—	—	—
03-04—Syracuse	AHL	44	2446	21	16	...	3	125	2	3.07	.907	3	142	1	2	12	0	5.07	.842
—Columbus	NHL	2	119	0	2	...	0	7	0	3.53	.899	—	—	—	—	—	—	—	—
04-05—Syracuse	AHL	14	844	5	6	...	...	33	2	2.35	.926	—	—	—	—	—	—	—	—
05-06—Syracuse	AHL	7	340	3	3	0	...	16	1	2.82	.920	5	288	2	3	11	1	2.29	.939
—Columbus	NHL	33	1804	11	15	3	...	97	0	3.23	.911	—	—	—	—	—	—	—	—
NHL Totals (2 years)		35	1923	11	17	3	0	104	0	3.24	.910								

LECLERC, MIKE LW/RW

PERSONAL: Born November 10, 1976, in Winnipeg. ... 6-2/208. ... Shoots left. ... Name pronounced luh-KLAIR.

TRANSACTIONS/CAREER NOTES: Selected by Anaheim Mighty Ducks in third round (third Mighty Ducks pick, 55th overall) of entry draft (July 8, 1995). ... Elbow surgery (October 29, 1999); missed 11 games. ... Elbow (December 17, 1999); missed two games. ... Knee (December 28, 2000); missed 15 games. ... Strained abdominal muscle (March 11, 2001); missed remainder of season. ... Right elbow (November 12, 2002); missed two games. ... Left knee (November 15, 2002); missed 11 games. ... Sore knee (January 3, 2003); missed 10 games. ... Sore knee (February 25, 2003); missed one game. ... Knee surgery (September 10, 2003); missed season's first 55 games. ... Reinjured knee (February 29, 2004); missed season's final 17 games. ... Traded by Mighty Ducks to Phoenix Coyotes for conditional pick in 2007 draft (August 23, 2005). ... Left knee (December 15, 2005); missed 18 games. ... Traded by Coyotes to Calgary Flames with G Brian Boucher for C Steve Reinprecht and G Philippe Sauve (February 1, 2006) ... Broken wrist (March 18, 2006); missed 13 games.

		REGULAR SEASON								PLAYOFFS				
Season Team	League	GP	G	A	Pts.	PIM	+/-	PP	SH	GP	G	A	Pts.	PIM
91-92—St. Boniface	Tier II Jr. A	43	16	12	28	25	...	...	...	—	—	—	—	—
—Victoria	WHL	2	0	0	0	0	...	...	...	—	—	—	—	—

Season Team	League	REGULAR SEASON GP	G	A	Pts.	PIM	+/-	PP	SH	PLAYOFFS GP	G	A	Pts.	PIM
92-93—Victoria	WHL	70	4	11	15	118	...	...	...	—	—	—	—	—
93-94—Victoria	WHL	68	29	11	40	112	...	...	...	—	—	—	—	—
94-95—Prince George	WHL	43	20	36	56	78	-13	6	1	—	—	—	—	—
—Brandon	WHL	23	5	8	13	50	3	1	0	18	10	6	16	33
95-96—Brandon	WHL	71	58	53	111	161	...	...	...	19	6	19	25	25
96-97—Baltimore	AHL	71	29	27	56	134	-10	11	0	—	—	—	—	—
—Anaheim	NHL	5	1	1	2	0	2	0	0	1	0	0	0	0
97-98—Cincinnati	AHL	48	18	22	40	83	-1	7	0	—	—	—	—	—
—Anaheim	NHL	7	0	0	0	6	-6	0	0	—	—	—	—	—
98-99—Cincinnati	AHL	65	25	28	53	153	12	13	0	3	0	1	1	19
—Anaheim	NHL	7	0	0	0	4	-2	0	0	1	0	0	0	0
99-00—Anaheim	NHL	69	8	11	19	70	-15	0	0	—	—	—	—	—
00-01—Anaheim	NHL	54	15	20	35	26	-1	3	0	—	—	—	—	—
01-02—Anaheim	NHL	82	20	24	44	107	-12	8	0	—	—	—	—	—
02-03—Anaheim	NHL	57	9	19	28	34	-8	1	0	21	2	9	11	12
03-04—Anaheim	NHL	10	1	3	4	4	-1	0	0	—	—	—	—	—
05-06—Phoenix	NHL	35	9	12	21	29	0	4	0	—	—	—	—	—
—Calgary	NHL	15	1	4	5	8	0	0	0	3	0	0	0	2
NHL Totals (9 years)		341	64	94	158	288	-43	16	0	26	2	9	11	14

LEETCH, BRIAN D

PERSONAL: Born March 3, 1968, in Corpus Christi, Texas. ... 6-1/190. ... Shoots left.

TRANSACTIONS/CAREER NOTES: Selected by New York Rangers in first round (first Rangers pick, ninth overall) of entry draft (June 21, 1986). ... Fractured left foot (December 1988). ... Hip pointer (March 15, 1989). ... Fractured left ankle (March 14, 1990). ... Ankle (November 21, 1992); missed one game. ... Stretched nerve in neck (December 17, 1992); missed 34 games. ... Fractured ankle (March 19, 1993) and had surgery; missed remainder of season. ... Nerve compression in right leg (January 4, 1998); missed two games. ... Head (April 5, 1998); missed four games. ... Fractured arm (November 24, 1999); missed 32 games. ... Injured ankle (December 3, 2002); missed 31 games. ... Traded by Rangers to Edmonton Oilers for G Jussi Markkanen and a fourth-round pick (traded to Toronto; Maple Leafs selected Roman Kukumberg) in 2004 draft (June 30, 2003). ... Signed as free agent by Rangers (July 30, 2003). ... Ankle (September 10, 2003); missed nine games. ... Traded by Rangers with fourth-round pick (Roman Kukumberg) to Toronto Maple Leafs for D Maxim Kondratiev, F Jarkko Immonen, first-round pick (traded to Calgary; Flames chose RW Kris Chucko) in 2004 draft and second-round pick (Michael Sauer) in 2005 draft (March 3, 2004). ... Signed as free agent by Boston Bruins (August 3, 2005). ... Strained right knee (November 1, 2005); missed 10 games. ... Groin (January 14, 2006); missed seven games). ... Aggravated groin injury (February 2, 2006); missed three games. ... Head (April 1, 2006); missed one game.

Season Team	League	REGULAR SEASON GP	G	A	Pts.	PIM	+/-	PP	SH	PLAYOFFS GP	G	A	Pts.	PIM
84-85—Avon Old Farms H.S.	Conn. H.S.	26	30	46	76	15	...	...	...	—	—	—	—	—
85-86—Avon Old Farms H.S.	Conn. H.S.	28	40	44	84	18	...	...	...	—	—	—	—	—
86-87—Boston College	Hockey East	37	9	38	47	10	...	...	...	—	—	—	—	—
87-88—U.S. national team	Int'l	60	13	61	74	38	...	...	...	—	—	—	—	—
—U.S. Olympic team	Int'l	6	1	5	6	4	2	...	...	—	—	—	—	—
—New York Rangers	NHL	17	2	12	14	0	5	1	0	—	—	—	—	—
88-89—New York Rangers	NHL	68	23	48	71	50	8	8	3	4	3	2	5	2
89-90—New York Rangers	NHL	72	11	45	56	26	-18	5	0	—	—	—	—	—
90-91—New York Rangers	NHL	80	16	72	88	42	2	6	0	6	1	3	4	0
91-92—New York Rangers	NHL	80	22	80	102	26	25	10	1	13	4	11	15	4
92-93—New York Rangers	NHL	36	6	30	36	26	2	2	1	—	—	—	—	—
93-94—New York Rangers	NHL	84	23	56	79	67	28	17	1	23	11	*23	*34	6
94-95—New York Rangers	NHL	48	9	32	41	18	0	3	0	10	6	8	14	8
95-96—New York Rangers	NHL	82	15	70	85	30	12	7	0	11	1	6	7	4
96-97—New York Rangers	NHL	82	20	58	78	40	31	9	0	15	2	8	10	6
97-98—New York Rangers	NHL	76	17	33	50	32	-36	11	0	—	—	—	—	—
—U.S. Olympic team	Int'l	4	1	1	2	0	-4	1	0	—	—	—	—	—
98-99—New York Rangers	NHL	82	13	42	55	42	-7	4	0	—	—	—	—	—
99-00—New York Rangers	NHL	50	7	19	26	20	-16	3	0	—	—	—	—	—
00-01—New York Rangers	NHL	82	21	58	79	34	-18	10	1	—	—	—	—	—
01-02—New York Rangers	NHL	82	10	45	55	28	14	1	0	—	—	—	—	—
—U.S. Olympic team	Int'l	6	0	5	5	0	...	...	...	—	—	—	—	—
02-03—New York Rangers	NHL	51	12	18	30	20	-3	5	0	—	—	—	—	—
03-04—New York Rangers	NHL	57	13	23	36	24	-5	4	1	—	—	—	—	—
—Toronto	NHL	15	2	13	15	10	11	1	0	13	0	8	8	6
05-06—Boston	NHL	61	5	27	32	36	-10	4	0	—	—	—	—	—
NHL Totals (18 years)		1205	247	781	1028	571	25	111	8	95	28	69	97	36

LEFEBVRE, GUILLAUME C

PERSONAL: Born May 7, 1981, in Amos, Que. ... 6-1/200. ... Shoots left. ... Name pronounced: gee-YOHM luh-FAYV

TRANSACTIONS/CAREER NOTES: Selected by Philadelphia Flyers in eighth round (sixth Flyers pick, 227th overall) of NHL entry draft (June 25, 2000). ... Traded by Flyers with third-round pick (C Tyler Redenbach) in 2003 entry draft and second-round pick (later traded to New York Rangers) in 2004 entry draft to Phoenix Coyotes for RW Tony Amonte (March 10, 2003). ... Traded by Coyotes with LW Ramzi Abid and D Dan Focht to Pittsburgh Penguins for C Jan Hrdina and D Francois Leroux (March 11, 2003). ... Signed as free agent by Wilkes-Barre/Scranton of the AHL (September 26, 2004).

Season Team	League	REGULAR SEASON GP	G	A	Pts.	PIM	+/-	PP	SH	PLAYOFFS GP	G	A	Pts.	PIM
98-99—Shawinigan	QMJHL	40	3	1	4	49	...	...	...	—	—	—	—	—
—Cape Breton	QMJHL	24	2	7	9	13	...	...	...	5	0	1	1	0

Season Team	League	GP	G	A	Pts.	PIM	+/-	PP	SH	GP	G	A	Pts.	PIM
		REGULAR SEASON								PLAYOFFS				
—Cape Breton	QMJHL	44	26	28	54	82	...	...	...	—	—	—	—	—
—Quebec	QMJHL	2	3	1	4	0	...	...	...	—	—	—	—	—
—Rouyn-Noranda	QMJHL	25	4	11	15	39	...	...	...	11	4	0	4	25
00-01—Rouyn-Noranda	QMJHL	61	24	43	67	160	...	...	...	9	3	1	4	22
01-02—Philadelphia	AHL	78	19	15	34	111	12	1	3	5	0	0	0	4
—Philadelphia	NHL	3	0	0	0	0	-1	0	0	—	—	—	—	—
02-03—Philadelphia	NHL	14	0	0	0	4	1	0	0	—	—	—	—	—
—Philadelphia	AHL	47	7	6	13	113	9	0	0	—	—	—	—	—
—Pittsburgh	NHL	12	2	4	6	0	1	0	0	—	—	—	—	—
—Wilkes-Barre/Scranton	AHL	1	1	0	1	0	2	0	0	5	0	0	0	6
03-04—Wilkes-Barre/Scranton	AHL	64	4	12	16	78	-4	0	0	14	1	0	1	19
04-05—Wilkes-Barre/Scranton	AHL	34	3	3	6	76	-5	0	0	11	1	0	1	23
05-06—Wilkes-Barre/Scranton	AHL	66	16	19	35	113	12	6	0	8	0	2	2	14
—Pittsburgh	NHL	9	0	0	0	9	-3	0	0	—	—	—	—	—
NHL Totals (3 years)		38	2	4	6	13	-2	0	0					

LEGACE, MANNY G

PERSONAL: Born February 4, 1973, in Toronto. ... 5-9/162. ... Catches left. ... Name pronounced LEH-guh-see.

TRANSACTIONS/CAREER NOTES: Selected by Hartford Whalers in eighth round (fifth Whalers pick, 188th overall) of NHL draft (June 26, 1993). ... Whalers franchise moved to North Carolina and renamed Carolina Hurricanes for 1997-98 season; NHL approved move on June 25, 1997. ... Traded by Hurricanes to Los Angeles Kings for future considerations (July 31, 1998). ... Signed as free agent by Detroit Red Wings (July 15, 1999). ... Claimed off waivers by Vancouver Canucks (September 30, 1999). ... Claimed off waivers by Red Wings (October 13, 1999). ... Injured (November 27, 2000); missed two games. ... Elbow (March 31, 2001); missed one game. ... Hip flexor (February 11, 2002); missed one game. ... Sprained knee (December 9, 2003); missed two games. ... Tore left knee ligament (November 1, 2005); missed 13 games.

Season Team	League	GP	Min.	W	L	OTL	T	GA	SO	GAA	SV%	GP	Min.	W	L	GA	SO	GAA	SV%
		REGULAR SEASON										PLAYOFFS							
89-90—Vaughan-Thornhill Jr. B	OHA	29	1660	...	...	...	...	119	1	4.30	...	—	—	—	—	—	—	—	—
90-91—Niagara Falls	OHL	30	1515	13	11	...	2	107	0	4.24	...	4	119	...	...	10	0	5.04	...
91-92—Niagara Falls	OHL	43	2384	21	16	...	3	143	0	3.60	...	14	791	...	...	56	0	4.25	...
92-93—Niagara Falls	OHL	48	2630	22	19	...	3	170	0	3.88	.897	4	240	0	4	18	0	4.50	.851
93-94—Canadian nat'l team	Int'l	16	859	8	6	...	0	36	2	2.51	...	—	—	—	—	—	—	—	—
94-95—Springfield	AHL	39	2169	12	17	...	6	128	2	3.54	.887	—	—	—	—	—	—	—	—
95-96—Springfield	AHL	37	2196	20	12	...	4	83	5	2.27	...	4	220	1	3	18	0	4.91	...
96-97—Springfield	AHL	36	2119	17	14	...	5	107	1	3.03	.897	12	746	9	3	25	2	2.01	.931
—Richmond	ECHL	3	157	2	1	...	0	8	0	3.06	...	—	—	—	—	—	—	—	—
97-98—Las Vegas	IHL	41	2107	18	16	...	4	111	1	3.16	.911	4	237	1	3	16	0	4.05	.887
—Springfield	AHL	6	345	4	2	...	0	16	0	2.78	.889	—	—	—	—	—	—	—	—
98-99—Long Beach	IHL	33	1796	22	8	...	1	67	2	2.24	.912	6	338	4	2	9	0	1.60	.944
—Los Angeles	NHL	17	899	2	9	...	2	39	0	2.60	.911	—	—	—	—	—	—	—	—
99-00—Manitoba	IHL	42	2409	20	18	...	5	104	2	2.59	...	2	141	0	2	7	0	2.98	...
—Detroit	NHL	4	240	4	0	...	0	11	0	2.75	.906	—	—	—	—	—	—	—	—
00-01—Detroit	NHL	39	2136	24	5	...	5	73	2	2.05	.920	—	—	—	—	—	—	—	—
01-02—Detroit	NHL	20	1117	10	6	...	2	45	1	2.42	.911	1	11	0	0	1	0	5.45	.500
02-03—Detroit	NHL	25	1406	14	5	...	4	51	0	2.18	.925	—	—	—	—	—	—	—	—
03-04—Detroit	NHL	41	2325	23	10	...	5	82	3	2.12	.920	4	220	2	2	8	0	2.18	.905
04-05—Khimik Voskresensk	Russian	2	89	...	...	...	...	10	0	6.73	...	—	—	—	—	—	—	—	—
05-06—Grand Rapids	AHL	1	60	1	0	0	...	2	0	2.00	.909	—	—	—	—	—	—	—	—
—Detroit	NHL	51	2905	37	8	3	...	106	7	2.19	.915	6	408	2	4	18	0	2.65	.884
NHL Totals (7 years)		197	11028	114	43	3	18	407	13	2.21	.917	11	639	4	6	27	0	2.54	.888

LEGWAND, DAVID C

PERSONAL: Born August 17, 1980, in Detroit. ... 6-2/190. ... Shoots left.

TRANSACTIONS/CAREER NOTES: Selected by Nashville Predators in first round (first Predators pick, second overall) of entry draft (June 27, 1998). ... Fractured left foot (January 13, 2000); missed 11 games. ... Back (January 30, 2002); missed 12 games. ... Strained back (March 30, 2002); missed remainder of season. ... Fractured collarbone (March 31, 2003); missed season's final 18 games. ... Sprained left knee (December 8, 2005), had surgery; missed 32 games. ... Knee (March 24, 2006); missed three games. ... Knee (April 6, 2006); missed two games.

Season Team	League	GP	G	A	Pts.	PIM	+/-	PP	SH	GP	G	A	Pts.	PIM
		REGULAR SEASON								PLAYOFFS				
96-97—Detroit	Jr. A	44	21	41	62	58	...	...	...	—	—	—	—	—
97-98—Plymouth	OHL	59	54	51	105	56	...	...	...	15	8	12	20	24
98-99—Plymouth	OHL	55	31	49	80	65	32	...	...	11	3	8	11	8
—Nashville	NHL	1	0	0	0	0	0	0	0	—	—	—	—	—
99-00—Nashville	NHL	71	13	15	28	30	-6	4	0	—	—	—	—	—
00-01—Nashville	NHL	81	13	28	41	38	1	3	0	—	—	—	—	—
01-02—Nashville	NHL	63	11	19	30	54	1	1	1	—	—	—	—	—
02-03—Nashville	NHL	64	17	31	48	34	-2	3	1	—	—	—	—	—
03-04—Nashville	NHL	82	18	29	47	46	9	5	1	6	1	0	1	8
04-05—Basel	Switzerland	3	6	2	8	2	...	1	0	12	11	19	30	10
05-06—Milwaukee	AHL	3	0	0	0	0	-1	0	0	—	—	—	—	—
—Nashville	NHL	44	7	19	26	34	3	0	0	5	0	1	1	8
NHL Totals (7 years)		406	79	141	220	236	6	16	3	11	1	1	2	16

LEHOUX, YANICK C

PERSONAL: Born April 8, 1982, in Montreal. ... 5-11/170. ... Shoots right.

TRANSACTIONS/CAREER NOTES: Selected by Los Angeles Kings in third round (third Kings pick, 86th overall) of entry draft (June 24, 2000). ... Claimed off waivers by Phoenix Coyotes (November 20, 2005). ... Claimed off waivers by Kings (November 25, 2005). ... Traded by Kings to Coyotes for D Tim Jackman (March 9, 2006).

		REGULAR SEASON								PLAYOFFS				
Season Team	**League**	**GP**	**G**	**A**	**Pts.**	**PIM**	**+/-**	**PP**	**SH**	**GP**	**G**	**A**	**Pts.**	**PIM**
99-00—Baie-Comeau	QMJHL	67	31	61	92	14	...	...	...	—	—	—	—	—
00-01—Baie-Comeau	QMJHL	70	67	68	135	62	26	15	13	11	8	16	24	0
01-02—Baie-Comeau	QMJHL	66	56	69	125	63	...	...	...	5	5	4	9	0
—Manchester	AHL	0	0	0	0	0	0	0	0	1	0	0	0	0
02-03—Manchester	AHL	78	16	21	37	26	...	...	...	1	0	0	0	0
03-04—Manchester	AHL	66	14	28	42	22	...	...	...	5	2	3	5	16
04-05—Manchester	AHL	38	23	31	54	16	13	8	0	0	0	0	0	0
05-06—Manchester	AHL	31	10	6	16	23	-3	5	0	—	—	—	—	—
—Phoenix	NHL	3	1	0	1	2	1	0	0	—	—	—	—	—
—San Antonio	AHL	23	8	6	14	13	-3	2	1	—	—	—	—	—
NHL Totals (1 year)		3	1	0	1	2	1	0	0					

LEHTINEN, JERE RW/LW

PERSONAL: Born June 24, 1973, in Espoo, Finland. ... 6-0/200. ... Shoots right. ... Name pronounced YAIR-ee LEH-tih-nehn.

TRANSACTIONS/CAREER NOTES: Selected by Minnesota North Stars in fourth round (third North Stars pick, 88th overall) of entry draft (June 20, 1992). ... North Stars franchise moved from Minnesota to Dallas and renamed Stars for 1993-94 season. ... Groin (December 21, 1995); missed six games. ... Groin (January 10, 1996); missed one game. ... Ankle (March 20, 1996); missed remainder of season. ... Knee (January 31, 1997); missed 13 games. ... Knee (March 5, 1997); missed five games. ... Separated shoulder (October 19, 1997); missed 10 games. ... Fractured thumb (November 14, 1998); missed five games. ... Ankle (March 25, 1999); missed two games. ... Ankle (October 16, 1999); missed 30 games. ... Injured ankle (January 19, 2000); missed 35 games. ... Flu (November 14, 2000); missed one game. ... Ankle (December 6, 2000); missed five games. ... Hip flexor (February 15, 2001); missed two games. ... Knee (January 29, 2002) and had surgery; missed one game. ... Bruised ankle (March 20, 2002); missed eight games. ... Hip (February 9, 2003); missed two games. ... Back spasms (October 13, 2003); missed 16 games. ... Flu (December 26, 2003); missed two games. ... Back spasms (March 22, 2004); missed six games. ... Flu (December 23, 2005); missed one game.

STATISTICAL PLATEAUS: Three-goal games: 2000-01 (1), 2002-03 (1). Total: 2.

		REGULAR SEASON								PLAYOFFS				
Season Team	**League**	**GP**	**G**	**A**	**Pts.**	**PIM**	**+/-**	**PP**	**SH**	**GP**	**G**	**A**	**Pts.**	**PIM**
90-91—Kiekko-Espoo	Finland	32	15	9	24	12	...	...	...	—	—	—	—	—
91-92—Kiekko-Espoo	Finland	43	32	17	49	6	...	...	...	—	—	—	—	—
92-93—Kiekko-Espoo	Finland	45	13	14	27	6	...	...	...	—	—	—	—	—
93-94—TPS Turku	Finland	42	19	20	39	6	...	...	...	11	11	2	13	2
—Fin. Olympic team	Int'l	8	3	0	3	11	5	1	0	—	—	—	—	—
94-95—TPS Turku	Finland	39	19	23	42	33	26	...	...	13	8	6	14	4
95-96—Dallas	NHL	57	6	22	28	16	5	0	0	—	—	—	—	—
—Michigan	IHL	1	1	0	1	0	...	...	...	—	—	—	—	—
96-97—Dallas	NHL	63	16	27	43	2	26	3	1	7	2	2	4	0
97-98—Dallas	NHL	72	23	19	42	20	19	7	2	12	3	5	8	2
—Fin. Olympic team	Int'l	6	4	2	6	2	1	1	0	—	—	—	—	—
98-99—Dallas	NHL	74	20	32	52	18	29	7	1	23	10	3	13	2
99-00—Dallas	NHL	17	3	5	8	0	1	0	0	13	1	5	6	2
00-01—Dallas	NHL	74	20	25	45	24	14	7	0	10	1	0	1	2
01-02—Dallas	NHL	73	25	24	49	14	27	7	1	—	—	—	—	—
—Fin. Olympic team	Int'l	4	1	2	3	2	...	...	...	—	—	—	—	—
02-03—Dallas	NHL	80	31	17	48	20	39	5	0	12	3	2	5	0
03-04—Dallas	NHL	58	13	13	26	20	0	4	1	5	0	0	0	0
05-06—Dallas	NHL	80	33	19	52	30	9	14	1	5	3	1	4	0
—Fin. Olympic team	Int'l	8	3	5	8	6	6	2	0	—	—	—	—	—
NHL Totals (10 years)		648	190	203	393	164	169	54	7	87	23	18	41	8

LEHTONEN, KARI G

PERSONAL: Born November 16, 1983, in Helsinki, Finland. ... 6-3/200. ... Catches left.

TRANSACTIONS/CAREER NOTES: Selected by Atlanta Thrashers in first round (first Thrashers pick, second overall) of entry draft (June 22, 2002). ... Strained groin (October 6, 2005); missed 35 games. ... Ankle sprain (April 7, 2006); missed final six games of regular season.

		REGULAR SEASON										PLAYOFFS							
Season Team	**League**	**GP**	**Min.**	**W**	**L**	**OTL**	**T**	**GA**	**SO**	**GAA**	**SV%**	**GP**	**Min.**	**W**	**L**	**GA**	**SO**	**GAA**	**SV%**
99-00—Jokerit Helsinki	Finland	2	...	...	...	...	...	...	...	...	...	—	—	—	—	—	—	—	—
00-01—Jokerit Helsinki	Finland	4	189	3	0	...	0	6	0	1.90	...	—	—	—	—	—	—	—	—
01-02—Jokerit Helsinki	Finland	23	1242	13	5	...	3	37	4	1.79	...	11	623	8	3	18	3	1.73	...
02-03—Jokerit Helsinki	Finland	49	...	...	...	...	...	...	...	...	...	—	—	—	—	—	—	—	—
03-04—Atlanta	NHL	4	240	4	0	...	0	5	1	1.25	.953	—	—	—	—	—	—	—	—
—Chicago	AHL	39	2192	20	14	...	2	88	3	2.41	.920	10	663	6	4	23	1	2.08	.939
04-05—Chicago	AHL	57	3378	38	17	...	...	128	5	2.27	.929	16	982	10	6	28	2	1.71	.939
05-06—Atlanta	NHL	38	2166	20	15	0	...	106	2	2.94	.906	—	—	—	—	—	—	—	—
NHL Totals (2 years)		42	2406	24	15	0	0	111	3	2.77	.910								

LEMIEUX, MARIO C/LW

PERSONAL: Born October 5, 1965, in Montreal. ... 6-4/230. ... Shoots right. ... Brother of Alain Lemieux, C for three NHL teams (1981-82 through 1986-87). ... Name pronounced luh-MYOO.

TRANSACTIONS/CAREER NOTES: Selected by Pittsburgh in first round (first Penguins pick, first overall) of entry draft (June 9, 1984). ... Sprained left knee (September 1984). ... Reinjured knee (December 2, 1984). ... Sprained right knee (December 20, 1986). ... Bruised right shoulder (November 1987). ... Sprained right wrist (November 3, 1988). ... Herniated disk (February 14, 1990); missed 21 games. ... Disc removed from back (July 11, 1990); missed first 50 games of season. ... Back spasms (October 1991); missed three games. ... Back spasms (January 4, 1992); missed three games. ... Injured back (January 29, 1992); missed six games. ... Flu (February 1992); missed one game. ... Fractured hand (May 5, 1992). ... Injured heel (December 1992); missed one game. ... Injured back (January 5, 1993); missed three games. ... Diagnosed with Hodgkin's disease (January 12, 1993) and had radiation treatment (February 1-March 2); missed 20 games. ... Injured back (September 1993); missed first 10 games of season. ... Injured back (October 28, 1993); missed one game. ... Injured back (November 2, 1993); missed one game. ... Flu (November 9, 1993); missed one game. ... Injured back (November 11, 1993); missed 38 games. ... Injured back (February 13, 1994); missed two games. ... Injured back (February 19, 1994); missed two games. ... Injured back (March 12, 1994); missed four games. ... Fined $500 for charging referee (April 6, 1994). ... Medical leave; missed 1994-95 season. ... Back spasms (November 9, 1996); missed one game. ... Back spasms (January 21, 1997); missed one game. ... Back spasms (February 4, 1997); missed one game. ... Strained hip flexor (March 4, 1997); missed one game. ... Strained hip flexor (March 14, 1997); missed two games. ... Retired (April 6, 1997). ... Inducted into Hockey Hall of Fame (November 17, 1997). ... Strained hip flexor (October 3, 2001); missed two games. ... Hip surgery (October 28, 2001); missed six games. ... Injured hip (November 17, 2001); missed 23 games. ... Reinjured hip (February 27, 2002); missed remainder of season. ... Injured groin (January 7, 2003); missed two games. ... Aggravated groin injury (January 13, 2003); missed eight games. ... Back spasms (March 25, 2003); missed two games. ... Injured hip (October 25, 2003) and had surgery; missed remainder of season. ... Stomach virus (November 16, 2005); missed one game. ... Stomach virus (November 27, 2005); missed two games. ... Irregular heartbeat (December 7, 2005); missed four games. ... Irregular heartbeat (December 17, 2005); missed 16 games. ... Retired (Jan 24, 2006).

STATISTICAL PLATEAUS: Three-goal games: 1986-87 (5), 1987-88 (3), 1988-89 (7), 1989-90 (3), 1990-91 (1), 1991-92 (1), 1992-93 (1), 1995-96 (4), 1996-97 (1), 2000-01 (1). Total: 27. ... Four-goal games: 1985-86 (1), 1986-87 (1), 1987-88 (2), 1988-89 (1), 1989-90 (1), 1992-93 (2), 1995-96 (1), 1996-97 (1). Total: 10. ... Five-goal games: 1988-89 (1), 1992-93 (1), 1995-96 (1). Total: 3. ... Total hat tricks: 40.

		REGULAR SEASON								PLAYOFFS				
Season Team	**League**	**GP**	**G**	**A**	**Pts.**	**PIM**	**+/-**	**PP**	**SH**	**GP**	**G**	**A**	**Pts.**	**PIM**
81-82—Laval	QMJHL	64	30	66	96	22	...	...	...	18	5	9	14	31
82-83—Laval	QMJHL	66	84	100	184	76	...	...	...	12	14	18	32	18
83-84—Laval	QMJHL	70	133	149	282	92	...	...	...	14	29	23	52	29
84-85—Pittsburgh	NHL	73	43	57	100	54	-35	11	0	—	—	—	—	—
85-86—Pittsburgh	NHL	79	48	93	141	43	-6	17	0	—	—	—	—	—
86-87—Pittsburgh	NHL	63	54	53	107	57	13	19	0	—	—	—	—	—
87-88—Pittsburgh	NHL	77	*70	98	*168	92	23	22	*10	—	—	—	—	—
88-89—Pittsburgh	NHL	76	*85	114	*199	100	41	*31	*13	11	12	7	19	16
89-90—Pittsburgh	NHL	59	45	78	123	78	-18	14	3	—	—	—	—	—
90-91—Pittsburgh	NHL	26	19	26	45	30	8	6	1	23	16	*28	*44	16
91-92—Pittsburgh	NHL	64	44	87	*131	94	27	12	4	15	*16	18	*34	2
92-93—Pittsburgh	NHL	60	69	91	*160	38	*55	16	6	11	8	10	18	10
93-94—Pittsburgh	NHL	22	17	20	37	32	-2	7	0	6	4	3	7	2
94-95—Pittsburgh	NHL	Did not play												
95-96—Pittsburgh	NHL	70	*69	92	*161	54	10	*31	*8	18	11	16	27	33
96-97—Pittsburgh	NHL	76	50	72	*122	65	27	15	3	5	3	3	6	4
97-98—Pittsburgh	NHL	Did not play												
98-99—Pittsburgh	NHL	Did not play												
99-00—Pittsburgh	NHL	Did not play												
00-01—Pittsburgh	NHL	43	35	41	76	18	15	16	1	18	6	11	17	4
01-02—Pittsburgh	NHL	24	6	25	31	14	0	2	0	—	—	—	—	—
—Can. Olympic team	Int'l	5	2	4	6	0	...	...	...	—	—	—	—	—
02-03—Pittsburgh	NHL	67	28	63	91	43	-25	14	0	—	—	—	—	—
03-04—Pittsburgh	NHL	10	1	8	9	6	-2	0	0	—	—	—	—	—
05-06—Pittsburgh	NHL	26	7	15	22	16	-16	3	0	—	—	—	—	—
NHL Totals (21 years)		915	690	1033	1723	834	115	236	49	107	76	96	172	87

LENEVEU, DAVID G

PERSONAL: Born May 23, 1983, in Fernie, B.C. ... 6-1/187. ... Catches left. ... Name pronounced: leh NEHV yoo

TRANSACTIONS/CAREER NOTES: Selected by Phoenix Coyotes in second round (third Coyotes pick, 46th overall) of entry draft (June 22, 2002).

		REGULAR SEASON										PLAYOFFS							
Season Team	**League**	**GP**	**Min.**	**W**	**L**	**OTL**	**T**	**GA**	**SO**	**GAA**	**SV%**	**GP**	**Min.**	**W**	**L**	**GA**	**SO**	**GAA**	**SV%**
01-02—Cornell	ECAC	14	842	11	2	...	1	21	2	1.50	...	—	—	—	—	—	—	—	—
02-03—Cornell	ECAC	32	1946	28	3	...	1	39	9	1.20	.940	—	—	—	—	—	—	—	—
03-04—Springfield	AHL	38	2219	16	19	...	3	102	1	2.76	.909	—	—	—	—	—	—	—	—
04-05—Utah	AHL	48	2702	11	32	...	3	132	0	2.93	.909	—	—	—	—	—	—	—	—
05-06—San Antonio	AHL	28	1646	10	16	2	...	80	2	2.92	.921	—	—	—	—	—	—	—	—
—Phoenix	NHL	15	814	3	8	2	...	44	0	3.24	.886	—	—	—	—	—	—	—	—
NHL Totals (1 year)		15	814	3	8	2	0	44	0	3.24	.886								

LEOPOLD, JORDAN D

PERSONAL: Born August 3, 1980, in Golden Valley, Minn. ... 6-1/205. ... Shoots left.

TRANSACTIONS/CAREER NOTES: Selected by Anaheim Mighty Ducks in second round (first Mighty Ducks pick, 44th overall) of entry draft (June 26, 1999). ... Traded by Mighty Ducks to Calgary Flames for LW Andrei Nazarov and second-round pick (traded back to Calgary) in 2001 draft (September 26, 2000). ... Concussion (October 4, 2002); missed season's first four games. ... Shoulder (November 27, 2002); missed six games. ... Groin (March 31, 2006); missed three games. ... Groin (April 7, 2006); missed five games. ... Traded by Flames with a second-round pick (C Codey Burki) in 2006 entry draft and a conditional draft choice to Colorado Avalanche for F Alex Tanguay (June 24, 2006).

		REGULAR SEASON								PLAYOFFS				
Season Team	League	GP	G	A	Pts.	PIM	+/-	PP	SH	GP	G	A	Pts.	PIM
97-98—U.S. National	NAHL	60	11	12	23	16	...	4	0	—	—	—	—	—
98-99—Minnesota	WCHA	39	7	16	23	20	...	...	...	—	—	—	—	—
99-00—Minnesota	WCHA	39	6	18	24	20	...	...	...	—	—	—	—	—
00-01—Minnesota	WCHA	42	12	37	49	38	...	...	...	—	—	—	—	—
01-02—Minnesota	WCHA	44	20	28	48	28	...	...	...	—	—	—	—	—
02-03—Saint John	AHL	3	1	2	3	0	-3	1	0	—	—	—	—	—
—Calgary	NHL	58	4	10	14	12	-15	3	0	—	—	—	—	—
03-04—Calgary	NHL	82	9	24	33	24	8	6	0	26	0	10	10	6
05-06—Calgary	NHL	74	2	18	20	68	6	2	0	7	0	1	1	4
—U.S. Olympic team	Int'l	6	1	0	1	4	1	0	0	—	—	—	—	—
NHL Totals (3 years)		214	15	52	67	104	-1	11	0	33	0	11	11	10

LESSARD, FRANCIS RW

PERSONAL: Born May 30, 1979, in Montreal. ... 6-3/225. ... Shoots right. ... Name pronounced luh-SAHRD.
TRANSACTIONS/CAREER NOTES: Selected by Carolina Hurricanes in third round (third Hurricanes pick, 80th overall) of NHL entry draft (June 21, 1997). ... Traded by Hurricanes to Philadelphia Flyers for eighth-round pick (G Antti Jokela) in 1999 entry draft (May 25, 1999). ... Traded by Flyers to Atlanta Thrashers for D David Harlock, third- (later traded to Phoenix Coyotes) and seventh-round (later traded to San Jose Sharks) picks in 2003 entry draft (March 15, 2002). ... Had back spasms (November 23, 2002); missed seven games. ... Suspended one game by NHL in spearing incident (November 14, 2003). ... Injured shoulder (March 15, 2004); missed one game.

		REGULAR SEASON								PLAYOFFS				
Season Team	League	GP	G	A	Pts.	PIM	+/-	PP	SH	GP	G	A	Pts.	PIM
96-97—Val-d'Or	QMJHL	66	1	9	10	287	...	...	...	—	—	—	—	—
97-98—Val-d'Or	QMJHL	63	3	20	23	338	...	...	...	19	1	6	7	101
98-99—Drummondville	QMJHL	53	12	36	48	295	-24	5	2	—	—	—	—	—
99-00—Philadelphia	AHL	78	4	8	12	416	...	...	...	5	0	1	1	7
00-01—Philadelphia	AHL	64	3	7	10	330	...	...	...	10	0	0	0	33
01-02—Philadelphia	AHL	60	0	6	6	251	-6	0	0	—	—	—	—	—
—Chicago	AHL	7	2	1	3	34	4	0	0	15	0	1	1	40
—Atlanta	NHL	5	0	0	0	26	0	0	0	—	—	—	—	—
02-03—Atlanta	NHL	18	0	2	2	61	1	0	0	—	—	—	—	—
—Chicago	AHL	50	2	5	7	194	3	0	0	1	0	0	0	0
03-04—Atlanta	NHL	62	1	1	2	181	-5	0	0	—	—	—	—	—
05-06—Chicago	AHL	36	2	3	5	161	-6	0	0	—	—	—	—	—
—Atlanta	NHL	6	0	0	0	0	-2	0	0	—	—	—	—	—
NHL Totals (4 years)		91	1	3	4	268	-6	0	0					

LESSARD, JUNIOR RW

PERSONAL: Born May 26, 1980, in St. Joseph deBeauce, Que. ... 6-0/195. ... Shoots right.
COLLEGE: Minnesota-Duluth.
TRANSACTIONS/CAREER NOTES: Signed as free agent by Dallas Stars (April 15, 2004).

		REGULAR SEASON								PLAYOFFS				
Season Team	League	GP	G	A	Pts.	PIM	+/-	PP	SH	GP	G	A	Pts.	PIM
00-01—Minnesota-Duluth	WCHA	36	4	8	12	12	...	...	...	—	—	—	—	—
01-02—Minnesota-Duluth	WCHA	39	17	13	30	50	...	...	...	—	—	—	—	—
02-03—Minnesota-Duluth	WCHA	40	21	16	37	20	...	...	...	—	—	—	—	—
03-04—Minnesota-Duluth	WCHA	45	32	31	63	34	...	...	...	—	—	—	—	—
04-05—Houston	AHL	71	11	11	22	25	-7	4	0	5	1	0	1	0
05-06—Iowa	AHL	66	26	32	58	30	4	8	0	7	3	4	7	4
—Dallas	NHL	5	1	0	1	12	0	0	0	—	—	—	—	—
NHL Totals (1 year)		5	1	0	1	12	0	0	0					

LETOWSKI, TREVOR RW/LW

PERSONAL: Born April 5, 1977, in Thunder Bay, Ont. ... 5-10/180. ... Shoots right.
TRANSACTIONS/CAREER NOTES: Selected by Phoenix Coyotes in seventh round (sixth Coyotes pick, 174th overall) of entry draft (June 22, 1996). ... Traded by Coyotes with LW Todd Warriner, RW Tyler Bouck and third-round pick (returned to Phoenix; Coyotes selected C Dimitri Pestunov) in 2003 to Vancouver Canucks for C Denis Pederson and D Drake Berehowsky (December 28, 2001). ... Signed as free agent by Columbus Blue Jackets (July 3, 2003). ... Fractured finger (October 11, 2003); missed seven games. ... Flu (March 5, 2006); missed one game. ... Signed as free agent by Carolina Hurricanes (July 6, 2006).

		REGULAR SEASON								PLAYOFFS				
Season Team	League	GP	G	A	Pts.	PIM	+/-	PP	SH	GP	G	A	Pts.	PIM
94-95—Sarnia	OHL	66	22	19	41	33	...	...	...	4	0	1	1	9
95-96—Sarnia	OHL	66	36	63	99	66	...	...	...	10	9	5	14	10
96-97—Sarnia	OHL	55	35	73	108	51	...	...	...	12	9	12	21	20
97-98—Springfield	AHL	75	11	20	31	26	...	...	...	4	1	2	3	18
98-99—Springfield	AHL	67	32	35	67	46	16	11	3	3	1	0	1	2
—Phoenix	NHL	14	2	2	4	2	1	0	0	—	—	—	—	—
99-00—Phoenix	NHL	82	19	20	39	20	2	3	4	5	1	1	2	4
00-01—Phoenix	NHL	77	7	15	22	32	-2	0	1	—	—	—	—	—
01-02—Phoenix	NHL	33	2	6	8	4	2	0	0	—	—	—	—	—
—Vancouver	NHL	42	7	10	17	15	2	1	0	6	0	1	1	8
02-03—Vancouver	NHL	78	11	14	25	36	8	1	1	6	0	1	1	0

Season Team	League	GP	G	A	Pts.	PIM	+/-	PP	SH	GP	G	A	Pts.	PIM
		REGULAR SEASON								PLAYOFFS				
03-04—Columbus	NHL	73	15	17	32	16	-12	4	0	—	—	—	—	—
04-05—Fribourg	Switzerland	9	4	5	9	6	...	2	2	—	—	—	—	—
05-06—Columbus	NHL	81	10	18	28	36	-2	1	1	—	—	—	—	—
NHL Totals (7 years)		480	73	102	175	161	-1	10	7	17	1	3	4	12

LEWIS, TREVOR C

PERSONAL: Born January 8, 1987, in Salt Lake City, Utah. ... 6-1/192. ... Shoots right.

TRANSACTIONS/CAREER NOTES: Selected by Los Angeles Kings in first round (second Kings pick; 17th overall) of NHL draft (June 24, 2006).

Season Team	League	GP	G	A	Pts.	PIM	+/-	PP	SH	GP	G	A	Pts.	PIM
		REGULAR SEASON								PLAYOFFS				
04-05—Des Moines	USHL	52	10	12	22	70	...	...	...	—	—	—	—	—
05-06—Des Moines	USHL	56	35	40	75	69	...	...	...	—	—	—	—	—

LIDSTROM, NICKLAS D

PERSONAL: Born April 28, 1970, in Vasteras, Sweden. ... 6-2/190. ... Shoots left. ... Name pronounced NIHK-luhs LIHD-struhm.

TRANSACTIONS/CAREER NOTES: Selected by Detroit Red Wings in third round (third Red Wings pick, 53rd overall) of entry draft (June 17, 1989). ... Back spasms (April 9, 1995); missed five games. ... Flu (April 14, 1996); missed one game. ... Flu (January 20, 1997); missed one game.

Season Team	League	GP	G	A	Pts.	PIM	+/-	PP	SH	GP	G	A	Pts.	PIM
		REGULAR SEASON								PLAYOFFS				
87-88—Vasteras	Sweden	3	0	0	0	0	...	...	...	—	—	—	—	—
88-89—Vasteras	Sweden	19	0	2	2	4	...	...	...	—	—	—	—	—
89-90—Vasteras	Sweden	39	8	8	16	14	...	...	...	—	—	—	—	—
90-91—Vasteras	Sweden	20	2	12	14	14	...	...	...	—	—	—	—	—
91-92—Detroit	NHL	80	11	49	60	22	36	5	0	11	1	2	3	0
92-93—Detroit	NHL	84	7	34	41	28	7	3	0	7	1	0	1	0
93-94—Detroit	NHL	84	10	46	56	26	43	4	0	7	3	2	5	0
94-95—Vasteras	Sweden	13	2	10	12	4	...	...	...	—	—	—	—	—
—Detroit	NHL	43	10	16	26	6	15	7	0	18	4	12	16	8
95-96—Vasteras	Sweden	13	2	10	12	4	...	...	...	—	—	—	—	—
—Detroit	NHL	81	17	50	67	20	29	8	1	19	5	9	14	10
96-97—Detroit	NHL	79	15	42	57	30	11	8	0	20	2	6	8	2
97-98—Detroit	NHL	80	17	42	59	18	22	7	1	22	6	13	19	8
—Swedish Oly. team	Int'l	4	1	1	2	2	4	1	0	—	—	—	—	—
98-99—Detroit	NHL	81	14	43	57	14	14	6	2	10	2	9	11	4
99-00—Detroit	NHL	81	20	53	73	18	19	9	4	9	2	4	6	4
00-01—Detroit	NHL	82	15	56	71	18	9	8	0	6	1	7	8	0
01-02—Detroit	NHL	78	9	50	59	20	13	6	0	23	5	11	16	2
—Swedish Oly. team	Int'l	4	1	5	6	0	...	...	...	—	—	—	—	—
02-03—Detroit	NHL	82	18	44	62	38	40	8	1	4	0	2	2	0
03-04—Detroit	NHL	81	10	28	38	18	19	3	1	12	2	5	7	4
05-06—Detroit	NHL	80	16	64	80	50	21	9	0	6	1	1	2	2
—Swedish Oly. team	Int'l	8	2	4	6	2	2	1	0	—	—	—	—	—
NHL Totals (14 years)		1096	189	617	806	326	298	91	10	174	35	83	118	44

LIFFITON, DAVID D

PERSONAL: Born October 18, 1984, in Windsor, Ont. ... 6-2/201. ... Shoots left.

TRANSACTIONS/CAREER NOTES: Selected by Colorado Avalanche in second round (first Avalanche pick, 63rd overall) of entry draft (June 21, 2003). ... Traded by Avalanche with D Chris McAllister and second-round pick (later traded to Florida; Panthers picked G David Shantz) in 2004 draft to New York Rangers for F Matthew Barnaby and third-round pick (LW Denis Parshin) in 2004 draft (March 8, 2004).

Season Team	League	GP	G	A	Pts.	PIM	+/-	PP	SH	GP	G	A	Pts.	PIM
		REGULAR SEASON								PLAYOFFS				
01-02—Plymouth	OHL	62	3	9	12	65	...	...	...	6	0	0	0	0
02-03—Plymouth	OHL	64	5	11	16	139	...	...	...	18	1	3	4	29
03-04—Plymouth	OHL	44	2	9	11	85	-5	2	0	9	0	0	0	12
04-05—Hartford	AHL	33	0	1	1	74	-4	0	0	—	—	—	—	—
—Charlotte	ECHL	16	0	2	2	18	...	...	...	15	1	4	5	27
05-06—Hartford	AHL	58	4	10	14	169	7	0	0	12	0	0	0	13
—New York Rangers	NHL	1	0	0	0	2	0	0	0	—	—	—	—	—
NHL Totals (1 year)		1	0	0	0	2	0	0	0					

LILES, JOHN-MICHAEL D

PERSONAL: Born November 25, 1980, in Zionsville, Ind. ... 5-10/185. ... Shoots left.

TRANSACTIONS/CAREER NOTES: Selected by Colorado Avalanche in fifth round (eighth Avalanche pick, 159th overall) of NHL entry draft (June 24, 2000). ... Bruised right knee (March 23, 2004); missed three games. ... Fractured foot (summer 2004).

Season Team	League	GP	G	A	Pts.	PIM	+/-	PP	SH	GP	G	A	Pts.	PIM
		REGULAR SEASON								PLAYOFFS				
99-00—Michigan State	CCHA	37	7	19	26	26	...	...	...	—	—	—	—	—
00-01—Michigan State	CCHA	42	7	18	25	28	...	...	...	—	—	—	—	—

Season Team	League	REGULAR SEASON GP	G	A	Pts.	PIM	+/-	PP	SH	PLAYOFFS GP	G	A	Pts.	PIM
01-02—Michigan State	CCHA	41	13	22	35	18	...	...	...	—	—	—	—	—
02-03—Michigan State	CCHA	39	16	34	50	46	...	...	...	—	—	—	—	—
—Hershey	AHL	5	0	1	1	4	-2	0	0	5	0	0	0	2
03-04—Colorado	NHL	79	10	24	34	28	7	2	0	11	0	1	1	4
04-05—Iserlohn	Germany	17	5	6	11	24	-3	3	1	...	...	...	...	...
05-06—Colorado	NHL	82	14	35	49	44	5	6	0	9	1	2	3	6
—U.S. Olympic team	Int'l	6	0	2	2	2	-3	0	0	—	—	—	—	—
NHL Totals (2 years)		161	24	59	83	72	12	8	0	20	1	3	4	10

LILJA, ANDREAS — D

PERSONAL: Born July 13, 1975, in Landskrona, Sweden. ... 6-4/222. ... Shoots left. ... Name pronounced LIHL-yuh.

TRANSACTIONS/CAREER NOTES: Selected by Los Angeles Kings in second round (second Kings pick, 54th overall) of entry draft (June 24, 2000). ... Left knee (October 13, 2001); missed 19 games. ... Traded by Kings with RW Jaroslav Bednar to Florida Panthers for D Dmitry Yushkevich and fifth-round pick (C Brady Murray) in 2003 (November 26, 2002). ... Foot (January 1, 2003); missed one game. ... Hand (January 25, 2003); missed two games. ... Shoulder (November 13, 2003); missed three games. ... Signed as free agent by Nashville Predators (July 25, 2004). ... Signed as free agent by Detroit Red Wings (August 24, 2005).

Season Team	League	REGULAR SEASON GP	G	A	Pts.	PIM	+/-	PP	SH	PLAYOFFS GP	G	A	Pts.	PIM
95-96—Malmo	Sweden	40	1	5	6	63	...	...	...	5	0	1	1	2
96-97—Malmo	Sweden	47	1	0	1	22	...	...	...	4	0	0	0	10
97-98—Malmo	Sweden	10	0	0	0	0	...	...	...	—	—	—	—	—
98-99—Malmo	Sweden	41	0	3	3	14	...	...	...	1	0	0	0	4
99-00—Malmo	Sweden	49	8	11	19	88	...	...	...	6	0	0	0	8
00-01—Lowell	AHL	61	7	29	36	149	...	...	...	4	0	6	6	6
—Los Angeles	NHL	2	0	0	0	4	-2	0	0	1	0	0	0	0
01-02—Los Angeles	NHL	26	1	4	5	22	3	1	0	5	0	0	0	6
—Manchester	AHL	4	0	1	1	4	1	0	0	—	—	—	—	—
02-03—Los Angeles	NHL	17	0	3	3	14	5	0	0	—	—	—	—	—
—Florida	NHL	56	4	8	12	56	8	0	0	—	—	—	—	—
03-04—Florida	NHL	79	3	4	7	90	-8	0	0	—	—	—	—	—
04-05—Mora	Sweden Dv. 1	44	3	8	11	67	-8	0	1	—	—	—	—	—
05-06—Detroit	NHL	82	2	13	15	98	18	0	0	6	0	1	1	6
NHL Totals (5 years)		262	10	32	42	284	24	1	0	12	0	1	1	12

L

LINDEN, TREVOR — C/RW

PERSONAL: Born April 11, 1970, in Medicine Hat, Alta. ... 6-4/220. ... Shoots right. ... Brother of Jamie Linden, RW with Florida Panthers organization (1993-97).

TRANSACTIONS/CAREER NOTES: Selected by Vancouver Canucks in first round (first Canucks pick, second overall) of entry draft (June 11, 1988). ... Hyperextended elbow (October 1989). ... Separated shoulder (March 17, 1990). ... Sprained knee (December 1, 1996); missed 24 games. ... Bruised ribs (March 8, 1997); missed eight games. ... Injured knee (April 5, 1997); missed one game. ... Strained groin (November 16, 1997); missed eight games. ... Sprained knee (January 26, 1998); missed six games. ... Traded by Canucks to New York Islanders for D Bryan McCabe, LW Todd Bertuzzi and third-round pick (LW Jarkko Ruutu) in 1998 entry draft (February 6, 1998). ... Traded by Islanders to Montreal Canadiens for first-round pick (D Branislav Mezei) in 1999 entry draft (May 29, 1999). ... Sprained ankle (December 1, 1999); missed 14 games. ... Reinjured ankle (January 6, 2000); missed six games. ... Fractured ribs (March 14, 2000); missed final 12 games of regular season. ... Bruised foot (December 8, 2000); missed one game. ... Bruised foot (December 30, 2000); missed 12 games. ... Traded by Canadiens with RW Dainius Zubrus and second-round pick (traded to Tampa Bay) in 2001 entry draft to Washington Capitals for F Jan Bulis, F Richard Zednik and first-round pick (C Alexander Perezhogin) in 2001 entry draft (March 13, 2001). ... Traded by Capitals with second-round pick (D Denis Grot) in 2003 entry draft to Canucks for first-round pick (RW Boyd Gordon) in 2002 entry draft and third-round pick (later traded to Edmonton Oilers) in 2003 entry draft (November 10, 2001). ... Sprained knee (October 10, 2002); missed six games. ... Cut above eye (December 15, 2002); mised five games.

STATISTICAL PLATEAUS: Three-goal games: 1988-89 (2), 1990-91 (1), 1995-96 (1), 1999-00 (1). Total: 5.

Season Team	League	REGULAR SEASON GP	G	A	Pts.	PIM	+/-	PP	SH	PLAYOFFS GP	G	A	Pts.	PIM
85-86—Medicine Hat	WHL	5	2	0	2	0	...	...	...	—	—	—	—	—
86-87—Medicine Hat	WHL	72	14	22	36	59	...	...	...	20	5	4	9	17
87-88—Medicine Hat	WHL	67	46	64	110	76	...	...	...	16	13	12	25	19
88-89—Vancouver	NHL	80	30	29	59	41	-10	10	1	7	3	4	7	8
89-90—Vancouver	NHL	73	21	30	51	43	-17	6	2	—	—	—	—	—
90-91—Vancouver	NHL	80	33	37	70	65	-25	16	2	6	0	7	7	2
91-92—Vancouver	NHL	80	31	44	75	101	3	6	1	13	4	8	12	6
92-93—Vancouver	NHL	84	33	39	72	64	19	8	0	12	5	8	13	16
93-94—Vancouver	NHL	84	32	29	61	73	6	10	2	24	12	13	25	18
94-95—Vancouver	NHL	48	18	22	40	40	-5	9	0	11	2	6	8	12
95-96—Vancouver	NHL	82	33	47	80	42	6	12	1	6	4	4	8	6
96-97—Vancouver	NHL	49	9	31	40	27	5	2	2	—	—	—	—	—
97-98—Vancouver	NHL	42	7	14	21	49	-13	2	0	—	—	—	—	—
—New York Islanders	NHL	25	10	7	17	33	-1	3	2	—	—	—	—	—
—Can. Olympic team	Int'l	6	1	0	1	10	2	0	0	—	—	—	—	—
98-99—New York Islanders	NHL	82	18	29	47	32	-14	8	1	—	—	—	—	—
99-00—Montreal	NHL	50	13	17	30	34	-3	4	0	—	—	—	—	—
00-01—Montreal	NHL	57	12	21	33	52	-2	6	0	—	—	—	—	—
—Washington	NHL	12	3	1	4	8	2	0	0	6	0	4	4	14
01-02—Washington	NHL	16	1	2	3	6	-2	1	0	—	—	—	—	—
—Vancouver	NHL	64	12	22	34	65	-3	2	0	6	1	4	5	0
02-03—Vancouver	NHL	71	19	22	41	30	-1	4	1	14	1	2	3	10

		REGULAR SEASON								PLAYOFFS				
Season Team	**League**	**GP**	**G**	**A**	**Pts.**	**PIM**	**+/-**	**PP**	**SH**	**GP**	**G**	**A**	**Pts.**	**PIM**
03-04—Vancouver	NHL	82	14	22	36	26	-6	4	0	7	0	0	0	6
05-06—Vancouver	NHL	82	7	9	16	15	3	1	1	—	—	—	—	—
NHL Totals (17 years)		1243	356	474	830	846	-58	114	16	112	32	60	92	98

LINDROS, ERIC C

PERSONAL: Born February 28, 1973, in London, Ont. ... 6-4/235. ... Shoots right. ... Brother of Brett Lindros, RW with New York Islanders (1994-96). ... Name pronounced LIHND-roez.

TRANSACTIONS/CAREER NOTES: Selected by Quebec Nordiques in first round (first Nordiques pick, first overall) of entry draft (June 22, 1991); refused to report. ... Traded by Nordiques to Philadelphia Flyers for G Ron Hextall, C Mike Ricci, C Peter Forsberg, D Steve Duchesne, D Kerry Huffman, first-round pick (G Jocelyn Thibault) in 1993 draft, cash and future considerations (June 20, 1992); Nordiques aquired LW Chris Simon and first-round pick (traded to Toronto Maple Leafs) in 1994 entry draft to complete deal (July 21, 1992). ... Sprained knee ligament (November 22, 1992); missed nine games. ... Injured knee (December 29, 1992); missed two games. ... Reinjured knee (January 10, 1993); missed 12 games. ... Torn right knee ligament (November 12, 1993); missed 14 games. ... Back spasms (March 6, 1994); missed one game. ... Sprained shoulder (April 4, 1994); missed remainder of season. ... Flu (January 29, 1995); missed one game. ... Bruised eye (April 30, 1995); missed final game of season and first three playoff games. ... Bruised left knee (November 2, 1995); missed seven games. ... Injured knee (April 5, 1996); missed two games. ... Injured right groin (October 1, 1996); missed 23 games. ... Bruised bone in back (February 13, 1997); missed two games. ... Charley horse (March 2, 1997); missed one game. ... Bruised calf (March 22, 1997); missed two games. ... Suspended two games and fined $2,000 for two high-sticking incidents (April 9, 1997). ... Bruised ribs (November 6, 1997); missed one game. ... Concussion (March 8, 1998); missed 18 games. ... Fined $1,000 for slashing incident (December 5, 1998). ... Concussion (December 29, 1998); missed two games. ... Suspended two games for high-sticking incident (March 28, 1999). ... Collapsed lung (April 1, 1999); missed remainder of season. ... Ill (October 28, 1999); missed two games. ... Bruised left hand (December 11, 1999); missed two games. ... Concussion (January 14, 2000); missed four games. ... Back spasms (February 20, 2000); missed five games. ... Concussion (March 13, 2000); missed final 14 games of regular season and 16 playoff games. ... Missed 2000-01 season in contract dispute. ... Rights traded by Flyers with future considerations to New York Rangers for LW Jan Hlavac, D Kim Johnsson, RW Pavel Brendl and third-round pick (LW Stefan Ruzicka) in 2003 entry draft (August 20, 2001). ... Sprained right knee (December 12, 2001); missed three games. ... Concussion (December 28, 2001); missed four games. ... Sprained right knee (January 28, 2002); missed one game. ... Bruised foot (March 9, 2002); missed two games. ... Suspended one game for high-sticking incident (October 12, 2002). ... Sprained left shoulder (October 20, 2003); missed seven games. ... Injured left eye (November 12, 2003); missed four games. ... Flu (January 22, 2004); missed one game. ... Concussion (January 29, 2004) and shoulder surgery (March 25, 2004); missed final 31 games of season. ... Signed as free agent by Maple Leafs (August 11, 2005). ... Torn ligament in right wrist (December 10, 2005); missed 27 games. ... Re-injured wrist (March 4, 2006); missed final 22 games of regular season. ... Signed as free agent by Dallas Stars (July 17, 2006).

STATISTICAL PLATEAUS: Three-goal games: 1992-93 (3), 1993-94 (1), 1994-95 (3), 1995-96 (1), 1997-98 (1), 1999-00 (1), 2001-02 (2). Total: 12. ... Four-goal games: 1996-97 (1). ... Total hat tricks: 13.

		REGULAR SEASON								PLAYOFFS				
Season Team	**League**	**GP**	**G**	**A**	**Pts.**	**PIM**	**+/-**	**PP**	**SH**	**GP**	**G**	**A**	**Pts.**	**PIM**
88-89—St. Michaels	MTHL	37	24	43	67	193	...	...	...	—	—	—	—	—
89-90—Detroit	NAJHL	14	23	29	52	123	...	...	...	—	—	—	—	—
—Oshawa	OHL	25	17	19	36	61	...	...	...	17	18	18	36	76
90-91—Oshawa	OHL	57	71	78	149	189	...	...	...	16	18	20	38	93
91-92—Oshawa	OHL	13	9	22	31	54	...	...	...	—	—	—	—	—
—Canadian nat'l team	Int'l	24	19	16	35	34	...	...	...	—	—	—	—	—
—Can. Olympic team	Int'l	8	5	6	11	6	...	...	...	—	—	—	—	—
92-93—Philadelphia	NHL	61	41	34	75	147	28	8	1	—	—	—	—	—
93-94—Philadelphia	NHL	65	44	53	97	103	16	13	2	—	—	—	—	—
94-95—Philadelphia	NHL	46	29	41	70	60	27	7	0	12	4	11	15	18
95-96—Philadelphia	NHL	73	47	68	115	163	26	15	0	12	6	6	12	43
96-97—Philadelphia	NHL	52	32	47	79	136	31	9	0	19	12	14	26	40
97-98—Philadelphia	NHL	63	30	41	71	134	14	10	1	5	1	2	3	17
—Can. Olympic team	Int'l	6	2	3	5	2	6	0	0	—	—	—	—	—
98-99—Philadelphia	NHL	71	40	53	93	120	35	10	1	—	—	—	—	—
99-00—Philadelphia	NHL	55	27	32	59	83	11	10	1	2	1	0	1	0
00-01—Philadelphia	NHL	Did not play — holdout												
01-02—New York Rangers	NHL	72	37	36	73	138	19	12	1	—	—	—	—	—
—Can. Olympic team	Int'l	6	1	0	1	8	...	...	...	—	—	—	—	—
02-03—New York Rangers	NHL	81	19	34	53	141	5	9	0	—	—	—	—	—
03-04—New York Rangers	NHL	39	10	22	32	60	7	3	0	—	—	—	—	—
05-06—Toronto	NHL	33	11	11	22	43	-3	4	0	—	—	—	—	—
NHL Totals (13 years)		711	367	472	839	1328	216	110	7	50	24	33	57	118

LINDSTROM, JOAKIM RW/LW

PERSONAL: Born December 5, 1983, in Skelleftea, Sweden. ... 6-0/187. ... Shoots left.

TRANSACTIONS/CAREER NOTES: Selected by Columbus Blue Jackets in second round (second Blue Jackets pick, 41st overall) of entry draft (June 22, 2002).

		REGULAR SEASON								PLAYOFFS				
Season Team	**League**	**GP**	**G**	**A**	**Pts.**	**PIM**	**+/-**	**PP**	**SH**	**GP**	**G**	**A**	**Pts.**	**PIM**
00-01—MoDo Ornskoldsvik	Sweden	10	2	3	5	2	...	...	...	7	0	1	1	0
01-02—MoDo Ornskoldsvik	Sweden	42	4	3	7	20	...	...	...	14	3	5	8	8
02-03—MoDo Ornskoldsvik	Sweden	29	4	2	6	6	...	...	...	6	1	1	2	2
03-04—MoDo Ornskoldsvik	Sweden	15	0	2	2	0	-4	...	...	—	—	—	—	—
04-05—Syracuse	AHL	13	4	4	8	0	-2	2	0	—	—	—	—	—
—MoDo Ornskoldsvik	Sweden	37	2	3	5	24	...	...	...	—	—	—	—	—
05-06—Syracuse	AHL	64	14	29	43	52	8	5	2	6	1	1	2	0
—Columbus	NHL	3	0	0	0	0	0	0	0	—	—	—	—	—
NHL Totals (1 year)		3	0	0	0	0	0	0	0					

LITTLE, BRYAN C

PERSONAL: Born November 12, 1987, in Edmonton. ... 5-10/190. ... Shoots right.
TRANSACTIONS/CAREER NOTES: Selected by Atlanta Thrashers in first round (first Thrashers pick; 12th overall) of NHL draft (June 24, 2006).

		REGULAR SEASON								PLAYOFFS				
Season Team	**League**	**GP**	**G**	**A**	**Pts.**	**PIM**	**+/-**	**PP**	**SH**	**GP**	**G**	**A**	**Pts.**	**PIM**
03-04—Barrie	OHL	64	34	24	58	18	22	...	...	12	5	5	10	7
04-05—Barrie	OHL	62	36	32	68	34	19	...	...	4	5	1	6	2
05-06—Barrie	OHL	64	42	67	109	99	26	...	...	14	8	15	23	19

LOMBARDI, MATTHEW C

PERSONAL: Born March 18, 1982, in Montreal. ... 6-0/190. ... Shoots left.
TRANSACTIONS/CAREER NOTES: Selected by Calgary Flames in third round (third pick of Flames, 90th overall) in 2002 entry draft (June 22, 2002). ... Head (May 9, 2004); missed final 13 playoff games. ... Sprained right ankle (October 17, 2005); missed 24 games.
STATISTICAL PLATEAUS: Three-goal games: 2003-04 (1).

		REGULAR SEASON								PLAYOFFS				
Season Team	**League**	**GP**	**G**	**A**	**Pts.**	**PIM**	**+/-**	**PP**	**SH**	**GP**	**G**	**A**	**Pts.**	**PIM**
00-01—Victoriaville	QMJHL	72	28	39	67	66	...	...	...	13	12	6	18	10
01-02—Victoriaville	QMJHL	66	57	73	130	70	...	...	...	22	17	18	35	18
02-03—Saint John	AHL	76	25	21	46	41	-6	7	1	—	—	—	—	—
03-04—Calgary	NHL	79	16	13	29	32	4	3	2	13	1	5	6	4
04-05—Lowell	AHL	9	3	1	4	9	0	0	1	11	0	3	3	16
05-06—Omaha Ak-Sar-Ben	AHL	1	1	1	2	0	1	0	0	—	—	—	—	—
—Calgary	NHL	55	6	20	26	48	-1	1	2	7	0	2	2	2
NHL Totals (2 years)		134	22	33	55	80	3	4	4	20	1	7	8	6

LOYNS, LYNN LW

PERSONAL: Born February 22, 1981, in Naicam, Sask. ... 5-11/205. ... Shoots left.
TRANSACTIONS/CAREER NOTES: Signed as free agent by San Jose Sharks (September 22, 2001). ... Traded by Sharks to Calgary Flames for fifth-round pick (traded to Florida; Panthers selected D Bret Nasby) in 2004 draft (January 9, 2004). ... Injured ankle (April 26, 2004); missed remainder of playoffs.

		REGULAR SEASON								PLAYOFFS				
Season Team	**League**	**GP**	**G**	**A**	**Pts.**	**PIM**	**+/-**	**PP**	**SH**	**GP**	**G**	**A**	**Pts.**	**PIM**
97-98—Spokane	WHL	49	1	12	13	8	...	...	...	13	1	4	5	2
98-99—Spokane	WHL	72	20	30	50	43	...	...	...	—	—	—	—	—
99-00—Spokane	WHL	71	20	29	49	47	...	...	...	14	3	2	5	12
00-01—Spokane	WHL	66	31	42	73	81	...	...	...	12	6	12	18	18
01-02—Cleveland	AHL	76	9	9	18	81	...	...	...	—	—	—	—	—
02-03—San Jose	NHL	19	3	0	3	19	-4	0	0	—	—	—	—	—
—Cleveland	AHL	36	7	8	15	39	...	...	...	—	—	—	—	—
03-04—San Jose	NHL	2	0	0	0	0	-1	0	0	—	—	—	—	—
—Cleveland	AHL	30	5	9	14	40	9	0	1	—	—	—	—	—
—Calgary	NHL	12	0	2	2	2	-2	0	0	—	—	—	—	—
—Lowell	AHL	18	6	6	12	9	1	0	0	—	—	—	—	—
04-05—Lowell	AHL	77	7	8	15	42	4	1	0	11	0	0	0	0
05-06—Omaha Ak-Sar-Ben	AHL	68	9	8	17	50	-4	1	1	—	—	—	—	—
—Calgary	NHL	1	0	0	0	0	0	0	0	—	—	—	—	—
NHL Totals (3 years)		34	3	2	5	21	-7	0	0					

LUCIC, MILAN LW

PERSONAL: Born June 7, 1988, in Vancouver. ... 6-2/204. ... Shoots left.
TRANSACTIONS/CAREER NOTES: Selected by Boston Bruins in second round (third Bruins pick; 50th overall) of NHL draft (June 24, 2006).

		REGULAR SEASON								PLAYOFFS				
Season Team	**League**	**GP**	**G**	**A**	**Pts.**	**PIM**	**+/-**	**PP**	**SH**	**GP**	**G**	**A**	**Pts.**	**PIM**
04-05—Coquitlam	BCHL	50	9	14	23	100	...	...	...	—	—	—	—	—
—Vancouver	WHL	1	0	0	0	2	...	...	...	2	0	0	0	0
05-06—Vancouver	WHL	62	9	10	19	149	4	...	...	18	3	4	7	23

LUKOWICH, BRAD D

PERSONAL: Born August 12, 1976, in Cranbrook, B.C. ... 6-1/200. ... Shoots left. ... Name pronounced LOO-kih-wihch.
TRANSACTIONS/CAREER NOTES: Selected by New York Islanders in fourth round (fourth Islanders pick, 90th overall) of entry draft (June 29, 1994). ... Traded by Islanders to Dallas Stars for third-round pick (D Robert Schnabel) in 1997 entry draft (June 1, 1996). ... Back spasms (December 6, 1999); missed one game. ... Traded by Stars with G Manny Fernandez to Minnesota Wild for third-round pick (C Joel Lundqvist) in 2000 entry draft and fourth-round pick (later traded back to Wild) in 2002 entry draft (June 12, 2000). ... Traded by Wild with third-(C Yared Hagos) and ninth-round (RW Dale Sullivan) picks in 2001 entry draft to Stars for C Aaron Gavey, C Pavel Patera, eighth-round pick (C Eric Johansson) in 2000 draft and fourth-round pick (later traded to Los Angeles Kings) in 2002 draft (June 25, 2000). ... Fractured finger (January 2, 2002); missed five games. ... Traded by Stars with seventh-round pick (D Jay Rosehill) in 2003 entry draft to Tampa Bay Lightning for second-round pick (G Tobias Stephan) in 2002 entry draft (June 22, 2002). ... Fractured facial bone (March 27, 2003); missed six games. ... Flu (March 16, 2004); missed two games. ... Injured upper body (May 13, 2004); missed two playoff games. ... Signed as free agent by New

York Islanders (August 11, 2005). ... Ribs (January 10, 2006); missed three games. ... Traded by Islanders to New Jersey Devils for third-round pick (traded to Phoenix; Coyotes selected D Jonas Ahnelov) in 2006 draft (March 9, 2006).

Season Team	League	REGULAR SEASON GP	G	A	Pts.	PIM	+/-	PP	SH	PLAYOFFS GP	G	A	Pts.	PIM
92-93—Cranbook	Tier II Jr. A	54	21	41	62	162	...	...	...	—	—	—	—	—
—Kamloops	WHL	1	0	0	0	0	...	...	...	—	—	—	—	—
93-94—Kamloops	WHL	42	5	11	16	166	...	0	0	16	0	1	1	35
94-95—Kamloops	WHL	63	10	35	45	125	53	2	0	18	0	7	7	21
95-96—Kamloops	WHL	65	14	55	69	114	...	...	...	13	2	10	12	29
96-97—Michigan	IHL	69	2	6	8	77	...	...	...	4	0	1	1	2
97-98—Michigan	IHL	60	6	27	33	104	-7	2	0	4	0	4	4	14
—Dallas	NHL	4	0	1	1	2	-2	0	0	—	—	—	—	—
98-99—Michigan	IHL	67	8	21	29	95	1	3	0	—	—	—	—	—
—Dallas	NHL	14	1	2	3	19	3	0	0	8	0	1	1	4
99-00—Dallas	NHL	60	3	1	4	50	-14	0	0	—	—	—	—	—
00-01—Dallas	NHL	80	4	10	14	76	28	0	0	10	1	0	1	4
01-02—Dallas	NHL	66	1	6	7	40	-1	0	0	—	—	—	—	—
02-03—Tampa Bay	NHL	70	1	14	15	46	4	0	0	9	0	1	1	2
03-04—Tampa Bay	NHL	79	5	14	19	24	29	0	0	18	0	2	2	6
04-05—Fort Worth	CHL	16	3	5	8	33	...	...	...	—	—	—	—	—
05-06—New York Islanders	NHL	57	1	12	13	32	-3	0	0	—	—	—	—	—
—New Jersey	NHL	18	1	7	8	8	3	0	0	9	0	0	0	4
NHL Totals (8 years)		448	17	67	84	297	47	0	0	54	1	4	5	20

LUNDMARK, JAMIE C/LW

PERSONAL: Born January 16, 1981, in Edmonton. ... 6-0/195. ... Shoots right.

TRANSACTIONS/CAREER NOTES: Selected by New York Rangers in first round (second Rangers pick, ninth overall) of entry draft (June 26, 1999). ... Flu (January 15, 2003); missed one game. ... Sprained right knee (December 4, 2003); missed 23 games. ... Traded by Rangers to Phoenix Coyotes for C Jeff Taffe (October 18, 2005). ... Hip (February 2, 2006); missed three games. ... Traded by Coyotes to Calgary Flames for fourth-round pick (traded to N.Y. Islanders; Islanders selected C Doug Rogers) in 2006 draft (March 9, 2006). ... Eye (March 31, 2006); missed four games.

Season Team	League	REGULAR SEASON GP	G	A	Pts.	PIM	+/-	PP	SH	PLAYOFFS GP	G	A	Pts.	PIM
97-98—St. Albert	Jr. A	53	33	58	91	176	...	...	...	—	—	—	—	—
98-99—Moose Jaw	WHL	70	40	51	91	121	-11	21	2	11	5	4	9	24
99-00—Moose Jaw	WHL	37	21	27	48	33	-7	8	1	—	—	—	—	—
00-01—Seattle	WHL	52	35	42	77	49	...	...	...	9	4	4	8	16
01-02—Hartford	AHL	79	27	32	59	56	-17	10	1	10	3	4	7	16
02-03—Hartford	AHL	22	9	9	18	18	2	2	1	—	—	—	—	—
—New York Rangers	NHL	55	8	11	19	16	-3	0	0	—	—	—	—	—
03-04—New York Rangers	NHL	56	2	8	10	33	-8	0	0	—	—	—	—	—
04-05—Bolzano	Italy	14	10	10	20	22	...	...	...	—	—	—	—	—
—Hartford	AHL	64	14	27	41	146	-1	5	2	6	2	4	6	8
05-06—San Antonio	AHL	4	1	2	3	2	1	0	1	—	—	—	—	—
—New York Rangers	NHL	3	1	0	1	6	-2	0	0	—	—	—	—	—
—Phoenix	NHL	38	5	13	18	36	-1	1	0	—	—	—	—	—
—Calgary	NHL	12	4	6	10	20	2	1	0	4	0	1	1	7
NHL Totals (3 years)		164	20	38	58	111	-12	2	0	4	0	1	1	7

LUNDQVIST, HENRIK G

PERSONAL: Born March 2, 1982, in Are, Sweden. ... 6-1/187. ... Catches left.

TRANSACTIONS/CAREER NOTES: Selected by New York Rangers in seventh round (20fifth pick overall) in 2000 entry draft (June 25, 2000). ... Hip flexor (April 4, 2006); missed seven games.

Season Team	League	REGULAR SEASON GP	Min.	W	L	OTL	T	GA	SO	GAA	SV%	PLAYOFFS GP	Min.	W	L	GA	SO	GAA	SV%
99-00—Vastra Frolunda	Sweden	35	...	...	...	...	...	...	...	2.37	...	—	—	—	—	—	—	—	—
00-01—Vastra Frolunda	Sweden	4	...	...	...	...	...	...	...	3.46	...	—	—	—	—	—	—	—	—
—Vastra Frolunda	Sweden Dv. 2	19	...	...	...	...	...	...	...	2.64	...	—	—	—	—	—	—	—	—
01-02—Vastra Frolunda	Sweden	20	...	...	...	...	...	...	...	2.71	...	8	...	8	0	...	...	2.21	...
—Vastra Frolunda	Sweden Dv. 2	1	...	...	...	...	...	4	...	4.00	...	—	—	—	—	—	—	—	—
02-03—Vastra Frolunda	Sweden	28	...	...	...	...	...	...	...	1.45	...	12	...	...	...	...	...	2.11	...
03-04—Vastra Frolunda	Sweden	48	2898	...	...	...	...	105	7	2.17	...	10	...	...	...	...	...	1.97	...
04-05—Frolunda	Sweden	44	...	33	8	...	3	...	6	1.79	...	—	—	—	—	—	—	—	—
05-06—New York Rangers	NHL	53	3112	30	12	9	...	116	2	2.24	.922	3	177	0	3	13	0	4.41	.835
—Swedish Oly. team	Int'l	6	...	...	...	...	...	...	0	2.33	.907	—	—	—	—	—	—	—	—
NHL Totals (1 year)		53	3112	30	12	9	0	116	2	2.24	.922	3	177	0	3	13	0	4.41	.835

LUONGO, ROBERTO G

PERSONAL: Born April 4, 1979, in Montreal. ... 6-3/205. ... Catches left. ... Name pronounced luh-WAHN-goh.

TRANSACTIONS/CAREER NOTES: Selected by New York Islanders in first round (first Islanders pick, fourth overall) of NHL draft (June 21, 1997). ... Traded by Islanders with C Olli Jokinen to Florida Panthers for RW Mark Parrish and LW Oleg Kvasha (June 24, 2000). ... Cut forearm (October 10, 2001); missed four games. ... Sprained right ankle (March 20, 2002); missed remainder of season. ... Back spasms (November 7, 2002); missed three games. ... Injured knee (March 26, 2003); missed one game. ... Traded by Panthers with D Lukas Krajicek and a sixth-round pick (W Sergei Shirokov) in the 2006 draft to Vancouver Canucks for F Todd Bertuzzi, G Alex Auld and D Bryan Allen (June 23, 2006).

Season Team	League	GP	Min.	W	L	OTL	T	GA	SO	GAA	SV%	GP	Min.	W	L	GA	SO	GAA	SV%
		REGULAR SEASON										PLAYOFFS							
95-96—Val-d'Or	QMJHL	23	1199	6	11	...	4	74	0	3.70	.878	3	68	0	1	5	0	4.41	...
96-97—Val-d'Or	QMJHL	60	3305	32	21	...	2	171	2	3.10	...	13	777	8	5	44	0	3.40	.904
97-98—Val-d'Or	QMJHL	54	3046	27	20	...	5	157	7	3.09	.899	17	1019	14	3	37	2	2.18	.933
98-99—Val-d'Or	QMJHL	21	1177	6	10	...	2	77	1	3.93	...	—	—	—	—	—	—	—	—
—Acadie-Bathurst	QMJHL	22	1341	14	7	...	1	74	0	3.31	...	23	1400	16	6	64	0	2.74	...
99-00—Lowell	AHL	26	1517	10	12	...	4	74	1	2.93	...	6	359	3	3	18	0	3.01	...
—New York Islanders	NHL	24	1292	7	14	...	1	70	1	3.25	.904	—	—	—	—	—	—	—	—
00-01—Florida	NHL	47	2628	12	24	...	7	107	5	2.44	.920	—	—	—	—	—	—	—	—
—Louisville	AHL	3	178	1	2	...	0	10	0	3.37	.917	—	—	—	—	—	—	—	—
01-02—Florida	NHL	58	3030	16	33	...	4	140	4	2.77	.915	—	—	—	—	—	—	—	—
02-03—Florida	NHL	65	3627	20	34	...	7	164	6	2.71	.918	—	—	—	—	—	—	—	—
03-04—Florida	NHL	72	4252	25	33	...	*14	172	7	2.43	.931	—	—	—	—	—	—	—	—
05-06—Florida	NHL	*75	4305	35	*30	9	...	*213	4	2.97	.914	—	—	—	—	—	—	—	—
—Canadian Oly. team	Int'l	2	...	...	...	...	...	...	0	1.51	.929	—	—	—	—	—	—	—	—
NHL Totals (6 years)		341	19134	115	168	9	33	866	27	2.72	.919								

LUPUL, JOFFREY RW

PERSONAL: Born September 23, 1983, in Edmonton. ... 6-1/200. ... Shoots right.
TRANSACTIONS/CAREER NOTES: Selected by Anaheim Mighty Ducks in first round (first Mighty Ducks pick, seventh overall) of NHL entry draft (June 22, 2002). ... Concussion (November 23, 2005); missed one game. ... Traded by Ducks with D Ladislav Smid and three future draft picks to Edmonton Oilers for D Chris Pronger (July 3, 2006).

Season Team	League	GP	G	A	Pts.	PIM	+/-	PP	SH	GP	G	A	Pts.	PIM
		REGULAR SEASON								PLAYOFFS				
00-01—Medicine Hat	WHL	69	30	26	56	39	...	...	...	—	—	—	—	—
01-02—Medicine Hat	WHL	72	56	50	106	95	...	...	...	—	—	—	—	—
02-03—Medicine Hat	WHL	50	41	37	78	82	...	...	...	11	4	11	15	20
03-04—Anaheim	NHL	75	13	21	34	28	-6	4	0	—	—	—	—	—
—Cincinnati	AHL	3	3	2	5	2	4	0	0	—	—	—	—	—
04-05—Cincinnati	AHL	65	30	26	56	58	10	10	1	12	3	9	12	27
05-06—Anaheim	NHL	81	28	25	53	48	-13	12	2	16	9	2	11	31
NHL Totals (2 years)		156	41	46	87	76	-19	16	2	16	9	2	11	31

LYDMAN, TONI D

PERSONAL: Born September 25, 1977, in Lahti, Finland. ... 6-1/200. ... Shoots left.
TRANSACTIONS/CAREER NOTES: Selected by Calgary Flames in fourth round (fifth Flames pick, 89th overall) of entry draft (June 22, 1996). ... Concussion (January 5, 2001); missed 12 games. ... Flu (December 26, 2001); missed two games. ... Flu (March 28, 2002); missed one game. ... Flu (December 27, 2002); missed one game. ... Injured shoulder (December 5, 2003); missed five games. ... Concussion (March 16, 2004); missed 10 games. ... Injured upper body (April 13, 2004); missed 20 playoff games. ... Traded by the Flames to Buffalo Sabres for third-round pick (C/RW John Armstrong) in 2006 (August 25, 2005). ... Strained groin (October 29, 2005); missed five games. ... Flu (January 12, 2006); missed one game.

Season Team	League	GP	G	A	Pts.	PIM	+/-	PP	SH	GP	G	A	Pts.	PIM
		REGULAR SEASON								PLAYOFFS				
93-94—Reipas Lahti	Finland Jr.	1	0	0	0	0	...	...	...	—	—	—	—	—
94-95—Reipas Lahti	Finland Jr.	26	6	4	10	10	...	...	...	—	—	—	—	—
95-96—Reipas Lahti	Finland Jr.	1	0	0	0	0	...	...	...	—	—	—	—	—
—Reipas Lahti	Finland	39	5	2	7	30	...	...	...	—	—	—	—	—
96-97—Tappara	Finland	49	1	2	3	65	...	...	...	3	0	0	0	6
97-98—Tappara Tampere	Finland	48	4	10	14	48	...	...	...	4	0	2	2	0
98-99—HIFK Helsinki	Finland	42	4	7	11	36	...	...	...	11	0	3	3	2
99-00—HIFK Helsinki	Finland	46	4	18	22	36	...	...	...	9	0	4	4	6
00-01—Calgary	NHL	62	3	16	19	30	-7	1	0	—	—	—	—	—
01-02—Calgary	NHL	79	6	22	28	52	-8	1	0	—	—	—	—	—
02-03—Calgary	NHL	81	6	20	26	28	-7	3	0	—	—	—	—	—
03-04—Calgary	NHL	67	4	16	20	30	6	2	0	6	0	1	1	2
04-05—HIFK Helsinki	Finland	8	1	2	3	2	6	...	...	5	0	3	3	0
05-06—Buffalo	NHL	75	1	16	17	82	9	0	0	18	1	4	5	18
—Fin. Olympic team	Int'l	8	1	0	1	10	4	0	0	—	—	—	—	—
NHL Totals (5 years)		364	20	90	110	222	-7	7	0	24	1	5	6	20

MACDONALD, CRAIG C/LW

PERSONAL: Born April 7, 1977, in Antigonish, N.S. ... 6-1/195. ... Shoots left.
TRANSACTIONS/CAREER NOTES: Selected by Hartford Whalers in fourth round (third Whalers pick, 88th overall) of entry draft (June 22, 1996). ... Whalers franchise moved to North Carolina and renamed Carolina Hurricanes for 1997-98 season; NHL approved move on June 25, 1997. ... Signed as free agent by Florida Panthers (August 14, 2003). ... Groin (November 18, 2003); missed five games. ... Claimed off waivers by Boston Bruins (January 20, 2004). ... Signed as free agent by Calgary Flames (August 11, 2005).

Season Team	League	GP	G	A	Pts.	PIM	+/-	PP	SH	GP	G	A	Pts.	PIM
		REGULAR SEASON								PLAYOFFS				
94-95—Lawrence Academy	Mass. H.S.	30	25	52	77	10	...	...	...	—	—	—	—	—
95-96—Harvard	ECAC	34	7	10	17	10	...	...	...	—	—	—	—	—
96-97—Harvard	ECAC	32	6	10	16	20	...	2	1	—	—	—	—	—
97-98—Canadian nat'l team	Int'l	51	15	20	35	133	...	...	...	—	—	—	—	—

M

		REGULAR SEASON								PLAYOFFS				
Season Team	League	GP	G	A	Pts.	PIM	+/-	PP	SH	GP	G	A	Pts.	PIM
98-99—New Haven	AHL	62	17	31	48	77	1	5	0	—	—	—	—	—
—Carolina	NHL	11	0	0	0	0	0	0	0	1	0	0	0	0
99-00—Cincinnati	IHL	78	12	24	36	76	...	...	...	11	4	1	5	8
00-01—Cincinnati	IHL	82	20	28	48	104	...	...	...	5	0	1	1	6
01-02—Lowell	AHL	64	19	22	41	61	1	2	1	—	—	—	—	—
—Carolina	NHL	12	1	1	2	0	-1	0	0	4	0	0	0	2
02-03—Lowell	AHL	27	7	20	27	38	-3	1	0	—	—	—	—	—
—Carolina	NHL	35	1	3	4	20	-3	0	0	—	—	—	—	—
03-04—Florida	NHL	34	0	3	3	25	-5	0	0	—	—	—	—	—
—San Antonio	AHL	2	0	0	0	4	0	0	0	—	—	—	—	—
—Boston	NHL	18	0	3	3	8	0	0	0	1	0	0	0	0
04-05—Lowell	AHL	71	10	18	28	104	-3	3	0	2	0	0	0	0
05-06—Omaha Ak-Sar-Ben	AHL	37	8	19	27	57	3	5	1	—	—	—	—	—
—Calgary	NHL	25	3	2	5	8	5	1	0	1	0	0	0	0
NHL Totals (5 years)		135	5	12	17	61	-4	1	0	7	0	0	0	2

MACKENZIE, DEREK C

PERSONAL: Born June 11, 1981, in Sudbury, Ont. ... 5-11/180. ... Shoots left.

TRANSACTIONS/CAREER NOTES: Selected by Atlanta Thrashers in fifth round (sixth Thrashers pick, 128th overall) of NHL entry draft (June 26, 1999).

		REGULAR SEASON								PLAYOFFS				
Season Team	League	GP	G	A	Pts.	PIM	+/-	PP	SH	GP	G	A	Pts.	PIM
97-98—Sudbury	OHL	59	9	11	20	26	...	...	...	10	0	1	1	6
98-99—Sudbury	OHL	68	22	65	87	74	...	...	...	4	2	4	6	2
99-00—Sudbury	OHL	68	24	33	57	110	1	5	4	12	5	9	14	16
00-01—Sudbury	OHL	62	40	49	89	89	25	8	5	12	6	8	14	16
01-02—Chicago	AHL	68	13	12	25	80	0	0	3	25	4	2	6	20
—Atlanta	NHL	1	0	0	0	2	-1	0	0	—	—	—	—	—
02-03—Chicago	AHL	80	14	18	32	97	14	0	4	9	0	0	0	4
03-04—Atlanta	NHL	12	0	1	1	10	0	0	0	—	—	—	—	—
—Chicago	AHL	63	19	16	35	67	8	0	2	10	7	1	8	13
04-05—Chicago	AHL	78	13	20	33	87	5	0	6	18	5	6	11	33
05-06—Chicago	AHL	36	10	12	22	48	-3	4	1	—	—	—	—	—
—Atlanta	NHL	11	0	1	1	8	0	0	0	—	—	—	—	—
NHL Totals (3 years)		24	0	2	2	20	-1	0	0					

MACLEAN, DON LW

PERSONAL: Born January 14, 1977, in Sydney, N.S. ... 6-3/208. ... Shoots left.

TRANSACTIONS/CAREER NOTES: Selected by Los Angeles Kings in second round (second Kings pick, 33rd overall) of entry draft (July 8, 1995). ... Traded by Kings to Toronto Maple Leafs for C Craig Charron (February 23, 2000). ... Signed as free agent by Columbus Blue Jackets (July 17, 2002). ... Neck (October 1, 2002); missed 57 games. ... Signed as free agent by Detroit Red Wings (August 25, 2005). ... Signed as free agent by Phoenix Coyotes (July 17, 2006).

		REGULAR SEASON								PLAYOFFS				
Season Team	League	GP	G	A	Pts.	PIM	+/-	PP	SH	GP	G	A	Pts.	PIM
94-95—Beauport	QMJHL	64	15	27	42	37	...	...	...	17	4	4	8	6
95-96—Beauport	QMJHL	1	0	1	1	0	...	...	...	—	—	—	—	—
—Laval	QMJHL	21	17	11	28	29	...	...	...	—	—	—	—	—
—Hull	QMJHL	39	26	34	60	44	...	...	...	17	6	7	13	14
96-97—Hull	QMJHL	69	34	47	81	67	...	...	...	14	11	10	21	29
97-98—Los Angeles	NHL	22	5	2	7	4	-1	2	0	—	—	—	—	—
—Fredericton	AHL	39	9	5	14	32	-8	2	0	4	1	3	4	2
98-99—Springfield	AHL	41	5	14	19	31	0	2	0	—	—	—	—	—
—Grand Rapids	IHL	28	6	13	19	8	-3	2	0	—	—	—	—	—
99-00—Lowell	AHL	40	11	17	28	18	...	...	...	—	—	—	—	—
—St. John's	AHL	21	14	12	26	8	...	...	...	—	—	—	—	—
00-01—Toronto	NHL	3	0	1	1	2	-2	0	0	—	—	—	—	—
—St. John's	AHL	61	26	34	60	48	...	...	...	4	2	1	3	2
01-02—St. John's	AHL	75	33	54	87	49	15	14	2	9	5	5	10	6
—Toronto	NHL	...	...	...	...	...	...	...	...	3	0	0	0	0
02-03—Syracuse	AHL	17	9	9	18	6	1	2	0	—	—	—	—	—
03-04—Columbus	NHL	4	1	0	1	0	-1	0	0	—	—	—	—	—
—Syracuse	AHL	77	27	42	69	50	-5	10	2	7	0	3	3	4
04-05—Espoo	Finland	51	22	21	43	46	...	...	...	—	—	—	—	—
05-06—Grand Rapids	AHL	76	56	32	88	63	18	21	0	14	6	2	8	8
—Detroit	NHL	3	1	1	2	0	2	1	0	—	—	—	—	—
NHL Totals (5 years)		32	7	4	11	6	-2	3	0	3	0	0	0	0

MADDEN, JOHN C

PERSONAL: Born May 4, 1973, in Barrie, Ont. ... 5-11/190. ... Shoots left.

TRANSACTIONS/CAREER NOTES: Signed as free agent by New Jersey Devils (June 26, 1997). ... Injured toe (January 20, 2001); missed one game. ... Injured groin (March 27, 2003); missed two games. ... Injured face (December 12, 2003); missed two games.

STATISTICAL PLATEAUS: Three-goal games: 2002-03 (1). ... Four-goal games: 2000-01 (1). ... Total hat tricks: 2.

Season Team	League	REGULAR SEASON GP	G	A	Pts.	PIM	+/-	PP	SH	PLAYOFFS GP	G	A	Pts.	PIM
92-93—Barrie	COJHL	43	49	75	124	62	...	...	...	—	—	—	—	—
93-94—Univ. of Michigan	CCHA	36	6	11	17	14	...	...	...	—	—	—	—	—
94-95—Univ. of Michigan	CCHA	39	21	22	43	8	...	...	...	—	—	—	—	—
95-96—Univ. of Michigan	CCHA	43	27	30	57	45	...	...	...	—	—	—	—	—
96-97—Univ. of Michigan	CCHA	42	26	37	63	56	...	...	...	—	—	—	—	—
97-98—Albany	AHL	74	20	36	56	40	35	3	2	13	3	13	16	14
98-99—Albany	AHL	75	38	60	98	44	24	8	6	5	2	2	4	6
—New Jersey	NHL	4	0	1	1	0	-2	0	0	—	—	—	—	—
99-00—New Jersey	NHL	74	16	9	25	6	7	0	*6	20	3	4	7	0
00-01—New Jersey	NHL	80	23	15	38	12	24	0	3	25	4	3	7	6
01-02—New Jersey	NHL	82	15	8	23	25	6	0	0	6	0	0	0	0
02-03—New Jersey	NHL	80	19	22	41	26	13	2	2	24	6	10	16	2
03-04—New Jersey	NHL	80	12	23	35	22	7	1	1	5	0	0	0	0
04-05—HIFK Helsinki	Finland	3	0	0	0	0	0	0	0	—	—	—	—	—
05-06—New Jersey	NHL	82	16	20	36	36	-7	0	1	9	4	1	5	8
NHL Totals (7 years)		482	101	98	199	127	48	3	13	89	17	18	35	16

MAIR, ADAM C

PERSONAL: Born February 15, 1979, in Hamilton, Ont. ... 6-2/215. ... Shoots right.
TRANSACTIONS/CAREER NOTES: Selected by Toronto Maple Leafs in fourth round (second Maple Leafs pick, 84th overall) of entry draft (June 21, 1997). ... Traded by Maple Leafs with second-round pick (C Mike Cammalleri) in 2001 entry draft to Los Angeles Kings for D Aki Berg (March 13, 2001). ... Suspended 10 games for leaving bench to fight (December 21, 2001). ... Traded by Kings with fifth-round pick (D Thomas Morrow) in 2003 draft to Buffalo Sabres for LW Erik Rasmussen (July 24, 2002). ... Bruised right foot (March 19, 2003); missed three games. ... Suspended one game for cross-checking incident (December 13, 2003). ... Strained groin (September 2005); missed first six games of season. ... Concussion (January 12, 2006); missed 31 games. ... Post-concussion syndrome (April 17, 2006); missed final five games of regular season and 15 playoff games.

Season Team	League	REGULAR SEASON GP	G	A	Pts.	PIM	+/-	PP	SH	PLAYOFFS GP	G	A	Pts.	PIM
94-95—Ohsweken	Jr. B	39	21	23	44	91	...	...	...	—	—	—	—	—
95-96—Owen Sound	OHL	62	12	15	27	63	...	...	...	6	0	0	0	2
96-97—Owen Sound	OHL	65	16	35	51	113	-17	5	1	4	1	0	1	2
97-98—Owen Sound	OHL	56	25	27	52	179	...	...	...	11	6	3	9	31
98-99—Owen Sound	OHL	43	23	41	64	109	21	...	...	16	10	10	20	47
—Saint John	AHL	24	5	12	17	31	...	...	...	3	1	0	1	6
—Toronto	NHL	...	...	...	...	...	...	...	...	5	1	0	1	14
99-00—St. John's	AHL	66	22	27	49	124	...	...	...	—	—	—	—	—
—Toronto	NHL	8	1	0	1	6	-1	0	0	5	0	0	0	8
00-01—St. John's	AHL	47	18	27	45	69	...	...	...	—	—	—	—	—
—Toronto	NHL	16	0	2	2	14	3	0	0	—	—	—	—	—
—Los Angeles	NHL	10	0	0	0	6	-3	0	0	—	—	—	—	—
01-02—Manchester	AHL	27	10	9	19	48	3	4	1	5	5	1	6	10
—Los Angeles	NHL	18	1	1	2	57	1	0	0	—	—	—	—	—
02-03—Buffalo	NHL	79	6	11	17	146	-4	0	1	—	—	—	—	—
03-04—Buffalo	NHL	81	6	14	20	146	-3	1	0	—	—	—	—	—
05-06—Buffalo	NHL	40	2	5	7	47	-2	0	0	3	0	0	0	0
NHL Totals (7 years)		252	16	33	49	422	-9	1	1	13	1	0	1	22

MAJESKY, IVAN D

PERSONAL: Born September 2, 1976, in Banska Bystrica, Czech. ... 6-5/230. ... Shoots right.
TRANSACTIONS/CAREER NOTES: Selected by Florida Panthers in ninth round (12th Panthers pick, 267th overall) of entry draft (June 24, 2001). ... Traded by Panthers to Atlanta Thrashers for second-round pick (C Kamil Kreps) in 2003 draft (June 20, 2003). ... Sprained left knee (November 29, 2003); missed five games. ... Reinjured left knee (December 13, 2003); missed nine games. ... Signed as free agent by Washington Capitals (August 10, 2005). ... Injured knee (September 2005); missed first 15 games of season.

Season Team	League	REGULAR SEASON GP	G	A	Pts.	PIM	+/-	PP	SH	PLAYOFFS GP	G	A	Pts.	PIM
95-96—Banska Bystrica	Slovakia	17	0	0	0	18	...	...	...	—	—	—	—	—
96-97—Banska Bystrica	Slovakia	49	2	4	6	...	...	...	...	—	—	—	—	—
97-98—Banska Bystrica	Slov. Div. 2	43	6	7	13	50	...	...	...	—	—	—	—	—
98-99—Hkm Zvolen	Slovakia	...	...	...	...	...	...	...	...	6	0	2	2	2
—Banska Bystrica	Slovakia Dv. 2	48	7	7	14	68	...	...	...	—	—	—	—	—
99-00—Hkm Zvolen	Slovakia	51	7	9	16	68	...	...	...	10	0	4	4	2
00-01—Ilves Tampere	Finland	54	2	14	16	99	...	...	...	9	0	1	1	6
01-02—Ilves Tampere	Finland	44	6	6	12	84	...	...	...	—	—	—	—	—
—Slovakian Oly. team	Int'l	4	0	1	1	4	...	...	...	—	—	—	—	—
02-03—Florida	NHL	82	4	8	12	92	-18	0	0	—	—	—	—	—
03-04—Atlanta	NHL	63	3	7	10	76	-7	0	0	—	—	—	—	—
04-05—Sparta Praha	Czech Rep.	28	2	6	8	40	12	...	...	5	2	1	3	6
05-06—Washington	NHL	57	1	8	9	66	-2	0	1	—	—	—	—	—
—Slovakian Oly. team	Int'l	6	0	0	0	4	-1	0	0	—	—	—	—	—
NHL Totals (3 years)		202	8	23	31	234	-27	0	1					

MAKAROV, IGOR RW

PERSONAL: Born September 19, 1987, in Moscow, Rus. ... 6-1/183. ... Shoots right.
TRANSACTIONS/CAREER NOTES: Selected by Chicago Blackhawks in second round (second Blackhawks pick; 33rd overall) of NHL draft (June 24, 2006).

Season Team	League	GP	G	A	Pts.	PIM	+/-	PP	SH		GP	G	A	Pts.	PIM
		REGULAR SEASON									PLAYOFFS				
04-05—Krylja Sov. Moscow....	Russian Jr.	6	2	2	4	4	...	...	...		1	0	0	0	0
05-06—Krylja Sov. Moscow....	Russian Jr.	35	9	7	16	20	...	...	...		—	—	—	—	—

MALAKHOV, VLADIMIR D

PERSONAL: Born August 30, 1968, in Ekaterinburg, U.S.S.R. ... 6-5/230. ... Shoots left. ... Name pronounced MAL-uh-kahf.
TRANSACTIONS/CAREER NOTES: Selected by New York Islanders in 10th round (12th Islanders pick, 191st overall) of entry draft (June 17, 1989). ... Sore groin; missed first two games of 1992-93 season. ... Injured right shoulder (January 16, 1993); missed eight games. ... Sprained shoulder (March 14, 1993); missed five games. ... Concussion (December 7, 1993); missed one game. ... Strained lower back (December 28, 1993); missed six games. ... Strained hip flexor (February 9, 1995); missed five games. ... Charley horse (March 14, 1995); missed two games. ... Traded by Islanders with C Pierre Turgeon to Montreal Canadiens for LW Kirk Muller, D Mathieu Schneider and C Craig Darby (April 5, 1995). ... Strained hip flexor (April 24, 1995); missed one game. ... Flu (October 25, 1995); missed two games. ... Bruised right leg (December 12, 1995); missed two games. ... Bruised ribs (October 24, 1996); missed one game. ... Fractured thumb (December 23, 1996); missed 16 games. ... Bruised lower back (October 29, 1997); missed one game. ... Sprained knee (December 10, 1997); missed four games. ... Shoulder tendinitis (February 28, 1998); missed three games. ... Back spasms (November 9, 1998); missed two games. ... Back spasms (December 5, 1998); missed six games. ... Back spasms (January 31, 1999); missed two games. ... Sprained knee (March 28, 1999); missed six games. ... Reinjured knee (April 10, 1999); missed final three games of season. ... Injured knee (September 17, 1999); missed first 53 games of 1999-2000 season. ... Injured knee (February 14, 2000); missed two games. ... Traded by Canadiens to New Jersey Devils for D Sheldon Souray, D Josh DeWolf and second-round draft pick (later traded to Washington Capitals) in 2001 entry draft (March 1, 2000). ... Signed as free agent by New York Rangers (July 10, 2000). ... Sprained knee (October 7, 2000); missed 14 games. ... Reinjured knee (November 15, 2000); missed remainder of season. ... Flu (February 6, 2002); missed one game. ... Back spasms (January 30, 2003); missed two games. ... Back spasms (February 8, 2003); missed two games. ... Injured shoulder (March 3, 2003); missed two games. ... Reinjured shoulder (March 26, 2003); missed five games. ... Injured wrist (January 26, 2004); missed 13 games. ... Traded by Rangers to Philadelphia Flyers for RW Rick Kozak and second-round pick in 2005 entry draft (March 8, 2004). ... Fractured jaw (March 18, 2004); missed six games. ... Concussion (May 2, 2004); missed final playoff game. ... Signed as free agent by Devils (August 4, 2005). ... Retired (December 19, 2005).
STATISTICAL PLATEAUS: Three-goal games: 1997-98 (1).

Season Team	League	GP	G	A	Pts.	PIM	+/-	PP	SH		GP	G	A	Pts.	PIM
		REGULAR SEASON									PLAYOFFS				
86-87—Spartak Moscow.........	USSR	22	0	1	1	12	...	...	...		—	—	—	—	—
87-88—Spartak Moscow.........	USSR	28	2	2	4	26	...	...	...		—	—	—	—	—
88-89—CSKA Moscow...........	USSR	34	6	2	8	16	...	...	...		—	—	—	—	—
89-90—CSKA Moscow...........	USSR	48	2	10	12	34	...	...	...		—	—	—	—	—
90-91—CSKA Moscow...........	USSR	46	5	13	18	22	...	...	...		—	—	—	—	—
91-92—CSKA Moscow...........	CIS	40	1	9	10	12	...	...	...		—	—	—	—	—
—Unif. Olympic team.....	Int'l	8	3	0	3	4	...	...	...		—	—	—	—	—
92-93—Capital District...........	AHL	3	2	1	3	11	6	0	0		—	—	—	—	—
—New York Islanders.....	NHL	64	14	38	52	59	14	7	0		17	3	6	9	12
93-94—New York Islanders.....	NHL	76	10	47	57	80	29	4	0		4	0	0	0	6
94-95—New York Islanders.....	NHL	26	3	13	16	32	-1	1	0		—	—	—	—	—
—Montreal....................	NHL	14	1	4	5	14	-2	0	0		—	—	—	—	—
95-96—Montreal....................	NHL	61	5	23	28	79	7	2	0		—	—	—	—	—
96-97—Montreal....................	NHL	65	10	20	30	43	3	5	0		5	0	0	0	6
97-98—Montreal....................	NHL	74	13	31	44	70	16	8	0		9	3	4	7	10
98-99—Montreal....................	NHL	62	13	21	34	77	-7	8	0		—	—	—	—	—
99-00—Montreal....................	NHL	7	0	0	0	4	0	0	0		—	—	—	—	—
—New Jersey................	NHL	17	1	4	5	19	1	1	0		23	1	4	5	18
00-01—New York Rangers......	NHL	3	0	2	2	4	0	0	0		—	—	—	—	—
01-02—New York Rangers......	NHL	81	6	22	28	83	10	1	0		—	—	—	—	—
—Russian Oly. team.......	Int'l	6	1	3	4	4	...	...	...		—	—	—	—	—
02-03—New York Rangers......	NHL	71	3	14	17	52	-7	1	0		—	—	—	—	—
03-04—New York Rangers......	NHL	56	3	15	18	53	-5	1	0		—	—	—	—	—
—Philadelphia...............	NHL	6	0	1	1	2	-1	0	0		17	1	5	6	12
05-06—New Jersey................	NHL	29	4	5	9	26	-9	3	0		—	—	—	—	—
NHL Totals (13 years)..........		712	86	260	346	697	48	42	0		75	8	19	27	64

MALEC, TOMAS D

PERSONAL: Born May 13, 1982, in Skalica, Czech. ... 6-2/193. ... Shoots left.
TRANSACTIONS/CAREER NOTES: Selected by Florida Panthers in third round (fourth Panthers pick, 64th overall) of entry draft (June 23, 2001). ... Traded by Panthers with D Bret Hedican, C Kevyn Adams and future considerations to Carolina Hurricanes for D Sandis Ozolinsh and C Byron Ritchie (January 16, 2002). ... Traded by Hurricanes with third-round pick (D Kyle Klubertanz) in 2004 draft to Anaheim Mighty Ducks for G Martin Gerber (June 18, 2004). ... Signed as free agent by Ottawa Senators (August 19, 2005).

Season Team	League	GP	G	A	Pts.	PIM	+/-	PP	SH		GP	G	A	Pts.	PIM
		REGULAR SEASON									PLAYOFFS				
00-01—Rimouski....................	QMJHL	64	13	50	63	198	...	...	...		11	0	11	11	26
01-02—Rimouski....................	QMJHL	51	14	32	46	164	...	...	...		7	3	1	4	10
—Lowell........................	AHL	...	...	...	...	...	...	...	...		4	0	0	0	4
02-03—Lowell........................	AHL	30	0	4	4	50	-6	0	0		—	—	—	—	—
—Carolina.....................	NHL	41	0	2	2	43	-5	0	0		—	—	—	—	—
03-04—Carolina.....................	NHL	2	0	0	0	2	-1	0	0		—	—	—	—	—
—Lowell........................	AHL	74	7	13	20	101	-11	0	1		—	—	—	—	—
04-05—Cincinnati..................	AHL	66	4	14	18	104	-17	1	0		6	0	2	2	10
05-06—Binghamton...............	AHL	79	1	27	28	118	-24	1	0		—	—	—	—	—
—Ottawa.......................	NHL	2	0	0	0	2	4	0	0		—	—	—	—	—
NHL Totals (3 years)...........		45	0	2	2	47	-2	0	0						

MALHOTRA, MANNY C/LW

PERSONAL: Born May 18, 1980, in Mississauga, Ont. ... 6-2/215. ... Shoots left. ... Name pronounced: mal HOH truh

TRANSACTIONS/CAREER NOTES: Selected by New York Rangers in first round (first Rangers pick, seventh overall) of entry draft (June 27, 1998). ... Sprained ankle (November 18, 1999); missed four games. ... Sprained ankle (November 6, 2001); missed three games. ... Traded by Rangers with LW Barrett Heisten to Dallas Stars for C Roman Lyashenko and LW Martin Rucinsky (March 12, 2002). ... Flu (April 14, 2002); missed one game. ... Claimed off waivers by Columbus Blue Jackets (November 21, 2003). ... Bruised ankle (March 26, 2004); missed remainder of regular season. ... Back spasms (December 1, 2005); missed two games. ... Shoulder (December 8, 2005); missed 22 games.

		REGULAR SEASON								PLAYOFFS				
Season Team	League	GP	G	A	Pts.	PIM	+/-	PP	SH	GP	G	A	Pts.	PIM
96-97—Guelph	OHL	61	16	28	44	26	...	...	...	18	7	7	14	11
97-98—Guelph	OHL	57	16	35	51	29	...	...	...	12	7	6	13	8
98-99—New York Rangers	NHL	73	8	8	16	13	-2	1	0	—	—	—	—	—
99-00—New York Rangers	NHL	27	0	0	0	4	-6	0	0	—	—	—	—	—
—Hartford	AHL	12	1	5	6	2	...	...	...	23	1	2	3	10
—Guelph	OHL	5	2	2	4	4	3	0	0	6	0	2	2	4
00-01—Hartford	AHL	28	5	6	11	69	...	...	...	5	0	0	0	0
—New York Rangers	NHL	50	4	8	12	31	-10	0	0	—	—	—	—	—
01-02—New York Rangers	NHL	56	7	6	13	42	-1	0	1	—	—	—	—	—
—Dallas	NHL	16	1	0	1	5	-3	0	0	—	—	—	—	—
02-03—Dallas	NHL	59	3	7	10	42	-2	0	0	5	1	0	1	0
03-04—Dallas	NHL	9	0	0	0	4	-2	0	0	—	—	—	—	—
—Columbus	NHL	56	12	13	25	24	-5	1	0	—	—	—	—	—
04-05—HV 71 Jonkoping	Sweden	20	5	2	7	16	-6	1	1	—	—	—	—	—
—Olimpija	Slovenia	26	13	14	27	36	...	...	...	—	—	—	—	—
05-06—Columbus	NHL	58	10	21	31	41	1	1	1	—	—	—	—	—
NHL Totals (7 years)		404	45	63	108	206	-30	3	2	5	1	0	1	0

MALIK, MAREK D

PERSONAL: Born June 24, 1975, in Ostrava, Czechoslovakia. ... 6-5/235. ... Shoots left. ... Name pronounced muh-REHK muh-LEEK.

TRANSACTIONS/CAREER NOTES: Selected by Hartford Whalers in third round (second Whalers pick, 72nd overall) of entry draft (June 26, 1993). ... Flu (January 20, 1997); missed three games. ... Bruised shin (March 20, 1997); missed four games. ... Whalers franchise moved to North Carolina and renamed Carolina Hurricanes for 1997-98 season; NHL approved move on June 25, 1997. ... Knee (April 7, 1999); missed one game. ... Whiplash (September 30, 2000); missed season's first six games. ... Cut face (December 15, 2002); missed one game. ... Traded by Hurricanes with LW Darren Langdon to Vancouver Canucks for LW Jan Hlavac and C Harold Druken (November 1, 2002). ... Sore back (March 8, 2004); missed two games. ... Signed as free agent by New York Rangers (August 2, 2005). ... Mild groin strain (October 8, 2005); missed one game. ... Shoulder (March 6, 2006); missed five games. ... Sore shoulder (April 11, 2006); missed two games.

		REGULAR SEASON								PLAYOFFS				
Season Team	League	GP	G	A	Pts.	PIM	+/-	PP	SH	GP	G	A	Pts.	PIM
91-92—TJ Vitkovice	Czech. Jrs	.Statistics unavailable												
92-93—TJ Vitkovice	Czech.	20	5	10	15	16	...	...	...	—	—	—	—	—
93-94—HC Vitkovice	Czech Rep.	38	3	3	6	...	...	...	...	3	0	1	1	...
94-95—Springfield	AHL	58	11	30	41	91	-1	5	1	—	—	—	—	—
—Hartford	NHL	1	0	1	1	0	1	0	0	—	—	—	—	—
95-96—Springfield	AHL	68	8	14	22	135	...	...	...	8	1	3	4	20
—Hartford	NHL	7	0	0	0	4	-3	0	0	—	—	—	—	—
96-97—Springfield	AHL	3	0	3	3	4	0	0	0	—	—	—	—	—
—Hartford	NHL	47	1	5	6	50	5	0	0	—	—	—	—	—
97-98—Malmoif	Sweden	37	1	5	6	21	...	...	...	—	—	—	—	—
98-99—HC Vitkovice	Czech Rep.	1	1	0	1	6	...	...	...	—	—	—	—	—
—New Haven	AHL	21	2	8	10	28	-7	1	0	—	—	—	—	—
—Carolina	NHL	52	2	9	11	36	-6	1	0	4	0	0	0	4
99-00—Carolina	NHL	57	4	10	14	63	13	0	0	—	—	—	—	—
00-01—Carolina	NHL	61	6	14	20	34	-4	1	0	3	0	0	0	6
01-02—Carolina	NHL	82	4	19	23	88	8	0	0	23	0	3	3	18
02-03—Carolina	NHL	10	0	2	2	16	-3	0	0	—	—	—	—	—
—Vancouver	NHL	69	7	11	18	52	23	1	1	14	1	1	2	10
03-04—Vancouver	NHL	78	3	16	19	45	†35	0	0	7	0	0	0	10
04-05—Vitkovice	Czech Rep.	42	1	9	10	50	10	...	...	7	0	0	0	37
05-06—New York Rangers	NHL	74	2	16	18	78	28	0	0	4	0	1	1	6
—Czech Rep. Oly. team	Int'l	8	0	0	0	8	-3	0	0	—	—	—	—	—
NHL Totals (10 years)		538	29	103	132	466	97	3	1	55	1	5	6	54

MALONE, RYAN C/LW

PERSONAL: Born December 1, 1979, in Pittsburgh. ... 6-4/215. ... Shoots left. ... Son of Greg Malone, player for Penguins (1976-77 through 1982-83), Hartford Whalers (1983-84 through 1985-86) and Quebec Nordiques (1985-86 through 1986-87).

TRANSACTIONS/CAREER NOTES: Selected by Pittsburgh Penguins in fourth round (fifth Penguins pick, 115th overall) of NHL draft (June 26, 1999). ... Re-signed by Penguins as restricted free agent (September 1, 2005).

		REGULAR SEASON								PLAYOFFS				
Season Team	League	GP	G	A	Pts.	PIM	+/-	PP	SH	GP	G	A	Pts.	PIM
97-98—Shattuck	USHS (West)	50	41	44	85	69	...	...	...	—	—	—	—	—
98-99—Omaha	USHL	51	14	22	36	81	...	...	...	—	—	—	—	—
99-00—St. Cloud State	WCHA	38	9	21	30	68	...	...	...	—	—	—	—	—
00-01—St. Cloud State	WCHA	36	7	18	25	52	...	...	...	—	—	—	—	—
01-02—St. Cloud State	WCHA	41	24	25	49	76	...	...	...	—	—	—	—	—
02-03—St. Cloud State	WCHA	27	16	20	36	85	...	...	...	—	—	—	—	—
—Wilkes-Barre/Scranton	AHL	3	0	1	1	2	-1	0	0	—	—	—	—	—

Season Team	League	REGULAR SEASON GP	G	A	Pts.	PIM	+/-	PP	SH	PLAYOFFS GP	G	A	Pts.	PIM
03-04—Pittsburgh	NHL	81	22	21	43	64	-23	5	3	—	—	—	—	—
04-05—Ambri-Piotta	Switzerland	—	—	—	—	—	—	—	—	1	0	0	0	2
—Blues Espoo	Finland	9	2	1	3	36	-2	...	...	—	—	—	—	—
—SV Renon	Italy	10	6	1	7	20	...	...	...	6	4	4	8	32
05-06—Pittsburgh	NHL	77	22	22	44	63	-22	10	5	—	—	—	—	—
NHL Totals (2 years)		158	44	43	87	127	-45	15	8					

MALTBY, KIRK LW/RW

PERSONAL: Born December 22, 1972, in Guelph, Ont. ... 6-0/190. ... Shoots right.

TRANSACTIONS/CAREER NOTES: Selected by Edmonton Oilers in third round (fourth Oilers pick, 65th overall) of entry draft (June 20, 1992). ... Chipped ankle bone (February 2, 1994); missed 13 games. ... Cut right eye (March 1, 1995); missed last game of season. ... Scratched left cornea (February 1, 1996); missed 16 games. ... Traded by Oilers to Detroit Red Wings for D Dan McGillis (March 20, 1996). ... Separated shoulder (September 24, 1997); missed 16 games. ... Abdominal pain (November 14, 1998); missed 19 games. ... Knee (December 31, 1998); missed five games. ... Ankle (March 31, 1999); missed one game. ... Suspended four games for slashing incident (March 17, 1999). ... Hernia (October 5, 1999); missed 41 games.

STATISTICAL PLATEAUS: Three-goal games: 1997-98 (1).

Season Team	League	REGULAR SEASON GP	G	A	Pts.	PIM	+/-	PP	SH	PLAYOFFS GP	G	A	Pts.	PIM
88-89—Cambridge Jr. B	OHA	48	28	18	46	138	...	...	...	—	—	—	—	—
89-90—Owen Sound	OHL	61	12	15	27	90	...	...	...	12	1	6	7	15
90-91—Owen Sound	OHL	66	34	32	66	100	...	...	...	—	—	—	—	—
91-92—Owen Sound	OHL	64	50	41	91	99	...	...	...	5	3	3	6	18
92-93—Cape Breton	AHL	73	22	23	45	130	9	3	4	16	3	3	6	45
93-94—Edmonton	NHL	68	11	8	19	74	-2	0	1	—	—	—	—	—
94-95—Edmonton	NHL	47	8	3	11	49	-11	0	2	—	—	—	—	—
95-96—Edmonton	NHL	49	2	6	8	61	-16	0	0	—	—	—	—	—
—Cape Breton	AHL	4	1	2	3	6	...	...	...	—	—	—	—	—
—Detroit	NHL	6	1	0	1	6	0	0	0	8	0	1	1	4
96-97—Detroit	NHL	66	3	5	8	75	3	0	0	20	5	2	7	24
97-98—Detroit	NHL	65	14	9	23	89	11	2	1	22	3	1	4	30
98-99—Detroit	NHL	53	8	6	14	34	-6	0	1	10	1	0	1	8
99-00—Detroit	NHL	41	6	8	14	24	1	0	2	8	0	1	1	4
00-01—Detroit	NHL	79	12	7	19	22	16	1	3	6	0	0	0	6
01-02—Detroit	NHL	82	9	15	24	40	15	0	1	23	3	3	6	32
02-03—Detroit	NHL	82	14	23	37	91	17	0	4	4	0	0	0	4
03-04—Detroit	NHL	79	14	19	33	80	24	1	4	12	1	3	4	11
05-06—Detroit	NHL	82	5	6	11	80	-9	0	1	6	2	1	3	4
NHL Totals (12 years)		799	107	115	222	725	43	4	20	119	15	12	27	127

M

MARA, PAUL D

PERSONAL: Born September 7, 1979, in Ridgewood, N.J. ... 6-4/219. ... Shoots left.

TRANSACTIONS/CAREER NOTES: Selected by Tampa Bay Lightning in first round (first Lightning pick, seventh overall) of entry draft (June 21, 1997). ... Fractured jaw (November 9, 1999); missed 13 games. ... Hip flexor (November 14, 2000); missed six games. ... Strained abdominal muscle (December 2, 2000); missed four games. ... Traded by Lightning with RW Mike Johnson, RW Ruslan Zainullin and second-round pick (D Matthew Spiller) in 2001 to Phoenix Coyotes for G Nikolai Khabibulin and D Stan Neckar (March 5, 2001). ... Wrist (October 30, 2001); missed two games. ... Foot (March 3, 2002); missed five games. ... Shoulder (February 28, 2003); missed nine games. ... Flu (December 12, 2003); missed one game. ... Flu (December 11, 2005); missed one game. ... Rib (March 2, 2006); missed one game. ... Knee (March 28, 2006); missed two games. ... Traded by Coyotes with an unconditional draft pick to Boston Bruins for D Nick Boynton and a fourth-round pick in 2007 entry draft (June 26, 2006).

Season Team	League	REGULAR SEASON GP	G	A	Pts.	PIM	+/-	PP	SH	PLAYOFFS GP	G	A	Pts.	PIM
94-95—Belmont Hill	Mass. H.S.	29	19	24	43	24	...	...	...	—	—	—	—	—
95-96—Belmont Hill	Mass. H.S.	28	18	20	38	40	...	...	...	—	—	—	—	—
96-97—Sudbury	OHL	44	9	34	43	61	-11	2	0	—	—	—	—	—
97-98—Sudbury	OHL	25	8	18	26	79	...	...	...	—	—	—	—	—
—Plymouth	OHL	25	8	15	23	30	...	...	...	15	3	14	17	30
98-99—Plymouth	OHL	52	13	41	54	95	25	...	...	11	5	7	12	28
—Tampa Bay	NHL	1	1	1	2	0	-3	1	0	—	—	—	—	—
99-00—Detroit	IHL	15	3	5	8	22	...	...	...	—	—	—	—	—
—Tampa Bay	NHL	54	7	11	18	73	-27	4	0	—	—	—	—	—
00-01—Tampa Bay	NHL	46	6	10	16	40	-17	2	0	—	—	—	—	—
—Detroit	IHL	10	3	3	6	22	...	...	...	—	—	—	—	—
—Phoenix	NHL	16	0	4	4	14	1	0	0	—	—	—	—	—
01-02—Phoenix	NHL	75	7	17	24	58	-6	2	0	5	0	0	0	4
02-03—Phoenix	NHL	73	10	15	25	78	-7	1	0	—	—	—	—	—
03-04—Phoenix	NHL	81	6	36	42	48	-11	1	0	—	—	—	—	—
04-05—Hannover	Germany	35	5	13	18	89	-6	3	0	...	...	...	...	...
05-06—Phoenix	NHL	78	15	32	47	70	-12	8	0	—	—	—	—	—
NHL Totals (7 years)		424	52	126	178	381	-82	19	0	5	0	0	0	4

MARCHANT, TODD C

PERSONAL: Born August 12, 1973, in Buffalo. ... 5-10/178. ... Shoots left. ... Brother of Terry Marchant, LW with Edmonton Oilers organization (1994-99). ... Name pronounced MAHR-shahnt.

TRANSACTIONS/CAREER NOTES: Selected by New York Rangers in seventh round (eighth Rangers pick, 164th overall) of entry draft (June 26, 1993). ... Traded by Rangers to Edmonton Oilers for C Craig MacTavish (March 21, 1994). ... Concussion (March 9, 1997); missed three games. ... Strained groin (November 10, 1997); missed four games. ... Scratched left eye (February 4, 1998); missed two games. ... Separated left shoulder (January 10, 2001); missed 10 games. ... Sprained right knee (February 12, 2001); missed one game. ... Virus (March 15, 2003); missed four games. ... Signed as free agent by Columbus Blue Jackets (July 2, 2003). ... Flu (November 14, 2003); missed one game. ... Injured groin (March 29, 2004); missed remainder of regular season. ... Claimed off waivers by Anaheim Mighty Ducks (November 21, 2005).

		REGULAR SEASON								PLAYOFFS				
Season Team	**League**	**GP**	**G**	**A**	**Pts.**	**PIM**	**+/-**	**PP**	**SH**	**GP**	**G**	**A**	**Pts.**	**PIM**
91-92—Clarkson	ECAC	33	20	12	32	32	...	...	...	—	—	—	—	—
92-93—Clarkson	ECAC	33	18	28	46	38	...	...	...	—	—	—	—	—
93-94—U.S. national team	Int'l	59	28	39	67	48	...	9	1	—	—	—	—	—
—U.S. Olympic team	Int'l	8	1	1	2	6	1	1	0	—	—	—	—	—
—Binghamton	AHL	8	2	7	9	6	-3	0	0	—	—	—	—	—
—New York Rangers	NHL	1	0	0	0	0	-1	0	0	—	—	—	—	—
—Edmonton	NHL	3	0	1	1	2	-1	0	0	—	—	—	—	—
—Cape Breton	AHL	3	1	4	5	2	4	0	0	5	1	1	2	0
94-95—Cape Breton	AHL	38	22	25	47	25	8	5	2	—	—	—	—	—
—Edmonton	NHL	45	13	14	27	32	-3	3	2	—	—	—	—	—
95-96—Edmonton	NHL	81	19	19	38	66	-19	2	3	—	—	—	—	—
96-97—Edmonton	NHL	79	14	19	33	44	11	0	4	12	4	2	6	12
97-98—Edmonton	NHL	76	14	21	35	71	9	2	1	12	1	1	2	10
98-99—Edmonton	NHL	82	14	22	36	65	3	3	1	4	1	1	2	12
99-00—Edmonton	NHL	82	17	23	40	70	7	0	1	3	1	0	1	2
00-01—Edmonton	NHL	71	13	26	39	51	1	0	4	6	0	0	0	4
01-02—Edmonton	NHL	82	12	22	34	41	7	0	3	—	—	—	—	—
02-03—Edmonton	NHL	77	20	40	60	48	13	7	1	6	0	2	2	2
03-04—Columbus	NHL	77	9	25	34	34	-17	4	0	—	—	—	—	—
05-06—Columbus	NHL	18	3	6	9	20	-1	0	0	—	—	—	—	—
—Anaheim	NHL	61	6	19	25	46	3	0	0	16	3	10	13	14
NHL Totals (12 years)		835	154	257	411	590	12	21	20	59	10	16	26	56

MARCHMENT, BRYAN D

PERSONAL: Born May 1, 1969, in Scarborough, Ont. ... 6-1/200. ... Shoots left.

TRANSACTIONS/CAREER NOTES: Selected by Winnipeg Jets in first round (first Jets pick, 16th overall) of entry draft (June 13, 1987). ... Sprained shoulder (March 1990). ... Back spasms (March 13, 1991). ... Traded by Jets with D Chris Norton to Chicago Blackhawks for C Troy Murray and LW Warren Rychel (July 22, 1991). ... Fractured cheekbone (December 12, 1991); missed 12 games. ... Suspended one preseason game and fined $500 for headbutting (September 30, 1993). ... Traded by Blackhawks with RW Steve Larmer to Hartford Whalers for LW Patrick Poulin and D Eric Weinrich (November 2, 1993). ... Suspended two games and fined $500 for illegal check (December 21, 1993). ... Sprained ankle (January 14, 1994); missed three games. ... Sprained ankle (February 19, 1994); missed remainder of season. ... Awarded to Edmonton Oilers as compensation for Whalers signing free agent RW Steven Rice (August 30, 1994). ... Suspended one game for game misconduct penalties (March 22, 1995). ... Suspended two games for game misconduct penalties (March 27, 1995). ... Strained lower back (April 15, 1995); missed two games. ... Suspended three games and fined $500 for leaving bench to fight (April 29, 1995). ... Suspended five games for kneeing player in preseason game (September 25, 1995). ... Injured ribs (October 22, 1996); missed two games. ... Flu (January 28, 1997); missed one game. ... Cracked ribs (February 13, 1997); missed eight games. ... Concussion (April 18, 1997); missed remainder of season. ... Suspended three games and fined $1,000 for striking another player (December 5, 1997). ... Traded by Oilers to Tampa Bay Lightning with C Steve Kelly and C Jason Bonsignore for D Roman Hamrlik and C Paul Comrie (December 30, 1997). ... Suspended three games for kneeing incident (February 6, 1998). ... Suspended eight games and fined $1,000 for kneeing incident (February 25, 1998). ... Traded by Lightning with D David Shaw and first-round pick (traded to Nashville; Predators selected C David Legwand) in 1998 draft to San Jose Sharks for LW Andrei Nazarov, first-round pick (later traded to Tampa Bay; Lightning selected C Vincent Lecavalier) in 1998 draft (March 24, 1998). ... Shoulder (January 7, 1999); missed 20 games. ... Suspended one game for unsportsmanlike conduct (April 6, 1999). ... Knee (October 2, 1999); missed nine games. ... Flu (December 8, 1999); missed one game. ... Ankle (January 5, 2000); missed 14 games. ... Groin (March 2, 2000); missed five games. ... Suspended three games for spearing incident (March 19, 2000). ... Neck (April 3, 2000); missed one game. ... Suspended three games for kneeing incident (March 13, 2001). ... Suspended six games for elbowing incident (November 10, 2001). ... Back (April 6, 2002); missed season's final four games. ... Traded by Sharks to Colorado Avalanche for third- (later traded to Calgary; Flames selected LW Ryan Donally) and fifth-round (later returned to Colorado; Avalanche selected C Brad Richardson) picks in 2003 draft (March 9, 2003). ... Signed as free agent by Toronto Maple Leafs (July 10, 2003). ... Groin (February 26, 2004); missed five games. ... Signed as free agent by Flames (October 11, 2005). ... Ribs (November 1, 2005); missed eight games. ... Torn left knee ligaments (January 6, 2006); missed 16 games.

		REGULAR SEASON								PLAYOFFS				
Season Team	**League**	**GP**	**G**	**A**	**Pts.**	**PIM**	**+/-**	**PP**	**SH**	**GP**	**G**	**A**	**Pts.**	**PIM**
84-85—Toronto Nationals	MTHL	...	14	35	49	229	...	...	...	—	—	—	—	—
85-86—Belleville	OHL	57	5	15	20	225	...	...	...	21	0	7	7	83
86-87—Belleville	OHL	52	6	38	44	238	...	...	...	6	0	4	4	17
87-88—Belleville	OHL	56	7	51	58	200	...	...	...	6	1	3	4	19
88-89—Belleville	OHL	43	14	36	50	198	...	...	...	5	0	1	1	12
—Winnipeg	NHL	2	0	0	0	2	0	0	0	—	—	—	—	—
89-90—Winnipeg	NHL	7	0	2	2	28	0	0	0	—	—	—	—	—
—Moncton	AHL	56	4	19	23	217	...	...	...	—	—	—	—	—
90-91—Winnipeg	NHL	28	2	2	4	91	-5	0	0	—	—	—	—	—
—Moncton	AHL	33	2	11	13	101	...	...	...	—	—	—	—	—
91-92—Chicago	NHL	58	5	10	15	168	-4	2	0	16	1	0	1	36
92-93—Chicago	NHL	78	5	15	20	313	15	1	0	4	0	0	0	12
93-94—Chicago	NHL	13	1	4	5	42	-2	0	0	—	—	—	—	—
—Hartford	NHL	42	3	7	10	124	-12	0	1	—	—	—	—	—
94-95—Edmonton	NHL	40	1	5	6	184	-11	0	0	—	—	—	—	—
95-96—Edmonton	NHL	78	3	15	18	202	-7	0	0	—	—	—	—	—
96-97—Edmonton	NHL	71	3	13	16	132	13	1	0	3	0	0	0	4
97-98—Edmonton	NHL	27	0	4	4	58	-2	0	0	—	—	—	—	—
—Tampa Bay	NHL	22	2	4	6	43	-3	0	0	—	—	—	—	—
—San Jose	NHL	12	0	3	3	43	2	0	0	6	0	0	0	10
98-99—San Jose	NHL	59	2	6	8	101	-7	0	0	6	0	0	0	4

Season Team	League	GP	G	A	Pts.	PIM	+/-	PP	SH		GP	G	A	Pts.	PIM
		REGULAR SEASON									PLAYOFFS				
99-00—San Jose	NHL	49	0	4	4	72	3	0	0		11	2	1	3	12
00-01—San Jose	NHL	75	7	11	18	204	15	0	1		5	0	1	1	2
01-02—San Jose	NHL	72	2	20	22	178	22	0	0		12	1	1	2	10
02-03—San Jose	NHL	67	2	9	11	108	-2	0	0		—	—	—	—	—
—Colorado	NHL	14	0	3	3	33	4	0	0		7	0	0	0	4
03-04—Toronto	NHL	75	1	3	4	106	4	0	0		13	0	0	0	8
05-06—Calgary	NHL	37	1	2	3	75	8	0	0		—	—	—	—	—
NHL Totals (17 years)		926	40	142	182	2307	31	4	2		83	4	3	7	102

MARJAMAKI, MASI — LW

PERSONAL: Born January 16, 1985, in Pori, Finland. ... 6-2/184. ... Shoots left. ... Name pronounced: MAW-see mahr-yuh-MAH-kee
TRANSACTIONS/CAREER NOTES: Selected by Boston Bruins in second round (third Bruins pick, 66th overall) of entry draft (June 20, 2003). ... Returned by Bruins to draft pool; selected by New York Islanders in fifth round (fourth Islanders pick, 144th overall) of entry draft (July 30, 2005).

Season Team	League	GP	G	A	Pts.	PIM	+/-	PP	SH		GP	G	A	Pts.	PIM
		REGULAR SEASON									PLAYOFFS				
02-03—Red Deer	WHL	65	15	20	35	56	...	...	...		23	1	2	3	20
03-04—Red Deer	WHL	28	6	8	14	46	-8	2	0		—	—	—	—	—
—Moose Jaw	WHL	35	15	10	25	57	4	4	1		10	1	3	4	15
04-05—Moose Jaw	WHL	51	14	32	46	49	-6	9	0		5	1	2	3	5
05-06—Bridgeport	AHL	75	9	22	31	77	-5	2	0		7	3	0	3	4
—New York Islanders	NHL	1	0	0	0	0	0	0	0		—	—	—	—	—
NHL Totals (1 year)		1	0	0	0	0	0	0	0						

MARKKANEN, JUSSI — G

PERSONAL: Born May 8, 1975, in Imatra, Finland. ... 6-0/182. ... Catches left. ... Name pronounced: YOO-see MAHR-kih-nehn
TRANSACTIONS/CAREER NOTES: Selected by Edmonton Oilers in fifth round (fifth Oilers pick, 133rd overall) of entry draft (June 23, 2001). ... Traded by Oilers with fourth-round pick (traded to Toronto; Maple Leafs selected RW Roman Kukumberg) in 2004 draft to New York Rangers for D Brian Leetch (June 30, 2003). ... Traded by Rangers with C Petr Nedved to Oilers for F Dwight Helminen, G Stephen Valiquette and second-round pick (LW Dane Byers) in 2004 draft (March 3, 2004). ... Signed as free agent by Oilers (August 5, 2005). ... Broken collarbone (September 2005); missed first two games of season. ... Flu (February 7, 2006); missed two games.

Season Team	League	GP	Min.	W	L	OTL	T	GA	SO	GAA	SV%	GP	Min.	W	L	GA	SO	GAA	SV%
		REGULAR SEASON										PLAYOFFS							
91-92—SaiPa	Finland Jr.	2	120	...	...	...	...	11	0	5.50	...	—	—	—	—	—	—	—	—
92-93—SaiPa	Finland Jr.	7	367	...	...	...	...	28	...	4.58	...	—	—	—	—	—	—	—	—
—SaiPa	Finland Div. 2	16	798	...	...	...	...	60	...	4.51	...	—	—	—	—	—	—	—	—
93-94—SaiPa	Finland Div. 2	30	1726	...	...	...	...	97	...	3.37	...	—	—	—	—	—	—	—	—
94-95—SaiPa	Finland Div. 2	43	2493	...	...	...	...	122	...	2.94	...	3	179	...	...	5	...	1.68	...
95-96—Tappara Tampere	Finland Jr.	5	298	...	...	...	...	21	...	4.23	...	—	—	—	—	—	—	—	—
—Tappara Tampere	Finland	23	1238	11	8	...	2	59	1	2.86	...	—	—	—	—	—	—	—	—
96-97—SaiPa	Finland	41	2340	9	24	...	7	132	0	3.38	...	—	—	—	—	—	—	—	—
97-98—SaiPa	Finland	48	2870	21	20	...	5	138	4	2.89	...	3	164	0	3	11	0	4.02	...
98-99—SaiPa	Finland	45	2633	21	19	...	4	105	4	2.39	...	7	366	3	3	21	0	3.44	...
99-00—SaiPa	Finland	48	2794	4	23	...	9	150	2	3.22	...	—	—	—	—	—	—	—	—
00-01—Tappara Tampere	Finland	52	3076	30	17	...	5	107	9	2.09	...	10	608	7	3	18	1	1.78	...
01-02—Edmonton	NHL	14	784	6	4	...	2	24	2	1.84	.929	—	—	—	—	—	—	—	—
—Hamilton	AHL	4	239	2	2	...	0	9	0	2.26	.914	—	—	—	—	—	—	—	—
02-03—Edmonton	NHL	22	1180	7	8	...	3	51	3	2.59	.904	1	14	0	0	1	0	4.29	.917
03-04—New York Rangers	NHL	26	1244	8	12	...	1	53	2	2.56	.913	—	—	—	—	—	—	—	—
—Edmonton	NHL	7	394	2	2	...	2	12	0	1.83	.934	—	—	—	—	—	—	—	—
04-05—Lada Togliatti	Russian	54	...	...	...	...	...	...	...	1.20	...	10	...	...	...	...	...	1.44	...
05-06—Edmonton	NHL	37	2016	15	12	6	...	105	0	3.13	.880	6	360	3	3	13	1	2.17	.905
NHL Totals (4 years)		106	5618	38	38	6	8	245	7	2.62	.903	7	374	3	3	14	1	2.25	.906

MARKOV, ANDREI — D

PERSONAL: Born December 20, 1978, in Voskresensk, U.S.S.R. ... 6-0/203. ... Shoots left.
TRANSACTIONS/CAREER NOTES: Selected by Montreal Canadiens in sixth round (sixth Canadiens pick, 16second overall) of entry draft (June 27, 1998). ... Injured thigh (December 21, 2002); missed one game. ... Injured knee (March 31, 2003); missed two games. ... Injured ankle (November 29, 2003); missed one game. ... Infected foot and sore hip (January 3, 2004); missed nine games. ... Left team for personal reasons (February 20, 2004); missed three games. ... Suspended three games for shoving linesman (November 26, 2005). ... Shoulder injury (January 19, 2006); missed eight games. ... Back spasms (March 13, 2006); missed three games. ... Back spasms (March 21, 2006); missed one game.

Season Team	League	GP	G	A	Pts.	PIM	+/-	PP	SH		GP	G	A	Pts.	PIM
		REGULAR SEASON									PLAYOFFS				
95-96—Khimik Voskresensk	CIS	36	0	0	0	14	...	...	...		—	—	—	—	—
96-97—Khimik Voskresensk	Russian	43	8	4	12	32	...	...	...		2	1	1	2	0
97-98—Khimik Voskresensk	Russian	43	10	5	15	83	...	...	...		—	—	—	—	—
98-99—Dynamo Moscow	Russian	38	10	11	21	32	...	...	...		16	3	6	9	6
99-00—Dynamo Moscow	Russian	29	11	12	23	28	...	...	...		17	4	3	7	8
00-01—Montreal	NHL	63	6	17	23	18	-6	2	0		—	—	—	—	—
—Quebec	AHL	14	0	5	5	4	...	...	...		7	1	1	2	2

Season Team	League	GP	G	A	Pts.	PIM	+/-	PP	SH	GP	G	A	Pts.	PIM
		REGULAR SEASON								PLAYOFFS				
01-02—Quebec	AHL	12	4	6	10	7	14	1	0	—	—	—	—	—
—Montreal	NHL	56	5	19	24	24	-1	2	0	12	1	3	4	8
02-03—Montreal	NHL	79	13	24	37	34	13	3	0	—	—	—	—	—
03-04—Montreal	NHL	69	6	22	28	20	-2	2	0	11	1	4	5	8
04-05—Dynamo Moscow	Russian	42	7	16	23	76	27	...	...	10	2	0	2	22
05-06—Montreal	NHL	67	10	36	46	74	13	6	1	6	0	1	1	4
—Russian Oly. team	Int'l	8	1	3	4	6	7	0	0	—	—	—	—	—
NHL Totals (5 years)		334	40	118	158	170	17	15	1	29	2	8	10	20

MARKOV, DANNY D

PERSONAL: Born July 30, 1976, in Moscow, U.S.S.R. ... 6-1/190. ... Shoots left.

TRANSACTIONS/CAREER NOTES: Selected by Toronto Maple Leafs in ninth round (seventh Maple Leafs pick, 223rd overall) of entry draft (July 8, 1995). ... Concussion (October 16, 1998); missed one game. ... Fractured foot (November 11, 1998); missed two games. ... Throat (November 23, 1998); missed two games. ... Back spasms (December 7, 1998); missed two games. ... Separated shoulder (December 16, 1998); missed 11 games. ... Injured (December 15, 1999); missed three games. ... Ankle (January 5, 2000); missed 10 games. ... Injured (March 15, 2000); missed one game. ... Foot (March 23, 2000); missed season's final eight games. ... Injured (January 6, 2001); missed one game. ... Back (January 31, 2001); missed 22 games. ... Traded by Maple Leafs to Phoenix Coyotes for C Robert Reichel, C Travis Green and RW Craig Mills (June 12, 2001). ... Fractured foot (March 24, 2002); missed remainder of season. ... Fractured forearm (December 28, 2002); missed 17 games. ... Traded by Coyotes with third-round pick (traded to New York Rangers; Rangers selected C Billy Ryan) to Carolina Hurricanes for D David Tanabe and D Igor Knyazev (June 22, 2003). ... Shoulder (January 9, 2004); missed two games. ... Traded by Hurricanes to Philadelphia Flyers for F Justin Williams (January 20, 2004). ... Suspended one game for receiving third game misconduct penalty of season (March 16, 2004). ... Traded by Flyers to Nashville Predators for a third-round pick (traded to L.A.; Kings selected C/RW Bud Holloway) in 2006 draft (August 2, 2005). ... Groin (October 22, 2005); missed four games. ... Groin (November 25, 2005); missed seven games. ... Knee (January 13, 2006); missed three games. ... Ankle (March 7, 2006); missed 10 games.

Season Team	League	GP	G	A	Pts.	PIM	+/-	PP	SH	GP	G	A	Pts.	PIM
		REGULAR SEASON								PLAYOFFS				
93-94—Spartak Moscow	Russian	13	1	0	1	6	...	...	...	1	0	0	0	0
94-95—Spartak Moscow	Russian	39	0	1	1	36	...	...	...	—	—	—	—	—
95-96—Spartak Moscow	Russian	38	2	0	2	12	...	...	...	2	0	0	0	2
96-97—Spartak Moscow	Russian	36	3	6	9	41	...	...	...	—	—	—	—	—
—St. John's	AHL	10	2	4	6	18	...	...	...	11	2	6	8	14
97-98—St. John's	AHL	52	3	23	26	124	11	0	0	2	0	1	1	0
—Toronto	NHL	25	2	5	7	28	0	1	0	—	—	—	—	—
98-99—Toronto	NHL	57	4	8	12	47	5	0	0	17	0	6	6	18
99-00—Toronto	NHL	59	0	10	10	28	13	0	0	12	0	3	3	10
00-01—Toronto	NHL	59	3	13	16	34	6	1	0	11	1	1	2	12
01-02—Phoenix	NHL	72	6	30	36	67	-7	4	0	—	—	—	—	—
—Russian Oly. team	Int'l	5	0	1	1	0	...	...	...	—	—	—	—	—
02-03—Phoenix	NHL	64	4	16	20	36	2	2	0	—	—	—	—	—
03-04—Carolina	NHL	44	4	10	14	37	-6	2	0	—	—	—	—	—
—Philadelphia	NHL	34	2	3	5	58	0	1	0	18	1	2	3	25
04-05—Vityaz Podolsk	Russian	26	5	7	12	16	7	...	...	12	0	3	3	6
05-06—Nashville	NHL	58	0	11	11	62	9	0	0	5	0	0	0	6
—Russian Oly. team	Int'l	8	0	1	1	4	7	0	0	—	—	—	—	—
NHL Totals (8 years)		472	25	106	131	397	22	11	0	63	2	12	14	71

MARLEAU, PATRICK C

PERSONAL: Born September 15, 1979, in Aneroid, Sask. ... 6-2/220. ... Shoots left. ... Name pronounced MAHR-loh.

TRANSACTIONS/CAREER NOTES: Selected by San Jose Sharks in first round (first Sharks pick, second overall) of NHL entry draft (June 21, 1997). ... Injured ankle (January 17, 2004); missed one game. ... Injured knee (January 21, 2004); missed one game. ... Re-signed by Sharks as restricted free agent (August 15, 2005).

STATISTICAL PLATEAUS: Three-goal games: 2001-02 (1).

Season Team	League	GP	G	A	Pts.	PIM	+/-	PP	SH	GP	G	A	Pts.	PIM
		REGULAR SEASON								PLAYOFFS				
93-94—Swift Current	Jr. A	53	72	95	167	...	...	...	...	—	—	—	—	—
94-95—Swift Current	Jr. A	30	30	22	52	20	...	...	...	—	—	—	—	—
95-96—Seattle	WHL	72	32	42	74	22	...	...	...	5	3	4	7	4
96-97—Seattle	WHL	71	51	74	125	37	14	7	9	15	7	16	23	12
97-98—San Jose	NHL	74	13	19	32	14	5	1	0	5	0	1	1	0
98-99—San Jose	NHL	81	21	24	45	24	10	4	0	6	2	1	3	4
99-00—San Jose	NHL	81	17	23	40	36	-9	3	0	5	1	1	2	2
00-01—San Jose	NHL	81	25	27	52	22	7	5	0	6	2	0	2	4
01-02—San Jose	NHL	79	21	23	44	40	9	3	0	12	6	5	11	6
02-03—San Jose	NHL	82	28	29	57	33	-10	8	1	—	—	—	—	—
03-04—San Jose	NHL	80	28	29	57	24	-5	9	0	17	8	4	12	6
05-06—San Jose	NHL	82	34	52	86	26	-12	20	1	11	9	5	14	8
NHL Totals (8 years)		640	187	226	413	219	-5	53	2	62	28	17	45	30

MARSHALL, GRANT RW

PERSONAL: Born June 9, 1973, in Mississauga, Ont. ... 6-1/200. ... Shoots right.

TRANSACTIONS/CAREER NOTES: Selected by Toronto Maple Leafs in first round (second Maple Leafs pick, 23rd overall) of NHL entry draft (June 20, 1992). ... Awarded to Dallas Stars with C Peter Zezel as compensation for Maple Leafs signing free-agent RW Mike Craig (August 10, 1994). ... Strained muscle (November 15, 1996); missed four games. ... Sprained shoulder (December 8, 1996); missed four games. ... Suffered concussion (January 4, 1997); missed two games. ... Strained groin (November 21, 1997); missed five games. ... Strained groin (April 16, 1998); missed one game. ... Fined $1,000 by NHL for elbowing incident (May 8, 1998). ... Injured groin; missed first four games of

1999-2000 season. ... Reinjured groin (October 13, 1999); missed 22 games. ... Reinjured groin (December 15, 1999); missed two games. ... Reinjured groin (December 27, 1999); missed five games. ... Reinjured groin (March 13, 2000); missed three games. ... Strained thigh (December 17, 2000); missed five games. ... Traded by Stars to Columbus Blue Jackets for second-round pick (LW Loui Eriksson) in 2003 entry draft (August 29, 2001). ... Injured foot (November 14, 2002); missed one game. ... Traded by Blue Jackets to New Jersey Devils for fourth-round pick (later traded to Carolina Hurricanes and Calgary Flames; Flames picked LW Kris Hogg) in 2004 draft (March 10, 2003). ... Injured back (October 28, 2003); missed 11 games. ... Bruised knee (March 21, 2003); missed five games. ... Injured back (October 28, 2003); missed 11 games. ... Injured groin (December 18, 2003); missed two games. ... Fractured right hand (March 28, 2004); missed final three games of regular season and playoffs. ... Groin (December 15, 2005); missed five games. ... Head injury (January 22, 2006); missed one game.

		REGULAR SEASON								PLAYOFFS				
Season Team	**League**	**GP**	**G**	**A**	**Pts.**	**PIM**	**+/-**	**PP**	**SH**	**GP**	**G**	**A**	**Pts.**	**PIM**
90-91—Ottawa	OHL	26	6	11	17	25	...	...	...	1	0	0	0	0
91-92—Ottawa	OHL	61	32	51	83	132	...	...	...	11	6	11	17	11
92-93—Newmarket	OHL	31	12	25	37	85	...	...	...	7	4	7	11	20
—Ottawa	OHL	30	14	28	42	83	...	...	...	—	—	—	—	—
—St. John's	AHL	2	0	0	0	0	-4	0	0	2	0	0	0	2
93-94—St. John's	AHL	67	11	29	40	155	1	1	1	11	1	5	6	17
94-95—Kalamazoo	IHL	61	17	29	46	96	24	3	5	16	9	3	12	27
—Dallas	NHL	2	0	1	1	0	1	0	0	—	—	—	—	—
95-96—Dallas	NHL	70	9	19	28	111	0	0	0	—	—	—	—	—
96-97—Dallas	NHL	56	6	4	10	98	5	0	0	5	0	2	2	8
97-98—Dallas	NHL	72	9	10	19	96	-2	3	0	17	0	2	2	*47
98-99—Dallas	NHL	82	13	18	31	85	1	2	0	14	0	3	3	20
99-00—Dallas	NHL	45	2	6	8	38	-5	1	0	14	0	1	1	4
00-01—Dallas	NHL	75	13	24	37	64	1	4	0	9	0	0	0	0
01-02—Columbus	NHL	81	15	18	33	86	-20	6	0	—	—	—	—	—
02-03—Columbus	NHL	66	8	20	28	71	-8	3	0	—	—	—	—	—
—New Jersey	NHL	10	1	3	4	7	-3	0	0	24	6	2	8	8
03-04—New Jersey	NHL	65	8	7	15	67	-9	5	0	—	—	—	—	—
05-06—New Jersey	NHL	76	8	17	25	70	-18	4	0	7	0	1	1	8
NHL Totals (11 years)		700	92	147	239	793	-57	28	0	90	6	11	17	95

MARSHALL, JASON — D/LW

PERSONAL: Born February 22, 1971, in Cranbrook, B.C. ... 6-2/196. ... Shoots right.

TRANSACTIONS/CAREER NOTES: Selected by St. Louis Blues in first round (first Blues pick, ninth overall) of entry draft (June 17, 1989). ... Traded by Blues to Anaheim Mighty Ducks for D Bill Houlder (August 29, 1994). ... Cut finger (November 24, 1996); missed two games. ... Bruised hand (March 19, 1997); missed five games. ... Separated right shoulder (December 19, 1997); missed eight games. ... Strained left hamstring (December 18, 1998); missed six games. ... Ill (March 17, 1999); missed one game. ... Traded by Mighty Ducks to Washington Capitals for D Alexei Tezikov and fourth-round pick (D Brandon Rogers) in 2001 draft (March 13, 2001). ... Signed as free agent by Minnesota Wild (July 2, 2001). ... Injured eye (November 21, 2002); missed three games. ... Concussion (December 7, 2002); missed 14 games. ... Traded by Wild to San Jose Sharks for fifth-round pick (D Jean-Claude Sawyer) in 2004 draft (March 3, 2004). ... Signed as free agent by New York Rangers (August 25, 2004). ... Signed as free agent by Mighty Ducks (August 8, 2005). ... Fractured nose (October 14, 2005); missed two games.

		REGULAR SEASON								PLAYOFFS				
Season Team	**League**	**GP**	**G**	**A**	**Pts.**	**PIM**	**+/-**	**PP**	**SH**	**GP**	**G**	**A**	**Pts.**	**PIM**
87-88—Columbia Valley	KIJHL	40	4	28	32	150	...	...	...	—	—	—	—	—
88-89—Vernon	BCHL	48	10	30	40	197	...	...	...	31	6	6	12	141
—Canadian nat'l team	Int'l	2	0	1	1	0	...	...	...	—	—	—	—	—
89-90—Canadian nat'l team	Int'l	72	1	11	12	57	...	...	...	—	—	—	—	—
90-91—Tri-City	WHL	59	10	34	44	236	...	...	...	7	1	2	3	20
—Peoria	IHL	...	...	...	...	...	...	...	...	18	0	1	1	48
91-92—Peoria	IHL	78	4	18	22	178	...	...	...	10	0	1	1	16
—St. Louis	NHL	2	1	0	1	4	0	0	0	—	—	—	—	—
92-93—Peoria	IHL	77	4	16	20	229	2	0	0	4	0	0	0	20
93-94—Peoria	IHL	20	1	1	2	72	-5	0	0	3	2	0	2	2
—Canadian nat'l team	Int'l	41	3	10	13	60	...	...	...	—	—	—	—	—
94-95—San Diego	IHL	80	7	18	25	218	-9	0	0	5	0	1	1	8
—Anaheim	NHL	1	0	0	0	0	-2	0	0	—	—	—	—	—
95-96—Baltimore	AHL	57	1	13	14	150	...	...	...	—	—	—	—	—
—Anaheim	NHL	24	0	1	1	42	3	0	0	—	—	—	—	—
96-97—Anaheim	NHL	73	1	9	10	140	6	0	0	7	0	1	1	4
97-98—Anaheim	NHL	72	3	6	9	189	-8	1	0	—	—	—	—	—
98-99—Anaheim	NHL	72	1	7	8	142	-5	0	0	4	1	0	1	10
99-00—Anaheim	NHL	55	0	3	3	88	-10	0	0	—	—	—	—	—
00-01—Anaheim	NHL	50	3	4	7	105	-12	2	1	—	—	—	—	—
—Washington	NHL	5	0	0	0	17	-1	0	0	—	—	—	—	—
01-02—Minnesota	NHL	80	5	6	11	148	-8	1	0	—	—	—	—	—
02-03—Minnesota	NHL	45	1	5	6	69	4	0	0	15	1	1	2	16
03-04—Minnesota	NHL	12	1	4	5	18	-1	1	0	—	—	—	—	—
—Houston	AHL	49	7	12	19	87	0	3	0	—	—	—	—	—
—San Jose	NHL	12	0	2	2	8	-2	0	0	17	0	1	1	25
04-05—Plzen	Czech Rep.	11	1	3	4	53	4	...	...	—	—	—	—	—
05-06—Portland	AHL	2	0	0	0	4	1	0	0	—	—	—	—	—
—Anaheim	NHL	23	0	4	4	34	2	0	0	—	—	—	—	—
NHL Totals (12 years)		526	16	51	67	1004	-34	5	1	43	2	3	5	55

MARTIN, PAUL — D

PERSONAL: Born March 5, 1981, in Minneapolis, Minn. ... 6-1/190. ... Shoots left.

TRANSACTIONS/CAREER NOTES: Selected by New Jersey Devils in second round (fifth Devils pick, 6second overall) of NHL draft (June 24, 2000). ... Flu (January 27, 2004); missed two games. ... Re-signed by Devils as restricted free agent (September 21, 2005). ... Bruised back (October 13, 2005); missed two games.

Season Team	League	GP	G	A	Pts.	PIM	+/-	PP	SH	GP	G	A	Pts.	PIM
		REGULAR SEASON								PLAYOFFS				
98-99—Elk River	USHS (West)	25	9	21	30	28	...	...	...	—	—	—	—	—
99-00—Elk River	USHS (West)	24	15	35	50	26	...	...	...	—	—	—	—	—
00-01—Minnesota	WCHA	38	3	17	20	8	...	...	...	—	—	—	—	—
01-02—Minnesota	WCHA	44	8	30	38	22	...	...	...	—	—	—	—	—
02-03—Minnesota	WCHA	45	9	30	39	32	...	...	...	—	—	—	—	—
03-04—New Jersey	NHL	70	6	18	24	4	12	2	0	—	—	—	—	—
04-05—Fribourg	Switzerland	11	3	4	7	2	...	0	0	—	—	—	—	—
05-06—New Jersey	NHL	80	5	32	37	32	1	3	0	9	0	3	3	4
NHL Totals (2 years)		150	11	50	61	36	13	5	0	9	0	3	3	4

MARTINEK, RADEK D

PERSONAL: Born August 31, 1976, in Havlicko Brod, Czech. ... 6-1/210. ... Shoots left.

TRANSACTIONS/CAREER NOTES: Selected by New York Islanders in eighth round (12th Islanders pick, 228th overall) of NHL entry draft (June 27, 1999). ... Sprained knee (November 8, 2001); missed seven games. ... Reinjured knee (December 11, 2001); missed remainder of season. ... Strained ribs (October 10, 2002); missed four games. ... Suffered concussion (November 18, 2003); missed three games. ... Fractured left ankle (February 21, 2004); missed 20 games. ... Re-signed by Islanders as restricted free agent (August 16, 2005). ... Signed by Islanders to two-year contract extension (March 7, 2006).

Season Team	League	GP	G	A	Pts.	PIM	+/-	PP	SH	GP	G	A	Pts.	PIM
		REGULAR SEASON								PLAYOFFS				
96-97—HC Ceske Budejovice	Czech Rep.	52	3	5	8	40	...	...	...	5	0	1	1	2
97-98—HC Ceske Budejovice	Czech Rep.	42	2	7	9	36	...	...	...	—	—	—	—	—
98-99—HC Ceske Budejovice	Czech Rep.	52	12	13	25	50	...	...	...	3	0	2	2	...
99-00—HC Ceske Budejovice	Czech Rep.	45	5	18	23	24	...	...	...	3	0	0	0	6
00-01—HC Ceske Budejovice	Czech.	44	8	10	18	45	...	...	...	—	—	—	—	—
01-02—New York Islanders	NHL	23	1	4	5	16	5	0	0	—	—	—	—	—
02-03—Bridgeport	AHL	3	0	3	3	2	3	0	0	—	—	—	—	—
—New York Islanders	NHL	66	2	11	13	26	15	0	0	4	0	0	0	4
03-04—New York Islanders	NHL	47	4	3	7	43	-9	0	0	5	0	1	1	0
04-05—Budejovice	Czech Dv.I	30	12	18	30	80	36	...	...	12	2	3	5	6
05-06—New York Islanders	NHL	74	1	16	17	32	-9	0	0	—	—	—	—	—
NHL Totals (4 years)		210	8	34	42	117	2	0	0	9	0	1	1	4

MARTINS, STEVE C

PERSONAL: Born April 13, 1972, in Gatineau, Que. ... 5-7/187. ... Shoots left.

TRANSACTIONS/CAREER NOTES: Selected by Hartford Whalers in first round (first Whalers pick, fifth overall) of supplemental draft (June 24, 1994). ... Whalers franchise moved to North Carolina and renamed Carolina Hurricanes for 1997-98 season; NHL approved move on June 25, 1997. ... Signed as free agent by Ottawa Senators (July 22, 1998). ... Back spasms (December 4, 1998); missed four games. ... Hip flexor (February 13, 1999); missed three games. ... Reinjured hip flexor (February 23, 1999); missed four games. ... Flu (March 24, 1999); missed four games. ... Claimed off waivers by Tampa Bay Lightning (October 29, 1999). ... Strained groin (November 13, 1999); missed one game. ... Sprained ankle (December 4, 1999); missed 12 games. ... Strained groin (November 14, 2000); missed three games. ... Traded by Lightning to New York Islanders for future considerations (January 4, 2001). ... Sprained chest muscle (January 16, 2001); missed one game. ... Signed as free agent by Senators (August 30, 2001). ... Right knee (March 2, 2002); missed final 21 games of regular season. ... Claimed off waivers by St. Louis Blues (January 15, 2003). ... Signed as free agent by Ottawa Senators (August 19, 2005).

Season Team	League	GP	G	A	Pts.	PIM	+/-	PP	SH	GP	G	A	Pts.	PIM
		REGULAR SEASON								PLAYOFFS				
91-92—Harvard	ECAC	20	13	14	27	26	...	...	...	—	—	—	—	—
92-93—Harvard	ECAC	18	6	8	14	40	...	...	...	—	—	—	—	—
93-94—Harvard	ECAC	32	25	35	60	93	...	...	...	—	—	—	—	—
94-95—Harvard	ECAC	28	15	23	38	93	...	7	2	—	—	—	—	—
95-96—Springfield	AHL	30	9	20	29	10	...	...	...	—	—	—	—	—
—Hartford	NHL	23	1	3	4	8	-3	0	0	—	—	—	—	—
96-97—Springfield	AHL	63	12	31	43	78	11	5	0	17	1	3	4	26
—Hartford	NHL	2	0	1	1	0	0	0	0	—	—	—	—	—
97-98—Chicago	IHL	78	20	41	61	122	14	6	0	21	6	14	20	28
—Carolina	NHL	3	0	0	0	0	0	0	0	—	—	—	—	—
98-99—Detroit	IHL	4	1	6	7	16	2	0	0	—	—	—	—	—
—Ottawa	NHL	36	4	3	7	10	4	1	0	—	—	—	—	—
99-00—Ottawa	NHL	2	1	0	1	0	-1	0	0	—	—	—	—	—
—Tampa Bay	NHL	57	5	7	12	37	-11	0	1	—	—	—	—	—
00-01—Tampa Bay	NHL	20	1	1	2	13	-9	0	0	—	—	—	—	—
—Detroit	IHL	8	5	4	9	4	...	...	...	—	—	—	—	—
—New York Islanders	NHL	39	1	3	4	20	-7	0	1	—	—	—	—	—
—Chicago	IHL	5	1	2	3	0	...	...	...	16	1	6	7	22
01-02—Ottawa	NHL	14	1	0	1	4	1	0	0	2	0	0	0	0
—Grand Rapids	AHL	51	10	21	31	66	4	4	2	3	0	0	0	0
02-03—Binghamton	AHL	26	5	11	16	31	9	0	1	—	—	—	—	—
—Ottawa	NHL	14	2	3	5	10	3	0	0	—	—	—	—	—
—St. Louis	NHL	28	3	3	6	18	-8	0	1	2	0	1	1	0
03-04—Worcester	AHL	22	4	9	13	16	0	1	0	—	—	—	—	—
—St. Louis	NHL	25	1	0	1	22	-7	0	1	1	0	0	0	0
04-05—JyP Jyvaskyla	Finland	54	13	12	25	66	4	...	...	3	0	0	0	4
05-06—Binghamton	AHL	76	22	58	80	80	-4	11	1	—	—	—	—	—
—Ottawa	NHL	4	1	1	2	0	2	0	0	—	—	—	—	—
NHL Totals (10 years)		267	21	25	46	142	-36	1	4	5	0	1	1	0

M

MASON, CHRIS — G

PERSONAL: Born April 20, 1976, in Red Deer, Alta. ... 6-0/195. ... Catches left.
TRANSACTIONS/CAREER NOTES: Selected by New Jersey Devils in fifth round (seventh Devils pick, 122nd overall) of entry draft (July 8, 1995). ... Signed as free agent by Anaheim Mighty Ducks (May 31, 1996). ... Traded by Mighty Ducks with D Marc Moro to Nashville Predators for G Dominic Roussel (October 5, 1998). ... Signed as free agent by Florida Panthers (August 16, 2002). ... Claimed by Predators in waiver draft (October 3, 2003). ... Groin (December 13, 2005); missed four games.

		REGULAR SEASON										PLAYOFFS							
Season Team	**League**	**GP**	**Min.**	**W**	**L**	**OTL**	**T**	**GA**	**SO**	**GAA**	**SV%**	**GP**	**Min.**	**W**	**L**	**GA**	**SO**	**GAA**	**SV%**
93-94 —Victoria	WHL	3	129	0	3	...	0	16	...	7.44	...	—	—	—	—	—	—	—	—
94-95 —Prince George	WHL	44	2288	8	30	...	1	192	1	5.03	...	—	—	—	—	—	—	—	—
95-96 —Prince George	WHL	59	3289	16	37	...	1	236	1	4.31	...	—	—	—	—	—	—	—	—
96-97 —Prince George	WHL	50	2851	19	24	...	4	172	2	3.62	.900	15	938	9	6	44	1	2.81	.914
97-98 —Cincinnati	AHL	47	2368	13	19	...	7	136	0	3.45	.903	—	—	—	—	—	—	—	—
98-99 —Milwaukee	IHL	34	1901	15	12	...	6	92	1	2.90	.906	—	—	—	—	—	—	—	—
—Nashville	NHL	3	69	0	0	...	0	6	0	5.22	.864	—	—	—	—	—	—	—	—
99-00 —Milwaukee	IHL	53	2952	27	21	...	8	137	2	2.78	...	3	252	1	2	11	0	2.62	...
00-01 —Nashville	NHL	1	59	0	1	...	0	2	0	2.03	.900	—	—	—	—	—	—	—	—
—Milwaukee	IHL	37	2226	17	14	...	5	87	5	2.35	...	4	239	1	3	12	0	3.01	...
01-02 —Milwaukee	AHL	48	2755	17	21	...	7	116	2	2.53	.910	—	—	—	—	—	—	—	—
02-03 —San Antonio	AHL	50	2914	25	18	...	6	122	1	2.51	.921	3	194	0	3	9	0	2.78	.926
03-04 —Nashville	NHL	17	744	4	4	...	1	27	1	2.18	.926	—	—	—	—	—	—	—	—
—Milwaukee	AHL	1	60	1	0	...	0	2	0	2.00	.929	—	—	—	—	—	—	—	—
04-05 —Valerengen	Norway	20	1204	...	...	...	...	36	1	1.79	.934	11	657	...	...	22	1	2.01	.936
05-06 —Nashville	NHL	23	1227	12	5	1	...	52	2	2.54	.913	5	296	1	4	17	0	3.45	.901
NHL Totals (4 years)		44	2099	16	10	1	1	87	3	2.49	.915	5	296	1	4	17	0	3.45	.901

MATTHIAS, SHAWN — C

PERSONAL: Born February 19, 1988, in Mississauga, Ont. ... 6-3/211. ... Shoots left.
TRANSACTIONS/CAREER NOTES: Selected by Detroit Red Wings in second round (second Red Wings pick; 47th overall) of NHL draft (June 24, 2006).

		REGULAR SEASON								PLAYOFFS				
Season Team	**League**	**GP**	**G**	**A**	**Pts.**	**PIM**	**+/-**	**PP**	**SH**	**GP**	**G**	**A**	**Pts.**	**PIM**
04-05 —Belleville	OHL	37	1	1	2	15	-14	...	...	3	0	0	0	0
05-06 —Belleville	OHL	67	13	21	34	42	-9	...	...	6	3	0	3	2

MATVICHUK, RICHARD — D

PERSONAL: Born February 5, 1973, in Edmonton. ... 6-2/215. ... Shoots left. ... Name pronounced MAT-vih-chuhk.
TRANSACTIONS/CAREER NOTES: Selected by Minnesota North Stars in first round (first North Stars pick, eighth overall) of 1991 NHL draft (June 22, 1991). ... Strained lower back (November 9, 1992); missed two games. ... Sprained ankle (December 27, 1992); missed 10 games. ... North Stars franchise moved from Minnesota to Dallas and renamed Stars for 1993-94 season. ... Bruised shoulder (April 5, 1994); missed one game. ... Tore knee ligaments (September 20, 1994) and had surgery; missed first 16 games of season. ... Had concussion (March 13, 1996); missed five games. ... Bruised shoulder (October 26, 1996); missed two games. ... Strained groin (February 18, 1997); missed 19 games. ... Tore knee ligament (January 21, 1998); missed eight games. ... Bruised thigh (December 31, 1998); missed one game. ... Has headaches (January 8, 1999); missed one game. ... Strained groin (March 14, 1999); missed two games. ... Reinjured groin (March 19, 1999); missed final 14 games of regular season and one playoff game. ... Injured knee (October 16, 1999); missed three games. ... Injured knee (November 10, 1999); missed three games. ... Flu (January 23, 2000); missed one game. ... Sprained thumb (February 2, 2000); missed one game. ... Sprained knee (March 1, 2000); missed one game. ... Fractured jaw (January 24, 2001); missed four games. ... Fractured left leg (January 11, 2003); missed 14 games. ... Injured knee (November 8, 2003); missed one game. ... Flu (November 29, 2003); missed one game. ... Injured knee (December 7, 2003); missed four games. ... Left team for personal reasons (April 4, 2004); missed one game. ... Signed as free agent by New Jersey Devils (July 12, 2004). ... Back injury (March 1, 2006); missed 14 games. ... Injured groin (April 9, 2006); missed three games.

		REGULAR SEASON								PLAYOFFS				
Season Team	**League**	**GP**	**G**	**A**	**Pts.**	**PIM**	**+/-**	**PP**	**SH**	**GP**	**G**	**A**	**Pts.**	**PIM**
88-89 —Fort Saskatchewan	AJHL	58	7	36	43	147	...	...	...	—	—	—	—	—
89-90 —Saskatoon	WHL	56	8	24	32	126	...	...	...	10	2	8	10	16
90-91 —Saskatoon	WHL	68	13	36	49	117	...	...	...	—	—	—	—	—
91-92 —Saskatoon	WHL	58	14	40	54	126	...	...	...	22	1	9	10	61
92-93 —Minnesota	NHL	53	2	3	5	26	-8	1	0	—	—	—	—	—
—Kalamazoo	IHL	3	0	1	1	6	1	0	0	—	—	—	—	—
93-94 —Kalamazoo	IHL	43	8	17	25	84	0	4	0	—	—	—	—	—
—Dallas	NHL	25	0	3	3	22	1	0	0	7	1	1	2	12
94-95 —Dallas	NHL	14	0	2	2	14	-7	0	0	5	0	2	2	4
—Kalamazoo	IHL	17	0	6	6	16	-9	0	0	—	—	—	—	—
95-96 —Dallas	NHL	73	6	16	22	71	4	0	0	—	—	—	—	—
96-97 —Dallas	NHL	57	5	7	12	87	1	0	2	7	0	1	1	20
97-98 —Dallas	NHL	74	3	15	18	63	7	0	0	16	1	1	2	14
98-99 —Dallas	NHL	64	3	9	12	51	23	1	0	22	1	5	6	20
99-00 —Dallas	NHL	70	4	21	25	42	7	0	0	23	2	5	7	14
00-01 —Dallas	NHL	78	4	16	20	62	5	2	0	10	0	0	0	14
01-02 —Dallas	NHL	82	9	12	21	52	11	4	0	—	—	—	—	—
02-03 —Dallas	NHL	68	1	5	6	58	1	0	0	12	0	3	3	8
03-04 —Dallas	NHL	75	1	20	21	36	0	0	0	5	0	1	1	8
05-06 —New Jersey	NHL	62	1	10	11	40	2	0	0	7	0	0	0	4
NHL Totals (13 years)		795	39	139	178	624	47	8	2	114	5	19	24	118

MAXWELL, BEN — C

PERSONAL: Born March 30, 1988, in North Vancouver, B.C. ... 6-0/177. ... Shoots left.
TRANSACTIONS/CAREER NOTES: Selected by Montreal Canadiens in second round (second Canadiens pick; 49th overall) of NHL draft (June 24, 2006).

		REGULAR SEASON								PLAYOFFS				
Season Team	League	GP	G	A	Pts.	PIM	+/-	PP	SH	GP	G	A	Pts.	PIM
03-04—Kootenay	WHL	3	0	1	1	2	2	...	...	1	...	...	...	...
04-05—Kootenay	WHL	68	8	10	18	37	6	...	...	16	0	1	1	6
05-06—Kootenay	WHL	69	28	32	60	52	17	...	...	6	3	5	8	0

MAY, BRAD — LW

PERSONAL: Born November 29, 1971, in Toronto. ... 6-1/217. ... Shoots left.
TRANSACTIONS/CAREER NOTES: Selected by Buffalo Sabres in first round (first Sabres pick, 14th overall) of entry draft (June 16, 1990). ... Fractured hand (March 11, 1995); missed 15 games. ... Injured left arm (March 3, 1996); missed one game. ... Suspended one game for accumulating three game misconduct penalties (March 31, 1996). ... Right shoulder surgery (October 14, 1996); missed 27 games. ... Fractured right hand (December 20, 1996); missed nine games. ... Fractured thumb (March 1, 1997); missed four games. ... Strained shoulder (September 27, 1997); missed first six games of season. ... Sprained knee (December 29, 1997); missed 11 games. ... Traded by Sabres with third-round pick (later traded to Tampa Bay; Lightning picked RW Jimmie Olvestad) in 1999 entry draft to Vancouver Canucks for LW Geoff Sanderson (February 4, 1998). ... Strained groin (October 30, 1998); missed five games. ... Fractured hand (March 26, 1999); missed final 10 games of season. ... Sprained knee (December 10, 1999); missed 13 games. ... Traded by Canucks to Phoenix Coyotes for future considerations (June 25, 2000). ... Suspended 20 games for slashing incident (November 15, 2000). ... Fractured rib (January 3, 2002); missed 10 games. ... Torn shoulder muscle (October 1, 2002) and had surgery; missed first 44 games. ... Injured groin (January 23, 2003); missed four games. ... Traded by Coyotes to Canucks for third-round pick (C/RW Dimitri Pestunov) in 2003 entry draft (March 11, 2003). ... Concussion (March 15, 2003); missed nine games. ... Suspended one game for fighting incident (October 21, 2003). ... Flu (November 29, 2003); missed one game. ... Injured foot (March 13, 2004); missed three games. ... Injured knee (March 27, 2004); missed two games. ... Signed as free agent by Colorado Avalanche (August 5, 2005). ... Groin injury (September 28, 2005); missed first five games of season. ... Groin injury (November 30, 2005); missed one game. ... Sprained knee (December 31, 2005); missed 11 games. ... Injured finger (March 4, 2006); missed two games. ... Groin injury (April 5, 2006); missed final six games of regular season and four playoff games..

		REGULAR SEASON								PLAYOFFS				
Season Team	League	GP	G	A	Pts.	PIM	+/-	PP	SH	GP	G	A	Pts.	PIM
87-88—Markham Jr. B	OHA	6	1	1	2	21	...	...	...	—	—	—	—	—
88-89—Niagara Falls	OHL	65	8	14	22	304	...	...	...	17	0	1	1	55
89-90—Niagara Falls	OHL	61	33	58	91	223	...	...	...	16	9	13	22	64
90-91—Niagara Falls	OHL	34	37	32	69	93	...	...	...	14	11	14	25	53
91-92—Buffalo	NHL	69	11	6	17	309	-12	1	0	7	1	4	5	2
92-93—Buffalo	NHL	82	13	13	26	242	3	0	0	8	1	1	2	14
93-94—Buffalo	NHL	84	18	27	45	171	-6	3	0	7	0	2	2	9
94-95—Buffalo	NHL	33	3	3	6	87	5	1	0	4	0	0	0	2
95-96—Buffalo	NHL	79	15	29	44	295	6	3	0	—	—	—	—	—
96-97—Buffalo	NHL	42	3	4	7	106	-8	1	0	10	1	1	2	32
97-98—Buffalo	NHL	36	4	7	11	113	2	0	0	—	—	—	—	—
—Vancouver	NHL	27	9	3	12	41	0	4	0	—	—	—	—	—
98-99—Vancouver	NHL	66	6	11	17	102	-14	1	0	—	—	—	—	—
99-00—Vancouver	NHL	59	9	7	16	90	-2	0	0	—	—	—	—	—
00-01—Phoenix	NHL	62	11	14	25	107	10	0	0	—	—	—	—	—
01-02—Phoenix	NHL	72	10	12	22	95	11	1	0	5	0	0	0	0
02-03—Phoenix	NHL	20	3	4	7	32	3	0	0	—	—	—	—	—
—Vancouver	NHL	3	0	0	0	10	1	0	0	14	0	0	0	15
03-04—Vancouver	NHL	70	5	6	11	137	-2	0	0	6	1	0	1	6
05-06—Colorado	NHL	54	3	3	6	82	-14	0	0	3	0	0	0	0
NHL Totals (14 years)		858	123	149	272	2019	-17	15	0	64	4	8	12	80

MAYERS, JAMAL — RW

PERSONAL: Born October 24, 1974, in Toronto. ... 6-1/212. ... Shoots right.
TRANSACTIONS/CAREER NOTES: Selected by St. Louis Blues in fourth round (third Blues pick, 89th overall) of entry draft (June 26, 1993). ... Suspended one playoff game for slashing (May 7, 1999). ... Flu (March 24, 2001); missed one game. ... Strained groin (October 3, 2001); missed first four games of season. ... Bruised left foot (January 17, 2002); missed one game. ... Knee (November 15, 2002); missed final 67 games of regular season and playoffs. ... Wrist (January 10, 2004); missed one game. ... Groin (October 19, 2005); missed one game. ... Fractured right foot (January 30, 2006); missed 13 games.

		REGULAR SEASON								PLAYOFFS				
Season Team	League	GP	G	A	Pts.	PIM	+/-	PP	SH	GP	G	A	Pts.	PIM
90-91—Thornhill	Jr. A	44	12	24	36	78	...	...	...	—	—	—	—	—
91-92—Thornhill	Jr. A	56	38	69	107	36	...	...	...	—	—	—	—	—
92-93—Western Michigan	CCHA	38	8	17	25	26	...	...	...	—	—	—	—	—
93-94—Western Michigan	CCHA	40	17	32	49	40	12	4	1	—	—	—	—	—
94-95—Western Michigan	CCHA	39	13	33	46	40	18	4	1	—	—	—	—	—
95-96—Western Michigan	CCHA	38	17	22	39	75	...	...	...	—	—	—	—	—
96-97—Worcester	AHL	62	12	14	26	104	-12	2	0	5	4	4	8	4
—St. Louis	NHL	6	0	1	1	2	-3	0	0	—	—	—	—	—
97-98—Worcester	AHL	61	19	24	43	117	-5	8	1	11	3	4	7	10
98-99—Worcester	AHL	20	9	7	16	34	-3	3	0	—	—	—	—	—
—St. Louis	NHL	34	4	5	9	40	-3	0	0	11	0	1	1	8
99-00—St. Louis	NHL	79	7	10	17	90	0	0	0	7	0	4	4	2
00-01—St. Louis	NHL	77	8	13	21	117	-3	0	0	15	2	3	5	8
01-02—St. Louis	NHL	77	9	8	17	99	9	0	1	10	3	0	3	2

Season Team	League	GP	G	A	Pts.	PIM	+/-	PP	SH	GP	G	A	Pts.	PIM
		REGULAR SEASON								PLAYOFFS				
02-03—St. Louis	NHL	15	2	5	7	8	1	0	0	—	—	—	—	—
03-04—St. Louis	NHL	80	6	5	11	91	-19	0	1	5	0	0	0	0
04-05—Hammarby	Sweden Dv. 2	10	7	8	15	10	10	1	0	9	2	5	7	26
—Missouri	UHL	13	5	2	7	68	-3	2	1	—	—	—	—	—
05-06—St. Louis	NHL	67	15	11	26	129	-22	0	2	—	—	—	—	—
NHL Totals (8 years)		435	51	58	109	576	-40	0	4	48	5	8	13	20

MCAMMOND, DEAN — C/LW

PERSONAL: Born June 15, 1973, in Grand Cache, Alta. ... 5-11/200. ... Shoots left.

TRANSACTIONS/CAREER NOTES: Selected by Chicago Blackhawks in first round (first Blackhawks pick, 22nd overall) of entry draft (June 22, 1991). ... Traded by Blackhawks with D Igor Kravchuk to Edmonton Oilers for RW Joe Murphy (February 25, 1993). ... Severed left Achilles' tendon (February 1, 1995); missed final 41 games of season. ... Fractured nose (November 11, 1996); missed two games. ... Flu (January 21, 1997); missed two games. ... Back spasms (March 1, 1997); missed remainder of season. ... Traded by Oilers with D Boris Mironov and D Jonas Elofsson to Blackhawks for C Chad Kilger, LW Daniel Cleary, LW Ethan Moreau and D Christian Laflamme (March 20, 1999). ... Bruised ribs (October 4, 1999); missed five games. ... Wrist (December 9, 1999); missed one game. ... Traded by Blackhawks to Philadelphia Flyers for third-round pick (later traded to Toronto; Maple Leafs selected C Nicolas Corbiel) in 2001 draft (March 13, 2001). ... Traded by Flyers to Calgary Flames for fourth-round pick (D Rosario Ruggeri) in 2002 draft (June 24, 2001). ... Back (January 19, 2002); missed one game. ... Ribs (January 24, 2002); missed eight games. ... Traded by Flames with D Derek Morris and C Jeff Shantz to Colorado Avalanche for LW Chris Drury and C Stephane Yelle (October 1, 2002). ... Back (October 18, 2002); missed 23 games. ... Traded by Avalanche to Flames for fifth-round pick (C Mark McCutheon) in 2003 draft (March 11, 2003). ... Ruled ineligible to play remainder of the 2002-03 season because of transaction violation by Flames (March 15, 2003). ... Concussion (October 25, 2003); missed five games. ... Back (March 11, 2004); missed final 13 games of regular season and playoffs. ... Signed as free agent by St. Louis Blues (August 9, 2005).

Season Team	League	GP	G	A	Pts.	PIM	+/-	PP	SH	GP	G	A	Pts.	PIM
		REGULAR SEASON								PLAYOFFS				
89-90—Prince Albert	WHL	53	11	11	22	49	...	...	...	14	2	3	5	18
90-91—Prince Albert	WHL	71	33	35	68	108	...	...	...	2	0	1	1	6
91-92—Prince Albert	WHL	63	37	54	91	189	...	...	...	10	12	11	23	26
—Chicago	NHL	5	0	2	2	0	-2	0	0	3	0	0	0	2
92-93—Prince Albert	WHL	30	19	29	48	44	-1	5	2	—	—	—	—	—
—Swift Current	WHL	18	10	13	23	29	-4	2	1	17	16	19	35	20
93-94—Edmonton	NHL	45	6	21	27	16	12	2	0	—	—	—	—	—
—Cape Breton	AHL	28	9	12	21	38	-3	3	0	—	—	—	—	—
94-95—Edmonton	NHL	6	0	0	0	0	-1	0	0	—	—	—	—	—
95-96—Edmonton	NHL	53	15	15	30	23	6	4	0	—	—	—	—	—
—Cape Breton	AHL	22	9	15	24	55	...	...	...	—	—	—	—	—
96-97—Edmonton	NHL	57	12	17	29	28	-15	4	0	—	—	—	—	—
97-98—Edmonton	NHL	77	19	31	50	46	9	8	0	12	1	4	5	12
98-99—Edmonton	NHL	65	9	16	25	36	5	1	0	—	—	—	—	—
—Chicago	NHL	12	1	4	5	2	3	0	0	—	—	—	—	—
99-00—Chicago	NHL	76	14	18	32	72	11	1	0	—	—	—	—	—
00-01—Chicago	NHL	61	10	16	26	43	4	1	0	—	—	—	—	—
—Philadelphia	NHL	10	1	1	2	0	-1	1	0	4	0	0	0	2
01-02—Calgary	NHL	73	21	30	51	60	2	7	0	—	—	—	—	—
02-03—Colorado	NHL	41	10	8	18	10	1	2	0	—	—	—	—	—
03-04—Calgary	NHL	64	17	13	30	18	9	4	1	—	—	—	—	—
04-05—Albany	AHL	79	19	42	61	72	-1	5	1	—	—	—	—	—
05-06—St. Louis	NHL	78	15	22	37	32	-25	4	0	—	—	—	—	—
NHL Totals (13 years)		723	150	214	364	386	18	39	1	19	1	4	5	16

MCBAIN, JAMIE — D

PERSONAL: Born February 25, 1988, in Edina, Minn. ... 6-2/190. ... Shoots right.

TRANSACTIONS/CAREER NOTES: Selected by Carolina Hurricanes in second round (first Hurricanes pick; 63rd overall) of NHL draft (June 24, 2006).

Season Team	League	GP	G	A	Pts.	PIM	+/-	PP	SH	GP	G	A	Pts.	PIM
		REGULAR SEASON								PLAYOFFS				
04-05—U.S. National	USHL	36	1	6	7	20	...	...	...	—	—	—	—	—
05-06—U.S. National	USHL	47	6	10	16	41	...	...	...	—	—	—	—	—

MCCABE, BRYAN — D

PERSONAL: Born June 8, 1975, in St. Catharines, Ont. ... 6-2/220. ... Shoots left.

TRANSACTIONS/CAREER NOTES: Selected by New York Islanders in second round (second Islanders pick, 40th overall) of entry draft (June 26, 1993). ... Traded by Islanders with LW Todd Bertuzzi and third-round pick (LW Jarkko Ruutu) in 1998 entry draft to Vancouver Canucks for C Trevor Linden (February 6, 1998). ... Missed first 13 games of 1998-99 season in contract dispute. ... Traded by Canucks with first-round pick (RW Pavel Vorobiev) in 2000 entry draft to Chicago Blackhawks for first-round pick (traded to Tampa Bay Lightning) in 1999 entry draft (June 26, 1999). ... Fractured facial bone (March 11, 2000); missed two games. ... Traded by Blackhawks to Toronto Maple Leafs for D Alexander Karpovtsev and fourth-round pick (D Vladimir Gusev) in 2001 entry draft (October 2, 2000). ... Bruised left hand (October 14, 2002); missed one game. ... Fractured right foot (November 19, 2002); missed six games. ... Injured knee (October 4, 2003) and had surgery; missed first seven games of season. ... Strained groin (January 7, 2006); missed nine games.

Season Team	League	GP	G	A	Pts.	PIM	+/-	PP	SH	GP	G	A	Pts.	PIM
		REGULAR SEASON								PLAYOFFS				
91-92—Medicine Hat	WHL	68	6	24	30	157	...	...	...	4	0	0	0	6
92-93—Medicine Hat	WHL	14	0	13	13	83	-10	0	0	—	—	—	—	—

Season Team	League	GP	G	A	Pts.	PIM	+/-	PP	SH	GP	G	A	Pts.	PIM
		REGULAR SEASON								PLAYOFFS				
—Spokane	WHL	46	3	44	47	134	-13	1	0	10	1	5	6	28
93-94—Spokane	WHL	64	22	62	84	218	13	6	3	3	0	4	4	4
94-95—Spokane	WHL	42	14	39	53	115	-6	3	1	—	—	—	—	—
—Brandon	WHL	20	6	10	16	38	4	0	3	18	4	13	17	59
95-96—New York Islanders	NHL	82	7	16	23	156	-24	3	0	—	—	—	—	—
96-97—New York Islanders	NHL	82	8	20	28	165	-2	2	1	—	—	—	—	—
97-98—New York Islanders	NHL	56	3	9	12	145	9	1	0	—	—	—	—	—
—Vancouver	NHL	26	1	11	12	64	10	0	1	—	—	—	—	—
98-99—Vancouver	NHL	69	7	14	21	120	-11	1	2	—	—	—	—	—
99-00—Chicago	NHL	79	6	19	25	139	-8	2	0	—	—	—	—	—
00-01—Toronto	NHL	82	5	24	29	123	16	3	0	11	2	3	5	16
01-02—Toronto	NHL	82	17	26	43	129	16	8	0	20	5	5	10	30
02-03—Toronto	NHL	75	6	18	24	135	9	3	0	7	0	3	3	10
03-04—Toronto	NHL	75	16	37	53	86	22	8	0	13	3	5	8	14
04-05—HV 71 Jonkoping	Sweden	10	1	0	1	30	-12	1	0	—	—	—	—	—
05-06—Toronto	NHL	73	19	49	68	116	-1	13	0	—	—	—	—	—
—Canadian Oly. team	Int'l	6	0	0	0	18	-3	0	0	—	—	—	—	—
NHL Totals (10 years)		781	95	243	338	1378	36	44	4	51	10	16	26	70

MCCARTHY, STEVE D

PERSONAL: Born February 3, 1981, in Trail, B.C. ... 6-1/198. ... Shoots left.

TRANSACTIONS/CAREER NOTES: Selected by Chicago Blackhawks in first round (first Blackhawks pick, 23rd overall) of entry draft (June 26, 1999). ... Injured groin (November 26, 2003); missed 54 games. ... Traded by Blackhawks to Vancouver Canucks for conditional pick in 2007 (August 22, 2005). ... Injured groin (November 10, 2005); missed eight games. ... Charley horse (February 8, 2006); missed one game. ... Traded by Canucks to Atlanta Thrashers for conditional seventh-round pick in 2007 draft (March 9, 2006).

Season Team	League	GP	G	A	Pts.	PIM	+/-	PP	SH	GP	G	A	Pts.	PIM
		REGULAR SEASON								PLAYOFFS				
96-97—Edmonton	WHL	2	0	0	0	0	...	...	...	—	—	—	—	—
97-98—Edmonton	WHL	58	11	29	40	59	...	...	...	—	—	—	—	—
98-99—Kootenay	WHL	57	19	33	52	79	6	11	0	6	0	5	5	8
99-00—Chicago	NHL	5	1	1	2	4	0	1	0	—	—	—	—	—
—Kootenay	WHL	37	13	23	36	36	18	11	0	—	—	—	—	—
00-01—Chicago	NHL	44	0	5	5	8	-7	0	0	—	—	—	—	—
—Norfolk	AHL	7	0	4	4	2	...	...	...	—	—	—	—	—
01-02—Chicago	NHL	3	0	0	0	2	-1	0	0	—	—	—	—	—
—Norfolk	AHL	77	7	21	28	37	-16	2	0	2	0	3	3	2
02-03—Chicago	NHL	57	1	4	5	23	-1	0	0	—	—	—	—	—
—Norfolk	AHL	19	1	6	7	14	4	0	0	9	0	4	4	0
03-04—Chicago	NHL	25	1	3	4	8	-9	0	0	—	—	—	—	—
05-06—Vancouver	NHL	51	2	4	6	43	3	0	0	—	—	—	—	—
—Atlanta	NHL	16	7	3	10	8	0	2	0	—	—	—	—	—
NHL Totals (6 years)		201	12	20	32	96	-15	3	0					

MCCARTY, DARREN LW

PERSONAL: Born April 1, 1972, in Burnaby, B.C. ... 6-1/215. ... Shoots right.

TRANSACTIONS/CAREER NOTES: Selected by Detroit Red Wings in second round (second Red Wings pick, 46th overall) of entry draft (June 20, 1992). ... Groin (January 29, 1994); missed five games. ... Shoulder (March 23, 1994); missed five games. ... Separated right shoulder (February 7, 1995); missed eight games. ... Right hand (March 30, 1995); missed two games. ... Left knee (April 9, 1995); missed five games. ... Right heel (November 7, 1995); missed one game ... Separated shoulder (December 2, 1995); missed six games. ... Cut right forearm (January 12, 1996); missed three games. ... Left hand (February 15, 1996); missed seven games. ... Hand (January 3, 1997); missed seven games. ... Bruised thigh (January 29, 1997); missed four games. ... Injured groin (April 5, 1997); missed two games. ... Fractured foot (January 11, 1998); missed eight games. ... Vertigo (April 4, 1998); missed three games. ... Strained groin (March 12, 1999); missed 10 games. ... Reinjured groin (April 5, 1999); missed three games. ... Strained groin (November 12, 1999); missed 39 games. ... Leg (March 5, 2000); missed final 17 games of regular season. ... Back spasms (December 1, 2000); missed one game. ... Sprained ankle (March 18, 2001); missed remainder of regular season. ... Shoulder (September 21, 2001); missed first two games of season. ... Sprained knee (October 13, 2001); missed 11 games. ... Infected finger (March 2, 2002); missed six games. ... Elbow (February 6, 2003); missed nine games. ... Back spasms (November 8, 2003); missed 39 games. ... Signed by Flames as free agent (August 2, 2005). ... Head (October 23, 2005); missed four games. ... Hip flexor (December 26, 2005); missed three games. ... Flu (March 7, 2006); missed one game. ... Back (March 26, 2006); missed two games. ... Groin (April 1, 2006); missed three games.

Season Team	League	GP	G	A	Pts.	PIM	+/-	PP	SH	GP	G	A	Pts.	PIM
		REGULAR SEASON								PLAYOFFS				
88-89—Peterborough Jr. B	OHA	34	18	17	35	135	...	...	...	—	—	—	—	—
89-90—Belleville	OHL	63	12	15	27	142	...	...	...	11	1	1	2	21
90-91—Belleville	OHL	60	30	37	67	151	...	...	...	6	2	2	4	13
91-92—Belleville	OHL	65	55	72	127	177	...	...	...	5	1	4	5	13
92-93—Adirondack	AHL	73	17	19	36	278	16	1	0	11	0	1	1	33
93-94—Detroit	NHL	67	9	17	26	181	12	0	0	7	2	2	4	8
94-95—Detroit	NHL	31	5	8	13	88	5	1	0	18	3	2	5	14
95-96—Detroit	NHL	63	15	14	29	158	14	8	0	19	3	2	5	20
96-97—Detroit	NHL	68	19	30	49	126	14	5	0	20	3	4	7	34
97-98—Detroit	NHL	71	15	22	37	157	0	5	1	22	3	8	11	34
98-99—Detroit	NHL	69	14	26	40	108	10	6	0	10	1	1	2	23
99-00—Detroit	NHL	24	6	6	12	48	1	0	0	9	0	1	1	12
00-01—Detroit	NHL	72	12	10	22	123	-5	1	1	6	1	0	1	2
01-02—Detroit	NHL	62	5	7	12	98	2	0	0	23	4	4	8	34

Season Team	League	GP	G	A	Pts.	PIM	+/-	PP	SH	GP	G	A	Pts.	PIM
		REGULAR SEASON								PLAYOFFS				
02-03—Detroit	NHL	73	13	9	22	138	10	1	0	4	0	0	0	6
03-04—Detroit	NHL	43	6	5	11	50	2	1	0	12	0	1	1	7
05-06—Calgary	NHL	67	7	6	13	117	-1	1	0	7	2	0	2	15
NHL Totals (12 years)		710	126	160	286	1392	64	29	2	157	22	25	47	209

MCCAULEY, ALYN C/LW

PERSONAL: Born May 29, 1977, in Brockville, Ont. ... 6-0/192. ... Shoots left.

TRANSACTIONS/CAREER NOTES: Selected by New Jersey Devils in fourth round (fifth Devils pick, 79th overall) of entry draft (July 8, 1995). ... Traded by Devils with D Jason Smith and C Steve Sullivan to Toronto Maple Leafs for C Doug Gilmour, D Dave Ellett and third-round pick (D Andre Lakos) in 1999 draft (February 25, 1997). ... Fractured ankle (December 31, 1997); missed 17 games. ... Strained shoulder (February 26, 1998); missed three games. ... Sprained left knee (December 30, 1998); missed 22 games. ... Concussion (March 3, 1999); missed remainder of season. ... Injured (October 9, 1999); missed one game. ... Flu (December 4, 1999); missed six games. ... Ill (January 11, 2000); missed one game. ... Sprained wrist (October 11, 2000); missed four games. ... Traded by Maple Leafs with C Brad Boyes and first-round pick (later traded to Boston; Bruins selected D Mark Stuart) in 2003 draft to San Jose Sharks for RW Owen Nolan (March 5, 2003). ... Lower body (March 30, 2006); missed one game. ... Lower body (April 9, 2006); missed five games. ... Signed as free agent by Los Angeles Kings (July 2, 2006).

STATISTICAL PLATEAUS: Three-goal games: 2003-04 (1).

Season Team	League	GP	G	A	Pts.	PIM	+/-	PP	SH	GP	G	A	Pts.	PIM
		REGULAR SEASON								PLAYOFFS				
92-93—Kingston Jr. A	MTHL	38	31	29	60	18	...	...	...	—	—	—	—	—
93-94—Ottawa	OHL	38	13	23	36	10	...	...	...	13	5	14	19	4
94-95—Ottawa	OHL	65	16	38	54	20	...	3	0	—	—	—	—	—
95-96—Ottawa	OHL	55	34	48	82	24	...	...	...	2	0	0	0	0
96-97—Ottawa	OHL	50	56	56	112	16	47	18	3	22	14	22	36	14
—St. John's	AHL	...	...	...	...	...	...	...	...	3	0	1	1	0
97-98—Toronto	NHL	60	6	10	16	6	-7	0	0	—	—	—	—	—
98-99—Toronto	NHL	39	9	15	24	2	7	1	0	—	—	—	—	—
99-00—Toronto	NHL	45	5	5	10	10	-6	1	0	5	0	0	0	6
—St. John's	AHL	5	1	1	2	0	...	...	...	—	—	—	—	—
00-01—Toronto	NHL	14	1	0	1	0	0	0	0	10	0	0	0	2
—St. John's	AHL	47	16	28	44	12	...	...	...	—	—	—	—	—
01-02—Toronto	NHL	82	6	10	16	18	10	0	1	20	5	10	15	4
02-03—Toronto	NHL	64	6	9	15	16	3	0	0	—	—	—	—	—
—San Jose	NHL	16	3	7	10	4	-2	3	0	—	—	—	—	—
03-04—San Jose	NHL	82	20	27	47	28	23	5	0	11	2	1	3	2
05-06—San Jose	NHL	76	12	14	26	30	-3	4	2	6	0	1	1	4
NHL Totals (8 years)		478	68	97	165	114	25	14	3	52	7	12	19	18

M

MCCLEMENT, JAY C

PERSONAL: Born March 2, 1983, in Kingston, Ont. ... 6-1/199. ... Shoots left.

TRANSACTIONS/CAREER NOTES: Selected by St. Louis Blues in second round (first Blues pick, 57th overall) of entry draft (June 23, 2001).

Season Team	League	GP	G	A	Pts.	PIM	+/-	PP	SH	GP	G	A	Pts.	PIM
		REGULAR SEASON								PLAYOFFS				
99-00—Brampton	OHL	63	13	16	29	34	...	...	...	6	0	4	4	8
00-01—Brampton	OHL	66	30	19	49	61	...	...	...	9	4	2	6	10
01-02—Brampton	OHL	61	26	29	55	43	...	...	...	—	—	—	—	—
02-03—Brampton	OHL	45	22	27	49	37	...	...	...	11	3	4	7	11
—Worcester	AHL	...	...	...	...	...	...	...	...	1	0	0	0	0
03-04—Worcester	AHL	69	12	13	25	20	...	...	...	10	0	3	3	0
04-05—Worcester	AHL	79	17	34	51	45	1	2	5	—	—	—	—	—
05-06—Peoria	AHL	11	4	5	9	4	-1	1	1	4	0	2	2	2
—St. Louis	NHL	67	6	21	27	30	-23	1	0	—	—	—	—	—
NHL Totals (1 year)		67	6	21	27	30	-23	1	0					

MCCORMICK, CODY C/RW

PERSONAL: Born April 18, 1983, in London, Ont. ... 6-2/200. ... Shoots right.

TRANSACTIONS/CAREER NOTES: Selected by Colorado Avalanche in fifth round (fourth Avalanche pick, 144th overall) of NHL entry draft (June 23, 2001). ... Fractured finger (November 30, 2003); missed one game.

Season Team	League	GP	G	A	Pts.	PIM	+/-	PP	SH	GP	G	A	Pts.	PIM
		REGULAR SEASON								PLAYOFFS				
00-01—Belleville	OHL	66	7	16	23	135	...	...	...	10	1	1	2	23
01-02—Belleville	OHL	63	10	17	27	118	...	...	...	11	2	4	6	24
02-03—Belleville	OHL	61	36	33	69	166	...	...	...	7	4	7	11	11
03-04—Hershey	AHL	32	3	6	9	60	-9	0	1	—	—	—	—	—
—Colorado	NHL	44	2	3	5	73	-4	0	0	—	—	—	—	—
04-05—Hershey	AHL	40	5	6	11	68	-8	2	1	—	—	—	—	—
05-06—Lowell	AHL	13	1	6	7	34	-2	0	0	—	—	—	—	—
—Colorado	NHL	45	4	4	8	29	1	0	0	—	—	—	—	—
NHL Totals (2 years)		89	6	7	13	102	-3	0	0					

MCDONALD, ANDY LW/C

PERSONAL: Born August 25, 1977, in Strathroy, Ont. ... 5-10/186. ... Shoots left.

TRANSACTIONS/CAREER NOTES: Signed as free agent by Anaheim Mighty Ducks (April 3, 2000). ... Concussion (January 12, 2001); missed seven games. ... Concussion (February 27, 2002); missed three games. ... Concussion (January 9, 2003); missed seven games. ... Concussion (February 7, 2003); missed 29 games. ... Concussion (October 6, 2003); missed three games.

		REGULAR SEASON								PLAYOFFS				
Season Team	League	GP	G	A	Pts.	PIM	+/-	PP	SH	GP	G	A	Pts.	PIM
96-97—Colgate	ECAC	33	9	10	19	19	...	...	...	—	—	—	—	—
97-98—Colgate	ECAC	35	13	19	32	26	...	...	...	—	—	—	—	—
98-99—Colgate	ECAC	35	20	26	46	42	...	...	...	—	—	—	—	—
99-00—Colgate	ECAC	34	25	33	58	49	...	...	...	—	—	—	—	—
00-01—Cincinnati	AHL	46	15	25	40	21	...	...	...	3	0	1	1	2
—Anaheim	NHL	16	1	0	1	6	0	0	0	—	—	—	—	—
01-02—Cincinnati	AHL	21	7	25	32	6	13	1	0	—	—	—	—	—
—Anaheim	NHL	53	7	21	28	10	2	2	0	—	—	—	—	—
02-03—Anaheim	NHL	46	10	11	21	14	-1	3	0	—	—	—	—	—
03-04—Anaheim	NHL	79	9	21	30	24	-13	2	1	—	—	—	—	—
04-05—Ingolstadt ERC	Germany	36	13	17	30	26	15	3	1	10	5	2	7	35
05-06—Anaheim	NHL	82	34	51	85	32	24	13	0	16	2	7	9	10
NHL Totals (5 years)		276	61	104	165	86	12	20	1	16	2	7	9	10

MCEACHERN, SHAWN RW

PERSONAL: Born February 28, 1969, in Waltham, Mass. ... 5-11/200. ... Shoots left. ... Name pronounced muh-KEH-kuhrn.

TRANSACTIONS/CAREER NOTES: Selected by Pittsburgh Penguins in sixth round (sixth Penguins pick, 110th overall) of draft (June 13, 1987). ... Traded by Penguins to Los Angeles Kings for D Marty McSorley (August 27, 1993). ... Traded by Kings to Penguins for D Marty McSorley and D Jim Paek (February 15, 1994). ... Suspended for first three games of 1994-95 season and fined $500 by NHL for slashing incident (September 21, 1994); suspension reduced to two games because of abbreviated 1994-95 season. ... Traded by Penguins with LW Kevin Stevens to Boston Bruins for C Bryan Smolinski and RW Glen Murray (August 2, 1995). ... Traded by Bruins to Ottawa Senators for RW Trent McCleary and third-round pick (LW Eric Naud) in 1996 draft (June 22, 1996). ... Fractured jaw (December 6, 1996); missed 17 games. ... Back spasms (February 7, 1998); missed one game. ... Injured wrist (April 3, 1999); missed one game. ... Injured groin (April 8, 1999); missed four games. ... Ill (February 1, 2000); missed one game. ... Bruised shoulder (February 26, 2000); missed four games. ... Fractured left thumb (March 25, 2000); missed season's final eight games. ... Injured groin (April 9, 2002); missed final two games of regular season. ... Traded by Senators with sixth-round pick (G Dan Turple) in 2004 draft to Atlanta Thrashers for D Brian Pothier (June 30, 2002). ... Injured groin (January 21, 2003: missed six games. ... Injured back (February 7, 2003); missed 30 games. ... Signed as free agent by Bruins (August 2, 2005). ... Back spasms (October 20, 2005); missed five games.

STATISTICAL PLATEAUS: Three-goal games: 1997-98 (1), 2002-03 (1). Total: 2.

		REGULAR SEASON								PLAYOFFS				
Season Team	League	GP	G	A	Pts.	PIM	+/-	PP	SH	GP	G	A	Pts.	PIM
85-86—Matignon	Mass. H.S.	20	32	20	52	...	...	...	...	—	—	—	—	—
86-87—Matignon	Mass. H.S.	16	29	28	57	...	...	...	...	—	—	—	—	—
87-88—Matignon	Mass. H.S.	22	52	40	92	...	...	...	...	—	—	—	—	—
88-89—Boston University	Hockey East	36	20	28	48	32	...	...	...	—	—	—	—	—
89-90—Boston University	Hockey East	43	25	31	56	78	...	...	...	—	—	—	—	—
90-91—Boston University	Hockey East	41	34	48	82	43	...	...	...	—	—	—	—	—
91-92—U.S. national team	Int'l	57	26	23	49	38	...	...	...	—	—	—	—	—
—U.S. Olympic team	Int'l	8	1	0	1	10	...	...	...	—	—	—	—	—
—Pittsburgh	NHL	15	0	4	4	0	1	0	0	19	2	7	9	4
92-93—Pittsburgh	NHL	84	28	33	61	46	21	7	0	12	3	2	5	10
93-94—Los Angeles	NHL	49	8	13	21	24	1	0	3	—	—	—	—	—
—Pittsburgh	NHL	27	12	9	21	10	13	0	2	6	1	0	1	2
94-95—Kiekko-Espoo	Finland	8	1	3	4	6	-2	...	...	—	—	—	—	—
—Pittsburgh	NHL	44	13	13	26	22	4	1	2	11	0	2	2	8
95-96—Boston	NHL	82	24	29	53	34	-5	3	2	5	2	1	3	8
96-97—Ottawa	NHL	65	11	20	31	18	-5	0	1	7	2	0	2	8
97-98—Ottawa	NHL	81	24	24	48	42	1	8	2	11	0	4	4	8
98-99—Ottawa	NHL	77	31	25	56	46	8	7	0	4	2	0	2	6
99-00—Ottawa	NHL	69	29	22	51	24	2	10	0	6	0	3	3	4
00-01—Ottawa	NHL	82	32	40	72	62	10	9	0	4	0	2	2	2
01-02—Ottawa	NHL	80	15	31	46	52	9	5	0	12	0	4	4	2
02-03—Atlanta	NHL	46	10	16	26	28	-27	4	1	—	—	—	—	—
03-04—Atlanta	NHL	82	17	38	55	76	5	5	1	—	—	—	—	—
04-05—Malmo	Sweden	6	0	1	1	14	-4	0	0	10	1	1	2	12
05-06—Providence	AHL	10	2	4	6	6	2	1	0	—	—	—	—	—
—Boston	NHL	28	2	6	8	22	-12	1	0	—	—	—	—	—
NHL Totals (14 years)		911	256	323	579	506	26	60	14	97	12	25	37	62

MCGILLIS, DAN D

PERSONAL: Born July 1, 1972, in Hawkesbury, Ont. ... 6-2/230. ... Shoots left.

TRANSACTIONS/CAREER NOTES: Selected by Detroit Red Wings in 10th round (10th Red Wings pick, 238th overall) of entry draft (June 20, 1992). ... Signed as free agent by Edmonton Oilers (September 6, 1996). ... Traded by Oilers with second-round pick (D Jason Beckett) in 1998 entry draft to Philadelphia Flyers for D Janne Niinimaa (March 24, 1998). ... Neck spasms (February 21, 1999); missed two games. ... Injured left knee (March 30, 1999); missed one game. ... Fractured right foot (November 28, 1999); missed four games. ... Strained groin (February 22, 2000); missed 10 games. ... Strained groin (November 3, 2001); missed one game. ... Strained lower back (January 19, 2002); missed six games. ... Traded by Flyers to San Jose Sharks for D Marcus Ragnarsson (December 6, 2002). ... Concussion (January 25, 2003); missed four games. ... Concussion (March 9, 2003); missed one game. ... Traded by Sharks to Boston Bruins for second-round pick (later traded to New York Rangers; Rangers selected D Ivan Baranka) in 2003 entry draft (March 11, 2003). ... Injured hip (February 3, 2004); missed two games. ... Signed as free agent by New Jersey Devils (August 4, 2005).

		REGULAR SEASON								PLAYOFFS				
Season Team	League	GP	G	A	Pts.	PIM	+/-	PP	SH	GP	G	A	Pts.	PIM
91-92—Hawkesbury	Tier II Jr. A	36	5	19	24	106	...	...	...	—	—	—	—	—
92-93—Northeastern Univ.	Hockey East	35	5	12	17	42	...	...	...	—	—	—	—	—
93-94—Northeastern Univ.	Hockey East	38	4	25	29	82	...	...	...	—	—	—	—	—
94-95—Northeastern Univ.	Hockey East	34	9	22	31	70	...	6	...	—	—	—	—	—
95-96—Northeastern Univ.	Hockey East	34	12	24	36	50	...	...	...	—	—	—	—	—
96-97—Edmonton	NHL	73	6	16	22	52	2	2	1	12	0	5	5	24
97-98—Edmonton	NHL	67	10	15	25	74	-17	5	0	—	—	—	—	—
—Philadelphia	NHL	13	1	5	6	35	-4	1	0	5	1	2	3	10
98-99—Philadelphia	NHL	78	8	37	45	61	16	6	0	6	0	1	1	12
99-00—Philadelphia	NHL	68	4	14	18	55	16	3	0	18	2	6	8	12
00-01—Philadelphia	NHL	82	14	35	49	86	13	4	0	6	1	0	1	6
01-02—Philadelphia	NHL	75	5	14	19	46	17	2	0	5	1	0	1	8
02-03—Philadelphia	NHL	24	0	3	3	20	7	0	0	—	—	—	—	—
—San Jose	NHL	37	3	13	16	30	-6	2	0	—	—	—	—	—
—Boston	NHL	10	0	1	1	10	2	0	0	5	3	0	3	2
03-04—Boston	NHL	80	5	23	28	65	-1	1	0	7	0	0	0	2
05-06—Albany	AHL	40	7	18	25	57	-5	6	0	—	—	—	—	—
—New Jersey	NHL	27	0	6	6	36	-5	0	0	—	—	—	—	—
NHL Totals (9 years)		634	56	182	238	570	40	26	1	64	8	14	22	76

MCGINN, JAMIE LW

PERSONAL: Born August 5, 1988, in Fergus, Ont. ... 5-11/179. ... Shoots left.

TRANSACTIONS/CAREER NOTES: Selected by San Jose Sharks in second round (second Sharks pick; 36th overall) of NHL draft (June 24, 2006).

		REGULAR SEASON								PLAYOFFS				
Season Team	League	GP	G	A	Pts.	PIM	+/-	PP	SH	GP	G	A	Pts.	PIM
04-05—Ottawa	OHL	59	10	12	22	35	4	...	...	18	4	7	11	0
05-06—Ottawa	OHL	65	26	31	57	113	-11	...	...	6	2	2	4	4

MCGRATTAN, BRIAN RW

PERSONAL: Born September 2, 1981, in Hamilton, Ont. ... 6-4/225. ... Shoots right.

TRANSACTIONS/CAREER NOTES: Selected by Los Angeles Kings in fourth round (fifth Kings pick, 104th overall) of NHL entry draft (June 26, 1999). ... Signed as free agent by Ottawa Senators (June 2, 2003). ... Right eye injury (February 6, 2006); missed six games.

		REGULAR SEASON								PLAYOFFS				
Season Team	League	GP	G	A	Pts.	PIM	+/-	PP	SH	GP	G	A	Pts.	PIM
97-98—Guelph	OHL	25	3	2	5	11	...	...	...	—	—	—	—	—
98-99—Guelph	OHL	6	1	3	4	15	...	...	...	—	—	—	—	—
—Sudbury	OHL	53	7	10	17	153	...	...	...	4	0	0	0	8
99-00—Sudbury	OHL	25	2	8	10	79	...	...	...	—	—	—	—	—
—Mississauga	OHL	42	9	13	22	166	...	...	...	—	—	—	—	—
00-01—Mississauga	OHL	31	20	9	29	83	-26	12	0	—	—	—	—	—
01-02—Mississauga	OHL	7	2	3	5	16	...	...	...	—	—	—	—	—
—Owen Sound	OHL	2	0	0	0	0	...	...	...	—	—	—	—	—
—Oshawa	OHL	25	10	5	15	72	...	...	...	—	—	—	—	—
—Sault Ste. Marie	OHL	26	8	7	15	71	...	...	...	6	2	0	2	20
02-03—Binghamton	AHL	59	9	10	19	173	9	4	0	1	0	0	0	0
03-04—Binghamton	AHL	66	9	11	20	327	...	...	...	1	0	0	0	0
04-05—Binghamton	AHL	71	7	1	8	551	-8	1	0	6	0	2	2	28
05-06—Ottawa	NHL	60	2	3	5	141	0	0	0	—	—	—	—	—
NHL Totals (1 year)		60	2	3	5	141	0	0	0					

MCKEE, JAY D

PERSONAL: Born September 8, 1977, in Kingston, Ont. ... 6-4/201. ... Shoots left.

TRANSACTIONS/CAREER NOTES: Selected by Buffalo Sabres in first round (first Sabres pick, 14th overall) of entry draft (July 8, 1995). ... Bruised stomach (March 29, 1998); missed two games. ... Bruised hand (October 30, 1998); missed one game. ... Bruised foot (February 13, 1999); missed six games. ... Flu (March 13, 1999); missed two games. ... Injured (November 25, 2000); missed five games. ... Injured hand (March 16, 2001); missed three games. ... Flu (January 23, 2002); missed one game. ... Injured knee (November 30, 2002); missed one game. ... Injured leg (December 21, 2002); missed one game. ... Flu (December 31, 2002); missed one game. ... Injured knee (February 15, 2003); missed 20 games. ... Injured knee (November 20, 2003); missed 13 games. ... Reinjured knee (January 9, 2004); missed six games. ... Reinjured knee (January 24, 2004); missed 18 games. ... Injured foot (November 5, 2005); missed six games. ... Leg infection (June 1, 2006); missed Game 7 of Eastern Conference finals. ... Signed as free agent by St. Louis Blues (July 1, 2006).

		REGULAR SEASON								PLAYOFFS				
Season Team	League	GP	G	A	Pts.	PIM	+/-	PP	SH	GP	G	A	Pts.	PIM
92-93—Ernestown	Jr. C	36	0	17	17	37	...	...	...	—	—	—	—	—
93-94—Sudbury	OHL	51	0	1	1	51	...	...	...	3	0	0	0	0
94-95—Sudbury	OHL	39	6	6	12	91	...	0	0	—	—	—	—	—
—Niagara Falls	OHL	26	3	13	16	60	...	2	0	6	2	3	5	10
95-96—Niagara Falls	OHL	64	5	41	46	129	...	...	...	10	1	5	6	16
—Rochester	AHL	4	0	1	1	15	...	...	...	—	—	—	—	—
—Buffalo	NHL	1	0	1	1	2	1	0	0	—	—	—	—	—

Season Team	League	GP	G	A	Pts.	PIM	+/-	PP	SH	GP	G	A	Pts.	PIM
		REGULAR SEASON								PLAYOFFS				
96-97—Buffalo	NHL	43	1	9	10	35	3	0	0	3	0	0	0	0
—Rochester	AHL	7	2	5	7	4	0	1	0	—	—	—	—	—
97-98—Buffalo	NHL	56	1	13	14	42	-1	0	0	1	0	0	0	0
—Rochester	AHL	13	1	7	8	11	6	0	0	—	—	—	—	—
98-99—Buffalo	NHL	72	0	6	6	75	20	0	0	21	0	3	3	24
99-00—Buffalo	NHL	78	5	12	17	50	5	1	0	1	0	0	0	0
00-01—Buffalo	NHL	74	1	10	11	76	9	0	0	8	1	0	1	6
01-02—Buffalo	NHL	81	2	11	13	43	18	0	0	—	—	—	—	—
02-03—Buffalo	NHL	59	0	5	5	49	-16	0	0	—	—	—	—	—
03-04—Buffalo	NHL	43	2	3	5	41	6	0	0	—	—	—	—	—
05-06—Buffalo	NHL	75	5	11	16	57	0	0	1	17	2	3	5	30
NHL Totals (10 years)		582	17	81	98	470	45	1	1	51	3	6	9	60

MCLAREN, KYLE D

PERSONAL: Born June 18, 1977, in Humboldt, Sask. ... 6-4/225. ... Shoots left.

TRANSACTIONS/CAREER NOTES: Selected by Boston Bruins in first round (first Bruins pick, ninth overall) of NHL entry draft (July 8, 1995). ... Injured back (November 21, 1995); missed one game. ... Injured knee (November 25, 1995); missed five games. ... Had the flu (January 3, 1996); missed one game. ... Suffered concussion (March 10, 1996); missed one game. ... Had charley horse (October 26, 1996); missed two games. ... Strained shoulder (February 2, 1997); missed 13 games. ... Injured foot (March 15, 1997); missed one game. ... Sprained thumb (March 27, 1997); missed remainder of season. ... Had hip pointer (November 1, 1997); missed five games. ... Injured knee (December 17, 1997); missed one game. ... Fractured foot (March 19, 1998); missed seven games. ... Strained groin (April 7, 1998); missed three games. ... Missed first 15 games of 1998-99 season in contract dispute. ... Separated shoulder (January 15, 1999); missed 14 games. ... Injured foot (April 10, 1999); missed one game. ... Strained thumb (November 18, 1999); missed seven games. ... Tore knee cartilage (April 1, 2000); missed final four games of season. ... Injured knee (October 20, 2000); missed 24 games. ... Sprained chest muscle (October 8, 2001); missed 12 games. ... Bruised right knee (November 17, 2001); missed one game. ... Tore right wrist ligament (December 22, 2001) and had surgery; missed 31 games. ... Suspended three playoff games by NHL for elbowing incident (April 26, 2002). ... Traded by Bruins with fourth-round pick (C Torrey Mitchell) in 2004 entry draft to San Jose Sharks as part of three-team trade in which Bruins acquired G Jeff Hackett and D Jeff Jillson and Montreal Canadiens acquired LW Niklas Sundstrom and third-round pick in 2004 draft (January 23, 2003); Canadiens later traded third-round pick to Los Angeles Kings (selected D Paul Baier). ... Injured foot (November 11, 2003); missed one game. ... Injured knee (November 26, 2003); missed two games. ... Injured knee (December 11, 2003); missed two games. ... Injured ribs (January 3, 2004); missed seven games. ... Had severe facial cuts (February 27, 2004); missed six games. ... Injured upper body (May 12, 2004); missed one playoff game. ... Re-signed by Sharks to multiyear contract extension (August 11, 2005). ... Injured left knee (December 15, 2005); missed five games.

Season Team	League	GP	G	A	Pts.	PIM	+/-	PP	SH	GP	G	A	Pts.	PIM
		REGULAR SEASON								PLAYOFFS				
93-94—Tacoma	WHL	62	1	9	10	53	...	...	...	6	1	4	5	6
94-95—Tacoma	WHL	47	13	19	32	68	29	5	0	4	1	1	2	4
95-96—Boston	NHL	74	5	12	17	73	16	0	0	5	0	0	0	14
96-97—Boston	NHL	58	5	9	14	54	-9	0	0	—	—	—	—	—
97-98—Boston	NHL	66	5	20	25	56	13	2	0	6	1	0	1	4
98-99—Boston	NHL	52	6	18	24	48	1	3	0	12	0	3	3	10
99-00—Boston	NHL	71	8	11	19	67	-4	2	0	—	—	—	—	—
00-01—Boston	NHL	58	5	12	17	53	-5	2	0	—	—	—	—	—
01-02—Boston	NHL	38	0	8	8	19	-4	0	0	4	0	0	0	20
02-03—San Jose	NHL	33	0	8	8	30	-10	0	0	—	—	—	—	—
03-04—San Jose	NHL	64	2	22	24	60	10	0	1	16	0	3	3	10
05-06—San Jose	NHL	77	2	21	23	66	6	0	0	11	0	3	3	4
NHL Totals (10 years)		591	38	141	179	526	14	9	1	54	1	9	10	62

MCLEAN, BRETT C

PERSONAL: Born August 14, 1978, in Comox, B.C. ... 5-11/794. ... Shoots left.

TRANSACTIONS/CAREER NOTES: Selected by Dallas Stars in ninth round (ninth Stars pick, 242nd overall) of entry draft (June 21, 1997). ... Signed as free agent by Calgary Flames (September 1, 1999). ... Signed as free agent by Minnesota Wild (July 13, 2000). ... Signed as free agent by Chicago Blackhawks (July 23, 2002). ... Concussion (February 29, 2004); missed three games. ... Signed as free agent by Colorado Avalanche (July 21, 2004).

Season Team	League	GP	G	A	Pts.	PIM	+/-	PP	SH	GP	G	A	Pts.	PIM
		REGULAR SEASON								PLAYOFFS				
94-95—Tacoma	WHL	67	11	23	34	33	...	...	...	4	0	1	1	0
95-96—Kelowna	WHL	71	37	42	79	60	...	...	...	6	2	2	4	6
96-97—Kelowna	WHL	72	44	60	104	96	...	...	...	4	4	2	6	12
97-98—Kelowna	WHL	54	42	46	88	91	25	10	6	7	4	5	9	17
98-99—Kelowna	WHL	44	32	38	70	46	...	...	...	—	—	—	—	—
—Brandon	WHL	21	15	16	31	20	...	...	...	5	1	6	7	8
—Cincinnati	AHL	7	0	3	3	6	-3	0	0	—	—	—	—	—
99-00—Saint John	AHL	72	15	23	38	115	...	...	...	3	0	1	1	2
—Johnstown	ECHL	8	4	7	11	6	...	...	...	—	—	—	—	—
00-01—Cleveland	IHL	74	20	24	44	54	...	...	...	4	0	0	0	18
01-02—Houston	AHL	78	24	21	45	71	-19	10	0	14	1	6	7	12
02-03—Chicago	NHL	2	0	0	0	0	-1	0	0	—	—	—	—	—
—Norfolk	AHL	77	23	38	61	60	14	4	3	9	2	6	8	9
03-04—Chicago	NHL	76	11	20	31	54	-11	5	1	—	—	—	—	—
—Norfolk	AHL	4	3	3	6	6	-2	2	0	—	—	—	—	—
04-05—Malmo	Sweden	38	7	6	13	102	0	1	0	9	1	1	2	16
05-06—Colorado	NHL	82	9	31	40	51	-7	1	0	8	0	1	1	4
NHL Totals (3 years)		160	20	51	71	105	-19	6	1	8	0	1	1	4

MCLENNAN, JAMIE G

PERSONAL: Born June 30, 1971, in Edmonton. ... 6-0/190. ... Catches left.

TRANSACTIONS/CAREER NOTES: Selected by New York Islanders in third round (third Islanders pick, 48th overall) of NHL draft (June 22, 1991). ... Signed as free agent by St. Louis Blues (July 3, 1996). ... Strained groin (October 29, 1997); missed two games. ... Strained groin (March 22, 1998); missed one game. ... Strained hip flexor (January 19, 1999); missed one game. ... Had the flu (March 11, 1999); missed two games. ... Selected by Minnesota Wild in expansion draft (June 23, 2000). ... Bruised forearm (November 11, 2000); missed one game. ... Ill (March 5, 2001); missed four games. ... Traded by Wild to Calgary Flames for ninth-round pick (F Mika Hannula) in 2002 draft (June 22, 2002). ... Injured back (November 29, 2002); missed two games. ... Fractured sternum (February 26, 2004); missed eight games. ... Traded by Flames with C Blair Betts and RW Greg Moore to New York Rangers for LW Chris Simon and seventh-round pick (C Matt Schneider) in 2004 draft (March 6, 2004). ... Signed as free agent by Florida Panthers (July 2, 2004). ... Signed as free agent by Calgary Flames (July 6, 2006).

		REGULAR SEASON										PLAYOFFS							
Season Team	League	GP	Min.	W	L	OTL	T	GA	SO	GAA	SV%	GP	Min.	W	L	GA	SO	GAA	SV%
88-89—Spokane	WHL	11	578	...	...	...	...	63	0	6.54	...	—	—	—	—	—	—	—	—
—Lethbridge	WHL	7	368	...	...	...	...	22	0	3.59	...	—	—	—	—	—	—	—	—
89-90—Lethbridge	WHL	34	1690	20	4	...	2	110	1	3.91	...	13	677	6	5	44	0	3.90	...
90-91—Lethbridge	WHL	56	3230	32	18	...	4	205	0	3.81	...	16	970	8	8	56	0	3.46	...
91-92—Capital District	AHL	18	952	4	10	...	2	60	1	3.78	...	—	—	—	—	—	—	—	—
—Richmond	ECHL	32	1837	16	12	...	2	114	0	3.72	...	—	—	—	—	—	—	—	—
92-93—Capital District	AHL	38	2171	17	14	...	6	117	1	3.23	.893	1	20	0	1	5	0	15.00	.583
93-94—Salt Lake City	IHL	24	1320	8	12	...	2	80	0	3.64	.889	—	—	—	—	—	—	—	—
—New York Islanders	NHL	22	1287	8	7	...	6	61	0	2.84	.905	2	82	0	1	6	0	4.39	.872
94-95—New York Islanders	NHL	21	1185	6	11	...	2	67	0	3.39	.876	—	—	—	—	—	—	—	—
—Denver	IHL	4	240	3	0	...	1	12	0	3.00	.906	11	641	8	2	23	1	2.15	.929
95-96—Utah	IHL	14	728	9	2	...	2	29	0	2.39	...	—	—	—	—	—	—	—	—
—New York Islanders	NHL	13	636	3	9	...	1	39	0	3.68	.886	—	—	—	—	—	—	—	—
—Worcester	AHL	22	1215	14	7	...	1	57	0	2.81	...	2	118	0	2	8	0	4.07	...
96-97—Worcester	AHL	39	2152	18	13	...	4	100	2	2.79	.903	4	262	2	2	16	0	3.66	.894
97-98—St. Louis	NHL	30	1658	16	8	...	2	60	2	2.17	.903	1	14	0	0	1	0	4.29	.750
98-99—St. Louis	NHL	33	1763	13	14	...	4	70	3	2.38	.891	1	37	0	1	0	0	0.00	1.000
99-00—St. Louis	NHL	19	1009	9	5	...	2	33	2	1.96	.903	—	—	—	—	—	—	—	—
00-01—Minnesota	NHL	38	2230	5	23	...	9	98	2	2.64	.905	—	—	—	—	—	—	—	—
01-02—Houston	AHL	51	2851	25	18	...	4	130	3	2.74	.895	14	879	8	6	31	2	2.12	.929
02-03—Calgary	NHL	22	1165	2	11	...	4	58	0	2.99	.892	—	—	—	—	—	—	—	—
03-04—Calgary	NHL	26	1446	12	9	...	3	53	4	2.20	.910	—	—	—	—	—	—	—	—
—New York Rangers	NHL	4	244	1	3	...	0	12	0	2.95	.876	—	—	—	—	—	—	—	—
04-05—Guildford	England	3	185	2	1	...	0	8	0	2.59	.927	7	385	4	3	13	0	2.02	.932
05-06—Florida	NHL	17	678	2	4	2	...	34	0	3.01	.906	—	—	—	—	—	—	—	—
NHL Totals (10 years)		245	13301	77	104	2	33	585	13	2.64	.898	4	133	0	2	7	0	3.16	.879

MCVICAR, ROBERT G

PERSONAL: Born January 15, 1982, in Brandon, Man. ... 6-4/195. ... Catches left.

TRANSACTIONS/CAREER NOTES: Selected by Vancouver Canucks in fifth round (sixth Canucks pick, 151st overall) of entry draft (June 23, 2002).

		REGULAR SEASON									PLAYOFFS							
Season Team	League	GP	Min.	W	L	T	GA	SO	GAA	SV%	GP	Min.	W	L	GA	SO	GAA	SV%
99-00—Brandon	WHL	14	687	5	6	0	43	0	3.76	...	—	—	—	—	—	—	—	—
00-01—Brandon	WHL	27	1537	12	10	2	76	0	2.97	...	—	—	—	—	—	—	—	—
01-02—Brandon	WHL	55	3276	33	18	2	151	1	2.77	...	—	—	—	—	—	—	—	—
02-03—Brandon	WHL	51	3026	31	15	5	136	2	2.70	...	—	—	—	—	—	—	—	—
03-04—Columbia	ECHL	19	1088	11	5	2	47	0	2.59	...	—	—	—	—	—	—	—	—
—Manitoba	AHL	10	513	4	3	2	25	0	2.92	...	—	—	—	—	—	—	—	—
04-05—Manitoba	AHL	1	61	0	1	...	3	0	2.95	.933	—	—	—	—	—	—	—	—
—Columbia	ECHL	34	2004	14	14	5	79	3	2.37	...	—	—	—	—	—	—	—	—
05-06—Vancouver	NHL	1	3	0	0	...	0	0	0.00	...	—	—	—	—	—	—	—	—
—Manitoba	AHL	6	337	3	3	...	17	0	3.03	.901	—	—	—	—	—	—	—	—
—Victoria	ECHL	33	1741	13	14	2	95	1	3.27	.902	—	—	—	—	—	—	—	—
NHL Totals (1 year)		1	3	0	0	0	0	0	0.00	...								

MELICHAR, JOSEF D

PERSONAL: Born January 20, 1979, in Ceske Budejovice, Czechoslovakia. ... 6-2/222. ... Shoots left. ... Name pronounced YOU-sehf mehl-ee-KHAHR.

TRANSACTIONS/CAREER NOTES: Selected by Pittsburgh Penguins in third round (third Penguins pick, 71st overall) of NHL draft (June 21, 1997). ... Bruised hip (December 6, 2001); missed one game. ... Dislocated shoulder (February 12, 2002); missed 15 games. ... Reinjured shoulder (April 4, 2002); missed remainder of season. ... Reinjured should (October 14, 2002); missed nine games. ... Reinjured shoulder (November 20, 2003); missed final 65 games of season. ... Re-signed by Penguins as restricted free agent (August 15, 2005).

		REGULAR SEASON								PLAYOFFS				
Season Team	League	GP	G	A	Pts.	PIM	+/-	PP	SH	GP	G	A	Pts.	PIM
95-96—HC Ceske Budejovice	Czech. Jrs.	38	3	4	7	...	...	...	...	—	—	—	—	—
96-97—HC Ceske Budejovice	Czech. Jrs.	41	2	3	5	10	...	...	...	—	—	—	—	—
97-98—Tri-City	WHL	67	9	24	33	152	-42	5	0	—	—	—	—	—
98-99—Tri-City	WHL	65	8	28	36	125	30	4	0	11	1	0	1	15
99-00—Wilkes-Barre/Scranton	AHL	80	3	9	12	126	...	...	...	—	—	—	—	—
00-01—Wilkes-Barre/Scranton	AHL	46	2	5	7	69	...	...	...	21	0	5	5	6
—Pittsburgh	NHL	18	0	2	2	21	-5	0	0	—	—	—	—	—

Season Team	League	REGULAR SEASON GP	G	A	Pts.	PIM	+/-	PP	SH	PLAYOFFS GP	G	A	Pts.	PIM
01-02—Pittsburgh	NHL	60	0	3	3	68	-1	0	0	—	—	—	—	—
02-03—Pittsburgh	NHL	8	0	0	0	2	-2	0	0	—	—	—	—	—
03-04—Pittsburgh	NHL	82	3	5	8	62	-17	0	0	—	—	—	—	—
04-05—Sparta Praha	Czech Rep.	13	0	4	4	8	4	...	...	5	0	0	0	6
05-06—Pittsburgh	NHL	72	3	12	15	66	-2	0	1	—	—	—	—	—
NHL Totals (5 years)		240	6	22	28	219	-27	0	1					

MELLANBY, SCOTT RW

PERSONAL: Born June 11, 1966, in Montreal. ... 6-1/208. ... Shoots right.

TRANSACTIONS/CAREER NOTES: Selected by Philadelphia Flyers in second round (first Flyers pick, 27th overall) of entry draft (June 9, 1984). ... Cut right index finger (October 1987). ... Severed nerve and damaged tendon in left forearm (August 1989); missed first 20 games of season. ... Virus (November 1989). ... Traded by Flyers with LW Craig Berube and C Craig Fisher to Edmonton Oilers for RW Dave Brown, D Corey Foster and rights to RW Jari Kurri (May 30, 1991). ... Injured shoulder (February 14, 1993); missed 15 games. ... Selected by Florida Panthers in expansion draft (June 24, 1993). ... Fractured nose and cut face (February 1, 1994); missed four games. ... Fractured finger (March 7, 1996); missed three games. ... Sprained left knee (January 9, 1998); missed three games. ... Strained groin (September 29, 1998); missed first nine games of season. ... Injured neck (January 16, 1999); missed one game. ... Reinjured neck (January 21, 1999); missed three games. ... Suspended one game for cross-checking incident (March 21, 1999). ... Slight concussion (April 5, 1999); missed one game. ... Concussion (October 12, 1999); missed three games. ... Flu (March 3, 2000); missed one game. ... Strained neck (October 28, 2000). ... Strained back (November 13, 2000); missed 12 games. ... Traded by Panthers to St. Louis Blues for RW David Morisset and fifth-round pick (C Vince Bellissimo) in 2002 draft (February 9, 2001). ... Fractured jaw (September 28, 2001); missed first 12 games of season. ... Flu (December 10, 2002); missed one game. ... Injured ribs (October 9, 2003); missed seven games. ... Concussion (October 29, 2003); missed four games. ... Flu (February 20, 2004); missed one game. ... Signed as free agent by Atlanta Thrashers (July 26, 2004). ... Strained groin (October 27, 2005); missed five games. ... Strained abdominal muscle (December 4, 2005); missed five games.

STATISTICAL PLATEAUS: Four-goal games: 2002-03 (1).

Season Team	League	REGULAR SEASON GP	G	A	Pts.	PIM	+/-	PP	SH	PLAYOFFS GP	G	A	Pts.	PIM
83-84—Henry Carr H.S.	MTHL	39	37	37	74	97	...	...	...	—	—	—	—	—
84-85—Wisconsin	WCHA	40	14	24	38	60	...	...	...	—	—	—	—	—
85-86—Wisconsin	WCHA	32	21	23	44	89	...	...	...	—	—	—	—	—
—Philadelphia	NHL	2	0	0	0	0	-1	0	0	—	—	—	—	—
86-87—Philadelphia	NHL	71	11	21	32	94	8	1	0	24	5	5	10	46
87-88—Philadelphia	NHL	75	25	26	51	185	-7	7	0	7	0	1	1	16
88-89—Philadelphia	NHL	76	21	29	50	183	-13	11	0	19	4	5	9	28
89-90—Philadelphia	NHL	57	6	17	23	77	-4	0	0	—	—	—	—	—
90-91—Philadelphia	NHL	74	20	21	41	155	8	5	0	—	—	—	—	—
91-92—Edmonton	NHL	80	23	27	50	197	5	7	0	16	2	1	3	29
92-93—Edmonton	NHL	69	15	17	32	147	-4	6	0	—	—	—	—	—
93-94—Florida	NHL	80	30	30	60	149	0	17	0	—	—	—	—	—
94-95—Florida	NHL	48	13	12	25	90	-16	4	0	—	—	—	—	—
95-96—Florida	NHL	79	32	38	70	160	4	19	0	22	3	6	9	44
96-97—Florida	NHL	82	27	29	56	170	7	9	1	5	0	2	2	4
97-98—Florida	NHL	79	15	24	39	127	-14	6	0	—	—	—	—	—
98-99—Florida	NHL	67	18	27	45	85	5	4	0	—	—	—	—	—
99-00—Florida	NHL	77	18	28	46	126	14	6	0	4	0	1	1	2
00-01—Florida	NHL	40	4	9	13	46	-13	1	0	—	—	—	—	—
—St. Louis	NHL	23	7	1	8	25	0	2	0	15	3	3	6	17
01-02—St. Louis	NHL	64	15	26	41	93	-5	8	0	10	7	3	10	18
02-03—St. Louis	NHL	80	26	31	57	176	1	13	0	6	0	1	1	10
03-04—St. Louis	NHL	68	14	17	31	76	-7	6	0	4	0	1	1	2
05-06—Atlanta	NHL	71	12	22	34	55	5	3	0	—	—	—	—	—
NHL Totals (20 years)		1362	352	452	804	2416	-27	135	1	132	24	29	53	216

MESZAROS, ANDREJ D

PERSONAL: Born October 13, 1985, in Povazska Bystrica, Czech. ... 6-2/193. ... Shoots right. ... Name pronounced: AHN-dray muh-ZAHR-ohz

TRANSACTIONS/CAREER NOTES: Selected by Ottawa Senators in first round (first Senators pick, 23rd overall) of NHL entry draft (June 26, 2004).

Season Team	League	REGULAR SEASON GP	G	A	Pts.	PIM	+/-	PP	SH	PLAYOFFS GP	G	A	Pts.	PIM
02-03—Trencin	Slovakia	23	0	1	1	4	...	...	...	—	—	—	—	—
03-04—Trencin	Slovakia	44	3	3	6	8	...	...	...	14	3	1	4	2
04-05—Vancouver	WHL	59	11	30	41	94	7	5	1	6	1	3	4	14
05-06—Ottawa	NHL	82	10	29	39	61	34	5	0	10	1	0	1	18
—Slovakian Oly. team	Int'l	6	0	2	2	4	5	0	0	—	—	—	—	—
NHL Totals (1 year)		82	10	29	39	61	34	5	0	10	1	0	1	18

MEYER, FREDDY D

PERSONAL: Born January 4, 1981, in Sanbornville, N.H. ... 6-1/195. ... Shoots left.

TRANSACTIONS/CAREER NOTES: Signed as free agent by Philadelphia Flyers (May 21, 2003). ... Broken right leg (September 28, 2005); missed 16 games.

Season Team	League	GP	G	A	Pts.	PIM	+/-	PP	SH	GP	G	A	Pts.	PIM
		REGULAR SEASON								PLAYOFFS				
99-00—Boston University	ECAC	25	1	11	12	52	...	...	...	—	—	—	—	—
00-01—Boston University	ECAC	28	6	13	19	82	...	...	...	—	—	—	—	—
01-02—Boston University	ECAC	37	5	15	20	78	...	...	...	—	—	—	—	—
02-03—Boston University	ECAC	36	5	16	21	76	...	...	...	—	—	—	—	—
03-04—Philadelphia	AHL	59	14	14	28	50	13	6	0	12	0	3	3	8
—Philadelphia	NHL	1	0	0	0	0	0	0	0	—	—	—	—	—
04-05—Philadelphia	AHL	59	6	9	15	71	15	2	0	21	3	9	12	34
05-06—Philadelphia	AHL	11	3	3	6	22	1	3	0	—	—	—	—	—
—Philadelphia	NHL	57	6	21	27	33	10	2	0	6	0	1	1	8
NHL Totals (2 years)		58	6	21	27	33	10	2	0	6	0	1	1	8

MEZEI, BRANISLAV D

PERSONAL: Born October 8, 1980, in Nitra, Czechoslovakia. ... 6-5/235. ... Shoots left. ... Name pronounced MEE-zy.
TRANSACTIONS/CAREER NOTES: Selected by New York Islanders in first round (third Islanders pick, 10th overall) of entry draft (June 26, 1999). ... Separated left shoulder (January 16, 2001); missed 13 games. ... Traded by Islanders to Florida Panthers for C Jason Wiemer (July 3, 2002). ... Fractured ankle (October 12, 2002); missed 27 games. ... Fractured foot (January 1, 2003); missed 43 games. ... Injured eye (November 24, 2003); missed 37 games. ... Knee injury (November 10, 2005); missed remainder of season.

Season Team	League	GP	G	A	Pts.	PIM	+/-	PP	SH	GP	G	A	Pts.	PIM
		REGULAR SEASON								PLAYOFFS				
96-97—Plastika Nitra	Slovakia Jrs.	40	8	17	25	42	...	...	...	—	—	—	—	—
97-98—Belleville	OHL	53	3	5	8	58	...	...	...	8	0	2	2	8
98-99—Belleville	OHL	60	5	18	23	90	44	...	...	18	0	4	4	29
99-00—Belleville	OHL	58	7	21	28	99	30	5	0	6	0	3	3	10
00-01—Lowell	AHL	20	0	3	3	28	...	...	...	—	—	—	—	—
—New York Islanders.....	NHL	42	1	4	5	53	-5	0	0	—	—	—	—	—
01-02—Bridgeport.....................	AHL	59	1	9	10	137	12	0	0	20	0	3	3	48
—New York Islanders.....	NHL	24	0	2	2	12	2	0	0	—	—	—	—	—
02-03—San Antonio	AHL	1	0	0	0	0	1	0	0	—	—	—	—	—
—Florida.........................	NHL	11	2	0	2	10	-2	0	0	—	—	—	—	—
03-04—Florida.........................	NHL	45	0	7	7	80	-4	0	0	—	—	—	—	—
04-05—Dukla Trencin.............	Slovakia	—	—	—	—	—	—	—	—	12	1	2	3	38
—Trinec..........................	Czech Rep.	41	1	2	3	68	-15	...	...	—	—	—	—	—
—Dukla Trencin.............	Slovakia	10	1	1	2	16	4	...	...	—	—	—	—	—
05-06—Florida.........................	NHL	16	0	1	1	37	3	0	0	—	—	—	—	—
NHL Totals (5 years)		138	3	14	17	192	-6	0	0					

MICHALEK, MILAN LW/RW

PERSONAL: Born December 7, 1984, in Jindrichuv Hradec, Czechoslovakia. ... 6-2/220. ... Shoots left.
TRANSACTIONS/CAREER NOTES: Selected by San Jose Sharks in first round (first Sharks pick, sixth overall) in 2003 NHL entry draft (June 23, 2003). ... Injured right knee (October12, 2003); missed 46 games. ... Injured knee (December 2, 2005); missed one game.

Season Team	League	GP	G	A	Pts.	PIM	+/-	PP	SH	GP	G	A	Pts.	PIM
		REGULAR SEASON								PLAYOFFS				
00-01—Budejovice	Czech. Jrs.	30	10	13	23	30	...	...	...	—	—	—	—	—
01-02—Budejovice	Czech.	47	6	11	17	12	...	...	...	—	—	—	—	—
02-03—Budejovice	Czech.	46	3	5	8	14	...	...	...	—	—	—	—	—
03-04—San Jose.....................	NHL	2	1	0	1	4	1	0	0	—	—	—	—	—
—Cleveland	AHL	7	2	2	4	4	1	1	0	—	—	—	—	—
04-05—Cleveland	AHL	0	0	0	0	0	0	0	0	—	—	—	—	—
05-06—San Jose.....................	NHL	81	17	18	35	45	1	4	0	9	1	4	5	8
NHL Totals (2 years)		83	18	18	36	49	2	4	0	9	1	4	5	8

MICHALEK, ZBYNEK D

PERSONAL: Born December 23, 1982, in Jindrchuv, Czech. ... 6-1/200. ... Shoots right. ... Name pronounced: zuh-BEEN-ihk muh-KAHL-ihk
TRANSACTIONS/CAREER NOTES: Signed as free agent by Minnesota Wild (September 29, 2001). ... Traded by Wild to Phoenix Coyotes for C Erik Westrum and D Dustin Wood (August 26, 2005).

Season Team	League	GP	G	A	Pts.	PIM	+/-	PP	SH	GP	G	A	Pts.	PIM
		REGULAR SEASON								PLAYOFFS				
00-01—Shawinigan	QMJHL	69	10	29	39	52	...	...	...	3	0	0	0	0
01-02—Shawinigan	QMJHL	68	16	35	51	54	...	...	...	10	8	7	15	10
02-03—Houston	AHL	62	4	10	14	26	...	...	...	23	1	1	2	6
03-04—Minnesota...................	NHL	22	1	1	2	4	-7	0	0	—	—	—	—	—
—Houston	AHL	55	5	16	21	32	-5	3	0	2	1	0	1	0
04-05—Houston	AHL	76	7	17	24	48	-10	5	0	5	1	2	3	4
05-06—Phoenix.......................	NHL	82	9	15	24	62	4	5	0	—	—	—	—	—
NHL Totals (2 years)		104	10	16	26	66	-3	5	0					

MIETTINEN, ANTTI RW/LW

PERSONAL: Born July 3, 1980, in Hameenlinna, Finland. ... 6-0/190. ... Shoots left. ... Name pronounced: AN-tee MYEHT-ih-nehn
TRANSACTIONS/CAREER NOTES: Selected by Dallas Stars in seventh round (10th Stars pick, 224th overall) of entry draft (June 24, 2000). ... Back spasms (October 27, 2003); missed two games. ... Flu (December 19, 2005); missed one game. ... Chest (February 9, 2006); missed two games.

Season Team	League	REGULAR SEASON GP	G	A	Pts.	PIM	+/-	PP	SH	PLAYOFFS GP	G	A	Pts.	PIM
99-00—HPK Hameenlinna	Finland	39	2	1	3	8	...	...	...	7	1	0	1	0
00-01—HPK Hameenlinna	Finland	55	13	11	24	28	...	...	...	—	—	—	—	—
01-02—HPK Hameenlinna	Finland	56	19	37	56	50	...	...	...	8	2	4	6	8
02-03—HPK Hameenlinna	Finland	53	25	25	50	54	...	...	...	10	1	7	8	29
03-04—Dallas	NHL	16	1	0	1	0	-9	0	0	—	—	—	—	—
—Utah	AHL	48	7	23	30	20	-17	4	1	—	—	—	—	—
04-05—Ilves Tampere	Finland	25	0	1	1	10	...	...	...	—	—	—	—	—
—Hamilton	AHL	35	8	20	28	21	11	3	0	4	1	1	2	6
05-06—Dallas	NHL	79	11	20	31	46	0	4	0	5	0	1	1	8
NHL Totals (2 years)		95	12	20	32	46	-9	4	0	5	0	1	1	8

MILLER, AARON D

PERSONAL: Born August 11, 1971, in Buffalo. ... 6-4/210. ... Shoots right.

TRANSACTIONS/CAREER NOTES: Selected by New York Rangers in fifth round (sixth Rangers pick, 88th overall) of entry draft (June 17, 1989). ... Traded by Rangers with fifth-round pick (LW Bill Lindsay) in 1991 to Quebec Nordiques for D Joe Cirella (January 17, 1991). ... Nordiques franchise moved to Colorado and renamed Avalanche for 1995-96 season (June 21, 1995). ... Concussion (October 24, 1998); missed one game. ... Knee (November 8, 1998); missed one game. ... Back spasms (March 17, 1999); missed three games. ... Sternum (November 17, 1999); missed 27 games. ... Right hand (November 22, 2000); missed five games. ... Traded by Avalanche with RW Adam Deadmarsh, first-round pick (C David Steckel) in 2001, a player to be named and first-round pick (C Brian Boyle) in 2003 to Los Angeles Kings for C Steve Reinprecht and D Rob Blake (February 21, 2001); Kings acquired C Jared Aulin to complete deal (March 22, 2001). ... Wrist (March 19, 2001); missed season's final nine games. ... Back spasms (October 20, 2001); missed eight games. ... Hernia (September 13, 2002) and had surgery; missed 13 games. ... Fractured foot (December 11, 2002); missed 18 games. ... Back (April 4, 2003); missed two games. ... Wrist (October 5, 2003); missed eight games. ... Cervical strain (December 11, 2003); missed 29 games. ... Back spasms (December 21, 2005); missed 16 games. ... Sore back (March 29, 2006), hip surgery (April 12, 2006); missed season's final 10 games.

Season Team	League	REGULAR SEASON GP	G	A	Pts.	PIM	+/-	PP	SH	PLAYOFFS GP	G	A	Pts.	PIM
87-88—Niagara	NAJHL	30	4	9	13	2	...	...	...	—	—	—	—	—
88-89—Niagara	NAJHL	59	24	38	62	60	...	...	...	—	—	—	—	—
89-90—Vermont	ECAC	31	1	15	16	24	...	...	...	—	—	—	—	—
90-91—Vermont	ECAC	30	3	7	10	22	...	...	...	—	—	—	—	—
91-92—Vermont	ECAC	31	3	16	19	36	...	...	...	—	—	—	—	—
92-93—Vermont	ECAC	30	4	13	17	16	...	...	...	—	—	—	—	—
93-94—Cornwall	AHL	64	4	10	14	49	2	0	0	13	0	2	2	10
—Quebec	NHL	1	0	0	0	0	-1	0	0	—	—	—	—	—
94-95—Cornwall	AHL	76	4	18	22	69	-8	2	0	—	—	—	—	—
—Quebec	NHL	9	0	3	3	6	2	0	0	—	—	—	—	—
95-96—Cornwall	AHL	62	4	23	27	77	...	...	...	8	0	1	1	6
—Colorado	NHL	5	0	0	0	0	0	0	0	—	—	—	—	—
96-97—Colorado	NHL	56	5	12	17	15	15	0	0	17	1	2	3	10
97-98—Colorado	NHL	55	2	2	4	51	0	0	0	7	0	0	0	8
98-99—Colorado	NHL	76	5	13	18	42	3	1	0	19	1	5	6	10
99-00—Colorado	NHL	53	1	7	8	36	3	0	0	17	1	1	2	6
00-01—Colorado	NHL	56	4	9	13	29	19	0	0	—	—	—	—	—
—Los Angeles	NHL	13	0	5	5	14	3	0	0	13	0	1	1	6
01-02—Los Angeles	NHL	74	5	12	17	54	14	0	1	7	0	0	0	0
—U.S. Olympic team	Int'l	6	0	0	0	4	...	...	...	—	—	—	—	—
02-03—Los Angeles	NHL	49	1	5	6	24	-7	0	0	—	—	—	—	—
03-04—Los Angeles	NHL	35	1	2	3	32	-3	0	0	—	—	—	—	—
05-06—Los Angeles	NHL	56	0	8	8	27	-6	0	0	—	—	—	—	—
NHL Totals (12 years)		538	24	78	102	330	42	1	1	80	3	9	12	40

MILLER, RYAN G

PERSONAL: Born July 17, 1980, in East Lansing, Mich. ... 6-2/170. ... Catches left.

TRANSACTIONS/CAREER NOTES: Selected by Buffalo Sabres in fifth round (seventh Sabres pick, 138th overall) of entry draft (June 26, 1999). ... Fractured right thumb (November 2, 2005); missed 18 games.

Season Team	League	REGULAR SEASON GP	Min.	W	L	OTL	T	GA	SO	GAA	SV%	PLAYOFFS GP	Min.	W	L	GA	SO	GAA	SV%
98-99 —Soo	NAHL	47	2711	31	14	...	1	104	8	2.30	.921	4	218	2	2	10	1	2.75	...
99-00 —Michigan State	CCHA	26	1525	16	4	...	3	39	8	1.53	...	—	—	—	—	—	—	—	—
00-01 —Michigan State	CCHA	40	2447	31	5	...	4	54	10	1.32	...	—	—	—	—	—	—	—	—
01-02 —Michigan State	CCHA	40	2411	26	9	...	5	71	8	1.77	...	—	—	—	—	—	—	—	—
02-03 —Buffalo	NHL	15	912	6	8	...	1	40	1	2.63	.902	—	—	—	—	—	—	—	—
—Rochester	AHL	47	2816	23	18	...	5	110	2	2.34	.920	3	189	1	2	13	0	4.13	.856
03-04 —Buffalo	NHL	3	178	0	3	...	0	15	0	5.06	.795	—	—	—	—	—	—	—	—
—Rochester	AHL	60	3578	27	25	...	7	132	5	2.21	.919	14	856	7	7	26	2	1.82	.929
04-05 —Rochester	AHL	63	3740	41	17	...	...	153	8	2.45	.922	9	547	5	4	24	0	2.63	.909
05-06 —Rochester	AHL	2	120	1	1	0	...	5	0	2.50	.889	—	—	—	—	—	—	—	—
—Buffalo	NHL	48	2862	30	14	3	...	124	1	2.60	.914	18	1123	11	7	*48	1	2.56	.908
NHL Totals (3 years)		66	3952	36	25	3	1	179	2	2.72	.907	18	1123	11	7	48	1	2.56	.908

MILLEY, NORM RW/LW

PERSONAL: Born February 14, 1980, in Toronto. ... 6-0/211. ... Shoots right.

TRANSACTIONS/CAREER NOTES: Selected by Buffalo Sabres in second round (third Sabres pick, 47th overall) of NHL draft (June 27, 1998). ... Signed as free agent by Tampa Bay Lightning (August 18, 2005).

		REGULAR SEASON								PLAYOFFS				
Season Team	**League**	**GP**	**G**	**A**	**Pts.**	**PIM**	**+/-**	**PP**	**SH**	**GP**	**G**	**A**	**Pts.**	**PIM**
95-96—Toronto Red Wings	MTHL	42	42	36	78	109	...	...	...	—	—	—	—	—
96-97—Sudbury	OHL	61	30	32	62	15	...	...	...	—	—	—	—	—
97-98—Sudbury	OHL	62	33	41	74	48	...	...	...	10	0	1	1	4
98-99—Sudbury	OHL	68	52	68	120	47	9	...	...	4	2	3	5	4
99-00—Sudbury	OHL	68	52	60	112	47	39	13	2	12	8	11	19	6
00-01—Rochester	AHL	77	20	27	47	56	...	...	...	4	0	0	0	2
01-02—Rochester	AHL	74	20	18	38	20	11	5	1	2	0	3	3	6
—Buffalo	NHL	5	0	1	1	0	0	0	0	—	—	—	—	—
02-03—Buffalo	NHL	8	0	2	2	6	-2	0	0	—	—	—	—	—
—Rochester	AHL	67	16	32	48	39	...	...	...	3	2	0	2	2
03-04—Rochester	AHL	77	18	19	37	60	2	2	0	16	7	6	13	10
—Buffalo	NHL	2	0	0	0	2	0	0	0	—	—	—	—	—
04-05—Rochester	AHL	72	12	21	33	46	1	1	0	9	1	2	3	4
05-06—Springfield	AHL	53	19	29	48	34	-18	9	2	—	—	—	—	—
—Tampa Bay	NHL	14	2	1	3	4	-2	1	0	—	—	—	—	—
NHL Totals (4 years)		29	2	4	6	12	-4	1	0					

MINK, GRAHAM LW

PERSONAL: Born May 12, 1979, in Stowe, Vt. ... 6-3/220. ... Shoots right.

TRANSACTIONS/CAREER NOTES: Signed as free agent by Washington Capitals (April 11, 2002). ... Signed as free agent by San Jose Sharks (July 14, 2006).

		REGULAR SEASON								PLAYOFFS				
Season Team	**League**	**GP**	**G**	**A**	**Pts.**	**PIM**	**+/-**	**PP**	**SH**	**GP**	**G**	**A**	**Pts.**	**PIM**
98-99—Vermont	ECAC	27	4	2	6	34	...	...	...	—	—	—	—	—
99-00—Vermont	ECAC	17	7	4	11	18	...	...	...	—	—	—	—	—
00-01—Vermont	ECAC	32	17	12	29	52	...	...	...	—	—	—	—	—
01-02—Richmond	ECHL	29	8	9	17	78	-2	...	...	—	—	—	—	—
—Portland	AHL	56	17	17	34	50	...	...	...	—	—	—	—	—
02-03—Portland	AHL	71	22	15	37	115	...	...	...	—	—	—	—	—
03-04—Portland	AHL	68	18	19	37	74	6	3	0	3	0	1	1	4
—Washington	NHL	2	0	0	0	2	-1	0	0	—	—	—	—	—
04-05—Portland	AHL	63	18	21	39	86	-10	7	1	—	—	—	—	—
05-06—Hershey	AHL	43	21	19	40	50	6	11	1	14	7	10	17	22
—Washington	NHL	3	0	0	0	0	0	0	0	—	—	—	—	—
NHL Totals (2 years)		5	0	0	0	2	-1	0	0					

M

MITCHELL, WILLIE D

PERSONAL: Born April 23, 1977, in Port McNeill, B.C. ... 6-3/205. ... Shoots left.

TRANSACTIONS/CAREER NOTES: Selected by New Jersey Devils in eighth round (12th Devils pick, 199th overall) of entry draft (June 22, 1996). ... Traded by Devils to Minnesota Wild for D Sean O'Donnell (March 4, 2001). ... Bruised right shoulder (October 16, 2001); missed five games. ... Strained groin (December 10, 2001); missed three games. ... Bruised left wrist (January 19, 2002); missed five games. ... Ribs (November 19, 2002); missed five games. ... Concussion (December 12, 2002); missed eight games. ... Knee (October 20, 2003); missed one game. ... Knee (November 21, 2003); missed 10 games. ... Flu (March 10, 2004); missed one game. ... Traded by Wild with second-round pick in 2007 to Dallas Stars for D Martin Skoula and D Shawn Belle (March 9, 2006). ... Upper body (April 11, 2006); missed two games. ... Upper body (April 18, 2006); missed one game. ... Signed as free agent by Vancouver Canucks (July 1, 2006).

		REGULAR SEASON								PLAYOFFS				
Season Team	**League**	**GP**	**G**	**A**	**Pts.**	**PIM**	**+/-**	**PP**	**SH**	**GP**	**G**	**A**	**Pts.**	**PIM**
95-96—Melfort	Jr. A	19	2	6	8	0	...	...	...	14	0	2	2	12
96-97—Melfort	Jr. A	64	14	42	56	227	...	...	...	4	0	1	1	23
97-98—Clarkson	ECAC	34	9	17	26	105	...	...	...	—	—	—	—	—
98-99—Clarkson	ECAC	34	10	19	29	40	...	...	...	—	—	—	—	—
—Albany	AHL	6	1	3	4	29	3	1	0	—	—	—	—	—
99-00—Albany	AHL	63	5	14	19	71	...	...	...	5	1	2	3	4
—New Jersey	NHL	2	0	0	0	0	1	0	0	—	—	—	—	—
00-01—Albany	AHL	41	3	13	16	94	...	...	...	—	—	—	—	—
—New Jersey	NHL	16	0	2	2	29	0	0	0	—	—	—	—	—
—Minnesota	NHL	17	1	7	8	11	4	0	0	—	—	—	—	—
01-02—Minnesota	NHL	68	3	10	13	68	-16	0	0	—	—	—	—	—
02-03—Minnesota	NHL	69	2	12	14	84	13	0	1	18	1	3	4	14
03-04—Minnesota	NHL	70	1	13	14	83	12	0	0	—	—	—	—	—
05-06—Minnesota	NHL	64	2	6	8	87	15	0	0	—	—	—	—	—
—Dallas	NHL	16	0	2	2	26	4	0	0	5	0	0	0	2
NHL Totals (6 years)		322	9	52	61	388	33	0	1	23	1	3	4	16

MITERA, MARK D

PERSONAL: Born October 22, 1987, in Royal Oak, Mich. ... 6-3/202. ... Shoots left.

TRANSACTIONS/CAREER NOTES: Selected by Anaheim Ducks in first round (first Ducks pick; 19th overall) of NHL draft (June 24, 2006).

		REGULAR SEASON								PLAYOFFS				
Season Team	**League**	**GP**	**G**	**A**	**Pts.**	**PIM**	**+/-**	**PP**	**SH**	**GP**	**G**	**A**	**Pts.**	**PIM**
04-05—U.S. National	USHL	42	5	12	17	80	...	...	...	—	—	—	—	—
05-06—Michigan	CCHA	39	0	10	10	59	5	...	...	—	—	—	—	—

MODANO, MIKE C

PERSONAL: Born June 7, 1970, in Livonia, Mich. ... 6-3/205. ... Shoots left. ... Name pronounced muh-DAH-noh.

TRANSACTIONS/CAREER NOTES: Selected by Minnesota North Stars in first round (first North Stars pick, first overall) of entry draft (June 11, 1988). ... Fractured nose (March 4, 1990). ... Groin (November 30, 1992); missed two games. ... North Stars franchise moved from Minnesota to Dallas and renamed Stars for 1993-94 season. ... Strained knee (January 6, 1994); missed six games. ... Concussion (February 26, 1994); missed two games. ... Bruised ankle (March 12, 1995); missed four games. ... Ruptured ankle tendons (April 4, 1995); missed remainder of season. ... Stomach muscle (November 9, 1995); missed four games. ... Flu (February 9, 1997); missed one game. ... Bruised ankle (November 12, 1997); missed one game. ... Torn knee ligament (December 5, 1997); missed 10 games. ... Knee (January 2, 1998); missed two games. ... Separated shoulder (March 13, 1998); missed 17 games. ... Strained groin (March 31, 1999); missed four games. ... Strained neck ligaments, concussion, fractured nose (October 2, 1999); missed three games. ... Concussion (January 12, 2000); missed one game. ... Strained hip flexor (March 28, 2000); missed one game. ... Strained back (October 10, 2000); missed one game. ... Bruised thigh (October 20, 2001); missed one game. ... Strained lower back (November 7, 2001); missed two games. ... Concussion (December 17, 2002); missed three games. ... Groin (January 2, 2004); missed six games. ... Knee (April 1, 2006); missed one game. ... Left knee (April 7, 2006); missed two games.

STATISTICAL PLATEAUS: Three-goal games: 1989-90 (1), 1993-94 (1), 1997-98 (1), 1998-99 (3). Total: 6. ... Four-goal games: 1995-96 (1). ... Total hat tricks: 7.

		REGULAR SEASON								PLAYOFFS				
Season Team	League	GP	G	A	Pts.	PIM	+/-	PP	SH	GP	G	A	Pts.	PIM
86-87—Prince Albert	WHL	70	32	30	62	96	...	...	...	8	1	4	5	4
87-88—Prince Albert	WHL	65	47	80	127	80	...	...	...	9	7	11	18	18
88-89—Prince Albert	WHL	41	39	66	105	74	...	...	...	—	—	—	—	—
—Minnesota	NHL	...	...	...	...	...	...	...	...	2	0	0	0	0
89-90—Minnesota	NHL	80	29	46	75	63	-7	12	0	7	1	1	2	12
90-91—Minnesota	NHL	79	28	36	64	65	2	9	0	23	8	12	20	16
91-92—Minnesota	NHL	76	33	44	77	46	-9	5	0	7	3	2	5	4
92-93—Minnesota	NHL	82	33	60	93	83	-7	9	0	—	—	—	—	—
93-94—Dallas	NHL	76	50	43	93	54	-8	18	0	9	7	3	10	16
94-95—Dallas	NHL	30	12	17	29	8	7	4	1	—	—	—	—	—
95-96—Dallas	NHL	78	36	45	81	63	-12	8	4	—	—	—	—	—
96-97—Dallas	NHL	80	35	48	83	42	43	9	5	7	4	1	5	0
97-98—Dallas	NHL	52	21	38	59	32	25	7	5	17	4	10	14	12
—U.S. Olympic team	Int'l	4	2	0	2	0	-2	0	0	—	—	—	—	—
98-99—Dallas	NHL	77	34	47	81	44	29	6	4	23	5	*18	23	16
99-00—Dallas	NHL	77	38	43	81	48	0	11	1	23	10	†13	23	10
00-01—Dallas	NHL	81	33	51	84	52	26	8	3	9	3	4	7	0
01-02—Dallas	NHL	78	34	43	77	38	14	6	2	—	—	—	—	—
—U.S. Olympic team	Int'l	6	0	6	6	4	...	...	...	—	—	—	—	—
02-03—Dallas	NHL	79	28	57	85	30	34	5	2	12	5	10	15	4
03-04—Dallas	NHL	76	14	30	44	46	-21	6	0	5	1	2	3	8
05-06—Dallas	NHL	78	27	50	77	58	23	12	1	5	1	3	4	4
—U.S. Olympic team	Int'l	6	2	0	2	6	-1	0	0	—	—	—	—	—
NHL Totals (17 years)		1179	485	698	1183	772	139	135	28	149	52	79	131	102

MODIN, FREDRIK LW

PERSONAL: Born October 8, 1974, in Sundsvall, Sweden. ... 6-4/220. ... Shoots left. ... Name pronounced moh-DEEN.

TRANSACTIONS/CAREER NOTES: Selected by Toronto Maple Leafs in third round (third Maple Leafs pick, 64th overall) of entry draft (June 29, 1994). ... Concussion (October 22, 1996); missed three games. ... Flu (March 10, 1997); missed one game. ... Strained groin (December 2, 1997); missed two games. ... Fractured collarbone (February 13, 1999); missed 15 games. ... Traded by Maple Leafs to Tampa Bay Lightning for D Cory Cross and seventh-round pick (F Ivan Kolozvary) in 2001 draft (October 1, 1999). ... Bruised thigh (December 8, 2000); missed one game. ... Flu (January 4, 2001); missed one game. ... Bruised hip (March 4, 2001); missed two games. ... Charley horse (November 29, 2001); missed two games. ... Injured right wrist (January 26, 2002); missed 26 games. ... Strained groin (October 10, 2002); missed two games. ... Injured back and ribs (November 17, 2002); missed four games. ... Lower-body injury (January 2, 2006); missed two games. ... Lower-body injury (March 25, 2006); missed three games. ... Traded by Lightning to with G Fredrik Norrena to Columbus Blue Jackets for G Marc Denis (June 30, 2006).

STATISTICAL PLATEAUS: Three-goal games: 2000-01 (1), 2003-04 (1). Total: 2.

		REGULAR SEASON								PLAYOFFS				
Season Team	League	GP	G	A	Pts.	PIM	+/-	PP	SH	GP	G	A	Pts.	PIM
91-92—Sundsvall Timra	Sweden Dv. 2	11	1	0	1	0	...	...	...	—	—	—	—	—
92-93—Sundsvall Timra	Sweden Dv. 2	30	5	7	12	12	...	...	...	—	—	—	—	—
93-94—Sundsvall Timra	Sweden Dv. 2	30	16	15	31	36	...	...	...	—	—	—	—	—
94-95—Brynas Gavle	Sweden	38	9	10	19	33	...	...	...	14	4	4	8	6
95-96—Brynas Gavle	Sweden	22	4	8	12	22	...	...	...	—	—	—	—	—
96-97—Toronto	NHL	76	6	7	13	24	-14	0	0	—	—	—	—	—
97-98—Toronto	NHL	74	16	16	32	32	-5	1	0	—	—	—	—	—
98-99—Toronto	NHL	67	16	15	31	35	14	1	0	8	0	0	0	6
99-00—Tampa Bay	NHL	80	22	26	48	18	-26	3	0	—	—	—	—	—
00-01—Tampa Bay	NHL	76	32	24	56	48	-1	8	0	—	—	—	—	—
01-02—Tampa Bay	NHL	54	14	17	31	27	0	2	0	—	—	—	—	—
02-03—Tampa Bay	NHL	76	17	23	40	43	7	2	1	11	2	0	2	18
03-04—Tampa Bay	NHL	82	29	28	57	32	31	5	1	23	8	11	19	10
04-05—Timra	Sweden	43	12	24	36	58	3	6	0	7	1	1	2	8
05-06—Tampa Bay	NHL	77	31	23	54	56	5	12	1	5	0	0	0	6
—Swedish Oly. team	Int'l	8	2	1	3	6	0	1	0	—	—	—	—	—
NHL Totals (9 years)		662	183	179	362	315	11	34	3	47	10	11	21	40

MODRY, JAROSLAV D

PERSONAL: Born February 27, 1971, in Ceske Budejovice, Czech. ... 6-2/226. ... Shoots left. ... Name pronounced MOH-dree.

TRANSACTIONS/CAREER NOTES: Selected by New Jersey Devils in ninth round (10th Devils pick, 179th overall) of entry draft (June 16,

1990). ... Ankle (January 31, 1995); missed two games. ... Reinjured ankle (February 18, 1995); missed three games. ... Traded by Devils to Ottawa Senators for fourth-round pick (C Alyn McCauley) in 1995 draft (July 8, 1995). ... Ruptured eardrum (December 27, 1995). ... Traded by Senators to Los Angeles Kings for RW Kevin Brown (March 20, 1996). ... Sprained left knee (January 14, 1997); missed one game. ... Strained hip flexor (January 5, 2002); missed one game. ... Flu (April 14, 2002); missed one game. ... Left team for personal reasons (February 16, 2004); missed one game. ... Signed as free agent by Atlanta Thrashers (July 1, 2004). ... Hamstring (April 13, 2006); missed final three games of regular season. ... Traded by Thrashers with F Patrik Stefan to Dallas Stars for F Niko Kapanen and a seventh-round pick (D Will O'Neill) in 2006 entry draft (June 24, 2006).

		REGULAR SEASON								PLAYOFFS				
Season Team	**League**	**GP**	**G**	**A**	**Pts.**	**PIM**	**+/-**	**PP**	**SH**	**GP**	**G**	**A**	**Pts.**	**PIM**
88-89—Budejovice	Czech.	28	0	1	1	...	...	...	...	—	—	—	—	—
89-90—Budejovice	Czech.	41	2	2	4	...	...	...	...	—	—	—	—	—
90-91—Dukla Trencin	Czech.	33	1	9	10	6	...	...	...	—	—	—	—	—
91-92—Dukla Trencin	Czech.	18	0	4	4	...	...	...	...	—	—	—	—	—
—Budejovice	Czech Dv.I	14	4	10	14	...	...	...	...	—	—	—	—	—
92-93—Utica	AHL	80	7	35	42	62	-17	3	0	5	0	2	2	2
93-94—New Jersey	NHL	41	2	15	17	18	10	2	0	—	—	—	—	—
—Albany	AHL	19	1	5	6	25	3	0	0	—	—	—	—	—
94-95—HC Ceske Budejovice	Czech Rep.	19	1	3	4	30	...	...	...	—	—	—	—	—
—New Jersey	NHL	11	0	0	0	0	-1	0	0	—	—	—	—	—
—Albany	AHL	18	5	6	11	14	11	1	0	14	3	3	6	4
95-96—Ottawa	NHL	64	4	14	18	38	-17	1	0	—	—	—	—	—
—Los Angeles	NHL	9	0	3	3	6	-4	0	0	—	—	—	—	—
96-97—Los Angeles	NHL	30	3	3	6	25	-13	1	1	—	—	—	—	—
—Phoenix	IHL	23	3	12	15	17	...	...	...	—	—	—	—	—
—Utah	IHL	11	1	4	5	20	...	...	...	7	0	1	1	6
97-98—Utah	IHL	74	12	21	33	72	13	4	0	4	0	2	2	6
98-99—Long Beach	IHL	64	6	29	35	44	16	1	0	8	4	2	6	4
—Los Angeles	NHL	5	0	1	1	0	1	0	0	—	—	—	—	—
99-00—Los Angeles	NHL	26	5	4	9	18	-2	5	0	2	0	0	0	2
—Long Beach	IHL	11	2	4	6	8	...	...	...	—	—	—	—	—
00-01—Los Angeles	NHL	63	4	15	19	48	16	0	0	10	1	0	1	4
01-02—Los Angeles	NHL	80	4	38	42	65	-4	4	0	7	0	2	2	0
02-03—Los Angeles	NHL	82	13	25	38	68	-13	8	0	—	—	—	—	—
03-04—Los Angeles	NHL	79	5	27	32	44	11	1	0	—	—	—	—	—
04-05—Liberec	Czech Rep.	19	3	7	10	24	12	...	...	12	0	4	4	22
05-06—Atlanta	NHL	79	7	31	38	76	-9	5	0	—	—	—	—	—
NHL Totals (11 years)		569	47	176	223	406	-25	27	1	19	1	2	3	6

MOEN, TRAVIS LW/RW

PERSONAL: Born April 6, 1982, in Swift Current, Sask. ... 6-3/210. ... Shoots left.

TRANSACTIONS/CAREER NOTES: Selected by Calgary Flames in fifth round (sixth Flames pick, 141st overall) of entry draft (June 24, 2000). ... Signed as free agent by Chicago Blackhawks (October 21, 2002). ... Traded by Blackhawks to the Anaheim Mighty Ducks for RW Michael Holmqvist (July 30, 2005). ... Injured knee (October 28, 2005); missed three games. ... Injured shoulder (January 26, 2006); missed 17 games.

		REGULAR SEASON								PLAYOFFS				
Season Team	**League**	**GP**	**G**	**A**	**Pts.**	**PIM**	**+/-**	**PP**	**SH**	**GP**	**G**	**A**	**Pts.**	**PIM**
98-99—Kelowna	WHL	4	0	0	0	0	...	...	...	—	—	—	—	—
99-00—Kelowna	WHL	66	9	6	15	96	...	...	...	—	—	—	—	—
00-01—Kelowna	WHL	40	8	8	16	106	...	...	...	—	—	—	—	—
01-02—Kelowna	WHL	71	10	17	27	197	...	...	...	13	1	0	1	28
02-03—Norfolk	AHL	42	1	2	3	62	-12	0	0	9	0	0	0	20
03-04—Chicago	NHL	82	4	2	6	142	-17	0	0	—	—	—	—	—
04-05—Norfolk	AHL	79	8	12	20	187	5	1	0	6	0	1	1	6
05-06—Anaheim	NHL	39	4	1	5	72	-3	0	0	9	1	0	1	10
NHL Totals (2 years)		121	8	3	11	214	-20	0	0	9	1	0	1	10

MOGILNY, ALEXANDER RW

PERSONAL: Born February 18, 1969, in Khabarovsk, U.S.S.R. ... 6-0/209. ... Shoots left. ... Name pronounced moh-GIHL-nee.

TRANSACTIONS/CAREER NOTES: Selected by Buffalo Sabres in fifth round (fourth Sabres pick, 89th overall) of entry draft (June 11, 1988). ... Flu (November 26, 1989). ... Missed games because of fear of flying (January 22, 1990); spent remainder of season using ground travel. ... Separated shoulder (February 8, 1991); missed six games. ... Flu (November 1991); missed two games. ... Flu (December 18, 1991); missed one game. ... Bruised shoulder (October 10, 1992); missed six games. ... Fractured leg and tore ankle ligaments (May 6, 1993); missed remainder of 1992-93 playoffs and first nine games of 1993-94 season. ... Sore ankle (February 2, 1994); missed four games. ... Inflamed ankle tendon (February 15, 1994); missed four games. ... Pinched nerve in neck (April 9, 1995); missed three games. ... Traded by Sabres with fifth-round pick (LW Todd Norman) in 1995 entry draft to Vancouver Canucks for C Michael Peca, D Mike Wilson and first-round pick (D Jay McKee) in 1995 entry draft (July 8, 1995). ... Injured hamstring (October 28, 1995); missed three games. ... Flu (December 3, 1996); missed two games. ... Strained groin (April 4, 1997); missed remainder of season. ... Missed first 16 games of 1997-98 season in contract dispute. ... Injured groin (December 15, 1997); missed 11 games. ... Strained back (February 24, 1998); missed four games. ... Sprained knee ligament (November 21, 1998); missed 17 games. ... Bruised kidney (January 4, 1999); missed two games. ... Strained abdominal muscle (February 20, 1999); missed four games. ... Injured back (November 26, 1999); missed eight games. ... Injured hip (January 12, 2000); missed seven games. ... Injured shoulder (February 12, 2000); missed eight games. ... Traded by Canucks to New Jersey Devils for C Brendan Morrison and C Denis Pederson (March 14, 2000). ... Injured neck (February 10, 2000); missed one game. ... Bruised abdomen (February 14, 2001); missed four games. ... Strained groin (April 4, 2001); missed one game. ... Signed as free agent by Toronto Maple Leafs (July 3, 2001). ... Back spasms (January 12, 2002); missed three games. ... Injured back (January 29, 2002); missed 13 games. ... Injured neck (November 19, 2002); missed one game. ... Injured foot (January 17, 2003); missed two games. ... Injured back (January 24, 2003); missed two games. ... Concussion (April 14, 2003); missed one playoff game. ... Injured groin (October 14, 2003); missed five games. ... Injured hip (November 22, 2003); missed 40 games. ... Hip surgery (September 27, 2004). ... Signed as free agent by Devils (August 16, 2005). ... Concussion (November 11, 2005); missed four games.

STATISTICAL PLATEAUS: Three-goal games: 1990-91 (1), 1991-92 (1), 1992-93 (5), 1993-94 (1), 1995-96 (3), 1996-97 (1), 2000-01 (1), 2002-03 (2). Total: 15. ... Four-goal games: 1992-93 (2). ... Total hat tricks: 17.

		REGULAR SEASON								PLAYOFFS				
Season Team	**League**	**GP**	**G**	**A**	**Pts.**	**PIM**	**+/-**	**PP**	**SH**	**GP**	**G**	**A**	**Pts.**	**PIM**
86-87—CSKA Moscow	USSR	28	15	1	16	4	...	...	...	—	—	—	—	—
87-88—CSKA Moscow	USSR	39	12	8	20	20	...	...	...	—	—	—	—	—
88-89—CSKA Moscow	USSR	31	11	11	22	24	...	...	...	—	—	—	—	—
89-90—Buffalo	NHL	65	15	28	43	16	8	4	0	4	0	1	1	2
90-91—Buffalo	NHL	62	30	34	64	16	14	3	3	6	0	6	6	2
91-92—Buffalo	NHL	67	39	45	84	73	7	15	0	2	0	2	2	0
92-93—Buffalo	NHL	77	76	51	127	40	7	27	0	7	7	3	10	6
93-94—Buffalo	NHL	66	32	47	79	22	8	17	0	7	4	2	6	6
94-95—Spartak Moscow	Russian	1	0	1	1	0	...	...	...	—	—	—	—	—
—Buffalo	NHL	44	19	28	47	36	0	12	0	5	3	2	5	2
95-96—Vancouver	NHL	79	55	52	107	16	14	10	5	6	1	8	9	8
96-97—Vancouver	NHL	76	31	42	73	18	9	7	1	—	—	—	—	—
97-98—Vancouver	NHL	51	18	27	45	36	-6	5	4	—	—	—	—	—
98-99—Vancouver	NHL	59	14	31	45	58	0	3	2	—	—	—	—	—
99-00—Vancouver	NHL	47	21	17	38	16	7	3	1	—	—	—	—	—
—New Jersey	NHL	12	3	3	6	4	-4	2	0	23	4	3	7	4
00-01—New Jersey	NHL	75	43	40	83	43	10	12	0	25	5	11	16	8
01-02—Toronto	NHL	66	24	33	57	8	1	5	0	20	8	3	11	8
02-03—Toronto	NHL	73	33	46	79	12	4	5	3	6	5	2	7	4
03-04—Toronto	NHL	37	8	22	30	12	9	4	1	13	2	4	6	8
05-06—Albany	AHL	19	4	10	14	17	-4	2	0	—	—	—	—	—
—New Jersey	NHL	34	12	13	25	6	-7	7	0	—	—	—	—	—
NHL Totals (16 years)		990	473	559	1032	432	81	141	20	124	39	47	86	58

MOJZIS, TOMAS — D

PERSONAL: Born May 2, 1982, in Kolin, Czechoslovakia. ... 6-1/186. ... Shoots left. ... Name pronounced: MOH jeez
TRANSACTIONS/CAREER NOTES: Selected by Toronto Maple Leafs in eighth round (11th Maple Leafs pick, 246th overall) of entry draft (June 24, 2001). ... Traded by Maple Leafs to Vancouver Canucks for RW Brad Leeb (September 4, 2002). ... Traded by Canucks with third-round pick (traded to New Jersey; Devils selected RW Vladimir Zharkov) in 2006 draft to St. Louis Blues for D Eric Weinrich (March 9, 2006).

		REGULAR SEASON								PLAYOFFS				
Season Team	**League**	**GP**	**G**	**A**	**Pts.**	**PIM**	**+/-**	**PP**	**SH**	**GP**	**G**	**A**	**Pts.**	**PIM**
00-01—Moose Jaw	WHL	72	11	25	36	115	...	...	...	4	0	1	1	8
01-02—Seattle	WHL	64	10	26	36	109	...	...	...	11	1	3	4	20
02-03—Seattle	WHL	62	21	49	70	126	...	...	...	15	1	6	7	36
03-04—Manitoba	AHL	63	5	13	18	50	...	...	...	—	—	—	—	—
04-05—Manitoba	AHL	80	7	23	30	62	1	1	0	14	0	2	2	28
05-06—Manitoba	AHL	37	5	13	18	52	0	3	1	—	—	—	—	—
—Vancouver	NHL	7	0	1	1	12	2	0	0	—	—	—	—	—
—Peoria	AHL	12	3	4	7	14	5	1	0	1	0	0	0	0
NHL Totals (1 year)		7	0	1	1	12	2	0	0					

MONTADOR, STEVE — D

PERSONAL: Born December 21, 1979, in Vancouver. ... 6-0/210. ... Shoots right.
TRANSACTIONS/CAREER NOTES: Signed as free agent by Calgary Flames (September 5, 2000). ... Injured upper body (March 22, 2004); missed six games. ... Traded by Flames with C Dustin Johner to Panthers for LW Kristian Huselius (December 2, 2005).

		REGULAR SEASON								PLAYOFFS				
Season Team	**League**	**GP**	**G**	**A**	**Pts.**	**PIM**	**+/-**	**PP**	**SH**	**GP**	**G**	**A**	**Pts.**	**PIM**
96-97—North Bay	OHL	63	7	28	35	129	...	...	...	—	—	—	—	—
97-98—North Bay	OHL	37	5	16	21	54	...	...	...	—	—	—	—	—
—Erie	OHL	26	3	17	20	35	...	...	...	7	1	1	2	8
98-99—Erie	OHL	61	9	33	42	114	...	...	...	5	0	2	2	9
99-00—Peterborough	OHL	64	14	42	56	97	...	...	...	5	0	2	2	4
00-01—Saint John	AHL	58	1	6	7	95	...	...	...	19	0	8	8	13
01-02—Saint John	AHL	67	9	16	25	107	-11	0	0	—	—	—	—	—
—Calgary	NHL	11	1	2	3	26	-2	0	0	—	—	—	—	—
02-03—Saint John	AHL	11	1	7	8	20	-4	0	0	—	—	—	—	—
—Calgary	NHL	50	1	1	2	114	-9	0	0	—	—	—	—	—
03-04—Calgary	NHL	26	1	2	3	50	-1	0	0	20	1	2	3	6
04-05—Mulhouse	France	15	1	7	8	69	...	...	...	—	—	—	—	—
05-06—Calgary	NHL	7	1	0	1	11	0	0	0	—	—	—	—	—
—Florida	NHL	51	1	5	6	68	4	0	0	—	—	—	—	—
NHL Totals (4 years)		145	5	10	15	269	-8	0	0	20	1	2	3	6

MOORE, DOMINIC — C/LW

PERSONAL: Born August 3, 1980, in Thornhill, Ont. ... 6-0/194. ... Shoots left. ... Brother of Steve Moore, C, Colorado Avalanche. Brother of Mark Moore, Pittsburgh Penguins organization.
TRANSACTIONS/CAREER NOTES: Selected by New York Rangers in third round (second Rangers pick, 95th overall) of NHL entry draft (June 24, 2000). ... Traded by Rangers to Nashville Predators for RW Adam Hall; then, traded by Predators with LW Libor Pivko to Pittsburgh Penguins for third-round pick in 2007 draft (July 19, 2006).

Season Team	League	GP	G	A	Pts.	PIM	+/-	PP	SH	GP	G	A	Pts.	PIM
		REGULAR SEASON								PLAYOFFS				
98-99—Aurora	OPJHL	51	34	53	87	70	...	...	...	—	—	—	—	—
99-00—Harvard	ECAC	28	12	8	20	28	...	...	...	—	—	—	—	—
00-01—Harvard	ECAC	32	15	28	43	40	...	...	...	—	—	—	—	—
01-02—Harvard	ECAC	32	13	16	29	37	...	...	...	—	—	—	—	—
02-03—Harvard	ECAC	34	24	27	51	30	...	...	...	—	—	—	—	—
03-04—New York Rangers	NHL	5	0	3	3	0	0	0	0	—	—	—	—	—
—Hartford	AHL	70	14	25	39	60	3	3	0	16	3	3	6	8
04-05—Hartford	AHL	78	19	31	50	78	14	8	2	6	1	1	2	4
05-06—New York Rangers	NHL	82	9	9	18	28	4	2	0	4	0	0	0	2
NHL Totals (2 years)		87	9	12	21	28	4	2	0	4	0	0	0	2

MORAN, IAN D/RW

PERSONAL: Born August 24, 1972, in Cleveland. ... 6-0/200. ... Shoots right. ... Name pronounced muh-RAN.

TRANSACTIONS/CAREER NOTES: Selected by Pittsburgh Penguins in sixth round (fifth Penguins pick, 107th overall) of entry draft (June 16, 1990). ... Bruised shoulder (November 22, 1995); missed nine games. ... Injured shoulder (February 21, 1996); missed one game. ... Shoulder surgery (March 21, 1996); missed remainder of season. ... Injured back and neck (April 10, 1997); missed two games. ... Bruised kneecap and had surgery (September 30, 1997); missed 34 games. ... Concussion (February 2, 1998); missed four games. ... Injured knee (March 21, 1998); missed five games. ... Injured ankle (October 26, 1998); missed five games. ... Reinjured ankle (November 7, 1998); missed nine games. ... Bruised ankle (January 5, 1999); missed two games. ... Bruised right testicle (February 5, 1999); missed three games. ... Injured ankle (April 3, 1999); missed one game. ... Fractured foot (December 2, 1999); missed two games. ... Flu (January 2, 2000); missed one game. ... Bruised ankle (April 7, 2000); missed final game of season. ... Injured knee (October 18, 2000); missed seven games. ... Fractured hand (November 10, 2000); missed 15 games. ... Flu (February 16, 2001); missed one game. ... Fractured thumb (February 19, 2001); missed 18 games. ... Fractured foot (December 8, 2001); missed 12 games. ... Injured hip (April 3, 2002); missed remainder of season. ... Traded by Penguins to Boston Bruins for fourth-round pick (D Paul Bissonette) in 2003 draft (March 11, 2003). ... Injured back (March 22, 2003); missed four games. ... Sprained ankle (December 23, 2003); missed final 47 games of season and playoffs. ... Injured left knee (October 27, 2005); missed final 69 games of season.

Season Team	League	GP	G	A	Pts.	PIM	+/-	PP	SH	GP	G	A	Pts.	PIM
		REGULAR SEASON								PLAYOFFS				
87-88—Belmont Hill	Mass. H.S.	25	3	13	16	15	...	...	...	—	—	—	—	—
88-89—Belmont Hill	Mass. H.S.	23	7	25	32	8	...	...	...	—	—	—	—	—
89-90—Belmont Hill	Mass. H.S.	...	10	36	46	0	...	...	...	—	—	—	—	—
90-91—Belmont Hill	Mass. H.S.	23	7	44	51	12	...	...	...	—	—	—	—	—
91-92—Boston College	Hockey East	30	2	16	18	44	...	...	...	—	—	—	—	—
92-93—Boston College	Hockey East	31	8	12	20	32	...	...	...	—	—	—	—	—
93-94—U.S. national team	Int'l	50	8	15	23	69	...	0	0	—	—	—	—	—
—Cleveland	IHL	33	5	13	18	39	-4	3	0	—	—	—	—	—
94-95—Cleveland	IHL	64	7	31	38	94	3	2	0	4	0	1	1	2
—Pittsburgh	NHL	...	...	...	...	...	...	...	...	8	0	0	0	0
95-96—Pittsburgh	NHL	51	1	1	2	47	-1	0	0	—	—	—	—	—
96-97—Cleveland	IHL	36	6	23	29	26	...	...	...	—	—	—	—	—
—Pittsburgh	NHL	36	4	5	9	22	-11	0	0	5	1	2	3	4
97-98—Pittsburgh	NHL	37	1	6	7	19	0	0	0	6	0	0	0	2
98-99—Pittsburgh	NHL	62	4	5	9	37	1	0	1	13	0	2	2	8
99-00—Pittsburgh	NHL	73	4	8	12	28	-10	0	0	11	0	1	1	2
00-01—Pittsburgh	NHL	40	3	4	7	28	5	0	0	18	0	1	1	4
01-02—Pittsburgh	NHL	64	2	8	10	54	-11	0	0	—	—	—	—	—
02-03—Pittsburgh	NHL	70	0	7	7	46	-17	0	0	—	—	—	—	—
—Boston	NHL	8	0	1	1	2	-1	0	0	5	0	1	1	4
03-04—Boston	NHL	35	1	4	5	28	3	0	0	—	—	—	—	—
04-05—Bofors	Sweden Dv. 2	7	0	4	4	22	-3	0	0	—	—	—	—	—
—Nottingham	England	14	2	6	8	8	...	...	...	5	0	1	1	2
05-06—Boston	NHL	12	1	1	2	10	0	0	0	—	—	—	—	—
NHL Totals (11 years)		488	21	50	71	321	-42	0	1	66	1	7	8	24

MOREAU, ETHAN LW

PERSONAL: Born September 22, 1975, in Huntsville, Ont. ... 6-2/220. ... Shoots left. ... Name pronounced MOHR-oh.

TRANSACTIONS/CAREER NOTES: Selected by Chicago Blackhawks in first round (first Blackhawks pick, 14th overall) of entry draft (June 28, 1994). ... Fractured knuckle (November 16, 1997); missed seven games. ... Fractured ankle (December 14, 1997); missed 20 games. ... Traded by Blackhawks with LW Daniel Cleary, C Chad Kilger and D Christian Laflamme to Edmonton Oilers for D Boris Mironov, LW Dean McAmmond and D Jonas Elofsson (March 20, 1999). ... Injured ribs (November 24, 1999); missed eight games. ... Flu (December 27, 1999); missed one game. ... Shoulder surgery (May 24, 2000); missed first 14 games of season. ... Bruised ankle (December 16, 2001); missed one game. ... Flu (December 11, 2002); missed two games. ... Injured shoulder (December 23, 2003); missed one game. ... Injured leg (January 31, 2006); missed seven games.

Season Team	League	GP	G	A	Pts.	PIM	+/-	PP	SH	GP	G	A	Pts.	PIM
		REGULAR SEASON								PLAYOFFS				
90-91—Orillia	OHA	42	17	22	39	26	...	...	...	—	—	—	—	—
91-92—Niagara Falls	OHL	62	20	35	55	39	...	...	...	17	4	6	10	4
92-93—Niagara Falls	OHL	65	32	41	73	69	...	...	...	4	0	3	3	4
93-94—Niagara Falls	OHL	59	44	54	98	100	...	11	...	—	—	—	—	—
94-95—Niagara Falls	OHL	39	25	41	66	69	...	11	1	—	—	—	—	—
—Sudbury	OHL	23	13	17	30	22	...	2	0	18	6	12	18	26
95-96—Indianapolis	IHL	71	21	20	41	126	...	...	...	5	4	0	4	8
—Chicago	NHL	8	0	1	1	4	1	0	0	—	—	—	—	—
96-97—Chicago	NHL	82	15	16	31	123	13	0	0	6	1	0	1	9
97-98—Chicago	NHL	54	9	9	18	73	0	2	0	—	—	—	—	—

Season Team	League	REGULAR SEASON								PLAYOFFS				
		GP	G	A	Pts.	PIM	+/-	PP	SH	GP	G	A	Pts.	PIM
98-99—Chicago	NHL	66	9	6	15	84	-5	0	0	—	—	—	—	—
—Edmonton	NHL	14	1	5	6	8	2	0	0	4	0	3	3	6
99-00—Edmonton	NHL	73	17	10	27	62	8	1	0	5	0	1	1	0
00-01—Edmonton	NHL	68	9	10	19	90	-6	0	1	4	0	0	0	2
01-02—Edmonton	NHL	80	11	5	16	81	4	0	2	—	—	—	—	—
02-03—Edmonton	NHL	78	14	17	31	112	-7	2	3	6	0	1	1	16
03-04—Edmonton	NHL	81	20	12	32	96	7	0	3	—	—	—	—	—
04-05—VSV	Austria	16	10	6	16	73	-8	4	1	3	4	0	4	0
05-06—Edmonton	NHL	74	11	16	27	87	6	2	4	21	2	1	3	19
NHL Totals (10 years)		678	116	107	223	820	23	7	13	46	3	6	9	52

MORGAN, JASON — C

PERSONAL: Born October 9, 1976, in St. John's, Newfoundland. ... 6-1/194. ... Shoots left.

TRANSACTIONS/CAREER NOTES: Selected by Los Angeles Kings in fifth round (fifth Kings pick, 118th overall) of entry draft (July 8, 1995). ... Signed as free agent by Calgary Flames (July 11, 2002). ... Claimed off waivers by Nashville Predators (December 31, 2003). ... Separated shoulder (January 7, 2004); missed 10 games. ... Claimed off waivers by Flames (February 19, 2004). ... Traded by Flames with future considerations to Chicago Blackhawks for LW Ville Nieminen (February 24, 2004). ... Signed as free agent by Minnesota Wild (July 17, 2006).

Season Team	League	REGULAR SEASON								PLAYOFFS				
		GP	G	A	Pts.	PIM	+/-	PP	SH	GP	G	A	Pts.	PIM
93-94—Kitchener	OHL	65	6	15	21	16	...	...	...	5	1	0	1	0
94-95—Kitchener	OHL	35	3	15	18	25	...	0	0	—	—	—	—	—
—Kingston	OHL	20	0	3	3	14	...	0	0	6	0	2	2	0
95-96—Kingston	OHL	66	16	38	54	50	...	...	...	6	1	2	3	0
96-97—Phoenix	IHL	57	3	6	9	29	...	...	...	—	—	—	—	—
—Mississippi	ECHL	6	3	0	3	0	...	...	...	3	1	1	2	6
—Los Angeles	NHL	3	0	0	0	0	-3	0	0	—	—	—	—	—
97-98—Springfield	AHL	58	13	22	35	66	13	4	1	3	1	0	1	18
—Los Angeles	NHL	11	1	0	1	4	-7	0	0	—	—	—	—	—
98-99—Long Beach	IHL	13	4	6	10	18	-2	0	0	—	—	—	—	—
—Springfield	AHL	46	6	16	22	51	-5	1	0	3	0	0	0	6
99-00—Florida	ECHL	48	14	25	39	79	...	...	...	5	2	2	4	16
—Cincinnati	IHL	15	1	3	4	14	...	...	...	—	—	—	—	—
00-01—Hamilton	AHL	11	2	0	2	10	...	...	...	—	—	—	—	—
—Springfield	AHL	16	1	4	5	19	...	...	...	6	0	1	1	2
—Florida	ECHL	37	15	22	37	41	...	...	...	5	2	3	5	17
01-02—Saint John	AHL	76	17	20	37	69	-19	10	1	—	—	—	—	—
02-03—Saint John	AHL	80	13	40	53	63	-2	3	2	—	—	—	—	—
03-04—Calgary	NHL	13	0	2	2	2	1	0	0	—	—	—	—	—
—Lowell	AHL	21	6	13	19	16	2	1	0	8	0	1	1	10
—Norfolk	AHL	19	6	8	14	16	-4	4	0	—	—	—	—	—
—Nashville	NHL	6	0	2	2	2	0	0	0	—	—	—	—	—
04-05—Norfolk	AHL	71	9	20	29	116	-8	2	0	6	2	2	4	8
05-06—Norfolk	AHL	51	8	31	39	58	9	4	0	—	—	—	—	—
—Chicago	NHL	7	1	1	2	6	1	0	0	—	—	—	—	—
NHL Totals (4 years)		40	2	5	7	14	-8	0	0					

MORRIS, DEREK — D

PERSONAL: Born August 24, 1978, in Edmonton. ... 6-0/220. ... Shoots right.

TRANSACTIONS/CAREER NOTES: Selected by Calgary Flames in first round (first Flames pick, 13th overall) of entry draft (June 22, 1996). ... Shoulder (February 22, 1999); missed 10 games. ... Concussion (December 14, 1999); missed three games. ... Missed first 27 games of 2000-01 season in contract dispute. ... Injured (November 8, 2001); missed one game. ... Wrist (November 29, 2001); missed 20 games. ... Traded by Flames with LW Dean McAmmond and C Jeff Shantz to Colorado Avalanche for LW Chris Drury and C Stephane Yelle (October 1, 2002). ... Eye (January 23, 2003); missed seven games. ... Traded by Avalanche with D Keith Ballard to Phoenix Coyotes for F Chris Gratton, D Ossi Vaananen and second-round pick (C Paul Stastny) in 2005 (March 9, 2004). ... Quadriceps muscle (October 5, 2005); missed three games. ... Rib (November 25, 2005); missed three games. ... Ankle (December 28, 2005), had surgery; missed 23 games.

Season Team	League	REGULAR SEASON								PLAYOFFS				
		GP	G	A	Pts.	PIM	+/-	PP	SH	GP	G	A	Pts.	PIM
95-96—Regina	WHL	67	8	44	52	70	...	...	...	11	1	7	8	26
96-97—Regina	WHL	67	18	57	75	180	10	8	0	5	0	3	3	9
—Saint John	AHL	7	0	3	3	7	-1	0	0	5	0	3	3	7
97-98—Calgary	NHL	82	9	20	29	88	1	5	1	—	—	—	—	—
98-99—Calgary	NHL	71	7	27	34	73	4	3	0	—	—	—	—	—
99-00—Calgary	NHL	78	9	29	38	80	2	3	0	—	—	—	—	—
00-01—Saint John	AHL	3	1	2	3	2	...	...	...	—	—	—	—	—
—Calgary	NHL	51	5	23	28	56	-15	3	1	—	—	—	—	—
01-02—Calgary	NHL	61	4	30	34	88	-4	2	0	—	—	—	—	—
02-03—Colorado	NHL	75	11	37	48	68	16	9	0	7	0	3	3	6
03-04—Colorado	NHL	69	6	22	28	47	4	2	0	—	—	—	—	—
—Phoenix	NHL	14	0	4	4	2	-5	0	0	—	—	—	—	—
05-06—Phoenix	NHL	53	6	21	27	54	-7	4	1	—	—	—	—	—
NHL Totals (8 years)		554	57	213	270	556	-4	31	3	7	0	3	3	6

MORRISON, BRENDAN — C

PERSONAL: Born August 15, 1975, in Pitt Meadows, B.C. ... 5-11/180. ... Shoots left.

TRANSACTIONS/CAREER NOTES: Selected by New Jersey Devils in second round (third Devils pick, 39th overall) of NHL draft (June 26,

1993). ... Missed first nine games of 1999-2000 season in contract dispute. ... Injured (October 29, 1999); missed two games. ... Traded by Devils with C Denis Pederson to Vancouver Canucks for RW Alexander Mogilny (March 14, 2000).
STATISTICAL PLATEAUS: Three-goal games: 2003-04 (1).

		REGULAR SEASON								PLAYOFFS				
Season Team	**League**	**GP**	**G**	**A**	**Pts.**	**PIM**	**+/-**	**PP**	**SH**	**GP**	**G**	**A**	**Pts.**	**PIM**
92-93—Penticton	BCJHL	56	35	59	94	45	...	...	...	—	—	—	—	—
93-94—Univ. of Michigan	CCHA	38	20	28	48	24	8	10	1	—	—	—	—	—
94-95—Univ. of Michigan	CCHA	39	23	53	76	42	28	5	1	—	—	—	—	—
95-96—Univ. of Michigan	CCHA	35	28	44	72	41	...	...	...	—	—	—	—	—
96-97—Univ. of Michigan	CCHA	43	31	57	88	52	39	14	0	—	—	—	—	—
97-98—Albany	AHL	72	35	49	84	44	11	8	4	8	3	4	7	19
—New Jersey	NHL	11	5	4	9	0	3	0	0	3	0	1	1	0
98-99—New Jersey	NHL	76	13	33	46	18	-4	5	0	7	0	2	2	0
99-00—HC Pardubice	Czech Rep.	6	5	2	7	2	...	...	...	—	—	—	—	—
—New Jersey	NHL	44	5	21	26	8	8	2	0	—	—	—	—	—
—Vancouver	NHL	12	2	7	9	10	4	0	0	—	—	—	—	—
00-01—Vancouver	NHL	82	16	38	54	42	2	3	2	4	1	2	3	0
01-02—Vancouver	NHL	82	23	44	67	26	18	6	0	6	0	2	2	6
02-03—Vancouver	NHL	82	25	46	71	36	18	6	2	14	4	7	11	18
03-04—Vancouver	NHL	82	22	38	60	50	16	5	1	7	2	3	5	8
04-05—Linkopings	Sweden	45	16	28	44	50	30	4	3	6	0	2	2	10
05-06—Vancouver	NHL	82	19	37	56	84	-1	8	0	—	—	—	—	—
NHL Totals (8 years)		553	130	268	398	274	64	35	5	41	7	17	24	32

MORRISON, MIKE G

PERSONAL: Born July 11, 1979, in Medford, Mass. ... 6-3/194. ... Catches left.
TRANSACTIONS/CAREER NOTES: Selected by Edmonton in seventh round (186th overall) of NHL entry draft (June 27, 1998). ... Claimed off waivers by Ottawa Senators (March 9, 2006). ... Signed as free agent by Phoenix Coyotes (July 2, 2006).

		REGULAR SEASON										PLAYOFFS							
Season Team	**League**	**GP**	**Min.**	**W**	**L**	**OTL**	**T**	**GA**	**SO**	**GAA**	**SV%**	**GP**	**Min.**	**W**	**L**	**GA**	**SO**	**GAA**	**SV%**
98-99 —Maine	Hockey East	11	347	3	0	...	1	10	1	1.73	...	—	—	—	—	—	—	—	—
99-00 —Maine	Hockey East	12	608	7	2	...	1	27	1	2.67	...	—	—	—	—	—	—	—	—
00-01 —Maine	Hockey East	10	490	2	3	...	3	16	1	1.96	...	—	—	—	—	—	—	—	—
01-02 —Maine	Hockey East	30	1645	20	3	...	4	60	2	2.19	...	—	—	—	—	—	—	—	—
02-03 —Columbus	ECHL	38	1948	9	18	...	6	113	1	3.48	...	—	—	—	—	—	—	—	—
03-04 —Toronto	AHL	27	1309	12	8	...	2	55	3	2.52	...	—	—	—	—	—	—	—	—
04-05 —Edmonton	AHL	14	728	2	5	...	5	21	2	1.73	...	—	—	—	—	—	—	—	—
—Greenville	ECHL	26	1576	13	10	...	2	72	1	2.74	...	3	150	1	1	9	0	3.61	...
05-06 —Edmonton	NHL	21	891	10	4	2	...	42	0	2.83	.884	—	—	—	—	—	—	—	—
—Ottawa	NHL	4	207	1	0	1	...	12	0	3.48	.875	—	—	—	—	—	—	—	—
NHL Totals (1 year)		25	1098	11	4	3	0	54	0	2.95	.882								

MORRISONN, SHAONE D

PERSONAL: Born December 23, 1982, in Vancouver. ... 6-3/205. ... Shoots left. ... Name pronounced: SHAWN MOHR-ih-suhn
TRANSACTIONS/CAREER NOTES: Selected by Boston Bruins in first round (first Bruins pick, 19th overall) of entry draft (June 23, 2001). ... Traded by Bruins with first- (D Jeff Schultz) and second-round (D Mikhail Yunkov) picks in 2004 draft to Washington Capitals for D Sergei Gonchar (March 3, 2004).

		REGULAR SEASON								PLAYOFFS				
Season Team	**League**	**GP**	**G**	**A**	**Pts.**	**PIM**	**+/-**	**PP**	**SH**	**GP**	**G**	**A**	**Pts.**	**PIM**
99-00—Kamloops	WHL	57	1	6	7	80	...	...	...	4	0	0	0	6
00-01—Kamloops	WHL	61	13	25	38	132	...	...	...	4	0	0	0	6
01-02—Kamloops	WHL	61	11	26	37	106	...	...	...	4	0	2	2	2
02-03—Providence	AHL	60	5	16	21	103	5	1	0	—	—	—	—	—
—Boston	NHL	11	0	0	0	8	0	0	0	—	—	—	—	—
03-04—Boston	NHL	30	1	7	8	10	10	0	0	—	—	—	—	—
—Providence	AHL	18	0	2	2	16	1	0	0	—	—	—	—	—
—Washington	NHL	3	0	0	0	0	0	0	0	—	—	—	—	—
—Portland	AHL	13	1	4	5	10	8	0	0	7	0	1	1	4
04-05—Portland	AHL	71	4	14	18	63	-17	3	0	—	—	—	—	—
05-06—Washington	NHL	80	1	13	14	91	7	0	0	—	—	—	—	—
NHL Totals (3 years)		124	2	20	22	109	17	0	0					

MORROW, BRENDEN LW

PERSONAL: Born January 16, 1979, in Carlyle, Sask. ... 5-11/200. ... Shoots left.
TRANSACTIONS/CAREER NOTES: Selected by Dallas Stars in first round (first Stars pick, 25th overall) of entry draft (June 21, 1997). ... Knee (December 1, 2001); missed 10 games. ... Groin (December 19, 2002); missed one game. ... Groin, charley horse (January 5, 2003); missed one game. ... Bruised chest (February 13, 2003); missed nine games. ... Shoulder (Jan 7, 2004); missed one game.
STATISTICAL PLATEAUS: Three-goal games: 2003-04 (1).

		REGULAR SEASON								PLAYOFFS				
Season Team	**League**	**GP**	**G**	**A**	**Pts.**	**PIM**	**+/-**	**PP**	**SH**	**GP**	**G**	**A**	**Pts.**	**PIM**
95-96—Portland	WHL	65	13	12	25	61	...	...	...	7	0	0	0	8
96-97—Portland	WHL	71	39	49	88	178	...	...	...	6	2	1	3	4
97-98—Portland	WHL	68	34	52	86	184	51	11	2	16	10	8	18	65

		REGULAR SEASON								PLAYOFFS				
Season Team	League	GP	G	A	Pts.	PIM	+/-	PP	SH	GP	G	A	Pts.	PIM
98-99—Portland	WHL	61	41	44	85	248	-1	19	1	4	0	4	4	18
99-00—Michigan	IHL	9	2	0	2	18	...	...	...	—	—	—	—	—
—Dallas	NHL	64	14	19	33	81	8	3	0	21	2	4	6	22
00-01—Dallas	NHL	82	20	24	44	128	18	7	0	10	0	3	3	12
01-02—Dallas	NHL	72	17	18	35	109	12	4	0	—	—	—	—	—
02-03—Dallas	NHL	71	21	22	43	134	20	2	3	12	3	5	8	16
03-04—Dallas	NHL	81	25	24	49	121	10	9	0	5	0	1	1	4
04-05—Oklahoma City	CHL	19	8	14	22	31	...	...	...	—	—	—	—	—
05-06—Dallas	NHL	81	23	42	65	183	30	8	1	5	1	5	6	6
NHL Totals (6 years)		451	120	149	269	756	98	33	4	53	6	18	24	60

MOTZKO, JOE RW/LW

PERSONAL: Born March 14, 1980, in Bemidji, Minn. ... 6-0/190. ... Shoots right.
TRANSACTIONS/CAREER NOTES: Signed as free agent by Columbus Blue Jackets (May 15, 2003).

		REGULAR SEASON								PLAYOFFS				
Season Team	League	GP	G	A	Pts.	PIM	+/-	PP	SH	GP	G	A	Pts.	PIM
99-00—St. Cloud State	WCHA	36	9	15	24	52	...	...	...	—	—	—	—	—
00-01—St. Cloud State	WCHA	41	17	20	37	56	...	...	...	—	—	—	—	—
01-02—St. Cloud State	WCHA	39	9	30	39	34	...	...	...	—	—	—	—	—
02-03—St. Cloud State	WCHA	38	17	25	42	59	...	...	...	—	—	—	—	—
—Syracuse	AHL	...	0	0	0	0	0	...	...	—	—	—	—	—
03-04—Syracuse	AHL	70	17	24	41	38	0	6	2	7	2	2	4	6
—Columbus	NHL	2	0	0	0	0	0	0	0	—	—	—	—	—
04-05—Syracuse	AHL	79	28	38	66	72	-8	9	2	—	—	—	—	—
05-06—Syracuse	AHL	61	27	34	61	54	-18	16	2	3	0	0	0	0
—Columbus	NHL	2	0	0	0	0	-2	0	0	—	—	—	—	—
NHL Totals (2 years)		4	0	0	0	0	-2	0	0					

MOWERS, MARK RW/C

PERSONAL: Born February 16, 1974, in Whitesboro, N.Y. ... 5-11/190. ... Shoots right.
TRANSACTIONS/CAREER NOTES: Signed as free agent by Nashville Predators (June 11, 1998). ... Knee (March 19, 2000); missed season's final nine games. ... Signed as free agent by Detroit Red Wings (August 5, 2002). ... Foot (March 29, 2004); missed final 10 games of season and playoffs. ... Signed as free agent by Boston Bruins (July 6, 2006).

		REGULAR SEASON								PLAYOFFS				
Season Team	League	GP	G	A	Pts.	PIM	+/-	PP	SH	GP	G	A	Pts.	PIM
94-95—New Hampshire	Hockey East	36	13	23	36	16	...	...	...	—	—	—	—	—
95-96—New Hampshire	Hockey East	34	21	26	47	18	...	...	...	—	—	—	—	—
96-97—New Hampshire	Hockey East	39	26	32	58	52	...	...	...	—	—	—	—	—
97-98—New Hampshire	Hockey East	35	25	31	56	32	...	...	...	—	—	—	—	—
98-99—Milwaukee	IHL	51	14	22	36	24	6	0	2	1	0	0	0	0
—Nashville	NHL	30	0	6	6	4	-4	0	0	—	—	—	—	—
99-00—Milwaukee	IHL	23	11	15	26	34	...	...	...	—	—	—	—	—
—Nashville	NHL	41	4	5	9	10	0	0	0	—	—	—	—	—
00-01—Milwaukee	IHL	63	25	25	50	54	...	...	...	58	1	2	3	2
01-02—Milwaukee	AHL	45	19	20	39	34	4	6	1	—	—	—	—	—
—Nashville	NHL	14	1	2	3	2	-2	0	0	—	—	—	—	—
02-03—Grand Rapids	AHL	78	34	47	81	47	26	9	2	15	3	4	7	4
03-04—Grand Rapids	AHL	16	8	6	14	4	5	3	1	—	—	—	—	—
—Detroit	NHL	52	3	8	11	4	3	1	0	11	1	0	1	16
04-05—Malmo	Sweden	9	2	0	2	0	-1	0	0	—	—	—	—	—
—Fribourg-Gotteron	Switzerland	3	2	0	2	0	...	...	...	9	9	8	17	12
05-06—Detroit	NHL	46	4	11	15	16	13	0	0	3	0	0	0	0
NHL Totals (5 years)		183	12	32	44	36	10	1	0	14	1	0	1	16

MUELLER, PETER C

PERSONAL: Born April 14, 1988, in Bloomington, Minn. ... 6-2/205. ... Shoots right.
TRANSACTIONS/CAREER NOTES: Selected by Phoenix Coyotes in first round (first Coyotes pick; eighth overall) of NHL draft (June 24, 2006).

		REGULAR SEASON								PLAYOFFS				
Season Team	League	GP	G	A	Pts.	PIM	+/-	PP	SH	GP	G	A	Pts.	PIM
04-05—U.S. National	USHL	40	26	26	52	56	...	...	...	—	—	—	—	—
05-06—Everett	WHL	52	26	32	58	44	4	...	...	15	7	6	13	10

MUIR, BRYAN D

PERSONAL: Born June 8, 1973, in Winnipeg. ... 6-4/220. ... Shoots left. ... Name pronounced MYOOR.
TRANSACTIONS/CAREER NOTES: Signed as free agent by Edmonton Oilers (April 30, 1996). ... Traded by Oilers with C Jason Arnott to New Jersey Devils for RW Bill Guerin and RW Valeri Zelepukin (January 4, 1998). ... Traded by Devils to Chicago Blackhawks for future considerations (November 13, 1998). ... Injured back (April 5, 1999); missed three games. ... Traded by Blackhawks with LW Reid Simpson to Tampa Bay Lightning for C Michael Nylander (November 12, 1999). ... Fractured ankle (November 17, 1999); missed 18 games. ... Injured ankle (March 12, 2000); missed 11 games. ... Traded by Lightning to Colorado Avalanche for eighth-round pick (LW Dimitri Bezrukov) in 2001 draft (January 23, 2001). ... Signed as free agent by Los Angeles Kings (July 31, 2003). ... Traded by Kings to Washington Capitals for future considerations (August 12, 2005). ... Groin injury (October 13, 2005); missed four games. ... Flu (March 20, 2006); missed one game.

		REGULAR SEASON								PLAYOFFS				
Season Team	League	GP	G	A	Pts.	PIM	+/-	PP	SH	GP	G	A	Pts.	PIM
91-92—Wexford	OJHL	50	11	35	46	...	...	...	...	—	—	—	—	—
92-93—New Hampshire	Hockey East	26	1	2	3	24	...	...	...	—	—	—	—	—
93-94—New Hampshire	Hockey East	36	0	4	4	48	...	...	...	—	—	—	—	—
94-95—New Hampshire	Hockey East	28	9	9	18	48	...	...	...	—	—	—	—	—
95-96—Canadian nat'l team	Int'l	42	6	12	18	36	...	...	...	—	—	—	—	—
—Edmonton	NHL	5	0	0	0	6	-4	0	0	—	—	—	—	—
96-97—Hamilton	AHL	75	8	16	24	80	-16	3	0	14	0	5	5	12
—Edmonton	NHL	...	...	...	...	...	...	...	...	5	0	0	0	4
97-98—Hamilton	AHL	28	3	10	13	62	9	2	0	—	—	—	—	—
—Edmonton	NHL	7	0	0	0	17	0	0	0	—	—	—	—	—
—Albany	AHL	41	3	10	13	67	6	0	0	13	3	0	3	12
98-99—New Jersey	NHL	1	0	0	0	0	0	0	0	—	—	—	—	—
—Albany	AHL	10	0	0	0	29	-7	0	0	—	—	—	—	—
—Chicago	NHL	53	1	4	5	50	1	0	0	—	—	—	—	—
—Portland	AHL	2	1	1	2	2	0	1	0	—	—	—	—	—
99-00—Chicago	NHL	11	2	3	5	13	-1	0	1	—	—	—	—	—
—Tampa Bay	NHL	30	1	1	2	32	-8	0	0	—	—	—	—	—
00-01—Tampa Bay	NHL	10	0	3	3	15	-7	0	0	—	—	—	—	—
—Detroit	IHL	21	5	7	12	36	...	...	...	—	—	—	—	—
—Hershey	AHL	26	5	8	13	50	...	...	...	—	—	—	—	—
—Colorado	NHL	8	0	0	0	4	0	0	0	3	0	0	0	0
01-02—Hershey	AHL	59	10	16	26	133	-6	6	0	—	—	—	—	—
—Colorado	NHL	22	1	1	2	9	1	0	0	21	0	0	0	2
02-03—Colorado	NHL	32	0	2	2	19	3	0	0	—	—	—	—	—
—Hershey	AHL	36	9	12	21	75	...	...	...	5	2	6	8	6
03-04—Los Angeles	NHL	2	0	1	1	2	1	0	0	—	—	—	—	—
—Manchester	AHL	73	13	36	49	141	24	5	0	6	2	3	5	12
04-05—MoDo Hockey	Sweden Jr.	26	1	5	6	36	4	0	0	—	—	—	—	—
05-06—Washington	NHL	72	8	18	26	72	-9	4	0	—	—	—	—	—
NHL Totals (10 years)		253	13	33	46	239	-23	4	1	29	0	0	0	6

MUNRO, ADAM G

PERSONAL: Born November 12, 1982, in St. George, Ont. ... 6-2/219. ... Catches left.

TRANSACTIONS/CAREER NOTES: Selected by Chicago Blackhawks in first round (second Blackhawks pick, 29th overall) of entry draft (June 23, 2001). ... Signed as free agent by Blackhawks (February 18, 2004). ... Concussion (March 4, 2004); missed three games.

		REGULAR SEASON										PLAYOFFS							
Season Team	League	GP	Min.	W	L	OTL	T	GA	SO	GAA	SV%	GP	Min.	W	L	GA	SO	GAA	SV%
99-00—Erie	OHL	22	948	8	7	...	1	48	1	3.04	...	1	5	0	0	1	0	12.00	...
00-01—Erie	OHL	41	2283	26	6	...	6	88	4	2.31	...	10	509	6	2	27	1	3.18	...
01-02—Erie	OHL	43	2277	24	13	...	1	128	3	3.37	...	6	361	4	2	17	0	2.83	...
02-03—Sault Ste. Marie	OHL	42	2494	20	20	...	2	160	...	3.85	...	4	240	0	4	12	0	3.00	...
03-04—Chicago	NHL	7	426	1	5	...	1	26	0	3.66	.880	—	—	—	—	—	—	—	—
—Norfolk	AHL	12	695	5	4	...	1	26	0	2.24	.891	—	—	—	—	—	—	—	—
04-05—Atlantic City	ECHL	5	271	2	2	...	...	9	0	1.99	.937	—	—	—	—	—	—	—	—
—Norfolk	AHL	30	1594	14	10	...	...	66	4	2.48	.905	—	—	—	—	—	—	—	—
05-06—Norfolk	AHL	28	1612	17	8	1	...	73	1	2.72	.909	4	239	0	4	15	0	3.77	.879
—Chicago	NHL	10	501	3	5	2	...	25	1	2.99	.893	—	—	—	—	—	—	—	—
NHL Totals (2 years)		17	927	4	10	2	1	51	1	3.30	.887								

MURLEY, MATT LW/RW

PERSONAL: Born December 17, 1979, in Troy, N.Y. ... 6-1/206. ... Shoots left.

TRANSACTIONS/CAREER NOTES: Selected by Pittsburgh Penguins in second round (second Penguins pick, 51st overall) of NHL entry draft (June 26, 1999). ... Left shoulder injury (December 23, 2005); missed three games. ... Torn labrum in left shoulder (January 16, 2006); missed final 36 games of regular season. ... Signed as free agent by Colorado Avalanche (July 12, 2006).

		REGULAR SEASON								PLAYOFFS				
Season Team	League	GP	G	A	Pts.	PIM	+/-	PP	SH	GP	G	A	Pts.	PIM
97-98—Syracuse	Jr. A	49	56	70	126	203	...	...	...	—	—	—	—	—
98-99—Rensselaer Poly. Inst.	ECAC	36	17	32	49	32	...	...	...	—	—	—	—	—
99-00—Rensselaer Poly. Inst.	ECAC	35	9	29	38	42	...	...	...	—	—	—	—	—
00-01—Rensselaer Poly. Inst.	ECAC	34	24	18	42	34	...	...	...	—	—	—	—	—
01-02—Rensselaer Poly. Inst.	ECAC	32	24	22	46	26	...	...	...	—	—	—	—	—
02-03—Wilkes-Barre/Scranton	AHL	73	21	37	58	45	-4	10	1	6	0	2	2	15
03-04—Pittsburgh	NHL	18	1	1	2	14	-6	0	0	—	—	—	—	—
—Wilkes-Barre/Scranton	AHL	63	10	27	37	69	2	5	0	24	7	6	13	17
04-05—Wilkes-Barre/Scranton	AHL	80	17	24	41	55	16	3	2	11	3	0	3	0
05-06—Pittsburgh	NHL	41	1	5	6	24	-9	0	0	—	—	—	—	—
NHL Totals (2 years)		59	2	6	8	38	-15	0	0					

MURRAY, DOUG D

PERSONAL: Born March 12, 1980, in Bromma, Sweden. ... 6-3/245. ... Shoots left.

COLLEGE: Cornell.

TRANSACTIONS/CAREER NOTES: Selected by San Jose Sharks in eighth round (sixth Sharks pick, 241st overall) of entry draft (June 24, 1999). ... Upper-body injury (February 6, 2006); missed four games. ... Upper-body injury (March 7, 2006); missed three games.

Season Team	League	GP	G	A	Pts.	PIM	+/-	PP	SH	GP	G	A	Pts.	PIM
		REGULAR SEASON								PLAYOFFS				
99-00—Cornell	ECAC	32	3	6	9	38	...	...	...	1	1	0	1	0
00-01—Cornell	ECAC	25	5	13	18	39	...	...	...	4	0	4	4	8
01-02—Cornell	ECAC	35	11	21	32	67	...	...	...	2	1	0	1	0
02-03—Cornell	ECAC	35	5	20	25	30	...	...	...	3	0	2	2	...
03-04—Cleveland	AHL	72	10	12	22	75	...	...	...	9	3	0	3	37
04-05—Cleveland	AHL	54	6	17	23	56	-7	4	0	—	—	—	—	—
05-06—Cleveland	AHL	20	1	7	8	37	-8	0	0	—	—	—	—	—
—San Jose	NHL	34	0	1	1	27	3	0	0	—	—	—	—	—
NHL Totals (1 year)		34	0	1	1	27	3	0	0					

MURRAY, GARTH C/LW

PERSONAL: Born September 17, 1982, in Regina, Sask. ... 6-1/207. ... Shoots left.
TRANSACTIONS/CAREER NOTES: Selected by New York Rangers in third round (third Rangers pick, 79th overall) of entry draft (June 23, 2001). ... Traded by Rangers to Montreal Canadiens for LW Marcel Hossa (September 30, 2005). ... Separated right shoulder (January 21, 2006); missed 15 games.

Season Team	League	GP	G	A	Pts.	PIM	+/-	PP	SH	GP	G	A	Pts.	PIM
		REGULAR SEASON								PLAYOFFS				
97-98—Regina	WHL	4	0	0	0	2	...	...	...	2	0	0	0	0
98-99—Regina	WHL	60	3	5	8	101	...	...	...	—	—	—	—	—
99-00—Regina	WHL	68	14	26	40	155	...	...	...	7	1	1	2	7
00-01—Regina	WHL	72	28	16	44	183	...	...	...	6	1	1	2	10
01-02—Regina	WHL	62	33	30	63	154	...	...	...	6	2	3	5	9
—Hartford	AHL	4	0	0	0	0	-5	0	0	9	1	3	4	6
02-03—Hartford	AHL	64	10	14	24	121	2	4	0	2	0	0	0	6
03-04—Hartford	AHL	63	11	11	22	161	4	0	1	16	0	4	4	29
—New York Rangers	NHL	20	1	0	1	24	-5	0	0	—	—	—	—	—
04-05—Hartford	AHL	55	4	5	9	182	0	0	0	5	1	0	1	8
05-06—Hamilton	AHL	26	1	1	2	46	-5	0	0	—	—	—	—	—
—Montreal	NHL	36	5	1	6	44	-2	0	0	6	0	0	0	0
NHL Totals (2 years)		56	6	1	7	68	-7	0	0	6	0	0	0	0

MURRAY, GLEN RW

PERSONAL: Born November 1, 1972, in Halifax, N.S. ... 6-3/225. ... Shoots right.
TRANSACTIONS/CAREER NOTES: Selected by Boston Bruins in first round (first Bruins pick, 18th overall) of entry draft (June 22, 1991). ... Injured elbow (December 15, 1993); missed two games. ... Traded by Bruins with C Bryan Smolinski to Pittsburgh Penguins for LW Kevin Stevens and LW Shawn McEachern (August 2, 1995). ... Separated shoulder (January 1, 1996); missed 10 games. ... Concussion (April 11, 1996); missed one game. ... Traded by Penguins to Los Angeles Kings for C Ed Olczyk (March 18, 1997). ... Flu (November 13, 1997); missed one game. ... Tore knee ligament (January 2, 1999); missed 19 games. ... Strained groin (March 28, 1999); missed two games. ... Bruised chest (January 13, 2000); missed three games. ... Strained quadriceps (November 18, 2000); missed 18 games. ... Traded by Kings with C Jozef Stumpel to Bruins for C Jason Allison and C/LW Mikko Eloranta (October 24, 2001). ... Flu (February 10, 2004); missed one game. ... Flu (November 8, 2005); missed one game. ... Strained groin (November 23, 2005); missed five games. ... Flu (December 11, 2005); missed one game. ... Bruised bone in right foot (January 12, 2006); missed 10 games. ... Flu (April 1, 2006); missed one game.
STATISTICAL PLATEAUS: Three-goal games: 1997-98 (1), 1999-00 (1), 2001-02 (1), 2002-03 (1), 2003-04 (1). Total: 5.

Season Team	League	GP	G	A	Pts.	PIM	+/-	PP	SH	GP	G	A	Pts.	PIM
		REGULAR SEASON								PLAYOFFS				
89-90—Sudbury	OHL	62	8	28	36	17	...	...	...	7	0	0	0	4
90-91—Sudbury	OHL	66	27	38	65	82	...	...	...	5	8	4	12	10
91-92—Sudbury	OHL	54	37	47	84	93	...	...	...	11	7	4	11	18
—Boston	NHL	5	3	1	4	0	2	1	0	15	4	2	6	10
92-93—Providence	AHL	48	30	26	56	42	15	3	0	6	1	4	5	4
—Boston	NHL	27	3	4	7	8	-6	2	0	—	—	—	—	—
93-94—Boston	NHL	81	18	13	31	48	-1	0	0	13	4	5	9	14
94-95—Boston	NHL	35	5	2	7	46	-11	0	0	2	0	0	0	2
95-96—Pittsburgh	NHL	69	14	15	29	57	4	0	0	18	2	6	8	10
96-97—Pittsburgh	NHL	66	11	11	22	24	-19	3	0	—	—	—	—	—
—Los Angeles	NHL	11	5	3	8	8	-2	0	0	—	—	—	—	—
97-98—Los Angeles	NHL	81	29	31	60	54	6	7	3	4	2	0	2	6
98-99—Los Angeles	NHL	61	16	15	31	36	-14	3	3	—	—	—	—	—
99-00—Los Angeles	NHL	78	29	33	62	60	13	10	1	4	0	0	0	2
00-01—Los Angeles	NHL	64	18	21	39	32	9	3	1	13	4	3	7	4
01-02—Los Angeles	NHL	9	6	5	11	0	5	4	0	—	—	—	—	—
—Boston	NHL	73	35	25	60	40	26	5	0	6	1	4	5	4
02-03—Boston	NHL	82	44	48	92	64	9	12	0	5	1	1	2	4
03-04—Boston	NHL	81	32	28	60	56	17	11	0	7	2	1	3	8
05-06—Boston	NHL	64	24	29	53	52	-8	6	1	—	—	—	—	—
NHL Totals (14 years)		887	292	284	576	585	30	67	9	87	20	22	42	64

MURRAY, REM C/LW

PERSONAL: Born October 9, 1972, in Stratford, Ont. ... 6-2/200. ... Shoots left.
COLLEGE: Michigan State
TRANSACTIONS/CAREER NOTES: Selected by Los Angeles Kings in sixth round (fifth Kings pick, 135th overall) of entry draft (June 20, 1992). ... Signed as free agent by Edmonton Oilers (August 17, 1995). ... Missed first five games of 1997-98 season recovering from wrist injury and

offseason appendectomy. ... Strained neck (March 17, 1998); missed one game. ... Flu (April 6, 1998); missed three games. ... Separated shoulder (October 7, 1999); missed seven games. ... Sprained knee (November 3, 1999); missed 28 games. ... Traded by Oilers with D Tom Poti to New York Rangers for C Mike York and fourth-round pick (D Ivan Koltsov) in 2002 draft (March 19, 2002). ... Traded by Rangers with D Tomas Kloucek and D Marek Zidlicky to Nashville Predators for G Mike Dunham (December 12, 2002). ... Strained neck (January 6, 2004); missed final 43 games of regular season and playoffs. ... Signed training camp tryout with Detroit Red Wings (September 2005). ... Released by Red Wings (October 3, 2005). ... Signed as free agent by Oilers (March 5, 2006).

STATISTICAL PLATEAUS: Three-goal games: 1996-97 (1).

		REGULAR SEASON								PLAYOFFS				
Season Team	League	GP	G	A	Pts.	PIM	+/-	PP	SH	GP	G	A	Pts.	PIM
90-91—Stratford Jr. B	OHA	48	39	59	98	22	...	...	...	—	—	—	—	—
91-92—Michigan State	CCHA	44	12	36	48	16	...	...	...	—	—	—	—	—
92-93—Michigan State	CCHA	40	22	35	57	24	...	...	...	—	—	—	—	—
93-94—Michigan State	CCHA	41	16	38	54	18	7	7	1	—	—	—	—	—
94-95—Michigan State	CCHA	40	20	36	56	21	18	4	0	—	—	—	—	—
95-96—Cape Breton	AHL	79	31	59	90	40	...	...	...	—	—	—	—	—
96-97—Edmonton	NHL	82	11	20	31	16	9	1	0	12	1	2	3	4
97-98—Edmonton	NHL	61	9	9	18	39	-9	2	2	11	1	4	5	2
98-99—Edmonton	NHL	78	21	18	39	20	4	4	1	4	1	1	2	2
99-00—Edmonton	NHL	44	9	5	14	8	-2	2	0	5	0	1	1	2
00-01—Edmonton	NHL	82	15	21	36	24	5	1	3	6	2	0	2	6
01-02—Edmonton	NHL	69	7	17	24	14	5	0	2	—	—	—	—	—
—New York Rangers	NHL	11	1	2	3	4	-9	0	0	—	—	—	—	—
02-03—New York Rangers	NHL	32	6	6	12	4	-3	1	1	—	—	—	—	—
—Nashville	NHL	53	6	13	19	18	1	1	0	—	—	—	—	—
03-04—Nashville	NHL	39	8	9	17	12	-1	0	2	—	—	—	—	—
05-06—Houston	AHL	54	11	24	35	8	-2	3	1	—	—	—	—	—
—Edmonton	NHL	9	1	1	2	2	1	0	0	24	0	4	4	2
NHL Totals (9 years)		560	94	121	215	161	1	12	11	62	5	12	17	18

NABOKOV, EVGENI G

PERSONAL: Born July 25, 1975, in Kamenogorsk, U.S.S.R. ... 6-0/200. ... Catches left. ... Name pronounced ehv-GEH-nee nuh-BAH-kahf.

TRANSACTIONS/CAREER NOTES: Selected by San Jose Sharks in ninth round (ninth Sharks pick, 219th overall) of entry draft (June 29, 1994). ... Injured chest (March 13, 2003); missed four games. ... Injured groin (November 21, 2003); missed six games. ... Left team for personal reasons (January 5, 2004); missed one game. ... Left team for personal reasons (January 19, 2004); missed one game. ... Injured shoulder (October 21, 2005); missed eight games. ... Strained groin (December 2, 2005); missed two games. ... Sore groin (January 16, 2006); missed two games. ... Re-signed by Sharks to multiyear contract extension (February 7, 2006). ... Abdominal injury (March 9, 2006); missed five games.

		REGULAR SEASON										PLAYOFFS							
Season Team	League	GP	Min.	W	L	OTL	T	GA	SO	GAA	SV%	GP	Min.	W	L	GA	SO	GAA	SV%
92-93—Torpedo Ust-Kam.	CIS	4	109	...	...	...	...	5	...	2.75	...	—	—	—	—	—	—	—	—
93-94—Torpedo Ust-Kam.	CIS	11	539	...	...	...	...	29	0	3.23	...	—	—	—	—	—	—	—	—
94-95—Dynamo Moscow	CIS	37	2075	...	...	...	...	70	...	2.02	...	—	—	—	—	—	—	—	—
95-96—Dynamo Moscow	CIS	37	1948	...	...	...	...	70	...	2.16	...	6	298	...	...	7	...	1.41	...
96-97—Dynamo Moscow	Russian	27	1588	...	...	...	...	56	2	2.12	...	4	255	...	...	12	0	2.82	...
97-98—Kentucky	AHL	33	1867	10	21	...	2	122	0	3.92	.872	1	23	0	0	1	0	2.61	.923
98-99—Kentucky	AHL	43	2429	26	14	...	1	106	5	2.62	.909	11	599	6	5	30	2	3.01	.907
99-00—Cleveland	IHL	20	1164	16	4	...	3	52	0	2.68	...	—	—	—	—	—	—	—	—
—San Jose	NHL	11	414	2	2	...	1	15	1	2.17	.910	1	20	0	0	0	0	0.00	1.00
—Kentucky	AHL	2	120	1	1	...	0	3	1	1.50	...	—	—	—	—	—	—	—	—
00-01—San Jose	NHL	66	3700	32	21	...	7	135	6	2.19	.915	4	218	1	3	10	1	2.75	.903
01-02—San Jose	NHL	67	3901	37	24	...	5	149	7	2.29	.918	12	712	7	5	31	0	2.61	.904
02-03—San Jose	NHL	55	3227	19	28	...	8	146	3	2.71	.906	—	—	—	—	—	—	—	—
03-04—San Jose	NHL	59	3456	31	19	...	8	127	9	2.20	.921	17	1052	10	7	30	3	1.71	.935
04-05—Metal. Magnitogorsk	Russian	14	808	...	...	...	...	27	3	2.00	...	5	307	...	...	13	0	2.53	...
05-06—San Jose	NHL	45	2575	16	19	7	...	133	1	3.10	.885	1	12	0	0	1	0	5.00	.750
—Russian Oly. team	Int'l	7	...	...	...	...	...	...	3	1.34	.940	—	—	—	—	—	—	—	—
NHL Totals (6 years)		303	17273	137	113	7	29	705	27	2.45	.911	35	2014	18	15	72	4	2.14	.920

NAGY, LADISLAV LW

PERSONAL: Born June 1, 1979, in Saca, Czechoslovakia. ... 5-11/192. ... Shoots left.

TRANSACTIONS/CAREER NOTES: Selected by St. Louis Blues in seventh round (eighth Blues pick, 177th overall) of entry draft (June 21, 1997). ... Traded by Blues with C Michal Handzus, C Jeff Taffe and first-round pick (LW Ben Eager) in 2002 to Phoenix Coyotes for LW Keith Tkachuk (March 13, 2001). ... Knee (October 24, 2001); missed seven games. ... Shoulder (November 10, 2001); missed one game. ... Groin (October 16, 2003); missed one game. ... Eye (January 14, 2004); missed two games. ... Fractured left wrist (February 17, 2004); missed remainder of season. ... Shoulder (September 30, 2005); missed first two games of season. ... Knee surgery (February 3, 2006); missed season's final 29 games.

STATISTICAL PLATEAUS: Three-goal games: 2003-04 (1).

		REGULAR SEASON								PLAYOFFS				
Season Team	League	GP	G	A	Pts.	PIM	+/-	PP	SH	GP	G	A	Pts.	PIM
96-97—Dragon Presov	Slov. Div.	11	6	5	11	...	...	...	...	—	—	—	—	—
97-98—HC Kosice	Slovakia	29	19	15	34	41	...	...	...	—	—	—	—	—
98-99—Halifax	QMJHL	63	71	55	126	148	55	14	13	5	3	3	6	18
—Worcester	AHL	...	...	...	...	...	...	...	...	3	2	2	4	0
99-00—Worcester	AHL	69	23	28	51	67	...	...	...	2	1	0	1	0
—St. Louis	NHL	11	2	4	6	2	2	1	0	6	1	1	2	0
00-01—St. Louis	NHL	40	8	8	16	20	-2	2	0	—	—	—	—	—
—Worcester	AHL	20	6	14	20	36	...	...	...	—	—	—	—	—
—Phoenix	NHL	6	0	1	1	2	0	0	0	—	—	—	—	—

Season Team	League	REGULAR SEASON								PLAYOFFS				
		GP	G	A	Pts.	PIM	+/-	PP	SH	GP	G	A	Pts.	PIM
01-02—Phoenix	NHL	74	23	19	42	50	6	5	0	5	0	0	0	21
02-03—Phoenix	NHL	80	22	35	57	92	17	8	0	—	—	—	—	—
03-04—Phoenix	NHL	55	24	28	52	46	11	11	0	—	—	—	—	—
04-05—HC Kosice	Slovakia	18	9	7	16	40	...	...	...	—	—	—	—	—
—Mora	Sweden Dv. 1	19	4	4	8	22	-12	0	0	—	—	—	—	—
05-06—Phoenix	NHL	51	15	41	56	74	8	7	1	—	—	—	—	—
NHL Totals (6 years)		317	94	136	230	286	42	34	1	11	1	1	2	21

NASH, RICK LW

PERSONAL: Born June 16, 1984, in Brampton, Ont. ... 6-4/206. ... Shoots left.
TRANSACTIONS/CAREER NOTES: Selected by Columbus Blue Jackets in first round (first Blue Jackets pick, first overall) of entry draft (June 22, 2002). ... Concussion, eye (October 14, 2003); missed one game. ... Bruised tailbone (December 9, 2002); missed four games. ... Hip pointer (January 23, 2003); missed three games. ... Bruised foot (January 31, 2004); missed two games. ... High ankle strain (September 14, 2005); missed 11 games. ... Sprained knee (November 3, 2005); missed 17 games.

Season Team	League	REGULAR SEASON								PLAYOFFS				
		GP	G	A	Pts.	PIM	+/-	PP	SH	GP	G	A	Pts.	PIM
00-01—London	OHL	58	31	35	66	56	...	...	...	4	3	3	6	8
01-02—London	OHL	54	32	40	72	88	...	...	...	12	10	9	19	21
02-03—Columbus	NHL	74	17	22	39	78	-27	6	0	—	—	—	—	—
03-04—Columbus	NHL	80	†41	16	57	87	-35	*19	0	—	—	—	—	—
04-05—Davos	Switzerland	44	26	20	46	81	...	10	1	15	9	2	11	26
05-06—Columbus	NHL	54	31	23	54	51	5	11	0	—	—	—	—	—
—Canadian Oly. team	Int'l	6	0	1	1	10	-2	0	0	—	—	—	—	—
NHL Totals (3 years)		208	89	61	150	216	-57	36	0					

NASH, TYSON LW

PERSONAL: Born March 11, 1975, in Edmonton. ... 5-11/191. ... Shoots left.
TRANSACTIONS/CAREER NOTES: Selected by Vancouver Canucks in 10th round (eighth Canucks pick, 247th overall) of entry draft (June 29, 1994). ... Signed as free agent by St. Louis Blues (July 24, 1998). ... Concussion (December 5, 1999); missed three games. ... Shoulder (March 11, 2000); missed season's final 13 games. ... Shoulder (December 5, 2000); missed one game. ... Knee (February 11, 2001); missed 16 games. ... Knee (March 22, 2001); missed remainder of season. ... Knee and abdominal surgery (summer 2001); missed season's first four games. ... Elbow (November 13, 2001); missed two games. ... Hip pointer (December 28, 2001); missed six games. ... Fractured nose (January 26, 2002); missed one game. ... Traded by Blues for fifth-round pick (RW Lee Stempniak) in 2003 to Phoenix Coyotes (June 22, 2003). ... Sprained right knee (January 16, 2004); missed four games. ... Suspended two games for slashing incident (February 10, 2004). ... Hip (November 5, 2005); missed nine games. ... Abdominal strain(December 3, 2005); missed 16 games. ... Right knee (April 10, 2006); missed season's final five games.

Season Team	League	REGULAR SEASON								PLAYOFFS				
		GP	G	A	Pts.	PIM	+/-	PP	SH	GP	G	A	Pts.	PIM
90-91—Kamloops	WHL	3	0	0	0	0	...	...	...	—	—	—	—	—
91-92—Kamloops	WHL	33	1	6	7	32	...	...	...	4	0	0	0	0
92-93—Kamloops	WHL	61	10	16	26	78	...	...	...	13	3	2	5	32
93-94—Kamloops	WHL	65	20	36	56	137	...	...	...	16	3	3	6	12
94-95—Kamloops	WHL	63	34	41	75	70	39	9	0	21	10	7	17	30
95-96—Syracuse	AHL	50	4	7	11	58	...	...	...	4	0	0	0	11
—Raleigh	ECHL	6	1	1	2	8	...	...	...	—	—	—	—	—
96-97—Syracuse	AHL	77	17	17	34	105	-17	2	1	3	0	2	2	0
97-98—Syracuse	AHL	74	20	20	40	184	-5	3	0	5	0	2	2	28
98-99—Worcester	AHL	55	14	22	36	143	-2	4	4	4	4	1	5	27
—St. Louis	NHL	2	0	0	0	5	-1	0	0	1	0	0	0	2
99-00—St. Louis	NHL	66	4	9	13	150	6	0	1	6	1	0	1	24
00-01—St. Louis	NHL	57	8	7	15	110	8	0	1	—	—	—	—	—
01-02—St. Louis	NHL	64	6	7	13	100	2	0	0	9	0	1	1	20
02-03—St. Louis	NHL	66	6	3	9	114	0	1	0	7	2	1	3	6
03-04—Phoenix	NHL	69	3	5	8	110	-6	0	0	—	—	—	—	—
05-06—Phoenix	NHL	50	0	6	6	84	-7	0	0	—	—	—	—	—
NHL Totals (7 years)		374	27	37	64	673	2	1	2	23	3	2	5	52

NASLUND, MARKUS LW

PERSONAL: Born July 30, 1973, in Ornskoldsvik, Sweden. ... 5-11/195. ... Shoots left. ... Name pronounced NAZ-luhnd.
TRANSACTIONS/CAREER NOTES: Selected by Pittsburgh Penguins in first round (first Penguins pick, 16th overall) of NHL draft (June 22, 1991). ... Traded by Penguins to Vancouver Canucks for LW Alex Stojanov (March 20, 1996). ... Flu (November 26, 1996); missed one game. ... Fractured leg (March 16, 2001); missed remainder of season. ... Injured groin (December 6, 2003); missed one game. ... Concussion (February 17, 2004); missed three games. ... Injured hip (January 26, 2006); missed one game.
STATISTICAL PLATEAUS: Three-goal games: 1995-96 (1), 1998-99 (1), 2000-01 (1), 2001-02 (3), 2002-03 (1). Total: 7. ... Four-goal games: 2002-03 (1), 2003-04 (1). Total: 2. ... Total hat tricks: 9.

Season Team	League	REGULAR SEASON								PLAYOFFS				
		GP	G	A	Pts.	PIM	+/-	PP	SH	GP	G	A	Pts.	PIM
89-90—MoDo Hockey	Sweden Jr.	33	43	35	78	20	...	...	...	—	—	—	—	—
90-91—MoDo Ornskoldsvik	Sweden	32	10	9	19	14	...	...	...	—	—	—	—	—
91-92—MoDo Ornskoldsvik	Sweden	39	22	18	40	54	...	...	...	—	—	—	—	—
92-93—MoDo Ornskoldsvik	Sweden	39	22	17	39	67	...	...	...	3	3	2	5	...
93-94—Pittsburgh	NHL	71	4	7	11	27	-3	1	0	—	—	—	—	—

Season Team	League	GP	G	A	Pts.	PIM	+/-	PP	SH	GP	G	A	Pts.	PIM
		REGULAR SEASON								PLAYOFFS				
—Cleveland	IHL	5	1	6	7	4	0	0	0	—	—	—	—	—
94-95—Pittsburgh	NHL	14	2	2	4	2	0	0	0	—	—	—	—	—
—Cleveland	IHL	7	3	4	7	6	4	0	0	4	1	3	4	8
95-96—Pittsburgh	NHL	66	19	33	52	36	17	3	0	—	—	—	—	—
—Vancouver	NHL	10	3	0	3	6	3	1	0	6	1	2	3	8
96-97—Vancouver	NHL	78	21	20	41	30	-15	4	0	—	—	—	—	—
97-98—Vancouver	NHL	76	14	20	34	56	5	2	1	—	—	—	—	—
98-99—Vancouver	NHL	80	36	30	66	74	-13	15	2	—	—	—	—	—
99-00—Vancouver	NHL	82	27	38	65	64	-5	6	2	—	—	—	—	—
00-01—Vancouver	NHL	72	41	34	75	58	-2	18	1	—	—	—	—	—
01-02—Vancouver	NHL	81	40	50	90	50	22	8	0	6	1	1	2	2
—Swedish Oly. team	Int'l	4	2	1	3	0	...	...	...	—	—	—	—	—
02-03—Vancouver	NHL	82	48	56	104	52	6	24	0	14	5	9	14	18
03-04—Vancouver	NHL	78	35	49	84	58	24	5	0	7	2	7	9	2
04-05—MoDo Ornskoldsvik	Sweden	13	8	9	17	8	1	3	0	6	0	1	1	10
05-06—Vancouver	NHL	81	32	47	79	66	-19	13	0	—	—	—	—	—
NHL Totals (12 years)		871	322	386	708	579	20	100	6	33	9	19	28	30

NASREDDINE, ALAIN D

PERSONAL: Born July 10, 1975, in Montreal. ... 6-1/201. ... Shoots left. ... Name pronounced AL-ain NAS-rih-DEEN.

TRANSACTIONS/CAREER NOTES: Selected by Florida Panthers in sixth round (eighth Panthers pick, 135th overall) of NHL entry draft (June 26, 1993). ... Traded by Panthers to Chicago Blackhawks for D Ivan Droppa (December 8, 1996). ... Traded by Blackhawks with G Jeff Hackett, D Eric Weinrich and fourth-round pick (D Chris Dyment) in 1999 draft to Montreal Canadiens for G Jocelyn Thibault, D Dave Manson and D Brad Brown (November 16, 1998). ... Suspended two games and fined $1,000 for physically demeaning a linesman (December 11, 1998). ... Traded by Canadiens with D Igor Ulanov to Edmonton Oilers for D Christian LaFlamme and D Mathieu Descoteaux (March 9, 2000). ... Signed as free agent by New York Islanders (October 2, 2002). ... Traded by Islanders to Pittsburgh Penguins for F Steve Webb (March 8, 2004). ... Signed as free agent by Wilkes-Barre/Scranton of the AHL (September 26, 2004).

Season Team	League	GP	G	A	Pts.	PIM	+/-	PP	SH	GP	G	A	Pts.	PIM
		REGULAR SEASON								PLAYOFFS				
91-92—Drummondville	QMJHL	61	1	9	10	78	...	...	...	4	0	0	0	17
92-93—Drummondville	QMJHL	64	0	14	14	137	...	...	...	10	0	1	1	36
93-94—Chicoutimi	QMJHL	60	3	24	27	218	11	1	0	26	2	10	12	118
94-95—Chicoutimi	QMJHL	67	8	31	39	342	10	4	0	13	3	5	8	40
95-96—Carolina	AHL	63	0	5	5	245	...	...	...	—	—	—	—	—
96-97—Carolina	AHL	26	0	4	4	109	2	0	0	—	—	—	—	—
—Indianapolis	IHL	49	0	2	2	248	...	...	...	4	1	1	2	27
97-98—Indianapolis	IHL	75	1	12	13	258	5	0	0	5	0	2	2	12
98-99—Chicago	NHL	7	0	0	0	19	-2	0	0	—	—	—	—	—
—Portland	AHL	7	0	1	1	36	-3	0	0	—	—	—	—	—
—Fredericton	AHL	38	0	10	10	108	7	0	0	15	0	3	3	39
—Montreal	NHL	8	0	0	0	33	1	0	0	—	—	—	—	—
99-00—Quebec	AHL	59	1	6	7	178	...	...	...	—	—	—	—	—
—Hamilton	AHL	11	0	0	0	12	...	...	...	10	1	1	2	14
00-01—Hamilton	AHL	74	4	14	18	164	...	...	...	—	—	—	—	—
01-02—Hamilton	AHL	79	7	10	17	154	9	1	0	12	1	3	4	22
02-03—New York Islanders	NHL	3	0	0	0	2	0	0	0	—	—	—	—	—
—Bridgeport	AHL	67	3	9	12	114	7	0	0	9	0	0	0	27
03-04—Bridgeport	AHL	53	1	6	7	70	-1	1	0	—	—	—	—	—
—Wilkes-Barre/Scranton	AHL	17	1	1	2	16	6	0	0	24	1	0	1	48
04-05—Wilkes-Barre/Scranton	AHL	75	3	15	18	129	5	1	0	11	0	1	1	18
05-06—Wilkes-Barre/Scranton	AHL	71	0	12	12	71	24	0	0	—	—	—	—	—
—Pittsburgh	NHL	6	0	0	0	8	2	0	0	—	—	—	—	—
NHL Totals (3 years)		24	0	0	0	62	1	0	0					

N

NAZAROV, ANDREI LW/RW

PERSONAL: Born May 22, 1974, in Chelyabinsk, U.S.S.R. ... 6-5/243. ... Shoots right. ... Name pronounced nuh-ZAH-rahf.

TRANSACTIONS/CAREER NOTES: Selected by San Jose Sharks in first round (second Sharks pick, 10th overall) of NHL draft (June 20, 1992). ... Suspended four games and fined $500 for head-butting (March 8, 1995). ... Fractured facial bones (February 5, 1997); missed 14 games. ... Suspended 13 games for physical abuse of officials (March 25, 1997). ... Knee (October 13, 1997); missed seven games. ... Traded by Sharks with first-round pick (C Vincent Lecavalier) in 1998 to Tampa Bay Lightning for D Bryan Marchment, D David Shaw and first-round pick (traded to Nashville; Predators selected C David Legwand) in 1998 (March 24, 1998). ... Finger (November 8, 1998); missed one game. ... Suspended seven games and fined $1,000 by NHL in cross-checking incident (November 19, 1998). ... Traded by Lightning to Calgary Flames for C Michael Nylander (January 19, 1999). ... Traded by Flames with second-round pick (returned to Calgary; Flames selected C Andrei Taratukhin) in 2001 to Anaheim Mighty Ducks for D Jordan Leopold (September 26, 2000). ... Traded by Mighty Ducks with D Patrick Traverse to Boston Bruins for C Samuel Pahlsson (November 18, 2000). ... Traded by Bruins to Phoenix Coyotes for fifth-round pick (G Peter Hamerlik) in 2002 (January 25, 2002). ... Suspended four games for receiving match penalty in game (March 10, 2003). ... Suspended two games for receiving match penalty in game (February 26, 2004). ... Signed as free agent by Minnesota Wild (August 1, 2005).

Season Team	League	GP	G	A	Pts.	PIM	+/-	PP	SH	GP	G	A	Pts.	PIM
		REGULAR SEASON								PLAYOFFS				
90-91—Mechel Chelyabinsk	USSR	2	0	0	0	0	...	...	...	—	—	—	—	—
91-92—Dynamo Moscow	CIS	2	1	0	1	2	...	...	...	—	—	—	—	—
92-93—Dynamo Moscow	CIS	42	8	2	10	79	...	...	...	10	1	1	2	8
93-94—Kansas City	IHL	71	15	18	33	64	-15	6	0	—	—	—	—	—
—San Jose	NHL	1	0	0	0	0	0	0	0	—	—	—	—	—
94-95—Kansas City	IHL	43	15	10	25	55	3	2	0	—	—	—	—	—

Season Team	League	REGULAR SEASON GP	G	A	Pts.	PIM	+/-	PP	SH	PLAYOFFS GP	G	A	Pts.	PIM
—San Jose	NHL	26	3	5	8	94	-1	0	0	6	0	0	0	9
95-96—San Jose	NHL	42	7	7	14	62	-15	2	0	—	—	—	—	—
—Kansas City	IHL	27	4	6	10	118	...	...	...	2	0	0	0	2
96-97—San Jose	NHL	60	12	15	27	222	-4	1	0	—	—	—	—	—
—Kentucky	AHL	3	1	2	3	4	-2	0	0	—	—	—	—	—
97-98—San Jose	NHL	40	1	1	2	112	-4	0	0	—	—	—	—	—
—Tampa Bay	NHL	14	1	1	2	58	-9	0	0	—	—	—	—	—
98-99—Tampa Bay	NHL	26	2	0	2	43	-5	0	0	—	—	—	—	—
—Calgary	NHL	36	5	9	14	30	1	0	0	—	—	—	—	—
99-00—Calgary	NHL	76	10	22	32	78	3	1	0	—	—	—	—	—
00-01—Anaheim	NHL	16	1	0	1	29	-9	0	0	—	—	—	—	—
—Boston	NHL	63	1	4	5	200	-14	0	0	—	—	—	—	—
01-02—Boston	NHL	47	0	2	2	164	-2	0	0	—	—	—	—	—
—Phoenix	NHL	30	6	3	9	51	7	0	0	3	0	0	0	2
02-03—Phoenix	NHL	59	3	0	3	135	-9	2	0	—	—	—	—	—
03-04—Phoenix	NHL	33	1	2	3	125	-7	0	0	—	—	—	—	—
04-05—Metallurg Novokuznetsk	Russian	9	0	0	0	20	-6	...	...	—	—	—	—	—
—Avangard Omsk	Russian	23	0	2	2	153	-4	...	...	10	0	0	0	10
05-06—Houston	AHL	1	0	0	0	0	0	0	0	—	—	—	—	—
—Minnesota	NHL	2	0	0	0	6	-1	0	0	—	—	—	—	—
NHL Totals (12 years)		571	53	71	124	1409	-69	6	0	9	0	0	0	11

NEDVED, PETR C/LW

PERSONAL: Born December 9, 1971, in Liberec, Czech. ... 6-3/196. ... Shoots left. ... Name pronounced NEHD-vehd.

TRANSACTIONS/CAREER NOTES: Selected by Vancouver Canucks in first round (first Canucks pick, second overall) of entry draft (June 16, 1990). ... Signed to offer sheet by St. Louis Blues (March 4, 1994); C Craig Janney and second-round pick (C Dave Scatchard) in 1994 draft awarded to Canucks as compensation (March 14, 1994). ... Traded by Blues to New York Rangers for LW Esa Tikkanen and D Doug Lidster (July 24, 1994); trade arranged as compensation for Blues signing coach Mike Keenan. ... Strained abdomen (February 27, 1995); missed two games. ... Traded by Rangers with D Sergei Zubov to Pittsburgh Penguins for LW Luc Robitaille and D Ulf Samuelsson (August 31, 1995). ... Bruised thigh (November 18, 1995); missed two games. ... Bruised tailbone (December 19, 1996); missed two games. ... Sprained wrist (January 14, 1997); missed two games. ... Charley horse (February 8, 1997); missed one game. ... Sprained wrist (March 20, 1997); missed three games. ... Missed all of 1997-98 season and first 18 games of 1998-99 season in contract dispute. ... Traded by Penguins with C Sean Pronger and D Chris Tamer to Rangers for RW Alexei Kovalev and C Harry York (November 25, 1998). ... Strained rib cage muscle (April 2, 1999); missed final seven games of season. ... Strained groin (December 2, 1999); missed four games. ... Bruised ribs (March 15, 2000); missed two games. ... Suspended three games for high-sticking incident (December 12, 2000). ... Concussion (October 31, 2001); missed four games. ... Hip pointer (December 21, 2002); missed four games. ... Strained lower back (November 2, 2003); missed one game. ... Traded by Rangers with G Jussi Markkanen to Edmonton Oilers for G Stephen Valiquette, C Dwight Helminen and a second-round pick (C Brandon Dubinsky) in 2004 draft (March 3, 2004). ... Signed as free agent by Phoenix Coyotes (August 26, 2004). ... Strained groin (October 5, 2005); missed three games. ... Injured elbow (October 30, 2005); missed nine games. ... Concussion (November 23, 2005); missed three games. ... Strained groin (December 26, 2005); missed four games. ... Traded by Coyotes to Philadelphia Flyers for D Dennis Seidenberg (January 20, 2006). ... Groin (February 4, 2006); missed one game. ... Groin (February 8, 2006); missed two games. ... Groin (April 2, 2006); missed four games.

STATISTICAL PLATEAUS: Three-goal games: 1998-99 (1), 1999-00 (3), 2000-01 (1), 2002-03 (1). Total: 6. ... Four-goal games: 1995-96 (1). ... Total hat tricks: 7.

Season Team	League	REGULAR SEASON GP	G	A	Pts.	PIM	+/-	PP	SH	PLAYOFFS GP	G	A	Pts.	PIM
88-89—Litvinov	Czech. Jrs.	20	32	19	51	12	...	...	...	—	—	—	—	—
89-90—Seattle	WHL	71	65	80	145	80	...	...	...	11	4	9	13	2
90-91—Vancouver	NHL	61	10	6	16	20	-21	1	0	6	0	1	1	0
91-92—Vancouver	NHL	77	15	22	37	36	-3	5	0	10	1	4	5	16
92-93—Vancouver	NHL	84	38	33	71	96	20	2	1	12	2	3	5	2
93-94—Canadian nat'l team	Int'l	17	19	12	31	16	...	...	...	—	—	—	—	—
—Can. Olympic team	Int'l	8	5	1	6	6	4	2	0	—	—	—	—	—
—St. Louis	NHL	19	6	14	20	8	2	2	0	4	0	1	1	4
94-95—New York Rangers	NHL	46	11	12	23	26	-1	1	0	10	3	2	5	6
95-96—Pittsburgh	NHL	80	45	54	99	68	37	8	1	18	10	10	20	16
96-97—Pittsburgh	NHL	74	33	38	71	66	-2	12	3	5	1	2	3	12
97-98—Sparta Praha	Czech Rep.	5	2	3	5	8	...	...	...	6	0	2	2	52
—Las Vegas	IHL	3	3	3	6	4	-4	2	0	—	—	—	—	—
98-99—Las Vegas	IHL	13	8	10	18	32	6	2	0	—	—	—	—	—
—New York Rangers	NHL	56	20	27	47	50	-6	9	1	—	—	—	—	—
99-00—New York Rangers	NHL	76	24	44	68	40	2	6	2	—	—	—	—	—
00-01—New York Rangers	NHL	79	32	46	78	54	10	9	1	—	—	—	—	—
01-02—New York Rangers	NHL	78	21	25	46	36	-8	6	1	—	—	—	—	—
02-03—New York Rangers	NHL	78	27	31	58	64	-4	8	3	—	—	—	—	—
03-04—New York Rangers	NHL	65	14	17	31	42	-9	5	0	—	—	—	—	—
—Edmonton	NHL	16	5	10	15	4	1	2	0	—	—	—	—	—
04-05—Sparta Praha	Czech Rep.	46	22	13	35	44	11	...	...	5	2	3	5	10
05-06—Phoenix	NHL	25	2	9	11	34	-6	1	0	—	—	—	—	—
—Philadelphia	NHL	28	5	9	14	36	-8	2	0	6	2	0	2	8
NHL Totals (14 years)		942	308	397	705	680	4	79	13	71	19	23	42	64

NEIL, CHRIS RW/LW

PERSONAL: Born June 18, 1979, in Markdale, Ont. ... 6-0/216. ... Shoots right.

TRANSACTIONS/CAREER NOTES: Selected by Ottawa Senators in sixth round (seventh Senators pick, 161st overall) of NHL entry draft (June 27, 1998). ... Injured hip (March 19, 2002); missed one game. ... Reinjured hip (March 24, 2002); missed three games. ... Fractured left leg (September 21, 2002); missed 12 games. ... Person absence (November 22, 2005); missed three games.

Season Team	League	GP	G	A	Pts.	PIM	+/-	PP	SH	GP	G	A	Pts.	PIM
		REGULAR SEASON								PLAYOFFS				
96-97—North Bay	OHL	65	13	16	29	150	...	...	...	—	—	—	—	—
97-98—North Bay	OHL	59	26	29	55	231	-8	...	...	—	—	—	—	—
98-99—North Bay	OHL	66	26	46	72	215	2	...	...	4	1	0	1	15
99-00—Grand Rapids	IHL	51	9	10	19	301	...	...	...	8	0	2	2	24
—Mobile	ECHL	4	0	2	2	39	...	...	...	—	—	—	—	—
00-01—Grand Rapids	IHL	78	15	21	36	354	...	...	...	10	2	2	4	22
01-02—Ottawa	NHL	72	10	7	17	231	5	1	0	12	0	0	0	12
02-03—Ottawa	NHL	68	6	4	10	147	8	0	0	15	1	0	1	24
03-04—Ottawa	NHL	82	8	8	16	194	13	0	0	7	0	1	1	19
04-05—Binghamton	AHL	22	4	6	10	132	10	1	0	6	1	1	2	26
05-06—Ottawa	NHL	79	16	17	33	204	9	8	0	10	1	0	1	14
NHL Totals (4 years)		301	40	36	76	776	35	9	0	44	2	1	3	69

NEUVIRTH, MICHAL G

PERSONAL: Born March 23, 1988, in Usti Labem, Cze. ... 6-0/174. ... Catches left.

TRANSACTIONS/CAREER NOTES: Selected by Washington Capitals in second round (third Capitals pick; 34th overall) of NHL draft (June 24, 2006).

Season Team	League	GP	Min.	W	L	OTL	T	GA	SO	GAA	SV%	GP	Min.	W	L	GA	SO	GAA	SV%
		REGULAR SEASON										PLAYOFFS							
04-05—Sparta Prague	Czech. Jrs.	10	501	...	...	...	...	20	1	2.40	.921	—	—	—	—	—	—	—	—
05-06—Sparta Prague	Czech. Jrs.	45	2695	...	...	...	...	91	5	2.02	.937	—	—	—	—	—	—	—	—

NICHOL, SCOTT C

PERSONAL: Born December 31, 1974, in Edmonton. ... 5-8/173. ... Shoots right.

TRANSACTIONS/CAREER NOTES: Selected by Buffalo Sabres in 11th round (ninth Sabres pick, 272nd overall) of entry draft (June 26, 1993). ... Signed as free agent by Calgary Flames (August 2, 2001). ... Hand (October 10, 2001); missed one game. ... Hip (October 25, 2001); missed one game. ... Suspended two games for unsportsmanlike conduct (December 10, 2001). ... Hip (January 5, 2002); missed three games. ... Knee (February 26, 2002); missed 14 games. ... Suspended five games for butt-ending (December 20, 2002). ... Signed by Chicago Blackhawks as free agent (July 1, 2003). ... Groin (January 27, 2004); missed five games. ... Suspended two games in slashing incident (March 27, 2004). ... Signed as free agent by Nashville Predators (August 6, 2005). ... Groin (October 4, 2005); missed one game. ... Broken foot (November 15, 2005); missed 27 games. ... Concussion (February 1, 2006); missed four games.

Season Team	League	GP	G	A	Pts.	PIM	+/-	PP	SH	GP	G	A	Pts.	PIM
		REGULAR SEASON								PLAYOFFS				
92-93—Portland	WHL	67	31	33	64	146	...	...	...	—	—	—	—	—
93-94—Portland	WHL	65	40	53	93	144	...	...	...	—	—	—	—	—
94-95—Rochester	AHL	71	11	16	27	136	-12	1	4	5	0	3	3	14
95-96—Rochester	AHL	62	14	17	31	170	...	...	...	19	7	6	13	36
—Buffalo	NHL	2	0	0	0	10	0	0	0	—	—	—	—	—
96-97—Rochester	AHL	68	22	21	43	133	9	1	4	10	2	1	3	26
97-98—Rochester	AHL	35	13	7	20	113	-10	1	1	—	—	—	—	—
—Buffalo	NHL	3	0	0	0	4	0	0	0	—	—	—	—	—
98-99—Rochester	AHL	53	13	20	33	120	19	1	0	—	—	—	—	—
99-00—Rochester	AHL	37	7	11	18	141	...	...	...	—	—	—	—	—
00-01—Detroit	IHL	67	7	24	31	198	...	...	...	—	—	—	—	—
01-02—Calgary	NHL	60	8	9	17	107	-9	2	1	—	—	—	—	—
02-03—Calgary	NHL	68	5	5	10	149	-7	0	1	—	—	—	—	—
03-04—Chicago	NHL	75	7	11	18	145	-16	0	0	—	—	—	—	—
04-05—London	England	15	7	12	19	86	...	1	0	—	—	—	—	—
05-06—Milwaukee	AHL	6	3	5	8	18	6	0	1	—	—	—	—	—
—Nashville	NHL	34	3	3	6	79	3	0	1	3	0	0	0	2
NHL Totals (6 years)		242	23	28	51	494	-29	2	3	3	0	0	0	2

NICKULAS, ERIC RW

PERSONAL: Born March 25, 1975, in Hyannis, Mass. ... 5-11/206. ... Shoots right. ... Name pronounced NICK-luhs.

TRANSACTIONS/CAREER NOTES: Selected by Boston Bruins in fourth round (third Bruins pick, 99th overall) of entry draft (June 29, 1994). ... Charley horse (September 22, 2000); missed season's first three games. ... Bruised ribs (October 14, 2000); missed two games. ... Signed as free agent by St. Louis Blues (July 16, 2002). ... Claimed off waivers by Chicago Blackhawks (February 24, 2004). ... Signed as free agent by Bruins (August 23, 2005). ... Signed by Hannover of German league (June 19, 2006).

Season Team	League	GP	G	A	Pts.	PIM	+/-	PP	SH	GP	G	A	Pts.	PIM
		REGULAR SEASON								PLAYOFFS				
91-92—Barnstable H.S.	Mass. Jr.	24	30	25	55	...	...	...	...	—	—	—	—	—
92-93—Tabor Academy	Mass. H.S.	28	25	25	50	...	...	...	...	—	—	—	—	—
93-94—Cushing Academy	Mass. H.S.	25	46	36	82	...	...	...	...	—	—	—	—	—
94-95—New Hampshire	Hockey East	33	15	9	24	32	...	1	1	—	—	—	—	—
95-96—New Hampshire	Hockey East	34	26	12	38	66	...	...	...	—	—	—	—	—
96-97—New Hampshire	Hockey East	39	29	22	51	80	...	7	1	—	—	—	—	—
97-98—Orlando	IHL	76	22	9	31	77	5	3	1	6	0	0	0	10
98-99—Providence	AHL	75	31	27	58	83	13	15	0	18	8	12	20	33
—Boston	NHL	2	0	0	0	0	0	0	0	1	0	0	0	2
99-00—Providence	AHL	40	6	6	12	37	...	...	...	12	2	3	5	20
—Boston	NHL	20	5	6	11	12	-1	1	0	—	—	—	—	—
00-01—Boston	NHL	7	0	0	0	4	-2	0	0	—	—	—	—	—
—Providence	AHL	62	20	23	43	100	...	...	...	12	4	4	8	24

Season Team	League	GP	G	A	Pts.	PIM	+/-	PP	SH	GP	G	A	Pts.	PIM
		REGULAR SEASON								PLAYOFFS				
01-02—Worcester	AHL	54	11	25	36	48	19	2	1	3	0	1	1	2
02-03—St. Louis	NHL	8	0	1	1	6	-2	0	0	—	—	—	—	—
—Worcester	AHL	39	17	16	33	40	7	7	2	3	0	0	0	2
03-04—St. Louis	NHL	44	7	11	18	44	-2	1	0	—	—	—	—	—
—Chicago	NHL	21	1	1	2	8	-6	0	0	—	—	—	—	—
04-05—Norfolk	AHL	53	11	11	22	32	-7	4	1	6	0	3	3	8
05-06—Providence	AHL	38	10	16	26	46	-1	3	2	5	1	1	2	4
—Boston	NHL	16	2	4	6	8	2	0	0	—	—	—	—	—
NHL Totals (6 years)		118	15	23	38	82	-11	2	0	1	0	0	0	2

NIEDERMAYER, ROB C/LW

PERSONAL: Born December 28, 1974, in Cassiar, B.C. ... 6-2/205. ... Shoots left. ... Brother of Scott Niedermayer, D, Anaheim Mighty Ducks. ... Name pronounced NEE-duhr-MIGH-uhr.

TRANSACTIONS/CAREER NOTES: Selected by Florida Panthers in first round (first Panthers pick, fifth overall) of NHL draft (June 26, 1993). ... Separated right shoulder (November 18, 1993); missed 17 games. ... Sprained knee ligament (November 22, 1996); missed 17 games. ... Strained groin (March 5, 1997); missed two games. ... Sprained wrist (March 20, 1997); missed three games. ... Concussion (October 1, 1997); missed 10 games. ... Dislocated right thumb (November 18, 1997); missed 15 games. ... Knee surgery during 1997-98 All-Star break; missed eight games. ... Postconcussion syndrome (March 19, 1998); missed remainder of season. ... Injured head (March 3, 2000); missed one game. ... Concussion (February 21, 2001); missed 15 games. ... Traded by Panthers with second-round pick (G Andrei Medvedev) in 2001 draft to Calgary Flames for RW Valeri Bure and C Jason Wiemer (June 23, 2001). ... Bruised hip (October 13, 2001); missed four games. ... Injured (November 17, 2001); missed one game. ... Sprained knee and ankle (January 8, 2002); missed 18 games. ... Injured (March 6, 2002); missed two games. ... Traded by Flames to Anaheim Mighty Ducks for D Mike Commodore and G J.F. Damphousse (March 11, 2003). ... Injured groin (December 2, 2003); missed 12 games. ... Reinjured groin (January 29, 2004); missed 14 games. ... Concussion (January 1, 2006); missed six games.

Season Team	League	GP	G	A	Pts.	PIM	+/-	PP	SH	GP	G	A	Pts.	PIM
		REGULAR SEASON								PLAYOFFS				
90-91—Medicine Hat	WHL	71	24	26	50	8	...	...	...	12	3	7	10	2
91-92—Medicine Hat	WHL	71	32	46	78	77	...	...	...	4	2	3	5	2
92-93—Medicine Hat	WHL	52	43	34	77	67	...	...	...	—	—	—	—	—
93-94—Florida	NHL	65	9	17	26	51	-11	3	0	—	—	—	—	—
94-95—Medicine Hat	WHL	13	9	15	24	14	-5	4	1	—	—	—	—	—
—Florida	NHL	48	4	6	10	36	-13	1	0	—	—	—	—	—
95-96—Florida	NHL	82	26	35	61	107	1	11	0	22	5	3	8	12
96-97—Florida	NHL	60	14	24	38	54	4	3	0	5	2	1	3	6
97-98—Florida	NHL	33	8	7	15	41	-9	5	0	—	—	—	—	—
98-99—Florida	NHL	82	18	33	51	50	-13	6	1	—	—	—	—	—
99-00—Florida	NHL	81	10	23	33	46	-5	1	0	4	1	0	1	6
00-01—Florida	NHL	67	12	20	32	50	-12	3	1	—	—	—	—	—
01-02—Calgary	NHL	57	6	14	20	49	-15	1	2	—	—	—	—	—
02-03—Calgary	NHL	54	8	10	18	42	-13	2	0	—	—	—	—	—
—Anaheim	NHL	12	2	2	4	15	3	1	0	21	3	7	10	18
03-04—Anaheim	NHL	55	12	16	28	34	-6	6	0	—	—	—	—	—
04-05—Ferencvaros	Hungary	5	2	1	3	14	...	...	...	—	—	—	—	—
05-06—Anaheim	NHL	76	15	24	39	89	-5	4	1	16	1	3	4	10
NHL Totals (12 years)		772	144	231	375	664	-94	47	5	68	12	14	26	52

NIEDERMAYER, SCOTT D

PERSONAL: Born August 31, 1973, in Edmonton. ... 6-1/200. ... Shoots left. ... Brother of Rob Niedermayer, C, Anaheim Mighty Ducks. ... Name pronounced NEE-duhr-MIGH-uhr.

TRANSACTIONS/CAREER NOTES: Selected by New Jersey Devils in first round (first Devils pick, third overall) of NHL draft (June 22, 1991). ... Sore back (December 9, 1992); missed four games. ... Injured knee (December 19, 1995); missed three games. ... Strained groin (February 12, 1997); missed one game. ... Flu (February 4, 1998); missed one game. ... Missed first nine games of 1998-99 season in contact dispute. ... Strained hip flexor (January 15, 2000); missed one game. ... Flu (January 26, 2000); missed one game. ... Suspended final nine games of regular season and one playoff game for high-sticking incident (March 21, 2000). ... Missed first 19 games of 2000-01 season in contract dispute. ... Injured knee (January 20, 2001); missed one game. ... Injured knee (February 8, 2001); missed five games. ... Strained lower back (October 5, 2001); missed first two games of season. ... Pinched nerve in neck (February 27, 2002); missed three games. ... Sore back (October 18, 2003); missed one game. ... Signed as free agent by Anaheim Mighty Ducks (August 4, 2005). ... Had arthroscopic knee surgery (February 13, 2006) during Olympic break; missed no games.

Season Team	League	GP	G	A	Pts.	PIM	+/-	PP	SH	GP	G	A	Pts.	PIM
		REGULAR SEASON								PLAYOFFS				
89-90—Kamloops	WHL	64	14	55	69	64	...	...	...	17	2	14	16	35
90-91—Kamloops	WHL	57	26	56	82	52	...	...	...	—	—	—	—	—
91-92—New Jersey	NHL	4	0	1	1	2	1	0	0	—	—	—	—	—
—Kamloops	WHL	35	7	32	39	61	...	...	...	17	9	14	23	28
92-93—New Jersey	NHL	80	11	29	40	47	8	5	0	5	0	3	3	2
93-94—New Jersey	NHL	81	10	36	46	42	34	5	0	20	2	2	4	8
94-95—New Jersey	NHL	48	4	15	19	18	19	4	0	20	4	7	11	10
95-96—New Jersey	NHL	79	8	25	33	46	5	6	0	—	—	—	—	—
96-97—New Jersey	NHL	81	5	30	35	64	-4	3	0	10	2	4	6	6
97-98—New Jersey	NHL	81	14	43	57	27	5	11	0	6	0	2	2	4
98-99—Utah	IHL	5	0	2	2	0	-5	0	0	—	—	—	—	—
—New Jersey	NHL	72	11	35	46	26	16	1	1	7	1	3	4	18
99-00—New Jersey	NHL	71	7	31	38	48	19	1	0	22	5	2	7	10
00-01—New Jersey	NHL	57	6	29	35	22	14	1	0	21	0	6	6	14
01-02—New Jersey	NHL	76	11	22	33	30	12	2	0	6	0	2	2	6

N

Season Team	League	GP	G	A	Pts.	PIM	+/-	PP	SH	GP	G	A	Pts.	PIM
		REGULAR SEASON								PLAYOFFS				
—Can. Olympic team	Int'l	6	1	1	2	4	...	...	...	—	—	—	—	—
02-03—New Jersey	NHL	81	11	28	39	62	23	3	0	24	2	*16	*18	16
03-04—New Jersey	NHL	81	14	40	54	44	20	9	0	5	1	0	1	6
05-06—Anaheim	NHL	82	13	50	63	96	8	9	0	16	2	9	11	14
NHL Totals (14 years)		974	125	414	539	574	180	60	1	162	19	56	75	114

NIEMINEN, VILLE — LW/RW

PERSONAL: Born April 6, 1977, in Tampere, Finland. ... 6-0/200. ... Shoots left. ... Name pronounced: VIHL-ee NEE-muh-nehn

TRANSACTIONS/CAREER NOTES: Selected by Colorado Avalanche in third round (fourth Avalanche pick, 78th overall) of entry draft (June 21, 1997). ... Concussion (October 13, 2001); missed six games. ... Traded by Avalanche with D Rick Berry to Pittsburgh Penguins for D Darius Kasparitis (March 19, 2002). ... Signed as free agent by Chicago Blackhawks (July 29, 2003). ... Traded by Blackhawks to Calgary Flames for C Jason Morgan and a conditional pick (February 24, 2004). ... Signed as unrestricted free agent by New York Rangers (August 4, 2005). ... Strained groin (September 29, 2005); missed first three games of season. ... Traded by Rangers to San Jose Sharks for third-round pick (traded to Anaheim; Ducks selected D John Degray) in 2006 draft (March 8, 2006).

Season Team	League	GP	G	A	Pts.	PIM	+/-	PP	SH	GP	G	A	Pts.	PIM
		REGULAR SEASON								PLAYOFFS				
94-95—Tappara Tampere	Finland Jr.	16	11	21	32	47	...	...	...	—	—	—	—	—
—Tappara Tampere	Finland	16	0	0	0	0	...	...	...	—	—	—	—	—
95-96—Tappara Tampere	Finland Jr.	20	20	23	43	63	...	...	...	—	—	—	—	—
—Tappara Tampere	Finland	4	0	1	1	8	...	...	...	—	—	—	—	—
—KooVee Tampere	Finland	7	2	1	3	4	...	...	...	—	—	—	—	—
96-97—Tappara Tampere	Finland	49	10	13	23	120	...	...	...	3	1	0	1	8
97-98—Hershey	AHL	74	14	22	36	85	6	2	0	—	—	—	—	—
98-99—Hershey	AHL	67	24	19	43	127	1	7	0	3	0	1	1	0
99-00—Hershey	AHL	74	21	30	51	54	...	...	...	9	2	4	6	6
—Colorado	NHL	1	0	0	0	0	0	0	0	—	—	—	—	—
00-01—Hershey	AHL	28	10	11	21	48	...	...	...	—	—	—	—	—
—Colorado	NHL	50	14	8	22	38	8	2	0	23	4	6	10	20
01-02—Colorado	NHL	53	10	14	24	30	1	1	0	—	—	—	—	—
—Fin. Olympic team	Int'l	4	0	1	1	2	...	...	...	—	—	—	—	—
—Pittsburgh	NHL	13	1	2	3	8	-2	0	0	—	—	—	—	—
02-03—Pittsburgh	NHL	75	9	12	21	93	-25	0	2	—	—	—	—	—
03-04—Chicago	NHL	60	2	11	13	40	-15	1	0	—	—	—	—	—
—Calgary	NHL	19	3	5	8	18	6	0	0	24	4	4	8	55
04-05—Tappara Tampere	Finland	26	14	13	27	32	3	...	...	8	2	4	6	12
05-06—New York Rangers	NHL	48	5	12	17	53	10	0	0	—	—	—	—	—
—San Jose	NHL	22	3	4	7	10	-3	0	1	11	0	2	2	24
—Fin. Olympic team	Int'l	8	0	1	1	4	1	0	0	—	—	—	—	—
NHL Totals (6 years)		341	47	68	115	290	-20	4	3	58	8	12	20	99

NIEUWENDYK, JOE — C

PERSONAL: Born September 10, 1966, in Oshawa, Ont. ... 6-2/205. ... Shoots left. ... Nephew of Ed Kea, D with two NHL teams (1973-83); and cousin of Jeff Beukeboom, D with two NHL teams (1985-99). ... Name pronounced NOO-ihn-dighk.

TRANSACTIONS/CAREER NOTES: Selected by Calgary Flames in second round (second Flames pick, 27th overall) of entry draft (June 15, 1985). ... Concussion (November 1987). ... Bruised ribs (May 25, 1989). ... Torn left knee ligament (April 17, 1990). ... Arthroscopic knee surgery (September 28, 1991); missed 12 games. ... Flu (November 19, 1992); missed one game. ... Strained right knee (March 26, 1993); missed four games. ... Charley horse (November 13, 1993); missed three games. ... Strained right knee ligaments (February 24, 1994); missed 17 games. ... Strained back (April 29, 1995); missed two games. ... Traded by Flames to Dallas Stars for C Corey Millen and rights to C/RW Jarome Iginla (December 19, 1995). ... Bruised chest (October 5, 1996); missed 12 games. ... Sprained knee (December 18, 1997); missed eight games. ... Reinjured knee (January 9, 1998); missed one game. ... Inflammed knee (January 10, 1999); missed five games. ... Sprained ankle (February 23, 1999); missed one game. ... Back spasms (March 16, 1999); missed one game. ... Injured knee (March 31, 1999); missed one game. ... Back spasms (October 20, 1999); missed three games. ... Bruised chest (December 17, 1999); missed 10 games. ... Separated shoulder (January 19, 2000); missed 21 games. ... Flu (January 4, 2001); missed two games. ... Strained groin (February 28, 2001); missed 11 games. ... Flu (February 10, 2002); missed one game. ... Traded by Stars with RW Jamie Langenbrunner to New Jersey Devils for C Jason Arnott, RW Randy McKay and first-round pick (traded to Columbus; traded to Buffalo; Sabres selected LW Dan Paille) in 2002 draft (March 19, 2002). ... Ill (March 13, 2003); missed one game. ... Injured hip (May 27, 2003); missed seven playoff games. ... Signed as free agent by Toronto Maple Leafs (September 9, 2003). ... Back spasms (November 2, 2003); missed seven games. ... Back spasms (November 20, 2003); missed four games. ... Injured ankle (December 13, 2003); missed one game. ... Injured rib cage (February 3, 2004); missed five games. ... Signed as free agent by Florida Panthers (August 1, 2005). ... Back spasms (October 18, 2005); missed 14 games. ... Injured back (November 26, 2005); missed one game. ... Injured back (December 13, 2005); missed two games.

STATISTICAL PLATEAUS: Three-goal games: 1987-88 (2), 1988-89 (1), 1989-90 (1), 1992-93 (1), 1993-94 (1), 1994-95 (1), 1997-98 (1), 2000-01 (1). Total: 9. ... Four-goal games: 1987-88 (2), 1997-98 (1). Total: 3. ... Five-goal games: 1988-89 (1). ... Total hat tricks: 13.

Season Team	League	GP	G	A	Pts.	PIM	+/-	PP	SH	GP	G	A	Pts.	PIM
		REGULAR SEASON								PLAYOFFS				
83-84—Pickering Jr. B	MTHL	38	30	28	58	35	...	...	...	—	—	—	—	—
84-85—Cornell	ECAC	23	18	21	39	20	...	...	...	—	—	—	—	—
85-86—Cornell	ECAC	21	21	21	42	45	...	...	...	—	—	—	—	—
86-87—Cornell	ECAC	23	26	26	52	26	...	...	...	—	—	—	—	—
—Canadian nat'l team	Int'l	5	2	0	2	0	...	...	...	—	—	—	—	—
—Calgary	NHL	9	5	1	6	0	0	2	0	6	2	2	4	0
87-88—Calgary	NHL	75	51	41	92	23	20	*31	3	8	3	4	7	2
88-89—Calgary	NHL	77	51	31	82	40	26	19	3	22	10	4	14	10
89-90—Calgary	NHL	79	45	50	95	40	32	18	0	6	4	6	10	4
90-91—Calgary	NHL	79	45	40	85	36	19	22	4	7	4	1	5	10
91-92—Calgary	NHL	69	22	34	56	55	-1	7	0	—	—	—	—	—

Season Team	League	GP	G	A	Pts.	PIM	+/-	PP	SH	Playoffs GP	G	A	Pts.	PIM
		REGULAR SEASON								PLAYOFFS				
92-93—Calgary	NHL	79	38	37	75	52	9	14	0	6	3	6	9	10
93-94—Calgary	NHL	64	36	39	75	51	19	14	1	6	2	2	4	0
94-95—Calgary	NHL	46	21	29	50	33	11	3	0	5	4	3	7	0
95-96—Dallas	NHL	52	14	18	32	41	-17	8	0	—	—	—	—	—
96-97—Dallas	NHL	66	30	21	51	32	-5	8	0	7	2	2	4	6
97-98—Dallas	NHL	73	39	30	69	30	16	14	0	1	1	0	1	0
—Can. Olympic team	Int'l	6	2	3	5	2	0	0	0	—	—	—	—	—
98-99—Dallas	NHL	67	28	27	55	34	11	8	0	23	*11	10	21	19
99-00—Dallas	NHL	48	15	19	34	26	-1	7	0	23	7	3	10	18
00-01—Dallas	NHL	69	29	23	52	30	5	12	0	7	4	0	4	4
01-02—Dallas	NHL	67	23	24	47	18	-2	6	0	—	—	—	—	—
—Can. Olympic team	Int'l	6	1	1	2	0	...	...	...	—	—	—	—	—
—New Jersey	NHL	14	2	9	11	4	2	0	0	5	0	1	1	0
02-03—New Jersey	NHL	80	17	28	45	56	10	3	0	17	3	6	9	4
03-04—Toronto	NHL	64	22	28	50	26	7	10	1	9	6	0	6	4
05-06—Florida	NHL	65	26	30	56	46	-2	7	0	—	—	—	—	—
NHL Totals (19 years)		1242	559	559	1118	673	159	213	12	158	66	50	116	91

NIINIMAA, JANNE D

PERSONAL: Born May 22, 1975, in Raahe, Finland. ... 6-1/220. ... Shoots left. ... Name pronounced YAH-nee NEE-nuh-muh.
TRANSACTIONS/CAREER NOTES: Selected by Philadelphia Flyers in second round (first Flyers pick, 36th overall) of entry draft (June 26, 1993). ... Traded by Flyers to Edmonton Oilers for D Dan McGillis and second-round pick (D Jason Beckett) in 1998 (March 24, 1998). ... Back spasms (November 4, 1998); missed one game. ... Back spasms (November 24, 1999); missed one game. ... Sprained knee (December 28, 2002); missed two games. ... Left knee, flu (January 13, 2003); missed three games. ... Traded by Oilers with second-round pick (C Evgeni Tunik) in 2003 to New York Islanders for LW Brad Isbister and LW Raffi Torres (March 11, 2003). ... Traded by Islanders with fifth-round pick in 2007 to Dallas Stars for D John Erskine and second-round pick (W Jesse Joensuu) in 2006 draft (January 10, 2006). ... Ankle (January 23, 2006); missed seven games. ... Ankle (March 26, 2006); missed two games.

Season Team	League	GP	G	A	Pts.	PIM	+/-	PP	SH	Playoffs GP	G	A	Pts.	PIM
		REGULAR SEASON								PLAYOFFS				
91-92—Karpat Oulu	Finland Div. 2	41	2	11	13	49	...	...	...	—	—	—	—	—
92-93—Karpat Oulu	Finland Div. 2	29	2	3	5	14	...	...	...	—	—	—	—	—
—Karpat	Finland Jr.	10	3	9	12	16	...	...	...	—	—	—	—	—
93-94—Jokerit Helsinki	Finland	45	3	8	11	24	...	...	...	12	1	1	2	4
94-95—Jokerit Helsinki	Finland	42	7	10	17	36	4	...	...	10	1	4	5	35
95-96—Jokerit Helsinki	Finland	49	5	15	20	79	...	...	...	11	0	2	2	12
96-97—Philadelphia	NHL	77	4	40	44	58	12	1	0	19	1	12	13	16
97-98—Philadelphia	NHL	66	3	31	34	56	6	2	0	—	—	—	—	—
—Fin. Olympic team	Int'l	6	0	3	3	8	1	0	0	—	—	—	—	—
—Edmonton	NHL	11	1	8	9	6	7	1	0	11	1	1	2	12
98-99—Edmonton	NHL	81	4	24	28	88	7	2	0	4	0	0	0	2
99-00—Edmonton	NHL	81	8	25	33	89	14	2	2	5	0	2	2	2
00-01—Edmonton	NHL	82	12	34	46	90	6	8	0	6	0	2	2	6
01-02—Edmonton	NHL	81	5	39	44	80	13	1	0	—	—	—	—	—
—Fin. Olympic team	Int'l	4	0	3	3	2	...	...	...	—	—	—	—	—
02-03—Edmonton	NHL	63	4	24	28	66	-7	2	0	—	—	—	—	—
—New York Islanders	NHL	13	1	5	6	14	-2	1	0	5	0	1	1	12
03-04—New York Islanders	NHL	82	9	19	28	64	12	4	0	5	1	2	3	2
04-05—Malmo	Sweden	10	0	3	3	34	-2	0	0	—	—	—	—	—
—Karpat Oulu	Finland	26	3	10	13	30	14	...	...	12	0	5	5	8
05-06—New York Islanders	NHL	41	1	9	10	62	-7	0	0	—	—	—	—	—
—Dallas	NHL	22	2	4	6	24	-5	1	1	4	0	1	1	8
NHL Totals (9 years)		700	54	262	316	697	56	25	3	59	3	21	24	60

N

NIITTYMAKI, ANTERO G

PERSONAL: Born June 18, 1980, in Turku, Finland. ... 6-1/192. ... Catches left. ... Name pronounced: an-TAIR-oh nih-tee-MAK-ee
TRANSACTIONS/CAREER NOTES: Selected by Philadelphia Flyers in sixth round (seventh Flyers pick, 168th overall) of NHL entry draft (June 27, 1998).

Season Team	League	GP	Min.	W	L	OTL	T	GA	SO	GAA	SV%	Playoffs GP	Min.	W	L	GA	SO	GAA	SV%
		REGULAR SEASON										PLAYOFFS							
96-97—TPS Turku	Finland Jr.	22	...	...	...	...	...	...	...	...	...	6	...	...	...	...	...	...	...
97-98—TPS Turku	Finland Jr.	33	...	...	...	...	...	...	...	...	...	—	—	—	—	—	—	—	—
98-99—TPS Turku	Finland Jr.	35	2095	...	...	...	...	60	0	1.72	...	—	—	—	—	—	—	—	—
99-00—TPS Turku	Finland	32	1899	23	6	...	2	68	3	2.15	...	8	453	6	1	13	0	1.72	...
00-01—TPS Turku	Finland	21	1112	10	6	...	1	46	2	2.48	...	—	—	—	—	—	—	—	—
01-02—TPS Turku	Finland	27	1498	16	8	...	1	46	3	1.84	...	4	295	2	2	11	0	2.24	...
02-03—Philadelphia	AHL	40	2283	14	21	...	2	98	0	2.58	.903	—	—	—	—	—	—	—	—
03-04—Philadelphia	NHL	3	180	3	0	...	0	3	0	1.00	.961	—	—	—	—	—	—	—	—
—Philadelphia	AHL	49	2730	24	13	...	6	92	7	2.02	.917	12	795	6	6	24	0	1.81	.920
04-05—Philadelphia	AHL	58	3452	33	21	...	...	119	6	2.07	.924	21	1269	15	5	37	3	1.75	.943
05-06—Philadelphia	NHL	46	2690	23	15	6	...	133	2	2.97	.895	2	73	0	0	5	0	4.11	.828
—Finland Oly. team	Int'l	6	...	...	...	...	...	...	3	1.34	.951	—	—	—	—	—			
NHL Totals (2 years)		49	2870	26	15	6	0	136	2	2.84	.899	2	73	0	0	5	0	4.11	.828

NILSON, MARCUS — LW/RW

PERSONAL: Born March 1, 1978, in Balsta, Sweden. ... 6-2/195. ... Shoots right.
TRANSACTIONS/CAREER NOTES: Selected by Florida Panthers in first round (first Panthers pick, 20th overall) of NHL draft (June 22, 1996). ... Suspended one game by NHL for slashing (March 16, 2002). ... Traded by Panthers to Calgary Flames for second-round pick (LW David Booth) in 2004 draft (March 8, 2004). ... Head (January 6, 2006); missed one game. ... Left knee (March 26, 2006); missed final 11 games of regular season and seven playoff games.

		REGULAR SEASON								PLAYOFFS				
Season Team	League	GP	G	A	Pts.	PIM	+/-	PP	SH	GP	G	A	Pts.	PIM
94-95—Djurgarden	Sweden Jr.	24	7	8	15	22	...	...	...	—	—	—	—	—
95-96—Djurgarden	Sweden Jr.	25	19	17	36	46	...	...	...	2	1	1	2	12
—Djurgarden Stockholm	Sweden	12	0	0	0	0	...	...	...	1	0	0	0	0
96-97—Djurgarden Stockholm	Sweden	37	0	3	3	33	...	...	...	4	0	0	0	0
97-98—Djurgarden Stockholm	Sweden	41	4	7	11	18	...	...	...	15	2	1	3	16
98-99—New Haven	AHL	69	8	25	33	10	-14	4	0	—	—	—	—	—
—Florida	NHL	8	1	1	2	5	2	0	0	—	—	—	—	—
99-00—Louisville	AHL	64	9	23	32	52	...	...	...	4	0	0	0	2
—Florida	NHL	9	0	2	2	2	2	0	0	—	—	—	—	—
00-01—Florida	NHL	78	12	24	36	74	-3	0	0	—	—	—	—	—
01-02—Florida	NHL	81	14	19	33	55	-14	6	1	—	—	—	—	—
02-03—Florida	NHL	82	15	19	34	31	2	7	1	—	—	—	—	—
03-04—Florida	NHL	69	6	13	19	26	-9	1	1	—	—	—	—	—
—Calgary	NHL	14	5	0	5	14	3	1	0	26	4	7	11	12
04-05—Djurgarden Stockholm	Sweden	48	17	22	39	110	11	7	2	7	1	2	3	10
05-06—Calgary	NHL	70	6	11	17	32	13	2	0	—	—	—	—	—
NHL Totals (7 years)		411	59	89	148	239	-4	17	3	26	4	7	11	12

NILSSON, ROBERT — RW

PERSONAL: Born January 10, 1985, in Calgary. ... 5-11/176. ... Shoots left. ... Son of Kent Nilsson, player with four NHL teams (1979-1987 and 1994-95).
TRANSACTIONS/CAREER NOTES: Selected by New York Islanders in first round (first Islanders pick, 15th overall) in 2003 NHL entry draft (June 23, 2003). ... Signed by Islanders to entry-level contract (August 30, 2005).

		REGULAR SEASON								PLAYOFFS				
Season Team	League	GP	G	A	Pts.	PIM	+/-	PP	SH	GP	G	A	Pts.	PIM
01-02—Leksand	Sweden Jr.	21	13	18	31	24	...	...	...	—	—	—	—	—
02-03—Leksand	Sweden Dv. 2	41	8	13	21	10	...	...	...	—	—	—	—	—
03-04—Leksand	Sweden Dv. 2	34	2	4	6	6	...	...	...	—	—	—	—	—
—Fribourg	Switzerland	7	1	3	4	2	...	...	...	4	1	0	1	2
04-05—Djurgarden	Sweden Jr.	8	8	4	12	12	4	3	0	—	—	—	—	—
—Djurgarden Stockholm	Sweden	23	2	4	6	6	0	1	0	3	0	0	0	0
—Hammarby	Sweden Dv. 2	7	0	4	4	4	2	0	0	—	—	—	—	—
05-06—Bridgeport	AHL	29	8	20	28	12	-1	2	0	7	1	4	5	0
—New York Islanders	NHL	53	6	14	20	26	-6	1	0	—	—	—	—	—
NHL Totals (1 year)		53	6	14	20	26	-6	1	0					

NODL, ANDREAS — RW

PERSONAL: Born February 28, 1987, in Vienna, Austria. ... 6-1/196. ... Shoots left.
TRANSACTIONS/CAREER NOTES: Selected by Philadelphia Flyers in second round (second Flyers pick; 39th overall) of NHL draft (June 24, 2006).

		REGULAR SEASON								PLAYOFFS				
Season Team	League	GP	G	A	Pts.	PIM	+/-	PP	SH	GP	G	A	Pts.	PIM
04-05—Sioux Falls	USHL	44	7	9	16	24	...	...	...	—	—	—	—	—
05-06—Sioux Falls	USHL	58	29	30	59	16	...	...	...	—	—	—	—	—

NOKELAINEN, PETTERI — C/RW

PERSONAL: Born January 16, 1986, in Imatra, Finland. ... 6-1/190. ... Shoots right. ... Name pronounced: PEHT-ree noh-kehl-LIGHN-ihn
TRANSACTIONS/CAREER NOTES: Selected by New York Islanders in first round (first Islanders pick, 16th overall) of entry draft (June 26, 2004). ... Signed by Islanders to entry-level contract (August 23, 2005). ... Sprained ankle (October 27, 2005); missed one game. ... Knee injury (November 3, 2005); missed 58 games. ... Knee (April 5, 2006); missed final eight games of regular season.

		REGULAR SEASON								PLAYOFFS				
Season Team	League	GP	G	A	Pts.	PIM	+/-	PP	SH	GP	G	A	Pts.	PIM
02-03—SaiPa	Finland	2	1	0	1	2	...	...	...	—	—	—	—	—
03-04—SaiPa	Finland	40	4	4	8	16	...	...	...	—	—	—	—	—
04-05—SaiPa	Finland	52	15	5	20	34	-12	...	...	—	—	—	—	—
05-06—New York Islanders	NHL	15	1	1	2	4	-1	0	0	—	—	—	—	—
NHL Totals (1 year)		15	1	1	2	4	-1	0	0					

NORDGREN, NIKLAS — LW/RW

PERSONAL: Born June 28, 1979, in Ornskoldsvik, Sweden. ... 5-11/183. ... Shoots right.
TRANSACTIONS/CAREER NOTES: Selected by Carolina Hurricanes in eighth round (seventh Hurricanes pick, 195th overall) of NHL entry draft

(June 21, 1997). ... Signed by Hurricanes to one-year contract (August 24, 2005). ... Traded by Hurricanes with C Krystofer Kolanos and second-round pick in 2007 draft to Penguins for LW Mark Recchi (March 9, 2006).

		REGULAR SEASON								PLAYOFFS				
Season Team	League	GP	G	A	Pts.	PIM	+/-	PP	SH	GP	G	A	Pts.	PIM
95-96—MoDo Hockey	Sweden Jr.	30	37	27	64	...	...	...	...	—	—	—	—	—
96-97—MoDo Hockey	Sweden Jr.	Statistics unavailable												
—MoDo Ornskoldsvik	Sweden	6	0	0	0	0	...	...	...	—	—	—	—	—
97-98—MoDo Hockey	Sweden Jr.	28	15	15	30	52	...	...	...	—	—	—	—	—
98-99—MoDo Ornskoldsvik	Sweden	7	0	0	0	2	...	...	...	—	—	—	—	—
99-00—Sundsvall Timra	Sweden Dv. 2	27	21	11	32	58	...	...	...	—	—	—	—	—
—MoDo Ornskoldsvik	Sweden	1	0	0	0	0	...	...	...	1	0	0	0	0
00-01—Sundsvall Timra	Sweden Dv. 2	35	22	19	41	45	...	...	...	—	—	—	—	—
01-02—Timra	Sweden	49	8	6	14	16	...	...	...	—	—	—	—	—
02-03—Timra	Sweden	47	20	23	43	40	...	...	...	10	1	4	5	4
03-04—Timra	Sweden	46	13	15	28	44	...	...	...	10	4	1	5	32
04-05—Timra	Sweden	46	19	17	36	71	...	...	...	7	0	2	2	6
05-06—Lowell	AHL	8	6	4	10	10	6	2	1	—	—	—	—	—
—Carolina	NHL	43	4	2	6	30	-4	0	0	—	—	—	—	—
—Pittsburgh	NHL	15	0	0	0	4	-4	0	0	—	—	—	—	—
NHL Totals (1 year)		58	4	2	6	34	-8	0	0					

NORONEN, MIKA G

PERSONAL: Born June 17, 1979, in Tampere, Finland. ... 6-2/196. ... Catches left. ... Name pronounced NO-rah-nehn.

TRANSACTIONS/CAREER NOTES: Selected by Buffalo Sabres in first round (first Sabres pick, 21st overall) of entry draft (June 21, 1997). ... Injured neck (December 9, 2003); missed one game. ... Injured groin (December 30, 2003); missed six games. ... Strained groin (November 22, 2005); missed two games. ... Traded by Sabres to Vancouver Canucks for second-round pick (G Jhonas Enroth) in 2006 draft (March 9, 2006).

		REGULAR SEASON										PLAYOFFS							
Season Team	League	GP	Min.	W	L	OTL	T	GA	SO	GAA	SV%	GP	Min.	W	L	GA	SO	GAA	SV%
95-96—Tappara Tampere	Finland Jr.	16	962	...	...	...	...	37	2	2.31	...	—	—	—	—	—	—	—	—
96-97—Tappara Tampere	Finland	5	215	...	...	...	...	17	0	4.74	...	—	—	—	—	—	—	—	—
97-98—Tappara Tampere	Finland	47	1703	14	12	...	3	83	1	2.92	...	4	196	1	2	12	0	3.67	...
98-99—Tappara Tampere	Finland	43	2494	18	20	...	5	135	2	3.25	...	—	—	—	—	—	—	—	—
99-00—Rochester	AHL	54	3089	33	13	...	4	112	6	2.18	...	21	1235	13	8	37	6	1.80	...
00-01—Buffalo	NHL	2	108	2	0	...	0	5	0	2.78	.872	—	—	—	—	—	—	—	—
—Rochester	AHL	47	2753	26	15	...	5	100	4	2.18	.913	4	250	1	3	11	0	2.64	...
01-02—Rochester	AHL	45	2763	16	17	...	12	115	3	2.50	.896	1	58	0	1	3	0	3.10	.870
—Buffalo	NHL	10	518	4	3	...	1	23	0	2.66	.894	—	—	—	—	—	—	—	—
02-03—Buffalo	NHL	16	891	4	9	...	3	36	1	2.42	.912	—	—	—	—	—	—	—	—
—Rochester	AHL	19	1168	5	9	...	5	55	2	2.83	.903	—	—	—	—	—	—	—	—
03-04—Buffalo	NHL	35	1796	11	17	...	2	77	2	2.57	.906	—	—	—	—	—	—	—	—
04-05—HPK Hameenlinna	Finland	27	1614	14	8	...	4	54	1	2.01	.927	9	482	4	4	21	1	2.61	.918
05-06—Rochester	AHL	2	121	0	2	0	...	6	0	2.98	.898	—	—	—	—	—	—	—	—
—Buffalo	NHL	4	169	1	2	0	...	12	0	4.26	.844	—	—	—	—	—	—	—	—
—Vancouver	NHL	4	170	1	1	0	...	10	0	3.53	.870	—	—	—	—	—	—	—	—
NHL Totals (5 years)		71	3652	23	32	0	6	163	3	2.68	.901								

NORSTROM, MATTIAS D

N

PERSONAL: Born January 2, 1972, in Stockholm, Sweden. ... 6-2/210. ... Shoots left. ... Name pronounced muh-TEE-uhz NOHR-struhm.

TRANSACTIONS/CAREER NOTES: Selected by New York Rangers in second round (second Rangers pick, 48th overall) of entry draft (June 20, 1992). ... Flu (April 28, 1995); missed two games. ... Shoulder (December 30, 1995); missed six games. ... Traded by Rangers with C Ray Ferraro, C Ian Laperriere, C Nathan LaFayette and fourth-round pick (D Sean Blanchard) in 1997 to Los Angeles Kings for RW Shane Churla, LW Jari Kurri and D Marty McSorley (March 14, 1996). ... Left wrist (November 7, 1996); missed one game. ... Suspended one game for illegal check (January 12, 1998). ... Ribs (April 11, 1999); missed four games. ... Ribs (October 13, 2001); missed three games. ... Chest (October 11, 2003); missed seven games. ... Personal absence (February 29, 2004); missed one game. ... Offseason left elbow surgery (April 6, 2004). ... Hamstring (September 27, 2005); missed two games. ... Neck strain (February 8, 2006); missed two games. ... Flu (March 11, 2006); missed one game.

		REGULAR SEASON								PLAYOFFS				
Season Team	League	GP	G	A	Pts.	PIM	+/-	PP	SH	GP	G	A	Pts.	PIM
91-92—AIK Solna	Sweden	39	4	4	8	28	...	...	...	—	—	—	—	—
92-93—AIK Solna	Sweden	22	0	1	1	16	...	...	...	—	—	—	—	—
93-94—New York Rangers	NHL	9	0	2	2	6	0	0	0	—	—	—	—	—
—Binghamton	AHL	55	1	9	10	70	-7	0	0	—	—	—	—	—
94-95—Binghamton	AHL	63	9	10	19	91	-1	0	1	—	—	—	—	—
—New York Rangers	NHL	9	0	3	3	2	2	0	0	3	0	0	0	0
95-96—New York Rangers	NHL	25	2	1	3	22	5	0	0	—	—	—	—	—
—Los Angeles	NHL	11	0	1	1	18	-8	0	0	—	—	—	—	—
96-97—Los Angeles	NHL	80	1	21	22	84	-4	0	0	—	—	—	—	—
97-98—Los Angeles	NHL	73	1	12	13	90	14	0	0	4	0	0	0	2
—Swedish Oly. team	Int'l	4	0	1	1	2	3	0	0	—	—	—	—	—
98-99—Los Angeles	NHL	78	2	5	7	36	-10	0	1	—	—	—	—	—
99-00—Los Angeles	NHL	82	1	13	14	66	22	0	0	4	0	0	0	6
00-01—Los Angeles	NHL	82	0	18	18	60	10	0	0	13	0	2	2	18
01-02—Los Angeles	NHL	79	2	9	11	38	-2	0	0	7	0	0	0	4
—Swedish Oly. team	Int'l	4	0	0	0	0	...	...	...	—	—	—	—	—
02-03—Los Angeles	NHL	82	0	6	6	49	0	0	0	—	—	—	—	—

Season Team	League	GP	G	A	Pts.	PIM	+/-	PP	SH	GP	G	A	Pts.	PIM
		REGULAR SEASON								PLAYOFFS				
03-04—Los Angeles	NHL	74	1	13	14	44	-3	0	0	—	—	—	—	—
04-05—AIK Solna	Sweden Dv. 2	8	1	0	1	4	...	...	...	—	—	—	—	—
05-06—Los Angeles	NHL	77	4	23	27	58	-3	2	1	—	—	—	—	—
NHL Totals (12 years)		761	14	127	141	573	23	2	2	31	0	2	2	30

NORTON, BRAD D/LW

PERSONAL: Born February 13, 1975, in Cambridge, Mass. ... 6-4/242. ... Shoots left. ... Brother of Jeff Norton, D with eight NHL teams (1987-2002).

TRANSACTIONS/CAREER NOTES: Selected by Edmonton Oilers in ninth round (ninth Oilers pick, 215th overall) of entry draft (June 26, 1993). ... Suspended three games by NHL for unsportsmanlike conduct (October 4, 2000). ... Strained hip flexor (October 11, 2000); missed 10 games. ... Signed as free agent by Florida Panthers (July 27, 2001). ... Ill (February 11, 2002); missed one game. ... Signed as free agent by Los Angeles Kings (October 8, 2002). ... Concussion (February 9, 2003); missed five games. ... Cervical injury (March 8, 2003); missed 14 games. ... Right arm (October 1, 2003); missed 37 games. ... Claimed off waivers by Washington Capitals (March 4, 2004). ... Injured hand (March 24, 2004); missed remainder of season. ... Signed as free agent by HIFK Helsinki of Finnish league (October 11, 2005). ... Claimed on waivers by AHL Binghamton (December 20, 2005). ... Signed as free agent by Ottawa Senators (March 8, 2006).

Season Team	League	GP	G	A	Pts.	PIM	+/-	PP	SH	GP	G	A	Pts.	PIM
		REGULAR SEASON								PLAYOFFS				
94-95—Massachusetts	Hockey East	30	0	6	6	89	-7	0	0	—	—	—	—	—
95-96—Massachusetts	Hockey East	34	4	12	16	99	...	...	...	—	—	—	—	—
96-97—Massachusetts	Hockey East	35	2	16	18	88	1	0	1	—	—	—	—	—
97-98—Massachusetts	Hockey East	20	2	13	15	28	...	...	...	—	—	—	—	—
—Detroit	IHL	33	1	4	5	56	1	0	0	22	0	2	2	87
98-99—Hamilton	AHL	58	1	8	9	134	8	0	0	11	0	1	1	6
99-00—Hamilton	AHL	40	5	12	17	104	...	...	...	10	1	4	5	26
00-01—Hamilton	AHL	46	3	15	18	114	...	...	...	—	—	—	—	—
01-02—Hershey	AHL	40	0	10	10	62	-8	0	0	2	0	0	0	6
—Florida	NHL	22	0	2	2	45	-2	0	0	—	—	—	—	—
02-03—Los Angeles	NHL	53	3	3	6	97	1	0	0	—	—	—	—	—
03-04—Los Angeles	NHL	20	0	1	1	77	-1	0	0	—	—	—	—	—
—Washington	NHL	16	0	1	1	17	-4	0	0	—	—	—	—	—
05-06—Binghamton	AHL	36	0	4	4	102	5	0	0	—	—	—	—	—
—Ottawa	NHL	7	0	0	0	31	1	0	0	—	—	—	—	—
NHL Totals (4 years)		118	3	7	10	267	-5	0	0					

NOVAK, FILIP D

PERSONAL: Born May 7, 1982, in Ceske Budejovice, Czechoslovakia. ... 6-1/174. ... Shoots left.

TRANSACTIONS/CAREER NOTES: Selected by New York Rangers in second round (first Rangers pick, 64th overall) of entry draft (June 24, 2000). ... Traded by Rangers with D Igor Ulanov, first- (later traded to Calgary; Flames picked LW Eric Nystrom) and second-round picks (C/RW Rob Globke) in 2002 draft and fourth-round pick (later traded to Atlanta; Thrashers picked RW Guillaume Desbiens) in 2003 draft to Florida Panthers for RW Pavel Bure and second-round pick (C Lee Falardeau) in 2002 draft (March 18, 2002). ... Ankle (October 8, 2003); missed entire season. ... Traded by Panthers to Ottawa Senators for sixth-round pick in 2007 draft (October 5, 2005).

Season Team	League	GP	G	A	Pts.	PIM	+/-	PP	SH	GP	G	A	Pts.	PIM
		REGULAR SEASON								PLAYOFFS				
98-99—Budejovice	Czech. Jrs.	68	8	10	18	34	...	...	...	—	—	—	—	—
99-00—Regina	WHL	47	7	32	39	70	...	...	...	7	1	4	5	5
00-01—Regina	WHL	64	17	50	67	75	...	...	...	6	1	4	5	6
01-02—Regina	WHL	60	12	46	58	125	...	...	...	6	2	2	4	19
02-03—San Antonio	AHL	57	10	17	27	79	5	4	0	1	0	0	0	0
03-04—San Antonio	AHL	Did not play — injured												
04-05—San Antonio	AHL	71	1	12	13	84	-8	1	0	—	—	—	—	—
05-06—Binghamton	AHL	64	8	44	52	58	0	4	1	—	—	—	—	—
—Ottawa	NHL	11	0	0	0	4	-2	0	0	—	—	—	—	—
NHL Totals (1 year)		11	0	0	0	4	-2	0	0					

N

NOVOTNY, JIRI C/LW

PERSONAL: Born August 12, 1983, in Pelhrimov, Czechoslovakia. ... 6-2/204. ... Shoots right. ... Name pronounced: JUHR-ee nuh-VAHT-nee

TRANSACTIONS/CAREER NOTES: Selected by Buffalo Sabres in first round (first Sabres pick, 22nd overall) of NHL entry draft (June 23, 2001).

Season Team	League	GP	G	A	Pts.	PIM	+/-	PP	SH	GP	G	A	Pts.	PIM
		REGULAR SEASON								PLAYOFFS				
99-00—Budejovice	Czech. Jrs.	39	11	12	23	14	...	...	...	—	—	—	—	—
00-01—Budejovice	Czech. Jrs.	33	10	10	20	...	...	...	...	—	—	—	—	—
—HC Ceske Budejovice	Czech Rep.	19	0	4	4	2	...	...	...	—	—	—	—	—
01-02—HC Ceske Budejovice	Czech Rep.	41	8	6	14	6	...	...	...	—	—	—	—	—
02-03—Rochester	AHL	43	2	9	11	14	-12	0	0	3	0	1	1	10
03-04—Rochester	AHL	48	1	14	15	16	-14	0	0	13	0	1	1	10
04-05—Rochester	AHL	61	5	20	25	36	8	1	0	9	2	2	4	4
05-06—Rochester	AHL	66	17	37	54	40	2	10	0	—	—	—	—	—
—Buffalo	NHL	14	2	1	3	0	-5	0	1	4	0	0	0	0
NHL Totals (1 year)		14	2	1	3	0	-5	0	1	4	0	0	0	0

NUMMINEN, TEPPO — D

PERSONAL: Born July 3, 1968, in Tampere, Finland. ... 6-2/197. ... Shoots right. ... Name pronounced TEH-poh NOO-mih-nehn.

TRANSACTIONS/CAREER NOTES: Selected by Winnipeg Jets in second round (second Jets pick, 29th overall) of entry draft (June 21, 1986). ... Separated shoulder (March 5, 1989). ... Fractured thumb (April 14, 1990). ... Fractured foot (January 28, 1993); missed 17 games. ... Dislocated thumb (February 9, 1994); missed remainder of season. ... Flu (January 23, 1995); missed one game. ... Stress fracture in right knee (February 22, 1995); missed five games. ... Separated shoulder (November 28, 1995); missed eight games. ... Jets franchise moved to Phoenix and renamed Coyotes for 1996-97 season; NHL approved move January 18, 1996. ... Strained hip flexor (March 1, 2000); missed two games. ... Sprained ankle (December 30, 2000); missed one game. ... Bruised foot (November 14, 2000); missed two games. ... Bruised foot (November 29, 2000); missed three games. ... Brused foot (March 6, 2001); missed one game. ... Strained hip flexor (March 15, 2001); missed two games. ... Bruised foot (April 6, 2001); missed one game. ... Fractured foot (November 4, 2001); missed six games. ... Bruised ankle (November 11, 2002); missed four games. ... Traded by Coyotes to Dallas Stars for C Mike Sillinger (July 22, 2003). ... Groin (November 8, 2003); missed two games. ... Fractured right foot (November 20, 2003); missed 12 games. ... Aggravated foot injury (December 20, 2003); missed one game. ... Heart ailment (March 20, 2004); missed five games. ... Signed as free agent by Buffalo Sabres (August 4, 2005). ... Hamstring (January 26, 2006); missed one game. ... Sprained knee (March 30, 2006); missed six games.

		REGULAR SEASON								PLAYOFFS				
Season Team	League	GP	G	A	Pts.	PIM	+/-	PP	SH	GP	G	A	Pts.	PIM
84-85—Tappara	Finland	30	14	17	31	10	...	...	...	—	—	—	—	—
85-86—Tappara	Finland	39	2	4	6	6	...	...	...	8	0	0	0	0
86-87—Tappara	Finland	44	9	9	18	16	...	...	...	9	4	1	5	4
87-88—Tappara	Finland	44	10	10	20	29	...	...	...	10	6	6	12	6
—Fin. Olympic team	Int'l	6	1	4	5	0	2	...	...	—	—	—	—	—
88-89—Winnipeg	NHL	69	1	14	15	36	-11	0	1	—	—	—	—	—
89-90—Winnipeg	NHL	79	11	32	43	20	-4	1	0	7	1	2	3	10
90-91—Winnipeg	NHL	80	8	25	33	28	-15	3	0	—	—	—	—	—
91-92—Winnipeg	NHL	80	5	34	39	32	15	4	0	7	0	0	0	0
92-93—Winnipeg	NHL	66	7	30	37	33	4	3	1	6	1	1	2	2
93-94—Winnipeg	NHL	57	5	18	23	28	-23	4	0	—	—	—	—	—
94-95—TuTu Turku	Finland	12	3	8	11	4	4	...	...	—	—	—	—	—
—Winnipeg	NHL	42	5	16	21	16	12	2	0	—	—	—	—	—
95-96—Winnipeg	NHL	74	11	43	54	22	-4	6	0	6	0	0	0	2
96-97—Phoenix	NHL	82	2	25	27	28	-3	0	0	7	3	3	6	0
97-98—Phoenix	NHL	82	11	40	51	30	25	6	0	1	0	0	0	0
—Fin. Olympic team	Int'l	6	1	1	2	2	-1	1	0	—	—	—	—	—
98-99—Phoenix	NHL	82	10	30	40	30	3	1	0	7	2	1	3	4
99-00—Phoenix	NHL	79	8	34	42	16	21	2	0	5	1	1	2	0
00-01—Phoenix	NHL	72	5	26	31	36	9	1	0	—	—	—	—	—
01-02—Phoenix	NHL	76	13	35	48	20	13	4	0	4	0	0	0	2
—Fin. Olympic team	Int'l	4	0	1	1	0	...	...	...	—	—	—	—	—
02-03—Phoenix	NHL	78	6	24	30	30	0	2	0	—	—	—	—	—
03-04—Dallas	NHL	62	3	14	17	18	-5	0	0	4	0	1	1	0
05-06—Buffalo	NHL	75	2	38	40	36	6	0	0	12	1	1	2	4
—Fin. Olympic team	Int'l	8	1	2	3	2	2	1	0	—	—	—	—	—
NHL Totals (17 years)		1235	113	478	591	459	43	39	2	66	9	10	19	24

NYLANDER, MICHAEL — C

PERSONAL: Born October 3, 1972, in Stockholm, Sweden. ... 6-1/195. ... Shoots left. ... Name pronounced NEE-lan-duhr.

TRANSACTIONS/CAREER NOTES: Selected by Hartford Whalers in third round (fourth Whalers pick, 59th overall) of NHL draft (June 22, 1991). ... Fractured jaw (January 23, 1993); missed 15 games. ... Traded by Whalers with D Zarley Zalapski and D James Patrick to Calgary Flames for D Gary Suter, LW Paul Ranheim and C Ted Drury (March 10, 1994). ... Fractured left wrist and forearm (January 24, 1995); missed 42 games. ... Injured wrist (January 16, 1996); missed three games. ... Injured left knee (March 26, 1998); missed final 11 games of season and first 23 games of 1998-99 season. ... Traded by Flames to Tampa Bay Lightning for RW Andrei Nazarov (January 19, 1999). ... Had concussion (April 8, 1999); missed final five games of season. ... Traded by Lightning to Chicago Blackhawks for D Bryan Muir and LW Reid Simpson (November 12, 1999). ... Traded by Blackhawks with third-round pick (RW Stephen Werner) in 2003 draft and future considerations to Washington Capitals for C Andrei Nikolishin and LW Chris Simon (November 1, 2002). ... Fractured right leg (October 3, 2003); missed first 63 games of the season. ... Traded by Capitals to Boston Bruins for second-round pick (RW Francois Bouchard) in 2006 draft and fourth-round pick (Patrick McNeill) in 2005 draft (March 4, 2004). ... Signed as free agent by New York Rangers (August 10, 2004).

STATISTICAL PLATEAUS: Three-goal games: 1992-93 (1). ... Four-goal games: 1999-00 (1). ... Total hat tricks: 2.

		REGULAR SEASON								PLAYOFFS				
Season Team	League	GP	G	A	Pts.	PIM	+/-	PP	SH	GP	G	A	Pts.	PIM
89-90—Huddinge	Sweden	31	7	15	22	4	...	...	...	—	—	—	—	—
90-91—Huddinge	Sweden	33	14	20	34	10	...	...	...	—	—	—	—	—
91-92—AIK Solna	Sweden	40	11	17	28	30	...	...	...	—	—	—	—	—
—Swedish Oly. team	Int'l	6	0	1	1	0	...	...	...	—	—	—	—	—
92-93—Hartford	NHL	59	11	22	33	36	-7	3	0	—	—	—	—	—
—Springfield	AHL	59	11	22	33	36	...	...	...	—	—	—	—	—
93-94—Hartford	NHL	58	11	33	44	24	-2	4	0	—	—	—	—	—
—Springfield	AHL	4	0	9	9	0	0	0	0	—	—	—	—	—
—Calgary	NHL	15	2	9	11	6	10	0	0	3	0	0	0	0
94-95—JyP HT	Finland	16	11	19	30	63	18	...	...	—	—	—	—	—
—Calgary	NHL	6	0	1	1	2	1	0	0	6	0	6	6	2
95-96—Calgary	NHL	73	17	38	55	20	0	4	0	4	0	0	0	0
96-97—Lugano	Switzerland	36	12	43	55	...	...	...	...	—	—	—	—	—
97-98—Calgary	NHL	65	13	23	36	24	10	0	0	—	—	—	—	—
—Swedish Oly. team	Int'l	4	0	0	0	6	1	0	0	—	—	—	—	—
98-99—Calgary	NHL	9	2	3	5	2	1	1	0	—	—	—	—	—
—Tampa Bay	NHL	24	2	7	9	6	-10	0	0	—	—	—	—	—
99-00—Tampa Bay	NHL	11	1	2	3	4	-3	1	0	—	—	—	—	—
—Chicago	NHL	66	23	28	51	26	9	4	0	—	—	—	—	—

Season Team	League	GP	G	A	Pts.	PIM	+/-	PP	SH	GP	G	A	Pts.	PIM
		REGULAR SEASON								PLAYOFFS				
00-01—Chicago	NHL	82	25	39	64	32	7	4	0	—	—	—	—	—
01-02—Chicago	NHL	82	15	46	61	50	28	6	0	5	0	3	3	2
—Swedish Oly. team	Int'l	4	1	2	3	0	...	...	...	—	—	—	—	—
02-03—Chicago	NHL	9	0	4	4	4	0	0	0	—	—	—	—	—
—Washington	NHL	71	17	39	56	36	3	7	0	6	3	2	5	8
03-04—Washington	NHL	3	0	2	2	8	1	0	0	—	—	—	—	—
—Boston	NHL	15	1	11	12	14	3	0	0	6	3	3	6	0
04-05—Karpat Oulu	Finland	23	5	15	20	22	9	...	...	—	—	—	—	—
—SKA St. Petersburg	Russian	8	2	5	7	0	-9	...	...	—	—	—	—	—
—Ak Bars Kazan	Russian	5	0	1	1	2	-1	...	...	—	—	—	—	—
05-06—New York Rangers	NHL	81	23	56	79	76	31	6	0	4	0	1	1	0
NHL Totals (12 years)		729	163	363	526	370	82	40	0	34	6	15	21	12

NYSTROM, ERIC — LW

PERSONAL: Born February 14, 1983, in Syosset, N.Y. ... 6-1/195. ... Shoots left. ... Son of Bobby Nystrom, RW with New York Islanders (1972-86).
COLLEGE: Michigan
TRANSACTIONS/CAREER NOTES: Selected by Calgary Flames in first round (first Flames pick, 10th overall) of entry draft (June 22, 2002).

Season Team	League	GP	G	A	Pts.	PIM	+/-	PP	SH	GP	G	A	Pts.	PIM
		REGULAR SEASON								PLAYOFFS				
00-01—U.S. National	USHL	66	15	17	32	102	...	...	...	—	—	—	—	—
01-02—Univ. of Michigan	CCHA	32	15	9	24	32	...	...	...	—	—	—	—	—
02-03—Univ. of Michigan	CCHA	39	15	11	26	24	...	...	...	—	—	—	—	—
03-04—Univ. of Michigan	CCHA	43	10	12	22	50	8	6	0	—	—	—	—	—
04-05—Univ. of Michigan	CCHA	38	13	19	32	33	...	...	...	—	—	—	—	—
05-06—Omaha Ak-Sar-Ben	AHL	78	15	18	33	37	-2	7	1	—	—	—	—	—
—Calgary	NHL	2	0	0	0	0	-1	0	0	—	—	—	—	—
NHL Totals (1 year)		2	0	0	0	0	-1	0	0					

O'BRIEN, DOUG — D

PERSONAL: Born February 16, 1984, in St. John's, Nfld. ... 6-1/200. ... Shoots left.
TRANSACTIONS/CAREER NOTES: Selected by Tampa Bay Lightning in sixth round (fourth Lightning pick, 192nd overall) of NHL entry draft (June 21, 2003).

Season Team	League	GP	G	A	Pts.	PIM	+/-	PP	SH	GP	G	A	Pts.	PIM
		REGULAR SEASON								PLAYOFFS				
00-01—Hull	QMJHL	47	1	6	7	16	...	...	...	5	0	1	1	0
01-02—Hull	QMJHL	46	1	5	6	36	...	...	...	12	0	0	0	14
02-03—Hull	QMJHL	71	10	34	44	102	35	9	0	19	3	12	15	18
03-04—Gatineau	QMJHL	66	17	46	63	146	52	7	0	15	1	8	9	16
04-05—Springfield	AHL	74	4	13	17	76	...	...	...	—	—	—	—	—
—Johnstown	ECHL	3	0	0	0	2	...	...	...	—	—	—	—	—
05-06—Springfield	AHL	74	7	25	32	70	-23	1	0	—	—	—	—	—
—Tampa Bay	NHL	5	0	0	0	2	0	0	0	—	—	—	—	—
NHL Totals (1 year)		5	0	0	0	2	0	0	0					

O'DONNELL, SEAN — D

PERSONAL: Born October 13, 1971, in Ottawa. ... 6-3/228. ... Shoots left.
TRANSACTIONS/CAREER NOTES: Selected by Buffalo Sabres in sixth round (sixth Sabres pick, 123rd overall) of NHL draft (June 22, 1991). ... Traded by Sabres to Los Angeles Kings for D Doug Houda (July 26, 1994). ... Bruised sternum (February 4, 1995); missed two games. ... Sprained left wrist (January 27, 1996); missed eight games. ... Sprained wrist (December 26, 1996); missed nine games. ... Suspended one game for an altercation while on the bench (January 30, 1997). ... Strained back (March 1, 1997); missed two games. ... Suspended two games for cross-checking and spearing incidents (April 14, 1999). ... Selected by Minnesota Wild in expansion draft (June 23, 2000). ... Flu (February 11, 2001); missed one game. ... Traded by Wild to New Jersey Devils for D Willie Mitchell (March 4, 2001). ... Signed as free agent by Boston Bruins (July 2, 2001). ... Back spasms (March 21, 2002); missed two games. ... Injured knee (February 6, 2003); missed 11 games. ... Signed as free agent by Phoenix Coyotes (July 6, 2004). ... Suspended two games by NHL for third instigator penalty (January 12, 2006). ... Traded by Coyotes to Anaheim Mighty Ducks for C Joel Perrault (March 9, 2006).

Season Team	League	GP	G	A	Pts.	PIM	+/-	PP	SH	GP	G	A	Pts.	PIM
		REGULAR SEASON								PLAYOFFS				
88-89—Sudbury	OHL	56	1	9	10	49	...	...	...	—	—	—	—	—
89-90—Sudbury	OHL	64	7	19	26	84	...	...	...	—	—	—	—	—
90-91—Sudbury	OHL	66	8	23	31	114	...	...	...	5	1	4	5	10
91-92—Rochester	AHL	73	4	9	13	193	...	...	...	16	1	2	3	21
92-93—Rochester	AHL	74	3	18	21	203	...	...	...	17	1	6	7	38
93-94—Rochester	AHL	64	2	10	12	242	...	...	...	4	0	1	1	21
94-95—Phoenix	IHL	61	2	18	20	132	13	0	0	9	0	1	1	21
—Los Angeles	NHL	15	0	2	2	49	-2	0	0	—	—	—	—	—
95-96—Los Angeles	NHL	71	2	5	7	127	3	0	0	—	—	—	—	—
96-97—Los Angeles	NHL	55	5	12	17	144	-13	2	0	—	—	—	—	—
97-98—Los Angeles	NHL	80	2	15	17	179	7	0	0	4	1	0	1	36
98-99—Los Angeles	NHL	80	1	13	14	186	1	0	0	—	—	—	—	—
99-00—Los Angeles	NHL	80	2	12	14	114	4	0	0	4	1	0	1	4
00-01—Minnesota	NHL	63	4	12	16	128	-2	1	0	—	—	—	—	—

Season Team	League	GP	G	A	Pts.	PIM	+/-	PP	SH	GP	G	A	Pts.	PIM
		REGULAR SEASON								PLAYOFFS				
—New Jersey	NHL	17	0	1	1	33	2	0	0	23	1	2	3	41
01-02—Boston	NHL	80	3	22	25	89	27	1	0	6	0	2	2	4
02-03—Boston	NHL	70	1	15	16	76	8	0	0	—	—	—	—	—
03-04—Boston	NHL	82	1	10	11	110	10	0	0	7	0	0	0	0
05-06—Phoenix	NHL	57	1	7	8	121	3	0	0	—	—	—	—	—
—Anaheim	NHL	21	1	2	3	26	3	0	0	16	2	3	5	23
NHL Totals (11 years)		771	23	128	151	1382	51	4	0	60	5	7	12	108

O'NEILL, JEFF RW/LW

PERSONAL: Born February 23, 1976, in Richmond Hill, Ont. ... 6-1/195. ... Shoots right.

TRANSACTIONS/CAREER NOTES: Selected by Hartford Whalers in first round (first Whalers pick, fifth overall) of NHL draft (June 28, 1994). ... Bruised foot (December 30, 1995); missed four games. ... Reinjured foot (January 10, 1996); missed four games. ... Injured shoulder (February 17, 1996); missed four games. ... Injured groin (January 2, 1997); missed one game. ... Sprained wrist (April 2, 1997); missed four games. ... Whalers franchise moved to North Carolina and renamed Carolina Hurricanes for 1997-98 season; NHL approved move on June 25, 1997. ... Concussion (December 20, 1997); missed one game. ... Fractured kneecap (April 13, 1998); missed three games. ... Strained neck (February 3, 1999); missed seven games. ... Back spasms (November 24, 1999); missed two games. ... Injured back (December 31, 2001); missed four games. ... Suspended one playoff game for checking from behind (May 4, 2002). ... Injured right shoulder (March 6, 2004) and had surgery (March 12, 2004); missed remainder of season. ... Traded by Hurricanes to Toronto Maple Leafs for a fourth-round pick (traded to St. Louis; Blues selected G Reto Berra) in the 2006 draft (July 30, 2005). ... Injured shoulder (October 8, 2005); missed two games.

STATISTICAL PLATEAUS: Three-goal games: 1996-97 (1), 2003-04 (1). Total: 2.

Season Team	League	GP	G	A	Pts.	PIM	+/-	PP	SH	GP	G	A	Pts.	PIM
		REGULAR SEASON								PLAYOFFS				
91-92—Thornhill	Tier II Jr. A	43	27	53	80	48	...	...	...	—	—	—	—	—
92-93—Guelph	OHL	65	32	47	79	88	...	...	...	5	2	2	4	6
93-94—Guelph	OHL	66	45	81	126	95	...	8	...	9	2	11	13	31
94-95—Guelph	OHL	57	43	81	124	56	...	6	1	14	8	18	26	34
95-96—Hartford	NHL	65	8	19	27	40	-3	1	0	—	—	—	—	—
96-97—Hartford	NHL	72	14	16	30	40	-24	2	1	—	—	—	—	—
—Springfield	AHL	1	0	0	0	0	0	0	0	—	—	—	—	—
97-98—Carolina	NHL	74	19	20	39	67	-8	7	1	—	—	—	—	—
98-99—Carolina	NHL	75	16	15	31	66	3	4	0	6	0	1	1	0
99-00—Carolina	NHL	80	25	38	63	72	-9	4	0	—	—	—	—	—
00-01—Carolina	NHL	82	41	26	67	106	-18	17	0	6	1	2	3	10
01-02—Carolina	NHL	76	31	33	64	63	-5	11	0	22	8	5	13	27
02-03—Carolina	NHL	82	30	31	61	38	-21	11	0	—	—	—	—	—
03-04—Carolina	NHL	67	14	20	34	60	-12	7	0	—	—	—	—	—
05-06—Toronto	NHL	74	19	19	38	64	-19	14	0	—	—	—	—	—
NHL Totals (10 years)		747	217	237	454	616	-116	78	2	34	9	8	17	37

ODELEIN, LYLE D

PERSONAL: Born July 21, 1968, in Quill Lake, Sask. ... 6-0/206. ... Shoots right. ... Brother of Selmar Odelein, defenseman with Edmonton Oilers (1985-86 through 1988-89). ... Name pronounced OH-duh-lighn.

TRANSACTIONS/CAREER NOTES: Selected by Montreal Canadiens in seventh round (eighth Canadiens pick, 141st overall) of entry draft (June 21, 1986). ... Bruised right ankle (January 22, 1991); missed five games. ... Twisted right ankle (February 9, 1991). ... Suspended one game for game misconduct penalties (March 1, 1993). ... Bruised shoulder (January 24, 1994); missed three games. ... Suspended two games without pay and fined $1,000 for shooting puck into the opposing team's bench (April 3, 1996). ... Traded by Canadiens to New Jersey Devils for RW Stephane Richer (August 22, 1996). ... Bruised knee (January 21, 1997); missed three games. ... Bruised shoulder (November 12, 1997); missed one game. ... Flu (January 11, 1999); missed two games. ... Bruised right knee (March 22, 1999); missed nine games. ... Injured back (November 5, 1999); missed three games. ... Flu (January 14, 2000); missed three games. ... Traded by Devils to Phoenix Coyotes for D Deron Quint and third-round pick (traded back to Phoenix; Coyotes selected D Beat Forster) in 2001 draft (March 7, 2000). ... Selected by Columbus Blue Jackets in expansion draft (June 23, 2000). ... Bruised knee (March 15, 2001); missed one game. ... Back spasms (January 16, 2002); missed three games. ... Traded by Blue Jackets to Chicago Blackhawks for D Jaroslav Spacek and second-round pick (C Dan Fritsche) in 2003 draft (March 19, 2002). ... Suspended one playoff game for cross-checking incident (April 22, 2002). ... Traded by Blackhawks to Dallas Stars for D Sami Helenius and seventh-round pick in 2004 entry draft (March 10, 2003). ... Injured foot (March 15, 2003); missed eight games. ... Signed as free agent by Florida Panthers (September 9, 2003). ... Signed by Penguins as unrestricted free agent (September 2, 2005). ... Knee injury (January 26, 2006) and surgery (February 28, 2006); missed final 31 games of regular season.

STATISTICAL PLATEAUS: Three-goal games: 1993-94 (1).

Season Team	League	GP	G	A	Pts.	PIM	+/-	PP	SH	GP	G	A	Pts.	PIM
		REGULAR SEASON								PLAYOFFS				
85-86—Moose Jaw	WHL	67	9	37	46	117	...	...	...	13	1	6	7	34
86-87—Moose Jaw	WHL	59	9	50	59	70	...	...	...	9	2	5	7	26
87-88—Moose Jaw	WHL	63	15	43	58	166	...	...	...	—	—	—	—	—
88-89—Sherbrooke	AHL	33	3	4	7	120	...	...	...	3	0	2	2	5
—Peoria	IHL	36	2	8	10	116	...	...	...	—	—	—	—	—
89-90—Sherbrooke	AHL	68	7	24	31	265	...	...	...	12	6	5	11	79
—Montreal	NHL	8	0	2	2	33	-1	0	0	—	—	—	—	—
90-91—Montreal	NHL	52	0	2	2	259	7	0	0	12	0	0	0	54
91-92—Montreal	NHL	71	1	7	8	212	15	0	0	7	0	0	0	11
92-93—Montreal	NHL	83	2	14	16	205	35	0	0	20	1	5	6	30
93-94—Montreal	NHL	79	11	29	40	276	8	6	0	7	0	0	0	17
94-95—Montreal	NHL	48	3	7	10	152	-13	0	0	—	—	—	—	—
95-96—Montreal	NHL	79	3	14	17	230	8	0	1	6	1	1	2	6
96-97—New Jersey	NHL	79	3	13	16	110	16	1	0	10	2	2	4	19
97-98—New Jersey	NHL	79	4	19	23	171	11	1	0	6	1	1	2	21
98-99—New Jersey	NHL	70	5	26	31	114	6	1	0	7	0	3	3	10

O

Season Team	League	REGULAR SEASON GP	G	A	Pts.	PIM	+/-	PP	SH	PLAYOFFS GP	G	A	Pts.	PIM
99-00—New Jersey	NHL	57	1	15	16	104	-10	0	0	—	—	—	—	—
—Phoenix	NHL	16	1	7	8	19	1	1	0	5	0	0	0	16
00-01—Columbus	NHL	81	3	14	17	118	-16	1	0	—	—	—	—	—
01-02—Columbus	NHL	65	2	14	16	89	-28	0	0	—	—	—	—	—
—Chicago	NHL	12	0	2	2	4	0	0	0	4	0	1	1	25
02-03—Chicago	NHL	65	7	4	11	76	7	0	0	—	—	—	—	—
—Dallas	NHL	3	0	0	0	6	0	0	0	2	0	0	0	0
03-04—Florida	NHL	82	4	12	16	88	-7	2	0	—	—	—	—	—
05-06—Pittsburgh	NHL	27	0	1	1	50	-10	0	0	—	—	—	—	—
NHL Totals (16 years)		1056	50	202	252	2316	29	13	1	86	5	13	18	209

OHLUND, MATTIAS D

PERSONAL: Born September 9, 1976, in Pitea, Sweden. ... 6-2/220. ... Shoots left. ... Name pronounced MAT-tee-uhz OH-luhnd.

TRANSACTIONS/CAREER NOTES: Selected by Vancouver Canucks in first round (first Canucks pick, 13th overall) of entry draft (June 28, 1994). ... Concussion (March 26, 1998); missed four games. ... Sprained shoulder (February 23, 1999); missed three games. ... Concussion (April 3, 1999); missed season's final five games. ... Eye (September 12, 1999); missed season's first 38 games. ... Groin (March 8, 2000); missed two games. ... Eye surgery (October 20, 2000); missed 17 games. ... Flu (October 6, 2001); missed one game. ... Sprained left knee (October 6, 2002); missed five games. ... Flu (December 28, 2002); missed one game. ... Knee (February 27, 2003); missed last 18 games of season and one playoff game. ... Ribs, shoulder (February 23, 2006); missed four games.

Season Team	League	REGULAR SEASON GP	G	A	Pts.	PIM	+/-	PP	SH	PLAYOFFS GP	G	A	Pts.	PIM
92-93—Pitea	Sweden Dv. 2	22	0	6	6	16	...	...	...	—	—	—	—	—
93-94—Pitea	Sweden Dv. 2	28	7	10	17	62	...	...	...	—	—	—	—	—
94-95—Lulea	Sweden	34	6	10	16	34	...	...	...	9	4	0	4	16
95-96—Lulea	Sweden	38	4	10	14	26	...	...	...	13	0	1	1	47
96-97—Lulea	Sweden	47	7	9	16	38	...	...	...	10	1	2	3	8
97-98—Vancouver	NHL	77	7	23	30	76	3	1	0	—	—	—	—	—
—Swedish Oly. team	Int'l	4	0	1	1	4	-1	0	0	—	—	—	—	—
98-99—Vancouver	NHL	74	9	26	35	83	-19	2	1	—	—	—	—	—
99-00—Vancouver	NHL	42	4	16	20	24	6	2	1	—	—	—	—	—
00-01—Vancouver	NHL	65	8	20	28	46	-16	1	1	4	1	3	4	6
01-02—Vancouver	NHL	81	10	26	36	56	16	4	1	6	1	1	2	6
—Swedish Oly. team	Int'l	4	0	2	2	2	...	...	...	—	—	—	—	—
02-03—Vancouver	NHL	59	2	27	29	42	1	0	0	13	3	4	7	12
03-04—Vancouver	NHL	82	14	20	34	73	14	5	0	7	1	4	5	13
04-05—Lulea	Sweden	2	1	0	1	4	-1	1	0	...	...	...	...	...
05-06—Vancouver	NHL	78	13	20	33	92	-6	8	1	—	—	—	—	—
—Swedish Oly. team	Int'l	6	0	2	2	2	2	0	0	—	—	—	—	—
NHL Totals (8 years)		558	67	178	245	492	-1	23	5	30	6	12	18	37

OKPOSO, KYLE RW

PERSONAL: Born April 16, 1988, in St. Paul, Minn. ... 6-0/195. ... Shoots right.

TRANSACTIONS/CAREER NOTES: Selected by New York Islanders in first round (first Islanders pick; seventh overall) of NHL draft (June 24, 2006).

Season Team	League	REGULAR SEASON GP	G	A	Pts.	PIM	+/-	PP	SH	PLAYOFFS GP	G	A	Pts.	PIM
04-05—Shattuck	USHS (West)	65	47	45	92	72	...	...	...	—	—	—	—	—
05-06—Des Moines	USHL	50	27	31	58	56	...	...	...	—	—	—	—	—

OLESZ, ROSTISLAV C

PERSONAL: Born October 10, 1985, in Bolivec, Czech. ... 6-2/205. ... Shoots left.

TRANSACTIONS/CAREER NOTES: Selected by Florida Panthers in first round (first Panthers pick, seventh overall) of entry draft (June 26, 2004). ... Sprained right MCL (October 18, 2005); missed 16 games. ... Shoulder injury (January 12. 2006); missed five games. ... Right knee injury (April 13, 2006); missed final two games of regular season.

Season Team	League	REGULAR SEASON GP	G	A	Pts.	PIM	+/-	PP	SH	PLAYOFFS GP	G	A	Pts.	PIM
00-01—Vitkovice	Czech Rep.	3	0	1	1	0	...	...	...	—	—	—	—	—
01-02—Vitkovice	Czech Rep.	11	1	2	3	0	...	...	...	—	—	—	—	—
02-03—Vitkovice	Czech Rep.	40	6	3	9	41	...	...	...	5	0	0	0	2
03-04—Vitkovice	Czech Rep.	35	1	11	12	10	...	...	...	6	2	1	3	4
04-05—Sparta Praha	Czech Rep.	47	6	7	13	12	...	...	...	—	—	—	—	—
05-06—Florida	NHL	59	8	13	21	24	-4	0	1	—	—	—	—	—
—Czech Rep. Oly. team	Int'l	8	0	0	0	2	1	0	0	—	—	—	—	—
NHL Totals (1 year)		59	8	13	21	24	-4	0	1					

OLIVER, DAVID RW

PERSONAL: Born April 17, 1971, in Sechelt, B.C. ... 6-0/190. ... Shoots right.

COLLEGE: Michigan

TRANSACTIONS/CAREER NOTES: Selected by Edmonton Oilers in seventh round (seventh Oilers pick, 144th overall) of entry draft (June 22, 1991). ... Hip pointer (January 24, 1997); missed one game. ... Claimed off waivers by New York Rangers (February 22, 1997). ... Signed as

free agent by Ottawa Senators (July 2, 1998). ... Signed as free agent by Phoenix Coyotes (July 16, 1999). ... Signed as free agent by Senators (August 2, 2000). ... Hip pointer (November 11, 2000); missed two games. ... Groin (November 19, 2000); missed five games. ... Signed as free agent by Dallas Stars (July 30, 2002). ... Throat (January 19, 2004); missed one game. ... Back (February 25, 2004); missed one game.
STATISTICAL PLATEAUS: Three-goal games: 1994-95 (1).

		REGULAR SEASON								PLAYOFFS				
Season Team	**League**	**GP**	**G**	**A**	**Pts.**	**PIM**	**+/-**	**PP**	**SH**	**GP**	**G**	**A**	**Pts.**	**PIM**
90-91—Univ. of Michigan	CCHA	27	13	11	24	34	...	...	...	—	—	—	—	—
91-92—Univ. of Michigan	CCHA	44	31	27	58	32	...	...	...	—	—	—	—	—
92-93—Univ. of Michigan	CCHA	40	35	20	55	18	...	...	...	—	—	—	—	—
93-94—Univ. of Michigan	CCHA	41	28	40	68	16	...	16	0	—	—	—	—	—
94-95—Cape Breton	AHL	32	11	18	29	8	-2	4	1	—	—	—	—	—
—Edmonton	NHL	44	16	14	30	20	-11	10	0	—	—	—	—	—
95-96—Edmonton	NHL	80	20	19	39	34	-22	14	0	—	—	—	—	—
96-97—Edmonton	NHL	17	1	2	3	4	-8	0	0	—	—	—	—	—
—New York Rangers	NHL	14	2	1	3	4	3	0	0	3	0	0	0	0
97-98—Houston	IHL	78	38	27	65	60	-5	18	1	4	3	0	3	4
98-99—Ottawa	NHL	17	2	5	7	4	1	0	0	—	—	—	—	—
—Houston	IHL	37	18	17	35	30	-1	4	0	19	10	6	16	22
99-00—Phoenix	NHL	9	1	0	1	2	0	1	0	—	—	—	—	—
—Houston	IHL	45	16	11	27	40	...	...	...	11	3	4	7	8
00-01—Grand Rapids	IHL	51	14	17	31	35	...	...	...	10	6	2	8	8
—Ottawa	NHL	7	0	0	0	2	0	0	0	—	—	—	—	—
01-02—Munich	Germany	59	20	14	34	30	...	...	...	9	2	2	4	6
02-03—Utah	AHL	37	11	14	25	14	-8	4	0	—	—	—	—	—
—Dallas	NHL	6	0	3	3	2	1	0	0	6	0	0	0	2
03-04—Utah	AHL	31	5	12	17	12	-2	2	1	—	—	—	—	—
—Dallas	NHL	36	7	5	12	12	6	3	0	1	0	0	0	0
04-05—Guildford	England	16	8	14	22	4	...	3	0	15	3	5	8	31
05-06—Iowa	AHL	54	21	13	34	26	-7	11	0	5	3	0	3	4
—Dallas	NHL	3	0	0	0	0	-1	0	0	—	—	—	—	—
NHL Totals (9 years)		233	49	49	98	84	-31	28	0	10	0	0	0	2

OLIWA, KRZYSZTOF LW/RW

PERSONAL: Born April 12, 1973, in Tychy, Poland. ... 6-5/245. ... Shoots left. ... Name pronounced KRIH-stahf OH-lee-vuh.
TRANSACTIONS/CAREER NOTES: Selected by New Jersey Devils in third round (fourth Devils pick, 65th overall) of entry draft (June 26, 1993). ... Injured foot (November 10, 1997); missed two games. ... Strained groin (November 28, 1998); missed one game. ... Sprained left knee (October 30, 1999); missed six games. ... Flu (January 11, 2000); missed one game. ... Injured left knee (April 2, 2000); missed final three games of season. ... Traded by Devils with future considerations (D Deron Quint) to Columbus Blue Jackets for third-round pick (C/LW Brandon Nolan) in 2001 draft and future considerations (June 12, 2000); Devils acquired RW Turner Stevenson to complete deal (June 23, 2000). ... Fractured arm (October 28, 2000); missed 23 games. ... Traded by Blue Jackets to Pittsburgh Penguins for third-round pick (D Aaron Johnson) in 2001 draft (January 14, 2001). ... Injured hamstring (March 20, 2001); missed five games. ... Traded by Penguins to New York Rangers for ninth-round pick (traded to Tampa Bay; Lightning selected RW Albert Vishnayako) in 2003 draft (June 22, 2002). ... Suspended five games for unsportsmanlike conduct (November 11, 2002). ... Traded by Rangers to Boston Bruins for future considerations (January 6, 2003). ... Signed as free agent by Calgary Flames (July 30, 2003). ... Suspended two games for high-sticking incident (November 21, 2003). ... Suspended three games for abuse of officials (March 21, 2004). ... Signed as free agent by Devils (July 15, 2004). ... Waived by Devils (October 24, 2005); cleared waivers.

		REGULAR SEASON								PLAYOFFS				
Season Team	**League**	**GP**	**G**	**A**	**Pts.**	**PIM**	**+/-**	**PP**	**SH**	**GP**	**G**	**A**	**Pts.**	**PIM**
90-91—GKS Katowice	Poland Jrs	5	4	4	8	10	...	...	...	—	—	—	—	—
91-92—GKS Tychy	Poland	10	3	7	10	6	...	...	...	—	—	—	—	—
92-93—Welland Jr. B	OHA	30	13	21	34	127	...	...	...	—	—	—	—	—
93-94—Albany	AHL	33	2	4	6	151	-6	0	0	—	—	—	—	—
—Raleigh	ECHL	15	0	2	2	65	-1	0	0	9	0	0	0	35
94-95—Albany	AHL	20	1	1	2	77	-2	0	0	—	—	—	—	—
—Detroit	IHL	4	0	1	1	24	-5	0	0	—	—	—	—	—
—Saint John	AHL	14	1	4	5	79	-4	0	0	—	—	—	—	—
—Raleigh	ECHL	5	0	2	2	32	-2	0	0	—	—	—	—	—
95-96—Albany	AHL	51	5	11	16	217	...	...	...	—	—	—	—	—
—Raleigh	ECHL	9	1	0	1	53	...	...	...	—	—	—	—	—
96-97—Albany	AHL	60	13	14	27	322	13	3	0	15	7	1	8	49
—New Jersey	NHL	1	0	0	0	5	-1	0	0	—	—	—	—	—
97-98—New Jersey	NHL	73	2	3	5	295	3	0	0	6	0	0	0	23
98-99—New Jersey	NHL	64	5	7	12	240	4	0	0	1	0	0	0	2
99-00—New Jersey	NHL	69	6	10	16	184	-2	1	0	—	—	—	—	—
00-01—Columbus	NHL	10	0	2	2	34	1	0	0	—	—	—	—	—
—Pittsburgh	NHL	26	1	2	3	131	-4	0	0	5	0	0	0	16
01-02—Pittsburgh	NHL	57	0	2	2	150	-5	0	0	—	—	—	—	—
02-03—New York Rangers	NHL	9	0	0	0	51	1	0	0	—	—	—	—	—
—Hartford	AHL	15	0	1	1	30	-7	0	0	—	—	—	—	—
—Boston	NHL	33	0	0	0	110	-4	0	0	—	—	—	—	—
03-04—Calgary	NHL	65	3	2	5	247	-8	0	0	20	2	0	2	6
04-05—Podhale Nowy Targ	Poland	...	...	...	...	...	...	...	...	2	0	0	0	12
05-06—New Jersey	NHL	3	0	0	0	0	-2	0	0	—	—	—	—	—
NHL Totals (9 years)		410	17	28	45	1447	-17	1	0	32	2	0	2	47

ONDRUS, BEN LW

PERSONAL: Born June 25, 1982, in Sherwood Park, Alta. ... 6-0/185. ... Shoots right.
TRANSACTIONS/CAREER NOTES: Signed as free agent by Toronto Maple Leafs (May 27, 2004).

Season Team	League	GP	G	A	Pts.	PIM	+/-	PP	SH	GP	G	A	Pts.	PIM
		REGULAR SEASON								PLAYOFFS				
98-99—Swift Current	WHL	46	4	4	8	58	...	...	...	6	0	1	1	8
99-00—Swift Current	WHL	67	14	15	29	138	...	...	...	12	1	0	1	22
00-01—Swift Current	WHL	69	13	17	30	151	...	...	...	—	—	—	—	—
01-02—Swift Current	WHL	67	30	41	71	153	...	...	...	12	4	3	7	18
02-03—Swift Current	WHL	67	33	36	69	98	...	...	...	3	0	1	1	11
—Idaho	WCHL	4	0	3	3	0	...	...	...	5	0	1	1	6
03-04—St. John's	AHL	60	6	11	17	102	...	...	...	—	—	—	—	—
04-05—St. John's	AHL	78	7	11	18	137	5	0	0	5	0	1	1	7
05-06—Toronto	AHL	53	12	18	30	104	0	5	0	5	1	2	3	4
—Toronto	NHL	22	0	0	0	18	-10	0	0	—	—	—	—	—
NHL Totals (1 year)		22	0	0	0	18	-10	0	0					

ORPIK, BROOKS D

PERSONAL: Born September 26, 1980, in San Francisco. ... 6-2/224. ... Shoots left.

TRANSACTIONS/CAREER NOTES: Selected by Pittsburgh Penguins in first round (first Penguins pick, 18th overall) of entry draft (June 24, 2000). ... Suspended one game for kneeing incident (October 11, 2003). ... Re-signed by Penguins as restricted free agent (September 13, 2005). ... Broken foot (December 27, 2005); missed 12 games. ... Suspended three games in boarding incident (March 6, 2006).

Season Team	League	GP	G	A	Pts.	PIM	+/-	PP	SH	GP	G	A	Pts.	PIM
		REGULAR SEASON								PLAYOFFS				
97-98—Thayer Academy	Mass. H.S.	22	0	7	7	...	...	...	...	—	—	—	—	—
98-99—Boston College	Hockey East	41	1	10	11	96	...	...	...	—	—	—	—	—
99-00—Boston College	Hockey East	38	1	9	10	100	...	...	...	—	—	—	—	—
00-01—Boston College	Hockey East	40	0	20	20	124	...	...	...	—	—	—	—	—
01-02—Wilkes-Barre/Scranton	AHL	78	2	18	20	99	2	1	0	—	—	—	—	—
02-03—Pittsburgh	NHL	6	0	0	0	2	-5	0	0	—	—	—	—	—
—Wilkes-Barre/Scranton	AHL	71	4	14	18	105	5	0	0	6	0	0	0	14
03-04—Wilkes-Barre/Scranton	AHL	3	0	0	0	2	1	0	0	24	0	4	4	53
—Pittsburgh	NHL	79	1	9	10	127	-36	0	0	—	—	—	—	—
05-06—Pittsburgh	NHL	64	2	7	9	124	-3	0	0	—	—	—	—	—
NHL Totals (3 years)		149	3	16	19	253	-44	0	0					

ORR, COLTON RW

PERSONAL: Born March 3, 1982, in Winnipeg, Manitoba. ... 6-3/210. ... Shoots right.

TRANSACTIONS/CAREER NOTES: Signed as free agent by Boston Bruins (September 19, 2001). ... Claimed on waivers by New York Rangers (November 29, 2005).

Season Team	League	GP	G	A	Pts.	PIM	+/-	PP	SH	GP	G	A	Pts.	PIM
		REGULAR SEASON								PLAYOFFS				
98-99—Swift Current	WHL	2	0	0	0	2	...	...	...	1	0	0	0	0
99-00—Swift Current	WHL	61	3	2	5	130	...	...	...	—	—	—	—	—
00-01—Swift Current	WHL	19	0	4	4	67	...	...	...	—	—	—	—	—
—Kamloops	WHL	41	8	1	9	179	...	...	...	3	0	0	0	20
01-02—Kamloops	WHL	1	0	0	0	7	...	...	...	2	0	0	0	2
02-03—Kamloops	WHL	3	2	0	2	17	...	...	...	—	—	—	—	—
—Regina	WHL	37	6	2	8	170	...	...	...	3	0	0	0	19
—Providence	AHL	1	0	0	0	7	0	0	0	—	—	—	—	—
03-04—Boston	NHL	1	0	0	0	0	-1	0	0	—	—	—	—	—
—Providence	AHL	64	1	4	5	257	-6	0	0	2	0	0	0	9
04-05—Providence	AHL	61	1	6	7	279	-6	0	0	17	1	0	1	44
05-06—Boston	NHL	20	0	0	0	27	0	0	0	—	—	—	—	—
—New York Rangers	NHL	15	0	1	1	44	1	0	0	1	0	0	0	2
NHL Totals (2 years)		36	0	1	1	71	0	0	0	1	0	0	0	2

ORSZAGH, VLADIMIR RW/LW

PERSONAL: Born May 24, 1977, in Banska Bystrica, Czech. ... 5-11/195. ... Shoots left. ... Name pronounced OHR-sahg.

TRANSACTIONS/CAREER NOTES: Selected by New York Islanders in fifth round (fourth Islanders pick, 106th overall) of NHL draft (July 8, 1995). ... Tendinitis (December 14, 1999); missed one game. ... Signed as free agent by Nashville Predators (June 1, 2001). ... Charley horse (March 2, 2002); missed two games. ... Rib muscle (December 23, 2002); missed three games. ... Bruised shoulder (March 31, 2003); missed one game. ... Torn right knee ligaments at world championships (May 2005). ... Signed as free agent by Phoenix Coyotes (December 29, 2005). ... Claimed on waivers by St. Louis Blues (December 30, 2005). ... Injured knee (March 5, 2006) and had surgery; missed season's final 24 games.

STATISTICAL PLATEAUS: Three-goal games: 2003-04 (1).

Season Team	League	GP	G	A	Pts.	PIM	+/-	PP	SH	GP	G	A	Pts.	PIM
		REGULAR SEASON								PLAYOFFS				
93-94—IS Banska Byst.	Slovakia Jrs.	...	38	27	65	...	...	...	...	—	—	—	—	—
94-95—Banska Bystrica	Slov. Div.	38	18	12	30	...	...	...	...	—	—	—	—	—
—Martimex ZTS Martin	Slovakia	1	0	0	0	0	...	...	...	—	—	—	—	—
95-96—Banska Bystrica	Slovakia	31	9	5	14	22	...	...	...	—	—	—	—	—
96-97—Utah	IHL	68	12	15	27	30	...	...	...	3	0	1	1	4
97-98—Utah	IHL	62	13	10	23	60	0	1	0	4	2	0	2	0
—New York Islanders	NHL	11	0	1	1	2	-3	0	0	—	—	—	—	—
98-99—Lowell	AHL	68	18	23	41	57	-6	7	2	3	2	2	4	2
—New York Islanders	NHL	12	1	0	1	6	2	0	0	—	—	—	—	—

Season Team	League	GP	G	A	Pts.	PIM	+/-	PP	SH	GP	G	A	Pts.	PIM
		REGULAR SEASON								PLAYOFFS				
99-00—Lowell	AHL	55	8	12	20	22	...	...	...	7	3	3	6	2
—New York Islanders	NHL	11	2	1	3	4	1	0	0	—	—	—	—	—
00-01—Djurgarden Stockholm	Sweden	50	23	13	36	62	...	...	...	16	7	3	10	20
01-02—Nashville	NHL	79	15	21	36	56	-15	5	0	—	—	—	—	—
02-03—Nashville	NHL	78	16	16	32	38	-1	3	0	—	—	—	—	—
03-04—Nashville	NHL	82	16	21	37	74	-4	2	2	6	2	0	2	4
04-05—Banska Bystrica	Slov. Div.	2	2	0	2	4	1	...	...	—	—	—	—	—
—Zvolen	Slovakia	38	16	14	30	50	40	...	...	17	5	2	7	24
05-06—Lulea	Sweden	19	8	5	13	42	...	...	...	—	—	—	—	—
—St. Louis	NHL	16	4	5	9	14	-2	1	0	—	—	—	—	—
NHL Totals (7 years)		289	54	65	119	194	-22	11	2	6	2	0	2	4

ORTMEYER, JED — RW

PERSONAL: Born September 3, 1978, in Omaha, Neb. ... 6-1/189. ... Shoots right.
COLLEGE: Michigan
TRANSACTIONS/CAREER NOTES: Signed as free agent by New York Rangers (May 10, 2003). ... Injured leg (March 20, 2004); missed remainder of season. ... Re-signed by Rangers as restricted free agent (September 6, 2005). ... Personal reasons (December 1, 2005); missed one game.

Season Team	League	GP	G	A	Pts.	PIM	+/-	PP	SH	GP	G	A	Pts.	PIM
		REGULAR SEASON								PLAYOFFS				
99-00—Univ. of Michigan	CCHA	41	8	16	24	24	40	...	...	—	—	—	—	—
00-01—Univ. of Michigan	CCHA	27	10	11	21	52	...	...	...	—	—	—	—	—
01-02—Univ. of Michigan	CCHA	41	15	23	38	40	...	...	...	—	—	—	—	—
02-03—Univ. of Michigan	CCHA	36	18	16	34	48	...	...	...	—	—	—	—	—
03-04—Hartford	AHL	13	2	8	10	4	8	0	0	16	5	2	7	6
—New York Rangers	NHL	58	2	4	6	16	-10	0	0	—	—	—	—	—
04-05—Hartford	AHL	61	7	20	27	63	11	1	0	6	0	1	1	4
05-06—New York Rangers	NHL	78	5	2	7	38	2	0	0	4	1	0	1	4
NHL Totals (2 years)		136	7	6	13	54	-8	0	0	4	1	0	1	4

OSGOOD, CHRIS — G

PERSONAL: Born November 26, 1972, in Peace River, Alta. ... 5-10/178. ... Catches left. ... Nickname: Ozzie.
TRANSACTIONS/CAREER NOTES: Selected by Detroit Red Wings in third round (third Red Wings pick, 54th overall) of entry draft (June 22, 1991). ... Hamstring (January 14, 1997); missed five games. ... Groin (March 14, 1998); missed four games. ... Hip flexor (November 19, 1998); missed six games. ... Right knee (April 27, 1999); missed four playoff games. ... Hand (November 24, 1999); missed 15 games. ... Claimed by New York Islanders in waiver draft (September 28, 2001). ... Tendinitis in wrist (January 22, 2002); missed three games. ... Ankle (January 24, 2002); missed 18 games. ... Traded by Islanders with third-round pick (G Konstantin Barulin) in 2003 to St. Louis Blues for C Justin Papineau and second-round pick (C Jeremy Colliton) in 2003 (March 11, 2003). ... Leg (December 30, 2003); missed two games. ... Hand (March 7, 2004); missed one game. ... Signed as free agent by Red Wings (August 8, 2005). ... Groin (September 15, 2005); missed season's first seven games. ... Groin (April 27, 2006); missed three playoff games.

Season Team	League	GP	Min.	W	L	OTL	T	GA	SO	GAA	SV%	GP	Min.	W	L	GA	SO	GAA	SV%
		REGULAR SEASON										PLAYOFFS							
89-90—Medicine Hat	WHL	57	3094	24	28	...	2	228	0	4.42	...	3	173	3	4	17	0	5.90	...
90-91—Medicine Hat	WHL	46	2630	23	18	...	3	173	2	3.95	...	12	714	7	5	42	0	3.53	...
91-92—Medicine Hat	WHL	15	819	10	3	...	0	44	0	3.22	...	—	—	—	—	—	—	—	—
—Brandon	WHL	16	890	3	10	...	1	60	1	4.04	...	—	—	—	—	—	—	—	—
—Seattle	WHL	21	1217	12	7	...	1	65	1	3.20	...	15	904	9	6	51	0	3.38	...
92-93—Adirondack	AHL	45	2438	19	19	...	2	159	0	3.91	.881	1	59	0	1	2	0	2.03	.920
93-94—Adirondack	AHL	4	240	3	1	...	0	13	0	3.25	.893	—	—	—	—	—	—	—	—
—Detroit	NHL	41	2206	23	8	...	5	105	2	2.86	.895	6	307	3	2	12	1	2.35	.891
94-95—Adirondack	AHL	2	120	1	1	...	0	6	0	3.00	.908	—	—	—	—	—	—	—	—
—Detroit	NHL	19	1087	14	5	...	0	41	1	2.26	.917	2	68	0	0	2	0	1.76	.920
95-96—Detroit	NHL	50	2933	*39	6	...	5	106	5	2.17	.911	15	936	8	7	33	2	2.12	.898
96-97—Detroit	NHL	47	2769	23	13	...	9	106	6	2.30	.910	2	47	0	0	2	0	2.55	.905
97-98—Detroit	NHL	64	3807	33	20	...	11	140	6	2.21	.913	*22	*1361	*16	6	48	2	2.12	.918
98-99—Detroit	NHL	63	3691	34	25	...	4	149	3	2.42	.910	6	358	4	2	14	1	2.35	.919
99-00—Detroit	NHL	53	3148	30	14	...	8	126	6	2.40	.907	9	547	5	4	18	2	1.97	.924
00-01—Detroit	NHL	52	2834	25	19	...	4	127	1	2.69	.903	6	365	2	4	15	1	2.47	.905
01-02—New York Islanders	NHL	66	3743	32	25	...	6	156	4	2.50	.910	7	392	3	4	17	0	2.60	.912
02-03—New York Islanders	NHL	37	1993	17	14	...	4	97	2	2.92	.894	7	417	3	4	17	1	2.45	.907
—St. Louis	NHL	9	532	4	3	...	2	27	2	3.05	.888	...	...	...	...	...	...	...	...
03-04—St. Louis	NHL	67	3861	31	25	...	8	144	3	2.24	.910	5	287	1	4	12	0	2.51	.890
05-06—Grand Rapids	AHL	3	180	2	1	0	...	10	0	3.33	.882	—	—	—	—	—	—	—	—
—Detroit	NHL	32	1846	20	6	5	...	85	2	2.76	.897	—	—	—	—	—	—	—	—
NHL Totals (12 years)		600	34450	325	183	5	66	1409	43	2.45	.907	87	5085	45	37	190	10	2.24	.910

OTT, STEVE — C/LW

PERSONAL: Born August 19, 1982, in Summerside, P.E.I. ... 6-0/185. ... Shoots left.
TRANSACTIONS/CAREER NOTES: Selected by Dallas Stars in first round (first Stars pick, 25th overall) of NHL draft (June 24, 2000). ... Sprained back (December 7, 2003); missed seven games. ... Fined $1,000 for penalties in game against Ottawa Senators (January 28, 2004).

Season Team	League	GP	G	A	Pts.	PIM	+/-	PP	SH	GP	G	A	Pts.	PIM
		REGULAR SEASON								PLAYOFFS				
98-99—Leamington	Jr. B	48	14	30	44	110	...	...	...	—	—	—	—	—
99-00—Windsor	OHL	66	23	39	62	131	...	...	...	12	3	5	8	21

Season Team	League	GP	G	A	Pts.	PIM	+/-	PP	SH	GP	G	A	Pts.	PIM
		REGULAR SEASON								PLAYOFFS				
00-01—Windsor	OHL	55	50	37	87	164	40	11	4	9	3	8	11	27
01-02—Windsor	OHL	53	43	45	88	178	...	...	...	14	6	10	16	49
02-03—Utah	AHL	40	9	11	20	98	-1	5	0	—	—	—	—	—
—Dallas	NHL	26	3	4	7	31	6	0	0	1	0	0	0	0
03-04—Dallas	NHL	73	2	10	12	152	-2	0	0	4	1	0	1	0
04-05—Hamilton	AHL	67	18	21	39	279	-1	1	0	4	0	0	0	20
05-06—Dallas	NHL	82	5	17	22	178	1	0	0	5	0	1	1	2
NHL Totals (3 years)		181	10	31	41	361	5	0	0	10	1	1	2	2

OUELLET, MAXIME G

PERSONAL: Born June 17, 1981, in Beauport, Que. ... 6-2/194. ... Catches left. ... Name pronounced: mak-SEEM wah-LEHT

TRANSACTIONS/CAREER NOTES: Selected by Philadelphia Flyers in first round (first Flyers pick, 22nd overall) of entry draft (June 26, 1999). ... Traded by Flyers with first- (traded to Dallas; Stars selected D Martin Vagner), second- (G Maxime Daigneault) and third-round (C Derek Krestanovich) picks in 2002 to Washington Capitals for C Adam Oates (March 19, 2002). ... Traded by Capitals to Vancouver Canucks for fifth-round pick (traded to New York Rangers; Rangers selected W Tomas Zaborsky) in 2006 draft (December 2, 2005).

Season Team	League	GP	Min.	W	L	OTL	T	GA	SO	GAA	SV%	GP	Min.	W	L	GA	SO	GAA	SV%
		REGULAR SEASON										PLAYOFFS							
97-98—Quebec	QMJHL	24	1199	12	7	...	1	66	0	3.30	...	7	305	3	1	16	0	3.15	...
98-99—Quebec	QMJHL	58	3447	40	12	...	6	155	3	2.70	...	13	803	6	7	41	1	3.06	...
99-00—Quebec	QMJHL	53	2984	31	16	...	4	133	2	2.67	.916	11	638	7	4	28	2	2.63	.912
00-01—Philadelphia	NHL	2	76	0	1	...	0	3	0	2.37	.889	—	—	—	—	—	—	—	—
—Philadelphia	AHL	2	86	1	0	...	0	4	0	2.79	.926	—	—	—	—	—	—	—	—
—Rouyn-Noranda	QMJHL	25	1471	18	6	...	1	65	3	2.65	.913	8	490	4	4	25	0	3.06	.894
01-02—Philadelphia	AHL	41	2294	16	13	...	8	104	1	2.72	.902	—	—	—	—	—	—	—	—
—Portland	AHL	6	358	3	3	...	0	17	0	2.85	.917	—	—	—	—	—	—	—	—
02-03—Portland	AHL	48	2773	22	16	...	7	111	7	2.40	.929	2	120	1	1	8	0	4.00	.889
03-04—Washington	NHL	6	365	2	3	...	1	19	1	3.12	.910	—	—	—	—	—	—	—	—
—Portland	AHL	52	3051	15	29	...	8	101	10	1.99	.925	5	302	2	2	8	0	1.59	.938
04-05—Portland	AHL	40	2304	15	20	...	...	111	0	2.89	.911	—	—	—	—	—	—	—	—
05-06—Hershey	AHL	1	41	0	0	0	...	5	0	7.32	.737	—	—	—	—	—	—	—	—
—Manitoba	AHL	16	946	9	7	0	...	46	0	2.92	.894	3	127	0	1	6	0	2.83	.919
—Vancouver	NHL	4	222	0	2	1	...	12	0	3.24	.894	—	—	—	—	—	—	—	—
NHL Totals (3 years)		12	663	2	6	1	1	34	1	3.08	.903								

OUELLET, MICHEL RW

PERSONAL: Born March 5, 1982, in Rimouski, Que. ... 6-1/201. ... Shoots right. ... Name pronounced: wuh LEHT

TRANSACTIONS/CAREER NOTES: Selected by Pittsburgh Penguins in fourth round (fourth Penguins pick, 124th overall) of NHL entry draft (June 24, 2000). ... Injured right knee (February 6, 2006); missed three games. ... Re-signed by Penguins as restricted free agent (August 18, 2005). ... Back injury (November 27, 2006); missed three games. ... Bruised right knee (February 6, 2006); missed three games.

Season Team	League	GP	G	A	Pts.	PIM	+/-	PP	SH	GP	G	A	Pts.	PIM
		REGULAR SEASON								PLAYOFFS				
98-99—Rimouski	QMJHL	28	7	13	20	10	...	...	...	—	—	—	—	—
99-00—Rimouski	QMJHL	72	36	53	89	38	...	...	...	—	—	—	—	—
00-01—Rimouski	QMJHL	63	42	50	92	50	-12	28	1	11	6	7	13	8
01-02—Rimouski	QMJHL	61	40	58	98	66	...	...	...	7	3	6	9	4
02-03—Wilkes-Barre/Scranton	AHL	4	0	2	2	0	1	0	0	—	—	—	—	—
—Wheeling	ECHL	55	20	26	46	40	-1	7	0	—	—	—	—	—
03-04—Wilkes-Barre/Scranton	AHL	79	30	19	49	34	0	12	0	22	2	10	12	6
04-05—Wilkes-Barre/Scranton	AHL	80	31	32	63	56	15	6	0	11	2	3	5	6
05-06—Wilkes-Barre/Scranton	AHL	19	10	20	30	12	12	6	1	—	—	—	—	—
—Pittsburgh	NHL	50	16	16	32	16	-13	11	0	—	—	—	—	—
NHL Totals (1 year)		50	16	16	32	16	-13	11	0					

OVECHKIN, ALEXANDER LW

PERSONAL: Born September 17, 1985, in Moscow, U.S.S.R. ... 6-2/212. ... Shoots right.

TRANSACTIONS/CAREER NOTES: Selected by Washington Capitals in first round (first Capitals pick, first overall) of NHL entry draft (June 26, 2004). ... Groin injury (January 31, 2006); missed one game.

Season Team	League	GP	G	A	Pts.	PIM	+/-	PP	SH	GP	G	A	Pts.	PIM
		REGULAR SEASON								PLAYOFFS				
01-02—Dynamo	Russian	22	2	2	4	4	...	...	...	3	0	0	0	0
—Dynamo-2	Russian Dv. 3	19	18	8	26	20	...	...	...	—	—	—	—	—
02-03—Dynamo	Russian	40	8	7	15	28	...	...	...	5	0	0	0	2
03-04—Dynamo	Russian	53	13	11	24	40	...	...	...	3	0	0	0	2
04-05—Dynamo	Russian	37	13	13	26	32	...	...	...	10	2	4	6	31
05-06—Washington	NHL	81	52	54	106	52	2	21	3	—	—	—	—	—
—Russian Oly. Team	Int'l	8	5	0	5	8	3	2	0	—	—	—	—	—
NHL Totals (1 year)		81	52	54	106	52	2	21	3					

OZOLINSH, SANDIS D

PERSONAL: Born August 3, 1972, in Riga, USSR. ... 6-3/215. ... Shoots left. ... Name pronounced SAN-dihz OH-zoh-lihnsh.

TRANSACTIONS/CAREER NOTES: Selected by San Jose Sharks in second round (third Sharks pick, 30th overall) of entry draft (June 22,

O

1991). ... Strained back (November 7, 1992); missed one game. ... Torn anterior cruciate ligament in knee (December 30, 1992); missed remainder of season. ... Injured knee (December 11, 1993); missed one game. ... Traded by Sharks to Colorado Avalanche for RW Owen Nolan (October 26, 1995). ... Separated left shoulder (December 7, 1995); missed four games. ... Fractured finger (February 23, 1996); missed two games. ... Back spasms (March 9, 1997); missed two games. ... Separated shoulder (October 7, 1997); missed two games. ... Injured knee (October 17, 1997) and had arthroscopic surgery; missed 13 games. ... Missed first 38 games of 1998-99 season in contract dispute. ... Bruised sternum (February 9, 1999); missed two games. ... Traded by Avalanche with second-round pick (LW Tomas Kurka) in 2000 draft to Carolina Hurricanes for D Nolan Pratt, first- (C Vaclav Nedorost) and two second-round (C Jared Aulin and D Argis Saviels) picks in 2000 draft (June 24, 2000). ... Injured knee (December 29, 2000) and had surgery; missed 10 games. ... Sprained knee (October 18, 2001); missed three games. ... Traded by Hurricanes with C Byron Ritchie to Florida Panthers for D Bret Hedican, C Kevyn Adams and D Tomas Malec (January 16, 2002). ... Traded by Panthers with D Lance Ward to Anaheim Mighty Ducks for C Matt Cullen, D Pavel Trnka and fourth-round pick (D James Pemberton) in 2003 draft (January 30, 2003). ... Injured ribs (December 5, 2003); missed four games. ... Strained shoulder (December 21, 2003) and had surgery (December 30, 2003); missed remainder of season. ... Strained chest muscle (October 10, 2005); missed two games. ... Flu (October 14, 2005); missed two games. ... Fractured ribs (October 25, 2005); missed nine games. ... Strained left knee (November 27, 2005); missed 14 games. ... Entered substance abuse and behavioral health program (December 29, 2005); missed 18 games. ... Traded by Mighty Ducks to New York Rangers for third-round pick (D John Degray) in 2006 draft (March 9, 2006).

STATISTICAL PLATEAUS: Three-goal games: 1999-00 (1), 2000-01 (1). Total: 2.

		REGULAR SEASON								PLAYOFFS				
Season Team	**League**	**GP**	**G**	**A**	**Pts.**	**PIM**	**+/-**	**PP**	**SH**	**GP**	**G**	**A**	**Pts.**	**PIM**
90-91—Dynamo Riga	USSR	44	0	3	3	49	...	...	...	—	—	—	—	—
91-92—HC Riga	CIS	30	5	0	5	42	...	...	...	—	—	—	—	—
—Kansas City	IHL	34	6	9	15	20	...	...	...	15	2	5	7	22
92-93—San Jose	NHL	37	7	16	23	40	-9	2	0	—	—	—	—	—
93-94—San Jose	NHL	81	26	38	64	24	16	4	0	14	0	10	10	8
94-95—San Jose	NHL	48	9	16	25	30	-6	3	1	11	3	2	5	6
95-96—San Francisco	IHL	2	1	0	1	0	...	...	...	—	—	—	—	—
—San Jose	NHL	7	1	3	4	4	2	1	0	—	—	—	—	—
—Colorado	NHL	66	13	37	50	50	0	7	1	22	5	14	19	16
96-97—Colorado	NHL	80	23	45	68	88	4	13	0	17	4	13	17	24
97-98—Colorado	NHL	66	13	38	51	65	-12	9	0	7	0	7	7	14
98-99—Colorado	NHL	39	7	25	32	22	10	4	0	19	4	8	12	22
99-00—Colorado	NHL	82	16	36	52	46	17	6	0	17	5	5	10	20
00-01—Carolina	NHL	72	12	32	44	71	-25	4	2	6	0	2	2	5
01-02—Carolina	NHL	46	4	19	23	34	-4	1	0	—	—	—	—	—
—Florida	NHL	37	10	19	29	24	-3	2	0	—	—	—	—	—
—Latvian Olympic team	Int'l	1	0	4	4	0	...	...	...	—	—	—	—	—
02-03—Florida	NHL	51	7	19	26	40	-16	5	0	—	—	—	—	—
—Anaheim	NHL	31	5	13	18	16	10	1	0	21	2	6	8	10
03-04—Anaheim	NHL	36	5	11	16	24	-7	1	0	—	—	—	—	—
05-06—Anaheim	NHL	17	3	3	6	8	-4	0	0	—	—	—	—	—
—New York Rangers	NHL	19	3	11	14	20	2	2	0	3	0	0	0	6
—Latvian Oly. team	Int'l	5	1	3	4	9	0	0	0	—	—	—	—	—
NHL Totals (13 years)		815	164	381	545	606	-25	65	4	137	23	67	90	131

PAETSCH, NATHAN D

PERSONAL: Born March 30, 1983, in Humboldt, Sask. ... 6-0/195. ... Shoots left. ... Name pronounced: PAYTCH

TRANSACTIONS/CAREER NOTES: Selected by Washington Capitals in second round (first Capitals pick, 58th overall) of NHL entry draft (June 23, 2001). ... Returned to draft pool by Capitals; selected by Buffalo Sabres in seventh round (eighth Sabres pick, 20second overall) of NHL entry draft (June 21, 2003).

		REGULAR SEASON								PLAYOFFS				
Season Team	**League**	**GP**	**G**	**A**	**Pts.**	**PIM**	**+/-**	**PP**	**SH**	**GP**	**G**	**A**	**Pts.**	**PIM**
98-99—Moose Jaw	WHL	2	0	0	0	0	...	...	...	—	—	—	—	—
99-00—Moose Jaw	WHL	68	9	35	44	48	...	...	...	4	0	1	1	0
00-01—Moose Jaw	WHL	70	8	54	62	118	...	...	...	4	1	2	3	6
01-02—Moose Jaw	WHL	59	16	36	52	86	...	...	...	12	0	4	4	16
02-03—Moose Jaw	WHL	59	15	39	54	81	...	...	...	13	3	10	13	6
03-04—Rochester	AHL	54	5	5	10	49	2	0	1	16	1	1	2	28
04-05—Rochester	AHL	80	4	19	23	150	15	1	0	9	1	1	2	16
05-06—Rochester	AHL	72	11	39	50	90	3	7	0	—	—	—	—	—
—Buffalo	NHL	1	0	1	1	0	-1	0	0	1	0	0	0	0
NHL Totals (1 year)		1	0	1	1	0	-1	0	0	1	0	0	0	0

PAHLSSON, SAMUEL C

PERSONAL: Born December 17, 1977, in Ornskoldsvik, Sweden. ... 6-0/208. ... Shoots left.

TRANSACTIONS/CAREER NOTES: Selected by Colorado Avalanche in seventh round (10th Avalanche pick, 176th overall) of draft (June 22, 1996). ... Traded by Avalanche with LW Brian Rolston, D Martin Grenier and first-round pick (LW Martin Samuelsson) in 2000 draft to Boston Bruins for D Ray Bourque and LW Dave Andreychuk (March 6, 2000). ... Traded by Bruins to Anaheim Mighty Ducks for LW Andrei Nazarov and D Patrick Traverse (November 18, 2000).

		REGULAR SEASON								PLAYOFFS				
Season Team	**League**	**GP**	**G**	**A**	**Pts.**	**PIM**	**+/-**	**PP**	**SH**	**GP**	**G**	**A**	**Pts.**	**PIM**
94-95—MoDo Ornskoldsvik	Sweden Jr.	30	10	11	21	26	...	...	...	—	—	—	—	—
95-96—MoDo Ornskoldsvik	Sweden	36	1	3	4	8	...	...	...	—	—	—	—	—
—MoDo Ornskoldsvik	Sweden Jr.	5	2	6	8	2	...	...	...	—	—	—	—	—
96-97—MoDo Ornskoldsvik	Sweden	49	8	9	17	83	...	...	...	—	—	—	—	—
97-98—MoDo Ornskoldsvik	Sweden	23	6	11	17	24	...	...	...	9	3	0	3	6
98-99—MoDo Ornskoldsvik	Sweden	50	17	17	34	44	...	...	...	13	3	3	6	10
99-00—MoDo Ornskoldsvik	Sweden	47	16	11	27	67	...	...	...	13	3	3	6	8
00-01—Boston	NHL	17	1	1	2	6	-5	0	0	—	—	—	—	—
—Anaheim	NHL	59	3	4	7	14	-9	1	1	—	—	—	—	—

Season Team	League	REGULAR SEASON GP	G	A	Pts.	PIM	+/-	PP	SH	PLAYOFFS GP	G	A	Pts.	PIM
01-02—Anaheim	NHL	80	6	14	20	26	-16	1	1	—	—	—	—	—
02-03—Cincinnati	AHL	13	1	7	8	24	7	0	0	—	—	—	—	—
—Anaheim	NHL	34	4	11	15	18	10	0	1	21	2	4	6	12
03-04—Anaheim	NHL	82	8	14	22	52	-2	1	0	—	—	—	—	—
04-05—Vastra Frolunda	Sweden	48	6	18	24	56	13	1	2	14	4	7	11	24
05-06—Anaheim	NHL	82	11	10	21	34	-1	0	3	16	2	3	5	18
—Swedish Oly. team	Int'l	8	2	2	4	8	-1	0	0	—	—	—	—	—
NHL Totals (5 years)		354	33	54	87	150	-23	3	6	37	4	7	11	30

PAILLE, DAN LW

PERSONAL: Born April 15, 1984, in Welland, Ont. ... 6-0/200. ... Shoots left. ... Name pronounced: PIGH yay

TRANSACTIONS/CAREER NOTES: Selected by Buffalo Sabres in first round (second Sabres pick, 20th overall) of NHL entry draft (June 22, 2002).

Season Team	League	REGULAR SEASON GP	G	A	Pts.	PIM	+/-	PP	SH	PLAYOFFS GP	G	A	Pts.	PIM
00-01—Guelph	OHL	64	22	31	53	57	...	...	...	4	2	0	2	2
01-02—Guelph	OHL	62	27	30	57	54	...	...	...	9	5	2	7	9
02-03—Guelph	OHL	54	30	27	57	57	...	...	...	11	8	6	14	6
03-04—Guelph	OHL	59	37	43	80	63	...	...	...	22	9	9	18	14
04-05—Rochester	AHL	79	14	15	29	54	4	0	3	9	2	2	4	6
05-06—Rochester	AHL	45	14	13	27	29	7	4	3	—	—	—	—	—
—Buffalo	NHL	14	1	2	3	2	5	0	0	—	—	—	—	—
NHL Totals (1 year)		14	1	2	3	2	5	0	0					

PALFFY, ZIGGY RW

PERSONAL: Born May 5, 1972, in Skalica, Czech. ... 5-10/180. ... Shoots left. ... Name pronounced PAL-fee.

TRANSACTIONS/CAREER NOTES: Selected by New York Islanders in second round (second Islanders pick, 26th overall) of NHL draft (June 22, 1991). ... Concussion (February 17, 1996); missed one game. ... Sprained shoulder (January 13, 1997); missed two games. ... Missed first 32 games of 1998-99 season in contract dispute. ... Traded by Islanders with C Bryan Smolinski, G Marcel Cousineau and fourth-round pick (C Daniel Johansson) in 1999 draft to Los Angeles Kings for C Olli Jokinen, LW Josh Green, D Mathieu Biron and first-round pick (LW Taylor Pyatt) in 1999 draft (June 20, 1999). ... Back spasms (December 4, 1999); missed four games. ... Back spasms (January 4, 2000); missed one game. ... Strained right shoulder (March 15, 2000); missed final 12 games of regular season. ... Strained hamstring (December 16, 2000); missed eight games. ... Flu (January 8, 2001); missed one game. ... Back spasms (October 26, 2001); missed five games. ... Fractured rib (December 1, 2001); missed 14 games. ... Strained groin (October 13, 2002); missed three games. ... Reinjured groin (October 25, 2002); missed three games. ... Facial injury (November 25, 2003); missed five games. ... Dislocated right shoulder (January 8, 2004) and had surgery; missed remainder of season. ... Signed as free agent by Pittsburgh Penguins (August 6, 2005). ... Pulled groin (December 1, 2005); missed one game. ... Retired (January 18, 2006).

STATISTICAL PLATEAUS: Three-goal games: 1995-96 (2), 1996-97 (1), 1997-98 (2), 1998-99 (1), 2000-01 (1), 2001-02 (1). Total: 8.

Season Team	League	REGULAR SEASON GP	G	A	Pts.	PIM	+/-	PP	SH	PLAYOFFS GP	G	A	Pts.	PIM
90-91—Nitra	Slovakia	50	34	16	50	18	...	...	...	—	—	—	—	—
91-92—Dukla Trencin	Czech.	32	23	25	48	...	...	...	...	—	—	—	—	—
92-93—Dukla Trencin	Czech.	43	38	41	79	...	...	...	...	—	—	—	—	—
93-94—Salt Lake City	IHL	57	25	32	57	83	1	6	2	—	—	—	—	—
—Slovakian Oly. team	Int'l	8	3	7	10	8	3	0	2	—	—	—	—	—
—New York Islanders	NHL	5	0	0	0	0	-6	0	0	—	—	—	—	—
94-95—Denver	IHL	33	20	23	43	40	8	4	0	—	—	—	—	—
—New York Islanders	NHL	33	10	7	17	6	3	1	0	—	—	—	—	—
95-96—New York Islanders	NHL	81	43	44	87	56	-17	17	1	—	—	—	—	—
96-97—New York Islanders	NHL	80	48	42	90	43	21	6	4	—	—	—	—	—
97-98—New York Islanders	NHL	82	45	42	87	34	-2	*17	2	—	—	—	—	—
98-99—HK 36 Skalica	Slovakia	9	11	8	19	6	...	...	...	—	—	—	—	—
—New York Islanders	NHL	50	22	28	50	34	-6	5	2	—	—	—	—	—
99-00—Los Angeles	NHL	64	27	39	66	32	18	4	0	4	2	0	2	0
00-01—Los Angeles	NHL	73	38	51	89	20	22	12	4	13	3	5	8	8
01-02—Los Angeles	NHL	63	32	27	59	26	5	15	1	7	4	5	9	0
—Slovakian Oly. team	Int'l	1	0	0	0	0	...	...	...	—	—	—	—	—
02-03—Los Angeles	NHL	76	37	48	85	47	22	10	2	—	—	—	—	—
03-04—Los Angeles	NHL	35	16	25	41	12	18	3	3	—	—	—	—	—
04-05—Skalica	Slovakia	8	10	3	13	6	5	...	...	—	—	—	—	—
—Praha	Czech.	41	21	19	40	30	8	...	...	7	5	2	7	2
05-06—Pittsburgh	NHL	42	11	31	42	12	5	2	0	—	—	—	—	—
NHL Totals (12 years)		684	329	384	713	322	83	92	19	24	9	10	19	8

PANDOLFO, JAY LW

P

PERSONAL: Born December 27, 1974, in Winchester, Mass. ... 6-1/190. ... Shoots left. ... Brother of Mike Pandolfo, LW, Columbus Blue Jackets (2003-04).

TRANSACTIONS/CAREER NOTES: Selected by New Jersey Devils in second round (second Devils pick, 3second overall) of NHL draft (June 26, 1993). ... Flu (January 14, 1999); missed two games. ... Bruised shoulder (March 17, 1999); missed 10 games. ... Facial lacerations (January 29, 2000); missed three games. ... Bruised shoulder (October 14, 2000); missed 13 games. ... Bruised ribs (December 19, 2001); missed six games. ... Bruised hip (January 21, 2002); missed 10 games. ... Injured groin (October 25, 2002); missed three games. ... Aggravated groin injury (November 9, 2003); missed seven games. ... Suffered concussion (January 13, 2003); missed four games.

Season Team	League	REGULAR SEASON GP	G	A	Pts.	PIM	+/-	PP	SH	PLAYOFFS GP	G	A	Pts.	PIM
89-90—Burlington H.S.	Mass. H.S.	23	33	30	63	18	...	...	...	—	—	—	—	—
90-91—Burlington H.S.	Mass. H.S.	20	19	27	46	10	...	...	...	—	—	—	—	—
91-92—Burlington H.S.	Mass. H.S.	20	35	34	69	14	...	...	...	—	—	—	—	—
92-93—Boston University	Hockey East	37	16	22	38	16	...	...	...	—	—	—	—	—
93-94—Boston University	Hockey East	37	17	25	42	27	24	6	1	—	—	—	—	—
94-95—Boston University	Hockey East	20	7	13	20	6	13	1	0	—	—	—	—	—
95-96—Boston University	Hockey East	39	38	29	67	6	...	...	...	—	—	—	—	—
—Albany	AHL	5	3	1	4	0	...	...	...	3	0	0	0	0
96-97—Albany	AHL	12	3	9	12	0	6	0	0	—	—	—	—	—
—New Jersey	NHL	46	6	8	14	6	-1	0	0	6	0	1	1	0
97-98—New Jersey	NHL	23	1	3	4	4	-4	0	0	3	0	2	2	0
—Albany	AHL	51	18	19	37	24	9	3	4	—	—	—	—	—
98-99—New Jersey	NHL	70	14	13	27	10	3	1	1	7	1	0	1	0
99-00—New Jersey	NHL	71	7	8	15	4	0	0	0	23	0	5	5	0
00-01—New Jersey	NHL	63	4	12	16	16	3	0	0	25	1	4	5	4
01-02—New Jersey	NHL	65	4	10	14	15	12	0	1	6	0	0	0	0
02-03—New Jersey	NHL	68	6	11	17	23	12	0	1	24	6	6	12	2
03-04—New Jersey	NHL	82	13	13	26	14	5	1	2	5	0	0	0	0
04-05—Salzburg	Austria	19	5	7	12	0	-9	2	1	—	—	—	—	—
05-06—New Jersey	NHL	82	10	10	20	16	2	0	0	9	1	4	5	0
NHL Totals (9 years)		570	65	88	153	108	32	2	5	108	9	22	31	6

PARISE, ZACH — C/LW

PERSONAL: Born July 28, 1984, in Minneapolis, Minn. ... 5-11/185. ... Shoots left.
TRANSACTIONS/CAREER NOTES: Selected by New Jersey Devils in first round (first Devils pick, 17th overall) in 2003 NHL entry draft (June 23, 2003).

Season Team	League	REGULAR SEASON GP	G	A	Pts.	PIM	+/-	PP	SH	PLAYOFFS GP	G	A	Pts.	PIM
02-03—Univ. of North Dakota	WCHA	39	26	35	61	34	...	...	...	—	—	—	—	—
03-04—Univ. of North Dakota	WCHA	37	23	32	55	24	...	...	...	—	—	—	—	—
04-05—Albany	AHL	73	18	40	58	56	-11	5	2	—	—	—	—	—
05-06—New Jersey	NHL	81	14	18	32	28	-1	2	0	9	1	2	3	2
NHL Totals (1 year)		81	14	18	32	28	-1	2	0	9	1	2	3	2

PARK, RICHARD — RW

PERSONAL: Born May 27, 1976, in Seoul, S. Korea. ... 5-11/190. ... Shoots right.
TRANSACTIONS/CAREER NOTES: Selected by Pittsburgh Penguins in second round (second Penguins pick, 50th overall) of entry draft (June 28, 1994). ... Traded by Penguins to Anaheim Mighty Ducks for RW Roman Oksiuta (March 18, 1997). ... Signed as free agent by Philadelphia Flyers (August 24, 1998). ... Signed as free agent by Minnesota Wild (June 6, 2000). ... Injured knee (October 5, 2003); missed five games. ... Injured elbow (December 18, 2003); missed two games. ... Signed as free agent by Vancouver Canucks (August 8, 2005). ... Injured leg (January 11, 2006); missed 13 games.

Season Team	League	REGULAR SEASON GP	G	A	Pts.	PIM	+/-	PP	SH	PLAYOFFS GP	G	A	Pts.	PIM
91-92—Williams Lake	PCJHL	76	49	58	107	91	...	...	...	—	—	—	—	—
92-93—Belleville	OHL	66	23	38	61	38	...	...	...	5	0	0	0	14
93-94—Belleville	OHL	59	27	49	76	70	...	10	...	12	3	5	8	18
94-95—Belleville	OHL	45	28	51	79	35	...	6	2	16	9	18	27	12
—Pittsburgh	NHL	1	0	1	1	2	1	0	0	3	0	0	0	2
95-96—Belleville	OHL	6	7	6	13	2	...	...	...	14	18	12	30	10
—Pittsburgh	NHL	56	4	6	10	36	3	0	1	1	0	0	0	0
96-97—Cleveland	IHL	50	12	15	27	30	...	...	...	—	—	—	—	—
—Pittsburgh	NHL	1	0	0	0	0	-1	0	0	—	—	—	—	—
—Anaheim	NHL	11	1	1	2	10	0	0	0	11	0	1	1	2
97-98—Cincinnati	AHL	56	17	26	43	36	-10	4	3	—	—	—	—	—
—Anaheim	NHL	15	0	2	2	8	-3	0	0	—	—	—	—	—
98-99—Philadelphia	AHL	75	41	42	83	33	32	11	8	16	9	6	15	4
—Philadelphia	NHL	7	0	0	0	0	-1	0	0	—	—	—	—	—
99-00—Utah	IHL	82	28	32	60	36	...	...	...	5	1	0	1	0
00-01—Cleveland	IHL	75	27	21	48	29	...	...	...	4	0	2	2	4
01-02—Houston	AHL	13	4	10	14	6	7	1	1	—	—	—	—	—
—Minnesota	NHL	63	10	15	25	10	-1	2	1	—	—	—	—	—
02-03—Minnesota	NHL	81	14	10	24	16	-3	2	2	18	3	3	6	4
03-04—Minnesota	NHL	73	13	12	25	28	0	4	0	—	—	—	—	—
04-05—Malmo	Sweden	9	1	3	4	4	2	0	0	—	—	—	—	—
—SC Langnau	Switzerland	10	3	0	3	8	...	1	0	6	4	1	5	6
05-06—Vancouver	NHL	60	8	10	18	29	-2	0	1	—	—	—	—	—
NHL Totals (9 years)		368	50	57	107	139	-7	8	5	33	3	4	7	8

PARKER, SCOTT — RW

PERSONAL: Born January 29, 1978, in Hanford, Calif. ... 6-5/230. ... Shoots right.
TRANSACTIONS/CAREER NOTES: Selected by New Jersey Devils in third round (sixth Devils pick, 63rd overall) of entry draft (June 22, 1996). ... Returned to draft pool by Devils; selected by Colorado Avalanche in first round (fourth Avalanche pick, 20th overall) of entry draft (June 27, 1998). ... Bruised shoulder (December 11, 2000); missed four games. ... Bruised foot (February 17, 2001); missed three games. ... Suspended

two games for unsportsmanlike conduct (October 15, 2001). ... Injured thumb and fractured nose (January 28, 2002); missed one game. ... Injured hand (November 25, 2002); missed two games. ... Fractured foot (December 23, 2002); missed 16 games. ... Injured arm (February 23, 2003); missed one game. ... Traded by Avalanche to San Jose Sharks for fifth-round pick (C Brad Richardson) in 2003 draft; (June 21, 2003). ... Flu (December 6, 2003); missed one game. ... Injured hip (December 26, 2003); missed three games. ... Reinjured hip (January 2, 2004); missed three games. ... Fractured forearm (January 15, 2004); missed one game. ... Reinjured hip (January 22, 2004); missed five games. ... Injured hand (March 20, 2004); missed remainder of season. ... Re-signed by Sharks as restricted free agent (August 15, 2005). ... Concussion (October 3, 2005); missed first 19 games of season. ... Postconcussion syndrome (December 3, 2005); missed 11 games. ... Postconcussion syndrome (December 27, 2005); missed 26 games. ... Suspended two games by NHL for misconduct (March 13, 2006).

		REGULAR SEASON								PLAYOFFS				
Season Team	League	GP	G	A	Pts.	PIM	+/-	PP	SH	GP	G	A	Pts.	PIM
94-95—Spokane	KIJHL	43	7	21	28	128	...	...	...	—	—	—	—	—
95-96—Kelowna	WHL	64	3	4	7	159	...	...	...	6	0	0	0	12
96-97—Kelowna	WHL	68	18	8	26	330	-14	6	0	6	0	2	2	4
97-98—Kelowna	WHL	71	30	22	52	243	-4	12	0	7	6	0	6	23
98-99—Hershey	AHL	32	4	3	7	143	-7	0	0	4	0	0	0	6
—Colorado	NHL	27	0	0	0	71	-3	0	0	—	—	—	—	—
99-00—Hershey	AHL	68	12	7	19	206	...	...	...	11	1	1	2	56
00-01—Colorado	NHL	69	2	3	5	155	-2	0	0	4	0	0	0	2
01-02—Colorado	NHL	63	1	4	5	154	0	0	0	—	—	—	—	—
02-03—Colorado	NHL	43	1	3	4	82	6	0	0	1	0	0	0	2
03-04—San Jose	NHL	50	1	3	4	101	0	0	0	—	—	—	—	—
05-06—San Jose	NHL	10	1	0	1	38	3	0	0	—	—	—	—	—
NHL Totals (6 years)		262	6	13	19	601	4	0	0	5	0	0	0	4

PARRISH, MARK RW

PERSONAL: Born February 2, 1977, in Edina, Minn. ... 5-11/200. ... Shoots right.

TRANSACTIONS/CAREER NOTES: Selected by Colorado Avalanche in third round (third Avalanche pick, 79th overall) of entry draft (June 22, 1996). ... Rights traded by Avalanche with third-round pick (D Lance Ward) in 1998 to Florida Panthers for RW/C Tom Fitzgerald (March 24, 1998). ... Back (February 14, 2000); missed one game. ... Traded by Panthers with LW Oleg Kvasha to New York Islanders for C Olli Jokinen and G Roberto Luongo (June 24, 2000). ... Right knee (February 9, 2001); missed 12 games. ... Ribs (January 15, 2002); missed four games. ... Flu (November 27, 2002); missed one game. ... Ankle (January 1, 2004); missed 23 games. ... Hip (October 22, 2005); missed four games. ... Traded by Islanders with D Brent Sopel to Los Angeles Kings for D Denis Grebeshkov and LW Jeff Tambellini (March 8, 2006). ... Signed as free agent by Minnesota Wild (July 1, 2006).

STATISTICAL PLATEAUS: Three-goal games: 2001-02 (2), 2002-03 (1). Total: 3. ... Four-goal games: 1998-99 (1). ... Total hat tricks: 4.

		REGULAR SEASON								PLAYOFFS				
Season Team	League	GP	G	A	Pts.	PIM	+/-	PP	SH	GP	G	A	Pts.	PIM
94-95—Thomas Jefferson	Minn. H.S.	27	40	20	60	42	...	...	...	—	—	—	—	—
95-96—St. Cloud State	WCHA	38	15	14	29	28	...	...	...	—	—	—	—	—
96-97—St. Cloud State	WCHA	35	27	15	42	60	...	11	2	—	—	—	—	—
97-98—Seattle	WHL	54	54	38	92	29	...	...	...	5	2	3	5	2
—New Haven	AHL	1	1	0	1	2	-1	0	0	—	—	—	—	—
98-99—Florida	NHL	73	24	13	37	25	-6	5	0	—	—	—	—	—
—New Haven	AHL	2	1	0	1	0	1	0	0	—	—	—	—	—
99-00—Florida	NHL	81	26	18	44	39	1	6	0	4	0	1	1	0
00-01—New York Islanders	NHL	70	17	13	30	28	-27	6	0	—	—	—	—	—
01-02—New York Islanders	NHL	78	30	30	60	32	10	9	1	7	2	1	3	6
02-03—New York Islanders	NHL	81	23	25	48	28	-11	9	0	5	1	0	1	4
03-04—New York Islanders	NHL	59	24	11	35	18	8	6	0	5	1	2	3	0
05-06—New York Islanders	NHL	57	24	17	41	16	-14	13	0	—	—	—	—	—
—Los Angeles	NHL	19	5	3	8	4	-9	3	0	—	—	—	—	—
—U.S. Olympic team	Int'l	6	0	0	0	4	-2	0	0	—	—	—	—	—
NHL Totals (7 years)		518	173	130	303	190	-48	57	1	21	4	4	8	10

PARROS, GEORGE RW

PERSONAL: Born December 29, 1979, in Washington, Pa. ... 6-4/210. ... Shoots right.

TRANSACTIONS/CAREER NOTES: Selected by Los Angeles Kings in eighth round (ninth Kings pick, 222nd overall) of entry draft (June 24, 1999). ... Right ankle sprain (November 17, 2005); missed 15 games. ... Sprained ankle (December 28, 2005); missed six games.

		REGULAR SEASON								PLAYOFFS				
Season Team	League	GP	G	A	Pts.	PIM	+/-	PP	SH	GP	G	A	Pts.	PIM
99-00—Princeton	ECAC	27	4	2	6	14	...	...	...	—	—	—	—	—
00-01—Princeton	ECAC	31	7	10	17	38	...	...	...	—	—	—	—	—
01-02—Princeton	ECAC	31	9	13	22	38	...	...	...	—	—	—	—	—
02-03—Princeton	ECAC	22	0	7	7	29	...	...	...	—	—	—	—	—
—Manchester	AHL	9	0	1	1	7	...	...	...	—	—	—	—	—
03-04—Manchester	AHL	57	3	6	9	126	...	...	...	5	0	0	0	4
04-05—Manchester	AHL	67	14	8	22	247	2	2	4	6	1	1	2	27
—Reading	ECHL	3	0	0	0	9	-2	0	0	—	—	—	—	—
05-06—Los Angeles	NHL	55	2	3	5	138	1	0	0	—	—	—	—	—
NHL Totals (1 year)		55	2	3	5	138	1	0	0					

P

PAYER, SERGE C

PERSONAL: Born May 9, 1979, in Rockland, Ont. ... 6-0/192. ... Shoots left.

TRANSACTIONS/CAREER NOTES: Signed as free agent by Florida Panthers (October 2, 1997). ... Traded by Panthers to Ottawa Senators for a ninth-round pick (D Luke Beaverson) in 2004 draft (September 10, 2003). ... Signed as free agent by Panthers (July 23, 2004). ... Signed as free agent by San Antonio of the AHL (September 26, 2004). ... Rib injury (November 28, 2005); missed six games.

Season Team	League	GP	G	A	Pts.	PIM	+/-	PP	SH	GP	G	A	Pts.	PIM
		REGULAR SEASON								PLAYOFFS				
95-96—Kitchener	OHL	66	8	16	24	18	...	...	...	12	0	2	2	2
96-97—Kitchener	OHL	63	7	16	23	27	...	...	...	13	1	3	4	2
97-98—Kitchener	OHL	44	20	21	41	51	...	...	...	6	3	0	3	7
98-99—Kitchener	OHL	40	18	19	37	22	10	...	...	—	—	—	—	—
99-00—Kitchener	OHL	44	10	26	36	53	-11	2	0	5	0	3	3	6
00-01—Louisville	AHL	32	6	6	12	15	...	...	...	—	—	—	—	—
—Florida	NHL	43	5	1	6	21	0	0	1	—	—	—	—	—
01-02—Utah	AHL	20	6	2	8	9	-2	3	0	—	—	—	—	—
02-03—San Antonio	AHL	78	10	31	41	30	9	2	3	1	0	0	0	2
03-04—Binghamton	AHL	67	14	21	35	91	-6	4	3	2	0	0	0	0
—Ottawa	NHL	5	0	1	1	2	1	0	0	—	—	—	—	—
04-05—San Antonio	AHL	3	1	1	2	4	0	0	0	—	—	—	—	—
05-06—Florida	NHL	71	2	4	6	26	-7	0	0	—	—	—	—	—
NHL Totals (3 years)		119	7	6	13	49	-6	0	1					

PEAT, STEPHEN RW

PERSONAL: Born March 10, 1980, in Princeton, B.C. ... 6-2/235. ... Shoots right.

TRANSACTIONS/CAREER NOTES: Selected by Mighty Ducks of Anaheim in second round (second Mighty Ducks pick, 3second overall) of entry draft (June 27, 1998). ... Traded by Mighty Ducks to Washington Capitals for fourth-round pick (RW Michel Ouellet) in 2000 draft (June 1, 2000). ... Strained groin (January 30, 2002); missed six games. ... Injured hand (November 9, 2002); missed 21 games. ... Injured foot (October 9, 2003); missed two games. ... Flu (January 23, 2004); missed one game. ... Upper-body injury (October 8, 2005); missed one game. ... Traded by Capitals to Carolina Hurricanes for LW Colin Forbes (December 28, 2005).

Season Team	League	GP	G	A	Pts.	PIM	+/-	PP	SH	GP	G	A	Pts.	PIM
		REGULAR SEASON								PLAYOFFS				
95-96—Red Deer	WHL	1	0	0	0	0	...	...	...	—	—	—	—	—
96-97—Red Deer	WHL	68	3	14	17	161	...	...	...	16	0	2	2	22
97-98—Red Deer	WHL	63	6	12	18	189	...	...	...	5	0	0	0	8
98-99—Red Deer	WHL	31	2	6	8	98	...	...	...	—	—	—	—	—
—Tri-City	WHL	5	0	0	0	19	...	...	...	—	—	—	—	—
99-00—Tri-City	WHL	12	0	2	2	48	...	...	...	—	—	—	—	—
—Calgary	WHL	23	0	8	8	100	19	0	0	13	0	1	1	33
00-01—Portland	AHL	6	0	0	0	16	...	...	...	—	—	—	—	—
01-02—Washington	NHL	38	2	2	4	85	-1	0	0	—	—	—	—	—
—Portland	AHL	17	2	2	4	57	-2	0	0	—	—	—	—	—
02-03—Portland	AHL	18	0	0	0	52	-5	0	0	—	—	—	—	—
—Washington	NHL	27	1	0	1	57	-3	0	0	—	—	—	—	—
03-04—Washington	NHL	64	5	0	5	90	-10	0	0	—	—	—	—	—
04-05—Danbury	UHL	7	0	1	1	45	-1	0	0	—	—	—	—	—
05-06—Hershey	AHL	5	0	1	1	7	3	0	0	—	—	—	—	—
—Washington	NHL	1	0	0	0	2	-2	0	0	—	—	—	—	—
—Lowell	AHL	3	1	1	2	23	-2	1	0	—	—	—	—	—
NHL Totals (4 years)		130	8	2	10	234	-16	0	0					

PECA, MICHAEL C

PERSONAL: Born March 26, 1974, in Toronto. ... 5-11/190. ... Shoots right. ... Name pronounced PEH-kuh.

TRANSACTIONS/CAREER NOTES: Selected by Vancouver Canucks in second round (second Canucks pick, 40th overall) of NHL draft (June 20, 1992). ... Fractured cheekbone (February 9, 1995); missed 12 games. ... Wrist (April 26, 1995); missed one game. ... Traded by Canucks with D Mike Wilson and first-round pick (D Jay McKee) in 1995 to Buffalo Sabres for RW Alexander Mogilny and fifth-round pick (LW Todd Norman) in 1995 (July 8, 1995). ... Back (October 29, 1995); missed six games. ... Bruised sternum (December 2, 1995); missed one game. ... Right knee (March 18, 1996); missed seven games. ... Shoulder (November 27, 1996); missed three games. ... Missed 1997-98 season's first 11 games in contract dispute. ... Hip (November 6, 1997); missed three games. ... Suspended three games and fined $1,000 inr elbowing incident (March 27, 1998). ... Reinjured hip (April 8, 1998); missed two games. ... Sprained knee (April 15, 1998); missed final two games of season and two playoff games. ... Dislocated shoulder (March 5, 2000); missed seven games. ... Suspended two games in elbowing incident (March 25, 2000). ... Missed 2000-01 season in contract dispute. ... Traded by Sabres to New York Islanders for C Tim Connolly and LW Taylor Pyatt (June 24, 2001). ... Concussion (October 11, 2001); missed two games. ... Knee (November 4, 2002); missed five games. ... Shoulder (October 19, 2002); missed 10 games. ... Groin (December 31, 2003); missed one game. ... Left leg (February 27, 2004); missed two games. ... Traded by Islanders to Edmonton Oilers for C Mike York and fourth-round pick (traded to Colorado; Avalanche selected D Kevin Montgomery) in 2006 (August 3, 2005). ... Concussion (November 2, 2005); missed four games. ... Sinusitis (January 29, 2006); missed one game. ... Hip (February 7, 2006); missed six games. ... Signed as free agent by Toronto Maple Leafs (July 18, 2006).

STATISTICAL PLATEAUS: Three-goal games: 1999-00 (1).

Season Team	League	GP	G	A	Pts.	PIM	+/-	PP	SH	GP	G	A	Pts.	PIM
		REGULAR SEASON								PLAYOFFS				
90-91—Sudbury	OHL	62	14	27	41	24	...	...	...	5	1	0	1	7
91-92—Sudbury	OHL	39	16	34	50	61	...	...	...	—	—	—	—	—
—Ottawa	OHL	27	8	17	25	32	...	...	...	11	6	10	16	6
92-93—Ottawa	OHL	55	38	64	102	80	...	...	...	—	—	—	—	—
—Hamilton	AHL	9	6	3	9	11	3	1	0	—	—	—	—	—
93-94—Ottawa	OHL	55	50	63	113	101	...	14	3	17	7	22	29	30
—Vancouver	NHL	4	0	0	0	2	-1	0	0	—	—	—	—	—
94-95—Syracuse	AHL	35	10	24	34	75	5	4	0	—	—	—	—	—
—Vancouver	NHL	33	6	6	12	30	-6	2	0	5	0	1	1	8
95-96—Buffalo	NHL	68	11	20	31	67	-1	4	3	—	—	—	—	—
96-97—Buffalo	NHL	79	20	29	49	80	26	5	*6	10	0	2	2	8
97-98—Buffalo	NHL	61	18	22	40	57	12	6	5	13	3	2	5	8
98-99—Buffalo	NHL	82	27	29	56	81	7	10	0	21	5	8	13	18
99-00—Buffalo	NHL	73	20	21	41	67	6	2	0	5	0	1	1	4

Season Team	League	REGULAR SEASON								PLAYOFFS				
		GP	G	A	Pts.	PIM	+/-	PP	SH	GP	G	A	Pts.	PIM
00-01—Buffalo	NHL	Did not play												
01-02—New York Islanders	NHL	80	25	35	60	62	19	3	6	5	1	0	1	2
—Can. Olympic team	Int'l	6	0	2	2	2	...	...	...	—	—	—	—	—
02-03—New York Islanders	NHL	66	13	29	42	43	-4	4	2	5	0	0	0	4
03-04—New York Islanders	NHL	76	11	29	40	71	17	0	1	5	0	0	0	6
05-06—Edmonton	NHL	71	9	14	23	56	-4	2	2	24	6	5	11	20
NHL Totals (12 years)		693	160	234	394	616	71	38	25	93	15	19	34	78

PENNER, DUSTIN LW

PERSONAL: Born September 28, 1982, in Winkler, Man. ... 6-4/230. ... Shoots left.
TRANSACTIONS/CAREER NOTES: Signed as free agent by Anaheim Mighty Ducks (May 12, 2004).

Season Team	League	REGULAR SEASON								PLAYOFFS				
		GP	G	A	Pts.	PIM	+/-	PP	SH	GP	G	A	Pts.	PIM
03-04—University of Maine	ECAC	43	11	12	23	52	...	...	...	—	—	—	—	—
04-05—Cincinnati	AHL	77	10	18	28	82	10	4	0	9	2	3	5	13
05-06—Portland	AHL	57	39	45	84	68	41	13	3	4	2	3	5	0
—Anaheim	NHL	19	4	3	7	14	3	2	0	13	3	6	9	12
NHL Totals (1 year)		19	4	3	7	14	3	2	0	13	3	6	9	12

PEREZHOGIN, ALEXANDER RW/LW

PERSONAL: Born August 10, 1983, in Ust-Kamenogorsk, U.S.S.R. ... 5-11/185. ... Shoots left. ... Name pronounced: pair ihz OH gihn
TRANSACTIONS/CAREER NOTES: Selected by Montreal Canadiens in first round (second Canadiens pick, 25th overall) of NHL entry draft (June 23, 2001). ... Suspended indefinitely by AHL for stick-swinging incident (April 30, 2004).

Season Team	League	REGULAR SEASON								PLAYOFFS				
		GP	G	A	Pts.	PIM	+/-	PP	SH	GP	G	A	Pts.	PIM
00-01—Avangard	Rus. Div.	41	47	24	71	40	...	...	...	—	—	—	—	—
01-02—Avangard Omsk	Russian	4	1	0	1	4	...	...	...	—	—	—	—	—
02-03—Avangard Omsk	Russian	48	15	6	21	28	...	...	...	—	—	—	—	—
03-04—Hamilton	AHL	77	23	27	50	52	19	6	0	5	3	3	6	16
04-05—Omsk	Russian	43	15	18	33	18	...	...	...	—	—	—	—	—
05-06—Hamilton	AHL	11	0	2	2	8	-4	0	0	—	—	—	—	—
—Montreal	NHL	67	9	10	19	38	5	3	0	6	1	1	2	4
NHL Totals (1 year)		67	9	10	19	38	5	3	0	6	1	1	2	4

PERRAULT, JOEL C/RW

PERSONAL: Born April 6, 1983, in Montreal. ... 6-2/165. ... Shoots right. ... Name pronounced PAIR-oh.
TRANSACTIONS/CAREER NOTES: Selected by Anaheim Mighty Ducks in fifth round (seventh Mighty Ducks pick, 137th overall) of entry draft (June 23, 2001). ... Traded by Mighty Ducks to Phoenix Coyotes for D Sean O'Donnell (March 9, 2006).

Season Team	League	REGULAR SEASON								PLAYOFFS				
		GP	G	A	Pts.	PIM	+/-	PP	SH	GP	G	A	Pts.	PIM
00-01—Baie-Comeau	QMJHL	68	10	14	24	46	...	...	...	11	1	1	2	10
01-02—Baie-Comeau	QMJHL	57	18	44	62	96	...	...	...	5	2	0	2	6
02-03—Baie-Comeau	QMJHL	70	51	65	116	93	...	...	...	12	3	7	10	14
03-04—Cincinnati	AHL	65	14	14	28	38	0	3	1	9	1	1	2	2
04-05—Cincinnati	AHL	51	9	19	28	40	-6	3	0	—	—	—	—	—
05-06—Portland	AHL	25	12	12	24	20	4	4	0	—	—	—	—	—
—San Antonio	AHL	12	1	6	7	4	5	0	0	—	—	—	—	—
—Phoenix	NHL	5	1	1	2	2	0	0	0	—	—	—	—	—
NHL Totals (1 year)		5	1	1	2	2	0	0	0					

PERREAULT, YANIC C

PERSONAL: Born April 4, 1971, in Sherbrooke, Que. ... 5-11/184. ... Shoots left. ... Name pronounced YAH-nihk puh-ROH.
TRANSACTIONS/CAREER NOTES: Selected by Toronto Maple Leafs in third round (first Maple Leafs pick, 47th overall) of entry draft (June 22, 1991). ... Signed as free agent by Los Angeles Kings (July 14, 1994). ... Abdominal muscle (December 13, 1996); missed 11 games. ... Kidney surgery (February 3, 1997); missed remainder of season. ... Traded by Kings to Maple Leafs for C/RW Jason Podollan and third-round pick (G Cory Campbell) in 1999 (March 23, 1999). ... Fractured arm (December 4, 1999); missed 23 games. ... Signed as free agent by Montreal Canadiens (July 4, 2001). ... Groin (January 25, 2003); missed eight games. ... Groin (December 18, 2003); missed four games. ... Ankle (January 4, 2004); missed one game. ... Signed as free agent by Nashville Predators (October 3, 2005). ... Strained knee (March 2, 2006); missed 11 games.
STATISTICAL PLATEAUS: Three-goal games: 1997-98 (2), 2001-02 (1). Total: 3. ... Four-goal games: 1998-99 (1). ... Total hat tricks: 4.

Season Team	League	REGULAR SEASON								PLAYOFFS				
		GP	G	A	Pts.	PIM	+/-	PP	SH	GP	G	A	Pts.	PIM
88-89—Trois-Rivieres	QMJHL	70	53	55	108	48	...	...	...	—	—	—	—	—
89-90—Trois-Rivieres	QMJHL	63	51	63	114	75	...	...	...	7	6	5	11	19
90-91—Trois-Rivieres	QMJHL	67	87	98	185	103	...	...	...	6	4	7	11	6
91-92—St. John's	AHL	62	38	38	76	19	...	...	...	16	7	8	15	4
92-93—St. John's	AHL	79	49	46	95	56	-19	20	0	9	4	5	9	2
93-94—St. John's	AHL	62	45	60	105	38	25	19	2	11	12	6	18	14
—Toronto	NHL	13	3	3	6	0	1	2	0	—	—	—	—	—
94-95—Phoenix	IHL	68	51	48	99	52	-18	19	1	—	—	—	—	—
—Los Angeles	NHL	26	2	5	7	20	3	0	0	—	—	—	—	—

Season Team	League	REGULAR SEASON								PLAYOFFS				
		GP	G	A	Pts.	PIM	+/-	PP	SH	GP	G	A	Pts.	PIM
95-96—Los Angeles	NHL	78	25	24	49	16	-11	8	3	—	—	—	—	—
96-97—Los Angeles	NHL	41	11	14	25	20	0	1	1	—	—	—	—	—
97-98—Los Angeles	NHL	79	28	20	48	32	6	3	2	4	1	2	3	6
98-99—Los Angeles	NHL	64	10	17	27	30	-3	2	2	—	—	—	—	—
—Toronto	NHL	12	7	8	15	12	10	2	1	17	3	6	9	6
99-00—Toronto	NHL	58	18	27	45	22	3	5	0	1	0	1	1	0
00-01—Toronto	NHL	76	24	28	52	52	0	5	0	11	2	3	5	4
01-02—Montreal	NHL	82	27	29	56	40	-3	6	0	11	3	5	8	0
02-03—Montreal	NHL	73	24	22	46	30	-11	7	0	—	—	—	—	—
03-04—Montreal	NHL	69	16	15	31	40	-10	5	0	9	2	2	4	0
05-06—Nashville	NHL	69	22	35	57	30	-3	10	0	1	0	0	0	2
NHL Totals (12 years)		740	217	247	464	344	-18	56	9	54	11	19	30	18

PERROTT, NATHAN RW

PERSONAL: Born December 8, 1976, in Owen Sound, Ont. ... 6-0/225. ... Shoots right. ... Name pronounced PAIR-iht.
TRANSACTIONS/CAREER NOTES: Selected by New Jersey Devils in second round (second Devils pick, 44th overall) of entry draft (July 8, 1995). ... Signed as free agent by Chicago Blackhawks (August 27, 1997). ... Traded by Blackhawks to Nashville Predators for future considerations (October 9, 2001). ... Traded by Predators to Toronto Maple Leafs for C Bob Wren (December 31, 2002). ... Traded by Maple Leafs to Stars for sixth-round pick in 2006 draft (November 6, 2005).

Season Team	League	REGULAR SEASON								PLAYOFFS				
		GP	G	A	Pts.	PIM	+/-	PP	SH	GP	G	A	Pts.	PIM
93-94—St. Mary's Jr. B	OHA	41	11	26	37	249	...	...	...	—	—	—	—	—
94-95—Oshawa	OHL	63	18	28	46	233	...	9	0	2	1	1	2	9
95-96—Oshawa	OHL	59	30	32	62	158	...	...	...	5	2	3	5	8
96-97—Sault Ste. Marie	OHL	42	19	23	42	137	10	8	0	11	5	5	10	60
97-98—Indianapolis	IHL	31	4	3	7	76	2	0	1	—	—	—	—	—
—Jacksonville	ECHL	30	6	8	14	135	...	...	...	—	—	—	—	—
98-99—Indianapolis	IHL	72	14	11	25	307	7	3	0	7	3	1	4	45
99-00—Cleveland	IHL	65	12	9	21	248	...	...	...	9	2	1	3	19
00-01—Norfolk	AHL	73	11	17	28	268	...	...	...	9	2	0	2	18
01-02—Norfolk	AHL	2	0	0	0	5	0	0	0	—	—	—	—	—
—Milwaukee	AHL	56	6	10	16	190	-5	0	0	—	—	—	—	—
—Nashville	NHL	22	1	2	3	74	-1	0	0	—	—	—	—	—
02-03—Milwaukee	AHL	27	1	2	3	106	1	0	0	—	—	—	—	—
—Nashville	NHL	1	0	0	0	5	0	0	0	—	—	—	—	—
—St. John's	AHL	36	7	8	15	97	-12	0	0	—	—	—	—	—
03-04—Toronto	NHL	40	1	2	3	116	-1	0	0	—	—	—	—	—
04-05—St. John's	AHL	60	16	12	28	276	6	1	0	2	0	0	0	6
05-06—Toronto	NHL	3	0	0	0	2	-5	0	0	—	—	—	—	—
—Dallas	NHL	23	2	1	3	54	2	0	0	—	—	—	—	—
NHL Totals (4 years)		89	4	5	9	251	-5	0	0					

PERRY, COREY RW

PERSONAL: Born May 16, 1985, in Peterborough, Ont. ... 6-2/184. ... Shoots right.
TRANSACTIONS/CAREER NOTES: Selected by Anaheim Mighty Ducks in first round (second Mighty Ducks pick, 28th overall) of entry draft (June 20, 2003). ... Concussion (October 28, 2005); missed five games.

Season Team	League	REGULAR SEASON								PLAYOFFS				
		GP	G	A	Pts.	PIM	+/-	PP	SH	GP	G	A	Pts.	PIM
01-02—London	OHL	60	28	31	59	56	...	...	...	12	2	3	5	30
02-03—London	OHL	67	25	53	78	145	...	...	...	14	7	16	23	27
03-04—London	OHL	66	40	73	113	98	...	...	...	15	7	15	22	20
—Cincinnati	AHL	3	1	1	2	4	...	...	...	—	—	—	—	—
04-05—London	OHL	60	47	83	130	117	66	18	4	18	11	27	38	46
05-06—Portland	AHL	19	16	18	34	32	7	4	1	—	—	—	—	—
—Anaheim	NHL	56	13	12	25	50	1	4	0	11	0	3	3	16
NHL Totals (1 year)		56	13	12	25	50	1	4	0	11	0	3	3	16

PERSSON, DENNIS D

PERSONAL: Born June 2, 1988, in Nykoping, Swe. ... 6-1/181. ... Shoots left.
TRANSACTIONS/CAREER NOTES: Selected by Buffalo Sabres in first round (first Sabres pick; 24th overall) of NHL draft (June 24, 2006).

Season Team	League	REGULAR SEASON								PLAYOFFS				
		GP	G	A	Pts.	PIM	+/-	PP	SH	GP	G	A	Pts.	PIM
05-06—Vasteras	Sweden Jr.	28	11	15	26	22	...	...	...	—	—	—	—	—
—Vasteras	Sweden Dv. 2	19	0	2	2	6	-4	...	...	—	—	—	—	—

PETERS, ANDREW LW

PERSONAL: Born May 5, 1980, in St. Catharines, Ont. ... 6-4/247. ... Shoots left.
TRANSACTIONS/CAREER NOTES: Selected by Buffalo Sabres in second round (second Sabres pick, 34th overall) of entry draft (June 27, 1998).

Season Team	League	REGULAR SEASON								PLAYOFFS				
		GP	G	A	Pts.	PIM	+/-	PP	SH	GP	G	A	Pts.	PIM
96-97—Georgetown	Tier II Jr. A	46	11	16	27	105	...	...	...	—	—	—	—	—
97-98—Oshawa	OHL	60	11	7	18	220	...	...	...	7	2	0	2	19
98-99—Oshawa	OHL	54	14	10	24	137	2	...	...	15	2	7	9	36
99-00—Kitchener	OHL	42	6	13	19	95	-1	2	0	4	0	1	1	14
00-01—Rochester	AHL	49	0	4	4	118	...	...	...	—	—	—	—	—
01-02—Rochester	AHL	67	4	1	5	388	-2	0	0	—	—	—	—	—
02-03—Rochester	AHL	57	3	0	3	223	-16	0	0	3	0	0	0	24
03-04—Buffalo	NHL	42	2	0	2	151	-3	0	0	—	—	—	—	—
04-05—Boden	Sweden Dv. 2	9	1	2	3	101	-2	1	0	13	1	2	3	95
05-06—Buffalo	NHL	28	0	0	0	100	-2	0	0	—	—	—	—	—
NHL Totals (2 years)		70	2	0	2	251	-5	0	0					

PETERSEN, TOBY C

PERSONAL: Born October 27, 1978, in Minneapolis. ... 5-10/196. ... Shoots left.
TRANSACTIONS/CAREER NOTES: Selected by Pittsburgh Penguins in ninth round (ninth Penguins pick, 244th overall) of entry draft (June 27, 1998). ... Dehydration (October 14, 2001); missed one game. ... Signed as free agent by Edmonton Oilers (July 30, 2004).
STATISTICAL PLATEAUS: Three-goal games: 2001-02 (1).

Season Team	League	REGULAR SEASON								PLAYOFFS				
		GP	G	A	Pts.	PIM	+/-	PP	SH	GP	G	A	Pts.	PIM
95-96—Thomas Jefferson	Minn. H.S.	25	29	30	59	...	...	...	...	—	—	—	—	—
96-97—Colorado College	WCHA	40	17	21	38	18	...	...	...	—	—	—	—	—
97-98—Colorado College	WCHA	34	13	15	28	30	...	...	...	—	—	—	—	—
98-99—Colorado College	WCHA	21	12	12	24	2	...	...	...	—	—	—	—	—
99-00—Colorado College	WCHA	37	14	19	33	8	...	...	...	—	—	—	—	—
00-01—Wilkes-Barre/Scranton	AHL	73	26	41	67	22	...	...	...	21	7	6	13	4
—Pittsburgh	NHL	12	2	6	8	4	3	0	0	—	—	—	—	—
01-02—Pittsburgh	NHL	79	8	10	18	4	-15	1	1	—	—	—	—	—
02-03—Wilkes-Barre/Scranton	AHL	80	31	35	66	24	-18	12	0	6	1	3	4	4
03-04—Wilkes-Barre/Scranton	AHL	62	15	29	44	4	...	...	...	21	2	10	12	12
04-05—Edmonton	AHL	78	14	15	29	21	-6	6	1	—	—	—	—	—
05-06—Edmonton	NHL	—	—	—	—	—	—	—	—	2	1	0	1	0
—Iowa	AHL	79	26	47	73	48	14	9	1	7	2	4	6	2
NHL Totals (3 years)		91	10	16	26	8	-12	1	1	2	1	0	1	0

PETIOT, RICHARD D

PERSONAL: Born August 20, 1982, in Daysland, Alta. ... 6-3/200. ... Shoots left.
TRANSACTIONS/CAREER NOTES: Selected by Los Angeles Kings in fourth round (fifth Kings pick, 116th overall) of entry draft (June 23, 2001). ... Bruised rib (September 27, 2005); missed season's first three games.

Season Team	League	REGULAR SEASON								PLAYOFFS				
		GP	G	A	Pts.	PIM	+/-	PP	SH	GP	G	A	Pts.	PIM
00-01—Camrose	AJHL	55	8	16	24	81	...	...	...	—	—	—	—	—
01-02—Colorado College	WCHA	39	4	6	10	35	...	...	...	—	—	—	—	—
02-03—Colorado College	WCHA	38	1	6	7	86	...	...	...	—	—	—	—	—
03-04—Colorado College	WCHA	39	3	5	8	61	...	...	...	—	—	—	—	—
04-05—Colorado College	WCHA	25	3	5	8	38	...	...	...	—	—	—	—	—
05-06—Manchester	AHL	63	4	10	14	52	15	0	0	7	1	0	1	6
—Los Angeles	NHL	2	0	0	0	2	-2	0	0	—	—	—	—	—
NHL Totals (1 year)		2	0	0	0	2	-2	0	0					

PETROVICKY, RONALD RW/LW

PERSONAL: Born February 15, 1977, in Zilina, Czech. ... 6-0/190. ... Shoots right.
TRANSACTIONS/CAREER NOTES: Signed as free agent by Calgary Flames (June 1, 1998). ... Injured wrist (October 5, 2000); missed 49 games. ... Claimed by New York Rangers in waiver draft (October 4, 2002). ... Injured ankle (January 6, 2003); missed 11 games. ... Claimed by Atlanta Thrashers in waiver draft (October 3, 2003). ... Suspended one game for kneeing (March 18, 2004). ... Strained oblique muscle (January 6, 2006); missed four games. ... Signed as free agent by Pittsburgh Penguins (July 24, 2006).

Season Team	League	REGULAR SEASON								PLAYOFFS				
		GP	G	A	Pts.	PIM	+/-	PP	SH	GP	G	A	Pts.	PIM
93-94—Dukla Trencin	Slovakia	36	28	27	55	42	...	...	...	—	—	—	—	—
94-95—Tri-City	WHL	39	4	11	15	86	-1	1	0	—	—	—	—	—
—Prince George	WHL	21	4	6	10	37	-14	2	0	—	—	—	—	—
95-96—Prince George	WHL	39	19	21	40	61	...	...	...	—	—	—	—	—
96-97—Prince George	WHL	72	32	37	69	119	-20	9	0	15	4	9	13	31
97-98—Regina	WHL	71	64	49	113	45	168	19	3	9	2	4	6	11
98-99—Saint John	AHL	78	12	21	33	114	-16	6	0	7	1	2	3	19
99-00—Saint John	AHL	67	23	33	56	131	...	...	...	3	1	1	2	6
00-01—Calgary	NHL	30	4	5	9	54	0	1	0	—	—	—	—	—
01-02—Calgary	NHL	77	5	7	12	85	0	1	0	—	—	—	—	—
02-03—New York Rangers	NHL	66	5	9	14	77	-12	2	1	—	—	—	—	—
03-04—Atlanta	NHL	78	16	15	31	123	-9	0	0	—	—	—	—	—
04-05—Brynas IF	Sweden	10	0	5	5	27	-5	0	0	9	0	2	2	0
—HK SKP PChZ Zilina	Slovakia	34	10	9	19	34	5	...	...	—	—	—	—	—
05-06—Atlanta	NHL	60	8	12	20	62	-8	2	0	—	—	—	—	—
—Slovakian Oly. team	Int'l	6	1	0	1	2	0	0	0	—	—	—	—	—
NHL Totals (5 years)		311	38	48	86	401	-29	6	1					

PETRY, JEFF D

PERSONAL: Born December 9, 1987, in Ann Arbor, Mich. ... 6-2/176. ... Shoots right.
TRANSACTIONS/CAREER NOTES: Selected by Edmonton Oilers in second round (first Oilers pick; 45th overall) of NHL draft (June 24, 2006).

		REGULAR SEASON								PLAYOFFS				
Season Team	League	GP	G	A	Pts.	PIM	+/-	PP	SH	GP	G	A	Pts.	PIM
05-06—Des Moines................	USHL	48	1	14	15	68	...	...	...	11	2	5	7	8

PETTINEN, TOMI D

PERSONAL: Born June 17, 1977, in Ylojarvi, Finland. ... 6-4/220. ... Shoots left.
TRANSACTIONS/CAREER NOTES: Selected by New York Islanders in ninth round (ninth Islanders choice, 267th overall) of NHL draft (June 25, 2000).

		REGULAR SEASON								PLAYOFFS				
Season Team	League	GP	G	A	Pts.	PIM	+/-	PP	SH	GP	G	A	Pts.	PIM
96-97—Ilves Tampere	Finland	16	1	0	1	12	...	...	...	—	—	—	—	—
97-98—Ilves Tampere	Finland	3	0	0	0	0	...	...	...	—	—	—	—	—
—Lukko Rauma	Finland	27	0	2	2	16	...	...	...	—	—	—	—	—
98-99—HIFK Helsinki	Finland	4	0	0	0	2	...	...	...	—	—	—	—	—
99-00—Ilves Tampere	Finland	51	1	6	7	78	...	...	...	3	1	2	3	2
00-01—Ilves Tampere	Finland	56	2	2	4	...	86	...	...	9	0	0	0	4
01-02—Ilves Tampere	Finland	48	5	4	9	51	...	...	...	3	0	0	0	4
—Bridgeport..................	AHL	...	...	...	...	...	...	...	...	9	0	1	1	0
02-03—New York Islanders.....	NHL	2	0	0	0	0	1	0	0	—	—	—	—	—
—Bridgeport..................	AHL	75	1	8	9	56	6	0	0	9	0	0	0	17
03-04—New York Islanders.....	NHL	4	0	0	0	2	-2	0	0	—	—	—	—	—
—Bridgeport..................	AHL	71	1	8	9	37	15	0	0	7	1	0	1	0
04-05—Lukko Rauma	Finland	56	6	14	20	49	10	...	...	9	0	2	2	33
05-06—Bridgeport..................	AHL	29	0	6	6	38	-6	0	0	7	0	1	1	14
—New York Islanders.....	NHL	18	0	0	0	16	-2	0	0	—	—	—	—	—
NHL Totals (3 years)...........		24	0	0	0	18	-3	0	0					

PETTINGER, MATT LW

PERSONAL: Born October 22, 1980, in Edmonton. ... 6-1/205. ... Shoots left. ... Nephew of Gord Pettinger, C with three NHL teams (1932-40).
TRANSACTIONS/CAREER NOTES: Selected by Washington Capitals in second round (second Capitals pick, 43rd overall) of NHL draft (June 24, 2000). ... Flu (January 14, 2002); missed two games. ... Had concussion (November 1, 2003); missed 11 games. ... Flu (January 10, 2006); missed four games. ... Chest injury (April 1, 2006); missed two games.

		REGULAR SEASON								PLAYOFFS				
Season Team	League	GP	G	A	Pts.	PIM	+/-	PP	SH	GP	G	A	Pts.	PIM
98-99—Denver........................	WCHA	38	14	6	20	52	...	...	...	—	—	—	—	—
99-00—Denver........................	WCHA	19	2	6	8	...	...	...	...	—	—	—	—	—
—Calgary	WHL	27	14	6	20	41	...	...	...	11	2	6	8	30
00-01—Portland......................	AHL	64	19	17	36	92	...	...	...	2	0	0	0	4
—Washington	NHL	10	0	0	0	2	-1	0	0	—	—	—	—	—
01-02—Portland......................	AHL	9	3	3	6	24	-1	2	0	—	—	—	—	—
—Washington	NHL	61	7	3	10	44	-8	1	0	—	—	—	—	—
02-03—Portland......................	AHL	69	14	13	27	72	-6	4	0	3	0	2	2	2
—Washington	NHL	1	0	0	0	0	0	0	0	—	—	—	—	—
03-04—Washington	NHL	71	7	5	12	37	-9	1	0	—	—	—	—	—
04-05—Olimpija	Slovenia	8	2	5	7	41	...	...	...	—	—	—	—	—
05-06—Washington	NHL	71	20	18	38	39	-2	4	5	—	—	—	—	—
NHL Totals (5 years)...........		214	34	26	60	122	-20	6	5					

PHANEUF, DION D

PERSONAL: Born April 10, 1985, in Edmonton. ... 6-2/200. ... Shoots left. ... Name pronounced FA-nuhf.
TRANSACTIONS/CAREER NOTES: Selected by Calgary Flames in first round (first Flames pick, ninth overall) of NHL entry draft (June 20, 2003).

		REGULAR SEASON								PLAYOFFS				
Season Team	League	GP	G	A	Pts.	PIM	+/-	PP	SH	GP	G	A	Pts.	PIM
01-02—Red Deer.....................	WHL	66	5	11	16	168	...	...	...	—	—	—	—	—
02-03—Red Deer.....................	WHL	71	16	14	30	185	...	...	...	—	—	—	—	—
03-04—Red Deer.....................	WHL	62	19	24	43	126	11	8	0	19	2	11	13	30
04-05—Red Deer.....................	WHL	55	24	32	56	73	15	12	0	7	1	4	5	12
05-06—Calgary	NHL	82	20	29	49	93	5	16	0	7	1	0	1	7
NHL Totals (1 year).............		82	20	29	49	93	5	16	0	7	1	0	1	7

PHILLIPS, CHRIS D

PERSONAL: Born March 9, 1978, in Calgary. ... 6-3/215. ... Shoots left. ... Nephew of Rod Phillips, Edmonton Oilers play-by-play announcer.
TRANSACTIONS/CAREER NOTES: Selected by Ottawa Senators in first round (first Senators pick, first overall) of entry draft (June 22, 1996). ... Bruised knee (November 13, 1997); missed two games. ... Bruised eye (February 25, 1998); missed five games. ... Back spasms (November

18, 1998); missed three games. ... Sprained right ankle (January 1, 1999); missed 21 games. ... Right ankle (February 20, 1999); missed 23 games. ... Right ankle (December 9, 1999), had surgery; missed 17 games. ... Back spasms (November 2, 2000); missed three games. ... Back spasms (December 2, 2000); missed two games. ... Left shoulder (April 1, 2001); missed final three games of season. ... Shoulder (September 19, 2001); missed first three games of season. ... Left elbow (December 18, 2001); missed 15 games. ... Right knee (December 7, 2002); missed three games. ... Flu (December 20, 2005); missed one game. ... Sprained thumb (February 9, 2006); missed one game. ... Left knee (March 29, 2006); missed final 11 games of regular season.

		REGULAR SEASON								PLAYOFFS				
Season Team	**League**	**GP**	**G**	**A**	**Pts.**	**PIM**	**+/-**	**PP**	**SH**	**GP**	**G**	**A**	**Pts.**	**PIM**
93-94—Fort McMurray	AJHL	56	6	16	22	72	...	...	...	—	—	—	—	—
94-95—Fort McMurray	AJHL	48	16	32	48	127	...	...	...	—	—	—	—	—
95-96—Prince Albert	WHL	61	10	30	40	97	...	...	...	18	2	12	14	30
96-97—Prince Albert	WHL	32	3	23	26	58	-8	1	0	—	—	—	—	—
—Lethbridge	WHL	26	4	18	22	28	16	1	0	19	4	21	25	20
97-98—Ottawa	NHL	72	5	11	16	38	2	2	0	11	0	2	2	2
98-99—Ottawa	NHL	34	3	3	6	32	-5	2	0	3	0	0	0	0
99-00—Ottawa	NHL	65	5	14	19	39	12	0	0	6	0	1	1	4
00-01—Ottawa	NHL	73	2	12	14	31	8	2	0	1	1	0	1	0
01-02—Ottawa	NHL	63	6	16	22	29	5	1	0	12	0	0	0	12
02-03—Ottawa	NHL	78	3	16	19	71	7	2	0	18	2	4	6	12
03-04—Ottawa	NHL	82	7	16	23	46	15	0	0	7	1	0	1	12
04-05—Brynas IF	Sweden	27	5	3	8	45	-15	2	0	9	1	2	3	2
05-06—Ottawa	NHL	69	1	18	19	90	19	0	0	9	2	0	2	6
NHL Totals (8 years)		536	32	106	138	376	63	9	0	67	6	7	13	48

PICARD, ALEXANDRE LW

PERSONAL: Born October 9, 1985, in Les Saules, Que. ... 6-2/190. ... Shoots left.
TRANSACTIONS/CAREER NOTES: Selected by Columbus Blue Jackets in first round (first Blue Jackets pick, eighth overall) of entry draft (June 26, 2004). ... Concussion (November 22, 2005); missed 18 games.

		REGULAR SEASON								PLAYOFFS				
Season Team	**League**	**GP**	**G**	**A**	**Pts.**	**PIM**	**+/-**	**PP**	**SH**	**GP**	**G**	**A**	**Pts.**	**PIM**
01-02—Sherbrooke	QMJHL	6	0	3	3	0	...	...	...	—	—	—	—	—
02-03—Sherbrooke	QMJHL	66	14	15	29	41	...	...	...	12	4	0	4	10
03-04—Lewiston	QMJHL	69	39	41	80	88	...	...	...	7	7	4	11	6
04-05—Lewiston	QMJHL	65	40	45	85	160	20	15	6	8	5	2	7	18
05-06—Syracuse	AHL	45	15	15	30	52	2	9	0	6	1	0	1	19
—Columbus	NHL	17	0	0	0	14	-2	0	0	—	—	—	—	—
NHL Totals (1 year)		17	0	0	0	14	-2	0	0					

PICARD, ALEXANDRE D

PERSONAL: Born July 5, 1985, in Gatineau, Que. ... 6-2/214. ... Shoots left.
TRANSACTIONS/CAREER NOTES: Selected by Philadelphia Flyers in third round (fifth Flyers pick, 85th overall) of NHL entry draft (June 20, 2003).

		REGULAR SEASON								PLAYOFFS				
Season Team	**League**	**GP**	**G**	**A**	**Pts.**	**PIM**	**+/-**	**PP**	**SH**	**GP**	**G**	**A**	**Pts.**	**PIM**
01-02—Halifax	QMJHL	59	2	12	14	28	...	...	...	13	2	3	5	6
02-03—Halifax	QMJHL	71	4	30	34	64	...	...	...	25	1	5	6	14
03-04—Cape Breton	QMJHL	57	10	2	12	44	23	9	0	5	0	0	0	0
04-05—Philadelphia	AHL	—	—	—	—	—	—	—	—	2	0	0	0	0
—Halifax	QMJHL	68	15	23	38	46	18	8	0	13	1	5	6	14
05-06—Philadelphia	AHL	75	7	26	33	82	6	4	0	—	—	—	—	—
—Philadelphia	NHL	6	0	0	0	4	-2	0	0	—	—	—	—	—
NHL Totals (1 year)		6	0	0	0	4	-2	0	0					

PIHLMAN, TUOMAS LW/RW

PERSONAL: Born November 13, 1982, in Espoo, Finland. ... 6-2/205. ... Shoots left. ... Name pronounced: TOH-mahz PEEL-muhn
TRANSACTIONS/CAREER NOTES: Selected by New Jersey Devils in second round (third Devils pick, 48th overall) of NHL entry draft (June 23, 2001).

		REGULAR SEASON								PLAYOFFS				
Season Team	**League**	**GP**	**G**	**A**	**Pts.**	**PIM**	**+/-**	**PP**	**SH**	**GP**	**G**	**A**	**Pts.**	**PIM**
00-01—JyP Jyvaskyla	Finland	47	3	6	9	59	...	...	...	—	—	—	—	—
01-02—JyP Jyvaskyla	Finland	44	9	2	11	93	...	...	...	—	—	—	—	—
02-03—JyP Jyvaskyla	Finland	53	19	15	34	58	...	...	...	1	0	0	0	0
03-04—New Jersey	NHL	2	0	0	0	2	0	0	0	—	—	—	—	—
—Albany	AHL	73	10	19	29	59	-11	2	1	—	—	—	—	—
04-05—Albany	AHL	68	9	13	22	48	-16	1	0	—	—	—	—	—
05-06—Albany	AHL	63	12	15	27	64	-1	4	1	—	—	—	—	—
—New Jersey	NHL	11	1	1	2	10	-1	0	0	—	—	—	—	—
NHL Totals (2 years)		13	1	1	2	12	-1	0	0					

PIRJETA, LASSE C/RW

PERSONAL: Born April 4, 1974, in Oulu, Finland. ... 6-4/225. ... Shoots left. ... Name pronounced PEER-yeh-tuh.
TRANSACTIONS/CAREER NOTES: Selected by Columbus Blue Jackets in fifth round (seventh Blue Jackets pick, 133rd overall) in NHL draft

(June 23, 2002). ... Separated shoulder (October 15, 2003); missed 16 games. ... Had concussion (January 4, 2003); missed four games. ... Injured throat (January 21, 2004); missed one game. ... Traded by Blue Jackets to Pittsburgh Penguins for C Brian Holzinger (March 9, 2004).

		REGULAR SEASON								PLAYOFFS				
Season Team	League	GP	G	A	Pts.	PIM	+/-	PP	SH	GP	G	A	Pts.	PIM
91-92—Tacoma	WHL	16	5	2	7	4	...	...	...	—	—	—	—	—
92-93—Karpat Oulu	Finland Jr.	24	13	19	32	34	...	...	...	—	—	—	—	—
—Karpat Oulu	Finland-2	20	4	3	7	6	...	...	...	—	—	—	—	—
93-94—TPS Turku	Finland	43	9	9	18	14	...	...	...	11	4	0	4	2
94-95—TPS Turku	Finland	49	7	13	20	64	...	...	...	8	0	1	1	29
95-96—TPS Turku	Finland	45	13	14	27	34	...	...	...	11	6	3	9	4
96-97—Vastra Frolunda	Sweden	50	14	8	22	36	...	...	...	3	0	1	1	4
97-98—Tappara	Finland	48	24	22	46	20	...	...	...	4	1	1	2	2
98-99—Tappara	Finland	54	22	19	41	32	...	...	...	—	—	—	—	—
99-00—HIFK Helsinki	Finland	54	18	25	43	24	...	...	...	9	2	3	5	10
00-01—HIFK Helsinki	Finland	55	15	18	33	24	...	...	...	—	—	—	—	—
01-02—Karpat Oulu	Finland	55	15	26	41	24	...	...	...	4	2	2	4	4
02-03—Columbus	NHL	51	11	10	21	12	-4	2	0	—	—	—	—	—
03-04—Columbus	NHL	57	2	8	10	20	-6	0	0	—	—	—	—	—
—Syracuse	AHL	5	1	2	3	2	2	0	0	—	—	—	—	—
—Pittsburgh	NHL	13	6	6	12	0	3	1	0	—	—	—	—	—
04-05—HIFK Helsinki	Finland	45	16	20	36	26	13	...	...	5	2	0	2	2
05-06—Wilkes-Barre/Scranton	AHL	8	1	4	5	6	0	0	0	—	—	—	—	—
—Pittsburgh	NHL	25	4	3	7	18	4	0	0	—	—	—	—	—
NHL Totals (3 years)		146	23	27	50	50	-3	3	0					

PISANI, FERNANDO RW/LW

PERSONAL: Born December 27, 1976, in Edmonton. ... 6-1/205. ... Shoots left. ... Name pronounced pih-ZAN-ee.
TRANSACTIONS/CAREER NOTES: Selected by Edmonton Oilers in eighth round (ninth Oilers pick, 195th overall) of entry draft (June 22, 1996). ... Right shoulder (December 16, 2003); missed three games. ... Ribs (January 20, 2004); missed two games. ... Ill (October 22, 2005); missed two games.
STATISTICAL PLATEAUS: Three-goal games: 2002-03 (1).

		REGULAR SEASON								PLAYOFFS				
Season Team	League	GP	G	A	Pts.	PIM	+/-	PP	SH	GP	G	A	Pts.	PIM
95-96—St. Albert	AJHL	58	40	63	103	134	...	...	...	18	7	22	29	28
96-97—Providence College	Hockey East	35	12	18	30	36	...	...	...	—	—	—	—	—
97-98—Providence College	Hockey East	36	16	18	34	20	...	...	...	—	—	—	—	—
98-99—Providence College	Hockey East	38	14	37	51	42	...	...	...	—	—	—	—	—
99-00—Providence College	Hockey East	38	14	24	38	56	...	...	...	—	—	—	—	—
00-01—Hamilton	AHL	52	12	13	25	28	...	...	...	—	—	—	—	—
01-02—Hamilton	AHL	79	26	34	60	60	24	11	0	15	4	6	10	4
02-03—Hamilton	AHL	41	17	15	32	24	14	7	0	—	—	—	—	—
—Edmonton	NHL	35	8	5	13	10	9	0	1	6	1	0	1	2
03-04—Edmonton	NHL	76	16	14	30	46	14	4	1	—	—	—	—	—
04-05—SC Langnau	Switzerland	7	1	3	4	0	...	0	0	—	—	—	—	—
—Asiago	Italy	12	1	5	6	6	...	...	...	9	4	6	10	0
05-06—Edmonton	NHL	80	18	19	37	42	5	4	1	24	*14	4	18	10
NHL Totals (3 years)		191	42	38	80	98	28	8	3	30	15	4	19	12

PITKANEN, JONI D

PERSONAL: Born September 19, 1983, in Oulu, Finland. ... 6-3/213. ... Shoots left.
TRANSACTIONS/CAREER NOTES: Selected by Philadelphia Flyers in first round (first Flyers pick, fourth overall) of entry draft (June 22, 2002). ... Stomach virus (December 18, 2003); missed four games. ... Concussion (January 8, 2004); missed two games. ... Concussion (March 6, 2004); missed two games. ... Torn abdominal muscle (December 3, 2005) and surgery (December 7, 2005); missed 21 games. ... Groin (January 21, 2006); missed two games.

		REGULAR SEASON								PLAYOFFS				
Season Team	League	GP	G	A	Pts.	PIM	+/-	PP	SH	GP	G	A	Pts.	PIM
00-01—Karpat Oulu	Finland	21	0	0	0	10	...	...	...	2	0	0	0	2
01-02—Karpat Oulu	Finland	49	4	15	19	65	...	...	...	4	0	0	0	12
02-03—Karpat Oulu	Finland	35	5	15	20	38	...	...	...	—	—	—	—	—
03-04—Philadelphia	NHL	71	8	19	27	44	15	5	0	15	0	3	3	6
04-05—Philadelphia	AHL	76	6	35	41	105	9	3	0	21	3	4	7	16
05-06—Philadelphia	NHL	58	13	33	46	78	22	5	0	6	0	2	2	2
NHL Totals (2 years)		129	21	52	73	122	37	10	0	21	0	5	5	8

PLATT, GEOFF C

PERSONAL: Born July 10, 1985, in Mississauga, Ont. ... 5-9/171. ... Shoots left.
TRANSACTIONS/CAREER NOTES: Signed as free agent by Columbus Blue Jackets (November 23, 2005).

		REGULAR SEASON								PLAYOFFS				
Season Team	League	GP	G	A	Pts.	PIM	+/-	PP	SH	GP	G	A	Pts.	PIM
01-02—North Bay	OHL	63	4	6	10	34	...	...	...	5	0	0	0	6
02-03—Erie	OHL	—	—	—	—	—	—	—	—	9	9	1	10	22
—Saginaw	OHL	62	32	22	54	79	...	...	...	—	—	—	—	—
03-04—Atlantic City	ECHL	—	—	—	—	—	—	—	—	3	0	0	0	0
—Saginaw	OHL	27	7	13	20	49	...	...	...	—	—	—	—	—
—Erie	OHL	28	18	11	29	22	...	...	...	6	2	3	5	16

Season Team	League	GP	G	A	Pts.	PIM	+/-	PP	SH	GP	G	A	Pts.	PIM
		REGULAR SEASON								PLAYOFFS				
04-05—Atlantic City	ECHL	2	0	2	2	0	...	...	...	—	—	—	—	—
—Erie	OHL	68	45	34	79	84	...	...	...	—	—	—	—	—
05-06—Syracuse	AHL	66	30	35	65	58	1	16	2	6	3	0	3	6
—Columbus	NHL	15	0	5	5	16	-4	0	0	—	—	—	—	—
NHL Totals (1 year)		15	0	5	5	16	-4	0	0					

PLEKANEC, TOMAS C/LW

PERSONAL: Born October 31, 1982, in Kladno, Czech. ... 5-10/189. ... Shoots left. ... Name pronounced pleh-KA-nyehts.

TRANSACTIONS/CAREER NOTES: Selected by Montreal Canadiens in third round (fourth Canadiens pick, 71st overall) of NHL entry draft (June 23, 2001). ... Injured knee (December 17, 2005); missed 13 games. ... Injured shoulder (March 7, 2006); missed one game.

Season Team	League	GP	G	A	Pts.	PIM	+/-	PP	SH	GP	G	A	Pts.	PIM
		REGULAR SEASON								PLAYOFFS				
00-01—HC Kladno	Czech Rep.	47	9	9	18	24	...	...	...	—	—	—	—	—
01-02—HC Kladno	Czech Rep.	48	7	16	23	28	...	...	...	—	—	—	—	—
02-03—Hamilton	AHL	77	19	27	46	74	5	6	0	13	3	2	5	8
03-04—Hamilton	AHL	74	23	43	66	90	21	5	3	10	2	5	7	6
—Montreal	NHL	2	0	0	0	0	0	0	0	—	—	—	—	—
04-05—Hamilton	AHL	80	29	35	64	68	4	11	1	4	2	4	6	6
05-06—Hamilton	AHL	2	0	0	0	2	0	0	0	—	—	—	—	—
—Montreal	NHL	67	9	20	29	32	4	1	0	6	0	4	4	6
NHL Totals (2 years)		69	9	20	29	32	4	1	0	6	0	4	4	6

POAPST, STEVE D

PERSONAL: Born January 3, 1969, in Cornwall, Ont. ... 6-0/199. ... Shoots left. ... Name pronounced POHPST.

TRANSACTIONS/CAREER NOTES: Signed as free agent by Washington Capitals (February 4, 1995). ... Signed as free agent by Chicago Blackhawks (July 27, 2000). ... Strained groin (April 1, 2001); missed three games. ... Concussion (January 8, 2004); missed 29 games. ... Signed as free agent by Pittsburgh Penguins (August 15, 2005). ... Traded by Penguins to St. Louis Blues for RW Eric Boguniecki (December 9, 2005).

Season Team	League	GP	G	A	Pts.	PIM	+/-	PP	SH	GP	G	A	Pts.	PIM
		REGULAR SEASON								PLAYOFFS				
86-87—Smith Falls	OJHL	54	10	27	37	94	...	...	...	—	—	—	—	—
87-88—Colgate	ECAC	32	3	13	16	22	...	...	...	—	—	—	—	—
88-89—Colgate	ECAC	30	0	5	5	38	...	...	...	—	—	—	—	—
89-90—Colgate	ECAC	38	4	15	19	54	...	...	...	—	—	—	—	—
90-91—Colgate	ECAC	32	6	15	21	43	...	...	...	—	—	—	—	—
91-92—Hampton Roads	ECHL	55	8	20	28	29	...	...	...	14	1	4	5	12
92-93—Hampton Roads	ECHL	63	10	35	45	57	...	...	...	4	0	1	1	4
—Baltimore	AHL	7	0	1	1	4	...	...	...	7	0	3	3	6
93-94—Portland	AHL	78	14	21	35	47	...	...	...	12	0	3	3	8
94-95—Portland	AHL	71	8	22	30	60	41	4	0	7	0	1	1	16
95-96—Portland	AHL	70	10	24	34	79	...	...	...	20	2	6	8	16
—Washington	NHL	3	1	0	1	0	-1	0	0	6	0	0	0	0
96-97—Portland	AHL	47	1	20	21	34	0	0	0	5	0	1	1	6
97-98—Portland	AHL	76	8	29	37	46	17	5	0	10	2	3	5	8
98-99—Portland	AHL	54	3	21	24	36	3	2	0	—	—	—	—	—
—Washington	NHL	22	0	0	0	8	-8	0	0	—	—	—	—	—
99-00—Portland	AHL	56	0	14	14	20	...	...	...	3	1	0	1	2
00-01—Norfolk	AHL	37	1	8	9	14	...	...	...	—	—	—	—	—
—Chicago	NHL	36	2	3	5	12	3	0	0	—	—	—	—	—
01-02—Chicago	NHL	56	1	7	8	30	6	0	0	5	0	0	0	0
02-03—Chicago	NHL	75	2	11	13	50	14	0	0	—	—	—	—	—
03-04—Chicago	NHL	53	2	2	4	26	-16	0	0	—	—	—	—	—
05-06—Pittsburgh	NHL	21	0	4	4	10	-5	0	0	—	—	—	—	—
—St. Louis	NHL	41	0	1	1	37	-21	0	0	—	—	—	—	—
NHL Totals (7 years)		307	8	28	36	173	-28	0	0	11	0	0	0	0

POCK, THOMAS D

PERSONAL: Born December 2, 1981, in Klagenfurt, Austria. ... 6-1/208. ... Shoots left.

TRANSACTIONS/CAREER NOTES: Signed as free agent by New York Rangers (March 23, 2004). ... Re-signed by Rangers (August 3, 2005).

Season Team	League	GP	G	A	Pts.	PIM	+/-	PP	SH	GP	G	A	Pts.	PIM
		REGULAR SEASON								PLAYOFFS				
00-01—Massachusetts	Hockey East	33	6	6	12	59	...	...	...	—	—	—	—	—
01-02—Massachusetts	Hockey East	23	5	7	12	26	...	...	...	—	—	—	—	—
02-03—Massachusetts	Hockey East	37	17	20	37	46	...	...	...	—	—	—	—	—
03-04—Massachusetts	Hockey East	37	16	25	41	48	...	...	...	—	—	—	—	—
—New York Rangers	NHL	6	2	2	4	0	-4	0	0	—	—	—	—	—
04-05—Hartford	AHL	50	1	5	6	55	9	1	0	6	0	1	1	8
—Charlotte	ECHL	3	0	2	2	2	1	0	0	—	—	—	—	—
05-06—Hartford	AHL	67	15	46	61	99	15	9	0	6	0	3	3	15
—New York Rangers	NHL	8	1	1	2	4	-3	0	0	—	—	—	—	—
NHL Totals (2 years)		14	3	3	6	4	-7	0	0					

POHL, JOHN C

PERSONAL: Born June 29, 1979, in Rochester, Minn. ... 6-1/194. ... Shoots right.

TRANSACTIONS/CAREER NOTES: Selected by St. Louis Blues in ninth round (eighth Blues pick, 255th overall) of entry draft (June 27, 1998). ... Traded by Blues to Toronto Maple Leafs for future considerations (August 24, 2005).

		REGULAR SEASON								PLAYOFFS				
Season Team	**League**	**GP**	**G**	**A**	**Pts.**	**PIM**	**+/-**	**PP**	**SH**	**GP**	**G**	**A**	**Pts.**	**PIM**
97-98—Red Wing H.S.	Minn. H.S.	28	30	77	107	18	...	...	...	—	—	—	—	—
—Twin Cities	USHL	10	5	3	8	10	...	...	...	—	—	—	—	—
98-99—Minnesota	WCHA	42	7	10	17	18	...	...	...	—	—	—	—	—
99-00—Minnesota	WCHA	41	18	49	67	26	...	...	...	—	—	—	—	—
00-01—Minnesota	WCHA	38	19	26	45	24	...	...	...	—	—	—	—	—
01-02—Minnesota	WCHA	44	27	52	79	26	...	...	...	—	—	—	—	—
02-03—Worcester	AHL	58	26	32	58	34	11	6	0	3	0	1	1	6
03-04—St. Louis	NHL	1	0	0	0	0	-2	0	0	—	—	—	—	—
—Worcester	AHL	65	16	25	41	65	-2	7	0	3	0	1	1	2
04-05—Worcester	AHL	13	3	6	9	2	-3	1	0	—	—	—	—	—
05-06—Toronto	AHL	60	36	39	75	42	4	18	2	5	1	5	6	10
—Toronto	NHL	7	3	1	4	4	2	1	0	—	—	—	—	—
NHL Totals (2 years)		8	3	1	4	4	0	1	0					

POLAK, VOJTECH LW

PERSONAL: Born June 27, 1985, in Ostrov nad Ohri, Czechoslovakia. ... 5-11/180. ... Shoots left.

TRANSACTIONS/CAREER NOTES: Selected by Dallas Stars in second round (second Stars pick, 36th overall) of entry draft (June 20, 2003). ... Signed by Stars (August 3, 2005).

		REGULAR SEASON								PLAYOFFS				
Season Team	**League**	**GP**	**G**	**A**	**Pts.**	**PIM**	**+/-**	**PP**	**SH**	**GP**	**G**	**A**	**Pts.**	**PIM**
99-00—Karlovy Vary	Czech. Jrs.	46	17	23	40	48	3	...	...	—	—	—	—	—
—Karlovy Vary	Czech. D-II	3	0	0	0	0	-2	...	...	—	—	—	—	—
00-01—Karlovy Vary	Czech. Jrs.	35	29	26	55	36	22	...	...	—	—	—	—	—
—Karlovy Vary	Czech. D-II	12	7	7	14	2	10	...	...	—	—	—	—	—
—Karlovy Vary	Czech Rep.	2	0	0	0	0	...	...	...	—	—	—	—	—
01-02—Karlovy Vary	Czech. Jrs.	2	1	2	3	4	1	...	...	—	—	—	—	—
—Karlovy Vary	Czech. D-II	37	11	14	25	26	11	...	...	—	—	—	—	—
—Karlovy Vary	Czech Rep.	9	1	1	2	2	...	...	...	—	—	—	—	—
02-03—Karlovy Vary	Czech Rep.	41	7	9	16	51	7	...	...	—	—	—	—	—
—Karlovy Vary	Czech. D-II	4	2	2	4	18	...	...	...	—	—	—	—	—
03-04—Karlovy Vary	Czech. D-II	5	8	4	12	2	0	...	...	—	—	—	—	—
—Karlovy Vary	Czech Rep.	44	0	8	8	42	-10	...	...	—	—	—	—	—
—Sparta Praha	Czech Rep.	1	1	0	1	0	...	...	...	—	—	—	—	—
04-05—Dukla Jihlava	Czech Rep.	16	1	2	3	12	...	...	...	—	—	—	—	—
—HC Karlovy Vary	Czech Rep.	26	1	5	6	4	...	...	...	—	—	—	—	—
05-06—Iowa	AHL	60	12	22	34	41	-5	2	1	3	0	1	1	0
—Dallas	NHL	3	0	0	0	0	-1	0	0	—	—	—	—	—
NHL Totals (1 year)		3	0	0	0	0	-1	0	0					

POMINVILLE, JASON RW

PERSONAL: Born November 30, 1982, in Repentigny, Que. ... 6-0/178. ... Shoots right.

TRANSACTIONS/CAREER NOTES: Selected by Buffalo Sabres in second round (fourth Sabres pick, 55th overall) of entry draft (June 23, 2001).

		REGULAR SEASON								PLAYOFFS				
Season Team	**League**	**GP**	**G**	**A**	**Pts.**	**PIM**	**+/-**	**PP**	**SH**	**GP**	**G**	**A**	**Pts.**	**PIM**
98-99—Shawinigan	QMJHL	2	0	0	0	0	...	...	...	—	—	—	—	—
99-00—Shawinigan	QMJHL	60	4	17	21	12	...	...	...	13	2	3	5	0
00-01—Shawinigan	QMJHL	71	46	61	107	24	...	...	...	10	6	6	12	0
01-02—Shawinigan	QMJHL	66	57	64	121	32	...	...	...	2	0	0	0	0
02-03—Rochester	AHL	73	13	21	34	16	5	3	0	3	1	1	2	0
03-04—Buffalo	NHL	1	0	0	0	0	0	0	0	—	—	—	—	—
—Rochester	AHL	66	34	30	64	30	1	22	0	16	9	10	19	6
04-05—Rochester	AHL	78	30	38	68	43	1	11	0	0	0	0	0	0
05-06—Rochester	AHL	18	19	7	26	11	2	9	1	—	—	—	—	—
—Buffalo	NHL	57	18	12	30	22	-4	10	2	18	5	5	10	8
NHL Totals (2 years)		58	18	12	30	22	-4	10	2	18	5	5	10	8

PONIKAROVSKY, ALEXEI LW

PERSONAL: Born April 9, 1980, in Kiev, U.S.S.R. ... 6-4/220. ... Shoots left. ... Name pronounced pahn-ih-kuh-RAHV-skee.

TRANSACTIONS/CAREER NOTES: Selected by Toronto Maple Leafs in fourth round (fourth Maple Leafs pick, 87th overall) of NHL draft (June 27, 1998).

		REGULAR SEASON								PLAYOFFS				
Season Team	**League**	**GP**	**G**	**A**	**Pts.**	**PIM**	**+/-**	**PP**	**SH**	**GP**	**G**	**A**	**Pts.**	**PIM**
95-96—Dynamo Moscow	CIS Jr.	70	14	10	24	20	...	...	...	—	—	—	—	—
96-97—Dynamo Moscow	Russian Jr.	60	12	15	27	30	...	...	...	—	—	—	—	—
—Dynamo Moscow	Rus. Div.	2	0	0	0	2	...	...	...	—	—	—	—	—

Season Team	League	REGULAR SEASON GP	G	A	Pts.	PIM	+/-	PP	SH	PLAYOFFS GP	G	A	Pts.	PIM
97-98—Dynamo Moscow........	Rus. Div.	24	1	2	3	30	...	...	...	—	—	—	—	—
98-99—Dynamo Moscow........	Russian	...	...	...	...	...	...	...	...	3	0	0	0	2
99-00—Dynamo Moscow........	Russian	19	1	0	1	8	...	...	...	1	0	0	0	0
00-01—St. John's....................	AHL	49	12	24	36	44	...	...	...	4	0	0	0	4
—Toronto	NHL	22	1	3	4	14	-1	0	0	—	—	—	—	—
01-02—St. John's....................	AHL	72	21	27	48	74	4	4	1	5	2	1	3	8
—Toronto	NHL	8	2	0	2	0	2	0	0	10	0	0	0	4
02-03—St. John's....................	AHL	63	24	22	46	68	18	5	2	—	—	—	—	—
—Toronto	NHL	13	0	3	3	11	4	0	0	—	—	—	—	—
03-04—Toronto	NHL	73	9	19	28	44	14	1	0	13	1	3	4	8
04-05—Khimik Voskresensk ...	Russian	19	1	5	6	16	4	...	...	—	—	—	—	—
05-06—Toronto	NHL	81	21	17	38	68	15	2	4	—	—	—	—	—
NHL Totals (5 years)...........		197	33	42	75	137	34	3	4	23	1	3	4	12

POPOVIC, MARK D

PERSONAL: Born October 11, 1982, in Stoney Creek, Ont. ... 6-1/207. ... Shoots left.

TRANSACTIONS/CAREER NOTES: Selected by Anaheim Mighty Ducks in second round (second Mighty Ducks pick, 35th overall) of entry draft (June 23, 2001). ... Traded by Mighty Ducks to Atlanta Thrashers for LW Kip Brennan (August 25, 2005).

Season Team	League	REGULAR SEASON GP	G	A	Pts.	PIM	+/-	PP	SH	PLAYOFFS GP	G	A	Pts.	PIM
98-99—Toronto St. Michael's..	OHL	60	6	26	32	46	...	...	...	—	—	—	—	—
99-00—Toronto St. Michael's..	OHL	68	11	29	40	68	...	...	...	—	—	—	—	—
00-01—Toronto St. Michael's..	OHL	61	7	35	42	54	...	...	...	18	3	5	8	22
01-02—Toronto St. Michael's..	OHL	58	12	29	41	42	...	...	...	15	1	11	12	10
02-03—Cincinnati....................	AHL	73	3	21	24	46	8	2	0	—	—	—	—	—
03-04—Anaheim	NHL	1	0	0	0	0	0	0	0	—	—	—	—	—
—Cincinnati....................	AHL	74	4	11	15	63	0	0	0	9	1	2	3	4
04-05—Cincinnati....................	AHL	74	1	17	18	47	16	0	0	11	2	3	5	6
05-06—Chicago........................	AHL	73	12	26	38	66	8	7	2	—	—	—	—	—
—Atlanta	NHL	7	0	0	0	0	-5	0	0	—	—	—	—	—
NHL Totals (2 years)...........		8	0	0	0	0	-5	0	0					

POTHIER, BRIAN D

PERSONAL: Born April 15, 1977, in New Bedford, Mass. ... 6-0/198. ... Shoots right. ... Name pronounced POH-thee-uhr.

TRANSACTIONS/CAREER NOTES: Signed as free agent by Atlanta Thrashers (April 8, 2000). ... Concussion (March 22, 2002); missed remainder of season. ... Traded by Thrashers to Ottawa Senators for LW Shawn McEachern and sixth-round pick (G Dan Turple) in 2004 entry draft (June 30, 2002). ... Concussion (December 14, 2003); missed 11 games. ... Bruised right foot (January 4, 2006); missed one game. ... Food poisoning (February 1, 2006); missed two games. ... Signed as free agent by Washington Capitals (July 1, 2006).

Season Team	League	REGULAR SEASON GP	G	A	Pts.	PIM	+/-	PP	SH	PLAYOFFS GP	G	A	Pts.	PIM
96-97—R.P.I.	ECAC	34	1	11	12	42	...	...	...	—	—	—	—	—
97-98—R.P.I.	ECAC	35	2	9	11	28	...	...	...	—	—	—	—	—
98-99—R.P.I.	ECAC	37	5	13	18	36	...	...	...	—	—	—	—	—
99-00—R.P.I.	ECAC	36	9	24	33	44	...	...	...	—	—	—	—	—
00-01—Orlando	IHL	76	12	29	41	69	...	...	...	16	3	5	8	11
—Atlanta	NHL	3	0	0	0	2	4	0	0	—	—	—	—	—
01-02—Atlanta	NHL	33	3	6	9	22	-19	1	0	—	—	—	—	—
—Chicago........................	AHL	39	6	13	19	30	2	1	0	—	—	—	—	—
02-03—Ottawa	NHL	14	2	4	6	6	11	0	0	1	0	0	0	2
—Binghamton	AHL	68	7	40	47	58	5	6	0	8	2	8	10	4
03-04—Ottawa	NHL	55	2	6	8	24	6	1	0	7	0	0	0	6
04-05—Binghamton	AHL	77	12	36	48	64	13	11	0	6	0	1	1	6
05-06—Ottawa	NHL	77	5	30	35	59	29	3	0	8	2	1	3	2
NHL Totals (5 years)...........		182	12	46	58	113	31	5	0	16	2	1	3	10

POTI, TOM D

PERSONAL: Born March 22, 1977, in Worcester, Mass. ... 6-3/215. ... Shoots left.

TRANSACTIONS/CAREER NOTES: Selected by Edmonton Oilers in third round (fourth Oilers pick, 59th overall) of entry draft (June 22, 1996). ... Bruised right knee (November 10, 1999); missed one game. ... Strained neck (December 4, 1999); missed two games. ... Bruised thumb (January 14, 2000); missed one game. ... Bruised ankle (February 13, 2000); missed one game. ... Reinjured ankle (February 29, 2000); missed one game. ... Fractured finger (December 21, 2001); missed seven games. ... Traded by Oilers with LW Rem Murray to New York Rangers for C Mike York and fourth-round pick (D Ivan Koltsov) in 2002 draft (March 19, 2002). ... Flu (December 21, 2002); missed one game. ... Neck (January 11, 2003); missed one game. ... Flu (November 4, 2003); missed two games. ... Thumb (November 20, 2003); missed one game. ... Back spasms (December 13, 2003); missed one game. ... Hip flexor (January 3, 2004); missed one game. ... Back (January 20, 2004); missed two games. ... Sore back (February 2, 2004); missed two games. ... Re-signed by Rangers as restricted free agent (August 15, 2005). ... Flu (October 31, 2005); missed one game. ... Strained groin (December 1, 2005); missed three games. ... Flu (December 31, 2005); missed one game. ... Upper body (April 9, 2006); missed two games. ... Signed as free agent by New York Islanders (July 8, 2006).

Season Team	League	REGULAR SEASON GP	G	A	Pts.	PIM	+/-	PP	SH	PLAYOFFS GP	G	A	Pts.	PIM
94-95—Cushing Academy.......	Mass. H.S.	36	16	47	63	35	...	...	...	—	—	—	—	—
95-96—Cushing Academy.......	Mass. H.S.	29	14	59	73	18	...	...	...	—	—	—	—	—
96-97—Boston University	Hockey East	38	4	17	21	54	10	1	0	—	—	—	—	—

Season Team	League	GP	G	A	Pts.	PIM	+/-	PP	SH	GP	G	A	Pts.	PIM
		REGULAR SEASON								PLAYOFFS				
97-98—Boston University	Hockey East	38	13	29	42	60	...	...	...	—	—	—	—	—
98-99—Edmonton	NHL	73	5	16	21	42	10	2	0	4	0	1	1	2
99-00—Edmonton	NHL	76	9	26	35	65	8	2	1	5	0	1	1	0
00-01—Edmonton	NHL	81	12	20	32	60	-4	6	0	6	0	2	2	2
01-02—Edmonton	NHL	55	1	16	17	42	-6	1	0	—	—	—	—	—
—U.S. Olympic team	Int'l	6	0	1	1	4	...	...	...	—	—	—	—	—
—New York Rangers	NHL	11	1	7	8	2	-4	1	0	—	—	—	—	—
02-03—New York Rangers	NHL	80	11	37	48	60	-6	3	0	—	—	—	—	—
03-04—New York Rangers	NHL	67	10	14	24	47	-1	4	0	—	—	—	—	—
05-06—New York Rangers	NHL	73	3	20	23	70	16	2	0	4	0	0	0	2
NHL Totals (7 years)		516	52	156	208	388	13	21	1	19	0	4	4	6

POTULNY, RYAN C

PERSONAL: Born September 5, 1984, in Grand Forks, N.D. ... 6-0/190. ... Shoots left. ... Brother of Grant Potulny of the Ottawa Senators organization.

COLLEGE: Minnesota.

TRANSACTIONS/CAREER NOTES: Selected by Philadelphia Flyers in third round (sixth Flyers pick, 87th overall) of entry draft (June 20, 2003).

Season Team	League	GP	G	A	Pts.	PIM	+/-	PP	SH	GP	G	A	Pts.	PIM
		REGULAR SEASON								PLAYOFFS				
01-02—Lincoln	USHL	60	23	34	57	65	...	...	...	4	0	1	1	2
02-03—Lincoln	USHL	54	35	43	78	18	...	...	...	10	6	11	17	8
03-04—Minnesota	WCHA	15	6	8	14	10	...	...	...	—	—	—	—	—
04-05—Minnesota	WCHA	44	24	17	41	20	...	...	...	—	—	—	—	—
05-06—Minnesota	WCHA	41	38	25	63	31	...	...	...	—	—	—	—	—
—Philadelphia	NHL	2	0	1	1	0	1	0	0	—	—	—	—	—
NHL Totals (1 year)		2	0	1	1	0	1	0	0					

POULIOT, MARC-ANTOINE C

PERSONAL: Born May 22, 1985, in Quebec City. ... 6-1/195. ... Shoots right. ... Name pronounced: MAHRK an-twahn POO-lee-aht

TRANSACTIONS/CAREER NOTES: Selected by Edmonton Oilers in first round (first Oilers pick, 22nd overall) of entry draft (June 20, 2003). ... Mononucleosis (April 26, 2006); missed playoffs.

Season Team	League	GP	G	A	Pts.	PIM	+/-	PP	SH	GP	G	A	Pts.	PIM
		REGULAR SEASON								PLAYOFFS				
01-02—Rimouski	QMJHL	28	9	14	23	32	...	...	...	5	0	0	0	4
02-03—Rimouski	QMJHL	65	32	41	73	100	...	...	...	—	—	—	—	—
03-04—Rimouski	QMJHL	42	25	33	58	62	...	...	...	9	5	7	12	12
04-05—Rimouski	QMJHL	70	45	69	114	83	46	22	0	13	4	15	19	8
05-06—Hamilton	AHL	65	15	30	45	63	-7	5	1	—	—	—	—	—
—Edmonton	NHL	8	1	0	1	0	1	0	0	—	—	—	—	—
NHL Totals (1 year)		8	1	0	1	0	1	0	0					

PRATT, NOLAN D

PERSONAL: Born August 14, 1975, in Fort McMurray, Alta. ... 6-2/215. ... Shoots left. ... Brother of Harlan Pratt, D, in Pittsburgh and Carolina organizations (1997-2003).

TRANSACTIONS/CAREER NOTES: Selected by Hartford Whalers in fifth round (fourth Whalers pick, 115th overall) of NHL entry draft (June 26, 1993). ... Whalers franchise moved to North Carolina and renamed Carolina Hurricanes for 1997-98 season; NHL approved move on June 25, 1997. ... Back spasms (December 21, 1998); missed eight games. ... Injured hip (December 20, 1999); missed two games. ... Injured hand (April 3, 2000); missed final two games of season. ... Traded by Hurricanes with first-(C Vaclav Nedorost) and two second-round (C Jared Aulin and D Argis Saviels) picks in 2000 draft to Colorado Avalanche for D Sandis Ozolinsh and second-round pick (LW Tomas Kurka) in 2000 draft (June 24, 2000). ... Injured wrist (October 4, 2000); missed two games. ... Traded by Avalanche to Tampa Bay Lightning for sixth-round pick (RW Scott Horvath) in 2001 draft (June 24, 2001). ... Fractured foot (September 29, 2001); missed first 11 games of season. ... Fractured right leg (December 31, 2001); missed 25 games. ... Dizziness (December 8, 2002); missed one game.

Season Team	League	GP	G	A	Pts.	PIM	+/-	PP	SH	GP	G	A	Pts.	PIM
		REGULAR SEASON								PLAYOFFS				
91-92—Portland	WHL	22	2	9	11	13	...	...	...	6	1	3	4	12
92-93—Portland	WHL	70	4	19	23	97	...	...	...	16	2	7	9	31
93-94—Portland	WHL	72	4	32	36	105	36	0	0	10	1	2	3	14
94-95—Portland	WHL	72	6	37	43	196	-22	3	0	9	1	6	7	10
95-96—Richmond	ECHL	4	1	0	1	2	...	...	...	—	—	—	—	—
—Springfield	AHL	62	2	6	8	72	...	...	...	2	0	0	0	0
96-97—Hartford	NHL	9	0	2	2	6	0	0	0	—	—	—	—	—
—Springfield	AHL	66	1	18	19	127	7	0	0	17	0	3	3	18
97-98—New Haven	AHL	54	3	15	18	135	-5	1	0	—	—	—	—	—
—Carolina	NHL	23	0	2	2	44	-2	0	0	—	—	—	—	—
98-99—Carolina	NHL	61	1	14	15	95	15	0	0	3	0	0	0	2
99-00—Carolina	NHL	64	3	1	4	90	-22	0	0	—	—	—	—	—
00-01—Colorado	NHL	46	1	2	3	40	2	0	0	—	—	—	—	—
01-02—Tampa Bay	NHL	46	0	3	3	51	-4	0	0	—	—	—	—	—
02-03—Tampa Bay	NHL	67	1	7	8	35	-6	0	0	4	0	1	1	0
03-04—Tampa Bay	NHL	58	1	3	4	42	11	0	0	20	0	0	0	8
04-05—EV Duisburg	German Dv. 2	10	2	2	4	14	...	...	...	12	0	3	3	10
05-06—Tampa Bay	NHL	82	0	9	9	60	7	0	0	5	0	0	0	7
NHL Totals (9 years)		456	7	43	50	463	1	0	0	32	0	1	1	17

PREISSING, TOM D

PERSONAL: Born December 3, 1978, in Rosemount, Minn. ... 6-0/205. ... Shoots right. ... Name pronounced PREH-sihng.
TRANSACTIONS/CAREER NOTES: Signed as free agent by San Jose Sharks (April 4, 2003). ... Injured upper body (February 23, 2004); missed two games. ... Re-signed by Sharks as restricted free agent (August 10, 2005). ... Pneumonia (December 23, 2005); missed five games. ... Traded by Sharks with D Josh Hennessy to Chicago Blackhawks for F Mark Bell in three-team trade in which Blackhawks then traded Preissing, Hennessy, D Michal Barinka and second-round pick in 2008 draft to Ottawa Senators for Fs Martin Havlat and Bryan Smolinski (July 10, 2006).

		REGULAR SEASON								PLAYOFFS				
Season Team	League	GP	G	A	Pts.	PIM	+/-	PP	SH	GP	G	A	Pts.	PIM
99-00—Colorado College	WCHA	36	4	14	18	20	...	...	...	—	—	—	—	—
00-01—Colorado College	WCHA	33	6	18	24	26	...	...	...	—	—	—	—	—
01-02—Colorado College	WCHA	43	6	26	32	42	...	...	...	—	—	—	—	—
02-03—Colorado College	WCHA	42	23	29	52	16	...	...	...	—	—	—	—	—
03-04—San Jose	NHL	69	2	17	19	12	8	2	0	11	0	1	1	0
04-05—Krefeld Pinguine	Germany	33	1	6	7	32	6	1	0	—	—	—	—	—
05-06—San Jose	NHL	74	11	32	43	26	17	2	0	11	1	6	7	4
NHL Totals (2 years)		143	13	49	62	38	25	4	0	22	1	7	8	4

PRIMEAU, KEITH C

PERSONAL: Born November 24, 1971, in Toronto. ... 6-5/220. ... Shoots left. ... Brother of Wayne Primeau, C, Boston Bruins. ... Name pronounced PREE-moh.
TRANSACTIONS/CAREER NOTES: Selected by Detroit Red Wings in first round (first Red Wings pick, third overall) of entry draft (June 16, 1990). ... Flu (January 13, 1993); missed two games. ... Sprained right shoulder (February 9, 1993); missed one game. ... Sprained right knee (March 2, 1993); missed two games. ... Sprained right knee (April 1, 1993); missed four games. ... Injured right thumb (February 10, 1995); missed one game. ... Flu (February 25, 1995); missed one game. ... Reinjured thumb (March 2, 1995); missed one game. ... Injured ribs (November 1, 1995); missed eight games. ... Injured left knee (January 13, 1996); missed one game. ... Traded by Red Wings with D Paul Coffey and first-round pick (D Nikos Tselios) in 1997 draft to Hartford Whalers for LW Brendan Shanahan and D Brian Glynn (October 9, 1996). ... Flu (December 3, 1996); missed one game. ... Concussion (December 21, 1996); missed one game. ... Suspended two games for slashing incident (January 3, 1997). ... Asthma (February 12, 1997); missed one game. ... Whalers franchise moved to North Carolina and renamed Carolina Hurricanes for 1997-98 season; NHL approved move on June 25, 1997. ... Strained hip flexor (November 13, 1997); missed one game. ... Injured wrist (February 13, 1999); missed one game. ... Strained lower back (April 10, 1999); missed three games. ... Missed first 47 games of 1999-2000 season in contract dispute. ... Rights traded by Hurricanes with fifth-round pick (traded to New York Islanders; Islanders selected RW Kristofer Ottosson) in 2000 draft to Philadelphia Flyers for C Rod Brind'Amour, G Jean-Marc Pelletier and second-round pick (traded to Colorado; Avalanche selected D Agris Saviels) in 2000 draft (January 23, 2000). ... Fractured rib (February 12, 2000); missed nine games. ... Reinjured ribs (March 4, 2000); missed three games. ... Headaches (October 29, 2000); missed two games. ... Bruised shoulder (December 27, 2000); missed three games. ... Sprained left knee (March 26, 2001); missed final six games of season and two playoff games. ... Sprained right ankle (October 13, 2001); missed three games. ... Strained muscle in ribs (March 4, 2002); missed two games. ... Reinjured ribs (March 18, 2002); missed two games. ... Bruised right ankle (October 12, 2002); missed two games. ... Injured wrist (December 10, 2003); missed one game. ... Fractured thumb (January 2, 2004); missed six games. ... Concussion (February 13, 2004); missed 21 games. ... Concussion (October 25, 2005); missed remainder of regular season.
STATISTICAL PLATEAUS: Three-goal games: 2000-01 (1).

		REGULAR SEASON								PLAYOFFS				
Season Team	League	GP	G	A	Pts.	PIM	+/-	PP	SH	GP	G	A	Pts.	PIM
87-88—Hamilton	OHL	47	6	6	12	69	...	...	...	11	0	2	2	2
88-89—Niagara Falls	OHL	48	20	35	55	56	...	...	...	17	9	6	15	12
89-90—Niagara Falls	OHL	65	57	70	127	97	...	...	...	16	16	17	33	49
90-91—Detroit	NHL	58	3	12	15	106	-12	0	0	5	1	1	2	25
—Adirondack	AHL	6	3	5	8	8	...	...	...	—	—	—	—	—
91-92—Detroit	NHL	35	6	10	16	83	9	0	0	11	0	0	0	14
—Adirondack	AHL	42	21	24	45	89	...	...	...	9	1	7	8	27
92-93—Detroit	NHL	73	15	17	32	152	-6	4	1	7	0	2	2	26
93-94—Detroit	NHL	78	31	42	73	173	34	7	3	7	0	2	2	6
94-95—Detroit	NHL	45	15	27	42	99	17	1	0	17	4	5	9	45
95-96—Detroit	NHL	74	27	25	52	168	19	6	2	17	1	4	5	28
96-97—Hartford	NHL	75	26	25	51	161	-3	6	3	—	—	—	—	—
97-98—Carolina	NHL	81	26	37	63	110	19	7	3	—	—	—	—	—
—Can. Olympic team	Int'l	6	2	1	3	4	3	0	1	—	—	—	—	—
98-99—Carolina	NHL	78	30	32	62	75	8	9	1	6	0	3	3	6
99-00—Philadelphia	NHL	23	7	10	17	31	10	1	0	18	2	11	13	13
00-01—Philadelphia	NHL	71	34	39	73	76	17	11	0	4	0	3	3	8
01-02—Philadelphia	NHL	75	19	29	48	128	-3	5	0	5	0	0	0	6
02-03—Philadelphia	NHL	80	19	27	46	93	4	6	0	13	1	1	2	14
03-04—Philadelphia	NHL	54	7	15	22	80	11	0	1	18	9	7	16	22
05-06—Philadelphia	NHL	9	1	6	7	6	0	1	0	—	—	—	—	—
NHL Totals (15 years)		909	266	353	619	1541	124	64	14	128	18	39	57	213

PRIMEAU, WAYNE C/LW

PERSONAL: Born June 4, 1976, in Scarborough, Ont. ... 6-4/230. ... Shoots left. ... Brother of Keith Primeau, C, Philadelphia Flyers. ... Name pronounced PREE-moh.
TRANSACTIONS/CAREER NOTES: Selected by Buffalo Sabres in first round (first Sabres pick, 17th overall) of entry draft (June 28, 1994). ... Bruised shoulder (November 4, 1998); missed four games. ... Reinjured shoulder (December 5, 1998); missed four games. ... Reinjured shoulder (January 11, 1999); missed one game. ... Strained groin (March 7, 1999); missed one game. ... Hip (January 1, 2000); missed 20 games. ... Traded by Sabres with C/RW Brian Holzinger, D Cory Sarich and third-round pick (RW Alexandre Kharitonov) in 2000 draft to Tampa Bay Lightning for C Chris Gratton and second-round pick (C Derek Roy) in 2001 draft (March 9, 2000). ... Suspended two games for slashing incident (January 23, 2001). ... Traded by Lightning to Pittsburgh Penguins for LW Matthew Barnaby (February 1, 2001). ... Neck (February 14, 2001); missed one game. ... Injured (March 21, 2001); missed one game. ... Heel (September 2001); missed season's first eight games. ...

Knee surgery (January 6, 2002); missed remainder of season. ... Traded by Penguins to San Jose Sharks for RW Matt Bradley (March 11, 2003). ... Back (March 21, 2003); missed five games. ... Groin (October 18, 2003); missed three games. ... Hip flexor (November 13, 2003); missed two games. ... Reinjured hip flexor (November 21, 2003); missed two games. ... Back spasms (November 2, 2005); missed two games. ... Traded by Sharks with D Brad Stuart and LW Marco Sturm to Boston Bruins for C Joe Thornton (November 30, 2005). ... Hip (April 6, 2006); missed final six games of regular season.

		REGULAR SEASON								PLAYOFFS				
Season Team	**League**	**GP**	**G**	**A**	**Pts.**	**PIM**	**+/-**	**PP**	**SH**	**GP**	**G**	**A**	**Pts.**	**PIM**
92-93—Owen Sound	OHL	66	10	27	37	110	...	...	...	8	1	4	5	0
93-94—Owen Sound	OHL	65	25	50	75	75	...	7	...	9	1	6	7	8
94-95—Owen Sound	OHL	66	34	62	96	84	...	10	1	10	4	9	13	15
—Buffalo	NHL	1	1	0	1	0	-2	0	0	—	—	—	—	—
95-96—Buffalo	NHL	2	0	0	0	0	0	0	0	—	—	—	—	—
—Owen Sound	OHL	28	15	29	44	52	...	...	...	—	—	—	—	—
—Oshawa	OHL	24	12	13	25	33	...	...	...	3	2	3	5	2
—Rochester	AHL	8	2	3	5	6	...	...	...	17	3	1	4	11
96-97—Rochester	AHL	24	9	5	14	27	-3	1	0	1	0	0	0	0
—Buffalo	NHL	45	2	4	6	64	-2	1	0	9	0	0	0	6
97-98—Buffalo	NHL	69	6	6	12	87	9	2	0	14	1	3	4	6
98-99—Buffalo	NHL	67	5	8	13	38	-6	0	0	19	3	4	7	6
99-00—Buffalo	NHL	41	5	7	12	38	-8	2	0	—	—	—	—	—
—Tampa Bay	NHL	17	2	3	5	25	-4	0	0	—	—	—	—	—
00-01—Tampa Bay	NHL	47	2	13	15	77	-17	0	0	—	—	—	—	—
—Pittsburgh	NHL	28	1	6	7	54	0	0	0	18	1	3	4	2
01-02—Pittsburgh	NHL	33	3	7	10	18	-1	0	1	—	—	—	—	—
02-03—Pittsburgh	NHL	70	5	11	16	55	-30	1	0	—	—	—	—	—
—San Jose	NHL	7	1	1	2	0	2	0	0	—	—	—	—	—
03-04—San Jose	NHL	72	9	20	29	90	4	0	1	17	1	2	3	4
05-06—San Jose	NHL	21	5	3	8	17	-6	1	1	—	—	—	—	—
—Boston	NHL	50	6	8	14	40	-10	0	0	—	—	—	—	—
NHL Totals (11 years)		570	53	97	150	603	-71	7	3	77	6	12	18	24

PRINTZ, DAVID D

PERSONAL: Born July 24, 1980, in Stockholm, Sweden. ... 6-5/220. ... Shoots left.
TRANSACTIONS/CAREER NOTES: Selected by Philadelphia Flyers in seventh round (ninth Flyers pick, 225th overall) of entry draft (June 24, 2001).

		REGULAR SEASON								PLAYOFFS				
Season Team	**League**	**GP**	**G**	**A**	**Pts.**	**PIM**	**+/-**	**PP**	**SH**	**GP**	**G**	**A**	**Pts.**	**PIM**
01-02—AIK Solna	Sweden	37	3	2	5	59	...	...	...	10	0	0	0	12
—AIK Solna	Sweden Jr.	8	2	3	5	20	...	...	...	—	—	—	—	—
02-03—Hameenlinna	Finland	17	1	0	1	10	...	...	...	—	—	—	—	—
—Ilves Tampere	Finland	23	1	2	3	10	...	...	...	—	—	—	—	—
03-04—AIK Solna	Sweden All.	27	0	4	4	38	...	...	...	—	—	—	—	—
—AIK Solna	Sweden Jr.	5	0	2	2	29	...	...	...	—	—	—	—	—
—AIK Solna	Sweden Sup.	14	0	3	3	4	...	...	...	15	4	2	6	22
04-05—Philadelphia	AHL	50	1	5	6	66	7	0	0	1	0	0	0	0
05-06—Philadelphia	AHL	80	6	14	20	135	-5	1	1	—	—	—	—	—
—Philadelphia	NHL	1	0	0	0	0	0	0	0	—	—	—	—	—
NHL Totals (1 year)		1	0	0	0	0	0	0	0					

PRONGER, CHRIS D

PERSONAL: Born October 10, 1974, in Dryden, Ont. ... 6-6/218. ... Shoots left. ... Brother of Sean Pronger, C with seven teams (1995-96 through 2003-04).
TRANSACTIONS/CAREER NOTES: Selected by Hartford Whalers in first round (first Whalers pick, second overall) of NHL draft (June 26, 1993). ... Left wrist (March 29, 1994); missed three games. ... Left shoulder (January 21, 1995); missed five games. ... Traded by Whalers to St. Louis Blues for LW Brendan Shanahan (July 27, 1995). ... Suspended four games in slashing incident (November 1, 1995). ... Hand (February 15, 1997); missed one game. ... Suspended four games in slashing incident (December 19, 1998). ... Ankle (February 11, 1999); missed 11 games. ... Back spasms (March 12, 2000); missed one game. ... Suspended one game in fighting incident (October 13, 2000). ... Knee surgery (January 21, 2001); missed 15 games. ... Fractured forearm (February 26, 2001); missed 15 games. ... Wrist (November 13, 2001); missed one game. ... Suspended two games for cross-checking incident (April 4, 2002). ... Offseason knee and wrist surgery; missed first 77 games of 2002-03 season. ... Suspended one game in kicking incident (March 16, 2004). ... Traded by Blues to the Edmonton Oilers for D Eric Brewer, D Jeff Woywitka and D Doug Lynch (August 3, 2005). ... Bruised left knee (November 25, 2005); missed one game. ... Traded by Oilers to Anaheim Ducks for RW Joffrey Lupul, D Ladislav Smid and three future draft picks (July 3, 2006).

		REGULAR SEASON								PLAYOFFS				
Season Team	**League**	**GP**	**G**	**A**	**Pts.**	**PIM**	**+/-**	**PP**	**SH**	**GP**	**G**	**A**	**Pts.**	**PIM**
90-91—Stratford	OPJHL	48	15	37	52	132	...	...	...	—	—	—	—	—
91-92—Peterborough	OHL	63	17	45	62	90	...	...	...	10	1	8	9	28
92-93—Peterborough	OHL	61	15	62	77	108	...	...	...	21	15	25	40	51
93-94—Hartford	NHL	81	5	25	30	113	-3	2	0	—	—	—	—	—
94-95—Hartford	NHL	43	5	9	14	54	-12	3	0	—	—	—	—	—
95-96—St. Louis	NHL	78	7	18	25	110	-18	3	1	13	1	5	6	16
96-97—St. Louis	NHL	79	11	24	35	143	15	4	0	6	1	1	2	22
97-98—St. Louis	NHL	81	9	27	36	180	*47	1	0	10	1	9	10	26
—Can. Olympic team	Int'l	6	0	0	0	4	0	0	0	—	—	—	—	—
98-99—St. Louis	NHL	67	13	33	46	113	3	8	0	13	1	4	5	28
99-00—St. Louis	NHL	79	14	48	62	92	*52	8	0	7	3	4	7	32
00-01—St. Louis	NHL	51	8	39	47	75	21	4	0	15	1	7	8	32
01-02—St. Louis	NHL	78	7	40	47	120	23	4	1	9	1	7	8	24
—Can. Olympic team	Int'l	6	0	1	1	2	...	...	...	—	—	—	—	—

Season Team	League	REGULAR SEASON GP	G	A	Pts.	PIM	+/-	PP	SH	PLAYOFFS GP	G	A	Pts.	PIM
02-03—St. Louis	NHL	5	1	3	4	10	-2	0	0	7	1	3	4	14
03-04—St. Louis	NHL	80	14	40	54	88	-1	7	0	5	0	1	1	16
05-06—Edmonton	NHL	80	12	44	56	74	2	10	0	24	5	16	21	26
—Can. Olympic team	Int'l	6	1	2	3	16	2	0	0	—	—	—	—	—
NHL Totals (12 years)		802	106	350	456	1172	127	54	2	109	15	57	72	236

PROSPAL, VACLAV LW

PERSONAL: Born February 17, 1975, in Ceske-Budejovice, Czech. ... 6-2/195. ... Shoots left. ... Name pronounced PRAHS-puhl. ... Nickname: Vinny.

TRANSACTIONS/CAREER NOTES: Selected by Philadelphia Flyers in third round (second Flyers pick, 71st overall) of NHL draft (June 26, 1993). ... Fractured left leg (January 3, 1998); missed 18 games. ... Traded by Flyers with RW Pat Falloon and second-round pick (LW Chris Bala) in 1998 draft to Ottawa Senators for RW Alexandre Daigle (January 17, 1998). ... Bruised thumb (April 2, 1998); missed two games. ... Bruised mouth (April 7, 1998); missed four games. ... Flu (November 29, 1998); missed one game. ... Traded by Senators to Florida Panthers for fourth-round pick (G Ray Emery) in 2001 draft and third-round pick (traded back to Ottawa) in 2002 draft (January 21, 2001). ... Traded by Panthers to Tampa Bay Lightning for C Ryan Johnson and sixth-round pick (traded back to Tampa Bay; Lightning selected D Doug O'Brien) in 2003 draft (July 10, 2001). ... Flu (December 26, 2001); missed one game. ... Suspended two games by NHL for cross-checking incident (January 21, 2003). ... Signed as free agent by Anaheim Mighty Ducks (July 17, 2003). ... Traded by Mighty Ducks to Lightning for second-round pick in 2005 draft (August 16, 2004). ... Upper-body injury (April 15, 2006); missed final game of regular season.

STATISTICAL PLATEAUS: Three-goal games: 2003-04 (1).

Season Team	League	REGULAR SEASON GP	G	A	Pts.	PIM	+/-	PP	SH	PLAYOFFS GP	G	A	Pts.	PIM
91-92—Motor-Ceske Bude.	Czech. Jrs.	36	16	16	32	12	...	...	...	—	—	—	—	—
92-93—Motor-Ceske Bude.	Czech. Jrs.	36	26	31	57	24	...	...	...	—	—	—	—	—
93-94—Hershey	AHL	55	14	21	35	38	-2	4	0	2	0	0	0	2
94-95—Hershey	AHL	69	13	32	45	36	-16	3	0	2	1	0	1	4
95-96—Hershey	AHL	68	15	36	51	59	...	...	...	5	2	4	6	2
96-97—Philadelphia	AHL	63	32	63	95	70	32	6	4	—	—	—	—	—
—Philadelphia	NHL	18	5	10	15	4	3	0	0	5	1	3	4	4
97-98—Philadelphia	NHL	41	5	13	18	17	-10	4	0	—	—	—	—	—
—Ottawa	NHL	15	1	6	7	4	-1	0	0	6	0	0	0	0
98-99—Ottawa	NHL	79	10	26	36	58	8	2	0	4	0	0	0	0
99-00—Ottawa	NHL	79	22	33	55	40	-2	5	0	6	0	4	4	4
00-01—Ottawa	NHL	40	1	12	13	12	1	0	0	—	—	—	—	—
—Florida	NHL	34	4	12	16	10	-2	1	0	—	—	—	—	—
01-02—Tampa Bay	NHL	81	18	37	55	38	-11	7	0	—	—	—	—	—
02-03—Tampa Bay	NHL	80	22	57	79	53	9	9	0	11	4	2	6	8
03-04—Anaheim	NHL	82	19	35	54	54	-9	7	0	—	—	—	—	—
04-05—Budejovice	Czech Dv.I	39	28	60	88	82	57	...	...	16	15	15	30	32
05-06—Tampa Bay	NHL	81	25	55	80	50	-3	10	0	5	0	2	2	0
—Czech Rep. Oly. team	Int'l	8	4	2	6	2	-1	0	1	—	—	—	—	—
NHL Totals (9 years)		630	132	296	428	340	-17	45	0	37	5	11	16	16

PRUCHA, PETR LW/RW

PERSONAL: Born September 14, 1982, in Chrudim, Czechoslovakia. ... 5-10/161. ... Shoots right.

TRANSACTIONS/CAREER NOTES: Selected by New York Rangers in eighth round (eighth Rangers pick, 240th overall) of NHL entry draft (June 23, 2002). ... Re-signed by Rangers (August 17, 2005). ... Right knee sprain (February 4, 2006); missed eight games.

Season Team	League	REGULAR SEASON GP	G	A	Pts.	PIM	+/-	PP	SH	PLAYOFFS GP	G	A	Pts.	PIM
01-02—HC Pardubice	Czech Rep.	20	1	1	2	2	...	...	...	5	0	0	0	0
02-03—HC Pardubice	Czech Rep.	49	7	9	16	12	...	...	...	17	2	6	8	8
03-04—HC Pardubice	Czech Rep.	48	11	13	24	24	...	...	...	7	4	3	7	2
04-05—HC Pardubice	Czech Rep.	47	7	10	17	24	...	...	...	16	6	7	13	2
05-06—Hartford	AHL	2	2	1	3	0	0	1	0	—	—	—	—	—
—New York Rangers	NHL	68	30	17	47	32	3	16	0	4	1	0	1	0
NHL Totals (1 year)		68	30	17	47	32	3	16	0	4	1	0	1	0

PRUSEK, MARTIN G

PERSONAL: Born December 11, 1975, in Ostrava, Czechoslovakia. ... 6-1/188. ... Catches left. ... Name pronounced PREW-sehk.

TRANSACTIONS/CAREER NOTES: Selected by Ottawa Senators in sixth round (sixth Senators pick, 164th overall) of NHL draft (June 26, 1999). ... Injured groin (January 2, 2003); missed five games. ... Concussion (March 15, 2003); missed four games. ... Back spasms (December 9, 2003); missed four games. ... Strained left knee (February 24, 2004); missed one game. ... Back spasms (March 17, 2004); missed three games. ... Signed as free agent by Columbus Blue Jackets (August 4, 2005).

Season Team	League	REGULAR SEASON GP	Min.	W	L	OTL	T	GA	SO	GAA	SV%	PLAYOFFS GP	Min.	W	L	GA	SO	GAA	SV%
94-95 —HC Vitkovice	Czech Rep.	4	232	...	...	...	...	18	...	4.66	...	—	—	—	—	—	—	—	—
95-96 —HC Vitkovice	Czech Rep.	40	...	...	...	...	...	114	1	...	...	4	...	...	...	10	...	...	...
96-97 —HC Vitkovice	Czech Rep.	49	...	...	...	...	...	109	8	...	...	9	...	...	...	19	1	...	...
97-98 —HC Vitkovice	Czech Rep.	50	...	...	...	...	...	129	...	...	...	9	...	...	...	26	...	...	...
98-99 —HC Vitkovice	Czech Rep.	37	1905	...	...	...	...	85	...	2.68	...	4	250	...	...	12	...	2.88	...
99-00 —HC Vitkovice	Czech Rep.	50	2647	...	...	...	...	132	...	2.99	...	—	—	—	—	—	—	—	—
00-01 —HC Vitkovice	Czech Rep.	30	1679	...	...	...	...	64	...	2.29	...	9	460	...	...	25	...	3.26	...
01-02 —Grand Rapids	AHL	33	1903	18	8	...	5	58	4	1.83	.925	5	277	2	3	10	0	2.17	.896
—Ottawa	NHL	1	62	0	1	...	0	3	0	2.90	.800	—	—	—	—	—	—	—	—

P

Season Team	League	REGULAR SEASON GP	Min.	W	L	OTL	T	GA	SO	GAA	SV%	PLAYOFFS GP	Min.	W	L	GA	SO	GAA	SV%
02-03 —Binghamton	AHL	4	242	1	2	...	1	7	1	1.74	.925	—	—	—	—	—	—	—	—
—Ottawa	NHL	18	935	12	2	...	1	37	0	2.37	.911	—	—	—	—	—	—	—	—
03-04 —Ottawa	NHL	29	1528	16	6	...	3	54	3	2.12	.917	1	40	0	0	1	0	1.50	.933
04-05 —Vitkovice	Czech Rep.	14	672	...	...	...	...	28	0	2.50	.931	—	—	—	—	—	—	—	—
—HC Znojemsti Orli	Czech Rep.	8	453	...	...	...	...	18	0	2.38	.933	—	—	—	—	—	—	—	—
05-06 —Syracuse	AHL	23	1203	12	7	1	...	60	2	2.99	.911	—	—	—	—	—	—	—	—
—Columbus	NHL	9	373	3	3	0	...	20	0	3.22	.879	—	—	—	—	—	—	—	—
NHL Totals (4 years)		57	2898	31	12	0	4	114	3	2.36	.909	1	40	0	0	1	0	1.50	.933

PUSHKAREV, KONSTANTIN C/RW

PERSONAL: Born February 12, 1985, in Ust-Kamenogorsk, U.S.S.R. ... 6-0/169. ... Shoots left.

TRANSACTIONS/CAREER NOTES: Selected by Los Angeles Kings in second round (fourth Kings pick, 44th overall) of entry draft (June 22, 2003).

Season Team	League	REGULAR SEASON GP	G	A	Pts.	PIM	+/-	PP	SH	PLAYOFFS GP	G	A	Pts.	PIM
02-03—Ust-Kamenogorsk	Russian	4	0	0	0	4	...	...	...	—	—	—	—	—
03-04—Omsk	Russian	5	1	0	1	0	...	...	...	—	—	—	—	—
04-05—Omsk	Russian	1	0	0	0	0	...	...	...	—	—	—	—	—
05-06—Manchester	AHL	77	19	19	38	95	-1	6	0	7	1	1	2	4
—Los Angeles	NHL	1	0	1	1	0	0	0	0	—	—	—	—	—
NHL Totals (1 year)		1	0	1	1	0	0	0	0					

PUSHOR, JAMIE D

PERSONAL: Born February 11, 1973, in Lethbridge, Alta. ... 6-3/218. ... Shoots right.

TRANSACTIONS/CAREER NOTES: Selected by Detroit Red Wings in second round (second Wings pick, 32nd overall) of entry draft (June 22, 1991). ... Strained groin (November 21, 1997); missed three games. ... Traded by Red Wings with fourth-round pick (C Viktor Wallin) in 1998 draft to Mighty Ducks of Anaheim for D Dmitri Mironov (March 24, 1998). ... Fractured right finger (April 15, 1998); missed remainder of season. ... Eye (January 6, 1999); missed two games. ... Bruised left shoulder and chest (February 14, 1999); missed four games. ... Selected by Atlanta Thrashers in expansion draft (June 25, 1999). ... Traded by Thrashers to Dallas Stars for LW Jason Botterill (July 15, 1999). ... Selected by Columbus Blue Jackets in expansion draft (June 23, 2000). ... Sprained knee (March 26, 2001); missed seven games. ... Traded by Blue Jackets to Pittsburgh Penguins for fourth-round pick (LW Kevin Jarman) in 2003 (March 15, 2002). ... Signed as free agent by the Columbus Blue Jackets (December 10, 2003). ... Traded by Blue Jackets to New York Rangers for eighth-round pick (W Matt Greer) in 2004 draft (January 23, 2004) . ... Signed as free agent by Columbus Blue Jackets (July 21, 2006).

Season Team	League	REGULAR SEASON GP	G	A	Pts.	PIM	+/-	PP	SH	PLAYOFFS GP	G	A	Pts.	PIM
88-89—Lethbridge	WHL	2	0	0	0	0	...	0	0	—	—	—	—	—
89-90—Lethbridge	WHL	10	0	2	2	2	...	...	...	—	—	—	—	—
90-91—Lethbridge	WHL	71	1	13	14	193	...	...	...	—	—	—	—	—
91-92—Lethbridge	WHL	49	2	15	17	232	...	...	...	5	0	0	0	33
92-93—Lethbridge	WHL	72	6	22	28	200	...	...	...	4	0	1	1	9
93-94—Adirondack	AHL	73	1	17	18	124	32	0	0	12	0	0	0	22
94-95—Adirondack	AHL	58	2	11	13	129	-12	0	0	4	0	1	1	0
95-96—Detroit	NHL	5	0	1	1	17	2	0	0	—	—	—	—	—
—Adirondack	AHL	65	2	16	18	126	...	...	...	3	0	0	0	5
96-97—Detroit	NHL	75	4	7	11	129	1	0	0	5	0	1	1	5
97-98—Detroit	NHL	54	2	5	7	71	2	0	0	—	—	—	—	—
—Anaheim	NHL	10	0	2	2	10	1	0	0	—	—	—	—	—
98-99—Anaheim	NHL	70	1	2	3	112	-20	0	0	4	0	0	0	6
99-00—Dallas	NHL	62	0	8	8	53	0	0	0	5	0	0	0	5
00-01—Columbus	NHL	75	3	10	13	94	7	0	1	—	—	—	—	—
01-02—Columbus	NHL	61	0	6	6	54	-10	0	0	—	—	—	—	—
—Pittsburgh	NHL	15	0	2	2	30	-3	0	0	—	—	—	—	—
02-03—Pittsburgh	NHL	76	3	1	4	76	-28	0	0	—	—	—	—	—
03-04—Columbus	NHL	7	0	0	0	2	-2	0	0	—	—	—	—	—
—Syracuse	AHL	17	1	4	5	24	1	0	0	...	...	...	...	...
—New York Rangers	NHL	7	0	0	0	0	-3	0	0	—	—	—	—	—
—Hartford	AHL	14	0	2	2	21	10	0	0	16	1	1	2	18
04-05—Syracuse	AHL	68	1	9	10	85	12	0	0	—	—	—	—	—
05-06—Syracuse	AHL	72	5	17	22	132	0	4	0	6	0	1	1	9
—Columbus	NHL	4	1	2	3	0	1	0	0	—	—	—	—	—
NHL Totals (10 years)		521	14	46	60	648	-52	0	1	14	0	1	1	16

PYATT, TAYLOR LW

PERSONAL: Born August 19, 1981, in Thunder Bay, Ont. ... 6-4/227. ... Shoots left. ... Son of Nelson Pyatt, C/LW with three NHL teams (1973-74 through 1979-80).

TRANSACTIONS/CAREER NOTES: Selected by New York Islanders in first round (second Islanders pick, eighth overall) of entry draft (June 26, 1999). ... Traded by Islanders with C Tim Connolly to Buffalo Sabres for C Michael Peca (June 24, 2001). ... Concussion (March 18, 2003); missed four games. ... Injured knee (January 7, 2004); missed 11 games. ... Separated collarbone (March 17, 2004); missed eight games. ... Re-signed to one-year contract by Buffalo as restricted free agent (August 4, 2005). ... Concussion (October 28, 2005); missed five games. ... Fractured right wrist (November 25, 2005); missed 36 games. ... Traded by Sabres to Canucks for fourth-round pick in 2007 draft (July 14, 2006).

STATISTICAL PLATEAUS: Three-goal games: 2002-03 (1).

Season Team	League	GP	G	A	Pts.	PIM	+/-	PP	SH	GP	G	A	Pts.	PIM
		REGULAR SEASON								PLAYOFFS				
97-98—Sudbury	OHL	58	14	17	31	104	...	...	...	10	3	1	4	6
98-99—Sudbury	OHL	68	37	38	75	95	-9	...	...	4	0	4	4	6
99-00—Sudbury	OHL	68	40	49	89	98	47	9	5	12	8	7	15	25
00-01—New York Islanders	NHL	78	4	14	18	39	-17	1	0	—	—	—	—	—
01-02—Rochester	AHL	27	6	4	10	36	-2	0	0	—	—	—	—	—
—Buffalo	NHL	48	10	10	20	35	4	0	0	—	—	—	—	—
02-03—Buffalo	NHL	78	14	14	28	38	-8	2	0	—	—	—	—	—
03-04—Buffalo	NHL	63	8	12	20	25	-7	1	2	—	—	—	—	—
04-05—Hammarby	Sweden Dv. 2	10	7	4	11	...	12	1	1	14	4	5	9	12
05-06—Buffalo	NHL	41	6	6	12	33	-1	0	0	14	0	5	5	10
NHL Totals (5 years)		308	42	56	98	170	-29	4	2	14	0	5	5	10

QUINCEY, KYLE D

PERSONAL: Born August 12, 1985, in Kitchener, Ont. ... 6-1/194. ... Shoots left.
TRANSACTIONS/CAREER NOTES: Selected by Detroit Red Wings in fourth round (second Red Wings pick, 132nd overall) of NHL entry draft (June 23, 2003).

Season Team	League	GP	G	A	Pts.	PIM	+/-	PP	SH	GP	G	A	Pts.	PIM
		REGULAR SEASON								PLAYOFFS				
02-03—London	OHL	66	6	12	18	77	6	3	0	14	3	4	7	11
03-04—London	OHL	3	0	2	2	4	3	0	0	—	—	—	—	—
—Mississauga	OHL	61	14	23	37	135	7	4	0	24	3	13	16	32
04-05—Mississauga	OHL	59	15	31	46	111	5	8	0	5	0	3	3	4
05-06—Grand Rapids	AHL	70	7	26	33	107	15	2	0	16	0	1	1	27
—Detroit	NHL	1	0	0	0	0	0	0	0	—	—	—	—	—
NHL Totals (1 year)		1	0	0	0	0	0	0	0					

RADIVOJEVIC, BRANKO RW

PERSONAL: Born November 24, 1980, in Piestany, Czech. ... 6-1/210. ... Shoots right. ... Name pronounced rah-dih-VOI-uh-vich.
TRANSACTIONS/CAREER NOTES: Selected by Colorado Avalanche in third round (third Avalanche pick, 93rd overall) of NHL draft (June 26, 1999). ... Signed as free agent by Phoenix Coyotes (June 19, 2001). ... Traded by Coyotes with G Sean Burke and rights to LW Ben Eager to Philadelphia Flyers for C Mike Comrie (February 9, 2004). ... Sprained ankle (January 25, 2006); missed eight games. ... Signed as free agent by Minnesota Wild (July 6, 2006).

Season Team	League	GP	G	A	Pts.	PIM	+/-	PP	SH	GP	G	A	Pts.	PIM
		REGULAR SEASON								PLAYOFFS				
97-98—Dukla Trencin	Slovakia Jrs.	52	30	33	63	50	...	...	...	—	—	—	—	—
98-99—Belleville	OHL	68	20	38	58	61	...	...	...	21	7	17	24	18
99-00—Belleville	OHL	59	23	49	72	86	27	7	1	16	5	8	13	32
00-01—Belleville	OHL	61	34	70	104	77	45	6	1	10	6	10	16	18
01-02—Springfield	AHL	62	18	21	39	64	-2	3	1	—	—	—	—	—
—Phoenix	NHL	18	4	2	6	4	1	0	0	1	0	0	0	2
02-03—Phoenix	NHL	79	12	15	27	63	-2	1	0	—	—	—	—	—
03-04—Phoenix	NHL	53	9	14	23	36	-5	2	1	—	—	—	—	—
—Philadelphia	NHL	24	1	8	9	36	0	0	0	18	1	1	2	32
04-05—HC Vsetin	Czech Rep.	31	7	11	18	114	4	...	...	—	—	—	—	—
—Lulea	Sweden	10	6	5	11	8	3	0	0	4	0	0	0	44
05-06—Philadelphia	NHL	64	8	6	14	44	-6	1	0	5	1	0	1	0
NHL Totals (4 years)		238	34	45	79	183	-12	4	1	24	2	1	3	34

RAFALSKI, BRIAN D

PERSONAL: Born September 28, 1973, in Dearborn, Mich. ... 5-10/190. ... Shoots right.
TRANSACTIONS/CAREER NOTES: Signed as free agent by New Jersey Devils (June 18, 1999). ... Suffered illness (January 3, 2000); missed one game. ... Bruised ribs (March 17, 2000); missed five games. ... Bruised left shoulder (February 8, 2001); missed three games. ... Sprained knee (January 24, 2002); missed four games. ... Bruised ribs (December 10, 2002); missed three games. ... Flu (April 24, 2003); missed one playoff game. ... Bruised knee (February 28, 2004); missed one game. ... Fractured right leg (March 9, 2004); missed 12 games. ... Signed as free agent by Devils (August 4, 2005).

Season Team	League	GP	G	A	Pts.	PIM	+/-	PP	SH	GP	G	A	Pts.	PIM
		REGULAR SEASON								PLAYOFFS				
91-92—Wisconsin	WCHA	34	3	14	17	34	...	...	...	—	—	—	—	—
92-93—Wisconsin	WCHA	32	0	13	13	10	...	...	...	—	—	—	—	—
93-94—Wisconsin	WCHA	37	6	17	23	26	...	...	...	—	—	—	—	—
94-95—Wisconsin	WCHA	43	11	34	45	48	...	...	...	—	—	—	—	—
95-96—Brynas Gavle	Sweden Dv. 2	18	3	6	9	12	...	...	...	9	0	1	1	2
—Brynas Gavle	Sweden	22	1	8	9	14	...	...	...	—	—	—	—	—
96-97—HPK Hameenlinna	Finland	49	11	24	35	26	...	...	...	10	6	5	11	4
97-98—HIFK Helsinki	Finland	40	13	10	23	24	...	...	...	9	5	6	11	0
98-99—HIFK Helsinki	Finland	53	19	34	53	18	...	...	...	11	5	9	14	4
99-00—New Jersey	NHL	75	5	27	32	28	21	1	0	23	2	6	8	8
00-01—New Jersey	NHL	78	9	43	52	26	36	6	0	25	7	11	18	7
01-02—New Jersey	NHL	76	7	40	47	18	15	2	0	6	3	2	5	4
—U.S. Olympic team	Int'l	6	1	2	3	2	...	...	...	—	—	—	—	—
02-03—New Jersey	NHL	79	3	37	40	14	18	2	0	23	2	9	11	8
03-04—New Jersey	NHL	69	6	30	36	24	6	2	0	5	0	1	1	0
05-06—New Jersey	NHL	82	6	43	49	36	0	3	0	9	1	8	9	2
—U.S. Olympic team	Int'l	5	0	2	2	0	-3	0	0	—	—	—	—	—
NHL Totals (6 years)		459	36	220	256	146	96	16	0	91	15	37	52	29

RANGER, PAUL D

PERSONAL: Born September 12, 1984, in North York, Ont. ... 6-3/198. ... Shoots left.
TRANSACTIONS/CAREER NOTES: Selected by Tampa Bay Lightning in sixth round (seventh Lightning pick, 183th overall) of entry draft (June 23, 2002). ... Concussion, hairline fracture of jaw (October 20, 2005); missed one game.

		REGULAR SEASON								PLAYOFFS				
Season Team	League	GP	G	A	Pts.	PIM	+/-	PP	SH	GP	G	A	Pts.	PIM
00-01—Oshawa	OHL	32	0	1	1	2	...	...	...	—	—	—	—	—
01-02—Oshawa	OHL	62	0	9	9	49	...	...	...	5	0	0	0	4
02-03—Oshawa	OHL	68	10	28	38	70	...	...	...	13	0	3	3	10
03-04—Oshawa	OHL	62	12	31	43	72	...	...	...	7	0	1	1	10
04-05—Springfield	AHL	69	3	8	11	46	-7	1	0	—	—	—	—	—
05-06—Springfield	AHL	1	1	2	3	0	2	0	0	—	—	—	—	—
—Tampa Bay	NHL	76	1	17	18	58	5	0	0	5	2	4	6	0
NHL Totals (1 year)		76	1	17	18	58	5	0	0	5	2	4	6	0

R

RASMUSSEN, ERIK C/LW

PERSONAL: Born March 28, 1977, in Minneapolis, Minn. ... 6-1/210. ... Shoots left. ... Name pronounced RAS-muh-suhn.
TRANSACTIONS/CAREER NOTES: Selected by Buffalo Sabres in first round (first Sabres pick, seventh overall) of NHL draft (June 22, 1996). ... Injured shoulder (October 26, 1997); missed one game. ... Injured foot (April 13, 1999); missed one game. ... Bruised hand (December 4, 1999); missed five games. ... Back spasms (March 23, 2000); missed one game. ... Injured knee (October 6, 2001); missed one game. ... Bruised knee (December 12, 2001); missed seven games. ... Injured shoulder (January 23, 2002); missed three games. ... Traded by Sabres to Los Angeles Kings for C Adam Mair and fifth-round (D Thomas Morrow) pick in 2003 draft (July 24, 2002). ... Signed as free agent by New Jersey Devils (July 27, 2003). ... Flu (December 13, 2003); missed one game. ... Injured shoulder (January 1, 2004); missed three games. ... Injured ankle (November 29, 2005); missed two games. ... Re-injured ankle (December 11, 2005); missed four games. ... Separated shoulder (February 7, 2006); missed two games. ... Injured shoulder (March 7, 2006); missed one game.

		REGULAR SEASON								PLAYOFFS				
Season Team	League	GP	G	A	Pts.	PIM	+/-	PP	SH	GP	G	A	Pts.	PIM
92-93—Saint Louis Park	Minn. H.S.	23	16	24	40	50	...	...	...	—	—	—	—	—
93-94—Saint Louis Park	Minn. H.S.	18	25	18	43	60	...	...	...	—	—	—	—	—
94-95—Saint Louis Park	Minn. H.S.	23	19	33	52	80	...	...	...	—	—	—	—	—
95-96—Minnesota	WCHA	40	16	32	48	55	...	...	...	—	—	—	—	—
96-97—Minnesota	WCHA	34	15	12	27	123	1	6	1	—	—	—	—	—
97-98—Buffalo	NHL	21	2	3	5	14	2	0	0	—	—	—	—	—
—Rochester	AHL	53	9	14	23	83	-11	5	0	1	0	0	0	5
98-99—Rochester	AHL	37	12	14	26	47	13	4	0	—	—	—	—	—
—Buffalo	NHL	42	3	7	10	37	6	0	0	21	2	4	6	18
99-00—Buffalo	NHL	67	8	6	14	43	1	0	0	3	0	0	0	4
00-01—Buffalo	NHL	82	12	19	31	51	0	1	0	3	0	1	1	0
01-02—Buffalo	NHL	69	8	11	19	34	-1	0	0	—	—	—	—	—
02-03—Los Angeles	NHL	57	4	12	16	28	-1	0	0	—	—	—	—	—
03-04—New Jersey	NHL	69	7	6	13	41	5	0	0	5	0	2	2	2
05-06—New Jersey	NHL	67	5	5	10	32	-4	1	0	9	0	0	0	8
NHL Totals (8 years)		474	49	69	118	280	8	2	0	41	2	7	9	32

RATCHUK, MICHAEL D

PERSONAL: Born February 20, 1988, in Buffalo, N.Y. ... 5-10/175. ... Shoots left.
TRANSACTIONS/CAREER NOTES: Selected by Philadelphia Flyers in second round (third Flyers pick; 42nd overall) of NHL draft (June 24, 2006).

		REGULAR SEASON								PLAYOFFS				
Season Team	League	GP	G	A	Pts.	PIM	+/-	PP	SH	GP	G	A	Pts.	PIM
04-05—U.S. National	USHL	31	3	4	7	12	...	...	...	—	—	—	—	—
05-06—U.S. National	USHL	47	11	15	26	50	...	...	...	—	—	—	—	—

RATHJE, MIKE D

PERSONAL: Born May 11, 1974, in Mannville, Alta. ... 6-5/237. ... Shoots left. ... Name pronounced RATH-jee. ... Nickname: Rat.
TRANSACTIONS/CAREER NOTES: Selected by San Jose Sharks in first round (first Sharks pick, third overall) of entry draft (June 20, 1992). ... Strained abdominal muscle (February 19, 1994); missed three games. ... Sprained knee (February 26, 1994); missed four games. ... Sprained knee (February 2, 1995); missed three games. ... Foot (February 15, 1995); missed one game. ... Hip flexor (April 25, 1995); missed two games. ... Strained abdominal muscle (October 6, 1995); missed first two games of season. ... Shoulder (November 14, 1995); missed 12 games. ... Groin (November 8, 1996); missed 50 games. ... Groin (November 12, 1999); missed 16 games. ... Missed first 28 games of 2001-02 season in contract dispute. ... Knee (January 23, 2002); missed two games. ... Wrist (November 13, 2003); missed one game. ... Eye (November 30, 2003); missed one game. ... Signed as free agent by Philadelphia Flyers (August 2, 2005). ... Groin (February 8, 2006); missed three games.

		REGULAR SEASON								PLAYOFFS				
Season Team	League	GP	G	A	Pts.	PIM	+/-	PP	SH	GP	G	A	Pts.	PIM
90-91—Medicine Hat	WHL	64	1	16	17	28	...	...	...	12	0	4	4	2
91-92—Medicine Hat	WHL	67	11	23	34	109	...	...	...	4	0	1	1	2
92-93—Medicine Hat	WHL	57	12	37	49	103	-1	7	0	10	3	3	6	12
—Kansas City	IHL	...	...	...	...	...	...	...	...	5	0	0	0	12
93-94—San Jose	NHL	47	1	9	10	59	-9	1	0	1	0	0	0	0
—Kansas City	IHL	6	0	2	2	0	-4	0	0	—	—	—	—	—
94-95—Kansas City	IHL	6	0	1	1	7	-3	0	0	—	—	—	—	—
—San Jose	NHL	42	2	7	9	29	-1	0	0	11	5	2	7	4

Season Team	League	GP	G	A	Pts.	PIM	+/-	PP	SH	GP	G	A	Pts.	PIM
		REGULAR SEASON								PLAYOFFS				
95-96—Kansas City	IHL	36	6	11	17	34	...	...	...	—	—	—	—	—
—San Jose	NHL	27	0	7	7	14	-16	0	0	—	—	—	—	—
96-97—San Jose	NHL	31	0	8	8	21	-1	0	0	—	—	—	—	—
97-98—San Jose	NHL	81	3	12	15	59	-4	1	0	6	1	0	1	6
98-99—San Jose	NHL	82	5	9	14	36	15	2	0	6	0	0	0	4
99-00—San Jose	NHL	66	2	14	16	31	-2	0	0	12	1	3	4	8
00-01—San Jose	NHL	81	0	11	11	48	7	0	0	6	0	1	1	4
01-02—San Jose	NHL	52	5	12	17	48	23	4	0	12	1	3	4	6
02-03—San Jose	NHL	82	7	22	29	48	-19	3	0	—	—	—	—	—
03-04—San Jose	NHL	80	2	17	19	46	18	0	1	17	1	5	6	13
05-06—Philadelphia	NHL	79	3	21	24	46	22	1	1	6	0	0	0	6
NHL Totals (12 years)		750	30	149	179	485	33	12	2	77	9	14	23	51

RAYCROFT, ANDREW G

PERSONAL: Born May 4, 1980, in Belleville, Ont. ... 6-1/185. ... Catches left.

TRANSACTIONS/CAREER NOTES: Selected by Boston Bruins in fifth round (fourth Bruins pick, 135th overall) of entry draft (June 27, 1998). ... Injured groin (March 22, 2003); missed six games. ... Strained hamstring (October 26, 2005); missed six games. ... Injured knee (January 19, 2006); missed five games. ... Traded by Bruins to Toronto Maple Leafs for rights to G Tuukka Rask (June 25, 2006).

Season Team	League	GP	Min.	W	L	OTL	T	GA	SO	GAA	SV%	GP	Min.	W	L	GA	SO	GAA	SV%
		REGULAR SEASON										PLAYOFFS							
96-97—Wellington	Tier II Jr. A	27	1402	...	...	...	...	92	0	3.94	...	—	—	—	—	—	—	—	—
97-98—Sudbury	OHL	33	1802	8	16	...	5	125	0	4.16	.898	2	89	0	1	8	0	5.39	.830
98-99—Sudbury	OHL	45	2528	17	22	...	5	173	1	4.11	.897	3	96	0	2	13	0	8.13	.812
99-00—Kingston	OHL	61	3340	33	20	...	5	191	0	3.43	.918	5	300	1	4	21	0	4.20	.897
00-01—Boston	NHL	15	649	4	6	...	0	32	0	2.96	.890	—	—	—	—	—	—	—	—
—Providence	AHL	26	1459	8	14	...	4	82	1	3.37	.891	—	—	—	—	—	—	—	—
01-02—Providence	AHL	56	3317	25	24	...	6	142	4	2.57	.908	—	—	—	—	—	—	—	—
—Boston	NHL	1	65	0	0	...	1	3	0	2.77	.897	—	—	—	—	—	—	—	—
02-03—Boston	NHL	5	300	2	3	...	0	12	0	2.40	.918	—	—	—	—	—	—	—	—
—Providence	AHL	39	2255	23	10	...	3	94	1	2.50	.917	4	264	1	3	6	1	1.36	.955
03-04—Boston	NHL	57	3420	29	18	...	9	117	3	2.05	.926	7	447	3	4	16	1	2.15	.924
04-05—Tappara Tampere	Finland	11	658	4	5	...	2	32	1	2.92	.912	3	104	0	2	11	0	6.36	.847
05-06—Providence	AHL	1	64	1	0	0	...	3	0	2.81	.870	—	—	—	—	—	—	—	—
—Boston	NHL	30	1619	8	19	2	...	100	0	3.71	.879	—	—	—	—	—	—	—	—
NHL Totals (5 years)		108	6053	43	46	2	10	264	3	2.62	.908	7	447	3	4	16	1	2.15	.924

READY, RYAN LW

PERSONAL: Born November 7, 1978, in Peterborough, Ont. ... 6-0/195. ... Shoots left.

TRANSACTIONS/CAREER NOTES: Selected by Calgary Flames in fourth round (eighth Flames pick, 100th overall) of NHL entry draft (June 21, 1997). ... Signed as free agent by Vancouver Canucks (June 16, 1999). ... Traded by Canucks to St. Louis Blues for LW Sergei Varlamov (March 9, 2004). ... Signed as free agent by Philadelphia Flyers (August 23, 2004). ... Injured groin (October 4, 2005); missed 21 games. ... Strained abductor (November 30, 2005); missed 13 games.

Season Team	League	GP	G	A	Pts.	PIM	+/-	PP	SH	GP	G	A	Pts.	PIM
		REGULAR SEASON								PLAYOFFS				
95-96—Peterborough	Jr. B	48	20	33	53	56	...	...	...	—	—	—	—	—
—Belleville	OHL	63	5	13	18	54	...	...	...	10	0	2	2	2
96-97—Belleville	OHL	66	23	24	47	102	-8	8	0	6	1	3	4	4
97-98—Belleville	OHL	66	33	39	72	80	1	...	...	10	5	2	7	12
98-99—Belleville	OHL	63	33	59	92	73	40	...	...	21	10	28	38	22
99-00—Syracuse	AHL	70	4	12	16	59	...	...	...	2	0	0	0	0
00-01—Kansas City	IHL	67	10	15	25	75	...	...	...	—	—	—	—	—
01-02—Manitoba	AHL	72	23	32	55	73	0	9	0	7	5	1	6	4
02-03—Manitoba	AHL	68	24	26	50	52	1	11	1	14	2	5	7	2
03-04—Manitoba	AHL	64	7	18	25	55	-16	2	1	—	—	—	—	—
—Worcester	AHL	16	2	5	7	10	-1	0	0	10	1	2	3	10
04-05—Philadelphia	AHL	72	7	18	25	104	8	2	1	19	2	11	13	6
05-06—Philadelphia	AHL	40	7	10	17	67	-1	3	1	—	—	—	—	—
—Philadelphia	NHL	7	0	1	1	0	0	0	0	—	—	—	—	—
NHL Totals (1 year)		7	0	1	1	0	0	0	0					

REASONER, MARTY C

PERSONAL: Born February 26, 1977, in Rochester, N.Y. ... 6-1/200. ... Shoots left.

TRANSACTIONS/CAREER NOTES: Selected by St. Louis Blues in first round (first Blues pick, 14th overall) of NHL entry draft (June 22, 1996). ... Traded by Blues with C Jochen Hecht and D Jan Horacek to Edmonton Oilers for C Doug Weight and LW Michel Riesen (July 1, 2001). ... Sprained left knee (January 23, 2002); missed four games. ... Fractured left ankle (November 10, 2003); missed 27 games. ... Injured right knee (January 15, 2004) and had arthroscopic surgery (January 21, 2004); missed remainder of season. ... Bruised hand (November 4, 2005); missed three games. ... Traded by Oilers with LW Yan Stastny and second-round pick (LW Milan Lucic) in 2006 draft to Boston Bruins for LW Sergei Samsonov (March 9, 2006). ... Signed as free agent by Oilers (July 4, 2006).

Season Team	League	GP	G	A	Pts.	PIM	+/-	PP	SH	GP	G	A	Pts.	PIM
		REGULAR SEASON								PLAYOFFS				
93-94—Deerfield Academy	Mass. H.S.	22	27	24	51	...	...	...	...	—	—	—	—	—
94-95—Deerfield Academy	Mass. H.S.	26	25	32	57	14	...	...	...	—	—	—	—	—

Season Team	League	GP	G	A	Pts.	PIM	+/-	PP	SH	GP	G	A	Pts.	PIM
		REGULAR SEASON								PLAYOFFS				
95-96—Boston College	Hockey East	34	16	29	45	32	...	...	...	—	—	—	—	—
96-97—Boston College	Hockey East	35	20	24	44	31	...	5	0	—	—	—	—	—
97-98—Boston College	Hockey East	42	33	40	73	56	...	...	...	—	—	—	—	—
98-99—St. Louis	NHL	22	3	7	10	8	2	1	0	—	—	—	—	—
—Worcester	AHL	44	17	22	39	24	-4	9	0	4	2	1	3	6
99-00—Worcester	AHL	44	23	28	51	39	...	...	...	—	—	—	—	—
—St. Louis	NHL	32	10	14	24	20	9	3	0	7	2	1	3	4
00-01—St. Louis	NHL	41	4	9	13	14	-5	0	0	10	3	1	4	0
—Worcester	AHL	34	17	18	35	25	...	...	...	—	—	—	—	—
01-02—Edmonton	NHL	52	6	5	11	41	0	3	0	—	—	—	—	—
02-03—Hamilton	AHL	2	0	2	2	2	0	0	0	—	—	—	—	—
—Edmonton	NHL	70	11	20	31	28	19	2	2	6	1	0	1	2
03-04—Edmonton	NHL	17	2	6	8	10	5	0	1	—	—	—	—	—
04-05—Salzburg	Austria	11	5	4	9	12	-6	1	0	—	—	—	—	—
05-06—Edmonton	NHL	58	9	17	26	20	-12	5	0	—	—	—	—	—
—Boston	NHL	19	2	6	8	8	-2	1	0	—	—	—	—	—
NHL Totals (7 years)		311	47	84	131	149	16	15	3	23	6	2	8	6

RECCHI, MARK — LW

PERSONAL: Born February 1, 1968, in Kamloops, B.C. ... 5-10/190. ... Shoots left. ... Name pronounced REH-kee.

TRANSACTIONS/CAREER NOTES: Selected by Pittsburgh Penguins in fourth round (fourth Penguins pick, 67th overall) of NHL draft (June 11, 1988). ... Injured left shoulder (December 23, 1990). ... Sprained right knee (March 30, 1991). ... Traded by Penguins with D Brian Benning and first-round pick (LW Jason Bowen) in 1992 draft to Philadelphia Flyers for RW Rick Tocchet, D Kjell Samuelsson, G Ken Wregget and third-round pick (C Dave Roche) in 1993 draft (February 19, 1992). ... Traded by Flyers with third-round pick (C Martin Hohenberger) in 1995 draft to Montreal Canadiens for D Eric Desjardins, LW Gilbert Dionne and LW John LeClair (February 9, 1995). ... Pneumonia (December 12, 1998); missed four games. ... Traded by Canadiens to Flyers for RW Dainius Zubrus and second-round pick (D Matt Carkner) in 1999 draft (March 10, 1999). ... Concussion (March 22, 1999); missed three games. ... Headaches (April 1, 1999); missed two games. ... Concussion (April 13, 1999); missed two games. ... Headaches (October 11, 2000); missed four games. ... Fatigue (October 24, 2000); missed nine games. ... Suspended two games for elbowing (March 8, 2002). ... Signed as free agent by Pittsburgh Penguins (July 9, 2004). ... Traded by Penguins to Hurricanes for D Niklas Nordgren, C Krystofer Kolanos and second-round pick in 2007 draft (March 9, 2006).

STATISTICAL PLATEAUS: Three-goal games: 1991-92 (1), 1996-97 (1), 1997-98 (1), 2001-02 (1), 2002-03 (1). Total: 5.

Season Team	League	GP	G	A	Pts.	PIM	+/-	PP	SH	GP	G	A	Pts.	PIM
		REGULAR SEASON								PLAYOFFS				
84-85—Langley Eagles	BCJHL	51	26	39	65	39	...	...	...	—	—	—	—	—
85-86—New Westminster	WHL	72	21	40	61	55	...	...	...	—	—	—	—	—
86-87—Kamloops	WHL	40	26	50	76	63	...	...	...	13	3	16	19	17
87-88—Kamloops	WHL	62	61	93	154	75	...	...	...	17	10	21	31	18
88-89—Pittsburgh	NHL	15	1	1	2	0	-2	0	0	—	—	—	—	—
—Muskegon	IHL	63	50	49	99	86	...	...	...	14	7	14	21	28
89-90—Muskegon	IHL	4	7	4	11	2	...	...	...	—	—	—	—	—
—Pittsburgh	NHL	74	30	37	67	44	6	6	2	—	—	—	—	—
90-91—Pittsburgh	NHL	78	40	73	113	48	0	12	0	24	10	24	34	33
91-92—Pittsburgh	NHL	58	33	37	70	78	-16	16	1	—	—	—	—	—
—Philadelphia	NHL	22	10	17	27	18	-5	4	0	—	—	—	—	—
92-93—Philadelphia	NHL	84	53	70	123	95	1	15	4	—	—	—	—	—
93-94—Philadelphia	NHL	84	40	67	107	46	-2	11	0	—	—	—	—	—
94-95—Philadelphia	NHL	10	2	3	5	12	-6	1	0	—	—	—	—	—
—Montreal	NHL	39	14	29	43	16	-3	8	0	—	—	—	—	—
95-96—Montreal	NHL	82	28	50	78	69	20	11	2	6	3	3	6	0
96-97—Montreal	NHL	82	34	46	80	58	-1	7	2	5	4	2	6	2
97-98—Montreal	NHL	82	32	42	74	51	11	9	1	10	4	8	12	6
—Can. Olympic team	Int'l	5	0	2	2	0	1	0	0	—	—	—	—	—
98-99—Montreal	NHL	61	12	35	47	28	-4	3	0	—	—	—	—	—
—Philadelphia	NHL	10	4	2	6	6	-3	0	0	6	0	1	1	2
99-00—Philadelphia	NHL	82	28	*63	91	50	20	7	1	18	6	12	18	6
00-01—Philadelphia	NHL	69	27	50	77	33	15	7	1	6	2	2	4	2
01-02—Philadelphia	NHL	80	22	42	64	46	5	7	2	4	0	0	0	2
02-03—Philadelphia	NHL	79	20	32	52	35	0	8	1	13	7	3	10	2
03-04—Philadelphia	NHL	82	26	49	75	47	18	14	1	18	4	2	6	4
05-06—Pittsburgh	NHL	63	24	33	57	56	-28	11	0	—	—	—	—	—
—Carolina	NHL	20	4	3	7	12	-8	2	0	25	7	9	16	18
NHL Totals (17 years)		1256	484	781	1265	848	18	159	18	135	47	66	113	77

REDDEN, WADE — D

PERSONAL: Born June 12, 1977, in Lloydminster, Sask. ... 6-2/208. ... Shoots left.

TRANSACTIONS/CAREER NOTES: Selected by New York Islanders in first round (first Islanders pick, second overall) of entry draft (July 8, 1995). ... Traded by Islanders with G Damian Rhodes to Ottawa Senators for G Don Beaupre, D Bryan Berard and C Martin Straka (January 23, 1996). ... Bruised left foot (January 29, 1998); missed one game. ... Back spasms (December 22, 1998); missed two games. ... Shoulder (March 4, 1999); missed eight games. ... Illness (February 1, 2000); missed one game. ... Bruised hand (September 25, 2000); missed first four games of season. ... Flu (April 8, 2002); missed final three games of season. ... Right hip flexor (November 8, 2002); missed three games. ... Flu (January 27, 2003); missed two games. ... Flu (February 5, 2004); missed one game. ... Knee injury (November 22, 2005); missed 10 games. ... Personal absence (March 30, 2006); missed seven games. ... Personal absence (April 23, 2006); missed one game.

Season Team	League	GP	G	A	Pts.	PIM	+/-	PP	SH	GP	G	A	Pts.	PIM
		REGULAR SEASON								PLAYOFFS				
92-93—Lloydminster	SJHL	34	4	11	15	64	...	...	...	—	—	—	—	—
93-94—Brandon	WHL	64	4	35	39	98	...	...	...	14	2	4	6	10

Season Team	League	REGULAR SEASON GP	G	A	Pts.	PIM	+/-	PP	SH	PLAYOFFS GP	G	A	Pts.	PIM
94-95—Brandon	WHL	64	14	46	60	83	49	4	0	18	5	10	15	8
95-96—Brandon	WHL	51	9	45	54	55	...	...	...	19	5	10	15	19
96-97—Ottawa	NHL	82	6	24	30	41	1	2	0	7	1	3	4	2
97-98—Ottawa	NHL	80	8	14	22	27	17	3	0	9	0	2	2	2
98-99—Ottawa	NHL	72	8	21	29	54	7	3	0	4	1	2	3	2
99-00—Ottawa	NHL	81	10	26	36	49	-1	3	0	—	—	—	—	—
00-01—Ottawa	NHL	78	10	37	47	49	22	4	0	4	0	0	0	0
01-02—Ottawa	NHL	79	9	25	34	48	22	4	1	12	3	2	5	6
02-03—Ottawa	NHL	76	10	35	45	70	23	4	0	18	1	8	9	10
03-04—Ottawa	NHL	81	17	26	43	65	21	12	0	7	1	0	1	2
05-06—Ottawa	NHL	65	10	40	50	63	35	8	0	9	2	8	10	10
—Canadian Oly. team	Int'l	6	1	0	1	0	2	0	0	—	—	—	—	—
NHL Totals (9 years)		694	88	248	336	466	147	43	1	70	9	25	34	34

REGEHR, RICHIE D

PERSONAL: Born January 17, 1983, in Bandung, Indonesia. ... 6-0/200. ... Shoots right. ... Brother of Robyn Regher, D, Calgary Flames. ... Name pronounced: rih GEER

TRANSACTIONS/CAREER NOTES: Signed as free agent by Calgary Flames (July 6, 2004).

Season Team	League	REGULAR SEASON GP	G	A	Pts.	PIM	+/-	PP	SH	PLAYOFFS GP	G	A	Pts.	PIM
98-99—Kelowna	WHL	2	0	0	0	0	...	...	...	—	—	—	—	—
99-00—Kelowna	WHL	50	6	8	14	22	...	...	...	5	0	1	1	0
00-01—Kelowna	WHL	71	10	27	37	68	...	...	...	6	0	1	1	4
01-02—Portland	WHL	52	8	36	44	62	...	...	...	7	2	5	7	8
02-03—Portland	WHL	67	16	45	61	115	...	...	...	7	2	2	4	8
03-04—Portland	WHL	65	9	34	43	88	...	...	...	5	0	1	1	6
04-05—Lowell	AHL	64	9	16	25	60	20	4	0	11	1	6	7	2
05-06—Omaha Ak-Sar-Ben	AHL	48	7	23	30	56	-4	5	1	—	—	—	—	—
—Calgary	NHL	14	0	2	2	6	0	0	0	—	—	—	—	—
NHL Totals (1 year)		14	0	2	2	6	0	0	0					

REGEHR, ROBYN D

PERSONAL: Born April 19, 1980, in Recife, Brazil. ... 6-2/226. ... Shoots left. ... Brother of Richie Regehr, D, Calgary Flames. ... Name pronounced: rih GEER.

TRANSACTIONS/CAREER NOTES: Selected by Colorado Avalanche in first round (1rd Avalanche pick, 19th overall) of entry draft (June 27, 1998). ... Traded by Avalanche to Calgary Flames (March 27, 1999); completing deal in which Flames traded RW Theo Fleury and LW Chris Dingman to Avalanche for LW Rene Corbet, D Wade Belak and second-round pick (Jarret Stoll) in 2000 draft (February 28, 1999). ... Fractured legs (summer 1999); missed first five games of season. ... Concussion (January 11, 2000); missed 11 games. ... Injured knee (November 4, 2000); missed six games. ... Injured knee (December 22, 2000); missed two games. ... Injured wrist (November 7, 2001); missed one game. ... Injured ribs, strained oblique muscle (February 4, 2003); missed six games. ... Sprained MCL in knee (September 29, 2005); missed first 14 games of season.

Season Team	League	REGULAR SEASON GP	G	A	Pts.	PIM	+/-	PP	SH	PLAYOFFS GP	G	A	Pts.	PIM
96-97—Kamloops	WHL	64	4	19	23	96	...	...	...	5	0	1	1	18
97-98—Kamloops	WHL	65	4	10	14	120	...	...	...	5	0	3	3	8
98-99—Kamloops	WHL	54	12	20	32	130	37	6	1	12	1	4	5	21
99-00—Saint John	AHL	5	0	0	0	0	...	...	...	—	—	—	—	—
—Calgary	NHL	57	5	7	12	46	-2	2	0	—	—	—	—	—
00-01—Calgary	NHL	71	1	3	4	70	-7	0	0	—	—	—	—	—
01-02—Calgary	NHL	77	2	6	8	93	-24	0	0	—	—	—	—	—
02-03—Calgary	NHL	76	0	12	12	87	-9	0	0	—	—	—	—	—
03-04—Calgary	NHL	82	4	14	18	74	14	2	0	26	2	7	9	20
05-06—Calgary	NHL	68	6	20	26	67	6	5	0	7	1	3	4	6
—Canadian Oly. team	Int'l	6	0	1	1	2	1	0	0	—	—	—	—	—
NHL Totals (6 years)		431	18	62	80	437	-22	9	0	33	3	10	13	26

REGIER, STEVE LW

PERSONAL: Born August 31, 1984, in Edmonton. ... 6-4/194. ... Shoots left.

TRANSACTIONS/CAREER NOTES: Selected by New York Islanders in fifth round (fifth Islanders pick, 148th overall) of NHL entry draft (June 28, 2004).

Season Team	League	REGULAR SEASON GP	G	A	Pts.	PIM	+/-	PP	SH	PLAYOFFS GP	G	A	Pts.	PIM
00-01—Medicine Hat	WHL	1	0	0	0	0	...	...	...	—	—	—	—	—
01-02—Medicine Hat	WHL	59	1	4	5	31	...	...	...	—	—	—	—	—
02-03—Medicine Hat	WHL	61	11	10	21	114	...	...	...	11	2	2	4	20
03-04—Medicine Hat	WHL	72	25	35	60	111	14	7	3	18	5	11	16	20
04-05—Bridgeport	AHL	75	7	15	22	43	6	0	0	—	—	—	—	—
05-06—Bridgeport	AHL	73	16	22	38	54	8	6	0	7	0	2	2	6
—New York Islanders	NHL	9	0	0	0	0	-1	0	0	—	—	—	—	—
NHL Totals (1 year)		9	0	0	0	0	-1	0	0					

REID, DARREN — RW

PERSONAL: Born May 8, 1983, in Lac La Biche, Alta. ... 6-2/185. ... Shoots right.
TRANSACTIONS/CAREER NOTES: Selected by Tampa Bay Lightning in eighth round (11th Lightning pick, 256th overall) of NHL entry draft (June 23, 2002).

		REGULAR SEASON								PLAYOFFS				
Season Team	League	GP	G	A	Pts.	PIM	+/-	PP	SH	GP	G	A	Pts.	PIM
01-02—Medicine Hat	WHL	37	8	9	17	70	...	...	...	—	—	—	—	—
02-03—Medicine Hat	WHL	63	14	30	44	163	...	...	...	11	5	0	5	19
03-04—Medicine Hat	WHL	67	33	48	81	194	...	...	...	20	13	8	21	31
04-05—Springfield	AHL	56	3	19	22	99	-10	0	1	—	—	—	—	—
05-06—Springfield	AHL	50	8	9	17	59	-16	2	1	—	—	—	—	—
—Tampa Bay	NHL	7	0	1	1	0	-2	0	0	—	—	—	—	—
NHL Totals (1 year)		7	0	1	1	0	-2	0	0					

REINPRECHT, STEVE — C/RW

PERSONAL: Born May 7, 1976, in Edmonton. ... 6-0/195. ... Shoots left. ... Name pronounced: RIGHN prehkt
TRANSACTIONS/CAREER NOTES: Signed as free agent by Los Angeles Kings (March 31, 2000). ... Traded by Kings with D Rob Blake to Colorado Avalanche for RW Adam Deadmarsh, D Aaron Miller, first-round pick (C David Steckel) in 2001, player to be named and future considerations (February 21, 2001); Kings acquired C Jared Aulin to complete deal (March 22, 2001). ... Knee (January 15, 2002); missed 13 games. ... Foot (March 21, 2002); missed one game. ... Shoulder (November 22, 2002); missed five games. ... Traded by Avalanche to Buffalo Sabres for D Keith Ballard (July 2, 2003). ... Traded by Sabres with D Rhett Warrener to Calgary Flames for C/LW Chris Drury and C Steve Begin (July 3, 2003). ... Shoulder (October 5, 2003); missed five games. ... Fractured left leg (December 2, 2003); missed 17 games. ... Flu (February 26, 2004); missed one game. ... Shoulder (March 2, 2004); misssed two games. ... Shoulder (March 9, 2004); missed remainder of season. ... Traded by Flames with G Philippe Sauve to Phoenix Coyotes for LW Mike Leclerc and G Brian Boucher (February 1, 2006)
STATISTICAL PLATEAUS: Three-goal games: 2001-02 (1), 2002-03 (1). Total: 2.

		REGULAR SEASON								PLAYOFFS				
Season Team	League	GP	G	A	Pts.	PIM	+/-	PP	SH	GP	G	A	Pts.	PIM
96-97—Wisconsin	WCHA	38	11	9	20	12	...	...	...	—	—	—	—	—
97-98—Wisconsin	WCHA	41	19	24	43	18	...	...	...	—	—	—	—	—
98-99—Wisconsin	WCHA	38	16	17	33	14	...	...	...	—	—	—	—	—
99-00—Wisconsin	WCHA	37	26	40	66	14	...	...	...	—	—	—	—	—
—Los Angeles	NHL	1	0	0	0	2	0	0	0	—	—	—	—	—
00-01—Los Angeles	NHL	59	12	17	29	12	11	3	2	—	—	—	—	—
—Colorado	NHL	21	3	4	7	2	-1	0	0	22	2	3	5	2
01-02—Colorado	NHL	67	19	27	46	18	14	4	0	21	7	5	12	8
02-03—Colorado	NHL	77	18	33	51	18	-6	2	1	7	1	2	3	0
03-04—Calgary	NHL	44	7	22	29	4	1	3	0	—	—	—	—	—
04-05—Mulhouse	France	22	20	27	47	6	...	...	...	10	7	6	13	2
05-06—Calgary	NHL	52	10	19	29	24	10	5	0	—	—	—	—	—
—Phoenix	NHL	28	12	11	23	8	1	4	1	—	—	—	—	—
NHL Totals (6 years)		349	81	133	214	88	30	21	4	50	10	10	20	10

REITZ, ERIK — D

PERSONAL: Born July 29, 1982, in Detroit. ... 6-0/192. ... Shoots right. ... Name pronounced RIGHTZ.
TRANSACTIONS/CAREER NOTES: Selected by Minnesota Wild in sixth round (fifth Wild pick, 170th overall) of entry draft (June 24, 2000).

		REGULAR SEASON								PLAYOFFS				
Season Team	League	GP	G	A	Pts.	PIM	+/-	PP	SH	GP	G	A	Pts.	PIM
99-00—Barrie	OHL	63	2	10	12	85	...	...	...	—	—	—	—	—
00-01—Barrie	OHL	68	5	21	26	178	6	0	0	5	1	0	1	21
01-02—Barrie	OHL	61	13	27	40	153	...	...	...	20	4	16	20	40
02-03—Houston	AHL	62	6	13	19	112	-6	2	0	11	0	3	3	31
03-04—Houston	AHL	69	5	19	24	148	-6	2	0	2	0	0	0	0
04-05—Houston	AHL	38	2	12	14	91	-1	1	0	—	—	—	—	—
05-06—Houston	AHL	72	5	23	28	139	4	1	1	8	0	5	5	20
—Minnesota	NHL	5	0	0	0	4	-2	0	0	—	—	—	—	—
NHL Totals (1 year)		5	0	0	0	4	-2	0	0					

RHEAUME, PASCAL — C/LW

PERSONAL: Born June 21, 1973, in Quebec City. ... 6-1/220. ... Shoots left. ... Name pronounced ray-OHM.
TRANSACTIONS/CAREER NOTES: Signed as free agent by New Jersey Devils (October 1, 1992). ... Claimed by St. Louis Blues in waiver draft (September 28, 1997). ... Concussion (February 28, 1999); missed 10 games. ... Shoulder surgery; missed first 62 games of 1999-2000 season. ... Signed as free agent by Chicago Blackhawks (July 31, 2001). ... Claimed off waivers by Atlanta Thrashers (November 14, 2001). ... Hamstring (December 3, 2001); missed 21 games. ... Pneumonia (April 7, 2002); missed two games. ... Flu (January 15, 2003); missed one game. ... Traded by Thrashers to Devils for future considerations (February 24, 2003). ... Signed as free agent by New York Rangers (October 22, 2003). ... Left knee (October 29, 2003); missed 24 games. ... Claimed off waivers by Blues (January 29, 2004). ... Hip flexor (March 16, 2004); missed three games. ... Signed as free agent by Devils (August 13, 2004). ... Traded by Devils with D Ray Schultz and D Steven Spencer to Phoenix Coyotes for D Brad Ference (November 25, 2005).
STATISTICAL PLATEAUS: Four-goal games: 2001-02 (1).

		REGULAR SEASON								PLAYOFFS				
Season Team	League	GP	G	A	Pts.	PIM	+/-	PP	SH	GP	G	A	Pts.	PIM
91-92—Trois-Rivieres	QMJHL	65	17	20	37	84	...	...	...	14	5	4	9	23
92-93—Sherbrooke	QMJHL	65	28	34	62	88	...	...	...	14	6	5	11	31

Season Team	League	REGULAR SEASON GP	G	A	Pts.	PIM	+/-	PP	SH	PLAYOFFS GP	G	A	Pts.	PIM
93-94—Albany	AHL	55	17	18	35	43	...	...	...	5	0	1	1	0
94-95—Albany	AHL	78	19	25	44	46	17	5	0	14	3	6	9	19
95-96—Albany	AHL	68	26	42	68	50	...	...	...	4	1	2	3	2
96-97—Albany	AHL	51	22	23	45	40	15	4	3	16	2	8	10	16
—New Jersey	NHL	2	1	0	1	0	1	0	0	—	—	—	—	—
97-98—St. Louis	NHL	48	6	9	15	35	4	1	0	10	1	3	4	8
98-99—St. Louis	NHL	60	9	18	27	24	10	2	0	5	1	0	1	4
99-00—St. Louis	NHL	7	1	1	2	6	-2	0	0	—	—	—	—	—
—Worcester	AHL	7	1	1	2	4	...	...	...	—	—	—	—	—
00-01—Worcester	AHL	56	23	36	59	63	...	...	...	11	2	4	6	2
—St. Louis	NHL	8	2	0	2	5	-1	2	0	3	0	1	1	0
01-02—Chicago	NHL	19	0	2	2	4	-1	0	0	—	—	—	—	—
—Atlanta	NHL	42	11	9	20	25	-3	6	0	—	—	—	—	—
02-03—Atlanta	NHL	56	4	9	13	24	-8	0	2	—	—	—	—	—
—New Jersey	NHL	21	4	1	5	8	3	0	1	24	1	2	3	13
03-04—New York Rangers	NHL	17	0	0	0	5	-3	0	0	—	—	—	—	—
—Hartford	AHL	3	1	0	1	0	0	0	0	—	—	—	—	—
—St. Louis	NHL	25	1	3	4	4	-3	0	0	3	0	0	0	2
04-05—Albany	AHL	78	24	25	49	85	-1	6	1	—	—	—	—	—
05-06—Albany	AHL	9	2	0	2	9	-6	1	0	—	—	—	—	—
—San Antonio	AHL	47	13	13	26	35	-6	5	1	—	—	—	—	—
—New Jersey	NHL	12	0	0	0	4	-6	0	0	—	—	—	—	—
—Phoenix	NHL	1	0	0	0	0	-1	0	0	—	—	—	—	—
NHL Totals (9 years)		318	39	52	91	144	-10	11	3	45	3	6	9	27

RIBEIRO, MIKE C

PERSONAL: Born February 10, 1980, in Montreal. ... 6-0/176. ... Shoots left. ... Name pronounced rih-bee-AIR-roh.
TRANSACTIONS/CAREER NOTES: Selected by Montreal Canadiens in second round (second Canadiens pick, 45th overall) of NHL entry draft (June 27, 1998). ... Injured collarbone (September 27, 2002); missed 13 games. ... Injured knee (February 21, 2003); missed four games.

Season Team	League	REGULAR SEASON GP	G	A	Pts.	PIM	+/-	PP	SH	PLAYOFFS GP	G	A	Pts.	PIM
97-98—Rouyn-Noranda	QMJHL	67	40	85	125	55	...	...	...	—	—	—	—	—
98-99—Rouyn-Noranda	QMJHL	69	67	100	167	137	50	24	8	11	5	11	16	12
—Fredericton	AHL	...	...	...	...	...	...	...	...	5	0	1	1	2
99-00—Montreal	NHL	19	1	1	2	2	-6	1	0	—	—	—	—	—
—Quebec	AHL	3	0	0	0	2	...	...	...	—	—	—	—	—
—Rouyn-Noranda	QMJHL	2	1	3	4	0	2	0	0	—	—	—	—	—
—Quebec	QMJHL	21	17	28	45	30	17	4	2	11	3	20	23	38
00-01—Quebec	AHL	74	26	40	66	44	...	...	...	9	1	5	6	23
—Montreal	NHL	2	0	0	0	2	0	0	0	—	—	—	—	—
01-02—Montreal	NHL	43	8	10	18	12	-11	3	0	—	—	—	—	—
—Quebec	AHL	23	9	14	23	36	7	2	2	3	0	3	3	0
02-03—Hamilton	AHL	3	0	1	1	0	1	0	0	—	—	—	—	—
—Montreal	NHL	52	5	12	17	6	-3	2	0	—	—	—	—	—
03-04—Montreal	NHL	81	20	45	65	34	15	7	0	11	2	1	3	18
04-05—Blues Espoo	Finland	17	8	9	17	4	7	...	...	—	—	—	—	—
05-06—Montreal	NHL	79	16	35	51	36	-6	8	0	6	0	2	2	0
NHL Totals (6 years)		276	50	103	153	92	-11	21	0	17	2	3	5	18

RICCI, MIKE C

PERSONAL: Born October 27, 1971, in Scarborough, Ont. ... 6-0/200. ... Shoots left. ... Name pronounced REE-chee.
TRANSACTIONS/CAREER NOTES: Selected by Philadelphia Flyers in first round (first Flyers pick, fourth overall) of entry draft (June 16, 1990). ... Fractured right index finger and thumb (October 4, 1990); missed nine games. ... Traded by Flyers with G Ron Hextall, C Peter Forsberg, D Steve Duchesne, D Kerry Huffman, first-round pick (G Jocelyn Thibault) in 1993, cash and future considerations to Quebec Nordiques for C Eric Lindros (June 20, 1992); Nordiques acquired LW Chris Simon and first-round pick (traded to Toronto; traded to Washington; Capitals selected D Nolan Baumgartner) in 1994 to complete deal (July 21, 1992). ... Wrist (November 3, 1992); missed four games. ... Flu (January 5, 1993); missed two games. ... Nordiques franchise moved to Colorado and renamed Avalanche for 1995-96 season (July 21, 1995). ... Sinus surgery (October 15, 1995); missed one game. ... Ankle (November 5, 1995); missed one game. ... Ankle (December 11, 1995); missed two games. ... Back spasms (January 4, 1996); missed 16 games. ... Shoulder (October 30, 1996); missed 11 games. ... Fractured thumb (January 6, 1997); missed four games. ... Shoulder surgery before 1997-98 season; missed first 16 games of season. ... Traded by Avalanche with second-round pick (RW Jonathan Cheechoo) in 1998 to San Jose Sharks for RW Shean Donovan and first-round pick (C Alex Tanguay) in 1998 (November 20, 1997). ... Back (March 3, 2002); missed one game. ... Shoulder (March 10, 2002); missed two games. ... Cut face (March 1, 2003); missed three games. ... Back (March 24, 2003); missed five games. ... Back (April 6, 2003); missed one game. ... Shoulder (February 26, 2004); missed 11 games. ... Signed as free agent by Phoenix Coyotes (July 9, 2004). ... Broken nose (October 9, 2005); missed three games.
STATISTICAL PLATEAUS: Three-goal games: 2000-01 (1). ... Five-goal games: 1993-94 (1). ... Total hat tricks: 2.

Season Team	League	REGULAR SEASON GP	G	A	Pts.	PIM	+/-	PP	SH	PLAYOFFS GP	G	A	Pts.	PIM
87-88—Peterborough	OHL	41	24	37	61	20	...	...	...	8	5	5	10	4
88-89—Peterborough	OHL	60	54	52	106	43	...	...	...	17	19	16	35	18
89-90—Peterborough	OHL	60	52	64	116	39	...	...	...	12	5	7	12	26
90-91—Philadelphia	NHL	68	21	20	41	64	-8	9	0	—	—	—	—	—
91-92—Philadelphia	NHL	78	20	36	56	93	-10	11	2	—	—	—	—	—
92-93—Quebec	NHL	77	27	51	78	123	8	12	1	6	0	6	6	8
93-94—Quebec	NHL	83	30	21	51	113	-9	13	3	—	—	—	—	—
94-95—Quebec	NHL	48	15	21	36	40	5	9	0	6	1	3	4	8

Season Team	League	GP	G	A	Pts.	PIM	+/-	PP	SH	GP	G	A	Pts.	PIM
		REGULAR SEASON								PLAYOFFS				
95-96—Colorado	NHL	62	6	21	27	52	1	3	0	22	6	11	17	18
96-97—Colorado	NHL	63	13	19	32	59	-3	5	0	17	2	4	6	17
97-98—Colorado	NHL	6	0	4	4	2	0	0	0	—	—	—	—	—
—San Jose	NHL	59	9	14	23	30	-4	5	0	6	1	3	4	6
98-99—San Jose	NHL	82	13	26	39	68	1	2	1	6	2	3	5	10
99-00—San Jose	NHL	82	20	24	44	60	14	10	0	12	5	1	6	2
00-01—San Jose	NHL	81	22	22	44	60	3	9	2	6	0	3	3	0
01-02—San Jose	NHL	79	19	34	53	44	9	5	2	12	4	6	10	4
02-03—San Jose	NHL	75	11	23	34	53	-12	5	1	—	—	—	—	—
03-04—San Jose	NHL	71	7	19	26	40	8	2	0	17	2	3	5	4
05-06—Phoenix	NHL	78	10	6	16	69	-22	5	1	—	—	—	—	—
NHL Totals (15 years)		1092	243	361	604	970	-19	105	13	110	23	43	66	77

RICHARDS, BRAD — C

PERSONAL: Born May 2, 1980, in Montague, Prince Edward Island. ... 6-1/198. ... Shoots left.
TRANSACTIONS/CAREER NOTES: Selected by Tampa Bay Lightning in third round (second Lightning pick, 64th overall) of NHL draft (June 27, 1998).

Season Team	League	GP	G	A	Pts.	PIM	+/-	PP	SH	GP	G	A	Pts.	PIM
		REGULAR SEASON								PLAYOFFS				
96-97—Notre Dame	SJHL	63	39	48	87	73	...	...	...	—	—	—	—	—
97-98—Rimouski	QMJHL	68	33	82	115	44	...	...	...	19	8	24	32	2
98-99—Rimouski	QMJHL	59	39	92	131	55	18	10	8	11	9	12	21	6
99-00—Rimouski	QMJHL	63	71	115	186	69	80	18	6	12	13	24	37	16
00-01—Tampa Bay	NHL	82	21	41	62	14	-10	7	0	—	—	—	—	—
01-02—Tampa Bay	NHL	82	20	42	62	13	-18	5	0	—	—	—	—	—
02-03—Tampa Bay	NHL	80	17	57	74	24	3	4	0	11	0	5	5	12
03-04—Tampa Bay	NHL	82	26	53	79	12	14	5	1	23	12	14	*26	4
04-05—Ak Bars Kazan	Russian	6	2	5	7	16	2	...	...	—	—	—	—	—
05-06—Tampa Bay	NHL	82	23	68	91	32	0	7	4	5	3	5	8	6
—Canadian Oly. team	Int'l	6	2	2	4	6	3	0	0	—	—	—	—	—
NHL Totals (5 years)		408	107	261	368	95	-11	28	5	39	15	24	39	22

RICHARDS, MIKE — C

PERSONAL: Born February 11, 1985, in Kenora, Ont. ... 5-11/199. ... Shoots left.
TRANSACTIONS/CAREER NOTES: Selected by Philadelphia Flyers in first round (first Flyers pick, 24th overall) of NHL entry draft (June 20, 2003). ... Sprained right wrist (November 22, 2005); missed one game. ... Concussion (December 16, 2005); missed two games.

Season Team	League	GP	G	A	Pts.	PIM	+/-	PP	SH	GP	G	A	Pts.	PIM
		REGULAR SEASON								PLAYOFFS				
01-02—Kitchener	OHL	65	20	38	58	52	...	...	...	4	0	1	1	6
02-03—Kitchener	OHL	67	37	50	87	99	...	...	...	21	9	18	27	24
03-04—Kitchener	OHL	58	36	53	89	82	...	...	...	1	0	0	0	0
04-05—Philadelphia	AHL	—	—	—	—	—	—	—	—	14	7	8	15	28
—Kitchener	OHL	—	—	—	—	—	—	—	—	15	11	17	28	36
—Kitchener	OHL	43	22	36	58	75	9	6	5	—	—	—	—	—
05-06—Philadelphia	NHL	79	11	23	34	65	6	1	3	6	0	1	1	0
NHL Totals (1 year)		79	11	23	34	65	6	1	3	6	0	1	1	0

RICHARDSON, BRAD — C/LW

PERSONAL: Born February 4, 1985, in Belleville, Ont. ... 5-11/178. ... Shoots left.
TRANSACTIONS/CAREER NOTES: Selected by Colorado Avalanche in fifth round (fourth Avalanche pick, 163rd overall) of NHL entry draft (June 21, 2003). ... Dislocated shoulder (November 1, 2003); missed remained of OHL season.

Season Team	League	GP	G	A	Pts.	PIM	+/-	PP	SH	GP	G	A	Pts.	PIM
		REGULAR SEASON								PLAYOFFS				
01-02—Owen Sound	OHL	58	12	21	33	20	-16	3	0	—	—	—	—	—
02-03—Owen Sound	OHL	67	27	40	67	54	-10	6	2	4	1	1	2	10
03-04—Owen Sound	OHL	15	7	9	16	4	2	5	0	—	—	—	—	—
04-05—Owen Sound	OHL	68	41	56	97	60	26	14	2	8	6	4	10	8
05-06—Lowell	AHL	29	4	13	17	20	-3	2	0	—	—	—	—	—
—Colorado	NHL	41	3	10	13	12	0	1	0	9	1	0	1	6
NHL Totals (1 year)		41	3	10	13	12	0	1	0	9	1	0	1	6

RICHARDSON, LUKE — D

PERSONAL: Born March 26, 1969, in Ottawa. ... 6-4/215. ... Shoots left.
TRANSACTIONS/CAREER NOTES: Selected by Toronto Maple Leafs in first round (first Maple Leafs pick, seventh overall) of entry draft (June 13, 1987). ... Traded by Maple Leafs with LW Vincent Damphousse, G Peter Ing and C Scott Thornton to Edmonton Oilers for G Grant Fuhr, LW Glenn Anderson and LW Craig Berube (September 19, 1991). ... Strained clavicular joint (February 11, 1992); missed three games. ... Flu (March 1993); missed one game. ... Fractured cheekbone (January 7, 1994); missed 15 games. ... Flu (February 28, 1995); missed two games. ... Signed as free agent by Philadelphia Flyers (July 14, 1997). ... Suspended two games for fighting incident (January 30, 2000). ... Bruised shoulder (February 24, 2000); missed five games. ... Fractured right foot (November 10, 2001); missed 10 games. ... Signed as free agent by Columbus Blue Jackets (July 4, 2002). ... Fractured finger (November 16, 2003); missed 17 games. ... Broken jaw (December 21, 2005);

missed 16 games. ... Traded by Blue Jackets to Maple Leafs for fifth-round pick (LW Nick Sucharski) and conditional pick in 2006 draft (March 8, 2006). ... Signed as free agent by Tampa Bay Lightning (July 11, 2006).

Season Team	League	REGULAR SEASON GP	G	A	Pts.	PIM	+/-	PP	SH	PLAYOFFS GP	G	A	Pts.	PIM
84-85—Ottawa Jr. B	ODHA	35	5	26	31	72	...	...	...	—	—	—	—	—
85-86—Peterborough	OHL	63	6	18	24	57	...	...	...	16	2	1	3	50
86-87—Peterborough	OHL	59	13	32	45	70	...	...	...	12	0	5	5	24
87-88—Toronto	NHL	78	4	6	10	90	-25	0	0	2	0	0	0	0
88-89—Toronto	NHL	55	2	7	9	106	-15	0	0	—	—	—	—	—
89-90—Toronto	NHL	67	4	14	18	122	-1	0	0	5	0	0	0	22
90-91—Toronto	NHL	78	1	9	10	238	-28	0	0	—	—	—	—	—
91-92—Edmonton	NHL	75	2	19	21	118	-9	0	0	16	0	5	5	45
92-93—Edmonton	NHL	82	3	10	13	142	-18	0	2	—	—	—	—	—
93-94—Edmonton	NHL	69	2	6	8	131	-13	0	0	—	—	—	—	—
94-95—Edmonton	NHL	46	3	10	13	40	-6	1	1	—	—	—	—	—
95-96—Edmonton	NHL	82	2	9	11	108	-27	0	0	—	—	—	—	—
96-97—Edmonton	NHL	82	1	11	12	91	9	0	0	12	0	2	2	14
97-98—Philadelphia	NHL	81	2	3	5	139	7	2	0	5	0	0	0	0
98-99—Philadelphia	NHL	78	0	6	6	106	-3	0	0	—	—	—	—	—
99-00—Philadelphia	NHL	74	2	5	7	140	14	0	0	18	0	1	1	41
00-01—Philadelphia	NHL	82	2	6	8	131	23	0	1	6	0	0	0	4
01-02—Philadelphia	NHL	72	1	8	9	102	18	0	0	5	0	0	0	4
02-03—Columbus	NHL	82	0	13	13	73	-16	0	0	—	—	—	—	—
03-04—Columbus	NHL	64	1	5	6	48	-11	0	0	—	—	—	—	—
05-06—Columbus	NHL	44	1	6	7	30	-18	0	0	—	—	—	—	—
—Toronto	NHL	21	0	3	3	41	-1	0	0	—	—	—	—	—
NHL Totals (18 years)		1312	33	156	189	1996	-120	3	4	69	0	8	8	130

RICHMOND, DANNY D

PERSONAL: Born August 1, 1984, in Chicago. ... 6-0/175. ... Shoots left.
COLLEGE: Michigan.
TRANSACTIONS/CAREER NOTES: Selected by Carolina Hurricanes in second round (second Hurricanes pick, 31st overall) of entry draft (June 21, 2003). ... Traded by Hurricanes with fourth-round pick (traded to Toronto; Maple Leafs selected G James Reimer) in 2006 draft to Chicago Blackhawks for D Anton Babchuk (January 20, 2006).

Season Team	League	REGULAR SEASON GP	G	A	Pts.	PIM	+/-	PP	SH	PLAYOFFS GP	G	A	Pts.	PIM
01-02—Chicago	USHL	56	8	45	53	129	...	...	...	4	0	4	4	20
02-03—Univ. of Michigan	CCHA	43	3	19	22	48	...	...	...	—	—	—	—	—
03-04—London	OHL	59	13	22	35	92	12	7	0	15	5	6	11	10
04-05—Lowell	AHL	63	4	9	13	139	4	0	0	6	0	2	2	8
05-06—Lowell	AHL	32	4	11	15	60	-11	2	0	—	—	—	—	—
—Norfolk	AHL	31	4	8	12	42	0	1	0	3	0	1	1	2
—Carolina	NHL	10	0	1	1	7	-3	0	0	—	—	—	—	—
—Chicago	NHL	10	0	0	0	18	-3	0	0	—	—	—	—	—
NHL Totals (1 year)		20	0	1	1	25	-6	0	0					

RINNE, PEKKA G

PERSONAL: Born November 3, 1982, in Kempele, Finland. ... 6-3/191. ... Catches left. ... Name pronounced PECK-ah REEN-eh.
TRANSACTIONS/CAREER NOTES: Selected by Nashville Predators in eighth round (10th Predators pick, 258th overall) of entry draft (June 28, 2004).

Season Team	League	REGULAR SEASON GP	Min.	W	L	OTL	T	GA	SO	GAA	SV%	PLAYOFFS GP	Min.	W	L	GA	SO	GAA	SV%
02-03—Karpat Oulu	Finland	1	60	0	1	...	0	7	0	7.00	...	—	—	—	—	—	—	—	—
03-04—Karpat Oulu	Finland	14	824	5	4	...	4	41	0	2.99	.897	2	59	1	0	3	0	3.05	...
04-05—Karpat Oulu	Finland	10	572	8	0	...	1	16	0	1.68	...	—	—	—	—	—	—	—	—
05-06—Nashville	NHL	2	63	1	1	0	...	4	0	3.81	.900	—	—	—	—	—	—	—	—
—Milwaukee	AHL	51	2960	30	18	2	...	139	2	2.82	.904	8	480	8	0	17	2	2.13	.931
NHL Totals (1 year)		2	63	1	1	0	0	4	0	3.81	.900								

RISSMILLER, PAT C/LW

PERSONAL: Born October 26, 1978, in Belmont, Mass. ... 6-4/210. ... Shoots left. ... Name pronounced RIGHZ-mih-luhr.
TRANSACTIONS/CAREER NOTES: Signed as free agent by San Jose Sharks (June 30, 2003). ... Re-signed by Sharks as restricted free agent (September 6, 2005).

Season Team	League	REGULAR SEASON GP	G	A	Pts.	PIM	+/-	PP	SH	PLAYOFFS GP	G	A	Pts.	PIM
02-03—Cincinnati	ECHL	2	2	2	4	0	...	...	...	—	—	—	—	—
—Cleveland	AHL	72	14	26	40	24	...	...	...	—	—	—	—	—
03-04—San Jose	NHL	4	0	0	0	0	0	0	0	—	—	—	—	—
—Cleveland	AHL	75	14	31	45	66	-7	3	1	9	0	1	1	8
04-05—Cleveland	AHL	69	21	23	44	50	-12	8	0	—	—	—	—	—
05-06—Cleveland	AHL	68	15	37	52	30	-12	8	0	—	—	—	—	—
—San Jose	NHL	18	3	3	6	8	1	1	0	11	2	1	3	6
NHL Totals (2 years)		22	3	3	6	8	1	1	0	11	2	1	3	6

RITA, JANI — LW

PERSONAL: Born July 25, 1981, in Helsinki, Finland. ... 6-1/206. ... Shoots right. ... Name pronounced YAH-nee REE-tah.

TRANSACTIONS/CAREER NOTES: Selected by Edmonton Oilers in first round (first Oilers pick, 13th overall) of NHL draft (June 26, 1999). ... Injured shoulder (March 6, 2002); missed one game. ... Re-signed to two-year contract by Edmonton as restricted free agent (August 10, 2005). ... Traded by Edmonton with D Cory Cross to Pittsburgh for Dick Tarnstrom (January 26, 2006).

		REGULAR SEASON								PLAYOFFS				
Season Team	League	GP	G	A	Pts.	PIM	+/-	PP	SH	GP	G	A	Pts.	PIM
96-97—Jokerit Helsinki	Finland Jr.	3	0	0	0	0	...	...	...	—	—	—	—	—
97-98—Jokerit Helsinki	Finland Jr.	36	15	9	24	2	...	...	...	8	4	1	5	0
—Jokerit Helsinki	Finland	...	...	...	...	...	...	...	...	1	0	0	0	0
98-99—Jokerit Helsinki	Finland	41	3	2	5	39	...	...	...	—	—	—	—	—
—Jokerit Helsinki	Finland Jr.	20	9	13	22	8	...	...	...	—	—	—	—	—
99-00—Jokerit Helsinki	Finland	49	6	3	9	10	...	...	...	11	1	0	1	0
00-01—Jokerit Helsinki	Finland	50	5	10	15	18	...	...	...	5	0	0	0	2
01-02—Hamilton	AHL	76	25	17	42	32	-10	4	1	15	8	4	12	0
—Edmonton	NHL	1	0	0	0	0	0	0	0	—	—	—	—	—
02-03—Edmonton	NHL	12	3	1	4	0	2	0	0	—	—	—	—	—
—Hamilton	AHL	64	21	27	48	18	12	4	0	23	3	4	7	2
03-04—Edmonton	NHL	2	0	0	0	0	0	0	0	—	—	—	—	—
—Toronto	AHL	64	17	24	41	18	7	4	0	1	1	0	1	0
04-05—HPK Hameenlinna	Finland	56	21	18	39	12	27	...	...	10	7	4	11	4
05-06—Edmonton	NHL	21	3	0	3	6	0	0	0	—	—	—	—	—
—Pittsburgh	NHL	30	3	4	7	4	-6	0	0	—	—	—	—	—
NHL Totals (4 years)		66	9	5	14	10	-4	0	0					

RITCHIE, BYRON — C

PERSONAL: Born April 24, 1977, in Burnaby, B.C. ... 5-10/195. ... Shoots left.

TRANSACTIONS/CAREER NOTES: Selected by Hartford Whalers in seventh round (sixth Whalers pick, 165th overall) of NHL draft (July 8, 1995). ... Whalers franchise moved to North Carolina and renamed Carolina Hurricanes for 1997-98 season; NHL approved move on June 25, 1997. ... Traded by Hurricanes with D Sandis Ozolinsh to Florida Panthers for D Bret Hedican, C Kevyn Adams, D Tomas Malec and conditional second-round draft pick in 2003 (January 16, 2002). ... Injured left knee (November 4, 2003); missed 15 games. ... Fractured collarbone (March 10, 2004); missed remainder of season. ... Signed as free agent by Calgary Flames (July 2, 2004). ... Injured right knee (January 3, 2006); missed 26 games.

		REGULAR SEASON								PLAYOFFS				
Season Team	League	GP	G	A	Pts.	PIM	+/-	PP	SH	GP	G	A	Pts.	PIM
93-94—Lethbridge	WHL	44	4	11	15	44	...	...	...	6	0	0	0	14
94-95—Lethbridge	WHL	58	22	28	50	132	-23	5	0	—	—	—	—	—
95-96—Lethbridge	WHL	66	55	51	106	163	...	...	...	4	0	2	2	4
—Springfield	AHL	6	2	1	3	4	...	...	...	8	0	3	3	0
96-97—Lethbridge	WHL	63	50	76	126	115	33	15	6	18	16	12	28	28
97-98—New Haven	AHL	65	13	18	31	97	-12	2	0	—	—	—	—	—
98-99—New Haven	AHL	66	24	33	57	139	-21	9	1	—	—	—	—	—
—Carolina	NHL	3	0	0	0	0	0	0	0	—	—	—	—	—
99-00—Carolina	NHL	26	0	2	2	17	-10	0	0	—	—	—	—	—
—Cincinnati	IHL	34	8	13	21	81	...	...	...	10	1	6	7	32
00-01—Cincinnati	IHL	77	31	35	66	166	...	...	...	5	3	2	5	10
01-02—Lowell	AHL	43	25	30	55	38	13	8	4	—	—	—	—	—
—Carolina	NHL	4	0	0	0	2	0	0	0	—	—	—	—	—
—Florida	NHL	31	5	6	11	34	-2	2	0	—	—	—	—	—
02-03—Florida	NHL	30	0	3	3	19	-4	0	0	—	—	—	—	—
—San Antonio	AHL	26	3	14	17	68	-8	0	1	3	1	0	1	0
03-04—Florida	NHL	50	5	6	11	84	-10	0	0	—	—	—	—	—
04-05—Rogle	Sweden Dv. 2	16	10	11	21	83	8	3	0	16	7	5	12	32
05-06—Calgary	NHL	45	4	2	6	69	-2	0	0	7	0	0	0	0
NHL Totals (6 years)		189	14	19	33	225	-28	2	0	7	0	0	0	0

RIVERS, JAMIE — D

PERSONAL: Born March 16, 1975, in Ottawa. ... 6-0/190. ... Shoots left. ... Brother of Shawn Rivers, defenseman with Tampa Bay Lightning (1992-93).

TRANSACTIONS/CAREER NOTES: Selected by St. Louis Blues in third round (second Blues pick, 63rd overall) of entry draft (June 26, 1993). ... Claimed by New York Islanders in waiver draft (September 27, 1999). ... Ankle (February 26, 2000); missed three games. ... Signed as free agent by Ottawa Senators (November 10, 2000). ... Claimed off waivers by Boston Bruins (October 13, 2001). ... Signed as free agent by Florida Panthers (December 16, 2002). ... Signed as free agent by Detroit Red Wings (July 29, 2003). ... Groin (October 9, 2005); missed two games. ... Traded by Red Wings to Phoenix Coyotes for seventh-round pick in 2006 (March 9, 2006). ... Foot (March 25, 2006); missed two games.

		REGULAR SEASON								PLAYOFFS				
Season Team	League	GP	G	A	Pts.	PIM	+/-	PP	SH	GP	G	A	Pts.	PIM
90-91—Ottawa	OHA Jr. A	55	4	30	34	74	...	...	...	—	—	—	—	—
91-92—Sudbury	OHL	55	3	13	16	20	...	...	...	8	0	0	0	0
92-93—Sudbury	OHL	62	12	43	55	20	...	...	...	14	7	19	26	4
93-94—Sudbury	OHL	65	32	89	121	58	...	22	1	10	1	9	10	14
94-95—Sudbury	OHL	46	9	56	65	30	...	6	0	18	7	26	33	22
95-96—St. Louis	NHL	3	0	0	0	2	-1	0	0	—	—	—	—	—
—Worcester	AHL	75	7	45	52	130	...	...	...	4	0	1	1	4
96-97—Worcester	AHL	63	8	35	43	83	-4	5	0	5	1	2	3	14
—St. Louis	NHL	15	2	5	7	6	-4	1	0	—	—	—	—	—

Season Team	League	GP	G	A	Pts.	PIM	+/-	PP	SH	GP	G	A	Pts.	PIM
		REGULAR SEASON								PLAYOFFS				
97-98—St. Louis	NHL	59	2	4	6	36	5	1	0	—	—	—	—	—
98-99—St. Louis	NHL	76	2	5	7	47	-3	1	0	9	1	1	2	2
99-00—New York Islanders	NHL	75	1	16	17	84	-4	1	0	—	—	—	—	—
00-01—Grand Rapids	IHL	2	0	0	0	2	...	...	...	—	—	—	—	—
—Ottawa	NHL	45	2	4	6	44	6	0	0	1	0	0	0	4
01-02—Ottawa	NHL	2	0	0	0	4	-3	0	0	—	—	—	—	—
—Boston	NHL	64	4	2	6	45	6	1	0	3	0	0	0	0
02-03—Florida	NHL	1	0	0	0	2	-2	0	0	—	—	—	—	—
—San Antonio	AHL	50	6	19	25	68	3	4	0	3	0	1	1	10
03-04—Grand Rapids	AHL	2	0	0	0	4	-1	0	0	—	—	—	—	—
—Detroit	NHL	50	3	4	7	41	9	0	0	2	0	0	0	2
04-05—Hershey	AHL	50	7	13	20	46	-13	5	0	—	—	—	—	—
05-06—Detroit	NHL	15	0	1	1	12	0	0	0	—	—	—	—	—
—Phoenix	NHL	18	0	5	5	26	2	0	0	—	—	—	—	—
NHL Totals (10 years)		423	16	46	62	349	11	5	0	15	1	1	2	8

RIVET, CRAIG D

PERSONAL: Born September 13, 1974, in North Bay, Ont. ... 6-3/201. ... Shoots right. ... Name pronounced REE-vay.
TRANSACTIONS/CAREER NOTES: Selected by Montreal Canadiens in third round (fourth Canadiens pick, 68th overall) of NHL draft (June 20, 1992). ... Separated shoulder (January 20, 1997); missed six games. ... Bruised back (November 1, 1997); missed one game. ... Had concussion (December 19, 1997); missed seven games. ... Sprained shoulder (November 9, 1998); missed five games. ... Back spasms and flu (January 18, 1999); missed three games. ... Strained groin (March 13, 1999); missed three games. ... Reinjured groin (March 24, 1999); missed five games. ... Fractured cheekbone (October 8, 1999); missed nine games. ... Flu (November 3, 1999); missed four games. ... Strained groin (January 4, 2000); missed eight games. ... Injured shoulder (November 29, 2000); missed five games. ... Reinjured shoulder (December 15, 2000) and had surgery; missed remainder of season. ... Injured ankle (February 5, 2004); missed two games.

Season Team	League	GP	G	A	Pts.	PIM	+/-	PP	SH	GP	G	A	Pts.	PIM
		REGULAR SEASON								PLAYOFFS				
90-91—Barrie Jr. B	OHA	42	9	17	26	55	...	...	...	—	—	—	—	—
91-92—Kingston	OHL	66	5	21	26	97	...	...	...	—	—	—	—	—
92-93—Kingston	OHL	64	19	55	74	117	...	...	...	16	5	7	12	39
93-94—Fredericton	AHL	4	0	2	2	2	-2	0	0	—	—	—	—	—
—Kingston	OHL	61	12	52	64	100	...	5	0	6	0	3	3	6
94-95—Fredericton	AHL	78	5	27	32	126	-5	1	0	12	0	4	4	17
—Montreal	NHL	5	0	1	1	5	2	0	0	—	—	—	—	—
95-96—Fredericton	AHL	49	5	18	23	189	...	...	...	6	0	0	0	12
—Montreal	NHL	19	1	4	5	54	4	0	0	—	—	—	—	—
96-97—Montreal	NHL	35	0	4	4	54	7	0	0	5	0	1	1	14
—Fredericton	AHL	23	3	12	15	99	6	1	0	—	—	—	—	—
97-98—Montreal	NHL	61	0	2	2	93	-3	0	0	5	0	0	0	2
98-99—Montreal	NHL	66	2	8	10	66	-3	0	0	—	—	—	—	—
99-00—Montreal	NHL	61	3	14	17	76	11	0	0	—	—	—	—	—
00-01—Montreal	NHL	26	1	2	3	36	-8	0	0	—	—	—	—	—
01-02—Montreal	NHL	82	8	17	25	76	1	0	0	12	0	3	3	4
02-03—Montreal	NHL	82	7	15	22	71	1	3	0	—	—	—	—	—
03-04—Montreal	NHL	80	4	8	12	98	-1	2	0	11	1	4	5	2
04-05—TPS Turku	Finland	18	3	1	4	28	3	...	...	6	0	0	0	39
05-06—Montreal	NHL	82	7	27	34	109	-5	5	0	6	0	2	2	2
NHL Totals (11 years)		599	33	102	135	738	6	10	0	39	1	10	11	24

ROACH, ANDY D

PERSONAL: Born August 22, 1973, in Mattawan, Mich. ... 5-11/185. ... Shoots left.
TRANSACTIONS/CAREER NOTES: Signed as free agent by St. Louis Blues (June 30, 2004).

Season Team	League	GP	G	A	Pts.	PIM	+/-	PP	SH	GP	G	A	Pts.	PIM
		REGULAR SEASON								PLAYOFFS				
93-94—Ferris State	CCHA	32	4	15	19	18	...	...	...	—	—	—	—	—
94-95—Ferris State	CCHA	36	11	19	30	26	...	...	...	—	—	—	—	—
95-96—Ferris State	CCHA	33	15	19	34	26	...	...	...	—	—	—	—	—
96-97—Ferris State	CCHA	37	12	34	46	18	...	...	...	—	—	—	—	—
97-98—San Antonio	IHL	67	8	16	24	30	-22	3	0	—	—	—	—	—
98-99—Long Beach	IHL	41	5	21	26	34	-9	2	1	—	—	—	—	—
—Utah	IHL	44	7	10	17	18	-17	4	0	—	—	—	—	—
99-00—Krefeld Pinguine	Germany	55	19	22	41	40	...	...	...	4	0	0	0	2
00-01—Mannheim	Germany	59	7	13	20	32	...	...	...	12	2	2	4	6
01-02—Mannheim	Germany	60	9	21	30	16	...	...	...	12	1	5	6	8
02-03—Mannheim	Germany	49	18	16	34	16	...	...	...	8	4	5	9	4
03-04—Mannheim	Germany	46	11	21	32	26	...	...	...	6	2	0	2	6
04-05—Lausanne HC	Switzerland	14	4	5	9	20	...	...	...	7	2	3	5	2
05-06—Peoria	AHL	10	2	3	5	6	-6	2	0	—	—	—	—	—
—St. Louis	NHL	5	1	2	3	10	0	1	0	—	—	—	—	—
NHL Totals (1 year)		5	1	2	3	10	0	1	0					

ROBERTS, GARY LW

PERSONAL: Born May 23, 1966, in North York, Ont. ... 6-2/215. ... Shoots left.
TRANSACTIONS/CAREER NOTES: Selected by Calgary Flames in first round (first Flames pick, 12th overall) of entry draft (June 9, 1984). ...

Injured back (January 1989). ... Whiplash (November 9, 1991); missed one game. ... Flu (January 19, 1993); missed one game. ... Left quadricep hematoma (February 16, 1993); missed 25 games. ... Suspended one game for high-sticking (November 19, 1993). ... Suspended four games and fined $500 for two slashing incidents and fined $500 for high-sticking (January 7, 1994). ... Fractured thumb (March 20, 1994); missed one game. ... Fractured thumb (April 3, 1994); missed last five games of season. ... Neck and spinal injury (February 4, 1995); had surgery and missed last 40 games of 1994-95 season and first 42 games of 1995-96 season. ... Injured neck (April 3, 1996); missed five games. ... Retired (June 17, 1996); did not play during 1996-97 season. ... Traded by Flames with G Trevor Kidd to Carolina Hurricanes for G Jean-Sebastien Giguere and C Andrew Cassels (August 25, 1997). ... Strained abdominal muscle (November 12, 1997); missed six games. ... Strained rib muscle (January 11, 1998); missed 10 games. ... Flu (March 31, 1998); missed one game. ... Injured groin (April 13, 1998); missed final three games of season. ... Sprained wrist (December 2, 1998); missed four games. ... Strained neck (April 14, 1999); missed one game. ... Strained shoulder (October 7, 1999); missed one game. ... Injured groin (October 23, 1999); missed four games. ... Flu (January 18, 2000); missed one game. ... Injured groin (February 12, 2000); missed seven games. ... Signed as free agent by Toronto Maple Leafs (July 4, 2000). ... Suffered injury (January 11, 2002); missed one game. ... Back spasms (January 24, 2002); missed two games. ... Strained rib muscle (March 25, 2002); missed final 10 games of season. ... Injured shoulder (October 10, 2002) and had surgery; missed 57 games. ... Injured groin (March 13, 2003); missed 11 games. ... Strained muscle (December 2, 2003); missed two games. ... Strained groin (February 16, 2004); missed eight games. ... Signed by Panthers as free agent (August 1, 2005). ... Groin injury (October 13, 2005); missed five games. ... Knee sprain (January 19, 2006); missed 19 games.

STATISTICAL PLATEAUS: Three-goal games: 1989-90 (1), 1991-92 (2), 1992-93 (2), 1993-94 (1), 1995-96 (3), 1997-98 (1), 2001-02 (1). Total: 11. ... Four-goal games: 1993-94 (1). ... Total hat tricks: 12.

		REGULAR SEASON								PLAYOFFS				
Season Team	**League**	**GP**	**G**	**A**	**Pts.**	**PIM**	**+/-**	**PP**	**SH**	**GP**	**G**	**A**	**Pts.**	**PIM**
82-83—Ottawa	OHL	53	12	8	20	83	...	...	...	5	1	0	1	19
83-84—Ottawa	OHL	48	27	30	57	144	...	...	...	13	10	7	17	62
84-85—Ottawa	OHL	59	44	62	106	186	...	...	...	5	2	8	10	10
—Moncton	AHL	7	4	2	6	7	...	...	...	—	—	—	—	—
85-86—Ottawa	OHL	24	26	25	51	83	...	...	...	—	—	—	—	—
—Guelph	OHL	23	18	15	33	65	...	...	...	20	18	13	31	43
86-87—Moncton	AHL	38	20	18	38	72	...	...	...	—	—	—	—	—
—Calgary	NHL	32	5	10	15	85	6	0	0	2	0	0	0	4
87-88—Calgary	NHL	74	13	15	28	282	24	0	0	9	2	3	5	29
88-89—Calgary	NHL	71	22	16	38	250	32	0	1	22	5	7	12	57
89-90—Calgary	NHL	78	39	33	72	222	31	5	0	6	2	5	7	41
90-91—Calgary	NHL	80	22	31	53	252	15	0	0	7	1	3	4	18
91-92—Calgary	NHL	76	53	37	90	207	32	15	0	—	—	—	—	—
92-93—Calgary	NHL	58	38	41	79	172	32	8	3	5	1	6	7	43
93-94—Calgary	NHL	73	41	43	84	145	37	12	3	7	2	6	8	24
94-95—Calgary	NHL	8	2	2	4	43	1	2	0	—	—	—	—	—
95-96—Calgary	NHL	35	22	20	42	78	15	9	0	—	—	—	—	—
96-97—Calgary	NHL	Did not play												
97-98—Carolina	NHL	61	20	29	49	103	3	4	0	—	—	—	—	—
98-99—Carolina	NHL	77	14	28	42	178	2	1	1	6	1	1	2	8
99-00—Carolina	NHL	69	23	30	53	62	-10	12	0	—	—	—	—	—
00-01—Toronto	NHL	82	29	24	53	109	16	8	2	11	2	9	11	0
01-02—Toronto	NHL	69	21	27	48	63	-4	6	2	19	7	12	19	*56
02-03—Toronto	NHL	14	5	3	8	10	-2	3	0	7	1	1	2	8
03-04—Toronto	NHL	72	28	20	48	84	9	11	1	13	4	4	8	10
05-06—Florida	NHL	58	14	26	40	51	4	4	0	—	—	—	—	—
NHL Totals (19 years)		1087	411	435	846	2396	243	100	13	114	28	57	85	298

ROBIDAS, STEPHANE D

PERSONAL: Born March 3, 1977, in Sherbrooke, Que. ... 5-11/189. ... Shoots right. ... Name pronounced ROE-bee-daw.

TRANSACTIONS/CAREER NOTES: Selected by Montreal Canadiens in seventh round (seventh Canadiens pick, 164th overall) of NHL draft (June 26, 1995). ... Bruised shoulder (December 16, 2000); missed two games. ... Claimed by Atlanta Thrashers in waiver draft (October 4, 2002). ... Traded by Thrashers to Dallas Stars for future considerations (October 4, 2002). ... Traded by Stars with second-round pick (C Jakub Sindel) in 2004 to Chicago Blackhawks for D Jon Klemm and fourth-round pick (RW Fredrik Naslund) in 2004 (November 17, 2003). ... Fractured left cheekbone (February 29, 2004); missed remainder of season. ... Signed by Stars as free agent (August 5, 2005).

		REGULAR SEASON								PLAYOFFS				
Season Team	**League**	**GP**	**G**	**A**	**Pts.**	**PIM**	**+/-**	**PP**	**SH**	**GP**	**G**	**A**	**Pts.**	**PIM**
93-94—Shawinigan	QMJHL	67	3	18	21	33	...	...	...	1	0	0	0	0
94-95—Shawinigan	QMJHL	71	13	56	69	44	...	...	...	15	7	12	19	4
95-96—Shawinigan	QMJHL	67	23	56	79	53	...	...	...	6	1	5	6	10
96-97—Shawinigan	QMJHL	67	24	51	75	59	...	...	...	7	4	6	10	14
97-98—Fredericton	AHL	79	10	21	31	50	0	6	0	4	0	2	2	0
98-99—Fredericton	AHL	79	8	33	41	59	20	2	1	15	1	5	6	10
99-00—Quebec	AHL	76	14	31	45	36	...	...	...	3	0	1	1	0
—Montreal	NHL	1	0	0	0	0	0	0	0	—	—	—	—	—
00-01—Montreal	NHL	65	6	6	12	14	0	1	0	—	—	—	—	—
01-02—Montreal	NHL	56	1	10	11	14	-25	1	0	2	0	0	0	4
02-03—Dallas	NHL	76	3	7	10	35	15	0	0	12	0	1	1	20
03-04—Dallas	NHL	14	1	0	1	8	-2	1	0	—	—	—	—	—
—Chicago	NHL	45	2	10	12	33	6	0	1	—	—	—	—	—
04-05—Frankfurt	Germany	51	15	32	47	64	14	12	0	6	1	2	3	6
05-06—Dallas	NHL	75	5	15	20	67	15	1	1	5	0	2	2	4
NHL Totals (6 years)		332	18	48	66	171	9	4	2	19	0	3	3	28

ROBINSON, NATHAN LW

PERSONAL: Born December 31, 1981, in Scarborough, Ont. ... 5-9/180. ... Shoots left.

TRANSACTIONS/CAREER NOTES: Signed by Detroit Red Wings as free agent (October 12, 2002). ... Signed as free agent by Boston Bruins (August 15, 2005).

Season Team	League	REGULAR SEASON								PLAYOFFS				
		GP	G	A	Pts.	PIM	+/-	PP	SH	GP	G	A	Pts.	PIM
98-99—Belleville	OHL	50	11	8	19	23	...	...	...	21	4	4	8	14
99-00—Belleville	OHL	61	19	18	37	45	...	...	...	15	3	4	7	10
00-01—Belleville	OHL	66	32	37	69	57	...	...	...	10	6	10	16	7
01-02—Belleville	OHL	67	47	63	110	74	...	...	...	11	8	6	14	10
02-03—Toledo	ECHL	9	5	9	14	29	...	...	...	—	—	—	—	—
—Grand Rapids	AHL	53	3	14	17	24	...	...	...	8	0	3	3	0
03-04—Detroit	NHL	5	0	0	0	2	-1	0	0	—	—	—	—	—
—Grand Rapids	AHL	69	24	26	50	41	8	11	2	3	0	0	0	2
04-05—Grand Rapids	AHL	50	8	16	24	10	-5	3	0	—	—	—	—	—
—Syracuse	AHL	19	6	14	20	18	9	1	0	—	—	—	—	—
05-06—Providence	AHL	70	29	31	60	55	6	7	1	6	4	5	9	2
—Boston	NHL	2	0	0	0	0	0	0	0	—	—	—	—	—
NHL Totals (2 years)		7	0	0	0	2	-1	0	0					

ROBITAILLE, LOUIS D

PERSONAL: Born March 16, 1982, in Montreal. ... 6-1/192. ... Shoots left. ... Name pronounced: ROH-bih-tigh
TRANSACTIONS/CAREER NOTES: Signed as nondrafted free agent by Washington Capitals (October 28, 2003).

Season Team	League	REGULAR SEASON								PLAYOFFS				
		GP	G	A	Pts.	PIM	+/-	PP	SH	GP	G	A	Pts.	PIM
99-00—Montreal	QMJHL	71	3	21	24	266	...	...	...	5	1	1	2	18
00-01—Montreal	QMJHL	69	2	10	12	269	...	...	...	—	—	—	—	—
01-02—Montreal	QMJHL	71	3	28	31	294	...	...	...	7	3	0	3	41
02-03—Montreal	QMJHL	60	7	23	30	191	...	...	...	7	0	10	10	12
03-04—Quad City	UHL	2	0	1	1	10	...	...	...	—	—	—	—	—
—Portland	AHL	58	1	5	6	103	...	...	...	5	1	0	1	17
04-05—Portland	AHL	59	2	3	5	186	-17	0	0	—	—	—	—	—
05-06—Hershey	AHL	65	7	12	19	334	2	1	0	14	0	1	1	45
—Washington	NHL	2	0	0	0	5	-1	0	0	—	—	—	—	—
NHL Totals (1 year)		2	0	0	0	5	-1	0	0					

ROBITAILLE, LUC LW

PERSONAL: Born February 17, 1966, in Montreal. ... 6-1/215. ... Shoots left. ... Name pronounced ROH-bih-tigh. ... Nickname: Lucky.
TRANSACTIONS/CAREER NOTES: Selected by Los Angeles Kings in ninth round (ninth Kings pick, 171st overall) of entry draft (June 9, 1984). ... Suspended four games in cross-checking incident (November 10, 1990). ... Right ankle surgery (June 15, 1994). ... Traded by Kings to Pittsburgh Penguins for RW Rick Tocchet and second-round pick (RW Pavel Rosa) in 1995 (July 29, 1994). ... Suspended for two games in high-sticking (February 7, 1995). ... Traded by Penguins with D Ulf Samuelsson to New York Rangers for D Sergei Zubov and C Petr Nedved (August 31, 1995). ... Stress fracture in ankle (December 15, 1995); missed five games. ... Fractured foot (March 12, 1997); missed regular season's final 13 games. ... Traded by Rangers to Kings for LW Kevin Stevens (August 28, 1997). ... Right groin and abdomen (February 25, 1998); had surgery; missed season's final 25 games. ... Fractured foot (November 3, 1999); missed 10 games. ... Signed as free agent by Detroit Red Wings (July 2, 2001). ... Signed as free agent by Kings (July 24, 2003). ... Groin (October 16, 2005); missed one game. ... Fractured leg (November 1, 2005); missed nine games. ... Announced retirement (April 10, 2006).
STATISTICAL PLATEAUS: Three-goal games: 1986-87 (1), 1987-88 (3), 1988-89 (1), 1989-90 (2), 1992-93 (2), 1998-99 (1), 1999-00 (1). Total: 11. ... Four-goal games: 1991-92 (1), 1993-94 (1), 1994-95 (1). Total: 3. ... Total hat tricks: 14.

Season Team	League	REGULAR SEASON								PLAYOFFS				
		GP	G	A	Pts.	PIM	+/-	PP	SH	GP	G	A	Pts.	PIM
83-84—Hull	QMJHL	70	32	53	85	48	...	...	...	—	—	—	—	—
84-85—Hull	QMJHL	64	55	94	149	115	...	...	...	5	4	2	6	27
85-86—Hull	QMJHL	63	68	123	191	93	...	...	...	15	17	27	44	28
86-87—Los Angeles	NHL	79	45	39	84	28	-18	18	0	5	1	4	5	2
87-88—Los Angeles	NHL	80	53	58	111	82	-9	17	0	5	2	5	7	18
88-89—Los Angeles	NHL	78	46	52	98	65	5	10	0	11	2	6	8	10
89-90—Los Angeles	NHL	80	52	49	101	38	8	20	0	10	5	5	10	12
90-91—Los Angeles	NHL	76	45	46	91	68	28	11	0	12	12	4	16	22
91-92—Los Angeles	NHL	80	44	63	107	95	-4	26	0	6	3	4	7	12
92-93—Los Angeles	NHL	84	63	62	125	100	18	24	2	24	9	13	22	28
93-94—Los Angeles	NHL	83	44	42	86	86	-20	24	0	—	—	—	—	—
94-95—Pittsburgh	NHL	46	23	19	42	37	10	5	0	12	7	4	11	26
95-96—New York Rangers	NHL	77	23	46	69	80	13	11	0	11	1	5	6	8
96-97—New York Rangers	NHL	69	24	24	48	48	16	5	0	15	4	7	11	4
97-98—Los Angeles	NHL	57	16	24	40	66	5	5	0	4	1	2	3	6
98-99—Los Angeles	NHL	82	39	35	74	54	-1	11	0	—	—	—	—	—
99-00—Los Angeles	NHL	71	36	38	74	68	11	13	0	4	2	2	4	6
00-01—Los Angeles	NHL	82	37	51	88	66	10	16	1	13	4	3	7	10
01-02—Detroit	NHL	81	30	20	50	38	-2	13	0	23	4	5	9	10
02-03—Detroit	NHL	81	11	20	31	50	4	3	0	4	1	0	1	0
03-04—Los Angeles	NHL	80	22	29	51	56	4	12	0	—	—	—	—	—
05-06—Los Angeles	NHL	65	15	9	24	52	-6	3	0	—	—	—	—	—
NHL Totals (19 years)		1431	668	726	1394	1177	72	247	3	159	58	69	127	174

ROBITAILLE, RANDY C/LW

PERSONAL: Born October 12, 1975, in Ottawa. ... 5-11/200. ... Shoots left. ... Name pronounced ROH-bih-tigh.
TRANSACTIONS/CAREER NOTES: Signed as free agent by Boston Bruins (March 27, 1997). ... Shoulder (March 27, 1997); missed remainder of season. ... Traded by Bruins to Atlanta Thrashers for RW Peter Ferraro (June 25, 1999). ... Traded by Thrashers to Nashville Predators

for LW Denny Lambert (August 16, 1999). ... Signed as free agent by Los Angeles Kings (July 6, 2001). ... Shoulder (December 3, 2001); missed 12 games. ... Claimed off waivers by Pittsburgh Penguins (January 4, 2002). ... Fractured foot (October 22, 2002); missed 10 games. ... Traded by Penguins to New York Islanders for fifth-round pick (RW Yevgeny Isakov) in 2003 (March 9, 2003). ... Signed as free agent by Thrashers (August 12, 2003). ... Knee (January 24, 2004); missed seven games. ... Signed as free agent by Predators (August 19, 2005). ... Claimed off waivers by Minnesota Wild (October 4, 2005). ... Flu (February 7, 2006); missed one game. ... Broken toe (February 12, 2006); missed one game. ... Knee (April 2, 2006); missed season's final eight games. ... Signed as free agent by Philadelphia Flyers (July 4, 2006).

		REGULAR SEASON								PLAYOFFS				
Season Team	**League**	**GP**	**G**	**A**	**Pts.**	**PIM**	**+/-**	**PP**	**SH**	**GP**	**G**	**A**	**Pts.**	**PIM**
94-95—Ottawa	CJHL	54	48	77	125	111	...	...	...	—	—	—	—	—
95-96—Miami (Ohio)	CCHA	36	14	31	45	26	...	...	...	—	—	—	—	—
96-97—Miami (Ohio)	CCHA	39	27	34	61	44	18	5	7	—	—	—	—	—
—Boston	NHL	1	0	0	0	0	0	0	0	—	—	—	—	—
97-98—Providence	AHL	48	15	29	44	16	-12	4	2	—	—	—	—	—
—Boston	NHL	4	0	0	0	0	-2	0	0	—	—	—	—	—
98-99—Providence	AHL	74	28	74	102	34	15	7	2	19	6	14	20	20
—Boston	NHL	4	0	2	2	0	-1	0	0	1	0	0	0	0
99-00—Nashville	NHL	69	11	14	25	10	-13	2	0	—	—	—	—	—
00-01—Milwaukee	IHL	19	10	23	33	4	...	...	...	—	—	—	—	—
—Nashville	NHL	62	9	17	26	12	-11	5	0	—	—	—	—	—
01-02—Los Angeles	NHL	18	4	3	7	17	-9	2	0	—	—	—	—	—
—Manchester	AHL	6	7	3	10	0	1	2	0	—	—	—	—	—
—Pittsburgh	NHL	40	10	20	30	16	-14	3	0	—	—	—	—	—
02-03—Pittsburgh	NHL	41	5	12	17	8	5	1	0	—	—	—	—	—
—New York Islanders	NHL	10	1	2	3	2	0	1	0	5	1	1	2	0
03-04—Atlanta	NHL	69	11	26	37	20	-12	5	0	—	—	—	—	—
04-05—ZSC Lions Zurich	Switzerland	36	22	45	67	56	...	10	1	15	2	17	19	10
05-06—Minnesota	NHL	67	12	28	40	54	-5	7	0	—	—	—	—	—
NHL Totals (9 years)		385	63	124	187	139	-62	26	0	6	1	1	2	0

ROENICK, JEREMY C

PERSONAL: Born January 17, 1970, in Boston. ... 6-1/196. ... Shoots right. ... Brother of Trevor Roenick, center with Hartford Whalers/Carolina Hurricanes organization (1993-94 through 1996-97). ... Name pronounced ROH-nihk.

TRANSACTIONS/CAREER NOTES: Selected by Chicago Blackhawks in first round (first Blackhawks pick, eighth overall) of entry draft (June 11, 1988). ... Knee (January 9, 1989); missed one month. ... Knee (April 2, 1995); missed remainder of regular season and first eight games of playoffs. ... Thigh (March 4, 1996); missed three games. ... Ankle (March 17, 1996); missed 12 games. ... Traded by Blackhawks to Phoenix Coyotes for C Alexei Zhamnov, RW Craig Mills and first-round pick (RW Ty Jones) in 1997 (August 16, 1996). ... Missed first four games of 1996-97 season in contract dispute. ... Knee (November 23, 1996); missed six games. ... Mild concussion (December 5, 1997); missed one game. ... Concussion (December 28, 1998); missed two games. ... Fractured jaw (April 14, 1999); missed final two games of regular season and six playoff games. ... Suspended five games for slashing incident (October 11, 1999). ... Injured (March 3, 2000); missed one game. ... Concussion (November 14, 2000); missed one game. ... Signed as free agent by Philadelphia Flyers (July 2, 2001). ... Right knee (March 18, 2002); missed seven games. ... Suspended two games for checking from behind (December 18, 2002). ... Suspended one game for misconduct incident involving a referee (January 13, 2004). ... Fractured jaw, concussion (February 12, 2004); missed 19 games. ... Traded by Flyers with third-round pick (C/RW Bud Holloway) in 2006 draft to Los Angeles Kings for future considerations (August 4, 2005). ... Concussion (September 25, 2005); missed remainder of preseason. ... Groin (October 23, 2005); missed one game. ... Pneumonia (December 1, 2005); missed two games. ... Fractured left ring finger (December 19, 2005), had surgery (December 22, 2005); missed 20 games. ... Fractured right ankle (March 25, 2006); missed one game. ... Signed as free agent by Phoenix Coyotes (July 4, 2006).

STATISTICAL PLATEAUS: Three-goal games: 1989-90 (1), 1990-91 (2), 1992-93 (1), 1999-00 (2), 2000-01 (1). Total: 7. ... Four-goal games: 1991-92 (1), 1993-94 (1). Total: 2. ... Total hat tricks: 9.

		REGULAR SEASON								PLAYOFFS				
Season Team	**League**	**GP**	**G**	**A**	**Pts.**	**PIM**	**+/-**	**PP**	**SH**	**GP**	**G**	**A**	**Pts.**	**PIM**
86-87—Thayer Academy	Mass. H.S.	24	31	34	65	...	...	...	...	—	—	—	—	—
87-88—Thayer Academy	Mass. H.S.	24	34	50	84	...	...	...	...	—	—	—	—	—
88-89—U.S. national team	Int'l	11	8	8	16	0	...	...	...	—	—	—	—	—
—Chicago	NHL	20	9	9	18	4	4	2	0	10	1	3	4	7
—Hull	QMJHL	28	34	36	70	14	...	...	...	—	—	—	—	—
89-90—Chicago	NHL	78	26	40	66	54	2	6	0	20	11	7	18	8
90-91—Chicago	NHL	79	41	53	94	80	38	15	4	6	3	5	8	4
91-92—Chicago	NHL	80	53	50	103	98	23	22	3	18	12	10	22	12
92-93—Chicago	NHL	84	50	57	107	86	15	22	3	4	1	2	3	2
93-94—Chicago	NHL	84	46	61	107	125	21	24	5	6	1	6	7	2
94-95—Koln	Germany	3	3	1	4	2	...	...	...	—	—	—	—	—
—Chicago	NHL	33	10	24	34	14	5	5	0	8	1	2	3	16
95-96—Chicago	NHL	66	32	35	67	109	9	12	4	10	5	7	12	2
96-97—Phoenix	NHL	72	29	40	69	115	-7	10	3	6	2	4	6	4
97-98—Phoenix	NHL	79	24	32	56	103	5	6	1	6	5	3	8	4
—U.S. Olympic team	Int'l	4	0	1	1	6	-1	0	0	—	—	—	—	—
98-99—Phoenix	NHL	78	24	48	72	130	7	4	0	1	0	0	0	0
99-00—Phoenix	NHL	75	34	44	78	102	11	6	3	5	2	2	4	10
00-01—Phoenix	NHL	80	30	46	76	114	-1	13	0	—	—	—	—	—
01-02—Philadelphia	NHL	75	21	46	67	74	32	5	0	5	0	0	0	14
—U.S. Olympic team	Int'l	6	1	4	5	2	...	...	...	—	—	—	—	—
02-03—Philadelphia	NHL	79	27	32	59	75	20	8	1	13	3	5	8	8
03-04—Philadelphia	NHL	62	19	28	47	62	1	10	1	18	4	9	13	8
05-06—Los Angeles	NHL	58	9	13	22	36	-5	2	0	—	—	—	—	—
NHL Totals (17 years)		1182	484	658	1142	1381	180	172	28	136	51	65	116	101

ROLOSON, DWAYNE G

PERSONAL: Born October 12, 1969, in Simcoe, Ont. ... 6-1/178. ... Catches left. ... Name pronounced ROH-luh-suhn.

TRANSACTIONS/CAREER NOTES: Signed as free agent by Calgary Flames (July 4, 1994). ... Signed as free agent by Buffalo Sabres (July 9,

1998). ... Selected by Columbus Blue Jackets in expansion draft (June 23, 2000). ... Signed as free agent by St. Louis Blues (July 14, 2000). ... Signed as free agent by Minnesota Wild (July 2, 2001). ... Ankle (February 12, 2003); missed two games. ... Left team for personal reasons (February 25, 2004); missed two games. ... Traded by Wild to Edmonton Oilers for first-round pick (traded to L.A.; Kings selected C Trevor Lewis) and a conditional pick in 2006 (March 8, 2006). ... Injured knee, elbow (June 5, 2006); missed remainder of playoffs.

		REGULAR SEASON										PLAYOFFS							
Season Team	League	GP	Min.	W	L	OTL	T	GA	SO	GAA	SV%	GP	Min.	W	L	GA	SO	GAA	SV%
90-91—Mass.-Lowell	Hockey East	15	823	5	9	...	0	63	0	4.59	...	—	—	—	—	—	—	—	—
91-92—Mass.-Lowell	Hockey East	12	660	3	8	...	0	52	0	4.73	...	—	—	—	—	—	—	—	—
92-93—Mass.-Lowell	Hockey East	39	2342	20	17	...	2	150	0	3.84	...	—	—	—	—	—	—	—	—
93-94—Mass.-Lowell	Hockey East	40	2305	23	10	...	7	106	0	2.76	...	—	—	—	—	—	—	—	—
94-95—Saint John	AHL	46	2734	16	21	...	8	156	1	3.42	.900	5	299	1	4	13	0	2.61	.897
95-96—Saint John	AHL	67	4026	33	22	...	11	190	1	2.83	...	16	1027	10	6	49	1	2.86	...
96-97—Calgary	NHL	31	1618	9	14	...	3	78	1	2.89	.897	—	—	—	—	—	—	—	—
—Saint John	AHL	8	481	6	2	...	0	22	1	2.74	.910	—	—	—	—	—	—	—	—
97-98—Saint John	AHL	4	245	3	0	...	1	8	0	1.96	.939	—	—	—	—	—	—	—	—
—Calgary	NHL	39	2205	11	16	...	8	110	0	2.99	.890	—	—	—	—	—	—	—	—
98-99—Buffalo	NHL	18	911	6	8	...	2	42	1	2.77	.909	4	139	1	1	10	0	4.32	.851
—Rochester	AHL	2	120	2	0	...	0	4	0	2.00	.922	—	—	—	—	—	—	—	—
99-00—Buffalo	NHL	14	677	1	7	...	3	32	0	2.84	.884	—	—	—	—	—	—	—	—
00-01—Worcester	AHL	52	3127	32	15	...	5	113	6	2.17	.929	11	697	6	5	23	1	1.98	...
01-02—Minnesota	NHL	45	2506	14	20	...	7	112	5	2.68	.901	—	—	—	—	—	—	—	—
02-03—Minnesota	NHL	50	2945	23	16	...	8	98	4	2.00	.927	11	579	5	6	25	0	2.59	.903
03-04—Minnesota	NHL	48	2847	19	18	...	11	89	5	1.88	†.933	—	—	—	—	—	—	—	—
04-05—Lukko Rauma	Finland	34	2049	20	10	...	4	70	4	2.05	.931	9	512	4	5	18	2	2.11	.941
05-06—Minnesota	NHL	24	1361	6	17	1	...	68	1	3.00	.910	—	—	—	—	—	—	—	—
—Edmonton	NHL	19	1163	8	7	4	...	47	1	2.42	.905	18	1160	12	5	45	1	2.33	.927
NHL Totals (8 years)		288	16233	97	123	5	42	676	18	2.50	.910	33	1878	18	12	80	1	2.56	.915

ROLSTON, BRIAN — LW

PERSONAL: Born February 21, 1973, in Flint, Mich. ... 6-2/210. ... Shoots left.

TRANSACTIONS/CAREER NOTES: Selected by New Jersey Devils in first round (second Devils pick, 11th overall) of entry draft (June 22, 1991). ... Loaned by Devils to U.S. Olympic Team (November 2, 1993). ... Fractured foot (October 17, 1995); missed 11 games. ... Hamstring (January 12, 1998); missed one game. ... Flu (January 28, 1998); missed one game. ... Traded by Devils with first-round pick in 2000 (later traded to Boston; Bruins selected RW Martin Samuelsson) to Colorado Avalanche for RW Claude Lemieux and first-round (D David Hale) and second-round pick (D Matt DeMarchi) in 2000 (November 3, 1999). ... Ankle (January 27, 2000); missed three games. ... Traded by Avalanche with D Martin Grenier, C Samuel Pahlsson and first-round pick (LW Martin Samuelsson) in 2000 to Boston Bruins for D Ray Bourque and LW Dave Andreychuk (March 6, 2000). ... Ribs (October 28, 2000); missed five games. ... Headaches (March 8, 2003); missed one game. ... Signed as free agent by Minnesota Wild (July 8, 2004).

STATISTICAL PLATEAUS: Three-goal games: 1996-97 (1).

		REGULAR SEASON								PLAYOFFS				
Season Team	League	GP	G	A	Pts.	PIM	+/-	PP	SH	GP	G	A	Pts.	PIM
89-90—Detroit	NAJHL	40	36	37	73	57	...	...	...	—	—	—	—	—
90-91—Detroit	NAJHL	36	49	46	95	14	...	...	...	—	—	—	—	—
91-92—Lake Superior St.	CCHA	41	18	28	46	16	...	...	...	—	—	—	—	—
92-93—Lake Superior St.	CCHA	39	33	31	64	20	...	...	...	—	—	—	—	—
—U.S. Jr. national team	Int'l	7	6	2	8	2	...	...	...	—	—	—	—	—
93-94—U.S. national team	Int'l	41	20	28	48	36	...	4	2	—	—	—	—	—
—U.S. Olympic team	Int'l	8	7	0	7	8	1	2	0	—	—	—	—	—
—Albany	AHL	17	5	5	10	8	-3	0	0	5	1	2	3	0
94-95—Albany	AHL	18	9	11	20	10	-3	3	0	—	—	—	—	—
—New Jersey	NHL	40	7	11	18	17	5	2	0	6	2	1	3	4
95-96—New Jersey	NHL	58	13	11	24	8	9	3	1	—	—	—	—	—
96-97—New Jersey	NHL	81	18	27	45	20	6	2	2	10	4	1	5	6
97-98—New Jersey	NHL	76	16	14	30	16	7	0	2	6	1	0	1	2
98-99—New Jersey	NHL	82	24	33	57	14	11	5	†5	7	1	0	1	2
99-00—New Jersey	NHL	11	3	1	4	0	-2	1	0	—	—	—	—	—
—Colorado	NHL	50	8	10	18	12	-6	1	0	—	—	—	—	—
—Boston	NHL	16	5	4	9	6	-4	3	0	—	—	—	—	—
00-01—Boston	NHL	77	19	39	58	28	6	5	0	—	—	—	—	—
01-02—Boston	NHL	82	31	31	62	30	11	6	*9	6	4	1	5	0
—U.S. Olympic team	Int'l	6	0	3	3	0	...	...	...	—	—	—	—	—
02-03—Boston	NHL	81	27	32	59	32	1	6	5	5	0	2	2	0
03-04—Boston	NHL	82	19	29	48	40	9	3	2	7	1	0	1	8
05-06—Minnesota	NHL	82	34	45	79	50	14	15	5	—	—	—	—	—
—U.S. Olympic team	Int'l	6	3	1	4	4	-1	3	0	—	—	—	—	—
NHL Totals (11 years)		818	224	287	511	273	67	52	31	47	13	5	18	22

ROURKE, ALLAN — D

PERSONAL: Born March 6, 1980, in Mississauga, Ont. ... 6-2/215. ... Shoots left.

TRANSACTIONS/CAREER NOTES: Selected by Toronto Maple Leafs in sixth round (sixth Maple Leafs pick, 154th overall) of entry draft (June 27, 1998). ... Traded by Toronto to Carolina Hurricanes for C Harold Druken (May 30, 2003). ... Signed as free agent by New York Islanders (August 12, 2005).

		REGULAR SEASON								PLAYOFFS				
Season Team	League	GP	G	A	Pts.	PIM	+/-	PP	SH	GP	G	A	Pts.	PIM
96-97—Kitchener	OHL	25	1	1	2	12	...	...	...	6	0	0	0	0
97-98—Kitchener	OHL	48	5	17	22	59	-8	...	...	6	1	1	2	6

Season Team	League	GP	G	A	Pts.	PIM	+/-	PP	SH	GP	G	A	Pts.	PIM
		REGULAR SEASON								PLAYOFFS				
98-99—Kitchener	OHL	66	11	28	39	79	-27	...	...	1	0	0	0	2
99-00—Kitchener	OHL	67	31	43	74	57	-9	13	1	5	0	6	6	13
00-01—St. John's	AHL	64	9	19	28	36	...	...	...	—	—	—	—	—
01-02—St. John's	AHL	62	2	9	11	48	-1	1	0	10	0	2	2	6
02-03—St. John's	AHL	65	12	19	31	49	5	3	1	—	—	—	—	—
03-04—Carolina	NHL	25	1	2	3	22	4	0	0	—	—	—	—	—
—Lowell	AHL	45	5	9	14	45	5	3	0	—	—	—	—	—
04-05—Lowell	AHL	60	7	9	16	75	11	2	2	11	1	2	3	40
05-06—Bridgeport	AHL	58	9	22	31	42	-7	4	1	1	1	0	1	0
—New York Islanders	NHL	6	0	1	1	0	1	0	0	—	—	—	—	—
NHL Totals (2 years)		31	1	3	4	22	5	0	0					

R

ROY, ANDRE — LW

PERSONAL: Born February 8, 1975, in Port Chester, N.Y. ... 6-3/221. ... Shoots left. ... Name pronounced WAH.

TRANSACTIONS/CAREER NOTES: Selected by Boston Bruins in sixth round (fifth Bruins pick, 151st overall) of NHL draft (June 29, 1994). ... Signed as free agent by Ottawa Senators (March 19, 1999). ... Injured right knee (November 18, 1999); missed one game. ... Back spasms (November 6, 2000); missed two games. ... Flu (January 13, 2001); missed two games. ... Suspended two games for unsportsmanlike conduct (February 26, 2001). ... Strained groin (March 30, 2001); missed one game. ... Injured left ankle (February 6, 2002); missed 11 games. ... Traded by Senators with sixth-round pick (D Paul Ranger) in 2002 draft to Tampa Bay Lightning for C Juha Ylonen (March 15, 2002). ... Suspended 13 games for leaving penalty box to fight (April 2, 2002); missed seven games at end of 2001-02 season and six games at start of 2002-03 season. ... Injured eye (December 29, 2002); missed one game. ... Suspended three games for abuse of official (February 9, 2003). ... Sprained knee (December 4, 2003); missed five games. ... Injured left knee (February 20, 2004); missed five games. ... Signed as free agent by Pittsburgh Penguins (August 4, 2005). ... Suspended two games (forfeiting $10,204.08) for repeatedly making inappropriate gestures toward Washington Capitals W Robin Gomez (September 29, 2005) during a preseason game; missed first two games of season. ... Broken orbital bone (October 25, 2005); missed 23 games. ... Hand injury (January 21, 2006); missed eight games.

Season Team	League	GP	G	A	Pts.	PIM	+/-	PP	SH	GP	G	A	Pts.	PIM
		REGULAR SEASON								PLAYOFFS				
93-94—Beauport	QMJHL	33	6	7	13	125	...	...	...	—	—	—	—	—
—Chicoutimi	QMJHL	32	4	14	18	152	...	...	...	25	3	6	9	94
94-95—Chicoutimi	QMJHL	20	15	8	23	90	...	...	...	—	—	—	—	—
—Drummondville	QMJHL	34	18	13	31	233	...	...	...	4	2	0	2	34
95-96—Providence	AHL	58	7	8	15	167	...	...	...	1	0	0	0	10
—Boston	NHL	3	0	0	0	0	0	0	0	—	—	—	—	—
96-97—Providence	AHL	50	17	11	28	234	11	0	0	—	—	—	—	—
—Boston	NHL	10	0	2	2	12	-5	0	0	—	—	—	—	—
97-98—Providence	AHL	36	3	11	14	154	-7	0	0	—	—	—	—	—
—Charlotte	ECHL	27	10	8	18	132	...	...	...	7	2	3	5	34
98-99—Fort Wayne	IHL	65	15	6	21	395	0	1	0	2	0	0	0	11
99-00—Ottawa	NHL	73	4	3	7	145	3	0	0	5	0	0	0	2
00-01—Ottawa	NHL	64	3	5	8	169	1	0	0	2	0	0	0	16
01-02—Ottawa	NHL	56	6	8	14	148	3	0	0	—	—	—	—	—
—Tampa Bay	NHL	9	1	1	2	63	-5	0	0	—	—	—	—	—
02-03—Tampa Bay	NHL	62	10	7	17	119	0	0	0	5	0	1	1	2
03-04—Tampa Bay	NHL	33	1	1	2	78	-5	0	0	21	1	2	3	61
05-06—Pittsburgh	NHL	42	2	1	3	116	-3	0	0	—	—	—	—	—
NHL Totals (8 years)		352	27	28	55	850	-11	0	0	33	1	3	4	81

ROY, DEREK — C

PERSONAL: Born May 4, 1983, in Ottawa, Ont. ... 5-9/187. ... Shoots left.

TRANSACTIONS/CAREER NOTES: Selected by Buffalo Sabres in second round (second Sabres pick, 32nd overall) of entry draft (June 23, 2001).

Season Team	League	GP	G	A	Pts.	PIM	+/-	PP	SH	GP	G	A	Pts.	PIM
		REGULAR SEASON								PLAYOFFS				
99-00—Kitchener	OHL	66	34	53	87	44	...	...	...	5	4	1	5	6
00-01—Kitchener	OHL	65	42	39	81	114	-20	22	6	—	—	—	—	—
01-02—Kitchener	OHL	62	43	46	89	92	...	...	...	4	1	2	3	2
02-03—Kitchener	OHL	49	28	50	78	73	...	...	...	21	9	23	32	14
03-04—Buffalo	NHL	49	9	10	19	12	-8	1	0	—	—	—	—	—
—Rochester	AHL	26	10	16	26	20	6	2	0	16	6	8	14	18
04-05—Rochester	AHL	67	16	45	61	60	-4	7	0	9	6	5	11	6
05-06—Rochester	AHL	8	7	13	20	10	-4	7	0	—	—	—	—	—
—Buffalo	NHL	70	18	28	46	57	1	5	1	18	5	10	15	16
NHL Totals (2 years)		119	27	38	65	69	-7	6	1	18	5	10	15	16

ROY, MATHIEU — D

PERSONAL: Born August 10, 1983, in St. Georges, Que. ... 6-2/200. ... Shoots right.

TRANSACTIONS/CAREER NOTES: Selected by Oilers in seventh round (10th Oilers pick, 215th overall) of entry draft (June 21, 2003).

Season Team	League	GP	G	A	Pts.	PIM	+/-	PP	SH	GP	G	A	Pts.	PIM
		REGULAR SEASON								PLAYOFFS				
99-00—Val-d'Or	QMJHL	48	1	4	5	66	...	...	...	—	—	—	—	—
00-01—Val-d'Or	QMJHL	30	0	7	7	60	...	...	...	17	0	0	0	4
01-02—Val-d'Or	QMJHL	53	7	26	33	103	...	...	...	7	0	2	2	19

Season Team	League	GP	G	A	Pts.	PIM	+/-	PP	SH	GP	G	A	Pts.	PIM
		REGULAR SEASON								PLAYOFFS				
02-03—Val-d'Or	QMJHL	52	11	21	32	164	...	...	...	7	1	0	1	8
03-04—Toronto	AHL	30	0	2	2	46	...	...	...	—	—	—	—	—
—Columbus	ECHL	10	1	2	3	13	...	...	...	—	—	—	—	—
04-05—Acadie-Bathurst	QMJHL	70	33	25	58	85	-33	17	0	—	—	—	—	—
—Edmonton	AHL	51	3	22	25	68	6	1	0	—	—	—	—	—
05-06—Hamilton	AHL	50	3	16	19	82	-8	2	0	—	—	—	—	—
—Edmonton	NHL	1	0	0	0	0	-1	0	0	—	—	—	—	—
NHL Totals (1 year)		1	0	0	0	0	-1	0	0					

ROZSIVAL, MICHAL D

PERSONAL: Born September 3, 1978, in Vlasim, Czech. ... 6-1/212. ... Shoots right. ... Name pronounced roh-ZIH-vahl.

TRANSACTIONS/CAREER NOTES: Selected by Pittsburgh Penguins in fourth round (fifth Penguins pick, 105th overall) of entry draft (June 22, 1996). ... Strained hip flexor (March 21, 2000); missed two games. ... Injured groin (April 4, 2002); missed two games. ... Sore groin (October 19, 2002); missed one game. ... Separated shoulder (November 18, 2002); missed 15 games. ... Injured head (February 23, 2003); missed three games. ... Bruised thumb (March 4, 2003); missed seven games. ... Aggravated thumb injury (March 31, 2003); missed three games. ... Injured right knee (October 3, 2003); missed 30 games. ... Reinjured right knee (December 24, 2003); missed remainder of season. ... Signed as free agent by New York Rangers (September 6, 2005).

Season Team	League	GP	G	A	Pts.	PIM	+/-	PP	SH	GP	G	A	Pts.	PIM
		REGULAR SEASON								PLAYOFFS				
94-95—Czech Rep.	Czech Rep.	31	8	13	21	...	...	...	...	—	—	—	—	—
95-96—Czech Rep.	Czech Rep.	36	3	4	7	...	...	...	...	—	—	—	—	—
96-97—Swift Current	WHL	63	8	31	39	80	23	4	0	10	0	6	6	15
97-98—Swift Current	WHL	71	14	55	69	122	24	8	1	12	0	5	5	33
98-99—Syracuse	AHL	49	3	22	25	72	-12	2	0	—	—	—	—	—
99-00—Pittsburgh	NHL	75	4	17	21	48	11	1	0	2	0	0	0	4
00-01—Pittsburgh	NHL	30	1	4	5	26	3	0	0	—	—	—	—	—
—Wilkes-Barre/Scranton	AHL	29	8	8	16	32	...	...	...	21	3	19	22	23
01-02—Pittsburgh	NHL	79	9	20	29	47	-6	4	0	—	—	—	—	—
02-03—Pittsburgh	NHL	53	4	6	10	40	-5	1	0	—	—	—	—	—
03-04—Wilkes-Barre/Scranton	AHL	1	0	0	0	2	0	0	0	—	—	—	—	—
04-05—Trinec	Czech Rep.	35	1	10	11	40	-10	...	...	—	—	—	—	—
—Pardubice	Czech Rep.	16	1	3	4	30	6	...	...	16	1	2	3	34
05-06—New York Rangers	NHL	82	5	25	30	90	35	3	0	4	0	1	1	8
NHL Totals (5 years)		319	23	72	95	251	38	9	0	6	0	1	1	12

RUCCHIN, STEVE C

PERSONAL: Born July 4, 1971, in Thunder Bay, Ont. ... 6-2/211. ... Shoots left. ... Name pronounced ROO-chihn.

TRANSACTIONS/CAREER NOTES: Selected by Mighty Ducks of Anaheim in first round (first Mighty Ducks pick, second overall) of supplemental draft (June 28, 1994). ... Flu (March 7, 1995); missed two games. ... Sprained left knee (November 27, 1995); missed 18 games. ... Strained groin (October 3, 1997); missed eight games. ... Strained left knee (April 9, 1998); missed two games. ... Groin (March 18, 1999); missed three games. ... Reinjured groin (March 31, 1999); missed seven games. ... Infected left ankle (December 28, 1999); missed 11 games. ... Fractured hand (September 22, 2000); missed six games. ... Fractured nose and cheekbone (November 15, 2000); missed 10 games. ... Concussion (December 13, 2001); missed remainder of season. ... Stress fracture in leg (November 11, 2001); missed 44 games. ... Traded by Mighty Ducks to New York Rangers for LW Trevor Gillies and a conditional pick in 2007 (August 24, 2005). ... Back (November 24, 2005); missed two games. ... Ankle (December 31, 2005); missed one game. ... Foot (April 6, 2006); missed final seven games of regular season. ... Signed as free agent by Atlanta Thrashers (July 3, 2006).

Season Team	League	GP	G	A	Pts.	PIM	+/-	PP	SH	GP	G	A	Pts.	PIM
		REGULAR SEASON								PLAYOFFS				
90-91—Univ. of W. Ontario	OUAA	34	13	16	29	14	...	...	...	—	—	—	—	—
91-92—Univ. of W. Ontario	OUAA	37	28	34	62	36	...	...	...	—	—	—	—	—
92-93—Univ. of W. Ontario	OUAA	34	22	26	48	16	...	...	...	—	—	—	—	—
93-94—Univ. of W. Ontario	OUAA	35	30	23	53	30	...	...	...	—	—	—	—	—
94-95—San Diego	IHL	41	11	15	26	14	-2	4	0	—	—	—	—	—
—Anaheim	NHL	43	6	11	17	23	7	0	0	—	—	—	—	—
95-96—Anaheim	NHL	64	19	25	44	12	3	8	1	—	—	—	—	—
96-97—Anaheim	NHL	79	19	48	67	24	26	6	1	8	1	2	3	10
97-98—Anaheim	NHL	72	17	36	53	13	8	8	1	—	—	—	—	—
98-99—Anaheim	NHL	69	23	39	62	22	11	5	1	4	0	3	3	0
99-00—Anaheim	NHL	71	19	38	57	16	9	10	0	—	—	—	—	—
00-01—Anaheim	NHL	16	3	5	8	0	-5	2	0	—	—	—	—	—
01-02—Anaheim	NHL	38	7	16	23	6	-3	4	0	—	—	—	—	—
02-03—Anaheim	NHL	82	20	38	58	12	-14	6	1	21	7	3	10	2
03-04—Anaheim	NHL	82	20	23	43	12	-14	9	1	—	—	—	—	—
05-06—New York Rangers	NHL	72	13	23	36	10	6	4	1	4	1	0	1	0
NHL Totals (11 years)		688	166	302	468	150	34	62	7	37	9	8	17	12

RUCINSKY, MARTIN LW

PERSONAL: Born March 11, 1971, in Most, Czech. ... 6-2/207. ... Shoots left. ... Name pronounced roo-SHIHN-skee.

TRANSACTIONS/CAREER NOTES: Selected by Edmonton Oilers in first round (second Oilers pick, 20th overall) of entry draft (June 22, 1991). ... Traded by Oilers to Quebec Nordiques for G Ron Tugnutt and LW Brad Zavisha (March 10, 1992). ... Flu (February 28, 1993); missed one game. ... Bruised buttocks (December 3, 1994); missed one game. ... Sprained right wrist (January 11, 1994); missed one game. ... Fractured left cheekbone (January 30, 1994); missed four games. ... Fractured right wrist (March 7, 1994); missed one game. ... Reinjured right wrist (March 21, 1994); missed six games. ... Reinjured right wrist (April 5, 1994); missed one game. ... Separated shoulder (February 25, 1995);

missed 17 games. ... Reinjured shoulder (April 6, 1995); missed remainder of season. ... Nordiques franchise moved to Colorado and renamed Avalanche for 1995-96 season (June 21, 1995). ... Injured groin (November 28, 1995); missed one game. ... Traded by Avalanche with G Jocelyn Thibault and RW Andrei Kovalenko to Montreal Canadiens for G Patrick Roy and RW Mike Keane (December 6, 1995). ... Sprained right knee (April 6, 1996); missed two games. ... Hand (October 19, 1996); missed one game. ... Strained knee (November 25, 1996); missed one game. ... Separated shoulder (December 28, 1996); missed 10 games. ... Bruised foot (October 17, 1997); missed one game. ... Sprained ankle (April 4, 1998); missed three games. ... Shoulder (March 6, 1999); missed three games. ... Concussion (November 16, 1999); missed one game. ... Back spasms (March 25, 2000); missed one game. ... Sprained knee (December 18, 2000); missed 21 games. ... Bruised left thigh (March 12, 2001); missed four games. ... Eye (November 3, 2001); missed two games. ... Traded by Canadiens with LW Benoit Brunet to Dallas Stars for RW Donald Audette and C Shaun Van Allen (November 21, 2001). ... Traded by Stars with C Roman Lyashenko to New York Rangers for C Manny Malhotra and LW Barrett Heisten (March 12, 2002). ... Signed as free agent by St. Louis Blues (October 24, 2002). ... Signed as free agent by Rangers (August 28, 2003). ... Traded by Rangers to Vancouver Canucks for C R.J. Umberger and D Martin Grenier (March 9, 2004). ... Signed as free agent by Rangers (August 3, 2005). ... Sprained left knee (October 29, 2005); missed 14 games. ... Knee (December 3, 2005); missed one game. ... Knee (March 15, 2006); missed three games. ... Broken finger (March 25, 2006); missed final 12 games of regular season.

STATISTICAL PLATEAUS: Three-goal games: 1995-96 (1), 1996-97 (1). Total: 2.

		REGULAR SEASON								PLAYOFFS				
Season Team	**League**	**GP**	**G**	**A**	**Pts.**	**PIM**	**+/-**	**PP**	**SH**	**GP**	**G**	**A**	**Pts.**	**PIM**
88-89—CHZ Litvinov	Czech.	3	1	0	1	2	...	...	...	—	—	—	—	—
89-90—CHZ Litvinov	Czech.	47	12	6	18	...	...	...	...	—	—	—	—	—
90-91—CHZ Litvinov	Czech.	49	23	18	41	79	...	...	...	—	—	—	—	—
—Czechoslovakia Jr.	Czech.	7	9	5	14	2	...	...	...	—	—	—	—	—
91-92—Cape Breton	AHL	35	11	12	23	34	...	...	...	—	—	—	—	—
—Edmonton	NHL	2	0	0	0	0	-3	0	0	—	—	—	—	—
—Halifax	AHL	7	1	1	2	6	...	...	...	—	—	—	—	—
—Quebec	NHL	4	1	1	2	2	1	0	0	—	—	—	—	—
92-93—Quebec	NHL	77	18	30	48	51	16	4	0	6	1	1	2	4
93-94—Quebec	NHL	60	9	23	32	58	4	4	0	—	—	—	—	—
94-95—Chem. Litvinov	Czech Rep.	13	12	10	22	34	...	...	...	—	—	—	—	—
—Quebec	NHL	20	3	6	9	14	5	0	0	—	—	—	—	—
95-96—HC Vsetin	Czech Rep.	1	1	1	2	0	...	...	...	—	—	—	—	—
—Colorado	NHL	22	4	11	15	14	10	0	0	—	—	—	—	—
—Montreal	NHL	56	25	35	60	54	8	9	2	—	—	—	—	—
96-97—Montreal	NHL	70	28	27	55	62	1	6	3	5	0	0	0	4
97-98—Montreal	NHL	78	21	32	53	84	13	5	3	10	3	0	3	4
—Czech Rep. Oly. team	Int'l	6	3	1	4	4	3	0	0	—	—	—	—	—
98-99—Montreal	NHL	73	17	17	34	50	-25	5	0	—	—	—	—	—
99-00—Montreal	NHL	80	25	24	49	70	1	7	1	—	—	—	—	—
00-01—Montreal	NHL	57	16	22	38	66	-5	5	1	—	—	—	—	—
01-02—Montreal	NHL	18	2	6	8	12	-1	1	0	—	—	—	—	—
—Dallas	NHL	42	6	11	17	24	3	2	0	—	—	—	—	—
—Czech Rep. Oly. team	Int'l	4	0	3	3	2	...	...	...	—	—	—	—	—
—New York Rangers	NHL	15	3	10	13	6	6	0	0	—	—	—	—	—
02-03—Litvinov	Czech Rep.	2	0	1	1	2	...	...	...	—	—	—	—	—
—St. Louis	NHL	61	16	14	30	38	-1	4	4	7	4	2	6	4
03-04—New York Rangers	NHL	69	13	29	42	62	13	0	1	—	—	—	—	—
—Vancouver	NHL	13	1	2	3	10	2	0	0	7	1	1	2	6
04-05—Chem. Litvinov	Czech Rep.	38	15	26	41	87	-1	...	...	—	—	—	—	—
05-06—New York Rangers	NHL	52	16	39	55	56	10	4	0	2	0	1	1	2
—Czech Rep. Oly. team	Int'l	8	1	3	4	0	0	0	1	—	—	—	—	—
NHL Totals (14 years)		869	224	339	563	733	58	56	15	37	9	5	14	24

RUPP, MICHAEL C/LW

PERSONAL: Born January 13, 1980, in Cleveland. ... 6-5/230. ... Shoots left.

TRANSACTIONS/CAREER NOTES: Selected by New York Islanders in first round (first Islanders pick, ninth overall) of entry draft (June 27, 1998). ... Returned to draft pool; selected by New Jersey Devils in third round (seventh Devils pick, 76th overall) of entry draft (June 24, 2000). ... Flu (February 5, 2003); missed three games. ... Traded by Devils with second-round pick in 2004 (later traded to Edmonton; Oilers selected LW Geoff Paukovich) to Phoenix Coyotes for C Jan Hrdina (March 5, 2004). ... Shoulder (March 10, 2004); missed nine games. ... Traded by Coyotes with D Cale Hulse and LW Jason Chimera to Columbus Blue Jackets for LW Geoff Sanderson and RW Tim Jackman (October 8, 2005). ... Ankle (January 18, 2006); missed 12 games. ... Irregular heartbeat (March 11, 2006); missed final 19 games of regular season. ... Signed as free agent by New Jersey Devils (July 10, 2006).

		REGULAR SEASON								PLAYOFFS				
Season Team	**League**	**GP**	**G**	**A**	**Pts.**	**PIM**	**+/-**	**PP**	**SH**	**GP**	**G**	**A**	**Pts.**	**PIM**
96-97—St. Edward's	USHS (East)	20	26	24	50	...	...	...	...	—	—	—	—	—
97-98—Windsor	OHL	38	9	8	17	60	...	...	...	—	—	—	—	—
—Erie	OHL	26	7	3	10	57	...	...	...	7	3	1	4	6
98-99—Erie	OHL	63	22	25	47	102	-2	...	...	5	0	2	2	25
99-00—Erie	OHL	58	32	21	53	134	4	10	0	13	5	5	10	22
00-01—Albany	AHL	71	10	10	20	63	...	...	...	—	—	—	—	—
01-02—Albany	AHL	78	13	17	30	90	-27	3	0	—	—	—	—	—
02-03—Albany	AHL	47	8	11	19	74	1	1	0	—	—	—	—	—
—New Jersey	NHL	26	5	3	8	21	0	2	0	4	1	3	4	0
03-04—New Jersey	NHL	51	6	5	11	41	-1	1	0	—	—	—	—	—
—Phoenix	NHL	6	0	1	1	6	-3	0	0	—	—	—	—	—
04-05—Danbury	UHL	14	5	5	10	30	4	1	0	—	—	—	—	—
05-06—Syracuse	AHL	3	1	2	3	12	1	0	0	—	—	—	—	—
—Phoenix	NHL	1	0	0	0	0	0	0	0	—	—	—	—	—
—Columbus	NHL	39	4	2	6	58	-3	0	0	—	—	—	—	—
NHL Totals (3 years)		123	15	11	26	126	-7	3	0	4	1	3	4	0

RUUTU, JARKKO RW/LW

PERSONAL: Born August 23, 1975, in Helsinki, Finland. ... 6-2/200. ... Shoots left. ... Brother of Tuomo Ruutu, C/RW, Chicago Blackhawks organization. ... Name pronounced ROO-too.

TRANSACTIONS/CAREER NOTES: Selected by Vancouver Canucks in third round (third Canucks pick, 68th overall) of NHL draft (June 27, 1998). ... Injured knee (March 19, 2004); missed 11 games. ... Signed as free agent by Pittsburgh Penguins (July 4, 2006).

		REGULAR SEASON								PLAYOFFS				
Season Team	**League**	**GP**	**G**	**A**	**Pts.**	**PIM**	**+/-**	**PP**	**SH**	**GP**	**G**	**A**	**Pts.**	**PIM**
91-92—HIFK Helsinki	Finland Jr.	1	0	0	0	0	...	...	...	—	—	—	—	—
92-93—HIFK Helsinki	Finland Jr.	34	26	21	47	53	...	...	...	—	—	—	—	—
93-94—HIFK Helsinki	Finland Jr.	19	9	12	21	44	...	...	...	—	—	—	—	—
94-95—HIFK Helsinki	Finland Jr.	35	26	22	48	117	...	...	...	—	—	—	—	—
95-96—Michigan Tech	WCHA	39	12	10	22	96	...	...	...	—	—	—	—	—
96-97—HIFK Helsinki	Finland	48	11	10	21	155	...	...	...	—	—	—	—	—
97-98—HIFK Helsinki	Finland	37	10	10	20	87	...	...	...	8	7	4	11	10
98-99—HIFK Helsinki	Finland	25	10	4	14	136	...	...	...	9	0	2	2	43
99-00—Syracuse	AHL	65	26	32	58	164	...	...	...	4	3	1	4	8
—Vancouver	NHL	8	0	1	1	6	-1	0	0	—	—	—	—	—
00-01—Kansas City	IHL	46	11	18	29	111	...	...	...	—	—	—	—	—
—Vancouver	NHL	21	3	3	6	32	1	0	1	4	0	1	1	8
01-02—Vancouver	NHL	49	2	7	9	74	-1	0	0	1	0	0	0	0
—Fin. Olympic team	Int'l	4	0	0	0	4	...	...	...	—	—	—	—	—
02-03—Vancouver	NHL	36	2	2	4	66	-7	0	0	13	0	2	2	14
03-04—Vancouver	NHL	71	6	8	14	133	-13	1	0	6	1	0	1	10
04-05—HIFK Helsinki	Finland	50	10	18	28	215	22	...	...	3	0	0	0	41
05-06—Vancouver	NHL	82	10	7	17	142	1	2	0	—	—	—	—	—
—Fin. Olympic team	Int'l	7	0	0	0	31	-1	0	0	—	—	—	—	—
NHL Totals (6 years)		267	23	28	51	453	-20	3	1	24	1	3	4	32

RUUTU, TUOMO C/LW

PERSONAL: Born February 16, 1983, in Vantaa, Finland. ... 6-0/208. ... Shoots left. ... Brother of Jarkko Ruutu, RW, Pittsburgh Penguins. ... Name pronounced ROO-too.

TRANSACTIONS/CAREER NOTES: Selected by Chicago Blackhawks in first round (first Blackhawks pick, ninth overall) of entry draft (June 23, 2001). ... Shoulder surgery (October 1, 2004); missed entire season. ... Back (October 15, 2005); missed five games. ... Aggravated back injury (November 1, 2005); missed 30 games. ... Cut tendon in right ankle (January 8, 2006); missed 37 games.

		REGULAR SEASON								PLAYOFFS				
Season Team	**League**	**GP**	**G**	**A**	**Pts.**	**PIM**	**+/-**	**PP**	**SH**	**GP**	**G**	**A**	**Pts.**	**PIM**
99-00—HIFK Helsinki	Finland Jr.	35	11	16	27	32	...	...	...	—	—	—	—	—
00-01—Jokerit Helsinki	Finland	47	11	11	22	86	...	...	...	5	0	0	0	4
01-02—Jokerit Helsinki	Finland	51	7	16	23	69	...	...	...	10	0	6	6	29
02-03—HIFK Helsinki	Finland	30	12	15	27	24	...	...	...	—	—	—	—	—
03-04—Chicago	NHL	82	23	21	44	58	-31	10	0	—	—	—	—	—
05-06—Chicago	NHL	15	2	3	5	31	-7	1	0	—	—	—	—	—
NHL Totals (2 years)		97	25	24	49	89	-38	11	0					

RUZICKA, STEFAN LW

PERSONAL: Born February 17, 1985, in Nitra, Czechoslovakia. ... 5-11/189. ... Shoots right. ... Name pronounced: steh-FAHN roo-ZEECH-kuh

TRANSACTIONS/CAREER NOTES: Selected by Philadelphia Flyers in third round (fourth Flyers pick, 81st overall) of NHL entry draft (June 20, 2003).

		REGULAR SEASON								PLAYOFFS				
Season Team	**League**	**GP**	**G**	**A**	**Pts.**	**PIM**	**+/-**	**PP**	**SH**	**GP**	**G**	**A**	**Pts.**	**PIM**
01-02—Nitra	Slovakia	19	0	5	5	29	-5	...	...	—	—	—	—	—
02-03—Nitra	Slovakia	17	5	7	12	4	22	...	...	—	—	—	—	—
03-04—Owen Sound	OHL	62	34	38	72	63	2	5	0	7	1	6	7	8
—Philadelphia	AHL	2	0	0	0	0	...	...	...	3	1	0	1	2
04-05—Owen Sound	OHL	62	37	33	70	61	21	10	0	8	3	3	6	14
05-06—Philadelphia	AHL	73	16	32	48	88	-8	11	0	—	—	—	—	—
—Philadelphia	NHL	1	0	0	0	2	0	0	0	—	—	—	—	—
NHL Totals (1 year)		1	0	0	0	2	0	0	0					

RYAN, JOE D

PERSONAL: Born October 19, 1987, in Winchester, Mass. ... 6-1/189. ... Shoots right.

TRANSACTIONS/CAREER NOTES: Selected by Los Angeles Kings in second round (third Kings pick; 48th overall) of NHL draft (June 24, 2006).

		REGULAR SEASON								PLAYOFFS				
Season Team	**League**	**GP**	**G**	**A**	**Pts.**	**PIM**	**+/-**	**PP**	**SH**	**GP**	**G**	**A**	**Pts.**	**PIM**
03-04—Quebec	QMJHL	57	0	9	9	98	1	...	...	5	0	0	0	8
04-05—Quebec	QMJHL	63	4	9	13	134	11	...	...	13	0	2	2	28
05-06—Quebec	QMJHL	61	6	18	24	202	4	...	...	23	2	8	10	29

RYAN, MATT C

PERSONAL: Born November 12, 1983, in Sharon, Ont. ... 6-0/185. ... Shoots left.
TRANSACTIONS/CAREER NOTES: Signed as free agent by Los Angeles Kings (August 3, 2004).

		REGULAR SEASON								PLAYOFFS				
Season Team	League	GP	G	A	Pts.	PIM	+/-	PP	SH	GP	G	A	Pts.	PIM
00-01—U. of Niagara	NCAA	32	7	12	19	32	...	...	...	—	—	—	—	—
01-02—U. of Niagara	NCAA	9	6	2	8	14	...	...	...	—	—	—	—	—
02-03—Guelph	OHL	48	14	11	25	34	...	...	...	—	—	—	—	—
03-04—Guelph	OHL	68	42	35	77	63	...	...	...	—	—	—	—	—
04-05—Manchester	AHL	77	9	15	24	59	-7	0	0	6	0	1	1	4
05-06—Manchester	AHL	68	12	12	24	79	4	0	2	7	1	1	2	8
—Los Angeles	NHL	12	0	1	1	2	-4	0	0	—	—	—	—	—
NHL Totals (1 year)		12	0	1	1	2	-4	0	0					

RYAN, PRESTIN D

PERSONAL: Born January 6, 1980, in Arcola, Sask. ... 6-0/195. ... Shoots left.
COLLEGE: Maine.
TRANSACTIONS/CAREER NOTES: Signed as free agent by Columbus Blue Jackets (April 12, 2004). ... Signed as free agent by Vancouver Canucks (August 30, 2006).

		REGULAR SEASON								PLAYOFFS				
Season Team	League	GP	G	A	Pts.	PIM	+/-	PP	SH	GP	G	A	Pts.	PIM
01-02—Maine	Hockey East	39	6	9	15	91	21	...	...	—	—	—	—	—
02-03—Maine	Hockey East	37	1	8	9	120	...	...	...	—	—	—	—	—
03-04—Maine	Hockey East	43	4	18	22	148	35	1	0	—	—	—	—	—
—Syracuse	AHL	...	...	...	...	...	...	...	...	3	0	0	0	2
04-05—Syracuse	AHL	59	3	6	9	161	7	0	0	—	—	—	—	—
05-06—Manitoba	AHL	64	11	12	23	63	0	4	0	13	1	1	2	25
—Vancouver	NHL	1	0	0	0	2	-1	0	0	—	—	—	—	—
NHL Totals (1 year)		1	0	0	0	2	-1	0	0					

RYCROFT, MARK RW/LW

PERSONAL: Born July 12, 1978, in Penticton, B.C. ... 5-11/194. ... Shoots right. ... Son of Al Rycroft, player for Cleveland of WHA. ... Brother of Travis Rycroft, St. Louis Blues organization.
COLLEGE: Denver.
TRANSACTIONS/CAREER NOTES: Signed as free agent by St. Louis Blues (May 15, 2000). ... Charley horse (March 11, 2004); missed 11 games. ... Signed as free agent by Colorado Avalanche (July 12, 2006).

		REGULAR SEASON								PLAYOFFS				
Season Team	League	GP	G	A	Pts.	PIM	+/-	PP	SH	GP	G	A	Pts.	PIM
97-98—Denver	WCHA	35	15	17	32	28	...	...	...	—	—	—	—	—
98-99—Denver	WCHA	41	19	18	37	36	...	...	...	—	—	—	—	—
99-00—Denver	WCHA	41	17	17	34	87	...	5	0	—	—	—	—	—
00-01—Worcester	AHL	71	24	26	50	68	...	...	...	11	2	5	7	4
01-02—St. Louis	NHL	9	0	3	3	4	0	0	0	—	—	—	—	—
—Worcester	AHL	66	12	19	31	68	-2	5	0	3	0	1	1	0
02-03—Worcester	AHL	45	8	18	26	35	1	1	0	1	0	0	0	0
03-04—St. Louis	NHL	71	9	12	21	32	2	0	0	3	0	0	0	2
04-05—Briancon	France	13	8	8	16	18	...	...	...	4	2	1	3	0
05-06—St. Louis	NHL	80	6	4	10	46	-14	0	1	—	—	—	—	—
NHL Totals (3 years)		160	15	19	34	82	-12	0	1	3	0	0	0	2

RYDER, MICHAEL RW/C

PERSONAL: Born March 31, 1980, in St. John's, Nfld. ... 6-0/196. ... Shoots right.
TRANSACTIONS/CAREER NOTES: Selected by Montreal Canadiens in ninth round (ninth Canadiens pick, 216th overall) of NHL draft (June 27, 1998). ... Virus (April 18, 2006); missed final game of regular season.

		REGULAR SEASON								PLAYOFFS				
Season Team	League	GP	G	A	Pts.	PIM	+/-	PP	SH	GP	G	A	Pts.	PIM
97-98—Hull	QMJHL	69	34	28	62	41	...	...	...	10	4	2	6	4
98-99—Hull	QMJHL	69	44	43	87	41	...	...	...	23	20	16	36	39
99-00—Hull	QMJHL	63	50	58	108	50	26	18	5	15	11	17	28	28
00-01—Quebec	AHL	61	6	9	15	14	...	...	...	—	—	—	—	—
—Tallahassee	ECHL	5	4	5	9	6	...	...	...	—	—	—	—	—
01-02—Quebec	AHL	50	11	17	28	9	17	0	0	3	0	1	1	2
—Mississippi	ECHL	20	14	13	27	2	0	2	2	—	—	—	—	—
02-03—Hamilton	AHL	69	34	33	67	43	15	10	1	23	11	6	17	8
03-04—Montreal	NHL	81	25	38	63	26	10	10	0	11	1	2	3	4
04-05—Leksand	Sweden Dv. 2	18	14	12	26	24	21	5	0	10	7	6	13	0
05-06—Montreal	NHL	81	30	25	55	40	-5	18	0	6	2	3	5	0
NHL Totals (2 years)		162	55	63	118	66	5	28	0	17	3	5	8	4

RYPIEN, RICK C

PERSONAL: Born May 16, 1984, in Coleman, Alb. ... 5-11/170. ... Shoots right.
TRANSACTIONS/CAREER NOTES: Signed as nondrafted free agent by Vancouver Canucks (March 22, 2005).

Season Team	League	REGULAR SEASON GP	G	A	Pts.	PIM	+/-	PP	SH	PLAYOFFS GP	G	A	Pts.	PIM
01-02—Regina	WHL	1	0	0	0	0	...	...	...	—	—	—	—	—
02-03—Regina	WHL	50	6	12	18	159	...	...	...	5	1	1	2	21
03-04—Regina	WHL	65	19	26	45	186	...	...	...	4	0	1	1	18
04-05—Regina	WHL	63	22	29	51	148	...	...	...	—	—	—	—	—
—Manitoba	AHL	8	1	1	2	5	...	...	...	14	0	0	0	35
05-06—Vancouver	NHL	5	1	0	1	4	1	0	0	—	—	—	—	—
—Manitoba	AHL	49	9	6	15	122	-1	0	1	13	1	1	2	22
NHL Totals (1 year)		5	1	0	1	4	1	0	0					

RYZNAR, JASON LW

PERSONAL: Born February 19, 1983, in Anchorage, Alaska. ... 6-3/205. ... Shoots left. ... Name pronounced: RIHZ nahr

COLLEGE: Michigan.

TRANSACTIONS/CAREER NOTES: Selected by New Jersey Devils in third round (third Devils pick, 64th overall) of NHL entry draft (June 22, 2002).

Season Team	League	REGULAR SEASON GP	G	A	Pts.	PIM	+/-	PP	SH	PLAYOFFS GP	G	A	Pts.	PIM
99-00—U.S. National	USHL	52	5	10	15	22	...	...	...	—	—	—	—	—
00-01—U.S. National	USHL	66	15	17	32	102	...	...	...	—	—	—	—	—
01-02—Univ. of Michigan	CCHA	40	9	7	16	22	...	...	...	—	—	—	—	—
02-03—Univ. of Michigan	CCHA	34	7	9	16	24	...	...	...	—	—	—	—	—
03-04—Univ. of Michigan	CCHA	36	6	11	17	28	...	...	...	—	—	—	—	—
04-05—Univ. of Michigan	CCHA	36	6	17	23	46	...	...	...	—	—	—	—	—
05-06—Albany	AHL	59	7	18	25	52	-4	1	0	—	—	—	—	—
—New Jersey	NHL	8	0	0	0	2	-1	0	0	—	—	—	—	—
NHL Totals (1 year)		8	0	0	0	2	-1	0	0					

S

SABOURIN, DANY G

PERSONAL: Born September 20, 1980, in Val d'Or, Que. ... 6-2/185. ... Catches left. ... Name pronounced SA-boo-rihn.

TRANSACTIONS/CAREER NOTES: Selected by Calgary Flames in fourth round (fifth Flames pick, 108th overall) of NHL draft (June 27, 1998). ... Signed as free agent by Wilkes-Barre/Scranton of the AHL (September 26, 2004).

Season Team	League	REGULAR SEASON GP	Min.	W	L	OTL	T	GA	SO	GAA	SV%	PLAYOFFS GP	Min.	W	L	GA	SO	GAA	SV%
97-98—Sherbrooke	QMJHL	37	1906	15	15	...	2	128	1	4.03	.877	—	—	—	—	—	—	—	—
98-99—Sherbrooke	QMJHL	30	1477	8	13	...	2	102	1	4.14	...	1	49	0	1	2	0	2.45	...
99-00—Sherbrooke	QMJHL	55	3066	25	22	...	5	181	1	3.54	.889	5	324	1	4	18	0	3.33	.888
00-01—Saint John	AHL	1	40	1	0	...	0	0	0	0.00	1.000	—	—	—	—	—	—	—	—
—Johnstown	ECHL	19	903	4	9	...	1	56	0	3.72	...	1	40	0	0	2	0	3.00	...
01-02—Johnstown	ECHL	27	1538	14	10	...	1	84	0	3.28	.879	3	137	0	2	5	0	2.19	.936
—Saint John	AHL	10	447	4	4	...	0	18	1	2.42	.899	—	—	—	—	—	—	—	—
02-03—Saint John	AHL	41	2219	15	17	...	4	100	4	2.70	.905	—	—	—	—	—	—	—	—
03-04—Calgary	NHL	4	169	0	3	...	0	10	0	3.55	.848	—	—	—	—	—	—	—	—
—Las Vegas	ECHL	10	613	6	3	...	1	24	0	2.35	.933	1	57	0	1	2	0	2.11	.941
—Lowell	AHL	14	820	5	7	...	2	39	0	2.85	.894	—	—	—	—	—	—	—	—
04-05—Wilkes-Barre/Scranton	AHL	20	1028	8	8	...	...	38	1	2.22	.921	0	0	0	0	0	0	...	...
—Wheeling	ECHL	27	1578	19	6	...	...	44	5	1.67	.942	—	—	—	—	—	—	—	—
05-06—Wilkes-Barre/Scranton	AHL	49	2943	30	14	4	...	111	4	2.26	.922	6	362	2	4	13	1	2.15	.927
—Pittsburgh	NHL	1	21	0	1	0	...	4	0	11.43	.714	—	—	—	—	—	—	—	—
NHL Totals (2 years)		5	190	0	4	0	0	14	0	4.42	.825								

SAKIC, JOE C

PERSONAL: Born July 7, 1969, in Burnaby, B.C. ... 5-11/195. ... Shoots left. ... Brother of Brian Sakic, LW with Washington Capitals (1990-91 and 1991-92) and New York Rangers organizations (1992-93 through 1994-95). ... Name pronounced SAK-ihk.

TRANSACTIONS/CAREER NOTES: Selected by Quebec Nordiques in first round (second Nordiques pick, 15th overall) of NHL draft (June 13, 1987). ... Sprained right ankle (November 28, 1988). ... Developed bursitis in left ankle (January 21, 1992); missed three games. ... Recurrence of bursitis in left ankle (January 30, 1992); missed eight games. ... Injured eye (January 2, 1993); missed six games. ... Nordiques franchise moved to Colorado and renamed Avalanche for 1995-96 season (June 21, 1995). ... Lacerated calf (January 4, 1997); missed 17 games. ... Injured knee (February 18, 1998); missed 18 games. ... Suspended one game and fined $1,000 by NHL for kneeing incident (April 21, 1998). ... Sprained right shoulder (December 17, 1998); missed seven games. ... Injured rib cartilage (November 8, 1999); missed six games. ... Reinjured rib cartilage (November 26, 1999); missed 13 games. ... Flu (January 18, 2000); missed one game. ... Injured groin (January 25, 2000); missed two games. ... Sprained ankle (December 13, 2002); missed nine games. ... Fractured foot (January 20, 2003); missed 15 games. ... Fractured jaw (January 4, 2004); missed one game.

STATISTICAL PLATEAUS: Three-goal games: 1988-89 (2), 1989-90 (1), 1990-91 (1), 1996-97 (1), 1998-99 (1), 1999-00 (2), 2000-01 (2), 2002-03 (1), 2003-04 (2). Total: 13. ... Four-goal games: 1991-92 (1). ... Total hat tricks: 14.

Season Team	League	REGULAR SEASON GP	G	A	Pts.	PIM	+/-	PP	SH	PLAYOFFS GP	G	A	Pts.	PIM
86-87—Swift Current	WHL	72	60	73	133	31	...	...	...	4	0	1	1	0
87-88—Swift Current	WHL	64	78	82	160	64	...	...	...	10	11	13	24	12
88-89—Quebec	NHL	70	23	39	62	24	-36	10	0	—	—	—	—	—
89-90—Quebec	NHL	80	39	63	102	27	-40	8	1	—	—	—	—	—
90-91—Quebec	NHL	80	48	61	109	24	-26	12	3	—	—	—	—	—
91-92—Quebec	NHL	69	29	65	94	20	5	6	3	—	—	—	—	—

Season Team	League	REGULAR SEASON GP	G	A	Pts.	PIM	+/-	PP	SH	PLAYOFFS GP	G	A	Pts.	PIM
92-93—Quebec	NHL	78	48	57	105	40	-3	20	2	6	3	3	6	2
93-94—Quebec	NHL	84	28	64	92	18	-8	10	1	—	—	—	—	—
94-95—Quebec	NHL	47	19	43	62	30	7	3	2	6	4	1	5	0
95-96—Colorado	NHL	82	51	69	120	44	14	17	6	22	*18	16	*34	14
96-97—Colorado	NHL	65	22	52	74	34	-10	10	2	17	8	*17	25	14
97-98—Colorado	NHL	64	27	36	63	50	0	12	1	6	2	3	5	6
—Can. Olympic team	Int'l	4	1	2	3	4	2	0	0	—	—	—	—	—
98-99—Colorado	NHL	73	41	55	96	29	23	12	†5	19	6	13	19	8
99-00—Colorado	NHL	60	28	53	81	28	30	5	1	17	2	7	9	8
00-01—Colorado	NHL	82	54	64	118	30	45	19	3	21	*13	13	*26	6
01-02—Colorado	NHL	82	26	53	79	18	12	9	1	21	9	10	19	4
—Can. Olympic team	Int'l	6	4	3	7	0	...	...	...	—	—	—	—	—
02-03—Colorado	NHL	58	26	32	58	24	4	8	0	7	6	3	9	2
03-04—Colorado	NHL	81	33	54	87	42	11	13	1	11	7	5	12	8
05-06—Colorado	NHL	82	32	55	87	60	10	10	0	9	4	5	9	6
—Canadian Oly. team	Int'l	6	1	2	3	0	-1	1	0	—	—	—	—	—
NHL Totals (17 years)		1237	574	915	1489	542	38	184	32	162	82	96	178	78

SALEI, RUSLAN D

PERSONAL: Born November 2, 1974, in Minsk, U.S.S.R. ... 6-1/212. ... Shoots left. ... Name pronounced ROO-slahn suh-LAY.

TRANSACTIONS/CAREER NOTES: Selected by Mighty Ducks of Anaheim in first round (first Mighty Ducks pick, ninth overall) of NHL draft (June 22, 1996). ... Charley horse (November 22, 1997); missed one game. ... Fractured left foot (December 10, 1997); missed one game. ... Suspended two games and fined $1,000 by NHL for head-butting incident (February 4, 1998). ... Suspended five games and fined $1,000 by NHL for illegal hit in preseason game (October 9, 1998). ... Injured shoulder (March 17, 1999); missed two games. ... Suspended 10 games by NHL for checking from behind incident (October 5, 1999). ... Injured foot (October 20, 2000); missed two games. ... Reinjured foot (October 23, 2000); missed six games. ... Injured back (December 17, 2000); missed one game. ... Headaches (January 21, 2001); missed 23 games. ... Bruised elbow, suffered back spasms (November 27, 2002); missed two games. ... Back spasms (December 4, 2002); missed seven games. ... Injured back (March 7, 2003); missed 11 games. ... Fractured facial bones (January 28, 2006); missed four games. ... Signed as free agent by Florida Panthers (July 2, 2006).

Season Team	League	REGULAR SEASON GP	G	A	Pts.	PIM	+/-	PP	SH	PLAYOFFS GP	G	A	Pts.	PIM
92-93—Tivali Minsk	CIS	9	1	0	1	10	...	...	...	—	—	—	—	—
93-94—Tivali Minsk	CIS	39	2	3	5	50	...	...	...	—	—	—	—	—
94-95—Tivali Minsk	CIS	51	4	2	6	44	...	...	...	—	—	—	—	—
95-96—Las Vegas	IHL	76	7	23	30	123	...	...	...	15	3	7	10	18
96-97—Anaheim	NHL	30	0	1	1	37	-8	0	0	—	—	—	—	—
—Baltimore	AHL	12	1	4	5	12	-1	1	0	—	—	—	—	—
—Las Vegas	IHL	8	0	2	2	24	...	...	...	3	2	1	3	6
97-98—Anaheim	NHL	66	5	10	15	70	7	1	0	—	—	—	—	—
—Cincinnati	AHL	6	3	6	9	14	1	2	0	—	—	—	—	—
—Belarus Oly. team	Int'l	7	1	0	1	4	-2	1	0	—	—	—	—	—
98-99—Anaheim	NHL	74	2	14	16	65	1	1	0	3	0	0	0	4
99-00—Anaheim	NHL	71	5	5	10	94	3	1	0	—	—	—	—	—
00-01—Anaheim	NHL	50	1	5	6	70	-14	0	0	—	—	—	—	—
01-02—Anaheim	NHL	82	4	7	11	97	-10	0	0	—	—	—	—	—
—Belarus Oly. team	Int'l	6	2	1	3	4	...	...	...	—	—	—	—	—
02-03—Anaheim	NHL	61	4	8	12	78	2	0	0	21	2	3	5	26
03-04—Anaheim	NHL	82	4	11	15	110	-1	0	1	—	—	—	—	—
04-05—Ak Bars Kazan	Russian	35	8	12	20	36	15	...	...	4	0	0	0	2
05-06—Anaheim	NHL	78	1	18	19	114	17	0	0	16	3	2	5	18
NHL Totals (9 years)		594	26	79	105	735	-3	3	1	40	5	5	10	48

SALO, SAMI D

PERSONAL: Born September 2, 1974, in Turku, Finland. ... 6-3/215. ... Shoots right.

TRANSACTIONS/CAREER NOTES: Selected by Ottawa Senators in ninth round (seventh Senators pick, 239th overall) of entry draft (June 22, 1996). ... Strained groin (Octoberr 17, 1998); missed five games. ... Strained groin (November 28, 1998); missed six games. ... Bruised thigh (February 18, 1999); missed one game. ... Strained shoulder (April 14, 1999); missed two games. ... Bruised chest (October 2, 1999); missed one game. ... Fractured left wrist (October 30, 1999); missed 23 games. ... Reinjured left wrist (December 29, 1999); missed 19 games. ... Sprained right knee ligament (February 29, 2000); missed one game. ... Flu (September 30, 2000); missed season's first two games. ... Injured left shoulder (November 16, 2000); missed six games. ... Reinjured left shoulder (December 9, 2000) and had surgery; missed 38 games. ... Bruised right foot (March 21, 2001); missed one game. ... Concussion (March 26, 2001); missed one game. ... Injured right knee (April 1, 2001); missed season's final three games. ... Injured groin (September 23, 2001); missed season's first three games. ... Flu (October 18, 2001); missed one game. ... Injured right hand (December27, 2001); missed six games. ... Back spasms (March 9, 2002); missed five games. ... Injured back (March 23, 2002); missed one game. ... Traded by Senators to Vancouver Canucks for LW Peter Schaefer (September 21, 2002). ... Injured groin (December 7, 2002); missed one game ... Injured shoulder (February 18, 2003); missed two games. ... Injured leg (December 26, 2003); missed eight games. ... Injured right shoulder and chest (February 23, 2006); missed final 23 games of season.

STATISTICAL PLATEAUS: Three-goal games: 1998-99 (1).

Season Team	League	REGULAR SEASON GP	G	A	Pts.	PIM	+/-	PP	SH	PLAYOFFS GP	G	A	Pts.	PIM
94-95—TPS Turku	Finland	7	1	2	3	6	...	...	...	—	—	—	—	—
—Kiekko-67	Finland Div. 2	19	4	2	6	4	...	...	...	—	—	—	—	—
95-96—TPS Turku	Finland	47	7	14	21	32	...	...	...	11	1	3	4	8
96-97—TPS Turku	Finland	48	9	6	15	10	...	...	...	10	2	3	5	4
97-98—Jokerit Helsinki	Finland	35	3	5	8	10	...	...	...	8	0	1	1	2
98-99—Ottawa	NHL	61	7	12	19	24	20	2	0	4	0	0	0	0
—Detroit	IHL	5	0	2	2	0	1	0	0	—	—	—	—	—

		REGULAR SEASON								PLAYOFFS				
Season Team	**League**	**GP**	**G**	**A**	**Pts.**	**PIM**	**+/-**	**PP**	**SH**	**GP**	**G**	**A**	**Pts.**	**PIM**
99-00—Ottawa	NHL	37	6	8	14	2	6	3	0	6	1	1	2	0
00-01—Ottawa	NHL	31	2	16	18	10	9	1	0	4	0	0	0	0
01-02—Ottawa	NHL	66	4	14	18	14	1	1	1	12	2	1	3	4
—Fin. Olympic team	Int'l	4	0	0	0	0	...	...	...	—	—	—	—	—
02-03—Vancouver	NHL	79	9	21	30	10	9	4	0	12	1	3	4	0
03-04—Vancouver	NHL	74	7	19	26	22	8	5	0	7	1	2	3	2
04-05—Vastra Frolunda	Sweden	41	6	8	14	18	10	1	1	14	1	6	7	2
05-06—Vancouver	NHL	59	10	23	33	38	9	9	0	—	—	—	—	—
—Fin. Olympic team	Int'l	6	1	3	4	0	4	0	1	—	—	—	—	—
NHL Totals (7 years)		407	45	113	158	120	62	25	1	45	5	7	12	6

SALVADOR, BRYCE D

PERSONAL: Born February 11, 1976, in Brandon, Man. ... 6-2/214. ... Shoots left.

TRANSACTIONS/CAREER NOTES: Selected by Tampa Bay Lightning in sixth round (sixth Lightning pick, 138th overall) of entry draft (June 29, 1994). ... Signed as free agent by St. Louis Blues (December 16, 1996). ... Strained hamstring (February 8, 2001); missed four games. ... Foot (March 6, 2001); missed one game. ... Wrist (March 20, 2001); missed one game. ... Strained rib muscle (October 10, 2001); missed seven games. ... Chest (February 7, 2002); missed one game. ... Concussion (March 28, 2002); missed eight games. ... Hamstring (December 7, 2002); missed two games. ... Injured in auto accident (January 2, 2003); missed two games. ... Bruised shoulder (February 22, 2003); missed two games. ... Wrist (October 2, 2003); missed eight games. ... Wrist (December 9, 2003); missed one game. ... Wrist (January 10, 2004); missed one game. ... Knee (November 26, 2005); missed one game. ... Flu (December 28, 2005); missed one game. ... Shoulder (January 20, 2006); missed two games. ... Re-injured shoulder (January 26, 2006); missed eight games. ... Aggravated shoulder (March 1, 2006); missed one game. ... Aggravated shoulder (March 6, 2006); missed season's final 17 games.

		REGULAR SEASON								PLAYOFFS				
Season Team	**League**	**GP**	**G**	**A**	**Pts.**	**PIM**	**+/-**	**PP**	**SH**	**GP**	**G**	**A**	**Pts.**	**PIM**
92-93—Lethbridge	WHL	64	1	4	5	29	...	...	...	4	0	0	0	0
93-94—Lethbridge	WHL	61	4	14	18	36	-6	0	0	9	0	1	1	2
94-95—Lethbridge	WHL	67	1	9	10	88	-33	0	0	—	—	—	—	—
95-96—Lethbridge	WHL	56	4	12	16	75	...	...	...	3	0	1	1	2
96-97—Lethbridge	WHL	63	8	32	40	81	19	6	0	19	0	7	7	14
97-98—Worcester	AHL	46	2	8	10	74	13	0	1	11	0	1	1	45
98-99—Worcester	AHL	69	5	13	18	129	-13	2	0	4	0	1	1	2
99-00—Worcester	AHL	55	0	13	13	53	...	...	...	9	0	1	1	2
00-01—St. Louis	NHL	75	2	8	10	69	-4	0	0	14	2	0	2	18
01-02—St. Louis	NHL	66	5	7	12	78	3	1	0	10	0	1	1	4
02-03—St. Louis	NHL	71	2	8	10	95	7	1	0	7	0	0	0	2
03-04—St. Louis	NHL	69	3	5	8	47	-4	0	0	5	0	0	0	2
—Worcester	AHL	2	0	1	1	0	0	0	0	—	—	—	—	—
04-05—Missouri	UHL	7	0	0	0	16	-8	0	0	—	—	—	—	—
05-06—St. Louis	NHL	46	1	4	5	26	-24	0	0	—	—	—	—	—
NHL Totals (5 years)		327	13	32	45	315	-22	2	0	36	2	1	3	26

SAMSONOV, SERGEI LW

PERSONAL: Born October 27, 1978, in Moscow, U.S.S.R. ... 5-8/194. ... Shoots right. ... Name pronounced sam-SAH-nahf.

TRANSACTIONS/CAREER NOTES: Selected by Boston Bruins in first round (second Bruins pick, eighth overall) of entry draft (June 21, 1997). ... Flu (December 20, 1997); missed one game. ... Bruised thigh (February 12, 1998); missed one game. ... Sinus infection (February 23, 1999); missed two games. ... Knee (January 4, 2000); missed five games. ... Knee (December 4, 2001); missed six games. ... Flu (December 28, 2001); missed two games. ... Wrist (October 19, 2002); missed 18 games. ... Groin (December 2, 2002); missed two games. ... Groin (December 8, 2002); missed four games. ... Wrist (December 19, 2002); missed season's final 50 games. ... Knee (December 12, 2003); missed nine games. ... Ribs (February 11, 2004); missed four games. ... Ribs (February 23, 2004); missed 11 games. ... Ribs (March 16, 2004); missed two games. ... Hand (December 4, 2005); missed two games. ... Ribs (December 28, 2005); missed one game. ... Flu (January 5, 2005); missed two games. ... Bruised foot (February 9, 2006); missed two games. ... Traded by Bruins to Edmonton Oilers for C Marty Reasoner, LW Yan Stastny and second-round pick (LW Milan Lucic) in 2006 (March 9, 2006). ... Signed as free agent by Montreal Canadiens (July 12, 2006).

STATISTICAL PLATEAUS: Three-goal games: 1997-98 (1).

		REGULAR SEASON								PLAYOFFS				
Season Team	**League**	**GP**	**G**	**A**	**Pts.**	**PIM**	**+/-**	**PP**	**SH**	**GP**	**G**	**A**	**Pts.**	**PIM**
94-95—CSKA Moscow	CIS	13	2	2	4	14	...	...	...	2	0	0	0	0
—CSKA Moscow Jrs.	CIS	50	110	72	182	...	...	...	...	—	—	—	—	—
95-96—CSKA Moscow	CIS	51	21	17	38	12	...	...	...	3	1	1	2	4
96-97—Detroit	IHL	73	29	35	64	18	...	...	...	19	8	4	12	12
97-98—Boston	NHL	81	22	25	47	8	9	7	0	6	2	5	7	0
98-99—Boston	NHL	79	25	26	51	18	-6	6	0	11	3	1	4	0
99-00—Boston	NHL	77	19	26	45	4	-6	6	0	—	—	—	—	—
00-01—Boston	NHL	82	29	46	75	18	6	3	0	—	—	—	—	—
01-02—Boston	NHL	74	29	41	70	27	21	3	0	6	2	2	4	0
—Russian Oly. team	Int'l	6	1	2	3	4	...	...	...	—	—	—	—	—
02-03—Boston	NHL	8	5	6	11	2	8	1	0	5	0	2	2	0
03-04—Boston	NHL	58	17	23	40	4	12	3	0	7	2	5	7	0
04-05—Dynamo Moscow	Russian	3	1	0	1	0	1	...	...	3	1	2	3	0
05-06—Boston	NHL	55	18	19	37	22	-3	6	0	—	—	—	—	—
—Edmonton	NHL	19	5	11	16	6	0	4	0	24	4	11	15	14
NHL Totals (8 years)		533	169	223	392	109	41	39	0	59	13	26	39	14

SAMUELSSON, MIKAEL RW/LW

PERSONAL: Born December 23, 1976, in Mariefred, Sweden. ... 6-1/205. ... Shoots left.

TRANSACTIONS/CAREER NOTES: Selected by San Jose Sharks in fifth round (seventh Sharks pick, 145th overall) of entry draft (June 27, 1998). ... Traded by Sharks with D Christian Gosselin to New York Rangers for LW Adam Graves (June 24, 2001). ... Traded by Rangers with RW Rico Fata, D Joel Bouchard, D Richard Lintner and cash to Pittsburgh Penguins for RW Alexei Kovalev, LW Dan LaCouture, D Janne Laukkanen and D Mike Wilson (February 10, 2003). ... Traded by Penguins with first-round pick (C Nathan Horton) and second-round pick (LW Stefan Meyer) in 2003 to Florida Panthers for first- (G Marc-Andre Fleury) and third- (LW Daniel Carcillo) round picks in 2003 (June 21, 2003). ... Fractured jaw (November 14, 2003); missed 22 games. ... Right hand (January 23, 2004); missed 21 games. ... Signed as free agent by Detroit Red Wings (September 24, 2005). ... Leg (December 23, 2005); missed one game. ... Wrist (March 4, 2006); missed nine games.

		REGULAR SEASON								PLAYOFFS				
Season Team	League	GP	G	A	Pts.	PIM	+/-	PP	SH	GP	G	A	Pts.	PIM
94-95—Sodertalje	Sweden Jr.	30	8	6	14	12	...	...	...	—	—	—	—	—
95-96—Sodertalje	Sweden Dv. 2	18	5	1	6	0	...	...	...	4	0	0	0	0
—Sodertalje	Sweden Jr.	22	13	12	25	20	...	...	...	—	—	—	—	—
96-97—Sodertalje	Sweden	29	3	2	5	10	...	...	...	—	—	—	—	—
—Sodertalje	Sweden Jr.	2	2	1	3	...	...	...	...	—	—	—	—	—
97-98—Sodertalje	Sweden	31	8	8	16	47	...	...	...	—	—	—	—	—
98-99—Sodertalje	Sweden	12	7	9	16	20	4	...	...	—	—	—	—	—
—Vastra Frolunda	Sweden	27	0	5	5	10	...	...	...	—	—	—	—	—
99-00—Brynas Gavle	Sweden	40	4	3	7	76	...	...	...	11	7	2	9	6
00-01—Kentucky	AHL	66	32	46	78	58	...	...	...	3	1	0	1	0
—San Jose	NHL	4	0	0	0	0	0	0	0	—	—	—	—	—
01-02—Hartford	AHL	8	3	6	9	12	0	1	0	—	—	—	—	—
—New York Rangers	NHL	67	6	10	16	23	10	1	2	—	—	—	—	—
02-03—New York Rangers	NHL	58	8	14	22	32	0	1	1	—	—	—	—	—
—Pittsburgh	NHL	22	2	0	2	8	-21	1	0	—	—	—	—	—
03-04—Florida	NHL	37	3	6	9	35	0	0	0	—	—	—	—	—
04-05—Geneva	Switzerland	12	2	4	6	14	...	2	0	—	—	—	—	—
—Sodertalje	Sweden	29	7	13	20	45	1	2	0	10	3	3	6	24
05-06—Detroit	NHL	71	23	22	45	42	27	7	0	6	0	1	1	6
—Swedish Oly. team	Int'l	8	1	3	4	2	0	1	0	—	—	—	—	—
NHL Totals (5 years)		259	42	52	94	140	16	10	3	6	0	1	1	6

S

SANDERSON, GEOFF C/LW

PERSONAL: Born February 1, 1972, in Hay River, N.W.T. ... 6-0/190. ... Shoots left.

TRANSACTIONS/CAREER NOTES: Selected by Hartford Whalers in second round (second Whalers pick, 36th overall) of entry draft (June 16, 1990). ... Shoulder (October 14, 1991); missed one game. ... Groin (November 13, 1991); missed three games. ... Knee (December 7, 1991); missed five games. ... Flu (February 1, 1994). ... Whalers franchise moved to North Carolina and renamed Carolina Hurricanes for 1997-98 season; NHL approved move on June 25, 1997. ... Traded by Hurricanes to Vancouver Canucks with D Enrico Ciccone and G Sean Burke for LW Martin Gelinas and G Kirk McLean (January 3, 1998). ... Shoulder (January 21, 1998); missed eight games. ... Traded by Canucks to Buffalo Sabres for LW Brad May and third-round pick (traded to Tampa Bay; Lightning selected LW Jimmie Olvestad) in 1999 (February 4, 1998). ... Hip (April 13, 1998); missed one game. ... Back (January 18, 1999); missed one game. ... Hip (February 19, 1999); missed one game. ... Knee (March 1, 2000); missed five games. ... Selected by Columbus Blue Jackets in expansion draft (June 23, 2000). ... Fractured finger (February 25, 2001); missed one game. ... Knee (March 14, 2001); missed 13 games. ... Back (November 1, 2001); missed 10 games. ... Hernia (December 6, 2001), had surgery; missed 24 games. ... Concussion (April 1, 2002); missed remainder of season. ... Shoulder (October 7, 2003); missed one game. ... Hip (October 25, 2003); missed one game. ... Traded by Blue Jackets to Canucks for third-round pick (G Daniel LaCosta) in 2004 (March 9, 2004). ... Claimed off waivers by Blue Jackets (June 28, 2004). ... Traded by Blue Jackets with RW Tim Jackman to Phoenix Coyotes for D Cale Hulse, LW Jason Chimera and C Mike Rupp (October 8, 2005). ... Hip flexor (December 20, 2005); missed two games. ... Hip (January 26, 2006); missed two games. ... Signed as free agent by Philadelphia Flyers (July 19, 2006).

STATISTICAL PLATEAUS: Three-goal games: 1992-93 (2), 1994-95 (1), 1995-96 (2), 1998-99 (1), 2000-01 (1). Total: 7. ... Four-goal games: 2002-03 (1). ... Total hat tricks: 8.

		REGULAR SEASON								PLAYOFFS				
Season Team	League	GP	G	A	Pts.	PIM	+/-	PP	SH	GP	G	A	Pts.	PIM
88-89—Swift Current	WHL	58	17	11	28	16	...	...	...	12	3	5	8	6
89-90—Swift Current	WHL	70	32	62	94	56	...	...	...	4	1	4	5	8
90-91—Swift Current	WHL	70	62	50	112	57	...	...	...	3	1	2	3	4
—Hartford	NHL	2	1	0	1	0	-2	0	0	3	0	0	0	0
—Springfield	AHL	...	...	...	...	...	...	...	...	1	0	0	0	2
91-92—Hartford	NHL	64	13	18	31	18	5	2	0	7	1	0	1	2
92-93—Hartford	NHL	82	46	43	89	28	-21	21	2	—	—	—	—	—
93-94—Hartford	NHL	82	41	26	67	42	-13	15	1	—	—	—	—	—
94-95—HPK Hameenlinna	Finland	12	6	4	10	24	-4	...	...	—	—	—	—	—
—Hartford	NHL	46	18	14	32	24	-10	4	0	—	—	—	—	—
95-96—Hartford	NHL	81	34	31	65	40	0	6	0	—	—	—	—	—
96-97—Hartford	NHL	82	36	31	67	29	-9	12	1	—	—	—	—	—
97-98—Carolina	NHL	40	7	10	17	14	-4	2	0	—	—	—	—	—
—Vancouver	NHL	9	0	3	3	4	-1	0	0	—	—	—	—	—
—Buffalo	NHL	26	4	5	9	20	6	0	0	14	3	1	4	4
98-99—Buffalo	NHL	75	12	18	30	22	8	1	0	19	4	6	10	14
99-00—Buffalo	NHL	67	13	13	26	22	4	4	0	5	0	2	2	8
00-01—Columbus	NHL	68	30	26	56	46	4	9	0	—	—	—	—	—
01-02—Columbus	NHL	42	11	5	16	12	-15	5	0	—	—	—	—	—
02-03—Columbus	NHL	82	34	33	67	34	-4	15	2	—	—	—	—	—
03-04—Columbus	NHL	67	13	16	29	34	-9	5	0	—	—	—	—	—
—Vancouver	NHL	13	3	4	7	4	-1	1	0	7	1	1	2	4
04-05—Geneva	Switzerland	9	4	1	5	29	...	0	0	—	—	—	—	—
05-06—Columbus	NHL	2	0	0	0	0	-1	0	0	—	—	—	—	—
—Phoenix	NHL	75	25	21	46	58	-14	11	1	—	—	—	—	—
NHL Totals (15 years)		1005	341	317	658	451	-77	113	7	55	9	10	19	32

SANFORD, CURTIS G

PERSONAL: Born October 5, 1979, in Owen Sound, Ont. ... 5-10/187. ... Catches left.
TRANSACTIONS/CAREER NOTES: Signed as free agent by St. Louis Blues (October 9, 2000). ... Hip flexor (December 16, 2005); missed seven games. ... Left knee sprain (March 13, 2006); missed season's final 19 games.

		REGULAR SEASON										PLAYOFFS							
Season Team	League	GP	Min.	W	L	OTL	T	GA	SO	GAA	SV%	GP	Min.	W	L	GA	SO	GAA	SV%
96-97—Owen Sound	OHL	19	847	4	8	...	1	77	0	5.45	...	—	—	—	—	—	—	—	—
97-98—Owen Sound	OHL	30	1542	13	10	...	2	114	1	4.44	...	9	456	4	4	30	1	3.95	...
98-99—Owen Sound	OHL	56	2998	30	16	...	5	191	2	3.82	...	16	960	9	7	58	0	3.63	...
99-00—Owen Sound	OHL	53	3124	18	26	...	6	198	1	3.80	...	—	—	—	—	—	—	—	—
—Missouri	UHL	6	237	3	1	...	0	6	0	1.52	...	—	—	—	—	—	—	—	—
00-01—Peoria	ECHL	27	1511	15	7	...	4	48	3	1.91	...	14	813	9	4	28	2	2.07	...
—Worcester	AHL	5	237	3	0	...	1	16	0	4.06	...	—	—	—	—	—	—	—	—
01-02—Peoria	ECHL	24	1418	13	8	...	2	58	1	2.45	...	—	—	—	—	—	—	—	—
—Worcester	AHL	9	537	5	4	...	0	22	0	2.46	...	—	—	—	—	—	—	—	—
02-03—Worcester	AHL	41	2316	18	14	...	8	93	3	2.41	.919	3	179	0	3	8	0	2.68	.924
—St. Louis	NHL	8	397	5	1	...	0	13	1	1.96	.912	—	—	—	—	—	—	—	—
03-04—Worcester	AHL	43	2367	20	16	...	3	84	5	2.13	...	9	569	4	5	24	0	2.53	...
04-05—Worcester	AHL	50	2742	19	25	...	...	123	2	2.69	.901	—	—	—	—	—	—	—	—
05-06—Peoria	AHL	6	358	4	2	0	...	11	2	1.84	.929	—	—	—	—	—	—	—	—
—St. Louis	NHL	34	1830	13	13	5	...	81	3	2.66	.908	—	—	—	—	—	—	—	—
NHL Totals (2 years)		42	2227	18	14	5	0	94	4	2.53	.909								

SANGUINETTI, BOBBY D

PERSONAL: Born February 29, 1988, in Trenton, N.J. ... 6-1/174. ... Shoots right.
TRANSACTIONS/CAREER NOTES: Selected by New York Rangers in first round (first Rangers pick; 21st overall) of NHL draft (June 24, 2006).

		REGULAR SEASON								PLAYOFFS				
Season Team	League	GP	G	A	Pts.	PIM	+/-	PP	SH	GP	G	A	Pts.	PIM
04-05—Owen Sound	OHL	67	4	20	24	12	16	...	...	5	0	2	2	0
05-06—Owen Sound	OHL	68	14	51	65	44	-6	...	...	11	5	10	15	4

SAPRYKIN, OLEG LW/RW

PERSONAL: Born February 12, 1981, in Moscow, U.S.S.R. ... 6-1/195. ... Shoots left. ... Name pronounced: OH-lehg suh-PREE-kihn
TRANSACTIONS/CAREER NOTES: Selected by Calgary Flames in first round (first Flames pick, 11th overall) of entry draft (June 26, 1999). ... Concussion (January 5, 2001); missed 11 games. ... Neck (September 16, 2001); missed season's first 12 games. ... Left knee (January 18, 2003); missed five games. ... Traded by Flames with D Denis Gauthier to Phoenix Coyotes for C Daymond Langkow (August 26, 2004). ... Knee (December 11, 2005); missed seven games. ... Shoulder (April 5, 2006); missed one game.

		REGULAR SEASON								PLAYOFFS				
Season Team	League	GP	G	A	Pts.	PIM	+/-	PP	SH	GP	G	A	Pts.	PIM
97-98—HC CSKA	Rus. Div.	15	0	3	3	6	...	...	...	—	—	—	—	—
—CSKA Moscow	Russian	20	0	2	2	8	...	...	...	—	—	—	—	—
98-99—Seattle	WHL	66	47	46	93	107	31	15	5	11	5	11	16	36
99-00—Calgary	NHL	4	0	1	1	2	-4	0	0	—	—	—	—	—
—Seattle	WHL	48	30	36	66	89	17	8	2	6	3	3	6	37
00-01—Calgary	NHL	59	9	14	23	43	4	2	0	—	—	—	—	—
01-02—Calgary	NHL	3	0	0	0	0	-2	0	0	—	—	—	—	—
—Saint John	AHL	52	5	19	24	53	-8	2	0	—	—	—	—	—
02-03—Saint John	AHL	21	12	9	21	22	-2	3	1	—	—	—	—	—
—Calgary	NHL	52	8	15	23	46	5	1	0	—	—	—	—	—
03-04—Calgary	NHL	69	12	17	29	41	1	4	0	26	3	3	6	14
04-05—CSKA Moscow	Russian	40	15	8	23	105	-7	...	...	—	—	—	—	—
05-06—Phoenix	NHL	67	11	14	25	50	-16	3	0	—	—	—	—	—
NHL Totals (6 years)		254	40	61	101	182	-12	10	0	26	3	3	6	14

SARICH, CORY D

PERSONAL: Born August 16, 1978, in Saskatoon, Sask. ... 6-3/204. ... Shoots right. ... Name pronounced SAIR-ich.
TRANSACTIONS/CAREER NOTES: Selected by Buffalo Sabres in second round (second Sabres pick, 27th overall) of NHL entry draft (June 22, 1996). ... Traded by Sabres with C Wayne Primeau, C/RW Brian Holzinger and third-round pick (RW Alexandre Kharitonov) in 2000 draft to Tampa Bay Lightning for C Chris Gratton and second-round pick (C Derek Roy) in 2001 draft (March 9, 2000). ... Bruised right knee (October 13, 2001); missed two games. ... Suffered concussion (October 27, 2001); missed one game. ... Bruised right shoulder (November 6, 2001); missed four games.

		REGULAR SEASON								PLAYOFFS				
Season Team	League	GP	G	A	Pts.	PIM	+/-	PP	SH	GP	G	A	Pts.	PIM
94-95—Saskatoon	WHL	6	0	0	0	4	...	...	...	3	0	1	1	0
95-96—Saskatoon	WHL	59	5	18	23	54	...	...	...	3	0	0	0	4
96-97—Saskatoon	WHL	58	6	27	33	158	-31	4	0	—	—	—	—	—
97-98—Seattle	WHL	46	8	40	48	137	-6	5	0	—	—	—	—	—
98-99—Rochester	AHL	77	3	26	29	82	30	3	0	20	2	4	6	14
—Buffalo	NHL	4	0	0	0	0	3	0	0	—	—	—	—	—
99-00—Buffalo	NHL	42	0	4	4	35	2	0	0	—	—	—	—	—
—Rochester	AHL	15	0	6	6	44	...	...	...	—	—	—	—	—
—Tampa Bay	NHL	17	0	2	2	42	-8	0	0	—	—	—	—	—

Season Team	League	GP	G	A	Pts.	PIM	+/-	PP	SH	GP	G	A	Pts.	PIM
		REGULAR SEASON								PLAYOFFS				
00-01—Tampa Bay	NHL	73	1	8	9	106	-25	0	0	—	—	—	—	—
—Detroit	IHL	3	0	2	2	2	...	...	...	—	—	—	—	—
01-02—Tampa Bay	NHL	72	0	11	11	105	-4	0	0	—	—	—	—	—
—Springfield	AHL	2	0	0	0	0	0	0	0	—	—	—	—	—
02-03—Tampa Bay	NHL	82	5	9	14	63	-3	0	0	11	0	2	2	6
03-04—Tampa Bay	NHL	82	3	16	19	89	5	0	1	23	0	2	2	25
05-06—Tampa Bay	NHL	82	1	14	15	79	-2	0	0	5	0	1	1	4
NHL Totals (7 years)		454	10	64	74	519	-32	0	1	39	0	5	5	35

SARNO, PETER C

PERSONAL: Born July 26, 1979, in Toronto. ... 5-11/185. ... Shoots left.

TRANSACTIONS/CAREER NOTES: Selected by Edmonton Oilers in sixth round (sixth Oilers pick, 141st overall) of NHL entry draft (June 21, 1997). ... Traded by Oilers to Vancouver Canucks for G Tyler Moss (February 16, 2004).

Season Team	League	GP	G	A	Pts.	PIM	+/-	PP	SH	GP	G	A	Pts.	PIM
		REGULAR SEASON								PLAYOFFS				
95-96—North York Flames	OPJHL	52	39	57	96	27	...	...	...	—	—	—	—	—
96-97—Windsor	OHL	66	20	63	83	59	14	5	0	5	0	3	3	6
97-98—Windsor	OHL	64	33	88	121	18	...	...	...	—	—	—	—	—
—Hamilton	AHL	8	1	1	2	2	2	0	0	—	—	—	—	—
98-99—Sarnia	OHL	68	37	93	130	49	32	...	...	6	1	7	8	2
99-00—Hamilton	AHL	67	10	36	46	31	...	...	...	—	—	—	—	—
00-01—Hamilton	AHL	79	19	46	65	64	...	...	...	—	—	—	—	—
01-02—Hamilton	AHL	76	12	40	52	38	6	2	0	15	6	7	13	4
02-03—Blues Espoo	Finland	45	17	23	40	34	...	...	...	7	2	1	3	2
03-04—Toronto	AHL	31	6	12	18	29	3	0	0	—	—	—	—	—
—Edmonton	NHL	6	1	0	1	2	2	0	0	—	—	—	—	—
—Manitoba	AHL	23	5	9	14	6	-8	2	0	—	—	—	—	—
04-05—Manitoba	AHL	80	16	66	82	53	11	6	0	14	1	8	9	4
05-06—Syracuse	AHL	39	12	39	51	20	11	5	0	6	0	5	5	8
—Columbus	NHL	1	0	0	0	0	0	0	0	—	—	—	—	—
NHL Totals (2 years)		7	1	0	1	2	2	0	0					

SATAN, MIROSLAV RW

PERSONAL: Born October 22, 1974, in Topolcany, Czech. ... 6-3/192. ... Shoots left. ... Name pronounced shuh-TAN.

TRANSACTIONS/CAREER NOTES: Selected by Edmonton Oilers in fifth round (sixth Oilers pick, 111th overall) of NHL draft (June 26, 1993). ... Collapsed lung (October 1, 1995); missed two games. ... Separated right shoulder (January 13, 1996); missed four games. ... Flu (March 9, 1997); missed one game. ... Traded by Oilers to Buffalo Sabres for D Craig Millar and LW Barrie Moore (March 18, 1997). ... Flu (November 28, 1998); missed one game. ... Injured foot (April 25, 1999); missed nine playoff games. ... Bruised hip, back (November 3, 2002); missed three games. ... Signed by Islanders as unrestricted free agent (August 3, 2005).

STATISTICAL PLATEAUS: Three-goal games: 1996-97 (1), 1997-98 (1), 1999-00 (1), 2002-03 (1), 2003-04 (1). Total: 5. ... Four-goal games: 2003-04 (1). ... Total hat tricks: 6.

Season Team	League	GP	G	A	Pts.	PIM	+/-	PP	SH	GP	G	A	Pts.	PIM
		REGULAR SEASON								PLAYOFFS				
91-92—VTJ Topolcany	Czech Dv.I	9	2	1	3	6	...	...	...	—	—	—	—	—
—VTJ Topolcany Jrs	Czech. Jrs.	31	30	22	52	...	...	...	...	—	—	—	—	—
92-93—Dukla Trencin	Czech.	38	11	6	17	...	...	...	...	—	—	—	—	—
93-94—Dukla Trencin	Slovakia	30	32	16	48	16	...	...	...	—	—	—	—	—
—Slovakian Oly. team	Int'l	8	9	0	9	0	-5	2	1	—	—	—	—	—
94-95—Detroit	IHL	8	1	3	4	4	-5	0	0	—	—	—	—	—
—San Diego	IHL	6	0	2	2	6	2	0	0	—	—	—	—	—
—Cape Breton	AHL	25	24	16	40	15	6	10	0	—	—	—	—	—
95-96—Edmonton	NHL	62	18	17	35	22	0	6	0	—	—	—	—	—
96-97—Edmonton	NHL	64	17	11	28	22	-4	5	0	—	—	—	—	—
—Buffalo	NHL	12	8	2	10	4	1	2	0	7	0	0	0	0
97-98—Buffalo	NHL	79	22	24	46	34	2	9	0	14	5	4	9	4
98-99—Buffalo	NHL	81	40	26	66	44	24	13	3	12	3	5	8	2
99-00—Dukla Trencin	Slovakia	3	2	8	10	2	...	...	...	—	—	—	—	—
—Buffalo	NHL	81	33	34	67	32	16	5	3	5	3	2	5	0
00-01—Buffalo	NHL	82	29	33	62	36	5	8	2	13	3	10	13	8
01-02—Buffalo	NHL	82	37	36	73	33	14	15	5	—	—	—	—	—
—Slovakian Oly. team	Int'l	2	0	1	1	0	...	...	...	—	—	—	—	—
02-03—Buffalo	NHL	79	26	49	75	20	-3	11	1	—	—	—	—	—
03-04—Buffalo	NHL	82	29	28	57	30	-15	11	1	—	—	—	—	—
04-05—Bratislava	Slovakia	18	11	9	20	14	8	4	1	18	15	7	22	16
05-06—New York Islanders	NHL	82	35	31	66	54	-8	17	0	—	—	—	—	—
—Slovakian Oly. team	Int'l	6	0	2	2	2	1	0	0	—	—	—	—	—
NHL Totals (10 years)		786	294	291	585	331	32	102	15	51	14	21	35	14

SAUER, KURT D

PERSONAL: Born January 16, 1981, in St. Cloud, Minn. ... 6-4/225. ... Shoots left. ... Name pronounced SAW-uhr.

TRANSACTIONS/CAREER NOTES: Selected by Colorado Avalanche in third round (fifth Avalanche pick, 88th overall) of NHL entry draft (June 24, 2000). ... Signed as free agent by Anaheim Mighty Ducks (June 6, 2002). ... Sprained left ankle (November 9, 2003); missed six games. ... Traded by Mighty Ducks with fourth-round pick (D Raymond Macias) in 2005 entry draft to Avalanche for D Martin Skoula (February 21, 2004).

Season Team	League	GP	G	A	Pts.	PIM	+/-	PP	SH	GP	G	A	Pts.	PIM
		REGULAR SEASON								PLAYOFFS				
99-00—Spokane	WHL	71	3	12	15	48	...	...	...	—	—	—	—	—
00-01—Spokane	WHL	48	5	10	15	85	...	...	...	3	1	0	1	2
01-02—Spokane	WHL	61	4	20	24	73	...	...	...	11	0	3	3	12
02-03—Anaheim	NHL	80	1	2	3	74	-23	0	0	21	1	1	2	6
03-04—Anaheim	NHL	55	1	4	5	32	-8	0	0	—	—	—	—	—
—Colorado	NHL	14	0	1	1	19	-3	0	0	3	0	0	0	0
05-06—Lowell	AHL	4	0	0	0	0	-1	0	0	—	—	—	—	—
—Colorado	NHL	37	1	4	5	24	5	0	0	9	0	0	0	4
NHL Totals (3 years)		186	3	11	14	149	-29	0	0	33	1	1	2	10

SAUVE, PHILIPPE G

PERSONAL: Born February 27, 1980, in Buffalo, N.Y. ... 6-0/180. ... Catches left.

TRANSACTIONS/CAREER NOTES: Selected by Colorado Avalanche in second round (sixth Avalanche pick, 38th overall) of entry draft (June 27, 1998). ... Traded by Avalanche to Calgary Flames for a conditional seventh-round pick in 2006 draft (August 9, 2005). ... Traded by Flames with C Steve Reinprecht to Phoenix Coyotes for LW Mike Leclerc and G Brian Boucher (February 1, 2006). ... Placed on waivers by Coyotes (March 8, 2006).

Season Team	League	GP	Min.	W	L	OTL	T	GA	SO	GAA	SV%	GP	Min.	W	L	GA	SO	GAA	SV%
		REGULAR SEASON										PLAYOFFS							
96-97—Rimouski	QMJHL	26	1332	11	9	...	2	84	0	3.78	...	1	14	0	0	3	0	12.86	...
97-98—Rimouski	QMJHL	40	2326	23	16	...	0	131	1	3.38	...	7	262	0	5	33	0	7.56	...
98-99—Rimouski	QMJHL	44	2401	16	19	...	4	155	0	3.87	...	11	595	6	4	30	1	3.03	...
99-00—Drummondville	QMJHL	28	1526	12	12	...	2	106	0	4.17	.864	—	—	—	—	—	—	—	—
—Hull	QMJHL	17	992	9	7	...	1	57	0	3.45	.903	12	735	6	6	47	0	3.84	.890
00-01—Hershey	AHL	42	2182	17	18	...	1	100	3	2.75	.914	3	218	0	3	10	0	2.75	...
01-02—Hershey	AHL	55	3129	25	20	...	6	111	6	2.13	.922	8	486	3	5	21	0	2.59	.915
02-03—Hershey	AHL	60	3394	26	20	...	12	134	5	2.37	.917	5	294	2	3	14	0	2.86	.914
03-04—Colorado	NHL	17	986	7	7	...	3	50	0	3.04	.896	—	—	—	—	—	—	—	—
—Hershey	AHL	10	578	3	7	...	0	25	2	2.60	.901	—	—	—	—	—	—	—	—
04-05—Mississippi	ECHL	21	1297	13	4	...	...	56	2	2.59	.923	4	226	1	3	16	...	4.23	.904
05-06—Calgary	NHL	8	402	3	3	0	...	22	0	3.28	.891	—	—	—	—	—	—	—	—
—Phoenix	NHL	5	187	0	4	0	...	17	0	5.45	.867	—	—	—	—	—	—	—	—
NHL Totals (2 years)		30	1575	10	14	0	3	89	0	3.39	.890								

SAVAGE, BRIAN LW/RW

PERSONAL: Born February 24, 1971, in Sudbury, Ont. ... 6-1/197. ... Shoots left. ... Name pronounced SA-vuhj.

TRANSACTIONS/CAREER NOTES: Selected by Montreal Canadiens in eighth round (11th Canadiens pick, 171st overall) of entry draft (June 22, 1991). ... Bruised knee (February 4, 1995); missed 10 games. ... Bruised knee (April 5, 1995); missed one game. ... Hip pointer (February 17, 1996); missed six games. ... Flu (April 1, 1996); missed one game. ... Pulled groin (October 26, 1996); missed one game. ... Fractured hand (October 1, 1997); missed seven games. ... Bruised thigh (November 26, 1997); missed one game. ... Fractured thumb (March 21, 1998); missed 10 games. ... Strained groin (November 4, 1998); missed one game. ... Reinjured groin (December 9, 1998); missed 11 games. ... Torn muscle in rib cage (January 21, 1999); missed 11 games. ... Fractured vertebrae in neck (November 20, 1999); missed 44 games. ... Fractured thumb (January 20, 2001); missed 20 games. ... Injured wrist (January 14, 2002); missed four games. ... Traded by Canadiens with third-round pick (D Matt Jones) in 2002 and future considerations to Phoenix Coyotes for LW Sergei Berezin (January 25, 2002). ... Strained hip flexor (April 10, 2002); missed final two games of season. ... Pulled groin (October 14, 2002); missed four games. ... Fractured thumb (November 17, 2002); missed five games. ... Concussion (December 15, 2002); missed 21 games. ... Fractured collarbone (March 24, 2003); missed last seven games of season. ... Fractured thumb (October 25, 2003); missed five games. ... Traded by Coyotes to St. Louis Blues for future considerations (March 9, 2004); returned to Coyotes to complete deal. ... Contract bought out by Coyotes (July 29, 2005). ... Signed as free agent by Philadelphia Flyers (September 15, 2005). ... Left knee injury (November 22, 2005); missed 11 games.

STATISTICAL PLATEAUS: Three-goal games: 1995-96 (1), 1996-97 (1), 1999-00 (2), 2000-01 (1), 2001-02 (1). Total: 6. ... Four-goal games: 1997-98 (1). ... Total hat tricks: 7.

Season Team	League	GP	G	A	Pts.	PIM	+/-	PP	SH	GP	G	A	Pts.	PIM
		REGULAR SEASON								PLAYOFFS				
89-90—Sudbury	OHA Mj. Jr	32	45	40	85	61	...	...	...	—	—	—	—	—
90-91—Miami (Ohio)	CCHA	28	5	6	11	26	...	...	...	—	—	—	—	—
91-92—Miami (Ohio)	CCHA	40	24	16	40	43	...	...	...	—	—	—	—	—
92-93—Miami (Ohio)	CCHA	38	37	21	58	44	23	10	2	—	—	—	—	—
—Canadian nat'l team	Int'l	9	3	0	3	12	...	...	...	—	—	—	—	—
93-94—Canadian nat'l team	Int'l	51	20	26	46	38	...	...	...	—	—	—	—	—
—Can. Olympic team	Int'l	8	2	2	4	6	2	0	0	—	—	—	—	—
—Fredericton	AHL	17	12	15	27	4	-7	4	0	—	—	—	—	—
—Montreal	NHL	3	1	0	1	0	0	0	0	3	0	2	2	0
94-95—Montreal	NHL	37	12	7	19	27	5	0	0	—	—	—	—	—
95-96—Montreal	NHL	75	25	8	33	28	-8	4	0	6	0	2	2	2
96-97—Montreal	NHL	81	23	37	60	39	-14	5	0	5	1	1	2	0
97-98—Montreal	NHL	64	26	17	43	36	11	8	0	9	0	2	2	6
98-99—Montreal	NHL	54	16	10	26	20	-14	5	0	—	—	—	—	—
99-00—Montreal	NHL	38	17	12	29	19	-4	6	1	—	—	—	—	—
00-01—Montreal	NHL	62	21	24	45	26	-13	12	0	—	—	—	—	—
01-02—Montreal	NHL	47	14	15	29	30	-14	7	0	—	—	—	—	—
—Phoenix	NHL	30	6	6	12	8	1	2	0	5	0	0	0	0
02-03—Phoenix	NHL	43	6	10	16	22	-4	1	0	—	—	—	—	—
03-04—Phoenix	NHL	61	12	13	25	36	-5	3	0	—	—	—	—	—
—St. Louis	NHL	13	4	3	7	2	-3	1	0	5	1	1	2	0
05-06—Philadelphia	NHL	66	9	5	14	28	-18	4	1	6	1	0	1	4
NHL Totals (12 years)		674	192	167	359	321	-80	58	2	39	3	8	11	12

SAVARD, MARC — C

PERSONAL: Born July 17, 1977, in Ottawa. ... 5-10/190. ... Shoots left. ... Name pronounced suh-VAHRD.
TRANSACTIONS/CAREER NOTES: Selected by New York Rangers in fourth round (third Rangers pick, 91st overall) of NHL draft (July 8, 1995). ... Traded by Rangers with first-round pick (C/LW Oleg Saprykin) in 1999 draft to Calgary Flames for rights to LW Jan Hlavac and first- (C Jamie Lundmark) and third-round (D Pat Aufiero) picks in 1999 draft (June 26, 1999). ... Concussion (January 8, 2000); missed two games. ... Missed first two games of 2000-01 season in contract dispute. ... Concussion (December 31, 2000); missed three games. ... Injured knee (October 10, 2001); missed 15 games. ... Injured head (March 23, 2002); missed remainder of season. ... Traded by Flames to Atlanta Thrashers for RW Ruslan Zainullan (November 15, 2002). ... Injured groin (November 28, 2002); missed five games. ... Injured hamstring (January 28, 2003); missed one game. ... Flu (March 13, 2003); missed one game. ... Injured left ankle and had surgery (November 4, 2003); missed nine games. ... Suspended one game for match penalty incident (November 28, 2003). ... Suffered concussion (January 4, 2004); missed three games. ... Sprained right knee (January 15, 2004); missed seven games. ... Injured knee (February 27, 2004); missed final 17 games of regular season. ... Signed as free agent by Boston Bruins (July 1, 2006).
STATISTICAL PLATEAUS: Three-goal games: 2001-02 (1). ... Four-goal games: 1999-00 (1). ... Total hat tricks: 2.

		REGULAR SEASON								PLAYOFFS				
Season Team	League	GP	G	A	Pts.	PIM	+/-	PP	SH	GP	G	A	Pts.	PIM
92-93—Metcalfe	Jr. B	31	46	53	99	26	...	...	...	—	—	—	—	—
93-94—Oshawa	OHL	61	18	39	57	24	...	...	...	5	4	3	7	8
94-95—Oshawa	OHL	66	43	96	139	78	...	12	3	7	5	6	11	8
95-96—Oshawa	OHL	48	28	59	87	77	...	...	...	5	4	5	9	6
96-97—Oshawa	OHL	64	43	87	130	94	22	10	3	18	13	24	37	20
97-98—New York Rangers	NHL	28	1	5	6	4	-4	0	0	—	—	—	—	—
—Hartford	AHL	58	21	53	74	66	16	5	0	15	8	19	27	24
98-99—Hartford	AHL	9	3	10	13	16	1	1	0	7	1	12	13	16
—New York Rangers	NHL	70	9	36	45	38	-7	4	0	—	—	—	—	—
99-00—Calgary	NHL	78	22	31	53	56	-2	4	0	—	—	—	—	—
00-01—Calgary	NHL	77	23	42	65	46	-12	10	1	—	—	—	—	—
01-02—Calgary	NHL	56	14	19	33	48	-18	7	0	—	—	—	—	—
02-03—Calgary	NHL	10	1	2	3	8	-3	0	0	—	—	—	—	—
—Atlanta	NHL	57	16	31	47	77	-11	6	0	—	—	—	—	—
03-04—Atlanta	NHL	45	19	33	52	85	-8	6	1	—	—	—	—	—
04-05—Bern	Switzerland	5	1	2	3	0	...	0	0	—	—	—	—	—
—Thurgau	Switz. Div. 2	13	9	19	28	10	...	3	0	—	—	—	—	—
05-06—Atlanta	NHL	82	28	69	97	100	7	14	1	—	—	—	—	—
NHL Totals (8 years)		503	133	268	401	462	-58	51	3					

SCATCHARD, DAVE — C/RW

PERSONAL: Born February 20, 1976, in Hinton, Alta. ... 6-2/224. ... Shoots right. ... Name pronounced SKATCH-uhrd.
TRANSACTIONS/CAREER NOTES: Selected by Vancouver Canucks in second round (third Canucks pick, 42nd overall) of entry draft (June 28, 1994). ... Hip pointer (December 15, 1997); missed two games. ... Ankle (October 13, 1999); missed five games. ... Traded by Canucks with G Kevin Weekes and RW Bill Muckalt to New York Islanders for G Felix Potvin, second- (traded to New Jersey; Devils selected RW Teemu Laine) and third-round (C Thatcher Bell) picks in 2000 (December 19, 1999). ... Concussion (March 22, 2000); missed final eight games of season. ... Neck (November 9, 2000); missed one game. ... Shoulder (October 20, 2003); missed 20 games. ... Signed as free agent by Boston Bruins (August 2, 2005). ... Groin (October 4, 2005); missed season's first four games. ... Traded by Bruins to Phoenix Coyotes for D David Tanabe (November 18, 2005). ... Groin (December 31, 200); missed one game. ... Groin (January 8, 2006); missed five games. ... Groin (January 26, 2006); missed one game. ... Bronchitis (March 28, 2006); missed seven games.
STATISTICAL PLATEAUS: Three-goal games: 2002-03 (2).

		REGULAR SEASON								PLAYOFFS				
Season Team	League	GP	G	A	Pts.	PIM	+/-	PP	SH	GP	G	A	Pts.	PIM
92-93—Kimberley	RMJHL	51	20	23	43	61	...	...	...	—	—	—	—	—
93-94—Portland	WHL	47	9	11	20	46	3	0	0	10	2	1	3	4
94-95—Portland	WHL	71	20	30	50	148	-23	5	1	8	0	3	3	21
95-96—Portland	WHL	59	19	28	47	146	...	...	...	7	1	8	9	14
—Syracuse	AHL	1	0	0	0	0	...	...	...	15	2	5	7	29
96-97—Syracuse	AHL	26	8	7	15	65	-1	4	0	—	—	—	—	—
97-98—Vancouver	NHL	76	13	11	24	165	-4	0	0	—	—	—	—	—
98-99—Vancouver	NHL	82	13	13	26	140	-12	0	2	—	—	—	—	—
99-00—Vancouver	NHL	21	0	4	4	24	-3	0	0	—	—	—	—	—
—New York Islanders	NHL	44	12	14	26	93	0	0	1	—	—	—	—	—
00-01—New York Islanders	NHL	81	21	24	45	114	-9	4	0	—	—	—	—	—
01-02—New York Islanders	NHL	80	12	15	27	111	-4	3	1	7	1	1	2	22
02-03—New York Islanders	NHL	81	27	18	45	108	9	5	0	5	1	0	1	6
03-04—New York Islanders	NHL	61	9	16	25	78	12	1	1	5	0	1	1	6
05-06—Boston	NHL	16	4	6	10	28	-2	1	0	—	—	—	—	—
—Phoenix	NHL	47	11	12	23	84	-11	4	0	—	—	—	—	—
NHL Totals (8 years)		589	122	133	255	945	-24	18	5	17	2	2	4	34

SCHAEFER, NOLAN — G

PERSONAL: Born January 15, 1980, in Yellow Grass, Sask. ... 6-2/195. ... Catches left. ... Name pronounced SHAY-fuhr.
TRANSACTIONS/CAREER NOTES: Selected by San Jose Sharks in fifth round (4rth Sharks pick, 166th overall) of entry draft (June 24, 2000).

		REGULAR SEASON										PLAYOFFS							
Season Team	League	GP	Min.	W	L	OTL	T	GA	SO	GAA	SV%	GP	Min.	W	L	GA	SO	GAA	SV%
99-00—Providence College	Hockey East	14	778	6	5	...	1	42	0	3.24	.904	—	—	—	—	—	—	—	—
00-01—Providence College	Hockey East	25	1529	15	8	...	2	63	3	2.47	...	—	—	—	—	—	—	—	—
01-02—Providence College	Hockey East	35	2062	11	18	...	5	113	0	3.29	...	—	—	—	—	—	—	—	—

Season Team	League	REGULAR SEASON GP	Min.	W	L	OTL	T	GA	SO	GAA	SV%	PLAYOFFS GP	Min.	W	L	GA	SO	GAA	SV%
02-03—Providence College	Hockey East	25	1440	13	8	...	2	71	0	2.96	...	—	—	—	—	—	—	—	—
03-04—Cleveland	AHL	27	1591	14	9	...	3	62	2	2.34	.919	9	572	4	5	24	0	2.52	.922
04-05—Cleveland	AHL	43	2417	17	23	...	...	110	3	2.73	.907	—	—	—	—	—	—	—	—
05-06—Cleveland	AHL	36	2059	12	21	2	...	118	2	3.44	.887	—	—	—	—	—	—	—	—
—San Jose	NHL	7	352	5	1	0	...	11	1	1.88	.920	—	—	—	—	—	—	—	—
NHL Totals (1 year)		7	352	5	1	0	0	11	1	1.88	.920								

SCHAEFER, PETER — LW

PERSONAL: Born July 12, 1977, in Yellow Grass, Sask. ... 5-11/194. ... Shoots left. ... Name pronounced SHAY-fuhr.

TRANSACTIONS/CAREER NOTES: Selected by Vancouver Canucks in third round (third Canucks pick, 66th overall) of NHL draft (July 8, 1995). ... Sprained shoulder (April 2, 1999); missed final six games of season. ... Flu (November 20, 1999); missed one game. ... Injured knee (February 14, 2000); missed three games. ... Reinjured knee (February 23, 2000); missed four games. ... Flu (April 2, 2000); missed one game. ... Missed 2001-02 season in contract dispute. ... Traded by Canucks to Ottawa Senators for D Sami Salo (September 21, 2002). ... Injured right knee (December 4, 2002); missed two games. ... Injured lower left leg (February 8, 2003); missed three games. ... Injured lower back (March 21, 2003); missed two games. ... Bruised foot (November 1, 2003); missed one game.

Season Team	League	REGULAR SEASON GP	G	A	Pts.	PIM	+/-	PP	SH	PLAYOFFS GP	G	A	Pts.	PIM
93-94—Brandon	WHL	2	1	0	1	0	...	...	...	—	—	—	—	—
94-95—Brandon	WHL	68	27	32	59	34	20	6	0	18	5	3	8	18
95-96—Brandon	WHL	69	47	61	108	53	...	...	...	19	10	13	23	5
96-97—Brandon	WHL	61	49	74	123	85	57	15	6	6	1	4	5	4
—Syracuse	AHL	5	0	3	3	0	2	0	0	3	1	3	4	14
97-98—Syracuse	AHL	73	19	44	63	41	-8	6	0	5	2	1	3	2
98-99—Syracuse	AHL	41	10	19	29	66	-17	5	1	—	—	—	—	—
—Vancouver	NHL	25	4	4	8	8	-1	1	0	—	—	—	—	—
99-00—Vancouver	NHL	71	16	15	31	20	0	2	2	—	—	—	—	—
—Syracuse	AHL	2	0	0	0	2	...	...	...	—	—	—	—	—
00-01—Vancouver	NHL	82	16	20	36	22	4	3	4	3	0	0	0	0
01-02—TPS Turku	Finland	33	16	15	31	93	...	...	...	8	1	2	3	2
02-03—Ottawa	NHL	75	6	17	23	32	11	0	0	16	2	3	5	6
03-04—Ottawa	NHL	81	15	24	39	26	22	2	2	7	0	2	2	4
04-05—Bolzano	Italy	15	11	14	25	10	...	...	...	10	1	7	8	12
05-06—Ottawa	NHL	82	20	30	50	40	16	4	4	10	2	5	7	14
NHL Totals (6 years)		416	77	110	187	148	52	12	12	36	4	10	14	24

SCHNEIDER, MATHIEU — D

PERSONAL: Born June 12, 1969, in New York City. ... 6-0/197. ... Shoots left.

TRANSACTIONS/CAREER NOTES: Selected by Montreal Canadiens in third round (fourth Canadiens pick, 44th overall) of entry draft (June 13, 1987). ... Left shoulder (February 1990). ... Left ankle (January 26, 1991); missed nine games. ... Ankle (January 27, 1993); missed 24 games. ... Separated shoulder (April 18, 1993); missed seven playoff games. ... Ankle (December 6, 1993); missed two games. ... Elbow surgery (March 29, 1994); missed five games. ... Flu (February 27, 1995); missed one game. ... Traded by Canadiens with LW Kirk Muller and C Craig Darby to New York Islanders for D Vladimir Malakhov and C Pierre Turgeon (April 5, 1995). ... Ribs (October 28, 1995); missed one game. ... Traded by Islanders with LW Wendel Clark and D D.J. Smith to Toronto Maple Leafs for LW Sean Haggerty, C Darby Hendrickson, D Kenny Jonsson and first-round pick (G Roberto Luongo) in 1997 (March 13, 1996). ... Suspended three games for elbowing incident (November 14, 1996). ... Groin (December 12, 1996); missed 27 games. ... Groin (February 12, 1997); had surgery; missed season's final 26 games. ... Concussion and facial cuts (December 2, 1997); missed two games. ... Shoulder (January 6, 1998); missed two games. ... Abdominal strain (February 2, 1998); missed one game. ... Groin (April 6, 1998); missed one game. ... Traded by Maple Leafs to New York Rangers for D Alexander Karpovtsev and fourth-round pick (LW Mirko Murovic) in 1999 (October 14, 1998). ... Flu (January 27, 2000); missed one game. ... Flu (March 26, 2000); missed one game. ... Selected by Columbus Blue Jackets in expansion draft (June 23, 2000). ... Signed as free agent by Los Angeles Kings (August 13, 2000). ... Back (November 16, 2000); missed one game. ... Groin (February 23, 2001); missed eight games. ... Hernia (November 9, 2001); missed 23 games. ... Strained left shoulder (January 28, 2002); missed two games. ... Traded by Kings to Detroit Red Wings for C Sean Avery, D Maxim Kuznetsov, first-round pick (RW Jeff Tambellini) in 2003 and second-round pick (traded to Boston; Bruins selected Martins Karsums) in 2004 (March 11, 2003). ... Suspended two games for high-sticking incident (January 10, 2004). ... Groin (March 21, 2004); missed two games. ... Groin (November 1, 2005); missed one game. ... Charley horse (December 17, 2005); missed one game. ... Groin (March 31, 2006); missed seven games. ... Groin (April 17, 2006); missed one game.

Season Team	League	REGULAR SEASON GP	G	A	Pts.	PIM	+/-	PP	SH	PLAYOFFS GP	G	A	Pts.	PIM
85-86—Mt. St. Charles H.S.	R.I.H.S.	19	3	27	30	...	...	...	...	—	—	—	—	—
86-87—Cornwall	OHL	63	7	29	36	75	...	...	...	5	0	0	0	22
87-88—Montreal	NHL	4	0	0	0	2	-2	0	0	—	—	—	—	—
—Cornwall	OHL	48	21	40	61	85	...	...	...	11	2	6	8	14
—Sherbrooke	AHL	...	...	...	...	...	...	...	...	3	0	3	3	12
88-89—Cornwall	OHL	59	16	57	73	96	...	...	...	18	7	20	27	30
89-90—Sherbrooke	AHL	28	6	13	19	20	...	...	...	—	—	—	—	—
—Montreal	NHL	44	7	14	21	25	2	5	0	9	1	3	4	31
90-91—Montreal	NHL	69	10	20	30	63	7	5	0	13	2	7	9	18
91-92—Montreal	NHL	78	8	24	32	72	10	2	0	10	1	4	5	6
92-93—Montreal	NHL	60	13	31	44	91	8	3	0	11	1	2	3	16
93-94—Montreal	NHL	75	20	32	52	62	15	11	0	1	0	0	0	0
94-95—Montreal	NHL	30	5	15	20	49	-3	2	0	—	—	—	—	—
—New York Islanders.....	NHL	13	3	6	9	30	-5	1	0	—	—	—	—	—
95-96—New York Islanders.....	NHL	65	11	36	47	93	-18	7	0	—	—	—	—	—
—Toronto	NHL	13	2	5	7	10	-2	0	0	6	0	4	4	8
96-97—Toronto	NHL	26	5	7	12	20	3	1	0	—	—	—	—	—
97-98—Toronto	NHL	76	11	26	37	44	-12	4	1	—	—	—	—	—
—U.S. Olympic team......	Int'l	4	0	0	0	6	-1	0	0	—	—	—	—	—

Season Team	League	GP	G	A	Pts.	PIM	+/-	PP	SH	GP	G	A	Pts.	PIM
		REGULAR SEASON								PLAYOFFS				
98-99—New York Rangers......	NHL	75	10	24	34	71	-19	5	0	—	—	—	—	—
99-00—New York Rangers......	NHL	80	10	20	30	78	-6	3	0	—	—	—	—	—
00-01—Los Angeles..............	NHL	73	16	35	51	56	0	7	1	13	0	9	9	10
01-02—Los Angeles..............	NHL	55	7	23	30	68	3	4	0	7	0	1	1	18
02-03—Los Angeles..............	NHL	65	14	29	43	57	0	10	0	—	—	—	—	—
—Detroit.........................	NHL	13	2	5	7	16	2	1	0	4	0	0	0	6
03-04—Detroit.........................	NHL	78	14	32	46	56	22	4	1	12	1	2	3	8
05-06—Detroit.........................	NHL	72	21	38	59	86	33	11	0	6	1	7	8	6
—U.S. Olympic team......	Int'l	6	1	2	3	16	0	1	0	—	—	—	—	—
NHL Totals (17 years)..........		1064	189	422	611	1049	38	86	3	92	7	39	46	127

SCHUBERT, CHRISTOPH — D

PERSONAL: Born February 5, 1982, in Munich, W. Germany. ... 6-3/219. ... Shoots left. ... Name pronounced SHOO-buhrt.
TRANSACTIONS/CAREER NOTES: Selected by Ottawa Senators in fourth round (fifth Senators pick, 127th overall) of NHL entry draft (June 23, 2001). ... Injured hamstring (Jan 12, 2006); missed one game. ... Injured back (February 3, 2006); missed one game.

Season Team	League	GP	G	A	Pts.	PIM	+/-	PP	SH	GP	G	A	Pts.	PIM
		REGULAR SEASON								PLAYOFFS				
00-01—Munchen.....................	Ger. Div. II	55	6	3	9	80	...	...	...	—	—	—	—	—
01-02—Munich	Germany	50	5	11	16	125	...	...	...	9	3	4	7	32
—German Oly. team.......	Int'l	7	0	1	1	6	...	...	...	—	—	—	—	—
02-03—Binghamton	AHL	70	2	8	10	102	18	0	0	8	0	1	1	2
03-04—Binghamton	AHL	70	2	10	12	69	-9	0	0	1	0	0	0	0
04-05—Binghamton	AHL	76	10	22	32	110	24	2	1	6	2	2	4	20
05-06—Ottawa	NHL	56	4	6	10	48	4	0	1	7	0	1	1	4
—German Oly. team.......	Int'l	5	0	1	1	2	0	0	0	—	—	—	—	—
NHL Totals (1 year).............		56	4	6	10	48	4	0	1	7	0	1	1	4

SCHULTZ, NICK — D

PERSONAL: Born August 25, 1982, in Strasbourg, Sask. ... 6-1/207. ... Shoots left.
TRANSACTIONS/CAREER NOTES: Selected by Minnesota Wild in second round (second Wild pick, 33rd overall) of entry draft (June 24, 2000). ... Bruised shoulder (February 6, 2002); missed one game.

Season Team	League	GP	G	A	Pts.	PIM	+/-	PP	SH	GP	G	A	Pts.	PIM
		REGULAR SEASON								PLAYOFFS				
98-99—Prince Albert..............	WHL	58	5	10	15	37	...	...	...	—	—	—	—	—
99-00—Prince Albert..............	WHL	72	11	33	44	38	...	...	...	6	0	3	3	2
00-01—Prince Albert..............	WHL	59	17	30	47	120	...	...	...	—	—	—	—	—
—Cleveland	IHL	4	1	1	2	2	...	...	...	3	0	1	1	0
01-02—Minnesota..................	NHL	52	4	6	10	14	0	1	0	—	—	—	—	—
—Houston.......................	AHL	0	0	0	0	0	0	0	0	14	1	5	6	2
02-03—Minnesota..................	NHL	75	3	7	10	23	11	0	0	18	0	1	1	10
03-04—Minnesota..................	NHL	79	6	10	16	16	12	1	0	—	—	—	—	—
04-05—Kassel	Germany	46	7	15	22	26	-15	3	0	7	0	4	4	6
05-06—Minnesota..................	NHL	79	2	12	14	43	2	0	0	—	—	—	—	—
NHL Totals (4 years)...........		285	15	35	50	96	25	2	0	18	0	1	1	10

SCUDERI, ROBERT — D

PERSONAL: Born December 30, 1978, in Syosset, N.Y. ... 6-0/214. ... Shoots left. ... Name pronounced SKUD-uhree.
TRANSACTIONS/CAREER NOTES: Selected by Pittsburgh Penguins in fifth round (fifth Penguins pick, 134th overall) of NHL entry draft (June 27, 1998). ... Signed as free agent by Wilkes-Barre/Scranton of the AHL (September 26, 2004). ... Re-signed by Penguins as free agent (August 9, 2005).

Season Team	League	GP	G	A	Pts.	PIM	+/-	PP	SH	GP	G	A	Pts.	PIM
		REGULAR SEASON								PLAYOFFS				
96-97—NY AppleCore	Jr. B	80	42	70	112	52	...	...	...	—	—	—	—	—
97-98—Boston College	Hockey East	42	0	24	24	12	...	...	...	—	—	—	—	—
98-99—Boston College	Hockey East	41	2	8	10	20	...	...	...	—	—	—	—	—
99-00—Boston College	Hockey East	42	1	13	14	24	...	...	...	—	—	—	—	—
00-01—Boston College	Hockey East	43	4	19	23	42	...	...	...	—	—	—	—	—
01-02—Wilkes-Barre/Scranton	AHL	75	1	22	23	66	-4	1	0	—	—	—	—	—
02-03—Wilkes-Barre/Scranton	AHL	74	4	17	21	44	5	2	0	6	0	1	1	4
03-04—Wilkes-Barre/Scranton	AHL	64	1	15	16	44	1	0	0	24	0	3	3	14
—Pittsburgh..................	NHL	13	1	2	3	4	2	0	0	6	0	1	1	4
04-05—Wilkes-Barre/Scranton	AHL	79	2	18	20	34	15	0	0	11	2	1	3	2
05-06—Wilkes-Barre/Scranton	AHL	13	0	8	8	8	11	0	0	—	—	—	—	—
—Pittsburgh..................	NHL	57	0	4	4	36	-18	0	0	—	—	—	—	—
NHL Totals (2 years)...........		70	1	6	7	40	-16	0	0	6	0	1	1	4

SEABROOK, BRENT — D

PERSONAL: Born April 20, 1985, in Richmond, B.C. ... 6-3/215. ... Shoots right.
TRANSACTIONS/CAREER NOTES: Selected by Chicago Blackhawks in first round (first Blackhawks pick, 14th overall) in entry draft (June 23, 2003). ... Sprained knee (December 21, 2005); missed 13 games.

Season Team	League	REGULAR SEASON GP	G	A	Pts.	PIM	+/-	PP	SH	PLAYOFFS GP	G	A	Pts.	PIM
00-01—Lethbridge	WHL	4	0	0	0	0	...	...	...	—	—	—	—	—
01-02—Lethbridge	WHL	67	6	33	39	70	...	...	...	4	1	1	2	2
02-03—Lethbridge	WHL	69	9	33	42	113	...	...	...	—	—	—	—	—
03-04—Lethbridge	WHL	61	12	29	41	107	...	...	...	—	—	—	—	—
04-05—Norfolk	AHL	3	0	0	0	2	-3	0	0	6	0	1	1	6
—Lethbridge	WHL	63	12	42	54	107	25	7	0	5	1	2	3	10
05-06—Chicago	NHL	69	5	27	32	60	5	1	0	—	—	—	—	—
NHL Totals (1 year)		69	5	27	32	60	5	1	0					

SEABROOK, KEITH D

PERSONAL: Born August 2, 1988, in Delta, B.C. ... 6-0/198. ... Shoots right.
TRANSACTIONS/CAREER NOTES: Selected by Washington Capitals in second round (fifth Capitals pick; 52nd overall) of NHL draft (June 24, 2006).

Season Team	League	REGULAR SEASON GP	G	A	Pts.	PIM	+/-	PP	SH	PLAYOFFS GP	G	A	Pts.	PIM
04-05—Coquitlam	BCHL	58	8	20	28	70	...	4	...	7	1	3	4	10
05-06—Burnaby	BCJHL	57	10	24	34	81	...	...	...	20	9	10	19	20

SEDIN, DANIEL LW

PERSONAL: Born September 26, 1980, in Ornskoldsvik, Sweden. ... 6-1/190. ... Shoots left. ... Twin brother of Henrik Sedin, C, Vancouver Canucks.
TRANSACTIONS/CAREER NOTES: Selected by Vancouver Canucks in first round (first Canucks pick, second overall) of NHL draft (June 26, 1999). ... Strained shoulder (November 30, 2000); missed four games. ... Injured back (March 25, 2001); missed two games. ... Reinjured back (April 2, 2001); missed one game. ... Sprained knee (December 19, 2001); missed two games.
STATISTICAL PLATEAUS: Four-goal games: 2003-04 (1).

Season Team	League	REGULAR SEASON GP	G	A	Pts.	PIM	+/-	PP	SH	PLAYOFFS GP	G	A	Pts.	PIM
96-97—MoDo Ornskoldsvik	Sweden Jr.	26	26	14	40	...	...	...	...	—	—	—	—	—
97-98—MoDo Ornskoldsvik	Sweden	45	4	8	12	26	...	...	...	9	0	0	0	2
—MoDo Ornskoldsvik	Sweden Jr.	4	3	3	6	4	...	...	...	—	—	—	—	—
98-99—MoDo Ornskoldsvik	Sweden	50	21	21	42	20	...	...	...	13	4	8	12	14
99-00—MoDo Ornskoldsvik	Sweden	50	19	26	45	28	...	...	...	13	8	6	14	18
00-01—Vancouver	NHL	75	20	14	34	24	-3	10	0	4	1	2	3	0
01-02—Vancouver	NHL	79	9	23	32	32	1	4	0	6	0	1	1	0
02-03—Vancouver	NHL	79	14	17	31	34	8	4	0	14	1	5	6	8
03-04—Vancouver	NHL	82	18	36	54	18	18	1	0	7	1	2	3	0
04-05—MoDo Ornskoldsvik	Sweden	49	13	20	33	40	5	4	1	6	0	3	3	6
05-06—Vancouver	NHL	82	22	49	71	34	7	11	0	—	—	—	—	—
—Swedish Oly. team	Int'l	8	1	3	4	2	2	0	0	—	—	—	—	—
NHL Totals (5 years)		397	83	139	222	142	31	30	0	31	3	10	13	8

SEDIN, HENRIK C

PERSONAL: Born September 26, 1980, in Ornskoldsvik, Sweden. ... 6-2/192. ... Shoots left. ... Twin brother of Daniel Sedin, LW, Vancouver Canucks.
TRANSACTIONS/CAREER NOTES: Selected by Vancouver Canucks in first round (second Canucks pick, third overall) of NHL draft (June 26, 1999). ... Injured shoulder (December 12, 2002); missed three games. ... Injured hand (February 25, 2003); missed one game. ... Strained abdominal muscle (March 13, 2004); missed four games.

Season Team	League	REGULAR SEASON GP	G	A	Pts.	PIM	+/-	PP	SH	PLAYOFFS GP	G	A	Pts.	PIM
96-97—MoDo Ornskoldsvik	Sweden Jr.	26	14	22	36	...	...	...	...	—	—	—	—	—
97-98—MoDo Ornskoldsvik	Sweden Jr.	8	4	7	11	6	...	...	...	—	—	—	—	—
—MoDo Ornskoldsvik	Sweden	39	1	4	5	8	...	...	...	7	0	0	0	0
98-99—MoDo Ornskoldsvik	Sweden	49	12	22	34	32	...	...	...	13	2	8	10	6
99-00—MoDo Ornskoldsvik	Sweden	50	9	38	47	22	...	...	...	13	5	9	14	2
00-01—Vancouver	NHL	82	9	20	29	38	-2	2	0	4	0	4	4	0
01-02—Vancouver	NHL	82	16	20	36	36	9	3	0	6	3	0	3	0
02-03—Vancouver	NHL	78	8	31	39	38	9	4	1	14	3	2	5	8
03-04—Vancouver	NHL	76	11	31	42	32	23	2	0	7	2	2	4	2
04-05—MoDo Ornskoldsvik	Sweden	44	14	22	36	50	9	4	1	6	1	3	4	6
05-06—Vancouver	NHL	82	18	57	75	56	11	5	1	—	—	—	—	—
—Swedish Oly. team	Int'l	8	3	1	4	2	2	0	0	—	—	—	—	—
NHL Totals (5 years)		400	62	159	221	200	50	16	2	31	8	8	16	10

SEIDENBERG, DENNIS D

PERSONAL: Born July 18, 1981, in Schwenningen, W. Germany. ... 6-0/200. ... Shoots left. ... Name pronounced ZIGH-dehn-buhrg.
TRANSACTIONS/CAREER NOTES: Selected by Philadelphia Flyers in sixth round (sixth Flyers pick, 172nd overall) of entry draft (June 24, 2001). ... Fractured leg (January 15, 2004); missed remained of season. ... Concussion (October 7, 2005); missed two games. ... Broken right wrist (November 22, 2005); missed seven games. ... Sprained left knee (January 6, 2006); missed two games. ... Traded by Flyers to Phoenix Coyotes for C Petr Nedved (January 20, 2006).

Season Team	League	GP	G	A	Pts.	PIM	+/-	PP	SH	GP	G	A	Pts.	PIM
		REGULAR SEASON								PLAYOFFS				
01-02—Mannheim	Germany	55	7	13	20	56	...	...	...	8	0	0	0	2
02-03—Philadelphia	AHL	19	5	6	11	17	-7	1	0	—	—	—	—	—
—Philadelphia	NHL	58	4	9	13	20	8	1	0	—	—	—	—	—
03-04—Philadelphia	NHL	5	0	0	0	2	-4	0	0	3	0	0	0	0
—Philadelphia	AHL	33	7	12	19	31	11	2	0	9	2	2	4	4
04-05—Philadelphia	AHL	79	13	28	41	47	18	6	0	18	2	8	10	19
05-06—Philadelphia	NHL	29	2	5	7	4	-4	1	0	—	—	—	—	—
—Phoenix	NHL	34	1	10	11	14	-9	1	0	—	—	—	—	—
—German Oly. team	Int'l	5	0	0	0	6	-2	0	0	—	—	—	—	—
NHL Totals (3 years)		126	7	24	31	40	-9	3	0	3	0	0	0	0

SEJNA, PETER — LW

PERSONAL: Born October 5, 1979, in Liptovsky Mikulas, Czech. ... 5-10/197. ... Shoots left. ... Name pronounced SHAY-nah.
TRANSACTIONS/CAREER NOTES: Signed as free agent by St. Louis Blues (April 6, 2003).

Season Team	League	GP	G	A	Pts.	PIM	+/-	PP	SH	GP	G	A	Pts.	PIM
		REGULAR SEASON								PLAYOFFS				
98-99—Des Moines	USHL	52	40	23	63	26	...	...	...	14	11	6	17	8
99-00—Des Moines	USHL	58	41	53	94	36	...	...	...	9	4	5	9	4
00-01—Colorado College	WCHA	41	29	29	58	10	...	...	...	—	—	—	—	—
01-02—Colorado College	WCHA	43	26	24	50	16	...	...	...	—	—	—	—	—
02-03—St. Louis	NHL	1	1	0	1	0	0	1	0	—	—	—	—	—
—Colorado College	WCHA	42	36	46	82	12	...	...	...	—	—	—	—	—
03-04—St. Louis	NHL	20	2	2	4	4	-9	2	0	—	—	—	—	—
—Worcester	AHL	59	12	29	41	13	8	5	1	10	3	3	6	10
04-05—Worcester	AHL	64	17	21	38	24	3	1	5	—	—	—	—	—
05-06—Peoria	AHL	44	19	31	50	18	3	14	1	4	3	0	3	2
—St. Louis	NHL	6	1	1	2	4	1	0	0	—	—	—	—	—
NHL Totals (3 years)		27	4	3	7	8	-8	3	0					

SELANNE, TEEMU — RW

PERSONAL: Born July 3, 1970, in Helsinki, Finland. ... 6-0/205. ... Shoots right. ... Name pronounced TAY-moo suh-LAH-nay. ... Nickname: The Finnish Flash.
TRANSACTIONS/CAREER NOTES: Selected by Winnipeg Jets in first round (first Jets pick, 10th overall) of entry draft (June 11, 1988). ... Severed ankle tendon (January 26, 1994); missed 33 games. ... Patella tendonitis (February 28, 1995); missed one game. ... Suspended two games and fined $500 (March 28, 1995). ... Traded by Jets with C Marc Chouinard and fourth-round pick (traded to Toronto; traded to Montreal; Canadiens selected C Kim Staal) in 1996 draft to Anaheim Mighty Ducks for C Chad Kilger, D Oleg Tverdovsky and third-round pick (D Per-Anton Lundstrom) in 1996 draft (Febraury 7, 1996). ... Strained abdominal muscle (March 23, 1997); missed four games. ... Strained abdominal muscle (February 7, 1998); missed five games. ... Strained groin (April 9, 1998); missed final four games of season. ... Strained thigh muscle (November 11,1998); missed six games. ... Reinjured thigh muscle (December 3, 1998); missed one game. ... Strained groin (November 14, 1999); missed three games. ... Strained groin (December 13, 2000); missed two games. ... Strained groin (December 22, 2000); missed two games. ... Injured knee (March 1, 2001); missed five games. ... Traded by Mighty Ducks to San Jose Sharks for LW Jeff Friesen, G Steve Shields and second-round pick (LW Vojtech Polak) in 2003 draft (March 5, 2001). ... Signed as free agent by Colorado Avalanche (July 3, 2003). ... Injured knee (October 28, 2003); missed one game. ... Injured neck (January 11, 2004); missed one game. ... Signed as free agent by Mighty Ducks (August 22, 2005). ... Strained groin (January 13, 2006); missed two games.
STATISTICAL PLATEAUS: Three-goal games: 1992-93 (4), 1993-94 (2), 1995-96 (2), 1996-97 (1), 1997-98 (3), 1998-99 (1), 1999-00 (1), 2000-01 (2). Total: 16. ... Four-goal games: 1992-93 (1), 1995-96 (1). Total: 2. ... Total hat tricks: 18.

Season Team	League	GP	G	A	Pts.	PIM	+/-	PP	SH	GP	G	A	Pts.	PIM
		REGULAR SEASON								PLAYOFFS				
87-88—Jokerit Helsinki	Finland Jr.	33	43	23	66	18	...	...	...	5	4	3	7	2
—Jokerit Helsinki	Finland	5	1	1	2	0	...	...	...	—	—	—	—	—
88-89—Jokerit Helsinki	Finland	34	35	33	68	12	...	...	...	5	7	3	10	4
89-90—Jokerit Helsinki	Finland	11	4	8	12	0	...	...	...	—	—	—	—	—
90-91—Jokerit Helsinki	Finland	42	33	25	58	12	...	...	...	—	—	—	—	—
91-92—Fin. Olympic team	Int'l	8	7	4	11	...	...	...	...	—	—	—	—	—
—Jokerit Helsinki	Finland	44	39	23	62	20	...	...	...	—	—	—	—	—
92-93—Winnipeg	NHL	84	†76	56	132	45	8	24	0	6	4	2	6	2
93-94—Winnipeg	NHL	51	25	29	54	22	-23	11	0	—	—	—	—	—
94-95—Jokerit Helsinki	Finland	20	7	12	19	6	3	...	...	—	—	—	—	—
—Winnipeg	NHL	45	22	26	48	2	1	8	2	—	—	—	—	—
95-96—Winnipeg	NHL	51	24	48	72	18	3	6	1	—	—	—	—	—
—Anaheim	NHL	28	16	20	36	4	2	3	0	—	—	—	—	—
96-97—Anaheim	NHL	78	51	58	109	34	28	11	1	11	7	3	10	4
97-98—Anaheim	NHL	73	†52	34	86	30	12	10	1	—	—	—	—	—
—Fin. Olympic team	Int'l	5	4	6	10	8	0	3	0	—	—	—	—	—
98-99—Anaheim	NHL	75	*47	60	107	30	18	*25	0	4	2	2	4	2
99-00—Anaheim	NHL	79	33	52	85	12	6	8	0	—	—	—	—	—
00-01—Anaheim	NHL	61	26	33	59	36	-8	10	0	—	—	—	—	—
—San Jose	NHL	12	7	6	13	0	1	2	0	6	0	2	2	2
01-02—San Jose	NHL	82	29	25	54	40	-11	9	1	12	5	3	8	2
—Fin. Olympic team	Int'l	4	3	0	3	2	...	...	...	—	—	—	—	—
02-03—San Jose	NHL	82	28	36	64	30	-6	7	0	—	—	—	—	—
03-04—Colorado	NHL	78	16	16	32	32	2	6	1	10	0	3	3	2
05-06—Anaheim	NHL	80	40	50	90	44	28	18	0	16	6	8	14	6
—Fin. Olympic team	Int'l	8	6	5	11	4	7	1	0	—	—	—	—	—
NHL Totals (13 years)		959	492	549	1041	379	61	158	7	65	24	23	47	20

SEMENOV, ALEXEI — D

PERSONAL: Born April 10, 1981, in Murmansk, U.S.S.R. ... 6-6/235. ... Shoots left. ... Name pronounced seh-MEH-nahv.

TRANSACTIONS/CAREER NOTES: Selected by Edmonton Oilers in second round (second Oilers pick, 36th overall) of entry draft (June 26, 1999). ... Injured shoulder (February 16, 2004); missed eight games. ... Traded by Oilers to Florida Panthers for fifth-round pick (G Bryan Pitton) in 2006 (November 19, 2005). ... Visa issues (November 19, 2005); missed five games.

		REGULAR SEASON								PLAYOFFS				
Season Team	League	GP	G	A	Pts.	PIM	+/-	PP	SH	GP	G	A	Pts.	PIM
97-98—Krylja Sovetov-2 Mos.	Rus. Div.	52	1	2	3	48	...	...	...	—	—	—	—	—
98-99—Sudbury	OHL	28	0	3	3	28	-11	0	0	2	0	0	0	4
99-00—Sudbury	OHL	65	9	35	44	135	21	6	1	12	1	3	4	23
—Hamilton	AHL	...	...	...	...	...	...	...	...	3	0	0	0	0
00-01—Sudbury	OHL	65	21	42	63	106	28	15	0	12	4	13	17	17
01-02—Hamilton	AHL	78	5	11	16	67	7	2	0	—	—	—	—	—
02-03—Hamilton	AHL	37	4	3	7	45	6	2	0	—	—	—	—	—
—Edmonton	NHL	46	1	6	7	58	-7	0	0	6	0	0	0	0
03-04—Edmonton	NHL	46	2	3	5	32	8	1	0	—	—	—	—	—
04-05—SKA St. Petersburg	Russian	50	0	8	8	26	-16	...	...	—	—	—	—	—
05-06—Rochester	AHL	3	0	0	0	7	-2	0	0	—	—	—	—	—
—Edmonton	NHL	11	1	1	2	17	-3	0	0	—	—	—	—	—
—Florida	NHL	16	1	1	2	21	-1	1	0	—	—	—	—	—
NHL Totals (3 years)		119	5	11	16	128	-3	2	0	6	0	0	0	0

SEVERSON, CAM — LW

PERSONAL: Born January 15, 1978, in Canora, Sask. ... 6-2/220. ... Shoots left.

TRANSACTIONS/CAREER NOTES: Selected by San Jose Sharks in eighth round (sixth Sharks pick, 192nd overall) of entry draft (June 21, 1997). ... Signed as free agent by Anaheim Mighty Ducks (August 22, 2002). ... Signed as free agent by Nashville Predators (July 22, 2004). ... Signed as free agent by Calgary Flames (August 11, 2005). ... Traded by Flames to Columbus Blue Jackets for D Cale Hulse (February 28, 2006).

		REGULAR SEASON								PLAYOFFS				
Season Team	League	GP	G	A	Pts.	PIM	+/-	PP	SH	GP	G	A	Pts.	PIM
98-99—Spokane	WHL	46	16	17	33	190	-25	4	0	—	—	—	—	—
—Oklahoma City	CHL	5	6	3	9	4	...	...	...	10	4	0	4	26
99-00—Louisiana	ECHL	7	0	2	2	22	...	...	...	—	—	—	—	—
—Peoria	ECHL	56	19	8	27	138	...	...	...	18	3	4	7	41
00-01—Portland	AHL	8	0	0	0	11	...	...	...	—	—	—	—	—
—Cincinnati	AHL	20	4	7	11	60	...	...	...	3	1	1	2	0
01-02—Hartford	AHL	65	11	10	21	116	-3	2	0	5	0	0	0	7
02-03—Cincinnati	AHL	71	12	9	21	156	-2	0	0	—	—	—	—	—
—Anaheim	NHL	2	0	0	0	8	0	0	0	1	0	0	0	0
03-04—Anaheim	NHL	31	3	0	3	50	-3	1	0	—	—	—	—	—
—Cincinnati	AHL	38	7	7	14	143	-2	1	0	—	—	—	—	—
04-05—Milwaukee	AHL	63	6	8	14	255	-12	1	0	4	0	0	0	12
05-06—Omaha Ak-Sar-Ben	AHL	54	13	7	20	146	-6	4	2	—	—	—	—	—
—Syracuse	AHL	12	4	3	7	28	-5	2	0	3	0	0	0	21
—Columbus	NHL	4	0	0	0	5	0	0	0	—	—	—	—	—
NHL Totals (3 years)		37	3	0	3	63	-3	1	0	1	0	0	0	0

SHANAHAN, BRENDAN — LW/RW

PERSONAL: Born January 23, 1969, in Mimico, Ont. ... 6-3/220. ... Shoots right.

TRANSACTIONS/CAREER NOTES: Selected by New Jersey Devils in first round (first Devils pick, second overall) of entry draft (June 13, 1987). ... Fractured nose (December 1987). ... Back spasms (March 1989). ... Suspended five games for stick-swinging incident (January 13, 1990). ... Lower abdominal strain (February 1990). ... Facial cuts (January 8, 1991), had surgery; missed five games. ... Signed as free agent by St. Louis Blues (July 25, 1991); D Scott Stevens awarded to Devils as compensation (September 3, 1991). ... Groin (October 24, 1992); missed 12 games. ... Suspended six off-days and fined $500 for hitting another player in face with his stick (January 7, 1993). ... Suspended one game for high-sticking incident (February 23, 1993). ... Viral infection (November 18, 1993); missed one game. ... Hamstring (March 22, 1994); missed two games. ... Viral infection (January 20, 1995); missed three games. ... Fractured ankle (May 15, 1995); missed last two playoff games. ... Traded by Blues to Hartford Whalers for D Chris Pronger (July 27, 1995). ... Wrist (November 11, 1995); missed eight games. ... Traded by Whalers with D Brian Glynn to Detroit Red Wings for C Keith Primeau, D Paul Coffey and first-round pick (D Nikos Tselios) in 1997 (October 9, 1996). ... Suspended one game and fined $1,000 for cross-checking incident (October 11, 1996). ... Groin (October 30, 1996); missed one game. ... Neck (October 12, 1997); missed four games. ... Back spasms (April 15, 1998); missed final game of season and two playoff games. ... Suspended two games for stick-swinging incident (November 9, 1999). ... Signed as free agent by New York Rangers (July 6, 2006).

STATISTICAL PLATEAUS: Three-goal games: 1988-89 (1), 1992-93 (1), 1993-94 (4), 1995-96 (1), 1996-97 (3), 1998-99 (2), 2001-02 (1), 2002-03 (1), 2003-04 (1). Total: 15. ... Four-goal games: 2000-01 (1). ... Total hat tricks: 16.

		REGULAR SEASON								PLAYOFFS				
Season Team	League	GP	G	A	Pts.	PIM	+/-	PP	SH	GP	G	A	Pts.	PIM
84-85—Mississauga	MTHL	36	20	21	41	26	...	...	...	—	—	—	—	—
85-86—London	OHL	59	28	34	62	70	...	...	...	5	5	5	10	5
86-87—London	OHL	56	39	53	92	128	...	...	...	—	—	—	—	—
87-88—New Jersey	NHL	65	7	19	26	131	-20	2	0	12	2	1	3	44
88-89—New Jersey	NHL	68	22	28	50	115	2	9	0	—	—	—	—	—
89-90—New Jersey	NHL	73	30	42	72	137	15	8	0	6	3	3	6	20
90-91—New Jersey	NHL	75	29	37	66	141	4	7	0	7	3	5	8	12
91-92—St. Louis	NHL	80	33	36	69	171	-3	13	0	6	2	3	5	14
92-93—St. Louis	NHL	71	51	43	94	174	10	18	0	11	4	3	7	18

Season Team	League	REGULAR SEASON GP	G	A	Pts.	PIM	+/-	PP	SH	PLAYOFFS GP	G	A	Pts.	PIM
93-94—St. Louis	NHL	81	52	50	102	211	-9	15	*7	4	2	5	7	4
94-95—Dusseldorf	Germany	3	5	3	8	4	...	...	...	—	—	—	—	—
—St. Louis	NHL	45	20	21	41	136	7	6	2	5	4	5	9	14
95-96—Hartford	NHL	74	44	34	78	125	2	17	2	—	—	—	—	—
96-97—Hartford	NHL	2	1	0	1	0	1	0	1	—	—	—	—	—
—Detroit	NHL	79	46	41	87	131	31	†20	2	20	9	8	17	43
97-98—Detroit	NHL	75	28	29	57	154	6	15	1	20	5	4	9	22
—Can. Olympic team	Int'l	6	2	0	2	0	3	1	0	—	—	—	—	—
98-99—Detroit	NHL	81	31	27	58	123	2	5	0	10	3	7	10	6
99-00—Detroit	NHL	78	41	37	78	105	24	13	1	9	3	2	5	10
00-01—Detroit	NHL	81	31	45	76	81	9	15	1	2	2	2	4	0
01-02—Detroit	NHL	80	37	38	75	118	23	12	3	23	8	11	19	20
—Can. Olympic team	Int'l	6	0	1	1	0	...	...	...	—	—	—	—	—
02-03—Detroit	NHL	78	30	38	68	103	5	13	0	4	1	1	2	4
03-04—Detroit	NHL	82	25	28	53	117	15	8	0	12	1	5	6	20
05-06—Detroit	NHL	82	40	41	81	105	29	14	0	6	1	1	2	6
NHL Totals (18 years)		1350	598	634	1232	2378	153	210	20	157	53	66	119	257

SHARP, PATRICK — C/RW

PERSONAL: Born December 27, 1981, in Thunder Bay, Ont. ... 6-0/197. ... Shoots right.
TRANSACTIONS/CAREER NOTES: Selected by Philadelphia Flyers in third round (second Flyers pick, 95th overall) of entry draft (June 23, 2001). ... Traded by Flyers with RW Eric Meloche to Chicago Blackhawks for RW Matt Ellison and third-round pick (traded to Montreal; Canadiens selected C Ryan White) in 2006 (December 5, 2005). ... Flu (January 17, 2006); missed five games.

Season Team	League	REGULAR SEASON GP	G	A	Pts.	PIM	+/-	PP	SH	PLAYOFFS GP	G	A	Pts.	PIM
98-99—Thunder Bay Flyers	USHL	55	19	24	43	48	...	...	...	3	1	1	2	0
99-00—Thunder Bay Flyers	USHL	56	20	35	55	41	...	...	...	—	—	—	—	—
00-01—Vermont	ECAC	30	11	13	24	34	...	...	...	—	—	—	—	—
01-02—Vermont	ECAC	31	13	13	26	50	...	...	...	—	—	—	—	—
02-03—Philadelphia	AHL	53	14	19	33	39	-5	6	0	—	—	—	—	—
—Philadelphia	NHL	3	0	0	0	2	0	0	0	—	—	—	—	—
03-04—Philadelphia	NHL	41	5	2	7	55	-3	0	0	12	1	0	1	2
—Philadelphia	AHL	35	15	14	29	45	5	7	0	1	2	0	2	0
04-05—Philadelphia	AHL	75	23	29	52	80	3	8	0	21	8	13	21	20
05-06—Philadelphia	NHL	22	5	3	8	10	4	1	0	—	—	—	—	—
—Chicago	NHL	50	9	14	23	36	1	0	1	—	—	—	—	—
NHL Totals (3 years)		116	19	19	38	103	2	1	1	12	1	0	1	2

SHELLEY, JODY — LW

PERSONAL: Born February 7, 1976, in Thompson, Man. ... 6-4/225. ... Shoots left.
TRANSACTIONS/CAREER NOTES: Signed as free agent by Calgary Flames (September 1, 1998). ... Signed as free agent by Columbus Blue Jackets (February 1, 2001). ... Suspended one game for fighting (December 5, 2002). ... Nose (November 20, 2003); missed one game. ... Throat (January 15, 2003); missed one game. ... Groin (March 1, 2003); missed two games. ... Abdomen (March 22, 2003) missed six games. ... Suspended three games for fighting (March 25, 2004).

Season Team	League	REGULAR SEASON GP	G	A	Pts.	PIM	+/-	PP	SH	PLAYOFFS GP	G	A	Pts.	PIM
94-95—Halifax	QMJHL	72	10	12	22	194	...	...	...	7	0	1	1	12
95-96—Halifax	QMJHL	50	13	19	32	319	...	...	...	6	0	2	2	36
96-97—Halifax	QMJHL	58	25	19	44	448	...	...	...	17	6	6	12	123
97-98—Dalhousie University	AUAA	19	6	11	17	145	...	...	...	—	—	—	—	—
—Saint John	AHL	18	1	1	2	50	...	...	...	—	—	—	—	—
98-99—Saint John	AHL	8	0	0	0	46	-1	0	0	—	—	—	—	—
—Johnstown	ECHL	52	12	17	29	325	-4	3	0	—	—	—	—	—
99-00—Johnstown	ECHL	36	9	17	26	256	...	...	...	—	—	—	—	—
—Saint John	AHL	22	1	4	5	93	...	...	...	3	0	0	0	2
00-01—Syracuse	AHL	69	1	7	8	357	...	...	...	5	0	0	0	21
—Columbus	NHL	1	0	0	0	10	0	0	0	—	—	—	—	—
01-02—Columbus	NHL	52	3	3	6	206	1	0	0	—	—	—	—	—
—Syracuse	AHL	22	3	5	8	165	4	1	0	—	—	—	—	—
02-03—Columbus	NHL	68	1	4	5	*249	-5	0	0	—	—	—	—	—
03-04—Columbus	NHL	76	3	3	6	228	-10	1	0	—	—	—	—	—
04-05—JyP Jyvaskyla	Finland	11	0	1	1	20	-3	...	...	3	0	0	0	25
05-06—Columbus	NHL	80	3	7	10	163	-4	0	0	—	—	—	—	—
NHL Totals (5 years)		277	10	17	27	856	-18	1	0					

SHEPPARD, JAMES — C

PERSONAL: Born April 25, 1988, in Halifax, Novia Scotia. ... 6-1/204. ... Shoots left.
TRANSACTIONS/CAREER NOTES: Selected by Minnesota Wild in first round (first Wild pick; ninth overall) of NHL draft (June 24, 2006).

Season Team	League	REGULAR SEASON GP	G	A	Pts.	PIM	+/-	PP	SH	PLAYOFFS GP	G	A	Pts.	PIM
04-05—Cape Breton	QMJHL	65	14	31	45	40	13	1	1	5	1	3	4	2
05-06—Cape Breton	QMJHL	66	30	54	84	78	3	14	1	9	2	5	7	12

S

SHIELDS, STEVE G

PERSONAL: Born July 19, 1972, in Toronto. ... 6-3/215. ... Catches left.

TRANSACTIONS/CAREER NOTES: Selected by Buffalo Sabres in fifth round (fifth Sabres pick, 10first overall) of entry draft (June 22, 1991). ... Traded by Sabres with fourth-round pick (RW Miroslav Zalesak) in 1998 draft to San Jose Sharks for G Kay Whitmore, second-round pick (RW Jaroslav Kristek) in 1998 draft and fifth-round pick (traded to Columbus; Blue Jackets selected C Tyler Kolarik) in 2000 draft (June 18, 1998). ... Sprained ankle (October 12, 2000); missed eight games. ... Traded by Sharks with LW Jeff Friesen and second-round pick (traded to Dallas; Stars selected LW Vojtech Polak) in 2003 draft to Mighty Ducks of Anaheim for RW Teemu Selanne (March 5, 2001). ... Injured ligaments in left shoulder and had surgery (March 7, 2001); missed remainder of season. ... Lacerated face and bruised jaw (April 3, 2002); missed remainder of season. ... Traded by Mighty Ducks to Boston Bruins for third-round pick (RW Shane Hynes) in 2003 draft (June 25, 2002). ... Traded by Bruins to Florida Panthers for a sixth-round pick in 2004 entry draft (October 5, 2003). ... Injured foot (February 12, 2004); missed one game. ... Signed by Atlanta Thrashers as free agent (October 26, 2005). ... Inured knee (November 9, 3005); missed six games. ... Knee injury (November 26, 2005); missed 19 games.

		REGULAR SEASON										PLAYOFFS							
Season Team	League	GP	Min.	W	L	OTL	T	GA	SO	GAA	SV%	GP	Min.	W	L	GA	SO	GAA	SV%
90-91—Univ. of Michigan	CCHA	37	1963	26	6	...	3	106	0	3.24	...	—	—	—	—	—	—	—	—
91-92—Univ. of Michigan	CCHA	37	2091	27	7	...	2	98	1	2.81	...	—	—	—	—	—	—	—	—
92-93—Univ. of Michigan	CCHA	39	2027	30	6	...	2	75	2	2.22	...	—	—	—	—	—	—	—	—
93-94—Univ. of Michigan	CCHA	36	1961	28	6	...	1	87	0	2.66	...	—	—	—	—	—	—	—	—
94-95—South Carolina	ECHL	21	1158	11	5	...	2	52	2	2.69	.912	3	144	0	2	11	0	4.58	.874
—Rochester	AHL	13	673	3	8	...	0	53	0	4.73	.830	1	20	0	0	3	0	9.00	.824
95-96—Rochester	AHL	43	2356	20	17	...	2	140	1	3.57	...	19	1126	15	3	47	1	2.50	...
—Buffalo	NHL	2	75	1	0	...	0	4	0	3.20	.875	—	—	—	—	—	—	—	—
96-97—Rochester	AHL	23	1331	14	6	...	2	60	1	2.70	.914	—	—	—	—	—	—	—	—
—Buffalo	NHL	13	789	3	8	...	2	39	0	2.97	.913	10	570	4	6	26	1	2.74	.922
97-98—Buffalo	NHL	16	785	3	6	...	4	37	0	2.83	.909	—	—	—	—	—	—	—	—
—Rochester	AHL	1	59	0	1	...	0	3	0	3.05	.885	—	—	—	—	—	—	—	—
98-99—San Jose	NHL	37	2162	15	11	...	8	80	4	2.22	.921	1	60	0	1	6	0	6.00	.833
99-00—San Jose	NHL	67	3797	27	30	...	8	162	4	2.56	.911	12	696	5	7	36	0	3.10	.889
00-01—San Jose	NHL	21	1135	6	8	...	5	47	2	2.48	.911	—	—	—	—	—	—	—	—
01-02—Anaheim	NHL	33	1777	9	20	...	2	79	0	2.67	.907	—	—	—	—	—	—	—	—
02-03—Boston	NHL	36	2112	12	13	...	9	97	0	2.76	.896	2	119	0	2	6	0	3.03	.897
03-04—Florida	NHL	16	732	3	6	...	1	42	0	3.44	.879	—	—	—	—	—	—	—	—
05-06—Chicago	AHL	4	240	2	2	0	...	9	0	2.25	.902	—	—	—	—	—	—	—	—
—Atlanta	NHL	5	266	1	2	1	...	19	0	4.29	.853	—	—	—	—	—	—	—	—
NHL Totals (10 years)		246	13630	80	104	1	39	606	10	2.67	.907	25	1445	9	16	74	1	3.07	.901

SHISHKANOV, TIMOFEI LW

PERSONAL: Born June 10, 1983, in Moscow, U.S.S.R. ... 6-1/213. ... Shoots right.

TRANSACTIONS/CAREER NOTES: Selected by Nashville Predators in second round (second Predators pick, 33rd overall) of entry draft (June 23, 2001). ... Traded by Predators to St. Louis Blues for C Mike Sillinger (January 30. 2006).

		REGULAR SEASON								PLAYOFFS				
Season Team	League	GP	G	A	Pts.	PIM	+/-	PP	SH	GP	G	A	Pts.	PIM
00-01—Spartak	Russian Jr.	12	0	0	0	2	...	...	...	—	—	—	—	—
01-02—HC CSKA Moscow	Rus. Div.	23	7	6	13	8	...	...	...	—	—	—	—	—
02-03—Quebec	QMJHL	51	36	46	82	60	...	...	...	11	5	12	17	14
03-04—Nashville	NHL	2	0	0	0	0	-1	0	0	—	—	—	—	—
—Milwaukee	AHL	63	23	20	43	46	23	3	0	22	2	6	8	17
04-05—Milwaukee	AHL	70	20	15	35	31	-3	6	0	6	1	0	1	2
05-06—Milwaukee	AHL	46	14	15	29	34	3	8	0	—	—	—	—	—
—St. Louis	NHL	22	3	2	5	6	-1	0	0	—	—	—	—	—
—Peoria	AHL	12	3	2	5	8	2	1	0	2	1	0	1	0
NHL Totals (2 years)		24	3	2	5	6	-2	0	0					

SIGALET, JORDAN G

PERSONAL: Born February 19, 1981, in New Westminster, B.C. ... 6-0/172. ... Catches left.

TRANSACTIONS/CAREER NOTES: Selected by Boston Bruins in seventh round (20ninth overall) of NHL draft (June 24, 2001).

		REGULAR SEASON										PLAYOFFS							
Season Team	League	GP	Min.	W	L	OTL	T	GA	SO	GAA	SV%	GP	Min.	W	L	GA	SO	GAA	SV%
01-02—Bowling Green	CCHA	13	657	2	6	...	2	38	0	3.47	...	—	—	—	—	—	—	—	—
02-03—Bowling Green	CCHA	20	1208	6	11	...	2	66	1	3.28	...	—	—	—	—	—	—	—	—
03-04—Bowling Green	CCHA	37	2210	10	17	...	9	101	2	2.74	...	—	—	—	—	—	—	—	—
04-05—Bowling Green	CCHA	32	1849	16	12	...	3	89	1	2.89	...	—	—	—	—	—	—	—	—
05-06—Providence	AHL	37	1955	19	11	2	...	83	1	2.55	.900	3	159	0	2	10	0	3.77	.882
—Boston	NHL	1	1	0	0	0	...	0	0	0.00	...	—	—	—	—	—	—	—	—
NHL Totals (1 year)		1	1	0	0	0	0	0	0	0.00	...								

SILLINGER, MIKE C

PERSONAL: Born June 29, 1971, in Regina, Sask. ... 5-11/195. ... Shoots right. ... Name pronounced SIHL-in-juhr.

TRANSACTIONS/CAREER NOTES: Selected by Detroit Red Wings in first round (first Red Wings pick, 11th overall) of entry draft (June 17, 1989). ... Fractured rib in training camp (September 1990). ... Flu (March 5, 1993); missed three games. ... Strained rotator cuff (October 9, 1993); missed four games. ... Eye (January 17, 1995); missed four games. ... Traded by Red Wings with D Jason York to Anaheim Mighty

Ducks for LW Stu Grimson, D Mark Ferner and sixth-round pick (LW Magnus Nilsson) in 1996 (April 4, 1995). ... Traded by Mighty Ducks to Vancouver Canucks for RW Roman Oksiuta (March 15, 1996). ... Concussion (March 26, 1997); missed two games. ... Traded by Canucks to Flyers for sixth-round pick (traded back to Philadelphia; Flyers selected C Garrett Prosofsky) in 1998 (February 5, 1998). ... Left knee (October 22, 1998); missed one game. ... Traded by Flyers with C Chris Gratton to Tampa Bay Lightning for RW Mikael Renberg and C Daymond Langkow (December 12, 1998). ... Traded by Lightning to Florida Panthers for C Ryan Johnson and LW Dwayne Hay (March 14, 2000). ... Fractured foot (November 8, 2000); missed 12 games. ... Groin (January 24, 2001); missed three games. ... Traded by Panthers to Ottawa Senators for future considerations (March 13, 2001). ... Signed as free agent by Columbus Blue Jackets (July 5, 2001). ... Concussion (November 1, 2001); missed one game. ... Knee (December 31, 2001); missed one game. ... Shoulder (December 9, 2002); missed two games. ... Groin (March 15, 2003); missed five games. ... Traded by Blue Jackets with second-round pick (D Johan Fransson) in 2004 for D Darryl Sydor; then traded by Stars to Phoenix Coyotes for D Teppo Numminen (July 22, 2003). ... Hernia surgery (October 10, 2003); missed five games. ... Traded by Coyotes to St. Louis Blues for G Brent Johnson (March 4, 2004). ... Flu (December 21, 2005); missed one game. ... Traded by Blues to Predators for LW Timofei Shishkanov (January 30, 2006). ... Signed as free agent by New York Islanders (July 2, 2006).

		REGULAR SEASON								PLAYOFFS				
Season Team	**League**	**GP**	**G**	**A**	**Pts.**	**PIM**	**+/-**	**PP**	**SH**	**GP**	**G**	**A**	**Pts.**	**PIM**
87-88—Regina	WHL	67	18	25	43	17	...	...	...	4	2	2	4	0
88-89—Regina	WHL	72	53	78	131	52	...	...	...	—	—	—	—	—
89-90—Regina	WHL	70	57	72	129	41	...	...	...	11	12	10	22	2
—Adirondack	AHL	...	...	...	...	...	...	...	...	1	0	0	0	0
90-91—Regina	WHL	57	50	66	116	42	...	...	...	8	6	9	15	4
—Detroit	NHL	3	0	1	1	0	-2	0	0	3	0	1	1	0
91-92—Adirondack	AHL	64	25	41	66	26	...	...	...	15	9	19	28	12
—Detroit	NHL	...	...	...	...	...	...	...	...	8	2	2	4	2
92-93—Detroit	NHL	51	4	17	21	16	0	0	0	—	—	—	—	—
—Adirondack	AHL	15	10	20	30	31	18	2	3	11	5	13	18	10
93-94—Detroit	NHL	62	8	21	29	10	2	0	1	—	—	—	—	—
94-95—Wien	Austria	13	13	14	27	10	...	...	...	—	—	—	—	—
—Detroit	NHL	13	2	6	8	2	3	0	0	—	—	—	—	—
—Anaheim	NHL	15	2	5	7	6	1	2	0	—	—	—	—	—
95-96—Anaheim	NHL	62	13	21	34	32	-20	7	0	—	—	—	—	—
—Vancouver	NHL	12	1	3	4	6	2	0	1	6	0	0	0	2
96-97—Vancouver	NHL	78	17	20	37	25	-3	3	3	—	—	—	—	—
97-98—Vancouver	NHL	48	10	9	19	34	-14	1	2	—	—	—	—	—
—Philadelphia	NHL	27	11	11	22	16	3	1	2	3	1	0	1	0
98-99—Philadelphia	NHL	25	0	3	3	8	-9	0	0	—	—	—	—	—
—Tampa Bay	NHL	54	8	2	10	28	-20	0	2	—	—	—	—	—
99-00—Tampa Bay	NHL	67	19	25	44	86	-29	6	3	—	—	—	—	—
—Florida	NHL	13	4	4	8	16	-1	2	0	4	2	1	3	2
00-01—Florida	NHL	55	13	21	34	44	-12	1	0	—	—	—	—	—
—Ottawa	NHL	13	3	4	7	4	1	0	0	4	0	0	0	2
01-02—Columbus	NHL	80	20	23	43	54	-35	8	0	—	—	—	—	—
02-03—Columbus	NHL	75	18	25	43	52	-21	9	3	—	—	—	—	—
03-04—Phoenix	NHL	60	8	6	14	54	-14	0	1	—	—	—	—	—
—St. Louis	NHL	16	5	5	10	14	4	0	1	5	3	1	4	6
05-06—St. Louis	NHL	48	22	19	41	49	-17	11	1	—	—	—	—	—
—Nashville	NHL	31	10	12	22	14	0	3	0	5	2	1	3	12
NHL Totals (15 years)		908	198	263	461	570	-181	54	20	38	10	6	16	26

SIM, JON — LW/RW

PERSONAL: Born September 29, 1977, in New Glasgow, N.S. ... 5-10/193. ... Shoots left.

TRANSACTIONS/CAREER NOTES: Selected by Dallas Stars in third round (second Stars pick, 70th overall) of NHL draft (June 22, 1996). ... Fractured shoulder blade (September 16, 2000); missed first six games of season. ... Traded by Stars to Nashville Predators for D Bubba Berenzweig and conditional pick in 2003 draft (February 17, 2003). ... Claimed by Los Angeles Kings off waivers from Predators (March 9, 2003). ... Claimed by Pittsburgh Penguins off waivers from Kings (March 4, 2004). ... Signed as free agent by Phoenix Coyotes (September 2, 2004). ... Signed as free agent by Philadelphia Flyers (August 2, 2005). ... Traded by Flyers to Panthers for sixth-round selection in 2007 draft (January 23, 2006). ... Signed as free agent by Atlanta Thrashers (July 13, 2006).

		REGULAR SEASON								PLAYOFFS				
Season Team	**League**	**GP**	**G**	**A**	**Pts.**	**PIM**	**+/-**	**PP**	**SH**	**GP**	**G**	**A**	**Pts.**	**PIM**
94-95—Laval	QMJHL	9	0	1	1	6	...	...	...	—	—	—	—	—
—Sarnia	OHL	25	9	12	21	19	...	...	...	4	3	2	5	2
95-96—Sarnia	OHL	63	56	46	102	130	...	...	...	10	8	7	15	26
96-97—Sarnia	OHL	64	56	39	95	109	0	29	2	12	9	5	14	32
97-98—Sarnia	OHL	59	44	50	94	95	...	...	...	5	1	4	5	14
98-99—Michigan	IHL	68	24	27	51	91	-19	12	1	5	3	1	4	18
—Dallas	NHL	7	1	0	1	12	1	0	0	4	0	0	0	0
99-00—Michigan	IHL	35	14	16	30	65	...	...	...	—	—	—	—	—
—Dallas	NHL	25	5	3	8	10	4	2	0	7	1	0	1	6
00-01—Dallas	NHL	15	0	3	3	6	-2	0	0	—	—	—	—	—
—Utah	IHL	39	16	13	29	44	...	...	...	—	—	—	—	—
01-02—Utah	AHL	31	21	6	27	63	-3	5	1	—	—	—	—	—
—Dallas	NHL	26	3	0	3	10	-3	1	0	—	—	—	—	—
02-03—Dallas	NHL	4	0	0	0	0	-1	0	0	—	—	—	—	—
—Utah	AHL	42	16	31	47	85	11	10	1	—	—	—	—	—
—Nashville	NHL	4	1	0	1	0	0	0	0	—	—	—	—	—
—Los Angeles	NHL	14	0	2	2	19	-3	0	0	—	—	—	—	—
03-04—Los Angeles	NHL	48	6	7	13	27	0	0	0	—	—	—	—	—
—Pittsburgh	NHL	15	2	3	5	6	-4	0	0	—	—	—	—	—
04-05—Philadelphia	AHL	63	35	26	61	66	29	7	3	21	10	7	17	44
—Utah	AHL	10	2	2	4	12	-8	2	0	—	—	—	—	—
05-06—Philadelphia	NHL	39	7	7	14	28	-6	4	0	—	—	—	—	—
—Florida	NHL	33	10	8	18	26	-1	4	0	—	—	—	—	—
NHL Totals (7 years)		230	35	33	68	144	-15	11	0	11	1	0	1	6

SIMON, BEN — C/LW

PERSONAL: Born June 14, 1978, in Shaker Heights, Ohio. ... 6-0/195. ... Shoots left.

TRANSACTIONS/CAREER NOTES: Selected by Chicago Blackhawks in fifth round (fifth Blackhawks pick, 110th overall) of entry draft (June 21, 1997). ... Rights traded by Blackhawks to Atlanta Thrashers for ninth-round pick (C Peter Flache) in 2000 draft (June 25, 2000). ... Signed as free agent by Nashville Predators (July 14, 2003). ... Traded to Thrashers with D Tomas Kloucek for C Simon Gamache and D Kirill Safronov (December 2, 2003). ... Signed as free agent by Columbus Blue Jackets (August 11, 2005).

		REGULAR SEASON								PLAYOFFS				
Season Team	League	GP	G	A	Pts.	PIM	+/-	PP	SH	GP	G	A	Pts.	PIM
92-93—Shaker Heights	Ohio H.S.	...	15	21	36	...	...	...	...	—	—	—	—	—
93-94—Shaker Heights	Ohio H.S.	...	45	41	86	...	...	...	...	—	—	—	—	—
94-95—Shaker Heights	Ohio H.S.	...	61	68	129	...	...	...	...	—	—	—	—	—
95-96—Cleveland	NAHL	50	45	46	91	...	...	...	...	—	—	—	—	—
96-97— Notre Dame	CCHA	30	4	15	19	79	...	...	...	—	—	—	—	—
97-98— Notre Dame	CCHA	37	9	28	37	91	...	...	...	—	—	—	—	—
98-99— Notre Dame	CCHA	37	18	24	42	65	...	...	...	—	—	—	—	—
99-00— Notre Dame	CCHA	40	13	19	32	53	...	...	...	—	—	—	—	—
00-01—Orlando	IHL	77	8	12	20	47	...	...	...	16	6	5	11	20
01-02—Chicago	AHL	74	11	23	34	56	3	0	1	25	2	3	5	24
—Atlanta	NHL	6	0	0	0	6	1	0	0	—	—	—	—	—
02-03—Atlanta	NHL	10	0	1	1	9	0	0	0	—	—	—	—	—
—Chicago	AHL	69	15	17	32	78	18	0	7	9	0	0	0	6
03-04—Milwaukee	AHL	18	1	3	4	6	-2	0	0	—	—	—	—	—
—Atlanta	NHL	52	3	0	3	28	-10	0	0	—	—	—	—	—
04-05—Chicago	AHL	53	11	10	21	58	2	3	0	18	1	5	6	44
05-06—Syracuse	AHL	66	13	24	37	93	-6	4	4	3	0	1	1	2
—Columbus	NHL	13	0	0	0	4	-4	0	0	—	—	—	—	—
NHL Totals (4 years)		81	3	1	4	47	-13	0	0					

SIMON, CHRIS — LW

PERSONAL: Born January 30, 1972, in Wawa, Ont. ... 6-4/235. ... Shoots left.

TRANSACTIONS/CAREER NOTES: Selected by Philadelphia Flyers in second round (second Flyers pick, 25th overall) of NHL entry draft (June 16, 1990). ... Traded by Flyers with first-round pick (traded to Toronto; traded to Washington; Capitals selected D Nolan Baumgartner) in 1994 draft to Quebec Nordiques (July 21, 1992) completing deal in which Flyers sent G Ron Hextall, C Mike Ricci, C Peter Forsberg, D Steve Duchesne, first-round pick (G Jocelyn Thibault) in 1993 draft and cash to Nordiques for C Eric Lindros (June 20, 1992). ... Flu (March 13, 1993); missed one game. ... Injured back (December 1, 1993); missed 31 games. ... Injured back (February 16, 1994); missed one game. ... Injured back (March 6, 1994); missed one game. ... Injured back (March 18, 1994); missed remainder of season. ... Injured back (January 31, 1995); missed six games. ... Injured shoulder (March 22, 1995); missed 13 games. ... Nordiques franchise moved to Colorado and renamed Avalanche for 1995-96 season (June 21, 1995). ... Back spasms (January 6, 1996); missed two games. ... Injured shoulder (February 5, 1996); missed four games. ... Traded by Avalanche with D Curtis Leschyshyn to Washington Capitals for RW Keith Jones and first- (D Scott Parker) and fourth-round (traded back to Washington; Capitals selected Krys Barch) picks in 1998 draft (November 2, 1996). ... Injured arm (December 20, 1996); missed two games. ... Back spasms (January 24, 1997); missed 17 games. ... Back spasms (March 22, 1997); missed one game. ... Strained shoulder (March 29, 1997); missed six games. ... Suspended three games for alleged racial remarks (November 9, 1997). ... Bruised shoulder (October 25, 1997); missed five games. ... Reinjured shoulder (December 20, 1997) and had shoulder surgery; missed remainder of season. ... Strained shoulder (December 5, 1998) and had shoulder surgery; missed remainder of season. ... Strained neck (November 27, 1999); missed six games. ... Reinjured neck (December 21, 1999); missed one game. ... Suspended one playoff game by NHL for cross-checking incident (April 14, 2000). ... Missed first nine games of 2000-01 season due to contract dispute. ... Injured shoulder (March 1, 2001); missed five games. ... Reinjured shoulder (March 19, 2001); missed five games. ... Suspended two games for elbowing incident (April 6, 2001). ... Traded by Capitals with C Andrei Nikolishin to Chicago Blackhawks for C Michael Nylander and conditional third-round pick in 2004 draft (November 1, 2002). ... Signed as free agent by New York Rangers (July 27, 2003). ... Suspended two games for cross-checking incident (January 11, 2004). ... Flu (February 23, 2004); missed one game. ... Traded by Rangers with seventh-round pick in 2004 draft to Calgary Flames for G Jamie McLennan, C Blair Betts and RW Greg Moore (March 6, 2004). ... Suspended two games for kneeing incident (March 23, 2004). ... Torso injury (October 27, 2005); missed six games. ... Signed as free agent by New York Islanders (July 11, 2006).

		REGULAR SEASON								PLAYOFFS				
Season Team	League	GP	G	A	Pts.	PIM	+/-	PP	SH	GP	G	A	Pts.	PIM
87-88—Sault Ste. Marie	OHA	55	42	36	78	172	...	...	...	—	—	—	—	—
88-89—Ottawa	OHL	36	4	2	6	31	...	...	...	—	—	—	—	—
89-90—Ottawa	OHL	57	36	38	74	146	...	...	...	3	2	1	3	4
90-91—Ottawa	OHL	20	16	6	22	69	...	...	...	17	5	9	14	59
91-92—Ottawa	OHL	2	1	1	2	24	...	...	...	—	—	—	—	—
—Sault Ste. Marie	OHL	31	19	25	44	143	...	...	...	11	5	8	13	49
92-93—Halifax	AHL	36	12	6	18	131	-9	1	0	—	—	—	—	—
—Quebec	NHL	16	1	1	2	67	-2	0	0	5	0	0	0	26
93-94—Quebec	NHL	37	4	4	8	132	-2	0	0	—	—	—	—	—
94-95—Quebec	NHL	29	3	9	12	106	14	0	0	6	1	1	2	19
95-96—Colorado	NHL	64	16	18	34	250	10	4	0	12	1	2	3	11
96-97—Washington	NHL	42	9	13	22	165	-1	3	0	—	—	—	—	—
97-98—Washington	NHL	28	7	10	17	38	-1	4	0	18	1	0	1	26
98-99—Washington	NHL	23	3	7	10	48	-4	0	0	—	—	—	—	—
99-00—Washington	NHL	75	29	20	49	146	11	7	0	4	2	0	2	24
00-01—Washington	NHL	60	10	10	20	109	-12	4	0	6	0	1	1	4
01-02—Washington	NHL	82	14	17	31	137	-8	1	0	—	—	—	—	—
02-03—Washington	NHL	10	0	2	2	23	-3	0	0	—	—	—	—	—
—Chicago	NHL	61	12	6	18	125	-4	2	0	—	—	—	—	—
03-04—New York Rangers	NHL	65	14	9	23	225	14	3	0	—	—	—	—	—
—Calgary	NHL	13	3	2	5	25	1	1	0	16	5	2	7	*74
05-06—Calgary	NHL	72	8	14	22	94	0	2	0	6	0	1	1	7
NHL Totals (13 years)		677	133	142	275	1690	13	31	0	73	10	7	17	191

SIMPSON, TODD — D

PERSONAL: Born May 28, 1973, in North Vancouver, B.C. ... 6-3/227. ... Shoots left.

TRANSACTIONS/CAREER NOTES: Signed as free agent by Calgary Flames (July 6, 1994). ... Injured knee (October 1, 1997) and underwent surgery; missed 10 games. ... Injured shoulder (November 15, 1997); missed four games. ... Concussion (March 19, 1998); missed final 15 games of season. ... Facial injury (March 13, 1999); missed nine games. ... Traded by Flames to Florida Panthers for LW Bill Lindsay (September 30, 1999). ... Fractured toe (October 9, 2000); missed five games. ... Concussion (December 4, 2000); missed 40 games. ... Traded by Panthers to Phoenix Coyotes for second-round draft pick (traded to New Jersey; Devils selected LW Tuomas Pihlman) in 2001 draft (March 13, 2001). ... Fractured foot (November 20, 2001); missed 15 games. ... Fractured right hand (October 12, 2002); missed 11 games. ... Suspended three games for high-sticking incident (November 27, 2002). ... Suspended two games for high-sticking incident (December 28, 2002). ... Claimed by Anaheim Mighty Ducks in waiver draft (October 3, 2003). ... Injured shoulder (January 30, 2004); missed three games. ... Traded by Mighty Ducks to Ottawa Senators for LW Petr Schastlivy (February 4, 2004). ... Injured shoulder (February 21, 2004); missed five games. ... Signed as free agent by Chicago Blackhawks (August 23, 2005). ... Injured knee (December 12, 2006); missed one game. ... Traded by Blackhawks to Montreal Canadiens for sixth-round pick (C Chris Auger) in 2006 draft (March 9, 2006).

		REGULAR SEASON								PLAYOFFS				
Season Team	League	GP	G	A	Pts.	PIM	+/-	PP	SH	GP	G	A	Pts.	PIM
91-92—Brown	ECAC	14	1	3	4	18	...	...	...	—	—	—	—	—
92-93—Tri-City	WHL	69	5	18	23	196	...	...	...	4	0	0	0	13
93-94—Tri-City	WHL	12	2	3	5	32	...	...	...	—	—	—	—	—
—Saskatoon	WHL	51	7	19	26	175	...	...	...	16	1	5	6	42
94-95—Saint John	AHL	80	3	10	13	321	-13	0	0	5	0	0	0	4
95-96—Calgary	NHL	6	0	0	0	32	0	0	0	—	—	—	—	—
—Saint John	AHL	66	4	13	17	277	...	...	...	16	2	3	5	32
96-97—Calgary	NHL	82	1	13	14	208	-14	0	0	—	—	—	—	—
97-98—Calgary	NHL	53	1	5	6	109	-10	0	0	—	—	—	—	—
98-99—Calgary	NHL	73	2	8	10	151	18	0	0	—	—	—	—	—
99-00—Florida	NHL	82	1	6	7	202	5	0	0	4	0	0	0	4
00-01—Florida	NHL	25	1	3	4	74	0	0	0	—	—	—	—	—
—Phoenix	NHL	13	0	1	1	12	-4	0	0	—	—	—	—	—
01-02—Phoenix	NHL	67	2	13	15	152	20	0	0	5	0	2	2	6
02-03—Phoenix	NHL	66	2	7	9	135	7	0	0	—	—	—	—	—
03-04—Anaheim	NHL	46	4	3	7	105	-6	0	0	—	—	—	—	—
—Ottawa	NHL	16	0	1	1	47	-1	0	0	—	—	—	—	—
04-05—Herning	Denmark	7	2	3	5	46	...	...	...	16	3	5	8	82
05-06—Chicago	NHL	45	0	3	3	116	-2	0	0	—	—	—	—	—
—Montreal	NHL	6	0	0	0	14	0	0	0	—	—	—	—	—
NHL Totals (10 years)		580	14	63	77	1357	13	0	0	9	0	2	2	10

SJOSTROM, FREDRIK — RW/LW

PERSONAL: Born May 6, 1983, in Fargelanda, Sweden. ... 6-1/217. ... Shoots left. ... Name pronounced: SHOO struhm

TRANSACTIONS/CAREER NOTES: Selected by Phoenix Coyotes in first round (first Coyotes pick, 11th overall) of entry draft (June 23, 2001). ... Cut foot (September 30, 2005); missed season's first two games.

		REGULAR SEASON								PLAYOFFS				
Season Team	League	GP	G	A	Pts.	PIM	+/-	PP	SH	GP	G	A	Pts.	PIM
99-00—MoDo Ornskoldsvik	Sweden Jr.	14	4	4	8	2	...	...	...	—	—	—	—	—
00-01—Vastra Frolunda	Sweden Jr.	7	2	5	7	6	...	...	...	—	—	—	—	—
—Vastra Frolunda	Sweden	31	2	3	5	6	...	...	...	5	0	0	0	2
01-02—Calgary	WHL	58	19	31	50	51	...	...	...	4	1	1	2	8
02-03—Calgary	WHL	63	34	43	77	95	...	...	...	5	1	3	4	4
—Springfield	AHL	2	1	0	1	0	-1	0	0	—	—	—	—	—
03-04—Springfield	AHL	17	0	7	7	8	-3	0	0	—	—	—	—	—
—Phoenix	NHL	57	7	6	13	22	-7	0	0	—	—	—	—	—
04-05—Utah	AHL	80	14	24	38	57	-14	3	1	—	—	—	—	—
05-06—Phoenix	NHL	75	6	17	23	42	1	1	0	—	—	—	—	—
NHL Totals (2 years)		132	13	23	36	64	-6	1	0					

SKOLNEY, WADE — D

PERSONAL: Born June 24, 1981, in Wynyard, Saskatchewan. ... 6-0/185. ... Shoots right.

TRANSACTIONS/CAREER NOTES: Signed as undrafted free agent by Philadelphia Flyers (Mary 31, 2002). ... Signed as free agent by Pittsburgh Penguins (July 21, 2006).

		REGULAR SEASON								PLAYOFFS				
Season Team	League	GP	G	A	Pts.	PIM	+/-	PP	SH	GP	G	A	Pts.	PIM
97-98—Brandon	WHL	42	1	11	12	49	...	...	...	...	0	0	0	0
98-99—Brandon	WHL	39	3	10	13	60	...	...	...	5	0	1	1	6
99-00—Brandon	WHL	14	0	2	2	23	...	...	...	—	—	—	—	—
00-01—Brandon	WHL	28	2	9	11	37	...	...	...	—	—	—	—	—
01-02—Brandon	WHL	49	4	12	16	179	...	...	...	19	2	7	9	56
02-03—Philadelphia	AHL	68	2	7	9	102	...	...	...	—	—	—	—	—
03-04—Philadelphia	AHL	56	1	8	9	106	...	...	...	12	0	0	0	23
04-05—Philadelphia	AHL	35	0	8	8	104	12	0	0	21	0	1	1	43
05-06—Philadelphia	AHL	56	0	5	5	197	-3	0	0	—	—	—	—	—
—Philadelphia	NHL	1	0	0	0	2	0	0	0	—	—	—	—	—
NHL Totals (1 year)		1	0	0	0	2	0	0	0					

SKOULA, MARTIN D

PERSONAL: Born October 28, 1979, in Litomerice, Czech. ... 6-2/220. ... Shoots left.

TRANSACTIONS/CAREER NOTES: Selected by Colorado Avalanche in first round (second Avalanche pick, 17th overall) of entry draft (June 27, 1998). ... Shoulder (January 5, 2000); missed two games. ... Shoulder (April 6, 2003); missed one game. ... Bruised foot (October 18, 2003); missed two games. ... Traded by Avalanche to Anaheim Mighty Ducks for D Kurt Sauer and fourth-round pick (D Raymond Macias) in 2005 (February 21, 2004). ... Signed as free agent by Dallas Stars (August 3, 2005). ... Traded by Stars with D Shawn Belle to Minnesota Wild for D Willie Mitchell and second-round pick in 2007 (March 9, 2006).

		REGULAR SEASON								PLAYOFFS				
Season Team	**League**	**GP**	**G**	**A**	**Pts.**	**PIM**	**+/-**	**PP**	**SH**	**GP**	**G**	**A**	**Pts.**	**PIM**
95-96—Litvinov	Czech. Jrs.	38	0	4	4	...	...	...	...	—	—	—	—	—
—Litvinov	Czech Rep.	...	...	...	...	...	...	...	...	1	0	0	0	0
96-97—Litvinov	Czech. Jrs.	38	2	9	11	...	...	...	...	—	—	—	—	—
—Litvinov	Czech Rep.	1	0	0	0	0	...	...	...	—	—	—	—	—
97-98—Barrie	COJHL	66	8	36	44	36	...	...	...	6	1	3	4	4
98-99—Barrie	OHL	67	13	46	59	46	58	...	...	12	3	10	13	13
—Hershey	AHL	...	...	...	...	...	...	...	...	1	0	0	0	0
99-00—Colorado	NHL	80	3	13	16	20	5	2	0	17	0	2	2	4
00-01—Colorado	NHL	82	8	17	25	38	8	3	0	23	1	4	5	8
01-02—Colorado	NHL	82	10	21	31	42	-3	5	0	21	0	6	6	2
—Czech Rep. Oly. team	Int'l	4	0	0	0	0	...	...	...	—	—	—	—	—
02-03—Colorado	NHL	81	4	21	25	68	11	2	0	7	0	1	1	4
03-04—Colorado	NHL	58	2	14	16	30	2	0	0	—	—	—	—	—
—Anaheim	NHL	21	2	7	9	2	3	1	0	—	—	—	—	—
04-05—Chem. Litvinov	Czech Rep.	47	4	15	19	101	-8	...	...	6	0	0	0	6
05-06—Dallas	NHL	61	4	11	15	36	6	3	0	—	—	—	—	—
—Minnesota	NHL	17	1	5	6	10	0	0	0	—	—	—	—	—
NHL Totals (6 years)		482	34	109	143	246	32	16	0	68	1	13	14	18

SKRASTINS, KARLIS D

PERSONAL: Born July 9, 1974, in Riga, U.S.S.R. ... 6-1/212. ... Shoots left. ... Name pronounced SKRAS-tinsh.

TRANSACTIONS/CAREER NOTES: Selected by Nashville Predators in ninth round (eighth Predators pick, 230th overall) of 1998 draft (June 27, 1998). ... Traded by Predators to Colorado Avalanche for third-round pick (later traded to Ottawa; Senators picked D Peter Regin) in 2004 draft (June 30, 2003).

		REGULAR SEASON								PLAYOFFS				
Season Team	**League**	**GP**	**G**	**A**	**Pts.**	**PIM**	**+/-**	**PP**	**SH**	**GP**	**G**	**A**	**Pts.**	**PIM**
92-93—Riga Stars	CIS	40	3	5	8	16	...	...	...	2	0	0	0	0
93-94—Riga Stars	CIS	42	7	5	12	18	...	...	...	2	1	0	1	4
94-95—Riga Stars	CIS	52	4	14	18	69	...	...	...	—	—	—	—	—
95-96—TPS Turku	Finland	50	4	11	15	32	...	...	...	11	2	2	4	10
96-97—TPS Turku	Finland	50	2	8	10	20	...	...	...	—	—	—	—	—
97-98—TPS Turku	Finland	48	4	15	19	67	...	...	...	—	—	—	—	—
98-99—Milwaukee	IHL	75	8	36	44	47	...	...	...	2	0	1	1	2
—Nashville	NHL	2	0	1	1	0	0	0	0	—	—	—	—	—
99-00—Milwaukee	IHL	19	3	8	11	10	...	...	...	—	—	—	—	—
—Nashville	NHL	59	5	6	11	20	-7	1	0	—	—	—	—	—
00-01—Nashville	NHL	82	1	11	12	30	-12	0	0	—	—	—	—	—
01-02—Nashville	NHL	82	4	13	17	36	-12	0	0	—	—	—	—	—
—Latvian Olympic team	Int'l	1	0	0	0	0	...	...	...	—	—	—	—	—
02-03—Nashville	NHL	82	3	10	13	44	-18	0	1	—	—	—	—	—
03-04—Colorado	NHL	82	5	8	13	26	18	0	1	11	0	2	2	2
04-05—Riga	Belarus	34	8	17	25	30	...	...	...	3	0	0	0	25
—Riga	Latvia	4	0	4	4	0	...	...	...	9	3	10	13	33
05-06—Colorado	NHL	82	3	11	14	65	-7	0	2	9	0	1	1	10
—Latvian Oly. team	Int'l	5	0	1	1	0	-1	0	0	—	—	—	—	—
NHL Totals (7 years)		471	21	60	81	221	-38	1	4	20	0	3	3	12

SLATER, JIM C/LW

PERSONAL: Born December 9, 1982, in Petoskey, Mich. ... 6-0/190. ... Shoots left.

TRANSACTIONS/CAREER NOTES: Selected by Atlanta Thrashers in first round (second Thrashers pick, 30th overall) of NHL entry draft (June 22, 2002).

		REGULAR SEASON								PLAYOFFS				
Season Team	**League**	**GP**	**G**	**A**	**Pts.**	**PIM**	**+/-**	**PP**	**SH**	**GP**	**G**	**A**	**Pts.**	**PIM**
00-01—Cleveland	NAHL	48	27	37	64	122	...	...	...	—	—	—	—	—
01-02—Michigan State	CCHA	32	9	18	27	48	...	...	...	—	—	—	—	—
02-03—Michigan State	CCHA	37	18	26	44	26	...	...	...	—	—	—	—	—
03-04—Michigan State	CCHA	42	19	29	48	38	...	...	...	—	—	—	—	—
04-05—Michigan State	CCHA	41	16	32	48	30	...	...	...	—	—	—	—	—
05-06—Chicago	AHL	4	0	2	2	2	2	0	0	—	—	—	—	—
—Atlanta	NHL	71	10	10	20	46	1	1	0	—	—	—	—	—
NHL Totals (1 year)		71	10	10	20	46	1	1	0					

SLEGR, JIRI — D

PERSONAL: Born May 30, 1971, in Jihlava, Czech. ... 6-1/210. ... Shoots left. ... Son of Jiri Bubla, defenseman with Vancouver Canucks (1981-82 through 1985-86). ... Name pronounced YIH-ree SLAY-guhr.

TRANSACTIONS/CAREER NOTES: Selected by Vancouver Canucks in second round (third Canucks pick, 23rd overall) of entry draft (June 16, 1990). ... Traded by Canucks to Edmonton Oilers for RW Roman Oksiuta (April 7, 1995). ... Sprained left knee ligaments (December 27, 1995); missed 19 games. ... Traded by Oilers to Pittsburgh Penguins for third-round pick (traded to New Jersey; Devils selected RW Brian Gionta) in 1998 draft (August 12, 1997). ... Hip pointer (November 14, 1997); missed four games. ... Flu (December 16, 1997); missed one game. ... Shoulder (March 2, 1998); missed one game. ... Fractured hand (November 5, 1998); missed 13 games. ... Bruised knee (April 1, 1999); missed one game. ... Sprained ankle (October 8, 1999); missed five games. ... Flu (November 20, 1999); missed one game. ... Sprained knee (November 26, 1999); missed two games. ... Traded by Penguins to Atlanta Thrashers for third-round pick (traded to Columbus; Blue Jackets selected D Aaron Johnson) in 2001 draft (January 14, 2001). ... Strained groin (March 28, 2001); missed five games. ... Strained hip (November 3, 2001). ... Herniated disk in back (November 19, 2001); missed 11 games. ... Strained knee (December 14, 2001); missed 15 games. ... Traded by Thrashers to Detroit Red Wings for C Yuri Butsayev and third-round pick (traded to Columbus; Blue Jackets selected LW Jeff Genovy) in 2002 draft (March 19, 2002). ... Signed as free agent by Vancouver Canucks (September 3, 2003). ... Traded by Canucks to Boston Bruins for future considerations (January 17, 2004). ... Back (October 18, 2005); missed four games. ... Sore back (January 2, 2006); missed five games. ... Sore back (January 19, 2006); missed final 26 games of regular season.

		REGULAR SEASON								PLAYOFFS				
Season Team	League	GP	G	A	Pts.	PIM	+/-	PP	SH	GP	G	A	Pts.	PIM
87-88—Litvinov	Czech Rep.	4	1	1	2	0	...	...	...	—	—	—	—	—
88-89—Litvinov	Czech.	8	0	0	0	0	...	...	...	—	—	—	—	—
89-90—Litvinov	Czech.	51	4	15	19	...	...	...	...	—	—	—	—	—
90-91—Litvinov	Czech.	39	10	33	43	26	...	...	...	—	—	—	—	—
91-92—Litvinov	Czech.	38	7	22	29	30	...	...	...	—	—	—	—	—
—Czech. Olympic Team	Int'l	8	1	1	2	...	...	...	...	—	—	—	—	—
92-93—Vancouver	NHL	41	4	22	26	109	16	2	0	5	0	3	3	4
—Hamilton	AHL	21	4	14	18	42	-12	2	0	—	—	—	—	—
93-94—Vancouver	NHL	78	5	33	38	86	0	1	0	—	—	—	—	—
94-95—Chem. Litvinov	Czech Rep.	11	3	10	13	43	...	...	...	—	—	—	—	—
—Vancouver	NHL	19	1	5	6	32	0	0	0	—	—	—	—	—
—Edmonton	NHL	12	1	5	6	14	-5	1	0	—	—	—	—	—
95-96—Edmonton	NHL	57	4	13	17	74	-1	0	1	—	—	—	—	—
—Cape Breton	AHL	4	1	2	3	4	...	...	...	—	—	—	—	—
96-97—Chem. Litvinov	Czech Rep.	1	0	0	0	0	...	...	...	—	—	—	—	—
—Sodertalje SK	Sweden	30	4	14	18	62	...	...	...	—	—	—	—	—
97-98—Pittsburgh	NHL	73	5	12	17	109	10	1	1	6	0	4	4	2
—Czech Rep. Oly. team	Int'l	6	1	0	1	8	2	0	0	—	—	—	—	—
98-99—Pittsburgh	NHL	63	3	20	23	86	13	1	0	13	1	3	4	12
99-00—Pittsburgh	NHL	74	11	20	31	82	20	0	0	10	2	3	5	19
00-01—Pittsburgh	NHL	42	5	10	15	60	-9	0	1	—	—	—	—	—
—Atlanta	NHL	33	3	16	19	36	-1	2	0	—	—	—	—	—
01-02—Atlanta	NHL	38	3	5	8	51	-21	1	0	—	—	—	—	—
—Detroit	NHL	8	0	1	1	8	1	0	0	1	0	0	0	2
02-03—Avangard Omsk	Russian	6	1	2	3	8	...	...	...	9	0	3	3	45
—Litvinov	Czech Rep.	10	2	3	5	14	...	...	...	—	—	—	—	—
03-04—Vancouver	NHL	16	2	5	7	8	6	1	1	—	—	—	—	—
—Boston	NHL	36	4	15	19	27	5	0	0	7	1	1	2	0
04-05—Chem. Litvinov	Czech Rep.	46	6	23	29	135	7	...	...	6	1	2	3	30
05-06—Boston	NHL	32	5	11	16	56	-2	4	0	—	—	—	—	—
NHL Totals (11 years)		622	56	193	249	838	32	14	4	42	4	14	18	39

SMITH, DAN — D

PERSONAL: Born October 19, 1976, in Fernie, B.C. ... 6-2/195. ... Shoots left.

COLLEGE: University of British Columbia.

TRANSACTIONS/CAREER NOTES: Selected by Colorado Avalanche in seventh round (seventh Avalanche pick, 181st overall) of entry draft (July 8, 1995). ... Signed as free agent by Phoenix Coyotes (August 8, 2002). ... Signed as free agent by Edmonton Oilers (August 21, 2003). ... Signed as free agent by Detroit Red Wings (July 13. 2006).

		REGULAR SEASON								PLAYOFFS				
Season Team	League	GP	G	A	Pts.	PIM	+/-	PP	SH	GP	G	A	Pts.	PIM
94-95—British Columbia	CWUAA	28	1	2	3	26	...	...	...	—	—	—	—	—
95-96—Tri-City	WHL	58	1	21	22	70	...	...	...	11	1	3	4	14
96-97—Tri-City	WHL	72	5	19	24	174	...	...	...	—	—	—	—	—
97-98—Hershey	AHL	50	1	2	3	71	4	0	0	6	0	0	0	4
98-99—Hershey	AHL	54	5	7	12	72	-2	3	0	5	0	1	1	0
—Colorado	NHL	12	0	0	0	9	5	0	0	—	—	—	—	—
99-00—Hershey	AHL	49	7	15	22	56	...	...	...	—	—	—	—	—
—Colorado	NHL	3	0	0	0	0	2	0	0	—	—	—	—	—
00-01—Hershey	AHL	58	2	12	14	34	...	...	...	12	0	1	1	4
01-02—Lukko Rauma	Finland	32	1	2	3	18	...	...	...	—	—	—	—	—
02-03—Springfield	AHL	69	1	14	15	53	0	0	0	6	0	2	2	0
03-04—Toronto	AHL	66	4	9	13	41	...	...	...	—	—	—	—	—
04-05—Edmonton	AHL	72	5	10	15	72	9	1	0	—	—	—	—	—
05-06—Hamilton	AHL	69	0	16	16	61	11	0	0	—	—	—	—	—
—Edmonton	NHL	7	0	0	0	7	1	0	0	—	—	—	—	—
NHL Totals (3 years)		22	0	0	0	16	8	0	0					

SMITH, JASON — D

PERSONAL: Born November 2, 1973, in Calgary. ... 6-3/212. ... Shoots right.

TRANSACTIONS/CAREER NOTES: Selected by New Jersey Devils in first round (first Devils pick, 18th overall) of entry draft (June 20, 1992). ... Right knee (November 5, 1994); missed 37 games. ... Hand (November 5, 1995); missed 15 games. ... Traded by Devils with C Steve Sullivan and C Alyn McCauley to Toronto Maple Leafs for C Doug Gilmour, D Dave Ellett and third-round pick (D Andre Lakos) in 1999 (February 25, 1997). ... Fractured toe (March 30, 1998); missed one game. ... Traded by Maple Leafs to Edmonton Oilers for fourth-round pick (D Jonathan Zion) in 1999 and second-round pick (C Kris Vernarsky) in 2000 (March 23, 1999). ... Shoulder (February 23, 2000); missed one game. ... Elbow (November 2, 2001); missed two games. ... Strained lower back (December 5, 2001); missed six games. ... Leg (January 29, 2003); missed two games. ... Shoulder (February 11, 2003); missed 12 games. ... Left ankle (December 30, 2003); missed 14 games. ... Toe (February 2, 2006); missed two games. ... Toe (February 7, 2006); missed four games

		REGULAR SEASON								PLAYOFFS				
Season Team	League	GP	G	A	Pts.	PIM	+/-	PP	SH	GP	G	A	Pts.	PIM
90-91—Calgary Canucks	AJHL	45	3	15	18	69	...	...	...	—	—	—	—	—
—Regina	WHL	2	0	0	0	7	...	...	...	—	—	—	—	—
91-92—Regina	WHL	62	9	29	38	168	...	...	...	—	—	—	—	—
92-93—Regina	WHL	64	14	52	66	175	-19	6	2	13	4	8	12	39
—Utica	AHL	...	...	...	...	...	...	...	...	1	0	0	0	2
93-94—New Jersey	NHL	41	0	5	5	43	7	0	0	6	0	0	0	7
—Albany	AHL	20	6	3	9	31	7	4	0	—	—	—	—	—
94-95—Albany	AHL	7	0	2	2	15	5	0	0	11	2	2	4	19
—New Jersey	NHL	2	0	0	0	0	-3	0	0	—	—	—	—	—
95-96—New Jersey	NHL	64	2	1	3	86	5	0	0	—	—	—	—	—
96-97—New Jersey	NHL	57	1	2	3	38	-8	0	0	—	—	—	—	—
—Toronto	NHL	21	0	5	5	16	-4	0	0	—	—	—	—	—
97-98—Toronto	NHL	81	3	13	16	100	-5	0	0	—	—	—	—	—
98-99—Toronto	NHL	60	2	11	13	40	-9	0	0	—	—	—	—	—
—Edmonton	NHL	12	1	1	2	11	0	0	0	4	0	1	1	4
99-00—Edmonton	NHL	80	3	11	14	60	16	0	0	5	0	1	1	4
00-01—Edmonton	NHL	82	5	15	20	120	14	1	1	6	0	2	2	6
01-02—Edmonton	NHL	74	5	13	18	103	14	0	1	—	—	—	—	—
02-03—Edmonton	NHL	68	4	8	12	64	5	0	0	6	0	0	0	19
03-04—Edmonton	NHL	68	7	12	19	98	13	0	1	—	—	—	—	—
05-06—Edmonton	NHL	76	4	13	17	84	1	0	0	24	1	4	5	16
NHL Totals (11 years)		786	37	110	147	863	45	1	3	51	1	8	9	56

SMITH, MARK — C/LW

PERSONAL: Born October 24, 1977, in Edmonton. ... 5-10/215. ... Shoots left.

TRANSACTIONS/CAREER NOTES: Selected by San Jose Sharks in ninth round (seventh Sharks pick, 219th overall) in NHL draft (June 21, 1997). ... Suffered concussion (November 5, 2000); missed seven games. ... Injured knee (February 26, 2001); missed three games. ... Flu (April 13, 2002); missed one game. ... Injured knee (October 28, 2005); missed one game. ... Injured chest (November 15, 2003); missed 15 games.

		REGULAR SEASON								PLAYOFFS				
Season Team	League	GP	G	A	Pts.	PIM	+/-	PP	SH	GP	G	A	Pts.	PIM
94-95—Lethbridge	WHL	49	3	4	7	25	...	...	...	—	—	—	—	—
95-96—Lethbridge	WHL	71	11	24	35	59	...	...	...	19	7	13	20	51
96-97—Lethbridge	WHL	62	19	38	57	125	...	...	...	19	7	13	20	51
97-98—Lethbridge	WHL	70	42	67	109	206	28	19	5	3	0	2	2	18
98-99—Kentucky	AHL	78	18	21	39	101	8	4	0	12	2	7	9	16
99-00—Kentucky	AHL	79	21	45	66	153	...	...	...	9	0	5	5	22
00-01—San Jose	NHL	42	2	2	4	51	2	0	0	—	—	—	—	—
—Kentucky	AHL	6	2	6	8	23	...	...	...	—	—	—	—	—
01-02—San Jose	NHL	49	3	3	6	72	-1	0	0	—	—	—	—	—
02-03—San Jose	NHL	75	4	11	15	64	1	0	0	—	—	—	—	—
03-04—San Jose	NHL	36	1	3	4	72	-5	0	0	10	1	0	1	11
04-05—Victoria	ECHL	20	6	9	15	41	-13	3	0	—	—	—	—	—
05-06—San Jose	NHL	80	9	15	24	97	3	2	1	11	3	0	3	6
NHL Totals (5 years)		282	19	34	53	356	0	2	1	21	4	0	4	17

SMITH, NATHAN — C

PERSONAL: Born February 9, 1982, in Strathcona, Alta. ... 6-2/200. ... Shoots left. ... Brother of Jarrett Smith, center, Mighty Ducks of Anaheim organization.

TRANSACTIONS/CAREER NOTES: Selected by Vancouver Canucks in first round (first Canucks pick, 23rd overall) of NHL entry draft (June 24, 2000).

		REGULAR SEASON								PLAYOFFS				
Season Team	League	GP	G	A	Pts.	PIM	+/-	PP	SH	GP	G	A	Pts.	PIM
98-99—Swift Current	WHL	47	5	8	13	26	...	...	...	—	—	—	—	—
99-00—Swift Current	WHL	70	21	28	49	72	...	...	...	12	1	6	7	4
00-01—Swift Current	WHL	67	28	62	90	78	...	...	...	19	4	3	7	20
01-02—Swift Current	WHL	47	22	38	60	52	...	...	...	12	3	6	9	18
02-03—Manitoba	AHL	53	9	8	17	30	6	3	0	14	1	3	4	25
03-04—Manitoba	AHL	76	4	16	20	71	-13	1	1	—	—	—	—	—
—Vancouver	NHL	2	0	0	0	0	-1	0	0	—	—	—	—	—
04-05—Manitoba	AHL	72	7	9	16	67	-11	0	0	14	2	4	6	20
05-06—Manitoba	AHL	20	5	4	9	57	-4	3	1	—	—	—	—	—
—Vancouver	NHL	1	0	0	0	0	0	0	0	—	—	—	—	—
NHL Totals (2 years)		3	0	0	0	0	-1	0	0					

SMITH, WYATT — C

PERSONAL: Born February 13, 1977, in Thief River Falls, Minn. ... 5-11/208. ... Shoots left.
TRANSACTIONS/CAREER NOTES: Selected by Phoenix Coyotes in ninth round (sixth Coyotes pick, 233rd overall) of entry draft (June 21, 1997). ... Signed as free agent by Nashville Predators (July 15, 2002). ... Injured shoulder (November 16, 2002); missed five games. ... Signed as free agent by New York Islanders (August 10, 2005). ... Signed as free agent by Minnesota Wild (July 19, 2006).

		REGULAR SEASON								PLAYOFFS				
Season Team	League	GP	G	A	Pts.	PIM	+/-	PP	SH	GP	G	A	Pts.	PIM
95-96—Minnesota	WCHA	32	4	5	9	32	...	...	...	—	—	—	—	—
96-97—Minnesota	WCHA	39	24	23	47	62	...	...	...	—	—	—	—	—
97-98—Minnesota	WCHA	39	24	23	47	62	...	...	...	—	—	—	—	—
98-99—Minnesota	WCHA	43	23	20	43	37	...	...	...	—	—	—	—	—
99-00—Springfield	AHL	60	14	26	40	26	...	...	...	5	2	3	5	13
—Phoenix	NHL	2	0	0	0	0	-2	0	0	—	—	—	—	—
00-01—Phoenix	NHL	42	3	7	10	13	7	0	1	—	—	—	—	—
—Springfield	AHL	18	5	7	12	11	...	...	...	—	—	—	—	—
01-02—Springfield	AHL	69	23	32	55	69	-5	9	0	—	—	—	—	—
—Phoenix	NHL	10	0	0	0	0	-5	0	0	—	—	—	—	—
02-03—Milwaukee	AHL	56	24	27	51	89	6	6	2	4	1	0	1	2
—Nashville	NHL	11	1	0	1	0	-1	0	0	—	—	—	—	—
03-04—Milwaukee	AHL	40	9	7	16	40	5	2	2	22	5	7	12	25
—Nashville	NHL	18	3	1	4	2	2	0	1	—	—	—	—	—
04-05—Milwaukee	AHL	69	19	28	47	89	4	11	0	7	1	4	5	10
05-06—Bridgeport	AHL	39	13	16	29	40	-8	6	0	—	—	—	—	—
—New York Islanders	NHL	42	0	8	8	26	-7	0	0	—	—	—	—	—
NHL Totals (6 years)		125	7	16	23	41	-6	0	2					

S

SMITHSON, JERRED — C/RW

PERSONAL: Born February 4, 1979, in Vernon, B.C. ... 6-2/200. ... Shoots right.
TRANSACTIONS/CAREER NOTES: Signed as free agent by Los Angeles Kings (February 18, 2000). ... Signed as free agent by Nashville Predators (July 22, 2004). ... Shoulder (November 19, 2005); missed one game.

		REGULAR SEASON								PLAYOFFS				
Season Team	League	GP	G	A	Pts.	PIM	+/-	PP	SH	GP	G	A	Pts.	PIM
00-01—Lowell	AHL	24	1	1	2	10	...	...	...	0	0	0	0	0
—Trenton	ECHL	3	0	1	1	2	...	...	...	0	0	0	0	0
01-02—Manchester	AHL	78	5	13	18	45	...	...	...	0	0	0	0	0
02-03—Manchester	AHL	38	4	21	25	60	...	...	...	3	0	0	0	4
—Los Angeles	NHL	22	0	2	2	21	-5	0	0	—	—	—	—	—
03-04—Los Angeles	NHL	8	0	1	1	4	0	0	0	—	—	—	—	—
—Manchester	AHL	66	7	13	20	51	-2	1	1	6	0	1	1	10
04-05—Milwaukee	AHL	80	11	11	22	92	3	1	1	5	0	0	0	4
05-06—Milwaukee	AHL	8	0	0	0	12	-3	0	0	—	—	—	—	—
—Nashville	NHL	66	5	9	14	54	9	0	0	3	0	0	0	4
NHL Totals (3 years)		96	5	12	17	79	4	0	0	3	0	0	0	4

SMOLINSKI, BRYAN — C/LW

PERSONAL: Born December 27, 1971, in Toledo, Ohio. ... 6-1/208. ... Shoots right. ... Name pronounced: smoh LIHN skee
TRANSACTIONS/CAREER NOTES: Selected by Boston Bruins in first round (first Bruins pick, 21st overall) of NHL entry draft (June 16, 1990). ... Injured knee (April 14, 1994); missed one game. ... Charley horse (April 1995); missed four games. ... Traded by Bruins with RW Glen Murray to Pittsburgh Penguins for LW Kevin Stevens and C Shawn McEachern (August 2, 1995). ... Bruised knee (January 16, 1996); missed one game. ... Traded by Penguins to New York Islanders for D Darius Kasparaitis and C Andreas Johansson (November 17, 1996). ... Traded by Islanders with RW Zigmund Palffy, G Marcel Cousineau and fourth-round pick (C Daniel Johansson) in 1999 draft to Los Angeles Kings for C Olli Jokinen, LW Josh Green, D Mathieu Biron and first-round pick (LW Taylor Pyatt) in 1999 draft (June 20, 1999). ... Sprained knee (April 3, 1999); missed final three games of season. ... Back spasms (April 3, 2001); missed final two games of season. ... Back spasms (October 26, 2001); missed one game. ... Flu (January 24, 2002); missed one game. ... Traded by Kings to Ottawa Senators for D Tim Gleason (March 11, 2003). ... Separated shoulder (November 23, 2003); missed two games. ... Injured right shoulder (November 19, 2005); missed one game. ... Traded by Senators with F Martin Havlat to Chicago Blackhawks in three-team deal in which San Jose Sharks traded D Tom Preissing and D Josh Hennessy to Blackhawks for F Mark Bell. Blackhawks then traded Preissing, Hennessy, D Michal Barinka and a second-round pick in 2008 draft (July 10, 2006).
STATISTICAL PLATEAUS: Three-goal games: 1994-95 (1), 2000-01 (1), 2002-03 (1). Total: 3.

		REGULAR SEASON								PLAYOFFS				
Season Team	League	GP	G	A	Pts.	PIM	+/-	PP	SH	GP	G	A	Pts.	PIM
87-88—Detroit Little Caesars	MNHL	80	43	77	120	...	...	...	...	—	—	—	—	—
88-89—Stratford Jr. B	OHA	46	32	62	94	132	...	...	...	—	—	—	—	—
89-90—Michigan State	CCHA	39	10	17	27	45	...	...	...	—	—	—	—	—
90-91—Michigan State	CCHA	35	9	12	21	24	...	...	...	—	—	—	—	—
91-92—Michigan State	CCHA	44	30	35	65	59	...	...	...	—	—	—	—	—
92-93—Michigan State	CCHA	40	31	37	68	93	...	...	...	—	—	—	—	—
—Boston	NHL	9	1	3	4	0	3	0	0	4	1	0	1	2
93-94—Boston	NHL	83	31	20	51	82	4	4	3	13	5	4	9	4
94-95—Boston	NHL	44	18	13	31	31	-3	6	0	5	0	1	1	4
95-96—Pittsburgh	NHL	81	24	40	64	69	6	8	2	18	5	4	9	10
96-97—Detroit	IHL	6	5	7	12	10	...	...	...	—	—	—	—	—
—New York Islanders	NHL	64	28	28	56	25	9	9	0	—	—	—	—	—
97-98—New York Islanders	NHL	81	13	30	43	34	-16	3	0	—	—	—	—	—
98-99—New York Islanders	NHL	82	16	24	40	49	-7	7	0	—	—	—	—	—

Season Team	League	GP	G	A	Pts.	PIM	+/-	PP	SH	GP	G	A	Pts.	PIM
		REGULAR SEASON								PLAYOFFS				
99-00—Los Angeles	NHL	79	20	36	56	48	2	2	0	4	0	0	0	2
00-01—Los Angeles	NHL	78	27	32	59	40	10	5	3	13	1	5	6	14
01-02—Los Angeles	NHL	80	13	25	38	56	7	4	1	7	2	0	2	2
02-03—Los Angeles	NHL	58	18	20	38	18	-1	6	1	...	...	...	...	...
—Ottawa	NHL	10	3	5	8	2	1	0	0	18	2	7	9	6
03-04—Ottawa	NHL	80	19	27	46	49	22	4	0	7	1	1	2	4
04-05—Motor City	UHL	21	9	23	32	18	20	1	1	—	—	—	—	—
05-06—Ottawa	NHL	81	17	31	48	46	8	4	0	10	3	3	6	2
NHL Totals (13 years)		910	248	334	582	549	45	62	10	99	20	25	45	50

SMYTH, RYAN — LW

PERSONAL: Born February 21, 1976, in Banff, Alta. ... 6-1/190. ... Shoots left. ... Brother of Kevin Smyth, LW with Hartford Whalers (1993-94 through 1995-96). ... Name pronounced SMIHTH.

TRANSACTIONS/CAREER NOTES: Selected by Edmonton Oilers in first round (second Oilers pick, sixth overall) of entry draft (June 28, 1994). ... Knee (January 20, 1998); missed 15 games. ... Thigh (December 27, 1998); missed one game. ... Jaw (March 10, 1999); missed seven games. ... Right ankle (November 16, 2001); missed 21 games. ... Shoulder (January 16, 2003); missed six games ... Shoulder (February 11, 2003); missed nine games. ... Knee (October 10, 2005); missed six games.

STATISTICAL PLATEAUS: Three-goal games: 1996-97 (1), 1999-00 (1), 2000-01 (2). Total: 4.

Season Team	League	GP	G	A	Pts.	PIM	+/-	PP	SH	GP	G	A	Pts.	PIM
		REGULAR SEASON								PLAYOFFS				
91-92—Moose Jaw	WHL	2	0	0	0	0	...	...	...	—	—	—	—	—
92-93—Moose Jaw	WHL	64	19	14	33	59	...	...	...	—	—	—	—	—
93-94—Moose Jaw	WHL	72	50	55	105	88	-30	22	0	—	—	—	—	—
94-95—Moose Jaw	WHL	50	41	45	86	66	21	14	5	10	6	9	15	22
—Edmonton	NHL	3	0	0	0	0	-1	0	0	—	—	—	—	—
95-96—Edmonton	NHL	48	2	9	11	28	-10	1	0	—	—	—	—	—
—Cape Breton	AHL	9	6	5	11	4	...	...	...	—	—	—	—	—
96-97—Edmonton	NHL	82	39	22	61	76	-7	†20	0	12	5	5	10	12
97-98—Edmonton	NHL	65	20	13	33	44	-24	10	0	12	1	3	4	16
98-99—Edmonton	NHL	71	13	18	31	62	0	6	0	3	3	0	3	0
99-00—Edmonton	NHL	82	28	26	54	58	-2	11	0	5	1	0	1	6
00-01—Edmonton	NHL	82	31	39	70	58	10	11	0	6	3	4	7	4
01-02—Edmonton	NHL	61	15	35	50	48	7	7	1	—	—	—	—	—
—Can. Olympic team	Int'l	6	0	1	1	0	...	...	...	—	—	—	—	—
02-03—Edmonton	NHL	66	27	34	61	67	5	10	0	6	2	0	2	16
03-04—Edmonton	NHL	82	23	36	59	70	11	8	2	—	—	—	—	—
05-06—Edmonton	NHL	75	36	30	66	58	-5	19	2	24	7	9	16	22
—Canadian Oly. team	Int'l	6	0	1	1	4	1	0	0	—	—	—	—	—
NHL Totals (11 years)		717	234	262	496	569	-16	103	5	68	22	21	43	76

SNEEP, CARL — D

PERSONAL: Born November 5, 1987, in St. Louis Park, Minn. ... 6-4/210. ... Shoots right.

TRANSACTIONS/CAREER NOTES: Selected by Pittsburgh Penguins in second round (second Penguins pick; 32nd overall) of NHL draft (June 24, 2006).

Season Team	League	GP	G	A	Pts.	PIM	+/-	PP	SH	GP	G	A	Pts.	PIM
		REGULAR SEASON								PLAYOFFS				
04-05—Brainerd	USHS (West)	26	20	21	41	25	...	...	...	—	—	—	—	—
05-06—Brainerd	USHS (West)	26	14	23	37	34	...	...	...	—	—	—	—	—

SNOW, GARTH — G

PERSONAL: Born July 28, 1969, in Wrentham, Mass. ... 6-3/200. ... Catches left. ... New York Islanders general manager.

TRANSACTIONS/CAREER NOTES: Selected by Quebec Nordiques in sixth round (sixth Nordiques pick, 114th overall) of entry draft (June 13, 1987). ... Nordiques franchise moved to Colorado and renamed Avalanche for 1995-96 season (June 21, 1995). ... Rights traded by Avalanche to Philadelphia Flyers for third- (traded to Washington; Capitals selected C Shawn McNeil) and sixth-round (G Kai Fischer) picks in 1996 draft (July 12, 1995). ... Injured groin (March 27, 1997); missed three games. ... Traded by Flyers to Vancouver Canucks for G Sean Burke (March 4, 1998). ... Strained hip flexor (March 18, 1998); missed three games. ... Strained hip flexor (October 31, 1998); missed two games. ... Injured finger (September 21, 1999); missed two games. ... Fractured finger (October 13, 1999); missed 15 games. ... Signed as free agent by Pittsburgh Penguins (October 10, 2000). ... Suspended two games for fighting (December 16, 2000). ... Strained groin (February 7, 2001); missed 25 games. ... Signed as free agent by New York Islanders (July 1, 2001). ... Suspended two games for attempting to injure a player (November 22, 2002). ... Injured groin (March 25, 2004); missed five games. ... Sprained MCL in left knee (January 4, 2006); missed 13 games. ... Announced retirement (July 18, 2006).

Season Team	League	GP	Min.	W	L	OTL	T	GA	SO	GAA	SV%	GP	Min.	W	L	GA	SO	GAA	SV%
		REGULAR SEASON										PLAYOFFS							
88-89—Maine	Hockey East	5	241	2	2	...	0	14	1	3.49	...	—	—	—	—	—	—	—	—
89-90—Maine	Hockey East	Did not play																	
90-91—Maine	Hockey East	25	1290	18	4	...	0	64	0	2.98	...	—	—	—	—	—	—	—	—
91-92—Maine	Hockey East	31	1792	25	4	...	2	73	2	2.44	...	—	—	—	—	—	—	—	—
92-93—Maine	Hockey East	23	1210	21	0	...	1	42	1	2.08	...	—	—	—	—	—	—	—	—
93-94—U.S. national team	Int'l	23	1324	13	5	...	3	71	1	3.22	...	—	—	—	—	—	—	—	—
—Quebec	NHL	5	279	3	2	...	0	16	0	3.44	.874	—	—	—	—	—	—	—	—
—U.S. Olympic team	Int'l	5	299	1	2	...	2	17	0	3.41	.881	—	—	—	—	—	—	—	—
—Cornwall	AHL	16	927	6	5	...	3	51	0	3.30	.891	13	790	8	5	42	0	3.19	.894

		REGULAR SEASON										PLAYOFFS							
Season Team	League	GP	Min.	W	L	OTL	T	GA	SO	GAA	SV%	GP	Min.	W	L	GA	SO	GAA	SV%
94-95—Cornwall	AHL	62	3558	32	20	...	7	162	3	2.73	.900	8	402	4	3	14	2	2.09	.944
—Quebec	NHL	2	119	1	1	...	0	11	0	5.55	.825	1	9	0	0	1	0	6.67	.667
95-96—Philadelphia	NHL	26	1437	12	8	...	4	69	0	2.88	.894	1	1	0	0	0	0	0.00	...
96-97—Philadelphia	NHL	35	1884	14	8	...	8	79	2	2.52	.903	12	699	8	4	33	0	2.83	.892
97-98—Philadelphia	NHL	29	1651	14	9	...	4	67	1	2.43	.902	—	—	—	—	—	—	—	—
—Vancouver	NHL	12	504	3	6	...	0	26	0	3.10	.901	—	—	—	—	—	—	—	—
98-99—Vancouver	NHL	65	3501	20	†31	...	8	†171	6	2.93	.900	—	—	—	—	—	—	—	—
99-00—Vancouver	NHL	32	1712	10	15	...	3	76	0	2.66	.902	—	—	—	—	—	—	—	—
00-01—Wilkes-Barre/Scranton	AHL	3	178	2	1	...	0	7	0	2.36	.920	—	—	—	—	—	—	—	—
—Pittsburgh	NHL	35	2032	14	15	...	4	101	3	2.98	.900	—	—	—	—	—	—	—	—
01-02—New York Islanders	NHL	25	1217	10	7	...	2	55	2	2.71	.900	1	26	0	0	2	0	4.62	.895
02-03—New York Islanders	NHL	43	2390	16	17	...	5	92	1	2.31	.918	5	305	1	4	12	1	2.36	.910
03-04—New York Islanders	NHL	39	2015	14	15	...	5	94	1	2.80	.899	—	—	—	—	—	—	—	—
04-05—SKA St. Petersburg	Russian	16	893	...	...	...	...	41	1	2.75	...	—	—	—	—	—	—	—	—
05-06—Bridgeport	AHL	1	60	1	0	0	...	1	0	1.00	.967	—	—	—	—	—	—	—	—
—New York Islanders	NHL	20	1096	4	13	1	...	68	0	3.72	.886	—	—	—	—	—	—	—	—
NHL Totals (12 years)		368	19837	135	147	1	43	925	16	2.80	.901	20	1040	9	8	48	1	2.77	.896

S

SOPEL, BRENT D

PERSONAL: Born January 7, 1977, in Calgary. ... 6-1/205. ... Shoots right. ... Name pronounced SOH-puhl.

TRANSACTIONS/CAREER NOTES: Selected by Vancouver Canucks in sixth round (sixth Canucks pick, 144th overall) of entry draft (July 8, 1995). ... Ankle (January 21, 2003); missed one game. ... Groin (October 30, 2003); missed two games. ... Traded by Canucks to New York Islanders for second-round pick (traded to Anaheim; Ducks selected RW Bryce Swan) in 2006 draft (August 3, 2005). ... Signed by Islanders as free agent (August 16, 2005). ... Wrist (October 22, 2005); missed three games. ... Traded by Islanders with LW Mark Parrish to Los Angeles Kings for D Denis Grebeshkov and LW Jeff Tambellini (March 8, 2006). ... Strained right knee (March 9, 2006); missed four games. ... Right knee (March 20, 2006); missed one game. ... Cracked right knee cap (April 13, 2006); missed season's final three games.

		REGULAR SEASON								PLAYOFFS				
Season Team	League	GP	G	A	Pts.	PIM	+/-	PP	SH	GP	G	A	Pts.	PIM
93-94—Saskatoon	WHL	11	2	2	4	2	...	...	...	—	—	—	—	—
94-95—Saskatoon	WHL	22	1	10	11	31	12	0	0	—	—	—	—	—
—Swift Current	WHL	41	4	19	23	50	3	3	0	3	0	3	3	0
95-96—Swift Current	WHL	71	13	48	61	87	...	...	...	6	1	2	3	4
—Syracuse	AHL	1	0	0	0	0	...	...	...	—	—	—	—	—
96-97—Swift Current	WHL	62	15	41	56	109	39	6	0	10	5	11	16	32
—Syracuse	AHL	2	0	0	0	0	0	0	0	3	0	0	0	0
97-98—Syracuse	AHL	76	10	33	43	70	-4	6	0	5	0	7	7	12
98-99—Syracuse	AHL	53	10	21	31	59	-33	6	1	—	—	—	—	—
—Vancouver	NHL	5	1	0	1	4	-1	1	0	—	—	—	—	—
99-00—Syracuse	AHL	50	6	25	31	67	...	...	...	4	0	2	2	8
—Vancouver	NHL	18	2	4	6	12	9	0	0	—	—	—	—	—
00-01—Vancouver	NHL	52	4	10	14	10	4	0	0	4	0	0	0	2
—Kansas City	IHL	4	0	1	1	0	...	...	...	—	—	—	—	—
01-02—Vancouver	NHL	66	8	17	25	44	21	1	0	6	0	2	2	2
02-03—Vancouver	NHL	81	7	30	37	23	-15	6	0	14	2	6	8	4
03-04—Vancouver	NHL	80	10	32	42	36	11	6	0	7	0	1	1	0
05-06—New York Islanders	NHL	57	2	25	27	64	-9	2	0	—	—	—	—	—
—Los Angeles	NHL	11	0	1	1	6	-4	0	0	—	—	—	—	—
NHL Totals (7 years)		370	34	119	153	199	16	16	0	31	2	9	11	8

SOURAY, SHELDON D

PERSONAL: Born July 13, 1976, in Elk Point, Alta. ... 6-4/227. ... Shoots left. ... Name pronounced SOOR-ay.

TRANSACTIONS/CAREER NOTES: Selected by New Jersey Devils in third round (third Devils pick, 71st overall) of entry draft (June 29, 1994). ... Injured head (September 27, 1997); missed five games. ... Bruised right wrist (October 17, 1997); missed four games. ... Flu (December 18, 1997); missed one game. ... Flu (January 30, 1998); missed one game. ... Traded by Devils with D Josh DeWolf and second-round pick (traded to Washington; traded to Tampa Bay; Lightning selected D Andreas Holmqvist) in 2001 draft to Montreal Canadiens for D Vladimir Malakhov (March 1, 2000). ... Strained abdominal muscle (September 23, 2000) and had surgery; missed first 29 games of season. ... Bruised ankle (February 10, 2001); missed one game. ... Strained groin (September 27, 2001); missed first three games of season. ... Bruised hip (November 6, 2001); missed one game. ... Sprained wrist (November 17, 2001); missed two games. ... Fractured left wrist (December 17, 2001); missed 41 games. ... Missed 2002-03 season recovering from wrist surgery. ... Injured left knee (February 10, 2004); missed 17 games. ... Injured shoulder (March 24, 2004); missed two games. ... Injured foot (November 10, 2005); missed one game. ... Strained groin (November 22, 2005); missed four games. ... Injured knee (January 13, 2006); missed one game. ... Injured groin (January 25, 2006); missed one game.

STATISTICAL PLATEAUS: Three-goal games: 2003-04 (1).

		REGULAR SEASON								PLAYOFFS				
Season Team	League	GP	G	A	Pts.	PIM	+/-	PP	SH	GP	G	A	Pts.	PIM
92-93—Fort Saskatchewan	AJHL	35	0	12	12	125	...	...	...	—	—	—	—	—
—Tri-City	WHL	2	0	0	0	0	...	...	...	—	—	—	—	—
93-94—Tri-City	WHL	42	3	6	9	122	-4	1	1	—	—	—	—	—
94-95—Tri-City	WHL	40	2	24	26	140	-5	0	0	—	—	—	—	—
—Prince George	WHL	11	2	3	5	23	-12	1	0	—	—	—	—	—
—Albany	AHL	7	0	2	2	8	-5	0	0	—	—	—	—	—
95-96—Prince George	WHL	32	9	18	27	91	...	...	...	—	—	—	—	—
—Kelowna	WHL	27	7	20	27	94	...	...	...	6	0	5	5	2
—Albany	AHL	6	0	2	2	12	...	...	...	4	0	1	1	4

Season Team	League	GP	G	A	Pts.	PIM	+/-	PP	SH	GP	G	A	Pts.	PIM
		REGULAR SEASON								PLAYOFFS				
96-97—Albany	AHL	70	2	11	13	160	11	0	1	16	2	3	5	47
97-98—New Jersey	NHL	60	3	7	10	85	18	0	0	3	0	1	1	2
—Albany	AHL	6	0	0	0	8	-2	0	0	—	—	—	—	—
98-99—New Jersey	NHL	70	1	7	8	110	5	0	0	2	0	1	1	0
99-00—New Jersey	NHL	52	0	8	8	70	-6	0	0	—	—	—	—	—
—Montreal	NHL	19	3	0	3	44	7	0	0	—	—	—	—	—
00-01—Montreal	NHL	52	3	8	11	95	-11	0	0	—	—	—	—	—
01-02—Montreal	NHL	34	3	5	8	62	-5	1	0	12	0	1	1	16
02-03—		Did not play												
03-04—Montreal	NHL	63	15	20	35	104	4	6	1	11	0	2	2	39
04-05—Farjestad Karlstad	Sweden	39	9	8	17	117	9	4	0	15	1	6	7	77
05-06—Montreal	NHL	75	12	27	39	116	-11	7	1	6	3	2	5	8
NHL Totals (7 years)		425	40	82	122	686	1	14	2	34	3	7	10	65

SPACEK, JAROSLAV D

PERSONAL: Born February 11, 1974, in Rokycany, Czechoslovakia. ... 5-11/204. ... Shoots left. ... Name pronounced: YAHR-uh-slahv SPAH-chehk

TRANSACTIONS/CAREER NOTES: Selected by Florida Panthers in fifth round (fifth Panthers pick, 117th overall) of entry draft (June 27, 1998). ... Flu (April 7, 1999); missed three games. ... Traded by Panthers to Chicago Blackhawks for D Anders Eriksson (November 6, 2000). ... Left shoulder (January 14, 2001); missed 18 games. ... Injured (November 13, 2001); missed two games. ... Fractured finger (November 25, 2001); missed eight games. ... Traded by Blackhawks with second-round pick (C Dan Fritsche) in 2003 to Columbus Blue Jackets for D Lyle Odelein (March 19, 2002). ... Hand (March 8, 2003); missed two games. ... Groin (November 29, 2003); missed 24 games. ... Signed as free agent by Blackhawks (August 4, 2005). ... Bruised ribs (October 5, 2005); missed two games. ... Suspended two games for clipping incident (January 2, 2006). ... Traded by Blackhawks to Edmonton Oilers for LW Tony Salmelainen (January 26, 2006) ... Signed as free agent by Buffalo Sabres (July 5, 2006).

Season Team	League	GP	G	A	Pts.	PIM	+/-	PP	SH	GP	G	A	Pts.	PIM
		REGULAR SEASON								PLAYOFFS				
92-93—Skoda Plzen	Czech.	16	1	3	4	...	...	...	...	—	—	—	—	—
93-94—Skoda Plzen	Czech Rep.	34	2	10	12	...	...	...	...	—	—	—	—	—
94-95—Interconex Plzen	Czech Rep.	38	4	8	12	14	...	...	...	3	1	0	1	2
95-96—ZKZ Plzen	Czech Rep.	40	3	10	13	42	...	...	...	3	0	1	1	4
96-97—ZKZ Plzen	Czech Rep.	52	9	29	38	44	...	...	...	—	—	—	—	—
97-98—Farjestad Karlstad	Sweden	45	10	16	26	63	...	...	...	12	2	5	7	14
98-99—Florida	NHL	63	3	12	15	28	15	2	1	—	—	—	—	—
—New Haven	AHL	14	4	8	12	15	-1	3	0	—	—	—	—	—
99-00—Florida	NHL	82	10	26	36	53	7	4	0	4	0	0	0	0
00-01—Florida	NHL	12	2	1	3	8	-4	1	0	—	—	—	—	—
—Chicago	NHL	50	5	18	23	20	7	2	0	—	—	—	—	—
01-02—Chicago	NHL	60	3	10	13	29	5	0	0	—	—	—	—	—
—Czech Rep. Oly. team	Int'l	4	0	0	0	0	...	...	...	—	—	—	—	—
—Columbus	NHL	14	2	3	5	24	-9	1	1	—	—	—	—	—
02-03—Columbus	NHL	81	9	36	45	70	-23	5	0	—	—	—	—	—
03-04—Columbus	NHL	58	5	17	22	45	-13	2	1	—	—	—	—	—
04-05—Plzen	Czech Rep.	30	3	8	11	26	-9	...	...	—	—	—	—	—
—Slavia Praha	Czech Rep.	17	4	9	13	29	12	...	...	7	0	2	2	8
05-06—Chicago	NHL	45	7	17	24	72	8	1	0	—	—	—	—	—
—Edmonton	NHL	31	5	14	19	24	3	3	0	24	3	11	14	24
—Czech Rep. Oly. team	Int'l	8	0	1	1	2	-4	0	0	—	—	—	—	—
NHL Totals (7 years)		496	51	154	205	373	-4	21	3	28	3	11	14	24

SPEZZA, JASON C

PERSONAL: Born June 13, 1983, in Mississauga, Ont. ... 6-2/206. ... Shoots right. ... Name pronounced SPEHT-zah.

TRANSACTIONS/CAREER NOTES: Selected by Ottawa Senators in first round (first Senators pick, second overall) of entry draft (June 23, 2001). ... Injured left knee (January 31, 2003); missed two games. ... Hip flexor (December 12, 2005); missed one game. ... Injured pectoral muscle (December 20, 2005); missed five games. ... Chest injury (January 4, 2005); missed seven games. ... Sore hip and back (March 21, 2006); missed one game.

Season Team	League	GP	G	A	Pts.	PIM	+/-	PP	SH	GP	G	A	Pts.	PIM
		REGULAR SEASON								PLAYOFFS				
98-99—Brampton	OHL	67	22	49	71	18	...	...	...	—	—	—	—	—
99-00—Mississauga	OHL	52	24	37	61	33	...	...	...	—	—	—	—	—
00-01—Mississauga	OHL	15	7	23	30	11	...	...	...	—	—	—	—	—
—Windsor	OHL	41	36	50	86	32	...	...	...	9	4	5	9	10
01-02—Windsor	OHL	27	19	26	45	16	...	...	...	—	—	—	—	—
—Belleville	OHL	26	23	37	60	26	...	...	...	11	5	6	11	18
—Grand Rapids	AHL	...	...	...	...	...	...	...	...	3	1	0	1	2
02-03—Binghamton	AHL	43	22	32	54	71	-5	5	0	2	1	2	3	4
—Ottawa	NHL	33	7	14	21	8	-3	3	0	3	1	1	2	0
03-04—Ottawa	NHL	78	22	33	55	71	22	5	0	3	0	0	0	2
04-05—Binghamton	AHL	80	32	85	117	50	18	10	3	6	1	3	4	6
05-06—Ottawa	NHL	68	19	71	90	33	23	7	0	10	5	9	14	2
NHL Totals (3 years)		179	48	118	166	112	42	15	0	16	6	10	16	4

SPILLER, MATTHEW D

PERSONAL: Born February 7, 1983, in Daysland, Alta. ... 6-5/233. ... Shoots left.

TRANSACTIONS/CAREER NOTES: Selected by Phoenix Coyotes in second round (second Coyotes pick, 31st overall) of entry draft (June 23, 2001).

Season Team	League	REGULAR SEASON GP	G	A	Pts.	PIM	+/-	PP	SH	PLAYOFFS GP	G	A	Pts.	PIM
99-00—Seattle	WHL	60	1	10	11	108	...	...	...	7	0	0	0	25
00-01—Seattle	WHL	71	4	7	11	174	...	...	...	9	1	0	1	22
01-02—Seattle	WHL	72	8	23	31	168	...	...	...	1	0	0	0	4
02-03—Seattle	WHL	68	11	24	35	198	...	...	...	15	2	7	9	36
03-04—Phoenix	NHL	51	0	0	0	54	-11	0	0	—	—	—	—	—
—Springfield	AHL	21	1	2	3	32	-8	0	0	—	—	—	—	—
04-05—Utah	AHL	79	4	7	11	160	-26	2	0	—	—	—	—	—
05-06—San Antonio	AHL	69	2	7	9	167	-20	2	0	—	—	—	—	—
—Phoenix	NHL	8	0	1	1	13	-1	0	0	—	—	—	—	—
NHL Totals (2 years)		59	0	1	1	67	-12	0	0					

ST. JACQUES, BRUNO D

PERSONAL: Born August 22, 1980, in Montreal. ... 6-2/204. ... Shoots left.

TRANSACTIONS/CAREER NOTES: Selected by Philadelphia Flyers in ninth round (12th Flyers pick, 253rd overall) of entry draft (June 27, 1998). ... Traded by Flyers with RW Pavel Brendl to Carolina Hurricanes for RW Sami Kapanen and D Ryan Bast (February 7, 2003). ... Injured shoulder (October 28, 2003); missed one game. ... Injured shoulder (November 1, 2003); missed nine games. ... Injured abdomen (November 29, 2003); missed 14 games. ... Strained abdomen (March 12, 2004); missed last 13 games of season. ... Traded by Hurricanes to Anaheim Mighty Ducks for RW Craig Adams (October 3, 2005).

Season Team	League	REGULAR SEASON GP	G	A	Pts.	PIM	+/-	PP	SH	PLAYOFFS GP	G	A	Pts.	PIM
97-98—Baie-Comeau	QMJHL	63	13	29	42	253	...	...	...	—	—	—	—	—
98-99—Baie-Comeau	QMJHL	49	1	21	22	138	...	...	...	—	—	—	—	—
99-00—Baie-Comeau	QMJHL	60	8	28	36	120	...	...	...	—	—	—	—	—
—Philadelphia	AHL	3	0	1	1	0	...	...	...	1	0	0	0	0
00-01—Philadelphia	AHL	45	1	16	17	83	...	...	...	10	1	0	1	16
01-02—Philadelphia	AHL	55	3	11	14	59	2	1	0	4	0	0	0	0
—Philadelphia	NHL	7	0	0	0	2	4	0	0	—	—	—	—	—
02-03—Philadelphia	NHL	6	0	0	0	2	-1	0	0	—	—	—	—	—
—Philadelphia	AHL	30	0	7	7	46	1	0	0	—	—	—	—	—
—Carolina	NHL	18	2	5	7	12	-3	0	0	—	—	—	—	—
—Lowell	AHL	8	1	1	2	8	-3	0	1	—	—	—	—	—
03-04—Carolina	NHL	35	0	2	2	31	-7	0	0	—	—	—	—	—
—Lowell	AHL	6	0	0	0	8	-4	0	0	—	—	—	—	—
04-05—Lowell	AHL	68	2	12	14	60	24	0	0	11	1	4	5	4
05-06—Portland	AHL	60	6	19	25	55	18	2	0	13	3	4	7	16
—Anaheim	NHL	1	1	0	1	0	1	0	0	—	—	—	—	—
NHL Totals (4 years)		67	3	7	10	47	-6	0	0					

ST. LOUIS, MARTIN RW

PERSONAL: Born June 18, 1975, in Laval, Que. ... 5-9/181. ... Shoots left.

TRANSACTIONS/CAREER NOTES: Signed as free agent by Calgary Flames (February 18, 1998). ... Concussion (March 15, 2000); missed two games. ... Signed as free agent by Tampa Bay Lightning (July 31, 2000). ... Bruised heel (November 6, 2001); missed one game. ... Fractured right leg (January 23, 2002); missed 26 games. ... Broken left ring finger (November 14, 2005); missed two games.

STATISTICAL PLATEAUS: Three-goal games: 2002-03 (1), 2003-04 (2). Total: 3.

Season Team	League	REGULAR SEASON GP	G	A	Pts.	PIM	+/-	PP	SH	PLAYOFFS GP	G	A	Pts.	PIM
93-94—Vermont	ECAC	33	15	36	51	24	...	...	...	—	—	—	—	—
94-95—Vermont	ECAC	35	23	48	71	36	...	...	...	—	—	—	—	—
95-96—Vermont	ECAC	35	29	56	85	36	...	...	...	—	—	—	—	—
96-97—Vermont	ECAC	35	24	26	50	65	...	...	...	—	—	—	—	—
97-98—Cleveland	IHL	56	16	34	50	24	-1	5	0	—	—	—	—	—
—Saint John	AHL	25	15	11	26	20	3	6	0	20	5	15	20	16
98-99—Calgary	NHL	13	1	1	2	10	-2	0	0	—	—	—	—	—
—Saint John	AHL	53	28	34	62	30	-2	4	4	7	4	4	8	2
99-00—Saint John	AHL	17	15	11	26	14	...	...	...	—	—	—	—	—
—Calgary	NHL	56	3	15	18	22	-5	0	0	—	—	—	—	—
00-01—Tampa Bay	NHL	78	18	22	40	12	-4	3	3	—	—	—	—	—
01-02—Tampa Bay	NHL	53	16	19	35	20	4	6	1	—	—	—	—	—
02-03—Tampa Bay	NHL	82	33	37	70	32	10	12	3	11	7	5	12	0
03-04—Tampa Bay	NHL	82	38	†56	*94	24	†35	8	*8	23	9	*15	24	14
04-05—Lausanne HC	Switzerland	23	9	16	25	16	...	4	1	—	—	—	—	—
05-06—Tampa Bay	NHL	80	31	30	61	38	-3	9	3	5	4	0	4	2
—Canadian Oly. team	Int'l	6	2	1	3	0	2	1	0	—	—	—	—	—
NHL Totals (7 years)		444	140	180	320	158	35	38	18	39	20	20	40	16

ST. PIERRE, MARTIN C

PERSONAL: Born August 11, 1983, in Emburn, Ont. ... 5-9/180. ... Shoots left.

TRANSACTIONS/CAREER NOTES: Signed as nondrafted free agent by Chicago Blackhawks (November 3, 2005).

Season Team	League	REGULAR SEASON GP	G	A	Pts.	PIM	+/-	PP	SH	PLAYOFFS GP	G	A	Pts.	PIM
00-01—Guelph	OHL	68	20	49	69	40	...	...	...	—	—	—	—	—
01-02—Guelph	OHL	66	32	53	85	68	...	...	...	—	—	—	—	—

Season Team	League	REGULAR SEASON								PLAYOFFS				
		GP	G	A	Pts.	PIM	+/-	PP	SH	GP	G	A	Pts.	PIM
02-03—Guelph	OHL	55	11	45	56	74	...	...	...	—	—	—	—	—
03-04—Guelph	OHL	68	45	65	110	95	...	...	...	—	—	—	—	—
04-05—Edmonton	AHL	18	4	3	7	8	-4	4	0	—	—	—	—	—
—Greenville	ECHL	45	14	39	53	55	...	...	...	—	—	—	—	—
05-06—Norfolk	AHL	77	23	50	73	98	0	6	0	4	0	3	3	2
—Chicago	NHL	2	0	0	0	0	-1	0	0	—	—	—	—	—
NHL Totals (1 year)		2	0	0	0	0	-1	0	0					

STAAL, ERIC C

PERSONAL: Born October 29, 1984, in Thunder Bay, Ont. ... 6-3/189. ... Shoots left. ... Brother of Marc Staal, D, New York Rangers; and Jordan Staal, C, Pittsburgh Penguins.

TRANSACTIONS/CAREER NOTES: Selected by Carolina Hurricanes in first round (first Hurricanes pick, second overall) in 2003 NHL entry draft (June 23, 2003).

Season Team	League	REGULAR SEASON								PLAYOFFS				
		GP	G	A	Pts.	PIM	+/-	PP	SH	GP	G	A	Pts.	PIM
00-01—Peterborough	OHL	63	19	30	49	23	...	...	...	7	2	5	7	4
01-02—Peterborough	OHL	56	23	39	62	40	...	...	...	6	3	6	9	10
02-03—Peterborough	OHL	66	39	59	98	36	...	...	...	7	9	5	14	6
03-04—Carolina	NHL	81	11	20	31	40	-6	2	1	—	—	—	—	—
04-05—Lowell	AHL	77	26	51	77	88	37	2	7	11	2	8	10	12
05-06—Carolina	NHL	82	45	55	100	81	-8	19	4	25	9	*19	*28	8
NHL Totals (2 years)		163	56	75	131	121	-14	21	5	25	9	19	28	8

STAAL, JORDAN C

PERSONAL: Born September 10, 1988, in Thunder Bay, Ont. ... 6-4/215. ... Shoots left. ... Brother of Eric Staal, C, Carolina Hurricanes; and Marc Staal, D, New York Rangers.

TRANSACTIONS/CAREER NOTES: Selected by Pittsburgh Penguins in first round (first Penguins pick, second overall) of NHL draft (June 24, 2006).

Season Team	League	REGULAR SEASON								PLAYOFFS				
		GP	G	A	Pts.	PIM	+/-	PP	SH	GP	G	A	Pts.	PIM
04-05—Peterborough	OHL	66	9	19	28	29	1	...	...	14	5	5	10	16
05-06—Peterborough	OHL	68	28	40	68	69	16	...	...	19	10	6	16	16

STAIOS, STEVE D

PERSONAL: Born July 28, 1973, in Hamilton, Ont. ... 6-1/200. ... Shoots right. ... Name pronounced STAY-ohz.

TRANSACTIONS/CAREER NOTES: Selected by St. Louis Blues in second round (first Blues pick, 27th overall) of entry draft (June 22, 1991). ... Traded by Blues with LW Kevin Sawyer to Boston Bruins for RW Steve Leach (March 8, 1996). ... Groin (November 6, 1996); missed 13 games. ... Claimed off waivers by Vancouver Canucks (March 18, 1997). ... Knee (February 24, 1999); missed 16 games. ... Selected by Atlanta Thrashers in expansion draft (June 25, 1999). ... Right knee (November 20, 1999); missed four games. ... Groin (December 30, 1999); missed 16 games. ... Groin (February 15, 2000); missed season's final 27 games. ... Traded by Thrashers to New Jersey Devils for ninth-round pick (C Simon Gamache) in 2000 (June 12, 2000). ... Traded by Devils to Thrashers for future considerations (July 10, 2000). ... Concussion (November 27, 2000); missed five games. ... Foot (December 22, 2000); missed two games. ... Hamstring (January 23, 2001); missed two games. ... Groin (February 7, 2001); missed three games. ... Signed as free agent by Edmonton Oilers (July 12, 2001). ... Foot (October 20, 2001); missed one game. ... Groin (February 5, 2002); missed four games. ... Concussion, thumb (December 30, 2002); missed six games.

Season Team	League	REGULAR SEASON								PLAYOFFS				
		GP	G	A	Pts.	PIM	+/-	PP	SH	GP	G	A	Pts.	PIM
89-90—Hamilton Jr. B	OHA	40	9	27	36	66	...	...	...	—	—	—	—	—
90-91—Niagara Falls	OHL	66	17	29	46	115	...	...	...	12	2	3	5	10
91-92—Niagara Falls	OHL	65	11	42	53	122	...	...	...	17	7	8	15	27
92-93—Niagara Falls	OHL	12	4	14	18	30	...	...	...	—	—	—	—	—
—Sudbury	OHL	53	13	44	57	67	...	...	...	11	5	6	11	22
93-94—Peoria	IHL	38	3	9	12	42	-9	1	0	—	—	—	—	—
94-95—Peoria	IHL	60	3	13	16	64	-3	1	0	6	0	0	0	10
95-96—Peoria	IHL	6	0	1	1	14	...	...	...	—	—	—	—	—
—Worcester	AHL	57	1	11	12	114	...	...	...	—	—	—	—	—
—Providence	AHL	7	1	4	5	8	...	...	...	—	—	—	—	—
—Boston	NHL	12	0	0	0	4	-5	0	0	3	0	0	0	0
96-97—Boston	NHL	54	3	8	11	71	-26	0	0	—	—	—	—	—
—Vancouver	NHL	9	0	6	6	20	2	0	0	—	—	—	—	—
97-98—Vancouver	NHL	77	3	4	7	134	-3	0	0	—	—	—	—	—
98-99—Vancouver	NHL	57	0	2	2	54	-12	0	0	—	—	—	—	—
99-00—Atlanta	NHL	27	2	3	5	66	-5	0	0	—	—	—	—	—
00-01—Atlanta	NHL	70	9	13	22	137	-23	4	0	—	—	—	—	—
01-02—Edmonton	NHL	73	5	5	10	108	10	0	0	—	—	—	—	—
02-03—Edmonton	NHL	76	5	21	26	96	13	1	3	6	0	0	0	4
03-04—Edmonton	NHL	82	6	22	28	86	17	1	0	—	—	—	—	—
04-05—Lulea	Sweden	7	2	1	3	12	3	0	0	—	—	—	—	—
05-06—Edmonton	NHL	82	8	20	28	84	10	1	0	24	1	5	6	28
NHL Totals (10 years)		619	41	104	145	860	-22	7	3	33	1	5	6	32

STAJAN, MATT C/LW

PERSONAL: Born December 19, 1983, in Mississauga, Ont. ... 6-1/180. ... Shoots left. ... Name pronounced STAY-juhn.
TRANSACTIONS/CAREER NOTES: Selected by Toronto Maple Leafs in second round (second Maple Leafs pick, 57th overall) of NHL draft (June 22, 2002).

		REGULAR SEASON								PLAYOFFS				
Season Team	**League**	**GP**	**G**	**A**	**Pts.**	**PIM**	**+/-**	**PP**	**SH**	**GP**	**G**	**A**	**Pts.**	**PIM**
00-01—Belleville	OHL	57	9	18	27	27	...	...	...	7	1	6	7	5
01-02—Belleville	OHL	68	33	52	85	50	...	...	...	11	3	8	11	14
02-03—St. John's	AHL	1	0	1	1	0	1	0	0	—	—	—	—	—
—Toronto	NHL	1	1	0	1	0	1	0	0	—	—	—	—	—
03-04—Toronto	NHL	69	14	13	27	22	7	0	0	3	0	0	0	2
04-05—St. John's	AHL	80	23	43	66	43	0	6	2	5	2	2	4	6
05-06—Toronto	NHL	80	15	12	27	50	5	3	4	—	—	—	—	—
NHL Totals (3 years)		150	30	25	55	72	13	3	4	3	0	0	0	2

STASTNY, YAN C/LW

PERSONAL: Born September 30, 1982, in Quebec City. ... 5-11/175. ... Shoots left. ... Son of Peter Stastny (Quebec Nordiques, 1980-90; New Jersey Devils, 1990-93; St. Louis Blues 1993-95); nephew of Marian (Quebec Nordiques, 1981-85; Toronto Maple Leafs, 1985-86); nephew of Anton Stastny (1980-89).
COLLEGE: Notre Dame.
TRANSACTIONS/CAREER NOTES: Selected by Boston Bruins in eighth round (sixth Bruins pick, 259th overall) of entry draft (June 23, 2002). ... Traded by Bruins to Edmonton Oilers for fourth-round pick in 2006 draft (August 30, 2005). ... Traded by Oilers with C Marty Reasoner and second-round pick (LW Milan Lucic) in 2006 draft to Bruins for LW Sergei Samsonov (March 9, 2006).

		REGULAR SEASON								PLAYOFFS				
Season Team	**League**	**GP**	**G**	**A**	**Pts.**	**PIM**	**+/-**	**PP**	**SH**	**GP**	**G**	**A**	**Pts.**	**PIM**
00-01—Omaha	USHL	44	17	14	31	101	...	...	...	11	6	6	12	12
01-02—Notre Dame	CCHA	33	6	11	17	38	...	...	...	—	—	—	—	—
02-03—Notre Dame	CCHA	39	14	9	23	44	...	...	...	—	—	—	—	—
03-04—Nurnberg	Germany	44	9	20	29	83	...	...	...	6	0	1	1	6
04-05—Nurnberg	Germany	51	24	30	54	60	...	...	...	6	2	1	3	8
05-06—Providence	AHL	—	—	—	—	—	—	—	—	6	0	5	5	12
—Iowa	AHL	51	14	17	31	42	4	4	1	—	—	—	—	—
—Edmonton	NHL	3	0	0	0	0	-2	0	0	—	—	—	—	—
—Boston	NHL	17	1	3	4	10	-2	0	0	—	—	—	—	—
NHL Totals (1 year)		20	1	3	4	10	-4	0	0					

STECKEL, DAVE C/LW

PERSONAL: Born May 15, 1982, in Milwaukee. ... 6-5/200. ... Shoots left.
TRANSACTIONS/CAREER NOTES: Selected by Los Angeles Kings in first round (second Kings pick, 30th overall) of entry draft (June 23, 2001). ... Signed as free agent by Washington Capitals (August 25, 2005).

		REGULAR SEASON								PLAYOFFS				
Season Team	**League**	**GP**	**G**	**A**	**Pts.**	**PIM**	**+/-**	**PP**	**SH**	**GP**	**G**	**A**	**Pts.**	**PIM**
99-00—U.S. National	USHL	52	13	13	26	94	...	...	...	—	—	—	—	—
00-01—Ohio State	CCHA	33	17	18	35	80	...	...	...	—	—	—	—	—
01-02—Ohio State	CCHA	36	6	16	22	75	...	...	...	—	—	—	—	—
02-03—Ohio State	CCHA	36	10	8	18	50	...	...	...	—	—	—	—	—
03-04—Ohio State	CCHA	41	17	13	30	44	...	...	...	—	—	—	—	—
04-05—Manchester	AHL	63	10	7	17	26	4	2	0	6	1	1	2	4
05-06—Hershey	AHL	74	14	20	34	58	1	2	4	14	9	3	12	14
—Washington	NHL	7	0	0	0	0	1	0	0	—	—	—	—	—
NHL Totals (1 year)		7	0	0	0	0	1	0	0					

STEEN, ALEXANDER C/LW

PERSONAL: Born March 1, 1984, in Winnipeg. ... 5-11/183. ... Shoots left. ... Son of Thomas Steen, center with Winnipeg Jets (1981-82 through 1994-95).
TRANSACTIONS/CAREER NOTES: Selected by Toronto Maple Leafs in first round (first Maple Leafs pick, 24th overall) of entry draft (June 22, 2002). ... Injured thumb (December 13, 2005); missed seven games.

		REGULAR SEASON								PLAYOFFS				
Season Team	**League**	**GP**	**G**	**A**	**Pts.**	**PIM**	**+/-**	**PP**	**SH**	**GP**	**G**	**A**	**Pts.**	**PIM**
01-02—Vastra Frolunda	Sweden	26	0	3	3	14	...	...	...	10	1	2	3	0
02-03—Vastra Frolunda	Sweden	45	5	10	15	18	...	...	...	16	2	3	5	4
03-04—Vastra Frolunda	Sweden	48	10	14	24	50	...	...	...	10	4	6	10	14
04-05—MoDo Ornskoldsvik	Sweden	50	9	8	17	26	-2	1	0	6	1	0	1	4
05-06—Toronto	NHL	75	18	27	45	42	-9	9	1	—	—	—	—	—
NHL Totals (1 year)		75	18	27	45	42	-9	9	1					

STEFAN, PATRIK C

PERSONAL: Born September 16, 1980, in Pribram, Czech. ... 6-2/210. ... Shoots left.
TRANSACTIONS/CAREER NOTES: Selected by Atlanta Thrashers in first round (first Thrashers pick, first overall) of NHL draft (June 26, 1999).

... Suffered concussion (November 19, 1999); missed two games. ... Back spasms (February 29, 2000); missed three games. ... Flu (March 22, 2000); missed two games. ... Injured groin (September 26, 2000); missed first five games of season. ... Flu (November 17, 2000); missed one game. ... Suffered concussion (November 22, 2000); missed three games. ... Injured head (December 29, 2000); missed one game. ... Strained groin (January 29, 2001); missed one games. ... Strained groin (February 7, 2001); missed three games. ... Flu (February 23, 2001); missed one game. ... Fractured jaw (October 6, 2001); missed eight games. ... Injured elbow (November 4, 2001); missed nine games. ... Injured ankle (March 19, 2003); missed 11 games. ... Strained oblique muscle (October 29, 2005); missed seven games. ... Had hernia surgery (February 13, 2006); missed 11 games. ... Traded by Thrashers with D Jaroslav Modry to Dallas Stars for F Niko Kapanen and a seventh-round pick (D Will O'Neill) in 2006 entry draft (June 24, 2006).

		REGULAR SEASON								PLAYOFFS				
Season Team	**League**	**GP**	**G**	**A**	**Pts.**	**PIM**	**+/-**	**PP**	**SH**	**GP**	**G**	**A**	**Pts.**	**PIM**
96-97—Sparta Praha	Czech Rep.	5	0	1	1	2	...	...	...	7	1	0	1	0
97-98—Sparta Praha	Czech Rep.	27	2	6	8	16	...	...	...	—	—	—	—	—
—Long Beach	IHL	25	5	15	20	10	...	...	...	10	1	1	2	2
98-99—Long Beach	IHL	33	11	24	35	26	...	...	...	—	—	—	—	—
99-00—Atlanta	NHL	72	5	20	25	30	-20	1	0	—	—	—	—	—
00-01—Atlanta	NHL	66	10	21	31	22	-3	0	0	—	—	—	—	—
01-02—Atlanta	NHL	59	7	16	23	22	-4	0	1	—	—	—	—	—
—Chicago	AHL	5	3	0	3	0	3	1	0	—	—	—	—	—
02-03—Atlanta	NHL	71	13	21	34	12	-10	3	0	—	—	—	—	—
03-04—Atlanta	NHL	82	14	26	40	26	-7	3	2	—	—	—	—	—
04-05—Ilves Tampere	Finland	37	13	28	41	47	13	...	...	7	1	6	7	4
05-06—Atlanta	NHL	64	10	14	24	36	3	2	0	—	—	—	—	—
NHL Totals (6 years)		414	59	118	177	148	-41	9	3					

STEMPNIAK, LEE RW/LW

PERSONAL: Born February 4, 1983, in Buffalo. ... 6-0/190. ... Shoots right. ... Name pronounced: STEHMP nee ak
COLLEGE: Darmouth.
TRANSACTIONS/CAREER NOTES: Selected by St. Louis Blues in fifth round (seventh Blues pick, 148th overall) of entry draft (June 21, 2003).

		REGULAR SEASON								PLAYOFFS				
Season Team	**League**	**GP**	**G**	**A**	**Pts.**	**PIM**	**+/-**	**PP**	**SH**	**GP**	**G**	**A**	**Pts.**	**PIM**
01-02—Dartmouth	ECAC	32	12	9	21	8	...	...	...	—	—	—	—	—
02-03—Dartmouth	ECAC	34	21	28	49	32	...	...	...	—	—	—	—	—
03-04—Dartmouth	ECAC	34	16	22	38	42	...	5	1	—	—	—	—	—
04-05—Dartmouth	ECAC	35	14	29	43	34	...	...	...	—	—	—	—	—
05-06—Peoria	AHL	26	8	7	15	32	5	2	0	3	0	3	3	2
—St. Louis	NHL	57	14	13	27	22	-10	5	0	—	—	—	—	—
NHL Totals (1 year)		57	14	13	27	22	-10	5	0					

STEVENSON, GRANT C/RW

PERSONAL: Born October 15, 1981, in Spruce Grove, Alta. ... 5-11/170. ... Shoots right.
TRANSACTIONS/CAREER NOTES: Signed as free agent by San Jose Sharks (April 18, 2003).

		REGULAR SEASON								PLAYOFFS				
Season Team	**League**	**GP**	**G**	**A**	**Pts.**	**PIM**	**+/-**	**PP**	**SH**	**GP**	**G**	**A**	**Pts.**	**PIM**
01-02—Minnesota State	WCHA	38	8	8	16	36	...	...	...	—	—	—	—	—
02-03—Minnesota State	WCHA	38	27	36	63	38	...	...	...	1	0	1	1	0
03-04—Cleveland	AHL	71	13	26	39	45	...	...	...	9	0	7	7	6
04-05—Cleveland	AHL	77	14	25	39	70	...	...	...	—	—	—	—	—
—Johnstown	ECHL	2	1	0	1	0	...	...	...	—	—	—	—	—
05-06—Cleveland	AHL	17	8	8	16	8	-1	3	0	—	—	—	—	—
—San Jose	NHL	47	10	12	22	14	-7	5	0	5	0	0	0	4
NHL Totals (1 year)		47	10	12	22	14	-7	5	0	5	0	0	0	4

STEVENSON, JEREMY LW/RW

PERSONAL: Born July 24, 1974, in San Bernardino, Calif. ... 6-1/215. ... Shoots left.
TRANSACTIONS/CAREER NOTES: Selected by Winnipeg Jets in third round (third Jets pick, 60th overall) of entry draft (June 20, 1992). ... Returned to draft pool by Jets; selected by Anaheim Mighty Ducks in 11th round (10th Mighty Ducks pick, 262nd overall) of entry draft (June 28, 1994). ... Fractured ankle (October 24, 1996); missed 33 games. ... Concussion (summer 1997); missed season's first four games. ... Signed as free agent by Nashville Predators (September 25, 2000). ... Signed as free agent by Minnesota Wild (November 26, 2002). ... Fractured cheekbone (November 2, 2003); missed 5 games. ... Shoulder (January 28, 2003); missed eight games. ... Claimed off waivers by Predators (October 22, 2003). ... Checkbone (November 4, 2003); missed five games. ... Shoulder (January 5, 2004); missed two games. ... Shoulder (January 24, 2004); missed five games. ... Injured knee (December 15, 2005) and had surgery; missed 13 games. ... Claimed off waivers by Dallas Stars (February 15, 2006).

		REGULAR SEASON								PLAYOFFS				
Season Team	**League**	**GP**	**G**	**A**	**Pts.**	**PIM**	**+/-**	**PP**	**SH**	**GP**	**G**	**A**	**Pts.**	**PIM**
90-91—Cornwall	OHL	58	13	20	33	124	...	...	...	—	—	—	—	—
91-92—Cornwall	OHL	63	15	23	38	176	...	...	...	6	3	1	4	4
92-93—Newmarket	OHL	54	28	28	56	144	...	...	...	5	5	1	6	28
93-94—Newmarket	OHL	9	2	4	6	27	...	1	0	—	—	—	—	—
—Sault Ste. Marie	OHL	48	18	19	37	183	...	7	0	14	1	1	2	23
94-95—Greensboro	ECHL	43	14	13	27	231	3	4	0	17	6	11	17	64
95-96—Baltimore	AHL	60	11	10	21	295	...	...	...	12	4	2	6	23
—Anaheim	NHL	3	0	1	1	12	1	0	0	—	—	—	—	—
96-97—Baltimore	AHL	25	8	8	16	125	5	1	0	3	0	0	0	8
—Anaheim	NHL	5	0	0	0	14	-1	0	0	—	—	—	—	—

Season Team	League	GP	G	A	Pts.	PIM	+/-	PP	SH	GP	G	A	Pts.	PIM
		REGULAR SEASON								PLAYOFFS				
97-98—Anaheim	NHL	45	3	5	8	101	-4	0	0	—	—	—	—	—
—Cincinnati	AHL	10	5	0	5	34	-1	2	0	—	—	—	—	—
98-99—Cincinnati	AHL	22	4	4	8	83	-7	2	0	3	1	0	1	2
99-00—Cincinnati	AHL	41	11	14	25	100	...	...	...	—	—	—	—	—
—Anaheim	NHL	3	0	0	0	7	-1	0	0	—	—	—	—	—
00-01—Milwaukee	IHL	60	16	13	29	262	...	...	...	5	2	1	3	12
—Nashville	NHL	8	1	0	1	39	-1	0	0	—	—	—	—	—
01-02—Milwaukee	AHL	53	12	7	19	192	8	1	0	—	—	—	—	—
—Nashville	NHL	4	0	0	0	9	0	0	0	—	—	—	—	—
02-03—Houston	AHL	18	6	7	13	77	8	2	0	—	—	—	—	—
—Minnesota	NHL	32	5	6	11	69	6	1	0	14	0	5	5	12
03-04—Minnesota	NHL	3	0	0	0	2	-1	0	0	—	—	—	—	—
—Nashville	NHL	53	5	4	9	103	-2	3	0	6	0	0	0	8
04-05—South Carolina	ECHL	42	9	20	29	140	3	4	1	3	1	0	1	2
05-06—Milwaukee	AHL	3	0	0	0	9	-2	0	0	—	—	—	—	—
—Nashville	NHL	35	4	3	7	74	0	0	0	—	—	—	—	—
—Dallas	NHL	16	1	0	1	21	-3	0	0	1	0	0	0	0
NHL Totals (9 years)		207	19	19	38	451	-6	4	0	21	0	5	5	20

STEVENSON, TURNER RW

PERSONAL: Born May 18, 1972, in Prince George, B.C. ... 6-3/235. ... Shoots right.

TRANSACTIONS/CAREER NOTES: Selected by Montreal Canadiens in first round (first Canadiens pick, 12th overall) of entry draft (June 16, 1990). ... Flu (October 21, 1995); missed two games. ... Sprained knee (October 7, 1996); missed five games. ... Sprained knee (October 26, 1996); missed four games. ... Sprained knee (November 11, 1996); missed seven games. ... Sprained left shoulder (November 12, 1997); missed eight games. ... Tore cartilage in ribs (December19, 1997); missed five games. ... Strained hamstring (April 15, 1998); missed three games. ... Suspended two games and fined $1,000 for elbowing incident (October 19, 1998). ... Back spasms (December 29, 1998); missed one game. ... Sprained ankle (December 31, 1998); missed 10 games. ... Back spasms (October 9, 1999); missed two games. ... Strained back (November 16, 1999); missed 13 games. ... Flu (January 11, 2000); missed three games. ... Selected by Columbus Blue Jackets in expansion draft (June 23, 2000). ... Traded by Blue Jackets to New Jersey Devils (June 23, 2000), completing deal in which Devils traded RW Krzysztof Oliwa to Blue Jackets for third-round pick (C/LW Brandon Nolan) in 2001 draft and future considerations (June 12, 2000). ... Sprained ankle (March 21, 2001); missed nine games. ... Injured right knee (October 17, 2001); missed 12 games. ... Reinjured knee (December 29, 2001); missed remainder of season. ... Bruised ankle (January 15, 2003); missed one game. ... Injured knee (February 15, 2003); missed four games. ... Injured groin (April 30, 2003); missed two playoff games. ... Reinjured groin (May 15, 2003); missed three playoff games. ... Reinjured groin (May 23, 2003); missed five playoff games. ... Injured groin (October 3, 2003); missed eight games. ... Injured groin (December 10, 2003); missed 12 games. ... Signed as free agent by Philadelphia Flyers (July 3, 2004). ... Right hip injury (October 11, 2005); missed one game. ... Torn labrum in right hip (October 14, 2005), underwent surgery (October 18, 2005); missed 12 games. ... Right hip injury (November 26, 2005); missed four games. ... Right hip flexor (December 10, 2005); missed 17 games. ... Injured hip (March 11, 2006); missed four games.

Season Team	League	GP	G	A	Pts.	PIM	+/-	PP	SH	GP	G	A	Pts.	PIM
		REGULAR SEASON								PLAYOFFS				
88-89—Seattle	WHL	69	15	12	27	84	...	...	...	—	—	—	—	—
89-90—Seattle	WHL	62	29	32	61	276	...	...	...	13	3	2	5	35
90-91—Seattle	WHL	57	36	27	63	222	...	...	...	6	1	5	6	15
—Fredericton	AHL	...	...	...	...	...	...	...	...	4	0	0	0	5
91-92—Seattle	WHL	58	20	32	52	264	...	...	...	15	9	3	12	55
92-93—Fredericton	AHL	79	25	34	59	102	15	6	2	5	2	3	5	11
—Montreal	NHL	1	0	0	0	0	-1	0	0	—	—	—	—	—
93-94—Fredericton	AHL	66	19	28	47	155	-2	5	2	—	—	—	—	—
—Montreal	NHL	2	0	0	0	2	-2	0	0	3	0	2	2	0
94-95—Fredericton	AHL	37	12	12	24	109	-2	2	0	—	—	—	—	—
—Montreal	NHL	41	6	1	7	86	0	0	0	—	—	—	—	—
95-96—Montreal	NHL	80	9	16	25	167	-2	0	0	6	0	1	1	2
96-97—Montreal	NHL	65	8	13	21	97	-14	1	0	5	1	1	2	2
97-98—Montreal	NHL	63	4	6	10	110	-8	1	0	10	3	4	7	12
98-99—Montreal	NHL	69	10	17	27	88	6	0	0	—	—	—	—	—
99-00—Montreal	NHL	64	8	13	21	61	-1	0	0	—	—	—	—	—
00-01—New Jersey	NHL	69	8	18	26	97	11	2	0	23	1	3	4	20
01-02—New Jersey	NHL	21	0	2	2	25	-3	0	0	1	0	0	0	4
02-03—New Jersey	NHL	77	7	13	20	115	7	0	0	14	1	1	2	26
03-04—New Jersey	NHL	61	14	13	27	76	0	4	0	5	0	0	0	0
05-06—Philadelphia	NHL	31	1	3	4	45	-2	0	1	—	—	—	—	—
NHL Totals (13 years)		644	75	115	190	969	-9	8	1	67	6	12	18	66

STEWART, ANTHONY C

PERSONAL: Born January 5, 1985, in LaSalle, Que. ... 6-1/225. ... Shoots right.

TRANSACTIONS/CAREER NOTES: Selected by Florida Panthers in first round (second Panthers selection, 25th overall) of entry draft (June 20, 2003). ... Wrist injury (November 11, 2005) and surgery (November 12); missed three months.

Season Team	League	GP	G	A	Pts.	PIM	+/-	PP	SH	GP	G	A	Pts.	PIM
		REGULAR SEASON								PLAYOFFS				
01-02—Kingston	OHL	65	19	24	43	43	...	...	...	1	0	0	0	0
02-03—Kingston	OHL	68	32	38	70	47	...	...	...	—	—	—	—	—
03-04—Kingston	OHL	53	35	23	58	76	...	...	...	5	3	4	7	7
04-05—San Antonio	AHL	10	1	2	3	14	1	0	0	—	—	—	—	—
—Kingston	OHL	62	32	35	67	70	-3	5	0	—	—	—	—	—
05-06—Rochester	AHL	4	2	3	5	0	0	0	0	—	—	—	—	—
—Florida	NHL	10	2	1	3	2	2	1	0	—	—	—	—	—
NHL Totals (1 year)		10	2	1	3	2	2	1	0					

STEWART, CHRIS — RW

PERSONAL: Born October 30, 1987, in Toronto. ... 6-1/228. ... Shoots right.
TRANSACTIONS/CAREER NOTES: Selected by Colorado Avalanche in first round (first Avalanche pick; 18th overall) of NHL draft (June 24, 2006).

		REGULAR SEASON								PLAYOFFS				
Season Team	League	GP	G	A	Pts.	PIM	+/-	PP	SH	GP	G	A	Pts.	PIM
04-05—Kingston	OHL	64	18	12	30	45	-8	...	...	—	—	—	—	—
05-06—Kingston	OHL	62	37	50	87	118	19	...	...	6	2	0	2	13

STEWART, KARL — LW/C

PERSONAL: Born June 30, 1983, in Aurora, Ontario. ... 5-10/175. ... Shoots left.
TRANSACTIONS/CAREER NOTES: Signed as undrafted free agent by Atlanta Thrashers (September 21, 2001).

		REGULAR SEASON								PLAYOFFS				
Season Team	League	GP	G	A	Pts.	PIM	+/-	PP	SH	GP	G	A	Pts.	PIM
00-01—Plymouth	OHL	68	9	14	23	67	...	...	...	19	3	4	7	14
01-02—Plymouth	OHL	65	20	23	43	104	...	...	...	6	0	2	2	21
02-03—Plymouth	OHL	68	35	50	85	120	...	...	...	17	7	10	17	31
03-04—Atlanta	NHL	5	0	1	1	4	0	0	0	—	—	—	—	—
—Chicago	AHL	72	10	32	42	188	24	1	1	10	2	3	5	29
04-05—Chicago	AHL	77	16	8	24	226	1	0	1	12	4	2	6	32
05-06—Chicago	AHL	71	22	18	40	184	17	1	6	—	—	—	—	—
—Atlanta	NHL	8	0	0	0	15	-3	0	0	—	—	—	—	—
NHL Totals (2 years)		13	0	1	1	19	-3	0	0					

STILLMAN, CORY — LW

PERSONAL: Born December 20, 1973, in Peterborough, Ont. ... 6-0/194. ... Shoots left. ... Second cousin of Cory Stillman, center, New York Islanders organization.
TRANSACTIONS/CAREER NOTES: Selected by Calgary Flames in first round (first Flames pick, sixth overall) of NHL draft (June 20, 1992). ... Flu (October 8, 1995); missed one game. ... Bruised knee (January 14, 1996); missed two games. ... Shoulder (December 16, 1996); missed five games. ... Bruised ribs (October 11, 1997); missed six games. ... Strained knee (December 27, 1998); missed five games. ... Shoulder (December 27, 1999); missed season's final 45 games. ... Shoulder (October 30, 2000); missed one game. ... Traded by Flames to St. Louis Blues for C Craig Conroy and seventh-round pick (LW David Moss) in 2001 draft (March 13, 2001). ... Knee (November 8, 2001); missed two games. ... Knee (December 20, 2002); missed three games. ... Traded by Blues to Tampa Bay Lightning for second-round draft pick (C David Backes) in 2003 draft (June 22, 2003). ... Flu (December 20, 2003); missed one game. ... Signed as free agent by Carolina Hurricanes (August 2, 2005). ... Foot (November 25, 2005); missed one game. ... Chest muscle strain (January 19, 2006); missed eight games. ... Lower body (April 8, 2006); missed one game.
STATISTICAL PLATEAUS: Three-goal games: 1997-98 (1), 2000-01 (1), 2001-02 (1). Total: 3.

		REGULAR SEASON								PLAYOFFS				
Season Team	League	GP	G	A	Pts.	PIM	+/-	PP	SH	GP	G	A	Pts.	PIM
89-90—Peterborough Jr. B	OHA	41	30	54	84	76	...	...	...	—	—	—	—	—
90-91—Windsor	OHL	64	31	70	101	31	...	...	...	11	3	6	9	8
91-92—Windsor	OHL	53	29	61	90	59	...	...	...	7	2	4	6	8
92-93—Peterborough	OHL	61	25	55	80	55	...	...	...	18	3	8	11	18
—Canadian nat'l team	Int'l	1	0	0	0	0	...	...	...	—	—	—	—	—
93-94—Saint John	AHL	79	35	48	83	52	-14	13	2	7	2	4	6	16
94-95—Saint John	AHL	63	28	53	81	70	-21	12	0	5	0	2	2	2
—Calgary	NHL	10	0	2	2	2	1	0	0	—	—	—	—	—
95-96—Calgary	NHL	74	16	19	35	41	-5	4	1	2	1	1	2	0
96-97—Calgary	NHL	58	6	20	26	14	-6	2	0	—	—	—	—	—
97-98—Calgary	NHL	72	27	22	49	40	-9	9	4	—	—	—	—	—
98-99—Calgary	NHL	76	27	30	57	38	7	9	3	—	—	—	—	—
99-00—Calgary	NHL	37	12	9	21	12	-9	6	0	—	—	—	—	—
00-01—Calgary	NHL	66	21	24	45	45	-6	7	0	—	—	—	—	—
—St. Louis	NHL	12	3	4	7	6	-2	3	0	15	3	5	8	8
01-02—St. Louis	NHL	80	23	22	45	36	8	6	0	9	0	2	2	2
02-03—St. Louis	NHL	79	24	43	67	56	12	6	0	6	2	2	4	2
03-04—Tampa Bay	NHL	81	25	55	80	36	18	11	1	21	2	5	7	15
05-06—Carolina	NHL	72	21	55	76	32	-9	10	0	25	9	17	26	14
NHL Totals (11 years)		717	205	305	510	358	0	73	9	78	17	32	49	41

STOLL, JARRET — C

PERSONAL: Born June 24, 1982, in Melville, Sask. ... 6-1/200. ... Shoots right.
TRANSACTIONS/CAREER NOTES: Selected by Calgary Flames in second round (third Flames pick, 46th overall) of entry draft (June 24, 2000). ... Returned to draft pool; selected by Edmonton Oilers in second round (third Oilers pick, 36th overall) of entry draft (June 22, 2002). ... Tonsillitis (October 30, 2003); missed five games. ... Tonsillitis (February 25, 2004); missed one game.

		REGULAR SEASON								PLAYOFFS				
Season Team	League	GP	G	A	Pts.	PIM	+/-	PP	SH	GP	G	A	Pts.	PIM
97-98—Saskatoon	SMHL	44	45	44	89	78	...	...	...	—	—	—	—	—
—Edmonton	WHL	8	2	3	5	4	...	...	...	—	—	—	—	—
98-99—Kootenay	WHL	57	13	21	34	40	...	...	...	4	0	0	0	2
99-00—Kootenay	WHL	71	37	38	75	64	...	...	...	20	7	9	16	24
00-01—Kootenay	WHL	62	40	66	106	105	...	...	...	11	5	9	14	22

Season Team	League	REGULAR SEASON GP	G	A	Pts.	PIM	+/-	PP	SH	PLAYOFFS GP	G	A	Pts.	PIM
01-02—Kootenay	WHL	47	32	34	66	64	...	...	...	22	6	13	19	35
02-03—Edmonton	NHL	4	0	1	1	0	-3	0	0	—	—	—	—	—
—Hamilton	AHL	76	21	33	54	86	...	...	...	23	5	8	13	25
03-04—Edmonton	NHL	68	10	11	21	42	8	1	1	—	—	—	—	—
04-05—Edmonton	AHL	66	21	17	38	92	13	7	0	—	—	—	—	—
05-06—Edmonton	NHL	82	22	46	68	74	4	11	1	24	4	6	10	24
NHL Totals (3 years)		154	32	58	90	116	9	12	2	24	4	6	10	24

STRAKA, MARTIN C/LW

PERSONAL: Born September 3, 1972, in Plzen, Czech. ... 5-9/178. ... Shoots left. ... Name pronounced STRAH-kuh.

TRANSACTIONS/CAREER NOTES: Selected by Pittsburgh Penguins in first round (first Penguins pick, 19th overall) of entry draft (June 20, 1992). ... Flu (February 14, 1995); missed four games. ... Traded by Penguins to Ottawa Senators for D Norm Maciver and C Troy Murray (April 7, 1995). ... Strained knee (April 19, 1995); missed remainder of season. ... Injured hamstring (November 11, 1995); missed one game. ... Traded by Senators with D Bryan Berard to New York Islanders for D Wade Redden and G Damian Rhodes (January 23, 1996). ... Claimed off waivers by Florida Panthers (March 15, 1996). ... Bruised buttocks (April 10, 1996); missed final two games of season. ... Strained groin (January 1, 1997); missed one game. ... Strained groin (January 8, 1997); missed two games. ... Strained groin (January 22, 1997); missed four games. ... Strained groin (March 5, 1997); missed nine games. ... Signed as free agent by Penguins (August 7, 1997). ... Fractured foot (December 29, 1997); missed seven games. ... Bruised shoulder (March 3, 1999); missed one game. ... Bruised shoulder (April 8, 1999); missed one game. ... Bruised knee (October 16, 1999); missed one game. ... Reinjured knee (October 27, 1999); missed two games. ... Bruised ribs (December 15, 1999); missed seven games. ... Bruised shin (April 5, 2000); missed one game. ... Fractured leg (October 28, 2001); missed 47 games. ... Fractured orbital and sinus bones (February 27, 2002); missed four games. ... Reinjured leg (March 7, 2002); missed remainder of season. ... Back injury (October 10, 2002); missed 11 games. ... Injured hamstring (November 29, 2002); missed two games. ... Reinjured hamstring (December 10, 2002); missed four games. ... Reinjured hamstring (February 12, 2003); missed five games. ... Traded to Los Angeles Kings for D Martin Strbak and F Sergei Anshakov (November 30, 2003). ... Sprained knee (January 11, 2004) and had surgery (February 13, 2004); missed 23 games. ... Signed as free agent by New York Rangers (August 2, 2005).

STATISTICAL PLATEAUS: Three-goal games: 1993-94 (1), 1997-98 (1), 1998-99 (1), 2000-01 (1). Total: 4.

Season Team	League	REGULAR SEASON GP	G	A	Pts.	PIM	+/-	PP	SH	PLAYOFFS GP	G	A	Pts.	PIM
89-90—Skoda Plzen	Czech.	1	0	3	3	...	...	...	...	—	—	—	—	—
90-91—Skoda Plzen	Czech.	47	7	24	31	6	...	...	...	—	—	—	—	—
91-92—Skoda Plzen	Czech.	50	27	28	55	20	...	...	...	—	—	—	—	—
92-93—Pittsburgh	NHL	42	3	13	16	29	2	0	0	11	2	1	3	2
—Cleveland	IHL	4	4	3	7	0	2	1	1	—	—	—	—	—
93-94—Pittsburgh	NHL	84	30	34	64	24	24	2	0	6	1	0	1	2
94-95—Interconex Plzen	Czech Rep.	19	10	11	21	18	...	...	...	—	—	—	—	—
—Pittsburgh	NHL	31	4	12	16	16	0	0	0	—	—	—	—	—
—Ottawa	NHL	6	1	1	2	0	-1	0	0	—	—	—	—	—
95-96—Ottawa	NHL	43	9	16	25	29	-14	5	0	—	—	—	—	—
—New York Islanders	NHL	22	2	10	12	6	-6	0	0	—	—	—	—	—
—Florida	NHL	12	2	4	6	6	1	1	0	13	2	2	4	2
96-97—Florida	NHL	55	7	22	29	12	9	2	0	4	0	0	0	0
97-98—Pittsburgh	NHL	75	19	23	42	28	-1	4	3	6	2	0	2	2
—Czech Rep. Oly. team	Int'l	6	1	2	3	0	1	0	0	—	—	—	—	—
98-99—Pittsburgh	NHL	80	35	48	83	26	12	5	4	13	6	9	15	6
99-00—Pittsburgh	NHL	71	20	39	59	26	24	3	1	11	3	9	12	10
00-01—Pittsburgh	NHL	82	27	68	95	38	19	7	1	18	5	8	13	8
01-02—Pittsburgh	NHL	13	5	4	9	0	3	1	0	—	—	—	—	—
02-03—Pittsburgh	NHL	60	18	28	46	12	-18	7	0	—	—	—	—	—
03-04—Pittsburgh	NHL	22	4	8	12	16	-16	1	0	—	—	—	—	—
—Los Angeles	NHL	32	6	8	14	4	-9	1	1	—	—	—	—	—
04-05—Plzen	Czech Rep.	45	16	18	34	76	5	...	...	—	—	—	—	—
05-06—New York Rangers	NHL	82	22	54	76	42	17	4	0	4	0	0	0	2
—Czech Rep. Oly. team	Int'l	8	2	6	8	6	4	0	0	—	—	—	—	—
NHL Totals (13 years)		812	214	392	606	314	46	43	10	86	21	29	50	34

STREIT, MARK D

PERSONAL: Born December 11, 1977, in Englisberg, Switz. ... 5-11/198. ... Shoots left.

TRANSACTIONS/CAREER NOTES: Selected by Montreal Canadiens in ninth round (eighth Canadiens pick, 262nd overall) of NHL entry draft (June 28, 2004). ... Flu (December 13, 2005); missed three games.

Season Team	League	REGULAR SEASON GP	G	A	Pts.	PIM	+/-	PP	SH	PLAYOFFS GP	G	A	Pts.	PIM
95-96—Fribourg	Switzerland	33	2	2	4	6	...	...	...	—	—	—	—	—
96-97—Davos	Switzerland	46	2	9	11	18	...	...	...	—	—	—	—	—
97-98—Ambri-Piotta	Switzerland	2	0	0	0	0	...	...	...	—	—	—	—	—
—Davos	Switzerland	38	4	10	14	14	...	...	...	—	—	—	—	—
98-99—Davos	Switzerland	44	7	18	25	42	...	...	...	—	—	—	—	—
99-00—Tallahassee	ECHL	14	0	5	5	16	...	...	...	—	—	—	—	—
—Utah	IHL	1	0	1	1	2	...	...	...	—	—	—	—	—
—Springfield	AHL	43	3	12	15	18	...	...	...	5	0	0	0	2
00-01—Zurich	Switzerland	44	5	11	16	48	...	...	...	16	2	5	7	37
01-02—Zurich	Switzerland	28	6	17	23	36	...	...	...	16	0	6	6	14
02-03—Zurich	Switzerland	37	4	20	24	62	...	...	...	—	—	—	—	—
03-04—Zurich	Switzerland	48	12	24	36	78	...	...	...	13	5	2	7	14
04-05—Zurich	Switzerland	44	14	29	43	46	...	...	...	15	4	11	15	20
05-06—Montreal	NHL	48	2	9	11	28	-6	2	0	1	0	0	0	0
—Swiss Olympic team	Int'l	6	2	1	3	6	1	1	0	—	—	—	—	—
NHL Totals (1 year)		48	2	9	11	28	-6	2	0	1	0	0	0	0

STRUDWICK, JASON D/RW

PERSONAL: Born July 17, 1975, in Edmonton. ... 6-3/225. ... Shoots left. ... Name pronounced STRUHD-wihk.

TRANSACTIONS/CAREER NOTES: Selected by New York Islanders in third round (third Islanders pick, 63rd overall) of NHL draft (June 29, 1994). ... Traded by Islanders to Vancouver Canucks for LW Gino Odjick (March 23, 1998). ... Injured back (November 17, 1999); missed 10 games. ... Strained knee (February 24, 2001); missed 11 games. ... Signed as free agent by Chicago Blackhawks (July 15, 2002). ... Injured wrist (November 1, 2003); missed 13 games. ... Injured shoulder (December 19, 2003); missed 10 games. ... Signed as free agent by New York Rangers (July 20, 2004). ... Personal leave (October 10, 2005); missed six games.

		REGULAR SEASON								PLAYOFFS				
Season Team	League	GP	G	A	Pts.	PIM	+/-	PP	SH	GP	G	A	Pts.	PIM
93-94—Kamloops	WHL	61	6	8	14	118	11	1	0	19	0	4	4	24
94-95—Kamloops	WHL	72	3	11	14	183	36	0	0	21	1	1	2	39
95-96—Worcester	AHL	60	2	7	9	119	...	...	...	4	0	1	1	0
—New York Islanders	NHL	1	0	0	0	7	0	0	0	—	—	—	—	—
96-97—Kentucky	AHL	80	1	9	10	198	-9	0	0	4	0	0	0	0
97-98—Kentucky	AHL	39	3	1	4	87	-12	0	0	—	—	—	—	—
—New York Islanders	NHL	17	0	1	1	36	1	0	0	—	—	—	—	—
—Vancouver	NHL	11	0	1	1	29	-3	0	0	—	—	—	—	—
—Syracuse	AHL	...	...	...	...	...	...	...	...	3	0	0	0	6
98-99—Vancouver	NHL	65	0	3	3	114	-19	0	0	—	—	—	—	—
99-00—Vancouver	NHL	63	1	3	4	64	-13	0	0	—	—	—	—	—
00-01—Vancouver	NHL	60	1	4	5	64	16	0	0	2	0	0	0	0
01-02—Vancouver	NHL	44	2	4	6	96	4	0	0	—	—	—	—	—
02-03—Chicago	NHL	48	2	3	5	87	-4	0	0	—	—	—	—	—
03-04—Chicago	NHL	54	1	3	4	73	-16	0	0	—	—	—	—	—
04-05—Ferencvaros	Hungary	6	1	2	3	8	...	...	...	—	—	—	—	—
05-06—New York Rangers	NHL	65	3	4	7	66	-10	0	0	3	0	0	0	0
NHL Totals (9 years)		428	10	26	36	636	-44	0	0	5	0	0	0	0

S

STUART, BRAD D

PERSONAL: Born November 6, 1979, in Rocky Mountain House, Alta. ... 6-2/215. ... Shoots left.

TRANSACTIONS/CAREER NOTES: Selected by San Jose Sharks in first round (first Sharks pick, third overall) of entry draft (June 27, 1998). ... Suspended two games for cross-checking incident (March 9, 2001). ... Injured ankle (January 6, 2003); missed eight games. ... Concussion (February 24, 2003); missed 21 games. ... Separated shoulder (October 3, 2003); missed five games. ... Traded by Sharks with C Wayne Primeau and LW Marco Sturm to Boston Bruins for C Joe Thornton (November 30, 2005). ... Flu (December 17, 2005); missed one game.

		REGULAR SEASON								PLAYOFFS				
Season Team	League	GP	G	A	Pts.	PIM	+/-	PP	SH	GP	G	A	Pts.	PIM
96-97—Regina	WHL	57	7	36	43	58	...	...	...	5	0	4	4	14
97-98—Regina	WHL	72	20	45	65	82	...	...	...	9	3	4	7	10
98-99—Regina	WHL	29	10	19	29	43	...	...	...	—	—	—	—	—
—Calgary	WHL	30	11	22	33	26	...	...	...	21	8	15	23	59
99-00—San Jose	NHL	82	10	26	36	32	3	5	1	12	1	0	1	6
00-01—San Jose	NHL	77	5	18	23	56	10	1	0	5	1	0	1	0
01-02—San Jose	NHL	82	6	23	29	39	13	2	0	12	0	3	3	8
02-03—San Jose	NHL	36	4	10	14	46	-6	2	0	—	—	—	—	—
03-04—San Jose	NHL	77	9	30	39	34	9	5	0	17	1	5	6	13
05-06—San Jose	NHL	23	2	10	12	14	-2	1	0	—	—	—	—	—
—Boston	NHL	55	10	21	31	38	-6	6	0	—	—	—	—	—
NHL Totals (6 years)		432	46	138	184	259	21	22	1	46	3	8	11	27

STUART, MARK D

PERSONAL: Born April 27, 1984, in Rochester, Minn. ... 6-1/209. ... Shoots left. ... Brother of Mike Stuart, D, St. Louis Blues.

COLLEGE: Colorado College

TRANSACTIONS/CAREER NOTES: Selected by Boston Bruins in first round (first Bruins pick, 21st overall) of entry draft (June 21, 2003).

		REGULAR SEASON								PLAYOFFS				
Season Team	League	GP	G	A	Pts.	PIM	+/-	PP	SH	GP	G	A	Pts.	PIM
02-03—Colorado College	WCHA	38	3	17	20	81	...	...	...	—	—	—	—	—
03-04—Colorado College	WCHA	37	4	11	15	100	...	...	...	—	—	—	—	—
04-05—Colorado College	WCHA	43	5	14	19	94	...	...	...	—	—	—	—	—
05-06—Providence	AHL	60	4	3	7	76	4	3	0	6	0	0	0	25
—Boston	NHL	17	1	1	2	10	-1	0	0	—	—	—	—	—
NHL Totals (1 year)		17	1	1	2	10	-1	0	0					

STUART, MIKE D

PERSONAL: Born August 31, 1980, in Rochester, Minn. ... 6-0/195. ... Shoots right. ... Brother of Mark Stuart, D, Boston Bruins.

COLLEGE: Colorado College

TRANSACTIONS/CAREER NOTES: Selected by Nashville Predators in fifth round (sixth Predators pick, 137th overall) of entry draft (June 24, 2000). ... Signed as free agent by St. Louis Blues (October 7, 2002).

		REGULAR SEASON								PLAYOFFS				
Season Team	League	GP	G	A	Pts.	PIM	+/-	PP	SH	GP	G	A	Pts.	PIM
98-99—Colorado College	WCHA	40	2	12	14	44	...	...	...	—	—	—	—	—
99-00—Colorado College	WCHA	32	2	5	7	26	...	...	...	—	—	—	—	—

Season Team	League	GP	G	A	Pts.	PIM	+/-	PP	SH	GP	G	A	Pts.	PIM
		REGULAR SEASON								PLAYOFFS				
—Colorado College	WCHA	33	1	13	14	36	...	...	...	—	—	—	—	—
01-02—Colorado College	WCHA	35	3	9	12	46	...	...	...	—	—	—	—	—
02-03—Worcester	AHL	41	1	5	6	19	-2	0	0	3	0	0	0	2
—Peoria	ECHL	19	2	7	9	12	3	0	0	—	—	—	—	—
03-04—St. Louis	NHL	2	0	0	0	0	0	0	0	—	—	—	—	—
—Worcester	AHL	30	0	4	4	20	-3	0	0	—	—	—	—	—
04-05—Worcester	AHL	70	1	10	11	26	5	0	0	—	—	—	—	—
05-06—Peoria	AHL	56	0	13	13	30	-10	0	0	4	0	2	2	0
—St. Louis	NHL	1	0	0	0	0	0	0	0	—	—	—	—	—
NHL Totals (2 years)		3	0	0	0	0	0	0	0					

STUMPEL, JOZEF — C/RW

PERSONAL: Born July 20, 1972, in Nitra, Czech. ... 6-3/225. ... Shoots right. ... Name pronounced JOH-sehf STUHM-puhl.

TRANSACTIONS/CAREER NOTES: Selected by Boston Bruins in second round (second Bruins pick, 40th overall) of entry draft (June 22, 1991). ... Injured shoulder (December 1992); missed nine games. ... Injured knee (March 17, 1994); missed nine games. ... Injured knee (April 1995). ... Fractured cheekbone (February 27, 1996); missed three games. ... Back spasms (January 4, 1997); missed one game. ... Back spasms (February 1, 1997); missed three games. ... Traded by Bruins with RW Sandy Moger and fourth-round pick (traded to New Jersey; Devils selected RW Pierre Dagenais) in 1998 draft to Los Angeles Kings for LW Dimitri Khristich and G Byron Dafoe (August 29, 1997). ... Flu (February 7, 1998); missed one game. ... Bruised kidney (March 5, 1998); missed four games. ... Strained hip flexor and abdominal muscle (October 18, 1998); missed 10 games. ... Sprained right ankle (November 16, 1998); missed three games. ... Sprained right knee (April 8, 1999); missed final five games of season. ... Hernia (November 3, 1999); missed 18 games. ... Bruised left knee (January 3, 2000); missed seven games. ... Missed first seven games of 2000-01 season in contract dispute. ... Fractured toe (December 14, 2000); missed two games. ... Strained right hamstring (February 10, 2001); missed two games. ... Fractured rib (March 4, 2001); missed seven games. ... Traded by Kings with RW Glen Murray to Bruins for C Jason Allison and C/LW Mikko Eloranta (October 24, 2001). ... Strained groin (March 26, 2002); missed one game. ... Injured wrist (November 19, 2002); missed three games. ... Injured hip (April 1, 2003); missed one game. ... Traded by Bruins with seventh-round pick in 2003 draft (traded to Nashville; Predators selected G Miroslav Hanulak) to Los Angeles Kings for fourth-round pick (C Patrick Valcak) in 2003 draft and second-round pick (RW Martins Karsums) in 2004 draft (June 22, 2003). ... Injured chest (October 26, 2003); missed 14 games. ... Signed as free agent by Florida Panthers (August 17, 2005). ... Hip flexor (March 29, 2006); missed seven games.

STATISTICAL PLATEAUS: Three-goal games: 1995-96 (1), 1997-98 (1). Total: 2.

Season Team	League	GP	G	A	Pts.	PIM	+/-	PP	SH	GP	G	A	Pts.	PIM
		REGULAR SEASON								PLAYOFFS				
89-90—Nitra	Slovakia	38	12	11	23	0	...	...	...	—	—	—	—	—
90-91—Nitra	Slovakia	49	23	22	45	14	...	...	...	—	—	—	—	—
91-92—Boston	NHL	4	1	0	1	0	1	0	0	—	—	—	—	—
—Koln	Germany	33	19	18	37	35	...	...	...	—	—	—	—	—
92-93—Providence	AHL	56	31	61	92	26	28	14	0	6	4	4	8	0
—Boston	NHL	13	1	3	4	4	-3	0	0	—	—	—	—	—
93-94—Boston	NHL	59	8	15	23	14	4	0	0	13	1	7	8	4
—Providence	AHL	17	5	12	17	4	0	2	0	—	—	—	—	—
94-95—Koln	Germany	25	16	23	39	18	...	...	...	—	—	—	—	—
—Boston	NHL	44	5	13	18	8	4	1	0	5	0	0	0	0
95-96—Boston	NHL	76	18	36	54	14	-8	5	0	5	1	2	3	0
96-97—Boston	NHL	78	21	55	76	14	-22	6	0	—	—	—	—	—
97-98—Los Angeles	NHL	77	21	58	79	53	17	4	0	4	1	2	3	2
98-99—Los Angeles	NHL	64	13	21	34	10	-18	1	0	—	—	—	—	—
99-00—Los Angeles	NHL	57	17	41	58	10	23	3	0	4	0	4	4	8
00-01—Slovan Bratislava	Slovakia	9	2	4	6	16	...	...	...	—	—	—	—	—
—Los Angeles	NHL	63	16	39	55	14	20	9	0	13	3	5	8	10
01-02—Los Angeles	NHL	9	1	3	4	4	1	0	0	—	—	—	—	—
—Boston	NHL	72	7	47	54	14	21	1	0	6	0	2	2	0
—Slovakian Oly. team	Int'l	2	2	1	3	0	...	...	...	—	—	—	—	—
02-03—Boston	NHL	78	14	37	51	12	0	4	0	5	0	2	2	0
03-04—Los Angeles	NHL	64	8	29	37	16	5	4	0	—	—	—	—	—
04-05—Slavia Praha	Czech Rep.	52	13	26	39	41	6	...	...	7	4	2	6	10
05-06—Florida	NHL	74	15	37	52	26	11	3	1	—	—	—	—	—
—Slovakian Oly. team	Int'l	3	0	0	0	0	-2	0	0	—	—	—	—	—
NHL Totals (14 years)		832	166	434	600	213	56	41	1	55	6	24	30	24

STURM, MARCO — LW/RW

PERSONAL: Born September 8, 1978, in Dingolfing, W. Germany. ... 6-0/195. ... Shoots left.

TRANSACTIONS/CAREER NOTES: Selected by San Jose Sharks in first round (second Sharks pick, 21st overall) of entry draft (June 22, 1996). ... Sprained wrist (April 1, 1998); missed six games. ... Injured foot (March 3, 1999); missed two games. ... Concussion (December 2, 1999); missed four games. ... Injured elbow (January 4, 2002); missed two games. ... Flu (January 27, 2002); missed one game. ... Injured hand (March 20, 2002); missed two games. ... Injured chest (January 15, 2004); missed two games. ... Left team for personal reasons (January 21, 2004); missed one game. ... Fractured left leg and dislocated ankle (March 5, 2004); missed remainder of season and playoffs. ... Traded by Sharks with C Wayne Primeau and D Brad Stuart to Boston Bruins for C Joe Thornton (November 30, 2005). ... Shoulder injury (February 4, 2006); missed four games. ... Flu (March 29, 2006); missed one game.

STATISTICAL PLATEAUS: Three-goal games: 1998-99 (1).

Season Team	League	GP	G	A	Pts.	PIM	+/-	PP	SH	GP	G	A	Pts.	PIM
		REGULAR SEASON								PLAYOFFS				
95-96—Landshut	Germany	47	12	20	32	50	...	...	...	—	—	—	—	—
96-97—Landshut	Germany	46	16	27	43	40	...	...	...	7	1	4	5	6
97-98—San Jose	NHL	74	10	20	30	40	-2	2	0	2	0	0	0	0
—German Oly. team	Int'l	2	0	0	0	0	0	0	0	—	—	—	—	—

Season Team	League	GP	G	A	Pts.	PIM	+/-	PP	SH	GP	G	A	Pts.	PIM
		REGULAR SEASON								PLAYOFFS				
98-99—San Jose	NHL	78	16	22	38	52	7	3	2	6	2	2	4	4
99-00—San Jose	NHL	74	12	15	27	22	4	2	4	12	1	3	4	6
00-01—San Jose	NHL	81	14	18	32	28	9	2	3	6	0	2	2	0
01-02—San Jose	NHL	77	21	20	41	32	23	4	3	12	3	2	5	2
—German Oly. team	Int'l	5	0	1	1	0	...	...	...	—	—	—	—	—
02-03—San Jose	NHL	82	28	20	48	16	9	6	0	—	—	—	—	—
03-04—San Jose	NHL	64	21	20	41	36	0	10	2	—	—	—	—	—
04-05—Ingolstadt ERC	Germany	45	22	16	38	56	14	6	1	11	3	4	7	12
05-06—San Jose	NHL	23	6	10	16	16	-8	3	0	—	—	—	—	—
—Boston	NHL	51	23	20	43	32	14	5	0	—	—	—	—	—
NHL Totals (8 years)		604	151	165	316	274	56	37	14	38	6	9	15	12

SUCHY, RADOSLAV D

PERSONAL: Born April 7, 1976, in Kezmarok, Czechoslovakia. ... 6-2/201. ... Shoots left. ... Name pronounced soo-KHEE.

TRANSACTIONS/CAREER NOTES: Signed as free agent by Phoenix Coyotes (September 25, 1997). ... Bruised finger (December 21, 2001); missed one game. ... Traded by Coyotes with sixth-round pick (D Derek Reinhart) in 2005 to Columbus Blue Jackets for fourth-round pick (G Jeremy Duchesne) in 2005 (July 6, 2004). ... Flu (January 20, 2006); missed three games.

Season Team	League	GP	G	A	Pts.	PIM	+/-	PP	SH	GP	G	A	Pts.	PIM
		REGULAR SEASON								PLAYOFFS				
94-95—Sherbrooke	QMJHL	69	12	32	44	30	...	...	...	7	0	3	3	2
95-96—Sherbrooke	QMJHL	68	15	53	68	68	...	...	...	7	0	3	3	2
96-97—Sherbrooke	QMJHL	32	6	34	40	14	...	...	...	—	—	—	—	—
—Chicoutimi	QMJHL	28	5	24	29	24	...	...	...	19	6	15	21	12
97-98—Las Vegas	IHL	26	1	4	5	10	0	0	0	—	—	—	—	—
—Springfield	AHL	41	6	15	21	16	13	0	1	4	0	1	1	2
98-99—Springfield	AHL	69	4	32	36	10	3	2	0	3	0	1	1	0
99-00—Springfield	AHL	2	0	1	1	0	...	...	...	—	—	—	—	—
—Phoenix	NHL	60	0	6	6	16	2	0	0	5	0	1	1	0
00-01—Phoenix	NHL	72	0	10	10	22	1	0	0	—	—	—	—	—
01-02—Phoenix	NHL	81	4	13	17	10	25	1	0	5	1	0	1	0
02-03—Phoenix	NHL	77	1	8	9	18	2	1	0	—	—	—	—	—
03-04—Phoenix	NHL	82	7	14	21	8	1	2	0	—	—	—	—	—
04-05—HC SKP Poprad	Slovakia	34	5	10	15	24	-1	...	...	5	0	0	0	2
05-06—Columbus	NHL	79	1	7	8	30	-8	0	0	—	—	—	—	—
—Slovakian Oly. team	Int'l	6	1	1	2	0	0	0	0	—	—	—	—	—
NHL Totals (6 years)		451	13	58	71	104	23	4	0	10	1	1	2	0

SUGLOBOV, ALEKSANDER RW

PERSONAL: Born January 15, 1982, in Elektrostal, U.S.S.R. ... 6-0/200. ... Shoots left. ... Name pronounced suh-GLOH-bahf.

TRANSACTIONS/CAREER NOTES: Selected by New Jersey Devils in second round (third Devils pick, 56th overall) of NHL draft (June 24, 2000). ... Traded by Devils to Maple Leafs for D Ken Klee (March 8, 2006).

Season Team	League	GP	G	A	Pts.	PIM	+/-	PP	SH	GP	G	A	Pts.	PIM
		REGULAR SEASON								PLAYOFFS				
98-99—Spartak Yekaterinburg	Russian	1	0	0	0	0	...	0	0	—	—	—	—	—
99-00—Torpedo Yaroslavl	Rus. Div.	38	23	10	33		...	...	...	—	—	—	—	—
—Torpedo Yaroslavl	Rus. Div.	2	0	0	0	0	...	0	0	—	—	—	—	—
00-01—Salavat Yulayev Ufa	Russian	6	0	0	0	4	...	...	...	—	—	—	—	—
—SKA St. Petersburg	Russian	8	1	0	1	6	...	...	...	—	—	—	—	—
—Lokomotiv Yaroslavl	Russian	4	0	0	0	2	...	...	...	11	1	2	3	6
01-02—Lokomotiv Yaroslavl	Russian	25	4	2	6	26	...	...	...	5	1	1	2	18
02-03—Yaroslavl	CIS	17	4	2	6	12	...	...	...	5	1	0	1	2
03-04—Albany	AHL	35	11	11	22	54	-9	4	0	—	—	—	—	—
—New Jersey	NHL	1	0	0	0	0	0	0	0	...	...	...	...	...
04-05—Albany	AHL	72	25	21	46	77	-15	7	0	—	—	—	—	—
05-06—Albany	AHL	51	25	23	48	52	4	11	0	—	—	—	—	—
—Toronto	AHL	15	8	2	10	21	1	5	0	5	5	2	7	2
—New Jersey	NHL	1	1	0	1	0	-2	1	0	—	—	—	—	—
—Toronto	NHL	2	0	0	0	0	-1	0	0	—	—	—	—	—
NHL Totals (2 years)		4	1	0	1	0	-3	1	0					

SULLIVAN, STEVE RW/LW

PERSONAL: Born July 6, 1974, in Timmins, Ont. ... 5-9/155. ... Shoots right.

TRANSACTIONS/CAREER NOTES: Selected by New Jersey Devils in ninth round (10th Devils pick, 233rd overall) of entry draft (June 29, 1994). ... Traded by Devils with D Jason Smith and C Alyn McCauley to Toronto Maple Leafs for C Doug Gilmour, D Dave Ellett and third-round pick (D Andre Lakos) in 1999 (February 25, 1997). ... Flu (March 7, 1998); missed three games. ... Back spasms (May 11, 1999); missed one playoff game. ... Claimed off waivers by Chicago Blackhawks (October 23, 1999). ... Flu (February 18, 2000); missed one game. ... Flu (December 13, 2000); missed one game. ... Shoulder (March 20, 2002); missed four games. ... Back (November 28, 2003); missed two games. ... Traded by Blackhawks to Nashville Predators for second-round pick (C Ryan Garlock) in 2004 and second-round pick (RW Michael Blunden) in 2005 (February 16, 2004). ... Groin (November 5, 2005); missed two games. ... Groin (November 18, 2005); missed two games. ... Groin (April 1, 2006); missed final nine games of regular season.

STATISTICAL PLATEAUS: Three-goal games: 2000-01 (1), 2002-03 (1), 2003-04 (1). Total: 3. ... Four-goal games: 1998-99 (1). ... Total hat tricks: 4.

		REGULAR SEASON								PLAYOFFS				
Season Team	League	GP	G	A	Pts.	PIM	+/-	PP	SH	GP	G	A	Pts.	PIM
91-92—Timmins	OJHL	47	66	55	121	141	...	...	...	—	—	—	—	—
92-93—Sault Ste. Marie	OHL	62	36	27	63	44	...	...	...	16	3	8	11	18
93-94—Sault Ste. Marie	OHL	63	51	62	113	82	...	...	...	14	9	16	25	22
94-95—Albany	AHL	75	31	50	81	124	41	8	0	14	4	7	11	10
95-96—Albany	AHL	53	33	42	75	127	...	...	...	4	3	0	3	6
—New Jersey	NHL	16	5	4	9	8	3	2	0	—	—	—	—	—
96-97—Albany	AHL	15	8	7	15	16	2	2	0	—	—	—	—	—
—New Jersey	NHL	33	8	14	22	14	9	2	0	—	—	—	—	—
—Toronto	NHL	21	5	11	16	23	5	1	0	—	—	—	—	—
97-98—Toronto	NHL	63	10	18	28	40	-8	1	0	—	—	—	—	—
98-99—Toronto	NHL	63	20	20	40	28	12	4	0	13	3	3	6	14
99-00—Toronto	NHL	7	0	1	1	4	-1	0	0	—	—	—	—	—
—Chicago	NHL	73	22	42	64	52	20	2	1	—	—	—	—	—
00-01—Chicago	NHL	81	34	41	75	54	3	6	*8	—	—	—	—	—
01-02—Chicago	NHL	78	21	39	60	67	23	3	0	5	1	0	1	2
02-03—Chicago	NHL	82	26	35	61	42	15	4	2	—	—	—	—	—
03-04—Chicago	NHL	56	15	28	43	36	-7	4	2	—	—	—	—	—
—Nashville	NHL	24	9	21	30	12	8	7	0	6	1	1	2	6
05-06—Nashville	NHL	69	31	37	68	50	2	13	4	5	0	2	2	0
NHL Totals (10 years)		666	206	311	517	430	84	49	17	29	5	6	11	22

SUMMERS, CHRIS D

PERSONAL: Born February 5, 1988, in Ann Arbor, Mich. ... 6-1/180. ... Shoots left.
TRANSACTIONS/CAREER NOTES: Selected by Phoenix Coyotes in first round (second Coyotes pick; 29th overall) of NHL draft (June 24, 2006).

		REGULAR SEASON								PLAYOFFS				
Season Team	League	GP	G	A	Pts.	PIM	+/-	PP	SH	GP	G	A	Pts.	PIM
04-05—U.S. National	USHL	35	1	4	5	18	...	...	...	—	—	—	—	—
05-06—U.S. National	USHL	51	5	10	15	56	...	...	...	—	—	—	—	—

SUNDIN, MATS C

PERSONAL: Born February 13, 1971, in Bromma, Sweden. ... 6-5/231. ... Shoots right. ... Name pronounced suhn-DEEN.
TRANSACTIONS/CAREER NOTES: Selected by Quebec Nordiques in first round (first Nordiques pick,first overall) of NHL draft (June 17, 1989). ... Separated right shoulder (January 2, 1993); missed three games. ... Suspended one game for second stick-related infraction (March 2, 1993). ... Traded by Nordiques with D Garth Butcher, LW Todd Warriner and first-round pick (traded to Washington; Capitals selected D Nolan Baumgartner) in 1994 draft to Toronto Maple Leafs for LW Wendel Clark, D Sylvain Lefebvre, RW Landon Wilson and first-round pick (D Jeffrey Kealty) in 1994 draft (June 28, 1994). ... Sprained shoulder (March 25, 1995); missed one game. ... Slightly tore knee cartilage (October 24, 1995); missed four games. ... Fractured ankle (October 9, 1999); missed nine games. ... Bruised left shoulder (December 27, 2002); missed six games. ... Facial cut (April 9, 2003); missed one game. ... Suspended one game for throwing stick into stands (January 6, 2004). ... Fractured lower left orbital bone (October 5, 2005); missed 12 games.
STATISTICAL PLATEAUS: Three-goal games: 1990-91 (2), 1992-93 (1), 1996-97 (1), 1998-99 (1). Total: 5. ... Five-goal games: 1991-92 (1). ... Total hat tricks: 6.

		REGULAR SEASON								PLAYOFFS				
Season Team	League	GP	G	A	Pts.	PIM	+/-	PP	SH	GP	G	A	Pts.	PIM
88-89—Nacka	Sweden	25	10	8	18	18	...	...	...	—	—	—	—	—
89-90—Djurgarden Stockholm	Sweden	34	10	8	18	16	...	...	...	8	7	0	7	4
90-91—Quebec	NHL	80	23	36	59	58	-24	4	0	—	—	—	—	—
91-92—Quebec	NHL	80	33	43	76	103	-19	8	2	—	—	—	—	—
92-93—Quebec	NHL	80	47	67	114	96	21	13	4	6	3	1	4	6
93-94—Quebec	NHL	84	32	53	85	60	1	6	2	—	—	—	—	—
94-95—Djurgarden Stockholm	Sweden	12	7	2	9	14	...	...	...	—	—	—	—	—
—Toronto	NHL	47	23	24	47	14	-5	9	0	7	5	4	9	4
95-96—Toronto	NHL	76	33	50	83	46	8	7	6	6	3	1	4	4
96-97—Toronto	NHL	82	41	53	94	59	6	7	4	—	—	—	—	—
97-98—Toronto	NHL	82	33	41	74	49	-3	9	1	—	—	—	—	—
—Swedish Oly. team	Int'l	4	3	0	3	4	1	0	0	—	—	—	—	—
98-99—Toronto	NHL	82	31	52	83	58	22	4	0	17	8	8	16	16
99-00—Toronto	NHL	73	32	41	73	46	16	10	2	12	3	5	8	10
00-01—Toronto	NHL	82	28	46	74	76	15	9	0	11	6	7	13	14
01-02—Toronto	NHL	82	41	39	80	94	6	10	2	8	2	5	7	4
—Swedish Oly. team	Int'l	4	5	4	9	10	...	...	...	—	—	—	—	—
02-03—Toronto	NHL	75	37	35	72	58	1	16	3	7	1	3	4	6
03-04—Toronto	NHL	81	31	44	75	52	11	11	1	9	4	5	9	8
05-06—Toronto	NHL	70	31	47	78	58	7	16	2	—	—	—	—	—
—Swedish Oly. team	Int'l	8	3	5	8	4	1	2	0	—	—	—	—	—
NHL Totals (15 years)		1156	496	671	1167	927	63	139	29	83	35	39	74	72

SUNDSTROM, NIKLAS RW/LW

PERSONAL: Born June 6, 1975, in Ornskoldsvik, Sweden. ... 6-0/191. ... Shoots left.
TRANSACTIONS/CAREER NOTES: Selected by New York Rangers in first round (first Rangers pick, eighth overall) of NHL draft (June 26, 1993). ... Fractured finger and sprained knee (December 5, 1997); missed 10 games. ... Traded by Rangers with G Dan Cloutier and first- (RW Nikita Alexeev) and third-round (traded to San Jose; traded to Chicago; Blackhawks selected LW Igor Radulov) picks in 2000 draft to Tampa Bay Lightning for first-round pick (RW Pavel Brendl) in 1999 draft (June 26, 1999). ... Traded by Lightning with third-round pick (traded to

Chicago; Blackhawks selected LW Igor Radulov) in 2000 draft to San Jose Sharks for D Andrei Zyuzin, D Bill Houlder, LW Shawn Burr and C Steve Guolla (August 4, 1999). ... Injured knee (November 29, 2001); missed one game. ... Injured knee (March 21, 2002); missed eight games. ... Traded by Sharks with third-round pick (later traded to Los Angeles; Kings picked D Paul Baier) in 2004 draft to Montreal Canadiens for G Jeff Hackett. (January 23, 2003). ... Injured shoulder (October 11, 2003); missed one game. ... Injured abdomen (January 4, 2004); missed four games. ... Had concussion (February 29, 2004); missed seven games. ... Injured groin (October 20, 2005); missed four games.

		REGULAR SEASON								PLAYOFFS				
Season Team	League	GP	G	A	Pts.	PIM	+/-	PP	SH	GP	G	A	Pts.	PIM
91-92—MoDo Ornskoldsvik	Sweden	9	1	3	4	0	...	...	...	—	—	—	—	—
92-93—MoDo Ornskoldsvik	Sweden	40	7	11	18	18	...	...	...	—	—	—	—	—
93-94—MoDo Ornskoldsvik	Sweden	37	7	12	19	28	...	...	...	11	4	3	7	2
94-95—MoDo Ornskoldsvik	Sweden	33	8	13	21	30	...	...	...	—	—	—	—	—
95-96—New York Rangers	NHL	82	9	12	21	14	2	1	1	11	4	3	7	4
96-97—New York Rangers	NHL	82	24	28	52	20	23	5	1	9	0	5	5	2
97-98—New York Rangers	NHL	70	19	28	47	24	0	4	0	—	—	—	—	—
—Swedish Oly. team	Int'l	4	1	1	2	2	3	0	0	—	—	—	—	—
98-99—New York Rangers	NHL	81	13	30	43	20	-2	1	2	—	—	—	—	—
99-00—San Jose	NHL	79	12	25	37	22	9	2	1	12	0	2	2	2
00-01—San Jose	NHL	82	10	39	49	28	10	4	1	6	0	3	3	2
01-02—San Jose	NHL	73	9	30	39	50	7	0	1	12	1	6	7	6
—Swedish Oly. team	Int'l	4	1	3	4	0	...	...	...	—	—	—	—	—
02-03—San Jose	NHL	47	2	10	12	22	-4	0	0	—	—	—	—	—
—Montreal	NHL	33	5	9	14	8	3	0	0	—	—	—	—	—
03-04—Montreal	NHL	66	8	12	20	18	3	0	0	4	1	0	1	2
04-05—Milano	Italy	33	9	27	36	40	...	...	...	—	—	—	—	—
05-06—Montreal	NHL	55	6	9	15	30	-6	0	0	5	0	3	3	4
NHL Totals (10 years)		750	117	232	349	256	45	17	7	59	6	22	28	22

SUROVY, TOMAS LW/RW

PERSONAL: Born September 24, 1981, in Banska Bystrica, Czechoslovakia. ... 6-1/191. ... Shoots left.
TRANSACTIONS/CAREER NOTES: Selected by Pittsburgh Penguins in fourth round (fifth Penguins pick, 120th overall) of NHL entry draft (June 23, 2001).

		REGULAR SEASON								PLAYOFFS				
Season Team	League	GP	G	A	Pts.	PIM	+/-	PP	SH	GP	G	A	Pts.	PIM
00-01—HC SKP Poprad	Slovakia	53	22	28	50	30	...	...	...	6	2	1	3	14
01-02—Wilkes-Barre/Scranton	AHL	65	23	10	33	37	-9	4	0	—	—	—	—	—
02-03—Pittsburgh	NHL	26	4	7	11	10	0	1	0	—	—	—	—	—
—Wilkes-Barre/Scranton	AHL	39	19	20	39	18	3	7	0	6	2	3	5	2
03-04—Wilkes-Barre/Scranton	AHL	30	14	13	27	14	13	4	0	24	6	11	17	8
—Pittsburgh	NHL	47	11	12	23	16	-8	3	0	—	—	—	—	—
04-05—Wilkes-Barre/Scranton	AHL	80	17	32	49	43	-10	3	0	11	2	6	8	9
05-06—Wilkes-Barre/Scranton	AHL	25	16	12	28	26	11	9	0	—	—	—	—	—
—Pittsburgh	NHL	53	12	13	25	45	-13	3	0	—	—	—	—	—
—Slovakian Oly. team	Int'l	6	0	1	1	2	0	0	0	—	—	—	—	—
NHL Totals (3 years)		126	27	32	59	71	-21	7	0					

SUTER, RYAN D

PERSONAL: Born January 21, 1985, in Madison, Wis. ... 6-1/191. ... Shoots left.
TRANSACTIONS/CAREER NOTES: Selected by Nashville Predators in first round (first Predators pick, seventh overall) in 2003 entry draft (June 23, 2003).

		REGULAR SEASON								PLAYOFFS				
Season Team	League	GP	G	A	Pts.	PIM	+/-	PP	SH	GP	G	A	Pts.	PIM
01-02—U.S. national team	Int'l	39	3	16	19	93	...	1	0	—	—	—	—	—
02-03—U.S. national team	Int'l	47	8	19	27	114	...	...	...	—	—	—	—	—
03-04—Wisconsin	WCHA	39	3	16	19	93	...	...	...	—	—	—	—	—
04-05—Milwaukee	AHL	63	7	16	23	70	10	4	0	7	1	5	6	16
05-06—Nashville	NHL	71	1	15	16	66	7	0	0	—	—	—	—	—
NHL Totals (1 year)		71	1	15	16	66	7	0	0					

SUTHERBY, BRIAN C/LW

PERSONAL: Born March 1, 1982, in Edmonton. ... 6-3/205. ... Shoots left.
TRANSACTIONS/CAREER NOTES: Selected by Washington Capitals in first round (first Capitals pick, 26th overall) of NHL entry draft (June 24, 2000). ... Strained lower back (November 18, 2004); missed five games. ... Lower-body injury (March 10, 2006); missed one game. ... Upper-body injury (April 7, 2006); missed four games.

		REGULAR SEASON								PLAYOFFS				
Season Team	League	GP	G	A	Pts.	PIM	+/-	PP	SH	GP	G	A	Pts.	PIM
98-99—Moose Jaw	WHL	66	9	12	21	47	...	...	...	11	0	1	1	0
99-00—Moose Jaw	WHL	47	18	17	35	102	...	...	...	4	1	1	2	12
00-01—Moose Jaw	WHL	59	34	43	77	138	...	...	...	4	2	1	3	10
01-02—Washington	NHL	7	0	0	0	2	-3	0	0	—	—	—	—	—
—Moose Jaw	WHL	36	18	27	45	75	...	...	...	12	7	5	12	33
02-03—Portland	AHL	5	0	5	5	11	1	0	0	—	—	—	—	—
—Washington	NHL	72	2	9	11	93	7	0	0	5	0	0	0	10
03-04—Washington	NHL	30	2	0	2	28	-5	0	0	—	—	—	—	—
—Portland	AHL	6	2	4	6	16	2	0	0	—	—	—	—	—

Season Team	League	GP	G	A	Pts.	PIM	+/-	PP	SH	GP	G	A	Pts.	PIM
		REGULAR SEASON								PLAYOFFS				
04-05—Portland	AHL	53	10	19	29	115	-3	3	1	—	—	—	—	—
05-06—Washington	NHL	76	14	16	30	73	-17	0	2	—	—	—	—	—
NHL Totals (4 years)		185	18	25	43	196	-18	0	2	5	0	0	0	10

SUTTON, ANDY D

PERSONAL: Born March 10, 1975, in Kingston, Ontario. ... 6-6/245. ... Shoots left.

TRANSACTIONS/CAREER NOTES: Signed as free agent by San Jose Sharks (March 20, 1998). ... Injured wrist (November 27, 1999); missed three games. ... Reinjured wrist (December 8, 1999); missed three games. ... Reinjured wrist (December 20, 1999); missed seven games. ... Reinjured wrist (January 12, 2000); missed 10 games. ... Traded by Sharks with seventh-round pick (RW/LW Peter Bartos) in 2000 draft and third-round pick (traded to Atlanta; traded to Pittsburgh; traded to Columbus; Blue Jackets selected D Aaron Johnson) in 2001 draft to Minnesota Wild for eighth-round pick (traded to Calgary; Flames selected D Joe Campbell) in 2001 draft and future considerations (June 12, 2000). ... Bruised knee (November 8, 2000); missed two games. ... Dislocated shoulder (March 6, 2001); missed one game. ... Separated right shoulder (October 30, 2001); missed 12 games. ... Strained groin (January 9, 2002); missed four games. ... Traded by Wild to Atlanta Thrashers for LW Hnat Domenichelli (January 22, 2002). ... Concussion (April 2, 2002); missed two games. ... Injured ankle (February 14, 2003); missed 27 games. ... Fractured left foot (January 1, 2004); missed 16 games. ... Re-signed by Thrashers as restricted free agent (August 11, 2005). ... Suspended four games (forfeiting $38,775.52) for deliberate attempt to injure match penalty (October 15, 2005). ... Flu (December 15, 2005); missed one game.

Season Team	League	GP	G	A	Pts.	PIM	+/-	PP	SH	GP	G	A	Pts.	PIM
		REGULAR SEASON								PLAYOFFS				
94-95—Michigan Tech	WCHA	19	2	1	3	42	...	1	0	—	—	—	—	—
95-96—Michigan Tech	WCHA	32	2	2	4	38	...	...	...	—	—	—	—	—
96-97—Michigan Tech	WCHA	32	2	7	9	73	...	...	...	—	—	—	—	—
97-98—Michigan Tech	WCHA	38	16	24	40	97	...	...	...	—	—	—	—	—
—Kentucky	AHL	7	0	0	0	33	-4	0	0	—	—	—	—	—
98-99—San Jose	NHL	31	0	3	3	65	-4	0	0	—	—	—	—	—
—Kentucky	AHL	21	5	10	15	53	9	3	0	5	0	0	0	23
99-00—San Jose	NHL	40	1	1	2	80	-5	0	0	—	—	—	—	—
—Kentucky	AHL	3	0	1	1	0	...	...	...	—	—	—	—	—
00-01—Minnesota	NHL	69	3	4	7	131	-11	2	0	—	—	—	—	—
01-02—Minnesota	NHL	19	2	4	6	35	-4	1	0	—	—	—	—	—
—Atlanta	NHL	24	0	4	4	46	0	0	0	—	—	—	—	—
02-03—Atlanta	NHL	53	3	18	21	114	-8	1	1	—	—	—	—	—
03-04—Atlanta	NHL	65	8	13	21	94	0	7	1	—	—	—	—	—
04-05—ZSC Lions Zurich	Switzerland	8	2	2	4	32	...	0	0	1	0	1	1	2
—Zurich	Switz. Div. 2	18	8	18	26	58	...	2	1	6	2	4	6	16
05-06—Atlanta	NHL	76	8	17	25	144	13	2	1	—	—	—	—	—
NHL Totals (7 years)		377	25	64	89	709	-19	13	3					

SVATOS, MAREK RW

PERSONAL: Born June 17, 1982, in Kosice, Czechoslovakia. ... 5-11/175. ... Shoots right. ... Name pronounced: MAIR-ihk suh-VAH-tohz

TRANSACTIONS/CAREER NOTES: Selected by Avalanche in seventh round (10th Avalanche pick, 227th overall) of NHL entry draft (June 24, 2001). ... Injured left shoulder and had surgery (October 14, 2003); missed 72 games. ... Right shoulder injury (March 5, 2006); missed remainder of regular season.

Season Team	League	GP	G	A	Pts.	PIM	+/-	PP	SH	GP	G	A	Pts.	PIM
		REGULAR SEASON								PLAYOFFS				
99-00—HC Kosice	Slovakia Jrs.	39	43	30	73	28	...	...	...	—	—	—	—	—
—HC Kosice	Slovakia	19	2	2	4	0	...	...	...	—	—	—	—	—
00-01—Kootenay	WHL	39	23	18	41	47	...	...	...	11	7	2	9	26
01-02—Kootenay	WHL	53	38	39	77	58	...	...	...	21	12	6	18	40
02-03—Hershey	AHL	30	9	4	13	10	...	...	...	—	—	—	—	—
03-04—Colorado	NHL	4	2	0	2	0	1	1	0	11	1	5	6	2
04-05—Hershey	AHL	72	18	28	46	69	9	3	0	—	—	—	—	—
05-06—Colorado	NHL	61	32	18	50	60	0	12	0	—	—	—	—	—
—Slovakian Oly. team	Int'l	6	0	0	0	0	-1	0	0	—	—	—	—	—
NHL Totals (2 years)		65	34	18	52	60	1	13	0	11	1	5	6	2

SVOBODA, JAROSLAV LW/RW

PERSONAL: Born June 1, 1980, in Cervenka, Czechoslovakia. ... 6-2/190. ... Shoots left. ... Name pronounced svah-BOH-duh.

TRANSACTIONS/CAREER NOTES: Selected by Carolina Hurricanes in eighth round (eighth Hurricanes pick, 20eighth overall) of entry draft (June 21, 1997). ... Dislocated shoulder (February 11, 2003); missed 25 games. ... Strained abdomal muscle (February 21, 2004); missed eight games. ... Torso (April 2, 2004); missed remainder of season. ... Traded by Hurricanes to Dallas Stars for fourth-round pick (D Jakub Vojta) in 2005 (June 29, 2004). ... Wrist (January 25, 2006); missed 15 games.

Season Team	League	GP	G	A	Pts.	PIM	+/-	PP	SH	GP	G	A	Pts.	PIM
		REGULAR SEASON								PLAYOFFS				
97-98—Olomouc	Czech. Jrs.	43	15	18	33	0	...	...	...	—	—	—	—	—
98-99—Kootenay	WHL	54	26	33	59	46	...	...	...	7	2	2	4	11
99-00—Kootenay	WHL	56	23	43	66	97	38	5	2	21	15	13	28	51
00-01—Cincinnati	IHL	52	4	10	14	25	...	...	...	—	—	—	—	—
01-02—Lowell	AHL	66	12	16	28	58	10	2	1	—	—	—	—	—
—Carolina	NHL	10	2	2	4	2	0	0	0	23	1	4	5	28
02-03—Lowell	AHL	9	1	1	2	10	-4	0	0	—	—	—	—	—
—Carolina	NHL	48	3	11	14	32	-5	1	0	—	—	—	—	—

Season Team	League	REGULAR SEASON GP	G	A	Pts.	PIM	+/-	PP	SH	PLAYOFFS GP	G	A	Pts.	PIM
03-04—Carolina	NHL	33	3	1	4	6	3	0	0	—	—	—	—	—
—Lowell	AHL	9	2	2	4	4	0	1	0	—	—	—	—	—
04-05—HC Trinec	Czech Rep.	9	0	2	2	14	-3	...	...	—	—	—	—	—
—Olomouc	Czech Dv.I	18	7	6	13	67	0	...	...	—	—	—	—	—
05-06—Dallas	NHL	43	4	3	7	22	-3	0	0	2	0	0	0	2
NHL Totals (4 years)		134	12	17	29	62	-5	1	0	25	1	4	5	30

SWAN, BRYCE RW

PERSONAL: Born October 6, 1987, in Alderpoint, Novia Scotia. ... 6-2/191. ... Shoots right.

TRANSACTIONS/CAREER NOTES: Selected by Anaheim Ducks in second round (second Ducks pick; 38th overall) of NHL draft (June 24, 2006).

Season Team	League	REGULAR SEASON GP	G	A	Pts.	PIM	+/-	PP	SH	PLAYOFFS GP	G	A	Pts.	PIM
04-05—Halifax	QMJHL	36	3	3	6	39	7	...	...	11	2	0	2	10
05-06—Halifax	QMJHL	34	14	11	25	54	-8	...	...	11	2	5	7	8

SYDOR, DARRYL D

S

PERSONAL: Born May 13, 1972, in Edmonton. ... 6-1/205. ... Shoots left. ... Name pronounced sih-DOHR.

TRANSACTIONS/CAREER NOTES: Selected by Los Angeles Kings in first round (first Kings pick, seventh overall) of NHL entry draft (June 16, 1990). ... Bruised hip (November, 1992); missed two games. ... Sprained right shoulder (March 15, 1993); missed two games. ... Traded by Kings with seventh-round pick (G Eoin McInerney) in 1996 draft to Dallas Stars for RW Shane Churla and D Doug Zmolek (February 17, 1996). ... Sprained knee (February 21, 1999); missed three games. ... Reinjured knee (March 7, 1999); missed five games. ... Fractured eye socket (October 2, 1999); missed three games. ... Injured groin (October 20, 1999); missed three games. ... Injured neck (March 26, 2000); missed two games. ... Flu (December 31, 2000); missed one game. ... Injured ankle (November 17, 2001); missed one game. ... Suffered concussion (December 14, 2001); missed three games. ... Injured shoulder (February 21, 2003); missed one game. ... Traded by Stars to Columbus Blue Jackets for C Mike Sillinger and second-round pick (D Johan Fransson) in 2004 entry draft (July 22, 2003). ... Traded by Blue Jackets with fourth-round pick (D Mike Lundin) in 2004 entry draft to Tampa Bay Lightning for C Alexander Svitov and third-round pick (later traded to Calgary Flames) in 2004 entry draft (January 27, 2004). ... Facial injury (January 28, 2006); missed two games. ... Traded by Lightning to Dallas Stars for a fourth-round pick in 2008 draft (July 3, 2006).

STATISTICAL PLATEAUS: Three-goal games: 1997-98 (1).

Season Team	League	REGULAR SEASON GP	G	A	Pts.	PIM	+/-	PP	SH	PLAYOFFS GP	G	A	Pts.	PIM
88-89—Kamloops	WHL	65	12	14	26	86	...	...	...	15	1	4	5	19
89-90—Kamloops	WHL	67	29	66	95	129	...	...	...	17	2	9	11	28
90-91—Kamloops	WHL	66	27	78	105	88	...	...	...	12	3	22	25	10
91-92—Kamloops	WHL	29	9	39	48	43	...	...	...	17	3	15	18	18
—Los Angeles	NHL	18	1	5	6	22	-3	0	0	—	—	—	—	—
92-93—Los Angeles	NHL	80	6	23	29	63	-2	0	0	24	3	8	11	16
93-94—Los Angeles	NHL	84	8	27	35	94	-9	1	0	—	—	—	—	—
94-95—Los Angeles	NHL	48	4	19	23	36	-2	3	0	—	—	—	—	—
95-96—Los Angeles	NHL	58	1	11	12	34	-11	1	0	—	—	—	—	—
—Dallas	NHL	26	2	6	8	41	-1	1	0	—	—	—	—	—
96-97—Dallas	NHL	82	8	40	48	51	37	2	0	7	0	2	2	0
97-98—Dallas	NHL	79	11	35	46	51	17	4	1	17	0	5	5	14
98-99—Dallas	NHL	74	14	34	48	50	-1	9	0	23	3	9	12	16
99-00—Dallas	NHL	74	8	26	34	32	6	5	0	23	1	6	7	6
00-01—Dallas	NHL	81	10	37	47	34	5	8	0	10	1	3	4	0
01-02—Dallas	NHL	78	4	29	33	50	3	2	0	—	—	—	—	—
02-03—Dallas	NHL	81	5	31	36	40	22	2	0	12	0	6	6	6
03-04—Columbus	NHL	49	2	13	15	26	-19	1	0	—	—	—	—	—
—Tampa Bay	NHL	31	1	6	7	6	3	0	0	23	0	6	6	9
05-06—Tampa Bay	NHL	80	4	19	23	30	-18	1	0	5	0	1	1	0
NHL Totals (14 years)		1023	89	361	450	660	27	40	1	144	8	46	54	67

SYKORA, PETR C/RW

PERSONAL: Born December 21, 1978, in Pardubice, Czech. ... 6-3/206. ... Shoots right.

TRANSACTIONS/CAREER NOTES: Selected by Detroit Red Wings in third round (second Red Wings pick, 76th overall) of entry draft (June 21, 1997). ... Traded by Red Wings with third-round pick (traded to Edmonton) in 1999 draft and future considerations to Nashville Predators for RW Doug Brown (July 14, 1998). ... Traded by Predators to Washington Capitals for third-round pick (RW Paul Brown) in 2003 entry draft (June 23, 2002). ... Signed as free agent by Capitals (August 23, 2005).

Season Team	League	REGULAR SEASON GP	G	A	Pts.	PIM	+/-	PP	SH	PLAYOFFS GP	G	A	Pts.	PIM
94-95—HC Pardubice	Czech. Jrs.	38	35	33	68	...	...	...	...	—	—	—	—	—
95-96—HC Pardubice	Czech. Jrs.	26	13	9	22	...	...	...	...	—	—	—	—	—
96-97—Pardubice	Czech Rep.	29	1	3	4	4	...	...	...	—	—	—	—	—
—Poji. Pardubice	Czech. Jrs.	12	14	4	18	...	...	...	...	—	—	—	—	—
97-98—Pardubice	Czech Rep.	39	4	5	9	8	...	...	...	3	0	0	0	0
98-99—Milwaukee	IHL	73	14	15	29	50	-7	3	0	2	1	1	2	0
—Nashville	NHL	2	0	0	0	0	-1	0	0	—	—	—	—	—
99-00—Milwaukee	IHL	3	0	1	1	2	...	...	...	—	—	—	—	—
—HC Pardubice	Czech Rep.	36	7	13	20	49	...	...	...	3	0	0	0	2
00-01—HC Pardubice	Czech Rep.	47	26	18	44	42	...	...	...	7	5	3	8	6
01-02—HC Pardubice	Czech Rep.	32	18	8	26	72	...	...	...	6	1	2	3	26

Season Team	League	GP	G	A	Pts.	PIM	+/-	PP	SH	Playoffs GP	G	A	Pts.	PIM
		REGULAR SEASON								PLAYOFFS				
02-03—HC Pardubice	Czech Rep.	45	18	18	36	86	...	...	...	19	7	7	14	39
03-04—HC Pardubice	Czech Rep.	48	23	23	46	20	...	...	...	7	1	0	1	6
04-05—HC Pardubice	Czech Rep.	43	25	10	35	28	...	...	...	16	3	2	5	33
05-06—HC Pardubice	Czech Rep.	28	11	14	25	46	...	...	...	—	—	—	—	—
—Washington	NHL	10	2	2	4	6	0	0	0	—	—	—	—	—
NHL Totals (2 years)		12	2	2	4	6	-1	0	0					

SYKORA, PETR — RW/LW

PERSONAL: Born November 19, 1976, in Plzen, Czech. ... 6-0/190. ... Shoots left. ... Name pronounced sih-KOHR-uh.

TRANSACTIONS/CAREER NOTES: Selected by New Jersey Devils in first round (first Devils pick, 18th overall) of entry draft (July 8, 1995). ... Injured back (February 21, 1996); missed two games. ... Injured groin (October 5, 1996); missed two games. ... Reinjured groin (November 9, 1996); missed four games. ... Reinjured groin (November 30, 1996); missed three games. ... Bruised shoulder (November 5, 1997); missed two games. ... Sprained left ankle (November 29, 1997); missed 20 games. ... Food poisoning (January 2, 1999); missed two games ... Flu (March 2, 2000); missed three games. ... Injured groin (October 26, 2000); missed three games. ... Reinjured groin (November 4, 2000); missed one game. ... Bruised shoulder (February 17, 2001); missed five games. ... Flu (December 26, 2001); missed three games. ... Bruised ribs (February 9, 2002); missed one game. ... Flu (March 20, 2002); missed five games. ... Traded by Devils with C Igor Pohanka, D Mike Commodore and G J.F. Damphousse to Anaheim Mighty Ducks for D Oleg Tverdovsky, LW Jeff Friesen and RW Maxin Balmochnykh (July 7, 2002). ... Strained groin (November 22, 2005); missed five games. ... Traded by Mighty Ducks to New York Rangers for D Maxim Kondratiev and fourth-round pick in 2007 draft (January 8, 2006).

Season Team	League	GP	G	A	Pts.	PIM	+/-	PP	SH	Playoffs GP	G	A	Pts.	PIM
		REGULAR SEASON								PLAYOFFS				
91-92—Skoda Plzen	Czech.	30	50	50	100	...	...	...	...	—	—	—	—	—
92-93—Skoda Plzen	Czech.	19	12	5	17	...	...	...	...	—	—	—	—	—
93-94—Skoda Plzen	Czech Rep.	37	10	16	26	...	...	...	...	4	0	1	1	...
—Cleveland	IHL	13	4	5	9	8	...	...	...	—	—	—	—	—
94-95—Detroit	IHL	29	12	17	29	16	10	3	0	—	—	—	—	—
95-96—Albany	AHL	5	4	1	5	0	...	...	...	—	—	—	—	—
—New Jersey	NHL	63	18	24	42	32	7	8	0	—	—	—	—	—
96-97—New Jersey	NHL	19	1	2	3	4	-8	0	0	2	0	0	0	2
—Albany	AHL	43	20	25	45	48	19	2	1	4	1	4	5	2
97-98—New Jersey	NHL	58	16	20	36	22	0	3	1	2	0	0	0	0
—Albany	AHL	2	4	1	5	0	...	...	...	—	—	—	—	—
98-99—New Jersey	NHL	80	29	43	72	22	16	15	0	7	3	3	6	4
99-00—New Jersey	NHL	79	25	43	68	26	24	5	1	23	9	8	17	10
00-01—New Jersey	NHL	73	35	46	81	32	36	9	2	25	10	12	22	12
01-02—New Jersey	NHL	73	21	27	48	44	12	4	0	4	0	1	1	0
—Czech Rep. Oly. team	Int'l	4	1	0	1	0	...	...	...	—	—	—	—	—
02-03—Anaheim	NHL	82	34	25	59	24	-7	15	1	21	4	9	13	12
03-04—Anaheim	NHL	81	23	29	52	34	-9	6	0	—	—	—	—	—
04-05—Metal. Magnitogorsk	Russian	45	18	13	31	46	20	...	...	5	2	3	5	8
05-06—Anaheim	NHL	34	7	13	20	28	1	1	0	—	—	—	—	—
—New York Rangers	NHL	40	16	15	31	22	5	7	0	4	0	0	0	0
NHL Totals (10 years)		682	225	287	512	290	77	73	5	88	26	33	59	40

SYVRET, DANNY — D

PERSONAL: Born June 13, 1985, in Millgrove, Ontario. ... 5-11/203. ... Shoots left.

TRANSACTIONS/CAREER NOTES: Selected by Edmonton Oilers in the 3rd round (81st overall) in NHL entry draft (July 30, 2005).

Season Team	League	GP	G	A	Pts.	PIM	+/-	PP	SH	Playoffs GP	G	A	Pts.	PIM
		REGULAR SEASON								PLAYOFFS				
02-03—London	OHL	68	8	14	22	31	...	...	...	14	1	6	7	11
03-04—London	OHL	68	3	28	31	32	...	...	...	15	1	6	7	4
04-05—London	OHL	62	23	46	69	33	...	...	...	18	5	15	20	4
05-06—Hamilton	AHL	62	0	20	20	38	-15	0	0	—	—	—	—	—
—Edmonton	NHL	10	0	0	0	6	-1	0	0	—	—	—	—	—
NHL Totals (1 year)		10	0	0	0	6	-1	0	0					

TAFFE, JEFF — C

PERSONAL: Born February 9, 1981, in Hastings, Minn. ... 6-3/201. ... Shoots left. ... Name pronounced TAYFE.

TRANSACTIONS/CAREER NOTES: Selected by St. Louis Blues in first round (first Blues pick, 30th overall) of entry draft (June 24, 2000). ... Traded by Blues with C Michal Handzus, RW Ladislav Nagy and first-round pick (LW Ben Eager) in 2002 to Phoenix Coyotes for LW Keith Tkachuk (March 13, 2001). ... Traded by Coyotes to New York Rangers for D Jamie Lundmark (October 18, 2005). ... Traded by Rangers to Phoenix for LW Martin Sonnenberg (January 24, 2006).

Season Team	League	GP	G	A	Pts.	PIM	+/-	PP	SH	Playoffs GP	G	A	Pts.	PIM
		REGULAR SEASON								PLAYOFFS				
98-99—Hastings H.S.	USHS (West)	25	38	48	86	26	...	...	...	—	—	—	—	—
99-00—Minnesota	WCHA	34	9	10	19	16	...	...	...	—	—	—	—	—
00-01—Minnesota	WCHA	38	12	23	35	56	...	...	...	—	—	—	—	—
01-02—Minnesota	WCHA	43	34	24	58	86	...	...	...	—	—	—	—	—
02-03—Springfield	AHL	57	23	26	49	44	-13	11	0	5	0	3	3	8
—Phoenix	NHL	20	3	1	4	4	-4	1	0	—	—	—	—	—
03-04—Phoenix	NHL	59	8	10	18	20	-8	5	0	—	—	—	—	—
—Springfield	AHL	15	10	6	16	19	-3	3	0	—	—	—	—	—
04-05—Utah	AHL	27	9	10	19	35	-19	4	0	—	—	—	—	—
05-06—Hartford	AHL	36	6	16	22	34	-6	3	0	—	—	—	—	—
—San Antonio	AHL	33	5	6	11	29	-13	3	0	—	—	—	—	—
—Phoenix	NHL	2	0	0	0	0	0	0	0	—	—	—	—	—
—New York Rangers	NHL	2	0	0	0	0	0	0	0	—	—	—	—	—
NHL Totals (3 years)		83	11	11	22	24	-12	6	0					

TALBOT, MAXIME C

PERSONAL: Born February 11, 1984, in Lemoyne, Que. ... 5-11/176. ... Shoots left.
TRANSACTIONS/CAREER NOTES: Selected by Pittsburgh Penguins in eighth round (ninth Penguins pick, 234th overall) of NHL entry draft (June 23, 2002).

		REGULAR SEASON								PLAYOFFS				
Season Team	League	GP	G	A	Pts.	PIM	+/-	PP	SH	GP	G	A	Pts.	PIM
00-01—Hull	QMJHL	24	6	7	13	60	...	...	...	—	—	—	—	—
—Rouyn-Noranda	QMJHL	40	9	15	24	78	...	...	...	—	—	—	—	—
01-02—Hull	QMJHL	65	24	36	60	174	...	...	...	—	—	—	—	—
02-03—Hull	QMJHL	69	46	58	104	130	...	...	...	20	14	30	44	33
03-04—Gatineau	QMJHL	51	25	73	98	41	...	...	...	15	11	16	27	0
04-05—Wilkes-Barre/Scranton	AHL	75	7	12	19	62	7	1	0	11	0	1	1	22
05-06—Wilkes-Barre/Scranton	AHL	42	12	20	32	80	12	2	2	11	3	6	9	16
—Pittsburgh	NHL	48	5	3	8	59	-12	0	2	—	—	—	—	—
NHL Totals (1 year)		48	5	3	8	59	-12	0	2					

TALLACKSON, BARRY RW

PERSONAL: Born April 14, 1983, in Grafton, N.D. ... 6-4/196. ... Shoots right.
COLLEGE: Minnesota.
TRANSACTIONS/CAREER NOTES: Selected by New Jersey Devils in second round (second Devils pick, 53rd overall) of entry draft (June 22, 2002).

		REGULAR SEASON								PLAYOFFS				
Season Team	League	GP	G	A	Pts.	PIM	+/-	PP	SH	GP	G	A	Pts.	PIM
99-00—U.S. National	USHL	53	14	6	20	90	...	...	...	—	—	—	—	—
00-01—U.S. National	USHL	63	23	24	47	77	...	...	...	—	—	—	—	—
01-02—Minnesota	WCHA	37	12	6	18	36	...	...	...	—	—	—	—	—
02-03—Minnesota	WCHA	32	9	14	23	18	...	...	...	—	—	—	—	—
03-04—Minnesota	WCHA	44	10	15	25	46	...	...	...	—	—	—	—	—
04-05—Albany	AHL	4	1	1	2	0	-1	0	0	—	—	—	—	—
—Minnesota	WCHA	36	11	8	19	54	...	...	...	—	—	—	—	—
05-06—Albany	AHL	60	14	23	37	62	-4	5	0	—	—	—	—	—
—New Jersey	NHL	10	1	1	2	2	-2	0	0	—	—	—	—	—
NHL Totals (1 year)		10	1	1	2	2	-2	0	0					

TALLINDER, HENRIK D

PERSONAL: Born January 10, 1979, in Stockholm, Sweden. ... 6-3/210. ... Shoots left.
TRANSACTIONS/CAREER NOTES: Selected by Buffalo Sabres in second round (second Sabres pick, 48th overall) of entry draft (June 21, 1997). ... Bruised shoulder (November 1, 2002); missed one game. ... Concussion, separated shoulder (November 7, 2002); missed 19 games. ... Sprained right ankle (February 8, 2003); missed 24 games. ... Broken arm (May 25); missed four playoff games.

		REGULAR SEASON								PLAYOFFS				
Season Team	League	GP	G	A	Pts.	PIM	+/-	PP	SH	GP	G	A	Pts.	PIM
96-97—AIK Solna Jrs.	Sweden	Statistics unavailable.												
—AIK Solna	Sweden	1	0	0	0	0	...	...	...	—	—	—	—	—
97-98—AIK Solna	Sweden	34	0	0	0	26	...	...	...	—	—	—	—	—
98-99—AIK Solna	Sweden	36	0	0	0	30	-5	...	...	—	—	—	—	—
99-00—AIK Solna	Sweden	50	0	2	2	59	...	...	...	—	—	—	—	—
00-01—TPS Turku	Finland	56	5	9	14	62	...	...	...	10	2	1	3	8
01-02—Rochester	AHL	73	6	14	20	26	11	1	0	2	0	0	0	0
—Buffalo	NHL	2	0	0	0	0	-1	0	0	—	—	—	—	—
02-03—Buffalo	NHL	46	3	10	13	28	-3	1	0	—	—	—	—	—
03-04—Buffalo	NHL	72	1	9	10	26	5	0	0	—	—	—	—	—
04-05—Bern	Switzerland	—	—	—	—	—	—	—	—	10	1	1	2	4
—Linkopings	Sweden	44	6	10	16	63	30	1	0	—	—	—	—	—
05-06—Buffalo	NHL	82	6	15	21	74	10	0	1	14	2	6	8	16
NHL Totals (4 years)		202	10	34	44	128	11	1	1	14	2	6	8	16

TAMBELLINI, JEFF LW

PERSONAL: Born April 13, 1984, in Calgary. ... 5-11/186. ... Shoots left. ... Son of Steve Tambellini, C, five NHL teams (1978-88) and current Canucks V.P. /assistant general manager.
COLLEGE: Michigan
TRANSACTIONS/CAREER NOTES: Selected by Los Angeles Kings in first round (third Kings pick, 27th overall) of entry draft (June 20, 2003). ... Signed by Kings to multiyear contract (August 15, 2005). ... Traded by Kings with D Denis Grebeshkov to New York Islanders for LW Mark Parrish and D Brent Sopel (March 8, 2006).

		REGULAR SEASON								PLAYOFFS				
Season Team	League	GP	G	A	Pts.	PIM	+/-	PP	SH	GP	G	A	Pts.	PIM
00-01—Chilliwack	BCJHL	54	21	30	51	13	...	...	...	—	—	—	—	—
01-02—Chilliwack	BCJHL	34	46	71	117	23	...	...	...	29	27	27	54	54
02-03—Univ. of Michigan	CCHA	43	26	19	45	24	...	...	...	—	—	—	—	—
03-04—Univ. of Michigan	CCHA	39	15	12	27	18	...	...	...	—	—	—	—	—
04-05—Univ. of Michigan	CCHA	42	24	33	57	32	...	...	...	—	—	—	—	—

Season Team	League	GP	G	A	Pts.	PIM	+/-	PP	SH	GP	G	A	Pts.	PIM
		REGULAR SEASON								PLAYOFFS				
05-06—Bridgeport	AHL	—	—	—	—	—	—	—	—	7	1	2	3	2
—Manchester	AHL	56	25	31	56	26	17	6	0	—	—	—	—	—
—Los Angeles	NHL	4	0	0	0	2	-1	0	0	—	—	—	—	—
—New York Islanders	NHL	21	1	3	4	8	2	0	0	—	—	—	—	—
NHL Totals (1 year)		25	1	3	4	10	1	0	0					

TANABE, DAVID D

PERSONAL: Born July 19, 1980, in White Bear Lake, Minn. ... 6-1/212. ... Shoots right. ... Name pronounced tuh-nah-BEE.
TRANSACTIONS/CAREER NOTES: Selected by Carolina Hurricanes in first round (first Hurricanes pick, 16th overall) of entry draft (June 26, 1999). ... Concussion (October 18, 2000); missed five games. ... Hip pointer (March 2, 2001); missed three games. ... Flu (October 13, 2001); missed one game. ... Injured oblique muscle (October 23, 2002); missed two games. ... Injured shoulder (November 15, 2002); missed seven games. ... Reinjured shoulder (December 4, 2002); missed five games. ... Traded by Hurricanes to Phoenix Coyotes with D Igor Knyazev for D Danny Markov and conditional fourth-round pick (RW Roman Tumanek) in 2004 draft (June 21, 2003). ... Injured knee (January 18, 2004) and had surgery (January 28, 2004); missed remainder of season. ... Traded by Coyotes to Boston Bruins for C Dave Scatchard (November 18, 2005). ... Pulled oblique muscle (March 14, 2006); missed two games. ... Torn ACL (April 6, 2006); missed final six games of regular season.

Season Team	League	GP	G	A	Pts.	PIM	+/-	PP	SH	GP	G	A	Pts.	PIM
		REGULAR SEASON								PLAYOFFS				
97-98—U.S. National	NAHL	73	8	21	29	96	...	1	0	—	—	—	—	—
98-99—Wisconsin	WCHA	35	10	12	22	44	...	...	...	—	—	—	—	—
99-00—Carolina	NHL	31	4	0	4	14	-4	3	0	—	—	—	—	—
—Cincinnati	IHL	32	0	13	13	14	...	...	...	11	1	4	5	6
00-01—Carolina	NHL	74	7	22	29	42	-9	5	0	6	2	0	2	12
01-02—Carolina	NHL	78	1	15	16	35	-13	0	0	1	0	1	1	0
02-03—Carolina	NHL	68	3	10	13	24	-27	2	0	—	—	—	—	—
03-04—Phoenix	NHL	45	5	7	12	22	4	2	0	—	—	—	—	—
04-05—Rapperswil	Switzerland	8	4	5	9	4	...	3	0	—	—	—	—	—
—Kloten	Switzerland	20	3	7	10	18	...	1	0	5	1	4	5	8
05-06—Phoenix	NHL	21	0	4	4	8	-5	0	0	—	—	—	—	—
—Boston	NHL	54	4	12	16	48	0	0	0	—	—	—	—	—
NHL Totals (6 years)		371	24	70	94	193	-54	12	0	7	2	1	3	12

T

TANGUAY, ALEX LW

PERSONAL: Born November 21, 1979, in Ste-Justine, Que. ... 6-1/190. ... Shoots left. ... Name pronounced tan-GAY.
TRANSACTIONS/CAREER NOTES: Selected by Colorado Avalanche in first round (first Avalanche pick, 12th overall) of entry draft (June 27, 1998). ... Strained neck (March 14, 2000); missed six games. ... Sinus infection (November 10, 2001); missed six games. ... Bruised ankle (December 23, 2001); missed one game. ... Reinjured ankle (December 27, 2001); missed three games. ... Bruised hip (January 29, 2002); missed two games. ... Groin (December 19, 2003); missed two games. ... Knee (March 12, 2004); missed 11 games. ... Hip flexor (February 12, 2006); missed one game. ... Sprained knee (March 21, 2006); missed 10 games. ... Traded by Avalanche to Calgary Flames for D Jordan Leopold and a second-round pick (C Codey Burki) in 2006 entry draft and a conditional draft choice (June 24, 2006).
STATISTICAL PLATEAUS: Three-goal games: 2002-03 (1), 2003-04 (1). Total: 2.

Season Team	League	GP	G	A	Pts.	PIM	+/-	PP	SH	GP	G	A	Pts.	PIM
		REGULAR SEASON								PLAYOFFS				
96-97—Halifax	QMJHL	70	27	41	68	50	...	...	...	12	4	8	12	8
97-98—Halifax	QMJHL	51	47	38	85	32	-6	13	3	5	7	6	13	4
98-99—Halifax	QMJHL	31	27	34	61	30	28	10	2	5	1	2	3	2
—Hershey	AHL	5	1	2	3	2	-2	0	0	5	0	2	2	0
99-00—Colorado	NHL	76	17	34	51	22	6	5	0	17	2	1	3	2
00-01—Colorado	NHL	82	27	50	77	37	35	7	1	23	6	15	21	8
01-02—Colorado	NHL	70	13	35	48	36	8	7	0	19	5	8	13	0
02-03—Colorado	NHL	82	26	41	67	36	34	3	0	7	1	2	3	4
03-04—Colorado	NHL	69	25	54	79	42	30	7	0	8	2	2	4	2
04-05—Lugano	Switzerland	6	3	3	6	4	...	1	0	—	—	—	—	—
05-06—Colorado	NHL	71	29	49	78	46	8	8	0	9	2	4	6	12
NHL Totals (6 years)		450	137	263	400	219	121	37	1	83	18	32	50	28

TARNASKY, NICK C

PERSONAL: Born November 25, 1984, in Caroline, Alta. ... 6-2/233. ... Shoots left.
TRANSACTIONS/CAREER NOTES: Selected by Tampa Bay Lightning in ninth round (11th Lightning pick, 287th overall) of NHL entry draft (June 21, 2003).

Season Team	League	GP	G	A	Pts.	PIM	+/-	PP	SH	GP	G	A	Pts.	PIM
		REGULAR SEASON								PLAYOFFS				
01-02—Vancouver	WHL	10	1	0	1	5	...	...	...	—	—	—	—	—
02-03—Kelowna	WHL	39	4	12	16	39	...	...	...	—	—	—	—	—
—Lethbridge	WHL	30	5	8	13	45	...	...	...	—	—	—	—	—
03-04—Lethbridge	WHL	71	26	23	49	108	...	...	...	—	—	—	—	—
04-05—Springfield	AHL	80	7	10	17	176	...	...	...	—	—	—	—	—
05-06—Springfield	AHL	68	14	9	23	100	-8	3	0	—	—	—	—	—
—Tampa Bay	NHL	12	0	1	1	4	-3	0	0	—	—	—	—	—
NHL Totals (1 year)		12	0	1	1	4	-3	0	0					

TARNSTROM, DICK — D

PERSONAL: Born January 20, 1975, in Sundbyberg, Sweden. ... 6-2/205. ... Shoots left.

TRANSACTIONS/CAREER NOTES: Selected by New York Islanders in 11th round (12th Islanders pick, 272nd overall) of entry draft (June 29, 1994). ... Wrist (March 27, 2002); missed seven games. ... Claimed off waivers by Pittsburgh Penguins (August 6, 2002). ... Foot (November 30, 2002); missed 15 games. ... Hamstring (January 7, 2003); missed two games. ... Hip (March 20, 2003); missed three games. ... Flu (January 3, 2004); missed one game. ... Flu (January 29, 2004); missed one game. ... Knee (October 27, 2005); missed 12 games. ... Flu (December 23, 2005); missed one game. ... Traded by Penguins to Edmonton Oilers for D Cory Cross and RW Jani Rita (January 26, 2006). ... Ill (February 4, 2006); missed one game. ... Respiratory infection (February 7, 2006); missed three games. ... Groin (March 12, 2006); missed five games. ... Hip (April 27, 2006); missed one playoff game.

		REGULAR SEASON								PLAYOFFS				
Season Team	League	GP	G	A	Pts.	PIM	+/-	PP	SH	GP	G	A	Pts.	PIM
92-93—AIK	Sweden	3	0	0	0	0	...	...	...	—	—	—	—	—
93-94—AIK	Sweden	33	1	4	5	...	...	...	...	—	—	—	—	—
94-95—AIK	Sweden	37	8	4	12	26	...	...	...	—	—	—	—	—
95-96—AIK	Sweden	40	0	5	5	32	...	...	...	—	—	—	—	—
96-97—AIK	Sweden	49	5	3	8	38	...	...	...	7	0	1	1	6
97-98—AIK Solna	Sweden	45	2	12	14	30	...	...	...	—	—	—	—	—
98-99—AIK Solna	Sweden	47	9	14	23	36	...	...	...	—	—	—	—	—
99-00—AIK Solna	Sweden	42	7	15	22	20	...	...	...	—	—	—	—	—
00-01—AIK Solna	Sweden	50	10	18	28	28	...	...	...	5	0	0	0	8
01-02—Bridgeport	AHL	9	0	2	2	2	3	0	0	—	—	—	—	—
—New York Islanders	NHL	62	3	16	19	38	-12	0	0	5	0	0	0	2
02-03—Pittsburgh	NHL	61	7	34	41	50	-11	3	0	—	—	—	—	—
03-04—Pittsburgh	NHL	80	16	36	52	38	-37	12	0	—	—	—	—	—
04-05—Sodertalje	Sweden Dv. 2	50	7	18	25	46	-5	2	0	9	1	0	1	6
05-06—Pittsburgh	NHL	33	5	5	10	52	-10	4	0	—	—	—	—	—
—Edmonton	NHL	22	1	3	4	24	-5	0	0	12	0	2	2	10
NHL Totals (4 years)		258	32	94	126	202	-75	19	0	17	0	2	2	12

TATICEK, PETR — C

PERSONAL: Born September 22, 1983, in Rakovnik, Czechoslovakia. ... 6-2/188. ... Shoots left. ... Name pronounced TA-tih-chehk.

TRANSACTIONS/CAREER NOTES: Selected by Florida Panthers in first round (second Panthers pick, ninth overall) of NHL entry draft (June 22, 2002). ... Traded by Panthers to Pittsburgh Penguins for D Richard Jackman (March 9, 2006).

		REGULAR SEASON								PLAYOFFS				
Season Team	League	GP	G	A	Pts.	PIM	+/-	PP	SH	GP	G	A	Pts.	PIM
00-01—HC Kladno	Czech Rep.	3	0	0	0	0	...	...	...	—	—	—	—	—
01-02—Sault Ste. Marie	OHL	60	21	42	63	32	...	...	...	6	3	3	6	4
02-03—Sault Ste. Marie	OHL	54	12	45	57	44	...	...	...	4	1	0	1	0
03-04—San Antonio	AHL	63	4	15	19	6	-10	1	0	—	—	—	—	—
04-05—San Antonio	AHL	67	7	15	22	21	-9	0	0	—	—	—	—	—
—Laredo	CHL	4	2	5	7	0	...	...	...	—	—	—	—	—
05-06—Houston	AHL	44	9	21	30	10	11	4	0	—	—	—	—	—
—Florida	NHL	3	0	0	0	0	0	0	0	—	—	—	—	—
—Wilkes-Barre/Scranton	AHL	17	4	4	8	7	0	4	0	1	0	0	0	2
NHL Totals (1 year)		3	0	0	0	0	0	0	0					

TAYLOR, TIM — C

PERSONAL: Born February 6, 1969, in Stratford, Ont. ... 6-1/190. ... Shoots left. ... Brother of Chris Taylor, C, Buffalo Sabres organization.

TRANSACTIONS/CAREER NOTES: Selected by Washington Capitals in second round (second Capitals pick, 36th overall) of NHL draft (June 11, 1988). ... Traded by Capitals to Vancouver Canucks for C Eric Murano (January 29, 1993). ... Signed as free agent by Detroit Red Wings (July 28, 1993). ... Injured right shoulder (April 5, 1996); missed three games. ... Sprained shoulder (October 15, 1996); missed 16 games. ... Flu (April 9, 1997); missed two games. ... Selected by Boston Bruins from Red Wings in waiver draft (September 28, 1997). ... Injured ribs (March 21, 1998); missed one game. ... Injured hip (March 22, 1998); missed two games. ... Sprained ankle (October 14, 1998); missed 12 games. ... Reinjured ankle (November 13, 1998); missed six games. ... Reinjured ankle (December 10, 1998); missed 14 games. ... Strained groin (April 17, 1999); missed final game of season. ... Signed as free agent by New York Rangers (July 15, 1999). ... Suffered concussion (October 2, 1999); missed two games. ... Injured hand (October 20, 1999); missed one game. ... Injured rib (November 24, 1999); missed one game. ... Flu (February 13, 2000); missed two games. ... Injured shoulder (November 28, 2000); missed one game. ... Tore abdominal muscle (December 31, 2000); missed remainder of season. ... Traded by Rangers to Tampa Bay Lightning for LW Nils Ekman and LW Kyle Freadrich (July 1, 2001). ... Strained groin (January 3, 2002); missed four games. ... Reinjured groin (January 18, 2002); missed four games. ... Reinjured groin (February 4, 2002); missed four games. ... Reinjured groin (March 2, 2002); missed remainder of season.

		REGULAR SEASON								PLAYOFFS				
Season Team	League	GP	G	A	Pts.	PIM	+/-	PP	SH	GP	G	A	Pts.	PIM
86-87—London	OHL	34	7	9	16	11	...	...	...	—	—	—	—	—
87-88—London	OHL	64	46	50	96	66	...	...	...	12	9	9	18	26
88-89—London	OHL	61	34	80	114	93	...	...	...	21	21	25	46	58
89-90—Baltimore	AHL	74	22	21	43	63	...	...	...	9	2	2	4	13
90-91—Baltimore	AHL	79	25	42	67	75	...	...	...	5	0	1	1	4
91-92—Baltimore	AHL	65	9	18	27	131	...	...	...	—	—	—	—	—
92-93—Baltimore	AHL	41	15	16	31	49	-7	2	1	—	—	—	—	—
—Hamilton	AHL	36	15	22	37	37	-10	5	1	—	—	—	—	—
93-94—Adirondack	AHL	79	36	81	117	86	23	13	3	12	2	10	12	12
—Detroit	NHL	1	1	0	1	0	-1	0	0	—	—	—	—	—
94-95—Detroit	NHL	22	0	4	4	16	3	0	0	6	0	1	1	12
95-96—Detroit	NHL	72	11	14	25	39	11	1	1	18	0	4	4	4
96-97—Detroit	NHL	44	3	4	7	52	-6	0	1	2	0	0	0	0

Season Team	League	GP	G	A	Pts.	PIM	+/-	PP	SH	GP	G	A	Pts.	PIM
		REGULAR SEASON								PLAYOFFS				
97-98—Boston	NHL	79	20	11	31	57	-16	1	3	6	0	0	0	10
98-99—Boston	NHL	49	4	7	11	55	-10	0	0	12	0	3	3	8
99-00—New York Rangers	NHL	76	9	11	20	72	-4	0	0	—	—	—	—	—
00-01—New York Rangers	NHL	38	2	5	7	16	-6	0	0	—	—	—	—	—
01-02—Tampa Bay	NHL	48	4	4	8	25	-2	0	1	—	—	—	—	—
02-03—Tampa Bay	NHL	82	4	8	12	38	-13	0	0	11	0	1	1	6
03-04—Tampa Bay	NHL	82	7	15	22	25	-5	0	0	23	2	3	5	31
05-06—Tampa Bay	NHL	82	7	6	13	22	-12	0	0	5	0	0	0	2
NHL Totals (12 years)		675	72	89	161	417	-61	2	6	83	2	12	14	73

TELLQVIST, MIKAEL G

PERSONAL: Born September 19, 1979, in Sundbyberg, Sweden. ... 5-11/185. ... Name pronounced TEHL-kvihst.
TRANSACTIONS/CAREER NOTES: Selected by Toronto Maple Leafs in third round (third Maple Leafs pick, 70th overall) of NHL entry draft (June 24, 2000).

Season Team	League	GP	Min.	W	L	OTL	T	GA	SO	GAA	SV%	GP	Min.	W	L	GA	SO	GAA	SV%
		REGULAR SEASON										PLAYOFFS							
98-99 —Djurgarden Stockholm	Sweden	3	124	...	...	...	...	8	0	3.87	...	4	240	...	...	11	0	2.75	...
99-00 —Djurgarden Stockholm	Sweden	30	1909	...	...	...	...	66	2	2.07	...	13	814	...	...	21	3	1.55	...
00-01 —Djurgarden Stockholm	Sweden	43	2622	...	...	...	...	91	5	2.08	...	16	1006	...	...	45	1	2.68	...
01-02 —St. John's	AHL	28	1521	8	11	...	6	79	0	3.12	.900	1	14	1	0	0	0	0.00	1.00
02-03 —St. John's	AHL	47	2651	17	25	...	3	148	1	3.35	.910	—	—	—	—	—	—	—	—
—Toronto	NHL	3	86	1	1	...	0	4	0	2.79	.895	—	—	—	—	—	—	—	—
03-04 —Toronto	NHL	11	647	5	3	...	2	31	0	2.87	.894	—	—	—	—	—	—	—	—
—St. John's	AHL	23	1342	10	11	...	1	60	1	2.68	.912	—	—	—	—	—	—	—	—
04-05 —St. John's	AHL	45	2599	24	16	...	...	115	0	2.65	.921	5	253	1	4	15	0	3.56	.899
05-06 —Toronto	NHL	25	1399	10	11	2	...	73	2	3.13	.895	—	—	—	—	—	—	—	—
—Swedish Oly. team	Int'l	1	...	...	...	...	...	...	...	3.00	.903	—	—	—	—	—	—	—	—
NHL Totals (3 years)		39	2132	16	15	2	2	108	2	3.04	.895								

TENUTE, JOEY C

PERSONAL: Born April 2, 1983, in Hamilton, Ont. ... 5-9/180. ... Shoots left.
TRANSACTIONS/CAREER NOTES: Selected by New Jersey Devils in eighth round (sixth Devils pick, 261st overall) of NHL entry draft (June 21, 2003). ... Signed as free agent by Washington Capitals (November 21, 2005).

Season Team	League	GP	G	A	Pts.	PIM	+/-	PP	SH	GP	G	A	Pts.	PIM
		REGULAR SEASON								PLAYOFFS				
00-01—Barrie	OHL	61	13	18	31	38	...	...	...	—	—	—	—	—
01-02—Barrie	OHL	66	19	31	50	76	...	...	...	20	7	7	14	28
02-03—Sarnia	OHL	68	41	71	112	75	...	...	...	3	1	2	3	0
03-04—Sarnia	OHL	58	22	56	78	70	8	8	1	3	2	2	4	17
04-05—South Carolina	ECHL	68	34	41	75	102	...	...	...	4	2	1	3	0
05-06—Hershey	AHL	61	20	30	50	60	3	7	0	13	0	2	2	8
—Washington	NHL	1	0	0	0	0	0	0	0	—	—	—	—	—
NHL Totals (1 year)		1	0	0	0	0	0	0	0					

THEODORE, JOSE G

PERSONAL: Born September 13, 1976, in Laval, Que. ... 5-11/180. ... Catches right. ... Name pronounced JO-zhay THEE-uh-dohr.
TRANSACTIONS/CAREER NOTES: Selected by Montreal Canadiens in second round (second Canadiens pick, 44th overall) of entry draft (June 28, 1994). ... Strained groin (March 29, 2000); missed three games. ... Concussion (October 26, 2001); missed four games. ... Injured hip (November 18, 2002); missed two games. ... Bruised left knee (December 17, 2005); missed one game. ... Fractured heel (February 16, 2006); missed 18 games. ... Traded by Canadiens to Avalanche for G David Aebischer (March 8, 2006).

Season Team	League	GP	Min.	W	L	OTL	T	GA	SO	GAA	SV%	GP	Min.	W	L	GA	SO	GAA	SV%
		REGULAR SEASON										PLAYOFFS							
92-93—St. Jean	QMJHL	34	1776	12	16	...	2	112	0	3.78	...	3	175	0	2	11	0	3.77	...
93-94—St. Jean	QMJHL	57	3225	20	29	...	6	194	0	3.61	.885	5	296	1	4	18	1	3.65	.910
94-95—Hull	QMJHL	58	3348	32	22	...	2	193	5	3.46	.890	21	1263	15	6	59	1	2.80	.898
—Fredericton	AHL	...	...	...	...	...	...	...	...	...	...	1	60	0	1	3	0	3.00	.897
95-96—Hull	QMJHL	48	2803	33	11	...	2	158	0	3.38	...	5	300	2	3	20	0	4.00	...
—Montreal	NHL	1	9	0	0	...	0	1	0	6.67	.500	—	—	—	—	—	—	—	—
96-97—Fredericton	AHL	26	1469	12	12	...	0	87	0	3.55	.898	—	—	—	—	—	—	—	—
—Montreal	NHL	16	821	5	6	...	2	53	0	3.87	.896	2	168	1	1	7	0	2.50	.935
97-98—Fredericton	AHL	53	3053	20	23	...	8	145	2	2.85	.918	4	237	1	3	13	0	3.29	.901
—Montreal	NHL	...	...	...	...	...	...	...	...	...	...	3	120	0	1	1	0	0.50	.971
98-99—Montreal	NHL	18	913	4	12	...	0	50	1	3.29	.877	—	—	—	—	—	—	—	—
—Fredericton	AHL	27	1609	12	13	...	2	77	2	2.87	.917	13	694	8	5	35	1	3.03	.926
99-00—Montreal	NHL	30	1655	12	13	...	2	58	5	2.10	†.919	—	—	—	—	—	—	—	—
00-01—Quebec	AHL	3	180	3	0	...	0	9	0	3.00	.886	—	—	—	—	—	—	—	—
—Montreal	NHL	59	3298	20	29	...	5	141	2	2.57	.909	—	—	—	—	—	—	—	—
01-02—Montreal	NHL	67	3864	30	24	...	10	136	7	2.11	*.931	12	686	6	6	35	0	3.06	.915
02-03—Montreal	NHL	57	3419	20	31	...	6	165	2	2.90	.908	—	—	—	—	—	—	—	—
03-04—Montreal	NHL	67	3961	33	28	...	5	150	6	2.27	.919	11	678	4	7	27	1	2.39	.919

T

Season Team	League	GP	Min.	W	L	OTL	T	GA	SO	GAA	SV%	GP	Min.	W	L	GA	SO	GAA	SV%
		REGULAR SEASON										PLAYOFFS							
04-05—Djurgarden Stockholm	Sweden	17	1024	...	...	...	...	42	0	2.46	.917	12	728	...	...	27	0	2.23	.922
05-06—Montreal	NHL	38	2114	17	15	5	...	122	0	3.46	.881	—	—	—	—	—	—	—	—
—Colorado	NHL	5	296	1	3	1	...	15	0	3.04	.887	9	573	4	5	29	0	3.04	.902
NHL Totals (10 years)		358	20350	142	161	6	30	891	23	2.63	.911	37	2225	15	20	99	1	2.67	.916

THERIEN, CHRIS D

PERSONAL: Born December 14, 1971, in Ottawa. ... 6-5/250. ... Shoots left. ... Name pronounced TAIR-ee-uhn.

TRANSACTIONS/CAREER NOTES: Selected by Philadelphia Flyers in 3ird round (seventh Flyers pick, 47th overall) of ntry draft (June 16, 1990). ... Flu (November 3, 1997); missed one game. ... Sprained left knee (April 8, 1998); missed three games. ... Strained shoulder (October 9, 1998); missed first three games of season. ... Bruised left thigh (December 13, 1998); missed three games. ... Back (September 14, 2000). ... Back (October 17, 2000); missed eight games. ... Concussion (November 15, 2001); missed five games. ... Strained back (November 23, 2002); missed six games. ... Concussion (January 3, 2003); missed four games. ... Strained trunk muscle (February 20, 2003); missed four games. ... Back spasms (December 6, 2003); missed three games. ... Back spasms (December 30, 2003); missed three games. ... Strained left shoulder (March 5, 2004); missed one game. ... Traded by Flyers to Dallas Stars for eighth-round pick (G Martin Houle) in 2004 draft and third-round pick (later traded to Tampa Bay; Lightning picked F Chris Lawrence) in 2005 draft (March 8, 2004). ... Signed as free agent by Flyers (August 2, 2005). ... Back spasms (October 7, 2005); missed three games. ... Sore back (January 9, 2006); missed two games. ... Concussion (February 4, 2006); missed one month.

Season Team	League	GP	G	A	Pts.	PIM	+/-	PP	SH	GP	G	A	Pts.	PIM
		REGULAR SEASON								PLAYOFFS				
89-90—Northwood School	N.Y. H.S.	31	35	37	72	54	...	...	...	—	—	—	—	—
90-91—Providence College	Hockey East	36	4	18	22	36	...	...	...	—	—	—	—	—
91-92—Providence College	Hockey East	36	16	25	41	38	...	...	...	—	—	—	—	—
92-93—Providence College	Hockey East	33	8	11	19	52	...	...	...	—	—	—	—	—
—Canadian nat'l team	Int'l	8	1	4	5	8	...	...	...	—	—	—	—	—
93-94—Canadian nat'l team	Int'l	59	7	15	22	46	...	...	...	—	—	—	—	—
—Can. Olympic team	Int'l	4	0	0	0	4	1	0	0	—	—	—	—	—
—Hershey	AHL	6	0	0	0	2	-2	0	0	—	—	—	—	—
94-95—Hershey	AHL	34	3	13	16	27	-2	1	0	—	—	—	—	—
—Philadelphia	NHL	48	3	10	13	38	8	1	0	15	0	0	0	10
95-96—Philadelphia	NHL	82	6	17	23	89	16	3	0	12	0	0	0	18
96-97—Philadelphia	NHL	71	2	22	24	64	27	0	0	19	1	6	7	6
97-98—Philadelphia	NHL	78	3	16	19	80	5	1	0	5	0	1	1	4
98-99—Philadelphia	NHL	74	3	15	18	48	16	1	0	6	0	0	0	6
99-00—Philadelphia	NHL	80	4	9	13	66	11	1	0	18	0	1	1	12
00-01—Philadelphia	NHL	73	2	12	14	48	22	1	0	6	1	0	1	8
01-02—Philadelphia	NHL	77	4	10	14	30	16	0	2	5	0	0	0	2
02-03—Philadelphia	NHL	67	1	6	7	36	10	0	0	13	0	2	2	2
03-04—Philadelphia	AHL	2	0	0	0	0	-1	0	0	—	—	—	—	—
—Philadelphia	NHL	56	1	9	10	50	2	0	0	—	—	—	—	—
—Dallas	NHL	11	0	0	0	2	4	0	0	5	2	0	2	0
05-06—Philadelphia	NHL	47	0	4	4	34	-7	0	0	—	—	—	—	—
NHL Totals (11 years)		764	29	130	159	585	130	8	2	104	4	10	14	68

THIBAULT, JOCELYN G

PERSONAL: Born January 12, 1975, in Montreal. ... 5-11/169. ... Catches left. ... Name pronounced TEE-boh.

TRANSACTIONS/CAREER NOTES: Selected by Quebec Nordiques in first round (first Nordiques pick, 10th overall) of entry draft (June 26, 1993). ... Sprained shoulder (March 28, 1995); missed 10 games. ... Nordiques franchise moved to Colorado and renamed Avalanche for 1995-96 season (June 21, 1995). ... Traded by Avalanche with LW Martin Rucinsky and RW Andrei Kovalenko to Montreal Canadiens for G Patrick Roy and RW Mike Keane (December 6, 1995). ... Bruised right hand (February 21, 1996); missed two games. ... Fractured finger (October 24, 1996); missed nine games. ... Flu (February 3, 1997); missed two games. ... Bruised collarbone (January 8, 1998); missed one game. ... Traded by Canadiens with D Dave Manson and D Brad Brown to Chicago Blackhawks for G Jeff Hackett, D Eric Weinrich, D Alain Nasreddine and fourth-round pick (D Chris Dyment) in 1999 draft (November 16, 1998). ... Fractured finger (November 27, 1999); missed six games. ... Flu (December 10, 2000); missed one game. ... Concussion (March 23, 2003); missed nine games. ... Injured hip (November 10, 2003) and had surgery (November 16, 2003); missed 60 games. ... Traded by Blackhawks to Penguins for fourth-round pick (D Ben Shutron) in 2006 draft (August 10, 2005). ... Knee injury (October 8, 2005); missed four games. ... Torn cartilage in left hip (January 4, 2006) and surgery (January 11, 2006); missed final 40 games of regular season.

Season Team	League	GP	Min.	W	L	OTL	T	GA	SO	GAA	SV%	GP	Min.	W	L	GA	SO	GAA	SV%
		REGULAR SEASON										PLAYOFFS							
91-92—Trois-Rivieres	QMJHL	30	1497	14	7	...	1	77	0	3.09	...	3	110	1	1	4	0	2.18	...
92-93—Sherbrooke	QMJHL	56	3190	34	14	...	5	159	3	2.99	.904	15	883	9	6	57	0	3.87	.862
93-94—Quebec	NHL	29	1504	8	13	...	3	83	0	3.31	.892	—	—	—	—	—	—	—	—
—Cornwall	AHL	4	240	4	0	...	0	9	1	2.25	.930	—	—	—	—	—	—	—	—
94-95—Sherbrooke	QMJHL	13	776	6	6	...	1	38	1	2.94	.903	—	—	—	—	—	—	—	—
—Quebec	NHL	18	898	12	2	...	2	35	1	2.34	.917	3	148	1	2	8	0	3.24	.895
95-96—Colorado	NHL	10	558	3	4	...	2	28	0	3.01	.888	—	—	—	—	—	—	—	—
—Montreal	NHL	40	2334	23	13	...	3	110	3	2.83	.913	6	311	2	4	18	0	3.47	.904
96-97—Montreal	NHL	61	3397	22	24	...	11	164	1	2.90	.910	3	179	0	3	13	0	4.36	.871
97-98—Montreal	NHL	47	2652	19	15	...	8	109	2	2.47	.902	2	43	0	0	4	0	5.58	.750
98-99—Montreal	NHL	10	529	3	4	...	2	23	1	2.61	.908	—	—	—	—	—	—	—	—
—Chicago	NHL	52	3014	21	26	...	5	136	4	2.71	.905	—	—	—	—	—	—	—	—
99-00—Chicago	NHL	60	3438	25	26	...	7	158	3	2.76	.906	—	—	—	—	—	—	—	—
00-01—Chicago	NHL	66	3844	27	32	...	7	†180	6	2.81	.895	—	—	—	—	—	—	—	—
01-02—Chicago	NHL	67	3838	33	23	...	9	159	6	2.49	.902	3	159	1	2	7	0	2.64	.909

Season Team	League	GP	Min.	W	L	OTL	T	GA	SO	GAA	SV%	GP	Min.	W	L	GA	SO	GAA	SV%
		REGULAR SEASON										PLAYOFFS							
02-03—Chicago	NHL	62	3650	26	28	...	7	144	8	2.37	.915	—	—	—	—	—	—	—	—
03-04—Chicago	NHL	14	821	5	7	...	2	39	1	2.85	.913	—	—	—	—	—	—	—	—
05-06—Pittsburgh	NHL	16	807	1	9	3	...	60	0	4.46	.876	—	—	—	—	—	—	—	—
NHL Totals (12 years)		552	31284	228	226	3	68	1428	36	2.74	.904	17	840	4	11	50	0	3.57	.891

THOMAS, BILL — RW

PERSONAL: Born June 20, 1983, in Pittsburgh, Pa. ... 6-1/185. ... Shoots right.
TRANSACTIONS/CAREER NOTES: Signed as free agent by Phoenix Coyotes (March 27, 2006).

Season Team	League	GP	G	A	Pts.	PIM	+/-	PP	SH	GP	G	A	Pts.	PIM
		REGULAR SEASON								PLAYOFFS				
03-04—Tri-City	USHL	60	31	38	69	30	...	...	...	9	8	6	14	4
04-05—U. of Neb.-Omaha	NCAA	39	19	26	45	12	...	...	...	—	—	—	—	—
05-06—Phoenix	NHL	9	1	2	3	8	-2	1	0	—	—	—	—	—
—U. of Neb.-Omaha	NCAA	41	27	23	50	43	...	...	...	—	—	—	—	—
NHL Totals (1 year)		9	1	2	3	8	-2	1	0					

THOMAS, TIM — G

PERSONAL: Born April 14, 1974, in Davison, Mich. ... 5-11/181. ... Catches left.
TRANSACTIONS/CAREER NOTES: Selected by Quebec Nordiques in ninth round (11th Nordiques pick, 217th overall) of entry draft (June 29, 1994). ... Nordiques franchise moved to Colorado and renamed Avalanche for 1995-96 season (June 21, 1995). ... Signed as free agent by Edmonton Oilers (June 4, 1998). ... Signed as free agent by Boston Bruins (August 8, 2002).

Season Team	League	GP	Min.	W	L	OTL	T	GA	SO	GAA	SV%	GP	Min.	W	L	GA	SO	GAA	SV%
		REGULAR SEASON										PLAYOFFS							
92-93 —Lakeland	Tier II	27	1580	...	...	...	...	87	...	3.30	...	—	—	—	—	—	—	—	—
93-94 —Vermont	ECAC	33	1863	15	11	...	6	95	1	3.06	...	—	—	—	—	—	—	—	—
94-95 —Vermont	ECAC	34	2011	18	14	...	2	90	3	2.69	.914	—	—	—	—	—	—	—	—
95-96 —Vermont	ECAC	37	2254	26	7	...	4	88	3	2.34	...	—	—	—	—	—	—	—	—
96-97 —Vermont	ECAC	36	2158	22	11	...	3	101	2	2.81	.914	—	—	—	—	—	—	—	—
97-98 —Birmingham	ECHL	6	360	4	1	...	1	13	1	2.17	...	—	—	—	—	—	—	—	—
—Houston	IHL	1	60	0	1	...	0	4	0	4.00	.852	—	—	—	—	—	—	—	—
—HIFK Helsinki	Finland	22	1035	22	4	...	1	28	2	1.62	...	9	551	9	0	14	3	1.52	...
98-99 —Hamilton	AHL	15	837	6	8	...	0	45	0	3.23	.905	—	—	—	—	—	—	—	—
—HIFK Helsinki	Finland	14	833	8	3	...	3	31	2	2.23	...	11	658	7	4	25	...	2.28	...
99-00 —Detroit	IHL	36	2020	15	21	...	3	120	1	3.56	...	—	—	—	—	—	—	—	—
00-01 —AIK Solna	Sweden	43	2542	...	...	...	...	105	3	2.48	...	5	299	...	...	20	0	4.01	...
01-02 —Karpat Oulu	Finland	32	1937	15	12	...	5	79	...	2.45	...	3	180	1	2	12	0	4.00	...
02-03 —Providence	AHL	35	2048	18	12	...	5	98	1	2.87	.906	—	—	—	—	—	—	—	—
—Boston	NHL	4	220	3	1	...	0	11	0	3.00	.907	—	—	—	—	—	—	—	—
03-04 —Providence	AHL	43	2549	20	16	...	6	78	9	1.84	.938	2	84	0	2	10	0	7.14	.474
04-05 —Jokerit Helsinki	Finland	54	3267	34	13	...	7	86	15	1.58	.946	12	721	8	4	22	0	1.83	.938
05-06 —Providence	AHL	26	1515	15	11	0	...	57	1	2.26	.923	—	—	—	—	—	—	—	—
—Boston	NHL	38	2187	12	13	10	...	101	1	2.77	.917	—	—	—	—	—	—	—	—
NHL Totals (2 years)		42	2407	15	14	10	0	112	1	2.79	.916								

THORBURN, CHRIS — C

PERSONAL: Born June 3, 1983, in Sault Ste. Marie, Ont. ... 6-3/207. ... Shoots right.
TRANSACTIONS/CAREER NOTES: Selected by Buffalo Sabres in second round (third Sabres pick, 50th overall) of NHL entry draft (June 23, 2001).

Season Team	League	GP	G	A	Pts.	PIM	+/-	PP	SH	GP	G	A	Pts.	PIM
		REGULAR SEASON								PLAYOFFS				
99-00—North Bay	OHL	56	12	8	20	33	...	...	...	6	0	2	2	0
00-01—North Bay	OHL	66	22	32	54	64	...	...	...	4	0	1	1	9
01-02—North Bay	OHL	67	15	43	58	112	...	...	...	5	1	2	3	8
02-03—Plymouth	OHL	27	11	22	33	56	...	...	...	18	11	9	20	10
—Saginaw	OHL	37	19	19	38	68	...	...	...	—	—	—	—	—
03-04—Rochester	AHL	58	6	16	22	77	0	2	0	16	3	2	5	18
04-05—Rochester	AHL	73	12	17	29	185	10	0	0	4	0	1	1	2
05-06—Rochester	AHL	77	23	27	50	134	-1	11	0	—	—	—	—	—
—Buffalo	NHL	2	0	1	1	7	-1	0	0	—	—	—	—	—
NHL Totals (1 year)		2	0	1	1	7	-1	0	0					

THORNTON, JOE — C

PERSONAL: Born July 2, 1979, in London, Ontario. ... 6-4/223. ... Shoots left. ... Cousin of Scott Thornton, LW, San Jose Sharks.
TRANSACTIONS/CAREER NOTES: Selected by Boston Bruins in first round (first Bruins pick, first overall) of entry draft (June 21, 1997). ... Fractured forearm before 1997-98 season; missed first three games. ... Injured ankle (December 13, 1997); missed 10 games. ... Viral infection (March 28, 1998); missed six games. ... Injured chest (April 17, 1999); missed final game of season and one playoff game. ... Bruised knee (November 20, 1999); missed one game. ... Charley horse (November 24, 2000); missed six games. ... Suspended two games for cross-checking incident (December 18, 2000). ... Suspended two games for cross-checking incident (February 6, 2001). ... Suspended three games

for cross-checking incident (March 1, 2002). ... Injured shoulder (March 7, 2002); missed 13 games. ... Injured elbow (January 7, 2003); missed five games. ... Injured cheekbone (January 19, 2003); missed three games. ... Injured ribs (April 3, 2004); missed final two games of regular season. ... Re-signed by Bruins as restricted free agent (August 11, 2005). ... Back spasms (October 10, 2005); missed one game. ... Traded by Bruins to San Jose Sharks for D Brad Stuart, LW Marco Sturm and C Wayne Primeau (November 30, 2005).

STATISTICAL PLATEAUS: Three-goal games: 2000-01 (1), 2001-02 (1). Total: 2.

MISCELLANEOUS: Led NHL in assists (96) and points (125) with two teams in 2005-06.

		REGULAR SEASON								PLAYOFFS				
Season Team	**League**	**GP**	**G**	**A**	**Pts.**	**PIM**	**+/-**	**PP**	**SH**	**GP**	**G**	**A**	**Pts.**	**PIM**
94-95—St. Thomas	Jr. B	50	40	64	104	53	...	...	...	—	—	—	—	—
95-96—Sault Ste. Marie	OHL	66	30	46	76	51	...	...	...	4	1	1	2	11
96-97—Sault Ste. Marie	OHL	59	41	81	122	123	29	11	0	11	11	8	19	24
97-98—Boston	NHL	55	3	4	7	19	-6	0	0	6	0	0	0	9
98-99—Boston	NHL	81	16	25	41	69	3	7	0	11	3	6	9	4
99-00—Boston	NHL	81	23	37	60	82	-5	5	0	—	—	—	—	—
00-01—Boston	NHL	72	37	34	71	107	-4	19	1	—	—	—	—	—
01-02—Boston	NHL	66	22	46	68	127	7	6	0	6	2	4	6	10
02-03—Boston	NHL	77	36	65	101	109	12	12	2	5	1	2	3	4
03-04—Boston	NHL	77	23	50	73	98	18	4	0	7	0	0	0	14
04-05—Davos	Switzerland	40	10	44	54	80	...	2	0	14	4	21	25	29
05-06—Boston	NHL	23	9	24	33	6	0	3	0	—	—	—	—	—
—San Jose	NHL	58	20	72	92	55	31	8	0	11	2	7	9	12
—Canadian Oly. team	Int'l	6	1	2	3	0	-1	1	0	—	—	—	—	—
NHL Totals (8 years)		590	189	357	546	672	56	64	3	46	8	19	27	53

THORNTON, SCOTT LW

PERSONAL: Born January 9, 1971, in London, Ont. ... 6-3/225. ... Shoots left. ... Cousin of Joe Thornton, C, Boston Bruins.

TRANSACTIONS/CAREER NOTES: Selected by Toronto Maple Leafs in first round (first Maple Leafs pick, third overall) of NHL draft (June 17, 1989). ... Separated shoulder (January 24, 1991); missed eight games. ... Traded by Maple Leafs with LW Vincent Damphousse, D Luke Richardson and G Peter Ing to Edmonton Oilers for G Grant Fuhr, W Glenn Anderson and LW Craig Berube (September 19, 1991). ... Concussion (November 23, 1991); missed one game. ... Sprained ankle (October 6, 1993); missed 13 games. ... Back spasms (November 21, 1993); missed one game. ... Bruised wrist (April 14, 1994); missed one game. ... Cytomegalo virus (January 9, 1996); missed three games. ... Traded by Oilers to Montreal Canadiens for RW Andrei Kovalenko (September 6, 1996). ... Bruised hand (December 28, 1996); missed three games. ... Flu (February 10, 1997); missed one game. ... Arthroscopic knee surgery (March 6, 1997); missed five games. ... Separated shoulder (January 3, 1998); missed two games. ... Injured neck (February 7, 1998); missed one game. ... Fractured rib (March 18, 1998); missed eight games. ... Injured shoulder (April 15, 1998); missed three games. ... Strained abdominal muscle (November 3, 1998) and had surgery; missed 31 games. ... Migraines (February 2, 1999); missed three games. ... Back spasms (April 13, 1999); missed one game. ... Injured tricep (September 20, 1999); missed first two games of 1999-2000 season. ... Reinjured tricep (October 8, 1999); missed three games. ... Strained groin (December 12, 1999); missed one game. ... Traded by Canadiens to Dallas Stars for LW Juha Lind (January 22, 2000). ... Flu (March 8, 2000); missed one game. ... Suspended for three games for high-sticking incident (March 22, 2000). ... Signed as free agent by San Jose Sharks (July 1, 2000). ... Injured neck (January 4, 2001); missed three games. ... Injured neck (January 30, 2001); missed five games. ... Injured wrist (March 10, 2002); missed one game. ... Injured shoulder (October 10, 2002); missed 14 games. ... Flu (February 17, 2003); missed two games. ... Injured eye (February 24, 2003); missed 21 games. ... Injured groin (November 8, 2003); missed one game. ... Strained groin (November 2, 2005); missed five games. ... Injured ribcage (March 13, 2006); missed five games. ... Signed as free agent by Los Angeles Kings (July 1, 2006).

STATISTICAL PLATEAUS: Three-goal games: 2000-01 (1).

		REGULAR SEASON								PLAYOFFS				
Season Team	**League**	**GP**	**G**	**A**	**Pts.**	**PIM**	**+/-**	**PP**	**SH**	**GP**	**G**	**A**	**Pts.**	**PIM**
86-87—London Diamonds	OPJHL	31	10	7	17	10	...	...	...	—	—	—	—	—
87-88—Belleville	OHL	62	11	19	30	54	...	...	...	6	0	1	1	2
88-89—Belleville	OHL	59	28	34	62	103	...	...	...	5	1	1	2	6
89-90—Belleville	OHL	47	21	28	49	91	...	...	...	11	2	10	12	15
90-91—Belleville	OHL	3	2	1	3	2	...	...	...	6	0	7	7	14
—Newmarket	AHL	5	1	0	1	4	...	...	...	—	—	—	—	—
—Toronto	NHL	33	1	3	4	30	-15	0	0	—	—	—	—	—
91-92—Edmonton	NHL	15	0	1	1	43	-6	0	0	1	0	0	0	0
—Cape Breton	AHL	49	9	14	23	40	...	...	...	5	1	0	1	8
92-93—Cape Breton	AHL	58	23	27	50	102	-17	7	0	16	1	2	3	35
—Edmonton	NHL	9	0	1	1	0	-4	0	0	—	—	—	—	—
93-94—Edmonton	NHL	61	4	7	11	104	-15	0	0	—	—	—	—	—
—Cape Breton	AHL	2	1	1	2	31	-2	1	0	—	—	—	—	—
94-95—Edmonton	NHL	47	10	12	22	89	-4	0	1	—	—	—	—	—
95-96—Edmonton	NHL	77	9	9	18	149	-25	0	2	—	—	—	—	—
96-97—Montreal	NHL	73	10	10	20	128	-19	1	1	5	1	0	1	2
97-98—Montreal	NHL	67	6	9	15	158	0	1	0	9	0	2	2	10
98-99—Montreal	NHL	47	7	4	11	87	-2	1	0	—	—	—	—	—
99-00—Montreal	NHL	35	2	3	5	70	-7	0	0	—	—	—	—	—
—Dallas	NHL	30	6	3	9	38	-5	1	0	23	2	7	9	28
00-01—San Jose	NHL	73	19	17	36	114	4	4	0	6	3	0	3	8
01-02—San Jose	NHL	77	26	16	42	116	11	6	0	12	3	3	6	6
02-03—San Jose	NHL	41	9	12	21	41	-7	4	0	—	—	—	—	—
03-04—San Jose	NHL	80	13	14	27	84	-6	1	0	12	2	2	4	22
04-05—Sodertalje	Sweden	12	2	5	7	10	-7	0	0	10	0	3	3	27
05-06—San Jose	NHL	71	10	11	21	84	-8	1	0	11	2	0	2	6
NHL Totals (15 years)		836	132	132	264	1335	-108	20	4	79	13	14	27	82

THORNTON, SHAWN RW

PERSONAL: Born July 23, 1977, in Oshawa, Ont. ... 6-1/209. ... Shoots right.

TRANSACTIONS/CAREER NOTES: Selected by Toronto Maple Leafs in seventh round (sixth Maple Leafs pick, 190th overall) of NHL entry draft

(June 21, 1997). ... Traded by Maple Leafs to Chicago Blackhawks for D Marty Wilford (September 30, 2001). ... Signed as free agent by Anaheim Ducks (July 14, 2006).

		REGULAR SEASON								PLAYOFFS				
Season Team	League	GP	G	A	Pts.	PIM	+/-	PP	SH	GP	G	A	Pts.	PIM
95-96—Peterborough	OHL	63	4	10	14	192	...	...	...	24	3	0	3	25
96-97—Peterborough	OHL	61	19	10	29	204	...	...	...	11	2	4	6	20
97-98—St. John's	AHL	59	0	3	3	225	-2	0	0	—	—	—	—	—
98-99—St. John's	AHL	78	8	11	19	354	6	2	0	5	0	0	0	9
99-00—St. John's	AHL	60	4	12	16	316	...	...	...	—	—	—	—	—
00-01—St. John's	AHL	79	5	12	17	320	...	...	...	3	1	2	3	2
01-02—Norfolk	AHL	70	8	14	22	281	-3	0	0	4	0	0	0	4
02-03—Chicago	NHL	13	1	1	2	31	-4	0	0	—	—	—	—	—
—Norfolk	AHL	50	11	2	13	213	-7	4	0	9	0	2	2	28
03-04—Chicago	NHL	8	1	0	1	23	2	0	0	—	—	—	—	—
—Norfolk	AHL	64	6	11	17	259	-7	0	0	8	1	1	2	6
04-05—Norfolk	AHL	71	5	9	14	253	-15	0	1	6	0	0	0	8
05-06—Norfolk	AHL	59	10	22	32	192	-8	2	2	4	0	0	0	35
—Chicago	NHL	10	0	0	0	16	-5	0	0	—	—	—	—	—
NHL Totals (3 years)		31	2	1	3	70	-7	0	0					

TIMONEN, KIMMO D

PERSONAL: Born March 18, 1975, in Kuopio, Finland. ... 5-10/196. ... Shoots left. ... Brother of Jussi Timonen, D, Philadelphia Flyers organization. ... Name pronounced KEE-moh TEE-muh-nehn.

TRANSACTIONS/CAREER NOTES: Selected by Los Angeles Kings in 10th round (11th Kings pick, 250th overall) of entry draft (June 26, 1993). ... Rights traded by Kings with D Jan Vopat to Nashville Predators for future considerations (June 26, 1998). ... Cut lip (January 26, 1999); missed one game. ... Abdominal strain (December 18, 1999); missed four games. ... Fractured wrist (January 11, 2000); missed 15 games. ... Fractured ankle (March 14, 2000); missed remainder of season. ... Left ankle (November 10, 2002); missed two games. ... Bruised calf (January 6, 2003); missed seven games. ... Bruised foot (January 17, 2004); missed two games. ... Knee (January 24, 2004); missed two games. ... Flu (December 3, 2005); missed one game. ... Bruised hand (March 7, 2006); missed one game.

		REGULAR SEASON								PLAYOFFS				
Season Team	League	GP	G	A	Pts.	PIM	+/-	PP	SH	GP	G	A	Pts.	PIM
91-92—KalPa Kuopio	Finland	5	0	0	0	0	...	...	...	—	—	—	—	—
92-93—KalPa Kuopio	Finland	33	0	2	2	4	...	...	...	—	—	—	—	—
93-94—KalPa Kuopio	Finland	46	6	7	13	55	...	...	...	—	—	—	—	—
94-95—TPS Turku	Finland	45	3	4	7	10	...	...	...	13	0	1	1	6
95-96—TPS Turku	Finland	48	3	21	24	22	...	...	...	9	1	2	3	12
96-97—TPS Turku	Finland	50	10	14	24	18	...	...	...	12	2	7	9	8
97-98—HIFK Helsinki	Finland	45	10	15	25	59	...	...	...	9	3	4	7	8
—Fin. Olympic team	Int'l	6	0	1	1	2	-3	0	0	—	—	—	—	—
98-99—Milwaukee	IHL	29	2	13	15	22	0	0	0	—	—	—	—	—
—Nashville	NHL	50	4	8	12	30	-4	1	0	—	—	—	—	—
99-00—Nashville	NHL	51	8	25	33	26	-5	2	1	—	—	—	—	—
00-01—Nashville	NHL	82	12	13	25	50	-6	6	0	—	—	—	—	—
01-02—Nashville	NHL	82	13	29	42	28	2	9	0	—	—	—	—	—
—Fin. Olympic team	Int'l	4	0	1	1	2	...	...	...	—	—	—	—	—
02-03—Nashville	NHL	72	6	34	40	46	-3	4	0	—	—	—	—	—
03-04—Nashville	NHL	77	12	32	44	52	-7	8	0	6	0	0	0	10
04-05—Lugano	Switzerland	3	0	1	1	0	...	0	0	—	—	—	—	—
—Brynas IF	Sweden	10	5	3	8	8	9	1	0	—	—	—	—	—
—KalPa Kuopio	Finland	12	4	13	17	6	14	...	...	—	—	—	—	—
05-06—Nashville	NHL	79	11	39	50	74	-3	8	0	5	1	3	4	4
—Fin. Olympic team	Int'l	8	1	4	5	2	2	1	0	—	—	—	—	—
NHL Totals (7 years)		493	66	180	246	306	-26	38	1	11	1	3	4	14

TJARNQVIST, DANIEL D

PERSONAL: Born October 14, 1976, in Umea, Sweden. ... 6-2/200. ... Shoots left. ... Brother of Mathias Tjarnqvist, LW, Dallas Stars. ... Name pronounced SCHAHRN-kvihst.

TRANSACTIONS/CAREER NOTES: Selected by Florida Panthers in fourth round (fifth Panthers pick, 88th overall) of entry draft (July 8, 1995). ... Traded by Panthers with D Gord Murphy, C Herbert Vasiljevs and sixth-round pick (traded to Dallas; Stars selected RW Justin Cox) in 1999 to Atlanta Thrashers for G Trevor Kidd (June 25, 1999). ... Hip pointer (April 2, 2003); missed three games. ... Signed as free agent by Minnesota Wild (August 15, 2005). ... Bruised foot (January 16, 2006); missed four games. ... Signed as free agent by Edmonton Oilers (July 6, 2006).

		REGULAR SEASON								PLAYOFFS				
Season Team	League	GP	G	A	Pts.	PIM	+/-	PP	SH	GP	G	A	Pts.	PIM
94-95—Rogle Angelholm	Sweden	33	2	4	6	2	...	...	...	—	—	—	—	—
95-96—Rogle Angelholm	Sweden	22	1	7	8	6	...	...	...	—	—	—	—	—
96-97—Jokerit Helsinki	Finland	44	3	8	11	4	...	...	...	9	0	3	3	4
97-98—Djurgarden Stockholm	Sweden	40	5	9	14	12	...	...	...	15	1	1	2	2
98-99—Djurgarden Stockholm	Sweden	40	4	3	7	16	18	...	...	4	0	0	0	2
99-00—Djurgarden Stockholm	Sweden	42	3	16	19	8	...	...	...	5	0	0	0	2
00-01—Djurgarden Stockholm	Sweden	45	9	17	26	26	...	...	...	16	6	5	11	2
01-02—Atlanta	NHL	75	2	16	18	14	-22	1	0	—	—	—	—	—
02-03—Atlanta	NHL	75	3	12	15	26	-20	1	0	—	—	—	—	—
03-04—Atlanta	NHL	68	5	15	20	20	-4	0	2	—	—	—	—	—
04-05—Djurgarden Stockholm	Sweden	49	12	12	24	30	-3	6	1	12	2	5	7	10
05-06—Minnesota	NHL	60	3	15	18	32	-11	3	0	—	—	—	—	—
—Swedish Oly. team	Int'l	8	2	1	3	4	2	0	0	—	—	—	—	—
NHL Totals (4 years)		278	13	58	71	92	-57	5	2					

TJARNQVIST, MATHIAS LW/RW

PERSONAL: Born April 15, 1979, in Umea, Sweden. ... 6-1/183. ... Shoots left. ... Brother of Daniel Tjarnqvist, D, Edmonton Oilers. ... Name pronounced: SCHAHRN-kvihst.

TRANSACTIONS/CAREER NOTES: Selected by Dallas Stars in third round (third Stars pick, 96th overall) of entry draft (June 26, 1999). ... Ankle (October 3, 2005); missed nine games.

		REGULAR SEASON								PLAYOFFS				
Season Team	**League**	**GP**	**G**	**A**	**Pts.**	**PIM**	**+/-**	**PP**	**SH**	**GP**	**G**	**A**	**Pts.**	**PIM**
99-00—Djurgarden Stockholm	Sweden	50	12	12	24	20	...	...	...	13	3	2	5	16
00-01—Djurgarden Stockholm	Sweden	47	11	8	19	53	...	...	...	16	1	2	3	6
01-02—Djurgarden Stockholm	Sweden	6	0	1	1	4	...	...	...	2	0	0	0	2
02-03—Djurgarden Stockholm	Sweden	38	11	13	24	30	...	...	...	9	4	1	5	12
03-04—Dallas	NHL	18	1	1	2	2	-6	0	0	—	—	—	—	—
—Utah	AHL	60	15	13	28	51	-17	6	1	—	—	—	—	—
04-05—HV 71 Jonkoping	Sweden	46	8	9	17	18	-6	4	0	—	—	—	—	—
05-06—Iowa	AHL	34	17	12	29	28	2	5	1	1	0	0	0	0
—Dallas	NHL	33	2	4	6	18	4	0	0	—	—	—	—	—
NHL Totals (2 years)		51	3	5	8	20	-2	0	0					

TKACHUK, KEITH LW

PERSONAL: Born March 28, 1972, in Melrose, Mass. ... 6-2/231. ... Shoots left. ... Cousin of Tom Fitzgerald, RW, Boston Bruins. ... Name pronounced kuh-CHUHK. ... Nickname: Walt.

TRANSACTIONS/CAREER NOTES: Selected by Winnipeg Jets in first round (first Jets pick, 19th overall) of entry draft (June 16, 1990). ... Cut forearm (November 12, 1993); missed one game. ... Strained groin (October 9, 1995); missed three games. ... Concussion (November 26, 1995); missed one game. ... Suspended two games and fined $1,000 for stick-swinging incident (March 16, 1996). ... Jets franchise moved to Phoenix and renamed Coyotes for 1996-97 season; NHL approved move on January 18, 1996. ... Flu (March 5, 1997); missed one game. ... Groin (March 2, 1998); missed two games. ... Fractured rib (March 12, 1998); missed seven games. ... Groin (December 14, 1998); missed two games. ... Fractured ribs (December 20, 1998); missed eight games. ... Strained lower back (February 2, 1999); missed two games. ... Neck (December 4, 1999); missed three games. ... Back spasms (December 26, 1999); missed four games. ... Sprained ankle (January 31, 2000); missed one game. ... Sprained ankle (February 12, 2000); missed 16 games. ... Suspended two games for high-sticking incident (March 24, 2000). ... Sprained ankle (March 29, 2000); missed final six games of regular season. ... Strained groin (October 12, 2000); missed one game. ... Injury (October 30, 2000); missed one game. ... Concussion (January 26, 2001); missed two games. ... Injury (February 9, 2001); missed one game. ... Traded by Coyotes to St. Louis Blues for C Michal Handzus, RW Ladislav Nagy, C Jeff Taffe and first-round pick (LW Ben Eager) in 2002 draft (March 13, 2001). ... Bruised thigh (February 16, 2002); missed eight games. ... Suspended one game for slashing incident (March 25, 2002). ... Fractured foot (November 2, 2002); missed 11 games. ... Suspended four games for cross-checking incident (February 25, 2003). ... Wrist (March 13, 2003); missed nine games. ... Suspended three games for high-sticking incident (November 15, 2003). ... Ankle (December 20, 2003); missed three games. ... Suspended by Blues for reporting to training camp overweight (September 16, 2005); missed two games. ... Strained groin (October 6, 2005); missed three games. ... Cracked ribs (October 15, 2005); missed 15 games. ... Fractured right hand (December 16, 2005); missed 22 games. ... Leg (April 11, 2006); missed one game.

STATISTICAL PLATEAUS: Three-goal games: 1993-94 (1), 1996-97 (1), 1997-98 (3), 1998-99 (1), 2000-01 (1). Total: 7. ... Four-goal games: 1995-96 (1), 1996-97 (1). Total: 2. ... Total hat tricks: 9.

		REGULAR SEASON								PLAYOFFS				
Season Team	**League**	**GP**	**G**	**A**	**Pts.**	**PIM**	**+/-**	**PP**	**SH**	**GP**	**G**	**A**	**Pts.**	**PIM**
88-89—Malden Catholic H.S.	Mass. H.S.	21	30	16	46	...	...	...	...	—	—	—	—	—
89-90—Malden Catholic H.S.	Mass. H.S.	6	12	14	26	...	...	...	...	—	—	—	—	—
90-91—Boston University	Hockey East	36	17	23	40	70	...	...	...	—	—	—	—	—
91-92—U.S. national team	Int'l	45	10	10	20	141	...	...	...	—	—	—	—	—
—U.S. Olympic team	Int'l	8	1	1	2	12	...	...	...	—	—	—	—	—
—Winnipeg	NHL	17	3	5	8	28	0	2	0	7	3	0	3	30
92-93—Winnipeg	NHL	83	28	23	51	201	-13	12	0	6	4	0	4	14
93-94—Winnipeg	NHL	84	41	40	81	255	-12	22	3	—	—	—	—	—
94-95—Winnipeg	NHL	48	22	29	51	152	-4	7	2	—	—	—	—	—
95-96—Winnipeg	NHL	76	50	48	98	156	11	20	2	6	1	2	3	22
96-97—Phoenix	NHL	81	*52	34	86	228	-1	9	2	7	6	0	6	7
97-98—Phoenix	NHL	69	40	26	66	147	9	11	0	6	3	3	6	10
—U.S. Olympic team	Int'l	4	0	2	2	6	-3	0	0	—	—	—	—	—
98-99—Phoenix	NHL	68	36	32	68	151	22	11	2	7	1	3	4	13
99-00—Phoenix	NHL	50	22	21	43	82	7	5	1	5	1	1	2	4
00-01—Phoenix	NHL	64	29	42	71	108	6	15	0	—	—	—	—	—
—St. Louis	NHL	12	6	2	8	14	-3	2	0	15	2	7	9	20
01-02—St. Louis	NHL	73	38	37	75	117	21	13	0	10	5	5	10	18
—U.S. Olympic team	Int'l	5	2	0	2	2	...	...	...	—	—	—	—	—
02-03—St. Louis	NHL	56	31	24	55	139	1	14	0	7	1	3	4	14
03-04—St. Louis	NHL	75	33	38	71	83	8	18	0	5	0	2	2	10
05-06—St. Louis	NHL	41	15	21	36	46	-15	10	0	—	—	—	—	—
—U.S. Olympic team	Int'l	6	0	0	0	8	-5	0	0	—	—	—	—	—
NHL Totals (14 years)		897	446	422	868	1907	37	171	12	81	27	26	53	162

TLUSTY, JIRI C

PERSONAL: Born March 16, 1988, in Slany, Cze. ... 6-0/196. ... Shoots left.

TRANSACTIONS/CAREER NOTES: Selected by Toronto Maple Leafs in first round (first Maple Leafs pick; 13th overall) of NHL draft (June 24, 2006).

		REGULAR SEASON								PLAYOFFS				
Season Team	**League**	**GP**	**G**	**A**	**Pts.**	**PIM**	**+/-**	**PP**	**SH**	**GP**	**G**	**A**	**Pts.**	**PIM**
05-06—HC Kladno	Czech.	44	7	3	10	51	-15	...	...	—	—	—	—	—

TOEWS, JONATHAN — C

PERSONAL: Born April 29, 1988, in Winnipeg, MB. ... 6-1/195. ... Shoots left. ... Name pronounced TAYVZ.
TRANSACTIONS/CAREER NOTES: Selected by Chicago Blackhawks in first round (first Blackhawks pick, third overall) of NHL draft (June 24, 2006).

		REGULAR SEASON								PLAYOFFS				
Season Team	League	GP	G	A	Pts.	PIM	+/-	PP	SH	GP	G	A	Pts.	PIM
04-05—Shattuck	USHS (West)	64	48	62	110	38	...	...	...	—	—	—	—	—
05-06—Univ. of North Dakota	WCHA	42	22	17	39	22	...	...	...	—	—	—	—	—

TOIVONEN, HANNU — G

PERSONAL: Born May 18, 1984, in Kalvola, Finland. ... 6-2/191. ... Catches left. ... Name pronounced HA-noo TOI-voh-nuhn.
TRANSACTIONS/CAREER NOTES: Selected by Boston Bruins in first round (first Bruins pick, 29th overall) of entry draft (June 22, 2002). ... Sprained right ankle (January 5, 2006); missed final 41 games of regular season.

		REGULAR SEASON										PLAYOFFS							
Season Team	League	GP	Min.	W	L	OTL	T	GA	SO	GAA	SV%	GP	Min.	W	L	GA	SO	GAA	SV%
01-02—HPK Hameenlinna	Finland Jr.	31	1877	...	...	...	...	103	2	3.29	...	—	—	—	—	—	—	—	—
02-03—HPK Hameenlinna	Finland	24	1432	16	2	...	4	54	2	2.26	...	...	...	1	1	3	1	...	...
03-04—Providence	AHL	36	2163	15	16	...	4	83	2	2.30	.915	—	—	—	—	—	—	—	—
04-05—Providence	AHL	54	3017	29	18	...	...	103	7	2.05	.932	17	1037	10	7	42	0	2.43	.923
05-06—Boston	NHL	20	1163	9	5	4	...	51	1	2.63	.914	—	—	—	—	—	—	—	—
NHL Totals (1 year)		20	1163	9	5	4	0	51	1	2.63	.914								

TOLLEFSEN, OLE-KRISTIAN — D

PERSONAL: Born March 29, 1984, in Oslo, Norway. ... 6-2/200. ... Shoots left.
TRANSACTIONS/CAREER NOTES: Selected by Columbus Blue Jackets in third round (third Blue Jackets pick, 65th overall) of entry draft (June 22, 2002).

		REGULAR SEASON								PLAYOFFS				
Season Team	League	GP	G	A	Pts.	PIM	+/-	PP	SH	GP	G	A	Pts.	PIM
02-03—Brandon	WHL	43	6	14	20	73	3	...	...	17	0	2	2	38
03-04—Brandon	WHL	53	3	27	30	94	17	...	...	11	0	4	4	15
04-05—Syracuse	AHL	64	0	3	3	115	2	0	0	—	—	—	—	—
05-06—Columbus	NHL	5	0	0	0	2	-2	0	0	—	—	—	—	—
—Syracuse	AHL	58	2	16	18	155	20	0	0	1	0	0	0	6
NHL Totals (1 year)		5	0	0	0	2	-2	0	0					

TOOTOO, JORDIN — RW

PERSONAL: Born February 2, 1983, in Churchill, Man. ... 5-9/194. ... Shoots right.
TRANSACTIONS/CAREER NOTES: Selected by Nashville Predators in fourth round (sixth Predators pick, 98th overall) of entry draft (June 23, 2001). ... Flu (February 20, 2004); missed three games. ... Back spasms (January 10, 2006); missed four games. ... Tailbone (April 5, 2006); missed four games.

		REGULAR SEASON								PLAYOFFS				
Season Team	League	GP	G	A	Pts.	PIM	+/-	PP	SH	GP	G	A	Pts.	PIM
99-00—Brandon	WHL	45	6	10	16	214	...	...	...	—	—	—	—	—
00-01—Brandon	WHL	60	20	28	48	172	...	...	...	6	2	4	6	18
01-02—Brandon	WHL	64	32	39	71	272	...	...	...	16	4	3	7	58
02-03—Brandon	WHL	51	35	39	74	216	...	...	...	17	6	3	9	49
03-04—Nashville	NHL	70	4	4	8	137	-6	2	0	5	0	0	0	4
04-05—Milwaukee	AHL	59	10	12	22	266	8	3	0	6	0	0	0	41
05-06—Milwaukee	AHL	41	13	14	27	133	6	3	0	9	8	1	9	14
—Nashville	NHL	34	4	6	10	55	9	0	0	3	0	0	0	0
NHL Totals (2 years)		104	8	10	18	192	3	2	0	8	0	0	0	4

TORRES, RAFFI — LW

PERSONAL: Born October 8, 1981, in Toronto. ... 6-0/216. ... Shoots left. ... Name pronounced TAN-rehs.
TRANSACTIONS/CAREER NOTES: Selected by New York Islanders in first round (second Islanders pick, fifth overall) of entry draft (June 24, 2000). ... Traded by Islanders with LW Brad Isbister to Edmonton Oilers for D Janne Niinimaa and second-round pick (C Yevgeny Tanik) in 2003 (March 11, 2003). ... Ankle (February 16, 2004); missed two games. ... Flu (May 21, 2006); missed two playoff games.

		REGULAR SEASON								PLAYOFFS				
Season Team	League	GP	G	A	Pts.	PIM	+/-	PP	SH	GP	G	A	Pts.	PIM
97-98—Thornhill	Jr. A	46	17	16	33	90	...	...	...	—	—	—	—	—
98-99—Brampton	OHL	62	35	27	62	32	...	...	...	—	—	—	—	—
99-00—Brampton	OHL	68	43	48	91	40	...	...	...	6	5	2	7	23
00-01—Brampton	OHL	55	33	37	70	76	16	12	5	8	7	4	11	19
01-02—Bridgeport	AHL	59	20	10	30	45	-5	7	0	20	8	9	17	26
—New York Islanders	NHL	14	0	1	1	6	2	0	0	—	—	—	—	—
02-03—New York Islanders	NHL	17	0	5	5	10	0	0	0	—	—	—	—	—
—Bridgeport	AHL	49	17	15	32	54	...	...	...	—	—	—	—	—
—Hamilton	AHL	11	1	7	8	14	...	...	...	23	6	1	7	29

Season Team	League	GP	G	A	Pts.	PIM	+/-	PP	SH	GP	G	A	Pts.	PIM
		REGULAR SEASON								PLAYOFFS				
03-04—Edmonton	NHL	80	20	14	34	65	12	5	0	—	—	—	—	—
04-05—Edmonton	AHL	67	21	25	46	165	4	8	0	—	—	—	—	—
05-06—Edmonton	NHL	82	27	14	41	50	4	6	0	22	4	7	11	16
NHL Totals (4 years)		193	47	34	81	131	18	11	0	22	4	7	11	16

TOSKALA, VESA G

PERSONAL: Born May 20, 1977, in Tampere, Finland. ... 5-10/195. ... Catches left. ... Name pronounced TAWS-koh-lah.

TRANSACTIONS/CAREER NOTES: Selected by San Jose Sharks in fourth round (fourth Sharks pick, 90th overall) of NHL draft (July 8, 1995). ... Injured groin (March 13, 2004); missed four games. ... Groin (October 26, 2005); missed five games. ... Groin (November 11, 2005); missed eight games. ... Re-signed by Sharks to two-year contract extension (February 27, 2006).

Season Team	League	GP	Min.	W	L	OTL	T	GA	SO	GAA	SV%	GP	Min.	W	L	GA	SO	GAA	SV%
		REGULAR SEASON										PLAYOFFS							
93-94—Ilves Jrs.	Finland	2	...	...	...	...	...	...	...	...	...	—	—	—	—	—	—	—	—
94-95—Ilves Jrs.	Finland	17	956	...	...	...	...	36	...	2.26	...	—	—	—	—	—	—	—	—
95-96—Ilves Tampere	Finland	37	2073	...	...	...	...	109	1	3.15	...	2	78	...	...	11	0	8.46	...
—Koo Vee	Finland	2	119	...	...	...	...	5	...	2.52	...	—	—	—	—	—	—	—	—
—Ilves Jrs.	Finland	3	180	...	...	...	...	3	...	1.00	...	—	—	—	—	—	—	—	—
96-97—Ilves Tampere	Finland	40	2270	22	12	...	5	108	0	2.85	...	8	479	3	5	29	0	3.63	...
97-98—Ilves Tampere	Finland	48	2555	26	13	...	3	118	1	2.77	...	9	519	6	3	18	1	2.08	...
98-99—Ilves Tampere	Finland	33	1966	21	12	...	0	70	5	2.14	...	4	248	1	3	14	...	3.39	...
99-00—Farjestad Karlstad	Sweden	44	2652	...	...	...	...	118	3	2.67	...	7	439	...	...	19	0	2.60	...
00-01—Kentucky	AHL	44	2466	22	13	...	5	114	2	2.77	.911	3	197	0	3	8	0	2.44	...
01-02—Cleveland	AHL	62	3574	19	33	...	7	178	3	2.99	.904	—	—	—	—	—	—	—	—
—San Jose	NHL	1	10	0	0	...	0	0	0	0.00	1.000	—	—	—	—	—	—	—	—
02-03—San Jose	NHL	11	537	4	3	...	1	21	1	2.35	.927	—	—	—	—	—	—	—	—
—Cleveland	AHL	49	2824	15	30	...	2	151	1	3.21	.474	—	—	—	—	—	—	—	—
03-04—San Jose	NHL	28	1541	12	8	...	4	53	1	2.06	.930	—	—	—	—	—	—	—	—
04-05—Ilves Tampere	Finland	3	186	0	1	...	2	8	0	2.58	.930	6	358	3	3	19	0	3.19	.920
05-06—Cleveland	AHL	1	65	0	0	1	...	0	1	0.00	1.000	—	—	—	—	—	—	—	—
—San Jose	NHL	37	2039	23	7	4	...	87	2	2.56	.901	11	686	6	5	28	1	2.45	.910
NHL Totals (4 years)		77	4127	39	18	4	5	161	4	2.34	.916	11	686	6	5	28	1	2.45	.910

TRAVERSE, PATRICK D

PERSONAL: Born March 14, 1974, in Montreal. ... 6-4/227. ... Shoots left.

TRANSACTIONS/CAREER NOTES: Selected by Ottawa Senators in third round (third Senators pick, 50th overall) of NHL entry draft (June 20, 1992). ... Suffered concussion (January 30, 1999); missed three games. ... Sprained shoulder (February 20, 1999); missed 13 games. ... Bruised right shoulder (February 17, 2000); missed seven games. ... Traded by Senators to Mighty Ducks of Anaheim for D Joel Kwiatkowski (June 12, 2000). ... Traded by Mighty Ducks with LW Andrei Nazarov to Boston Bruins for C Samuel Pahlsson (November 19, 2000). ... Traded by Bruins to Montreal Canadiens for D Eric Weinrich (February 21, 2001). ... Injured neck (April 5, 2001); missed final game of season. ... Sprained knee (November 5, 2001); missed 12 games. ... Suffered concussion (January 10, 2002); missed 12 games. ... Flu (February 27, 2003); missed one game. ... Signed as free agent by Dallas Stars (September 9, 2004). ... Injured ankle (January 26, 2006); out indefinitely. ... Signed as free agent by San Jose Sharks (July 10, 2006).

Season Team	League	GP	G	A	Pts.	PIM	+/-	PP	SH	GP	G	A	Pts.	PIM
		REGULAR SEASON								PLAYOFFS				
91-92—Shawinigan	QMJHL	59	3	11	14	12	...	...	...	10	0	0	0	4
92-93—Shawinigan	QMJHL	53	5	24	29	24	...	...	...	—	—	—	—	—
—New Haven	AHL	2	0	0	0	2	2	0	0	—	—	—	—	—
—St. Jean	QMJHL	15	1	6	7	0	...	...	...	4	0	1	1	2
93-94—Prince Edward	AHL	3	0	1	1	2	-3	0	0	—	—	—	—	—
—St. Jean	QMJHL	66	15	37	52	30	8	3	0	5	0	4	4	4
94-95—Prince Edward	AHL	70	5	13	18	19	-7	1	0	7	0	2	2	0
95-96—Prince Edward	AHL	55	4	21	25	32	...	...	...	5	1	2	3	2
—Ottawa	NHL	5	0	0	0	2	-1	0	0	—	—	—	—	—
96-97—Worcester	AHL	24	0	4	4	23	-2	0	0	—	—	—	—	—
—Grand Rapids	IHL	10	2	1	3	10	...	...	...	2	0	1	1	2
97-98—Hershey	AHL	71	14	15	29	67	-11	11	0	7	1	3	4	4
98-99—Ottawa	NHL	46	1	9	10	22	12	0	0	—	—	—	—	—
99-00—Ottawa	NHL	66	6	17	23	21	17	1	0	6	0	0	0	2
00-01—Anaheim	NHL	15	1	0	1	6	-6	0	0	—	—	—	—	—
—Boston	NHL	37	2	6	8	14	4	1	0	—	—	—	—	—
—Montreal	NHL	19	2	3	5	10	-8	0	0	—	—	—	—	—
01-02—Montreal	NHL	25	2	3	5	14	-7	2	0	—	—	—	—	—
—Quebec	AHL	4	0	2	2	4	-4	0	0	—	—	—	—	—
02-03—Montreal	NHL	65	0	13	13	24	-9	0	0	—	—	—	—	—
03-04—Hamilton	AHL	80	5	21	26	31	16	2	1	10	1	2	3	0
04-05—Houston	AHL	72	6	9	15	28	0	3	0	5	0	0	0	2
05-06—Iowa	AHL	40	3	21	24	16	6	2	0	7	1	2	3	2
—Dallas	NHL	1	0	0	0	0	0	0	0	—	—	—	—	—
NHL Totals (7 years)		279	14	51	65	113	2	4	0	6	0	0	0	2

TUCKER, DARCY RW/LW

PERSONAL: Born March 15, 1975, in Castor, Alta. ... 5-10/178. ... Shoots left.

TRANSACTIONS/CAREER NOTES: Selected by Montreal Canadiens in sixth round (eighth Canadiens pick, 151st overall) of entry draft (June

26, 1993). ... Bruised knee (December 16, 1996); missed one game. ... Traded by Canadiens with RW Stephane Richer and D David Wilkie to Tampa Bay Lightning for C Patrick Poulin, RW Mick Vukota and D Igor Ulanov (January 15, 1998). ... Suspended two games for spearing incident (December 28, 1999). ... Traded by Lightning with fourth-round pick (RW Miguel Delisle) in 2000 draft to Toronto Maple Leafs for RW Mike Johnson, D Marek Posmyk and fifth- (RW Pavel Sedov) and sixth- (D Aaron Gionet) round picks in 2000 draft (February 9, 2000). ... Concussion (November 19, 2001); missed three games. ... Suspended five games for unsportsmanlike conduct (March 5, 2003). ... Injured leg (April 9, 2003); missed one game. ... Injured left eye (January 21, 2004); missed five games. ... Strained abdomen (March 9, 2004); missed remainder of season. ... Left team for personal reasons (November 25, 2005); missed two games. ... Rib injury (January 14, 2006); missed six games.

		REGULAR SEASON								PLAYOFFS				
Season Team	**League**	**GP**	**G**	**A**	**Pts.**	**PIM**	**+/-**	**PP**	**SH**	**GP**	**G**	**A**	**Pts.**	**PIM**
91-92—Kamloops	WHL	26	3	10	13	42	...	...	...	9	0	1	1	16
92-93—Kamloops	WHL	67	31	58	89	155	...	...	...	13	7	6	13	34
93-94—Kamloops	WHL	66	52	88	140	143	60	20	2	19	9	18	27	43
94-95—Kamloops	WHL	64	64	73	137	94	55	22	3	21	16	15	31	19
95-96—Fredericton	AHL	74	29	64	93	174	...	...	...	7	7	3	10	14
—Montreal	NHL	3	0	0	0	0	-1	0	0	—	—	—	—	—
96-97—Montreal	NHL	73	7	13	20	110	-5	1	0	4	0	0	0	0
97-98—Montreal	NHL	39	1	5	6	57	-6	0	0	—	—	—	—	—
—Tampa Bay	NHL	35	6	8	14	89	-8	1	1	—	—	—	—	—
98-99—Tampa Bay	NHL	82	21	22	43	176	-34	8	2	—	—	—	—	—
99-00—Tampa Bay	NHL	50	14	20	34	108	-15	1	0	—	—	—	—	—
—Toronto	NHL	27	7	10	17	55	3	0	2	12	4	2	6	15
00-01—Toronto	NHL	82	16	21	37	141	6	2	0	11	0	2	2	6
01-02—Toronto	NHL	77	24	35	59	92	24	7	0	17	4	4	8	38
02-03—Toronto	NHL	77	10	26	36	119	-7	4	1	6	0	3	3	6
03-04—Toronto	NHL	64	21	11	32	68	4	8	1	12	2	0	2	14
05-06—Toronto	NHL	74	28	33	61	100	-12	18	0	—	—	—	—	—
NHL Totals (10 years)		683	155	204	359	1115	-51	50	7	62	10	11	21	79

TURCO, MARTY G

PERSONAL: Born August 13, 1975, in Sault Ste. Marie, Ont. ... 5-11/183. ... Catches left.

TRANSACTIONS/CAREER NOTES: Selected by Dallas Stars in fifth round (fourth Stars pick, 124th overall) of entry draft (June 29, 1994). ... Suspended one game by NHL for high-sticking (January 21, 2003). ... Ankle (February 11, 2003); missed 18 games. ... Suspended four games by NHL for high-sticking (March 25, 2004). ... Flu (December 26, 2005); missed one game. ... Lower-body injury (January 16, 2006); missed one game.

		REGULAR SEASON										PLAYOFFS							
Season Team	**League**	**GP**	**Min.**	**W**	**L**	**OTL**	**T**	**GA**	**SO**	**GAA**	**SV%**	**GP**	**Min.**	**W**	**L**	**GA**	**SO**	**GAA**	**SV%**
93-94 —Cambridge Jr. B	OHA	34	1937	...	...	...	...	114	0	3.53	...	—	—	—	—	—	—	—	—
94-95 —Univ. of Michigan	CCHA	37	2064	27	7	...	1	95	1	2.76	.894	—	—	—	—	—	—	—	—
95-96 —Univ. of Michigan	CCHA	42	2334	34	7	...	1	84	5	2.16	...	—	—	—	—	—	—	—	—
96-97 —Univ. of Michigan	CCHA	41	2296	33	4	...	4	87	4	2.27	.894	—	—	—	—	—	—	—	—
97-98 —Univ. of Michigan	CCHA	45	2640	33	10	...	1	95	3	2.16	...	—	—	—	—	—	—	—	—
98-99 —Michigan	IHL	54	3127	24	17	...	10	136	1	2.61	.920	5	300	2	3	14	0	2.80	.918
99-00 —Michigan	IHL	60	3399	28	27	...	7	139	7	2.45	...	—	—	—	—	—	—	—	—
00-01 —Dallas	NHL	26	1266	13	6	...	1	40	3	*1.90	*.925	—	—	—	—	—	—	—	—
01-02 —Dallas	NHL	31	1519	15	6	...	2	53	2	2.09	.921	—	—	—	—	—	—	—	—
02-03 —Dallas	NHL	55	3203	31	10	...	10	92	7	*1.72	*.932	12	798	6	6	25	0	1.88	.919
03-04 —Dallas	NHL	73	4359	37	21	...	13	144	9	1.98	.913	5	325	1	4	18	0	3.32	.849
04-05 —Djurgarden Stockholm	Sweden	6	356	...	...	...	...	12	1	2.02	.932	—	—	—	—	—	—	—	—
05-06 —Dallas	NHL	68	3910	41	19	5	...	166	3	2.55	.898	5	319	1	4	18	0	3.39	.868
NHL Totals (5 years)		253	14257	137	62	5	26	495	24	2.08	.915	22	1442	8	14	61	0	2.54	.892

TURGEON, PIERRE C

PERSONAL: Born August 28, 1969, in Rouyn, Que. ... 6-1/200. ... Shoots left. ... Brother of Sylvain Turgeon, LW with four NHL teams (1983-84 through 1994-95). ... Name pronounced TUHR-zhaw.

TRANSACTIONS/CAREER NOTES: Selected by Buffalo Sabres in first round (first Sabres pick, 1rst overall) of entry draft (June 13, 1987). ... Traded by Sabres with RW Benoit Hogue, D Uwe Krupp and C Dave McLlwain to New York Islanders for C Pat LaFontaine, LW Randy Wood, D Randy Hillier and future considerations; Sabres later received fourth-round pick (D Dean Melanson) in 1992 draft to complete deal (October 25, 1991). ... Injured right knee (January 3, 1992); missed three games. ... Separated shoulder (April 28, 1993); missed six playoff games. ... Tendinitis in right wrist (October 5, 1993); missed one game. ... Flu (December 29, 1993); missed one game. ... Fractured cheekbone (January 26, 1994); missed 12 games. ... Traded by Islanders with D Vladimir Malakhov to Montreal Canadiens for LW Kirk Muller, D Mathieu Schneider and C Craig Darby (April 5, 1995). ... Strained shoulder (November 8, 1995); missed two games. ... Bruised thigh (October 24, 1996); missed one game. ... Traded by Canadiens with C Craig Conroy and D Rory Fitzpatrick to St. Louis Blues for LW Shayne Corson, D Murray Baron and fifth-round pick (D Gennady Razin) in 1997 draft (October 29, 1996). ... Fractured right forearm (October 4, 1997); missed 22 games. ... Fractured hand (December 14, 1998); missed 14 games. ... Back spasms (November 20, 1999); missed four games. ... Flu (January 11, 2000); missed one game. ... Injured thumb (January 29, 2000); missed 24 games. ... Concussion (January 11, 2001); missed three games. ... Signed as free agent by Dallas Stars (July 1, 2001). ... Sprained ankle (October 29, 2001); missed 12 games. ... Strained shoulder (March 12, 2002); missed four games. ... Strained hip (February 8, 2003); missed three games. ... Fractured ankle (March 8, 2003); missed 12 games. ... Sprained neck (November 15, 2003); missed three games. ... Injured hip (November 29, 2003); missed two games. ... Flu (December 12, 2003); missed one game. ... Placed on waivers by Stars (July 27, 2005). ... Signed as free agent by Colorado Avalanche (August 3, 2005). ... Injured hip (November 14, 2005); missed one game. ... Strained groin (November 25, 2005); missed three games. ... Injured shoulder (January 7, 2006); missed 16 games.

STATISTICAL PLATEAUS: Three-goal games: 1989-90 (1), 1990-91 (1), 1991-92 (2), 1992-93 (4), 1993-94 (2), 1994-95 (1), 1995-96 (1), 1998-99 (1), 1999-00 (1), 2000-01 (1). Total: 15.

T

		REGULAR SEASON								PLAYOFFS				
Season Team	League	GP	G	A	Pts.	PIM	+/-	PP	SH	GP	G	A	Pts.	PIM
85-86—Granby	QMJHL	69	47	67	114	31	...	...	...	—	—	—	—	—
86-87—Granby	QMJHL	58	69	85	154	8	...	...	...	7	9	6	15	15
87-88—Buffalo	NHL	76	14	28	42	34	-8	8	0	6	4	3	7	4
88-89—Buffalo	NHL	80	34	54	88	26	-2	19	0	5	3	5	8	2
89-90—Buffalo	NHL	80	40	66	106	29	10	17	1	6	2	4	6	2
90-91—Buffalo	NHL	78	32	47	79	26	14	13	2	6	3	1	4	6
91-92—Buffalo	NHL	8	2	6	8	4	-1	0	0	—	—	—	—	—
—New York Islanders	NHL	69	38	49	87	16	8	13	0	—	—	—	—	—
92-93—New York Islanders	NHL	83	58	74	132	26	-1	24	0	11	6	7	13	0
93-94—New York Islanders	NHL	69	38	56	94	18	14	10	4	4	0	1	1	0
94-95—New York Islanders	NHL	34	13	14	27	10	-12	3	2	—	—	—	—	—
—Montreal	NHL	15	11	9	20	4	12	2	0	—	—	—	—	—
95-96—Montreal	NHL	80	38	58	96	44	19	17	1	6	2	4	6	2
96-97—Montreal	NHL	9	1	10	11	2	4	0	0	—	—	—	—	—
—St. Louis	NHL	69	25	49	74	12	4	5	0	5	1	1	2	2
97-98—St. Louis	NHL	60	22	46	68	24	13	6	0	10	4	4	8	2
98-99—St. Louis	NHL	67	31	34	65	36	4	10	0	13	4	9	13	6
99-00—St. Louis	NHL	52	26	40	66	8	30	8	0	7	0	7	7	0
00-01—St. Louis	NHL	79	30	52	82	37	14	11	0	15	5	10	15	2
01-02—Dallas	NHL	66	15	32	47	16	-4	7	0	—	—	—	—	—
02-03—Dallas	NHL	65	12	30	42	18	4	3	0	5	0	1	1	0
03-04—Dallas	NHL	76	15	25	40	20	17	6	0	5	1	3	4	2
05-06—Colorado	NHL	62	16	30	46	32	1	7	0	5	0	2	2	6
NHL Totals (18 years)		1277	511	809	1320	442	140	189	10	109	35	62	97	36

TVERDOVSKY, OLEG D

PERSONAL: Born May 18, 1976, in Donetsk, U.S.S.R. ... 6-1/205. ... Shoots left. ... Name pronounced OH-lehg teh-vuhr-DAHV-skee.

TRANSACTIONS/CAREER NOTES: Selected by Mighty Ducks of Anaheim in first round (first Mighty Ducks pick, second overall) of entry draft (June 28, 1994). ... Pink eye (March 15, 1995); missed two games. ... Traded by Mighty Ducks with C Chad Kilger and third-round pick (D Per-Anton Lundstrom) in 1996 draft to Winnipeg Jets for C Marc Chouinard, RW Teemu Selanne and fourth-round pick (traded to Toronto) in 1996 draft (February 7, 1996). ... Jets franchise moved to Phoenix and renamed Coyotes for 1996-97 season; NHL approved move on January 18, 1996. ... Pulled rib muscle (December 23, 1997); missed one game. ... Traded by Coyotes to Mighty Ducks for C Travis Green and first-round pick (C Scott Kelman) in 1999 draft (June 26, 1999). ... Strained groin (March 24, 2002); missed remainder of season. ... Traded by Mighty Ducks with LW Jeff Friesen and RW Maxim Balmochnykh to New Jersey Devils for RW Petr Sykora, C Igor Pohanka, D Mike Commodore and G J.F. Damphousse (July 7, 2002). ... Bruised back (November 16, 2002); missed one game. ... Flu (December 23, 2002); missed two games. ... Viral illness (January 3, 2003); missed five games. ... Recurrence of viral illness (January 17, 2003); missed 20 games. ... Signed as free agent by Carolina Hurricanes (August 5, 2005). ... Concussion (November 25, 2005); missed five games. ... Upper body injury (January 28, 2006); missed five games.

		REGULAR SEASON								PLAYOFFS				
Season Team	League	GP	G	A	Pts.	PIM	+/-	PP	SH	GP	G	A	Pts.	PIM
92-93—Soviet Wings	CIS	21	0	1	1	6	...	...	...	6	0	0	0	...
93-94—Soviet Wings	CIS	46	4	10	14	22	...	...	...	3	1	0	1	2
94-95—Brandon	WHL	7	1	4	5	4	1	0	0	—	—	—	—	—
—Anaheim	NHL	36	3	9	12	14	-6	1	1	—	—	—	—	—
95-96—Anaheim	NHL	51	7	15	22	35	0	2	0	—	—	—	—	—
—Winnipeg	NHL	31	0	8	8	6	-7	0	0	6	0	1	1	0
96-97—Phoenix	NHL	82	10	45	55	30	-5	3	1	7	0	1	1	0
97-98—Hamilton	AHL	9	8	6	14	2	12	1	2	—	—	—	—	—
—Phoenix	NHL	46	7	12	19	12	1	4	0	6	0	7	7	0
98-99—Phoenix	NHL	82	7	18	25	32	11	2	0	6	0	2	2	6
99-00—Anaheim	NHL	82	15	36	51	30	5	5	0	—	—	—	—	—
00-01—Anaheim	NHL	82	14	39	53	32	-11	8	0	—	—	—	—	—
01-02—Anaheim	NHL	73	6	26	32	31	0	2	0	—	—	—	—	—
—Russian Oly. team	Int'l	6	1	1	2	0	...	...	...	—	—	—	—	—
02-03—New Jersey	NHL	50	5	8	13	22	2	2	0	15	0	3	3	0
03-04—Avangard Omsk	Russian	57	16	17	33	58	8	...	...	11	0	2	2	2
04-05—Avangard Omsk	Russian	48	5	15	20	65	8	...	...	11	0	3	3	35
05-06—Carolina	NHL	72	3	20	23	37	-1	0	0	5	0	0	0	0
NHL Totals (10 years)		687	77	236	313	281	-11	29	2	45	0	14	14	6

TYUTIN, FEDOR D

PERSONAL: Born July 19, 1983, in Izhevsk, U.S.S.R. ... 6-2/207. ... Shoots left. ... Name pronounced TOOT-ihn.

TRANSACTIONS/CAREER NOTES: Selected by New York Rangers in second round (second Rangers pick, 40th overall) of NHL draft (June 23, 2001). ... Injured finger (November 17, 2005); missed four games.

		REGULAR SEASON								PLAYOFFS				
Season Team	League	GP	G	A	Pts.	PIM	+/-	PP	SH	GP	G	A	Pts.	PIM
00-01—SKA St. Petersburg	Russian	34	2	4	6	20	...	...	...	—	—	—	—	—
01-02—Guelph	OHL	53	19	40	59	54	...	...	...	9	2	8	10	8
02-03—Kazan	Rus. Div.	10	0	0	0	8	...	...	...	—	—	—	—	—
—SKA-2 St. Petersburg	Rus. Div.	10	1	1	2	16	...	...	...	5	0	0	0	4
03-04—New York Rangers	NHL	25	2	5	7	14	-4	0	1	—	—	—	—	—
—Hartford	AHL	43	5	9	14	48	7	0	0	16	0	5	5	18
04-05—Hartford	AHL	13	2	1	3	10	0	1	0	—	—	—	—	—
—SKA St. Petersburg	Russian	35	5	3	8	24	-3	...	...	—	—	—	—	—
05-06—New York Rangers	NHL	77	6	19	25	58	1	4	0	4	0	1	1	0
—Russian Oly. team	Int'l	8	0	1	1	4	2	0	0	—	—	—	—	—
NHL Totals (2 years)		102	8	24	32	72	-3	4	1	4	0	1	1	0

ULANOV, IGOR — D

PERSONAL: Born October 1, 1969, in Krasnokamsk, U.S.S.R. ... 6-3/215. ... Shoots left. ... Name pronounced EE-gohr yoo-LAH-nahf.

TRANSACTIONS/CAREER NOTES: Selected by Winnipeg Jets in 10th round (eighth Jets pick, 20third overall) of entry draft (June 22, 1991). ... Back spasms (March 7, 1992); missed five games. ... Fractured foot (March 16, 1995); missed 19 games. ... Traded by Jets with C Mike Eagles to Washington Capitals for third-round (traded to Dallas; Stars selected Sergey Gusev) and fifth-round (G Brian Elder) picks in 1995 (April 7, 1995). ... Traded by Capitals to Chicago Blackhawks for third-round pick (G Dave Weninger) in 1996 (October 17, 1995). ... Traded by Blackhawks with LW Patrick Poulin and second-round pick (D Jeff Paul) in 1996 to Tampa Bay for D Enrico Ciccone (March 20, 1996). ... Ribs (October 5, 1996); missed three games. ... Groin (February 14, 1997); missed six games. ... Traded by Lightning with C Patrick Poulin and RW Mick Vukota to Montreal Canadiens for RW Stephane Richer, C Darcy Tucker and D David Wilkie (January 15, 1998). ... Left knee (January 21, 1998); missed remainder of season. ... Fractured left foot (November 3, 1999); missed 13 games. ... Traded by Canadiens with D Alain Nasreddine to Edmonton Oilers for D Christian Laflamme and D Mathieu Descoteaux (March 9, 2000). ... Ankle (November 19, 2000); missed one game. ... Right hand (December 2, 2000); missed two games. ... Suspended two games by NHL in cross-checking incident (December 14, 2000). ... Left eye (February 24, 2001); missed three games. ... Left eye (March 2, 2001); missed six games. ... Signed as free agent by New York Rangers (July 1, 2001). ... Suspended seven games in cross-checking incident (October 12, 2001). ... Traded by Rangers with D Filip Novak, first- (traded to Calgary; Flames selected LW Eric Nystrom) and second-round (C/RW Rob Globke) picks in 2002 and fourth-round pick (traded to Atlanta; Thrashers selected RW Guillaume Desbiens) in 2003 to Florida Panthers for RW Pavel Bure and second-round pick (C Lee Falardeau) in 2002 (March 18, 2002). ... Toe (March 5, 2003); missed two games. ... Signed as free agent by Oilers (January 5, 2004). ... Groin (January 17, 2004); missed one game. ... Rib (October 8, 2005); missed three games. ... Broken toe (October 28, 2005); missed 10 games. ... Knee (January 7, 2006); missed six games. ... Rib (February 10, 2006); missed one game.

		REGULAR SEASON								PLAYOFFS				
Season Team	League	GP	G	A	Pts.	PIM	+/-	PP	SH	GP	G	A	Pts.	PIM
90-91—Khimik	USSR	41	2	2	4	52	...	...	...	—	—	—	—	—
91-92—Khimik	CIS	27	1	4	5	24	...	...	...	—	—	—	—	—
—Winnipeg	NHL	27	2	9	11	67	5	0	0	7	0	0	0	39
—Moncton	AHL	3	0	1	1	16	...	...	...	—	—	—	—	—
92-93—Moncton	AHL	9	1	3	4	26	6	0	0	—	—	—	—	—
—Fort Wayne	IHL	3	0	1	1	29	1	0	0	—	—	—	—	—
—Winnipeg	NHL	56	2	14	16	124	6	0	0	4	0	0	0	4
93-94—Winnipeg	NHL	74	0	17	17	165	-11	0	0	—	—	—	—	—
94-95—Winnipeg	NHL	19	1	3	4	27	-2	0	0	—	—	—	—	—
—Washington	NHL	3	0	1	1	2	3	0	0	2	0	0	0	4
95-96—Indianapolis	IHL	1	0	0	0	0	...	...	...	—	—	—	—	—
—Chicago	NHL	53	1	8	9	92	12	0	0	—	—	—	—	—
—Tampa Bay	NHL	11	2	1	3	24	-1	0	0	5	0	0	0	15
96-97—Tampa Bay	NHL	59	1	7	8	108	2	0	0	—	—	—	—	—
97-98—Tampa Bay	NHL	45	2	7	9	85	-5	1	0	—	—	—	—	—
—Montreal	NHL	4	0	1	1	12	-2	0	0	10	1	4	5	12
98-99—Montreal	NHL	76	3	9	12	109	-3	0	0	—	—	—	—	—
99-00—Montreal	NHL	43	1	5	6	76	-11	0	0	—	—	—	—	—
—Edmonton	NHL	14	0	3	3	10	-3	0	0	5	0	0	0	6
00-01—Edmonton	NHL	67	3	20	23	90	15	1	0	6	0	0	0	4
01-02—New York Rangers	NHL	39	0	6	6	53	-4	0	0	—	—	—	—	—
—Hartford	AHL	6	1	1	2	2	2	0	0	—	—	—	—	—
—Florida	NHL	14	0	4	4	11	-3	0	0	—	—	—	—	—
02-03—San Antonio	AHL	5	1	0	1	4	-2	0	0	—	—	—	—	—
—Florida	NHL	56	1	1	2	39	7	0	0	—	—	—	—	—
03-04—Edmonton	NHL	42	5	13	18	28	19	1	0	—	—	—	—	—
—Toronto	AHL	10	0	5	5	8	4	0	0	—	—	—	—	—
05-06—Edmonton	NHL	37	3	6	9	29	-11	1	0	—	—	—	—	—
NHL Totals (14 years)		739	27	135	162	1151	13	4	0	39	1	4	5	84

UMBERGER, R.J. — C/LW

PERSONAL: Born May 3, 1982, in Pittsburgh. ... 6-2/215. ... Shoots left.

TRANSACTIONS/CAREER NOTES: Selected by Vancouver Canucks in first round (first Canucks pick, 16th overall) of NHL draft (June 23, 2001). ... Traded by Canucks with D Martin Grenier to New York Rangers for LW Martin Rucinsky (March 9, 2004). ... Missed 2003-04 season in contract dispute. ... Signed as free agent by Philadelphia Flyers (June 16, 2004).

		REGULAR SEASON								PLAYOFFS				
Season Team	League	GP	G	A	Pts.	PIM	+/-	PP	SH	GP	G	A	Pts.	PIM
99-00—U.S. National	USHL	57	33	35	68	20	...	...	...	—	—	—	—	—
00-01—Ohio State	CCHA	32	14	23	37	18	...	...	...	—	—	—	—	—
01-02—Ohio State	CCHA	37	18	21	39	31	...	...	...	—	—	—	—	—
02-03—Ohio State	CCHA	43	26	27	53	16	...	...	...	—	—	—	—	—
03-04—	Did not play													
04-05—Philadelphia	AHL	80	21	44	65	36	19	2	0	21	3	7	10	12
05-06—Philadelphia	AHL	8	3	7	10	8	4	0	1	—	—	—	—	—
—Philadelphia	NHL	73	20	18	38	18	9	5	0	5	1	0	1	2
NHL Totals (1 year)		73	20	18	38	18	9	5	0	5	1	0	1	2

UPSHALL, SCOTTIE — LW/RW

PERSONAL: Born October 7, 1983, in Fort McMurray, Alta. ... 6-0/187. ... Shoots left.

TRANSACTIONS/CAREER NOTES: Selected by Nashville Predators in first round (first Predators pick, sixth overall) of entry draft (June 22, 2002). ... Knee (December 23, 2003); missed nine games. ... Hip (March 5, 2006); missed three games.

		REGULAR SEASON								PLAYOFFS				
Season Team	League	GP	G	A	Pts.	PIM	+/-	PP	SH	GP	G	A	Pts.	PIM
00-01—Kamloops	WHL	70	42	45	87	111	...	...	...	4	0	2	2	10
01-02—Kamloops	WHL	61	32	51	83	139	...	...	...	4	1	2	3	21

Season Team	League	REGULAR SEASON GP	G	A	Pts.	PIM	+/-	PP	SH	PLAYOFFS GP	G	A	Pts.	PIM
02-03—Kamloops	WHL	42	25	31	56	111	...	...	...	6	0	2	2	34
—Milwaukee	AHL	2	1	0	1	2	0	0	0	6	0	0	0	2
—Nashville	NHL	8	1	0	1	0	2	0	0	—	—	—	—	—
03-04—Milwaukee	AHL	31	13	11	24	42	1	3	0	8	3	0	3	4
—Nashville	NHL	7	0	1	1	0	-2	0	0	—	—	—	—	—
04-05—Milwaukee	AHL	62	19	27	46	108	9	8	2	5	2	2	4	8
05-06—Milwaukee	AHL	23	17	16	33	44	11	5	1	8	3	9	12	12
—Nashville	NHL	48	8	16	24	34	14	1	0	2	0	0	0	0
NHL Totals (3 years)		63	9	17	26	34	14	1	0	2	0	0	0	0

VAANANEN, OSSI D

PERSONAL: Born August 18, 1980, in Vantaa, Finland. ... 6-4/215. ... Shoots left. ... Name pronounced OH-see VAH-nih-nehn.

TRANSACTIONS/CAREER NOTES: Selected by Phoenix Coyotes in second round (second Coyotes pick, 43rd overall) of NHL draft (June 27, 1998). ... Bruised shoulder (March 17, 2002); missed six games. ... Bruised foot (October 24, 2002); missed one game. ... Strained right knee (February 1, 2003); missed 14 games. ... Sore neck (December 7, 2003); missed one game. ... Traded by Coyotes with C Chris Gratton and second-round pick (C Paul Stastny) in 2005 draft to Colorado Avalanche for D Derek Morris and D Keith Ballard (March 9, 2004). ... Ankle (February 2, 2006) and surgery (February 3, 2006); missed final 28 games of regular season and eight playoff games.

Season Team	League	REGULAR SEASON GP	G	A	Pts.	PIM	+/-	PP	SH	PLAYOFFS GP	G	A	Pts.	PIM
95-96—Jokerit Helsinki	Finland Jr. B	2	0	0	0	0	...	...	...	—	—	—	—	—
96-97—Jokerit Helsinki	Finland Jr. B	17	1	2	3	43	...	...	...	—	—	—	—	—
97-98—Jokerit Helsinki	Finland Jr.	31	0	6	6	24	...	...	...	—	—	—	—	—
98-99—Jokerit Helsinki	Finland	48	0	1	1	42	...	...	...	3	0	1	1	2
99-00—Jokerit Helsinki	Finland	49	1	6	7	46	...	...	...	11	1	1	2	2
00-01—Phoenix	NHL	81	4	12	16	90	9	0	0	—	—	—	—	—
01-02—Phoenix	NHL	76	2	12	14	74	6	0	1	5	0	0	0	6
—Fin. Olympic team	Int'l	2	0	1	1	0	...	...	...	—	—	—	—	—
02-03—Phoenix	NHL	67	2	7	9	82	1	0	0	—	—	—	—	—
03-04—Phoenix	NHL	67	2	4	6	87	-10	0	0	—	—	—	—	—
—Colorado	NHL	12	0	0	0	2	-4	0	0	11	0	1	1	18
04-05—Jokerit Helsinki	Finland	—	—	—	—	—	—	—	—	12	0	0	0	26
—Jokerit Helsinki	Finland	28	2	2	4	30	6	...	...	—	—	—	—	—
05-06—Colorado	NHL	53	0	4	4	56	10	0	0	1	0	0	0	0
NHL Totals (5 years)		356	10	39	49	391	12	0	1	17	0	1	1	24

VAN RYN, MIKE D

PERSONAL: Born May 14, 1979, in London, Ont. ... 6-1/202. ... Shoots right. ... Name pronounced van RIGHN.

TRANSACTIONS/CAREER NOTES: Selected by New Jersey Devils in first round (first Devils pick, 26th overall) of NHL entry draft (June 27, 1998). ... Signed as free agent by St. Louis Blues (June 30, 2000). ... Traded by Blues to Florida Panthers for RW Valeri Bure and conditional fifth-round pick in 2004 draft (March 11, 2003). ... Suffered concussion (January 23, 2004); missed three games. ... Hip flexor (November 11, 2005); missed one game. ... Thigh injury (January 4, 2006); missed one game.

Season Team	League	REGULAR SEASON GP	G	A	Pts.	PIM	+/-	PP	SH	PLAYOFFS GP	G	A	Pts.	PIM
95-96—London Jr. B	OHA	44	9	14	23	24	...	...	...	—	—	—	—	—
96-97—London Jr. B	OHA	46	14	31	45	32	...	...	...	—	—	—	—	—
97-98—Univ. of Michigan	CCHA	25	4	14	18	36	...	...	...	—	—	—	—	—
98-99—Univ. of Michigan	CCHA	37	10	13	23	52	...	...	...	—	—	—	—	—
99-00—Sarnia	OHL	61	6	35	41	34	-2	5	0	7	0	5	5	4
00-01—St. Louis	NHL	1	0	0	0	0	-2	0	0	—	—	—	—	—
—Worcester	AHL	37	3	10	13	12	...	...	...	7	1	1	2	2
01-02—Worcester	AHL	24	2	7	9	17	8	0	0	—	—	—	—	—
—St. Louis	NHL	48	2	8	10	18	10	0	0	9	0	0	0	0
02-03—Worcester	AHL	33	2	8	10	16	-2	2	0	—	—	—	—	—
—St. Louis	NHL	20	0	3	3	8	3	0	0	—	—	—	—	—
—San Antonio	AHL	11	0	3	3	20	2	0	0	3	0	0	0	0
03-04—Florida	NHL	79	13	24	37	52	-16	6	1	—	—	—	—	—
05-06—Florida	NHL	80	8	29	37	90	15	3	0	—	—	—	—	—
NHL Totals (5 years)		228	23	64	87	168	10	9	1	9	0	0	0	0

VANDENBUSSCHE, RYAN RW

PERSONAL: Born February 28, 1973, in Simcoe, Ont. ... 6-0/205. ... Shoots right. ... Name pronounced VAN-dehn-buhsh.

TRANSACTIONS/CAREER NOTES: Selected by Toronto Maple Leafs in eighth round (173rd overall) of NHL draft (June 20, 1992). ... Signed as free agent by New York Rangers (August 22, 1995). ... Traded by Rangers to Chicago Blackhawks for D Ryan Risidore (March 24, 1998). ... Suspended one game for head-butting incident (March 28, 1999). ... Elbow surgery before 1999-2000 season; missed first six games of season. ... Sore back (December 3, 1999); missed five games. ... Cut left hand (March 3, 2000); missed 10 games. ... Injured wrist (January 5, 2003); missed 14 games. ... Injured wrist (November 29, 2003); missed six games. ... Strained neck (January 29, 2004); missed three games. ... Signed as free agent by Pittsburgh Penguins (July 12, 2004). ... Cervical strain (December 28, 2005); missed final 46 games of regular season.

Season Team	League	REGULAR SEASON GP	G	A	Pts.	PIM	+/-	PP	SH	PLAYOFFS GP	G	A	Pts.	PIM
90-91—Cornwall	OHL	49	3	8	11	139	...	...	...	—	—	—	—	—
91-92—Cornwall	OHL	61	13	15	28	232	...	...	...	6	0	2	2	9

Season Team	League	GP	G	A	Pts.	PIM	+/-	PP	SH	GP	G	A	Pts.	PIM
		REGULAR SEASON								PLAYOFFS				
92-93—Newmarket	OHL	30	15	12	27	161	...	...	...	—	—	—	—	—
—Guelph	OHL	29	3	14	17	99	...	...	...	5	1	3	4	13
—St. John's	AHL	1	0	0	0	0	...	...	...	—	—	—	—	—
93-94—St. John's	AHL	44	4	10	14	124	...	...	...	—	—	—	—	—
—Springfield	AHL	9	1	2	3	29	...	...	...	5	0	0	0	16
94-95—St. John's	AHL	53	2	13	15	239	...	...	...	—	—	—	—	—
95-96—Binghamton	AHL	68	3	17	20	240	...	...	...	4	0	0	0	9
96-97—Binghamton	AHL	38	8	11	19	133	...	...	...	—	—	—	—	—
—New York Rangers	NHL	11	1	0	1	30	-2	0	0	—	—	—	—	—
97-98—New York Rangers	NHL	16	1	0	1	38	-2	0	0	—	—	—	—	—
—Hartford	AHL	15	2	0	2	45	-2	0	0	—	—	—	—	—
—Chicago	NHL	4	0	1	1	5	0	0	0	—	—	—	—	—
—Indianapolis	IHL	3	1	1	2	4	3	0	0	—	—	—	—	—
98-99—Indianapolis	IHL	34	3	10	13	130	-11	1	0	—	—	—	—	—
—Portland	AHL	37	4	1	5	119	-12	0	0	—	—	—	—	—
—Chicago	NHL	6	0	0	0	17	0	0	0	—	—	—	—	—
99-00—Chicago	NHL	52	0	1	1	143	-3	0	0	—	—	—	—	—
00-01—Chicago	NHL	64	2	5	7	146	-8	0	0	—	—	—	—	—
01-02—Chicago	NHL	50	1	2	3	103	-10	0	0	1	0	0	0	0
02-03—Norfolk	AHL	4	0	1	1	5	1	0	0	—	—	—	—	—
—Chicago	NHL	22	0	0	0	58	0	0	0	—	—	—	—	—
03-04—Chicago	NHL	65	4	1	5	120	-10	2	0	—	—	—	—	—
04-05—Wilkes-Barre/Scranton	AHL	23	4	7	11	67	1	2	0	11	2	2	4	11
05-06—Pittsburgh	NHL	20	1	0	1	42	0	0	0	—	—	—	—	—
NHL Totals (9 years)		310	10	10	20	702	-35	2	0	1	0	0	0	0

VANDERMEER, JIM D

PERSONAL: Born February 21, 1980, in Caroline, Alta. ... 6-1/218. ... Shoots left.

TRANSACTIONS/CAREER NOTES: Signed as free agent by Philadelphia Flyers (July 6, 2001). ... Dislocated shoulder (January 20, 2004); missed six games. ... Traded by Flyers with C Colin Fraser and second-round pick in 2004 entry draft (LW Bryan Bickell) to Chicago Blackhawks for C Alexei Zhamnov and fourth-round pick in 2004 entry draft (February 19, 2004). ... Injured groin (October 29, 2005); missed two games. ... Injured ankle (November 19, 2005); missed two games. ... Suspended two games in high-sticking incident (March 3, 2006).

Season Team	League	GP	G	A	Pts.	PIM	+/-	PP	SH	GP	G	A	Pts.	PIM
		REGULAR SEASON								PLAYOFFS				
97-98—Red Deer	WHL	35	0	3	3	55	...	...	...	2	0	0	0	0
98-99—Red Deer	WHL	70	5	23	28	258	...	...	...	9	0	1	1	24
99-00—Red Deer	WHL	71	8	30	38	221	...	...	...	4	0	1	1	16
00-01—Red Deer	WHL	65	28	37	65	180	...	...	...	22	0	13	13	43
01-02—Philadelphia	AHL	74	1	13	14	88	-8	0	0	5	0	2	2	14
02-03—Philadelphia	NHL	24	2	1	3	27	9	0	0	8	0	1	1	9
—Philadelphia	AHL	48	4	8	12	122	-9	2	0	—	—	—	—	—
03-04—Philadelphia	NHL	23	3	2	5	25	-5	0	0	—	—	—	—	—
—Philadelphia	AHL	26	1	6	7	118	-8	0	0	—	—	—	—	—
—Chicago	NHL	23	2	10	12	58	-6	1	1	—	—	—	—	—
04-05—Norfolk	AHL	52	3	10	13	164	13	2	0	—	—	—	—	—
05-06—Chicago	NHL	76	6	18	24	116	-2	2	0	—	—	—	—	—
NHL Totals (3 years)		146	13	31	44	226	-4	3	1	8	0	1	1	9

VANEK, THOMAS LW/RW

PERSONAL: Born January 19, 1984, in Vienna, Austria. ... 6-2/207. ... Shoots right.

TRANSACTIONS/CAREER NOTES: Selected by Buffalo Sabres in first round (first Sabres pick, fifth overall) of entry draft (June 20, 2003).

Season Team	League	GP	G	A	Pts.	PIM	+/-	PP	SH	GP	G	A	Pts.	PIM
		REGULAR SEASON								PLAYOFFS				
02-03—Minnesota	WCHA	45	31	31	62	60	...	...	...	—	—	—	—	—
03-04—Minnesota	WCHA	38	26	25	51	72	...	...	...	—	—	—	—	—
04-05—Rochester	AHL	74	42	26	68	62	-3	25	0	5	2	3	5	10
05-06—Buffalo	NHL	81	25	23	48	72	-11	11	0	10	2	0	2	6
NHL Totals (1 year)		81	25	23	48	72	-11	11	0	10	2	0	2	6

VARADA, VACLAV LW/RW

PERSONAL: Born April 26, 1976, in Vsetin, Czech. ... 6-0/208. ... Shoots left. ... Name pronounced vuh-RAH-duh.

TRANSACTIONS/CAREER NOTES: Selected by San Jose Sharks in fourth round (fourth Sharks pick, 89th overall) of entry draft (June 29, 1994). ... Traded by Sharks with LW Martin Spahnel and fourth-round pick (D Mike Martone) in 1996 draft to Buffalo Sabres for D Doug Bodger (November 16, 1995). ... Fractured left hand (February 2, 1997); missed 15 games. ... Sprained ankle (February 9, 1999); missed 10 games. ... Injured ear (January 18, 2000); missed three games. ... Concussion (February 25, 2001); missed six games. ... Suspended one game for unsportsmanlike conduct (October 27, 2001). ... Suspended three games for high-sticking incident (November 10, 2001). ... Suspended one game for checking from behind (January 20, 2002). ... Sprained right knee (January 7, 2003); missed 17 games. ... Traded by Sabres with fifth-round pick (C Tim Cook) in 2003 draft to Ottawa Senators for C Jakub Klepis (February 25, 2003). ... Sprained knee (March 4, 2003); missed seven games. ... Injured knee (December 13, 2003) and had surgery; missed 52 games. ... Injured knee (September 2005); missed first five games of season.

Season Team	League	GP	G	A	Pts.	PIM	+/-	PP	SH	GP	G	A	Pts.	PIM
		REGULAR SEASON								PLAYOFFS				
92-93—TJ Vitkovice	Czech.	1	0	0	0	...	...	...	...	—	—	—	—	—
93-94—HC Vitkovice	Czech Rep.	24	6	7	13	...	...	...	...	5	1	1	2	...
94-95—Tacoma	WHL	68	50	38	88	108	7	21	4	4	4	3	7	11
—Czech. Jr. nat'l team	Int'l	7	6	4	10	25	...	...	...	—	—	—	—	—
95-96—Kelowna	WHL	59	39	46	85	100	...	...	...	6	3	3	6	16
—Rochester	AHL	5	3	0	3	4	...	...	...	—	—	—	—	—
—Buffalo	NHL	1	0	0	0	0	0	0	0	—	—	—	—	—
—Czech. Jr. nat'l team	Int'l	6	5	1	6	8	...	...	...	—	—	—	—	—
96-97—Rochester	AHL	53	23	25	48	81	8	3	1	10	1	6	7	27
—Buffalo	NHL	5	0	0	0	2	0	0	0	—	—	—	—	—
97-98—Rochester	AHL	45	30	26	56	74	20	14	2	—	—	—	—	—
—Buffalo	NHL	27	5	6	11	15	0	0	0	15	3	4	7	18
98-99—Buffalo	NHL	72	7	24	31	61	11	1	0	21	5	4	9	14
99-00—HC Vitkovice	Czech Rep.	5	2	3	5	12	...	...	...	—	—	—	—	—
—Buffalo	NHL	76	10	27	37	62	12	0	0	5	0	0	0	8
00-01—Buffalo	NHL	75	10	21	31	81	-2	2	0	13	0	4	4	8
01-02—Buffalo	NHL	76	7	16	23	82	-7	1	0	—	—	—	—	—
02-03—Buffalo	NHL	44	7	4	11	23	-2	1	0	—	—	—	—	—
—Ottawa	NHL	11	2	6	8	8	3	1	0	18	2	4	6	18
03-04—Ottawa	NHL	30	5	5	10	26	2	0	0	7	1	1	2	4
04-05—Vitkovice	Czech Rep.	44	8	19	27	83	13	...	...	11	3	3	6	37
05-06—Ottawa	NHL	76	5	16	21	50	2	1	0	8	0	2	2	12
NHL Totals (10 years)		493	58	125	183	410	19	7	0	87	11	19	30	82

VARLAMOV, SEMEN G

PERSONAL: Born April 27, 1988, in Samara, Rus. ... 6-1/183. ... Catches left.
TRANSACTIONS/CAREER NOTES: Selected by Washington Capitals in first round (second Capitals pick; 23rd overall) of NHL draft (June 24, 2006).

Season Team	League	GP	Min.	W	L	OTL	T	GA	SO	GAA	SV%	GP	Min.	W	L	GA	SO	GAA	SV%
		REGULAR SEASON										PLAYOFFS							
05-06—Lokomotiv Yaroslavl	Russian	33	1782	...	...	...	...	54	8	1.82	...	—	—	—	—	—	—	—	—

VASICEK, JOSEF C/LW

PERSONAL: Born September 12, 1980, in Havlickuv Brod, Czechoslovakia. ... 6-4/200. ... Shoots left. ... Name pronounced VAHSH-ih-chehk.
TRANSACTIONS/CAREER NOTES: Selected by Carolina Hurricanes in fourth round (fourth Hurricanes pick, 91st overall) of NHL draft (June 27, 1998). ... Injured knee (January 14, 2002); missed four games. ... Left knee injury (November 12, 2005) and surgery (December 5, 2005); missed 59 games. ... Traded by Hurricanes to Nashville Predators for F Scott Walker (July 18, 2006).
STATISTICAL PLATEAUS: Three-goal games: 2003-04 (1).

Season Team	League	GP	G	A	Pts.	PIM	+/-	PP	SH	GP	G	A	Pts.	PIM
		REGULAR SEASON								PLAYOFFS				
95-96—Havlickuv Brod	Czech. Jrs.	36	25	25	50	...	...	...	...	—	—	—	—	—
96-97—Slavia Praha	Czech. Jrs.	37	20	40	60	...	...	...	...	—	—	—	—	—
97-98—Slavia Praha	Czech. Jrs.	34	13	20	33	...	...	...	...	—	—	—	—	—
98-99—Sault Ste. Marie	OHL	66	21	35	56	30	7	...	...	5	3	0	3	10
99-00—Sault Ste. Marie	OHL	54	26	46	72	49	16	9	1	17	5	15	20	8
00-01—Carolina	NHL	76	8	13	21	53	-8	1	0	6	2	0	2	0
—Cincinnati	IHL	...	...	...	...	...	...	...	...	3	0	0	0	0
01-02—Carolina	NHL	78	14	17	31	53	-7	3	0	23	3	2	5	12
02-03—Carolina	NHL	57	10	10	20	33	-19	4	0	—	—	—	—	—
03-04—Carolina	NHL	82	19	26	45	60	-3	6	0	—	—	—	—	—
04-05—Slavia Praha	Czech Rep.	52	20	23	43	42	13	...	...	7	1	6	7	10
05-06—Carolina	NHL	23	4	5	9	8	3	0	0	8	0	0	0	2
NHL Totals (5 years)		316	55	71	126	207	-34	14	0	37	5	2	7	14

VASYUNOV, ALEXANDER LW

PERSONAL: Born April 22, 1988, in Yaroslavl, Rus. ... 6-0/189. ... Shoots right.
TRANSACTIONS/CAREER NOTES: Selected by New Jersey Devils in second round (second Devils pick; 58th overall) of NHL draft (June 24, 2006).

Season Team	League	GP	G	A	Pts.	PIM	+/-	PP	SH	GP	G	A	Pts.	PIM
		REGULAR SEASON								PLAYOFFS				
05-06—Lokomotive Yaroslavl	Russian Jr.	29	29	6	35	14	...	...	...	—	—	—	—	—
—Lokomotiv Yaroslavl	Russian	2	0	0	0	2	...	...	...	—	—	—	—	—

VEILLEUX, STEPHANE C/LW

PERSONAL: Born November 16, 1981, in Beauceville, Que. ... 6-1/181. ... Shoots left. ... Name pronounced STEH-fan VAY-oo.
TRANSACTIONS/CAREER NOTES: Selected by Minnesota Wild in third round (fourth Wild pick, 93rd overall) of entry draft (June 23, 2001).

Season Team	League	GP	G	A	Pts.	PIM	+/-	PP	SH	GP	G	A	Pts.	PIM
		REGULAR SEASON								PLAYOFFS				
98-99—Victoriaville	QMJHL	65	6	13	19	35	...	...	...	6	1	3	4	2
99-00—Victoriaville	QMJHL	22	1	4	5	17	...	...	...	—	—	—	—	—

Season Team	League	GP	G	A	Pts.	PIM	+/-	PP	SH	GP	G	A	Pts.	PIM
		REGULAR SEASON								PLAYOFFS				
—Val-d'Or	QMJHL	50	14	28	42	100	...	...	...	—	—	—	—	—
00-01—Val-d'Or	QMJHL	68	48	67	115	90	...	...	...	21	15	18	33	42
01-02—Houston	AHL	77	13	22	35	113	5	0	2	14	2	4	6	20
02-03—Minnesota	NHL	38	3	2	5	23	-6	1	0	—	—	—	—	—
—Houston	AHL	29	8	4	12	43	1	2	0	23	7	11	18	12
03-04—Minnesota	NHL	19	2	8	10	20	0	1	1	—	—	—	—	—
—Houston	AHL	64	13	25	38	66	-11	3	4	2	1	1	2	2
04-05—Houston	AHL	59	15	24	39	35	5	7	1	0	0	0	0	0
05-06—Minnesota	NHL	71	7	9	16	63	-13	0	0	—	—	—	—	—
NHL Totals (3 years)		128	12	19	31	106	-19	2	1					

VERMETTE, ANTOINE LW/C

PERSONAL: Born July 20, 1982, in St. Agapit, Que. ... 6-0/184. ... Shoots left.

TRANSACTIONS/CAREER NOTES: Selected by Ottawa Senators in second round (third Senators pick, 55th overall) of NHL entry draft (June 24, 2000). ... Separated shoulder (January 9, 2004); missed nine games. ... Injured shoulder (February 3, 2004); missed eight games.

Season Team	League	GP	G	A	Pts.	PIM	+/-	PP	SH	GP	G	A	Pts.	PIM
		REGULAR SEASON								PLAYOFFS				
98-99—Quebec	QMJHL	57	9	17	26	32	...	...	...	13	0	0	0	2
99-00—Victoriaville	QMJHL	71	30	41	71	87	...	...	...	6	0	1	1	6
00-01—Victoriaville	QMJHL	71	57	62	119	102	50	17	3	9	4	6	10	14
01-02—Victoriaville	QMJHL	4	0	2	2	6	...	...	...	22	10	16	26	10
02-03—Binghamton	AHL	80	34	28	62	57	-2	13	3	14	2	9	11	10
03-04—Ottawa	NHL	57	7	7	14	16	5	0	1	4	0	1	1	4
—Binghamton	AHL	3	0	0	0	6	-3	0	0	—	—	—	—	—
04-05—Binghamton	AHL	78	28	45	73	36	20	7	4	6	1	4	5	10
05-06—Ottawa	NHL	82	21	12	33	44	17	1	6	10	2	0	2	4
NHL Totals (2 years)		139	28	19	47	60	22	1	7	14	2	1	3	8

VIGIER, J.P. RW/LW

PERSONAL: Born September 11, 1976, in Notre Dame de Lourdes, Man. ... 6-0/200. ... Shoots right. ... Name pronounced vih-ZHAY.

TRANSACTIONS/CAREER NOTES: Signed as free agent by Atlanta Thrashers (March 24, 2000). ... Injured cheekbone (January 22, 2004); missed three games. ... Rib (February 21, 2004); missed seven games. ... Facial cuts (April 3, 2004); missed remainder of regular season. ... Signed as free agent by AHL Chicago (September 27, 2004). ... Broken foot (October 19, 2005); missed 14 games. ... Torn ACL (February 9, 2006) and surgery (February 12, 2006); missed final 25 games of regular season.

Season Team	League	GP	G	A	Pts.	PIM	+/-	PP	SH	GP	G	A	Pts.	PIM
		REGULAR SEASON								PLAYOFFS				
96-97—Northern Michigan	CCHA	36	10	14	24	54	...	...	...	—	—	—	—	—
97-98—Northern Michigan	CCHA	36	12	15	27	60	...	...	...	—	—	—	—	—
98-99—Northern Michigan	CCHA	42	21	18	39	80	...	...	...	—	—	—	—	—
99-00—Northern Michigan	CCHA	39	18	17	35	72	...	...	...	—	—	—	—	—
—Orlando	IHL	1	0	0	0	0	...	...	...	—	—	—	—	—
00-01—Orlando	IHL	78	23	17	40	66	...	...	...	16	6	6	12	14
—Atlanta	NHL	2	0	0	0	0	-2	0	0	—	—	—	—	—
01-02—Chicago	AHL	62	25	16	41	26	4	9	0	21	7	7	14	20
—Atlanta	NHL	15	4	1	5	4	-5	0	0	—	—	—	—	—
02-03—Chicago	AHL	63	29	27	56	54	13	11	2	9	3	1	4	4
—Atlanta	NHL	13	0	0	0	4	-13	0	0	—	—	—	—	—
03-04—Atlanta	NHL	70	10	8	18	22	-18	2	2	—	—	—	—	—
04-05—Chicago	AHL	76	29	41	70	56	26	11	1	18	5	6	11	19
05-06—Atlanta	NHL	41	4	6	10	40	-4	1	1	—	—	—	—	—
NHL Totals (5 years)		141	18	15	33	70	-42	3	3					

V

VISHNEVSKI, VITALY D

PERSONAL: Born March 18, 1980, in Kharkov, U.S.S.R. ... 6-2/200. ... Shoots left. ... Name pronounced vihsh-NEHV-skee.

TRANSACTIONS/CAREER NOTES: Selected by Anaheim Mighty Ducks in first round (first Mighty Ducks pick, fifth overall) of NHL draft (June 27, 1998). ... Injured (April 5, 2000); missed final two games of season. ... Strained hip muscle (January 30, 2001); missed three games. ... Strained shoulder (March 16, 2001); missed three games. ... Back spasms (December 23, 2001); missed one game. ... Sprained left wrist (December 26, 2001); missed five games. ... Suspended two games for elbowing incident (March 15, 2002).

Season Team	League	GP	G	A	Pts.	PIM	+/-	PP	SH	GP	G	A	Pts.	PIM
		REGULAR SEASON								PLAYOFFS				
95-96—Torpedo Yaroslavl	CIS Div. II	40	4	4	8	20	...	...	...	—	—	—	—	—
96-97—Torpedo Yaroslavl	Rus. Div.	45	0	2	2	30	...	...	...	—	—	—	—	—
97-98—Torpedo Yaroslavl	Rus. Div.	47	8	9	17	164	...	...	...	—	—	—	—	—
98-99—Torpedo Yaroslavl	Russian	34	3	4	7	38	...	...	...	10	0	0	0	4
99-00—Cincinnati	AHL	35	1	3	4	45	...	...	...	—	—	—	—	—
—Anaheim	NHL	31	1	1	2	26	0	1	0	—	—	—	—	—
00-01—Anaheim	NHL	76	1	10	11	99	-1	0	0	—	—	—	—	—
01-02—Anaheim	NHL	74	0	3	3	60	-10	0	0	—	—	—	—	—
02-03—Anaheim	NHL	80	2	6	8	76	-8	0	1	21	0	1	1	6
03-04—Anaheim	NHL	73	6	10	16	51	0	0	0	—	—	—	—	—
04-05—Khimik Voskresensk	Russian	51	7	17	24	92	-6	...	...	—	—	—	—	—
05-06—Anaheim	NHL	82	1	7	8	91	8	0	0	16	0	4	4	10
—Russian Oly. team	Int'l	8	0	1	1	4	2	0	0	—	—	—	—	—
NHL Totals (6 years)		416	11	37	48	403	-11	1	1	37	0	5	5	16

VISHNEVSKIY, IVAN D

PERSONAL: Born February 18, 1988, in Barnaul, Rus. ... 5-11/176. ... Shoots left.
TRANSACTIONS/CAREER NOTES: Selected by Dallas Stars in first round (first Stars pick; 27th overall) of NHL draft (June 24, 2006).

		REGULAR SEASON								PLAYOFFS				
Season Team	League	GP	G	A	Pts.	PIM	+/-	PP	SH	GP	G	A	Pts.	PIM
04-05—Lada Togliatti	Russian	50	39	32	71	...	...	...	...	—	—	—	—	—
05-06—Rouyn-Noranda	QMJHL	54	13	35	48	57	1	...	...	5	2	1	3	2

VISNOVSKY, LUBOMIR D

PERSONAL: Born August 11, 1976, in Topolcany, Czech. ... 5-10/188. ... Shoots left. ... Name pronounced LOO-boh-mihr vihsh-NAWV-skee.
TRANSACTIONS/CAREER NOTES: Selected by Los Angeles Kings in fourth round (fourth Kings pick, 118th overall) of entry draft (June 24, 2000). ... Back spasms (December 3, 2000); missed one game. ... Back spasms (November 19, 2002); missed one game. ... Back (November 23, 2002); missed nine games. ... Left knee (January 18, 2003); missed 12 games. ... Ankle (March 20, 2003); missed one game. ... Concussion (December 20, 2003); missed six games. ... Shoulder (January 31, 2004); missed 17 games. ... Cervical strain (Jan 12, 2006); missed two games.

		REGULAR SEASON								PLAYOFFS				
Season Team	League	GP	G	A	Pts.	PIM	+/-	PP	SH	GP	G	A	Pts.	PIM
94-95—Bratislava	Slovakia	36	11	12	23	10	...	...	...	9	1	3	4	2
95-96—Bratislava	Slovakia	35	8	6	14	22	...	...	...	13	1	5	6	2
96-97—Bratislava	Slovakia	44	11	12	23	...	...	...	...	2	0	1	1	...
97-98—Bratislava	Slovakia	36	7	9	16	16	...	...	...	11	2	4	6	8
98-99—Bratislava	Slovakia	40	9	10	19	31	...	...	...	10	5	5	10	0
99-00—Bratislava	Slovakia	52	21	24	45	38	...	...	...	8	5	3	8	16
00-01—Los Angeles	NHL	81	7	32	39	36	16	3	0	8	0	0	0	0
01-02—Los Angeles	NHL	72	4	17	21	14	-5	1	0	4	0	1	1	0
—Slovakian Oly. team	Int'l	3	1	2	3	0	...	...	...	—	—	—	—	—
02-03—Los Angeles	NHL	57	8	16	24	28	2	1	0	—	—	—	—	—
03-04—Los Angeles	NHL	58	8	21	29	26	8	5	0	—	—	—	—	—
04-05—Bratislava	Slovakia	43	13	24	37	40	12	8	0	14	2	10	12	10
05-06—Los Angeles	NHL	80	17	50	67	50	7	10	0	—	—	—	—	—
—Slovakian Oly. team	Int'l	6	1	1	2	0	3	1	0	—	—	—	—	—
NHL Totals (5 years)		348	44	136	180	154	28	20	0	12	0	1	1	0

VOKOUN, TOMAS G

PERSONAL: Born July 2, 1976, in Karlovy Vary, Czech. ... 6-0/197. ... Catches right. ... Name pronounced voh-KOON.
TRANSACTIONS/CAREER NOTES: Selected by Montreal Canadiens in ninth round (11th Canadiens pick, 226th overall) of entry draft (June 29, 1994). ... Selected by Nashville Predators in expansion draft (June 26, 1998). ... Neck (January 19, 1999); missed one game. ... Injured (March 31, 2000); missed season's final four games. ... Foot (October 16, 2000); missed three games. ... Ankle (April 6, 2002); missed remainder of season. ... Flu (January 14, 2003); missed one game. ... Flu (January 8, 2004); missed two games. ... Strained left knee (December 9, 2005); missed three games. ... Sore back, blood clots (April 3, 2006); missed regular season's final eight games and playoffs.

		REGULAR SEASON										PLAYOFFS							
Season Team	League	GP	Min.	W	L	OTL	T	GA	SO	GAA	SV%	GP	Min.	W	L	GA	SO	GAA	SV%
93-94 —Poldi Kladno	Czech Rep.	1	20	...	...	...	...	2	0	6.00	...	—	—	—	—	—	—	—	—
94-95 —Poldi Kladno	Czech Rep.	26	1368	...	...	...	...	70	...	3.07	...	5	240	...	...	19	...	4.75	...
95-96 —Wheeling	ECHL	35	1911	20	10	...	2	117	0	3.67	...	7	436	4	3	19	0	2.61	...
—Fredericton	AHL	...	...	...	...	...	...	...	...	...	...	1	59	0	1	4	0	4.07	...
96-97 —Fredericton	AHL	47	2645	12	26	...	7	154	2	3.49	.902	—	—	—	—	—	—	—	—
—Montreal	NHL	1	20	0	0	...	0	4	0	12.00	.714	—	—	—	—	—	—	—	—
97-98 —Fredericton	AHL	31	1735	13	13	...	2	90	0	3.11	.907	—	—	—	—	—	—	—	—
98-99 —Milwaukee	IHL	9	539	3	2	...	4	22	1	2.45	.920	2	149	0	2	8	0	3.22	.909
—Nashville	NHL	37	1954	12	18	...	4	96	1	2.95	.908	—	—	—	—	—	—	—	—
99-00 —Nashville	NHL	33	1879	9	20	...	1	87	1	2.78	.904	—	—	—	—	—	—	—	—
—Milwaukee	IHL	7	364	6	2	...	0	17	0	2.80	...	—	—	—	—	—	—	—	—
00-01 —Nashville	NHL	37	2088	13	17	...	5	85	2	2.44	.910	—	—	—	—	—	—	—	—
01-02 —Nashville	NHL	29	1471	5	14	...	4	66	2	2.69	.903	—	—	—	—	—	—	—	—
02-03 —Nashville	NHL	69	3974	25	31	...	11	146	3	2.20	.918	—	—	—	—	—	—	—	—
03-04 —Nashville	NHL	73	4221	34	29	...	10	178	3	2.53	.909	6	356	2	4	12	1	2.02	†.939
04-05 —HIFK Helsinki	Finland	—	—	—	—	...	—	—	—	—	—	4	205	0	3	12	0	3.51	.846
—HC Znojemsti Orli	Czech Rep.	27	1599	10	14	...	3	69	3	2.59	.927	—	—	—	—	—	—	—	—
05-06 —Nashville	NHL	61	3601	36	18	7	...	160	4	2.67	.919	—	—	—	—	—	—	—	—
—Czech Oly. team	Int'l	7	...	...	...	...	...	...	1	2.46	.897	—	—	—	—	—	—	—	—
NHL Totals (8 years)		340	19208	134	147	7	35	822	16	2.57	.912	6	356	2	4	12	1	2.02	.939

VOLCHENKOV, ANTON D

PERSONAL: Born February 25, 1982, in Moscow, U.S.S.R. ... 6-1/227. ... Shoots left. ... Name pronounced: vohl CHEHN kahf
TRANSACTIONS/CAREER NOTES: Selected by Ottawa Senators in first round (first Senators pick, 21st overall) of NHL draft (June 24, 2000). ... Dental surgery (December 27, 2002); missed one game. ... Injured groin (February 27, 2003); missed four games. ... Injured left shoulder (March 21, 2003); missed seven games. ... Had concussion (October 3, 2003); missed seven games. ... Injured right shoulder (December 9, 2003) and had surgery; missed 52 games. ... Injured rib (November 1, 2005); missed two games. ... Concussion (March 21, 2006); missed three games. ... Neck injury (April 5, 2006); missed two games.

Season Team	League	REGULAR SEASON GP	G	A	Pts.	PIM	+/-	PP	SH	PLAYOFFS GP	G	A	Pts.	PIM
99-00—CSKA	Rus. Div.	30	2	9	11	36	...	...	...	—	—	—	—	—
00-01—Krylja Sovetov	Rus. Div.	34	3	4	7	56	...	...	...	—	—	—	—	—
01-02—Kryla Sov. Moscow	Russian	47	4	16	20	50	...	...	...	3	0	0	0	29
02-03—Ottawa	NHL	57	3	13	16	40	-4	0	0	17	1	1	2	4
03-04—Ottawa	NHL	19	1	2	3	8	1	0	0	5	0	0	0	6
04-05—Binghamton	AHL	69	10	35	45	62	24	3	0	6	0	3	3	0
05-06—Ottawa	NHL	75	4	13	17	53	21	0	0	9	0	4	4	8
—Russian Oly. team	Int'l	8	0	0	0	2	2	0	0	—	—	—	—	—
NHL Totals (3 years)		151	8	28	36	101	18	0	0	31	1	5	6	18

VOROBIEV, PAVEL RW/LW

PERSONAL: Born May 5, 1982, in Karaganda, U.S.S.R. ... 6-0/194. ... Shoots left.
TRANSACTIONS/CAREER NOTES: Selected by Chicago Blackhawks in first round (second Blackhawks pick, 11th overall) of entry draft (June 24, 2000). ... Bruised ankle (November 18, 2005); missed three games. ... Aggravated bruised ankle (November 27, 2005); missed four games.

Season Team	League	REGULAR SEASON GP	G	A	Pts.	PIM	+/-	PP	SH	PLAYOFFS GP	G	A	Pts.	PIM
98-99—Torpedo Yaroslavl	Rus. Div.	17	0	1	1	0	...	...	...	—	—	—	—	—
99-00—Torpedo Yaroslavl	Russian	8	2	0	2	4	...	...	...	—	—	—	—	—
—Torpedo Yaroslavl	Rus. Div.	40	19	15	34	8	...	...	...	—	—	—	—	—
00-01—Lokomotiv Yaroslavl	Russian	36	8	8	16	28	...	...	...	10	4	1	5	8
01-02—Lokomotiv Yaroslavl	Russian	9	3	2	5	6	...	...	...	7	0	0	0	4
02-03—Lokomotiv Yaroslavl	Russian	44	10	18	28	10	...	...	...	—	—	—	—	—
03-04—Chicago	NHL	18	1	3	4	4	1	1	0	—	—	—	—	—
—Norfolk	AHL	57	13	16	29	8	4	0	0	4	0	0	0	0
04-05—Norfolk	AHL	79	19	25	44	48	-1	6	2	6	2	1	3	4
05-06—Norfolk	AHL	32	9	16	25	23	4	0	1	4	1	2	3	0
—Chicago	NHL	39	9	12	21	34	-2	2	0	—	—	—	—	—
NHL Totals (2 years)		57	10	15	25	38	-1	3	0					

VRBATA, RADIM RW

PERSONAL: Born June 13, 1981, in Mlada Boleslav, Czech. ... 6-1/190. ... Shoots right. ... Name pronounced ra-DEEM vuhr-BA-tuh.
TRANSACTIONS/CAREER NOTES: Selected by Colorado Avalanche in eighth round (10th Avalanche pick, 212th overall) of entry draft (June 26, 1999). ... Injured ribs (December 21, 2001); missed eight games. ... Flu (March 6, 2002); missed one game. ... Injured wrist (March 7, 2003); missed one game. ... Traded by Avalanche to Carolina Hurricanes for LW Bates Battaglia (March 11, 2003). ... Flu (March 4, 2003); missed two games. ... Traded by Hurricanes to Chicago Blackhawks for future considerations (December 30, 2005).
STATISTICAL PLATEAUS: Three-goal games: 2001-02 (1), 2003-04 (1). Total: 2.

Season Team	League	REGULAR SEASON GP	G	A	Pts.	PIM	+/-	PP	SH	PLAYOFFS GP	G	A	Pts.	PIM
98-99—Hull	QMJHL	64	22	38	60	16	...	...	...	23	6	13	19	6
99-00—Hull	QMJHL	58	29	45	74	26	...	...	...	15	3	9	12	8
00-01—Shawinigan	QMJHL	55	56	64	120	67	...	...	...	10	4	7	11	4
—Hershey	AHL	...	...	...	...	...	...	...	...	1	0	1	1	2
01-02—Hershey	AHL	20	8	14	22	8	5	2	0	—	—	—	—	—
—Colorado	NHL	52	18	12	30	14	7	6	0	9	0	0	0	0
02-03—Colorado	NHL	66	11	19	30	16	0	3	0	—	—	—	—	—
—Carolina	NHL	10	5	0	5	2	-7	3	0	—	—	—	—	—
03-04—Carolina	NHL	80	12	13	25	24	-10	4	0	—	—	—	—	—
04-05—Mlada-Boleslav	Czech Rep.	2	0	1	1	6	-2	...	...	—	—	—	—	—
—Liberec	Czech Rep.	45	18	21	39	91	26	...	...	12	3	2	5	0
05-06—Carolina	NHL	16	2	3	5	6	0	1	0	—	—	—	—	—
—Chicago	NHL	45	13	21	34	16	4	5	0	—	—	—	—	—
NHL Totals (4 years)		269	61	68	129	78	-6	22	0	9	0	0	0	0

VYBORNY, DAVID C/RW

PERSONAL: Born June 2, 1975, in Jihlava, Czechoslovakia. ... 5-10/189. ... Shoots left. ... Name pronounced vih-BOHR-nee.
TRANSACTIONS/CAREER NOTES: Selected by Edmonton Oilers in second round (third Oilers pick, 33rd overall) of entry draft (June 26, 1993). ... Signed as free agent by Columbus Blue Jackets (June 7, 2000). ... Strained hip flexor (February 20, 2001); missed one game. ... Strained groin (April 1, 2001); missed two games. ... Strained hip flexor (November 29, 2001); missed one game. ... Sprained knee (January 24, 2002); missed three games. ... Rib (December 21, 2005); missed two games.
STATISTICAL PLATEAUS: Three-goal games: 2003-04 (1).

Season Team	League	REGULAR SEASON GP	G	A	Pts.	PIM	+/-	PP	SH	PLAYOFFS GP	G	A	Pts.	PIM
90-91—Sparta Prague	Czech.	3	0	0	0	0	...	...	...	—	—	—	—	—
91-92—Sparta Prague	Czech.	32	6	9	15	2	...	...	...	—	—	—	—	—
92-93—Sparta Prague	Czech.	52	20	24	44	...	...	...	...	—	—	—	—	—
93-94—Sparta Prague	Czech Rep.	44	15	20	35	...	...	...	...	6	4	7	11	...
94-95—Cape Breton	AHL	76	23	38	61	30	-12	7	0	—	—	—	—	—
95-96—Sparta Praha	Czech Rep.	52	19	36	55	42	...	...	...	—	—	—	—	—
96-97—Sparta Praha	Czech Rep.	47	20	29	49	14	...	...	...	—	—	—	—	—
97-98—MoDo Ornskoldsvik	Sweden	45	16	21	37	34	...	...	...	—	—	—	—	—
98-99—Sparta Praha	Czech Rep.	52	24	46	70	22	...	...	...	8	1	3	4	...
99-00—Sparta Praha	Czech Rep.	50	25	38	63	30	...	...	...	9	3	8	11	4
00-01—Columbus	NHL	79	13	19	32	22	-9	5	0	—	—	—	—	—

Season Team	League	GP	G	A	Pts.	PIM	+/-	PP	SH		GP	G	A	Pts.	PIM
		REGULAR SEASON									PLAYOFFS				
01-02—Columbus	NHL	75	13	18	31	6	-14	6	0		—	—	—	—	—
02-03—Columbus	NHL	79	20	26	46	16	12	4	1		—	—	—	—	—
03-04—Columbus	NHL	82	22	31	53	40	-26	8	4		—	—	—	—	—
04-05—Sparta Praha	Czech Rep.	51	12	34	46	10	12	...	...		5	2	5	7	4
05-06—Columbus	NHL	80	22	43	65	50	-9	5	2		—	—	—	—	—
—Czech Rep. Oly. team	Int'l	8	1	3	4	0	3	0	0		—	—	—	—	—
NHL Totals (5 years)		395	90	137	227	134	-46	28	7						

WALKER, MATT D

PERSONAL: Born April 7, 1980, in Beaverlodge, Alta. ... 6-3/227. ... Shoots right. ... Nickname: Walks.

TRANSACTIONS/CAREER NOTES: Selected by St. Louis Blues in third round (third Blues pick, 83rd overall) of entry draft (June 27, 1998). ... Groin (September 23, 2003); missed season's final 51 games. ... Foot (October 5, 2005); missed five games. ... Separated right shoulder (December 8, 2005); missed eight games. ... Sprained knee (January 4, 2006); missed 13 games.

Season Team	League	GP	G	A	Pts.	PIM	+/-	PP	SH		GP	G	A	Pts.	PIM
		REGULAR SEASON									PLAYOFFS				
97-98—Portland	WHL	64	2	13	15	124	...	...	...		16	0	0	0	21
98-99—Portland	WHL	64	1	10	11	151	-16	0	0		—	—	—	—	—
99-00—Portland	WHL	38	2	7	9	97	...	...	...		—	—	—	—	—
—Kootenay	WHL	69	6	26	32	150	-1	6	0		—	—	—	—	—
00-01—Worcester	AHL	61	4	8	12	131	...	...	...		11	0	0	0	6
—Peoria	ECHL	8	1	0	1	70	...	...	...		—	—	—	—	—
01-02—Worcester	AHL	49	2	11	13	164	5	0	0		3	0	0	0	8
02-03—Worcester	AHL	40	1	8	9	58	15	0	0		—	—	—	—	—
—St. Louis	NHL	16	0	1	1	38	0	0	0		—	—	—	—	—
03-04—St. Louis	NHL	14	0	1	1	25	0	0	0		4	0	0	0	0
—Worcester	AHL	4	0	1	1	7	-2	0	0		—	—	—	—	—
04-05—Worcester	AHL	20	2	4	6	44	1	0	0		—	—	—	—	—
05-06—St. Louis	NHL	54	0	2	2	79	-7	0	0		—	—	—	—	—
NHL Totals (3 years)		84	0	4	4	142	-7	0	0		4	0	0	0	0

WALKER, SCOTT RW

PERSONAL: Born July 19, 1973, in Cambridge, Ont. ... 5-10/196. ... Shoots right.

TRANSACTIONS/CAREER NOTES: Selected by Vancouver Canucks in fifth round (fourth Canucks pick, 124th overall) of entry draft (June 26, 1993). ... Abdominal strain (October 12, 1996); missed eight games. ... Groin (December 13, 1996); missed six games. ... Fractured nose (November 16, 1997); missed four games. ... Selected by Nashville Predators in expansion draft (June 26, 1998). ... Shoulder (November 19, 1998); missed nine games. ... Ear infection (January 26, 1999); missed two games. ... Concussion (December 6, 1999); missed 10 games. ... Foot (January 21, 2000); missed three games. ... Left shoulder (January 19, 2001); missed eight games. ... Concussion (November 13, 2001); missed three games. ... Concussion (December 1, 2001); missed 12 games. ... Postconcussion syndrome (January 10, 2002); missed remainder of season. ... Torn rib cartilage (October 16, 2002); missed 17 games. ... Neck (January 4, 2003); missed two games. ... Knee (January 14, 2003); missed three games. ... Groin (November 13, 2003); missed six games. ... Sports hernia (October 22, 2005); missed 33 games. ... Wrist (February 8, 2006); missed 16 games. ... Traded by Predators to Carolina Hurricanes for C Josef Vasicek (July 18, 2006).

STATISTICAL PLATEAUS: Three-goal games: 2000-01 (1), 2003-04 (1). Total: 2.

Season Team	League	GP	G	A	Pts.	PIM	+/-	PP	SH		GP	G	A	Pts.	PIM
		REGULAR SEASON									PLAYOFFS				
89-90—Kitch.-Cambridge Jr.	OHA	33	7	27	34	91	...	...	...		—	—	—	—	—
90-91—Cambridge Jr. B	OHA	45	10	27	37	241	...	...	...		—	—	—	—	—
91-92—Owen Sound	OHL	53	7	31	38	128	...	...	...		5	0	7	7	8
92-93—Owen Sound	OHL	57	23	68	91	110	...	...	...		8	1	5	6	16
—Canadian nat'l team	Int'l	2	3	0	3	0	...	...	...		—	—	—	—	—
93-94—Hamilton	AHL	77	10	29	39	272	-16	2	0		4	0	1	1	25
94-95—Syracuse	AHL	74	14	38	52	334	6	5	0		—	—	—	—	—
—Vancouver	NHL	11	0	1	1	33	0	0	0		—	—	—	—	—
95-96—Vancouver	NHL	63	4	8	12	137	-7	0	1		—	—	—	—	—
—Syracuse	AHL	15	3	12	15	52	...	...	...		16	9	8	17	39
96-97—Vancouver	NHL	64	3	15	18	132	2	0	0		—	—	—	—	—
97-98—Vancouver	NHL	59	3	10	13	164	-8	0	1		—	—	—	—	—
98-99—Nashville	NHL	71	15	25	40	103	0	0	1		—	—	—	—	—
99-00—Nashville	NHL	69	7	21	28	90	-16	0	1		—	—	—	—	—
00-01—Nashville	NHL	74	25	29	54	66	-2	9	3		—	—	—	—	—
01-02—Nashville	NHL	28	4	5	9	18	-13	1	0		—	—	—	—	—
02-03—Nashville	NHL	60	15	18	33	58	2	7	0		—	—	—	—	—
03-04—Nashville	NHL	75	25	42	67	94	4	9	3		6	0	1	1	6
04-05—Cambridge	OHA Sr.	5	2	6	8	4	...	...	...		—	—	—	—	—
—Dundas	OHA Sr.	1	1	1	2	17	...	...	...		—	—	—	—	—
05-06—Nashville	NHL	33	5	11	16	36	2	1	0		5	0	0	0	6
NHL Totals (11 years)		607	106	185	291	931	-36	27	10		11	0	1	1	12

W

WALLIN, NICLAS D

PERSONAL: Born February 20, 1975, in Boden, Sweden. ... 6-3/220. ... Shoots left. ... Name pronounced VAH-leen.

TRANSACTIONS/CAREER NOTES: Selected by Carolina Hurricanes in fourth round (third Hurricanes pick, 97th overall) of entry draft (June 24, 2000). ... Fractured wrist (October 5, 2000); missed six games. ... Strained shoulder (January 29, 2001); missed five games. ... Wrist injury (November 11, 2005); missed three games. ... Wrist surgery (November 19, 2005), missed 17 games. ... Lower-body injury (March 11, 2006); missed three games. ... Groin injury (March 21, 2006); missed nine games.

Season Team	League	REGULAR SEASON GP	G	A	Pts.	PIM	+/-	PP	SH	PLAYOFFS GP	G	A	Pts.	PIM
96-97—Brynas Gavle	Sweden	47	1	1	2	16	...	...	...	—	—	—	—	—
97-98—Brynas Gavle	Sweden	44	2	3	5	57	...	...	...	3	0	1	1	4
98-99—Brynas Gavle	Sweden	46	2	4	6	52	...	...	...	14	0	0	0	8
99-00—Brynas Gavle	Sweden	48	7	9	16	73	...	...	...	—	—	—	—	—
00-01—Carolina	NHL	37	2	3	5	21	-11	0	0	3	0	0	0	2
—Cincinnati	IHL	8	1	2	3	4	...	...	...	—	—	—	—	—
01-02—Carolina	NHL	52	1	2	3	36	1	0	0	23	2	1	3	12
02-03—Carolina	NHL	77	2	8	10	71	-19	0	0	—	—	—	—	—
03-04—Carolina	NHL	57	3	7	10	51	-8	0	0	—	—	—	—	—
04-05—Lulea	Sweden	39	6	7	13	89	-15	4	0	3	0	1	1	6
05-06—Carolina	NHL	50	4	4	8	42	2	0	0	25	1	4	5	14
NHL Totals (5 years)		273	12	24	36	221	-35	0	0	51	3	5	8	28

WALTER, BEN — C

PERSONAL: Born May 11, 1984, in Beaconsfield, Que. ... 6-1/195. ... Shoots left. ... Son of Ryan Walter, center with three teams (1978-1993).
COLLEGE: Massachusetts-Lowell.
TRANSACTIONS/CAREER NOTES: Selected by Boston Bruins in fifth round (fifth Bruins pick, 160th overall) of NHL entry draft (June 28, 2004).

Season Team	League	REGULAR SEASON GP	G	A	Pts.	PIM	+/-	PP	SH	PLAYOFFS GP	G	A	Pts.	PIM
00-01—Langley	BCHL	50	8	22	30	19	...	...	...	—	—	—	—	—
02-03—Mass.-Lowell	Hockey East	35	5	12	17	12	...	...	...	—	—	—	—	—
03-04—Mass.-Lowell	Hockey East	36	18	16	34	18	-1	8	1	—	—	—	—	—
04-05—Mass.-Lowell	Hockey East	36	26	13	39	28	...	...	...	—	—	—	—	—
05-06—Providence	AHL	62	16	24	40	33	0	8	1	3	2	0	2	2
—Boston	NHL	6	0	0	0	4	2	0	0	—	—	—	—	—
NHL Totals (1 year)		6	0	0	0	4	2	0	0					

WALZ, WES — C

PERSONAL: Born May 15, 1970, in Calgary. ... 5-10/180. ... Shoots right.
TRANSACTIONS/CAREER NOTES: Selected by Boston Bruins in third round (third Bruins pick, 57th overall) of entry draft (June 17, 1989). ... Traded by Bruins with D Garry Galley and third-round pick (Milos Hoban) in 1993 to Philadelphia Flyers for D Gord Murphy, RW Brian Dobbin and third-round pick (LW Sergei Zholtok) in 1992 (January 2, 1992). ... Signed as free agent by Calgary Flames (August 31, 1993). ... Hip (February 26, 1995); missed one game. ... Signed as free agent by Detroit Red Wings (August 11, 1995). ... Signed as free agent by Minnesota Wild (June 28, 2000). ... Ankle (October 7, 2001); missed eight games. ... Left shoulder (February 25, 2002); missed 10 games. ... Flu (January 4, 2003); missed one game. ... Flu (October 18, 2003); missed two games. ... Left shoulder (January 7, 2004); missed 11 games. ... Abdomen (February 27, 2004); missed one game. ... Abdominal strain (March 3, 2004); missed six games.

Season Team	League	REGULAR SEASON GP	G	A	Pts.	PIM	+/-	PP	SH	PLAYOFFS GP	G	A	Pts.	PIM
87-88—Prince Albert	WHL	1	1	1	2	0	...	...	...	—	—	—	—	—
88-89—Lethbridge	WHL	63	29	75	104	32	...	...	...	8	1	5	6	6
89-90—Boston	NHL	2	1	1	2	0	-1	1	0	—	—	—	—	—
—Lethbridge	WHL	56	54	86	140	69	...	...	...	19	13	24	37	33
90-91—Maine	AHL	20	8	12	20	19	...	...	...	2	0	0	0	21
—Boston	NHL	56	8	8	16	32	-14	1	0	2	0	0	0	0
91-92—Boston	NHL	15	0	3	3	12	-3	0	0	—	—	—	—	—
—Maine	AHL	21	13	11	24	38	...	...	...	—	—	—	—	—
—Hershey	AHL	41	13	28	41	37	...	...	...	6	1	2	3	0
—Philadelphia	NHL	2	1	0	1	0	1	0	0	—	—	—	—	—
92-93—Hershey	AHL	78	35	45	80	106	-2	5	5	—	—	—	—	—
93-94—Calgary	NHL	53	11	27	38	16	20	1	0	6	3	0	3	2
—Saint John	AHL	15	6	6	12	14	6	2	1	—	—	—	—	—
94-95—Calgary	NHL	39	6	12	18	11	7	4	0	1	0	0	0	0
95-96—Adirondack	AHL	38	20	35	55	58	...	...	...	—	—	—	—	—
—Detroit	NHL	2	0	0	0	0	0	0	0	—	—	—	—	—
96-97—Zug	Switzerland	41	24	22	46	67	...	...	...	—	—	—	—	—
97-98—Zug	Switzerland	38	18	34	52	32	...	...	...	20	16	12	28	18
98-99—Zug	Switzerland	42	22	27	49	75	...	...	...	10	3	9	12	2
99-00—Long Beach	IHL	6	4	3	7	8	...	...	...	—	—	—	—	—
—Lugano	Switzerland	13	7	11	18	14	...	...	...	5	3	4	7	4
00-01—Minnesota	NHL	82	18	12	30	37	-8	0	7	—	—	—	—	—
01-02—Minnesota	NHL	64	10	20	30	43	0	0	2	—	—	—	—	—
02-03—Minnesota	NHL	80	13	19	32	63	11	0	0	18	7	6	13	14
03-04—Minnesota	NHL	57	12	13	25	32	5	0	3	—	—	—	—	—
05-06—Minnesota	NHL	82	19	18	37	61	7	1	1	—	—	—	—	—
NHL Totals (11 years)		534	99	133	232	307	25	8	13	27	10	6	16	16

W

WANVIG, KYLE — RW

PERSONAL: Born January 29, 1981, in Calgary. ... 6-2/219. ... Shoots right. ... Name pronounced WAHN-vihg.
TRANSACTIONS/CAREER NOTES: Selected by Boston Bruins in third round (third Bruins pick, 89th overall) of entry draft (June 26, 1999). ... Returned to draft pool by Bruins; selected by Minnesota Wild in second round (second Wild pick, 36th overall) of entry draft (June 23, 2001). ... Suspended one game for instigating an altercation with Penguins D Brooks Orpik (December 8, 2005). ... Signed as free agent by Atlanta Thrashers (July 18, 2006).

Season Team	League	GP	G	A	Pts.	PIM	+/-	PP	SH	GP	G	A	Pts.	PIM
		REGULAR SEASON								PLAYOFFS				
97-98—Edmonton	WHL	62	17	12	29	69	...	...	...	—	—	—	—	—
98-99—Kootenay	WHL	71	12	20	32	119	...	...	...	7	1	3	4	18
99-00—Kootenay	WHL	6	2	2	4	12	...	...	...	—	—	—	—	—
—Red Deer	WHL	58	21	18	39	123	2	5	0	4	1	0	1	4
00-01—Red Deer	WHL	69	55	46	101	202	...	...	...	22	10	12	22	47
01-02—Houston	AHL	34	6	7	13	43	-7	1	0	9	0	1	1	23
02-03—Houston	AHL	57	13	16	29	137	...	...	...	21	6	4	10	27
—Minnesota	NHL	7	1	0	1	13	0	0	0	—	—	—	—	—
03-04—Minnesota	NHL	6	0	1	1	10	-2	0	0	—	—	—	—	—
—Houston	AHL	72	25	16	41	147	0	10	0	2	0	1	1	0
04-05—Houston	AHL	76	13	17	30	158	-12	7	1	5	1	2	3	8
05-06—Minnesota	NHL	51	4	8	12	64	-8	1	0	—	—	—	—	—
NHL Totals (3 years)		64	5	9	14	87	-10	1	0					

WARD, AARON D

PERSONAL: Born January 17, 1973, in Windsor, Ont. ... 6-2/225. ... Shoots right.

TRANSACTIONS/CAREER NOTES: Selected by Winnipeg Jets in first round (first Jets pick, fifth overall) of entry draft (June 22, 1991). ... Traded by Jets with fourth-round pick (D John Jakopin) in 1993 draft and future considerations to Detroit Red Wings for RW Paul Ysebaert (June 11, 1993); Red Wings acquired RW Alan Kerr to complete deal (June 18, 1993). ... Bronchitis (December 22, 1996); missed three games. ... Flu (October 26, 1997); missed two games. ... Bruised knee (November 26, 1997); missed one game. ... Fractured right foot (December 3, 1997); missed 19 games. ... Sprained shoulder (February 7, 1998); missed two games. ... Strained rotator cuff (November 21, 1998); missed two games. ... Injured ribs (October 22, 1999); missed seven games. ... Injured (December 4, 1999); missed four games. ... Injured shoulder (January 22, 2000); missed final 35 games of regular season. ... Flu (January 7, 2001); missed two games. ... Traded by Red Wings to Carolina Hurricanes for second-round pick (C Jiri Hudler) in 2002 draft (July 9, 2001). ... Flu (December 12, 2001); missed one game. ... Injured arm (March 8, 2002); missed one game. ... Injured back (October 29, 2002); missed two games. ... Injured hip (March 15, 2003); missed three games. ... Infection (October 28, 2003); missed seven games. ... Injured upper body (November 26, 2003); missed two games. ... Injured knee (December 9, 2003); missed two games. ... Injured left wrist and had surgery (January 20, 2004); missed 20 games. ... Sports hernia (January 10, 2006); missed 10 games. ... Chest injury (March 18, 2006); missed one game. ... Signed as free agent by New York Rangers (July 3, 2006).

Season Team	League	GP	G	A	Pts.	PIM	+/-	PP	SH	GP	G	A	Pts.	PIM
		REGULAR SEASON								PLAYOFFS				
88-89—Nepean	COJHL	56	2	17	19	44	...	...	...	—	—	—	—	—
89-90—Nepean	COJHL	52	6	33	39	85	...	...	...	—	—	—	—	—
90-91—Univ. of Michigan	CCHA	46	8	11	19	126	...	...	...	—	—	—	—	—
91-92—Univ. of Michigan	CCHA	42	7	12	19	64	...	...	...	—	—	—	—	—
92-93—Univ. of Michigan	CCHA	30	5	8	13	73	...	...	...	—	—	—	—	—
—Canadian nat'l team	Int'l	4	0	0	0	8	...	...	...	—	—	—	—	—
93-94—Detroit	NHL	5	1	0	1	4	2	0	0	—	—	—	—	—
—Adirondack	AHL	58	4	12	16	87	31	0	0	9	2	6	8	6
94-95—Adirondack	AHL	76	11	24	35	87	2	2	0	4	0	1	1	0
—Detroit	NHL	1	0	1	1	2	1	0	0	—	—	—	—	—
95-96—Adirondack	AHL	74	5	10	15	133	...	...	...	3	0	0	0	6
96-97—Detroit	NHL	49	2	5	7	52	-9	0	0	19	0	0	0	17
97-98—Detroit	NHL	52	5	5	10	47	-1	0	0	—	—	—	—	—
98-99—Detroit	NHL	60	3	8	11	52	-5	0	0	8	0	1	1	8
99-00—Detroit	NHL	36	1	3	4	24	-4	0	0	3	0	0	0	0
00-01—Detroit	NHL	73	4	5	9	57	-4	0	0	—	—	—	—	—
01-02—Carolina	NHL	79	3	11	14	74	0	0	0	23	1	1	2	22
02-03—Carolina	NHL	77	3	6	9	90	-23	0	0	—	—	—	—	—
03-04—Carolina	NHL	49	3	5	8	37	1	2	0	—	—	—	—	—
04-05—Ingolstadt ERC	Germany	8	0	3	3	16	-5	0	0	11	1	1	2	16
05-06—Carolina	NHL	71	6	19	25	62	2	0	0	25	2	3	5	18
NHL Totals (11 years)		552	31	68	99	501	-40	2	0	78	3	5	8	65

WARD, CAM G

PERSONAL: Born February 29, 1984, in Sherwood Park, Alta. ... 6-0/176. ... Catches left.

TRANSACTIONS/CAREER NOTES: Selected by Carolina Hurricanes in first round (first Hurricanes pick, 25th overall) of NHL entry draft (June 22, 2002).

Season Team	League	GP	Min.	W	L	OTL	T	GA	SO	GAA	SV%	GP	Min.	W	L	GA	SO	GAA	SV%
		REGULAR SEASON										PLAYOFFS							
00-01—Red Deer	WHL	1	60	1	0	...	0	0	1	0.00	...	—	—	—	—	—	—	—	—
01-02—Red Deer	WHL	46	2694	30	11	...	4	102	1	2.27	...	23	1502	14	9	53	2	2.12	...
02-03—Red Deer	WHL	57	3368	40	13	...	3	118	5	2.10	...	—	—	—	—	—	—	—	—
03-04—Red Deer	WHL	56	3338	31	16	...	8	114	4	2.05	...	—	—	—	—	—	—	—	—
04-05—Lowell	AHL	50	2828	27	17	...	...	94	6	1.99	.937	11	663	5	6	28	2	2.53	.918
05-06—Lowell	AHL	2	118	0	2	0	...	5	0	2.54	.915	—	—	—	—	—	—	—	—
—Carolina	NHL	28	1484	14	8	2	...	91	0	3.68	.882	*23	*1320	*15	*8	47	2	2.14	.920
NHL Totals (1 year)		28	1484	14	8	2	0	91	0	3.68	.882	23	1320	15	8	47	2	2.14	.920

WARD, JASON RW/C

PERSONAL: Born January 16, 1979, in Chapleau, Ont. ... 6-3/203. ... Shoots right.

TRANSACTIONS/CAREER NOTES: Selected by Montreal Canadiens in first round (first Canadiens pick, 11th overall) of entry draft (June 21, 1997). ... Fractured cheekbone (February 10, 2000); missed seven games. ... Injured knee (January 12, 2001); missed remainder of season.

... Injured elbow (March 27, 2003); missed four games ... Fractured ankle (November 1, 2003); missed 19 games. ... Separated left shoulder (January 24, 2004); missed two games. ... Signed as free agent by New York Rangers (August 4, 2005).

		REGULAR SEASON								PLAYOFFS				
Season Team	League	GP	G	A	Pts.	PIM	+/-	PP	SH	GP	G	A	Pts.	PIM
94-95—Oshawa	Tier II Jr. A	47	30	31	61	75	...	...	...	—	—	—	—	—
95-96—Niagara Falls	OHL	64	15	35	50	139	...	...	...	10	6	4	10	23
96-97—Erie	OHL	58	25	39	64	137	6	4	3	5	1	2	3	2
97-98—Erie	OHL	21	7	9	16	42	...	...	...	—	—	—	—	—
—Windsor	OHL	26	19	27	46	34	...	...	...	—	—	—	—	—
—Fredericton	AHL	7	1	0	1	2	3	0	0	1	0	0	0	2
98-99—Windsor	OHL	12	8	11	19	25	...	...	...	—	—	—	—	—
—Plymouth	OHL	23	14	13	27	28	...	...	...	11	6	8	14	12
—Fredericton	AHL	...	...	...	...	...	...	...	...	10	4	2	6	22
99-00—Quebec	AHL	40	14	12	26	30	...	...	...	3	2	1	3	4
—Montreal	NHL	32	2	1	3	10	-1	1	0	—	—	—	—	—
00-01—Quebec	AHL	23	7	12	19	69	...	...	...	—	—	—	—	—
—Montreal	NHL	12	0	0	0	12	3	0	0	—	—	—	—	—
01-02—Quebec	AHL	78	24	33	57	128	0	4	1	3	0	0	0	2
02-03—Montreal	NHL	8	3	2	5	0	3	0	0	—	—	—	—	—
—Hamilton	AHL	69	31	41	72	78	20	10	4	23	12	9	21	20
03-04—Hamilton	AHL	2	0	3	3	17	1	0	0	—	—	—	—	—
—Montreal	NHL	53	5	7	12	21	3	2	0	5	0	2	2	2
04-05—Hamilton	AHL	77	20	34	54	66	7	9	1	4	2	1	3	2
05-06—New York Rangers	NHL	81	10	18	28	44	-4	0	2	1	0	0	0	2
NHL Totals (5 years)		186	20	28	48	87	4	3	2	6	0	2	2	4

WARRENER, RHETT D

PERSONAL: Born January 27, 1976, in Shaunavon, Sask. ... 6-2/217. ... Shoots right. ... Name pronounced REHT WAHR-ihn-nuhr.

TRANSACTIONS/CAREER NOTES: Selected by Florida Panthers in second round (second Panthers pick, 27th overall) of entry draft (June 28, 1994). ... Strained groin (October 20, 1996); missed four games. ... Reinjured groin (November 11, 1996); missed two games. ... Reinjured groin (December 22, 1996); missed 10 games. ... Strained groin (November 2, 1998); missed 12 games. ... Traded by Panthers with fifth-round pick (G Ryan Miller) in 1999 draft to Buffalo Sabres for D Mike Wilson (March 23, 1999). ... Shoulder (October 30, 1999); missed two games. ... Strained hip muscle (January 1, 2000); missed four games. ... Groin (February 21, 2000); missed eight games. ... Concussion (November 17, 2000); missed five games. ... Groin (October 26, 2001); missed 14 games. ... Wrist (January 8, 2002); missed one game. ... Suspended two games for receiving third instigator penalty in one season (March 29, 2002). ... Strained abdominal muscle (December 1, 2002); missed three games. ... Groin (December 20, 2002); missed nine games. ... Fractured foot (January 10, 2003); missed 10 games. ... Inner-ear imbalance (March 18, 2002); missed one game. ... Traded by Sabres to Calgary Flames with C Steve Reinprecht for C Steve Begin and C/LW Chris Drury (July 2, 2003). ... Groin (November 4, 2003); missed two games. ... Mouth (January 30, 2004); missed two games. ... Knee (January 6, 2006); missed three games. ... Sprained knee (March 9, 2006); missed 17 games.

		REGULAR SEASON								PLAYOFFS				
Season Team	League	GP	G	A	Pts.	PIM	+/-	PP	SH	GP	G	A	Pts.	PIM
91-92—Saskatoon	WHL	2	0	0	0	0	...	...	...	—	—	—	—	—
92-93—Saskatoon	WHL	68	2	17	19	100	...	...	...	9	0	0	0	14
93-94—Saskatoon	WHL	61	7	19	26	131	25	6	0	16	0	5	5	33
94-95—Saskatoon	WHL	66	13	26	39	137	52	4	0	10	0	3	3	6
95-96—Carolina	AHL	9	0	0	0	4	...	...	...	—	—	—	—	—
—Florida	NHL	28	0	3	3	46	4	0	0	21	0	3	3	10
96-97—Florida	NHL	62	4	9	13	88	20	1	0	5	0	0	0	0
97-98—Florida	NHL	79	0	4	4	99	-16	0	0	—	—	—	—	—
98-99—Florida	NHL	48	0	7	7	64	-1	0	0	—	—	—	—	—
—Buffalo	NHL	13	1	0	1	20	3	0	0	20	1	3	4	32
99-00—Buffalo	NHL	61	0	3	3	89	18	0	0	5	0	0	0	2
00-01—Buffalo	NHL	77	3	16	19	78	10	0	0	13	0	2	2	4
01-02—Buffalo	NHL	65	5	5	10	113	15	0	0	—	—	—	—	—
02-03—Buffalo	NHL	50	0	9	9	63	1	0	0	—	—	—	—	—
03-04—Calgary	NHL	77	3	14	17	97	8	0	1	24	0	1	1	6
05-06—Calgary	NHL	61	3	3	6	54	7	0	1	7	0	0	0	14
NHL Totals (10 years)		621	19	73	92	811	69	1	2	95	1	9	10	68

WEAVER, MIKE D

PERSONAL: Born May 2, 1978, in Bramalea, Ont. ... 5-9/182. ... Shoots right.

TRANSACTIONS/CAREER NOTES: Signed as free agent by Atlanta Thrashers (June 15, 2000). ... Signed as free agent by Los Angeles Kings (July 16, 2004). ... Foot (October 29, 2005); missed seven games. ... Hip flexor (December 29, 2005); missed six games.

		REGULAR SEASON								PLAYOFFS				
Season Team	League	GP	G	A	Pts.	PIM	+/-	PP	SH	GP	G	A	Pts.	PIM
96-97—Michigan State	CCHA	39	0	7	7	46	...	...	...	—	—	—	—	—
97-98—Michigan State	CCHA	44	4	22	26	68	...	...	...	—	—	—	—	—
98-99—Michigan State	CCHA	42	1	6	7	54	...	...	...	—	—	—	—	—
99-00—Michigan State	CCHA	37	0	8	8	34	...	...	...	—	—	—	—	—
00-01—Orlando	IHL	68	0	8	8	34	...	...	...	16	0	2	2	8
01-02—Chicago	AHL	58	2	8	10	67	-9	1	0	25	1	3	4	21
—Atlanta	NHL	16	0	1	1	10	0	0	0	—	—	—	—	—
02-03—Atlanta	NHL	40	0	5	5	20	-5	0	0	—	—	—	—	—
—Chicago	AHL	33	2	2	4	32	2	0	0	9	0	3	3	4
03-04—Atlanta	NHL	1	0	0	0	0	-1	0	0	—	—	—	—	—
—Chicago	AHL	78	3	14	17	89	20	0	0	9	2	2	4	20

W

Season Team	League	GP	G	A	Pts.	PIM	+/-	PP	SH		GP	G	A	Pts.	PIM
		REGULAR SEASON									PLAYOFFS				
04-05—Manchester	AHL	79	1	22	23	61	35	0	0		6	0	1	1	0
05-06—Los Angeles	NHL	53	0	9	9	14	-3	0	0		—	—	—	—	—
NHL Totals (4 years)		110	0	15	15	44	-9	0	0						

WEBER, MIKE D

PERSONAL: Born December 16, 1987, in Pittsburgh, Pa. ... 6-2/199. ... Shoots left.
TRANSACTIONS/CAREER NOTES: Selected by Buffalo Sabres in second round (third Sabres pick; 57th overall) of NHL draft (June 24, 2006).

Season Team	League	GP	G	A	Pts.	PIM	+/-	PP	SH		GP	G	A	Pts.	PIM
		REGULAR SEASON									PLAYOFFS				
03-04—Windsor	OHL	65	0	2	2	49	-9	...	...		—	—	—	—	—
04-05—Windsor	OHL	68	2	6	8	132	-17	...	...		11	0	1	1	18
05-06—Windsor	OHL	68	5	21	26	181	17	...	...		7	0	0	0	12

WEBER, SHEA D

PERSONAL: Born August 14, 1985, in Sicamous, B.C. ... 6-3/195. ... Shoots right.
TRANSACTIONS/CAREER NOTES: Selected by Nashville Predators in second round (fourth Predators pick, 49th overall) of entry draft (June 20, 2003).

Season Team	League	GP	G	A	Pts.	PIM	+/-	PP	SH		GP	G	A	Pts.	PIM
		REGULAR SEASON									PLAYOFFS				
01-02—Kelowna	WHL	5	0	0	0	0	...	...	...		—	—	—	—	—
—Sicamous	KIJHL	47	9	33	42	87	...	...	...		—	—	—	—	—
02-03—Kelowna	WHL	70	2	16	18	167	...	...	...		19	1	4	5	26
03-04—Kelowna	WHL	60	12	20	32	126	23	8	0		17	3	14	17	16
04-05—Kelowna	WHL	55	12	29	41	95	12	7	0		18	9	8	17	25
05-06—Milwaukee	AHL	46	12	15	27	49	1	9	1		8	5	2	7	8
—Nashville	NHL	28	2	8	10	42	8	2	0		4	2	0	2	8
NHL Totals (1 year)		28	2	8	10	42	8	2	0		4	2	0	2	8

WEEKES, KEVIN G

PERSONAL: Born April 4, 1975, in Toronto. ... 6-0/195. ... Catches left. ... Name pronounced WEEKS.
TRANSACTIONS/CAREER NOTES: Selected by Florida Panthers in second round (second Panthers pick, 41st overall) of enttry draft (June 26, 1993). ... Sprained right knee (March 19, 1998); missed remainder of season. ... Traded by Panthers with D Ed Jovanovski, C Dave Gagner, C Mike Brown and first-round pick (C Nathan Smith) in 2000 draft to Vancouver Canucks for RW Pavel Bure, D Bret Hedican, D Brad Ference and third-round pick (RW Robert Fried) in 2000 draft (January 17, 1999). ... Injured knee (October 28, 1999); missed three games. ... Traded by Canucks with C Dave Scatchard and RW Bill Muckalt to New York Islanders for G Felix Potvin, second- (traded to New Jersey; Devils selected RW Teemu Laine) and third-round (C Thatcher Bell) picks in 2000 draft (December 19, 1999). ... Sore neck (April 9, 2000); missed final game of season. ... Traded by Islanders with D Kristian Kudroc and second-round pick (traded to Phoenix; Coyotes selected D Matthew Spiller) in 2001 draft to Tampa Bay Lightning for first- (LW Raffi Torres), fourth- (RW/LW Vladimir Gorbunov) and seventh-round (D Ryan Caldwell) picks in 2000 draft (June 24, 2000). ... Injured knee (December 2, 2000); missed three games. ... Strained groin (January 7, 2001); missed three games. ... Strained groin (April 4, 2001); missed final three games of season. ... Traded by Lightning to Carolina Hurricanes for RW Shane Willis and LW Craig Dingman (March 5, 2002). ... Concussion (December 11, 2002); missed eight games. ... Signed as free agent by New York Rangers (August 26, 2004). ... Strained groin (October 12, 2005); missed four games. ... Bruised right ankle (November 24, 2005); missed six games.

Season Team	League	GP	Min.	W	L	OTL	T	GA	SO	GAA	SV%	GP	Min.	W	L	GA	SO	GAA	SV%
		REGULAR SEASON										PLAYOFFS							
91-92 —Toronto St. Mikes	OJHL	35	1575	...	...	...	...	68	4	2.59	...	—	—	—	—	—	—	—	—
—St. Michael's	Tier II Jr. A	2	127	...	...	...	...	11	0	5.20	...	—	—	—	—	—	—	—	—
92-93 —Owen Sound	OHL	29	1645	9	12	...	5	143	0	5.22	...	1	26	0	0	5	0	11.54	...
93-94 —Owen Sound	OHL	34	1974	13	19	...	1	158	0	4.80	.880	—	—	—	—	—	—	—	—
94-95 —Ottawa	OHL	41	2266	13	23	...	4	154	1	4.08	.879	—	—	—	—	—	—	—	—
95-96 —Carolina	AHL	60	3403	24	25	...	8	229	2	4.04	...	—	—	—	—	—	—	—	—
96-97 —Carolina	AHL	51	2899	17	28	...	4	172	1	3.56	.895	—	—	—	—	—	—	—	—
97-98 —Fort Wayne	IHL	12	719	9	2	...	1	34	1	2.84	.918	—	—	—	—	—	—	—	—
—Florida	NHL	11	485	0	5	...	1	32	0	3.96	.870	—	—	—	—	—	—	—	—
98-99 —Detroit	IHL	33	1857	19	5	...	7	64	4	2.07	.919	—	—	—	—	—	—	—	—
—Vancouver	NHL	11	532	0	8	...	1	34	0	3.83	.868	—	—	—	—	—	—	—	—
99-00 —Vancouver	NHL	20	987	6	7	...	4	47	1	2.86	.898	—	—	—	—	—	—	—	—
—New York Islanders	NHL	36	2026	10	20	...	4	115	1	3.41	.902	—	—	—	—	—	—	—	—
00-01 —Tampa Bay	NHL	61	3378	20	*33	...	3	177	4	3.14	.898	—	—	—	—	—	—	—	—
01-02 —Tampa Bay	NHL	19	830	3	9	...	0	40	2	2.89	.915	—	—	—	—	—	—	—	—
—Carolina	NHL	2	120	2	0	...	0	3	0	1.50	.927	8	408	3	2	11	2	1.62	.939
02-03 —Carolina	NHL	51	2965	14	24	...	9	126	5	2.55	.912	—	—	—	—	—	—	—	—
03-04 —Carolina	NHL	66	3765	23	30	...	11	146	6	2.33	.912	—	—	—	—	—	—	—	—
05-06 —New York Rangers	NHL	32	1850	14	14	3	...	91	0	2.95	.895	1	60	0	1	4	0	4.00	.840
NHL Totals (8 years)		309	16938	92	150	3	33	811	19	2.87	.903	9	468	3	3	15	2	1.92	.927

WEIGHT, DOUG C

PERSONAL: Born January 21, 1971, in Warren, Mich. ... 5-11/201. ... Shoots left. ... Name pronounced WAYT.
TRANSACTIONS/CAREER NOTES: Selected by New York Rangers in second round (second Rangers pick, 34th overall) of entry draft (June

16, 1990). ... Sprained elbow (October 14, 1991); missed three games. ... Damaged ligaments (January 11, 1991). ... Suspended four off-days and fined $500 for cross-checking incident (November 5, 1992). ... Traded by Rangers to Edmonton Oilers for LW Esa Tikkanen (March 17, 1993). ... Sprained ankle (February 15, 1997); missed one game. ... Injured ankle (February 21, 1997); missed one game. ... Sprained left shoulder (March 15, 1998); missed two games. ... Torn right knee ligament (October 28, 1998); missed 34 games. ... Fractured ribs (December 14, 1999); missed five games. ... Traded by Oilers with LW Michel Riesen to St. Louis Blues for C Marty Reasoner, C Jochen Hecht and D Jan Horacek (July 1, 2001). ... Sprained knee and injured hip (February 28, 2002); missed 20 games. ... Injured ankle (February 5, 2003); missed two games. ... Fractured facial bone (February 11, 2003); missed 10 games. ... Suspended four games for high-sticking incident (November 7, 2003). ... Injured groin (November 16, 2003); missed one game. ... Injured groin (December 23, 2003); missed one game. ... Sublexed left shoulder (September 27, 2005); missed remainder of preseason. ... Concussion (October 29, 2005); missed two games. ... Traded with LW Erkki Rajamaki by Blues to Carolina Hurricanes for RW Jesse Boulerice, LW Magnus Kahnberg, C Mike Zigomanis, first-round pick (traded to New Jersey; Devils selected D Matthew Corrente) in 2006 draft, fourth-round pick in 2006 (G Reto Berra) and fourth-round pick in 2007 (January 30, 2006). ... Groin injury (March 18, 2006); missed seven games. ... Signed as free agent by Blues (July 2, 2006).

STATISTICAL PLATEAUS: Three-goal games: 1995-96 (1), 2003-04 (1). Total: 2.

		REGULAR SEASON								PLAYOFFS				
Season Team	**League**	**GP**	**G**	**A**	**Pts.**	**PIM**	**+/-**	**PP**	**SH**	**GP**	**G**	**A**	**Pts.**	**PIM**
88-89—Bloomfield	NAJHL	34	26	53	79	105	...	...	...	—	—	—	—	—
89-90—Lake Superior St.	CCHA	46	21	48	69	44	...	...	...	—	—	—	—	—
90-91—Lake Superior St.	CCHA	42	29	46	75	86	...	...	...	—	—	—	—	—
—New York Rangers	NHL	...	...	...	...	...	...	...	...	1	0	0	0	0
91-92—New York Rangers	NHL	53	8	22	30	23	-3	0	0	7	2	2	4	0
—Binghamton	AHL	9	3	14	17	2	...	...	...	4	1	4	5	6
92-93—New York Rangers	NHL	65	15	25	40	55	4	3	0	—	—	—	—	—
—Edmonton	NHL	13	2	6	8	10	-2	0	0	—	—	—	—	—
93-94—Edmonton	NHL	84	24	50	74	47	-22	4	1	—	—	—	—	—
94-95—Rosenheim	Germany	8	2	3	5	18	...	...	...	—	—	—	—	—
—Edmonton	NHL	48	7	33	40	69	-17	1	0	—	—	—	—	—
95-96—Edmonton	NHL	82	25	79	104	95	-19	9	0	—	—	—	—	—
96-97—Edmonton	NHL	80	21	61	82	80	1	4	0	12	3	8	11	8
97-98—Edmonton	NHL	79	26	44	70	69	1	9	0	12	2	7	9	14
—U.S. Olympic team	Int'l	4	0	2	2	2	-3	0	0	—	—	—	—	—
98-99—Edmonton	NHL	43	6	31	37	12	-8	1	0	4	1	1	2	15
99-00—Edmonton	NHL	77	21	51	72	54	6	3	1	5	3	2	5	4
00-01—Edmonton	NHL	82	25	65	90	91	12	8	0	6	1	5	6	17
01-02—St. Louis	NHL	61	15	34	49	40	20	3	0	10	1	1	2	4
—U.S. Olympic team	Int'l	6	0	3	3	4	...	...	...	—	—	—	—	—
02-03—St. Louis	NHL	70	15	52	67	52	-6	7	0	7	5	8	13	2
03-04—St. Louis	NHL	75	14	51	65	37	-3	6	0	5	2	1	3	6
04-05—Frankfurt	Germany	7	6	9	15	26	8	3	0	11	2	10	12	8
05-06—St. Louis	NHL	47	11	33	44	50	-11	7	0	—	—	—	—	—
—Carolina	NHL	23	4	9	13	25	-6	2	0	23	3	13	16	20
—U.S. Olympic team	Int'l	6	0	3	3	4	0	0	0	—	—	—	—	—
NHL Totals (15 years)		982	239	646	885	809	-53	67	2	92	23	48	71	90

WEINHANDL, MATTIAS RW/LW

PERSONAL: Born June 1, 1980, in Ljungby, Sweden. ... 6-0/195. ... Shoots right. ... Name pronounced maa-TEE-us WIGHN-hahn-duhl.

TRANSACTIONS/CAREER NOTES: Selected by New York Islanders in third round (fifth Islanders pick, 78th overall) of entry draft (June 26, 1999). ... Shoulder (November 29, 2002); missed eight games. ... Ankle (September 10, 2003); missed season's first 12 games. ... Claimed off waivers by Minnesota Wild (March 4, 2006).

		REGULAR SEASON								PLAYOFFS				
Season Team	**League**	**GP**	**G**	**A**	**Pts.**	**PIM**	**+/-**	**PP**	**SH**	**GP**	**G**	**A**	**Pts.**	**PIM**
97-98—Troja-Ljungby	Sweden Dv. 2	29	4	2	6	10	...	...	...	—	—	—	—	—
98-99—Troja-Ljungby	Sweden Dv. 2	38	20	20	40	30	...	...	...	—	—	—	—	—
99-00—MoDo Ornskoldsvik	Sweden	32	15	9	24	6	...	...	...	13	5	3	8	8
00-01—MoDo Ornskoldsvik	Sweden	48	16	16	32	14	...	...	...	6	1	3	4	6
01-02—MoDo Ornskoldsvik	Sweden	50	18	16	34	10	...	...	...	14	4	11	15	4
02-03—Bridgeport	AHL	23	9	12	21	14	2	2	1	—	—	—	—	—
—New York Islanders	NHL	47	6	17	23	10	-2	1	0	—	—	—	—	—
03-04—New York Islanders	NHL	55	8	12	20	26	9	4	0	5	0	0	0	2
—Bridgeport	AHL	10	3	6	9	10	7	0	0	—	—	—	—	—
04-05—MoDo Ornskoldsvik	Sweden	50	26	20	46	18	3	14	0	6	0	0	0	4
05-06—New York Islanders	NHL	53	2	4	6	14	-4	0	0	—	—	—	—	—
—Minnesota	NHL	15	2	3	5	10	0	0	0	—	—	—	—	—
NHL Totals (3 years)		170	18	36	54	60	3	5	0	5	0	0	0	2

W

WEINRICH, ERIC D

PERSONAL: Born December 19, 1966, in Roanoke, Va. ... 6-1/207. ... Shoots left. ... Name pronounced WIGHN-rihch.

TRANSACTIONS/CAREER NOTES: Selected by New Jersey Devils in second round (third Devils pick, 32nd overall) of NHL draft (June 15, 1985). ... Traded by Devils with G Sean Burke to Hartford Whalers for RW Bobby Holik and second-round pick (LW Jay Pandolfo) in 1993 draft (August 28, 1992). ... Concussion (November 25, 1992); missed two games. ... Sprained knee (September 22, 1993); missed five games. ... Injured right knee (October 5, 1993); missed five games. ... Traded by Whalers with LW Patrick Poulin to the Chicago Blackhawks for RW Steve Larmer and D Bryan Marchment (Nov, 2, 1993). ... Fractured jaw (February 24, 1994); missed 17 games. ... Eye (November 1, 1995); missed three games. ... Cut thigh (December 31, 1996); missed one game. ... Traded by Blackhawks with G Jeff Hackett, D Alain Nasreddine and fourth-round pick (D Chris Dyment) in 1999 draft to Montreal Canadiens for G Jocelyn Thibault, D Dave Manson and D Brad Brown (November 16, 1998). ... Fractured foot (March 22, 2000); missed five games. ... Traded by Canadiens to Boston Bruins for D Patrick Traverse (February 21, 2001). ... Signed as free agent by Philadelphia Flyers (July 5, 2001). ... Strained left shoulder (October 30, 2001); missed two games, ... Bruised foot (February 4, 2004); missed three games. ... Traded by Flyers to St. Louis Blues for fifth-round pick (RW Gino Pisellini) in 2004 draft (February 9, 2004). ... Played in Europe during 2004-05 lockout. ... Traded by Blues to Vancouver Canucks for D Tomas Mojzis and third-round pick (traded to New Jersey; Devils selected RW Vladimir Zharkov) in 2006 draft (March 9, 2006).

Season Team	League	REGULAR SEASON GP	G	A	Pts.	PIM	+/-	PP	SH	PLAYOFFS GP	G	A	Pts.	PIM
83-84—North Yarmouth Acad.	Maine H.S.	17	23	33	56	...	...	...	...	—	—	—	—	—
84-85—North Yarmouth Acad.	Maine H.S.	20	6	21	27	...	...	...	...	—	—	—	—	—
85-86—Maine	Hockey East	34	0	15	15	26	...	...	...	—	—	—	—	—
86-87—Maine	Hockey East	41	12	32	44	59	...	...	...	—	—	—	—	—
87-88—Maine	Hockey East	8	4	7	11	22	...	...	...	—	—	—	—	—
—U.S. national team	Int'l	39	3	9	12	24	...	...	...	—	—	—	—	—
—U.S. Olympic team	Int'l	3	0	0	0	24	2	...	...	—	—	—	—	—
88-89—Utica	AHL	80	17	27	44	70	...	...	...	5	0	1	1	8
—New Jersey	NHL	2	0	0	0	0	-1	0	0	—	—	—	—	—
89-90—Utica	AHL	57	12	48	60	38	...	...	...	—	—	—	—	—
—New Jersey	NHL	19	2	7	9	11	1	1	0	6	1	3	4	17
90-91—New Jersey	NHL	76	4	34	38	48	10	1	0	7	1	2	3	6
91-92—New Jersey	NHL	76	7	25	32	55	10	5	0	7	0	2	2	4
92-93—Hartford	NHL	79	7	29	36	76	-11	0	2	—	—	—	—	—
93-94—Hartford	NHL	8	1	1	2	2	-5	1	0	—	—	—	—	—
—Chicago	NHL	54	3	23	26	31	6	1	0	6	0	2	2	6
94-95—Chicago	NHL	48	3	10	13	33	1	1	0	16	1	5	6	4
95-96—Chicago	NHL	77	5	10	15	65	14	0	0	10	1	4	5	10
96-97—Chicago	NHL	81	7	25	32	62	19	1	0	6	0	1	1	4
97-98—Chicago	NHL	82	2	21	23	106	10	0	0	—	—	—	—	—
98-99—Chicago	NHL	14	1	3	4	12	-13	0	0	—	—	—	—	—
—Montreal	NHL	66	6	12	18	77	-12	4	0	—	—	—	—	—
99-00—Montreal	NHL	77	4	25	29	39	4	2	0	—	—	—	—	—
00-01—Montreal	NHL	60	6	19	25	34	-1	2	0	—	—	—	—	—
—Boston	NHL	22	1	5	6	10	-8	1	0	—	—	—	—	—
01-02—Philadelphia	NHL	80	4	20	24	26	27	0	0	5	0	0	0	4
02-03—Philadelphia	NHL	81	2	18	20	40	16	1	1	13	2	3	5	12
03-04—Philadelphia	NHL	54	2	7	9	32	11	1	0	—	—	—	—	—
—St. Louis	NHL	26	2	8	10	14	1	1	0	5	0	1	1	0
04-05—VSV	Austria	10	3	8	11	8	7	1	0	3	0	1	1	6
05-06—St. Louis	NHL	59	1	16	17	44	-10	1	0	—	—	—	—	—
—Vancouver	NHL	16	0	0	0	8	-13	0	0	—	—	—	—	—
NHL Totals (17 years)		1157	70	318	388	825	56	24	3	81	6	23	29	67

WEISS, STEPHEN C

PERSONAL: Born April 3, 1983, in Toronto. ... 5-11/191. ... Shoots left.

TRANSACTIONS/CAREER NOTES: Selected by Florida Panthers in first round (first Panthers pick, fourth overall) of entry draft (June 23, 2001). ... Fractured toe (February 18, 2003); missed five games. ... Sprained knee (February 1, 2004); missed 16 games. ... Fractured leg (March 29, 2004); missed remaineder of season. ... Torn ligament in left wrist (January 3, 2006) and wrist surgery (January 16, 2006); missed final 41 games of regular season.

Season Team	League	REGULAR SEASON GP	G	A	Pts.	PIM	+/-	PP	SH	PLAYOFFS GP	G	A	Pts.	PIM
99-00—Plymouth	OHL	64	24	42	66	35	...	...	...	23	8	18	26	18
00-01—Plymouth	OHL	62	40	47	87	45	...	...	...	18	7	16	23	10
01-02—Plymouth	OHL	46	25	45	70	69	...	...	...	6	2	7	9	13
—Florida	NHL	7	1	1	2	0	0	1	0	—	—	—	—	—
02-03—Florida	NHL	77	6	15	21	17	-13	0	0	—	—	—	—	—
03-04—Florida	NHL	50	12	17	29	10	-10	3	0	—	—	—	—	—
—San Antonio	AHL	10	6	3	9	14	-1	3	0	—	—	—	—	—
04-05—San Antonio	AHL	62	15	23	38	38	-1	7	0	—	—	—	—	—
—Chicago	AHL	18	7	9	16	12	8	1	0	18	2	7	9	17
05-06—Florida	NHL	41	9	12	21	22	-2	5	0	—	—	—	—	—
NHL Totals (4 years)		175	28	45	73	49	-25	9	0					

WELCH, NOAH D

PERSONAL: Born August 26, 1982, in Boston. ... 6-4/212. ... Shoots left.

HIGH SCHOOL: St. Sebastian's (Needham. Mass.).

COLLEGE: Harvard.

TRANSACTIONS/CAREER NOTES: Selected by Pittsburgh Penguins in second round (second Penguins pick, 54th overall) of NHL draft (June 23, 2001).

Season Team	League	REGULAR SEASON GP	G	A	Pts.	PIM	+/-	PP	SH	PLAYOFFS GP	G	A	Pts.	PIM
01-02—Harvard	ECAC	26	5	5	10	54	...	1	0	—	—	—	—	—
02-03—Harvard	ECAC	34	6	22	28	70	...	2	0	—	—	—	—	—
03-04—Harvard	ECAC	34	6	13	19	58	...	...	...	—	—	—	—	—
04-05—Harvard	ECAC	34	6	12	18	36	...	...	...	—	—	—	—	—
05-06—Pittsburgh	NHL	5	1	3	4	2	0	0	0	—	—	—	—	—
—Wilkes-Barre/Scranton	AHL	77	9	20	29	99	15	6	1	11	1	0	1	18
NHL Totals (1 year)		5	1	3	4	2	0	0	0					

WELLWOOD, KYLE C/RW

PERSONAL: Born May 16, 1983, in Windsor, Ont. ... 5-10/180. ... Shoots right.

TRANSACTIONS/CAREER NOTES: Selected by Toronto Maple Leafs in sixth round (sixth Maple Leafs pick, 134th overall) of NHL entry draft (June 23, 2001).

Season Team	League	REGULAR SEASON GP	G	A	Pts.	PIM	+/-	PP	SH	PLAYOFFS GP	G	A	Pts.	PIM
98-99—Tecumseh	Jr. B	51	22	41	63	12	...	...	...	—	—	—	—	—
99-00—Belleville	OHL	65	14	37	51	14	...	...	...	16	3	7	10	6
00-01—Belleville	OHL	68	35	83	118	24	...	...	...	10	3	16	19	4
01-02—Belleville	OHL	28	16	24	40	4	...	...	...	—	—	—	—	—
—Windsor	OHL	26	14	21	35	0	...	...	...	16	12	12	24	0
02-03—Windsor	OHL	57	41	59	100	0	...	...	...	7	5	9	14	0
03-04—Toronto	NHL	1	0	0	0	0	-1	0	0	—	—	—	—	—
—St. John's	AHL	76	20	35	55	6	-14	8	0	—	—	—	—	—
04-05—St. John's	AHL	80	38	49	87	20	11	11	0	5	2	2	4	2
05-06—Toronto	NHL	81	11	34	45	14	0	3	0	—	—	—	—	—
NHL Totals (2 years)		82	11	34	45	14	-1	3	0					

WESLEY, GLEN D

PERSONAL: Born October 2, 1968, in Red Deer, Alta. ... 6-1/205. ... Shoots left. ... Brother of Blake Wesley, D with four NHL teams (1979-80 through 1985-86).

TRANSACTIONS/CAREER NOTES: Selected by Boston Bruins in first round (first Bruins pick, third overall) of entry draft (June 13, 1987). ... Sprained left knee (October 1988). ... Fractured foot (November 24, 1992); missed 14 games. ... Injured groin (February 1993); missed one game. ... Injured groin (March 1993); missed three games. ... Injured groin (April 1993); missed two games. ... Injured kidney (March 3, 1994); missed three games. ... Traded by Bruins to Hartford Whalers for first-round picks in 1995 (D Kyle McLaren), 1996 (D Johnathan Aitken) and 1997 (C Sergei Samsonov) drafts (August 26, 1994). ... Bruised shin (November 4, 1995); missed two games. ... Injured groin (December 28, 1995); missed three games. ... Sprained knee (January 6, 1996); missed three games. ... Injured groin (January 17, 1996); missed four games. ... Injured groin (January 25, 1996); missed three games. ... Strained hip flexor (November 4, 1996); missed one game. ... Fractured foot (November 16, 1996); missed 10 games. ... Flu (February 5, 1997); missed one game. ... Whalers franchise moved to North Carolina and renamed Carolina Hurricanes for 1997-98 season; NHL approved move on June 25, 1997. ... Sprained ankle (March 24, 1999); missed eight games. ... Strained groin (November 22, 1999); missed two games. ... Eye injury (February 17, 2000); missed two games. ... Fractured jaw (March 4, 2001); missed 11 games. ... Injured shoulder (April 3, 2002); missed final five games of season. ... Traded by Hurricanes to Toronto Maple Leafs for second-round pick in 2004 draft (March 9, 2003). ... Injured groin (October 11, 2002); missed three games. ... Injured groin (January 25, 2003); missed three games. ... Fractured left ankle (March 25, 2003); missed eight games. ... Signed as free agent by Hurricanes (July 8, 2003). ... Injured shoulder (November 19, 2003); missed seven games. ... Signed as free agent by Hurricanes (August 16, 2005). ... Injured groin (November 5, 2005); missed eight games. ... Sprained MCL (December 31, 2005); missed 10 games.

STATISTICAL PLATEAUS: Three-goal games: 1993-94 (1).

Season Team	League	REGULAR SEASON GP	G	A	Pts.	PIM	+/-	PP	SH	PLAYOFFS GP	G	A	Pts.	PIM
83-84—Red Deer	AJHL	57	9	20	29	40	...	...	...	—	—	—	—	—
—Portland	WHL	3	1	2	3	0	...	...	...	—	—	—	—	—
84-85—Portland	WHL	67	16	52	68	76	...	...	...	6	1	6	7	8
85-86—Portland	WHL	69	16	75	91	96	...	...	...	15	3	11	14	29
86-87—Portland	WHL	63	16	46	62	72	...	...	...	20	8	18	26	27
87-88—Boston	NHL	79	7	30	37	69	21	1	2	23	6	8	14	22
88-89—Boston	NHL	77	19	35	54	61	23	8	1	10	0	2	2	4
89-90—Boston	NHL	78	9	27	36	48	6	5	0	21	2	6	8	36
90-91—Boston	NHL	80	11	32	43	78	0	5	1	19	2	9	11	19
91-92—Boston	NHL	78	9	37	46	54	-9	4	0	15	2	4	6	16
92-93—Boston	NHL	64	8	25	33	47	-2	4	1	4	0	0	0	0
93-94—Boston	NHL	81	14	44	58	64	1	6	1	13	3	3	6	12
94-95—Hartford	NHL	48	2	14	16	50	-6	1	0	—	—	—	—	—
95-96—Hartford	NHL	68	8	16	24	88	-9	6	0	—	—	—	—	—
96-97—Hartford	NHL	68	6	26	32	40	0	3	1	—	—	—	—	—
97-98—Carolina	NHL	82	6	19	25	36	7	1	0	—	—	—	—	—
98-99—Carolina	NHL	74	7	17	24	44	14	0	0	6	0	0	0	2
99-00—Carolina	NHL	78	7	15	22	38	-4	1	0	—	—	—	—	—
00-01—Carolina	NHL	71	5	16	21	42	-2	3	0	6	0	0	0	0
01-02—Carolina	NHL	77	5	13	18	56	-8	1	0	22	0	2	2	12
02-03—Carolina	NHL	63	1	7	8	40	-5	1	0	—	—	—	—	—
—Toronto	NHL	7	0	3	3	4	3	0	0	5	0	1	1	2
03-04—Carolina	NHL	74	0	6	6	32	18	0	0	—	—	—	—	—
05-06—Carolina	NHL	64	2	8	10	46	10	0	0	25	0	2	2	16
NHL Totals (18 years)		1311	126	390	516	937	58	50	7	169	15	37	52	141

WESTCOTT, DUVIE D

PERSONAL: Born October 30, 1977, in Winnipeg, Man. ... 5-11/197. ... Shoots right. ... Name pronounced DOO-vee WEHST-kaht.

TRANSACTIONS/CAREER NOTES: Signed as free agent by Columbus Blue Jackets (May 10, 2001). ... Bruised ankle (October 14, 2003); missed eight games. ... Bruised ankle (November 16, 2003); missed 24 games. ... Fractured hand (February 2, 2004); missed 16 games. ... Bruised sternum (December 30, 2005); missed one game. ... Head (April 13, 2005); missed one game.

Season Team	League	REGULAR SEASON GP	G	A	Pts.	PIM	+/-	PP	SH	PLAYOFFS GP	G	A	Pts.	PIM
96-97—Winnipeg	MJHL	52	12	47	59	...	...	...	...	—	—	—	—	—
97-98—Alaska-Anchorage	WCHA	25	3	5	8	43	...	...	...	—	—	—	—	—
—Omaha	USHL	12	3	3	6	31	...	...	...	14	0	8	8	84
98-99—St. Cloud State	WCHADid not play—transfer student													
99-00—St. Cloud State	WCHA	36	1	18	19	67	...	...	...	—	—	—	—	—
00-01—St. Cloud State	WCHA	38	10	24	34	116	...	...	...	—	—	—	—	—
01-02—Syracuse	AHL	68	4	29	33	99	3	1	1	10	0	1	1	12
—Columbus	NHL	4	0	0	0	2	-2	0	0	—	—	—	—	—
02-03—Columbus	NHL	39	0	7	7	77	-3	0	0	—	—	—	—	—
—Syracuse	AHL	22	1	10	11	54	...	...	...	—	—	—	—	—

Season Team	League	GP	G	A	Pts.	PIM	+/-	PP	SH	GP	G	A	Pts.	PIM
		REGULAR SEASON								PLAYOFFS				
03-04—Columbus	NHL	34	0	7	7	39	-15	0	0	—	—	—	—	—
04-05—JyP Jyvaskyla	Finland	46	11	7	18	106	6	...	...	2	0	2	2	25
05-06—Columbus	NHL	78	6	22	28	133	1	1	1	—	—	—	—	—
NHL Totals (4 years)		155	6	36	42	251	-19	1	1					

WESTRUM, ERIK C

PERSONAL: Born July 26, 1979, in Minneapolis, Minn. ... 6-0/204. ... Shoots left.

TRANSACTIONS/CAREER NOTES: Selected by Phoenix Coyotes in seventh round (ninth pick by Coyotes, 187th overall) of entry draft (June 27, 1998). ... Traded with D Dustin Wood to Minnesota Wild for D Zbynek Michalek (August 26, 2005). ... Signed as free agent by Toronto Maple Leafs (July 13, 2006).

Season Team	League	GP	G	A	Pts.	PIM	+/-	PP	SH	GP	G	A	Pts.	PIM
		REGULAR SEASON								PLAYOFFS				
96-97—Apple Valley	Minn. H.S.	25	23	33	56	...	...	...	...	—	—	—	—	—
97-98—Minnesota	WCHA	39	6	12	18	43	...	...	...	—	—	—	—	—
98-99—Minnesota	WCHA	41	10	26	36	81	...	...	...	—	—	—	—	—
99-00—Minnesota	WCHA	39	27	26	53	99	...	...	...	—	—	—	—	—
00-01—Minnesota	WCHA	42	26	35	61	84	...	...	...	—	—	—	—	—
01-02—Springfield	AHL	73	13	29	42	116	-17	4	1	—	—	—	—	—
02-03—Springfield	AHL	—	—	—	—	—	—	—	—	6	0	4	4	6
—Springfield	AHL	70	10	22	32	65	2	4	2	—	—	—	—	—
03-04—Phoenix	NHL	15	1	1	2	20	-3	0	0	—	—	—	—	—
—Springfield	AHL	56	14	17	31	81	-1	3	1	—	—	—	—	—
04-05—Utah	AHL	80	18	15	33	117	-16	3	3	—	—	—	—	—
05-06—Houston	AHL	71	34	64	98	138	11	17	0	8	1	7	8	20
—Minnesota	NHL	10	0	1	1	2	-1	0	0	—	—	—	—	—
NHL Totals (2 years)		25	1	2	3	22	-4	0	0					

WHITE, COLIN D

PERSONAL: Born December 12, 1977, in New Glasgow, Nova Scotia. ... 6-4/215. ... Shoots left.

TRANSACTIONS/CAREER NOTES: Selected by New Jersey Devils in second round (fifth Devils pick, 49th overall) of NHL draft (June 22, 1996). ... Suffered injury (January 28. 2000); missed two games. ... Stiff neck (March 10, 2000); missed three games. ... Injured neck (December 26, 2001); missed two games. ... Reinjured neck (January 3, 2002); missed two games. ... Strained neck (January 23, 2002); missed two games. ... Injured neck (April 1, 2002); missed one game. ... Sprained knee (February 19, 2003); missed seven games. ... Sore neck (March 28, 2003); missed two games. ... Bruised knee (December 2, 2003); missed four games. ... Stiff neck (March 15, 2004); missed two games. ... Re-signed by Devils as restricted free agent (September 21, 2005). ... Injured groin (October 15, 2005); missed eight games. ... Injured ankle (April 18, 2006); missed final game of regular season.

Season Team	League	GP	G	A	Pts.	PIM	+/-	PP	SH	GP	G	A	Pts.	PIM
		REGULAR SEASON								PLAYOFFS				
94-95—Laval	QMJHL	7	0	1	1	32	...	...	...	—	—	—	—	—
—Hull	QMJHL	5	0	1	1	4	...	...	...	12	0	0	0	23
95-96—Hull	QMJHL	62	2	8	10	303	...	...	...	18	0	4	4	42
96-97—Hull	QMJHL	63	3	12	15	297	...	...	...	14	3	12	15	65
97-98—Albany	AHL	76	3	13	16	235	10	0	0	13	0	0	0	55
98-99—Albany	AHL	77	2	12	14	265	19	0	0	5	0	1	1	8
99-00—Albany	AHL	52	5	21	26	176	...	...	...	—	—	—	—	—
—New Jersey	NHL	21	2	1	3	40	3	0	0	23	1	5	6	18
00-01—New Jersey	NHL	82	1	19	20	155	32	0	0	25	0	3	3	42
01-02—New Jersey	NHL	73	2	3	5	133	6	0	0	6	0	0	0	2
02-03—New Jersey	NHL	72	5	8	13	98	19	0	0	24	0	5	5	29
03-04—New Jersey	NHL	75	2	11	13	96	10	0	0	5	0	0	0	4
05-06—New Jersey	NHL	73	3	14	17	91	-2	1	0	4	0	0	0	4
NHL Totals (6 years)		396	15	56	71	613	68	1	0	87	1	13	14	99

WHITE, IAN D

W

PERSONAL: Born June 4, 1984, in Winnipeg. ... 5-10/185. ... Shoots right.

TRANSACTIONS/CAREER NOTES: Selected by Toronto Maple Leafs in sixth round (sixth Maple Leafs pick, 191st overall) of NHL entry draft (June 23, 2002).

Season Team	League	GP	G	A	Pts.	PIM	+/-	PP	SH	GP	G	A	Pts.	PIM
		REGULAR SEASON								PLAYOFFS				
00-01—Swift Current	WHL	69	12	31	43	24	...	...	...	19	1	4	5	6
01-02—Swift Current	WHL	70	32	47	79	40	...	...	...	12	4	5	9	12
02-03—Swift Current	WHL	64	24	44	68	44	...	...	...	4	0	4	4	0
03-04—St. John's	AHL	8	0	4	4	2	...	...	...	—	—	—	—	—
—Swift Current	WHL	43	9	23	32	32	...	...	...	5	1	3	4	8
04-05—St. John's	AHL	—	—	—	—	—	—	—	—	5	0	2	2	2
—St. John's	AHL	78	4	22	26	54	12	1	1	—	—	—	—	—
05-06—Toronto	NHL	12	1	5	6	10	2	0	0	—	—	—	—	—
—Toronto	AHL	59	8	30	38	42	12	5	0	5	1	4	5	4
NHL Totals (1 year)		12	1	5	6	10	2	0	0					

WHITE, TODD C/LW

PERSONAL: Born May 21, 1975, in Kanata, Ont. ... 5-10/194. ... Shoots left.

TRANSACTIONS/CAREER NOTES: Signed as free agent by Chicago Blackhawks (August 6, 1997). ... Charley horse (October 4, 1997); missed one game. ... Bruised ribs before 1998-99 season; missed first six games. ... Traded by Blackhawks to Philadelphia Flyers for future considerations (January 26, 2000). ... Signed as free agent by Ottawa Senators (July 12, 2000). ... Concussion (January 15, 2002); missed one game. ... Hip flexor (March 11, 2003); missed two games. ... Shoulder (October 11, 2003); missed one game. ... Shoulder (October 23, 2003); missed two games. ... Shoulder (November 7, 2003); missed four games. ... Fractured right foot (February 17, 2004); missed 22 games. ... Traded by Senators to Minnesota Wild for fourth-round pick (C Cody Bass) in 2005 (July 30, 2005). ... Knee (October 12, 2005); missed one game. ... Groin (November 5, 2005); missed five games. ... Broken left leg (March 21, 2006); missed season's final 14 games.

		REGULAR SEASON								PLAYOFFS				
Season Team	**League**	**GP**	**G**	**A**	**Pts.**	**PIM**	**+/-**	**PP**	**SH**	**GP**	**G**	**A**	**Pts.**	**PIM**
93-94—Clarkson	ECAC	33	10	12	22	28	...	...	...	—	—	—	—	—
94-95—Clarkson	ECAC	34	13	16	29	44	...	...	...	—	—	—	—	—
95-96—Clarkson	ECAC	38	29	43	72	36	...	...	...	—	—	—	—	—
96-97—Clarkson	ECAC	37	38	36	74	22	...	...	...	—	—	—	—	—
97-98—Chicago	NHL	7	1	0	1	2	0	0	0	—	—	—	—	—
—Indianapolis	IHL	65	46	36	82	28	18	21	1	5	2	3	5	4
98-99—Chicago	IHL	25	11	13	24	8	4	2	0	10	1	4	5	8
—Chicago	NHL	35	5	8	13	20	-1	2	0	—	—	—	—	—
99-00—Cleveland	IHL	42	21	30	51	32	...	...	...	—	—	—	—	—
—Chicago	NHL	1	0	0	0	0	0	0	0	—	—	—	—	—
—Philadelphia	AHL	32	19	24	43	12	...	...	...	5	2	1	3	8
—Philadelphia	NHL	3	1	0	1	0	-1	0	0	—	—	—	—	—
00-01—Grand Rapids	IHL	64	22	32	54	20	...	...	...	10	4	4	8	10
—Ottawa	NHL	16	4	1	5	4	5	0	0	2	0	0	0	0
01-02—Ottawa	NHL	81	20	30	50	24	12	4	0	12	2	2	4	6
02-03—Ottawa	NHL	80	25	35	60	28	19	8	1	18	5	1	6	6
03-04—Ottawa	NHL	53	9	20	29	22	12	1	1	7	1	0	1	4
04-05—Sodertalje	Sweden	1	0	1	1	4	-1	0	0	—	—	—	—	—
05-06—Minnesota	NHL	61	19	21	40	18	-1	5	0	—	—	—	—	—
NHL Totals (8 years)		337	84	115	199	118	45	20	2	39	8	3	11	16

WHITFIELD, TRENT C

PERSONAL: Born June 17, 1977, in Estevan, Sask. ... 5-11/205. ... Shoots left.

TRANSACTIONS/CAREER NOTES: Selected by Boston Bruins in fourth round (fifth Bruins pick, 100th overall) of NHL draft (June 22, 1996). ... Signed as free agent by Washington Capitals (September 1, 1998). ... Claimed off waivers by New York Rangers (January 16, 2002). ... Claimed off waivers by Capitals (February 1, 2002). ... Chest (March 8, 2004); missed five games. ... Signed as free agent by St. Louis Blues (August 2, 2005).

		REGULAR SEASON								PLAYOFFS				
Season Team	**League**	**GP**	**G**	**A**	**Pts.**	**PIM**	**+/-**	**PP**	**SH**	**GP**	**G**	**A**	**Pts.**	**PIM**
93-94—Spokane	WHL	5	1	1	2	0	...	...	...	—	—	—	—	—
94-95—Spokane	WHL	48	8	17	25	26	-7	2	0	11	7	6	13	5
95-96—Spokane	WHL	72	33	51	84	75	...	...	...	18	8	10	18	10
96-97—Spokane	WHL	58	34	42	76	74	15	12	4	9	5	7	12	10
97-98—Spokane	WHL	65	38	44	82	97	22	11	3	18	9	10	19	15
98-99—Portland	AHL	50	10	8	18	20	-11	1	0	—	—	—	—	—
—Hampton Roads	ECHL	19	13	12	25	12	13	2	1	4	2	0	2	14
99-00—Portland	AHL	79	18	35	53	52	...	...	...	3	1	1	2	2
—Washington	NHL	...	...	...	...	...	...	...	...	3	0	0	0	0
00-01—Portland	AHL	19	9	11	20	27	...	...	...	—	—	—	—	—
—Washington	NHL	61	2	4	6	35	3	0	0	5	0	0	0	2
01-02—New York Rangers	NHL	1	0	0	0	0	1	0	0	—	—	—	—	—
—Portland	AHL	45	14	20	34	24	-9	8	0	—	—	—	—	—
—Washington	NHL	24	0	1	1	28	-3	0	0	—	—	—	—	—
02-03—Portland	AHL	64	27	34	61	42	3	7	5	—	—	—	—	—
—Washington	NHL	14	1	1	2	6	1	0	0	6	0	0	0	10
03-04—Washington	NHL	44	6	5	11	14	-2	0	1	—	—	—	—	—
—Portland	AHL	24	8	7	15	22	-5	4	0	—	—	—	—	—
04-05—Portland	AHL	67	17	38	55	75	-9	8	2	—	—	—	—	—
05-06—Peoria	AHL	41	19	34	53	18	5	12	1	—	—	—	—	—
—St. Louis	NHL	30	2	5	7	14	-3	1	0	—	—	—	—	—
NHL Totals (6 years)		174	11	16	27	97	-3	1	1	14	0	0	0	12

WHITNEY, RAY LW

PERSONAL: Born May 8, 1972, in Ft. Saskatchewan, Alta. ... 5-10/178. ... Shoots right.

TRANSACTIONS/CAREER NOTES: Selected by San Jose Sharks in second round (second Sharks pick, 23rd overall) of NHL draft (June 22, 1991). ... Sprained knee (October 30, 1993); missed 18 games. ... Flu (December 15, 1993); missed one game. ... Ankle (February 20, 1995); eye infection (February 28, 1995); missed seven games. ... Eye infection (March 21, 1995); missed one game. ... Flu (April 9, 1995); missed one game. ... Groin (December 15, 1995); missed three games. ... Wrist (February 18, 1996); missed 17 games. ... Signed as free agent by Edmonton Oilers (October 1, 1997). ... Claimed off waivers by Florida Panthers (November 6, 1997). ... Strained groin (October 22, 1999); missed one game. ... Groin (November 10, 2000). ... Strained back (January 17, 2001); missed six games. ... Strained back (February 9, 2001); missed 28 games, ... Traded by Panthers with future considerations to Columbus Blue Jackets for C Kevyn Adams and fourth-round pick (RW Michael Woodford) in 2001 draft (March 13, 2001). ... Strained chest muscle (October 12, 2001); missed 11 games. ... Flu (December 8, 2001); missed one game. ... Strained lower back (March 25, 2002); missed one game. ... Flu (February 12, 2003); missed one game. ... Signed as free agent by Detroit Red Wings (July 30, 2003). ... Groin (November 19, 2003); missed 10 games. ... Injured groin (December 9, 2003);

missed five games. ... Signed as free agent by Carolina Hurricanes (August 6, 2005). ... Strained groin (October 5, 2005); missed season's first six games. ... Strained groin (November 22, 2005); missed six games. ... Groin (April 5, 2006); missed final six games of regular season and one playoff game.

STATISTICAL PLATEAUS: Three-goal games: 2002-03 (1).

		REGULAR SEASON								PLAYOFFS				
Season Team	**League**	**GP**	**G**	**A**	**Pts.**	**PIM**	**+/-**	**PP**	**SH**	**GP**	**G**	**A**	**Pts.**	**PIM**
88-89—Spokane	WHL	71	17	33	50	16	...	...	...	—	—	—	—	—
89-90—Spokane	WHL	71	57	56	113	50	...	...	...	6	3	4	7	6
90-91—Spokane	WHL	72	67	118	185	36	...	...	...	15	13	18	31	12
91-92—San Diego	IHL	63	36	54	90	12	...	...	...	4	0	0	0	0
—San Jose	NHL	2	0	3	3	0	-1	0	0	—	—	—	—	—
—Koln	Germany	10	3	6	9	4	...	...	...	—	—	—	—	—
92-93—Kansas City	IHL	46	20	33	53	14	-2	6	1	12	5	7	12	2
—San Jose	NHL	26	4	6	10	4	-14	1	0	—	—	—	—	—
93-94—San Jose	NHL	61	14	26	40	14	2	1	0	14	0	4	4	8
94-95—San Jose	NHL	39	13	12	25	14	-7	4	0	11	4	4	8	2
95-96—San Jose	NHL	60	17	24	41	16	-23	4	2	—	—	—	—	—
96-97—Kentucky	AHL	9	1	7	8	2	-3	0	0	—	—	—	—	—
—Utah	IHL	43	13	35	48	34	...	...	...	7	3	1	4	6
—San Jose	NHL	12	0	2	2	4	-6	0	0	—	—	—	—	—
97-98—Edmonton	NHL	9	1	3	4	0	-1	0	0	—	—	—	—	—
—Florida	NHL	68	32	29	61	28	10	12	0	—	—	—	—	—
98-99—Florida	NHL	81	26	38	64	18	-3	7	0	—	—	—	—	—
99-00—Florida	NHL	81	29	42	71	35	16	5	0	4	1	0	1	4
00-01—Florida	NHL	43	10	21	31	28	-16	5	0	—	—	—	—	—
—Columbus	NHL	3	0	3	3	2	-1	0	0	—	—	—	—	—
01-02—Columbus	NHL	67	21	40	61	12	-22	6	0	—	—	—	—	—
02-03—Columbus	NHL	81	24	52	76	22	-26	8	2	—	—	—	—	—
03-04—Detroit	NHL	67	14	29	43	22	7	3	1	12	1	3	4	4
05-06—Carolina	NHL	63	17	38	55	42	0	12	0	24	9	6	15	14
NHL Totals (14 years)		763	222	368	590	261	-85	68	5	65	15	17	32	32

WHITNEY, RYAN D

PERSONAL: Born February 19, 1983, in Boston. ... 6-4/202. ... Shoots left.

TRANSACTIONS/CAREER NOTES: Selected by Pittsburgh Penguins in first round (first Penguins pick, fifth overall) of entry draft (June 22, 2002). ... Fined $1,500 by NHL in spearing incident (January 27, 2006). ... Strained neck (March 19, 2006); missed two games.

		REGULAR SEASON								PLAYOFFS				
Season Team	**League**	**GP**	**G**	**A**	**Pts.**	**PIM**	**+/-**	**PP**	**SH**	**GP**	**G**	**A**	**Pts.**	**PIM**
00-01—U.S. National	USHL	60	9	31	40	86	...	...	...	—	—	—	—	—
01-02—Boston University	Hockey East	31	4	15	19	44	...	...	...	—	—	—	—	—
02-03—Boston University	Hockey East	34	3	10	13	48	...	...	...	—	—	—	—	—
03-04—Boston University	Hockey East	38	9	16	25	56	...	...	...	—	—	—	—	—
—Wilkes-Barre/Scranton	AHL	...	...	...	...	...	...	...	...	20	1	9	10	0
04-05—Wilkes-Barre/Scranton	AHL	80	6	35	41	101	-12	4	0	11	2	7	9	12
05-06—Wilkes-Barre/Scranton	AHL	9	5	9	14	6	7	3	0	11	1	4	5	8
—Pittsburgh	NHL	68	6	32	38	85	-7	2	0	—	—	—	—	—
NHL Totals (1 year)		68	6	32	38	85	-7	2	0					

WIDEMAN, DENNIS D

PERSONAL: Born March 20, 1983, in Elmira, Ont. ... 5-11/200. ... Shoots right.

TRANSACTIONS/CAREER NOTES: Selected by Buffalo Sabres in eighth round (ninth Sabres pick, 241th overall) of entry draft (June 23, 2002). ... Signed as free agent by St. Louis Blues (June 30, 2004).

		REGULAR SEASON								PLAYOFFS				
Season Team	**League**	**GP**	**G**	**A**	**Pts.**	**PIM**	**+/-**	**PP**	**SH**	**GP**	**G**	**A**	**Pts.**	**PIM**
99-00—Sudbury	OHL	63	10	26	36	64	...	...	...	12	1	2	3	22
00-01—Sudbury	OHL	25	7	11	18	37	...	...	...	—	—	—	—	—
—London	OHL	24	8	8	16	38	...	...	...	5	0	4	4	6
01-02—London	OHL	65	27	42	69	141	...	...	...	12	4	9	13	26
02-03—London	OHL	55	20	27	47	83	...	...	...	14	6	6	12	10
03-04—London	OHL	60	24	41	65	85	...	...	...	15	7	10	17	17
04-05—Worcester	AHL	79	13	30	43	65	-22	7	0	—	—	—	—	—
05-06—Peoria	AHL	12	2	4	6	31	-1	2	0	—	—	—	—	—
—St. Louis	NHL	67	8	16	24	83	-31	5	1	—	—	—	—	—
NHL Totals (1 year)		67	8	16	24	83	-31	5	1					

WIEMER, JASON C/LW

PERSONAL: Born April 14, 1976, in Kimberley, B.C. ... 6-1/225. ... Shoots left. ... Name pronounced WEE-muhr.

TRANSACTIONS/CAREER NOTES: Selected by Tampa Bay Lightning in first round (first Lightning pick, eighth overall) of NHL draft (June 28, 1994). ... Flu (March 2, 1995); missed one game. ... Injured jaw (November 3, 1995); missed one game. ... Injured back (April 12, 1996);

missed one game. ... Broke bursa sac in elbow (November 30, 1996); missed 14 games. ... Traded by Lightning to Calgary Flames for RW Sandy McCarthy and third- (LW Brad Richards) and fifth-round (D Curtis Rich) picks in 1998 draft (March 24, 1998). ... Injured hand (March 30, 1999); missed three games. ... Injured knee before start of 1999-2000 season; missed first 10 games of season. ... Reinjured knee (October 28, 1999); missed three games. ... Injured (March 31, 2000); missed final five games of season. ... Concussion (December 31, 2000); missed 17 games. ... Traded by Flames with RW Valeri Bure to Florida Panthers for C Rob Niedermayer and second-round pick (G Andrei Medvedev) in 2001 draft (June 23, 2001). ... Suspended seven games by NHL for butt-ending opponent (November 20, 2001). ... Concussion (April 5, 2002); missed remainder of season. ... Traded by Panthers to New York Islanders for D Branislav Mezei (July 3, 2002). ... Bruised ribs (March 13, 2003); missed one game. ... Claimed off waivers by Minnesota Wild (November 13, 2003). ... Bruised thigh (December 5, 2003); missed two games. ... Signed as a free agent by Calgary Flames (August 5, 2004). ... Traded by Flames to New Jersey Devils for fourth-round pick (C Hugo Carpentier) in 2006 draft (March 9, 2006).

STATISTICAL PLATEAUS: Three-goal games: 1995-96 (1).

		REGULAR SEASON								PLAYOFFS				
Season Team	**League**	**GP**	**G**	**A**	**Pts.**	**PIM**	**+/-**	**PP**	**SH**	**GP**	**G**	**A**	**Pts.**	**PIM**
91-92—Kimberley	RMJHL	45	34	33	67	211	...	...	...	—	—	—	—	—
—Portland	WHL	2	0	1	1	0	...	...	...	—	—	—	—	—
92-93—Portland	WHL	68	18	34	52	159	...	...	...	16	7	3	10	27
93-94—Portland	WHL	72	45	51	96	236	46	17	4	10	4	4	8	32
94-95—Portland	WHL	16	10	14	24	63	-7	6	0	—	—	—	—	—
—Tampa Bay	NHL	36	1	4	5	44	-2	0	0	—	—	—	—	—
95-96—Tampa Bay	NHL	66	9	9	18	81	-9	4	0	6	1	0	1	28
96-97—Tampa Bay	NHL	63	9	5	14	134	-13	2	0	—	—	—	—	—
—Adirondack	AHL	4	1	0	1	7	-2	0	0	—	—	—	—	—
97-98—Tampa Bay	NHL	67	8	9	17	132	-9	2	0	—	—	—	—	—
—Calgary	NHL	12	4	1	5	28	-1	1	0	—	—	—	—	—
98-99—Calgary	NHL	78	8	13	21	177	-12	1	0	—	—	—	—	—
99-00—Calgary	NHL	64	11	11	22	120	-10	2	0	—	—	—	—	—
00-01—Calgary	NHL	65	10	5	15	177	-15	3	0	—	—	—	—	—
01-02—Florida	NHL	70	11	20	31	178	-4	5	1	—	—	—	—	—
02-03—New York Islanders	NHL	81	9	19	28	116	5	0	1	5	0	0	0	23
03-04—New York Islanders	NHL	13	1	3	4	24	-1	0	0	—	—	—	—	—
—Minnesota	NHL	62	7	11	18	106	-6	1	0	—	—	—	—	—
05-06—Calgary	NHL	33	1	2	3	65	-3	0	0	—	—	—	—	—
—New Jersey	NHL	16	1	0	1	38	-1	0	0	8	0	0	0	16
NHL Totals (11 years)		726	90	112	202	1420	-81	21	2	19	1	0	1	67

WILLIAMS, JASON C/RW

PERSONAL: Born August 11, 1980, in London, Ont. ... 5-11/185. ... Shoots right.

TRANSACTIONS/CAREER NOTES: Signed as free agent by Detroit Red Wings (September 22, 2000). ... Flu (November 1, 2003); missed one game. ... Injured groin (November 8, 2003); missed two games. ... Lower body (April 14, 2006); missed two games.

		REGULAR SEASON								PLAYOFFS				
Season Team	**League**	**GP**	**G**	**A**	**Pts.**	**PIM**	**+/-**	**PP**	**SH**	**GP**	**G**	**A**	**Pts.**	**PIM**
96-97—Peterborough	OHL	60	4	8	12	8	...	...	...	10	1	0	1	2
97-98—Peterborough	OHL	55	8	27	35	31	...	...	...	4	0	1	1	2
98-99—Peterborough	OHL	68	26	48	74	42	...	...	...	5	1	2	3	2
99-00—Peterborough	OHL	66	36	37	73	64	...	...	...	5	2	1	3	2
00-01—Cincinnati	AHL	76	24	45	69	48	...	...	...	1	0	0	0	2
—Detroit	NHL	5	0	3	3	2	1	0	0	2	0	0	0	0
01-02—Cincinnati	AHL	52	23	27	50	27	-4	6	1	3	0	1	1	6
—Detroit	NHL	25	8	2	10	4	2	4	0	9	0	0	0	2
02-03—Detroit	NHL	16	3	3	6	2	3	1	0	—	—	—	—	—
—Grand Rapids	AHL	45	23	22	45	18	5	9	1	15	1	7	8	16
03-04—Detroit	NHL	49	6	7	13	15	1	0	0	3	0	0	0	2
04-05—Assat Pori	Finland	43	26	17	43	52	-5	...	...	2	1	1	2	4
05-06—Detroit	NHL	80	21	37	58	26	4	6	0	6	1	1	2	6
NHL Totals (5 years)		175	38	52	90	49	11	11	0	20	1	1	2	10

WILLIAMS, JEREMY C/RW

PERSONAL: Born January 26, 1984, in Glenavon, Sask. ... 5-11/184. ... Shoots right.

TRANSACTIONS/CAREER NOTES: Selected by Toronto Maple Leafs in seventh round (fifth Maple Leafs pick, 220th overall) of NHL entry draft (June 21, 2003).

		REGULAR SEASON								PLAYOFFS				
Season Team	**League**	**GP**	**G**	**A**	**Pts.**	**PIM**	**+/-**	**PP**	**SH**	**GP**	**G**	**A**	**Pts.**	**PIM**
00-01—Swift Current	WHL	2	0	0	0	2	...	...	...	—	—	—	—	—
01-02—Swift Current	WHL	32	6	7	13	30	...	...	...	12	1	0	1	4
02-03—Swift Current	WHL	72	41	52	93	117	...	...	...	4	1	0	1	6
03-04—Swift Current	WHL	68	52	49	101	82	19	24	0	5	2	1	3	12
—St. John's	AHL	4	0	2	2	0	...	...	...	—	—	—	—	—
04-05—St. John's	AHL	75	16	20	36	24	0	5	0	5	0	0	0	0
05-06—Toronto	AHL	55	23	33	56	77	2	8	0	5	1	0	1	6
—Toronto	NHL	1	1	0	1	0	0	0	0	—	—	—	—	—
NHL Totals (1 year)		1	1	0	1	0	0	0	0					

WILLIAMS, JUSTIN RW

PERSONAL: Born October 4, 1981, in Cobourg, Ont. ... 6-1/190. ... Shoots right.

TRANSACTIONS/CAREER NOTES: Selected by Philadelphia Flyers in first round (first Flyers pick, 28th overall) of NHL draft (June 24, 2000). ... Fractured hand (February 19, 2001); missed 12 games. ... Flu (November 10, 2001); missed one game. ... Strained right shoulder (December 8, 2001); missed two games. ... Sprained knee (September 27, 2002); missed three preseason games. ... Strained left shoulder (November 15, 2002); missed five games. ... Injured knee (January 18, 2003) requiring surgery; missed 36 games. ... Traded by Flyers to Carolina Hurricanes for D Danny Markov (January 20, 2004). ... Fractured left wrist (February 13, 2004); missed three games.

		REGULAR SEASON								PLAYOFFS				
Season Team	League	GP	G	A	Pts.	PIM	+/-	PP	SH	GP	G	A	Pts.	PIM
97-98—Colborne	Jr. C	36	32	35	67	26	...	...	...	—	—	—	—	—
—Cobourg	Tier II Jr. A	17	0	3	3	5	...	...	...	—	—	—	—	—
98-99—Plymouth	OHL	47	4	8	12	28	...	...	...	7	1	2	3	0
99-00—Plymouth	OHL	68	37	46	83	46	...	...	...	23	14	16	30	10
00-01—Philadelphia	NHL	63	12	13	25	22	6	0	0	—	—	—	—	—
01-02—Philadelphia	NHL	75	17	23	40	32	11	0	0	5	0	0	0	4
02-03—Philadelphia	NHL	41	8	16	24	22	15	0	0	12	1	5	6	8
03-04—Philadelphia	NHL	47	6	20	26	32	10	3	0	—	—	—	—	—
—Carolina	NHL	32	5	13	18	32	2	1	0	—	—	—	—	—
04-05—Lulea	Sweden	49	14	18	32	61	-5	2	0	4	0	1	1	29
05-06—Carolina	NHL	82	31	45	76	60	1	8	4	25	7	11	18	34
NHL Totals (5 years)		340	79	130	209	200	45	12	4	42	8	16	24	46

WILLIAMS, NIGEL D

PERSONAL: Born April 18, 1988, in Aurora, Ill. ... 6-4/226. ... Shoots left.

TRANSACTIONS/CAREER NOTES: Selected by Colorado Avalanche in second round (second Avalanche pick; 51st overall) of NHL draft (June 24, 2006).

		REGULAR SEASON								PLAYOFFS				
Season Team	League	GP	G	A	Pts.	PIM	+/-	PP	SH	GP	G	A	Pts.	PIM
05-06—U.S. National	USHL	48	6	9	15	41	...	...	...	—	—	—	—	—

WILLSIE, BRIAN RW/LW

PERSONAL: Born March 16, 1978, in London, Ont. ... 6-1/195. ... Shoots right.

TRANSACTIONS/CAREER NOTES: Selected by Colorado Avalanche in sixth round (seventh Avalanche pick, 146th overall) of NHL draft (June 22, 1996). ... Claimed by Washington Capitals in waiver draft (October 3, 2003). ... Had concussion (December 27, 2003); missed 21 games. ... Signed as free agent by Portland of the AHL (December 15, 2004). ... Signed as free agent by Los Angeles Kings (July 4, 2006).

		REGULAR SEASON								PLAYOFFS				
Season Team	League	GP	G	A	Pts.	PIM	+/-	PP	SH	GP	G	A	Pts.	PIM
95-96—Guelph	OHL	65	13	21	34	18	...	...	...	16	4	2	6	6
96-97—Guelph	OHL	64	37	31	68	37	3	10	2	18	15	4	19	10
97-98—Guelph	OHL	57	45	31	76	41	28	...	...	12	9	5	14	18
98-99—Hershey	AHL	72	19	10	29	28	-8	3	1	3	1	0	1	0
99-00—Hershey	AHL	78	20	39	59	44	...	...	...	12	2	6	8	8
—Colorado	NHL	1	0	0	0	0	0	0	0	—	—	—	—	—
00-01—Hershey	AHL	48	18	23	41	20	...	...	...	12	7	2	9	14
01-02—Colorado	NHL	56	7	7	14	14	4	2	0	4	0	1	1	2
02-03—Hershey	AHL	59	29	28	57	49	2	11	4	—	—	—	—	—
—Colorado	NHL	12	0	1	1	15	0	0	0	6	1	0	1	2
03-04—Washington	NHL	49	10	5	15	18	-7	1	1	—	—	—	—	—
04-05—Olimpija	Slovenia	14	7	9	16	38	...	...	...	—	—	—	—	—
—Portland	AHL	53	23	17	40	47	-8	7	0	—	—	—	—	—
05-06—Washington	NHL	82	19	22	41	77	-19	8	1	—	—	—	—	—
NHL Totals (5 years)		200	36	35	71	124	-22	11	2	10	1	1	2	4

W

WILM, CLARKE C/LW

PERSONAL: Born October 24, 1976, in Central Butte, Sask. ... 6-0/202. ... Shoots left.

TRANSACTIONS/CAREER NOTES: Selected by Calgary Flames in sixth round (fifth Flames pick, 150th overall) of NHL entry draft (July 8, 1995). ... Suffered concussion (November 27, 1998); missed two games. ... Injured eye (January 26, 2002); missed two games. ... Suffered injury (March 9, 2001); missed two games. ... Injured ankle (March 18, 2002); missed remainder of season. ... Signed as free agent by Nashville Predators (July 11, 2002). ... Signed as free agent by Toronto Maple Leafs (October 28, 2003).

		REGULAR SEASON								PLAYOFFS				
Season Team	League	GP	G	A	Pts.	PIM	+/-	PP	SH	GP	G	A	Pts.	PIM
91-92—Saskatoon	WHL	...	...	...	...	...	...	...	...	1	0	0	0	0
92-93—Saskatoon	WHL	69	14	19	33	71	...	...	...	9	4	2	6	13
93-94—Saskatoon	WHL	70	18	32	50	181	...	...	...	16	0	9	9	19
94-95—Saskatoon	WHL	71	20	39	59	179	30	4	3	10	6	1	7	21
95-96—Saskatoon	WHL	72	49	61	110	83	...	...	...	4	1	1	2	4
96-97—Saint John	AHL	62	9	19	28	107	-4	1	0	5	2	0	2	15
97-98—Saint John	AHL	68	13	26	39	112	7	7	0	21	5	9	14	8
98-99—Calgary	NHL	78	10	8	18	53	11	2	2	—	—	—	—	—

Season Team	League	REGULAR SEASON GP	G	A	Pts.	PIM	+/-	PP	SH	PLAYOFFS GP	G	A	Pts.	PIM
99-00—Calgary	NHL	78	10	12	22	67	-6	1	3	—	—	—	—	—
00-01—Calgary	NHL	81	7	8	15	69	-11	2	0	—	—	—	—	—
01-02—Calgary	NHL	66	4	14	18	61	-1	0	1	—	—	—	—	—
02-03—Nashville	NHL	82	5	11	16	36	-11	0	0	—	—	—	—	—
03-04—St. John's	AHL	47	16	17	33	97	5	3	2	—	—	—	—	—
—Toronto	NHL	10	0	0	0	7	0	0	0	5	0	1	1	2
04-05—St. John's	AHL	69	11	16	27	145	-13	2	0	5	2	2	4	8
05-06—Toronto	NHL	60	1	7	8	43	-15	0	0	—	—	—	—	—
NHL Totals (7 years)		455	37	60	97	336	-33	5	6	5	0	1	1	2

WINCHESTER, BRAD — LW/C

PERSONAL: Born March 1, 1980, in Madison, Wis. ... 6-5/208. ... Shoots left.
COLLEGE: Wisconsin.
TRANSACTIONS/CAREER NOTES: Selected by Edmonton Oilers in second round (second Oilers pick, 35th overall) of entry draft (June 24, 2000).

Season Team	League	REGULAR SEASON GP	G	A	Pts.	PIM	+/-	PP	SH	PLAYOFFS GP	G	A	Pts.	PIM
98-99—U.S. National	USHL	68	21	36	57	...	...	...	...	—	—	—	—	—
99-00—Wisconsin	WCHA	29	8	8	16	48	...	...	...	—	—	—	—	—
00-01—Wisconsin	WCHA	41	7	9	16	71	...	...	...	—	—	—	—	—
01-02—Wisconsin	WCHA	38	14	20	34	38	...	...	...	—	—	—	—	—
02-03—Wisconsin	WCHA	38	10	6	16	58	...	...	...	—	—	—	—	—
03-04—Toronto	AHL	65	13	6	19	85	-10	0	1	3	0	0	0	2
04-05—Edmonton	AHL	76	22	18	40	143	2	10	0	—	—	—	—	—
05-06—Hamilton	AHL	40	26	14	40	118	-8	16	0	—	—	—	—	—
—Edmonton	NHL	19	0	1	1	21	-2	0	0	10	1	2	3	4
NHL Totals (1 year)		19	0	1	1	21	-2	0	0	10	1	2	3	4

WISEMAN, CHAD — LW

PERSONAL: Born March 25, 1981, in Burlington, Ont. ... 6-1/201. ... Shoots left.
TRANSACTIONS/CAREER NOTES: Selected by San Jose Sharks in eighth round (eighth Sharks pick, 246th overall) in 2000 NHL draft (June 25, 2000). ... Traded by Sharks to New York Rangers for LW Nils Ekman (August 12, 2003).

Season Team	League	REGULAR SEASON GP	G	A	Pts.	PIM	+/-	PP	SH	PLAYOFFS GP	G	A	Pts.	PIM
98-99—Mississauga	OHL	64	11	25	36	29	...	...	...	—	—	—	—	—
99-00—Mississauga	OHL	68	23	45	68	53	...	...	...	—	—	—	—	—
00-01—Mississauga	OHL	30	15	29	44	22	...	...	...	—	—	—	—	—
—Plymouth	OHL	32	11	16	27	12	...	...	...	19	12	8	20	22
01-02—Cleveland	AHL	76	21	29	50	61	-21	4	3	—	—	—	—	—
02-03—San Jose	NHL	4	0	0	0	4	-2	0	0	—	—	—	—	—
—Cleveland	AHL	77	17	35	52	44	...	...	...	—	—	—	—	—
03-04—New York Rangers	NHL	4	1	0	1	0	-1	0	0	—	—	—	—	—
—Hartford	AHL	62	25	27	52	45	15	7	4	15	5	6	11	12
04-05—Hartford	AHL	60	17	16	33	74	3	7	1	6	1	1	2	6
05-06—Hartford	AHL	69	19	36	55	65	3	4	1	11	3	6	9	22
—New York Rangers	NHL	1	0	1	1	4	2	0	0	1	0	0	0	2
NHL Totals (3 years)		9	1	1	2	8	-1	0	0	1	0	0	0	2

WISHART, TY — D

PERSONAL: Born May 19, 1988, in Belleville, Ont. ... 6-4/205. ... Shoots left.
TRANSACTIONS/CAREER NOTES: Selected by San Jose Sharks in first round (first Sharks pick; 16th overall) of NHL draft (June 24, 2006).

Season Team	League	REGULAR SEASON GP	G	A	Pts.	PIM	+/-	PP	SH	PLAYOFFS GP	G	A	Pts.	PIM
04-05—Prince George	WHL	58	1	7	8	41	-14	...	...	—	—	—	—	—
05-06—Prince George	WHL	70	5	32	37	68	12	...	...	5	0	0	0	4

W

WISNIEWSKI, JAMES — D

PERSONAL: Born February 21, 1984, in Canton, Mich. ... 6-0/206. ... Shoots right. ... Name pronounced wihz-NOO-skee.
TRANSACTIONS/CAREER NOTES: Selected by Chicago Blackhawks in fifth round (fifth Blackhawks pick, 156th overall) of NHL entry draft (June 23, 2002).

Season Team	League	REGULAR SEASON GP	G	A	Pts.	PIM	+/-	PP	SH	PLAYOFFS GP	G	A	Pts.	PIM
00-01—Plymouth	OHL	53	6	23	29	72	...	...	...	19	3	10	13	34
01-02—Plymouth	OHL	62	11	25	36	100	...	...	...	6	1	2	3	6
02-03—Plymouth	OHL	52	18	34	52	60	...	...	...	18	2	10	12	14
03-04—Plymouth	OHL	50	17	53	70	63	...	...	...	9	3	7	10	8

Season Team	League	REGULAR SEASON								PLAYOFFS				
		GP	G	A	Pts.	PIM	+/-	PP	SH	GP	G	A	Pts.	PIM
04-05—Norfolk	AHL	66	7	18	25	110	4	3	1	5	1	3	4	2
05-06—Chicago	NHL	19	2	5	7	36	0	0	0	—	—	—	—	—
—Norfolk	AHL	61	7	28	35	67	4	3	1	4	1	2	3	6
NHL Totals (1 year)		19	2	5	7	36	0	0	0					

WITT, BRENDAN D

PERSONAL: Born February 20, 1975, in Humboldt, Sask. ... 6-2/219. ... Shoots left.

TRANSACTIONS/CAREER NOTES: Selected by Washington Capitals in first round (first Capitals pick, 11th overall) of entry draft (June 26, 1993). ... Missed 1994-95 season in contract dispute. ... Fractured wrist (January 28, 1996); missed 34 games. ... Flu (November 15, 1996); missed five games. ... Shoulder (November 27, 1997); missed seven games. ... Flu (January 6, 1998); missed three games. ... Wrist (April 6, 1998); missed regular season's final six games and five playoff games. ... Knee (October 18, 1998); missed one game. ... Hip flexor (October 28, 1998); missed five games. ... Left team for personal reasons (January 26, 1999); missed one game. ... Wrist (February 3, 1999); missed 15 games. ... Knee (October 16, 1999); missed two games. ... Back (November 26, 1999); missed one game. ... Groin (March 11, 2000); missed one game. ... Thigh (March 25, 2000); missed one game. ... Left arm (October 17, 2000); missed one game. ... Flu (December 16, 2000); missed three games. ... Shoulder (December 29, 2000); missed five games. ... Leg (October 10, 2001); missed two games. ... Leg (November 6, 2001); missed five games. ... Thumb (January 3, 2002); missed seven games. ... Groin (October 26, 2002); missed three games. ... Shoulder (November 9, 2002); missed four games. ... Ribs (March 14, 2003); missed two games. ... Ribs (March 29, 2003); missed four games. ... Concussion (October 11, 2003); missed two games. ... Shoulder (December 11, 2003); missed 11 games. ... Lower body (March 24, 2004); missed one game. ... Personal leave (October 26, 2005); missed one game. ... Leg (November 27, 2005); missed one game. ... Traded by Capitals to Nashville Predators for C Kris Beech and first-round pick (G Semen Varlamov) in 2006 draft (March 9, 2006). ... Suspended one game by NHL in kneeing incident (April 4, 2006). ... Signed as free agent by New York Islanders (July 3, 2006).

Season Team	League	REGULAR SEASON								PLAYOFFS				
		GP	G	A	Pts.	PIM	+/-	PP	SH	GP	G	A	Pts.	PIM
90-91—Seattle	WHL	...	...	...	...	...	...	...	...	1	0	0	0	0
91-92—Seattle	WHL	67	3	9	12	212	...	...	...	15	1	1	2	84
92-93—Seattle	WHL	70	2	26	28	239	-14	2	0	5	1	2	3	30
93-94—Seattle	WHL	56	8	31	39	235	18	5	0	9	3	8	11	23
94-95—	Did not play													
95-96—Washington	NHL	48	2	3	5	85	-4	0	0	—	—	—	—	—
96-97—Washington	NHL	44	3	2	5	88	-20	0	0	—	—	—	—	—
—Portland	AHL	30	2	4	6	56	1	0	0	5	1	0	1	30
97-98—Washington	NHL	64	1	7	8	112	-11	0	0	16	1	0	1	14
98-99—Washington	NHL	54	2	5	7	87	-6	0	0	—	—	—	—	—
99-00—Washington	NHL	77	1	7	8	114	5	0	0	3	0	0	0	0
00-01—Washington	NHL	72	3	3	6	101	2	0	0	6	2	0	2	12
01-02—Washington	NHL	68	3	7	10	78	-1	0	0	—	—	—	—	—
02-03—Washington	NHL	69	2	9	11	106	12	0	0	6	1	0	1	0
03-04—Washington	NHL	72	2	10	12	123	-22	0	0	—	—	—	—	—
04-05—Bracknell	England	3	1	4	5	0	...	...	...	—	—	—	—	—
05-06—Washington	NHL	58	1	10	11	141	-5	0	0	—	—	—	—	—
—Nashville	NHL	17	0	3	3	68	5	0	0	5	0	0	0	12
NHL Totals (10 years)		643	20	66	86	1103	-45	0	0	36	4	0	4	38

WOLSKI, WOJTEK LW

PERSONAL: Born February 24, 1986, in Zabrize, Poland. ... 6-3/200. ... Shoots left. ... Name pronounced: VOY-tehk VOHL-skee

TRANSACTIONS/CAREER NOTES: Selected by Colorado Avalanche in first round (first Avalanche pick, 21st overall) of NHL entry draft (June 26, 2004).

Season Team	League	REGULAR SEASON								PLAYOFFS				
		GP	G	A	Pts.	PIM	+/-	PP	SH	GP	G	A	Pts.	PIM
02-03—Brampton	OHL	64	25	32	57	26	...	...	...	11	5	0	5	6
03-04—Brampton	OHL	66	29	41	70	30	...	...	...	12	5	3	8	8
04-05—Brampton	OHL	67	29	44	73	41	-6	13	2	6	2	5	7	6
05-06—Brampton	OHL	56	47	81	128	46	...	...	...	11	7	11	18	4
—Colorado	NHL	9	2	4	6	4	-5	2	0	8	1	3	4	2
NHL Totals (1 year)		9	2	4	6	4	-5	2	0	8	1	3	4	2

WOOLLEY, JASON D

PERSONAL: Born July 27, 1969, in Toronto. ... 6-0/206. ... Shoots left.

TRANSACTIONS/CAREER NOTES: Selected by Washington Capitals in third round (fourth Capitals pick, 61st overall) of entry draft (June 17, 1989). ... Fractured wrist (October 12, 1992); missed 24 games. ... Torn abdominal muscle (January 2, 1994). ... Signed as free agent by IHL Detroit (October 7, 1994). ... Contract sold by IHL Detroit to Florida Panthers (February 14, 1995). ... Separated left shoulder (October 15, 1995); missed two games. ... Fractured left thumb (November 18, 1995); missed 13 games. ... Traded by Panthers with C Stu Barnes to Pittsburgh Penguins for C Chris Wells (November 19, 1996). ... Groin (November 22, 1996); missed one game. ... Groin (February 27, 1997); missed one game. ... Groin (March 4, 1997); missed two games. ... Bruised wrist (March 18, 1997); missed two games. ... Traded by Penguins to Buffalo Sabres for fifth-round pick (D Robert Scuderi) in 1998 (September 24, 1997). ... Fractured thumb (October 1, 1997); missed nine games. ... Flu (February 15, 1999); missed one game. ... Groin (April 14, 1999); missed one game. ... Rib (November 12, 1999); missed four games. ... Flu (March 4, 2000); missed two games. ... Groin (December 12, 2000); missed four games. ... Knee (February 25, 2001); missed two games. ... Flu (November 11, 2001); missed three games. ... Traded by Sabres to Detroit Red Wings for future considerations (November 17, 2002). ... Bruised foot (December 28, 2003); missed one game. ... Back (February 18, 2004); missed season's final 21 games. ... Groin (October 22, 2005); missed 10 games. ... Groin (November 15, 2005); missed five games.

Season Team	League	REGULAR SEASON								PLAYOFFS				
		GP	G	A	Pts.	PIM	+/-	PP	SH	GP	G	A	Pts.	PIM
87-88—St. Michael's Jr. B	ODHA	31	19	37	56	22	...	...	...	—	—	—	—	—
88-89—Michigan State	CCHA	47	12	25	37	26	...	...	...	—	—	—	—	—
89-90—Michigan State	CCHA	45	10	38	48	26	...	...	...	—	—	—	—	—
90-91—Michigan State	CCHA	40	15	44	59	24	...	...	...	—	—	—	—	—
91-92—Canadian nat'l team	Int'l	60	14	30	44	36	...	...	...	—	—	—	—	—
—Can. Olympic team	Int'l	8	0	5	5	4	...	...	...	—	—	—	—	—
—Baltimore	AHL	15	1	10	11	6	...	...	...	—	—	—	—	—
—Washington	NHL	1	0	0	0	0	1	0	0	—	—	—	—	—
92-93—Baltimore	AHL	29	14	27	41	22	4	5	0	1	0	2	2	0
—Washington	NHL	26	0	2	2	10	3	0	0	—	—	—	—	—
93-94—Portland	AHL	41	12	29	41	14	15	5	0	9	2	2	4	4
—Washington	NHL	10	1	2	3	4	2	0	0	4	1	0	1	4
94-95—Detroit	IHL	48	8	28	36	38	7	0	0	—	—	—	—	—
—Florida	NHL	34	4	9	13	18	-1	1	0	—	—	—	—	—
95-96—Florida	NHL	52	6	28	34	32	-9	3	0	13	2	6	8	14
96-97—Florida	NHL	3	0	0	0	2	1	0	0	—	—	—	—	—
—Pittsburgh	NHL	57	6	30	36	28	3	2	0	5	0	3	3	0
97-98—Buffalo	NHL	71	9	26	35	35	8	3	0	15	2	9	11	12
98-99—Buffalo	NHL	80	10	33	43	62	16	4	0	21	4	11	15	10
99-00—Buffalo	NHL	74	8	25	33	52	14	2	0	5	0	2	2	2
00-01—Buffalo	NHL	67	5	18	23	46	0	4	0	8	1	5	6	2
01-02—Buffalo	NHL	59	8	20	28	34	-6	6	0	—	—	—	—	—
02-03—Buffalo	NHL	14	0	3	3	29	-1	0	0	—	—	—	—	—
—Detroit	NHL	62	6	17	23	22	12	1	0	4	1	0	1	0
03-04—Detroit	NHL	55	4	15	19	28	19	0	0	4	0	0	0	0
04-05—UHL	UHL	9	4	2	6	4	2	2	0	—	—	—	—	—
05-06—Detroit	NHL	53	1	18	19	28	3	0	0	—	—	—	—	—
NHL Totals (14 years)		718	68	246	314	430	65	26	0	79	11	36	47	44

WOYWITKA, JEFF D

PERSONAL: Born September 1, 1983, in Vermillion, Alta. ... 6-2/197. ... Shoots left. ... Name pronounced: woy WIHT kuh

TRANSACTIONS/CAREER NOTES: Selected by Philadelphia Flyers in first round (first Flyers pick, 27th overall) of entry draft (June 23, 2001). ... Traded by Flyers with first-round pick (C Robbie Schremp) in 2004 and third-round pick (D Danny Syvret) in 2005 to Edmonton Oilers for C Mike Comrie (December 16, 2003). ... Traded by Oilers with D Eric Brewer and D Doug Lynch to St. Louis Blues for D Chris Pronger (August 2, 2005).

Season Team	League	REGULAR SEASON								PLAYOFFS				
		GP	G	A	Pts.	PIM	+/-	PP	SH	GP	G	A	Pts.	PIM
99-00—Red Deer	WHL	67	4	12	16	40	...	...	...	4	0	3	3	2
00-01—Red Deer	WHL	72	7	28	35	113	...	...	...	22	2	8	10	25
01-02—Red Deer	WHL	72	14	23	37	109	...	...	...	23	2	10	12	22
02-03—Red Deer	WHL	57	16	36	52	65	...	...	...	23	1	9	10	25
03-04—Philadelphia	AHL	29	0	6	6	51	...	...	...	—	—	—	—	—
—Toronto	AHL	53	4	18	22	41	-5	2	0	3	0	0	0	0
04-05—Edmonton	AHL	80	6	20	26	84	-7	1	0	—	—	—	—	—
05-06—Peoria	AHL	53	1	14	15	58	3	0	0	4	0	0	0	4
—St. Louis	NHL	26	0	2	2	25	-12	0	0	—	—	—	—	—
NHL Totals (1 year)		26	0	2	2	25	-12	0	0					

WOZNIEWSKI, ANDY D

PERSONAL: Born May 25, 1980, in Buffalo Grove, Ill. ... 6-5/221. ... Shoots left. ... Name pronounced: wahs NOO skee

COLLEGE: Massachusetts-Lowell, then Wisconsin.

TRANSACTIONS/CAREER NOTES: Signed as free agent by Toronto Maple Leafs (May 27, 2004).

Season Team	League	REGULAR SEASON								PLAYOFFS				
		GP	G	A	Pts.	PIM	+/-	PP	SH	GP	G	A	Pts.	PIM
99-00—Mass.-Lowell	Hockey East	17	1	1	2	8	...	...	...	—	—	—	—	—
00-01—Texas	NAJHL	54	10	34	44	98	...	...	...	8	2	7	9	12
01-02—Wisconsin	WCHA	39	3	13	16	54	...	...	...	—	—	—	—	—
02-03—Wisconsin	WCHA	33	1	7	8	47	...	...	...	—	—	—	—	—
03-04—St. John's	AHL	3	0	1	1	0	...	...	...	—	—	—	—	—
—Wisconsin	WCHA	43	6	8	14	104	...	...	...	—	—	—	—	—
04-05—St. John's	AHL	28	1	4	5	20	2	0	0	0	0	0	0	0
05-06—Toronto	NHL	13	0	1	1	13	-8	0	0	—	—	—	—	—
—Toronto	AHL	31	4	11	15	42	-2	1	0	—	—	—	—	—
NHL Totals (1 year)		13	0	1	1	13	-8	0	0					

WRIGHT, TYLER C/RW

PERSONAL: Born April 6, 1973, in Kamsack, Sask. ... 6-1/190. ... Shoots right.

TRANSACTIONS/CAREER NOTES: Selected by Edmonton Oilers in first round (first Oilers pick, 12th overall) of entry draft (June 22, 1991). ... Traded by Oilers to Pittsburgh Penguins for seventh-round pick (RW Brandon LaFrance) in 1996 draft (June 22, 1996). ... Bruised ribs (December 13, 1996); missed one game. ... Back spasms (January 18, 2000); missed two games. ... Strained knee (April 3, 2000); missed

two games. ... Selected by Columbus Blue Jackets in expansion draft (June 23, 2000). ... Bruised ribs (December 23, 2000); missed five games. ... Flu (February 21, 2001); missed one game. ... Concussion (November 1, 2001); missed five games. ... Concussion (October 23, 2002); missed one game. ... Fractured hand (November 14, 2002); missed nine games. ... Bruised thigh (March 6, 2003); missed one game. ... Hyperextended elbow (October 14, 2003); missed six games. ... Traded by Blue Jackets with D Francois Beauchemin to Anaheim Mighty Ducks for C Sergei Fedorov and fifth-round pick (D Maxime Frechette) in 2006 draft (November 15, 2005).
STATISTICAL PLATEAUS: Three-goal games: 2000-01 (1), 2002-03 (2). Total: 3.

		REGULAR SEASON								PLAYOFFS				
Season Team	**League**	**GP**	**G**	**A**	**Pts.**	**PIM**	**+/-**	**PP**	**SH**	**GP**	**G**	**A**	**Pts.**	**PIM**
89-90—Swift Current	WHL	67	14	18	32	119	...	...	...	4	0	0	0	12
90-91—Swift Current	WHL	66	41	51	92	157	...	...	...	3	0	0	0	6
91-92—Swift Current	WHL	63	36	46	82	295	...	...	...	8	2	5	7	16
92-93—Swift Current	WHL	37	24	41	65	76	-7	14	2	17	9	17	26	49
—Edmonton	NHL	7	1	1	2	19	-4	0	0	—	—	—	—	—
93-94—Cape Breton	AHL	65	14	27	41	160	-20	2	3	5	2	0	2	11
—Edmonton	NHL	5	0	0	0	4	-3	0	0	—	—	—	—	—
94-95—Cape Breton	AHL	70	16	15	31	184	-16	2	2	—	—	—	—	—
—Edmonton	NHL	6	1	0	1	14	1	0	0	—	—	—	—	—
95-96—Edmonton	NHL	23	1	0	1	33	-7	0	0	—	—	—	—	—
—Cape Breton	AHL	31	6	12	18	158	...	...	...	—	—	—	—	—
96-97—Pittsburgh	NHL	45	2	2	4	70	-7	0	0	—	—	—	—	—
—Cleveland	IHL	10	4	3	7	34	...	...	...	14	4	2	6	44
97-98—Pittsburgh	NHL	82	3	4	7	112	-3	1	0	6	0	1	1	4
98-99—Pittsburgh	NHL	61	0	0	0	90	-2	0	0	13	0	0	0	19
99-00—Wilkes-Barre/Scranton	AHL	25	5	15	20	86	...	...	...	—	—	—	—	—
—Pittsburgh	NHL	50	12	10	22	45	4	0	0	11	3	1	4	17
00-01—Columbus	NHL	76	16	16	32	140	-9	4	1	—	—	—	—	—
01-02—Columbus	NHL	77	13	11	24	100	-40	4	0	—	—	—	—	—
02-03—Columbus	NHL	70	19	11	30	113	-25	3	2	—	—	—	—	—
03-04—Columbus	NHL	68	9	9	18	63	-19	2	0	—	—	—	—	—
04-05—Biel-Bienne	Switz. Div. 2	7	3	4	7	4	...	1	0	12	8	8	16	44
05-06—Columbus	NHL	18	0	4	4	20	-3	0	0	—	—	—	—	—
—Anaheim	NHL	25	2	2	4	31	2	0	0	—	—	—	—	—
NHL Totals (13 years)		613	79	70	149	854	-115	14	3	30	3	2	5	40

YAKUBOV, MIKHAIL C

PERSONAL: Born February 16, 1982, in Barnaul, U.S.S.R. ... 6-3/202. ... Shoots left. ... Name pronounced YAK-oo-bahf.
TRANSACTIONS/CAREER NOTES: Selected by Chicago Blackhawks in first round (first Blackhawks pick, 10th overall) of NHL entry draft (June 24, 2000). ... Claimed off waivers by Panthers (January 29, 2006).

		REGULAR SEASON								PLAYOFFS				
Season Team	**League**	**GP**	**G**	**A**	**Pts.**	**PIM**	**+/-**	**PP**	**SH**	**GP**	**G**	**A**	**Pts.**	**PIM**
99-00—Lada Togliatti	Rus. Div.	26	12	19	31	14	...	...	...	—	—	—	—	—
00-01—Lada Togliatti	Russian	25	0	0	0	4	...	...	...	4	0	0	0	0
01-02—Red Deer	WHL	71	32	57	89	54	...	...	...	23	14	9	23	28
02-03—Norfolk	AHL	62	6	5	11	36	-7	3	1	9	0	0	0	8
03-04—Chicago	NHL	30	1	7	8	8	-12	0	0	—	—	—	—	—
—Norfolk	AHL	51	9	18	27	22	10	1	0	8	0	3	3	2
04-05—Norfolk	AHL	59	12	15	27	43	-1	3	0	3	0	0	0	0
05-06—Norfolk	AHL	8	1	3	4	8	-4	1	0	—	—	—	—	—
—Chicago	NHL	10	1	2	3	8	0	0	0	—	—	—	—	—
—Florida	NHL	13	0	1	1	4	-1	0	0	—	—	—	—	—
NHL Totals (2 years)		53	2	10	12	20	-13	0	0					

YASHIN, ALEXEI C

PERSONAL: Born November 5, 1973, in Sverdlovsk, U.S.S.R. ... 6-3/220. ... Shoots right. ... Name pronounced uh-LEK-see YA-shihn.
TRANSACTIONS/CAREER NOTES: Selected by Ottawa Senators in first round (first Senators pick, second overall) of NHL draft (June 20, 1992). ... Strep throat (December 4, 1993); missed one game. ... Missed 1999-2000 season in contract dispute. ... Traded by Senators to New York Islanders for RW Bill Muckalt, D Zdeno Chara and first-round pick (C Jason Spezza) in 2001 draft (June 23, 2001). ... Strained groin (April 6, 2002); missed final four games of season. ... Cut right forearm (December 23, 2003); missed 35 games.
STATISTICAL PLATEAUS: Three-goal games: 1993-94 (1), 1994-95 (1), 1995-96 (1), 1997-98 (1), 1998-99 (1), 2000-01 (1), 2001-02 (1). Total: 7. ... Four-goal games: 2002-03 (1). ... Total hat tricks: 8.

		REGULAR SEASON								PLAYOFFS				
Season Team	**League**	**GP**	**G**	**A**	**Pts.**	**PIM**	**+/-**	**PP**	**SH**	**GP**	**G**	**A**	**Pts.**	**PIM**
90-91—Avtomo. Sverdlovsk	USSR	26	2	1	3	10	...	...	...	—	—	—	—	—
91-92—Dynamo Moscow	CIS	35	7	5	12	19	...	...	...	—	—	—	—	—
92-93—Dynamo Moscow	CIS	27	10	12	22	18	...	...	...	10	7	3	10	18
93-94—Ottawa	NHL	83	30	49	79	22	-49	11	2	—	—	—	—	—
94-95—Las Vegas	IHL	24	15	20	35	32	19	4	0	—	—	—	—	—
—Ottawa	NHL	47	21	23	44	20	-20	11	0	—	—	—	—	—
95-96—Ottawa	NHL	46	15	24	39	28	-15	8	0	—	—	—	—	—
96-97—Ottawa	NHL	82	35	40	75	44	-7	10	0	7	1	5	6	2
97-98—Ottawa	NHL	82	33	39	72	24	6	5	0	11	5	3	8	8
—Russian Oly. team	Int'l	6	3	3	6	0	6	1	0	—	—	—	—	—
98-99—Ottawa	NHL	82	44	50	94	54	16	19	0	4	0	0	0	10
99-00—Ottawa	NHL	Did not play.												
00-01—Ottawa	NHL	82	40	48	88	30	10	13	2	4	0	1	1	0
01-02—New York Islanders	NHL	78	32	43	75	25	-3	15	0	7	3	4	7	2
—Russian Oly. team	Int'l	6	1	1	2	0	...	...	...	—	—	—	—	—

Season Team	League	GP	G	A	Pts.	PIM	+/-	PP	SH	GP	G	A	Pts.	PIM
		REGULAR SEASON								PLAYOFFS				
02-03—New York Islanders.....	NHL	81	26	39	65	32	-12	14	0	5	2	2	4	2
03-04—New York Islanders.....	NHL	47	15	19	34	10	-1	3	0	5	0	1	1	0
04-05—Lokomotiv Yaroslavl ...	Russian	10	3	3	6	14	4	...	...	9	3	7	10	10
05-06—New York Islanders.....	NHL	82	28	38	66	68	-14	10	0	—	—	—	—	—
—Russian Oly. team.......	Int'l	8	1	3	4	4	1	0	0	—	—	—	—	—
NHL Totals (12 years)..........		792	319	412	731	357	-89	119	4	43	11	16	27	24

YELLE, STEPHANE C

PERSONAL: Born May 9, 1974, in Ottawa. ... 6-1/190. ... Shoots left. ... Name pronounced STEH-fan YEHL.

TRANSACTIONS/CAREER NOTES: Selected by New Jersey Devils in eighth round (ninth Devils pick, 186th overall) of NHL draft (June 20, 1992). ... Traded by Devils with 11th-round pick (D Stephen Low) in 1994 draft to Quebec Nordiques for 11th-round pick (C Mike Hansen) in 1994 draft (June 1, 1994). ... Nordiques franchise moved to Colorado and renamed Avalanche for 1995-96 season (June 21, 1995). ... Pulled groin (February 15, 1996); missed nine games. ... Strained hip flexor (December 14, 1996); missed three games. ... Sprained right wrist (November 28, 1998); missed nine games. ... Sprained knee (May 3, 1999); missed nine playoff games. ... Injured sternum (January 25, 2000); missed two games. ... Strained hip flexor (March 7, 2000); missed one game. ... Injured ankle (October 25, 2000); missed one game. ... Strained groin (November 18, 2000); missed three games. ... Injured back (November 20, 2000); missed three games. ... Herniated disk in back (October 27, 2000); missed 10 games. ... Injured knee (February 17, 2001); missed nine games. ... Sprained knee (March 24, 2001); missed six games. ... Injured ankle (November 16, 2001); missed one game. ... Flu (November 27, 2001); missed one game. ... Bruised foot (December 23, 2001); missed one game. ... Bruised knee (January 3, 2001); missed one game. ... Injured shoulder (March 14, 2002); missed five games. ... Traded by Avalanche with LW Chris Drury to Calgary Flames for D Derek Morris, LW Dean McAmmond and C Jeff Shantz (October 1, 2002). ... Injured head (October 14, 2003); missed one game. ... Injured shoulder (November 15, 2004); missed two games. ... Injured left eye (January 6, 2004); missed three games. ... Sprained right knee (January 16, 2004); missed 18 games. ... Injured ankle (December 19, 2005); missed eight games.

Season Team	League	GP	G	A	Pts.	PIM	+/-	PP	SH	GP	G	A	Pts.	PIM
		REGULAR SEASON								PLAYOFFS				
91-92—Oshawa.......................	OHL	55	12	14	26	20	...	...	...	7	2	0	2	1
92-93—Oshawa.......................	OHL	66	24	50	74	20	...	...	...	10	2	4	6	4
93-94—Oshawa.......................	OHL	66	35	69	104	22	...	...	...	5	1	7	8	2
94-95—Cornwall	AHL	40	18	15	33	22	3	11	0	13	7	7	14	8
95-96—Colorado.....................	NHL	71	13	14	27	30	15	0	2	22	1	4	5	8
96-97—Colorado.....................	NHL	79	9	17	26	38	1	0	1	12	1	6	7	2
97-98—Colorado.....................	NHL	81	7	15	22	48	-10	0	1	7	1	0	1	12
98-99—Colorado.....................	NHL	72	8	7	15	40	-8	1	0	10	0	1	1	6
99-00—Colorado.....................	NHL	79	8	14	22	28	9	0	1	17	1	2	3	4
00-01—Colorado.....................	NHL	50	4	10	14	20	-3	0	1	23	1	2	3	8
01-02—Colorado.....................	NHL	73	5	12	17	48	1	0	1	20	0	2	2	14
02-03—Calgary	NHL	82	10	15	25	50	-10	3	0	—	—	—	—	—
03-04—Calgary	NHL	53	4	13	17	24	1	1	0	23	3	3	6	16
05-06—Calgary	NHL	74	4	14	18	48	10	1	1	7	1	0	1	8
NHL Totals (10 years)..........		714	72	131	203	374	6	6	8	141	9	20	29	78

YONKMAN, NOLAN D

PERSONAL: Born April 1, 1981, in Punnichy, Sask. ... 6-6/245. ... Shoots right.

TRANSACTIONS/CAREER NOTES: Selected by Washington Capitals in second round (fifth Capitals pick, 37th overall) of NHL draft (June 26, 1999). ... Hip pointer (November 4, 2005); missed seven games.

Season Team	League	GP	G	A	Pts.	PIM	+/-	PP	SH	GP	G	A	Pts.	PIM
		REGULAR SEASON								PLAYOFFS				
97-98—Kelowna......................	WHL	65	0	2	2	36	...	...	...	7	0	0	0	2
98-99—Kelowna......................	WHL	61	1	6	7	129	-33	0	0	6	0	0	0	6
99-00—Kelowna......................	WHL	71	5	7	12	153	-30	2	0	5	0	0	0	8
00-01—Kelowna......................	WHL	7	0	1	1	19	...	...	...	—	—	—	—	—
—Brandon......................	WHL	51	6	10	16	94	...	...	...	6	0	1	1	12
01-02—Portland......................	AHL	59	4	3	7	116	0	0	0	—	—	—	—	—
—Washington	NHL	11	1	0	1	4	3	0	0	—	—	—	—	—
02-03—Portland......................	AHL	24	1	4	5	40	4	0	0	3	0	1	1	2
03-04—Washington	NHL	1	0	0	0	0	0	0	0	—	—	—	—	—
—Portland......................	AHL	4	0	0	0	11	3	0	0	—	—	—	—	—
04-05—Portland......................	AHL	32	0	3	3	68	-6	0	0	—	—	—	—	—
05-06—Hershey	AHL	6	0	0	0	15	-1	0	0	—	—	—	—	—
—Washington	NHL	38	0	7	7	86	1	0	0	—	—	—	—	—
NHL Totals (3 years)...........		50	1	7	8	90	4	0	0					

YORK, MIKE C

PERSONAL: Born January 3, 1978, in Waterford, Mich. ... 5-10/185. ... Shoots right.

TRANSACTIONS/CAREER NOTES: Selected by New York Rangers in sixth round (seventh Rangers pick, 136th overall) of NHL draft (June 21, 1997). ... Bruised ribs (January 22, 2001); missed one game. ... Left shoulder (February 9, 2001); missed two games. ... Flu (March 13, 2002); missed one game. ... Traded by Rangers with fourth-round pick (D Ivan Koltsov) in 2002 draft to Edmonton Oilers for D Tom Poti and LW Rem

Murray (March 19, 2002). ... Flu (November 15, 2002); missed one game. ... Flu (February 18, 2003); missed one game. ... Fractured wrist (February 25, 2003); missed two games. ... Reinjured wrist (March 6, 2003); missed five games. ... Fractured finger (January 16, 2004); missed 16 games. ... Finger (March 10, 2004); missed four games. ... Traded by Oilers with fourth-round pick (traded to Colorado; Avalanche selected D Kevin Montgomery) in 2006 draft to New York Islanders for Michael Peca (August 3, 2005). ... Re-signed by Islanders as restricted free agent (August 13, 2005). ... Concussion (March 17, 2006); missed two games. ... Eye (March 28, 2006); missed one game. ... Broken toe (April 11, 2006); missed final four games of regular season.

		REGULAR SEASON								PLAYOFFS				
Season Team	**League**	**GP**	**G**	**A**	**Pts.**	**PIM**	**+/-**	**PP**	**SH**	**GP**	**G**	**A**	**Pts.**	**PIM**
95-96—Michigan State	CCHA	39	12	27	39	20	...	...	...	—	—	—	—	—
96-97—Michigan State	CCHA	37	18	29	47	42	...	...	...	—	—	—	—	—
97-98—Michigan State	CCHA	40	27	34	61	38	...	...	...	—	—	—	—	—
98-99—Michigan State	CCHA	42	22	32	54	41	...	...	...	—	—	—	—	—
—Hartford	AHL	3	2	2	4	0	2	1	0	6	3	1	4	0
99-00—New York Rangers	NHL	82	26	24	50	18	-17	8	0	—	—	—	—	—
00-01—New York Rangers	NHL	79	14	17	31	20	1	3	2	—	—	—	—	—
01-02—New York Rangers	NHL	69	18	39	57	16	8	2	0	—	—	—	—	—
—U.S. Olympic team	Int'l	6	0	1	1	0	...	...	...	—	—	—	—	—
—Edmonton	NHL	12	2	2	4	0	-1	1	0	—	—	—	—	—
02-03—Edmonton	NHL	71	22	29	51	10	-8	7	2	6	0	2	2	2
03-04—Edmonton	NHL	61	16	26	42	15	18	1	2	—	—	—	—	—
04-05—Iserlohn	Germany	52	16	46	62	77	-6	9	1	—	—	—	—	—
05-06—New York Islanders	NHL	75	13	39	52	30	-9	4	1	—	—	—	—	—
NHL Totals (6 years)		449	111	176	287	109	-8	26	7	6	0	2	2	2

YOUNG, SCOTT RW

PERSONAL: Born October 1, 1967, in Clinton, Mass. ... 6-1/200. ... Shoots right.

TRANSACTIONS/CAREER NOTES: Selected by Hartford Whalers in first round (first Whalers pick, 11th overall) of entry draft (June 21, 1986). ... Cut above right eye (October 8, 1988). ... Cut face (February 18, 1990). ... Traded by Whalers to Pittsburgh Penguins for RW Rob Brown (December 21, 1990). ... Traded by Penguins to Quebec Nordiques for D Bryan Fogarty (March 10, 1992). ... Rib (February 14, 1993); missed one game. ... Bruised ribs (February 23, 1993); missed one game. ... Sprained right ankle (October 5, 1993); missed eight games. ... Nordiques franchise moved to Colorado and renamed Avalanche for 1995-96 season (June 21, 1995). ... Bruised right shoulder (December 23, 1996); missed five games. ... Traded by Avalanche to Anaheim Mighty Ducks for third-round pick (traded to Florida; Panthers selected D Lance Ward) in 1998 draft (September 17, 1997). ... Bruised right foot (November 22, 1997); missed two games. ... Bruised right foot (November 29, 1997); missed five games. ... Eye abrasion (March 9, 1998); missed two games. ... Signed as free agent by St. Louis Blues (July 16, 1998). ... Back (February 8, 1999); missed one game. ... Back (January 28, 2000); missed three games. ... Separated shoulder (April 5, 2000); missed regular season's final two games. ... Shoulder (December 5, 2000); missed one game. ... Back spasms (October 13, 2001); missed four games. ... Eye (January 8, 2002); missed 11 games. ... Signed as free agent by Dallas Stars (July 5, 2002). ... Hip flexor (March 7, 2003); missed one game. ... Suspended two games for high-sticking incident (March 12, 2003). ... Back spasms (January 19, 2004); missed five games. ... Fined $1,000 for high-sticking incident (January 28, 2004). ... Back spasms (February 27, 2004); missed remained of season. ... Signed as free agent by Blues (September 13, 2005). ... Hip (December 1, 2005); missed one game. ... Back (December 8, 2005); missed two games.

STATISTICAL PLATEAUS: Three-goal games: 1992-93 (1), 1993-94 (1), 1994-95 (1), 1996-97 (1). Total: 4.

		REGULAR SEASON								PLAYOFFS				
Season Team	**League**	**GP**	**G**	**A**	**Pts.**	**PIM**	**+/-**	**PP**	**SH**	**GP**	**G**	**A**	**Pts.**	**PIM**
84-85—St. Marks H.S.	Mass. H.S.	23	28	41	69	...	...	...	...	—	—	—	—	—
85-86—Boston University	Hockey East	38	16	13	29	31	...	...	...	—	—	—	—	—
86-87—Boston University	Hockey East	33	15	21	36	24	...	...	...	—	—	—	—	—
87-88—U.S. Olympic team	Int'l	59	13	53	66	...	...	...	...	—	—	—	—	—
—Hartford	NHL	7	0	0	0	2	-6	0	0	4	1	0	1	0
88-89—Hartford	NHL	76	19	40	59	27	-21	6	0	4	2	0	2	4
89-90—Hartford	NHL	80	24	40	64	47	-24	10	2	7	2	0	2	2
90-91—Hartford	NHL	34	6	9	15	8	-9	3	1	—	—	—	—	—
—Pittsburgh	NHL	43	11	16	27	33	3	3	1	17	1	6	7	2
91-92—U.S. national team	Int'l	10	2	4	6	21	...	...	...	—	—	—	—	—
—U.S. Olympic team	Int'l	8	2	1	3	2	...	...	...	—	—	—	—	—
—Bolzano	Italy	18	22	17	39	6	...	...	...	—	—	—	—	—
92-93—Quebec	NHL	82	30	30	60	20	5	9	6	6	4	1	5	0
93-94—Quebec	NHL	76	26	25	51	14	-4	6	1	—	—	—	—	—
94-95—Frankfurt	Germany	1	1	0	1	0	...	...	...	—	—	—	—	—
—Landshut	Germany	4	6	1	7	6	...	...	...	—	—	—	—	—
—Quebec	NHL	48	18	21	39	14	9	3	3	6	3	3	6	2
95-96—Colorado	NHL	81	21	39	60	50	2	7	0	22	3	12	15	10
96-97—Colorado	NHL	72	18	19	37	14	-5	7	0	17	4	2	6	14
97-98—Anaheim	NHL	73	13	20	33	22	-13	4	2	—	—	—	—	—
98-99—St. Louis	NHL	75	24	28	52	27	8	8	0	13	4	7	11	10
99-00—St. Louis	NHL	75	24	15	39	18	12	6	1	6	6	2	8	8
00-01—St. Louis	NHL	81	40	33	73	30	15	14	3	15	6	7	13	2
01-02—St. Louis	NHL	67	19	22	41	26	11	5	0	10	3	0	3	2
—U.S. Olympic team	Int'l	6	4	0	4	2	...	...	...	—	—	—	—	—
02-03—Dallas	NHL	79	23	19	42	30	24	5	1	10	4	3	7	6
03-04—Dallas	NHL	53	8	8	16	14	-15	2	0	4	1	0	1	2
04-05—Memphis	CHL	3	2	1	3	0	...	...	...	—	—	—	—	—
05-06—St. Louis	NHL	79	18	31	49	52	-32	10	0	—	—	—	—	—
NHL Totals (17 years)		1181	342	415	757	448	-40	108	21	141	44	43	87	64

YZERMAN, STEVE C

PERSONAL: Born May 9, 1965, in Cranbrook, B.C. ... 5-11/185. ... Shoots right. ... Name pronounced IGH-zuhr-muhn.

TRANSACTIONS/CAREER NOTES: Selected by Detroit Red Wings in first round (first Red Wings pick, fourth overall) of entry draft (June 8, 1983). ... Fractured collarbone (January 31, 1986). ... Right knee (March 1, 1988) and had surgery. ... Right knee i(April 8, 1991). ... Herniated disc (October 21, 1993); missed 26 games. ... Sprained knee (May 27, 1995); missed three playoff games. ... Flu (March 17, 1996); missed one game. ... Bruised ankle (April 9, 1997); missed one game. ... Sprained knee (January 28, 1998); missed three games. ... Strained groin (April 11, 1998); missed three games. ... Cut forehead, nose; fractured nose (January 21, 1999); missed one game. ... Sprained knee (March 29, 2000); missed regular season's final four games. ... Sprained knee (September 28, 2000); missed first two games of season. ... Knee surgery (October 13, 2000); missed 23 games. ... Bruised ankle (December 26, 2001); missed three games. ... Right knee surgery (January 27, 2002); missed six games. ... Knee (February 26, 2002); missed 19 games. ... Offseason knee surgery; missed first 66 games of 2002-03 season. ... Groin (December 6, 2003); missed six games. ... Eye (May 1, 2004); missed remainder of playoffs. ... Strained groin (September 2005); missed first four games of season. ... Groin (October 15, 2005); missed four games. ... Tore groin muscle (December 11, 2005); missed nine games. ... Groin (April 13, 2006); missed three games. ... Back (April 27, 2006); missed two playoff games. ... Announced retirement (July 3, 2006).

STATISTICAL PLATEAUS: Three-goal games: 1983-84 (1), 1984-85 (1), 1987-88 (2), 1988-89 (2), 1989-90 (2), 1990-91 (3), 1991-92 (3), 1992-93 (3). Total: 17. ... Four-goal games: 1989-90 (1). ... Total hat tricks: 18.

		REGULAR SEASON								PLAYOFFS				
Season Team	**League**	**GP**	**G**	**A**	**Pts.**	**PIM**	**+/-**	**PP**	**SH**	**GP**	**G**	**A**	**Pts.**	**PIM**
81-82—Peterborough	OHL	58	21	43	64	65	...	...	...	6	0	1	1	16
82-83—Peterborough	OHL	56	42	49	91	33	...	...	...	4	1	4	5	0
83-84—Detroit	NHL	80	39	48	87	33	-17	13	0	4	3	3	6	0
84-85—Detroit	NHL	80	30	59	89	58	-17	9	0	3	2	1	3	2
85-86—Detroit	NHL	51	14	28	42	16	-24	3	0	—	—	—	—	—
86-87—Detroit	NHL	80	31	59	90	43	-1	9	1	16	5	13	18	8
87-88—Detroit	NHL	64	50	52	102	44	30	10	6	3	1	3	4	6
88-89—Detroit	NHL	80	65	90	155	61	17	17	3	6	5	5	10	2
89-90—Detroit	NHL	79	62	65	127	79	-6	16	†7	—	—	—	—	—
90-91—Detroit	NHL	80	51	57	108	34	-2	12	6	7	3	3	6	4
91-92—Detroit	NHL	79	45	58	103	64	26	9	*8	11	3	5	8	12
92-93—Detroit	NHL	84	58	79	137	44	33	13	†7	7	4	3	7	4
93-94—Detroit	NHL	58	24	58	82	36	11	7	3	3	1	3	4	0
94-95—Detroit	NHL	47	12	26	38	40	6	4	0	15	4	8	12	0
95-96—Detroit	NHL	80	36	59	95	64	29	16	2	18	8	12	20	4
96-97—Detroit	NHL	81	22	63	85	78	22	8	0	20	7	6	13	4
97-98—Detroit	NHL	75	24	45	69	46	3	6	2	22	6	*18	*24	22
—Can. Olympic team	Int'l	6	1	1	2	10	4	0	0	—	—	—	—	—
98-99—Detroit	NHL	80	29	45	74	42	8	13	2	10	9	4	13	0
99-00—Detroit	NHL	78	35	44	79	34	28	15	2	8	0	4	4	0
00-01—Detroit	NHL	54	18	34	52	18	4	5	0	1	0	0	0	0
01-02—Detroit	NHL	52	13	35	48	18	11	5	1	23	6	17	23	10
—Can. Olympic team	Int'l	6	2	4	6	2	...	...	...	—	—	—	—	—
02-03—Detroit	NHL	16	2	6	8	8	6	1	0	4	0	1	1	2
03-04—Detroit	NHL	75	18	33	51	46	10	7	0	11	3	2	5	0
05-06—Detroit	NHL	61	14	20	34	18	8	4	0	4	0	4	4	4
NHL Totals (22 years)		1514	692	1063	1755	924	185	202	50	196	70	115	185	84

ZANON, GREG D

PERSONAL: Born June 5, 1980, in Burnaby, B.C. ... 5-11/200. ... Shoots left.

COLLEGE: Nebraska-Omaha.

TRANSACTIONS/CAREER NOTES: Selected by Ottawa Senators in fifth round (fifth Senators pick, 156th overall) of entry draft (June 25, 2000). ... Signed as free agent by Nashville Predators (July 9, 2004).

		REGULAR SEASON								PLAYOFFS				
Season Team	**League**	**GP**	**G**	**A**	**Pts.**	**PIM**	**+/-**	**PP**	**SH**	**GP**	**G**	**A**	**Pts.**	**PIM**
95-96—Burnaby	BCJHL	49	16	27	43	142	...	...	...	—	—	—	—	—
96-97—Victoria	BCJHL	53	4	13	17	124	...	...	...	—	—	—	—	—
97-98—Victoria	BCJHL	59	11	21	32	108	...	...	...	7	0	2	2	10
98-99—South Surrey	BCHL	59	17	54	71	154	...	...	...	—	—	—	—	—
99-00—U. of Neb.-Omaha	CCHA	42	3	26	29	56	...	...	...	—	—	—	—	—
00-01—U. of Neb.-Omaha	CCHA	39	12	16	28	64	...	...	...	—	—	—	—	—
01-02—U. of Neb.-Omaha	CCHA	41	9	16	25	54	...	...	...	—	—	—	—	—
02-03—U. of Neb.-Omaha	CCHA	32	6	19	25	44	...	...	...	—	—	—	—	—
03-04—Milwaukee	AHL	62	4	12	16	59	...	...	...	22	2	6	8	31
04-05—Milwaukee	AHL	80	2	17	19	59	...	...	...	7	0	1	1	10
05-06—Milwaukee	AHL	71	8	27	35	55	17	3	0	15	1	7	8	18
—Nashville	NHL	4	0	2	2	6	0	0	0	—	—	—	—	—
NHL Totals (1 year)		4	0	2	2	6	0	0	0					

Z

ZEDNIK, RICHARD RW/LW

PERSONAL: Born January 6, 1976, in Bystrica, Czech. ... 6-1/196. ... Shoots left. ... Name pronounced ZEHD-nihk.

TRANSACTIONS/CAREER NOTES: Selected by Washington Capitals in 10th round (10th Capitals pick, 249th overall) of entry draft (June 29, 1994). ... Flu (November 6, 1996); missed two games. ... Flu (December 12, 1997); missed one game. ... Concussion (March 18, 1998); missed six games. ... Strained abdominal muscle (April 2, 1998); missed final eight games of regular season and four playoff games. ... Bruised shoulder (October 21, 1998); missed 10 games. ... Suspended four games and fined $1,000 for high-sticking (November 20, 1998). ... Strained groin (December 19, 1998); missed 19 games. ... Concussion (February 23, 2000); missed 13 games. ... Suspended four games for cross-checking (October 19, 2000). ... Sprained foot (January 12, 2001); missed two games. ... Traded by Capitals with C Jan Bulis and first-round pick (C Alexander Perezhogin) in 2001 draft to Montreal Canadiens for C Trevor Linden, RW Dainius Zubrus and second-round pick (traded to Tampa Bay; Lightning selected D Andreas Holmqvist) in 2001 draft (March 13, 2001). ... Injured groin (October 14, 2002); missed one game. ... Injured groin (November 15, 2002); missed one game. ... Personal leave (December 6, 2003); missed one game. ... Strained groin (October 6, 2005); missed eight games. ... Flu (December 20, 2005); missed one game. ... Injured thumb (January 16, 2006); missed one game. ... Flu (February 9, 2006); missed one game. ... Traded by Canadiens to Capitals for a third-round pick in 2007 draft (July 12, 2006).

STATISTICAL PLATEAUS: Three-goal games: 2000-01 (1).

		REGULAR SEASON								PLAYOFFS				
Season Team	**League**	**GP**	**G**	**A**	**Pts.**	**PIM**	**+/-**	**PP**	**SH**	**GP**	**G**	**A**	**Pts.**	**PIM**
93-94—Banska Bystrica	Slovakia	25	3	6	9	...	...	...	...	—	—	—	—	—
94-95—Portland	WHL	65	35	51	86	89	3	15	0	9	5	5	10	20
95-96—Portland	WHL	61	44	37	81	154	...	...	...	7	8	4	12	23
—Portland	AHL	1	1	1	2	0	...	...	...	21	4	5	9	26
—Washington	NHL	1	0	0	0	0	0	0	0	—	—	—	—	—
96-97—Washington	NHL	11	2	1	3	4	-5	1	0	—	—	—	—	—
—Portland	AHL	56	15	20	35	70	5	0	0	5	1	0	1	6
97-98—Washington	NHL	65	17	9	26	28	-2	2	0	17	7	3	10	16
98-99—Washington	NHL	49	9	8	17	50	-6	1	0	—	—	—	—	—
99-00—Washington	NHL	69	19	16	35	54	6	1	0	5	0	0	0	5
00-01—Washington	NHL	62	16	19	35	61	-2	4	0	—	—	—	—	—
—Montreal	NHL	12	3	6	9	10	-2	1	0	—	—	—	—	—
01-02—Montreal	NHL	82	22	22	44	59	-3	4	0	4	4	4	8	6
02-03—Montreal	NHL	80	31	19	50	79	4	9	0	—	—	—	—	—
03-04—Montreal	NHL	81	26	24	50	63	5	7	0	11	3	3	6	2
04-05—Zvolen	Slovakia	37	15	20	35	56	30	...	...	17	9	10	19	12
05-06—Montreal	NHL	67	16	14	30	48	-2	6	0	6	2	0	2	4
—Slovakian Oly. team	Int'l	6	1	0	1	12	-3	0	0	—	—	—	—	—
NHL Totals (10 years)		579	161	138	299	456	-7	36	0	43	16	10	2633@hd2	

ZETTERBERG, HENRIK LW

PERSONAL: Born October 9, 1980, in Njurunda, Sweden. ... 6-0/190. ... Shoots left.

TRANSACTIONS/CAREER NOTES: Selected by Detroit Red Wings in seventh round (fourth Red Wings pick, 210th overall) of entry draft (June 27, 1999). ... Groin (October 25, 2002); missed three games. ... Fractured leg (November 4, 2003); missed 17 games. ... Hip (January 18, 2006); missed two games. ... Upper body (April 7, 2006); missed one game.

		REGULAR SEASON								PLAYOFFS				
Season Team	**League**	**GP**	**G**	**A**	**Pts.**	**PIM**	**+/-**	**PP**	**SH**	**GP**	**G**	**A**	**Pts.**	**PIM**
97-98—Timra	Sweden Jr.	18	9	5	14	4	...	...	...	—	—	—	—	—
—Timra	Sweden Dv. 2	16	1	2	3	4	...	...	...	4	0	1	1	0
98-99—Timra	Sweden Dv. 2	37	15	13	28	2	...	...	...	4	2	1	3	2
99-00—Timra	Sweden Dv. 2	11	4	6	10	0	...	...	...	10	10	4	14	4
00-01—Timra	Sweden	47	15	31	46	24	...	...	...	—	—	—	—	—
01-02—Timra	Sweden	48	10	32	42	20	...	...	...	—	—	—	—	—
—Swedish Oly. team	Int'l	4	0	1	1	0	...	...	...	—	—	—	—	—
02-03—Detroit	NHL	79	22	22	44	8	6	5	1	4	1	0	1	0
03-04—Detroit	NHL	61	15	28	43	14	15	7	1	12	2	2	4	4
04-05—Timra	Sweden	50	19	31	50	24	15	5	1	7	6	2	8	2
05-06—Detroit	NHL	77	39	46	85	30	29	17	1	6	6	0	6	2
—Swedish Oly. team	Int'l	8	3	3	6	0	3	1	0	—	—	—	—	—
NHL Totals (3 years)		217	76	96	172	52	50	29	3	22	9	2	11	6

ZHAMNOV, ALEXEI C

PERSONAL: Born October 1, 1970, in Moscow, U.S.S.R. ... 6-1/201. ... Shoots left. ... Name pronounced ZHAM-nahf.

TRANSACTIONS/CAREER NOTES: Selected by Winnipeg Jets in fourth round (fifth Jets pick, 77th overall) of NHL draft (June 16, 1990). ... Strained hip flexor (November 2, 1992); missed two games. ... Back spasms (January 27, 1993); missed one game. ... Back spasms (February 3, 1993); missed one game. ... Back spasms (February 12, 1993); missed 12 games. ... Bruised leg (October 26, 1993); missed three games. ... Sprained back (December 27, 1993); missed eight games. ... Back spasms (March 19, 1994); missed remainder of season. ... Fractured leg (October 12, 1995); missed eight games. ... Flu (January 5, 1996); missed one game. ... Bruised back (March 7, 1996); missed four games. ... Injured back (March 16, 1996); missed remainder of season. ... Jets franchise moved to Phoenix and renamed Coyotes for 1996-97 season; NHL approved move on January 18, 1996. ... Traded by Coyotes with RW Craig Mills and first-round pick (RW Ty Jones) in 1997 draft to Chicago Blackhawks for C Jeremy Roenick (August 16, 1996). ... Fractured toe (November 2, 1997); missed four games. ... Concussion (November 29, 1997); missed one game. ... Concussion (March 3, 1998); missed four games. ... Bruised back (April 4, 1998); missed one game. ... Fractured finger (April 15, 1998); missed two games. ...

Bruised ankle (November 10, 1998); missed one game. ... Flu (December 26, 1998); missed one game. ... Injured back (February 6, 1999); missed four games. ... Strained groin (November 7, 1999); missed three games. ... Strained hamstring (January 15, 2000); missed eight games. ... Fractured larynx (January 21, 2001); missed 18 games. ... Hip pointer (March 3, 2002); missed four games. ... Injured hand (January 17, 2003); missed two games. ... Injured hand (March 7, 2003); missed six games ... Back surgery (October 14, 2003); missed 35 games. ... Traded by Blackhawks with fourth-round pick (D Michael R.J. Anderson) in 2004 draft to Philadelphia Flyers for D Jim Vandermeer, C Colin Fraser and second-round pick (LW Bryan Bickell) in 2004 draft (February 19, 2004). ... Signed as free agent by Boston Bruins (August 4, 2005). ... Bruised shoulder (October 5, 2005); missed first 17 games of season. ... Broken ankle (January 7, 2006); missed final 41 games of regular season.

STATISTICAL PLATEAUS: Three-goal games: 1993-94 (2), 1994-95 (1), 1995-96 (1), 1996-97 (1). Total: 5. ... Five-goal games: 1994-95 (1). ... Total hat tricks: 6.

		REGULAR SEASON								PLAYOFFS				
Season Team	League	GP	G	A	Pts.	PIM	+/-	PP	SH	GP	G	A	Pts.	PIM
88-89—Dynamo Moscow	USSR	4	0	0	0	0	...	...	...	—	—	—	—	—
89-90—Dynamo Moscow	USSR	43	11	6	17	23	...	...	...	—	—	—	—	—
90-91—Dynamo Moscow	USSR	46	16	12	28	24	...	...	...	—	—	—	—	—
91-92—Dynamo Moscow	CIS	39	15	21	36	28	...	...	...	—	—	—	—	—
—Unif. Olympic team	Int'l	8	0	3	3	8	...	...	...	—	—	—	—	—
92-93—Winnipeg	NHL	68	25	47	72	58	7	6	1	6	0	2	2	2
93-94—Winnipeg	NHL	61	26	45	71	62	-20	7	0	—	—	—	—	—
94-95—Winnipeg	NHL	48	30	35	65	20	5	9	0	—	—	—	—	—
95-96—Winnipeg	NHL	58	22	37	59	65	-4	5	0	6	2	1	3	8
96-97—Chicago	NHL	74	20	42	62	56	18	6	1	—	—	—	—	—
97-98—Chicago	NHL	70	21	28	49	61	16	6	2	—	—	—	—	—
—Russian Oly. team	Int'l	6	2	1	3	2	7	1	0	—	—	—	—	—
98-99—Chicago	NHL	76	20	41	61	50	-10	8	1	—	—	—	—	—
99-00—Chicago	NHL	71	23	37	60	61	7	5	0	—	—	—	—	—
00-01—Chicago	NHL	63	13	36	49	40	-12	3	1	—	—	—	—	—
01-02—Chicago	NHL	77	22	45	67	67	8	6	0	5	0	0	0	0
—Russian Oly. team	Int'l	6	1	0	1	4	...	...	...	—	—	—	—	—
02-03—Chicago	NHL	74	15	43	58	70	0	2	3	—	—	—	—	—
03-04—Chicago	NHL	23	6	12	18	14	-8	1	0	—	—	—	—	—
—Philadelphia	NHL	20	5	13	18	14	7	0	0	18	4	10	14	8
04-05—Vityaz Podolsk	Russian	24	5	22	27	20	11	...	...	16	7	7	14	10
05-06—Boston	NHL	24	1	9	10	30	-4	0	0	—	—	—	—	—
NHL Totals (13 years)		807	249	470	719	668	10	64	9	35	6	13	19	18

ZHERDEV, NIKOLAI RW

PERSONAL: Born November 5, 1984, in Kiev, U.S.S.R. ... 6-1/197. ... Shoots right. ... Name pronounced ZHAIR-dev.

TRANSACTIONS/CAREER NOTES: Selected by Columbus Blue Jackets in first round (first Blue Jackets pick, fourth overall) in entry draft (June 23, 2003). ... Left team for personal reasons (February 25, 2004); missed two games. ... Knee sprain (April 2, 2006); missed final eight games of regular season.

		REGULAR SEASON								PLAYOFFS				
Season Team	League	GP	G	A	Pts.	PIM	+/-	PP	SH	GP	G	A	Pts.	PIM
00-01—Elektrostal	Russian Jr.	18	5	8	13	12	...	...	...	—	—	—	—	—
01-02—Elektrostal	Russian Jr.	53	13	15	28	60	...	...	...	—	—	—	—	—
02-03—HC CSKA Moscow	Russian	44	12	12	24	34	...	...	...	—	—	—	—	—
03-04—CSKA Moscow	Russian	20	2	2	4	14	...	...	...	—	—	—	—	—
—Columbus	NHL	57	13	21	34	54	-11	5	0	—	—	—	—	—
04-05—CSKA Moscow	Russian	51	19	21	40	62	17	...	...	—	—	—	—	—
05-06—Syracuse	AHL	2	1	0	1	0	1	0	0	—	—	—	—	—
—Columbus	NHL	73	27	27	54	50	-13	10	0	—	—	—	—	—
NHL Totals (2 years)		130	40	48	88	104	-24	15	0					

ZHITNIK, ALEXEI D

PERSONAL: Born October 10, 1972, in Kiev, U.S.S.R. ... 5-11/214. ... Shoots left. ... Name pronounced ZHIHT-nihk.

TRANSACTIONS/CAREER NOTES: Selected by Los Angeles Kings in fourth round (third Kings pick, 81st overall) of NHL draft (June 22, 1991). ... Flu (January 12, 1993); missed five games. ... Suspended one game for cross-checking incident (November 30, 1993). ... Traded by Kings with D Charlie Huddy, G Robb Stauber and fifth-round pick (D Marian Menhart) in 1995 draft to Buffalo Sabres for G Grant Fuhr, D Philippe Boucher and D Denis Tsygurov (February 14, 1995). ... Fractured thumb (February 19, 1995); missed three games. ... Reinjured thumb (March 8, 1995); missed one game. ... Ruptured calf muscle (March 19, 1995); missed 11 games. ... Suspended two games and fined $1,000 for high-sticking incident (November 1, 1996). ... Missed first four games of 1997-98 season due to contract dispute. ... Bruised chest (November 29, 1998); missed one game. ... Eye injury (October 17, 1999); missed one game. ... Fractured finger (March 8, 2000); missed six games. ... Suspended one playoff game for high-sticking incident (April 19, 2000). ... Suspended four games for high-sticking incident (October 18, 2000). ... Suspended one game for kneeing incident (November 8, 2002). ... Fractured foot (November 22, 2002); missed 10 games. ... Bruised shoulder (March 10, 2004); missed last 14 games of season. ... Signed as free agent by New York Islanders (August 2, 2005). ... Ankle sprain (January 31, 2006); missed five games. ... Broken ankle (March 15, 2006); missed final 18 games of regular season.

		REGULAR SEASON								PLAYOFFS				
Season Team	League	GP	G	A	Pts.	PIM	+/-	PP	SH	GP	G	A	Pts.	PIM
89-90—Sokol Kiev	USSR	31	3	4	7	16	...	...	...	—	—	—	—	—
90-91—Sokol Kiev	USSR	40	1	4	5	46	...	...	...	—	—	—	—	—
91-92—CSKA Moscow	CIS	36	2	7	9	48	...	...	...	—	—	—	—	—
—Unif. Olympic team	Int'l	8	1	0	1	0	...	...	...	—	—	—	—	—
92-93—Los Angeles	NHL	78	12	36	48	80	-3	5	0	24	3	9	12	26
93-94—Los Angeles	NHL	81	12	40	52	101	-11	11	0	—	—	—	—	—
94-95—Los Angeles	NHL	11	2	5	7	27	-3	2	0	—	—	—	—	—
—Buffalo	NHL	21	2	5	7	34	-3	1	0	5	0	1	1	14

Season Team	League	GP	G	A	Pts.	PIM	+/-	PP	SH	GP	G	A	Pts.	PIM
		REGULAR SEASON								PLAYOFFS				
95-96—Buffalo	NHL	80	6	30	36	58	-25	5	0	—	—	—	—	—
96-97—Buffalo	NHL	80	7	28	35	95	10	3	1	12	1	0	1	16
97-98—Buffalo	NHL	78	15	30	45	102	19	2	3	15	0	3	3	36
—Russian Oly. team	Int'l	6	0	2	2	2	1	0	0	—	—	—	—	—
98-99—Buffalo	NHL	81	7	26	33	96	-6	3	1	21	4	11	15	*52
99-00—Buffalo	NHL	74	2	11	13	95	-6	1	0	4	0	0	0	8
00-01—Buffalo	NHL	78	8	29	37	75	-3	5	0	13	1	6	7	12
01-02—Buffalo	NHL	82	1	33	34	80	-1	1	0	—	—	—	—	—
02-03—Buffalo	NHL	70	3	18	21	85	-5	0	0	—	—	—	—	—
03-04—Buffalo	NHL	68	4	24	28	102	-13	2	0	—	—	—	—	—
04-05—Ak Bars Kazan	Russian	23	1	8	9	30	9	...	...	4	0	0	0	2
05-06—New York Islanders	NHL	59	5	24	29	88	4	3	0	—	—	—	—	—
NHL Totals (13 years)		941	86	339	425	1118	-46	44	5	94	9	30	39	164

ZIDLICKY, MAREK D

PERSONAL: Born February 3, 1977, in Most, Czech. ... 5-11/190. ... Shoots right. ... Name pronounced MAIR-ehk zhihd-LIHTS-kee.

TRANSACTIONS/CAREER NOTES: Selected by New York Rangers in sixth round (sixth Rangers pick, 176th overall) of entry draft (June 25, 2001). ... Traded by Rangers with LW Rem Murray and D Tomas Kloucek to Nashville Predators for G Mike Dunham (December 12, 2002). ... Hand (January 6, 2006); missed one game. ... Hand (January 28, 2006); missed three games. ... Shoulder (March 28, 2006); missed regular season's final 11 games and first three playoff games.

Season Team	League	GP	G	A	Pts.	PIM	+/-	PP	SH	GP	G	A	Pts.	PIM
		REGULAR SEASON								PLAYOFFS				
94-95—HC Kladno	Czech.	30	2	2	4	38	...	...	...	11	1	1	2	10
95-96—HC Poldi Kladno	Czech.	37	4	5	9	74	...	...	...	7	1	1	2	8
96-97—HC Poldi Kladno	Czech.	49	5	16	21	60	...	...	...	2	0	0	0	0
97-98—Kladno	Czech.	51	2	13	15	121	...	...	...	—	—	—	—	—
98-99—Kladno	Czech	50	10	12	22	94	...	...	...	—	—	—	—	—
99-00—HIFK Helsinki	Finland	47	11	10	21	18	...	...	...	9	3	1	4	6
00-01—HIFK Helsinki	Finland	51	12	25	37	146	...	...	...	5	0	1	1	6
01-02—HIFK Helsinki	Finland	56	11	29	40	107	...	...	...	—	—	—	—	—
02-03—HIFK Helsinki	Finland	54	10	37	47	79	...	...	...	4	0	0	0	4
03-04—Nashville	NHL	82	14	39	53	82	-16	9	0	1	0	0	0	0
04-05—HIFK Helsinki	Finland	49	11	20	31	91	2	...	...	5	0	3	3	14
05-06—Nashville	NHL	67	12	37	49	82	8	10	0	2	0	1	1	2
—Czech Oly. team	Int'l	7	4	1	5	16	0	3	0	—	—	—	—	—
NHL Totals (2 years)		149	26	76	102	164	-8	19	0	3	0	1	1	2

ZIGOMANIS, MIKE C/RW

PERSONAL: Born January 17, 1981, in North York, Ont. ... 6-1/200. ... Shoots right. ... Name pronounced zih-goh-MAH-nuhz.

TRANSACTIONS/CAREER NOTES: Selected by Buffalo Sabres in second round (fourth Sabres pick, 64th overall) of NHL draft (June 22, 1999). ... Returned to draft pool by Sabres; selected by Carolina Hurricanes in second round (second Hurricanes pick, 46th overall) of draft (June 23, 2001). ... Traded by Hurricanes with RW Jesse Boulerice, LW Magnus Kahnberg, first-round (traded to New Jersey; Devils selected D Matthew Corrente) and fourth-round (G Reto Berra) picks in 2006 and fourth-round pick in 2007 to St. Louis Blues for C Doug Weight and LW Erkki Rajamaki (January 30, 2006). ...Signed as free agent by Phoenix Coyotes (July 21, 2006).

Season Team	League	GP	G	A	Pts.	PIM	+/-	PP	SH	GP	G	A	Pts.	PIM
		REGULAR SEASON								PLAYOFFS				
97-98—Kingston	OHL	62	23	51	74	30	...	...	...	12	1	6	7	2
98-99—Kingston	OHL	67	29	56	85	36	-11	...	...	5	1	7	8	2
99-00—Kingston	OHL	59	40	54	94	49	21	13	3	5	0	4	4	0
00-01—Kingston	OHL	52	40	37	77	44	21	6	3	—	—	—	—	—
01-02—Lowell	AHL	79	18	30	48	24	-1	4	0	5	1	1	2	2
02-03—Lowell	AHL	38	13	18	31	19	-2	2	0	—	—	—	—	—
—Carolina	NHL	19	2	1	3	0	-4	1	1	—	—	—	—	—
03-04—Carolina	NHL	17	0	3	3	2	-1	0	0	—	—	—	—	—
—Lowell	AHL	61	17	35	52	56	1	5	2	—	—	—	—	—
04-05—Lowell	AHL	76	29	31	60	71	7	7	2	11	4	7	11	8
05-06—Lowell	AHL	11	6	7	13	19	-2	3	0	—	—	—	—	—
—Carolina	NHL	21	1	0	1	4	1	0	0	—	—	—	—	—
—Peoria	AHL	28	10	18	28	16	2	4	2	4	2	4	6	6
—St. Louis	NHL	2	0	0	0	0	0	0	0	—	—	—	—	—
NHL Totals (3 years)		59	3	4	7	6	-4	1	1					

ZUBOV, SERGEI D

PERSONAL: Born July 22, 1970, in Moscow, U.S.S.R. ... 6-1/200. ... Shoots right. ... Name pronounced SAIR-gay ZOO-bahf.

TRANSACTIONS/CAREER NOTES: Selected by New York Rangers in fifth round (sixth Rangers pick, 85th overall) of entry draft (June 16, 1990). ... Concussion (February 26, 1993); missed one game. ... Flu (February 4, 1995); missed one game. ... Wrist surgery (February 27, 1995); missed nine games. ... Traded by Rangers with C Petr Nedved to Pittsburgh Penguins for LW Luc Robitaille and D Ulf Samuelsson (August 31, 1995). ... Fractured finger (October 9, 1995); missed nine games. ... Finger (November 11, 1995); missed seven games. ... Bruised shoulder (March 31, 1996); missed one game. ... Traded by Penguins to Dallas Stars for D Kevin Hatcher (June 22, 1996). ... Flu (November 20, 1996); missed one game. ... Back spasms (January 24, 1997); missed two games. ... Neck (March 4, 1998); missed nine games. ... Wrist (April 14, 1999); missed one game. ... Knee (March 29, 2000); missed final five games of season. ... Bruised shoulder (January 6, 2001); missed two games. ... Sprained shoulder (December 2, 2001); missed two games. ... Charley horse (March 22, 2004); missed five games. ... Back spasms (October 16, 2005); missed two games. ... Lower-body injury (March 29, 2006); missed two games.

Season Team	League	REGULAR SEASON GP	G	A	Pts.	PIM	+/-	PP	SH	PLAYOFFS GP	G	A	Pts.	PIM
88-89—CSKA Moscow..........	USSR	29	1	4	5	10	...	...	...	—	—	—	—	—
89-90—CSKA Moscow..........	USSR	48	6	2	8	16	...	...	...	—	—	—	—	—
90-91—CSKA Moscow..........	USSR	41	6	5	11	12	...	...	...	—	—	—	—	—
91-92—CSKA Moscow..........	CIS	36	4	7	11	6	...	...	...	—	—	—	—	—
—Unif. Olympic team...	Int'l	8	0	1	1	0	...	...	...	—	—	—	—	—
92-93—CSKA Moscow..........	CIS	1	0	1	1	0	...	...	...	—	—	—	—	—
—Binghamton..............	AHL	30	7	29	36	14	31	0	1	11	5	5	10	2
—New York Rangers....	NHL	49	8	23	31	4	-1	3	0	—	—	—	—	—
93-94—New York Rangers....	NHL	78	12	77	89	39	20	9	0	22	5	14	19	0
—Binghamton..............	AHL	2	1	2	3	0	-2	0	0	—	—	—	—	—
94-95—New York Rangers....	NHL	38	10	26	36	18	-2	6	0	10	3	8	11	2
95-96—Pittsburgh................	NHL	64	11	55	66	22	28	3	2	18	1	14	15	26
96-97—Dallas.......................	NHL	78	13	30	43	24	19	1	0	7	0	3	3	2
97-98—Dallas.......................	NHL	73	10	47	57	16	16	5	1	17	4	5	9	2
98-99—Dallas.......................	NHL	81	10	41	51	20	9	5	0	23	1	12	13	4
99-00—Dallas.......................	NHL	77	9	33	42	18	-2	3	1	18	2	7	9	6
00-01—Dallas.......................	NHL	79	10	41	51	24	22	6	0	10	1	5	6	4
01-02—Dallas.......................	NHL	80	12	32	44	22	-4	8	0	—	—	—	—	—
02-03—Dallas.......................	NHL	82	11	44	55	26	21	8	0	12	4	10	14	4
03-04—Dallas.......................	NHL	77	7	35	42	20	0	4	1	5	1	1	2	0
05-06—Dallas.......................	NHL	78	13	58	71	46	20	9	0	5	1	5	6	6
NHL Totals (13 years).......		934	136	542	678	299	146	70	5	147	23	84	107	56

ZUBRUS, DAINIUS C/LW

PERSONAL: Born June 16, 1978, in Elektrenai, U.S.S.R. ... 6-4/231. ... Shoots left. ... Name pronounced DIGH-nuhz ZOO-bruhz.

TRANSACTIONS/CAREER NOTES: Selected by Philadelphia Flyers in first round (first Flyers pick, 15th overall) of NHL draft (June 22, 1996). ... Bruised right hand (October 8, 1997); missed two games. ... Reinjured right hand (October 15, 1997); missed five games. ... Suspended two games and fined $1,000 in slashing incident (April 2, 1998). ... Strained left hamstring (December 15, 1997); missed one game. ... Traded by Flyers with second-round pick (D Matt Carkner) in 1999 draft to Montreal Canadiens for RW Mark Recchi (March 10, 1999). ... Strained hip flexor (October 20, 1999); missed one game. ... Injured back (October 27, 1999); missed one game. ... Back spasms (January 4, 2000); missed one game. ... Had concussion (February 27, 2000); missed six games. ... Injured rib cage (September 27, 2000); missed first two games of season. ... Had concussion (December 21, 2000); missed 19 games. ... Traded by Canadiens with C Trevor Linden and second-round pick (traded to Tampa Bay; Lightning selected D Andreas Holmqvist) in 2001 draft to Washington Capitals for C Jan Bulis, RW Richard Zednik and first-round pick (C Alexander Perezhogin) in 2001 draft (March 13, 2001). ... Strained groin (December 13, 2001); missed five games. ... Injured foot (January 22, 2002); missed one game. ... Injured right arm (February 26, 2002); missed five games. ... Bruised hand (November 27, 2002); missed 14 games. ... Had concussion (January 17, 2003); missed three games. ... Injured right foot (January 1, 2004); missed 10 games. ... Injured upper body (February 13, 2004); missed two games. ... Injured upper body (February 19, 2004); missed four games. ... Injured chest (March 6, 2004); missed two games. ... Injured chest (March 13, 2004); missed final 11 games of season. ... Groin injury (November 3, 2005); missed three games. ... Groin injury (November 15, 2005); missed seven games. ... Right arm injury (January 31, 2006); missed one game.

STATISTICAL PLATEAUS: Three-goal games: 2000-01 (1).

Season Team	League	REGULAR SEASON GP	G	A	Pts.	PIM	+/-	PP	SH	PLAYOFFS GP	G	A	Pts.	PIM
95-96—Pembroke.................	CJHL	28	19	13	32	73	...	...	...	—	—	—	—	—
—Caledon....................	Jr. A	7	3	7	10	2	...	...	...	17	11	12	23	4
96-97—Philadelphia..............	NHL	68	8	13	21	22	3	1	0	19	5	4	9	12
97-98—Philadelphia..............	NHL	69	8	25	33	42	29	1	0	5	0	1	1	2
98-99—Philadelphia..............	NHL	63	3	5	8	25	-5	0	1	—	—	—	—	—
—Montreal..................	NHL	17	3	5	8	4	-3	0	0	—	—	—	—	—
99-00—Montreal..................	NHL	73	14	28	42	54	-1	3	0	—	—	—	—	—
00-01—Montreal..................	NHL	49	12	12	24	30	-7	3	0	—	—	—	—	—
—Washington..............	NHL	12	1	1	2	7	-4	1	0	6	0	0	0	2
01-02—Washington..............	NHL	71	17	26	43	38	5	4	0	—	—	—	—	—
02-03—Washington..............	NHL	63	13	22	35	43	15	2	0	6	2	2	4	4
03-04—Washington..............	NHL	54	12	15	27	38	-16	6	1	—	—	—	—	—
04-05—Lada Togliatti............	Russian	42	8	11	19	85	9	...	...	10	3	1	4	22
05-06—Washington..............	NHL	71	23	34	57	84	3	13	0	—	—	—	—	—
NHL Totals (9 years).........		610	114	186	300	387	19	34	2	36	7	7	14	20

ZYUZIN, ANDREI D

PERSONAL: Born January 21, 1978, in Ufa, U.S.S.R. ... 6-1/215. ... Shoots left. ... Name pronounced ZYOO-zihn.

TRANSACTIONS/CAREER NOTES: Selected by San Jose Sharks in first round (first Sharks pick, second overall) of entry draft (June 22, 1996). ... Suspended for remainder of season for leaving team without permission (April 1, 1999) ... Suspended two playoff games for slashing (April 19, 1999). ... Traded by Sharks with D Bill Houlder, LW Shawn Burr and C Steve Guolla to Tampa Bay Lightning for LW Niklas Sundstrom and third-round pick (traded to Chicago; Blackhawks selected LW Igor Radulov) in 2000 (August 4, 1999). ... Shoulder (October 28, 1999); missed five games. ... Shoulder (January 11, 2000); missed remainder of season. ... Concussion (November 20, 2000); missed five games. ... Concussion (December 1, 2000); missed five games. ... Shoulder (January 30, 2001); missed two games. ... Ankle (March 15, 2001); missed one game. ... Concussion (March 21, 2001); missed three games. ... Traded by Lightning to New Jersey Devils for D Josef Boumedienne, D Sascha Goc and LW Anton But (November 9, 2001). ... Shoulder (December 5, 2001); missed four games. ... Bruised foot (February 27, 2002); missed three games. ... Claimed off waivers by Minnesota Wild (November 3, 2002). ... Flu (December 12, 2002); missed one game. ... Back spasms (October 28, 2003); missed two games. ... Ankle (December 18, 2003); missed one game. ... Groin (January 16, 2004); missed two games. ... Groin

Z

(January 21, 2004); missed 10 games. ... Facial cuts (October 5, 2005); missed two games. ... Right knee (November 5, 2005); missed nine games. ... Knee (December 13, 2005); missed three games. ... Stomach virus (December 26, 2005); missed one game. ... Face (January 26, 2006); missed two games. ... Groin (April 9, 2006); missed season's final four games. ... Signed as a free agent by Calgary Flames (July 1, 2006).

		REGULAR SEASON								PLAYOFFS				
Season Team	**League**	**GP**	**G**	**A**	**Pts.**	**PIM**	**+/-**	**PP**	**SH**	**GP**	**G**	**A**	**Pts.**	**PIM**
94-95—Salavat Yulayev Ufa ..	CIS	30	3	0	3	16	...	...	...	—	—	—	—	—
95-96—Salavat Yulayev Ufa ..	CIS	41	6	3	9	24	...	...	...	2	0	0	0	4
96-97—Salavet Yulayev Ufa ..	USSR	32	7	10	17	28	...	...	...	7	1	1	2	4
97-98—San Jose	NHL	56	6	7	13	66	8	2	0	6	1	0	1	14
—Kentucky	AHL	17	4	5	9	28	-2	2	0	—	—	—	—	—
98-99—San Jose	NHL	25	3	1	4	38	5	2	0	—	—	—	—	—
—Kentucky	AHL	23	2	12	14	42	9	1	0	—	—	—	—	—
99-00—Tampa Bay	NHL	34	2	9	11	33	-11	0	0	—	—	—	—	—
00-01—Tampa Bay	NHL	64	4	16	20	76	-8	2	1	—	—	—	—	—
—Detroit	IHL	2	0	1	1	0	...	...	...	—	—	—	—	—
01-02—Tampa Bay	NHL	9	0	2	2	6	-6	0	0	—	—	—	—	—
—New Jersey	NHL	38	1	2	3	25	1	1	0	—	—	—	—	—
—Albany	AHL	3	0	1	1	2	-5	0	0	—	—	—	—	—
02-03—New Jersey	NHL	1	0	1	1	2	-1	0	0	—	—	—	—	—
—Minnesota	NHL	66	4	12	16	34	-7	2	0	18	0	1	1	14
03-04—Minnesota	NHL	65	8	13	21	48	4	4	0	—	—	—	—	—
04-05—Salavat Yulayev Ufa ..	Russian	14	2	1	3	6	-2	...	...	—	—	—	—	—
—Severstal Cherepovets	Russian	10	2	1	3	8	-2	...	...	—	—	—	—	—
05-06—Minnesota	NHL	57	7	11	18	50	-12	4	0	—	—	—	—	—
NHL Totals (8 years)		415	35	74	109	378	-27	17	1	24	1	1	2	28

HEAD COACHES

BABCOCK, MIKE — RED WINGS

PERSONAL: Born April 29, 1963, in Manitouwadge, Ont.

HEAD COACHING RECORD

BACKGROUND: Coach, Red Deer (Alta.) College (1988-91). ... Coach, University of Lethbridge, Alta. (1993-94). ... Coach, Spokane of the WHL (1994-95 through 1999-2000). ... Coach, Cincinnati of the AHL (2000-01 through 2001-02). ... Coach, Anaheim Mighty Ducks (May 22, 2002, to June 30, 2005). ... Named coach, Detroit Red Wings (July 15, 2005).

		REGULAR SEASON						PLAYOFFS		
Season Team	League	W	L	T	OL	Pct.	Finish	W	L	Pct.
91-92—Moose Jaw	WHL	33	36	3	...	.479	6th/East Division	0	4	.000
92-93—Moose Jaw	WHL	27	42	3	...	.396	8th/East Division	—	—	—
94-95—Spokane	WHL	32	36	4	...	.472	5th/West Division	3	1	.750
95-96—Spokane	WHL	50	18	4	...	.722	1st/West Division	9	9	.500
96-97—Spokane	WHL	35	33	4	...	.514	3rd/West Division	4	5	.444
97-98—Spokane	WHL	45	23	4	...	.653	2nd/West Division	10	8	.556
98-99—Spokane	WHL	19	44	9	...	.326	7th/West Division	—	—	—
99-00—Spokane	WHL	47	21	4	...	.681	1st/West Division	10	5	.667
00-01—Cincinnati	AHL	41	26	9	4	.569	2nd/Southern Division	1	3	.250
01-02—Cincinnati	AHL	33	33	11	3	.481	3rd/Central Division	1	2	.333
02-03—Anaheim	NHL	40	27	9	6	.543	2nd/Pacific Division	15	6	.714
03-04—Anaheim	NHL	29	35	10	8	.415	4th/Pacific Division	—	—	—
05-06—Detroit	NHL	58	16	...	8	.707	1st/Central Division	2	4	.333
NHL Totals (3 years)		127	78	19	22	.555	**NHL Totals (2 years)**	17	10	.630

NOTES:

91-92—Lost to Prince Albert in East Division preliminary round.
94-95—Lost to Tri-City in West Division quarterfinals.
95-96—Defeated Portland in division quarterfinals; defeated Kamloops in division finals; lost to Brandon in WHL Finals.
96-97—Defeated Kelowna in division quarterfinals; lost to Prince George in division semifinals.
97-98—Defeated Kelowna in division quarterfinals; defeated Prince George in division semifinals; lost to Portland in division finals.
99-00—Defeated Tri-City in division quarterfinals; defeated Prince George in division finals; lost to Kootenay in WHL finals.
00-01—Lost to Norfolk in conference quarterfinals of Calder Cup playoffs.
01-02—Lost to Chicago in qualifying round of Calder Cup playoffs.
02-03—Defeated Detroit in Western Conference quarterfinals; defeated Dallas in Western Conference semifinals; defeated Minnesota in Western Conference finals; lost to New Jersey in Stanley Cup Finals.
05-06—Lost to Edmonton Oilers, 4-2, in Western Conference quarterfinals.

CARBONNEAU, GUY — CANADIENS

PERSONAL: Born March 18, 1960, in Sept-Iles, Que. ... 5-11/190. ... Shoots right. ... Played center ... Name pronounced GEE KAHR-buh-noh.
TRANSACTIONS/CAREER NOTES: Selected by Montreal Canadiens as underage junior in third round (fourth Canadiens pick, 44th overall) of NHL entry draft (August 9, 1979). ... Strained right knee ligaments (October 7, 1989); missed nine games. ... Fractured nose (October 28, 1989). ... Suffered concussion (October 8, 1990). ... Fractured rib (January 13, 1992); missed six games. ... Injured elbow (March 2, 1992); missed one game. ... Suffered right knee tendinitis (October 1, 1992); missed five games. ... Fractured finger (November 14, 1992); missed three games. ... Suffered knee tendinitis (February 4, 1993); missed 15 games. ... Suffered from the flu (February 11, 1994); missed one game. ... Traded by Canadiens to St. Louis Blues for C Jim Montgomery (August 19, 1994). ... Underwent knee surgery (March 31, 1995); missed six games. ... Traded by Blues to Dallas Stars for RW Paul Broten (October 2, 1995). ... Injured groin (October 17, 1995); missed five games. ... Strained groin (December 8, 1996); missed one game. ... Bruised forearm (March 31, 1997); missed two games. ... Sprained neck (October 14, 1997); missed one game. ... Strained back (October 25, 1997); missed three games. ... Strained groin (October 22, 1998); missed one game. ... Bruised ankle (February 17, 1999); missed one game. ... Injured knee (March 14, 1999); missed two games. ... Sprained ankle (March 31, 1999); missed one game. ... Strained neck (February 21, 2000); missed two games. ... Fractured wrist (March 5, 2000); missed seven games. ... Announced retirement (July 2, 2000).
STATISTICAL PLATEAUS: Three-goal games: 1982-83 (1), 1993-94 (1). Total: 2.

		REGULAR SEASON								PLAYOFFS				
Season Team	League	GP	G	A	Pts.	PIM	+/-	PP	SH	GP	G	A	Pts.	PIM
76-77—Chicoutimi	QMJHL	59	9	20	29	8	...	...	...	4	1	0	1	0
77-78—Chicoutimi	QMJHL	70	28	55	83	60	...	...	...	—	—	—	—	—
78-79—Chicoutimi	QMJHL	72	62	79	141	47	...	...	...	4	2	1	3	4
79-80—Chicoutimi	QMJHL	72	72	110	182	66	...	...	...	12	9	15	24	28
—Nova Scotia	AHL	...	...	...	...	...	...	...	...	2	1	1	2	2
80-81—Montreal	NHL	2	0	1	1	0	0	0	0	—	—	—	—	—
—Nova Scotia	AHL	78	35	53	88	87	...	...	...	6	1	3	4	9
81-82—Nova Scotia	AHL	77	27	67	94	124	...	...	...	9	2	7	9	8
82-83—Montreal	NHL	77	18	29	47	68	18	0	5	3	0	0	0	2
83-84—Montreal	NHL	78	24	30	54	75	5	3	7	15	4	3	7	12
84-85—Montreal	NHL	79	23	34	57	43	28	0	4	12	4	3	7	8
85-86—Montreal	NHL	80	20	36	56	57	18	1	2	20	7	5	12	35
86-87—Montreal	NHL	79	18	27	45	68	9	0	0	17	3	8	11	20
87-88—Montreal	NHL	80	17	21	38	61	14	0	3	11	0	4	4	2
88-89—Montreal	NHL	79	26	30	56	44	37	1	2	21	4	5	9	10
89-90—Montreal	NHL	68	19	36	55	37	21	1	1	11	2	3	5	6
90-91—Montreal	NHL	78	20	24	44	63	-1	4	1	13	1	5	6	10
91-92—Montreal	NHL	72	18	21	39	39	2	1	1	11	1	1	2	6
92-93—Montreal	NHL	61	4	13	17	20	-9	0	1	20	3	3	6	10
93-94—Montreal	NHL	79	14	24	38	48	16	0	0	7	1	3	4	4

Season Team	League	GP	G	A	Pts.	PIM	+/-	PP	SH	GP	G	A	Pts.	PIM
		REGULAR SEASON								PLAYOFFS				
94-95—St. Louis	NHL	42	5	11	16	16	11	1	0	7	1	2	3	6
95-96—Dallas	NHL	71	8	15	23	38	-2	0	2	—	—	—	—	—
96-97—Dallas	NHL	73	5	16	21	36	9	0	1	7	0	1	1	6
97-98—Dallas	NHL	77	7	17	24	40	3	0	1	16	3	1	4	6
98-99—Dallas	NHL	74	4	12	16	31	-3	0	0	17	2	4	6	6
99-00—Dallas	NHL	69	10	6	16	36	10	0	1	23	2	4	6	12
NHL Totals (19 years)		1318	260	403	663	820	186	12	32	231	38	55	93	161

HEAD COACHING RECORD

BACKGROUND: Assistant coach, Montreal Canadiens (November 2000 through 2001-02). ... Named coach of Montreal Canadiens (May 5, 2006).

CARLYLE, RANDY — DUCKS

PERSONAL: Born April 19, 1956, in Sudbury, Ont. ... 5-10/200. ... Shoots left. ... Played defense.
TRANSACTIONS/CAREER NOTES: Selected by Toronto Maple Leafs from Sudbury Wolves in second round (first Maple Leafs pick, 30th overall) of entry draft (June 1, 1976). ... Broken ankle; missed parts of 1978-79 season. ... Traded by Maple Leafs with C George Ferguson to Pittsburgh Penguins for D Dave Burrows (June 14, 1978). ... Injured back (October 1982). ... Injured knee (January 1983). ... Injured knee (March 1984). ... Traded by Penguins to Winnipeg Jets for first-round pick in 1984 draft (D Doug Bodger) and player to be named after the 1983-84 season (D Moe Mantha) (March 5, 1984). ... Injured thigh (November 12, 1985); missed eight games. ... Whiplash (November 1986); missed nine games. ... Strained neck muscles (January 18, 1989). ... Bruised left knee (November 5, 1989); missed nine games. ... Missed 10 games due to death of parents (December 1989). ... Torn ligaments in right knee (March 15, 1990). ... Strained groin and bruised thigh (November 11, 1990); missed five games. ... Strained triceps (February 20, 1991); missed seven games. ... Bruised ribs (October 29, 1991); missed three games. ... Strained abdomen (December 14, 1991); missed six games. ... Ankle contusion (January 4, 1992); missed two games. ... Quad strain (October 10, 1992); missed eight games. ... Quad strain (November 2, 1992); missed four games. ... Strained shoulder (December 5, 1992); missed two games. ... Strained groin (December 11, 1992); missed seven games. ... Quad strain (January 8, 1993); missed six games. ... Pulled groin (February 28, 1993); missed three games.

Season Team	League	GP	G	A	Pts.	PIM	+/-	PP	SH	GP	G	A	Pts.	PIM
		REGULAR SEASON								PLAYOFFS				
73-74—Sudbury	OHA Mj. Jr	12	0	8	8	21	...	...	...	—	—	—	—	—
74-75—Sudbury	OHA Mj. Jr	67	17	47	64	118	...	...	...	15	3	6	9	21
75-76—Sudbury	OHA Mj. Jr	60	15	64	79	126	...	...	...	17	6	13	19	50
76-77—Dallas	CHL	26	2	7	9	63	...	...	...	—	—	—	—	—
—Toronto	NHL	45	0	5	5	51	...	...	...	9	0	1	1	20
77-78—Dallas	CHL	21	3	14	17	31	...	...	...	—	—	—	—	—
—Toronto	NHL	49	2	11	13	31	...	...	...	7	0	1	1	8
78-79—Pittsburgh	NHL	70	13	34	47	78	...	...	...	7	0	0	0	12
79-80—Pittsburgh	NHL	67	8	28	36	45	...	...	...	5	1	0	1	4
80-81—Pittsburgh	NHL	76	16	67	83	136	...	...	...	5	4	5	9	9
81-82—Pittsburgh	NHL	73	11	64	75	131	...	...	...	5	1	3	4	16
82-83—Pittsburgh	NHL	61	15	41	56	110	...	...	...	—	—	—	—	—
83-84—Pittsburgh	NHL	50	3	23	26	82	...	...	...	—	—	—	—	—
—Winnipeg	NHL	5	0	3	3	2	...	...	...	3	0	2	2	4
84-85—Winnipeg	NHL	71	13	38	51	98	...	...	...	8	1	5	6	13
85-86—Winnipeg	NHL	68	16	33	49	93	...	...	...	—	—	—	—	—
86-87—Winnipeg	NHL	71	16	26	42	93	...	...	...	10	1	5	6	18
87-88—Winnipeg	NHL	78	15	44	59	210	...	...	...	5	0	2	2	10
88-89—Winnipeg	NHL	78	6	38	44	78	...	...	...	—	—	—	—	—
89-90—Winnipeg	NHL	53	3	15	18	50	8	2	0	—	—	—	—	—
90-91—Winnipeg	NHL	52	9	19	28	44	...	...	...	—	—	—	—	—
91-92—Winnipeg	NHL	66	1	9	10	54	...	...	...	5	1	0	1	6
92-93—Winnipeg	NHL	22	1	1	2	14	-6	0	0	—	—	—	—	—
NHL Totals (17 years)		1055	148	499	647	1400	2	2	0	69	9	24	33	120

HEAD COACHING RECORD

BACKGROUND: Assistant coach, Winnipeg (1995). ... Coach, Manitoba of IHL (1996-97 through 1999-2000). ... President/general manager, Washington (2001-02). ... Assistant coach, Washington (2002-03 through 2003-04) ... Coach, Manitoba of the AHL (2004-05). ... Named coach of the Anaheim Mighty Ducks (August 1, 2005).

Season Team	League	W	L	T	OL	Pct.	Finish	W	L	Pct.
		REGULAR SEASON						PLAYOFFS		
05-06—Anaheim	NHL	43	27	...	12	.524	3rd/Pacific Division	9	7	.563
NHL Totals (1 year)		43	27	...	12	.524	**NHL Totals (1 year)**	9	7	.563

NOTES:

05-06—Defeated Calgary Flames, 4-3, in Western Conference quarterfinals; defeated Colorado Avalanche, 4-0, in Western Conference semifinals; lost to Edmonton Oilers, 4-1, in Western Conference finals.

CRAWFORD, MARC — KINGS

PERSONAL: Born February 13, 1961, in Belleville, Ont. ... Shoots left. ... Played left wing. ... Brother of Bob Crawford, RW with four NHL teams (1979-80 and 1981-87).
TRANSACTIONS/CAREER NOTES: Selected by Vancouver Canucks in fourth round (third Canucks pick, 70th overall) of NHL draft (June 11, 1980). ... Suspended three games for leaving bench to fight (February 3, 1987).

Season Team	League	GP	G	A	Pts.	PIM	+/-	PP	SH	GP	G	A	Pts.	PIM
		REGULAR SEASON								PLAYOFFS				
79-80—Cornwall	OHL	54	27	36	63	127	...	...	...	18	8	20	28	48
80-81—Cornwall	OHL	63	42	57	99	242	...	...	...	19	20	15	35	27

Season Team	League	REGULAR SEASON GP	G	A	Pts.	PIM	+/-	PP	SH	PLAYOFFS GP	G	A	Pts.	PIM
81-82—Dallas	CHL	34	13	21	34	71	...	...	...	—	—	—	—	—
—Vancouver	NHL	40	4	8	12	29	0	0	0	14	1	0	1	11
82-83—Vancouver	NHL	41	4	5	9	28	-3	0	0	3	0	1	1	25
—Fredericton	AHL	30	15	9	24	59	...	...	...	9	1	3	4	10
83-84—Vancouver	NHL	19	0	1	1	9	0	0	0	—	—	—	—	—
—Fredericton	AHL	56	9	22	31	96	...	...	...	7	4	2	6	23
84-85—Vancouver	NHL	1	0	0	0	4	-4	0	0	—	—	—	—	—
85-86—Vancouver	NHL	54	11	14	25	92	-7	0	0	3	0	1	1	8
—Fredericton	AHL	26	10	14	24	55	...	...	...	—	—	—	—	—
86-87—Vancouver	NHL	21	0	3	3	67	-8	0	0	—	—	—	—	—
—Fredericton	AHL	25	8	11	19	21	...	...	...	—	—	—	—	—
87-88—Fredericton	AHL	43	5	13	18	90	...	...	...	2	0	0	0	14
88-89—Milwaukee	IHL	53	23	30	53	166	...	...	...	11	2	5	7	26
NHL Totals (6 years)		176	19	31	50	229	-22	0	0	20	1	2	3	44

HEAD COACHING RECORD

BACKGROUND: Player/assistant coach, AHL Fredericton (1987-88). ... Coach, Cornwall of OHL (1989-91). ... Head coach, Quebec Nordiques (1994-95). ... Nordiques franchise moved to Denver for 1995-96 season and renamed Colorado Avalanche. ... Head coach, Colorado Avalanche (1995-1998). ... Head coach, Vancouver Canucks (1998-99 through 2005-06). ... Named head coach of Los Angeles Kings (May 22, 2006).

Season Team	League	REGULAR SEASON W	L	T	OL	Pct.	Finish	PLAYOFFS W	L	Pct.
89-90—Cornwall	OHL	24	38	4	...	.394	6th/Leyden Division	2	4	.333
90-91—Cornwall	OHL	23	42	1	...	.356	7th/Leyden Division	—	—	—
91-92—St. John's	AHL	39	29	12	...	.563	2nd/Atlantic Division	11	5	.688
92-93—St. John's	AHL	41	26	13	...	.594	1st/Atlantic Division	4	5	.444
93-94—St. John's	AHL	45	23	12	...	.638	1st/Atlantic Division	6	5	.545
94-95—Quebec	NHL	30	13	5	...	.677	1st/Northeast Division	2	4	.333
95-96—Colorado	NHL	47	25	10	...	.634	1st/Pacific Division	16	6	.727
96-97—Colorado	NHL	49	24	9	...	.652	1st/Pacific Division	10	7	.588
97-98—Colorado	NHL	39	26	17	...	.579	1st/Pacific Division	3	4	.429
98-99—Vancouver	NHL	8	23	6	...	.297	4th/Northwest Division	—	—	—
99-00—Vancouver	NHL	30	29	15	8	.457	3rd/Northwest Division	—	—	—
00-01—Vancouver	NHL	36	28	11	7	.506	3rd/Northwest Division	0	4	.000
01-02—Vancouver	NHL	42	30	7	3	.555	2nd/Northwest Division	2	4	.333
02-03—Vancouver	NHL	45	23	13	1	.628	2nd/Northwest Division	7	7	.500
03-04—Vancouver	NHL	43	24	10	5	.585	1st/Northwest Division	3	4	.429
05-06—Vancouver	NHL	42	32	...	8	.512	4th/Northwest Division	—	—	—
NHL Totals (11 years)		411	277	103	32	.562	**NHL Totals (8 years)**	43	40	.518

NOTES:

89-90—Lost to Oshawa in Leyden Division quarterfinals.
91-92—Defeated Cape Breton in first round of Calder Cup playoffs; defeated Moncton in second round of Calder Cup playoffs; lost to Adirondack in Calder Cup finals.
92-93—Defeated Moncton in first round of Calder Cup playoffs; lost to Cape Breton in second round of Calder Cup playoffs.
93-94—Defeated Cape Breton in first round of Calder Cup playoffs; lost to Moncton in second round of Calder Cup playoffs.
94-95—Lost to New York Rangers in Eastern Conference quarterfinals.
95-96—Defeated Vancouver in Western Conference quarterfinals; defeated Chicago in Western Conference semifinals; defeated Detroit in Western Conference finals; defeated Florida in Stanley Cup finals.
96-97—Defeated Chicago in Western Conference quarterfinals; defeated Edmonton in Western Conference semifinals; lost to Detroit in Western Conference finals.
97-98—Lost to Edmonton in Western Conference quarterfinals.
98-99—Replaced Mike Keenan as head coach (January 24).
00-01—Lost to Colorado in Western Conference quarterfinals.
01-02—Lost to Detroit in Western Conference quarterfinals.
02-03—Defeated St. Louis in Western Conference quarterfinals; lost to Minnesota in Western Conference semifinals.
03-04—Lost to Calgary in Western Conference quarterfinals.

GALLANT, GERARD — BLUE JACKETS

PERSONAL: Born September 2, 1963, in Summerside, P.E.I. ... 5-10/190. ... Shoots left. ... Played left wing. ... Name pronounced: guh-LANT.

TRANSACTIONS/CAREER NOTES: Selected by Detroit Red Wings in sixth round (fourth Red Wings pick, 107th overall) of NHL draft (June 10, 1981). ... Broke jaw (December 11, 1985); missed 25 games. ... Fined $500 for stick-swinging incident (April 8, 1989). ... Suspended five games for slashing (October 7, 1989). ... Suspended three games for hitting linesman (January 13, 1990). ... Suffered sore back (November 1990); missed eight games. ... Back spasms (December 1990); missed 18 games. ... Underwent surgery to remove bone spur in back (March 14, 1991); missed remainder of season. ... Injured hand (February 1992); missed five games. ... Strained back (March 20, 1992); missed five games. ... Injured hip (December 15, 1992); missed three games. ... Flu (January 17, 1993); missed one game. ... Signed as free agent by Tampa Bay Lightning (July 21, 1993). ... Sprained back (November 17, 1993); missed four games. ... Sprained back (April 1, 1994); missed six games.

STATISTICAL PLATEAUS: Three-goal games: 1987-88 (3), 1988-89 (1). Total: 4.

Season Team	League	REGULAR SEASON GP	G	A	Pts.	PIM	+/-	PP	SH	PLAYOFFS GP	G	A	Pts.	PIM
79-80—Summerside	PEIHA	45	60	55	115	90	...	...	...	—	—	—	—	—
80-81—Sherbrooke	QMJHL	68	41	60	101	220	...	...	...	14	6	13	19	46
81-82—Sherbrooke	QMJHL	58	34	58	92	260	...	...	...	22	14	24	38	84
82-83—St. Jean	QMJHL	33	28	25	53	139	...	...	...	—	—	—	—	—
—Verdun	QMJHL	29	26	49	75	105	...	...	...	15	14	19	33	84
83-84—Adirondack	AHL	77	31	33	64	195	...	...	...	7	1	3	4	34
84-85—Adirondack	AHL	46	18	29	47	131	...	...	...	—	—	—	—	—
—Detroit	NHL	32	6	12	18	66	...	...	...	3	0	0	0	11

Season Team	League	GP	G	A	Pts.	PIM	+/-	PP	SH		GP	G	A	Pts.	PIM
		REGULAR SEASON									PLAYOFFS				
85-86—Detroit	NHL	52	20	19	39	106	...	...	...		—	—	—	—	—
86-87—Detroit	NHL	80	38	34	72	216	...	...	...		16	8	6	14	43
87-88—Detroit	NHL	73	34	39	73	242	...	...	...		16	6	9	15	55
88-89—Detroit	NHL	76	39	54	93	230	...	...	...		6	1	2	3	40
89-90—Detroit	NHL	69	36	44	80	254	-6	12	3		—	—	—	—	—
90-91—Detroit	NHL	45	10	16	26	111	...	...	...		—	—	—	—	—
91-92—Detroit	NHL	69	14	22	36	187	...	...	...		11	2	2	4	25
92-93—Detroit	NHL	67	10	20	30	188	20	0	0		6	1	2	3	4
93-94—Tampa Bay	NHL	51	4	9	13	74	-6	1	0		—	—	—	—	—
94-95—Atlanta	IHL	16	3	3	6	31	-8	0	0		—	—	—	—	—
—Tampa Bay	NHL	1	0	0	0	0	0	0	0		—	—	—	—	—
95-96—Detroit	IHL	3	2	1	3	6	...	...	...		—	—	—	—	—
NHL Totals (11 years)		615	211	269	480	1674	8	13	3		58	18	21	39	178

HEAD COACHING RECORD

BACKGROUND: Named Columbus Blue Jackets interim coach (January 1, 2004). ... Named Blue Jackets coach (June 25, 2004).

Season Team	League	W	L	T	OL	Pct.	Finish		W	L	Pct.
		REGULAR SEASON							PLAYOFFS		
03-04—Columbus	NHL	16	24	4	1	.400	4th/Central Division		—	—	—
05-06—Columbus	NHL	35	43	...	4	.427	3rd/Central Division		—	—	—
NHL Totals (2 years)		51	67	4	5	.417					

GRETZKY, WAYNE — COYOTES

PERSONAL: Born January 26, 1961, in Brantford, Ont. ... 6-0/180. ... Shoots left. ... Brother of Brent Gretzky, center with Tampa Bay Lightning (1993-94 and 1994-95).

TRANSACTIONS/CAREER NOTES: Signed as underage junior by Indianapolis Racers to multiyear contract (May 1978). ... Traded by Racers with LW Peter Driscoll and G Ed Mio to Edmonton Oilers for cash and future considerations (November 1978). ... Bruised right shoulder (January 28, 1984). ... Underwent surgery on left ankle to remove benign growth (June 1984). ... Twisted right knee (December 30, 1987). ... Corneal abrasion to left eye (February 19, 1988); missed three games. ... Traded by Oilers with RW/D Marty McSorley and LW/C Mike Krushelnyski to Los Angeles Kings for C Jimmy Carson, LW Martin Gelinas, first-round picks in 1989 (traded to New Jersey; Devils selected Jason Miller), 1991 (LW Martin Rucinsky) and 1993 (D Nick Stajduhar) drafts and cash (August 9, 1988). ... Injured groin (March 17, 1990). ... Strained lower back (March 22, 1990); missed five regular-season games and two playoff games. ... Left team for personal reasons (October 1991); missed five games. ... Sprained knee (February 25, 1992); missed one game. ... Herniated thoracic disc (summer 1992); missed first 39 games of season. ... Sprained left knee (April 9, 1994). ... Traded by Kings to St. Louis Blues for LW Craig Johnson, C Patrice Tardiff, C Roman Vopat, 5th-round pick (D Peter Hogan) in 1996 draft and first-round pick (LW Matt Zultek) in 1997 draft (February 27, 1996). ... Bruised lower back (April 4, 1996); missed three games. ... Signed as free agent by New York Rangers (July 21, 1996). ... Bulging disc in neck (February 22, 1999); missed 12 games. ... Retired (April 16, 1999).

STATISTICAL PLATEAUS: Three-goal games: 1979-80 (2), 1980-81 (2), 1981-82 (6), 1982-83 (2), 1983-84 (6), 1984-85 (5), 1985-86 (3), 1986-87 (3), 1987-88 (1), 1988-89 (2), 1989-90 (1), 1990-91 (2), 1991-92 (1), 1997-98 (1). Total: 37. ... Four-goal games: 1980-81 (1), 1981-82 (3), 1983-84 (4), 1986-87 (1). Total: 9. ... Five-goal games: 1980-81 (1), 1981-82 (1), 1984-85 (1), 1987-88 (1). Total: 4. ... Total hat tricks: 50.

Season Team	League	GP	G	A	Pts.	PIM	+/-	PP	SH		GP	G	A	Pts.	PIM
		REGULAR SEASON									PLAYOFFS				
76-77—Peterborough	OMJHL	3	0	3	3	0	...	...	...		—	—	—	—	—
77-78—Sault Ste. Marie	OMJHL	64	70	112	182	14	...	...	...		13	6	20	26	0
78-79—Indianapolis	WHA	8	3	3	6	0	...	...	...		—	—	—	—	—
—Edmonton	WHA	72	43	61	104	19	...	...	...		13	10	10	20	2
79-80—Edmonton	NHL	79	51	*86	†137	21	15	13	1		3	2	1	3	0
80-81—Edmonton	NHL	80	55	*109	*164	28	41	15	4		9	7	14	21	4
81-82—Edmonton	NHL	80	*92	*120	*212	26	*81	18	†6		5	5	7	12	8
82-83—Edmonton	NHL	80	*71	*125	*196	59	60	18	*6		16	12	*26	*38	4
83-84—Edmonton	NHL	74	*87	*118	*205	39	*76	*20	*12		19	13	*22	*35	12
84-85—Edmonton	NHL	80	*73	*135	*208	52	*98	8	*11		18	17	*30	*47	4
85-86—Edmonton	NHL	80	52	*163	*215	46	71	11	3		10	8	11	19	2
86-87—Edmonton	NHL	79	*62	*121	*183	28	*70	13	*7		21	5	*29	*34	6
87-88—Edmonton	NHL	64	40	*109	149	24	39	9	5		19	12	*31	*43	16
88-89—Los Angeles	NHL	78	54	†114	168	26	15	11	5		11	5	17	22	0
89-90—Los Angeles	NHL	73	40	*102	*142	42	8	10	4		7	3	7	10	0
90-91—Los Angeles	NHL	78	41	*122	*163	16	30	8	0		12	4	11	15	2
91-92—Los Angeles	NHL	74	31	*90	121	34	-12	12	2		6	2	5	7	2
92-93—Los Angeles	NHL	45	16	49	65	6	6	0	2		24	15	†25	*40	4
93-94—Los Angeles	NHL	81	38	*92	*130	20	-25	14	4		—	—	—	—	—
94-95—Los Angeles	NHL	48	11	37	48	6	-20	3	0		—	—	—	—	—
95-96—Los Angeles	NHL	62	15	66	81	32	-7	5	0		—	—	—	—	—
—St. Louis	NHL	18	8	13	21	2	-6	1	1		13	2	14	16	0
96-97—New York Rangers	NHL	82	25	†72	97	28	12	6	0		15	10	10	20	2
97-98—New York Rangers	NHL	82	23	†67	90	28	-11	6	0		—	—	—	—	—
—Can. Olympic team	Int'l	6	0	4	4	2	3	0	0		—	—	—	—	—
98-99—New York Rangers	NHL	70	9	53	62	14	-23	3	0		—	—	—	—	—
NHL Totals (20 years)		1487	894	1963	2857	577	518	204	73		208	122	260	382	66

HEAD COACHING RECORD

BACKGROUND: Named coach of the Phoenix Coyotes (August 8, 2005). ... Left team for personal reasons (December 17, 2005); missed one month.

Season Team	League	W	L	T	OL	Pct.	Finish		W	L	Pct.
		REGULAR SEASON							PLAYOFFS		
05-06—Phoenix	NHL	38	39	...	5	.463	5th/Pacific Division		—	—	—
NHL Totals (1 year)		38	39	...	5	.463					

HANLON, GLEN — CAPITALS

PERSONAL: Born February 20, 1957, in Brandon, Man. ... 6-0/185. ... Shoots right. ... Played goal.

TRANSACTIONS/CAREER NOTES: Selected by Vancouver Canucks from Brandon Wheat Kings in third round (third Canucks pick, 40th overall) of NHL entry draft (June 14, 1977). ... Tore ankle ligaments; missed part of 1977-78 season. ... Injured shoulder; missed part of 1979-80 season. ... Stretched knee ligaments (October 18, 1980). ... Suffered shoulder separation (March, 1981). ... Traded by Canucks to St. Louis Blues for RW Tony Currie, RW Jim Nill, G Rick Heinz and fourth-round pick (G Shawn Kilroy) in 1982 draft (March 9, 1982). ... Traded by Blues with C Vaclav Nedomansky to New York Rangers for D Andre Dore and future considerations (January 4, 1983). ... Traded by Rangers with third-round picks in 1987 (C Dennis Holland) and 1988 (D Guy Dupuis) drafts and future considerations to Detroit Red Wings for C Kelly Kisio, RW Lane Lambert and D Jim Leavins and fifth-round pick in 1988 draft (July 29, 1986). ... Lacerated finger (October 16, 1987). ... Broke left index finger (January, 1988). ... Injured hip (March, 1989). ... Fractured right hand (January 21, 1991); missed eight games.

		REGULAR SEASON								PLAYOFFS				
Season Team	League	GP	G	A	Pts.	PIM	+/-	PP	SH	GP	G	A	Pts.	PIM
73-74—Brandon	MJHL	20	...	0	...	5	...	...	...	—	—	—	—	—
74-75—Brandon	WCHL	43	...	1	...	6	...	...	...	5	...	...	...	...
75-76—Brandon	WCHL	64	...	2	...	35	...	...	...	5	...	...	...	...
76-77—Brandon	WCHL	65	...	5	...	8	...	...	...	16	...	...	...	...
77-78—Tulsa	CHL	53	...	4	...	30	...	...	...	2	...	...	...	...
—Vancouver	NHL	4	...	0	...	2	...	...	...	—	—	—	—	—
78-79—Vancouver	NHL	31	...	1	...	30	...	...	...	—	—	—	—	—
79-80—Vancouver	NHL	57	...	1	...	43	...	...	...	2	...	...	...	...
80-81—Dallas	CHL	4	...	1	...	0	...	...	...	—	—	—	—	—
—Vancouver	NHL	17	...	1	...	10	...	...	...	—	—	—	—	—
81-82—Vancouver	NHL	28	...	0	...	22	...	...	...	—	—	—	—	—
—St. Louis	NHL	2	...	0	...	0	...	...	...	3	...	...	...	...
82-83—St. Louis	NHL	14	...	0	...	0	...	...	...	—	—	—	—	—
—New York Rangers	NHL	21	...	0	...	2	...	...	...	1	...	...	...	...
83-84—New York Rangers	NHL	50	...	2	...	30	...	...	...	5	...	...	...	...
84-85—New York Rangers	NHL	44	...	0	...	4	...	...	...	3	...	...	...	...
85-86—Adirondack	AHL	10	...	0	...	2	...	...	...	—	—	—	—	—
—New Haven	AHL	5	...	1	...	4	...	...	...	—	—	—	—	—
—New York Rangers	NHL	23	...	1	...	4	...	...	...	3	...	...	...	...
86-87—Detroit	NHL	36	...	0	...	20	...	...	...	8	...	...	...	...
87-88—Detroit	NHL	47	...	1	...	30	...	...	...	8	...	...	...	...
88-89—Detroit	NHL	39	...	1	...	12	...	...	...	2	...	...	...	...
89-90—Detroit	NHL	45	...	3	...	24	...	...	...	—	—	—	—	—
90-91—Detroit	NHL	19	...	0	...	4	...	...	...	—	—	—	—	—
—San Diego	IHL	11	...	0	...	2	...	...	...	—	—	—	—	—
NHL Totals (14 years)		477	0	11	0	237	0	0	0	35	...	...	...	...

HEAD COACHING RECORD

BACKGROUND: Head coach, Portland of the AHL (1999-2000 through 2001-02). ... Named coach of Washington Capitals (December 10, 2003).

		REGULAR SEASON						PLAYOFFS		
Season Team	League	W	L	T	OL	Pct.	Finish	W	L	Pct.
99-00—Portland	AHL	46	23	10	1	.638	2nd/Northeast Division	1	3	.250
00-01—Portland	AHL	34	40	4	2	.450	5th/Northeast Division	0	3	.000
01-02—Portland	AHL	30	31	15	4	.469	4th/Northern Division	—	—	—
03-04—Washington	NHL	15	28	9	2	.361	5th/Southeast Division	—	—	—
05-06—Washington	NHL	29	41	...	12	.354	5th/Southeast Division	—	—	—
NHL Totals (2 years)		44	69	9	14	.357				

NOTES:

99-00—Lost in first round of AHL playoffs.

00-01—Lost in first round of AHL playoffs.

HARTLEY, BOB — THRASHERS

PERSONAL: Born September 7, 1960, in Hawkesbury, Ont.

HEAD COACHING RECORD

BACKGROUND: Coach, Hawkesbury Hawks of the CJHL (1987-1991) ... Coach, Laval of the QMJHL (1991-93). ... Assistant coach, Cornwall of the AHL (1993-94). ... Coach, Cornwall of AHL (1994-96). ... Coach, Hershey of the AHL (1996-98). ... Coach, Colorado Avalanche (June 30, 1998 to December 18, 2002). ... Named coach of Atlanta Thrashers (January 14, 2003).

		REGULAR SEASON						PLAYOFFS		
Season Team	League	W	L	T	OL	Pct.	Finish	W	L	Pct.
87-88—Hawkesbury	CJHL	9	39	0	...	.188	...	1	4	.200
88-89—Hawkesbury	CJHL	35	20	1	...	.634	...	6	6	.500
89-90—Hawkesbury	CJHL	15	15	1	...	.500	...	12	3	.800
90-91—Hawkesbury	CJHL	42	10	4	...	.786	...	12	0	1.000
91-92—Laval	QMJHL	38	27	5	...	.579	...	4	6	.400
92-93—Laval	QMJHL	43	25	2	...	.629	1st/Robert Le Bel Division	12	1	.923
94-95—Cornwall	AHL	38	33	9	...	.531	2nd/Southern Division	8	6	.571
95-96—Cornwall	AHL	34	39	7	...	.469	4th/Central Division	3	5	.375
96-97—Hershey	AHL	43	22	10	...	.640	2nd/Mid-Atlantic Division	15	8	.652
97-98—Hershey	AHL	36	31	7	...	.534	2nd/Mid-Atlantic Division	3	4	.429
98-99—Colorado	NHL	44	28	10	...	.598	1st/ Northwest Division	11	8	.579
99-00—Colorado	NHL	42	28	11	1	.579	1st/Northwest Division	11	6	.647
00-01—Colorado	NHL	52	16	10	4	.695	1st/Northwest Division	16	7	.696
01-02—Colorado	NHL	45	28	8	1	.598	1st/Northwest Division	11	10	.524

Season Team	League	REGULAR SEASON W	L	T	OL	Pct.	Finish	PLAYOFFS W	L	Pct.
02-03—Colorado	NHL	10	8	9	4	.468				
—Atlanta	NHL	19	14	5	1	.551	3rd/Southeast Division	—	—	—
03-04—Atlanta	NHL	33	37	8	4	.451	2nd/Southeast Division	—	—	—
05-06—Atlanta	NHL	41	33	...	8	.500	3rd/Southeast Division	—	—	—
NHL Totals (7 years)		286	192	61	23	.563	**NHL Totals (4 years)**	49	31	.613

NOTES:

92-93—Defeated Verdun in quarterfinals of President Cup playoffs; defeated Drummondville in semifinals of President Cup playoffs; defeated Sherbrooke in finals of President Cup playoffs.

94-95—Defeated Hershey in division semifinals in Calder Cup playoffs; defeated Binghamton in division finals in Calder Cup playoffs; lost to Fredericton in league semifinals in Calder Cup playoffs.

95-96—Defeated Albany in conference quarterfinals in Calder Cup playoffs; lost to Rochester in conference finals in Calder Cup playoffs.

96-97—Defeated Kentucky in conference quarterfinals in Calder Cup playoffs; defeated Phliadelphia in conference semifinals in Calder Cup playoffs; defeated Springfield in conference finals in Calder Cup playoffs; defeated Hamilton in Calder Cup finals.

97-98—Defeated Kentucky in conference quarterfinals in Calder Cup playoffs; lost to Philadelphia in conference semifinals in Calder Cup playoffs.

98-99—Defeated San Jose in Western Conference quarterfinals; defeated Detroit in Western Conference semifinals; lost to Dallas in Western Conference finals.

99-00—Defeated Phoenix in Western Conference quarterfinals; defeated Detroit in Western Conference semifinals; lost to Dallas in Western Conference finals.

00-01—Defeated Vancouver in Western Conference quarterfinals; defeated Los Angeles in Western Conference semifinals; defeated St. Louis in Western Conference finals; defeated New Jersey in Stanley Cup finals.

01-02—Defeated Los Angeles in Western Conference quarterfinals; defeated San Jose in Western Conference semifinals; lost to Detroit in Western Conference finals.

HITCHCOCK, KEN — FLYERS

PERSONAL: Born December 17, 1951, in Edmonton.

HEAD COACHING RECORD

BACKGROUND: Assistant coach, Philadelphia Flyers (1990-93). ... Coach, Dallas Stars (January 8, 1996, through 2001-02). ... Associate coach, Canadian Olympic team (2002). ... Named coach of Flyers (May 14, 2002).

Season Team	League	REGULAR SEASON W	L	T	OL	Pct.	Finish	PLAYOFFS W	L	Pct.
84-85—Kamloops	WHL	52	17	2	...	.746	1st/West Division	10	5	.667
85-86—Kamloops	WHL	49	19	4	...	.708	1st/West Division	14	2	.875
86-87—Kamloops	WHL	55	14	3	...	.785	1st/West Division	8	5	.615
87-88—Kamloops	WHL	45	26	1	...	.632	1st/West Division	12	6	.667
88-89—Kamloops	WHL	34	33	5	...	.507	3rd/West Division	8	8	.500
89-90—Kamloops	WHL	56	16	0	...	.778	1st/West Division	14	3	.824
93-94—Kalamazoo	IHL	48	26	7	...	.636	1st/Atlantic Division	1	4	.200
94-95—Kalamazoo	IHL	43	24	14	...	.617	2nd/Northern Division	10	6	.625
95-96—Michigan	IHL	19	10	11	...	.613	...	—	—	—
—Dallas	NHL	15	23	5	...	.407	6th/Central Division	—	—	—
96-97—Dallas	NHL	48	26	8	...	.634	1st/Central Division	3	4	.429
97-98—Dallas	NHL	49	22	11	...	.665	1st/Central Division	10	7	.588
98-99—Dallas	NHL	51	19	12	...	.695	1st/Pacific Division	16	7	.696
99-00—Dallas	NHL	43	23	10	6	.585	1st/Pacific Division	14	9	.609
00-01—Dallas	NHL	48	24	8	2	.634	1st/Pacific Division	4	6	.400
01-02—Dallas	NHL	23	17	6	4	.520	...	—	—	—
02-03—Philadelphia	NHL	45	20	13	4	.628	2nd/Atlantic Division	6	7	.462
03-04—Philadelphia	NHL	40	21	15	6	.579	1st/Atlantic Division	11	7	.611
05-06—Philadelphia	NHL	45	26	...	11	.549	2nd/Atlantic Division	2	4	.333
NHL Totals (10 years)		407	221	88	33	.602	**NHL Totals (8 years)**	66	51	.564

NOTES:

84-85—Defeated Portland in West Division semifinals; defeated New Westminster in West Division finals; lost to Prince Albert in WHL finals.

85-86—Defeated Seattle in West Division semifinals; defeated Portland in West Division finals; defeated Medicine Hat in WHL finals.

86-87—Defeated Victoria in West Division semifinals; lost to Portland in West Division finals.

87-88—Defeated New Westminster in West Division semifinals; defeated Spokane in West Division finals; lost to Medicine Hat in WHL finals.

88-89—Defeated Victoria in West Division semifinals; lost to Portland in West Division finals.

89-90—Defeated Spokane in West Division semifinals; defeated Seattle in West Division finals; defeated Lethbridge in WHL finals.

93-94—Lost to Cincinnati in Eastern Conference quarterfinals.

94-95—Defeated Chicago in Eastern Conference quarterfinals; defeated Cincinnati in Eastern Conference semifinals; lost to Kansas City in Eastern Conference finals.

95-96—Replaced Bob Gainey as head coach (January 8).

96-97—Lost to Edmonton in Western Conference quarterfinals.

97-98—Defeated San Jose in Western Conference quarterfinals; defeated Edmonton in Western Conference semifinals; lost to Detroit in Western Conference finals.

98-99—Defeated Edmonton in Western Conference quarterfinals; defeated St. Louis in Western Conference semifinals; defeated Colorado in Western Conference finals; defeated Buffalo in Stanley Cup finals.

99-00—Defeated Edmonton in Western Conference quarterfinals; defeated San Jose in Western Conference semifinals; defeated Colorado in Western Conference finals; lost to New Jersey in Stanley Cup finals.

00-01—Defeated Edmonton in Western Conference quarterfinals; lost to St. Louis in Western Conference semifinals.

01-02—Replaced as head coach by Rick Wilson (January 25).

02-03—Defeated Toronto in Eastern Conference quarterfinals; lost to Ottawa in Eastern Conference semifinals.

03-04—Defeated New Jersey in Eastern Conference quarterfinals; defeated Toronto in Eastern Conference semifinals; lost to Tampa Bay in Eastern Conference finals.

05-06—Lost to Buffalo Sabres, 4-2, in Eastern Conference quarterfinals.

JULIEN, CLAUDE — DEVILS

PERSONAL: Born November 11, 1958, in Orleans, Ont. ... 6-0/195. ... Shoots right. ... Played defense.

TRANSACTIONS/CAREER NOTES: Signed as free agent by St. Louis Blues (September 1981). ... Sent with D Gordon Donnelly to Quebec Nordiques as compensation for Blues signing coach Jacques Demers (August 1983). ... Broke nose (February 1, 1986). ... Signed by Fredericton Express after completing a season in Europe (March 1987).

Season Team	League	REGULAR SEASON GP	G	A	Pts.	PIM	+/-	PP	SH	PLAYOFFS GP	G	A	Pts.	PIM
77-78—Newmarket	OHA	45	18	26	44	137	...	...	...	—	—	—	—	—
—Oshawa	OMJHL	11	0	5	5	14	...	...	...	—	—	—	—	—
78-79—	Did not play													
79-80—Windsor	OMJHL	68	14	37	51	148	...	...	...	16	5	11	16	23
80-81—Windsor	OMJHL	3	1	2	3	21	...	...	...	—	—	—	—	—
—Port Huron	IHL	77	15	40	55	153	...	...	...	4	1	1	2	4
81-82—Salt Lake City	IHL	70	4	18	22	134	...	...	...	5	1	4	5	0
82-83—Salt Lake City	IHL	76	14	47	61	176	...	...	...	6	3	3	6	16
83-84—Milwaukee	IHL	5	0	3	3	2	...	...	...	—	—	—	—	—
—Fredericton	AHL	57	7	22	29	58	...	...	...	7	0	4	4	6
84-85—Fredericton	AHL	77	6	28	34	97	...	...	...	6	2	4	6	13
—Quebec	NHL	1	0	0	0	0	...	...	...	—	—	—	—	—
85-86—Quebec	NHL	13	0	1	1	25	...	...	...	—	—	—	—	—
—Fredericton	AHL	49	3	18	21	74	...	...	...	6	1	4	5	19
86-87—Fredericton	AHL	17	1	6	7	22	...	...	...	—	—	—	—	—
87-88—Fredericton	AHL	35	1	14	15	52	...	...	...	13	1	3	4	30
—Baltimore	AHL	30	6	14	20	22	...	...	...	—	—	—	—	—
88-89—Halifax	AHL	79	8	52	60	72	...	...	...	4	0	2	2	4
89-90—Halifax	AHL	77	6	37	43	65	...	...	...	4	0	1	1	7
90-91—Kansas City	IHL	54	7	16	23	43	...	...	...	—	—	—	—	—
91-92—Moncton	AHL	48	2	15	17	10	...	...	...	4	0	1	1	4
NHL Totals (2 years)		14	0	1	1	25	0	0	0					

HEAD COACHING RECORD

BACKGROUND: Coach of Montreal Canadiens (January 17, 2003-January 14, 2006). ... Fired by Canadiens (January 14, 2006). ... Named coach of New Jersey Devils (June 13, 2006).

Season Team	League	REGULAR SEASON W	L	T	OL	Pct.	Finish	PLAYOFFS W	L	Pct.
96-97—Hull	QMJHL	48	19	3	...	.707	1st/Lebel Conference	—	—	—
97-98—Hull	QMJHL	32	37	1	...	.464	6th/Lebel Conference	—	—	—
98-99—Hull	QMJHL	23	38	9	...	.393	6th/Lebel Conference	—	—	—
99-00—Hull	QMJHL	42	24	6	...	.625	1st/Western Division	—	—	—
00-01—Hamilton	AHL	28	41	6	...	.413	4th/Canadian Division	—	—	—
01-02—Hamilton	AHL	37	30	10	3	.525	2nd/Canadian Division	—	—	—
02-03—Hamilton	AHL	33	6	3	3	.767	...	—	—	—
—Montreal	NHL	12	16	3	5	.389	4th/Northeast Division	—	—	—
03-04—Montreal	NHL	41	30	7	4	.543	4th/Northeast Division	4	7	.364
05-06—Montreal	NHL	19	16	...	6	.463		—	—	—
NHL Totals (3 years)		72	62	10	15	.484	**NHL Totals (1 year)**	4	7	.364

NOTES:

96-97—Won QMJHL championship; won Memorial Cup.
02-03—Left team to coach Montreal Canadiens.
02-03—Replaced Michel Therrien as head coach (January 18).
03-04—Defeated Boston in Eastern Conference quarterfinals; lost to Tampa Bay in Eastern Conference semifinals.
05-06—Replaced by Bob Gainey as head coach (January 14).

KITCHEN, MIKE — BLUES

PERSONAL: Born February 1, 1956, in Newmarket, Ont. ... Nickname: Kitch. ... Played Defense.

Season Team	League	REGULAR SEASON GP	G	A	Pts.	PIM	+/-	PP	SH	PLAYOFFS GP	G	A	Pts.	PIM
73-74—Toronto Young Nats	OHA	69	3	17	20	145	...	...	...	—	—	—	—	—
74-75—Toronto Young Nats	OHA	68	5	30	35	136	...	...	...	—	—	—	—	—
75-76—Toronto Young Nats	OHA	65	6	18	24	148	...	...	...	—	—	—	—	—
76-77—Rhode Island	AHL	14	0	10	10	14	...	...	...	—	—	—	—	—
—Colorado Rockies	NHL	60	1	8	9	36	...	...	...	—	—	—	—	—
77-78—Colorado Rockies	NHL	61	2	17	19	45	...	...	...	2	0	0	0	2
78-79—Colorado Rockies	NHL	53	1	4	5	28	...	...	...	—	—	—	—	—
79-80—Fort Worth	CHL	30	0	9	9	22	...	...	...	15	0	1	1	16
—Colorado Rockies	NHL	42	1	6	7	25	...	...	...	—	—	—	—	—
80-81—Colorado Rockies	NHL	75	1	7	8	100	...	...	...	—	—	—	—	—
81-82—Fort Worth	CHL	13	1	5	6	16	...	...	...	—	—	—	—	—
—Colorado Rockies	NHL	63	1	8	9	60	...	...	...	—	—	—	—	—
82-83—New Jersey	NHL	77	4	8	12	52	...	...	...	—	—	—	—	—
83-84—New Jersey	NHL	43	1	4	5	24	...	...	...	—	—	—	—	—
84-85—Maine	AHL	12	0	1	1	10	...	...	...	—	—	—	—	—
NHL Totals (8 years)		474	12	62	74	370	0	0	0	2	0	0	0	2

HEAD COACHING RECORD

BACKGROUND: Assistant coach, AHL Newmarket (1988-89). ... Assistant coach, Toronto Maple Leafs (1989-98). ... Assistant coach, St. Louis Blues (Sept. 1, 1998 through Feb. 24, 2004). ... Named head coach, Blues (Feb. 24, 2004).

		REGULAR SEASON						PLAYOFFS		
Season Team	League	W	L	T	OL	Pct.	Finish	W	L	Pct.
03-04—St. Louis	NHL	10	7	4	0	.571	2nd/Central Division	1	4	.200
05-06—St. Louis	NHL	21	46	...	15	.256	5th/Central Division	—	—	—
NHL Totals (2 years)		31	53	4	15	.320	**NHL Totals (1 year)**	1	4	.200

NOTES:

03-04—Lost to San Jose in Western Conference quarterfinals.

LAVIOLETTE, PETER — HURRICANES

PERSONAL: Born December 7, 1964, in Franklin, Mass. ... 6-2/200. ... Shoots left.
TRANSACTIONS/CAREER NOTES: Signed as free agent by New York Rangers (August 12, 1987). ... Signed as free agent by Boston Bruins (September 8, 1992).

		REGULAR SEASON								PLAYOFFS				
Season Team	League	GP	G	A	Pts.	PIM	+/-	PP	SH	GP	G	A	Pts.	PIM
85-86—Westfield State	NCAA	19	12	8	20	44	...	...	...	—	—	—	—	—
86-87—Indianapolis	IHL	72	10	20	30	146	...	...	...	5	0	2	2	12
87-88—U.S. national team	Int'l	56	3	22	25	...	...	...	...	—	—	—	—	—
—U.S. Olympic team	Int'l	5	0	2	2	4	2	...	...	—	—	—	—	—
—Colorado	IHL	19	2	5	7	27	...	...	...	9	3	5	8	7
88-89—Denver	IHL	57	6	19	25	120	...	...	...	3	0	0	0	4
—New York Rangers	NHL	12	0	0	0	6	2	0	0	—	—	—	—	—
89-90—Flint	IHL	62	6	18	24	82	...	...	...	4	0	0	0	4
90-91—Binghamton	AHL	65	12	24	36	72	...	...	...	10	2	7	9	30
91-92—Binghamton	AHL	50	4	10	14	50	...	...	...	11	2	7	9	9
92-93—Providence	AHL	74	13	42	55	64	-3	0	1	6	0	4	4	10
93-94—U.S. national team	Int'l	56	10	25	35	63	...	5	0	—	—	—	—	—
—U.S. Olympic team	Int'l	8	1	0	1	6	0	0	0	—	—	—	—	—
—San Diego	IHL	17	3	4	7	20	-4	0	0	9	3	0	3	6
94-95—Providence	AHL	65	7	23	30	84	11	2	0	13	2	8	10	17
95-96—Providence	AHL	72	9	17	26	53	...	...	...	4	1	1	2	8
96-97—Providence	AHL	41	6	8	14	40	-1	1	0	—	—	—	—	—
NHL Totals (1 year)		12	0	0	0	6	2	0	0					

HEAD COACHING RECORD

BACKGROUND: Coach, ECHL Wheeling (1997-98) ... Named assistant coach of the Boston Bruins, June 30, 2000. ... Coach, AHL Providence (1998-2000); named AHL's most outstanding coach (1999) ... Assistant coach, Boston Bruins (2000-01). ... Coach, New York Islanders (May 23, 2001 to June 3, 2003) ... Named coach of Carolina Hurricanes (December 15, 2003).

		REGULAR SEASON						PLAYOFFS		
Season Team	League	W	L	T	OL	Pct.	Finish	W	L	Pct.
97-98—Wheeling	ECHL	37	24	9	...	.593	2nd/Northeast Division	8	7	.533
98-99—Providence	AHL	56	16	4	...	.763	1st/New England Division	15	4	.789
99-00—Providence	AHL	33	38	6	3	.450	5th/New England Division	10	4	.714
01-02—New York Islanders	NHL	42	28	8	4	.561	2nd/Atlantic Division	3	4	.429
02-03—New York Islanders	NHL	35	34	11	2	.494	3rd/Atlantic Division	1	4	.200
03-04—Carolina	NHL	20	26	6	4	.411	3rd/Southeast Division	—	—	—
05-06—Carolina	NHL	52	22	...	8	.634	1st/Southeast Division	16	9	.640
NHL Totals (4 years)		149	110	25	18	.535	**NHL Totals (3 years)**	20	17	.541

NOTES:

97-98—Defeated Dayton in preliminary round of playoffs; defeated Toledo in quarterfinals; lost to Hampton Roads in semifinals.
98-99—Defeated Worcester in conference quarterfinals of Calder Cup playoffs; defeated Hartford in conference semifinals of Calder Cup playoffs; defeated Fredericton in conference finals of Calder Cup playoffs; defeated Rochester in Calder Cup finals.
99-00—Defeated Quebec in conference quarterfinals of Calder Cup playoffs; defeated Lowell in conference semifinals of Calder Cup playoffs; lost to Hartford in conference finals of Calder Cup playoffs.
01-02—Lost to Toronto in Eastern Conference quarterfinals.
02-03—Lost to Ottawa in Eastern Conference quarterfinals.
03-04—Replace Paul Maurice as head coach (December 23).
05-06—Defeated Montreal Canadiens, 4-2, in Eastern Conference quarterfinals; defeated New Jersey Devils, 4-1, in Eastern Conference semifinals; defeated Buffalo, 4-3, in Eastern Conference finals; defeated Edmonton, 4-3, in Stanley Cup finals.

LEMAIRE, JACQUES — WILD

PERSONAL: Born September 7, 1945, in Ville LaSalle, Que. ... Shoots left. ... Uncle of Manny Fernandez, G, Minnesota Wild. ... Name pronounced luh-MAIR.
STATISTICAL PLATEAUS: Three-goal games: 1977-78 (1), 1978-79 (2). Total: 3.

		REGULAR SEASON								PLAYOFFS				
Season Team	League	GP	G	A	Pts.	PIM	+/-	PP	SH	GP	G	A	Pts.	PIM
62-63—Lachine	QJHL	42	41	63	104	...	...	...	...	—	—	—	—	—
63-64—Montreal Jr. Can.	OHA Jr. A	42	25	30	55	...	...	...	...	—	—	—	—	—
64-65—Montreal Jr. Can.	OHA Jr. A	56	25	47	72	...	...	...	...	—	—	—	—	—
—Quebec	AHL	1	0	0	0	0	...	...	...	—	—	—	—	—
65-66—Montreal Jr. Can.	OHA Jr. A	48	41	52	93	69	...	...	...	—	—	—	—	—
66-67—Houston	CPHL	69	19	30	49	19	...	...	...	6	0	1	1	0

Season Team	League	REGULAR SEASON GP	G	A	Pts.	PIM	+/-	PP	SH	PLAYOFFS GP	G	A	Pts.	PIM
67-68—Montreal	NHL	69	22	20	42	16	15	3	1	13	7	6	13	6
68-69—Montreal	NHL	75	29	34	63	29	31	5	0	14	4	2	6	6
69-70—Montreal	NHL	69	32	28	60	16	19	13	0	—	—	—	—	—
70-71—Montreal	NHL	78	28	28	56	18	0	6	0	20	9	10	19	17
71-72—Montreal	NHL	77	32	49	81	26	37	8	0	6	2	1	3	2
72-73—Montreal	NHL	77	44	51	95	16	59	9	0	17	7	13	20	2
73-74—Montreal	NHL	66	29	38	67	10	4	10	0	6	0	4	4	2
74-75—Montreal	NHL	80	36	56	92	20	25	12	0	11	5	7	12	4
75-76—Montreal	NHL	61	20	32	52	20	26	6	0	13	3	3	6	2
76-77—Montreal	NHL	75	34	41	75	22	70	5	2	14	7	12	19	6
77-78—Montreal	NHL	75	36	61	97	14	54	6	0	15	6	8	14	10
78-79—Montreal	NHL	50	24	31	55	10	9	6	1	16	11	12	23	6
NHL Totals (12 years)		852	366	469	835	217	349	89	4	145	61	78	139	63

HEAD COACHING RECORD

BACKGROUND: Assistant coach, University of Plattsburgh (1981-82). ... Assistant coach, Montreal Canadiens (October 1982-February 1983). ... Interim coach, Montreal Canadiens (1984) ... Assistant to managing director/director of player personnel, Canadiens (1985-88). ... Assistant to managing director of Verdun Canadiens (1988-89). ... Assistant to managing director, Canadiens (1989-91). ... Assistant to managing director of Fredericton Canadiens (1991-93). ... Served as interim coach of Montreal Canadiens while Jacques Demers was hospitalized with chest pains (March 10-11, 1993; team went 1-1). ... Coach, New Jersey Devils (1993-98) ... Consultant to general manager, Canadiens (1998-2000). ... Named head coach of Minnesota Wild (June 29, 2000). ... Fined $10,000 as result of RW Kyle Wanvig instigating an altercation with Pittsburgh D Brooks Orpik (December 8, 2005).

Season Team	League	REGULAR SEASON W	L	T	OL	Pct.	Finish	PLAYOFFS W	L	Pct.
79-80—Sierre Swiss	Switzerland	...	...	...	...	...	Record unavailable.	—	—	—
80-81—Sierre Swiss	Switzerland	...	...	...	...	...	Record unavailable.	—	—	—
82-83—Longueuil	QMJHL	37	29	4	...	.557	3rd/LeBel Division	8	7	.533
83-84—Montreal	NHL	7	10	0	...	.412	4th/Adams Division	9	6	.600
84-85—Montreal	NHL	41	27	12	...	.588	1st/Adams Division	6	6	.500
93-94—New Jersey	NHL	47	25	12	...	.631	2nd/Atlantic Division	11	9	.550
94-95—New Jersey	NHL	22	18	8	...	.542	2nd/Atlantic Division	16	4	.800
95-96—New Jersey	NHL	37	33	12	...	.524	5th/Atlantic Division	—	—	—
96-97—New Jersey	NHL	45	23	14	...	.634	1st/Atlantic Division	5	5	.500
97-98—New Jersey	NHL	48	23	11	...	.652	1st/Atlantic Division	2	4	.333
00-01—Minnesota	NHL	25	39	13	5	.384	5th/Northwest Division	—	—	—
01-02—Minnesota	NHL	26	35	12	9	.390	5th/Northwest Division	—	—	—
02-03—Minnesota	NHL	42	29	10	1	.573	3rd/Northwest Division	8	10	.444
03-04—Minnesota	NHL	30	29	20	3	.488	5th/Northwest Division	—	—	—
05-06—Minnesota	NHL	38	36	...	8	.463	5th/Northwest Division	—	—	—
NHL Totals (12 years)		408	327	124	26	.531	**NHL Totals (7 years)**	57	44	.564

NOTES:

82-83—Defeated Chicoutimi in President Cup quarterfinals; defeated Laval in President Cup semifinals; lost to Verdun in President Cup finals.
83-84—Defeated Boston in Adams Division semifinals; defeated Quebec in Adams Division finals; lost to New York Islanders in Wales Conference finals.
84-85—Defeated Boston in Adams Division semifinals; lost to Quebec in Adams Division finals.
93-94—Defeated Buffalo in Eastern Conference quarterfinals; defeated Boston in Eastern Conference semifinals; lost to New York Rangers in Eastern Conference finals.
94-95—Defeated Boston in Eastern Conference quarterfinals; defeated Pittsburgh in Eastern Conference semifinals; defeated Philadelphia in Eastern Conference finals; defeated Detroit in Stanley Cup finals.
96-97—Defeated Montreal in Eastern Conference quarterfinals; lost to New York Rangers in Eastern Conference semifinals.
97-98—Lost to Ottawa in Eastern Conference quarterfinals.
02-03—Defeated Colorado in Western Conference quarterfinals; defeated Vancouver in Western Conference semifinals; lost to Anaheim in Western Conference finals.

LEWIS, DAVE — BRUINS

PERSONAL: Born July 3, 1953, in Kindersley, Sask. ... 6-2/205. ... Shoots left.

TRANSACTIONS/CAREER NOTES: Selected by New York Islanders in third round (second Islanders pick, 33rd overall) of 1973 NHL entry draft. ... Traded by Islanders to with RW Billy Harris Los Angeles Kings for C Butch Goring (March 10, 1980). ... Traded by Kings to Minnesota North Stars for C Steve Christoff and D Fred Barrett (October 3, 1983). ... Traded by North Stars to New Jersey Devils for LW Brent Ashton (October 3, 1983). ... Released by Devils (July 1, 1986). ... Signed as free agent by Detroit Red Wings (July 27, 1986).

Season Team	League	REGULAR SEASON GP	G	A	Pts.	PIM	+/-	PP	SH	PLAYOFFS GP	G	A	Pts.	PIM
71-72—Saskatoon	WCJHL	52	2	9	11	68	...	...	...	8	2	3	5	4
72-73—Saskatoon	WCJHL	67	10	35	45	89	...	...	...	16	3	12	15	44
73-74—New York Islanders	NHL	66	2	15	17	58	-7	1	1	—	—	—	—	—
74-75—New York Islanders	NHL	78	5	14	19	98	8	0	0	17	0	1	1	28
75-76—New York Islanders	NHL	73	0	19	19	54	29	0	0	13	0	1	1	44
76-77—New York Islanders	NHL	79	4	24	28	44	29	0	1	12	1	6	7	4
77-78—New York Islanders	NHL	77	3	11	14	58	32	0	1	7	0	1	1	11
78-79—New York Islanders	NHL	79	5	18	23	43	43	0	0	10	0	0	0	4
79-80—New York Islanders	NHL	62	5	16	21	54	10	0	0	—	—	—	—	—
—Los Angeles	NHL	11	1	1	2	12	3	0	0	4	0	1	1	2
80-81—Los Angeles	NHL	67	1	12	13	98	25	0	0	4	0	2	2	4
81-82—Los Angeles	NHL	64	1	13	14	75	-19	0	0	10	0	4	4	36
82-83—Los Angeles	NHL	79	2	10	12	53	-22	0	0	—	—	—	—	—
83-84—New Jersey	NHL	66	2	5	7	63	-19	...	...	—	—	—	—	—
84-85—New Jersey	NHL	74	3	9	12	78	-29	0	0	—	—	—	—	—
85-86—New Jersey	NHL	69	0	15	15	81	0	0	0	—	—	—	—	—
86-87—Detroit	NHL	58	2	5	7	66	12	0	0	14	0	4	4	10
87-88—Detroit	NHL	6	0	0	0	18	-3	0	0	—	—	—	—	—
NHL Totals (15 years)		1008	36	187	223	953	92	1	3	91	1	20	21	143

HEAD COACHING RECORD

BACKGROUND: Associate coach, Detroit Red Wings (1988-2002). ... Head coach of the Detroit Red Wings (2002-05). ... Scout, Detroit Red Wings (2005-06). ... Named coach of Boston Bruins (June 30, 2006).

		REGULAR SEASON						PLAYOFFS		
Season Team	**League**	**W**	**L**	**T**	**OL**	**Pct.**	**Finish**	**W**	**L**	**Pct.**
02-03—Detroit	NHL	48	20	10	4	.646	1st/Central Division	0	4	.000
03-04—Detroit	NHL	48	21	11	2	.652	1st/Central Division	6	6	.500
NHL Totals (2 years)		96	41	21	6	.649	**NHL Totals (2 years)**	6	10	.375

NOTES:

02-03—Lost to Anaheim in Western Conference finals.
03-04—Defeated Nashville, 4-2, in Western Conference quarterfinals; lost to Calgary, 4-2, in Western Conference semifinals.

MACTAVISH, CRAIG — OILERS

PERSONAL: Born August 15, 1958, in London, Ont. ... 6-1/195. ... Shoots left.
TRANSACTIONS/CAREER NOTES: Selected by Boston Bruins in ninth round (ninth Bruins pick, 153rd overall) of NHL draft (June 15, 1978). ... Signed as free agent by Edmonton Oilers (February 1, 1985). ... Strained lower back (January 1993); missed one game. ... Suffered concussion (March 10, 1993); missed one game. ... Strained wrist (October 18, 1993); missed one game. ... Reinjured wrist (December 7, 1993); missed one game. ... Suffered whiplash (December 15, 1993); missed four games. ... Bruised foot (December 30, 1993); missed one game. ... Traded by Oilers to New York Rangers for C Todd Marchant (March 21, 1994). ... Signed as free agent by Philadelphia Flyers (July 6, 1994). ... Injured foot (January 24, 1995); missed one game. ... Bruised foot (April 14, 1995); missed two games. ... Underwent knee surgery (September 25, 1995); missed first eight games of season. ... Traded by Flyers to St. Louis Blues for C Dale Hawerchuk (March 15, 1996). ... Announced retirement (April 29, 1997).
STATISTICAL PLATEAUS: Three-goal games: 1985-86 (1), 1990-91 (1). Total: 2.

		REGULAR SEASON								PLAYOFFS				
Season Team	**League**	**GP**	**G**	**A**	**Pts.**	**PIM**	**+/-**	**PP**	**SH**	**GP**	**G**	**A**	**Pts.**	**PIM**
77-78—University of Lowell	ECAC-II	24	26	19	45	...	...	...	...	—	—	—	—	—
78-79—University of Lowell	ECAC-II	31	36	52	88	...	...	...	...	—	—	—	—	—
79-80—Binghamton	AHL	34	17	15	32	20	...	...	...	—	—	—	—	—
—Boston	NHL	46	11	17	28	8	...	0	0	10	2	3	5	7
80-81—Boston	NHL	24	3	5	8	13	-1	0	0	—	—	—	—	—
—Springfield	AHL	53	19	24	43	89	...	...	...	7	5	4	9	8
81-82—Erie	AHL	72	23	32	55	37	...	...	...	—	—	—	—	—
—Boston	NHL	2	0	1	1	0	...	...	...	—	—	—	—	—
82-83—Boston	NHL	75	10	20	30	18	15	0	0	17	3	1	4	18
83-84—Boston	NHL	70	20	23	43	35	9	7	0	1	0	0	0	0
84-85—Boston	NHL	Did not play												
85-86—Edmonton	NHL	74	23	24	47	70	17	4	1	10	4	4	8	11
86-87—Edmonton	NHL	79	20	19	39	55	9	1	4	21	1	9	10	16
87-88—Edmonton	NHL	80	15	17	32	47	-3	0	3	19	0	1	1	31
88-89—Edmonton	NHL	80	21	31	52	55	10	2	4	7	0	1	1	8
89-90—Edmonton	NHL	80	21	22	43	89	13	1	6	22	2	6	8	29
90-91—Edmonton	NHL	80	17	15	32	76	-1	2	6	18	3	3	6	20
91-92—Edmonton	NHL	80	12	18	30	98	-1	0	2	16	3	0	3	28
92-93—Edmonton	NHL	82	10	20	30	110	-16	0	3	—	—	—	—	—
93-94—Edmonton	NHL	66	16	10	26	80	-20	0	0	—	—	—	—	—
—New York Rangers	NHL	12	4	2	6	11	6	1	0	23	1	4	5	22
94-95—Philadelphia	NHL	45	3	9	12	23	2	0	0	15	1	4	5	20
95-96—Philadelphia	NHL	55	5	8	13	62	-3	0	0	—	—	—	—	—
—St. Louis	NHL	13	0	1	1	8	-6	0	0	13	0	2	2	6
96-97—St. Louis	NHL	50	2	5	7	33	-12	0	0	1	0	0	0	2
NHL Totals (18 years)		1093	213	267	480	891	18	18	29	193	20	38	58	218

HEAD COACHING RECORD

BACKGROUND: Assistant coach, New York Rangers (1997-98 and 1998-99). ... Assistant coach, Edmonton Oilers (1999-2000). ... Named coach of the Oilers (June 22, 2000).

		REGULAR SEASON						PLAYOFFS		
Season Team	**League**	**W**	**L**	**T**	**OL**	**Pct.**	**Finish**	**W**	**L**	**Pct.**
00-01—Edmonton	NHL	39	28	12	3	.549	2nd/Northwest Division	2	4	.333
01-02—Edmonton	NHL	38	28	12	4	.537	3rd/Northwest Division	—	—	—
02-03—Edmonton	NHL	36	26	11	9	.506	4th/Northwest Division	2	4	.333
03-04—Edmonton	NHL	36	29	12	5	.512	4th/Northwest Division	—	—	—
05-06—Edmonton	NHL	41	28	...	13	.500	3rd/Northwest Division	15	9	.625
NHL Totals (5 years)		190	139	47	34	.521	**NHL Totals (3 years)**	19	17	.528

NOTES:

00-01—Lost to Dallas in Western Conference quarterfinals.
02-03—Lost to Dallas in Western Conference quarterfinals.
05-06—Defeated Detroit Red Wings, 4-2, in Western Conference quarterfinals; defeated San Jose Sharks, 4-2, in Western Conference semifinals; defeated Anaheim Mighty Ducks, 4-1, in Western Conference finals; lost to Carolina Hurricanes, 4-3, in Stanley Cup finals

MARTIN, JACQUES — PANTHERS

PERSONAL: Born October 1, 1952, in Rockland, Ont.

HEAD COACHING RECORD

BACKGROUND: Coach, St. Louis Blues (1986-87 through 1987-88). ... Assistant coach, Chicago Blackhawks (1988-89 through 1989-90). ... Assistant coach, Quebec Nordiques (1990-91 through 1992-93 and 1994-95). ... Assistant coach, Colorado Avalanche (1995 through January

24, 1996). ... Coach, Ottawa Senators (January 24, 1996 through April 22, 2004). ... Associate coach, Canadian Olympic team (2002). ... Named coach of Florida Panthers (May 27, 2004).

		REGULAR SEASON						PLAYOFFS		
Season Team	League	W	L	T	OL	Pct.	Finish	W	L	Pct.
85-86—Guelph	OHL	41	23	2	...	.636	2nd/Emms Division	15	3	.833
86-87—St. Louis	NHL	32	33	15	...	.494	1st/Norris Division	2	4	.333
87-88—St. Louis	NHL	34	38	8	...	.475	2nd/Norris Division	5	5	.500
93-94—Cornwall	AHL	33	36	11	...	.481	T3rd/Southern Division	4	2	.667
95-96—Ottawa	NHL	10	24	4	...	.316	6th/Northeast Division	—	—	—
96-97—Ottawa	NHL	31	36	15	...	.470	T3rd/Northeast Division	3	4	.429
97-98—Ottawa	NHL	34	33	15	...	.506	5th/Northeast Division	5	6	.455
98-99—Ottawa	NHL	44	23	15	...	.628	1st/Northeast Division	0	4	.000
99-00—Ottawa	NHL	41	28	11	2	.567	2nd/Northeast Division	2	4	.333
00-01—Ottawa	NHL	48	21	9	4	.640	1st/Northeast Division	0	4	.000
01-02—Ottawa	NHL	38	26	9	7	.531	3rd/Northwest Division	7	5	.583
02-03—Ottawa	NHL	52	21	8	1	.683	1st/Northeast Division	11	7	.611
03-04—Ottawa	NHL	43	23	10	6	.585	3rd/Northeast Division	3	4	.429
05-06—Florida	NHL	37	34	...	11	.451	4th/Southeast Division	—	—	—
NHL Totals (12 years)		444	340	119	31	.539	**NHL Totals (10 years)**	38	47	.447

NOTES:

85-86—Defeated Sudbury in OHL quarterfinals; defeated Windsor in OHL semifinals; defeated Belleville in J. Ross Robertson Cup finals.
86-87—Lost to Toronto in Norris Division semifinals.
87-88—Defeated Chicago in Norris Division semifinals; lost to Detroit in Norris Division finals.
93-94—Defeated Hamilton in quarterfinals of Calder Cup playoffs; defeated Hershey in division finals of Calder Cup playoffs; lost to Moncton in semifinals of Calder Cup playoffs.
95-96—Replaced Rick Bowness as head coach (January 24).
96-97—Lost to Buffalo in Eastern Conference quarterfinals.
97-98—Defeated New Jersey in Eastern Conference quarterfinals; lost to Washington in Eastern Conference semifinals.
98-99—Lost to Buffalo in Eastern Conference quarterfinals.
99-00—Lost to Toronto in Eastern Conference quarterfinals.
00-01—Lost to Toronto in Eastern Conference quarterfinals.
01-02—Defeated Philadelphia in Eastern Conference quarterfinals; lost to Toronto in Eastern Conference semifinals.
02-03—Defeated New York Islanders in Eastern Conference quarterfinals; defeated Philadelphia in Eastern Conference semifinals; lost to New Jersey in Eastern Conference finals.
03-04—Lost to Toronto in Eastern Conference quarterfinals.

MAURICE, PAUL — MAPLE LEAFS

PERSONAL: Born January 30, 1967, in Sault Ste. Marie, Ont.

HEAD COACHING RECORD

BACKGROUND: Assistant coach, Hartford Whalers (June 9-November 6, 1995). ... Whalers franchise moved to North Carolina and renamed Carolina Hurricanes for 1997-98 season; NHL approved move on June 25, 1997. ... Fired by Hurricanes (December 15, 2003) ... Coach, Toronto Marlies of AHL (2005-06). ... Named head coach of Toronto Maple Leafs (May 12, 2006).

		REGULAR SEASON						PLAYOFFS		
Season Team	League	W	L	T	OL	Pct.	Finish	W	L	Pct.
93-94—Detroit	OHL	42	20	4	...	.667	1st/West Division	11	6	.647
94-95—Detroit	OHL	44	18	4	...	.697	1st/West Division	16	5	.762
95-96—Hartford	NHL	29	33	8	...	.471	4th/Northeast Division	—	—	—
96-97—Hartford	NHL	32	39	11	...	.457	5th/Northeast Division	—	—	—
97-98—Carolina	NHL	33	41	8	...	.451	6th/Northeast Division	—	—	—
98-99—Carolina	NHL	34	30	18	...	.524	1st/Southeast Division	2	4	.333
99-00—Carolina	NHL	37	35	10	0	.512	3rd/Southeast Division	—	—	—
00-01—Carolina	NHL	38	32	9	3	.518	2nd/Southeast Division	2	4	.333
01-02—Carolina	NHL	35	26	16	5	.524	1st/Southeast Division	13	9	.591
02-03—Carolina	NHL	22	43	11	6	.335	5th/Southeast Division	—	—	—
03-04—Carolina	NHL	8	12	8	2	.400		—	—	—
05-06—Toronto	AHL	41	29	4	6	.538	4th/North Division	1	4	.200
NHL Totals (9 years)		268	291	99	16	.464	**NHL Totals (3 years)**	17	17	.500

NOTES:

93-94—Defeated Owen Sound in quarterfinals of OHL playoffs; defeated Sault Ste. Marie in semifinals of OHL playoffs; lost to North Bay in OHL finals.
94-95—Defeated London in first round of OHL playoffs; defeated Peterborough in second round of OHL playoffs; defeated Sudbury in third round of OHL playoffs; defeated Guelph in J. Ross Robertson Cup finals.
95-96—Replaced Paul Homgren as head coach (November 6) with club in third place.
98-99—Lost to Boston in Eastern Conference quarterfinals.
00-01—Lost to New Jersey in Eastern Conference quarterfinals.
01-02—Defeated New Jersey in Eastern Conference quarterfinals; defeated Montreal in Eastern Conference semifinals; defeated Toronto in Eastern Conference finals; lost to Detroit in Stanley Cup finals.
03-04—Replaced as head coach by Peter Laviolette (December 15).
05-06—Lost in first round of AHL playoffs.

MURRAY, BRYAN — SENATORS

PERSONAL: Born December 5, 1942, in Shawville, Que. ... Brother of Terry Murray, D with four NHL teams (1972-73 through 1981-82) and head coach of three NHL teams (1989-90 through 1996-97 and 1998-99 through December 10, 2000).

HEAD COACHING RECORD

BACKGROUND: Coach, Washington Capitals, 1981-1990). ... General manager, Detroit Red Wings (1990-94). ... Vice president and general manager, Florida Panthers (1994-95 through December 28, 2000). ... Coach, Anaheim Mighty Ducks (2001-02). ... General manager, Anaheim Mighty Ducks (2002-04). ... Named coach of Ottawa Senators (June 8, 2004). ... Fined $10,000 after D Zdeno Chara instigated an altercation with Kings D Tim Gleason in the last five minutes of play (December 3, 2005).

		REGULAR SEASON						PLAYOFFS		
Season Team	League	W	L	T	OL	Pct.	Finish	W	L	Pct.
78-79—Regina	WHL	18	47	7	...	.299	4th/East Division	—	—	—
79-80—Regina	WHL	47	24	1	...	.660	1st/East Division	14	4	.778
80-81—Hershey	AHL	47	24	9	...	.644	1st/Southern Division	6	4	.600
81-82—Hershey	AHL	6	7	0	...	.462	...	—	—	—
—Washington	NHL	25	28	13	...	.477	5th/Patrick Division	—	—	—
82-83—Washington	NHL	39	25	16	...	.582	3rd/Patrick Division	1	3	.250
83-84—Washington	NHL	48	27	5	...	.631	2nd/Patrick Division	4	4	.500
84-85—Washington	NHL	46	25	9	...	.631	2nd/Patrick Division	2	3	.400
85-86—Washington	NHL	50	23	7	...	.669	2nd/Patrick Division	5	4	.556
86-87—Washington	NHL	38	32	10	...	.538	2nd/Patrick Division	3	4	.429
87-88—Washington	NHL	38	33	9	...	.531	2nd/Patrick Division	7	7	.500
88-89—Washington	NHL	41	29	10	...	.575	1st/Patrick Division	2	4	.333
89-90—Washington	NHL	18	24	4	...	.435	...	—	—	—
90-91—Detroit	NHL	34	38	8	...	.475	3rd/Norris Division	3	4	.429
91-92—Detroit	NHL	43	25	12	...	.613	1st/Norris Division	4	7	.364
92-93—Detroit	NHL	47	28	9	...	.613	2nd/Norris Division	3	4	.429
97-98—Florida	NHL	17	31	11	...	.381	6th/Atlantic Division	—	—	—
01-02—Anaheim	NHL	29	42	8	3	.402	5th/Pacific Division	—	—	—
05-06—Ottawa	NHL	52	21	...	9	.634	1st/Northeast Division	5	5	.500
NHL Totals (15 years)		565	431	131	12	.553	**NHL Totals (11 years)**	39	49	.443

NOTES:

79-80—Defeated Lethbridge in East Division semifianls; eliminated Brandon in East Division round-robin series; defeated Medicine Hat in East Division finals; defeated Victoria in Monsignor Athol Murray Memorial Trophy finals.
80-81—Defeated New Haven in Calder Cup quarterfinals; lost to Adirondack in Calder Cup semifinals.
82-83—Lost to New York Islanders in Patrick Division semifinals.
83-84—Defeated Philadelphia in Patrick Division semifinals; lost to New York Islanders in Patrick Division finals.
84-85—Lost to New York Islanders in Patrick Division semifinals.
85-86—Defeated New York Islanders in Patrick Division semifinals; lost to to New York Rangers in Patrick Division finals.
86-87—Lost to New York Islanders in Patrick Division semifinals.
87-88—Defeated Philadelphia in Patrick Division semifinals; lost to New Jersey in in Patrick Division finals.
88-89—Lost to Philadelphia in Patrick Division semifinals.
89-90—Replaced as head coach by Terry Murray (January 15).
90-91—Lost to St. Louis in Norris Division semifinals.
91-92—Defeated Minnesota in Norris Division semifinals; lost to Chicago in Norris Division finals.
92-93—Lost to Toronto in Norris Division semifinals.
97-98—Replaced Doug Maclean as head coach on an interim basis (November 24).
05-06—Defeated Tampa Bay Lightning, 4-1, in Eastern Conference quarterfinals; lost to Buffalo Sabres, 4-1, in Eastern Conference semifinals.

NOLAN, TED — ISLANDERS

PERSONAL: Born April 7, 1958, in Sault Ste. Marie, Ont. ... 6-0/185. ... Shoots left. ... Father of Brandon Nolan, center, Vancouver Canucks organization.

TRANSACTIONS/CAREER NOTES: Selected by Detroit Red Wings in fifth round (seventh Red Wings pick, 78th overall) of NHL amateur draft (June 15, 1978). ... Injured knee (October 1983). ... Signed as free agent by Buffalo Sabres (March 7, 1985). ... Traded by Sabres to Pittsburgh Penguins for future considerations (September 1985). ... Injured knee (October 1983). ... Injured back (January 25, 1986). ... Signed as free agent by Sabres (August 1986).

		REGULAR SEASON								PLAYOFFS				
Season Team	League	GP	G	A	Pts.	PIM	+/-	PP	SH	GP	G	A	Pts.	PIM
76-77—Sault Ste. Marie	OHA	60	8	16	24	109	...	...	...	9	1	2	3	19
77-78—Sault Ste. Marie	OHA	66	14	30	44	106	...	...	...	13	1	3	4	20
78-79—Kansas City	CHL	73	12	38	50	66	...	...	...	4	1	2	3	0
79-80—Adirondack	AHL	75	16	24	40	106	...	...	...	5	0	1	1	0
80-81—Adirondack	AHL	76	22	28	50	86	...	...	...	18	6	10	16	11
81-82—Adirondack	AHL	39	12	18	30	81	...	...	...	—	—	—	—	—
—Detroit	NHL	41	4	13	17	45	...	...	...	—	—	—	—	—
82-83—Adirondack	AHL	78	24	40	64	103	...	...	...	6	2	5	7	14
83-84—Detroit	NHL	19	1	2	3	26	...	...	...	—	—	—	—	—
—Adirondack	AHL	31	10	16	26	76	...	...	...	7	2	3	5	18
84-85—Rochester	AHL	65	28	34	62	152	...	...	...	5	4	0	4	18
85-86—Pittsburgh	NHL	18	1	1	2	34	...	...	...	—	—	—	—	—
—Baltimore	AHL	10	4	4	8	19	...	...	...	—	—	—	—	—
NHL Totals (3 years)		78	6	16	22	105	0	0	0					

HEAD COACHING RECORD

BACKGROUND: Assistant coach, Hartford Whalers (June 29, 1994 through July 17, 1995). ... Coach, Buffalo Sabres (1995-97). ... Coach, Moncton of QMJHL (2005-06). ... Named coach of New York Islanders (June 9, 2006).

		REGULAR SEASON						PLAYOFFS		
Season Team	League	W	L	T	OL	Pct.	Finish	W	L	Pct.
88-89—Sault Ste. Marie	OHL	21	43	2	...	.333	8th/Emms Division	—	—	—
89-90—Sault Ste. Marie	OHL	18	42	6	...	.318	7th/Emms Division	—	—	—
90-91—Sault Ste. Marie	OHL	42	21	3	...	.659	1st/Emms Division	12	2	.857

Season Team	League	W	L	T	OL	Pct.	Finish	W	L	Pct.
		REGULAR SEASON						PLAYOFFS		
91-92—Sault Ste. Marie	OHL	41	19	6	...	.667	1st/Emms Division	12	7	.632
92-93—Sault Ste. Marie	OHL	38	23	5	...	.614	1st/Emms Division	9	5	.643
93-94—Sault Ste. Marie	OHL	35	24	7	...	.583	2nd/Emms Division	10	4	.714
95-96—Buffalo	NHL	33	42	7	...	.445	5th/Northeast Division	—	—	—
96-97—Buffalo	NHL	40	30	12	...	.561	1st/Northeast Division	5	7	.417
05-06—Moncton	QMJHL	52	15	3	0	.743	1st/Eastern Division	16	5	.762
NHL Totals (2 years)		73	72	19	...	.503	**NHL Totals (1 year)**	5	7	.417

NOTES:

88-89—Replaced Don Boyd as Greyhounds coach.
90-91—Defeated Hamilton in OHL quarterfinals; defeated Niagara Falls in semifinals; defeated Oshawa in J. Ross Roberston Cup finals.
91-92—Defeated Kitchener in OHL semifinals; defeated Niagara Falls in finals; defeated North Bay in J. Ross Roberston Cup finals.
92-93—Defeated Owen Sound in OHL semifinals; defeated Detroit in semifinals; lost to Peterborough in J. Ross Roberston Cup finals.
93-94—Defeated Windsor in OHL quarterfinals; defeated Guelph in semifinals; lost to Detroit in J. Ross Roberston Cup finals.
96-97—Defeated Ottawa, 4-3, in Eastern Conference quarterfinals; lost to Philadelphia, 4-1, in Eastern Conference semifinals.
05-06—Defeated Victoriaville, 4-1, in Eastern Division first round; defeated Halifax, 4-1, in Eastern quarterfinals; defeated Gatineau, 4-1, in semifinals; defeated Quebec, 4-2, in President's Cup final.

PLAYFAIR, JIM — FLAMES

PERSONAL: Born May 22, 1964, in Vanderhoof, B.C. ... 6-4/200. ... Shoots left. ... Brother of Larry Playfair, defenseman with Buffalo Sabres (1978-79 through 1985-86, 1988-89 and 1989-90) and Los Angeles Kings (1986-86 through 1988-89).

TRANSACTIONS/CAREER NOTES: Selected by Edmonton Oilers in first round (first Oilers pick, 20th overall) of NHL entry draft (June 9, 1982). ... Suffered severe groin pull (November 1984). ... Bruised liver (February 1987). ... Signed as free agent by Chicago Blackhawks (July 31, 1987). ... Bruised left shoulder (October 18, 1988). ... Strained back (November 1988). ... Suffered sore back (March 1990). ... Injured back (December 20, 1990); missed 10 weeks. ... Suffered detached retina (March 3, 1991); missed remainder of season. ... Fired as assistant coach of Indianapolis Ice (March 16, 1993).

Season Team	League	GP	G	A	Pts.	PIM	+/-	PP	SH	GP	G	A	Pts.	PIM
		REGULAR SEASON								PLAYOFFS				
80-81—Fort Saskatchewan	AJHL	31	2	17	19	105	...	...	...	—	—	—	—	—
81-82—Portland	WHL	70	4	13	17	121	...	...	...	15	1	2	3	21
82-83—Portland	WHL	63	8	27	35	218	...	...	...	14	0	5	5	16
83-84—Portland	WHL	16	5	6	11	38	...	...	...	—	—	—	—	—
—Calgary	WHL	44	6	9	15	96	...	...	...	4	0	1	1	2
—Edmonton	NHL	2	1	1	2	2	...	...	...	—	—	—	—	—
84-85—Nova Scotia	AHL	41	0	4	4	107	...	...	...	—	—	—	—	—
85-86—Nova Scotia	AHL	73	2	12	14	160	...	...	...	—	—	—	—	—
86-87—Nova Scotia	AHL	60	1	21	22	82	...	...	...	—	—	—	—	—
87-88—Saginaw	IHL	50	5	21	26	133	...	...	...	—	—	—	—	—
—Chicago	NHL	12	1	3	4	21	...	...	...	—	—	—	—	—
88-89—Saginaw	IHL	23	3	6	9	73	...	...	...	6	0	2	2	20
—Chicago	NHL	7	0	0	0	28	...	...	...	—	—	—	—	—
89-90—Indianapolis	IHL	67	7	24	31	137	...	...	...	14	1	5	6	24
90-91—Indianapolis	IHL	23	3	4	7	31	...	...	...	—	—	—	—	—
91-92—Indianapolis	IHL	23	1	1	2	53	...	...	...	—	—	—	—	—
NHL Totals (3 years)		21	2	4	6	51	...	...	...					

HEAD COACHING RECORD

BACKGROUND: Assistant coach, Michigan K-Wings of IHL (1996-2000). ... Assistant coach, Calgary Flames (2003-06). ... Named head coach of Flames (July 12, 2006).

Season Team	League	W	L	T	OL	Pct.	Finish	W	L	Pct.
		REGULAR SEASON						PLAYOFFS		
93-94—Dayton	ECHL	29	31	...	8	.485	5th/North Division	1	2	.333
94-95—Dayton	ECHL	42	17	...	9	.684	2nd/North Division	5	4	.556
95-96—Dayton	ECHL	35	28	...	7	.550	5th/North Division	0	3	.000
00-01—Saint John	AHL	44	24	7	5	.625	1st/Canadian Division	15	4	.789
01-02—Saint John	AHL	29	34	13	4	.469	5th/Canadian Division	—	—	—
02-03—Saint John	AHL	10	19	2	1	.359		—	—	—

NOTES:

93-94—Lost in first round of playoffs.
94-95—Lost in second round of playoffs.
95-96—Lost in first round of playoffs.
00-01—Defeated Portland in first round of playoffs; defeated Quebec in second round; defeated Providence in semifinals; defeated Wilkes-Barre Scranton in finals.
02-03—Replaced by Ron Wilson as head coach.

QUENNEVILLE, JOEL — AVALANCHE

PERSONAL: Born September 15, 1958, in Windsor, Ont. ... 6-1/200. ... Shoots left. ... Played defense.

TRANSACTIONS/CAREER NOTES: Selected by Toronto Maple Leafs in second round (first Maple Leafs pick, 21st overall) of NHL amateur draft (June 15, 1978). ... Traded by Maple Leafs with RW Lanny McDonald to Colorado Rockies for RW Wilf Paiement and LW Pat Hickey (December 1979). ... Injured ribcage (March 1980). ... Underwent surgery to repair torn ligaments in ring finger of left hand (March 1980). ... Sprained ankle, twisted knee and suffered facial lacerations (January 4, 1982). ... Rockies franchise moved to New Jersey and became the Devils (June 30, 1982). ... Traded by Devils with C Steve Tambellini to Calgary Flames for C Mel Bridgman and D Phil Russell (July 1983). ... Traded by Flames with D Richie Dunn to Hartford Whalers for D Mickey Volcan and third-round pick in 1984 draft (August 1983). ... Fractured right shoulder (December 18, 1986); missed 42 games. ... Separated left shoulder (January 19, 1989); missed nine games. ... Traded by Whalers to Washington Capitals for cash (October 3, 1990). ... Signed as free agent by Maple Leafs (July 30, 1991).

Season Team	League	REGULAR SEASON GP	G	A	Pts.	PIM	+/-	PP	SH	PLAYOFFS GP	G	A	Pts.	PIM
75-76—Windsor	OHA Mj. Jr	66	15	33	48	61	...	...	...	—	—	—	—	—
76-77—Windsor	OMJHL	65	19	59	78	169	...	...	...	9	6	5	11	112
77-78—Windsor	OMJHL	66	27	76	103	114	...	...	...	6	2	3	5	17
78-79—Toronto	NHL	61	2	9	11	60	7	0	0	6	0	1	1	4
—New Brunswick	AHL	16	1	10	11	10	...	...	...	—	—	—	—	—
79-80—Toronto	NHL	32	1	4	5	24	-2	1	0	—	—	—	—	—
—Colorado Rockies	NHL	35	5	7	12	26	-21	1	0	—	—	—	—	—
80-81—Colorado Rockies	NHL	71	10	24	34	86	-24	3	0	—	—	—	—	—
81-82—Colorado Rockies	NHL	64	5	10	15	55	-29	0	0	—	—	—	—	—
82-83—New Jersey	NHL	74	5	12	17	46	-13	0	1	—	—	—	—	—
83-84—Hartford	NHL	80	5	8	13	95	-11	0	2	—	—	—	—	—
84-85—Hartford	NHL	79	6	16	22	96	-15	0	0	—	—	—	—	—
85-86—Hartford	NHL	71	5	20	25	83	20	1	0	10	0	2	2	12
86-87—Hartford	NHL	37	3	7	10	24	8	0	1	6	0	0	0	0
87-88—Hartford	NHL	77	1	8	9	44	-13	0	0	6	0	2	2	2
88-89—Hartford	NHL	69	4	7	11	32	3	0	0	4	0	3	3	4
89-90—Hartford	NHL	44	1	4	5	34	9	0	0	—	—	—	—	—
90-91—Washington	NHL	9	1	0	1	0	-8	0	0	—	—	—	—	—
—Baltimore	AHL	59	6	13	19	58	...	...	...	6	1	1	2	6
91-92—St. John's	AHL	73	7	23	30	58	...	...	...	16	0	1	1	10
NHL Totals (13 years)		803	54	136	190	705	-89	6	4	32	0	8	8	22

HEAD COACHING RECORD

BACKGROUND: Player/coach, St. John's of the AHL (1991-92). ... Assistant coach, St. John's (1992-93). ... Assistant coach, Quebec Nordiques (1994-95). ... Quebec franchise moved in summer 1995 to Denver and renamed Colorado Avalanche. ... Assistant coach, Colorado Avalanche (1995-96 through January 5, 1997). ... Coach, St. Louis Blues (January 7, 1997 through February 24, 2004). ... Named coach of Colorado Avalanche (July 7, 2004).

Season Team	League	REGULAR SEASON W	L	T	OL	Pct.	Finish	PLAYOFFS W	L	Pct.
93-94—Springfield	AHL	29	38	13	...	.444	4th/Northern Division	2	4	.333
96-97—St. Louis	NHL	18	15	7	...	.538	4th/Central Division	2	4	.333
97-98—St. Louis	NHL	45	29	8	...	.598	3rd/Central Division	6	4	.600
98-99—St. Louis	NHL	37	32	13	...	.530	2nd/Central Division	6	7	.462
99-00—St. Louis	NHL	51	19	11	1	.689	1st/Central Division	3	4	.429
00-01—St. Louis	NHL	43	22	12	5	.598	2nd/Central Division	9	6	.600
01-02—St. Louis	NHL	43	27	8	4	.573	2nd/Central Division	5	5	.500
02-03—St. Louis	NHL	41	24	11	6	.567	2nd/Central Division	3	4	.429
03-04—St. Louis	NHL	29	23	7	2	.534	...	—	—	—
05-06—Colorado	NHL	43	30	...	9	.524	2nd/Northwest Division	4	5	.444
NHL Totals (9 years)		350	221	77	27	.576	**NHL Totals (8 years)**	38	39	.494

NOTES:

93-94—Lost to Adirondack in division semifinals of Calder Cup playoffs.
96-97—Replaced Mike Keenan as coach (January 6); lost to Detroit in Western Conference quarterfinals.
97-98—Defeated Los Angeles in Western Conference quarterfinals; lost to Detroit in Western Conference semifinals.
98-99—Defeated Phoenix in Western Conference quarterfinals; lost to Dallas in Western Conference semifinals.
99-00—Lost to San Jose in Western Conference quarterfinals.
00-01—Defeated San Jose in Western Conference quarterfinals; defeated Dallas in Western Conference semifinals; lost to Colorado in Western Conference finals.
01-02—Defeated Chicago in Western Conference quarterfinals; lost to Detroit in Western Conference semifinals.
02-03—Lost to Vancouver in Western Conference quarterfinals.
03-04—Replaced by Mike Kitchen (February 24).
05-06—Defeated Dallas Stars, 4-1, in Western Conference quarterfinals; lost to Anaheim Mighty Ducks, 4-0, in Western Conference semifinals.

RENNEY, TOM — RANGERS

PERSONAL: Born March 1, 1955, in Cranbrook, B.C.

HEAD COACHING RECORD

BACKGROUND: Assistant coach, Canadian national team (1992). ... Coach, Canadian national team (1993-94 through 1995-96). ... Coach, Vancouver Canucks (June 1996 through November 1997). ... Coach, Canadian national team (1999-2000). ... Assistant coach, New York Rangers (July 21, 2003 through February 24, 2004). ... Named interim coach, Rangers (February 25, 2004). ... Named coach, Rangers (July 6, 2004).

Season Team	League	REGULAR SEASON W	L	T	OL	Pct.	Finish	PLAYOFFS W	L	Pct.
90-91—Kamloops	WHL	50	20	2	...	.708	1st/West Division	5	7	.417
91-92—Kamloops	WHL	51	17	4	...	.736	1st/West Division	12	5	.706
96-97—Vancouver	NHL	35	40	7	...	.470	4th/Pacific Division	—	—	—
97-98—Vancouver	NHL	4	13	2	...	.263	...	—	—	—
03-04—New York Rangers	NHL	5	11	0	4	.250	4th/Atlantic Division	—	—	—
05-06—New York Rangers	NHL	44	26	...	12	.537	3rd/Atlantic Division	0	4	.000
NHL Totals (4 years)		88	90	9	16	.456	**NHL Totals (1 year)**	0	4	.000

NOTES:

90-91—Defeated Tri-City in West Division semifinals; lost to Spokane in West Division Finals.
91-92—Defeated Tacoma in West Division preliminary round; defeated Seattle in West division finals; defeated Saskatoon in WHL finals.

97-98—Replaced as head coach by Mike Keenan (November 13) with club in seventh place.
03-04—Named interim coach, replacing Glen Sather (February 25, 2004).
05-06—Lost to New Jersey Devils, 4-0, in Eastern Conference quarterfinals.

RUFF, LINDY — SABRES

PERSONAL: Born February 17, 1960, in Warburg, Alta. ... 6-2/202. ... Shoots left.

TRANSACTIONS/CAREER NOTES: Selected by Buffalo Sabres in second round (second Sabres pick, 32nd overall) of NHL entry draft (August 9, 1979). ... Fractured ankle (December 1980). ... Fractured hand (March 1983). ... Injured shoulder (January 14, 1984). ... Separated shoulder (October 26, 1984). ... Fractured left clavicle (March 5, 1986). ... Sprained shoulder (November 1988). ... Traded by Sabres to New York Rangers for fifth-round pick (D Richard Smehlik) in 1990 draft (March 7, 1989). ... Fractured rib (January 23, 1990); missed seven games. ... Fractured nose (March 21, 1990). ... Bruised left thigh (April 1990). ... Signed as free agent by Sabres (September 1991).

		REGULAR SEASON								PLAYOFFS				
Season Team	League	GP	G	A	Pts.	PIM	+/-	PP	SH	GP	G	A	Pts.	PIM
76-77—Taber	AJHL	60	13	33	46	112	...	...	...	—	—	—	—	—
—Lethbridge	WCHL	2	0	2	2	0	...	...	...	—	—	—	—	—
77-78—Lethbridge	WCHL	66	9	24	33	219	...	...	...	8	2	8	10	4
78-79—Lethbridge	WHL	24	9	18	27	108	...	...	...	6	0	1	1	0
79-80—Buffalo	NHL	63	5	14	19	38	-2	1	0	8	1	1	2	19
80-81—Buffalo	NHL	65	8	18	26	121	3	1	0	6	3	1	4	23
81-82—Buffalo	NHL	79	16	32	48	194	1	3	0	4	0	0	0	28
82-83—Buffalo	NHL	60	12	17	29	130	14	2	0	10	4	2	6	47
83-84—Buffalo	NHL	58	14	31	45	101	15	3	0	3	1	0	1	9
84-85—Buffalo	NHL	39	13	11	24	45	-1	2	0	5	2	4	6	15
85-86—Buffalo	NHL	54	20	12	32	158	8	5	1	—	—	—	—	—
86-87—Buffalo	NHL	50	6	14	20	74	-12	0	0	—	—	—	—	—
87-88—Buffalo	NHL	77	2	23	25	179	-9	0	0	6	0	2	2	23
88-89—Buffalo	NHL	63	6	11	17	86	-17	0	0	—	—	—	—	—
—New York Rangers	NHL	13	0	5	5	31	-6	0	0	2	0	0	0	17
89-90—New York Rangers	NHL	56	3	6	9	80	-10	0	0	8	0	3	3	12
90-91—New York Rangers	NHL	14	0	1	1	27	-2	0	0	—	—	—	—	—
91-92—Rochester	AHL	62	10	24	34	110	...	...	...	13	0	4	4	16
92-93—San Diego	IHL	81	10	32	42	100	43	0	1	14	1	6	7	26
NHL Totals (12 years)		691	105	195	300	1264	-18	17	1	52	11	13	24	193

HEAD COACHING RECORD

BACKGROUND: Assistant coach, Florida Panthers (1993-94 through 1996-97). ... Named head coach, Buffalo Sabres (July 21, 1997).

		REGULAR SEASON						PLAYOFFS		
Season Team	League	W	L	T	OL	Pct.	Finish	W	L	Pct.
97-98—Buffalo	NHL	36	29	17	...	.543	3rd/Northeast Division	10	5	.667
98-99—Buffalo	NHL	37	28	17	...	.555	3rd/Northeast Division	14	7	.667
99-00—Buffalo	NHL	35	32	11	4	.494	3rd/Northeast Division	1	4	.200
00-01—Buffalo	NHL	46	30	5	1	.591	2nd/Northeast Division	7	6	.538
01-02—Buffalo	NHL	35	35	11	1	.494	5th/Northeast Division	—	—	—
02-03—Buffalo	NHL	27	37	10	8	.390	5th/Northeast Division	—	—	—
03-04—Buffalo	NHL	37	34	7	4	.494	5th/Northeast Division	—	—	—
05-06—Buffalo	NHL	52	24	...	6	.634	2nd/Northeast Division	11	7	.611
NHL Totals (8 years)		305	249	78	24	.524	**NHL Totals (5 years)**	43	29	.597

NOTES:

97-98—Defeated Philadelphia in Eastern Conference quarterfinals; defeated Montreal in Eastern Conference semifinals; lost to Washington in Eastern Conference finals.
98-99—Defeated Ottawa in Eastern Conference quarterfinals; defeated Boston in Eastern Conference semifinals; defeated Toronto in Eastern Conference finals; lost to Dallas in Stanley Cup finals.
99-00—Lost to Philadelphia in Eastern Conference quarterfinals.
00-01—Defeated Philadelphia in Eastern Conference quarterfinals; lost to Pittsburgh in Eastern Conference semifinals.
05-06—Defeated Philadelphia Flyers, 4-2, in Eastern Conference quarterfinals; defeated Ottawa Senators, 4-1, in Eastern Conference semifinals; lost to Carolina Hurricanes, 4-3, in Eastern Conference finals.

THERRIEN, MICHEL — PENGUINS

PERSONAL: Born November 4, 1963, in Montreal.

HEAD COACHING RECORD

BACKGROUND: Pro scout, Canadiens (2003). ... Hired as coach of Pittsburgh Penguins (December 15, 2005).

		REGULAR SEASON						PLAYOFFS		
Season Team	League	W	L	T	OL	Pct.	Finish	W	L	Pct.
93-94—Laval	QMJHL	49	22	1	...	.688	1st/Robert LeBel Divsion	6	4	.600
94-95—Laval	QMJHL	48	22	2	...	.681	1st/Robert LeBel Division	5	5	.500
95-96—Granby	QMJHL	56	12	2	...	.814	1st/Robert LeBel Division	12	3	.800
96-97—Granby	QMJHL	44	20	6	...	.671	2nd/Robert LeBel Division	1	3	.250
97-98—Fredericton	AHL	33	32	10	...	.507	2nd/Atlantic Division	1	3	.250
98-99—Fredericton	AHL	33	36	6	...	.480	3rd/Atlantic Division	9	6	.600
99-00—Quebec	AHL	37	34	5	4	.494	1st/Atlantic Division	0	3	.000
00-01—Quebec	AHL	12	6	1	0	.658	...	—	—	—
—Montreal	NHL	23	27	6	6	.419	5th/Northeast Division	—	—	—
01-02—Montreal	NHL	36	31	12	3	.512	4th/Northeast Division	6	6	.500
02-03—Montreal	NHL	18	19	4	5	.489	...	—	—	—
03-04—Wilkes/Barre	AHL	34	28	10	8	.537	3rd/East Division	12	12	.500
04-05—Wilkes/Barre	AHL	39	27	7	7	.537	4th/East Division			
05-06—Wilkes/Barre	AHL	21	1	2	1	.880				
—Pittsburgh	NHL	14	29	...	8	.353	5th/Atlantic Division	—	—	—
NHL Totals (4 years)		73	87	18	19	.416	**NHL Totals (1 year)**	6	6	.500

NOTES:

93-94—Defeated Beauport in President Cup semifinals; lost to Chicoutimi in President Cup finals.
94-95—Defeated Shawnigan in President Cup semifinals; lost to Hull in President Cup finals.
95-96—Defeated St. Hyacinthe in President Cup quarterfinals; defeated Chicoutimi in President Cup semifinals; defeated Beauport in President Cup finals.
96-97—Lost to Val d'Or in President Cup quarterfinals.
97-98—Lost to Portland in Calder Cup quarterfinals.
98-99—Defeated St. John's in quarterfinals of Calder Cup playoffs; defeated Saint John in division semifinals of Calder Cup playoffs; lost to Providence in conference finals of Calder Cup playoffs.
99-00—Lost to Providence in quarterfinals of Calder Cup playoffs.
00-01—Replaced Alain Vigneault as head coach (November 20).
01-02—Defeated Boston in Eastern Conference quarterfinals; lost to Carolina in Eastern Conference semifinals.
02-03—Fired January 17, 2003.
03-04—Defeated Bridgeport in first round of Calder Cup playoffs; defeated Philadelphia in divisional semifinals; defeated Hartford in semifinals; lost to Milwaukee in Calder Cup finals.
05-06—Replaced Ed Olczyk as coach of Penguins (December 15).

TIPPETT, DAVE — STARS

PERSONAL: Born August 25, 1961, in Moosomin, Sask. ... 5-10/173. ... Shoots left. ... Played center or left wing.

TRANSACTIONS/CAREER NOTES: Signed as a free agent by Hartford Whalers (February 29, 1984). ... Injured right thumb tendons (October 8, 1989). ... Traded by Whalers to Washington Capitals for sixth-round pick (C Jarret Reid) in 1992 draft (September 30, 1990). ... Separated shoulder (November 28, 1990); missed 11 games. ... Signed as free agent by Pittsburgh Penguins (August 28, 1992). ... Fractured thumb (November 20, 1992); missed six games. ... Signed as free agent by Philadelphia Flyers (August 2, 1993). ... Broken bone in left foot (November 27, 1993); missed eight games.

		REGULAR SEASON								PLAYOFFS				
Season Team	League	GP	G	A	Pts.	PIM	+/-	PP	SH	GP	G	A	Pts.	PIM
79-80—Prince Albert	SJHL	85	72	95	167	...	...	...	...	—	—	—	—	—
80-81—Prince Albert	SJHL	84	62	93	155	...	...	...	...	—	—	—	—	—
81-82—North Dakota	WCHA	43	13	28	41	24	...	...	...	—	—	—	—	—
82-83—North Dakota	WCHA	36	15	31	46	44	...	...	...	—	—	—	—	—
83-84—Can. Olympic team	Int'l	66	14	19	33	24	...	...	...	—	—	—	—	—
—Hartford	NHL	17	4	2	6	2	...	...	...	—	—	—	—	—
84-85—Hartford	NHL	80	7	12	19	12	...	...	...	—	—	—	—	—
85-86—Hartford	NHL	80	14	20	34	18	...	...	...	10	2	2	4	4
86-87—Hartford	NHL	80	9	22	31	42	...	...	...	6	0	2	2	4
87-88—Hartford	NHL	80	16	21	37	32	...	...	...	6	0	0	0	2
88-89—Hartford	NHL	80	17	24	41	45	...	...	...	4	0	1	1	0
89-90—Hartford	NHL	66	8	19	27	32	0	0	1	7	1	3	4	2
90-91—Washington	NHL	61	6	9	15	24	...	...	...	10	2	3	5	8
91-92—Washington	NHL	30	2	10	12	16	...	...	...	7	0	1	1	0
—Canadian nat'l team	Int'l	1	0	0	0	4	...	...	...	—	—	—	—	—
—Can. Olympic team	Int'l	6	1	2	3	10	...	...	...	—	—	—	—	—
92-93—Pittsburgh	NHL	74	6	19	25	56	5	0	1	12	1	4	5	14
93-94—Philadelphia	NHL	73	4	11	15	38	-20	0	2	—	—	—	—	—
94-95—Houston	IHL	75	18	48	66	56	-6	6	0	4	1	2	3	4
NHL Totals (11 years)		721	93	169	262	317	-15	0	4	62	6	16	22	34

HEAD COACHING RECORD

BACKGROUND: Assistant coach, Houston Aeros (1994-95). ... General manager, Aeros (1998-99). ... Assistant coach, Los Angeles Kings (1999-2002). ... Named coach of Dallas Stars (May 16, 2002).

		REGULAR SEASON						PLAYOFFS		
Season Team	League	W	L	T	OL	Pct.	Finish	W	L	Pct.
95-96—Houston	IHL	29	45	8	...	.402	5th/Central Division	—	—	—
96-97—Houston	IHL	44	30	8	...	.585	2nd/Southwest Division	8	5	.615
97-98—Houston	IHL	50	22	10	...	.671	2nd/Southwest Division	1	3	.250
98-99—Houston	IHL	54	15	13	...	.738	1st/Southwest Division	11	8	.579
02-03—Dallas	NHL	46	17	15	4	.652	1st/Pacific Division	6	6	.500
03-04—Dallas	NHL	41	26	13	2	.579	2nd/Pacific Division	1	4	.200
05-06—Dallas	NHL	53	23	...	6	.646	1st/Pacific Division	1	4	.200
NHL Totals (3 years)		140	66	28	12	.626	**NHL Totals (3 years)**	8	14	.364

NOTES:

96-97—Defeated Las Vegas in conference quarterfinals of Turner Cup playoffs; defeated San Antonio in conference semifinals of Turner Cup playoffs; lost to Long Beach in conference finals of Turner Cup playoffs.
97-98—Lost to Milwaukee in conference quarterfinals of Turner Cup playoffs.
98-99—Defeated Long Beach in conference semifinals of Turner Cup playoffs; defeated Chicago in conference finals of Turner Cup playoffs; defeated Orlando in Turner Cup finals.
02-03—Defeated Edmonton in Western Conference quarterfinals; lost to Anaheim in Western Conference semifinals.
03-04—Lost to Colorado Avalanche in Western Conference quarterfinals.
05-06—Lost to Colorado Avalanche, 4-1, in Western Conference quarterfinals.

TORTORELLA, JOHN — LIGHTNING

PERSONAL: Born June 24, 1958, in Boston.

		REGULAR SEASON								PLAYOFFS				
Season Team	League	GP	G	A	Pts.	PIM	+/-	PP	SH	GP	G	A	Pts.	PIM
79-80—University of Maine	ECAC	31	14	22	36	71	...	...	...	—	—	—	—	—
82-83—Hampton Roads	ACHL	1	1	0	1	2	...	...	...	—	—	—	—	—
—Erie	ACHL	12	2	10	12	4	...	...	...	—	—	—	—	—

Season Team	League	REGULAR SEASON GP	G	A	Pts.	PIM	+/-	PP	SH	PLAYOFFS GP	G	A	Pts.	PIM
83-84—Virginia-Erie	ACHL	64	25	37	62	77	...	...	...	4	1	1	2	18
84-85—Virginia	ACHL	63	33	54	87	66	...	...	...	4	3	4	7	0
85-86—Virginia	ACHL	60	37	59	96	153	...	...	...	5	1	3	4	60

HEAD COACHING RECORD

BACKGROUND: General Manager, Virginia Lancers ACHL (1986-87 and 1987-88). ... Assistant coach, New Haven Nighthawks AHL (1988-89). ... Assistant coach, Buffalo Sabres (1989-90 through 1994-95). ... Assistant coach, Phoenix Coyotes (1997-98 and 1998-99). ... Assistant coach, New York Rangers (1999-March 28, 2000). ... Associate coach, Tampa Bay Lightning (July 7, 2000-January 6, 2001). ... Named coach of Lightning (January 6, 2001).

Season Team	League	REGULAR SEASON W	L	T	OL	Pct.	Finish	PLAYOFFS W	L	Pct.
86-87—Virginia	ACHL	36	19	3	...	.647	1st overall	8	4	.667
87-88—Virginia	AAHL	37	5	1	...	.872	1st overall	3	5	.375
95-96—Rochester	AHL	37	38	5	...	.494	3rd/Central Division	15	4	.789
96-97—Rochester	AHL	40	30	9	...	.563	1st/Empire State Division	6	4	.600
99-00—New York Rangers	NHL	0	4	0	0	.000	4th/Atlantic Division	—	—	—
00-01—Tampa Bay	NHL	12	27	1	3	.291	5th/Southeast Division	—	—	—
01-02—Tampa Bay	NHL	27	40	11	4	.396	3rd/Southeast Division	—	—	—
02-03—Tampa Bay	NHL	36	25	16	5	.537	1st/Southeast Division	5	6	.455
03-04—Tampa Bay	NHL	46	22	8	6	.610	1st/Southeast Division	16	7	.696
05-06—Tampa Bay	NHL	43	33	...	6	.524	2nd/Southeast Division	1	4	.200
NHL Totals (6 years)		164	151	36	24	.485	**NHL Totals (3 years)**	22	17	.564

NOTES:

86-87—Defeated Carolina in ACHL semifinals; defeated Mohawk Valley in ACHL finals.
87-88—Defeated Johnstown in round-robin series; lost to Carolina in AAHL finals.
95-96—Defeated Adirondack in conference quarterfinals of Calder Cup playoffs; defeated Cornwall in conference semifinals of Calder Cup playoffs; defeated Syracuse in conference finals of Calder Cup playoffs; defeated Portland in Calder Cup finals.
96-97—Defeated Syracuse in conference quarterfinals of Calder Cup playoffs; lost to Albany in conference semifinals of Calder Cup playoffs.
99-00—Replaced John Muckler as head coach on interim basis (March 28).
00-01—Replaced Steve Ludzik as head coach (January 6).
02-03—Defeated Washington in Eastern Conference quarterfinals; lost to New Jersey in Eastern Conference semifinals.
03-04—Defeated New York Islanders in Eastern Conference quarterfinals; defeated Montreal in Eastern Conference semifinals; defeated Philadelphia in Eastern Conference finals; defeated Calgary in Stanley Cup finals.
05-06—Lost to Ottawa Senators, 4-1, in Eastern Conference quarterfinals.

TROTZ, BARRY — PREDATORS

PERSONAL: Born July 15, 1962, in Winnipeg.

Season Team	League	REGULAR SEASON GP	G	A	Pts.	PIM	+/-	PP	SH	PLAYOFFS GP	G	A	Pts.	PIM
79-80—Regina	WHL	41	4	8	12	42	...	...	...	—	—	—	—	—
80-81—Regina	WHL	62	4	13	17	115	...	...	...	—	—	—	—	—
81-82—Regina	WHL	50	6	28	34	155	...	...	...	20	1	7	8	79

HEAD COACHING RECORD

BACKGROUND: Player/assistant coach, University of Manitoba (1983-84). ... Coach/general manager, Dauphin Kings junior team (1984-87). ... Assistant coach, University of Manitoba (1987-88). ... Scout, Washington Capitals (1988-91). ... Assistant coach, Baltimore Skipjacks of the AHL (1991-92). ... Scout, Nashville Predators (1997). ... Coach, Predators (August 6, 1997).

Season Team	League	REGULAR SEASON W	L	T	OL	Pct.	Finish	PLAYOFFS W	L	Pct.
92-93—Baltimore	AHL	28	40	12	...	.425	4th/Southern Division	3	4	.429
93-94—Portland	AHL	43	27	10	...	.600	2nd/Northern Division	12	5	.706
94-95—Portland	AHL	46	22	12	...	.650	2nd/Northern Division	3	4	.429
95-96—Portland	AHL	32	38	10	...	.463	3rd/Northern Division	14	10	.583
96-97—Portland	AHL	37	26	10	...	.575	3rd/New England Division	2	3	.400
98-99—Nashville	NHL	28	47	7	...	.384	4th/Central Division	—	—	—
99-00—Nashville	NHL	28	40	7	7	.384	4th/Central Division	—	—	—
00-01—Nashville	NHL	34	36	9	3	.470	3rd/Central Division	—	—	—
01-02—Nashville	NHL	28	41	13	0	.421	4th/Central Division	—	—	—
02-03—Nashville	NHL	27	35	13	7	.409	4th/Central Division	—	—	—
03-04—Nashville	NHL	38	29	11	4	.530	3rd/Central Division	2	4	.333
05-06—Nashville	NHL	49	25	...	8	.598	2nd/Central Division	1	4	.200
NHL Totals (7 years)		232	253	60	29	.456	**NHL Totals (2 years)**	3	8	.273

NOTES:

92-93—Lost to Binghamton in the first round of Calder Cup playoffs.
93-94—Defeated Albany in Northern Division semifinals; defeated Adirondack in Northern Division finals; defeated Moncton in Calder Cup finals.
94-95—Lost to Providence in Northern Division semifinals.
95-96—Defeated Worcester in Eastern Conference quarterfinals; defeated Springfield in Eastern Conference semifinals; defeated Saint John in Eastern Conference finals; lost to Rochester in Calder Cup finals.
96-97—Lost to Springfield in Southern Conference quarterfinals.
03-04—Lost to Detroit in Western Conference quarterfinals.
05-06—Lost to San Jose Sharks, 4-1, in Western Conference quarterfinals.

VIGNEAULT, ALAIN — CANUCKS

PERSONAL: Born May 14, 1961, in Quebec City. ... Shoots right. ... Played defense. ... Name pronounced: vin-YOE
TRANSACTIONS/CAREER NOTES: Selected by St. Louis Blues in eighth round (seventh Blues pick, 167th overall) of NHL entry draft (June 1981).

Season Team	League	REGULAR SEASON GP	G	A	Pts.	PIM	+/-	PP	SH	PLAYOFFS GP	G	A	Pts.	PIM
79-80—Hull	QMJHL	35	5	34	39	82	...	...	...	—	—	—	—	—
—Trois Riv. Flambeaux.	QJHL	28	6	19	25	93	...	...	...	—	—	—	—	—
80-81—Trois Riv. Flambeaux.	QJHL	67	7	55	62	181	...	...	...	—	—	—	—	—
81-82—Salt Lake City	CHL	64	2	10	12	266	...	...	...	—	—	—	—	—
—St. Louis	NHL	14	1	2	3	43	-1	0	0	—	—	—	—	—
82-83—Salt Lake City	CHL	33	1	4	5	189	...	...	...	—	—	—	—	—
—St. Louis	NHL	28	1	3	4	39	-4	0	0	—	—	—	—	—
83-84—Montana	CHL	47	2	14	16	139	...	...	...	—	—	—	—	—
—Maine	AHL	11	0	1	1	46	...	...	...	—	—	—	—	—
NHL Totals (2 years)		42	2	5	7	82	-5	0	0					

HEAD COACHING RECORD

BACKGROUND: Assistant coach, Canadian junior national team (1989 and 1991). ... Assistant coach, Ottawa Senators (1992-93 through November 20, 1995). ... Coach, Manitoba of AHL (2005-06). ... Named coach of Canucks (June 21, 2006).

Season Team	League	REGULAR SEASON W	L	T	OL	Pct.	Finish	PLAYOFFS W	L	Pct.
86-87—Trois-Rivieres	QMJHL	26	37	2	...	.415	5th/Frank Dilio Division	—	—	—
87-88—Hull	QMJHL	43	23	4	...	.643	1st Robert Le Bel Division	12	7	.632
88-89—Hull	QMJHL	40	25	5	...	.607	3rd/Robert Le Bel Division	5	4	.556
89-90—Hull	QMJHL	36	29	5	...	.550	T5th/Robert Le Bel Division	4	7	.364
90-91—Hull	QMJHL	33	25	7	...	.562	2nd/Robert Le Bel Division	2	4	.333
91-92—Hull	QMJHL	40	23	5	...	.625	2nd/Robert Le Bel Division	2	4	.333
95-96—Beauport	QMJHL	19	7	5	...	.694	1st/Frank Dilio Division	13	7	.650
96-97—Beauport	QMJHL	24	44	2	...	.357	6th/Frank Dilio Division	1	3	.250
97-98—Montreal	NHL	37	32	13	...	.530	4th/Northeast Division	4	6	.400
98-99—Montreal	NHL	32	39	11	...	.457	5th/Northeast Division	—	—	—
99-00—Montreal	NHL	35	38	9	4	.459	4th/Northeast Division	—	—	—
00-01—Montreal	NHL	5	9	2	0	.375	...	—	—	—
03-04—Prince Edward	QMJHL	40	19	5	6	.650	3rd/Atlantique Division	—	—	—
04-05—Prince Edward	QMJHL	24	39	7	0	.393	4th/Atlantique Division	—	—	—
05-06—Manitoba	AHL	44	24	7	5	.633	3rd/North Division	7	6	.538
NHL Totals (4 years)		109	118	35	4	.476	**NHL Totals (1 year)**	4	6	.400

NOTES:

87-88—Defeated Granby in quarterfinals of President Cup playoffs; defeated Laval in semifinals of President Cup playoffs; defeated Drummondville in President Cup finals.
88-89—Defeated St. Jean in quarterfinals of President Cup playoffs; lost to Victoriaville in semifinals of President Cup playoffs.
89-90—Defeated Longueuil in quarterfinals of President Cup playoffs; lost to Laval in semifinals of President Cup playoffs.
90-91—Lost to Laval in quarterfinals of President Cup playoffs.
91-92—Lost to Laval in quarterfinals of President Cup playoffs.
95-96—Defeated Rimouski in quarterfinals of President Cup playoffs; defeated Hull in semifinals of President Cup playoffs; lost to Granby in President Cup finals.
96-97—Lost to Halifax in quarterfinals of President Cup playoffs.
97-98—Defeated Pittsburgh in Eastern Conference quarterfinals; lost to Buffalo in Eastern Conference semifinals.
00-01—Replaced as Canadiens coach by Michel Therrien.
05-06—Defeated Syracuse in first round of Calder Cup playoffs; lost to Grand Rapids in second round.

WILSON, RON — SHARKS

PERSONAL: Born May 28, 1955, in Windsor, Ont. ... 5-11/175. ... Shoots right. ... Son of Larry Wilson, C with Detroit Red Wings (1949-50, 1951-53) and Chicago Blackhawks (1953-56) and coach with Red Wings (1976-77); and nephew of Johnny Wilson, LW with four NHL teams (1949-62) and coach with four NHL teams and two WHA teams (1969-80). ... Played defense.

TRANSACTIONS/CAREER NOTES: Selected by Toronto Maple Leafs in seventh round (seventh Maple Leafs pick, 132nd overall) in NHL draft (June 3, 1975). ... Loaned by Davos HC to Minnesota North Stars for remainder of NHL season and playoffs (March 1985). ... Loaned by Davos HC to Minnesota North Stars for remainder of NHL season and playoffs (March 1986). ... Traded by Davos HC to Minnesota North Stars for D Craig Levie (May 1986). ... Separated shoulder (March 9, 1987).

Season Team	League	REGULAR SEASON GP	G	A	Pts.	PIM	+/-	PP	SH	PLAYOFFS GP	G	A	Pts.	PIM
73-74—Providence	ECAC	26	16	22	38	...	...	...	...	—	—	—	—	—
74-75—Providence	ECAC	27	26	61	87	12	...	...	...	—	—	—	—	—
—U.S. national team	Int'l	27	5	32	37	42	...	...	...	—	—	—	—	—
75-76—Providence	ECAC	28	19	47	66	44	...	...	...	—	—	—	—	—
76-77—Providence	ECAC	30	17	42	59	62	...	...	...	—	—	—	—	—
—Dallas	CHL	4	1	0	1	2	...	...	...	—	—	—	—	—
77-78—Dallas	CHL	67	31	38	69	18	...	...	...	—	—	—	—	—
—Toronto	NHL	13	2	1	3	0	-5	1	0	—	—	—	—	—
78-79—New Brunswick	AHL	31	11	20	31	13	...	...	...	—	—	—	—	—
—Toronto	NHL	46	5	12	17	4	-10	4	0	3	0	1	1	0
79-80—New Brunswick	AHL	43	20	43	63	10	...	...	...	—	—	—	—	—
—Toronto	NHL	5	0	2	2	0	-2	0	0	3	1	2	3	2
80-81—EHC Kloten	Switzerland	38	22	23	45	...	...	...	...	—	—	—	—	—
81-82—Davos HC	Switzerland	38	24	23	47	...	...	...	...	...	...	...	...	...
82-83—Davos HC	Switzerland	36	32	32	64	...	...	...	...	...	...	...	...	...
83-84—Davos HC	Switzerland	36	33	39	72	...	...	...	...	...	...	...	...	...
84-85—Davos HC	Switzerland	38	39	62	101	...	...	...	...	...	...	...	...	...
—Minnesota	NHL	13	4	8	12	2	-1	0	0	9	1	6	7	2
85-86—Davos HC	Switzerland	27	28	41	69	...	...	...	...	...	...	...	...	...
—Minnesota	NHL	11	1	3	4	8	-2	1	0	5	2	4	6	4
86-87—Minnesota	NHL	65	12	29	41	36	-9	6	0	—	—	—	—	—
87-88—Minnesota	NHL	24	2	12	14	16	-4	1	0	—	—	—	—	—
NHL Totals (7 years)		177	26	67	93	66	-33	13	0	20	4	13	17	8

HEAD COACHING RECORD

BACKGROUND: Assistant coach, Milwaukee of the IHL (1989-90). ... Served as Milwaukee interim coach while Ron Lapointe underwent cancer treatments (February and March 1990; team went 9-10). ... Assistant coach, Vancouver Canucks (1990-91 through 1992-93). ... Named coach of San Jose Sharks (December 4, 2002).

		REGULAR SEASON						PLAYOFFS		
Season Team	**League**	**W**	**L**	**T**	**OL**	**Pct.**	**Finish**	**W**	**L**	**Pct.**
93-94—Anaheim	NHL	33	46	5	...	.423	4th/Pacific Division	—	—	—
94-95—Anaheim	NHL	16	27	5	...	.385	6th/Pacific Division	—	—	—
95-96—Anaheim	NHL	35	39	8	...	.476	4th/Pacific Division	—	—	—
96-97—Anaheim	NHL	36	33	13	...	.518	2nd/Pacific Division	4	7	.364
97-98—Washington	NHL	40	30	12	...	.561	3rd/Atlantic Division	12	9	.571
98-99—Washington	NHL	31	45	6	...	.415	3rd/Southeast Division	—	—	—
99-00—Washington	NHL	44	24	12	2	.610	1st/Southeast Division	1	4	.200
00-01—Washington	NHL	41	27	10	4	.561	1st/Southeast Division	2	4	.333
01-02—Washington	NHL	36	33	11	2	.506	2nd/Southeast Division	—	—	—
02-03—San Jose	NHL	19	25	7	6	.395	5th/Pacific	—	—	—
03-04—San Jose	NHL	43	21	12	6	.598	1st/Pacific Division	10	7	.588
05-06—San Jose	NHL	44	27	...	11	.537	2nd/Pacific Division	6	5	.545
NHL Totals (12 years)		418	377	101	31	.505	**NHL Totals (6 years)**	35	36	.493

NOTES:

96-97—Defeated Phoenix in Western Conference quarterfinals; lost to Detroit in Western Conference semifinals.

97-98—Defeated Boston in Eastern Conference quarterfinals; defeated Ottawa in Eastern Conference semifinals; defeated Buffalo in Eastern Conference finals; lost to Detroit in Stanley Cup finals.

99-00—Lost to Pittsburgh in Eastern Conference quarterfinals.

00-01—Lost to Pittsburgh in Eastern Conference quarterfinals.

02-03—Replaced Darryl Sutter as head coach (Decemeber 4).

03-04—Defeated St. Louis in Western Conference quarterfinals; defeated Colorado in Western Conference semifinals; lost to Calgary in Western Conference finals.

05-06—Defeated Nashville, 4-1, in Western Conference quarterfinals; lost to Edmonton Oilers, 4-2, in Western Conference semifinals.

YAWNEY, TRENT — BLACKHAWKS

PERSONAL: Born September 29, 1965, in Hudson Bay, Sask. ... 6-3/195. ... Shoots left. ... Played defense.

TRANSACTIONS/CAREER NOTES: Selected by Chicago Blackhawks as underage junior in 3rd round (2nd Blackhawks pick, 45th overall) of entry draft (June 9, 1984). ... Bruised left shoulder (March 1989). ... Strained right knee (April 24, 1989). ... Bruised kidney (November 11, 1989). ... Bruised thigh (January 1990). ... Strained knee (October 1990). ... Traded by Blackhawks to Calgary Flames for LW Stephane Matteau (December 16, 1991). ... Fractured right clavicle (September 26, 1992); missed first 20 games of season. ... Tore muscle in shoulder (September 9, 1993); missed 25 games. ... Strained left thumb ligaments (January 28, 1995); missed five games. ... Reinjured left thumb (February 11, 1995); missed two games. ... Strained right thumb ligaments (March 22, 1995); missed one game. ... Suffered from the flu (November 8, 1995); missed two games. ... Lacerated hand (January 5, 1996); missed one game. ... Injured knee (February 3, 1996); missed one game. ... Signed as free agent by St. Louis Blues (July 6, 1996). ... Signed as free agent by Blackhawks (September 25, 1997). ... Sprained thumb (March 14, 1998); missed eight games. ... Fractured arm (January 9, 1999); missed 19 games. ... Announced retirement to become assistant coach with Blackhawks (February 22, 1999).

		REGULAR SEASON								PLAYOFFS				
Season Team	**League**	**GP**	**G**	**A**	**Pts.**	**PIM**	**+/-**	**PP**	**SH**	**GP**	**G**	**A**	**Pts.**	**PIM**
81-82—Saskatoon	WHL	6	1	0	1	0	...	...	...	—	—	—	—	—
82-83—Saskatoon	WHL	59	6	31	37	44	...	...	...	6	0	2	2	0
83-84—Saskatoon	WHL	72	13	46	59	81	...	...	...	—	—	—	—	—
84-85—Saskatoon	WHL	72	16	51	67	158	...	...	...	3	1	6	7	7
85-86—Canadian nat'l team	Int'l	73	6	15	21	60	...	...	...	—	—	—	—	—
86-87—Canadian nat'l team	Int'l	51	4	15	19	37	...	...	...	—	—	—	—	—
87-88—Canadian nat'l team	Int'l	60	4	12	16	81	...	...	...	—	—	—	—	—
—Can. Olympic team	Int'l	8	1	1	2	6	1	...	...	—	—	—	—	—
—Chicago	NHL	15	2	8	10	15	1	2	0	5	0	4	4	8
88-89—Chicago	NHL	69	5	19	24	116	-5	3	1	15	3	6	9	20
89-90—Chicago	NHL	70	5	15	20	82	-6	1	0	20	3	5	8	27
90-91—Chicago	NHL	61	3	13	16	77	6	3	0	1	0	0	0	0
91-92—Indianapolis	IHL	9	2	3	5	12	...	...	...	—	—	—	—	—
—Calgary	NHL	47	4	9	13	45	-5	1	0	—	—	—	—	—
92-93—Calgary	NHL	63	1	16	17	67	9	0	0	6	3	2	5	6
93-94—Calgary	NHL	58	6	15	21	60	21	1	1	7	0	0	0	16
94-95—Calgary	NHL	37	0	2	2	108	-4	0	0	2	0	0	0	2
95-96—Calgary	NHL	69	0	3	3	88	-1	0	0	4	0	0	0	2
96-97—St. Louis	NHL	39	0	2	2	17	2	0	0	—	—	—	—	—
97-98—Chicago	NHL	45	1	0	1	76	-5	0	0	—	—	—	—	—
98-99—Chicago	NHL	20	0	0	0	32	-6	0	0	—	—	—	—	—
NHL Totals (12 years)		593	27	102	129	783	7	11	2	60	9	17	26	81

HEAD COACHING RECORD

BACKGROUND: Named coach of the Chicago Blackhawks (July 7, 2005).

		REGULAR SEASON						PLAYOFFS		
Season Team	**League**	**W**	**L**	**T**	**OL**	**Pct.**	**Finish**	**W**	**L**	**Pct.**
00-01—Norfolk	AHL	36	26	13	5	.531	3rd/Southern Division	4	5	.444
01-02—Norfolk	AHL	38	26	12	4	.550	1st/South Division	1	3	.250
02-03—Norfolk	AHL	37	26	12	5	.538	1st/South Division	5	4	.556
03-04—Norfolk	AHL	35	36	4	5	.463	5th/East Division	4	4	.500
04-05—Norfolk	AHL	43	30	6	1	.575	3rd/East Division	2	4	.333
05-06—Chicago	NHL	26	43	...	13	.317	4th/Central Division	—	—	—
NHL Totals (1 year)		26	43	0	13	.317